HANDBOOK OF DEVELOPMENTAL PSYCHOLOGY

Benjamin B. Wolman
Editor

George Stricker
Associate Editor

Steven J. Ellman
Patricia Keith-Spiegel
David S. Palermo
Consulting Editors

Prentice-Hall, Inc.   Englewood Cliffs, New Jersey 07632

Library of Congress Cataloging in Publication Data

Main entry under title:

HANDBOOK OF DEVELOPMENTAL PSYCHOLOGY

   Bibliography: p.
   Includes index.
   1. Developmental psychology. I. Wolman,
Benjamin B. II. Stricker, George. [DNLM:
1. Human development. 2. Psychology.
BF 713 H236 (P)]
BF713.H363   155   81-13830
ISBN 0-13-372599-5   AACR2

*Editorial/production supervision and interior
   design by Linda Schuman*
Case design by Edsal Enterprises
Jacket design by Tony Ferrara Studio
Manufacturing buyer: Edmund W. Leone

Printed in the United States of America

10 9 8 7 6 5 4 3 2 1

ISBN 0-13-372599-5

PRENTICE-HALL INTERNATIONAL, INC., *London*
PRENTICE-HALL OF AUSTRALIA PTY. LIMITED, *Sydney*
PRENTICE-HALL OF CANADA, LTD., *Toronto*
PRENTICE-HALL OF INDIA PRIVATE LIMITED, *New Delhi*
PRENTICE-HALL OF JAPAN, INC., *Tokyo*
PRENTICE-HALL OF SOUTHEAST ASIA PTE. LTD., *Singapore*
WHITEHALL BOOKS LIMITED, *Wellington, New Zealand*

*This Handbook is dedicated
to the memory of*
Jean Piaget,
friend and teacher.

Contents

Preface

Developmental psychology has come of age. Its origins go far back to the naturalistic observations by J. H. Pestalozzi (1774) and D. V. Tiedman (1787). Toward the end of the nineteenth century W. Preyer (1882) and Charles Darwin (1887) published developmental reports of their own sons, followed by Wilhelm and Klara Stern who described the childhood of their daughter Eva (I have met Eva Stern in her advanced years).

G. Stanley Hall was undoubtedly the pioneer of scientific research technique in child psychology. G. Stanley Hall was the founder and the first president of the American Psychological Association (1892), founder of *Pedagogical Seminar,* the first scholarly journal in child psychology (1893), and author of the first systematic studies in childhood (1891), adolescence (1904), and old age (1922). Hall's *questionnaire method* was applied by a great many students of developmental psychology for years to come, including my own early research.

Alfred Binet's intelligence tests (first published in 1905) opened new vistas in developmental psychology. Binet's work was followed by that of Wilhelm Stern in Germany, Cyril Burt in Great Britain, and Lewis M. Terman in the United States. The worldwide acclaimed Terman's Stanford-Binet Tests, first published in 1916, have spanned decades of research in developmental psychology and have been followed by the works of a great many prominent psychologists, culminating in David Wechsler's superb intelligence scales.

Research in developmental psychology has continued unabated irrespective of theoretical viewpoints. Sigmund Freud's (1856–1939) pioneering work on psychosexual child development broke down the barriers of Victorian prudishness. New and daring theoretical concepts have been developed by C. G. Jung, A. Adler, Melanie Klein, S. Ferenczi, O. Rank, K. Horney, H. S. Sullivan, and

scores of Freudian and non-Freudian psychoanalysts. The hitherto unknown aspects of emotional life, conscious and unconscious, have been unraveled by detailed case-study methods, and clinical data have been scrutinized by scores of American research workers, among them R. R. Sears, D. H. Mowrer, and in later years R. R. Holt, E. Peter Freund, I. Sarnoff, and many others, and the annually published volumes *Psychoanalytic Study of the Child* contain a wealth of empirical data and theoretical constructs.

Psychoanalytic and related research was certainly not the only avenue of developmental psychology. The behavioristic school has made a major and valid contribution to the research methods and substantive data in developmental psychology. John Broadus Watson's (1878–1958) daring approach has opened new vistas in research and introduced the highly important aspect of learning processes. While the psychoanalysts emphasized natural developmental phases, the leading behaviorists, among them B. F. Skinner and others, stressed the relevance of learning in human change. Several leading psychoanalysts, among them Heinz Hartmann and Erik Erikson, have incorporated some concepts of learning theory in their works.

It is impossible to do justice to this enormous field in a few pages of a preface. To describe the development of developmental psychology is like painting the sea. It would take a huge volume to describe the works of all prominent men and women who devoted their lives to the study of developmental psychology and have enriched our understanding of human change from cradle to grave.

The last decade saw an upsurge of interest in this rapidly expanding field. The *International Encyclopedia of Psychiatry, Psychology, Psychoanalysis and Neurology* published in 1977 has 300(!) articles in developmental psychology. The huge special October 1979 issue of the *American Psychologist* is devoted to *Psychology of Children: Current Research and Practice.*

The *Handbook of Developmental Psychology* is a product of collective effort of 75 men and women. The fifty chapters were written especially for this *Handbook* by leading experts. The editors of the *Handbook* are George Stricker, Associate Editor, Steven J. Ellman, Patricia Keith-Spiegel, and David S. Palermo, Consulting Editors, and myself.

The *Handbook* covers the entire span of human life. The first part includes ten chapters devoted to the various research methods and theories. Part Two is devoted to prenatal life and infancy, Part Three deals with childhood, Part Four with adolescence, Part Five with adult years, and Part Six with aging.

The present *Handbook* is a product of three years of planning, writing, and editing. This volume could not have been created without the brilliant and efficient work of my associate editor, Dr. George Stricker, to whom I am profoundly indebted. I am also indebted to Mr. Ted Jursek, Editor of Professional and Reference Books at Prentice-Hall, for his patience and encouragement; to Ms. Jean Evans, the Managing Editor of the *International Encyclopedia of Psychiatry, Psychology, Psychoanalysis and Neurology* for her wise and efficient help; and to Ms. Linda Schuman, Production Editor, for her patience, constructive effort, and most efficient planning and execution of this major project. The *Handbook* is dedicated to the memory of Jean Piaget.

Benjamin B. Wolman

Contributors

LINDA P. ACREDOLO, Ph.D. (Chapter 15) is Assistant Professor of Psychology, University of California, Davis, CA.

LEONORE LOEB ADLER, Ph.D. (Chapter 6) is Professor of Psychology, Molloy College, Rockville Centre, NY.

JAMES L. ALEXANDER, Ph.D. (Chapter 8) is Assistant Professor of Rehabilitation, Baylor College of Medicine, Houston, TX.

VERN L. BENGTSON, Ph.D. (Chapter 49) is Professor of Sociology, University of California, Los Angeles, CA., and Chief, Social Science Division, Research Institute of the Andrus Gerontology Center, Los Angeles, CA.

HENRY B. BILLER, Ph.D. (Chapter 39) is Professor of Psychology, University of Rhode Island, Kingston, RI.

MICHAEL BOYES, M.A. (Chapter 22) is Graduate Student of Psychology, University of British Columbia, Vancouver, B.C. Canada.

CARLFRED B. BRODERICK, Ph.D. (Chapter 40) is Professor of Sociology and Executive Director of Marriage and Family Therapy Program, University of Southern California, Los Angeles, CA.

NANCY A. BUSCH-ROSSNAGEL, Ph.D. (Chapter 25) is Assistant Professor of Human Development and Family Studies, Colorado State University, Fort Collins, CO.

PATRICIA L. CARRELL, Ph.D. (Chapter 17) is Associate Professor of Linguistics, Southern Illinois University, Carbondale, IL.

JAMES L. CARROLL, Ph.D. (Chapter 24) is Associate Professor of Educational Psychology, Arizona State University, Tempe, AZ.

MICHAEL CHANDLER, Ph.D. (Chapter 22) is Professor of Psychology, University of British Columbia, Vancouver, B.C. Canada.

WM. CAMERON CHUMLEA, Ph.D. (Chapter 26) is Fels Assistant Professor of Pediatrics and Research Scientist, Fels Research Institute and Wright State University School of Medicine, Yellow Springs, OH.

ROBERT A. COOKE, Ph.D. (Chapter 10) is Associate Research Scientist, Institute for Social Research, University of Michigan, Ann Arbor, MI.

NANCY WADSWORTH DENNEY, Ph.D. (Chapter 45) is Professor of Psychology, University of Kansas, Lawrence, KS.

NINA DIAMOND, Ph.D. (Chapter 1) is Assistant Professor of Psychology, Central Michigan University, Mount Pleasant, MI.

WILLIAM J. DOHERTY, Ph.D. (Chapter 37) is Assistant Professor of Family Practice, College of Medicine, University of Iowa, Iowa City, IA.

PHILIP H. DREYER, Ph.D. (Chapter 32) is Associate Professor of Education and Psychology, Claremont Graduate School, Claremont, CA.

TIFFANY MARTINI FIELD, Ph.D. (Chapter 38) is Associate Professor of Pediatrics and Psychology, University of Miami Medical School, Miami, FL.

GEORGE W. GOETHALS, Ed.D., Postdoctoral diploma in Clinical Psychology (Chapter 2) is Senior Lecturer, Harvard Medical School, Cambridge Hospital; and Consultant in Psychology, Harvard University Health Service, Cambridge, MA.

JOHN WILLIAM HAGEN, Ph.D. (Chapter 20) is Professor and Chairman, Developmental Program, and Research Scientist, Center for Human Growth and Development, University of Michigan, Ann Arbor, MI.

JANET L. HAKE, B.A. (Chapter 15) is Master of Science candidate in Child Development, University of California, Davis, CA.

ANTONIA HALTON, M.A. (Chapter 11) is Infant Therapist, Infant Developmental Unit, Solomon Carter Fuller Mental Health Center, Boston, MA.

ROBERT J. HAVIGHURST, Ph.D. (Chapter 43) is Professor of Education and Human Development, The University of Chicago, Chicago, IL.

CHRISTOPHER HERTZOG, Ph.D. (Chapter 7) is Research Associate and Senior Fellow, Department of Psychology, University of Washington, Seattle, WA.

REGINA O'CONNELL HIGGINS, M.Ed. (Chapter 2) is Assistant Professor of Counseling Psychology, Lesley Graduate School, Cambridge, MA.

RICHARD HIRSCHMAN, D.M.D., Ph.D. (Chapter 14) is Professor of Psychology, Kent State University, Kent, OH.

ROBERT M. HODAPP, B.A. (Chapter 16) is a doctoral candidate in the Developmental Program of the Department of Psychology, Boston University, Boston, MA.

JOHN L. HORN, Ph.D. (Chapter 47) is Professor of Psychology, University of Denver, Denver, CO.

NEIL S. JACOBSON, Ph.D. (Chapter 37) is a full-time faculty member in the Department of Psychology, University of Washington, Seattle, WA.

LISSY F. JARVIK, M.D., Ph.D. (Chapter 44) is Professor of Psychiatry, University of California, Los Angeles, CA; and Chief of the Psychogenetic Laboratory at the Brentwood Veterans Administration Medical Center, Los Angeles, CA.

LYLE STEVEN JOFFE, Ph.D. (Chapter 12) is Staff Psychologist and Clinical Supervisor, Michael Reese Hospital and Medical Center—Nicholas J. Pritzker Children's Psychiatric Unit, Chicago, IL.

BOAZ KAHANA, Ph.D. (Chapter 48) is Professor of Psychology, Oakland University, Rochester, MI; and Director of the Mental Health and Aging Training Program, Wayne State University, Detroit, MI.

ROBERT KAIL, Ph.D. (Chapter 20) is Associate Professor of Psychological Sciences, Purdue University, West Lafayette, IN.

JOAN B. KELLY, Ph.D. (Chapter 41) is Director and Co-Founder of the Northern California Mediation Center, Greenbrae, CA.

ERICH W. LABOUVIE, Ph.D. (Chapter 4) is Associate Professor of Psychology, Center of Alcohol Studies, Rutgers University, New Brunswick, NJ.

GISELA LABOUVIE-VIEF, Ph.D. (Chapter 46) is Professor of Psychology, Wayne State University, Detroit, MI.

ASENATH LA RUE, Ph.D. (Chapter 44) is Assistant Professor, Department of Psychiatry and Biobehavioral Sciences, University of California, Los Angeles, CA; and Research Psychologist, Psychogenetics Unit, Brentwood Veterans Administration Medical Center, Los Angeles, CA.

RICHARD M. LERNER, Ph.D. (Chapters 28, 33) is Professor of Child Development in the College of Human Development, Pennsylvania State University, University Park, PA.

BARBARA K. LINDAUER, Ph.D. (Chapter 19) is Research Scientist, Denver Research Institute, Social Systems Research and Evaluation Division, University of Denver, Denver, CO.

JOHN PAUL McKINNEY, Ph.D. (Chapter 31) is Professor of Developmental Psychology, Michigan State University, East Lansing, MI.

LAWRENCE E. MELAMED, Ph.D. (Chapter 14) is Professor of Psychology, Kent State University, Kent, OH.

DENNIS L. MOLFESE, Ph.D. (Chapter 17) is Professor of Psychology, Southern Illinois University, Carbondale, IL.

VICTORIA J. MOLFESE, Ph.D. (Chapter 17) is Associate Professor of Psychology, Southern Illinois University, Carbondale, IL.

DEWAYNE MOORE, Ph.D. (Chapter 31) is Visiting Assistant Professor of Psychology, Clemson University, Clemson, SC.

EDWARD MUELLER, Ph.D. (Chapter 16) is Associate Professor of Psychology, Boston University, Boston, MA.

BERNARD I. MURSTEIN, Ph.D. (Chapter 36) is Professor of Psychology, Connecticut College, New London, CT.

EDITH D. NEIMARK, Ph.D. (Chapter 27) is Professor of Psychology, Douglass College, Rutgers, The State University of New Jersey, New Brunswick, NJ.

BARBARA M. NEWMAN, Ph.D. (Chapter 34) is Chairperson and Associate Professor in the Department of Family Relations and Human Development, The Ohio State University, Columbus, OH.

PHILIP R. NEWMAN, Ph.D. (Chapter 29) is Psychologist, Columbus, OH.

GIL G. NOAM, Dipl. Psych. (Chapter 2) is Assistant Psychologist, McClean Hospital, Belmont, MA; and Lecturer, Harvard Medical School, Boston, MA.

STEVEN L. NOCK, Ph.D. (Chaper 35) is Assistant Professor of Sociology, University of Virginia, Charlottesville, VA.

JUM C. NUNNALLY, Ph.D. (Chapter 9) is Professor of Psychology, Vanderbilt University, Nashville, TN.

CONSTANCE M. OLIVER, Ph.D. (Chapter 14) is Staff Psychologist, Lee Mental Health Center, Fort Myers, FL.

SCOTT G. PARIS, Ph.D. (Chapter 19) is Associate Professor in the Combined Program in Education and Psychology, University of Michigan, Ann Arbor, MI.

GAIL A. PETERSEN, Ph.D. (Chapter 18) is Assistant Professor of Psychology, Institute of Advanced Psychological Studies, Adelphi University, Garden City, NY.

ROBERT M. PRINCE, Ph.D. (Chapter 42) is Administrator of Continuing Education in Psychology at the Queens Hospital Center Affiliation of Long Island Jewish Hillside Medical Center; and Adjunct Supervisor of Psychotherapy at Yeshiva University, New York, NY.

JAMES R. REST, Ph.D. (Chapter 24) is Professor of Educational Psychology, University of Minnesota, Minneapolis, MN.

LEONARD A. ROSENBLUM, Ph.D. (Chapter 5) is Professor of Psychiatry and Director of the Primate Behavior Laboratory, Downstate Medical Center, Brooklyn, NY.

K. WARNER SCHAIE, Ph.D. (Chapter 7) is Professor of Psychology and Director of the Gerontology Research Institute, University of Southern California, Los Angeles, CA.

DAVID A. SCHELL, M.A. (Chapter 46) is Graduate Student, Wayne State University, Detroit, MI.

GARY G. SCHWARTZ, B.A. (Chapter 5) is Teaching Assistant in the Program in Biological Psychology, Downstate Medical Center, Brooklyn, NY.

JUDY A. SHEA, M.S. (Chapter 28) is Doctoral Student, The Pennsylvania State University, University Park, PA.

OZZIE SIEGEL, Ph.D. (Chapter 30) is Chief Psychologist, Queens Hospital Center Affiliation of Long Island Jewish Hillside Medical Center; and Assistant Clinical Professor of Psychology, Adelphi University, Garden City, NY.

DEE L. SHEPHERD-LOOK, Ph.D. (Chapter 23) is Professor of Psychology, California State University, Northbridge, CA.

GERALD STECHLER, Ph.D. (Chapter 11) is Professor and Chairman, Department of Child Psychiatry and Child Development, Boston University School of Medicine, Boston, MA.

GEORGE STRICKER, Ph.D. is Associate Editor of the *Handbook* and Professor and Assistant Dean, Institute of Advanced Psychological Studies, Adelphi University, Garden City, NY.

LILLIAN E. TROLL, Ph.D. (Chapter 49) is Professor and Program Director, Department of Psychology, University College, Rutgers, The State University of New Jersey, New Brunswick, NJ.

BARBARA F. TURNER, Ph.D. (Chapter 50) is Associate Professor of Human Development and Psychology, University of Massachusetts, Amherst, MA.

ANNETTE K. VANCE, M.Sc. (Chapter 25) is Assistant Professor of Education, University of New Brunswick, Fredericton, N.B. Canada.

BRIAN E. VAUGHN, Ph.D. (Chapter 12) is Research Psychologist, University of California, Los Angeles, CA.

FRED W. VONDRACEK, Ph.D. (Chapter 33) is Associate Professor of Human Development and Head, Department of Individual and Family Studies, The Pennsylvania State University, University Park, PA.

GLENN E. WEISFELD, Ph.D. (Chapter 13) is Assistant Professor of Psychology, Wayne State University, Detroit, MI.

GROVER J. WHITEHURST, Ph.D. (Chapter 21) is Associate Professor of Psychology, State University of New York, Stony Brook, NY.

SUSAN M. WIDMAYER, Ph.D. (Chapter 30) is Assistant Professor of Pediatrics and Psychology, University of Miami School of Medicine, Miami, FL.

EDWIN P. WILLEMS, Ph.D. (Chapter 8) is Professor of Psychology and Associate Dean of Social Sciences, University of Houston Central Campus, Houston, TX; and Professor of Rehabilitation, Baylor College of Medicine, Houston, TX.

BENJAMIN B. WOLMAN, Ph.D. (Chapter 3) is Professor Emeritus, Long Island University, Brooklyn, NY, Editor of the *Handbook,* and Editor-in-Chief, *International Encyclopedia of Psychiatry, Psychology, Psychoanalysis and Neurology.*

CAROL R. ZEITS, Ph.D. (Chapter 42) is Psychologist, New York, NY and Great Neck, NY.

Research Methods
and Theories

PART ONE

1

Cognitive Theory

NINA DIAMOND

Identical objects and events are relatively rare in the world; variation in one or another aspect is the rule. The area of human understanding that proceeds by reason and whose purpose is to make the unknown known is based on the act of recognizing a set of things to be alike when they are not identical. Jacob Bronowski illustrates this in *The Common Sense of Science*. He refers to the simple question which is said to have turned Isaac Newton's attention to the problem of gravitation: Why does an apple when it leaves the tree fall to the ground? Thinkers of the Middle Ages answered that question in the tradition of Aristotle by saying that the apple falls because it is the nature of apples to do so. Unsophisticated and misleading as their answer seems to us, it represents, as Bronowski said, "a bold and remarkable extension of the mind" (1953, p. 23). Its importance lies in the fact that it did not make a statement about a particular apple of a particular variety at a particular time but involved the creation of a permanent class of apples—the generalization of the concept of *apple*. Newton in turn was able to see the likeness which no one else had seen between the fall of the apple and the swing of the moon in its orbit around the earth. The theory of gravitation rests on this notion.

Bronowski's comments address the role of categorization in what have traditionally been referred to as the "higher" mental processes. William James, though, was impressed with the fundamental nature of the act of creating equivalence classes; he wrote that the "sense of sameness is the very keel and backbone of our thinking" (1950, p. 459, first published in 1890). James emphasized that he was speaking of perceived sameness, sameness imposed by the mind's structure, rather than "real" sameness of things in the universe (a clarification rendered almost superfluous by nature's reluctance to provide us with identical objects and events). He viewed the recognition that something new is like something previously encountered, the "feeling of 'Hollo! Thingumbob again!'" (p. 463), as the basis of all cognitive activity.

The notion that human beings respond to categories of things, rather than to individual instances, possesses a kind of intuitive validity. This is so because alternative assumptions are obviously untenable. We do not respond in the same way to all apprehended stimuli. On the other hand, if we were to experience as unique every event that was nonidentical to those previously encountered and respond accordingly, we would soon be unable to function in our complex world. Like other living things the human organism possesses an ability to adapt to the environment—that is, it can profit from experience. The ability to benefit from experience implies that we store traces of past events and that incoming information must somehow make contact with these traces. Association between old and new, moreover, depends upon the recognition that a given stimulus is like some previously experienced event (Neisser, 1967, p. 50).

Human beings' utilization of past experience in responding effectively to novel events is generally attributed to our capacity for conceptualization. The term *concept* is employed in the psychological literature to denote a rather wide variety of phenomena. Although its meaning admits of many interpretations, most users of the term would concur with the following statement by Elkind (1969):

Psychologically speaking, concepts are mechanisms by which we attempt to cope with the multiplicity of nature. By means of concepts, we are able to deal with new events in terms of past experience, and thus effect a psychic economy through the avoidance of additional efforts at adaptation. (p. 172)

A corollary of the proposition that it is conceptual ability that accounts for the occurrence of some previously learned reaction to some novel event is the statement that conceptual categories serve a predictive function. If, for example, on the basis of sensory information some novel object is inferred to be an apple, then we can be confident that certain motor patterns will be appropriate for grasping and lifting it from the table. We know that it may be eaten, cut with a knife, transformed into applesauce, and (to return to Bronowski) that it is likely to fall from the tree to the ground for the same reason that other apples do. The act of placing some event in an identity class constitutes a first step in the direction of "rendering the environment generic" (Bruner, 1957, p. 43) and thereby achieving predictability as well as economy of effort.

As indicated earlier, it is almost intuitively obvious that we store traces of past events and make use of this information at some later time in order to respond adequately to novelty. However, the answers to questions about the way in which this is accomplished—what it is that is abstracted from experience and how the stored information is accessed and used to allow us to recognize nonidentical recurrences of events—are far from obvious. This is the reason for the semantic confusion that surrounds the term *concept*. To the psychologist attempting to characterize the human organism as an information-processing mechanism, questions which concern concepts and the abstraction process are extremely important, partly because concepts are implicated in ratiocination, as Bronowski pointed out, or in the words of Jerome Kagan (1966), they "are the fundamental agents of intellectual work . . . whose theoretical significance parallels the seminal role of valence in chemistry, gene in biology, or energy in physics" (p. 97). What endows questions about conceptual knowlege with greater significance, however, is their tendency to subsume others concerning the human organism as a mechanism capable of being modified by experience—questions about memory and learning.[1]

For developmentalists the issue of conceptual abstraction must be of particular concern. Young children and animals are capable of discriminating and responding to classes of things, yet it is apparent that profound differences exist between the conceptual abilities of adults and those of immature or nonhuman organisms. Any theory of conceptual abstraction must inevitably make broad claims about the organism as an information-processing mechanism, addressing questions of what must be "built in" to allow the organism to be modified by experience and of how the process of modification actually works (see Bransford, Note 1, pp. 13–14). Therefore the explication by such a theory of observed age-related changes in the process of forming and using concepts can take us a long way toward a relatively complete understanding of cognitive development.

There is another important reason for affording a central role to the problem of conceptual abstraction in the study of age-related cognitive change. It has to do with

the fact that conceptual categories form the basis for dealing adaptively with novelty. An important step toward understanding human development consists in recognizing the extent to which a young child's world is composed of novel objects and events and how important for the child is the acquisition of cognitive structures that can endow the world with a degree of predictability. As Nelson (1977) says,

The essential task of cognitive organization for the first several years of life is to form concepts about . . . objects and events and the larger contexts in which they occur, in order to be able to make accurate predictions about more and more recurrent experiences. The more complete the prediction at any given time, the less effort that must be spent in processing new information and the more new information that can be taken in from the present context for future use. (p. 220)

The world of the adult, on the other hand, is largely familiar. It is rare that we encounter something entirely new. The decreasing extent to which the environment of the developing child is experienced as novel implies what Trabasso (1973, p. 449) describes as a shift in the relative importance of internal versus external sources of knowledge. Because they lack an internal knowledge store, it is reasonable to suppose that the energies of young children are directed toward the extraction of information from regularities of occurrence in the environment. In contrast the adult uses minimal external inputs to access and operate upon a large and highly organized store of internal knowledge. Theories intended to explicate age-related changes in human beings as information-processing systems and to show how the complex knowledge of the adult is derived from a base established in early childhood cannot be complete without a specification of how concepts are acquired, organized, and accessed to make possible the recognition of nonidentical recurrences of events.

PIAGET'S THEORY

The latter portion of this chapter will be devoted to an exploration of the notion of the concept and the process of concept acquisition as depicted in Piaget's theory of development. The name of Jean Piaget has been known in this country since around 1930. His early studies of child thought were highly regarded and were given a particularly enthusiastic reception by child psychologists. There followed a period of nearly a quarter century, however, during which the results of his investigations were looked upon with a great deal of skepticism or were passed over entirely by the American psychological establishment. The mid-1950s saw a burgeoning of interest in Piaget, but it would be another decade before the work that had for many years constituted a very substantial part of the available theory and experimentation in developmental psychology would receive anything resembling the recognition and understanding it deserved. There are a number of reasons for what Flavell (1963, p. 10) refers to as the long-prevailing "under-assimilation" of Piaget's system in the English-speaking professional world.

First, Piaget writes in French. For many years only his

---

[1] The implications of the problem of conceptual abstraction for theories of learning and memory are dealt with in an unpublished, but highly influential, paper written by Bransford in 1970. Since in many respects this chapter relies heavily on Bransford's analysis, his article will be cited frequently.

very early works were available in translation. Second, most of the writings are difficult to understand; Piaget himself admits that he is "not an easy author" and that comprehension of his theory requires a great deal of effort. Third, many behavioral scientists are overwhelmed by the sheer volume of Piaget's output. His published works are so numerous and so widely dispersed that there are few people who can claim to have read them all. Although there are a large number of books and articles available which seek to explicate various aspects of the theory for the benefit of psychologists or lay persons, nobody has yet attempted a comprehensive summary of Piaget's life's work. This is probably just as well, since the theory has continued to evolve and to be subjected by Piaget to minor and not-so-minor modifications.

In addition to those cited above, there is another factor responsible for the relative lack of appreciation afforded the work of the world's foremost contributor to the field of intellectual development. It is Piaget's position on issues regarding the nature of knowledge and the process of knowledge acquisition—in particular, his contention that knowledge is not bestowed upon a passive observer but is constructed by the individual in the course of his/her interaction with the world. The questions which Piaget asks are not those with which American psychologists have traditionally occupied themselves. He is less concerned with the content of knowledge than with its structure and less interested in the environmental conditions under which knowledge is acquired than in the innately determined capacity of the human mind to create structure and to assimilate external events to that structure. This position is very much at odds with the behaviorist view that dominated American psychology for a long time.

Before further considering Piaget's theory of development and undertaking a discussion of the notion of the concept implicit in his work, I would like to describe three divergent views of the nature of concepts and the abstraction process represented in the general psychological literature of the last half-century. The decision to begin by examining these various views of concepts is not prompted by an Aristotelian concern for specifying exactly what it is to have a concept before asking about the genesis or ontogeny of conceptual knowledge. It is instead determined by a conviction that the particular way in which the problem of conceptual knowledge is viewed affects the type of developmental theory that is believed necessary. A particular epistemological point of view, in other words, predisposes us to ask certain questions about development and not to ask (or even acknowledge the existence of) others.

The advent of cognitive psychology in the early 1960s and the Chomskian revolution in linguistics which took place at about the same time effected an ideological shift on the part of a large number of experimental psychologists. This change in perspective has given rise to a psychological *Zeitgeist* much more in tune with, and receptive to, Piaget's thinking about development than that which prevailed before 1960. It is possible to trace the course of this ideological shift by examining the notion of the concept which has dominated the field of experimental psychology from the 1920s to the present. The brief historical account of "the concept of the concept" presented in this chapter is based in part on Jenkins's (1966)

delineation of three general classes of concepts and on Cambeilh's (Note 2) review of the literature pertaining to each of them.

THE S-R VIEW

The study of conceptual behavior as an independent domain of investigation within experimental psychology can be said to have begun about sixty years ago. The philosophy and methodology of the initial research conducted on problems in the area were those of American behavioral psychology as espoused by Watson in 1913 (Watson, 1948). Essentially, behaviorism arose as a protest against psychology as defined and practiced by Wundt, Titchener, and others of the structural school (see Boring, 1950). For the structuralists the proper object of psychological study was conscious mental experience. The method of introspection was used to gain access to the structure of subjects' knowledge of the world. Radical behaviorists from Watson to Skinner (1963), on the other hand, have maintained that behavior is the only concern of psychology, and they have sought to study the observable responses of human and infrahuman organisms to objectively defined stimuli. Any attempt to introspect on the nature of what is known or perceived is condemned as unscientific and misleading, as is any reference to unobserved mental processes in descriptions or explanations of behavior. The traditional *S-R* or "nonmediated" view of conceptual behavior is thus one which defines such behavior functionally with reference to a stimulus and from which mention of organismic processes intervening (mediating) between an extra-subjective physical event and the response to that event is conspicuously absent.

The process of conceptual abstraction is considered by *S-R* theorists to be a complex form of discrimination learning. In the typical discrimination learning experiment, continuous reinforcement is used to maintain the response to an original conditioned stimulus, while a generalized conditioned response is extinguished. In other words, as a result of differential reinforcement, a particular response is made to only one of a pair of stimulus events that initially elicited the response. From the nonmediated point of view, concept learning is similar to discrimination learning, except that what is being discriminated are classes of stimuli rather than individual instances. Class membership is determined by the presence of certain stimulus features. Subjects must therefore learn to discriminate common elements in stimuli belonging to a class and, on the basis of their experience, respond to those elements when they appear in a new context. When behavior has come under the control of one or more features of a set of otherwise dissimilar stimuli, the behavior itself is designated as abstract and therefore conceptual. Adherence to this view of the nature of concepts and the abstraction process is characteristic of Hull's 1920 study, after which much of the early work on conceptual behavior was patterned, of Skinner's views as expressed in *Verbal Behavior* (1957), and of the mathematical model of concept identification proposed by Bourne and Restle (1959).

The methodology of Hull's pioneering study (Woodworth & Schlosberg, 1960, p. 610) was derived from the standard simple discrimination learning task and from verbal learning studies that utilized the paired-associates paradigm. For the purposes of Hull's research, nonsense names were assigned to twelve Chinese characters, each containing a unique smaller character called a "radical." The characters were written on cards and assembled into a pack; the subject was required to learn to associate each character with its assigned name (i.e., identify the concept presented). Following the learning trials with the first pack, a new pack of cards was produced. The subject was told that the same names would be used and that s/he was to try to "guess" the name of each character the first time around. The twelve characters in the new pack were different from those in the pack that had previously been learned, but each contained one of the original twelve radicals. The task of the subject was thus to recognize the acquired concept in a new stimulus context. After s/he had learned to identify each character in the second pack correctly, a third, fourth, fifth, and sixth were presented in which each of the same twelve radicals was represented in a novel character. The subject learned to respond to the characters in each deck with their designated names. Analysis of data consisting of the percent of correct first trial responses for each of the six decks indicated a marked increase in the subjects' ability to identify new members of a class. According to Hull, subjects had learned to discriminate the common element, the radical, in the otherwise dissimilar stimulus figures. They were subsequently able to utilize these elements in responding accurately to novel instances of the concept. Hull argued that "real-life" concepts were acquired in the same way. The meaning of a concept such as *round* is abstracted from a set of diverse experiences which have in common the element of roundness. The individual is then able to recognize roundness in unfamiliar situations.

Skinner (1957) takes a similar view of the way in which a class response is acquired. He refers to such a response as an "abstract tact," where *tact* is defined as a verbal operant—a given response evoked by a particular object or event or by a property of an object or event (pp. 81–82). According to Skinner, the abstract tact evolves through differential reinforcement of selected stimulus properties by the "verbal community," with the level of abstraction being equivalent to the ratio of unreinforced to reinforced responses (p. 114). Bourne and Restle's (1959) mathematical model of concept identification is also associationistic in spirit. It assumes conditioning of relevant stimulus elements to the conceptual response and, in addition, postulates simultaneous neutralization of, or adaptation to, irrelevant stimulus features. Informative feedback is the presumed reinforcer within this system.

Implicit in all of these formulations is the notion of a passive organism that is the target of constant stimulus bombardment. In the course of experience, associative bonds are formed between particular stimulus elements and the categorizing or conceptual response. When those elements reappear in a new stimulus context, the category response is likely to be elicited.

Many continued to adhere to the traditional nonmediated view of conceptual behavior, and a large literature concerned with the effects of such factors as stimulus complexity and delayed or misinformative feedback was amassed (see Dominowski, 1970; and Glanzer et al., 1963 for a concise treatment of this literature). But the shape of behaviorism had begun to change as S-R theorists took to "inventing hypothetical mechanisms with vigor and enthusiasm and only faint twinges of conscience" (Neisser, 1967, p. 5). A number of behaviorists undertook their investigation and analyses of conceptual behavior with these new mediational entities in mind.

THE MEDIATIONAL VIEW

One of the first proponents of a mediated view of behavior was Woodworth (1929) who suggested that the "empty-organism" S-R formulation be replaced by a new S-O-R format. Woodworth felt that knowledge of stimulus conditions alone might be inadequate for the prediction of responses. Somewhat later, Tolman formulated the notion of intervening variables. These were characteristics of the organism like age, heredity, and experience that (in theory, at least) could be manipulated as independent variables for the purpose of assessing their effect on environmental-behavioral relations. In the years following, Hull (who had by then made the transition from a traditional to a mediated point of view), Spence, and many others proposed "symbolic constructs," "hypothetical constructs," or "hypothetical entities" that were all in some general way related to Tolman's intervening variables (Watson, 1971, pp. 581–583).

Although considerable confusion regarding the nature of mediating variables continued to exist (see e.g., MacCorquodale & Meehl, 1948), many behaviorists came to acknowledge the inadequacy of the classical S-R position for explaining various psychological phenomena. In recent years the rationale for a mediated position has been broadened and has received support from a variety of sources (see e.g., Bourne, 1966; Bousfield, 1961; Osgood, 1956). Within the realm of conceptual behavior, the findings most pertinent to questions about the relative merit of the traditional and mediated positions come from studies which require subjects to solve concept problems involving solution shifts.

In a typical solution shift experiment (e.g., Kendler & Kendler, 1962), pairs of stimuli presented to subjects differ simultaneously on two dimensions—e.g., brightness (stimuli may be black or white) and size (stimuli may be large or small). Initially subjects are reinforced for responding to all stimuli that occupy a particular value on one dimension (e.g., they must always choose the black stimulus, regardless of its size). After this discrimination has been learned, the attribute to which subjects must respond in order to be rewarded is changed without warning. In one variation they are rewarded for choosing the value opposite to that previously reinforced. If choice of the black stimulus was originally reinforced, it is selection of the white one that is rewarded following the solution shift. This is called a reversal shift because the dimension (brightness) is the same, but the value rewarded has been reversed (white, rather than black). In the other variation the basis for reward is suddenly shifted to a value on the other, previously irrelevant, dimension. Rather than choosing all black stimuli, regardless of size, the subject must choose all large stimuli, regardless of whether they are black or white. This is called a nonreversal shift.

If concept formation is equivalent to a process by which associative links are formed between stimulus attributes and overt responses (the traditional *S-R* interpretation), the reversal shift should prove more difficult than the nonreversal variation. This is the case because in the nonreversal condition, half of the associations learned in the first discrimination task remain "correct" once the solution shift has been effected (i.e., choice of the large black stimulus still is reinforced; selection of the small white one still is not). Adequate performance in the reversal condition, on the other hand, requires that all the associative connections acquired in the first discrimination task be broken.

Mediation theory, however, makes the opposite prediction regarding the relative difficulty of the reversal and nonreversal shifts. According to the mediation model, "external stimulation (*S*) is translated into an implicit cue (*s*) that controls behavior. In essence, the implicit cue (*s*) represents the external environment (*S*). By representation is meant the substitution of one set of cues for another" (Kendler, 1976, p. 485). In regard to the solution shift problem, the same mediational response is used in the second discrimination task of a reversal shift as in the first, although a new overt response is required. In the nonreversal variation, a new mediational response must be acquired if the subject is to perform adequately on the second task, as well as a new overt response. Because of this additional requirement, mediation theory predicts that the nonreversal shift should prove more difficult than the reversal shift. The mediation hypothesis (Kendler & Kendler, 1962) has inspired an extensive body of research and can call upon an impressive amount of supporting data (see Harrow & Friedman, 1958; Kendler & D'Amato, 1955). It has become clear that the *S-R* interpretation of conceptual behavior is inadequate for explaining the performance of human adults on solution shift problems.

Despite what appears to be, and in some respects actually is, a significant difference between the original *S-R* and mediated positions, the latter does not really constitute a major theoretical or methodological deviation from the constraints of classical behaviorism (Fodor, 1966; Osgood, 1966) on questions pertaining to concepts and the abstraction process. Within both formulations the essence of a concept consists of the commonalities among a number of otherwise diverse stimulus events. Organisms are able to form concepts to the extent that they are capable of detecting these commonalities. In the course of the abstraction process, associative bonds (mediated by representational responses on the part of the organism, or not) are formed among stimulus attributes of successive perceptions and between these attributes and the class response. Features which differentiate successive stimulus events are ignored or forgotten. Discrimination and attention are thus key issues for the traditional *S-R* and mediational theories of conceptual behavior.

The question of how novel instances of an acquired concept are recognized also receives similar treatment within the *S-R* and mediational frameworks. The essence of the concept, the attributes that characterize all exemplars to which the organism has been exposed, are stored in memory. Novel instances of the concept are then recognized to the extent that they are perceived to possess these common attributes. The *S-R* and mediational approaches thus share an elementaristic, particularistic view of conceptual knowledge. Consistent with their emphasis on the analysis of stimuli into component elements, they show a marked lack of concern for the problem of structure. This is the case in regard to structure that prevails among stimulus events in the world, as well as structure of stored knowledge that has been abstracted from experience.

Bransford (Note 1) makes it clear that the lack of concern for external structure that is manifested by the *S-R* and mediational accounts of conceptual behavior implies some serious inadequacies on the part of those views. The difficulties posed by this failure to consider the problem of structure are summarized under two headings (pp. 26–34): (1) "Different exemplars can be instances of the same concept and yet have no elements in common"; and (2) "an adequate characterization of a particular concept . . . involves more than simply listing the elements of which it is composed." Some of the evidence presented in support of these two related statements serves to demonstrate that a perceptual order or structure involves elements plus certain relations between them and that organisms recognize and respond to similarity of patterns or structures. This is the case even when the structures are composed of different elements. Perceived similarity thus cannot be assumed to reside in distinct particulars but is necessarily abstract. It becomes clear, in the course of Bransford's argument, that the traditional and mediational views of conceptual behavior are inadequate in that they are unable to capture this abstractness.

Bransford also points out that, although they appear to, the *S-R* mediational theories do not really address the question of what a concept is. He asks how the attributes which define the essence of an acquired concept are themselves defined within these frameworks and finds that attributes are alleged to be primitive concepts. Bransford notes that, in this respect, traditional views of the concept actually presuppose the problem at hand.

Finally Bransford calls our attention to what is probably the most critical aspect of the *S-R* and mediated views of the concept. This is the set of claims they make ". . . about the relationship between experience and knowledge; about what organisms learn when they learn concepts and how that knowledge is related to what was actually experienced during acquisition of the concept" (pp. 34–37). Such claims have important implications for the type of information-processing mechanism an organism is inferred to be. According to *S-R* and mediational theory, what is retained in memory are only those features common to all instances of a concept. Elements which differentiate exemplars from one another are likely to be lost. Therefore the relationship between knowledge and experience is equivalent to that between subset and set; it is less than one-to-one. This view of the knowledge-experience relation is not shared by a third theory of conceptual behavior. Cognitive theory provides an alternative framework within which to consider concepts and the abstraction process and defines both in a manner substantially different from the way in which they were traditionally defined.

THE COGNITIVE VIEW

From a historical perspective, the cognitive psychological viewpoint may be considered most closely allied with that of Gestalt psychology in that both are "non-mechanical and focused on organized and differentiated conscious experience such as is involved in perception and thinking" (Anderson & Ausubel, 1965, p. 4). However, as Leeper (1970) points out, elements from several diverse subject areas—animal psychology, physiological psychology, psychiatry, and personality theory—united with features of Gestalt psychology to form the basis of the cognitive approach. According to the tenets of cognitive psychology, both overt behavior and conscious mental experience are appropriate phenomena for psychological study. The organism is viewed as active rather than reactive (Reese & Overton, 1970) in relation to external stimulation, and the term *cognition* is used to refer to all of the processes by which ". . . sensory input is transformed, reduced, elaborated, stored, recovered and used" by the active organism (Neisser, 1967, p. 4). Thus the distinction traditionally maintained between the "higher" and the less exalted functions of the human mind is erased. Reality is viewed as being "constructed" and "reconstructed" through the application of these cognitive operations to data provided by the senses. Whereas the goal of *S-R* psychology is the description of relations existing between concrete, particularistic environmental and behavioral events, cognitive psychologists direct their efforts toward the solution of problems concerning principles of organization and function which govern differentiated states of consciousness. From the cognitive point of view, adherence to the theories and methods of behaviorism precludes the study of some of the phenomena that are most worthwhile and requires oversimplification of a number of other psychological processes (Anderson & Ausubel, 1965).

As noted previously, *S-R* and mediation theory entail a common elements view of the concept, where the abstraction process is assumed to consist in a distillation of the attributes shared by exemplars. Contemporary cognitive theory, on the other hand, describes the concept as an abstract relational system and emphasizes the symbolic, rule-learning nature of the abstraction process. In this respect, it may be said that the cognitive viewpoint has been influenced by the work of Chomsky (1964, 1972) who holds that linguistic competence involves the ability to relate the superficial (surface) phonological structure of sentences to the underlying (deep) meaning structure. According to the tenets of transformational linguistics, possession of the concept of a grammatical sentence in a particular language and the capacity for understanding and producing such sentences is predicated on the acquisition and use of a generative rule system rather than on knowledge of individual word meanings or on experience-derived associative connections among words.

The cognitive orientation posits the existence of an inductive mechanism, similar to that which operates on rule-governed linguistic input, by which organisms acquire knowledge of the regularities of structured sequences of environmental events. Experiences are "used as examples from which general rule systems . . . which capture the regularities of these expressions are induced"

(Bransford, Note 1, p. 49). Generality is achieved, not through the loss of "irrelevant" information, but from the coding of information into more abstract form. Organisms induce general propositions that go beyond their specific experiences. The knowledge-experience relation, which was described as being less than one-to-one within the traditional view of the concept, is thus considered by cognitive theorists to be greater than one-to-one; the organism knows something more than what it has experienced. In addition the individual who has acquired a concept is said to have knowledge *from* experience, but not necessarily *of* past events (ibid.). This is the case because what has been stored is assumed to be an abstract rule system, rather than individual stimulus events or properties of stimuli. Just as knowledge of the rules of transformational grammar allows an individual to generate and understand sentences he has never heard before, the system learned when a concept has been acquired is capable of generating novel instances as well as those from which it was induced. It may therefore be difficult to distinguish old from new exemplars of a concept.

The results of two independent lines of research conducted during the last two decades indicate rather unambiguously that what is abstracted from experience is a rule or a relational system. These findings demonstrate that learning of a set of stimuli entails an internal integration of the structural parameters of the set. They also provide evidence that the learning of structure determines learning and remembering of individual stimulus items and may even preempt the learning of individual stimuli.

One such series of studies (henceforth referred to as "the Garner studies") was conducted by Garner and his associates over several years (Garner & Degerman, 1967; Garner & Whitman, 1965; Whitman & Garner, 1962, 1963) and employed the method of free-recall learning. In a free-recall learning experiment, subjects are exposed to a group of stimuli, such as visual forms or nonsense syllables, and are later asked to reproduce in any order all stimuli presented during acquisition. Only one of these studies (Whitman & Garner, 1963) was undertaken to explore conceptual behavior per se, but the results of all of them shed light on the relation between knowledge and experience and are thus directly relevant to the problem of conceptual abstraction.

The Garner studies were designed to investigate the effects of form and amount of relational set structure on free-recall learning. By orthogonally combining the values on a small number of stimulus dimensions, a hypothetical set of stimuli was generated. Subjects were then exposed to specially selected subsets of the total set. These subsets were chosen in such a way that all attributes characterizing stimuli in the larger set were also represented in the subset. But because not every arrangement of attributes contained in the total set was present in the subset, an internal constraint or correlational structure could be said to have been imposed on the subset. Under these conditions the *form* of structure depends on which particular stimuli are selected from the total set, since the selection procedure defines the relations existing among the attributes. The *amount* of internal structure is determined by the size of the subset in relation to the size of the total set. The greater the differences in size between the total set and the subset to be learned, the greater the amount of internal structure possessed by the subset.

The subsets selected by Garner from his total stimulus sets assumed one of two forms of internal structure: simple paired contingencies or more complex interactions among stimulus characteristics. The effects of structure on free-recall learning were explored most fully in a study by Garner and Whitman (1965). This research employed nonsense words generated by using two alternative letters in each of four positions. The total stimulus set thus had sixteen members. Various subsets of size four or eight were then formed. All of the subsets containing four stimuli had the same simple correlational structure; two simple contingencies existed in that the first two letters were correlated and the last two letters were correlated. The four-member subsets were then combined into subsets of eight in such a way as to give the larger subsets either a simple or a complex form of structure. Following is a summary of the results of the learning experiments carried out with these stimuli.

1. As had been demonstrated in a previous study which employed geometric stimuli (Whitman & Garner, 1962), the form of internal structure was found to be an important determinant of performance on the free-recall task. Subsets of eight stimuli characterized by simple contingencies between variables were learned much more quickly than were eight-member subsets in which interactive contingencies prevailed.

2. It was found that slightly fewer trials were required to learn the total set of sixteen words than to learn subsets of eight words with simple structure. This finding stands in contradiction to the traditionally held notion that learning is a direct function of list length. The authors interpreted their findings as indicating that the internal structure of a set of stimuli is as important a determinant of learning as is the number of stimuli contained in the set. They wrote, "... a subset of words should be more difficult to learn than the total set itself, even though it is a small set of words, because the internal structure of the subset gives ... [the subject] something to learn which the total set does not" (Garner & Whitman, 1965, p. 262). In other words learning a subset requires that a subject learn the dimensional components of the total set and, in addition, learn the correlational structure of the subset itself.

3. The amount of time taken by a group of subjects to learn a subset of eight words with simple structure was not diminished by having previously learned the total set of sixteen words. This result is startling if one fails to consider the factor of internal structure, since when a subject has initially learned a total set of sixteen words, it is reasonable to expect that s/he already knows the eight words comprising the subset to be learned in the following task. But, if learning of a subset is assumed to involve apprehending the structure of the subset, rather than learning the individual items, then it becomes apparent that learning the whole set does not necessarily help in learning a subset. It was found, however, that learning an eight-word subset did facilitate learning of the total set. This finding is consistent with the notion that in learning a subset, one implicitly learns the whole set from which it has been drawn.

Free-recall learning was used by Whitman and Garner (1963) to study concept acquisition. The decision to employ this method is explained by Garner (1974).

... [T]he important part of a concept problem is not to tell the positive instances from the negative ones or the A's from the B's but rather to learn what goes together to form the single class—in other words, to learn what the subset is that is called "A" or "yes" or is the righthand button. If the concept problem is really more a matter of learning subsets within defined total sets, rather than discriminating subset from subset, then learning techniques more like free recall are the appropriate ones, and just possibly the use of the paired associates paradigm inappropriately changes the nature of the problem for the subject. (p. 83)

For Garner, then, solving a concept problem is tantamount to learning both a stuctured subset and the larger set within which it is contained. If this is a valid way of viewing the subject's task, then structure may be expected to play an important role in concept learning.

Whitman and Garner (1963) found that if the amount of internal structure was held constant, the introduction of constraint in the form of simple paired contingencies facilitated concept attainment, whereas learning was impeded when the internal stucture of the subset assumed the form of interactions involving three or more variables. The results of studies by Peters and Denney (1971) and by Gottwald (1971) also indicate that concept and classification learning is most appropriately considered in terms of the learning of subsets of stimuli with specifiable structure. On the basis of his own work and that of these investigators, Garner (1974) concludes,

While the ability of a subject to discriminate between positive and negative instances or just between different classes of stimuli is an ultimate consequence of a subject's learning what stimuli go into each class, it is a secondary consequence that does not define or establish the essence of concept learning. (p. 86)

Garner's view of the nature of concept learning thus differs in important respects from traditional views within which the processes of discrimination and attention are of primary significance and the factor of structure is virtually ignored.

A second set of findings corroborates the notion that what is derived from experience and stored for later use in recognizing exemplars of a concept cannot be viewed as a series of individual stimulus events or characteristics shared by the members of such a series. The research to be described deals with the question of what is learned when one is exposed to meaningful verbal material. As was the case with the Garner studies, the findings demonstrate that exposure to a set of stimuli (here a set of sentences, rather than letter configurations) results in an internal integration of the structural parameters of the set. A "wholistic semantic description" or idea (concept) is constructed from the individual elements which make up the input *and from the individual's store of previously acquired knowledge.* Subsequent stimulus events qualify as "exemplars" of the acquired idea or concept to the extent that they are consistent with its meaning. The rationale of these studies adheres to the general tenets of cognitive psychology but derives more directly from Bartlett's work on memory.

Bartlett's theory of memory, presented in his classic text *Remembering* (1932), differed in essential respects from those popular in his time. Bartlett studied the phenomenon of distortion in recall and maintained that remembering is a process of active imaginative reconstruction rather than one which consists in the excitation or calling forth of static traces laid down on some previous occasion. Departing from the tradition established by researchers such as Ebbinghaus who employed unrelated words or nonsense syllables as stimuli, Bartlett presented his subjects with meaningful material. They read stories a paragraph or two in length and were tested for recall at various intervals afterward. Bartlett observed that although the subjects believed they were recalling the material accurately, their research protocols contained frequent errors of a systematic kind. Many details, especially those perceived as meaningless or inconsistent, were omitted from the subjects' accounts of what had been presented and often only an overall impression or general idea was retained. While the stories produced were likely to be shorter and more concrete than the originals, Bartlett noted that certain story elements had been elaborated. The nature of these elaborations indicated that the theme of the material and a small number of particulars had been used as a basis for reconstructing the remaining details according to subjects' expectations about what must have been the case.

To explain his findings Bartlett invoked the notion of *schemata,* integrated organized representations of past experience and behavior to which meaningful material becomes assimilated. These knowledge structures were assumed to become activated at the time of recall and to guide the individual in reconstructing a previously encountered series of events. Bartlett believed that his subjects' prior knowledge of the world had been used to produce a coherent, meaningful construction from the sometimes meager information they retained as a result of exposure to the acquisition material. Distortion thus resulted from what he called "effort after meaning." Bartlett's work received little notice until cognitive psychology, with its emphasis on the active organism and its recognition of the interaction between memorial and other functions of the human mind, came into being.

While the theoretical underpinnings of recent research concerned with the question of what it is that is acquired and stored when one learns verbal material came from Bartlett, its methodology is essentially that of an experiment carried out by Franks and Bransford (reported in Bransford, Note 1) which employed visual patterns as stimuli. For the purposes of this study, various spatial arrangements of colored figures were used to form visual configurations. A total hypothetical set was generated from all possible combinations of all figures in all four spatial quadrants. By placing constraints on the randomness inherent in the total set, a subset was formed. The constraints were such that each configuration in the subset had to be related to all other configurations by a specified group of transformations (e.g., substitutions, deletions). Subjects were then exposed to selected members of this subset and asked to reproduce them. Following acquisition the subjects were shown patterns of three distinct types and were asked whether they had seen each configuration before. They were also requested to assign confidence ratings to each of their responses. The pattern types were (1) "old" (presented during acquisition), (2) "novel" (not presented during

acquisition but related transformationally to the acquisition stimuli), and (3) "noncase" (not presented during acquisition and not transformationally related to the acquisition stimuli). The results demonstrated that experience with selected stimuli from the subset resulted in tacit knowledge of the relational system which prevailed among the members of this group of stimuli. Ratings assigned to novel configurations were as high as, or higher than, those given to old patterns. Subjects were quite confident that they had seen the novel stimuli before, although they actually had not been exposed to these stimuli during acquisition. Noncase stimuli received very low ratings, relative to the other types of configurations.

Like Garner's results these findings indicate that subjects perceive and respond to relations existing among acquisition stimuli. The integrated representation of the system governing these relations is then used in deciding whether or not configurations encountered later are instances of the acquired concept. The fact that patterns derived by means of transformations permissible within the system were "recognized," despite the fact that subjects had never seen them before, provides strong evidence that in learning the acquisition stimuli they also gained knowledge of the stuctured subset from which these patterns were drawn. The results of the Franks and Bransford study receive confirmation from those of semantic integration experiments whose methodology is similar but in which sentences are employed instead of visual patterns. Although Bransford did not conduct all of the semantic integration experiments, many of them are his and for the sake of convenience I will refer to this body of work as "the Bransford studies."

The typical semantic integration study begins with an acquisition phase consisting in the consecutive presentation of a set of simple sentences which, taken together, express a complex idea. Subjects are later asked to indicate whether or not each of a number of test sentences had been included in the acquisition set and to assign confidence ratings to their judgments. Stimuli are of three types: (1) "old" (presented during acquisition), (2) "novel" (not presented during acquisition but consistent with the expressed idea), and (3) "noncase" (not presented during acquisition nor consistent with the expressed idea).

Employing this paradigm, Bransford and Franks (1971) found that subjects had difficulty distinguishing "old" from "novel" sentences but readily rejected "noncase" test stimuli. In addition it was discovered that the degree of confidence expressed in regard to judgments about a particular sentence reflected the extent to which the complete idea contained in the acquisition material was represented in that sentence. It appeared that what had been learned as a result of exposure to the acquisition material and stored in memory was a wholistic representation of the material—the complete idea rather than a set of partial meanings expressed by individual acquisition sentences. Subjects' memory representations seemed to have originated from the integration of information contained in several sentences and to include ideas not directly expressed in any one of them. Further research by Franks and Bransford (1972) and by Marschark and Paivio (1977) demonstrated that this strategy was not limited to the processing of material which could be easily imaged; evidence for semantic integration was found using material of an abstract nature as well.

As research on semantic integration continued, it became clear that the process utilizes an individual's general knowledge of the world, as well as information presented within the framework of a specific acquisition task. Experiments designed to investigate semantic integration as a joint function of prior knowledge and present input do so by varying the amount of context provided and the sequencing of contextual information with respect to the acquisition material.

In their research Bransford and Johnson (1972, 1973) employed a prose passage whose overall meaning was unclear, although the vocabulary items were familiar and the sentences which comprised the passage followed rules of normal English construction. This material was presented to three independent groups of subjects. Those in one group were given a topic designed to activate knowledge relevant to the content of the passage. They were told what the topic was before being exposed to the acquisition material. A second group was provided with the same contextual information, but the topic was not disclosed until after the subjects had read the passage. A third group was given no contextual information. Recall was much better and comprehensibility ratings considerably higher in the first group than in the other two, suggesting that the activation of relevant contextual knowledge was a prerequisite for the encoding of the prose information. Similar results were obtained in another experiment by the same investigators (1972) in which pictures, instead of topics, were used to activate knowledge relevant to the acquisition material. This study included a "partial context" condition in which the picture shown to subjects before they read the passage contained all objects represented in the "appropriate context" picture, but the objects were arranged in such a way that the picture did not specify the nature of the relations existing among the concrete story elements. Subjects in the partial context condition experienced as much difficulty comprehending and remembering the passage as did those who received no contextual information.

These findings demonstrate that "attention to semantic properties alone will not guarantee the availability of an adequate context for the comprehension of prose" (Bransford & Johnson, 1972, p. 724). New material is integrated with prior knowledge of related material to form a wholistic idea or relational concept which is then stored in memory. Individual items of new information function jointly with previously acquired knowledge to allow the construction of an integrated semantic description. For prior knowledge to aid comprehension and recall, it must be activated and be present during the ongoing process of comprehension. Contextual cues serve to "address" that portion of the previously existing knowledge structure to which new information will be assimilated. When contextual cues are not available or when such cues fail for some reason to activate a suitable cognitive framework, integration is hampered and comprehension and recall are poor.

An additional group of studies provides further insight into the nature of what is acquired and stored as a result of exposure to a series of linguistic events (Barclay, 1973; Bransford, Barclay, & Franks, 1972; Doolings &

Christiaansen, 1977; Fredriksen, 1975; Harris, Teske, & Ginns, 1975; Potts, 1974; Thorndyke, 1976). Their results indicate that subjects not only store an integrated representation of new material, but in addition store information that can be logically deduced from the original material or that can be inferred based on a particular domain of world knowledge. Thus, the integrated representation often contains more information than was given during acquisition. These findings, and those of the previously described studies on the effects of semantic and perceptual structure, do not allow us to specify exactly what it is that is extracted from experience and stored for later use in recognizing nonidentical recurrences of events. However it is clear that this acquired knowledge cannot be adequately characterized as a copy of previous experience or as a set of elements common to a sequence of experienced stimulus events.

Summary

This section explored three theories of the nature of concepts and the abstraction process. It was suggested that the *S-R* and mediation theories, which view concepts as sets of elements common to a number of otherwise diverse stimulus events, were inadequate in several respects. The perspective from which cognitive theory views concepts and the abstraction process was shown to be quite different. Although at the moment the answers which this theory provides to questions about concepts and the abstraction process are less clearcut than those given within the *S-R* and mediational frameworks, a number of empirical findings indicate that the cognitive approach is a valid one.

Cognitive theory views the concept as an abstract relational system from which specific exemplars may be derived. These include, but are not limited to, that group of exemplars from which the system was induced. The system is said to be abstract in that information has been coded into general terms which specify permissible variations among exemplars, rather than on the grounds that a small portion of the input has been retained, while the rest has been ignored or forgotten. Cognitive theory assumes that novel events are judged to be instances of a concept to the extent that they can be generated from the relational structure acquired.

Very different inferences are likely to be drawn about the organism as an information-processing mechanism based on each of these views of the conceptual abstraction process (see Bransford, Note 1, p. 54). The *S-R* and mediated views emphasize the processes of discrimination and attention necessary for isolating features common to a series of exemplars of a concept. Cognitive theory, on the other hand, assumes an organism capable of apprehending the regularities inherent in its experience and of inducing a relational system which captures those regularities and has the power to predict. In order to construct such a rule or relational system, the organism must be capable of integrating information from a number of temporally disparate stimulus events (Bransford, Note 1, pp. 69–73).

Age-related change in conceptual functioning is also described very differently by those who subscribe to the various views of concepts and the abstraction process. *S-*

R theorists have, for the most part, shown little concern with developmental research; their aim has been to identify general laws of behavior which hold across all age groups. Complex behavior like thinking is interpreted within the *S-R* framework as being reducible to simple associative connections between environmental stimuli and behavioral responses. To the extent that development is discussed at all, it is described in terms of a gradual increase with age in the number and strength of such connections as a result of reinforcement. Children learn from experience to discriminate and respond selectively to particular features of stimuli that they encounter in the environment. Age-related change is thus viewed as being quantitative rather than qualitative.

The fact that nonreversal shifts on concept attainment problems are easier for young children than are reversal shifts (Kendler & Kendler, 1970; Kendler, Kendler, & Learnard, 1962) while the converse is true for older children and adults has led mediation theorists to postulate a developmental shift during childhood from external to internal control of behavior (see Kendler, 1976). The single-unit *S-R* theory which assumes direct association between external stimulus and overt response is viewed as appropriate for predicting the behavior of young children on concept problems that require a solution shift, whereas the performance of adults requires a mediation model. The external-internal shift is attributed to an age-related increase in the ability to generate symbolic representational responses; older children, but not younger ones, are capable of translating an external stimulus into an implicit cue that more effectively controls behavior than the stimulus itself does. While other interpretations of the solution shift data are possible (see Osler & Madden, 1973), the description of age-related change in conceptual behavior put forth by the mediation theorists themselves is similar to that given by proponents of traditional *S-R* theory in that it does not involve a qualitative change in the nature of the concept or the abstraction process.

Cognitive theory posits an inherently active organism which does not simply respond to environmental events but transforms incoming information and incorporates it into the structure of things already known. Mental functioning is interpreted in organic terms; the analogy is to a living organism composed of a number of interrelated systems of action rather than a machine whose complex behavior can ultimately be reduced to simple cause-effect phenomena. From this perspective, development is seen as the outcome of a series of qualitative changes in the structure of a system of knowledge.

THE PIAGETIAN NOTION OF THE CONCEPT

Piaget, the principal proponent of the cognitive view of development, offers a theory that represents an integration of the disciplines of biology and epistemology. Piaget was trained as a biological scientist, and his thinking has been deeply influenced by Darwinian evolutionary theory, particularly the notion that processes and states can best be understood in terms of their developmental course. Also evident in his work is the fascination with

mind that is the hallmark of the French intellectual tradition. Furth (1969, p. 9) points out that Piaget has primarily been concerned with two questions: (1) What is the nature of intelligence? and (2) What is the source of knowledge? For Piaget these are empirical questions rather than philosophical issues warranting armchair analysis.

Central to Piaget's investigation has been the biological concept of adaptation. Adaptation on the part of any living thing involves a restructuring of its activity in response to the demands of the environment. Such restructuring frequently results in a lasting alteration of form. According to Piaget (1971), intelligence is a process of continuous active psychological adaptation to a complex physical and social world—a special case, as it were, of general biological adaptation. Action, whether direct or executed on the representational plane, is thus the essence of intelligence. Actions cannot be understood in isolation from one another, however, nor does a thorough knowledge of the stimulus conditions under which they occur constitute an adequate basis for inferring their significance. Piaget believes that underlying all human behavior is coherent, meaningful structure. This structure, which is accessible to logical analysis, reflects the fundamental nature of human thought and therefore the biological structure of the human mind. A reaction on the part of an organism is also the response of the underlying structure within the organism. In order to understand intelligent action, it is necessary to investigate the underlying cognitive structures that render such action possible and adaptively appropriate (Furth, 1969, p. 13). Even the stimulus is not something external, "out there," but rather something that is actively constructed by the subject who assimilates environmental events to his/her own previously existing cognitive structures.

Piaget holds that behavior at all levels is characterized by structure, but that structure takes different forms at different ages. The overt behavioral schemes of the infant (coherent patterns of action derived from innate reflexes) are elaborated, coordinated, and internalized to give rise to the reversible mental operations that can be applied to concrete objects by the eight-year-old. These eventually become the logically organized systems of formal operations that constitute adult intelligence. The cognitive structures change gradually in the course of the subject's interaction with the world by *accommodating* to environmental events. However, the structures originate from within the organism, and their integrity is maintained throughout development by a series of internal coordinations whose aim is the achievement of a harmonious balance or equilibrium between assimilation and accommodation. Knowledge, then, which is identified with cognitive structures, is not imposed on the organism from the outside, nor does it inhere in the individual from the outset. It is instead constructed through continuous interaction between the subject and the external world. Knowledge of objects and of relations among them is the result of a subject's actions upon them. Piaget (1970) writes,

From the most elementary sensorimotor actions (such as pushing and pulling) to the most sophisticated intellectual operations, which are interiorized actions carried out mentally (e.g., joining together, putting in order, putting into one-to-one correspondence), knowledge is constantly linked with actions or operations. (p. 704)

To my knowledge Piaget does not have a general "theory of the concept"; his ideas regarding the nature of concepts and the abstraction process must be distilled from his writings on other topics. Such a distillation process makes evident basic similarities between Piaget's thinking over the last forty years on the subject of conceptual development and that of cognitive theorists conducting experiments with adult subjects during the mid-1960s and 1970s.

Three areas of Piaget's work seem to be most revealing of his point of view regarding concepts: (1) memory, (2) object permanence and conservation, and (3) classification. While I will not offer a comprehensive treatment of Piaget's ideas on these topics, I will present some of the major theoretical notions involved, as well as a small amount of the research on which they are based. I will also point out the relations that seem to me to be extant between Piaget's theoretical formulations and those which receive support from the experimental findings of Garner and Bransford.

Memory

The research conducted by Bransford and his colleagues and by Garner addressed the question of what is acquired and stored for subsequent use as a result of exposure to a series of environmental events. The findings indicate that subjects construct a wholistic idea or relational system from the isolated stimulus elements with which they are presented. The nature of this internal representation is partially determined by the individual's store of previously acquired knowledge. Piaget's investigation of memory in children (e.g., Piaget, 1968; Piaget & Inhelder, 1973) is concerned with the same question, and the answer which Piaget provides is strikingly similar to that which was arrived at by Bransford working with adult subjects.

Piaget holds that the form in which experience will be stored is determined by the level of a child's intelligence as embodied in the cognitive structures he has evolved. The individual's level of understanding of a concept influences the memory representation of an encountered instance of that concept. Reference to some of Piaget's writings may help to clarify the meaning of these statements.

Piaget's previous work on the child's concept of number (1952a) established that an understanding of ordinal relations develops only gradually. Until the stage of concrete operations is reached (at about age seven), children are unable to construct an ordered series of objects which differ on a single dimension. To investigate the influence of knowing on remembering, Piaget (1968) presented children of various ages with a series of ten wooden rods that had been arranged in size order without the children's assistance. His subjects were asked to look closely at the series and to try to remember what they saw. One week later each child was requested to recall the series by drawing it. The experimenter subsequently determined the child's stage of development with respect to seriation

by administering the standard tests designed by Piaget for that purpose. It was found that children at the preoperational level of development, who did not possess mature seriation schemes, produced distorted reproductions of the configuration, whereas those at a more advanced level reproduced the series correctly. In addition after eight months during which time they had no experience with the series of rods, a number of children who had been unable to produce a veridical representation of the series one week after seeing it demonstrated an ability to do so.

Piaget interpreted these and other of his findings as indicating that remembering is not a process by which discrete environmental events are passively recorded and stored. Human beings actively construct an integrated representation whose nature is determined by the scheme with which the stimulus material is associated. If a mature scheme is present, assimilation of stimulus events to this structure will result in an accurate representation of the events. If such a scheme has not been completely evolved, assimilation to the existing scheme will produce a distorted representation of the stimuli.

A distinction is drawn by Piaget between memory "in the strict sense" and memory "in the wider sense." The latter refers to "the conservation of the entire past, or at least of everything in the subject's past that serves to inform his present action or understanding" (Piaget & Inhelder, 1973, p. 1). Memory in the wider sense really has to do with conservation of schemes, the functional units of intelligence. This type of memory involves aspects of past experience which are generalizable over many specific cases. Memory in the strict sense, on the other hand, refers to memory for particular objects or events from the past. This aspect of memory does not involve general concepts but pertains to "particular situations we ourselves have encountered and which we can localize in time more or less accurately" (Piaget & Inhelder, 1973, p. 5).

According to Piaget, memory in the strict sense is dependent on memory in the wider sense. The conservation of any given memory is dependent on the conservation of the scheme to which it has been assimilated. With time the scheme develops, and the memory representation is altered in the direction of greater accuracy. This explains why the recall of some of Piaget's subjects actually improved over time. These children, whose level of intelligence (here defined as their existing schemes for seriation) initially prevented them from ordering the materials accurately, had during the eight months coordinated the mental operations necessary for performing the task.

The behavioral schemes of infancy and the "intuitive" sequences of action executed on the representational plane by the preoperational child are not considered by Piaget to be concepts per se. This is because they do not exhibit the coherent structure of the systems of intellectual operations which appear later on in the course of development. Nonetheless Piaget recognizes similarities between schemes and concepts, even at the sensorimotor level: "The scheme as it appears to us constitutes a sort of sensorimotor concept or, more broadly, the motor equivalent of a system of classes and relations" (Piaget, 1952b, p. 385). Within Piaget's theoretical framework, that which is derived from experience and used in dealing with subsequently occurring events is presumed to be a set of actions or mental operations that can be applied to these events. The scheme or concept may be viewed as a set of rules for acting in relation to things in the milieu—a "mobile frame" of physical or mental action that is successively applied to various contents. For example, to possess the concept of an ordered series is to recognize the necessity for comparing each element in a set with its neighbor in one direction and its neighbor in the other direction. This strategy is a general one that must be employed irrespective of the dimension along which a particular series is to be ordered.

It is clear that the notion of the concept implicit in Piaget's writings on memory has a good deal in common with that described more explicitly by Garner and Bransford. For Piaget, as for these investigators, what is stored is neither a copy of past experience nor individual elements common to a sequence of stimulus events but a general system from which specific exemplars may be derived. Individuals acquire knowledge *from* past experience, but not necessarily *of* the particular events that constitute experience and from which the system has been induced. A newly encountered series of stimulus events is perceived in terms of the relations existing among its members. The nature of the integrated description of these events which the subjects construct is dictated by their store of previously acquired conceptual knowledge. Environmental events are transformed in the process of assimilation to existing cognitive structures. When appropriate structures do not yet exist, are inadequate, or are not properly "addressed" by the stimulus context, the material cannot be assimilated, and comprehension and recall are poor.

Object Permanence and Conservation

Adults possess many different kinds of concepts of greater or lesser abstractness and generality, but undoubtedly the most important is the concept of the single unitary object. Piaget has established that the object concept is not present at birth and does not appear fully formed at some later time. Instead it develops gradually during the first two years of life as a result of the child's continuous interaction with the environment. In order to understand the evolution of the object concept, it is necessary to know something about the end state toward which it progresses—that is, about the mature object concept as it is defined by Piaget. An *object*, according to Piaget, is something which moves in a space common to it and to the subject who observes it (Flavell, 1963, p. 129). However the object is an entity in its own right whose continued existence is independent of the subject's immediate perceptions of it. Individuals who possess such an object concept believe that things continue to exist even when they can no longer see them and, in their search for an object which has disappeared, are able to take into account various invisible displacements of the object in the common space.

Since the core of the Piagetian object concept is the understanding that things continue to exist when one can no longer see or act directly upon them, Piaget's exploration of the development of the concept of a permanent object (1954) has focused on the way in which infants behave when an object is removed from sight. He has identified six stages in the formation or construction of the concept of the permanent object. During the first stage the infant reacts only to events which impinge directly on his/her senses. When an object appears, the child is likely to stare or smile at it, but when the object is withdrawn the infant stops looking and occupies him/herself with whatever remains in the perceptual field. The fact that the young infant exhibits no special behavior when objects vanish suggests that s/he does not view the universe as being divided into things which have substance and are external to the self. Instead s/he perceives images or "pictures" (ibid., p. 8) which have no relation to one another. At this stage the infant cannot separate the object from the sensorimotor schemes to which s/he assimilates it.

During Stage 2 the infant begins to move in the direction of a mature object concept. The infant coordinates various perceptual schemes which previously functioned in an independent manner and, upon hearing a sound, will now turn in the direction from which it comes in order to see what produced it. S/he also follows an object visually (i.e., accommodates the "looking scheme" to a moving object). However when the object disappears, the infant continues to stare at the place where it was last seen. It is not until Stage 3 that the child possesses sufficient expectations regarding the continued existence of things that s/he is moved to action when a desired object disappears from sight.

In the third stage the infant becomes capable of anticipating an object's movement even though s/he may be unable to see it—for example looking on the floor for an object which s/he has seen dropped from above. When the child is looking at or manipulating an object and his/her attention is directed elsewhere, the interrupted action is often resumed spontaneously as though the infant takes for granted the continuing availability of the object. If a toy at which the infant is looking is partially covered by a cloth, s/he tries to lift the cloth to discover the rest of the object. While this behavior may suggest to a casual observer that the child already perceives objects as having a permanent, independent existence, further investigation reveals that the object concept remains subjective in that it is still closely tied to the infant's own actions. The "search" for a vanished object, for example, consists only in a continuation of movements of the eyes or hands that were initiated while the object was still in view. The infant's aim in continuing these actions, according to Piaget, is to somehow recapture an interesting experience, rather than to locate the object per se.

Stage 4 brings an active search for vanished objects. The infant begins to look for objects outside his/her perceptual field and studies the displacements of moving objects. However, the child still identifies the object with a particular location, generally the one in which s/he has been successful in finding it before. This becomes apparent when an object that has previously been hidden and found in a particular spot is hidden there again but is subsequently moved to a second location while the child is watching. Under these circumstances the infant is unable to take note of the successive displacements s/he has witnessed and searches for the object in the original place. For the Stage 4 child, the object cannot move to a variety of locations and remain the same object.

During the next stage the ability to follow an object through a visible sequence of movements is finally manifested. The child understands positional relations between the object and other elements in the environment, including him/herself, and no longer connects the object with a particular location or situation (e.g., previous success in finding it). The permanence conferred by the infant on the object, however, is still conditional in that it is limited to situations in which the movement of the object is visible. If the Stage 5 child must imagine or infer such movement, s/he reverts to the response that was characteristic of the previous stage, looking for the object where it was successfully found in the past.

By the end of the second year of life, the sensorimotor schemes have become internalized, and the child is able to use mental symbols and words to represent absent objects. In doing so s/he begins to be free from domination by the concrete situation in all aspects of mental life. This freedom is manifested in the realm of object permanence by the ability to locate an object which has undergone a series of invisible displacements. The child is able to do this because s/he has formed a mental representation of the object and can imagine a series of possible loci which it might occupy in the common space.

Piaget's account of the development of the object concept is really a description of how the child learns that things retain their identity despite certain changes and transformations. The infant gradually comes to understand that objects continue to exist in a particular form, regardless of the sensorimotor schemes to which s/he happens to be assimilating them at the moment and irrespective of whether their disappearance from the perceptual field prevents the child from acting on them at all. The existence and nature of the object become independent of the locus at which the child has just seen it disappear or has found it in the past. The development of an object concept that is resistant to variations of appearance due to position in space is the result of the child's continuous interaction with the environment. When an infant lifts the cloth partially covering a toy which s/he has seen hidden, for example, this is done because previous sensorimotor experience with the toy has taught him/her something about its properties and about the many different appearances it may take. The child has handled it and viewed it from various distances and visual angles and is therefore able to recognize it as the same object, even though only a portion of it is in view at the moment.

The development of the concept of a permanent object, then, represents an adaptation on the part of the child to several kinds of transformations that things may undergo. These variations go unnoticed by adults and certainly pose no problems of conception for the mature individual, but Piaget's work on the origins of intelligence, conducted during the late 1920s and early 1930s, showed that they do pose such problems for the infant. The young child must learn to deal with these variations to negotiate successfully in a world where objects continually change position in relation to him/her and to one another and periodically leave and reenter the perceptual field. The studies of the child's ability to conserve physical properties (quantity, weight, volume) which Piaget conducted somewhat later as part of an investigation of the ontogeny of scientific thinking are concerned

with a related, but more subtle, achievement on the part of the child—learning that certain attributes of objects themselves remain invariant despite readily observable changes in other attributes.

One of Piaget's most striking findings in connection with the capacity for scientific thought was that it is not until the age of seven or eight, the advent of the stage of concrete operations, that the child can be said to have a concept of physical quantity. A thorough understanding of weight is not developed until age ten or eleven and possession of the concept of volume is not common until age twelve. Since for Piaget, thought is closely bound to action on the environment (especially in school-age children), he explores the development of these concepts by posing problems to children of various ages which require them to manipulate and answer questions about objects and substances that are present before them. (This work is discussed most completely in Piaget & Inhelder, 1941; see also Inhelder & Piaget, 1958; Piaget, 1952a.)

For example the child is given a ball of clay and asked to make another just like it, just as big and heavy. The experimenter retains one of the balls as a standard of comparison and while the child watches alters the other in some way: rolls the ball into a sausage, flattens it into a cake, or cuts it into several pieces. The experimenter then employs several procedures, whose nature depends on the type of concept being investigated, to see whether the child believes that the alteration in form has resulted in a change in the amount, weight, or volume of clay, or whether s/he is aware that these properties have remained invariant (been conserved).

For the purpose of investigating the notion of substance or quantity, the child is simply asked if there is as much clay in the transformed piece as in the standard. In the case of weight, a scale balance is used; the experimenter inquires as to whether the standard and altered pieces weigh the same, i.e., would balance the scale or make the arm horizontal if they were placed on opposite sides. In assessing conservation of volume, the experimenter uses a pair of identical beakers containing equal quantities of liquid. After the child has formed two balls of clay and has asserted that they are equally large and heavy, the experimenter shows that when the balls are placed in the containers they displace an equal volume of liquid (cause the water level to rise to the same height). Then the experimenter alters the appearance of one of the balls and asks whether it will still make the water level rise to that height.

Conservation may also be assessed using other substances. To study the conservation of liquid quantity, the experimenter pours water into two identically shaped containers and gains the child's assent that both have the same amount of liquid in them. Then either s/he or the child pours the water from one of the containers into a vessel of a completely different shape, e.g., one much taller and thinner than the original. Following this procedure the child is asked whether the first container, in which the liquid has remained, and the new, differently shaped container each have the same amount of water or if one has more than the other.

Piaget's investigation revealed similar developmental trends for quantity, weight, and volume although, as mentioned before, these concepts are not acquired at the same time. Initially there is no conservation. For example the child asserts that the sausage has more clay than the standard because "it is longer" or that the tall, thin container has more liquid because "the water goes higher." It is useless to try to convince the child otherwise. Even if s/he eventually concedes that there is the same amount in each piece of clay or in each container, the child will make a similar error on subsequent conservation tasks. Additional procedures can be used to verify that the child actually believes a change in quantity has occurred. If asked to pour the same amount of liquid into a tall, narrow and a short, wide container, s/he will pour the water to the same level, despite the disproportion in amount that results from this action.

The total lack of ability to conserve is followed by a tenuous, empirically based conservation. The child asserts that the quantity, weight, or volume is the same after some transformations but not others. Finally there exists evidence for the existence of a logical, almost axiomatic conservation. The child expresses certainty that no change in quantity, weight, or volume has occurred as a result of any of the transformations s/he has witnessed and, in fact, seems to regard as absurd the experimenter's questions regarding the possibility of such change.

Piaget explains the achievement of conservation in terms of perceptual decentration and the reversibility that is characteristic of concrete operations. The child initially attends exclusively to, or *centers* on, a single perceptual attribute of the situation (e.g., the greater length of the sausage as compared with the standard) and bases judgments on this one factor. Later the child is able to note other factors as well (e.g., the comparatively smaller width of the sausage) but is incapable of systematically coordinating these perceptions. S/he cannot take them both into account in making a judgment and does not yet understand that a decrease in one dimension is exactly compensated by an increase in the other. The eventual grasp of these relations indicates that there has been a shift of conceptual focus from states alone to the transformations that lead from one state to the next. Not only does the child see that every change in one dimension is compensated by an inversely proportionate change in another, but also comes to realize that every actual transformation has associated with it a potential transformation that annuls it—the sausage can be rolled back into a ball, the liquid can be returned to the original vessel. The outcome of this developmental process is a rigorous conservation of physical properties.

There is a clear analogy between the conservation problems posed to children of preschool and school age and the problem confronting the infant engaged in constructing an object concept. In the latter case the child must discover that the sheer existence of an object remains invariant despite the fact that it has moved to a new position in space. The conservation tasks require that the child recognize the invariance of particular attributes of objects in the face of changes in other attributes (Flavell, 1963, p. 299). The essence of both achievements is an ability to construct concepts that capture permissible variations. The formation of such concepts allows the child to deal adaptively with environmental transformations.

Every concept has two different kinds of content (see Elkind, 1969). The first of these, *extensive content,* is de-

scribed by listing the objects that the concept points to or denotes. The second kind of content is referred to as *intensive content* and has to do with the basis on which a group of things are regarded as belonging together. Extensive content is assessed by presenting a subject with a group of exemplars that vary widely among themselves and asking him/her to classify them. Access to the intensive content of concepts is generally gained through verbal definition procedures.

The *S-R* and mediated views of conceptual behavior are primarily concerned with the extensive content of concepts. Possession of a concept is evidenced by a "common response to dissimilar stimuli" (Kendler & Kendler, 1962), and, as Bransford pointed out, there is minimal concern on the part of traditional theorists with the question of what has been learned that enables the subject to discriminate between exemplars and nonexemplars. To the extent that this question is addressed by the traditional theory of the concept, it is answered inadequately in that the essence of a concept, its defining property, is itself considered to be a concept.

The experimental procedures of cognitive theorists like Garner and Bransford, on the other hand, are designed to assess the intensive content of concepts. For Bransford the problem is one of finding out how various events must be related to each other to count as instances of the same concept. Garner (1974, p. 83) makes it clear that he is also concerned with intensive content. He says that concept acquisition cannot be considered equivalent to a process by which one learns to distinguish the *A*'s from the *B*'s or the *yes*'s from the *no*'s but is instead a matter of learning what goes together to form the single class or of learning what the subset is that is called *A* or *yes*. The processes of attention and discrimination are considered by these theorists to be important for concept formation, but a description of the way in which particular exemplars are discriminated from nonexemplars does not in their view constitute an adequate theory of the concept. A complete account of what goes on when a concept is acquired must include a characterization of what is learned as well as what is ignored—it is necessary to specify how "different exemplars might be interrelated in such a manner that a concept would emerge" (Bransford, Note 1, p. 40).

Piaget's writings on the acquisition of the object concept and the various conservations are also concerned with the assessment of intensive conceptual content— with what the child has learned when s/he possesses a mature object concept or a thorough understanding of quantity. The question in regard to the object concept is: On what basis are a number of diverse experiences involving an object grouped together to form the infant's notion of the object? A common-elements approach to the problem clearly will not do, since this set of experiences must eventually include instances where the object is not present in the visual field.

The substance-conservation tasks also represent an attempt to learn about the intensive content of concepts. Elkind (1969) writes,

If the child says that the sausage has more clay than the ball, that two objects have the same amount only when they have the same shape, then we know that the intensive content of the child's concept of substance is form. On the other hand, if he says that the ball and the sausage have the same amount, we know that he has a units concept of substance. (p. 181)

So although the methodology employed by these investigators is not that traditionally used for assessing intensive content of concepts (verbal definition), it is clear that their work addresses the question of what individuals know that enables them to perceive a group of things as belonging together. In addition the answers which all three theorists provide to this question are similar. What is learned when one acquires a concept, according to Garner, Bransford, and Piaget, is not an element or set of elements common to a group of conceptual instances. Rather the individual learns a rule or relational system which is abstract in that it captures in general terms permissible variations among exemplars of a concept or specifies acceptable and unacceptable transformations of a hypothetical prototype.

The results of Garner's work demonstrated that in learning a structured subset of stimuli subjects learned the total set (which contained all possible permutations of the stimulus components) and, in addition, learned a rule for determining which permutations resulted in stimuli that belonged to the acquisition subset. In the Franks and Bransford study which employed visual patterns as stimuli, subjects also learned a system within which some arrangements of the stimulus elements were permissible while others were not. Subjects in the semantic integration experiments were highly confident that they had seen stimuli which represented certain types of transformations of actual acquisition stimuli (those which did not violate the meaning of the acquisition material), whereas stimuli produced by means of other transformations were immediately identified as nonmembers of the acquisition set.

It has frequently been noted that our perception of an object is not tied to the flux of impressions that it engenders on the various occasions of our contact with it. We transcend variability of sensation in order to formulate a notion of a single object that can be considered responsible for all of our different experiences with the object. Bransford (Note 1) makes explicit the role played by an understanding of transformations in the construction of such an object concept: "The concept of an object entails knowledge of the various appearances it may take. The essence of the object must thus be defined relative to any of these particular values . . . [i.e.] to the transformations that leave it invariant" (p. 60).

Bransford then points out that characterization of a class concept (the representation of a class of different individual objects) also involves the specification of possible changes that things may undergo. The same process which allows recognition of the individual object is essential to the formation of the class concept.

For the class concept, variable terms are substituted for individual values. Thus a particular cube may be a particular color. The class of all cubes can comprehend all colors possible. In short, there are certain transformations that leave an object invariant. There is a larger set of variable specifications that leave an object a member of a generic class. (p. 61)

The transformations that are so central to the thinking of Garner and Bransford on issues pertaining to con-

cepts do not play a role in the traditional theory of the concept. However they are very much in evidence in Piaget's description of the development of the object concept and in his work on the conservations characteristic of the concrete-operational stage of development.

It is useful to think of the particular object, property, relation, and so on with which the conservation problems are concerned as an exemplar of a class of such objects, relations, and such like. In the most general sense the conservation problems ask the child whether certain transformations affect the exemplar's membership in the class. With respect to the substance-conservation task . . . , the child is in effect asked whether a particular exemplar of the class of relations "same amount" is still a member of that class after one of the components of the relation is changed in appearance. (Elkind, 1969, p. 181)

For Piaget, intensive conceptual content is always defined in terms of the changes in appearance that things tend to undergo. His theory of development describes the process by which human beings acquire the ability to deal adaptively with environmental transformations.

Classification

If concept formation is considered to be an adaptive mechanism by which the environment is rendered generic, then Piaget's work on classification is clearly pertinent to questions concerning the nature of concepts. According to Piaget true classification does not occur until a child reaches the age of seven or eight. The act of constructing or posing a class is considered to be an operation. As such it cannot be understood in isolation but must be viewed as part of an integrated system. Operations gain their meaning from the cognitive structures of which they are part. Piaget argues, in other words, that the operation of regarding objects as members of a class is impossible without possession of a more general classificatory orientation. Such an orientation involves the ability to pose other classes, to subtract one class from another, and so on. The single class is an abstraction from a total system of classes. Posing a class represents the actualization of one of several potential operations that adhere together to form a cognitive structure (Flavell, 1963).

The roots of classificatory behavior are found in infancy (Piaget, 1952b). Sensorimotor schemes like sucking require exercise in order to consolidate themselves, and the infants search out objects in the environment to which these schemes can be applied. They assimilate a wide variety of things to the organized action patterns which they have available. With experience, however, and especially when highly motivated, infants show selectivity or discrimination. They exercise their schemes on some objects and not on others. For example, when hungry they will suck on the nipple and reject the area surrounding it, although initially they evidenced a tendency to suck on whatever came in contact with their lips. Piaget labels this selectivity *recognitory assimilation* and considers it to be a crude form of recognition. The infants' actions show that, when necessary, they can perceive the difference between the nipple and other things. Recognitory assimilation is not classification, but it constitutes a first move in that direction. A special type of recognitory assimilation which is observed somewhat later in the course of development represents another step in the formation of classes.

It is frequently the case that a chance action on the part of an infant produces an advantageous or interesting result involving an object in the external world. When the child perceives a connection between his/her own movements and the result, s/he attempts by trial and error to reproduce it. Piaget refers to this behavior as a *secondary circular reaction.* Later when the object is again encountered, the child often fails to apply to it the circular reaction previously observed but instead goes through only a partial enactment of the appropriate scheme. The behavior is not an automatic or mechanical "response" to an external "stimulus," nor is its purpose to amuse the child. It appears quite serious and intentional but at the same time does not seem designed to produce the effect which has in the past resulted from execution of the entire scheme. Because the child responds with the abbreviated action only to a specific object with which s/he has previously interacted in a particular manner and does not display the entire scheme when it would be feasible to do so, Piaget regards these abbreviated actions as precursors of classification. Of course the infant is not yet operating on a mental level, and the abbreviated schemes apply only to individual objects over a period of time, not to a collection of objects. Nonetheless the child's actions signify that s/he recognizes the object as something to be acted upon in a particular way, and in that sense they may be viewed as a beginning attempt to classify the object.

In order to study classificatory behavior in older children, Piaget presented them with an array of flat geometric shapes made of plastic or wood in several different colors (Inhelder & Piaget, 1964). The shapes included squares, triangles, rings, and half-rings. Children were told to put together things that were alike or to place things that were the same in one pile and those that were different in another. Piaget also employed a set of non-geometric stimuli composed of toy houses, animals, people, and so on. His results pointed to the existence of three stages in the development of classification ability.

Young children approximately two through five years of age typically included only some of the stimuli in the collections they created. They did not consistently use a clear rule or defining property to determine which objects were placed in a particular class. Frequently their sorting was based on the spatial proximity of items in the original array. When these children did place several objects in the same class because of some physical similarity among them, subsequent classification responses were likely to be made on some other basis. A four-year-old might put a blue ring and a yellow ring together because they were both rings, but then add a yellow triangle because its color was the same as that of the yellow ring. The child seemed to forget the property that was initially employed to define class membership. Another strategy common among young children was to use the stimulus objects to construct an interesting arrangement or picture.

Children who were somewhat older produced configurations which had the appearance of real classes. A child at this stage of development might construct one group of curvilinear forms and another of polygons using all of the stimuli in the array. These supraordinate groups were often further subdivided according to color or form in such a way that at a particular level all classifications were based on the same criterion. The groups of objects that the children formed, in other words, were mutually exclusive, internally consistent, and hierarchically organized. According to Piaget, though, true classification must be based upon a thorough understanding of inclusion relations. Consider the case in which an individual constructs a hierarchy involving supraordinate classes that differ on the dimension of form (e.g., rings and triangles) and subordinate classes based on color (e.g., blue and red). Looking at the system the person should be able to conclude that all the rings are either red or blue, that there are more rings than blue rings, that if the red rings were removed the blue rings would remain, and so on.

Using colored beads and pictures of flowers, Piaget explored the extent to which inclusion relations were understood by children five through eleven years of age. He first permitted them to group the objects in any way they wished and then asked his subjects questions regarding the inclusion relations that existed within the classification systems they had created. He found that the younger children were unable to answer these questions correctly. Given seven beads of which five were white and two were black and asked whether there were more beads or more white beads, children between the ages of five and seven insisted that there were more white beads because there were only two black ones. They did not make the requested comparison between the whole set and a subset because, according to Piaget, they were unable at this age to maintain a simultaneous awareness of the whole and a part.

Comparison of the number of white and the number of black beads in the situation previously described merely involves sorting light from dark and evaluating the relative size of the two piles. Comparing the class of all beads with that of white beads, however, is more difficult because physical comparison of a set with one of its subsets is impossible. Once the subset has been isolated, the set no longer exists in its original state. In order to compare the set and subset, a mental operation must be performed. Before the age of seven or eight, young children are incapable of such an operation, and so they focus or center upon the subset that they can see and ignore the total set. They reinterpret the question so that it can be answered by physical inspection.

After age seven or eight, however, children not only construct hierarchical classification systems but also demonstrate by correctly answering class inclusion questions that they can think simultaneously about wholes and parts. They are able to reconstruct the whole set mentally in order to compare it with a part that is visible. Although they have difficulty with class inclusion questions that refer to hypothetical objects, children between the ages of seven and eleven are considered by Piaget to be capable of mature classification on the concrete level.

It is apparent that this work addresses the question of what is known by an individual who possesses a concept or is capable of creating a class, rather than what such an individual does. Although a five-year-old and a nine-year-old may respond in the same manner to an array of objects that vary on one or more dimensions, i.e., both may exhibit a "common response to dissimilar stimuli," Piaget has shown that their understanding of the class concept involved is substantially different. What is learned when one acquires a concept, according to Piaget, is not a feature that distinguishes exemplars from nonexemplars; in fact, the essence of a concept cannot be said to inhere in any of its exemplars. In order to pose a class or respond to a number of diverse things as instances of a single concept, one must possess knowledge of an abstract system which specifies the relations existing among members of a particular class, as well as those which prevail between that class and other supraordinate and subordinate classes.

The knowledge-experience relation implicated in Piaget's work on classification is greater than one-to-one, as it is in that of Garner and Bransford on concept acquisition. Evidence accumulated by these cognitive theorists indicates that human beings construct an integrated representation of nonconsecutively experienced stimulus events. The representation contains more information than is present in any or all of the events themselves. We can say with respect to Piaget's findings, for example, that the children who produced hierarchical classification systems of flowers or beads are unlikely to have done so on the basis of previous experience with such an arrangement of those objects. It is even more unlikely that children who responded correctly to the class inclusion questions had ever before been asked or given answers to such questions. Piaget's subjects actively constructed an abstract relational system on the basis of their experience with individual class exemplars. They then used the system in grouping stimuli with which they were presented and in answering the class inclusion questions.

Piagetian theory implicates the processes of selective attention and discrimination in concept learning at all levels, and they are considered to play a primary role in the classificatory behavior of infants and very young children. However, mature conceptual functioning is based on the ability to perform a group of mental operations which relate individual stimuli and groups of stimuli to one another. Since what is abstracted from experience and stored is not a set of features common to the exemplars of a concept, attempts to explain concept learning solely in terms of selective attention and discrimination must of necessity be inadequate. Garner seems to be expressing a similar view of what is involved in acquiring a concept when he says that it is a matter of learning subsets within defined total sets, rather than of discriminating the members of one subset from those of another. According to both Garner and Piaget, discrimination of positive from negative instances or of one class from another is a consequence of learning what stimuli go in each class but does not constitute the essence of concept learning.

Because Piaget believes that for scientific purposes ordinary language is overly ambiguous and subject to misinterpretation, he provides formal logicomathematical descriptions of the cognitive structures whose existence is indicated by the results of his studies (Inhelder & Piaget, 1964; Piaget, 1957). Cambeilh (Note 2) points out that one aspect of Piaget's formal description of the structure of classification seems to provide an appropiate context within which to understand the results of Garner's research on free recall learning. The reasoning behind this assertion is described in the following section.

According to Piaget a child's thinking at the concrete-operational stage is characterized by nine different operational modes called "groupings," the first four of which describe the logic involved in class inclusion. These groupings, which have some of the properties of the mathematical "group" and some of the "lattice," consist of elements (classes in a hierarchy), an operator such as additon or multiplication, and five properties which govern the application of the operator to the elements. Grouping 3, called bi-univocal multiplication of classes, has to do with the capacity for finding the intersect or logical product of two or more classes. A simple example from Piaget (Inhelder & Piaget, 1964, p. 151) may be used to illustrate.

Consider a set of wooden blocks which differ with respect to form and color. One can divide the set into subclasses according to color, e.g., $A_1 =$ red, $A'_1 =$ blue. The union of these two subclasses constitutes the class of colors $(A_1 + A'_1 = B_1)$. One can then take the same set of blocks, now called B_2, and subdivide it according to shape, e.g., $A_2 =$ circle, $A'_2 =$ square, $A_2 + A'_2 = B_2$. Once these series have been constructed, it is possible to multiply logically a member of one series by a member of another to obtain the largest class which contains the defining attributes of both subclasses. One can perform multiplicative operations such as $A_1 \times A_2 = A_1 A_2$ (the class of blocks that are both red and circular) and $A'_1 \times A_2 = A'_1 A_2$ (blocks that are both blue and circular). It is also possible to multiply the two series as wholes: $B_1 \times B_2 = B_1 B_2 = A_1 A_2 + A'_1 A_2 + A_1 A'_2 + A'_1 A'_2$. The four subclasses yielded by this procedure may be represented as a 2×2 matrix or table with the component classes of B_1 on one axis and those of B_2 on the other. When more variables are represented in the total set, the matrix can be expanded.

Much of the experimental evidence adduced by Piaget in support of Grouping 3 involves the use of tasks which require that the subject find the intersect or logical product of two or more classes. For example, s/he is shown a row of pictures of different colored cats which forms a right angle with a column of pictures of yellow objects of different kinds. S/he is asked to select a picture that can be appropriately placed at the point where the row and column intersect—that is, s/he must choose a yellow cat from an array of other pictures which do not possess both the attribute of "catness" *and* that of "yellowness." The ability to solve such problems is not acquired until the age of seven or eight, at which time the child is capable of integrating new and old exemplars of a concept in order to abstract the relations existing among a coordinated set of attributes.

Garner's findings indicate that subjects acquire knowledge of a total set of stimuli as a result of experience with a structured subset. Cambeilh (Note 2, p. 39) notes that Garner does not explicitly discuss the mechanism by which this might occur and suggests that when stimuli not previously experienced are learned, it is reasonable to assume that the subject combines attributes (in Garner's study, letters and positions) multiplicatively so as to generate those items not present in the acquisition subset. In other words, construction of the whole set, on the basis of experience with a structured subset in which all attributes are represented, may be viewed as dependent on the application of this rule: "Combine every attribute of the stimuli with every other attribute." The ability to apply such a rule is precisely that which is described by Piaget's Grouping 3.

CONCLUSIONS

Like other scientists most of those who study cognitive development are aware that what Thomas Kuhn (1970) refers to as "normal science" is science centered on a paradigm—one or more achievements within a discipline that define for its practitioners admissible research problems and methods. The achievements that generate the corpus of theory, application, and instrumentation on which future efforts of a particular scientific community will be based are those "sufficiently unprecedented to attract an enduring group of adherents away from competing modes of scientific activity" and "sufficiently open ended to leave all sorts of problems for the redefined group of practitioners to resolve" (p. 10). The essence of the paradigm inheres in its theoretical component which is of the type called "formal theory" (Marx, 1976). The paradigm theory is a relatively final and polished explanatory structure that affords in-depth understanding of a large number of the phenomena with which those in the field are concerned. The object of normal science is not the invention of new theories; in fact, it is important for continued progress within a discipline that the paradigm not be viewed as an object for validation. Scientists instead engage in activities that result in the further articulation of those formulations supplied by the paradigm.

The field of developmental psychology does not have a paradigm. Sheldon White (1979) recently described what we do have as a "polyglot empiricism," representing in microcosm the research traditions of nearly all the subspecialties of psychology, juxtaposed with some "cosmic theorizing" whose products are very broad in scope and of a form that renders them difficult to validate. The productive links that some developmentalists claim to have established between the cosmic theories, which have been around in one form or another for two-and-a-half centuries, and the more recently acquired hard data are all but invisible to a considerable number of the field's practitioners.

The sense of White's evaluation is not very different from that of some remarks made by Zigler (1963) some two decades ago. Zigler indicated that theory construction in developmental psychology was at a very primitive level. Theoretical formulations were either so close to a particular set of data as to constitute nothing more than a shorthand description of them or so far removed from the results of empirical investigation that they descriptively encompassed large amounts of data without providing much in the way of explanation. The field was characterized by an overreliance on naturalistic observation, and theories formulated to explain developmental phenomena observed in the real world were incapable of generating specific predictions about relations that should and should not hold in various experimenter-created worlds. The theories were thus of little use since

they were equally refractory to confirmation and disproof.

Some may believe that developmental psychology is better off now with a "grab-bag" full of methodological approaches than it was in the late 1950s when we tended to rely on a single method of investigation. Most, however, would agree that there has been no great leap forward in the construction and general acceptance within the field of elegant, comprehensive, theoretical structures capable of explaining the changes in psychological functioning (including those in the cognitive realm) that take place over the course of human development.

Kuhn points out that "the road to a firm research consensus is extraordinarily arduous" (1970, p. 15). A state of affairs similar to the one which prevails in developmental psychology is historically typical of all sciences. The lack of a paradigm does not preclude discovery and advance within a discipline. However, "until the paradigm comes," it would seem critically important for the practitioners of a young science to keep metatheoretical issues firmly in mind—that is, to devote a great deal of attention to a consideration of the types of questions which ought to be asked instead of looking for answers to those which have traditionally been of interest. The business of the scientist in an undeveloped area of investigation is to strive toward a set of terms or concepts with which to think productively about nature. Empirical investigation is, under these circumstances, used to determine the extent to which particular constructs are relevant and applicable, rather than to bear out or refute specific predictions about natural or behavioral phenomena.

Inquiring as to the kinds of questions that ought to be asked and the terms in which they can most profitably be posed is not easy. Such an endeavor requires that the scientist step back from, and consider anew, a body of work which has become familiar and whose premises have come to be taken for granted. The process is made more difficult by decisions to limit one's thinking to a particular area or mode of investigation. If one is concerned with cognitive development, it is neither necessary nor desirable to exclude from consideration the methods and findings of research that employs adult subjects in an effort to explore the nature of conceptual knowledge and the process of knowledge acquisition.

Implicit in Piaget's theoretical framework is the notion that an analysis of conceptual knowledge cannot succeed in isolation from a consideration of its ontogeny. I would contend that the converse is also true. In thinking about development, it is important to look closely at the system that is eventually acquired—to find out what it is, how it is used, what mechanisms underlie performance, and so on. The results of investigations of what it is to have a certain form of understanding and of those whose purpose is to study the development of that form of understanding can inform one another so as to generate a set of terms or concepts useful and appropriate for posing questions of both types.

What I am suggesting is certainly not new. In fact my position is very similar to that taken by Garner, Hake, and Eriksen (1956) in their classic article on the role of converging operations in research on perception. Since perceptual phenomena constitute processes intervening between stimuli and responses, they cannot be observed directly. These phenomena come to be known as concepts whose properties are induced from objectively determined relations between stimuli and responses. According to the article if conclusions regarding perception are based on the results of a single experimental operation, they cannot be more than a restatement of those results. However, a set of operations which yields data on a variety of inputs and outputs can converge on a perceptual concept that has a reality independent of any single experimental context. Garner et al. are, of course, referring to experimental operations employed within a single field of endeavor. However it is reasonable to expect that the principle which they are elucidating can be applied more broadly with the same beneficial results.

Although Piaget's popularity has increased dramatically in recent years, there is a great deal of concern among developmental psychologists that the terms and concepts invoked by his theory more closely reflect Piaget's own cognitive structures and unique methodological approach than they do the real world of mental and behavioral phenomena. Many would probably concur with White's inclusion of Piaget within the category of "cosmic theorists"; they believe that his constructs have not yet been sufficiently validated by the results of empirical investigation, and they fear that the nature of the system is such that its components may not even be subject to such validation. It must be admitted, however, that most empirical studies based on Piaget's theory can best be described as replications of his experiments, rather than attempts to bring other theoretical constructs and methods to bear on questions concerning the validity of the system. It is important to recognize that there is more than one way to validate a theory.

Ideally the method of converging operations described by Garner, Hake, and Eriksen serves the function of preventing reification of perceptual constructs by the cognitive psychologist. To the extent that the operations converging on a concept are sufficiently varied in terms of subjects employed, stimuli presented, and responses required, the likelihood of peremptorily and incorrectly invoking that concept to explain performance is minimized. This is precisely the function that studies of adult cognition can serve in regard to constructs subsumed within our developmental theories. The Garner and Bransford studies, as well as those conducted by a number of other cognitive psychologists, have succeeded in providing an intellectual climate within which Piaget's theory can be understood and appreciated by rendering the questions he asks less alien and more comprehensible (although that was not, of course, their purpose). Additionally, and more importantly, such research is capable of contributing hard evidence regarding the validity of Piaget's terms and concepts as vehicles which can be used to arrive at an understanding of cognitive development. I have tried to demonstrate that this is the case in regard to one aspect of the theoretical framework which Piaget has evolved; his position on very important issues concerning the nature and acquisition of conceptual knowledge appears to receive confirmation from the results of studies whose methods and subject populations are quite different from those which Piaget himself used.

It would seem that the same approach could be employed in exploring the validity of other aspects of the system, as well as that of terms and concepts invoked by other theories of development.

While it is certainly the case that the field of cognitive development lacks a paradigm theory, we can be said to have a candidate or two for that position. To the extent that developmental psychologists are willing to allow knowledge from several sources to cross-fertilize, we are likely to arrive at a comprehensive and satisfactory account of the age-related phenomena in which we are interested that will serve to guide our thinking and experimentation for a long time to come. Theoretical hybrids, like those belonging to the world of living things, tend to be hardier.

REFERENCE NOTES

1. Bransford, J. D. The problem of conceptual abstraction: Implications for theories of learning and memory. Unpublished manuscript, University of Minnesota, 1970. (Available from J. D. Bransford, Vanderbilt University.)

2. Cambeilh, P. Developmental aspects of abstraction underlying free recall. Unpublished doctoral dissertation, Adelphi University, 1973.

REFERENCES

ANDERSON, R. C., & AUSUBEL, D. P. (Eds.). *Readings in the psychology of cognition.* New York: Holt, Rinehart & Winston, 1965.

BARCLAY, J. R. The role of comprehension in remembering sentences. *Cognitive Psychology,* 1973, *4,* 229–254.

BARTLETT, F. C. *Remembering: A study in experimental and social psychology.* Cambridge, England: Cambridge University Press, 1932.

BORING, E. G. *A history of experimental psychology* (2nd ed.). Englewood Cliffs, N.J.: Prentice-Hall, 1950.

BOURNE, L. E. *Human conceptual behavior.* Boston: Allyn & Bacon, 1966.

BOURNE, L. E., & RESTLE, F. Mathematical theory of concept identification. *Psychological Review,* 1959, *66,* 278–296.

BOUSFIELD, W. A. The problem of meaning in verbal learning. In C. N. Cofer (Ed.), *Verbal learning and verbal behavior.* New York: McGraw-Hill, 1961.

BRANSFORD, J. D., BARCLAY, J. R., & FRANKS, J. Sentence memory: A constructive versus interpretive approach. *Cognitive Psychology,* 1972, *3,* 193–209.

BRANSFORD, J. D., & FRANKS, J. The abstraction of linguistic ideas. *Cognitive Psychology,* 1971, *2,* 331–350.

BRANSFORD, J. D., & JOHNSON, M. Contextual prerequisites for understanding: Some investigations of comprehension and recall. *Journal of Verbal Learning and Verbal Behavior,* 1972, *11,* 717–726.

BRANSFORD, J. D., & JOHNSON, M. Considerations of some problems of comprehension. In W. G. Chase (Ed.), *Visual information processing.* New York: Academic Press, 1973.

BRONOWSKI, J. *The common sense of science.* New York: Random House, 1953.

BRUNER, J. Going beyond the information given. In H. E. Gruber, K. R. Hammond, & R. Jessor (Eds.), *Contemporary Approaches to Cognition.* Cambridge, Mass.: Harvard University Press, 1957.

CHOMSKY, N. Review of *Verbal behavior* by B. F. Skinner. In J. Fodor & J. Katz (Eds.), *The structure of language; Readings in the philosophy of language.* Englewood Cliffs, N.J.: Prentice-Hall, 1964.

CHOMSKY, N. *Language and mind.* New York: Harcourt Brace Jovanovich, 1972.

DOMINOWSKI, R. L. Concept attainment. In M. Marx (Ed.), *Learning: Interactions.* New York: Macmillan, 1970.

DOOLINGS, D., & CHRISTIAANSEN, R. Episodic and semantic aspects of memory for prose. *Journal of Experimental Psychology: Human Learning and Memory*, 1977, *3*, 428–436.

ELKIND, D. Conservation and concept formation. In D. Elkind & J. H. Flavell (Eds.), *Studies in cognitive development*. New York: Oxford University Press, 1969.

FLAVELL, J. H. *The developmental psychology of Jean Piaget*. Princeton, N.J.: D. Van Nostrand, 1963.

FODOR, J. A. More about mediators: A reply to Berlyne and Osgood. *Journal of Verbal Learning and Verbal Behavior*, 1966, *5*, 412–415.

FRANKS, J., & BRANSFORD, J. D. The acquisition of abstract ideas. *Journal of Verbal Learning and Verbal Behavior*, 1972, *11*, 311–315.

FREDERIKSEN, C. Effects of context-induced processing operations on semantic information acquired from discourse. *Cognitive Psychology*, 1975, *7*, 139–166.

FURTH, H. G. *Piaget and knowledge: Theoretical foundations*. Englewood Cliffs, N.J.: Prentice-Hall, 1969.

GARNER, W. R. *The processing of information and structure*. Hillsdale, N.J.: Lawrence Erlbaum Associates, 1974.

GARNER, W. R., & DEGERMAN, R. L. Transfer in free recall learning of overlapping lists of nonsense words. *Journal of Verbal Learning and Verbal Behavior*, 1967, *6*, 922–927.

GARNER, W. R., HAKE, H. W., & ERIKSEN, C. W. Operationism and the concept of perception. *The Psychological Review*, 1956, *63*, 149–159.

GARNER, W. R., & WHITMAN, J. R. Form and amount of internal structure as factors in free recall learning of nonsense words. *Journal of Verbal Learning and Verbal Behavior*, 1965, *4*, 257–266.

GLANZER, M., HUTTENLOCHER, J., & CLARK, W. Systematic operations in solving concept problems: A parametric study of a class of problems. *Psychological Monographs*, 1963, *77* (1, Whole No. 564).

GOTTWALD, R. L. Effects of response labels in concept attainment. *Journal of Experimental Psychology*, 1971, *91*, 30–33.

HARRIS, R., TESKE, R., & GINNS, M. Memory for pragmatic implications from courtroom testimony. *Psychonomic Science Bulletin*, 1975, *6*, 494–496.

HARROW, M., & FRIEDMAN, G. B. Comparing reversal and nonreversal shifts in concept formation with partial reinforcement controlled. *Journal of Experimental Psychology*, 1958, *55*, 592–597.

INHELDER, B., & PIAGET, J. *The growth of logical thinking from childhood to adolescence*. New York: Basic Books, 1958.

INHELDER, B., & PIAGET, J. *The early growth of logic in the child*. New York: Harper & Row, Pub., 1964.

JAMES, W. *The principles of psychology*. New York: Dover, 1950. (Originally published, 1890.)

JENKINS, J. J. Meaningfulness and concepts: Concepts and meaningfulness. Pp. 65–79 in H. Klausmeier & C. Harris (Eds.), *Analyses of concept learning*. New York: Academic Press, 1966.

KAGAN, J. A developmental approach to conceptual growth. In H. J. Klausmier & C. W. Harris (Eds.), *Analyses of concept learning*. New York: Academic Press, 1966.

KENDLER, H. H. Environmental and cognitive control of behavior. In N. S. Endler, L. R. Boulter, & H. Osser (Eds.), *Contemporary issues in developmental psychology*. New York: Holt, Rinehart and Winston, 1976.

KENDLER, H. H., & D'AMATO, M. F. A comparison of reversal shifts and nonreversal shifts in human conceptual behavior. *Journal of Experimental Psychology*, 1955, *49*, 165–174.

KENDLER, H. H., & KENDLER, T. S. Vertical and horizontal processes in problem solving. *Psychological Review*, 1962, *69*, 1–16.

KENDLER, T. S. The concept of a concept. In A. W. Melton (Ed.), *Categories of human learning*. New York: Academic Press, 1964.

KENDLER, T. S., & KENDLER, H. H. An ontogeny of optional shift behavior. *Child Development*, 1970, *41*, 1–27.

KENDLER, T. S., KENDLER, H. H., & LEARNARD, B. Mediated responses to size and brightness as a function of age. *American Journal of Psychology*, 1962, *75*, 571–586.

KUHN, T. *The structure of scientific revolutions*. Chicago: University of Chicago Press, 1970.

LEEPER, R. W. Cognitive learning theory. In M. H. Marx (Ed.), *Learning: Theories*. New York: Macmillan, 1970.

MACCORQUODALE, K., & MEEHL, P. On a distinction between hypothetical constructs and intervening variables. *Psychological Review*, 1948, *55*, 95–107.

MARSCHARK, M., & PAIVIO, A. Integrative processing of concrete and abstract sentences. *Journal of Verbal Learning and Verbal Behavior*, 1977, *16*, 217–231.

MARX, M. H. Formal theory. In M. H. Marx & F. E. Goodson (Eds.), *Theories in contemporary psychology*. New York: Macmillan, 1976.

NEISSER, U. *Cognitive psychology*. Englewood Cliffs, N.J.: Prentice-Hall, 1967.

NELSON, K. Cognitive development and the acquisition of knowledge. In R. C. Anderson, R. J. Spiro, & W. E. Montague (Eds.), *Schooling and the acquisition of knowledge*. Hillsdale, N.J.: Lawrence Erlbaum Associates, 1977.

OSGOOD, C. E. Behavior theory and the social sciences. *Behavioral Sciences*, 1956, *1*, 167–185.

OSGOOD, C. E. Meaning cannot be an r_m? *Journal of Verbal Learning and Verbal Behavior*, 1966, *5*, 402–407.

OSLER, S. F., & MADDEN, J. The verbal label: Mediator or classifier? *Journal of Experimental Child Psychology*, 1973, *16*, 303–317.

PETERS, D. G., & DENNEY, J. P. Labeling and memory effects on categorizing and hypothesizing behavior for biconditional and conditional conceptual rules. *Journal of Experimental Psychology*, 1971, *87*, 229–233.

PIAGET, J. *The child's conception of number*. Atlantic Highlands, N.J.: Humanities Press, 1952a.

PIAGET, J. *The origins of intelligence in children*. New York: International Universities Press, 1952b.

PIAGET, J. *The construction of reality in the child*. New York: Basic Books, 1954.

PIAGET, J. *Logic and psychology*. New York: Basic Books, 1957.

PIAGET, J. *On the development of memory and identity*. Worcester, Mass.: Clark University Press, 1968.

PIAGET, J. Piaget's theory. In P. H. Mussen (Ed.), *Carmichael's manual of child psychology* (3rd ed.). New York: John Wiley, 1970.

PIAGET, J. *Biology and knowledge: An essay on the relations between organic regulations and cognitive processes*. Chicago: The University of Chicago Press, 1971.

PIAGET, J., & INHELDER, B. *Le développement des quantités physiques chez l'enfant*. Paris: Delachaux et Niestlé, 1941.

PIAGET, J., & INHELDER, B. *Memory and intelligence*. New York: Basic Books, 1973.

POTTS, G. Storing and retrieving information about ordered relationships. *Journal of Experimental Psychology*, 1974, *103*, 431–439.

REESE, H. W., & OVERTON, W. F. Models of development and theories of development. In L. R. Goulet & P. B. Baltes (Eds.), *Lifespan developmental psychology: Research and theory*. New York: Academic Press, 1970.

SKINNER, B. F. *Verbal behavior*. Englewood Cliffs, N.J.: Prentice-Hall, 1957.

SKINNER, B. F. Behaviorism at fifty. *Science*, 1963, *140*, 951–958.

THORNDYKE, P. The role of inferences in discourse comprehension. *Journal of Verbal Learning and Verbal Behavior*, 1976, *15*, 437–446.

TRABASSO, T. Language and cognition. In W. G. Chase (Ed.), *Visual information processing*. New York: Academic Press, 1973.

WATSON, J. B. Psychology as the behaviorist views it. In W. Dennis (Ed.), *Readings in the history of psychology*. New York: Appleton-Century-Crofts, 1948.

WATSON, R. I. *The great psychologists*. Philadelphia: Lippincott, 1971.

WHITE, S. Children in perspective. *American Psychologist*, 1979, *34*, 812–814.

WHITMAN, J. R., & GARNER, W. R. Free recall learning of visual figures as a function of form of internal structure. *Journal of Experimental Psychology*, 1962, *64*, 558–564.

WHITMAN, J. R., & GARNER, W. R. Concept learning as a function of form of internal structure. *Journal of Verbal Learning and Verbal Behavior*, 1963, *2*, 195–202.

WOLMAN, B. B. *Contemporary theories and systems in psychology* (rev. ed.). New York: Plenum, 1981.

WOODWORTH, R. S. *Psychology*. New York: Holt, Rinehart & Winston, 1929.

WOODWORTH, R. S., & SCHLOSBERG, T. T. *Experimental psychology*. New York: Holt, Rinehart & Winston, 1960.

ZIGLER, E. Metatheoretical issues in developmental psychology. In M. H. Marx (Ed.), *Theories in contemporary psychology*. New York: Macmillan, 1963.

2

Psychoanalytic Approaches to Developmental Psychology

GIL G. NOAM
REGINA O'CONNELL HIGGINS
GEORGE W. GOETHALS

Psychoanalysis is a broad field which encompasses nearly every domain of human activity, whether that activity is pathological or normal, conscious or unconscious, performed waking or sleeping. This chapter will focus on a limited aspect of the field: what psychoanalysis can provide for the scholar interested in developmental psychology. We will review both historical and contemporary facets of psychoanalytic theory using two criteria. The first is that an idea has led to theoretical elaboration relevant to developmental psychology. The second is that an idea has generated or produced empirical research.

We will do three things in this chapter: We will discuss basic principles which originate with Freud and are important theoretical contributions to developmental psychology; we will discuss the elaborations of these ideas in the United States; and we will suggest how, in the 1980s, psychoanalytic theory may be useful to those interested in developmental psychology, especially in its connection to personality development and interpersonal relationships.

FREUD'S LEGACY

We begin this chapter by asking the question: What theoretical ideas of Freud's have had the greatest effect on the study of personality development and on developmental psychology in general? Freud wrote many papers that *could* be construed as having relevance to developmental psychology; but we believe that Freud's Lectures XX and XXXI (written in 1916–1917 and 1933 respectively) have been the point of departure for creative refinements of psychoanalytic thinking and have had the greatest historical importance.

Special thanks to Barbara Turner and Petra Pogge-Hesse for comments and editorial help and David Miranda who helped prepare the bibliography and contributed to the description of theory and research of ego psychology.

Theory of Psychosexual Development

Lecture XX contains a discussion of the relationship between so-called sexual perversion and infantile sexuality. Two different themes are encompassed: sexual perversion and its genesis and the development of sexual capacities in a growing human being. We will look at some statements of particular importance in this essay, beginning with the following quotation. We can see the emphasis Freud places on the mother-child attachment, which he interprets in developmental terms.

Sucking for nourishment becomes the point of departure from which the whole sexual life develops, the unattainable prototype of every later sexual satisfaction, to which in times of need phantasy often enough reverts. The desire to suck includes within it the desire for the mother's breast, which is therefore the first *object* of sexual desire; I cannot convey to you any adequate idea of the importance of this first object in determining every later object adopted, of the profound influence it exerts, through transformation and substitution, upon the most distant fields of mental life. (Freud, 1935, p. 275)[1]

This statement of Freud's ideas on development anticipates many concepts that psychoanalysts and developmental psychologists have followed. There are a number of important conceptions in this compressed statement. The following is a list of ideas extracted from the Lecture with a brief discussion of their implications for developmental psychology.

1. *Sucking for nourishment becomes the point of departure from which the whole sexual life develops.*

This emphatic statement underscores an extremely important issue: The mother-infant nursing relationship

[1]Quotations from Lectures XX and XXXI are reprinted from *New Introductory Lectures on Psychoanalysis* by Sigmund Freud, tr. by James Strachey, by permission of W. W. Norton & Company, Inc., Sigmund Freud Copyrights Ltd., The Institute of Psycho-Analysis, and The Hogarth Press Ltd. Copyright © 1965, 1964 by James

is the point from which the sexual life of an individual takes its "departure." Because this involves the mother, by implication Freud is stressing the paramount importance of "mother-infant bonding" for the total development not only of sexuality but of personality.

2. *The unattainable prototype of every later sexual satisfaction to which in times of need fantasy often reverts.*

This statement indirectly operationalizes Freud's concept of the defense of regression. This is critical historically; it implies the possibility of psychoanalytic theory being used in interdisciplinary research. Defenses are learned; thus, the concept of defenses itself becomes a point at which academic psychology and its research on learning can be expanded. This statement also anticipates some of Freud's central ideas on adolescent development: that object-finding is really object-refinding. It seems certain that the statement anticipates not only Erikson's ideas about the crisis involved in weaning but also his theoretical position on basic trust and mistrust, the central theoretical idea in *Childhood and Society*.

3. *The desire to suck includes within it the desire for the mother's breast, which is therefore the first object of sexual desire.*

In this observation is the implication of Freud's theory of zonal eroticism, here, of course, specifically oral eroticism. However the phrase about the breast's being "the first *object* of sexual desire" anticipates the core of British object-relations theory and its discussion, developmentally, of whole and part objects, a theoretical idea which has been elaborated in recent years in the work of Otto Kernberg.

4. *I cannot convey to you any adequate idea of the importance of this first object in determining every later object adopted, of the profound influence it exerts, through transformation and substitution, upon the most distant fields of mental life.*

One of the major controversies within developmental psychology is whether a personality is a continuous or discontinuous process—that is, does one develop—using the word metaphorically—by accretion, or does one develop through a series of *critical incidents* which cause one to go through periods of rapid and profound personality *change* in the course of development? In this statement Freud is implying that the totality of an individual's life is going to be affected by this first object relationship; thus he anticipates the work of Binstock (1973) and the work of Dicks (1963) on marriage and marital tensions.

In summary Lecture XX is the genesis of what we now call attachment theory and anticipates some, but not all, of the issues in object-relations theory; tangentially it also contributes to a theory of defensive operations. We also see Freud standing foursquare on the issue of sexual motivation and development as being the source of all human behavior.

Freud and Object Loss

If one examines overall psychoanalytic theory and asks what is its most important concept, one would find a popular answer to be the unconscious determination of behavior. Considering psychoanalytic theory in relation

to developmental psychology, one finds this idea reviewed, both directly and indirectly, in Lecture XXXI. This is one of Freud's most fascinating and interesting essays; it is an emendation of ideas set forth approximately ten years earlier in his monograph "The Ego and the Id" and shows Freud in the process of thinking and revising his thoughts. The essay has the peculiar quality of being lucid yet simultaneously having *apparent* contradictions.

The unconscious motivation of behavior is the key to psychoanalytic thinking generally. In Lecture XXXI those of us interested in developmental psychology are shown that life for human beings originates in a complex lifelong dynamic process involving the strategies which develop in loving and coping with the inevitable loss of love objects. The Lecture focuses on Freud's final definitions of the id, ego, and superego and the dynamic relationships that exist among these three domains of the psyche. It is his discussion of the formation of the superego—a special case of loving and losing—that is central to our understanding of psychoanalysis as a possible approach to developmental psychology.

Freud's statement on the centrality of this idea in his thinking is,

If one has lost a love-object or has to give it up, one often compensates oneself by identifying oneself with it; one sets it up again inside one's ego, so that in this case object-choice regresses, as it were, to identification.

When the Oedipus complex passes away the child must give up the intense object-cathexes which it has formed towards its parents, and to compensate for this loss of object, its identifications with its parents, which have probably long been present, become greatly intensified. Identifications of this kind, which may be looked upon as precipitates of abandoned object-cathexes, will recur often enough in the later life of the child; but it is in keeping with the emotional importance of this first instance of such a transformation that its product should occupy a special position in the ego. (Freud, 1933, pp. 91–92)

Freud describes a continual dynamic related to loving and losing. One compensates (defends oneself) when one loses a love-object by setting that object up again inside of one's own ego: "object-choice regresses, as it were, to identification." It must be emphasized that this critical, highly dynamic, and inevitable relationship between loving and losing is, in our estimation, the key developmental concept in Freud's theory. His elucidation of this relationship, not only in Lecture XXXI but also in his essay "Mourning and Melancholia," reveals an emotional dynamic, axiomatic in its explicitness. Thus the first major theme that Lecture XXXI presents is that defending oneself against love objects in complex ways is the human condition. This is done by incorporating into one's personality those objects that one has had to give up during one's life.

Freud, Superego, and Identification

It can be argued that man's concern with some concept which defines the *self* has been a preoccupation since the time of Greek philosophy if not before. As important as the discussion of the ego is in Freud's work, it is the idea of the superego in Lecture XXXI which is in some ways his most important contribution, especially as one regards the course of contemporary psychology. There are several all-important reasons for this.

Freud begins his discussion of the superego with the following statement:

No sooner have we got used to the idea of the superego, as something which enjoys a certain independence, pursues its own ends, and is independent of the ego as regards the energy at its disposal, than we are faced with a clinical picture which throws into strong relief the severity and even cruelty of this function, and the vicissitudes through which its relations with the ego may pass. I refer to the condition of melancholia, or more accurately the melancholic attack, of which you have often heard. . . . Conscience is no doubt something within us, but it has not been there from the beginning. In this sense it is the opposite of sexuality, which is certainly present from the very beginning of life and not a thing that only comes in later. (Ibid., p. 87)

Freud is saying that at times parts of the personality can be in violent opposition to each other. The superego, when it operates, can often lead a person to feel a sense of loss of self-esteem, which is in its extreme form a sense of melancholy. By identifying the conscience—that is, one of the functions of the superego—as something that arrives later, Freud is suggesting that at least part of the personality is *learned*. He has thus created the possibility of a relationship between behavior psychology and instinct psychology. This becomes explicit when he discusses how the superego is formed.

The basis of the process is what we call an identification. That is to say that one ego becomes like another, one which results in the first ego behaving itself in certain respects in the same way as the second; it imitates it, and as it were takes it into itself. This identification has been not inappropriately compared with the oral-cannibalistic incorporation of another person. Identification is a very important kind of relationship with another person, probably the most primitive, and is not to be confused with object choice. One can express the difference between them in this way: when a boy identifies himself with his father he wants to *be like* his father; when he makes him the object of his choice, he wants to have him, to possess him; in the first case, his ego is altered on the model of his father, in the second case that is not necessary. Identification and object choice are broadly speaking independent of each other, but one can identify oneself with a person and alter one's ego accordingly, and take the same person as one's sexual object. (Ibid., pp. 91–92)

There are a number of ideas here of great importance to developmental psychologists. The first is that, although Freud does not say it directly, the superego is formed as a consequence of identification, which in turn is the defensive strategy used to deal with object loss. The second is that the concept of identification is essentially the way one deals with another person who may be threatening; incorporating him/her into oneself can, in a magical way, cause that person to disappear. The third important idea is that Freud sees identification as "the most primitive kind of relationship" a human being has. He is implying that phase in life when one has not yet differentiated oneself as a separate being from parental objects. Finally Freud is suggesting what has become almost axiomatic: One cathects (identifies). He implies that, in adult relationships at least, one can not only

cathect, but also identify with the object. Thus adult relationships at least in part are matters both of external object choice and internalization of the object that one loves.

After defining the superego's formation, Freud continues,

We have allocated to it the activities of self-observation, conscience, and the holding up of ideals. It follows from our account of its origin that it is based upon an overwhelmingly important biological fact no less than upon a momentous psychological fact, namely the lengthy dependence of the human child on its parents and the Oedipus complex; these two facts moreover are closely bound up with each other. (Ibid., pp. 94–95)

In his biography of Freud, Ernest Jones remarks that Freud saw his discussions of the Oedipus complex as the key to his whole theory of personality development. In Lecture XXXI he reemphasizes that theme and anticipates the complex relationship between the biological nature of man with his lengthy dependence on the parent—itself an anticipation of both object-relation and attachment theories—and the psychological complexity of breaking that dependency and attachment through the crisis of the Oedipus complex. In a sense this one quotation from Freud sums up his whole theory.

When he says we have allotted to the superego "the functions of self-observation, conscience, and the holding up of ideals," he has put in final form something he had begun to develop in his earlier writings: the notion of splits within the personality. The superego is not a single entity; it is "split" into three segments. The ego can be seen as having been "split" into the helpless, hemmed-in, anxiety-ridden part of the personality as well as the executive part of the personality. In a sense, then, the ego's final topology, according to Freud, is a five-way "split": the executive ego, the derivative ego, the conscience, self-observation, and the holding up of ideals.

Freud and the Ego

Possibly no conceptualization of Freud's is more important *historically* than the implicit notion of ego splits, which are brought into full focus in this Lecture. One of the intriguing and puzzling aspects of his discussion of the ego and superego as parts of the personality is the way in which Freud seems to be writing in a highly contradictory manner; he appears to define the ego as both a derivative part of the personality and as a highly executive, autonomous part of it. The juxtaposition of two famous quotations will illustrate these different approaches. The first is the idea of the derivative and possibly passive ego.

One can hardly go wrong in regarding the ego as that part of the id which has been modified by its proximity to the external world and the influence that the latter has had on it, and which serves the purpose of receiving stimuli and protecting the organism from them, like the cortical layer with which a particle of living substance surrounds itself. (Ibid., p. 106)

It has to serve three harsh masters, and has to do its best to reconcile the claims and demands of all three. These demands are always divergent and often seem quite incompatible; no wonder that the ego so frequently gives way under its task. The three tyrants are the external world, the superego, and the id. When one watches the efforts of the ego to satisfy them all, or rather, to obey them all simultaneously, one cannot regret having personified the ego, and established it as a separate being. It feels itself hemmed in on three sides and threatened by three kinds of danger, towards which it reacts by developing anxiety when it is too hard pressed.

In this way, goaded on by the id, hemmed in by the superego, and rebuffed by reality, the ego struggles to cope with its economic task of reducing the forces and influences which work in it and upon it to some kind of harmony; and we may well understand how it is that we so often cannot repress the cry: "Life is not easy." When the ego is forced to acknowledge its weakness, it breaks out into anxiety: reality anxiety in the face of the external world, moral anxiety in the face of the superego, and neurotic anxiety in the face of the strength of the passions in the id. (Ibid., pp. 108–109)

However there is in the same discussion an entirely different picture of the ego.

This relation to the external world is decisive for the ego. The ego has taken over the task of representing the external world for the id, and so of saving it; for the id, blindly striving to gratify its instincts in complete disregard of the superior strength of outside forces, could not otherwise escape annihilation. In the fulfilment of this function, the ego has to observe the external world and preserve a true picture of it in the memory traces left by its perceptions, and, by means of the reality-test, it has to eliminate any element in this picture of the external world which is a contribution from internal sources of excitation. On behalf of the id, the ego controls the path of access to motility, but it interpolates between desire and action the procrastinating factor of thought, during which it makes use of the residues of experience stored up in memory. In this way it dethrones the pleasure-principle, which exerts undisputed sway over the processes in the id, and substitutes for it the reality-principle, which promises greater security and greater success.

The ego advances from the function of perceiving instincts to that of controlling them, but the latter is only achieved through the mental representative of the instinct becoming subordinated to a larger organisation, and finding its place in a coherent unity. In popular language, we may say that the ego stands for reason and circumspection, while the id stands for the untamed passions. (Ibid., pp. 106–107)

Ultimately what Freud discusses here is the ego's dual task of dealing with both *external* and *internal* object relationships. The ego may be seen largely in terms of its adaptive functions and coping styles; it can also be seen in terms of its attempts—sometimes successful and sometimes not—to serve as an integrative force within the personality.

Without these conceptualizations, without the implication of the primary nature of the early cannibalistic identification with the parent, the work of Melanie Klein and W.R.D. Fairbairn would not have been possible. In a parallel fashion Freud's discussion of the adaptive functions of the ego and the superego developed the line which leads to viewing personality development largely in terms of defenses and coping mechanisms. Thus Freud left us two legacies. One became ego psychology, represented by the work of Anna Freud, Hartmann, Kris, Loewenstein, and Erikson. The other became British object-relations theory, represented by the works of Melanie Klein, W.R.D. Fairbairn, J. D. Sutherland, and Donald Winnicott, among others. Freud did not contradict himself; instead, he left future thinkers two quite different paths. The following of each has been of enormous historical importance.

EGO PSYCHOLOGY

The previous section of this chapter concerned the Freudian basis upon which both adaptive ego psychology and object-relations theory are built. These two schools within psychoanalytic theory have had very different histories. The following section will explore the development of American ego psychology and empirical research based on its various concepts. We begin with a review of the four major phases of ego psychology, as described by Rapaport (1967), to provide further historical context and to consider connections to Freudian thought.

The first phase arises from Freud's early writings in which he equated the terms *self* and *consciousness* with a rudimentary, limited concept of the ego. He developed a first theory of defenses at a time when the role of reality occupied a major place in his thinking. Defenses warded off affect associated with memories and with past and present reality experiences.

The second phase, however, is marked by Freud's lesser emphasis of the reality experience. He discovered that infantile sexual experiences, as reported by patients in analysis, were not necessarily based on reality but on fantasy. His center of interest shifted to the agent which creates the fantasies and the processes by which this agent works. The discovery of the instinctual drive followed, and its exploration dominated the second phase. Theoretical issues important to ego psychology at this stage were the concepts of secondary process (1900), the reality principle (1911), and the analysis of the process of repression.

The third phase concerns the Freudian description of the ego as a coherent organization of mental processes. Although the ego is structured around the "conscious" and "preconscious" systems, it includes unconscious forces similar to those from the id. Although the ego can transform id energies to ego energies, it is also made up of neutral energies. Rapaport describes the limitations of the ego concept of the third phase: The ego is controlled by the prompts of id, superego, and reality; the ego is "the helpless rider of the id horse." In *The Problem of Anxiety* (1926), Freud gave the ego a more important place in the psychic apparatus and suggested autonomous defensive styles in the face of danger; thus, he reintroduced the importance of external reality.

Rapaport's fourth stage deals with the theoretical formulations of modern ego psychology. This is the subject of the following review.

Anna Freud and the Ego's Defense Mechanisms

Anna Freud's book *The Ego and the Mechanisms of Defense* provides the foundation for much of modern ego psychology though her ideas remain within the theoretical bounds Sigmund Freud had set. Her work has become an important bridge between psychoanalysis and developmental psychology, both theoretically and empirically. She writes of the traditional overemphasis, in both psychoanalytic theory and practice, on drives, the id, and the unconscious: "The view held was that the term psychoanalysis should be reserved for the new discoveries relating to the unconscious psychic life, i.e., the study of repressed instinctual impulses, affects, and fantasies" (p. 31). Anna Freud argued that adjustment to the outside world had been underemphasized; she posits a more comprehensive definition.

At the present time, we should probably define the task of analysis as follows: to acquire the fullest possible knowledge of all three institutions of which we believe psychic personality to be constituted and to learn what are their relations to one another and to the outside world. That is to say: in relation to the ego, to explore its contents, its boundaries, and its functions, and to trace the history of its dependence on the outside world, the id, and the superego; and in relation to the id, to give an account of the instincts, i.e., of the id contents, and to follow them through the transformations which they undergo. (1936, pp. 4–5)

Anna Freud sees the analysis of the ego as more difficult than the traditional psychoanalytic analysis of the id because the ego is the source of resistance. She classifies the ego's defenses and adds to the list Sigmund Freud created. New mechanisms include regression, reaction formation, isolation, undoing, projection, introjection, turning against the self, displacement, and reversal. Anna Freud links different neuroses to characteristic defenses, e.g., undoing and isolation to obsessional neurosis. By doing so she underlines the developmental aspect of psychoanalytic thought about psychopathology as well as about defenses. She traces defenses to their developmental origins.

It is meaningless to speak of repression where the ego is still merged with the id. Similarly, we might suppose that projection and introjection were methods which depended on the differentiation of the ego from the outside world. The expulsion of ideas or affects from the ego and their relegation to the outside world would be a relief to the ego only when it had learned to distinguish itself from that world. (p. 51)

To this day the focus on defense mechanisms as adaptive as well as pathological has been one of the most fruitful contributions of psychoanalysis to both psychotherapy and developmental research. The list of defenses has been further expanded (by Bibring, Dwyer, Hunington, & Valenstein, 1967; Laughlin, 1979; Wallenstein, 1956; and others), and the definitions have varied; but the systematizing process itself originated with Anna Freud.

Empirical research based on the theory of ego defense mechanisms has shown its relevance to overall assessment of psychological functioning. Measures of adaptive and defensive ego functions have been developed. Haan (1977), for example, created a Q-sort to measure coping, defensive, and fragmentation processes.

Because it is beyond the scope of this chapter to describe all attempts to measure defenses, we will select the most important recent contribution in order to demonstrate the importance of such a line of research for psychoanalysis and developmental psychology. Vaillant (1978) studied a sample of undergraduates from a major eastern U.S. university from the years 1942 to 1944. They were chosen to be part of a comprehensive longitudinal study using psychological, sociological, and health mea-

sures. Subjects were interviewed and tested by clinicians; every two years until 1955 they were sent questionnaires about employment, family, health habits, and political views. They were interviewed again in 1950–1952 and in the early 1970s. Blind raters interpreted protocols collected for each case using detailed definitions of defensive functions based on Anna Freud's descriptions.

With this data Vaillant established an empirically useful hierarchical classification of defensive behavior: psychotic, immature, neurotic, and mature defenses. He found a general trend toward more mature defenses with age, a trend toward regression during times of crisis, and a great variability of adaptive patterns which inherent capacities and early life advantages did not predict. He also found a moderate correlation between maturity of defenses and adjustment in the areas of work, family relations, and physical and psychological health. Vaillant's study has shown that defenses are useful tools to study psychological development over the lifespan.

Heinz Hartmann and the Autonomous Ego

Heinz Hartmann follows the tradition of Anna Freud: She specified the ego's defense mechanisms; he broadened the conception of ego functions beyond defense. He believed that analytic theory can and should be applied to normal functioning and adaptation and borrowed models from other natural and social sciences to emphasize this point.

Classic psychoanalytic theory holds that the ego develops from the id's acting in conflict with reality. Hartmann proposed, however, that many of the functions that constitute the ego develop from innate abilities, independent of conflict. "The individual does not acquire all the apparatuses which are put into service of the ego in the course of development: perception, motility, intelligence, etc., rest on emotional givens" (Hartmann, 1958, p. 101). Furthermore neither the ego nor the id exists at birth, but they become differentiated from a "matrix" of undifferentiated functions as development proceeds.

Strictly speaking, there is no ego before the differentiation of ego and id, but there is no id either, since both are products of differentiation. We may consider as inborn ego apparatuses those apparatuses which, after this differentiation, are unequivocally in the service of the ego. (Ibid., pp. 102–103)

Hartmann defined the ego in terms of a newly expanded range of functions, ones which act for purposes other than defense and coping with conflict. They are part of the "conflict-free ego sphere." Many functions develop in this sphere.

Perception, intention, object comprehension, thinking, language, recall-phenomena, productivity, to the well-known phases of motor development, grasping, crawling, walking, and to the maturation and learning processes implicit in all of these and many others. (Ibid., p. 8)

In fact these ego functions include such abstract notions as the differentiation and synthesis (the "organizing function") of the personality.

Ego functions such as those mentioned previously are labeled *apparatuses of primary autonomy*, for they are neither derived from conflict nor directly dependent on the drives. These contrast with ego functions which originally serve a specific defense need but later become independent adaptational skills. "An ego function, such as curiosity or rationalization, may arise as a defense against drives but come to serve adaptation or even become a goal in its own right; then it is said to have secondary autonomy" (Loevinger, 1976, p. 366).

The development from defense to autonomous function is called a *change of function*. Loevinger describes altruism as an example of this process.

In altruism, or at least one form of it, the person signs over to someone else his own desires, for which he has come to expect frustration . . . by identification one substitutes gratification for frustration, and one exchanges the passive role of the rejected one for the active role of the benefactor. (Ibid., pp. 365–366)

A parallel transformation of the drives occurs. Hartmann expanded the function of sublimation to a deinstinctualization of all drives: "We call neutralization the change of both libidinal and aggressive energy away from the instinctual and toward a non-instinctual mode . . . a mode of energy more appropriate to the functions of the ego" (Hartmann, 1964, pp. 227, 235; noted in Schafer, 1968, p. 45). This psychic energy, now deinstinctualized, is used by the ego to "feed" all ego functions.

"Neutralization of psychic energy" is also useful for understanding both mental disorders and psychological development. Hartmann hypothesized that psychosis is a lack of neutralization and ineffective functioning of the ego. The developments of object relations and neutralization are intertwined; they each contribute to the other.

. . . full object relations . . . presuppose, as one contribution from the ego, some degree of neutralization of libidinal as well as aggressive energy which secures constancy of the objects independent of the need situation. . . . But it has also been emphasized . . . that good object relations benefit neutralization. (Hartmann, 1964, p. 199)

By this process, object relations develop from an objectless state, through one in which the object is recognized in relation to self, and finally to a state in which the object has independent existence. Thus ego development involves an interaction between the ego functions, neutralization, and object relations.

Another important component of Hartmann's theory of the ego is its role in adaptation. Just as the ego itself has been expanded, its role has been broadened. Earlier its primary role was that of defense; now it includes adaptation. Adaptation is the development of motor skills of language. It is learning and memory, and it is defense as well.

This concept is derived from biology and emphasizes the reciprocity between individual and environment, child and mother, and individuals and society. Hartmann said he would call a man well adapted (to an "average expectable stimulation") "if his productivity, his ability to enjoy life and his mental equilibrium are undisturbed" (1939, p. 23). He noted that the adaptational processes in animals are served primarily by the drives, but in humans, ego functions adaptively regulate the often conflicting drives or those which are nonadaptive in the immediate environment.

One should note the multiple influences, both internal and external, on the ego. Hartmann recognized these in the biological concept of maintaining equilibrium—what he calls "fitting together." He recognizes four types: those between the individual and the environment, the individual and his/her instinctual drives ("vital equilibrium"), the self and mental institutions ("structural equilibrium"), and that between the synthetic function (integrating the personality) and the rest of the ego.

Hartmann also describes what he calls *regressive adaptation*. This means that "reality adaptation cannot alone guarantee an optimal total adaptation" and that it is sometimes necessary to make a "detour through regression" (Hartmann, 1939, p. 36). Adaptive regression, especially its role in creativity, humor, and wit is an idea developed by Rapaport (1967) and Kris (1934). Examples of adaptive regression—"in service of the ego"—are maternal and paternal behavior as compared to usual adult functioning (Blanck & Blanck, 1974, p. 31); creative endeavors, humor, myth, rituals (Loevinger, 1976, p. 336); and "productive fantasy and imaginative processes, problem solving, the capacity for orgiastic experience, ego-building identifications, empathic writing, love, and the therapeutic process" (Bellak, Hurvich, & Gediman, 1973, p. 185).

Criticisms of ego psychology have come from many sources and include work by theorists from the same tradition. The metapsychological insight of George Klein is one example.

One of Klein's criticisms is that the relationship between drive and ego in Hartmann's model is untenable. Although Hartmann did not question instinct theory, he emphasized both aggressive and libidinal energies. The ego transforms these energies through neutralization for a broad range of functions. As Klein (1970) stated,

The ego has had to take account of the plasticity of behavior, of such phenomena as cognitive "autonomy" from stimulation of capacities for choice and volition, and of the development of abilities and intelligence. It has become an exceedingly acrobatic feat to relate these to a libidinal drive development that has its own *directional* mechanisms prior to an ego, while assuming at the same time an independent ego agency whose main function is to control the workings of highly structured drives. (pp. 518–521)

Another criticism of ego psychology, by Schafer, concerns the lack of consistency in defining intrapsychic structures, especially the ego. Beyond the issue of a process or motivational explanation of "function," Hartmann contradicted his definition of the ego in terms of its function. "He spoke of the ego as being defined by its functions. . . . At the same time, he noted that thinking, perception and action frequently serve the id (and) superego, in opposition to the ego" (Schafer, 1970, p. 435). For example the superego neutralizes aggressive energy to prevent cruelty, though this is supposedly an ego function.

The list of the ego's duties has also continued to increase. According to Freud the ego's functions included self-preservation, awareness of an attention to external stimuli, control of voluntary movement, memory, and intrapsychic mediation. Anna Freud added the functions of relating to reality, reality testing, and the synthesis of the personality (Hartmann's "organizing function"). Hartmann emphasized the barrier to stimuli and certain cognitive functions. Bellak (1949) added tolerance of frustration, and Beres (1965) emphasized object relations (Bellak et al., 1973, pp. 52–53).

One wonders, with Klein, "Has anything in the standard subject matter of university psychology laboratories been left out of this list of functions allegedly specific to the 'ego'?" (Klein, 1970, p. 516). Ego psychologists, however, have not only revised analytic theory, but they have also tried to clarify psychoanalytic constructs. The adaptational model and concepts of neutralization and the primary and secondary autonomy of the ego have broadened the scope of psychoanalysis, making it more relevant to the study of normal functioning and development.

Much fruitful research in psychoanalysis and dynamic psychiatry has come from work derived from Hartmann's conceptualizations of the ego and its functions. Although much research in the area has been done, we only have space enough to review three: Bellak et al. (1973), Prelinger and Zimet (1964), and Grinker, Werble, and Drye (1968) which attempt to operationalize ego functions.[2]

Bellak et al. (1973) assessed 25 normals, 25 neurotics, and 50 schizophrenics for ego functioning, using a semistructured interview and a battery of psychological tests. They sought to find patterns of functioning in each group. Ego functions were labelled (1) reality testing, (2) judgment, (3) sense of reality of self and of world, (4) regulation and control (of drives, affects, impulses), (5) object relations, (6) thought processes, (7) adaptive regression in the service of the ego, (8) defense, (9) stimulus barrier, (10) autonomous functioning, (11) synthesis, and (12) mastery-competence. A semistructured interview using a number of questions relevant to each ego function produced data rated on a 13-point scale.

The subjects also took a battery of psychological tests which consisted of the TAT, the Rorschach, the WAIS, the Figure Drawing test and the Bender Gestalt. Due to the small number of subjects, the investigators limited their analyses to ego functioning in schizophrenics. These patients were grouped by factor analysis of function scores in these areas: (1) reality orientation, (2) socialization, (3) adaptive thinking, and (4) integrative capacity. Schizophrenics revealed a variety of ego-function disorders, although thought disorder was not the most prominent nor uniformly present.

Prelinger and Zimet (1964) were careful to provide a uniform assignment of numerical scores. Test and interview material was interpreted by a rater on 78 scales. These scales were grouped in the following areas: (1) ideational styles, (2) prominent affects, (3) prominent defenses, (4) superego, (5) adaptational strengths, (6) sense of self, (7) psychosocial modalities, and (8) character elaborations. The authors used a five-point scale and a guide which was often quite detailed regarding assignment to each of the five levels. An example is the cue for a maximal (5) rating on regression in service of the ego: "Frequent and intense immersion in personal, irrational

material, encroachment of ego-alien material, difficulty in recovering realistic orientation, only spotty utilization of the material for adaptive solutions" (p. 57).

Grinker et al. (1968) were explicitly behavioral in their orientation to measuring ego functions. Their approach is due to their desire to establish empirically the validity of the psychiatric diagnosis of "borderline." The ward and therapy behavior of 51 psychiatric patients was rated on 280 variables, although with only 93 explicit ego-function variables. Areas assessed were outward behaviors (toward other people, environment, tasks), perception, messages (verbal and nonverbal), affects and defenses (including relationships with people), and ego integrity or synthesis. The investigators applied the variables producing sufficient data to cluster-, factor-, and component-analysis, deriving four coherent subgroups of borderline patients, as well as a set of behaviors and ego functions which characterize each of the groups and the patient sample as a whole.

Grinker points to two important practical problems. First, the measurement of ego functions and the validity of those measurements are problematic, especially those of highly abstract functions (e.g., synthesis of the ego or integrity of personality) when rated from observable behaviors. Second, all the investigators used large numbers of items and yet found many items did not produce enough data for analysis. These problems, combined with the lack of consistent definitions and standardized lists of functions and measurement techniques, leave the comparative evaluation of ego functions research tentative and controversial.

The classic model of psychic conflict was of an ego mediating the opposing demands of the id and superego. Ego psychology, as a theory and an empirical approach, expands this model especially in the area of adapting to the demands of reality. Furthermore as Klein (1970) pointed out, adaptation itself has a developmental context, a viewpoint adhered to by much of modern psychology.

Where previously the resolution of crisis was taken to mean resolution of conflict, equal emphasis is now given to *developmental crises* that arise when adaptational modes of one stage are no longer suited to the unfolding requirements of a succeeding biological stage. . . . It is now a recognized principle in the psychoanalytic theory of *normal* development that crisis and dilemma are inescapable, indeed, they are *positive*, conditions of normal psychological growth. (p. 512)

This conception is specifically described by a major innovator in American ego psychology, Erik Erikson.

Erik Erikson and the Transforming Ego

Erikson builds on Hartmann's adaptational theory with its biological and social concept of individuals being born preadapted to an "average expectable environment." He specifies the preadaptedness by introducing new principles of development—growth by epigenetic steps through psychosocial crisis. His life-cycle concept, first presented in *Childhood and Society* (1950), made it necessary to describe not the expectable environment but a series which corresponds to the eight stages of man: ". . . the human environment as a whole must permit and safeguard a series of more or less discontinuous and yet

---

[2] For a review of this literature, see Hauser and Daffner, 1980.

culturally and psychologically consistent developments, each extending further along the radius of life tasks. All of this makes man's so-called biological adaptation a matter of life cycles developing within their community's changing history" (Erikson, 1968, p. 222).

Thus the epigenetic stage model bridges internal psychological forces and the social context. Each stage is defined according to age-specific crises, and each crisis is defined as the intersection of cognitive, psychosexual, and interpersonal development in which the self interacts with others in a crisis-specific, historically contextualized way. The stage model is functional—that is, it is connected to the choices an individual makes.

We might call this a "functional" rather than a structural analysis of a cognitive process. Such a functional analysis will always be an "ego psychology" analysis. It will always specify what the process means in terms of the relations between a self and ego and others or the world. It will always define the process as it springs from and has consequences for the individual's self-esteem or sense of competence. (Noam, Snarey, & Kohlberg, in press)

Even so Erikson remains within the bounds of Freudian instinct theory. Guntrip (1971) claims that Erikson takes the same position as Freud regarding early infancy. Erikson focuses on the id, but much of what Freud treated as the id, Erikson defines as ego reactions.

Our clinical work indicates that this point in the individual's early history [how to continue sucking at the time that teeth have grown from within] is the origin of an evil dividedness, where anger against annoying teeth, and anger against the withdrawing mother, and anger with one's impotent anger all lead to a forceful experience of sadistic and masochistic confusion, leaving the general impression that once upon a time, one destroyed one's unity with the maternal matrix. (Erikson, 1950, p. 74)

Here are both the basic Freudian statement of the meaning of the mother-child relationship and Erikson's agreement and elaboration. Erikson's work, however, despite attempts to build social and interpersonal flexibility into his theory of the life cycle, still has some of the heavy-handed determinism that characterizes Freud's work. Erikson has expanded Freud's original five stages—three infantile, a stage of latency, and a stage of genitality—to eight stages and has attempted to go beyond Freud in his thinking about adolescence. Like Freud, however, Erikson places a tremendous emphasis upon the meaning of the mother-infant contact because it is the first interpersonal experience.

Erikson's theory presumes the following sequence of major points in the life cycle: Basic trust is a prerequisite for *identity formation,* and *identity formation* in its turn is a prerequisite for an individual to form sexual relationships. It is clear from Erikson's writing that *identity versus identity diffusion* precedes the critical stage of *intimacy versus isolation.* Again, a quotation from Erikson (1968) is helpful.

It is only when identity formation is well on its way that true intimacy—which is really a counterpointing as well as a fusing of identities—is possible. Sexual intimacy is only part of what I have in mind, for it is obvious that sexual intimacies often precede the capacity to develop a true and mutual psychosocial intimacy with another person, be it in friendship, in erotic encounters, or in joint inspiration. The youth who is not sure of his identity shies away from interpersonal intimacy or throws himself into acts of intimacy which are promiscuous without true fusion or real self-abandon. (p. 135)

Erikson goes further in another statement, from his paper published in 1959. The focus here is on a limited and a specific part of the life cycle.

For where an assured sense of identity is missing, even friendships and affairs become desperate attempts at delineating the fuzzy outlines of identity by mutual narcissistic mirroring: to fall in love then often means to fall into one's mirror image, hurting oneself and damaging the mirror. During lovemaking or in sexual fantasies, a loosening of sexual identity threatens: it even becomes unclear whether sexual excitement is experienced by the individual or by his partner, and this in either heterosexual or homosexual encounters. The ego thus loses its flexible capacity for abandoning itself to sexual and affectual sensations, in a fusion with another individual who is both partner to the sensation and guarantor of one's continuing identity: fusion with another becomes identity loss. (p. 125)

We can ask, nonetheless, how does one reach a stage of sexual maturity so that one can behave like a sexually mature adult? Consistently throughout Erikson's work the sequence is clear: Adult sexuality follows identity formation. The foundation of identity is basic trust, the ability to see oneself as having continuity and sameness, and acting accordingly. Erikson's theory of the stages leading to sexual maturity can be summarized as follows: (1) Infancy (oral sensory): Trust vs. Mistrust; (2) Early Childhood (muscular-anal): Autonomy vs. Shame, Doubt; (3) Play Age (locomotor-genital): Initiative vs. Guilt; (4) School Age (latency): Industry vs. Inferiority; (5) Puberty and Adolescence: Identity vs. Role Confusion; (6) Young Adulthood: Intimacy vs. Isolation; (7) Adulthood: Generativity vs. Stagnation; and (8) Maturity: Ego Integrity vs. Despair.

We also note that while Erikson acknowledges the importance of the mother-infant bond and views it as a critical event, he joins Anna Freud in seeing adolescence as a time when, using Sullivan's phrase, the "warps" of earlier experience could be not only addressed but redressed. Erikson's contribution to developmental psychology is his use of a redefinition of psychoanalytic theory as a point of departure for studying the whole life of the individual. By viewing the human condition over a lifetime, he anticipates the work of George Vaillant, Daniel Levinson, and Robert White.

There have been many empirical applications of Erikson's developmental model, although Erikson himself has been skeptical regarding attempts at statistical analysis based on his clinical and developmental theory (Erikson & Erikson, 1981). Marcia (1978) reviews the area of identity formation. The measures include a semantic differential procedure (Bronson, 1972), adjective-ranking technique (Block, 1961), various uses of the Q-sort to measure discrepancies between perceived and ideal self (Gruen, 1960) and between familial figures and perceived self (Hauser, 1971). Marcia (1966) operationally defined Erikson's four identity statuses in terms of the central concepts of crisis and commitment. *Identity achievement* represents post-crisis commitment to ideological, religious, and occupational life areas. *Foreclosure* is commitment without consideration of alternatives to socially—to be specific, parentally—offered positions. *Identity-diffusion* is neither commitment nor present investment in a period of choice. *Moratorium* denotes a current crisis or the consideration of identity issues.

The measurement of Marcia's concepts of identity status consisted of two parts. First, subjects were interviewed within a semistructured format. The questions concerned commitment and present or past consideration or crisis about issues. Tapes of the interviews were rated by judges familiar with model examples of the answers appropriate to each status.

The second part of the measurement was an overall identity assessment using 23 projective sentence-completion stems ("When I let myself go, I . . ."). There were three point ratings, with model responses for each stem, to assess the degree of security of identity.

The relationships between Marcia's identity statuses and other ego states and ego functions have been studied with results of theoretical consistency. Such correlates include anxiety levels (Byrne, 1961; Mahler, 1959; Marcia, 1967; Oshman & Manosevitz, 1974; Podd, Marcia, & Rubin, 1970; Stark & Traxler, 1974), self-esteem (Breuer, 1973; Rosenfeld, 1972), moral reasoning (Hayes, 1977; Poppen, 1974; Rowe, 1978), and styles of cognition (Kirby, 1977; Tzuriel & Klein, 1977). Correlations to intimacy were made by Kinsler (1972), Constantinople (1969), and Orlofsky, Marcia, and Lesser (1973).

The number of investigations which translate Eriksonian concepts into productive research is remarkable. The studies mentioned above are but a fraction of the studies which examine only one stage of this developmental model. Psychological research which studies the relationship between the epigenetic stages, psychological states, and social phenomena will yet continue, a fact that is a further testimony to the importance of Erikson's thought.

OBJECT-RELATIONS THEORY

This section of the chapter will present basic concepts from the works of W.R.D. Fairbairn and Donald Winnicott. Their contributions, central to object-relations theory, are a structural mapping of the psyche, where objects are assumed to be an integral part of the ego itself, and descriptions of early interactions which would allow the child to retain more or less ego integrity or unity. The Freudian tenet that conflicts experienced during adulthood are foreshadowed by early childhood experiences is maintained by these men. They see difficulties in early relationships, and the consequences for psychic development, as the shapers of adult developmental processes. These ideas are particularly valuable because of the implications for normal adult development; they are also relevant to specific areas of empirical work within developmental psychology.

Both theorists derive their ideas from extensive clinical work. Donald Winnicott's years as a pediatrician providing well-baby care and his emphasis on therapeutic consultations with children and their parents have made his theoretical work relevant and intellectually accessible to parents and others who have contact with children. Both authors have used their conceptions of early interpersonal relations to help adults in clinical situations.

W.R.D. Fairbairn and the Central Ego

The Central Ego and Internalization. Freud maintained that the id is the oldest structural aspect of the psyche, containing all that is present at birth and inherited. Fairbairn believes that the oldest structure of the psyche is what he calls the central ego.

In the case of "the central ego," the correspondence to Freud's "ego" is fairly close from a functional standpoint; but there are important differences between the two concepts. Unlike Freud's "ego," the "central ego" is not conceived as originating out of something else (the "id") or as constituting a passive structure dependent for its activity upon impulses proceeding from the matrix out of which it originated, and on the surface of which it rests. On the contrary, the "central ego" is conceived as a primary and dynamic structure from which . . . the other mental structures are subsequently derived. (1952, p. 106)

In this scheme, impulses do not exist in the absence of an ego structure, thus distinguishing the id and the ego is unnecessary.

Fairbairn asserts that the libido is fundamentally object-seeking and therefore directed toward another individual in a manner that is progressively more discriminating and specific. "Any theory of ego development that is to be satisfactory must be conceived of in terms of relationships with objects, and in particular relationships with objects which have been internalized during early life under the pressure of deprivation and frustration" (ibid.). He believes that an infant begins with a pristine, unitary ego; he stressed the child's capacity for relatedness with another, based on the intrinsic pleasure of those interactions.

Presumably the satisfaction of visceral needs does have some role in determining the child's experience of relatedness with the caregiver. But Fairbairn's hypotheses create a larger role for the effect of playful, exploratory, and otherwise relaxed interactions which occur for progressively longer periods during the first several months of life. Thus in his scheme, attachment does not evolve merely because the primary figure is associated with impulse gratification. He asserts that the ego is object-relational from the beginning, and its energies are directed toward negotiating the vicissitudes of interpersonal experiences. The ego ultimately represents various aspects of relationships with significant individuals within the psyche itself.

For Fairbairn the structural aspects of the psyche do not emerge according to a biologically based timetable or from the infant's attempts to control his/her own overwhelming impulses toward need-gratification. The central ego is inborn and maintains unity until it is disrupted under the pressure of the infant's attempt to cope with unsatisfying interpersonal experiences. Gratification specifically refers to pleasurable experiences which happen within, and are identified with, the interpersonal field (the "infant-caregiver matrix"). The infant's tendency to represent the caregiver as an other in relation to him/herself within his/her own psyche is critical. This process is called internalization and appeared originally in Freud's discussion of superego formation. The internalization of benevolent interactions tends to strengthen and expand the child's original central ego.

The central system, or ego,

... has assimilated and organized much of the experience with significant people in the early environment and hence much of the cultural pattern in which the individual is reared. This central organization (the ego) is characterized by its relatively much greater capacity to learn and by its unique feature, namely, that its integrative functions appear closely connected with consciousness. . . . In the healthy adult, the main needs are ego-syntonic and of such a character that a manifold set of personal relationships is sought and maintained. The relatively free transactions between the need systems themselves (greater communication) in the healthy person also means that he responds more as a whole, is more integrated in assessing inner and outer reality. The central ego in such a person is therefore being enriched throughout life and this *constant enrichment provides motivational growth and support*. The capacity of the central ego to tolerate conflicting needs and to organize them appears to be largely an acquired property. Certain kinds of early experience make or mar this capacity in a profound way. What starts off the ego as an adequate independent organizer, i.e., what lays the foundation for an organizing ego, independent of the mother who has been the first organizer, is particularly important. (Sutherland, 1963, p. 116)

The infant and caregiver participate in a series of interactions which are like a continuum going, broadly speaking, from the infant's pressing need for visceral gratification to play dialogues—relaxed "conversations." However, self and other are not clearly delineated by the infant at the time s/he first experiences both relatively satisfying and depriving interactions with the caregiver. Thus the contours of the emerging self become dependent, to some extent, upon the nature of the internal representation of self and other as existing in an interactional field—the matrix.

To explain this situation Fairbairn posits subsidiary egos which emerge within the originally unitary ego. These are structures which correspond to the exciting and depriving aspects of experiences within the matrix. For example the appearance of the mother after a brief period of separation is inherently exciting to the infant who may have become distressed by her absence. The infant may anticipate visual recognition, tactile contact, or a greeting; these are forms of contact which generally comfort and relieve distress. They also allow him/her to resume interest in other aspects of the environment. Should the infant seem ready for contact and be rebuffed, s/he perceives and "stores" this experience along with other rejecting ones. These gradually are organized around one version or internal image of the caregiver. Conversely the initial anticipation of excitement is also stored, along with other exciting or anticipatory experiences. They are loosely organized around a second parental image within the child's psyche.

Fairbairn refers to internalized representations of the experience of the other as the exciting (or libidinal) object and the rejecting (or antilibidinal) objects; each has a corresponding internal representation of self: the excit-

ing (libidinal) ego and the rejecting (antilibidinal) ego. Because "bad" objects and corresponding egos threaten the security of the internal world, they are repressed. If the infant's experiences are *overly* exciting and *overly* frustrating, the structures which represent these experiences tend to remain split off from the central ego and are therefore not experienced as a part of the self. As long as the structures remain unintegrated with the central or observing portion of the self, they are relatively immune to modification. In normal development a certain level of deprivation and frustration during the early years is considered reasonable, and the infant can generally reintegrate the "bad" aspects by continuing to experience a generally satisfying relationship with another.

Assuming that the caregiver's central ego is relatively well integrated and his/her perception of the infant is not distorted by projecting the repressed internalized "bad" aspects of his/her own psyche onto the child, the child can gradually integrate split-off "bad" parts of his/her internal world back into the central ego and tolerate the ambivalence of loving another who is neither all good nor all bad but at least "good enough." This tolerance occurs as the capacity of the child's central ego to observe itself and to integrate more complex, discrepant information increases. The child's essential task at this point is to experience both him/herself and the other as differentiated individuals who are essentially good and satisfying to one another despite some frustrating or depriving interactions. The child's chances of achieving reparation during subsequent developmental phases are thereby increased.

Although this process of differentiation is complex and protracted, Fairbairn believes that the ability to reintegrate "bad" aspects of the early relationship into one relatively continuous, unitary conception of oneself and the other—hence tolerating the ambivalence of perceiving good and bad aspects simultaneously—is an essential achievement during the early years. If the store of early experiences weighs too strongly on the frustrating and the depriving side, the child's central ego is not sufficiently strong or well enough supported by the external caregiving environment to achieve the reintegration.

Integration of the Psychic Structures and Implications for Later Intimate Relationships.

Structures are conceived as interrelated dynamic psychological systems; constantly in active relationship with each other and with the outer world. Each structure has a great complexity in depth into which is built a history. The particular experiences of the person will contribute many subsystems. . . . There is a tendency for these constituent subsystems to group or assume a hierarchical order around the image of one person, even if only loosely. (Sutherland, 1963, p. 115)

After the structural system develops, "these structures are organized and seek to effect certain kinds of relationships" (ibid.). The extent to which the systems of the self are within the individual's awareness may vary; nonetheless, all parts of the personality emerge sooner or later, especially in later intimate relationships. The individual's tendency is to seek out relationships in which the repressed, as well as the known, parts of the personality can emerge. It is as if a re-creation of the original depriving or frustrating situation is sought, with interactions akin to those in the original relationships occurring again. The largely unconscious purpose of this re-creation is the effort to achieve reparation and closure, allowing the individual to reintegrate split-off parts of him/herself. Fairbairn stresses that because the structures were originally segregated within the context of an interpersonal relationship, the most likely arena for their reemergence and integration is also interpersonal. Ideally, most intimate relationships are

fashioned predominantly by the central ego so that the identity and the reality of the other is fully accepted, i.e., the overall acceptance of this person raises the threshold tolerance for unfulfilled expectancies so that the relationship is maintained. If the frustrations in the relationship are too great despite mutual adaptation attempts, it can be ended without destructive behavior. The concern for the other in adult relationships stems from many sources, one being the patterning of the central ego's actions by the tendency, even though this be a latent process, to make real relationships approximate to that of the ideal ego with its ideal object. (Ibid., p. 117)

Some aspects of later intimate relationships are also fashioned by the repressed, segregated portions of the ego system. The balance of the interactions more likely occurs as an outgrowth of each partner's central ego strengths, especially if early experiences allowed each to reintegrate split-off, negative portions of the system to a significant extent. Most personalities, however, retain some amount of dissociated structural terrain in adulthood, experiences which are "bad" enough that they cannot be held ambivalently within the central ego. Normally if object choice stems primarily from the strengths of the central ego, an intimate relationship can tolerate the reemergence of "bad" objects and "bad" ego as they attempt reparation. Ideally the other partner does not participate in re-creating the original cycle of excitement and frustration. Reintegration is more likely if the first partner's original deprivation was not so great as to swamp the central ego's efforts to observe the discrepancy between the original perceptions of the other and the distorted perceptions which erupt when the "bad" objects reemerge. Also reintegration is more likely if the current object has enough observing central-ego function to appeal to the central-ego strength of the first partner; both partners may then be able to address the source of the distortion and facilitate the process of reparation.

H. V. Dicks has expanded and applied clinically Fairbairn's particular approach to object-relations theory. He envisions the process of reintegration as a normal and inevitable part of adult intimacy.

Marriage is the nearest adult equivalent to the original parent-child relationship. Thus its success must revolve around the freedom to regress. The freedom to bring into the adult relation the deepest elements of infantile object-relations is a condition of growth. To be able to regress to mutual childlike dependence, in flexible role exchanges, without censure or loss of dignity, in the security of knowing that the partner accepts because he or she can properly identify with, or tolerate as a good parent this "little needy ego" when it peeps out—this is the promise people seek when they search for one person who will be unconditionally loving, permissive and strong—who will enable one to fuse all part-object relations

into a meaningful whole and be enhanced by it. The search for this in heterosexuality determines the persistence with which people seek their "ideal mate." They may divorce only to re-enact the pattern again. Or they may desperately cling together and repeat the old frustrating object-relations using each other as victim and aggressor. (Dicks, 1963, p. 129)

Donald W. Winnicott and the Holding Ego

Winnicott agrees with Fairbairn that individuals internalize relationships and that early "object relations" have a potent effect on the specific contours of an individual's internalized world. He is interested in the nature of early interactions which ultimately lead to the normal capacity for interpersonal relations and a clear differentiation of the self.

Winnicott once heard himself saying to the British Psychoanalytic Society, " 'There is no such thing as a baby' . . . I was alarmed to hear myself utter these words and tried to justify myself by pointing out that if you show me a baby you certainly show me also someone caring for the baby, or at least a pram with someone's eyes and ears glued to it. One sees a 'nursing couple' " (Winnicott, 1958, p. 99). Explaining more theoretically, Winnicott writes,

We sometimes loosely assume that before the two-body object relationship there is a one-body relationship, but this is wrong, and obviously wrong if we look closely. The capacity for the one-body relationshp *follows* that of a two-body relationship, through the introjection of the object . . . before object relationships the state of affairs is this: that the unit is not the individual, the unit is an environment-individual set-up. The center of gravity of the being does not start off in the individual. It is the total set-up. By good-enough childcare, technique, holding, and general management the shell becomes gradually taken over and the kernel (which has looked all the time like a human baby to us) can begin to be an individual. . . . The good-enough infant care technique neutralizes the external persecutions, and prevents the feelings of disintegraton and loss of contact between psyche and soma.

In other words, without a good-enough technique of infant care the new human being has no chance whatever. With a good-enough technique the center of gravity of being in the environment-individual set-up can afford to lodge in the centre, in the kernel rather than in the shell. The human being now developing an entity from the centre can become localized in the baby's body and so can begin to create an external world at the same time as acquiring a limiting membrane and an inside. According to this theory there was no external world at the beginning although we as observers could see an infant in an environment. How deceptive this can be is shown through analysis at a later date that what we ought to have seen was an environment developing falsely into a human being, hiding within itself a potential individual. (Ibid., pp. 99–100)

Characteristics of the Infant-Mother Matrix. Both Winnicott and Fairbairn stress the relatedness of the infant and his/her active contribution to a two-person relationship. Even prior to rudimentary self-object differentiation, the infant's responsiveness elicits responsiveness from the caregiver. Thus the caregiver is dependent upon the infant to provide signals or cues which shape the adapted interventions; this Winnicott believes is the essence of "good-enough mothering."

Findings from a number of sources suggest that the

infant's "entering repertoire" (gestures, movements, etc.) and even his/her physical characteristics maximize the chances of receiving maternal and paternal care. Harper (1975) observes that the physiological and psychological changes during pregnancy shift maternal focus to the infant and lay the groundwork for subsequent maternal preoccupation with the child. Klaus and Kennell (1976) have outlined a system of reciprocity which operates during the immediate postpartum period and may serve to intensify the bond between mother and neonate. Some aspects are initiated more directly by the infant and others by the mother, but all are maintained interactively.

What Winnicott calls "good-enough mothering" initially entails a careful matching of the mother's interventions with the needs of the baby, a responsiveness as finely tuned as possible. The caregiver gradually "deadapts" at a pace tolerated by the infant without overtaxing him/her. Winnicott views both close adaptation ("good-enough mothering") and gradual de-adaptation as critical components of self-object differentiation.

The mother, at the beginning, by an almost 100 percent adaptation affords the infant the opportunity for the *illusion* that her breast is part of the infant. It is, as it were, under the baby's magical control. The same can be said in terms of infant care in general, in the quiet times between excitements. Omnipotence is nearly a fact of experience. The mother's eventual task is gradually to disillusion the infant, but she has no hope of success unless at first she has been able to give opportunity for illusion . . . the mother's adaptation to the infant's needs, when good enough, gives the infant the *illusion* that there is an external reality that corresponds to the infant's own capacity to create. In other words, there is an overlap between what the mother supplied and what the infant might conceive of. (Winnicott, 1971, pp. 11–12)

The infant's experiences with measured discontinuity allow him/her to feel some separateness and give him/her the chance to extend his/her own coping repertoire. If frustration, including delayed visceral gratification as well as a greater lag in interpersonal responsiveness and a slow providing of new sensory-perceptual experiences, is brief, then the infant can either learn to wait and/or discover ways to meet some of his/her own needs. The mother's less-than-complete responsiveness provides a circumscribed opportunity for the infant to encounter novel situations and develop the internal resources to deal with them. Unless the mother does curtail full adaptation, the world appears magically created, and the infant's inner resources are not realized.

Winnicott discusses the way the infant comes to realize that feelings originate within and are directed at another and that it is the same other toward whom s/he feels both love and hate. This process enables the infant to evolve gradually a differentiated sense of him/herself and the other, as well as some basic tolerance for ambivalence.

The infant is beginning to relate himself to objects that are less and less subjective phenomena, and more and more objectively perceived "not me" elements. He has begun to establish a self. . . . The mother has now become—in the child's mind—a coherent image, and the term "the whole object" now becomes applicable. This development implies an ego that begins to be independent of the mother's auxiliary ego

. . . the infant now feels that personal richness resides within the self. (Winnicott, 1965, pp. 74–75)

Winnicott's concept of the "holding environment" is an interesting elaboration on the work of other object-relation theorists, such as Melanie Klein and W.R.D. Fairbairn. Initially the caregiver provides both literal and metaphorical holding. The latter occurs when the caregiver intervenes in such a way that "unthinkable anxiety" is avoided. This is particularly necessary when the baby has no idea or only a shadowy conception that s/he has not created the world. When the infant has distinguished a rudimentary boundary between him/herself and the caregiver, the "holding environment" serves another function: The mother provides a consistent presence and "benevolent" boundaries. Continuity in the psychological field provides a framework of external stability within which the child moves, going along a continuum of integration and lack of integration. Winnicott believes this allows the child to achieve reparation and the consequent internalization of a more discrete and continuous relationship between him/herself and the other.

There are two specific areas in which the caregiver's actions directly facilitate differentiation: interactive play and the child's playing alone while in the presence of the mother. The caregiver's interventions occur within an interpersonal context and pave the way for the child's internalizing the primary relationship more fully. Once this internalization is achieved, the child is better able to be physically alone because s/he can derive comfort from an internalized store of good experiences with the object. Essential components of a comforting internalized world include the sense that s/he is a separate entity with thoughts, feelings, motivations, and preference and a recognition of his/her ability to make autonomous choices. Ideally the caregiver is internalized as a continuous presence who sponsors, guides, and celebrates the child's autonomy.

Winnicott stresses that interactional play is not an expression of instinctual drives; the excitement which arises from play stems from creating a reality which is intermediate between inner psychic reality and the external world.

Into this play area the child gathers objects of phenomena from external reality and uses these in the service of some sample derived from inner or personal reality. Without hallucinating the child puts out a sample of dream potential and lives with this sample in a chosen setting of fragments from external reality . . . playing is inherently exciting and precarious. This characteristic derives *not* from instinctual arousal but from the precariousness that belongs to the interplay in the child's mind of that which is subjective (near hallucination) and that which is objectively perceived (actual, or shared reality). (Winnicott, 1971, pp. 51–52)

"Playing creates an interpersonal psychological field in which the baby can move between personal psychic reality and the experience of controlling actual objects. Within this field the baby can enjoy a 'marriage' of the omnipotence of intrapsychic process and his/her control of the actual" (Ibid., pp. 47–48).

Two developmental research teams have investigated the nature of reciprocal interactions during "play dialogues" between mothers and their infants during approximately the first six months of life. Stern's (1974) work focuses on the role of gaze in the mutual regulation of social interaction, and Brazelton, Koslowski, and Main's (1974) observations include a broader inventory of the activities which trigger and sustain play.

During mutual interactions, both mother and infant balance their activities around the infant's thresholds and preferences for discrepancy, habituation, and stimulus overload.

The presence of the infant's gaze, especially in combination with other expressive behavior, tends to elicit unique maternal facial and vocal behaviors and tends to hold the mother's gaze on the infant. The mother then modulates the stimulus configuration of her facial and· vocal performance, using as cues the infant's state of arousal and affect and quality of his visual attention. (Stern, 1974, p. 207)

Stern describes a mutual regulatory system, in which the infant gazes away when his/her internal state is changing, and the mother both waits for him/her to resume contact and modifies her actions to prevent stimulus overload or habituation. She maintains the system within an optimal range defined by the infant, who initiates and terminates nearly all the mutual gazes.

Any self-correcting system such as this is set to operate within a given tolerance range ... the array of stimuli the mother provides and infant's level of arousal and affect repeatedly fall below some optimal level where active aversion is executed ... the clinical import of this situation is that the infant acquires experience with the regulation of his state of arousal and affect on the basis of another person's interpersonal behavior. (Ibid., pp. 209–210)

Brazelton et al., in observations of cyclical interactional patterns, stress that the strength of the dyadic interaction dominates the meaning of each member's behavior. The behavior of one member of the dyad becomes part of a cluster of behaviors which interact with a cluster of behaviors from the other. "No single behavior can be separated from the cluster for analysis without losing its meaning in the sequence ... in the same way the dyadic nature of the interaction superseded the importance of an individual member's clusters and sequences" (Brazelton et al., 1974, p. 56).

The reports of Stern and Brazelton et al. discuss the organizational patterns governing the interacting pair and the fruitlessness of trying to pinpoint one agent of control. Their observations seem to indicate that infants are fundamentally object-seeking, an idea Fairbairn also suggests. The infants in the studies were a few months old and demonstrated a rather sophisticated capacity for relatedness, apparently because of the intrinsic pleasure of interpersonal contact. The complexity, depth, and richness of the dyadic interactions is far removed from the need for visceral gratification; their sophisticated organization is also difficult to explain by secondary reinforcement or association alone. Brazelton et al. and Stern's observations are reminiscent of Winnicott's more colloquial point that "there is no such thing as a baby ... one sees a nursing couple" (Winnicott, 1958, p. 99). Since both studies examined this complex organization or interactions during play dialogues, they support Winni-

cott's notion that during play the mother and infant create a psychological field in which each contributes creatively to what emerges. As he suggests, both partners are extending their interactive repertoires in a manner that involves mutual reflection. Thus the infant receives differentiated feedback on his/her effect on another; s/he uses these reflections to organize his/her concept of him/herself, and this process occurs in the context of a relationship. Play allows an active, vital attachment to form and extends the basis of the bond beyond passive dependence.

The optimal range of stimuli circumscribed by the infant corresponds to Winnicott's notion that the infant enters with a repertoire to which the mother must closely adapt. The descriptions of the thresholds for engagement and overstimulation suggest the boundaries of the "holding environment" that the mother can provide, boundaries which probably become broader and more flexible as the infant's flexibility itself increases. Thus the infant benefits from the mother's gradual de-adaptation. In fact Brazelton et al.'s description of the mother's activities is similar to Winnicott's discussion of an acceptable "holding environment."

The mother tends to provide a "holding framework" for her own cues, that is, she holds the infant with her hands, with her eyes, with her voice and smile, and with changes from one modality to another as he habituates to one or another. All these holding experiences are opportunities for the infant to learn how to control motor responses, and how to attend for longer and longer periods. They amount to a kind of learning about organization of behavior in order to attend. (Brazelton et al., 1974, p. 70)

Addressing the quality of modulation that the mother provides within the boundaries of the infant's repertoire, Fairbairn and Winnicott both say that the interactions which become the substrate for internalized, differentiated structures of the ego occur before the infant distinguishes him/herself from his/her mother. Differentiation is dependent on relating with another and having oneself reflected back within that context. The well-modulated stimulation offered by mothers who both wait for the baby to initiate contact and allow him/her to terminate before reengaging exemplify Winnicott's idea that the "good-enough" mother must wait for the spontaneous gesture of the infant.

An important feature of Winnicott's conception of interactional play is his insistence that it does not emerge unless the infant's visceral needs (i.e., food, warmth, physical comfort, literal holding) are in the background. Play facilitates the development of an active, vital attachment and allows different facets of each interactant's personality to emerge. Play also allows both mother and baby to expand their interactive repertoire and spontaneously create novel combinations or sequences of activities. Because the interactants repeat and elaborate upon the actions of one another, a great deal of mutual reflection occurs. Thus in a relatively relaxed arena, the infant actively participates in a process which can offer him/her differentiated information about him/herself as well as his/her effect on the reaction of another. The outstanding feature of Winnicott's conception of attachment is his inclusion of an active and creative wellspring in the maternal-infant bond; attachment is extended beyond nurturance. The caregiver becomes more than an emblem of visceral satisfaction; s/he is a partner in a creative process.

The periods in which the child plays alone in the presence of the mother, without the two individuals either communicating directly, focusing their attention on one another, or encroaching on one another's privacy, are also critical to self-object differentiation. In a relatively relaxed situation, the infant is free to drift among various levels of integration and focus, peripherally aware of the mother's presence.

Being alone in the presence of someone can take place at a very early stage, when the *ego immaturity is naturally balanced by ego-support* from the mother. In the course of time the individual introjects the ego-supportive mother and in this way becomes able to be alone without frequent reference to the mother or mother symbol. (Winnicott, 1965, p. 32)

Winnicott writes that in the context of "ego relatedness" relatively unintegrated states can emerge.

I think it will be generally agreed that id-impulse is significant only if it is contained in ego living. An id-impulse either disrupts a weak ego or else strengthens a strong one. It is possible to say that id-relationships strengthen the ego when they occur in a framework of ego-relatedness. If this is to be accepted, then an understanding of the importance of the capacity to be alone follows. It is only when alone (that is to say, in the presence of someone) that the infant can discover his own personal life . . . [he can] become unintegrated, to flounder, to be in a state where there is no orientation, to be able to exist for a time without being either a reactor to an external impingement or an active person with a direction of interest or movement. The stage is set for an id experience. In the course of time there arrives a sensation or impulse. In this setting the sensation or impulse will feel real and be truly a personal experience. The individual who has developed the capacity to be alone is constantly able to rediscover the personal impulse, and the personal impulse is not wasted because the state of being alone is something which (though paradoxically) always implies that someone else is there. . . . In the course of time the individual becomes able to forgo the *actual* presence of a mother or mother-figure. This has been referred to in such terms as the establishment of an "internal environment." (Ibid., pp. 33–34)

Implications for Intimacy: The True and False Selves. Winnicott postulates that all individuals start out with a True Self which at the earliest stage

is the theoretical position from which comes the spontaneous gesture and the personal idea. The spontaneous gesture is the True Self in action. Only the True Self can be creative and only the True Self can feel real. Whereas a True Self feels real, the existence of a False Self results in a feeling unreal or a sense of futility. (Ibid., p. 148)

Winnicott believes that the False Self emerges if the child's early experiences with others do not provide a climate conducive to the emergence of the True Self. "The False Self, if successful in its function, hides the True Self, or else finds a way of enabling the True Self to start to live" (Ibid.). The False may be present to a

low or high degree . . . ranging from the healthy polite aspect of the Self to the truly split-off compliant False Self which is

mistaken for the whole child . . . where there is a high degree of split between the True Self and the False Self which hides the True Self, there is found a poor capacity for using symbols, and a poverty of cultural living . . . one observes in such persons extreme restlessness, an inability to concentrate and a need to collect impingements from external reality so that the living-time of the individual can be filled by reactions to these impingements. (Ibid., p. 150)

He presents a continuum which describes the degree to which the compliant False Self may be hiding the True Self.

1. At one extreme: the False Self sets up as real and it is this that observers tend to think is the real person. In living relationships, work relationships, and friendships, however, the False Self begins to fail. In situations in which what is expected is a whole person the False Self has some essential lacking. At this extreme the True Self is hidden.
2. Less extreme: the False Self defends the True Self; the True Self is, however, acknowledged as a potential and is allowed a secret life. Here is the clearest example of clinical illness as an organization with a positive aim, the preservation of the individual in spite of abnormal environmental conditions.
3. More towards health: the False Self has as its main concern a search for conditions which will make it possible for the True Self to come into its own. If conditions cannot be found then there must be reorganized a new defence against exploitation of the True Self, and if there be doubt then the clinical result is suicide. . . .
4. Still further towards health: the False Self is built on identifications. . . .
5. In health: the False Self is represented by the whole organization of the polite and mannered social attitude, a "not wearing the heart on the sleeve," as might be said. Much has gone to the individual's ability to forgo omnipotence and the primary process in general, the gain being the place in society which can never be attained or maintained by the True Self alone. (Ibid., pp. 142–143)

Winnicott assumes that well-placed maternal interventions foster the baby's emerging repertoire of spontaneous gestures. "Not-good-enough mothering" imposes gestures, pacing, movement, meaning, and the initiation and termination of contact upon the child. Such mothering creates conditions in which the child must develop a compliant False Self to hide and protect the True Self, and his/her personality is more likely to resemble the initial stages in Winnicott's continuum. If the holding environment continues to be lacking in empathy, it is likely that the False Self will continue to eclipse the True Self and compromise an individual's subsequent capacity for intimacy.

In his discussion of the functions of play, Winnicott also mentions the emergence of the True Self. If the patterns of interactive play are rigidly circumscribed or there is insufficient opportunity to play alone in the mother's presence, it is difficult for the child to experience a spontaneous source of action and impulse within him/herself. Winnicott assumes that negotiations with the interpersonal relationships are the raw material for the child's initial organization of "self vs. other." If sensorimotor and perceptual experiences fail to delineate the interactants because the activities which the infant initiates are not reflected back to him/her as his/her own, the child can only internalize a poorly defined relationship.

The boundaries of the self within later intimate relationships may remain similarly obscure. It may be difficult for the individual to distinguish from which partner impulses, feelings, activities, motivations, values, or beliefs originate. The capacity to be alone in a manner that is relaxed and fruitful or the ability to be alone in the presence of another without either partner intruding while they relax together are both contingent on the clarity and security of the initial relationships each person has internalized. "It is perhaps fair to say that after satisfactory intercourse each partner is alone and is contented to be alone, being able to enjoy being alone along with another person who is also alone, is in itself an experience of health" (ibid., p. 31). In this state two whole individuals can safely become unintegrated for a time and simply *be* without needing to *do*. Such a state assumes that each person has had a protective holding environment when the ego was not strong enough to bind itself and lapse into unintegration. By encountering some essentially individual experience in this state and emerging with ego integrity, the individual can then internalize the process of having had this experience with another present. This internalized holding environment both serves as a referential context when the person is actually alone and allows for ego autonomy within the context of ego relatedness in subsequent intimate situations.

Thus the individual continues to differentiate or remain in touch with his/her True Self while with another. In the Freudian conception, self-differentiation occurred when one went away from another and not when one was "relating" closely with another. Winnicott's conception allows adults to use an interpersonal context for individuation as well as for cooperative communication; he sees the goals as mutually enhancing.

OUTLOOK

In the previous sections, we have described the Freudian legacy upon which both American ego psychology and British object-relations theory are based. These two schools within psychoanalytic theory have had very different traditions, due partly to the historical events that led a group of Austrian and German analysts (e.g., Erikson, Hartmann, Horney, Kris, and Loewenstein) to immigrate to the United States during Hitler's rise to power.

In a 1963 issue of the *British Journal of Medical Psychology*, J. D. Sutherland writes, in honor of W.R.D. Fairbairn,

To the British it is striking how far apart these two areas of work have remained (for some years it seemed that the work of Klein had been declared an un-American activity!). There are now signs that this situation is changing. I believe this trend is due to a growing realization that some of the apparent differences do not represent incompatible lines of work, but, on the contrary, can be seen in substantial measure as complementary. (Sutherland, 1963, p. 109)

Sutherland foresaw a change of direction in the United States, leading to very productive attempts at synthesis of ego psychology and object-relations theory. This trend has culminated with the theoretical work of both Otto Kernberg (1979) and Heinz Kohut (1971). While leading to major debates within the psychoanalytic movement, their contributions enhance its vitality. Building on Freud's discoveries, they are searching for a more encompassing metapsychology and theory, better capable of explaining both clinical and developmental phenomena. In the process, psychoanalysis finds itself in a turbulent reevaluation of its basic premises, a process we have focused on historically in this chapter.

In our conclusion, we deal with those changes by discussing the importance of *psychoanalysis as a developmental psychology*. Subsequently, we deal with the interface between *psychoanalysis and academic developmental psychology*.

PSYCHOANALYSIS AS A DEVELOPMENTAL PSYCHOLOGY

The theory of psychoanalysis has been developed based on clinical treatment and observation of primarily adult patients who free-associate to present problems, past experiences, and relationships to important others. Such an approach has contributed to both the development of a treatment modality and to an understanding of the process of development itself. The paramount contribution of psychoanalysis has been the attempt to understand psychopathology in developmental terms. In traditional psychoanalytic treatment, the patient transfers thoughts and feelings that are part of the representational world of the past onto the therapist. This transference becomes the central tool in uncovering early developmental process and unconscious influences. Thus, the therapeutic context creates a process of "microgenesis" (Werner, 1957), which can recapitulate ontogenesis. In other words, what happens in therapy is a quasi-repetition of development. The reconstruction of the past points to arrests and fixations in development, as well as to unintegrated conflicts from developmental transitions in the past.

Generalizing from reconstructions of the past, from the adult patient's vantage point, to an actual model of human development poses great dangers. Major psychoanalytic theorists have considered this issue (cf. Hartmann, Anna Freud, Erikson) as psychoanalysis and psychotherapy were applied to the growing child. Thus clinical intervention became at the same time a method of child observation. However, the focus was still primarily on the child in need of help. Only when psychoanalysts and psychoanalytically informed psychologists began to observe well-adapted children, often in their natural environments, did the data begin to fit the more universal claims of psychoanalytic developmental theory. Some of the important concepts of psychoanalysis were rejected or verified based on these observations. The distinctions among these sources of data (i.e., psychoanalysis, child-psychotherapy, and child observation) have remained ambiguous and present the field of psychoanalysis and developmental psychology with confusing results.

Clinical Observations:
The Examples of Kernberg and Kohut

Otto Kernberg and Heinz Kohut are two major contributors to the field of psychoanalysis whose developmental theories are based on clinical reconstructions. In terms of adult development, Kernberg (1974a, 1974b, 1976a), in his three articles on love, considers how in the therapeutic processes infantile introjects can be transformed so that the adult may form an intimate and integrated relationship with a "whole object." He maintains that we have spent far too much time on the psychopathology of sex and far too little time on the psychopathology of love.

Kernberg focuses on what he, along with Kohut, conceives as the single most important psychopathology: the borderline condition and pathological narcissism, isolating the individual from meaningful, deep relationships with others. Both Erikson and Sullivan have dealt with the question of adult intimacy and have implied its relationship to what occurred between mother and infant. Kernberg shows how these "warps" can be treated and love relationships formed. In the same spirit as Fairbairn and Balint, Kernberg acknowledges the effect upon adult loving that the mother-infant bond can have. He points out how adult intimacy can be a transcendent form of development. This development propels the individual to new stages of integration in becoming a fuller person as a differentiated individual, not only in the dyadic relationship with the beloved but also as a consequence of that dyadic relationship.

Kohut and his collaborators have also developed object-relations theory further, rejecting classical Freudian drive and trauma theory. They have new insights into the personality structure, treatment process, and metapsychology through analyses with patients characterized by fragile self-esteem, extreme vulnerability to failures and disappointment, and narcissistic disorders of the self. Kohut observed in his patients more archaic transference reactions than those described by classical analysis. He divided these transfers of early object constellations onto the analyst into two groups: the mirror transference which recapitulates the need of the child for greatness, perfection, and grandiosity; and the idealizing transference which repeats the need for merging with a source of power and omnipotence (Kohut & Wolf, 1978). The term *self-object* is used to describe how important others are experienced as part of the self; the term *self-object transference* refers to the narcissistic transference. The process through which the person takes into the self as "building blocks" what is external to the self at first is called *transmuting internalization.* Implicit in object-relations theory is the need for a clear knowledge of how the self develops; Kohut has begun this process. He calls his developmental model of the self the *self-objects,* and the process of transmuting internalization, the *psychology of the self.*

Although Kohut and Kernberg's theories are still controversial within psychoanalysis, they share its emphasis on infancy and early childhood as keys to understanding development over the life span.

Child Observation:
The Example of Ainsworth

There is a long tradition of child observation in psychoanalysis. Anna Freud's Hampstead Clinic perpetuates a strong emphasis on child observational studies (A. Freud, 1951) and research on child psychoanalysis (Sandler, 1962), employing a paradigm that interprets child psychopathology as a deviation from a path of normal development.

Similarly, Spitz (1945, 1946) observed infants who had not received adequate parenting due to early separation. The outcome of his classic longitudinal study was the description of the syndrome of hospitalism. Mahler's (1975) studies on the process of separation-individuation of the pre-Oedipal child had invaluable import to the fields of human development and psychoanalysis.

Empirical studies of child observation, when examined in an object-relations theory framework, provide evidence that the behavior of mother and infant must be considered as a system in which each partner's concept of self emerges from a history of mutual influence. Object-relations theorists postulate that relationships are internalized; this process of self-differentiation proceeds from the infant's having first represented experiences with another within the psyche before s/he has clearly discerned "who is doing what to whom."

Child observation has been a significant avenue exploring and illuminating the role of these early relationships and their effect on thought, feeling, and interaction. John Bowlby (1969), a major figure in the field of child observation, perceived the mother-infant bond in a broader form than Freud's classical psychoanalytic view. Freud characterized the bond between mother and child as an outgrowth of visceral gratification: The child loves the mother because she feeds him/her; this love for her is mediated by gratification. Bowlby believed that the propensity for attachment is biologically based. In his scheme, attachment refers to an affective tie between the infant and caregiver and to a behavioral system which flexibly operates in terms of set goals, mediated by feeling and in interaction with other behavioral systems. It is *adaptive* for the child to be in proximity to the mother and to explore his/her environment; these are the set goals. Bowlby believed that attachment as a behavioral system enhanced the survival of the species. If the child has a propensity to attach, then the child is more likely to benefit from the mother's protection from predators; s/he also benefits from her nurturance. Therefore it is biologically adaptive, in a broad sense, for the child to attach. This extends Freud's narrower definition of attachment, also biologically based, which says the tie forms *because* the mother meets some of the child's specific visceral needs, specifically the need for food.

Ainsworth et al. (1978) provide empirical evidence derived from child observation about patterns of attachment. Her work has focused on the behavior of infants in a so-called "strange situation" in which the quality of their attachment is assessed by their reactions to a separation from and reunion with their caregivers. Ainsworth has developed a classification scheme for three general patterns: security, avoidance, and resistance in the attachment behavior of one-year-olds (Ainsworth, Bell, &

Stayton, 1971; Ainsworth et al., 1978). Of further interest from an object relations perspective is Ainsworth's work in isolating two types of childhood bonding characterized by mothering which fosters either securely or insecurely attached children. Securely attached children try to maintain proximity to the mother, establishing contact with the mother upon reunion by smiling or vocalizing over a distance. When distressed, they cry and/or seek proximity. Following refueling through this contact, the child is subsequently able to resume active exploration and play. Mothers of securely attached children tend to be more expressive and respond more appropriately to the needs of other children.

Children in the avoidant group seek little or no proximity with the mother, ignoring and/or avoiding her in the reunion episode. Resistant children tend to seek proximity to their mothers but also display contact-resisting behaviors, indicating an ambivalent attachment to their mother.

Mothers of insecurely attached children, particularly avoidant children, are more rejecting and are portrayed as harboring submerged forms of anger.

Using an object-relations theory framework, we may postulate that infants in the securely attached group had internalized relationships marked by continuity of responsiveness and reciprocity. When the physical presence of the mother is inaccessible, the infant has access to an internal world that provides a secure "holding environment" for him/her. Because internalization is not firm at this stage, the child is distressed by separation; however, a concrete experience with the caretaker can quickly establish his/her outer equilibrium by stabilizing his/her inner experience of that relationship. Apparently lacking such an internalized holding environment, the less securely attached group of infants had difficulty regaining their internal equilibrium even when their caregivers returned. Child observations interpreted by object-relations theory can provide the necessary theoretical formulations to guide future research and can document or refute certain psychoanalytic models.

PSYCHOANALYSIS AND ACADEMIC DEVELOPMENTAL PSYCHOLOGY

Historically academic psychology has had an ambivalent relationship with psychoanalysis. Nonetheless important psychodynamic concepts have become integrated into a developmental discipline as psychoanalytic language is translated into concepts more consistent with the academic psychological tradition. The coping literature in social psychology exemplifies this movement. Although rejecting the underlying psychodynamic model, the field has been influenced by psychoanalytic concepts of defense. Learning theorists have also reinterpreted psychoanalytic constructs in terms of psychological theory. Piaget, the most influential developmental psychologist of the twentieth century, acknowledges psychoanalysis in itself, while emphasizing the need for a general psychology that would integrate the findings of cognitive developmental psychology with psychoanalytic psychology. In an address to the American Psychoanalytic Association in 1973, he stated,

A day will come when the psychology of cognitive functions and psychoanalysis will have to fuse in a general theory which will improve both, through mutual correction, and starting right now we should be preparing for that prospect by showing the relations which could exist between them. (Piaget, 1973, p. 250)

Psychoanalysts and psychotherapists employ an understanding of individual development and focus on individual differences. The process of biographical reconstruction is a personal one guided by theory and enhancing psychoanalytic thought. Psychoanalysts and psychotherapists analyze their patients' experiences and internalized relationships from within the overarching conceptualization of the dynamic interplay of the structures of personality (ego, id, superego). Specific life situations and family constellations that fostered or hindered past development as well as the process of change in the present are focal realms in the treatment. Freud and subsequent generations of psychoanalytic theorists generalized from their clinical cases to a universalistic theory of development.

Structural-developmental psychology has characteristically been concerned mainly with formulating general constructs of development that are universal to all of the species. Thus when Piaget observed his own three children, he focused on aspects of their development which have universal qualities in a cognitive developmental progression. The study of individual life histories and individual differences has never been in the center of interest of Piagetian psychology.

In the past decade academic developmental psychology has broadened its scope to include the study of cognitive, social, moral, and emotional development. This growth has brought academic psychology closer to areas traditionally pursued by psychoanalysts. Life-span developmental psychology has provided a methodology for the rigorous study of developmental patterns over the life cycle. Conceptually the field owes much to the pioneering contribution of Erik Erikson. The recent interest in psychopathology from an academic-developmental perspective has led to more overlap of psychoanalytic and Piagetian constructs (Kegan, 1979; Noam, 1979). Now when developmental psychologists are more interested in applying developmental theories to individuals in kindergartens, schools, hospitals, or prisons, they can learn from psychoanalytically oriented researchers and clinicians important dynamics of the processes of development.

One example of a psychoanalytic concept yet to be explored within the field of applied developmental psychology is *regression*. Typically, if acknowledged at all, regression is perceived in only one form: the return to an earlier stage of development in time of stress. The frustrated child on the playground "regresses" to the oral stage of development behaviorally and sucks his/her thumb. But the concept can be viewed in other ways. Anna Freud, in *The Ego and the Mechanisms of Defense*, points out that regression paradoxically may be the way in which, from time to time, we go forward in our development. She calls this function *regression in the service of the ego*. Psychoanalysis has also contributed by connecting adulthood to the development of the person in childhood and adolescence. Here, the concept of regression forms an important theoretical and clinical link.

An interesting discussion of regression appears in the works of Michael Balint, a member of the British object-relations school. Balint (1966) sees the human condition as a constant attempt to return to, or find, the equivalent of what he terms "the harmonious interpenetrating mixup" of the mother-child attachment. Throughout our lives we seek an equivalent of the primary, unambivalent love that exists between mother and infant. He views adult sexual intimacy as a "playful" way to return to earlier states with someone with whom one has formed a trusting relationship. The experience of orgasm—i.e., a return to a helpless state—is the end adult analogue: One trusts one's helplessness to another. Helplessness, then, is regression in that one returns to the infantile state of helplessness in a trusting adult sexual relationship. Balint balances this helplessness by indicating that only the "intact" adult has the courage and trust to be helpless in the face of another. Thus regression becomes a highly adaptive way of dealing with growth. It is multifaceted and enters many parts of our experience. Academic developmental psychology should make far more use of this extremely valuable idea.

Developmental psychology provides an understanding of important personality transformations beyond childhood. These shifts occur in such domains as intellectual, moral, and ego development. Since psychoanalysis interprets psychopathology mainly in terms of early childhood experiences, developmental psychology's examination of adolescent and adult transformations can bring to psychoanalysis a new understanding of the relationship between early childhood experiences and adult ego development.

Growth in both fields demands a new look at the similarities and differences of the two paradigms. A new synthesis of ego development will influence preventative and clinical intervention and significantly encompass all aspects of human development and interpersonal relations. Psychoanalysis alone is not able to address all pertinent questions, especially important cognitively based personality changes. Similarly, developmental theory is insufficient to address the fundamental issues of a person's thoughts and actions in the social world as well as the person's struggles with early experiences which are not yet integrated into the personality. Both theories will need further elaboration.

Ultimately, however, both psychoanalysis and developmental psychology need to consider the context in which an individual grows. Erikson comments in *Childhood and Society* that historians can no longer be innocent of human psychological processes and psychoanalysts can no longer ignore social and historical factors that affect the individual. He is insisting that psychoanalytic theory cannot deal with an individual in a vacuum. In reading this book, it is very easy to be caught up in his elucidation of psychosexual development, his original concept of the eight epigenetic stages comprising the life span, his substitution of identity for sexuality as the key to understanding health and illness. It is possible to overlook some of what Erikson saw as necessities for twentieth-century thinking about developmental processes. His approach serves as an outline for developmental psychologists who have not considered the larger historical and social context of development. Much of developmental psychology arising from Piaget's structural paradigm is based on the interactionist view that organisms assimilate and accommodate to their environments. But the structures within the environment have remained formal and need a social reconstruction. Psychoanalysis and developmental psychology must join with other social sciences to study the social and relational aspects of development as they appear within the specific conditions of the social and historical context.

REFERENCES

Ahrens, R. Beitrag zur Entwicklung des Physiognomie und Mimkekehnens. *Zeitschrift für experimentelle und angewandte Psychologie*, 1964, *2*, 412–454.

Ainsworth, M. S. Object relations, dependency, and attachment: A theoretical review of the infant-mother relationship. *Child Development*, 1969, *40*, 969–1025.

Ainsworth, M. S. The development of infant-mother attachment. In B. Caldwell & H. Ricciuti (Eds.), *Review of child development research* (Vol. 3). Chicago: University of Chicago Press, 1973.

Ainsworth, M. S. Infant-mother attachment and social development: Socialization as a product of reciprocal responsiveness to signals. In M.P.M. Richards (Ed.), *The integration of the child into the social world*. Cambridge, England: Cambridge University Press, 1974.

Ainsworth, M. S., & Bell, S. M. Attachment, exploration, and separation: Illustrated by the behavior of one-year-olds in a strange situation. *Child Development,*1970, *41*, 49–67.

Ainsworth, M. S., Bell, S. M., & Stayton, D. Individual differences in strange situation behavior of one-year-olds. In H. Schaffer (Ed.), *The origins of human social interactions*. London: Academic Press, 1971.

Ainsworth, M. S., Blehar, M. C., Waters, E., & Wall, S. Patterns of attachment: A psychological study of the strange situation. New York: John Wiley, 1978.

Anthony, E. J., & Benedek, T. (Eds.). *Parenthood: Its psychology and psychopathology*. Boston: Little, Brown, 1970.

Apfelbaum, B. Some problems in contemporary ego psychology. *Journal of the American Psychoanalytic Association*, 1962, *10*, 526–537.

Balint, M. *Primary love and psychoanalytic technique*. London: Tavistock Publications, 1966. (Originally published, 1952.)

Belenky, M. F., & Gilligan, C. *Predicting clinical outcomes: A longitudinal study of the impact of the abortion crisis on moral development and life crisis on moral development and life circumstance*. Unpublished manuscript, Harvard University, 1979.

Bell, J. E. *The family in the hospital*. Bethesda, Md.: National Institute of Mental Health, 1960.

Bell, R. Q. Stimulus control of parent or caretaker behavior by offspring. *Developmental Psychology*, 1971, *4*, 61–72.

Bellak, L. A multiple factor psychosomatic theory of schizophrenia. *Psychiatric Quarterly*, 1949, *23*, 738–755.

Bellak, L., & Rosenberg, S. The effects of antidepressant drugs on psychodynamics. *Psychosomatics*, 1966, *7*, 106–114.

Bellak, L., Hurvich, M., & Gediman, H. K. *Ego functions in schizophrenics, neurotics, and normals*. New York: John Wiley, 1973.

Beres, D. Structure and function in psychoanalysis. *International Journal of Psychoanalysis*, 1965, *46*, 53–63.

Bibring, G., Dwyer, T., Hunington, D., & Valenstein, A. A study of the psychological processes in pregnancy and of the earliest mother-child relationship: II Methodological considerations. *The Psychoanalytic Study of the Child*, 1967, *16*, 25–72.

Bijou, S. W., & Baer, D. M. *Child Development* (Vol. 2). New York: Appleton-Century-Crofts, 1965.

Binstock, W. A. On two forms of intimacy. *Journal of the American Psychoanalytic Association*, 1973, *21*, 93–107.

Blanck, R., & Blanck, G. *Ego psychology: Theory and practice*. New York: Columbia University Press, 1974.

BLOCK, J. Ego identity, role variability, and adjustment. *Journal of Consulting Psychology*, 1961, *25*, 392–397.

BOWLBY, J. *Attachment and loss.* (Vol. 1: Attachment). New York: Basic Books, 1969.

BRAZELTON, T. B. Personal communication. Cited in M. Klaus & J. Kennell, *Maternal infant bonding.* St. Louis, Mo.: C. V. Mosby, 1976.

BRAZELTON, T. B., KOSLOWSKI, B., & MAIN, M. The origins of reciprocity: The early mother-infant interaction. In M. Lewis & M. Rosenblum (Eds.), *The effect of the infant on its caregiver.* New York: John Wiley, 1974.

BRETHERTON, I., & AINSWORTH, M. S. Responses of one-year-olds to a stranger. In M. Lewis & M. Rosenblum (Eds.), *The origins of fear.* New York: John Wiley, 1974.

BREUER, H. *Ego identity status in late adolescent college males, as measured by a group-administered incomplete sentences blank, and related to inferred stance toward authority.* Unpublished doctoral dissertation, New York University, 1973.

BRONSON, G. W. Infants' reactions to unfamiliar persons and novel objects. *Monographs of the Society for Research in Child Development*, 1972, *37*(Serial No. 148).

BYRNE, P. The repression-sensitization scale: rationale, reliability, and validity. *Journal of Personality*, 1961, *29*, 334–349.

CANDEE, D. Ego development aspects of new left ideology. *Journal of Personality and Social Psychology*, 1974, *30*, 620–630.

CARPENTER, W. T., GUNDERSON, J. G., & STRAUSS, J. S. Considerations of the borderline syndrome: A longitudinal comparative study of borderline and schizophrenic patients. In P. Hartocollis (Ed.), *Borderline personality disorders.* New York: International Universities Press, 1977.

CASSEL, Z. K., & SANDER, L. W. *Neonatal recognition processes and attachment: The masking experiment.* Paper presented at meeting of the Society for Research in Child Development, Denver, 1975.

CHODOROW, N. *The reproduction of mothering.* Berkeley: University of California Press, 1978.

CONDON, W. S., & SANDER, L. W. Neonate movement is synchronized with adult speech: Interactional participation and language acquisition. *Science*, 1974, *183*, 99–101.

CONNELL, D. B. *Individual difference in infant attachment related to habituation to a redundant stimulus.* Unpublished doctoral dissertation, Syracuse University, 1974.

CONSTANTINOPLE, A. An Eriksonian measure of personality development in college students. *Developmental Psychology*, 1969, *1*, 357–372.

COX, N. Prior help, ego development, and helping behavior. *Child Development*, 1974, *45*, 594–603.

DICKS, H. V. Object relations theory and marital studies. *British Journal of Medical Psychology*, 1963, *36*, 125–129.

ERIKSON, E. *Identity, youth and crisis.* New York: W. W. Norton & Co., Inc., 1968.

ERIKSON, E. *Childhood and Society.* New York: W. W. Norton & Co., Inc., 1950.

ERIKSON, E., & ERIKSON, J. On generativity and identity. Interview by D. Hulsizer, M. Murphy, G. Noam, & C. Taylor. *Harvard Educational Review*, 1981, *51*(No. 2).

FAIRBAIRN, W.R.D. *Psychoanalytic studies of the personality.* London: Routledge and Kegan Paul, 1952.

FREUD, A. *The ego and the mechanisms of defense.* New York: International Universities Press, 1936.

FREUD, A. Aggression in relation to emotional development: Normal and pathological. *Psychoanalytic Study of the Child*, 1949, *3/4*, 37–48.

FREUD, A., with DANN, S. Experiment in group upbringing. In *Psychoanalytical study of the child* (Vol. 6). New York: International Universities Press, 1951.

FREUD, S. "Civilized" sexual morality and modern nervous illness. In J. Strachey (Ed.), *The complete psychological works of Sigmund Freud* (Vol. 9). London: Hogarth Press, 1959. (Originally published, 1908.)

FREUD, S. The sexual life of man. (Lecture XX) In *A general introduction to psychoanalysis.* (J. Riviere, Trans.) New York: Liveright, 1935. (Originally published, 1916–1917.)

FREUD, S. The ego and the id. In J. Strachey (Ed.), *The complete psychological works of Sigmund Freud* (Vol. 19). London: Hogarth Press, 1961. (Originally published, 1923.)

FREUD, S. *The problem of anxiety.* New York: Psychoanalytic Quarterly Press and W. W. Norton & Co., Inc., 1936. (Originally published, 1926, as *Hemmung, symptom und angst.*)

FREUD, S. [The anatomy of the mental personality, Lecture XXXI.] In *New introductory lectures on psycho-analysis.* (W.J.H. Sprott, Trans.) New York: W. W. Norton & Co., Inc., 1933.

FROMM, E. Psychoanalytic characterology and its application to the understanding of culture. In S. S. Sargent & M. W. Smith (Eds.), *Culture and personality.* New York: Viking Fund, 1949.

GEWIRTZ, J. L. Mechanisms of social learning: Some roles of stimulation and behavior in early human development. In D. A. Goslen (Ed.), *Handbook of socialization theory and research.* Skokie, Ill.: Rand McNally, 1969.

GIOVACCHINI, P. Effects of adaptive and disruptive aspects of early object relations upon later parental functioning. In E. J. Anthony & T. Benedek (Eds.), *Parenthood: Its psychology and psychopathology.* Boston: Little, Brown, 1970.

GOETHALS, G. W. Symbiosis and the life cycle. *British Journal of Medical Psychology,* 1973, *46*, 91–96.

GOETHALS, G. W. The evolution of sexual and genital intimacy: A comparison of the views of Erik H. Erikson and Harry Stack Sullivan. *Journal of the American Academy of Psychoanalysis*, 1976, *4* (No. 4), 529–544.

GOLDBLUM, R., AHLSTEDT, S., CARLSSON, B., & HANSON, L. Antibody production by human colostrum cells. *Pediatric Research*, 1975, *9*, 330.

GOREN, C., SARTY, M., & WU, P. Visual following and pattern discrimination of face-like stimuli by newborn infants. *Pediatrics*, 1975, *56*, 544–549.

GREEN, S. The evaluation of ego adequacy. *Journal of Hillside Hospital*, 1954, *3*, 199–203.

GRINKER, R. R., WERBLE, B., & DRYE, R. C. *The borderline syndrome: A behavioral study of ego functions.* New York: Basic Books, 1968.

GRUEN, W. Rejection of false informatin about oneself as an indication of ego-identity. *Journal of Consulting Psychology*, 1960, *24*, 231–233.

GUNDERSON, J. G. Characteristics of borderlines. In P. Hartocollis (Ed.), *Borderline personality disorders.* New York: International Universities Press, 1977a.

GUNDERSON, J. G. *Diagnostic interview for borderlines.* Unpublished, McLean Hospital, 1977b.

GUNDERSON, J. G., & SINGER, M. T. Defining borderline patients: An overview. *The American Journal of Psychiatry*, 1975, *1324*, 1–10.

GUNTRIP, H. *Psychoanalytic theory, therapy, and the self.* New York: Basic Books, 1971.

HAAN, N. *Coping and defending—Processes of self-environment organization.* New York: Academic Press, 1977.

HABERMAS, J. Moral development and ego identity. In *Communication and the evolution of society.* Boston: Beacon Press, 1979.

HARLOW, H. The development of affectional patterns in infant monkeys. In B. M. Foss (Ed.), *Determinants of infant behavior* (Vol. 1). New York: John Wiley, 1961.

HARPER, R., CONCEPCION, S., & SOKOL, S. Is parental contact with infants in the neonatal intensive care unit really a good idea? *Pediatric Research*, 1975, *9*, 259.

HARTMANN, H. The development of the ego concept in Freud's work. *International Journal of Psychoanalysis*, 1956, *37*, 425–438.

HARTMANN, H. *Ego psychology and the problem of adaptation.* New York: International Universities Press, 1958. (Originally published, 1939.)

HARTMANN, H. Comments on the psychoanalytic theory of the ego. In H. Hartmann (Ed.), *Essays on ego psychology: Selected problems in psychoanalytic theory.* New York: International Universities Press, 1964a.

HARTMANN, H. Mutual influences in the development of the ego and the id. In H. Hartmann (Ed.), *Essays on ego psychology.* New York: International Universities Press, 1964b.

HARTMANN, H., KRIS, E., & LOEWENSTEIN, R. M. Papers on psychoanalysis: A concept in search of identity. *Psychoanalytic Review*, 1970, *56*, 511–525.

HAUSER, S. T. *Black and white identity formation.* New York: Wiley Interscience, 1971.

HAUSER, S. T. Loevinger's model and measure of ego development: A critical review. *Psychological Bulletin,* 1976, *83*, 928–955.

HAUSER, S. T., & DAFFNER, K. Ego functions and development: Empirical research and clinical relevance. *McLean Hospital Journal*, 1980, *5*(No. 2), 87–109.

HAYES, J. M. *Ego identity and moral character development in male college students.* Unpublished doctoral dissertation, Catholic University of America, 1977.

HOFFMAN, H. S. Fear mediated processes in the context of imprinting. In M. Lewis & L. Rosenblum (Eds.), *The origins of fear.* New York: John Wiley, 1974.

HOPPE, C. *Ego development and conformity behavior.* Unpublished doctoral dissertation, Washington University, 1972.

JACOBSEN, E. *The self and the object world.* New York: International Universities Press, 1964.

KAILA, E. Die Reaktionen des Säuglings auf das menschliche Gesicht. *Zeitschrift für Psychologie,* 1935, *135,* 156–163.

KARUSH, A., ESSER, B., COOPER, A., & SWERDLOFF, B. The evaluation of ego strength. I: A profile of adaptive balance. *Journal of Nervous and Mental Disease,* 1964, *139,* 236–253.

KEGAN, R. A neo-Piagetian approach to object relations. In B. Lee with G. Noam (Eds.), *New approaches to the self.* New York: Plenum Press, in press.

KEGAN, R. The evolving self: A process conception for ego psychology. *Counseling Psychologist,*1979, *8*(No. 2), 5–34.

KERNBERG, O. Structural derivatives of object relationships. *International Journal of Psychoanalysis,* 1966, *47,* 236–253.

KERNBERG, O. Borderline personality organization. *Journal of the American Psychoanalytic Association,* 1967, *15,* 641–685.

KERNBERG, O. Factors in the psychoanalytic treatment of narcissistic personalities. *Journal of the American Psychoanalytic Association,* 1970a, *18,* 51–85.

KERNBERG, O. A psychoanalytic classification of character pathology. *Journal of the American Psychoanalytic Association,* 1970b, *18,* 800–822.

KERNBERG, O. *New developments in psychoanalytic object relations theory.* Paper presented at 58th annual meeting of the American Psychoanalytic Association, May 1971a.

KERNBERG, O. The course of the analysis of a narcissistic personality with hysterical and compulsive features. *Journal of the American Psychoanalytic Association,* 1971b, *19,* 451–471.

KERNBERG, O. Early ego integration and object relations. *Annals of the New York Academy of Sciences,* 1972, *193,* 233–247.

KERNBERG, O. Barriers to falling and remaining in love. *Journal of the American Psychoanalytic Association,* 1974a, *22,* 486–511.

KERNBERG, O. Mature love: Prerequisites and characteristics. *Journal of the American Psychoanalytic Association,* 1974b, *22,* 743–768.

KERNBERG, O. Boundaries and structure in love relations. *Journal of the American Psychoanalytic Association,*1976a, *25,* 81–114.

KERNBERG, O. *Object relations theory and clinical psychoanalysis.* New York: Jason Aronson, 1976b.

KERNBERG, O. The structural diagnoses of borderline personality organization. In P. Hartocollis (Ed.), *Borderline personality disorders.* New York: International Universities Press, 1977.

KERNBERG, O. *Borderline conditions and pathological narcissism.* New York: Jason Aronson, 1979.

KETY, S. S. Mental illness in the biological and adoptive families of adopted individuals who have become schizophrenic. Pp. 19–26 in H. M. Praag (Ed.), *On the origin of schizophrenic psychoses.* Amsterdam: De Erven Bohn B.V., 1975.

KINSLER, P. *Ego-identity and intimacy.* Unpublished doctoral dissertation. State University of New York at Buffalo, 1972.

KIRBY, C. S. *Complexity-simplicity as a dimension of identity formation.* Unpublished doctoral dissertation, Michigan State University, 1977.

KLAUS, M. H., & KENNELL, J. H. *Maternal infant bonding.* St. Louis, Mo.: C. V. Mosby, 1976.

KLAUS, M. H., KENNELL, J. H., PLUMB, N., & ZUEHLKE, S. Human maternal behavior at first contact with her young. *Pediatrics,* 1970, *46,* 187–192.

KLEIN, G. S. The ego in psychoanalysis—A concept in search of identity. *Psychoanalytic Review,* 1970, *56,* 511–525.

KLEIN, M. *Contributions to psycho-analysis 1921–1945.* London: Hogarth Press and the Institute of Psychoanalysis, 1968. (Originally published, 1948.)

KNIGHT, R. Borderline states. *Bulletin of the Menninger Clinic,* 1953, *17,* 1–12.

KOHUT, H. *The analysis of the self.* New York: International Universities Press, 1971.

KOHUT, H. *Restoration of the self.* New York: International Universities Press, 1977.

KOHUT, H., & WOLF, E. S. The disorders of the self and their treatment: An outline. *International Journal of Psychoanalysis,* 1978, *54,* 413–425.

KORNER, A. F. Mother-child interaction: One- or two-way street? *Social Work,* 1965, *10,* 47–51.

KORNER, A. F. Individual differences at birth: Implications for early experience and later development. *American Journal of Orthopsychiatry,* 1971, *41,* 608–619.

KORNER, A. F. The effect of the infant's state, level of arousal, sex, and ontogenetic state on the caregiver. In M. Lewis & L. Rosenblum (Eds.), *The effect of the infant on the caregiver.* New York: John Wiley, 1974.

KRIS, E. The psychology of caricature. In E. Kris (Ed.), *Psychoanalytic explorations in art.* New York: International Universities Press, 1952. (Originally published, 1934.)

LANG, R. *Birthbook.* Ben Lomond, Calif.: Genesis Press, 1972.

LAUGHLIN, H. P. *The ego and its defenses.* New York: Jason Aronson, 1979.

LEWIS, M. & ROSENBLUM, L. *The effect of the infant on its caregiver.* New York: John Wiley, 1974.

LICHTENSTEIN, H. *The dilemma of human identity.* New York: Jason Aronson, 1977.

LOEVINGER, J. The meaning and measurement of ego development. *American Psychologist,* 1966, *21*(No. 3), 195–206.

LOEVINGER, J. *Ego development: Conceptions and theories.* San Francisco: Jossey-Bass, 1976.

LOEVINGER, J., & WESSLER, R. *Measuring ego development* (Vol. 1). San Francisco: Jossey-Bass, 1970.

LUBORSKY, L., FABIAN, M., HALL, B., TICHO, E., & TICHO, G. Treatment variables. *Bulletin of the Menninger Clinic,* 1958, *22,* 126–147.

MAHLER, C. *The assessment and evaluation of the coping styles of two ego identity status groups: Moratorium and foreclosure, to identity conflict arousing stimuli.* Unpublished master's thesis, State University of New York at Buffalo, 1959.

MAHLER, M. S., PINE, F., & BERGMAN, A. *The psychological birth of the human infant.* New York: Basic Books, 1975.

MAIN, M. *Exploration, play, and level of cognitive functioning as related to child-mother attachment.* Unpublished doctoral dissertation, Johns Hopkins University, 1973.

MAIN, M. Sicherheit und Wissen. In K. E. Grossman (Ed.), *Entwicklung der Lernfähigkeit in der Sozialen Umvielt.* München: Kindler Verlag, 1977.

MARCIA, J. E. Development and validation of ego identity status. *Journal of Personality and Social Psychology,* 1966, *3*(No. 5), 551–558.

MARCIA, J. E. Ego identity status: Relation to change in self-esteem, "general maladjustment," and authoritarianism. *Journal of Personality,* 1967, *35*(No. 1), 119–133.

MARCIA, J. E. Identity six years after: A follow-up study. *Journal of Youth and Adolescence,* 1976, 5, 145–160.

MARCIA, J. E. Identity in adolescence. In J. Adelson (Ed.), *Handbook of adolescence.* New York: John Wiley, 1978.

MARCIA, J. E., & FRIEDMAN, M. L. Ego identity status in college women. *Journal of Personality,* 1970, *38*(No. 2), 249–263.

MASTERSON, J. F. *Psychotherapy of the borderline adult.* New York: Brunner/Mazel, 1976.

MATA, L. Personal communication, 1974. Cited in M. H. Kennell & J. H. Klaus, *Maternal infant bonding.* St. Louis, Mo.: C. V. Mosby, 1976.

MATAS, L. *Consequences of the quality of infant-mother attachment for the adaptation of two-year-olds.* Paper presented at meeting of the Society for Research in Child Development, New Orleans, March 1977.

MATTESON, D. D. Alienation vs. exploration and commitment: Personality and family correlates of adolescent identity statuses. Report from the Project for Youth Research. Copenhagen: Royal Danish School of Educational Studies, 1974.

MEISSNER, W. W. Notes on some conceptual aspects of borderline personality organization. *International Review of Psychoanalysis,* 1978a, *5,* 297–311.

MEISSNER, W. W. Theories of personality. In A. M. Nicholi, Jr. (Ed.), *The Harvard guide to modern psychiatry.* Cambridge, Mass.: Belknap Press, 1978b.

MORGAN, G., & RICCIUTI, H. N. Infants' response to strangers during the first year. In B. M. Foss (Ed.), *Determinants of infant behavior* (Vol. 4). New York: John Wiley, 1969.

MURRAY, H. *The assessment of men.* New York: Holt, Rinehart & Winston, 1948.

NEUBER, K. A., & GENTHER, R. W. The relationship between ego identity, personal responsibility, and facilitative communication. *Journal of Psychology*, 1977, *95*, 45–49.

NOAM, G., SNAREY, J. & KOHLBERG, L. Ego development. In B. Lee with G. Noam (Eds.), *New approaches to the self.* New York: Plenum Press, in press.

NOAM, G. *Object relations theory and structural developmental psychology: The borderline conditions.* Unpublished, Harvard University, 1979.

ORLOFSKY, J. L., MARCIA, J. E., & LESSER, I. M. Ego identity status and the intimacy vs. isolation crisis of young adulthood. *Journal of Personality and Social Psychology*, 1973, *27* (No. 2), 211–219.

OSHMAN, H., & MANOSEVITZ, M. The impact of the identity crisis on the adjustment of late adolescent males. *Journal of Youth and Adolescence*, 1974, *3*, 207–216.

PARSONS, T. The superego and the theory of social systems. *Psychiatry*, 1952, *15*, 15–25.

PENN, H. *The history of the borderline concept.* Unpublished manuscript, Harvard Medical School.

PIAGET, J. The affective unconscious and the cognitive unconscious. *Monograph of the Journal of the American Psychoanalytic Association*, 1973, *21*.

PODD, M., MARCIA, J. E., & RUBIN, B. M. The effects of ego identity and partner perception on a prisoner's dilemma game. *Journal of Social Psychology*, 1970, *82*, 117–126.

POPPEN, P. J. The development of sex differences in moral judgment for college males and females. Unpublished doctoral dissertation, Cornell University, 1974.

PRELINGER, E., & ZIMET, C. *An ego psychological approach to character assessment.* New York: The Free Press, 1964.

RAPAPORT, D. An historical survey of psychoanalytic ego psychology. In M. Gill (Ed.), *The collected papers of David Rapaport.* New York: Basic Books, 1967.

RHEINGOLD, H. L. The effect of a strange environment on the behavior of infants. In B. M. Foss (Ed.), *Determinants of infant behavior* (Vol. 4). New York: John Wiley, 1969.

RICCIUTI, H. N. Fear and the development of social attachments. In M. Lewis & L. Rosenblum (Eds.), *The origins of fear.* New York: John Wiley, 1974.

RICHTER, H. E. *Eltern kind und neurose.* Stuttgart: Klett-Verlag, 1963.

ROBSON, K. S. The role of eye to eye contact in maternal infant attachment. *Journal of Child Psychology and Psychiatry*, 1967, *8*, 13–25.

ROSENFELD, R. U. *The relationship of ego-identity to similarity among self, ideal self, and probable occupational role concept among college males.* Unpublished doctoral dissertation, University of Maryland, 1972.

ROWE, I. *Ego identity status, cognitive development and levels of moral reasoning.* Master's thesis, Simon Fraser University, 1978.

RUBIN, R. Maternal touch. *Nursing Outlook,* 1963, *11*, 828–831.

SANDLER, J. The Hampstead Index as an instrument of psychoanalytic research. *International Journal of Psychoanalysis*, 1962, *43*, 287–291.

SARGENT, H., MODLIN, H., FARIS, M., & VOTH, H. The psychotherapy research project of the Menninger Foundation: Situational variables. *Bulletin of the Menninger Foundation*, 1958, *22*, 148–166.

SCHAFER, R. *Aspects of internalization.* New York: International Universities Press, 1968.

SCHAFER, R. An overview of Heinz Hartmann's contributions to psychoanalysis. *International Journal of Psychoanalysis*, 1970, *51*(No. 4), 425–446.

SCHENKEL, S., & MARCIA, J. E. Attitudes toward premarital intercourse in determining ego identity status in college women. *Journal of Personality*, 1972, *3*, 472–482.

SHAPIRO, E. R. The psychodynamics and developmental psychology of the borderline patient: A review of the literature. *American Journal of Psychiatry*, 1978, *135*, 1305–1315.

SPITZ, R. Hospitalism: An inquiry into the genesis of psychiatric conditions in early childhood. Pp. 53–74 in *Psychoanalytical study of the child* (Vol. 1). New York: International Universities Press, 1945.

SPITZ, R. A follow-up report. Pp. 113–117 in *Psychoanalytic study of the child* (Vol. 2). New York: International Universities Press, 1946.

SPITZ, R. A., & WOLFF, K. M. The smiling response: A contribution to the ontogenesis of social relations. *Genetic Psychology Monographs*, 1946, *34*, 57–125.

SPITZER, R. L., ENDICOTT, J., & GIBBON, M. Crossing the border into borderline personality and borderline schizophrenia. *Archives of General Psychiatry*, 1979, *36*, 17–23.

SROUFE, L. A. Wariness of strangers and the study of infant development. *Child Development*, 1977, *48*, 731–746.

SROUFE, L. A., & WATERS, E. Heart rate as a convergent measure in clinical and developmental research. *Merrill Palmer Quarterly*, 1977, *23*, 3–28.

STARK, P. A., & TRAXLER, A. J. Empirical validation of Erikson's theory of identity crises in late adolescence. *The Journal of Psychology*, 1974, *86*, 25–33.

STERN, A. Psychoanalytic investigation of and therapy in the borderline group of neurosis. *Psychoanalytic Quarterly*, 1938, *7*, 467–489.

STERN, D. Mother and infant at play: The dyadic interaction involving facial, vocal, and gaze behaviors. In M. Lewis & L. Rosenblum (Eds.), *The effect of the infant on its caregiver.* New York: John Wiley, 1974.

STIERLIN, H., & RAVENSCROFT, K. Variations of adolescent separation conflicts. *British Journal of Medical Psychology*, 1972, *45*, 299–313.

SUTHERLAND, J. D. Object relations theory and the conceptual model of psychoanalysis. *British Journal of Medical Psychology,* 1963, *36*, 109–124.

TURKLE, S. *Psychoanalytic politics.* New York: Basic Books, 1978.

TZURIEL, D., & KLEIN, M. M. Ego identity: Effects of ethnocentrism, ethnic identification, and cognitive complexity in Israeli, Oriental and Western ethnic groups. *Psychological Reports*, 1977, *40*, 1099–1110.

VAILLANT, G. E. *Adaptation to life.* Boston: Little, Brown, 1978.

VOLKAN, V. D. *Primitive internalized object relations.* New York: International Universities Press, 1976.

WALKER, A. Immunology of the gastrointestinal tract. *Journal of Pediatrics.* 1973, *83*, 517–530.

WALLERSTEIN, R., ROBBINS, L., SARGENT, H., & LUBORSKY, L. The psychotherapy research project of the Menninger Foundation; Rationale, method, and sample size. *Bulletin of the Menninger Foundation*, 1956, *20*, 221–278.

WERNER, H. The concept of development from a comparative and organismic point of view. In D. Harris (Ed.), *The Concept of development.* Minneapolis: University of Minnesota Press, 1957.

WINNICOTT, D. W. The depressive position in normal emotional development. *British Journal of Medical Psychology*, 1954, *28*, 89–100.

WINNICOTT, D. W. *Collected papers: Through pediatrics to psycho-analysis.* London: Tavistock Publications, 1958.

WINNICOTT, D. W. *The maturational processes and the facilitating environment.* New York: International Universities Press, 1965.

WINNICOTT, D. W. *Playing and reality.* New York: Basic Books, 1971.

YARROW, L. Attachment and dependency: A developmental perspective. In J. Gewirtz (Ed.), *Attachment and dependency.* Washington, D.C.: D. H. Winston & Sons, 1972.

3

Interactional Theory

BENJAMIN B. WOLMAN

The dichotomy of nature versus nurture is of a particular significance for any theory of child development. There is no doubt that all human beings undergo far-reaching changes during their life span from conception to grave. The question is: Are these changes, all or some of them, genetically determined or a product of environmental, sociocultural influences? Moreover even genetic factors are not inflexible (Schecter, Toussieng, Sternloff, & Pollack, 1972). There was not much substance to Lamarck's theory that environmentally acquired changes are carried from generation to generation, but significant changes may take place in conception and in prenatal life (Rainer, 1977; Thompson & Wilde, 1973).

Thus the very idea of clearcut developmental phases, whether Gesell's, Freud's, Piaget's, or the one introduced in the following pages, must be viewed, at the best, as an approximation or as a not-too-precise generalization with many exemptions and possible loopholes.

The idea of biologically determined developmental phases need not omit environmental influences, for even biology leaves room for variations, and the members of the same species may go through quite different developmental phases if they live in different environments. In short it is a poor biology that ignores ecology.

There are highly significant differences among the developmental processes of the various species. One may safely assume that the lower the species is on the evolutionary ladder, the simpler and the more rigid are the developmental processes in the life span of an individual organism. Consider protozoa. There are no breathtaking differences at the start and the end of their lives.

The higher the species, the more complex are the changes from the start to the end of their lives and the more flexible are their developmental phases. Consider insects. Their developmental phases are clearly determined in the sequence of egg, larva, cocoon, and adult insect. Hardly any insect remains "fixated" on one of the early phases and hardly, if ever, does an insect become an "immature adult." Short of a major physical impairment, all insects follow developmental phases common to their particular biological species.

A somewhat more flexible statement could be applied to higher biological species. Consider mammals. All of them are sexually reproduced and go through periods of various duration in the intrauterine, prenatal life. No newly born mammal is capable of procuring food and shelter for itself, and all the neonates require a considerable period of parental care before they reach maturity and can adequately function on their own.

The higher the species, the longer and more complex is the road from birth to maturity. Human neonates compare unfavorably with other mammals. They are, as it were, born prematurely, totally unable to survive unless taken care of (Carmichael, 1954). Human infants need a long time before they attain any degree of self-sufficiency.

This period of transition from infancy to adulthood seems to become more and more prolonged in modern societies (Wolman, 1973b). Primitive tribes practiced puberty rites that celebrated a quick transition. The rites were sort of a test of adulthood, and the young who passed them were admitted to the community of adults.

POWER AND ACCEPTANCE

In observing overt behavior one cannot overlook two fundamental patterns. The first is the struggle for survival. Some people are forceful and strong, while others are weak and helpless. The second is that some individuals use whatever power they have for helping others in cooperation and friendliness, while others act in a destructive and hostile manner (Wolman, 1974).

Apparently there are *two* dimensions of behavior. The first is the strong-weak or *power* dimension. The amount of power an individual has indicates how well s/he can protect life and satisfy his/her own needs and the needs of others. Whoever can satisfy needs and protect life is strong; whoever cannot is weak. Power is related to vitality and ability to survive, and the dimension of power includes all levels and degrees of one's ability to satisfy needs, from omnipotence to a complete decline of power to death.

The second dimension, which I call *acceptance*, points to the way in which the available amount of power is used. One may use power to *satisfy the needs of others or to prevent their satisfaction.* One may be friendly or hostile. The terms *friendly* and *hostile* indicate the *direction* in which power is used. *Power may be defined as the ability to satisfy needs, and acceptance as the willingness to do so.* A strong individual *can* satisfy needs, the most basic of which is to stay alive.

The term *acceptance* is isomorphic to Freud's libido and destrudo cathexes, for whoever has power may use it *for* or *against* others. Whenever s/he uses his/her power *for* the satisfaction of others' needs, s/he is friendly. Whenever s/he uses it *against* the satisfaction of others' needs, s/he is destructive and hostile. In the first case it is object cathexis of the libido; in the second, the destrudo is object-cathected.

The terms *friendly* and *hostile* describe one's attitude toward other people; *A*, for example, may be friendly or hostile toward *B*. These terms can also be used in regard to oneself. For example, *A* may like or hate him/herself. Whenever the terms *friendly* and *hostile* are used to indicate one's attitude toward others, it is *interindividual cathexis* of libido or destrudo respectively. Whenever we speak of one's attitude toward oneself, it is *intraindividual cathexis,* to be explained in a later section.

One can be friendly and strong, friendly and weak, and hostile and strong, or hostile and weak.

The term *aggressiveness* often indicates both hostility and forcefulness; one may be a weak enemy or a strong friend, and *forcefulness* does not necessarily indicate hostility. A forceful, decisive, competent surgeon saves the lives of his/her patients and is, in regard to them, strong and friendly.

Accordingly interindividual relationships may be divided into four observable patterns, depending upon the aims of the participants. I call them *H* (hostile), *I* (instrumental), *M* (mutual), and *V* (vectorial).

Whenever an individual seeks to harm or destroy the other participant(s) in the encounter, s/he displays *hostility.* Whenever s/he wants to use the other(s) to gain benefits and to have his/her own needs satisfied, this is *instrumentalism.* Whenever the aim is to satisfy both him/herself and the partner(s) in a give-and-take relationship, this is *mutualism.* Whenever his/her aim is to satisfy the needs of others without expecting anything in return, this is *vectorialism* (Wolman, 1966, 1973a).

The infant's attitude toward his/her mother is exploitative, parasitic, and instrumental; marital partners usually seek mutual gratification, and a mother's attitude toward her infant is vectorial. An infant is *weak,* s/he has nothing to give; s/he must be instrumental, s/he must receive supplies from without, or s/he will not survive. As a child grows, develops, and learns, s/he acquires strength and becomes capable of giving. Sexual and nonsexual friendships, by definition, involve a give-and-take or mutual relationship. A mature adult is capable of giving vectorial love and care to his/her children without asking anything in return. A normal and well-adjusted individual combines all four attitudes in a balanced manner. S/he is reasonably hostile whenever attacked (defensive type of hostility), reasonably instrumental in livelihood-procuring activities, reasonably mutual in sex and marriage, and reasonably vectorial in regard to his/her children, to those who need his/her help, and to things s/he believes in. S/he is neither an angel nor an animal but a balanced human being (Hartmann, 1958).

There seem to be definite, though not rigidly circumscribed, developmental stages from the onset of life toward a balanced maturity (Abraham, 1949; Bühler, Keith-Spiegel, & Thomas, 1973; Erikson, 1963; Piaget, 1969).

INTERINDIVIDUAL CATHEXIS

Before I describe the developmental stages of interindividual behavior, I would like to compare it to Freud's conceptual system. Freud's model of personality includes *topography*—that is, the mental strata (unconscious, preconscious, and conscious), *dynamics* of the driving forces (libido and destrudo), and the *structure* of mental apparatus (id, ego, and superego). Yet Freud's model does not do justice to the problems of social relations as the neoanalytic schools of Horney (1939) and Sullivan (1953) do. I suggest therefore some modification in Freud's concept of cathexis in the hope that such a modification will increase the understanding of social relations (Freud, 1938; Hartmann & Loewenstein, 1962).

Freud described the individual who cathects his/her libido in others, but he did not explain what happens to the one who receives the cathected libido. When a mother loves her child, her libido is cathected in the child; the loving mother "gives love" to her child, and some amount of emotional energy, libido, is given away. Freud dealt with the giving mother but did not study what happened to the receiving child. Does the child "receive" the love that is "given" him/her? What happens to the child whose mother does not love him/her? What happens when the mother demands love from her child?

The sociologically oriented psychoanalyst Karen Horney (1939) stressed *the need to be loved.* When a child feels loved and accepted, s/he experiences the feeling of *safety.* When a child feels rejected, *basic anxiety* develops. Human activities are guided by both pleasure, related to satisfaction of basic needs, and safety, related to human relationships. According to Horney (1939) people would rather renounce pleasure than safety. Instead of promoting Freudian love, sexual or aim-inhibited, Horney introduced the concepts of *protection* and *safety;* in place of Freud's active cathexis of libido—the need to give love—she emphasized the need to be loved.

H. S. Sullivan went even further. His theory is rightly

called a theory of *interpersonal relations*. According to Sullivan (1953) personality can never be isolated from the complexity of interpersonal relations in which the person lives. Sullivan stressed the concept of *empathy*, described by him as a kind of "emotional contagion or communion" between a child and his/her parental figures. Thus the infant shows a curious relationship or connection with the significant adult, ordinarily the mother. When the feeding mother is upset, the infant may develop feeding difficulty and indigestion.

Freud dealt with the person who invests his/her libido in others; I suggest broadening the concept and studying the cathected person and the *interindividual cathexis*. The concept of interindividual cathexis is merely a theoretical concept; there are no neurological counterparts to it. It may, however, resemble Pavlov's explanation of reflex. According to Pavlov (1928) an external stimulus is "transformed into a nervous process and transmitted along a circuitous route (from the peripheral endings of the centripetal nerve, along its fibers to the apparatus of the central nervous system, and out along the centrifugal path until, reaching one or another organ, it excites its activity)" (p. 121). Pavlov's description can be explained in terms of cathexis of physical energy; the external stimulus transmits a part of its energetic load in the peripheral endings of the centripetal nerve, cathects or charges this nerve ending, and through the circuitous route it cathects the nerve center (Ansell & Bradley, 1973; Essman, 1977; Reitan & Davison, 1974).

One may but speculate about the interindividual cathexis of mental energy, for there is no empirical proof of cathexis of mental energy, nor can one be sure that a cathexis of mental energy follows the same rules as the cathexis of physical energy. The term *interindividual cathexis* is thus introduced as a theoretical construct and not as an empirical fact.

This new construct can serve as a bridge between psychoanalytic studies of personality and observable social interaction. The objective of instrumental relationships is to receive libidinal cathexis from others. The individual's own libido is self-cathected, and s/he expects the libido of others to be object-cathected into him/her. All neonates are instrumental and narcissistic and want to be loved. An infant's attitude is instrumental, for s/he wishes to receive cathexes and to become a libido-cathected object. The same applies to any other instrumental relationship.

The objective of mutual relationships is to give and to take—that is, to receive libidinal cathexes as well as to give them to others. Mature and satisfactory sexual relations are mutual. Nonsexual friendship is also mutual, for each partner desires to object-cathect his/her desexualized libido in his/her partner and expects the same from that partner.

A dysbalance in interindividual libido and destrudo cathexes caused by faulty interaction between the individual and his/her environment creates a dysbalance of libido and destrudo in *oneself*. Since this kind of dysbalance leads to behavior disorders, it is reasonable to assume that faulty social relations may be the main cause underlying such disorders. If these faulty social relationships start early in childhood, the damage caused to one's personality can be quite serious (Wolman, 1973a).

There is neither a clearcut criterion nor a precise and wholly objective yardstick for the measurement of cathectic dysbalances. All efforts of quantification of libido and destrudo are doomed to fail because libido and destrudo are not empirical data but theoretical constructs. However, an isomorphic theoretical framework derived from descriptive data may open new vistas in the direction of precise and quantitative diagnostic techniques based on overt interactional behavior.

DEVELOPMENTAL PROCESSES

The entire process of development evolves according to the law of *negative acceleration*. Negative acceleration means a sequence of decreased increments. The child's progress, be it physical height or intellectual development, gradually slows down. The developmental process has an immanent, built-in goal which is maturity. The progress toward the goal is rapid in prenatal and early life, and it becomes slower and slower toward the end of the developmental process.

While the physical goal of maturity includes several clearly definable areas such as anatomy and physiology of the human organism, the concept of psychological maturity hinges on several factors of development and learning related to interaction with one's social environment.

There is an apparent gulf between physical and sociocultural maturity. People reach their full height and full development of anatomical structure and physiological functions in late adolescence. Their mental development takes usually much longer, and it reaches maturity in postadolescent years, in adulthood. Adult, mature individuals do not "grow" any longer, but they do *learn*. The learning process may continue until one's last breath.

The fact of continuous learning contradicts earlier hypotheses that implied that most aspects of personality structure are shaped in childhood. Apparently in accordance with Gesell's (1928) structure-function principle, certain periods are best suited for certain types of learning—e.g., ballet dancing, violin playing, and some other talents must be trained in childhood and, if missed, cannot be recaptured in later life. A gifted person can start painting, however, at practically any time in life, following in the footsteps of Gauguin, Grandma Moses, and a few other artists. The emotional development is probably more complex.

As a rule the older one is, the more difficult it is to condition new behavioral patterns and uncondition the old ones; but difficult as it may be, it is not impossible. The cathectic processes of love (libido) and hate (destrudo) continue uninterrupted, and new likes and dislikes come and go throughout one's life. Certain aspects of personality can undergo changes even late in life.

The changes in conditioning and cathexes are caused by *interaction* with other people. *Changes in interindividual libido and destrudo cathexes inevitably cause changes in the intraindividual balance of cathexes—that is, personality changes.* An older person may feel isolated, harbor resentment against others, and hate oneself. A significant personality change can take place when an active, busy, self-assured man is forced to retire and suddenly feels useless, helpless, and lonely. The bitter old man is in some cases a product of hardening of the arteries, but in many cases his bitterness may be an artefact of a culture that discriminates against old age.

The fact that minority groups have a higher ratio of antisocial behavior is certainly not a product of genetic factors, but it is a result of discrimination which evokes resentment in them, leading, in some instances, to antisocial behavior.

I have treated men and women of all ages, some of them very young and some very old. I cannot say that all older people have always been more difficult patients than the young ones. Some elderly people displayed mental alertness and willingness to change, and they underwent considerable personality changes in the process of psychotherapy.

Psychotherapy, as I shall explain in the forthcoming volume *Interactional Psychotherapy*, is a *field-process*, just as any other interactional relationship. The relative *balance of power* of interacting people determines the degree of influence one can exercise. The same principle applies to all human relations, and especially to the child-parent interaction in which the parents wield considerable influence on the child's behavior and development.

BETWEEN PARENTS AND CHILDREN

There are two main reasons why children are less capable than adults of coping with their environment. Children are physically weaker and smaller, less experienced and less wise than adults, and therefore less capable of making rational decisions and implementing them. *The younger they are, the less power they have.* They are less capable of sustaining themselves and conducting a successful struggle for survival. The second reason is their dependence—that is, the need to be accepted by others. Children's need for support and allies is much greater than that of adults. Small children cannot survive unless an adult takes care of them and supplies them with food, water, shelter, and protection against potential dangers. The dependence on outside support makes little children fear rejection and abandonment (Wolman, 1978).

In addition to these two main reasons, children have no say in choosing their environment and influencing their opportunities. Adults have some degree of mobility: They can change jobs, places of residence, marital relations, religion, business association, or political affiliation. Children are born to and brought up by people they did not choose, and they are, indeed, the captive audience in their parents' homes.

Adults can create a more or less stable environment of their choice. Excluding major catastrophes such as earthquakes and wars, adults can live all their years in a certain neighborhood, practice a certain occupation, develop friendly relations with business associates and relatives, and establish structured daily routines. Children do not have these options. They must move to a new neighborhood and attend a new school whenever their parents decide so and accept a new, and in some cases unfriendly, physical and social environment not of their choice. Children may feel uprooted whenever their parents decide to change their place of residence, their family relationships, or any other social contacts.

Adults remain adult as long as they live, whether they are young or middle-aged or old, and their behavior patterns are more or less circumscribed by their sex, age, occupation, and religion. Children's behavioral patterns are continuously changing. *No child is allowed to remain a child, and no child is allowed to be an adult.* Growth and maturation are processes of change, and the terms of change are arbitrarily and often whimsically determined by their parents.

Children have very little power of their own, and their parents have all the power to promote or destroy their mental health. A self-confident person reacts to a danger with mobilization of his/her resources, but rejection, isolation, and abandonment adversely affect a child who has very little self-confidence and practically no self-reliance.

Traumatized, hurt, and anxious children may *regress* to an earlier phase of development where they might feel better protected and more secure. A kindergarten-age child may regress to baby talk, and a school-age child may become a bed-wetter.

Mature adults *first* count on themselves and *then* on their friends, relatives, and others. Children must count *first* on others, on the loving and protecting parents or parental substitutes. *Adults' security depends on power first and acceptance second; children's security depends on acceptance by others first and their own power next.* Power has been defined as the ability to satisfy needs, and survival is all encompassing and universal. Acceptance has been defined as the willingness to do so—that is, to satisfy the needs of other people—by helping and protecting them.

Immature adults may believe that somebody somehow will take care of them. They avoid rational risks and much more by their passive attitude and waiting for nonexisting saviors.

Every child must receive an adequate amount of protection which will enable him/her to function as a child. A child has the right to be a child and, as such, needs parental protection that gives a feeling of security based on being accepted by his/her strong and friendly parents. The presence of loving parents or parental substitutes is necessary for his/her mental health and development into a well-adjusted adult. A child needs cathecting supplies of parental libido in order to develop his/her own intraindividual balance of cathexes. Children need help in the process of growing up and reaching maturity. They must grow stronger and wiser and develop a realistic estimate of their physical and mental resources. They need help and encouragement in the natural process of shifting from depending on others toward a growing self-reliance.

Mentally healthy individuals are realistic, and their perception of life is reasonably close to the actuality. They are capable of distinguishing wish from reality, and whenever they err, they test again and rectify their findings. The picture they have of themselves and others closely corresponds to the truth.

Children gradually develop the ability for reality testing. Children learn and mature gradually, and every child has his/her own biologically determined speed of maturational and innate ability to learn and profit from experience. Parents can provide the best possible opportunities for growth. They should protect the child from diseases and prevent malformations, but they must be aware of the fact that there is no power in the world that can make a child into a mature adult overnight.

The process of growth is rarely a straight vertical line. There are ups and downs; some feelings temporarily disappear and come back at a later time. As the child's cognitive abilities improve, s/he may fear things s/he did not fear before because there was no awareness of that potential threat. However at the same time, s/he may be afraid or not afraid at all of familiar things. As his/her imaginative abilities develop, imaginary creatures and situations may arouse fear.

Children need not be rushed into adulthood nor be infantilized. They should be helped to go through the necessary steps until they reach maturity. They must be helped to overcome infantile behavioral patterns and to develop gradually the skill of coping with life's problems in a rational way.

DEVELOPMENTAL PHASES

One can stress different aspects in child development. Piaget (1969) dealt with several aspects such as cognitive and moral issues. There is no precise synchronic order in child development. A child can be well advanced in physical growth, less developed in cognitive functions, and underdeveloped in moral behavior. Freud (1938) stressed psychosexual aspects and saw in them the core issues in personality development. Certainly one may find considerable links between the various aspects of human growth, but there is no reason to assume that any one of them is the only one or unquestionably the most important aspect of personality development.

The next part of this chapter describes what seems to be a series of significant steps in social adjustment. I believe that *interactional patterns* play a highly important role (although not the exclusive role) in personality development and are related to Freud's developmental phases.

My schedule of social development stresses the child's increasing ability to relate to other people within the framework of the four possible interactional patterns—hostility [*H*], instrumentalism [*I*], mutualism [*M*] and vectorialism [*V*]. I assume that well-adjusted, mature individuals act *rationally* in all four directions. They can display hostile behavior in self-defense; they are instrumental (takers) in the pursuit of livelihood; they are mutual (givers and takers) with friends, sex partners, and spouses; and they are vectorial (givers) toward children and in charitable and idealistic activities (Wolman, 1974).

Since unlimited, unrestrained hostility is destructive and prevents any social order, the ability to control it is a prerequisite for social adjustment. No society, no matter how primitive it is, can tolerate war of all against all. Dictatorial societies practice all freedom for some individuals at the expense of everyone else. Democratic societies practice *some freedom for all*, which implies some degree of socially agreed-upon limitation of freedom. Ultimately, mature adults practice voluntary self-restraint.

The Anomous Phase

One can distinguish five developmental phases leading from birth toward social maturity. The first phase is a state of *anomia* or total lack of any self-restraint. Life starts in a state of extreme instrumentalism, unlimited selfishness, and parasitic narcissism.

The very survival of the neonates depends upon their ability to continue the *parasitic-narcissistic* position of their prenatal life. As a rule the most parasitic infants have the best chances for survival. To take everything and to *give nothing* in return is the survival device of the newborn child who voraciously grabs mother's breast or the milk bottle and displays instrumental vitality. At this stage of life there is no love for anyone except for oneself, and the narcissistic-parasitic self-love is a prerequisite for survival. Most probably neonates are endowed with libido and destrudo energies and "built-in" releasing forces of Eros and Ares. All libido is self-cathected in primary narcissism, and all destrudo is ready for discharge in a primary, self-defense hostility.

Everything is supplied in intrauterine life, but after birth the situation is quite grave. "Sink or swim" are the alternatives. Threat to the infant's life, whether physical threat or a disruption of narcissistic supplies, elicits an immediate discharge of destrudo.

Threat produces *fear,* the alarm bell of the system. Fear produces one or both of the reactions, fight or flight. Those who don't fear don't hate. People who fear they may die unless they devour someone fight aggressors or react as defenders who fear death inflicted by aggressors. Those who fear, hate. Those who hate, fear.

In neonates at the anomia stage, hostile reactions are not tempered by a control apparatus. Infants' actions are id-action, without brakes. Fear in infants means panic, and fight means furious rage. In catatonics (Wolman, 1966) there is no self-control, no avoidance of dangers, no goal-directed assault on enemies. Catatonics are often driven by blind panic or wild rage, senseless and indiscriminate.

Destrudo is archaic, primordial, primary. There cannot be any developmental stages analogous to Freud's developmental stages of libido. Destrudo serves survival. When object-love fails, part of it turns into secondary narcissistic love, part into destrudo. Destrudo and libido could be pictured as two kinds of mental energy, like two kinds of fuel transformable into each other. When the supply of libido is exhausted, the organism uses the lower type of fuel. In states of emergency, prolonged deprivation, exhaustion, and severe pain, destrudo takes over. It is as if hate is called in when love cannot help. Destrudo is more primitive, and it is always present. It may lead to outbursts of rage in animals and to temper tantrums in infants. In mature adults it is put under the control of the ego and used for self-defense. In infants the id-seated destrudo has no restraints. It is *anomous*.

Freud wrote in "Why War,"

The death instinct turns into destructive instinct if it is directed outwards, on to objects. The living creature preserves it own life, so to say, by destroying an extraneous one. Some portion of the death instinct, however, remains operative within the living being, and we have sought to trace quite a number of normal and pathological phenomena to this internalization of the destructive instinct. We have even been guilty of the heresy of attributing the origin of conscience to this diversion inwards of aggressiveness. You will notice that it by no means is a trivial matter if this process is carried too far: it is positively unhealthy. On the other hand if these forces are turned to destruction in the external world, the living creature will be relieved and the effect must be beneficial. This would serve as a biological justification for all the ugly and dangerous impulses against which we are struggling. It must be admitted that they stand nearer to Nature than does our resistance to them, for which an explanation also needs to be found. (1932, pp. 282–283)

Were Freud right, all life would have ended in suicide unless or until some external outlets were found. Animal and human infants fight for their *own* lives. Hostility and destructiveness are servants not of Thanatos, the god of death, but of Ares, the god of war. Death is never the goal of fight; the goal of fight is destruction either for eating or for the prevention of being eaten. All hostility is initially *outward-directed*. Infants are born with the innate tendency to self-direct their libido and to direct their destrudo against the outer world.

Objects serving the child's survival foster the development of object-cathexis of libido, and all objects threatening the infant activate object-cathexis of destrudo.

Infants are destructive. Their oral love is a fusion of object-libido and object-destrudo with the obvious predominance of destrudo. At the anal stage libido object-cathexis becomes somewhat stronger (Abraham's "tenderness"). The possessive-protection love of the phallic stage represents an additional gain of libido over destrudo. In well-adjusted adults destrudo is partially sublimated, partially aim-inhibited, and partially suppressed. In normal adults "binding and neutralizing" of the destrudo has taken place.

Regression is a reverse process. People who failed to grow up are aggressive. Manic-depressives and schizophrenics display excessive destructiveness.

The Phobonomous Phase

Hartmann's ego psychology has introduced a valuable modification to Freud's developmental theory. Hartmann assumed that the development of the ego, being partly based on the process of maturation, is not entirely traceable to the interaction of drives and environment; indeed, it can become partly independent from the drives in a secondary way. Hartmann terms these factors in ego development *primary* and *secondary autonomy,* respectively. The secondary autonomy of ego functions has a bearing on the stability of its developmental acquisitions.

The autonomous factors may also come to be involved in the ego's defense against instinctual tendencies, against the outer reality, and against the superego. What developed as a result of defense against an instinctual drive may grow into a more or less independent, and more or less structured, pattern of behavior. These relatively stable patterns are referred to by Hartmann as *secondary autonomy* (Hartmann, 1958).

The relative independence of the ego from the id pressures can be expressed in terms of distance from ego-id conflicts or distance from the regressive trends exerted by the id determinants. The newly acquired ego functions, the secondarily autonomous, show a high degree of reversibility in the child who uses special devices in his/her effort to counteract regression.

Hartmann stressed the importance of environmental factors in personality development. While taking into consideration genetic and cultural-historical factors, Hartmann related the development of the ego and superego to the process of adaptation to one's social environment. The fabric of social interactions, the process of division of labor, and the individual's social position determine the possibilities of adaptation; these qualities also regulate the elaboration of instinctual drives and the ego's development. Social structure determines which behavioral forms will have the greatest adaptive chance. The relation of the individual to his/her environment is "disrupted" from moment to moment and must constantly be returned to an equilibrium. Every organism is capable of maintaining or reestablishing its equilibrium, and according to Hartmann, "we can picture the process as an oscillation around the equilibrium" (1958, p. 38).

Hartmann believed that the superego emerges in the Oedipal conflict, but though genetically related to earlier anal phenomena, it must not be confused with them. The superego is not a part of the system ego, but it does include the ego-ideal. The contents of the superego are differentiated from superego functions; certainly the same applies to their respective cathexes. There may be, moreover, tensions and conflicts between the major systems (id, ego, and superego), as well as conflicts within the superego itself (Hartmann & Loewenstein, 1962).

My developmental studies, reported in several volumes, have led me to a further modification of the psychoanalytic theory and emphasis on the power and acceptance factors. The early development of ego signals early awareness of dangers and a dim awareness of power and acceptance relations. The early ego somehow dimly perceives threats and support and reacts to them.

At the oral stage the infant usually receives the necessary narcissistic supplies. Parents or parental substitutes relate to him/her in a vectorial way. They give him/her food in a kind, protective, loving manner. The infant is a taker and puts into his/her mouth whatever is given to him/her—hence the name, the *oral* stage. The oral stage shows a "devouring affection" toward love objects, and this love is "cannibalistic."

In terms of the power and acceptance theory, the oral stage is an early form of instrumentalism. It is an interindividual relationship in which the desire to be helped (to get) is combined with a great deal of fear and hostility. The "weak" infant must receive food and tries to receive it at any cost. When refused s/he attacks. All four forms of hostility—aggression, defense, panic, and horror—are easily elicited at this stage. Fear is the sole deterrent. As soon as the infantile ego is capable of perceiving external threats, the child enters the *phobonomic phase*—that is, fear of retaliation and of being hurt may restrain him/her from hostile behavior. Hostile object-directed behavior is present in every neonate, but object-directed friendly behavior develops as a reaction to a friendly environment.

Freud wrote,

Sadistic impulses already begin to occur sporadically during the oral phase along with the appearance of the teeth. Their extent increases greatly during the second phase, which we described as the sadistic anal phase, because satisfaction is then sought in aggression and in the excretory function. We justify our inclusion of aggressive impulses in the libido by supposing that sadism is an instinctual fusion which thenceforth persists without interruption. (1938, pp. 28–29)

Hostility never disappears entirely. The initial prenatal and neonatal position of the infant dictated by *Lust for Life* is motivated by Ares. At this early stage hostility, not love, is the choice weapon needed for survival. Love is giving, and the neonate has nothing to give. S/he has a long way to go through the oral-cannibalistic, anal-retentive, phallic-possessive, latent-aim-inhibited, pubertal-genital toward the mature give-and-take love of marriage (mutual) and the giving-without-taking love of parenthood (vectorial). In order to give, one must have something to give. The progress toward adulthood is a gradual victory of power over weakness and of love over hate.

The entire oral stage is instrumental and hostile. The lower the personality structure, the more hostility. Weakness produces fear, and fear of retaliation inhibits hostile behavior.

The anal stage brings not only toilet training but also walking and talking. The erect position and walking around permits the child to use his/her hands and manipulate objects to a much greater extent than s/he could have done in the oral stage. The child can explore distant places, walk around, disappear from mother's sight, and reach into new places hitherto forbidden. What an increase of power!

The beginning of speech is another source of ever-increasing power. To be able to comprehend and be comprehended, to call and be called, to exchange wishes and demands—all this gives the infant a new feeling of power. Perhaps infants hallucinate power, but the toddlers who babble nonstop obviously enjoy the torrent of talk. With the increased mastery of words, they flood their environment with a tidal wave of questions (*Fragenwut*) that they do not necessarily expect to be answered.

The third source of power lies in toilet training. Here, for the first time, the parent-child power relationship is reversed. At the oral stage the infant was at his/her mother's mercy. At the anal stage many a mother is at the mercy of the child. Feces are the child's indisputable possession, the prototype of money and of any future property, and the child can use them to gain control over his/her mother. S/he may retain them for "future use" and also for a future increase of pleasure. The child can give them generously or withhold or use delayed giving for building up his/her powers. Extortion of concessions and dictatorships are derivatives of the anal-retentive attitudes. In face-to-face relationships, anal retentiveness can be used as revenge, cold and silent attitude, withholding of affection, and ignoring and rejecting.

Anal-sadistic behavior can take on the shape of active-expulsiveness. The smell of feces is offensive, and spiteful elimination is a hostile act. One can show hostile disrespect by using the word "shit." Anal-expulsive actions, such as elimination or passing gas, and their verbal equivalents are hostile acts.

The anal phase belongs to the instrumental pattern of interaction. It is a kind of advanced instrumentalism, where one does not devour immediately but keeps for future use. Adults with strong oral fixations are selfish; they are prone to use others instantly and recklessly. Anally fixated individuals are more sophisticated; they do not

destroy their slaves but care for them in order to get more out of them. Abraham's (1955) "tenderness" is merely a higher level of instrumentalism.

Instrumental attitude readily leads to hostile behavior whenever one's wishes are not satisfied. Oral instrumentalism operates on the "pleasure principle" and demands immediate gratification; anal instrumentalism can postpone gratification in accordance with the "reality principle," which is a definite span of progress. At both developmental phases the fear of being hurt, abandoned, punished, or rejected is the main, if not only, factor that inhibits hostile behavior. Thus both oral and anal phases are *phobonomic*.

The Heteronomous Phase

Social adjustment is predetermined by the ability to control one's id-seated impulses of libido and, even more, of destrudo. The neonate has no control apparatus, and his/her behavior is motivated by the need for immediate discharge of energy, called by Freud *Lustprinzip*, erroneously translated into English as the pleasure principle. The neonate's social behavior is *anomous*, with no restraints whatsoever.

The early development of the ego brings with it a growing awareness of dangers. Fear has survival value, for a reckless, uninhibited behavior may lead to disaster. Fear of being hurt signals the beginning of the *phobonomous phase* which brings a decrease of blind acting-out and an increased use of the *reality principle,* which implies concern with possible consequences of one's deeds. Fear of anticipated consequences brings a gradual inhibition of hostile acting-out.

In a newborn child all libido is self-cathected and all destrudo ready for object-cathexis against outside threats. A friendly and protective environment which displays abundant interindividual object-cathexis toward the child stimulates the child's development toward a reciprocal libido object-cathexis. The infant begins to "love" his/her parents, although this love is originally extremely instrumental. Receiving libido cathexes from without fosters the child's readiness to an initially limited cathexis of his/her libido in those who love him/her—that is, supply libido cathexes.

According to Freud, at the phallic stage object-love is channeled into genital desires directed toward the parent of the opposite sex. For the first time in the child's life, the object-directed libido becomes the dominating force, stronger than destrudo. At the oral stage the cannibalistic object-relationship is dominated by destrudo. Infants eat, and eating is destruction.

There are, probably, some beginnings of love at the anal stage, but real love, defined as behavior aimed at the protection of life, does not exist at that stage. Abraham's "tenderness" is, at best, a delay in destruction, for the sake of a greater pleasure at a later stage. A child holds on to feces to derive increased pleasure later on and enjoys his/her newly acquired powers. Both the oral and anal phases reflect instrumentalism and the phobonomous attitude.

The *heteronomous attitude* that usually starts at the phallic stage develops out of combination of fear with love. It starts as fear of losing love, and gradually love becomes the dominant factor.

Love is always possessive; it implies taking care. It is not easy to take care of remote objects and people. Hugging, kissing, and caressing are pleasurable for both the one who hugs and the one who is being hugged. It is an interactional process of interindividual libido cathexis. Mother's affectionate embraces and kind words are reassuring and comforting. When mother holds him/her in her arms, the child feels loved and happy. The earliest love experiences are narcissistic. The infant "loves" to take in, to incorporate, and to aggrandize him/herself by this intake. S/he loves what s/he can hold and holds on to what s/he loves. S/he uses his/her mouth to incorporate and possess things that will become part of him/herself through incorporation. Later on s/he holds on to mother and toys, and physical proximity gives him/her the feeling of security.

The processes of growth and learning enable the child to give back some of the love that has been cathected onto him/her by his/her parents. The more the child has received libido cathexis (of course, desexualized, nondemanding libido) from his/her parents, the sooner s/he becomes capable to object-cathect his/her own libido. Children who received much parental love are better prepared to give love to others; children who suffered love deprivation may remain love-hungry addicts.

The phallic love, while still instrumental, is the forerunner of mutualism. Both cathexis and conditioning contribute to this development. In interaction with other children, the child holds on to his/her own possessions while trying to grab the playmate's toys. The playground, the sandbox, and the nursery school break the ground for mutuality.

The child's attitude toward the parent of the opposite sex undergoes a deeper metamorphosis. The shift toward the genital and masturbatory activities makes the child aware of pleasure derived respectively from the penis and the clitoris.

The phallic phase is full of possessiveness and jealousy. These two feelings are rooted in the fact that sexual organs determine monogamous relations, and no child has more than one father and one mother.

The Oedipal love for the mother leads to ambivalent feelings toward the chief competitor, the father, as the Oedipal love for the father, called the Electra complex, leads to ambivalent feelings toward the mother. For the first time the child loves one parent and loves and hates the other one. The child derives pleasure and security from possessing the beloved parent and wishes to get rid of the competing one. Both Eros and Ares serve the child's needs.

The hostile feeling toward the competing parent of the same sex is defensive-aggressive. The little boy wishes to annihilate the competitor, but at the same time he fears the castrating father.

The father is the main provider and satisfier of needs. If father is perceived by the child as a strong (capable of satisfying needs) and friendly (willing to do so) person, the child wishes the strong and friendly father to be ever stronger and friendlier. The Oedipal conflict may be rooted in the genitals, in masturbation and castration fear, but it transgresses its sexual origins. It is a conflict between the desire to protect and to destroy, to love and to hate. The child's attitude to his father is a combination of love and fear, and this is the beginning of the *het-*

eronomous phase. Identification with someone the child loves and fears signals the beginning of superego and inner inhibition of hostile and sexual impulses.

The early beginnings of the superego can be traced to parental prohibitions at toilet training at the anal stage. The child who accepted parental prohibitions becomes ready for introjecting the parental images. These "forerunners of superego" develop into a superego at the phallic phase when the child introjects the image of the parent of the same sex. The undischarged hostility directed against the parent does not disappear, but it becomes stored in the superego and is usually directed against oneself. According to Freud the superego criticizes the ego. The superego, reflecting parental criticism, pursues the line of monitoring, censoring, and rebuking the ego.

This self-directed hostility is a highly important personality trait. Mature adults practice self-criticism and experience guilt feelings whenever they act in a manner offensive to their own superego norms. The superego developed out of fear and love becomes the inner restraining force, based on identification with parents or other authority figures. It is no longer fear of outside forces, but a willing acceptance of restrictions imposed by those one loves and fears; it is *heteronomy.*

The Socionomous Phase

The child's adjustment follows certain distinct patterns. It starts with the zero point at the anomous phase when the entire behavior is impulsive, unrestrained, motivated by the urge for an instant satisfaction of needs, according to the *Lustprinzip.* The newborn is amoral and has no consideration or love for anyone.

With the development of the primitive ego, the *reality principle* acts as a restraining factor. Fear of being hurt and a growing ability to anticipate the sad consequences of one's actions are indicative of the beginning of the *phobonomous* phase.

The next phase starts with one's identification with authority figures and introjection of their rules and prohibitions. This is the *heteronomous* phase.

Interactions with peers lead to the fourth phase of social adjustment. Social relations enter the phase of *mutualism,* and the inner force of *we-ego* emerges.

Identification with a group and sharing responsibility for the social norms indicate the beginning of a higher phase of development. Instead of abiding by heteronomous rules imposed from without, the individual takes part in setting rules for him/herself and others. This *socionomous phase* also leads to a higher level of moral development.

Morality starts with interaction between I and Thou. Consider an imaginary and totally isolated individual, living alone on an unreachable island. Whatever s/he does cannot be related to, nor subject to, moral judgment. An isolated individual may be described as bright or dull, quick or slow, quiet or temperamental, diligent or lazy, neat or sloppy; all these adjectives have no moral connotation. His/her behavior is neither moral nor immoral, and whatever s/he does cannot be defined as being right or wrong.

One is, however, morally right or wrong in regard to other human beings. The fundamental rule of morality is self-evident, and it was expressed in simple words by the ancient Jewish sage, Hillel: "Don't do unto thy neighbor what you don't want him to do unto you." Justice, equal rights, and consideration are the main tenets of morality.

Whatever people do, they do it on a certain level. Some people make noise, other people make music. Some people play piano with one finger, but some are Van Cliburn, Horowitz, and Rubinstein. Some people smear canvasses, while some others create immortal paintings.

There are clearly distinguishable levels in moral behavior. Some people act with no regard for anyone except themselves. They are immoral: anomous. Other people refrain from hurting others only when restrained by fear. Legal systems and their enforcement represent this lowest common denominator of morality. It is a phobonomous morality imposed from without and defended by police and courts.

People brought up by strong and friendly parents reach a higher level of morality based on a combination of love and fear which leads to the formation of the superego. Parental norms incorporated in the superego undergo gradual changes. The child interacts with other children; s/he learns in school and attends a church or a temple. In addition to parental authority, s/he faces the authority of the teachers and other adults whom s/he learns to respect and obey.

Religion may play a significant role in the development of moral principles based on a combination of love and fear. It suggests a higher level of moral behavior for there is no immediate and tangible punishment for immoral behavior.

The legal and religious systems are voluntary; they are based on social agreement. No one forces anyone to join a particular, or any, denomination, and all democratic nations allow free emigration. Sharing a country's social and political system implies a willing acceptance of its laws, and belonging to a religious community can be indicative of sharing its moral values. Belonging to a group allows the individual to feel accepted and to accept, and the spirit of mutualism fosters and reinforces unity of beliefs and goals.

Identification with the group, belonging, and being a member of the "in-group" increase one's feeling of security and power. The group may develop a group-spirit (esprit de corps) and may make the individual feel not as a child who obeys his/her parent but as an individual who obeys the rules s/he took part in establishing.

The individual's consideration for the others gains additional force—i.e., the in-group or we-ego. The formation of the we-ego follows a similar pattern to the formation of the superego. Sharing of group norms is a paradoxical phenomenon. The group members attain a higher level of personality development by taking part in setting the values of their group and willingly honoring them, though the content of their values is not necessarily higher than those advocated by the parents.

The Autonomous Phase

The feeling of responsibility is the highest level of social development and of morality. Responsibility is the core concept of moral behavior. Infants cannot be held responsible for their deeds. They are weak anomous unable to restrain their id-seated impulses. The parents or pa-

rental substitutes must assume responsibility for their children and impose rational restraint. This is the phobonomous phase.

As the children grow and become stronger, they identify with their parents and other significant adults and willingly accept the parental dos and don'ts. Their behavior becomes heteronomous, and their responsibility is a borrowed one. As they become more mature and capable of group-identification, they take an active part in setting rules and norms. Their behavior becomes socionomous, and they share responsibility with their group.

This is a totally different type of morality. It outgrows the survival interests of a particular group or society. It is universal for it encompasses the entire human race. It is a new level of personality development—it transcends the heteronomous superego and the socionomous we-ego. It is the vector-ego that implies courage of one's own convictions and moral commitment to one's brothers, to all human brothers.

The vector-ego is the supreme personality agency of mature, self-confident, and self-respecting individuals. A person who has developed a vector-ego feels that s/he is his/her brother's keeper and, from his/her own volition, has assumed moral responsibility for whatever goes on in and around him/her.

One must be strong to be able to give. Children and immature adults cannot be parents. Being weak they tend to be takers, and they emotionally rob their children. Mature parenthood is the basis for all moral systems and, by being vectorial, facilitates the child's growth toward vectorial morality.

Moral growth need not be restricted to childhood and adolescence. Human life can be a process of continuous growth. The vectorial-ego may start with parenthood and assumption of responsibility for one's children, but it can grow and encompass all humanity.

Becoming is synonymous with moral development which proceeds from irresponsible anomia through the borrowed responsibility of heteronomy toward the shared responsibility of socionomy. The next and the highest level of becoming is the individual's own responsibility—autonomy.

Autonomy means rules and commandments imposed from within. It implies a total and unreserved responsibility for whatever is going on. It is the moral obligation to humankind—to all men, women, and children. It is the ever-present readiness to be of help to those in need.

The ancient Persian religion of Zarathustra did not use punishment and reward as moral devices. It appealed to the innermost feeling of responsibility. According to this religion the world is divided between the forces of light—symbolized by Ormuzd, the lofty God of Light—and the forces of darkness—symbolized by Ahriman, the evil God of Darkness. The struggle between right and wrong, just and evil, love and hatred goes on in every human heart. Good deeds support Ormuzd; evil deeds help Ahriman. Whose victory do you, the individual, want to bring? It is up to every human being to take sides in this struggle, and every single individual is responsible for its outcome. Every human being is free to choose between love and hate. There is no reward nor punishment but only moral responsibility. It is the moral obligation to serve the God of Light and to give oneself to this task, even when no one else joins in. Even—alone.

Jeremiah condemned his sinful compatriots. The ancient Egyptian king Akhnaton introduced monotheistic faith in a single god, Aton, against the powerful pagan priests. Christ proclaimed love and charity against the materialistic and oppressive Roman Empire. Johann Huss was burned alive when he called for revival of Christ's moral principles. Martin Luther fought against papal corruption. Giving does not impoverish those who give. Responsible parenthood, as the prototype of vectorialism, proves beyond a doubt the idea that giving is enriching to the giver. A man who takes care of his family is more manly than he was ever before. Loving parents are not emotionally impoverished; the more love they give, the more love they have.

The more energy one uses, the more access one gains to the deeper layers of one's psyche. Consider a gold mine; those who trample on the surface picking the bared gold pieces do not obtain all gold resources, but those who dig deep gain access to real treasures.

Heteronomous individuals who obey orders from without use as much energy as is required of them. More energy is used by socionomous individuals who take an active part in the group decision-making process. Maximum energy is revealed by autonomous individuals who are free to use all their energies at will.

In economic life, slaves are the least efficient workers, hired labor is more efficient, and free enterprise is the most efficient. No one works as hard and is as productive as the person who works on his/her own.

Multiply this rule a million times and you discover the value of freedom, autonomy, and vector-ego. Free spirits can produce many times more than mental slaves. People who have the courage to be themselves, who are free to live the way they want and set their own goals, gain access to their hidden energy sources.

People who yield to every temptation, unable to control themselves, are not free. They may become slaves to alcohol, drugs, and violent behavior. Their conscious ego has no power, and they float on the waves of life like a ship without a rudder. They are at the mercy of their momentary impulses, pushed around by their own weakness.

Some of the contemporary advocates of excessive hedonism and disinhibition advertise their shabby ideas under the disguise of freedom. Floating on impulse, license, and indulgence in selfish, parasitic, and antisocial behavior are advertised as freedom devices.

Freedom means the freedom to make one's own decisions. Freedom means the power to control one's behavior, to set goals in life, and to pursue them vigorously. Freedom to think, to develop new ideas, and to choose one's way in life must not be confused with regression to infantile modes of behavior. One cannot reverse the developmental process, and whoever tries to turn a tree into a sapling will ruin the tree. Immature men and women do not turn into children but become disturbed, maladjusted adults.

Genuine freedom is attained through autonomy of the human mind. People capable of giving orders to themselves and exercising full control over their cravings and desires, capable of reasoning and deciding, are free human beings.

REFERENCES

ABRAHAM, K. *Selected papers on psychoanalysis.* London: Hogarth Press, 1949; New York: Basic Books, 1955.
ANSELL, G. B., & BRADLEY, P. B. (Eds.). *Macromolecules and behavior.* London: Macmillan, 1973.
BÜHLER, C., KEITH-SPIEGEL, P., & THOMAS, K. Developmental psychology. Pp. 861–917 in B. B. Wolman (Ed.), *Handbook of general psychology.* Englewood Cliffs, N.J.: Prentice-Hall, 1973.
CARMICHAEL, L. The onset and early development of behavior. In L. Carmichael (Ed.), *Manual of child psychology.* New York: John Wiley, 1954.
ERIKSON, E. *Childhood and society.* New York: W. W. Norton & Co., Inc. 1963.
ESSMAN, W. B. Biochemistry of learning and memory. Pp. 348–358 in B. B. Wolman (Ed.), *International encyclopedia of psychiatry, psychology, psychoanalysis, and neurology* (Vol. 2). New York: Aesculapius Publishers, 1977.
FREUD, S. *An outline of psychoanalysis.* New York: W. W. Norton & Co., Inc. 1938.
FREUD, S. Why war? In *Collected papers* (Vol. 5). London: Hogarth Press, 1950. (Originally published, 1932)
GESELL, A. *Infancy and human growth.* New York: Macmillan, 1928.
HARTMANN, H. *Ego psychology and the problem of adaptation.* New York: International Universities Press, 1958.
HARTMANN, H., & LOEWENSTEIN, R. M. Notes on the superego. *Psychoanalytic Study of the Child,* 1962, *17,* 42–81.
HORNEY, K. *New ways in psychoanalysis.* New York: W. W. Norton & Co., Inc. 1939.
PAVLOV, I. P. *Lectures on conditioned reflexes.* New York: Liveright, 1928.
PIAGET, J. *The psychology of the child.* New York: Basic Books, 1969.
RAINER, J. D. Genetics and psychopathology. Pp. 188–191 in B. B. Wolman (Ed.), *International encyclopedia of psychiatry, psychology, psychoanalysis, and neurology* (Vol. 5). New York: Aesculapius Publishers, 1977.
REITAN, R. M., & DAVISON, L. A. (Eds.). *Clinical neuropsychology.* Washington, D. C.: D. H. Winston & Sons, 1974.
RUSSELL, R. W., & WARBURTON, D. M. Biochemical bases of behavior. In B. B. Wolman (Ed.), *Handbook of general psychology.* Englewood Cliffs, N.J.: Prentice-Hall, 1973.
SCHECHTER, M.D., TOUSSIENG, P. W., STERNLOFF, R. E., & POLLACK, E. A. Etiology of mental disorders: Prenatal, natal, and postnatal organic factors. Pp. 129–149 in B. B. Wolman (Ed.), *Manual of child psychopathology.* New York: McGraw-Hill, 1972.
SULLIVAN, H. S. *Interpersonal theory of psychiatry.* New York: W. W. Norton & Co., Inc., 1953.
THOMPSON, W. R., & WILDE, G.J.S. Behavior genetics. Pp. 206–229 in B. B. Wolman (Ed.), *Handbook of general psychology.* Englewood Cliffs, N.J.: Prentice-Hall, 1973.
WOLMAN, B. B. *Vectoriasis praecox or the group of schizophrenias.* Springfield, Ill.: Chas. C Thomas, 1966.
WOLMAN, B. B. *Call no man normal.* New York: International Universities Press, 1973a.
WOLMAN, B. B. The rebellion of youth. *International Journal of Social Psychiatry,* 1973b, *18,* 11–19.
WOLMAN, B. B. Power and acceptance as determinants of social relations. *International Journal of Group Tensions,* 1974, *4,* 151–183.
WOLMAN, B. B. *Children's fears.* New York: Grosset and Dunlap, 1978.
WOLMAN, B. B. *Interactional psychotherapy,* in press.

4

Issues
in Life-Span
Development

ERICH W. LABOUVIE

Although life-span developmental approaches to the study of human behavior are not new, past efforts (Bayley, 1968; Bloom, 1964; Brim, 1966; Bühler, 1959; Bühler & Massarik, 1968; Erikson, 1959; Havighurst, 1948; Keniston, 1971; Neugarten, 1968; Pressey & Kuhlen, 1957; Thomae, 1959, 1968) have had relatively little impact on the mainstream of American developmental psychology. Reasons for this lack of recognition may well be found in an interplay between a long-standing and dominant preference for experimental, short-term manipulative research methods (Huston-Stein & Baltes, 1976) and cognitive economics (Mischel, 1979) that both scientists and people in general engage in to reduce and simplify incoming information and to avoid an overwhelming overload.

Without trying to identify particular causes for recent changes in this state of affairs, it is fair to conclude that arguments on behalf of a life-span approach and its usefulness appear to attract increasing numbers of developmentalists (Baltes & Schaie, 1973a; Datan & Ginsberg, 1975; Datan & Reese, 1977; Goulet & Baltes, 1970; Nesselroade & Reese, 1973). Given the fact that the life-span approach is only in its beginnings, both at the level of conceptual frameworks and of empirical data, it would seem premature to characterize it in terms of a finite and fixed set of issues. Instead it is suggested that these issues are emerging and changing at the same time that the life-span point of view is emerging and changing. However it is also clear that age-specific research programs and researchers do not become truly life-span–oriented by merely including wider age ranges in their designs and studies. The last statement is based on the notion of factual relativity accepted by most scientists (Weimer, 1979). According to that notion facts are conceptual in nature, and the activities of science can be fact correcting

and fact refuting—that is, as conceptual points of view change, so do the facts themselves change. Consequently the facts of age-specific developmental approaches are not necessarily the facts of a life-span developmental perspective, and vice versa. It remains to be seen whether life-span approaches are quantitatively or qualitatively different from age-specific frameworks in both theory and method (see also Baltes, 1973; Huston-Stein & Baltes, 1976).

Since our basic argument suggests that relevant issues emerge as the life-span developmental perspective itself continues to emerge, it would be misleading to introduce any set of issues and their treatment as comprehensive and final rather than selective and illustrative. For that same reason it would also be unsatisfactory merely to repeat what has already been said before. Instead what is to follow is intended to add to previous discussions of theoretical and methodological issues that are often neglected or not even experienced by proponents of age-specific approaches (Baltes, 1973; Baltes, Cornelius, & Nesselroade, 1979; Baltes, Reese, & Nesselroade, 1977; Baltes & Schaie, 1973b; Baltes & Willis, 1977; Huston-Stein & Baltes, 1976; Riegel, 1972, 1976). Therefore the reader is referred to these sources as the relevant context for the following discussion.

THE LIFE-SPAN DEVELOPMENTAL
POINT OF VIEW

In *A Theory of Data* Coombs (1964) proposed to distinguish among behavior, raw data, and data. *Behavior* is defined as everything that is potentially observable about a person or event. *Raw data* is all that which is selected and constructed by an investigator as empirical fact for further analysis. *Data* refers to a chosen conceptual interpretation of the raw data. As a general framework this distinction is useful in the sense that it points to two facets of scientific activities. One involves the discovery, selection, and construction of raw data out of the total pool of behaviors; the other is concerned with the mapping of raw data onto data—that is, procedures for empirical verification and falsification (Baltes & Cornelius, 1977).

A point that is as important as the distinction itself is the fact that more specific definitions of the three categories, of their lines of demarcation, and of their interrelationships are likely to differ for different philosophical views and metamodels. According to Weimer (1979), this fact is increasingly recognized by the community of social scientists and has led to a movement away from socalled *justificationism,* a stance that identifies knowledge with *proof* and *authority.* It reflects an increasing awareness that facts cannot be obtained without having a prior theory. Because facts are conceptual in nature, people with different conceptual schemes are likely to live in different spheres of experience and to construct different notions of what events or phenomena are to be noticed and recorded (White, 1977). For instance Mischel (1977) suggested that, as a function of one's goals and objectives, the study of human behavior may either focus on *environmental conditions* that control and modify behavior, on mediating *person variables* such as competencies, expectancies, values, and rules, or on *phenomenological impacts* such as affects and thoughts. At a more general and abstract level, Reese and Overton (1970; Overton & Reese, 1973) compared the mechanistic and organismic paradigms and their associated notions of what constitutes relevant raw data for each. Thus it is appropriate to view not only theories but also facts or raw data to be embedded in a context of more general theories and models (see also Baltes & Willis, 1977).

Because science is not a private, but a social, enterprise, scientific practice cannot be understood solely in terms of criteria that are internal to the scientific method itself but must also be related to the social-psychological context of scientific and cultural developments (Baltes & Willis, 1977; Riegel, 1973; Weimer, 1979). It is neither necessary nor desirable to portray the ideal of scientific practice as a monolithic enterprise. Instead actual science manifests a plurality of points of view (Baltes & Willis, 1977). According to Weimer (1979), scientists are confronted with arguments rather than data in the context of constructive rhetoric and a position of comprehensive rational criticism. For this rhetoric to be constructive, scientists need to rely on either relatively explicit social proof structures (White, 1977) or on some shared tacit knowledge that is learned via commands in a master-apprentice relationship and/or from exemplary puzzles and their solutions (Weimer, 1979).

Implications of the preceding considerations for the present discussion are twofold. First, it should be obvious that it is not intended here to portray the life-span approach as better or superior to an age-specific one. Both are seen as complementary to each other, each being useful in relation to different goals and purposes. Second, while it is possible to explicate certain puzzles and issues as exemplary for a life-span approach, full appreciation

of their flavor and complexity is probably gained only in actual scientific practice.

Definition and Construction of a Life-Span Perspective

In light of what has been said before about factual relativity, it seems advisable to approach the definition of a life-span developmental perspective via a methodologically oriented prescription similar to the one proposed by Baltes (1973; see also Baltes et al., 1977). Specifically, the prescription to be adopted here provides a general guideline (1) for the selection and construction of raw data that are relevant from a life-span, though not necessarily from an age-specific, point of view and (2) for the construction of strategies that are used to map raw data onto data. The proposed definition reads as follows:

Life-span oriented views of human development deal with the study of *long-term* sequences and patterns of change in human behavior. The sequences and patterns may be studied as (1) interindividual differences in long-term sequences and patterns of intraindividual changes or (2) long-term sequences and patterns of changes in interindividual differences.

This definition corresponds to the one by Baltes (1973) in terms of its emphasis on long-term, rather than short-term, changes as the relevant domain of raw data. Both definitions differ from each other with regard to the strategies that are considered for the mapping of raw data onto data. The present definition, in contrast to the one given by Baltes (1973), distinguishes explicitly between a focus on differences in intraindividual changes versus an emphasis on changes in interindividual differences. The relevance of this distinction will be discussed in more detail later.

Table 4–1 represents an attempt to illustrate the domain of raw data as defined above. Although the categories of responses-behaviors [R], organismic variables [O], and environmental-stimulus variables [S] are employed, no suggestion is made as to how the categories are to be used conceptually. In other words, Table 4–1 is not intended to reflect a bias in favor of a mechanistic-behavioristic world view. Proponents of organismic and dialectical paradigms may interpret the categories in reference to Riegel's (1977) terminology with [R] representing the individual-psychological, [O] the inner-biological, and [S] the cultural-sociological and outer-physical levels. In accordance with the definition given before, it is simply left open how the individual researcher goes about to

Table 4–1 Raw Data for a Life-Span Developmental Point of View

VARIABLE DOMAIN	SELECTED TIME SEQUENCE						
	t_1	t_2	t_3	·	·	·	t_n
R-variables	$[R]_1$	$[R]_2$	$[R]_3$	·	·	·	$[R]_n$
O-variables	$[O]_1$	$[O]_2$	$[O]_3$	·	·	·	$[O]_n$
S-variables	$[S]_1$	$[S]_2$	$[S]_3$	·	·	·	$[S]_n$

Selected Relationships
  (a) within-domain versus cross-domain relationships
  (b) concurrent versus time-lagged relationships

Note: The construction of long-term developmental sequences and patterns involves the selection of time points, of variables, and of relationships to be investigated.

construct—that is, to describe and explain—temporal sequences within and between categories and levels.

The following points should be noted in the presentation of Table 4–1:

1. Each category, [R], [O], or [S], can be constructed in terms of multiple sets of empirical measures and variables;
2. Within and across categories, sets of variables are sequentially ordered in reference to the same individuals or groups of individuals;
3. For a given individual or group of individuals, sequences are initiated at a particular point in *historical time* and extended over a time interval that is comparable to the length of the total human life span.

The first two points are, of course, not unique to a life-span orientation. Only the third one clearly demarcates it from age-specific approaches by emphasizing its focus on the study of long-term change sequences in a historical context. Therefore it is not surprising that this particular emphasis permeates the formulation and discussion of issues in the area of developmental psychology whenever a life-span perspective is adopted (Baltes, 1973; Baltes et al., 1977; Baltes & Willis, 1977; Huston-Stein & Baltes, 1976).

Previous theoretical and methodological considerations have focused primarily on (1) the nature of change and its relation to both ontogenetic and historical-evolutionary sources of change and (2) the role of structures and transitions in relation to corresponding notions of descriptive and explanatory continuity versus discontinuity. On a theoretical level these discussions have helped to explicate metamodels of development (Gergen, 1977; Looft, 1973; Overton & Reese, 1973; Reese & Overton, 1970; Sterns & Alexander, 1977) as well as models of the interaction between ontogenetic and historical sources of change (Baltes et al., 1979; Bengtson & Black, 1973; Brim, 1966; Buss, 1974a; Elder, 1975; Neugarten & Datan, 1973; Riegel, 1972, 1976, 1977). On a methodological level there are efforts to design appropriate methodologies for the analysis of long-term change sequences. They include the formulation of sequential designs (Baltes, 1968; Baltes et al., 1977; Buss, 1973; Schaie, 1965; Wohlwill, 1973) and of strategies for the analysis of long-term sequences of proximal and distal causal relationships (Jöreskog, 1979; Kenny, 1973; Labouvie, 1974; Rogosa, 1979).

The present discussion is not intended merely to repeat what has been stated in the earlier literature. Instead it seems more profitable to complement previous discussions by directing attention to those facets of the issues that, in this writer's opinion, have not yet been explicated in sufficient detail. In particular we will consider issues related to (1) the construction of causal explanations, (2) the generality versus specificity of variables, and (3) the distinction between interindividual differences in intraindividual changes and changes in interindividual differences as the basis of different strategies used to map raw data onto data.

Explanatory Paradigms and the Construction of Explanations

When considering the nature of scientific explanations in developmental psychology, it has become almost cus-

tomary to refer to Aristotle's categories of material, efficient, formal, final, and incidental causes (e.g., Baltes et al., 1977). These categories have served to outline differences between organismic and mechanistic world views (Overton & Reese, 1973; Reese & Overton, 1970). Within the life-span framework, differential emphasis on the various categories has been of interest in reference to the question of explanatory continuity versus discontinuity (Baltes, 1973; Baltes & Willis, 1977; Looft, 1973) as well as a possible integration and synthesis between both metamodels (Baltes & Schaie, 1973b; Flavell, 1970; Kohlberg, 1973; Labouvie, 1975; Merlino, 1975). Amidst all those discussions, however, life-span developmentalists seem to share a growing belief that the focus of their debates may be somewhat misdirected.

According to Mischel (1977), it can be argued that a consideration of metamodels is of little use if developmentalists fail to specify explanatory goals and objectives. In line with this argument, previous explorations of this problem have led to definitions that characterize explanatory objectives primarily in terms of the causal categories mentioned before. For instance the distinction between structure-function and antecedent-consequent relationships as representing different explanatory goals is mainly accounted for in terms of a differential emphasis on different categories of causes (e.g., Baltes & Willis, 1977). What is essentially left unanswered is the question of whether it is more useful or appropriate to define categories of causes first and then to specify explanatory goals in terms of the former, rather than the other way around. The position offered here maintains that it may well be less confusing to begin with a clear specification of explanatory goals before considering different types and categories of causes.

A survey of psychological theories and research suggests that the objectives of explaining human behavior may differ in terms of at least two distinct features that are often left implicit. One of them relates to the definition and construction of the *explanandum*, that which is explained; the second concerns the status assigned to the relationship between the explanandum and the *explanans*, that which explains.

It appears that change in human behavior, the explanandum of interest, has generally been defined in one of two ways—namely, either as the occurrence of some specified form or as the form of some occurrence. Therefore the study of change has been approached from two different perspectives that, it should be noted, are not contradictory but complementary to each other. According to the first the form of change is given, and an attempt is made to link its occurrence to a set of causes. We may ask: What spatio-temporal conditions cause an increase or a decrease in intellectual performance? According to the second approach, the occurrence of change is given, and an attempt is made to relate its form to some set of causes. Thus we may ask: What causes the change in intellectual performance to be an increase rather than a decrease, or vice versa? This comparison suggests that one may either select certain forms of change as given and explain their occurrence, or one may take the occurrence of change as given and explain its form.

This distinction between the form of occurrences and the occurrence of forms is reflected in the two world views known as mechanistic and organismic paradigms

(Overton & Reese, 1973; Reese & Overton, 1970). While the mechanistic view focuses on the occurrence of selected forms, the organismic perspective emphasizes the form of selected occurrences. According to our view the two paradigms are simply concerned with the construction of different, though complementary, aspects of change in human behavior. Whether the dialectical perspective proposed by Riegel (1977) can achieve a synthesis of the two remains to be seen.

Given the distinction between the occurrence of a form and the form of an occurrence, it is convenient to propose corresponding categories of causes by defining (1) incidental causes as all those causes that are linked to the occurrence of a specified form and (2) formal causes as those that are related to the form of an occurrence. What may motivate individual researchers to focus on one aspect of change rather than the other is not relevant here, except to say that it may, at least in part, depend on whether one is more impressed by the uniformity or the variety of change in human behavior.

Some form of synthesis between both perspectives is particularly desirable from a life-span point of view which assumes that change patterns across the life span do not represent invariant and universal forms but are the result of a dialectical interaction between ontogenetic and historical sources of change. Part of this synthesis will require a more flexible conceptualization of the locus of both incidental and formal causes. In contrast to the mechanistic and organismic paradigms (e.g., Looft, 1973), it is not necessary to locate all incidental causes exclusively in the environment of the organism and all formal causes exclusively within the organism.

The second feature that characterizes explanatory objectives can be considered separately from the first. It concerns the status of the explanans in relation to the explanandum. More concretely it relates to the question of whether a given cause, be it incidental or formal, is assumed to be a determinant that is necessary or sufficient or both with regard to the explanandum.

If, as the life-span view suggests, behaviors and behavioral changes are generally influenced by a multitude of incidental and formal causes, the search for single determinants that are both necessary and sufficient to account for either the form of an occurrence or the occurrence of a form becomes highly illusory and futile. Instead it would seem more appropriate to expect both age- and history-related sources of change to represent, at best, either necessary *but not* sufficient or sufficient *but not* necessary determinants. A separation of the two characteristics (being necessary versus being sufficient) raises some conceptual and methodological issues. Conceptually it follows that the status of a particular determinant as being necessary or sufficient or both in reference to a given change phenomenon is not invariant but must be seen in relation to a much broader spatio-temporal context of determinants in which it is embedded. Since that context is subject to historical change, the causal status of a given determinant may exhibit historical changes as well (Labouvie, Note 1).

This conclusion has important implications if one is interested in defining the purpose and validity of experimental methods within a life-span perspective. Traditionally, the goal of experiments has been seen as one of documenting via elimination of alternative hypotheses that a specific manipulation represents, within the context of the experiment, a necessary and sufficient determinant of the changes that are observed in the dependent variable and that this relationship can be generalized to other contexts. From a life-span point of view this interpretation is of very limited usefulness. More specifically the task is not so much one of identifying a particular determinant as necessary and sufficient but rather one of specifying the contexts in which a single determinant or a multiple set of determinants are (1) necessary and sufficient, (2) only necessary but not sufficient, (3) only sufficient but not necessary, and (4) neither necessary nor sufficient in reference to the occurrence or form of behavioral changes that are being studied.

Methodologically the rigidity of the traditional interpretation is reflected by the kind of strategies that are used to analyze data. To illustrate this point, the reader is referred to Table 4–2. For simplicity it is assumed that the hypothesized causal relationship is formulated in terms of an association between dichotomies and represented empirically in the form of a contingency table. Analyses of such data typically involve all four frequencies simultaneously, a strategy that is appropriate only if it is hypothesized that the determinant is both necessary and sufficient. In contrast only subsets of these frequencies are logically relevant in the case where the determinant is conceptualized as only necessary but not sufficient or as only sufficient but not necessary. A similar criticism can also be raised with regard to analysis of variance procedures and the use of correlation coefficients, all of which are essentially insensitive to differences in the causal status of determinants.

The proposed distinctions between different aspects of the explanandum and different qualities of causal relationships also have a certain relevance for two other issues—namely, the problem of descriptive and explanatory continuity versus discontinuity (Baltes & Schaie, 1973b; Beilin, 1971; Emmerich, 1964, 1968; Huston-Stein & Baltes, 1976; Kagan, 1969; Neugarten, 1969; Overton & Reese, 1973: Reese & Overton, 1970) and the question of how to structure and analyze long-term sequences of both proximal and distal, causal relationships (Baltes et al., 1977; Huston-Stein & Baltes, 1976; Labouvie, 1974; Wohlwill, 1973). Descriptive and explanatory discontinuity may obtain simply because of shifts in one's perspective from one that focuses on the

Table 4–2 Qualities of a Causal Relationship: Expected Frequencies

Cause	Outcome	
	$y < y_c$	$y \unrhd y_c$
H_o: $x \unrhd x_c$ is necessary and sufficient for $y \unrhd y_c$ and $x < x_c$ is necessary and sufficient for $y < y_c$.		
$x < x_c$	$f_a > 0$	$f_b = 0$
$x \unrhd x_c$	$f_c = 0$	$f_d > 0$
H_o: $x \unrhd x_c$ is necessary but not sufficient for $y \unrhd y_c$.		
$x < x_c$	$f_a > 0$	$f_b = 0$
$x \unrhd x_c$	irrelevant	irrelevant
H_o: $x \unrhd x_c$ is sufficient but not necessary for $y \unrhd y_c$.		
$x < x_c$	irrelevant	irrelevant
$x \unrhd x_c$	$f_c = 0$	$f_d > 0$

Note: f_a, f_b, f_c, and f_d are expected frequencies.

form of change to one that emphasizes the occurrence of a particular form of change, and vice versa. If one believes that change is most pronounced and most uniform in the early and late parts of life, the resulting empirical-theoretical formulations are likely to concentrate on a description and explanation of the form of those changes as illustrated by the conceptual frameworks of Piaget (1970), Kohlberg (1973), or Cumming and Henry (1961). If middle adulthood is seen as a period of relative stability and of considerable heterogeneity of individual change patterns, the focus is likely to shift to a description and explanation of the occurrence of particular forms of change within particular contexts. As far as the life-span point of view is concerned, however, such shifts in perspectives are not necessary or desirable. Instead both foci are needed simultaneously to understand the phenomenon of developmental change across the total life span.

The structuring and analysis of long-term sequences of causal relationships needs to take into account that any proximal or distal determinant is embedded in a temporally ordered set of determinants. Thus whether a particular determinant is necessary or sufficient may depend on the total set of determinants and its temporal structure. While each of several determinants may be only necessary when considered separately, a particular temporal sequencing of them may, nevertheless, represent a sufficient condition for the occurrence of some behavioral change. On the other hand each of several determinants may be sufficient in itself without any combination of them representing a condition that is both necessary and sufficient. As stated earlier, analytical methods available to developmentalists are by and large not suited to allow such a detailed analysis of the causal quality of proximal and distal determinants.

Generality versus Specificity of Concepts and Measures

It was stated earlier that facts are conceptual in nature. This should not be taken to imply that the relevant concepts are always sufficiently explicated or to suggest that empirical measures can always be assumed to relate to the concepts of interest. As every reader knows there is a considerable amount of literature which has dealt with this issue in terms of concepts such as reliability, validity, and equivalence of measures in relation to underlying concepts (e.g., Baltes et al., 1977; Eckensberger, 1973; Labouvie, 1980a; Wohlwill, 1973). What is somewhat surprising, however, is the fact that these discussions have given comparatively little systematic consideration to a problem that is perhaps more basic. It is more basic in the sense that it concerns the construction and selection of concepts and measures in terms of their generality or specificity. It would appear that most of the attention given to this problem has thus far been generated in the context of debates between the perspectives of situationism and personologism (e.g., Fiske, 1979; Mischel, 1968, 1977, 1979). Life-span developmentalists have begun to recognize the relevance of this issue for the study of long-term change (e.g., Baltes & Labouvie, 1973; Labouvie, Note 1; Schaie, 1978; Scheidt & Schaie, 1978).

According to Fishbein and Ajzen (1975) and Mischel

(1977, 1979) it is useful to consider both concepts and measures in reference to a spatio-temporal context of situations and times (see also Buss, 1974b; Cattell, 1946). As illustrated in Table 4–3 the relevant time frames and situational contexts that are associated with concepts and measures may range from very specific to very general. In line with the proposed distinction between intra-situational stability and cross-situational consistency (Mischel, 1968, 1977), levels of specificity-generality along the time and the situation dimension are not necessarily related to each other. In other words the concepts that are invented and the measures that are constructed may be highly specific in reference to time or situation or both; on the other hand, they may represent a relatively high level of generality if they are based on large time frames or aggregates of situations or both. In a somewhat simplified fashion one may categorize concepts and measures as (1) both time- and situation-specific, (2) situation-specific but time-free, (3) situation-free but time-specific, and (4) both time- and situation-free. More important than the descriptive framework itself are, of course, the implications that follow from it.

Probably the most general and most basic implication is related to the problem of establishing a reasonable degree of congruence in specificity-generality between corresponding concepts and measures. If a given concept is intended to have a high degree of temporal and situational generality, it does not make sense to employ a single measure that is highly time- and situation-specific. Instead the concept's generality needs to be matched by using a multiple set or battery of measures (Baltes & Nesselroade, 1970; Baltes et al., 1977; Bentler & Speckart, 1979). On the other hand if a particular concept is constructed with a high degree of temporal and situational specificity, it is not desirable to use a measure that is relatively general in terms of its time frame and situational context. According to Fishbein and Ajzen (1975) the level of specificity-generality of measures in the behavioral domain [R] can be manipulated by choosing either single-act criteria, repeated-observation criteria, or multiple-act criteria. However it should be recognized that the problem of congruence between measures and concepts is not unique to the domain of behaviors but applies equally to organismic [O] and environmental-situational [S] measures and concepts. Thus similar categories may be proposed for the latter two domains. Finally the problem of congruence is one that permeates all empirical research. In order to recognize its full salience within the context of a life-span developmental perspec-

Table 4–3 Specificity versus Generality of Concepts and Measures: Time Frames and Situational Contexts

SITUATIONAL CONTEXT	TIME FRAME	
	Short	Long
Narrow; specific	Time-specific Situation-specific	Time-free Situation-specific (Intrasituational stability)
Broad; general	Time-specific Situation-free (Cross-situational consistency)	Time-free Situation-free

tive, it should be seen in conjunction with the issue considered next.

A second implication that is suggested by the descriptive framework in Table 4–3 concerns one's choice of the level(s) of specificity-generality for the concepts of interest. At one extreme it is possible to opt only for concepts (and associated measures) that are highly situation- and time-specific. When focusing on relatively short units of behavior in specific situations, the distinction between concepts and measures becomes almost redundant (Fiske, 1979). This approach is perhaps best exemplified by situationism (Mischel, 1968, 1977) and interactional contextualism (e.g., Hartup & Lempers, 1973) which prefer to study "what people do in specific situations" and "how they change their behavior under specific conditions" (e.g., Baer, 1973). Although there can be no doubt about the value of these approaches (Fiske, 1979), their usefulness is somewhat questionable if one is interested in the study of long-term change sequences. To construct such sequences in terms of highly time- and situation-specific concepts and measures would seem to be too cumbersome and inefficient to be a practical possibility.

In comparison, alternatives that tend toward the other extreme of the specificity-generality dimension will emphasize concepts that have a high degree of generality with regard to the time dimension, the situation dimension, or both. Construction of concepts and measures that are time-free in the sense that they represent central tendencies over relatively large time frames may be useful for certain purposes and is perhaps best exemplified by psychometric models of personality and intelligence. However such an approach is of little interest to developmentalists because it reflects a one-sided focus on stability rather than change and in that sense is both adevelopmental and ahistorical.

The alternative that has had more appeal for developmentalists is based on the selection and construction of concepts that are situation-free and represent central tendencies (or consistencies) across many different situations, though not across many points in time. Wohlwill (1973) advocated this approach in order to distinguish between developmental and nondevelopmental phenomena. This position is exemplified by the theoretical frameworks of Erikson (1963), Kohlberg (1973), and Piaget (1960). According to Mischel (1977) it should be pointed out that it is perfectly appropriate and legitimate to study how "people change in general" if one is interested in such a question. However according to the definition given earlier, it is *not* the question that is of foremost interest for the life-span developmental point of view. Although the use of situation-free concepts and measures lends itself very easily to an efficient description and construction of long-term change sequences, it is, nevertheless, of only limited usefulness if one is interested in the description and explanation of individual long-term change in a changing historical context.

The foregoing discussion of alternatives suggests that the life-span developmental approach may benefit most by relying on concepts that are constructed at an intermediate level of generality with regard to both time frames and situational contexts. In that sense they would be similar or correspond to middle level concepts discussed by Mischel (1979; see also Rosch, Mervis, Gray,

Johnson, & Boyes-Braem, 1976). If intermediate-level concepts are assumed to represent limited time intervals and limited sets of situational contexts, it becomes important that corresponding measures of such concepts reflect both the time frames and the range of situations that are of interest, in a representative fashion. This requirement, in turn, provides an additional facet for the analysis of the problem of measurement equivalence (Labouvie, 1980a). Besides questioning whether formally identical measures tap the same concept in different age or cohort populations, one may also ask whether the time frames and situational contexts of the measures are equivalent across groups. For instance peer ratings obtained from groups of old and young individuals may be conceptually equivalent in terms of their relationship to underlying concepts; however, the ratings of the older group, as compared to those of the younger one, may well be based on longer time frames and a broader range of situational contexts.

The choice of specificity-generality of one's concepts and their associated measures is also likely to have a bearing on the relative contribution and usefulness of both proximal and distal causal relationships in explaining a given change phenomenon. If the change is described at a relatively high level of temporal or situational specificity, it is reasonable to expect that proximal or concurrent relationships are generally stronger and more easily documented than distal ones. On the other hand if change is conceptualized at a high level of situational or temporal generality, distal relationships, especially in the form of *R-R* connections, are probably much more easily obtained. Thus a choice of intermediate-level concepts and measures, as proposed above, may be most appropriate for a simultaneous consideration of both proximal and distal relationships in the context of long-term change sequences.

Differences in Intraindividual Changes versus Changes in Interindividual Differences

As stated earlier the distinction between differences in intraindividual changes versus changes in interindividual differences can be interpreted as one between different strategies for the mapping of raw data onto data. One can also view it as an issue of specificity-generality not along the time or situation dimension but along the person dimension. A focus on differences in intraindividual changes emphasizes specificity and may be seen as *person-centered;* in contrast, a focus on changes in interindividual differences is *group-centered* and emphasizes generality along the person dimension (Mischel, 1977).

It is evident that the bulk of developmental research has been the result of a preoccupation with the study of changes in interindividual differences (Wohlwill, 1973). This assessment is also valid for the majority of empirical investigations that were carried out with a life-span perspective in mind (e.g., Baltes, Baltes, & Reinert, 1970; Nesselroade & Baltes, 1974; Schaie, Labouvie, & Buech, 1973; Schaie & Strother, 1968).

The rather one-sided focus on changes in interindividual differences is reflected in the common practice of constructing change patterns and sequences in the form of (1) differences and trends in group means and group frequencies or (2) a set of synchronous, auto-, and cross-lagged correlations or covariances. By relating interindividual differences at any one point in time to differences at other points in time via means-averages or correlations-covariances, it is change in interindividual differences rather than differences in intraindividual change that is constructed and interpreted.

There is no reason to suggest that one approach is always better and more useful than the other. Obviously it will depend on one's purposes and goals. It would seem clear that a better balance between both strategies is needed, especially if the study of differential intraindividual change is claimed to be an important goal of the life-span developmental point of view. Based on recent simulation studies (Baltes & Nesselroade, 1973; Baltes, Nesselroade, & Cornelius, 1978), Labouvie (1980b, 1981) has attempted to document more explicitly the complementarity of the two approaches. It is somewhat unfortunate that psychometric discussions of change measurement (e.g., Bereiter, 1963; Cronbach & Furby, 1970) seem to have biased most developmentalists toward an almost exclusive focus on changes in interindividual differences.

To illustrate this point more concretely, consider the following example (see Table 4-4). For simplicity assume that intraindividual changes in some target behavior R_i of individual i over a specified time interval $[t_1, t_n]$ can be expressed in a formal mathematical equation as follows:

$$R_i(t) = a_i + b_i t + c_i t^2;$$
$$i = 1, 2, \ldots, N;$$
$$t_1 \leq t \leq t_n$$

If the focus is on differences in intraindividual changes, each person i is described in terms of a characteristic set of change coefficients (a_i, b_i, c_i) that is fixed and invariant across the time interval of interest (see Table 4-4). Analyses will proceed by first estimating the coefficients a_i, b_i, and c_i for all individuals and then relating individual differences in all three coefficients to each other as well as to differences in potential antecedent conditions.

In comparison if the focus is on the study of changes in interindividual differences, a series of time points t_1, t_2, $\ldots$, t_n is described in terms of a corresponding series of interindividual differences R_{1i}, R_{2i}, $\ldots$, R_{ni}. Subsequent analyses will estimate series of means and sets of cross-lagged correlations or covariances and attempt to relate changes in means and covariances to potential antecedents.

As Table 4-4 illustrates, changes in means, variances, and covariances of interindividual differences are simply a function of time. In other words information contained in those changes is trivial as far as the analysis of differences in intraindividual changes is concerned.

This example is not intended to suggest that the analysis of changes in interindividual differences is always less informative than that of differences in intraindividual changes. Instead it points out that a more balanced utilization of both approaches is needed to provide a better and more complete description and understanding of developmental change phenomena across the life span.

Table 4-4 Individual Differences in Intraindividual Changes versus Changes in Interindividual Differences

FOCUS	RELEVANT INFORMATION
Assumed Model: $R_i(t) = a_i + b_i t + c_i t^2$ for individual i and (t_l, t_n)	
Individual Differences in Intraindividual Changes	(a) intraindividual change coefficients a_i, b_i, and c_i (b) individual differences in a_i, b_i, c_i
Changes in Interindividual Differences	(a) means at time points t_k $(k = 1, \ldots, n)$ $\bar{R}(t_k) = \bar{a} + \bar{b} t_k + \bar{c} t_k^2$ (b) covariances between times t_k and t_l $\text{Cov}(R_i(t_k), R_i(t_l)) =$ $Var(a_i) + t_k t_l \text{Var}(b_i) + t_k^2 t_l^2 \text{Var}(c_i) +$ $(t_k + t_l)\text{Cov}(a_i b_i) + (t_k^2 + t_l^2)\text{Cov}(a_i c_i) +$ $(t_k t_l^2 + t_k^2 t_l)\text{Cov}(b_i c_i)$

Note: Var = variance; Cov = covariance.

CONCLUSIONS

The thesis presented here is that life-span and age-specific developmental points of view should not be interpreted as competing but as complementary approaches with complementary goals and objectives. This complementarity does not merely imply a difference in conceptual frameworks. According to the notion of factual relativity, the facts of a life-span perspective may not be the facts of age-specific frameworks, and vice versa.

The life-span developmental point of view is emerging and so are its relevant issues. As the study of long-term change sequences in continuously changing historical contexts, it cannot develop without considering issues that involve the choice of explanatory paradigms and the construction of explanations, the selection and construction of concepts and measures, and the choice of representational modes for the construction and description of change itself. Each of these issues is a multifaceted one, and previous discussions have focused on some facets more than on others. Illumination of as many facets as possible helps both to refine the objectives of the life-span developmental approach and to document its usefulness.

REFERENCE NOTES

1. Labouvie, E. W. *Methodological issues in the prediction of psychopathology: A life span perspective.* Paper presented at the meeting of the Society for Life History Research in Psychopathology and the Society for the Study of Social Biology, New York, 1979.

REFERENCES

BAER, D. M. The control of developmental process: Why wait? In J. R. Nesselroade & H. W. Reese (Eds.), *Life-span developmental psychology. Methodological issues.* New York: Academic Press, 1973.

BALTES, P. B. Longitudinal and cross-sectional sequences in the study of age and generation effects. *Human Development,* 1968, *11,* 145–171.

BALTES, P. B. Prototypical paradigms and questions in life-span research on development and aging. *Gerontologist,* 1973, *13,* 458–567.

BALTES, P. B., BALTES, M. M., & REINERT, G. The relationship between time of measurement and age in cognitive development of children. *Human Development,* 1970, *13,* 258–268.

BALTES, P. B., & CORNELIUS, S. W. The status of dialectics in developmental psychology: Theoretical orientation versus scientific method. In N. Datan & H. W. Reese (Eds.), *Life-span developmental psychology. Dialectical perspectives on experimental research.* New York: Academic Press, 1977.

BALTES, P. B., CORNELIUS, S. W., & NESSELROADE, J. R. Cohort effects in developmental psychology. In J. R. Nesselroade & P. B. Baltes (Eds.), *Longitudinal research in the study of behavior and development.* New York: Academic Press, 1979.

BALTES, P. B., & LABOUVIE, G. V. Adult development of intellectual performance: Description, explanation, modification. In C. Eisdorfer & M. P. Lawton (Eds.), *The psychology of adult development and aging.* Washington, D.C.: American Psychological Association, 1973.

BALTES, P. B., & NESSELROADE, J. R. Multivariate longitudinal and cross-sectional sequences for analyzing ontogenetic and generational change: A methodological note. *Developmental Psychology,* 1970, *2,* 163–168.

BALTES, P. B., & NESSELROADE, J. R. The developmental analysis of individual differences on multiple measures. In J. R. Nesselroade & H. W. Reese (Eds.), *Life-span developmental psychology. Methodological issues.* New York: Academic Press, 1973.

BALTES, P. B., NESSELROADE, J. R., & CORNELIUS, S. W. Multivariate antecedents of structural change in development: A simulation of cumulative environmental patterns. *Multivariate Behavioral Research,* 1978, *13,* 127–152.

BALTES, P. B., REESE, H. W., & NESSELROADE, J. R. *Life-span developmental psychology: Introduction to research methods.* Monterey, Calif.: Brooks/Cole, 1977.

BALTES, P. B., & SCHAIE, K. W. (Eds.). *Life-span developmental psychology: Personality and socialization.* New York: Academic Press, 1973a.

BALTES, P. B. & SCHAIE, K. W. On life-span developmental research paradigms: Retrospects and prospects. In P. B. Baltes & K. W. Schaie (Eds.), *Life-span developmental psychology: Personality and socialization.* New York: Academic Press, 1973b.

BALTES, P. B., & WILLIS, S. L. Toward psychological theories of aging and development. In J. E. Birren & K. W. Schaie (Eds.), *Handbook of the psychology of aging.* New York: Van Nostrand Reinhold, 1977.

BAYLEY, N. Behavioral correlates of mental growth: Birth to thirty-six years. *American Psychologist,* 1968, *23,* 1–17.

BEILIN, H. Developmental stages and developmental processes. In D. R. Green, M. P. Ford, & G. P. Flamer (Eds.), *Measurement and Piaget.* New York: McGraw-Hill, 1971.

BENGTSON, V. L., & BLACK, K. D. Intergenerational relations and continuities in socialization. In P. B. Baltes & K. W. Schaie (Eds.), *Life-span developmental psychology: Personality and socialization.* New York: Academic Press, 1973.

BENTLER, P. M., & SPECKART, G. Models of attitude-behavior relations. *Psychological Review,* 1979, *86,* 452–464.

BEREITER, C. Some persisting dilemmas in the measurement of change. In C. W. Harris (Ed.), *Problems in measuring change.* Madison: University of Wisconsin Press, 1963.

BLOOM, M. Life-span analysis: A theoretical framework for behavioral science research. *Human Relations,* 1964, *12,* 538–554.

BRIM, O. G. Socialization through the life cycle. In O. G. Brim & S. Wheeler (Eds.), *Socialization after childhood: Two essays.* New York: John Wiley, 1966.

BÜHLER, C. *Der menschliche Lebenslauf als psychologisches Problem* (2nd ed.). Göttingen: Hogrefe, 1959.

BÜHLER, C., & MASSARIK, F. (Eds.). *The course of human life.* New York: Springer-Verlag, 1968.

BUSS, A. R. An extension of developmental models that separate ontogenetic changes and cohort differences. *Psychological Bulletin,* 1973, *80,* 466–479.

BUSS, A. R. Generational analysis: Description, explanation, and theory. *Journal of Social Issues,* 1974a, *30,* 55–71.

BUSS, A. R. A general developmental model for interindividual differences, intraindividual differences, and intraindividual changes. *Developmental Psychology,* 1974b, *10,* 70–78.

CATTELL, R. B. *The description and measurement of personality.* New York: World Book, 1946.

COOMBS, C. H. *A theory of data.* New York: John Wiley, 1964.

CRONBACH, L. J., & FURBY, L. How should we measure "change"—or should we? *Psychological Bulletin,* 1970, *74,* 68–80.

CUMMING, E., & HENRY, W. E. *Growing old: The process of disengagement.* New York: Basic Books, 1961.

DATAN, N., & GINSBERG, L. H. (Eds.). *Life-span developmental psychology. Normative life crises.* New York: Academic Press, 1975.

DATAN, N., & REESE, H. W. (Eds.). *Life-span developmental psychology. Dialectical perspectives on experimental research.* New York: Academic Press, 1977.

ECKENSBERGER, L. H. Methodological issues of cross-cultural research in developmental psychology. In J. R. Nesselroade & H. W. Reese (Eds.), *Life-span developmental psychology. Methodological issues.* New York: Academic Press, 1973.

ELDER, G. Age-differentiation in a life course perspective. *Annual Review of Sociology,* 1975, *1,* 165–190.

EMMERICH, W. Continuity and stability in early social development. *Child Development,* 1964, *35,* 311–332.

EMMERICH, W. Personality development and concepts of structure. *Child Development,* 1968, *39,* 671–690.

ERIKSON, E. H. Identity and the life cycle. *Psychological Issues,* 1959, *1*(Whole No. 1).

ERIKSON, E. H. *Childhood and society.* New York: W. W. Norton & Co., Inc., 1963.

FISHBEIN, M., & AJZEN, I. *Belief, attitude, intention and behavior: An introduction to theory and research.* Reading, Mass.: Addison-Wesley, 1975.

FISKE, D. W. Two worlds of psychological phenomena. *American Psychologist,* 1979, *34,* 733–739.

FLAVELL, J. H. Cognitive changes in adulthood. In L. R. Goulet & P. B. Baltes (Eds.), *Life-span developmental psychology. Research and theory.* New York: Academic Press, 1970.

GERGEN, K. J. Stability, change, and chance in understanding human development. In N. Datan & H. W. Reese (Eds.), *Life-span developmental psychology. Dialectical perspectives on experimental research.* New York: Academic Press, 1977.

GOULET, L. R., & BALTES, P. B. (Eds.). *Life-span developmental psychology. Research and theory.* New York: Academic Press, 1970.

HARTUP, W. W., & LEMPERS, J. A problem in life-span development: The interactional analysis of family attachments. In P. B. Baltes & K. W. Schaie (Eds.), *Life-span developmental psychology: Personality and socialization.* New York: Academic Press, 1973.

HAVIGHURST, R. J. *Developmental tasks and education.* New York: D. McKay, 1948.

HUSTON-STEIN, A., & BALTES, P. B. Theory and method in life-span developmental psychology: Implications for child development. *Advances in Child Development and Behavior,* 1976, *11,* 169–188.

JÖRESKOG, K. G. Statistical estimation of stuctural models in longitudinal-developmental investigations. In J. R. Nesselroade & P. B. Baltes (Eds.), *Longitudinal research in the study of behavior and development.* New York: Academic Press, 1979.

KAGAN, J. The three faces of continuity in human development. In D. A. Goslin (Ed.), *Handbook of socialization theory and research.* Skokie, Ill.: Rand McNally, 1969.

KENISTON, K. Psychological development and historical change. *Journal of Interdisciplinary History,* 1971, *2,* 330–345.

KENNY, D. A. Cross-lagged and synchronous common factors in panel data. In A. S. Goldberger & O. D. Duncan (Eds.), *Structural equation models in the social sciences.* New York: Seminar Press, 1973.

KOHLBERG, L. Continuities in childhood and adult moral development revisited. In P. B. Baltes & K. W. Schaie (Eds.), *Life-span developmental psychology: Personality and socialization.* New York: Academic Press, 1973.

LABOUVIE, E. W. Developmental causal structures of organism-environment interactions. *Human Development,* 1974, *17,* 444–452.

LABOUVIE, E. W. The dialectical nature of measurement activities in the behavioral sciences. *Human Development,* 1975, *18,* 396–403.

LABOUVIE, E. W. Identity versus equivalence of psychological measures and constructs. In L. W. Poon (Ed.), *Aging in the 1980's: Selected contemporary issues in the psychology of aging.* Washington, D.C.: American Psychological Association, 1980a.

LABOUVIE, E. W. Measurement of individual differences in intraindividual changes. *Psychological Bulletin,* 1980b, *88,* 54–59.

LABOUVIE, E. W. The study of multivariate change structures: A conceptual perspective. *Multivariate Behavioral Research,* 1981, *16,* 23–35.

LOOFT, W. R. Socialization and personality throughout the life span: An examination of contemporary psychological approaches. In P. B. Baltes & K. W. Schaie (Eds.), *Life-span developmental psychology: Personality and socialization.* New York: Academic Press, 1973.

MERLINO, F. J. Metatheoretical isolationism reconsidered: Its impact for developmental theories. *Human Development,* 1975, *18,* 391–395.

MISCHEL, W. *Personality and assessment.* New York: John Wiley, 1968.

MISCHEL, W. On the future of personality measurement. *American Psychologist,* 1977, *32,* 246–254.

MISCHEL, W. On the interface of cognition and personality: Beyond the person-situation debate. *American Psychologist,* 1979, *34,* 740–754.

NESSELROADE, J. R., & BALTES, P. B. Adolescent personality development and historical change: 1970–1972. *Monographs of the Society for Research in Child Development,* 1974, *39*(1, Whole No. 154).

NESSELROADE, J. R., & REESE, H. W. (Eds.). *Life-span developmental psychology. Methodological issues.* New York: Academic Press, 1973.

NEUGARTEN, B. L. Toward a psychology of the life cycle. In B. L. Neugarten (Ed.), *Middle age and aging: A reader in social psychology.* Chicago: University of Chicago Press, 1968.

NEUGARTEN, B. L. Continuities and discontinuities of psychological issues into adult life. *Human Development,* 1969, *12,* 121–130.

NEUGARTEN, B. L., & DATAN, N. Sociological perspectives on the life cycle. In P. B. Baltes & K. W. Schaie (Eds.), *Life-span developmental psychology: Personality and socialization.* New York: Academic Press, 1973.

OVERTON, W. F., & REESE, H. W. Models of development: Methodological implications. In J. R. Nesselroade & H. W. Reese (Eds.), *Lifespan developmental psychology. Methodological issues.* New York: Academic Press, 1973.

PIAGET, J. *Psychology of intelligence.* Totowa, N.J.: Littlefield & Adams, 1960.

PIAGET, J. Piaget's theory. In P. H. Mussen (Ed.), *Carmichael's manual of child psychology.* New York: John Wiley, 1970.

PRESSEY, S. L., & KUHLEN, R. G. *Psychological development through the life span.* New York: Harper & Row, Pub., 1957.

REESE, H. W., & OVERTON, W. F. Models of development and theories of development. In L. R. Goulet & P. B. Baltes (Eds.), *Life-span developmental psychology. Research and theory.* New York: Academic Press, 1970.

RIEGEL, K. F. Time and change in the development of the individual and society. In H. W. Reese (Ed.), *Advances in child development and behavior* (Vol. 7). New York: Academic Press, 1972.

RIEGEL, K. F. Developmental psychology and society: Some historical and ethical considerations. In J. R. Nesselroade & H. W. Reese (Eds.), *Life-span developmental psychology. Methodological issues.* New York: Academic Press, 1973.

RIEGEL, K. F. The dialectics of human development. *American Psychologist,* 1976, *31,* 689–700.

RIEGEL, K. F. The dialectics of time. In N. Datan & H. W. Reese (Eds.), *Life-span developmental psychology. Dialectical perspectives on experimental research.* New York: Academic Press, 1977.

ROGOSA, D. Causal models in longitudinal research. In J. R. Nesselroade & P. B. Baltes (Eds.), *Longitudinal research in the study of behavior and development.* New York: Academic Press, 1979.

ROSCH, E., MERVIS, C., GRAY, W., JOHNSON, D., & BOYES-BRAEM, P. Basic objects in natural categories. *Cognitive Psychology,* 1976, *8,* 382–439.

SCHAIE, K. W. A general model for the study of developmental problems. *Psychological Bulletin,* 1965, *64,* 92–107.

SCHAIE, K. W. External validity in the assessment of intellectual development in adulthood. *Journal of Gerontology,* 1978, *33,* 695–701.

SCHAIE, K. W., LABOUVIE, G. V., & BUECH, B. V. Generational and cohort-specific differences in adult cognitive functioning: A fourteen-year study of independent samples. *Developmental Psychology,* 1973, *9,* 151–166.

SCHAIE, K. W., & STROTHER, C. R. A cross-sequential study of age changes in cognitive behavior. *Psychological Bulletin,* 1968, *70,* 671–680.

SCHEIDT, R. J., & SCHAIE, K. W. A taxonomy of situations for an elderly population: Generating situational criteria. *Journal of Gerontology,* 1978, *33,* 848–857.

STERNS, H. L., & ALEXANDER, R. A. Cohort, age, and time of measurement: Biomorphic considerations. In N. Datan & H. W. Reese (Eds.), *Life-span developmental psychology. Dialectical perspectives on experimental research.* New York: Academic Press, 1977.

THOMAE, H. (Ed.). *Entwicklungspsychologie.* Göttingen: Hogrefe, 1959.

THOMAE, H. *Das Individuum und seine Welt.* Göttingen: Hogrefe, 1968.

WEIMER, W. B. *Notes on the methodology of scientific research.* Hillsdale, N.J.: Lawrence Erlbaum Associates, 1979.

WHITE, S. H. Social proof structures: The dialectic of method and theory in the work of psychology. In N. Datan & H. W. Reese (Eds.), *Life-span developmental psychology. Dialectical perspectives on experimental research.* New York: Academic Press, 1977.

WOHLWILL, J. F. *The study of behavioral development.* New York: Academic Press, 1973.

5

Primate Infancy:
Problems
and Developmental Strategies

GARY G. SCHWARTZ
LEONARD A. ROSENBLUM

Of all living creatures, "the ape is closest to man." So wrote Galen of Pergamum who, in A.D. 130, capitalized on this observation by using simian primates as substitutes for human cadavers. Despite the astuteness of Galen's taxonomic judgment—the great apes are indeed our closest living relations—the use of monkeys and apes as models for human psychological development ideally requires a more explicit conceptualization of man's phylogenetic relationship to the nonhuman primates. While few psychologists today would subscribe to the popular misbelief that human beings "descended" from the modern apes, the evolutionary bases for humanity's affinities with their primate relations, and thus the foundation for meaningful comparisons across species, are often mis- or incompletely understood. In setting the stage for our discussion of infant primate psychological development then, it will be helpful to focus first on the backdrop of primate phylogeny and on the nature of the comparative approach.

"I confess freely to you," penned William Congreve, "I could never look long upon a monkey, without very mortifying reflections." Written more than 150 years before Darwin's *The Origin of Species,* Congreve's insight remains an acute testimony to the monkey's ability to mirror human psychology. Although the fascination that monkeys and apes hold for us is certainly much older (the Bible, for instance, records ships laden with silver, ivory, and apes), the explicit scientific evidence for our kinship with the primates can be dated from the publication of Thomas Henry Huxley's *Evidence of Man's Place*

in Nature in 1863. Since that time the study of primate phylogeny, once the exclusive domain of comparative anatomy and paleontology, has benefited by the addition of new systematic, behavioral, and biochemical techniques. Ironically these new methods are seldom in complete agreement with one another with regard to the precise time course or branching pattern of primate phylogeny (see Washburn, 1973, and Simpson, 1975, for insightful analyses of this problem). In the following section we attempt to sketch only in broad outline some of the major features of primate evolution. Reviews of the paleontological evidence of primate phylogeny may be found in Simons (1976), Simpson (1945), and Walker (1976), and of the newer molecular approaches in Goodman and Tashian (1976).

PHYLOGENY

Phylogeny is the historical study of the true genealogical relationships of organisms and is thus never completely knowable. Most primatologists, however, are in agreement that the ancestry of present-day primates is traceable through a common arboreal insectivore which probably resembled the modern tree shrew. The most direct living descendants of this stem insectivore are the modern prosimians: the lemuroids, lorises, galagos, and tarsiers. Aptly called *Halbaffen* in German, meaning half-monkeys, these pre–monkey-like primates comprise the suborder Prosimii of the order Primates. The prosimians represent an early major departure from the lineage which later led to the suborder Anthropoidea, or the true monkeys and apes. Prosimians survive today largely through an insular distribution (three of the five prosim-

Preparation of this chapter was supported by Grant #MH15965 from USPHS and from funds provided by the State University of New York.

ian families are restricted to Madagascar) and their ability to avoid competition with more advanced primates successfully.

Some 50 million years ago, two major lineages diverged from a prosimian stock and gave rise to the New World families, whose members now range from southern Mexico to South America, and the Old World families inhabiting Africa and Asia. The most common representatives of the New World, or Neotropical, families are the squirrel monkey and the once-familiar organ grinder's monkey, the capuchin. Old World monkey families include the leaf-eating colobines and the more massive, predominantly terrestrial, African baboons and their Asian cousins, the macaques. Ape and human families, more recent branches of the Old World lineage, together comprise the superfamily Hominoidea consisting of the apes of Asia, the gibbon and siamang (the so-called lesser apes), the orangutan, and the great apes of Africa, the gorilla and chimpanzee. Man is the sole member of a separate family, the Hominidae, represented by the single worldwide polytypic species, *Homo sapiens*. As Simpson (1972) notes, the most important implication of this last zoological statement is that all men are, *in fact*, brothers. Similarly in genealogical perspective, the apes, Old World monkeys, New World monkeys, and prosimians are, in order of recency of separation, our cousins once removed.

NEOTENY

These genetical relationships alone would make the nonhuman primates invaluable models for psychological observation and experimentation. However the whole of modern primate evolution has been characterized by a consistent evolutionary trend—one realized most fully in humans—that is of tremendous developmental significance. That trend is known as *neoteny*. By neoteny we mean a general retardation of somatic development (e.g., gestation time, postnatal growth, sexual maturity, etc.) such that characteristics of early periods of development in an ancestral species are retained in later ontogenetic stages in their descendants. Neoteny has profoundly influenced human evolution (see Gould, 1977); a good example is seen in the paedomorphic, or child-shaped, appearance of the human skull. A large inflated cranium is characteristic of infant and juvenile macaques for example, but not of adults; the accelerated growth of the jaw in later ontogeny reduces the monkey's cranial dimensions relative to the face and produces the "dental muzzle" characteristic of mature macaques. Humans, by contrast, retain a relatively inflated cranium throughout their life span. Because of the prolongation of fetal growth rates in humans, the positive allometry, or relative growth, of the jaw appears much later in ontogeny and to a far lesser degree, with the result that adult human crania appear to be only slightly modified magnifications of fetal forms.

In more behavioral terms neoteny means that patterns of early development, for example those seen in macaques, are prolonged in the apes in general and protracted even more so in humans. Thus a pigtail macaque may be relatively independent of its mother by the time it is slightly over a year old. A chimpanzee infant does

not achieve the same degree of independence of mother until it is three or four, and depending on the nature of our assessment, a human child may not attain comparable autonomy until the age of nine or ten or even older. The progressive deceleration of developmental rates as one moves from the prosimian to the anthropoid to the hominoid primates (see Figure 5–1) offers psychologists an evolutionary "time-lapse photography" of sorts through which, at different speeds and with "species-specific modifications," one may catch glimpses of the processes involved in human psychological development.

The tremendous diversity in the psychological development of primates of different species poses a sobering problem for scientists who aspire to derive basic developmental processes common to the primates as a whole. This difficulty is compounded further by the literature's underrepresentation in studies of normative development (but see Fossey, 1979; Goodall, 1968; Rosenblum, 1961, 1971a). Just as the proliferation of increasingly sensitive biochemical techniques has clouded rather than clarified the overall picture of primate phylogeny (Washburn, 1973), so have the relatively narrow foci of pathology and deprivation-rearing obscured the major evolutionary trends in primate infancy.

Rather than recount the data on primate development that has ably been presented elsewhere (see especially Harlow & Mears, 1979; Konner, 1975), we hope instead to place those data in different perspective—to re-view them, as it were, from the twin vantage points of adaptation and of the infants' strategies for survival. In the present, somewhat heterodox, overview, we will focus on general "pan-specific" problems: birth, thermoregulation, mother-recognition, and social autonomy. These are problems that, in one form or another, all developing primates must face. Drawing on examples from the macaque species with which we are most familiar, we attempt to illustrate the means through which these developmental problems are resolved ontogenetically by either or both members of the mother-infant dyad. Spe-

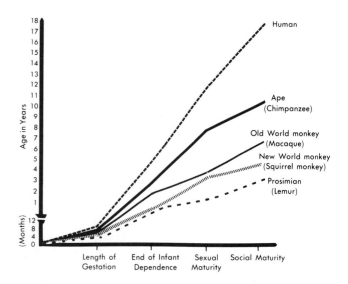

Figure 5-1 Neoteny in primate evolution evidenced by a general retardation of the rate of somatic and psychological development. Human ontogeny represents an extreme "deceleration" of a basic primate pattern.

cifically we will offer some comparisons of the macaque patterns and those of different primate species, for just as there are many ways to skin a felid, there are many different ways to grow up a primate. By combining the general and specific approaches, we hope to highlight the continuities in comparative primate development without depriving the subject of its fascinating variability.

THE NATURE OF PROBLEMS

Our use of the word *problem* in the preceding paragraph refers not to some immediate specific puzzle that confronts the organism but rather to a class of inveterate difficulties, the "solutions" to which are manifest through natural selection. The task of distinguishing between a red square and a blue triangle is not a problem for an infant primate in the same way that staying alive is. In an engineering sense the infant's imperative, global problem of staying alive may be conceptualized as embracing a set of necessary sub-problems, some of which are clearly, while others may be only, betrayed by their solutions. Rooting behaviors and clinging behaviors are examples of each of these kinds of solutions. While rooting represents the neonate's reflexive solution to the unmistakable biological problem of nutrition, clinging, we argue, may reflect a more cryptic solution to the less widely appreciated problem of the thermoregulation. In the phraseology of evolutionary biology, "solutions" are adaptations, and "problems" are selection pressures.

Williams (1966) advocates a restriction of the term *adaptation* to those cases in which the structure or behavior in question appears to be designed for a certain goal or function and has been perfected by natural selection for that purpose. Other fortuitous manifestations of that behavior are properly termed *effects*.

Thus I would say that reproduction and dispersal are the goals or functions or purposes of apples as a means or mechanism by which such goals are realized by apple trees. By contrast, the apple's contributions to Newtonian inspiration and the economy of Kalamazoo County are merely fortuitous effects. (p. 9)

Similarly not all infant or all maternal behaviors are adaptations; some are manifestly effects, and others, the majority perhaps, are as yet not readily assignable to either category. Returning to our earlier example, the laboratory primate's facility in geometric discriminations is almost certainly an effect of selection for visual acuity and memory in organisms whose survival depends upon the accuracy of their discriminations among resources and conspecifics.

In short the principle of adaptation includes the biological concepts of design and its improvement by natural selection. Adaptation is a powerful explanatory tool but not one that should be invoked (or believed!) without special deliberation. Voltaire's Dr. Pangloss, whose name has come to signify an uncritical faith in the ubiquity of this principle, saw the world overflowing with adaptation. Everything, apparently, was created for the purpose which we see for it; thus, "Our noses were made to carry spectacles, so we have spectacles. Legs were clearly intended for breeches, and we wear them" (see

Gould & Lewontin, 1979). The reader is advised to recall the pitfalls of the Panglossian fallacy wherever adaptations are described in the psychological or evolutionary literature, and the present contribution, naturally, is no exception.

AUTONOMY

Autonomy, used here to mean a generalized independence from biological caretakers, is a state achieved only after considerable delay and with considerable difficulty by most primate infants. In order to understand just why this should be so, it would be well to consider some of the problems faced by other altricial animals—those organisms of which most primates are excellent examples—that are relatively helpless at birth. Imperative biological problems—thermoregulation, nutrition, and protection from the environment—threaten the newborn primate from the very moment of birth, and our ultimate discussion of social autonomy must accordingly begin with the biological capacities and difficulties of the neonate.

Apart from protection from predators, probably the most immediate and ubiquitous threat faced by mammalian neonates is hypothermia—a perilous drop in deep-body temperature. Whereas prior to birth mammalian embryos are swathed in warm intrauterine fluids, in order to survive in the extrauterine environment, newborn mammals must maintain their core body temperature within a high and narrow range—a struggle made all the more difficult by their small size, poor thermal insulation, and relative helplessness. (For an excellent introduction to the thermoenergetics of young mammals, see Adolph, 1951; Hull, 1973.)

The special problems encountered by primate infants can be best placed in perspective through comparison with the problems and solutions of mammalian infants in general. The thermoregulatory capacities of mammals, young or old, are constrained by their thermal insulation and by the area of exposed surface; the smaller the mammal, the greater its exposed surface (relative to body mass), and the greater the rate of heat loss. At 5 grams, for example, a newborn rat could not maintain homeothermy ($37°C$) even at the moderately warm environmental temperature of $24°C$. To do so would require a six-fold increase in metabolic rate—a thermogenesis hopelessly beyond the capabilities of a day-old rat pup. Moreover the infant rat could not consume, nor could its mother provide, enough milk to fuel such a metabolic feat for more than a few minutes each day. Instead the limitations of size and thermal insulation of the rat neonate are overcome by behavioral responses of mother and young. The mother constructs a well-insulated nest and periodically visits the huddling pups to incubate them with her own body heat. Nest construction in rats is itself a thermoregulatory behavior in that this behavior is initiated by peripheral body cooling and inhibited by peripheral body heating (Kinder, 1927). After three weeks the now 30- to 40-gram rat pups are weaned. In response to cold stress the 21-day-old pup can increase its metabolic rate fourfold and is no longer dependent on the nest for protection (Hull, 1973). Remarkably the stimuli eliciting the cyclic pattern of nest-entering and nest-leaving by the mother rat are themselves thermal. (See Leon,

Croskerry, & Smith, 1978, and Woodside & Leon, 1980, for a series of fascinating experiments on the thermal control of maternal behavior in this species.) Primate neonates, even among representatives of the largest size ranges, are still dependent upon the thermal protection of mother, surrogate or otherwise. Carpenter, an unusually gifted early observer of wild primate groups, noted that the infant gibbon must be particularly dependent on the mother for warmth as at birth the body of this small ape (400g) is virtually hairless. The gibbon mother compensates for its poorly insulated offspring by swaddling it between her flexed thighs and abdomen: "A furry enclosure is thus arranged which may be of considerable importance as a temperature regulating arrangement for the young infant. In a sense, the mother forms a nest for her young from her own trunk and limbs" (1940, p. 144; see Ibscher, 1967, p. 60 for a photograph of this "maternal-nest").

Although clinical observations of the newborn rhesus monkey (weight at birth approximately 480g) reveal that it is capable of nearly doubling its heat production upon cold exposure, this temporary increase in thermogenesis would be insufficient for an infant lacking maternal support to maintain a stable body temperature even under favorable climatic conditions (Dawes, Jacobson, Mott, & Shelly, 1960).

These data prompt a rekindling of Harlow's now classical demonstration that infant rhesus monkeys will cling tenaciously to nonfeeding terrycloth surrogates in favor of nutritive "mothers" constructed of bare wire (Harlow, 1958). It is tempting to view this phenomenon, known widely as "contact comfort" (though perhaps more appropriately described here as contact clinging), as a behavioral mechanism which has evolved, at least partially, in the service of thermoregulaton. Given the tendency toward hypothermia in an isolated primate infant, the thermal qualities of the terrycloth surrogate would undoubtedly make for a "warmer," more insulating (and hence more comforting) mother than would an equally claspable but thermally bankrupt wire surrogate. Up until 15 days of age (when the preference reverses), newborn monkeys prefer a heated, wire surrogate to a room-temperature, cloth one (Harlow & Suomi, 1970). Jeddi (1970, 1972) has reported similar findings for puppies. This thermal interpretation of contact clinging becomes more compelling as the temperature differential between the laboratory test environment and the normothermic temperature of the infant monkey increases. "Contact comfort," upon further reinvestigation, may prove to be an incarnation of thermal comfort in terrycloth disguise.

PARTURITIONAL PATTERNS AND EARLY MATERNAL BEHAVIOR

Short of cataloguing the behavior of each species (and we question the didactic utility of such an approach), any attempt to summarize the birth process in "the primate" courts the risk of dangerous oversimplification. Here descriptions of parturitional and peri-parturitional behavior from representatives of three anthropoid families are compared to illustrate a primate evolutionary leitmotif—the pervasive trend, recognizable even in the neonate, toward an increase in maternal dependence among longer-lived, more neotenous, primate species. (For a taxonomic overview of birth-related behavior in primates, see Brandt & Mitchell, 1971.)

Marmosets and tamarins (family Callitrichidae) are small (150–650g), precocial (that is, relatively mature at birth), densely furred primates of South America whose reproductive biology has attracted concerted scientific attention only recently (Eisenberg, 1977). Two reasons for the renewed psychobiological interest in callitrichids are the monogamous pair-bond of mated adults (a phenomenon rare among primates) and the female's production of multiple births, usually twins. (For details of the conservation and evolutionary biology of this group see Hershkovitz, 1977, and Kleiman, 1977.)

Detailed observations of parturitional and early infant behavior in the common marmoset (Callithrix jacchus) are taken from Rothe (1977) and follow the four-phase classification of parturition of Naaktgeboren and Slijper (1970). The estimated length of gestation in marmoset species is about 130 days, and females are usually sexually mature by 18 months. During the gestation period Rothe's pregnant marmosets showed no obvious changes in social interaction with their mates or other group members until briefly before the first contractions occurred, when females characteristically withdrew from the common sleeping box to prepare for birth. Typically preparation for birth, or Phase 1, began at night. (Although perhaps of small comfort to human parents faced with the mad dash to the hospital in the wee hours, the pattern of nighttime births is characteristic of primates.) During Phase 2, the dilation phase, laboring marmoset females assume characteristic postures, including a freezing of locomotion, raised tail, closed eyes, and heavy breathing. After a series of increasingly convulsive contractions, the rupture of the amniotic sac marks the end of the dilation phase. Phase 3, the expulsive phase, follows and extends from the first expulsive contractions to the complete extrusion of all fetuses. Save for one infant, all births observed by Rothe presented in the vertex position. Females were never observed to manipulate the fetus manually to assist in the expulsion. Phase 4 spans the period from the completed delivery of all infants to the placenta's expulsion and includes the time when, starting at the placental end, the mother consumes the placenta and the umbilical cord.

One of the most striking aspects of marmoset delivery is the degree to which the marmoset neonate negotiates the transition to extrauterine life independently of the mother. Immediately after the hands and arms emerge, the newborn marmoset responds with rowing, rotating, and clutching motions in an attempt to establish a hold on the mother's fur. These grasping motions may begin even before the infant has been completely expelled. Several minutes after it has effected a strong hold on the mother's fur and while still connected to the placenta by the umbilical cord, the infant must reach the mother's nipples entirely unaided. This dramatic self-delivery on the part of the marmoset infant is in marked contrast to the behavior of its observant but reciprocally unassisting mother. Maternal care of the newborn marmoset immediately following delivery is limited to a few cursory lickings of the face. The mother does not actively help the newborn to grasp her fur nor does she attempt to grasp the infant even if, suspended by the umbilical cord, it lies dangling beneath her.

The degree to which a mother will intercede on the behalf of a weak or defective infant offers a revealing index of phylogenetic changes in the quality of maternal care. In this regard marmosets probably represent a "primitive" grade.[1] Rothe notes,

Infants born in poor physical condition receive more pronounced care only if they move and especially if they vocalize (distress and contact calls). The mother's behavior, however, depends essentially on that of the infant's. If the neonate does not vocalize or if it lies motionless beside or under its mother, she shows no further interest.

In summary, if the newborn *Callithrix jacchus* succeeds in clinging unaided to its mother after expulsion, it has a fair chance of survival. Infants who fail to cling have no chance or at best a very reduced one. (p. 201)

Parturitional behavior in the squirrel monkey (*Saimiri sciureus,* the primate in greatest laboratory currency among New World species, Figure 5–2) is similar in many structural details to that of the marmoset. The gestation period in squirrel monkeys is approximately 180 days, and females are sexually mature by about 3 years (Rosenblum, 1968). Unlike chimpanzees in which extrusion of the cervical plug (the blood-tinged vaginal exudate referred to as "show" in humans) indicates that delivery will occur within a few days (usually within 24 hours in human females), squirrel monkeys evince few reliable signs of approaching delivery. Like the marmoset the mother's posturing during Phase 2[2] includes a dramatic "locomotor freezing." During the expulsive stage squirrel monkey mothers, unlike marmosets, were observed to lick and nuzzle the half-expelled fetus, although not to pull at it. In a breech presentation described by Bowden et al., however, one laboring mother

tugged over 60 times at the fetus' tail during the 18 h between its emergence and the emergence of the limbs, trunk, and head. She also gently tugged the body when all but the head had emerged. These observations suggest that pulling the half exposed infant is a much weaker element in the squirrel monkey's delivery behavior than in such species as rhesus. (p. 21)

Within a few minutes of expulsion, the single infant climbs onto the mother's back. After delivery of the afterbirth, the squirrel monkey mother, like the females of all placental mammals, consumes part or all of the placenta. (The human female may be an exception; however, pla-

Figure 5–2 Squirrel monkey (*Saimiri sciureus*) mother with several week old infant in typical dorso-ventral clinging position

centophagia has been described by Harms [1956] in at least some primitive tribes.)

Although structural elements of *Saimiri* parturition depart little from the marmoset plan, the squirrel monkey mother is capable of surprising compensatory behavior, a clear adaptive grade beyond the marmoset mother, as is evidenced by a natural experiment by Rumbaugh (1965). Reasoning that the passive maternal care that the squirrel monkey typically gives its young is appropriate to the infant's needs and thus is a reflection not of indifference but of economy, Rumbaugh questioned: How might the mother behave if the newborn squirrel monkey needed *greater* care? To effect an infant in need of care, Rumbaugh separated a week-old squirrel monkey from its mother and taped its arms behind its back, thereby preventing it from grasping its mother's fur. Seeing the screeching infant upon the floor,

The mother pressed down with her abdomen upon the young, an action which normally would have facilitated its grasp of her hair. This behavior gave way to visual inspection of the infant, particularly its face, coupled with successive lifting movements using one arm at a time in a manner that positioned the infant ventrally. When the infant still failed to grasp the mother, the predicted maternal behavior occurred; the mother picked up the infant with both arms, cradled it, then walked bipedally away from E for a distance of 4 ft. and a total of 13 steps by count of two observers. At no time did the mother attempt to remove the tape that rendered the infant's arms useless. (p. 174)

The squirrel monkey maternal repertoire then, although designed "economically" to satisfy the minimal requirements of the normal infant, also includes some "emergency provisions" which emerge only when they are evoked by the extraordinary needs of debilitated young.

The solicitous behavior of the squirrel monkey mother toward her temporarily incapacitated infant adumbrates, in many respects, the intensive care that is char-

[1] While they decidedly *do not* reflect phylogeny, grades are useful evolutionary metaphors that describe successive levels of organization in the improvement of an organic design for some specified function (Gould, 1976). The sequence, marmoset-capuchin-chimpanzee-human, for example, represents a reasonable sequence of grades in the evolution of the primate cortex defined by an increase in cortical volume relative to body size. The same sequence would obviously be inappropriate for an analysis, say, of brachiation.

[2] We should note that Bowden, Winter, and Ploog (1967), whose paper on pregnancy and delivery behavior illustrates many of the behaviors reviewed here, use a different classification of parturitional stages. We have regrouped their stages in accordance with Naaktgeboren and Slijper (1970) only to facilitate comparisons. See also the descriptions by Rumbaugh (1965) and Takeshita (1961).

acteristic of most Old World primate mothers. Parturition in macaque species has been detailed vividly in two classic papers by Tinklepaugh and Hartman (1930, 1932). Macaques comprise the most widespread primate genus save for humans and are thus good examples of Old World taxa.[3] Like squirrel monkeys the mean gestation length in macaque species is about 170 days, and females reach reproductive maturity between 3 and 4 years of age. Macaque females apparently remain fertile for all or most of their adult life (which, in captivity at least, may exceed 20 years)—a fact, we later note, that has important consequences for the mother-infant relationship.

The approach of labor in rhesus and crab-eating macaques as observed by Tinklepaugh and Hartman (and this is true also of our observations of pigtail and bonnet macaques) is forecast only by a general reduction of activity in the final days of pregnancy. A number of hours and, occasionally, a number of days prior to the onset of labor, manual exploration of the vagina with subsequent sniffing and attendant licking of the fingers may be observed. Phase 2, the onset of labor, is evidenced by the female's periodic assumption of a squatting posture—a behavior characteristic of all anthropoids except "civilized" humans. The expulsive stage may span from less than an hour to more than a day; Tinklepaugh and Hartman report a female who showed more than 1200 contractions over a 32-hour period. The possibility that mechanical stimulation of the mother by the fetus and its membranes may function as releaser mechanisms for the mother's parturitional behavior was clearly expressed by these authors.

At each successive stage in the process of birth-giving, the behavior is nearly always appropriate. The swelling and irritation of the genital region lead to manual exploration. The presence of mucous, urine, and fecal matter calls forth the posture and straining common to the eliminatory processes. . . . As labor progresses . . . the eliminatory position is taken more often, straining is more intense and, facilitating the latter, the animals seize hold of the walls or floor of the cage. The fetus advances in the canal, causing the perineum to bulge from the pressure. Then what have been manual exploratory movements, change to manual eliminatory movements—namely, efforts to remove the source of irritation, and the licking of the fluids from the hands continues. The head of the baby eventually appears . . . and then the manual efforts become effective. The wet, newborn baby is drawn forth and around one side to the mother's breast. The fluid is licked from both baby and maternal hands. During the washing process the genitals are again irritated by the frequent tautness of the cord when the baby is shifted from one position to another. . . . These events result in further exploration and finally in the drawing forth of the afterbirth—a mass of tissue . . . covered with fetal fluids. It is licked then eaten. (Tinklepaugh & Hartman, 1930, pp. 94–95)

It is of comparative interest to note that although the mother manually assists the infant to her ventrum after it is expelled, she makes no attempt to adjust its physical orientation; the infant accomplishes the proper ventral-ventral orientation itself via its strong righting reflexes

Figure 5-3 Pigtail macaque (*Macaca nemestrina*) devouring the placenta and umbilical cord following the birth of her ventrally-clinging infant

and negative geotropism (Mowbray & Cadell, 1962). If the infant is somehow unable to perform these adjustments, the mother will attempt to compensate and may clasp her disoriented infant for long periods. Indeed the ability of the macaque mother to countervail the disabilities of her infant represents a grade of maternal care manifestly superior to that of callitrichid or squirrel monkey mothers.[4] Lindburg's (1969) description of the behavior of mothers of rhesus infants with thalidomide-induced phocomelia provides elegiac testimony of macaque mothers' efforts to care for severely abnormal offspring. Similarly Berkson (1977) has detailed the solicitous maternal care afforded by a crab-eating macaque toward her visually handicapped infant. The mother's compensatory care for her blind young included keeping the infant within the group, maintaining its access to food, and generally protecting it from the dangers toward which its awkward sightlessness impelled it.

Perhaps the most dramatic displays of generalized maternal protectiveness coupled with apparently pathologic maternal response are observed when newborns or infants die. It is quite common for macaque mothers to guard fiercely, transport, and even groom dead infants and stillborns (see Figure 5–4). In many cases for the first day or two following the death, the mother carries the corpse constantly. A gradual decrease in protection and interest ensues over several days, but care often does not cease until the body is extremely decomposed. During

[3] Taxa (singular, taxon) are any group of organisms recognized as a formal unit at any level of a hierarchical classification (Mayr, 1963). For example rhesus macaques, macaques, primates, mammals, and chordates all constitute progressively higher (i.e., more inclusive) taxa.

[4] There can be little doubt that human parental care, in which heroic societal efforts may be extended to ensure the viability of even the most profoundly defective individuals, represents the most advanced grade in this primate pattern of maternal compensation.

this period of protecting the dead infant, the mother sets it before her as she rests and carries it by its limbs, tail, body, or head as she moves. Typically this behavior occurs without any obvious effort to sustain the infant at the ventrum, although McKenna (1980) has reported an attempt of a langur mother to pump milk manually from her breast into the mouth of her dead infant.

This "graded series" of maternal compensation for debilitated infants is only a special manifestation of the trend apparent in normal maternal care. While a macaque mother will initially place her infant to the ventrum, the normal infant is capable of achieving the proper orientation and holding fast. However this is not true of the more neotenous apes, which routinely require maternal assistance. Schaller, in his field study of the mountain gorilla, notes that "newborn infants appeared to lack the strength to clasp hair securely, and the mothers had continually to support them with at least one arm" (1963, p. 263). The human newborn, by comparison, can do little more toward its own support than to wrap its tiny hands about a parental finger.

Whatever the unique problems to which primate mothers and infants show varying behavioral adaptations, all primate, and indeed most mammalian, neonates share a common thermal problem to which maternal care has been adapted.

At birth, newborn mammals are wet with fetal fluids, and thus rapid heat loss due to evaporation occurs at a time when the mammal is least able to compensate and when it can expect to receive least assistance from mother. Newborn mammals have a lively desire to suckle as soon as they are born. It is probable that they are rewarmed by their mother while they take their first feed. The "old-fashioned" practice of giving the newborn human infant to its mother so that he can suckle may well have immediate advantages to the infant as well as encouraging uterine contractions, stimulating milk secretion, and contributing to the future psychological welfare of mother and child. (Hull, 1973, p. 197)

BIOLOGICAL SOLUTIONS

Since the primates we are normally most familiar with—the monkeys of the Old World, the apes, and ourselves—usually produce but a single offspring at a time, there is a tendency to regard this pattern as somehow "right" or "natural" without questioning why, in fact, single births should be the rule. It is only when we are faced with the pattern of multiple births characteristic of the marmosets and tamarins and of certain prosimian families that the question of "Why one young per pregnancy?" presents itself. Leutenegger (1979) has recently suggested an intriguing hypothesis to explain the reduction in the number of primate offspring per litter, implicating a ubiquitous biological variable—body size. Leutenegger's hypothesis conjoins two patterns of relative, or allometric, growth. The first of these is a classical observation; relative to overall body size, smaller animals have greater cranial dimensions than do similarly shaped, larger forms. The second trend is the negative allometry of neonatal-maternal weight. By this we mean that the neonates of smaller primate species represent increasingly greater percentages of maternal weight. The intersection of these two trends, the negative allometries of head-

Figure 5-4 Bonnet mother (*Macaca radiata*) clinging to her stillborn infant. Note the mother's incorrect positioning of the infant.

body size and of neonatal-maternal weight, results in fetal head dimensions in small primate species which exceed the dimensions of the maternal birth canal. In the 6000-gram howler monkey, for example, the diameter of the female's pelvic canal is comfortably in excess of the corresponding dimensions of the neonate's head, and the 500-gram infant is easily delivered. By contrast the 600-gram squirrel monkey mother gives birth to a 100-gram infant that represents 17 percent of her own nonpregnant weight. The diameter of the newborn squirrel monkey's head exceeds considerably that of the mother's pelvis, and the strenuous delivery is accomplished only through dilation of the pelvic ligaments (Bowden et al., 1967). Apparently the squirrel monkey represents the lower critical size for the production of single births in anthropoid primates. At a smaller body size the cranial dimensions of a single fetus would exceed so greatly the dimensions of the birth canal as to render delivery impossible. Leutenegger proposes that anthropoids smaller than the squirrel monkey, the marmosets and tamarins, have "solved" this problem by the architectural expedient of multiple births. By producing twins and, on occasion, triplets, callitrichids effectively reduce the size of an individual newborn to a size commensurate with maternal architecture. Despite the production of twins fetal head dimensions still exceed pelvic dimensions in the common marmoset by about 4 percent (Leutenegger, 1970), demonstrating even more dramatically the selective advantage of smaller, multiple births (Leutenegger, 1979).[5]

Although the status of the newborn primate as a relatively helpless organism is often stressed, it is instructive to note some important exceptions to this generalization. As if by strategy the newborn primate is equipped with a

[5] Here we should note that difficulties encountered during parturition in the human female do not stem from these allometric trends per se but rather from the forward restructuring of the pelvic canal that accompanied the evolution of human's increasingly erect posture. Parturition in the largely quadrupedal gorilla, by comparison, is unstrained (Schaller, 1963).

repertory of responses, comparatively well developed at birth, which help to compensate for its physiological immaturity and consequent dependency. Many of these behaviors fall under the general heading of contact reflexes. A light touch to the cheek or lips of an infant macaque, for example, will elicit a turning of the head in the same direction as the touch, followed by an opening and closing of the mouth. This behavior, referred to as the "rooting" or head-turning response, disappears in macaques by the ninth or tenth day of life (see Mowbray & Cadell, 1962, for a detailed description of newborn rhesus reflexes). Interestingly the head-turning response is neotenously preserved in human infants and is a trick employed successfully by professional photographers. Knowledgeable portraitists can get an otherwise uncooperative infant to "pose" in the desired direction simply by applying a light touch to the appropriate cheek. Although the term *rooting* is often used to include the related sucking reflex, the two patterns may profitably be separated. The opening and closing of the mouth seen in macaque, baboon, and langur infants during the head-turning reflex effects a "jawhold" on the mother's fur or nipple and is a means of support independent of the sucking response (Chance & Jolly, 1970). Other contact reflexes include the grasping reflex, in which stimulation of the plantar surface of the hand or foot elicits vigorous grasping of any object within reach (normally the mother's fur) and the clasping reflex, whereby the infant rotates both arms and legs towards an object and wraps itself around it in a tight embrace. The clasping reflex of week-old macaques is so strong that most rhesus infants tested by Mowbray and Cadell would not relinquish their hold even when lifted off the ground on a cylinder covered with coarse sandpaper! Similarly the newborn monkey placed in ventral contact with a claspable, cylindrical object will initially make no effort to release its hold even when the cylinder, with infant tenaciously attached, is placed on a flat surface. Several days after birth, however, the infant will release its hold in order to reposition itself in ventral contact with the table surface. This response is known as releasing and righting. Releasing and righting, like the other contact reflexes, represent an obvious adaptation to maintaining the maternal contact upon which, literally at times, the infant's survival depends.

Although properly termed "reflexive," there appears to be a sort of "orderly variability" in the manifestation and duration of these early behavioral responses among representatives of different primate taxa. As with the trend for increasing maternal assistance of the newborn observed in altricial primates, the extent of infantile expression of these early behavior patterns mirrors the reciprocal abilities of the mother and infant. Thus while probably all neurologically normal primate infants exhibit the grasp reflex, the trend is toward a decrease in its measured duration. The recorded maximum duration of the grasp reflex in the rhesus monkey is 33 minutes; it is reduced to 5 minutes in the chimpanzee, and the human infant grasps for only 2 minutes (Mason, 1965).[6]

In concluding this section on the adaptations of newborn primates, we should note that primate neonates, like neonates of most mammalian taxa, can evidently tolerate hypothermia to a degree and for a duration that cannot be weathered by adult mammals (Adolph, 1951). Although data on the limits of experimentally cold-exposed primate infants are few (but see Chaffee, Allen, Brewer, Horvath, Mason, & Smith, 1966), numerous accounts attest that apparently lifeless and nearly frozen callitrichid infants may revive upon gradual reheating (summarized in Hershkovitz, 1977). While it is surely tempting to view this dramatic hypothermia as a thermal adaptation, it remains to be demonstrated that under natural conditions this ability would actually improve an infant marmoset's chances of survival.[7] Whereas a hypothermic macaque infant, under normal conditions at least, could expect to be rewarmed by its mother, an infant macaque would approach fatal hypothermia relatively more rapidly (that is, at a higher core temperature) than would the infant marmoset. Indeed the lowest environmental temperature that a naked human infant can withstand and still maintain a safe, high, deep-body temperature is about 25°C—a temperature well above that of the average environment in most climatic conditions (Adamsons, 1966; Buetow & Klein, 1964).

Unlike hibernating mammals, newborn mammals which become hypothermic are unable to rewarm themselves, and it is unlikely that environmental conditions will change sufficiently to reanimate them; they are therefore dependent on warmth from their parents. Could this be the reason, Hull (1973) suggests, why some adult mammals lie on their weak and dying young?

RECOGNITION AND AUTONOMY: "SOCIAL" SOLUTIONS

The liberation from the requirements of biological sustenance from caregivers, incorporated in our definition of autonomy, should not be taken to mean that the infant attains a capacity to function entirely free of group support, especially when confronted with potentially endangering situations. By the time an infant has achieved an adult homeothermic capacity and might even be capable of autonomous foraging, it may still, for example, be incapable of following its natal troop over a large home range or difficult terrain. Isolated, the infant would present a particularly vulnerable target for predators (Berkson, 1977), and in this sense its dependence upon the group for social support is as critical to its survival as is its biological dependence on mother. Although the formulations of modern kinship theory predict that various troop members should provide support to the infant proportional to their degree of relatedness (Chapais & Schulman, 1980; Trivers, 1974), this has yet to be demonstrated experimentally. Rather, in virtually all primate species, it is the mother who

[6] An exception to this generalization is the orangutan whose infants can apparently cling for hours (Nadler, personal communication). The peculiar endurance of the infant orangutan may reflect an adaptation to the almost exclusively arboreal habitat of these solitary great apes.

[7] Since human infants can withstand temperatures too low for adult survival, deep hypothermia with total circulatory arrest may be a viable procedure for infant open-heart surgery (Gonzalez, 1979). This is certainly a fortuitous effect, however, and one would not argue that infant hypothermia is an adaptation to surgery.

assumes this crucial protective function on behalf of her developing offspring.[8]

At this point an apparent paradox emerges in the early phases of the gradual shift from infant dependence to infant autonomy. While the infant clings continuously to mother and remains dependent upon her for thermal, nutritive, and physical (not to mention psychological!) support, it has little need to differentiate her from conspecific individuals who surround the mother-infant dyad. Indeed even in the earliest stages of the infant's attempts to move from the mother (which may occur as early as the first week in macaques), the mother typically maintains at least some form of partial contact with her infant and frequently "retrieves" the exploring infant to her ventrum. These "guarding and retrieval patterns" directed selectively by the mother toward her own infant are at their highest levels during the first two to three months of the infant's life and then wane to much lower levels in ensuing months (Rosenblum, 1971a). It would appear then that even the infant's earliest efforts toward separation do not require that the infant attain an ability to discriminate mother either from others in its social group or from those individuals with whom it makes less frequent contact. Protection and support will be provided at the mother's watchful initiative. As the length and duration of the infant's excursions increase, however, and as its locomotive skills and the diversity of its activity burgeon in the following weeks, it becomes increasingly encumbent upon the infant to maintain a constant awareness of the location of its mother. It must be able, when needed, to move unerringly to the reassuring protection of her ventrum.

Although in at least some species (the squirrel monkey, for example, Kaplan, Cubicciotti, & Redican, 1977), infants that are regularly in intimate proximity to the mother may show olfactory-assisted recognition, it is clear that distance reception through vision, in Old World primates especially, becomes the primary mode of discrimination as the infant matures. Early anecdotal reports suggested that such visual recognition in macaques might emerge as early as two to three weeks of life, i.e., the age at which first movements from mother appear. It now appears that such pseudodiscriminations (see Bowlby, 1969) were misinterpreted by early observers. It seems clear that the described infant responses reflected not the recognition of mother as a specific individual independent of her behavior (a capacity we now know develops at a considerably later date) but rather approach behaviors elicited by differential maternal behavior (a "releaser" effect).

Detailed experimental work during the past decade (focusing, regrettably, on a limited number of species) has shed considerable new light on this intriguing and unanticipated problem of early social development. Three major findings have been established. First, and

despite the fact that macaques can perform simple geometric discriminations by two weeks of age (Zimmerman, 1962), infant macaques raised with their mothers in social groups do not reliably differentiate their mothers from conspecific strangers until after the second month of life. This fact becomes evident when tests are conducted under experimental conditions which preclude differential responses of the stimulus animals toward the infant. (See Rosenblum & Alpert [1974] for details of the infant-mother recognition paradigm.) As mentioned before, after the age of two to three months the mother-initiated retrieval-protective patterns begin to wane and are supplanted by an increasingly infant-initiated self-protective pattern. Fearful affects also emerge at about the same age (see Rosenblum & Alpert, 1974).

Second, data on group-reared infants have shown that females evidence the differentiation of mother from others several weeks earlier than males do. Compared to their male counterparts females demonstrate both more consistent and overwhelming response to mother and a relatively greater avoidance of strangers than males do during the first six to ten months of life (Alpert & Rosenblum, 1974). These early gender differences anticipate sex differences later in development, both in females' earlier attainment of puberty (e.g., at two to three years for female macaques and *Saimiri*, compared to four to five years for males) and in the greater tendency of females to maintain life-long propinquity to mother while males, particularly as puberty approaches, tend to leave their natal groups.

Third, and most significantly, these new findings indicate that the course of development of these visual-recognition capacities in macaques are markedly influenced by the social milieu within which the infant and its mother live (see Rosenblum & Paully, 1980). In the bonnet macaque, for example, an uncommonly gregarious species in which from birth onward infants have considerable opportunity for contact and interactive experience with numerous nonmother figures, clear, strong recognition of mother appears at 10 to 14 weeks. In the pigtail macaque, a closely related form but one in which social groups are characterized by considerable group tension and by greater spatial and social distancing between nonrelated adults, a different trend emerges. In pigtails, where early infant-mother interactions are largely precluded by mothers' protective efforts, discriminative responses to mother appear several weeks later than in bonnets. Distinctions between mothers and strangers in pigtails are not nearly as definitive in either sex as we have seen in bonnets raised in identical laboratory settings. Contrary to the intuitive speculations of early animal-attachment theorists (cf. Cairns, 1972), rearing of an infant with its mother in isolation from other conspecifics does not support the contention that ". . . mutual discrimination develops most readily in the course of insulated and exclusive interactions" (p. 54). Infant bonnets raised by their mothers in a single-dyad situation without other conspecifics do not evidence reliable distinctions between their mothers and an unfamiliar conspecific adult female before eight months of age!

The infant macaque then, in the absence of either the "need or opportunity" to learn the distinguishing characteristics of mother, fails to do so until well after the

---

[8] Curiously in marmosets it is the father who adopts primary responsibility for infant care, carrying the young on his back and returning them to the mother only intermittently for nursing. While this may reflect a compensatory adaptation to the mother's high energetic investment in twinning, we should note that the marmoset father, by mating monogamously, has nearly equal "parental investment" in the infants as does his mate. The male gibbon, a monogamous ape, also exhibits an "unusual" degree of parental care (Carpenter, 1940).

***Figure* 5-5** Bonnet macaque mothers with their infants in typical proximity

cortical apparatus which normally mediates its development has matured (see Zimmerman & Torrey, 1965). There is, moreover, nothing "Lamarkian" in this apparent development in response to need. Rather it is in keeping with the plasticity and the economy of behavioral development that infants learn a series of specific discriminations between mother and others but do so only as a function of the discriminative opportunities that are available.

Only later as a result of processes probably similar to those described in other contexts as "learning-set" (Harlow, 1958) does the infant establish the class distinctions of "mother" and "nonmother." When infant bonnets are raised from birth with their mother in the presence of only one other adult female, the infants do indeed discriminate mother from familiar female by the usual age of about two to three months. However these same infants do not distinguish between mother and complete stranger until about five months and roughly one-third of the infants reared in this fashion fail to differentiate mother and stranger even as late as eight months of age.

These experiments illustrate that the development of the infant's social-perceptual skills, an essential step in its progress toward autonomy, depends not only on the behavioral reciprocity of mother and infant but also on the dyad's interaction with the social environment—what some have termed *the ecology of development* (Bronfenbrenner, 1979). Altering the normal social ecology of bonnets by placing the mother and infant alone, a condition that resembles in more extreme form the natural social ecology of pigtails, results in a delay of social perceptual abilities in bonnets that mimics or even exceeds in latency the normal ontogeny of these perceptual abilities in pigtails. These findings complement greatly those of field primatologists (e.g., Gartlan, 1969; Struhsaker, 1969) whose detailed observations of primate populations in varying habitats caused them to conclude that ecology,

rather than phylogeny, may be a more potent determinant of primate social organization.

As the normal infant attains the capacity to differentiate mother from others and move at first tentatively and then more confidently into the surrounding physical and social environment, further social differentiation ensues. Discriminations among conspecifics of different age and sex classes become increasingly clear during the first six to eight months of life. Invitations to "rough and tumble" play, for example, are not distributed randomly among adults, juveniles, and infants; the infant's play initiatives are directed selectively toward peers. As the infant matures these initiatives become increasingly selective and are directed overwhelmingly toward same-sexed partners. Like the human child the primate infant interacts with an increasingly differentiated social network as it emerges from its initially circumscribed focus about mother (see Lewis & Rosenblum, 1975). That the social differentiations originate with the young infants themselves and are not explicable solely by differential responses directed toward them by others has recently been demonstrated experimentally through the use of videotape techniques (Plimpton, Swartz, & Rosenblum, 1981).

Similarly just as the macaque infant comes to apportion specific responses to the different classes of social stimuli in its world, the infant's own gender and status roles take shape during the first six months of life. Determined largely by hormonal factors in prenatal life (Goy & Phoenix, 1972), play patterns, choice of partners, and emerging aggressive and precopulatory sexual patterns show clear gender distinctions well before infant autonomy is achieved and several years prior to puberty. Young male infants move from their mothers more readily (Rosenblum, 1971a), engage in more vigorous contact play patterns (i.e., "rough and tumble" play, Goy & Phoenix, 1972; Rosenblum, 1961), and increasingly select male play partners with whom to do so. Males also exhibit elements of adult threat gestures and fragments of adult male copulatory patterns more frequently than their young female age-mates. In addition to these gender roles, the hierarchical status within the group reflects a clear transmission of maternal status to the young quite early in life, with the result that offspring of more dominant mothers achieve higher peer-group status than those of more subordinate females—a nongenic but clearly heritable transmission of rank (see Chapais & Schulman, 1980).

Experimental evidence suggests that the opportunities for these early "social experiments" can influence subsequent adult behavior. Early isolate rearing in rhesus monkeys appears to debilitate the normal capacity for peer relations, sexual behavior, and parental care (Mason, 1965). Theories abound regarding the crucial role early play and related patterns may have as rehearsal for the infant's subsequent behaviors in the group or as opportunities essential for the infant's neurobehavioral maturation. Recent evidence in the wild (Baldwin & Baldwin, 1974) suggests that, in squirrel monkeys at least, lack of social play in the young of a social group (the result of a nutritively impoverished environment) did not alter any salient patterns of adult behavior. Even early rearing in complete social isolation may not permanently deter social responsiveness in some species (Sackett, Holm, & Ruppenthal, 1976). Thus the tendency to see these early patterns as the building blocks of later behavior remains a seductive assumption rather than a proven generalization at present.

WEANING STRATEGIES

Reviewing the emerging sociality of the developing primate, one is struck by the interplay of forces acting upon the mother-infant dyad which effect the infant's dramatic shift toward autonomy. Despite their variously intimate attentions to one another in the early postparturient period, mother and infant are soon confronted with a multiplicity of needs whose fulfillments may not be met by the dyadic partner. The mother, for example, must attend not only to her own nutritive and hygienic needs but must also maintain a social position within her group which facilitates the meeting of those immediate requirements and which ensures her future ability to reproduce successfully. Since her youngest infant is generally one of a series of her progeny and the survival of each to reproductive maturity (the Neo-Darwinist's shorthand for socialization) is her vital concern, the mother's social support on behalf of previous young, as well as her biological preparation for future ones, compete for the resources that can be apportioned to her newest infant. An optimum breeding strategy for an iteroparous, or repeatedly breeding, female can be formulated employing Hamilton's (1964) concept of "inclusive fitness"—a kind of census of an individual's shared genes. More precisely, inclusive fitness denotes the sum of an individual's own fitness (measured in the currency of offspring) plus "the sum of all the effects it causes to the related part of the fitness of all its relatives" (Wilson, 1975, p. 118). An investment plan for maximizing the inclusive fitness of the mother, then, would involve a balancing of her investments in the elements just described: her own health and future reproduction, her social support to previous offspring (as well as support to her nonuterine kin), and her biological support for her youngest infant.

The infant's behavior may be viewed similarly as a reflection of competing demands on its time and energy. While its requirements for maternal protective and nutritive support must be met, the infant's curiosity, its opportunities for expanded motoric expression, and if Harlow, Harlow, & Hansen (1963) are correct, its primary motivations for peer interaction, all draw the infant into the extradyadic milieu. The fitness of the infant and its future reproductive success may predispose it toward increased sociality. While the infant's maintenance of mother as the primary source of nourishment and support is advantageous for a time at least, it is probable that social experience gained from early interaction with the extradyadic environment will contribute significantly to its subsequent reproductive success.

In the course of the infant's maturation, each member of the dyad is confronted with a similar problem in its life-history strategy—the shifting balance between the costs and benefits of sustained investment in the dyadic partner versus investment in other offspring and kin. In his classic analysis of the "fitness economics" of this problem, Trivers (1974) hypothesized that conflict between mother and offspring should ensue when the value of the mother-offspring investment acquires a different valence for the ultimate fitness of each partner. Since on the average the mother shares half her genes with her current offspring and half with other surviving offspring (in addition to a smaller fraction shared with each nonuterine kin), the mother should seek to maximize her inclusive fitness by withdrawing support from her present infant relatively early and reinvesting elsewhere. The infant, however, whose primary genetic identification is with itself (especially since the mother's subsequent offspring will generally be the infant's half-siblings and share only one-fourth of its genes), should seek selfishly to maximize its own fitness by persisting in demands for supportive care from the mother. "If cost and benefit are measured in the same units," Trivers summed up, "then at some point the cost to the mother will exceed the benefit to her young and the net reproductive success of the mother decreases if she continues to nurse" (1974, p. 260). Thus in primates (and likely in any species exhibiting sexual reproduction, iteroparity, and slowly maturing young), the onset of weaning and the subsequent termination of infant dependency may represent part of the mother's solution to the ultimate biological problem of ensuring her genetic representation in subsequent generations.

The behavioral manifestations of this conflict in each partner show almost a seesaw pattern. The mother of the four- to eight-month-old macaque infant, for example, will alternate between overt weaning and rejecting behaviors which deter contact, like biting and hair pulling, and bouts of protection, retrieval, nursing, and maternally supportive contact. The infant, in turn, will actively seek its play partners and the attractive features of its environment by spending and initiating increasingly prolonged departures from mother. Yet these same infants will strive militantly to return to mother, clinging to any available body surface if necessary, and displaying frank and protracted distress ("tantrums") when rebuffed. Although earlier interpretations of this pattern debated the relative prepotence of "maternal rejection" versus "infant leaving" in effecting the shift towards infant autonomy, it now appears that this debate may represent a "nonproblem" (Williams, 1966). A host of developmental data, including the emergence of the infant's nascent sexual behavior, suggests that the changing deployment of infant and maternal reproductive strategies together emancipate the growing infant from its initially exclusive and dependent filial pattern (see Rosenblum, 1971a). It is vital to note, and very much in keeping with the fitness strategies described, that long after nursing, physical dependence, and sustained contact between the dyad has ended, a unique bond between mother and infant endures throughout the remainder of their lives. This bond, expressed with remarkable ethological insight by Pope, is the result of the neotenous development that is the hallmark of primate development.

> The beast and bird their common charge attend
> The mothers nurse it, and the sires defend;
> The young dismissed, to wander earth or air,
> There stops the instinct, and there ends the care.
> A longer care man's helpless kind demands,
> That longer care contracts more lasting bands.

Alexander Pope, *Essay on Man*, 1733

REFERENCES

ADAMSONS, K., JR. The role of thermal factors in fetal and neontal life. *The Pediatric Clinics of North America*, 1966, *13*, 599–619.

ADOLPH, E. F. Responses of hypothermia in several species of infant mammals. *American Journal of Physiology*, 1951, *166*, 75–91.

ALPERT, S., & ROSENBLUM, L. A. The influence of gender and rearing conditions on attachment and response to strangers. *Symposium of the 5th Congress of the International Primatological Society*, 1974, 217–231.

BALDWIN, J. D., & BALDWIN, J. I. Exploration and social play in squirrel monkeys (*Saimiri*). *American Zoologist*, 1974, *14*, 303–315.

BERKSON, G. The social ecology of defects in primates. Pp. 189–204 in S. Chevalier-Skolnikoff and F. E. Poirier (Eds.), *Primate bio-social development*. New York: Garland, 1977.

BOWDEN, D., WINTER, P., & PLOOG, D. Pregnancy and delivery behavior in the squirrel monkey (*Saimiri sciureus*) and other primates. *Folia primatologica*, 1967, *5*, 1–42.

BOWLBY, J. *Attachment and loss* (Vol. 1). New York: Basic Books, 1969.

BRANDT, E. M., & MITCHELL, G. Parturition in primates. Behavior related to birth. Pp. 178–223 in L. A. Rosenblum (Ed.), *Primate behavior: Developments in field and laboratory research* (Vol. 2). New York: Academic Press, 1971.

BRONFENBRENNER, U. *The ecology of human development, experiments by nature and design*. Cambridge, Mass.: Harvard University Press, 1979.

BUETOW, K. C., & KLEIN, S. W. Effect of maintenance of "normal" skin temperature on survival of infants of low birth weight. *Pediatrics*, 1964, *34*, 163–181.

CAIRNS, R. B. Attachment and dependency: A psychobiological and social learning synthesis. In J. L. Gewirtz (Ed.), *Attachment and dependency*. New York: John Wiley, 1972.

CARPENTER, C. R. A field study in Siam of the behavior and social relations of the gibbon (*Hylobates lar*). *Comparative Psychology Monographs*, 1940, *16*, 1–212.

CHAFFEE, R. J., ALLEN, J. R., BREWER, M., HORVATH, S. M., MASON, C., & SMITH, R. E. Cellular physiology of cold- and heat-exposed squirrel monkeys (*Saimiri sciurea*). *Journal of Applied Physiology*, 1966, *21*, 151–157.

CHANCE, M., & JOLLY, C. *Social groups of monkeys, apes and men*. New York: Dutton, 1970.

CHAPAIS, B., & SCHULMAN, S. R. An evolutionary model of female dominance relations in primates. *Journal of Theoretical Biology*, 1980, *82*, 47–89.

CHEVALIER-SKOLNIKOFF, S., & POIRIER, F. E. (Eds.). *Primate bio-social development*. New York: Garland, 1977.

DARWIN, C. *The descent of man and selection in relation to sex*. London: Murray, 1871.

DAWES, G. S., JACOBSON, H. N., MOTT, J. C., & SHELLY, H. J. Some observations on foetal and new-born rhesus monkeys. *Journal of Physiology* (*London*), 1960, *152*, 271–298.

EISENBERG, J. Comparative ecology and reproduction of New World monkeys. Pp. 11–22 in D. G. Kleiman (Ed.), *The biology and conservation of the Callitrichidae*. Washington, D.C.: Smithsonian Institution, 1977.

FOSSEY, D. Development of the mountain gorilla (*Gorilla gorilla beringei*): The first thirty-six months. Pp. 139–184 in D. A. Hamburg & E. R. McCown (Eds.), *The great apes*. Menlo Park, Calif.: Benjamin/Cummings, 1979.

GARTLAN, J. A. Structure and function in primate society. *Folia primatologica*, 1969, *8*, 89–120.

GONZALEZ, E. R. Deep hypothermia for infant open heart surgery: Pros and cons. *Journal of the American Medical Association*, 1979, *241*, 2585–2596.

GOODALL, J. The behaviour of free-living chimpanzees in the Gombe Stream Reserve. *Animal Behaviour Monographs*, 1968, *1*, 165–301.

GOODMAN, M., & TASHIAN, R. E. *Molecular anthropology, genes and proteins in the evolutionary ascent of the primates*. New York: Plenum, 1976.

GOULD, S. J. Grades and clades revisited. Pp. 115–122 in R. B. Masterson, W. Hodos, & H. Jerison (Eds.), *Evolution, brain, and behavior: Persistent problems*. Hillsdale, N.J.: Lawrence Erlbaum Associates, 1976.

GOULD, S. J. *Ontogeny and phylogeny*. Cambridge, Mass.: Belknap Press, 1977.

GOULD, S. J., & LEWONTIN, R. C. The spandrels of San Marco and the Panglossian paradigm: A critique of the adaptationist programme. *Proceedings of the Royal Society of London*, 1979, *B 205*, 581–598.

GOY, R. W., & PHOENIX, C. H. The effects of testosterone propionate administered before birth on the development of behavior in genetic female rhesus monkeys. In C. Sawyer & R. Gorski (Eds.), *Steroid hormones and brain function*. Berkeley: University of California Press, 1972.

HAMILTON, W. D. The genetic evolution of social behavior. *Journal of Theoretical Biology*, 1964, *7*, 1–52.

HARLOW, H. F. The nature of love. *American Psychologist*, 1958, *13*, 673–685.

HARLOW, H. F., HARLOW, M. K., & HANSEN, E. W. The maternal affectional system of rhesus monkeys. Pp. 254–281 in H. L. Rheingold (Ed.), *Maternal behavior in mammals*. New York: John Wiley, 1963.

HARLOW, H. F., & SUOMI, S. J. The nature of love—simplified. *American Psychologist*, 1970, *25*, 161–168.

HARLOW, H. F., & MEARS, C. *The human model: Primate perspectives*. New York: Halstead Press, 1979.

HARMS, J. W. Schwangerschaft und Geburt. Pp. 661–722 in H. Hofer, A. H. Schultz, & D. Starck (Eds.), *Primatologia* (Vol. I.). Basel: Karger, 1956.

HERSHKOVITZ, P. *Living New World monkeys* (Platyrrhini) *with an introduction to the primates* (Vol. I). Chicago: University of Chicago Press, 1977.

HULL, D. Thermoregulation in young mammals. Pp. 167–200 in G. C. Whittow (Ed.), *Comparative physiology of thermoregulation* (Vol. III). New York: Academic Press, 1973.

HUXLEY, T. H. *Evidence of man's place in nature*. London: Williams and Norgate, 1863.

IBSCHER, L. Geburt und frühe entwicklung zweier gibbons (*Hylobates lar 1.*) *Folia primatologica*, 1967, *5*, 43–69.

JEDDI, E. Confort du contact et thermorégulation comportementale. *Physiology and Behavior*, 1970, *5*, 1487–1493.

JEDDI, E. Thermoregulatory efficiency of neonatal rabbit search for fur comfort contact. *International Journal of Biometeorology*, 1972, *15*, 105.

KAPLAN, J., CUBICCIOTTI, D. D., III, & REDICAN, W. K. Olfactory discrimination of squirrel monkey mothers by their infants. *Developmental Psychobiology*, 1977, *10*, 447–453.

KINDER, E. F. A study of the nest building activity of the albino rat. *Journal of Experimental Zoology*, 1927, *47*, 117–161.

KLEIMAN, D. G. (Ed.). *The biology and conservation of the Callitrichidae*. Washington, D.C.: Smithsonian Institution, 1977.

KONNER, M. Relationships among infants and juveniles in comparative perspective. In M. Lewis & L. A. Rosenblum (Eds.), *Friendship and peer relations*. New York: John Wiley, 1975.

LEON, M., CROSKERRY, P., & SMITH, G. Thermal control of mother-young contact in rats. *Physiology and Behavior*, 1978, *21*, 793–811.

LEWIS, M., & ROSENBLUM, L. A. (Eds.). *Friendship and peer relations*. New York: John Wiley, 1975.

LEUTENEGGER, W. Beziehungen zwischen der Neugeborengrösse und dem Sexual-dimorphismus am Becken bei simischen Primaten. *Folia Primatologica*, 1970, *12*, 224–235.

LEUTENEGGER, W. Evolution of litter size in primates. *American Naturalist*, 1979, *114*, 525–531.

LINDBURG, D. Behavior of infant rhesus monkeys with thalidomide-induced malformations. *Psychonomic Science*, 1969, *15*, 55–56.

McKENNA, J. J. Postmortem infant caregiving among captive Indian langurs. *American Journal of Physical Anthropology*, 1980, *52*, 251.

MASON, W. A. The social development of monkeys and apes. Pp. 514–543 in I. DeVore (Ed.), *Primate behavior, field studies of monkeys and apes*. New York: Holt, Rinehart & Winston, 1965.

MAYR, E. *Animal species and evolution*. Cambridge, Mass.: Belknap Press, 1963.

MOWBRAY, J. B., & CADELL, T. E. Early behavior patterns in rhesus monkeys. *Journal of Comparative and Physiological Psychology*, 1962, *55*, 350–357.

NAAKTGEBOREN, C., & SLIJPER, E. J. *Biologie der Geburt. Eine Einführung in die vergleichende Geburtskunde*. Berlin: Parey, 1970.

PLIMPTON, E. H., SWARTZ, K. B., & ROSENBLUM, L. A. Responses of juvenile bonnet macaques to social stimuli presented through color videotapes. *Developmental Psychobiology*, 1981, *14*, 109–115.

ROSENBLUM, L. A. The development of social behavior in the rhesus monkey. Unpublished Ph.D. dissertation, The University of Wisconsin, 1961.

ROSENBLUM, L. A. Mother-infant relations and early behavioral development in the squirrel monkey. Pp. 207–233 in L. A. Rosenblum & R. W. Cooper (Eds.), *The squirrel monkey.* New York: Academic Press, 1968.

ROSENBLUM, L. A. The ontogeny of mother-infant relations in macaques. In H. Moltz (Ed.), *The ontogeny of vertebrate behavior.* New York: Academic Press, 1971a.

ROSENBLUM, L. A. Kinship interaction patterns in pigtail and bonnet macaques. *Proceedings of the 3rd Congress of the International Primatological Society.* Basel: Karger, 1971b.

ROSENBLUM, L. A., & ALPERT, S. Fear of strangers and specificity of attachment in monkeys. Pp. 165–193 in M. Lewis & L. A. Rosenblum (Eds.), *Origins of fear.* New York: John Wiley, 1974.

ROSENBLUM, L. A., & ALPERT, S. Response to mother and stranger: A first step in socialization. Pp. 463–477 in S. Chevalier-Skolnikoff & F. E. Poirier (Eds.), *Primate bio-social development.* New York: Garland, 1977.

ROSENBLUM, L. A., & PAULLY, P. W., JR. The social milieu of the developing monkey: Studies of the development of social perception. *Reproduction, Nutrition and Development,* 1980, *20,* 827–840.

ROSENBLUM, L. A., & YOUNGSTEIN, K. P. Developmental changes in compensatory dyadic response in mother and infant monkeys. In M. Lewis & L. A. Rosenblum (Eds.), *The effect of the infant on its caregiver.* New York: John Wiley, 1974.

ROTHE, H. Parturition and related behavior in *Callithrix jacchus* (Ceboidea, Callitrichidae). Pp. 193–206 in D. G. Kleiman (Ed.), *The biology and conservation of the Callitrichidae.* Washington, D.C.: Smithsonian Institution, 1977.

RUMBAUGH, D. M. Maternal care in relation to infant behavior in the squirrel monkey. *Psychological Reports,* 1965, *16,* 171–176.

SACKETT, G. P., HOLM, R. A., & RUPPENTHAL, G. C. Social isolation rearing: Species differences in behavior of macaque monkeys. *Developmental Psychology,* 1976, *12,* 283–288.

SCHALLER, G. B. *The mountain gorilla.* Chicago: University of Chicago Press, 1963.

SIMONS, E. L. The fossil record of primate phylogeny. Pp. 35–62 in M. E. Goodman & R. E. Tashian (Eds.), *Molecular anthropology, genes and proteins in the evolutionary ascent of the primates.* New York: Plenum, 1976.

SIMPSON, G. G. The principles of classification and a classification of mammals. *Bulletin of the American Museum of Natural History,* 1945, *85,* 1–350.

SIMPSON, G. G. The evolutionary concept of man. Pp. 17–37 in B. Campbell (Ed.), *Sexual selection and the descent of man 1871–1971.* Chicago: Aldine, 1972.

SIMPSON, G. G. Recent advances in methods of phylogenetic inference. Pp. 3–19 in W. P. Luckett & F. S. Szalay (Eds.), *Phylogeny of the primates, a multidisciplinary approach.* New York: Plenum, 1975.

STRUHSAKER, T. T. Correlates of ecology and social organization among African cercopithecines. Folia primatologica, 1969, *11,* 80–118.

TAKESHITA, H. On the delivery behavior of squirrel monkeys (*Saimiri sciurea*) and a mona monkey (*Cercopithecus mona*). *Primates,* 1961, *3,* 59–72.

TINKLEPAUGH, O. L., & HARTMAN, K. G. Behavioral aspects of parturition in the monkey (*Macaca rhesus*). *Comparative Psychology,* 1930, *11,* 63–98.

TINKLEPAUGH, O. L., & HARTMAN, K. G. Behavior and maternal care of the newborn monkey (*Macaca mulatta*). *Journal of Genetic Psychology,* 1932, *40,* 257–286.

TRIVERS, R. L. Parent-offspring conflict. *American Zoologist,* 1974, *14,* 249–264.

WALKER, A. Splitting times among hominoids deduced from the fossil record. Pp. 63–77 in M. Goodman & R. E. Tashian (Eds.), *Molecular anthropology, genes and proteins in the evolutionary ascent of the primates.* New York: Plenum, 1976.

WASHBURN, S. L. Primate studies and human evolution. Pp. 467–485 in G. H. Bourne (Ed.), *Nonhuman primates and medical research.* New York: Academic Press, 1973.

WILLIAMS, G. C. *Adaptation and natural selection, a critique of some current evolutionary thought.* Princeton, N.J.: Princeton University Press, 1966.

WILSON, E. O. *Sociobiology: The new synthesis.* Cambridge, Mass.: Belknap Press, 1975.

WOODSIDE, B., & LEON, M. Thermoendocrine influences on maternal nesting behavior in rats. *Journal of Comparative and Physiological Psychology,* 1980, *94,* 41–60.

ZIMMERMAN, R. R. Form generalization in the infant monkey. *Journal of Comparative and Physiological Psychology,* 1962, *55,* 918–923.

ZIMMERMAN, R. R., & TORREY, C. C. Ontogeny of learning. Pp. 405–477 in A. M. Schrier, H. F. Harlow, & F. Stollnitz (Eds.), *Behavior of nonhuman primates.* New York: Academic Press, 1965.

6

Cross-Cultural Research and Theory

LEONORE LOEB ADLER

Within the last decade or two cross-cultural psychology has become an important branch of psychology generally and developmental psychology specifically. With this new emphasis on culture and ethnicity, a great deal of activity ensued among the behavioral scientists. While such investigations previously compared differences in observable customs and traditional manners from culture to culture or country to country, cross-cultural research now focuses not only on the discovery of differences but also pays equal attention to the findings of similarities across cultures. "Cross-cultural research recognizes that while the discovery of differences may be significant, the finding of similarities may provide even more meaningful information. Because of the ever-increasing spread of Western culture, special emphasis should be placed on such aspects" (Adler, 1977).

Values and attitudes may change slowly or quickly, depending in part on the social situation and the economic conditions. Life styles may undergo modification because of existing modernizing trends which are influenced by current mass communication systems in addition to the widespread dissemination of educational material within local communities and extending across distant populations. Thus one can speculate about the outcomes or anticipate the answers to this question: What are the effects of this continuing Westernization on human development in both traditional and modern cultures? It is with different methods of cross-cultural research that many of the answers about human development can be found, recognizing that this development is based on the interactions of the genetic endowment and the early socialization processes which take place within the surrounding environment of society and culture.

Cross-cultural research can provide the insight so necessary to evaluate whether accepted relationships and observable behaviors are valid universally or if they occur only in a modern or in a traditional culture or society. Many of the developmental aspects that were investigated by cross-cultural psychologists yielded some predictable but also some unexpected outcomes in the behavior patterns of different groups of people. However the prognoses of gradual growth, both for mental and physical phenomena, could occur under favorable environmental and hereditary conditions. Yet some situations could exist in which the outcomes produced questions to which no easy answers could be found. For instance testing children and/or adults in traditional cultures with Western or modern methods frequently came up with results different from those found in the country where the testing procedure originated. The answer to the question "Why did the results turn out so different?" is an important issue in cross-cultural research. It stimulated a great amount of research activity during recent years. All aspects used in the investigation came under scrutiny. In addition the current milieu and earlier experiences of the children tested were meaningful in terms of individual backgrounds and education.

The discovery of better methods to test existing theories or to formulate new principles in the development of different types of personality, in terms of the rate of cognitive growth as well as the acquisition of special motor skills, was just part of the cross-cultural developmental investigator's routine. How much of the social and emotional development of a child depends on the type and quality of the relationship with its mother? How important or meaningful are the effects of father absence in the moral development of children? In order to arrive at satisfactory answers, it is expedient to employ the most efficient methods for the cross-cultural investigations. Most of them were gleaned from experimental research procedures and modified to fit the circumstances.

Emic versus Etic Approaches

A vital issue in cross-cultural research, which has been repeatedly discussed in the literature (Berry, 1980; Triandis, Malpass, & Davidson, 1971; Werner, 1979; among others), is that of the *emic* or the *etic* approach to investigations. Perhaps a better way to explain it is to say that there is a difference which occurs stemming from two contrasting orientations. The first approach, emic, looks at only one culture (and therefore is *not* a cross-cultural method, by definition) with a "from within" orientation. The second approach, etic, is used to study several cultures but compares the behaviors from the vantage point of an outsider "looking in." Theoretically speaking the best approach would be if a team of cross-cultural scientists would collaborate in their research. It would mean that (1) some members of the team who live in the society would have the familiarity with the culture and the knowledge to explain the behavior or interpret the data on their own terms, and (2) other members of the team from other cultures or countries would observe, compare, and then interpret the actions with an outsider's point of view. In this way the interpretations of the data will not take on an ethnocentric slant which would cause a definite bias. With such a team effort it is possible to find out whether developmental relationships and interactions are valid only in a specific culture or whether the effects are found universally in many or all societies in the world. In short a cross-cultural perspective offers the opportunity for broader kinds of investigations in which the range or the scope of the variables includes a considerably larger focus (Whiting, 1968).

PHYSICAL DEVELOPMENT

Just as in other fields, many areas are being investigated in cross-cultural developmental psychology. While this topic deals with the full span of human life, most cross-cultural studies in developmental psychology deal with the earliest interactions. There exists a strong mutual relationship, as well as a reciprocal interrelationship, between the physical growth and the social and environmental factors that produce effects or influence the rate of progress of intellectual functioning.

The most rapid progress in physical development occurs during the first two years in the life of a human being, although the growth rate is even greater *in utero*, right after conception. Nevertheless the neonate is very helpless and is completely dependent, not only on the mother's care but also on the environment. Of course in a feedback relationship, the baby exerts a definite power to control the people in its immediate surroundings. Certain universals are found in comparisons of early behavior patterns. All newborn babies respond to specific stimuli with a set of reflexes. Among these are the "rooting reflex" in which the baby turns its head and mouth in the direction of stimulation when corners of the mouth or the cheek are gently stroked. The "grasping reflex," which lasts only a short time, occurs when one places an object (or a finger) into the hand of a neonate; the baby will grasp it and will not let it loose. Other reflexes could be included also. Sucking seems to have a reflex as a basis of the behavior that becomes more efficient through experience.

Among the systematic studies of growth and development are those that deal with three basic principles: (1) *The cephalocaudal development* refers to the progression of growth from head to foot; a baby's head develops and grows before the other parts of the body, such as the arms and then the legs. (2) *The proximodistal development* includes both the physical growth and motor development. In this case the growth progresses from the center of the torso toward the periphery; a baby learns how to control the movements of the shoulders and then gains control over the arms and then the fingers. The same sequence is found in the development of the leg and the toes. (3) *Differentiation and integration* means that a baby's abilities become more and more distinct and specific. Werner (1948) termed the procedure in which infants have to combine and integrate several specific and differentiated skills into making complex responses as "hierarchic integration."

Looking at the normal development from birth to toddlerhood, cross-cultural comparisons uncover ethnic and racial, as well as gender, differences. Newborn baby boys are somewhat larger and weigh more than newborn baby girls, though females reveal a greater skeletal development. This distinction increases with age (Munroe & Munroe, 1975). A comparison of the disposition of neonates disclosed that Chinese-Americans were much calmer than their Euro-American counterparts (Freedman, 1971). Birth weights of Western neonates were heavier than those of non-Western newborn babies (Achar & Yankauer, 1962). Another cross-cultural investigation of body size of one-year-olds showed that Western babies were larger in stature and body weight, as well as in head and chest circumference, than non-Western infants (Meredith, 1970).

In the area of motor development, Western children's pattern starts with sitting and progresses to creeping, crawling, standing, walking, and then squatting (Munroe & Munroe, 1975), while Balinese babies go from sitting to squatting before progressing to standing (Mead & Macgregor, 1951).

Meredith (1969) found that eight-year-old children's weight and height were greater in modern societies than in traditional societies. Of course there are individual differences, but generally this trend remains during the school-age years.

Initiation Rites

During the adolescents' growth spurts, not only the reproductive systems change. During puberty the skeletal and muscular dimensions increase greatly in size and strength, though more so in boys than in girls (Tanner, 1961). Before the onset of puberty, initiation ceremonies take place, depending on the demands of the cultural rituals. Among the Gusii in Kenya, girls (at about eight or nine years) will submit eagerly to clitoridectomies; just as the Gusii boys (at about ten to twelve years) will demonstrate their readiness to be circumcised (LeVine & Le-

Vine, 1963). In both these situations these initiations signal the beginning of assuming adult behavior and responsibility which includes premarital sexual relationships among the Gusii. It has been suggested that the effects of *low male saliency* include circumstances of father absence, mother-infant sleeping arrangements, and mother-child households, among others. These conditions can lead to young boys being exposed to low male salience. Whiting, Kluckhohn, and Anthony (1958) showed that exclusive mother-infant sleeping arrangements are strongly associated with intense, male initiation rites at puberty. Munroe and Munroe (1975) concur with this view and point out that cross-cultural correlations between

societies with low male salience in infancy, followed by strong sex differentiation and male social dominance, practice male initiation ceremonies that include circumcision. The rites can be interpreted as an attempt to expunge unacceptably feminine tendencies in young males. (pp. 124–125)

Other cultures and different ethnic groups follow a variety of procedures of circumcision or subincision at various ages during infancy or childhood. The latter ritual was discussed by Cawte in *Medicine Is the Law* (1974). He suggested that ". . . with the literature on subincision and the notion of vulva-envy, it conveyed that men made themselves bleed to simulate women" (p. 148). Various other explanations within each group are offered for these rituals.

DEVELOPMENTAL THEORIES

Physical growth and muscular development bring a relatively basic acquisition of motor skills, which may be related to hereditary factors. However, environmental factors, such as nutrition and socioeconomic status, are also important for intellectual as well as physical development during early childhood. Lack of adequate nutrition has been blamed, in part, for the poor results of children's performances on cognitive tasks.

Social-Learning Theories

While nutrition may be one significant aspect in the early development of cognitive functions, other factors, important in infantile experiences, enter into the discussion as well. Interaction and feedback relationships in the home environment are most meaningful in social-learning theory. Cross-cultural research is sparse in the field of social-learning theory. However, in their book *Children of Six Cultures,* Whiting and Whiting (1975) described the application of reinforcement theory in terms of rewards, nonrewards, or punishment to modify behavior patterns or direct children to conform to societal norms and standards. The rewards are used to reinforce desirable or appropriate behavior. Behavior-modification methods have been used by parents throughout the ages to strengthen good (adaptive) behavior and reduce or eliminate bad (maladaptive) behavior.

Another type of social-learning theory follows the outlines of Bandura's (1969) observational-learning or modeling theory. This theory states that learning can take place without direct rewards or reinforcers, by imitation of another person who acts as the demonstrator or model. Acquisition or learning of a variety of social behaviors can occur from watching television, looking at fights or aggressive acts of other people, or experiencing the contagious effects of specific emotional demonstrations and behaviors. The effects of covert learning by observation remain to be tested cross-culturally.

Psychosexual Theory

Another developmental approach, Sigmund Freud's theory of psychosexual development, was one of the most influential for many years. Freud's theory of personality development emphasized how critical the period of early childhood was in terms of the socialization of the individual. During the psychosexual stages—*oral, anal, phallic, latent,* and *genital*—extending from birth to adolescence, the child seeks to gratify its sensual desires. However during this process the child may experience a conflict with the parent of the opposite sex, which will become resolved when the child identifies with the same-sex parent. How the parents respond, affectionately and warm or cold and distant, will affect the personality development of the child. Guthrie (1979) related how Malinowski (1927) originated the idea to test a theory cross-culturally to establish or reject its merits universally. Malinowski investigated whether Freud's Oedipus Complex would prevail. Because of the family structure among the Trobrianders, Malinowski rejected the universality of Freud's theory. However after a debate with Jones (1928) in the journals, Malinowski withdrew from his point of view. Guthrie suggested that "it also established the doctrine that data from other societies did not bear on Freud's theories unless they were collected under conditions of psychoanalytic investigation or treatment" (1979, p. 352). Guthrie also suggested that because psychoanalytic theory was so prominent for such a long time, data collected in other cultures or societies had essentially no effect on other personality theories or on psychopathology. He proposed that this is the reason why very few indications of cross-cultural investigations can be found in such textbooks today.

Cognitive Development

Piaget's theory of cognitive development appears to be one of the most popular and most frequently tested hierarchical stage theories. The stages start at birth, move through toddlerhood to childhood, and end eventually with a stage that starts at preadolescence and goes to adulthood. The four stages are identified as *sensorimotor, preoperational, concrete operations,* and *formal operations.* The last stage was described by Inhelder and Piaget (1958) as reaching the ability to think in terms of hypothetical possibilities. This cognitive level is one of the most important achievements differentiating adolescents from children. Yet they predicted that this last stage, or the highest level, might not be reached by all individuals in all societies. It appears that cross-cultural research confirmed this statement. Piaget felt that a sign of intelligence is the ability to adapt to the environment through assimilation. The child assimilates new experiences to those structures that already exist, which in turn are accommodated (modified) on the bases of these new experiences. Cognitive development proceeds through the series of stages, progressing toward higher levels of equilibrium between the individual and the environment. Cross-cultural research is being used to test the universality of Piaget's theory by Dasen, one of the research scientists who worked closely with Piaget and Inhelder in Geneva, Switzerland. He also conducts excellent research programs in the field and writes comprehensive summaries of the investigations by Piagetian followers. In *Piagetian Psychology: Cross-Cultural Contributions* which Dasen (1977) edited, he wrote,

The first question I have asked is how universal Piaget's theory is, or what is universal in his theory? Piaget (1974) in fact makes no formal claims in this respect and looks toward cross-cultural, empirical data to provide the answer. . . . One may notice the expectation that the qualitative aspects of the theory (the basic cognitive processes, the structural properties of the stages, and their hierarchical ordering) should be universal, if not the quantitative aspects (the ages at which children develop through the various levels of the sequence). (p. 3)

Moral Development

Part of Piaget's theory of cognitive development relies on evaluations and interpretations of moral rules and moral behavior with ethical implications. Both Piaget (1965) and Kohlberg (1969) look at moral judgment as part of children's level of cognitive development. Both realize that the importance of social learning (e.g., observational learning of behavior displayed by models in specific situations that may lead to rewards or punishment) is based on some moral values. White and Speisman (1977) feel that cross-cultural differences in moral codes are a reflection of the societies or the social groups' promoting or hindering cognitive development. In both theories there are stages, though the highest level need not be reached by everybody. During a trip to China, Honig (1978) observed that moral teachings permeate every aspect of their educational program. The children are constantly told by their teachers how to love and care for each other. Moral development is promoted in a variety of ways and is taught by means of playlets and dramatizations in addition to posters and other methods. Bronfenbrenner (1970), in a cross-national comparison within the Western world, reports that in the Soviet Union children sometimes act as the socializing person, rather than the adult. In a set of *Propositions* Bronfenbrenner (1979) suggests that there are other parameters in a child-rearing environment beyond the dyadic level.

ASSESSMENT OF COGNITIVE DEVELOPMENT

Field Dependent versus Field Independent

Another completely different approach was followed by Berry who sought to assess in his exemplary studies the relationship between such variables as the performance in perceptual tasks and local culture which comprise, among others, the traditional socialization practices that shape perceptions and attitudes regarding events and occurrences of daily life. Berry's approach was to identify the cognitive styles that originated with child-rearing practices and/or environmental conditions leading to (1) a field-dependent or (2) a field-independent perception. In the former approach the surrounding field and parts of the field fuse and are experienced globally. The latter, on the other hand, means that the perception is more articulated, as parts of the field are perceived discretely from the ground. Berry selected groups that differed in socialization practices as well as in ecological conditions. He compared the Eskimos of Baffin Bay, who practice extremely permissive child-rearing methods, with the Temne of Sierra Leone, who have very strict child-rearing practices. The results showed that the Eskimos, who were hunters, were much more field independent than the agricultural Temne. Dawson's (1969a) study supported these findings by showing that mothers exerting strict control in raising their children promoted a field-dependent perception in their children.

The methods most frequently used to measure field-dependence/field-independence which originated with Witkin and his co-workers are (1) the Rod and Frame Test and (2) the Embedded Figure Test (Witkin, Oltman, Raskin, & Karp, 1971). In both these tests the underlying notion is that individuals differ in the ability to extract a figure from its surrounding field. The greater the ease with which the person perceives the discreteness of the figure, the more articulated is the individual's field-independent personality. Studies in the United States and Europe, in developing countries, in Asia, and with Australian Aboriginals have shown that significant differences were observed after early adolescence between boys and girls, the latter being more field dependent than their male counterparts (Maccoby & Jacklin, 1974).

Assessment of Research Methods

Ciborowski (1979) granted

. . . the great bulk of the data base (is) stemming from the Embedded Figure Test. What we are faced with is the near classic cross-cultural approach of taking a relatively simple test that was generated in a technological society and administering that test to traditional, nontechnological groups for which the test may have but minimal meaning and cultural relevance. The grave shortcomings of such a basically methodologically etic approach have been echoed by many researchers, particularly Cole and Scribner (1974), Ciborowski (1976), as well as Berry (1974) himself. (pp. 110–111)

Ciborowski proceeds to describe a study by Irwin, Schafer, and Freiden (1974) in which people of the Mano tribe in Liberia had to perform the same task as American undergraduates. The latter were not familiar with the material; the former were accustomed to it and turned out to be significantly "superior." This research shows the importance of testing subjects on their own terms.

Assessment of Cognitive Development in Traditional Environment

Many methods are used to test cognitive development and the relationship between culture and cognition. Cole and his co-workers (1971) used a variety of research methods. Among these were some standard paradigms which they used to investigate how Liberian farmers handle mathematical knowledge. Card-sort techniques were employed to test cognitive functions. Free recall served to investigate the effects of memory. Open-ended tasks helped to assess language skills and evaluate the ability to deal with syllogisms and logical solutions. The subjects, Kpelle people, were drawn from different age groups. Some had secondary school background and were students, while others had little or no formal schooling and belonged to the village elders. Cole with Gay, Glick, and Sharp (1971) found that the Liberian and the American high-school students responded pretty much in the same way. However this was not the case with the adult farmers. A large number of investigators, including Cole and Lave (1979) have "... demonstrated that schooling enhances cognitive performance on a wide range of developmentally sensitive tasks; indeed, to some people it seems that cognitive-developmental research in the United States has been measuring *years of schooling* using age as its proxy variable" (The Laboratory of Comparative Human Cognition, 1979, p. 830).

Different Cross-Cultural Approaches to Cognitive Development

The research scientists from the Laboratory of Comparative Human Cognition, of which Cole is a member, feel that any discussion about *which* is the better approach—either laboratory or field investigations—to study behavior has outlived its usefulness. They feel it no longer matters which method is chosen. They suggest that

whatever other disagreements psychologists have, they all agree that the specification of psychological processes represents a specification of environment-organism interactions. In order to exploit the potential of cross-cultural research we must vastly increase our power to describe environments for behaving. (Ibid., p. 832)

They specifically mention that *culture* or *schooling* are used as surrogates for environmental variation and are often invalidated in a laboratory setting. The team of scientists advanced as their goal to have more observations of children outside a laboratory setting, thereby increasing the range of contexts to which they can legitimately generalize.

Education and experience are important factors in the schooling of children. In a widely quoted study by Price-Williams, Gordon, and Ramirez (1969), it was shown that six- to nine-year-old Mexican schoolchildren, including some who were children of potters, responded quite differentially in a test of Piaget's conservation. In each case the potters' children who were exposed to the pottery making were doing significantly better on the conservation of substance (clay) tasks.

Another perspective to cross-cultural cognitive research is generated by Schmidt (1978) from the German Democratic Republic. He follows a dialectic-materialistic determinism, which is part of the Marxist point of view. One of his main purposes is to accomplish a better understanding of the theories of general psychology and to help to create a bridge by explaining the theories and methods of developmental psychology.

Another approach, also cognitive, is pursued by Svendsen (1978; with Kinge, 1979) from Norway, who looks for the connection among intellectual functioning, achievement motivation, and social-class background of schoolchildren and then extends it to young adults and their intellectual ability, education, and occupation. His investigations showed, however, that only a few women were economically active so that no conclusions could be drawn. On the other hand results from the men demonstrated that the three variables were interrelated and in agreement with studies from other countries (Matarazzo, 1972).

After her return, Honig (1978) reported her observations in Japan and China.

I found it personally amusing that nowhere in our travels did I encounter a child-care person who, when I inquired, was familiar with Erikson or Piaget's work. Yet everywhere I saw the evidence of a superb "equilibration" process by which the ideas of both theoreticians were applied in ingenious and creative ways to the rearing of children. (p. 25)

PERCEPTUAL DEVELOPMENT

How a person perceives the world plays an important part from the earliest time in an infant's life throughout the life span. Research pursued in Great Britain (reported on the 1970s television series, "Nova") showed that an infant who is two weeks old can recognize the face and voice of the mother and establish eye contact with her. There is less eye contact when a "stranger" is taking the mother's place. However when the "stranger's" face is paired with the mother's voice, the infant has practically no eye contact but instead looks away from the unfamiliar stimulus. Most of the perceptual tests are based on visual development, though hearing and language are areas of investigation as well. Werner (1979) cited four, possibly five, types of perceptual processes. The first one was presented by Gibson (1969) who felt that perceptual development occurred with increasing differentiation through sensory processes by using the cues that were present in the environment. The second view was advanced by Brunswik (1956) who thought of the perceptual process in terms of evaluating the various cues in the environment, as with a judgmental process based on past experience. The third point of view was introduced by Whorf (1956) who said that the structure and expression of languages influence the perception of the environment and can shape the culture. The fourth view was presented by Dawson (1969b) who talked about perceptual skills as an adaptation through interaction between the physiological and psychological processes which are influenced by the sociocultural systems in the environment. Another, possibly fifth, perceptual process has not yet been fully established. This one, proposed by Jahoda (1971), stated that the effects of pigmentation of the retina, involving to a greater degree the blue end of the spectrum or the short wave lengths, affected the spatial perception of visual illusions. In another study Jahoda (1975) presented Ghanian and Scottish children with both red and blue illusion figures but failed to replicate the previous results. Werner (1979) suggested that it is most likely that the susceptibility to a variety of optical illusions was probably an adaptive response involving both environmental and biological factors.

Visual (Optical) Illusions

During the past decades cross-cultural research was used to demonstrate that individuals from different cultures responded in various ways to the presentation of visual illusions. Segall, Campbell, and Herskovits (1966) tested both children and adults in different locations on three continents. The responses varied depending on the degree of "carpenteredness," a structural byproduct of modernity that belongs to a technically developed environment. In modern societies the scenery is dominated by straight lines—houses and roofs, roads and streets, trucks, trains, and railroad tracks. Contrarily, different levels of unorganized and unstructured effects are the bases to a natural environment with less rectilinearity. The curved lines of the thatched roof huts in warm climates and the crammed clutter of the tropical jungle demonstrate a lack of "carpenteredness."

The "horizontal-vertical illusion" is created when a vertical line of the same length as a horizontal line intersects that line in the center and forms an upside-down "T." The illusion that the vertical line is longer should be stronger to people who live in the steppes than to those who live among a thick tangled mass of tropical vegetation.

A strong effect in "carpentered" environment was obtained with the Müller-Lyer illusion which consists of two (vertical or horizontal) lines, same size, presented side by side. Both lines have arrowheads intersecting at both ends; however, in one figure they point toward the inside while in the other the arrowheads point toward the outside. Berry (1968) tested this illusion with the Temne tribe in Sierra Leone in Africa as well as with the Eskimos in Baffin Bay, confirming the original findings by Segall et al. (1966).

These studies provided support for the hypothesis that a cognitive factor is responsible for the difference in perception of illusions. Kilbride and Leibowitz (1977, 1981) tested rural Baganda villagers of Uganda. They found that these rural subjects did not perceive the Ponzo illusion of a three-dimensional (3D) perspective. However, this illusion, which is caused by the horizontal, parallel lines that are familiar from a ladder or railroad tracks that vanish at a distance, was perceived by urban Ugandan college students. It seemed to be based in an experiential factor of depth perception. They found that if their subjects perceived photographs of local roads, ladders, etc. as a three-dimensional presentation, these subjects perceived the Ponzo illusion. Those who perceived the pictures as two-dimensional did not see the illusion. However some people were "mixed," i.e., varied in their responses from trial to trial. The results may be influenced not only by environmental factors but also by the level of education of the subjects.

Another frequently quoted research on 3D perception (not with illusions) was that by Hudson (1967). In a sequence of pictures the subjects are to report whether a native hunter is about to spear an antelope or an elephant. These two animals, the hunter, and the tree are presented at various parts of the pictures, with or without a road. Among "cues" for depth perception are size, overlap, and converging lines. It appeared, though, that in order to perceive depth, informal pictorial experience is essential (Mundy-Castle, 1966).

SOCIAL DEVELOPMENT

Child-Rearing Practices

Nurturance was the most frequent reaction to infants by adults and children as observed in their six-culture study and reported by the Whitings (1975). However while studying some Wolof babies in Senegal, Lusk and Lewis (1972) found that the pattern of caretaker-infant interaction varied depending on the age of the children. However the age of the caretaker did not matter in the behavior toward the infant.

In a longitudinal research of child-mother (caretaker) interaction, Caudill and Weinstein (1969) reported the comparisons between Japanese and United States mothers. The former had more physical contact, while the latter spent less time in physical contact but emphasized verbal interaction. Honig (1978) reported her personal view in her comparison of child-rearing practices between Japan and the People's Republic of China. In both societies the very young were most often held in the arms by adults and were "treated in Asian settings with gentleness and a sense of genuine pleasure" (p. 7).

In most cases it is still considered an important family function to raise children. Breast-feeding, therefore, is very widespread. If a mother in China works, she is given an hour off in the morning and in the afternoon to breast-feed her baby at the infant-nursery across the street from her workplace. Breast-feeding customs vary in length of time. Some of these are dependent on the day-and-night constancy in mother-infant interaction, like the Trobriand islanders (Munroe & Munroe, 1975). For the first few months mother and baby are constantly together, and thereafter they still keep on sharing the sleeping quarters. Such an arrangement provides ample opportunity for an extensive social exchange between mother and infant.

For studies of child-rearing practices, questionnaire methods were augmented with observational studies by Kirk (1981) of motion picture records and analyses of mother-child teaching interaction which showed the relationship between the caretaker's nonverbal communicative behavior and the child's rate of cognitive development. The interaction may be a feedback system though Kirk suggested that it did not necessarily involve both sides with equal strength in terms of exerting influence on the other. In other words a change in the caretaker's behavior will result in a change in the child's behavior as well.

An extensive three-country research, which includes Japan, the Philippines, and Thailand, is being conducted by Shirai of Japan and her co-workers. The behavior of two-year-old children, who are in the "negative period," is evaluated and analyzed, especially with regard to the mother's interaction. The experiment is being used to observe the mother-child interactions. The mother is given a transparent box which contains an attractive reward but is securely closed at the top with a cellophane tape so that the child can never open it. The mother is told that if her child can open the box by him/herself, s/he can keep the contents. The dyad is observed for the resulting interaction. It is an ingenious approach not only to study the social interaction but also to get insight into each participant's motivation—and frustration. These are important aspects in the socialization process.

Most of the current social developmental theories pay much attention to the early interrelationship between mother and child. In psychoanalytic theory, the earliest period is a stage which serves to gratify "instinctive" needs and is conducive to create significant positive feelings in the infant. Erikson (1950) emphasizes this period's new social interactions that lead to trusting other people rather than mistrusting them. When the infant's needs are met and feelings of discomfort are removed, safety and dependability are expressed in attitudes of trust. In all such theories it is the maternal relationship with the child that lays the foundations for both cognitive and personality developments.

Acceptance or Rejection of Children

It seems only reasonable to assume that most cultures would want to create a congenial home environment for infancy and early childhood. However styles do differ. In one comprehensive investigation parents' attitudes of acceptance or rejection of their children came under scrutiny. It was found that the societies which tolerated the rejection and neglect of children produced different personalities than those societies where children were warmly accepted and affectionately loved. Rohner (1975) found that the Alorese, a society living in what was known as the Dutch East Indies, now called Indonesia, would score very low on his acceptance-rejection rating scale and infant satisfaction scale, as compiled by Barry, Bacon and Child (1967). Cross-cultural investigations revealed that the composition of the household members is an important point in the family's interrelationships. Acceptance and rejection depend on many different aspects. When a mother can get help or assistance from another person, such as a grandparent, rejection is less likely to occur. Children will also be more likely to be accepted when fathers are home on a daily basis during the first year of the baby's life.

Father Absence

Generally it was found that the absence of the father often results in negative consequences. It does not matter whether this life style is caused by desertion, divorce, death, or single parenting or whether the child is growing up in a polygynous society or with a cultural background that admonishes prolonged postpartum sexual taboos. Munroe and Munroe (1975) suggest that the cause for the many sex-typing problems by men are due to the low exposure to adult men during childhood. Women seem to have fewer sex stereotype problems since their focus is directed more at the status attributes of the male role. It has also been shown by Hoffman (1971) that seventh-grade boys in the United States who grew up without a father figure in the household scored significantly lower on all moral judgments on Kohlbergian tasks, compared to father-present boys. In another study Burton (1972) observed the effects of father absence with the projective technique of the "Draw-a-Person Test." The results showed that the average size of the man drawn was directly related to the degree of father presence during the boy's infancy. A very good review on the topic of father absence cross-culturally is presented by Spires and Robin (1981) who show the impact of fatherless homes on (1) sex role behavior, (2) masculine "protest" behavior, and (3) achievement motivation and cognitive development.

Working Mothers

In families where the mother is working and contributing a great deal to the subsistence of the society, she also rears her children so that she can function in her economic role. She must be able to depend on the children's behavior while she is away from home. Therefore obedience is necessary. Another important point which is stressed is the responsibility of the children to contribute their share to the household. Whiting and Whiting (1975) found altruistic behavior, consisting of "offering help, support, suggesting responsibility to others," was common among the children of women who carried heavy work schedules. Frequently children helped with childcare chores, herding animals, food cultivation, and preparation of meals. On the other hand children in societies where they did not have to help or contribute with the household chores turned out much more egotistic (Okinawans and Americans from New England communities).

Communal Living: The Kibbutz

Many different approaches to the socialization of infants and children can be found; however, space limitations do not permit extensive documentation. Still an important change in family patterning came about in *kibbutz* living in Israel, which was based on a pattern of communal housing and socializing the infants and children in collectivist ideology. This feature is one of the most essential in any kibbutz and differs greatly from the agricultural settlement, the *moshav,* which provides a combination of "collectivized production with private consumption in nuclear-family-based households" (Endleman, 1977). While familial sleeping arrangements for children exist, the most frequent pattern in kibbutz living is that children under five years old spend the nights in the children's houses, children up to puberty sleep in the parents' apartment, and adolescents move to youth dormitories. However during times of danger of enemy attacks on the kibbutz, all children sleep in the centrally located children's houses.

Accounts of children growing up in communal households report that the major part of the socialization of infants and children is taken over by caretakers and later by teachers, but not by parents. The outcome of such child-rearing patterns of the traditional kibbutz showed that the children think and feel in terms of being one of the group, rather than as an individual raised in a nuclear family (Bettelheim, 1969).

PERSONALITY VARIABLES

Achievement Motivation

The only outstanding research with children testing achievement motivation in a traditional setting was undertaken by LeVine (1966) in Nigeria with secondary-school boys from the Hausa, the Yoruba, and the Ibo tribes. He analyzed stories of the boys' dreams. LeVine suggested that the three tribes had different socioeconomic practices and values, which were reflected in the societies' child-rearing practices. These in turn led to different personality development, including those of achievement motivation.

Among the comparable research activities are the studies by McClelland (1971), who for more than two decades devoted his efforts to investigations of achievement motivation. He proposed that greater opportunities in employment and education would lead to greater achievement motivation. He wrote that for high achievement motivation, a greater opportunity to achieve must also be present.

Competitive and Cooperative Behavior

To some extent both competition and cooperation are related to achievement motivation. As success is rewarding in achievement motivation, so is it possible for other types of personality traits—e.g., competitive or cooperative behavior—to be explained in terms of reinforcement theory and the milieu in which the children grow up (Madsen, 1967). If the child grows up in an agricultural setting, cooperation with the family to produce crops for the market and food for the table is essential. However, in a middle-class milieu where the father's job or position is based on competition in order to keep the job and to assure economic survival, aggressive and competitive behavior is indeed appropriate and desirable. In an Israeli study Shapira (1976) investigated the competitive and cooperative behavior of four- to eleven-year-old kibbutz children and city children. The results showed that the kibbutz children were consistently more cooperative and the city children more competitive. Honig (1978) wrote about the Chinese children who learned cooperation in all phases of their upbringing at home, in school, and at work and play. On the other hand, competition is often prevalent for the Japanese children who have to achieve high grades to get admitted to the schools of their choice or to universities. The sta-

tistics for suicide (to save face) among youngsters who do not make the grade is of concern.

Assertiveness

Competitiveness may be developmentally related to assertiveness. Kagan and Carlson (1975) investigated this aspect of personality development through socialization in Mexican and Anglo-American children. The children had to perform a task, an assertiveness-pull scale, which was set up so that the pulls were monitored. Naturalistic observation of the urban middle-class Anglo-American children showed that they responded significantly more assertively than the semirural lower-class Anglo-American and the Mexican-American children. However both of the latter groups were more assertive than rural Mexican children. The two psychologists found that assertiveness increased with age, though more so among the Anglo-American children.

It can be concluded that with such traits as cooperativeness, competitiveness, and assertiveness, the effect of the interpersonal relationship is important. Peer influence, with or without direct support by parents and teachers, seems to transmit a lasting effect on the social values of children. Werner (1979) proposes that "the young, as role models for still younger children, become important pacesetters in the developing world and in human evolution" (p. 324).

Compliance

A similar situation exists with compliance. Draguns (1979) wrote that "behavior, under conditions of compliance or brought about by external constraint, is of peripheral interest to the student of personality. A personality investigator is concerned with actions that result from identification, imitation, or internalization" (p. 180).

Aggressive Behavior

Aggressive behavior also seems to be a product of social learning. It is generally accepted that it is a behavior pattern acquired through socialization (Carmichael, 1946). Frequently this behavior is learned through observational learning, i.e., imitation (Bandura & Walters, 1963). Although it was previously believed that frustration would lead to aggressive behavior, today's thought is that other than aggressive responses can be resorted to after a frustrating experience. The "instinctive" approach to aggression is also no longer accepted. Since it was shown (Segall, 1976, pp. 199–213) that aggressive responding was modeled after others displayed such behavior, the instinct theory is rejected.

LANGUAGE DEVELOPMENT

Among the cognitive processes that are investigated by psychologists are the relationships of language to concept formation. Whorf (1956), following Sapir's (1921/1949) point of view, postulated that linguistic relativity contributes to a great extent to the perception of culture. Whorf visualized that languages are like molds that shape people's perception of the world, stir their thoughts, guide their expressions, and consequently direct their behaviors. In Whorf's view differences in languages, expressions or concepts, and words are bound to affect people and consequently their modes of living in different ways. However this view is too extreme for some scientists, who prefer to follow Brown's (1965) theory, which deals with generic terms quite differently. For example an English-speaking person has one word for "rice," but the Hanunoo of the Philippines can choose among 92 different words. Chomsky (1968) and Lenneberg (1967) proposed a theory of grammar that could be applied to cross-cultural linguistics. Chomsky's Language Acquisition Device (LAD) is an innate mechanism. Its existence, though, can be neither proven nor disproven. Still another position is advanced by Cole and Scribner (1974) who feel that languages can be defined in terms of meanings that are specified with regard to social roles, norms, or standards as they are perceived in their cultures.

Language Acquisition

While the rates of language development may vary greatly, the sequence of stages seems to follow a universal progression. Certain changes occur because of the infant's interaction with people in the immediate environment in general, and with the caregivers specifically. Institutionalized babies do not babble as frequently as noninstitutionalized infants. Children who grow up in a bilingual household start to develop their language skills later than those who grow up in a household where just one language is spoken (Rheingold, 1960, 1961). In the United States the middle-class child showed speech sound superiority over the lower- (working) class child (Irwin, 1948).

EDUCATION AND SCHOOLING

The great importance of formal education has been recognized and continues to increase following the spread of Western education. The influence formal schooling has on shaping cognitive development has been recognized in many countries and cultures, not only among the technological societies but in traditional settings as well.

Is TV a Help to Education?

In modern societies education does not only take place in the traditional ways through schooling or practical experience; education can be gained via viewing TV programs. Shirai (1980) investigated the TV viewing of Japanese preschool children between two and five years old. Social class (fathers' white- or blue-collar work and working or nonworking mothers) in different environmental settings (urban uptown and downtown, as well as rural) was taken into consideration. The results show that the rural children spend the least time looking at TV; the most viewing is done by the children of blue-collar workers and working mothers who live in the urban downtown neighborhoods. The mothers' opinions (questionnaire method) were analyzed, and it was found that mothers from all three environments have the same attitudes with regard to TV viewing and programs. They differ, however, in their answers to questions on "morality" (*positive:* "TV promotes moral sentiments of justice, honesty, and gentleness"; *negative:* "TV may make children apathetic to violence"). Uptown mothers tend to be negative while the downtown mothers are definitely positive.

The Effects of Social Class

Social class was also a factor in the analysis of school problems in a study of *special classes* in Norway by Svendsen (1980). He found that there was a clear relationship between social background and individual interviews (examinations) by psychologists. Children whose parents were among the "high status group" were rarely seen by school psychologists compared to children of "workers." The parents' social groups were divided into three categories by education or equivalents: Group 1 included university graduates, as well as business executives, etc.; Group 2 included college graduates and farmers, office personnel, etc.; and Group 3 included high school graduates and blue-collar workers, farmhands, etc. The children of the last two groups needed more visits to the school psychologists and placements into special classes.

Social status also makes a significant difference in the preschool education of Turkish children as reported by Vassaf (1980). Rich families can provide private kindergartens and nursery training for their children. These programs are geared to teach the children to become "little gentlemen and ladies." On the other hand most of the government nurseries serve the working population. Yet these facilities are understaffed with a ratio of about fifty children to one caretaker. This means that most of the attention will be directed toward maintenance rather than toward the education of the children. However some working mothers have made arrangements with a nonworking woman to provide child care as well as food, toys, and educational material. This arrangement with a "day mother" is not too expensive, and the parents have a chance to give some input into their children's behavior and activities.

Considering that the literacy rate among Turkish women is about 48 percent (and about 70 percent in rural areas), Vassaf reported that many women should receive state support to help with the upbringing of their children.

Nearly 51 percent of all deaths in Turkey occur among infants and children. Accidental death is the third largest cause among infants and children from birth to four years of age. One out of every five children in Turkey suffers from malnutrition. This is due to lack of material resources and to ignorance of preventive measures. It should be the responsibility of the caretakers to handle health and safety precautions. Therefore Vassaf suggests intervention programs would be informative and educational at the same time.

United Nation's Help to Education

Garcia-Chafardet (1978) reported that

the history of development, to date since the early 1950's including the history of United Nations development organizations' programming policies, had produced an overwhelming concentration on the transfer of new technologies *to men;* on the provision of training in virtually all developing fields (except Domestic Sciences and Maternal-Child Health) *to men;* on the expansion of basic public schooling overwhelmingly *for boys;* and on the massive concentration of family planning by persuading girls and women, while disregarding the general influence of male decisions on birth control. (p. 108) (Italics added.)

Do Textbooks Further Education and Modernization?

Subtle and obvious gender differences were recorded by Denmark and Waters (1976). They counted the stereotypical sex role behaviors which were assigned to girls and boys in primary school readers from several countries: France, Rumania, Spain, Sweden, and the U.S.S.R. Their analyses showed that all the countries in their survey subscribed to typical sex-role stereotypical behaviors. All texts, except those from Sweden, represented fewer female characters than males. While some girls and women in the Russian, Rumanian, and Swedish texts were depicted in less traditional roles, only the Swedish text showed men or boys in nurturant or nontraditional roles. The authors proposed a concerted effort on the part of the publishers to rectify this overt and covert sexual biasing in children's primary school books.

GENDER DIFFERENCES

Gender Differences and Stereotypes

The ever-pervading differential effect of sex roles through early socialization was recognized and carefully considered by Denmark in her paper: "What Sigmund Freud did not know about boys and girls" (1971). She concluded that all cultures and societies assign different sex roles to the two genders.

In the literature there are many reports (e.g., Super, 1977) of the dichotomy of treatment of boy babies and girl babies. Some of these discussions centered around thirteen different African societies; in addition, there were many accounts of several geographic locations in India (Graves, 1978; Kumar, 1978) and numerous reports in the U.S., among others. In all these descriptions boy babies received preferential treatment.

The effects of mother-infant interaction are more intense after infant sons' gross motor behavior begins than after the daughters' (Lewis, 1972). In another research a study was made of the selection of toys by adults of both genders, when the gender of the baby was *not* known but was ascribed either male, female, or no (neutral) sex. These ascriptions resulted in sex-stereotypical selections of toys for the infants by the subjects (Sidorowicz & Lunney, 1980).

Gender differences were also found with US-American caretakers who were consistently more likely to punish boys by spanking and other forms of physical punishment (Maccoby & Jacklin, 1974) while girls generally received (soft-spoken) verbal reprimands (Servin, O'Leary, Kent, & Tonick, 1973).

Garcia-Chafardet (1978) reported that in many parts of the world females are discriminated against because of gender. As an example she mentioned that in India the death rates of infant girls are much higher compared to those of boys. Indian parents prefer feeding their meager rations to their sons who will provide security in old age, rather than to their daughters who will leave when they get married. Garcia-Chafardet related that in Mexico midwives charge twice as much for the delivery of a boy than for a girl.

Since African women in Third World countries have a heavy workload (they produce and process 80 percent of the food [Garcia-Chafardet, 1978]), it is not surprising that Nigerian children (Zaïdi, 1979) drew pictures that represented a leisure value system (Adler, 1981), i.e., nonworking women and working men. At the present time these pictures represent rather "wishful thinking" instead of general occurrences, though it seems to be the drift of the modernization trend.

ASSESSMENT OF DEVELOPMENTAL PROGRESS

Intelligence Testing

In order to assess the developmental progress in children, both physically and cognitively, cross-cultural scientists set out to test the children in a variety of ways by many different procedures. During the past decades many discussions have centered around the meaning and the causes of "intelligence." Suggestions were often made in favor of either genetics or the environment. More recently there was frequent agreement in favor of an interrelationship of both heredity and environment, a nature-nurture interaction. However, the way to arrive at a valid and reliable answer is the problem for cross-cultural psychologists. The answers to the simple question *"What* is measured?" and *"How* is it measured?" are quite complex. A cross-cultural scientist might get good and reliable indices in one culture or society but not in another. On the other hand does the test really measure what it is supposed to measure—is it valid? The IQ tests were developed to measure general ability but apply mainly to the culture or society in which they were constructed.

As previously stated, Piaget's stages are an assessment of intelligence (see p. 78) which is widely used in cross-cultural research.

Caution Needed for Interpretation of Tests

Bayley (1969) constructed a scale to assess the developmental progress of infants with regard to the norms or to the scores of a large sample within their culture. Generally African children from birth to two years seem more precocious than their American and European counterparts. However Kilbride (1978) reported in a longitudinal study that the affect was not as great as earlier reports had suggested. As it turned out specific aspects were valued in the infant behavior and consequently reinforced by their parents during their interaction with the babies. This would seem an important point in keeping with the reinforcement theory discussed earlier (see p. 78). Segall (1979) also offers a word of warning:

It is possible that both the precocity and its decline are to some extent artifactual. . . . And, with regard to the measured decline in precocity, it is very likely—indeed almost certain—that the tests used to measure performance from age two onward are composed of items that favor Western children. (p. 107)

Other studies may, inadvertently, interpret results with a nonfactual conclusion.

In another study by Marmorale and Brown (1981), Wechsler Intelligence Scale for Children (WISC) IQ scores of US–American children with different ethnic backgrounds were compared. The results of the Puerto Rican children did not remain constant over a period of several years, while those of the white and black children remained unchanged. English-language competence was not a factor because the Puerto Rican children were tested each time in Spanish while the two other groups received the test in English. All the children were tested during the first and at the end of the third year of school. The increments for the Puerto Rican children between the first and the second series of tests reached a significant level ($p<.01$) in all retest IQs. The investigators suggest a number of important implications. The results showed that great caution is needed for the interpretation of the scores. It is also highly questionable whether low IQ Puerto Rican children should be placed in the traditionally "slow" classes. The two scientists suggest that the Puerto Rican children's intellectual deficit is only apparent as a reflection of ethnically acquired modes of responding to the highly verbal cognitive demands of the typical school. Furthermore they believe that repeated testing throughout childhood and adolescence would be necessary to determine whether the Puerto Rican children are genuinely lacking in ability.

SOME TESTS USED IN CROSS-CULTURAL RESEARCH

Some cross-cultural studies in intellectual development investigate the rate of development. This can be evaluated with the help of psychological tests that provide information on specific skills and adaptive behavior. However, a problem existed, brought about by the tests which were developed in Western-culture countries and standardized there. Differences occurred in psychomotor development during infancy in favor of traditional cultures. This advantage was soon lost, and by the age of two years, the Western children scored higher than the non-Western. Such results should not be interpreted to infer that Western babies are neglected or deprived, though they receive less "contact comfort" than do non-Western infants. Several studies have reported that this early developmental slowness has no permanent effects unless social deprivation continues. With regard to testing, when the child is approximately two years old, there is a gradual changeover from the motor skills to the cognitive skills on test items.

For a long time the Porteus Mazes were used to assess the intellectual level of children and adults from modern and traditional countries. However this type of examination depends not only on familiarity with such tests and general testing procedures but also on performance skills and speed in carrying out the task. It is for that reason that the Australian Aboriginals did not perform as well as the American subjects.

Culture-Fair Tests

In recent years special types of tests have been administered more frequently. These tasks were said to be more or less "culture-fair." This means that, for example, an intelligence test is equally as *fair* to children who speak English as to those who do not. It means that children are neither advantaged nor disadvantaged when a test requires hearing or reading instructions. Meanings or connotations of words could vary depending on the children's backgrounds, such as social and economic standing and ethnic origin. To eliminate culture bias is the endeavor of every responsible cross-cultural psychologist. However scientists like Frijda and Jahoda (1966) warn that "the notion of 'fairness' looks suspiciously as though there were an underlying feeling that, given appropriate measures, cultural differences ought to disappear" (p. 118). Among the more frequently presented tests are the (Kohs) Block Design test and the Kuhlmann-Anderson (an Omnibus) test.

Another point can be made: What is considered "culture-appropriate" in one group may not be quite so appropriate in another culture or society. Segall (1979) advanced a reminder when he talked about culture-fairness: "Different things are being measured in different cultures and to an unknown degree" (p. 53).

Projective Techniques

While it seems difficult to achieve the goal for a culture-fair test, the use of pictures or symbols, instead of words, comes closest.

Frequently projective techniques rely on the use of pictures, among them: the Human Figure Drawing Tests, the Fruit-Tree Test, the House-Tree-Person Test, the Make a Picture-Story Test, the Holtzman Inkblot Technique, the Rorschach Technique, the Rosenzweig Picture Frustration Test, the Thematic Apperception Test, the Tomkins-Horn Picture Arrangement Test, the Figure-Placement Task, and the Play Assessment Techniques. In such projective tests there are no "right" nor "wrong" answers. Frequently the projective method is used in clinical work to measure attitudes in such a way that does not need to be articulated or recognized by the subjects and therefore can tap attitudes at variance with the subjects' verbally stated beliefs. Mead (1977) pointed out that a drawing could be called an objective test, because "it does not need to be mediated by words. . . . Children's drawings are all particularly useful as the independent analyst does not need a delicate knowledge of the language. . . . All such materials can be very useful to both experimentalists and clinicians" (p. 502).

Familiarity versus Values in Children's Drawings

Children's drawings can be used not only as a projective technique but also as an index of children's preferences. Adler (1981) reported on her programmatic study in which 4314 children from all types of geographical areas on six continents were asked to "draw a picture—any scene—with a fruit-tree in it." Boys and girls, ages 5 to 12 years old, contributed one picture each. In highest rank, all over, was the apple tree, which represented a larger category than the next eight fruit-tree varieties together.

Adler continued the program investigating different aspects in the study to find out what would exert an influence on the imagery of children. Among the sequence was a cross-cultural study in which children from Central Europe, East Asia, and North America responded differentially to the availability—or unavailability—of a specific color (such as red or orange). Though many drew indigenous trees, most of them responded to the cues in a similar manner.

The latest phase was to evaluate these "scenes" by the children from Central Europe, Eastern Asia, and North America in terms of the *familiarity hypothesis* versus the *value hypothesis*. The value hypothesis proposes that children draw scenes in which the themes have culturally desirable goal qualities and are socially acceptable. The attitudes toward the persons (and animals) represented in the pictures incorporate positive affects, and in addition they mirror positive social values. The familiarity hypothesis, however, suggests that children reflect their environment or that which the children have knowledge of or have experienced. Not everything with which the children are equally familiar is drawn—unpleasant themes and persons are not represented in the drawings (or very infrequently) such as a dentist, who is unpopular but not unfamiliar to children.

While the pictures may mirror the environment, they also reflect existing value systems by presenting preferences. Since the apple tree can only grow in a temperate climate and most of the countries in the temperate zone are "modern" or "Westernized," the apple tree could be representative of the spread of Westernization as well as of the desirability of modernization.

EFFECTS OF MALNUTRITION AND DISEASE

All areas of development are involved when an infant or child is well-fed. On the other hand the effects of malnutrition, while not necessarily leading to death, can leave permanent damage, physically, emotionally, or mentally. Cognitive development, such as language structures, can suffer. Among the most widespread conditions for which hospitalization may become necessary are marasmus (the "wasting away" disease) and kwashiorkor. In addition the social-psychological consequences of hospitalization of an infant or young child have to be dealt with. Effects of these conditions may result in mental re-

tardation, disturbance of intellectual as well as social development, or both. The most dangerous deficit—or rather nonutilization—is the protein or calorie intake during the first and second years of life. Also more information is needed on the chronic condition of mild protein-calorie malnutrition (PCM). The best test to evaluate the intellectual deficit is still under discussion (Ricciuti, 1970; Werner, 1979).

Termination of Breast-Feeding

Werner (1979) reported that the abrupt termination of breast-feeding by a working mother results in a drastic effect on the developmental progress of the baby. The precocious effect that infants in traditionally reared preindustrial environments demonstrated will stop or be reversed. The deficit in sensorimotor development has been found to occur earlier among illiterates of the lower socioeconomic classes who live in city slums in the developing countries. There the working mothers spend less time or no time breast-feeding their babies. A current program to provide formula milk is *not* easily established since clean water and sanitary conditions are important conditions for its success. Also if mothers cannot read the instructions, the proportions of the formula's ingredients may not be accurate for the age of the infant.

Some Prevention Measures for Diseases

Acute malnutrition is one of the greatest scourges of the Third World countries especially when it occurs within the first three years of life. A strong correlation exists between PCM conditions and a reduction in intellectual levels at school age.

Byproducts of malnutrition are conditions of gastrointestinal problems and respiratory diseases. These conditions result from poverty and unsanitary environments, as well as ignorance of methods to prevent, at least in part, such unfortunate conditions. Clean water is one of the most urgent requirements for preventing sickness and avoiding the spreading of diseases. Werner (1979) reported that in developing countries tuberculosis is active among children. Infants and children have to fight bouts with whooping cough, measles, and other childhood diseases. In comparison there are encouraging signs from the children in North America and Western and Central Europe who follow a program of vaccinations and booster shots, as well as X-ray checkups. Blood tests and eye tests during regular medical examinations help prevent a future epidemic of diseases. Medical visits for the pregnant mother, good diets, her delivery and after-care will help in giving infants a better start.

CONCLUSIONS

The aim of the present chapter on cross-cultural research and theory in developmental psychology is to familiarize the reader with some of the topics and ideas that are under investigation. It would have been a herculean task to cite *all* aspects of research being studied. Even within each area that is mentioned in this chapter, an intense and careful search was conducted for appropriate examples from all over the world.[1] Cross-cultural activities are booming, judging by the enormous number of studies in books and journals. New interest in cross-cultural research is rampant, not only in the laboratory but also in the field. This, of course, is a good turn of events for developmental cross-cultural psychology. Laboratory research has an important place in the sciences, but with field work in different environments, more provocative dimensions are added. While research may find answers to existing questions, it also may raise new queries. Cross-cultural research is an exciting branch of science with new actions and interactions that deal with already familiar societies and investigate rarely visited cultures. It is exhilarating not only to find obvious differences between the groups but also to observe similarities in the behavior of individuals from different cultures and countries. This is the underlying and continuously driving force that spurs on the uninterrupted quest to find universalities, not only in the developmental stages set forth by Piaget, among others, but also in areas of socialization and value systems (see Graubert & Adler, 1981).

A case in point is the trend toward modernization in many of the industrialized nations, in which men and women both have opportunities to contribute to the upkeep of the household. This is the reason why Whiting and Edwards (1973) found that there is a minimum of sex differences in the behavior among young children in these societies. Especially in the modern countries, boys and girls are dressed alike and participate in the same games and sports activities. However Adler (1981) noticed that the pictures by European and North American girls showed a greater androgynous effect than did the pictures by the boys from the same countries. The boys' drawings were more stereotyped. With the increase of women seeking and receiving equality in work and pay, stereotypical differences may diminish in children's drawings in the future.

To discover the explanations or to test theories and come up with new hypotheses to be tested next time around—that is the life of a research psychologist! Most of the topics of research fall into specific categories. Some can be studied in the laboratory, while field work is a better approach for special areas that are in urgent need of local investigation. With better communication between the traditional cultures and societies and the modern countries and communities, the concern for prevailing conditions becomes more acute. It is necessary to achieve a better understanding not only of the local occurrences but also of the historical and economic background as well. Greater compassion and concerted regard are needed to deal with existing widespread conditions. It is a sorrowful fact that there are too many sick and sad children in this world, rather than a prevalence of healthy and happy ones. More frequent interactions and interpretations of the findings will lead to better feedback and improved social relationships.

This chapter has as its scope to survey the status of cross-cultural developmental psychology. It represents a summary of current research, theories, and practices.

[1] At the time of the writing of this chapter "Developmental Psychology," Volume 4, *Handbook of Cross-Cultural Psychology,* H. C. Triandis, Ed., was still in press and could not serve as a reference work.

Hopefully it will promote better assessment of the development of behavior in a variety of social situations and in different environmental settings in terms of ecology and culture.

REFERENCES

ACHAR, S. T., & YANKAUER, A. Studies on the birth weight of South Indian infants. *Indian Journal of Child Health,* 1962, *11,* 157–167.

ADLER, L. L. A plea for interdisciplinary cross-cultural research: Some introductory remarks. Pp. 1–2 in L. L. Adler (Ed.), *Issues in cross-cultural research* (Vol. 285). New York: Annals of the New York Academy of Sciences, 1977.

ADLER, L. L. The effects of calm and emotional behavior on projected social distances: A cross-cultural comparison. *International Journal of Group Tensions,* 1978, *8* (Nos. 1, 2), 49–63.

ADLER, L. L. Children's drawings as an indicator of individual preferences reflecting group values: A programmatic study. In L. L. Adler (Ed.), *Cross-cultural research at issue.* New York: Academic Press, 1981.

BANDURA, A. *Principles of behavior modification.* New York: Holt, Rinehart & Winston, 1969.

BANDURA, A., & WALTERS, R. H. *Social learning and personality.* New York: Holt, Rinehart & Winston, 1963.

BAYLEY, N. *Manual for the Bayley scales of infant development.* New York: Psychological Corporation, 1969.

BARRY, H., III, BACON, M. K., & CHILD, I. L. Definitions, ratings and bibliographic sources of child-training practices of 110 cultures. Pp. 293–331 in C. S. Ford (Ed.), *Cross-cultural approaches.* New Haven, Conn.: HRAF Press, 1967.

BERRY, J. W. Ecology, perceptual development and the Müller-Lyer illusion. *British Journal of Psychology,* 1968, *59,* 205–210.

BERRY, J. W. Radical cultural relativism and the concept of intelligence. Pp. 225–229 in J. W. Berry & P. Dasen (Eds.), *Culture and cognition.* London: Methuen, 1974.

BERRY, J. W. Introduction to methodology. Pp. 1–28 in H. C. Triandis & J. W. Berry (Eds.), *Handbook of cross-cultural psychology* (Vol. 2). Boston: Allyn & Bacon, 1980.

BETTELHEIM, B. *The children of the dream.* New York: Macmillan, 1969

BRONFENBRENNER, U. *Two worlds of childhood: U.S. and U.S.S.R.* New York: Clarion, 1970.

BRONFENBRENNER, U. Contexts of child rearing: Problems and prospects. *The American Psychologist,* 1979, *34* (No. 10), 844–850.

BROWN, R. *Social Psychology.* New York: Free Press, 1965.

BRUNSWIK, E. *Perception and the representative design of psychological experiments.* Berkeley: University of California Press, 1956.

BURTON, R. V. Cross-sex identity in Barbados. *Developmental Psychology,* 1972, *6*(No. 3), 365–374.

CARMICHAEL, L. (Ed.). *Manual of child psychology.* New York: John Wiley, 1946.

CAUDILL, W., & WEINSTEIN, H. Maternal care and infant behavior in Japan and America. *Psychiatry,* 1969, *32,* 12–43.

CAWTE, J. *Medicine is the law.* Honolulu: University Press of Hawaii, 1974.

CHOMSKY, N. *Language and mind.* New York: Harcourt Brace Jovanovich, 1968.

CIBOROWSKI, T. J. Cultural and cognitive discontinuities of school and home: Remedialism revisited. In D. McElwain & G. Kearney (Eds.), *Aboriginal cognition.* Atlantic Highlands, N.J.: Humanities Press, 1976.

CIBOROWSKI, T. J. Cross-cultural aspects of cognitive functioning: Culture and knowledge. Pp. 101–116 in A. J. Marsella, R. G. Tharp, & T. J. Ciborowski (Eds.), *Perspectives on cross-cultural psychology.* New York: Academic Press, 1979.

COLE, M., GAY, J., GLICK, J. A., & SHARP, D. W. *The cultural context of learning and thinking.* New York: Basic Books, 1971.

COLE, M., & SCRIBNER, S. *Culture and thought.* New York: John Wiley, 1974.

DASEN, P. R. (Ed.). *Piagetian psychology: Cross-cultural contributions.* New York: Gardner Press, 1977.

DAWSON, J.L.M. Attitude change and conflict among Australian aborigines. *Australian Journal of Psychology,* 1969a, *21,* 101–116.

DAWSON, J.L.M. Theoretical and research base of bio-social psychology. *University of Hong Kong Supplement to the Gazette*, 1969b, *16*, 1–10.

DENMARK, F. L. *What Sigmund Freud did not know about boys and girls.* Paper presented at the Convocation at St. Olaf College, North Field, Minn., January 1977.

DENMARK, F. L., & WATERS, A. *The male and female in children's readers: A cross-cultural analysis.* Paper presented at the 3rd International Congress of the International Association for Cross-Cultural Psychology, Tilburg, Holland, July 1976.

DRAGUNS, J. G. Culture and personality. In A. J. Marsella, R. G. Tharp, & T. J. Ciborowski (Eds.), *Perspectives on cross-cultural psychology.* New York: Academic Press, 1979.

ENDLEMAN, R. Familistic social change on the Israeli kibbutz. Pp. 605–611 in L. L. Adler (Ed.), *Issues in cross-cultural research.* New York: Annals of the New York Academy of Sciences, 1977.

ERIKSON, E. *Childhood and society.* New York: W. W. Norton & Co., Inc. 1950.

FREEDMAN, D. G. Genetic influences on development of behavior. Pp. 208–233 in G.B.A. Stoelinge & J. J. Van der Werff Ten Bosch (Eds.), *Normal and abnormal development of behavior.* Leiden, Holland: Leiden University Press, 1971.

FRIJDA, N. H., & JAHODA, G. On the scope and methods of cross-cultural research. *International Journal of Psychology*, 1966, *1*, 110–127.

GARCIA-CHAFARDET, I. Effects of sexist policies on the process of development. *International Journal of Group Tensions*, 1978, *8* (Nos. 1, 2), 98–111.

GIBSON, E. J. *Principles of perceptual learning and development.* Englewood Cliffs, N.J.: Prentice-Hall, 1969.

GRAUBERT, J. G., & ADLER, L. L. Attitudes toward stigma-related and stigma-free stimuli: A cross-national perspective. In L. L. Adler (Ed.), *Cross-cultural research at issue.* New York: Academic Press, 1981.

GRAVES, P. L. Infant behavior and maternal attitudes: Early sex differences in West Bengal India. *Journal of Cross-Cultural Psychology*, 1978, *9*, 45–80.

GUTHRIE, G. M. A cross-cultural odyssey: Some personal reflections. Pp. 349–368 in A. J. Marsella, R. G. Tharp, & T. J. Ciborowski (Eds.), *Perspectives on cross-cultural psychology.* New York: Academic Press, 1979.

HOFFMAN, M. L. Father absence and conscience development. *Developmental Psychology*, 1971, *4*, 400–405.

HONIG, A. S. Comparison of child-rearing practices in Japan and in the People's Republic of China: A personal view. *International Journal of Group Tensions*, 1978, *8* (Nos. 1, 2), 6–32.

HUDSON, W. The study of the problem of pictorial perception among unacculturated groups. *International Journal of Psychology*, 1967, *2*, 90–107.

INHELDER, B., & PIAGET, J. *The growth of logical thinking from childhood to adolescence.* New York: Basic Books, 1958.

IRWIN, M., SCHAFER, G., & FREIDEN, C. Emic and unfamiliar category sorting of Mano farmers and U.S. undergraduates. *Journal of Cross-Cultural Psychology*, 1974, *5*, 407–423.

IRWIN, O. C. Infant speech: The effect of family occupational status and of age on sound frequency. *Journal of Speech and Hearing Disorders*, 1948, *13*, 320–323.

JAHODA, G. Retinal pigmentation, illusion susceptibility and space perception. *International Journal of Psychology*, 1971, *6*, 199–208.

JAHODA, G. Retinal pigmentation and space perception: A failure to replicate. *Journal of Social Psychology*, 1975, *97*, 133–134.

JONES, E. Review of *Sex and repression in savage society* by B. Malinowski. *International Journal of Psycho-Analysis*, 1928, *4*, 364–374.

KAGAN, S., & CARLSON, H. Development of adaptive assertiveness in Mexican and United States children. *Developmental Psychology*, 1975, *11*, 71–78.

KILBRIDE, J. E. *The African precocity issue: Recent findings from Uganda.* Paper presented at the 7th Annual Meeting of the Society for Cross-Cultural Research. New Haven, Conn., February 24, 1978. (Abstract in the *SCCR Newsletter*, 1978, *6* [No. 1], 10.)

KILBRIDE P. L., & LEIBOWITZ, H. W. The Ponzo illusion among the Baganda of Uganda. Pp. 408–417 in L. L. Adler (Ed.), *Issues in cross-cultural research* (Vol. 285). New York: Annals of the New York Academy of Sciences, 1977.

KILBRIDE, P. L., & LEIBOWITZ, H. W. The Ponzo illusion among the Baganda; Implications for ecological and perceptual theory. In L. L. Adler (Ed.), *Cross-cultural research at issue.* New York: Academic Press, 1981.

KIRK, L. Role of nonverbal maternal behavior in the learning process. In L. L. Adler (Ed.), *Cross-cultural research at issue.* New York: Academic Press, 1981.

KOHLBERG, L. *Stages in the development of moral thought and action.* New York: Holt, Rinehart & Winston, 1969.

KUMAR, U. The functional and the dysfunctional role of interpersonal communication patterns of the Hindu joint family in India. *International Journal of Group Tensions*, 1978, *8* (Nos. 1, 2), 120–129.

Laboratory of Comparative Human Cognition, The. Cross-cultural psychology's challenge to our ideas of children and development. *American Psychologist*, 1979, *34* (No. 10), 827–833.

LENNEBERG, E. H. *Biological foundations of language.* New York: John Wiley, 1967.

LEVINE, R. A. *Dreams and deeds.* Chicago: University of Chicago Press, 1966.

LEVINE, R. A., & LEVINE, B. B. Nyansongo: A Gusii community in Kenya. In B. B. Whiting (Ed.), *Six cultures: Studies of child rearing.* New York: John Wiley, 1963.

LEWIS, M. State as an infant-environmental interaction: An analysis of mother-infant behavior as a function of sex. *Merrill-Palmer Quarterly*, 1972, *18*, 95–211.

LUSK, D., & LEWIS, M. Mother-infant interaction and infant development among the Wolof of Senegal. *Human Development*, 1972, *15*, 58–69.

MACCOBY, E. E., & JACKLIN, C. N. *The psychology of sex differences.* Stanford, Calif.: Stanford University Press, 1974.

MADSEN, M. C. Cooperative and competitive motivation of children in three Mexican subcultures. *Psychological Reports*, 1967, *20*, 1307–1320.

MALINOWSKI, B. *Sex and repression in savage society.* London: Kegan Paul, 1927.

MARMORALE, A. M., & BROWN, F. Constancy of WISC IQs of Puerto Rican, White and Black children. In L. L. Adler (Ed.), *Cross-cultural research at issue.* New York: Academic Press, 1981.

MATARAZZO, J. D. *Wechsler's measurement and appraisal of adult intelligence* (5th ed.). Baltimore, Md.: Williams & Wilkins, 1972.

McCLELLAND, D. C. *Motivational trends in society.* New York: General Learning Press, 1971.

MEAD, M. Comments from an anthropologist. Pp. 501–504 in L. L. Adler (Ed.), *Issues in cross-cultural research* (Vol. 285). New York: Annals of the New York Academy of Sciences, 1977.

MEAD, M., & MACGREGOR, F. C. *Growth and culture.* New York: Putnam's, 1951.

MEREDITH, H. V. Body size of contemporary groups of eight-year-old children studied in different parts of the world. *Monographs of the Society for Research in Child Development*, 1969, *34* (No. 1).

MEREDITH, H. V. Body size of contemporary groups of one-year-old infants studied in different parts of the world. *Child Development*, 1970, *41*, 551–600.

MUNDY-CASTLE, A. Pictorial depth perception in Ghanain children. *International Journal of Psychology*, 1966, *1*, 290–300.

MUNROE, R. L., & MUNROE, R. H. *Cross-cultural human development.* Monterey, Calif.: Brooks/Cole, 1975.

PIAGET, J. *The moral judgment of the child.* New York: The Free Press, 1965.

PIAGET, J. Need and significance of cross-cultural studies in genetic psychology. In J. W. Berry & P. R. Dasen (Eds.), *Culture and cognition: Readings in cross-cultural psychology.* London: Methuen, *1974.*

PRICE-WILLIAMS, D. R., GORDON, W., & RAMIREZ, M., III. Skill and conservation. *Developmental Psychology*, 1969, *1*, 769.

RHEINGOLD, H. L. The measurement of maternal care. *Child Development*, 1960, *31*, 565–575.

RHEINGOLD, H. L. The effect of environmental stimulation upon social and exploratory behavior in the human infant. Pp. 143–171 in B. M. Foss (Ed.), *Determinants of infant behavior* (Vol. 1). New York: John Wiley, 1961.

RICCIUTI, H. N. Malnutrition, learning and intellectual development: Research and remediation. Pp. 237–253 in F. F. Korton, S. W. Cook, & J. I. Lacey (Eds.), *Psychology and the problem of society.* Washington, D.C.: American Psychological Association, 1970.

ROHNER, R. P. *They love me, they love me not: A study of the world-wide effects of parental acceptance and rejection.* New Haven, Conn.: HRAF Press, 1975.

SAPIR, E. *Language: An introduction to the study of speech.* New York: Harvest Books, 1949. (Originally published by Harcourt Brace and Co., 1921.)

SCHMIDT, H.-D. *Allgemeine Entwicklungs-Psychologie.* Berlin, DDR: VEB Deutscher Verlag der Wissenschaft, 1978.

SEGALL, M. H. *Human behavior and public policy: A political psychology.* Elmsford, N.Y.: Pergamon Press, 1976.

SEGALL, M. H. *Cross-cultural psychology: Human behavior in global perspective.* Monterey, Calif.: Brooks/Cole, 1979.

SEGALL, M., CAMPBELL, D. T., & HERSKOVITS, M. *The influence of culture on visual perception.* Indianapolis: Bobbs-Merrill, 1966.

SERVIN, L., O'LEARY, K., KENT, R., & TONICK, I. A comparison of teacher response to the pre-academic and problem behavior of boys and girls. *Child Development,* 1973, *44,* 796–804.

SHAPIRA, A. Developmental differences in competitive behavior of kibbutz and city children in Israel. *Journal of Social Psychology,* 1976, *98,* 19–26.

SHARP, D., COLE, M., & LAVE, C. Cognitive consequences of education. *Monographs of the Society for Research in Child Development,* 1979, *44* (Serial No. 178), 1–2.

SHIRAI, T. *Television problems of preschool children in Japan.* Paper presented at the 38th Annual Convention of the International Council of Psychologists, Bergen, Norway, June 30, 1980.

SHIRAI, T. *Three-country research: In Japan, the Philippines and Taiwan.* In progress.

SIDOROWICZ, L. S., & LUNNEY, G. S. Baby X revisited. *Sex Roles,* 1980, *6* (No. 1), 67–72.

SPIRES, R. C., & ROBIN, M. W. Father absence cross-culturally: A review of the literature. In L. L. Adler (Ed.), *Cross-cultural research at issue.* New York: Academic Press, 1981.

SUPER, C. M. *Differences in the care of male and female infants: Data from non-American samples.* Worcester, Mass.: Clark University (Mimeograph), October 1977.

SVENDSEN, D. Testresultster og sosial bakgrunn ved skolestart. *Norisk Pedagogisk Tidskrift,* 1978, *62* (No. 9), 334–339.

SVENDSEN, D. *School problems and family background: A Norwegian follow-up study.* Paper presented at the 38th Annual Convention of the International Council of Psychologists, Bergen, Norway, July 1, 1980.

SVENDSEN, D., & KINGE, F. O. Work and disability at the age of 30 years. *Scandinavian Journal of Social Medicine,* 1979, *7,* 119–126.

TANNER, J. M. *Education and physical growth.* New York: International Universities Press, 1961.

TRIANDIS, H. C., MALPASS, R. S., & DAVIDSON, A. R. Cross-cultural psychology. Pp. 1–84 in *Biennial Review of Anthropology.* Palo Alto: Annual Reviews, Inc., 1971.

VASSAF, G. Y. H. *Preschool education in Turkey: The failings of a non-community approach.* Paper presented at the International Council of Psychologists Meeting, in Conjunction of the 22nd International Congress of Psychology, Leipzig, D.D.R., July 9, 1980.

WERNER, E. E. *Cross-cultural child development: A view from the planet earth.* Monterey, Calif.: Brooks/Cole, 1979.

WERNER, H. *Comparative psychology of mental development.* E. B. Garside, trans. New York: International Universities Press, 1948.

WHITE, K. M. & SPEISMAN, J. C. *Adolescence.* Monterey, Calif.: Brooks/Cole, 1977.

WHITING, B. B., & EDWARDS, C. P. A cross-cultural analysis of sex differences in the behavior of children aged three through eleven. *Journal of Social Psychology,* 1973, *91,* 171–188.

WHITING, B. B., & WHITING, J. W. M. *Children of six cultures: A psychocultural analysis.* Cambridge, Mass.: Harvard University Press, 1975.

WHITING, J. W. M. Methods and problems in cross-cultural research. Pp. 693–728 in G. Lindzey & E. Aronson (Eds.), *The handbook of social psychology* (Vol. 2) (2nd ed.). Reading, Mass.: Addison-Wesley, 1968.

WHITING, J. W. M., KLUCKHOHN, F., & ANTHONY, A. S. The function of male initiation ceremonies at puberty. Pp. 359–370 in E. E. Maccoby, T. Newcomb, & E. Hartley (Eds.), *Readings in social psychology.* New York: Holt, Rinehart & Winston, 1958.

WITKIN, H. A., OLTMAN, P. K., RASKIN, E., & KARP, S. A. *A manual for the embedded figure test.* Palo Alto, Calif.: Consulting Psychologists Press, 1971.

WHORF, B. L. *Language, thought and reality: Selected writings.* Cambridge, Mass.: Technology Press, 1956.

ZAÏDI, S. M. H. Values expressed in Nigerian children's drawings. *International Journal of Psychology,* 1979, *14,* 163–169.

7

Longitudinal Methods

K. WARNER SCHAIE
CHRISTOPHER HERTZOG

INTRODUCTION

Investigators studying problems in the developmental sciences, particularly developmental psychologists, have long felt that the explication of lawful relations in developmental processes of necessity requires observing the same organisms over that period of time during which developmental phenomena of interest are likely to occur. However because most developmental phenomena of interest in humans occur relatively slowly (with the exception of early infancy and the period prior to death in old age), it is not generally practical for developmental research designs to follow subjects over the entire developmental period. Thus a variety of developmental research designs have been devised to finesse the problem by assuming that some estimate of developmental change from an experimental or quasi-experimental design may be substituted for the long-term observation. Many investigators have tried to model developmental phenomena with more economical designs, whether by experimental induction of change, by retrospective analysis, or by comparisons of individuals of differing developmental levels at one point in time. These more economical developmental designs all have merit depending upon whether the assumptions necessary to apply the design are accurate and whether the design is best suited for the specific questions to be asked. It is often the case that the status of these designs as quasi-experiments is ill defined and that the enabling assumptions have not been explicitly formulated.

It is the purpose of this chapter to discuss three topics

involved in the correct understanding and application of research design method to the study of developmental processes. The first topic places the various developmental methods within the context of the broad group of quasi-experimental designs (Campbell & Stanley, 1967) useful in developmental research. The second topic concerns explication of the interdependence of developmental theory and selection of the best suited research designs, such that data collection and analysis are properly derived from theory and thus capable of testing theory-derived hypotheses. The third topic involves the description of statistical models and estimating techniques currently available for the modeling of developmental processes. Here special emphasis will be given to the recently developed methods permitting the application of factor analysis and linear structural equation systems to developmental data.

As will become clear upon reading this chapter, these three topics are interrelated in many ways and a number of different approaches could be chosen for their presentation. We begin with a discussion of the relation between developmental theory and longitudinal methods, including a set of definitions and principles, a discussion of the advantages and disadvantages of the longitudinal methods, and some guidelines for the suitability of alternate theoretical models in attaining parsimonious design choices. We next explicate the types of quasi-experimental designs common in developmental psychology. In this context we consider the methodological problems intrinsic to the common developmental designs, present expanded sequential strategies to reduce limitations of the more traditional developmental designs, consider the remaining confounds and their impact, and assess the applicability of proposals for the simultaneous estimation of confounded parameters coming from sociological research. The final section on statistical techniques for lon-

Preparation of this chapter was greatly facilitated by research support of the first author from the National Institute of Aging (AG–480) and a postdoctoral fellowship support for the second author, also from the National Institute of Aging (AG–5150).

gitudinal analysis briefly highlights methods for the test of hypotheses concerning means and covariance structures. Space limitations prevent us from elaborating on these methods in any detail, but the interested reader is directed to the relevant reference materials.

DEVELOPMENTAL THEORY AND LONGITUDINAL METHODS

Definition and Principles

In general, the goal of longitudinal methods in developmental psychology is to obtain valid measures of developmental change for descriptive and explanatory purposes. This section will attempt to link the application of longitudinal methods with underlying developmental theory by highlighting current views of development as a time-dependent process, indicating alternate models of development, and offering some definitions of what is or is not included in the term "longitudinal methods."

Development as a Time Dependent Process. Although development consists of intraindividual change over time, not all such change should, in principle, be developmental; indeed, there has been some controversy as to the attributes which would enable one to posit behavioral change as truly *developmental* (cf. Baer, 1970; Baltes & Nesselroade, 1979; Baltes & Willis, 1977; Reese & Overton, 1970). *Organismic* conceptions of development demand that developmental change have the attributes of universality, fixed sequentiality, structural and qualitative transformations and orientation toward an end state (see McCall, 1977, or Wohlwill, 1973 as representatives of this position). Such *strong* conception of development is contrasted by the operant position which might be characterized as a *weak* model. Here in its extreme form any reliably observed form of behavior change might be viewed as development (cf. Baer, 1970; Bandura, 1971). Generally, however, most developmental researchers would agree with Baltes and Nesselroade (1979) that there are some minimal criteria needed to label change as being developmental. They suggest "one needs a theory-based or empirically derived behavior change process on the descriptive level ... [and] ... the use of historical time-ordered paradigms of influences for the explanation of developmental change" (p. 15).

We may start then with Kessen's (1960) formulation that "a characteristic is said to be developmental if it can be related to age in an orderly way" (p. 36), or $B = f(A)$. Kessen also specified that a response in a developmental model should be seen generally as a function of age as well as a special population and an environment. In earlier work (Schaie, 1965, 1973) we have explicated this expanded notion by a model where $B = f[A,C,T]$. It should be noticed that the three items involved are strictly *descriptive* parameters. Their definition implies that *age* [A] will refer to the number of time units elapsed between the birth (entrance into the environment) of the organism and the point in time at which the dependent variable is measured. The special population in this expanded model is generally defined as *cohort* [C], which

implies the total population of individuals entering the specified environment at the same point or interval in time.[1] Environment is for descriptive purposes more precisely defined by the term *time of measurement* [T] (equivalent to the term *period* in the sociological literature)—that is, the point in time at which the response of interest is actually recorded.

The critical problem in working with the model $B = f[A,C,T]$ is that although the three effects are conceptually independent, the three variables are in fact linearly dependent. If we define C by birth year, then $T = C + A$; if year of birth and age are known, then the current year may be specified with complete certainty. As we shall see, the research designs to be discussed in this chapter aid in the estimation of these three effects, but they do not eliminate the indeterminacy due to the linear dependence except by making assumptions about the presence or absence of some of the effects in question. Thus application of the methods described here may, in principle, disentangle the effects of A, C, and T (although the validity of the approach depends directly on the veracity of the assumptions which must be made to enable estimation of the various effects).

It cannot be emphasized enough that a descriptive model based on these methods can do nothing more than identify those effects which are *correlated* with A, C, or T, independent of other parameters. Given an organismic conception of development, we cannot conclude that effects associated with A, and not C or T, represent developmental change in the strong sense referred to above unless there are theoretically sound justifications and additional evidence for concluding that the age-correlated change is truly representing ontogenetic development. From a life-span perspective the justification for inferring ontogenetic change from significant A effects might be generally stronger in child development than in adult development, although this position would be vigorously debated by child psychologists and gerontologists alike. In any case one cannot conclude that A effects imply inevitably the existence of ontogenetic change. For example a study of attitudes and life-satisfaction after age 65 would probably be able to isolate age-correlated change, common to a range of cohorts and times of measurement. Yet such change might not necessarily be a function of ontogenetic development since it could also be specific to retirement and related to A only by virtue of the fixed retirement age prevalent in the society over the period of measurement. As such the changes might well be due to an age-correlated but event- or sequence-relevant phenomenon (Baltes & Willis, 1977).

It follows then that developmental analysis only begins with the parametric description of age-correlated change, and understanding of development also requires an attempt to provide explanations of behavioral development from a process-oriented perspective. A process-oriented explanation of development requires specification of antecedent-consequent relationships at a causal

[1] It should be noted that cohort can also be defined by entry into a common environment by individuals of different ages, e.g., a college class or the initial work force of a new factory. Restrictions regarding the nature of the population and latitude in defining the boundaries of a given cohort will depend upon the special assumptions appropriate to the problem being investigated (see also Rosow, 1978).

level. The specification and testing of alternative process-oriented models of behavioral development is obviously a principal goal of developmental psychology and yet is its most difficult task, since developmental phenomena are generally produced by complex interactions among a set of underlying processes which may produce a range of developmental phenotypes depending upon the environmental milieu in which their genotypes operate. Thus validation of process-oriented models of development must inevitably require the analysis of a multivariate system of variables measuring the behavioral domain of interest and the putative processes determining developmental change in this domain (Baltes & Nesselroade, 1973; Nesselroade, 1977).

It is rather implausible to assume that behavioral development could be encapsulated in any univariate causal model. Much of our discussion of longitudinal methods must then focus on the design and analysis of behavioral investigations from a multivariate perspective as it affects measurement of relevant constructs and specification of causal relations among these constructs.

In order to begin to provide an accurate descriptive and explanatory account of developmental phenomena, we must begin by specifying a set of competing models which account for these phenomena. These models must obviously be directed toward an explanation of change within individuals (intraindividual change), as emphasized by most developmental theorists (e.g., Baltes & Nesselroade, 1979; Wohlwill, 1973). The models must also allow for differences among individuals at any given point in time (interindividual differences) and interindividual differences in the course of intraindividual change (see Baltes & Nesselroade, 1979; Baltes & Willis, 1977). The power of such models will be directly related to their ability to account for systematic age-related intraindividual change *and* interindividual differences in intraindividual change on the basis of a set of causal processes varying between individuals. When all is said and done, we are concerned with deriving estimates for populations and their subtypes, as well as definitions of the range within which intraindividual variability about such parameters may be found (for further discussion of these issues see Baltes & Nesselroade, 1979; Buss, 1974).

Models of Development. The selection of a longitudinal design for a developmental study depends critically upon the developmental model believed applicable to the phenomenon (Schaie, 1973). Thus it is important to consider the (often implicit) developmental models used by behavioral scientists and their salient characteristics vis-à-vis design selection.

A distinction must first be drawn between developmental models implying either quantitative or qualitative change. Quantitative change implies continuous incremental or decremental change in some measures of behavior, given the assumption that the underlying processes determining the behavior remain fixed or static. Quantitative models of development need not be linear (and might even be recursive); the assumption of linearity and unidirectionality is usually made only as a simplifying convenience for data analysis. The critical factor in a quantitative model is that development is represented only in changes in the performance level on

some behavioral scale. By contrast qualitative change is often considered to require discrete shifts from one stage to another (e.g., the Piagetian cognitive stages); qualitative developmental change implies that behavior at a later stage of development cannot be accounted for as a simple function of behavior at an earlier state of development—rather some structural metamorphosis among determining processes is hypothesized to have produced a new function relating process to behavior (see Wohlwill, 1973, for a useful account of these concepts and of criteria for inferring qualitative change).

Developmental models are not necessarily exclusively quantitative or qualitative in nature since in qualitative models continuous changes are said to occur within a given stage until a threshold level is reached, at which point the transformation to the next stage occurs. As pointed out by Baltes and Nesselroade (1970, 1973), the distinction between qualitative and quantitative developmental change is critical in determining the adequacy of longitudinal methods in a given application. It makes little sense to make purely quantitative comparisons of behavior on a given performance measure at two different levels of development if qualitative change has occurred because the likelihood is high that qualitative change will impose a qualitative difference in the relationship of the behavioral scale to the underlying constructs the scale supposedly measures.

If we expect qualitative differences in antecedent-consequent relationships due to development, our analysis must be designed concomitantly to characterize the nature of the qualitative change and to estimate the extent of quantitative change over the age range where the process-behavior relationships may be assumed static and thus characterized as a continuous quantitative function. Whether our model is quantitative or qualitative, it is obvious that the ages of development studied in our model will have implications as to the kind of data needed for full description of the developmental process. With respect to development during childhood, it is usually true that, where quantitative models are sufficient to account for a developmental phenomenon, an *incremental* model will fit most variables. The incremental model implies monotonic increases in performance level on a behavioral scale, although the function describing the behavioral increment may not be linear but rather a slowly decelerating growth rate and young adult asymptote as specified by a Gompertzian growth curve. Whether a continuous or stage model is assumed to apply to childhood development, interindividual differences about the normative developmental rates and the temporal latitude of stages are generally assumed to be narrow.

Studies of adult development have, for the most part, implicitly assumed an *irreversible decrement* model. This model, common to analyses in areas such as intelligence, creativity, and achievement, assumes that maximal level of function is reached in young adulthood followed by a linearly accelerating and irreversible decline. The irreversible decrement model implicitly assumes that adult development may be characterized by a purely quantitative model of decline secondary to the aging process; it generally emphasizes the process of biological decrement with aging (Baltes & Willis, 1977; Schaie, 1973). Another implicit specification of the irreversible decrement model is that age changes occur as a function of maturational (ontogenetic) events which are affected but slightly by environmental variation.

Research in adult psychological development has been dominated by the irreversible decrement model, to the exclusion of other models of potential explanatory power (Baltes & Willis, 1977; Barton, Plemons, Willis, & Baltes, 1975; Labouvie-Vief, 1977; Labouvie-Vief & Chandler, 1978). It has generally been the case that age-correlated effects are assumed to be evidence of irreversible decrement, even in the absence of corroborative evidence that processes other than biological decrement due to aging cannot account for the age-correlated effects. The irreversible decrement model is a valid model for some psychological processes, most notably those functions which are directly related to the biological integrity of the central nervous system; however, we must echo the concerns of Baltes and Willis (1977) and others that research in adult psychological development should not axiomatically postulate the irreversible decrement model as a theoretical basis for all research questions of interest.

Given the position that alternative models for adult psychological development other than the irreversible decrement model should be developed and tested, what alternative models might be specified? Two simple alternatives (Schaie, 1973) are the *adult stability* and the *decrement with compensation* models. The adult stability model postulates that once an adult asymptote is reached, behavior remains stable throughout the remaining life span. However cyclical changes might still occur about an optimal level as the result of both external and internal events (cf. Goulet, Hay, & Barclay, 1974; Schaie, 1973). The stability model has been assumed to hold in the study of personality traits, and it may also fit components of cognitive development such as crystallized intelligence.

The decrement with compensation model, increasingly popular as a result of gerontological intervention studies, expects decline past maturity but argues that environmental intervention may compensate for maturationally programmed deficits. This model might fit concepts such as fluid intelligence or measures of performance where decline is to be expected due to correlated decremental biological events but where environmental input might have significant moderating effects. An excellent example in the area of physiology is the research by DeVries (1974) which suggests that programmed exercise for the elderly may ameliorate muscular and cardiovascular decline previously assumed to be irreversible.

Another important model for adult development is the *sequence-relevant* model (Baltes & Willis, 1977), which posits that age-correlated change is specific to a programmed sequence of processes which are correlated with age but not isomorphic with ontogenetic change—that is, a sequence of processes which are not inevitably associated with the aging process. One of the implications of the sequence-relevant model is that developmental psychologists must differentiate normative from nonnormative age change (cf. Baltes & Nesselroade, 1979), which can be an extremely difficult theoretical problem. Nevertheless the distinction of sequence-relevant change from age-relevant change is an important one for it is quite possible that effects which have been

assumed to be a function of ontogenetic decline might be better described by an adult stability model coupled with a probabilistic occurrence of sequence-relevant change. An example would be the terminal decline or terminal drop hypothesis of Riegel and others (e.g., Riegel & Riegel, 1972; Siegler, 1975) which posits stability of adult intelligence until impending death when physiological pathology compromises the functional efficiency of the nervous system.

Finally we must recognize that no one developmental model need be valid for all individuals. One of the characteristics of human development is the ever-increasing range of individual differences; thus developmental psychologists need to specify models which take into account the wide variety of multidimensional and multidirectional possibilities for patterns of developmental change. It is unlikely that a life-span–oriented approach can, for any variable system, sufficiently account for development with a single developmental model. Alternate patterns of change are highly likely for the stages of late maturation, adulthood, and senescence.

Longitudinal Methods. The term *longitudinal methods* has been used in a variety of ways. Hindley (1972), for example, claims that "there is no hard and fast definition of what constitutes a longitudinal study" (p. 23), although Baltes and Nesselroade (1979) contend that one requirement of a longitudinal inquiry must be that "the entity under investigation is observed repeatedly and evolves over time" (p. 4). For our purposes, however, we would like to include within the general category of longitudinal methods at least that variant of a longitudinal study which does not involve repeated measurement of the same individual—namely, sampling procedures in which a cohort is observed repeatedly by means of successive random samples from the parent population.

Longitudinal methods traditionally involve age-based parametric models in which chronological age is the predictor variable of central importance. However it would be quite feasible to include designs which might address hypotheses where there is a directional time sequence, even one which is uncorrelated with chronological age. Indeed such designs might well be required in order to address questions as to the cross-cultural congruence of universal developmental stages. Thus our discussion of longitudinal methods will include designs which are not technically "longitudinal" by the stricter criteria of others; we consider designs which are longitudinal only in the sense that they model age-correlated effects by sampling across a sequence of points.

In the past, longitudinal methods have been utilized primarily for the purpose of describing developmental phenomena, and much of our discussion of longitudinal method focuses on descriptive applications. However these methods can be readily applied to explanation and intervention by specifying prediction systems of process variables or introducing design extensions which can handle treatment effects (e.g., Labouvie, 1974, 1978).

Advantages of Longitudinal Methods

The primary advantage of the longitudinal methods, of course, is the fact that they emphasize intraindividual change (IAC) while cross-sectional approaches can make statements only about interindividual variability (IEV). Even in the case where independent samples are studied over time from a given cohort, the emphasis is then on change within the populations examined rather than upon differences between samples possibly coming from noncomparable populations. Obviously most longitudinal approaches permit analyses of IEV in addition to IAC.

Following Baltes and Nesselroade (1979) we can identify five distinct rationales for longitudinal studies of behavioral development. Of these, three involve developmental descriptions while the other two are explanatory in nature. As indicated previously, the first rationale is concerned with the *direct identification of IAC*. Such change can be quantitative and continuous, or it can involve transformation of one behavior to another or changes in the patterns of observed variables as they measure theoretical constructs. Observations based on a single occasion are simply not appropriate for this purpose. To be explicit, if cross-sectional data are to be used to estimate IAC, the assumptions to be met would include that (1) subjects must be matched across age levels, (2) different-aged subjects must come from the same parent population at birth, and (3) different-aged subjects must have experienced identical life histories. Such assumptions cannot be met in human studies.

The second rationale concerns the direct *identification of IEV in IAC*—that is, we are here interested in the degree of variability displaced by different individuals in their behavioral course over time. Examination of similarities and differences in developmental patterns requires the availability of measures of longitudinal change *within* individuals. Unless such data are available, it is not possible to answer the question of whether or not group parameters are characteristic of the development of any individual. Of course the valuable hypothesis-generating source of single-subject research depends upon longitudinal analyses (cf. Shontz, 1976).

Third, longitudinal data permit the *analysis of interrelations among IAC* within a multivariate behavioral domain of variables. Only when several individual behaviors have been followed over time is it then possible to discover constancy and change of the entire organism, particularly where a wholistic or structural approach is taken to human development (e.g., Riegel & Rosenwald, 1975). Longitudinal studies alone, by means of multiple observations over time, permit the discovery of structural relations among changes in behavior. Such approaches are obviously essential for the meaningful identification of systems and progressive differentiation processes as essential concepts in the understanding of human growth and development (cf. Lund, 1978; Urban, 1978).

The fourth rationale for longitudinal studies involves the *analysis of determinants of IAC*. Here we are concerned with the identification of time-ordered antecedents and consequents as necessary, albeit not sufficient, conditions for causal inference. Longitudinal data alone can provide the necessary data when the causal process involves discontinuity (e.g., sleeper effects), is multidirectional, or contains a multivariate pattern of influences (cf. Baltes, Reese, & Nesselroade, 1977; Heise, 1975).

Fifth and finally, longitudinal studies permit the *analysis of IEV in the determinants of IAC*. What is at issue here is the fact that many individuals can show similar patterns in intraindividual change which may be determined by different change processes. This may be the case for persons at different levels in the range of talent or other personality attributes. But interindividual differences in patterns of change may also be due to the operation of alternate combinations of causal sequences.

Importance of Strong Developmental Theory

The inherent confounds implicit in the longitudinal methods require strong, clearly specified developmental theories in order to generate meaningful hypotheses and, in fact, to permit design economies which make certain longitudinal inquiries logistically feasible. Some of the major objections of recent papers critical of Schaie's sequential methods (Adam, 1978; Buss, 1979–1980) are related primarily to the conceptual difficulties an investigator encounters when attempting to apply sequential strategies using a totally atheoretical approach. While we will consider these strategies and their limitations in detail, it should be mentioned here that it is certainly unprofitable for developmental psychologists (or any other scientists) to pursue descriptive paradigms in a theoretical vacuum; such an approach is not merely weak science but highly prone to the "discovery" and perpetuation of misleading inferences.

The critical problem (one which, quite frankly, remains to be satisfactorily solved) is how plausible rival models of development may be tested when confounds inherent in longitudinal methods appear to preclude designs which make the alternative model's assumptions directly falsifiable. The following methods do not resolve this problem; however, we would argue that they provide a method of matching a developmental model to research design in a way which produces valid estimates of hypothesized effects, given that the model is valid and, further, that their assumptions are less restrictive (and more likely to hold true) than the assumptions enabling the simpler, more traditional designs. The developmental psychologist should be acutely sensitive to the fact that the parameter estimates from a chosen design are no more valid than the model assumptions which permit their estimation. There is simply no substitute for an explicitly defined developmental model; even a misspecified model, if explicitly formulated, at least provides a basis for understanding the potential consequences of the misspecified sources of effects.

LONGITUDINAL METHODS AS QUASI-EXPERIMENTAL RESEARCH DESIGN

Multiple Observations with or without Experimental Treatments: Methodological Problems

Internal and External Validity. Because age is a subject attribute which cannot be experimentally assigned (at least not without a time machine), longitudinal studies cannot conform to the rules for true experiments and hence are subject to all the problems inherent in what Campbell and Stanley (1967) term *quasi-experiments*.

These problems may be categorized as either threats to the *internal validity* or the *external validity* of a given quasi-experiment. Internal validity is upheld if the factors analyzed in a given design are truly measures of the hypothesized construct and are not confounded by other factors not explicitly included in the design. External validity defines the limits of valid generalization from the findings of a given study.

Campbell and Stanley (1967) enumerated eight different threats to the internal validity of a pretest-posttest design: effects of history, maturation, testing, instrumentation, statistical regression, mortality, selection, and the selection-maturation interaction. For the developmental psychologist, history and maturation have special meaning above and beyond the internal validity threat posed for a pretest-posttest design. Maturation is quite obviously not a threat in developmental studies but rather the specific variable of interest. The fact that maturation is the primary effect of interest to developmental psychologists does not imply that the measurement of maturational effects is inevitably straightforward; given a specific developmental model, it may be crucial to not merely test the null hypothesis of no maturational effects but rather some explicit alternative hypothesis specifying the direction and magnitude of the expected maturational effect.

Historical effects, on the other hand, are the primary source of internal validity problems for the developmental psychologist. History is directly tied to both cohort and time-of-measurement effects. A cohort, as we have defined it, is a group of individuals born in the same historical period who therefore share the same environmental circumstances at the same point in their maturational sequence. Time-of-measurement effects represent the events which affect all members of the population living at a given period of history. In both cases historical events may modify the range of person-environment interactions and limit the external validity of any internally valid estimate of maturational change. However, as we shall see shortly, historical effects, operating as either cohort or time-of-measurement effects, may threaten the internal validity of designs attempting to measure maturation per se.

Since the traditional longitudinal design is a special case of the pretest-posttest design in that it repeatedly measures the same individuals over time, the other six internal validity threats listed by Campbell and Stanley are important threats to the validity of longitudinal designs as well. The validity threats are discussed in greater detail later, but we now supply their definitions: *Testing* refers to the effects of the measurement process itself, which may be confused with maturational effects. There are two major effects of testing per se—practice and reactivity. The act of testing itself provides practice on the test, which should in general lead to improvements in performance with each new retest. *Reactivity* refers to the possible effects of being tested on subsequent behavior because the subjects react to being tested by behaving differently than had they not been tested. Such effects could also be confused with maturation. *Instrumentation* refers to any differences in the measurement techniques which covary with the measurement occasions. *Statistical regression* refers to the tendency for variables containing measurement error to regress toward their mean from

one occasion to the next. *Mortality* refers to the attrition of subjects from a sample between measurement occasions; it is termed *experimental mortality* so as to include attrition due to biological mortality, morbidity, and other psychological and sociocultural factors. *Selection* refers to the process of obtaining a sample from the population, and the *selection-by-maturation interaction* refers to the possibility that variation in the method of sample selection may produce variation in the maturational effects to be estimated (see also Cook & Campbell, 1975).

In addition to the threats to the internal validity of quasi-experiments, Campbell and Stanley (1967) call attention also to a number of limitations (threats to external validity) with respect to how widely findings from such studies can be generalized. These limitations are concerned with questions regarding the *experimental units,* the extent to which longitudinal data collected on one sample can permit inference to other populations; *experimental settings,* the extent to which findings have cross-situational validity (cf. Scheidt & Schaie, 1978); *treatment variables,* limitations imposed by specific settings of measurement-implicit reinforcement schedules (cf. Birkhill & Schaie, 1975; Schaie & Goulet, 1977); and *measurement variables,* the extent to which task characteristics are appropriate at different developmental stages in a longitudinal study (cf. Schaie, 1977–1978; Sinnott, 1975).

Longitudinal methods as defined in this paper are generally designed to estimate the expanded function $B = f[A,C,T]$ in an economical manner. As discussed previously by many (e.g., Kessen, 1960; Schaie, 1965), developmental psychologists cannot afford to wait a lifetime to produce answers to the research questions that interest them. The problem is particularly acute for life-span studies of human development, where explication of A, C, and T parameters over a wide range of C and T values would require the impossible: that the experimenter outlive his or her subjects by at least one (or more) lifetimes! Hence one needs designs which compromise the conflicting goals of maximal external validity over possible variables in A, C, and T and minimal investment of time in data collection.

The most economical design in terms of time investment is the simple *cross-sectional* design, which samples a range of individuals of varying chronological ages at a single point in time. In the simple cross-sectional design, too much may have been given up in the name of economy since the effect of A is completely confounded with C (cf. Schaie, 1965). Thus the estimates of C obtained from the cross-sectional design are internally invalid unless the strong assumption of no effects for A may be made (Baltes, 1968; Kuhlen, 1963; Schaie, 1965, 1973, 1977).

The cross-sectional design, when applied to the study of development, represents an attempt to estimate IAC functions from IEV data which, taken in isolation, may result in incorrect inferences about developmental functions. Thus the simple cross-sectional design is not the design of choice for developmental research. Given that the focus of this chapter is upon longitudinal methods, we shall have little else to say about the simple cross-sectional design. Our attention now turns to the discussion of the economy and validity problems of other developmental designs.

Traditional, Single–Cohort Longitudinal Designs. The classic longitudinal design was developed for the purpose of explicitly estimating development as IAC—emphasizing that the most valid estimates of development measure change over time in the same individuals. Explicitly this design represents a time series with an initial pretest, a subsequent intervention (traditionally the maturational events occurring over time), and a posttest, all on the same individual organisms. If the longitudinal study is continued over more than a single time interval, there is simply a further succession of alternating treatments (read maturational events) and further posttests. Traditionally the longitudinal design was only applied to one group of individuals of relatively homogenous chronological age at first testing and, therefore, to a single birth cohort.

As pointed out repeatedly (Schaie, 1965, 1972a, 1973, 1977) the single-cohort longitudinal design is highly susceptible to validity threats and should be avoided unless (1) experimental isolation can be achieved or (2) it can be shown that the dependent variable is not influenced by external environmental events. Barring such strong assumptions (which will rarely hold for studies of human development), several of the threats to internal validity enumerated above are likely to provide alternative explanations for the observed behavioral change (or lack thereof) which are as plausible as sources of the effect as is maturation itself. First, T and A are completely confounded, and thus any period effects related to the dependent variable will render estimates of A internally invalid. These period effects may either mimic or suppress maturational changes occurring over the particular age span measured depending upon whether A and T covary positively or negatively. Second, the single-cohort longitudinal design does not directly control for other internal validity threats which plague test-retest designs—namely, testing, instrumentation, experimental mortality, and statistical regression. The careful researcher can eliminate the confound of instrumentation by taking steps to assure that the measurement procedures are as consistent as possible, and statistical-regression effects can be minimized by including at least two retest occasions (Baltes & Nesselroade, 1979); however, there is simply no way for the single-cohort longitudinal design to circumvent the confounds of testing and experimental mortality effectively. Repeated testing must inevitably introduce the possibility of practice effects or reactivity to the testing situation, and the requirement of multiple test occasions virtually insures an attrition of some subjects who participated at the initial testing but who are unavailable, for whatever reason, for subsequent retesting. To the extent that experimental mortality simply produces a positively biased sample, then the problem is one of external validity—i.e., the overall level of performance of the attrited sample is higher than that of the population. However if the attrition effect interacts with maturation such that returning subjects have different developmental functions than attrited subjects, then the developmental function estimated by the single-cohort longitudinal design is internally invalid.

The single-cohort sampling of the traditional longitudinal design also limits the external validity of the design. Given that cohorts may differ in person-environment interactions due to historical effects (e.g., the children of the great depression; cf. Elder, 1974), descriptions of maturational change derived from a single cohort may well be unreplicable (i.e., externally invalid) for other cohorts.

Considering the problems inherent in the single cohort longitudinal design, one of us has explicitly wondered whether this design is ever a completely valid design for developmental research (Schaie, 1972a), a position which has evoked a spirited defense of traditional longitudinal methods (McCall, 1977). In fairness we should emphasize that the single-cohort longitudinal design, while deficient as a general method for studying developmental phenomena, may prove useful in particular applications, such as defining typologies of developmental patterns for a specifically targeted, single cohort population. Moreover the single cohort design may provide preliminary evidence regarding developmental functions which will later be replicated for additional cohorts and measurement occasions. Exclusive use of the single cohort longitudinal design for discovering normative laws of development is ill-advised unless the (probably unrealistic) assumptions of no period effects and no cohort-by-maturation interactions can be theoretically justified, a priori, for a specific population and behavior.

Sequential Strategies

Definitions. In order to reduce the limitations inherent in the single-cohort longitudinal design, several alternative *sequential* strategies have been suggested (Baltes, 1968; Schaie, 1965, 1970, 1977). The term *sequential* derives from the fact that the sampling frame for these designs requires a sequence of samples taken across multiple measurement occasions. In order to explicate the various possible sequential designs, we must first differentiate the *sampling design* from the *analysis design*. The two concepts are heavily interrelated; sampling design refers to the particular cells of a cohort-by-age (time) matrix to be sampled in a developmental study, while analysis design refers to the ways in which the cells which have been sampled may be organized to analyze for the effects of A, C, and T. Figure 7–1 provides a prototypical cohort-by-age matrix, which may be used to illustrate the various sequential designs. Note that, given the inherent confounding of A, C, and T discussed earlier, the cohort-by-age matrix in Figure 7–1 represents all three parameters: A and C as rows and columns of the matrix, and T as a parameter contained within the cells of the matrix.

We may distinguish two types of sampling designs: those which use repeated measurements on the same individuals to fill the cells of the matrix and those which use independent samples of individuals to fill the cells of the matrix; either sampling method could be used to provide the matrix given in Figure 7–1. Restricting our discussion (for the present) to the sampling design, we may use Baltes's (1968; Baltes, Reese, & Nesselroade, 1977) terminology to define these two designs as *longitudinal* and *cross-sectional sequences*. As shown in the diagonals in Figure 7–1, a cross-sectional sequence involves the replication of a cross-sectional study in that the same age range of interest is assessed for at least two different time periods. As a consequence the estimate for each age level

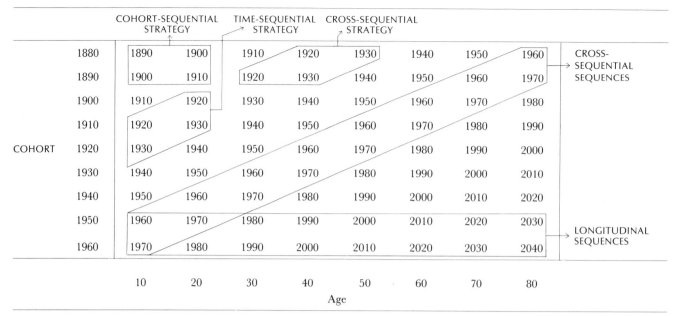

Figure 7-1 Schematic showing cross-sectional and longitudinal sequences and the modes of analysis deduced from the general developmental model. (Note: Entries represent times of measurement [period].)

is obtained for multiple cohorts. Each estimate, however, is obtained from an ideally random sample of its age-cohort and measured only once. By contrast the longitudinal sequence (bottom rows in Figure 7–1) represents the repeated measurement of at least two cohorts over the age range of interest. Here again estimates from each cohort are obtained at two different points in time. A critical distinction is the fact that only the longitudinal sequence provides data which permit evaluation of IAC and IEV in IAC.[2]

Schaie's General Developmental Model. It was pointed out earlier (Schaie, 1965) that data matrices like Figure 7–1 contained information permitting a variety of alternate strategies of analyses.[3] To be specific, each row can be treated as a longitudinal study, each diagonal as a cross-sectional study, and each column would represent a time-lag study (i.e., comparison of behavior at a specific age for successive cohorts). The sequential sampling designs cannot disentangle all components of the $B = f [A,C,T]$ function, given the linear dependence among the three factors. However, Schaie (1965) suggested that, given the $B = f [A,C,T]$ model, three distinct analysis designs exist which are created by considering the separate effects of two of the three components while assuming the constancy or irrelevance of the third. Consequently we suggested (as exemplified in Figure 7–1) that the *cohort-sequential* strategy would permit separation of age

change from cohort differences, under the assumption of no time effects; the *time-sequential* strategy permits the separation of age differences from period differences, assuming no cohort effects; and the *cross-sequential* strategy permits the separation of age-cohort differences from period differences, assuming no age effects. The time-sequential strategy is not a truly longitudinal approach (i.e., one cannot do a time-sequential analysis on repeated measures data, since a given individual cannot be the same age at two different points in time—see Figure 7–1) and will not therefore be considered further except to note that it has merit for the estimation of reliable age differences, for social policy purposes, and for dependent variables where cohort effects are likely to be minimal.

Longitudinal Sequences. When data are collected in the form of longitudinal sequences (which should rightly be emphasized in developmental studies of IAC), it is possible to apply both the cohort sequential [CS] and cross-sequential [XS] designs. There is now general agreement that the CS design is of greatest interest to developmental psychologists because it explicitly differentiates IAC within cohorts from IEV between cohorts (cf. Baltes & Nesselroade, 1979; Schaie & Baltes, 1975). Not only does the CS design disentangle the effects of A and C, completely confounded in simple cross-sectional designs, but it also permits a check of the consistency of age functions across successive cohorts, thus proving to be of greater external validity than the single cohort longitudinal design.

Again the critical assumption in the CS design is that there are no time-of-measurement effects present in the data; this assumption is most parsimonious for developmental psychologists for whom age and cohort are likely to be of primary interest. Nevertheless there may be period-specific effects present in the data, either because of "true" period effects or because of confounding of occasion-related internal validity threats such as differences in instrumentation between occasions. We may therefore

---

[2] It would, of course, be possible to construct row entries in Figure 7–1 by means of successive independent samples from the cohorts under observation. Such data would use age correlated IEV to provide estimates on averaged IAC but would no longer be "truly" longitudinal—i.e., repeated observations on the same organisms. Such data (frequently used in survey research) are important in controlling for various threats to the validity of repeated measurement designs (see following for details).

[3] Baltes (1968) conceptualized cross-sectional and longitudinal sequences as both sampling and analysis designs and disputed the validity of the analysis designs suggested in Schaie's general developmental model. This apparent disagreement was reconciled by Schaie and Baltes (1975).

ask: How would the assumption violation of no T effects be reflected in the CS analysis? Although the specific perturbations depend upon the particular data matrix and the sources of effects in that matrix, confounded T effects will generally affect both (1) the estimates of A, reflected in an analysis of variance design as the main effect for A and the C by A interaction and (2) the estimates of the C effects, since the different cohorts will be sampled at different time periods. In short all estimated effects are likely to be perturbed. A simple confounded main effect for T would most likely be reflected in a significant C by A interacton (Schaie, 1973), for (given a confounded T effect) we would be likely to discover that the cohorts differed in maturational pattern simply because they were sampled at different time periods.

This conclusion leads to an interpretational paradox: We cannot distinguish a true C by A interaction from a confounded T main effect, once a C by A interaction has been obtained in the CS analysis, unless we have a *strong theory* which not only hypothesizes a true A by C interaction but also specifies (1) the cohorts over which the interaction holds and (2) the direction of the A effect in each cohort. When such specification is possible, we may examine the pattern of effects to determine if the obtained C by A interaction matches our theoretical specification; if it does not, then some time-related confound is relatively more likely. While a significant C by A interaction which is inconsistent with, or not predicted by, our theory may indicate the presence of a time-related confound, it could also be a reflection of a true C by A interaction which is not of the form specified by our model. The absence of a C by A interaction is not sufficient evidence to conclude that no confounded T effects exist; the power of our test of interaction may not detect its presence, or the effects might be localized to a small subset of occasions, in which case our estimates of A, C, and A by C effects will be biased. This is the essence of the interpretational indeterminacy in sequential analysis: If the assumptions which justify the design are violated, the effect estimates obtained are to some degree inaccurate. Given a strong theory about the nature and direction of estimated and confounded effects, the interpretational problem may be reduced to estimating the relative likelihood of confounded T effects; given the pattern of effect estimates, but in the absence of strong theory, the meaning of the pattern of results from the CS (or any other sequential design) may remain obscure.

One of the positive implications of the relationship of strong theory to the interpretation of sequential designs is that the theory may sufficiently specify the pattern of effects so that an invalid design (i.e., one in which the major assumption is violated) may actually provide useful information about the confounded effect. Consider the cross-sequential [XS] design, which crosses C and T under the assumption of no A effects. A developmental psychologist might well ask: Why should I estimate such a design if effects of A are my primary interest? There are two points to be made in answering this question: (1) The XS design may be applied when longitudinal data are available only for a limited number of measurement occasions (time periods) but a wide range of cohort groups and (2) given a strong developmental theory about the nature of the confounded A effects, a misspecified XS design (in the sense that A effects are nonzero)

may provide valuable information about the significance of A effects in both the T and the C by T effects. With regard to the first point, the XS design is feasible with only two measurement occasions, while a CS design requires at least three. The number of measurement occasions required to estimate CS designs which span a relatively large age and/or cohort range can be prohibitive were we to insist that no analysis of the data should be performed until the CS design appropriate to the research question was possible.

To illustrate this point consider again Figure 7–1. A CS design following three cohorts (1880 to 1900, say) over an equivalent 20-year age range (10 to 30, say) would require sampling from 1890 through 1930; an XS design following subjects longitudinally for 20 years would initially be possible in 1910. The CS design is still the method of choice, in that it provides convergent information on the age span 10 to 30 over three separate cohorts, but the misspecified XS design provides some information about development in that age span which, accompanied by theoretical notions about the developmental phenomenon, may be used to make preliminary inferences on the pattern of age effects as represented (confounded) in the T and C by T parameters. Schaie's early work on the sequential analysis of intelligence began by assuming misspecification in an XS design and attempting to draw preliminary inferences regarding C and A effects (cf. Schaie, Labouvie, & Buech, 1973; Schaie & Strother, 1968). It is always preferable to estimate the "true" parameter effects from the appropriate design—i.e., one which makes the correct limiting assumptions; however, it will often be the case that the developmental psychologist must settle for something less than the optimal design, if only temporarily.

Schaie's "Most Efficient Design." Once we allow for a stepwise approximation to the CS design as measurement occasions are added to the data matrix, the question arises on the best way to sample from the age-by-cohort matrix. Most investigators who wish to ask questions with respect to both IAC and IEV nevertheless would like to limit the time course of their longitudinal sampling. In addition theoretical notions about different developmental models applying differentially to subsets of variables in a multivariate set of measures may suggest the need to apply alternative sequential designs to different subsets of dependent variables. Schaie (1965) initially proposed a sequential *sampling* design termed the "most efficient design," which maximizes the potential design applications, given that sampling must begin at some occasion, defined as Time 1. It is as follows:

1. Draw a random sample from each cohort within the age range of interest and measure at Time 1. (Score 11)
2. Obtain a second measurement on as many subjects as possible who were initially tested at Time 1 at Time 2. (Score 12)
3. Draw a new random sample from each cohort tested at Time 1 plus a sample from the next younger cohort and measure at Time 2. (Score 22)
4. Get a third measurement on as many subjects as possible that were measured at Time 1 and Time 2 at Time 3. (Score 13)
5. Obtain a second measurement on as many subjects as

possible who were first tested at Time 2 at Time 3. (Score 23)

6. Draw a third random sample from each cohort tested at Time 2 plus a sample from the next younger cohort and measure at Time 3. (Score 33)

Note that Scores 11, 22, and 33 provide a cross-sectional sequence while Scores 11, 12, and 13, or 22 and 23, will provide longitudinal sequences. Given such data collection it is possible to examine the cohort-sequential model for each set of two cohorts (Scores 11, 12, 22, and 23) or to examine the cross-sequential model for two replications (Scores 11 and 12 as well as 22 and 23). Scores 13 and 33 will permit controls for practice and experimental mortality (see following and Schaie, 1972b, 1977).

Remaining Confounds in Longitudinal Sequences: Possible Solutions

Confounds Not Directly Resolved by the Cohort-Sequential Strategy. In their pure form the previously described approaches will aid the developmental psychologist to estimate maturational effects while controlling for confounds due to history and certain simple selection effects. Other threats to validity of developmental studies can often be controlled by further design refinements.

Experimental mortality. As discussed briefly before, human panels are rarely maintained in their entirety during a longitudinal study. One must check therefore whether subject attrition has been random or systematic with respect to the dependent variables. The most straightforward approach is upon completion of the first follow-up test to segregate Time 1 scores into those for subjects who were successfully retested at Time 2 and those who failed to reappear. Although most investigators of this issue have found that dropouts are, on the average, less able and have different personality characteristics, it does not follow that dropouts will have different age patterns than do the retest survivors (e.g., Schaie, Labouvie, & Barrett, 1973). It does not follow either that systematic dropouts will be maintained upon subsequent retests (Gribbin & Schaie, 1978). Whether or not attrition is subject to secular trends or to cohort effects can be assessed by suitable modifications of the simple sequential models (cf. Schaie, 1977; Schaie & Parham, 1974). The most straightforward control for experimental mortality involves the comparison of cross-sectional sequences (e.g., following successive samples tested only once from the same cohort such as Scores 11, 22, and 33). The problem here is in increased sampling variation and the inability to consider IEV in IAC.

Testing effects. When ability tests are given repeatedly, it is possible that substantial practice effects occur (e.g., Hofland, Willis, & Baltes, 1981). Also the administration of attitude scales or personality tests may tend to produce modification of attitudes or social desirability values of questionnaire items. A direct test of practice effects is possible by comparing performance of individuals of the same age at the same point in time but who differ in level of practice (e.g., comparison of Scores 12 and 22). Interaction of practice with age, cohort, or time-of-measurement effects can be studied, as well as the possible in-

teraction of practice and experimental mortality. All such designs, however, require addition of further follow-up data collection and a combination of cross-sectional and longitudinal sequences (cf. Schaie, 1977, for details).

Changes in instrumentation. The need to maintain the same methods of data-collection reduction and analysis across measurement occasions is obvious, since changes in instrumentation will introduce time-of-measurement effects in the data. An additional instrumentation problem in longitudinal studies conducted over extensive periods of time is that it may become unavoidable to change part or all of the assessment battery. This may be the case because tests given to subjects when they were children may no longer be valid for the same subjects as adults. Batteries may also require change when tests shift in validity due to cultural change affecting their construct validity (cf. Gribbin & Schaie, 1977). In such cases control samples may be needed to whom both old and new instruments have been administered. Alternately it may be possible to compare factor scores upon the application of appropriate techniques of comparative factor analysis (Jöreskog & Sörbom, 1979).

Statistical regression. Observed changes in level in longitudinal studies may be no more than consequences of insufficient reliability of measurement instruments. Particularly in the case where comparison of several levels of ability or standing on other classificatory dimensions is sought, regression effects need to be examined. A general discussion of this problem is provided by Furby (1973), and a method proposed by Baltes, Nesselroade, Schaie, & Labouvie (1972) may be useful in assessing the extent of the problem. In that method, bottom and top scores are divided at Time 1 and compared at Time 2; if performance gradients are not parallel, bottom and top scorers are then divided at Time 2 and compared at Time 1. Regression effects are demonstrated if the gradients obtained under the two methods show opposite direction.

True time-of-measurement effects. When secular trends are expected as in short-term studies, it may be reasonable to switch to one of the alternate strategies deduced from the general developmental model. For example for periods of the life span where little developmental change is expected, the *XS* model might then be appropriate. Likewise where cohorts are defined as narrow bands with little likelihood of substantial cohorts shifts, the *TS* model may then be reasonable to test for time-of-measurement effects as contrasted to age differences (see Schaie & Parham, 1974).

Sampling bias and volunteer behavior. Here only collateral studies or knowledge of the relation between parent population and obtained samples will help. One such collateral study might be to investigate volunteer behavior under alternate conditions both with respect to rate of responding and performance on the dependent variables of interest. An example of such a collateral study has been reported by Gribbin and Schaie (1976) as to the effect of offering or not offering a monetary incentive. In the latter study no differences were found in rate of volunteering or performance in intelligence tests, but some personality questionnaire differences were noted.

Effects of changing populations. Secular changes in the demographic composition of a population present difficulties for obtaining comparable samples in sequential designs. Any changes over time in population characteristics will tend to produce samples which cannot be assumed to differ only in age, birth year, or time tested. If the population is changing, it may be desirable to shift a sampling without replacement to a sampling with replacement model (e.g., Gribbin, Stone, & Schaie, 1976). It may even be appropriate to attempt to match samples on certain characteristics (although matching often creates as many problems as it solves). In any case, it becomes most important in sequential sampling for the researcher to have good demographic information about the population from which a panel is drawn, as well as information about shifts in population characteristics over the time frame of the longitudinal study.

Additional Design Considerations

In addition to attending to the confounds inherent in designs analyzing longitudinal and cross-sectional data matrices, the developmental psychologist must consider several other issues relevant to selection of a sequential design for a given research application. Several of these theoretical and practical considerations are discussed in this section.

Unequal Sampling Intervals. A potential source of problems for data analysis and interpretation in sequential designs is the use of unequal sampling intervals over time, where disproportionate numbers of years intervene between occasions of measurement. An example would be a study in which the initial measurement occasion was, say, 1980, and subsequent testings occurred in 1985, 1986, 1990, and 1995. These unequal intervals of measurement require special analytic techniques if age is to be treated as an interval scale in estimating aging or growth-curve parameters (see following); moreover, the unequal intervals will have the effect of "deorthogonalizing" the age or time factor with the cohort factor. Unequal intervals of measurement do not produce insurmountable analysis problems, but they increase the complexity of the analysis procedure and should be avoided in the name of parsimony unless special considerations relevant to the problem area require them.

Unequal Factor Intervals. Another design problem in sequential strategies arises when the two factors included in the design involve different time spans. This issue is not isomorphic with the unequal sampling intervals problem, for here we refer to different numbers of levels of each factor (be it A, C, or T) even when the time interval for each of the factors is held constant. Figure 7–2 illustrates the distinction; in the lower panel (Figure 7–2B) the unequal factor interval problem arises because more levels of C are measured than are levels of T. This type of unequal interval will be quite common in sequential sampling, because it is always possible to sample a wide range of birth cohorts at a single point in time, and replicate sampling over time would result in a matrix which contains a wider cohort range than a time range (at least) until the time span (in years) between first and most recent measurement occasions equaled the time span (in years of birth) between the most recent and

A.   An equal time interval CS design (3 cohorts, 3 ages, 20 year span)

COHORT						
1880	1890	1900	1910	1920	1930
1890	1900	1910	1920	1930	1940
1900	1910	1920	1930	1940	1950
1910	1920	1930	1940	1950	1960
1920	1930	1940	1950	1960	1970
1930	1940	1950	1960	1970	1980
	10	12	30	40	50

Age

B.   An unequal time interval CS design (4 cohorts, 2 ages, 30 year cohort span, 10 year age span)

COHORT						
1880	1890	1900	1910	1920	1930
1890	1900	1910	1920	1930	1940
1900	1910	1920	1930	1940	1950
1910	1920	1930	1940	1950	1960
1920	1930	1940	1950	1960	1970
1930	1940	1950	1960	1970	1980
	10	20	30	40	50

Age

Figure 7-2 Schematic illustrating the unequal time interval problem for a cohort-sequential design

most remote cohorts initially sampled. Thus a cross-sequential analysis after two times of measurement will probably contain disparate time spans, with more cohorts than times of measurement in the design. In fact the cross-sequential analyses of intelligence by Schaie and co-workers (e.g., Schaie, Labouvie, & Buech, 1973; Schaie & Labouvie-Vief, 1974; Schaie & Strother, 1968) involve analyses of such disparate time spans.

Unequal time spans produce a type of "bias" in sequential designs—namely, that the expected value of the variance components for each factor will be unequal and in direct proportion to the ratio of the different time spans (Adam, 1977; Botwinick & Arenberg, 1976). Thus the differences in time spans in the factors will be reflected in an analysis of variance as in differences in the size of omnibus F-ratios (that is, F-ratio testing the null hypothesis of equivalence of all the marginal means for the factors) or in different values for proportion of variance estimates such as the intraclass correlation or ω^2. If the cohort factor is sampled over 20 years of birth and the time factor is sampled over five years of measurement, then we would expect that the omnibus F-test testing the hypothesis of no cohort effects would be roughly four times larger than the omnibus F-test for no time effects even if the two factors had roughly the same magnitude of effect for each unit of time on our interval scales (i.e., years).

This effect is a natural consequence of the unequal time intervals and is not a source of bias in the statistical sense of bias in estimators. The omnibus F-test in both cases is the proper test of the null hypothesis of no effects across all levels of the factors involved; as the number of levels of the factor increases, the likelihood also increases that at least two of the subclass means are reliably different. Thus the unequal time intervals do not "bias" the results and do not in any way limit the investigator to using equal time spans in sequential designs. The primary effect of unequal intervals is that the magnitude of F-ratios or proportion of variance estimates cannot be used in a direct comparison of the relative importance of the two factors under study. Using our previous example it would be erroneous to claim that a cohort effect is more important than the time effect simply because the proportion of variance for cohort was greater, since that pattern would be predicted by the unequal time intervals alone. A better test of the hypothesis would be that the ratio of variance accounted for exceeds a level reliably greater than that expected by the disproportionate time spans alone.[4] In the presence of unequal time spans, the investigator should be careful not to make mistaken inferences on the relative importance of the two effects being estimated; however, there need be no worry that the significance tests are invalidated by the unequal intervals.

Age, Cohort, and Time as Continuous Variables. The argument could be made that descriptive inferences

using the time-related variables age, cohort, and time are less than maximally powerful unless these variables are treated as continuous and not as categorical variables. Under this argument the sequential designs discussed above should not arbitrarily categorize these variables and use analysis of variance but treat them as continuous and use multiple regression (e.g., Buss, 1979–1980). Since multiple regression and analysis of variance are functionally isomorphic (Cohen & Cohen, 1975; Kerlinger & Pedhazur, 1973) the question is not one of appropriate analysis technique but whether too much information is lost by pooling the continuous time intervals into discrete categories. The loss of information obviously depends on the size of the categorical intervals pooled and the within-category covariation thereby ignored. In general we suspect that the regression approach is not likely to yield vastly different inferences from the analysis of variance approach in practice as long as sample sizes are not small (say not less than ten per cell) and the time intervals defining age or cohort are not large (say, less than ten years). Part of the reason for our conclusion is that chronological age per se is an imperfect measure of biological, psychological, and social aging (Wohlwill, 1973); hence, pooling over small intervals is not likely to lose a great deal of predictive power, given the measurement error inherent in the chronological age variable. We recognize that regression approach has probably been underused in sequential data analysis, primarily because the sampling procedures (measurement at discrete time intervals) used in longitudinal research led directly to the use of categorical analysis (i.e., analysis of variance) methods.

Practical Issues. The preceding discussion leads directly into consideration of the following questions: (1) How large a time interval should exist between measurement occasions? (2) How wide a range of ages and/or cohorts should be sampled? and (3) How large should the sample size be? General answers to these questions cannot be given since they depend directly on the content area of interest, the developmental hypothesis to be tested, and the level of prior knowledge about the phenomenon under study. Consideration of the length of time interval in longitudinal sampling depends upon the tradeoff between the need to measure change in the minimum time possible and the concern that repeated testing in short periods of time will greatly increase the probability of unwanted practice effects. Consideration of the size of the age or cohort range to be sampled similarly depends upon the hypotheses the investigator has about the critical developmental periods and the range of birth years over which generational differences are expected. In general it is probably desirable to include a wider range of ages and/or cohorts than are hypothesized to show differences, particularly in an initial exploratory study, so that the hypothesis may be falsified with respect to certain ages and/or cohorts; however, the inclusion of additonal levels of cohort and age must be weighed against the cost of including additional subjects and measurement occasions in the design. With respect to sample size, the investigator may wish to perform a power analysis (Cohen, 1977) to predict how many subjects will be required to yield statistical significance for a lower bound estimate of effect size (assuming one is

---

[4] Botwinick and Arenberg (1976) criticized Schaie and co-workers for direct comparisons in cross-sequential analysis using disparate time spans. Their criticism was recognized by Schaie and Parham (1977) as valid (with respect to the disparate time spans only). The latter paper reported on equal time-span cohort-sequential analyses, in which unweighted comparison of F ratios was justified.

available); however, in longitudinal sampling one should allow for a rate of experimental mortality in developing this estimate. The attrition rate will depend upon the nature of the population and the sampling procedure (e.g., Rosenthal & Rosnow, 1975); in Schaie's studies of unpaid volunteers from a prepaid health plan, sampled at seven-year intervals, attrition rate in the longitudinal sequences has been roughly 40 percent (Schaie, 1979).

Decision Rules for Age, Cohort, and Time Effects. As discussed before, one of the problems in implementing a sequential design approach is the consequence of model misspecification and the difficulty in drawing valid inferences on the presence of age, cohort, and period effects in the absence of strong theoretical posture on the likelihood of these effects being present in the data. Originally Schaie (1965) attempted to formulate some decision rules for deciding on the presence or absence of the three effects by comparing the results from different sequential analyses of the same data matrix, a procedure criticized by Baltes (1968) and Buss (1973), among others. Schaie's decision rules were based upon an intuitive rationale for teasing apart effects which, quite frankly, has been shown to be of questionable validity—and these decision rules should no longer be taken seriously. The critical problem is that in the presence of effects for all three factors, and in the concurrent absence of strong theoretical specification of the pattern and magnitude of some of the effects, there is at present (and in the foreseeable future) no method available for estimating all the three effects and their interactions simultaneously. The decision rules by Schaie (1965) will not generally lead to the "true" model—that is, the one which produces unbiased estimates of all the effects operating in a given domain of study. An *atheoretical* exploratory study attempting to estimate effects for all levels of age, cohort, and period and their joint interactions is unlikely to be a fruitful enterprise.[5]

Additional Between-Subjects Factors. The investigator may wish to partition the between-subjects portion of the sequential design according to additional individual difference variables of interest. This partition may be either a priori (that is, the factor is explicitly included in the sampling design) or a posteriori (the partition is based upon individual differences determined during or after the first measurement occasion). Examples of such

grouping factors are sex, experimental mortality (Schaie, 1977), or health status (Hertzog, Schaie, & Gribbin, 1978). In some cases (e.g., experimental mortality) the partition must be a posteriori since it is based upon events occurring after the first measurement occasion. The major problem with a posteriori group definitions is that they will usually result in a loss of statistical power caused by the reduction in subgroup size. It is therefore preferable, wherever possible, to include additional grouping factors at the time of initial design so that sampling may be done with respect to all subgroups.

The investigator should be aware that the inclusion of additional groups also incurs the risk of additional sampling by treatment interactions, which may have ramifications for the age effects being estimated. It might be the case, for example, that middle-aged women and middle-aged men would be differentially representative of their respective populations due to differential availability for sampling (determined obviously by the type of sampling procedure employed).

Alternative Designs for Sequential Data Analysis

Simultaneous Estimation of A, C, and T. An important alternative type of sequential designs eschews Schaie's standard sequential designs in an attempt to simultaneously estimate components for all three factors, A, C, and T, in a single design. These designs operate on the same sequential data matrices (i.e., cross-sectional and longitudinal sequences) but do not use traditional analysis of variance designs or analysis techniques to estimate effects of only two of the three factors, as in the *XS, TS,* and *CS* designs. We refer to these alternative models as *additive effects models* since the basic procedure is to postulate no interaction components involving any of the three factors, A, C, and T. Under this additivity assumption, it is possible to simultaneously estimate parameters for some of the A, C, and T effects if enough suitable assumptions (in the form of restrictions on the effects that are present in the analysis) are imposed to make all remaining parameters estimable.

The approach was first discussed by Mason, Mason, Winsborough, and Poole (1973) and later modified and advocated by Donaldson (1979) and Horn and McArdle (1980). Consider a cross-sectional data sequence of the type shown in Figure 7–1. Under the additivity assumption, the cell means in the population may be represented by the following equation:

$$\mu_{ijk} = \alpha_i + \beta_j + \gamma_k \qquad (1)$$

where α refers to effects for age i, β to effects for cohort j, and γ to effects for time k. For any individual, the linear model will also contain an individual differences error component:

$$\mu_{ijkm} = \alpha_i + \beta_j + \gamma_k + e_{ijkm} \qquad (2)$$

In normal ANOVA applications, we might impose side conditions of the form $\Sigma_{\alpha i} = 0$, etc., in order to uniquely define the parameters, and to enable the usual ANOVA tests of the null hypotheses:

$$H_\alpha: \text{all } \alpha_i = 0; \; H_\beta: \text{all } \beta_j = 0; \; H_\gamma: \text{all } \gamma_k = 0 \qquad (3)$$

---

[5] In her critique of sequential strategies and Schaie's (1965) decision rules, Adam (1978) demonstrated that the expected value for C in a 2 by 2 cross-sequential analysis was equivalent to the expected value for A in a 2 by 2 time-sequential analysis involving the same cells of a cross-sectional sequence. Adam's point is well taken, although it depends upon the assumption that all A, C, and T effects are nonzero, and it is limited to the 2 by 2 case. However Adam goes well beyond this demonstration to infer that it somehow validates criticisms of Schaie's work by Horn and Donaldson (1976) and that it would be preferable to use some two-factor sequential design in exploratory situations. Adam is incorrect on both points; in the latter case her assumption that all A, C, and T effects are nonzero insures that no sequential design will produce unbiased estimates of the various effects. Since Adam does not specify her two-factor design, we cannot be more explicit as to the confounds inherent in the two-factor design she seems to prefer. Her model is explicitly additive, and thus she would be able to estimate all but two of the A, C, and T effects under the additive effects model we describe later (although violation of the additivity assumption would also produce biased estimates).

However, given the linear dependency among the three factors, A, C, and T, no solution exists for all $\alpha_i \beta_j$, and γ_k. Mason, Mason, Winsborough, and Poole (1973) showed, however, that if an a priori assumption could be made regarding the equality of two parameters (e.g., $\alpha_1 = \alpha_2$), this assumption would be sufficient to remove the indeterminacy and to just identify the other parameters. Then statistical estimates for these parameters could be found. They also pointed out that additional assumptions of the same type would place further restrictions on the model leading to overidentification of the remaining parameters (which has desirable properties in statistical hypothesis testing of the models). The parameter estimates in such a procedure are, of course, completely dependent upon the accuracy of the equality assumptions used to enable the estimation procedure; different assumptions would produce different estimates for the effects.

Donaldson (1979) extended the Mason approach by treating it under the framework of full rank linear modeling (Searle, 1971; Timm & Carlson, 1975). Horn and McCardle (1980) further generalized the approach to restricted modeling of mean and covariance structures. In the process of extolling the virtues of the additive effects models, these authors have been highly critical of both Schaie's sequential designs and traditional ANOVA applications to analyze them, stating explicitly that the model testing approach is superior to the "traditional" sequential strategies approach. It has become important to consider the advantages and disadvantages of the simultaneous additive effects model by itself and in comparison to sequential strategies; if the additive effects approach could be considered invariably superior to the traditional sequential designs of Schaie, it should obviously supplant them as the method of choice.

Before proceeding with an evaluation of the additive effects model, let us recognize that there are two separate criticisms inherent in the Donaldson-Horn-McArdle critique: (1) that the parametric model of Schaie's sequential approach is invalid and (2) that the statistical analysis procedures employed by Schaie in his empirical applications of sequential strategies are invalid. With regard to the second point, the critique is pointed toward the application of standard ANOVA techniques. There is no question that the ANOVA procedures used by Schaie (e.g., Schaie & Labouvie-Vief, 1974; Schaie and Strother, 1968)—namely, use of unweighted means, univariate ANOVA on multiple dependent measures—are dated by more sophisticated multivariate approaches (of the kind we outline later). Moreover it is certainly true that Schaie and colleagues' previous application of traditional ANOVA techniques emphasized interpretation of omnibus F-tests and did not focus on estimation of individual effects (i.e., the αs etc.] or on a priori or a posteriori contrasts among cell means in order to delineate more precisely the source of the significant differences. Comparisons among individual-cell means were done on the basis of longitudinal or cross-sectional gradients across observed means. The use of classic univariate ANOVA models is no longer the staple of Schaie's statistical analyses; in any case it should not be the focus of a discussion of the merits of the parametric models of the additive effects approach. Having now confessed past "sins," we turn to the issue at hand!

In our view the additive effects model represents an important contribution to the area of sequential methodology, but it is just as flawed and imperfect as Schaie's traditional sequential designs, for it is no more or less valid than the assumptions invoked to enable estimation of the A, C, and T effects. In the case of the additive effects model, there are two sets of assumptions: (1) All interaction effects are zero and (2) at least two, and possibly more, main effect contrasts are equal. Donaldson (1979) and Horn and McArdle (1980) are both quite explicit on the dependence of the estimates of the additive effects model on the validity of the assumptions of the second type, but they completely ignore the importance (in our view, the more critical importance) of the validity of the assumptions of the first type. Similarly the validity of the XS, TS, and CS designs is contingent upon the assumption that the unanalyzed components are all zero. Both the traditional sequential strategies and the additive effects model suffer from a common problem: Given invalid assumptions, we obtain inappropriately biased and invalid effect estimates.

We may formalize the problem in the following way. Given a fixed range of ages, cohorts, and periods of measurement, a general linear model for the means in the population is:

$$\mu_{ijk} = \alpha_i + \beta_j + \gamma_k + (\alpha\beta)_{ij} + (\alpha\gamma)_{ik} + (\beta\gamma)_{jk} + (\alpha\beta\gamma)_{ijk} \tag{4}$$

where the joint terms (e.g., $\alpha\beta$) denote interactions. For a given population and construct(s), some or all of the effects may be zero, but the preceding equation describes the general case in which all effects are nonzero. In the equation we are indicating true population parameters, not statistical estimates of those parameters. The problem is that, although the effects for all the terms in Equation 4 may be present in the population (all are in principle theoretically distinct), the linear dependency among the measures of A, C, and T makes it impossible to estimate all the effects independently. In fact the linear dependency precludes one from ever estimating the three-way interaction among A, C, and T, even though it might be theoretically meaningful. If one wishes to estimate all the possible effects for any given two-way interaction, say $(\alpha\beta)_{ij}$, then none of the other effects for either of the remaining two-way interactions is estimable. If one wishes to estimate all the effects for two of the main effects, then none of the effects for the remaining factor is estimable. In all cases the design is limited by the degrees of freedom contained in the sampling design, which is of "deficient rank" with respect to A, C, T because of the linear dependence among the factors.

Given this state of affairs, the investigator may only obtain valid effect estimates for some of the population parameters under the assumption that the parameters not estimated are in fact zero in the population. An XS design assumes all terms involving α_i—i.e., α_i, $(\alpha\beta)_{ij}$, $(\alpha\gamma)_{ik}$, and $(\alpha\beta\gamma)_{ijk}$—to be zero; a CS design assumes all terms involving γ_k to be zero. The additive effects model assumes all interactions—i.e., $(\alpha\beta)_{ij}$, $(\alpha\gamma)_{ik}$, $(\beta\gamma)_{jk}$, and $(\alpha\beta\gamma)_{ijk}$—to be zero and imposes at least one additional assumption on the main effects (of the form $\alpha_i = \alpha_j$ etc.) in order to estimate the remaining effects. When all is said and done, none of these models is applicable to all developmental problems. Theorists are likely to differ on the merits of any of these models to a given problem; Glenn (1976) and Baltes, Cornelius, and Nesselroade (1979) doubt the usefulness of the additive effects model because they suspect that the hypothesis of no interactions is rarely, if ever, likely to be true, while Donaldson (1979) and Horn and McArdle (1980) question the validity of sequential strategies because they doubt that all effects attributable to one of the A, C, and T factors are ever likely to be zero in the population. This is the dilemma of descriptive research designs involving parametric treatment of A, C, and T effects; we must make limiting assumptions to estimate any of the effects, and these assumptions must be theoretically sound for the estimates to have maximal utility. As pointed out by Baltes et al. (1979), there just is no purely statistical solution to the problem.

Before concluding this section we should note another potential problem with the additive effects model. The simultaneous estimation of A, C, and T effects might mislead one into assuming that meaningful estimates of all A and C effects could be obtained from simply taking two cross-sectional samples (i.e., the smallest possible cross-sectional sequence). In fact a just-identified solution attempting to estimate all A and C effects (except two which are set equal) is unlikely to lead to useful estimates because of the presence of a high degree of nonorthogonality among the effect contrasts used in the statistical analysis. There will be a powerful suppressor effect operating if all the estimates are made simultaneously. If the investigator is interested in estimating A and C effects, there is no better matrix of observations than the age-by-cohort matrix discussed previously in the context of CS designs. As the cross-sectional sequence increases in measurement occasions, then an additive effects design estimating A and C effects will experience a decreasing problem with suppression with respect to A and C effects (the same principle applies to longitudinal sequences). Thus it is not the case that the additive effects model obviates the need for extended sequential sampling.

As stated before we believe the additive effects model to be a significant contribution to the area of sequential methodology, not because it should supplant other sequential designs but because its proponents have demonstrated how the sequential designs of Schaie are only one way of partitioning a sequential sampling matrix. Given theoretical justification other types of designs may also be formulated. Indeed one possibility (which we have not thought through in any detail) is that, under a theoretically sound set of restrictions on different A, C, and T effects, it may be possible to also estimate some partial interaction effects (cf. Boik, Note 1) in the same design. The fact that individual effects may be explicitly represented in linear models by a set of vectors of contrast coefficients describing relations among the cell means increases the investigator's flexibility in matching theory to design and estimation.

Replacement of Age, Cohort, and Time

Since age, cohort, and time actually represent marker variables (Wohlwill, 1973; see preceding) for underlying causal processes, it is undoubtedly the goal of develop-

mental explanation to replace these variables with the process-oriented variables thought to actually determine the A, C, and T effects. As pointed out by several authors (e.g., Baltes et al., 1979; Buss, 1979–1980; Schaie, 1977–1978), such replacement requires a valid theory for the source of the underlying effects and a suitable method for measuring the processes under study.

The advantage of study of the "real meaning" of cohort membership (Baltes et al., 1979; Rosow, 1978) or age from a strictly descriptive viewpoint is that it implicitly removes the linear dependency among A, C, and T by replacing A or C with process variables which are applicable to all levels of the other two factors (see Mason et al., 1976). One could then proceed to estimate descriptive parameters for A, C, and T effects without the constraints discussed in the previous section.

The ultimate goal, however, would be to replace all three factors with process variables and to account for change over time in behavior on the basis of explicit knowledge of antecedent-consequence relationships (Baltes & Willis, 1977, 1979). The ideal method for proceeding from construct and variable definition to statistical estimation in such causal models is the use of structural regression (Baltes, Reese, & Nesselroade, 1977; Buss, 1979–1980; Rogosa, 1979) as outlined by many behavioral scientists and mathematical statisticians (e.g., Duncan, 1975; Goldberger & Duncan, 1973; Heise, 1975; Jöreskog, 1973). Structural regression methods provide the most comprehensive means by which causal influences may be modeled among nonmanipulable individual-differences variables of the type inherent in developmental research. A detailed examination of the issues inherent in causal modeling is beyond the scope of this chapter; the reader is referred to the references just cited. Further discussion of structural regression approaches in the context of developmental analysis is given in the following sections.

STATISTICAL METHODS FOR DEVELOPMENTAL ANALYSIS

Developmental Hypotheses about Means

The majority of developmental studies are interested in testing hypotheses about change in level of performance over time. When the hypothesis involves developmental change in the population, interest focuses on change in the population means with age, which may be summarized in an average growth curve. With respect to the population means, the developmental psychologist wishes to know (1) the direction of change in mean levels with age (time) and (2) the magnitude of developmental change, expressed in the unit of measurement of the interval scale X. Developmental patterns in performance level could be multidirectional (nonmonotonic), monotonically increasing, monotonically decreasing, or stable with increasing age. Knowledge of the direction of developmental change will rarely suffice, however; usually the investigator requires an estimate of the magnitude of such change.

The sufficiency of any set of summary statistics describing the average developmental function is dependent upon the complexity of that function. When the change in means is linearly increasing or decreasing over time, the magnitude and direction of change may be economically expressed as the slope of the linear function—i.e., change in X per unit time (age). When the developmental function is nonlinear, description of direction and magnitude of change is more complex. When the developmental function may be specified, the summary statistics derive from the parameters of a fitted function (e.g., a Gompertz curve). Given a nonlinear developmental function whose exact form is left unspecified, the direction and magnitude of change may be represented in any set of summary statistics which encapsulate the mean difference between ages. Two common sets of statistics are mean contrasts among adjacent ages (occasions) or the regression weights from an orthogonal polynomial equation.

In the multivariate case the investigator would be interested in the consistency of the developmental function across variates—that is, the extent to which the means vary in direction and magnitude of change across different measures. When the data have been collected for multiple groups from the population, the investigator's interest focuses on the consistency of the developmental function across groups. Different groups might have coincident functions (a single developmental function in common, such that the curves lie on top of one another), parallel functions (equivalent changes with age but constant mean differences between groups at each age [occasion]), or divergent functions (group differences in developmental change, with or without group differences in means at the initial age measured).

Developmental Hypotheses about Covariance Matrices

Although most developmental studies have focused on developmental changes in mean performance levels, developmental hypotheses about changes in the range and ordering of individual differences with age may be tested by examining the appropriate elements of the covariance matrix of the observations. The variance parameter reflects the magnitude of the dispersion of individuals around the population mean; thus changes in variances with age indicate age change in interindividual variability (IEV). The covariance elements among repeated measures of a single variable reflect the extent to which the ordering of individuals about the means is consistent across measurement occasions. If individuals maintained fixed positions relative to the mean, the covariance between the measure at any two occasions would equal the product of the variances, and the correlation between the two measures would be 1. Thus the covariances reflect the stability of IEV with age.

The interpretation of developmental changes in variance and covariance parameters with age depends in part upon the ordering of such changes. A systematic increase in variability over time might well imply IEV in intraindividual change (IAC) since the increasing dispersion of individuals about the average developmental function might reflect divergence of individual developmental functions from the average developmental function. Many complex developmental hypotheses may be modeled explicitly in terms of their implications for the

covariance structure of the measurement variable over occasions.

For the multivariate case the investigator may be interested in the consistency of developmental changes in variance and covariance elements across multiple measures, which would be reflected in the similarity of changes in variance and covariance elements over occasions. If the design involves measurement of multiple subgroups from the population, interest will also focus on the consistency of the changes on variance and covariance elements between the different groups. As with group comparisons on means, one can ask whether the groups show equivalent changes in individual differences at each point of the developmental function.

Statistical Tests of Hypotheses concerning Means

As discussed previously most developmental research questions focus on age changes in the means of a group of subjects over time. Hypotheses regarding age changes in mean levels have usually been tested by means of classical analysis of variance (ANOVA), as have most hypotheses in recent psychological research. Increasingly, however, methods of multivariate regression have begun to supplant traditional ANOVA as the statistical approach, fueled by the increasing awareness that the ANOVA and regression approaches are basically the same, ANOVA being a special case of regression with categorical independent variables and an orthogonal experimental design (Cohen & Cohen, 1975). Indeed most statistical packages which now perform ANOVA actually use regression as the computational technique. One of the major advantages of using multivariate regression to analyze ANOVA designs (i.e., categorical sampling designs) is that it is particularly appropriate for the analysis of nonorthogonal sampling designs, wherein the cell sizes are unequal. In sequential data where orthogonality with respect to the subclass subject frequencies is rarely, if ever, obtained, the generality of the regression method for testing hypotheses about the subclass means makes it the method of choice.

The General Multivariate Regression Model. The model for multivariate regression (also known as the general linear model) has been extensively treated in a number of texts (e.g., Bock, 1975; Searle, 1971; Timm, 1975). The general multivariate model for an individual in the population is:

$$\underset{\sim}{y} = \underset{\sim}{x} \cdot \beta + \underset{\sim}{\varepsilon} \tag{5}$$

where $\underset{\sim}{y}$ is a $p \times 1$ vector of dependent variables, $\underset{\sim}{x}$ is a $q \times 1$ vector of independent (predictor) variables, β is a $p \times q$ matrix of regression coefficients, and $\underset{\sim}{\varepsilon}$ is a $p \times 1$ vector of error components.

The interpretation of the regression coefficients in β depends upon how the independent variables are structured in $\underset{\sim}{x}$. If, as in the present case, we are concerned with the analysis of categorical sampling designs, the independent variables in $\underset{\sim}{x}$ must be structured to reflect the classifications of the design matrix. Generally the method is to fill $\underset{\sim}{x}$ with any set of independent (not necessarily orthogonal) contrasts among the cells in the design by using the method of dummy coding (Cohen & Cohen, 1975; Searle, 1971; Timm, 1975). Often this is accomplished by defining x as a model matrix, A, consisting of a matrix of ones and zeroes, indicating one effect of the linear model (i.e., each α_j, etc.) in each column of A. A design matrix of this type is of deficient rank; not all such effects may be estimated. In fact, when the grand mean vector μ is unknown and must be estimated, none of the individual effects are separately identified, only differences among the effects may be estimated (Searle, 1971). The general procedure is to reparameterize A and B in terms of a new basis matrix K and a parameter matrix θ, where the elements of K represent difference contrasts among the effects of the form $\theta_1 \alpha_1 - \alpha_2$, etc. The basis matrix may be selected on the basis of a priori planned comparisons among the means, in terms of effects specified by hypothesis, in accord with the "usual ANOVA constraints," or by specifying certain effects to be zero; in each case it is necessary to reduce the number of independent linear functions of the effects to the rank of the matrix A (which is equivalent to the degrees of freedom in the categorical sampling design).

Once the model is reparameterized to full rank, estimation of the regression coefficients and significance tests for these effects in terms of hypotheses about the means follows. The most common method of estimation is the familiar least squares method. The procedures for multivariate significance testing are too complex to be detailed here (see Bock, 1975 or Timm, 1975); the logic corresponds closely to significance testing procedures for univariate regression analysis of categorical designs (Cohen & Cohen, 1975).

We have to this point ignored the complications introduced by the use of longitudinal (repeated measures) designs. Before considering longitudinal sequences, we should point out that the model as specified is well suited to the analysis of sequential designs using cross-sectional sequences, where all A, C, or T effects are represented as between-subjects effects. The basis matrix simply reflects the contrasts among the cells for the sequential design selected. A particularly useful set of contrasts for cross-sectional sequences is the set of orthogonal polynomial coefficients; A or T effects may be represented in terms of a polynomial model of a specified degree (see Bock, 1975, 1979).

The presence of nonorthogonality in the sequential design complicates the analysis considerably. Nonorthogonality among the effects arises from two sources: (1) the subclass frequences (cell sizes) are unequal and (2) the linear contrasts in K are not orthogonal. The first source is by far the most common and is the rule rather than the exception in sequential sampling designs. The second source would arise if the contrasts were not orthogonal in the sampling design, as in the case for the additive effects model. In the orthogonal case where the cell sizes are equal and the contrasts mutually independent, the main effect estimates are all orthogonal to one another. The order of entry of effects into the regression equation is then arbitrary and has no effect on the sums of squares partition among the effects. As is well known, however, when the design is nonorthogonal, the expected-mean squares of the main effects are not independent but certain terms involve the sum of effects over the levels of the other factors (Bock, 1975; Searle, 1971). The

confounding of the main effects and interactions implies that the order of entry of contrasts in the regression equation affects the sums of squares associated with each effect. Thus the usual hierarchical (stepwise) fitting of effects must consider the consequences of fitting α_j before β_k, say.

These issues have been considered in detail by several authors (e.g., Appelbaum & Cramer, 1974; Cramer & Appelbaum, 1980; Herr & Gaebelein, 1978; Overall, Spiegel, & Cohen, 1975), and there is no consensus on how the problem should be handled. One approach is to specify on a priori grounds the order of effects entry into the regression equation. This hierarchical model requires that the precedence of certain effects over others may be specified on theoretical grounds. An alternative approach is to adjust each main effect by entering its effect contrasts as the last set of main effects, eliminating the effects of preceding main effects. This approach is advocated by Searle (1971) and others (e.g., Overall & Spiegel, 1969; Overall et al., 1975) as the most valid, especially when the source of nonorthogonality in the cell sizes is nonrandom with respect to the factors in the design. An alternative approach is to use a simultaneous estimation procedure which includes all effects in the design. This approach, termed the *experimental design model* by Overall and Spiegel (also termed the *standard parametric model*, STP, by Herr and Gaebelein) adjusts all effects by simultaneously eliminating the sums of squares shared by the other effects in the design. This method is not available in most multivariate analysis packages using least squares methods to estimate the linear model. It is the model available in the maximum likelihood program LISREL discussed later.

The problem of nonorthogonality is particularly acute for analyses with cross-sectional sequences, where all effects are between-subjects and selection of the nonorthogonal method may affect partition of the sums of squares among A, C, and T effects. For analyses of longitudinal sequences, the longitudinal effect (either A or T) is generally orthogonal to other between-subjects factors (e.g., C, or sex), and the sampling design may be partitioned into mutually orthogonal subspaces of between- and within-subjects effects. Then the selection of nonorthogonal analysis methods affects only the between-subjects effects.

Longitudinal Sequences. The analysis of sequential designs for cross-sectional sequences involves traditional applications of MANOVA techniques to between-subjects designs; we will not consider this application further (see Bock, 1975; Timm, 1975). Analyses of longitudinal data are complicated by the presence of the within-subjects factors, which requires special statistical treatment. There are several possible statistical approaches to the analysis of a longitudinal data matrix, including (1) classical mixed model ANOVA (see Winer, 1971), (2) unweighted or weighted MANOVA (Bock, 1979), or (3) analysis of covariance structures (Jöreskog, 1974; Wiley, Schmidt, & Bramble, 1973). The reader will probably be most familiar with the classical mixed model ANOVA, which in fact was used by Schaie and co-workers in many previous analyses of sequential designs. Advances in statistical treatment of longitudinal data over the last decade have badly dated the classical mixed model

ANOVA, however, and we no longer advocate its use except in unusually favorable circumstances. Indeed in the following sections mixed model ANOVA is discussed mainly to provide a background for preferred alternative methods.

General considerations. As discussed before, two sequential designs are possible, given data from a longitudinal sequence: the *XS* design, crossing *C* with *T* (repeated measures on *T*), and the *CS* design, crossing *C* with *A* (repeated measures on *A*). We focus on the analysis of the *CS* design; the generalization to the *XS* design is straightforward. The presence of the repeated measures facet of the *CS* design introduces the random factor *subjects* into the design (nested within *C* groups). Restricting our consideration of the *CS* design for the moment to the univariate case, the linear model for this design is:

$$Y_{ijk} = \mu + \alpha_j + \beta_k + \tau_{i(k)} + \alpha\beta_{jk} + \beta\tau_{ij(k)} + \varepsilon_{ijk} \quad (6)$$

where α_j are the $j = (1 ...., {}_j)$ age effects, β_k are the $k = (1, ..., k)$ cohort effects, $\tau_{i(k)}$ are the effects for the $i = (1, ...i_k)$ subjects, nested in the kth group, and the remaining effects are the associated interactions and the individual error component.

Mixed-model analysis. As is well known the virtue of the repeated measures design is the increased power of the statistical tests due to the removal of the subjects effect from the error term. With more than two levels of the age factor, the conventional mixed model approach requires pooling of the error *SS* over the multiple degree of freedom error subspaces. Unfortunately the assumption of sphericity in the error space necessary for this procedure is often violated and the traditional mixed model significance tests for the age and cohort-by-age interaction will often have inflated Type I error rate (Greenhouse & Geisser, 1959; McCall & Appelbaum, 1973).[6] The two major solutions to the problem are (1) use of corrected *F*-ratios (by adjusting the degrees of freedom) as recommended by Greenhouse and Geisser (1959) or (2) use of a *multivariate* significance test for the *univariate* repeated measures effects (McCall & Appelbaum, 1973). There is some debate as to which of these options is preferable for univariate data (e.g., Rogan et al. 1979); however, given multiple dependent measures, the multivariate approach is superior as a method of protecting against the experiment-wise Type I error rate (Bock, 1975).

Multivariate ANOVA for repeated measures. The multivariate approach involves the multiplication of the data (or the matrix of means) by orthogonal contrasts representing the structure of the repeated measures factor. Any orthogonal decomposition of the repeated measures effects will suffice, but for use with sequential data we recommend the Fisher-Tchebycheff orthogonal polynomials for trend (Bock, 1975). The use of a polynomial model places the multivariate ANOVA approach in the general class of polynomial growth curve models (e.g., see Guire and Kowalski, 1979; Pottloff & Roy, 1964).

We consider first the univariate case for a *CS* design.

The linear model is more complex (see Bock, 1979; Timm, 1975); it essentially reduces to the following equation for the matrix of observed means:

$$\bar{\underset{\sim}{Y}} = \underset{\sim}{K}\Theta P \quad (7)$$

(Bock, 1979; Finn, 1969), where $\underset{\sim}{K}$ is a full rank basis matrix of effect contrasts for between-subjects factors, $\underset{\sim}{P}$ is a J-1 order matrix of orthogonal polynomials for trend over age, and Θ is the matrix of effects to be estimated. There are several methods of estimating the effects in Θ. The simplest is to select directly a basis matrix $\underset{\sim}{K}$ of orthogonal contrasts, representing the effects of cohort, and to use the J-1 matrix of orthogonal polynomials, $\underset{\sim}{P}$. As shown by Finn (1969) and McCall and Appelbaum (1973), the procedure is then to create explicitly a new matrix of observations by postmultiplying the matrix of original observations by the orthonormalized transform of $\underset{\sim}{P}$, creating a new vector of variables, say *Z*, of order *J*. This vector is then partitioned into two exclusive parts. Since the first column of $\underset{\sim}{P}$ is a column of ones (for the grand mean), the leading element of $\underset{\sim}{Z}$ is the weighted average of all *J* repeated measures. An analysis of the between-subjects factorial using z_1 as a dependent measure tests the main effects and interactions of the between-subjects effects. In the *CS* design, this analysis involves the *K*-1 effects for cohort represented in $\underset{\sim}{K}$. The remaining *J*-1 variates in $\underset{\sim}{Z}$ are the repeated measures weighted by the coefficients for the corresponding polynomial terms (i.e., linear, quadratic, cubic, etc.). Under the null hypothesis of no age effects, the expected value of these weighted variates is zero; hence a test of the hypothesis that the constant terms equal zero provides a test of the main effects hypothesis for age (Guire & Kowalski, 1979; McCall & Appelbaum, 1973). The test of the effects for cohort on the transformed variates provides a test of the cohort-by-age interaction. The null hypotheses are tested by a MANOVA using the *J*-1 transformed variates as multiple dependent measures. The multivariate significance tests provide omnibus significance tests analogous to the omnibus tests in the mixed model ANOVA. The critical point is that testing the main effect for age is accomplished by testing the constant terms for the polynomial transforms of the original measures; usually the test of the constant term (in untransformed data) is of little interest because the magnitude of the constant is arbitrary. Examples of this type of analysis are found in Finn (1969), Finn and Mattsson (1978), and McCall and Appelbaum (1973). McCall and Appelbaum (1973) provide examples of more than one within-subjects factors as well. Schaie and Hertzog (Note 2) have used this method in the analysis of *CS* designs.

The assumptions required for the MANOVA treatment of the univariate data are much less restrictive than those of the mixed model approach—namely, that the between-subjects groups have the same general population covariance matrix $\underset{\sim}{\Sigma}$. The MANOVA approach to repeated measures analysis may be generalized to the case of *P* dependent variates by simply performing the transformation on the *P* variates simultaneously, making $\underset{\sim}{Z}$ a $J \times P$ matrix. Then the multivariate test of the hypothesis that the $(J$-1$) \times P$ submatrix of means of $\underset{\sim}{Z}$ is null provides an omnibus test of the hypothesis that all age effects are zero (for all *P* variates simultaneously).

---

[6] The sphericity assumption is necessary for mixed model analysis; the more frequently cited compound symmetry assumption is sufficient but not necessary—it is in fact overly restrictive (see Rogan, Keselman, & Mendoza, 1979).

Questions as to how any significant effects might be localized in some subset of polynomial terms or in some subset of the dependent measures may be handled by inspecting the univariate F-tests following a significant multivariate F, but this procedure provides no protection of Type I error rate for the multiple comparisons. A more elegant procedure is to employ step-down testing procedures (Bock, 1975; Finn, 1969), provided that the transformed variates may be ordered in such a way as to make the step-down test meaningful with respect to a priori hypotheses about localization of the significant effects. The step-down procedure consists essentially of a multivariate analysis of covariance, where the preceding P-1 variates are covaried on the pth variate. Ordering the variates is thus a critical part of the step-down analysis. The interested reader should consult Bock (1975, Chap. 7) for detailed discussion of the application of the step-down procedures to the multivariate repeated-measures design.

Statistical Tests of Hypotheses concerning Covariance Structures

Many developmental hypotheses are best tested by formulating statistical models regarding the structure of covariance matrices taken from longitudinal or cross-sectional sequences. As discussed in the section on statistical methods, many hypotheses regarding individual differences in developmental patterns involve examination of variances and covariances among observed measures. Furthermore the problems of measurement imprecision and the inability to manipulate human development directly have begun to force developmental psychologists to follow the lead of economists and sociologists and to consider the utility of causal modeling among latent variables by means of structural regression techniques. It is not unreasonable to expect that the next decade will see a methodological explosion in the form of increased use and appreciation of methods of modeling covariance structures by developmental psychologists, particularly those concerned with life-span developmental phenomena.

Much of the credit for this explosion, if it does indeed occur, will be given to the Swedish statistician Jöreskog, whose contributions to the methods of covariance structures analysis, especially in their application to factor analysis and structural equations models for longitudinal data, have been noteworthy. Jöreskog and co-workers, most notably Sörbom, have not only extended extant statistical models for covariance structures analysis but have also contributed an important method of statistical estimation and testing of the parameters from those covariance-structure models. We do not mean to belittle the contribution of many other scientists to the theory and methods of covariance structures analysis (see Bentler & Weeks, 1979, and Bentler, 1980, for reviews and a historical perspective on this topic). Nevertheless Jöreskog's contributions, as exemplified in a generation of computer programs designed for covariance structures analysis, seem of primary importance.

The LISREL Model. Jöreskog and Sörbom (1978) have developed a highly general model for structural equations: LISREL (LInear Structural RELations). The LISREL model consists of a system of linear structural regression equations describing the relationships among sets of observed and unobserved variables. The use of structural equations systems has been advocated as a method of assessing the putative cause-and-effect relations among correlated observed variables when experimental manipulation to achieve causal inference is not possible (see Duncan, 1975; Heise, 1975). Wright is generally credited with the development of this approach (e.g., Wright, 1954), initially termed *path analysis,* and his methods have been most frequently utilized in sociological research (Duncan, 1975). *Path analysis* is the term commonly applied when causal relations are specified among observed variables. The term *structural equations* is used when the variables in the causal system are not necessarily directly measured but may also be hypothetical construct or latent variables which may or may not be related to other observed variables (Heise, 1975).

The power of structural equations is that the usual matrix of regression coefficients among observed or latent variables is not used as an indicator of direct influences among constructs; instead, the investigator is required to specify a model regarding a causal sequence among variables. In general this will imply direct effects of some variables upon others, indirect effects for some variables upon others—implying that the usual regression coefficients reflect association through an intervening variable, and no direct or indirect effects of some variables on others—thus implying the correlation between variables to be spurious in a causal sense (see Duncan, 1975; Heise, 1975; Land, 1968). Structural equations models are particularly useful for longitudinal analyses (Duncan, 1975; Jöreskog & Sörbom, 1977; Rogosa, 1979) when certain causal sequences are known to be required by the time-structuring of the data and the causal axiom, "if *a* precedes *b*, *b* cannot cause *a*." Jöreskog and Sörbom's LISREL program is a particularly powerful method for specifying and estimating structural equations models. It represents in essence a union of restricted maximum likelihood factor analysis with multivariate structural regression equations (Jöreskog, 1973; Jöreskog & Sörbom, 1978). The procedure estimates the unknown parameters in a set of linear equations regressing endogenous dependent latent variables (the variances of which are accounted for by the model) upon exogenous independent latent variables (the variances of which lie outside the prediction of the model). Relationships may also be specified among endogenous latent variables. The latent variables are estimated through the use of maximum likelihood factor analysis. The model allows for errors in the structural regression equations (regression residuals) and errors in the regressions of latent variables on observed variables (errors of measurement). Provided that a given model is identified—that is, it is a model specifying a unique solution for all parameters—given a set of observed variables, the LISREL program will estimate all unknown regression coefficients, covariance matrices among latent variables, the residual covariance matrix, and the measurement error covariance matrices.

The LISREL model consists of two parts, the measurement model and the structural equations model. The measurement model specifies how the latent variables (factors) are measured in terms of the observed variables; it is the factor analysis model. The structural equations model specifies the "causal" relationships among the latent variables; it is the regression model. Space limitation precludes a detailed specification of the LISREL equations (see Jöreskog & Sörbom, 1978).

There are three types of parameters in LISREL: (1) *fixed parameters* have values which are fixed in advance, (2) *free parameters* are unknowns which are to be estimated, and (3) *constrained parameters* are two or more unknowns which are constrained to have the same value. LISREL is thus a restricted model, for it is necessary to restrict (i.e., fix or constrain) a sufficient number of parameters in advance in order to uniquely identify all the freely estimated parameters. A model is identified if it produces a unique population covariance matrix Σ— that is, there is no arbitrary linear transformation of the LISREL parameters which produce the same Σ. A necessary, but not sufficient, condition for identification is that the number of unknowns in the linear equations are equal to or less than the number of observed variances and covariances. The other conditions for identification depend upon the model that is specified; treatment of the identification problem in structural equations may be found in Jöreskog (1979), Jöreskog & Sörbom (1977), Werts, Jöreskog, and Linn (1973), and Wiley (1973).

The estimation of the unknown parameters in LISREL is accomplished by maximum likelihood methods. The maximum likelihood solution is obtained by an interactive algorithm which uses the first and second derivatives of the fitting function, F (with respect to the parameter matrices) to find estimates which simultaneously minimize F. Details may be found in Jöreskog (1973). One of the chief advantages of LISREL is that the goodness of fit of the model to the sample data may be assessed by the value of the fitting function, F, at its minimum. Given the large sample assumption, F may be multiplied by the sample size to obtain a value that is asymptotically distributed as χ^2 with degrees of freedom equal to the number of elements in S, minus the number of unknown parameters fitted in the model. In exploratory situations, where the true model is unknown and several alternatives are to be compared, the improvement in fit between two models may be assessed by computing the difference in χ^2 between them, which is also asymptotically distributed as χ^2 with degrees of freedom equal to the difference in degrees of freedom between the models. This procedure is only viable if the models are nested—that is, if the parameter specification of one model is the same as the parameter specification of the other, excepting some additional free parameters. There are two important qualifications to this procedure. First, the sampling distribution of F under repeated model testings on the same data is unknown, and thus the significance tests for χ^2 have unknown Type I error rate. Repeated model modifications may be capitalizing on chance fluctuations in sample data to an unacceptable degree, and any final model should be confined (validated) in an independent sample, whenever possible. Second, the χ^2 test is highly dependent upon sample size and is sensitive to departures from multivariate normality in the data. Hence it is possible to obtain a large and significant χ^2 value when the model fits relatively well by other standards and is, in fact, an acceptable model.

Absolute χ^2 should not be taken as the only or the ultimate criterion for model acceptance (Jöreskog, 1971).

The most recent version of LISREL (LISREL IV) has been extended to the simultaneous analysis of multiple groups. The chief advantage of the simultaneous analysis in multiple groups is that parameters may be fixed or constrained to equality across groups. The ability to constrain parameters across groups is particularly useful, for an investigator may then systematically test hypotheses about the equivalence of unknown parameters across groups of subjects. The basic procedure is to estimate the same model in all groups with parameters of interest constrained to equality between groups, and then to estimate the same model with the parameters free to vary between groups. Then the difference in χ^2 between the two models represents a test of the null hypothesis of group equivalance in the parameters.

Analysis of Repeated Measures Designs. Covariance structures analysis of repeated measures designs involves the use of contrast coefficients to define latent variables, for which means (effects) and variances (variance components) may be estimated. LISREL may be used as a general model to analyze repeated measures designs by specifying the model as outlined by Bock and Bargmann (1966), Jöreskog (1974), Scheifley and Schmidt (1978), and Wiley, Schmidt, and Bramble (1973). The basic procedure is to use a matrix of contrasts to define the latent variables in the measurement equations, then the variance of the latent variables are the variance components associated with the effects (see Jöreskog, 1974).

In order to analyze longitudinal sequences, multiple cohort groups must be introduced into the model. There are several ways in which this type of analysis may be performed. Jöreskog (1979) describes the analysis of growth-curve models in multiple groups by means of structural analysis, but by using a model other than LISREL. The model leaves the covariance matrix Σ unrestricted and models only the means in terms of polynomial constraints. An alternative method of estimating the growth curve model for multiple cohorts involves using the simultaneous multiple groups option in LISREL. With this approach the variance components model described above is formed by using polynomial contrasts. The variance components are estimated simultaneously across cohort groups. The null hypothesis of no cohort effects may be tested by fitting a model constraining the variance components to between-cohort equality versus a model which leaves them free to vary.

The covariance structures approach allows greater ranges of model specification than does, say, the MANOVA approach. It also does not require the assumption of homogenous covariance matrices over cohorts. Another advantage of the covariance structures approach is that the simultaneous estimation procedure eliminates the need for concern about ordering of effects to be tested—the variance components will be invariant with respect to ordering of the latent variables in the equations.

Horn and McArdle (1980) present a method of modeling additive effects models for repeated designs using structural analysis of the moment matrix. The method is similar to Jöreskog (1979) in that it is left unrestricted, only the mean vector is structured. Horn and McArdle

(1980) use equality constraints to specify the *A, C, T* effects over the different groups and occasions.

Restricted Factor Analysis. One of the more important LISREL applications for developmental research is its use for estimating a restricted factor analysis model. There are two major factor analysis applications that may be of interest to developmental psychologists: (1) analysis of measurement properties (reliability) over different age groups and (2) longitudinal factors analysis.

Measurement properties. The use of covariance structures analysis for estimation of the psychometric properties of tests has been detailed by Jöreskog (1974) and by Rock, Werts, and Flaugher (1978). The application is based upon the fact that different models for psychometric properties may be expressed in terms of a factor analysis model (Lord & Novick, 1968). The measures are said to be congeneric if a single factor accounts for the common variance of the variables. If the factor loadings may be constrained to be equal, the true score variances of the tests are equal, and the measures are said to be tau-equivalent. If both the factor loadings and the unique variances may be constrained equal, then the measures are said to be parallel forms, because both true score variances and error variances are equal (Jöreskog, 1974).

Tests of the psychometric properties of tests across different age or cohort groups is an important procedure if there is reason to suspect that the tests may have different measurement properties in the groups. Quantitative comparisons of mean differences in scores have little meaning if the tests have fundamentally different measurement properties. A minimal requirement is that the tests be congeneric measures of the hypothesized construct in all groups with the same units of measurement (scale). As shown by Rock et al. (1978), the tenability of the equivalent scales hypothesis rests upon the plausibility of a model constraining the factor loadings to equivalence between the groups. Provided that the equivalent scales hypothesis is not rejected, the groups may be compared for quantitative differences in true score means. Rock et al. provide a detailed description of how hypotheses concerning the psychometric properties of tests may be estimated using a restricted factor analysis model.

Simultaneous factor analysis in multiple groups. A similar application of restricted factor analysis involves testing the hypothesis of equivalent factor structures in multiple age groups. Hypotheses of age changes in the factor structure of intelligence and personality have been advanced by many (see Reinert, 1970, for a review). The most common hypothesis is the age-differentiation-dedifferentiation hypothesis, which states that intellectual structure is initially nearly unidimensional, differentiates during childhood and adolescence to a more complex multidimensional structure, and then dedifferentiates into a less complex structure in old age. Factor analytic studies have been cited as evidence for and against differentiation in childhood and dedifferentiation in adulthood; much of the contradictory evidence may be attributed to differing methods of exploratory factor analysis (Reinert, 1970).

A paper by Meredith (1964) bears directly upon the issue of appropriate criteria for assessing group differences in factor structure. Specifically Meredith used Lawley's selection theorem to show that, if a factor analysis model holds for a given population, then selection of subgroups from the population should still yield an invariant factor pattern matrix of raw score regressions of observed variables on factors. However, the covariance matrices of observed variables, unique components, and factors would not generally be equivalent across groups. Meredith's paper is of critical importance with regard to the hypothesis of structural change with age, for it suggests that (1) age differences in standardized factor loadings or in factor covariance matrices would be expected by age selection alone—and therefore cannot be taken as evidence that the age groups derive from separate populations in which different factor analysis models hold and (2) only group differences in the raw score factor pattern matrix constitute evidence of qualitative age differences in factor structure (Mulaik, 1972).

The LISREL model represents the ideal method of comparing groups in factor structure, since the analysis enables tests of between-groups equivalence in different parameters using equality constraints between groups and since the simultaneous analysis uses covariance matrices and not correlation matrices as input data. Examples of multiple group factor analysis of this type may be found in Jöreskog (1971), McGaw and Jöreskog (1971), and Bechtoldt (1974). Recent studies using these methods to analyze age differences in factor structure include Cunningham (1980), Horn and McArdle (1980), and Hertzog and Schaie (Note 3).

Longitudinal factor analysis. One of the major benefits of restricted factor analysis models is their application to longitudinal factor analysis. Given a matrix of multiple measures at several occasions, usual exploratory factor analysis procedures will be dominated by the high covariances among replicated measures across occasions, and will tend to recover what may be termed "test-specific" factors, one for each measure. Although such a model has some interesting properties, it does not represent the optimal model for assessing changes in factor structure over occasions. Several authors (e.g., Bentler, 1980; Corballis, 1973; Corballis & Traub, 1970) have suggested alternative longitudinal factor analysis models which better preserve the longitudinal nature of the data. The most general longitudinal factor analysis model seems to be the one specified by Jöreskog and Sörbom (1977). Their model is similar to Corballis's (1973) model except that Corballis's model is more restrictive in requiring standardized variables and factors. The general approach is to specify an occasion-specific model—i.e., one in which a particular factor analytic model is hypothesized to account for the within-occasion covariance matrix, and with the same factors replicated over occasions.

The invariance of the solution across occasions can be assessed by comparing (1) the invariance in the relationship between observed variables and factors across occasions and (2) the stability of factors across occasions. The hypothesis of cross-occasion invariance in factor loadings applies only to the maximum likelihood estimators for the unstandardized factor loadings. Standardized loadings will not be invariant unless the factors have the same variance across occasions. This is one of the limitations of the Corballis-Traub type longitudinal factor analysis.

The stability of individual differences across occasions is indicated in the elements in the factor covariance matrix. Differences in the factor variances would indicate that the variability of individuals around the factor mean differed between occasions. The magnitude of the factor covariances would indicate the extent of consistence in individuals' relative ranking about the factor mean; when this matrix is postscaled to a correlation matrix, then the factor correlations should approach unity as individuals approach exact maintenance of position relative to the factor mean. Thus the occasion-specific model supplies the parameters which were indicated earlier as being crucial for hypotheses regarding changes in IEV and of IEV in IAC but in terms of the latent variables. The fact that these parameters are estimated from latent variables, thereby eliminating contaminating influences of measurement error, is an important and useful property of the occasion-specific longitudinal factor analysis model. Hertzog and Schaie (Note 3), Jöreskog and Sörbom (Note 4), and Olsson and Bergman (1977) provide examples of this approach.

An important additional feature of this longitudinal factor analysis model is that it can include covariances among the residual elements. Several authors (e.g., Corballis, 1973; Sörbom, 1975) have suggested that local independence of the residuals for replicated variables is unlikely; the regression residual (or unique components) from the factor analysis model will contain both random error and reliable variance, albeit variance specific to the measure of "true" variance of a trait not common to all indicators of a factor. Failure to include autocorrelated residuals in a model where they hold in the population will perturb all other parameter estimates.

Jöreskog and Sörbom's longitudinal factor analysis model serves as the measurement model for a structural equations system designed to estimate the causal influences among latent constructs. Jöreskog and Sörbom (1977) discuss this LISREL model in detail. It has two important features: (1) an autoregressive model among the longitudinal latent variables and (2) the introduction of exogenous and endogenous predictor variables (e.g., measures of *SES*, health status). The first-order autoregressive model states that between-subjects variation about the factor mean at a given occasion $t + 1$ is predicted only by between-subjects variation about the mean of a latent variable, η, at the previous occasion, t:

$$\eta_{t+1} = \beta_{t+1} \eta_t + \zeta_{t+1} \qquad (8)$$

This model is consistent with a simplex (Jöreskog, 1974) pattern in the correlations among η's; correlations decrease monotonically as one moves away from the diagonal (correlations are highest for adjacent η's). This type of model has found extensive use in time-series modeling (see Frederiksen & Rotondo, 1979).

The application of multiple occasion structural models to longitudinal research is discussed extensively by Kenny (1979) and Rogosa (1979). One of the more important applications of modeling structural regressions in multiple occasion models is the cross-lagged re-

gression model. In this model the prediction system for replicated latent variables conforms to the first-order autoregressive pattern described previously, but cross-lagged regressions are permitted between nonreplicate latent variables at adjacent occasions. The use of cross-lagged regressions is intended to isolate a causal sequence by determining which latent variable provides the greatest prediction of subsequent nonreplicate latent variables. The logic is the same as in cross-lagged correlation analysis, except that the structural regression approach has several major advantages: (1) It disattenuates the relationships among latent variables of measurement error in the observed variables; (2) it allows for simultaneous estimation of a system of lagged regressions of any order of occasions; and (3) it does not force a standardized solution, thereby preventing any cross-occasion changes in the variance of the latent variables from affecting the magnitude of prediction, as reflected in the unstandardized structural regression coefficients (Rogosa, 1979). These properties of structural regression systems make the cross-lagged regression system a better general model for studying causal influences in longitudinal data, although simple cross-lagged correlations may provide a useful "quick and dirty" test of whether the relationships are of sufficient magnitude (and of the proper form) to justify the added time and expense of structural regression analysis.

LISREL models with means. Jöreskog and Sörbom (1980) have described the introduction of means into the general LISREL model. LISREL may now be used to estimate means of latent variables, which is extremely useful for developmental analysis (Jöreskog & Sörbom, Note 4).

REFERENCE NOTES

1. Boik, Robert J. Interactions, partial interactions, and interaction contrasts in the analysis of variance. Unpublished manuscript.

2. Schaie, K. W., & Hertzog, C. Estimates of ontogenetic change in intelligence during adulthood: A fourteen-year cohort-sequential study. Unpublished manuscript.

3. Hertzog, C., & Schaie, K. W. *Aging and structural invariance in intelligence.* Paper presented at the 87th annual convention of the American Psychological Association, New York, September 1979.

4. Jöreskog, K. G., & Sörbom, D. *Simultaneous analysis of longitudinal data from several cohorts.* Paper presented at the SSRC Conference, *Analyzing Longitudinal data for Age, Period, and Cohort Effects.* Snowmass, Colorado, June 1979.

REFERENCES

ADAM, J. Statistical bias in cross-sequential studies of aging. *Experimental Aging Research*, 1977, *3*, 325–333.

ADAM, J. Sequential strategies and the separation of age, cohort, and time-of-measurement contributions to developmental data. *Psychological Bulletin*, 1978, *85*, 1309–1316.

APPELBAUM, M. I., & CRAMER, E. M. Some problems in the nonorthogonal analysis of variance. *Psychological Bulletin*, 1974, *81*, 335–343.

BAER, D. M. An age-irrelevant concept of development. *Merrill-Palmer Quarterly*, 1970, *16*, 238–246.

BALTES, P. B. Longitudinal and cross-sectional sequences in the study of age and generation effects. *Human Development*, 1968, *11*, 145–171.

BALTES, P. B., CORNELIUS, S. W., & NESSELROADE, J. R. Cohort effects in developmental psychology. Pp. 61–87 in J. R. Nesselroade & P. B. Baltes (Eds.), *Longitudinal research in the study of behavior and development.* New York: Academic Press, 1979.

BALTES, P. B., & NESSELROADE, J. R. Multivariate longitudinal and cross-sectional sequences for analyzing ontogenetic and generational change: A methodological note. *Developmental Psychology,* 1970, *2,* 163–168.

BALTES, P. B., & NESSELROADE, J. R. The developmental analysis of individual differences on multiple measures. Pp. 219–252 in J. R. Nesselroade & H. W. Reese (Eds.), *Life-span developmental psychology: Methodological issues.* New York: Academic Press, 1973.

BALTES, P. B., & NESSELROADE, J. R. History and rationale of longitudinal research. Pp. 1–39 in J. R. Nesselroade & P. B. Baltes (Eds.), *Longitudinal research in the study of behavior and development.* New York: Academic Press, 1979.

BALTES, P. B., NESSELROADE, J. R., SCHAIE, K. W., & LABOUVIE, E. W. On the dilemma of regression effects in examining ability-level related differentials in ontogenetic patterns of intelligence. *Developmental Psychology,* 1972, *6,* 78–84.

BALTES, P. B., REESE, H. W., & NESSELROADE, J. R. *Life-span developmental psychology: Introduction to research methods.* Monterey, Calif.: Brooks/Cole, 1977.

BALTES, P. B., & WILLIS, S. L. Toward psychological theories of aging and development. Pp. 128–154 in J. E. Birren & K. W. Schaie (Eds.), *Handbook of the psychology of aging.* New York: Van Nostrand Reinhold, 1977.

BALTES, P. B., & WILLIS, S. L. The critical importance of appropriate methodology in the study of aging: The sample case of psychometric intelligence. In F. Hoffmeister, C. Mueller, & H. P. Krause (Eds.), *Brain function in old age.* Heidelberg, Germany: Springer-Verlag, 1979.

BANDURA, A. *Social learning and theory.* New York: General Learning Press, 1971.

BARTON, E. M., PLEMONS, J. K., WILLIS, S. L., & BALTES, P. B. Recent findings on adult and gerontological intelligence: Changing a stereotype of decline. *American Behavioral Scientist,* 1975, *19,* 224–236.

BECHTOLDT, H. P. A confirmatory analysis of the factor stability hypothesis. *Psychometrica,* 1974, *39,* 319–326.

BENTLER, P. M. Assessment of developmental factor change at the individual and group level. Pp. 145–174 in J. R. Nesselroade & H. W. Reese (Eds.), *Life-span developmental psychology: Methodological issues.* New York: Academic Press, 1973.

BENTLER, P. M. Multivariate analysis with latent variables: Causal modeling. *Annual Review of Psychology,* 1980, *31,* 332–456.

BENTLER, P. M., & WEEKS, D. G. Interrelations among models for the analysis of moment structures. *Multivariate Behavior Research,* 1979, *14,* 169–185.

BIRKHILL, W. R., & SCHAIE, K. W. The effect of differential reinforcement of cautiousness in the intellectual performance of the elderly. *Journal of Gerontology,* 1975, *30,* 578–583.

BOCK, R. D. *Multivariate statistical methods in behavioral research.* New York: McGraw-Hill, 1975.

BOCK, R. D. Univariate and multivariate analysis of variance of time-structured data. Pp. 199–231 in J. R. Nesselroade & P. B. Baltes (Eds.), *Longitudinal research in the study of behavior and development.* New York: Academic Press, 1979.

BOCK, R. D., & BARGMANN, R. E. Analysis of covariance structures. *Psychometrica,* 1966, *31,* 507–534.

BOTWINICK, J., & ARENBERG, D. Disparate time-spans in sequential studies of aging. *Experimental Aging Research,* 1976, *2,* 55–66.

BUSS, A. R. An extension of developmental models that separate ontogenetic change and cohort differences. *Psychological Bulletin,* 1973, *80,* 466–479.

BUSS, A. R. A general developmental model for interindividual differences and intraindividual changes. *Developmental Psychology,* 1974, *10,* 70–78.

BUSS, A. R. Methodological issues in life-span developmental psychology from a dialectical perspective. *Journal of Aging and Human Development,* 1979–1980, *10,* 121–163.

CAMPBELL, D. T., & STANLEY, J. C. *Experimental and quasi-experimental designs for research.* Skokie, Ill.: Rand McNally, 1967.

COHEN, J. *Statistical power analysis for the behavioral sciences,* rev. ed. New York: Academic Press, 1977.

COHEN, J., & COHEN, P. *Applied multiple regression/correlation analysis for the behavioral sciences.* Hillsdale, N.J.: Lawrence Erlbaum Associates, 1975.

COOK, T. C., & CAMPBELL, D. T. The design and conduct of quasi-experiments and true experiments in field setting. In M. D. Dunnette (Ed.), *Handbook of industrial and organizational research.* Skokie, Ill.: Rand McNally, 1975.

CORBALLIS, M. C. A factor model for analyzing change. *British Journal of Mathematical and Statistical Psychology,* 1973, *26,* 90–97.

CORBALLIS, M. C., & TRAUB, R. E. Longitudinal factor analysis. *Psychometricka,* 1970, *35,* 79–93.

CRAMER, E. M., & APPELBAUM, M. I. Nonorthogonal analysis of variance-once again. *Psychological Bulletin,* 1980, *87,* 51–57.

CUNNINGHAM, W. R. Age comparative factor analysis of ability variables in adulthood and old age. *Intelligence,* 1980, *4,* 133–149.

DEVRIES, H. A. *Vigor regained.* Englewood Cliffs, N.J.: Prentice-Hall, 1974.

DONALDSON, G. *On the formulation, estimation, and testing of a developmental model of human abilities specifying age, cohort, and time parameters.* Unpublished doctoral dissertation, University of Denver, 1979.

DUNCAN, O. D. *Introduction to structural equations models.* New York: Academic Press, 1975.

ELDER, G. H., JR. *Children of the great depression.* Chicago: University of Chicago Press, 1974.

FINN, J. D. Multivariate analysis of repeated measures data. *Multivariate Behavior Research,* 1969, *4,* 391–413.

FINN, J. D., & MATTSSON, I. *Multivariate analysis in educational research.* Chicago: National Educational Resources, 1978.

FREDERIKSON, C. H., & ROTONDO, J. A. Time-series models and the study of longitudinal change. Pp. 111–153 in J. R. Nesselroade & P. B. Baltes (Eds.), *Longitudinal research in the study of behavior and development.* New York: Academic Press, 1979.

FURBY, L. Interpreting regression toward the mean in developmental research. *Developmental Psychology,* 1973, *8,* 172–179.

GLENN, N. D. Cohort analysts' futile quest: Statistical attempts to separate age, cohort, and period effects. *American Sociological Review,* 1976, *41,* 900–904.

GOLDBERGER, A., & DUNCAN, O. D. (Eds.). *Structural equations models in the social sciences.* New York: Seminar Press, 1973.

GOULET, L. R., HAY, C. M., & BARCLAY, C. R. Sequential analysis and developmental research methods: Descriptions of cyclical phenomena. *Psychological Bulletin,* 1974, *81,* 517–521.

GREENHOUSE, S. W., & GEISSER, S. On methods in the analysis of profile data. *Psychometrika,* 1959, *24,* 95–112.

GRIBBIN, K., & SCHAIE, K. W. Monetary incentive, age, and cognition. *Experimental Aging Research,* 1976, *2,* 461–468.

GRIBBIN, K., & SCHAIE, K. W. *The aging of tests: A methodological problem of longitudinal studies.* Paper presented at the 30th annual meeting of the Gerontological Society, San Francisco, 1977.

GRIBBIN, K., & SCHAIE, K. W. *Selective attrition in longitudinal studies: A cohort-sequential approach.* Paper presented at the International Congress of Gerontology, Tokyo, 1978.

GRIBBIN, K., STONE, V., & SCHAIE, K. W. *Ability differences between established and redefined populations in sequential studies.* Paper presented at the annual meeting of the American Psychological Association, Washington, D.C., 1976.

GUIRE, K. E., & KOWALSKI, C. J. Mathematical description and representation of developmental change functions on the intra- and interindividual levels. In J. R. Nesselroade & P. B. Baltes (Eds.), *Longitudinal research in the study of behavior and development.* New York: Academic Press, 1979.

HEISE, D. R. *Causal analysis.* New York: John Wiley, 1975.

HERR, D. G., & GAEBELEIN, J. Nonorthogonal two-way analysis of variance. *Psychological Bulletin,* 1978, *85,* 207–216.

HERTZOG, C., SCHAIE, K. W., & GRIBBIN, K. Cardiovascular disease and changes in intellectual functioning from middle to old age. *Journal of Gerontology,* 1978, *33,* 872–883.

HINDLEY, C. B. The place of longitudinal methods in the study of development. Pp. 23–50 in F. J. Moenks, W. W. Hartup, & J. deWit (Eds.), *Determinants of behavioral development.* New York: Academic Press, 1972.

HOFLAND, B. F., WILLIS, S. L., & BALTES, P. B. Fluid intelligence performance in the elderly: Retesting and intraindividual variability. *Journal of Educational Psychology,* 1981, *73,* in press.

HORN, J. L., & DONALDSON, G. On the myth of intellectual decline in adulthood. *American Psychologist,* 1976, *31,* 701–719.

HORN, J. L., & MCARDLE, J. J. Perspectives on mathematical/statistical model building (MASMOB) in research on aging. Pp. 503–541 in L. F. Poon (Ed.), *Aging in the 1980's: Selected contemporary issues in the psychology of aging.* Washington, D.C.: American Psychological Association, 1980.

JÖRESKOG, K. G. Simultaneous factor analysis in several populations. *Psychometrika,* 1971, *36,* 409–426.

JÖRESKOG, K. G. A general method for estimating a linear structural-equations system. In A. S. Goldberger & O. D. Duncan (Eds.), *Structural equations models in the social sciences.* New York: Seminar Press, 1973.

JÖRESKOG, K. G. Analyzing psychological data by structural analysis of covariance matrices. Pp. 1–56 D. H. Krantz, R. C. Atkinson, R. D. Luce, & P. Suppes (Eds.), *Contemporary developments in mathematical psychology.* San Francisco: W. H. Freeman & Company Publishers, 1974.

JÖRESKOG, K. G. Statistical estimation of structural models in longitudinal developmental investigations. Pp. 303–351 in J. R. Nesselroade & P. B. Baltes (Eds.), *Longitudinal research in the study of behavior and development.* New York: Academic Press, 1979.

JÖRESKOG, K. G., & SÖRBOM, D. Statistical models and methods for analyses of longitudinal data. Pp. 285–325 in D. S. Aigner & A. S. Goldberger (Eds.), *Latent variables in socioeconomic models.* Amsterdam: North Holland Publishing, 1977.

JÖRESKOG, K. G., & SÖRBOM, D. *LISREL IV: Analysis of linear structural relationships by the method of maximum likelihood.* Chicago: National Educational Resources, 1978.

JÖRESKOG, K. G., & SÖRBOM, D. *Advances in factor analysis and structural equations models.* Cambridge, Mass.: Abt Associates, 1979.

JÖRESKOG, K. G., & SÖRBOM, D. *LISREL IV appendices.* Chicago: National Educational Resources, 1980.

KENNY, D. A. *Correlation and causality.* New York: John Wiley, 1979.

KERLINGER, F. N., & PEDHAZUR, E. J. *Multiple regression in behavioral research.* New York: Holt, Rinehart & Winston, 1973.

KESSEN, W. Research design in the study of developmental problems. In P. H. Mussen (Ed.), *Handbook of research methods in child development.* New York: John Wiley, 1960.

KUHLEN, R. G. Age and intelligence: The significance of cultural change in longitudinal vs. cross-sectional findings. *Vita Humana,* 1963, *6,* 113–124.

LABOUVIE, E. W. Developmental causal structures of organism-environment interactions. *Human Development,* 1974, *17,* 444–452.

LABOUVIE, E. W. Experimental sequential structures for the exploration of ontogenetic and socio-historical changes. *Human Development,* 1978, *21,* 161–169.

LABOUVIE-VIEF, G. Adult cognitive development: In search of alternative explanations. *Merrill-Palmer Quarterly,* 1977, *23,* 227–263.

LABOUVIE-VIEF, G., & CHANDLER, M. J. Cognitive development and life-span developmental theories: Idealistic versus contextual perspectives. Pp. 181–210 in P. B. Baltes (Ed.), *Life-span development and behavior* (Vol. 1). New York: Academic Press, 1978.

LAND, K. C. Principles of path analysis. In E. F. Borgatta & G. W. Bohrnstedt (Eds.), *Sociological methodology, 1969.* San Francisco: Jossey-Bass, 1968.

LORD, F. M., & NOVICK, M. N. *Statistical theories of mental test scores.* Reading, Mass.: Addison-Wesley, 1968.

LUND, R. D. *Development and plasticity of the brain.* New York: Oxford University Press, 1978.

McCALL, R. B. Challenges to a science of developmental psychology. *Child Development,* 1977, *48,* 333–344.

McCALL, R. B., & APPELBAUM, M. I. Bias in the analysis of repeated measures designs: Some alternative approaches. *Child Development,* 1973, *44,* 401–415.

McGAW, B., & JÖRESKOG, K. G. Factorial invariance of ability measures in groups differing in intelligence and socioeconomic status. *British Journal of Mathematical Psychology,* 1971, *24,* 154–168.

MASON, K. O., MASON, W. M., WINSBOROUGH, H. H., & POOLE, W. K. Some methodological issues in cohort analyses of archival data. *American Sociological Review,* 1973, *38,* 242–258.

MASON, W. M., MASON, K. O., & WINSBOROUGH, H. H. Reply to Glenn. *American Sociological Review,* 1976, *41,* 904–905.

MEREDITH, W. Notes on factorial invariance. *Psychometrika,* 1964, *29,* 177–185.

MULAIK, S. A. *Foundations of factor analysis.* New York: McGraw-Hill, 1972.

NESSELROADE, J. R. Issues in studying developmental change in adults from a multivariate perspective. Pp. 59–69 in J. E. Birren & K. W. Schaie (Eds.), *Handbook of the psychology of aging.* New York: Van Nostrand Reinhold, 1977.

OLSSON, V., & BERGMAN, L. R. A longitudinal factor model for studying change in ability structure. *Multivariate Behaviorial Research,* 1977, *12,* 221–241.

OVERALL, J. E., & SPIEGEL, D. K. Concerning least squares analysis of experimental data. *Psychological Bulletin,* 1969, *72,* 311–327.

OVERALL, J. E., SPIEGEL, D. K., & COHEN, J. Equivalence of orthogonal and nonorthogonal analysis of variance. *Psychological Bulletin,* 1975, *82,* 182–186.

POTTLOFF, R. F., & ROY, S. N. A generalized multivariate analysis of variance model useful especially for growth curve problems. *Biometrika,* 1964, *51,* 313–326.

REESE, H. W., & OVERTON, W. F. Models of development and theories of development. Pp. 116–149 in L. R. Goulet & P. B. Baltes (Eds.), *Life-span development: Research and theory.* New York: Academic Press, 1970.

REINERT, G. Comparative factor analytic studies of intelligence throughout the human life-span. Pp. 115–145 in L. R. Goulet & P. B. Baltes (Eds.), *Life-span developmental psychology: Research and theory.* New York: Academic Press, 1970.

RIEGEL, K. F. *Psychology of development and history.* New York: Plenum, 1976.

RIEGEL, K. F., & RIEGEL, R. M. Development, drop and death. *Developmental Psychology,* 1972, *6,* 306–319.

RIEGEL, K. F., & ROSENWALD, G. C. (Eds.). *Structure and functions: Developmental and historical aspects.* New York: John Wiley, 1975.

RILEY, M. W., JOHNSON, W., & FONER, A. (Eds.). *Aging and society: A sociology of age stratification.* New York: Russell Sage Foundation, 1972.

ROCK, D. A., WERTS, C. E., & FLAUGHER, R. L. The use of analysis of covariance structures for comparing the psychometric properties of multiple variables across populations. *Multivariate Behavioral Research,* 1978, *13,* 403–418.

ROGAN, J. C., KESELMAN, H. J., & MENDOZA, J. L. Analysis of repeated measurements. *British Journal of Mathematic and Statistical Psychology,* 1979, *32,* 269–286.

ROGOSA, D. Causal models in longitudinal research: Rationale, formulation, and interpretation. Pp. 263–302 in J. R. Nesselroade & P. B. Baltes (Eds.), *Longitudinal research in the study of behavior and development.* New York: Academic Press, 1979.

ROSENTHAL, R., & ROSNOW, R. L. *The volunteer subject.* New York: Wiley Interscience, 1975.

ROSOW, I. What is a cohort and why? *Human Development,* 1978, *21,* 65–75.

SCHAIE, K. W. A general model for the study of developmental problems. *Psychological Bulletin,* 1965, *64,* 92–107.

SCHAIE, K. W. A reinterpretation of age-related changes in cognitive structure and functioning. Pp. 485–507 in L. R. Goulet & P. B. Baltes (Eds.), *Life-span developmental psychology: Research and theory.* New York: Academic Press, 1970.

SCHAIE, K. W. Can the longitudinal method be applied to psychological studies of human development? Pp. 3–22 in F. Z. Moenks, W. W. Hartup, & J. DeWitt (Eds.), *Determinants of behavioral development.* New York: Academic Press, 1972a.

SCHAIE, K. W. Limitations on the generalizability of growth curves of intelligence. *Human Development,* 1972b, *15,* 141–152.

SCHAIE, K. W. Methodological problems in descriptive developmental research on adulthood and aging. Pp. 253–280 in J. R. Nesselroade & H. W. Reese (Eds.), *Life-span developmental psychology: Methodological issues.* New York: Academic Press, 1973.

SCHAIE, K. W. Quasi-experimental research designs in the psychology of aging. Pp. 39–58 in J. E. Birren & K. W. Schaie (Eds.), *Handbook of the psychology of aging.* New York: Van Nostrand Reinhold, 1977.

SCHAIE, K. W. Toward a stage theory of adult cognitive development. *Journal of Aging and Human Development,* 1977–1978, *8,* 129–138.

SCHAIE, K. W. The primary mental abilities in adulthood: An exploration in the development of psychometric intelligence. In P. B. Baltes & O. G. Brim, Jr. (Eds.), *Life-span development and behavior.* Vol. 2. New York: Academic Press, 1979.

SCHAIE, K. W., & BALTES, P. B. On sequential strategies in developmental research: Description or explanation. *Human Development,* 1975, *18,* 384–390.

SCHAIE, K. W., & GOULET, L. R. Trait theory and verbal learning processes. Pp. 567–584 in R. B. Cattell & R. M. Dreger (Eds.), *Handbook of modern personality theory.* New York: Hemisphere/Halsted, 1977.

SCHAIE, K. W., LABOUVIE, G., & BARRETT, T. J. Selective attrition effects in a fourteen-year study of adult intelligence. *Journal of Gerontology,* 1973, *28,* 328–334.

SCHAIE, K. W., LABOUVIE, G., & BUECH, B. U. Generational and cohort-specific differences in adult cognitive functioning. *Developmental Psychology,* 1973, *9,* 151–166.

SCHAIE, K. W., & LABOUVIE-VIEF, G. Generational versus ontogenetic components of change in adult cognitive behavior: A fourteen year cross-sequential study. *Developmental Psychology,* 1974, *10,* 305–320.

SCHAIE, K. W., & PARHAM, I. A. Social responsibility in adulthood: Ontogenetic and sociocultural change. *Journal of Personality and Social Psychology,* 1974, *30,* 483–492.

SCHAIE, K. W., & PARHAM, I. A. Cohort-sequential analyses of adult intellectual development. *Developmental Psychology,* 1977, *13,* 649–653,

SCHAIE, K. W., & STROTHER, C. R. A cross-sequential study of age changes in cognitive behavior. *Psychological Bulletin,* 1968, *70,* 671–680.

SCHEIDT, R. J., & SCHAIE, K. W. Taxonomy of situations for the aged: Generating situational criteria. *Journal of Gerontology,* 1978, *33,* 848–857.

SCHEIFLEY, V. M., & SCHMIDT, W. H. Analyses of repeated measures data: A simulation study. *Multivariate Behavioral Research,* 1978, *13,* 347–362.

SEARLE, S. R. *Linear models.* New York: John Wiley, 1971.

SHONTZ, F. C. Single-organism designs. In P. M. Bentler, D. J. Lettieri, & G. A. Austin (Eds.), *Data analysis, strategies and designs for substance abuse research.* Washington, D.C.: U.S. Government Printing Office, 1976.

SIEGLER, I. The terminal drop hypothesis: Fact or artifact? *Experimental Aging Research,* 1975, *1,* 169–185.

SINNOTT, J. D. Everyday thinking and Piagetian operativity in adults. *Human Development,* 1975, *18,* 430–443.

SÖRBOM, D. Detection of correlated errors in longitudinal data. *British Journal of Mathematical and Statistical Psychology,* 1975, *28,* 138–151.

TIMM, N. H. *Multivariate analysis with applications in education and psychology.* Monterey, Calif.: Brooks/Cole, 1975.

TIMM, N. H., & CARLSON, J. C. Analysis of variance through full rank models. *Multivariate Behavioral Research Monographs,* 1975, No. 75–1.

URBAN, H. B. The concept of development from a systems perspective. Pp. 46–85 in P. B. Baltes (Ed.), *Life-span development and behavior* (Vol. 1). New York: Academic Press, 1978.

WERTS, C. E., JÖRESKOG, K. G., & LINN, R. L. Identification and estimation in path analysis with unmeasured variables. *American Journal of Sociology,* 1973, *78,* 1469–1484.

WILEY, D. E. The identification problem for structural equation models with unmeasured variables. Pp. 69–83 in A. S. Goldberger & O. D. Duncan (Eds.), *Structural equations models in the social sciences.* New York: Academic Press, 1973.

WILEY, D. E., SCHMIDT, W. H., & BRAMBLE, W. J. Studies of a class of covariance structure models. *Journal of the American Statistical Association,* 1973, *68,* 317–323.

WINER, B. J. *Statistical principles in experimental design* (2nd ed.). New York: McGraw-Hill, 1971.

WOHLWILL, J. F. *The study of behavioral development.* New York: Academic Press, 1973.

WRIGHT, S. The interpretation of multivariate systems. Pp. 11–23 in O. Kempthorne (Ed.), *Statistics and mathematics in biology.* Ames: Iowa State University Press, 1954.

8

The Naturalistic Perspective in Research

EDWIN P. WILLEMS

JAMES L. ALEXANDER

This chapter presents a set of relatively fundamental assumptions and arguments which, taken together, will represent a rationale for naturalistic research.

To many students of human development, experimental analysis is still the highest and most fruitful form of activity to which the psychologist can aspire. Most professionals qualify their enthusiasm for the experimental method with recognition of the complexity of behavior. Even though a great deal of human activity does not lend itself at present to experimental analysis, many psychologists believe that the most important issues in complex behavior will one day be solved through experimental procedures. Despite the qualifiers and doubts that have been raised about this set of beliefs (Bronfenbrenner, 1979; Willems, 1969, 1973), experimental analysis still resides at the top of the procedural pecking order.

"In psychology, as in any science, the heart of the experimental method is the direct control of the thing studied. When we say, 'Let us do an experiment,' we mean, 'Let us do something and see what happens.' The order is important: we do something first and then see what happens" (Skinner, 1947, p. 20). What the investigator *makes* happen and what s/he allows or does not allow to happen are the major stylistic earmarks of the experiment. In other words an experiment is a *deliberately* contrived, simplified, and artificial situation in which the investigator varies some factors and minimizes the functioning of other factors in which s/he is not interested in order to measure changes in behavior that result from what s/he manipulates. The experiment is generally characterized by purposeful limitation of complexity, and the optimal setting for the experiment is a special location chosen and arranged by the investigator. All of these procedural strengths, sometimes executed partially and sometimes totally, lead investigators to the experiment as the strategy of choice, sometimes in principle, and sometimes because their phenomena cannot be studied by any other means. Control is the guiding principle, and precision of inference and test are the accompaniments. Each of the major dimensions of the experiment—degree of manipulation of independent variables, degree of control over other variables, and degree of restriction and demarcation of the dependent variables—can vary from study to study, but the underlying logic remains the same: Control as much as possible. For most investigators, these earmarks of the experiment are the criteria for ideal research. With intermittent exceptions, both singly and collectively, these investigators often feel guilty and apologetic when they do anything else in their research—as if they are conducting studies that fall short of the ideal.

Even though the solidarity of the experimental bias and its imperialism in human development have been waning, the process has been too slow. To accelerate and consolidate the appropriate kind of pluralism in methods, the logic, criteria, and impact of naturalistic research must be firmed up in substantive ways. That is the purpose of this chapter. After some statements about methodological assumptions and some definitions, the major purposes of naturalistic research will be discussed. Rather than offering a shopping list of techniques of specific projects or a review of naturalistic studies, this chapter will focus on the more generic naturalistic perspective.

METHODOLOGICAL CONTEXT

Discussions of the relative merits and usefulness of naturalistic research methods, as against controlled laboratory methods, tend to deteriorate into polemics and petulant argumentation. It is common to hear words like "rigor" versus "sloppiness," "control of variance" versus "meaningfulness," "sterile" versus "true-to-life," "rich" versus "nit-picking," and "scientific" versus "anecdotal." There are at least two reasons for the frequent disputation about naturalistic methods as against other kinds, usually experimental ones. The first reason is the law of the hammer: If you give a child a hammer, things to be pounded become the most important things around. The principle involved is that not only do we often allow methods and techniques to dictate the choice and merits of our own research problems, but we also often let our own methods dictate and evaluate the merits of someone else's research problem, rather than the issues and purposes of the investigator in combination with his/her methods and techniques. Believing in the inherent correctness and scientific efficacy of certain techniques, we prescribe and proscribe, praise and blame. A second reason for much of the empty disputation about methods is the troublesome word, *natural*. Too often we hear *natural* used in the sense of real and true, as against unreal, or even unnatural. Is the finding from a nonlaboratory, field study more true or more real than the finding from a laboratory experiment? We don't know, but it is this question that stimulates much of the heat of methodological argument. There seems to be some agreement on what characterizes naturalistic *methods,* but little consensus and much controversy over the naturalness of findings. There can be specifiable differences in the empirical findings from the two modes of research, and these differences suggest some important scientific issues.

In *Personal Knowledge* (1958) Polanyi argues that when all our formal talk is said and done, "Scientists . . . spend their lives trying to guess right" (p. 143). Although most investigators recognize that research involves much guesswork, most of us would hesitate to call our work a guessing game, at least in its long-range perspective. We prefer to see ourselves as mapping nature *factually* and observing and explaining events *objectively*—that is, logic and objective observation are the earmarks we usually wish to ascribe to our efforts in research.

Polanyi would agree that logic and observation are indeed characteristics of the activity of research, but he would ask us to recognize that some crucial scientific processes never have been, and perhaps never will be, subject to canons of strict logical necessity. The relation between a scientific question and what one considers appropriate or adequate evidence, or the relation between a question and evidence, on the one hand, and what one considers an appropriate or adequate interpretation, on the other, are not strictly impersonal, logical matters. What is logical to one person is illogical to another, what closes one person's curiosity piques another's, and what is true-blue observation to one person is hunch, inference, biased statement, or plain junk to another. Such disagreements and what they motivate in terms of exchange and activity provide much of the excitement, satisfaction, and even progress of research. More importantly, however, in view of the guesswork inherent in research and the disagreement originating from differences in personal tastes and working styles, scientists agree—in the sense of arriving at consensual agreement—upon various procedures and rules for minimizing personal bias and for optimizing reliability in the process of trying to guess right.

In human development, as in other areas of science, these agreed-upon guidelines and rules fall at numerous points along a spectrum ranging from great generality to extreme specificity. At the former pole is the philosophy of science—that is, consideration of the general functions, maxims, presuppositions, strengths, and limitations of science. At the latter pole are rules, prescriptions, and catalogues for the use of very specific techniques and methods of measurement and observation, such as interviews, questionnaires, phenomenological reports, standard adjustments, Q sorts, electronic monitoring, and so on. Somewhere in the midrange between the general earmarks or the philosophy of science on the one hand, and the choice and application of particular techniques, measurements, and conditions of research on the other, is a wide band of concern that is commonly called *methodology*. Despite the fact that the boundaries of methodology are difficult to determine with precision, there are two basic questions that provide the springboards for most methodological discussion and represent its focal concerns: (1) "How do I obtain interpretable data?" or "How do I obtain data for which the ambiguity of evaluation is reduced to the lowest possible degree?" and (2) "Given a purpose or set of purposes, a question or set of questions, what kinds of investigative exercises, operations, and strategies should I embark upon to fulfill the purposes and answer the questions?" Frequently the second question is harder to answer than the first. However it is also more important, because it probes directly into the issue of appropriateness, adequacy, or suitability of strategies of research, where appropriateness must be evaluated in part against what the investigator is looking for—that is, what his/her questions are.

In order to make the argument more concrete, one working assumption must be made explicit. We assume that psychological research is a quest and that investigators of behavior are after something. We assume that those persons whose interests and activities constitute that diverse aggregate, psychological research, believe they are contributing to the understanding of behavior in everyday settings—in nature, so to speak—and we assume that it is this faith that keeps the work going, no matter how esoteric and rarified it may appear at any particular time. Given that belief we can develop the rationale for naturalistic research. However some definitions are in order.

NATURALISTIC RESEARCH

One immediate problem in discussing naturalistic research is to sharpen the meaning of the adjective, *naturalistic,* so that it denotes something relevant to the process of empirical investigation. It is common to define naturalistic research as research on natural phenomena. Not only does this definition stumble on a circularity, but it is also fruitless to look for the criteria of naturalness in the events and phenomena that one is studying. Frequency of occurrence is one such phenomenon-based criterion that leads nowhere. For example tonsillectomies might occur more frequently than paralysis-inducing accidents but would not necessarily be judged more natural. Degree of human artifice is a second phenomenon-based criterion that breaks down. For example a visit to a dentist involves a high degree of human instigation and arrangement but probably would not be judged less natural than a tornado, at least for purposes of research. Finally the degree to which a situation or event is true to human nature might be invoked. However, this criterion begs the question of what is true to human nature.

One of the issues running through the search for phenomenon-based criteria of naturalness is that, for some people, that which is natural is good and that which is artificial is bad. In behavioral research naturalness or naturalism, if we can speak of it at all, is a function of what the investigator does. When discussing behavioral research we should disavow the value judgments and their accompanying search for phenomenon-based criteria of naturalness and rather focus descriptively upon the conduct of research itself. On this view, phenomena that are highly unusual, occur very infrequently, and involve a high degree of human artifice and arrangement can be the targets of naturalistic investigation. In other words it is possible to differentiate research activities in terms of the part the researcher plays, or where the researcher is placed, in the process of research. Since we can then speak jointly of what an investigator does and what is found, this differentiation is more useful than focusing only on the phenomena studied.

In terms of the investigator's role, naturalistic methods can be distinguished with some precision. Pure naturalistic approaches "have input only: there is one-way communication between them and the phenomena to which they are applied; they disclose things and events unchanged by the techniques used to observe them" (Barker, 1964, p. 268). This is the most basic principle or characteristic of naturalistic research. Naturalistic methods discover and reveal occurrences that are free of the influences of the investigator. The investigator functions as a passive recipient or observer of data from a world functioning according to its own laws.

Psychological phenomena are scanned by the psychologist [investigator] who functions with respect to them as a transducer, transforming them in accordance with coding categories into data. This data-generating system is, in effect, a translating machine; it translates psychological phenomena into data. The data it generates are operative images of the phenomena, prepared in retrievable form for storage and further analysis. (Barker, 1965, p. 1)

In contrast, with experimental methods there is a direct, causal, or instigating relationship between the methods themselves and the phenomena they deal with or observe. What they discover are results of the conditions imposed or created by the investigator. In an experiment the investigator ". . . is coupled into the psychological unit as an operative part of it, regulating input, and/or influencing interior conditions, and/or constraining output. The psychologist [investigator] dominates this system; as operator, he sends messages via the unit [phenomena] to himself as receiver and transducer" (Barker, 1965, p. 3).

These definitions can be made more precise by developing a framework that characterizes the actual execution of research. Such a framework will aid in generating correspondence between research purposes and methods on relatively nonspeculative and nonpolemical grounds.

The activities an investigator actually engages in while carrying out a piece of research fall somewhere in a two-dimensional descriptive space. The first dimension describes the degree of investigator influence upon, or manipulation of, the antecedent conditions of the behavior studied, on the assumption that the degree of such influence may vary from high to low, or from much to none. The second dimension describes the degree to which units are imposed by the investigator upon the behavior studied in the act of measuring it. Conceiving of the two dimensions as orthogonal, with hypothetical variation from maximal to minimal on each, allows one to describe research activities as rating somewhere from high to low on investigator manipulation of antecedent conditions (independent variables) and also on imposition of units on the data by the investigator.

Figure 8–1 displays these descriptive dimensions in orthogonal relation. Assuming that the target of an investigation is some behavioral phenomenon, it is possible to describe two separate, though often interdependent, ways in which the investigator may function in the process of obtaining behavioral data: (1) by influencing or arranging the antecedent conditions of the behavior and (2) by imposing restrictions or limitations on the range or spectrum of responses—that is, the behavior itself. Furthermore, as described by Figure 8–1, each of these functions can vary on a continuum.

Studies commonly labeled naturalistic observation (Low-Low), field experimentation (Med-Med), and laboratory experimentation (High-High) probably fall on the main diagonal. Some of the other combinations are less obvious and would benefit from illustration. For example a study by Bechtel (1967) can be placed at Low-High. Bechtel developed an electronic apparatus called a *hodometer* to record the use of space in an art gallery. The hodometer is composed of mats, each one-foot square and sensitive to pressure. The mats, each with a micro switch connected to a counter, are laid on the floor and covered by a carpet, thereby offering an unobtrusive tab-

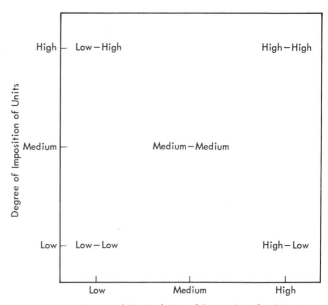

Figure 8–1 A description of the investigator's role in data gathering procedures

ulation of the occupancy of space in the room. The important point for present purposes is that under conditions where he did not manipulate or arrange the room environment, as in his study of an art gallery, Bechtel's program rates low on manipulation of antecedent conditions and high on imposition of units—i.e., the number of micro switch contacts per room area. Barker, Dembo, and Lewin's (1943) classic study of frustration and regression exemplifies High-Low on the figure. Here the investigators carefully sequentialized and manipulated the antecedents of play and goal blockage but obtained rich, open-ended, descriptive records of behavior from which to infer frustration and constructiveness of play.

There are implications of viewing research activities in general, and naturalism in particular, in terms of what the investigator does. First, as traditionally conceived, the laboratory experiment is a strategy through which an investigator produces phenomena and makes them occur at his/her behest, at will, in a setting whose purpose is investigation. In contrast naturalistic study is a strategy by which an investigator records, or commits to a researchable form, phenomena that s/he does not produce or bring about, in settings whose purposes are determined by other persons. In the controversies over the merits of manipulated laboratory research and naturalistic research, what is usually called laboratory experimentation falls in the High-High sector, and what is usually called naturalistic research falls in the Low-Low sector. The controversies usually focus on the most extreme cases that represent only a small portion of the possibilities.

Second, and perhaps more important, the descriptive space avoids arbitrary dichotomies and suggests that the manner in which the investigator functions in the process of generating data—and therefore what is often called the degree of naturalness—falls on continua whose various points are so difficult to differentiate that they cannot be defended with finality and rigor. McGuire (1967) reminds us that "experiment," in its etymologically correct usage, means "to test, to try" (p. 128), pointing up the arbitrary nature of most attempts to encapsulate research strategies. The degree of "quasi-ness" in Campbell and Stanley's (1963) treatment of experimental and quasi-experimental design refers to a similar continuum. However it is clear that the main diagonal describes only a small portion of the possible set of research activities—that is, the usual categories correlate manipulation and imposition of units too highly and exclude a great number of possibilities. The usual way of viewing the alternatives of naturalistic research and other modes is far too restricted.

The physical sciences frequently are cited as disciplines more mature scientifically than the social and behavioral sciences. In psychology's self-conscious effort to attain scientific respectability, there has been a tendency to identify scientific with controlled experimentation, and the laboratory experiment in physics often is held up as a model for psychology. Physicists accept the data from pure observation as a necessary complement to the data produced in experimental laboratories. If we were to place the research activities of physics into the two-dimensional descriptive framework, we probably would have little trouble filling the entire space. It is interesting to speculate that the maturity of a science might be gauged by the amount of space in the framework that is actually filled by investigations in the discipline. In other words the mark of a mature science is the use of the full spectrum of research methods and some consensus about the functions served by each.

With the two-dimensional characterization of research in mind, the remainder of this chapter deals with the question: So what? Naturalistic research uniquely serves certain scientific purposes. The reasons for choosing naturalistic methods, or the rationale for naturalistic methods, can be stated in terms of what works for investigative purposes. Some of the components of such a rationale will be discussed in this chapter.

CHOICE OF NATURALISTIC METHODS

It is requisite to any science that it concern itself with how its phenomena are distributed in the real world and how its findings, laws, and theories match the real world—the world of conditions that have not been created by experimental designs. The naturalistic side of science makes this possible. If one of the ultimate goals of human development is to apply its findings, laws, and theories to the real world, a naturalistic approach is required, because the conditions for application cannot be found through experimentation alone. Naturalistic research requires a methodological orientation which is in many ways the antithesis of an experimental orientation, requiring a sort of disciplined naïveté on the part of the investigator. Naturalistic research is not defective or sloppy experimentation; in fact, it is not experimentation at all because it leaves behavior and its contexts intact.

One form of contextual disturbance of behavior is to wrench it out of its environmental context. Another fundamental source of distortion of behavior by contrivance is taking bits of it out of its normal temporal sequence. It is often thought that behavior in its natural course is so complicated and unstable that the only way to make it amenable to study is to restrain it by experimental controls. However there is a naturally occurring robustness, interdependence, and order in behavior along its temporal dimension, and research techniques are being developed to study such interdependence and order. Paralleling the concern with the intact continuity of behavior is the concern for ways to deal with the continuous, ongoing matrix of environmental events with which behavior intermingles and interacts.

A basic concern of naturalistic research is to specify the environment in which the behavior of organisms is distributed. Brunswik called this "textural ecology" (Postman & Tolman, 1959, p. 551). Bronfenbrenner (1979) has provided a profound elaboration of these principles, including a classification of levels of analysis for the environment. The point here is that in order to specify the environmental regularities to which the organism must adapt and within which it behaves, it is necessary to measure and describe the external environment—the environmental offerings, so to speak.

What, then, are some issues, concerns, or components that would lead an investigator to choose methods tending toward the low manipulation—low imposition parts of the descriptive space presented in Figure 8–1? This section will focus on one set of such issues or purposes, a set which is neither necessarily independent nor exhaustive. For convenience we shall use the term *naturalistic* to refer to studies and methods that tend toward the low end on either or both of the two dimensions in Figure 8–1.

Artificiality

One question in this highly interrelated set of issues is the question of artificiality of findings and conditions of investigation. One of the favorite arguments against laboratory research by the proponents of naturalistic research is that the conditions of investigation, and therefore the findings, are artificial in the typical laboratory study. The problem with this accusation is that it is value laden and difficult to document. What are the criteria of artificiality? Perhaps more important, when would one choose to engage in research that rates high or low on so-called artificiality? Brunswik dwelt at length with this problem and stated it in terms of tying and untying of variables.

Artificial Tying. In his critiques of systematic, carefully arranged, experimental research, Brunswik made much of what he called *artificial tying of variables* (Postman & Tolman, 1959, p. 517). In experiments variables are often allowed or made to vary together in ways that persons never confront in their everyday circumstances. An example of this problem, reported by Gump and Kounin (1959–1960), illustrates the point.

Gump and Kounin wanted to test the effects of various kinds of control techniques by teachers upon nontarget students in college classes—that is, they wanted to see what effects control techniques, focused upon particular students, had upon other students in the classroom. Student confederates were instructed to come late to classes. Teachers were trained to try supportive, friendly, control techniques at some times and threatening, punitive ones at others. The investigators found that punitive, as compared to supportive, techniques resulted in lowered evaluations of the instuctor's competence, likeability, and fairness. However on later questionnaires they found that most students were surprised that one of their college instructors would take time out to correct a student for coming late to class. What they found was how students evaluate instructors using two kinds of control techniques when the students are surprised or when they see the teachers' behavior as atypical. In their efforts to produce a reasonably clean experiment, the investigators had taken a phenomenon out of its everyday context and combined several factors artificially. A naturalistic approach is necessary to uncover the patterning and structure of variables in the real lives of persons and to discover how the phenomena are actually distributed in nature. More about this later.

Klinghammer (1967), discussing early experience, imprinting, and mate selection in altricial birds, points out that the theoretical controversy over what is a substitute imprinting object and what is a primary imprinting object has resulted from experimental procedures that provide animals with "additional experiences" (p. 39), or tied variables, that they never confront in a natural, nonexperimental situation. According to Klinghammer, exposure to a potential mate from the birds' own species *and* exposure to an object outside the birds' species "is bound to have a disruptive effect on behavior" (p. 39).

Artificial Untying. Brunswik discusses another way in which carefully contrived experiments distort the relationships that persons face in their natural environments. He calls this *artificial untying of variables* (Postman & Tolman, 1959, p. 519), which occurs when natural covariations among variables are eliminated through experimental control. When variables are artificially untied in research, the extent to which the results can be generalized to real-life behavior is limited. Gump and Sutton-Smith (1955) reported a study in which a naturalistic orientation uncovered an artificial untying of variables in an experiment.

The study investigated the reactions of poorly skilled players when they were placed in more or less difficult positions or roles in children's games. In the experimental game chosen, a person who was "It" worked in the center of a rectangular playing field and attempted to tag other players who ran to and from safe areas at each end of the rectangle. High power was given to the "It" position by having the child who was "It" call the turns; he said when the others could run. Another condition gave low power to the "It" position; the other players could run whenever they chose. Preselected slow runners were assigned to high- and low-power "It" positions. Results confirmed the research hypotheses: In low-power as opposed to high-power "It" positions, poorly skilled boys experienced more tagging failures and uttered more defeatist and distress comments. They were teased and combined against only in the low-power positions.

When the authors adopted a naturalistic approach and observed what happened in gyms, playgrounds, and camps, where they had not arranged the environment, they found that

... (a) poorly skilled boys do not often get into games they cannot manage; (b) if they do get involved, they tend to avoid difficult roles by not trying to win such a position or by quitting if they cannot avoid it; and (c) if they occupy the role and are having trouble, the game often gets so boring to opponents that these opponents let themselves be caught in order to put the game back on a more zestful level. (Gump & Kounin, 1959–1960, p. 148)

The arranged experiment yielded interesting results and supported the investigators' hypotheses, but it did not measure what occurs in the everyday lives of children. "It showed what happens under somewhat desperate circumstances—circumstances created and sustained by interfering adults" (Gump & Kounin, 1959–1960, p. 148). In their experiment the investigators had artificially untied variables to produce a condition that seldom, if ever, occurs in everyday life. The observations in the investigator-free context demonstrated what boys actually do when left to their own resources; the experimental data did not show this. However, the experimental data, with the environmental variables arranged, offered an explanation for the naturalistic data. The experimental data suggested *why* slow runners seldom, if ever, behave in certain roles.

All of these examples illustrate tying and untying of variables as a basis for choice among methods, but they also point to another issue—namely, the interplay, or interdependence, of experimental and naturalistic research. In fact for human development Bronfenbrenner (1979) and Willems (1973) have outlined strategies toward research that weaken the old distinctions. Manipulated experimentation has explored the range and extent of object substitution in imprinting in a way that naturalistic research cannot. In Gump and Sutton-Smith's studies the naturalistic methods documented what boys actually do in games, while the experiment, by forcing poorly skilled boys into difficult roles, suggested *why* they do what they do in games. The manipulational research suggested that experiences of failure and negative social feedback upon performance are factors that keep poorly skilled boys out of the difficult roles. This reciprocity and interdependence of research strategies needs continuous reemphasis. Neither strategy, manipulational nor naturalistic, is a weak derivative, poor second cousin, or second-rate supplement of the other. For example field workers have observed hundreds of hours devoted to social play among monkeys and apes in the wild, thus documenting the occurrence and range of play in nature. However it was Harlow's experiments that showed just how essential social play is to the development of behavior (see Mason, 1965).

The Problem of Yield

Another issue in a discussion of naturalistic methods is closely related to the distribution of phenomena (discussed later) and is important because it is often turned into a criticism of naturalistic research. The criticism often runs something like this: As scientists we are seeking general laws of behavior; therefore, we must assure ourselves of adequate empirical yield from our studies in terms of frequency and intensity of occurrences. Many, if not all, naturalistic studies, when compared to laboratory experiments, involve a disproportionate amount of time and effort relative to data yield. *Ergo,* the optimal methods are laboratory experiments.

A demonstration of just this problem is a study reported by Gump and Kounin (1959–1960). These investigators had made extensive studies of classroom settings, seeking what effects disciplinary or control techniques had upon children other than the target child, and they wished to extend the study to other contexts, such as a public camp. They chose two camp settings for study—a cabin clean-up period and a rest period. One observer noted the behavior of adult cabin leaders, and other observers made records of individual campers. Over a six-week period involving six observers, about 46 hours of camper behavior were recorded. The total yield of responses by nontarget children was about one incident for every 18 pages of verbal record. Such a low frequency is interesting in itself, but it fits the criticism of economy of effort and yield.

How shall such a criticism be answered? In a rationale for naturalistic methods, the answer should be an empirical one, and the answer is that the economy-of-yield argument is not unidirectional; it does not apply uniquely to naturalistic studies. Sometimes it is impossible to produce in the laboratory even a minimal trace of a condition analogous to a circumstance in the real world. Kounin has reported such an incident (Kounin, 1961). The investigators wanted to study the effects of

various control techniques, or types of discipline, by teachers upon students who ranged from low to high on commitment to a task. After training their experimental teachers, they contracted a sample of adolescents to come to the campus of Wayne State University during the summer, for pay, to serve as experimental students. However the investigators could not induce low commitment, or noncommitment, in any group of students. The yield for that cell of the design was zero. The typical real-life school has its few who lack commitment to the tasks at hand, and these investigators were able to fill that research cell only by studying students in actual classes. This is an instance in which it was possible to discover through a naturalistic orientation a phenomenon that could not be produced experimentally. The problem of ratio of effort to yield is not unique to naturalistic studies.

Generalization

One of the most important scientific issues that a discussion of naturalistic research should include is the problem of generalizing findings and laws to everyday circumstances. This has an empirical root in the problem of discrepant findings. It is one thing to have an investigator's purpose lead to a choice of naturalistic or experimental methods, but it is another matter when two different approaches are used to study what is assumed to be the same phenomenon and discrepant findings are the outcome. Such discrepancies point to an important scientific function for naturalistic methods, as several examples will suggest.

Kortlandt (1962), in a summary of his observations of chimpanzees in the wild, offers a number of comparisons between what one would conclude about the behavior of chimps from studies of captive animals and from naturalistic studies. First, according to Kortlandt, one would conclude from captive chimps that infants are spoiled and frequently disobey parental calls. In the wild, on the other hand, even with all their freedom, infant chimps do not appear spoiled, and they almost always obey their mothers at the first hint. Second, whereas one would conclude from studies of captives that chimps appear increasingly "dull and vacant" (p. 131) with passing years; older chimps in the wild, if anything, become more lively, alert, and curious. Third, from studies of captive chimps, one would generalize that they live in harem groups of five to fifteen. Kortlandt saw no such grouping in the wild. Fourth, one would probably conclude from captive chimps that they are essentially arboreal, whereas "in the wild they behave like such basically terrestrial animals as baboons" (p. 133). Finally, compared to captive animals, behavior of young chimps in the wild is markedly retarded, developing humanlike characteristics much later than captives. Despite the fact that Kortlandt's captive baselines are from chimps in zoos and not in experimental laboratories, the point remains that the investigator of chimp behavior would be in error on at least five counts if s/he generalized from captive chimps to the wild state.

Washburn (1963) reports that baboons have been studied frequently in captivity, as in zoos and primate laboratories. One of the most common findings in these conditions is that, almost invariably, when two or more baboons are confined together, one emerges as the leader. This finding in itself is not surprising. However, it is important to take note of how the leaders emerge while in confinement. Leaders in confinement emerge by intimidation—that is, by comparative brute power—and they maintain their leadership positions in the same manner.

In the wild, leaders emerge among the baboons, but in their natural habitats and in their natural groupings, these leaders do not emerge through physical intimidation. In fact the leaders seldom, if ever, resort to brute force, even in discipline. Leadership is ascribed to them on the basis of superior cunning, sexual expertise, and, apparently, attractiveness. Unlike their counterparts in confinement, the leaders in the uncontrived circumstances seemingly need to make no show of force and brutality.

It is clear that the investigator of leadership behavior in baboons would be seriously mistaken if s/he were to generalize from the factors producing leadership in confinement to those producing it in the natural, day-to-day world of the baboon. The problem of generalization to what exists in the everyday lives of organisms requires a naturalistic approach. In this case no amount of caution would have made the generalizations from studies in captivity fit the everyday world accurately. A different research orientation directed at documenting the distribution and occurrence of phenomena in natural settings is required.

We could argue indefinitely about the relative merits of research with animals such as rats for generalizing to human behavior. However there is some suggestion that experimental research with rats does not even generalize to rats. Kavanau (1964, 1969) has provided some evidence on this issue. His statement focuses on the special factors which are unique to laboratory studies with rats and the special breeds of rats used.

A few generalizations emerging from ethologically oriented laboratory studies of wild rodents have important bearings on the rationale and design of experiments on learning and reinforcements. Depriving animals of natural outlets for activity by confining them in small and barren enclosures greatly influences their behavior. Thus, when given the means to modify their environment in ways that do not subject them to great stress, captive rodents exercise this control repeatedly. These animals find it rewarding to attain and to exercise a high degree of control over their environment, perhaps in partial substitution for the freedom of action enjoyed in the wild but denied by confinement.... The initial responses of rodents in laboratory enclosures do not reflect the preferences or behavior of animals adapted to the experimental situation, but rather those of animals forced to endure unnatural and completely arbitrary conditions and schedules of confinement and experimentation. The time required for animals to adapt to the "insults" of laboratory experimentation is measured not in minutes or hours but in days or weeks. Thus, even in experiments for which the design and analysis do not penetrate beyond regarding the animal as a convenient experimental machine or black box, the responses to daily short experimental sessions generally give information only about the initial, and often rebellious, reactions of the "machine" to abnormal and enforced working conditions. (1964, p. 490)

Kavanau implies that it is impossible to generalize from carefully contrived experimental conditions to real-

life behavior. However, one might ask: What if the investigator waits to allow the animals to adapt to the artificial conditions or uses laboratory-bred animals? This makes the laboratory researcher's quandary double-edged. As Kavanau says,

Using such atypical species representatives as domestic rats and mice for laboratory studies of behavior narrows the animal response spectrum to a point where its significance for adaptation, survival, and evolution becomes highly questionable. The selectively inbred animals are hundreds of generations removed from the wild. Their bland behavior tells us mainly how animals react to experimental regimes after many of the characteristic adaptive responses of the species have been largely or completely lost. Domestic animals remain convenient vegetalized strains for physiological studies, but only wild animals provide the full range and vigor of responses upon which solutions to the central problems of behavior must be based. (p. 490) (Quotes from Kavanau, 1964 © 1964 by the American Association for the Advancement of Science.)

Kavanau seems to be saying that if the ultimate concern of the behavioral scientist is to generalize about the everyday, real-life behavior and adaptations of organisms, then the carefully controlled but contrived conditions of the experiment will not yield appropriate data. Furthermore he says that if we wait until laboratory conditions become natural to the organism, we will have then produced a different organism, which again will not yield generalizable data.

In an investigation of decision-making procedures in groups, Hall and Williams (1966) combined variations in manipulation of antecedent conditions in a single study. They were investigating the effect of group conflict upon processes and outcomes in group decisions, and they compared the performances of 20 established, intact groups of management trainees to 20 ad hoc groups, groups with no history as groups outside the laboratory. Hall and Williams explicitly set out to assess the generalizability of findings from ad hoc laboratory groups to established groups, and their finding was that such generalization is precarious business. The ad hoc groups differed from the established groups in their processes of making decisions, the nature of their decisions, and especially in the way they dealt with conflict. Apart from common sense and speculation, there are now data to suggest that on several dimensions, generalization from ad hoc experimental assemblies to established groups would be in error.

Other examples of the problem of generalizing from the laboratory to everyday life could be cited, but the issues seem fairly clear. It should be emphasized that the findings for Washburn's confined baboons, Hall and Williams's ad hoc groups, and the captive chimps to which Kortlandt refers were accurate and reliable for those subjects and those conditions—that is, the internal validity of those data is not under question here. It is also clear that the investigators would have been in error if they had made straightforward generalizations to everyday occurrences on the basis of those subjects alone. Bauer (1964), in a review of research on social communication and social influence, does not hesitate to conclude flatly, ". . . the characteristic behavior of the audience in the natural habitat is such as to bring about crucial modifications of the results seen in the laboratory" (p. 321). It is seductively easy to be content with results obtained in manipulated laboratory experiments and to assume that caution is the only requirement for generalizing. The examples cited and an extensive literature on external validity (Bronfenbrenner, 1979; Campbell & Stanley, 1963; Cook & Campbell, 1976; Willems, 1973) indicate that caution is not the only requirement and that naturalistic methods perform a unique function in generalization. The point is that any program of research that includes generalization as one of its aims should purposefully include data yielded by methods that tend toward low manipulation and low imposition of units. This is an empirical matter rather than a speculative one.

Pointing to discrepancies in findings, stating the problem of generalizing and asserting that naturalistic methods perform a unique function represent only a beginning and tell investigators little about how to view the functions of manipulational and naturalistic research, when to use methods falling into either strategy, or how to dovetail their functions in the problem of generalizing. One very readable and informative early treatment of the matter of dovetailing is offered by Breland and Breland (1966), especially in their conception of the laboratory as a surrogate of an organism's ecological niche (pp. 62–69). The Brelands propose a number of guidelines and implications for generalizing in the study of animal behavior, and they conclude that it is no longer feasible for psychologists to generate complete theories, taxonomies, and generalizations from the strictures of the laboratory and that one of the most pressing needs is to relate what organisms do in the laboratory to what they do in the wild. Menzel (1969) has developed this theme further with more examples.

In this same vein Scott and Wertheimer (1962) conclude,

When it comes to generalizing research findings to the normal, everyday behavior of the organism, naturalistic observation would appear to enjoy a clear lead over the other methodologies—assuming, of course, that it is based on an adequate sampling of the behaviors under study. Not only can the investigator be sure that the relationships he has observed occur in the subject's natural habitat, but through time-sampling of behavior he can determine the relative frequencies with which the events appear. This can provide an index of the "importance" of a functional relationship to the organism in its natural ecology. In laboratory studies, on the other hand, the particular functional relationship observed may be in large part a product of the special, artificial conditions of the experiment. Such a restriction in generality is likely to be particularly serious in those "hold constant" experiments in which control of extraneous variables artificially places them at levels that would hardly be encountered in the subject's normal activity. A given experiment may show conclusively a relationship between the independent and dependent variables, which, however, is demonstrated only under such peculiar circumstances that the result is uninteresting, except as a curiosity. (pp. 95–96)

Relevant to the problem of generalization, as well as to the issue of artificiality and tying of variables discussed earlier, is Pugh's (1966) discussion of strategies for studying human behavior in organizations. Pugh says,

One may ask why it is considered less artificial to study men getting paid for standing on the assembly line at a motor factory screwing on car-door handles than to study men getting paid for taking part in a laboratory ergograph experiment. The answer is that it is not so much the actual laboratory task itself that is artificial . . . as the social situation in which it is performed. The social role of mass production operator is far removed from that of laboratory subject. The enormous disparity in the duration of role occupancy is sufficient to ensure differences in sanctions and motivations, with consequent divergence in performance. (p. 236)

Pugh is pointing to two descriptive properties of laboratory studies that limit generalization to everyday phenomena. First, he mentions the global social situation in which the experimental task is performed. Pugh's use of words here reminds one of the more extensive treatment by Orne (1962), who showed that persons do unique things in the social situation of the experimental laboratory. Second, Pugh mentions the difference in time perspective, or duration of role occupancy, between lab and everyday circumstance and how it might affect the results of research. Kounin's (1961) failure to induce low commitment mentioned earlier might be an example of the effects of differing time perspective. Argyris (1968, 1976) has expanded on Pugh's arguments.

We often can, and often should, press our explorations into phenomena by changing, interrupting, or producing them at our behest. However the argument here is that any program of research that includes generalization as one of its aims should purposefully include data yielded by methods that tend toward low manipulation and low imposition of units—in other words, naturalistic methods. Stated in a slightly different way, the argument goes as follows: Appropriate generalization to everyday events is a problem of ecological validity. Ecological validity is not used here in Brunswik's technical sense but in the more intuitive sense of correspondence between our generalizing statements and what occurs in the organism's natural habitat. Achievement of ecological validity requires, at least in part, an ecological or contextual perspective in research. It is widely accepted that an ecological perspective requires naturalistic methods. Therefore naturalistic methods are important in any program of generalizing. Much work remains to be done in explicating the factors and guidelines for such a program beyond the bare hints offered by the Brelands, Scott and Wertheimer, Pugh, Orne, and this chapter. Bronfenbrenner (1979) offers an excellent beginning.

DISTRIBUTION OF PHENOMENA IN NATURAL SYSTEMS

Roger Barker reported that he once had trouble with a well on his farm. The water was affected by nitrates, which can be a serious problem in a well. He consulted a county agricultural extension agent who referred him to a data sheet on nitrates in water. The sheet contained detailed information on nitrates—their overall abundance, their geographical distribution, and the geological conditions under which they occur. This information provided Barker with a basis to plan some remedial steps and also to decide where a new well should be located. However this experience also puzzled and troubled Barker as a behavioral scientist. He wondered where he could go to find analogous data sheets on significant human behavior and experience—frustration, failure, reward, punishment, and so on. There are no such data sheets, of course, at least not on a large scale. It is a curious collective oversight, if not a distinct embarrassment, that the social and behavioral sciences have not developed detailed, systematic tables of information on the distribution, range, and frequency of behavior and behavior-environment relations.

If professionals in other areas proceeded in the way most social and behavioral scientists do, we would question their competence and judgment. We assume that geologists and other scientists have plotted out the characteristics of the earth's crust in such a way that they know the distribution of layers and the relationship between subsurface crustal formations and occurrence of crude oil, and we assume that a company in search of oil will use that information to reduce the likelihood of drilling a dry hole. We expect the planners of buildings and roads to benefit from systematic information on the distributions and characteristics of soils, rocks, subsurface moisture, and fault lines to avoid expensive and tragic mistakes. We would scarcely feel sorry for the person who did not take advantage of what hydrologists know about rainfall and subsurface water sources before putting in a large and expensive pecan orchard.

Social and behavioral scientists can assimilate all of that and still not realize its implications for the understanding of human behavior. We fail to recognize a two-part problem: (1) Studying the distributions of behavior and behavior-environment relations in natural systems is a perfectly meritorious and important scientific activity in its own right and (2) the planning, execution, and success of plans and programs of change often suffer from the lack of such distributional information. Such information is one of the most central contributions of ecological and naturalistic research.

The Times We Are In

Extensive, careful description and classification of the location, range, frequency, and intensity of behavioral phenomena in natural systems is accepted as crucial in other areas of science but is relegated to second-rate status in behavioral science by the prevailing norms and standards of our time. Why should this important part of behavioral science have so little status and popularity outside of public opinion polling and choice behavior in voting trends and marketing of products? An example will illustrate the problem. Following on the work of Stoner (1961) and the conceptualization by Brown (1965), a great number of investigators produced several hundred studies to test the proposition that participation in a group changes individual preferences and behaviors in the direction of greater risk. These studies, which staged the conditions in experiments, disentangled so many aspects of social risk taking that it would be almost impossible to review them all. However almost all of the research was of a particular type: Given a certain set of conditions as arranged by an experimenter, certain kinds of risk-taking behavior occur. Why, in all of this investment of effort, time, and money, was not an extensive, descriptive documentation of the distribution of risk taking in natural systems undertaken? What are the conditions, situations, problems, and tasks that involve risk in everyday life? What is the frequency of risk taking in various circumstances and by persons at various points along the span of chronological age? Do drivers in car pools take more risks than persons driving alone? How often and under what conditions do postcardiac patients engage in the risks of strenuous programs of exercise? When, how often, and under what conditions do handicapped persons in wheelchairs or on crutches take the risks of negotiating environments that involve slopes, curbs, stairways, doorways, and the absence of other persons to help them? The many if-then experiments that have been conducted are intriguing. However perspective on how the phenomena of risk taking are distributed in natural social and environmental systems is just as important to social and behavioral scientists as perspective on the distribution of crude oil in natural geological systems is to scientists, businesses, and policy planners involved in the energy problem.

One major step in the right direction has been reported by Ebbesen and Haney (1973), who made more than 13,600 observations of drivers at intersections and the circumstances under which the drivers took the risk of turning in front of oncoming traffic. Not only are the resulting tables of raw frequency interesting and full of implications for understanding the everyday behavior of drivers, but Ebbesen and Haney were also able to identify the following factors that increase such risk taking: (1) long waiting time at the intersection, (2) sex (males take more risks than females), (3) presence of other cars behind the car in question, and (4) driver alone in the car (other riders present lowered the rate of risk taking). Complete understanding requires descriptive information on rates, contexts, and distributions just as much as it requires testing of single hypotheses in a series of separate studies.

There are a number of reasons why American behavioral science has not emphasized the study of the distributions of behavioral phenomena in natural systems. First, many investigators seem to believe that behavior cannot really be studied reliably—*scientifically*—except when its occurrence and its conditions are subject to the investigator's control. Human behavior is often thought to be too ephemeral, too variable, too malleable without such control, and the experiment is often seen as the best way, or only way, to make behavior tractable and amenable to scientific study. Second, extensive descriptive work on natural systems is often seen as too mundane, time-consuming, and boring. Third, perhaps even more importantly and perniciously, it is easy to emphasize short-term theoretical and model-testing payoff in research and lose sight of long-range payoff for humanity.

Fourth, while the purpose of this section is to present the scientific and practical importance of naturalistic research and extensive descriptions of the distribution of investigator-free phenomena, there is another common aspect that permeates such research and often sets the persons involved in it apart from others. Among those scientists there is a compelling and clear quality that can best be called love for their subject matter. It is almost as if they are more enamored of complete and careful descriptive data and more in love with their subject matter, or even with their subjects, than they are with fame, research grants, nice offices, and competition. In their brief summary of the history of ethology, Crook and Goss-Custard (1972) note that

The pleasing truth seems to be that the founding fathers of classical ethology were all more in love with their animals than with the art of competition or controversy. They were ... "starers at animals," pure observers whose theories only gradually crystallized as an almost inductive necessity from the mountains of acutely perceptive observations they collected. Indeed the direct intellectual ancestors ... were all primarily observers in the tradition of natural history.... Only gradually did experimentation join observation in ethology. (p. 280)

Finally, one of the major reasons why extensive descriptive research on distributions of behavioral phenomena is not widely accepted or conducted in behavioral sciences is that, by and large, behavioral scientists have not taken the ecological perspective on behavior seriously enough. Ecological research begins with *extensive* research—the description and measurement of distributions in natural systems—and then elaborates the process of investigation to include *intensive* research—that is, the more discrete study of parts of the systems and the testing of specific hypotheses (Southwood, 1966). In discussing the structure of ecological research, Watt (1966) concludes that it always contains the following categories of activity: (1) systems measurement, the development of procedures for basic observation and the gathering of descriptive data, (2) systems description, the development of systematic tables and archives of descriptive data, and (3) systems analysis, or plotting the relationships among variables. For Watt these steps are so important that advanced models and hypotheses cannot be developed until the basic descriptive work is done.

... by far the most time-consuming in almost all ecological research programs, is the process of collecting data.... The rate at which ecology can progress is limited by the slowest activity in ecological research programs, namely systems measurement and systems analysis.... systems measurement is clearly identified as the step in the ecological research programs which limits the present rate of development in ecology, and we have the most powerful motivation for doing something about this problem. (1966, p. 255)

The naturalistic perspective involves the kind of descriptive research that creates data pools and archives of data that allow investigators to characterize the systems in which they are interested before they manipulate parts of the systems, experiment on them, or recommend policies for them. Thus we can see why extensive descriptive research is not highly valued in behavioral science. If the ecological perspective were widely accepted, extensive description would achieve the status of important scientific activity because it would be seen as necessary. As things stand now, without the acceptance of the naturalistic-ecological perspective, such research is often relegated to the second-rate status of "only descriptive research." It is also easier to understand why so few behavioral scientists have followed the pioneering example of investigators like Barker (1963, 1965, 1968), Barker and Schoggen (1973), Barker and Wright (1955), Gump (1967, 1969), Gump and Kounin (1959–1960), Kounin (1967), Willems (1972a, 1972b, 1976, 1977), and Wright

(1967, 1969–1970) in developing extensive descriptions of human behavior in schools, classrooms, camps, treatment facilities, and communities.

Data gathered continuously over extended periods of time are crucial to the naturalistic perspective. The issues of longitudinal research over extended periods of time and distributions of phenomena in intact systems are intertwined in important ways. This is so because extensive documentation of distributions not only means extensiveness in terms of size and number of variables; it can often mean extensiveness in time as well. Berrien (1968) discusses some reasons why a systems-oriented view of behavior and environment has not received the attention it should. He argues that one reason

... for the paucity of empirical support stems from the fact that the requisite research designs involve frequently, or better yet, continuously measured observations over an extended period on bona fide systems. Most of the social experiments conducted in laboratories are on groups with no history and a short life using cross-sectional rather than longitudinal measures. The variables are generally taken on comparable groups before and after some experimental manipulation.... We need a major change in the kind of data we collect.... Malthus' vision of an underemployment equilibrium had to wait a hundred years before the requisite national economic statistics were available to permit Keynes to revive and elaborate the Malthusian theory. I fervently hope that the general systems approach to social systems will not have to wait that long. (p. 122)

Behavioral Examples

In the early 1960s there were a number of controversies about the processes by which the developing child acquires a first language. Was it by means of a progressive set of associations between specific verbal units, such as words and phrases? By learning intact semantic or syntactic structures? By learning rules that would allow him/her to generate new and appropriate utterances? Not only was the controversy raging, but investigators were also conducting many studies to test their favorite hunches. Into the midst of all this activity, Weir (1962) injected a very reasonable set of data by recording, night after night, the presleep monologues (verbalizations) of her two-and-a-half-year-old son. Weir's book contained the descriptive analysis of the boy's speech and presented the entire set of 2600 utterances in an appendix. For one highly renowned psycholinguist, G. A. Miller, this extensive description of the naturally occurring verbal behavior of a small boy provided some important perspectives on the process of language learning.

After the many years of reading psychological theories about the environmental events that strengthen or weaken various stimulus-response associations, I was completely unprepared to encounter a two-year-old boy who—all alone—corrected his own pronunciations, drilled himself on consonant clusters, and practiced substituting his small vocabulary into fixed sentence frames. (Weir, 1962, Foreword)

Dyck (1963) used over 200 hours of direct observations of children in their natural habitats to measure the distributions of social contacts the children experienced. Dyck found that when the children engaged in contacts with their parents, the parents initiated 34 percent of the contacts. In contrast teachers initiated 73 percent of the child-teacher contacts by the same children. Such data do not sound earthshaking except when we realize that complete understanding of the process of socialization must take account of who does what, when, and where with developing children in their everyday lives.

The same observational protocols analyzed by Dyck have yielded many other descriptions of the rates and frequencies of the naturally occurring behavior of children (Barker & Wright, 1955; Wright, 1967). For example 67 percent of the children's behavior units were social units—that is, they involved direct input from others. Among the social behaviors 60 percent involved adults, and 67 percent involved females as the other persons. Among social behaviors involving adults 33 percent were dominated by the adults. Among social behaviors involving other children, the other children dominated 17 percent of the behaviors. Fawl (1963) found that disruptions of a child's behavior occurred at a median rate of 5.4 per hour, and that 50 percent of these disruptions came about through the loss of something the children were occupied with or valued.

In similar, extensive observations conducted in England and America, Schoggen, Barker, and Barker (1963) found that the average behavioral act of the American child was much shorter in duration than the average act of the English child. Barker and Barker (1963) showed that in contacts with children, English adults made devaluative inputs four times as often as American adults.

Wright (1969–1970) has demonstrated that analogous extensive studies of situations, or behavior settings, provide a picture of the scope of activities by children. He has shown how wide a range of activities children in midwestern American communities participate in, how often they participate in them, how often they have relatively responsible and important functions in the activities, how often they meet acquaintances and strangers, how frequently they are exposed to and interact with various classes of objects and persons, and how much time they spend with various kinds of activities, various classes of persons, and various classes of objects.

The importance of such information can be illustrated with an analogy and a concrete example. Geologists, hydrologists, and petroleum engineers have developed hypotheses regarding the relationships between properties of the earth's crust and the quality and occurrence of water and crude oil. The hydrologist's hypotheses might be of the following form: In geological formations of type A, water with impurities (nitrates, minerals, metals) of rate M will be found. For the pertroleum engineer: Crude oil with sulphur content of rate P will be found in geological formations of type C. When they are buttressed by research, such hypotheses (if-then models) are very important, but hydrologists and petroleum engineers know that such hypotheses are only part of the picture. In order to *find* potable water and sulphur-free crude oil and in order to *understand* why water and crude oil of high quality are found in some places and not in others, the picture must be completed with extensive descriptive data on the frequencies and distributions of geological formations of type A and C, as well as the larger contexts in which they occur. Geologists, hydrologists, and petroleum engineers get paid to know that kind of thing.

Analogously, developmental psychologists often generate specific hypotheses regarding the relationship between the kinds of persons to whom the developing child is exposed and the characteristic behavior patterns acquired by the child: (1) Exposure by the child to socializing agents of both sexes will lead to behavior pattern A, while restriction to female socializing agents will result in behavior pattern B or (2) involvements with a wide range of nonfamily adults will produce behavior pattern C, while relative restriction of involvements to parents will result in behavior pattern D. Such if-then models are important, but they are only part of the picture, no matter how firmly they are supported by experiments. In order to predict what kinds of behavior patterns will emerge in the current socioenvironmental system and in order to understand why a given type of behavior pattern emerges in some conditions and not in others, the picture must be completed with descriptive data on the distributions and frequencies of various social, environmental, and behavioral conditions in which developing children live.

Wright (1969–1970) has provided some of those data in his massive descriptions of the community lives of children. Where do children become behaviorally involved with nonfamily adults, and where do children become behaviorally involved with the greatest variety of persons? Where do social greetings by others lead to extended interactions with the child? On a community-wide basis Wright has found that, for children aged six to eleven, such events occur much more often in small towns than large towns. Children in large towns see more persons, but children in small towns become behaviorally involved, beyond fleeting exposure and greetings, with larger numbers and a greater variety of persons. How are sex-typed involvements distributed? Wright finds that children in large towns spend much more time with women only (e.g., mothers, female teachers, female group leaders) than children in small towns. Furthermore although children in large towns enter more settings than small-town children, small-town children have responsible leadership functions in more settings and participate in a much wider variety of settings.

These data only exemplify the system-wide distributions provided by Wright. Not only do some of Wright's data violate common sense and conventional social wisdom, but they also provide a much larger context in which to evaluate specific hypotheses regarding social development and other aspects of community life for children. Barker and Schoggen (1973) have offered a similar series of studies of English and American towns that represents one of the most extensive behavioral and socioenvironmental compendia ever gathered by behavioral scientists. The work of Barker, Wright, and their associates represents a demanding scientific model for behavioral scientists, but the substance of their data is also so extensive that the authors of scientific hypotheses and theories of personality development, socialization, person-environment interaction, adult-child relations, and culture and personality will be able to use the data sets as sounding boards for the appropriateness of their hypotheses for years to come. We can also understand better what Barker (1965) was trying to say some years ago.

I read . . . that potassium (K) ranks seventh in order of abundance of elements, and constitutes about 2.59% of the igneous rocks of the earth's crust; that its compounds are widely distributed in primary rocks, the oceans, the soil, plants, and animals; and that soluble potassium salts are present in all fertile soils. . . . The fact that there is no equivalent information in the literature of scientific psychology (about playing, about laughing, about talking, about being valued and devalued, about conflict, about failure) confronts psychologists with a monumental incompleted task. (p. 6)

Since the middle 1960s, behavioral and social scientists' acceptance of relatively nontheoretical extensive descriptions of the naturally occurring distributions of behavioral phenomena seems to have grown, as several further examples will help to illustrate. Studies by Schmitt (1971) and Ronnebeck (1972) have provided a new perspective on the behavior of disfigured children. Partly on the basis of common sense and partly on the basis of earlier writings by behavioral scientists (e.g., Goffman, 1963; Seligman, Macmillan, & Carroll, 1971; Vigliano, Hart, & Singer, 1958), a particular view of the effects of disfigurement had developed. For facial disfigurement as a result of a severe facial burn, for example, that view may be schematized as follows. The trauma of treatment and physical recovery affects the child's self-concept and social relationships in negative ways. More importantly the salience of the face as a social stimulus, the stigma attached to facial disfigurement, the aversion that persons feel and express toward facial disfigurement, and the various forms of negative social feedback that disfigured persons experience combine to restrict their social lives by limiting their status, attractiveness, and interpersonal relations. Schmitt (1971) obtained detailed data on the public (nonhome) behavior of 8 children whose faces were severely disfigured as the result of burns and 8 matched, nondisfigured children. The children were aged 6 to 12, and data were obtained for 28 consecutive days. The results of these extensive descriptions were surprising because, contrary to the popular hypothesis, there were no significant differences between the two groups in the number of settings they entered, the number of leadership functions they performed, the types of companions they had, and so on, for a number of measures of public behavior. There were some nonsignificant trends that favored the nondisfigured children, but others favored the disfigured group. In other words the notion of severe curtailment of social life because of facial disfigurement was hardly borne out by Schmitt's data.

One likely response to such data—in fact an interpretation offered by Schmitt himself—is that the traditional hypothesis is still really true, but that the negative social effects of facial disfigurement simply show up later. Even though the effects do not show up in children aged 6 to 12, they will surely show up among adolescents because adolescence is the period during which heterosexual issues and cosmetic and esthetic issues become particularly important. In order to extend the base of descriptive data and provide a context for answering such questions, Ronnebeck (1972) used Schmitt's method to study 13-to-19-year-old (postpubertal) adolescents. From 22 facially disfigured subjects and 22 matched, nondisfigured subjects, Ronnebeck obtained data on all public behavior for 28 consecutive days. Ronnebeck found some differences, but again the differences were relatively few in number. Among comparisons on 96 measures, only 12 favored the nondisfigured group significantly. Again the hypothesis of dramatic constriction of public social life was not borne out. Furthermore although one might argue that facial disfigurement would affect adolescent girls more than boys, Ronnebeck found just the opposite; the differences he found between disfigured and nondisfigured adolescents occurred mainly for boys and not for girls.

These studies offer a clear demonstration of how important it is to obtain extensive descriptions of behavior in natural, everyday community systems. How, where, and in what ways does facial deformity produce negative effects in the social lives of developing persons? Schmitt and Ronnebeck have provided the basis for a two-part answer: (1) not very often and not in very many places; (2) the few effects that do occur are found mainly in the case of adolescent boys, for whom facial deformity leads to some restriction of the number of settings participated in. However even those boys seem to compensate by participating more intensively in the settings they enter. Stuart (1973) conducted a similar study of wheelchair-bound students for a period of seven days at school, at home, and abroad in the community. This is the first time anyone has provided an extensive, detailed, quantitative description of the daily behavior of persons confined to wheelchairs, and the picture is highly illuminating. The overall frequencies of various types of behavior, participation in various settings, and time spent in various activities and places for the wheelchair-bound student is nearly indistinguishable from the typographies of matched, nondisabled students. Not only do the studies by Schmitt, Ronnebeck, and Stuart support the feasibility and general importance of extensive descriptive research on human behavior, but they also suggest that when we leave our preoccupation with person-based, psychological hypotheses and predictions and describe the behavior of persons in everyday systems, we will often find that what we thought must be the case simply is not the case at all.

Paris and Cairns (1972) report an interesting series of studies of the effects of positive and negative feedback on the behavior of retarded children. In a controlled experiment Paris and Cairns found that negative feedback (unpleasant, punishing consequences) achieved results more effectively on the behaviors to which it was applied than did positive feedback on the behaviors to which it was applied. Extensive observations of the retarded children in natural, nonexperimental settings provided a partial explanation. Naturalistic observation of how frequent and how contingent (how precisely following the behavior) the two types of feedback were revealed that positive feedback occurred more frequently than negative feedback in the daily lives of children. However, the negative feedback was provided in a more regularly contingent fashion (more precisely). In other words the social environment gave the retarded children more positive inputs but gave them diffusely, or in a less predictable way. Negative inputs came less often but were applied more strictly to specific negative behaviors.

Littlewood and Sale (1972) report the results of about 50,000 observations of British children at play in and around 16 housing developments in five different cities.

Observers made rounds at fixed intervals during the summer holidays and recorded the type of activity, its location, and the sex and estimated age of participating children. This is a very rich source of data with some intriguing findings, including the following. (1) On the average about 20 percent of a housing complex's children were found to be outdoors at any one time. (2) Five-to-ten-year-olds were seen most often (30 percent of them were usually outdoors). (3) The proportion of children playing outside at a complex was positively correlated with the proportion of children living in apartments on the ground floor. (4) The proportion of children playing outside was *negatively* correlated with the density of persons per acre in the complex. (5) Seventy-five percent of play took place near the dwellings, even when the playing surface near the buildings was poorly suited to play—e.g., roads, pavements, gardens, and ·planted areas. (6) Places with conventional play equipment (swings, slides, etc.) were used much more than places with less conventional, avant garde equipment (concrete mazes, pyramids, etc.). Data such as these provided by Littlewood and Sale and by Holme and Massie (1970) on the relationship between rate of use of play areas and distance from children's residences have implications for planners and administrators of residential systems.

Just as much as hydrologists, geologists, petroleum engineers, and public health professionals, behavioral scientists get paid for having a complete, contextual understanding of their phenomena of interest. The only way for behavioral science to achieve such complete understanding is to recognize the importance of studying distributions of behavioral phenomena in natural systems. The only way to obtain such distributional data is with naturalistic research methods.

Nonbehavioral Analogies and Arguments

One of the most telling indications of the backward state of the art and the lack of acceptance of naturalistic and distributional research in behavioral science is the fact that clear examples of its scientific and practical merits are so hard to find and summarize. The common reaction by behavioral scientists to such research is to ask: So what? What difference does it make when someone simply describes the rate, intensity, and frequency of behavior X and the manner in which it is distributed among persons, among groups, among places, and over time? There is a twofold problem in the sciences of behavior. First, behavioral scientists generally have not formulated the viewpoints and models that would lead to understanding the kind of information that is provided by distributional measures and to attaching theoretical and inferential values to them. Second, behavioral scientists generally have not come to realize that distributional data are worthwhile in themselves. Extensive compendia and handbooks of such data are a major mark of the maturity of a science.

Empirical Analogies. A professor of entomology at the University of Arizona counts ants. For some time he has been marking off square units of space in various places and then carefully, slavishly counting the number of ants per unit of space and describing their distributions and paths. Such data are interesting in their own right to entomologists. More importantly such distributional data answer some important questions. For example knowing the number, distributions, and paths of ants allows one to calculate how many grass seeds are being taken from an area by ants for food. The distribution of ants affects the distribution of grass seeds and, therefore, the distribution and viability of grass.

Second, since lead aerosols are atmospheric pollutants, it is important to determine their average, maximum, and minimum rates of occurrence in various locales. Procedures have been developed to measure such rates and the distributions are being monitored carefully in relation to altitudes, geographical formations, and layers of thermal inversion around cities (Chow, Early, & Snyder, 1972). Maintenance of human health in various areas makes it imperative that such descriptive work be conducted for lead aerosols and other pollutants in the air we breathe (e.g., carbon monoxide, asbestos).

Third, the distributions of mercury and lead are being measured in the Greenland ice sheet (Dickson, 1972). Is this a wasteful and stupid hobby, conducted by some strange folks who simply like to count weird things? The answer is no, for several reasons. (1) It is imperative that the natural background content of mercury in the environment be determined. (2) The Greenland ice sheet has been found to be an ideal spot in which to measure whether the concentration of mercury in the atmosphere correlates with human industrial activity, probably because the ice sheet is relatively free of mercury contamination from nonindustrial sources. (3) Both the distributional content of mercury in the environment and a place to achieve unbiased descriptions of its accumulations are important because much is known by now about the biological effects of mercury that makes its way into plant and animal tissue.

Finally, as Chase (1971) points out, careful descriptive records have been kept for many years on the causes of death in the United States. The resulting tables of frequency and distribution are fascinating. The top three causes of death in 1900 were pneumonia and influenza, tuberculosis, and diarrhea and enteritis, while the top three causes in 1967 were diseases of the heart, cancer, and strokes. In 1900 the top three caused 31.4 percent of the deaths, but the new top three killers in 1967 accounted for 66.7 percent, more than twice as many. Furthermore only one of the ten leading causes of death in 1900 (pneumonia and influenza) even appeared among the top ten in 1967. These data indicate some dramatic shifts in causes of death in the 67-year period. Not only are such data important in understanding what is happening in the ecosystem, but they are necessary in order to plan changes in preventive and remedial health care. When we consider the fact that such information is also available for the various regions of the country, we begin to see how far behind the behavioral sciences are.

Conceptual Analogies. Behavioral scientists have much to learn from examples like those just cited. In addition to these data-based illustrations, scientists in other areas have developed more abstract and conceptual rationales for distributional research. For example carbon monoxide, vanadium, iron, manganese, cobalt, nickel, copper, zinc, arsenic, tin, fluoride, and lead are among the substances that have various effects in environmental and biological systems (Horne, 1972). What makes such substances interesting is that, while all of them are necessary for life, each of them can also be an illness-dealing and death-dealing pollutant. The important scientific and practical issues are to determine the critical concentrations of each substance and, knowing their critical concentrations, to measure their distributions in natural systems. Both the determination of critical concentrations and the measurement of natural distributions are very complex problems. For any of the substances mentioned, there is no simple, linear relationship between degree of benefit or injury and rate of concentration. Small concentrations may be necessary to support life, and concentrations below those levels may be injurious or lethal. A great deal is already known about higher concentrations that produce noticeably injurious and lethal effects. Much of the hue and cry we hear these days is about high concentrations beyond which various substances become toxic. However almost nothing is known about the concentrations below which lethal deficits occur or about optimal concentrations. The critical threshold concentrations and the shapes of the curves must be spelled out for the various substances. Just as importantly the natural distributions of the substances must be measured before we do too much cleaning up and rearranging of the environment. Otherwise, thinking we are removing a pollutant, we may actually be reducing its concentration below the threshold necessary to sustain life in healthy form.

Why mention these issues in a discussion of naturalistic research? Part of the reason is to point out that professionals in nonbehavioral disciplines are raising conceptual issues that behavioral scientists have not even dreamed of. What kinds of behaviors, occurring where and with what frequency in natural systems, fall at various points on dimensions of concentration? What are the thresholds of behavioral concentration that sustain healthy behavioral functioning and below and above which there are injurious effects? By and large, behavioral scientists have not even conceived of this problem. Not having conceived of the problem, they have not attached importance or value to research that describes and measures the distributions and concentrations of behavioral phenomena.

Asimov (1963) presents a model and a set of data from which we can learn much by analogy. As a simple case consider the ocean as an environment and consider *copepods*—common, tiny crustaceans—as organisms in that environment. For both it is possible to calculate the percentage, by weight, of each constituent element. The percent of oxygen is about 86 in the ocean and lower, at about 80, in the copepod. If we calculate the ratio of the percent composition of oxygen in the copepod to the percent composition in ocean water, the ratio (called the *concentration factor*) is about 0.93. One way to understand the implications of the concentration factor is to imagine a conversion of ocean to the living tissue of copepods. Since oxygen is found in smaller percentage concentrations in copepod tissue than in ocean water, oxygen cannot be the limiting factor in the conversion process. Whenever the concentration factor for any substance is less than one, this means that the substance will not be a limiting factor in the multiplication of living things.

Corresponding percent compositions and concentration factors can be calculated for all the essential elements. The important issue here is that a concentration factor greater than one sets up the possibility of a bottleneck and the essential element with the highest concentration factor is the first one to be used up. That element, therefore, is *life's bottleneck* because its percent composition in living tissue exceeds the percent composition in ocean water by the greatest amount. Going through the concentration factors for 15 essential elements in the copepod case, we find, surprisingly, that phosphorous has the highest concentration factor, at 12,000. Because its percent composition in living tissue is 12,000 times higher than its percent composition in the environment, phosphorous is life's bottleneck in the ocean system.

It would be possible to debate some of the specific numbers in these tables of concentration and some of the conditions under which the various conversions might or might not occur. However two things are fascinating about Asimov's thesis. The first is that there is a conceptual model in terms of which we can deduce and understand the relative functional weights of various elements in the life process. We have nothing comparable in the sciences of behavior. We do not have the faintest beginnings of a comprehensive model that allows us to attach theoretical weights to the adaptive importance of various behaviors. In what proportions and frequencies should laughing, cooperating, solving problems, playing, fighting, resting, and becoming angry be engaged in by developing children? We do not know. In what proportions and frequencies should various kinds of behaviors occur around them or be delivered to them? Again we have no idea.

The second fascinating aspect of Asimov's presentation is the simple fact that actual data, actual tables of concentration and distribution, are already available. Great numbers of scientists have considered it scientifically worthwhile to go out and simply observe, describe, count, measure, and classify the distributions of elements and compounds in large environments and in animal tissues. Again we have nothing comparable in human development. By and large we favor manipulations, demonstrations, experiments, and questionnaire surveys of attitudes and preferences that tell us nothing about natural distributions of behavior. Some behavioral scientists have been warning us for years that it is important for the behavioral sciences to have detailed documentation of the everyday distributions of behavioral phenomena (e.g., Barker, 1965, 1968, 1969; Henry, 1971; Sells, 1969, 1971; Willems, 1965, 1969, 1973, 1976), but the idea has not really caught on as yet.

Asimov's argument regarding life's chemical bottlenecks could not be carried off without either the conceptual model or the available tables of descriptive data. It is clear that if one wished to intervene and modify the bottleneck problem in the chemical sphere, there are a few precisely defined points to which the model would lead one for the intervention. The general implications of the Asimov illustration for our present discussion are straightforward. If we are to continue our attempts to accelerate, decelerate, produce, eliminate, and shape behaviors, and especially if such attempts are going to intensify and spread, then we must at some point end our blind tinkering with them. We must grow far beyond the hit-or-miss grounds we now use for deciding where and when to intervene and tinker. We must begin taking account of (1) the much larger organism-behavior-environment systems within which our activities take place, (2) concentration factors of behavior within those systems, and (3) optimal proportions of behaviors across populations and subpopulations. We must improve our ability to prescribe remedial action and avoid the removal of vital behaviors or the inadvertent addition of dysfunctional ones. It is true that in order to develop that capability we must acquire more theoretical insight into the various kinds of adaptive value that behavior serves. It is also true that one necessary condition for developing that capability will be to value, promote, encourage, and conduct research on the naturally occurring distributions of the phenomena of behavior. Barker argues (1968),

Entomologists know the biological vectors of malaria, and they also know much about the occurrence of these vectors over the earth. In contrast, psychologists know little more than laymen about the distribution and degrees of occurrence of their basic phenomena: of punishment, of hostility, of friendliness, of social pressure, of reward, of fear, of frustration. Although we have daily records of the oxygen count of river water, of the ground temperature of cornfields, of the activity of volcanoes, of the behavior of nesting robins, of the rate of sodium iodide absorption by crabs, there have been few scientific records of how human mothers care for their young, how teachers behave in the classroom (and how the children respond), what families actually do and say during mealtime, or how children live their lives from the time they wake in the morning until they go to sleep at night. Because we have lacked such records, we have been able only to speculate about many important questions. . . . Before we can answer these kinds of questions, we must know more than the laws of behavior. We must know how the relevant conditions are distibuted among men. (pp. 2–3)

Implications

When we realize how long we as psychologists and other behavioral scientists have been testing, treating, and studying various aspects of human behavior, it is disconcerting to discover that we are far behind in some fundamental parts of science. If we had been paying attention to the scientific strategies and modes of investigation that led other sciences to the kind of understanding that allows them to deal effectively with natural systems, we might not be so far behind. It is critical that we know a great deal about the distributions of behavior in natural systems. Such research can only be conducted with naturalistic methods. Behavioral scientists must come to value such research as the strongest possible mode of inquiry for some basic scientific tasks. Persons must be trained to carry out such research. Funds, initiatives, incentives, and organizational and administrative arrangements must be mobilized for the execution of such research, the storage of appropriate data, and for the use of the data. Methods of sampling, observation, measurement, classification, quality control, and monitoring must be developed. Appropriate new theories of human behavior and its contexts must be developed so that distributional indices of behavior can be weighted and interpreted in useful ways.

One of the ways in which we evade the necessary descriptive work on distributions is to complain that we do not have the hypotheses that will guide the work. We can argue that pediatricians and neurologists first hypothesized that lack of protein in the mother's diet during pregnancy leads to damage to the child's central nervous system and that only then did it become important to go out and document the distribution of eating habits in various parts of the population. We can argue that the hypothesized relationships between grass seeds and ants is what made it important to study the distribution of ants. Yet as demonstrated by the cases of geology and the availability of water and crude oil, Asimov's bottleneck case, and the distribution of trace substances that can be both beneficial and harmful, that ordered sequence from hypothesized importance to distributional study does not always occur or need it occur. Often the monitoring and tallying of natural distributions comes first, and often it is done independently, just because the phenomena are there to be described. If this is true in other areas, then it can be true in human development. We need no longer be patient with those who insist that we hypothesize that interaction with a wide range of adults is important to a child before we go out and describe the array of adults with whom children interact; that we have a definitive hypothesis regarding the developmental importance of various types of play before we simply describe the freestanding distributions of children's play; that we hypothesize the long-range significance of participation in community activities before we measure the rates and depths of participation in community activities by various parts of the population and in various parts of the society; or that we know something about the long-range significance of independence before we describe the frequency of behavioral independence in spinal-cord-injured adults.

It is true that science needs hypotheses and theoretical justifications. However we will never lack hypotheses and theories. What we really need is to eliminate some of our overweening dependence on the comfort and pseudo-status of hypotheses, remove the blinders and limitations they create, and do more observing, describing, and tallying of behavioral phenomena in natural systems.

CONCLUDING COMMENTS

We have argued that naturalistic research fulfills certain major scientific purposes in unique ways. Two such purposes are the documentation of external validity or generalizability and the documentation of distributions of phenomena in natural systems. Since naturalistic research is the only way to achieve those purposes, it cannot be argued that naturalistic research is second best or falls short of any ideals.

Writers such as Breland and Breland (1966), Bronfenbrenner (1979), Lockard (1971), and Menzel (1969) suggest that naturalistic research is the most generic and that experimental procedures are the specialty procedures that one uses only to answer some specific questions. This suggests the reversal of a time-honored principle in methodology, in terms of which most psychologists are socialized in their training: Always control as much as you possibly can in your research. The more current and more mature principle that is emerging is: Never control any more than you absolutely have to in order to answer your question clearly.

REFERENCES

ARGYRIS, C. Some unintended consequences of rigorous research. *Psychological Bulletin*, 1968, *70*, 185–197.

ARGYRIS, C. Problems and new directions for industrial psychology. Pp. 151–184 in M. D. Dunnette (Ed.), *Handbook of industrial and organizational psychology.* Skokie, Ill.: Rand McNally, 1976.

ASIMOV, I. *Fact and fancy.* New York: Pyramid Books, 1963.

BARKER, R. G. (Ed.). *The stream of behavior.* New York: Appleton-Century-Crofts, 1963.

BARKER, R. G. Observation of behavior: Ecological approaches. *Journal of Mt. Sinai Hospital*, 1964, *31*, 268–284.

BARKER, R. G. Explorations in ecological psychology. *American Psychologist*, 1965, *20*, 1–14.

BARKER, R. G. *Ecological psychology.* Stanford, Calif.: Stanford University Press, 1968.

BARKER, R. G. Wanted: An eco-behavioral science. Pp. 31–43 in E. P. Willems & H. L. Raush (Eds.), *Naturalistic viewpoints in psychological research.* New York: Holt, Rinehart and Winston, 1969.

BARKER R. G., & BARKER, L. S. Social actions in the behavior streams of American and English children. Pp. 127–159 in R. G. Barker (Ed.), *The stream of behavior.* New York: Appleton-Century-Crofts, 1963.

BARKER, R. G., DEMBO, T., & LEWIN, K. Frustration and regression. Pp. 441–458 in R. G. Barker, J. S. Kounin, & H. F. Wright (Eds.), *Child behavior and development.* New York: McGraw-Hill, 1943.

BARKER, R. G., & SCHOGGEN, P. *Qualities of community life.* San Francisco: Jossey-Bass, 1973.

BARKER, R. G., & WRIGHT, H. F. *Midwest and its children.* New York: Harper & Row, Pub., 1955.

BAUER, R. A. The obstinate audience: The influence process from the point of view of social communication. *American Psychologist*, 1964, *19*, 319–328.

BECHTEL, R. B. Hodometer research in architecture. *Milieu*, 1967, *1* (No. 2), 1–9.

BERRIEN, F. K. *General and social systems.* New Brunswick, N.J.: Rutgers University Press, 1968.

BRELAND, K., & BRELAND, M. *Animal behavior.* New York: Macmillan, 1966.

BRONFENBRENNER, U. *The ecology of human development.* Cambridge, Mass.: Harvard University Press, 1979.

BROWN, R. *Social psychology.* New York: Free Press, 1965.

CAMPBELL, D. T., & STANLEY, J. C. *Experimental and quasi-experimental designs for research.* Skokie, Ill.: Rand McNally, 1963.

CHASE, A. *The biological imperatives.* New York: Holt, Rinehart & Winston, 1971.

CHOW, T. J., EARL, J. L., & SNYDER, C. B. Lead aerosol baseline: Concentration at White Mountain and Laguna Mountain, California. *Science*, 1972, *178*, 401–402.

COOK, T. P., & CAMPBELL, D. T. The design and conduct of quasi-experiments and true experiments in field settings. Pp. 223–326 in M. D. Dunnette (Ed.), *Handbook of industrial and organizational psychology.* Skokie, Ill.: Rand McNally, 1976.

CROOK, J. H., & GOSS-CUSTARD, J. D. Social ethology. Pp. 277–312 in P. H. Mussen & M. R. Rosenzweig (Eds.), *Annual review of psychology.* Palo Alto, Calif.: Annual Reviews, Inc., 1972.

DICKSON, E. M. Mercury and lead in the Greenland ice sheet: A reexamination of the data. *Science*, 1972, *177*, 536–538.

DYCK, A. J. The social contacts of some Midwest children with their parents and teachers. Pp. 78–98 in R. G. Barker (Ed.), *The stream of behavior.* New York: Appleton-Century-Crofts, 1963.

EBBESEN, E. P., & HANEY, M. Flirting with death: Variables affecting risk taking at intersections. *Journal of Applied Social Psychology*, 1973, *3*, 303–324.

FAWL, C. L. Disturbances experienced by children in their natural habitats. Pp. 99–126 in R. G. Barker (Ed.), *The stream of behavior.* New York: Appleton-Century-Crofts, 1963.

GOFFMAN, E. *Stigma.* Englewood Cliffs, N.J.: Prentice-Hall, 1963.

GUMP, P. V. *The classroom behavior setting: Its nature and relation to student behavior.* Final Report to U.S. Office of Education, Project No. 5-0334, Contract No. OE-4-10-107, 1967.

GUMP, P. V. Intra-setting analysis: The third grade classroom as a special but illustrative case. Pp. 200–220 in E. P. Willems & H. L. Raush (Eds.), *Naturalistic viewpoints in psychological research.* New York: Holt, Rinehart & Winston, 1969.

GUMP, P. V., & KOUNIN, J. S. Issues raised by ecological and "classical" research efforts. *Merrill-Palmer Quarterly*, 1959–1960, *6*, 145–152.

GUMP P. V., & SUTTON-SMITH, B. The "it" role in children's games. *The Group*, 1955, *17*, 3–8.

HALL, J., & WILLIAMS, M. S. A comparison of decision-making performances in established and ad hoc groups. *Journal of Personality and Social Psychology*, 1966, *3*, 214–222.

HENRY, J. *Pathways to madness.* New York: Random House, 1971.

HOLME, A., & MASSIE, P. *Children's play: A study of needs and opportunities.* London: Michael Joseph, Ltd., 1970.

HORNE, R. A. Biological effects of chemical agents (Letter). *Science*, 1972, *177*, 1152–1153.

KAVANAU, J. L. Behavior: Confinement, adaptation, and compulsory regimes in laboratory studies. *Science*, 1964, *143*, 490.

KAVANAU, J. L. Behavior of captive white-footed mice. Pp. 221–270 in E. P. Willems & H. L. Raush (Eds.), *Naturalistic viewpoints in psychological research.* New York: Holt, Rinehart & Winston, 1969.

KLINGHAMMER, E. Factors influencing choice of mate in altricial birds. Pp. 5–42 in H. W. Stevenson, E. H. Hess, & H. L. Rheingold (Eds.), *Early behavior: Comparative and developmental approaches.* New York: John Wiley, 1967.

KORTLANDT, A. Chimpanzees in the wild. *Scientific American*, 1962, *205* (No. 5), 128–138.

KOUNIN, J. S. *Dimensions of adult-child relationships in the classroom.* Paper presented to the Topology Meeting, New York, August 1961.

KOUNIN, J. S. An analysis of teachers' managerial techniques. *Psychology in the Schools*, 1967, *4*, 221–227.

LEE, R. E., JR. The size of suspended particulate matter in air. *Science*, 1972, *178*, 567–575.

LITTLEWOOD, J., & SALE, R. *Children at play: A look at where they play and what they do on housing estates.* London: Department of Environment, 1972.

LOCKARD, R. B. Reflections on the fall of comparative psychology: Is there a message for us all? *American Psychologist*, 1971, *26*, 168–179.

MASON, W. A. The social development of monkeys and apes. Pp. 514–543 in I. DeVore (Ed.), *Primate behavior: Field studies of monkeys and apes.* New York: Holt, Rinehart & Winston, 1965.

McGUIRE, W. J. Some impending reorientations in social psychology: Some thoughts provoked by Kenneth Ring. *Journal of Experimental Social Psychology*, 1967, *3*, 124–139.

MENZEL, E. W., JR. Naturalistic and experimental approaches to primate behavior. Pp. 78–121 in E. P. Willems & H. L. Raush (Eds.), *Naturalistic viewpoints in psychological research.* New York: Holt, Rinehart & Winston, 1969.

ORNE, M. T. On the social psychology of the psychological experiment: With particular reference to demand characteristics and their implications. *American Psychologist*, 1962, *17*, 776–783.

PARIS, S. G., & CAIRNS, R. B. An experimental and ethological analysis of social reinforcement with retarded children. *Child Development*, 1972, *43*, 717–729.

POLANYI, M. *Personal knowledge.* Chicago: University of Chicago Press, 1958.

POSTMAN, L., & TOLMAN, E. C. Brunswik's probabilistic functionalism. Pp. 502–564 in S. Koch (Ed.), *Psychology: A study of a science* (Vol. 1). New York: McGraw-Hill, 1959.

PUGH, D. S. Modern organizational theory: A psychological and sociological study. *Psychological Bulletin*, 1966, *66*, 235–251.

RONNEBECK, R. W. *A naturalistic investigation of community adjustment of facially disfigured burned teenagers.* Unpublished doctoral dissertation, University of Houston, 1972.

SCHMITT, R. C. *Some ecological variables of community adjustment in a group of facially disfigured burned children.* Unpublished doctoral dissertation, University of Houston, 1971.

SCHOGGEN, P., BARKER, L. S., & BARKER, R. G. Structure of the behavior of American and English children. Pp. 160–168 in R. G. Barker (Ed.), *The stream of behavior.* New York: Appleton-Century-Crofts, 1963.

SCOTT, W. A., & WERTHEIMER, M. *Introduction to psychological research.* New York: John Wiley, 1962.

SELIGMAN, R., MACMILLAN, B. G., & CARROLL, S. S. The burned child: A neglected area of psychiatry. *American Journal of Psychiatry.* 1971, *128,* 84–89.

SELLS, S. B. Ecology and the science of psychology. Pp. 15–30 in E. P. Willems & H. L. Raush (Eds.), *Naturalistic viewpoints in psychological research.* New York: Holt, Rinehart & Winston, 1969.

SELLS, S. B. *Environmental assessment: A context for the study of human behavior.* Institute of Behavioral Research, Texas Christian University. Presidential address, Division of Military Psychology, American Psychological Association, 1971.

SKINNER, B. F. Experimental psychology. Pp. 16–49 in W. Dennis (Ed.), *Current trends in psychology.* Pittsburgh: University of Pittsburgh Press, 1947.

SOUTHWOOD, T.R.E. *Ecological methods.* London: Methuen, 1966.

STONER, J.A.F. *A comparison of individual and group decisions involving risk.* Unpublished master's thesis, Massachusetts Institute of Technology, 1961.

STUART, D. G. *A naturalistic study of the daily activities of disabled and nondisabled college students.* Unpublished master's thesis, University of Houston, 1973.

VIGLIANO, A., HART, L. W., & SINGER, F. Psychiatric sequelae of old burns of children and their parents. *American Journal of Orthopsychiatry,* 1958, *28,* 85–97.

WASHBURN, S. L. Phi Beta Kappa Lecture. University of Kansas, 1963.

WATT, K.E.F. Ecology in the future. Pp. 253–267 in K.E.F. Watt (Ed.), *Systems analysis in ecology.* New York: Academic Press, 1966.

WEIR, R. H. *Language in the crib.* The Hague: Mouton, 1962.

WILLEMS, E. P. An ecological orientation in psychology. *Merrill-Palmer Quarterly,* 1965, *11,* 317–343.

WILLEMS, E. P. Toward an explicit rationale for naturalistic research methods. *Human Development,* 1967, *10,* 138–154.

WILLEMS, E. P. Planning a rationale for naturalistic research. Pp. 44–71 in E. P. Willems & H. L. Raush (Eds.), *Naturalistic viewpoints in psychological research.* New York: Holt, Rinehart & Winston, 1969.

WILLEMS, E. P. The interface of the hospital environment and patient behavior. *Archives of Physical Medicine and Rehabilitation,* 1972a, *53,* 115–122.

WILLEMS, E. P. Place and motivation: Complexity and independence in patient behavior. Pp. 4-3-1 to 4-5-8 in W. J. Mitchell (Ed.), *Environmental design: Research and practice.* Los Angeles: University of California at Los Angeles, 1972b.

WILLEMS, E. P. Behavioral ecology and experimental analysis: Courtship is not enough. Pp. 195–217 in J. R. Nesselroade & H. W. Reese (Eds.), *Life-span developmental psychology: Methodological issues.* New York: Academic Press, 1973.

WILLEMS, E. P. Behavioral ecology, health status, and health care: Application to the rehabilitation setting. Pp. 211–263 in I. Altman & J. F. Wohlwill (Eds.), *Human behavior and environment: Advances in theory and research.* New York: Plenum, 1976.

WILLEMS, E. P. Behavioral ecology. Pp. 39–68 in D. Stokols (Ed.), *Perspectives on environment and behavior.* New York: Plenum, 1977.

WOLMAN, B. B. Concerning psychology and the philosophy of science. Pp. 22–48 in B. B. Wolman (Ed.), *Handbook of general psychology.* Englewood Cliffs, N.J.: Prentice-Hall, 1973.

WRIGHT, H. F. *Recording and analyzing child behavior.* New York: Harper & Row, Pub., 1967.

WRIGHT, H. F. *Children's behavior in communities differing in size* (5 vols.). Lawrence: University of Kansas, 1969–1970.

9

The Study of Human Change: Measurement, Research Strategies, and Methods of Analysis

JUM C. NUNNALLY

It is not difficult to make the case that most scientific theories and related research activities are concerned with some form of natural or experimentally induced change. This is evident in research on the "big bang" theory of the origin of the universe, natural selection in the evolution of animal species, and the growth-and-decline prototheory that guides much of the research on human development and eventual aging. There is a place in science for the descriptive study concerned with the characteristics and distributions of "objects" at a particular point in time, such as a geological survey of a particular region or a "survey" of opinions about a particular set of social issues, but even there the apparent "static" findings usually are interpreted in the light of what has gone on earlier and might transpire later. Of course the effort in all experiments is to induce changes, in a neat and orderly way, rather than sift through observations of natural changes that might provide circumstantial evidence with respect to a hypothesis. In this chapter the study of change will be concerned with (1) people, (2) psychological attributes such as abilities and personality traits, (3) "natural" changes over the life span, or (4) experiments intended to modify such natural evolvements, and (5) individual differences and differences among groups in both life-span research and experiments pertaining thereto.

The literature concerning methodology for the study of human psychological growth and change is massive by now. The volume edited by Harris (1963) congealed a broad spectrum of ideas about research strategies in this area, opened up the possibility of employing a variety of statistical methods that had not been used previously, and left strewn in its path a large number of nagging questions. Numerous methodologists subsequently published papers relating to one or more issues that had been brought to focus by the Harris volume. Nunnally (1973,

1975), as have others, cautioned against use of covariance analysis as a proper tool in life-span research. Cronbach and Furby (1970), in a microscopic analysis of "change scores," essentially came to the conclusion that the methodological issues were so formidable that it might be best not to study such change scores at all. Many papers on research methodology have appeared in the yearly volumes of *Life-Span Developmental Psychology* and in journals relating to developmental research. A number of relatively recent books are devoted mainly to the study of human change, one of the more comprehensive of these being the book by Wohlwill (1973). The author has written before on these topics (Nunnally, 1973, 1975). With this glut of literature concerning methodology on the shelf and apparently much of it being ignored in research practice, is there really need for a chapter such as this at this time? I think so, because some important issues should be brought to a head.

TYPES OF DEVELOPMENTAL STUDIES

As most readers know, a very wide variety of studies are included in books and professional journals relating to "developmental" or to "life-span" research. Many different disciplines are involved in these types of investigations; consequently, even within the context of one research enterprise, many different-appearing technologies of investigation might be pursued. The discussion here will be related most directly to psychological variables, but most of the major issues cut across similar studies made by other professional groups.

A great deal of dust was kicked up in the 1960s and early 1970s regarding methodology in life-span research, and enough of the dust has settled now to make some challenging statements. The major issues in life-span research are by no means statistical but relate to other nagging problems. The first of these problems is a lack of adequate measurement methods for most of the interesting psychological constructs. The second is that we seldom have enough of the right kind of data to grace the available armamentarium of mathematical models and statistical methods for analysis. Third, a welter of stopgap and partial solutions in statistical analysis could easily be replaced by more powerful general approaches—ones that will be discussed here. Fourth, many of the would-be conundrums regarding picking apart life-span data into meaningful components could easily have been answered with statistical methods that were available long ago—and particularly I am thinking of a method for resolving numerous developmental curves into component curves. Fifth, no one seems to know why it is important to study individual differences in life-span research. Now let us look at these and other important issues.

Observational versus Experimental Studies

Traditionally most developmental studies were mainly observational in character rather than experimental, as was evidenced in textbooks and journal articles relating to the topic up until circa 1950. The last twenty or so years have seen a marked growth in experimental studies of issues in human development. The advent of relatively precise theories of cognitive development and social learning probably has nourished such experimentation.

Longitudinal and Cross-Sectional Studies

So far it has not been explicitly stated, but one would gather that life-span research is concerned with testing the *same* people on at least several and perhaps many occasions. In contrast one finds in the literature many cross-sectional studies comparing responses of different age groups who are all tested at approximately the same time and frequently tested only once. For example one frequently sees in newspapers and other periodicals voting preferences by people of different age levels. Such cross-sectional studies are performed by numerous government agencies on issues relating to age differences in income, recreational activities, health-related matters, and numerous other circumstances of living. Such ahistorical cross-sectional studies of age differences in preferences, values, economic circumstances, styles of life, and other characteristics are quite important for understanding people now in terms of the age dimension.

As important as cross-sectional studies of age groups are in their own right, they provide only gross approximations to true longitudinal trends. This is discussed and illustrated in Nunnally (1973) and Wohlwill (1973). Few people these days would even argue that it is sensible to construe purely cross-sectional data as definitive of longitudinal trends, but efforts have been made to piece together different segments of longitudinal data (e.g., each covering several years of actual longitudinal data) into an approximation of what would have been obtained had the same subjects been followed from beginning to end. This effort leads one into a quagmire of assumptions and dubious statistical practices. Even on logical grounds the practice would fail, because with most developmental variables one expects some "generation effects." Consequently it simply would not be possible to gauge the growth and decline of an attribute over a lifetime when all of the data were collected in no more than a fourth of that time and then pieced together statistically like Frankenstein. This does not mean that some fragments of developmental data would not be of interest in and of themselves, such as some sharp changes that might be evidenced in older age groups taken separately, but any effort to piece together a precise developmental function from a hodgepodge of partially longitudinal strands is doomed to failure.

Long-Term Surveys

When people who work in other areas hear the term "developmental psychology," they are most likely to envision a curve showing the relationship between some type of ability and chronological age ranging from early childhood up to young adulthood. The term *life span* suggests a broader range of chronological age, with a concern for changes above the age of 65. In either case chronological age is on the X-axis of the graph, the broader the span of age investigated the better, and the shape of the function is the major matter of interest. Actually very few broad-spectrum surveys of growth and change throughout major portions of the life span have been undertaken. The few major ones are summarized by Wohlwill (1973). The logistics of performing womb-to-tomb studies over "even" a decade or more are usually out of the question. Much of the long-range information about development and change in relation to chronological age has been obtained incidentally in the course of studies for other purposes or from accrued records in schools or governmental or medical files. Rightly or wrongly, the ongoing long-range developmental surveys of psychological attributes have been criticized as being poorly planned, unimaginative, and too "gross" in terms of measurements to permit fine documentation of changing cognitive and affective processes.

Aging

For several reasons one might anticipate increased surveying of cognitive and affective functions in the age range from 55 onward. This is becoming an age range of intense interest (e.g., as regards retirement from employment), and one can expect increasing sources of research support. Unlike the difficulties that frequently are encountered at the other end of the age spectrum in the study of young children, older adults usually are able to give meaningful responses to the same types of measures that typically are applied to younger age groups.

Critical Periods

In contrast to the long-range surveys, the study of critical periods focuses on rather circumscribed portions of the life span in which particularly interesting changes are thought to occur. Considerable interest has been shown in stages of sensorimotor development in young children relating to walking, talking, attentional mechanisms, and others. Research also has been focused on a series of developments in the period from two to about eight which is particularly potent for the development of "cognitive structures" and for certain aspects of socialization. There is not much in the way of investigation of critical periods from that point on, except with respect to the drastic physical and psychological turbulence of puberty. Other than for the stage of puberty, which in most individuals is time-bound within several years, there is no easy way to denote critical periods throughout adulthood from that point onward.

In addition to the intrinsic value of results from studies of critical periods, the analyses of data have made it obvious that chronological age per se need not always be the X-axis for the developmental function. Even with developmental functions where a nearly infallible sequence of evolving behaviors in rank order is anticipated, children enter those stages and substages at different ages, and they vary in terms of in-out time. Thus in motor development, even if two children eventually go through the same stages by the age of six, they might have started and stopped the various substages at different ages. This opens up the possibility of scaling the X-axis in terms of junctures in the developmental sequence, either expressed simply as rank order or with an attempt being made to generate a sensible, sensitive ipsative scale. There has been a good bit of controversy as to how this might be done (see discussion in Wohlwill, 1973), but at least there is the possibility of individualizing developmental periods for subjects and investigating functional relations with other variables on that basis. However simple chronological age still dominates the scene as regards the analysis of developmental functions.

Processes and Individual Differences

The term *processes* is used here to refer to sequences of cognitive and affective changes evidenced in the average response of a group of subjects. Such average responses are shown in typical age functions—e.g., changes in brain structure during the first six months of life and increase in vocabulary from age four to adulthood. Whenever one investigates average responses in those ways, inevitably there are individual differences in overall levels of developmental functions and perhaps differences also in curve shapes. In the investigation of various aspects of personality, socialization, and other noncognitive variables, an examination of an age function may obscure the fact that a small number of the children actually are going "the other way"—e.g., becoming more dependent and manifesting a more "external locus of control" as time goes on. Whichever the case individual differences are a fact of life in developmental as in all research, and frequently the variance related to individual differences actually overwhelms the variance manifested in the mean trend. This is frequently recognized in developmental research, either out of alarm for taking the usual growth function as an oversimplification of what actually happens to individuals or in pointing to a potentially useful line of research in the study of such individual differences in their own right. Later a method will be discussed for finding and properly assembling subgroups of individuals who manifest growth functions that are

markedly different from that of the trend as a whole. More important at this point, however, is to recognize some problems regarding the investigation of individual differences in the context of developmental studies. Admitting that large, reliable individual differences usually do exist, other than for documenting that such is the case, no one seems to be quite sure what should be done about this matter. If such individual differences are mainly in terms of "level" rather than "shape," then the mean trend does no real injustice to the data as a whole. In developmental studies how does one investigate individual differences? In a narrow sense the answer is to correlate, and certainly there is no shortage of highly elaborate statistical methods for examining correlational structures. A much more important question is: "What does one hope to find from such analyses?"

FUNDAMENTAL ISSUES IN RESEARCH DESIGN AND ANALYSIS

The very difficult problem of adequate measurement will be considered later, but before then it will be assumed that such measurement methods are available when discussing research design and analysis. Different types of designs and different methods of analysis are required depending upon the type of developmental investigation at issue; however, all developmental investigations have some points in common, which are discussed as follows.

The Temporal Dimension

In order to be classified as a developmental investigation, at least one independent variable must concern *time*. In some cases this is the only independent variable, as would be the case in depicting the functional relationship between vocabulary and chronological age. As mentioned previously, in some cases attempts have been made to ipsatively rescale chronological age with respect to critical periods or other particularities of the individual's maturational process, but this still represents a scaling of time. Time can be stated in rank order as regards to a sequence of testing, in which intervals of time are not judged to be important. This would be the case in applying dependent measures before an experiment, during an experiment, afterwards, and perhaps a week later. There is a sequential flow of time, and the rank ordering of testing times makes a difference; but amount of time per se may be of only incidental importance.

Within-Subjects Research Designs

Whatever else may be involved in developmental studies, they necessarily concern repeated-measurements or within-subjects research designs. In an experiment the repetition of measures may be only once, as before the treatment and afterward. In a true longitudinal study, the same test or other measure might need to be applied as many as 20 or more times over a period of years. Such repeated-measurements (within-subjects) designs have some special advantages and some special problems in behavioral research.

In terms of problems one certainly worries about "reactivity of measurement," in which the measurements taken on earlier occasions influence measurements taken on later occasions, and there are many ways in which this can happen. If the measurements require some type of skilled performance, as in motor skills, the individual may improve primarily because of practice on the first measure rather than because of maturation or any effect of experimental treatments. If the measure concerns attitudes or other noncognitive variables, the individual might be alerted to his/her own attitudes, think and change on his/her own over time in a way that does not mirror either maturational effects or effects of any experimental treatments. There are many other ways in which measurements can be "reactive."

To get around the problems caused by reactivity of measurements, a number of things have been suggested—none of which is entirely satisfactory. One suggestion has been to employ alternative forms of the measuring instrument rather than to apply the same test or other measuring device over and over. This possibility fails on both grounds of feasibility and in terms of experimental logic. With respect to the former, very few measuring instruments have alternative forms, or if they do have alternative forms, there are seldom more than two versions of the test. To circumvent this difficulty some truly randomized tests will be discussed later that can be given over and over without some of the reactivity that would be present from taking the same test repeatedly.

On logical grounds the use of alternative forms of tests fails because no matter how strenuous the efforts to match alternative forms, their employment in research would require a tedious type of counterbalancing of the order in which they were used. Even then additional sources of error would be added to the results because it would be necessary to extract the error variance relating to forms from that which could be attributable to developmental trends or to experimental treatments. Such uses of alternative forms for only a before-and-after study relating to developmental issues would be feasible, but this would not be feasible for testing on a half-dozen or more occasions.

Trends in Experiments

A simple illustration of an experimental trend is given in Figure 9–1. The dependent measure might concern a cognitive variable such as the ability to detect a "target" geometrical configuration in the context of distracting configurations, or the dependent measure might concern a noncognitive variable such as *locus of control*. The treatment condition is interposed between the third and fourth testing occasions. The treatment for the perceptual variable could concern practice in the underlying skills necessary to perform the task as a whole. With the noncognitive variable the treatment might concern the possible impact of a month's summer-camp experience that is intended to help emotionally disturbed children learn to cope with their environments. The design depicted in Figure 9–1 is different from that which would usually be employed. First, there is no control group or groups, or alternative treatment conditions, with which to compare this one type of summer-camp experience. Second, it is not usually feasible to test on three occasions

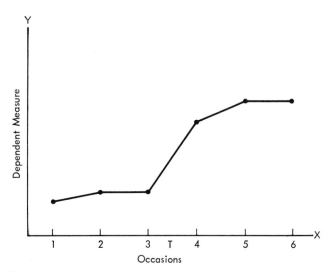

Figure 9-1 Developmental function at three testing times before and three testing times after an experimental treatment (*T*)

before and three occasions after the treatment. More typically one would be testing only before and after the treatment, although important information might be obtained from the additional testings.

Several suggestions are obtained by looking at the means in Figure 9–1. First, there appears to be a small "practice effect." Much more striking is the apparent treatment effect, evidenced in the big "jump" in the curve between occasions three and four. One would want to employ inferential statistics to gain assurance regarding the "reality" and size of the change—more about that will be discussed later. It also is instructive to look at what happens in the two follow-up testing occasions at points five and six. It appears from looking at the graph that the perceptual ability in the hypothetical example keeps "growing" but also appears to level off after occasion five. With the example of *locus of control*, the average child continues to shift toward an internal locus of control, even after the summer-camp experience is over. Assuming that these observations are supported by inferential statistics (discussed later), the story as just told would neatly summarize the results.

In addition to inspecting and analyzing the mean differences in Figure 9–1, it is instructive to inspect the correlations among individual differences obtained on the six occasions, as shown in Table 9–1. An inspection of the table provides some useful information regarding consistency of individual differences over the time of the experiment: reliability as evidenced in the first three occasions, the altering of individual differences as a function of the treatment interposed between occasions three and four, and the stability of the new ordering of individual differences on occasions four, five, and six. Two warnings should be given in looking at this table. First, one would not likely find such neatly sectioned results as regards the different parts of an experiment. Second, unless the number of subjects in the study was well over 100, there would be so much sampling error as to obscure any "real" pattern that would be found in whatever population is being "sampled."

A very important point is that if one can assume multivariate normality for the six sets of scores depicted in Figure 9–1 (or in any developmental study), then the

Table 9-1 Correlations among Six Testing Occasions Depicted in Figure 9-1

	OCCASION					
	1	2	3	4	5	6
1	—	.92	.88	.65	.63	.66
2		—	.94	.71	.65	.73
3			—	.75	.71	.65
4				—	.89	.84
5					—	.87
6						—

means are entirely independent of the correlations depicted in Table 9-1. Even if strict multivariate normality does not hold, the plot of means and the table of correlations have no direct bridges of interpretation. One encounters numerous discussions of developmental data in which the conversation glides in subtle ways from implications regarding correlations to implications regarding mean differences, and vice versa.

The Error Term

In the within-subjects designs that typify developmental investigations (frequently with some between-group factors also), the interaction of subjects and occasions constitutes the primary error term. Measurement error is one of the major contributors to that interaction term—the higher the reliability, the lower the interaction, and vice versa. The size of that interaction term is influenced by numerous forms of error introduced in the experimental setting; whether or not one wants to refer to these all as constituting measurement error depends upon the choice of words. Sampling error regarding numbers of subjects enters the picture in relation to degrees of freedom available for converting sums of squares due to interaction into the mean square for interaction. Thus a large amount of sampling error due to a small number of persons sampled would combine with measurement error and related forms of experimental error to create a large mean square for interaction; since this would serve as the error term for developmental trends, a large mean square for interaction always is "bad."

Other than for questions of feasibility, it is easy to tell one how to reduce that critical mean square for interaction. The most straightforward way is to increase substantially the number of subjects. The second way to reduce that error is to increase substantially the number of test items. Total test scores usually are compounded of item scores, the term *item* being used quite generally to refer to scores on typical psychological tests and also to the component scores that are added to obtain total scores in measures of learning, perception, social, and even physiological investigations (see Nunnally, 1978, for a more detailed discussion of this matter). The remaining aspects of the mean square for interaction in a within-subjects design are frequently quite illusive as regards variations in equipment and procedures in experiments, and variations in testing environments and examiner-related variations with respect to test administration and scoring.

It is easy to sit on high and advise people to standardize everything as much as possible that might contribute to experimental or measurement error, but that frequently is difficult to do in practice. Of course it would be most unwise to undertake a protracted and expensive developmental investigation when the measured data will depend substantially on the skill and judgment of particular researchers or for other reasons there are "tricky" aspects of carrying out the experimental procedures or measurement operations in such a way as to either artifactually influence mean scores or to inject randomness into the variance of individual differences.

Change Scores

The author would like to take a strong stand on the contention that all studies of change, including developmental investigations, are necessarily based on the actual changes or gains that are observed rather than on any transformations of such scores. Arguments on this point were hot and heavy in the late 1950s. Much of this and later thinking was summarized in the Harris volume (1963); Cronbach and Furby (1970) dissected the issue to a point of confusion; and this author (1973, 1975) and others in recent years have not entirely resolved the question.

The original concern and controversy started because of several characteristics of change scores, or gain scores as they frequently are called. To put the issue in perspective, imagine that in one investigation we are making a longitudinal study of standing height and vocabulary from the years 6 through 26. Of course what one wants to investigate are the changes or gains from age to age. If this is a within-subjects design, as the term *longitudinal* implies, there not only are changes in mean scores from occasion to occasion, but there are also changes in the scores of individuals which can be written down, inspected, and statistically analyzed. Several characteristics of these change scores from occasion to occasion become obvious. First, the change score itself is correlated to a predictable extent with both the first and second measure, or the pre- and posttest measures when referring to an experiment. This means that any interpretation of the change score is "confounded" by pre- and posttest scores. Second, unless the correlation between the two measures is substantial, the variance of change scores will be larger than the variance of scores on either of the two occasions. If this variance represents error, the situation would be "bad"; consequently, some investigators thought that something should be done about the matter. A third point that can be deduced from a further consideraton of the variance of change scores is that the measurement error from the first and second occasions accumulates, which tends to make change scores less reliable than the two measures from which they were derived (see Nunnally, 1978, for an extensive discussion of this point and for related equations). This also looks "bad" because no one wants to deal with a measure that might be unreliable.

The fourth observation relates to the correlation between the pretest and posttest. The two measures can be correlated like any other two variables can, and the character of the relationship can be seen visually in the typical scatter diagram. If one looks at such a scatter diagram, a linear regression toward the mean usually is observed. Having gone this far the methodologist becomes worried because it is obvious that change scores are partially estimable from the regression line, but by this point, the methodologist has probably worried him/herself into some improper deductions.

Regardless of how one may analyze change scores in terms of their components, they constitute the only real data to be investigated. It is immaterial whether or not such change scores correlate substantially with before measures and after measures; it is immaterial that first and second measures show a regression effect; it is immaterial that the measurement error in change scores is a combination of the measurement errors of the two variables taken separately. Change scores are what they are when we find them, and they are at the very heart of the study of effects in developmental investigations. This author recommended before (1973, 1975) and here recommends again that longitudinal data and studies of change in experiments be conceptualized as and analyzed as within-subjects designs with ANOVA and with some additional statistics which will be discussed later. Actually one would obtain exactly the same statistical results from applying such within-subjects ANOVA statistics as would be obtained from computing difference scores and reanalyzing the data as though it were a between-groups study. One could do this by subtracting the overall mean for each person from scores obtained on each occasion. The analysis of the change scores would produce exactly the same "significance level" as would the within-subject analysis of the six original sets of scores. In performing within-subject ANOVA computations, we in effect hide from ourselves the fact that we actually are analyzing difference, change, or gain scores. What appears to be perfectly sensible when looked at in one way (the correct way, so I say) looks somehow disturbing to some people when looked at in a more molecular way.

STUDIES OF TRENDS IN DEVELOPMENTAL RESEARCH

A simple example of an experimental trend imposed on a developmental sequence was given in Figure 9-1; a simple example of a purely longitudinal study showing growth rates in a dependent variable for males and females is given in Figure 9-2. These examples are, of course, oversimplifications because in most developmental investigations there would be a variety of treatment conditions and/or a variety of groups among which comparisons would be made. These simple examples, however, allow us to look at some general principles of experimental design and analysis in developmental investigations.

Study of Trends with ANOVA

This author spent a considerable amount of time prior to writing this chapter in searching through books and journal articles on mathematical statistics and research methodology for developmental studies—looking for "what is new" as general approaches to the analysis of developmental trends. The conclusion that I came to is that major reliance still should be placed on classical approaches to the analysis of variance, as is described in

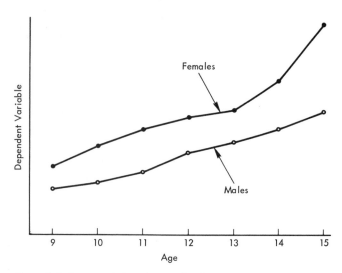

Figure 9-2 Age trends in a longitudinal study

detail in a plethora of good sources (e.g., Hays, 1973; Kirk, 1968; Winer, 1971). As for the applicability of ANOVA concepts to the analysis of complex research designs in psychology, a milestone was that of the widely quoted article by Grant (1962). Anyone who wants to understand trend analysis (in addition to just reading the computer printout) would be fortunate to lay hands on the basic text by Lewis (1960), now out of print. Some possible alternatives to ANOVA for the study of developmental trends and for experiments relating to such development will be discussed later, but before such alternatives are discussed, let it be said that there is really nothing currently that challenges within-subjects (repeated-measurements) ANOVA as a companion to the design and analysis of research.

The use of ANOVA designs and approaches to analysis are well known in all the disciplines that perform developmental studies, and consequently it is not necessary to go into great detail here. Instead the issues will be illustrated, and some general principles stated. What has proven to be helpful to the research worker during the last ten or more years is the advent of highly elaborate computer packages for taking apart developmental trends in intricate detail and in essence doing such analyses for the experimenter at the push of a button.

Statistical Properties. Here it is still assumed that by developmental research we are referring to studies that have chronological age as one important dimension of investigation or some variable that correlates with age, such as grades in school. In some developmental studies, of course, the total time span of the investigation is not large, and one is concerned mainly with measurements before and after some treatment condition. In either case a major concern is with changes of subjects either naturally over time or in conjunction with some type of treatment condition. All such designs then are typified as being within-subject (W-S) or repeated-measurements, at least as regards the cardinal independent variable of time periods for taking measurements. There are some particular characteristics and some advantages and disadvantages of employing W-S ANOVA rather than ANOVA among intact different age groups. This matter was discussed previously in relation to true longitudinal studies as contrasted with mainly cross-sectional studies of age groups. In addition to the *W-S* design being more interpretable as regards truly developmental functions, the statistical properties of the two types of analysis are somewhat different. Whereas in the employment of ANOVA to compare different groups of subjects the error term consists of residual within cell variance after main effects and interactions are assessed, in the *W-S* design the error term for each temporal trend consists of an interaction of individual differences with other facets of the design. (If there are facets of the design concerning comparisons of different groups of subjects, e.g., males and females or experimental treatment groups, the choice of a proper error term is somewhat more complicated, as discussed and illustrated in Winer, 1971, Chap. 7.)

In addition to the *W-S* design being logically the one to employ in developmental studies, there can be some dividends. The major one is the considerably smaller error term that would be obtained in comparison to ANOVA with randomized groups *if* in the *W-S* design there are substantial correlations between individual differences obtained at different times of measurement, e.g., different age levels. If all correlations among adjacent age levels were 1.00, then the error term would be zero, and any differences at all in central tendency would be infinitely "significant." At the other extreme if all correlations among age levels were zero, then the sums of squares for error would be the same size as in a between-groups ANOVA applied to the same data (although the degrees of freedom for the error term would be larger in the latter case). These relationships regarding correlations among testing times and the size of the error term in the statistical design have led some authors to discuss which design is "better," as though there were a simple choice. If one intends to investigate people over time, either naturally or in relation to an experimental treatment, then there is no choice but to employ a *W-S* design. The issues then concern the encumbrances of such designs upon the planning and analysis of research activities.

Assumptions. The really hard questions about employing *W-S* designs in developmental studies concern the meeting of assumptions required in assessing research results in relation to *F*-distributions, *t*-tests for contrasts among means, and related statistics. In all ANOVA designs, it is assumed that measurements in a particular study are randomly sampled from either a very large or conceptually infinite population (or domain, or universe) of such measurements. It frequently is said that we sample people, but it is not really the people as such that we sample but rather measurements taken on people—height, weight of a particular gland, and scores on tests of human competence and personality. In employing statistics relating to the *F*-distribution, it is assumed that the different samples of measurements at different age levels have approximately the same variance, but this is quite likely not to be the case in a great deal of developmental research. There are two reasons for such heterogeneity of variance. First, no matter how one would "scale" an attribute, it is logical that the variance would not be the same at different points on an age continuum or different points before and after an experimental treatment. This would be the case with height, for exam-

ple, where individuals are expected not only to increase in height as they mature but also to become progressively more diverse in that regard. Similarly on a test of word knowledge, it is expected not only that the average number of words understood by children would increase as they mature, but that the standard deviation would increase also. While this is not the place to argue about the meaning of such increases in sizes of standard deviations during the maturing process, it is a common observation that standard deviations are not the same throughout a period of age in which an investigation is undertaken or potentially not the same before and after treatment conditions are imposed as part of an experiment. A second reason why homogeneity of variance is not a tenable assumption in much developmental research is that measurement instruments frequently are constructed in such a way as to artifactually induce heterogeneity of variance, along with having some effects on mean values also. The simplest example is that of an instrument that has too low a "ceiling," such as in a test of word knowledge in which sufficiently difficult items are not included to measure higher and higher levels of word knowledge throughout years of schooling. This heterogeneity of variance can be offset to some extent by various scale transformations, but that usually is neither necessary nor wise unless there is a firm convention for rescaling variables, as in the customary log transformation made of latency scores in tests that concern quick responses. Ad hoc transformations purely for statistical purposes may prove more confusing than helpful in the long run. It is known that statistics based on the *F* distribution are "robust" with respect to the assumption of homogeneity of variance, particularly when there are equal numbers of subjects in each group being compared—as necessarily is the case in true longitudinal studies.

The real concern as regards assumptions for ANOVA in developmental research is that of *independence of errors.* Of course this does not mean that successive measurement periods must be uncorrelated, because indeed it is actually hoped that such correlations will be substantial. What is required is that the portion of leftover variance that is designated the error term contains variation that can be attributed only to pure randomness and not to a failure of the data to "fit the model." In order to fit the model for a *W-S* ANOVA properly, it is assumed that the correlation from occasion to occasion is the same "in the population" and that such differences in correlation as are witnessed in the data could be attributed only to chance. It is a simple fact of life in performing developmental studies that this assumption is blatantly incorrect. Why this is the case is illustrated in Table 9–2, which depicts a pattern of correlations that would be reasonable to find among measures of either aggressiveness or word knowledge taken at five times from age 7 through 15. The table shows the *simplex pattern* that is so typically found in correlating traits at different age levels. When a simplex pattern is found among the correlations (or any other discernible pattern), it is clear evidence that errors are not independent, and unlike the assumption of homogeneity of variance, a lack of independence in the error term is a serious violation of ANOVA. Various suggestions have been made for avoiding this problem by a form of profile analysis which will be discussed subsequently or by adjustments in the

Table 9–2 A Simplex Pattern of Correlations for a Trait Measured at Five Age Levels

Age	7	9	11	13	15
7	—	.80	.70	.60	.50
9		—	.80	.70	.60
11			—	.80	.70
13				—	.80
15					—

degrees of freedom for employing the *F* test (see Morrison, 1976; Wallenstein & Fleiss, 1979; Winer, 1971).

The likelihood of finding serious departures from the assumption of equal correlation throughout times of repeated measurement is why this author set off on several months of looking for possible alternative designs and methods of analysis for developmental studies, particularly for truly longitudinal studies over more than a half-dozen years. My conclusion is that it would be better generally to live with what problems this breach of assumptions gives us than to employ potential alternative approaches. The alternatives have their own problems as regards assumptions, some of their statistical properties are matters of dispute, and they certainly are not as well known and easy to work with as is trend analysis with ANOVA. For that reason it is recommended that ANOVA designs and procedures of analysis continue to be employed as the mainstay of developmental research, but the presence of correlated errors in such designs provides one more reason for being quite cautious in interpreting borderline cases of statistical significance or in placing faith in confidence intervals derived from *W-S* ANOVA.

Trends in Longitudinal Studies

The analysis of trends in longitudinal studies presents no major statistical problems other than for the concern mentioned previously about an expected simplex patterning of correlations for responses obtained on different testing occasions. The simple comparison of age functions for males and females in Figure 9–2 illustrates the problem. In this case there would be a quantitatively ordered facet of fixed effects for age, a fixed effects facet for sex, and a random facet for subjects, with such subjects being nested within the male and female groups. One need only take out the nearest reference source on the computation of analysis of variance to find the routines for taking apart the relevant sums of squares.

If differences with respect to age and sex were as clear as in Figure 9–2, it would be almost a waste of time to compute the levels of statistical significance. However one would probably obtain such statistics incidentally in the course of performing more incisive analyses, or the particular computer program would probably "output" them even if they were thought to be nonessential. More to the point here, and typically the case in most longitudinal studies, is to "fit" the two trends, examine differences in the curve form over different regions of the age continuum, and obtain a combined fit for males and females if the two curves were not highly disparate.

One is in a good position to perform trend analysis when working with an age continuum because age con-

stitutes a reasonable quantitative variable for indexing such trends. The procedure would be to fit orthogonal polynomials to the curves successively until higher order terms provided negligible decreases in the sums of squares relating to deviations of means about the curve. If there are *J* points on the quantitative continuum, then a curve of the order of *J* − 1 would fit the means exactly but trivially so. Usually the intention is to fit the curve reasonably well with linear, second-order, and no more than third-order curves. Anything more than that not only is gilding the lily but may be attributable to artifacts in the way that the dependent variable is measured. How to fit curves with orthogonal polynomials and to study differences within and between curves is described in Hays (1973), Winer (1971), and in numerous other advanced texts on applied statistics. The general approach can be carried to the investigation of numerous groups of persons over any number of age levels.

Several matters are important to consider with respect to the analysis of age trends as illustrated in Figure 9–2. First, one is usually looking for some type of interaction in the results. In most longitudinal investigations it would come as no surprise that curves go upward or downward in terms of however the variable is measured, and usually also it is no surprise that a linear trend will do a reasonably good job of fitting the means in any one group considered separately and of groups combined when effects due to overall group differences are removed. What is important to look at are interactions of points on each curve about the linear trend, and interactions or deviations of points about higher order trends. In comparing groups the real meat of the matter is to look at interactions between slopes of curves subtending different points in time. How such variance components are partitioned into main effects and interactions can become complicated in practice when there are more than two fixed effects (in the present example sex and years of age) and when subjects are "within" on some factors and "between" on other factors. However all that one needs to do is to "plug in" the characteristics of the design and supply the data for either the standard computational routines (e.g., Hays, 1973; Kirk, 1968; Winer, 1971) or have the data analyzed with one of the omnibus computer routines for multifactor ANOVA.

In the course of performing analyses of trends with ANOVA, it would be wise also to obtain confidence intervals for each developmental curve and measures of degree of relationship. The confidence intervals would provide guidelines with respect to the safety of interpreting apparent differences of means over the age continuum for one group considered separately and for apparent interactions of groups with respect to differences in means at different age levels. Measures of degree of relationship will tell the experimenter how much, in an absolute sense, the fixed facets of the design explain variance in the dependent variable (see Dodd & Schultz, 1970; Dwyer, 1974). Of primary importance in most developmental studies is amount of variance explained by age. Measures of degree of relationship could also be obtained for the random factor of repeated measurements on subjects, showing the tendency of subjects within a factor to remain consistent with respect to individual differences over different age levels. For the fixed factors in a design, the measure of degree of relationship is *omega-*

squared, and for the random factor due to repeated measurements on subjects, the measure is the *intraclass correlation* coefficient. Good discussions on the basic logic of employing such measures of degree of relationship are in Hays (1973) and Winer (1971); computational procedures for complex designs are discussed in Dodd and Schultz (1970) and in Dwyer (1974).

ANOVA Designs for Randomized Experimental Groups

From the standpoint of statistics per se, there really are no problems in the analysis of experiments where it is feasible to assign members randomly from a larger group of subjects to one or more treatment groups and control groups. An example would be in studying three approaches to special education in mathematics at the fourth-grade level in a large school being employed for the purpose. There are three fourth-grade classrooms, providing ample subjects for the study. There are two treatment groups, each of which will study from a different type of programmed text in mathematics. The control group in each class will receive the usual mode of instruction instead of working from a programmed text. Comparisons are made of male and female students within treatment conditions. Classrooms would be a "control factor" to test for any interaction of that factor with others in the design and to reduce the "error term" appropriately. An equal number of boys and girls from each class would be assigned to the two treatment conditions and the control group, and it would be desirable to arrange the assignment of subjects such that there was an equal number in each possible "cell" of the design. Of course this design could be elaborated in numerous ways, but it is already complicated enough to illustrate some important points.

Primary attention with this illustrative design would be focused on the before-after comparison of achievement in mathematics. One could make comparisons of "after" measurements only, and if the results were striking, to have chosen that route might have been the better part of wisdom. However, one is likely to be "swamped" with large individual differences in achievement in mathematics after the experiment is completed, so much so that any apparent differences would be obscured by the large amount of error. Such error probably could be reduced considerably by employing a *W-S* design.

If treatment conditions exist for only several months and comparisons of repeated-measures are only from before to after the treatment, one could argue that this is not really a developmental study at all. It would be a waste of time to quibble over the semantics of the issue, but at least at a minimal level of examining developmental functions, experiments of this kind should be considered here. A wider question is that of whether or not any changes produced by the treatments are particular to the segment of chronological age, or grade level, investigated. Whether or not the experimenter intended to investigate the age or grade time continuum, without some knowledge of what went on well before and well after the experiment, it would be difficult to interpret the results. This is true not only of a simple experiment of this kind but also in all experiments undertaken on dependent measures that are important in experimental

studies of change and with variables that are known to change naturally as a function of time. Even if no experimental conditions are imposed, one could draw all kinds of interesting graphs to depict different possible extensions of the curve before and after the experiment to show that very different interpretations would be given if more extensive information were available about the changing shape of the curve.

As with the study of "natural" developmental trends, the trends investigated in the hypothetical experiment would be picked apart in terms of components of variance attributable to the fixed factors of treatment conditions, testing periods, sex, and classroom. There would be a random factor relating to subjects which would be repeated on before-after measurements or on more frequent occasions before and after. Consistent individual differences on the several repeated measurements would allow one to reduce the error term for assessing changes. In such designs for experiments on developmental issues, one inevitably is studying interactions—interactions of individuals on each curve at various points before and after the treatment, interactions of boys and girls in terms of such changes, and interactions of curves obtained from different classrooms.

Quasi-Experiments

Where issues relating to experimental design, analysis, and interpretation become very difficult indeed is with respect to circumstances in which it is not possible to assign subjects randomly to treatment groups. This is the case, for example, in some rather casual preexperimental studies, such as in comparing two approaches to special instruction in which one method of instruction is given only to girls and the other only to boys. Of course no sane person would perform such an "experiment," but it does serve to illustrate the problems dramatically. At a more sophisticated level of research, groupings of subjects are frequently "given" to the experimenter, and there simply is no choice of randomly assigning subjects to treatments. An example would be in studying effects of nursing-home living for the aged as compared to older people who remain in their home environments. In this case living in a nursing home can be thought of as a type of experimental treatment, but of course the persons who go to a nursing home are likely to be dissimilar to those who do not. Regardless of what the dependent measures are, the two groups would probably differ at the outset of the "experiment." Even if such differences were not substantial initially, the two groups probably would differ on numerous variables that would tend to interact with "treatments."

At the other end of the age continuum, one frequently encounters studies of nonrandomized groups of children in relation to special education. One or several forms of special education are studied in a number of different groups. For obvious reasons it is frequently not possible to randomly assign subjects to such treatment conditions. The treatment conditions are not applied to "normal" children because they would not make sense with them; and their educational progress might be slowed by working with materials and exercises that would seem trivial. Based on measurements of achievement administered before and afterwards, the unfortunate experimenter attempts to make sense of the conceptual and statistical jungle by applying whatever special methods of analysis seem appropriate. This is an unpleasant thicket for either the experimentalist or the research methodologist who wanders in, because the effort to obtain clean answers from messy data are frustrating to say the very least. Volumes now have been written on special research designs and special methods of analysis that provide some help in dealing with quasi-experiments (see Cook & Campbell, 1979).

In any experiment where intact groups of subjects must be given different treatments as a part of a quasi-experiment, conclusions must necessarily be based on a wealth of circumstantial evidence. To provide such circumstantial evidence, it helps if there are numerous testing periods before and after the treatment, several dependent measures that provide different perspectives on the results of the experiment, and potentially a variety of control groups. Some of the requirements in this regard are discussed in Nunnally (1975); a more detailed coverage is given by Cook and Campbell (1979). What it all amounts to is that with a great deal of effort one can reach quasi-conclusions about the results of quasi-experiments. However the burden here is on the design and the assurance therein that such comparisons are possible as to rule out some of the major competing interpretations that could be given for different types of results. This is really not a statistical game in which clean conclusions can be reached with elaborate methods of analysis. However in some very important issues in life-span research, one is forced into studying experimental comparisons made on nonrandomized groups.

Covariance Analysis

In looking through the statistics books for possible methods to employ in developmental research, one who does not spend time in dealing with statistics might fasten on covariance analysis for possible use in developmental research. Covariance analysis represents one of those statistical tools that looks both reasonable and attractive until the logic is picked apart and one looks at some horrible examples of what can happen when it is employed (see Werts & Linn, 1969, 1970, 1971). At first glance one might consider covariance analysis as a possible substitute for the use of repeated-measurements ANOVA as discussed and illustrated before. An example would be in the experiment discussed previously concerning three different methods of instruction applied to three randomized groups within classrooms and to boys and girls. Rather than employ within-subject ANOVA in that instance, one could have employed covariance analysis, covarying the first measurement from subsequent measurements. Whatever the research issues and no matter how complex the fixed facets of the design, the first step would be to determine regression slopes within all cells of the design. If the regression slope were approximately the same (one of the assumptions for applying ANCOVA), then the average of such regression slopes would be taken as the regression slope to use in making "corrections." The next step would be to pool all scores on the first dependent measure (the covariate) including therein the mean score for each cell. One would multiply

all of the scores (including the cell means) by the regression slope and subtract these score by score from the second and later dependent measurements. Essentially one analyzes such regressed scores by ANOVA in the usual way. This sounds very simple and harmless, but it can lead to some very confusing results.

First, one must look at some of the major assumptions that are necessary for the analysis to rest on firm statistical foundations. In addition to the assumption of homogeneity of regression slopes (which frequently is tenuous in developmental investigations), it is assumed that only linear regressions are at work among test scores, which also may not be a good assumption in developmental research. It is assumed that measures are perfectly reliable, both the covariate and the dependent measure, which is seldom even approximately correct. There are those who argue that perfect reliability is not a requirement for employing ANCOVA and that some sensible corrections can be made (e.g., Overall & Woodard, 1977), but this author is unconvinced. These problems in employing covariance analysis have been elaborated on in numerous places (e.g., Werts & Linn, 1969, 1970, 1971).

The purpose here is not to write off COVARAN entirely as a statistical concept and statistical tool; admittedly the burden of assumptions is heavy, and the logic is frequently questionable even when a "sensible" concomitant variable is partialled from *randomized* groups. When the technique is applied to nonrandomized groups, as frequently must be the case in developmental research, it is clearly hazardous. If scores are available before and after an experiment or available at numerous points in a longitudinal study, it is far better to work directly with the actually obtained scores in *W-S* ANOVA and not adjust them in any way by one or more covariates.

Profile Analysis

There is a potential competitor to ANOVA for the analysis of developmental studies. This is called *profile analysis*, which is based on a somewhat different statistical rationale than ANOVA. Potentially it has some real advantages but also has some problems of its own. What one does in profile analysis is to treat the successive repeated measurements as a problem in multivariate analysis of variance (MANOVA) and analyze the data accordingly (see Harris, 1975; Morrison, 1976; Tatsuoka, 1971). How such analyses are performed can be illustrated with the example in Figure 9-2. Although the methods apply when there are only two groups, here males and females, the application of MANOVA would be more important when there are more than two groups—e.g., if in this case males and females were subdivided into two ethnic groups. Measures taken at each age level would be analagous to *different* measures, as is more typically the case in the employment of MANOVA.

Profile analysis allows one to take apart, in a surgical way, components of trends such as those shown in Figure 9-2. First, one could test for significant differences of overall means. Thus it is clearly seen in Figure 9-2 that females are higher than males on this particular dependent variable. If there were any doubt, an overall test of significance could be computed, and confidence intervals could be asserted for this overall difference. In effect one would draw both curves through the mean of the means, and then there would be no differences in overall height of curves. Next, one could compare the interaction of the two curves. Even if they were at the same overall height, they could still vary from point to point. With two groups this would be tested by Hotelling's T-test. One would take the mean of the two means at each age level and make a statistical test for "flatness," which again would involve the T-test. Of course, just looking at the upward slopes would make the results of such a test obvious. Next, one can perform trend analysis by fitting the combined means for females and males with orthogonal polynomials. One can keep elaborating this procedure to form any kinds of post hoc contrasts among overall means, among the means within each group, and contrasts of the means in different groups (see Morrison, 1976, as to how this is done).

Profile analysis with statistical procedures relating to MANOVA potentially has some attractive advantages over the use of ANOVA for the same purposes. First, with profile analysis one finds highly flexible methods for taking apart differences between and within curves, for ascertaining confidence intervals both planned and post hoc, and for curve-fitting. One finds all of the statistical tools that are needed for developmental investigations, including the analysis of the results of experiments. The second potential advantage is that the statistical methods related to profile analysis and MANOVA *do not* rest on the assumption of homogeneity of variance within developmental trends. The reader will remember that this was raised as a major problem in employing *W-S* ANOVA with respect to developmental functions. Third, and relatedly, it does not matter whether there is a discernible patterning of correlations among sources of individual differences at various points on the curve. Thus the appearance of the inevitable simplex pattern among correlations at different ages would pose no problem for profile analysis. Both homogeneity of variance and homogeneity of regression slopes between ages are not assumptions for the employment of profile analysis within any one curve considered separately.

Since profile analysis has essentially the same power as ANOVA (depending upon which statistical distribution function is used with the former), everything seems to be in favor of employing profile analysis rather than *W-S* ANOVA for the analysis of developmental functions. Before concluding that profile analysis is better than repeated-measurement ANOVA, three potential problems with the former should be mentioned. First, although profile analysis does not assume homogeneity of variances and homogeneity of correlations within a developmental trend for one group considered separately, it assumes homogeneity of covariance matrices between different groups. The assumption would then be that the whole covariance matrix for males would be the same as that for females in Figure 9–2. The methods are apparently robust for small departures from equality of covariance matrices, but quite spurious results can be obtained if this assumption is patently incorrect.

A second problem, one related to the first, is that there is quite a bit of uncertainty and controversy regarding *which* type of statistical-distribution theory to employ in

multivariate analysis generally. There are several alternative approaches. The one usually employed with MANOVA is in relation to Wilk's *lamda* statistic, or the function there of the U statistic. Another approach is with the so-called *trace statistics*. By far the most flexible approach is with statistics concerning the *greatest characteristic root* (GCR). With such GCR statistics one has available a whole toolbox of convenient approaches for taking apart developmental studies in fine grain. One could not only examine differences in means within the profile for particular groups relating to the first GCR, but one could also look at successive GCR's. Each GCR is related not only to statistical tests of significance and to confidence intervals, but also each produces a discriminant function. Thus one could perform a multiple discriminant function analysis of the successive points within any one developmental trend. The flexibility provided by such GCR analyses is far more than could be obtained from repeated-measurements ANOVA. None of the competing statistical-distribution theories relating to MANOVA or to profile analysis in the dissecting of developmental trends has the same flexibility as the GCR statistics (Harris, 1975). Essentially the former statistics are good for saying "something happened," but they provide no tools for further determining exactly what happened. The GCR statistics are somewhat less powerful in many cases than statistics based on other statistical distributions (which is not really a major problem), but far worse they seem to be more sensitive to the assumption of equality of covariance matrices among different groups which are compared.

If the GCR statistics cannot be employed in surgically taking apart the data relating to developmental trends, the use of MANOVA alone based on Wilk's *lamda* or the trace statistics would provide very little, if any, advantage over repeated-measurements ANOVA. A number of prominent statisticians have attempted to extend tests based on Wilk's *lamda* and trace statistics to take apart within-subjects studies in detail, but Harris (1975) argues persuasively that this is not statistically legitimate (in so doing, Harris makes a cogent argument that statistical tests frequently employed with the multiple discriminant function and with canonical correlational analysis are not legitimate).

Obviously the practicing researcher who borrows statistics rather than invents them will want some dust to settle among statistically oriented theorists before s/he can feel comfortable with problems concerning (1) the robustness of profile analysis with respect to the assumption of homogeneity of covariance matrices and (2) the propriety and validity of employing one, rather than another, distribution theory for the analysis of results. The overall conclusion that this author reached after studying methods of profile analysis related to MANOVA (the same methods being related to canonical correlation and the discriminant function) is that whereas they are mathematically elegant and potentially might allow one to circumvent some of the untenable assumptions in employing *W-S* ANOVA, a rush to profile analysis should be held in abeyance. My own working rule for the present is to stick with repeated-measurements ANOVA until methods of profile analysis (hopefully based on GCR statistics) are more fully understood.

STATISTICAL INDUCTION OF TRENDS

As many persons have lamented, the study of an overall developmental trend anywhere in the age continuum may obscure potential differences among people in their individual trends. If there are obvious groupings of people (e.g., sex or ethnic groups), these can be recognized initially and investigated with appropriate designs such as those discussed previously. If either the differences among groups are statistically removed or no groups are hypothesized initially, one still finds considerable variability at each point in the developmental sequence. If the correlation from one testing point to another is high, this means that curves for individuals tend to be parallel; consequently, other than for the elevation factor, there really are no differences in curve forms for individuals. If correlations are near zero, then individuals are laws unto themselves as regards trends. Of course the situation is usually in between these two extremes, with correlations expected somewhere in the range betwen .40 and .80 for many types of attributes. This leaves the possibility that what appears to be a general trend in the data "hides" meaningful differences in trends for latent groups of people. The possibility of recovering such latent groups and statistically determining their separable trends has occasioned a great deal of discussion and statisticizing (Harris, 1963; Nesselroade & Reese, 1973). Statistical modeling with respect to the recovery of latent groups in developmental data has gone on since that time, but really not much has been added and really nothing much needs to be.

The mathematical solution to the recovery of latent groups in any W-S research design was settled long ago by this author (1962) and by Tucker (1966). Both authors gave essentially the same mathematical solution—Nunnally illustrating the solution with respect to analysis of score profiles and Tucker with respect to learning curves. The solution quite simply is to factor analyze the raw scores. This can be done by forming a matrix of cross-products of raw scores in the same way that one would form cross-products of deviation scores to obtain covariances or cross-products of standard scores to obtain correlations. Factor analysis can be applied to such matrices of raw-score cross-products in the same way as they can to matrices of covariances or correlations. (The results are more interpretable if each sum of cross-products is divided by the number of measures, these being analogous to covariances and correlations.)

Raw-score factor analysis in developmental studies would be applied to the cross-products of scores for individuals over the number of occasions on which measurements are made. If in a longitudinal study measurements are made with respect to height, or vocabulary, or anything else once a year over a period of ten years, then one would simply take the matrix of raw scores with respect to the particular dependent variable, compute sums of cross-products of those scores, and submit them to any form of factor analysis. What one is doing by this approach is to factor analyze growth functions for individuals. If indeed there are latent growth functions in a group of persons, they will appear in factor analysis. Each factor obtained will be a different developmental curve. One can rotate those factors either by eye or with the use of any of the analytical methods of rotation. The demon-

stration by Tucker of how raw-score factor analysis would be applied to learning curves illustrates what could be done with the analysis of curves obtained in developmental investigations.

The availability of raw-score factor analysis for "detecting" latent developmental functions obviates a wide variety of piecemeal approaches. Numerous approaches to cluster analysis or typal analysis are intended to do the same thing that is done much better by raw-score factor analysis. The use of the D statistic for measuring distance between persons has been advocated as a way to specify latent groups of individuals in terms of growth functions and in many other multivariate problems, but there is absolutely nothing that can be obtained from such D measures that could not be obtained and mathematized much more easily with raw-score factor analysis (Nunnally, 1978).

One could elaborate this discussion of statistical methods for detecting latent developmental functions, but alas, it would not be worth the effort. The reason is that almost never does one have sufficient amounts of data as regards measurement at different points in time to justify application of factor analytic techniques or anything else that would do much the same. If one has developmental curves for, say, 200 persons at ten points in time, one would have to contend with a 200-by-200 matrix of cross-product terms, with each cross-product term being obtained over only ten points of measurement. Each sum of cross-products would be based on only ten degrees of freedom, which puts one in much the same bind as one would have if one examined a correlation matrix for 200 tests in which the correlations were obtained over only ten individuals. This obviously is an impossible situation in which to work as regards the opportunities for taking advantage of chance. There simply would be no way to perform meaningful analyses with so many people and so few data points as would be involved in almost any conceivable developmental study.

The same problem of insufficient data plagues all attempts to perform factor analytic investigations of covariant tendencies of growth functions. The problem occurs in P technique, T technique, and the alphabet soup of within-person and between-person approaches to factor analysis such as those that have been delineated by Cattell (see Nunnally, 1978). As clever as such designs for person-factoring are, in developmental investigations no one has ever produced enough data points (measured at enough points in time) to allow any of the statistical procedures to be employed sensibly. There is nothing wrong with the statistical procedures—the data simply does not merit the analyses.

In looking at the number of data points (occasions of measurement) that would be required in order to obtain meaningful results from statistical methods for estimating latent developmental functions, it becomes quite apparent that the study of differences in such developmental functions in relation to differences among groups of people will need to depend almost exclusively on the experimenter's wisdom in hypothesizing such groups initially. When an experiment is undertaken, the experimental design itself states the way in which groups are to be formed. In studies of natural development, however, what are some of the dimensions along which groups should be formed and investigated for potential differences in developmental functions? An old standby is to include the two sexes as one such classification, and ethnic differences frequently constitute another potentially important classification (e.g., with respect to maturation of teeth); but it is hard to find any old standbys after that point, particularly in relation to psychological dependent variables such as word knowledge and extraversion. Without being able to hypothesize such groups initially based either on formal theory or just common sense, there is very little hope afterwards of detecting statistically stable latent growth functions no matter how elaborate the statistical method which is applied.

STUDIES OF INDIVIDUAL DIFFERENCES

Individual differences in growth function were discussed in the previous section; here will be discussed other possible investigations of individual differences. Large individual differences are the rule throughout developmental research, and it is only natural to wonder what statistical and conceptual models apply to them. In the same way that studies of trends are usually thought of in terms of W-S ANOVA designs, studies of individual differences are usually thought of with respect to patterns of correlations. Gorsuch (1974) provides a comprehensive discussion of the analysis of correlation structures, particularly with respect to factor analysis. Theories relating to the study of individual differences and numerous mathematical models relating to the design and analysis of research are discussed in Nunnally (1978). Some interesting mathematical models and inferential statistics for the analysis of patterned covariance and correlation structures are discussed by Morrison (1976). Numerous special issues concerning the analysis of correlation structures in developmental research are discussed in the volume edited by Nesselroade and Baltes (1978). Still other approaches and illustrative problems are discussed in the volume edited by Harris (1963). Obviously the person who wants advice on how to design and analyze correlation structures in developmental research will find no end of advice and a super abundance of high-powered statistical methods. A discussion of some of the most important issues and related mathematical models follows.

Correlations within Developmental Trends

The employment of within-subjects designs for longitudinal studies was discussed previously, and it was said that the correlations of individual differences among age groups served to reduce the amount of error in studying such trends. As a byproduct of longitudinal studies (e.g., of height or of vocabulary), one obtains matrices of correlations showing, for example, correlations among measurements at a half-dozen or more age levels for the same group. Such matrices of correlations can be analyzed by any of the approaches that are available in general for that purpose—e.g., multiple correlation, partial correlation, factor analysis, path analysis, and numerous other approaches. As mentioned previously the correlation patterns found in longitudinal data tend to have a monotonous sameness about them—namely, tending to fit the simplex pattern illustrated in Table 9-2. Although

the matter does not seem very central for developmental research, considerable theorizing and math-modeling have been done to statistically "fit" the simplex (Morrison, 1976). The simplex pattern is the most elementary of a hierarchy of patterns discussed by Guttman (summarized in Nunnally, 1978). Rather than witness only the monotonous waning of sizes of correlations as time between testing occasions increases, it is possible, at least theoretically, that such correlations would grow larger and smaller in "batches" in ways that would be predictable from mathematical models. However this author has never observed anything more complex than the simplex in longitudinal data.

Where the investigation of temporal trends in correlation patterns might be more interesting would be with respect to experiments intended to alter developmental trends, as discussed previously and illustrated in Figure 9-1 and Table 9-1. It is to be expected that individual differences at one point in time will be "disturbed" by experimental treatments, or to put it in statistical language, for the treatment effect to interact with individual differences. A dramatic treatment effect would be expected to be evidenced not only in a marked change in the trendline but also in a substantially *lower* correlation from immediately before to immediately after the treatment than among a number of measurements made before the treatment and a number of measurements made after the treatment. Such junctures in correlation matrices would be interesting, but this author has not yet seen a clear example.

Longitudinal Study of Factor Structures

Rather than examine patterns of correlations over time for one variable, another set of issues concerns factor structures found among different measures at different points in time. Few studies of this kind are available, but essentially what they entail is administering a variety of tests (or any other types of measures) on a number of occasions. There has been considerable controversy as to the logic and method of performing such investigations (see Nunnally, 1973, 1978), and consequently some clarifying comments should be made. First, clearcut comparisons of factor structures at different points in time can be made only if exactly the same measures are administered to exactly the same people at all points in time for which comparisons are to be made. If some people are different or some measures are different on various occasions of testing, there simply is no way to compare clearly factor structures obtained at different points in time. As the author has elaborated on elsewhere (1973, 1975, 1978), the only firm foundation for comparing factor structures at different points in time is by correlating factor scores at those points and not correlating or otherwise statistically comparing factor loadings obtained on different occasions. Comparisons of sets of loadings may be of interest in their own right, but they cannot tell one whether factors are the *same* at different points in time. Proposals have been made for comparing sets of factor loadings to answer questions about "invariance" of factors in *different* samples of people, but it is easily demonstrated that all such approaches can be laughed off the front porch with some truly crushing counter examples—e.g., the various measures of "factorial similarity" based on comparisons of factor loadings can, by example, lead one to the conclusion that two orthogonal factors in the *same* analysis are really highly related. Proper approaches to comparing stability or invariance of factors in different analyses are discussed in Nunnally (1978).

Rather than simply perform factor analyses at different age levels and hope that the factor structures appear to be quite similar (as regards correlations of factor scores on different occasions), numerous approaches have been advocated for simultaneously analyzing correlations obtained at different points in time or for "forcing" patterns of factor loadings to look as much alike as possible by optimum methods of rotation. Some of these approaches are quite useful, and others are downright dangerous (Nunnally, 1978). One useful approach is with "extension methods," by which the factor analysis would be conducted within one age group (say within an 18-year-old group), and the correlations for earlier age levels on the same subjects would be carried along as an extension (Gorsuch, 1974). This would allow one to compute factor loadings and factor scores for all age groups in the same analysis. One could obtain the same result by a conceptually simpler but computationally no easier method—namely, by obtaining factor scores at the 18-year age level and simply correlating scores at other age levels with those. The concept of an extension analysis provides a useful way of thinking about stability and change of factor structures over time (Gorsuch, 1974). To look at the stability of factor structures in this way requires one to specify a *reference year* for which comparisons would be made backward and forward in time, which is a method of working statistically that has some logic on its side (Nunnally, 1973).

Rather than declare one year as a standard by which comparisons of factor structures would be made for different age levels, an alternative approach is to factor simultaneously in all of the age levels under consideration. The most thorough approach for doing this is that developed by Jöreskog (1978). These methods are quite complex, and their workings probably would be understandable only to persons who are highly familiar with factor analysis.

Theoretical Classification Schemes

Most of the discussion so far in this section on studies of individual differences has been with respect to statistical models which, in and of themselves, have no necessary relevance to substantive theory concerning the attributes of people. It is perhaps a sad commentary that most of the so-called theory in the study of individual differences is largely of that character. There are some conceptual schemes as regards structures of human abilities and personality characteristics that are based in psychologizing rather than statisticizing (see Nunnally, 1978). The best known of these "rational" schemes for the study of individual differences is that of Guilford's Structure of Intellect, which is intended to explain many types of human abilities in terms of content facets. The effort is to explain the mental activity of people when they are solving problems of many different kinds. That classification scheme has generated a wealth of research, and although the original theory has met with many dif-

ficulties, the overall enterprise is quite laudatory. Until we have such rational classification schemes based in psychological theory, there is very little chance of understanding individual differences in abilities or personality characteristics at any one age level, in any group of people, much less to chart the growth and change of individual differences over time.

The problem with individual differences is that they are illusively like the holes in doughnuts. In studying individual differences, one does not really investigate persons but rather the statistical spaces between them. Such spaces between people do lead to covariance and correlation matrices and permit one to perform all manner of complicated statistics upon them, but somehow in the process, the individual and people as a group can become lost. What is needed before we can have a thorough psychology of individual differences is to have a psychology of individuation. Efforts along those lines are occurring with respect to Freudian personality development and social learning theory, with both cases being concerned with the psychology of how people get to be different from one another. Only by tying in statistical and measurement technology with such interesting theories of maturation would there be much chance of gathering proper data and analyzing it in proper ways so as to provide important results.

MEASUREMENT PROBLEMS

By far the most intractable problems in developmental psychology, as well as psychology and the behavioral sciences generally, is that of adequate measurement of constructs—such constructs as ego strength, self-acceptance, dogmatism, locus of control, creativity, various kinds of motivation, and numerous types of cognitive styles. Our theories are populated with interesting-sounding construct names for which measurements are either lacking altogether or are surely being measured only in gross approximation.

Developmental studies in psychology are faced not only with all the usual difficulties of measuring anything important, but also with some special difficulties of their own. If one is investigating developmental trends over a considerable portion of the life span, it is necessary to measure the same thing at each age level. In some longitudinal studies this has resulted in giving the same test over and over at many age levels, such as in studying changes on the Stanford-Binet test. The possibilities for practice effects and other types of reactivity of measurement are quite obvious when exactly the same measuring instrument is given over and over. Even if one wanted to employ exactly the same items at different age levels, some very difficult problems of measurement would arise. With many of the types of tests that one would want to employ, younger subjects would simply not know how to respond, as would be the case with some personality inventories. Many of the items on ability tests that would be appropriate for children below age ten would seem silly to college students. Below age six, it is not usually possible to get meaningful responses from children to printed, self-explanatory tests, and consequently individual testing usually must be employed. But such individual testing probably would be both prohibitively expensive and might seem odd to older age groups.

Rather than give the same tests (the same set of items) over and over across some section of the life span, it is at least theoretically possible to give alternative forms. But in terms of the way that we usually think about such alternative forms, one would need to have many alternative forms, and such alternative forms simply are not available for any widely used test.

Another problem with testing over and over throughout the life span is that some types of test items become "dated," as would be the case in having subjects respond to pictorial material, responses to which would be determined in part by styles of clothing, automobiles, and even time-bound slogans, magazine titles, and many other cultural artifacts. Because words tend to take on new meanings over time, even the wording of some items might prove to be archaic if numerous alternative forms were developed before an investigation was set in motion and groups are administered alternative forms that had been constucted twenty years earlier.

For many types of measurement problems in developmental research, one can almost write off children below the age of six, and with other types of measures below the age of ten, as regards any possibility of strictly comparable measurement for developmental trends thereafter. This is because of the problems of language in employing printed forms for children below six and the problems of obtaining meaningful responses to complex test content below the age of about ten (e.g., in making sociometric ratings or in giving meaningful responses to items relating to reasoning factors, where a certain level of sophistication is required even to be able to take the tests).

The situation is not nearly so bad on the other end of the age continuum, which is a blessing in longitudinal studies of old age. Older adults are usually literate enough to work with printed tests and whatever types of paraphernalia that might be required to obtain measurements. They are accustomed to filling out printed forms for so many purposes in life and thus are not stymied in trying to express themselves in that medium. Also there is no real problem in employing the same type of item or testing instrument over numerous years in older age. If they understood and could work with the measurement procedure earlier, there is no reason why they could not do that later. One finds that the opportunities for comparable measurement in longitudinal studies are really much better at the older rather than the younger end of the age spectrum.

Computerized Testing

For the last several years the author has been working on a new technology of measurement which exemplifies some of the ways in which measurements can be improved for developmental investigations. The purpose of this line of investigation is to develop a computerized technology that would allow any investigator to have available at the push of a button measures of a wide variety of tests of human ability and personality characteristics. However one would want to count them, evidence has accrued over the last half-century for the existence of at least 40 factors of intellect, 15 factors of personality as evidence in printed tests, and scattered findings regard-

ing numerous factors of expressed emotion, values, interests, and other noncognitive attributes.

The purpose of the computerized testing system is to develop and refine measures of human ability and personality gradually, starting with the better known factors and working out toward the fringe of less well-known quantities. Developed so far have been eight tests of classical types of human abilities, and measures of approximately nine emotional states, as exhibited in self-ratings. The tests are all computer administered, scored, and statistically analyzed in terms of specially constructed programs. (This research has not been discussed before in print.)

With some of our computerized tests that exemplify what is needed in developmental studies, there really is no one test as such, but rather a set of instructions to the computer to "invent" items of a particular type. The simplest illustration is with respect to arithmetic problems. In one type of item the subject is presented with two-by-two addition problems—e.g., to add the numbers 28 and 36. The subject punches out the correct answer on a simple keyboard, and time taken to get the correct answer is the major dependent measure. Items are presented serially on a video screen, and all instructions are presented in the same mode. The computer composes items one after the other while the subject is responding. This is done on a random basis with respect to programmed instructions. In the example of the addition problem, the computer is "instructed" to fill in the two-by-two problem with random numbers. Obviously there then would be 10,000 possible ways to fill in the digits zero through nine in the four spaces. This then gives us a "test" with 10,000 items from which we can randomly sample.

Another example is our Matrix Scanning Test, which concerns the ability to detect a visual pattern in a field of competing stimuli. On each item, the subjects see a four-by-four matrix of one-digit numbers, the numbers from zero to nine. The computer is instructed to make one, and only one, of the numbers appear at three random places in the matrix. The other numbers are drawn entirely at random from the remaining digits, with the only restriction being that none of them is triplicated. The subject pushes the correct numbered key when the triplicated digit is detected. The number of possible items in this test is truly astronomical.

We are in the process of developing numerous computerized tests. Such tests have a number of attractive advantages, only some of which will be discussed here in relation to developmental research. First, there is no problem at all with testing people at different age levels as regards having enough alternative forms. Second, as regards practice effects and other forms of reactivity, the availability of such huge item pools allows one to let the individual have a great deal of practice initially before developmental studies are undertaken. Third, although we do not know what difficulties might be encountered in studying children below the age of ten, tests of this kind should be usable with most people from ten years to ripe old age. Fourth, one avoids many of the problems of having trained testers and many sources of unreliability by having testing, scoring, and analysis entirely automated. Fifth, the availability of huge item pools from which one can actually sample items allows a direct tie-in with fundamental psychometric principles relating to the domain-sampling model for the study of measurement error (Nunnally, 1978). Only if such truly randomized assembling of tests is possible can the technology of testing be brought in line with the psychometric foundations on which good tests are supposedly built, used, and studied. Our excursions into computerized testing so far are only suggestive of some of the things that could be done to develop better measurement technologies for psychology and, in the present instance, for life-span research.

CONCLUSIONS

In the study of human development we are spending far too much time worrying about elaborate statistical methods (plenty are available) to apply to frequently nonexistent or nonimportant data and not spending nearly enough time in (1) operationalizing our theories in terms of adequate measurement methods and subsequently (2) employing them in substantial experiments or with respect to significant portions of the life span.

REFERENCES

COOK, D. C., & CAMPBELL, D. T. *Quasi-experimentation.* Skokie, Ill.: Rand McNally, 1979.

CRONBACH, L. J., & FURBY, L. How should we measure "change"—or should we? *Psychological Bulletin,* 1970, *74,* 68–80.

DODD, D. H., & SCHULTZ, R. F. Computational procedures for estimating magnitude of effect for some analysis of variance designs. *Psychological Bulletin,* 1970, *79,* 17–22.

DWYER, J. H. Analysis of variance and the magnitude of effects: A general approach. *Psychological Bulletin,* 1974, *81,* 731–737.

GORSUCH, R. L. *Factor analysis.* Philadelphia: Saunders, 1974.

GRANT, D. A. Testing the null hypothesis and the strategy and tactics of investigating theoretical models. *Psychological Review,* 1962, *69,* 54–61.

HARRIS, C. W. *Problems in measuring change.* Madison: University of Wisconsin Press, 1963.

HARRIS, R. J. *A primer of multivariate statistics.* New York: Academic Press, 1975.

HAYS, W. L. *Statistics for the social sciences* (2nd ed.). New York: Holt, Rinehart & Winston, 1973.

JÖRESKOG, K. G. Structural analysis of covariance and correlation matrices. *Psychometrika,* 1978, *43,* 443–478.

KIRK, R. E. *Experimental design: Procedures for the behavioral sciences.* Monterey, Calif.: Brooks/Cole, 1968.

LEWIS, D. *Quantitative methods in psychology.* New York: McGraw-Hill, 1960.

MORRISON, D. F. *Multivariate statistical methods* (2nd ed.). New York: McGraw-Hill, 1976.

NESSELROADE, J. R., & BALTES, P. B. *Longitudinal research in the behavioral sciences: Design and analysis.* New York: Academic Press, 1978.

NESSELROADE, J. R., & REESE, H. W. *Life-span developmental psychology.* New York: Academic Press, 1973.

NUNNALLY, J. C. The analysis of profile data. *Psychological Bulletin,* 1962, *59,* 311–319.

NUNNALLY, J. C. Research strategies and measurement methods for investigating human development. In J. R. Nesselroade & H. W. Reese (Eds.), *Life-span developmental psychology.* New York: Academic Press, 1973.

NUNNALLY, J. C. The study of change in evaluation research. In E. L. Struening & M. Guttentag (Eds.), *Handbook of evaluation research* (Vol. 1). Beverly Hills, Calif.: Sage Publications, Inc., 1975.

NUNNALLY, J. C. *Psychometric theory* (2nd ed.). New York: McGraw-Hill, 1978.

OVERALL, J. E., & WOODWARD, J. A. Nonrandom assignment and the analysis of covariance. *Psychological Bulletin,* 1977, *84,* 588–594.

SHAFFER, J. P., & GILLO, M. W. A multivariate extension of the correlation ratio. *Educational and Psychological Measurement,* 1974, *34,* 521–524.

TATSUOKA, M. T. *Multivariate analysis.* New York: John Wiley, 1971.

TUCKER, L. R. Learning theory and multivariate experiments: Illustrations by determination of generalized learning curves. In R. B. Cattell (Ed.), *Handbook of multivariate experimental psychology.* Skokie, Ill.: Rand-McNally, 1966.

WALLANSTEIN, S., & FLEISS, J. L. Repeated measurements analysis of variance when the correlations have a certain pattern. *Psychometrika,* 1979, *44,* 229–234.

WERTS, C. E., & LINN, R. L. Lord's paradox: A generic problem. *Psychological Bulletin,* 1969, *72,* 423–425.

WERTS, C. E., & LINN, R. L. A general linear model for studying growth. *Psychological Bulletin,* 1970, *73,* 17–22.

WERTS, C. E., & LINN, R. L. Problems with inferring treatment effects from repeated measures. *Educational and Psychological Measurement,* 1971, *31,* 857–866.

WINER, B. J. *Statistical principles in experimental design* (2nd ed.). New York: McGraw-Hill, 1971.

WOHLWILL, J. F. *The study of behavioral development.* New York: Academic Press, 1973.

WOLMAN, B. B. (Ed.). *International encyclopedia of psychiatry, psychology, psychoanalysis and neurology.* New York: Aesculapius Publishers, 1977.

10

The Ethics and Regulation
of Research involving Children

ROBERT A. COOKE

Research that requires the involvement of children presents a variety of difficult issues that must be addressed by investigators, others in the scientific community, and society at large. Such issues concern the adequacy of the procedures to be used for obtaining permission for the subjects' participation, the fairness of the methods for selecting subjects, and the acceptablity of the balance of risks to benefits for subjects. Additionally questions can arise regarding whether the research does in fact require the participation of children and whether sufficient previous research has been carried out with adults to ascertain the risk to which the children might be exposed. These and other questions must be answered in light of the sometimes conflicting practical requirements of research and the ethical standards of the scientific and lay communities. The research, for example, might require that some information about the study be withheld from subjects while ethical standards might call for full disclosure and informed consent. Answers to these questions can be further complicated by inconsistencies and ambiguities in societal values and the applicable laws of the jurisdiction in which the research is to be conducted. Relevant legislation and court decisions suggest that permission for the participation of minors must be obtained from their parents or guardians, but some recent decisions and emerging societal norms require that the rights of children be respected and assent be obtained directly from them.

Questions regarding the involvement of human subjects in research (Freund, 1969; Gray, 1975; Katz, 1972) and the regulaton of this research (Barber, 1980; Barber, Lally, Makarushka, & Sullivan, 1973, 1979; Gray, 1978;

Gray, Cooke, & Tannenbaum, 1978; Grossman & Morris, 1970) have been examined in some detail. Questions specifically concerning research that requires the involvement of children also have been addressed, albeit in ways that have led to some inconsistent answers (Curran & Beecher, 1969; Hauerwas, 1977; Ramsey, 1970; Worsfold, 1974). Despite these inconsistencies somewhat similar sets of ethical standards and guidelines have been developed by various research-oriented associations, including the American Academy of Pediatrics (1977), the Division on Developmental Psychology of the American Psychological Association (1968), and the Society for Research in Child Development (1975).

Concurrent with the development of guidelines by professional associations has been the establishment of policies for the protection of human subjects by the National Institutes of Health (NIH) and the Department of Health, Education and Welfare (DHEW) (Michael & Weinberger, 1977). By early 1966 the Surgeon General of the Public Health Service (PHS) issued a policy statement on the protection of human subjects of clinical research and investigations (Curran, 1970; Levine, 1976). Later that year clarifications and revisions of the statement extended the applicability of the policy to all PHS grants, including those for behavioral research (Levine, 1976; Staff of the National Commission, 1978). In 1971, DHEW published *The Institutional Guide to DHEW Policy on Protection of Human Subjects,* which applied to the entire department and all grants.

Subsequently the National Research Act of 1974 (5 USC 33) was passed, authorizing regulations on the protection of human subjects (DHEW, 1974). These regulations were not a code of research ethics but rather, with few exceptions, a mechanism for making such determinations (Michael & Weinberger, 1977). The regulations specified, for example, the establishment of institutional

This chapter was written while the author was a Visiting Scholar at the Institute for Research on Educational Finance and Governance, Stanford University.

review boards (IRB's) within organizations where research was conducted to review the acceptability of proposed projects with respect to risks and benefits, informed consent, and related issues (Levine, 1976). The 1974 Research Act also called for the establishment of the National Commission for the Protection of Human Subjects of Biomedical and Behavioral Research (hereafter referred to as the National Commission). Under Public Law 93-348, this commission was mandated to develop ethical guidelines for the conduct of research involving human subjects and to make recommendations for the application of such guidelines (Culliton, 1974). Particular attention was to be directed toward special classes of research subjects, including children. Recommendations for research involving children were sent to the president, Congress, and the secretary of Health, Education and Welfare in 1977 (National Commission, 1977). These recommendations, with minor changes, were accepted by DHEW and published in 1978 (DHEW, 1978, pp. 31786–31794).

The recommendations of the National Commission are likely to have a significant impact over the next decade on the regulation and conduct of behavioral and biomedical research involving children. These recommendations will be highlighted in this chapter, along with some of the legal (Annas, Glantz, & Katz, 1977), ethical (Bartholome, 1977b; Hauerwas, 1977) and psychological (Ferguson, 1977) perspectives considered in the deliberations and reports of the National Commission. Also to be presented are the results of a survey conducted for the National Commission on informed consent, risks and benefits, and review procedures in research involving children (Tannenbaum & Cooke, 1977). This survey, which was conducted by The University of Michigan's Survey Research Center, will be referred to throughout this chapter as the IRB survey. National Commission recommendations and the survey results will be presented in the context of guidelines previously developed by NIH and DHEW, ethical statements of selected professional associations, and recent papers on the ethics of research with children.

This chapter begins with some definitions of children and a review of the types of research in which children have been involved as subjects in recent years. Five of the major ethical positions considered by the National Commission are then summarized. Next, the chapter focuses on issues related to beneficence, justice, and respect—three ethical principles which (according to the National Commission, 1977) should underlie research involving children. These issues involve the risks and benefits of research, the selection of subjects, and informed consent and consent forms. Finally, the procedures used by biomedical and behavioral institutions to review and regulate research involving children are discussed.

CHILDREN

A variety of definitions of the term *children* has been proposed in writings on the ethics and regulation of research involving human subjects. One frequently cited definition is found in the 1973 draft of policies and procedures for the protection of human subjects developed by the National Institutes of Health. Children are defined in this draft as "individuals who have not attained the legal age of consent to participate in research as determined under the applicable law of the jurisdiction in which the proposed research is to be conducted" (NIH, 1973, p. 31739). Definitions of this type, however, do not provide a clear guide for researchers since little legislation and few court cases directly apply to the involvement of children in either therapeutic or nontherapeutic research.

The definition proposed more recently by the National Commission refers to the "legal age of consent to medical care" rather than the age of consent to participate in research (National Commission, 1977, p. xix). The legal age of consent to medical treatment is 18 in most states; in some states this age is as low as 14 and in others as high as 21 (Bartholome, 1977b; National Commission, 1977, pp. 85–87). While parental consent is normally a necessary and sufficient condition for the treatment of persons under these ages, courts and legislatures are granting children the capacity to receive health care services without parental consent under certain circumstances (Annas et al., 1977). Parental consent is not required in some states if an emergency exists, if the child is emancipated (by marriage, judicial decree, consent of the parents, or a failure of the parents to meet their responsibilities), or if the child is sufficiently "mature" to understand the nature of the procedures and the risks. Additionally many states permit children to consent for the treatment of addiction, pregnancy, or venereal disease, and certain other states permit children to receive treatment for other conditions (e.g., rape and infectious or communicable diseases) without parental approval (National Commission, 1977, pp. 85–87).

In summarizing the way that courts view the consent of children to medical care and the taking of risks, Annas et al. conclude that "the general rule concerning majority and the age of consent is not based on scientific or logical rationale" but rather "is the result of generally irrelevant feudal law doctrine" (1976, p. 2.19). Nevertheless this area of law (i.e., that which is relevant to the participation of children in research of benefit to them) is more specific than that relevant to the participation of children in research not involving direct benefit. Pertinent cases in the latter area involve the donation by minors of kidneys, skin grafts, and bone marrow (e.g., *Bonnner* v. *Moran*) and include one decision regarding the participation of children in an experimental program on drug abuse (*Merriken* v. *Cressman*). Such cases, however, provide insights into specific consent issues rather than definitions of majority.

An alternative approach to defining children in the context of research is based on stages of development and the capacity to understand. Ferguson (1977, 1978), for example, refers to four different development groups: (1) infants and preverbal toddlers, (2) preschool and beginning school-age children—generally those below the age of seven, (3) preadolescent children, and (4) adolescents. Although variation in the cognitive growth of individuals precludes defining these groups in terms of specific age spans, the groups are nevertheless useful for establishing consent procedures for different research activities. Similar groupings or distinctions between children at different developmental stages have been proposed by others. Recommendations by the National Minority Conference on Human Experimentation (1976) distinguish between children over and under the age of 7 with respect to participation in nontherapeutic research. Based on legal considerations the British Medical Research Council (1962–1963) differentiates children of 12 years or younger from those over this age. Bartholome (1976) cites 5 to 7 years as the "age of reason," 14 to 16 years as the age range when it becomes possible to obtain informed consent (Allen, 1974), and 18 to 21 years as the range up to which parental consent should also be required.

TYPES OF RESEARCH INVOLVING CHILDREN

Although considered inappropriate as subjects for many research projects, there are certain circumstances that justify and require the participation of children of all ages in behavioral and biomedical studies (Lockhart, 1977). It is necessary to study children to ascertain their physiologic responses both to drugs and disease since their responses often differ from those of adults. Similarly studies of normal physiology and behavior can provide significant benefit to children suffering from disease and "children are the only subjects from whom these data can be obtained" (NIH, 1973, p. 31740). The general orientation of NIH (1973, p. 31738) and other organizations (e.g., the American Academy of Pediatrics, 1977) has been that research activities involving children are often essential if the health of young people is to be maintained and improved.

Neither researchers nor federal decision makers (e.g., divisions of the Office of Management and Budget, congressional committees, interagency departments, and external advisory groups) have agreed to a theoretical or operational definition of research on children or to a set of goals for this research (Kiesler, 1979). Nevertheless the available statistics indicate that a significant amount of research involving young people was carried out during the 1970s. A census of research commissioned by the Federal Interagency Panels on Early Childhood and Adolescent Research and Development lists 5,000 research, development, and demonstration projects with $474 million in funding during 1977. About 25 to 30 percent of this funding was for basic, applied, evaluation, and policy research—a total for research on children of approximately $130 million. The largest funders were the Office of Education (e.g., the Bureau of Education for the Handicapped and the Bureau of Elementary and Secondary Education), the National Institute of Education, the Office of Human Development Services (especially the Administration for Children, Youth, and Families), the National Institute of Child Health and Human Development, and the National Institute of Mental Health (Kiesler, 1979, p. 1009).

Focusing on research involving children funded by federal agencies in 1975, 3,460 projects were counted by the chief of the Research Documentation Branch, Division of Research Grants, NIH, and by the Social Research Group at the George Washington University (National Commission, 1977, p. 39). More than half of these projects (56 percent) were funded by the Education Di-

vision, which defines research involving children to include literature surveys, statistical analyses, research conferences, and material development, as well as studies directly involving children as subjects. A substantial percentage of the projects was sponsored by the National Institutes of Health (24 percent) and the Alcohol, Drug Abuse, and Mental Health Administration (5 percent). (These latter projects represent only those that directly involve children as subjects.) The remaining projects were funded by other components of DHEW (10 percent) and other federal agencies (4 percent), including sections of the Departments of Agriculture, Justice, and Labor (National Commission, 1977, pp. 38–39).

In the IRB survey 471 research projects were identified in which at least 25 percent of the subjects were under 19 years of age (Tannenbaum & Cooke, 1977). These projects represent 28 percent of all those that passed through a sample of institutional review boards during the period of July 1, 1974, to June 30, 1975. Approximately 14 percent of the projects involving children were reviewed by boards in children's hospitals and, in most cases, were carried out in these organizations; 52 percent were reviewed by boards in other biomedical institutions (medical schools, universities sharing medical school review boards, general hospitals, schools of nursing and dentistry, and biomedical research institutions); and the remaining 34 percent were reviewed in universities, institutions for the mentally infirm, and behavioral research institutions.

Behavioral research accounted for approximately 40 percent of the projects in the sample that involved children. About a fifth of this behavioral research entailed the study of an intervention of some kind, such as social or psychological therapy, behavior modification, or educational innovations. The behavioral research that did not entail the study of such interventions included primarily psychological or educational testing, interviews or questionnaires, or behavioral observation. Approximately half of the projects were biomedical, most frequently involving (1) the clinical evaluation of bodily tissues or fluids or (2) the administration of a drug, chemical agent, or blood product. An additional 3 percent of the projects involving children focused on the secondary analysis of existing data and the third-party evaluation of bodily fluids or tissues obtained for other purposes. The primary intervention or procedure used in each of the research projects involving children is shown in Table 10–1 along with comparison data for all projects in the IRB survey sample. As shown in the table a relatively high proportion of the projects involving children used behavioral observation techniques or psychological-educational testing.

The principal investigator of each research project involving children was asked about the kinds of subjects that were selected for the experimental group of the study. The subjects selected for the biomedical projects involving children were most often patients (Table 10–2). In certain cases, these patients were selected specifically because they were children or were mentally retarded. The kinds of subjects selected most frequently for the behavioral projects were patients and children under 18 (not necessarily patients). Additionally college students were among the kinds of subjects selected in a significant number of the behavioral studies.

Table 10-1 The Primary Intervention or Procedure of Research Projects (Percent of Projects)

	PROJECTS INVOLVING CHILDREN (N = 471)	ALL PROJECTS (N = 2039)
Behavioral Intervention		
Educational intervention	2%	2%
Modification of an organization or a service delivery system	2	1
Behavior modification or experimentation	3	2
Social or psychological therapy	1	1
Other	—[a]	1
Other Behavioral		
Interviews-questionnaires	7	11
Psychological or educational testing	13	6
Behavioral observations	14	6
Interviews with patients (e.g., medical histories)	2	2
Biomedical	53	62
Secondary Analysis	3	6

[a] Indicates less than 0.5%.

Source: Based on data presented in Cooke, Tannenbaum, & Gray, 1978, and Tannenbaum & Cooke, 1977.

THE INVOLVEMENT OF CHILDREN IN RESEARCH: SOME ETHICAL CONSIDERATIONS[1]

The substantial amount of research involving children over the past decade has been carried out amidst an on-going debate regarding the appropriateness of using children as subjects—particularly in studies not intended to benefit subjects. This debate has focused mainly on the conditions under which the participation of children is justified, given their limited capacity to provide informed consent.

Background

When research is conducted primarily to benefit the subjects, the potential benefits to children can justify their involvement (Ramsey, 1970). However some of the research carried out with children carries little or no possibility of direct benefit to the subjects and, instead, is primarily intended to benefit other children or to contribute to scientific knowledge. The conditions under which this type of research is justified can be difficult to define. Literal interpretation of the Nuremberg Code appears to preclude under any circumstances the participation of children in research without benefit to the subjects. "The voluntary consent of the human subject is absolutely essential. This means that the person involved should have the legal capacity to give consent" (Trials of War Criminals before the Nuremberg Military Tribunals, 1949, p. 181). If children are assumed not to have this capacity, they should not be the subjects of research. The code, however, may not pertain to children because they were not involved in the specific cases under trial (Alexander, 1970). Additionally, the chief medical consultant to the War Crimes Trial notes that the ethical principles for mentally incompetent and mentally competent persons are the same, but the former are likened to children in an ethical and legal sense and the consent of a guardian is required (Beecher, 1970; Ivy, 1948).

The Declaration of Helsinki, published in 1964 by the World Medical Association, states that the consent of a legal guardian should be secured if the subject is not legally competent. The 1975 revision states, "When the

[1] This discussion is largely based on Chapter 8 of the National Commission's *Report and Recommendations: Research Involving Children* (1977, pp. 91–121), supplemented by the early NIH recommendations (1973) and reviews by Bartholome (1977b) and others.

Table 10-2 Kinds of Subjects Selected[a] (Percent of Projects)[b]

	TYPE OF RESEARCH			
	Biomedical (N = 219)	Behavioral Intervention (N = 45)	Other Behavioral (N = 147)	Secondary Analysis (N = 14)
"General population"[c]	8%	21%	19%	38%
Children under 18	15	35	34	11
Persons with specific condition, characteristic[c]	7	21	15	9
Patients	81	46	33	54
Children who are patients	21	1	8	9
Other patients[c]	58	28	12	38
Mentally retarded[c]	1	17	5	0
Mentally ill[c]	0	4	0	0
Pregnant women	1	0	4	3
Fetus	0	0	0	4
Professional, institutional, or other staff	4	2	4	0
College students	3	19	20	0
Other categories	4	6	6	4

[a] Based on investigators' responses to the question: What kinds of subjects were selected for the experimental group in your study, that is, were they from the general population or were they patients, prisoners, college students, or from some other category?

[b] Totals may add to more than 100% since respondents could mention more than one kind of subject.

[c] Age not specified by investigator.

Source: Adapted from Tannenbaum & Cooke, 1977, p. 1.46.

subject is a minor, permission from the responsible relative replaces that of the subject in accordance with national legislation" (National Commission, 1977, p. 93). The early code was accepted by various groups—including the American Medical Association—and this resulted in the general acceptance throughout this country of third-party permission for research employing interventions that are not for an incompetent subject's direct benefit (Beecher, 1970; National Commission, 1977).

The conduct of nontherapeutic (as well as therapeutic) research involving children is supported also by early federal guidelines and drafts thereof regarding the protection of human subjects. Draft guidelines developed by NIH (1973) include special policy considerations pertaining directly to children and others with limited ability to give truly informed and fully autonomous consent. The aim of these special guidelines "is to set standards which are both comprehensive and equitable, in order to provide protection and, to the extent consistent with such protection, maintain an environment in which clinical research may continue to thrive" (NIH, 1973, p. 31739). Clinical research is defined as an investigation involving the biological, behavioral, or psychological study of a person, his/her body, or his/her surroundings. In addition to studies intended to benefit the subject or other people with similar conditions, clinical research includes "investigative, nontherapeutic studies in which there is no intent or expectation of treating an illness from which the patient is suffering, or in which the subject is a 'normal control' who is not suffering from an illness but who volunteers to participate for the potential benefit of others" (Bartholome, 1977b; NIH, 1973, p. 31739). This type of research is not necessarily harmful and is needed, for example, to recognize deviations from the normal that define disease.

Participants in nontherapeutic research (and in other types of clinical studies) may be "at risk" due to their involvement—that is, subjects may be exposed to the possibility of physical, psychological, sociological, or other harm due to a research activity that goes beyond the application of accepted and established methods necessary to meet their needs. According to the NIH draft guidelines, research that places children at risk is justified only when certain conditions are met. These conditions include the obtaining of consent from both parents (since the research entails the possibility of additional burdens of care and support) and providing children who have attained the "age of discretion" (7 years) the opportunity to refuse to participate (NIH, 1973, p. 31742). The draft guidelines also specify that the research must be reviewed by the institutional review boards at the organization at which the research is to be conducted, the appropriate agency Primary Review Committee, and the Ethical Review Board (NIH, 1973, p. 31741).

Research with children, under certain conditions, also is permitted in *The Institutional Guide to DHEW Policy on Protection of Human Subjects* (DHEW, 1971). The guide emphasizes that consent is required from the subject or his/her authorized representative. The institutional review board is charged with determining whether potential representatives can be presumed to have the necessary interest and concern with the subjects' rights and welfare and whether these third parties are legally au-

thorized to expose the subjects to the risk involved. The proposal that children of the age of discretion be provided the opportunity to refuse to participate was adopted by NIH after the publication of *The Institutional Guide* (The Clinical Center, 1975).

Ethical Positions

While nontherapeutic research with children was acceptable under the federal guidelines of the 1970s, this position was not shared by all those concerned with the ethics of research. This divergence in perspectives is illustrated by the five ethical positions on the involvement of children in research considered in the deliberations and recommendations of the National Commission (1977). These positions, along with the National Commission's reaction to each position, are summarized here.

The most restrictive position, presented by Ramsey (1970, 1976, 1977), is that research that does not directly benefit the participating children is always ethically impermissible. Nontherapeutic research should not be conducted without the informed consent of the subject; young children are not capable of giving informed consent; and therefore children should not participate in such research. Their participation is inconsistent with the right of people to determine for themselves the nature, timing, and extent to which they will share themselves with others. Although participation in research with benefits to subjects is permissible, participation in nontherapeutic research represents the use of children as a means to the ends of researchers and is a violation of respect for persons.

Various problems with the restrictive position taken by Ramsey are cited by the National Commission (1977, pp. 96–99). First, although children are not fully qualified to consent, many give their assent and are willingly involved in research. Second, this position does not adequately consider the level of risk and would exclude much biomedical and behavioral research involving no more risk than that encountered in the daily lives of children. Third, Ramsey assumes that all research can be classified as beneficial or not beneficial to subjects; however, it is sometimes difficult or impossible to predict the benefits subjects will realize.

A second and less restrictive position is based on the assumptions that children have obligations to participate in research and that such participation is expressive of basic values of human nature or purposes of human life (McCormick, 1975, 1976). McCormick contends that children would be likely to consent to therapeutic research because they ought to promote their own health; also, they would be likely to consent to nontherapeutic research because they ought to contribute to the health of others. Proxy consent or parental permission for children's participation is acceptable because such participation is right—as members of the human community, people should share in research experimentation for the good of all.

One problem with McCormick's position is that it does not follow from the wide sharing of human beings of certain values or purposes (e.g., health and happiness) that all persons ought to promote these values or purposes (National Commission, 1977, p. 101). A second problem is that consent cannot necessarily be presumed just because there is an underlying obligation. Due to individual differences it cannot be presumed that all adults *would* consent merely because they *ought* to consent to participate in research. There is little reason, therefore, to presume that all children would consent under the same circumstances.

A third position considered by the National Commission is derived from the work of Toulmin (1976) on fetal research and that of Worsfold (1974) on children. Toulmin focuses on what a person could not reasonably object to if s/he were able to understand what is at stake and make a decision in his/her own right. Worsfold emphasizes what a reasonable child would approve of (e.g., a consent decision made by others on his/her behalf) in retrospect and with the development of rational powers. These views would permit, with proper third-party permission, research involving children who have not attained the age of reason. Worsfold adds, however, that children of sufficient understanding have the right to make their own decisions and that the preferences of younger children should be considered by those deciding on their behalf.

Worsfold's position is based on the language of children's rights and deemphasizes parents' responsibilities and duties toward children. In reacting to this position Hauerwas (1977) suggests that the latter rather than the former be emphasized; policy could be based on notions of children as family members who need care and love rather than on notions of children's rights. This position can also be challenged given its focus on reasonableness. The fact that something seems reasonable is not sufficient for involving persons in research; there are many things that would not be permitted to be done to nonconsenting subjects even though the subjects could not reasonably object to these things. The lack of a reasonable objection may be a necessary but not sufficient condition for involving children in research (National Commission, 1977, pp. 107–108).

A fourth position suggests that the participation of children in certain types of research can be justified by the moral development provided by such participation (Bartholome, 1977b; Beecher, 1970). Parents are obligated to provide moral instruction to their children, and moral growth can be provided by participation in research. Parents should therefore decide whether participation in a particular project would be a beneficial learning experience, and their children can then assent (or refuse) to participate (see Bartholome, 1976, 1977b). While children over the age of 5 or 7 should influence decisions regarding their involvement in research activities, younger children do not have a moral obligation to the community and should not be included in nontherapeutic research with serious invasive procedures.

A problem with this position is that it excludes nontherapeutic research involving uninstructable children yet fails to show why such research would be immoral (National Commission, 1977, p. 113). Another problem is that young people are required to be adults in order to be respected. This requirement is inconsistent with the assumption that children have rights, not as adults but as members of a family unit with claims against parents and society for the provision of care (Hauerwas, 1977).

The final position summarized and reported by the National Commission is that research on children is jus-

tified in light of its beneficial consequences to the class of children in general. Engelhardt (1975) argues that infants, although often willful, have no free will and are not objects of respect as are adults. There is no obligation, therefore, to respect the autonomy of infants but rather an obligation to protect them from harm and to preserve their physiological and psychological integrity. Although research leaving a residual amount of damage to children cannot be allowed, research involving risks not greater than those of normal activities can be justified in terms of the minimal duties that each person owes to society. Similar arguments are presented by Veatch (1976), who contends that, when there is no risk or minimal risk, certain obligations to the common welfare may be presupposed even if consent cannot be obtained. Veatch applies this position only to young children and does not suggest that social benefits can cancel out individual rights. Nevertheless it could be argued that this social benefit approach fails to respect persons—it exposes them to risks without apparent benefits or their consent. Furthermore this position specifies neither the scope of research that is permissible nor the point at which individual rights outweigh social benefits. Finally, the social benefit approach does not allow for research with somewhat more than minimal risks but with potentially substantial benefits to others (National Commission, 1977, pp. 116–118).

Commission Recommendations

The position taken by the National Commission is that research involving children is important for the health and well-being of all young persons; such research can be carried out in an ethical manner; and therefore this research should be conducted and supported. Research with children is necessary, for example, to "learn more about normal development as well as disease states in order to develop methods of diagnosis, treatment and prevention of conditions that jeopardize the health of children, interfere with optimal development, or adversely affect well-being in later years" (National Commission, 1977, pp. 1–2). The conditions under which this research is justified, however, become more numerous and restrictive as the benefits to subjects decrease and the risks to which they are exposed increase.

The recommendations of the National Commission are presented in Table 10–3 and appear in the *Federal Register* (DHEW, 1978, pp. 31786–94) as guidelines to be issued as regulations. The published guidelines are consistent with the National Commission's recommendations, with the following exceptions: (1) the objections of children to participate in research are not held as binding; (2) no specific age is set after which the assent of children is mandatory—rather institutional review boards are asked to consider age on a case-by-case basis; and (3) the Secretary of DHEW may appoint an ad hoc panel to consider difficult research projects, rather than necessarily relying upon the National Ethics Advisory Board (McCartney, 1978).

These recommendations and guidelines are based on the conclusion that three ethical principles—beneficence, respect for persons, and justice—should underlie the conduct of research involving human subjects. With respect to research involving children, "the challenge is

Table 10-3 Recommendations of the National Commission

Recommendation (1): Since the Commission finds that research involving children is important for the health and well-being of all children and can be conducted in an ethical manner, the Commission recommends that such research be conducted and supported, subject to the conditions set forth in the following recommendations.

Recommendation (2): Research involving children may be conducted or supported provided an Institutional Review Board has determined that:
(A) the research is scientifically sound and significant;
(B) where appropriate, studies have been conducted first on animals and human adults, then on older children, prior to involving infants;
(C) risks are minimized by using the safest procedures consistent with sound research design and by using procedures performed for diagnostic or treatment purposes whenever feasible;
(D) adequate provisions are made to protect the privacy of children and their parents, and to maintain confidentiality of data;
(E) subjects will be selected in an equitable manner; and
(F) the conditions of all applicable subsequent recommendations are met.

Recommendation (3): Research that does not involve greater than minimal risk to children may be conducted or supported provided an Institutional Review Board has determined that:
(A) the conditions of Recommendation (2) are met; and
(B) adequate provisions are made for assent of the children and permission of their parents or guardians, as set forth in Recommendations (7) and (8).

Recommendation (4): Research in which more than minimal risk to children is presented by an intervention that holds out the prospect of direct benefit for the individual subjects, or by a monitoring procedure required for the well-being of the subjects, may be conducted or supported provided that an Institutional Review Board has determined that:
(A) such risk is justified by the anticipated benefit to the subjects;
(B) the relation of anticipated benefit to such risk is at least as favorable to the subjects as that presented by available alternative approaches;
(C) The conditions of Recommendation (2) are met; and
(D) adequate provisions are made for assent of the children and permission of their parents or guardians, as set forth in Recommendations (7) and (8).

Recommendation (5): Research in which more than minimal risk to children is presented by an intervention that does not hold out the prospect of direct benefit for the individual subjects, or by a monitoring procedure not required for the well-being of the subjects, may be conducted or supported provided an Institutional Review Board has determined that:
(A) such risk represents a minor increase over minimal risk;
(B) such intervention or procedure presents experiences to subjects that are reasonably commensurate with those inherent in their actual or expected medical, psychological, or social situations, and is likely to yield generalizable knowledge about the subjects' disorder or condition;
(C) the anticipated knowledge is of vital importance for understanding or amelioration of the subjects' disorder or condition;
(D) the conditions of Recommendation (2) are met; and
(E) adequate provisions are made for assent of the children and permission of their parents or guardians as set forth in Recommendations (7) and (8).

Recommendation (6): Research that cannot be approved by an Institutional Review Board under Recommendations (3), (4), and (5), as applicable, may be conducted or supported provided an Institutional Review Board has determined that the research presents an opportunity to understand, prevent, or alleviate a serious problem affecting the health or welfare of children and, in addition, a national ethical advisory board and, following opportunity for public review and comment, the secretary of the responsible federal department (or highest official of the responsible federal agency) has determined either (A) that the research satisfies the conditions of Recommendations (3), (4), and (5), as applicable, or (B) the following:
(i) the research presents an opportunity to understand, prevent or alleviate a serious problem affecting the health or welfare of children;
(ii) the conduct of the research would not violate the principles of respect for persons, beneficence and justice;
(iii) the conditions of Recommendation (2) are met; and
(iv) adequate provisions are made for the assent of the children and permission of their parents or guardians, as set forth in Recommendations (7) and (8).

Recommendation (7): In addition to the determinations required under the foregoing recommendations, as applicable, the Institutional Review Board should determine that adequate provisions are made for: (A) soliciting the assent of children (when capable) and the permission of their parents or guardians; and, when appropriate, (B) monitoring the solicitation of assent and permission, and involving at least one parent or guardian in the conduct of the research. A child's objection to participation in research should be binding unless the intervention holds out a prospect of direct benefit that is important to the health or well-being of the child and is available only in the context of the research.

Recommendation (8): If the Institutional Review Board determines that a research protocol is designed for conditions or a subject population for which parental or guardian permission is not a reasonable requirement to protect the subjects, it may waive such requirement provided an appropriate mechanism for protecting the children who will participate as subjects in the research is substituted. The choice of an appropriate mechanism should depend upon the nature and purpose of the activities described in the protocol, the risk and anticipated benefit to the research subjects, and their age, status and condition.

Recommendation (9): Children who are wards of the state should not be included in research approved under Recommendations (5) or (6) unless such research is: (A) related to their status as orphans, abandoned children, and the like; or (B) conducted in a school or similar group setting in which the majority of children involved as subjects are not wards of the state. If such research is approved, the Institutional Review Board should require that an advocate for each child be appointed, with an opportunity to intercede that would normally be provided by parents.

Recommendation (10): Children who reside in institutions for the mentally infirm or who are confined in correctional facilities should participate in research only if the conditions regarding research on the institutionalized mentally infirm or on prisoners (as applicable) are fulfilled in addition to the conditions set forth herein.

Source: National Commission for the Protection of Human Subjects of Biomedical and Behavioral Research, 1977, pp. 1–20.

to find a proper balance in applying these principles and to establish priorities among these principles when they appear to be in conflict" (Height, King, Louisell, Ryan, & Seldin, 1977, p. 123). The National Commission's efforts to balance and set priorities among these principles are reflected in those aspects of the recommendations pertaining to the selection of subjects, the risks and benefits of the research, and procedures for obtaining permission and assent for the subjects' participation.

SUBJECT SELECTION

The moral principle of justice requires a fair distribution of risks and benefits in a given population (Lebacqz, 1980). This principle has two major implications for research involving children and, specifically, for the selection of subjects for this research (Height et al., 1977, pp. 131–132). First, research programs should be designed so as not to overutilize any particular groups of children due to their availability; the risks of research, as well as its benefits, should be distributed equally to all groups. Second, children should not be selected as subjects unless they are the only appropriate population of subjects, and studies on adults and animals have been previously conducted (Height et al., 1977; NIH, 1973, p. 31740).

Equity

No group of children should be overutilized as subjects based on administrative convenience or the availability of a population living in conditions of economic deprivation (National Commission, 1977, p. 4; see also the recommendations of the Workshop on Children of the National Minority Conference on Human Experimentation, 1976). The possibility of overutilizing a particular group of children can arise if subjects are chosen because they are clients of organizations to which researchers have access *and* if these organizations are frequented mainly by one socioeconomic, racial, or ethnic group (American Academy of Pediatrics, 1977).

As shown in Table 10–4, investigators in the IRB survey most frequently mentioned institutions (e.g., schools and hospitals) to which they had professional access when asked about their source(s) of subjects. Despite the predominance of this approach to selecting subjects, data from the larger survey (on research involving adults as well as research involving children) indicate that disadvantaged groups are not overutilized in research entailing risks to subjects (Cooke, Tannenbaum, & Gray, 1978, p. 65). Projects involving large percentages of minorities or children under 18 (excluding newborns) were less likely than other projects to entail above-average risk. Projects in which investigators reported relatively high proportions of (1) males, (2) persons between 41 and 64 years of age, or (3) higher- or middle-income persons were more likely than other projects to be above average in risk. Furthermore projects involving high proportions of males or persons between 19 and 40 years of age were more likely than others to entail risks that outweighed benefits to subjects (although the number of such projects was small).

Selection of Children versus Adults

Research risks should be allocated to adults rather than to children whenever possible because adults can be more meaningfully informed about the risks involved. Adults can also more accurately report their feelings or physiological responses to investigators, inform investigators if something unusual occurs, and thus reduce the probability and severity of harmful effects. "Accordingly, infants might be at greater risk than adults participating in the same research" (Grotberg, 1976; Height et al., 1977, p. 132). There are, however, research topics that require the participation of children (Curran & Beecher, 1969; Lockhart, 1977). Whenever possible the participation of children in such studies should be preceded by research on adults (Bartholome, 1977b; NIH, 1973). Similarly research on young children and infants should be preceded by research on older children (NIH, 1973).

Criteria Used in the Selection of Subjects

The systematic selection of certain groups of children for participation in research may be inappropriate unless certain conditions are met. Children who are wards of the state should not be selected for research with more than minimal risk unless the study is directly related to the status of orphans or abandoned children (National Commission, 1977, p. 20). It also has been advocated that "incarcerated children should not be used for experimentation" when disproportionately large numbers of these children are from minority groups (National Minority Conference on Human Experimentation, 1976). Furthermore it has been argued, contrary to one interpretation of a National Commission recommendation (1977, Recommendation 5), that sick children should not be singled out as the only group of children who may participate in research with no benefit to subjects and with more than minimal risk (Turtle, 1977).

Whereas research on particular groups of subjects is sometimes viewed as inappropriate, the existence of a specific criterion for subject selection can indicate some prospect of direct benefit to subjects. The presence of a selection criterion can mean that the research is related to the subjects' condition and that some benefit may accrue to them, even when the research is not directly intended to benefit subjects (Bartholome, 1976). Based on the reports of investigators in the IRB survey, subjects

Table 10-4 The Sources Used to Obtain Subjects (Percent of Projects)[a]

	TYPE OF RESEARCH			
	Biomedical (N = 219)	Behavioral Intervention (N = 45)	Other Behavioral (N = 147)	Secondary Analysis (N = 14)
Institutional population via professional access	44%	28%	16%	46%
Referrals by other physicians, professionals	46	16	9	27
Information from records	7	11	12	27
Referrals by other subjects	11	7	11	0
Formal groups, organizations	3	10	15	0
Advertisement or notice	3	7	14	0
Blood samples	1	0	0	12
Other sources[b]	2	—	10	0

[a] Percentages may add to more than 100% since respondents could mention more than one source of subjects.

[b] Including general population, friends, and relatives.

Source: Based on data presented in Tannenbaum & Cooke, 1977, p. 1.48.

were selected on the basis of a particular condition or characteristic in the large majority of the projects. Subject selection was related to the presence of a specific condition or characteristic in 93 percent of the biomedical studies, 87 percent of the behavioral intervention studies, 80 percent of the behavioral projects, and 79 percent of the secondary analysis studies (Tannenbaum & Cooke, 1977). Subjects of biomedical research were selected most often due to the presence of endocrine, nutritional, or metabolic diseases; diseases of the nervous system and sense organs; and neoplasms (see Table 10–5). The criteria most frequently used for the selection of subjects of behavioral intervention studies were mental disorders, diseases of the nervous system and sense organs, and other diseases or conditions such as congenital anomalies and personal adjustment problems. Educational situation, age, and mental disorders were the criteria most frequently used for the selection of subjects in other behavioral studies.

RISKS AND BENEFITS

The principal of beneficence, which requires both the provision of benefit and the avoidance of harm, has been used to justify the conduct of research involving children (Height et al., 1977). This research can promote the health of young people as a class—e.g., by improving methods to treat diseases or abnormal conditions—and can reduce the possibility of harm to them—e.g., by

evaluating the safety of procedures in standard practice (Lockhart, 1977: NIH, 1973). Similarly the children participating in this research often can receive benefits—medical, physiological, or moral—from their involvement (Bartholome, 1976). Beneficence, however, also requires that those participating in the research be protected from harm by limiting the risks to which they are exposed (Height et al., 1977, pp. 123–124). The objectives of minimizing risks to subjects and achieving an acceptable balance of risks and benefits are emphasized in practically every ethical discussion of research with children (e.g., Bartholome, 1977b; Beecher, 1970; Ramsey, 1977). These objectives have been emphasized also in the ethical statements or guidelines developed by various professional groups (e.g., American Academy of Pediatrics, 1977; Society for Research in Child Development, 1975).

Risks and Benefits of Recent Projects

In most of the IRB survey projects that involved children, the risks to subjects were low both in terms of probability and severity. The potential benefits to subjects were somewhat greater, though the probability of such benefits (and the associated risks) appeared to vary with the purpose of the research. Based on data provided by investigators, the projects involving children were divided into four groups: (1) research primarily intended to benefit the subjects directly and/or entailing at least a moderate probability of medical or psychological bene-

Table 10-5 Conditions Used as a Basis for Subject Selection (Percent of Projects)[a]

	TYPE OF RESEARCH			
	Biomedical	Behavioral Intervention	Other Behavioral	Secondary Analysis
Disease or Medical Condition	96%	60%	38%	80%
Infective and parasitic diseases	5	8	2	3
Neoplasms	10	5	2	18
Disease of nervous system and sense organs	10	10	1	3
Endocrine, nutritional, metabolic diseases	11	0	0	0
Other diseases, complications, injuries	62	10	11	18
Mental disorders	3	26	16	15
Medical characteristics	5	1	11	26
Behavioral Problem	—[b]	12	8	0
Educational problem	—	4	2	0
Personal adjustment problem	0	8	4	0
Other behavioral or legal problem	0	0	2	0
Demographic Characteristic	14	23	68	3
Age	8	5	16	0
Sex	—	4	3	3
Race	—	1	6	0
Genetic or kinship ties	1	0	1	0
Income	2	0	3	0
Social class	0	1	3	0
Educational situation	0	4	19	0
Life/family situation	1	2	9	0
Other demographic or personal characteristic	2	6	8	0
Other Selection Criteria	0	10	3	0

[a] Percent of those projects in which subjects were selected because of a specific condition or characteristic. Percentages may add to more than 100% since respondents could mention more than one condition.

[b] Indicates less than 0.5%.

Source: Adapted and revised from data presented in Tannenbaum & Cooke, 1977, pp. 1.52–1.58.

fits—24 percent of the projects, (2) research primarily intended to benefit in the future persons with psychological or medical conditions similar to those of the subjects—26 percent, (3) research conducted primarily for other purposes with subjects selected on the basis of a particular condition or characteristic—23 percent, and (4) research conducted primarily for other purposes in which subjects were not selected on the basis of a particular condition—9 percent. The most frequent "other purpose" for which these latter projects were conducted was to contribute to scientific knowledge. (Eighteen percent of the projects could not be classified due to insufficient data.)

The primary purpose of most biomedical projects involving children was reported to be to benefit either the subjects or others with similar conditions (Table 10–6). Studies of behavioral interventions were even more likely to be reported as intended primarily to benefit subjects. Other behavioral studies, as well as secondary analysis projects, were more likely to have been conducted mainly for other purposes such as the development of knowledge.

This grouping of projects on the basis of their primary purpose generates categories of research that loosely parallel four types of research procedures identified by NIH. These procedures are (1) studies that represent a deviation from accepted practice but are directly aimed at improved diagnosis, prevention, or treatment of a patient, (2) studies that are related to a patient's disease but from which he or she will not necessarily receive any direct benefit, (3) research in which there is no intent or expectation of treating an illness from which the patient is suffering, and (4) investigative, nontherapeutic research in which subjects are "normal controls" or are not selected on the basis of any particular medical condition or characteristic (NIH, 1973, p. 31739).

NIH distinguishes between the first type of study, in which subjects are not considered to be at special risk, and the latter three types, in which subjects might be "at risk" by virtue of their participation. Bartholome (1977b) makes a further distinction between the third and fourth types. Studies in the third category are not necessarily therapeutic, but direct benefit can (and often does) accrue to the subjects of such investigations; studies in the fourth category are nontherapeutic. Ethical considerations may be most complicated for the last type of procedure since, if any risk is involved, benefits to sub-

jects might not outweigh this risk. From another perspective, however, the third type of research can pose the most complex problems. Such research potentially could subject sick children to greater risks than other children, even though the former would require greater protection than the latter (see Turtle, 1977).

Given the ethical complications associated with the third and fourth types of procedures, it would be expected that these procedures would entail a lower probability of risk than research intended to benefit subjects or others with similar conditions. Data on the probability of specific risks and benefits (as expected by investigators prior to involving subjects in the research) for the four groupings of projects are shown in Table 10–7. Many of the projects intended primarily to benefit subjects entailed at least a low probability of medical and/or psychological benefits to subjects. A substantial percentage of these projects also had at least a low probability of risk to subjects, usually minor psychological stress or minor medical complications. A smaller percentage of the projects primarily intended to benefit persons other than the subjects involved at least a low probability of risks and benefits to subjects, and an even smaller proportion of the projects conducted for other purposes entailed such risks and benefits. However even some of these latter projects were expected to benefit subjects and also to expose them to certain minor risks.

Balance of Risks and Benefits

Ethical guidelines for research involving children typically stress that benefits should outweigh risks to subjects. The benefits to be considered, however, usually go beyond those derived by subjects. For example the guidelines of the American Academy of Pediatrics state that studies that promise no demonstrable benefit should not be conducted, irrespective of the minimal nature of the attendant risks (1977). Benefits here include the development of new treatment modalities for children as well as the benefits derived directly by the subjects (such as close medical scrutiny, better nursing attention, and more effective therapeutic interventions). These benefits must be weighed against such risks as the known and predictable effects of the procedures (as determined by previous studies on animals, adults, or older children), the potential for psychological or social damage, and other effects that

Table 10-6 Primary Purpose of Projects (Percent of Projects)

	TYPE OF RESEARCH			
	Biomedical (N = 220)	Behavioral Intervention (N = 45)	Other Behavioral (N = 147)	Secondary Analysis (N = 14)
Benefit subjects	35%	46%	11%	17%
Benefit others	30	24	29	21
Other purpose (subjects selected by condition)	19	10	37	47
Other purpose (subjects not selected by condition)	4	10	17	15
No information[a]	12	10	6	0
TOTAL	100%	100%	100%	100%

[a] Includes projects for which investigators did not answer the relevant questions or responded with "don't know," uncodable, or uncertain responses.

Source: Based on data presented in Tannenbaum & Cooke, 1977, p. 1.55.

Table 10-7 Projects with at Least a Low Probability of Selected Risks and Benefits to Subjects (Percent of Projects)

	RESEARCH PRIMARILY INTENDED TO BENEFIT SUBJECTS (N = 119)	RESEARCH PRIMARILY INTENDED TO BENEFIT OTHERS (N = 123)	RESEARCH CONDUCTED FOR OTHER PURPOSES	
			Subjects Selected by Condition (N = 115)	Subjects Not Selected by Condition (N = 41)
Medical benefits	68%	40%	20%	2%
Psychological benefits	41	25	20	27
Other benefits	28	15	21	21
Minor psychological stress	18	20	16	22
Serious psychological stress	3	0	4	0
Minor medical complications	26	—	2	0
Serious medical complications	11	0	0	0
Fatal complications	7	0	0	0
Embarrassment (breach of confidentiality)	1	7	4	1
Legal risk (breach of confidentiality)	1	0	6	0
Other risks	6	3	1	3

Source: Based on data presented in Tannenbaum & Cooke, 1977, pp. 1.58–1.61.

could remain latent for long periods. The risks involved in drug research under therapeutic conditions must be minimized by, for example, limiting the number and types of evasive tests. The risks involved in nontherapeutic research would prohibit such research regardless of its potential for advancing knowledge for the benefit of other people (American Academy of Pediatrics, 1977).

NIH draft policies and procedures specify two judgments that must be made concerning the ethical propriety of research: (1) whether it is possible to assess the risk and (2) what the acceptable limits of risk are to which children can be subjected given the potential benefits of the research (NIH, 1973, p. 31741). First, research in adult and animal populations must be available to provide a base for assessing the risks to children. If risks cannot be assessed, the research cannot be conducted. Data from the IRB survey (which focuses on projects conducted after the publication of the NIH guidelines) show that almost all investigators were very certain or fairly certain that they knew all of the risks to subjects before involving them in the research. (Investigators conducting behavioral intervention studies were somewhat less certain about the risks than were other investigators.) Additionally the majority of investigators reported that, based

on what they learned during the study, the risks to subjects were as expected. Some investigators reported less risk than expected; very few reported more risk than expected (Tannenbaum & Cooke, 1977).

Second, the risks to subjects must be acceptable in view of the benefits—presumably not only the benefits to subjects but also those to other persons with similar conditions and to scientific knowledge. Judgments about the acceptable balance of risks and benefits transcend scientific issues and require interaction among individuals with diverse background and training (NIH, 1973). Such individuals, as members of review boards, approved all the research included in the IRB survey. The risks involved in this research were rarely seen by the investigators as outweighing benefits to subjects (Table 10–8). The reported balance of benefits to risks probably would be yet more favorable if other types of benefits (e.g., to persons with conditions similar to the subjects') had been considered by the investigators.

Compared to the 1973 procedures developed by NIH, the recommendations of the National Commission provide somewhat more specific parameters for decisions concerning the balance of risks and benefits in research. This greater specificity is due in part to the definition of

Table 10-8 Balance of Risks and Benefits to Subjects[a] (Percent of Projects)

	TYPE OF RESEARCH			
	Biomedical (N = 220)	Behavioral Intervention (N = 45)	Other Behavioral (N = 147)	Secondary Analysis (N = 14)
Much more risk than benefit	—%	0%	—%	0%
Somewhat more risk than benefit	1	0	—	0
Equal risk and benefit	4	1	3	3
Somewhat more benefit than risk	8	3	8	0
Much more benefit than risk	47	72	36	6
No risk or benefit	20	2	41	69
Assessment cannot be made	3	16	3	0
No information	17	6	9	22
TOTAL	100%	100%	100%	100%

[a] Based on data provided by the investigators in response to the question: Before you began involving subjects in this study, which one of the following statements best describes your assessment of the balance of risks and benefits to the average subject (aside from any financial benefit)?

Source: Tannenbaum & Cooke, 1977, p. 1.75.

certain critical terms such as *risk*. *"Minimal risk* is the probability and magnitude of physical and phychological harm that is normally entailed in the daily lives, or in the routine medical or psychological examination, of healthy children" (National Commission, 1977, p. xx). Generally no more than minimal risk is posed by the routine methods of behavioral research, such as most questionnaires, observational techniques, noninvasive psychological monitoring, and psychological tests and puzzles. More than minimal risk is involved, however, when questionnaires focus on anxiety-provoking topics, when information gathered can be harmful if disclosed and no provisions are made for preserving confidentiality, or when data will be shared with persons who may use such information against the subjects (ibid., p. xxi; also see Reatig, 1981).

The relative specificity of the guidelines is due also to the structure of the Commission's recommendations (see Table 10–3). Guidelines for research that does not involve greater than minimal risk to children (Recommendation 3) are separated from those for research with more than minimal risk (Recommendations 4, 5, and 6). Similarly guidelines for research that hold out the prospect of direct benefit for the individual subjects (Recommendation 4) are separated from those for research that does not hold out this prospect but that can lead to knowledge of vital importance for understanding or ameliorating the subjects' disorder (Recommendation 5) or can help to understand, prevent, or alleviate a serious problem affecting the health or welfare of children. As the balance of benefits (for subjects) to risks becomes less favorable, the guidelines become more strict with respect to the ethical review of the research, the obtaining of consent, and the acceptable probability and magnitude of the potential contribution of the research to the health and welfare of children.

Confidentiality

The most serious risk to which subjects are exposed in many projects within the social or behavioral sciences is embarrassment or the possibility of legal complications due to a breach of confidentiality (Cooke et al., 1977; Mosteller, 1980). Given the prevalence of this risk, ethical guidelines for social research typically have highlighted the issue of confidentiality and the responsibilities of investigators in this area. For example the ethical standards of the Society for Research in Child Development (1975) state that the investigator should keep in confidence all information obtained about research participants. Furthermore the identity of participants should be concealed in written and oral reports of the research findings and in informal discussions between the researcher and students or colleagues (Division on Developmental Psychology, 1968; Society for Research in Child Development, 1975). These guidelines are similar to the recommendations of the National Commission: "Adequate measures should be taken to protect the privacy of children and their families and to maintain the confidentiality of data" (1977, p. 4). Investigators should implement strategies for protecting confidentiality— such as coding or removing identifiers as soon as possible, limiting access to data, and storing information in locked filing cabinets—depending on the degree of sensitivity of the data to be collected (National Commission, 1978, p. 31).

Guidelines of the American Psychological Association Division on Developmental Psychology state that investigators have a duty to report general findings to parents but should not assume the role of diagnostician or counselor in carrying out this responsibility. Investigators should exercise caution in reporting results or making evaluative statements since their opinion may carry unintended weight with children and their parents (Society for Research in Child Development, 1975). Care must be taken to avoid "labeling" children or stigmatizing them with diagnostic characterizations, particularly when the results are based on tests that are being studied to obtain information on their reliability or validity (Reatig, 1981). However, when investigators become aware of information about problems that may seriously affect the child's well-being, they bear the responsibility of discussing this information with those expert in the field in order that parents may arrange the necessary assistance for their child (Society for Research in Child Development, 1975).

Financial Compensation

A significant minority of the research investigators (26 percent) and review board members (37 percent) interviewed in the IRB survey felt that compensation should not be given to subjects for the purpose of inducing participation. About the same percentages of investigators (23 percent) and board members (40 percent) opposed the practice of "giving compensation commensurate with the degree of risk to subjects." Both groups of respondents were more accepting of the practice of compensating subjects for time spent in research not intended to benefit them directly (Cooke et al., 1977). These survey items, however, pertained to the payment of research subjects in general rather than to payment for the participation of children specifically. Responses to similar questions concerning children might indicate lower acceptance of these practices.

A major concern with financial compensation is that it might almost force parents in economic distress to make decisions they would not otherwise make regarding the participation of their children in research (Frankel, 1978). It therefore has been recommended that payments to adults on behalf of minors should not be large enough to induce the parent or guardian to allow the child to participate in a study or to subject them to painful or invasive procedures (American Academy of Pediatrics, 1977). Payments to the children themselves should not be so large as to outweigh legitimate reasons for reluctance to participate (Ferguson, 1977). Additionally when payment is made (whether in money, gifts, or services) for the participation of children, this payment should not annul ethical principles regarding informed consent, confidentiality, and the avoidance of harm to subjects (Division on Developmental Psychology, 1968).

CONSENT

The ethical principle of respect for persons requires that the permission of autonomous individuals be asked prior to involving them in research and that their choices be honored (Height et al., 1977). It is this principle that is difficult—and, according to some, impossible—to uphold when children are to be included in research. Children are among those potential research subjects who have diminished autonomy and an incapacity (or low capacity) to give valid consent. This problem with consent has led some researchers, as noted before, to take the position that children should be excluded from research unless they are likely to benefit from participation (Frenkel, 1977; Ramsey, 1976, 1977). Many others, however, view as permissible the participation of children in research without direct benefits to subjects if certain conditions are met (Bartholome, 1976; McCormick, 1976). These conditions include permission by parents for the child's participation and assent from the child. Permission by parents recognizes the general role of parents, as caretakers, to guide decisions affecting their dependent children's lives and activities. Assent of children recognizes the developing autonomy of children (7 years or older) and their capacity of some degree of understanding (Height et al., 1977).

Recent Guidelines

Recommendations of the National Commission state that adequate provisions must be made for soliciting the assent of children (when they are capable), obtaining the permission of their parents or guardians, monitoring the solicitation of assent and permission, and involving at least one parent in the conduct of the research (Recommendation 7). The term *permission* (i.e., what one may do on behalf of another) is used by the National Commission to distinguish parental agreement from *consent* (i.e., what a person may do autonomously). Also, the term *assent* is used to distinguish a child's agreement from legally valid consent (National Commission, 1977, pp. 12–13).

The recommendations require the permission of parents, legally appointed guardians, or others who care for a child in a normal family setting (e.g., stepparents or relatives such as grandparents who have a close relationship with the child). In most cases, the permission of at least one parent is recommended. The permission of both parents—if competent and reasonably available—is advised when the proposed research involves more than minimal risk and does not hold out the prospect of direct benefit to the subject. There are, however, certain circumstances under which parental permission can be replaced by another "appropriate mechanism" for protecting prospective subjects who are children. These circumstances include research related to those conditions for which children might legally receive treatment without parental consent (e.g., drug addiction and venereal disease), research on neglected or abused children, or research involving children whose parents are legally or functionally incompetent (Recommendation 8). An appropriate alternative mechanism under such circumstances might be a social worker or nurse acting as a surrogate parent with the approval of a review board (National Commission, 1977, pp. 12–19).

In addition to parental permission the assent of children 7 years of age or older also is recommended. While this assent would not be necessary from infants or children over 6 who are incapacitated (so they cannot be reasonably consulted), the objection of a child of any age should be respected. Objections of young children to participation may be overridden only under special circumstances. Such a circumstance is exemplified by a study that includes an intervention that is available only in research context and from which the subject might derive significant benefit (ibid., p. 16).

The recommendation of the National Commission that parents or guardians be involved in the consent process is consistent with guidelines developed by various groups. The consent of parents or those who act *in loco parentis*, as well as the assent of their children, is specified by the Society for Research in Child Development (1975), the Division on Developmental Psychology of the American Psychological Association (1968), and the American Academy of Pediatrics Committee on Drugs (1977). The recommendation that parental consent should not be required under certain conditions—for example, when the child is emancipated or when the research focuses on drug addiction—is consistent with various court cases and state laws regarding medical treatment (Annas et al., 1977).

Recommendations that the assent of children under 7 years of age should not be mandatory and that the objection of children of any age should be respected are consistent with research on the ability of children to understand (Ferguson, 1977). However, the position of the National Commission and others (e.g., American Academy of Pediatrics, 1977; Ferguson, 1978; NIH, 1973, p. 31742; Rosen, Rekers, & Bentler, 1978) that assent should be obtained from children of at least 7 years of age has been questioned. Ackerman (1979), for example, argues that assent should not always be required and that parents have the moral duty to make choices for children that will contribute to helping the child become the right kind of person. Children, especially those with catastrophic illnesses, need and follow their parents' or physicians' guidance (ibid.). The recommendations of the National Commission pertaining to assent and the objections of children are among the few which are not included in the guidelines subsequently presented by the Department of Health, Education and Welfare and the Food and Drug Administration (1978). These guidelines, as noted above, specify (1) that the objection of a child is not held as binding and (2) that review boards should set the age after which the assent of children is mandatory on a case-by-case basis.

Circumstances under which consent requirements might be waived are not delineated in the National Commission's recommendations for research involving children. However, the Commission's report on institutional review boards (1978) specifies certain types of research for which a board may deem informed consent unnecessary. This research includes the study of documents, records, or pathological specimens where the subjects are identified.[2] Consistent with the conclusions of the Privacy Protection Study Commission, the National Commission for the Protection of Human Subjects permits such research without the explicit authorization of the individuals involved if the subjects' interests are protected and certain conditions are met. These conditions include, for example, that the organization providing the

---

[2] When subjects are not identified, the research does not need to be considered as involving human subjects.

records or specimens determines that such use or disclosure does not violate any limitations under which the information or specimens were collected and that the importance of the research warrants the risks to the individuals from exposure to the researchers of records or specimens (National Commission, 1978, p. 29). Requirements for informed consent may be waived also for observational studies supplemented by interaction with the persons being studied (see Wax, 1977). The review board, however, must determine that the behavior to be studied is "public" (e.g., social behavior in public places), that nondisclosure is essential to the methodological soundness of the research and is justified by the importance or scientific merit of the study, and that the research presents no more than minimal risk and is unlikely to cause embarrassment to the subjects (National Commission, 1978, pp. 30–31).

In research where consent is required, it should be sought "under circumstances that provide sufficient opportunity for subjects to consider whether or not to participate and that minimize the possibility of coercion or undue influence" (National Commission, 1978, p. 20; also see DHEW, 1974; National Bureau of Standards, 1976). Consent is obtained by communicating to subjects, in language they can understand, information they may reasonably be expected to desire in considering whether or not to participate, including:

(i) that an Institutional Review Board has approved the solicitation of subjects to participate in the research, that such research is voluntary, that refusal to participate will involve no penalties or loss of benefits to which subjects are otherwise entitled, that participation can be terminated at any time, and that the conditions of such termination are stated;

(ii) the aims and specific purposes of the research, whether it includes procedures designed to provide direct benefit to subjects, and available alternative ways to pursue any such benefit;

(iii) what will happen to subjects in the research, and what they will be expected to do;

(iv) any reasonably foreseeable risks to subjects, and whether treatment or compensation is available if harm occurs;

(v) who is conducting the study, who is funding it, and who should be contacted if harm occurs or there are complaints; and

(vi) any additional costs to subjects or third parties that may result from participation. (National Commission, 1978, pp. 20–21)

Consent Processes

Investigators sometimes complain that the usual consent model does not fit well with certain types of research—including observational studies, survey research, studies involving tissue or blood samples that have been obtained for other purposes, secondary analyses of records, and applied studies involving the modification of a service delivery system (Duster, Matza, & Wellman, 1979; Gray & Cooke, 1980; Wax, 1977). Furthermore consent in some settings is viewed as a legalistic device more for the protection of researchers than of subjects and as a procedure that can unnecessarily raise the salience to subjects of unlikely harmful effects (Loftus & Fries, 1979). Nevertheless some type of consent was obtained in the large majority of the projects included in the IRB survey.

Written and/or oral consent was obtained from subjects (and/or others acting on their behalf) in 95 percent of the biomedical, 92 percent of the behavioral intervention, 29 percent of the secondary analysis, and 92 percent of the other behavioral projects involving children. Principal investigators of over 80 percent of all the projects said they provided an oral explanation of the study to subjects or their proxies. Although written consent was obtained in most projects, oral consent only was obtained in 18 percent of the nonintervention behavioral studies. Neither written nor oral consent was obtained in certain studies because, according to the investigators: (1) the return of questionnaires implied consent; (2) only routine treatments or procedures were being used; (3) names of subjects were not available to the researchers; (4) consent was obtained elsewhere; (5) no risks to subjects were involved; or (6) the review board did not require that consent be obtained (Tannenbaum & Cooke, 1977).

Investigators had either exclusive or partial responsibility for obtaining consent in the majority of projects. Persons other than the principal investigators had this responsibility in 21 percent of the biomedical, 25 percent of the behavioral intervention, and 17 percent of the other behavioral projects in which consent was obtained. A professional colleague of the principal investigator, either on or off the study staff, was the other person most likely to obtain consent. Less frequently nurses, interns, students, and research assistants were responsible for this activity.

Under certain circumstances it is advisable that a third party not connected with the research be present when consent is obtained (Bartholome, 1976; British Medical Research Council, 1962–1963; Lowe, Alexander, & Mishkin, 1974). A review board may determine that a third party is needed as an advocate for the subject when risk is high and subject autonomy is low (Faden, Lewis, & Rimer, 1980; National Commission, 1977, p. 17; Pocaro, 1979). A third party such as a social worker may be needed when there exist language barriers between the investigator and the subjects (Foster, 1977). With respect to the projects in the IRB survey, third parties were present when consent was sought in approximately half the studies involving children. In behavioral studies the other person present was usually a research assistant or a member of the subject's family; in biomedical studies the other person was most often a nurse or a family member (see Table 10–9). It is unclear whether these third parties served primarily to facilitate the consent process, witness the obtaining of consent, or serve as an advocate for the subjects.

Proxy Consent

Proxy consent or permission from parents or guardians, as recommended by such groups as the American Medical Association (1967), was obtained in the large majority of the projects involving children. This permission was obtained in 88 percent of the biomedical and 76 percent of the behavioral projects in which some procedure was used to gain a written and/or oral agreement for the participation of children. Parents, relatives, or legal guardians of the subjects were the persons who

Table 10-9 Presence of Other Persons during Consent Process[a] (Percent of Projects)

	TYPE OF RESEARCH			
	Biomedical (N = 219)	Behavioral Intervention (N = 45)	Other Behavioral (N = 147)	Secondary Analysis (N = 14)
Other persons present	58%	52%	49%	13%
Family member	27	15	22	6
Physician or dentist	18	8	3	6
Nurse	37	10	3	12
Research assistant	22	29	17	0
Other	9	21	15	6
No other person present	24	22	31	0
Question not applicable[b]	9	13	10	81
No information	9	13	10	6
TOTAL	100%	100%	100%	100%

[a] Based on investigators' responses to the question: Aside from yourself and the subject (and/or the proxy), is anyone else usually present when consent is sought?

[b] E.g., because consent was not obtained.

Source: Tannenbaum & Cooke, 1977, p. 1.86.

served most frequently as proxies. In a small percentage of projects, permission for the participation of at least some subjects was obtained from the subject's physician, an institutional representative, or the courts (see Table 10–10). In the studies where proxy consent was used, consent was obtained from *proxies only* twice as often as it was obtained from *proxies as well as subjects*.

Intellect and degree of illness sometimes were used by investigators for determining whether permission would be obtained from the subject's parents or guardians. More frequently the subject's age was the criterion. The age *above* which no proxy consent was obtained ranged from 4 years, in rare cases, to 21 years, more frequently. The median age above which no proxy consent was obtained was 18 years. This is the age at which persons can legally consent to medical treatment in most states (National Commission, 1978, pp. 85–87) and within the age range (18 to 21 years) up to which parental permission for participation in clinical research typically is recommended (e.g., Bartholome, 1977b). The age *below* which consent was not obtained from the subject as well as the proxy ranged from 1 year to 21 years. The median age below which consent was not obtained from the subject as well as the proxy was 7 years.

The propriety of proxy consent, including that ob-

tained from the parents of children, has been challenged from various perspectives. The use of proxy consent, according to Ramsey, treats the child not as a child but as an adult person who has become a joint adventurer in the common cause of medical research. "If the grounds for this are alleged to be the presumptive or implied consent of the child, that must simply be characterized as a violent or false presumption" (Ramsey, 1970, p. 14). Even when the general principle of proxy consent is accepted, its practice under certain circumstances may afford inadequate protection to children (Pocaro, 1979). Economic and social pressures can force parents to make choices of questionable value when their child's welfare is concerned. Parents may give their permission, when they would not otherwise do so, if the expected quality and amount of treatment appears to be contingent on their child's participation, if there has been difficulty in securing treatment for the child, or if payments for participation are excessive (Frankel, 1978).

Most investigators reported in the IRB survey that proxy consent protected subjects "very well" or "fairly well." Some, however, indicated that proxy consent protects the interests of subjects "not well at all" or "not very well." This latter group included 3 percent of the investigators interviewed in children's hospitals, 7 per-

Table 10-10 Persons Serving as Proxies[a] (Percent of Projects)[b]

	TYPE OF RESEARCH			
	Biomedical (N = 219)	Behavioral Intervention (N = 45)	Other Behavioral (N = 147)	Secondary Analysis (N = 14)
Parent or other relatives	75%	52%	63%	12%
Legal guardian	23	33	23	6
Subject's own physician	2	0	0	0
Institutional representative	2	1	2	0
Courts	—	4	5	6
Someone else	0	1	0	0
Question not applicable[c]	19	32	31	88
No information	5	13	1	0

[a] Based on investigators' responses to the question: Who is asked to give proxy consent for subjects in your study?

[b] Percentages may add to more than 100% since more than one response could be checked.

[c] No consent or no proxy consent obtained in the study.

Source: Tannenbaum & Cooke, 1977, p. 1.102.

cent of those in other biomedical institutions (e.g., general hospitals and medical schools), and 14 percent of those in universities and other behavioral research organizations. The main reasons given for the inadequacy of proxy consent were: (1) When only proxy consent is used, subjects may not be able to decide themselves whether or not they wish to participate in the research; (2) the proxy may not be able to understand the research; and (3) the proxy might not care about protecting the rights of the subject. Other problems concerned the subjects and the proxies not being adequately informed about the research or its risks (Tannenbaum & Cooke, 1977).

Incomplete Disclosure and Deception

While informed consent typically requires the presentation of all pertinent information to subjects and their proxies, the design of certain research projects requires that some information not be divulged to subjects (Duster et al., 1979). Other projects require that subjects be deceived as to the purpose or procedures of the study. Ethical standards developed by the Society for Research in Child Development (1975) permit concealment or deception if the investigator satisfies a committee of peers that these practices are necessary for a particular study. When such practices are used, the Society prescribes that measures be taken after the study to ensure that participants understand the reasons for concealment or deception.

There remains considerable disagreement regarding the appropriateness of deception and incomplete disclosure in research and, in particular, in research involving children. The continuing use of these practices may merely teach investigators how to lie and produce research results based on the behavior of people who do not trust authority figures (Murray, 1980). Research designs based on deception might lead children to believe that investigators frequently lie, cannot be trusted, and will provide invalid information in future studies (Ferguson, 1977). Deception and, to a lesser extent, incomplete disclosure potentially have negative conse-

quences for research investigators as well as for subjects (Baumrind, 1979).

Despite the possible dysfunctional consequences of these practices, deception or incomplete disclosure was required by the design of some of the projects included in the IRB survey. Subjects were told things which were not true in 7 percent of the nonintervention behavioral projects involving children. The false information usually centered around the purpose or specific procedures of the study, and the reason for deceiving subjects was to prevent the biasing of results. None of the biomedical or behavioral intervention studies involved deception. Information was withheld from subjects in many of the behavioral studies and a small minority of the biomedical studies (see Table 10–11). The information not divulged most often concerned the purpose or procedures of the study, the treatment or medication being used, and the possible benefits to subjects. The reasons for incomplete disclosure paralleled those for deception—avoiding bias in the results.

While deception has been defended on the basis of both paternalistic and utilitarian grounds, both of these defenses can be challenged. The paternalistic defense is that deceptive procedures can be therapeutic for subjects. This defense, however, assumes that the deception (rather than the other research procedures) is beneficial and that subjects would agree that the deception is beneficial to them. Additionally the paternalistic defense carries the danger of "justifying not only ineliminable deception but also deception motivated by a concern to conserve time, effort, and expense" (Soble, 1978, p. 41). The utilitarian defense is that deception not causing harm is acceptable because the knowledge gained is socially valuable. Nevertheless deception is inconsistent with moral principles, is not valued by most people, and potentially can lead to decreased public support for research (ibid.).

Various strategies have been proposed for obtaining some consent from subjects while still deceiving them. Consent with full disclosure could be obtained from subjects after the fact, prior consent could be obtained from

Table 10–11 Information Not Divulged to Subjects[a] (Percent of Projects)

	TYPE OF RESEARCH			
	Biomedical (N = 219)	Behavioral Intervention (N = 45)	Other Behavioral (N = 147)	Secondary Analysis (N = 14)
Yes, certain information not divulged	8%	21%	41%	0%
Purpose of study	—	10	24	0
Purpose of specific procedures	1	9	24	0
Medication or treatment being used	4	2	4	0
Possible benefits to subjects	0	0	7	0
Existence of study	1	2	—	0
Possible risks or discomforts to subjects	0	0	1	0
Other	2	2	14	0
No, not required by study design or all information divulged	92	78	58	97
No information	—	1	1	3
TOTAL	100%	100%	100%	100%

[a] Based on investigators' responses to the question: In some research the design of the study requires that certain information not be divulged to subjects. Is that the case in this study? The figures in the offset columns reflect the percentage of projects in which information was not divulged about specific aspects of the study (e.g., its purpose or benefits). In certain projects, information was not divulged about two or more of these aspects.

Source: Tannenbaum & Cooke, 1977, p. 1.91.

persons similar to the subjects (Veatch, 1975), or subjects could be informed that they will be deceived without specifying the exact nature of the deception (Milgram, 1977). While each of these strategies alone has ethical or scientific limitations, the joint application of the two later strategies may be a viable option (Soble, 1978).

The withholding or altering of information, though not mentioned in the National Commission's recommendations for research involving children, is discussed in the report and recommendations on institutional review boards (1978). A review board can approve incomplete disclosure or deception if it determines that (1) these practices are not likely to be harmful to subjects, (2) sufficient information will be disclosed to give prospective subjects an opportunity to decide whether they want to participate, (3) no information about the risk of harm or discomfort is withheld when such risk is present, and (4) information is not withheld for the purpose of eliciting the cooperation of subjects. Furthermore investigators must truthfully answer any questions by subjects prior to their participation and should debrief subjects after their participation (National Commission, 1978, pp. 26–27).

WRITTEN CONSENT

Documentation of consent is recommended by the National Commission since it provides the investigator with evidence of consent and the subjects with a readily available source of information about the research (National Commission, 1978, p. 27). There are circumstances, however, for which a review board may determine that written consent is not necessary or appropriate. For example the existence of a signed consent form might place subjects at risk if the research focuses on illegal or stigmatizing characteristics or behavior (ibid., pp. 21, 27). In such cases a written record of consent linking subjects to the research might be viewed as inappropriate. Written consent may be viewed as unnecessary if the research presents no more than minimal risk and involves no procedures for which written consent is normally required (ibid., p. 21). This type of research is exemplified by studies using a mailed questionnaire or a telephone interview. A written description of the project would be appropriate in the former case and an oral explanation in the latter. Neither case would automatically require signatures from subjects (ibid., pp. 28–29).

These recommendations pertain to research involving human subjects in general rather than to research involving children specifically. The guidelines regarding children mention only that the review board "should pay particular attention to the explanation and consent form, if any, to assure that appropriate language is used" (National Commission, 1977, p. 17). Nevertheless a review board may require that written permission from parents or guardians be obtained for the involvement of children in research, even when the routine nature of the research procedures would render consent from adult subjects unnecessary.

Earlier guidelines formulated by federal agencies typically called for written consent without specifying the circumstances under which this form of consent might not be necessary. DHEW regulations state that a consent form must be signed by each subject or a legally authorized representative and that copies of the information disclosed to subjects must be filed with the review board (Public Law 93-348, 1974; 45 CFR 46 revised as of April 1, 1967). Department of Commerce guidelines require that subjects sign a consent form that explains the responsibilities of both subjects and investigators (National Bureau of Standards, 1976). Similarly, policies of the Veterans Administration (1975) specify that subjects must sign consent forms and each sheet of multipage forms. Guidelines developed by professional associations generally have been more flexible than the early guidelines of federal agencies. Ethical standards of the Division on Developmental Psychology of the American Psychological Association (1968) and the Society for Research in Child Development (1975) state only that informed consent should be obtained, "preferably in writing."

Consent Forms

As noted in the previous section, consent was obtained in writing in most of the projects involving children in the IRB survey. Consent forms were used in 92 percent of the projects carried out in children's hospitals, 78 percent of those conducted in other biomedical institutions, and 78 percent of those in universities and behavioral research organizations. At least two-thirds of these forms were developed specifically for the particular project in which they were used; the others were based on a standardized form provided by the institutions. About 70 percent of the forms were short in length and contained less than 300 words. These forms, short and long, varied greatly in terms of the comprehensiveness of the information provided to subjects.

Informed consent, according to Levine (1975), involves providing subjects (and/or those giving permission for the subject's participation) with various elements of information, including (1) statements concerning the overall purpose of the research, the role of the subjects, discomforts and risks, benefits, and alternatives, (2) reasons why the subject has been selected, (3) descriptions of the procedures—including the setting of the research, the time involved, and the people with whom the subject will interact, (4) offers to answer questions and to provide consultation to the subject, and (5) a statement that refusal or withdrawal will not prejudice future interactions with the investigator. As defined by the Society for Research in Child Development (1975), informed consent requires that information be provided about all features of the research, the professional and institutional affiliation of the investigator, and the responsibilities of the investigator and research participants.

The Institutional Guide to DHEW Policy on Protection of Human Subjects (1971) specifies six items pertinent to informed consent: (1) the purpose of the research, (2) procedures involved, (3) risks, (4) benefits, (5) a statement that subjects are free to withdraw from the research, and (6) an invitation to subjects to ask questions about participating in the research. Content analyses of the consent forms used by investigators in the IRB survey indicate that relatively few of these forms mentioned all six of these items in any detail (see Table 10–12). Statements regarding risks and benefits (or the lack thereof) were

Table 10–12 Items Covered by Consent Forms (Percent of Projects)

ITEM	CHILDREN'S HOSPITALS (N = 35)			OTHER BIOMEDICAL INSTITUTIONS (N = 158)			UNIVERSITIES (N = 94)		
	No Mention	Brief Mention[a]	Detailed Description	No Mention	Brief Mention[a]	Detailed Description	No Mention	Brief Mention[a]	Detailed Description
Purpose	13%	66%	21%	25%	66%	9%	29%	60%	11%
Procedures	9	68	23	4	71	23	18	54	28
Benefits	50	16	34	34	40	26	74	16	10
Risks	16	32	52	37	35	28	74	15	11
Withdrawal	46	34	20	23	45	32	14	62	24
Questions[b]	63	—	37	47	—	53	50	—	50

[a] Consent forms which make some reference to the item or which include an unspecified certified statement (e.g., "I certify that I have been informed about the purpose, procedures, and risks of this study").

[b] Coded dichotomously—either the form did or did not include a statement inviting questions.

Source: Based on data presented in Tannenbaum & Cooke, 1977, p. 1.113.

particularly likely to be missing from forms used in universities and other behavioral research organizations.

Other elements of informed consent, beyond those listed in *The Institutional Guide,* often were omitted from consent forms. The availability of alternative procedures (DHEW, 1974; Levine, 1975) was mentioned in less than 15 percent of the forms used in projects designed primarily to benefit subjects. (These alternatives were mentioned in oral statements to subjects in an additional 13 percent of the projects.) Only 14 percent of the projects in which some information would be withheld from subjects mentioned this in their consent forms. The expected duration of subjects' participation (Levine, 1975) was mentioned in 32 percent of the forms. Discussions of confidentiality (Society for Research in Child Development, 1975) were found in 39 percent of the forms.

Readability of Consent Forms

Informed consent requires that the information given to the subjects and/or persons acting on their behalf must be written in a language that can be understood by them (American Academy of Pediatrics, 1977). This requirement apparently is a difficult one for research investigators to meet. The purposes, procedures, and risks of projects may be too abstract or complex for many researchers to communicate in a simple manner.

The reading level of most of the consent forms analyzed during the IRB survey was difficult or very difficult (see Table 10–13). Readability was assessed through the use of the Flesch Yardstick, a formula based on the number of syllables per 100 words and the number of words per sentence (Flesch, 1948). Reading ease scores based on this formula thus consider both the complexity of sentences (as reflected by the number of words) and the abstractness of the terms used (as approximated by the number of syllables per word). Flesch readability scores have been shown to be related to tests of comprehension (Flesch, 1948; Klare, 1952), reading speed (Brown, 1952; Rothkopf & Coatney, 1974), and certain other measures of readability (Klare, 1952).

As shown in Table 10–13, most short consent forms—those under 300 words—were written at an academic or scientific reading level. The majority of the longer forms also were fairly difficult, difficult, or very difficult to read. Passages concerning the purpose of the project in long forms tended to be more difficult to read than passages concerning the procedures or risks of the study (Cooke, Tannenbaum, & Gray, 1978). Although medical and technical terms comprised substantially less than 5 percent of the words in most consent forms, the use of such terms rendered certain forms difficult to read. Many other forms, which did not include such terms, were difficult to read due to their sentence structure and use of lengthy nontechnical words.

REGULATION AND REVIEW OF RESEARCH

The principal mechanism for regulating research for the protection of human subjects has been review committees or institutional review boards (IRB's). The evolution and history of IRB's—documented elsewhere (Curran, 1970; Levine, 1976; Veatch, 1975)—revolve primarily around medical research rather than psychological or educational research. Surveys conducted in the early 1960s indicate that committees were then in use in various university departments of medicine to review human experimentation (see Katz, 1972; Levine, 1976). By 1966 policy statements of the U.S. Public Health Service (PHS) required peer review of the judgment of principal investigators by a committee of institutional associates. This review of applications for clinical research grants was to focus on the rights and welfare of subjects, the methods used to obtain consent, and the risks and benefits of the research (Curran, 1970). Revisions of these policy statements extended the review requirement to all PHS grants, required institutions to file statements of assurance of compliance with PHS policies (including policies pertaining to prior review by a committee), and made grantee institutions responsible for assuring that research investigations were in accordance with community laws and that due consideration was given to pertinent ethical issues (Levine, 1976). In 1971, DHEW published similar guidelines that applied to all grantee institutions (DHEW, 1971; Michael & Weinberger, 1977).

After further modifications, these policy statements and guidelines were revised and issued as DHEW regulations. The National Research Act of 1974 (Public Law 93–348) required that each institution applying for a grant or contract involving human subjects establish an IRB to review the proposed research and protect the

Table 10-13 Readability of Short Consent Forms[a] (Percent of Projects) (N = 216)

	VERY EASY (COMICS)	EASY (PULP FICTION)	FAIRLY EASY (SLICK FICTION)	STANDARD (*TIME*)	FAIRLY DIFFICULT (*ATLANTIC*)	DIFFICULT (SCHOLARLY, ACADEMIC)	VERY DIFFICULT (SCIENTIFIC, PROFESSIONAL)	TOTAL
Children's hospitals	0%	0	1	12	0	60	27	100%
Other bio-medical institutions	0%	1	0	9	12	56	22	100%
Universities	0%	—	4	19	20	51	6	100%
All projects	0%	1	1	13	13	55	17	100%

[a] Table based on projects using consent forms with less than 300 words. The overall readability of each form was assessed by applying the Flesch formula (1948) to all sentences included in the form.

Source: Tannenbaum & Cooke, 1977, p. 1.117.

rights of subjects. The wording of this act, the implementing regulations (DHEW, 1974), and subsequent technical amendments (DHEW, 1975) resulted in many institutions requiring IRB approval of not only activities supported by DHEW but of all research, development, and related activities carried out within the institution (Staff of the National Commission, 1978).

The regulations introduced in 1974 required each institution conducting DHEW research to develop a statement of principles to govern the review of research and to establish an IRB with members of diverse backgrounds. The members could not have a direct interest in the research under review, could not all be employees or agents of the institution, and could not be members of a single professional group. The review of proposals by board members was to be supplemented by reviews by the funding agency staff, scientific advisory committees, and interdisciplinary councils for (1) scientific merit, (2) potential benefits to subjects, and (3) the importance of the knowledge to be gained (ibid.).

IRB's under the National Research Act are required to review all research proposed within the institution to determine whether subjects would be at risk. For the projects involving risk the IRB must determine whether the risk to subjects is outweighed by the sum of benefits to subjects and the knowledge to be gained and whether the rights and welfare of subjects will be protected. Additionally the board must determine whether adequate methods are planned for obtaining legally effective informed consent—i.e., the knowing consent of an individual (or a legally authorized representative) so situated as to be able to exercise free power of choice without undue inducement or any element of force, fraud, deceit, duress, or other form of constraint or coercion.

These policies, initially developed for NIH and the Alcohol, Drug Abuse, and Mental Health Administration, were later adopted by various other offices within DHEW. Compliance with 45 CRF 46 was required by the Office of the Secretary for Planning and Evaluation, the Office of Human Development Services, and the Health Services Administration (Staff of the National Commission, 1978). Somewhat different policies for the ethical review of research were adopted by other components of DHEW, including the Center for Disease Control and the Education Division. One important difference was that these policies specified that IRB review is required only when the investigator determines that subjects in his/her project will be at risk. Various federal

agencies and offices in departments other than DHEW adopted review policies similar to those in 45 CFR 46 (e.g., the Army and Air Force within the Department of Defense, the National Science Foundation, the Department of Energy, and the Consumer Product Safety Commission). Other federal departments and agencies adopted policies based on the 1971 *Institutional Guide to DHEW Policy on Protection of Human Subjects* (e.g., the Department of Agriculture and the Navy) or informal guidelines based on the American Psychological Association's 1973 *Ethical Principles in the Conduct of Research with Human Participants* (e.g., the Internal Revenue Service, the Civil Service Commission, and the Commission on Civil Rights).

The Activities and Performance of IRB's

While much has been written about review boards since the National Research Act was passed (e.g., Barber, 1980; Dalglish, 1976; Gray, 1978; Gray & Cooke, 1980), relatively little of this literature has focused specifically on the activities of boards regarding research with children. Some relevant data are available, however, from the IRB survey and the investigators whose projects involved children. These data concern the changes in projects required by IRB's and the reactions of investigators to the review procedure (Tannenbaum & Cooke, 1977).

Review boards frequently required some formal action on the part of investigators before approving their research proposals (Table 10–14). Boards requested more information (about, for example, consent procedures and risks and benefits) from investigators conducting well over a third of the biomedical and behavioral intervention studies. Modifications in consent procedures and/or forms were required in 40 percent of the secondary analysis projects and in approximately a quarter of the biomedical projects and behavioral studies not involving an intervention. In the secondary analysis projects these changes most frequently required that written consent be obtained from subjects. The most frequently required changes in behavioral studies were the obtaining of written (rather than oral) consent and the provision of additional information to subjects (Tannenbaum & Cooke, 1977). Other requested modifications—such as those in scientific design, subject selection, risks and discomforts, and confidentiality—occurred relatively infrequently. In addition to these formal modifications, changes in proj-

Table 10-14 Actions Formally Required of Principal Investigator by Review Boards (Percent of Projects)[a]

	TYPE OF RESEARCH			
	Biomedical (N = 220)	Behavioral Intervention (N = 45)	Other Behavioral (N = 147)	Secondary Analysis (N = 14)
More information	38%	46%	29%	22%
Modification in consent forms and procedures	27	12	23	40
Modification in scientific design	3	6	0	0
Modification in subject selection	4	2	0	0
Modification regarding risks, discomforts	6	7	4	0
Modification regarding confidentiality	1	2	9	9
Other modifications	5	8	5	0

[a] Percentages need not add to 100% since respondents might indicate fewer or more than one action required.

Source: Tannenbaum & Cooke, 1977, p. 1.41.

ects also resulted from informal discussions between the researchers and board members prior to the submission of the proposal to the IRB. About a third of the investigators reported such discussions, and over half of these reported making changes in their proposals as a result of the discussions (Tannenbaum & Cooke, 1977).

Investigators' attitudes toward review boards were, for the most part, more favorable than unfavorable (Table 10-15). However, a number of respondents in all types of institutions felt that the procedures caused at least some problems. Investigators cited, particularly, committee actions in areas not appropriate to its function and judgments made by the committee that it is not qualified to make. A fairly high percentage of investigators doing research involving children outside of children's hospitals felt that the procedures were impeding the progress of research at least to some extent. Many investigators doing research outside of biomedical institutions (i.e., in universities and behavioral research organizations) also

felt that the procedures were an unwarranted intrusion on the investigator's autonomy.

The finding that researchers in universities and behavioral research settings viewed the review procedure less favorably than did those in biomedical institutions was not unexpected. The review process was initially developed for medical research and may not be completely appropriate for research in the social sciences (Mosteller, 1980). Furthermore though many studies in the social sciences involve no unusual risks for subjects, these projects must nevertheless be reviewed by IRB's. This has placed social scientists in a position where their freedom to observe and communicate with other persons is more restricted than that of other professional groups such as journalists (Pattullo, 1980). The results of the IRB survey show that investigators whose research involved children saw various problems with the review process as well as various ways in which the process could be improved. Difficulties mentioned most frequently by researchers in

Table 10-15 Attitudes of Investigators toward Review Procedures and Committees[a]

	CHILDREN'S HOSPITALS (N = 31)[b]	OTHER BIOMEDICAL (N = 212)[b]	UNIVERSITIES (N = 144)[b]
Procedures protect rights of subjects—at least to some extent	99%	97%	99%
Procedures improve quality of research—at least to some extent	91	81	56
Procedures are an unwarranted intrusion on investigator's autonomy—at least to some extent	10	17	38
Procedures run with reasonable efficiency—at least to some extent	100	98	90
Committee gets into areas not appropriate to its function—at least to some extent	62	51	42
Committee makes judgments it is not qualified to make—at least to some extent	50	41	50
Procedures impede progress of research—at least to some extent	14	40	48

[a] Three response options were provided for each question: (1) to a large extent, (2) to some extent, and (3) not at all. The figures in this table show the percentage of respondents answering either "to a large extent" or "to some extent."

[b] The number of respondents varies across items due to missing data.

Source: Based on data presented in Tannenbaum & Cooke, 1977, pp. 1.222–1.224.

universities and other behavioral research settings were the process takes too long, review procedures are too complicated, low risk projects are reviewed in the same way as higher risk projects, and the ethical guidelines are incomplete or unclear. Nevertheless, most investigators—92 percent of all those interviewed during the IRB survey—felt that the benefits to subjects from the review procedures outweighed or balanced any difficulties caused by these procedures (Gray & Cooke, 1980, p. 40).

The Future of Review Processes

The recommendations of the National Commission (1978) strongly support the use of IRB's for the regulation of research. The National Commission's recommendations clarify and specify in some detail the role of IRB's, simplify the review process in certain ways, and eliminate the duplication and/or inconsistencies of current federal guidelines for the protection of human subjects.[3] The recommendations would establish DHEW as the single cognizant agency for the promulgation of regulations pertaining to the protection of human research subjects (ibid., p. 4) and for the accreditation of all IRB's (ibid., p. 5). IRB's would be responsible for reviewing all research involving human subjects sponsored or conducted by institutions that receive any federal support for research involving human subjects, for the provision of health care, or for the conduct of health-related research. This review could be carried out prior to or within a specified time after the submission of an application for a grant or contract but always would have to precede the initiation of a project involving human subjects.

An IRB should consist of at least five persons of diverse backgrounds and "sufficient maturity, experience and competence to assure that the Board will be able to discharge its responsibilities and that its determination will be accorded respect by investigators and the community served by the institution" (ibid., p. 13). The board must also include at least one member who is not otherwise affiliated with the institution. Under the proposed guidelines, the IRB would have the authority to review and approve, require modifications in, or disapprove all scientific research involving human subjects. (Scientific research is defined as a formal investigation designed to develop or contribute to generalizable knowledge and human subjects as persons about whom an investigator conducting research obtains (1) data through intervention or interaction with the persons or (2) identifiable private information [ibid., p. xx].)

IRB's would be responsible for reviewing each research proposal in terms of the various issues discussed throughout this chapter—the equity of subject selection, the acceptability of risks to subjects in relation to anticipated benefits to subjects and the knowledge to be gained, and the appropriateness of procedures for obtaining informed consent. Boards would be responsible also for determining that the research methods are appropriate to the objectives of the research and the field to be studied and that risks to subjects are minimized by using the safest procedures consistent with sound research design. Proposals must be reviewed at convened meetings at which a majority of board members are present, and the consensus of a majority of the members present is required for the approval of a project. For proposals that are not approved as submitted, boards must inform investigators of the basis of decisions to disapprove or require modification and give investigators an opportunity to respond in person or in writing (ibid., p. 32). Finally, IRB's would be responsible for the continued review of approved research—including, for example, requiring reports from investigators, soliciting information from subjects about their participation, and observing the recruitment of subjects and the conduct of research (ibid., p. 16).

IRB's would be permitted to arrange with DHEW expedited review procedures for certain categories of research that recur with some regularity, present no more than minimal risk to subjects, and present no serious ethical issue requiring IRB deliberation. Examples of the kinds of research for which expedited review might be appropriate are (1) projects involving survey research instruments, standard psychological tests, or similar procedures when subjects are normal volunteers—providing that the data will be gathered anonymously or that confidentiality will be protected by measures appropriate to the sensitivity of the data, (2) program evaluation projects that entail no deviation for subjects from the normal requirements of their involvement in the program being evaluated or benefits related to their participation in such programs, and (3) research using standard protocols or noninvasive procedures generally accepted as presenting no more than minimal risk, even when done by students (National Commission, 1978, pp. 34–35). With the prior approval of DHEW, proposals in such categories can be reviewed by an IRB chairperson or by an experienced reviewer designated by the chairperson. Proposals reviewed in this expedited manner should be referred to the full committee if the individual reviewer determines that the proposal falls outside the defined category of research, presents problems regarding such issues as informed consent or level of risk, or includes multiple procedures that in combination may expose subjects to more than minimal risk (ibid., p. 33).

In general the guidelines proposed by the National Commission support the strategy of local review of research in favor of a more centralized strategy (e.g., review at the regional or national level). While the guidelines represent a national and centralized policy for the protection of research subjects, many of the National Commission recommendations would strengthen IRB's as a mechanism for making local determinations regarding the ethical propriety of research projects.[4] IRB's would be at least partly supported by federal funds, their members would be granted protection in connection with any liability arising out of their performance of duties, and the boards would be provided with meeting

---

[3] The proposed regulations published by DHEW (1979) differ from the National Commission's recommendations in a number of significant ways. These differences—and some criticisms of the DHEW proposals—are discussed by Gray (1980).

[4] Reviews of research proposals by federal agencies might nevertheless consider the adequacy with which the rights of subjects are protected. Within the Department of Health and Human Services (formerly DHEW), the Initial Review Group (study section) and the National Advisory Council may focus on human subject protection issues when reviewing a proposed project (Reatig, 1981).

space and sufficient staff to support their activities. This reinforcement of the review process is consistent with the National Commission's initial premise "that investigators should not have the sole responsibility for determining whether research involving human subjects fulfills ethical standards" (National Commission, 1978, p. 1). This responsibility must be shared by others because investigators are always in a position of potential conflict by virtue of their concern with the pursuit of knowledge as well as the welfare of the subjects of their research.

In working to ensure that this responsibility will be shared, the National Commission's recommendations follow and perpetuate a trend that has made the review requirement increasingly more encompassing. This trend has led, according to Pattullo (1980), to a situation where institutions must review even "trivial" research and have reacted by honoring the regulations "more in the breach than in the observance" (p. 16). In response to the National Commission's recommendations and DHEW's proposed regulations, some major professional and university associations have urged review only for those social science projects that involve significant risks of harm (Mosteller, 1980).[5]

The IRB system, however, has been defended by others (e.g., Swazey, 1980), who contend that the problem has been that social researchers and review board members are not conversant with the regulations. Regulation has been defended also by those who feel that in this society moral regulations have to some large degree broken down and individual responsibility has been replaced by organizational or corporate responsibility. The regulation of organizations is needed as a substitute for morality, given that certain organizations "undertake courses of action that individuals within the corporation would be deeply shocked by if it was proposed that they as individuals do what the corporation does" (MacIntyre, 1980, p. 33). Barber (1980) argues that although social scientists have reacted as conservatively as those in most professions to new regulations that involve even small reductions in their present large autonomy, they have done little to creatively balance their own values with changing social values. Nevertheless he concludes,

the professions probably will have to face more regulations and can live with it. They will live more successfully with it by adapting constructively to it, by standing firm, but never rigid, on their own values, which are indeed among those that are essential for the welfare and improvement of our society, but also respecting new values and the old values newly insisted upon by less powerful groups in our society. (Barber, 1980, p. 36)[6]

[5] In fact the National Commission's proposals would provide for the expedited review of research unlikely to entail significant harm—partly for the purpose of determining that no more than minimal risks are involved and that a full review is unnecessary.

[6] Final regulations on the review of research, effective as of July 21, 1981, have recently been approved by the Department of Health and Human Services (DHHS). The regulations require the review by IRB's of DHHS-funded projects but exclude from this requirement research that entails little or no risk for subjects. Exempted projects include those based on the secondary analysis of data, the observation of public behavior, or standard survey research techniques—unless such projects involve risks associated with a breach of confidentiality. The regulations permit IRB's to establish local procedures for exempting appropriate projects from the review process.

REFERENCES

ACKERMAN, T. F. Fooling ourselves with child autonomy and assent in nontherapeutic clinical research. *Clinical Research,* 1979, *27,* 345–348.

ALEXANDER, L. Psychiatry: Methods and processes for investigation of drugs. *Annals of the New York Academy of Science,* 1970, *169,* 347.

ALLEN, J. L. A theological approach to moral rights. *Journal of Religious Ethics,* 1974, *2,* 119–141.

American Academy of Pediatrics (Committee on Drugs). Guidelines for the ethical conduct of studies to evaluate drugs in pediatric populations. *Pediatrics,* 1977, *60*(No. 1).

American Medical Association. Ethical guidelines for clinical investigation. *Annals of Internal Medicine,* 1967, *67*(No. 3, pt. 2, Suppl. 7), 73–78.

ANNAS, G. J., GLANTZ, L. H., & KATZ, B. F. Law of informed consent in human experimentation: Children. In the National Commission for the Protection of Human Subjects of Biomedical and Behavioral Research (Eds.), *Appendix to report and recommendations on research involving children* [DHEW Publication (OS) 77-0005]. Washington, D.C.: U. S. Government Printing Office, 1977.

BARBER, B. Regulation and the professions. *Hastings Center Report,* 1980, *10*(No. 1), 34–36.

BARBER, B., LALLY, J., MAKARUSHKA, J., & SULLIVAN, D. *Research on human subjects.* New Brunswick, N.J.: Transaction Books, 1979. (Originally published, 1973.)

BARTHOLOME, W. G. Parents, children, and the moral benefits of research. *Hastings Center Report,* 1976, *6*(No. 6), 44–45.

BARTHOLOME, W. G. Proxy consent in the medical context: The infant as person. In the National Commission for the Protection of Human Subjects of Biomedical and Behavioral Research (Eds.), *Appendix to report and recommendations on research involving children* [DHEW Publication (OS)77-0005]. Washington, D.C.: U.S. Government Printing Office, 1977a.

BARTHOLOME, W. G. The ethics of nontherapeutic clinical research on children. In the National Commission for the Protection of Human Subjects of Biomedical and Behavioral Research (Eds.), *Appendix to report and recommendations on research involving children* [DHEW Publication (OS)77-0005]. Washington, D.C.: U.S. Government Printing Office, 1977b.

BAUMRIND, D. The costs of deception. *IRB: A Review of Human Subjects Research,* 1979, *1*(No. 6), 1–4.

BEECHER, H. K. *Research and the individual: Human studies.* Boston: Little, Brown, 1970.

BONNER v. *MORAN,* 126 F.2d 121 (D.C. Cir. 1941).

British Medical Research Council. Responsibility in investigations on human subjects. *Report of the Medical Research Council for 1962–1963,* Cmnd. 2382, 21–25.

BROWN, J. L. The Flesch formula "through the looking glass." *College English,* 1952, *13,* 393–394.

The Clinical Center. *Policy and Communications Bulletin,* 1975, No. 75–5.

COOKE, R. A., TANNENBAUM, A. S., & GRAY, B. H. A survey of institutional review boards and research involving human subjects, 1977. In the National Commission for the Protection of Human Subjects of Biomedical and Behavioral Research (Eds.), *Appendix to report and recommendations on institutional review boards* [DHEW Publications (OS)78-0009]. Washington, D.C.: U.S. Government Printing Office, 1978.

CULLITON, B. J. National Research Act: Restores training, bans fetal research. *Science,* 1974, *185,* 426–427.

CURRAN, W. J. Government regulation of the use of human subjects in medical research: The approach of two federal agencies. In P. A. Freund (Ed.), *Experimentation with human subjects.* New York: Braziller, 1970.

CURRAN, W. J., & BEECHER, H. K. Experimentation in children: A recommendation of legal ethical principles. *Journal of the American Medical Association,* 1969, *210,* 77–83.

DALGLISH, T. K. *Protecting human subjects in social and behavioral research: Ethics, law, and the DHEW rules: A critique.* Unpublished doctoral dissertation, University of California at Berkeley, 1976.

Department of Health, Education and Welfare. *The institutional guide to DHEW policy on protection of human subjects* [DHEW Publication (NIH) 72-102]. Washington, D.C.: U.S. Government Printing Office, 1971.

Department of Health, Education and Welfare. Protection of human subjects, 45 CFR 46. *Federal Register,* 1974, *39,* 18917.

Department of Health, Education and Welfare. Protection of human subjects: Technical amendments, 45 CFR 46. *Federal Register,* 1975, *40,* 11854.

Department of Health, Education and Welfare. *Federal Register,* 1978, *43,* 31786–31794.

Department of Health, Education and Welfare. Proposed regulations amending basic HEW policy for protection of human research subjects. *Federal Register,* 1979, *44,* 47688–47698.

Division on Developmental Psychology of the American Psychological Association. Ethical standards for research with children. *Newsletter,* 1968, 1–3.

Duster, T., Matza, D., & Wellman, D. Field work and the protection of human subjects. *The American Sociologist,* 1979, *14,* 136–142.

Englehardt, H. T., Jr. Basic ethical principles in the conduct of biomedical and behavioral research involving human subjects. Paper prepared for the National Commission for the Protection of Human Subjects of Biomedical and Behavioral Research, December 1975.

Faden, R. R., Lewis, C., & Rimer, B. Monitoring informed consent: An exploratory record review. *IRB: A Review of Human Subjects Research,* 1980, *2*(No. 8), 9–10.

Ferguson, L. R. The competence and freedom of children to make choices regarding participation in biomedical and behavioral research. In the National Commission for the Protection of Human Subjects of Biomedical and Behavioral Research (Eds.), *Appendix to report and recommendations on research involving children* [DHEW Publication (OS) 77-0005]. Washington, D.C.: U.S. Government Printing Office, 1977.

Ferguson, L. R. The competence and freedom of children to make choices regarding participation in research: A statement. *Journal of Social Issues,* 1978, *34*(No. 2), 114–121.

Flesch, R. A new readability yardstick. *Journal of Applied Psychology,* 1948, *32,* 221–233.

Foster, H. W., Jr. Children and the institutionalized mentally infirm. In the National Commission for the Protection of Human Subjects of Biomedical and Behavioral Research (Eds.), *Appendix to report and recommendations on research involving children* [DHEW Publication (OS) 77-0005]. Washington, D.C.: U.S. Government Printing Office, 1977.

Frankel, M. S. Social, legal, and political responses to ethical issues in the use of children as experimental subjects. *Journal of Social Issues,* 1978, *34*(No. 2), 101–113.

Frenkel, D. A. Consent of incompetents (minor and mentally ill) to medical treatment. *Legal Medical Quarterly,* 1977, *1,* 187–192.

Freund, P. A. (Ed.). *Experimentation with human subjects.* New York: Braziller, 1969.

Gray, B. H. Institutional review boards as an instrument of assessment. *Science, Technology, and Human Values,* Fall 1978, 34–46.

Gray, B. H. *Human subjects in medical experimentation.* New York: Wiley Interscience, 1975.

Gray, B. H. Social research and the proposed DHEW regulations. *IRB: A Review of Human Subjects Research,* 1980, *2*(No. 1), 1–5.

Gray, B. H., & Cooke, R. A. The impact of institutional review boards on research. *Hasting Center Report,* 1980, *10*(No. 1), 36–41.

Gray, B. H., Cooke, R. A., & Tannenbaum, A. S. Research involving human subjects. *Science,* 1978, *201,* 1094–1101.

Grossman, M., & Morris, R. C., Jr. Emerging assets and liabilities of a committee on human welfare and experimentation. *New England Journal of Medicine,* 1970, *282,* 427–431.

Grotberg, E. *The role of federal agencies in the protection of children as research subjects.* Paper presented at the Rights of Children Conference at the University of Illinois, Champaign-Urbana, October 1976.

Hauerwas, S. Rights, duties, and experimentation on children: A critical response to Worsfold and Bartholome. In the National Commission for the Protection of Human Subjects of Biomedical and Behavioral Research (Eds.), *Appendix to report and recommendations on research involving children* [DHEW Publication (OS)77-0005]. Washington, D.C.: U.S. Government Printing Office, 1977.

Height, D. I., King, P., Louisell, D. W., Ryan, K. J., & Seldin, D. W. Deliberations and conclusions. In the National Commission for the Protection of Human Subjects of Biomedical and Behavioral Research (Eds.), *Report and recommendations on research involving children* [DHEW Publication (OS)77-0004]. Washington, D.C.: U.S. Government Printing Office, 1977.

Ivy, A. The history of the use of human subjects in medical experiments. *Science,* 1948, *108,* 1.

Katz, J. *Experimentation with human beings.* New York: Russell Sage, 1972.

Kiesler, S. B. Federal policies for research on children. *American Psychologist,* 1979, *34,* 1009–1016.

Klare, G. R. Measures of the readability of written communication: An evaluation. *Journal of Educational Psychology,* 1952, *43,* 385–399.

Lebacqz, K. Beyond respect for persons and beneficence: Justice in research. *IRB: A Review of Human Subjects Research,* 1980, *2*(No. 7), 1–4.

Levine, R. J. *The nature and definition of informed consent in various research settings.* Washington, D.C.: National Commission for the Protection of Human Subjects of Biomedical and Behavioral Research, 1975.

Levine, R. J. The institutional review board, 1976. In the National Commission for the Protection of Human Subjects of Biomedical and Behavioral Research (Eds.), *Appendix to report and recommendations: Institutional review boards* [DHEW Publication (OS)78-0009]. Washington, D.C.: U.S. Government Printing Office, 1978.

Lockhart, J. D. Pediatric drug testing: Is it a risk? *Hastings Center Report,* 1977, *7*(No. 3), 8–10.

Loftus, E. F., & Fries, J. F. Informed consent may be hazardous to health. *Science,* 1979, *204,* 11.

Lowe, C. U., Alexander, D., & Mishkin, B. Nontherapeutic research in children: An ethical dilemma. *Journal of Pediatrics,* 1974, *84,* 468–473.

McCartney, J. J. Research on children: National commission says "Yes, if . . ." *Hastings Center Report,* 1978, *8*(No. 5), 26–31.

McCormick, R. Experimentation on the fetus: Policy proposals, 1975. In the National Commission for the Protection of Human Subjects of Biomedical and Behavioral Research (Eds.), *Appendix: Research on the fetus* [DHEW Publication (OS)76–128]. Washington, D.C.: U.S. Government Printing Office, 1976.

McCormick, R. A. Experimentation in children: Sharing in sociality. *Hastings Center Report,* 1976, *6*(No. 6), 41–46.

MacIntyre, A. Regulation: A substitute for morality. *Hastings Center Report,* 1980, *10*(No. 1), 31–33.

Merriken v. Cressman, 364 F. Supp. 913 (E.D. Pa. 1973).

Michael, J. A., & Weinberger, J. A. Federal restrictions on educational research: Protection for research participants. *Educational Researcher,* 1977, *6*(No. 1), 3–7.

Milgram, S. Subject reactions: The neglected factor in the ethics of experimentation. *Hastings Center Report,* 1977, *1*(No. 5), 19–23.

Mosteller, F. Regulation of social research. *Science,* 1980, *208,* 1219.

Murray, T. H. Learning to deceive. *Hastings Center Report,* 1980, *10*(No. 2), 11–14.

National Bureau of Standards. *Administrative manual 3.01, appendix A.* Washington, D.C.: U.S. Department of Commerce, 1976.

National Commission for the Protection of Human Subjects of Biomedical and Behavioral Research (Eds.). *Report and recommendations: Research involving children* [DHEW Publication (OS)77-0004]. Washington, D.C.: U.S. Government Printing Office, 1977.

National Commission for the Protection of Human Subjects of Biomedical and Behavioral Research (Eds.). *Report and recommendations; Institutional review boards* [DHEW Publication (OS)78-0008]. Washington, D.C.: U.S. Government Printing Office, 1978.

National Institutes of Health, Department of Health, Education and Welfare. Protection of human subjects: Policies and procedures. *Federal Register,* 1973, *38,* 31738–31749.

National Minority Conference on Human Experimentation. Resolution and recommendations of the workshop on children, 1976. In the National Commission for the Protection of Human Subjects of Biomedical and Behavioral Research (Eds.), *Appendix to report and recommendations on research involving children* [DHEW Publication (OS)77-0005]. Washington, D.C.: U.S. Government Printing Office, 1977.

Pattullo, E. L. Who risks what in social research? *Hastings Center Report,* 1980, *10*(No. 2), 15–18.

Pocaro, E. T. Experimentation with children: The "pawns" of medical technology. *Medicolegal News,* 1979, *7,* 6–16.

Ramsey, P. *The patient as person.* New Haven: Yale University Press, 1970.

Ramsey, P. The enforcement of morals: Nontherapeutic research on children. *Hastings Center Report,* 1976, *6*(No. 4), 21–24.

Ramsey, P. Children on research subjects: A reply. *Hastings Center Report,* 1977, *7,* 40–41.

Reatig, N. DHHS internal policies for reviewing research involving children. *IRB: A Review of Human Subjects Research,* 1981, *3*(No. 1), 1–4.

Rosen, A. C., Rekers, G. A., & Bentler, P. M. Ethical issues in the treatment of children. *Journal of Social Issues,* 1978, *34*(No. 2), 122–136.

Rothkopf, E. Z., & Coatney, R. P. Effects of readability of context passages on subsequent inspection rates. *Journal of Applied Psychology,* 1974, *59,* 679–682.

Soble, A. Deception in social science research: Is informed consent possible? *Hastings Center Report,* 1978, *8*(No. 5), 40–46.

Society for Research in Child Development (Development Interest Group). *Ethical standards for research with children.* 1975.

Staff of the National Commission for the Protection of Human Subjects of Biomedical and Behavioral Reseach. Existing mechanisms for applying ethical guidelines to research involving human subjects. In the National Commission for the Protection of Human Subjects of Biomedical and Behavioral Research (Eds.), *Report and recommendations: Institutional review boards* [DHEW Publication (OS)78-0008]. Washington, D.C.: U.S. Government Printing Office, 1978.

Swazey, J. P. Professional protectionism rides again. *Hastings Center Report,* 1980, *10*(No. 2), 18–19.

Tannenbaum, A. S., & Cooke, R. A. Research involving children. In the National Commission for the Protection of Human Subjects of Biomedical and Behavioral Research (Eds.), *Appendix to report and recommendations on research involving children* [DHEW Publication (OS)77-0005]. Washington, D.C.: U.S. Government Printing Office, 1977.

Toulmin, S. Fetal experimentation: Moral issues and institutional controls, 1975. In the National Commission for the Protection of Human Subjects of Biomedical and Behavioral Research (Eds.), *Appendix: Research on the fetus* [DHEW Publication (OS)76-128]. Washington, D.C.: U.S. Government Printing Office, 1976.

Trials of war criminals before the Nuremberg military tribunals, U.S. v. Karl Brandt (Vol. 2). Washington, D.C.: U.S. Government Printing Office, 1949.

Turtle, R. H. Dissenting statement. In the National Commission for the Protection of Human Subjects of Biomedical and Behavioral Research (Eds.), *Report and recommendations on research involving children* [DHEW Publication (OS)77-0004]. Washington, D.C.: U.S. Government Printing Office, 1977.

Veatch, R. M. Ethical principles in medical experimentation. In A. M. Rulin & P. M. Timpane (Eds.), *Ethical and legal issues of social experimentation.* Washington, D.C.: Brookings Institution, 1975.

Veatch, R. M. Human experimentation committees: Professional or representative? *Hastings Center Report,* 1975, *5*(No. 5), 31–40.

Veatch, R. M. Three theories of informed consent: Philosophical foundations and policy implications. Paper prepared for the National Commission for the Protection of Human Subjects of Biomedical and Behavioral Research, February 1976.

Veterans Administration. V.A. issue M–3, chap. 1. Washington, D.C., 1975.

Wax, M. L. Field workers and research subjects: Who needs protection? *Hastings Center Report,* 1977, *7*(No. 4), 29–32.

World Medical Association. Declaration of Helsinki, 1964. In H. K. Beecher, *Research and the individual: Human studies.* Boston: Little, Brown, 1970.

Worsfold, V. L. A philosophical justification of children's rights. *Harvard Education Review,* 1974, *44*(No. 1), 29–44.

Infancy

PART TWO

11

Prenatal Influences
on Human Development

GERALD STECHLER
ANTONIA HALTON

The human fetus is closely linked to the mother through a myriad of connections that are necessary for the normal pattern of morphogenesis. These connections can also become the route by which disturbances in embryonic and fetal development can take place. From very early times interest in morphogenesis has been keen. The preformist vs. epigenetic controversy was one manifestation of the profound interest and curiosity in embryology. Legal and moral issues around the meaning of congenital anomalies and the fate of the bearers were another source of interest.

A rudimentary model of normal embryology, with a fascinating interactive hypothesis, is found in the Talmud.

What does an embryo resemble when it is in the bowels of its mother? Folded writing tablets.... Its head lies between its knees, its mouth is closed and its navel is open, and it eats what its mother eats and drinks what its mother drinks, but produces no excrements because otherwise it might kill its mother. As soon, however, as it went out to the air space of the world, the closed organ opens and the open one closes, for if that had not happened, the embryo could not live even one single hour. (*Niddah* 30b)

The risks of pregnancy for mother and child have been a source of concern throughout recorded history. In our time, shifts in life style, in medical knowledge, and in the quality of our environment have brought the issue of congenital hazards to the level of headline attention. Newer hazards such as radiation, obstetrical analgesia and anesthesia, and medications such as tranquilizers and hormones have joined older, longstanding hazards such as infectious illnesses, genetic and chromosomal deviations, and malnutrition. Another important factor has

been the increased sophistication and availability of special-care nurseries, so that babies born with marginal health status are more likely to survive. The chance of central nervous system (CNS) defects and ultimate behavioral problems is above average for these compromised infants. Furthermore the conditions of early postnatal life may be so aberrant because of these infants' medical needs that another layer of psychological insult is imposed.

PROSPECTIVE VERSUS RETROSPECTIVE STUDY DESIGNS

Our review highlights some of the classic and some of the more recent studies in selected risk areas. In some of the categories of research included, both prospective and retrospective studies are cited. At times the conclusions drawn from representative studies within each design category may be at variance with each other. Several factors can contribute to this variance of findings. The retrospective studies are usually done first for reasons of speed and economy in checking out an hypothesis. The slower, more expensive, longitudinal prospective study may then not confirm the strength of the relationship originally established through the retrospective studies. The prospective study may show a strong postnatal effect which dwindles with increasing age. In the retrospective design one starts with a base of poorly functioning older children, and so one does not encounter attenuation of effect related to increased age. One might expect that in a retrospective study the older the cohort the higher the correlation with early events, whereas exactly the opposite situation would prevail in a prospective study. Given a range of severity of damage at birth and the possibility of compensatory structural and functional mechanisms, this discrepancy is exactly what one would expect.

In the prospective studies, if the less severely damaged individuals are recovering or compensating, less of a residual effect will be seen on the whole for the initially at-risk group. In the retrospective study, if the same model applies, the subjects are likely to be the originally most severely damaged individuals and would therefore tend to implicate prenatal factors strongly as producing long-lasting trauma.

A prospective viewpoint of prenatal influences on development is likely to be organized around the agents which are known to increase risk to the fetus and neonate, while a retrospective viewpoint is likely to be organized around syndromes such as certain forms of mental retardation.

We are faced with a situation in which, even if we adhere to a linear causal model, each catalogued antecedent event may show up as one or more of a large array of outcome events. Conversely any given outcome event, seen singly or as part of a syndrome, may be the final common pathway of a large number of antecedent events. The nature of reality is such that both antecedent and consequent events occur in confounded clusters rendering almost impossible the teasing apart of elemental influences or outcomes.

LINEAR VERSUS ORGANISMIC
MODELS OF DEVELOPMENT

At another level the linear model of development is itself rejected as an inadequate approximation of the known self-organizing, self-regulating, and in some instances, self-correcting properties of a complex living system. Development, when viewed from the organismic, general systems theory platform, can in no way be approximated by stacking one brick on top of another or tracing a red thread through a labyrinth.

The profound difficulty we encounter is that we know that the general systems approach is a better approximation of developmental and life processes, but the systematic evidence that is available has been gathered almost completely via quasi-experimental methods and linear models of causality.

Sameroff and Chandler (1975) in a review of this area distinguish between linear and organismic models of development, clearly favoring the latter, and yet are reduced to the former in the detailed presentation of the evidence. There is a good chance that we will not be able to do much better, but we will struggle to move toward that goal where we can.

FACTORS INFLUENCING
INFERENCES ABOUT BEHAVIOR

Another problem we face in trying to unravel the behavioral or psychological effects of prenatal events is the nature of structure-function relationships in complex developing organisms. A congenital anomaly manifested in some external feature of the body will be noticed and recorded at birth and therefore is going to be the feature

most often associated with some prior toxic or stressful event. An internal anatomical feature if it grossly interferes with functioning, such as an esophageal atresia or a patent ductus, will also be picked up quickly and associated with antecedent events.

Behavior is much more amorphous, is most often not manifest until later in human development, and is related to a very large array of causal events. While the vast bulk of anatomical stuctures are formed prenatally, only the most rudimentary of behaviors appear during this period. Therefore this aspect of development of the individual is the most difficult to relate to prenatal factors. During gestation the embryo is developing quasi-behaviors vital to life, such as heartbeats. Other simple behaviors preparatory to postnatal life, such as sucking movements, swallowing, limb movements, and some sensory functions, are also in evidence (Hooker, 1952/1969; Humphrey, 1972). A few suggestive studies indicate that some shaping of intrauterine behaviors may be under environmental influence (Smith & Steinschneider, 1975; Spelt, 1948).

To help bridge the chasm between anatomy and behavior, certain propositions must be kept in mind, particularly since many of the studies to be cited are referenced with respect to physical anomalies and not behavior.

1. If a physical defect is noted, there may also be a behavioral effect even if it is not noted.
2. The behavioral effect may be direct, in the sense that some alteration of the CNS is part of the congenital anomaly syndrome, even if not easily observable.
3. The behavioral effect may be indirect, as in the case of thalidomide which, let us say for argument's sake, has no direct effect on the CNS. Thalidomide produces such gross anatomical defects that mother-infant relationships, other social relationships, self-image, and exploratory activities leading to cognitive functions are profoundly affected. In less obvious instances it may be almost impossible to differentiate between direct and indirect effects, as in the case of cerebral palsy.
4. The absence of an observable physical defect cannot rule out what may be profound behavioral effects—e.g., the biochemical lesion model of schizophrenia would not lead us to expect any anatomically observable stigma either early or later in life.
5. The CNS is so complex and so largely hidden from view that we must be particularly careful about not accepting null hypotheses. Perhaps more so than in any other field, a failure to show an observable outcome of an antecedent event may be more a function of our primitive methods than of the true absence of an effect.

HORMONES

Normal embryonic and fetal development includes the secretion of hormones by the fetus, and these hormones play an important role in the development of the reproductive organs. The process of differentiation into male or female fetus starts with a chromosomal difference in the fertilized ova. If testes develop, much of the further development appears to be strongly influenced by the hormones secreted by the testes.

The undifferentiated gonad, in the normal genetic male embryo, begins to develop into testes in the sixth and seventh weeks of gestation. This appears to be the one major step in the development of reproductive organs occurring prior to hormonal influence. In the female the ovary begins to differentiate much later, in the eleventh or twelfth week. The testes begin to secrete testosterone, which in a modified form influences the differentiation of the vas deferens, prostate, and seminal vesicle. The testes also secrete an inhibiting substance that prevents the development of Fallopian tubes, uterus, and vagina. If testosterone is not secreted, as in a normal female fetus, the male stuctures do not develop, and female reproductive tracts develop. They will develop even if an ovary is not present (Grumbach & Van Wyk, 1974).

Irregularities in the amount of testosterone (androgen) present during periods of fetal development will result in a variety of structural abnormalities. Too little androgen produces feminization of male fetuses because the female structures are not suppressed. Too much androgen produces masculinization of female fetuses, as in the adrenogenital syndrome where a fetus is exposed to excess androgen because of a malfunction in the adrenal system. The secretion of progesterone and estrogen by the ovaries does not seem to influence normal fetal development of internal and external female genitalia, but less is known about the prenatal function of these hormones at this time. It appears that external genitalia will develop in female form, except in those fetuses (male or female) where testosterone and other androgens are present early in development. The time differences in differentiation of sexual organs and the tendency for the fetus to develop as a female if left unstimulated by androgen thus allows for the development of hermaphrodites and individuals with partially male and partially female reproductive organs.

Fetuses are also exposed to synthetic hormones through treatments prescribed to prevent miscarriages, through hormone pregnancy tests, or through oral contraceptives. Such exposures are associated with cardiovascular defects (Heinonen, Slone, Monson, Hook, & Shapiro, 1977; Janerich, Marin, Dugan, Standfast, & Strite, 1977; Rothman, Fyler, Goldblatt, & Kreidberg, 1979) as well as abnormal development of sexual structures. Between 1945 and 1970 one particular synthetic estrogen, diethylstilbestrol (DES), was used extensively to maintain pregnancies in the early months when spontaneous abortions are frequent. Then a relationship between prenatal exposure to DES and malignant tissue growth in the offspring was detected. Some of the daughters of mothers given DES in early pregnancy developed clear-cell carcinoma of the vagina or cervix. In one study of 292 cases of this rare cancer, 182 were exposed to DES prenatally, 27 to an unknown drug, 7 to another hormone, and 75 were not exposed to any hormone (Herbst, Scully, Robboy, & Welch, 1978). Males exposed to DES prenatally also have abnormalities of the reproductive organs (Bibbo, Gill, & Azizi, 1977). A histologic autopsy study of the genital tracts of almost 300 stillborn and newborn females demonstrated that the effect of the hormone is present at birth. Abnormal vaginal cells were found in 70 percent of DES-exposed female neonates as contrasted with 4 percent of those who had not been exposed. The time of exposure and dosage were important: The likelihood of vaginal adenosis was highest when exposure was at 21 days gestational age or less, and when the dose was large (Johnson, Driscoll, Hertig, Cole, & Nickerson, 1979).

Although only a small number of the DES daughters actually develop cancer, the effects of their prenatal exposure have now manifested themselves in yet another way. Many of the DES-exposed daughters have now reached the childbearing age, and their pregnancies are significantly more likely to result in an unfavorable outcome than women who were not exposed to DES (Barnes et al., 1980). This is true for women whose mothers had a history of complicated pregnancies and for women whose mothers had no history of complicated pregnancies, indicating that it is probably not a genetic defect that the mother passed on to the daughter.

Not only do hormones influence the development of primary and secondary sex characteristics, but they also influence brain development and thus may affect the behavior of children (Money, 1973; Reinisch & Karow, 1977). For example, girls who have been exposed prenatally to an excess of male hormones—the adrenogenital syndrome—have been described as developing into "tomboys." They are physically energetic, active, and not interested in playing with dolls or identifying with Mommy (Money & Ehrhardt, 1972). At first it was suggested that androgen also influenced the higher-than-average intelligence of these girls, but Baker and Ehrhardt (1974) did a careful study using normal siblings as controls and found no evidence for an elevated IQ associated with the adrenogenital syndrome.

It should be noted that other factors aside from hormonal levels contribute to the gender development of human beings. The culture socializes the child from the moment of birth to behave like a boy or girl. As Money and colleagues have described (1972, 1973), in some cases where a mistake is made—for example a genetic female whose external sex organs lead others to raise her as a boy—the gender identity is harder to change than the anatomy. Such cases are often treated hormonally or surgically, e.g., preventing the "boy" from developing breasts by giving testosterone, while the psychological male identity is maintained or reinforced.

Prenatal exposure to progestins and estrogen has also been shown to affect the personality development of boys and girls, as measured by the Cattell Personality Questionnaires (Reinisch, 1977). Subjects exposed to progestin alone or in combination with varying amounts of estrogen were compared with unexposed siblings, and significant differences were found. Those who had been exposed to progestin alone or in combination with low doses of estrogen were more independent, individualistic, self-assured, and self-sufficient than their siblings. Those who had been exposed to more estrogen than progestin were significantly more group-oriented and group-dependent. No differences were found on intelligence tests.

Evidence of long-term effects of in utero exposure to progesterone is supplied by Dalton (1976). She found that a group of progesterone-exposed children were developmentally advanced at one year and throughout their school years had significantly better achievement records than the control groups. The greatest effects were manifested in those who were exposed early (in this study before the sixteenth week of gestation) and for a longer duration (more than eight weeks).

NUTRITION

Prenatal malnutrition is probably the most widespread of all potential hazards, yet it has been only sparsely studied in humans. Stein, Susser, Saenger, and Marolla (1975) conducted a retrospective study of males subjected to famine conditions while in utero during the Dutch hunger winter of 1944–1945. The pregnant women who were exposed to a level of famine postulated to cause prenatal nutritional deprivation were compared with a control group. When the food rations were most limited, the birthrate was quite low, with a rapid rise coming after the liberation. Babies who were born to the deprived mothers with the peak of the famine having occurred during the third trimester of their gestation had low birthweight and reduced head circumference. The mothers' own body weight and the weight of the placenta were also reduced. There was not as clear an effect on size if the famine coincided with the first trimester of gestation, although those babies did show a significant increase in deathrate during the first postnatal week. The third-trimester deprivation group did not show an elevated deathrate for that first postnatal week. Their elevated deathrate occurred between 7 and 89 days. The mental performance of the male survivors at age 19 showed no residual effects of the famine; however, sampling bias is likely to have eliminated severely retarded individuals.

Another World War II study (Antonov, 1947) stemming from the siege of Leningrad found no increase in congenital anomalies; but there was a high rate of premature births, and both stillbirths and neonatal deaths were more frequent than normal. We found no follow-up study of the survivors.

A few studies (Burke, Beal, Kirkwood, & Stuart, 1943; Burke & Stuart, 1948; Jeans, Smith, & Stearns, 1955) report lower birthweight and/or greater premature birth in children of malnourished mothers. No follow-up is reported.

In chronically malnourished populations, there is no doubt that the developmental potentiality of the children is compromised. This is considered to be one of the major health problems in the world today. It is possible and perhaps likely that prenatal malnutrition plays a significant role in this complex matter. However, in these poverty and disease-stricken areas of the world, the contribution of other prenatal, postnatal, physical, and psychological factors is so confounded with a variable such as prenatal malnutrition that there is little that can be said about that variable alone.

An example of a more recent and sharply defined attempt to assay the immediate effects of inferred prenatal malnutrition is a study (Bhatia, Katiyar, & Agarwal, 1979) in which the newborn's neuromotor behavior is the measured outcome. The inference of the intrauterine malnutrition was based on low hemoglobin and low serum albumin levels in the mothers and on a low maternal weight for height index. The weight of the babies, the weight of the placenta, and the placental protein content were all significantly below the values obtained for a normal control group. As a group, the undernourished babies were significantly more immature in neuromotor functioning than the controls.

Goggin, Holmes, Hassanein, and Lansky (1978) used the ponderal index, a ratio of weight to height, in the newborn to identify a group of babies with inferred intrauterine malnutrition. At birth they have little or no subcutaneous fat and appear malnourished. At follow-up well-baby visits up to one year of age, general developmental functions were compared with normal and obese babies. There were no differences found with respect to amount of motor activity, amount of exploratory behavior, and level of specific coordinated acts. The only significant difference was a greater amount of babbling in the malnourished group, which is difficult to interpret with respect to developmental norms.

The animal literature is replete with specific and general nutritional effects on fetal development (Hurley, 1977). The relatively weak findings in the human literature may in part be due to the overall paucity of studies; to the complexity of confounding factors, such as subsequent postnatal malnutrition; and to the poor control over, or even knowledge of, the complete prenatal nutritional history. Dobbing (1974) cautions against generalizing from animal models to human development because of differences in embryological patterns and differences in degree of brain maturation at birth.

SMOKING

In 1935 Sontag and Wallace first reported that the fetal heartrate rose as the mother smoked. Cigarette smoking by the pregnant woman has now been found to be related to a number of serious consequences for the fetus and neonate, including spontaneous abortion (Himmelberger, Brown, & Cohen, 1978; U.S. Department of Health, Education and Welfare, chap. 8, 1979), major congenital anomalies such as anencephaly (Evans, Newcombe, & Campbell, 1979), and an increased perinatal deathrate (Butler, Goldstein, & Ross, 1972; Hardy & Mellits, 1972; Naeye, 1978; Niswander & Gordon, 1972).

In an effort to determine what mechanisms are involved, some investigators recently drew blood samples every 2½ minutes from 8 pregnant smokers as they puffed through a straw for 10 minutes ("sham smoking") and then as they smoked 2 cigarettes for 10 minutes (Quigley, Sheehan, Wilkes, & Yen, 1979). Pulse rate and blood pressure were recorded continuously. The cigarette smoking produced a rapid rise in the women's pulse rate, blood pressure, and carboxyhemoglobin levels. Norepinephrine and epinephrine levels both rose significantly within 2½ minutes of the onset of cigarette smoking. After the women had smoked 7½ minutes, the fetal heartrate also rose significantly, and it continued rising to an average peak increase of 23 beats per minute at 17½ minutes after the onset of the women's cigarette smoking.

The investigators concluded that the fetus is deprived of oxygen in two ways. Nicotine causes maternal increases in epinephrine and norepinephrine, which produce vasoconstriction. The blood supply from the uterus to the placenta is thus reduced, producing a transient hypoxia. The increased carbon monoxide inhaled while smoking leads to a prolonged increase in carboxyhemoglobin levels in the mother. The average basal level for a nonsmoker ranges from 0.4 percent to 2.6 percent, whereas for a smoker it ranges from 2 percent to 14 percent. The higher levels of carboxyhemoglobin reduce oxygenation of the blood, producing a longlasting fetal hypoxia (Quigley et al., 1979).

The decrease in oxygen available during fetal development may lead to the brain abnormalities associated with smoking (Evans et al., 1979; Naeye, 1978) and to the frequent finding of reduced head circumference. Cleft lip and palate are also associated with maternal smoking during pregnancy (Ericson, Kallén, & Westerholm, 1979). Lower-than-average birthweight is consistently found for the newborn infants of smoking mothers. In the Collaborative Perinatal Project, a prospective study of more than 50,000 pregnant women, women who smoked more than 30 cigarettes per day had more than twice as many low birthweight babies as nonsmoking women (Niswander & Gordon, 1972). Lowered birthweight and reduced head circumference are in turn related to many other negative outcome variables, including high neonatal mortality rates and lower IQ at age 4 (Broman, Nichols, & Kennedy, 1975).

Smoking is also a risk factor for spontaneous abortion in the early months of pregnancy. A questionnaire study of 27,000 nurses and anesthetists found that the spontaneous abortion rate was significantly higher for smokers at all ages (Himmelberger et al., 1978).

Slight behavioral differences have been noted in apparently healthy newborn infants of smoking mothers. The infants cried more during a neonatal assessment than infants of nonsmoking women (Woodson, Woodson, Blurton-Jones, Pollock, & Evans, 1980); in another study they scored lower on autonomic regulation and orientation to an auditory stimulus, and they habituated faster to an auditory stimulus (Picone, Allen, Olsen, Schramm, & Ferris, 1980). These behavioral differences can influence the interactions between the neonate and its physical and social environment, possibly leading to further problems. Such behaviors may also be subtle signs of slight brain damage, which might manifest itself more clearly later.

Some long-term follow-up studies have explored the possibility of behavioral influences in intellectual development. A study of 17,000 British children revealed that children whose mothers had smoked during pregnancy were significantly shorter and scored significantly lower on reading tests (given at both ages 7 and 11) and tests of general ability (given at age 11) (Butler & Goldstein, 1973). The differences were small but consistent, and they held when other factors were taken into account in the statistical analysis, such as mother's age and height, social class, sex, and number of older and younger children in the household.

Another follow-up study found that infants of smokers were not different physically or cognitively than infants of nonsmokers, tested at 4 and 7 years of age (Hardy & Mellits, 1972). However their inner-city sample generally had low IQ scores; the mean scores for smoking and nonsmoking groups were 92 and 93. Lower socioeconomic status and its concomitants may have such an overwhelming influence on development that in its presence other factors become relatively unimportant.

Another serious behavioral problem related to smoking during pregnancy has been detected in the population of the Collaborative Perinatal Project. In this large prospective study, 125 infants died of sudden infant death syndrome (SIDS). This is an as yet unexplained syndrome in which an infant, usually under six months of age, dies during sleep. Presumably because of respiratory problems, the infant stops breathing, but there is no recognizable cause of death (Lipsitt, 1978). When the SIDS infants were matched with a control group (n = 375) for gestational age, sex, race, socioeconomic status (SES), place of birth, and date of delivery, one of the significant differences ($p < .001$) between the two groups was that 46 percent of the mothers of SIDS victims smoked more than six cigarettes per day and only 25 percent of the control group mothers smoked (Naeye, Ladis, & Drage, 1976).

Although infants with major congenital anomalies were excluded from this analysis, many of the SIDS infants had minor signs of abnormal functioning at the time of birth, including lower Apgar scores, respiratory difficulties, or problems with body temperature regulation. These frequently accompany lowered birthweight, which is another characteristic of the SIDS infants. After birth the SIDS infants often were found to be developing abnormally in areas such as bones, brain, and other organs. Naeye et al. (1976) suggest that this abnormal growth pattern is similar to that seen in laboratory studies of animals with chronic hypoxia.

ALCOHOL

In Biblical times they knew that alcohol was not healthy for the unborn child (Judges 13:7), but only recently has the medical world become aware of the numerous teratogenic effects of alcohol on the physical and mental development of the fetus. In their excellent review of the fetal alcohol syndrome, Clarren and Smith (1978) describe the four basic kinds of abnormalities that characterize children who have been exposed to alcohol in utero.

1. *Central nervous system dysfunctions:* including microcephaly, retardation, irritability in infancy, and hyperactivity in childhood.
2. *Growth deficiency:* smaller than normal both prenatally and postnatally in height and weight.
3. *Facial appearance:* short palpebral fissures, thin upper lip, undeveloped or absent philtrum, short nose, and so on.
4. *Variable major and minor anomalies:* malformations of the eyes, ears, and mouth, and cardiac murmurs, for example.

Alcohol has been shown to have a direct influence on the behavior of the fetus. A small group of pregnant women who were not heavy drinkers but drink occasionally were given an ounce of 80 proof vodka in a glass of diet ginger ale, while the control group drank only ginger ale. All the women were in their third trimester, between 37 and 39 weeks of gestation. The researchers recorded fetal breathing movements and maternal blood alcohol levels for 30 minutes before and 60 minutes after the women drank their drinks. Fetal breathing movements ceased in all subjects who drank alcohol, beginning anytime from 3 to 30 minutes after the alcohol was consumed. The apneic period lasted for more than half an hour in many of the fetuses. The blood alcohol level in the mothers was generally low, but nevertheless as it decreased, the percent of breathing movements by the fetus increased (Fox, Steinbrecher, Pessel, Inglis, Medvid, & Angel, 1978). It can be seen that fetal physiology is highly sensitive to even mild acute alcohol exposure. This could be one route to abnormal prenatal development.

Mental retardation has been documented by a number of researchers (e.g., Jones, Smith, Streissguth, & Myrianthopoulos, 1974; Shurygin, 1974). Clarren and Smith (1978) conclude that substantial evidence now points to the direct prenatal effect of alcohol on the fetal brain and that much of the mental retardation associated with maternal alcoholism is attributable to that cause. A study by Streissguth, Herman, and Smith (1978) found that those patients with more of the abnormalities characteristic of the fetal alcohol syndrome had lower IQ scores, suggesting that the alcohol had produced both. Jones et al. (1974) found that children of alcoholics raised by relatives or in foster homes had below-normal IQ scores at the age of 7. However, the mean score for those living with their chronic alcoholic mothers was 73, while those who were not with their mothers had a mean IQ of 84. Although this was not a statistically significant difference, we think that the higher scores may indicate the effect of postnatal factors on the total system.

Finally, neuropathological studies show structural alterations of the brains of infants who have been exposed prenatally. Certain similarities appear, such as failure or interruption in neuronal and glial migrations, although not necessarily in the same areas (Clarren & Smith, 1978). This may be the clearest unconfounded evidence for prenatal effects.

Alcohol may have its most severe effect on the fetus in the last trimester of pregnancy. During this period the fetal brain is developing cerebral convolutions and fissures, myelinization is beginning, and the rate of brain growth is greatest. If heavy drinkers are able to abstain or reduce their alcohol consumption throughout the third trimester, they give birth to significantly fewer infants below the tenth percentile in weight, length, and/or head circumference than women who continue to drink (Rosett, Weiner, Zuckerman, McKinlay, & Edelin, 1980). Rosett et al. found that 27 percent of the infants born to heavy drinkers had a head circumference below the tenth percentile, while only 4 percent of the infants whose mothers moderated their drinking in the third trimester were below the tenth percentile. In regard to birthweight, 45 percent were extremely low in weight, as compared to 8 percent for the infants of mothers who reduced their alcohol intake.

A study of almost 3500 embryos (obtained by abortion in the first trimester) found no evidence that malformations would be more likely to occur if the woman drank (Matsunaga & Shiota, 1980). This suggests that the effects of alcohol are more severe during the fetal period—the second and third trimesters.

Behavioral aftereffects, such as hyperactivity or learning difficulties, are not yet well documented. One retrospective study (Shaywitz, Cohen, & Shaywitz, 1980) finds that out of a group of 85 children referred for a range of learning disorders, 15 children (coming from 10 families) had histories of high prenatal exposure to alcohol. This is undoubtedly a higher percentage than would be found in a random population, but there is no adequate way of unconfounding the prenatal and postnatal

factors. The families of these children showed severe disruption with two maternal deaths, two current maternal hospitalizations, and five divorces.

This study, along with others (see Clarren & Smith, 1978), reports hyperactivity and associated learning problems. Many of the cases show the facial attributes of the fetal alcohol syndrome, but there has been no correlation of concomitant severity in the two domains, which if present would lend support to the prenatal hypothesis.

In addition many other risk factors are often present prenatally, such as malnutrition, smoking, or toxemia during the pregnancy. One epidemiologic study reported that the risk of a growth-retarded infant is doubled if the woman drinks or smokes; if she does both, the risk is quadrupled (Sokol, Miller, & Reed, 1980).

DRUGS

A seemingly harmless sedative, thalidomide, has become a classic example of the influence a foreign substance can have on the embryo, while the mother remains unharmed. The ingestion of the drug during a specific gestational period produces major deformities. When thalidomide is taken between 21 and 36 days after conception, the arms, legs, and ears of the embryo develop in a grossly deformed way. The dramatic increase in the number of infants born with these defects alerted physicians to the possibility of a teratogenic agent, and thalidomide was identified as being responsible. In many instances the influence of a particular drug, be it beneficial or harmful, is much less noticeable, if indeed it has any effect at all on the fetus.

The placenta was once believed to be a barrier that prevented many substances from entering the fetal circulatory system, but it is now known that any substance dissolved in the mother's blood plasma can pass into the fetus. The fetus may not be able to metabolize the drug or may respond to it differently than an adult.

The main protection afforded by the placenta is to slow the transfer of the substance, which thereby provides more time for the maternal organism to metabolize and excrete the substance before the concentration in the embryo or fetus becomes injurious. The results of several studies indicate that this might not be the case with psychoactive drugs. (Coyle, Wayner, & Singer, 1976, p. 192)

Drugs may interfere with normal prenatal development at any point in the process, from preventing ovulation, fertilization, or implantation to producing direct or indirect damage to the embryo or fetus. Some effects may not be apparent at birth, especially damage to the fetal brain which may contribute to defective or atypical behavior that emerges later in development.

Most pregnant women take a variety of drugs during their pregnancy, especially analgesics (such as aspirin), antibiotics, antinauseants, antihistamines, barbiturates, diuretics, caffeine, iron, and vitamins (Heinonen, Slone, Shapiro et al., 1977; Schardein, 1976). The number of drug products being used by pregnant women in the United States is steadily increasing. The data from the Collaborative Perinatal Project, covering more than 50,000 pregnancies, showed an increase from an average use of

2.6 drug products in 1958 to 4.5 in 1965, not including iron and most vitamins. In 1965, more than a third of all pregnant women in this study took from five to ten drug products, and many of these products contained a combination of drugs. As Heinonen et al. (1977) point out, a steady increase in drug use occurred despite the wide publicity being given the drug thalidomide and its teratogenic influence on fetal development in 1961 and 1962. However, they found no concurrent rise in the rate of birth defects during the years of the study, suggesting that many of these drugs do not influence the physical development of the fetus. From their extensive analyses Heinonen et al. (1977) reasoned that very few substances are teratogenic; many of the frequently used drugs, such as aspirin and antinauseants, seemed to be "reasonably safe." They concluded that "congenital anomalies can seldom be attributed predominantly to a single factor. Occasionally some overwhelming factor (e.g., rubella, thalidomide) can be identified, but it appears to be much more the rule that birth defects have a multifactorial etiology" (p. 419).

One problem with the data base in the Collaborative Perinatal Project is that two-thirds of the women registered for the study after the fourth month of pregnancy. Their drug use in the first trimester may not have been accurately recalled or recorded. Since the first six weeks are critical in evaluating the influence of some drugs, the unavailability of this information may have prevented some associations from being detected. Heinonen et al. (1977) failed to confirm a number of reports that had implicated specific drugs as causing birth defects when ingested in the first two months of pregnancy. A study of 19,000 pregnancies found that meprobamate and chlordiazepoxide (generic names for Miltown, Equanil, and Librium) caused serious congenital anomalies (Milkovich & van den Berg, 1974). In this study the health records from a comprehensive medical care plan (Kaiser-Permanente) were analyzed, so that drugs prescribed for women before they knew they were pregnant were included in the analysis. All the records of women who had been diagnosed as anxious were analyzed. If in the first 42 days of gestation meprobamate was taken, the rate of severe congenital anomalies was 12.1 per 100 live births; for chlordiazepoxide, the rate was 11.4; for other drugs, 4.6; and for no drug, 2.6. If a drug was first taken after 43 days of gestation, the rate of congenital anomalies was much lower, and not significantly higher for those women who took meprobamate and chlordiazepoxide. The fetal death rate was also quite high for these drugs; it was significantly higher for deaths before 20 weeks' gestation. One may wonder why such a clearcut association did not turn up in the Collaborative Perinatal Project's data. One reason may be methodological: The data on drug use in the first six weeks are not complete or accurate enough. In addition the women from the Kaiser-Permanente study live in one region of the country, and environmental factors specific to this locale may have contributed to the rate of anomalies. Although it is probably impossible to specify the network of influences that were acting upon these women, the evidence clearly points to a relationship between meprobamate or chlordiazepoxide and prenatal difficulties in this sample.

Other drugs that are found to be teratogenic include anticonvulsants given to epileptics (Lowe, 1973), anti-neoplastic drugs, such as chlorambucil and methotrexate; certain drugs given to diabetics, specifically tolbutamide and chlorpropamide; and some antibiotics, especially streptomycin and tetracycline (Howard & Hill, 1979). The diseases for which these drugs are prescribed may themselves be detrimental to embryonic and fetal development, but sometimes a choice of drugs is possible. For example with diabetic pregnant women, insulin does not appear to be as risky for the fetus as tolbutamide and chlorpropamide (Howard & Hill, 1979). The effects are often quite specific—e.g., procaine is associated with eye and ear malformations, tetracycline with stained teeth. The dose and duration of ingestion of the drug, the stage of development when the embryo or fetus is exposed to it, and the susceptibility of the individual to the drug are all factors that may influence the drug's effect. The changes in the system produced by any one drug may be ameliorated or exacerbated by other substances or factors acting concurrently on the system.

Excessively large intakes of specific substances have been associated with severe developmental problems—e.g., a woman taking 10 to 15 aspirin tablets daily during the first trimester, as well as smoking two packs of cigarettes per day, gave birth to a grossly deformed infant who lived only 1½ hours (Benawra, Mangurten, & Duffell, 1980). Salicylate has been shown to be teratogenic in animal studies but appears to be relatively harmless to the embryo when not used excessively. Tolbutamide and chlorpropamide when taken in large doses are associated with fetal death (Tuchman-Duplessis, 1975).

In addition to congenital malformations, drugs taken by the pregnant woman may cause behavioral abnormalities in the infant after birth. Both heroin and methadone are associated with retarded growth in utero. Postnatally many of these infants also exhibit withdrawal symptoms because they have become physiologically addicted to these drugs during gestation. The most frequent symptoms noted are hyperactivity, tremors, irritability, vomiting, fever, and a shrill cry. These symptoms may not appear until three or four days after birth (Zelson, 1973), after many newborns have been discharged from the hospital. This could account for the reports by some investigators that methadone does not produce severe withdrawal symptoms in the neonate.

A study comparing a group of 46 infants born to mothers maintained on methadone during pregnancy with a group of 45 infants born to mothers who took heroin found that both groups of infants exhibited severe withdrawal symptoms. In fact significantly more of the methadone babies had a larger number of withdrawal signs (Zelson, Lee, & Casalino, 1973).

Neonates with withdrawal symptoms are given chlorpromazine, phenobarbital, or some other tranquilizer, and if treated, the symptoms gradually disappear in the first months. However, the mothers may have a difficult time coping with the jittery, irritable behavior of the babies, especially because these mothers have so many problems of their own. Thus prenatal exposure to the drug influences the behavior of the newborn; that in turn will influence the interactions of the infant with its mother and also with its physical environment—with the infant's response to visual, auditory, and tactile stimuli. A follow-up study of black newborns found a significant difference between addicted and nonaddicted infants on the psychomotor score of the Bayley Scales of Infant Development at one year. Over the first year the psychomotor scores of addicted infants declined by 16 points, significantly more than for nonaddicted infants (Strauss, Starr, Ostrea, Chavez, & Stryker, 1976).

Another complication of prenatal addiction is that these infants are more likely to die from SIDS. One large study of more than 1000 infants, two-thirds born to addicted mothers, found a significant increased risk for SIDS (Chavez, Ostrea, Stryker, & Smialek, 1979). The SIDS infants were also significantly more likely to exhibit moderate-to-severe withdrawal symptoms in the neonatal period. Other investigators have also noted the increased risk for SIDS in prenatally addicted infants (Finnegan & Reeser, 1978; Rajegowda, Kandell, & Falciglia, 1976).

ENVIRONMENTAL HAZARDS

The environment in which a pregnant woman lives may present the developing embryo with challenging and even life-threatening conditions. Radiation can result in fetal death; produce major anomalies, especially microcephaly; and in surviving infants cause mental retardation (Murphy, 1929; Plummer, 1952; Yamazaki, Wright, & Wright, 1954). Chemicals that may have no harmful effects on adults have been found to cause birth defects and behavioral abnormalities in prenatally exposed organisms. Longitudinal animal studies have demonstrated that prenatal exposure to low levels of chemicals has a toxic effect on behavior, manifesting itself later in life, in the absence of conspicuous birth defects (Spyker, 1975).

For most environmental pollutants no documentation of toxicity to human embryos exists (Wilson & Fraser, 1977). One important exception is methyl mercury, inadvertently ingested by pregnant women who eat contaminated meat or fish. The exposed fetus suffers damage, especially to the nervous system, which manifests itself after birth by abnormal movements (tremor, nystagmus, chorea), convulsions, irritability, and an abnormal EEG pattern (Snyder, 1971). Another verified toxic chemical is hexachlorophene, which is associated with a high rate of severe congenital malformations when pregnant women wash their hands frequently with it (Halling, 1979).

Maternal fever during the early months of pregnancy has been reported to result in birth defects (Fraser & Skelton, 1978; Layde, Edmonds, & Erickson, 1980; Miller, Smith, & Shepard, 1978). However, these abnormalities may arise from the medication prescribed to treat the fever or from a virus causing the fever. An unusual environmental hazard reported by Miller et al. (1978) is exposure to a hot sauna, which may raise the body temperature. If this occurs during the third or fourth week of gestation, it may result in anencephaly.

ANOXIA

Perinatal brain damage appears to be a major determining factor in a large number of children showing substantial cerebral dysfunction (Benton, 1973; Strother, 1973). This includes major clinical syndromes, such as epilepsy (Amiel-Tison, 1969), cerebral palsy (Towbin, 1960), and some forms of mental retardation (Schreiber, 1939).

Knobloch and Pasamanick (1959) point out that in addition to the fetal and neonatal deaths caused by cerebral damage, there are sublethal insults "which give rise to a series of clinical neuro-psychiatric syndromes depending on the degree and location of the damage" (p. 1384).

Towbin (1978), reviewing a number of studies, points out a series of basic concepts which have emerged.

1. Hypoxia is the most common cause of damage to the brain of the fetus or neonate. There is a wide range of factors impinging upon the pregnant woman and fetus that have the final effect of reducing the oxygen supply to the fetal or neonatal central nervous system (CNS). Mechanically induced injuries to the infant's brain at delivery do indeed occur but are of less significance than hypoxia. The great range of other causal agents impacting on the fetal CNS such as genetic, metabolic, infectious, or toxic processes—some of which are discussed in this chapter—are much less frequently found in cases of neonatal neuropathology. Of all of the antecedents of neonatal brain damage, hypoxia is the most frequent cause.

2. The location of the damage in the brain is related to whether the insult occurs at term or earlier. In full-term babies the damage is most frequently found in the cerebral cortex. In premature fetuses and babies damage to deeper cerebral tissue is more common.

3. The timing of the damaging events is often removed by days or weeks from the moment of birth. Even when the delivery appears clinically uncomplicated, the hypoxic insult may have been developing "silently" for some period. Problems involving the placenta, whether premature detachment, infarction, or infection, if not causing death, may lead to a damaged brain through reduced oxygenation.

The most readily observable anoxic condition occurs immediately after birth. The newborn infant may fail to breathe spontaneously and thereby reduce oxygen to the brain. Apnea, the absence of respiratory movements, can be momentary or extend over many minutes. Newborns survive periods that would be fatal to adults, but they probably start to have measurable brain damage after about three minutes of apnea.

Retrospective studies as early as 1939 showed a strong relationship between mental retardation and anoxia at birth. Schreiber (1939) found that 70 percent of a group of mental retardates had such histories. This and other retrospective studies have been reviewed by Sameroff and Chandler (1975). They point out some of the serious methodological problems with this design including selective sampling, inadequate controls, and a questionable data base for the birth histories.

A "prospective-retrospective" design exemplified by the early studies of Darke (1944) and Preston (1945) seeks to overcome the selective bias by starting with birth records rather than a current cohort of malfunctioning children. Remaining for both of these studies is the problem of the unreliability of old records and inadequate or absent control groups.

This same basic design was used by Benaron, Tucker, Andrews, Boshes, Cohen, Fromm, and Yacorzynski

(1960). Starting from a very large sample of birth records (40,000 babies), 43 who had extremely long latencies to onset of respiration (12 minutes or greater) were identified. The age range at follow-up extended from 3 to 19 years. The IQ scores were lower than for matched controls, but some of the anoxic children scored higher than the controls, indicating that the deleterious effect is far from universal.

Prospective studies of the consequences of perinatal hypoxia point to a measurable effect lasting for several years. For periods of delayed resuscitation at birth lasting as little as three minutes, Stechler (1964a) reports generalized retardation of development that is measurable until age 1½. There is also a greater variability in test-retest scores among the hypoxic children as compared with normal children, which might indicate a greater emotional or state-dependent factor influencing their performance.

The child with the most prolonged apnea, 16 minutes, later had the highest developmental quotient (DQ) of the entire sample. This is similar to the variable outcome reported by Benaron et al. (1960) in their group of babies with extremely long resuscitation times.

Graham and colleagues began a large prospective study in the mid-1950s. They used broadly based outcome measures including perceptual-motor, neurological, and personality, to tap into later functioning. One of the important criticisms of earlier studies was that they were too dependent on IQ.

The examinations done during the newborn period showed that the babies who were anoxic were impaired on indices of maturation level, visual responsiveness, irritability, muscle tension, and pain threshold (Graham, Pennoyer, Caldwell, Greenman, & Hartman, 1957). The degree of impairment was related to a prognostic score which was in turn based on a composite of pre- and postnatal anoxia and the clinical assessment of CNS disturbance. Overall they found a correlation of .46 between the composite prognostic score and the composite of the five behavioral scales. An unfortunate aspect of this important research is that the assessment of the CNS status of the neonate was pooled with the pre- and postnatal anoxia estimates to arrive at the prognostic score. The CNS assessment contains some items, such as irritability, which are virtually identical with items on the behavioral scale. Thus instead of correlating data from two domains—that is, anoxia and behavior—there is an undetermined amount of intermixing of the two domains.

A follow-up study of these same children at age three (Graham, Ernhart, Thurston, & Craft, 1962) showed them to score lower than the controls on all of the tests of cognitive functions, but they did not score significantly lower on the perceptual-motor tests. There were more positive neurological findings in the anoxic group and some differences on the personality measures. Within the anoxic group virtually all of the contribution to later effects came from the children who had sustained the postnatal anoxia. The prenatal anoxic group did not differ from the controls.

There was a subsequent follow-up at seven years of age (Corah, Anthony, Painter, Stern, & Thurston, 1965). Only a scattering of significant differences remained, not enough to claim a measurable residual deficit.

The largest sample ever collected to study pre- and perinatal influences on development is contained in the Collaborative Perinatal Project. Broman et al. (1975) reported a follow-up at age 4 of over 25,000 cases. The Revised Stanford-Binet was administered. A number of variables correlated with the IQ of the children; among them were maternal IQ which, not surprisingly, was the most predictive of all variables. In this sample the failure to breathe spontaneously in the first two minutes after birth was predictive of lower IQ.

Although there are some prospective studies which report negative findings on the relationship between perinatal anoxia and later developmental measures (Fraser & Wilks, 1959; Usdin & Weil, 1952), the weight of evidence seems to point in the direction of a significant relationship which affects broad areas of cognitive functioning, as well as some areas of personality. The prospective studies point toward a lessened effect with increasing age. Given the nature of measurements of central tendencies, this could indicate that all subjects reduce their deficit with age or that a portion of the subjects show fairly dramatic improvements.

The growing concern about the long-range effects of intrapartum hypoxia has led to a widespread use of external and internal fetal monitoring devices, and a substantial increase in the rate of Cesarean sections. Predictably there has now been a reaction to possible damaging side effects of the internal fetal monitors—e.g., risks of scalp infection in the infant or subsequent maternal infection. Another concern is that undue alarm over fetal heartrate changes picked up by the monitoring device has led to an overuse of Cesarean section, with the known and unknown risks that may be attendant to that procedure. Fetal monitoring itself does not seem to account for the increase in Cesarean sections.

A Task Force on Predictors of Intrapartum Fetal Distress established by the National Institute of Child Health and Human Development recently reported on this issue (Zuspan, Quilligan, Iams, & van Geijn, 1979). They found that current estimates of intrapartum risks are less than earlier ones. The best estimate now is that 20 to 40 percent of cerebral palsy and 10 percent of severe mental retardation are accounted for by intrapartum events. They believe that current outcome measures are inadequate to assess the subclinical effects of intrapartum hypoxia. They also believe that fetal distress in labor cannot be assessed adequately by a single measure such as heartrate. Intervention in labor to alleviate fetal hypoxia requires careful consideration of a range of clinical and laboratory information.

ANESTHESIA AND ANALGESIA

The last hours during which the fetus is tied to the maternal circulatory and respiratory systems are critical ones for the survival of the infant. During these hours the fetus is often subjected to anesthesia or analgesia given to the mother to ease obstetrical pain. Childbirth practices aim to minimize the stress for both mother and child, by facilitating rapid access through the birth canal and thereby lessening the risks of suffocation or anoxia. However, many of the drugs cross the placenta and enter the fetal blood stream, producing a depressed state in the newborn.

Many basic functions of the newborn infant have been shown to be influenced by anesthesia or analgesia used in childbirth. Visual attention (Stechler, 1964b), sucking (Kron, Stein, & Goddard, 1966), first day of weight gain (Brazelton, 1961), smiling (Emde & Koenig, 1969), irritability and motor movements (Standley, Soule, Copans, & Duchowny, 1974), and orientation (Tronick, Wise, Als, Adamson, Scanlon, & Brazelton, 1976) are all negatively influenced by anesthesia, barbiturates, narcotics, or other analgesics. As with any other drug, dosage and timing of ingestion are critical variables affecting the result, and those studies finding little or no drug effects on the neonate's behavior (e.g., Horowitz, Ashton, Culp, Gaddis, Levin, & Reichmann, 1977; Tronick et al., 1976) usually note that their sample received light levels of medication. In addition the Tronick study excluded infants with Apgar scores less than seven, which may have eliminated some of the newborns who were most affected by obstetric medication.

Recently a number of studies document the depressed state of neonates whose mothers have been given meperidine (e.g., Demerol) during labor (Brackbill, Kane, Manniello, & Abramson, 1974; Hodgkinson, Bhatt, Grewal, & Marx, 1978). Neurobehavioral responses remain depressed for at least two days. Hodgkinson et al. (1978) found that naloxone, injected into the mother shortly before delivery, counteracts the effects of meperidine in lowering the neonate's response, but the effects of naloxone appear to be quite transitory. By 24 hours after birth, those newborns experiencing both meperidine and naloxone score significantly lower on pinprick responses, rooting, sucking, and response to sound than the no-narcotics group. Incidentally all of the infants in this study were delivered under general anesthesia as well.

Epidural anesthesia has also been shown to reduce the newborn's responsiveness, especially motor abilities (such as head control while being pulled to sitting), muscle tone, rooting, and the Moro reflex (Scanlon, Brown, Weiss, & Alper, 1974). The babies were tested during the first eight hours of life, and so the duration of the effects is indeterminate. Some investigators claim that the effects of obstetric medication persist for longer periods of time, although the influences on behavior have not been shown to be dramatic (Aleksandrowicz & Aleksandrowicz, 1974; Brackbill, 1977).

Because of the prodigious and diverse number of factors that also contribute to the development of the individual and because we may look at the wrong variables when trying to detect long-term effects, it is not surprising that few are discovered. However, neonates who are not very responsive and tend to be irritable will interact with their mothers and other aspects of their environment in a less alert way than the normal undrugged newborn. Thus mother-neonate interaction will be different in the first days of life. A study of mother-neonate interaction with three-day-olds found that the infants whose mothers received more medication had their eyes open significantly less often during the feeding observation (Brown, Bakeman, Snyder, Fredrickson, Morgan, & Hepler, 1975). These infants also were less responsive to auditory stimulation. The feedback provided by mother to the baby and by baby to the mother creates a continuing transactional process so that events in the

first days of life may have enduring influence on development.

Long-Term Exposure to Anesthesia. Anesthesia has also been shown to be an environmental hazard affecting prenatal development. Women who are frequently exposed to anesthesia (anesthetists in operating rooms) have difficulties in pregnancy. Women have an increased risk of abortion and congenital malformations, and the wives of men who are exposed also have an increased risk of reproductive problems (Tuchman-Duplessis, 1975).

EMOTIONAL STRESS

The influence of maternal emotions on the developing fetus is even more difficult to evaluate than other factors. As we have seen, the determination of the influence of any one specific factor is nearly always tentative because of the enormous number of factors impinging on the mother-fetus system. The subjective nature of emotions and the unlikelihood of their being recorded further complicate the methodology in this area of prenatal influences. However, several retrospective studies have used the occurrence during pregnancy of objectively stressful events and have found a significant association between these events and pre- or postnatal abnormalities. It has been suggested that maternal emotional stress can result in Down's syndrome (Drillien & Wilkinson, 1964), infantile pyloric stenosis (Revill & Dodge, 1978), and behavior problems in children (Stott & Latchford, 1976). Prospective studies have related subjective maternal anxiety during pregnancy with neonatal irritability (Ottinger & Simmons, 1964), with neonatal behavioral "deviance" (Ferreira, 1960), and with use of anesthesia during childbirth and neonatal motor maturity—two variables which are themselves related (Standley, Soule, & Copans, 1979). Most recently it has been reported that during childbirth the presence of a supportive companion significantly reduced length of labor and the signs of fetal distress such as meconium staining (Sosa, Kennell, Klaus, Robertson, & Urrutia, 1980).

The mechanisms by which these influences could be transmitted include chemical and endocrine disturbances that may damage chromosomes or alter the mother's physiology in ways that are detrimental to the developing fetus. A stressful situation stimulates the production of adrenaline (epinephrine) in the mother, causing her blood flow to be diverted from the uterus to other organs in her body. A drop in circulating blood to the placenta may result in a deficient supply of oxygen to the fetus.

Some cases of Down's syndrome appear to be related to severe emotional stress of several months' duration, usually originating before conception and present in the first trimester. A study of over 200 children with IQ's under 60 compared the incidence of such stress in a group of mothers of children with Down's syndrome and a group of mothers whose retarded children had no evidence of Down's. More than a third of the Down's mothers reported events believed to be severely stressful that occurred in early pregnancy, while only 13 percent of the mothers of other mental defectives reported such stress. This was true for mothers under 29 as well as over 39, although the incidence of Down's was considerably greater in the older women (Drillien & Wilkinson, 1964). This study replicates a report by Stott (1961) that also implicated stress as a risk factor for Down's syndrome.

Another structural defect that has been attributed to emotional stress is infantile pyloric stenosis. This congenital condition involves a tightening of the stomach outlet due to an enlarged muscle; it is treated surgically. A Life Events Inventory Checklist was given to 100 mothers of infants with pyloric stenosis, as well as to normal and spina bifida control groups (Revill & Dodge, 1978). The life events are weighted in terms of amount of stress they are likely to produce (Cochrane & Robertson, 1973).

The mean number of weighted events occurring during pregnancy was significantly greater for the mothers of infants with pyloric stenosis than for either of the control groups. During the last trimester, mothers of infants with pyloric stenosis experienced almost four times as many weighted events as the normal control group.

One of the most extensive studies of prenatal antecedents for behavioral problems and chronic ill-health in children was conducted by Stott and Latchford (1976). They interviewed 1300 mothers, asking for factual information about events that occurred during the pregnancy, as well as obtaining a history of the child from birth to five years. They selected 63 birth and postnatal child variables to represent morbidity, including reports of neonatal respiratory difficulty, vomiting, bronchitis (examples of physical health), immature speech, bedwetting at 5 years of age (habit disorder), and "would never settle at anything long, soon lost interest in new toy or game" (behavior disturbance). Then for each of 150 prenatal variables, Stott and Latchford determined the presence or absence of the child morbidity variables. They found suggestive relationships among many of the pre- and postnatal variables.

Marital discord during the pregnancy, fears about the marriage, moving to a new locality, own father becoming ill or dying, unwanted pregnancy, smoking during pregnancy, acute gastrointestinal symptoms, respiratory infections, and collapsing and fainting during pregnancy all were strongly associated with child morbidity. Prenatal events such as experiencing a burn, fall, or painful medical treatment, being lonely because husband was absent, and witnessing an accident were not related to child morbidity.

However, many of the prenatal conditions that were found to be associated with the child's health and behavior may have continued to influence the child's environment postnatally, so that one cannot conclude that the etiology of the children's problems is congenital.

An example of an attempt to unconfound the prenatal and postnatal influences is an epidemiologic study in Finland of loss of father (Huttunen & Niskanen, 1978). Families in which the husband died during the prenatal period were compared with a control group of families in which the husband died during the first year of the child's life. A significantly higher incidence of psychiatric and behavior disorders was found for the children whose father died during their prenatal period. No significant difference was found for pregnancy and birth complications for the two groups. In a specific subgroup made up of the subjects with psychiatric disturbances, those in the control group (n = 7) had a high frequency of birth and

pregnancy complications, whereas the psychiatric cases in the prenatal-loss group (n = 16) had a significantly lower mean score for pregnancy and birth complications. Once again this suggests the possibility that a variety of physical and emotional stresses can lead to a similar outcome. Of course a possible confounding element remains in this study, because as the authors themselves say, the early interactions between the newborn infant and its recently widowed mother may be "disordered" (Huttunen & Niskanen, 1978).

Several studies have used neonatal assessments in an attempt to distinguish between the mother's postnatal influence on her infant and the prenatal anxiety that may have influenced fetal development. One prospective study gave expectant mothers the IPAT anxiety scale during pregnancy and then selected two groups composed of the highest and lowest scorers. Crying of their newborn infants was recorded for 30 minutes before and after each feeding on the second to fourth days of life. Infants of high-anxiety mothers cried significantly more than low-anxiety mothers before feedings, but after feedings the amount of crying, which was low for both groups, did not differ (Ottinger & Simmons, 1964). The authors believe that because the two groups of infants were not different in crying after feedings, the excessive preprandial crying by the infants of high-anxiety mothers was not due to the mothers' handling during the feedings.

There is another way to explain the results in this study. The infants of anxious mothers may have been temporarily satisfied by a feeding that was only partly successful, and so they did not cry much after feeding. Although these infants go back to sleep, it is possible that they wake up earlier than the infants of low-anxiety mothers, resulting in more preprandial crying. The postnatal anxiety of the mother may have produced the effect rather than her prenatal anxiety. It is unfortunate that the feedings were not observed and rated to provide some information about the mothers' actual behavior.

Another prospective study found a relationship between the mother's fear of harming the baby, determined in the last month of the pregnancy, and the infant's behavior in the first five days of life (Ferreira, 1960). Infants rated by nurses as being deviant had mothers who scored significantly higher on this measure of anxiety. Ferreira's suggestion that the deviant behavior is not the result of the mothers' handling is based in part on his failure to find an increase in the number of babies judged deviant over the five-day period.

Standley et al. (1979) followed the first pregnancies of a group of women and using questionnaires and interviews rated the anxiety level of the mothers during the last month of pregnancy. Maternal anxiety was correlated with a higher use of local and regional anesthesia during childbirth and with the infant's motor maturity on a neonatal assessment. In this case the somewhat depressed behavior of the anxious mother's newborn infant may be the result of being subjected to more anesthesia. The study restricted its sample to uncomplicated pregnancies and may thereby have eliminated other relationships between prenatal maternal anxiety and infant outcome.

A striking example of such an effect is reported by Sosa et al. (1980), who studied the childbirth experiences of a group of healthy women in Guatemala. Hospital routine prohibited any relative or friend of the expectant mother to be present on the maternity ward. The study randomly assigned a supportive companion to some of the mothers as they were admitted to the maternity unit, and this untrained woman stayed with them until the delivery, talking to them, rubbing their backs, and holding their hands. The women provided with this emotional support experienced significantly fewer problems during childbirth (e.g., fewer Cesarean sections or less use of oxytocin), and their newborn infants were less likely to experience fetal distress, such as that indicated by meconium staining. Mothers and infants who experienced these complications or interventions were then excluded from the study, and it was necessary to admit more than three times as many women to the control group to obtain equal numbers in each group. In the final sample of uncomplicated pregnancies, the group of women who had a supportive companion delivered their infants in significantly less time than the control group (who had no supportive companion). The mean length of labor was 19.3 hours for the control group and 8.7 hours for the experimental (and presumably less anxious) group.

CONCLUSIONS

The perspective one gains concerning prenatal influences on later development is very much shaped by the model or models of development that are implicit in one's thinking. The simplest kind of cause-effect model assumes that some discrete event, such as the ingestion of a toxic substance, can produce a definable lesion in the fetal brain—the size and location of the lesion depending on the nature of the toxin, the amount taken in, and its gestational timing. Once the lesion has been created, a specific behavioral effect can be expected relative to the kind of behavior that is under the control of that portion of the brain which sustained the lesion.

In reality the situation is dramatically more complicated, and that complexity has made the sorting out of cause-effect relationships an incredibly difficult task. Occasionally, as in the oft-cited thalidomide example, the outcome effects are so prominent and clearcut and the causal agents so specific and unconfounded, that identification and removal of the offending agent is a relatively straightforward matter. More often than not the causal events are multiple and interact with each other in complex and undefined ways. For instance maternal alcoholism is rarely an isolated event. It often coexists with other health hazards such as poor nutrition, tobacco smoking, emotional stress, and perhaps the use of other drugs. The health status of the father may complicate the situation to an as yet unknown degree. Furthermore the causal agents do not occur only once during pregnancy but are often a chronic condition. An additional factor is the possibility of secondarily triggered events such as more complicated labor and delivery, each adding its own measure of risk.

Finally, the continuum of risk is extended into the postnatal environment via the mother-child interaction and the general environmental conditions. The variability introduced by this enormous range of factors is usually treated as error variance in most studies of prenatal influence. Yet to the extent that the postnatal environment consists of factors which are correlated with the prenatal risk, such as the family life style which spans the pre- and postnatal period, it is not simply a source of error but a source of confounding and confusion.

Beyond all of these considerations is the recognition that a complex developing system, not just a dynamically balanced organism, is being influenced. The developmental concept implies *organized radical change*. It implies that as new organs, functions, and systems emerge during the pre- and postnatal epochs, nonlinear transformations are taking place. It implies that the relative continuity or discontinuity of elements across organizational levels is not a simple quantitative relationship, that effects do not merely grow stronger or weaker with the passage of time but can alter the very manner by which they operate.

No single or comprehensive model is available by which to understand these complexities. Certain principles have been known for a long while—e.g., it is during the period of most rapid growth and differentiation of a system or organ that it is most vulnerable to insult. This is best understood by noting that incorporation of elements from the surround is most rapid at these times, so that the presence of toxic substances or the lack of nutrients is most influential.

This version of a sensitive-phase hypothesis is preferable to one which relies mainly on the idea of residual plasticity. The latter notion, if applied too broadly, leads to the untenable idea that the earlier an insulting event occurs the less will be its long-range effect, because the residual plasticity of the system will allow for greater compensation. A model of dynamic embryology takes compensatory actions into account, but that is by no means the only principle operating.

One of the curiosities of our thinking within psychology is that we may keep contradictory hypotheses side by side. Some of our models imply that early events are the least influential in the long run, while others imply that early events are most influential. No single or simple answer will suffice. We lack both sufficient empirical knowledge as well as adequate models of how complex self-organizing systems operate.

We need truly developmental models, ones which at their core have mechanisms of organized radical change. The homeostatic mechanisms must be well represented within the models as must the mechanisms of readjustment to external shifts, because without these life cannot be maintained. However, neither of these sets of mechanisms can form the basis for explaining development. Development is a departure from these cybernetic stabilization functions. Development is the process of maintaining organization while at the same time radically altering it.

It is only when substantial progress has been made in these directions that clear answers to the questions about the long-term consequences of prenatal events can be found. With such models we will be able to plot how earlier epochs influence continuity across the boundaries of major qualitative reorganizations. Then prediction, in prospective studies, can advance beyond an actuarial, gross correlational design.

It is the nature of self-organizing systems (Prigogine, 1978) that they cannot be understood deterministically on the basis of their prior states or on the basis of current input-output relationships (Maturana & Varela, 1980). Nevertheless with sufficiently detailed data they can be modeled, and the shaping influence of new interactions as well as initial state conditions can be incorporated into a developmental approach.

On a more pragmatic level, one of the major goals of trying to establish antecedent-consequent relationships around prenatal events is to reduce the risk to the pregnant woman and the fetus. As certain environmental hazards, medical procedures, eating, drinking, and smoking habits have been identified as related to birth or developmental defects, steps have been taken to reduce those risk factors. The reduction of analgesia and anesthesia during labor and delivery, special labeling procedures regarding the unsafe or untested nature of certain medications in relation to pregnancy, and an attempt to upgrade prenatal and perinatal care have all been prominent over the past 20 years.

Infant mortality figures represent far more than the influence of prenatal events. Even healthy newborns are at risk during the first postnatal year depending on rudimentary aspects of sanitation, nutrition, and medical care. Thus comparative infant mortality figures for different countries are not meant here to be an indicator of relative prenatal risks but only as a convenient and available index of the range of support for maternal-infant health in various locales. For 1974 the under-one-year deaths per 1000 live births ranged, among the countries reporting, from a low of 9.6 in Sweden to a high of 115.5 for the black population of South Africa (*Demographic Yearbook*, 1979). Between 1974 and 1977 the United States showed a steady decline in infant mortality from 16.7 to 14.0, but the 1977 figure is still far behind Sweden's 8.0 or Japan's 8.9 for that year.

Some of the hazards to maternal-fetal-infant health are poorly understood and therefore almost impossible to control; some are fairly well understood but for economic, political, or cultural reasons have been difficult to control. Others have yielded with remarkable rapidity. Research to enlarge the understanding of hazards and medical-political action to reduce the risk from known hazards must be taken. Such work may be one of the hallmarks of the civilized quality of a society.

REFERENCES

ALEKSANDROWICZ, M. K., & ALEKSANDROWICZ, D. R. Obstetrical pain-relieving drugs as predictors of infant behavior variability. *Child Development*, 1974, *45*, 935–945.

AMIEL-TISON, C. Cerebral damage in full-term newborn, aetiological factors, neonatal status and long-term follow-up. *Biology of the Neonate*, 1969, *14*, 234–250.

ANTONOV, A. N. Children born during the siege of Leningrad in 1942. *Journal of Pediatrics*, 1947, *30*, 250.

BAKER, S. W., & EHRHARDT, A. A. Prenatal androgen, intelligence, and cognitive sex differences. In R. C. Friedman, R. M. Richart, & R. L. Vande Wiele (Eds.), *Sex differences in behavior.* New York: John Wiley, 1974.

BARNES, A. B., COLTON, T., GUNDERSEN, J., NOLLER, K. L., TILLEY, B. C., STRAMA, T., TOWNSEND, D. E., HATAB, P., & O'BRIEN, P. C. Letter. *New England Journal of Medicine*, 1980, *303*(No. 5), 281.

BENARON, H. B. W., TUCKER, B. E., ANDREWS, J. P., BOSHES, B., COHEN, J., FROMM, E., & YACORZYNSKI, G. K. Effects of anoxia during labor and immediately after birth on the subsequent development of the child. *American Journal of Obstetrics and Gynecology*, 1960, *80*, 1129–1142.

BENAWRA, R., MANGURTEN, H. H., & DUFFELL, D. R. Cyclopia and other anomalies following maternal ingestion of salicylates. *Journal of Pediatrics*, 1980, *96*, 1069–1071.

BENTON, A. L. Minimal brain dysfunction from a neuro-psychological point of view. In F. F. de la Cruz, B. H. Fox, & R. H. Roberts (Eds.), *Minimal brain dysfunction* (Annals of the New York Academy of Science, Vol. 205) New York: Scholarly Reprints, 1973.

BHATIA, V. P., KATIYAR, G. P., & AGARWAL, K. N. Effect of intrauterine nutritional deprivation on neuromotor behaviour of the newborn. *Acta Paediatrica Scandinavia*, 1979, *68*, 561–566.

BIBBO, M., GILL, W., & AZIZI, F. Follow-up study of male and female offspring of DES-exposed mothers. *Obstetrics and Gynecology*, 1977, *49*, 1.

BRACKBILL, Y. Long-term effects of obstetrical anesthesia on infant autonomic function. *Developmental Psychobiology*, 1977, *10*, 529–535.

BRACKBILL, Y., KANE, J., MANNIELLO, R. L., & ABRAMSON, D. Obstetric meperidine usage and assessment of neonatal status. *Anesthesiology*, 1974, *40*, 116–120.

BRAZELTON, T. B. Psychophysiologic reaction in the neonate, II: The effects of maternal medication on the neonate and his behavior. *Journal of Pediatrics*, 1961, *58*, 513–518.

BROMAN, S. H., NICHOLS, P. L., & KENNEDY, W. A. *Preschool IQ: Prenatal and early developmental correlates.* Hillsdale, N.J.: Lawrence Erlbaum Associates, 1975.

BROWN, J., BAKEMAN, R., SNYDER, P. A., FREDRICKSON, W. T., MORGAN, S. T., & HEPLER, R. Interactions of black inner-city mothers with their newborn infants. *Child Development*, 1975, *46*, 677–686.

BURKE, B. S., BEAL, V. S., KIRKWOOD, S. B., & STUART, H. C. The influence of nutrition during pregnancy upon the conditions of the infant at birth. *Journal of Nutrition*, 1943, *26*, 569–583.

BURKE, B. S., & STUART, H. C. Nutritional requirements during pregnancy and lactation. *Journal of the American Medical Association*, 1948, *137*, 119–128.

BUTLER, N. R., & GOLDSTEIN, H. Smoking in pregnancy and subsequent child development. *British Medical Journal*, 1973, *4*, 573–575.

BUTLER, N. R., GOLDSTEIN, H., & ROSS, E. M. Cigarette smoking in pregnancy: Its influence on birth weight and perinatal mortality. *British Medical Journal*, 1972, *2*, 127–130.

CHAVEZ, C. J., OSTREA, E. M., STRYKER, J. C., & SMIALEK, Z. Sudden infant death syndrome among infants of drug-dependent mothers. *Journal of Pediatrics*, 1979, *95*, 407–409.

CLARREN, S. K., & SMITH, D. W. The fetal alcohol syndrome. *New England Journal of Medicine*, 1978, *298*, 1063–1067.

COCHRANE, R., & ROBERTSON, A. The life events inventory: A measure of the relative severity of psychosocial stresses. *Journal of Psychosomatic Research*, 1973, *17*, 135–139.

CORAH, N. L., ANTHONY, E. J., PAINTER, P., STERN, J. A., & THURSTON, D. L. Effects of perinatal anoxia after seven years. *Psychological Monographs*, 1965, *79* (Whole No. 596), 3.

COYLE, I., WAYNER, M. J., & SINGER, G. Behavioral teratogenesis: A critical evaluation. *Pharmacology, Biochemistry & Behavior*, 1976, *4*, 191–200.

DALTON, K. Prenatal progesterone and educational attainment. *British Journal of Psychiatry*, 1976, *129*, 438–442.

DARKE, R. A. Late effect of severe asphyxia neonatorum. *Journal of Pediatrics*, 1944, *24*, 148–158.

Demographic Yearbook 1978. United Nations Statistical Office. New York: U.N., 1979.

DOBBING, J. Prenatal nutrition and neurological development. In J. Cravioto, L. Hambraeus, & B. Vahlquist (Eds.), *Early malnutrition and mental development.* Uppsala, Sweden: Almquist & Wiksell, 1974.

DRILLIEN, C. M., & WILKINSON, E. M. Emotional stress and mongoloid births. *Developmental Medicine and Child Neurology*, 1964, *6*, 140–143.

EMDE, R. N., & KOENIG, K. L. Neonatal smiling and rapid eye movement states. *Journal of the American Academy of Child Psychiatry*, 1969, *8*, 57–67.

ERICSON, A., KALLÉN, B., & WESTERHOLM, P. Cigarette smoking as an etiologic factor in cleft lip and palate. *American Journal of Obstetrics and Gynecology*, 1979, *35*, 348–351.

EVANS, D. R., NEWCOMBE, R. G., & CAMPBELL, H. Maternal

smoking habits and congenital malformations: A population study. *British Medical Journal*, 1979, *2*, 171–173.

FERREIRA, A. J. The pregnant mother's emotional attitude and its reflection upon the newborn. *American Journal of Orthopsychiatry*, 1960, *30*, 553–561.

FINNEGAN, L. P., & REESER, D. S. The incidence of sudden death in infants born to women maintained on methadone. *Pediatric Research*, 1978, *12*, 405.

FOX, H. E., STEINBRECHER, M., PESSEL, D., INGLIS, J., MEDVID, L., & ANGEL, E. Maternal ethanol ingestion and the occurrence of human fetal breathing movements. *American Journal of Obstetrics and Gynecology*, 1978, *132*, 354–358.

FRASER, F. C., & SKELTON, J. Possible teratogenicity of maternal fever. Letter. *Lancet*, 1978, *2*, 634.

FRASER, M. S., & WILKS, J. The residual effects of neonatal asphyxia. *Journal of Obstetrics and Gynecology of the British Commonwealth*, 1959, *66*, 748–752.

GOGGIN, J. E., HOLMES, G. E., HASSANEIN, K., & LANSKY, S. B. Observations of postnatal developmental activity in infants with fetal malnutrition. *Journal of Genetic Psychology*, 1978, *132*, 247–253.

GRAHAM, F. K., ERNHART, C. B., THURSTON, D. L., & CRAFT, M. Development three years after perinatal anoxia and other potentially damaging newborn experiences. *Psychological Monographs*, 1962, *76* (Whole No. 522), 3.

GRAHAM, F. K., PENNOYER, M. M., CALDWELL, B. M., GREENMAN, M., & HARTMAN, A. F. Relationship between clinical status and behavior test performance in a newborn group with histories suggesting anoxia. *Journal of Pediatrics*, 1957, *50*, 177–189.

GRUMBACH, M. M., & VAN WYK, J. J. Disorders of sex differentiation. In R. H. Williams (Ed.), *Textbook of endocrinology* (5th ed.). Philadelphia: Saunders, 1974.

HALLING, H. Suspected link between exposure to hexachlorophene and malformed infants. *Annals of the New York Academy of Sciences*, 1979, *320*, 426–435.

HARDY, J. M., & MELLITS, D. E. Does maternal smoking during pregnancy have a long-term effect on the child? *Lancet*, 1972, *2*, 1332–1336.

HEINONEN, O. P., SLONE, D., MONSON, R. R., HOOK, E. B., & SHAPIRO, S. Cardiovascular birth defects and antenatal exposure to female sex hormones. *New England Journal of Medicine*, 1977, *296*, 67–70.

HEINONEN, O. P., SLONE, D., SHAPIRO, S., GAETANA, L. F., HARTZ, S. C., MITCHELL, A. A., MONSON, R. R., ROSENBERG, L., SISKIND, V., & KAUFMAN, D. W. *Birth defects and drugs in pregnancy*. Littleton, Mass.: PSG Pub., 1977.

HERBST, A. L., SCULLY, R. E., ROBBOY, S. J., & WELCH, W. R. Complications of prenatal therapy with diethylstilbestrol. *Pediatrics*, 1978, *62*, 1151–1159.

HIMMELBERGER, D. V., BROWN, B. W., JR., & COHEN, E. N. Cigarette smoking during pregnancy and the occurrence of spontaneous abortion and congenital abnormality. *American Journal of Epidemiology*, 1978, *108*, 470–479.

HODGKINSON, R., BHATT, M., GREWAL, G., & MARX, G. F. Neonatal neurobehavior in the first 48 hours of life: Effect of the administration of meperidine with and without naloxone in the mother. *Pediatrics*, 1978, *62*, 294–298.

HOOKER, D. *The prenatal origin of behavior*. New York: Hafner, 1969. (Originally published, 1952.)

HOROWITZ, F. D., ASHTON, J., CULP, R. E., GADDIS, E., LEVIN, S., & REICHMANN, B. The effect of obstetrical medication on the behavior of Israeli newborns and some comparisons with American and Uruguayan infants. *Child Development*, 1977, *48*, 1607–1623.

HOWARD, F. M., & HILL, J. M. Drugs in pregnancy. *Obstetrical and Gynecological Survey*, 1979, *34*, 643–653.

HUMPHREY, T. Central representation of the oral and facial areas of human fetuses. In J. F. Bosma (Ed.), *Third symposium on oral sensation and perception: The mouth of the infant*. Springfield, Ill.: Chas. C Thomas, 1972.

HURLEY, L. S. Nutritional deficiencies and excesses. In J. G. Wilson & F. C. Fraser (Eds.), *Handbook of teratology* (Vol. 1). New York: Plenum, 1977.

HUTTUNEN, M. O., & NISKANEN, P. Prenatal loss of father and psychiatric disorders. *Archives of General Psychiatry*, 1978, *35*, 429–431.

JANERICH, D. T., DUGAN, J. M., STANDFAST, S. J., & STRITE, L.

Congenital heart disease and prenatal exposure to exogenous sex hormones. *British Medical Journal*, 1977, *1*, 1058–1060.

JEANS, P. C., SMITH, M. B., & STEARNS, G. Incidence of prematurity in relation to maternal nutrition. *Journal of the American Dietetic Association*, 1955, *31*, 576–581.

JOHNSON, L. D., DRISCOLL, S. G., HERTIG, A. T., COLE, P. T., & NICKERSON, R. J. Vaginal adenosis in stillborns and neonates exposed to diethylstilbestrol and steroidal estrogens and progestins. *Obstetrics and Gynecology*, 1979, *53*, 671–679.

JONES, K. L., SMITH, D. W., STREISSGUTH, A. P., & MYRIANTHOPOULOS, N. C. Outcome in offspring of chronic alcoholic women. *Lancet*, 1974, *1*, 1076–1078.

KNOBLOCH, H., & PASAMANICK, B. Syndrome of minimal cerebral damage in infancy. *Journal of the American Medical Association*, 1959, *170*, 1384–1387.

KRON, R. D., STEIN, M., & GODDARD, K. E. Newborn sucking behavior affected by obstetric sedation. *Pediatrics*, 1966, *37*, 1012–1016.

LAYDE, P. M., EDMONDS, L. D., & ERICKSON, J. D. Maternal fever and neural tube defects. *Teratology*, 1980, *21*, 105–118.

LIPSITT, L. P. Perinatal indicators and psychophysiological precursors of crib death. In F. D. Horowitz (Ed.), *Early developmental hazards: Predictors and precautions*. Boulder, Colo.: Westview Press, 1978.

LOWE, C. R. Congenital malformations among infants born to epileptic women. *Lancet*, 1973, *1*, 9–10.

MATSUNAGA, E., & SHIOTA, K. Search for maternal factors associated with malformed human embryos: A prospective study. *Teratology*, 1980, *21*, 323–331.

MATURANA, H. R., & VARELA, F. J. *Autopoeisis and cognition*. Boston: Reidel Publishing Co., 1980.

MILKOVICH, L., & VAN DEN BERG, B. J. Effects of meprobamate and chlordiazepoxide on human embryonic and fetal development. *New England Journal of Medicine*, 1974, *291*, 1268–1271.

MILLER, P., SMITH, D. W., & SHEPARD, T. H. Maternal hyperthermia as a possible cause of anencephaly. *Lancet*, 1978, *1*, 519–520.

MONEY, J. Prenatal hormones and postnatal socialization in gender identity differentiation. *Nebraska Symposium on Motivation*, 1973, *21*, 221–295.

MONEY, J., & EHRHARDT, A. *Man and woman: Boy and girl*. Baltimore, Md.: Johns Hopkins University Press, 1972.

MONEY, J., & LEWIS, V. IQ, genetics and accelerated growth: Adrenogenital syndrome. *Bulletin of the Johns Hopkins Hospital*, 1966, *118*, 365–373.

MURPHY, D. P. The outcome of 625 pregnancies in women subjected to pelvic radium or roentgen irradiation. *American Journal of Obstetrics and Gynecology*, 1929, *18*, 179–187.

NAEYE, R. L. Relationship of cigarette smoking to congenital anomalies and perinatal death. *American Journal of Pathology*, 1978, *90*, 289–294.

NAEYE, R. L., LADIS, B., & DRAGE, J. S. Sudden infant death syndrome: A prospective study. *American Journal of Diseases of Children*, 1976, *130*, 1207–1210.

NISWANDER, K. R., & GORDON, M. (Eds.). *The collaborative perinatal study of the National Institute of Neurological Diseases and Stroke: The women and their pregnancies*. Washington, D.C.: U.S. Government Printing Office, 1972.

OTTINGER, D., & SIMMONS, J. Behavior of human neonates and prenatal · maternal anxiety. *Psychological Reports*, 1964, *14*, 391–394.

PICONE, T. A., ALLEN, L. H., OLSEN, P. N., SCHRAMM, M., & FERRIS, M. *The effects of maternal weight gain and smoking during pregnancy on human neonatal behavior*. Paper read at the International Conference of Infant Studies, New Haven, Conn., April 1980.

PLUMMER, G. Anomalies occurring in children exposed *in utero* to the atomic bomb in Hiroshima. *Pediatrics*, 1952, *10*, 687–693.

PRESTON, M. I. Late behavioral aspects found in cases of prenatal, natal, and postnatal anoxia. *Journal of Pediatrics*, 1945, *26*, 353–366.

PRIGOGINE, I. Time, structure and fluctuations. *Science*, 1978, *201*, 777–785.

QUIGLEY, M. E., SHEEHAN, K. L., WILKES, M. M., & YEN, S.S.C. Effects of maternal smoking on circulating catecholamine levels and fetal heart rates. *American Journal of Obstetrics and Gynecology*, 1979, *133*, 685–690.

RAJEGOWDA, B. K., KANDELL, S. R., & FALCIGLIA, H. SIDS in infants of narcotic-addicted mothers. *Pediatric Research,* 1976, *10,* 334.

REINISCH, J. M. Prenatal exposure of human foetuses to synthetic progestin and estrogen affects personality. *Nature,* 1977, *266,* 561–562.

REINISCH, J. M., & KAROW, W. G. Prenatal exposure to synthetic progestins and estrogens: Effects on human development. *Archives of Sexual Behavior,* 1977, *6,* 257–288.

REVILL, S. I., & DODGE, J. A. Psychological determinants of infantile pyloric stenosis. *Archives of Disease in Childhood,* 1978, *53,* 66–68.

ROSETT, H. L., WEINER, L., ZUCKERMAN, B., McKINLAY, S., & EDELIN, K. C. Reduction of alcohol consumption during pregnancy with benefits to the newborn. *Alcoholism: Clinical and Experimental Research,* 1980, *4,* 178–184.

ROTHMAN, K. J., FYLER, D. C., GOLDBLATT, A., & KREIDBERG, M. B. Exogenous hormones and other drug exposures of children with congenital heart disease. *American Journal of Epidemiology,* 1979, *109,* 433–439.

SAMEROFF, A. J., & CHANDLER, M. J. Reproductive risk and the continuum of caretaking casualty. In F. D. Horowitz (Ed.), *Review of child development research* (Vol. 4). Chicago: University of Chicago Press, 1975.

SCANLON, J. W., BROWN, W. V., WEISS, J. B., & ALPER, M. H. Neurological responses of newborn infants after maternal epidural anesthesia. *Anesthesiology,* 1974, *40,* 121–128.

SCHARDEIN, J. L. *Drugs as teratogens.* Cleveland: CRC Press, 1976.

SCHREIBER, F. Mental deficiency from paranatal asphyxia. *Proceedings of the American Association of Mental Deficiency,* 1939, *63,* 95–100.

SHAYWITZ, S. E., COHEN, D. J., & SHAYWITZ, B. A. Behavior and learning difficulties in children of normal intelligence born to alcoholic mothers. *Journal of Pediatrics,* 1980, *96,* 978–982.

SHURYGIN, G. I. Ob osobennostiiakh psikhickeskogo razvitiia detei ot materei stradaiushchikh khronicheskim alkogolizmom. *Pediatriia,* 1974, *11,* 71–73.

SMITH, C. J., & STEINSCHNEIDER, A. Differential effects of prenatal rhythmic stimulation on neonatal arousal states. *Child Development,* 1975, *46,* 574–578.

SNYDER, R. D. Congenital mercury poisoning. *New England Journal of Medicine,* 1971, *284,* 1014–1016.

SOKOL, R. J., MILLER, S. I., & REED, G. Alcohol abuse during pregnancy: An epidemiologic study. *Alcoholism,* 1980, *4,* 135–145.

SONTAG, L. W., & WALLACE, R. F. The effect of cigarette smoking during pregnancy upon the fetal heart rate. *American Journal of Obstetrics and Gynecology,* 1935, *29,* 77–83.

SOSA, R., KENNELL, J., KLAUS, M., ROBERTSON, S., & URRUTIA, J. The effect of a supportive companion on perinatal problems, length of labor, and mother-infant interaction. *New England Journal of Medicine,* 1980, *303*(No. 11), 597–600.

SPELT, D. K. The conditioning of the human fetus *in utero. Journal of Experimental Psychology,* 1948, *38,* 338–346.

SPYKER, J. M. Assessing the impact of low level chemicals on development: Behavioral and latent effects. *Federation Proceedings,* 1975, *34,* 1835–1844.

STANDLEY, K., SOULE, B., & COPANS, S. A. Dimensions of prenatal anxiety and their influence on pregnancy outcome. *American Journal of Obstetrics and Gynecology,* 1979, *135,* 22–26.

STANDLEY, K., SOULE, A. B., COPANS, S. A., & DUCHOWNY, M. S. Local-regional anesthesia during childbirth: Effect on newborn behavior. *Science,* 1974, *186,* 634–635.

STECHLER, G. A longitudinal follow-up of neonatal apnea. *Child Development,* 1964a, *35,* 333–348.

STECHLER, G. Newborn attention as affected by medication during labor. *Science,* 1964b, *144,* 315–317.

STEIN, Z., SUSSER, M., SAENGER, G., & MAROLLA, F. *Famine and human development: The Dutch hunger winter of 1944–1945.* New York: Oxford University Press, 1975.

STOTT, D. H. Mongolism related to emotional shock in early pregnancy. *Vita Humana,* 1961, *4,* 57–76.

STOTT, D. H., & LATCHFORD, S. A. Prenatal antecedents of child health, development, and behavior: An epidemiological report of incidence and association. *Journal of the American Academy of Child Psychiatry,* 1976, *15,* 161–191.

STRAUSS, M. E., STARR, R. H., OSTREA, E. M., CHAVEZ, C. J., & STRYKER, J. C. Behavioral concomitants of prenatal addiction to narcotics. *Journal of Pediatrics,* 1976, 89, 842–846.

STREISSGUTH, A. P., HERMAN, C. S., & SMITH, D. W. Intelligence, behavior, and dysmorphogenesis in the fetal alcohol syndrome: A report on 20 patients. *Journal of Pediatrics,* 1978, *92,* 363–367.

STROTHER, C. R. Minimal brain dysfunction: A historical overview. In F. F. de la Cruz, B. H. Fox, & R. H. Roberts (Eds.), *Minimal brain dysfunction* (Annals of the New York Academy of Sciences, Vol. 205). New York: Scholarly Reprints, 1973.

TOWBIN, A. *The pathology of cerebral palsy.* Springfield, Ill.: Chas. C Thomas, 1960.

TOWBIN, A. Cerebral dysfunctions related to perinatal organic damage: Clinical-neuropathologic correlations. *Journal of Abnormal Psychology,* 1978, *87,* 617–635.

TRONICK, E., WISE, S., ALS, H., ADAMSON, L., SCANLON, J., & BRAZELTON, T. B. Regional obstetric anesthesia and newborn behavior: Effect over the first ten days of life. *Pediatrics,* 1976, *58,* 94–100.

TUCHMAN-DUPLESSIS, H. *Drug effects on the fetus.* Littleton, Mass.: PSG Pub., 1975.

U.S. Department of Health, Education and Welfare. *Smoking and health: A report of the Surgeon General.* Washington, D.C.: U.S. Government Printing Office, 1979.

USDIN, G. L., & WEIL, M. L. Effect of apnea neonatorium on intellectual development. *Pediatrics,* 1952, *9,* 387–394.

WEATHERSBEE, P. S., & LODGE, J. R. Alcohol, caffeine, and nicotine as factors in pregnancy. *Postgraduate Medicine,* 1979, *66* (No. 3), 165–171.

WILSON, J. G., & FRASER, F. C. (Eds.). *Handbook of teratology* (4 vols.). New York: Plenum, 1977.

WOODSON, E. M. da COSTA, WOODSON, R. H., BLURTON-JONES, N. G., POLLOCK, S. B., & EVANS, M. A. *Maternal smoking and newborn behavior.* Paper read at the International Conference on Infant Studies, New Haven, Conn., April 1980.

YAMAZAKI, J. N., WRIGHT, S. W., & WRIGHT, P. M. Outcome of pregnancy in women exposed to the atomic bomb in Nagasaki. *American Journal of Diseases of Children,* 1954, *87,* 448–463.

ZELSON, C. Infant of the addicted mother. *New England Journal of Medicine,* 1973, *288,* 1393–1395.

ZELSON, C., LEE, S. J., & CASALINO, M. Neonatal narcotic addiction: Comparative effects of maternal intake of heroin and methadone. *New England Journal of Medicine,* 1973, *289,* 1216–1220.

ZUSPAN, F. P., QUILLIGAN, F. J., IAMS, J. D., & van GEIJN, H. P. Predictors of intrapartum fetal distress: The role of electronic fetal monitoring. Report of the NICHHD Consensus Development Task Force. *American Journal of Obstetrics and Gynecology,* 1979, *135,* 287–291.

12

Infant-Mother Attachment:
Theory, Assessment,
and Implications for Development

LYLE STEVEN JOFFE
BRIAN E. VAUGHN

The role of the infant-mother relationship in the formation and development of personality has long been a focal point for intense debate and empirical investigation. It was Freud's (1949) view that the mother-infant relationship served as a prototype for all later social relations, continuing to exert its influence throughout childhood and into adulthood. Perhaps unfortunately neither Freud nor his followers in the traditional psychoanalytic tradition provided behavioral operational definitions of this hypothesized affective bond. Consequently the extreme position taken by psychoanalysts has seldom been deemed to fall within the parvenu of traditional personality research, and there have not been specific tests of this position. Recently the shift to interactional analysis of behavior, combined with the contributions of ethology and sociobiology, has rekindled an interest in the relationship between infant and caregiver which is likely to have a significant impact on our understanding of the developmental tasks of infancy and the relationship between early experience and later interpersonal competence.

Despite the rapidly growing pace of research concerned with the origins and development of early social relations, remarkably little consensus remains as to the nature of the child's tie to significant adults, nor is there consensus regarding the appropriate criteria for inferring the existence of such a tie (see Rajecki, Lamb, & Obmascher, 1978, for a recent review). Researchers from a social learning perspective have maintained that such constructs do not derive from behavioral observation and, therefore, have little (or no) scientific merit (e.g., Masters & Wellman, 1974; Weinraub, Brooks, & Lewis, 1977). Other investigators, employing modified *S-R* theories, suggest that everything implied in the notion of a mother-infant "bond" may be captured in the pattern-

ing of interactive behavior (e.g., Cairns, 1972; Gewirtz, 1972; Rosenthal, 1973).

In the present chapter the nature of the infant-toddler's tie to the mother figure is examined in light of current theoretical perspectives and in terms of current empirical research. The first major section of the chapter is devoted to the presentation of several major theories of attachment formation and development, their historical grounding, and current status. Second, there is a discussion concerning the assessment strategies proposed by the several theoretical formulations with an extended treatment of an assessment technique that has proved most useful in identifying individual differences in infant-mother attachment relationships (that is, Ainsworth's *strange situation technique*). Finally, the significance of attachment will be underscored by examining its contemporary correlates and its implications for subsequent development. It will be argued that the perspective provided by the ethological-organizational model (e.g., Ainsworth, 1973; Bowlby, 1969, 1973; Sroufe & Waters, 1977) has been and continues to be the most useful framework from which to examine this developmental phenomenon.

THEORETICAL PERSPECTIVES

Social Learning and Dependency

In the history of developmental research concerning the origins of the mother-infant relationship, the concept of *dependency* preceded the more recent introduction of *attachment*. A thorough review of dependency research is provided by Maccoby and Masters (1970) and an authoritative critique by Sears (1972). It seems sufficient for our present purpose to note that dependency was originally conceived to be a secondary drive acquired through the gratification of basic physiological needs. It is most often defined as a generalized tendency to rely on other people for approval, affection, and guidance (Maccoby & Masters, 1970). The origins of the infant's tie to the mother was, in essence, conceived to rest upon the fact that she gratified the baby's basic drives, and all later social dependency relations were seen as a generalization of this initial dependency relation with the mother-figure. Freud (1949) viewed love as having its origins in the satisfied need for nourishment. Less definitively, Dollard and Miller (1950) conceptualized this relationship in terms of the feeding experience providing the occasion for the child to like to be with others. From Freud onward such thinking has dominated much of psychoanalytic writing and has also provided a common assumption for social learning theorists who have attempted to integrate Freud's insights with learning theory process formulations. This perspective is to be found in the writings of Beller (1955, 1957); Heathers (1955); Sears (1957, 1963, 1965); and Stendler (1954), to name but a few.

The secondary drive model, however, did not go long unchallenged and has generally been rejected as both unhelpful and misleading. Harlow's now famous experiments with rhesus monkeys (1961, 1963) demonstrated the importance of "contact comfort" in fostering the development of attachment behavior, providing evidence completely at variance with a drive reduction model of early affectional development. It has also been demonstrated that infants may become attached to other infants their own age (Freud & Dann, 1951; Schaffer & Emerson, 1964a); that attachment behavior may develop under conditions of serious mistreatment by the attachment figure (Rosenblum & Harlow, 1963; Seay, Alexander, & Harlow, 1964); and that human infants respond readily to social stimuli or social interaction without the requirement that food or bodily care be involved (Brackbill, 1958; Rheingold, Gewirtz, & Ross, 1959). This drive model has also lost support because of criticisms implicit in other emerging variants of learning theory. Gewirtz (1961) has criticized this position for its implication that infants are passive and unresponsive once their biological needs have been met. Walters and Foote (1962) criticized it for emphasizing states of deprivation and distress, choosing instead to stress the notion of "competence motivation" introduced by White (1959). Finally Sears (an original proponent of the acquired drive model) acknowledged its doubtful usefulness as a construct stating: "If we acknowledge as we must, that there is not critical evidence to support the drive contention, then we must ask what alternative explanations can be used to account for these phenomena" (1963, p. 28).

Bijou and Baer (1965) and Gewirtz (1961, 1969) have described the origins of the child's relationship with his/her mother in terms of the reinforcement of operant behaviors, considering dependency as neither a drive nor a trait but simply a convenient label for certain kinds of learned behaviors. The central concept for instrumental conditioning theorists is the reinforcing stimulus. Gewirtz (1969) uses this concept to account for both de-

pendency and attachment, suggesting that they are best conceptualized as abstractions for classes of functional relationships involving the positive stimulus control of a wide variety of an individual's reponses by stimuli provided either by a class of persons (dependency) or by a particular person (attachment). The greater the number of behaviors under the stimulus control of a particular person relative to the number of behaviors under the control of others, and the greater number of settings in which the control operates, the stronger the attachment is said to be.

Among instrumental conditioning theorists, Gewirtz (1969) has demonstrated more interest in integrating his system with those of the ethologically oriented theorists to be discussed shortly. Although he acknowledges that there may be genetically determined biases and species-specific behaviors in humans, he questions whether any of the responses implicated in the acquisition of attachment are species characteristic. Furthermore he draws an unduly sharp distinction between learned behavior and that which is innate, suggesting that if learning can be implicated, behaviors cannot be labeled as species characteristic. Such a distinction runs counter to contemporary thinking in genetics and ethology and seems only to revive the rather outdated nature-nurture dispute. The dichotomy carried to its logical extreme would define innate behavior as that which requires no organism. Nevertheless Gewirtz (1961, 1969) has characterized ethological approaches to attachment as "prelearning" approaches and has implied that once learning takes over, any initial facilitation that might have been offered by genetic bias is totally overshadowed. For the majority of learning theorists, the intactness of the organism is the only contribution of genetic endowment to behavior.

Cairns (1966a) has advanced a dramatically different theory of attachment based on a contiguity learning model (Guthrie, 1935, 1946). The central feature of this model is that the organism, regardless of age and species, becomes attached to an object, whether animate or inanimate, which is constantly in the organism's environment, by means of associative conditioning. Reinforcement is not viewed as essential for attachments to occur, but rather the object of attachment gains control over the animal's behavior by virtue of being present during many of its responses. In support of this position Cairns (1966b) has demonstrated that lambs could become attached to television sets if kept in isolation from other animals but in proximity to a set in operation. Bateson (1966) demonstrated that chicks could become imprinted to a static object under similar conditions. Cairns, however, rests much of his argument on evidence that disturbance occasioned by separation from the object of attachment diminishes as separation continues, and thus separation reduces attachment strength. That continuing separation diminishes disturbance is supported by research with both young children and non-human primates, and as Ainsworth (1972) notes, there is support for Cairns's claim that the separated infant may, under favorable circumstances, form other attachments while separated from the mother. Cairns, however, fails to reconcile the paradox that once attachments are formed, they can and usually are maintained over quite prolonged periods of separation and that both human infants and nonhuman primates show a pronounced heightening of attachment behavior upon reunion with the mother, whether immediately or after some period of delay (Ainsworth, 1972). The point of concern is simply that attachments seem capable of surviving a rather extensive period during which the infant's behaviors are not supported by the absent attachment figure. This observation is of sufficient importance to be dealt with in greater detail at a later point in this text and seriously calls into question the notion that the "strength" of attachment should be inversely related to the length of separation from the object.

Still other learning theorists have shifted from a view of attachment (or, dependency) as a generalized acquired drive to viewing it as a generalized personality trait (Maccoby & Masters, 1970). Generally traits have been viewed as both psychological realities that exist in some tangible form in the person and also as causes of behavior (Allport, 1966; Cattell, 1950). A chief aim of the trait approach is to infer the underlying personality structure of individuals and to then compare persons and groups on trait dimensions. Underlying traits are inferred from behavior and, in turn, are used to account for the observed behavioral consistencies. In an attempt to assimilate attachment to the earlier dependency paradigm, Maccoby and Masters (1970) suggested that attachment might be viewed as such a central motive state. In keeping with a traditional definition of a trait, this implied that a major dimension of attachment was its strength, and this was to be inferred from the strength of the various behaviors generally agreed to be indices of attachment. They suggested ten possible measures of behavior strength, including the number of persons toward which the behavior is shown, as well as the frequency with which the behavior is emitted. Ainsworth (1972), in discussing this attempt to encompass attachment within the framework of the dependency paradigm, notes that the traditional criteria for assessing the validity of the concept of a generalized trait were then considered applicable to attachment. Thus to support a trait hypothesis of attachment, Maccoby and Masters (1970) suggested that all behavioral indices of attachment should be positively correlated, that there should be stability of such measures across time, and that there should be stability of measures of attachment across situations. The evidence for such a trait approach to attachment will be discussed later.

When considering the contributions of operant conditioning and social learning theorists to the problem at hand, it seems well to remember that different levels of analysis are both useful and necessary if a complete understanding of the infant-mother attachment relation is to be achieved. Contemporary ethological and organizational perspectives do not, in fact, detail the learning processes implicated in the development of attachment or the functional relationships between stimulus and response. However while Cairns, Gewirtz, and Bijou and Baer have proposed formulations which do not invoke the concept of "acquired drive," they seem to go to an equally misleading extreme by minimizing or completely ignoring the strong biological basis that (ethological formulations hold) each partner brings to the relationship. The entire emphasis here is on the environment and the

relative potencies of different stimulus events to increase the strength of any behavior the organism happens to emit. The only condition within the organism which is acknowledged as an important influence is whatever may be represented by its reinforcement history. Ainsworth (1969) notes that such a bias may lead to the view that every behavioral system is environmentally labile to an infinite degree which may result in potentially damaging effects on practice.

Waters (1980), in discussing such approaches to attachment, has strongly argued that such an analysis may not provide an adequate description of the infant's experience. He points out that interaction is not usually viewed as an end in itself, nor does the description of interaction seem to provide a comprehensive description of the infant's experience. For their part social learning theorists tend to have difficulty incorporating into their systems any view of inner structure. Both Lewin (1935) and Piaget (1936/1952) have implied that all developmental changes and all learning comes about through the modification of structures already present in the organism as a result of its interaction with the environment. As will be discussed in detail in the following section, both control systems theory and the ethological approach postulate a structured organism and that all behavior and development come about through the interaction of the structured organism with those aspects of the environment which its structure is sensitive to receive as input (Ainsworth, 1972).

The Intraorganismic Perspective: Ethology and Control Systems

During the last decade this traditional and essentially unidirectional emphasis has been challenged by the notion of reciprocity between infant and caregiver (e.g., Bell, 1968, 1974; Brazelton, Koslowski, & Main, 1974; Stern, 1974), as well as by a renewed interest in how that which lies inside the organism contributes to organism-environment interaction. In the domain of infant research in general, such an intraorganismic perspective has been favored both by cognitive psychologists concerned with the foundations and transformations of cognitive structures and by those who view attachment as having both an inner organization *and* an outward behavioral manifestation. Advances in the biological sciences have drawn attention to intraorganismic conditions for the activation, termination, and organization of behavior. The influence of ethology on both developmental and comparative psychology, the new relevance of Darwin's evolutionary theory and the principle of natural selection, the fundamentally biological influence of Piaget on cognitive psychology, as well as advances in control systems and computer models, have all contributed to an increasing interest in what is inside the organism to begin with, how this inner programming affects the response to environmental input, and how the organism itself becomes transformed as a result of this fundamental interaction.

Contemporary attachment theory was given its first preliminary statement in Bowlby's 1958 paper entitled "The Nature of a Child's Tie to His Mother" and more fully explicated in *Attachment and Loss* (1969, 1973, 1980). An initial psychoanalytic orientation was integrated with the biological discipline of ethology, psychobiology, control systems theory, and Piaget's structural approach to the development of cognition. While this integration was undertaken primarily to understand the origin, function, and development of an infant's early social relations, that part of Bowlby's theory that deals specifically with attachment is embedded in a general theory of behavior that owes much to these varied origins.

Bowlby's concept of attachment (1958, 1969) breaks dramatically with other theoretical approaches in a number of important respects. First, attachment behavior is conceived within the framework of a behavioral system (see Baerends, 1976) and not equated with any particular discrete behavior, as has been the case with those approaches to attachment previously described. When conceived of in terms of a behavior system, observable behavioral components are not the only components of the system; there are intraorganismic, organizational components as well. Also a variety of behaviors may serve the same system, and any specific behavioral component may come to serve more than one behavior system. Nevertheless several behaviors may be classed together as serving a particular behavioral system because they usually have a common outcome. The behaviors classified in this fashion may, therefore, be diverse in form, and each is essential only insofar as it represents a component of a series of behaviors that lead to the outcome.

Bowlby also places major emphasis on the biological function of behavior and the Darwinian principle that structures and behavioral systems characteristic of the species (as well as the underlying genotypes) are represented in the population because they gave survival advantage in the environment of evolutionary adaptedness. The biological function of a behavior system is, therefore, that outcome of the system which originally gave it survival advantage. The primary function of attachment behavior, and of reciprocal maternal behavior, is conceived to be the protection of the infant from harm. While the biological function of the behavioral system may or may not give special survival advantage in one or another of the various environments in which populations now live, unless changes in the average expectable environment render the behavioral system a liability, it will be maintained in the repertoire of the species (Ainsworth, Blehar, Waters, & Wall, 1978). Bowlby (1969) proposes that the infant's tie to its mother is mediated by just such species characteristic behavior patterns and not by the mother's role in satisfying the infant's biological needs. Attachment behavior is regarded as a class of social behavior equivalent in importance to that of mating or parental behavior and is deemed to have a function specific to itself. The origins of attachment are, therefore, not to be found in feeding per se but in mother-infant interaction, and no reference to "needs" or "drives" is required. Attachment behavior is simply regarded as that which occurs when certain behavioral systems are activated. Such species characteristic behaviors as smiling and crying are presumed to possess a signaling function that serves to activate maternal behavior and bring the adult into proximity to the child. By means of such behavior as sucking, following, and clinging, the child plays an active role in seeking proximity and contact, and in the course of development, these behavior patterns become coordinated and focused on the mother to form the basis of attachment.

In Bowlby's scheme the behavioral hallmark of the attachment system is the seeking of proximity to or contact with the attachment figure. The control system which is said to mediate this behavior regulates the infant's signaling, approach, and contact maintaining behavior by reference to an internal parameter referred to as the "set goal." This is not a goal object in the conventional sense but represents a degree of proximity or access to the mother which is maintained by periodic activation of attachment (e.g., proximity promoting) behavior. By specifying a number of internal and environmental inputs that can influence the calibration of the set goal, the model is able to encompass certain observations that are otherwise not readily explained. For example infants are known to desire closer contact with the attachment figure when they are ill, tired, frightened, or in certain prepotent situations such as an unfamiliar environment or darkness.

Despite Bowlby's insistence that human infants are genetically predisposed toward becoming attached to some person if given the opportunity, it is not predetermined to whom they will become attached, nor is attachment present at birth. Consequently although contemporary attachment theory does not specify in great detail the experiences involved in the development of attachment, learning is clearly implicated. The human infant, it would appear, cannot form an attachment before a certain degree of cognitive development has occurred and cannot become attached without having experienced a substantial number of transactions with the attachment figure (Ainsworth, 1972; Bowlby, 1969; Schaffer & Emerson, 1964b). (Only under very unusual circumstances, such as long term institutionalization, do infants encounter conditions such that their attachment behavior does not result in the formation of an attachment [e.g., Goldfarb, 1943; Provence & Lipton, 1962].)

According to Bowlby's (1969) model, attachment develops through a number of phases, beginning with an initial "pre-attachment" phase occupying the period from birth through the first few weeks of life. From birth the infant appears disposed to respond readily to stimuli emanating from other members of the species and especially from adult females (Bowlby, 1969; Wolff, 1969). From the beginning the infant's behavioral repertoire includes behaviors which promote proximity and/or contact with the mother. These behaviors may be roughly divided into two classes: those that have the usual outcome of attracting the adult such as smiling and crying, and those that are more actively contact promoting such as rooting, sucking, grasping, and following with the eyes. Such behaviors, so far as may be ascertained, are universal in the species (i.e., species characteristic), appearing in all cultures, and following a predictable and regular schedule of development. These behaviors, as well as those more complex behaviors to which they eventually give rise in the course of development, have been labeled attachment behaviors. Due to the undifferentiated and undiscriminating nature of these early behaviors, one cannot yet speak of the infant as being attached at this time.

With the increasingly discriminative and differential development of these early behaviors, a second phase of "attachment in the making" is entered. At the end of this phase the infant may be described as clearly attached to a specific figure. It is generally agreed that this occurs sometime during the second half of the first year of life (Ainsworth, 1969; Bowlby, 1969; Schaffer, 1958; Schaffer & Callender, 1959; Spitz & Wolff, 1946). It is during this phase of developing attachment that behaviors such as smiling to a familiar figure begin to occur much more frequently, while smiles to unfamiliar figures dramatically decline. It is important to note, however, that it is not yet necessary to invoke an elaborate control systems model to account for the infant's behavior up to this point since the complexity involved does not exceed the explanatory power of stimulus-response chaining.

Soon after discriminating and differential behavior has become established, the infant enters the phase of "clearcut" attachment. It is during this time that the onset of locomotion is achieved, and active proximity seeking behavior begins to augment (not replace) the discriminative signaling characteristic of the previous phase. It is also during this period that the infant enters Piaget's fourth stage of the development of the object concept and develops the cognitive capacity to conceive of absent objects (Bell, 1970). The attachment figure can then be cognitively represented in a sense, and one may speak of the infant as attached to a certain individual. By this point infants have developed a reasonably large repertoire of behaviors through which they may attempt to approximate a particular "set-goal." An infant may, for example, respond to his/her mother's return from a brief absence by an active approach, signaling, smiling, vocalizing, or crying, and any of these behaviors (alone or in combination) may achieve the set-goal of proximity or contact with the attachment figure. Once the infant is capable of such behavioral diversity, the component behaviors lose much of their original significance and, as stated earlier, become important only insofar as they contribute to the desired outcome. For Bowlby it is this increase in the flexibility of behavioral organization that necessitates the invocation of a control systems model.

The fourth phase of a "goal-corrected" partnership, beginning no earlier than the infant's second year of life (12–24 months), becomes increasingly complex. Previously the coordination of the infant's plans and set-goals with his/her mother's behavior was primarily an empirical matter. With the growing ability to see things form the mother's point of view, the infant begins to be able to infer something of her behavior. The infant may now go beyond a mere accommodation of his/her behavior to hers and can begin to initiate attempts to influence her behavior in much more sophisticated ways. This phase has not, however, received much systematic investigation.

Perhaps the major conceptual limitation of Bowlby's model lies in its singularity of function. In Bowlby's (1969) control systems model, the set-goal mediating the child's attachment behavior is the maintenance of a certain degree of proximity. Waters (1980) points out that although this has the advantage of accounting for the "goal-corrected" aspect of the infant's behavior, it places too little emphasis on the child's complex motivation toward the environment. In this very basic sense Bowlby's model would seem to lack the necessary flexibility to integrate attachment behavior with the development and operation of other behavioral systems. As Waters (1980) states: "It seems fair to suggest that if the evolution of this behavioral system reflects nothing more than the advantages of being close to adults, the goal could be more effectively accomplished by a tendency to cling unremittingly" (p. 36).

Engel (1971) notes that while a number of internal inputs can modify the set-goal of Bowlby's control system, external events relevant to mother-infant are the major stimuli. Waters (1980) observes that when the set-goal of the attachment behavioral system is viewed as a degree of proximity, it is difficult to see how the infant's tendency to be more readily upset by repetitions of a separation-reunion experience can be explained, nor is the effectiveness of alternatives to proximity (e.g., distal interaction) easily understood.

Ainsworth (e.g, 1963, 1967, 1969, 1972, 1973) has collected an extensive body of data relevant to Bowlby's theory which has resulted in a reformulation of that model more able to account for the infant's complex motivation to explore the environment. Ainsworth (1973) notes that a major function of the attachment behavioral system is to mediate the infant's excursions into the world and to shift the balance of behavior from exploration to proximity seeking in response to various contingencies. To this end Ainsworth postulates two related concepts: the *attachment-exploration balance* and the *secure base phenomenon*. The attachment-exploration balance is, in fact, so characteristic of the infant-mother relationship that it has been suggested that clear evidence of this kind of organization in the infant's behavior in a variety of situations is the best criteria for the presence of an attachment (Ainsworth, 1973; Stayton, Ainsworth, & Main, 1973; Waters, 1980). Both concepts are introduced to account for the well documented fact that infant exploratory behavior is disrupted in the absence of the attachment figure and that the infant may spontaneously approach the mother for affection as much as for comforting (Ainsworth, 1969; Schaffer & Emerson, 1964b).

For Ainsworth the set-goal of the attachment behavioral system is not simply the coordination of interpersonal distance with an internal criteria but rather the congruence of the infant's appraisal of a wide variety of internal and external inputs with a criterion of "felt security" (Ainsworth, 1975; Sroufe, 1979a). Bischoff (1975) has presented an elaborate control systems formulation of the attachment-exploration balance which also incorporates the notion of "felt security." The information upon which the control system functions is, therefore, no longer based upon a simple discrepancy between distance and the set-goal of proximity or contact but includes some consideration of the "meaning" of that discrepancy.

The Attachment Construct: Attachment and Attachment Behaviors

The distinction between attachment as a bond or enduring relationship between infants and their mothers and attachment behaviors by means of which such a bond is formed and later mediated occupies a central position in the organizational approach to attachment (Ainsworth, 1969, 1972; Ainsworth et al., 1978; Sroufe & Waters, 1977; Waters, 1980). Bowlby (1969) devoted the majority of his attention to attachment as a behavior system and, in doing so, also discussed the specific behaviors that serve that system in infancy and early childhood. While he devoted relatively little attention to the relation between such behaviors and attachment as a bond, the way in which he described the attachment behavioral system as becoming internally organized with respect to a specific figure may be interpreted as reflecting his understanding of the nature of the attachment bond.

In many respects the failure of those working within the confines of other theoretical perspectives to grasp the organizational significance of the concept of a behavior system has led to the erroneous conclusion that attachment and overt attachment behavior are one and the same (e.g., Masters & Wellman, 1974). As Ainsworth et al. (1978) note, the failure to make this crucial distinction has implications for a variety of theoretical misconceptions. It may be reasoned, for example, that attachment has disappeared if attachment behavior is no longer overtly observed, that the intensity with which a child shows attachment behavior in a given situation may be taken as an index of the strength of his/her attachment, or that attachment consists in nothing more than the contingencies of the interaction between mother and infant (Ainsworth et al., 1978).

The necessity of viewing attachment as a construct rather than in terms of the discrete behaviors which mediate the mother-infant relationship is most clearly illustrated in Ainsworth's (1973) observation that despite striking vicissitudes of attachment behavior, attachments seem to bridge time and distance. As has been previously pointed out, attachment behaviors (i.e., behaviors that promote proximity or contact) are manifest during the very earliest months of life, long before the infant may be described as attached to anyone. Even after infants have become attached, they do not manifest attachment behavior continuously. Under some circumstances attachment behavior is more strongly activated than under other circumstances, and at times, it is wholly overridden by other behavioral systems. Waters (1980) notes that a behavior is an attachment behavior by virtue of, and only insofar as it is employed in the service of, the attachment behavioral system. Behaviors become integrated with the attachment behavioral system or they do not on the basis of experience (Ainsworth, 1973). Ainsworth goes on to state,

We must infer the existence of an attachment bond from a stable propensity over time to seek proximity and contact with a specific figure, even though attachment behavior may appear only intermittently or, in the case of major separations, be absent for long periods. The term attachment refers to the class of diverse behaviors which promote proximity and contact, at first without discrimination of the figure, but later with increasing specificity in regard to the figure to whom the child is becoming attached. (p. 123)

Evidence in support of this enduring affective bond comes primarily from the observation of infants during prolonged periods of separation (Bowlby, 1969, 1973; Robertson & Robertson, 1971). In a paper describing the origins and sequelae of separation anxiety, Bowlby (1960) describes the response of young children to prolonged separation from the attachment figure as occurring in three major stages: *protest, despair,* and *detachment.* In the initial phase of response to separation, the young child is wholly concentrated on the mother and her whereabouts. Protesting the separation and trying any means to regain proximity and/or contact with the attachment figure are characteristic. Depending upon the length of separation, the child's attachment behavior may then become more infrequently manifested, or it may cease altogether. Were one guided entirely by overt behavior, it might reasonably be concluded that the child has ceased to be attached; however, the fact that the bond endures is most vividly demonstrated in most children when reunited with the attachment figure. If reunited with the attachment figure in these early phases of separation, the child experiences a strong heightening of attachment behavior which may persist for a rather extended period of time. As Ainsworth et al. (1978) note, were attachment identical with attachment behavior, one would be forced to conclude that separation first strengthens the bond, then weakens it, and finally destroys it. If one holds that the bond has altogether disappeared, it then becomes quite impossible to account for the fact that it apparently undergoes such rapid revitalization so quickly after reunion.

There may be some delay in the emergence of attachment behavior after a long period of separation, and this delay is associated with the length and extent of disappearance of overt attachment behavior during the separation itself (Ainsworth et al., 1978). Upon reunion the child may not only fail to show distress but may also fail to show anger and does not cling. It seems as if the infant does not know his/her mother and, in fact, to have lost all interest in her. Bowlby (1960) does not suggest that the attachment bond has disappeared, but rather that a repressive, defensive process has emerged. Should the child be left too long in this phase of detachment or if too many separations are suffered, s/he may in time come to act as if neither mothering nor contact with humans is of much significance. The repeated observations of children whose detachment suddenly gives way to intense attachment behavior implies most dramatically that the attachment, the bond, has not disappeared. Ainsworth et al. (1978) also note that the presence or absence of overt attachment behavior and the intensity with which it is manifest is most certainly dependent on numerous situational factors including hunger, fatigue, and illness. It is difficult to conceive that this bond with the mother varies in strength from day to day or moment to moment, even though the intensity of activation of attachment may vary.

To view attachment as a construct means to treat it as an inner organization of behavioral systems which not only controls the "stable propensity" to seek proximity to the attachment figure but also as responsible for the distinctive quality of the organization of specific attachment behaviors through which proximity with the attachment figure is promoted. Such a hypothesis implies a stable intraorganismic basis for individual differences in the organization of attachment behavior (Ainsworth, 1973; Ainsworth et al., 1978; Sroufe, 1979a, 1979b; Sroufe & Waters, 1977; Waters, 1980). As a reflection of the organization of behavior, attachment occupies the status of an "intervening variable" (Ainsworth, Bell, & Stayton, 1974) or a developmental organizational construct (Sroufe & Waters, 1977). The term *affective bond* is meant as a metaphorical description of this construct and pointedly suggests that there is a stable, enduring quality to the attachment relation (Ainsworth, 1973). It is the pattern of behavioral organization, the quality of attachment, the affective bond that endures.

Assessing Attachment: Techniques and Controversies

The failure to distinguish between attachment as an emotional bond and attachment behaviors, as well as the disinclination of many theorists to employ higher order constructs, has led to considerable disagreement concerning the appropriate measures to be employed in the assessment of attachment, nor is there consensus among researchers on the appropriate criteria relevant to possible construct validation. As Waters (1980) notes, this situation has arisen not so much from the inability of diverse theoretical perspectives to find common ground as from the failure to make explicit the kinds of constructs which have been chosen in building theories of attachment.

In many respects the theoretical shift from *drive* to *trait* seems to have had very little impact on either the measures employed or the criteria deemed appropriate for validating the attachment concept. Secondary drive theories, as well as trait theories, share in common an emphasis on behaviors as indices of underlying causal constructs and in the expectation that the major individual differences in attachment are largely differences in degree, which may be conveniently operationalized in terms of the intensity of behavioral manifestation (see Ainsworth, 1969; Maccoby & Masters, 1970; Waters, 1980). From this perspective attachment is conceived as a trait governing the expression of a class of behaviors. It is assumed that the validity of the construct is demonstrated if all behaviors believed to be governed by the trait are positively correlated, if individual differences in the exhibition of these behaviors remain stable over situations, and if individual differences in the frequency and intensity of these behaviors remain stable across the course of development. Should these criteria not be met, then the construct and the body of theory surrounding the construct may be called into question (Cronbach & Meehl, 1955).

Several studies in the literature (e.g., Coates, Anderson, & Hartup, 1972a, 1972b; Maccoby & Feldman, 1972) as well as an influential critique of the then available evidence by Masters and Wellman (1974) suggest that the validity criteria implicit in trait formulations of attachment are not easily met. Discrete attachment behaviors have not been found to be stable across situations or over relatively short periods of time, nor have the observed intercorrelations among behavioral indices of attachment been consistently high. In their critique of the research from this perspective, Masters and Wellman (1974) concluded that,

The correlational analysis of human infant attachment behaviors does not provide support for the concept of attachment as a psychological trait or central motive state. The stability and functional equivalence of theoretically relevant behaviors required by such conceptualizations is not found consistently in the empirical data. (p. 228)

Waters (1980), in a review of the Masters and Wellman critique and the empirical evidence upon which the critique was based, notes that while such *negative results* most certainly do not reflect upon an organizational approach to attachment, they also need not reflect poorly on psychometric-trait formulations. As Cronbach and Meehl (1955) make clear, seemingly negative results may be obtained by employing measures that do not adequately measure the construct in question or by experimental designs which fail to provide an adequate test of the theory. A strong case can be made that most studies in which correlations of behavioral frequencies have been used as assessments of the coherence of the causal trait formulation of attachment have used inadequate behavioral samples and, therefore, could not have fairly tested the trait formulation theory (see Waters, 1980).

There are some other problems with the trait-formulation assessments of attachment, over and above the questions of reliability raised by Masters and Wellman (1974) which derive from the almost atheoretical perspective taken by researchers adopting the social learning methodology to the study of infant-mother attachment. If sufficiently long samples of behavior were collected to assure reliability and stability of discrete attachment behaviors, the researcher would still be faced with the question of whether or not the analysis of such laboratory observations of behavior or the detailing of such observations truly capture important individual differences with respect to attachment. This fundamental concern applies both to causal trait formulations and to the modified *S-R* approach previously discussed. While the notion of the *strength* of attachment does mean something (see Ainsworth, 1969), it does not correspond to the dimensions of individual differences most pertinent to developmental research. Furthermore operationally defining attachment in terms of the presence or absence of a few criterion behaviors has led to the notion that attachments emerge fully formed toward the end of the first year of life (i.e., attachment is present when its strength is greater than zero) which leaves little for the developmentalist to do beyond observing the increase in frequency of attachment behaviors during the first two years and watching their decline thereafter.

The view that attachments emerge fully formed and change only in intensity is not consistent with the view that attachment is based on the operation of a behavioral system and carries with it the added disadvantage of implying that beyond the second year of life, attachments must either be attenuated or become a developmental liability. Flexibility, rather than dependency, is the hallmark of the typical infant-adult relationship during the end of the first and beginning of the second year of life, and it seems important to work toward a conceptualization in which the infant-adult tie and later adult-adult ties can be viewed as assets in the development of interpersonal competence rather than as liabilities.

The Strange Situation: An Assessment of the Infant-Mother Relationship

When faced with separation from the mother, infants older than seven or eight months of age often demonstrate intense, long-lasting distress, directed toward the recovery of the attachment figure. This distress is not readily reduced by attention from substitute caretakers. In such situations the infant may attempt to regain the mother by crying, calling, or searching, and with increasing age such actions become coordinated and goal directed (Bowlby, 1953, 1960b; Robertson & Bowlby, 1952; cf., Ainsworth, 1972). Such findings lead quite naturally to the assumption that the critical criteria of whether a child has become attached to a specific figure is his/her unequivocal distress when definitely separated from that figure.

As Ainsworth notes, the undesirability of engineering such major separation experiences for the purpose of either diagnostic or research assessment gave rise to the search for dependable criteria of attachment other than the distress engendered by major mother-infant separations. Spitz (1959) proposed the phenomenon of "eight-month-anxiety" as the criterion of attainment of true object relations. Schaffer and Emerson (1964b), in a pioneer study of the development of attachment among Glasgow infants, used separation protest in minor, everyday situations as the criteria for judging age of onset of attachments. Ainsworth (1963, 1967), in her study of Ganda infants, used multiple criteria including separation protest. Yet a number of infants in her Ganda sample appeared to be clearly attached without manifesting consistent distress in everyday separation situations in the home environment. This finding led Ainsworth to doubt the validity of distress in minor separations as the sole criterion of attachment and led her to emphasize the use of multiple criteria.

Ainsworth (1963, 1967) identified a number of attachment behaviors relevant to the assessment of whether or not an infant has become attached. These behaviors include the following: crying and/or following when the mother leaves the room, greeting responses, active contact behaviors, the use of the mother as a secure base from which to explore, and clinging. In order to be considered indices of attachment, however, such behaviors must be manifest in a discriminating and differential way. The possible behavioral combinations, as well as the wide range of individual differences in the way attachment behavior was organized in her Ganda sample (differences apparently related to differences among mothers in their infant-care practices), led to the development of the *strange situation* (Ainsworth & Wittig, 1969) to explore this issue further.

The strange situation is à brief (20-minute) procedure held in a laboratory room filled with toys. The experimental situation is composed of eight episodes presented in a fixed order in which the infant faces an unfamiliar environment and person, both with the mother present and absent. The situation is described as follows (Ainsworth, Bell, & Stayton, 1971; Ainsworth et al., 1978; Ainsworth & Wittig, 1969). During episodes one and two the mother and child are in the laboratory room alone. The first episode is introductory; the second is intended to elicit the extent of the infant's exploratory behavior prior to separation from the mother. In episode three a female stranger enters the room and sits quietly reading a magazine for one minute, engages the mother in conversation for one minute, and then attempts to engage the baby in interactive play for the final minute of the episode. The first separation occurs in episode four when the mother leaves the room for the first time. If the baby is distressed the stranger attempts to distract or console him/her; if s/he is not distressed the stranger does not intrude. Episode five marks the first reunion of mother and infant, at which point the stranger leaves mother and child alone. The baby's greeting behavior upon reunion is noted as well as his/her ability to settle if distressed and to return to exploration. In episode six the baby is left entirely alone, followed by the return of the stranger in episode seven, and the second reunion with the mother in episode eight.

The original strange situation study (Ainsworth & Wittig, 1969), as well as later replications (Ainsworth, Bell, & Stayton, 1971, 1972; Bell, 1970), revealed that some infants were minimally distressed by minor separations but, in ordinary interactions with their mother, seemed clearly attached. When separated briefly from her in the strange situation, however, they tended to show distress, as well as heightened proximity and contact maintaining behavior when she returned. Other infants showed frequent and intense distress in ordinary separation experiences at home. In the strange situation these infants often cried frequently even with the mother present, greeted the mother with a fuss or other signs of ambivalence, responded negatively to physical contact with her, or lacked active contact seeking behavior. These infants also tended to fuss when put down, while those who responded positively to contact were easily put down after being held and readily returned to exploratory activity. Some infants who showed separation distress and who cried frequently at home did not cry when the mother left them in the strange situation and failed to seek proximity and contact upon her return.

These findings have led Ainsworth (e.g., 1972) and others to stress not only the importance of multiple criteria for assessing the presence of an infant-parent attachment but also the desirability of assessing the quality (as opposed to the strength) of the attachment bond. Ainsworth (1972) notes that by one set of criteria or another, all of the infants in the original sample were attached. Nonetheless, there were striking differences in the manner in which their attachments were organized. The recommendation for employing multiple criteria for the assessment of attachment is not intended to omit such indices as crying upon separation from mother or attempting to follow her but is simply intended to draw attention to supplementary criteria which may be of significance in the case of infants whose attachment relationship is secure enough that they may not consistently display either distress or anxious search under conditions of relatively minor and nonstressful separations.

The strange situation procedure affords an opportunity to assess the balance of exploration and attachment behaviors under a cumulative stress condition. The ways in which attachment behavior is seen to be organized under stress provide a basis for classifying the infants in terms of a qualitative dimension (security vs. anxiety) descriptive of their attachments to their mothers. Infants are classified into one of three groups (labeled *A*, *B*, *C*) chiefly on the basis of their behavior toward the mother in the reunion episodes of the strange situation. The classification system first distinguishes between infants who are, or who are not, securely attached to the mother (the *B* vs. non-*B* groups). Ainsworth and associates (see

Ainsworth et al., 1978) have provided extensive validity data for this distinction based on observations of the behavior of the secure and anxiously attached infants in their homes. A second distinction between groups is provided by the behaviors shown by the anxiously attached infants in the strange situation. This distinction (the *A* vs. *C* groups) is in terms of the ways in which the anxiety of the nonsecure infants is expressed. The details of the strange situation classification system have been described in detail by Ainsworth and associates (e.g., Ainsworth et al., 1978) and by Sroufe (e.g., Sroufe & Waters, 1977).

Infants are classified as secure in their attachments (group *B*) if they greet the mother positively, actively attempt to reestablish proximity or interaction with her, and display few or no negative behaviors toward her during the reunion episodes of the strange situation. Group *B* is the normative group for white middle-class one-year-olds, both in terms of the percentage of infants so classified (about two-thirds of the infants in a given sample) and in the sense of representing a secure attachment. Group *B* infants usually explore the room during the preseparation episodes of the strange situation, showing that they find the mother's presence a source of security. It is, however, the behaviors cited before rather than their exploratory behavior that provide the basis for classification.

Infants are assigned to the anxious (non-*B*) groups, *A* and *C*, if they show substantial negative behavior toward the mother during the strange situation and especially during reunion. Infants are classified in group *C* if they show angry resistance toward the mother upon reunion. The anger in the behavior is sometimes rather subtle, as in slight pushing away in the context of apparently wanting to be held. Some group *C* infants display heightened attachment behaviors upon reunion and are often highly distressed by separation and, occasionally, by the unfamiliar situation itself. To both the casual and the practiced observer, the group *C* infant seems anxious and immature. Again it is primarily the ambivalence implicit in both seeking and resisting the mother that is the distinguishing characteristic of the group *C* infant.

Infants are classified in group *A* if they ignore the mother's entrance in the reunion episodes or if they actively avoid her attempts to reestablish contact and/or interaction during the reunion episodes. Avoidance may consist of looking away, turning away, making an "abortive" approach to the mother, or simply ignoring the mother altogether. While resistant behavior such as pushing away from the mother or dropping toys in an angry manner indicate to even the casual observer that something is amiss (at least from the baby's point of view), behaviors such as looking away or turning away hardly seem indicative of disturbance. The avoidant group *A* baby may in fact strike the observer (or the parent) as socially independent and even precociously mature. Avoidance and resistance may, however, be better understood if considered in conjunction with anxiety, conflict, physical contact, and the final response to major separations witnessed in young children.

According to Bowlby (1973), anxiety may occur whenever attachment behavior is strongly activated and the attachment figure is inaccessible and/or unresponsive. Thus anxiety is likely to occur in young children when separation from the mother is *involuntary* and especially if it occurs in an unfamiliar environment, which may itself be alarming. Anxiety may also occur in any situation in which a young child's attachment behavior is activated but s/he is apprehensive that the mother may not be responsive or remain inaccessible (Hinde, 1974; Spencer-Booth & Hinde, 1966). According to Hinde (1970) the simultaneous activation of competing systems may result in the "disinhibition" of a behavior not related to those systems. This is especially true if the behavior is of high priority in the behavioral repertoire. Exploration is such a behavior, and it is frequently witnessed in conflict situations such as those which the avoidant (group *A*) infants have experienced. As part of the study of the mother-infant physical contact relation (Main, 1973), the attitudes toward physical contact with their infants expressed by the mothers of Ainsworth's Baltimore sample were investigated. While not conclusive the data suggested that the mothers of avoidant (group *A*) infants differ from those of resistant (group *C*) infants in that they express dislike of establishing physical contact with their infants.

It seems safe to conclude, therefore, that while both the avoidant and resistant infants suffer some anxiety due to the psychological and sometimes physical inaccessibility of the attachment figure, the infants whose mothers reject them will suffer the greatest anxiety. Such infants will repeatedly find themselves in conflict whether to approach the mother in response to the activation of their attachment system or to move away from her in response to maternal rejection. For these infants there is both the anxiety rising from maternal unresponsiveness and a conflict arising from the activation of competing systems. When conflict causes attachment behavior to be blocked by the child looking or moving away, the reaction has been described as defensive behavior (Ainsworth & Bell, 1970) and seems remarkably reminiscent of the response of young children to major separations described by Bowlby (1960).

In sum, in exhibiting resistance toward the mother in the strange situation, infants exhibit a focal concern with her—one which may take precedence over exploration and learning. At the same time they show that they have not lost the ability to be interested in people and that they are still able to express all the anger that they feel. Avoidant infants are, in contrast, at least superficially freed of their interest in the mother by reason of defensive behavior. These infants may, however, be in the process of losing the capacity for intimacy and forming relationships in general. This, of course, is an area in need of further research if we are to attempt to evaluate these analogic relations adequately.

Despite the possible criticisms and statistical disadvantages of applying a fine-grained classificatory system to an initially small sample, the original provision of groups seems justified on two interrelated counts; differences in configurational patterns of behavior among the groups and internal consistency within each group. Analysis of strange situation protocols reveals clearcut differences in the behavioral configuration exhibited by infants in the three main groups. In other words specific types of behavior in response to the cumulative stresses of the strange situation clearly distinguish between groups. Internal consistency of the group refers to the high degree of similarity in the strange situation behavior of the individual members of each group. In regard to the criterion behaviors mentioned above, infants classified in a particular group do, in fact, resemble one another more closely than they resemble infants in other groups. It is also important to stress the fact that despite the laboratory-based nature of the strange situation test it is not without considerable concurrent validity assessed in terms of usual behavior in the home (Ainsworth et al., 1978). Although this relation represents only a first step toward validation, it is an attractive notion that one might, in a twenty-minute laboratory procedure, obtain a reliable and valid assessment of the nature of the relationship that has developed between an infant and the mother over the course of the first year.

Recent research (Sroufe & Waters, 1977; Vaughn et al., 1979; Waters, 1978) has begun to address the problems of reliability and generalizability of attachment classifications more directly. Following Ainsworth's procedures Sroufe and Waters (1977) classified 70 twelve-month infants in the strange situation. They reported that 90 percent of the infants were readily classified with interrater agreement of 0.94 for the three main categories and 0.88 for the eight subcategories. The proportion of infants falling into each category compared favorably with Ainsworth's original Baltimore sample.

Waters (1978) provides some additional evidence concerning the reliability and stability of this classification system. Fifty infants who had been classified at 12 months of age were reclassified at 18 months by two coders, blind to the earlier classifications. He found that 48 of 50 infants fell into the same major category, despite many changes in the frequency of discrete attachment behaviors. In a recent study reported by Vaughn et al. (1979), this finding of significant stability was found in a large sample of infants from an economically disadvantaged population.

As Sroufe (1979b) notes, demonstrating coherence in individual development does not rest on continuity alone; change in adaptation should be comprehended as well. Whereas Waters (1978) demonstrated that 96 percent of the middle-class infants in his sample received the same attachment classifications when assessed at an interval of six months, Vaughn et al. (1979) found considerably less stability in their sample of economically disadvantaged infants and mothers. In the Vaughn et al. sample, only 62 of 100 infants received the same major classification at 18 months. Of particular importance, however, was the finding that stressful life events were related to the quality of infant-mother attachments. Mothers of anxiously attached infants reported significantly greater life stresses than mothers of securely attached infants at 18 months. Mothers of those infants whose classification changed from secure at 12 months to anxious at 18 months reported significantly more stressful events than did mothers of those infants who were classified as securely attached at both ages. In a reanalysis of some of the data presented by Vaughn et al. (1979), Rosenberg et al. (1979) examined actual *changes* in stress levels from 12 to 18 months. They found that the mothers of securely attached 18-month-olds report significant *reductions* in stress levels over the 12- to 18-month period and that these reductions are significantly *greater* than for mothers of anxiously attached infants (who

either increase or show only marginal reductions in stress levels). Vaughn et al. (1979) note that the specification of circumstances associated with changes in the quality of attachment are as important for attachment theory as the finding of significant continuity in the attachment relationships.

Several important points can be made from these investigations. First, discrete behavioral indices of attachment were not found to be stable in any of the studies cited above. Touching and looking at the mother, for example, demonstrated zero stability. *Behavioral categories* (e.g., avoidance and resistance), however, demonstrated substantial stability, although the manner in which such behavior was manifested may have varied from 12 to 18 months. Whereas the avoidant infant may have demonstrated one type of avoidance at 12 months (e.g., turning away), avoidance at 18 months may have taken the form of ignoring the mother after a reunion. Similarly, securely attached infants consistently demonstrated their ability to use the mother as a secure base from which to explore and were always found to be interested in reestablishing contact (either by physically making contact or by increasing interactions across a distance) with their mothers upon reunion. Although the behavioral expression may vary, the meaning of the behaviors in question was remarkably clear. This is the second point: It is the quality of the affective bond which remains stable and not discrete behaviors. It is the security derived from the attachment relationship around which attachment behaviors are organized that is reflected in the Strange Situation assessment, not the supposed strength of the bond.

Validity Data from the First-Year: Observations of Infant-Mother Interaction

The ultimate validity of the strange situation, as with any laboratory-based assessment procedure, must lie in its relationship to external variables. To this end Ainsworth, Bell, and Stayton (1971) reported their findings comparing infant-mother interaction in the home situation during the last quarter of the first year of life with infant behavior in the strange situation for the 23 babies in Ainsworth's original Baltimore sample. They compared the mothers of group *B* infants with the mothers of non-*B* infants in terms of the mothers' "sensitivity to the signals and communications of the infant," which Ainsworth believes to be the central variable for assessing mothering during the first year of life. All mothers rated above scale midpoint had group *B* infants; all those rated below scale midpoint had group *A* or *C* infants. The mothers of group *A* and *C* infants did not differ on the average in the extent to which they were insensitive to their infants' signals. Infant behavior in the home situation was also coded. Infants later to be classified in group *B* behaved in the home situation as if they were securely attached, crying less than other infants and responding more positively to being held.

In several studies, Ainsworth (cf. Ainsworth et al., 1978) has related the quality of attachment to various patterns of caretaking during the first year. In a study of the mother-infant relationship in the feeding situation during the first three months of life, a significant relationship was found between early feeding patterns and the infant's strange situation classification at 12 months. Feeding patterns have also been clearly related to both the amount and pattern of infant crying behavior during the first quarter of the infant's first year of life (Ainsworth & Bell, 1969). Blehar, Lieberman, and Ainsworth (1977) reported that 12-month strange situation classifications could be predicted from maternal behaviors as early as 6 to 15 weeks of age. Bell and Ainsworth (1972) concluded that maternal behavior throughout the first year of life had more influence on how much the infant cried at the end of the first year than did the infant's initial tendency to cry. Ainsworth and Bell (1974) reported that in the third and fourth quarters of the first year of life, infants who cried more had mothers who more frequently ignored their crying. It was also found that infants who cried little had a wider range of differentiated modes of communication than did babies who cried a great deal.

In sum, the strange situation does not appear to be as situation-bound as some would suggest. It has, in fact, proved to be a reliable and valid assessment technique for describing the quality of the infant-mother attachment relation.

THE IMPLICATIONS
OF INFANT-MOTHER ATTACHMENT
FOR OTHER AREAS OF DEVELOPMENT

A major function of the attachment behavioral system is to mediate the infant's excursions into the world and to shift the balance of behavior from exploration to proximity seeking in response to a variety of internal and external contingencies (Ainsworth, 1973; Waters, 1980). As such, the relationship between the attachment and exploration behavioral systems is one of dynamic equilibrium best understood in terms of the ordering of behavioral priorities.

Under conditions of stress, such as illness, fatigue, hunger, fear of separation from the primary caretaker, attachment behavior becomes dominant and, therefore, incompatible wih exploration. Conversely, under other conditions, the presence of the attachment figure serves to support and encourage exploration of a novel environment (Ainsworth & Bell, 1970). Hinde (1970) observed that while the stimulus conditions which give rise to infant curiosity and exploration are closely allied with those producing fear and avoidance, the presence of the attachment figure may influence the infant's internal state in such a way that sways the relative balance of behavior from avoidance to exploration. In a study concerned with exploring this relationship in primates, Harlow and Zimmerman (1959) demonstrated that even the presence of a cloth-covered surrogate mother had the effect of allaying anxiety and reducing fear of the unknown, providing a degree of comfort compatible with exploration. In the presence of the surrogate mother, infant monkeys were able to venture forth and explore the environment in much the same fashion as if in the presence of the natural mother.

Subsequent studies indicate that human infants also use the mother as a secure base from which to explore the environment, normally exhibiting exploratory behavior

and attachment behavior in regular, smoothly alternating bouts (Ainsworth & Bell, 1970). This balance between attachment and exploration is, in fact, so characteristic of the infant-mother relationship that it has been suggested that clear evidence of such behavioral organization is the best criteria for inferring the existence of an attachment relationship (Ainsworth, 1973; Waters, 1980). Similarly, it has been demonstrated that separation from the mother has a suppressing effect upon exploration. When separated from their mothers for a brief period, most one-year-old infants will explore the environment somewhat when reunited. Following the stress induced by a second separation, however, most one-year-olds become increasingly preoccupied with attachment behavior in the mother's presence with a consequent reduction in exploratory activity (Ainsworth & Bell, 1970). That it is the infant's response to the *mother's* presence which is crucial is consistent with the observation that infants left in an unfamiliar situation with someone other than the mother will tend to cry (Rheingold, 1969). Moreover, such findings strongly suggest that the mother's presence will not necessarily support exploration if the infant has reason to distrust her constancy or physical accessibility.

Studies have also demonstrated that separation from the mother may have long-term effects as well. Spencer-Booth and Hinde (1966) conducted a study in which the mothers of four young macaque monkeys were removed from their infants for a period of six days. When assessed two years later, the experimental group continued to show deficits in exploratory behavior as compared to that of control subjects who had not undergone such a separation (Spencer-Booth & Hinde, 1971). In terms of the human infant, the relationship between prolonged separation from the mother and subsequent exploration per se has not been systematically investigated. It has, however, been amply demonstrated that sustained early separations may inhibit or prevent the formation of an attachment (Goldfarb, 1943; Provence & Lipton, 1962) and that following the establishment of a primary attachment relationship, prolonged separations may lead to apathy and psychological detachment (Bowlby, 1960a). Studies which directly address the issue of exploration as related to early separation from the caregiver would be of great interest since the investigations of Spencer-Booth and Hinde (1966, 1971) would suggest that even relatively brief separations may have potentially damaging effects for some time to come.

While the majority of studies concerned with this relationship have examined the effects of the physical accessibility of the mother, individual differences in the overall quality of attachment have also been related to subsequent exploratory competence. Just as the level of anxiety may be influenced by the mother's physical absence or inconstancy, the psychological uncertainty engendered by an anxious attachment relationship also appears to arouse attachment behavior at the expense of exploration.

Ainsworth and Bell (1970) measured three aspects of infant exploratory behavior during the strange situation: locomotion, object manipulation, and visual exploration. They demonstrated that the mother's presence was essential for the maintenance of all three aspects of exploration and that even brief separations tipped the behavioral balance from exploration to attachment. Ainsworth, Bell, and Stayton (1971) explored the relationship between individual differences in the way infants balance exploratory behavior with attachment behavior in the home situation and obtained results consistent with expectation. Infants judged secure in their primary attachment relationship with the mother were able to use the mother as a secure base from which to explore. Infants who had been judged anxiously attached did not. Predictable differences were also found between the nature of the infant's exploratory activity and 12 month strange situation classifications. Securely attached (group *B*) infants were found to use the mother as a secure base from which to explore the experimental room, but separation heightened attachment behavior and dramatically curtailed exploration in subsequent episodes. Anxious-resistant (group *C*) infants were found to resemble securely attached infants in their exploratory behavior, although there was also found to be a group of passive group *C* infants who explored little. Anxious-avoidance (group *A*) infants were found to maintain relatively high levels of exploration throughout the strange situation. Main (1973) reviewed Ainsworth's narrative records of visits to 26 mother-infant pairs and was able to demonstrate differences in regard to their behavior with objects. As compared to anxiously attached infants, those secure in their attachment were found to take more pleasure in object exploration.

These findings were replicated in part by Joffe (1977), who employed factor analytic techniques to clarify the structural differences in exploratory behavior in the context of the strange situation. As expected, it was found that the presence of the stranger significantly inhibited exploration in both securely and anxiously attached groups of infants. In addition, it was demonstrated that securely attached (group *B*) infants were the only infants to demonstrate the attachment-exploration balance first described by Ainsworth and Bell (1970). Securely attached infants were also found to engage in higher quality object exploration and to employ significantly more fine motor manipulations in their investigations of the object world than did either anxious-avoidant (group *A*) or anxious-resistant (group *C*) infants. Although anxious-avoidant infants maintained conspicuously high levels of exploration throughout, qualitative differences were observed. In comparison to securely attached infants, anxious-avoidant infants displayed less detailed object exploration and tended to engage in a great deal of "locomotor wandering." Anxious-resistant infants, on the other hand, were characterized by either unusual passivity and immaturity of object exploration or frequent hitting, banging, and throwing of toys.

Several additional studies have also confirmed this relationship between security of attachment and exploration. Bretherton and Ainsworth (1974) reported that securely attached one-year-olds were more attracted to available toys and tended to be more curious, although they became somewhat reticent in the presence of the stranger. Main (1973) found that infants classified as securely attached at 12 months played significantly longer, more intensely, and with more positive affect as toddlers than did anxiously attached infants.

When viewed in terms of interrelated behavioral systems, these findings are consistent with the assumption that the infant must order his/her behavioral priorities and that such ordering is highly dependent upon a number of internal and external factors. To the extent that the infant is preoccupied with either the physical or emotional accessibility of the attachment figure, attachment behavior will predominate. To the extent that the infant comes to know his/her world through exploration and play, the effect of maternal inaccessibility may be expected to have predictable effects on subsequent learning. Studies specifically addressing this issue are presently lacking and, consequently, clarification of this potentially interesting relationship must await future confirmation.

Attachment and Cognitive Functioning

Beginning with the interest of psychoanalysts in the concept of object constancy (Beres, 1968; Frosch, 1966; Hartmann, 1952; Werner, 1957) and the observation that children showing disturbances in their relations with others often exhibited deficits in the scheme of the object (Anthony, 1956), several attempts have been made to demonstrate an association between the libidinal and cognitive aspects of human attachment in infancy.

Decarie (1965) first attempted to reconcile the psychoanalytic criteria for mental representation of the mother (e.g., evocative memory) and the concept of object constancy with the development of object permanence as set forth by Piaget (1937). Based on psychoanalytic criteria, Decarie developed an objectal scale to assess the development of libidinal object relations, as well as an object permanence scale to assess the development of the scheme of objects as permanent. While a generally positive association was reported between an infant's standing on these two scales, there were many problems with the objectal scale that prevented any firm conclusions. Most importantly, Decarie found that the sequence obtained through the administration of the objectal scale was highly variable in over half the sample to whom the scale was administered. It was only through subsequent analysis of the homogeneous protocols and a revision of Piaget's criteria which allowed any relationship to be demonstrated.

Coblinger (1965) also attempted to reconcile psychoanalytic data with that reported by Piaget but, again, was unable to do so without stretching the evidence in ways that were uncongenial to both Piaget and psychoanalysis. Generally, these studies indicate that there does not appear to be a one-to-one correspondence between psychoanalytic criteria of object relations and the development of object permanence defined in cognitive terms.

Later studies, however, have been successful in demonstrating certain interesting relationships between the development of the concept of objects as permanent and the infant's relations with important human figures. Bell (1970) employed the strange situation with a white middle-class sample of infants and was able to demonstrate successfully that for infants judged secure in their primary attachment relationship the scheme of the permanence of persons develops *more rapidly* than does the scheme of the permanence of objects. She was also able to demonstrate that for infants exhibiting this relative difference in rate of development the entire scheme of the permanence of objects develops more rapidly. These data are consistent with earlier analytic investigations insofar as demonstrating the existence of a relationship between object permanence and the infant's relationship with the mother. These findings also suggest, however, that the relationship is likely to be complex and that the development of person permanence and object permanence may develop at different rates and along somewhat different developmental lines.

Studies employing more traditional tests of cognitive development have also explored the relationship between differences in infant-mother interaction and level of cognitive development. A significant positive association was shown between a mother's "sensitivity to the signals and communications of her infant" and the infant's developmental quotient measured during the last quarter of the first year of life (Ainsworth & Bell, 1970). Similarly, Stayton, Hogan, and Ainsworth (1971) found maternal sensitivity, acceptance, and cooperation to predict IQ significantly during the last quarter of the first year. Main (1973) found significant differences between securely and anxiously attached infants at 20 months of age on the *Bayley Scales of Infant Development* in favor of the securely attached group. Longitudinal studies have shown an association between maternal behavior during the first three years of life and intelligence through age 18 (Bayley & Schaefer, 1964). Strikingly, Bayley reports a highly negative association between maternal hostility during the first three years and intelligence at age 36 and, conversely, positive associations between maternal love and understanding and intelligence at age 36.

Recently, the relationship between infant-mother interaction and subsequent problem-solving style has begun to be investigated and the results have proven extremely interesting. Matas, Arend, and Sroufe (1978) related security of attachment at 18 months to performance in a problem-solving situation at two years of age. Two-year-olds, with the mother present, were exposed to three problem-solving situations of graduated difficulty and rated on such variables as enthusiasm in approaching the problems, positive and negative affect, frustration behavior, time away from task, compliance, ignoring, or noncompliance with the mother's suggestions. Each of these measures distinguished securely from anxiously attached toddlers. Overall, securely attached toddlers were found to be significantly more effective problem solvers in this situation.

While the data available to date does support an association between the quality of infant-mother interaction and cognitive development, the relationship is not a simple one and cannot be said to be accurately understood at the present time. As Sroufe (1979a) has said, affect and cognition are inseparable and each influences the other. It is as descriptively accurate to say that emotional experience and expression promote cognitive growth as it is to say that cognitive factors underlie emotional development (Sroufe & Waters, 1976). It is largely due to the reciprocal effects of affect and cognition that the nature of the relationships involved are likely to be very difficult to investigate although recent work has been encouraging (see Emde, Gaensbauer, & Harmon, 1976).

Attachment and Subsequent Social-Personality Development

As has been previously discussed some important links between attachment and other behavioral systems such as exploration and cognitive functioning have begun to be investigated. The implications of the early infant-mother attachment relation for subsequent development, however, have only begun to be explored although such influences are expected from the organizational point of view. Yarrow (1972) has suggested that a child who has developed confident expectations toward his/her mother and sees the environment as essentially predictable may be more capable of developing independence and better able to form new social relationships. Sroufe and Waters (1977) state, "Establishing a secure adaptive relationship with the mother may be viewed as a major developmental task of the first year of life, having consequences for subsequent tasks such as exploration and mastery of the inanimate environment, achieving a concept of the autonomous self, and competence in the peer group" (p. 1195).

In regard to the influence of infant-mother attachment on early socialization, Main and Londerville (1977) conducted a short-term longitudinal investigation concerned with the infant's obedience to the mother, evidence for the establishment of internalized controls, the mother's verbal commands, and the mother's physical interventions. The toddler's compliance was observed not only with respect to the mother but with two other persons as well, maternal report as well as direct observation were utilized, and active disobedience or acts of physical aggression were also considered. Security of attachment was found to be related to socialization: Infants classified as securely attached at 12 months of age were found to be more compliant and cooperative at 21 months than were anxiously attached infants. Negative behavior toward the mother was related to negative behavior toward unfamiliar persons at 21 months. Similar results have been reported by Stayton, Hogan, and Ainsworth (1971).

In a recent study concerned with the relation between mother-infant attachment and early socialization, Joffe (1980) observed 117 mother-infant pairs in the context of an experimental, laboratory-based, *prohibition situation* (Egeland, Taraldson, Brunnquell, & Joffe, 1978). The experimental situation was designed to encourage the infants' exploration of a novel environment, and maternal style of control or limit setting was also assessed. Infants who were classified as securely attached at 12 months of age demonstrated substantially greater compliance with maternal commands and prohibitions than did infants judged to be anxiously attached. Securely attached infants were, however, also observed to engage in more active exploration of the environment. Mothers of securely attached infants were found to demonstrate cooperative, sensitive interaction with their infants, imposing behavioral controls only when absolutely necessary and directing the infants' activity in a manner that was nonintrusive and readily accepted. Both groups of anxiously attached infants (anxious-avoidant group *A* and anxious-resistant group *C*) were found to be equally noncompliant with maternal wishes; however, the mothers of these two groups of infants were observed to differ in their behavior within the prohibition situation. Mothers of anxiously attached (group *C*) infants were observed to engage in a great deal of physical intrusion, expressed their impatience readily, and generally seemed at a loss as to the successful means to direct their infant's ongoing activities. Mothers of anxiously attached (group *A*) infants, on the other hand, were found to be low on involvement throughout. When observed again at 18 months of age, these original differences were found to be quite stable, implying that the patterns of infant-mother interaction developed in the context of the attachment relation have observable and relatively stable implications for later infant compliance and maternal style of control.

Attachment as an affective bond would also have consequences for other aspects of social development. Main (1973) demonstrated certain individual differences in willingness to engage in social interaction and turn-taking in a group of 18-month-old infants. Using a simple game of ball, she found that securely attached toddlers approached an adult playmate when she first entered the room and that they more frequently returned the ball to her in a "game-like" manner than did insecurely attached infants. The securely attached group also laughed more during the game than did the anxiously attached group and were more frequently described as being playful, although these differences did not reach conventional levels of significance.

The relationship between the quality of infant-mother attachment and initial responsiveness to peers is illustrated in a recent report by Pastor (in press). He found that toddlers earlier identified as securely attached were more sociable and more positively oriented toward peers in a play situation than were children identified as anxiously attached. In this study the quality of attachment had been assessed at 18 months, and the play interactions were observed at 20–23 months of age. Thus the attachment classifications were predictive of later social behavior across time, across situations, and across interactional systems (peer vs. mother).

Leach (1972) examined the relationship between the ability to separate from the mother and the quality of peer relations in the early years. She observed the behavior of six preschoolers who had been referred to a psychological clinic because of reported difficulties separating from the mother and compared their behavior to 18 children with no such difficulties attending the same nursery school. The six index children demonstrated reduced, unsatisfactory interactions with both peers and their mothers. They initiated less overall behavior and were less responsive to other children than were controls.

Lieberman (1977) explored the influence of attachment to the mother and social experience with peers on the social competence of three-year-olds in a play session with a strange peer. The quality of infant-mother attachment was assessed by several measures in the home. Information concerning each child's early experiences with peers prior to his/her current nursery school or daycare attendance was obtained from maternal report. Lieberman found that security of attachment as assessed at home was positively correlated with peer experience. Partial correlations demonstrated that security of attachment was correlated only with nonverbal measures of peer competence, whereas peer experience was corre-

lated only with verbal measures. She concluded that security of attachment and peer experience were related to different aspects of peer competence. This study is consistent with Pastor's (in press) report in establishing links between the attachment relation and early interaction with peers.

Waters, Wippman, and Sroufe (1979) have demonstrated that the quality of attachment at 15 months was related to independent *Q*-sort descriptions of children in nursery school at age 3½ years. Securely attached children were later described as peer leaders, socially involved, attracting the attention of others, curious and actively engaged in their surroundings. Overall differences between securely attached infants in "peer competence" and "personal competence" were highly significant and not due to IQ.

In a more recent study (Arend, Gove, & Sroufe, 1979), this work was linked to important work on two dimensions of personality organization, ego control and ego resiliency (Block & Block, 1980). *Ego control* refers to the degree of control the child maintained over impulses, wishes, and desires. Overcontrol leads to rigidity and lack of spontaneity, while undercontrol is related to the inability to delay gratification and to engage in purposeful behavior. *Ego resiliency* refers to flexibility of control such that the resilient child can plan and delay when circumstances require but can also exhibit spontaneity, enthusiasm, and curiosity when appropriate. Using the Blocks' *Q*-sort measure, Arend et al. (1979) demonstrated that children who were securely attached (at 18 months of age) were independently described by their preschool teachers (at age 4–5 years) as highly resilient. Items typically placed in the "most characteristic" category for the securely attached children included *resourceful in initiating activities, curious and exploring,* and *self-reliant, confident.* Items in the "least characteristic" category included *inhibited and constricted, tends to disengage under stress,* and *becomes anxious when the environment is unpredictable.* Securely attached children were also described as being moderate on control, neither over- nor undercontrolled. Infants classified in either of the two anxiously attached groups were significantly lower on resiliency, with those in the anxious-avoidant (group *A*) group tending to be overcontrolled and those in the anxious-resistant (group *C*) group tending to be undercontrolled.

In a controversial paper Bowlby (1977) has recently ventured beyond the current empirical data to embrace the original hypothesis proposed by Freud (1938) concerning the relationship between early infant-mother attachment and later love relationships. Bowlby (1977) suggests that there is a strong causal tie between the experiences of an individual with his/her parents during infancy and the later capacity to form affectional bonds in general. Bowlby proposes the initial secure base grounded in infancy leads to the later development of security, self-reliance, trust, cooperation, and generally helpful attitudes toward others. In the psychoanalytic literature such a person is said to have a strong ego and may be described as showing "basic trust" (Erikson, 1950), or "mature dependence" (Fairbairn, 1952). In terms of attachment theory such an individual is described as having built up a representational model of self as being both able to perform effectively and to be worthy of being helped by others should the need arise.

While data prelevant to this hypothesis are by no means complete, the study reported by Matas, Arend, and Sroufe (1978) does suggest that securely attached infants are both more enthusiastic in approaching a difficult problem and more accessible to parental help in solving such problems.

In the absence of security Bowlby (1977) believes that the child may grow up to be anxious, insecure, overdependent, and generally immature. Under stress such persons are apt to develop neurotic symptoms, depression, or phobia. Alternatively such persons may develop symptoms which seemingly are the opposite of immaturity. Parkes (1973) described this constellation of behavioral responses as *compulsive self-reliance*. Rather than seek the love and care of others, a person exhibiting this pattern insists on doing everything alone, under all conditions. Bowlby (1977) suggests that these people most often respond to increasing levels of stress by developing psychosomatic symptoms.

To explain why individual differences in infant-mother relationships should continue to influence interpersonal relationships throughout the lifetime, it seems necessary to postulate that representational models of attachment figures and of self built during infancy and childhood persist relatively unchanged, as the core of personality, throughout adult life. As a result the individual tends to assimilate any new person with whom a bond is formed (e.g., a spouse or a child) to an existing model and continues to do so in spite of evidence that the model is inappropriate. Similarly the individual expects to be perceived and treated by others in ways that are consistent with the self-model and to continue with such expectations in the face of contrary evidence. Such biased perceptions and expectations lead to various misconceptions about others, to false expectations about the way they will behave, and to inappropriate actions intended to forestall those expected behaviors.

Although Bowlby's speculations concerning the sequelae of infant-mother attachment are intriguing, we must recognize that at the present time they do not have empirical support. This is not, however, because there is a body of evidence inconsistent with his hypotheses but because they have not yet been tested. Indeed the empirical research confirming the impact of infant-mother attachment on development in late infancy and toddlerhood has only recently been reported (see Sroufe, 1979b). We suggest that Bowlby's speculations, though presently extending far beyond the available empirical research evidence, will prove to be rich theoretical sources for researchers conducting longitudinal studies of personality and social development.

CONCLUSIONS

Within the ethological-organizational view of attachment (Ainsworth, 1973; Bowlby, 1969; Sroufe, 1979a; Sroufe & Waters, 1977) attachment is conceived to be an enduring affective bond between infant and caregiver, a position in marked contrast to the social learning formulation that attachment is really nothing more than the interaction between infant and caregiver (Cairns, 1972; Rosenthal, 1973), that attachment can be defined in terms of discrete behaviors independent of meaning or context (Feldman & Ingham, 1975), and that stable individual differences in attachment cannot be found or are simply irrelevant to an understanding of attachment (e.g., Masters & Wellman, 1974). Neither is attachment viewed as simply another relationship having little scientific merit (Weinraub et al., 1977).

In many respects the preceding discussion touches on an issue central to scientific investigation and having implications extending far beyond the study of infant-adult attachment per se. More specifically one must address the issue of the nature of the models employed and the subsequent implications of model selection for what are and are not considered meaningful problems for investigations, the types of methods employed, and the explanations to be applied in the interpretation of the data generated. As representations, models aid in the understanding and explanation of the subject matter and provide a lens through which the subject matter is viewed in a new way. Models of inquiry establish the basic categories which determine the introduction of certain classes of theoretical construct and exclude others, define meaningful problems for inquiry, suggest methods for exploring these problems, provide types of explanations for exploring these problems, and provide types of explanations for interpreting data.

Differences in such criteria as the meaning of *explanation*, and even *fact*, would strongly suggest that attempts to synthesize fundamentally different approaches are futile and that any attempt to do so inevitably results in the type of theoretical synthesis or eclecticism that breeds more confusion than clarity. Attachment theory, as conceived within the ethological-organizational perspective, has been described as "programmatic" and open ended (Ainsworth et al., 1978). It does not purport to be a tight network of propositions on the basis of which hypotheses may be formulated, any one of which in the event of an inadequate and unsuccessful test could invalidate the theory as a whole. Instead this is an explanatory theory serving as a guide to understanding data already at our disposal and a guide to further research. As such the perspective presented here has served its function laudably. The ethological-organizational approach to infant-adult attachment is replete with predictions and implications, subject to empirical study, which other approaches to the same problem simply do not provide. An examination of the available evidence leaves little doubt as to the significance of this shift in perspective for the understanding of the development tasks of infancy and the relationship between early experience and later interpersonal competence.

REFERENCES

AINSWORTH, M. The development of mother-infant interaction among the Ganda. In B. M. Foss (Ed.), *Determinants of infant behavior.* London: Methuen & Company, Ltd., 1963.

AINSWORTH, M. *Infancy in Uganda: Infant care and the growth of love.* Baltimore, Md.: Johns Hopkins University Press, 1967.

AINSWORTH, M. Object relations, dependency, and attachment: A theoretical view of the infant-mother relationship. *Child Development,* 1969, *40,* 969–1025.

AINSWORTH, M. Attachment and dependency: A comparison. Pp. 97–137 in J. Gewirtz (Ed.), *Attachment and dependency.* Washington, D.C.: V. H. Winston & Sons, 1972.

AINSWORTH, M. The development of infant-mother attachment. In B. Caldwell & H. Ricciuti (Eds.), *Review of child development research* (Vol. 3). Chicago: University of Chicago Press, 1973.

AINSWORTH, M. *Infant development and mother-infant interaction among Ganda and American families.* Paper presented at Wenner-Gren Conference on Cultural and Social Influences in Early Infancy and Childhood. Burg Wartenstein, West Germany, June 1975.

AINSWORTH, M., & BELL, S. M. Some contemporary patterns of mother-infant interaction in the feeding situation. In A. Ambrose (Ed.), *Stimulation in early infancy.* London: Academic Press, 1969.

AINSWORTH, M., & BELL, S. Attachment, exploration and separation: Illustrated by the behavior of one-year-olds in a strange situation. *Child Development,* 1970, *41,* 49–67.

AINSWORTH, M., & BELL, S. Mother-infant interaction and the development of competence. In K. J. Connally & J. S. Bruner (Eds.), *The growth of competence.* New York: Academic Press, 1974.

AINSWORTH, M., BELL, S., & STAYTON, D. Individual differences in strange situation behavior of one-year-olds. In H. Schaffer (Ed.), *The origins of human social relations.* London: Academic Press, 1971.

AINSWORTH, M., BELL, S., & STAYTON, D. Individual differences in the development of some attachment behaviors. *Merrill-Palmer Quarterly of Behavior and Development,* 1972, *18,* 123–143.

AINSWORTH, M., BELL, S., & STAYTON, D. Infant-mother attachment and social development: Socialization as a product of reciprocal responsiveness to signals. In M. Richards (Ed.), *The integration of the child into the social world.* Cambridge, England: Cambridge University Press, 1974.

AINSWORTH, M., BLEHAR, M., WATERS, E., & WALL, S. *Strange-situation behavior of one-year-olds: Its relation to mother-infant interaction in the first year and to qualitative differences in the infant-mother attachment relationship.* Hillsdale, N.J.: Lawrence Erlbaum Associates, 1978.

AINSWORTH, M., & WITTIG, B. Attachment and exploratory behavior of one-year-olds in a strange situation. In B. M. Foss (Ed.), *Determinants of infant behavior* (Vol. 4). New York: Barnes & Noble Books, 1969.

ALLPORT, G. W. Traits revisited. *American Psychology,* 1966, *21,* 1–10.

ANTHONY, E. J. The significance of Jean Piaget for child psychiatry. *British Journal of Medical Psychology,* 1956, *29,* 20–34.

AREND, D., GOVE, F., & SROUFE, L. A. Continuity of individual adaptation from infancy to kindergarten: A predictive study of ego-resiliency and curiosity in preschoolers. *Child Development,* 1979, *50,* 950–959.

ARSENIAN, J. M. Young children in an insecure situation. *Journal of Abnormal and Social Psychology,* 1943, *38,* 225–249.

BAERENDS, G. P. A model of the functional organization of incubation behavior. In G. P. Baerands & R. H. Drent (Eds.), *The Herring Gull and its egg. Behaviour Supplement,* 1976, *17,* 261–310.

BATESON, P.P.G. The characteristics and context of imprinting. *Biological Review,* 1966, *41,* 177–220.

BAYLEY, N., & SCHAEFER, E. S. Correlations of maternal and child behaviors with the development of mental abilities: Data from the Berkeley Growth Study. *Monographs of the Society for Research in Child Development,* 1964, *29*(6, Whole No. 97).

BELL, R. Q. A reinterpretation of the direction of effects in socialization. *Psychological Review,* 1968, *75,* 81–95.

BELL, R. Q. Contributions of human infants to caregiving and social interaction. Pp. 1–19 in H. Lewis & L. A. Rosenblum (Eds.), *The effect of the infant on its caregivers.* New York: John Wiley, 1974.

BELL, S. The development of the concept of object as related to infant-mother attachment. *Child Development,* 1970, *41,* 291–311.

BELL, S., & AINSWORTH, M. Infant crying and maternal responsiveness. *Child Development,* 1972, *43,* 1171–1190.

BELLER, E. K. Dependency and independence in young children. *Journal of Genetic Psychology,* 1955, *87,* 25–35.

BELLER, E. K. Dependency and autonomous achievement striving related to orality and anality in early childhood. *Child Development,* 1957, *28,* 287–315.

BERES, D. The humanness of human beings: Psychoanalytic considerations. *Psychoanalytic Quarterly,* 1968, *37,* 487–522.

BIJOU, S. W., & BAER, D. M. *Child development* (Vol. 2). Universal stage of infancy. New York: Appleton-Century-Crofts, 1965.

BISCHOFF, N. A systems approach towards the functional connections of fear and attachment. *Child Development,* 1975, *46,* 801–817.

BLEHAR, M. C., LIEBERMAN, A., & AINSWORTH, M. Early face-to-face interaction and its relation to later infant-mother attachment. *Child Development,* 1977, *48,* 182–194.

BLOCK, J. *Recognizing the coherence of personality.* Unpublished manuscript, University of California, 1976.

BLOCK, J. H., & BLOCK, J. The role of ego-control and ego-resiliency in the organization of behavior. In W. A. Collins (Ed.), *Minnesota Symposium on Child Psychology* (Vol. 11). Hillsdale, N.J.: Lawrence Erlbaum Associates, 1980.

BLURTON-JONES, N. G. *Ethological studies of child behavior.* Cambridge, England: Cambridge University Press, 1972.

BOWLBY, J. Some pathological processes set in train by early mother-child separation. *Journal of Mental Science,* 1953, *99,* 265–272.

BOWLBY, J. The nature of the child's tie to his mother. *International Journal of Psycho-Analysis,* 1958, *39,* 350–373.

BOWLBY, J. Grief and mourning in infancy and early childhood. *Psychoanalytic study of the child,* 1960a, *15,* 9–52.

BOWLBY, J. Separation anxiety. *International Journal of Psycho-Analysis,* 1960b, *41,* 89–113.

BOWLBY, J. *Attachment and loss* (Vol. 1). Attachment. New York: Basic Books, 1969.

BOWLBY, J. *Attachment and loss* (Vol. 2). Separation, anxiety and anger. New York: Basic Books, 1973.

BOWLBY, J. The making and breaking of affectional bonds: Etiology and psychopathology in the light of attachment theory. *British Journal of Psychiatry,* 1977, *130,* 201–210.

BOWLBY, J. *Attachment and loss* (Vol. 3). Sadness and depression. New York: Basic Books, 1980.

BRACKBILL, Y. Extinction of the smiling response in infants as a function of reinforcement schedule. *Child Development,* 1958, *29,* 115–124.

BRAZELTON, T. B., KOSLOWSKI, B., & MAIN, H. The origins of reciprocity: The early infant-mother interaction. Pp. 49–76 in M. Lewis & L. A. Rosenblum (Eds.), *The effect of the infant on its caregiver.* New York: Wiley-Interscience, 1974.

BRETHERTON, I., & AINSWORTH, M. Responses of one-year-olds to a stranger in a strange situation. In M. Lewis & L. Rosenblum (Eds.), *The origins of fear.* New York: John Wiley, 1974.

CAIRNS, R. B. Attachment behavior of mammals. *Psychological Review,* 1966a, *73,* 409–426.

CAIRNS, R. B. The development, maintenance, and extinction of social attachment behavior in sheep. *Journal of Comparative and Physiological Psychology,* 1966b, *62,* 298–306.

CAIRNS, R. B. Attachment and dependency: A psychobiological and social learning synthesis. Pp. 29–80 in J. Gewirtz (Ed.), *Attachment and dependency.* Washington, D.C.: V. H. Winston & Sons, 1972.

CATTELL, R. B. *Personality: A systematic theoretical and factual study.* New York: McGraw-Hill, 1950.

COATES, B., ANDERSON, E. P., & HARTUP, W. W. Interrelations in the attachment behavior of human infants. *Developmental Psychology,* 1972a, *6,* 218–230.

COATES, B., ANDERSON, E. P., & HARTUP, W. W. The stability of attachment behaviors in the human infant. *Developmental Psychology,* 1972b, *6,* 231–237.

COBLINGER, W. G. The Geneva school of genetic psychology and psychoanalysis: Parallels and counterparts. Pp. 301–356 of appendix to R. A. Spita, *The first year of life.* New York: International Universities Press, 1965.

COX, F., & CAMPBELL, D. Young children in a new situation with and without their mothers. *Child Development,* 1968, *39,* 123–131.

CRONBACH, L., & MEEHL, P. E. Construct validity in psychological tests. *Psychological Bulletin,* 1955, *58,* 281–302.

DECARIE, T. G. *Intelligence and affectivity in early childhood.* New York: International Universities Press, 1965.

DOLLARD, J., & MILLER, N. E. *Personality and psychotherapy.* New York: McGraw-Hill, 1950.

EGELAND, B., TARALDSON, B., BRUNNQUELL, D., & JOFFE, L. S. *Rating scales for prohibition of forbidden objects.* Unpublished manuscript, University of Minnesota, 1978.

EMDE, R., GAENSBAUER, T., & HARMON, R. Emotional expression in infancy: A biobehavioral study. *Psychological Issues Monograph Series,* 1976, *10* (Monog. No. 37).

ENGEL, G. Attachment behavior, object relations and the dynamic-economic points of view: Critical review of Bowlby's *At-*

tachment and loss. International Journal of Psychoanalysis, 1971, 52, 183–96.

ERIKSON, E. H. *Childhood and society.* New York: W. W. Norton & Co., Inc., 1950.

FAIRBAIRN, W. R. *Psychoanalytic studies of the personality.* London: Tainstock/Routlege, 1952.

FELDMAN, S., & INGHAM, M. Attachment behavior: A validation study in two age groups. *Child Development,* 1975, 46, 319–330.

FREUD, A., & DANN, S. An experiment in group upbringing. In *The psychoanalytic study of the child* (Vol. 6). New York: International Universities Press, 1951.

FREUD, S. *An outline of psychoanalysis.* New York: W. W. Norton and Company, 1949.

FROSCH, J. A note on reality constancy. In R. M. Lowenstein, L. M. Newman, M. Schur, & A. J. Solnit (Eds.), *Psychoanalysis—A general psychology.* New York: International Universities Press, 1966, 349–376.

GEWIRTZ, J. A learning analysis of the effects of normal stimulation, privation, and deprivation on the acquisition of social motivation and attachment. Pp. 213–298 in B. H. Foss (Ed.), *Determinants of infant behaviour.* London: Methuen (New York: John Wiley), 1961.

GEWIRTZ, J. Mechanisms of social learning: Some roles of stimulation and behavior in early human development. Pp. 57–212 in D. A. Goslin (Ed.), *Handbook of socialization theory and research.* Skokie, Ill.: Rand McNally, 1969.

GEWIRTZ, J. Attachment, dependence, and distinction in terms of stimulus control. Pp. 139–177 in J. Gewirtz (Ed.), *Attachment and dependency.* Washington, D.C.: V. H. Winston & Sons, 1972.

GOLDFARB, W. Effects of early institutional care on adolescent personality. *Journal of Experimental Education,* 1943, 12, 106–129.

GUTHRIE, E. R. *Psychology of learning.* New York: Harper, 1935.

GUTHRIE, E. R. Psychological facts and psychological theory. *Psychological Bulletin,* 1946, 43, 1–20.

HARLOW, H. F. The development of affectional patterns in infant monkeys. Pp. 75–97 in B. M. Foss (Ed.), *Determinants of infant behaviour.* London: Methuen, 1961.

HARLOW, H. F. The maternal affectional system. Pp. 3–34 in B. M. Foss (Ed.), *Determinants of infant behaviour.* London: Methuen, 1963.

HARLOW, H. F., & ZIMMERMAN, R. R. Affectional responses in the infant monkey. *Science,* 1959, 130, 421–432.

HARTMANN, H. The mutual influences in the development of ego and id. Pp. 155–182 in *Essays on ego psychology.* New York: International Universities Press, 1964 (1952).

HEATHERS, G. Emotional dependence and independence in nursery school play. *Journal of Genetic Psychology,* 1955, 87, 37–57.

HINDE, R. A. *Animal behavior: A snythesis of ethology and comparative psychology* (2nd ed.). New York: McGraw-Hill, 1970.

HINDE, R. A. *Biological bases of human social behavior.* New York: McGraw-Hill, 1974.

HINDE, R. A., & SPENCER-BOOTH, Y. Effects of brief separation from mother on rhesus monkeys. *Science,* 1971, 173, 111–118.

JOFFE, L. S. *Attachment, exploration and cognitive functioning.* Unpublished master's thesis, University of Wisconsin, 1977.

JOFFE, L. S. *The relation between mother-infant attachment and compliance with maternal commands and prohibitions.* Unpublished doctoral dissertation, University of Minnesota, 1980.

LEACH, G. M. A comparison of the social behavior of some normal and problem children. In N. Blurton-Jones (Ed.), *Ethological studies of child behavior.* Cambridge, England: Cambridge University Press, 1972.

LEWIN, K. *A dynamic theory of personality.* New York: McGraw-Hill, 1935.

LIEBERMAN, A. F. Preschoolers' competence with a peer: Influence of attachment and social experience. *Child Development,* 1977, 48, 1277–1287.

MACCOBY, E., & FELDMAN, S. Mother-attachment and stranger-reactions in the third year of life. *Monographs of the Society for Research in Child Development,* 1972, 37(1, Whole No. 146).

MACCOBY, E., & MASTERS, J. Attachment and dependency. In P. H. Mussen (Ed.), *Carmichael's manual of child psychology* (Vol. 2). New York: John Wiley, 1970.

MAIN, M. Analysis of a peculiar form of reunion behavior seen in some day-care children: Its history and sequelae in children who are home reared. In R. Webb (Ed.), *Social development in daycare.* Baltimore, Md.: Johns Hopkins University Press, 1973.

MAIN, M., & LONDERVILLE, S. *Compliance and aggression in toddler-hood: Precursors and correlates.* Unpublished manuscript, University of California, 1978.

MASTERS, J., & WELLMAN, H. Human infant attachment: A procedural critique. *Psychological Bulletin,* 1974, 81, 218–237.

MATAS, L., AREND, R. A., & SROUFE, L. A. Continuity of adaptation in the second year: The relationship between quality of attachment and later competence. *Child Development,* 1978, 49, 547–556.

PARKES, C. M. *Bereavement: Studies of grief in adult life.* London: Tavistock, 1972.

PASTOR, D. The quality of the mother infant attachment and its relationship to toddlers' initial sociability and peers. *Developmental Psychology,* in press.

PIAGET, J. *The origins of intelligence in children* (2nd ed.). New York: International Universities Press, 1952. (Originally published 1936.)

PIAGET, J. *The construction of reality in the child.* New York: Basic Books, 1954 (1937).

PROVENCE, S., & LIPTON, R. C. *Infants in institutions.* New York: International Universities Press, 1962.

RAJECKI, D. W., LAMB, M. E., & OBMASCHER, P. Toward a general theory of infantile attachment: A comparative review of aspects of the social bond. *The Behavioral and Brain Sciences,* 1978, 3, 417–464.

RHEINGOLD, H. L. The social and socializing infant. Pp. 779–799 in D. A. Goslin (Ed.), *Handbook of socialization theory and research.* Skokie, Ill.: Rand McNally, 1969.

RHEINGOLD, H. L., GEWIRTZ, J. L., & ROSS, H. W. Social conditioning of vocalizations in the infant. *Journal of Comparative and Physiological Psychology,* 1959, 52, 68–73.

ROBERTSON, J., & BOWLBY, J. Responses of young children to separation from their mother. Observations of the sequences of response of children aged 16 to 24 months during the course of separation. *Courier, Center International de l'Enfance,* 1952, 2, 131–142.

ROBERTSON, J., & ROBERTSON, J. Young children in brief separation: A fresh look. *Psychoanalytic Study of the Child,* 1971, 26, 264–315.

ROSENBLUM, L. A., & HARLOW, H. F. Approach-avoidance conflict in the mother surrogate situation. *Psychological Reports,* 1963, 12, 83–85.

ROSENBERG, D., WATERS, E., EGELAND, B., & VAUGHN, B. *The effects of environmental change on the stability of strange situation classifications.* Paper presented at the meeting of the American Psychological Association, New York, September 1979.

ROSENTHAL, M. Attachment and mother-infant interaction: Some research impasses and a suggested change in orientation. *Journal of Child Psychology, Psychiatry, and Allied Disciplines,* 1973, 14, 201–207.

SCHAFFER, H. R. Objective observations of personality development in early infancy. *British Journal of Medical Psychology,* 1958, 31, 174–183.

SCHAFFER, H. R., & CALLENDER, W. M. Psychological effect of hospitalization in infancy. *Pediatrics,* 1959, 24, 528–539.

SCHAFFER, H. R., & EMERSON, P. E. Patterns of response to physical contact in early human development. *Journal of Child Psychology and Psychiatry,* 1964a, 5, 1–13.

SCHAFFER, H. R., & EMERSON, P. E. The development of social attachments in infancy. *Monographs of the Society for Research in Child Development,* 1964b, 29(No. 3).

SEARS, R. R. Dependency motivation. *Nebraska Symposium on Motivation,* 1963, 11, 25–64.

SEARS, R. R., MACCOBY, E. E., & LEVIN, H. *Patterns of child rearing.* Evanston, Ill.: Row, Peterson, 1957.

SEARS, R. R., RAU, L., & ALPERT, R. *Identification and child rearing.* Stanford, Calif.: Stanford University Press, 1965.

SEAY, B., ALEXANDER, B. K., & HARLOW, H. F. Maternal behavior of socially deprived rhesus monkeys. *Journal of Abnormal and Social Psychology,* 1964, 69, 345–354.

SPENCER-BOOTH, Y., & HINDE, R. A. The effects of separating rhesus monkeys from their mothers for six days. *Journal of Child Psychology and Psychiatry,* 1966, 7, 179–198.

SPENCER-BOOTH, Y., & HINDE, R. A. Effects of brief separations from mothers during infancy on behavior of rhesus monkeys 6–24 months later. *Journal of Child Psychology and Psychiatry,* 1971, 12, 157–172.

SPITZ, R. A. *A genetic field theory of ego formation.* New York: International Universities Press, 1959.

SPITZ, R. A., & WOLFF, K. M. Anaclitic depression. *Psychoanalytic Study of the Child*, 1946, *2*, 313–342.

SROUFE, L. A. Socioemotional development. In J. D. Osotsky (Ed.), *Handbook of infant development.* New York: John Wiley, 1979a.

SROUFE, L. A. The coherence of individual development: Early care, attachment, and subsequent developmental issues. *American Psychologist*, 1979b, *34*, 834–841.

SROUFE, L. A., & WATERS, E. The ontogenesis of smiling and laughter: A perspective on the organization of development in infancy. *Psychological Review*, 1976, *83*, 173–189.

SROUFE, L. A., & WATERS, E. Attachment as an organizational construct. *Child Development*, 1977, *48*, 1184–1199.

STAYTON, D., AINSWORTH, M., & MAIN, M. The development of separation behavior in the first year of life: Protest, following and greeting. *Developmental Psychology*, 1973, *9*, 213–225.

STAYTON, D. J., HOGAN, R., & AINSWORTH, M. Infant obedience and maternal behavior: The origins of socialization reconsidered. *Child Development*, 1971, *41*, 1057–1069.

STENDLER, C. B. Possible causes of overdependency in young children. *Child Development*, 1954, *25*, 125–146.

STERN, D. N. Mother and infant at play: The dyadic interaction involving facial, vocal, and gaze behaviors. Pp. 187–213 in M. Lewis & L. A. Rosenblum (Eds.), *The effect of the infant on its caregiver.* New York: John Wiley, 1974.

VAN LAWICK-GOODALL, J. The behavior of free-living chimpanzees in the Gombe Stream reserve. *Animal Behavior Monograph*, 1968, *1*(No. 3), 165–311.

VAUGHN, B., EGELAND, B., SROUFE, L. A., & WATERS, E. Individual differences in infant-mother attachment at 12 and 18 months: Stability and change in families under stress. *Child Development*, 1979, *50*, 971–975.

WALTERS, R. H., & FOOTE, A. A study of reinforcer effectiveness with children. *Merrill-Palmer Quarterly*, 1962, *8*, 149–157.

WATERS, E. The reliability and stability of individual differences in infant-mother attachment. *Child Development*, 1978, *49*, 483–494.

WATERS, E. Traits, relationships and behavioral systems: The attachment construct and the organization of behavior and development. In K. Immelman, E. Barlow, M. Main, & L. Petrinovich (Eds.), *Development of behavior.* New York: Cambridge University Press, 1980.

WATERS, E., WIPPMAN, J., & SROUFE, L. A. Attachment, positive affect, and competence in the peer group: Two studies in construct validation. *Child Development*, 1979, *50*, 821–829.

WEINRAUB, M., BROOKS, J., & LEWIS, M. The social network: A reconsideration of the concept of attachment. *Human Development*, 1977, *20*, 31–47.

WERNER, H. *Comparative psychology and mental development.* New York: International Universities Press, 1957.

WHITE, R. W. Motivation reconsidered: The concept of competence. *Psychological Review*, 1959, *66*, 297–333.

WOLFF, P. H. The natural history of crying and other vocalization in infancy. In B. H. Foss (Ed.), *Determinants of infant behavior IV.* London: Methuen, 1969.

YARROW, L. Attachment and dependency: A developmental perspective. In J. Gewirtz (Ed.), *Attachment and dependency.* Washington, D.C.: V. H. Winston & Sons, 1972.

13

The Nature-Nurture Issue
and the Integrating Concept
of Function

GLENN E. WEISFELD

The nature-nurture issue—the relative contributions of genes and environment to behavior—constitutes a central paradigm in developmental psychology as well as other behavioral sciences. The simplistic either-or formulation of the question has been superseded by the concept of interactionism, which will be our starting point in this chapter. Subsequently we shall argue for recasting the nature-nurture question in terms of distinguishing behaviors that have evolved under specific selection pressures from those that are made possible by the organism's general capacities for flexible responding. The principal research strategies for identifying evolved behaviors will then be discussed. Lastly we shall suggest that functional analysis may be applied not just to species-wide evolved behaviors but also to cultural and other variants. Throughout the chapter the perspectives and research of learning theorists, cognitive developmentalists, and ethologists will be compared, with a view toward demonstrating the ultimate compatibility and complementarity of these approaches.

INTERACTIONISM

Interactionism is the position that behavior, like any other phenotypic trait, is compounded of both genetic and environmental factors which are interactive rather than additive. Genes must play a role in all behavior because behavior is mediated by nervous systems that differentiate and function under genetic influence. Whereas the information that a person learns is provided through

experience in the environment, the capacity to modify one's behavior in response to environmental input is genetically based. Conversely environment necessarily plays a role in behavior since every organism develops, exists, and behaves in a milieu. The nerves themselves are guided to their embryonic destinations by the chemical gradients that surround them. Even a strongly canalized phenotype, such as the development of visually directed reaching in infancy, will be delayed if the environment fails to provide a modicum of visual and tactile stimulation (White & Held, 1966).

One example of the complexity of genome-environment interaction is that of snail-smashing behavior in the song thrush (Henty, cited by Barlow, 1977). The bird holds the snail by the foot and smashes it against a rock by means of a rhythmic sideways motion of the head. A long period of trial-and-error learning during a critical period is required for young song thrushes to master the behavior. However the European blackbird, a morphologically similar relative of the song thrush that also relishes escargots, cannot be taught to smash them open. "The difference between the two species in their capacity to learn how to open the snail is therefore genetic. One could say that *learning* to smash snails in the song thrush is *instinctive,* or vice versa" (Barlow, p. 244). Additional provocative examples of interaction are provided by Lorenz (1965).

Several problems concerning the nature-nurture issue need to be resolved before proceeding further. For example the idea that genetically based behaviors cannot be modified by environmental influences, that genes alone "determine" some behaviors, runs directly counter to the principle of interactionism. Genes always operate in a context, and that context can in theory always be altered, thereby modifying the resulting behavioral pheno-

The author gratefully acknowledges the assistance of Drs. Sandor B. Brent, Joseph L. Jacobson, Sandra W. Jacobson, Laurence J. Stettner, Francine Wehmer, and Carol C. Weisfeld. He also absolves them of responsibility for the views expressed herein.

type. Thus even behaviors that are characterized, for the sake of simplicity, as innate or instinctual can be modified by experience. For instance gull chicks peck at the parents' beaks shortly after hatching. This prompts the parent to regurgitate food. Particular features of the parent's beak (sign stimuli) release the chick's pecking response, but the response does not develop properly in chicks reared in the dark rather than in the wild. Thus experience acts upon the genetic basis of the behavior (Hailman, 1967).

An example in humans is phenylketonuria (PKU), a genetic condition that results in mental retardation and other behavioral anomalies. PKU is caused by an enzyme deficiency that leads to an inability to metabolize phenylalanine, an amino acid present in milk and other foods. Phenylalanine accumulates in the brain, causing damage. If diagnosed, PKU can be effectively treated by eliminating foods high in phenylalanine from the child's diet. Here we see a genetically based, originally inflexible behavioral condition that can now be modified by environmental intervention and whose treatment came about by understanding its biological basis.

Paradoxically, then, the more we learn about the genetic basis of a phenotypic trait, the more effectively we can intervene. For example it has been suggested that a sensitive period for bonding to the group occurs during the "gang stage" before puberty and that this may explain why racial integration seems to be more difficult to effect thereafter (Fiske, 1974). If such a sensitive period were to be demonstrated empirically, this knowledge would be useful for policy makers, who might then devise more effective integration programs—e.g., by focusing more extensively on the elementary school years.

The biological approach to behavior is not inherently conservative. Like other forms of knowledge it can be used or abused in the service of any political ideology. In the past everyone from social Darwinists (e.g., Spencer) to communists (e.g., Kropotkin) has appealed to various "facts" about the genetic basis of human behavior to buttress his/her philosophy. Similarly the viewpoint that human nature is extremely malleable has been espoused by exponents of techniques ranging from torture and brainwashing through advertising and propaganda to education and child-rearing practices. In recent years some liberals (e.g., Sahlins, 1976) have condemned biological approaches categorically, especially sociobiology. Much of the current antagonism of liberals to the biological approach seems to be founded on the notion that to acknowledge that genes play a role in human behavior is to admit that environment plays little or no role and hence that intervention is futile. As we have seen, this is doubtful. If anything, ignoring genetic influences deprives one of knowledge about effective intervention and therefore favors the status quo. "For instance, the belief that human aggression is based not on phylogenetic adaptation but on learning implies a tremendous underassessment of its dangers" (Lorenz, 1965, p. 20). Other critics of the evolutionary approach to human behavior (e.g., Allen et al., 1975) fear that intervention will be effective—all too effective—in the hands of the power elite. Konner's (1977) reply to this stance is that "if responsible scientists fail to consider the biology of behavior, irresponsible ones will do so" (p. 71). A related misconception (Allen et al., 1975) is that behavioral biologists argue

that genetically based behaviors are natural and hence ethically ideal. Wilson (1975a) and others reject this inference, which is known as the naturalistic fallacy of ethics. For further discussion of these important political and epistemological issues, see Charlesworth (1972), Crawford (1979), Konnor (1977), and van den Berghe (1977).

Another problematical belief is that the factor of culture somehow completely overrides the role of genes in behavior. First of all this would seem to be patently false for the various nonhuman species that might make a claim to culture—i.e., that transmit behaviors by observational learning or active instruction, that use tools, or that transmit locally varying behavioral practices to their offspring. For example young jackdaws acquire fear of cats from their parents (Nash, 1978), but we would hardly wish to conclude that genes play no role in jackdaw behavior or even in the transmission of this particular behavior from parent to offspring.

On the human level, technology has permitted our species to pervade the entire globe. However this display of brain power is a tribute in part to the capacities of man's cerebral cortex, which develops at the direction of genes. The language centers in the cortex that are involved in the acquisition and transmission of cultural information are shaped by genes. So too are the premotor cortex, which allows primates such as ourselves to learn to perform various manual tasks dexterously, and the prefrontal cortex, which is involved in performing delayed and serial responses. In other words man's capacities for flexible, inventive, and socially influenced behaviors have a genetic basis.

Subcortical structures appear to mediate genetically based, "instinctual" behaviors such as aggression, sex, fear, and exploration. Because the cerebral cortex increased tremendously in size during hominid evolution, some theorists have assumed that culturally acquired behavior has eclipsed genetically based behavior. However certain subcortical structures also grew progressively through primate-hominid evolution, suggesting that genetically based behaviors are not merely vestigial in man. These structures include the amygdala (Andy & Stephan, 1974), thalamus, and hippocampus (Fishbein, 1976). Human behavior is obviously more flexible than that of a frog or rat, but it is still influenced by biological needs that are monitored by the hypothalamus and other subcortical structures. Man's cortex provides great flexibility in satisfying these needs—capacity for skilled movements, perceptual discrimination, memory, symbolic thought, foresight, collective action—but the behavioral product, whether it be playing a piano or suckling, constitutes an interaction of genes and experience. Moreover the precise relative contributions of genes and environment to any behavioral act are unknowable. Both types of factor are always essential and inextricably related. Quantification of genetic and environmental factors is meaningful only with reference to the variability of a trait across individuals, as explained later.

A related notion (e.g., Kantor, 1958) is that, although genes may play a role in human infancy as in neonatal reflexes, by early childhood cultural influences effectively override genetic factors. It is true that a neonate has little experience on which to draw, whereas an elderly person has a great deal. However, many heritable human behaviors typically develop in adolescence or adulthood, such as schizophrenia, Huntington's chorea, and the sex drive. Genetic inputs change, rather than recede, through the life span. Cairns's (1979) comparative approach to human social development emphasizes this perspective. Similarly the belief that neonatal behavior is preset and inflexible is being laid to rest by investigations of the effects of intrauterine experience on neonatal behavior (e.g., Strauss, Lessen-Firestone, Starr, & Ostrea, 1975; Streissguth, 1977) and of parent-infant reciprocal interactions (e.g., Bell & Harper, 1977; Lewis & Rosenblum, 1974).

Lastly, it should be emphasized that establishing that socialization or other environmental factors shape a behavior in no way diminishes the possibility that genes are also involved. For example both socialization and genetic factors appear to be responsible for human sex differences in aggression (Hoyenga & Hoyenga, 1979).

POINTS OF VIEW ON THE NATURE-NURTURE ISSUE

Interactionism is accepted in principle by virtually all developmental psychologists, be they learning theorists (e.g., Bandura, 1973), ethologists (e.g., Blurton Jones, 1972; Charlesworth, 1972), or cognitive developmentalists (e.g., Kagan, Kearsley, & Zelazo, 1977; Piaget, 1971). They differ not on the principle of interactionism but rather on the emphasis of their research. An attempt will now be made to characterize these different perspectives.

Learning Theory Outlook

Learning theorists acknowledge that the capacity to learn is genetically based but tend to seek explanations for human behavior by examining the subject's experience: available models, instruction, cultural background, reinforcement history, practice effects, etc. Language acquisition, for example, is explained with reference to input from the environment and to practice. In the extreme form of learning theory, behaviorism, even species differences in behavior have been downplayed in order to extend the theory as widely as possible (Skinner, 1938).

Most contemporary learning theorists, however, especially those with a true comparative perspective, remain cognizant of the effect of genetic influences on learning capacity. They have offered many demonstrations that species differ in their sensory, cognitive, perceptual, mnemonic, and motoric abilities (Seligman, 1970). Along these lines research has been conducted comparing the learning capacities of children and apes of various ages.

Cognitive Outlook

Cognitive developmental psychologists make relatively few references to nonhuman species; nonetheless, many are committed to maturational models. Cognitive theorists explain language development, for instance, in maturational as well as experiential terms (Brown, 1973). Some investigators, such as Kagan (1977), envision cognitive capacities as emerging rather abruptly, as though genetic programs "kick in" relatively independently of

experience. Others, such as Piaget, emphasize the effect of experience cumulating over time to shape each emerging capacity. This latter sort of dynamic interaction between current phenotype and experience is referred to as *epigenesis* (Waddington, 1960).

Most cognitive developmentalists tend to relegate individual differences to secondary importance. Since they are trying to establish the existence of invariant stage sequences, individual differences constitute error variance. Where it exists this variance is usually explained in terms of differences in instruction and practice rather than genes.

Thus learning theorists and cognitive developmentalists tend to downplay genetic differences in same-age individuals. They also share an interest in cognitive rather than emotional, or motivational, explanations of behavior. A case in point is infants' avoidance of strangers. A learning theorist typically would explain an infant's fear of strangers in terms of reinforcement history: The infant learns to avoid the type of individual—a stranger—that has been punitive in the past. Cognitive developmentalists explain the emergence of fear of strangers in terms of some cognitive maturational process. Schaffer (1974) hypothesized that the appearance of fear of strangers is made possible by the development of several new general cognitive competences, such as the ability to recall a stimulus that is not perceptually present and the ability to consider two stimuli simultaneously. The emergence of these cognitive capacities would explain why infants of this age (seven to nine months) are able to distinguish strangers from familiar others, but it does not explain why strangers evoke fear rather than tranquility or some other emotion. Perhaps the infant's experience with strangers is usually negative and leads to conditioned fear, or perhaps fear of strangers is an example of the general tendency toward neophobia in animals. In any event maturation of the motivational aspect of the behavior is, characteristically, left unspecified. The closest thing to a motivational factor in Piaget's (1970) theory may be his principle of equilibration—i.e., the assumption that cognitive processes tend to increase in coherence and stability over time. Other cognitive theorists take the position that cognitive processes can be intimately involved in shaping human motivations. Kohlberg (1966) hypothesizes that a tendency to value what one is can lead a child to identify with the same-sex parent and to adopt sex-appropriate behaviors. Similarily Kagan (1972) cites the resolution of uncertainty, and White (1959), the need for effectance, as important motivational forces in human behavior.

Ethological Outlook

Ethologists postulate the existence of specific emotions, motives, or instincts more liberally; cognitive processes are seldom specified. Whereas most other theorists seldom mention evolutionary considerations, ethologists stress the maturation of evolved motivational tendencies. For example, Bowlby (1969) maintains that infants' fear of strangers was selected for specifically in human evolution. Individual genetic differences, as well as experience, are seen as modifying these species-wide, genetically based behaviors.

Ethologists construct *ethograms,* which are inventories

of the behaviors observed in the species under investigation. The behaviors included in an ethogram are species-wide: All feral populations of the species exhibit them. The study of population and individual differences is postponed until the basic units of behavior have been identified.

Because of their focus on biological adaptation, ethologists usually categorize behaviors according to their functions—i.e., the ways in which they contribute to the survival of the species. A human ethogram might therefore begin with five functional categories: (1) feeding, (2) rest, (3) defense, (4) reproduction, and (5) elimination. Every organism, indeed every cell, must perform these functions. Different species, however, perform them in different ways. Some animals, for instance, reproduce without exhibiting any parental behaviors, whereas others show elaborate care of the young. It is therefore necessary to break down these general functions into species-specific behaviors—e.g., feeding might include foraging, ingestion, mastication, and swallowing behaviors.

If we were developing an ethogram for a nonhuman species, we would then break down each of these general behavioral categories into still smaller units. We might, for example, analyze the foraging behavior of the cat into detection of prey, stalking, freezing, pouncing, and neck-biting. Human behavior, however, is extremely flexible; to try to catalogue the various behaviors involved in hunting with weapons would be a very lengthy and probably pointless task. An alternative approach is to take advantage of the fact that motivated behaviors are associated with particular emotional states—e.g., hunger, thirst, smell, taste, and sucking pleasure are emotions that accompany behaviors associated with feeding. Pugh (1977), Izard (1971), and others have stressed the role of emotion in human behavioral development.

The principal research method of the ethologist is unobtrusive observation. This method has become popular with many behavioral scientists of various theoretical perspectives, especially developmental psychologists. Observational methods have been applied to a wide range of behaviors in numerous settings. These methods are favored in large part because they minimize the artificiality of laboratory manipulations and survey techniques. Ethologists, however, are particularly interested in another advantage of this method: ecological validity. Since they focus primarily on species-typical behaviors, ethologists conduct their observations in the animal's natural habitat. They reason that if the environment exerts selective pressure which molds behavior, then the best place to view these evolved behaviors is in the animal's natural surroundings or, in the case of humans, in settings that resemble the conditions that prevailed during most of human evolution. Thus while observing children unobtrusively in a classroom carries certain advantages over experimental techniques, ethologists would prefer to observe them in free play since classrooms are artificial from an evolutionary standpoint.

Even when ethologists attempt to go beyond the descriptive, ethographic stage of research to the use of experimental manipulations, as in studying the effects of artificial releasers with various stimulus features, they are attempting to elucidate behavioral phenomena that occur in the wild. Thus the hallmark of the ethological approach is not the method of unobtrusive observation but the theory of natural selection (see Martin, 1974). The initial focus on species-wide behaviors follows from the fact that these behaviors are more likely to be genetically based than are behaviors that vary across populations or individuals. Ethologists, then, are interested primarily in long-term gene-environment interactions—namely the influence of ecological factors on genetically based behaviors.

Synthesis

Many of the above statements about the perspectives of various types of theorists may be overly general, but it is necessary to run this risk in order to make the point that these various approaches to developmental psychology emphasize different aspects of behavior. Each has important research findings to contribute since each has a different bias toward the nature-nurture issue. To take the development of perception as an example, learning theorists such as Brunswik (1956) stress the factor of experience in matching stimulus cues with environmental realities. Cognitive developmentalists such as Gibson (1969) focus on the increasing differentiation of sensory information. Ethologically oriented investigators such as Dawson (1969) have emphasized the adaptive value of particular perceptual skills. These views are complementary and integrative, rather than being competing explanations.

NEURAL MEDIATION

It may be helpful at this point to attempt to translate these three theoretical perspectives into physiological terms. This will highlight the complementarity of these outlooks, as well as the artificiality of the nature-nurture distinction.

In brief, ethologists focus on the subcortically mediated aspects of behavior—i.e., motivated behaviors such as flight, defense, feeding, and sex. Learning theorists and cognitive developmentalists concentrate on cortically mediated behaviors—i.e., the modification of these motivated behaviors by experience and maturation.

Subcortically Mediated Behaviors

Ethologists' emphasis on observable, motivated behaviors stems from the understandable reluctance of animals to trust a researcher with their private thoughts and from the difficulty of studying higher-order cognitive processes without the aid of artificial manipulations of low ecological validity. Also the cognitive capacities of such favorite ethological subjects as the herring gull and the stickleback are less developed than those of humans. In neurophysiological terms ethologists have concentrated on basic, essential behaviors that are mediated by the subcortical structures which are fairly standard across the vertebrate classes (MacLean, 1964). This is in keeping with ethologists' desire to derive general rules of behavior before going on to specific variations. By studying essential, motivated behaviors such as feeding, defense, and reproduction that occur in all animals, they hope to derive global principles concerning the relationship between behavior and habitat. An emphasis on cortically mediated behaviors would necessarily confine itself mainly to the larger mammals, especially primates and carnivores. This would limit the comparative scope of ethology.

Furthermore an emphasis on cortical processes would be inconsistent with the view that cortically mediated behaviors are phylogenetically and ontogenetically sequential to, and hence in a sense less basic than, subcortical processes. The vast majority of animal species have little or no cortex. Having relatively short life spans, these animals can usually adjust to environmental changes rapidly enough by genetic mutation; they need not modify their behavior radically through experience during the life span. Moreover even in animals with a well-developed cortex, this brain stucture is less essential to life than are subcortical structures such as the brainstem and hypothalamus. Finally in comparative perspective, the cortex evolved as a means of adding flexibility to the animal's perceptual and motoric behavior capacities for meeting its instinctual—i.e., subcortically based—survival needs. Nevertheless the subcortex, particularly the hypothalamus, may be said to still monitor the organism's internal needs, mediate the perception and memory of pain and pleasure, set behavioral priorities, and recruit the perceptual and motoric capacities of the cortex for its own homeostatic ends. In this view also, cognition is subordinate to motivation. A cat that exhibits great cunning in catching its prey is motivated by hunger no less than is a frog that snaps up insects in a fixed, stereotypic manner. Without a feeding motive even the most erudite cat would perish as fast as the frog. In fact in stable environments, inflexible, consistent behavior is more adaptive than flexible but potentially erratic responding.

The functioning of subcortical structures, however, is influenced by environmental conditions. If a cat that has been raised in social isolation has its amygdala electrically stimulated, it is no more likely to attack a mouse than to attack an inanimate object. Furthermore the elicitation of subcortical, motivated behaviors such as predation, sleep, feeding, and sex depends in part on deprivation state—i.e., recent experience.

Cortically Mediated Behaviors

The learning theorist or cognitive psychologist is more concerned with humans as they differ from other species, with individual and population variability, and with the elements of behavioral experience and their contributions to variability. S/he focuses on cortically mediated processes because of an interest in the distinguishing characteristics of human beings. Whereas the ethologist views cortically mediated behavioral flexibility as evolving gradually in long-lived species to enable them to adjust to environmental factors within their lifetimes, the learning theorist perceives a qualitative distinction in man's degree of flexibility.

There is no denying man's great behavioral flexibility. The cortex grows progressively in the phylogenetic series leading to man, especially the prefrontal cortex. Finally to the great flexibility in facial expression and bodily control that are hallmarks of primate behavior is added the hominid capacity for linguistic symbolization.

Man's convoluted cortex allows him not only to execute a variety of responses but also to develop in various ways. Some individuals become food gatherers, others artisans or priests. This intra- and interindividual flexibility is made possible by the capacities of the cortex, combined with socializaton and practice experiences.

Initially learning theorists viewed the black box of the brain as a rather undifferentiated memory store that received informational inputs indiscriminately and could make virtually any possible response. This cybernetic model of the brain is consistent with an extreme behaviorist view, a view that minimizes genetically based instincts or motivated behaviors, as well as species differences in learned behaviors.

Contemporary learning theorists and cognitive developmentalists recognize, of course, that each species—not just man—possesses unique sensory, perceptual, motivational, cognitive, and motoric capacities. This recognition has come about by observing species differences in behavior and neurophysiology. By peering into the black box, neural scientists have learned that, while the localization of function is a very tricky business, nevertheless the cortex itself is highly differentiated. Even the "silent areas" of the cortex are yielding their secrets. In so doing they are progressively obscuring the nature-nurture distinction. Let us examine the development of the major cortical areas in this light.

The major sensory cortices—visual, auditory, and somesthetic—are organized to respond to various types of physical energy—e.g., light, sound, heat, and pressure. This input comes from the sensory receptors to the primary sensory areas of the cortices. This sensory information then undergoes various perceptual transformations that render it biologically—i.e., functionally—meaningful. These transformations occur in the secondary and association sensory areas.

The best understood of these is the visual cortex. Physical elements such as lines, edges, colors, and motion in various planes are transformed into contours, shapes, solids, and finally, recognizable objects. These perceptions, however, require and are modifiable by experience. We cannot recognize the functional category *knife* without exposure to various examples of it. Even the ganglion cells of the retina require exposure to light in order to proliferate normally (Reisen, 1950). Numerous other effects of experience on the physical, chemical, and functional properties of the visual cortex have been documented. Throughout the cortex, dendritic connections continue to form during the entire life span (Buell & Coleman, 1979), presumably in response to individual experience.

A lesion in the secondary area of one of the sensory cortices impairs the ability to recognize objects by means of that modality. For example one patient was shown a drawing of a pair of eyeglasses. He studied its two circles and connecting segments and concluded that it must be a bicycle (Luria, 1973). Lesions in the right hemisphere can interfere with the ability to recognize faces, even one's own. Thus the secondary areas integrate more elementary perceptions.

At the borders of the visual, auditory, and somesthetic areas, the perception of objects across sensory modalities is mediated. A lesion in the parieto-occipital association area can compromise the ability to visualize the form of an object on the basis of touch. At the confluence of these three sensory fields lies Wernicke's area, the center for receptive language. This seems eminently appropriate since language elements constitute cross-modality symbolic abstractions from the various stimulus properties of objects.

The motor cortex, similarly, transforms movements from isolated elements into coherent, functional combinations. Mild electrical stimulation of the primary motor areas sometimes produces movements of single muscles. More intense stimulation can give rise to movement of a body part to a particular final position regardless of its initial position. Stimulation can also cause rhythmic movements as agonist and antagonist muscles contract alternately.

Farther anterior, in the premotor area, stimulation elicits acquired, skilled movements such as turning the hand or moving the thumb and fingers toward each other. Presumably cellular connections in the premotor area are assembled as the subject practices particular motions. Myelination can also be affected by perceptual and motoric experience. A lesion to the premotor area can cause impairment of the ability to perform particular skilled movements. A lesion to the premotor area that represents the tongue, lips, and larynx (Broca's area) results in motor aphasia.

Farther forward still, the prefrontal cortex mediates the ability to perform complex sequences of movements protracted over time. A person with a prefrontal lesion is typically highly distractible.

Synthesis

Complex human behaviors seem to be mediated by both cortical and subcortical structures acting in combination to satisfy survival needs. Neurophysiological processes on both levels are shaped by genetic and environmental factors. The resulting behavioral output represents an integrated product of nature and nurture. Behavior patterns such as aggression or sex are neither innate nor acquired; they are both. Biological organisms do not learn how to experience a sex drive. However, human beings and other primates do learn how and when to satisfy it. Similarly we do not learn how to experience hunger, anger, pride, shame, or loneliness, although these emotions may be conditioned to occur under particular circumstances.

Experience operates upon an organism with genetically based constraints at every level: sensory, perceptual, cognitive, motivational, and motoric. Human newborns, like other organisms, are highly attentive to movement, intensity, and contour contrast (Kagan, 1970) and prefer complex patterns to solid colors (Fantz, 1961). Similarly human infants are especially responsive to high-pitched voices in the female range (Wolff, 1969), a bias with obvious functional value.

Biological factors also shape man's motoric capacities. Some bodily parts, such as the fingers, mouth, and tongue, are more finely innervated than others. Moreover, man seems to possess certain species-wide fixed action patterns, as in the domain of facial expressions (Eibl-Eibesfeldt, 1975; Ekman, 1971; Izard, 1971). These, however, can sometimes be suppressed in accordance with cultural norms, as in the Japanese (Ekman, 1971).

Each species learns particular responses readily; it is said to be *prepared* to acquire these responses. Barlow (1977) speaks of the "naturalness" of the conditioning stimulus affecting the ease of learning. In humans the actual content of learning is largely supplied by the culture, but there are built-in biases favoring the acquisition of certain responses—e.g., walking is acquired more readily than brachiating, and children learn languages more easily before than after puberty. Harlow (1958), Lorenz (1965), and others have asserted further that aspects of learning, such as transfer, extinction, spontaneous recovery, and various reinforcement schedules, can be analyzed in terms of the efficient acquisition and maintenance of rewarded responses.

GENE-BEHAVIOR PATHWAYS

One difficulty concerning the topic of genetic influences on behavior is ethologists' use of a sort of shorthand in referring to hypothesized genetically based behaviors. An ethologist might say that hunting behavior is genetically based, or innate, in humans. This does not mean that they possess genes for performing such movements as pulling an arrow from a quiver or drawing a bowstring. The genetic influences are envisioned as being indirect and subtle. In the case of hunting, perhaps human beings possess genes for visually tracking moving targets, for hurling projectiles accurately with practice, for making weapons, and for enjoying the taste of meat. These genetically based abilities and motivational propensities would be sharpened by natural selection once hunting began to be practiced. No single gene or combination of genes for hunting behavior per se need be postulated.

The objection that natural selection could not have engineered genes for highly complex abilities and that, therefore, genes cannot influence any but the simpler behaviors is usually not relevant. Evolution is often amazingly ingenious in solving difficult problems by means of simple elements, as illustrated by the waggle dance of bees communicating the location of flowers (von Frisch, 1953).

A well-documented example of how this objection to the operation of genes on grounds of complexity proved irrelevant is the history of the Westermarck (1891) hypothesis. Westermarck proposed that incest avoidance in humans was due not solely to cultural taboos but also to a biologically based sexual aversion that arises between people reared together in childhood. Westermarck's hypothesis remained largely ignored for 50 years because most people assumed that incest avoidance had to occur through some higher cognitive process: the learning of a taboo or recognition of the harmful biological effects of inbreeding. We now have good evidence, however, in favor of Westermarck's idea. Spiro (1954) and Shepher (1971), studying Israeli kibbutzniks, and Wolf (1970), studying Chinese live-in child brides, have demonstrated that close social contact during childhood tends to reduce mutual sexual interest at maturity. This aversion develops in these cases not because of cultural taboos but despite cultural pressures encouraging romantic involvement and despite the stated wishes of the principals.

With present-day knowledge of such phenomena as critical periods and imprinting, we are now in a position to suggest plausible mechanisms for incest avoidance, which is well documented in nonhuman primates as well. Demarest (1977) explains the behavior in terms of the role of the amygdala in narrowing the subject's range of sexual objects, as demonstrated originally by the Klüver and Bucy (1939) research on hypersexuality, and in mediating differential behavioral responses as a function of stimulus novelty.

The gene-behavior pathway, then, need not be of the simple, fixed-action-pattern variety, nor need higher cognitive or conscious processes be involved. The effects of many genes may support a single behavioral tendency (*polygenism*); moreover, a single gene can have multiple effects (*pleiotropy*). This means that one-to-one correspondence between gene and behavior is probably too simple in most cases, even on a purely genetic level and neglecting the role of environment. It therefore becomes simplistic to talk about selective pressure favoring a particular gene for a specific evolved behavior. It may be preferable to speak of selective pressure favoring a particular behavior whose genetic and environmental bases are complex and are embedded within the general capacities of the organism. We shall follow this practice later.

This more interactive perspective, however, brings problems of its own. How do we know, for example, that the abilities that facilitate hunting were selected for specifically? Perhaps they were favored because they facilitated other behaviors as well, such as tool-making, scavenging for meat, and hurling projectiles for defense against predators or human rivals. Because human behavior is so flexible, it lacks the discrete, analyzable character of that of simpler species. It is relatively easy to discern the adaptive value of a fixed action pattern, but it is difficult to know just which human abilities and inclinations were selected for to promote which utilitarian behaviors.

In a sense the learning theorist is correct in his/her view that natural selection favored human flexibility itself: a highly undifferentiated capacity for perceiving, planning, and executing. In another sense, however, the ethological view is supported: Man's complex, flexible nervous system provided him with great possibilities for multiplier effects—i.e., for exquisite refinement through the evolutionary process of numerous behavior patterns as the need for each arose. The more complex man's perceptual, cognitive, and motoric capacities, the greater their potential for subtle but far-reaching modifications, both ontogenetic and phylogenetic.

IDENTIFYING SPECIES-WIDE EVOLVED BEHAVIORS

Since both environment and genes are essential for any behavior, it is meaningless to debate their relative quantitative contributions. All behaviors, from the simplest reflex to a clearly culture-bound practice, require some input from both genes and environment.

An alternative approach to the nature-nurture issue is to identify behavior patterns in a particular species that seem to have an evolved basis—i.e., seem to have a genetic component that has been selected for specifically.

In the remainder of the chapter we shall follow this ethological strategy of identifying the species-wide, evolved behavior patterns first and subsequently analyzing within-species variation.

Let us take an example to illustrate the rationale of this evolutionary approach. Ethologists assume that pigeons peck at food because this type of feeding behavior was adaptive in their evolution. It is assumed that genes for making pecking movements were selected for specifically. Other behaviors are made possible not because specific genes for them evolved, but because the general behavioral capacities of the animal allow the behaviors to be performed. For instance pigeons can be taught to play ping-pong. We assume that specific genes for playing ping-pong did not evolve in the pigeon. Intuitively we can distinguish behaviors such as food pecking from behaviors such as ping-pong on the basis of the assumption that the former are evolved—that is, mediated by specific genetic programs that were selected for by species-specific adaptive forces. For any given behavior pattern, the question is not "Do genes play a role in the behavior?" or "Which wields more influence, genes or environment?" For the ethologist the key question here is "Did this behavior evolve in response to a specific selective pressure in this species?" Answering this question not only tells us something about the way the behavior develops but also aids us in analyzing its function, as explained later.

The distinction between evolved and nonevolved species-wide behaviors is not as clearcut as this example may suggest. One might argue that the pigeon's ability to learn novel behaviors was selected for and that therefore even playing ping-pong has an evolved basis. It seems more constructive to draw a distinction between the evolved capacity for learning new behaviors and the particular behaviors that depend upon that capacity, some of which may be evolved and some of which may not be. In this view playing ping-pong, since it did not occur in the evolution of pigeons that exhibit this trait, has no specific evolved basis.

Whether or not a given behavior evolved in a particular species is a meaningful empirical question. Several research strategies have been developed, mostly by Darwin (1872), to help answer it. No one of these strategies yields definitive results. Confidence of the evolved basis of a particular behavior can be increased, however, by cumulating evidence derived from more than one strategy.

Cross-Cultural Prevalence

A finding that a particular behavior is universal provides some evidence that it is evolved. If the behavior varies from locale to locale, then the possibility of an evolved basis is less likely. For example the song of male white-crowned sparrows contains certain elements that occur in all populations of the species. These elements probably are mediated by a specific genetic program. Other song elements vary across sparrow populations—i.e., local dialects exist. These elements appear not to be evolved, because the birds need to hear them in order to sing them. Since members of the same species can be regarded as having essentially the same genes, any intraspecific variation is assumed to be acquired, or "cultural." This assumption is invalid in some cases because animals as well as humans show certain genetically based local and individual variations in phenotype. Nevertheless as a general rule of thumb, if an anatomical or a behavioral trait is species-wide, most evolutionary biologists (e.g., Barlow, 1977; Eibl-Eibesfeldt, 1975) assume that it probably evolved. If it varies from population to population, the likelihood is less that these differences have a specific genetic basis.

Various developmental psychologists, including those who downplay the role of genes (e.g., Maccoby & Jacklin, 1974), endorse these generalizations for humans also. A trait is unlikely to be maintained throughout the human species by cultural diffusion alone. As Charlesworth (1972) puts it, "Species universal behaviors that occur with high frequency in many different environments not in communication with each other are generally considered as having an innate basis until proven otherwise" (p. 13).

A less direct argument is offered by Mayr (1976), who points out that taxonomies based upon behavioral traits tend to parallel those based upon morphological traits. The simplest explanation for these congruencies is that they reflect common genotypes—i.e., the behavioral as well as morphological traits are genetically based. In many instances behavioral characteristics have enabled taxonomists to distinguish among sibling species, which are virtually identical morphologically.

On the other hand Maier and Schneirla (1964) have pointed out that in theory the cause of a species-wide behavior can be environmental rather than genetic. However even if the development of a behavior depends upon certain features of the environment, the behavior can still have a genetic basis—i.e., it can still have been selected for. Tinbergen (1951) cites the example of some species of nightingales in which the identical song is learned by all males as a result of exposure to it as juveniles. The fact that experience is necessary for the behavior to be exhibited does not rule out the existence of some genetically based predisposition to acquire the song; in fact, it is rather likely that genetic programs mesh with environmental givens.

This strategy can be applied to a human behavior, then, by examining its cross-cultural prevalence. Finding that the behavior is universal suggests an evolved basis. If it is not universal the behavior is more likely to be a product of culture. Ideally, widely scattered cultures are investigated so as to gain a representative sample and to minimize the possibility of a localized phenomenon or cultural diffusion.

One illustration of this strategy is provided by studies of separation protest. Separation protest has been found to emerge, peak, and decline at approximately the same ages in five very diverse cultures: the African Bushmen, a hunter-gatherer group; a relatively isolated Guatemalan Indian village; an Israeli kibbutz, where child-rearing practices deviate substantially from those in most cultures; an urban Guatemalan slum; and an American middle-class sample (Kagan, 1976). The probable universality of these aspects of separation protest, then, suggests that they have a specific evolved basis.

In seeking human universals it is often useful to attempt to look back into prehistory by studying contemporary hunter-gatherer cultures. Since man practiced this way of life for virtually all of his evolutionary history, the behavior of isolated contemporary hunter-gatherers is thought to be conservative in general, to be relatively pristine in the sense that it is only minimally distorted by technological changes. However, contemporary hunter-gatherer cultures are cultures and hence do show considerable variation from each other (cf. Bicchieri, 1972), so it is best to sample more than one such culture when seeking clues to commonalities in human behavior. Hunter-gatherer peoples are also of special interest because they provide an ecologically valid model for speculating about the adaptive value of particular human universals.

Perhaps the most cogent alternative explanation of human universals is that certain practices are beneficial to all societies and were therefore independently invented in multiple cultural foci from which they spread by cultural diffusion. This approach is taken by D'Andrade (1966) to explain the apparent uniformity of certain sex differences in the division of labor among various cultures. According to D'Andrade all cultures take cognizance of the physical differences between the sexes, assigning physically strenuous tasks to males and nurturing tasks to females. In assigning tasks which could be performed by either sex, cultures tend to generalize from observable physical differences. Thus males both hunt and make the weapons needed for hunting, even though physical strength is not necesary to make most weapons. It is not really necessary that the inventors appreciate the logic or utility of the practice; they could acquire it by some serendipitous process and retain it in their culture by means of a magical or superstitious belief system. The essence of this explanation of universals is that certain practices are retained in all cultures because of their general adaptive value to human societies.

Evolutionary biologists such as Waddington (1953) and Mayr (1963) would reply to this explanation by maintaining that, given enough time, a behavioral practice that arises purely as a nongenetic, acquired habit will eventually evolve a genetic basis. This is sometimes referred to as the *Baldwin effect*. Let us consider a hypothetical example in humans. Assume that a single innovative youth began to eat tomatoes. Eventually other members of the tribe picked up the habit, and it was transmitted to subsequent generations. Because of random genetic differences among members of the population, tomatoes would taste better to, and be chewed and digested more easily by, some individuals than others. In a tomato-rich environment the tomato lovers would enjoy a selective advantage over the tomato haters. In other words genes promoting tomato eating would spread through the population. Even if the habit also spread as a cultural value, favorable genes would tend to support the behavior as insurance against the vagaries of cultural values and their transmission and acquisition.

Anthropologists generally accept the *age-area principle* that the more widespread a cultural practice is, the older it is (Ember & Ember, 1973). Therefore most universals must be very old, perhaps dating back to the time when man was evolving as a species in East Africa. Those behavioral practices that were generally conducive to the hominid way of life were buttressed by appropriate mutations that were retained as man dispersed throughout the world. The ethologist argues that if a practice is universal it is unlikely that man got along without it for millions of years before culturally acquiring it, and if it has existed for millions of years, genetic supports have probably evolved to buttress it.

Nevertheless it is conceivable that a particular behavior occurs universally without any specific genetic supports. Perhaps mothers worldwide tend to hold their infants on the left side (Salk, 1960) because the heartbeat is louder there, and they have learned (probably unconsciously) that this position is more effective in quieting an infant. The effect has been reported for left-handers also (Freedman, 1979).

Another possible explanation for human universals is that they are products of modern telecommunications methods and have been transmitted wherever the cinema has been introduced. Ekman (1971) addressed this possibility in his research on emotional expression. After establishing that seven emotions are expressed in comparable ways in Argentina, Brazil, Chile, Japan, and the U.S., he confirmed his conclusions that these emotional expressions have specific genetic bases by documenting their existence in two isolated New Guinea cultures: the Fore and the Grand Valley Dani.

Certain ambiguities occur when a particular behavior is found in *almost* all cultures. In these cases the behavior may have an evolved basis that is obscured in the exceptional culture by some other factor. Mead (1935) described the Tchambuli as providing an exception to certain widespread temperamental sex differences such as in aggressiveness. This exception can be explained by cultural contact with Europeans, which changed the Tchambuli men from fierce, domineering headhunters into idle, ineffectual anachronisms (Freedman, 1974). To ignore the recent history of the Tchambuli in favor of "counting" their way of life during a time when the culture was dying out is inappropriate and shows that the universality rule has to be interpreted judiciously. Similarly Ekman (1971) argues that a universal genetically based tendency, such as to display a certain emotion in a particular way, might be obscured in certain cultures that discourage overt expressions or substitute alternative expressions.

The Possibility of Experiential Acquisition Is Precluded

This strategy is based on the notion that if the influence of environmental factors on a behavior is minimal, then the behavior is likely to be strongly canalized by a specific genetic program. Several variations on this strategy are practiced.

Early Onset. If a behavior first occurs before a crucial experience can have taken place, then the experience cannot be necessary for the behavior. If, for example, a behavior is seen shortly after birth, then socialization cannot be responsible—although socialization factors may subsequently affect the form, circumstances, or frequency of its occurrence. This test, even if applied at birth, does not eliminate the possibility that prenatal experience shapes the behavior—e.g., ducklings recognize their species-specific vocalization after hatching, in large part because of exposure to the sound while still in the egg (Gottlieb, 1975). However, this behavior by duck-

lings is presumably evolved, requiring only that the appropriate vocalization be plugged in prenatally.

Anybody thinking it possible that the bird learns, within the egg, behavior which fits exigencies not encountered until later in life, automatically has to assume the existence of a teaching apparatus which contains the phylogenetically acquired information concerning those exigencies. (Lorenz, 1965, p. 24)

An early onset does not *automatically* imply that the behavior is evolved; it merely eliminates the possibility that some particular subsequent experience is critical.

Let us take an example to emphasize this point. Because languages vary in the number of color words and in the range of colors to which any particular term applies, Whorf (1956) hypothesized that color categories are learned along with other category labels as part of the process of language acquisition. However research by Bornstein, Kessen, and Weiskopf (1976) using a habituation-dishabituation paradigm shows that four-month-olds categorize color much like adults. After habituating to a yellow stimulus, infants dishabituated more to orange than to a greener yellow, even though wavelength differences between the habituation and dishabituation stimuli were the same in the two cases. Thus color categorization cannot depend on language acquisition, since it precedes language mastery by several years. By process of elimination this suggests—but does not demonstate directly—that this behavioral capacity has a specific evolved basis.

Similarly Bower (1966) has argued that size constancy does not depend on prolonged perceptual experience since it can be shown to be present at four months. Since retinal image size varies according to distance, subtle mechanisms such as binocular disparity and motion parallax seem to be required. These mechanisms apparently develop before the infant has had the opportunity to explore its perceptual environment by manipulating toys and locomoting across distances. However, some form of input from the environment doubtless is necessary for this capacity to unfold normally.

Sensory Deprivation. If a particular competence develops normally even though the organism has been prevented from perceiving an apparently crucial environmental event, the importance of that experience can be discounted. This test is widely used in studies in which animals are reversibly or permanently deprived of the crucial sensory input. Most research using this test on humans has involved individuals who have been blind or deaf from birth. Evidence that blind children begin to smile at the same age as sighted children (Eibl-Eibesfeldt, 1975) suggests a genetic basis for smiling and rules out modeling as a causal factor for this capacity. Whether or not this genetic basis was selected for specifically—i.e., whether or not smiling is an evolved behavior—is best tested for by using other research strategies. Ruling out the necessity of a particular environmental factor merely renders more probable the reliance of the behavior on a specific genetic program.

Occasionally instances of early sensory exposure can also be informative. It has been found that premature infants, who are exposed to human faces at an earlier point in development than full-term infants, begin to smile at faces at the same conceptual age as full-term infants (Dittrichova, 1969). These data suggest that the onset of smiling to faces is influenced by genes, although perhaps not by a specific genetic program: general control over the facial musculature may simply emerge at this time.

Experimentally induced sensory deprivation can also be used to test the hypothesis that a certain experiential input is critical to a particular developmental process. Chimps that had been prevented since birth from seeing other chimps failed to show the fear of a decapitated chimp that is exhibited with normal visual experience (Hebb, 1946). These data support Hebb's hypothesis that visual experience and the opportunity to develop a schema for a normal chimp are necessary for the development of fear of the decapitated chimp. However they do not infer that this behavior has no evolved basis. A genetic program for neophobia presumably depends upon exposure to various stimuli so that novel ones can be distinguished.

Cognitive Deprivation. If the subject lacks the cognitive capacity that is hypothesized to contribute to the behavior, then the possibility of cognitive–process-dependent acquisition can be ruled out. In animal research the brain can be transected below the neocortex to eliminate the possibility of cortically mediated learning. In human research mentally retarded children and normal children who are considered too young to possess the crucial cognitive capacity are frequently employed as subjects. Heckhausen (1967), studying normal children and retarded adults, determined that achievement motivation emerges at the mental age of 3½ years, thus precluding the necessity of later cognitive abilities.

Social Deprivation. The possibility of social transmission of a behavior pattern can be eliminated by raising an animal in isolation. While few types of deprivation experiment can ethically be performed on humans, feral children and children who have been isolated by deranged parents and guardians occasionally provide this type of evidence.

Usually, however, nonhuman subjects are used. Sackett (1966) isolated a sample of rhesus monkeys from visual contact with conspecifics and humans and observed their responses to a set of photographs on a weekly basis from birth through nine months. The monkeys began to exhibit an intense fear response to the photo of a threatening adult male at 2½–3 months, the age at which rhesus monkeys first exhibit fear in the wild. Although Sackett did not perform systematic experiments to determine which specific properties of the stimulus were critical—e.g., height, facial configuration, body posture—a genetic basis is likely due to the lack of opportunity for observational learning. Fear of the threatening photograph subsided after a few weeks. While the emergence of this fear is genetically based, some experience is apparently necessary for its maintenance—a typical example of interaction.

Even if the results of a deprivation experiment are negative, the operation of specific genes is not precluded. Animal ethologists have found that both a particular experience and some genetically controlled sensitive period are required for the development of many behaviors—

e.g., imprinting phenomena. A deprivation experiment can demonstrate the necessity of a particular experience, but it cannot eliminate the possibility of a specific genetic basis.

Another problem with deprivation experiments is that the experience in question is not simply eliminated but rather is replaced by another that may differ in unanticipated ways from the organism's normal experience. For example social deprivation may necessarily be accompanied by an artificially low level of perceptual variety. Some researchers have attempted to control for this factor but probably imperfectly so because of our ignorance of the crucial properties of social objects.

Even if gross deprivation prevents the development of a behavior, we still have learned little about the crucial factor deleted. Consider Harlow's conclusion that rhesus infants that are deprived of contact with conspecifics develop inadequate sexual and parental behavior as adults (Harlow & Harlow, 1965). Far greater specificity regarding this phenomenon is provided by the finding that monkeys that were reared in isolation but were allowed to see and hear conspecifics in neighboring cages could mate and rear young successfully (Meier, 1965a, 1965b).

The effects that are obtained from a deprivation experiment may be due to the stress that the organism experiences while living in, or upon being suddenly released from, the impoverished environment (Fuller, 1976). For a thorough analysis of this research strategy, see Lorenz (1965).

Stereotypy

If a behavior pattern is relatively fixed in form, especially from its first occurrence, it may be a *fixed action pattern.* Fixed action patterns are characterized by an automaticity that contrasts with the gradually developed smoothness of learned voluntary movement patterns. Elements of stereotypy commonly include a characteristic tempo, sequence, intensity, duration, and time of onset. Human coitus has been observed to contain certain invariant, stereotypic sequential phases (Masters & Johnson, 1966). Stereotypy suggests the operation of a specific genetic program that controls a complex of interrelated behavioral elements.

Fixed action patterns are typically exhibited in response to specific releasing stimuli. For example, during courtship periods, all that is needed to release aggressive behavior in English robins is the sight of a red breast or a bunch of red feathers (Lack, 1953). The sight of a male robin whose breast has been dyed brown will not release the aggressive response. As this example suggests, the response need not constitute a fixed action pattern to be evolved. In this case it is the releaser that is stereotypic—i.e., that contains certain features that elicit the behavior promptly and automatically.

Evidence that a specific releaser can stimulate a particular behavioral response in humans suggests an *innate releasing mechanism* similar to those found in animals. For example a newborn infant will protrude its tongue in response to the sight of any oblong object moving toward its mouth, such as an adult's tongue or a pen (Jacobson, 1979).

Research on fear of strangers has shown that the infant's overall evaluation of a particular situation will influence the degree to which the fear response is expressed (Sroufe, Waters, & Matas, 1974). However, Weinraub and Putney (1978) found that 10½-month-old infants responded significantly more fearfully to strangers who towered over them than to strangers whom they viewed at eye level. Since the appearance and demeanor of the stranger were held constant, these data suggest that certain cues, such as towering, may be specific releasers of the fear response in human infants. These data lend support to Bowlby's (1969) hypothesis that fear of strangers is not simply a response to discrepant events (cf. Kagan, 1974) but that it evolved specifically to protect infants from potentially harmful unfamiliar individuals of superior size.

A high degree of specificity of the releaser is no guarantee that the behavior is evolved. To the contrary, releasers need only be specific enough to initiate the necessary response under natural conditions, as in imprinting on the mother. Subsequently the response typically comes to be elicited by a more specific stimulus through experience. Thus in many avian and mammalian species the maternal-offspring bond progresses from species-wide to individual. A rhesus mother will accept any infant rhesus during the first week or two after parturition, but thereafter she accepts only her own infant. By this time the infant is mobile, and the mother needs to be able to identify it if it wanders off. Reciprocally the infant can identify its mother by this time also.

Prevalence in Related Species

Phylogenetic Continuity. If a behavior or other trait occurs in most members of a group of closely related species—i.e., throughout a taxon—this implies a single evolutionary origin and hence an evolved basis. All mammals have the same basic forelimb anatomy, and so this feature is presumed to have evolved before mammals differentiated into their various orders. This phenomenon is referred to as *homologous* evolution; the forelimb of the whale, for example, is homologous to that of the wolf. *Homology* means having a common evolutionary, or genetic, origin. The trait may serve different functions in different species. Usually, however, the trait will serve the same function—e.g., the forelimb of most mammals (all except adult man) functions in locomotion.

To test a human trait for homologous evolution, one determines whether or not it occurs in man's close relatives—that is, in species belonging to the ancestral line leading to hominids. If the trait appears to be a general primate, Old World primate, or anthropoid characteristic, then its presence in man is probably due to homologous rather than independent evolution. It is unlikely in these cases that man's primate ancestors possessed the trait but that man lost it for a time, only to reacquire it subsequently on either an evolved or a cultural basis.

This test can be misapplied by generalizing about all primates from a single one, such as the rhesus macaque. Harlow and associates (e.g., Suomi & Harlow, 1975) have concluded that contact with mothers and peers is important for the development of competent social behavior in rhesus monkeys. They go on to speculate that this conclusion may also apply to humans. However a very closely related monkey, pigtail macaques, showed few enduring effects from total social isolation (Sackett,

Holm, & Ruppenthal, 1976). In order to apply the test for homologous evolution properly to a human trait, one must survey enough species to conclude that the pattern was present in one of man's direct ancestors and not just in a single closely related contemporary species.

Convergent Evolution. Of course phylogenetic continuity cannot be demonstrated for all species-wide evolved traits. Some traits presumably evolved in response to uniquely hominid selective pressures that man did not share with his primate ancestors. For example in all cultures the nuclear family occurs and takes the form of the one-male unit (monogamy or polygyny). Because this form is universal it is likely to have an evolved basis. Nevertheless it is absent from man's closest relatives: the chimpanzee, gorilla, orangutan, and most other primates. If we assume that it has an evolved basis, the nuclear family must have arisen de novo in hominid evolution.

The test to apply in these cases is to try to identify the selective pressure that gives rise to the trait wherever it occurs. For instance in precocial birds and primates there is an extended period early in life during which the young tend to remain in proximity to the parent. In precocial birds this tendency is established by imprinting; in primates a more gradual attachment process occurs. Because this form of behavior is not found in any common reptilian ancestor of these two taxa, we assume that it evolved independently in response to similar selection pressures. Because these behavior patterns are merely analogous, we would not necessarily expect to find the same stereotypy or stability in attachment behavior as has been demonstrated for the imprinting phenomenon.

Blurton Jones (1972) refers to an instance of analogous, or *convergent,* evolution to provide evidence that evolving humans carried their babies about with them. Generally speaking, herbivorous mammals take their offspring with them while they search for food, whereas carnivores, which require speed and agility for stalking their prey, tend to cache their offspring while foraging. Blurton Jones points out that among species that cache their young the protein and fat content of milk, as well as infant sucking rates, tend to be high in order to ensure that the cached offspring's nutritional needs can be met quickly. Specific data on sucking rates and fat and protein content can be collected to construct a matrix that includes a wide variety of unrelated species. When our species' place in this matrix is determined, it is clear that fat, protein, and sucking rate are all very low so that man falls among the species that carry their young. Thus this approach suggests that infants were carried rather than cached in human evolution.

Lorenz (1965) argues that even if a trait is found in only one species, if it is of obvious adaptive advantage, then it probably evolved. However, captive raccoons have been observed to wash food before eating it, and yet this behavior has not been reliably reported in the wild (Burton & Burton, 1970). Therefore this "argument from design" is probably best recast in terms of the species universality test. If applied to a single population of the human species, which possesses great ability to modify its behavior over the life span toward adaptive ends, this argument is weak indeed.

Specific Physiological Basis

Another strategy for identifying a species-wide evolved behavior is to demonstrate that particular biological structures mediate the trait. If the operation of a particular neural, hormonal, or genetic entity can be demonstrated, this may constitute the product of a specific selective pressure.

Nervous System. If a specific neural structure mediates the behavior, this implies a genetic basis simply because a particular constellation of genes must have programmed the differentiation of the neural structure. Even Piaget (1977), who generally emphasized the role of experience in development, concluded that eye-hand coordination is genetically specified as a result of evidence that the development of this coordination is associated with "the myelinization of certain new nerve paths in the pyramidal tract" (p. 7). Of course experience can stimulate and enhance myelination. Experiments with rats have demonstrated that environmental stimulation can affect the weight, chemistry, and structural complexity of the brain itself (Rosenzweig & Bennett, 1970). Genetic endowment prepares the organism for development, but specific experiential input is critical for at least some outcomes.

The trick in using this research strategy is to differentiate between neural structures that evolved to mediate the behavior in question specifically and those structures that mediate the behavior because of their general plasticity. For example piano playing probably involves the portion of the premotor cortex adjacent to the hand area of the primary motor cortex. This is a specific neural structure, and yet obviously we are not justified in saying that this behavior therefore evolved under a specific selective pressure. The problem is that the cortex—and even various subcortical structures—exhibit plasticity in that the behaviors they mediate can be modified by experience, in the case of piano playing by practice. Thus behavior may actually be shaping the structure of the brain, rather than the reverse.

In order to rule out this type of acquired skill, one might stipulate that the correspondence between neural structure and behavior must be strictly one-to-one—that is, the neural structure should mediate the behavior in all individuals regardless of learning experience. The corresponding area of the brain of a nonpianist might mediate typing, thereby ruling out an evolved basis for either behavior. On the other hand the lateral hypothalamus mediates feeding behavior in many, if not all, mammals, so one would correctly conclude that this behavior evolved.

Problems still remain however. Electrical stimulation of the same neural structure can give rise to different behaviors, depending upon the intensity of stimulation. A weak current applied to a point in the amygdala might evoke a threat response, and a strong current might evoke attack. Perhaps such ambiguities will eventually be clarified by research involving the use of lesions that localize the mediation of these behaviors to discrete, different neural circuits. Given our present state of knowledge about the brain, this strategy is of limited value. It should be applied only by carefully considering such factors as the plasticity of the particular neural structure, its specificity, and its role in related species.

An additional example may make the problem clearer. The secondary areas of the auditory cortex in the temporal lobe are involved in the comprehension of speech sounds. Did this area evolve specifically for this function? The problem is that the corresponding cortical area in other mammals, such as the dog, presumably allows it to comprehend a range, albeit limited, of human vocal commands. Perhaps this structure is highly elaborated in man, but at what point does a quantitative evolutionary change become qualitative?

Endocrine System. If the level of some hormone affects a behavior, then presumably the hormone acts upon a specific neural substrate, which in turn was shaped by specific genes. Money and Ehrhardt (1972) have reported increases in "tomboy" behavior (roughhousing, preferring functional to decorative clothes) and decreases in maternal behavior (doll play, interest in marriage and children) in girls who had been subjected to masculinizing hormonal influences prenatally. This does not imply, of course, that a particular neural structure mediates doll play; perhaps girls were simply more inclined toward sedentary play in general.

Again we encounter the problem of specificity. Perhaps the actions of the hormone are so general that numerous behaviors, including some that are not evolved, are affected. For example adrenalin raises activity level generally. Among the behaviors whose frequency or intensity is increased may be nail-biting, which presumably is not evolved. To guard against drawing erroneous conclusions of this type, it is helpful to consider the specificity of the action of the hormone and the uniformity of the resulting behavior across human and animal subjects.

Genes. The role of genes in behavior can be demonstrated by breeding animals selectively for a particular trait, such as aggressiveness. In humans, familial and pedigree studies, especially twin studies, have been used to establish a genetic basis for numerous cognitive and personality factors (Mittler, 1971). For example Freedman (1965) found greater concordance between identical than fraternal twins in the age of onset of both social smiling and fear of strangers, indicating that these developmental milestones are under genetic control. Again the specificity of these genetic influences is a separate question.

It is often argued that heritability cannot be established by showing greater concordance between monozygotic twin pairs because parents may treat monozygotics more similarly than dizygotics. However, evidence from several sources weakens that argument. Scarr (1968) found that identical twins mistaken by their parents to be fraternal twins were behaviorally as similar as other identical twins, and misjudged fraternal twins were no more similar than other fraternal twins. In addition identical twins reared apart are often almost as similar in personality as identical twins reared together (Shields, 1962), suggesting that the influence of parental expectations concerning the similarity of identical twins is relatively small.

Plomin and Rowe (1979) recently used the twin method to examine infant behavior vis-à-vis mother and stranger in seven brief, structured situations. The responses of the identical twins to the stranger were significantly more similar than those of the fraternal twins, while behaviors toward the mother were equally similar in both groups. These data indicate a genetic basis for the observed variability in fear of strangers in contrast to mother-child relationships, where variability seems to be more heavily influenced by experience (cf. Ainsworth, Bell, & Stayton, 1971). The existence of genetically based variability implies that the behavior itself is under genetic control of some sort.

In applying the twin method, one must recognize that if a given trait exhibits zero heritability, the operation of specific genes is not ruled out. The trait may be so vital that no surviving member of the species lacks it in full measure—that is, the full-blown genetic program is present in all living individuals and hence shows no variation as a function of genetic relatedness. For example all subjects in a twin study will show evidence of possessing a medulla oblongata; therefore, heritability will be zero even though it is clear that genes play a great role in the differentiation of this neural structure.

Again it is meaningless to try to quantify the relative contributions of genes and environment to a behavior. The formula Phenotype = Genotype + Environment + (Genotype × Environment Interaction) is incorrect; all is interaction. By way of illustration Barash (1978) cites the absurdity of trying to break down the height of a six-foot man into five feet of genes, eight inches of environment, and four inches of interaction. On the other hand it is meaningful to quantify the contributions of genes and environment to the variability of a trait in a particular population: Phenotypic Variance = Genotypic Variance + Environmental Variance + Interaction Variance.

However, a statement such as this must be carefully qualified. It depends upon the population sampled and the ranges of its genetic and environmental variabilities. The apparent role of genes will be lessened by using a highly inbred population, and the role of environment by using a homogeneous culture. Moreover technological advances can alter the picture. If certain children in the population experience an enriched environment that raises IQ whereas others do not, heritability will be lowered. If all the children in the population experience this enriched environment uniformly, the role of genes will appear to be magnified. Thus we may speak of highly flexible behavioral systems that give rise to great interindividual variability, but the relative contributions of genes and environment to this variability are difficult to quantify in any absolute sense. Other limitations of the concept of heritability are discussed by Hirsch (1972).

Synthesis

These, then, are the principal research strategies that have been used to identify species-wide behaviors with specific evolved bases. The use of these strategies has been limited, in part, by the paucity of our knowledge in many areas, especially cross-cultural studies, ethological research on key species, and physiological factors. Interest in the hypothesis that specific behaviors have an evolved basis has increased among developmental psychologists in recent years, so that it is no longer necessary to look exclusively to animal behavior for examples to illustrate each of these strategies. For at least one developmental phenomenon in infancy, fear of strangers, there is convergent evidence of an evolved basis from studies using several very different approaches: (1) social isolation of rhesus monkeys; (2) infant responsiveness to towering, a stereotyped releaser; and (3) comparisons of identical and fraternal twins. As these strategies become increasingly popular among developmental psychologists, we may discover that the role of evolution in shaping human behavior is far more significant than most investigators have assumed.

FURTHER ANALYSIS OF SPECIES-WIDE EVOLVED BEHAVIORS

Identifying an evolved behavior is merely a first step. Tinbergen (1951) has argued that in order to understand a behavior pattern completely it must be analyzed on four levels: (1) evolutionary pattern, or *phylogeny;* (2) adaptive value, or *function;* (3) development over the life span, or *ontogeny;* and (4) causation by internal and external factors, or *immediate elicitors.* The developmental psychologist, for example, should not be content with knowing the chronological development of a behavior but should also seek to understand its evolutionary history, its function, and how various stimuli elicit it. Textbooks by Nash (1978) and Fishbein (1976) exemplify this approach.

These four levels for analyzing a given behavior are interrelated because they constitute different aspects of the same evolved systems, of gene-environment interactions. Therefore knowledge about the ontogeny of a given behavior, for example, can be gleaned indirectly by studying the behavior on the other three levels.

Again we see the potential complementarity of the different approaches to developmental psychology. Ethologists are especially interested in phylogeny and function—the evolutionary, or *ultimate,* causation of behavior. Learning theorists and cognitive developmentalists, on the other hand, deal more with *proximate* causation—ontogeny and immediate elicitors. Ultimate causation represents evolutionary gene-environment interaction, and proximate causation represents life-span interactions. We shall now consider some of the kinds of relationship that can be described between pairs of these four levels.

Phylogeny and Function

Suppose that we have identified a particular behavior as evolved. How do we determine its function? The most direct method is to consider its taxonomic distribution. Those species that exhibit the trait should share some feature that accounts for its functional value. For example good night vision is characteristic of nocturnal species, while postnatal precocity is a characteristic of migratory prey species.

Sometimes any of several selective factors promote the evolution of a particular behavior pattern. For instance monogamy is associated with (1) the need for two parents to defend or maintain a valuable resource; (2) a difficult environment, again necessitating two parents; and (3) a large advantage obtained from breeding early in the season, which monogamous pairs can do since they are perennially mated and do not have to spend time finding new partners (Wilson, 1975b).

Many human behaviors can probably be explained in terms of selection pressures that operate on all large, group-living terrestrial mammals. For this reason ethologists have paid particular attention to species with analogous ecological characteristics, such as the group-living terrestrial lions, wolves, and baboons. In addition primates are studied closely, since humans can be expected to share many homologous characteristics with our direct primate ancestors and their present-day representatives. For example the human infant's notoriously poor sphincter control can be understood, even if not appreciated, as typical of arboreal primates which have no hygienic need for continence the way den-dwelling or nesting mammals do. Thus the methods of both analogy and homology are employed to elucidate adaptive functions. In both cases clues to functional value are to be found in phyletic analysis.

Ontogeny and Immediate Elicitors

Various factors elicit developmental changes in behavior. Tinbergen (1951) distinguished between internal and external factors causing ontogenetic changes. Biopsychologists have focused on internal—e.g., neuroembryological—causes of maturational changes. Learning theorists, on the other hand, concentrate on environmental factors in behavior, such as perceptual, social, and cultural experience. For instance exposure to an aggressive model may have long-term (ontogenetic) effects on behavior, as well as short-term ones.

Lehrman's (1961) studies of the reproductive behavior of ring doves provided a classic demonstration of the interaction of internal factors—i.e., hormones—and external releasers in a developmental sequence. When a pair is placed together, the male begins to court the female. His displays trigger the release of gonadotropins in her, which in turn stimulate egg production and estrogen secretion, which prepares her for sexual and nest-building behavior. The male's presence also causes her to secrete progesterone, which initiates incubation behavior, and prolactin, which stimulates growth of the crop. The presence of nesting materials and of the hatchlings also act as releasers.

The connection between ontogeny and immediate elicitation also figures prominently in the work of cognitive developmental psychologists. They try to establish links between the emergence of a particular cognitive capacity and the appearance of a behavior that is thought to depend upon that capacity. For example Piaget argues that separation protest depends upon the infant's developing a capacity for object permanence (Flavell, 1977).

Ontogeny and Function

Ontogeny reflects functional considerations because the organism must survive as well as develop. Developmental changes in behavior must of course reflect design constraints—i.e., certain changes must occur in order to attain a particular level of complexity at maturity. Behavioral changes must also reflect age-specific selection pressures since natural selection occurs throughout the life span. The question of adaptive value is therefore an especially complex one for the developmental psychologist, who must ask what the function of a given behavior is at the particular stage of life at which it occurs. For example why does weaning typically occur at two or three years in humans? Why not earlier or later? Why is menarche triggered or at least paralleled by attainment of a certain body size? Has the synchrony between social and physical development been disrupted by the acceleration of menarche that has accompanied dietary improvements in the West over the last century?

This type of question presents new challenges and new opportunities for our discipline. For one thing it calls for the replacement of culture-relative developmental stage designations—e.g., preschool years—with more biologically relevant markers, such as independent locomotion, weaning, and puberty. It also calls attention to the fact that the organism has to meet multiple survival exigencies at every point in development, rather than being preoccupied with a single crisis, task, or theme. Needs such as hunger, warmth, and safety may change markedly through the life span in their intensity and in how they are met, but they are present in all stages.

Ontogeny and Phylogeny

Haeckel's law that "ontogeny recapitulates phylogeny" is illustrated by the familiar example of the frog, whose aquatic evolutionary past is repeated in every generation as it develops from tadpole to air-breathing land-dweller. Biologists have found that evolutionary changes tend to occur late rather than early in ontogenetic development. This phenomenon is known as *terminal addition*. In the frog, the legs and lungs were added to the mature tadpole precursor, rather than to an early embryonic stage. Terminal addition is believed to be the principal form of evolutionary change, because a radical change late in ontogeny can build upon the earlier stages. In contrast a radical change early in ontogeny could be too drastic, thereby endangering survival. Nature seems to be conservative and opportunistic, to modify mature organisms by accretion rather than starting over from scratch.

A second feature associated with recapitulation is *condensation*. This is the elimination of superfluous intervening stages and the resulting acceleration of maturation. Thus the human embryo passes rapidly through the equivalents of the invertebrate, fish, amphibian, and reptilian stages of prehominid evolution because many nonessential features, such as fins, can be bypassed. They do not contribute to the hominid design. Only those features that are essential building blocks are retained, such as the first three gill arches, which develop/evolved into part of the mandible, the malleus, the incus, the styloid process, and the hyoid bone. By contrast the fourth and fifth arches persist only as rudiments.

While most evolutionary changes appear to involve terminal addition, some do affect early points in ontogeny. Placentation occurs early in fetal development even though it evolved late in vertebrate evolution, with the mammals. Similarly the smile appears early in ontogeny but late in the evolutionary line leading to hominids. Thus ontogeny does not parallel phylogeny perfectly. In fact one common type of evolved change is a simple, conservative adjustment in timing, known in embryology as *heterochrony*. For example humans reach reproductive maturity and independence later in the life span than their primate ancestors did (see Gould, 1977).

Child development, then, does not provide a clearcut sequential synopsis of man's evolutionary history. Age two does not correspond to the Mesozoic Era; some traits of two-year-olds may correspond to much earlier or much later periods, depending upon the function of those traits in hominid survival. Nevertheless if we examine a particular aspect of behavior, such as language, its development may accurately represent the sequence of its evolution because of design constraints—that is, each individual needs to pass through the phylogenetically simpler stages before being able to master the more complex aspects of language.

Phylogeny and Immediate Elicitors

According to Plotkin (1979) there have been few attempts to study physiological causation comparatively. In one such endeavor Masterson and Skeen (1972) tried to implicate the prefrontal system (nucleus medialis dorsalis of the thalamus, its projection in prefrontal cortex, and the caudate nucleus) in delayed response tasks. It is known that lesions to this system interfere with this capacity in higher primates. Masterson and Skeen did not lesion any animals. They merely compared the size of this system in three species in the primate phylogenetic series (hedgehog, tree shrew, bushbaby) with these species' performance on this type of task. A statistically significant trend resulted. The authors suggested that this trend continues through to man, who excells at delayed response tasks and has a very large prefrontal cortex.

Another example of this sort of relationship concerns testosterone and sex differences in aggression. In most primates the male is more aggressive than the female, a sex difference that appears to be due in large part to the male's producing more testosterone, both before birth and after the onset of puberty (Hutt, 1972). The implication is that this sex difference in humans has a long phylogenetic history.

Function and Immediate Elicitors

Understanding a physiological process is akin to appreciating its adaptive value. Indeed, the term *function* is used in both types of explanation.

Nursing provides a good illustration of one such functional system. Behaviorally nursing begins because the infant possesses rooting and sucking reflexes and a sucking drive; these evolved tendencies obviate the necessity for trial-and-error learning in response to the hunger drive, which by itself would be an inefficient system for initiating feeding (Pugh, 1977). Nursing also helps to maintain contact between mother and infant so that she can provide her child with protection and teach new behaviors by example and instruction (Ainsworth, 1977). Nutritionally, mother's milk is ideal and requires the helpless infant to do little to obtain it. Immunologically nursing transmits some of the mother's lymphocytes, macrophages, and antibodies, plus some of her benign bacterial flora which take up residence in the infant and thereby preempt invasion by foreign bacteria against which the infant has no antibodies (Klaus & Kennell,

1976). Physiologically the infant's suckling releases oxytocin, which transports the milk to the nipple area (let down reflex), and prolactin, which replenishes the supply in accordance with need. Oxytocin also aids in the shrinking of the uterus after parturition. The release of oxytocin and prolactin can be conditioned through repeated pairing of nursing with, say, the infant's hunger cry. Similarly the infant's cry has been shown to increase the blood supply to the breasts. Last but not least, lactation provides a natural form of birth spacing by inhibiting the resumption of ovulation, at least for a time.

Synthesis

Recently a group of researchers has provided a good demonstration of the relationships among the ontogeny, phylogeny, elicitation, and function of various behaviors belonging to Piaget's sensorimotor period.

Parker (1977) and Chevalier-Skolnikoff (1977) have described the similarities and differences in the development of these behaviors in infants of three species (stumptail macaque, chimpanzee, and man) and analyzed the functional significance of these behaviors. Stumptail macaques show highly developed (Stages 4–6 in Piaget's sensorimotor series) tactile and kinesthetic sensitivity compared with more rudimentary (Stage 3) development of other sensory modalities. Chevalier-Skolnikoff (1977) suggests that these well-developed tactile and kinesthetic abilities allow this species to acquire copulatory skills when relatively young—i.e., to reach reproductive age quickly. The chimpanzee differs from the macaque in having well-developed auditory and visual perception and gestural ability. These capacities are thought to allow this animal to communicate by voice and gesture and to make and use tools. Human infants are relatively advanced in prehension, vocal ability, and vision.

Gibson (1977) draws convincing parallels between the development of these behaviors and the maturation of various cortical structures in stumptail macaque and human infants—that is, the size of certain cortical areas in these and other primates seems to correspond to the degree of development of particular behavioral capacities. For example humans eventually surpass other primates in performing sequential or delayed movements, capacities which correspond to man's large prefrontal cortex. Humans also excel in cross-modality perception, corresponding to the large association areas, and in perceiving sequential actions and causality, mediated by the temporal association area. This research demonstrates the degree to which a comparative perspective can enhance our understanding of cognitive development in our own species.

BEHAVIORAL VARIABILITY

Although the study of individual differences has been generally deemphasized by ethologists (Medawar, 1976), within-species variation can also be understood in terms of biological principles, especially the notion of adaptive function. The remainder of the chapter will be devoted to explaining how this can be done. Let us begin by examining a familiar case of variation, that in human feeding behavior.

Why are some but not all people obese? Recent research has shown that infants who are overfed often develop relatively large and abundant adipose cells, which subsequently remain filled with fat, thereby causing permanent obesity (Rodin, 1977). A person who has been obese throughout childhood and adolescence has only one chance in 29 of maintaining normal body weight in adulthood (Bray, 1970). A substantial majority of obesity cases seem to occur in this way; relatively few seem to be hormonally based, and the personality problems of obese individuals in our society appear to be sequelae rather than causes of obesity (Rodin, 1977).

The physiological basis for this clinical condition is fairly well established. But does this form of obesity have an evolved basis? The strategies for testing whether a trait is evolved are intended for use on normal populations. If obesity is a pathological condition, we need not explain its prevalence in evolutionary terms. However because obesity is quite prevalent in some human populations, we may want to consider the hypothesis that it could confer some survival advantage upon those populations that manifest it.

In trying to determine the adaptive value, or function, of an evolved characteristic, we need to consider its distribution. Obesity is very rare among feral animals (except for hibernating ones). What is distinct about our species that might account for our susceptibility to obesity? One possible explanation relates to our sedentary way of life. Unlike other species we can rely on agriculture and technology for food and defense; we need not keep in shape to survive. However, we are still vulnerable to starvation; therefore, a tendency toward obesity may have evolved, especially in populations that have been prone to starvation pressure, such as those dwelling in the cold climate of Northern Europe.

If so, we would expect obesity to be inherited to some degree; indeed, the condition does tend to run in certain families and ethnic groups. But the proximate causation of obesity is more than just a matter of genes. Experience plays a role, specifically food intake during infancy. This makes it possible for a population to adjust rapidly to changes in the food supply, without having to wait for a favorable mutation to occur and spread through the group. In populations that are under chronic starvation pressure, the cultural practice of overfeeding infants whenever the food supply permits might, therefore, be advantageous. These children would develop vigorous appetites, thereby affording them an increased lifetime protection against starvation, a "spare tire." If food is abundant, however, overfeeding might be maladaptive even with a sedentary way of life because of the health hazards of obesity—e.g., diabetes and hypertension. Obesity is adaptive under starvation pressure and maladaptive under conditions of abundance, if this model is correct. Consistent with this explanation, obesity is more common among poor people, at least in the West, than among the more affluent (Stunkard, 1968). Obesity that is observed during periods of abundance could be due to the exposure of relatively recent generations to the threat of starvation, a form of historical "lag."

This example suggests that a genetically based behavior may, in some cases, be triggered or adjusted by environmental input. Moreover this environmental input may be "purely" cultural. The biological system would allow a given population to "plug in" the appropriate cultural attitude toward feeding its infants and thereby to adjust fairly rapidly to a change in food supply. In this way a culturally based practice could enhance the survival of a population and hence can be regarded as adaptive, or functional, in the biological sense.

This approach, whereby evolutionary theory is applied to anthropological data, is sometimes known as *ecological anthropology*. Harris (1968, 1974), for example, takes puzzling cultural practices, such as Hindu cow worship, and tries to explain them in terms of their economic advantage to the society's ecology. Harris emphasizes that people do not necessarily comprehend the adaptive advantages of their own cultural practices. A culture typically evolves an elaborate religious belief system, rather than teleological explanations, to ensure enforcement of its mores (LeVine, 1977). In a similar vein Durham (1979) bases his work on the premise that the selection of cultural traits can be best explained in terms of the individual's survival and reproduction, rather than in terms of group survival, economic prosperity, maintenance of the social structure, or ease of transmission—criteria that have been traditionally employed in anthropology. In casting his analysis on the individual rather than group level, Durham is following the prevailing attitude on this question. Evolutionary biologists generally look first to the level of the individual organism to account for an evolved behavior. Group selection is considered as an alternative explanation when selection on the individual level seems implausible, and most evolutionary biologists agree that group selection is probably rare (Williams, 1971).

The approach taken by ecological anthropologists illustrates the degree to which a functional perspective can overcome the traditional nature-nurture dichotomy. Since genes and environment necessarily interact, it makes little sense to try to determine the adaptive value of a gene acting in isolation. It is more appropriate to consider the adaptive value of the gene-environment combination that emerges in the phenotype.

Since human genes depend for their existence upon the survival of the cultural organism that carries them and since cultures are dependent on the survival of their individual members, it follows that genes and culture are more likely to be cooperative than antagonistic in their effects. One example is that of production of lactase, the enzyme that allows digestion of milk sugar. This enzyme is present in adults of those populations, including Northern Europeans, that practice dairy farming, and it allows them to digest dairy products. It is essentially absent in other populations of adults that do not drink milk. Lactase is present in high amounts in populations that consume whole milk; low amounts suffice to allow digestion of milk products in other societies. Whole milk tends to be consumed in cold climates with little sunlight: Milk products are consumed nearer the equator. Durham (1980) explains that lactase, which is highly concentrated in whole milk but less so in milk products, aids the absorption of calcium from the small intestine—as does vitamin D, whose synthesis is promoted by sunlight. Societies with little sunlight appear to have evolved the alternative of high lactase levels and consumption of whole milk in order to absorb calcium.

Despite current optimism about the explanatory powers of ecological anthropology, many features of a given culture doubtless bear no discernible relationship to its ecology and may even be alien to the population's interests (Hinde, 1980). Many cultural traits can probably never be explained except as historical accidents— e.g., as due to cultural diffusion analogous to genetic drift. One example is the practice, handed down from the Romans, of throwing rice at newlyweds. Other cultural traits may persist because, although harmful in themselves, they are linked historically or functionally to some beneficial cultural trait. For example, war making may have been functional for some societies until the advent of nuclear weapons. Nevertheless a functional approach suggests that most cultural practices are probably adaptive. If not they would die out along with their carriers, just as deleterious mutations do.

ADAPTIVENESS OF BEHAVIORAL VARIATION

Whenever the members of a population vary with respect to a trait, the variation can, in theory, be classified as: (1) *pathological,* or maladaptive; (2) *neutral,* a product of genetic or cultural drift; (3) *linked* to some other, adaptive trait; or (4) *adaptive,* a product of natural selection.

Pathological Variation

Examples of pathological variants include congenital malformations and mass suicide. Evolutionary theory implies that this type of variant will be relatively rare, since it should tend to be selected out.

Neutral Variation

A possible example of a neutral variant is hair color in humans, because it does not affect fitness in any apparent way. Kimura (1979) argues that neutral variants are common. However, Mayr (1970) maintains that it is unlikely that any two alleles would have identical selective values. It is possible, for example, that hair color did serve some adaptive function at some time in the past. Thus perfectly neutral variants are probably rare.

Linked Variation

Evolutionary theory suggests that some behavioral variants survive, not because they are adaptive in themselves, but because they are linked to other adaptive traits. The best-known example of this is sickle cell anemia, which has survived in some populations because heterozygous carriers of the gene for sickling possess immunity to malaria. The heterozygotes are fitter than either homozygous state, a phenomenon known as *overdominance.*

Overdominance has been proposed to explain the puzzling fact that male homosexuality is common in numerous cultures. It is difficult to understand why so many individuals of low reproductive fitness (success at leaving viable offspring, the ultimate biological test)

continue to appear, especially given the strong possibility from twin data of a genetic basis (Kallman, 1952). Hutchinson (1959) has proposed that male homosexuality is linked to some other trait that raises fitness superordinately in heterozygotes. Alternative sociobiological explanations for homosexuality are reviewed in Wilson (1975b).

Schizophrenia is another enigma for biologists. It, too, occurs at a stable, appreciable frequency across various cultures, is at least moderately heritable, and its victims have relatively low reproductive rates. Here, too, overdominance may be operating: The normal siblings of schizophrenics leave more offspring than do members of the general population (McClearn & DeFries, 1973). The hypothesized gene for schizophrenia would persist because it lent the siblings of its bearers a selective advantage in reproduction fitness that outweighed the disadvantage to the schizophrenics themselves.

Adaptive Variation

Human behavior appears to be highly variable, and most of this variation is probably *adaptive.* Selection seems to have favored variability in temperament and specialization of labor both within and between societies. Judging from twin studies and ethnographic reports, this variability is probably promoted by both genetic and socialization factors.

It may seem contrary to evolutionary theory that the fittest variant does not eventually eliminate all the others from a population. However there are several advantages to variability within a breeding population. One benefit is that competition among population members is lowered if the variants occupy somewhat different ecological niches—they may eat different foods or occupy different territories. Another advantage is that a variable population is better equipped to survive in the event of a catastrophic environmental change, in that at least one of the variants may be adapted to the new situation. Furthermore the existence of different genotypes makes it possible for natural selection to continue to improve the population even under relatively stable environmental conditions. Finally the variability may entail specialization of labor. For example among African wild dogs, some adults remain behind with the pups while others hunt and, upon returning, regurgitate meat for the pups. This variability benefits each member of the pack.

DETERMINING THE FUNCTION OF A BEHAVIORAL VARIANT

As in the case of species-wide evolved behaviors, the function of a behavioral variant is assessed by first identifying the level—e.g., culture or individual—on which selection has taken place. Once this is done hypotheses about the nature of the selective force operating on that level can be proposed and tested.

Cultural Variation

The behavior may vary across cultures. This means that selection has occurred on the local, or ecological, level. The mechanism may be genetic, cultural, or both.

Freedman (1974) and others have reported that Navajo and Chinese infants perform more passively on neonatal behavioral assessment scales, relative to Caucasians. Similarly African and American infants of sub–Saharan African descent demonstrate "motoric precocity" in head control, visual pursuit, sitting, standing, and walking, when compared with Caucasians. The early onset of these behavioral differences, together with their distribution along ethnic lines, suggests that genes are at least partly responsible.

Another example is provided by LeVine (1977), who maintains that in cultures with high infant mortality rates the infant is kept constantly in contact with the caretaker so that she can monitor his/her health status and take remedial action if illness occurs. Cultures with lower infant mortality rates, LeVine argues, evolve child-rearing practices that favor other considerations, such as preparing the child for his/her future economic role. LeVine argues that people in a traditional society not only are not cognizant of these functional considerations but would be at a selective disadvantage if they deliberated about them rather than just following the dictates of custom or religion. Various other examples are presented by Werner (1979).

Individual Variation

A second possibility is that the behavior varies across individuals within a culture. Genetic or environmental factors or both may play major roles. If heritability is high, genes are implicated. If heritability is low, environmental factors are relatively important in determining the observed variation.

Even a behavioral variant that has no evolved basis, such as birds learning to open milk bottles on front porches, may be justifiably regarded as adaptive if it enhances survival and reproduction. The same might even be said of pigeons playing ping-pong in a psychology laboratory.

LeVine (1977) furnishes us with another example in humans. He reports that mothers in Nigeria and elsewhere usually delay weaning if their child is small. In so doing, he maintains, they are guided by cultural dictates, rather than by an understanding of nutritional consequences.

Kinship

Behavior toward kin sometimes differs from that toward other conspecifics. Trivers (1974) has suggested an explanation of "weaning conflict" in terms of *kin altruism*. Sociobiological theory assumes that natural selection will favor a behavior that aids the individual in passing genes on to the next generation. This can be accomplished either directly, by reproducing, or indirectly, by aiding kin with whom s/he has genes in common. The latter phenomenon is referred to as *kin altruism*. Trivers begins by noting that a great many, and perhaps all, mammalian offspring protest being weaned. It therefore seems appropriate to explain this behavior on the mammalian level, rather than analyzing it in exclusively human terms. Trivers then asks why the mother and offspring should oppose each other's efforts during weaning or at any other time. As close kin they should tend to practice

mutual altruism. However their genomes are not identical; they share one-half, but not all, of their genes. This discrepancy in consanguinity can be used to explain *parent-offspring conflict*.

Trivers goes on to recognize that the mother and offspring are in agreement early in the nursing period that nursing should continue. Without this behavior the offspring would die, to the detriment of both parties. Later on the mother will find it in her biological self-interest to terminate nursing so that she can go on to raise new litters. The offspring also stands to benefit biologically from having siblings, but it is biased in its own favor vis-à-vis them—that is, the infant wishes to prolong nursing and its nutritional advantages somewhat beyond the point dictated by the mother's wishes. She is related equally to her present and future offspring. The infant is related to itself by unity but to future siblings by only one-half.

Trivers suggests that various degrees of cooperation and competition should characterize other family relationships. Studies of stepparents vs. biological parents, identical vs. fraternal twins, and so forth could be used to test this hypothesis further.

Gender

Many behavioral sex differences have been documented. Division of labor by sex is universal and therefore may have some general adaptive value to our species. On the other hand which particular forms of labor will be performed by which sex seems to be determined in large measure at the cultural or ecological level. Biological factors are more likely to play a role in those forms of labor that are consistently performed by one of the sexes cross-culturally. Similarly sex differences in temperament, cognitive abilities, and other behaviors have been reported (Hoyenga & Hoyenga, 1979). Some of these appear to reflect mainly socialization factors whereas others seem to be genetically based.

In his analysis of behavioral sex differences, Trivers (1972) has found some striking similarities over a wide variety of species, ranging from fruit flies and birds to man. In general females spend more time caring for the young—both during gestation and after—and tend to be less promiscuous and more selective in choosing a mate. Males tend to compete vigorously for mates. Trivers suggests that these commonalities can be explained in terms of a theory of *parental investment*. In the case of mammals, which is the vertebrate class for which these sex differences are the most pronounced, the female necessarily makes the greater parental investment in that she carries the offspring in utero and meets its nutritional needs first via the placenta and later via lactation. By the time the mammalian young is weaned, the female has invested far more biological resources than the male; in some species she even cares for her offspring after weaning. Consequently, Trivers argues, she tends to be more selective initially in choosing a mate, in order to protect her greater investment against input from undesirable genes. Males, on the other hand, compete vigorously for females because, after the female has been impregnated, she will bear more of the effort in assuring the offspring's survival. It is in his interest to impregnate a large number of females since each offspring requires relatively little effort on his part. In those few (nonmammalian) vertebrates in which the male makes the greater total parental investment, the female competes more actively for mates—i.e., she is the courting sex.

This reasoning leads to a number of predictions for a primate such as man in which the male makes a substantial investment in the young (although less than the female's). These predictions include the predominance of polygyny over polyandry and greater concern on the part of the males with their mates' fidelity. Daly and Wilson (1978) have tested these predictions by reviewing anthropological and sociological data on human sex differences, and the predictions are generally supported.

Age

Strictly speaking, age alone is the domain of the developmental psychologist. To the extent that qualitative changes in behavior occur as a function of age, genetic effects may be implicated. The terms *maturation, stages,* and *sensitive periods* all suggest a genetically based, evolved ontogenetic program. Alternatively age-related developmental changes may be based on an epigenetic process (Piaget, 1970), whereby qualitatively new behaviors emerge as a consequence of structural reorganization. To the extent that behavior changes gradually through the life span, the role of learning is implicated.

Earlier we made the point that culturally arbitrary designations of stages are of little value to a cross-cultural science of human development. A similar criticism may be made of the use of chronological age, which is objective on the physical level but somewhat irrelevant to biological organisms, for which diurnal, lunar, and seasonal cycles are more salient. Age, like gender, does not in itself shape behavior (Lipsitt & Reese, 1979). It is merely a rough concomitant or marker of the genetic and environmental factors that actually mold behavior. Many important temporal units are sequential or relational, rather than chronological. We need to learn which behaviors occur synchronously and which ones occur serially and to explain their relations in terms of proximate and ultimate causal factors.

Developmental changes can be triggered by brain maturation, hormones, releasers, models, tutors, peers, practice, nutrition, pathogens, and serendipitous experiences. The method of choice in understanding the proximate causation of individual variability over time is the longitudinal study, which allows us to predict future individual differences on the basis of present individual differences in experience or attributes. For example longitudinal research has revealed that a boy's "toughness" as recognized by his first-grade peers is predictive of his popularity, leadership, and dominance in high school (Weisfeld, Omark, & Cronin, 1980). Cross-sectional research can reveal age-related changes and correlations between variables measured at the same time but cannot link possible causal factors over time, inasmuch as age per se is not causal.

On the level of ultimate causation, some developmental psychologists (e.g., Brent, 1978; Konner, 1977; LeVine, 1977; Weisfeld, 1979) are considering the roles played by various age grades in the functioning of the whole population. Each age grade can be regarded as depending upon and contributing to the others in char-

acteristic ways. Sociobiologists refer to this notion as *age polyethism.* It follows from this perspective that each age grade should possess not only distinctive cognitive, perceptual, and motoric capacities but also unique motivational and emotional profiles.

Synthesis

In summary whether the variation occurs across populations or among individuals within a population or both, it may be caused by either genes or environment or both. All we can infer is that genetically based variability is likely to be older than exclusively culturally based variability and therefore that the relevant selective pressure is probably older too. The question of the specific function of the variability can be addressed only after determining the level on which selection has occurred, by trying to identify the relevant selective factors.

One complex variant, the avunculate, has been examined extensively from a functional perspective by Kurland (1979). The avunculate is a social system in which men tend to care for their sisters' children more than for their wives' children. It is most common in matrilineal societies. In matrilineal cultures women are usually more economically independent of their husbands, which may explain the reportedly higher rate of extramarital liaisons in such cultures. In cases of widespread sexual infidelity, a husband cannot be very certain of the paternity of his wife's children. From the perspective of reproductive fitness, a man would waste his effort by caring for another man's offspring. Under these conditions selection appears to have favored the appearance of the avunculate. By caring for his sister's children, a man can indirectly aid (practice kin altruism toward) children to whom he is certain to be related.

The fact that the avunculate tends to be found in matrilineal societies is an example of selection on the population level. Selection for the avunculate may also have occurred on the individual level. Husbands who devote their efforts to aiding their sister's children will be more successful in transmitting their genes than husbands who aid their putative children under conditions of low certainty of paternity.

Whether selection for this practice occurred primarily on the group or the individual level, one might expect that all husbands in a given society would aid their sisters' children in preference to their wives'. However, Kurland discovered considerable variation within these cultures. It appears that, when a husband's certainty of paternity is high, he tends to care for his own child rather than his sister's. This is adaptive for him since if he really is the father he will share one-half of its genes whereas he is related to his sister's child by a coefficient of only one-fourth. Also consistent with this theory is evidence that the husband's wife, sister, other relatives, and in-laws in these societies try to influence his behavior in a direction favorable to their offspring.

How do these people know how to act in accordance with their individual biological self-interests? First it should be recognized that it is not necessary for them to understand what they are trying to accomplish, so long as they behave in a manner consistent with their biological interests. Obviously they do not understand sociobiology and do not perform the necessary calculations in determining which child to aid and by how much. Nevertheless on some level their suspicions about their wives and other relevant information do shape behavior along adaptive lines. This could occur in several ways. Genes favoring suspiciousness, the ability to recognize one's offspring on the basis of facial characteristics, or a predisposition for jealousy might be selected for. So might sensitivity to being ridiculed as a cuckold. In addition a husband might acquire certain relevant skills during his lifetime—e.g., the ability to detect infidelity in his wife when it occurred. Similarly a family might develop a tradition of protecting its male members against being cuckolded. Regardless of the proximate mechanism, the behavior appears to be adaptive.

CONCLUSIONS

Genes and environment interact inextricably to produce behavioral phenotypes. Interactionism is capable of clarifying the role of genes in human behavior.

Developmental psychologists of different theoretical bents—learning theorists, cognitive developmentalists, and ethologists—emphasize the relative roles of genes and environment to different degrees in their research, but these differences are ultimately reconcilable. Each type of theorist focuses on a different aspect of human behavior, as revealed by considering their perspectives in neurophysiological terms.

An alternative to trying to quantify the relative contributions of nature and nurture to behavior is to identify evolved behaviors—i.e., species-specific products of natural selection that represent the interaction of genes and environment. Various research strategies for doing so were critically reviewed.

Evolutionary analysis of behavior includes description on four levels: phylogeny, function, ontogeny, and immediate elicitors. These levels are interrelated since they constitute different aspects of the same products of gene-environment interaction. Therefore each level contributes to our understanding of the others.

Like species-wide behavior patterns, behavioral variability can be analyzed in terms of functional value by determining the level on which selection for the behavior has occurred. These levels include: species, culture, individual, kinship, gender, and age. A particular variant need not be a product of natural selection, in the usual sense, to be analyzed in terms of its biological utility. Thus the concept of functional value potentially can illuminate any nonpathological behavioral variant, even a "purely" cultural one.

REFERENCES

AINSWORTH, M.D.S. Attachment theory and its utility in cross-cultural research. In P. H. Leiderman, S. R. Tulkin, & A. Rosenfeld (Eds.), *Culture and infancy: Variations in the human experience.* New York: Academic Press, 1977.

AINSWORTH, M.D.S., BELL, S.M.V., & STAYTON, D. J. Individual differences in strange-situation behavior of one-year-olds. In H. R. Schaffer (Ed.), *The origins of human social relations.* New York: Academic Press, 1971.

ALLEN, E. et al. Letter to *New York Review of Books,* November 13, 1975.

ANDY, O. J., & STEPHAN, H. Comparative primate neuroanatomy of structures relating to aggressive behavior. In R. L. Holloway (Ed.), *Primate aggression, territoriality, and xenophobia.* New York: Academic Press, 1974.

BANDURA, A. *Aggression: A social learning analysis.* Englewood Cliffs, N.J.: Prentice-Hall, 1973.

BARASH, D. P. Sociobiology: The underlying concept. *Science,* 1978, *200,* 1106–1107.

BARLOW, G. W. Issues and concepts in ethology. In K. Immelman (Ed.), *Grzimek's encyclopedia of ethology* (English ed.). New York: Van Nostrand Reinhold, 1977.

BELL, R. Q., & HARPER, L. V. *Child effects on adults.* Hillsdale, N.J.: Lawrence Erlbaum Associates, 1977.

BICCHIERI, M. G. *Hunters and gatherers today.* New York: Holt, Rinehart & Winston, 1972.

BLURTON JONES, N. (Ed). *Ethological studies of child behavior.* Cambridge, England: Cambridge University Press, 1972.

BLURTON JONES, N. G. Growing points in human ethology: Another link between ethology and the social sciences? In P.P.G. Bateson & R. A. Hinde (Eds.), *Growing points in ethology.* Cambridge, England: Cambridge University Press, 1976.

BORNSTEIN, M. H., KESSEN, W., & WEISKOPF, S. The categories of hue in infancy. *Science,* 1976, *191,* 201–202.

BOWER, T.G.R. The visual world of infants. *Scientific American,* 1966, *215,* 80–92.

BOWLBY, J. *Attachment and loss* (Vol. 1). Attachment. New York: Basic Books, 1969.

BRAY, G. A. The myth of diet in the management of obesity. *American Journal of Clinical Nutrition,* 1970, *23,* 1141–1148.

BRENT, S. B. Individual specialization, collective adaptation and rate of environmental change. *Human Development,* 1978, *21,* 21–33.

BROWN, R. *A first language: The early stages.* Cambridge, Mass.: Harvard University Press, 1973.

BRUNSWIK, E. *Perception and the representative design of psychological experiments.* Berkeley: University of California Press, 1956.

BUELL, S. J., & COLEMAN, P. D. Dendritic growth in the aged human brain and failure of growth in senile dementia. *Science,* 1979, *206,* 854–856.

BURTON, M., & BURTON, R. *The international wildlife encyclopedia.* New York: Marshall Lavendish, 1970.

CAIRNS, R. B. *Social Development: The origins and plasticity of interchanges.* San Francisco: W. H. Freeman & Company Publishers, 1979.

CHARLESWORTH, W. R. Developmental psychology: Does it offer anything distinctive? In W. R. Looft (Ed.), *Developmental psychology: A book of readings.* Hinsdale, Ill.: Dryden Press, 1972.

CHEVALIER-SKOLNIKOFF, S. A Piagetian model for describing and comparing socialization in monkey, ape, and human infants. In S. Chevalier-Skolnikoff & F. E. Poirier (Eds.), *Primate bio-social development: Biological, social, and ecological determinants.* New York: Garland, 1977.

CRAWFORD, C. George Washington, Abraham Lincoln, and Arthur Jensen: Are they compatible? *American Psychologist,* 1979, *34,* 664–672.

DALE, M., & WILSON, M. *Sex, evolution and behavior.* North Scituate, Mass.: Duxbury, 1978.

D'ANDRADE, R. Cross-cultural studies of sex differences in behavior. In E. E. Maccoby (Ed.), *The development of sex differences.* Stanford, Calif.: Stanford University Press, 1966.

DARWIN, C. *The expression of the emotions in man and animals.* London: Murray, 1872.

DAWSON, J.L.M. Theoretical and research base of bio-social psychology. *University of Hong Kong, Supplement to the Gazette,* 1969, *16,* 1–10.

DEMAREST, W. J. Incest avoidance among human and nonhuman primates. In S. Chevalier-Skolnikoff & F. E. Poirier (Eds.), *Primate bio-social development: Biological, social, and ecological determinants.* New York: Garland, 1977.

DITTRICHOVA, J. The development of premature infants. In R. J. Robinson (Ed.), *Brain and early development.* London: Academic Press, 1969.

DURHAM, W. H. Toward a coevolutionary theory of human biology and culture. In N. A. Chagnon & W. Irons (Eds.), *Evolutionary biology and human social behavior: An anthropological perspective.* North Scituate, Mass.: Duxbury, 1979.

DURHAM, W. H. *Interactions of genetics and culture: A case study of dairying.* Paper presented at the American Anthropological Society meeting, Washington, D.C., December 1980.

EIBL-EIBESFELDT, I. *Ethology: The biology of behavior.* New York: Holt, Rinehart & Winston, 1975.

EKMAN, P. Universals and cultural differences in facial expression of emotion. Pp. 207–283 in J. K. Cole (Ed.), *Nebraska Symposium on Motivation.* Lincoln: University of Nebraska Press, 1971.

EMBER, C. R., & EMBER, M. E. *Cultural anthropology.* Englewood Cliffs, N.J.: Prentice-Hall, 1973.

FANTZ, R. L. The origin of form perception. *Scientific American,* 1961, *204,* 66–72.

FISHBEIN, H. B. *Evolution, development, and children's learning.* Santa Monica, Calif.: Goodyear, 1976.

FISKE, A. P. *A sensitive period in group bonding in humans.* Unpublished manuscript, University of Chicago, 1974.

FLAVELL, J. H. *Cognitive development.* Englewood Cliffs, N.J.: Prentice-Hall, 1977.

FREEDMAN, D. G. Hereditary control of early social behavior. In B. M. Foss (Ed.), *Determinants of infant behavior* (Vol. 3). London: Methuen, 1965.

FREEDMAN, D. G. *Human infancy: An evolutionary perspective.* Hillsdale, N.J.: Lawrence Erlbaum Associates, 1974.

FREEDMAN, D. G. *Human sociobiology.* New York: Free Press, 1979.

FREEDMAN, D. G., & DeBOER, M. M. Biological and cultural differences in early child development. *Annual Review of Anthropology,* 1979, *8,* 579–600.

FULLER, J. L. Experiential deprivation and later behavior. *Science,* 1976, *158,* 1645–1652.

GIBSON, E. J. *Principles of perceptual learning and development.* Englewood Cliffs, N.J.: Prentice-Hall, 1969.

GIBSON, K. R. Brain structure and intelligence in macaques and human infants from a Piagetian perspective. In S. Chevalier-Skolnikoff & F. E. Poirier (Eds.), *Primate bio-social development: Biological, social, and ecological determinants.* New York: Garland, 1977.

GOTTLIEB, G. Development of species identification in ducklings. *Journal of Comparative and Physiological Psychology,* 1975, *89,* 387–399, 675–684, 899–912.

GOULD, S. J. *Ontogeny and phylogeny.* Cambridge, Mass.: Harvard University Press, 1977.

HAILMAN, J. P. The ontogeny of an instinct. *Behaviour,* Supplement 15, 1967.

HARLOW, H. The evolution of learning. In A. Roe & G. G. Simpson (Eds.), *Behavior and evolution.* New Haven, Conn.: Yale University Press, 1958.

HARLOW, H. F., & HARLOW, M. K. The affectional systems. In A. M. Schrier, H. F. Harlow & F. Stollnitz (Eds.), *Behavior of nonhuman primates.* New York: Academic Press, 1965.

HARRIS, M. *The rise of anthropological theory.* New York: Thomas Y. Crowell, 1968.

HARRIS, M. *Cows, pigs, wars, and witches: The riddles of culture.* New York: Random House, 1974.

HEBB, D. O. On the nature of fear. *Psychological Review,* 1946, *53,* 250–275.

HECKHAUSEN, H. *The anatomy of achievement motivation.* New York: Academic Press, 1967.

HINDE, R. A. *Ethology and the social sciences.* Address to the Animal Behavior Society, Ft. Collins, Colo., June 11, 1980.

HIRSCH, J. Behavior-genetic analysis and its biosocial consequences. In W. R. Looft (Ed.), *Developmental psychology: A book of readings.* Hinsdale, Ill.: Dryden Press, 1972.

HOYENGA, K. G., & HOYENGA, K. T. *The question of sex differences: Psychological, cultural, and biological issues.* Boston: Little, Brown, 1979.

HUTCHINSON, G. E. A speculative consideration of certain possible forms of sexual selection in man. *American Naturalist,* 1959, *93,* 81–91.

HUTT, C. *Males and females.* Baltimore, Md.: Penguin, 1972.

IZARD, C. E. *Face of emotion.* New York: Appleton-Century-Crofts, 1971.

JACOBSON, S. W. Matching behavior in the young infant. *Child Development,* 1979, *50,* 425–430.

KAGAN, J. Attention and psychological change in the young child. *Science,* 1970, *170,* 826–832.

KAGAN, J. Motives and development. *Journal of Personality & Social Psychology,* 1972, *22,* 51–66.

KAGAN, J. Discrepancy, temperament and infant distress. In M. Lewis & L. A. Rosenblum (Eds.), *The origins of fear.* New York: John Wiley, 1974.

KAGAN, J. Emergent themes in human development. *American Scientist,* 1976, *64,* 186–196.

KAGAN, J. The uses of cross-cultural research in early development. In P. H. Leiderman, S. R. Tulkin, & A. Rosenfeld (Eds.), *Culture and infancy: Variations in the human experience.* New York: Academic Press, 1977.

KAGAN, J., KEARSLEY, R. B., & ZELAZO, P. R. The effects of infant day care on psychological development. *Educational Quarterly,* 1977, *1,* 109–142.

KALLMAN, F. J. Twin and sibship study of overt male homosexuality. *American Journal of Human Genetics,* 1952, *4,* 136–146.

KANTOR, J. R. *Interbehavioral psychology.* Bloomington, Ind.: Principia Press, 1958.

KIMURA, M. The neutral theory of molecular evolution. *Scientific American,* 1979, *241,* 98–126.

KLAUS, M. H., & KENNELL, J. H. *Maternal-infant bonding.* St. Louis, Mo.: C. V. Mosby, 1976.

KLÜVER, H., & BUCY, P. C. Preliminary analysis of functions of the temporal lobes in monkeys. *Archives of Neurology and Psychiatry,* 1939, *42,* 979–1000.

KOHLBERG, L. A. A cognitive-developmental analysis of children's sex role concepts and attitudes. In E. E. Maccoby (Ed.), *The development of sex differences.* Stanford, Calif.: Stanford University Press, 1966.

KOHLBERG, L., & GILLIGAN, C. The adolescent as a philosopher: The discovery of the self in a postconventional world. *Daedalus,* Fall 1971, *100,* 1051–1086.

KONNER, M. J. Aspects of the developmental ethology of a foraging people. In N. Blurton Jones (Ed.), *Ethological studies of child behaviour.* Cambridge, England: Cambridge University Press, 1972.

KONNER, M. Evolution of human behavior development. In P. H. Leiderman, S. R. Tulkin, & A. Rosenfeld (Eds.), *Culture and infancy: Variations in the human experience.* New York: Academic Press, 1977.

KURLAND, J. A. Paternity, mother's brother, and human sociality. In N. A. Chagnon & W. Irons (Eds.), *Evolutionary biology and human social behavior: An anthropological perspective.* North Scituate, Mass.: Duxbury, 1979.

LACK, D. *The life of the robin.* Harmondsworth, England: Pelican, 1953.

LEHRMAN, D. S. The presence of the mate and of nesting material as stimuli for the development of incubation behavior in the ring dove (*Streptopelia risoria*). *Behaviour,* 1961, *7,* 241–286.

LeVINE, R. A. Child rearing as cultural adaptation. In P. H. Leiderman, S. R. Tulkin, & A. Rosenfeld (Eds.), *Culture and infancy: Variations in the human experience.* New York: Academic Press, 1977.

LEWIS, M., & ROSENBLUM, L. A. *The effect of the infant on its caregiver.* New York: John Wiley, 1974.

LIPSITT, L. P., & REESE, H. W. *Child development.* Glenview, Ill.: Scott, Foresman, 1979.

LORENZ, K. *Evolution and modification of behavior.* Chicago: University of Chicago Press, 1965.

LURIA, A. R. *The working brain.* Baltimore, Md.: Penguin, 1973.

McCLEARN, G. E., & DeFRIES, J. C. (Eds.), *Introduction to behavioral genetics.* San Francisco: W. H. Freeman & Company Publishers, 1973.

MACCOBY, E. E., & JACKLIN, C. N. *The psychology of sex differences.* Stanford, Calif.: Stanford University Press, 1974.

MacLEAN, P. D. Psychosomatic disease and the "visceral brain": Recent developments bearing on the Papez theory of emotion. In R. L. Isaacson (Ed.), *Basic readings in neuropsychology.* New York: Harper & Row, Pub., 1964.

MAIER, N.R.F., & SCHNEIRLA, T. C. *Principles of animal psychology.* New York: Dover, 1964.

MARTIN, R. D. The biological basis of human behaviour. In W. B. Broughton (Ed.), *The biology of brains.* London: Institute of Biology, 1974.

MASTERS, W. H., & JOHNSON, V. E. *Human sexual response.* Boston: Little, Brown, 1966.

MASTERSON, B., & SKEEN, L. C. Origins of anthropoid intelligence. *Journal of Comparative and Physiological Psychology,* 1972, *81,* 423–433.

MAYR, E. *Animal species and evolution.* Cambridge, Mass.: Harvard University Press, 1963.

MAYR, E. *Populations, species, and evolution.* Cambridge, Mass.: Harvard University Press, 1970.

MAYR, E. *Evolution and the diversity of life.* Cambridge, Mass.: Harvard University Press, 1976.

MEAD, M. *Sex and temperament in three primitive societies.* New York: Morrow, 1935.

MEDAWAR, P. B. Does ethology throw any light on human behaviour? In P.P.G. Bateson & R. A. Hinde (Eds.), *Growing points in ethology.* Cambridge, England: Cambridge University Press, 1976.

MEIER, G. W. Maternal behaviour of feral- and laboratory-reared monkeys following the surgical delivery of their infants. *Nature,* 1965a, *206,* 492–493.

MEIER, G. W. Other data on the effects of social isolation during rearing upon adult reproductive behaviour in the rhesus monkey (*Macaca mulatta*). *Animal Behaviour,* 1965b, *13,* 228–231.

MITTLER, P. *The study of twins.* New York: Penguin, 1971.

MONEY, J., & EHRHARDT, A. A. *Man and woman, boy and girl.* Baltimore, Md.: Johns Hopkins University Press, 1972.

NASH, J. *Developmental psychology: A psychobiological approach.* Englewood Cliffs, N.J.: Prentice-Hall, 1978.

OAKLEY, D. A. Cerebral cortex and adaptive behaviour. In D. A. Oakley & H. C. Plotkin (Eds.), *Brain, behaviour and evolution.* London: Methuen, 1979.

PARKER, S. T. Piaget's sensorimotor series in an infant macaque: A model for comparing unstereotyped behavior and intelligence in human and nonhuman primates. In S. Chevalier-Skolnikoff & F. E. Poirier (Eds.), *Primate bio-social development: Biological, social, and ecological determinants.* New York: Garland, 1977.

PIAGET, J. Piaget's theory. In P. H. Mussen (Ed.), *Carmichael's manual of child psychology.* New York: John Wiley, 1970.

PIAGET, J. *Biology and knowledge.* Chicago: University of Chicago Press, 1971.

PIAGET, J. Problems of equilibration. In M. H. Appel & L. S. Goldberg (Eds.), *Topics in cognitive development* (Vol. 1). New York: Plenum, 1977.

PLOMIN, R., & ROWE, D. C. Genetic and environmental etiology of social behavior in infancy. *Developmental Psychology,* 1979, *15,* 62–72.

PLOTKIN, H. C. Brain-behaviour studies and evolutionary biology. In D. A. Oakley & H. C. Plotkin (Eds.), *Brain, behaviour and evolution.* London: Methuen, 1979.

PUGH, G. E. *The biological basis of human values.* New York: Basic Books, 1977.

REISEN, A. H. Arrested vision. *Scientific American,* 1950, *183,* 16–19.

RODIN, J. Bidirectional influences of emotionality, stimulus responsivity, and metabolic events in obesity. In J. D. Maser & M.E.P. Seligman (Eds.), *Psychopathology: Experimental models.* San Francisco: W. H. Freeman & Company Publishers, 1977.

ROSENZWEIG, M. R., & BENNETT, E. L. Effects of differential environments on brain weights and enzyme activities in gerbils, rats, and mice. *Developmental Psychobiology,* 1970, *2,* 87–95.

SACKETT, G. P. Monkeys reared in isolation with pictures as visual input: Evidence for an innate releasing mechanism. *Science,* 1966, *154,* 1468–1473.

SACKETT, G. P., HOLM, R. A., & RUPPENTHAL, G. C. Social isolation rearing: Species differences in behavior of macaque monkeys. *Developmental Psychology,* 1976, *12,* 283–288.

SAHLINS, M. The use and abuse of biology: An anthropological critique of sociobiology. Ann Arbor: University of Michigan Press, 1976.

SALK, L. Effects of normal heartbeat sound on behavior of newborn infant: Implications for mental health. *World Mental Health,* 1960, *12,* 4.

SCARR, S. Environmental bias in twin studies. *Eugenics Quarterly,* 1968, *15,* 34–40.

SCHAFFER, H. R. Cognitive components of the infant's response to strangeness. In M. Lewis & L. A. Rosenblum (Eds.), *The origins of fear.* New York: John Wiley, 1974.

SELIGMAN, M.E.P. On the generality of the laws of learning. *Psychological Review,* 1970, *77,* 406–418.

SHEPHER, J. Mate selection among second generation kibbutz adolescents and adults: Incest avoidance and negative imprinting. *Archives of Sexual Behavior,* 1971, *1,* 293–307.

SHIELDS, J. *Monozygotic twins brought up together and apart.* Oxford, England: Oxford University Press, 1962.

SKINNER, B. F. *The behavior of organisms: An experimental analysis.* Englewood Cliffs, N.J.: Prentice-Hall, 1966.

SPIRO, M. E. Is the family universal? *American Anthropologist,* 1954, *56,* 839–846.

SROUFE, L. A., WATERS, E., & MATAS, L. Contextual determinants of infant affectional response. In M. Lewis & L. Rosenblum (Eds.), *Origins of fear.* New York: John Wiley, 1974.

STRAUSS, M. E., LESSEN-FIRESTONE, J. K., STARR, R. H., & OSTREA, E. M. Behavior of narcotics-addicted newborns. *Child Development,* 1975, *46,* 887–893.

STREISSGUTH, A. P. Maternal alcoholism and the outcome of pregnancy. In M. Greenwealth (Ed.), *Alcohol problems in women and children.* New York: Grune & Stratton, 1977.

STUNKARD, A. J. Environment and obesity: Recent advances in our understanding of regulation of food intake in man. *Federation Proceedings,* 1968, *27,* 1367.

SUOMI, S. J., & HARLOW, H. F. The role and reason of peer relationships in rhesus monkeys. In M. Lewis & L. A. Rosenblum (Eds.), *Friendship and peer relations.* New York: John Wiley, 1975.

TINBERGEN, N. *The study of instinct.* Oxford, England: Clarendon Press, 1951.

TRIVERS, R. L. Parental investment and sexual selection. In B. Campbell (Ed.), *Sexual selection and the descent of man 1871–1971.* Chicago: Aldine, 1972.

TRIVERS, R. L. Parent-offspring conflict. *American Zoologist,* 1974, *14,* 249–264.

VAN DEN BERGHE, P. Sociobiology, dogma, and ethics. *Wilson Quarterly,* Summer 1977, pp. 121–126.

VON FRISCH, K. *The dancing bees.* New York: Harcourt Brace Jovanovich, 1953.

WADDINGTON, C. H. Genetic assimilation of an acquired character. *Evolution,* 1953, *7,* 118.

WADDINGTON, C. H. Genetic assimilation. In E. W. Caspari & J. W. Thoday (Eds.), *Advances in genetics.* New York: Academic Press, 1960.

WEINRAUB, M., & PUTNEY, E. The effect of height on infants' social responses to unfamiliar persons. *Child Development,* 1978, *49,* 598–603.

WEISFELD, G. E. An ethological view of human adolescence. *Journal of Nervous & Mental Disease,* 1979, *167,* 38–55.

WEISFELD, G. E., OMARK, D. R., & CRONIN, C. L. A longitudinal and cross-sectional study of dominance in boys. In D. R. Omark, F. F. Strayer, & D. G. Freedman (Eds.), *Dominance relations: An ethological view of human conflict and social interaction.* New York: Garland, 1980.

WERNER, E. E. *Cross-cultural child development: A view from the planet earth.* Monterey, Calif.: Brooks/Cole, 1979.

WESTERMARCK, E. A. *The history of human marriage.* London: Macmillan, 1891.

WHITE, B. L., & HELD, R. Plasticity of sensorimotor development in the human infant. In J. Rosenblith & W. Allinsmith (Eds.), *The causes of behavior: Readings in child development and educational psychology.* Boston: Allyn & Bacon, 1966.

WHITE, R. W. Motivation reconsidered: The concept of competence. *Psychological Review,* 1959, *66,* 297–333.

WHORF, B. L. *Language, thought and reality: Selected writings.* Cambridge, Mass.: Technology Press, 1956.

WILLIAMS, G. C. *Group selection.* Chicago: Aldine, 1971.

WILSON, E. O. Human decency is animal. *New York Times Magazine,* October 12, 1975a, pp. 38–50.

WILSON, E. O. *Sociobiology: The new synthesis.* Cambridge, Mass.: Harvard University Press, 1975b.

WOLF, A. P. Childhood association and sexual attraction: A further test of the Westermarck hypothesis. *American Anthropologist,* 1970, *72,* 503–515.

WOLFF, P.H. The natural history of crying and other vocalizations in early infancy. In B. Foss (Ed.), *Determinants of infant behavior* (Vol. 4). London: Methuen, 1969.

14

The Psychophysiology
of Infancy

RICHARD HIRSCHMAN
LAWRENCE E. MELAMED
CONSTANCE M. OLIVER

Numerous analyses of psychophysiological functioning in infancy have appeared in recent years, partly in response to the relative difficulty in delineating specific infant behaviors. First, the infant has few functional modes of communication. It cannot tell with words when it has perceived or processed stimuli. Second, physiological responses are particularly sensitive to changes in psychological state and often are more sensitive than behavioral measures (Rose, Schmidt, & Bridger, 1978). Third, physiological responses can be used in longitudinal studies in ways behavioral responses cannot, either because the physiological response is already functional at birth or because the emergence of the response may be indicative of significant biological milestones or more general maturational changes (Campos, 1976).

Of particular interest has been the relationship between the central nervous system and the autonomic nervous system. This interest has been catalyzed by the work of the Soviets on the orienting response and conditioning (Sokolov, 1960, 1963) and by the work of the Laceys (Lacey, 1956; Lacey & Lacey, 1978) on the relationship between cardiovascular activity and cognitive processing in mature subjects. On the basis of this work, it is reasonable to assume that an analysis of autonomic functioning might help to clarify the development of central nervous system functioning in the neonate.

The purpose of this chapter is to review the literature concerning psychophysiological activity in the neonate and then to relate this to more complex processes (e.g., attention, arousal, and emotion) which reflect the development of the central nervous system. Regrettably limitations of space prevent exhaustive coverage of these topics and require the omission of a number of related

topics. For example recently a substantial amount of research has been done on cortical activity and state cycles in the neonate and some interest shown as well in the environmental adaptation of the neonate. The reader is referred to Berg and Berg (1978) for a review of the first two topics and to Hirschman and Katkin (1974) for a review of the latter topic. Also there have been assessments of autonomic functioning in utero (Copher & Huber, 1967; Welford & Sontag, 1969). However, investigators in this area have been limited by the inaccessibility of the systems of interest. Thus our discussion will focus on autonomic functioning postpartum.

We shall first review the literature on the peripheral autonomic response capabilities of the neonate. Then we shall examine how these capabilities are related to the emergence of arousal, orienting, attention, and learning. Finally we shall explore a relatively virgin area—the psychophysiology of neonatal emotional states.

AUTONOMIC CAPABILITY

Spontaneous Responses

In order to examine higher order central nervous system processing in the neonate, it is necessary to first delineate the psychophysiological repertoire during the first year of life. Most of the studies in this area have focused on cardiovascular functioning.

In a longitudinal study of 40 full-term newborns, Contis and Lind (1963) found that for the first hour after birth, the infant heartrate decreases. They interpreted this as a transition from the fetal rate to a lower rate. However during the first few days, the infant heartrate is in a period of gradual, constant acceleration to about 120

Preparation of this chapter was supported in part by N.I.D.R. Grant DE 04769 awarded to the first author.

beats per minute. In support of this Graham, Clifton, and Hatton (1968) also found that the infant heartrate increases during the first five days of life.

Two studies provide longitudinal data on infant heartrate levels through the first several months of life. In a study of 14 infants, Lipton, Steinschneider, and Richmond (1966) reported that the mean heartrate at 2 to 5 days of age was substantially lower than at 2½ or 5 months and that there was no significant difference in heartrate between the ages of 2½ and 5 months. In another related study, Lewis, Wilson, Ban, and Baumel (1970) found that between 2 and 56 weeks of age there was a linear decrease in infant heartrate. Considering these two studies, the status of infant heartrate past the first week of life is uncertain. In addition an analysis of the records of 16 newborns by Clifton and Graham (1968) indicated that the mean infant heartrate does not remain stable during the first 5 days of life. Clifton and Graham computed a second index of heartrate, a "low rate" derived from the computation of the slowest heartrate of all prestimulus periods on a given day. This rate showed substantial stability during the first 5 days postpartum.

A potential difficulty in tracking heartrate is that it appears to covary with the state of the neonate. Bridger, Birns, and Blank (1965) and Campos and Brackbill (1973) found substantial correlations between heartrate measures and levels of overall excitation. Likewise Harper and colleagues found a reduction of heartrate during sleep states relative to awake states (Harper, Hoppenbrouwers, Sterman, McGinty, & Hodgman, 1976) and sleep-awake differences in cardiac waveform (Harper, Kelly, Walter, & Hoppenbrouwers, 1976). Heartrate differences between the active (REM) and quiet (NREM) sleep states were not observed. They did find significant differences in the shape of the cardiac waveform during active and quiet sleep in infants ranging in age from one day to five weeks. Studies such as these consistently indicate that cardiovascular functioning and infant state are highly related. However the relationship between heartrate and state is not such that one can infer state from heartrate level alone; two infants with the same heartrate are not necessarily in the same state.

Although evaluations of spontaneous psychophysiological activity in the infant typically have focused on cardiac rate, a few attempts have been made to investigate electrodermal activity, particularly as a function of sleep state. Apparently skin potential responses increase significantly during periods of active sleep in full-term infants (Bell, 1970). Also skin potential responses occur more frequently during active sleep than during quiet sleep in full-term newborns (Curzi-Dascalova, Pajot, & Dreyfus-Brisac, 1973). This distribution is opposite to that seen in adults where skin potential responses are more numerous during quiet sleep than during active sleep (Lester, Burch, & Dosset, 1967). With the development of EEG sleep spindles during the second month of life, the response frequency in quiet sleep increases rapidly to exceed frequencies observed in active sleep and approaches levels typical of the quiet sleep state in adults (Curzi-Dascalova & Dreyfus-Brisac, 1976). In one of the few studies of the resting skin conductance in the newborn, Kaye (1964) found progressive increases in conductance

from the palmar and plantar regions as well as from the upper calf during the first few days of life. Kaye concluded that these changes represented a general increase in arousal level.

Throughout much of this discussion on resting level, it has been assumed that autonomic activity in the absence of stimulation is, in fact, spontaneous. However this may not be the case. Brackbill (1970) found that 30-day-old infants were more aroused (heartrate, respiration, and motor indicants) during an eight-minute period of no stimulation than during an eight-minute period of continuous auditory stimulation. Paradoxically continuous stimulation may exert a more calming effect on infants than silence. What stimulates an infant during silence and what effect somatic influences have on spontaneous activity in infants have yet to be determined. This latter issue has been discussed in detail with respect to the mature organism by Obrist and his colleagues (Obrist, 1968, 1976; Obrist, Webb, Sutterer, & Howard, 1970).

Stimulated Responses

Brief Stimulation-Heartrate. Neonatal heartrate is responsive to a variety of stimuli. In the initial studies of cardiac functioning during the first week of life, the cardiac response to discrete stimuli typically was reported as a monophasic heartrate acceleration (Bartoshuk, 1962b; Bridger & Reiser, 1959; Clifton, Graham, & Hatton, 1968; Gray & Crowell, 1968; Lipton & Steinschneider, 1964; Lipton et al., 1966). Bridger and Reiser (1959) reported monophasic acceleration in three- to five-day-old infants in response to air puffs delivered to the abdomen. Bartoshuk (1962b) obtained monophasic heartrate acceleration to auditory stimuli in two- to three-day-old infants. Likewise Gray and Crowell (1968) found that two-day-old infants responded with cardiac accelerations to auditory clicks, the smell of acetic acid, and a puff of nitrogen delivered to the abdomen.

In a series of seminal papers, Graham and her colleagues (Graham & Clifton, 1966; Graham & Jackson, 1970; Keen, Chase, & Graham, 1965) reported that cardiac decelerations do not occur or occur minimally in the newborn. However Lipsitt and Jacklin (1971) found that infants two to four days old responded with cardiac deceleration to an olfactory stimulus. They postulated that this deceleration was attributable to the physiological maturity of the olfactory system relative to other sensory systems. Unfortunately Jacklin (1972) was unable to replicate this finding.

In contrast older infants are capable of decelerative responses to discrete stimuli (Berg, 1972; Clifton & Meyers, 1969; Gray & Crowell, 1968; Lewis & Spaulding, 1967; Lipton et al., 1966). Lewis and Spaulding (1967) obtained monophasic cardiac deceleration to auditory and visual stimuli from a group of six-month-old infants. In three longitudinal studies (Clifton & Meyers, 1969; Gray & Crowell, 1968; Lipton et al., 1966), stimuli which consistently had elicited accelerative responses in newborns produced decelerative responses exclusively or complex responses with decelerative components in infants six weeks to five months of age. Prior to the present decade there was little dispute regarding the form of the neonatal heartrate response to stimulation (Hirschman & Katkin, 1974). The heartrate response to stimulation during the first weeks of life supposedly was accelerative. After the first six weeks of life, the heartrate response also could be decelerative. This increase in response capability was thought to be a function of physiological (Lipton et al., 1966; Obrist, Wood, & Perez-Reyes, 1965) or behavioral (Graham & Jackson, 1970) changes over time.

In 1971 Sameroff suggested that the early accelerative response may not necessarily be a function of the maturational level of the newborn but rather may reflect specific experimental conditions. Previous studies had typically used loud auditory stimuli with sudden onsets and may have activated a sensory system that is less mature in the newborn than other sensory systems (Graham & Jackson, 1970). In Sameroff's view many stimuli may be intense for the newborn. He proposed that stimuli of different intensities and modalities would elicit differential cardiac responses.

Since that time investigators have attempted to determine more precisely the effects of various stimulus parameters on the heartrate response of the newborn. Jackson, Kantowitz, and Graham (1971) found that the quality and onset characteristics of auditory stimuli may exert a critical influence. In one- to three-day-old infants, 75 db tones produced short latency heartrate accelerations as compared to the immediate accelerations observed in response to 75 db rectangular pulses in earlier work (Clifton, Graham, & Hatton, 1968). The heartrate response in the most recent study also developed more gradually, and the peak heartrate was reduced.

Schachter, Williams, Khachaturian, Tobin, Kruger, and Kerr (1971) were able to elicit a decelerative response to auditory clicks from six-, two- and three-day-old infants. The response was attenuated, however, and was followed by heartrate acceleration. In a study in which intensity, frequency, and rise time of auditory stimuli were varied (Kearsley, 1973), monophasic heartrate deceleration was obtained but in a nonpredictable fashion. Infants one to three days of age responded with deceleration to auditory stimuli with frequencies of 500 and 2000 H_z. In contrast cardiac acceleration occurred in response to frequencies of 1000 H_z. Kearsley (1973) concluded that the neonatal heartrate response to auditory stimuli is a function of specific combinations of intensities and rise times applied to particular frequencies. Eisenberg, Marmarou, and Giovachino (1974) also reported sustained auditory-evoked heartrate decelerations in a 13-day-old infant using a synthetically produced vowel *ah*, which is a prominent component of the young infant's verbal repertoire. On the basis of extensive exploration of many stimulus conditions (Eisenberg, 1965; Eisenberg, Griffin, Coursin, & Hunter, 1964; Eisenberg et al., 1974), Eisenberg concluded that heartrate deceleration is a salient functional concomitant of synthetically produced speech sounds. Eisenberg's conclusion is supported by recent evidence by Clarkson and Berg (1979) who also obtained a decelerative response to synthetically produced vowels. Clarkson and Berg (1979) noted, too, that the temporal pattern of such stimuli is an especially important parameter. In their study pulsed vowels elicited a significant heartrate deceleration while continuous vowels did not.

With respect to visual stimuli Sameroff, Cashmore, and Dykes (1973) presented two- and three-day-old infants with patterned and blank field stimuli. Heartrate deceleration occurred in response to the patterned stimuli but not in response to the blank field stimuli. They concluded that a decelerative response to visual stimulation may occur in the newborn but only to moderately complex, nonstartling stimuli. In another study utilizing visual stimuli, Adkinson and Berg (1976) monitored the heartrate of one- to four-day-old infants during the gradual onset and offset of colored lights of mild intensity. The infants responded to both stimulus onset and offset with significant heartrate decelerations.

In one of the few recent studies using tactile stimulation, Yang and Douthitt (1974) examined heartrate change as a function of stimulus intensity. They used air puff stimulation similar to that used by Bridger and Reiser (1959) and Lipton et al. (1966). Two-day-old infants were subjected to increasing intensities until a threshold behavioral response occurred. No specific heartrate response occurred to any of the intensities below threshold. At the threshold level all infants displayed accelerative responses; relative to the previous studies utilizing tactile stimulation, the accelerative responses were gradual and small.

Taken together the studies since 1970 of neonatal heartrate response to stimulation have created a somewhat ambiguous picture of cardiac functioning in the infant. Decelerative responses as well as accelerative responses can be elicited during the first week of life. However it has been difficult, if not impossible, to make general predictive comments regarding the magnitude of the cardiac response as a function of certain stimulus parameters, especially when two or more parameters are considered simultaneously. The issue may be complicated by the possibility that descending feedback from immature brain centers in neonates may disrupt the activity from lower centers which presumably are able to sustain cardiac orienting to certain stimuli (Graham, Leavitt, & Strock, 1978).

The indeterminate status of the neonatal cardiac response to stimulation is seen most clearly in investigations linking cardiac response to infant state. After a thorough review of many state-oriented, physiological studies of the neonate, Hutt, Lenard, and Prechtl (1969) concluded that state has a strong influence on the neonate's response to stimulation. Unfortunately the effects of state cannot be systematically inferred. In the opinion of Hutt et al. (1969), neonatal responsivity is not only a function of state but also a function of the type of stimulation. Ashton (1973) summarized this perspective.

It is not possible to predict the effects of state upon reactivity on the basis of the spurious assumption that a particular state can categorically be said to be a reflection of a point on an arousal continuum. Thus, it can only be said that the neonate reacts *differently* when in one state than when in another. The effects of the state variable can only be meaningfully interpreted in terms of the stimulus parameters employed. (p. 13)

In an important investigation of the influence of state upon cardiac reactivity, Berg, Berg, and Graham (1971) monitored the heartrate responses of four-month-old infants to auditory stimulation. When the heartrate responses of all infants were averaged without regard to state, the heartrate curve was similar to the decelerative curves obtained in earlier work by Clifton and Meyers (1969). However, the results were strikingly affected when the state of the infant was considered. In alert infants the heartrate decelerations were more pronounced than in the total group. In less alert infants who showed increasing agitation or increasing somnolence, the decelerative trends were attenuated, and acceleration appeared. Thus the infants exhibited significantly different reactions to the same stimuli in different states. The interactive effects of stimulus and state on neonatal heartrate have been confirmed by Rewey (1973) for auditory, tactile, and vestibular stimulation. It appears that stimulated heartrate responses of alert infants, even during the first weeks of life, may be decelerative. In contrast the stimulated heartrate responses of infants in any nonalert state are largely accelerative. Furthermore the effects of state on reactivity are not straightforward in that they interact with stimulus parameters in ways that are not yet fully predictable. Investigators who study infant state agree, though, that a clearer picture of neonatal heartrate capability emerges when controlling for the state of the infant (Berg, 1974; Berg et al., 1971; Pomerleau-Malcuit & Clifton, 1973; Rewey, 1973).

Continuous Stimulation-Heartrate. Brackbill (1971, 1973, 1975) has studied the infant's level of autonomic functioning over a relatively long period of time as distinct from the infant's more transient responses to discrete stimuli. She discovered that continuous stimulation modified the arousal level of one-month-old infants—i.e., there were rapid decreases in heartrate, respiration rate, crying, and motor activity. This effect was not restricted to one sensory modality but rather was a general characteristic across auditory, visual, proprioceptive-tactile, and temperature modalities. The effect was also cumulative across modalities. Continuous stimulation of four modalities lowered arousal level more effectively than continuous stimulation of three modalities; three were more effective than two, and so on (Brackbill, 1971). Finally the effectiveness of continuous stimulation in reducing arousal level increased directly with stimulus intensity (Brackbill, 1975) and endured over a relatively long period of time (Brackbill, 1973). This continuous stimulation effect probably involves central nervous system sites that initially are relatively primitive but show functional change with postnatal development (Brackbill, 1973).

AROUSAL AND ORIENTING BEHAVIOR

As indicated in the previous sections, much effort has been directed toward determining the nature of the neonatal heartrate response to stimulation. The most significant reason for this effort is that heartrate seems to be inextricably linked to cognitive functioning in adults. A primary impetus for this view is the Laceys' hypothesis that the direction of heartrate change reflects different interactions with the environment (Lacey, 1959; Lacey & Lacey, 1962, 1978; Lacey, Kagan, Lacey, & Moss, 1963). Situations involving sensory intake evoke cardiac deceleration while situations involving rejection of irrelevant or painful stimuli evoke heartrate acceleration. Graham and Clifton (1966) related this hypothesis to Sokolov's (1963) concepts of orienting and defensive responses. Sokolov proposed that the orienting response serves to enhance stimulus intake while the defensive response serves

to limit the effects of noxious or distracting stimuli. Graham and Clifton (1966) concluded that heartrate deceleration is a component of the orienting response and that heartrate acceleration is a component of the defensive response. Insofar as these two responses modulate incoming information, an understanding of cardiac activity in early life may be crucial to an analysis of the development of central nervous system capabilities.

Prior to Graham and Jackson's (1970) review of infant cardiac responding, no clear evidence of heartrate deceleration in the newborn had been reported. The capacity of the newborn to process information was presumed to be limited by the protective defensive response and the relative inaccessibility of the orienting response. Reports of age-related change in cardiac responsiveness to stimulation (Clifton & Meyers, 1969; Gray & Crowell, 1968; Lipton et al., 1966) were often interpreted as evidence of a simple developmental shift in stimulus receptivity. Thus the newborn was considered to be unreceptive relative to older infants and adults (Graham & Clifton, 1966; Graham & Jackson, 1970).

Although there have been recent reports that the newborn is capable of eliciting a decelerative heartrate response (Berg & Berg, 1978; Clifton, 1974a), the response is specific to certain types of stimuli during certain states. However, the specificity of the heartrate response cannot be explained by state and stimulus parameters alone. Decelerative responses are more difficult to elicit in the newborn than in the older infant and adult. Heartrate appears to vary with developmental stage as well as with stimulus and state. This may be an indication that the infant reacts adaptively and attentively to stimuli that are biologically significant if they occur when the infant is ready to process them (Pomerleau-Malcuit & Clifton, 1973).

Evidence of a decelerative response in newborns has required modification of the earlier interpretations of cardiac activity vis-à-vis central processing. According to Sokolov, stimulus integration presupposes orientation. Prior to the reports of neonatal heartrate deceleration, the newborn was assumed to have limited abilities to process information. However the appearance of cardiac deceleration is not sufficient to assume the existence of orienting and the concomitant central processing of information during the first weeks of life. According to Clifton (1974a), "HR deceleration is multidetermined, and the presence of such deceleration does not necessarily imply an orienting response (OR). In a subject suspected of an inability to orient, HR deceleration should not be assumed to be an OR component" (p. 487). Changes in cardiac responses simply might be related to the general development of peripheral autonomic nervous system mechanisms rather than to the development of central orienting processes (Lipton et al., 1966). Without additional evidence heartrate deceleration may not necessarily be an indicant of central orienting.

Berg and Berg (1978) identified two indirect strategies for determining the likelihood that heartrate deceleration is an indication of the development of central orienting processes in the newborn. The first strategy is to show that the neonate's cardiovascular system is capable of a specific type of decelerative response typical of more mature infants and adults. The second strategy is to determine the extent to which one can predict the likelihood of heartrate deceleration from specific concepts of orienting. Evidence relevant to each of these strategies will be briefly reviewed.

The decelerative responses observed during the first days of life have typically taken two forms: a brief initial deceleration preceding an acceleration above baseline (Lipsitt & Jacklin, 1971; Schachter et al., 1971) and a longer *sustained* deceleration (Adkinson & Berg, 1976; Clarkson & Berg, 1979; Pomerleau-Malcuit & Clifton, 1973; Sameroff et al., 1973). There have been few, if any, examples of responses intermediate between these two forms. These two forms of heartrate deceleration also have been observed in adults and older infants. The brief deceleration is typical of sleeping subjects (Berg, Jackson, & Graham, 1975; Rewey, 1973). The sustained monophasic deceleration is typical of alert subjects (Berg & Chan, 1973; Jackson, 1974; Raskin, Kotses, & Bever, 1969) and is a concomitant of adult orientation.

It may be that only the sustained monophasic deceleration observed in studies of newborns clearly qualifies as a component of the mature orienting response (Berg & Berg, 1978). Thus the decelerative response observed by Lipsitt and Jacklin (1971) and by Schachter et al. (1971) may not have been "true" orienting. Other reports of sustained deceleration in newborns (Adkinson & Berg, 1976; Clarkson & Berg, 1979; Pomerleau-Malcuit & Clifton, 1973; Sameroff et al., 1973) indicate that the newborn is capable of producing decelerative orienting responses like those of mature adults. Furthermore the sustained decelerations do not seem to be limited in the newborn to particular stimulus modalities, as they can be elicited by auditory, visual, and vestibular stimuli. Although the newborn produces the sustained decelerative response with relatively great reluctance (Clifton, 1974a), the capability to produce the response is present as early as the first week of life.

Sokolov's definition (1963) of the orienting response includes responses occurring to the offset of stimulation as well to the onset. Cardiac decelerations to the offset of auditory stimuli are displayed by adult subjects (Chase & Graham, 1967) and thus would be indicative of mature orienting. Similar responses have been observed in infants of at least three months of age (Berg, 1974; Clifton & Meyers, 1969; Lewis, 1971; Rewey, 1973). Reports of offset decelerations in newborn infants would provide additional evidence for the existence of a mature orienting system immediately postpartum. This evidence has been provided by the following investigators. Porges, Arnold, and Forbes (1973) found sustained heartrate decelerations to the offset of an auditory stimulus in one- to three-day-old infants. Adkinson and Berg (1976) found sustained decelerations to the offset of mild intensity colored lights in newborns. Porges, Stamps, and Walter (1974) also found similar but more modest decelerative responses to the offset of room illumination in one- to three-day-old infants.

With respect to Berg and Berg's (1978) second strategy, there are several recent findings of newborn cardiac responding which are predictable from concepts of central orienting. According to Berg and Berg (1978), the effects of state, stimulus, perinatal, and somatic variables may be expected to influence cardiac responding of newborns in a predictable fashion. Although not all of the investigators to be mentioned in this discussion have made a priori predictions addressing the issue of central versus peripheral mediation of cardiac response in early life, nevertheless they have provided valuable data that bear on the issue.

The nonalert state is one of the conditions not favorable for orienting (Graham & Jackson, 1970). Thus awake subjects should display larger decelerations than sleepy or otherwise nonalert subjects. Given that newborns spend proportionately greater amounts of time in nonalert states, past studies reporting differences in heartrate responses between newborns and older infants may have reflected this factor. In recent studies controlling for state (Adkinson & Berg, 1976; Pomerleau-Malcuit & Clifton, 1973), infants one to four days old showed heartrate decelerations of a magnitude equivalent to those obtained in studies of older infants (Berg, 1974; Rewey, 1973). The decelerative response of newborns appears to be sensitive to state variations which would be expected from an organism possessing central mechanisms capable of facilitating information processing. The newborn decelerative response is sensitive to state transitions as well as the aforementioned fixed state categories of alert and nonalert (Nelson, Clifton, Dowd, Appleton, & Little, 1975). As infants begin the transition from wakefulness to sleep, the evoked heartrate response changes from deceleration to acceleration.

Another characteristic which may influence the orienting response is whether the eliciting stimulus is turned on and left on for its duration (continuous) or whether it is interrupted periodically (pulsed). The pulsed stimulus with its multiple alterations in intensity would be expected to elicit greater orienting (Berg & Berg, 1978). Pulsed auditory stimuli have been found to elicit significantly larger decelerations than continuous stimuli (Berg, 1972, 1974; Clarkson & Berg, 1979; Clifton & Meyers, 1969; Leavitt, Brown, Morse, & Graham, 1976; Rewey, 1973). That decelerative responses in infants six weeks of age and less have been reported only when stimuli were intermittent suggests that a developmental change in central processing may occur at this time. Prior to six weeks of age the ability to process temporal transitions possibly may help the infant to attend to auditory stimuli (Leavitt et al., 1976).

In similar fashion the effects of a number of high risk and perinatal factors such as low birthweight, maternal disease, nonoptimal obstetrical procedures, and malnutrition should decrease the likelihood of eliciting central orienting in the newborn. The assumption is that such factors do not provide optimal conditions for the central processing of sensory information and that an attenuation of central orienting should be a consequence. In this regard Stamps (1979) studied the relationship between cardiac orienting and birthweight in 8 normal full-term newborns between the ages of 40 and 65 hours. A median split was used to divide the infants into heavy and light birthweight groups. Subjects received six 20-second auditory stimuli. Stamps found significant heartrate changes for only the heavyweight subjects. They showed accelerative responses on trials 1 and 6 and decelerative responses on trials 2 through 5. Kittner and Lipsitt (1976) studied 16 clinically normal newborns differing in the number of nonoptimal factors in their obstetrical history (e.g., maternal chronic disease, Cesarean section delivery, and cardiac irregularity). There was a significant difference between the low risk and high risk groups in the direction of their heartrate responses to a series of auditory stimuli. Compared to the low risk group, the high risk group displayed more heartrate acceleration and less heartrate deceleration. Brackbill (1977) also found that anesthetics administered to mothers during delivery affected infants' heartrate responses for at least 8 postnatal months. In response to auditory stimulation, infants born to mothers who were not medicated showed a decelerative response while those born to mothers who were medicated showed a biphasic, decelerative-accelerative response. In another study which supports the presence of centrally controlled orienting in infancy, Lester (1975) found that one-year-old malnourished infants showed an attenuation or absence of the decelerative response relative to well-nourished infants.

Perhaps the strongest evidence for linking central processing and autonomic activity in infancy is provided by studies of cardiac-somatic coupling. Obrist (1976) proposed that the cardiovascular system functions primarily to satisfy general metabolic demands and secondarily to accommodate to other processes (e.g., orienting). If age-related changes in the form of the heartrate response are simply a function of autonomic development, then concomitant age-related increases in the relationship between cardiac and somatic responses would be expected. If cardiac-somatic coupling can be increasingly overridden with age (e.g., by demonstrating orienting while the infant is engaged in somatic activity), then concomitant age-related changes in cardiac responsivity probably are due to the modification of central nervous system mechanisms and probably are indicative of changes in central processing capabilities (Berg & Berg, 1978). The following studies support the latter position.

Pomerleau-Malcuit, Malcuit, and Clifton (1975) used facial stimulation to determine the extent of cardiac-somatic coupling during orienting and defensive reactions in two- and three-day-old infants. The first stimulus, stroking the cheek near the mouth, produced ipsilateral head-turning, an approach or orienting response. The second stimulus, a light pinch on the ear, produced contralateral head-turning, a defensive response. Regardless of stimulation type, heartrate accelerations accompanied head-turning (somatic activity). When no overt behavioral response was observed, cheek stimulation elicited heartrate deceleration and ear stimulation elicited heartrate acceleration. The effect of facial stimulation (and presumably its consequent meaning to the infant) on cardiac activity, relative to the effect of movement, was demonstrated by the larger acceleration to the aversive stimulus (pinch on the ear) when no movement was present than to the approach stimulus (stroke on the cheek) when movement was present. Furthermore orienting was demonstrated in that the cheek stimulation elicited a decelerative response when there was no overt head-turning by the infant. Pomerleau-Malcuit et al. (1975) concluded that movement itself did not produce the observed heartrate responses; rather, central processing of the signal value of the stimulus determined both behavioral and cardiac responding.

Studies of heartrate and sucking activity also support the central processing hypothesis. Typically sucking activity in neonates is accompanied by heartrate acceleration—i.e., cardiac-somatic coupling occurs (Crook &

Lipsitt, 1976; Lipsitt, Reilly, Butcher, & Greenwood, 1976); thus the use of pacifiers in previous studies may have prevented the appearance of heartrate deceleration, indicative of orienting. In this regard Gregg, Clifton, and Haith (1976) discovered that an earlier failure to obtain cardiac deceleration to a visual stimulus in one- to four-day-old newborns may have resulted from the use of pacifiers in their experiment. When they reanalyzed their data to consider the effects of sucking, they found that infants who were sucking on a pacifier during visual tracking displayed heartrate accelerations. This response failed to occur in those infants who were not sucking. More recently Clarkson and Berg (1978) reported that the use of a pacifier attenuated decelerative responses to auditory stimuli in newborns. By nine weeks of age the effects of sucking and other somatic activity on tempering cardiac orienting (heartrate deceleration) apparently is less potent (Berg & Berg, 1978). Infants at nine weeks of age showed decelerative heartrate responses to auditory stimuli, even while they were sucking (Brown, Leavitt, & Graham, 1977).

In summary both orienting and defensive responses exist soon after birth. The evidence reviewed here is consistent with Clifton's (1974a) hypothesis that development starts as an interactive process, with orienting occurring only in specific circumstances. Age and stimulus characteristics interact in a complex fashion so that some stimuli are effective in eliciting orientation soon after birth while others become effective at later stages of development. Orienting in the newborn occurs only under the most optimal conditions, while in later infancy and adulthood, orienting occurs more readily and in response to a greater range of stimuli.

ATTENTION

Attention as a construct generally has been used in infant psychophysiological research to refer to two aspects of behavior. The first aspect refers to a selective recognition response. Fagan's (1977) model of infant recognition behavior, although not specifically derived from psychophysiological data, offers a succinct example of this approach. In recognition testing, after an infant becomes familiar with a visual stimulus, s/he is presented with a recognition test pairing the familiar stimulus with a novel one. Preference is ordinarily found for the novel stimulus. Fagan proposed that in successful recognition the infant's looking behavior consists of two linked covert responses. The first is an attentional observing response to a stimulus dimension, particularly to one that makes differentiation of the novel and familiar stimulus possible. The second is a fixation response to a specific cue. Presumably the novel stimulus recruits all of the infant's fixation. The psychophysiological translation of this model of infant recognition is that an orienting response occurs to novel (nonfamiliar) stimuli as a result of previous habituation to another stimulus discriminably different on at least one dimension. In discussing attention Fagan referred to Jeffrey's (1976) serial habituation model in which the infant becomes familiar with a stimulus by repeatedly orienting and habituating to stimulus dimensions in order of their saliency.

The second aspect of the construct of attention as it

appears in infant psychophysiological research concerns what might be called the infant's depth of processing. This refers to the infant's intensity of regard, perhaps to how sustained is his/her processing of the stimulus. Thus Kagan and Lewis (1965) argued that "... one might assume that fixations of a stimulus accompanied by heart rate decreases indicated more intense scanning than a fixation of equal length without a cardiac change" (p. 96). Lewis and Spaulding (1967) referred to an "absorption phase" in responding to a stimulus. Both of these concepts include a process that requires not only orienting towards the stimulus but also includes taking in and, presumably, utilizing the stimulus information. It will be apparent from the review that follows that cardiac deceleration is the primary dependent variable in both types of attentional studies. The impetus for its use when attention is equated with sensory intake is, of course, the Laceys' (1978) hypothesis relating cardiac deceleration to such activity.

Attention as Recognition

As noted previously Fagan's attention model of infant recognition includes an observing or orienting response to a stimulus dimension followed by fixation upon a novel stimulus cue. Using four-month-old infants, McCall and Kagan (1967) found support for the hypothesis that the fixation or "attention-recruiting power" of a stimulus is a function of its discrepancy relative to a familiar stimulus. One group, the experienced subjects, were provided with a mobile representing a particular geometric pattern for one month prior to testing. The testing involved the standard plus three patterns representing a small to large range of discrepancy from the standard as rated by adults. Partial support for the discrepancy hypothesis was obtained for experienced female infants. McCall and Kagan found a pattern of cardiac deceleration that, for the majority of these infants, showed increasing deceleration as the discrepancy of the stimulus from the standard increased. The difficulty in using cardiac deceleration as a measure of the strength of attention was highlighted by the fact that male infants did not show this pattern. Furthermore first fixation responses did not support the discrepancy hypothesis for infants of either sex.

Subsequently Melson and McCall (1970) examined the discrepancy hypothesis in five-month-old girls using auditory stimuli. In order to tease out the individual differences that occur in response patterns, cardiac decelerations to small and large changes in a tone sequence were evaluated separately for slow and rapidly habituating infants. Subjects were further classified on the basis of their general looking behavior toward a series of achromatic patterns—i.e., short versus long fixators. Although the infants generally showed cardiac deceleration to the discrepant tonal sequences, these responses were enhanced for the infants showing rapid habituation. These infants also showed greater deceleration to the more discrepant tonal sequence. Quite independent of habituation rate, infants who showed short fixations in the visual pretest were also more likely to show enhanced cardiac deceleration for discrepant tonal sequences. The independence of the two predictors of the rate of cardiac de-

celeration was supported by the rank-order correlation of +.03 between them.

These two studies seem to indicate that stimulus parameters must be examined closely in defining novel and familiar stimuli. Apparently quantitatively defined stimulus discrepancy is a predictor of autonomic responsivity, at least for certain female infants. The complexity of the sex variable is highlighted by McCall and Melson's (1970) finding that the cardiac response to visual discrepancy correlated −.70 with the cardiac response to auditory discrepancy in 5½-month-old boys.

In spite of the difficulty in conceptualizing the role of cardiac deceleration in stimulus recognition, as indicated by its dependencies on stimulus, sex, and procedural variables, cardiac deceleration has been used consistently as a dependent measure to investigate specific problems in child development. Chang and Trehub (1977) examined the auditory pattern perception capabilities of 4½- to 5½-month-old infants using a dishabituation paradigm. Following the lead of Melson and McCall, they preselected their subjects by using only fast habituators, dropping 12 of 43 subjects. The variable of interest was the temporal grouping of tonal patterns. The infants were first habituated to six tone patterns with a long pause between the second and third stimulus (a 2, 4 grouping). Dishabituation in the form of significant cardiac deceleration occurred when the infants were presented with a 4, 2 grouping of the same tones. Further data replicated Melson and McCall's finding that changing the component tones of an auditory pattern produces significant cardiac deceleration.

Goldberg (1976) evaluated the cardiac responses of four- to five-month-old infants in the context of Bower's (1967) concept of existence constancy. Bower had proposed that infants have an expectation that objects, temporarily occluded, continue to exist as stable objects. He based this on the increased anticipatory looking behavior of infants when previously viewed objects did not reappear from behind an occluding screen as they had been trained to expect. Goldberg found a cardiac deceleration only to stimulus novelty in her version of this paradigm. The only discriminative cardiac response occurred to the novel stimulus when it was used either as the disappearing and reappearing stimulus or as the stimulus that just disappeared. Goldberg also measured fixation time but found nothing other than evidence for a decline in attention over trials. Although Goldberg argued that cardiac deceleration is a more sensitive measure of cognitive abilities, perhaps the more defensible position is that multiple dependent measures are needed in evaluating cognitive development in infancy.

Attention as Processing

The importance of Kagan and Lewis's (1965) elaborate study of attentional processes in infants has not diminished in the 15 years since its publication. The positive features of their study were the use of several measures of attention and three different classes of stimuli. One drawback was a focus on only one age group of infants, 24 weeks. The indicants of attention were heart-rate, total fixation time, and certain behavioral measures of orientation, such as arm movement. The consistency of findings for these measures varied with the class of stimuli employed. When the stimuli to be attended to were film strips of faces and geometric designs, there were no significant differences in cardiac responses among the stimuli although there were differences in fixation time and in some of the behavioral measures. The correlation between fixation time and cardiac deceleration was not significant for these stimuli. When the subjects were divided into high and low visual fixation groups for each stimulus, two of the ten *t*-tests were significant. When auditory stimuli (e.g., voices, tones, music) were employed, no habituation of the heartrate was obtained. Furthermore none of the correlations between behavioral measures of attention and cardiac deceleration were significant. Stimulus preferences were discernible using the cardiac deceleration measure. There were differences between boys and girls in the type of auditory stimulus to which they showed greatest deceleration. Girls attended most to music while the boys attended most to tones. In response to the light matrix stimuli, there were significant correlations between length of fixation and the degree of cardiac deceleration. Furthermore there was a tendency for more complex patterns to lead to significantly greater cardiac deceleration. This was especially true when cardiac deceleration was evaluated during the last ten seconds of the exposure trial.

Using the responses to the light matrix stimuli for support, Kagan and Lewis proposed that cardiac deceleration could be used to indicate the degree to which a stimulus maintains the attention of the infant. This conclusion is reinforced by the findings of Lewis, Kagan, Campbell, and Kalafat (1966), who also obtained significant correlations between length of fixation and degree of cardiac deceleration in response to light matrix stimuli. This was true for both boys and girls. Again the subjects were 24 weeks of age. Kagan (1971) presented some evidence that the correlation between length of fixation and degree of deceleration may only be true during the first six months of life.

The complexity of Kagan and Lewis's data does not lead to straightforward conclusions. Cardiac deceleration was a successful dependent variable in discriminating preferences only for a limited number of stimuli. It correlated well with other measures only when the light matrix was used. In fact arm movement was a more consistent measure of attention across stimuli than cardiac deceleration. It would seem premature to consider cardiac deceleration as a better or more valid indicator of sustained attention than other measures. Like other measures it seems to have areas of unique applicability. As mentioned previously multiple dependent measures are needed to identify attentional phenomena. Lewis and Spaulding's (1967) findings support this point. They measured behavioral orientation and cardiac deceleration to both auditory and visual stimuli in six-month-old infants. Steeper deceleration occurred to the auditory stimulus. However, cardiac responses in the presence of behavioral orientation to the visual stimuli were comparable to the deceleration that occurred to the auditory stimuli. It may be that cardiac deceleration is particularly useful as a measure of attention for the auditory modality for which receptor orientation is not critical whereas a combination of a behavioral orientation measure and cardiac deceleration is most useful for the visual modality.

In contrast to the aforementioned conceptual orientation, Field (1979) argued that enhanced information processing may occur during periods of increased heartrate rather than during periods of decreased heartrate. She proposed an information processing/arousal-modulation interpretation of infant looking-away behavior. Infants from two to four months of age will fixate for longer periods of time on a doll's face than they will on their mother's face (Field, 1978). This also is true if the mother's face and the doll's face are comparable in animation. Field (1979) recorded tonic heartrate in four-month-old infants during three-minute presentations of either a mother's or a doll's face. Tonic heartrate was significantly greater than base line during the "animate" mother's face situation and significantly lower than base line during the still doll's face situation. Looking-away behavior was significantly enhanced in response to the animated mother's face. These data could be interpreted to mean that a doll's face is processed more effectively than the mother's face at this age. This interpretation would be consistent with the use of cardiac deceleration as an indication of stimulus intake and the fact that the mother's animate face is a much more complex stimulus than the still doll's face. On the other hand Field suggested that the infant may be modulating arousal by looking away during the animated mother's face condition while at the same time processing the information obtained during the previous look at the mother's face. This hypothesis is intriguing in that cardiac acceleration heretofore has been considered to be only an indicant of arousal or defense. Cardiac acceleration also has been shown to accompany other internal processing states, such as when doing mental arithmetic (Lacey et al., 1963). Obviously attention is directed inward in these states. It would be interesting to see a replication of this finding with a series of novel patterns varying along some informational parameter. The typical fixation/cardiac deceleration paradigm using a novel stimulus for dishabituation probably would not reveal this phenomenon.

LEARNING

It was noted previously in this chapter that psychophysiological responses need to be evaluated in light of the infant's sex, state, and maturation. This is especially appropriate in the context of learning paradigms. As will be evident further on, the particular constraints on the young infant's ability to respond autonomically in learning paradigms affect fundamental questions about the nature of learning, particularly within the classical conditioning paradigm. Before examining the literature on classical conditioning in the infant, it is necessary to point out that autonomic habituation in newborns also has been considered as evidence of learning, perhaps as an indicant of a cognitive stimulus schema (Bartoshuk, 1962a). Regardless of the merits of this point of view (see Hirschman & Katkin, 1974), this chapter is concerned only with demonstrations of learning within classical conditioning paradigms.

Classical Conditioning in the Newborn

Classical conditioning of the newborn infant's heart-rate has been an intense recent interest of infant psychophysiologists. One reason for this is that heartrate ordinarily is a very reliable and tractable response and should be as appropriate an indicant of learning as any autonomic measure. Also heartrate conditioning has been demonstrated in older infants (Fitzgerald & Brackbill, 1976). Another reason, alluded to numerous times in this chapter, is that heartrate may affect information processing. Clifton (1974b) suggested that one value of demonstrating classical conditioning with an autonomic response is that any discontinuities between autonomic responses and motor responses may reflect immaturity of the central nervous system. She referred to a study by Polikanina (1961) with prematures in which autonomic responses were elicited before defensive motor responses were established to a noxious unconditional stimulus (UCS) of ammonia vapor. This discontinuity disappeared when the prematures were tested at an older age.

Clifton (1974a) examined the classical conditioning of heartrate in one- to four-day-old infants. The conditioning group was presented with a conditional stimulus (CS) of a 72 db, 300 H_z square wave auditory stimulus and a UCS of a 5 percent glucose solution. All infants were maintained in a noncrying, awake state for 30 conditioning trials. Comparisons of heartrate were made between the conditioning groups and a random control group during the interstimulus interval (ISI) and during the absence of the UCS on extinction trials. The control group received tones at the same intertrial intervals as the conditioning group, but the UCS was presented at random times on each trial. The cardiac response to both the CS and UCS was acceleration. No group differences were found for the CS on conditioning trials. The only positive finding was a large deceleration that occurred on the first extinction trial at the point where the UCS would have been presented. As this response was a deceleration and not the acceleration of the conditioning trials, Clifton interpreted it as a "what happened?" or orienting response. She argued that the infants showed an expectancy of the UCS based on the previous association with the CS—i.e., S-S learning (Bolles, 1972). Neither in this study nor in any of those reviewed subsequently in this section did infants show acquisition and extinction of the conditional response (CR) typical of a traditional classical conditioning paradigm.

A very thoughtful exposition of the S-S learning position was presented by Stamps and Porges (1975). These investigators obtained data that also supported the argument that the newborn learns to anticipate the UCS through its previous association with the CS. The state and age of these infants were comparable to those in the Clifton study. However the CS was a pure tone, and the UCS was a pattern of blinking colored lights. Only 12 conditioning trials were used although a much longer ISI was used than in the Clifton study. The variables of sex and preexperimental heartrate variability also were explored. Conditioning was examined by looking for heartrate changes coincident with the CS, immediately before the UCS, and during the absence of the UCS on extinction trials. With respect to the heartrate variability fac-

tor, high variance subjects showed a deceleration to the CS that changed in a complicated way over trial blocks. Females tended to show a small deceleration to the CS whereas males showed a small acceleration. The females showed significant heartrate deceleration in anticipation of the UCS. When the UCS was absent the conditioning group as a whole, in comparison to a random control group, showed significant deceleration. These latter data clearly support Clifton's view that the newborn is learning to anticipate the UCS. The anticipatory responses for the female newborns were replicated in a temporal conditioning study conducted by Stamps (1977). The experimental group was presented with a buzzer as the UCS at fixed 20-second intervals. The 20 seconds served as a temporal CS. The only straightforward finding was that experimental group females showed significantly lower heartrates than the control group females during the response intervals immediately preceding the UCS on later trial blocks.

The delay paradigm employed by Clifton (1974a) and the delay trace procedure used by Stamps and Porges (1975) have both been used by Crowell et al. (1976) to examine heartrate conditioning in two-day-old infants. Only the data from the delay paradigm were consistent with predictions about the form of the conditioned CR. The paradigm consisted of a flashing light CS and a buzzer UCS with a three-second ISI. The initial response to the CS was a monophasic acceleration. On extinction trials the same response was obtained, but its amplitude was enhanced. Crowell et al. argued that this enhancement indicated the establishment of a CR in the sense of Dykman's (1967) sensitization hypothesis. Sensitization refers to modifications which occur in the response to the CS due to increases in the activity in its associated neural pathways, presumably caused by the subsequent activation of the unconditional response (UCR) by the UCS. According to this view the UCR and the CR need not be similar in form. The former only initiates the sensitization necessary for enhancing the normal response to the CS.

Unfortunately in none of the aforementioned studies was there a demonstration of newborn heartrate conditioning in which a formerly "neutral" stimulus acquired a CR that replicated the response to the UCS and which extinguished when the CS-UCS pairing terminated. In three of the reviewed studies anticipatory "what happened" decelerative responses during extinction were used as indicants of conditioning while the fourth study used a "sensitized" accelerative response to the CS as the CR. If one's definition of classical conditioning precludes S-S learning, then these studies have not demonstrated classical conditioning of heartrate in the newborn. This is essentially the position of Clifton (1974a). There are some additional concerns. For example it is not clear what the base rate is for successful autonomic conditioning in newborns. Also the reviewed studies included some evidence for the failure to condition. Nevertheless the quite disparate stimuli, paradigms, and statistical evaluation procedures (not a minor point but beyond the scope of this review) used in these studies have all provided evidence of the CS being able to elicit a response that can be directly attributed to its association with the UCS.

Classical Conditioning Later in the First Year of Life

Fitzgerald and Brackbill (1976) have provided a comprehensive review of the American and Russian work on classical conditioning in infancy. Although they did not specifically focus on psychophysiological variables, they reviewed all pre-1976 research in which an autonomic UCR was used. Specifically they presented four working hypotheses about classical conditioning in infancy.

(1) Early conditionability is a synergistic or interactive function of the sensory modality giving rise to the CS and the neurological system innervating the response. (2) Conditionability is a function of the young organism's biobehavioral state. (3) Individual differences in conditionability are related to individual differences in the infant's initial response to stimulation (i.e., to orienting). (4) Early conditioning is also a function of the degree of complexity of the associations required by experimental conditions. (p. 354)

In order to point out how limited our knowledge of infant classical conditioning is, it is important to note that no modern study has used infants older than about five months of age. Further, only one new study has been presented in the literature since 1976. This chapter includes studies in which heartrate was used as the CR and those studies in which other autonomic responses were used as CR's. With regard to the latter the study reported by Brackbill and Fitzgerald (1969) is a good example of Fitzgerald and Brackbill's (1976) point that there must be a specific synergism—i.e., CS and CR specificity—for conditioning to occur. Four different types of stimuli served as the CS in various procedures: auditory, time (a constant 20-second ISI), tactile, and a compound of a tone and a fixed ISI. All four types of CS were used to condition pupillary dilation and constriction. The subjects were two-month-old infants. Interestingly temporal conditioning was very successful for both pupil responses. The compound CS (tone and 20-second ISI) was also successful in producing conditioned dilation and constriction. Neither the tactile stimulus nor the tone alone were successful as CS's.

Brackbill and Fitzgerald (1972) extended their research on temporal conditioning to include stereotype temporal conditioning. This type of temporal conditioning involves the presentation of a pattern or sequence of temporal intervals (ISI's). In their experiment the pattern consisted of a 20-second ISI followed by a 4-second UCS and then a 30-second ISI followed by the same 4-second UCS. The UCS was a light bulb either being turned on or off to produce the desired UCR of pupil constriction or dilation, respectively. The infants were approximately the same age as in the earlier study. Subjects were presented conditioning and test trials (no UCS) on an approximate ratio of 3.5:1. The pupil dilation response was significantly increased during the four seconds of the test trials compared to the preceding four-second intervals. Brackbill and Fitzgerald were not successful in conditioning the constriction response. These data stand in contrast to the data presented previously in which these investigators found evidence for the conditioning of both pupil dilation and constriction with a temporal CS. Both types of conditioning were ob-

tained by Brackbill and Fitzgerald in a follow-up temporal conditioning study with 16 of their original 30 subjects.

The relationship of the infant's sex, state, and orienting magnitude to the degree of conditioned discrimination and discrimination reversal was explored by Ingram and Fitzgerald (1974). Using the skin potential response (SPR) as the UCR, three-month-old infants were conditioned to discriminate between a $500 H_z$ and a $1000 H_z$ square wave tone CS. The UCS was an air puff delivered to the infant's cheek. A delay paradigm was used in which the CS and UCS terminated together after a five-second ISI. The infants were presented with the UCS after one of the tones but not after the other on discrimination trials. For discrimination reversal the identity of these tones was switched. Both discrimination and discrimination reversal training was successful in that the magnitude of the SPR was significantly greater for the CS+ tone in both procedures. Surprisingly only 6 of the 12 infants showed such significance in their individual data for the discrimination task. For discrimination reversal, the proportion was only 3 of 12. In order to examine these individual differences further, Ingram and Fitzgerald divided their subjects into high and low orienting groups using a median split based on subjects' responses to the first stimulus presentation. In the high orienting group, 5 of 6 infants showed conditioned discrimination whereas only 1 of 6 showed conditioned discrimination in the low orienting group. An equally impressive finding was a significant correlation of −.71 between orienting response magnitude and the number of trials required to reach the criterion of conditioned discrimination. Neither the infant's state, as measured by the Brackbill and Fitzgerald (1969) state scale, nor sex was related to conditioning performance.

The studies reviewed so far in this section support Fitzgerald and Brackbill's (1976) contention that "If there is any emergent theme to the contemporary learning literature, it is not the generality of the principles of learning but rather the extent to which the principles of learning are constrained in their generality" (p. 353). The data from heartrate conditioning further amplify this conclusion. Consider the following: Stamps and Porges (1975) found evidence of conditioned deceleration to the CS in female newborns. On the other hand Turco and Stamps (1979) found evidence of a conditioned deceleration to the CS only for their male subjects. They used infants with a mean age of 4.5 months. The modality of the CS and UCS in their study was opposite to that used in the Stamps and Porges study. Clearly, simple parametric studies are needed to aid in interpreting these findings.

Clifton (1974a) reported on two heartrate conditioning studies with older infants in which the findings were similar to that obtained with newborns. Appleton (Note 1) used a tonal CS and a glucose UCS in attempting to condition a transformed heartrate CR in 2½ to 3-month-old infants. The initial cardiac deceleration to the CS habituated over trials. The UCR was cardiac acceleration. The only evidence for conditioning was a pronounced deceleration that occurred during extinction for the conditioning group. This deceleration only occurred on the second extinction trial, but it did occur, as it had for the newborns, at the approximate point in time at which the infants would have received the glucose.

Pomerleau-Malcuit, Malcuit, and Clifton (Note 2) replicated Appleton's study using a gentle rocking motion of the infant's cradle as the UCS. The CS was again a tone. The response to the tone was a deceleration that habituated over trials as in the Appleton study. The response to the rocking (the UCR) was a deceleration rather than an acceleration such as had occurred to the glucose presentation. However as with the former UCR, it did not habituate over trials. Pomerleau-Malcuit et al. reported that there was no reliable evidence of conditioning in this study. Given the weak evidence for conditioning in the Appleton study, it would be premature to conclude that the change to the rocking UCS was critical to the findings of Pomerleau-Malcuit et al.

There are only sketchy conclusions to be drawn from the postneonatal classical conditioning studies. The demonstrations of conditioning using pupillary and SPR measures seem solid. Certainly they are less tenuous than the heartrate studies with newborns. As noted previously the evidence for conditioning of heartrate is, of course, equally slim for the older infants. The "holy grail" that seems to be sought in infant conditioning is consistent evidence for cardiac conditioning. It is apparently not yet available. What is most evident, in both newborn and older infant studies, is the need for more data. As Fitzgerald and Brackbill (1976) emphasized, successful classical conditioning seems to depend upon many subtle aspects of the paradigm used—e.g., infant's state, sex, OR magnitude, CS-UCS synergy, ISI, and delay vs. trace procedures. Perhaps the field of psychophysiological assessment of learning in infants is still in such an early stage of infancy that we must simply await further development before describing the creature.

EMOTION

An intriguing but yet relatively unexplored possibility is that autonomic measures might be used to validate early developmental shifts in affective response capabilities. This type of analysis might be most appropriate for situations in which overt behavior is difficult to detect or for situations in which the behavior is observable but ambiguous or subtle—e.g., changes in facial expression (Clifton, 1977). Obviously affective states in infants often satisfy these criteria. One of the more interesting examples is the research by Campos and his colleagues on the development of distress-danger responses to the visual cliff (Campos, Langer, & Krowitz, 1970; Haith & Campos, 1977; Schwartz, Campos, & Baisel, 1973; Schwartz, Campos, Baisel, & Amatore, 1971). Inferring neonatal sensitivity to depth or danger from autonomic activity is dependent upon the application of Sokolov's distinction between the orienting response and the defense response (Yonas & Pick, 1975). The defense response (e.g., heartrate acceleration) may be indicative of a biological adaptation to danger. Thus to the extent that a neonate can perceive danger, placing the neonate on the deep side of a visual cliff should elicit cardiac acceleration. Campos and his colleagues discovered that when 55-day-old infants were placed on the deep side of the visual

cliff, they responded with attention rather than with distress. Placement on the deep side resulted in a reliable cardiac deceleration while placement on the shallow side resulted in a small, nonsignificant cardiac response. Placement on the deep side also resulted in less crying and less motor activity than placement on the shallow side. Thus infants at less than three months of age appear to discriminate the two sides of the visual cliff—i.e., they orient to the deep side.

Campos discovered a somewhat different pattern with five- and nine-month-old infants. Five-month-old infants showed a nonsignificant decelerative response on the deep side while nine-month-old infants showed a reliable accelerative response on the deep side. In Sokolovian terms this accelerative-decelerative shift with age may represent a change in response capability from attention (orienting) to distress (defense). However this conclusion is tempered by the following. Infants also may show cardiac acceleration in nonaversive states—e.g., laughter (Schwartz et al., 1973). Campos was unable to find expected differences in negative and positive vocalizations as a function of deep or shallow side placement on the visual cliff. Without a concomitant behavioral measure of distress, it is difficult to assume that the developmental heartrate changes reported by Campos necessarily reflect affective changes. Even if overt behavioral changes were elicited, there still would be an interpretive problem. Cardiac acceleration may occur simply in response to the increase in somatic activity associated with overt behavior (Clifton, 1977).

One resolution has been to opt for the "lesser of two evils" by demonstrating concomitant autonomic and behavioral changes in other stressful contexts. To some extent this would offer additional support for the aforementioned interpretation of heartrate responses to the visual cliff. Such evidence has been provided from studies of stranger anxiety. Stranger anxiety may be defined by specific overt behavioral reactions (Clifton, 1977)—e.g., "wary" facial expressions. Sroufe and his colleagues (Sroufe, Waters, & Matas, 1974; Waters, Matas, & Sroufe, 1975) found that in response to a stranger, larger heartrate increases were shown by infants with "wary" facial expressions than by infants with "nonwary" facial expressions.

In a comprehensive examination of the developmental shift in reactions to a stranger, Campos, Emde, Gaensbauer, and Henderson (1975) found that 5- and 9-month-old infants who were behaviorally distressed by a stranger showed accelerative cardiac responses while infants who were undistressed showed decelerative cardiac responses. Behavioral distress to a stranger occurred more frequently at 9 months of age than at 5 months of age. As expected accelerative responses typically were seen at 9 months of age while decelerative responses typically were seen at 5 months of age. Similar age-dependent changes also were reported by Skarin (1977), who used 5- to 7- and 10- to 12-month-old infants.

Taken together these studies suggest that a developmental shift in affective response capability may occur at seven to nine months of age. It may be that during this stage indiscriminate attentional responses are transformed into more specific affective responses. Whether these changes reflect a maturational change in cognitive processing or the development of peripheral mechanisms affecting sensory intake and central nervous system feedback still is unresolved.

REFERENCE NOTES

1. Appleton, C. *Classical reward conditioning of the heart rate response to auditory stimuli in three-month-old infants.* Unpublished master's thesis, University of Massachusetts, 1972.

2. Pomerleau-Malcuit, A., Malcuit, G., & Clifton, R. *An evidence of cardiac orienting in human newborns: Heart rate response to facial stimulations eliciting approach and escape behaviors.* Unpublished manuscript, University of Massachusetts, 1972.

REFERENCES

ADKINSON, C. D., & BERG, W. K. Cardiac deceleration in newborns: Habituation, dishabituation, and offset responses. *Journal of Experimental Child Psychology,* 1976, *21,* 46–60.

ASHTON, R. The state variable in neonatal research: A review. *Merrill-Palmer Quarterly,* 1973, *19,* 3–20.

BARTOSHUK, A. K. Human neonatal cardiac acceleration to sound: Habituation and dishabituation. *Perceptual and Motor Skills,* 1962a, *15,* 15–27.

BARTOSHUK, A. K. Response decrement with repeated elicitation of human neonatal cardiac acceleration to sound. *Journal of Comparative and Physiological Psychology,* 1962b, *55,* 9–13.

BELL, R. Q. Sleep cycles and skin potential in newborns studied with a simplified observation and recording system. *Psychophysiology,* 1970, *6,* 778–786.

BERG, K. M., BERG, W. K., & GRAHAM, F. K. Infant heart rate response as a function of stimulus and state. *Psychophysiology,* 1971, *8,* 30–44.

BERG, W. K. Habituation and dishabituation of cardiac responses in four-month-old, awake infants. *Journal of Experimental Child Psychology,* 1972, *14,* 92–107.

BERG, W. K. Cardiac orienting responses of 6- and 16-week old infants. *Journal of Experimental Child Psychology,* 1974, *17,* 303–312.

BERG, W. K., & BERG, K. M. Psychophysiological development in infancy: State, sensory function and attention. In J. Osofsky (Ed.), *Handbook of infant development.* New York: John Wiley, 1978.

BERG, W. K., & CHAN, S. HR responses to equivalent stimulus onsets and offsets. *Psychophysiology,* 1973, *10,* 192.

BERG, W. K., JACKSON, J. C., & GRAHAM, F. K. Tone intensity and rise-decay time effects on cardiac responses during sleep. *Psychophysiology,* 1975, *12,* 254–261.

BOLLES, R. C. Reinforcement, expectancy and learning. *Psychological Review,* 1972, *79,* 394–407.

BOWER, T.G.R. The development of object permanence: Sonic studies of existence constancy. *Perception & Psychophysics,* 1967, *2,* 411–418.

BRACKBILL, Y. Acoustic variation and arousal level in infants. *Psychophysiology,* 1970, *6,* 517–526.

BRACKBILL, Y. Cumulative effects of continuous stimulation on arousal level in infants. *Child Development,* 1971, *42,* 17–26.

BRACKBILL, Y. Continuous stimulation reduces arousal level: Stability of the effect over time. *Child Development,* 1973, *44,* 43–46.

BRACKBILL, Y. Psychophysiological measures of pharmacological toxicity in infants: Perinatal and postnatal effects. In P. L. Morselli, S. Garattini, & F. Serini (Eds.), *Basic and therapeutic aspects of perinatal pharmacology.* New York: Raven Press, 1975.

BRACKBILL, Y. Long-term effects of obstetrical anesthesia on infant autonomic function. *Developmental Psychobiology,* 1977, *10,* 529–535.

BRACKBILL, Y., & FITZGERALD, H. E. Development of the sensory analyzers during infancy. In L. P. Lipsitt & H. W. Reese (Eds.), *Advances in child development and behavior* (Vol. 4). New York: Academic Press, 1969.

BRACKBILL, Y., & FITZGERALD, H. E. Stereotype temporal conditioning in infants. *Psychophysiology,* 1972, *9,* 569–577.

BRIDGER, W. H., BIRNS, B. M., & BLACK, M. A comparison of behavioral ratings and heart rate measurements in human neonates. *Psychosomatic Medicine,* 1965, *27,* 123–134.

BRIDGER, W. H., & REISER, M. F. Psychophysiologic studies of the neonate: An approach toward the methodological and theoretical problems involved. *Psychosomatic Medicine,* 1959, *21,* 265–276.

BROWN, J. W., LEAVITT, L. A., & GRAHAM, F. K. Response to auditory stimuli in 6- and 9-week-old human infants. *Developmental Psychobiology,* 1977, *10,* 255–266.

CAMPOS, J. J. Heart rate: A sensitive tool for the study of emotional development. In L. Lipsitt (Ed.), *Developmental psychobiology: The significance of infancy.* Hillsdale, N.J.: Lawrence Erlbaum Associates, 1976.

CAMPOS, J. J., & BRACKBILL, Y. Infant state: Relationship to heart rate, behavioral response and response decrement. *Developmental Psychobiology,* 1973, *6,* 9–19.

CAMPOS, J. J., EMDE, R. N., GAENSBAUER, T., & HENDERSON, C. Cardiac and behavioral interrelationships in the reactions of infants to strangers. *Developmental Psychology,* 1975, *11,* 589–601.

CAMPOS, J. J., LANGER, A., & KROWITZ, A. Cardiac responses on the visual cliff in prelocomotor human infants. *Science,* 1970, *170,* 196–197.

CHANG, H. W., & TREHUB, S. E. Infants' perception of temporal grouping in auditory patterns. *Child Development,* 1977, *48,* 1666–1670.

CHASE, W., & GRAHAM, F. K. Heart rate response to nonsignal tones. *Psychonomic Science,* 1967, *9,* 181–182.

CLARKSON, M. G., & BERG, W. K. Cardiac deceleration in neonates as influenced by temporal pattern and spectral complexity of auditory stimuli. *Psychophysiology,* 1978, *15,* 284–285.

CLARKSON, M. G., & BERG, W. K. Temporal pattern as a determinant of cardiac orienting to auditory stimuli in neonates. *Psychophysiology,* 1979, *16,* 191.

CLIFTON, R. K. Cardiac conditioning and orienting in the infant. In P. A. Obrist, A. H. Black, J. Brener, & L. V. DiCara (Eds.), *Cardiovascular psychophysiology.* Chicago: Aldine, 1974a.

CLIFTON, R. K. Heart rate conditioning in the newborn infant. *Journal of Experimental Child Psychology,* 1974b, *18,* 9–21.

CLIFTON, R. K. The relation of infant cardiac responding to behavioral state and motor activity. In W. A. Collins (Ed.), *Minnesota symposia on child psychology* (Vol. 2). Chicago: Thomas Y. Crowell, 1977.

CLIFTON, R. K., & GRAHAM, F. K. Stability of individual differences in heart rate activity during the newborn period. *Psychophysiology,* 1968, *5,* 37–50.

CLIFTON, R. K., GRAHAM, F. K., & HATTON, H. M. Newborn heart-rate response and response habituation as a function of stimulus duration. *Journal of Experimental Child Psychology,* 1968, *6,* 265–278.

CLIFTON, R. K., & MEYERS, W. J. The heart-rate response of four-month-old infants to auditory stimuli. *Journal of Experimental Child Psychology,* 1969, *7,* 122–135.

CONTIS, G., & LIND, J. Study of systolic blood pressure, heart rate, body temperature of normal newborn infants through the first week of life. *Acta Peadiatrica Supplement,* 1963, *146,* 41–47.

COPHER, D. E., & HUBER, C. P. Heart-rate response of the human fetus to induced maternal hypoxia. *American Journal of Obstetrics and Gynecology,* 1967, *98,* 320–335.

CROOK, C. K., & LIPSITT, L. P. Neonatal nutritive sucking: Effects of taste stimulation upon sucking rhythm and heart rate. *Child Development,* 1976, *47,* 518–522.

CROWELL, D. H., BLURTON, L. B., KOBAYASHI, L. R., McFARLAND, J. L., & YANG, R. K. Studies in early infant learning: Classical conditioning of the neonatal heart rate. *Developmental Psychology Monograph,* 1976, *12,* 373–397.

CURZI-DASCALOVA, L., & DREYFUS-BRISAC, C. Distribution of skin potential responses according to state of sleep during the first months of life in human babies. *Electroencephalography and Clinical Neurophysiology,* 1976, *41,* 339–407.

CURZI-DASCALOVA, L., PAJOT, N., & DREYFUS-BRISAC, C. Spontaneous skin potential responses in sleeping infants between 24 and 41 weeks of conceptual age. *Psychophysiology,* 1973, *10,* 478–487.

DYKMAN, R. A. On the nature of classical conditioning. In C. C. Brown (Ed.), *Methods in psychophysiology.* Baltimore, Md.: Waverly Press, 1967.

EISENBERG, R. B. Auditory behavior in the neonate. I. Methodological problems and the logical design of research procedures. *Journal of Auditory Research,* 1965, *5,* 159–177.

EISENBERG, R. B., GRIFFIN, E. J., COURSIN, D. B., & HUNTER, M.

A. Auditory behavior in the human neonate: A preliminary report. *Journal of Speech and Hearing Research*, 1964, *7*, 245–269.

EISENBERG, R. B., MARMAROU, A., & GIOVACHINO, P. Infant heart rate changes to a synthetic speech sound. *Journal of Auditory Research*, 1974, *14*, 21–28.

FAGAN, J. F. An attention model of infant recognition. *Child Development*, 1977, *48*, 345–359.

FIELD, T. Interaction patterns of preterm and term infants. In T. Field, A. Sostek, S. Goldberg, & H. H. Shuman (Eds.), *Infants born at risk*. Jamaica, N.Y.: Spectrum, Publ., 1978.

FIELD, T. M. Visual and cardiac responses to animate and inanimate faces by young term and preterm infants. *Child Development*, 1979, *50*, 188–194.

FITZGERALD, H. E., & BRACKBILL, Y. Classical conditioning in infancy: Development and constraints. Psychological Bulletin, 1976, *83*, 353–375.

GOLDBERG, S. Visual tracking and existence constancy in 5-month-old infants. *Journal of Experimental Child Psychology*, 1976, *22*, 478–491.

GRAHAM, F. K., & CLIFTON, R. K. Heart rate change as a component of the orienting response. *Psychological Bulletin*, 1966, *65*, 305–320.

GRAHAM, F. K., CLIFTON, R. K., & HATTON, H. M. Habituation of heart rate response to repeated auditory stimulation during the first five days of life. *Child Development*, 1968, *39*, 35–52.

GRAHAM, F. K., & JACKSON, J. C. Arousal systems and infant heart rate responses. In L. P. Lipsitt & H. W. Reese (Eds.), *Advances in child development and behavior* (Vol. 5). New York: Academic Press, 1970.

GRAHAM, F. K., LEAVITT, L. A., & STROCK, B. D. Precocious cardiac orienting in a human anencephalic infant. *Science*, 1978, *199*, 322–324.

GRAY, M. L., & CROWELL, D. H. Heart rate changes to sudden peripheral stimuli in the human during early infancy. *Journal of Pediatrics*, 1968, *72*, 807–814.

GREGG, C., CLIFTON, R. K., & HAITH, M. A possible explanation for the frequent failure to find cardiac orienting in the newborn infant. *Developmental Psychology*, 1976, *12*, 75–76.

HAITH, M. M., & CAMPOS, J. J. Human infancy. In M. R. Rosenzweig & L. W. Porter (Eds.), *Annual review of psychology*. Palo Alto, Calif.: Annual Reviews, 1977.

HARPER, R. M., HOPPENBROUWERS, T., STERMAN, M. B., McGINTY, D. J., & HODGMAN, J. Polygraphic studies of normal infants during the first six months of life: I. Heart rate and variability as a function of state. *Pediatric Research*, 1976, *10*, 945–956.

HARPER, R. M., KELLY, D. S., WALTER, D. O., & HOPPENBROUWERS, T. Cardiac waveform alterations during sleep in the infant. *Psychophysiology*, 1976, *13*, 318–322.

HIRSCHMAN, R., & KATKIN, E. S. Psychophysiological functioning, arousal, attention and learning during the first year of life. In H. W. Reese (Ed.), *Advances in child development and behavior* (Vol. 9). New York: Academic Press, 1974.

HUTT, S. J., LENARD, H. G., & PRECHTL, H.F.R. Psychophysiological studies in newborn infants. In L. P. Lipsitt & H. W. Reese (Eds.), *Advances in child development and behavior* (Vol. 4). New York: Academic Press, 1969.

INGRAM, E. M., & FITZGERALD, H. E. Individual differences in infant orienting and autonomic conditioning. *Developmental Psychobiology*, 1974, *7*, 359–367.

JACKLIN, C. N. *The pattern of cardiac response to olfactory stimulation in neonates*. Unpublished doctoral dissertation, Brown University, 1972.

JACKSON, J. C. Amplitude and habituation of the orienting reflex as a function of stimulus intensity. *Psychophysiology*, 1974, *11*, 647–659.

JACKSON, J. C., KANTOWITZ, S. R., & GRAHAM, F. K. Can newborns show cardiac orienting? *Child Development*, 1971, *42*, 107–121.

JEFFREY, W. E. Habituation as a mechanism for perceptual development. In T. J. Tighe & R. N. Leaton (Eds.), *Habituation: Perspectives from child development, animal behavior, and neurophysiology*. Hillsdale, N.J.: Lawrence Erlbaum Associates, 1976.

KAGAN, J. *Change and continuity in infancy*. New York: John Wiley, 1971.

KAGAN, J., & LEWIS, M. Studies of attention in the human infant. *Merrill-Palmer Quarterly*, 1965, *11*, 95–127.

KAYE, H. Skin conductance in the human neonate. *Child Development*, 1964, *35*, 1297–1305.

KEARSLEY, R. B. The newborn's response to auditory stimulation: A demonstration of orienting and defensive behavior. *Child Development*, 1973, *44*, 582–590.

KEEN, R. E., CHASE, H. H., & GRAHAM, F. K. Twenty-four hour retention by neonates of an habituated heart rate response. *Psychonomic Science*, 1965, *2*, 265–266.

KITTNER, S., & LIPSITT, L. P. Obstetric history and the heart-rate response of newborns to sound. *Developmental Medicine and Child Neurology*, 1976, *18*, 460–470.

LACEY, B. C., & LACEY, J. I. Two-way communication between the heart and the brain. Significance of time within the cardiac cycle. *American Psychologist*, 1978, *33*, 99–113.

LACEY, J. I. The evaluation of autonomic responses: Toward a general solution. *Annals of the New York Academy of Sciences*, 1956, *67*, 125–163.

LACEY, J. I. Psychophysiological approaches to the evaluation of psychotherapeutic process and outcome. In E. A. Rubenstein & M. B. Parloff (Eds.), *Research in psychotherapy*. Washington, D.C.: American Psychological Association, 1959.

LACEY, J. I., KAGAN, J., LACEY, B. C., & MOSS, H. A. The visceral level: Situational determinants and behavioral correlates of autonomic response patterns. In P. H. Knapp (Ed.), *Expression of the emotions in man*. New York: International Universities Press, 1963.

LACEY, J. I., & LACEY, B. C. The law of initial value in the longitudinal study of autonomic constitution: Reproducibility of autonomic responses and response patterns over a four year interval. *Annals of the New York Academy of Sciences*, 1962, *98*, 1257–1290.

LEAVITT, L. A., BROWN, J. W., MORSE, P. A., & GRAHAM, F. K. Cardiac orienting and auditory discrimination in 6-week-old infants. *Developmental Psychology*, 1976, *12*, 514–523.

LESTER, B.M.K., BURCH, N. R., & DOSSET, R. C. Noctural EEG-GSR profiles: The influence of presleep states. *Psychophysiology*, 1967, *3*, 238–248.

LESTER, B. M. Cardiac habituation of the orienting response to an auditory signal in infants of varying nutritional states. *Developmental Psychology*, 1975, *11*, 432–442.

LEWIS, M. A developmental study of the cardiac response to stimulus onset and offset during the first year of life. *Psychophysiology*, 1971, *8*, 689–698.

LEWIS, M., KAGAN, J., CAMPBELL, H., & KALAFAT, J. The cardiac response as a correlate of attention in infants. *Child Development*, 1966, *37*, 63–71.

LEWIS M., & SPAULDING, S. J. Differential cardiac response to visual and auditory stimulation in the young child. *Psychophysiology*, 1967, *3*, 229–237.

LEWIS, M., WILSON, C. D., BAN, P., & BAUMEL, M. H. An exploratory study of resting cardiac rate and variability from the last trimester of prenatal life through the first year of postnatal life. *Child Development*, 1970, *41*, 799–811.

LIPSITT, L. P., & JACKLIN, C. N. Cardiac deceleration and its stability in human newborns. *Developmental Psychology*, 1971, *5*, 535.

LIPSITT, L. P., REILLY, B. M., BUTCHER, M. J., & GREENWOOD, M. M. The stability and interrelationships of newborn sucking and heart rate. *Developmental Psychobiology*, 1976, *9*, 305–310.

LIPTON, E. L., & STEINSCHNEIDER, A. Studies on the psychophysiology of infancy. *Merrill-Palmer Quarterly*, 1964, *10*, 102–117.

LIPTON, E. L., STEINSCHNEIDER, A., & RICHMOND, J. B. Autonomic function in the neonate. VII. Maturational changes in cardiac control. *Child Development*, 1966, *37*, 1–16.

McCALL, R. B., & KAGAN, J. Stimulus schema discrepancy and attention in the infant. *Journal of Experimental Child Psychology*, 1967, *5*, 381–390.

McCALL, R. B., & MELSON, W. H. Complexity, contour, and area as determinants of attention in infants. *Developmental Psychology*, 1970, *3*, 343–349.

MELSON, W. H., & McCALL, R. B. Attentional responses of five-month-old girls to discrepant auditory stimuli. *Child Development*, 1970, *41*, 1159–1171.

NELSON, M. N., CLIFTON, R. K., DOWD, J. M., APPLETON, T., & LITTLE, A. *Heart rate and sucking responses to tones in neonates: New state controls suggest a possible explanation for previous failures to obtain orienting responses*. Paper presented at Society for Psychological Research, Toronto, Canada, 1975. (Clifton, R. K. The relation of infant cardiac responding to behavioral state and motor activity. In A. Collins (Ed.), *Minnesota symposium on child psychology* (Vol. 2). Hillsdale, N.J.: Lawrence Erlbaum Associates, 1978.)

OBRIST, P. A. Heart rate and somatic motor coupling during classical aversive conditioning in humans. *Journal of Experimental Psychology*, 1968, *77*, 180–193.

OBRIST, P. A. The cardiovascular-behavioral interaction—as it appears today. *Psychophysiology*, 1976, *13*, 95–107.

OBRIST, P. A., WEBB, R. A., SUTTERER, J. R., & HOWARD, J. L. The cardiac-somatic relationship: Some reformulations. *Psychophysiology*, 1970, *6*, 569–587.

OBRIST, P. A., WOOD, D. M., & PEREZ-REYES, M. Heart rate during conditioning in humans: Effects of UCS intensity, vagal blockage, and adrenergic block of vasomotor activity. *Journal of Experimental Psychology*, 1965, *70*, 32–42.

POLIKANINA, R. The relationship between autonomic and somatic components during development of a defensive conditioned reflex in premature children. *Pavlov Journal of Higher Nervous Activity*, 1961, *11*, 72–82.

POMERLEAU-MALCUIT, A., & CLIFTON, R. K. Neonatal heart-rate response to tactile, auditory, and vestibular stimulation in different stages. *Child Development*, 1973, *44*, 485–496.

POMERLEAU-MALCUIT, A., MALCUIT, G., & CLIFTON, R. K. An attempt to elicit cardiac orienting and defense responses in the newborn to two types of facial stimulation. *Psychophysiology*, 1975, *12*, 527–535.

PORGES, S. W., ARNOLD, W. R., & FORBES, E. J. Heart rate variability: An index of attentional responsivity in human newborns. *Developmental Psychology*, 1973, *8*, 85–92.

PORGES, S. W., STAMPS, L. E., & WALTER, G. F. Heart rate variability and newborn heart rate responses to illumination changes. *Developmental Psychology*, 1974, *10*, 507–513.

RASKIN, D. C., KOTSES, H., & BEVER, J. Autonomic indicators of orienting and defensive responses. *Journal of Experimental Psychology*, 1969, *80*, 423–432.

REWEY, H. H. Developmental change in infant heart rate response during sleeping and waking states. *Developmental Psychology*, 1973, *8*, 35–41.

ROSE, S. A., SCHMIDT, K., & BRIDGER, W. H. Changes in tactile responsivity during sleep in the human newborn infant. *Developmental Psychology*, 1978, *14*, 163–172.

SAMEROFF, A. J. Can conditioned responses be established in the newborn infant: 1971? *Developmental Psychology*, 1971, *5*, 1–12.

SAMEROFF, A. J., CASHMORE, T. F., & DYKES, A. C. Heart rate deceleration during visual fixation in human newborns. *Developmental Psychology*, 1973, *8*, 117–119.

SCHACHTER, J., WILLIAMS, T. A., KHACHATURIAN, Z., TOBIN, M., KRUGER, R., & KERR, J. Heart rate responses to auditory clicks in neonates. *Psychophysiology*, 1971, *8*, 163–179.

SCHWARTZ, A.N., CAMPOS, J. J., & BAISEL, E. J. The visual cliff: Cardiac and behavioral correlates on the deep and shallow sides at five and nine months of age. *Journal of Experimental Child Psychology*, 1973, *15*, 86–99.

SCHWARTZ, A. N., CAMPOS, J. J., BAISEL, E. J., & AMATORE, B. *Cardiac and behavioral correlates of infant distress: Visual cliff and maternal separation.* Paper presented at the meetings of the Society for Research and Child Development, Minneapolis, April 1971.

SKARIN, K. Cognitive and contextual determinants of stranger fear in six- and eleven-month-old infants. *Child Development*, 1977, *48*, 537–544.

SOKOLOV, E. N. Neuronal models and the orienting reflex. In M.A.B. Brazier (Ed.), *The central nervous system and behavior*. New York: Josiah Macy, Jr. Foundation, 1960.

SOKOLOV, E. N. *Perception and the conditioned reflex.* London: Pergamon, 1963.

SROUFE, L. A., WATERS, E., & MATAS, L. Contextual determinants of infant affective response. In M. Lewis & L. Rosenblum (Eds.), *The origins of fear*. New York: John Wiley, 1974.

STAMPS, L. E. Temporal conditioning of heart rate responses in newborn infants. *Developmental Psychology*, 1977, *13*, 624–629.

STAMPS, L. E. Relationships between cardiac orienting and birth weight in normal full term newborns. *Psychophysiology*, 1979, *16*, 181.

STAMPS, L. E., & PORGES, S. W. Heart rate conditioning in newborn infants: Relationships among conditionability, heart rate variability, and sex. *Developmental Psychology*, 1975, *11*, 424–431.

TURCO, T. L., & STAMPS, L. E. Classical conditioning of heart rate in young infants. *Psychophysiology*, 1979, *16*, 185.

WATERS, E., MATAS, L., & SROUFE, L. A. Infants' reactions to an approaching stranger: Description, validation and functional significance of wariness. *Child Development*, 1975, *46*, 348–356.

WELFORD, N. T., & SONTAG, L. W. Recording fetal heart rate as a behavioral measure. *American Psychologist*, 1969, *24*, 276–279.

YANG, R. K., & DOUTHITT, T. C. Newborn responses to threshold tactile stimulation. *Child Development*, 1974, *45*, 237–242.

YONAS, A., & PICK, H. L. An approach to the study of infant space perception. In L. B. Cohen & P. Salapatek (Eds.), *Infant perception: From sensation to cognition* (Vol. 42). New York: Academic Press, 1975.

15

Infant Perception

LINDA P. ACREDOLO

JANET L. HAKE

The topic of infant perception is generating an astounding amount of research these days. The reason for this surge is primarily methodological. Although the questions have been around for centuries, the tools for obtaining the answers have not. The infant's notoriously limited behavioral repertoire posed a particular challenge, and it was not until Fantz (1958) demonstrated the effectiveness of a simple preference technique that researchers began to view the area of infant perception as a conquerable frontier. With true pioneer spirit the quest began, first in laboratories at a few major universities, but then as the students trained there moved out on their own and news of success spread, the number of laboratories grew at a geometric rate. The methodological barrier holding back the curious had finally been breached, and the result was an exhilarating rush toward solution of the nature-nurture questions so long as the heart of psychological and philosophical debate. Despite our efforts many of the answers still elude us; however, the feeling of being on the threshold is very strong. As each piece of the puzzle is added the feeling of exhilaration grows. It is our hope that the following sections will engender in the reader some of this same excitement.

METHODOLOGICAL TECHNIQUES AND ISSUES

As mentioned, the burgeoning interest in infant perception is due in large part to the discovery of effective techniques for assessing perceptual capacities at very young ages. A number of excellent discussions of these methods are already available (Cohen, DeLoache, & Strauss, 1979; Cohen & Gelber, 1975; Mauer, 1975; Teller, 1979); however, a brief summary is necessary here to facilitate the reader's understanding of the research findings in subsequent sections. In addition to describing the major dependent variables and experimental designs, brief attention will also be given to several important methodological issues that have arisen as our knowledge of the infant's response systems has become more extensive.

Dependent Measures

Although their behavioral repertoire is quite limited in comparison to older children and adults, infants still do look, search, reach, touch, and suck. Fortunately researchers have drawn quite successfully from this limited list. Probably the most commonly used is the first: the tendency of infants to look at—to fixate—visual stimuli. Fixation time has generally been measured with some variation of a technique introduced by Fantz (1958). In his corneal reflection technique, fixation of an object is assumed to coincide with the appearance of the reflection of the object on the infant's pupil. Although it has proven to be extremely useful for determining looking versus nonlooking and general scanning patterns, the technique's precision in assessing exact points of fixation has been questioned (Mauer, 1975). The fovea in adults is not exactly on a straight line path from the pupil, and the same is probably true for infants. In addition interpretation of the measure is made difficult by the occurrence of "blank stares" during which time the infant's eyes may be centered on an object without any real processing taking place (Cohen, DeLoache, & Strauss, 1979). There is one important advantage of the corneal reflection procedure according to Mauer (1975): Its accuracy is not easily affected by head movement. As a consequence its popularity continues unabated among researchers.

Visual activity is also frequently assessed electrophysiologically. The most common measures include (1) the *visually evoked potential* (VEP)—a measure of cortical activity in response to visual stimuli; (2) the *electroretinogram* (ERG)—a measure of electrical potential produced by the retina that includes both a component originating from the cones and a component originating from the rods; and (3) the *electrooculogram* (EOG)—a measure of eye movement derived from changes in the position of the eye relative to the electrodes placed around the eye. A variation of the first of these three, called the *auditory evoked potential,* is used to assess reception of auditory stimuli at the cortical level. A final commonly used electrophysiological measure is heartrate. Presentation of a stimulus in any modality can result in a change in heartrate—acceleration or deceleration, depending on the age and state of the infant and the nature of the stimulus (Berg & Berg, 1979).

The infant's tendency to reach for objects has also provided a useful tool for assessing perceptual capacities. Reaching has been particularly useful in the study of depth perception, the assumption being that a tendency to reach for near rather than far objects is an indication that distance cues have been processed (e.g., Bower, 1972; Bower, Broughton, & Moore, 1970a; Cruikshank, 1941; DiFranco, Muir, & Dodwell, 1978; Field, 1976, 1977; Gordon & Yonas, 1976; Yonas, Cleaves, & Pettersen, 1978). Reaching has also been used as a measure of the infant's recognition of a familiar stimulus. When an infant reaches for a novel stimulus paired with one that has been encountered previously, it is an indication that information from that previous encounter has in fact been processed. Used in this way reaching has been particularly effective to assess the ability of infants to process form information cross-modally (e.g., Bryant, Jones, Claxton, & Perkins, 1972; Rose, Gottfried, & Bridger, 1978) and tactually (e.g., Soroka, Corter, & Abramovitch, 1979).

The measures described so far—visual fixation, electrophysiological measures, and reaching—certainly do not exhaust the list of dependent variables available to researchers. Other measures used somewhat less frequently, but still quite successfully, include: sucking as an index of attention (e.g., Milewski, 1976, 1978, 1979) and taste preference (e.g., Crook, 1978; Crook & Lipsitt, 1976); crawling as an index of depth perception (e.g., Gibson & Walk, 1960) and spatial orientation (e.g., Corter, Zucker, & Galligan, 1980); head turning as an index of searching (e.g., Acredolo, 1978; Acredolo & Evans, 1980; Muir & Field, 1979); and smiling as an index of pleasure (e.g., MacDonald & Silverman, 1978; Steiner, 1979).

Experimental Designs

The designs used to study infant perception range from very simple to quite complex. Perhaps the simplest procedures are those in which a single stimulus is presented and the infant's reactions, such as eye movements, facial expressions, vocalizations, and reaching behaviors, are recorded. From the application of this simple technique we have learned such divergent things as how scanning of visual stimuli changes with age (e.g., Mauer & Salapatek, 1976; Salapetek & Kessen, 1966), when in development infants begin to recognize themselves in mirrors (e.g., Lewis & Brooks, 1978; Mans, Cicchetti, &

Sroufe, 1978), the degree to which infants can localize sound (Mendelson & Haith, 1976; Muir & Field, 1979), and the remarkable ability of infants to imitate pitch (Kessen, Levine, & Wendrich, 1979).

A slight alteration of the single stimulus procedure gives us one of the two most frequently used paradigms—the preference method. In this case two stimuli are simultaneously presented to the infant, and any preference for one stimulus over the other is noted as an indication that the two stimuli were in fact discriminable. Total visual fixation time, latency to fixation, and number of initial fixations across trials are the most typically used measures of preference. The method was promoted most successfully by Fantz (1958, 1961, 1963) who established beyond doubt that even newborn infants prefer to look at something rather than nothing, thus indicating that some visual capacity is present from the very beginning of life. The one important drawback to the method is the difficulty inherent in interpreting a lack of preference for one stimulus over the other. Although it is possible that such an outcome indicates a failure to discriminate between the stimuli, it could just as logically stem from equal interest in the two. One way out of this dilemma is to increase the likelihood that a real preference will exist, either by using a second stimulus clearly established as unpopular by past researchers (e.g., a homogeneous gray stimulus as in Salapatek, Bechtold, & Bushnell's 1976 study of infant acuity) or by decreasing the interest value of one of the stimuli during the experiment itself. This latter technique constitutes the second very popular method of assessing perceptual capacities, the habituation method.

In the habituation method infants are familiarized with one of two stimuli during either one trial of long duration or a series of trials. Attention, as indexed by visual fixation, heartrate, or sucking rate, typically declines over time. After either a set number of trials or a set degree of decline in attention (e.g., three successive trials during which the average fixation time was less than one-half the average fixation time on the first three trials), the familiarized stimulus is replaced with a second stimulus. The assumption is that if this second stimulus is discriminable from the first, then a recovery in attention should result. The novel stimulus should be preferred to the familiar one, as indicated by an increase in fixation time, heartrate change, reaching, or by a decrease in sucking. This method has been used successfully in nearly every domain of infant perception, including among others shape constancy (e.g., Caron, Caron, & Carlson, 1979), face perception (e.g., Fagan & Singer, 1979), temporal perception (e.g., Chang & Trehub, 1977a, 1977b), concept formation (Cohen & Strauss, 1979), perception of rigid versus elastic motion (Gibson, Owsley, & Johnston, 1978) and recognition of mirror image rotations (Bornstein, Gross, & Wolf, 1978).

Although the three methods described so far are the most commonly used, several others appear from time to time in the literature. Operant conditioning, for example, has been used to test the infant's capacity to recognize aspects of a stimulus. The infant typically is trained to make a specific response in the presence of a particular stimulus. That stimulus is then replaced by other stimuli which differ in theoretically interesting ways from the original. The tendency of the infant to generalize the learned response to each of these is assessed. When infants trained to turn their heads to a triangle with a bar across it were presented with variations of the triangle without the bar, they responded most strongly to a perfect triangle (Bower, 1966c). These results were interpreted as evidence of the priority, even for infants, of the Gestalt law of good continuation.

Classical conditioning has also recently made an appearance as a methodological tool. Acredolo (1978) trained infants to anticipate the appearance of an event (unconditioned stimulus, UCS) following a buzzer (conditioned stimulus, CS). The event elicited visual fixation (unconditioned response, UCR). Once this expectation was established, the infants' understanding of the location of the event was assessed by moving them to another location in the same room, sounding the buzzer alone, and watching where the infants looked in anticipation of the event's occurrence (conditioned response, CR). The results indicated a strong tendency to simply repeat the learned response rather than take the change of position into consideration.

A final method worthy of note represents an innovative combination of operant conditioning and habituation. It is most commonly referred to as the *high amplitude sucking* (HAS) method and has been found useful with infants as young as one month of age, a time when regular habituation and operant conditioning methods work less effectively (Eimas, 1975; Eimas, Siqueland, Jusczyk, & Vigorito, 1971, Milewski, 1976, 1978, 1979; Trehub & Rabinovitch, 1972). Typically the HAS method involves reinforcing high amplitude sucking with presentation of a stimulus event. Responding at first increases as the infant learns the contingency and maintains interest in the event. However the infant's interest gradually declines. This habituation is then followed by presentation of a second stimulus. Any revival of high amplitude sucking in response to the change is interpreted as evidence that the second stimulus has been discriminated from the first.

Methodological Issues

Effective utilization of the methods outlined above depends more and more on the researcher's knowledge of and concern about certain methodological issues. Brief mention of a few of these will hopefully facilitate the reader's evaluation of research to be described in the remainder of this chapter.

1. Researchers have now fairly firmly established the existence of a direction bias in infants in the form of a preference toward looking to the right. This preference is not only prevalent among newborns (Turkewitz, Gordon, & Birch, 1965; Turkewitz, Moreau, & Birch, 1966) but also among three-month-olds (Coryell & Michel, 1978; Gesell, 1938) and four-month-olds (DeLoache, Rissman, & Cohen, 1978). Consequently researchers must be extremely careful to counterbalance the position of simultaneously presented stimuli.

2. Another very important factor for researchers to consider is the state of the infant at the time of testing. Whether the infant is alert or not can affect the direction of heartrate change in response to a stimulus (Berg & Berg, 1979) and the degree of recovery to the novel stimulus in the high amplitude sucking paradigm (Williams & Golenski, 1979),

as well as more obvious measures such as auditory thresholds (Berg & Berg, 1979; Eisenberg, 1976, 1979).

3. A final issue concerns the frequent practice of allowing an infant to suck on something while stimuli are presented. Evidence is accumulating that the sucking may actually alter the infant's processing of auditory and visual information. Berg and Berg (1979), after reviewing the literature on heartrate change, concluded that sucking on a pacifier can decrease the likelihood of heartrate deceleration in response to stimuli. In addition Mendelson (1979) reports evidence suggesting that sucking is related to better oculomotor control, although the reason for this correlation remains a puzzle. At any rate it is clear that researchers can no longer blithely place pacifiers into the mouths of their subjects without considering the impact on their data.

VISUAL PERCEPTION

Development of the eye is first evident at about the fourth week of gestation as invaginations of the embryonic brain form the optic vesicles which lie beneath the surface ectoderm of the head. The optic vesicle induces the ectoderm layer to thicken and form the lens placode which invaginates to form the lens vesicle. Concomitant with the formation of the lens vesicle, the optic vesicles invaginate to form the optic cups from which the retina eventually develops. All these structures are apparent by about 30 days of gestation. Further differentiation of the retinal layers is completed by about seven months of gestation. According to Tuchmann-Duplessis, Auroux, and Haegel (1975), the eye is sensitive to light from this time on, although the fovea centralis does not complete differentiation until four months postnatally. This estimation appears to be in agreement with other traditional embryological sources on the visual system (Duke-Elder & Cook, 1963; Mann, 1964). Mauer (1975) states that by seven months of gestation the visual pathway is anatomically complete and functional and that the fovea has begun to differentiate. Further Mauer (1975) indicates that by 23 weeks of gestation, rods and cones can be identified, and by 36 weeks the photoreceptor cells become structurally fairly similar to those of the adult.

There were several studies that raised questions regarding the validity of some of these traditional conclusions about development of the human visual system. Mauer (1975) cautioned against relying too heavily on human anatomical-histological material since the specimens were examined postmortem and subject to the conditions necessary for histological preparation. Both these factors could lead to artifactual results. Haith (1978) has also raised the issue that many of the original anatomical studies based their findings on a few newborn babies who had died of unknown causes and could have been developmentally retarded. Use of such infants would lead to an underestimation of the degree of development of the retina at birth. Evidence suggesting that such underestimation has occurred comes from studies of postnatal retinal development in rhesus monkeys, whose visual system is anatomically and electrophysiologically similar to that of humans and well developed by birth. Haith (1978) points out a variety of evidence suggesting that, if anything, the visual system of rhesus monkeys should be *less* well developed at birth than that of humans. Horsten and Winkelman (1964) have reported limited histological data on the newborn retina suggesting the human retina may be more advanced developmentally than generally thought.

In summary anatomical-histological studies of the development of the human retina are incomplete and the reliability of some of the observations is suspect. Some results from human and comparative studies suggest the human retina is functional at birth but exactly how functional may be up to behavioral scientists to determine.

Relatively little is known about the maturation of the visual pathways beyond the eye in the human fetus and infant. In general it appears that peripheral components of the primary visual system mature earlier than more central components. The optic nerve, for example, is incompletely myelinated at birth. Estimates of time of completion for this process range from three weeks (Last, 1968) to four months postnatally (Duke-Elder & Cook, 1963). The lateral geniculate and superior colliculus show limited myelination in the late fetal period, and the process is completed by about 1 month postnatal age. Temporal lobe areas associated with vision do not begin to myelinate until a few months after birth, and the process continues for about ten years (Yakovlev & LeCours, 1967). The anatomical studies of Conel (1939, 1941, 1947, 1951, 1955, 1959) on the development of the infant cortex indicate that the visual cortex of the human infant is poorly developed at birth. Bronson (1974) has pointed out that the maturational sequence of the components of primary visual pathway approximates the order in which visual information is processed. He also presented evidence to suggest that the secondary visual pathway develops in advance of the primary visual pathway.

Acuity

Once Fantz (1958) had established beyond doubt that infants were not blind at birth, attention turned to determining exactly how well they could see. Assessment of visual acuity, the resolving power of the eye, has resulted in a variety of estimates, all of which indicate that vision at birth is not nearly as fine-grained as it is in adulthood. While normal acuity in adults is about 1′ of arc, the estimates of acuity in the first two months range from 8′ to 40′ (Cohen, DeLoache, & Strauss, 1979). The estimates have varied due to a number of factors: the area of the retina tested (central versus peripheral), the type of stimuli used (single lines versus grating or stripe patterns), and the method of assessment (use of the optokinetic nystagmus response versus reliance on the infant's preference for looking at something over nothing). Several good reviews of this literature are available (Cohen et al., 1979; Dobson & Teller, 1978); consequently, the following discussion will focus on recent studies by Mauer and her associates that have demonstrated just about the finest levels of both central and peripheral acuity to date. These studies will also serve to acquaint the reader with typical methodological techniques used by researchers in the area.

If infants *can* see a stimulus, they tend to look at it. This is the basis of a popular procedure used by Lewis, Mauer, and Kay (1978). Single lines varying in width from 4′ to 3°18′ were presented 33 cm from the left eye of 1- to 7-day-old infants. The lines also varied in position across trials, appearing either centrally or 10°, 20°, or 30° from center. As each trial started, a column of red lights designed to direct gaze to the center of the visual field was turned off, and a stimulus appeared. The direction of gaze of the left eye was recorded on film, the assumption being that the proportion of gaze directed at the target location would be significantly greater when the stimulus was present than absent as long as it was visible. The results indicated better central and peripheral acuity than had previously been found, a result Lewis et al. attribute in part to the use of single lines instead of stripes or gratings. A line as thin as 8′ was perceivable centrally; peripheral detection was found for the 33′ line at 10° and 20°, and the 1°6′ line at 30°. The argument that the central line may have been intruding into the periphery, and therefore really may have been testing nonfoveal vision, was countered by pointing out that the infants did not shift their gaze to the peripheral ends of the line as would have been the case if the central section were not visible. One final pattern of interest was the tendency for acuity to be better for stimuli presented to the left than to the right. Recalling that only the left eye was tested, Lewis et al. suggested that the pattern may indicate better temporal than nasal vision at birth.

In contrast to the focus by Lewis et al. on the ability to *detect* peripheral stimuli, Mauer and Lewis (1979) assessed the ability of newborns to discriminate between patterns presented nonfoveally. Pairs of patterns were presented, each containing one pattern determined in pilot testing to be strongly preferred over the other. After a central band of lights was turned off, the pairs appeared, one to the right, one to the left, at either 10°, 20°, or 30° from center. The stimuli toward which the infant turned was recorded, and a predominance of turns toward the normally preferred stimulus pattern was interpreted as an indication that discrimination had occurred. The results indicated some discrimination at all distances, but finer-grained discrimination closer to center. When the patterns differed on many attributes, discrimination occurred at all distances. However when they differed on only one dimension, discrimination occurred at 10° but not at 20° or 30°.

It is evident from both these studies that infant acuity is better than had previously been determined. It is not, however, comparable to the adult norm of 1′ of arc. When is this norm achieved? The only evidence to date suggests that acuity approaches this level by six months for some infants (Fantz, Ordy, & Udelf, 1962). Given the fact that estimates of acuity at birth have changed radically with the advent of new methods, the acuity estimates across the first year can be expected to do the same. It will probably be some time before the final developmental picture is clear.

Pattern Perception

With the possible exception of depth perception, more research has been conducted on the development of the perception of pattern than on any other facet of infant perception. Once Fantz (1958) had established beyond doubt that even newborn infants could see patterns, research on the parameters of this ability began in earnest.

Since a complete review of this vast literature is beyond the scope of this chapter, interested readers are urged to consult excellent reviews already available elsewhere (Bond, 1972; Cohen et al., 1979; Fantz, Fagan, & Miranda, 1975; Karmel & Maisel, 1975; Salapatek, 1975; Thomas, 1973). The following discussion will focus on evidence uncovered since these reviews and will be categorized to address three issues of particular interest to researchers: (1) developmental changes in scanning patterns, (2) the nature of the information abstracted from patterned stimuli, and (3) stimulus attributes affecting pattern preference.

Scanning Patterns. Along with the advent of techniques for charting eye movements came an interest in evaluating scanning patterns at different ages. The cornerstone of this literature is the now classic study by Salapatek and Kessen (1966) that indicated that many newborn infants tend to concentrate their fixations on single, high contrast features of simple geometric forms. Subsequent research (see Salapatek, 1975, for discussion) has generally confirmed this finding and added to it evidence that scanning for the first two months tends to be strongly limited to features of the outer contours of complex as well as simple forms. Mauer and Salapatek (1976), for example, presented one- and two-month-old infants with three real but stationary and expressionless human faces: their mother, a strange man, and a strange woman. Eye movement records indicated that at two months the infant scanned a significantly greater number of features than at one month, and the features which were fixated were significantly more likely to be internal to the face, especially the eyes. The one-month-olds concentrated on the periphery of the face, particularly segments of the hairline and chin, or looked away altogether. These results are consistent with findings reported by Donnee (1973) and Hainline (1978) for photographs of real faces and Bergmann, Haith, and Mann (1971) for line drawings of faces. Despite their limited scanning, the one-month-old infants in the study were apparently processing enough information to allow them to distinguish their mother's face from the others. The infants at this age were significantly more likely to look away from their mother's face than from the other two, a pattern Mauer and Salapatek suggest may be attributable to the infants' distress at the discrepancy between their mother's face as they typically encounter it and its stationary, expressionless presentation in the experiment.

Additional evidence of an externality effect in early infant scanning was provided by Milewski (1976). Using a high amplitude sucking procedure, he demonstrated that one-month-old infants were sensitive to changes in the external but not the internal features of a compound form—a square inside a circle. After habituation to the compound configuration, either one or the other form was changed to a triangle. Although a change of the outer circle was detected by both one- and four-month-old infants, only the older subjects showed renewed interest when the inner figure was altered; Milewski concluded that insufficient scanning of interior segments was responsible for the results at one month.

Subsequent studies have focused on possible explanations for the externality effect. One hypothesis recently advanced is that the effect is partially an artifact of the stationary nature of the stimuli typically used to assess infant scanning (Bushnell, 1979; Girton, 1979). Infants even at birth are capable of tracking a moving stimulus, although somewhat inefficiently (Kremenitzer, Vaughan, Kurtzberg, & Dowling, 1979), and have even been shown to prefer moving over stationary representations of human faces (Carpenter, 1974). Perhaps the addition of movement to internal features would elicit fixation even among very young infants. Girton (1979) tested this hypothesis for five-week-old infants using a schematic face with oscillating eye circles within the outlines of the eyes. The same eye configuration was also presented in isolation. The results indicated greater attention, in the form of decreased sucking, to stimuli with intrastimulus motion. Interest was a function of the speed of the movement: The faster the eye moved, the greater the attention. However attention was not influenced by the presence or absence of the facial outline, indicating indirectly that the motion had indeed been seen even when it was an internal feature. Unfortunately even Girton concedes that without actual eye movement data these results do not prove that the moving eyes were the *focus* of attention. They do suggest, however, that internal movement is at least picked up peripherally and does indeed influence the perceptual behavior of infants as young as five weeks of age.

Additional support for the hypothesis that movement enhances the scanning of internal features was provided by Bushnell (1979). In his first experiment he replicated Milewski's (1976) results using a regular habituation-recovery method based on visual fixation time in place of Milewski's high amplitude sucking procedure. Infants at one month of age were still sensitive to changes in the outer, but not inner, contour of a compound form. He then demonstrated that allowing the inner form to move or to flash on and off during familiarization trials resulted in one-month-old infants being able to detect a change of the inner form to another geometric shape. Thus the addition of movement did draw attention to internal features. In view of these results criticisms of the stationary nature of the stimuli typically used do seem to have validity.

But the question still remains: Why, in the absence of movement, do infants under two months of age tend to limit scanning to external contours? Three hypotheses have been advanced: limited processing capacity, greater salience of larger elements, and preference for defined, bounded figures-against-ground in the Gestalt sense. Bower and Dunkeld (1973) suggest that infants are limited in the sheer number of features they can attend to and simply pick the outer contour because it is the more salient of the two. Although limitations on processing capacity no doubt exist, Bushnell (1979) has demonstrated that the processing capacity of one-month-old infants is not as limited as Bower and Dunkeld contend. He found that even with attention-getting movement added to the interior form of a compound stimulus his infants were still able to detect a change in the shape of the outer form. His subjects were capable of attending to both forms when they chose to.

It is still possible, however, that salience is a factor and that the larger size of the external form makes it more attention-grabbing. There is a good deal of evidence to support this hypothesis. Fantz, Fagan, and Miranda (1975) report that up through six months of age element size is an important factor in determining attention, with infants showing a preference for larger elements. Vurpillot, Ruel, and Castrec (1977) demonstrated that two- and four-month-old infants when presented with a cross-shaped configuration composed of tiny individual crosses were influenced by the size of the individual elements. When these elements were large, attention was drawn to them, and a change in the larger configuration went undetected. However when the individual elements were small, attention was drawn to the larger configuration, and change in its shape was detected, while change in the individual elements was not. Milewski (1978) reported that the placement of a small form adjacent to, rather than within, a larger form still did not elicit the attention of one-month-old infants. Infants familiarized to a small circle next to a large triangle did not dishabituate when the small form was changed to a square. In contrast familiarization of the subjects to two small forms, instead of one large and one small, did result in detection of a change in one of the two forms by half the infants. The equal size of the two forms appears to have increased the likelihood that attention would be drawn to both of them.

Unfortunately the strong case just presented for the importance of size is weakened somewhat by the results of another experiment in the series by Bushnell (1979). Unlike Milewski (1978) his use of a small form next to a large form did result in detection of a change in the small form by one-month-old infants. This pattern lead Bushnell to conclude that the boundedness of a form, rather than its size, is the crucial factor affecting its salience. The reason for the contradictory findings in these two studies is not clear, although the fact that Milewski used a high amplitude sucking procedure while Bushnell used decline in visual fixation to measure habituation may be a contributing factor. Obviously a definitive explanation of the externality effect in the absence of movement awaits resolution of this conflict.

Information Abstracted from Patterns. The information abstracted from a stimulus depends in part, of course, on the extensiveness with which the stimulus is scanned. Even given total scanning there is the possibility of different impressions of what has been seen. In this regard Cohen has repeatedly discussed evidence suggesting a developmental shift from abstraction of the separable components of a compound configuration to abstraction of the total configuration as a unit (Cohen, 1979a, 1979b; Cohen et al., 1979). His theory is based mainly on habituation studies in which compound stimuli are presented in a familiarization phase followed by changes in one or all of the components in a dishabituation test (Bower, 1966a; Cohen & Gelber, 1975; Cohen, Gelber, & Lazar, 1971; Cornell & Strauss, 1973; Fagan, 1977; Miller, 1972; Miller, Ryan, Sinnod, & Wilson, 1976). Cohen concludes that perception of configurational units is not pervasive until five months of age. Before this age the ability to abstract the overall configuration depends heavily on the complexity of the form, no doubt in part due to limited scanning patterns. High contrast lines and angles are the units from one to two months, simple dimensions such as color or form can be processed as units between two and four or five months, but it is not until approximately five months that more complex combinations of forms and colors are perceived as unified wholes in a Gestalt sense.

Several recent studies provide additional support for Cohen's developmental sequence. Schwartz and Day (1979) report a series of nine habituation studies showing that infants as young as two months of age (the youngest tested) are highly sensitive to *relations* among high contrast edges, an indication that they are attentive to more than simply the isolated elements of the pattern. The priority given to relational information was revealed by habituating infants to very simple two-dimensional forms and then comparing the degree of dishabituation to variants of these forms. The nine studies tested a range of simple forms from single angles to squares, rectangles, diamonds, and triangles. The variants used to test recognition were based on changes in the relations among the elements (e.g., new angle values), changes in the size of elements (e.g., from a rectangle to a square), and changes in the orientation of the whole unit (e.g., 90° rotation). By far the most consistent and strongest recovery of attention was to changes in angle values. Orientation changes evoked the lowest levels of recovery. Although Schwartz and Day argue, based on their data, that the ability to abstract the relational information constituting perception of form is probably innate, Cohen (1979a) cautions that such a conclusion is not justified until infants younger than those in their study are tested.

Milewski (1979) has also recently provided data indicating sensitivity to relational information among young infants. Through use of the high amplitude sucking method, three-month-old infants were habituated to either a linear or triangular arrangement of three dots. Once the habituation criterion had been reached, half the infants were presented with the novel arrangement, and half continued to receive the familiar one. Comparison of these two groups revealed significantly more high amplitude sucking in response to the novel arrangement, indicating that the change in the relationship of the three dots had been perceived. In a second experiment infants were habituated to a series of displays, each presenting dots of equal size in either a linear or triangular arrangement. The position and size of the arrangement on the screen was varied from trial to trial. The only variable constant across the series was the arrangement. The results of dishabituation trials with a novel arrangement indicated clearly that these three-month-old infants had abstracted the invariant relationship among the dots, again evidence of a response to the total Gestalt.

The abstraction of relations among dots was also the focus of a recent study by Lasky and Gogel (1978). The dots in this case, however, were moving rather than stationary. Five-month-old infants were presented with a display in which two dots moved horizontally back and forth in parallel trajectories while a third dot moved vertically up and down between them. This display, when viewed by adults, produces an illusion of diagonal movement of the third dot, the direction (NW to SE versus NE to SW) dependent on the phase of motion between the vertical and horizontal elements. In order to determine whether infants are sensitive to the relative motion of these elements, Lasky and Gogel habituated the infants to one phase relationship and then changed to the other and looked for attention recovery. According to the researchers the actual change in the individual motion of the dots accompanying phase alteration is very subtle. Consequently they felt justified in concluding that the dishabituation produced by the phase change was due to their infants having perceived the illusion and having detected a change in the direction of the illusory diagonal. Lasky and Gogel concluded that relational responding is strong at five months, a conclusion quite consistent with the developmental sequence suggested by Cohen. Testing with younger infants is an obvious next step.

There is, however, some reason to suspect that younger infants would not respond in the same way to Lasky and Gogel's illusion. The problem would not necessarily stem from insensitivity to the relative motion. Instead the infants might simply be unable to distinguish between the two diagonal lines produced by the different phase relationships. Evidence supporting this contention is provided by Bornstein et al. (1978) in a study of the ability of three- to four-month-old infants to distinguish between mirror image rotations. Using habituation procedures they determined that their infants could discriminate orthogonal lines from oblique lines and could discriminate among oblique lines at various levels of slant. They could not, however, discriminate between mirror image oblique lines (/ versus \). The same was true for slightly more complicated line arrangements and for human faces. In the latter case the infants could discriminate between right profiles of two different faces but not between right and left profiles of the same face. The reason, they argue, is that mirror images in nature are usually aspects of the same object and therefore need not be discriminated. Whatever the reason for the effect, it would seem to pose a problem for younger subjects exposed to Lasky and Gogel's (1978) illusion. Should such infants still show evidence of recovery to phase changes, one might justifiably question Lasky and Gogel's contention that it was the illusory diagonal their infants were responding to rather than changes in the movement of the individual dots.

Most of the studies described above have demonstrated abstraction by the infant of relations among elements of a pattern. Going one step beyond, Milewski (1979) showed that his infants could abstract a relational invariant from a series of different patterns with just their spatial arrangement in common. Studies using similar procedures have also demonstrated that five-month-old infants can abstract the invariant of rigid as opposed to elastic motion from a series of different rigid movements (Gibson, Owsley, & Johnston, 1978), that seven-month-old infants can abstract a facial expression denoting happiness from a series of different models showing the expression (Nelson, Morse, & Leavitt, 1979), and that five- to six-month-old infants can abstract the sex of a human face from a series of different individuals (Cornell, 1974; Fagan, 1976). These studies all indicate an ability to perceive similarities among different displays and to categorize the displays together. They do not, however, provide much information on the process of categorization.

A recent study by Strauss (1979) does provide data relevant to this categorization question. Rosch (1975a, 1975b, 1975c) has argued that, among adults, category membership is judged by comparison to a category prototype abstracted from the various members already encountered. With this hypothesis in mind Strauss designed a study to reveal the nature of any category prototype abstracted by ten-month-old infants. The stimuli used were schematic human faces containing four features that varied from trial to trial: length of the nose, width of the nose, length of the face, and distance between the eyes. These features all varied along a continuous scale divided into values of 1 to 5. In a familiarization phase the infants saw 16 different faces carefully composed so that the extreme values of each feature (e.g., 1 and 5) were represented three times as often as the middle value (i.e., 3). The goal was to determine whether the infants would form a prototype face based on the values that had occurred most frequently (a model prototype) or based on the average of all the values experienced (an average prototype). To find out, Strauss followed the familiarization trials with presentation of pairs of faces, one composed of extreme values, the other of middle values. In each case the infants spent more time looking at the face representing modal values, thus indicating that the other face, the one representing average values, had actually been seen three times less frequently. Strauss succeeded in demonstrating a tendency for ten-month-old infants to average feature values as various category members were encountered. It will be interesting to see if this same strategy typifies infant processing of other kinds of stimuli as well.

In summary, evidence to date suggests that even infants as young as two months of age are abstracting relational information from the patterns they see (Schwartz & Day, 1979). The relations are at first apparently limited to simple arrangements of high contrast lines, dots, and simple forms, with the ability to abstract more complex configurations coming later in development, around the age of five months. The ability to categorize individual displays by abstracting the invariants among them appears to be within the repertoire of three-month-old infants for very simple patterns (Milewski, 1979) and of five-month-old and older infants for more complex displays. We even have some preliminary evidence suggesting that the categorization of at least some patterned stimuli proceeds through a process of averaging stimulus values to produce a prototype (Strauss, 1979). However a great deal of additional evidence will be needed to determine if this same strategy is really pervasive during infancy.

Stimulus Attributes. Interest in infant preferences for some patterns over others began with Fantz's observation (1958, 1961) that his one- to six-week-old infants looked longer at a bull's eye than at horizontal stripes. Since that time researchers have been busy both determining preferences at different ages and trying to explain them. Several excellent discussions of this extensive literature are already available (Cohen et al., 1979; Karmel & Maisel, 1975; Fantz, Fagan, & Miranda, 1975). Consequently only the highlights and very recent additions to the literature will be included here.

The major finding of this literature is that as infants get older they show a tendency to prefer more and more complex stimuli. Since checkerboards have been used in a large proportion of the studies, this statement has often been translated to mean a trend with age toward checkerboards with greater numbers of squares. Brennan, Ames, and Moore (1966), for example, tested 3-, 8-, and

14-week-old infants with 2 x 2, 8 x 8, and 24 x 24 square checkerboards and found the simplest pattern preferred by younger infants and the intermediate pattern by older infants. More recently, DeLoache et al. (1978) used 2 x 2 and 24 x 24 checkerboard patterns to explore Cohen's (1972) theory that infant visual activity is divisible into attention-getting and attention-keeping processes. In order to examine the first of these, they measured latency to look in addition to total fixation and found their four-month-old infants turning more quickly to the more complex pattern. Moreover the speed of turning increased over trials both with stimulus presentation independent of the infant's response and contingent on head-turning toward the stimulus's location. Based on these latency changes, DeLoache et al. concluded that attention-getting, at least at four months, is neither a simple reflex behavior elicited by stimulus onset or a result of arousal; rather, it seems to reflect an active search process enabling infants to modulate their own visual experiences.

Although it is clear from these studies and others like them (Cohen, 1972; Greenberg, 1971; Greenberg & O'Donnell, 1972) that complexity preference changes with age, it is far from clear exactly what "complexity" is, and why such preference changes occur. Several suggestions have been made. Greenberg (1971) suggests complexity is information, and preferences change as information processing capacity increases. Karmel and Maisel (Karmel, 1969a, 1969b; Karmel & Maisel, 1975) argue that complexity is contour density, defined specifically as a ratio of the sum of lengths of all black and white transitions to the total area of the figure. Preference change occurs, according to this theory, because of a decrease in the size of neurological receptive fields as development proceeds.

The possibility that neurological development is playing a role in complexity preference has also been suggested by Hoffman (1978). When six- and ten-week-old infants were presented with stimuli varying in amount of contour, visually evoked potential (VEP) recordings indicated an age difference in the relative contributions of cortical and subcortical regions. The wave component contributed by cortical activity varied with the amount of contour for the older infants but not the younger infants. The subcortical component, in contrast, varied with stimulus change at both ages. Hoffman concludes that an important neurological shift is taking place at about two months of age and may be responsible for changes in response to contour density.

Fantz and his colleagues have also contributed to the complexity debate by pointing out that many of the patterns used to represent different degrees of complexity contain individual parts whose size decreases as their number increases. Consequently a preference by young infants for a 2 x 2 over a 24 x 24 checkerboard is ambiguous. Are the infants showing a preference for patterns with few elements or patterns whose elements are large? Their own research, based on comparisons of stimuli in which only one of the dimensions is varied, indicates that both size and number are important but that the younger the infant, the more important the role of size. Specifically, younger infants prefer large over small elements. A similar size effect has also been found for patterns other than checkerboards (Maisel & Karmel, 1978). Both

neurological maturation and changes in visual acuity have been suggested as possible explanations (Cohen et al., 1979).

The impact of stimulus attributes on responses other than visual fixation has also been studied. McGuire and Turkewitz (1978) varied the size, brightness, and distance of a cone and measured finger extension (approach) and flexion (withdrawal) in 10- to 15- and 20- to 25-week-old infants. Consistent with the visual fixation literature, the results here suggest an increase with age in the attractiveness of stimuli which McGuire and Turkewitz describe as more intense. The younger, but not the older, infants showed a tendency to approach weak stimuli and withdraw from strong. Additional evidence suggesting an intensity effect has been supplied by Field (1979). Three-month-old infants showed more gaze aversion and heartrate acceleration to a very animated face than to a less animated or still face. It appears that intensity continues to be an important stimulus attributed as processing capacities continue to develop in the infant.

In summary the pattern perception literature has been consistent in showing increased preference for more complex and intense stimuli as the infant grows older. Most researchers agree that the explanation probably lies in part with changes in neurology underlying visual behavior. However the specific nature of these changes is still unclear. Changes in preference may be, as Karmel and Maisel suggest, a function of increased definition of receptive fields with increasing age, and as Hoffman (1978) suggests, they may result from a shift from subcortical to cortical processing. Bornstein (1978b) even suggests that the perceptual preferences evidenced during infancy probably have adaptive value, thus accounting for their relationship to the neurological substratum. Although it is clear that additional data are necessary before any of these suggestions can be regarded as definitive, the existing evidence is consistent in indicating that, far from being blind, the young infant is often awake, alert, and searching.

Depth Perception

The mystery of how perception of the third dimension is achieved given the constraints of a two-dimensional retina has fascinated philosophers for centuries. It is, in fact, the focus of one of our oldest nature-nurture debates. Are infants born with the capacity to see in three dimensions or must they, as Bishop Berkeley (1709) contended, learn to interpret retinal information as depth by fumbling about in the three-dimensional world around them? These are the two most familiar hypotheses; however, two additional possibilities are also important to consider. First, the nature position can be, and indeed should be, expanded to include the possibility that depth perception may be absent at birth due to immaturity of the visual system but develop in the first few months through innately programmed maturational processes. Many people overlook this possibility, assuming wrongly that the nature position hinges solely on demonstration of depth perception in the neonate. It is also important to consider the possibility that depth perception, like most behaviors, reflects both innate and learned components. An innately given knowledge of relative distance, for example, may be honed with practice into fairly precise knowledge of absolute distance.

With the advent of new methodological techniques for assessing the infant's perceptual experience, psychologists interested in these hypotheses were finally able to leave their armchairs and head for their laboratories. The result has been a rapid accumulation of information relevant to depth perception in young infants. The following discussion will focus on a variety of subtopics including: (1) sensitivity to primary cues for depth, (2) defensive reactions to impending collision, and (3) the ability to reach for objects at different distances.

Primary Cues: Accommodation. *Accommodation* refers to the process by which the shape of the lens of the eye is changed in order to bring objects at different distances into focus. The changing shape of the lens, as indicated by feedback from the ciliary muscles that control it, provides information about the relative distance of objects. One of the "facts" about infant perception most frequently cited in textbooks is that the infant's lens is constantly focused at one distance, about 19 cm from the eye. The belief that the infant is initially unable to accommodate to objects nearer or farther than this distance stems from classic studies by Haynes, White, and Held (1965) and White and Zolot (cited in White, 1971) using dynamic retinoscopy. The same studies report that accommodation improves rapidly, reaching adult levels by about four months.

More recent research by Banks (1980), however, has provided evidence contradicting this rather pessimistic view of accommodative capacities in the first few months. Banks suggests that the failure of infants to accommodate in previous studies may have been due to the use of a single stimulus which, as it was moved farther from the infant's eyes, subtended a smaller and smaller visual angle. In view of the poor level of acuity typical at these ages, it is quite possible that the visual array at some distances simply failed to stimulate accommodation because it was not seen clearly enough. Banks also points out that the subjects in these studies were institutionalized infants and therefore may have been somewhat slower than home-reared infants in the development of visual capacities.

In his own studies of infant accommodation Banks avoided these problems by using home-reared one-, two-, and three-month-old infants who were presented with checkerboard patterns that increased in size with increasing distance. The results indicated that accommodation improves significantly between one and two months of age, but not much after that. In other words, accommodation approaches adult levels by two months. Moreover, accommodation at one month is considerably better than the total lack of accommodation attributed to infants of this age by Haynes et al. (1965) in previous studies.

The fact remains, however, that accommodation does improve significantly over the first two months. Based on measures of acuity and pupil size Banks attributes the change to a gradual decrease in the "depth of focus" in the infant eye. Depth of focus refers to the range of distances from the fixation point across which no detectable blurring occurs. It appears that infants at one month have a much larger depth of focus than is found for adults, thus rendering them oblivious to many accommo-

dative errors. They fail to accommodate because they are unaware that they need to do so. Thus, the old view of the young infant as capable of seeing clearly at one distance (19 cm) and not at others, needs some revision. In view of the work by Banks it seems more likely that the one-month-old infant sees equally *un*clearly across a wide range of distances. This description of accommodation also helps explain why acuity does not change with increasing distance from the supposed fixed focal length of 19 cm, a fact demonstrated recently by Salapatek, Bechtold, and Bushnell (1976). Quite simply, acuity does not change because the stimuli are equally unclear with increasing distance rather than less clear.

What then accounts for the rapid improvement in accommodation from one to two months of age? Banks suggests that increases in acuity, primarily due to refinements at neurological levels, result in a decline in depth of focus, which in turn creates noticeable blur when accommodative errors are made. Accommodative processes are then invoked by the infant to reduce the blur, and we have a more nearly adult-like accommodation profile. At the same time that better acuity is stimulating better accommodation, the reverse is also occurring. Improved accommodation increases the probability of the infant receiving visual images with less blur, images that would in turn stimulate the development of the high-resolution elements at the retinal and cortical levels that are necessary for even greater strides in acuity. These two visual processes, then, are involved in what Banks (1980) calls a case of reciprocal dependency.

In summary recent research indicates that accommodation is present in rudimentary form at one month of age and improves to nearly adult standards by two months. At that point, presumably, accommodation is available as a reliable cue for depth. Unfortunately, the degree to which it exists in infants younger than one month and the role it plays in depth perception in these very early days have yet to be determined. With this in mind, we now turn to the question of convergence.

Primary Cues: Convergence. The convergence of our two eyes onto a single target provides a wealth of information about depth: The degree of turn as the eyes focus on the same object is greater for near objects than far, and the binocular disparity produced upon complete convergence produces well-known stereoptic effects. But to what degree do the infant's eyes converge? One of the variety of techniques available to answer this question involves corneal photography. When the target object is seen reflected at the center of both pupils, convergence is assumed. Based on results from this technique both Wickelgren (1967, 1969) and Mauer (1974) concluded that convergence is rare in the first month of life. One major problem with the technique, unfortunately, is that the actual fixation point of the fovea can not be determined using corneal photography beyond an error range of 3° to 6°. Since, for adults, it takes a disparity of only 10 minutes of a degree between the two eyes to prevent fusion, it is impossible with such photography to tell if fusion is really occurring (Aslin, 1977; Haith, 1978). However since this accuracy problem would result in over- rather than under-estimations of convergence, the pessimistic conclusion drawn by Wickelgren and Mauer may still be justified.

A second technique for assessing convergence involves moving a stimulus toward and away from the infant and noting any appropriate convergent movements of the eyes. Aslin (1977) moved a cross back and forth from 57 cm to within 12 to 15 cm of the eyes at two rates of speed, 12 and 23 cm/sec. The results indicated an increase with age in the percentage of trials eliciting appropriate convergence movements: 37 percent, 52 percent, and 69 percent at 1, 2, and 3 months respectively. In addition the speed of approach was important. The faster rate resulted in delays in convergence at both 1 and 2 months. By 3 months, however, binocular convergence was attained within ½ sec of the end-of-target movement for both rates of speed. In general the results are consistent with those of Ling (1942) who reported successful convergence at 7 weeks with an object approaching the infant even more slowly (5 cm/sec).

Despite the relative sophistication of the three-month-old revealed in Aslin's study, the development of convergence is apparently not complete by this age. In a second study Aslin (1977) found that three-month-old infants did not respond with saccadic eye movements to prism-induced disparity. The eye movements, which occurred on 8 percent of the trials at three months, 13 percent at four months, and 72 percent at six months, represent an attempt to reinstate alignment of the two eyes. These results were consistent with those of an earlier study by Parks (1966). Aslin offers three possible reasons for the poor showing of the three-month-olds in this task: (1) an inability to detect such rapidly produced disparity; (2) some deficiency in the saccadic process so that a movement, although deemed necessary, cannot be produced; or (3) the existence at three months of a larger fusion area than normally found in adults so that the nonalignment created by the prisms was not sufficient to actually produce disparity at this age. Whatever the eventual explanation, it is clear from Aslin's study that convergence ability is not an all-or-none affair and continues to undergo refinement through the first six months of life.

This general conclusion received further support from a study by Fox, Aslin, Shea, and Dumais (1980) in which 2½-, 3½-, and 4½-month-old infants were presented with moving random dot patterns, one to each eye. When viewed without binocular fusion, the patterns are indeed random; however, when complete convergence occurs, a stereoscopic form is perceived. In order to determine whether or not the infants were seeing the form, the researchers took advantage of the tendency of the infants to track a moving object. The stereoscopic form was moved across the visual field, and any appropriate eye movements were noted. The results indicated significant eye movement and, therefore, binocular fusion at both 3½ and 4½ months, but not at 2½ months. Fox et al. suggest that the problem at the younger ages may be a failure to maintain the *consistent* binocular fusion necessary to perceive the stimulus event.

One final technique used to assess the stereoptic effects that can accompany convergence involves production of a virtual object. Similar to the Fox et al. procedure, creation of a virtual object is accomplished by providing the two eyes with slightly disparate views which, when merged through binocular convergence, produce the illusion of a three-dimensional object in space. In one of the original virtual object studies, Bower, Broughton, and Moore (1970a) placed polarized goggles on infants as young as eight days in order to produce the illusion. The illusory object was slowly moved toward the infants from 40 cm away. Reaching began at about 20 cm, according to Bower et al., and was accompanied by emotional upset when no object was encountered tactually. In contrast to much of the work on convergence just described, these results seem to indicate the presence of fairly consistent binocular fixation within the first month.

An attempt by Field (1977) to replicate the Bower et al. study with slightly older infants was not successful, perhaps due to a different method for producing the illusion. Field (1977) used a Fresnel lens, which requires no goggles, and tested infants at three, five, and seven months of age. Infants at the two younger ages showed no upset at all and very few reaches toward the objects. These results are supported in part by those of Yonas, Oberg, and Norcia (1978) who also tested infants about three and five months of age. In this case the virtual object was loomed at the infants, and any defensive behaviors were interpreted as evidence of binocular convergence. Although the older infants (20 weeks) did show such reactions, the younger infants (14 weeks) did not. In contrast to Field's results, however, some evidence of convergence at the younger age was produced. These infants did fixate toward the center of the visual field significantly longer in the loom condition than in a control condition without polarized goggles, in which the same two disparate views were available but side by side rather than fusible. The need to look for such subtle indications of convergence was also demonstrated by Gordon and Yonas (1976) in a study in which 5½-month-old infants were presented with a virtual object at three distances. Although the infants failed to reach accurately, they did show more reach and grasp behaviors toward the object at the closer distance and also leaned farther forward when the object was the farthest away. These differential responses to the different illusory distances suggest strongly that some degree of binocular fusion was in fact taking place.

What are we to conclude about binocular convergence from all these studies during infancy? Although the picture is far from clear as yet, the best bet seems to be that some degree of convergence is probably present at birth (Bower et al., 1970a; Slator & Findlay, 1975); however, both its prevalence, consistency, and precision increase greatly across the first six months. With so many techniques now available to study the problem, additional data will no doubt continue to appear.

Primary Cues: Motion Parallax. One behavior we know to be within the infant's repertoire is head movement; when head movement is possible, motion parallax is potentially available as information about depth. As the head moves from side to side, slightly different perspectives of a scene are perceived. The amount and speed of object displacement in these perspectives depends on object distance; Near objects are displaced faster and farther than far objects. Such information is available even when a scene is viewed monocularly and may therefore be especially useful to infants who have trouble coordinating the two eyes.

Despite its potential value our knowledge of the role of motion parallax in infancy is very limited. Bower (1966c) reported evidence of motion parallax in six- and eight-week-old infants presented with his classic size constancy procedure. Like those in the original experiment, these infants were operantly conditioned to turn their heads in response to a certain size cube at a certain distance. They were then tested with other cubes whose size and/or distance varied from the original. Unlike the initial group of infants, however, these subjects viewed the cubes monocularly. When their responses mirrored those of the original binocular group in showing sensitivity to distance information, Bower concluded that motion parallax was the important contributing factor.

Evidence of motion parallax among slightly older infants is provided by Yonas, Cleaves, and Petterson (1978). As part of a study of pictorial cues for depth, they presented 20- to 22-week-old infants with a real window rotated 45° so that one end was closer to the infants than the other. Despite monocular viewing these infants reached to the close end more often than the far end, thus indicating sensitivity to their relative distances. Although by this age accommodation may have been playing a role, too, it seems quite likely that motion parallax was a major contributor.

With this necessarily brief discussion of motion parallax, our coverage of the primary cues for depth comes to a close. Obviously the picture is still incomplete and, as usual, the call is for more research. Motion parallax, in particular, seems due for further investigation at younger ages. Perhaps some fresh ideas will be generated from a look at the next group of studies, a series in which defensive reactions to depth situations are sought.

Defensive Reactions. The strategy of evoking defensive reactions as evidence of depth perception began with the classic study by Gibson and Walk (1960) using the visual cliff. Although their demonstration of avoidance of the cliff by seven- to nine-month-olds did not answer the question of whether depth perception is innate in humans, their work with newborns of other species (e.g., goats and chickens) did demonstrate that it *could* be innate in an organism. Unfortunately subsequent studies with the visual cliff using younger human infants have brought us little closer to an answer for our own species. Campos, Langer, and Krowitz (1970) tested two-month-olds by laying them face down on both sides and noting heartrate change. Significant change occurred on the deep but not the shallow side, indicating that the two sides had been discriminated. However, the direction of change, deceleration, suggested that the infants were more interested in the cliff than frightened by it. The absence of a fear response at this age is not, however, proof that depth perception does not exist. It is equally possible that the infants were indeed perceiving the situation in three dimensions but simply had not yet learned to interpret the stimulus event as potentially dangerous. Seeing depth and understanding its meaning for bodily safety are two separable things.

The search for defensive reactions indicating sensitivity to depth continued on another front. In the loom-zoom procedure an object, either real or illusory, is loomed rapidly on a collision course toward the infant and then zoomed away again. The assumption is that if infants are capable of interpreting the expansion of the retinal image accompanying the loom as a change in distance, then they may show concern about the impending collision. Some of the initial results of loom-zoom studies with neonates were very promising. Both Bower, Broughton, and Moore (1970b) and Ball and Tronick (1971) observed a seemingly defensive retraction of the head as the object loomed toward the infant. In addition, Bower et al. reported interposition of hands in front of the face, eye widening, and general emotional upset. Of these four behaviors the head retraction was the most reliable and seemed to provide convincing evidence of a defensive reaction to impending collision. Whether this was simply a reflexive response to a specific stimulus event or true knowledge of depth seemed to be the only question remaining.

Recently, however, the explanation of this head retraction in terms of innate depth perception has been challenged. Yonas (1979; Yonas & Pettersen, 1979) has reported evidence indicating that the infants, rather than moving their heads to avoid collision, may simply have retracted their heads in order to watch the upper edge of the image rise as it expanded over the visual field. Perception of a change in distance might not have been involved at all. Support for this explanation comes from a study (Yonas & Pettersen, 1979) in which the reaction of three- to six-week-old infants to two looming objects were compared: a diamond shape whose upper edge rose during the loom and a triangle whose upper edge stayed at the same level relative to the infant's eyes. Head retraction occurred to the diamond but not the triangle, thus supporting an interpretation in terms of infant attention rather than fear.

Both Bower (1977b) and Yonas (1979) have used another procedure to test the interest hypothesis. The procedure involves an upright rectangular form which appears to fall forward 90° on a collision course with the infant's head. The motion is then reversed, and the form moves back to its original upright position. In a reverse of the typical loom-zoom situation, the loom phase in this case involves a falling contour and the zoom phase a rising contour. According to the interest hypothesis, we should also see a reverse in the behavior of the infants: attention to the upper edge should result in head retraction during the nonthreatening zoom phase and *not* the loom phase. This is exactly what Yonas found with his three- to six-week-old infants. Unfortunately, however, Bower reports exactly the opposite results and, therefore, support for a depth perception explanation of head retraction: The loom phase elicited head retraction while the zoom phase did not! The reason for the contradiction between these two studies is not yet clear; obviously, a definitive decision on depth perception in the loom-zoom situation awaits its resolution.

In the meantime it is important to note that even if Yonas is correct in his interpretation of head retraction it still would not prove that depth perception is absent in the first month of life. The infants may in fact actually be perceiving the expanding retinal image as an approaching surface but simply be more interested than afraid. In this sense the results of the loom-zoom procedures leave us in the same quandary as the studies of young infants on the visual cliff. Depth perception may be present prior to realization of its potential danger. The reader is referred to Yonas (1979) for further discussion of this literature.

Distance-Regulated Reaching. Sensitivity to distance information has also been assessed by evaluating infant motor behaviors in response to real objects placed at different distances from the infant. The results have been fairly consistent in showing such sensitivity at three months of age (Field, 1976, 1977), with a study by Bower (1972) indicating its presence even in newborns.

Field (1976) presented 15-, 19-, and 24-week old infants with objects at three distances. In order to control for retinal image size the farther the object, the larger it was. The results indicated a tendency to reach less often and pay less attention to the far object, even at 15 weeks. A subsequent study by Field (1977) yielded similar results.

The study by Bower (1972) with newborn infants involved the same basic procedure. Two objects were used: a 3 cm foam rubber square presented just beyond the infant's reach and a 6 cm foam rubber sphere presented at twice that distance. As in the Field studies there were significantly more attempts to reach the small object than the large far object, an indication that the two stimulus events were distinguishable. Whether it is truly the nearer distance that makes the closer object more attractive or some other factor (e.g., the greater image displacement produced by motion parallax) is, unfortunately, not yet clear.

Summary. As even casual perusal of the previous sections will reveal, firm conclusions about depth perception in infancy are not yet possible. Unfortunately the literature, like many in infant perception, is plagued with two difficult problems: ambiguous findings and conflicting results. The loom-zoom literature provides good examples of each. Researchers were initially delighted with reports of head retraction in reaction to impending collision. Here at last was what appeared to be unambiguous evidence that newborn infants were responding to the depth information being relayed by the cues for depth· rather than changes in the cues themselves; but just as plaudits were being offered and textbooks rewritten, along came another interpretation: The infants may have simply been following the upper contour of the expanding images. In fact a subsequent study by Yonas and Pettersen (1979) supported this interpretation. And where does their study leave us? Once again the situation is ambiguous: Depth perception may or may not be present; Yonas and Pettersen's results neither confirm it nor rule it out.

The problem of conflicting results, although hardly restricted to the depth perception literature, seems to be particularly salient here. A striking example is the conflict between the loom-zoom studies of Bower (1977b) and Yonas (1979) discussed earlier. Other examples are found in the binocular fixation literature where some studies report convergence much earlier than other studies. How are we to explain these contradictions? Many possibilities come to mind when one considers the nature of the organism under study. Human infants are a very unpredictable, uncooperative lot whose behaviors differ radically depending on factors such as state of alertness, general health, circumcision, socioeconomic status (SES), prematurity, temperament, fear of strangers, and birth order. In fact even the availability of a pacifier can change perceptual responding (Berg & Berg, 1979). Is it any wonder that studies produce conflicting results? Obviously the only answer is to keep collecting data in the hope that common denominators will begin to appear.

Despite the problems enumerated above, a few things are already clear. Perhaps the most obvious is that a strong nature position, positing adult level depth perception at birth, is just not accurate. Although some sensitivity to optical expansion and motion parallax may exist at that point, three other important cues—accommodation, binocular convergence, and binocular disparity—all undergo substantial development during the first six months. Given the immaturity of the infant's visual and motor systems, such maturational changes are hardly surprising. Experience in the world, however, also plays a role. Bishop Berkeley would be delighted with the studies indicating that, at the very least, infants must acquire knowledge of the potential dangers of depth-related situations (e.g., the visual cliff).

Other Space Perception Issues

Picture Perception. Interest in picture perception during infancy stems from the desire to understand the ontogeny of two phenomena: depth perception and symbolic representation. A picture is, after all, most commonly a two-dimensional representation of a three-dimensional object or scene. The way infants react to pictures can tell us (1) at what point in development visual capacities are keen enough to detect the dimensional difference and (2) when it is that infants begin to understand the representational relation between pictures and the objects depicted. Research to date divides fairly cleanly along these lines, with some studies assessing the ability of infants to discriminate two-dimensional from three-dimensional stimuli and others focusing on the capacity to recognize the objects pictorially represented. One exception to this dichotomy is the work of Yonas and his associates whose prime interest is in the interface between the two broad categories, specifically, development of the ability to recognize pictorial representations of depth—the classic "painter's cues" of depth perception. Each of these approaches will be discussed later.

Most studies of the ability of infants to discriminate between two-dimensional and three-dimensional stimuli indicate that the ability is present very early in life, although the basis upon which the discrimination is made is unclear. In one of the oldest studies, Fantz (1961) reported that infants as young as one month of age preferred to look at a solid sphere over a flat circle of the same diameter, thus indicating that the two were discriminable on some dimension. The ability of one-month-old infants was also assessed more recently by Pipp and Haith (1977). Using *L*-shaped forms either flush with the background or extending 2.5 cm inward or outward, the reseachers found a significant preference for the recessed *L* over the two-dimensional *L*. Discrimination was also found at two months, this time, however, in the form of a preference for the raised *L* over the two-dimensional form.

Three-month-old infants have been studied in two experiments. In a study primarily devoted to shape constancy, Day and McKenzie (1973) found more rapid habituation to a cube shown in various orientations than to photos depicting the same orientations. Cook, Field, & Griffiths (1978), in a follow-up of the Day and McKenzie experiment, found faster habituation to trials with a real cube alone than to trials where the cube was alternated with a photo. The infants were apparently interpreting the alternating series as containing more than single repeated stimulus. Although the bases of the discrimination remain unknown, the data are fairly consistent in showing an ability to distinguish two-dimensional from three-dimensional stimuli.

The data for infants younger than one month were not quite so consistent. Bower (1972) started the controversy by reporting significantly more reaches by newborn infants toward a real object compared to a photo of the real object. The apparently successful use of reaching to index the discrimination was particularly important since it suggested that the infants were interpreting the real object as "graspable" and the photo as "nongraspable"—an indication of true knowledge of a difference in depth. Unfortunately Dodwell, Muir, and DiFranco (1976) failed in their effort to replicate Bower's results. A reanalysis of their data, however, did turn up some evidence to support Bower (DiFranco et al., 1978). When the criterion for "directed reach" was relaxed by removing the requirement that the reach cover more than half the distance to the object, the results indicated significantly more directed reaches to the real object than to the photo. However the difference was not nearly of the magnitude reported by Bower. In addition DiFranco et al. found that the real object elicited a significantly higher number of visual orientations than did the photo. At the very least, therefore, the study indicates an ability to differentiate the object from the photo. Whether or not the object's graspability is discerned at this age remains unclear pending more successful replication of Bower's results.

Studies of the representational nature of pictures have been even fewer in number and have not involved infants younger than five months of age. One of the first of these studies was the report of Hochberg and Brooks (1962) that their 19-month-old son had been able to identify verbally objects in photos and line drawings even though he had been denied exposure to pictures up until that age. This monumental effort provided the first clue that interpretation of two-dimensional representations might not need to be learned. In a study using much younger infants and much simpler stimulus patterns, Rose (1977) found that six-month-old infants could both discriminate two-dimensional from three-dimensional presentations of geometrical forms and transfer information from one to the other. Infants who had been familiarized with a geometric pattern presented three-dimensionally were then presented with two-dimensional representations of both the familiar stimulus and a novel stimulus. Despite the change in dimensionality, the infants still showed a preference for the novel pattern. The familiar stimulus had been recognized in the photo. Similar transfer also occurred in the opposite direction—from two-dimensional to three-dimensional representation.

The trend toward younger infants continued with Dirks and Gibson (1977) who also substituted human faces for the simple geometrical designs used by Rose.

Five-month-old infants were first habituated to a live woman's face and then presented with either a picture of the familiar face or a picture of a novel face. The infants dishabituated to the picture of the new, but not the old, face, thus indicating that they had recognized the familiar face from the photo. The level at which recognition had occurred was assessed in a second experiment. Unlike the novel photo in the initial experiment, the novel photo this time was of a face quite similar in features (sex, hair style, etc.) to the familiar face. The result was a failure of the infants to dishabituate to either test stimuli, indicating that recognition in the initial study had probably been based on gross physiognomic features. This limitation, however, does not detract from the important finding that the infants were capable of treating the photos as equivalent at some level to the real faces they had seen.

These results were extended both to another object and to other types of two-dimensional representations by DeLoache, Strauss, and Maynard (1979). In the first of a series of three experiments, five-month-old infants were familiarized for 60 seconds to two identical real dolls. Three pairs of test items were then presented: the familiar doll and a novel doll, colored photos of both dolls, and black and white photos of both dolls. In all three cases the infants showed a significant preference for the novel doll, thus indicating that the real doll was recognizable in both kinds of photos. In the second experiment a colored photo of a female face was the familiarization stimulus, and black and white photos and line drawings of the familiar face and a novel face were the test stimuli. Again significant preferences were found in each case for the novel face, this time indicating recognition of a photographed face with a line drawing. The final experiment was an important control condition. All possible combinations of all the stimuli from both experiments were presented to infants in pairs. The fact that significant preferences for the more realisitic member of each pair were found indicated that the infants could in fact discriminate between the various representational formats. True transfer of information rather than a failure to discriminate had been occurring in the initial experiments. This study, along with those of Rose (1977) and Dirks and Gibson (1977), provides strong evidence that the representational nature of pictures is grasped by five months of age. Studies with younger infants will no doubt be appearing soon.

The final literature to be discussed concerns infant sensitivity to pictorial representations of depth. One of the earliest contributors to the literature was Bower (1966c). In a study of size constancy with six- to eight-week-old infants, Bower reported that all signs of size constancy disappeared when the real cubes used in the other conditions were replaed with colored slides. Bower concluded that infants at this age were not sensitive to the depth information in the slides. Yonas (1979), however, argues that Bower was in essence stacking the deck against the pictorial depth information by allowing the infants binocular vision and the ability to move their heads. Any clear perception of flatness provided by these cues might simply have overridden pictorial depth information that had been observed.

In his own studies of pictorial depth (Yonas, 1979; Yonas, Cleaves, & Pettersen, 1978) Yonas has assessed both monocular and binocular perception of a classical piece of apparatus—Ames's trapezoidal window (Ames, 1951). Instead of an actual window the trapezoidal window is a two-dimensional picture of a window which has been rotated 45° about the vertical axis creating a trapezoidal-shaped image. When presented in the frontoparallel plane, the picture creates a powerful illusion of a rectangular window with six panes, slanted so that one side is closer to the viewer than the other—an illusion created solely by the pictorial depth cue of linear perspective. Are infants sensitive to this cue? In order to find out, Yonas presented both a real window slanted 45° and the trapezoidal window to infants at two ages, 20 to 22 weeks and 24 to 26 weeks. At both ages the response to the *real* window was a significant tendency to reach more often to the close side—even with one eye covered to eliminate binocular disparity. Some combinations of accommodation, motion parallax, and pictorial information was enabling the infants to perceive the relative distances of the two sides. The next step was to isolate the pictorial information by using the trapezoidal window (with one eye still covered). In this case only the older infants showed a tendency to reach more often to the side represented pictorially as closer. The younger infants reached equally to both sides. An important control condition consisted of a two-dimensional display of a large and a small window side by side in the frontoparallel plane. The fact that infants at neither age reached more to the larger window indicates that the results with the trapezoidal window cannot be attributed merely to a preference at 24 to 26 weeks for the larger of two portions of a display. The results with the trapezoidal window indicate that by 24 to 26 weeks infants are in fact quite sensitive to pictorially presented information about depth. Conclusions about the younger infants are more difficult to draw. Although it is possible that they lack any sensitivity at all to linear perspective, it is also possible that such sensitivity exists but to a degree easily overridden by the conflicting flatness information provided by accommodation and motion parallax. Additional work will hopefully indicate which description is the more accurate.

In summary the research on picture perception has proceeded fairly successfully on three fronts. First, sufficient data now exist to support the conclusion that one-month-old infants for sure, and newborn infants quite probably, are capable of discriminating pictures from the objects they depict. The basis of this discrimination remains unspecified, although the research on early sensitivity to depth cues would indicate motion parallax as a more likely contributor than binocular parallax or accommodation. Unfortunately it is quite possible that the different information emanating from an object and its pictorial representation is not even interpreted by the infants in terms of differences in depth. Additional data suggesting, as Bower's did, that infants perceive a real object as more graspable would help resolve the question. In regard to the second major issue in the literature, we know that by five months of age (if not earlier) infants are also aware of the representational nature of pictures. Infants at this age who have been familiarized with a real object proceed to show a preference for a picture of a novel object over a picture of a familiar object. The object and its pictorial representations are treated as equiv-

alent. Finally, the work on recognition of depth information portrayed pictorially indicates the presence of such sensitivity at five months. Whether younger infants are less sensitive to these "painters' cues" or simply more easily swayed by information from the primary cues remains to be determined.

Object Constancy. As spatial relations between objects and perceivers change due to movement of one or the other or both, perceptions of object size and shape remain the same. These object constancies are crucial to our perception of a stable world since, without them, objects would be perceived as constantly expanding and contracting and perpetually contorting from one shape to another. Is this, perhaps, an accurate description of the world of the infant? Or are even newborn infants capable of abstracting the invariants of size and shape from the flow of retinal images? Unfortunately the question remains unanswered for the newborn, although there is increasing evidence that at least by three months the infant is capable of abstracting some information about shape from the changing perceptual array. Day and McKenzie (1977) have summarized and evaluated much of the research relevant to this issue from the 1960s and early 1970s. Rather than duplicating this review, we shall focus attention on their major conclusions and more recent evidence.

The size constancy question was considered by many to have been resolved by Bower in the 1960s, at least for six- to eight-week-old infants (Bower, 1966c). Using operant conditioning procedures, Bower trained infants to turn their heads in the presence of a 12-inch cube placed one meter away in order to receive social reinforcement. He then measured the transfer of this learning to four test stimuli: the original stimulus, the same size cube placed three times farther away, a cube three times bigger placed the same distance as the training stimulus, and a cube three times bigger placed three times farther away. This last stimulus presented a retinal image of the same size as the training stimulus, and when the infants responded least to this cube, Bower concluded that they were not dependent on retinal image projection and therefore were capable of size constancy. This certainly is a possibility; however, the fact that the infants also responded significantly more to any stimulus at one meter than to any at three meters may indicate that his infants were demonstrating a preference for near objects. Although such a preference is interesting evidence of sensitivity to distance information, it weakens Bower's conclusion that the bigger cube placed farther away was rejected because it was perceived to be a different size than the training stimulus. Indeed support for this distance preference explanation was provided by McKenzie and Day (1972) who found that infants between 6 and 20 weeks responded little to any objects beyond 1 meter regardless of their projected size on the retina. Day and McKenzie (1977) summarize other attempts to replicate Bower's original study, many of which report a preference for near objects, but none of which have found evidence of size constancy. Although the existence of size constancy in infants remains an open question, these studies have contributed to our knowledge by indicating that distance is a salient dimension for infants as young as 6 to 8 weeks of age.

Our knowledge of shape constancy in infancy also began with a study by Bower (1966b). Once again operant conditioning was used, this time to show that seven- to nine-week-old infants were more likely to generalize a learned response (a head turn to a rectangle rotated 45° from the frontoparallel plane) to test stimuli of the same objective shape at different slants than to test stimuli of the same projective shape (trapezoidal). Bower concluded that this rejection of retinal image shape in favor of real shape was evidence of shape constancy.

A similar conclusion was advanced by Day and McKenzie (1973) based on their use of the habituation method. Infants 6 to 16 weeks old were habituated to either a cube in a constant orientation or to a cube whose orientation changed from trial to trial. A third group was exposed to photographs of the varying orientations instead of the cube itself. Habituation occurred in both conditions with the real cube but not in the condition with the pictures, thus indicating some ability of infants to discriminate three-dimensional from two-dimensional stimuli. In regard to shape constancy, however, the important comparison was of the two conditions with the real cube. When these two groups showed the same rate of habituation, Day and McKenzie concluded that the infants seeing the series of varying orientations were abstracting the real shape of the cube from the various perspectives and quickly tiring of it. Shape constancy was said to have been demonstrated.

Unfortunately several problems prevent acceptance of the Day and McKenzie study as strong evidence of shape constancy. First, as a number of researchers have pointed out (Caron, Caron, & Carlson, 1978; Cohen et al., 1979), the failure of the two real cube groups to differ in their habituation rates may have been due to a floor effect. Neither group was very interested in the cubes to begin with, averaging only 3.5 seconds of fixation during the initial 20-second trial. Given such meager interest to start with, it is not surprising that the groups failed to differ in their habituation times. Caron et al. (1978) also argue that the Day and McKenzie study was weakened by their failure to include a condition in which infants saw a series of stimuli projecting the same retinal shape but differing in real shape. If shape constancy is really present in these infants, such a series of stimuli should hold their interest considerably longer than the condition that Day and McKenzie did include in which only one object was presented. One final criticism was advanced by Cook et al. (1978). No evidence, they argued, had been supplied to show that the infants seeing the series of varying orientations of the cube were even capable of discriminating one perspective from the next. A failure to discriminate in this case would mean that the infants were perceiving essentially the same stimulus on each trial. Consequently a habituation rate comparable to the other group, which was also seeing an unchanging stimulus (the stationary cube), would be expected.

With this criticism in mind Cook et al. (1978) conducted their own habituation study with three-month-old infants. The infants were familiarized either to a cube alone or to a cube alternating with another stimulus. In each case the orientation of the forms varied from trial to trial. The other stimuli included a wedge, a truncated pyramid, photographs of the cube, and an L-shaped concave solid. When habituation rates were compared the results showed comparable rates for the cube alone, the cube alternating with the wedge, and the cube alternating with the truncated pyramid. Only the conditions with the photographs and the L-form elicited significantly longer looking times than the cube alone, thus suggesting that these were the only cases where two forms were being perceived instead of one. These results do replicate Day and McKenzie's findings of discrimination between two-dimensional and three-dimensional forms. However, the failure of the Cook et al. subjects to discriminate between a cube and similar forms calls into question Day and McKenzie's conclusion that shape constancy was the reason for the comparable habituation rates of the stationary cube and the rotating cube in their study.

Fortunately, a series of studies by Caron et al. (1978, 1979; Caron, Caron, Carlson, & Cobb, 1979) has provided more definitive evidence of shape constancy. In their first study (Caron et al., 1978), 11- to 13-week-old infants were habituated to one of six stimuli. All subjects were then tested for recovery to a square presented at 0° slant. The habituation stimuli included the same 0° square, the square tilted back 30°, the square tilted back 60°, a large trapezoid tilted 60° to produce the same retinal image as the 0° square, a small trapezoid presented at 0° slant to produce the same area as the square, and a large square. Their reasoning was that if shape constancy does exist at this age, the subjects in the first three conditions, all of whom habituated to the square, should show little, if any, recovery to the test square. Recovery, however, should occur to the trapezoids, even in the case of the tilted trapezoid projecting a square as the retinal image. The results, unfortunately, were rather puzzling. The subjects familiarized to the trapezoids did indeed show recovery, thus suggesting that the infants were not relying solely on projective shape. However the infants showed the same amount of recovery in all the other conditions as well (with the obvious exception of the first condition where habituation and test stimulus were identical). The infants appeared to be sensitive to changes in slant in addition to, or perhaps even instead of, changes in shape. The latter possibility was ruled out in a subsequent study (Caron, Caron, Carlson, & Cobb, 1979) in which slant was held constant across habituation and test trials while shape (or shape and size) was varied. Since subjects did show recovery to the test stimuli despite the constant slant, the researchers concluded that infants at this age are sensitive to more than slant and, therefore, that the results of the initial study were not due to changes in slant alone. However the possibility remained that the subjects were showing dependency on slant plus retinal image rather than slant plus objective shape. Their recovery in the tilted trapezoid condition could have been due to detected change in slant alone (through parallax and disparity information), while their recovery in the tilted square conditions could have been due to slant and retinal image changes combined. Obviously additional data were necessary before firm conclusions could be drawn.

Fortunately such data are provided in their third and most recent study (Caron, Caron, & Carlson, 1979). In this case 12-week-old infants were habituated to either a square or a trapezoid presented at a variety of nonfrontal slants (60°, 40°, 20°, −20°, −40°). After the habituation criterion was reached, the infants were exposed for two trials to the familiar shape presented at a new slant (0°) and for two trials to the novel shape at the same new slant (0°). The order of presentation of familiar and novel stimuli was counterbalanced across subjects. Their assumption was that if infants are indeed capable of shape constancy at this age then they should abstract the real shape of the object from its presentation at various slants during the habituation trials and show less interest in that shape then in the totally novel shape during the test trials. This is exactly what happened. Both those habituated to the square and those habituated to the trapezoid looked significantly longer at the novel shape than at the familiar shape, even though they had never encountered the familiar shape at that slant before. The preference for the trapezoid by those habituated to the square is particularly striking since the habituation stimulus they had seen actually had projected retinal images in the shape of trapezoids. The objection to the Day and McKenzie (1973) study raised by Cook et al. (1978) that infants may be showing failure to discriminate instead of shape constancy cannot be raised here. The very fact that the infants were showing differential fixation to the novel and familiar forms during the test trials indicates that the infants were capable of discriminating between them. After a long series of attempts, we finally have additional evidence to support the contention, raised over a decade ago by Bower, that shape constancy exists for infants as young as 12 weeks of age.

All of the shape constancy studies described so far have two things in common: the use of simple rather than complex geometrical forms and the use of stationary presentations of the various perspectives instead of actual rotation. For these reasons one might argue that the shape constancy abilities demonstrated so far are of little use to an infant whose world is more fully stocked with complex moving objects. Fortunately we also have some information about these other kinds of simulus events. The ability of infants to abstract objective shape from a moving stimulus was assessed by Owlsey (1979). Four-month-old infants with one eye covered were habituated to either a stationary wedge, which projected as a cube, or a rotating wedge. The results suggested that the infants had been able to abstract the wedge shape from the changing optical array: The infants who had habituated to the rotating wedge increased attention when shown the cube but not the wedge, while the infants who had habituated to the stationary wedge did not increase attention in either case. The use of monocular viewing conditions in this study suggests that shape constancy is not dependent on binocular disparity.

The result of using complex rather than simple form is illustrated in a study by Cohen and Strauss (1979). Using the same basic design as Caron, Caron, and Carlson (1979) but with photographs of faces instead of squares and trapezoids, Cohen and Strauss habituated 18-, 24-, and 30-week-old infants to one of three series of stimuli: repeated presentations of one face in one orientation, presentations of one face in four orientations, or presentations of different faces in four orientations. All infants were then tested with a novel face and the familiar face in a novel orientation. The results indicated shape constancy at 30 weeks but not at the younger ages. In contrast to the younger infants who dishabituated to both

stimuli in each condition, the 30-week-old infants did not dishabituate to the familiar face in the new orientation if they had been exposed to the sequence of that face in four different orientations. They had apparently abstracted the structure of the face to a degree which allowed them to recognize it even from a totally new perspective. The results of this study suggest that, although the rudiments of shape constancy may be present at three months, its application to very complex stimuli such as the human face awaits further development. Given the literature already discussed on the ability of infants to perceive objects as wholes rather than as collections of elements, this age pattern is hardly surprising.

One final study relevant to shape constancy is a study by Ruff with six-month-old infants in which both a complex object and real movement were used (Ruff, 1978, 1980). A variety of different kinds of movement were included. The object was a complex rigid form which was presented with a novel complex form following habituation. The results in general suggested that the facilitative effect of movement on shape recognition was a *U*-shaped function. Little movement of the form resulted in poor recognition, but so also did complex rotation. A right-to-left movement and a simple rotation were the most effective, with the former producing recognition faster than the latter. Based on the work of Gibson (1966), Ruff suggests that a moderate level of overlap from one perspective to the next is the most helpful at this stage of development.

In summary, evidence to date seems sufficiently strong to conclude that shape constancy, at least in a rudimentary form, is present by three months. Whether or not it is there earlier remains to be seen, although the accumulating data on depth perception in general indicates that it may not be there much before two months. But even after three months, the infant's shape constancy abilities probably continue to undergo refinement. As indicated by the studies just discussed, both the type of object involved and the type of transformation it undergoes make a difference; as each increases in complexity, so probably also does the age at which successful object constancy is achieved. Unfortunately our knowledge of size constancy in infancy is not even this far advanced.

Spatial Orientation. The challenge of space perception does not stop with the successful acquisition of depth perception, picture perception, or size and shape constancy. Infants must also be ready to cope with the consequences of their own movements through space. They must recognize that their position relative to objects will be altered with such movement—that it is the world that is stable and they who are mobile rather than the other way around. The possibility that this knowledge is acquired rather than inborn was first raised by Piaget (1971). He suggested that during the first year infants are egocentric—that is, they code the location of objects in terms of the objects' spatial relationship to their bodies and their past actions toward the objects rather than in terms of objective relations among objects themselves. Although Piaget contributed observational data to support this contention, it is only recently that researchers have been interested in providing systematic data relevant to the issue.

Most researchers have approached the problem by

creating a conflict, a situation in which the infants must choose between reliance on egocentric information or objective spatial relations. Acredolo (1978) retested a group of infants at 6, 11, and 16 months in a situation where they were taught to anticipate the appearance of an experimenter at one or two windows whenever they heard a buzzer. The windows were to the left and right of the infant on the walls of a fair-sized (3.2 x 3.2 m) room. Once the infants had learned to expect the event at the window, they were rotated to the opposite end of the room, the buzzer was sounded, and the direction in which they looked to find the event was recorded. Repetition of the originally correct response led to the incorrect window and was evidence of reliance on egocentric information; a turn toward the correct window was evidence of the ability to maintain spatial orientation. The results indicated heavy reliance on egocentric information at both 6 and 11 months. It was not until 16 months that the infants turned consistently to the correct window. More recent data (Acredolo & Evans, 1980) indicate that the impact of egocentricity can be somewhat attenuated by the presence of salient landmarks even at six months and that the influence of the landmarks increases with increasing age.

The conclusions by Acredolo and her associates that egocentrism is a feature of spatial orientation in young infants has received additional support recently from a study by Rieser (1979). In this case six-month-old infants were placed on their backs with a visual display of four windows over their heads: one 20° to the left of their line of sight, one 20° to the right, one 20° above, and one 20° below. As in the Acredolo studies, the infants were taught to expect an event at one of the windows, were moved (this time only 90° around their midline), and were observed as they searched for the event from their new position. Each infant was tested in one of six conditions varying in the brightness of the environment, the presence or absence of discriminable landmarks, and the relevance of gravitational cues. The results indicated strong egocentric responding in all but two of the conditions. Infants fixated the egocentric window first and longest (1) when the environment was so dim that only bodily movement information was available; (2) when texture information was visible as a clue to movement but no landmarks were present; (3) when the target door and the egocentic door were marked by landmarks of different colors; and (4) when the target door was the only door without landmarks. The only cases where responses to the correct door predominated were when the target door, but not the egocentric door, was marked and when the infants were tilted so that gravity provided a cue to the correct door. These results are not only consistent with those of Acredolo but also help counter the criticism (Cohen et al., 1979) that the failure of Acredolo's infants to maintain their orientation was due to the use of left-right directions in the task—directions notoriously difficult for children to distinguish. Since Rieser included the window above the infants' heads as a target window, the egocentric responding that resulted cannot be so easily dismissed.

A related line of research has involved a small-scale version of the conflict paradigm described above. Bremner and Bryant (1977) presented nine-month-old babies with an object that was hidden under one of two covers on a table, one to the left and one to the right of midline. After the infants had successfully recovered the object for five trials, the infants were rotated to the other side of the table, and the object was hidden under the same cover. Instead of retrieving it there, however, the infants tended strongly to repeat the action that had led them to the object in initial trials. In a subsequent study (Bremner, 1978a), egocentrism of this type was found to be much rarer when distinguishably different covers were used, thus once again indicating that salient landmarks are useful sources of information. That the landmarks must be in close proximity to the object itself was indicated by the high levels of egocentrism still found when the tablecloths *under* the covers rather than the covers themselves were made distinguishable. These results are consistent with the discovery by Acredolo and Evans (1980) that a landmark indirectly marking a target location is not useful to infants under 11 months of age.

In the studies just described, the hidden object has not been of particular significance to the subjects. Perhaps had the mother been the hidden object, increased motivation to keep track of her would have resulted in less egocentric responding. Corter et al. (1980) tested this hypothesis by placing nine-month-old infants in a room with two doors. After placing her infant on the floor so that one door was to the right and one to the left, each mother exited through one of the doors. In most cases the infants looked at and proceeded toward the appropriate door. On the next trial the mother left again but this time through the opposite door. Despite the mother's status as a valuable object, the infants still demonstrated egocentric behavior by returning to the *first* door instead of the second. Thus egocentrism seems to be a high priority strategy even when motivation to be correct is strong.

A final issue that has arisen in this literature concerns whether the egocentrism manifested in these studies is simply the result of a motor habit established in repeated training trials or the result of real dependence on a spatial reference system centered on the child's body. Evidence suggesting the former was provided by Bremner (1978b) who eliminated training trials by simply rotating the infants to the opposite side of a table as soon as an object was hidden on the first trial. The result was a drop in the proportion of egocentric responders from .88 with training trials to .38 without them. Acredolo (1979), however, discovered that these results were at least partially attributable to the fact that Bremner's infants were tested in their homes. When the task without training trials was repeated in the home, a low level of egocentic responding (15 percent of subjects) was found once again; when the task was repeated in two laboratory environments—a landmark-free enclosure and an unfamiliar office—the levels of egocentrism rose dramatically (76 percent in each). These results are important for three reasons. First, they indicate that true reliance on an egocentric frame of reference (as opposed to a motor habit) does occur during infancy, at least in unfamiliar environments. Second, they indicate that the familiarity of the home environment is operating in some way to facilitate spatial orientation. Whether this facilitation is due to increased knowledge of the spatial environment outside the boundaries of the task or simply to a greater ability to concentrate on the task when in a reassuring environment remains to be determined. Third, these results stand as a warning to researchers that generalizations from the testing environment to other environments must be made with caution.

In summary the research on spatial orientation in infancy has been fairly consistent in showing, as Piaget predicted, that egocentrism is a problem during the first year. Its influence, however, declines after the first year and is increasingly mitigated even during the first year by the presence of salient landmarks directly marking target locations. Additional variables that have proven important include the environment in which testing occurs and the presence of training trials from the infant's initial location. The significance to the child of the object whose location is being noted has not been found to have an impact. What is still needed is investigaton of how all these variables interact. Perhaps, for example, the use of the mother as the hidden object would facilitate dependence on landmarks. In addition attention needs to be directed toward discovery of the correlates of spatial orientation. Is successful orientation at an early age the result of advanced cognitive development, freedom of exploration in the home, or the presence of sibs? Knowledge of these correlates may help us explain the individual differences invariably seen among the subjects in these studies.

Conclusion

The literature pertaining to visual perception in infants is really too extensive to be covered adequately in one review chapter, let alone in one subsection of such a chapter. Although we have done our best to highlight the most recent important findings in the field, some interesting issues had to be sacrificed to space limitations. That is the reason why, for example, the topics of color vision and face perception were neglected. Research is progressing on both these fronts, but in-depth discussions just could not be included.

Readers interested in color perception are urged to consult two excellent reviews by Bernstein (1978a) and Werner and Wooten (1979). Although these authors disagree on the extent and organization of color vision in infants, they do agree that at least dichromatic vision is present as early as two months of age. Given this foundation, researchers are now exploring the role color vision plays in infant perception—particularly how it affects what infants look at and what they retain. Recent relevant articles include Bornstein (1978b, 1979), Burnham and Day (1979), and Kessen and Bornstein (1978).

A review of the face perception literature is available in Cohen et al. (1979). Their conclusion is that the face has no special status at birth; it is merely one complex pattern among many. Development of the ability to differentiate among faces is now a major concern among researchers. Recent articles relevant to this issue include Fagan (1978), Fagen and Shepherd (1979), Fagan and Singer (1979), and Watson, Hayes, Vietze, and Becker (1979).

AUDITORY PERCEPTION

Anatomy and Embryology

The adult ear consists of three major sections. The external ear serves to funnel sound waves from the external environment to the eardrum or tympanic membrane. The canal through which the sounds are transmitted also introduces resonant frequencies. In the middle ear, vibrations of the tympanic membrane are transferred through a series of bony ossicles, the malleus, incus, and stapes. The footplate of the stapes, in turn, impinges on a membranous structure, the oval window, and causes it to vibrate and set up fluid waves in the inner ear. Since there is a considerable energy loss when sound vibrations in air encounter water, the middle ear serves as an impedance matching device. The two main factors involved in overcoming the energy loss include (1) the lever arrangement of the ossicles which serves to increase the forcefulness of the vibrations and more importantly (2) the ratio of the area of the tympanic membrane to that of the stapes footplate or oval window. The inner ear functions to transform the movements of the stapedial footplate (and oval window) into fluid vibrations. The fluid waves are transduced into neural activity as a result of shearing forces acting on the sensory receptor cells (called hair cells) found in the cochlea of the inner ear (organ of Corti). Fibers of the acoustic nerve then carry the output from these receptors to various parts of the central nervous system.

From this very superficial introduction to the structure and function of the ear, it can be seen that a number of structural factors in development could be relevant to an understanding of auditory development. For example changes in the length of the external ear canal may shift the resonance frequencies produced. Residual mesenchymal tissue in the middle ear cavity could reduce the efficiency of vibration transfer in the middle ear, differential growth rates of the tympanic membrane and stapes footplate could relate to changing auditory thresholds, or hair cell maturation may be incomplete. These factors have been summarized very well by Hecox (1975) and will only be briefly reiterated here.

Although formation of external ear structures begins early in embryonic life, growth continues postnatally through puberty. The tympanic membrane reaches adult position and dimensions by the age of one year. In the middle ear the ossicles appear at about seven weeks of gestation and reach their final size by six to eight months of gestation. There has been disagreement about the relative freedom of movement of the ossicles. Embryological studies suggest that connective tissue in the middle ear cavity is not completely resorbed until some time after birth, giving rise to the notation of an abnormally stiffened middle ear function in neonates. Keith (1973, 1975), however, tested middle ear function in neonates and found capacities similar to those in older children. The middle ear cavity appeared free of mucus or other fluids within a few hours of birth. Keith's results suggest that any unresorbed connective tissue that may remain in the cavity is probably not playing a major role in any hearing impairment at birth.

The middle ear cavity, however, does continue to elongate for a period after birth. Thus developmental changes in the size of the external and middle ear cavities probably produce shifts in their resonating characteristics, and the impedance matching function of the middle ear could be altered by the relative area changes in the tympanic membrane and stapedial footplate.

Major structural features of the inner ear are discernible by six months of gestation. There are several postnatal changes in the organ of Corti. Bredberg (1968) observed that the number of hair cells in the newborn is approximately the same as in the adult, but he also observed that the outermost row of hair cells matures last and is not complete by birth. Bredberg also reports that the most basal portion of the cochlea may not be fully mature at birth. Johnsson and Hawkins (1972) found evidence of hair cell loss in the basal turn of the cochlea of newborn and infants and suggests that the high tone loss usually associated with aging may even begin in utero. According to Hecox (1975), development of the auditory nerve in humans is incompletely understood but apparently starts early and is well myelinated in the human newborn. At the level of the inferior colliculus, however, there is evidence that "immature" myelination patterns exist in the neonate.

Prenatal Responses

Auditory responses in the fetus and neonate have recently been reviewed by Bench (1978) and Bench and Mentz (1975). Since the early studies of Sontag and Wallace (1935), it has been generally agreed that the fetus can respond to auditory stimuli. In spite of the inherent difficulties of stimulating and recording responses in the human fetus in utero, there is evidence that a variety of auditory stimuli will elicit movement and heartrate acceleration before birth (Bench, 1978).

By taking advantage of the accessibility of the fetal scalp during birth, Scibetta, Rosen, Hochberg, and Chik (1971) developed a method for measuring fetal EEG changes in response to sound stimuli. Electrodes were placed on the fetal scalp during labor to record EEG changes in response to audiofrequency stimuli administered via a small transducer positioned alongside the fetal ear, thus enabling the experiment to proceed without obstruction by maternal structures. Their results suggested that fetal EEG responses to sound stimuli are similar to that of the neonate.

Neonatal Responses

There is a vast literature relating to the auditory responses of neonates. Studies of auditory stimuli can be divided into two broad categories, physiological and behavioral, based on the nature of the response being measured. The goal of many of the studies has been to determine intensity and frequency thresholds at birth.

Physiological Responses. In these studies changes in various physiological parameters are measured following presentation of an auditory stimulus. Earlier studies in this area, reviewed by Spears and Hohle (1967), examined changes in respiration rate and skin resistance. More recent studies have focused on electrophysiological responses located in three areas: (1) the electrocardiographic (ECG) or cardiac response; (2) measurement of middle and inner ear function including acoustic impedance, tympanometry, and the electrocochleographic response, and (3) the electroencephalographic (EEG) response.

The cardiac response to auditory stimuli has generally been interpreted in relation to two reflex systems be-

lieved to reflect how a stimulus is processed. Sokolov (1963) described two general reflex systems operating in response to stimulation: (1) the *defensive reflex,* which functions to limit the effects of the stimulation and to protect the organism and (2) the *orienting reflex,* which occurs in reponse to novel or interesting stimuli that convey information to the organism. Cardiac acceleration is usually viewed as part of the defensive or protective reflex, whereas cardiac deceleration is usually associated with the orienting reflex (Graham & Clifton, 1966; Graham & Jackson, 1970).

In contrast to infants two months of age and older for whom heartrate deceleration predominates, the response of neonates to most auditory stimuli is reported to be heartrate acceleration. Recently, however, Berg and Berg (1979) critically reviewed the literature dealing with neonatal cardiac responses and concluded that it is possible to demonstrate deceleration in neonates, albeit with much more difficulty. They cite two important conditions that need to be satisfied. One important parameter is the state of the subject. Sleeping infants ranging in age from neonates to four months of age have a predominantly accelerative cardiac response, whereas sustained decelerative responses generally can be elicited from alert infants under appropriate conditions (Berg, Berg, & Graham, 1971; Jackson, Kantowitz, & Graham, 1971; Lewis, Bartels, & Goldberg, 1967; Rewey, 1973). One of the other important conditions is the nature of the auditory stimulus, especially the intensity, rise time, and whether or not the stimulus is continuous or pulsed. Generally decelerative responses to auditory stimuli in infants less than six weeks of age have been observed only when stimuli were intermittent (Berg & Berg, 1979).

Physiological changes in middle and inner ear ("end-organ") function can be measured by techniques such as acoustic impedance, tympanometry, and stapedial reflexes or by the recording of electrical activity of the hair cells of the cochlea (the cochlear microphonic). Details of the methods and interpretation of tympanograms have been reviewed by Feldman (1976). Measurement by Keith (1973, 1975) of acoustic compliance of the tympanic membrane, tympanometry, and acoustic impedance established that both newborns and older infants have normal middle ear pressures and mobility. The presence of a stapedial reflex in newborns, the contraction of the stapedius muscle in response to sound, was only inconsistently observed by Keith (1973), apparently because it was sometimes masked by a generalized body movement. Lamb and Dunckel (1976) have reviewed the use of reflexes and tympanograms in neonatal, infant, and child auditory screening procedures. Detailed studies of tympanometry in normal neonates have also been carried out by Himelfarb, Popelka, and Shanon (1979).

Another type of electrophysiological measure used in evaluating the auditory response is the electroencephalogram (EEG) based on the recording of small electrical potentials generated by the activity of the nervous system. EEG data are usually recorded from electrodes placed on the scalp and reflect variations in the electrical potentials in underlying regions of the brain. These variations give rise to waveforms that can be analyzed with respect to frequency, amplitude, time characteristics, and spatial distribution (Eisenberg, 1976). Changes in waveform associated with different types of sensory stimuli are referred to as the *sensory evoked potential* (SEP) and are believed to result from the sequential activation of nuclei and neural pathways as the evoked response travels through the brain. The particular wave form associated with an auditory stimulus is called the *auditory (or acoustic) evoked response* (AER), and clinical procedures for measuring AER are sometimes referred to as *electroencephalic response audiometry* (ERA) (Eisenberg, 1976). The term *auditory evoked potential* (AEP) is also used by some investigators. Auditory brainstem potentials are a result of the electrical activity generated in the auditory pathway in its course through the brain (Starr, Amlie, Martin, & Saunders, 1977).

The components of the AER include an early, brainstem evoked response (0–10 msec latency); a middle response (10–50 msec latency), and a late, long-latency (50–500 msec) response, also known as the cortical evoked response (Picton, Hillyard, Krausz, & Galambos, 1974). Because of the small amplitudes involved in the AER, the recordings use computer averaging techniques to sample the activity at the electrodes for a period of time following each stimulus. The potentials are divided into seven waveforms. Wave 1 is believed to represent the action potential of the auditory nerve; Wave 2, the activity of the cochlear nuclei; Wave 3, the activity of the superior olivary nuclei; and Waves 4 and 5, the activity of the inferior colliculus. The precise origins of Waves 6 and 7 remain to be established.

Recordings of brainstem responses in premature and term, newborn, and older infants have shown that the auditory system of these groups is immature compared to that of the adult. Hecox and Galambos (1974) reported a developmental trend toward decreased latency of Wave 5 with increasing age, adult latencies appearing by about 12 to 18 months of age. It was suggested that continued myelination of the neural pathway may have been responsible for the increased impulse conduction. Salamy, McKean, and Buda (1975) also compared brainstem evoked potentials in newborns, young infants, and adults and observed a decrease in latency from birth to adulthood. Furthermore they found that different components of the response matured at different rates. Peripheral transmission, defined as the time from stimulus initiation to the peak of Wave 1, attained functional maturity during the first few months of life. In contrast central transmission, defined as the time difference between the peaks of Waves 1 and 5, did not mature until later. Salamy and McKean (1976) further refined these initial observations and reported that auditory processes related to peripheral transmission reached adult latency levels by six weeks of age. Central transmission through the brainstem did not reach adult values until about one year of age.

Schulman-Galambos and Galambos (1975) measured brainstem auditory evoked responses in premature and term infants (34 to 42 weeks gestational age) and found that as age increased there was a systematic decrease in the latency of the response at each sound intensity level. They also observed that at a given age the latency of response increased with decreasing stimulus intensity. Starr et al. (1977) studied responses in infants from 25 to 44 weeks of gestational age and found that reliable components in response to a 65 db sound level click stimulus could first be recorded at about 28 weeks of gestational age. Decreasing latencies with increasing maturation were once again observed, this time with a maximal rate of change between weeks 28 and 34. However auditory function was present earlier than 28 weeks as evidenced by a response to a signal of increased intensity.

The importance of the AER for identifying auditory problems was demonstrated by Schulman-Galambos and Galambos (1979). The infants they studied included some with severe sensorineural hearing loss, all of whom could be identified as a result of their brainstem evoked auditory responses. Abnormal AER have also been found in infants 3 to 12 months of age suffering from severe malnutrition (Barnet, Weiss, Sotillo, Ohlrich, Shkurovich, & Cravioto, 1978). Thus the AER appears to be useful for clinical evaluations throughout the first year (cf., Galambos & Hecox, 1977).

The components of the AER that follow the early, brainstem evoked response are divided into mid-latency ($\simeq$ 10–50 msec) and late or long-latency (50–500 msec) responses (Picton et al., 1974). In contrast to the studies on the brainstem component, relatively little attention has been devoted to the middle component. One exception is Engel (1971) who studied middle and late components of the AER in infants and found repeatable middle components in only 3 of 24 infants tested. Subsequently McRandle, Smith, and Goldstein (1974) elicited stable, repeatable middle components with click stimuli from normal sleeping newborns. Mendel, Adkinson, and Harker (1977) recorded middle components of the AER in response to tonal stimuli in 18 infants at one, four, and eight months of age during natural sleep. The infant responses obtained by McRandle et al. and Mendel et al. were similar to those obtained from adult subjects, except that amplitudes were smaller than those of adults. In one final study Wolf and Goldstein (1978) reported that latencies of the middle component decreased and amplitudes increased as the magnitude of the stimulus increased, a situation similar to that for adults.

The long-latency component (50–500 msec) of the AER is sometimes referred to as the *cortical evoked response* (CER). Because of the apparent lack of clinical utility, relatively few studies have been carried out on infants. What evidence there is suggests that infants have higher thresholds of response than adults (Barnet & Goodwin, 1965; Rapin & Graziani, 1967: Taguchi, Picton, Orpin, & Goodman, 1969) and that latencies decrease with age (Barnet, Olrich, Weiss, & Shanks, 1975; Olrich, Barnet, Weiss, & Shanks, 1978).

Behavioral Responses. According to Bench (1978), it is generally agreed that the most reliably observed behavioral response in the neonate to a loud, complex stimulus is a gross startle or jumping reaction. Less complex and quieter sound stimuli elicit milder motor responses. The auropalpebral reflex (reflex blinking when the eyes are open or tightening of the eyelids when the eyes are closed) has also been frequently observed in response to loud sound or to stimuli with sudden onsets, such as click stimuli. Other responses include kicking, turning of the head or eyes, and either onset or cessation of crying. The startle response of neonates reported in the literature has typically been described as a Moro or Moro-like reflex, thus implying that the response involves symmetrical movements primarily of the shoulders, arms, elbows, and fingers. Bench, Collyer, Langford, and Toms (1972), in a detailed comparison of the sound evoked startle response and the Moro reflex, found that the sound evoked startle was a gross, sudden outburst of movement involving most or all of the limbs in a comparatively diffuse manner. Accordingly the authors concluded that the term *Moro reflex* has been somewhat inappropriately applied to neonatal auditory responses.

More recently studies have centered on discriminating between stimulus-response activity and ongoing, spontaneous activity of the infant (see Eisenberg, 1976, for a review). Efforts have been made to measure more carefully and control various characteristics of the sound stimuli employed, to assess the prestimulus psychophysiological state of the infant, and to assess the physical and physiological factors of the infant's testing environment (e.g., Bench, Collyer, Mentz, & Wilson, 1976). Recent evidence has indicated that neonates generally are not very responsive behaviorally to pure tones or to narrow-band noise. In contrast responsivity is reliably elicited by relatively loud, broad-spectrum noise stimuli.

Intensity Thresholds. The threshold of response is the minimum level of stimulus intensity required to elicit a response. Responsivity is not dependent on intensity alone; variations in stimulus frequency and bandwidth also play a role. Although threshold of intensity can be ascertained either behaviorally or electrophysiologically, recent research has emphasized the latter as the more sensitive of the two types of measures.

Brainstem auditory evoked potentials are reliably elicited in subjects ranging from prematurely born infants to adults and appear to be independent of the the the physiological or psychological state of the subject (Picton & Hillyard, 1974; Schulman-Galambos & Galambos, 1979). Upon recording brainstem AER's to click stimuli filtered beteen 150 and 1500 H_z, Schulman-Galambos and Galambos (1979) reported that threshold sensitivity in sleeping newborns resembled that of adults. While the normal adults produced brainstem AER's to clicks of 5 to 10 db, the normal newborns, all tested within 72 hours of birth, responded to stimuli of 10 to 20 db. Similar thresholds were reported by Hecox (1975), who obtained recognizable brainstem AER's to 27 db clicks in neonates compared to 20 db for older children (up to three years of age), and 10 db for adults. Measurement of brainstem AER's to click stimuli in sleeping premature infants of various ages have indicated that the responses first appear at about week 28 of gestation and progressively approach adult threshold values near term (Starr et al., 1977; Schulman-Galambos & Galambos, 1979).

Middle components of the averaged auditory evoked responses have been recorded in sleeping infants one, four, and eight months of age by Mendel, Adkinson, and Harker (1977). Tone bursts centered at 1000 H_z were presented at intensities ranging from 15 to 60 db. Responses were reported in all infants at 60 db, in 75 percent of the infants at 30 db, and in 18 percent of the subjects at 15 db. Also employing tonal stimuli at 1000 H_z at low intensities, Wolf and Goldstein (1978) studied middle component AER's obtained from five neonates ranging from birth to four days of age. An identifiable response was reported in all subjects to intensities as low as

30 db, and three of the neonates responded to 10 db level.

Barnet and Goodwin (1965) recorded cortical evoked potentials (the long-latency component of the AER) in two- to four-day-old sleeping neonates upon presentation of a series of clicks at intensities ranging from 35 to 65 db. All subjects produced an identifiable response at 45 db, while 75 percent of the infants responded at 35 db. Taguchi et al. (1969) found sleep-state dependency of cortical evoked responses in neonates when employing tone burst stimuli. Infants 4 to 12 days old tested during active and quiet sleep had the lowest thresholds during quiet sleep, approximately 30 db. Intensity thresholds for cortical evoked responses have been found to be a function of sleep state in adults as well (Weitzman & Kremen, 1965).

Studies examining the heartrate responses in infants have generally reported higher and more variable threshold values than those reported for auditory evoked responses. Bartoshuk (1964) found significant responses to intensities of 48 to 58 db for a 1000 H_z tonal stimulus. Consistent with psychoacoustic work with adults, Bartoshuk also found that the logarithm of the cardiac response was linearly related to intensity. Steinschneider, Lipton, and Richmond (1966) presented nine newborns with broad-spectrum noise stimuli of 55 to 100 db and found all subjects responded to 55 db. In addition the magnitude of the cardiac response increased with increasing sound pressure level, suggesting the neonates were capable of stimulus intensity discrimination. In contrast Schulman (1973), employing a relatively strict response criterion, estimated the threshold for 500 to 3000 H_z to be at 90 db for newborns.

In summary electrophysiological measures based on the AER have yielded intensity thresholds from 10 db to 45 db at birth, compared to the norm of 5 db to 10 db for adults. Using heartrate measures the estimates have been slightly higher, 48 db to 55 db. The median threshold overall is about 20 to 30 db, with important individual differences occurring among infants.

Speech Perception

Having established during the 1960s that infants could indeed hear a wide variety of sounds, interest in the 1970s turned to a particular category of sounds—those characterizing human speech. The time was ripe for such a shift. Interest in language acquisition was beginning to surge as a result of reinterpretations of classic positions (e.g., Bloom, 1970); with this interest came the suspicion that if 12- and 18-month-old infants were more linguistically sophisticated than had been assumed, perhaps the same might be true of even younger infants. The lateralization literature was also a stimulus. The decade of the 1970s was characterized by great interest in the differential functioning of the two hemispheres of the brain, especially the localization of language in the left hemisphere. The question of the developmental history of this specialization naturally arose. Developmental psychologists also turned with great enthusiasm in the 1970s to the ontogeny of the attachment bond between mother and infant. Although the emphasis was on emotional components, increasing attention was given to nonemotional facets of behavior, including maternal speech, which might help draw mother to infant and infant to mother in reciprocal patterns. Finally the availability of better techniques for assessing infant perception, particularly the habituation paradigm, provided researchers with much needed tools to help in the search for answers to the new questions being asked.

What was the consequence of all this interest in infant speech perception? Perhaps the basic discovery so far has been that from their earliest days infants are quite sensitive to the acoustical patterns characteristic of speech and tend to respond differently to speech and nonspeech signals. A physiological foundation for language sensitivity this early in life has been provided by a growing body of evidence indicating that, contrary to previous theory (Lenneberg, 1967), hemispheric asymmetries exist even in early infancy. Many indices have been used to demonstrate this lateralization: differences in auditory evoked potentials across the hemispheres (Molfese, Freeman, & Palermo, 1975; Molfese & Molfese, 1979), difference in EEG distributions across the hemispheres (Davis & Wada, 1977; Gardiner & Walter, 1977), heartrate habituation and dichotic listening (Glanville, Best, & Levenson, 1977), and anatomical examination (Wada, Clarke, & Hamm, 1975; Witelson & Pallie, 1973). Molfese et al. (1975) found asymmetries in auditory evoked potentials across the two hemispheres for words and nonsense syllables when compared to nonspeech stimuli (white noise, musical chords). More recently Molfese and Molfese (1979) have attempted to discover the exact nature of the acoustical information in speech to which the left hemisphere is differentially sensitive. Newborn infants were presented with consonant-vowel combinations that varied acoustically in terms of their second formant transitions ([b] vs. [g]) and formant structure. Measurement of auditory evoked potential in the two hemispheres indicated a mechanism in the left hemisphere uniquely sensitive to the second formant transition information and mechanisms in both hemispheres sensitive to formant structure. Even at birth the left hemisphere is more heavily engaged than the right hemisphere in processing acoustical patterns characteristic of human speech.

Behavioral manifestations of the special status of speech sounds are also present from birth. On a general level research indicates lower thresholds for sounds within the range (1000 to 3000 H_z) most important for speech perception (Eisenberg, 1965, 1979; Hoversten & Moncur, 1969). Greater sensitivity at birth to the wideband sounds typical of speech in comparison to pure sine waves has also been reported (Hutt, Hutt, Lenard, Von Bernuth, & Muntjewerff, 1968). On a more specific level Eisenberg (1976, 1979) cites evidence from her own extensive work with newborns indicating different behavioral reactions to patterned and nonpatterned acoustical signals. Constant, nonpatterned signals, such as tones and band noises, elicit mostly gross motor responses (either increasing or decreasing) and heartrate acceleration. They often result in eye widening but very seldom elicit vocalization. In contrast, patterned signals, including ascending and descending tonal sequences and speech, elicit more fine-grained motor reflexes (e.g., facial grimacing or displacement of single digits), crying or

cessation of crying, pupillary dilation, and visual search.

Eisenberg (1979) also reports that heartrate data indicate differences in reaction even within the category of patterned signals. While tonal sequences elicit acceleration followed by deceleration, synthetic speech sounds are usually followed instead by deceleration. Response latencies are also considerably longer for speech than tonal patterns, even when measured with auditory evoked potentials.

The production of fine-grained motor behavior in reaction to speech has also been noted by Condon and Sander (1974). They also report that the motor movements tend to be timed to coincide with major fluctuations in the speech signals. They describe the rhythmic relationship as an entrainment process—the infant moving in involuntary response to verbal stimulation. The rhythmic movements they observed occurred in response to both male and female voices, both English and Chinese utterances, and both live and taped presentations. The last finding is significant because it indicates that the response was to the acoustical signal itself rather than to visual or tactile stimuli from the speaker. Since disconnected vowel and tapping sounds did not elicit any rhythmic movements, Condon and Sander concluded that they had uncovered further evidence of special sensitivity to speech or speech-like sounds during infancy, a sensitivity which may facilitate the acquisition of very basic linguistic structuring. The possibility has also been raised that this entrainment process plays a significant role in attachment formation by providing mothers with positive reinforcement for verbal interactions with their infants (Klaus & Kennell, 1976).

Having established that infants differentiate between speech (or at least speech-like) and nonspeech signals, what evidence is there of discrimination within the broad category of speech? Fortunately quite a lot of evidence bearing on this question has accumulated (see Eimas, 1975b, 1978, and Eimas & Tartter, 1979, for thorough reviews). In a groundbreaking study by Moffitt (1971), a heartrate habituation-dishabituation procedure was used to show that 4½- to 5½-month-old infants could distinguish between two synthetic speech sounds differing only in place of articulation ([ba] vs. [ga]). In a subsequent study Morse (1972) demonstrated the same discrimination at an even younger age (1½ months) using high amplitude sucking procedures. Since these early studies the number of place of articulation distinctions young infants have been shown capable of making has grown to include [ma] vs. [na] (Eimas & Miller, 1978), [bae] vs. [dae] (Eimas, 1974), [d] vs. [g], and [m] vs. [g] occurring at the end of syllables (Jusczyk, 1977) and [b] vs. [g] occurring in the middle of polysyllabic patterns (Jusczyk & Thompson, 1978). Infants have also been found capable of discriminating speech sounds differing on the voicing dimension. The list of discriminations in this case includes [pa] vs. [ba] (Eimas et al., 1971), [s] vs. [z], and [t] vs. [d] occurring at the end of syllables (Eilers, 1977; Eilers, Wilson, & Moore, 1977), and a prevoiced vs. voiced distinction that adult English ignores (Eimas, 1975b). Distinctions of other types reported in the literature to date include [ra] vs. [la] (Eimas, 1975a), [ba] vs. [ma] (Eimas & Miller, 1978), [ba] vs. [fa], and [sa] vs. [sha] (Eilers, 1977; Eilers & Minifie, 1975; Eilers, Wilson, &

Moore, 1977), and various vowel distinctions (Swoboda et al., 1976; Trehub, 1973b). Five-month-old infants have even been shown capable of distinguishing a synthesized from a naturally produced [baba], attending significantly longer to the latter than the former (Trehub & Curran, 1979). Given this impressive list of discriminations, one wonders if there are any distinctions infants are *not* capable of making. There are a few. Eilers and her associates (Eilers, 1977; Eilers & Minifie, 1975) reported failure to distinguish [sa] from [za] until 6 months and [θa] from [fa] until 12 months.

The list of distinctions available to the child in the first three months is quite impressive. However, does this ability to make such fine-grained distinctions indicate anything more than keen auditory capacities? Does it, for example, indicate that the acoustic sounds comprising speech are receiving differential treatment in comparison to nonspeech sounds? The discrimination literature alone cannot tell us. Several related types of evidence do in fact suggest that speech and nonspeech signals are processed in qualitatively different ways. In one of the earliest demonstrations, Morse (1972) found that the ability of his 1½-month-old infants to distinguish [ba] from [ga] depended on whether the sounds were presented in a speech or nonspeech context. Parallel findings for adults have also been reported (Mattingly, Liberman, Syrdal, & Halwes, 1971).

Most of the other support for the theory of a special speech mode comes from studies of categorical perception of speech sounds. *Categorical perception* refers to the tendency for adults to divide acoustical signals in speech into categories (e.g., [pa] vs. [ba]) and to treat those signals falling within a category as more similar to each other than to signals falling into other categories. This seems reasonable until one realizes that the acoustical signals upon which the categories are imposed actually constitute a *continuous* series of values along various dimensions—e.g., voice onset time (VOT). Consequently a stimulus from one category (e.g., −40 msec VOT) might differ from a stimulus in its own category (e.g., −100 msec VOT) by the same amount of VOT (60 msec) that it differs from a stimulus in another category (e.g., +20 msec VOT). Yet because of categorical perception, the equal acoustical differences result in vast perceptual differences, both the first stimuli being perceived as [pa] and the second stimulus as [ba]. Since categorical perception tends not to characterize nonspeech sounds, demonstrations of categorical perception in infants would support the existence of special processing of speech.

Does categorical perception exist in infancy? The first affirmative answer came from Eimas et al. (1971) using categories based on VOT, infants as young as one month of age, and a high amplitude sucking procedure to produce a habituation-dishabituation situation. The stimuli all differed by 20 msec of VOT; three were perceived by adults as [b] (VOT values of −20, 0, and +20 msec), and three were perceived as [p] (VOT values of +40, +60, and +80). After two minutes of response habituation with one stimulus, a different stimulus was presented, and any response recovery was noted. The results produced strong evidence of categorical responding. Recovery was significantly stronger to stimuli from another category than to stimuli from within the same category. Eimas (1975a) found the same type of evidence for cate-

gorical perception of the alveolar consonant categories [d] and [t], and Eimas (1974) demonstrated that categorical perception exists for two- to three-month-olds based on place of articulation ([dae]) vs. [gae]) as well as VOT. Perhaps most impressive were the results of the second experiment by Eimas (1974) in which a component of each speech sound used in the study (representatives of [bae] and [gae] was isolated and used as a nonspeech stimulus. The component in each case was the very brief, second formant transition of the total acoustic signal. Despite the fact that this component is a crucial contributor to the speech sounds, its isolation resulted in an absence of categorical perception. Even at two to three months, it seems that acoustical signals comprising speech are treated differently from even very similar nonspeech patterns. Other demonstrations of categorical perception include fairly convincing evidence for [r] vs. [l] (Eimas, 1975a), and the prevoiced-voiced distinction of Thai (Lasky, Syrdal-Lasky, & Klein, 1975).

The evidence discussed so far suggests that the infant comes into the world already well prepared to process acoustic patterns characteristic of human speech, at least at a phonological level. There is also reason to suspect, however, that at some point down the road the specific language environment in which the child is reared has an influence on the perceptual capacities just described. The best evidence so far comes from a study by Trehub (1973a) in which infants from English-speaking families were found capable of discriminating a stridency contrast ([a] vs. [ʒa]) not found in English. English-speaking adults, in contrast, reported great difficulty in making this same distinction. Although more studies are needed which directly contrast infants and adults from the same language environments, Trehub's results suggest that the language environment may operate in part to diminish rather than enhance discriminatory capacities. Once the existence of such a shaping process is more fully established, attention will likely turn to determining exactly when and precisely how the process proceeds.

In summary the evidence to date suggests that infants quite early in life are sensitive to the acoustical patterns characterizing human speech. Even at birth their motor responses and heartrate reactions differ depending on the patterned versus nonpatterned nature of the signal, and by one to three months they are perceiving many speech signals categorically. Furthermore a physical foundation for all these skills is already present at birth in the form of hemispheric asymmetry. Many important questions, however, still remain. Although we know the infant is in a sense primed for speech, we do not yet know the precise role these early perceptual skills play in language comprehension or production nor the extent of the impact of the specific language environment in which the infant is reared. Also to be determined is the contribution this sensitivity to speech makes to other aspects of development such as attachment, auditory-visual coordination, and perhaps even object permanence. Finally the question of individual differences among infants needs to be addressed. Some sex differences have already been reported in the lateralization literature (Molfese & Molfese, 1979), and it seems likely that other differences exist as well, for example between preterm and full-term infants. Since excitement seems to build with each new discovery in this area, we should not have long to wait for some answers.

TASTE PERCEPTION

Four primary taste qualities are generally considered to exist for adults: sweet, sour, salt, and bitter. The sense of taste is mediated by groups of cells (taste buds) located primarily on small raised areas (papillae) on the upper surface of the tongue. Other areas sensitive to taste include the palate at the top of the throat, the epiglottis at the back of the throat, and even the mucous membranes of the cheeks and floor of the mouth. In order to be an effective taste stimulus, a substance must be soluble in water (or an equivalent medium such as saliva). While in solution with water, a substance can then come into contact with the taste receptors. Taste, however, is not the only sensation to which the oral cavity is sensitive. Also present are pain, pressure, and temperature receptors that provide information on the texture and consistency of substances placed there (Brown & Deffenbacher, 1979).

Anatomical research has shown that taste buds have a more extensive distribution in neonates and children than in adults (Parker, 1922), suggesting that the sense of taste may be well developed even before birth. Based on microscopic morphological examination of tongue specimens from fetuses of six weeks gestational age to near term, Bradley and Stearn (1967) concluded that taste buds were mature enough to function at about 13 to 15 weeks of gestation. A more pessimistic note was voiced by Spears and Hohrle (1967) who argued that it is unlikely that adequate stimulation of taste receptors would occur in utero since the source of stimulation (amniotic fluid) is essentially unchanging during pregnancy. A large body of recent evidence, however, has clearly shown that amniotic fluid is a very complex, constantly changing chemical environment (Fairweather & Eskes, 1978). The mouth of the fetus opens at approximately 9.5 weeks of gestation, with tongue movements and swallowing observed somewhat later (Humphrey, 1978). Thus there is every reason to suspect that adequate stimulation of taste buds could take place in the fetus. This view is further supported by the observation that the addition of saccharin to the amniotic fluid of fetuses near term results in increased swallowing (Windle, 1940).

It has been suggested that taste buds in different parts of the upper digestive tract may have different functions (Bradley, Cheal, & Kim, 1980). Recently evidence has been provided that indicates the epiglottis is chemosensitive in the newborn monkey, calf, lamb, and pig (Downing & Lee, 1975; Johnson, Robinson, & Salisbury, 1973). Various solutions, including water, cow's milk, and glucose, interrupted breathing when introduced into the larynx of neonatal animals, while a saltwater solution did not. These investigators suggest that the taste buds on the laryngeal surface of the epiglottis may function as specialized receptors mediating protective laryngeal reflexes. If this is the case, the epiglottal taste buds are involved in a functional role different from that of oral taste buds.

The findings of Johnson and Salisbury (1975, 1977) provide further support for the existence of specialized taste receptors in the human neonate for the prevention of inhalation of fluids when swallowing. Their studies concerned effects of different feeding solutions on patterns of sucking, swallowing, and breathing. They found that when cow's milk or water was ingested the fluids were not inhaled; however, when saltwater was introduced, the infant's breathing was poorly suppressed. In a separate experiment four-day-old neonates fed breast milk were observed to have undisturbed patterns of breathing during ingestion, while neonates fed artificial milk exhibited disturbed breathing, often markedly so, during ingestion. No disturbance was observed in the sucking patterns during either feeding situation. While inhalation of fluid into the lungs should be quite minimal for infants fed natural milk or water, Johnson and Salisbury suggest that inhalation may occur when neonates are fed artificial fluids containing critical concentrations of salt. Moreover they conclude that taste is an important component of the reflex defense mechanism of the upper airway during ingestion.

Research on taste perception in infants up to the 1950s, as reviewed by Peiper (1963) and Lipsitt (1977), focused on whether young infants can detect and discriminate various taste stimuli. Equivocal findings emerged from these studies due, at least in part, to a lack of standardization of stimuli, apparatus, and methods. As noted by Lipsitt (1977), interpretation is further complicated by the fact that any kind of stimulation of the oral cavity and lips can evoke sucking behavior. Some aspect of sucking or mouthing behavior was observed in a majority of these studies and was considered to reflect neonatal reaction to taste properties of the stimuli. Unfortunately it remained unclear whether the infants were actually differentiating the four taste qualities. Generally the evidence from early studies suggested that neonates react positively to sweet stimuli and negatively to sour, salt, and bitter stimuli.

In order to observe the effects of differing taste qualities on the intake of fluids by infants, recent studies have involved measurements of both sucking behavior and amount of fluid ingested. It has been demonstrated that infants from birth to four days of age ingest more sweetened fluid than water and that consumption increases with increasing sugar concentration (Desor, Maller, & Turner, 1973; Engen, Lipsitt, & Peck, 1974). In addition, Desor et al. (1973) found that neonates will respond differentially to various types of sugar, with fructose and sucrose being more effective in increasing ingestion than lactose or glucose. Similar patterns of preferences have emerged from intake measurements of infants 5 to 11 and 20 to 28 weeks of age (Desor, Maller & Greene, 1977). Comparable sugar preferences have been reported for adults as well (Moskowitz, 1971). Nisbett and Gurwitz (1970), who controlled for possible confounding effects of viscosity and texture, found birthweight-related preferences in neonates when measuring ingestion of sweetened and unsweetened formula. Neonates of heavy birthweight consumed a significantly greater amount of sweetened formula, but only slightly more unsweetened formula, than infants of medium or light birthweight. Their data also indicated that female neonates consumed significantly more sweetened formula than males.

In a similar vein, Engen, Lipsitt, and Robinson (1978) observed neonates from birth to four days of age and reported a significant correlation between birthweight and rate of sucking for a sugar solution. By measuring the total number of sucks per minute, they demonstrated that heavy infants sucked a sweet solution at faster rates than did light infants. Birthweight was found to affect the total number of sucks per minute for all fluids to some extent, although its greatest effect was on the intake of sweet fluid. Finally, though heavy mothers tended to give birth to heavy infants, it was found that the weight of the infant, not the weight of the mother, was related to greater responsiveness to sweet stimulation. These findings are consistent with Nisbett and Gurwitz's (1970) data on ingestion, except that no significant sex difference in amount of sweetened fluids ingested was observed.

As a result of increased understanding of the underlying organization of sucking in general, the measurements of total intake and sucking frequency discussed before have been supplanted by more detailed observations of sucking behavior. (The interested reader is referred to Crook, 1979, for a complete discussion of the literature concerning the organization and control of infant sucking.) The sucking rhythm of the infant typically consists of a sequence of response bursts separated by resting periods or pauses. Various aspects of the underlying fine structure of the sucking response may be observed in a given period of testing. These include the number of bursts, the average number of sucks within a burst, and the average duration of pause. Still finer analysis may focus on the temporal separation of sucks within a burst. Although this last measure is sometimes described in the literature as the "rate" of sucking, it actually is a measure of within-burst rate only and should not be confused with the absolute frequency of response observed over longer periods involving both bursts and pauses (Crook, 1979). Clarity in the literature might best be achieved if *rate* were used for frequency per unit time (inclusive of pauses) and within-burst rate were referred to as *pace* of sucking (exclusive of pauses).

A longitudinal study by Lipsitt, Reilly, Butcher, and Greenwood (1976) has demonstrated stability in measures of the total number of sucks, burst lengths, and pause durations for undisturbed nonnutritive (dry) sucking by neonates between the second and third days of life. When sucking delivered a 15 percent sucrose solution, the duration of sucking bursts increased, and the number and duration of pauses decreased. Furthermore sucking pace was slower and heartrate faster during sucking for sucrose solution than during nonnutritive sucking.

Nutritive sucking rhythm has also been shown to be sensitive to differences in the sucrose concentration of the fluids being ingested. Crook (1977) compared changes in the response rhythms of separate groups of infants two to five days old who sucked either for water or 5 percent, 10 percent or 15 percent sucrose solutions. Longer bursts and shorter pauses were observed for the greater sucrose concentrations. The within-burst structure of the response was also affected: The fastest pace of response was for water and the 5 percent sucrose solution, while the pace slowed significantly for the greater sucrose concentrations. These results were replicated by Crook and Lipsitt (1976) using a within-subjects comparison of infants two to three days old who sucked for 5 percent or 15

percent sucrose solutions. In addition to sucking rhythm, the heartrate of the infants was monitored. An inverse relationship was found such that increasing the sweetness of the fluid resulted in both a decrease of sucking pace and an increase in heartrate. This heartrate pattern is consistent with the results of Lipsitt et al. (1976) who compared sucking for a single sweet solution with nonnutritive sucking.

It may be concluded from these studies that sweeter fluids increase the total amount of sucking within a given period and sweeter fluids tend to maintain slower within-burst responses. If total intake of fluid reflects taste preference, why does the infant respond more slowly to something it presumably prefers? In all cases the infants received only small and fixed amounts of fluid per suck so that as sucking pace slowed and less effort was exerted heartrate would also be expected to slow. This apparently paradoxical relationship between sucking and heartrate may be due in part to the influence of swallowing on the organization of sucking. Burke (1977), comparing intake of 5 percent and 10 percent sucrose solutions, demonstrated that the frequency of swallowing in neonates two to four days old increased significantly as a function of increasing concentration of sucrose given per suck. It is also possible that slower responding involves more vigorous sucking. Support for this explanation is provided by Nowlis and Kessen (1976) who found that anterior tongue movements of neonates increased in amplitude as concentration of glucose and sucrose increased. It has been suggested that these findings indicate that sweet solutions have positive hedonic properties for neonates and that the various effects of sweet stimulation upon sucking and heartrate may reflect a form of "savoring" (Crook & Lipsitt, 1976; Lipsitt et al., 1976).

There is little recent information available concerning the effects of taste qualities other than sweetness upon sucking rhythm and fluid ingestion. Maller and Desor (1973) fed neonates solutions of salt, urea, and citric acid in weak to moderate concentrations and observed no significant difference in intake compared to water despite the fact that the concentrations were well above adult taste thresholds. In addition the findings of Johnson and Salisbury (1977), discussed previously in terms of taste bud function, indicate that the gross sucking patterns of neonates remain undisturbed during ingestion of saltwater solutions.

Changes in sucking rhythm and total ingestion have been measured most often under experimental conditions in which taste stimuli are contingent upon individual sucks by the infant. More recently Crook (1978) has employed an alternative method in which a minute "pulse" of fluid was presented intraorally to two- to three-day-old infants during the pauses in their nonnutritive (dry) sucking rhythm. Following the delivery of sucrose solution, the next burst of sucking was found to be initiated sooner and to be of longer length than bursts recorded during unstimulated, randomly interspersed control trials. Burst length also increased as the concentration of the sucrose in the solution was increased to a moderate level. Concentrations beyond this level resulted in shortening of the bursts. In contrast to these results for sugar solutions, introduction of any level of salt into the solution resulted in shortening of the bursts. The latency of response, or the time between onset of stimulation and the next suck, was consistently observed to be very short (often within a second of stimulation) for all fluid stimuli investigated compared to control trial latencies. It has been suggested by Crook that response latency is independent of taste stimulation, dependent instead on the tactile properties of the stimulus. Taste properties of the fluid stimulus are then reflected in burst length. Finally Crook has suggested that these results reflect hedonic processes and provide support for the conclusion that even at birth the sweet taste is hedonically positive and the salt taste hedonically negative.

Lateral tongue movements have also been used to assess taste perception. Weiffenbach and Thach (1973) have described such movements in three-day-old neonates presented with small quantities of sugar solutions. Using the tendency of the response to habituate, the investigators demonstrated differential responses by neonates to concentrations of glucose plus water as compared to water alone. Each tongue movement observed was discrete and reflexive in nature, suggesting its potential as a measure for taste discrimination. The sensitivity measure remains uncertain, however, since relatively high concentrations of sucrose were necessary to elicit differential responding.

Stimulation of the tongue with minute quantities of fluid has provided another measurable response. Upon administering small quantities of sweet, sour, and bitter solutions to infants, Steiner (1979) observed changes in facial expressions which differed markedly from those induced by distilled water (the control stimulus). Sweet stimulation led to a retraction of the mouth angles (resembling a smile) and relaxation of the face, followed typically by licking of the upper lip and a burst of sucking movements. Sour stimulation induced protrusion or pursing of the lips, while bitter stimulation led to depression of the mouth angles or arching of the mouth opening. In contrast distilled water induced a quick swallow without any facial expression. These motor reactions were readily elicited from newborns tested within the first hours after birth, prior to exposure to any nutrients or feeding, as well as from neonates three to seven days of age. The sour stimulus was also administered to premature infants who displayed the same lip-pursing reaction observed in the full-term infants. The same changes in facial expressions induced by the three taste stimuli were observed in anencephalic and hydroanencephalic neonates. Autopsies later performed on these developmentally malformed neonates revealed only the brainstem intact, thus indicating that the reflex-like reaction did not require cortical participation. Although these gustofacial reflexes are of considerable interest, the taste solutions used by Steiner were strong, and the question remains whether the measure is sufficiently sensitive for studies of taste discrimination. Finally methodological problems are involved in using facial expressions as an index of taste responsivity since, as Crook (1978) noted, expressions are difficult to scale.

In summary recent evidence is consistent in showing that newborn infants, both term and preterm, are sensitive to taste. Both measures of solution intake and sucking patterns have shown that mild to moderately sweet solutions are preferred over saline solutions and distilled water, with this preference exhibited particularly strongly among heavy birthweight infants. In contrast to sweet solutions reaction to sour and bitter stimuli are negative, at least as assessed through changes in facial expressions. In view of these results it seems safe to conclude with Crook (1979) and Steiner (1979) that the hedonistic aspects of tasting are present at birth; savoring one's food is apparently one of life's earliest pleasures.

OLFACTORY PERCEPTION

The basic physical characteristics that determine whether or not a substance is odorous are not fully known. A substance must first be present as individual molecules in the air; it must be volatile. In order to stimulate the olfactory receptors inside the nose, the volatile molecules must then adhere to the receptors or, perhaps, to the immediately surrounding substances. In order to do so the volatile molecules must be soluble to some extent. Yet substances can meet the necessary requirements of volatility and solubility and not be odorous. Other physical characteristics of a substance, such as chemical composition, are important, although molecular size, composition, and shape have yielded only moderate correlations with odorousness. Given the uncertainty concerning the physical properties necessary for detection of odors, it is hardly surprising that knowledge of the way in which such characteristics might differentially stimulate olfactory receptors remains even more limited.

The olfactory system first appears at about 30 days of gestation with the formation of the nasal placodes, two oval-shaped areas of thickened tissue on either side of the midline of the head (Tuchmann-Duplessis et al., 1975). The placodes rapidly invaginate and differentiate into the olfactory epithelium which contains the neurosensory cells that, in some unknown manner, discriminate among odors. By the fetal period (seventh week) of development, the olfactory epithelium is located in the uppermost reaches of the nasal cavities, and nerve processes have made contact with the olfactory bulbs (the two bulb-shaped structures on the forward ventral surface of the brain) and olfactory areas of the cerebral cortex.

With the opening of the nostrils at about six months of gestation, it is conceivable that fluid currents could pass over the olfactory epithelium bringing with them potentially odorous substances. Whether the neural pathways are functional at this early stage in the human is difficult to determine experimentally. However, developing olfactory neurons of fetal rats, placed in organ cultures, do evoke neurophysiological responses similar to those recorded from adult rats (Farbman & Gesteland, 1975). Indirect evidence of human fetal functioning is provided by Sarnat (1978) who found that both pre- and full-term infants responded to a strong peppermint extract stimulus. Tested during active sleep the infants were observed to initiate sucking, increase general motor activity, or both. Presumably this indicates that, given a sufficiently strong stimulus, even premature infants as young as 28 weeks of age can detect odor.

After birth, of course, air is inspired through the nostrils. The flow of respiratory air generally takes a low pathway through the nasal cavity on its way to the trachea, but a small amount of air (5 to 10 percent of total flow) reaches the area of the olfactory epithelium (Brown

& Deffenbacher, 1979). Currents, set up by the air moving past a series of elevated folds or cochae on the wall of each nasal passage, flow past the neurosensory cells of the olfactory epithelium. If odorous substances are contained in the air in sufficient quantity, the chemicals in some manner stimulate the sensory cells thereby generating an electrical impulse. This impulse is carried via nerve processes to the olfactory bulb and on to olfactory areas of the cerebral cortex.

The literature dealing with olfaction in infancy has been critically reviewed through 1965 by Spears and Hohle (1967) who conclude that studies prior to 1930 were hampered by a lack of both objective response measures and systematic variation of stimulus intensity. A further complication, still present in more recent studies, is the use of test substances considered to be olfactory stimuli which, in fact, are also irritants. The problem arises because the olfactory epithelium also contains the free endings of the trigeminal nerve which are affected by chemical irritants and are independent of the olfactory receptors (Moncrieff, 1967). Historically the term *odor* has been used loosely in the literature to refer to test substances which are olfactory stimulators, irritants of the trigeminal nerve endings, or both. The only general agreement reached in these early studies was that neonates were capable of responding to substances such as ammonia, menthol, and acetic acid and that the responses were largely due to irritation of the trigeminal nerve rather than to stimulation of olfactory receptors. Controversy remained as to whether the infant was capable of responding purely olfactorially to odors at all, let alone capable of discriminating among them. Moncrieff (1955) suggested that both the olfactory and trigeminal systems of the adult are equally sensitive to ammonia, and subsequent researchers appear to have assumed that test substances, such as acetic acid and ammonia, stimulate both systems in infants as well (e.g., Engen, Lipsitt, & Kaye, 1963; Rieser, Yonas, & Wikner, 1976). Unfortunately even substances considered to be "pure" olfactory stimuli, such as phenylethyl alcohol, may actually be activating both sensory nerves when presented in high concentrations (Tucker, 1971).

After a hiatus of nearly 30 years, a series of studies appeared which finally offered clear evidence that neonates do indeed detect the presence of odors. Recording general body activity, leg movements, and respiration changes, Lipsitt, Engen, and Kaye (1963) demonstrated that infants respond to an unpleasant odor (asafoetida) within 24 hours of birth. During their second, third, and fourth days, the infants were presented first with a nondorous (control) stimulus, followed by a series of concentrations of asafoetida of ascending strength until a response greater than that to the control stimulus was elicited. Sensory adaptation was minimized by presenting only one above-threshold stimulus per day to each infant. The strength of the odor stimulus needed to elicit a response drastically declined within the first few days of life, suggesting the occurrence of important refinements within the olfactory system.

Using recordings of activity and respiration, Engen et al. (1963) demonstrated that infants 32 to 68 hours old respond differentially to different odors. In the first of two experiments, subjects received either ten presentations of full-strength acetic acid followed by ten presen-

tations of full-strength phenylethyl alcohol, or the reverse. Control (nonodorous) trials were alternated with stimulus trials and were used as base line for responses. In order to be judged positive, a stimulus response had to be greater than its accompanying control trial. Significant numbers of responses were obtained for both stimuli, but acetic acid produced a higher percentage of responses. No reliable diminution of responses over ten trials occurred for either stimulus, nor was a reliable effect of presentation order observed. In a second experiment full-strength anise oil and asafoetida were presented using the same procedure except that the odor presented during the first ten trials was reintroduced for two trials immediately following the ten presentations of the second odor. Asafoetida produced a greater percentage of responses than anise oil. In addition a decrement in response over the ten trials was observed for both odors regardless of the order of presentation, although frequency of response was lower for either odor when presented second. Following the ten presentations of the second odor, reintroduction of the first odor stimulus resulted in recovery in response frequencies to levels observed during the early trials of its initial presentation. Finally Engen et al. (1963) observed that successive presentations of acetic acid or asafoetida, both unpleasant odors, resulted in a progressive refinement of motor responses manifested by a change from initial diffuse responses to smooth and efficient movements away from the unpleasant odors.

The observed decrement in response as a function of repeated stimulation by asafoetida and anise oil cannot clearly be explained since, as Engen et al. (1963) point out, it could be due either to sensory adaptation (i.e., receptor or neural fatigue produced by repeated stimulation) or to response habituation or adaptation (i.e., extinction of interest in an initially effective stimulus). Moreover the recovery of response observed following stimulation with a second qualitatively different odor is consistent with interpretations of either sensory adaptation or response habituation to the initial odor stimulus. The issue of sensory adaptation versus response habituation has been pursued in a related experiment by Engen and Lipsitt (1965), who used differentiated breathing patterns following presentation of olfactory stimuli as their response measure. Infants, ranging in age from 27 to 77 hours, first received ten presentations of a stimulus, a mixture of amyl acetate and heptanal in diluent diethyl phthalate. A decrement in responsiveness was observed over the ten trials, at which point one of the two component odors was presented singly in solution with the diluent. A significant increase in response frequency was observed in the posttest trials for both amyl acetate and heptanal. If response decrement had been due to sensory fatigue (sensory adaptation), the change from the compound stimulus to one of the two component odorants would not be expected to produce response recovery on the posttest trials. Response recovery in the form of change in respiration was produced, however, upon change from the first to the second stimulus. Consequently the results were interpreted in terms of response habituation, and the response recovery, or dishabituation, was considered to be the result of the "novelty" stimulus. This conclusion was supported by the additional finding that amyl acetate produced a greater response recovery than heptanal in the posttest trials. Amyl acetate was judged by a group of adults to be less similar to the amyl acetate-heptanal mixture than heptanal and is consistent with its being a more effective (more novel) stimulus.

Infant reaction to odorous substances varying in molecular length have also been assessed. Engen (1965) demonstrated that infants from birth to five days of age will respond differentially to an homologous series of alcohols of increasing chain length. Change in the infant's respiration was used as an index of the intensity, or stimulus efficiency, of each alcohol in the series. The results indicated that the shorter chain alcohols were more intense or efficient stimuli than the longer chain alcohols when presented at 100 percent (undiluted) concentration. However when presented at threshold concentrations, the longer chain alcohols were the more efficient stimuli in producing responsiveness. These results were consistent with psychophysical scaling data from verbal reports of adult subjects in response to the same range of stimuli. In the same vein Rovee (1969) used integrated stabilimeter activity as her measure of response magnitude and presented infants 30 to 107 hours old with graded concentrations of a series of aliphatic alcohols. The results, consistent with those of Engen (1965), demonstrated that magnitude of response varies directly with stimulus intensity and inversely with molecular chain length. In addition the longer chain alcohols were the more effective (intense) stimuli in producing response when the alcohols were presented at threshold concentrations, although the corresponding stimulus values reported were higher over all concentrations than those reported by Engen (1965). Rovee (1969) concluded that more intense stimulation may be needed to produce movement compared to respiratory disruption or, alternatively, that the swaddling used during stimulus presentation may have obscured minimal motor responses.

In an innovative approach to the question of olfactory development, MacFarlane (1975) studied the development of social preference of neonates by observing head-turn responses to breast pads. In the initial experiment responses of neonates two to seven days old were observed when two breast pads, one clean and one from the infant's own mother, were suspended on either side of the infant's cheek. As a group the neonates spent significantly more time turned toward their own mother's breast pads than turned toward a clean breast pad. However in a separate experiment, two-day-old neonates did not show a differential response to their own mother's breast pad over a strange mother's breast pad. By six days neonates did show a differential response which became most pronounced by eight to ten days. The possibility remains that neonates aged two to four days are capable of discrimination but do not demonstrate it by head-turning. Alternatively the developmental decrease in olfactory thresholds reported by Lipsitt et al. (1963) may have contributed to the results. Changes in neonatal olfactory responsiveness across the first few days may also be related to changes known to occur in the neonate's hormonal milieu after birth (Orti, 1978). Gonadal steroid hormones, for example, have been shown to affect the olfactory threshold of the rat (Pietras & Moulton, 1975).

In a series of studies parallel to his studies of taste perception, Steiner (Steiner, 1974, 1977; Steiner & Finnegan, 1975) demonstrated that neonates will exhibit well-defined facial reflexes to pleasant and aversive odors. Full-term infants less than 12 hours old who had not yet had contact with nutrients or food odors were tested. Food-related odors, previously classified as pleasant or unpleasant by an adult panel, elicited facial expressions of two distinct types. Facial relaxation, a smile-like retraction of the mouth, and initiation of sucking and licking were induced by pleasant odors. Unpleasant odors elicited arching of the lips or depression of the corners of the mouth and often spitting and salivation. One hydroanencephalic infant was also tested with food odor and displayed facial expressions identical to those of the normal neonates. Since an autopsy revealed that cortical structures of the brain were not present in this infant, Steiner tentatively concluded that the facial response did not require cortical processing. Furthermore he viewed the differential responses of neonates as indicative of an innate, reflexive capacity to discriminate odors according to their hedonic dimension. He termed the response the *nasofacial reflex*.

One final olfactory issue that has been addressed is the ability of infants to locate the source of an odor in space. Bower (1974) suggested that the study of olfactory preference by Engen et al. (1963) offered some evidence of an innate localization capacity. It remained unclear, however, whether the infants were purposefully moving away from the location of the noxious odors or merely moving in a general response to their presence. More recently neonatal capacity for radial localization of the odor ammonia was demonstrated by Rieser et al. (1976). As a group the neonates were observed more frequently to turn away from the odor source as it was presented at a number of different positions on either side of the facial midline. Unlike Engen et al. (1963), no systematic change in the form of response was observed over repeated trials. Although Rieser et al. concluded that the newborn posesses innate sensitivity to the radial localization of an odor, the question remains whether this capacity is simply a crude centering response reflexive in nature or really does involve some sort of spatial representation of the environment external to the infant.

THE CUTANEOUS SENSES

Prenatal Development

The nerve terminations involved in sensations of touch, pressure, pain, and temperature are located in the skin. To the extent they have been studied, sensitivity to these sensations appears to develop early in fetal life. These studies, recently reviewed by Humphrey (1978), have been carried out on previable human fetuses removed by Cesarean section when the therapeutic termination of pregnancy was necessary. The fetuses must be examined quickly since anoxia begins shortly after placental separation. In view of the source of the subjects, three factors must be kept in mind in evaluating the data of these studies: (1) the possibility that anoxia had begun before testing; (2) the presence of anesthetics or other drugs administered to the mother prior to delivery; (3) the status of the subjects as aborted fetuses that may not have been developing normally. With these cautions in mind, the data indicate that areas around the lips are sensitive to light touch as early as 7½ weeks of gestation. Comparisons of all parts of the body indicate in general that the oral area and genital area become sensitive to stimulation before intervening regions. Also the palms of the hands and soles of the feet become sensitive before the other regions of the extremities. This is not surprising in view of the fact that these areas correspond to the cutaneous areas in adults that contain the greatest number and variety of sensory receptors.

Temperature sensitivity also appears to develop early in fetal life, and studies indicate that the fetus, like the newborn, may be more sensitive to stimuli colder than body temperature than to stimuli that are warmer (Humphrey, 1978). Unfortunately the development of sensations of pain in utero has received little direct experimental study. In summary there is good evidence to support the view that most, if not all, of the cutaneous sensations are structurally and functionally developed well before birth.

Postnatal Responses

Tactile Stimulation. Newborns are obviously sensitive to touch, as indicated by the presence of many touch evoked reflexes. A touch on the cheek, for example, will usually cause an infant to turn its head; a touch on the lips will usually start sucking actions. Even premature infants show various touch evoked reflexes (Saint-Anne Dargassies, 1966). A number of experimental studies also have shown the full-term infant to be responsive, in terms of heartrate and motor behavior, to both strong tactile stimulation (Bell & Costello, 1964; Bridger & Reiser, 1959; Lamper & Eisdorfer, 1971; Lipton, Steinschneider, & Richmond, 1966) and mild tactile stimulation (Wolff, 1967; Yang & Douthill, 1974).

Comparisons between term and preterm infants have also been made. Rose, Schmidt, & Bridger (1976) demonstrated both behavioral responses and heartrate acceleration to tactile stimulation among full-term infants but only weak behavioral responses and no cardiac response among premature infants. A sex difference indicated that the weak behavioral responses were due mainly to the male preterm subjects. The cause of these differences between full- and preterm infants is unclear. It may stem from either higher thresholds for stimulation, an inability to maintain vigorous responding even when perceiving the stimulus, or both these factors.

Pain. The few studies on the sensitivity of infants to pain have been summarized by Spears and Hohle (1967) and indicate (1) that the infant is more responsive to a pinprick stimulus in the head region compared to the limbs and (2) that the number of pinpricks required to elicit a response decreases as the age of the subjects increases. Lipsitt and Levy (1959) studied pain thresholds in infants by measuring motor responses to electrotactual stimulation (shock). Consistent with the conclusion drawn by Spears and Hohle, they showed a systematic decrease in the response thresholds of infants over the first four days of life. The mean thresholds decreased from about 85 to 90 volts on the first postnatal day to 70 volts by day four.

Some inferences about infant response to pain can be derived from reports on circumcision. Routine circumcision is often performed without anesthesia on about the third day of life and appears to be a painful process (Weiss, 1964; 1968). Emde, Harmon, Metcalf, Koenig, and Wagonfeld (1971) observed that circumcision without anesthesia was followed by an increase in the amount of quiet sleep. The latency period to the onset of quiet sleep was decreased, and the number and length of quiet sleep episodes increased. The authors suggested the observations could be interpreted as a response to stress. Anders and Chalemian (1974), on the other hand, found an increase in prolonged wakefulness with fussing and crying during a one-hour observation period following circumcision, and no significant quiet sleep changes were observed up to seven hours after the procedures. They suggested that later quiet sleep state shifts were secondary to changes in wakefulness and pointed out that differing techniques were used for circumcision in the two studies. However it should be noted that both Emde et al. (1971) and Anders and Chalemian (1974) observed an increase in fussing and crying *during* the circumcision procedure, suggesting that the infants were sensitive to pain at this age.

INTERCONNECTIONS AMONG THE SENSES

In typical fashion our discussion of perception has until now presented the senses one by one: sight, hearing, taste, smell, and touch. Such an organization ignores a very important fact about human perceptions. The various sensory systems do not always operate in isolation from one another; they are very often closely intertwined. We expect to be able to see something we hear, feel something we see, or smell something we taste. We frequently use information gained through one sensory system to "inform" our other sensory systems. This cross-modal transfer of information is what enables us to identify objects by touch which we have previously only seen or to reach out in the correct direction to touch an object we cannot see but can hear.

How do these interconnections come about? Must the connections be learned one by one through a gradual process of association? Some researchers believe this to be the case. Piaget (1971) argues that infants learn to link vision with touch only through the repeated visual observation of hand movements, and they learn to link vision with hearing only through repeated efforts to visually locate the sources of sounds. The general developmental trend, according to this hypothesis, is from isolation of the senses to gradual intercoordination.

As appealing as Piaget's hypothesis is on a logical basis, evidence is now accumulating which suggests that development may actually proceed, at least in part, in the opposite direction. Coordination of the senses may be present at birth, and the task of infancy may actually be one of learning to differentiate the senses one from another (Bower, 1974, 1979; Bruner & Koslowski, 1972; Gibson, 1969; Spelke, 1979a). In the following discussions we will focus on the intermodal relations that have received the most attention: coordination of sight with sound and sight with touch.

Auditory-Visual Coordination

The question of the degree to which auditory and visual experiences are integrated in infancy is divisible into at least two sub-questions, each of which has received attention from researchers. The first of these is the issue of whether the infant attributes a position in space to a sound that is heard. The answer to this question has typically been sought in demonstrations of the presence or absence of auditory localization—the ability to turn appropriately toward the source of an auditory stimulus. The second question concerns the degree to which auditory and visual information are perceived as part of a unified, multimodal, perceptual experience. For some objects or events, this translates into whether or not infants are sensitive to the information invariant across the two modalities (e.g., invariants in the rhythms of auditory and visual information from a beating drum). For other objects, in contrast, the problem becomes one of learning a connection rather than abstracting it, and the questions for researchers become when and how the connection is achieved (e.g., associating mother's voice with her visual image). Evidence relevant to each of these issues is accumulating, although as usual, definitive answers still elude us.

Of the two major questions auditory localization is the one that received the earliest attention. In one now famous study Wertheimer (1961) reported roughly appropriate eye movements on the part of an infant only minutes old in response to soft clicks presented laterally. Subsequent studies with greater numbers of infants, however, produced contradictory results. Fortunately some of the factors responsible for the conflicting results have now been identified. The intensity of the sound, for example, was found by Turkewitz, Birch, Moreau, Levy, and Cornwell (1966) to affect the direction of initial eye movements in response to an auditory stimulus. Loud sounds produced a reflexive glance away from the source during the first second, whereas soft sounds produced the same response but toward the source.

The duration of the stimulus and the duration of the response time allotted the infant apparently also make a difference. Both Mendelson and Haith (1976) and Muir and Field (1979) provide strong evidence of auditory localization in newborns with auditory events lasting a good deal longer than the brief clicks and tones used by some researchers reporting unsuccessful attempts (e.g., McGurk, Turnure, & Creighton, 1977, Experiment 1). The use of sustained stimuli automatically also provides the infant with longer response times. Mendelson and Haith (1976) presented infants with a male voice that lasted 40 seconds. The infants' eye movements were recorded throughout that time, and results revealed initial fixations toward the source followed by turns away from the source. When Muir and Field (1979) actually measured latencies in response to their 20-second presentations of a rattle, they found a median time of 2.5 seconds before movement was started and 5.75 seconds until it was completed. Field, DiFranco, Dodwell, and Muir (1979) report that latencies remain slow even at 2½ months. They found a median of 1.98 seconds for a voice paired with a face and 3.95 for the voice presented alone. These studies, therefore, indicate the importance of looking beyond the initial brief, jerking movements of the eyes reported by Turkewitz et al. (1966), often termed the *oculogyric reflex*. Both Mendelson and Haith (1976) and Muir and Field (1979) describe the later, longer lasting responses as investigative in nature—as though the infant is actually seeking the visual source of the sound.

The study by Muir and Field (1979) is also instructive for several other reasons. Unlike past studies the infants in this case were allowed to move their heads as well as their eyes. In addition constant efforts were made to maintain the infants in an alert state. Combined with the use of a sustained stimulus, the result was the most convincing evidence to date of auditory localization in newborns. In the more rigorously controlled Experiment 2, 12 infants between two and four days of age turned toward the sound of a rattle presented 90° to the left or right on 74 percent of the trials, away from it on 17 percent of the trials, and failed to turn at all on only 9 percent of the trials. The accuracy of the turns was also fairly impressive, with 8 of 12 subjects turning the full 90° on nearly every trial. Permitting the infants to move their heads as well as their eyes proved very important since the general pattern of behavior was widening of the eyes at sound onset, followed by turning of the head with the eyes somewhat closed. The eyes were then reopened when the turn was complete.

Based on these results as well as those of Mendelson and Haith (1976) and Butterworth and Castillo (1976), it seems safe to conclude that healthy, alert newborn infants are capable of turning in the direction appropriate to a laterally presented sound. Of course establishing this fact still leaves important questions unresolved. Besides the obvious issue of the precision of these movements, there is also the difficult matter of determining whether they indicate true recognition of the fact that auditory events should have a source in space or simply the presence of an innate reflex upon which true auditory-visual coordination will later be built. Whatever the final answer, it is clear even from existing data that infants respond in very active ways to their environments—ways which predispose them to start learning quite early just how the external world operates.

Being able to locate the source of a sound is not the only way in which an integration of the visual and auditory systems can manifest itself. In a clever series of studies, Spelke (1976, 1978, 1979a, 1979b) has demonstrated that at four months of age infants can also detect invariants in each modality which link them together into a unified, multimodal experience. The basic procedure used to demonstrate this ability is the simultaneous presentation of two separate films with a sound track matching one of them emitted from a speaker located between the two film screens. A preference for the film which matches the sound is interpreted as evidence that the infant has detected the properties common to both. Spelke (1979b) presented four-month-old infants one film of a toy kangaroo and another of a toy donkey. In each case the animal was bouncing up and down; however, one bounced at a faster rate than the other. In the first experiment a sound track matching and synchronized with the rhythm of one of the animals was presented between the films. Analysis of visual fixation indicated a preference for the synchronized film on the first of two 100-second presentations and significantly more and faster initial looks to the synchronized film on a set of 24 five-second trials. Thus four-month-old infants were detecting properties common to the auditory and visual events.

Was it the similarity in rate that they were detecting or the co-occurrence of the visual impact and the sound? A second experiment in which the rates depicted in the movie and its sound track were matched, but not synchronized, indicated a preference for the more appropriate film. The infants were abstracting the tempo information. In a third study the two animals were filmed moving at the same rate but out of synchrony with one another. A sound track matching one of the two was again presented in between them; the results indicated a preference for the film whose movement was in synchrony with the sound. In other words four-month-old infants are apparently sensitive to a variety of information. They are able to match on the basis of either tempo, synchrony, or both. In each case a unified episode was sought. Whether or not this same capacity exists at younger ages remains to be seen.

As Spelke and Owsley (1979) point out, not all sound-producing objects emit sounds containing invariant properties linking them logically to their visual sources as was the case with the bouncing animals. Some object-sound relations are arbitrary and must be learned. An example is the link between a certain face and voice or between a car and its horn. The age at which such learning can be demonstrated is important theoretically because its presence in the repertoire of the very young infant might indicate an innate predisposition to link sights with sounds. So far the youngest age at which such learning has been found is 15 weeks. Spelke and Owsley (1979) reported that infants at this age showed evidence of linking a parent's voice to the correct parent. Lyons-Ruth (1977) demonstrated a similar capacity among four-month-old infants using a novel object instead of a known person. After a brief familiarization period with a sound-emitting toy, the infants showed gaze aversion when the sound and the toy were no longer presented contiguously. Evidently this ability to learn an association between sight and sound is present at least as early as 3½ to 4 months.

In summary there is strong evidence of auditory localization of at least rough accuracy among newborn infants. They move both their heads and their eyes in efforts to locate the source of sounds, particularly when the sounds are patterned and of long duration. They also are capable by 15 weeks, if not earlier, of learning an association between a sound and the object that produces it (Spelke & Owsley, 1979). Finally four-month-old infants show sensitivity to qualities like rhythm and synchrony which cut across both sound and sight and unite them into a unified perceptual event. It is, of course, possible that these last two intermodal capacities are acquired during the first four months of experience in the world. Evidence from younger infants will be necessary for a definitive answer to this nature-nurture question.

Vision and Touch

As should be abundantly clear from the number of categories included under visual perception in this chapter, the visual system supplies many types of information

about the external environment. At least three of these—distance, size, and shape—have been the focus of researchers interested in the extent to which information is shared between vision and touch during infancy. The first of these three, perception of object distance, was covered in the discussion of depth perception. In brief the evidence overall is fairly consistent showing an impact of visual depth information on reaching behavior in infants within the first three months. The second of these three, perception of object size, was the focus of studies by Bruner and Koslowski (1972) and Bower (1972). In the study by Bruner and Koslowski, infants were tested every two weeks from the age of 8 weeks to 22 weeks. On each occasion they were shown two balls, one of graspable size and one too large to grasp, presented one at a time at the same 4- to 5-inch distance within touching range. All bodily movements were filmed, and analyses revealed that even before successful reach and grasp behaviors developed, the infants were responding differently to the two balls. The small ball elicited significantly more movements of one or both clenched hands to the midline (adduction to midline) and more midline activity. In contrast the large ball elicited more forward swiping behavior. Based on these results Bruner and Koslowski contended that the infants were making use of visual information to regulate their early attempts to reach and grasp; they were behaving as if they interpreted the small ball as graspable and the large ball as hittable but *not* graspable. Since the age of these infants precludes extensive grasping experience, Bruner and Koslowski concluded that visual-motor integration is the starting point of development, with gradual differentiation of the two and refinement of action sequences being the tasks facing the infant during the first year of life.

Bower (1972) came to a similar conclusion based on a study of thumb-finger separation in response to large and small objects. Infants as young as two weeks of age were found to differentiate between the stimuli, this time opening their hands wider in response to the large but still graspable objects than to the smaller objects. Both these studies, therefore, suggest that the size information provided by the visual system is used even at very young ages to modulate motor responses.

The integration of vision and touch in the perception of object shape has received an increasing amount of attention recently but has not yet involved infants younger than six months of age. The typical procedure is a cross-modal one in which objects are presented in one modality for a certain length of time followed by a test of recognition in another modality. The ground-breaking study in the area involved nine-month-old infants who were first shown two three-dimensional shapes, then made to feel one of the two without being able to see it, and finally once again presented the two shapes visually (Bryant et al., 1972). In a clever attempt to increase the infant's interest in the object being felt, this object was designed to make sounds while in the infant's hands. Evidence of cross-modal transfer did result for one pair of shapes: an egg-shaped form paired with an identical form whose top had been notched. The evidence consisted of a tendency on the part of the infants to choose the object they had held when both were presented visually in the final phase of the experiment. No cross-modal transfer was found with cube forms, one of which had a notch cut in the top. Thus although such transfer exists at nine months, it may be partially a function of the specific shapes used. It is also possible, of course, that the infants could tell the two cubes apart but simply liked them equally well.

The work by Bryant et al. (1972) has been extended by Gottfried, Rose, and Bridger (1977, 1978; Rose, Gottfried, & Bridger, 1978, 1979). All their studies have been consistent in showing cross-modal transfer at 12 months, as long as the infants are middle or high SES and full-term. They have also consistently reported an absence of such transfer at six and nine months. The negative impact of prematurity was demonstrated in two studies comparing full-term and premature middle SES infants of the same age as measured from expected dates of birth. In the first study (Rose et al., 1978), 12-month-old infants were familiarized for 30 seconds, either orally, tactually, or visually, to a simple three-dimensional form. This form was then presented visually with a novel form, and both visual fixation and reaching preferences were noted. For the full-term infants recognition of the familiar form, as manifested in a preference for the novel form, occurred whether their initial experience had been oral (mouthing), tactual (handling), or visual. However, the premature infants showed recognition only in the nontransfer case of visual familiarization. The importance of SES was also demonstrated in the same experiment when a group of low SES, full-term infants behaved just as the premature infants had.

In a second study involving premature infants, Rose et al. (1979) compared visual familiarization with visual plus haptic familiarization. The haptic experience was of two types: either handling of the form itself or handling of the form enclosed in a transparent cube so that distinctive features could be seen but not felt. The familiarization phase lasted until 20 seconds of visual fixation to the frontal perceptive had accumulated and was followed by a test in which preference for a novel form over the familiar form was assessed. Both 6- and 12-month-old premature and full-term infants were tested, with each subject experiencing each condition. The results indicated that the 12-month-old premature infants were behaving like the 6-month-old full-term infants. For both these groups the only condition which produced evidence of recognition was the visual-only condition. The addition of haptic experiences did not appear to facilitate performance at all. In contrast the 12-month-old full-term infants did show recognition in all conditions, although the strongest preference data resulted from visual-only familiarization. Just why premature and low SES infants did more poorly in these cross-modal tasks is not clear. Rose et al. (1978) suggest three possibilities: (1) deficits in acquiring or retaining tactual information, (2) slower information processing so that longer familiarization times are needed, and/or (3) deficits in the capacity to integrate information from the two modalities.

Two recent studies of visual recognition among preterm infants provide support for the second of these three possibilities (Cornell, 1979; Rose, 1980). In both studies preterm and full-term infants were first familiarized with one visual stimulus and then presented with that stimulus paired with a novel stimulus. Preference for the novel stimulus during this second phase was interpreted as evidence that recognition of the first stimulus had occurred.

The results in both studies indicated that the preterm infants were capable of processing visual information but that longer familiarization times were needed to bring them to the level of recognition shown by the full-term infants. However slow information processing is apparently not inevitable among preterm infants, since Rose (1980; Rose, Schmidt, Riese, & Bridger, 1980) also reports that a short neonatal intervention program was sufficient to eliminate the performance difference between the preterm and full-term infants. Exactly how the program, a mixture of tactual, proprioceptive, and vestibular stimuli, operated to facilitate visual recognition is not clear. Whatever the eventual explanation, the results certainly are encouraging.

As noted above, Rose et al. (1979) did not find evidence at six months of any contribution being made by tactual experience with an object. In fact the addition of physical manipulation seemed, if anything, to detract from the level of recognition achieved with vision alone. Similar results were reported for nine-month-olds as well as six-month-olds in another study by these same researchers (Gottfried et al., 1978). However not all research has painted such a pessimistic view of the six-month-old infant's cross-modal capacities. Ruff and Kohler (1978) familiarized six-month-old infants for 30 seconds, either visually or haptically, to a cube or a ball. Recognition was then tested by presenting both objects visually and noting preference. Contrary to the studies just discussed, infants in both familiarization conditions showed evidence of recognition, this time in terms of a preference for the familiar shape. Thus the infants were apparently modulating their visual behavior on the basis of previous tactile experiences. The choice of the familiar stimulus over the novel one is also interesting since it suggests that failures to find preferences, as in the Gottfried et al. (1978) study, could quite possibly be due to equal preferences for the familiar and novel objects instead of an absence of discrimination.

Additional evidence of cross-modal transfer at six months is provided in another study by Ruff (1980). In this case infants were allowed either just visual familiarization or visual plus tactile manipulation over a series of trials in which the form was constant but the color of the object varied. In contrast to the results of Rose et al. (1979), recognition occurred here only for the condition involving both modalities. Vision alone did not suffice.

Why the apparent contradictions at six months of age? One factor may be the use of different shapes. As was discovered in the very earliest study (Bryant et al., 1972), cross-modal transfer may be elicited for some stimulus pairs but not others, perhaps due to the confusability of the particular distinctive features in each or to equal attractiveness which masks cross-modal transfer in the typical test phase. Ruff's success at six months with visual plus haptic familiarization may have been due to the fact that her stimulus was a cube with bumps (or indentations) in each side which was presented over trials in different colors. It is possible that the bumps were more detectable haptically than visually and that the change of color distracted visual attention to form in the vision-only condition. Another possible explanation for the contradictory evidence at six months is that greater familiarization time may be necessary to facilitate integration of the two modalities at this age. Some support for such an explanation comes from the fact that the two studies showing no cross-modal transfer at six months used a familiarization period of 20 seconds of accumulated fixation (Gottfried et al., 1978; Rose et al., 1979), while the two that did show transfer used either a 30-second familiarization period (Ruff & Kohler, 1978) or a series of familiarization trials (Ruff, 1980). Other evidence relevant to this possibility is provided by Lasky (1980) who reports that, even in visual-visual tasks, length of the familiarization phase can have an important impact on recognition of an object as manifested in preference for a novel stimulus.

In summary the literature on the coordination of haptic and visual systems indicates rough integration for size and distance information at very early ages, and integration of shape information by at least six months under some conditions. Cross-modal transfer of shape information may in fact exist at even younger ages, and its demonstration will be important to the final decision about the relationship among the perceptual systems at birth.

Sensory Plasticity

For a number of years now, engineers have been working on an ultrasonic device designed to help blind infants perceive the layout of the world around them (Bower, 1977a, 1978, 1979). The device, which is worn on the infant's head, operates similarly to the echolocation systems of dolphins and bats. One component of the device continuously irradiates the environment around the infant with ultrasonic waves which bounce off objects and are reflected back to the child's head. Other components of the system pick them up there and translate them into auditory signals which hold clues to the layout of the environment:

1. Pitch signals the distance of the reflecting surface. A low pitch indicates an object is near; a high pitch indicates that it is far away.
2. Loudness signals the size of the reflecting surface. A loud sound indicates the object is large; a quiet sound indicates the object is small.
3. Clarity of the sound indicates the texture of the reflecting surface. A clear sound means the surface is hard; a fuzzy sound means it is soft.
4. Finally the left-right position of the surface relative to the child's body is given by the varying arrival time of the sounds at the infant's two ears. Sounds signifying an object to the right are made to arrive at the right ear before the left, and sounds signifying an object to the left are made to arrive at the left ear before the right.

The fact that scientists have been able to devise a device to produce such a complex series of translations is certainly remarkable; but this fact of engineering genius pales next to the achievement shown by the infants themselves. According to Bower's latest report the device has been tried on six blind infants ranging in age from 5 to 16 months. All of them demonstrated the ability to translate the auditory signals back into information about the visual world—one child showing evidence of use within two minutes. Bower described the infants' re-

actions: They begin reaching for objects; they become fascinated with moving their own hands in front of them (a behavior analogous to the visual-hand-regard seen so commonly in sighted infants); and older ones even go through doorways without mistakes. All of this is accompanied by great joy—as if the infants themselves were grasping the miraculous nature of it all.

The practical implications of this work are clear. What may be less obvious is that these results also have theoretical implications in terms of what they indicate about the nature of perception during infancy. These infants are demonstrating an ability to respond to very abstract properties of the sounds they are hearing and to sense automatically the counterparts of these properties in visual space. The ease of their translation from one modality to the other is important evidence of intersensory coordination in infancy. Unfortunately this coordination seems to decline once infancy is passed. As a consequence blind adults must work for weeks and even months to learn to use the same ultrasonic information that takes an infant only minutes to conquer.

CONCLUSIONS

We have tried in this chapter to present an overview of some of the most recent research on perception in infancy. Although still incomplete the picture that emerges is of an active organism predisposed to seek stimulation from the environment. However the stimulation sought is not random; certain preferences are already present when the child enters the world. Newborn infants prefer to look at high contrast edges, to scan external contours of patterns, to taste sweet solutions, to smell pleasant odors, and to search for pulsating sounds. By one to two months of age, if not earlier, patterns are examined much more thoroughly, color vision is present, relations among edges receive priority, and a great number of phonological distinctions are perceived, some categorically. By three months binocular convergence, acuity, and accommodation are all considerably improved, shape constancy is well established, complexity of preferred patterns has increased, spatial arrangements among isolated elements are abstracted, and associations between specific sights and sounds are retained. Months four and five reveal an infant capable of responding to compound forms as whole Gestalts, matching sights and sounds based on common temporal attributes, and recognizing objects depicted two-dimensionally. Cross-modal transfer of information between hand and eye is present under some conditions at six months (and perhaps earlier), and spatial orientation is present, although heavily dependent on egocentric relations.

Perhaps the most remarkable part of this litany of development is not that the infant accomplishes all this so quickly, but that psychologists have uncovered all these milestones in such a short length of time. Given the same rate of discovery in future years, it will not be long before the once impenetrable "frontier" of infant perception will be a well-charted, familiar landscape to parents and scholars alike. We hope this review will have contributed to the attainment of this goal.

REFERENCES

ACREDOLO, L. P. The development of spatial orientation in infancy. *Developmental Psychology*, 1978, *14*, 224–234.

ACREDOLO, L. P. Laboratory versus home: The effect of environment on the 9-month-old infant's choice of spatial reference system. *Developmental Psychology*, 1979, *15*, 666–667.

ACREDOLO, L. P., & EVANS, D. Developmental changes in the effects of landmarks on infant spatial behavior. *Developmental Psychology*, 1980, *16*, 312–318.

ALBERTI, P. W. The diagnostic role of stapedius reflex estimations. *Otolaryngologic Clinics of North America*, 1978, *11*, 251–261.

AMES, A. Visual perception and the rotating trapezoidal window. *Psychological Monographs*, 1951, *65*(1, Whole No. 324).

ANDERS, T. F., & CHALEMIAN, R. J. The effect of circumcision on sleep-wake states in human neonates. *Psychosomatic Medicine*, 1974, *36*, 174–179.

ASLIN, R. N. Development of binocular fixation in human infants. *Journal of Experimental Child Psychology*, 1977, *23*, 133–150.

BALL, W., & TRONICK, E. Infant responses to impending collisions: Optical and real. *Science*, 1971, 818–820.

BANKS, M.S. The development of visual accommodation during early infancy. *Child Development*, 1980, *51*, 646–666.

BARNET, A., & GOODWIN, R. Averaged evoked electroencephalic responses to clicks in the human newborn. *Electroencephalography and Clinical Neurophysiology*, 1965, *18*, 441–450.

BARNET, A. B., OHLRICH, E. S., WEISS, I. P., & SHANKS, B. Auditory evoked potentials during sleep in normal children from ten days to three years of age. *Electroencephalography and Clinical Neurophysiology*, 1975, *39*, 29–41.

BARNET, A. B., WEISS, I. P., SOTILLO, M. V., OHLRICH, E. S., SHKUROVICH, Z. M., & CRAVIOTO, J. Abnormal auditory evoked potentials in early infancy malnutrition. *Science*, 1978, *201*, 450–452.

BARTOSHUK, A. K. Human neonatal cardiac responses to sound: A power function. *Psychonomic Science*, 1964, *1*, 151–152.

BELL, T. Q., & COSTELLO, N. S. Three tests for sex differences in tactile sensitivity in the newborn. *Biologia Neonatorum*, 1964, *7*, 335–346.

BENCH, J. The auditory response. In V. Stave (Ed.), *Perinatal physiology*. New York: Plenum, 1978.

BENCH, J., COLLYER, Y., LANGFORD, C., & TOMS, R. A comparison between the neonatal sound-evoked startle response and the head-drop (Moro) reflex. *Developmental Medicine and Child Neurology*, 1972, *14*, 308–317.

BENCH, J., COLLYER, Y., MENTZ, L., & WILSON, I. Studies in infant behavioural audiometry: I. Neonates. *Audiology*, 1976, *15*, 85–105.

BENCH, R. J., & MENTZ, D. L. On the measurement of the foetal auditory response. In R. J. Bench, A. Pye, & J. D. Pye (Eds.), *Sound reception in mammals*, Symposium of the Zoological Society of London (No. 37). New York: Academic Press, 1975.

BERG, K. M., BERG, W. K., & GRAHAM, F. K. Infant heart rate response as a function of stimulus and state. *Psychophysiology*, 1971, *8*, 30–44.

BERG, W. K., & BERG, K. M. Psychophysiological development in infancy: State, sensory function, and attention. In J. Osofsky (Ed.), *Handbook of infant development*. New York: John Wiley, 1979.

BERGMAN, T., HAITH, M., & MANN, L. *Development of eye contact and facial scanning in infants*. Paper presented at the meeting of the Society for Research in Child Development, Minneapolis, 1971.

BERKELEY, G. An essay towards a new theory of vision. In A. C. Fraser (Ed.), *Selections from Berkeley*. Oxford, England: Clarendon, 1910.

BLOOM, L. *Language development: Form and function in emerging grammars*. Cambridge, Mass.: M.I.T. Press, 1970.

BOND, E. K. Perception of form by the human infant. *Psychological Bulletin*, 1972, *77*, 225–245.

BORNSTEIN, M. H. Chromatic vision in infancy. In H. W. Reese & L. Lipsitt (Eds.), *Advances in child development and behavior* (Vol. 12). New York: Academic Press, 1978a.

BORNSTEIN, M. H. Visual behavior of the young human infant: Relationships between chromatic and spatial perceptions and the activity of the underlying brain mechanisms. *Journal of Experimental Child Psychology*, 1978b, *26*, 174–192.

BORNSTEIN, M. H. Effects of habituation experience on post-ha-
bituation behavior in young infants: Discrimination and generalization among colors. *Developmental Psychology*, 1979, *15*, 348–349.

BORNSTEIN, M. H., GROSS, C. G., & WOLF, J. Z. Perceptual similarity of mirror images in infancy. *Cognition*, 1978, *6*, 89–116.

BORNSTEIN, M., & KESSEN, W. *Psychological development from infancy: Image to intention*. Hillsdale, N.J.: Lawrence Erlbaum Associates, 1979.

BOWER, T.G.R. Heterogeneous summation in human infants. *Animal Behaviour*, 1966a, *14*, 395–398.

BOWER, T.G.R. Slant perception and shape constancy in infants. *Science*, 1966b, *151*, 832–834.

BOWER, T.G.R. The visual world of infants. *Scientific American*, 1966c, *215*, 80–92.

BOWER, T.G.R. Object perception in infants. *Perception*, 1972, *1*, 15–30.

BOWER, T.G.R. *Development in infancy*. San Francisco: W. H. Freeman & Company Publishers, 1974.

BOWER, T.G.R. Blind babies see with their ears. *New Scientist*, 1977a, *73*, 256–257.

BOWER, T.G.R. Comment on Yonas et al., "Development of sensitivity to information for impending collision." *Perception and Psychophysics*, 1977b, *21*, 281–282.

BOWER, T.G.R. Visual development in the blind child. In A. MacFarlane (Ed.), *Clinic in developmental medicine on vision*. London: Spastics International Medical Publication, 1978.

BOWER, T.G.R. The origins of meaning in perceptual development. In A. Pick (Ed.), *Perception and its development: A tribute to Eleanor J. Gibson*. Hillsdale, N.J.: Lawrence Erlbaum Associates, 1979.

BOWER, T.G.R., BROUGHTON, J. M., & MOORE, M. Demonstrations of intention in the reaching behavior of neonate humans. *Nature*, 1970a, *228*, 5272.

BOWER, T.G.R., BROUGHTON, J. M., & MOORE, M. Infant response to approaching objects: An indication of response to distal variables. *Perception and Psychophysics*, 1970b, *9*, 193–196.

BOWER, T.G.R., & DUNKELD, J. *Perceptual development*. Unpublished manuscript, 1973.

BRADLEY, R. M., CHEAL, M. L., & KIM, Y. H. Quantitative analysis of developing epiglottal taste buds in sheep. *Journal of Anatomy*, 1980, *130*, 25–32.

BRADLEY, R. M., & STEARN, I. B. The development of the human taste bud during the foetal period. *Journal of Anatomy*, 1967, *101*, 743–752.

BRADLEY-JOHNSON, S., & TRAVERS, R.M.W. Cardiac change of retarded and nonretarded infants to an auditory signal. *American Journal of Mental Deficiency*, 1979, *83*, 631–636.

BREDBERG, G. Cellular pattern and nerve supply to the human organ of Corti. *Acta Oto-Laryngologica*, 1968, suppl. 236.

BREMNER, J. G. Egocentric versus allocentric spatial coding in nine-monthh-old infants: Factors influencing the choice of code. *Developmental Psychology*, 1978a, *14*, 346–355.

BREMNER, J. G. Spatial errors made by infants: Inadequate spatial cues or evidence of egocentrism? *British Journal of Psychology*, 1978b, *69*, 77–84.

BREMNER, J. G., & BRYANT, P. E. Place versus response as the basis of spatial errors made by young infants. *Journal of Experimental Child Psychology*, 1977, *23*, 162–171.

BRENNAN, W. M., AMES, E. W., & MOORE, R. W. Age differences in infants' attention to patterns of different complexities. *Science*, 1966, *151*, 354–356.

BRIDGER, W. H., & REISER, M. F. Psychophysiologic studies of the neonate: An approach toward the methodological and theoretical problems involved. *Psychosomatic Medicine*, 1959, *21*, 265–276.

BRONSON, G. W. The postnatal growth of visual capacity. *Child Development*, 1974, *45*, 873–890.

BROWN, E. L., & DEFFENBACHER, K. *Perception and the senses*. New York: Oxford University Press, 1979.

BROWN, J. W., LEAVITT, L. A., & GRAHAM, F. K. Response to auditory stimuli in 6- and 9-week-old human infants. *Developmental Psychobiology*, 1977, *10*, 255–266.

BRUNER, J. S., & KOSLOWSKI, B. Visually preadapted constituents of manipulatory action. *Perception*, 1972, *1*, 3–14.

BRYANT, P. E., JONES, P., CLAXTON, V., & PERKINS, G. M. Recognition of shapes across modalities by infants. *Nature*, 1972, *240*, 303–304.

BURKE, P. M. Swallowing and the organization of sucking in the human newborn. *Child Development*, 1977, *48*, 523–531.

BURNHAM, D. K., & DAY, R. H. Detection of color in rotating objects by infants and its generalization over changes in velocity. *Journal of Experimental Child Psychology*, 1979, *28*, 191–204.

BUSHNELL, I.W.R. Modification of the externality effect in young infants. *Journal of Experimental Child Psychology*, 1979, *28*, 211–229.

BUTTERWORTH, C., & CASTILLO, M. Coordination of auditory and visual space in newborn infants. *Perception*, 1976, *5*, 155–167.

CAMPOS, J. J., LANGER, A., & KROWITZ, A. Cardiac responses on the visual cliff in prelocomotor human infants. *Science*, 1970, *170*, 195–196.

CARON, A. J., CARON, R. F., & CARLSON, V. R. Do infants see objects or retinal images? Shape constancy revisited. *Infant Behavior and Development*, 1978, *1*, 229–243.

CARON, A. J., CARON, R. F., & CARLSON, V. R. Infant perception of the invariant shape of objects varying in slant. *Child Development*, 1979, *50*, 716–721.

CARON, R. F., CARON, A. J., CARLSON, V. R., & COBB, L. S. Perception of shape-at-a-slant in the young infant. *Bulletin of the Psychonomic Society*, 1979, *1*, 229–243.

CARPENTER, G. C. Visual regard of moving and stationary faces in early infancy, *Merrill-Palmer Quarterly*, 1974, *20*, 187–194.

CHANG, H-W., & TREHUB, S. E. Auditory processing of relational information by young infants. *Journal of Experimental Child Psychology*, 1977a, *24*, 324–331.

CHANG, H-W., & TREHUB, S. E. Infants' perception of temporal grouping in auditory patterns. *Child Development*, 1977b, *48*, 1666–1670.

CLIFTON, R. K., & GRAHAM, F. K. Stability of individual differences in heart rate activity during the newborn period. *Psychophysiology*, 1968, *5*, 37–50.

COHEN, L. B. Attention-getting and attention-holding processes of infant visual preferences. *Child Development*, 1972, *43*, 869–879.

COHEN, L. B. Commentary. *Monograph of the Society for Research in Child Development*, 1979a, *44*(No. 182).

COHEN, L. B. Our developing knowledge of infant perception. *American Psychologist*, 1979b, *34*, 894–899.

COHEN, L. B., DELOACHE, J. S., & RISSMAN, M. W. The effect of stimulus complexity on infant visual attention and habituation. *Child Development*, 1975, *46*, 611–617.

COHEN, L. B., DELOACHE, J. S., & STRAUSS, M. Infant visual perception. In J. Osofsky (Ed.), *Handbook of infant development*. New York: John Wiley, 1979.

COHEN, L. B., & GELBER, E. R. Infant visual memory. Pp. 347–403 in L. Cohen & P. Salapatek (Eds.), *Infant perception: From sensation to cognition: Basic visual processes* (Vol. 1). New York: Academic Press, 1975.

COHEN, L. B., GELBER, E. R., & LAZAR, M. A. Infant habituation and generalization to differing degrees of stimulus novelty. *Journal of Experimental Child Psychology*, 1971, *11*, 379–389.

COHEN, L. B., & SALAPATEK, P. *Infant perception: From sensation to cognition*. New York: Academic Press, 1975.

COHEN, L. B., & STRAUSS, M. S. Concept acquisition in the human infant. *Developmental Psychology*, 1979, *50*, 410–424.

CONDON, W. S., & SANDER, L. W. Neonate movement is synchronized with adult speech. *Science*, 1974, *183*, 99–100.

CONEL, J. L. *The postnatal development of the human cerebral cortex* (Vol. 1). The cortex of the newborn. Cambridge, Mass.: Harvard University, 1939.

CONEL, J. L. *The postnatal development of the human cerebral cortex* (Vol. 2). The cortex of the one-month-old infant. Cambridge, Mass.: Harvard University, 1941.

CONEL, J. L. *The postnatal development of the human cerebral cortex* (Vol. 3). The cortex of the three-month infant. Cambridge, Mass.: Harvard University, 1947.

CONEL, J. L. *The postnatal development of the human cerebral cortex* (Vol. 4). The cortex of the six-month infant. Cambridge, Mass.: Harvard University, 1951.

CONEL, J. L. *The postnatal development of the human cerebral cortex* (Vol. 5). The cortex of the fifteen-month infant. Cambridge, Mass.: Harvard University, 1955.

CONEL, J. L. *The postnatal development of the human cerebral cortex* (Vol. 6). The cortex of the twenty-four month infant. Cambridge, Mass.: Harvard University, 1959.

COOK, M., FIELD, J., & GRIFFITHS, K. The perception of solid form in early infancy. *Child Development*, 1978, *49*, 866–869.

COPENHHAVER, W. M., KELLY, D. E., & WOOD, R. L. *Bailey's textbook of histology* (17th ed.). Baltimore, Md.: Williams & Wilkins, 1978.

CORNELL, E. H. Infants' discrimination of faces following redundant presentations. *Journal of Experimental Child Psychology*, 1974, *18*, 98–106.

CORNELL, E. H. Infants' recognition memory, forgetting and savings. *Journal of Experimental Child Psychology*, 1979, *28*, 359–374.

CORNELL, E. H., & STRAUSS, M. Infants' responsiveness to compounds of habituated visual stimuli. *Developmental Psychology*, 1973, *9*, 73–78.

CORTER, C. M., ZUCKER, K. J., & GALLIGAN, R. F. Patterns in the infant's search for mother during brief separation. *Developmental Psychology*, 1980, *16*, 62–69.

CORYELL, J., & MICHEL, G. F. How supine postural preference of infants can contribute towards the development of handedness. *Infant Behavior and Development*, 1978, *1*, 245–257.

CROOK, C. K. Modification of the temporal organization of neonatal sucking by taste stimulation. In J. M. Weiffenbach (Ed.), *Taste and development: The genesis of sweet preference*. Washington, D.C.: U.S. Government Printing Office, 1977.

CROOK, C. K. Taste perception in the newborn infant. *Infant Behavior and Development*, 1978, *1*, 52–69.

CROOK, C. K. The organization and control of infant sucking. *Advances in Child Development and Behavior*, 1979, *14*, 209–252.

CROOK, C. K., & LIPSITT, L. P. Neonatal nutritive sucking: Effects of taste stimulation upon sucking rhythm and heart rate. *Child Development*, 1976, *47*, 518–522.

CRUIKSHANK, R. M. The development of visual size constancy in early infancy. *Journal of Genetic Psychology*, 1941, *58*, 327–351.

DAVIS, A. E., & WADA, J. A. Hemispheric asymmetries in human infants: Spectral analysis of flash and click evoked potentials. *Brain and Language*, 1977, *4*, 23–31.

DAY, R. H., & McKENZIE, B. E. Perceptual shape constancy in early infancy. *Perception*, 1973, *2*, 315–320.

DAY, R. H., & McKENZIE, B. E. Constancies in the perceptual world of the infant. In W. Epstein (Ed.), *Stability and constancy in visual perception. Mechanisms and Processes*. New York: John Wiley, 1977.

DELOACHE, J. S., RISSMAN, M. D., & COHEN, L. B. An investigation of the attention-getting process in infants. *Infant Behavior and Development*, 1978, *1*, 11–25.

DELOACHE, J. S., STRAUSS, M. S., & MAYNARD, J. Picture perception in infancy. *Infant Behavior and Development*, 1979, *2*, 77–89.

DESOR, J. A., MALLER, O., & GREENE, L. S. Preference for sweet in humans: Infants, children and adults. In J. Weiffenbach (Ed.), *Taste and development: The ontogeny of sweet preference*. Washington, D.C.: U.S. Government Printing Office, 1977.

DESOR, J. A., MALLER, O., & TURNER, R. Taste in acceptance of sugars by human infants. *Journal of Comparative and Physiological Psychology*, 1973, *84*, 496–501.

DiFRANCO, D., MUIR, D. W., & DODWELL, P. C. Reaching in very young infants. *Perception*, 1978, *7*, 385–392.

DIRKS, J., & GIBSON, E. Infants' perception of similarity between live people and their photographs. *Child Development*, 1977, *48*, 124–130.

DITTRICHOVA, J., & PAUL, K. Responsivity in newborns during sleep. *Activitas Nervosa Superior*, 1974, *16*, 112–113.

DOBSON, V., & TELLER, D. Visual acuity in human infants: A review and comparison of behavioral and electrophysiological studies. *Vision Research*, 1978, *18*, 1469–1483.

DODWELL, P. C., MUIR, D., & DiFRANCO, D. Responses of infants to visually presented objects. *Science*, 1976, *194*, 209–211.

DONNEE, L. H. *Infants' developmental scanning patterns to face and non-face stimuli under various auditory conditions*. Paper presented at the meeting of the Society for Research in Child Development, Philadelphia, 1973.

DOWNING, S. E., & LEE, J. C. Laryngeal chemo-sensitivity: A possible mechanism of sudden infant death. *Pediatrics*, 1975, *55*, 640–649.

DUKE-ELDER, S., & COOK, C. *Systems of ophthalmology* (Vol. 3). St. Louis, Mo.: C. V. Mosby, 1963.

EILERS, R. E. Context-sensitive perception of naturally produced stop and fricative consonants by infants. *Journal of the Acoustical Society of America*, 1977, *61*, 1321–1336.

EILERS, R. E., & MINIFIE, F. D. Fricative discrimination in early infancy. *Journal of Speech and Hearing Research*, 1975, *18*, 158–167.

EILERS, R. E., WILSON, W. R., & MOORE, J. M. Developmental changes in speech discrimination in three-, six-, and twelve-month-old infants. *Journal of Speech and Hearing Research*, 1977, *20*, 766–780.

EIMAS, P. D. Auditory and linguistic processing of cues for place of articulation by infants. *Perception & Psychophysics*, 1974, *16*, 513–521.

EIMAS, P. D. Auditory and phonetic coding of the cues for speech: Discrimination of the [r-l] distinction by young infants. *Perception & Psychophysics*, 1975a, *18*, 341–347.

EIMAS, P. D. Speech perception in early infancy. In L. B. Cohen & P. Salapatek (Eds.), *Infant perception* (Vol. 2). New York: Academic Press, 1975b.

EIMAS, P. D. Developmental aspects of speech perception. In R. Held, H. Leibowitz, & H-L. Teuber (Eds.), *Handbook of sensory physiology* (Vol. 8). New York: Springer-Verlag, 1978.

EIMAS, P. D., & MILLER, J. L. Effects of selective adaptation on the perception of speech and visual patterns: Evidence for feature detectors. In R. D. Walk & H. L. Pick, Jr. (Eds.), *Perception and experience*. New York: Plenum, 1978.

EIMAS, P. D., & TARTTER, V. C. The development of speech perception. In H. W. Reese & L. P. Lipsitt (Eds.), *Advances in child development and behavior* (Vol. 13). New York: Academic Press, 1979.

EIMAS, P. D., SIQUELAND, E. R., JUSCZYK, P., & VIGORITO, J. Speech perception in infants. *Science*, 1971, *171*, 303–306.

EISENBERG, R. B. Auditory behavior in the human neonate. I. Methodologic problems and the logical design of research procedures. *Journal of Auditory Research*, 1965, *5*, 159–177.

EISENBERG, R. B. *Auditory competence in early life: The roots of communicative behavior*. Baltimore, Md.: University Park Press, 1976.

EISENBERG, R. B. Stimulus significance as a determinant of infant responses to sound. In E. B. Thoman (Ed.), *Origins of the infant's social responsiveness*. Hillsdale, N.J.: Lawrence Erlbaum Associates, 1979.

EMDE, R., HARMON, R., METCALF, D., KOENIG, K., & WAGONFELD, S. Stress and neonatal sleep. *Psychosomatic Medicine*, 1971, *33*, 491–497.

ENGEL, R. Early waves of the electroencephalic auditory response in neonates. *Neuropaediatrie*, 1971, *3*, 147–154.

ENGEN, T. Psychophysical analysis of the odor intensity of homologous alcohols. *Journal of Experimental Psychology*, 1965, *70*, 611–616.

ENGEN, T., & LIPSITT, L. P. Decrement and recovery of responses to olfactory stimuli in the human neonate. *Journal of Comparative and Physiological Psychology*, 1965, *59*, 312–316.

ENGEN, T., LIPSITT, L. P., & KAYE, H. Olfactory responses and adaptation in the human neonate. *Journal of Comparative and Physiological Psychology*, 1963, *56*, 73–77.

ENGEN, T., LIPSITT, L. P., & PECK, M. B. Ability of newborn infants to discriminate sapid substances. *Developmental Psychology*, 1974, *10*, 741–746.

ENGEN, T., LIPSITT, L. P., & ROBINSON, D. O. The human newborn's sucking behavior for sweet fluids as a function of birthweight and maternal weight. *Infant Behavior and Development*, 1978, *1*, 118–121.

FAGAN, J. F. Infants' recognition of invariant features of faces. *Child Development*, 1976, *47*, 627–638.

FAGAN, J. F. An attention model of infant recognition. *Child Development*, 1977, *48*, 345–359.

FAGAN, J. F., III. Facilitation of infant's recognition memory. *Child Development*, 1978, *49*, 1066–1075.

FAGAN, J. F., III, & SHEPHERD, P. A. Infants' perception of face orientation. *Infant Behavior and Development*, 1979, *2*, 227–234.

FAGAN, J. F., & SINGER, L. T. The role of simple feature differences in infants' recognition of faces. *Infant Behavior and Development*, 1979, *2*, 39–48.

FAIRWEATHER, D.V.I., & ESKES, T.K.A.B. *Amniotic fluid. Research and clinical application* (2nd ed.). Amsterdam: Excerpta Medica, 1978.

FANTZ, R. L. Pattern vision in young infants. *Psychological Record*, 1958, *8*, 43–49.

FANTZ, R. L. The origin of form perception. *Scientific American*, 1961, *204*, 66–72.

FANTZ, R. L. Pattern vision in newborn infants. *Science*, 1963, *140*, 296–297.

FANTZ, R. L., FAGAN, J. F., & MIRANDA, S. Early visual selectivity. Pp. 249–341 in L. Cohen & P. Salapatek (Eds.), *Infant perception: From sensation to cognition*. New York: Academic Press, 1975.

FANTZ, R. L., ORDY, J. M., & UDELF, M. S. Maturation of pattern vision in infants during the first six months. *Journal of Comparative and Physiological Psychology*, 1962, *55*, 907–917.

FARBMAN, A. I., & GESTELAND, R. C. Developmental and electrophysiological studies of olfactory mucosa in organ culture. In D. A. Denton & J. P. Coghlan (Eds.), *Olfaction and taste*. New York: Academic Press, 1975.

FELDMAN, A. S. Tympanometry-procedures, interpretations and variables. In A. S. Feldman & L. A. Wilber (Eds.), *Acoustic impedance and admittance—The measurement of middle ear function*. Baltimore, Md.: Williams & Wilkins, 1976.

FIELD, J. Relation of young infants' reaching behavior to stimulus distance and solidarity. *Developmental Psychology*, 1976, *12*, 444–448.

FIELD, J. Coordination of vision and prehension in infants. *Child Development*, 1977, *48*, 97–103.

FIELD, J., DiFRANCO, D., DODWELL, P., & MUIR, D. Auditory-visual coordination in 2½ month old infants. *Infant Behavior and Development*, 1979, *2*, 113–122.

FIELD, T. M. Visual and cardiac responses to animate and inanimate faces by young term and preterm infants. *Child Development*, 1979, *50*, 188–194.

FOX, R., ASLIN, R., SHEA, S. L., & DUMAIS, S. Stereopsis in human infants. *Science*, 1980, *207*, 323–324.

GALAMBOS, R., & HECOX, K. Clinical applications of the brain stem auditory evoked potentials. In J. E. Desmedt (Ed.), *Auditory evoked potentials in man*. New York: Karger, 1977.

GARDINER, M. F., & WALTER, D. O. Evidence of hemispheric specialization from infant EEG. In S. Harnad, R. Doty, L. Goldstein, J. Jaynes, & G. Krauthamer (Eds.), *Lateralization in the nervous system*. New York: Academic Press, 1977.

GARDNER, E., GRAY, D. J., & O'RAHILLY, R. *Anatomy. A regional study of human structure* (2nd ed.). Philadelphia: Saunders, 1963.

GESELL, A. The tonic neck reflex in the human infant. *Journal of Pediatrics*, 1938, *13*, 455–464.

GIBSON, E. J. *Principles of perceptual learning and development*. Englewood Cliffs, N.J.: Prentice-Hall, 1969.

GIBSON, E. J., OWSLEY, C. J., & JOHNSTON, J. Perception of invariants by 5-month-old infants: Differentiation of two types of motion. *Developmental Psychology*, 1978, *14*, 407–415.

GIBSON, E. J., & WALK, R. The "visual cliff." *Scientific American*, 1960, *202*, 64–71.

GIBSON, J. J. *The senses considered as perceptual systems*. Boston: Houghton-Mifflin, 1966.

GIRTON, M. Infants' attention to intrastimulus motion. *Journal of Experimental Child Psychology*, 1979, *28*, 416–423.

GLANVILLE, B., BEST, C., & LEVENSON, R. A cardiac measure of cerebral asymmetries in infant auditory perception. *Developmental Psychology*, 1977, *13*, 54–59.

GORDON, F. R., & YONAS, A. Sensitivity to binocular depth information in infants. *Journal of Experimental Child Psychology*, 1976, *22*, 413–422.

GOTTFRIED, A. W., ROSE, S. A., & BRIDGER, W. H. Cross-modal transfer in human infants. *Child Development*, 1977, *48*, 118–123.

GOTTFRIED, A. W., ROSE, S. A., & BRIDGER, W. H. Effects of visual, haptic, and manipulatory experiences on infants' visual recognition memory of objects. *Developmental Psychology*, 1978, *14*, 305–312.

GRAHAM, F. K., & CLIFTON, R. K. Heart-rate change as a component of the orienting response. *Psychological Bulletin*, 1966, *65*, 305–320.

GRAHAM, F. K., & JACKSON, J. C. Arousal systems and infant heart rate responses. In L. P. Lipsitt & W. H. Reese (Eds.), *Advances in child development and behavior* (Vol. 5). New York: Academic Press, 1970.

GRAHAM, F. K., LEAVITT, L. A., STROCK, B. D., & BROWN, J. W. Precocious cardiac orienting in human anencephalic infants *Science*, 1978, *199*, 322–324.

GREENBERG, D. J. Accelerating visual complexity levels in the human infant. *Child Development*, 1971, *42*, 905–918.

GREENBERG, D. J., & O'DONNELL, W. J. Infancy and the optimal level of stimulation. *Child Development*, 1972, *43*, 639–645.

HAINLINE, L. Developmental changes in visual scanning of face and nonface patterns by infants. *Journal of Experimental Child Psychology*, 1978, *25*, 90–115.

HAITH, M. M. Visual competence in early infancy. In R. H. Held, H. Leibowitz, & H. L. Teuber (Eds.), *Handbook of sensory physiology* (Vol. 8). New York: Springer-Verlag, 1978.

HAYNES, H., WHITE, B. L., & HELD, R. Visual accommodation in human infants. *Science*, 1965, *148*, 528–530.

HECOX, K. Electrophysiological correlates of human auditory development. In L. B. Cohen & P. Salapatek (Eds.), *Infant perception: From sensation to cognition. II.* Perception of space, speech and sound. New York: Academic Press, 1975.

HECOX, K., & GALAMBOS, R. Brain stem auditory evoked responses in human infants and adults. *Archives of Otolaryngology*, 1974, *99*, 30–33.

HIMELFARB, M. Z., POPELKA, G. R., & SHANON, E. Tympanometry in normal neonates. *Journal of Speech and Hearing Research*, 1979, *22*, 179–191.

HOCHBERG, J. E., & BROOKS, V. Pictorial recognition as an unlearned ability: A study of one child's performance. *American Journal of Psychology*, 1962, *75*, 624–628.

HOFFMAN, R. F. Developmental changes in human infant visual-evoked potentials to patterned stimuli recorded at different scalp locations. *Child Development*, 1978, *49*, 110–118.

HOLLINGSHEAD, W. H. *Textbook of anatomy* (3rd ed.). Hagerstown, Md.: Harper & Row, 1974.

HORSTEN, G., & WINKELMAN, J. Electro-retinographic critical fusion frequency of the retina in relation to histological development in man and animals. *Documenta Opthalmologica*, 1964, *18*, 515–521.

HOVERSTEN, G. H., & MONCUR, J. P. Stimuli and intensity factors in testing infants. *Journal of Speech and Hearing Research*, 1969, *12*, 687–702.

HUMPHREY, T. Function of the nervous system during prenatal life. In U. Stave (Ed.), *Perinatal physiology*. New York: Plenum, 1978.

HUTT, S., HUTT, C., LENARD, H., VON BERNUTH, H., & MUNTJEWERFF, W. Auditory responsivity in the human neonate. *Nature*, 1968, *218*, 888–890.

JACKSON, J. C., KANTOWITZ, S. R., & GRAHAM, F. K. Can newborns show cardiac orienting? *Child Development*, 1971, *42*, 107–121.

JOHNSON, P., ROBINSON, J. S., & SALISBURY, D. The onset and control of breathing after birth. In K. S. Comline, K. W. Cross, G. S. Dawes, & P. W. Nathaniels (Eds.), *Foetal and neonatal physiology*. Cambridge, England: Cambridge University Press, 1973.

JOHNSON, P., & SALISBURY, D. M. Breathing and sucking during feeding in the newborn. In *Parent-infant interaction*. Amsterdam: CIBA Foundation Symposium 33, new series, ASP, 1975.

JOHNSON, P., & SALISBURY, D. M. Preliminary studies on feeding and breathing in the newborn. In J. M. Weiffenbach (Ed.), *Taste and development: The genesis of sweet preference*. Washington, D.C.: U.S. Government Printing Office, 1977.

JOHNSSON, L.-G., & HAWKINS, J. E., JR. Sensory and neural degeneration with aging, as seen in microdissections of the human inner ear. *Annals of Otology, Rhinology and Laryngology*, 1972, *81*, 179–193.

JUSCZYK, P. W. Perception of syllable-final stop consonants by 2-month-old infants. *Perception and Psychophysics*, 1977, *21*, 450–454.

JUSCZYK, P. W., & THOMPSON, E. Perception of a phonetic contrast in multi-syllabic utterances by two-month-old infants. *Perception and Psychophysics*, 1978, *23*, 105–109.

KARMEL, B. Z. The effect of age, complexity, and amount of contour on pattern preferences in human infants. *Journal of Experimental Child Psychology*, 1969a, *7*, 339–354.

KARMEL, B. Z. Complexity, amount of contour, and visually dependent preference behavior in hooded rats, domestic chicks, and human infants. *Journal of Comparative and Physiological Psychology*, 1969b, *69*, 649–657.

KARMEL, B. Z., & MAISEL, E. B. A neuronal activity model for infant visual attention. In L. B. Cohen & P. Salapatek (Eds.), *Infant perception: From sensation to cognition: Basic visual processes* (Vol. 1). New York: Academic Press, 1975.

KEITH, R. W. Impedance audiometry with neonates. *Archives of Otolaryngology*, 1973, *97*, 248–257.

KEITH, R. W. Middle ear function in neonates. *Archives of Otolaryngology*, 1975, *101*, 375–379.

KESSEN, W., & BORNSTEIN, M. H. Discriminability of brightness change for infants. *Journal of Experimental Child Psychology*, 1978, *25*, 526–530.

KESSEN, W., LEVINE, J., & WENDRICH, K. A. The imitation of pitch in infants. *Infant Behavior and Development*, 1979, *2*, 93–100.

KLAUS, M. H., & KENNELL, J. H. *Maternal-infant bonding*. St. Louis, Mo.: C. V. Mosby, 1976.

KREMENITZER, J., VAUGHAN, A. G., KURTZBERG, D., & DOWLING, K. Smooth-pursuit movements in the newborn infant. *Child Development*, 1979, *50*, 442–448.

LAMB, L. E., & DUNCKEL, D. C. Acoustic impedance measurement with children. In A. S. Feldman & L. A. Wilber (Eds.), *Acoustic impedance and admittance—The measurement of middle ear function*. Baltimore, Md.: Williams & Wilkins, 1976.

LAMPER, K., & EISDORFER, J. Prestimulus activity level and responsivity in the neonate. *Child Development*, 1971, *42*, 465–473.

LASKY, R. Length of familiarization and preference for novel and familiar stimuli. *Infant Behavior and Development*, 1980, *3*, 15–28.

LASKY, R. E., & GOGEL, W. C. The perception of relative motion by young infants. *Perception*, 1978, *7*, 617–623.

LASKY, R. E., SYRDAL-LASKY, A., & KLEIN, R. E. VOT discrimination by four and six and a half month old infants from Spanish environments. *Journal of Experimental Child Psychology*, 1975, *20*, 215–225.

LAST, P. *Eugene Wolff's anatomy of the eye and orbit*. London: Lewis, 1968.

LENNENBERG, E. *Biological foundations of language*. New York: John Wiley, 1967.

LEWIS, M., BARTELS, B., & GOLDBERG, S. State as a determinant of infant's heart rate response to stimulation. *Science*, 1967, *155*, 486–488.

LEWIS, M., & BROOKS, J. Self-knowledge and emotional development. In M. Lewis & L. Rosenblum (Eds.), *The development of affect*. New York: Plenum, 1978.

LEWIS, T. L., MAUER, D., & KAY, D. Newborns' central vision: Whole or hole? *Journal of Experimental Child Psychology*, 1978, *26*, 193–203.

LING, B. C. A genetic study of sustained visual fixation and associated behavior in the human infant from birth to six months. *Journal of Genetic Psychology*, 1942, *61*, 227–277.

LIPSITT, L. P. Taste in human neonates: Its effects on sucking and heart rate. In J. M. Weiffenbach (Ed.), *Taste and development: The genesis of sweet preference*. Washington, D.C.: U.S. Government Printing Office, 1977.

LIPSITT, L. P., ENGEN, T., & KAYE, H. Developmental changes in the olfactory threshold of the neonate. *Child Development*, 1963, *34*, 371–376.

LIPSITT, L. P., & LEVY, N. Electrotactual threshold in the neonate. *Child Development*, 1959, *30*, 547–554.

LIPSITT, L. P., REILLY, B. M., BUTCHER, M. J., & GREENWOOD, M. M. The stability and interrelationships of newborn sucking and heart rate. *Developmental Psychobiology*, 1976, *9*, 305–310.

LIPTON, E. L., STEINSCHNEIDER, A., & RICHMOND, J. B. Autonomic function in the neonate. VII: Maturational changes in cardiac control. *Child Development*, 1966, *37*, 1–16.

LYONS-RUTH, K. Bimodal perception in infancy: Response to auditory-visual incongruity. *Child Development*, 1977, *48*, 820–827.

MACDONALD, N. E., & SILVERMAN, I. W. Smiling and laughter in infants as a function of level of arousal and cognitive evaluation. *Developmental Psychology*, 1978, *14*, 235–241.

MACFARLANE, A. Olfaction in the development of social preferences in the human neonate. In *Parent-infant interaction*. Amsterdam: CIBA Foundation Symposium 33, new series, ASP, 1975.

MCGUIRE, I., & TURKEWITZ, G. Visually-elicited finger movements in infants. *Child Development*, 1978, *49*, 362–370.

MCGURK, H., TURNURE, C., & CREIGHTON, S. J. Auditory-visual coordination in neonates. *Child Development*, 1977, *48*, 138–143.

MCKENZIE, B. E., & DAY, R. H. Distance as a determinant of visual fixation in early infancy. *Science*, 1972, *178*, 1108–1110.

MCRANDLE, C. C., SMITH, M. A., & GOLDSTEIN, R. Early averaged electroencephalic responses to clicks in neonates. *Annals of Otology, Rhinology, and Laryngology*, 1974, *83*, 695–702.

MAISEL, E. B., & KARMEL, B. Z. Contour density and pattern configuration in visual preferences of infants. *Infant Behavior and Development*, 1978, *1*, 127–140.

MALLER, O., & DESOR, J. A. Effect of taste on ingestion by human newborns. In J. F. Rosma (Ed.), *Fourth symposium on oral sensation and perception*. Washington, D. C.: U.S. Government Printing Office, 1973.

MANN, I. *The development of the human eye*. London: British Medical Association, 1964.

MANS, L., CICCHETTI, D., & SROUFE, L. A. Mirror reaction of Down's syndrome infants and toddlers: Cognitive underpinnings of self-recognition. *Child Development*, 1978, *49*, 1247–1250.

MATTINGLY, I. G., LIBERMAN, A. M., SYRDAL, A. K., & HALWES, T. Discrimination in speech and nonspeech modes. *Cognitive Psychology*, 1971, *2*, 131–157.

MAUER, D. *The development of binocular convergence in infants.* Doctoral dissertation, University of Minnesota, 1974.

MAUER, D. Infant visual perception: Methods of study. In L. B. Cohen & P. Salapatek (Eds.), *Infant perception: From sensation to cognition: Basic visual processes* (Vol. 1). New York: Academic Press, 1975.

MAUER, D., & LEWIS, T. Peripheral discrimination by 3-month-old infants. *Child Development*, 1979, *50*, 276–279.

MAUER, D., & SALAPATEK, P. Developmental changes in the scanning of faces by young infants. *Child Development*, 1976, *47*, 523–527.

MENDEL, M. I., ADKINSON, C. D., & HARKER, L. A. Middle components of the auditory evoked potentials in infants. *Annals of Otology, Rhinology and Laryngology*, 1977, *86*, 293–299.

MENDELSON, M. J. Oculomotor activity and nonnutritive sucking are coordinated at birth. *Infant Behavior and Development*, 1979, *2*, 341–353.

MENDELSON, M. J., & HAITH, M. The relation between audition and vision in the human newborn. *Monograph of the Society for Research in Child Development*, 1976, *41*(Whole No. 167).

MILEWSKI, A. E. Infants' discrimination of internal and external pattern elements. *Journal of Experimental Child Psychology*, 1976, *22*, 229–246.

MILEWSKI, A. E. Young infants' visual processing of internal and adjacent shapes. *Infant Behavior and Development*, 1978, *1*, 359–371.

MILEWSKI, A. E. Visual discrimination and detection of configurational and invariance in 3-month-old infants. *Developmental Psychology*, 1979, *15*, 357–363.

MILLER, D. J. Visual habituation in the human infant. *Child Development*, 1972, *43*, 481–493.

MILLER, D. J., RYAN, E. B., SINNOTT, J. P., & WILSON, M. A. Serial habituation in two-, three-, and four-month-old infants. *Child Development*, 1976, *47*, 341–349.

MOFFITT, A. R. Consonant cue perception by twenty to twenty-four week old infants. *Child Development*, 1971, *42*, 717–731.

MOLFESE, D. L., FREEMAN, R. B., JR., & PALERMO, D. S. The ontogeny of brain lateralization for speech and nonspeech stimuli. *Brain and Language*, 1975, *2*, 356–368.

MOLFESE, D. L., & MOLFESE, V. J. Hemisphere and stimulus differences as reflected in the cortical responses of newborn infants to speech stimuli. *Developmental Psychology*, 1979, *15*, 505–511.

MONCRIEFF, R. W. A technique for comparing the threshold concentrations for olfactory, trigeminal and ocular irritations. *Quarterly Journal of Experimental Psychology*, 1955, *7*, 128–132.

MONCRIEFF, R. W. *The chemical senses* (3rd ed.). Cleveland: CRC Press, 1967.

MORSE, P. A. The discrimination of speech and nonspeech stimuli in early infancy. *Journal of Experimental Child Psychology*, 1972, *14*, 477–492.

MOSKOWITZ, H. R. The sweetness and pleasantness of sugars. *American Psychologist*, 1971, *84*, 387–405.

MUIR, D., & FIELD, J. Newborn infants' orientation to sound. *Child Development*, 1979, *50*, 431–436.

NELSON, C. A., MORSE, P. A., & LEAVITT, L. A. Recognition of facial expression by seven-month-old infants. *Child Development*, 1979, *50*, 1239–1242.

NISBETT, R., & GURWITZ, S. Weight, sex, and the eating behavior of human newborns. *Journal of Comparative and Physiological Psychology*, 1970, *73*, 245–253.

NORTHERN, J. L., & DOWNS, M. P. *Hearing in children.* Baltimore, Md.: Williams & Wilkins Co., 1974.

NOWLIS, G. H., & KESSEN, W. Human newborns differentiate differing concentrations of sucrose and glucose. *Science*, 1976, *191*, 865–866.

OHLRICH, E. S., BARNET, A. B., WEISS, I. P., & SHANKS, B. L. Auditory evoked potential development in childhood: A longitudinal study. *Electroencephalography and Clinical Neurophysiology*, 1978, *44*, 411–423.

ORDY, J. M., SAMORAJSKI, T., COLLINS, R. L., & NAGY, A. R. Postnatal development of vision in a subhuman primate (*Macaca mulatta*). *Archives of Ophthalmology*, 1965, *73*, 674–686.

ORTI, E. Steroid hormone formation and metabolism. In U. Stave (Ed.), *Perinatal physiology* (2nd ed.). New York: Plenum, 1978.

OWSLEY, C. J. *Extracting invariance from changing stimulation in infancy.* Paper presented at a Celebration in Honor of Eleanor Gibson, Cornell University, Ithaca, June 1979.

PARKER, G. H. *Smell, taste and allied senses in the vertebrates.* Philadelphia: Lippincott, 1922.

PARKS, M. M. Growth of the eye and development of vision. In S. Liebman & S. Gellis (Eds.), *The pediatrician's ophthalmology*. St. Louis, Mo.: C. V. Mosby, 1966.

PEIPER, A. *Cerebral function in infancy and childhood.* New York: Consultants Bureau, 1963.

PIAGET, J. *The construction of reality in the child.* New York: Ballantine, 1971; New York: Basic Books, 1954.

PICTON, T. W., & HILLYARD, S. A. Human auditory evoked potentials. II: Effects of attention. *Electroencephalography and Clinical Neurophysiology*, 1974, *36*, 191–199.

PICTON, T. W., HILLYARD, S. A., KRAUSZ, H. I., & GALAMBOS, R. Human auditory evoked potentials. I: Evaluation of components. *Electroencephalography and Clinical Neurophysiology*, 1974, *36*, 179–190.

PIETRAS, R. J., & MOULTON, D. G. Effects of gonadal steroids on odor detection performance in the rat. In D. A. Denton & J. P. Coghlan (Eds.), *Olfaction and taste*. New York: Academic Press, 1975.

PIPP, S., & HAITH, M. M. Infant visual scanning of two and three-dimensional forms. *Child Development*, 1977, *48*, 1640–1644.

RAPIN, I., & GRAZIANI, L. Auditory evoked responses in normal, brain damaged, and deaf infants. *Neurology*, 1967, *17*, 881–894.

REWEY, H. H. Developmental change in infant heart rate response during sleep and waking states. *Developmental Psychology*, 1973, *8*, 35–41.

RICHARDS, M.P.M., BERNAL, J. F., & BRACKBILL, Y. Early behavioral differences: Gender or circumcision? *Developmental Psychobiology*, 1976, *9*, 89–95.

RIESER, J. Spatial orientation of six-month-old infants, *Child Development*, 1979, *50*, 1078–1087.

RIESER, J., YONAS, A., & WIKNER, K. Radial localization of odors by human neonates. *Child Development*, 1976, *47*, 856–859.

ROSCH, E. Cognitive representations of semantic categories. *Journal of Experimental Child Psychology: General*, 1975a, *104*, 192–233.

ROSCH, E. The nature of mental codes for color categories. *Journal of Experimental Psychology: Human Perception and Performance*, 1975b, *1*, 303–322.

ROSCH, E. Universals and cultural specifics in human categorization. In R. BRISLIN, S. BOCHNER, & W. LONNER (Eds.), *Cross-cultural perspectives on learning*. New York: Halsted Press, 1975c.

ROSE, S. A. Infants' transfer of response between 2-dimensional and 3-dimensional stimuli. *Child Development*, 1977, *48*, 1086–1091.

ROSE, S. A. Enhancing visual recognition memory in preterm infants. *Developmental Psychology*, 1980, *16*, 85–92.

ROSE, S. A., GOTTFRIED, A. W., & BRIDGER, W. H. Cross-modal transfer in infants: Relationship to prematurity and SES background. *Developmental Psychology*, 1978, *14*, 643–652.

ROSE, S. A., GOTTFRIED, A. W., & BRIDGER, W. H. Effects of haptic cues on visual recognition memory in fullterm and preterm infants. *Infant Behavior and Development*, 1979, *2*, 55–67.

ROSE, S. A., SCHMIDT, K., & BRIDGER, W. H. Cardiac and behavioral responsivity to tactile stimulation in premature and fullterm infants. *Developmental Psychology*, 1976, *12*, 311–320.

ROSE, S. A., SCHMIDT, K., & BRIDGER, W. H. Changes in tactile responsivity during sleep in the human newborn infant. *Developmental Psychology*, 1978, *14*, 163–172.

ROSE, S. A., SCHMIDT, K., RIESE, M. L., & BRIDGER, W. H. Effects of prematurity and early intervention on responsivity to tactual stimuli: A comparison of preterm and fullterm infants. *Child Development*, 1980, *51*, 416–425.

ROVEE, C. K. Psychophysical scaling of olfactory response to the aliphalic alcohols in human neonates. *Journal of Experimental Child Psychology*, 1969, *7*, 245–254.

RUFF, H. Infant recognition of the invariant form of objects. *Child Development*, 1978, *49*, 293–306.

RUFF, H. A. The development of perception and recognition of objects. *Child Development*, 1980, *51*, 981–992.

RUFF, H. A., & KOHLER, C. J. Tactual-visual transfer in six-month-old infants. *Infant Behavior and Development*, 1978, *1*, 259–264.

SAINT-ANNE DARGASSIES, S. Part V: Neurological maturation of the premature infant of 28 to 41 weeks gestational age. In F. Falkner (Ed.), *Human development*. Philadelphia: Saunders, 1966.

SALAMY, A., & McKEAN, C. M. Postnatal development of human brainstem potentials during the first year of life. *Electroencephalography and Clinical Neurophysiology*, 1976, *40*, 418–426.

SALAMY, A., McKEAN, C. M., & BUDA, F. Maturational changes in auditory transmission as reflected in human brainstem potentials. *Brain Research*, 1975, *96*, 361–366.

SALAPATEK, P. Pattern perception in early infancy. In L. B. Cohen & P. Salapatek (Eds.), *Infant perception: From sensation to cognition: Basic visual processes* (Vol. 1). New York: Academic Press, 1975.

SALAPATEK, P., & BANKS, M. Infant sensory assessment: Vision. In F. D. du Minifie & L. L. Lloyd (Eds.), *Communicative and cognitive abilities: Early behavioral assessment*. Baltimore, Md.: University Park Press, 1978.

SALAPATEK, P., BECHTOLD, A. G., & BUSHNELL, E. W. Infant acuity as a function of viewing distance. *Child Development*, 1976, *47*, 860–863.

SALAPATEK, P., & KESSEN, W. Visual scanning of triangles by the human newborn. *Journal of Experimental Child Psychology*, 1966, *3*, 155–167.

SARNAT, H. B. Olfactory reflexes in the newborn infant. *The Journal of Pediatrics*, 1978, *92*, 624–626.

SCHMIDT, K., & BIRNS, B. The behavioral arousal threshold in infant sleep as a function of time and sleep state. *Child Development*, 1971, *42*, 269–277.

SCHULMAN, C. A. Heart rate audiometry. Part I. An evaluation of heart rate response to auditory stimuli in newborn hearing screening. *Neuropediatrie*, 1973, *4*, 362–374.

SCHULMAN-GALAMBOS, C., & GALAMBOS, R. Brain stem auditory-evoked responses in premature infants. *Journal of Speech and Hearing Research*, 1975, *18*, 456–465.

SCHULMAN-GALAMBOS, C., & GALAMBOS, R. Brain stem evoked response audiometry in newborn hearing screening. *Archives of Otolaryngology*, 1979, *105*, 86–90.

SCHWARTZ, M., & DAY, R. H. Visual shape perception in early infancy. *Monograph of the Society for Research in Child Development*, 1979, *44*,(Whole No. 182).

SCIBETTA, J. J., ROSEN, M. G., HOCHBERG, C. J., & CHIK, L. Human fetal brain response to sound during labor. *American Journal of Obstetrics and Gynecology*, 1971, *109*, 82–85.

SIMMONS, F. B. Identification of hearing loss in infants and young children. *Otolaryngologic Clinics of North America*, 1978, *11*, 19–28.

SLATOR, A. M., & FINDLAY, F. M. Binocular fixation in the newborn baby. *Journal of Experimental Child Psychology*, 1975, *20*, 248–273.

SOKOLOV, E. N. *Perception and the conditioned reflex*. New York: Macmillan, 1963.

SONTAG, L. W., & WALLACE, R. F. The movement response of the human fetus to sound stimuli. *Child Development*, 1935, *6*, 253–258.

SOROKA, S. M., CORTER, C. M., & ABRAMOVITCH, R. Infants' tactual discrimination of novel and familiar tactual stimuli. *Child Development*, 1979, *50*, 1251–1253.

SPEARS, W. C., & HOHLE, R. H. Sensory and perceptual processes in infants. In Y. Brackbill (Ed.), *Infancy and early childhood. A handbook and guide to human development*. New York: Free Press, 1967.

SPELKE, E. Infants' intermodal perception of events. *Cognitive Psychology*, 1976, *8*, 553–560.

SPELKE, E. *Intermodal exploration by four-month-old infants: Perception and knowlege of auditory-visual events*. Unpublished doctoral dissertation, Cornell University, 1978.

SPELKE, E. Exploring audible and visible events in infancy. In A. D. Pick (Ed.), *Perception and its development: A tribute to Eleanor J. Gibson*. Hillsdale, N.J.: Lawrence Erlbaum Associates, 1979a.

SPELKE, E. Perceiving bimodally specified events in infancy. *Developmental Psychology*, 1979b, *15*, 626–636.

SPELKE, E. S., & OWSLEY, C. J. Intermodal exploration and knowledge in infancy. *Infant Behavior and Development*, 1979, *2*, 13–27.

STARR, A., AMLIE, R. N., MARTIN, W. H., & SAUNDERS, S. Devel-

opment of auditory function in newborn infants revealed by auditory brainstem potentials. *Pediatrics*, 1977, *60*, 831–839.

STEINER, J. E. The gustofacial response: Observation on normal and anencephalic newborn infants. In J. F. Bosma (Ed.), *Oral sensation and perception: Development in the fetus and infant*. Washington, D.C.: U.S. Government Printing Office, 1973.

STEINER, J. E. Innate discriminative human facial expression to taste and smell stimulation. (Discussion paper.) *Annals of the New York Academy of Sciences*, 1974, *237*, 229–233.

STEINER, J. E. Facial expressions of the neonate infant indicating the hedonics of food-related chemical stimuli. In J. M. Weiffenbach (Ed.), *Taste and development: The genesis of sweet preference*. Washington, D.C.: U.S. Government Printing Office, 1977.

STEINER, J. E. Human facial expressions in response to taste and smell stimulation. In H. Reese & L. Lipsitt (Eds.), *Advances in child development and behavior* (Vol. 13). New York: Academic Press, 1979.

STEINER, J. E., & FINNEGAN, L. Innate discriminative facial expression to food related odorants in the neonate infant. *Israel Journal of Medical Sciences*, 1975, *11*, 858.

STEINSCHNEIDER, A., LIPTON, E. L., & RICHMOND, J. B. Auditory sensitivity in the infant: Effect of intensity on cardiac and motor responsivity. *Child Development*, 1966, *37*, 233–252.

STRAUSS, M. S. The abstraction of prototypical information by adults and 10-month-old infants. *Journal of Experimental Child Psychology: Human Learning and Memory*, 1979, *5*, 618–632.

SWOBODA, P. J., DASS, J., MORSE, P. A., & LEAVITT, L. A. Memory factors in vowel discrimination of normal and at-risk infants. *Child Development*, 1978, *49*, 332–339.

SWOBODA, P. J., MORSE, P. A., & LEAVITT, L. A. Continuous vowel discrimination in normal and at-risk infants. *Child Development*, 1976, *47*, 459–465.

TAGUCHI, K., PICTON, T., ORPIN, J., & GOODMAN, W. Evoked response audiometry in newborn infants. *Acta Oto-Laryngologica Supplementum*, 1969, *252*, 5–17.

TELLER, D. Y. The forced choice preferential looking procedure: A psychophysical technique for use with human infants. *Infant Behavior and Development*, 1979, *2*, 135–153.

THOMAS, H. Unfolding the baby's mind: The infant's selection of visual stimuli. *Psychological Review*, 1973, *80*, 468.

TREHUB, S. E. *Auditory-linguistic sensitivity in infants*. Unpublished doctoral dissertation, McGill University, Montreal, Canada, 1973a.

TREHUB, S. E. Infants' sensitivity to vowel and tonal contrasts. *Developmental Psychology*, 1973b, *9*, 91–96.

TREHUB, S. E., & CURRAN, S. Habituation of infants' cardiac response to speech stimuli. *Child Development*, 1979, *50*, 1247–1250.

TREHUB, S. E., & RABINOVITCH, M. S. Auditory-linguistic sensitivity in early infancy. *Developmental Psychology*, 1972, *6*, 74–77.

TUCHMANN-DUPLESSIS, H., AUROUX, M., & HAEGEL, P. *Illustrated human embryology* (Vol. 3). Nervous system and endocrine glands. New York: Springer-Verlag, 1975.

TUCKER, D. Nonolfactory responses from the nasal cavity: Jacobsen's organ and the trigeminal system. In L. B. Beidler (Ed.), *Handbook of sensory physiology IV*: Chemical senses. New York: Springer-Verlag, 1971.

TURKEWITZ, G., BIRCH, H. B., MOREAU, T., LEVY, L., & CORNWELL, A. C. Effect of intensity of auditory stimulation on directional eye movements in the human neonate. *Animal Behavior*, 1966, *14*, 93–101.

TURKEWITZ, G., GORDON, E. W., & BIRCH, H. G. Head turning in the human neonate: Spontaneous patterns. *Journal of Genetic Psychology*, 1965, *107*, 143–158.

TURKEWITZ, G., MOREAU, T., & BIRCH, H. G. Head position and receptor organization in the human neonate. *Journal of Experimental Child Psychology*, 1966, *4*, 169–177.

VURPILLOT, E., RUEL, J., & CASTREC, A. L'organisation perceptive chez le nourrisson: Réponse au tout ou à ses éléments. *Bulletin de Psychologie*, 1977, *327*, 396–405.

WADA, J. A., CLARKE, R., & HAMM, A. Cerebral hemispheric asymmetry in humans. *Archives of Neurology*, 1975, *32*, 239–246.

WATSON, J. S., HAYES, L. A., VIETZE, P., & BECKER, J. Discriminative infant smiling to orientations of tackling faces of mother and stranger. *Journal of Experimental Child Psychology*, 1979, *28*, 92–99.

WEIFFENBACH, J. F., & THACH, B. T. Elicited tongue movements: Touch and taste in the newborn human. In J. F. Bosma (Ed.),

Oral sensation and perception development in the fetus and infant. Washington, D.C.: U.S. Government Printing Office, 1973.

WEISS, C. Routine non-ritual circumcision in infancy: A new look at an old operation. *Clinical Pediatrics,* 1964, *3,* 560–562.

WEISS, C. Does circumcision of the newborn require an anesthetic? *Clinical Pediatrics,* 1968, *7,* 128–129.

WEITZMAN, E., & GRAZIANI, L. Maturation and topography of the auditory evoked response of the prematurely born infant. *Developments in Psychobiology,* 1968, *1,* 79–89.

WEITZMAN, E. D., & KREMEN, H. Auditory evoked responses during different stages of sleep in man. *Electroencephalography and Clinical Neurophysiology,* 1965, *18,* 65–70.

WERNER, J. S., & WOOTEN, B. R. Human infant color vision and color perception. *Infant Behavior and Development,* 1979, *2,* 241–274.

WERTHEIMER, M. Psychomotor co-ordination of auditory-visual space at birth. *Science,* 1961, *134,* 1962.

WHITE, B. L. *Human infants.* Englewood Cliffs, N.J.: Prentice-Hall, 1971.

WICKELGREN, L. Convergence in the human newborn. *Journal of Experimental Child Psychology,* 1967, *5,* 74–85.

WICKELGREN, L. The ocular response of human newborns to intermittent visual movement. *Journal of Experimental Child Psychology,* 1969, *8,* 469–482.

WILLIAMS, L., & GOLENSKI, J. Infant behavioral state and speech sound discrimination. *Child Development,* 1979, *50,* 1243–1246.

WINDLE, W. F. *Physiology of the fetus. Origin and extent of function in prenatal life.* Philadelphia: Saunders, 1940.

WITELSON, S. F., & PALLIE, W. Left hemisphere specialization for language in the newborn: Neuroanatomical evidence of asymmetry. *Brain,* 1973, *96,* 641–647.

WOLF, K. E., & GOLDSTEIN, R. Middle component averaged electroencephalic responses to tonal stimuli from normal neonates. *Archives of Otolaryngology,* 1978, *104,* 508–513.

WOLFF, P. H. The causes, control and organization of behavior in the neonate. *Psychological Issues,* 1967, *5,* 1–105.

YAKOVLEV, P., & LeCOURS, A. The myelogenetic cycles of regional maturation of the brain. In A. Minkowski (Ed.), *Regional development of the brain in early life.* Oxford: Blackwell, 1967.

YANG, R. K., & DOUTHITT, T. C. Newborn responses to threshold tactile stimulation. *Child Development,* 1974, *45,* 237–242.

YONAS, A. Studies of spatial perception in infants. In A. D. Pick (Ed.), *Perception and its development: A tribute to Eleanor J. Gibson.* Hillsdale, N.J.: Lawrence Erlbaum Associates, 1979.

YONAS, A., CLEAVES, W., & PETTERSON, L. Development of sensitivity to pictorial depth. *Science,* 1978, *200,* 77–79.

YONAS, A., OBERG, C., & NORCIA, A. Development of sensitivity to binocular information for the approach of an object. *Developmental Psychology,* 1978, *14,* 147–152.

YONAS, A., & PETTERSEN, L. *Responsiveness in newborns to optical information for collision.* Paper presented at the Biennial Meeting of the Society for Research in Child Development, San Francisco, March 1979.

16

Early Social Development

ROBERT M. HODAPP
EDWARD MUELLER

Few areas of developmental psychology have expanded as rapidly or in as interesting a fashion as the field of early social development. The number of new topics of research increases yearly, just as the total number of studies in social development multiplies at an almost exponential rate. Just a brief mention of some works in early social development can provide an inkling of the current excitement in this field. There is, first, the recent finding that mother-infant "skin-to-skin" contact, directly following birth, has powerful, lasting effects on the later quality of the mother-infant relationship (Kennell et al., 1974). Mothers who experienced increased contact with their newborns (one hour right after birth, fifteen extra hours within the first three days) were more responsive to their babies one month and even one year later than were "normal (hospital) contact" mothers.

A second, more general, finding is that mothers seem to know how to be "in tune with" their infant's developmental level at each time period. Mothers facilitate infant social skills by successfully eliciting and holding their baby's eye gazes at the three- to four-month period (Stern, 1974a). Similarly when the child is ten months of age and mastering the idea of linguistic intentionality (commands, statements), mothers respond to their infant's pointing to an object with statements like, "Oh, you *want* it," stressing the demand aspects of the message. Later at 16 months when the child's understanding of intentionality has presumably been mastered, mothers say things like, "Oh, you want the *ball*," stressing the object of reference in similar situations (Bruner, 1978).

Another interesting finding comes from the growing field of early peer relations. Infants 12 to 24 months old learn to interact with their same-aged peers in ways strikingly different from their behaviors with mother. A more motor, as opposed to verbal (seen in the parent-child system), mode predominates (Mueller, 1979). In fact skills learned through peer-peer interactions serve at times to teach *parents* how to act, a total shake-up to the traditional socialization process model (Vandell, 1979).

Just as important as the preceding examples, however, are the theoretical assumptions underlying much of the current research. These assumptions, to be stressed in this chapter, serve to anchor advances in the field and, as such, are of importance in their own right.

The first of these principles is that of a *developmental perspective*. This directly contrasts with a learning theory view of development (Reese & Overton, 1970) and, to some extent, also with more psychoanalytic and ethological (i.e., genetically determined, maturational) viewpoints. The developmental perspective, then, involves the analysis of an organism's qualitative (and not simply quantitative) changes over time as it advances to its preferred state of maturity. This process is assumed to involve two complementary processes—differentiation of an existing skill or structure into more finely specified skills (or structures) and subsequent integration of these skills or structures at higher levels of organization (Werner & Kaplan, 1964).

A good example of this developmental approach occurs in the first few days after birth. Examining four subsystems of newborn behavioral functioning, Als (1979) suggests that

the differentiation of the alert state depends on the infant's facility in autonomic functioning, his motoric regulation, and his state regulation. When these are integrated the infant can accomplish sophisticated interactions with a social or inani-

We would like to thank Stephen Wirtz, Cheryl Bragg, and Deborah Lowe Vandell for their thoughtful and detailed comments on earlier versions of this chapter.

mate stimulus without manifesting disruptions in his more basic systems. (p. 25)

Mastery of three basic systems and their integration into a smooth (higher level) mode of functioning allows for the differentiation of the alert state, the only behavioral state in which sophisticated mother-child interaction is possible.

The second major principle underlying much early social developmental research is the concept of *interaction*. This simply means that both participants in a dyadic interaction, be they parent-infant or peer-peer, affect the behavior of the other member.

The main implication of this viewpoint concerns the direction of causality (Bell, 1968). No longer can one solely speak of the mother's actions causing the infant's behavior (as in the traditional "attachment" concept). Both participants in an interaction are considered to cause the other's behavior mutually. Mothers, for example, are thought to be influenced by some sort of infant "feedback loop" (e.g., demonstrating attention, happiness, boredom), just as they influence their infants by offering them their first human contact, warmth, love, and nourishment.

The interactional view is also compatible with the naturalistic-ecological trend now current throughout psychology. It provides a theoretical basis for such research as mother-newborn interactional studies in hospitals (Kennell et al., 1974), mother-infant studies in play situations (Stern, 1974a) and peer-peer studies in play-groups (Mueller & Brenner, 1977).

It may appear, to some extent at least, that the twin perspectives of development and interaction clash, for the developmental task of assessing a single infant's social skills cannot be divorced from the interactive environment from which that skill arises. Furthermore it can be argued that one need only talk of behaviors produced by the infant in the interactive setting, thereby avoiding the issue of skills altogether.

It is our view, however, that interaction by itself does not cause development (i.e., "talking to dogs may not ever produce a talking dog"). An infant's interaction with either the social or nonsocial world has a beneficial effect only if that interaction can be used as a workshop to develop infant skills. It is in this sense that development and interaction go hand-in-hand; it is also in this sense that we feel that the study of the development of infant skills, seen within the interactive setting and employing interactive assumptions (e.g., bidirectionality of effects), is still the most important task of the developmental psychologist.

While using slightly different terminology, Sameroff's (1975) transactional model of development captures this interrelatedness between the developmental and interactional viewpoints. As he explains,

... if developmental processes are to be understood, it will not be through continuous assessment of the child alone, but through a continuous assessment of the transactions between the child and his environment to determine how these transactions facilitate or hinder adaptive integration as both the child and his surroundings change and evolve. (p. 283)

It is this notion of a continuous interplay between development and interactive setting, of change and evolution

in *both* the child and his/her surroundings, which forms the basis of the developmental-interactional analysis. While specific instances of this theoretical point will appear later in this chapter (e.g., pacing and matching concepts), in a more general sense these two complementary viewpoints will be used to characterize all aspects of early social development. It is our view that the joint perspective of development and interaction is the most productive orientation in the field today.

EARLIEST PARENT-CHILD RELATIONS, BIRTH TO SIX MONTHS

Relations between the Mother and Her Newborn

Surrounded by its mother, father, and other interested adults, the human neonate enters a world which is distinctly social in nature. Every bodily need and desire is provided for by this small group of caring adults. Indeed it is probably fair to say that the human neonate is among the least lonely of all people of any age.

In particular the role of the mother in the infant's social world will be emphasized in this section. While the infant-mother dyad is not the sole interpersonal interaction in early infancy, it *is* an important relationship, and one which has produced the greatest body of social developmental literature.

It is instructive to note the work of Klaus and Kennell (Kennell et al., 1974; Klaus & Kennell, 1976) in this context. For while few would deny the importance of the initial mother-infant dyad, these researchers have demonstrated the importance of early mother-infant contact for the later course of this relationship. In an experimental study of 28 hospital-born infants, "extended contact" mothers, or those who experienced 16 extra hours of skin-to-skin contact with their newborns during the first three days after birth, were more responsive than normal hospital contact mothers (who had only 20- to 30-minute feeding sessions with their infants every four hours) at one-month and one-year intervals. At one month this conclusion is based on the differential result of the two groups on (1) questions to the mother, (2) behavior ratings of the mother during a standardized medical exam, and (3) time-lapse film analysis of mothers feeding their babies. At one year, differences were found in the answers of the two groups of mothers to an interview question ("How do you feel about having worked or gone back to school since the birth of your baby?"), in the number of mothers in each group who spent most of the medical examination assisting the physician, in the amount of time spent soothing their crying infants, and in the infants' median scores on the Bayley test (Kennell et al., 1974).

Besides demonstrating the importance of early physical contact, the Klaus and Kennell team, in a paper by Hales, Lozoff, Sosa, and Kennell (1977), attempts to demonstrate the limits of this early sensitive period for mother-infant relations. They first separated 60 Guatemalan mother-infant dyads into three groups, an early contact group (45 minutes of skin-to-skin contact directly after birth), a delayed contact group (45 minutes, but 12 hours after delivery) and a control group (some limited contact starting at 12 hours after birth). They then made time-sampling observations of maternal behavior 36 hours after birth in the areas of affectionate behavior, proximity maintaining behavior, and caretaking behaviors.

The results of this study are somewhat inconclusive. No significant early contact-delayed contact differences were found (although the means of the early contact group were greater than those of the delayed contact group on all three measures), and only the affectionate behavior category distinguished the early contact from the control conditions. On examining the data further, the amount of time the mother spent in holding her baby in the *en face* position did differ depending on the timing of the mother-infant physical contact (early contact greater than delayed contact); additionally, nonnursing, proximity maintaining scores also showed some (nonsignificant) differences between the two groups.

The assertion that there is a sensitive period for mother-infant relations directly following birth is an overly strong claim. Concerning the Hales et al. (1977) study, there are the problems of inconclusive results and of a rather short-term effect (at 36 hours) which could easily be explained in other ways (e.g., infants and mothers are always alert right after birth, the early contact condition, but neither may be as alert 12 hours later, the delayed condition). It may be that *any* contact with the infant in the alert, awake state (the explanation for the postpartum sensitive period, see Klaus & Kennell, 1976, p. 66) occurring in the first few days after birth gets the mother-infant interaction "off on the right foot," as the original Kennell et al. (1974) results suggest.

If mother-infant contact produces some long-range effects, it also shows interactional qualities and effects early on. Even from birth the system is one in which causality operates in both directions. Recent naturalistic studies of newborn-mother interactions demonstrate how, to a large extent, it is the neonate who, however unwittingly, controls the mother's behavior. An awake, alert baby is thus likely to elicit talking, smiling, *en face* holding, and feeding behaviors from the mother. A distressed infant will rarely be taken into the *en face* position but will be moved, cuddled, and rocked by the mother. In this same responsive way mothers generally do not talk to, hum, stimulate feeding, or in other ways disturb their sleeping babies (Als, 1977).

Each of these maternal behaviors, while interactional in nature, allows for the infant's development of a smooth transition from one state to another (Als, 1979; Sander, 1976). A crying baby, or an infant in one of Wolff's (1966) six behavioral states, will often be soothed by the mother until s/he reaches a state of alert inactivity. Similarly a periodically sleeping infant (or an infant in the sleep state in between deep and light sleep) will often be gently moved to a more comfortable position when its body position changes or when its breathing becomes too irregular.

This pattern of mother-infant interactions also shows short-term development over time. In a study of infants who roomed-in with their mothers during their first two weeks (Sander et al., 1970), both parties showed a progressively increasing co-occurrence of behavioral state. Infants who were alert only 25 percent of the time when held by their mothers on the second day were alert 57 percent of the time they were held at eight days. Over a longer time period it has been shown that the methods used by mothers to soothe their crying infants changes with development. Soon after birth a predominantly proximal method of soothing (involving touching, holding) is used; gradually, more distal, and less proximal, contact occurs (Beckwith, 1971).

There are, then, important short-term (Sander et al., 1970) as well as long-term (Kennell et al., 1974) effects of early mother-infant interaction. These short-term effects most likely stem from the fact that mothers, even in this early period, have begun to help their infants in the solution of their particular developmental problems (Sander, 1976). The problem of neonatal state transitions serves as both the developmental task of the newborn (Als, 1979) and as the content upon which the mother-newborn relationship revolves. As such it is simply the first of a long series of problems through which development proceeds and interactions center.

Infant Behaviors and General Principles of Development

Having spoken of the early mother-newborn interaction and its importance for the future and short-term course of the infant-mother relationship, we now turn to the infant's contribution to social development. Far from being helpless organisms which simply react to their mothers' ministrations, young infants are rapidly developing skills which they quickly learn to "plug in" to the original social system.

Possibly the most social of these early developmental phenomena are the smile and the cry. An infant's smile serves as a social reward to its parents, making them feel as if the child knows and appreciates their loving care. In a similar way the baby's cry attunes its parents to the pains and discomforts of the young infant.

Like many early infant abilities, the smile is not, at first, strictly social. Endogenous, or spontaneous (i.e., internally controlled), smiles occur during sleep in the first week and seem to be the direct result of central nervous system activity (Wolff, 1963). The first elicited smiles, which occur soon after, seem to be similar in nature. Elicited smiles occur when "stimulation increases the level of excitation above some threshold, with the smile occurring as relaxation follows, between 6 and 8 seconds after stimulation" (Sroufe & Waters, 1976, p. 175).

Soon after, usually in the second week, smiling occurs when the infant's eyes are open. At first only when the infant is satiated with food, with the child having a "glassy," "drunken" look (Wolff, 1963), the smile at this age may occur either spontaneously or as a response to the mother's voice.

Smiling in the alert, awake state occurs in the third week. A seemingly focused, attentive infant now smiles more to the human voice, marking the entrance of the first "social smile" (Wolff, 1963). By the fourth week eye-to-eye contact and such moderate tactile stimulation as the first "pat-a-cake" games increase the social function of the smile.

Also at about this time (four to five weeks), external stimuli gradually outweigh internal stimuli in their ability to control smiling. The infant will often interrupt feeding and smile upon hearing the mother's voice. As

Wolff notes, "During the early weeks the balance is generally in favor of internal causes of behavior, and the baby behaves as if he were compelled to react to the inner stimulations. . . . [Gradually] the smile becomes stimulus-bound in a new way, namely to external stimulation" (Wolff, 1963, p. 129). Eye-to-eye contact, "pat-a-cake" games, and other mild stimulations now serve to control the smiling behavior externally.

By eight to ten weeks the infant goes beyond even this external control to personally master the smiling behavior. A *recognitory assimilation*, or essentially cognitive, principle now operates (Piaget, 1952; Zelazo, 1972). Infants must first assimilate, or cognitively understand, a new stimulus before they can smile at it. In a series of experiments in which infants were repeatedly exposed to a novel stimulus, Zelazo (1972) predicted a "curvilinear trend" (no smiling, then much smiling, then few smiles) in smiling behavior.

Initially, no smiling should occur as schemata are formed—a process perhaps more akin to accommodation. Smiling should emerge and increase on subsequent trials where some effort is necessary to match the newly formed schema to the stimulus. Repeated stimulus exposures beyond this point, however, should be too easily assimilable and smiling should decline. (Zelazo, 1972, p. 354)

While the studies reviewed by Zelazo (Zelazo & Kagan, 1972; Zelazo & Komer, 1971) do not irrefutably demonstrate the recognitory assimilation hypothesis as the explanation of infant smiling, the idea does seem reasonable. As Sroufe and Waters (1976) note, however, this type of cognitive hypothesis is not opposed to the "tension release" explanation, or the idea that smiling occurs after some excitatory threshold has been attained and relaxation follows. For the infant older than two months, smiling may occur after the stimulus has been fully assimilated (cognitively) and the concomitant tension brought on by this attempt to master the stimulus has been relieved (physiologically). This may simply be a case where an infant behavior is susceptible to several "acceptable" explanations in differing domains (see Michel & Moore, 1978, Chap. 2, for a discussion of this problem in psychology and biology).

Like smiling, the development of crying also shows an "endogenous to external" progression. Many of the cries in the first week are "probably related to lack of gastric filling rather than to an unsatisfied need for sucking or for oral stimulation" (Wolff, 1969, p. 88). By the third week there is an interaction between the infant's behavioral state and external stimulation such that "stimulus configurations which elicit only indifference or smiling when the baby is content may precipitate crying when presented while the infant is crying or fussy" (Wolff, 1969, p. 97). The same stimulus, such as a "pat-a-cake" game, now elicits different responses depending on the infant's state. In this sense a particular stimulus can have different psychological meaning on different occasions.

An interesting suggestion concerning crying is that this behavior may be the origin of such noncry vocalizations as gurgling, high-pitched squeals, and *ga-ga* and *da-da* sounds. "Every new non-cry pattern seems to appear for the first time as the infant gets fussy, and shortly before he begins to cry" (Wolff, 1969, p. 99). If so this would be a clear example of developmental differentiation, here of a social-emotional behavior, into more finely separated and specified behaviors, each still relating to a social, communicative context.

Still, this differentiation approach to early vocal phenomena is probably not totally correct in that features from two sorts of "primitive" vocalizations,—distress and "vegetative" (i.e., belching, coughing, swallowing) sounds—are now thought to be combined to form cooing behaviors at 7½ to 10 weeks (Stark, 1978). These two studies (Stark, 1978; Wolf, 1969) do, however, suggest the utility of the two notions of differentiation and integration (coordination) in explaining development.

Smiling and crying are, then, two infant behaviors which follow similar developmental paths. Both progress from a pattern of mainly internal to mainly external control (to cognitive mastery of external stimuli in smiling), such that both behaviors are elicited by different stimuli at different times. Both also demonstrate several developmental-interactional principles. While partially overlapping, these ideas help to summarize the first six months of development.

The first of these principles, *intersystems relationships*, simply asserts that, at least early in infancy, the cognitive, affective, and motor systems are essentially fused. Especially in these early months it is risky to state that one particular behavior is "cognitive," or that another is "affective." Thus, in smiling, an essentially affective behavior has cognitive (recognitory assimilation) and physiological components starting at two months.

A second principle, also demonstrated by smiling, is that of *pacing* (Cairns, 1979), the idea that it is the infant, by his/her ability to handle only certain stimuli at each particular stage in development, who determines the general nature of a social interaction at any given time. Smiling is optimally elicited by auditory stimuli (voice) at about two to three weeks, by the visual stimulation of faces by the fourth week, and by any new, novel stimuli by 8 to 10 weeks. In crying, "frustration" to the one-week-old consists of giving the baby a pacifier for 30 seconds, removing it for 15 to 20 seconds, and then repeating this pattern again and again. By 2 to 3 months, however, teasing with a pacifier no longer brings on frustration (Wolff, 1969, p. 105); at this point taking preferred toys away from the visual field, reintroducing them, and then taking them away again produces crying.

While this concept can be seen in the 0- to 6-month period through smiling and crying, pacing is important throughout the infancy period (and presumably beyond). Sander (1976), in a clinical study of mothers and infants, found that there are roughly five periods from 0 to 18 months, each centered around a dominant issue in the infant's development. The job of the mother in each period is to coordinate her behavior with the actual capabilities of her infant. In a global way this means that in the 0- to 2½-month period, the period of *initial adaptation*, she must try to "achieve a suitable meshing of mothering activities with cues the baby gives of his state" (Sander, 1976, p. 131); more specifically she must not overstimulate her baby by introducing overly complex stimuli at three weeks or understimulate her baby by introducing overly simple stimuli at four months.

A third principle is that of *organizational rules*. The infant is "organized" according to the principles of *action*, *selection, repetition,* and *contingency* (Hubbs-Tait, 1975a). S/he is an active organism which selects those stimuli on which it will act. The infant then repeats those actions which have produced interesting results.

The infant, starting at eight to ten weeks, actively appraises the stimulus before smiling. It selects those stimuli to which it will optimally smile at any particular time (voice at three weeks, new and interesting stimuli after two months). Similarly it selects those stimuli to which it will cry at any particular time; crying at the pacifier teasing (described before) at one week but not at a later age. Finally the concepts of *repetition* and *contingency,* along with Schaffer's (1978) concept of *internally controlled rhythmicity* in infants, are useful in understanding much of what occurs in infant-mother interactions. These three ideas, *repetition, contingency,* and *rhythmicity,* help explain why mother-infant interactions are cyclic in nature, involving such things as looking-nonlooking (Brazelton, Koslowski, & Main, 1974; Stern, 1974a), "you go, I go" turn-taking routines (Bruner, 1977; Kaye, 1977), and other continually repeating patterns of interaction.

Qualities of Early Mother-Infant Interactions

The mother-infant interactional system is an extremely popular area of research as it concerns the nature of the social interaction itself and reveals the possible precursors of future skills (e.g., language). Although our focus will be primarily on the nature of the mother-infant interactional system, we will also begin to touch on the wider-ranging issue of social precursors to later skills.

Most of the "free play" studies of the mother-infant interactional system focus on the three- to four-month period. This time span has not been chosen haphazardly. By the third to fourth month of life, the infant has become remarkably social, with an established repertoire of vocalizations (Bullowa, 1972; Rheingold, Gewirtz, & Ross, 1959) and facial expressions, especially smiles (Ambrose, 1961; Emde & Harmon, 1972; Spitz & Wolf, 1946). His/her control of gaze is by then almost functionally mature (White, Castle, & Held, 1964). At this age several major lines of social behavioral development converge (gaze, smiling, vocalization) and are integrated in the performance of the play activity (Stern, 1974b, p. 403).

This is not to say that many important developments have not begun to occur before three months. Mothers and infants have started to vocalize by turns in the 1½- to 3-month period (Bateson, 1975). Similar to this proto-dialogue phenomenon, the cyclic mother-infant interactions (described later) can first be seen around two months (Brazelton et al., 1975). Even by four weeks of age strikingly different patterns of infant behavior in response to social and nonsocial stimuli are seen (Brazelton et al., 1974). Infants generally become "hooked" on objects, showing a slow buildup of tension for a long period of time before turning away. In contrast mother-infant interactions show a more gradual cycle of attention and withdrawal, building and subsiding in a smoother fashion. Brazelton et al. (1974) have mapped the mother-infant interactional system at three to four months as fol-

lows. The mother first produces actions, such as vocalizations or vestibular contacts of various sorts, in an effort to elicit her infant's attention. Having achieved eye contact the mother then slowly accelerates the number and intensity of her behaviors. This, in turn, leads to a corresponding acceleration in the infant's degree of tension (as exemplified by arms and legs moving, smiling, vocalizations), which gradually reaches a point of peak excitement when the infant is extremely tense and his/her actions are jerky. This period of high excitation is then followed by a period of gradual deceleration, after which the infant looks away and goes into the negative part of the cycle (performing more and more actions while looking at nonsocial objects). Finally when the mother elicits eye contact, the cycle of synchronous mother-infant behaviors begins again (Brazelton et al., 1974).

It takes a skilled and sensitive mother to elicit interaction patterns even approximating the preceding. She must be comfortable in allowing her infant to break eye contact and correspondingly lower or totally stop her behaviors. Mothers who insist upon not allowing their infants to break contact (by increasing the number or intensity of their behaviors) only push their infants into larger periods of gazing at nonsocial objects (Brazelton et al., 1974, Fig. 3). On the other hand mothers who are too passive, either by letting their infants lead the interaction or by possessing too few interactive techniques (only the "peek-a-boo" game, for example), also fail to achieve a mutually satisfying pattern of mother-infant interaction (Stern, 1974b).

The main issue and paradox of these early mother-infant interactions is that of control. The mother, for her part, has a much wider repertoire of behaviors, determines when and where the interaction will occur, and thus seems to control the interaction. The infant, through his/her bestowal of attention on the mother (possibly in part due to its internal rhythmic pattern of attention, Schaffer, 1978), also seems to possess the power position in the dyad. Thus, both participants seem to be the controller of mother-infant interaction.

The paradox can in some sense be solved by thinking of the mother-infant interaction as operating through a series of hierarchically organized levels (Stern, 1974b). At the lowest level, that of the behaviors of infant and mother, the mother dominates. Her "baby talk" style, exaggerated facial expressions, and movements all serve to attract and hold the baby's interest.

At the next level, that of the *episode,* the infant is clearly in control. Episodes, or those periods of time in which infants and mothers engage in mutual eye gazing, usually occur when the infant looks at the mother and are broken off when it looks away. Stern (1974a) found that a full 94 percent of all mutual gazes are initiated (in that the infant looks at the mother who is already looking) and terminated (infant looks away from mutual gaze situation) by the infant. Brazelton et al. also note the need for mothers to be sensitive to their infant's gaze behaviors; increasing the level of behaviors to an already uninterested infant simply did not elicit eye contact (Brazelton et al., 1974, Fig. 3). Finally Fafouti-Milenkovic and Uzgiris (1979) noted that the infant looking at and acting toward the mother most often (60 percent of the time) ended with the mother acting alone; thus the infant had stopped acting toward the mother and looked away (leaving the mother still trying to elicit infant social behavior).

Stern's final two levels are those of games and of the play period itself. While little work has been done in these areas at the three- to four-month period, mothers possess a wider variety of games, or behavioral combinations, than infants do. Similarly mothers probably control when a particular play period will begin and end, although lack of attention or drowsiness on the part of the infant undoubtedly influences this decision.

It should be noted, in passing, that not all social interaction is of the sort just described. Most of the studies reviewed before concentrate on mother-infant play periods at three to four months in a laboratory setting. While this may account for some of the difficulties over the control issue in that the mother is constantly trying to elicit infant social behavior for the researchers, this type of study also misses other social interactions. Collis and Schaffer (1975) noted that mothers follow their six- and eight-month-old infants' nonsocial visual gazes and then comment on the objects seen by the infant. This sort of indirect social interaction bridges the gap between the infant's cognitive and social worlds; even when looking away (a nonsocial act in dyadic play research), the infant is indirectly involved in social interaction through the efforts of the sensitive mother.

There are, then, important social interactions involving the mother and her infant well before the six-month period. The question arises, however, as to just how much of this seemingly smooth, reciprocal interaction is based on the efforts of the infant and not simply on the effects of the sensitive mother. From this view comes the idea that interaction need not mean that both participants are equal on skill level or on their agreement concerning the goal of the interaction.

The problem of the infant's contribution to the interactive process has received careful attention from several researchers. Cairns (1979), in a discussion of a study by Tronick, Als, and Brazelton (1977) in which the infant is referred to as a "skillful communicator," notes the many possible explanations for mother-infant synchrony. First, there is the possibility of response limitations, such that the infant can only do so many possible behaviors in a certain situation. Faced with the nipple, the infant sucks. A second possibility is that the mother matches her behavior to that of the infant. This type of matching behavior is seen repeatedly in the literature (Als, 1977; Brazelton et al., 1974), especially as regards the matching of maternal behaviors to the infant's rhythmic pattern of attention (Schaffer, 1978; Stern, 1974a). Finally, there is the possibility of mutual contributions in an interaction (Tronick et al., 1977).

While not mentioned by Cairns, it seems possible that each of these three possibilities could be operating simultaneously and the infant could still be a skillful communicator. The infant behavioral repertoire is limited (Stern, 1974b), mothers do match their behaviors to infant attentional rhythms (Brazelton et al., 1974; Stern, 1974a), and yet both participants mutually (if not equally) engage in socially directed actions (Brazelton et al., 1974). While Tronick et al. (1977) may indeed speak in terms which give the infant too much credit for the achievement of social interaction, the infant is still a skillful communicator. For this, it seems to us, the baby need only possess (1) a set of behaviors which are actively produced and (2) an intention to engage in social interaction.

To start with the latter point, the intentional quality of the infant can be demonstrated clinically and experimentally. In a study by Tronick, Als, Adamson, Wise, & Brazelton (1978), it was found that when mothers do not react to the infant, remaining still and expressionless, two-month-old infants become wary and begin to withdraw and engage in self-comforting behaviors. Clinically this behavior is summarized as follows:

As in the normal interaction, the infant orients toward the mother and greets her. But when she fails to respond, he sobers and looks wary. He stares at her, gives her a brief smile, and then looks away from her. He then alternates brief glances toward her with glances away from her, thus monitoring her behavior. He occasionally smiles briefly, yet warily in less and less convinced attempts to get the interaction back on track. As these attempts fail, the infant eventually withdraws, orients his face and body away from his mother with hopeless expression, and stays turned away from her. None of the infants cried, however. (Tronick et al., 1978, p. 8)

Combined with the statistical findings of less smiling and less head orientation toward the mother and more slumping down in the seat (all in the "still face" as opposed to the "normal interaction" condition), a picture of active withdrawal emerges. At least on the "intention to engage in social interaction" level, the infant is a communicator.

The skill aspect of infant communication at this age is more difficult to assess. Fafouti-Milenkovic and Uzgiris (1979), by using a systems theory (Bertalannfy, 1968) approach, have attempted to solve the problem by pairing an unfamiliar mother (of a same-aged child) with the young infant. Their findings indicate that, in the presence of the unfamiliar mother, infants spend more time observing and more strictly adhere to the pattern of adult initiate–infant observe–adult escalate–infant participate, the original pattern on the mother-infant system. While infants are not equal, they are still skillful in the interactive setting. They observe the mother (Stern, 1974a) and, to some extent, alternate vocal (Bateson, 1975; Lewis & Freedle, 1972) and game (Watson, 1972) behaviors. If not equivalent in skill level, they still show themselves to be intentionally active participants in early interpersonal interactions.

A final question of this period concerns the possibility of social precursors to later skills. It has been postulated that infant-mother turn-taking is the precursor to later language dialogue skills in both its temporal ("we do not both speak at once") and reciprocal ("I speak, you listen," then vice versa) aspects.

This possibility of early social precursors, of a proto-dialogue in early mother-infant interactions, comes from many sources. There is the finding of mother-infant interactions in the feeding situation. When the infant is in the "burst" phase (sucking on nipple), mothers remain quiet. When the infant has paused, however, mothers talk to, jiggle, and stroke their babies, at which time the infants tend to pause longer. This phenomenon, occurring at two weeks, is thought to be among the first of the proto-dialogue interactions.

Similar infant-mother patterns are found in the alternating vocal behaviors of 1½- to 3-month-old infants and their mothers (Bateson, 1975) and in the game phenomenon (Watson, 1972) starting in the first few months. In each of these behaviors both participants are actors in turn, presenting ample opportunities for the first learning of dialogue-like skills.

But as Bretherton and Bates (1979) point out, caution is warranted. Dialogue-like behaviors in early infant-mother interactions may be analogous to later dialogue skills, but this could simply reflect limits on the possible ways two people can communicate with each other. Coaction and alternation may be the only possibilities, and thus the appearance of alternation (i.e., proto-dialogue) at one point in development is not necessary for the reappearance of that same way of communicating in a different domain (i.e., language) at a later time. At present only the gross analogy that early infant proto-dialogue at 1 to 3 months seems similar to dialogue skills at 1 to 1½ years has been postulated. Clearly more work needs to be done on this aspect of early mother-infant interaction.

EMERGENT SOCIAL INTERACTIONS: TOPICS IN THE PERIOD BEYOND SIX MONTHS

Developing Infant Skills

In a whole host of ways, the six-month-old baby is different from the same infant only a few months earlier. Development in several areas is proceeding at a rapid pace. These developments produce the effect of changing the infant's interpersonal interactions in important ways, allowing the child to enter fully several interpersonal worlds (mother-, father-, and peer-child) by the end of infancy.

It is impossible to look at the social interactional system of six-month and older infants without appreciating their developmental accomplishments. Developments in the cognitive, social, and linguistic domains deserve mention (albeit with the warning that they are still somewhat fused), for it is from these three areas that important prerequisites for later social interactive skills arise.

The cognitive, or nonsocial, world of the infant is centered about the developing concepts of *permanent objects, means-ends relationships,* and notions of *causality* (Piaget, 1954). This simply means that the child is coming to understand that objects (and people) continue to exist when out of sight, that one can use several means to achieve a particular goal (e.g., a stick to attain an out-of-reach object), and that people actively cause events to happen (instead of being hands which the infant moves). While not exhaustive of infant cognitive achievements, it now seems evident that at least these three skills are important prerequisites to later social skills.

Object permanence, probably the most studied of all cognitive skills, is thought to affect social development (and interactions) in three ways. First, there is the notion that the infant's attachment to the mother (to be discussed later) can only come about when the baby begins to realize that objects are permanent. Sensorimotor stage 4 object permanence, the retrieval of an object when hidden behind one screen, is thought to be an attach-

ment prerequisite (Bowlby, 1969). While this is probably too simplistic a notion, in that the object *concept* (including such things as identity) and not simply a specific stage of permanence is more important (Decarie, 1978), the idea of some sort of "object precursor" to attachment behaviors seems reasonable.

Second, there is the idea of the person permanence–object permanence decalage, or the finding that, in general, infants reach sensorimotor stage 4 permanence with people (i.e., the mother) before they accomplish stage 4 permanence with objects (Decarie, 1978). While even the decalage itself has recently been questioned (Jackson, Campos, & Fischer, 1978), Bell (1970) found that children who show an object-before-person decalage (a "negative" decalage) are either overly or not enough attached to the mother in the "strange situation" condition. In contrast infants with the "normal" pattern of decalage, or person permanence before object permanence, are correctly attached to the mother.

Finally, there is the possibility that the person permanence–object permanence decalage could be a useful tool in finding stable personality characteristics. There is the possibility that object-before-person permanence children at ten months are the same children who speak about objects ("referential") as opposed to speaking about people ("expressive," Nelson, 1973) at 1½ to 2 years. While this search for gross (and somewhat enduring) personality styles may be too simplistic, especially in light of Bretherton and Bates's (1979) search for stage-to-stage transitions (and Sameroff's transactional model of development), some sort of research along this line seems promising.

The means-ends and causality achievements have implications of a more social-linguistic sort. It has been found (Bates, Camaioni, & Volterra, 1975) that some understanding (stage 5) of the means-ends and causality relationships significantly correlates with the onset of gestural language (pointing to receive an object or pointing and showing to "talk about" an object). The ten-month-old infant thus uses "new means to achieve an end" (the achievement of stage 5 means-ends) in a new way, using gestural language (the new means) to get the mother's attention or action (the ends). In related studies the acquisition of stage 5 means-ends and causality skills have been shown to be prerequisites to language acquisition in both autistic (Curcio, 1978) and retarded (Kahn, 1975) children, lending further support to the importance of these two skills for later language.

Important social developments also take place soon after six months. Infants begin to experience a concept of the self by the end of the first year (Lewis & Brooks-Gunn, 1979). A study by Stechler and Kaplan (1980) suggests that this developing self-concept is acquired throughout the first-year period as a result of a series of conflicts between the infant and its caretakers. Based on observational data Stechler and Kaplan "look for instances in which an expressed wish or desire of the infant runs up not just against a parental prohibition, but against a prohibition which has already become internalized to some extent, so that the tug is felt within the infant" (p. 88). Through these experiences of infant-parental conflict, the infant simultaneously becomes actor, observer of its own actions, and perceiver of an internal conflict—or a being with a true concept of its own "self."

Finally, also in the social sphere, there is the notion of the *coordinated socially directed behavior* (SDB) (Mueller & Brenner, 1977). This measure of social skill involves a look at the mother (or peer) while simultaneously performing two or more actions. Infants have been found to increase their use of this behavior proportionally (in comparison to simple SDB's, or one action + look) in peer-peer interaction as they develop in the interaction from one to two years (Mueller & Brenner, 1977). This increased use of coordinated, as opposed to simple, SDB's is thought to be a manifestation, in the social sphere, of the cognitive concept (Piaget, 1954) of coordination. The infant increasingly develops the ability to combine two or more behaviors while looking at the mother (Mueller, 1979).

Mother-Infant Interactions beyond Six Months

It seems reasonable to consider the mother-infant interaction first. Besides the greater volume of literature, however, the mother is now thought to be the center of a much discussed developmental phenomenon: the attachment relationship of the infant to the mother. Even today with the downfall of the strict attachment concept, the idea lives on in many circles, no less alive as a concept, a research idea, or as a prevailing theme of social development than it was 15 years ago.

Attachment is the idea that between approximately six and eight months the infant forms a strong affectional bond toward the mother. This bond is unique in that "the object of attachment serves a special psychological function for which others cannot substitute" (Cohen, 1974, p. 207). Additionally attachment manifests itself in certain specific behaviors (e.g., proximity maintaining behaviors, distress at the mother's absence) and has, for the most part, been looked at in a unidirectional (infant attached to mother) way. The purpose of this bond, in an evolutionary sense, is thought to be the protection of the young of the species by keeping it close to its primary caretaker (Bowlby, 1969).

At first glance the concept seems reasonable, if simply for the observations that infants do protest their mothers' departures and for the simplicity of the "evolutionary" model. On closer analysis, however, the attachment concept is open to question on many grounds. First, the "unique" relationship of the infant to the mother is debatable. Infants form close and enduring bonds to their fathers (Cohen & Campos, 1974; Lamb, 1977a) and possibly with siblings (Lamb, 1978) and peers (Mueller & Lucas, 1975) as well. It may simply be the case that in our culture, as presently constituted, mothers more often take care of young infants, resulting in closer, but not qualitatively different, bonds to the mother figure.

The data on mother- versus father-infant relationships do not support the "uniqueness" hypothesis. In strange situation experiments infants decrease amount of play activities, increase amount of crying, and engage in proximity maintaining behaviors upon the departure of either parent (Kotelchuck et al., 1975). While it may be that mothers receive more attachment behaviors than fathers, "the father is clearly an object of attachment for most infants of 10 months of age or older" (Cohen & Campos, 1974, p. 152).

In a similar way the behavioral manifestations of attachment are open to question. As Weinraub, Brooks, and Lewis (1977) note, attachment behaviors (e.g., proximity maintaining, touching, distress at departure) are very much situationally determined and variable from one time to another (Coates, Anderson, & Hartup, 1972). Additionally individual attachment behaviors may not correlate with each other (Rosenthal, 1973) and may change over time (Cohen, 1974). While these findings may not be criticisms of the attachment bond so much as of the way in which that bond is assessed (Lamb, 1974), they do serve to make the attachment concept somewhat nebulous.

Attachment is generally studied as a unidirectional phenomenon. The infant is thought to be attached to the mother, thus engaging in attachment behaviors in various settings. Recent research, however, suggests that mothers, too, are attached to their infants (Klaus & Kennell, 1976) and, indeed, that causality in social interactions is a complex phenomenon (Bell, 1968; Clarke-Stewart, 1978; Parke, 1979).

Finally, if attachment is (1) not specific to the mother, (2) behaviorally unclear, variable and situationally specific, and (3) not unidirectional, but interactional, in nature, then what *is* it? More importantly what is its utility for social developmental research? For if it is simply another term for "love" or "affectional bond," then its nature as a theoretical construct has been vastly overrated.

Still our criticism is primarily of the strongest version of the attachment concept. Recent work suggests that some aspects of the theory may be predictively useful. Sroufe and his colleagues (Arend, Gove, & Sroufe, 1979; Sroufe, 1979), have begun to suggest that the attachment bond itself (at 24 months) is a useful predictor of personality organization (on ego control and ego resiliency measures) at four years. However, other studies (Vaughan, Egeland, Sroufe, & Waters, 1979) have shown that infants from low socioeconomic families less often show stable attachment patterns at six-month intervals (12 to 18 months). In all cases a simple (i.e., static) interactional view that predicts outcome at *B* from an observation (attachment relationship) at *A* would seem to be insufficient to explain complex developmental phenomena.

Our own view, in line with Rheingold and Eckerman (1974) and Weinraub et al. (1977), is that a more "social network"—dynamically interactional perspective comes closer to explaining the infant's relations to other people. These researchers assert that different people, who have as their common feature their "peopleness," populate the child's world. S/he, in turn, responds to these people in certain ways, producing certain subsamples of behavior to any one person at any one time. This, in essence, accounts for the variable and situational nature of attachment behaviors and for the presence of attachment relationships to more than one person.

In addition we feel that attachment behaviors to mother, father, and other (usually adult) figures may be a function of infant feelings of trust (Erikson, 1950) in that person. In this view infants will become attached to persons from whom they have a history of positive contingent actions—that is, infants trust any person who, throughout many interactions over a sustained period of time, has responded to their needs and helped them to organize their cognitive and social worlds (e.g., Collis & Schaffer, 1975). Feelings of trust are in this way bound up with notions of mastery over the external environment (Lewis, 1976), one of the major developmental tasks of infancy in both the object and social domains.

With the deemphasis of attachment, other areas of mother-infant interaction have begun to be studied. In contrast to the attachment literature, however, the more interactional studies of this period have tended to focus on the specific behaviors of mothers and infants in naturalistic (i.e., home) or "natural task" settings, thereby totally avoiding the trickier issue of postulating abstract relationships altogether.

Among the most comprehensive studies of mother-infant interactions in the post–six-month period is a monograph by Clarke-Stewart (1973). Examining 43 lower-class mother-infant pairs from the New Haven, Connecticut, area throughout the 9- to 18-month period, Clarke-Stewart found several interesting results. First, an "optimal maternal care" variable, which included such behaviors as the amount of positive emotion shown toward the baby and the amounts of maternal stimulation and responsiveness, correlated with infant developments in the cognitive, linguistic, and social areas. Additionally infant cognitive development was not related to the physical environment per se, but rather to the amount of time in which the mother engaged in object play. Again in a finding similar to that of Collis and Schaffer (1975), mothers mediated their infants' object environments by commenting on objects or manipulating them, for example.

In an effort to establish causal relationships between maternal behaviors and infant skills and development, a series of cross-lagged correlations was also performed. While a cluster of maternal behaviors (optimal maternal care factor) seemed to predict later infant cognitive development, this finding did not hold in the area of social relations. As Clarke-Stewart explains,

In the area of social interaction, unlike the relation between maternal stimulation and the child's intellectual development, the influence of the child's behavior on his mother's activities was strongly felt. The process of reciprocal mother-child influence was clearly demonstrated. The more often the child looked, smiled, or vocalized to his mother, the more affectionate and attached to the child she became and the more responsive she was to his distress and demands. (Clarke-Stewart, 1973, p. 93)

While the pattern of mothering may affect such cognitive abilities as the infant's intellectual level and such social-emotional behaviors as the amount of infant negative behaviors (which correlates with amount of maternal rejection), the infant, at least in the social sphere, also has an important impact on the interaction. In essence, then, from this somewhat global, comprehensive study, mother-child relationship beyond six months can be seen to be developmental-interactional in nature.

Another, more specific, area of study during this period is the "task literature" of 6- to 12-month-old infants and their mothers. Kaye (1976), in a study of six-month-olds, looked at the types of maternal teaching strategies involved in instructing infants to reach around an obstruction to get a hidden object. He found that mothers

have three general styles of teaching, *showing* (modeling the task), *shaping* (breaking the task into component parts), and *shoving* (pushing the infant's hand around the barrier to retrieve the object). While equally effective (or ineffective, as few children were able to learn the task), mothers' styles were highly dependent on their infants' ability to perform the task on the pretest. Infants who looked away and never reached for the hidden object in the pretest "produced" mothers who shaped the task, first making the object visible to the child, then partially putting it behind the barrier. In contrast mothers whose infants already showed some ability to perform the task in the pretest generally modeled the task behavior for their infants, reaching around the barrier themselves in an attempt to elicit infant imitation.

The Kaye (1976) study shows how the skill level (and subsequent behaviors) of infants determines the nature of the interactive sequence. In an elaboration on this type of finding, Hubley and Trevarthen (1979) longitudinally studied "cooperative task" situations with 8- to 12-month-old infants and their mothers. Mothers played with their babies with and without toys, watched as their infants played alone with toys, and in the fourth section of each experimental session, tried to teach their infants to put three wooden figures into a truck. Dividing infant behaviors into interpersonal acts, or social behaviors that make no reference to objects (smiling, laughing, looking at mother), and acts of joint praxis, or "actions on objects oriented to the attention or action of the other person" (pointing, showing), Hubley and Trevarthen found that 31 percent of all interactive sequences contained both types of behaviors by 54 weeks. Instead of separating social and cognitive-social behaviors, one-year-olds do both together, demonstrating a "greater proficiency in combining attention to a task and attention to a person" (Hubley & Trevarthen, 1979, p. 69). In a finding consonant with Kaye's results, mothers less often modeled the "put-in" behavior as the age of their infant increased; eventually (by 54 weeks) it was sufficient for the mother to indicate another object to be put into the truck ("Here's another one") or to indicate where the object was ("What about over here?") for the infant to accomplish the task (Hubley & Trevarthen, 1979, Fig. 4).

A second specific area of interactional reseach in this period concerns the study of mother-infant games. Bruner and associates (Bruner, 1975, 1977; Ratner & Bruner, 1978) have shown how the play of mothers and infants helps in structuring the infant's world, especially in a linguistically analogous way. Ratner and Bruner (1978) longitudinally studied the structure and development of a game involving the disappearance of an object in two mother-infant pairs. Abstracting the "grammar" (i.e., rule structure) of the game, they demonstrated how mothers vary optional elements in an effort to sustain their infants' attention. At times only the most basic elements of this particular game, hiding and "discovering" the clown, were used; at other times a whole host of optional elements, including a preparatory phase (holding the clown and saying to the infant, "Look what I've got here! Who's this?") were employed.

The two infants gradually developed from passive spectators to active initiators of the game. One infant smiled at the reappearance of the clown at six months, began to passively understand the game by seven months and, by eight months, was attempting to "hide" and "discover" the·clown. At this point the mother had to allow the game to be simplified into its two most basic components for the child could only produce the hiding (which she verbally marked with such statements as "Gone!") and reappearance ("Boo!") parts of the game.

A third and related area of research in this period is that of mother input language. Mothers have been shown to focus on those aspects of the language which infants are learning at any particular time. In another study by Bruner (1978), mothers' responses to their infants' pointing behaviors changed with age. At 10 to 14 months mothers commented about infant intentions ("Oh, you want it!"); at 15 months statements about the object of reference ("Oh, you want the ball!") were made.

It has been found that mothers' speech to infants lengthens and becomes more complex with age throughout infancy (Phillips, 1973). This finding of increasingly complex maternal speech may itself be more complicated. A study by Furrow, Nelson and Benedict (1979) suggests that specific maternal inputs have specific effects at specific times. In their study the number of verbs in the mothers' speech when the child was aged one year six months was negatively correlated with the child's mean length of utterance (MLU) at two years three months (i.e., fewer verbs by mother—better language by child). Comparing the mothers' speech and the children's speech, both at two years three months, the opposite relationship was found; more verbs by mothers correlated with higher MLU's for their children. Thus a specific input (verbs) on the part of the mother may have a different effect at two periods of development. While this is only one study, the possibility of employing the concepts of pacing and matching in the language domain now seems reasonable. It may even be possible to turn the process around by looking at changes in maternal input as indications that some components of the child's language learning task have changed. These two complementary ideas, viewing language input from the child's perspective (i.e., pacing) and viewing language development from the adult's perspective (i.e., matching), seem to be among the exciting possibilities foreshadowed by this study.

At the risk of repetition, these three specific areas of mother-infant interaction can be summarized by stating that, at least in a general way, mothers react to their infant's particular developmental "issue" at every turn. In a task situation they modify their teaching strategies to match their infant's abilities. If s/he seems to need the breaking down of the reach-around task into simpler parts, they do it; if not they model the task or (as in Hubley & Trevarthen, 1979) they simply verbally instruct the child in what to do ("How about putting that one in?"). In game situations mothers vary their presentations (just as they do in nonobject games at three months, Stern, 1974a) in order to keep their infants' interest. Mothers also, however, allow their infants to take over (even if that means a simplified game for a while) when their infants are developmentally ready. Finally, in the language input domain, mothers vary both the semantic content and linguistic complexity of their utterances to match their infants' competencies.

Again while the mother-infant relationship in the be-

yond-six-month period seems, from the preceding, to be a series of perfectly coordinated interactions in which the mother matches her behaviors to the infant's developing needs, this state of affairs is more the ideal than the norm. As in the pre–six-month stage, maternal matching is not always perfect. Indeed some amount of mother-infant conflict situations or instances of inexact maternal matching may be necessary in order for certain developments (e.g., personality growth) to occur (Stechler & Kaplan, 1980). While the concepts of matching and pacing are useful in explaining development, they should be looked at in a general way, even in this, the most intimate of the infant's early relationships.

Father-Infant Interaction

Examination of the role of the father in the infant's life is new material for the field of early social development. While fathers, like siblings, peers, and other adults, have been acknowledged as being physically present in infancy, their importance as socially interactive beings has only recently been appreciated. Research in the areas of mother-infant interactions, attachment to the mother-figure, and differentiation from the mother have all stressed the primacy of the mother-infant dyad, to the virtual exclusion of all other interactive systems. Indeed it is a valid observation that "in some child development texts, more space is devoted to the infant's relationship to his toys than to his father" (Cohen & Campos, 1974, p. 146).

This general lack of interest in the father can be traced to three principal causes (Parke, 1979). First, mothers have historically been the primary caretakers of young children and, in accordance with sex-role stereotypes, this has generally been considered appropriate. Second, research on rats has shown short-term hormonal changes presumably associated with maternal behaviors. Finally, the theoretical importance of the maternal figure is stressed in both psychoanalytic and behavioristic theories of infant development. The mother is thought to affect the primary emotional bond (Freudian theory) or, in behavioristic theories, to be the source of "secondary reinforcement" through her association with the feeding (primary reinforcement) situation.

It is probably more than a coincidence that a slight diminution of the hold of each of these three forces has at least coincided with the new interest in father-infant interactions. Presently societal sex-role stereotypes are being questioned, as is the use of hormonal changes in animals to predict human behaviors. In addition the finding that "contact comfort," as opposed to food, has primary reinforcing qualities for infant monkeys (Harlow, 1959) has weakened the argument for the unique secondary reinforcing qualities of the mother. Indeed fathers can now, theoretically, be as reinforcing as mothers and can thus serve as potential equals in interactions with their infants.

The question arises, however, as to the competence versus the actual performance of the fathers (Parke, 1979). The distinction is relevant both conceptually and methodologically in the father-infant literature. Conceptually it spells the difference between what fathers actually do, the amount of time that they spend with their babies, and how well fathers *can* do certain tasks, irrespective of the actual incidence of their doing these tasks in the everyday setting. As Parke and Sawin (1976) note, "Too often the fact of low father involvement throughout history in the caretaking of children has been extended to the conclusion that the low level of involvement was equivalent to a low level of competence [in caretaking]" (p. 366). Clearly the two need not go together, although data concerning both the competence and performance of fathers are important in order to ascertain the father's role in infant development.

Methodologically, too, the competence-performance distinction has merit for the ordering of research, although the two types of studies show much overlap. While it is somewhat of an overgeneralization, performance studies employ either naturalistic (Rebelsky & Hanks, 1971) or questionnaire (Pederson & Robson, 1969) methods. Competence studies (those interested in the higher, lower, or *different* abilities of fathers versus mothers), on the other hand, are often more manipulative. They tend to look at mother-infant versus father-infant interactions by experimentally producing such results (e.g., Parke & O'Leary, 1976); thus, skill level or possibly different styles of father- versus mother-infant interaction (not a "competence" notion per se) are observed, regardless of the actual occurrence of such interactions in the natural environment.

Fathers have generally been found to interact little with their infants, at least in comparison to mothers. Rebelsky and Hanks (1971) found that fathers talk to their three-month-old infants only one minute per day. This estimate may be low, however, as the (mother report) questionnaire of Pederson and Robson (1969) found that fathers spent slightly less than eight hours a week in play with their 9½-month-old infants. The overall availability of fathers, the number of hours per week that the father is home when the baby is awake, averaged 26 hours (with a range from 5 to 47 hours!) in this study. Kotelchuck (1976), in a direct (questionnaire-based) comparison of maternal to paternal involvement with their 6- to 21-month-old infants, found that, as expected, mothers participate more in the lives of their infants than do fathers. The middle-class, Boston mothers of his sample (Kotelchuck, 1972) spent 9.0 hours per day with their children, in comparison to the 3.2 hours per day spent by the fathers. They also spent more time feeding (1.45 to 0.25 hours per day) and playing (2.3 to 1.2 hours per day) with their infants and, in most cases (64 percent of sample), were totally responsible for the care of the infant. Thus it seems fairly well established that fathers interact less often with their infants than mothers do. Even on these purely quantitative measures, however, fathers do interact a fair amount with their infants (playing with them about eight hours per week), making the long-held assumption that fathers rarely participate in the lives of their infants unjustifiable.

Over a wide age range throughout infancy, fathers when placed in a dyadic situation with their babies interact as well as (if differently from) mothers. In a two-part study by Parke and O'Leary (1976), parental interactions with their newborns were examined in three conditions: with mother, father, and infant present; with the mother and infant alone; and with the father and infant alone. In both parts of the study, with a group of Lamaze-trained fathers who were present at delivery and

with a group of lower-class fathers, few mother versus father differences were found. While in both groups mothers smiled at their babies more than fathers did, all other behaviors were essentially equal (although lower-class fathers held and stimulated their infants more than the mothers did). From this study fathers seem to be competent, involved interactors with their newborns.

In another competence study Parke and Sawin (1976) investigated the degree to which fathers are sensitive to their newborn's cues in the feeding context. Using a comparison of the conditional probabilities of a specific parental behavior following a particular infant behavior, few maternal-paternal sensitivity differences were found. When the infant coughed or spit up ("auditory distress signal"), the conditional probability of either parent stopping their feeding of the child was similar (0.27 for mothers, 0.35 for fathers). In another measure the amount of milk consumed by the bottle-fed infants when fed by father versus mother was compared. The results of this measure also showed that both parents are nearly identical (1.3 ounces for mother feeding versus 1.2 ounces for father feeding) in their ability to feed their baby.

A similar type of study, this one involving the microanalysis of five father- and mother-infant pairs (Yogman, Dixon, Tronick, Als, & Brazelton, 1977), found that the structure of father- and mother-infant play interactions is similar in the period from two weeks to six months. Infant-father interactions, similar to interactions with the mother, were mutually regulated in the same attention-nonattention, buildup-withdrawal pattern shown in mother-infant interactions before six months (Brazelton et al., 1974). While father-infant interactions were characterized by more "peaks and valleys" in infant attention as compared to the smoother, more "flowing" mother-infant interactions, the two interactions were similar in structure.

There were, however, important differences in the Yogman et al. (1977) study, differences which seem to characterize father-infant (as opposed to mother-infant) interactions in general. Even when the infants were two and three months old, fathers were more likely (14 percent of the time in father-infant interactions, 0 percent in mother-infant interactions) to engage in physical "tapping" games with their infants, whereas mothers (27 percent to 1 percent of the time) were more likely to engage in vocal games with the baby. Even at this early age fathers and mothers, while both competent in their interactions with their infants, seem to show different styles of interaction.

This type of "competent, but different" quality of father-infant interactions is seen in other studies as well. Lamb (1977a) found that, at 7 to 13 months, mothers were more likely to engage in conventional play ("peek-a-boo" and "pat-a-cake" games) whereas fathers showed more physical (rough-and-tumble games) play with their infants (see Clarke-Stewart, 1978, for similar results with 15- to 30-month-olds). Additionally mothers and fathers held their infants for different reasons, mothers for caretaking purposes and fathers for play. Infant reactions to parent play initiatives also differed, fathers eliciting more positive affect during play than mothers (as measured by observer ratings). While mothers actually spend more time playing with their infants than fathers do, there is a "playful" quality to father-infant interactions, where proportionally more of the interaction time (37.5 percent to 25.8 percent of mother-infant time, Kotelchuck, 1976) is spent on playful interactions and less on caretaking activities.

A second major difference between the two systems concerns the father's fostering of sex roles in infants, especially in boys. While this sex-role function of father-child interactions seems to heighten after infancy, its origin seems to occur in the one- to two-year period. Fathers, although they do touch first-born boys more than later-born boys or girls in the neonatal period (Parke & O'Leary, 1976), generally do not differ in their interactive styles with their male and female infants before one year (Rendina & Dickerscheid, 1976). Starting at about 15 months, however, boys are addressed more than girls and experience father interaction twice as often as girls do (Lamb & Lamb, 1976). A clear preference of boys for their fathers (as measured by more touching, approaching, asking to be picked up) is then shown by the end of the second year. Similarly while not as powerful an effect (as sex-role pressure is assumed to be more intense on boys than on girls), girls by the end of the second year are beginning to prefer their mothers differentially (Lamb, 1977b).

There are, then, two important differences between the mother-child and the father-child systems. First, there is the physically playful and exciting (more intense pleasure) quality of father-infant interaction as opposed to the slightly more task-oriented, verbal nature of mother-infant interactions. This may be partly due to the father's limited amount of interactions and general lack of caretaking duties (in Kotelchuck, 1976, 43 percent of fathers reported that they *never* changed the infant's diapers). The second difference, that of the differential interactive patterns with their male and female infants, is still a somewhat tentative finding as concerns the infancy period. It may be, however, that as Parke and Sawin (1976) note, "Fathers really do prefer boys—especially first born boys" (p. 370).

Finally, there is the question of the direction of effects, now not only in the father-infant system but in the father-mother-infant system as well. For the mother's role as primary caretaker has generally been interpreted as meaning that the father's influence is, at best, indirect; he supports the mother who interacts with the baby. Clarke-Stewart (1978), in one of the few triadic, interactive, *and* longitudinal studies, found that the direction of causality is not so simple. Using cross-lagged correlations she found that the mothers' verbal stimulation and play at 15 months was closely related to children's intellectual performance (as measured by Minnesota scale) at 18 months. For fathers the opposite was true: Children's intellectual performance at 15 months correlated with paternal talk and play at 30 months. The amount that the father talked and played at one age was associated with mother's talking and playing at later ages. Thus Clarke-Stewart's findings suggest that "the most plausible causal direction—if such can be inferred—is mother influencing child, child influencing father and father influencing mother" (1978, p. 476). There seems to be a complex, multidirectional pattern of interactive effects in the mother-father-infant triad, a pattern which causes one to be cautious in attributing any one, simple role to the father in the life of his infant.

Peer-Peer Interactions

The study of the relationships of infants to their same-aged peers is a relatively new field of early social developmental research. However, the questioning of attachment and the newly discovered role of the father undoubtedly helped to pave the way for this new area. In addition the ever-increasing number of working women with young children has made the possibility of infant-infant relations an established sociological fact which continues to grow in importance.

Theoretically, too, the study of infant peer interaction has posed a host of newly considered questions and problems. How do the mother- (and father-) infant and peer-peer systems differ, and how are they alike? How is it that two infants, equally skilled (or unskilled) in their ability to interact socially with others, engage in social interactions at all, especially in light of the fact that neither can match his/her behavior to that of the other? Indeed, this "problem" of maternal skill advantage and tendency to match behavior to that of the infant is totally eliminated in interactions between similar-aged peers. As such the system is optimal from a research standpoint (i.e., no artificially produced social interactions; see earlier discussion of Cairns, 1979; Tronick et al., 1977), although the peer system may lag behind the adult-infant system in its ability to "draw out" high level social behaviors at an early age.

These are, then, some of the important practical and theoretical problems which have helped make the recent study of early peer relations an interesting and popular field. Unfortunately this new interest has led to a certain amount of confusion as to how one *does* peer-peer research and, consequently, what one finds (Mueller & Vandell, 1979). Studies have focused on dyadic and group interactions with familiar and unfamiliar peers and have been undertaken in playgroups, homes, and daycare centers. One, two, and no toys have been introduced into the (dyadic) interactive setting in experimental studies or, in naturalistic research, a well-equipped room has been provided; the infants themselves have determined their object-related preferences and behaviors. Both younger (below one year) and older (one to two years) infants have been studied in most of the preceding situations. Each of these variables—amount of peer familiarity, interactive setting, age of infants, type of study, and number of interactors—has an important effect on the conclusions one draws about the nature of early peer-peer interactions.

To oversimplify somewhat, most studies have centered on the one- to two-year period and employed familiar peers in dyadic interactions. Familiarity and a two-person interaction, in particular, seem to be important. The early studies of peer relations (Bridges, 1933) using unfamiliar peers showed little interaction and even less interaction of a positive kind. More recent studies using familiar peers, on the other hand, show a considerable amount of positive (and neutral) interactions of a sophisticated nature.

Similarly infants produce more interactive behaviors when in a dyad as opposed to a group (three or more) setting (Bronson, 1975; Vandell, 1976). When considering the parent-infant literature, this seems reasonable; even parents (especially mothers) produce less social behaviors to their infants when another adult (Clarke-Stewart, 1978) or infant (Rubenstein & Howes, 1976) is also present.

Mueller and Lucas (1975) have described a three-stage sequence of interactions in the one- to two-year period. First, object-focused interactions occur. Here both toddlers interact simultaneously on an object but are more interested in eliciting an interesting display from the object than in influencing the other toddler's behavior. For example a pull train can elicit simultaneous behaviors from the two children, one pulling, the other tooting or following. The second stage, that of "simple and complex contingency interchanges," is similar to Watson's (1972) parent-infant games. One child says *da* and the other laughs, a sequence which is repeated again and again. Finally, a stage of complementary interchanges occurs and as in the run-chase and offer-receive games, both children can take either role in an interaction. Role complementarity occurs when the "giver" becomes the "receiver" at a later point in the game, demonstrating his/her knowledge of reciprocity.

In general this development from object-centered, to contingent, to reciprocal stages seems to characterize the development of peer interactions in the one- to two-year period, the most studied age range in the peer relations literature. There is, however, some preliminary evidence that peer-peer interactions at earlier ages may not follow this sequence (Hubbs-Tait, 1975b; Vandell, Wilson, & Buchanan, 1980). First, in a little-known diary study of twin infants by Lichtenberger (1965), "object-less" interactions were found by three months of age. Thus the following sequence occurred at three months, four days.

Sigrid lies on the changing table next to Horst. S. crows and peeks at H.; she turns her head away, looks again, turns her head away anew, laughs again. . . . H. looks on at the game and joins in her laughter. (Lichtenberger, 1965, p. 14, from—and translated by—Hubbs-Tait, 1975b, p. 22)

A second source of object-less social interactions below one year comes from a study by Vandell et al. (1980). Examining the same pairs of (unfamiliar) infants at 6½, 9, and 12 months, she found that when put in a "toy absent" condition peers directed more social behaviors (mainly smiles and vocalizations) to each other than when in a "toy present" condition (Vandell et al., 1980, Table 3). Vandell also notes, however, that the toy absent condition (as opposed to the toy present condition) was a more stressful situation for her infants and had to be limited to five minutes in duration (the toy present condition lasted ten minutes). "Thus, it may be that the toy absent condition represents a special situation which momentarily enhances sociability but lacks ecological validity" (Vandell et al., 1980, p. 487).

Age seems to be an important variable, especially as concerns the type of peer interactions. It seems possible that at first *all* social interactions, like those in the mother-infant system at three months (Brazelton et al., 1974), are not concerned with objects. Gradually the object and social worlds come to coexist (e.g., DeStefano's [1976] finding of more object-centered social behaviors with toddlers when objects are *present*, but much object-less interactions when they are not, from Mueller, 1979,

Table 4). Finally the two worlds are combined, leading to proto-linguistic behaviors (Bates et al., 1975) of infants toward adults at ten months and the three-stage object-mediated exchanges with toddlers from one to two years (Mueller & Lucas, 1975).

A second issue in the analysis of the peer interaction system concerns the presence of "shared meanings" in dyads. These meanings, or themes, of peer interactions are measurable based "on behavioral evidence of inter-child *agreement* regarding the topic of an interaction. Both toddlers must perform behaviors indicative of a single definable theme. In this sense the theme or meaning is said to be 'shared' " (Brenner & Mueller, in preparation, p. 6).

For the playgroups studied by Brenner and Mueller, 12 shared meanings emerged. The six most common meanings consisted of motor copy (which occurred in 25 percent of the instances of shared meaning), object possession struggle (19 percent), vocal copy (13 percent), shared positive affect (11 percent), object exchange (10 percent), and aggression (9 percent). Interestingly not every peer interaction, at any age studied (12 to 18 months), revolved around a shared meaning; the percentage of shared meaning interactions rose from 14 percent at 12.5 months to 40 percent of the interactions of 18-month-old toddlers. This ability to coordinate their meanings did, however, once achieved, facilitate longer interactions, as sustained interactive sequences (four or more interactions) tended to consist of interactions about one of the 12 shared meanings, while shorter interactions were far less likely to be topical in nature. This preliminary evidence suggests that infant peers move from having elicitation control over each other to engaging in reciprocal, theme-governed play, with the side benefit that longer sequences of interactions can occur when a shared theme is present.

Finally there is the comparison between the peer-peer and adult-child interactive systems. The question itself can be broken into structural and content areas. Structurally it remains unclear whether the two systems are essentially similar or dissimilar in nature. The object-focused to contingent to reciprocal structural sequence, found in one- to two-year-old toddlers (Mueller & Lucas, 1975), does not appear to fit with the interactive sequence with adults, where object-less interactions are predominant in the two- to six-month period and where contingent games also occur at an early age. Recent evidence of early (below one year) peer contacts (Hubbs-Tait, 1975b; Vandell et al., 1980) seems to imply that peers engage in object-less interactions at very young ages (in much the same way that infants interact with their mothers).

While the question of structural similarity versus dissimilarity remains an unsolved problem, two points should be made. First, even if the general structural developmental progression is identical in the two systems, the peer system probably lags behind the adult system. Infants engage in reciprocal, role reversible, give-and-take games with their mothers at 8 to 10 months (e.g., Ratner & Bruner, 1978), while similar types of activity with familiar peers do not occur until 16 to 18 months. It is also true, however, that playgroup toddlers (as opposed to homecare children) more competently interact with their parents, initiating interactions more and terminating less. They also seem to elicit less sophisticated (i.e., more closely matching) interactive behaviors from their mothers, leading to a greater percentage of successful interactions (Vandell, 1979). While it may be true that the peer system lags behind the parent-child system, it also causes profound changes in both parental and infant behaviors in that system. In this context more studies on this type of "second order effect" (Bronfenbrenner, 1979), in which one interactor or interactive setting (e.g., playgroup) causes changes which then affect a third party (e.g., mother's behavior toward child), would seem to be badly needed.

A second point is that all differences found between the adult-infant system versus the peer-peer system have generally been considered to be due solely to systems differences. In most studies, however, degree of familiarity with the familiar adults (all of the infant's life) has vastly differed from familiarity with the infant peer (usually only a few months). Only more, detailed studies of infant twins, or of peers familiar from birth, will disentangle this confounding of degree of familiarity with systems differences.

The two systems do seem to differ. Vandell (1976) found that toddlers (aged 16 to 22 months) are more vocal with their mothers and more motoric with their peers. Similarly more behaviors which were termed "agonistic," "looking alone responses," and "object taking" were found in the peer, as opposed to the mother-infant, system. A more motoric style, a type of interaction which may foster infants' object skills (Rubenstein & Howes, 1976), seems to be characteristic of the peer system.

It is interesting to speculate that there may be a hierarchy of infant interactive systems. Mothers seem predominantly more verbal and educational (as far as labeling, object-centered play) with their infants. Fathers are more physically playful but still retain the competence (and contingent qualities) of the mother-figure. Finally peers are most motoric and least advanced in their interactive skills. With development (and experience in interactions) throughout the second year, mothers become more verbal to their infants, while infants become more motoric with their same-aged peers (Vandell, 1977, from Mueller, 1979, Table 5). Only fathers remain as vocal and motoric as at earlier ages, holding down their position as intermediate figure in the diverse and complex array of social worlds which develop for the child throughout infancy.

SOME CURRENT QUESTIONS

We end our review of the field of early social development with a series of questions for two reasons. First, this sort of review, by its very nature, stresses the new findings which best describe the area. Unfortunately a byproduct of this focus is the impression that social developmental researchers do know a great deal, an impression which is as false as it is true. Second, an area's questions, possibly more than anything else, *define* that area, presupposing where it has been and hinting at where it may go in the future.

Tentatively, then, here are several of the current and, we feel, interesting questions in the field of early social development.

How Do the Social, Cognitive, and Linguistic Systems Go Together throughout the Infant's Development? While this is, strictly speaking, solely a developmental question, it underlies much of the current thinking in several fields. This chapter, for example, has often blurred the lines among these several areas. Specifically we have spoken of dialogue-like social behaviors in three-month-olds, cognitive analogues and prerequisites to social behaviors (e.g., coordination of cognitive schemas as the analogue for coordinated SDB's and object permanence as the prerequisite for attachment behaviors); the "grammar" of mother-infant games; and the cognitive assimilation hypothesis of infant smiling.

It may be that these three systems are often so interlinked that separation, even for heuristic purposes, is unproductive. However in the field of early communication (itself a social linguistic phenomenon), the separation of two of these systems, the cognitive from the linguistic, has proven useful (Bates, Benigni, Bretherton, Camaioni, & Volterra, 1977). What the results of the untangling of these three systems may be as it concerns other areas remains to be seen.

Are Social "Skills" Stable Phenomena or Situationally Determined Events? This question is probably most apparent in the area of infant peer relations. If such variables as peer familiarity, number of interactors, situation under which study was carried out, number of toys introduced *all* affect how one infant acts toward another, is there such a thing as an underlying social "skill" or competence in young infants?

Obviously one need not strongly hold that behaviors always reflect stable underlying competencies or that they are always only situational responses. As much of the Piagetian-based literature has shown (e.g., Brainerd & Hooper, 1975), task variables often help or hinder performance. As such there is probably some sort of flexible, developing competency in a particular area for quite a while. During these transitional stages, behaviors seen in one situation may not generalize to another; the skills are simply not yet fully in place.

What Is the Role of "Social Styles" in Social Development? Aside from our earlier discussion of "expressive" versus "referential" children, this chapter has generally ignored the issue of individual differences. As Nelson (1978) has attempted to demonstrate, "social styles" may reflect the fused or separate nature of the cognitive and interpersonal skills of a particular infant at a certain period of development. Indeed the issue of styles is ubiquitous in the early language development literature, where different strategies of infants in their attempts to "break into" the language (Bowerman, 1976) have important implications about the speed of acquisition of grammar.

On another level the "style" of fathers' interactions with their male and female infants may be one cause of sex-role development, even in infancy. Here again the idea of the continuing interaction between the personality and behaviors of the parent and the infant's developing skills and personality style seems important. Brazelton and colleagues also find mother-infant miscommunication due to inadequate strategies or physical disabilities in the mother (Brazelton et al., 1974; Brazelton et al., 1975) or to disabilities (e.g., blindness) on the part of the infant (Als, Tronick, & Brazelton, 1980).

How Do the Infant's Different Interpersonal Worlds Coexist and Which Types of Behaviors (from Which People) Help Cause Which Further Developments? This may be the toughest question for the interactional view of early social development to handle. While the differential and second order effects of the father-mother-infant system have begun to be addressed (Clarke-Stewart, 1978), the role of peers and siblings in the infant's social world is largely unknown.

Yet if social interaction consists of more than dyadic interaction, second and even third order effects (as defined by Bronfenbrenner, 1979) must be addressed. For example siblings probably do affect the way in which a mother relates to her newborn infant, but this type of fairly clearcut second order effect has not yet been examined. Hopefully some larger, more general theory will eventually encompass all possible numbers and types of interactions while still possessing enough of a "systems quality" to realize that, when a particular interactor is absent (the mother, for example), another can probably take over behaviors typical of the missing person (the father giving "maternal" social behaviors to the infant).

Are Developments during the Infancy Period Unique and Critical for All Later Development? While not explored in detail this question runs throughout our discussion of several topics. The findings of Klaus and Kennell, the work of the attachment researchers (Bowlby, 1969; Sroufe, 1979) and the work of several theorists (e.g., Freud), all assert that there is a critical importance to the child's social interactions and relations in the infancy period.

In line with the developmental-interactional perspective, however, no time period would seem, a priori, to be of unique and irreversible importance. Findings of stability, for example, of stable attachment categories for individual children throughout time (see Sroufe, 1979) is explained in this view not as an interaction at a particular time having a lasting effect, but rather as the first indication that a particular style of interaction between the child and its environment has continued over many different interactions. Still, more work in this area obviously needs to be done to lend support to either the "static" interactional-critical age (i.e., strong attachment) view or to a more developmental-interactional (i.e., transactional) view of development.

These are, then, some of the findings and questions concerning social development in infancy. Obviously we have been somewhat selective in our perceptions of the relevant research, guided as we have been by the developmental-interactional framework. While we cannot predict the future, we would hope that this framework can be profitably employed to begin to solve questions like the preceding ones. If and when this happens (and all indications are that this is *already* happening), an interesting field will have been made even more exciting.

REFERENCES

ALS, H., The newborn communicates. *Journal of Communication*, 1977, *27*, 66–73.

ALS, H. Social interaction: Dynamic matrix for developing behavioral organization. In I. Uzgiris (Ed.), *Social interaction and communication during infancy*. San Francisco: Jossey-Bass, 1979.

ALS, H., TRONICK, E., & BRAZELTON, T. B. Stages of early behavioral organization: The study of a sighted infant and of a blind infant in interaction with their mothers. In T. M. Field, D. Stern, A. Sostek, & S. Goldberg (Eds.), *Interactions of high-risk infants and children: Disturbances and interventions*. New York: Academic Press, 1980.

AMBROSE, J. A. The development of the smiling response in early infancy. In B. M. Foss (Ed.), *Determinants of infant behavior* (Vol. 1). New York: John Wiley, 1961.

AREND, R., GOVE, F. L., & SROUFE, L. A. Continuity of individual adaptation from infancy to kindergarten: A predictive study of ego-resiliency and curiosity in preschoolers. *Child Development*, 1979, *50*, 950–959.

BATES, E., BENIGNI, L., BRETHERTON, I., CAMAIONI, L., & VOLTERRA, V. From gesture to the first word: On cognitive and social prerequisites. In M. Lewis & L. A. Rosenblum (Eds.), *Interaction, conversation and the development of language*. New York: John Wiley, 1977.

BATES, E., CAMAIONI, L., & VOLTERRA, V. The acquisition of performatives prior to speech. *Merrill-Palmer Quarterly*, 1975, *21*, 205–226.

BATESON, M. C. Mother-infant exchanges: The epigenesis of conversational interaction. *Annals of the New York Academy of Science*, 1975, *263*, 101–113.

BECKWITH, L. Relationship between infant's vocalizations and their mothers' behavior. *Merrill-Palmer Quarterly*, 1971, *17*, 211–226.

BELL, R. Q. A reinterpretation of the direction of effects in studies of socialization. *Psychological Review*, 1968, *75*, 81–95.

BELL, S. The development of the concept of object as related to infant-mother attachment. *Child Development*, 1970, *41*, 291–311.

BERTALANNFY, L. V. *General systems theory*. New York: Braziller, 1968.

BOWERMAN, M. Semantic factors in the acquisition of rules for word use and sentence construction. In D. Morehead & A. Morehead (Eds.), *Normal and deficient child language*. Baltimore, Md.: University Park Press, 1976.

BOWLBY, J. *Attachment and Loss* (Vol. 1). Attachment. New York: Basic Books, 1969.

BRAINERD, C., & HOOPER, F. A methodological analysis of developmental studies in identity conservation and equivalence conservation. *Psychological Bulletin*, 1975, *82*, 725–737.

BRAZELTON, T. B., KOSLOWSKI, B., & MAIN, M. The origins of reciprocity: The early mother-infant interaction. In M. Lewis & L. A. Rosenblum (Eds.), *The effect of the infant on its caretaker*. New York: John Wiley, 1974.

BRAZELTON, T. B., TRONICK, E., ADAMSON, L., ALS, H., & WISE, S. Early mother-infant reciprocity. In M. A. Hofer (Ed.), *Parent-infant interaction*. Amsterdam: Elsevier, 1975.

BRENNER, J., & MUELLER, E. The development of shared meaning in boy toddlers. *Child Development*, in press.

BRETHERTON, I., & BATES, E. The emergence of intentional communication. In I. Uzgiris (Ed.), *Social interaction and communication during infancy*. San Francisco: Jossey-Bass, 1979.

BRIDGES, K.M.B. A study of social development in early infancy. *Child Development*, 1933, *4*, 36–49.

BRONFENBRENNER, U. Contexts of child rearing: Problems and prospects. *American Psychologist*, 1979, *34*, 844–850.

BRONSON, W. Peer-peer interactions in the second year of life. In M. Lewis & L. A. Rosenblum (Eds.), *Friendship and peer relations*. New York: John Wiley, 1975.

BRUNER, J. The ontogenesis of speech acts. *Journal of Child Language*, 1975, *2*, 1–19.

BRUNER, J. Early social interaction and language interaction. In H. R. Schaffer (Ed.), *Studies in mother-infant interaction*. New York: Academic Press, 1977.

BRUNER, J. Learning the mother tongue. *Human Nature*, September 1978, pp. 42–49.

BULLOWA, M. Epigenesis of conversational interaction. *Quarterly Progress Report No. 100*. Cambridge, Mass.: MIT Research Laboratory of Electronics, 1972.

CAIRNS, R. B. *Social development: The origins and plasticity of interchanges.* San Francisco: W. H. Freeman and Company, Publishers, 1979.

CLARKE-STEWART, A. Interactions between mothers and their young children: Characteristics and consequences. *Monographs of the Society of Research in Child Development,* 1973, *38.*

CLARKE-STEWART, A. And Daddy makes three: The father's impact on mother and young child. *Child Development,* 1978, *49,* 466–478.

COATES, B., ANDERSON, E. P., & HARTUP, W. W. The stability of attachment behaviors in the human infant. *Developmental Psychology,* 1972, *6,* 231–237.

COHEN, L. The operational definition of human attachment. *Psychological Bulletin,* 1974, *81,* 207–217.

COHEN, L., & CAMPOS, J. Father, mother and stranger as elicitors of attachment behaviors in infancy. *Developmental Psychology,* 1974, *10,* 146–154.

COLLIS, G. M., & SCHAFFER, H. M. Synchronization of visual attention in mother-infant pairs. *Journal of Child Psychiatry and Psychology,* 1975, *16,* 315–320.

CURCIO, F. Sensorimotor functioning and communication in mute autistic children. *Journal of Autism and Childhood Schizophrenia,* 1978, *8,* 281–292.

DECARIE, T. G. Affect development and cognition in a Piagetian context. In M. Lewis & L. A. Rosenblum (Eds.), *The development of affect.* New York: Plenum, 1978.

DESTEFANO, C. T. *Environmental determinants of peer social activity in 18 month old males.* Unpublished Ph.D. dissertation, Boston University, 1976.

EMDE, R.N., & HARMON, R. J. Endogenous and exogenous smiling systems in early infancy. *Journal of Child Psychiatry,* 1972, *11,* 177–200.

ERIKSON, E. *Childhood and society.* New York: W. W. Norton & Co., Inc., 1950.

FAFOUTI-MILENKOVIC, M., & UZGIRIS, I. The mother-infant communication system. In I. Uzgiris (Ed.), *Social interaction and communication during infancy.* San Francisco: Jossey-Bass, 1979.

FURROW, D., NELSON, K., & BENEDICT, H. Mothers' speech to children and syntactic development: Some simple relationships. *Journal of Child Language,* 1979, *6,* 423–442.

HALES, D., LOZOFF, B., SOSA, R., & KENNELL, J. Defining the limits of the sensitive period. *Developmental Medicine and Child Neurology,* 1977, *19,* 454–461.

HARLOW, H. Love in infant monkeys. *Scientific American,* July, 1959.

HUBBS-TAIT, L. *Infant-infant interaction.* Unpublished paper, Boston University, 1975.

HUBLEY, P., & TREVARTHEN, C. Sharing a task in infancy. In I. Uzgiris (Ed.), *Social interaction and communication during infancy.* San Francisco: Jossey-Bass, 1979.

JACKSON, E., CAMPOS, J., & FISCHER, K. The question of decalage between object permanence and person permanence. *Developmental Psychology,* 1978, *14,* 1–10.

KAHN, J. V. Relationship of Piaget's sensorimotor period to language acquisition of profoundly retarded children. *American Journal of Mental Deficiency,* 1975, *79,* 640–643.

KAYE, K. Infants' effects upon their mothers' teaching strategies. In J. C. Glidewell (Ed.), *The social context of learning and development.* New York: Gardner Press, 1976.

KAYE, K. Toward the origin of dialogue. In H. R. Schaffer (Ed.), *Studies in mother-infant interaction.* New York: Academic Press, 1977.

KENNELL, J. H., JERAULD, R., WOLFE, J., CHESLER, D., KREGER, N., McALPINE, W., STEFFA, N., & KLAUS, M. Maternal behavior one year after early and extended post-partum contact. *Developmental Medicine and Child Neurology,* 1974, *16,* 172–179.

KLAUS, M. H., & KENNELL, J. H. *Maternal-infant bonding.* St. Louis, Mo.: C. V. Mosby, 1976.

KOTELCHUCK, M. *The nature of the child's tie to his father.* Unpublished Ph.D. dissertation, Harvard University, 1972.

KOTELCHUCK, M. The infant's relationship to the father: Experimental evidence. In M. E. Lamb (Ed.), *The role of the father in child development.* New York: John Wiley, 1976.

KOTELCHUCK, M., ZELAZO, P., KAGEN, J., & SPELKE, E. Infant reaction to parental separations when left with familiar and unfamiliar adults. *Journal of Genetic Psychology,* 1975, *126,* 255–262.

LAMB, M. A defense of the concept of attachment. *Human Development,* 1974, *17,* 376–385.

LAMB, M. Father-infant and mother-infant interactions in the first year of life. *Child Development,* 1977a, *48,* 167–181.

LAMB, M. The development of parental preferences in the first two years of life. *Sex Roles,* 1977b, *3,* 494–497.

LAMB, M. The development of sibling relationships in infancy: A short-term longitudinal study. *Child Development,* 1978, *49,* 1189–1196.

LAMB, M., & LAMB, J. The nature and importance of the father-infant relationship. *Family Coordinator,* 1976, *25,* 373–379.

LEWIS, M. E. *The origins of self-competence.* Paper presented at the NIMH conference on Mood Development, Washington, D.C., November 1976.

LEWIS, M. E., & BROOKS-GUNN, J. Toward a theory of social cognition: The development of self. In I. Uzgiris (Ed.), *Social interactions and communication during infancy.* San Francisco: Jossey-Bass, 1979.

LEWIS, M. E., & FREEDLE, R. *Mother-infant dyad: The cradle of meaning.* Paper presented at the Symposium on "Language and Thought: Communication and Affect," Erindale College, University of Toronto, March 1972.

LICHTENBERGER, W. *Mitmenschliches Verhalten eines Zwillingspaares in seinen ersten Lebensjahren.* Munich: Ernst Reinhardt, 1965.

MICHEL, G., & MOORE, C. *Biological perspectives in developmental psychology.* Belmont, Calif.: Wadsworth, 1978.

MUELLER, E. (Toddlers + toys) = (an autonomous social system). In M. Lewis & L. A. Rosenblum (Eds.), *The child and its family.* New York: Plenum, 1979.

MUELLER, E., & BRENNER, J. The growth of social interactions in a toddler playgroup: The role of peer experience. *Child Development,* 1977, *48,* 854–861.

MUELLER, E., & LUCAS, T. A developmental analysis of peer interactions among toddlers. In M. Lewis & L. A. Rosenblum (Eds.), *Friendship and peer relations.* New York: John Wiley, 1975.

MUELLER, E., & VANDELL, D. L. Infant-infant interaction. In J. D. Osofsky (Ed.), *Handbook of infant development.* New York: John Wiley, 1979.

NELSON, K. Structure and strategy in learning to talk. *Society for Research in Child Development Monographs,* 1973, *38* (Nos. 1–2).

NELSON, K. The role of language in infant development. In M. H. Bornstein & W. Kessen (Eds.), *Psychological development from infancy: Image to intention.* Hillsdale, N.J.: Lawrence Erlbaum Associates, 1978.

PARKE, R. D. Perspectives in father-infant development. In J. D. Osofsky (Ed.), *Handbook of infant development.* New York: John Wiley, 1979.

PARKE, R. D., & O'LEARY, S. Father-mother-infant interaction in the newborn period: Some feelings, some observations and some unresolved issues. In K. Riegel & J. Meacham (Eds.), *The Developing Individual in a Changing World* (Vol. 2). Social and environmental issues. The Hague: Mouton, 1976.

PARKE, R. D., & SAWIN, D. B. The father's role in infancy: A reevaluation. *The Family Coordinator,* 1976, *25,* 365–371.

PEDERSON, F. A., & ROBSON, K. S. Father participation in infancy. *American Journal of Orthopsychiatry,* 1969, *39,* 466–472.

PHILLIPS, J. R. Syntax and vocabulary of mothers' speech to young children: Age and sex comparisons. *Child Development,* 1973, *44,* 182–185.

PIAGET, J. *The origins of intelligence in children.* New York: Routledge and Kegan Paul, 1952.

PIAGET, J. *The construction of reality in the child.* New York: Basic Books, 1954.

RATNER, N., & BRUNER, J. Games, social exchange and the acquisition of language. *Journal of Child Language,* 1978, *5,* 391–401.

REBELSKY, F., & HANKS, C. Fathers' vocal interactions with infants in the first three months of life. *Child Development,* 1971, *42,* 63–68.

REESE, W. H., & OVERTON, W. F. Models of development and theories of development. In L. R. Goulet & P. B. Baltes (Eds.), *Life-span developmental psychology.* New York: Academic Press, 1970.

RENDINA, I., & DICKERSCHEID, J. D. Father involvement with first-born infants. *The Family Coordinator,* 1976, *25,* 373–379.

RHEINGOLD, H. L., & ECKERMAN, C. O. General issues in the study of peer relations. In M. Lewis & L. A. Rosenblum (Eds.), *Friendship and peer relations.* New York: John Wiley, 1974.

RHEINGOLD, H. L., GEWIRTZ, J. L., & ROSS, H. W. Social conditioning of vocalizations in the infant. *Journal of Comparative Physiological Psychology*, 1959, *52*, 68–73.

ROSENTHAL, M. Attachment and mother-infant interaction: Some research impasses and a suggested change in orientation. *Journal of Child Psychiatry and Psychology*, 1973, *14*, 201–207.

RUBENSTEIN, J., & HOWES, C. The effects of peers on toddler interactions with mother and toys. *Child Development*, 1976, *47*, 597–605.

SAMEROFF, A. Early influences on development: Fact or fancy? *Merrill-Palmer Quarterly*, 1975, *21*, 267–294.

SANDER, L. W. Issues in early mother-child interaction. In E. N. Rexford, L. W. Sander, & T. Shapiro (Eds.), *Infant psychiatry: A new synthesis*. New Haven, Conn.: Yale Press, 1976.

SANDER, L. W., STECHLER, G., JULIA, M., & BURNS, P. Early mother-infant interactions and 24-hour patterns of activity and sleep. *Journal of the American Academy of Child Psychiatry*, 1970, *9*, 103–123.

SCHAFFER, H. R. Acquiring the concept of the dialogue. In M. H. Bornstein & W. Kessen (Eds.), *Psychological development from infancy: Image to intention*. Hillsdale, N.J.: Lawrence Erlbaum Associates, 1978.

SPITZ, R. A. & WOLF, K. M. The smiling response. *Genetic Psychology Monographs*, 1946, *34*, 57–125.

SROUFE, L. A. The coherence of individual development: Early care, attachment and subsequent developmental issues. *American Psychologist*, 1979, *34*, 834–841.

SROUFE, L. A., & WATERS, E. The ontogenesis of smiling and laughter: A perspective on the organization of development in infancy. *Psychological Review*, 1976, *83*, 173–189.

STARK, R. E. Features of infant sounds: The emergence of cooing. *Journal of Child Language*, 1978, *5*, 378–390.

STECHLER, G., & KAPLAN, S. The development of the self: A psychoanalytic perspective. *The Psychoanalytic Study of the Child*, 1980, *35*, 85–105.

STERN, D. Mother and infant at play: The dyadic interaction involving facial, vocal and gaze behaviors. In M. Lewis & L. A. Rosenblum (Eds.), *The effect of the infant on its caretaker*. New York: John Wiley, 1974a.

STERN, D. The goal and structure of mother-infant play. *Journal of the American Academy of Child Psychiatry*, 1974b, *13*, 402–421.

TRONICK, E., ALS, H., & BRAZELTON, T. B. The infant's capacity to regulate mutuality in face-to-face interaction. *Journal of Communication*, 1977, *27*, 74–80.

TRONICK, E., ALS, H., ADAMSON, L., WISE, S., & BRAZELTON, T. B. The infant's responses to entrapment between contradictory messages in face-to-face interaction. *Journal of the American Academy of Child Psychiatry*, 1978, *17*, 1–13.

VANDELL, D. L. *Toddler sons' interactions with mothers, fathers and peers.* Unpublished Ph.D. dissertation, Boston University, 1976.

VANDELL, D. L. Effects of a playgroup experience on mother-son and father-son interaction, *Developmental Psychology*, 1979, *15*, 379–385.

VANDELL, D. L., WILSON, K. S., & BUCHANAN, N. R. Peer interaction in the first year of life: An examination of its structure, content and sensitivity to toys. *Child Development*, 1980, *51*, 481–488.

VAUGHAN, B., EGELAND, B., SROUFE, L. A., & WATERS, E. Individual differences in infant-mother attachment at twelve and eighteen months: Stability and change in families under stress. *Child Development*, 1979, *50*, 971–975.

WATSON, J. Smiling, cooing and "the game." *Merrill-Palmer Quarterly*, 1972, *4*, 323–339.

WEINRAUB, M., BROOKS, J., & LEWIS, M. The social network: A reconsideration of the concept of attachment. *Human Development*, 1977, *20*, 31–47.

WERNER, H., & KAPLAN, B. *Symbol formation.* New York: John Wiley, 1964.

WHITE, B. L., CASTLE, P., & HELD, R. Observations on the development of visually-directed reaching. *Child Development*, 1964, *35*, 349–365.

WOLFF, P. Observations on the early development of smiling. In B. Foss (Ed.), *Determinants of infant behavior* (Vol. 2). London: Methuen, 1963.

WOLFF, P. The causes, controls and organizations of behavior in the neonate. *Psychological Issues*, 1966, *5* (Whole No. 17).

WOLFF, P. Crying and vocalization in infancy. In B. Foss (Ed.), *Determinants of infant behavior* (Vol. 4). New York: John Wiley, 1969.

YOGMAN, M., DIXON, S., TRONICK, E., ALS, H., & BRAZELTON, T. B. *The goals and structure of face-to-face interaction between infants and fathers.* Paper presented at the biennial meeting of SRCD, New Orleans, 1977.

ZELAZO, P. Smiling and vocalizing: A cognitive emphasis. *Merrill-Palmer Quarterly*, 1972, *18*, 349–365.

ZELAZO, P., & KAGAN, J. Infant smiling to sequential visual stimuli: Trial and age effects. Unpublished manuscript, 1972.

ZELAZO, P., & KOMER, M. Infant smiling to non-social stimuli and the recognition hypothesis. *Child Development*, 1971, *42*, 1327–1339.

17

Early Language Development

DENNIS L. MOLFESE
VICTORIA J. MOLFESE
PATRICIA L. CARRELL

The study of infant language development has emerged as an important area in developmental psycholinguistics. One sign of the newness of this area is reflected by the fact that much of the work reviewed in this chapter was conducted during the last decade. With few exceptions the research problems addressed in the chapter were not addressed before 1965. Although striking gains have been made in virtually every area of infant language, much is still unknown concerning the environmental, linguistic, cognitive, and physiological factors that surround the early development of language.

Areas remain in which methodological limitations restrict the information obtained from research studies. For example infant research continues to be plagued by small sample sizes as in much of the "motherese" and semantic development work. Subject attrition rates are very high for some paradigms as in the infant speech perception area (30 percent to 60 percent depending on the paradigm employed). Here as in other areas researchers have become almost exclusively reliant on cross-sectional designs. What longitudinal work has been conducted is usually of short duration and involves small numbers of infants. Different groups generally receive different treatments, and within-subject designs are rare. In addition many studies are either atheoretical or loosely tied to a theoretical base. More attention is given to the building of a data base and replicating the findings of others than to testing, extending, or building theories. While the choice of such tactics does not preclude the drawing of inferences concerning infant language development, the advantages normally gained from the use of a variety of subject designs and theoretical orientations have to some extent been lost.

The present chapter is divided into three major sections—the first concerns the phonological aspects of early language production and perception, the second treats the environmental and social factors that surround the interactions between the infant and parents, while the third focuses on the cognitive-semantic issues of prelinguistic and early linguistic development. The research reviewed here is restricted to infants from birth to approximately 18 months of age.

SOUND PRODUCTION DEVELOPMENT: THE PRELINGUISTIC PERIOD

Little descriptive or experimental data were available on infant vocalizations and auditory perception prior to 1940 (Irwin, 1941; Irwin & Chen, 1943). The importance of work prior to that time was severely limited by the small sample sizes, absence of reliability estimates across observers, the lack of standard recording techniques (both for characterizing and for recording sounds), and the absence of statistical analyses. Irwin and Chen (1941) were the first to utilize the International Phonetic Alphabet (IPA) as a notational system for characterizing infant vocalization. Irwin and his associates were really the first to study systematically the vocalizations of infants in a largely cross-sectional sample (some infants were followed longitudinally) that spanned the period from birth to 30 months of age. The children (with a median birthweight of 3390 grams) were sampled from monolingual middle-class families and were tested during afternoons following the noon feeding in their homes. The vocalizations were transcribed usually by one examiner (except when tests were conducted for reliability, see Irwin, 1945, and Irwin & Chen, 1941) using the IPA from spontaneous speech sound vocalizations of the child. This system and examples of the sounds which the characters represent are presented in Figure 17–1. The vocalizations were recorded within what Irwin described as *breath units*—exhalations that contained noncry vocalizations. The standard sample for an infant consisted of sounds produced during 30 such breath units although those units were not necessarily recorded consecutively. The data were later grouped and reported in 15 two-month intervals or age levels beginning with one and two months (age level 1) and ending with months 29–30 (age level 15). The series of studies conducted by Irwin using these techniques covered nearly three decades—from the early 1940s until the mid-1960s—and dealt with changes in the place of articulation (Irwin, 1946, 1951), manner of articulation (Irwin, 1947), vowel and consonant frequency, and the developmental progression in the production of vowels and consonants (Chen & Irwin, 1946; Irwin & Chen, 1946).

Irwin and Chen (1946) reported that all vocalization sounds (consonants and vowels) increased from a mean of 7.2 sounds at 1 to 2 months of age to a mean of 21 sounds at 17 to 18 months of age and then to 27.2 sounds at 29 to 30 months of age. These data are based on sample sizes ranging from 62 to 80 children and 41 to 181 transcriptions of 30 breaths each. Chen and Irwin (1946) computed means for vowel and consonant types on the same data set described by Irwin and Chen (1946). They noted production rates of 4.5 vowel sounds at 1 to 2 months of age, 7.1 vowels at 5 to 6 months, and 10 vowels at 13 to 14 months of age. After this age the number of different vowel sounds seemed to stabilize, only gradually increasing to 11.4 sounds at 29 to 30 months of age. Consonant sounds, though few initially with only 2.7 consonant sounds at 1 to 2 months of age, showed a more accelerated expansion rate with 5.2 different consonant sounds produced at 5 to 6 months, 10.9 sounds at 17 to 18 months, and 15.8 consonants at 29 to 30 months of age. Irwin (1947), in a paper on manner of articulation, noted that of the 2.7 consonant sounds produced at 1 to 2 months of age, most were voiceless (96.4 percent), with the majority of these consonant sounds being plosives (52 percent) and fricatives (44.4 percent). By 5 to 6 months of age Irwin noted a sharp reduction in the percentage of plosives (down to 29.8 percent) with about equal numbers being voiced and voiceless. Fricative sounds, however, continued to be largely voiceless (62.9 percent) and constituted the greater percentage of consonant sounds. Interestingly it is at approximately 5 to 6 months of age that Irwin noted the initial emergence and increase in other speech sounds such as glides, nasals, and semivowels. By 17 to 18 months of age plosive sounds again predominate in the infant's vocalizations (50.4 percent) but with the majority being voiced (thus making a major reversal from the pattern present at 1 to 2 months of age). The percentage of sounds that are fricatives is sharply reduced by this time (27.5 percent), but the majority (25.7 percent) continue to be voiceless. By 30 months of age equal numbers of voiced (25.7 percent) and voiceless (23.2 percent) sounds are produced while more voiceless fricatives (17.4 percent) were noted than voiced fricatives (2.7 percent). Plosives at this stage characterize nearly half of the consonant sound samples.

When Irwin (1947) plotted changes in place of articulation (where in the vocal tract the different sounds were produced), several interesting patterns were noted. Initially most consonant sounds were produced in the back (i.e., velar and glottal sounds) of the vocal tract (98.7 percent at 1 to 2 months of age). By 5 to 6 months, however, there was a 12 percent decline in these velar and glottal sounds while the number of consonant sounds produced in the front of the vocal tract (labial, labial-dental, lingual-dental, and postdental) increased by a factor of 10. From this time on there was an increase in the percentage of consonant sounds produced in the front two-thirds of the vocal tract (70 percent at 18 months and 80.7 percent at 30 months). The contribution of the back consonants to total consonant production declined even further with age (30 percent at 18 months and 19.3 percent at 30 months).

When Irwin (1951) plotted developmental changes in consonant position in the infants' vocalizations, he found that in general the number of different consonants produced in the front of the vocal tract increased linearly, the number of different medial consonant sounds declined, and the number of final consonant sounds increased (although the latter were largely absent until 10 to 12 months of age).

In an attempt to identify if such place and manner patterns occurred consistently for words, Winitz and Irwin (1958) sampled the vocalizations of infants between 13 and 18 months of age. Generally the infants produced more two syllable words initially at 13 to 14 months (51.8 percent) than monosyllable words (24 percent). These multisyllable words included words consisting of a repeated syllable such as *beebee* (17.52 percent) and words consisting of two syllables in which one sound is common and one sound varies as in *baby* (31.39 percent). The monosyllable words were usually consonant-vowel (18.25 percent) and occasionally consonant-vowel-consonant (5.8 percent) in form. By 15 to 16 months the

ɪ	in EAT	hʍ	in WHICH
ɪ	in IT	ʍ	in WITCH
eɪ,e	in EIGHT	f	in FEW
ɛ	in ED	v	in VIEW
æ	in AT	θ	in THIN
ʌ	in UTTER	ð	in THEN
ə	in ABOUT	t	in TOP
ɝ	in EARLY	d	in DAD
ɚ	in EARLIER	n	in KNACK
ɑ	in ROT	s	in SOUP
ɔ	in OUGHT	z	in ZIPPERS
oʊ,o	in OAT	ʃ	in SHIP
ʊ	in CROOK	ʒ	in ROUGE
u	in OOPS	tʃ	in CHIP
jᵘ	in USE	dʒ	in GYP
ɪu	in FEW	r	in RED
ɑu	in OUT	l	in LED
aɪ	in I	j	in YELL
ɔɪ	in VOID	k	in CAT
p	in PAPA	g	in GAME
b	in BABY	ŋ	in BANK
m	in MAMA	h	in HEIGH

Figure 17-1 International Phonetic Alphabet (IPA)

majority of words were monosyllabic consonant-vowel (44.2 percent) and consonant-vowel-consonant (20.1 percent) in form with a marked reduction in two syllable words (22.3 percent). This trend continues at 17 to 18 months of age with productions including approximately 50 percent monosyllabic words and 38 percent disyllabic words. The manner and place of articulation information utilized in these early words was similar to that reported above. Winitz and Irwin (1973) noted that the use of particular back vowels in words a, ɔ, o, u, ʊ, increased from 35.3 percent at 13 months to 53.75 percent at 18 months while the percentage of front vowels declined from 45.5 percent to 37 percent over this same period. The front consonants occurred the most frequently in words at all ages. The voiced labial consonant /b/ was used in words more frequently than other consonants with the voiced dental postdental /d/ as the next most frequently used consonant. The back consonants at 13 to 14 months contributed only a small percentage of the consonants used in words (6.78 percent). This increased somewhat by 15 to 16 months (15.55 percent) with little change later. The majority of the consonants in words noted by Winitz and Irwin are voiced plosives at all ages (59.3 percent, 50.9 percent, and 61.2 percent at 14, 16, and 18 months respectively). Voiceless fricatives increased from 2.9 percent at 14 months to 7.3 percent at 16 months but then changed little afterwards. Nasals declined slightly from 18.6 percent at 14 months to 12.6 percent at 18 months.

Irwin's research represented an initial yet systematic attempt to characterize the changes in the infant's vocalizations over time. Yet because this work was the first of its kind, it has been subjected to criticisms stemming from forty years of methodological and theoretical hindsight. The major problems concern (1) the limitations of the notational system (IPA) used by Irwin to characterize the children's vocalizations (Ervin & Miller, 1963); (2) the failure to report or consider the nature of the larger utterances in which the sounds occurred (Ervin & Miller, 1963); (3) the acoustic differences between the infant vocalizations and the sounds the IPA was designed to classify (Lynip, 1951); and (4) the absence of high resolution recording and spectral analysis equipment during the era of Irwin's work. Despite these problems, however, Irwin's data continue to have value for the infant language scientist today:

The consonantal and vowel profiles obtained by Irwin and his colleagues might well have been altered if different transcription measures were used, but his findings probably give a fairly good picture of the development of infant prelanguage utterances within the first year and a half. (Winitz, 1969, p. 28)

SOUND PRODUCTION DEVELOPMENT: THE LINGUISTIC PERIOD

At the time that Irwin began his research program on infant vocalizations, Jakobson (1941) proposed a system that characterized speech sounds in terms of acoustic as well as articulatory characteristics (Chomsky & Halle, 1968; Jakobson, 1968; Jakobson, Fant, & Halle, 1952; Jakobson & Halle, 1956). In this system, phonemes, the

speech sounds of a language, consist of a set of attributes or features. The speech sounds of all languages can be described in terms of these features. This system has been used primarily to describe language sounds rather than prelanguage vocalizations (Ringwall, Reese, & Markel, 1965, 1970).

Approximately 12 to 15 features have been used to define the sounds in any language. A partial list of these features and their characteristics follows in Table 17–1. Each feature is dichotomous—it is either present (e.g., the feature +voice indicates vocal chord vibration. + voice is a characteristic of speech sound such as /b/) or absent (e.g., −voice indicates a lack of initial vocal chord vibration or voicing as in the case of /p/). The features, in addition, are defined in terms of acoustic and articulatory characteristics.

A particular distinctive feature either characterizes a certain phoneme (+) or does not (−). Most consonant sounds, since they generally involve a closure or restriction in the size of the vocal tract opening, are characterized as +consonantal while vowel sounds, which involve a larger vocal tract opening, contain the feature −consonantal. Voiced consonants, such as /b, d, g/ in which laryngeal pulsing or vocal chord vibration occurs during production, contain the features +consonantal, +voiced while other consonants such as /p, t, k/ which lack the voicing quality, contain the features +consonantal, −voiced. By assigning to the different speech sounds the appropriate features, each phoneme can be distinguished from all other phonemes on the basis of one or more features.

Jakobson postulated that the child begins to acquire language by dichotomizing all the speech sounds on the basis of a single feature. The child, then, has two groups of sounds, those that contain a + on some feature and those that are − on that same feature. The child can then discriminate between these two sets of sounds. Gradually the child adds additional features, progressively separating the speech sounds until all have been identified on the basis of their distinctive features.

Table 17-1 Phonological Distinctive Features and Their Attributes

FEATURE	POSITIVE (+)	NEGATIVE (−)
Continuant	Gradual onset	Abrupt onset
Consonantal	Occlusion of vocal tract	Open vocal tract
Diffuse	One or more noncentral formants	One central formant dominates
Grave	Lower frequencies predominate	High frequencies predominate
Nasal	Air stream bifurcated to use nasal and oral cavities as resonators	Air stream through oral cavity only
Strident	Irregular sound waveforms	Patterned waveforms
Tense	Long sound interval; large energy	Short interval; less energy
Vocalic	Single harmonic structure; gradual onset	Noise structure; abrupt onset
Voice	Strong low frequency sound component; vibration of vocal cords	No vibration of vocal bands

If the child has identified the features vocalic, consonantal, diffuse, strident, nasal, continuant, and voiced but not the feature grave, he should correctly understand and produce the differences between *pear* and *bear*, which differ in terms of the voicing feature of the initial consonant, but he should produce and respond to *pear* and *tear* as if they were the same because the initial phonemes differ only on the basis of the grave feature. (Palermo, 1971, p. 431)

Jakobson suggested that the first word produced by the child is formed from phonemes composed of features that are polar opposites. For example the initial word /pa/ consists of the two phonemes /p/ and /a/ which differ along every feature category from each other. The /p/ phoneme has the features +consonant, −voice, +diffuse since its production involves an initially occluded vocal tract that begins without vocal chord vibration. The acoustic energy from the /p/ is not concentrated in any specific frequency range. The /a/ phoneme, however, contains the features −consonant, +voice, −diffuse. The /a/ is produced with an open vocal tract, is voiced, and contains clearly demarcated formants. The word /pa/, for Jakobson, is the most likely first word for the child since it contains phonemes that contrast maximally with each other. Words produced later in development involve distinctions among other finer feature distinctions such as +grave (to distinguish /p/ from /t/). The development of speech sounds proceeds from this initial optimal consonant-vowel contrast that produces a maximal sound difference to gradually finer and finer distinctions in which the consonant sounds become more compact (−diffuse) and vowel-like (−consonant) while the vowels become more diffuse (+diffuse) and consonant-like (+consonant).

The order in which features are acquired, Jakobson argues, relates to the number of languages that contain that feature. The most common features are acquired first while those features which are idiosyncratic to only a few languages are mastered last.

Each feature is thought to be acquired in an all-or-none fashion rather than gradually over a long time period. When it is acquired it becomes a characteristic of all the sounds for which it is relevant. The acquisition of the voicing feature by the infant should be characterized by the appearance of the /g/−/k/ distinction as well as the /b/−/p/, /d/−/t/, and /f/−/v/ distinctions.

Although the research on infant word productions using a feature system is sketchy, some generalizations have been noted for infant language:

(a) The contrast between vowel and consonant—[+vocalic, −consonantal] versus [−vocalic, +consonantal]—is probably the earliest contrast to be observed.

(b) A stop-continuant contrast—[−continuant] versus [+continuant]—is quite early for all children, the continuant being a fricative [+strident] or a nasal [+nasal]. For example, the stop /p/ is contrasted with the fricative continuant /f/ and the nasal continuant /m/ at an early age.

(c) Stops precede fricatives; that is, [−continuant, −strident] precedes [+continuant, +strident].

(d) If two consonants are alike in manner of articulation (i.e., have the same markings on the features continuant and strident), one will be labial and the other alveolar or dental, that is, one will be [+grave] and the other [−grave]. For example, /p/ and /t/ are both [−continuant, −strident], but /p/ is [+grave] and /t/ is [−grave]. At this level of child de-

velopment, there is no distinction between [+diffuse] and [−diffuse]; hence, the distinction between /k/ and /t/ is not present.

(e) Contrasts involving place of articulation (i.e., contrasts involving the features grave and diffuse) precede voicing contrasts. For example, the distinction between /p/ and /k/, involving [+diffuse] versus [−diffuse], precedes the distinction between /b/ and /p/, involving [+voiced] versus [−voiced].

(f) Affricates—[−continuant, +strident]—and liquids—[+vocalic, +consonantal]—usually appear later than stops and nasals. For example, the affricates /c/ as in chip and /j/ as in jet, and the liquids /l/ and /r/ appear later than the stop /p/ and the nasal /m/.

(g) The vowel distinctions based on the diffuse-compact feature appear before those based on the flat-plain and grave-acute features. That is, the high versus low contrast in vowels, such as between /i/ and /ae/, precedes the front versus back distinctions, such as between /i/ and /u/. (Palermo, 1971, pp. 432–433)

INFANT SPEECH PERCEPTION

While Irwin and Jakobson addressed the vocalizations and speech sound production in the prelinguistic and linguistic infant, researchers in the areas of acoustic and linguistic sciences succeeded in identifying some of the cues that are important to human speech perception. It is now known that the human adult's perception of speech sounds is based on the perception of a complex code that is subject to a variety of acoustic, physiological, and cognitive constraints (Liberman, Cooper, Shankweiler, & Studdert-Kennedy, 1967). The reader is referred to Liberman et al. for a review of this literature.

Methodology

Within the last decade developmental researchers have utilized this information gained from adult speech perception to study the developmental pattern of speech perception abilities from birth. Current research suggests that infants very early in life are able to discriminate many, if not all, of the phonological features that characterize human speech.

The four procedures that have been largely responsible for the advances in our understanding of infant speech perception include the operant, nonnutritive, high amplitude sucking procedure (HAS), the heartrate deceleration response technique (HR), the visually reinforced, head-turning procedure (HT), and more recently the use of auditory evoked response recording techniques (AER).

In the HAS paradigm the infant's sucking on a blind nipple controls the presentation, rate of presentation, and/or loudness of a speech stimulus. As the rate of the infant's suck increases, the presentation rate or loudness increases. In response to the stimulus, the rate (per minute) of sucking initially increases. As the infant begins to habituate to the sound, the sucking rate declines. If the sucking rate decreases to some predetermined level (usually to some percentage below base line levels that were recorded before any stimulus was presented), the sound is changed. If the sucking rate for a "sound change" condition increased relative to a "no-change" control condition, it is interpreted as evidence of discrimination.

In the HR procedure the infant generally responds to stimulus sound onset with heartrate deceleration (which is assumed to reflect orientation). This orienting response (OR) tends to habituate with repeated presentation of the sounds. After a fixed number of trials to permit habituation of the cardiac OR, a novel sound is presented. If the heartrate increases to the new sounds, discrimination of the stimulus contrast is inferred.

For the HT procedure the infant is seated on the parent's lap and entertained by an assistant seated directly across from the infant. A speech stimulus is presented at a constant rate through a speaker located in front and to the side of the infant. Intermittently a few tokens of a novel stimulus are presented. If the infant turns its head toward the speaker when the change occurs, a visual reinforcer is illuminated for the infant to see. If the infant turns more frequently on trials when a change occurs, compared to no-change control trials, discrimination is inferred.

The fourth procedure involves the recording of auditory evoked brain responses (the brain response that is elicited by an auditory stimulus) from the scalp of infants while a series of speech sounds is presented. Differences in the auditory evoked responses (AER) elicited by different stimuli are interpreted as evidence for sound discrimination.

Research with these four techniques has enabled researchers to determine whether infants at various ages can discriminate between various speech and nonspeech sounds. The review that follows will be restricted to those discriminations which are related to the perception of speech-related cues.

Stop Consonant Perception: Place of Articulation

Moffitt (1968, 1971), using an HR procedure, was the first to demonstrate that 4- to 5-month-old infants could perform a simple auditory discrimination of place of articulation for the syllables /ba/ vs. /ga/. Morse (1972) demonstrated this place contrast as early as six weeks of age with an HAS procedure. This effect was later replicated by Leavitt, Brown, Morse, and Graham (1976) and Miller, Morse, and Dorman (1977) using the HR procedures. Molfese and Molfese (1979a), using AER procedures to study the responses of newborn infants, reported that the brain responses elicited by /b/ initial syllables differed from those elicited by /g/ initial syllables. Thus it appears that the ability to discriminate simple place of articulation contrasts is present from birth.

More recent work indicates that infants can discriminate these place contrasts when they occur in other positions besides the initial position. Jusczyk (1977) reported that two-month-old infants discriminated the /d/-/g/ contrast in the final position of consonant-vowel-consonant and vowel-consonant syllables. Jusczyk and Thompson (1978) reported a similar effect for place contrasts which occurred in the second syllable of two-syllable stimuli (e.g., /bada/ vs. /baga/). Moreover such effects were not affected by syllable stress. Williams (1977)

noted a similar effect for place contrasts in the medial position for vowel-consonant-vowel syllables.

Eimas (1947a), using a HAS procedure, was the first to demonstrate that young infants (two to three months of age) could discriminate the place continuum categorically. *Categorical perception* refers to the situation that occurs when two stimuli that are acoustic variations of the same phonetic category (they are assigned the same speech sound label by a language user) cannot be discriminated from each other while two stimuli separated by the same acoustic difference but are labeled so members of different phonetic categories can be discriminated.

Eimas synthesized on a computer a set of stimuli that were evenly spaced along a continuum. Adults classified the consonant sounds on one side of the continuum as /b/ while the other side was identified as /d/. Eimas then selected pairs of stimuli from this /b–d/ continuum such that all pairs differed in equal acoustic amounts. These stimulus pairs were then presented to three groups of infants.

Group D heard two stimuli, one during the initial habituation phase from the adult phonetic category /d/ and the other during the post shift phase from the category /b/. Group S received two stimuli that were acoustic variations of the same adult phonetic category /d/. Infants in the control condition, Group C, were assigned one of the four stimuli presented to Groups D and S. The overall acoustic differences between the two stimuli used for Group D were nearly identical to the differences between stimuli for Group S. Thus when Eimas found that Group D increased sucking rate over the post shift period while Groups S and C showed a decrease in sucking rate, Eimas inferred that *categorical discrimination* of /b/ and /d/ had been demonstrated. In Experiment 2 of this study, Eimas demonstrated that the infants could not categorically discriminate the critical cues for place contrasts (second formant transition cues) when these cues were isolated from the rest of the speech information. Each isolated pattern corresponded exactly to one of the second formant transitions of the speech stimuli. Using the HAS Eimas found that Groups D and S did not differ in their responses to the isolated patterns but that they did differ for the complete speech stimuli.

Several attempts have thus far been made to assess the presence of perceptual constancy for place contrasts. Fodor, Garrett, and Brill (1975) found that they could condition HT more readily in infants three to five and four to five months if syllables with the same initial consonant (/pi, pa/ vs. /ku/) were grouped together rather than if different consonants were reinforced (/pi, ku/ vs. /pa/). Molfese and Molfese (1981), in a study in which brain responses were elicited in response to the synthesized syllables /bi, bae, bɔ, gi, gae, gɔ/, reported finding a component of the newborn's brain response which reflected differences between the /b, g/ initial phonemes independent of the final vowel sounds. Similar effects have now also been noted with one- and two-month-old infant rhesus monkeys (Molfese, Morse, Taylor, & Erwin, 1981). In light of these last two studies, it would appear that some types of perceptual constancy for speech sounds may be innate and have some homologue in non-human organisms.

Stop Consonant Perception: Voicing Contrasts

The now classic study by Eimas, Siqueland, Jusczyk, and Vigorito (1971) was the first to demonstrate categorical speech perception for voicing contrasts in young infants. Eimas, using the HAS procedure, found that one- and four-month-old infants discriminated the voicing contrast /p/vs. /b/ categorically. This effect was later replicated by Eimas (1974a) for two- and three-month-olds with the HAS procedure and the contrasts /d/ vs. /t/. Miller (1974) reported similar effects with six- to eight-week-old infants, and Trehub and Rabinovitch (1972) demonstrated an auditory discrimination of /ba/ and /pa/ for both synthetic and normal speech stimuli.

Although HR measures were successfully used to demonstrate place of articulation discrimination by young infants, studies employing this measure to study categorical perception of voicing contrasts have failed to find such effects (Doty, 1974; Miller & Hankes-Ruzicka, 1978; Roth & Morse, 1975). Molfese and Molfese (1979b), using AER procedures with newborn infants and with infants from two to five months of age, reported no categorical effects in newborn infants. Brain response patterns did mirror a categorical effect, however, in the older infants. They interpreted these effects to suggest that the ability to detect voicing contrasts categorically develops some time after birth.

Although the question as to the developmental appearance of voicing contrasts remains open, researchers have in recent years attempted to address the issue of environmental influences on the development of voicing contrast discriminations. Some languages such as English employ two voicing categories—a *voiced* category and a *voiceless* one. In the voiced category the vocal folds begin to vibrate at the time that the articulators such as the lips release the sound (as in the case of /b/). For the voiceless sounds, lip release occurs some time before the vocal chords begin to vibrate (e.g., /p/). In some other languages, however, there is a third voicing category known as *prevoicing*—the vocal folds begin to vibrate some time before release. By studying infants from various language environments, one may derive some information concerning (1) the basic voicing boundaries that are present early in life and (2) how such boundaries change with experience in certain language environments. Lasky, Syrdal-Lasky, and Klein (1975) utilized HR procedures to assess voicing discrimination in 4- to 6½-month-old infants living in Guatemala. The parents spoke only Spanish, a language with a prevoiced-voiced, but no voiced-voiceless, contrast. Lasky et al. reported that these infants discriminated the English voiced-voiceless contrast but not the contrasts of their environment. Eilers, Gavin, and Wilson (1979), using the HT procedure with 6-month-old Cuban infants, supported the Lasky et al. findings for the English boundary. However they also found evidence for the Spanish contrast (unlike Lasky et al.). The English environment infants discriminated only the voiced-voiceless boundary (see also Eilers, Wilson, & Moore, 1977). Streeter (1976) conducted a HAS study with 2-month-old infants in Kenya whose parents spoke only Kikuyu, a language that employs the prevoiced-voiced distinction. These infants discriminated both the English contrast (voiced-

voiceless) as well as the Kikuyu prevoiced-voiced contrast.

Eimas (1975b) in a HAS test with American infants with stimuli which involved a prevoiced-voiced contrast failed to find reliable categorical discrimination of the foreign contrast. The cross-language studies, then, suggest that infants are able to discriminate the voiced-voiceless contrast whether it is part of their normal language environment or not. If the prevoiced-voiced contrast is part of the infant's (6-months old) language environment, they will also discriminate this contrast categorically. If the contrast involves the prevoiced-voiced distinction and it is not part of the infant's language environment, then the infant will not categorically discriminate this boundary.

As with place of articulation contrasts, researchers have investigated the development of the voicing contrast in two- and three-syllable contexts. Trehub (1973), employing HAS procedures, noted that 4- to 17-week-old infants discriminated voicing contrasts for consonants in the case of /aba/ vs. /apa/ but not /ataba/ vs. /atapa/. Eilers (1977) and Eilers et al. (1977), using HAS and HT procedures, noted that infants from 2 to 14 months of age could discriminate voicing contrasts in syllables' final consonants that involved both voicing and vowel duration cues.

Vowel Perception

Trehub (1973) was the first to report that young infants (4 to 17 weeks of age) could discriminate a series of vowel contrasts such as /i/-/u/, /i/-/a/, /pa/-/pi/, and /ta/-/ti/. In an experiment designed to assess infant categorical perception of vowels, Swoboda, Morse, and Leavitt (1976) found that 8-week-olds discriminated /i/ from /I/ in a continuous, noncategorical manner. However when vowel duration was shortened, Swoboda, Kass, Morse, and Leavitt (1978) reported that infants discriminated the vowels categorically, much in the manner that adults do under similar circumstances. In addition Kuhl (1976b, 1976c, 1977, 1979) showed that infants have some perceptual constancy for vowel categories over different intonation patterns and speakers.

In general the infant's discrimination of vowel sounds seems somewhat similar to that of an adult. The infant appears to possess a number of skills early in life which enable it to discriminate vowel sounds, perceive them categorically under certain circumstances, and differentiate these vowel sounds in spite of changes in other acoustic cues.

Other Speech Contrasts

While infants from one month of age seem able to discriminate a number of contrasts, their perceptual abilities may not match those of adults for all speech contrasts. Eilers and Minifie (1975) and Eilers (1977) found that infants between 4 and 17 weeks of age could discriminate fricative contrasts (/sa/ vs. /va/) but not the voiced-voiceless fricative contrasts (/sa/ vs. /za/). By 6 to 8 months of age infants were able to discriminate these fricative voicing contrasts (Eilers et al., 1977). However, these infants could not discriminate the /fi/ vs. /θi/ or the /fa/ vs. /θa/ contrasts. The 12- to 14-month-olds tested in this same study could discriminate /fi/ vs. /θi/ but not /fa/ vs. /θa/. Holmberg, Morgan, and Kuhl (1977) also reported some difficulty in training the /f/ vs. /θ/ distinction to 6-month-olds.

Eimas (1975a) reported that 2- to 3-month-olds categorically discriminated /ra/ vs. /la/. Trehub (1976) found that 5- to 17-week-old English infants could discriminate the Czech /ra/–/za/ contrast which English-speaking adults find difficult to discriminate. For semivowel glides Jusczyk, Copan, and Thompson (1978) found that 2-month-olds could discriminate /wa/ vs. /ga/ regardless of position or stress in two-syllable stimuli.

Suprasegmental Cues

Kaplan (1969) noted that infants as young as four months of age can change their heartrate when presented sentences in which the intonation pattern changed. Morse, using the HAS procedure, found that six-week-olds could discriminate rising versus falling intonation contours for consonant-vowel syllables. Spring and Dale (1977) found that four-month-olds could discriminate differences in stress in two-syllable stimuli.

Concluding Remarks

The infant early in life possesses many of the speech discrimination abilities that characterize an adult language user. Some of the skills include the ability not only to discriminate between speech sounds but to perceive categorically the sounds as well. As noted the infant is able to respond to some speech sound contrasts such as place of articulation and voicing, as in the case of stop consonants and vowels. The perception of sounds such as fricatives, especially when combined with other contrasts, appears to develop somewhat later. The context in which speech sounds are heard, as well as intonation and speaker voice, has also been found to have some influence on the perception of speech sounds.

MOTHERESE: FORM, MEANING, AND FUNCTION

Only a little more than ten years ago, it was thought possible to study language acquisition without studying the linguistic environment of the child. The only work being done at that time on the nature of linguistic input to children was carried out by linguists and anthropologists studying "baby talk"—i.e., the special lexicon used with infants viewed as simplified forms of adult words (Ferguson, 1964; also reviewed in Ferguson, 1977). Other fairly widely observed features of baby talk were mainly prosodic—including high pitch and exaggerated intonation contours (cf. Blount & Padgug, 1977; Garnica, 1975, 1977). The focus of this research, however, was primarily on describing baby talk as a certain type of "simplified" speech register and not on trying to discover its relationship and relevance to language acquisition (though some research in this tradition noted that informants justified their use of baby talk with the motive of "making the language easier to learn").

Since the late 1960s psychologists and linguists in-terested in language acquisition have studied the nature of the language environment of the child. To a great extent this recent trend has been motivated by efforts to refute the earlier prevailing view that language acquisition was largely innate, facilitated by a rich *language acquisition device* (LAD), and that it occurred independently of the language environment. In fact the results of recent research on mothers' speech have contributed significantly to the widespread abandonment of the nativist view of language acquisition and to the growing recognition of other important factors in language acquisition. Snow has pointed out that recent acceptance of the following three basic assumptions about language acquisition has been advanced by the results of mothers' speech research:

1. Language acquisition is the result of a process of interaction between mother and child which begins early in infancy, to which the child makes as important a contribution as the mother, and which is crucial to cognitive and emotional development as well as to language acquisition.
2. Language acquisition is guided by and is the result of cognitive development.
3. Producing simplified speech registers is one of the many communicative skills whose acquisition is as interesting as the acquisition of syntax or phonology. (Snow, 1977a, pp. 31–32)

The continued study of "motherese"[1] has also come about as part of an increased awareness on the part of linguists, psychologists, and anthropologists that such phenomena constitute an interesting area of research which is relevant not only to the study of language acquisition, but to the whole question of paying more attention to the general environment in which language acquisition occurs and to the social-interactional nature of what is acquired and how it is acquired. Motherese has led to the study of the language acquisition process in the same way it occurs—within the context of social interactions.

Methodological Preliminaries

The body of research conducted in the area of motherese is already quite large and is growing steadily. Yet in terms of rigorous research methods and reliable, valid, conclusive results, the field is still very much in its infancy. The field has experienced a number of theoretical and methodological shifts in its short life with the result that no single methodology or theoretical focus has been in vogue long enough to generate a coherent body of research replete with sound research designs, conclusive findings, and replications.

By far the greater proportion of the research has been on extremely small sample sizes studied longitudinally for relatively brief periods of time. Sample size has varied upward from 2 mother-child dyads (Lieven, 1978a,

[1] For ease and simplicity the term "motherese" was chosen as the label for the study of the language addressed to children, thereby avoiding both the longer, more clumsy descriptive phrases like "the speech addressed to children" and the more awkward (but admittedly sex neutral and more general) terms such as "caregiver" or "caretaker." All of these alternative labels are included as part of "motherese." Research conducted comparing fathers' and mothers' speech to their young children has reported fathers' input to be quite similar to the mothers' (Gleason, 1975).

1978b) to 4 mothers (Holzman, 1974), 5 mothers (Sachs, Brown, & Salerno, 1976), 8 mothers (Remick, 1971), 10 mothers (Broen, 1972; Ringler, 1973), 12 mothers (Cherry & Lewis, 1978), and 16 mothers (Cross, 1978). Larger sample sizes have been used in only a few studies—e.g., 42 mothers in Snow (1972), 57 mothers in Phillips (1973), and 80 mothers in Lewis and Freedle (1973).

Due to the inherent nature of the object of investigation—i.e., motherese—the data and the situations in which they have been generated and collected have been fairly consistent among the various studies. Most of the data have been mothers' speech samples generated and collected from free play situations of mothers with their children (Broen, 1972; Phillips, 1973). Sometimes the location of the free play activity varied between laboratory playroom (Cherry & Lewis, 1978) and the child's own home (Cross, 1978); sometimes the location of the free play activity is not specified, other than an assurance that it was a "naturalistic setting" (Lewis & Freedle, 1973). A minority of studies have also included comparisons of mother-child speech to mother-adult speech; the mother-adult speech has usually been informal conversations with an adult, usually the experimenter (Broen, 1972). As Grimshaw (1977) points out, however, little control has been placed on the so-called spontaneous mother-adult speech to make it comparable to the mother-child speech; for example, there are various differences in the two situations related to topic, social relationships between the participants, and other social aspects of the context.

One important variable in the study of motherese has been the age of the child whom the mother is addressing. The broad range of values that this variable has taken is at once a positive and a negative aspect of research in the field. The range of children's ages has varied quite broadly, from infants as young as a few days (Jones & Moss, 1971), one month (Cohen & Beckwith, 1976), or three months (Snow, 1977b) to two- to four-year-olds (the so-called young language-acquiring child). Studies which have investigated "stages" of motherese, as directed to children of varying ages and levels of language proficiency, have included groups of children of various ages (e.g., Phillips, 1973, had three groups of children, ages 8, 18, and 28 months). In other studies which have compared motherese to language addressed to older people, the "older" subjects have varied from ten-year-old children (Snow, 1972) to adults (Remick, 1971; Ringler, 1973). The negative aspect of this broad range of children's ages is that it makes comparing studies and generalizing findings problematical.

In deciding which research to include for review in this chapter on motherese, we chose as an operational upper limit to include only those studies in which the target children to whom the motherese was addressed were under the age of two years or below 2.0 MLU (mean length of utterance)—at least at the beginning of the study if it was longitudinal or as the age of one of the child groups if more than one target group was included.

The most common variables studied have been the phonological-prosodic—e.g., pitch, rate of speech, intonation contour (Broen, 1972; Garnica, 1977; Sachs et al., 1976); certain syntactic measures—e.g., sentence type, such as declarative, *yes-no* and *wh-* interrogative and im-perative (Newport, Gleitman, & Gleitman, 1977; Sachs et al., 1976); MLU (Cross, 1977, 1978); and measures of syntactic complexity (Newport, 1976; Phillips, 1973; Sachs et al., 1976; Snow, 1972). Another common variable has been the mothers' use of expansions and repetitions (Broen, 1972; Cazden, 1965; Lieven, 1978a; Newport et al., 1977). However the vast majority of the variables studied have been studied one time only and appear to be idiosyncratic to a particular study. In one of the largest studies reported in this chapter, Cross (1977, 1978) studied 60 different motherese variables, grouped as "syntactic," "referentiality," "speech style" or "discourse" types; most of her variables are unique to her study. Cross (1977) includes a useful appendix which describes each motherese variable and indicates whether it has been used by other researchers. The studies with large numbers of motherese variables, however, encounter additional methodological difficulties in the face of their small sample sizes. For example Cross (1977, 1978) studied 60 different motherese parameters with a sample of only 16 mothers.

Studies relating features of motherese to features of the child's language are even more difficult to compare due to the added differences among them in terms of the child variables studied. About the only child language variable common to these studies is the child's MLU (Cross, 1977, 1978; Newport et al., 1977).

The major methodological shortcoming of research on motherese is the extent to which the purpose behind the study is lost. The strongest implicit motivation behind research into the nature of the speech addressed to children is to determine whether the use of the special speech style has any effect on the course of language acquisition. Too often, however, this purpose is not reflected in the research design. Very few studies have been done in which language acquisition is the dependent variable and features of motherese the independent variables. Lewis & Freedle (1973), Newport (1976; Newport et al., 1977), and Cross (1977, 1978) are among the few exceptions.

Early Studies of Motherese: Focus on Form

As mentioned before, the motivation behind the early research on motherese was to refute the strong nativist view of language acquisition. In particular its focus was to question the view that a large innate component was necessary to buffer the language acquisition process against the supposed sparseness, complexity, and confusion in the "primary linguistic data." In other words the research set out to show that, although adult-to-adult speech might be largely ill formed, ungrammatical, fragmentary, replete with false starts, hesitation, and slips of the tongue (Bever, Fodor, & Weksel, 1965; Chomsky, 1967; McNeill, 1966; Miller & Chomsky, 1963), input to children was not like that (contrary to Fodor, 1966). Thus the first task undertaken by motherese researchers was simply to describe the characteristics of mothers' speech; the focus was on describing various aspects of the form of that speech. These studies have been reviewed in detail by Farwell (1973) and Vorster (1975).

Results of these early studies (e.g., Broen, 1972; Drach, 1969; Kobashigawa, 1969; Phillips, 1973; Remick, 1976;

Sachs et al., 1976; Snow, 1972) very easily confirmed the view that the language addressed to children is different in form from that addressed to adults. Every measure used in these studies of grammatical complexity (MLU, incidence of subordinate clauses, mean preverb length, incidence of conjunctions) or of prosodic and syntactic well-formedness (incidence of hesitations, disfluencies, utterance fragments, false starts) showed that the speech addressed to infants between 18 and 36 months of age was much simpler, more redundant, and much more grammatical than the speech addressed to children or adults (see Snow, 1977a, pp. 33–35, for tables of the variables included in each study). A major shortcoming of these early studies of motherese is that, although a large number of different variables have been studied, and a few of these (e.g., MLU) ubiquitously, in general very few measures have really been studied intensively.

However the broad outlines of mothers' speech to children—that it is simple, redundant, that it contains many questions, many imperatives, few past tenses, little coordination or subordination, and few disfluencies, is higher pitched, and has an exaggerated intonation pattern (Garnica, 1975, 1977)—are by now quite well established and generally widely accepted.

The general conclusion of these early studies of motherese was that the speech addressed to children of language learning age was well adapted to the children's own linguistic level. Consequently, it could also be concluded that the role of an innate LAD might be considerably less than was earlier proposed. Information about the structure of language was available to the child in the primary linguistic data.[2]

The findings of these early studies were purely descriptive. No one had yet undertaken to sort out just what it was about talking to children that caused such simplification, redundancy, and grammaticality. Was it, for example, the age of the children, their cuteness, their low status, or their inability to speak correctly? However, there were indications in some of the early research that the mothers' speech is a product of a delicately balanced interactional process. Phillips (1973) found that true motherese does not appear reliably until children are old enough to respond to adults' speech. Snow (1972) found that even an experienced mother is not capable of producing fully adequate motherese when the child is not present to cue her. Although the mothers in Snow's study did speak more slowly, simply, and redundantly when asked to make tapes which would later be played to their children, they did not simplify their language as much as they did when the child was present with them. This suggests that at least some of the characteristics of motherese are adjustments made in response to cues from the child. An implication of this suggestion was that the form of mothers' speech would be quite well adapted to the linguistic level of the child. Thus the characteristics of maternal speech would be expected to change

abruptly in the direction of simplicity, well-formedness, and redundancy at 12 to 14 months when the child first showed signs of understanding and then gradually reapproach the normal adult levels over the next several years.

The findings mentioned before on the structured simplicity of motherese led to two common misinterpretations. One was the view that mothers were providing mini-language lessons for their children. Such an interpretation is an unjustified extrapolation from the evidence. Although mothers often do try to teach their children various aspects of their language, what they are doing most of the time is merely trying to communicate with their children. The simplifications found are a side effect of their efforts to communicate. Garnica (1977) has elicited some interesting comments from mothers about why they think they talk to young children as they do. Any mini-language lessons provided by mothers' simplifications are incidental to, and not the cause of, those simplifications.

Another misinterpretation of the early findings was the conclusion that there was no innate component to language acquisition. An overzealous reaction against the rich, powerful, innate LAD was the conclusion that everything the child needed to acquire language successfully was present in the structurally simple primary linguistic data revealed by these early studies of motherese. Of course it is absurd to argue that any complex behavior is entirely innate or entirely learned; innate and environmental factors always interact in the development of complex skills. However it is not absurd to ask how large or how small a role is played by innate versus environmental factors. Since the advent of the early findings on motherese, the role of environmental factors in language acquisition has been focused on to such a great extent that researchers often lose sight of, or at least fail to recognize any longer, the contributions of an innate linguistic capacity.

The proper conclusion to be drawn from these early studies was that Chomsky's position regarding the unimportance of the linguistic input was unproven. Since all children, in addition to possessing an innate linguistic capacity, also receive simple, redundant, and well-formed input, the relative contributions of the innate and the environmental factors cannot be determined. Only if the prediction could be proven that children without access to such simplified input *ceteris paribus* are unsuccessful or retarded in their language development could we conclude that the innate component is relatively less important than Chomsky hypothesized. Only if providing a simplified, redundant, and well-formed input enabled nonhumans with human-like cognitive abilities (e.g., young chimpanzees) as well as human children to acquire language could we conclude that the innate component is of no importance at all.

Recently Newport (1976; Newport, Gleitman, & Gleitman, 1975) has attempted to provide new support for Chomsky's position of a rich LAD by showing that the speech addressed to children is really syntactically complex rather than simple. The basis for saying that such speech is complex, despite the earlier findings of short utterance length and absence of complex sentences, is that questions and imperatives are used very frequently in addition to declaratives. How, argues New-

---

[2] An interesting additional finding was that not only mothers, but also all adults and even children aged 4 to 5, produced simplified, redundant speech when addressing 16- to 36-month-olds (Anderson & Johnson, 1973; Sachs & Devin, 1976; Shatz & Gelman, 1973). Thus simplified speech could be assumed to be universally available to language learning children; not just children growing up in middle-class North America and cared for by their doting mothers but also children living in extended families and cared for by siblings have simplified forms of language as input.

port, could a child learn the underlying subject-verb-object (S-V-O) order in English from an input corpus of motherese utterances consisting of about 40 percent to 60 percent of such deformed syntactic types as interrogatives (with inverted aux-subject) and imperatives (with deleted subject)? It is, of course, clear that English-speaking children do operate with a general S-V-O rule, since not only their declaratives but also their early interrogatives exhibit this order of elements.

The fact that children are exposed to high percentages of these "complex" syntactic patterns does not rule out, of course, other bases the children may have for distinguishing among these orders and keeping them distinct (e.g., intonational contours differentiating interrogatives and imperatives from declaratives; the fact that auxiliary verbs are unstressed and may not be attended to by the children, thus making interrogatives appear similar to declaratives in retaining S-V-O patterns).

Later Studies of Motherese: Focus on Meaning

One serious shortcoming of the early studies of motherese was that they concentrated almost exclusively on the form of the mothers' speech but neglected to describe what mothers were talking about. This is comprehensible when we realize that these early studies of motherese were done in the late 1960s and early 1970s when analyses of child speech were similarly primarily concerned with children's acquisition of syntactic knowledge. Therefore it seemed natural to analyze maternal form to determine how it might influence the child's acquisition of form. The child's task was seen as one of testing many different innately based hypotheses about the syntax of the language being acquired against the observed input. In this view acquiring semantics was looked upon as a separate task before the child.

In 1972 MacNamara argued against this view and maintained that acquisition of syntax could be explained only if it is recognized that children figure out the rules underlying syntactic structure by using semantic cues in the adult's utterance. MacNamara suggested that knowledge of the meanings of important lexical items (content words, especially) plus knowledge of what is likely to be said about the entities or actions in a given situation enables the child to guess correctly what the utterance means. Not only must the child be a good guesser, but the adult also has to talk about things the child expects to hear about. MacNamara argued that adult utterances have no syntax as far as the young child is concerned and that a child in the early stages of language acquisition must interpret adult utterances the same way adults interpret the young child's utterances—i.e., by relating the words used to aspects of the situation being talked about. After many opportunities of observing the referential meaning of a word and the relative order in which those meanings occur (e.g., that the word referring to the agent precedes the word referring to the action), the child begins to induce a semantic-word order rule. Later upon encountering other evidence (e.g., sentences—like passives in which the word referring to the agent does not occur in first position), the child is forced to abandon his/her semantic-word order rule for a truly syntactic rule.

In this model there must be severe semantic limitations on the mothers' linguistic input to the child. Reanalysis of motherese in light of this view reveals that the semantic content of motherese is indeed severely restricted. Mothers tend to restrict their utterances to the present tense, to concrete nouns, to comments on what the child is doing and on what is going on around the child at the time (Phillips, 1972; Snow, Arlman-Rupp, Hassing, Jobse, Joosten, & Vorster, 1976). The semantic content of motherese tends to consist of statements and questions about what objects are called, what noises they make, what color they are, what actions they are performing, where they are located, and who they belong to, but very little else (Snow, 1977a). These limitations on the semantic content of motherese may also provide the explanation of the syntactic simplicity mentioned before. The syntactic simplicity can be thought of as a consequence of semantic simplicity.

As mentioned before, it has also been demonstrated that there is no high correlation between the child's linguistic level and most measures of the syntactic complexity of motherese. Although mothers may speak more simply to infants than they do to four- or eight-year-olds, there is no strong evidence of mothers precisely grading the formal, syntactic complexity of their speech. This may very well be because there are no natural ways for mothers to fine-tune their syntactic complexity and gradually increase it a step at a time as the child's abilities mature. Speakers are, however, able to control the semantic complexity of their speech more precisely through choice of lexical items or topics to discuss. One might expect that semantic complexity would be more closely related to the child's linguistic abilities. In this area however the crucial experiments have yet to be performed.

Most Recent Studies of Motherese: Focus on Function

The most recent evolution of the study of motherese focuses is not on what form or content the mother is directing *at* her child, but rather on what the mother is doing *with* her child—namely, interacting socially via conversations. Although the partners in these conversations have differing linguistic abilities, the child may nonetheless play an important role in eliciting speech from the mother. Commonly the child introduces a topic, and the mother follows the child's lead in providing a comment on that topic. Topic-introduction, commenting, and expanding are common conversational patterns between mothers and even very young infants. In all of this the mother's speech is very much determined by the child's linguistic level, cognitive abilities, and, above all, his/her ideas and interests.

Various researchers have begun to analyze motherese in terms of such views of mother-child conversational interaction. Shugar (1978) analyzed mother-child conversations as dyadic interactions striving to "create text." She described how mothers of three children (1, 7, MLU 1.2; 2, 0, MLU 2.0; 2, 0, MLU 1.7) produce utterances which create a context within which even the most rudimentary child's utterance becomes a meaningful part.

Cross (1977, 1978) in two studies of 16 mother-child dyads (children aged 19 to 33 months) found that while there were no significant differences in measures of mothers' syntactic modification for a group of "normally developing" children and a group of "accelerated" children, there were significant differences in the two groups in the incidence of utterances in mothers' speech that were semantically similar to the semantic intention of the child's preceding utterance. These findings tend to support the view that children who learn to talk early and well have greater access to such semantically, interactionally related maternal utterances.

Lieven (1978a, 1978b) found some interesting individual differences in the kinds of mother-child dyadic interactions. In her longitudinal study of two such pairs (the children were 18 and 20 months at the start of the study), Lieven described how the children's and mother's speech differed in each dyad. While the children were similar in terms of MLU, they appeared to use language for different purposes. Kate talked slowly and clearly, usually about objects and events in her immediate environment; she used many locative and attributive expressions. Beth, on the other hand, Lieven claimed, spoke more to engage her mother's interest and attention; her utterances fell into the categories of "notice," "existence," and "recurrence." Her speech was difficult to interpret and was highly repetitive and uninformative. These child characteristics Lieven relates to differences in the mothers' speech. Kate's mother was highly responsive to what her child said, and her utterances appeared to be closely related to her child's utterances. There was considerably more turn-taking, more commenting on the child-nominated topics, more extension and expansion by Kate's mother. Beth's mother often did not respond to her child's utterances, and when she did, her responses were often semantically unrelated to the child utterances (e.g., "Oh, really."). Yet despite receiving very little semantically relevant speech from her mother, Beth did eventually learn to talk normally. Therefore although the amount of semantically and interactionally relevant motherese a child receives may vary considerably, it has not been proven that access to such speech is crucial to the normal development of language. It also seems plausible that although a child's access to such relevant motherese may vary greatly, as would seem to be suggested by Lieven's findings, only the most socially deprived children would have no access at all to such input.

Although the main emphasis in the study of motherese has been on mothers' speech to children who are talking, semantically and interactionally relevant speech begins long before children first use language. Snow (1977b, 1978), in her longitudinal study of two mothers talking to their female infants from 3 months to 20 months, has uncovered some interactional, discourse characteristics of motherese which are present in mothers' speech to infants as young as 3 months and which remain constant throughout the period studied. Some of the characteristics (e.g., questions) occurred with even greater frequency in the speech directed to the younger children. The most striking feature of motherese that remained constant over the period of study was the extent to which the mother's speech was directed by the child's activities. The wide range of the infant's behavior—reaching for something, changing gaze direction, laughing, smiling, vocalizing, and even in the youngest infant's

burping, yawning, coughing, sneezing—can always evoke a specific relevant response from the mother. Much of the mother's speech to infants and young children can be described as an attempt to establish a conversation and to keep the conversation going by giving the child the maximum opportunity to function as a conversational partner and by accepting even the most minimal of the child's behavior as an adequate "turn." What does change over time is what the mother's utterances refer to, and these changes seem to result from the child's ability to function as a conversational partner and from resultant changes in the mother's definition of acceptable child responses. At three months of age the majority of maternal utterances refer only to the infant, but by the time the infant is six to eight months of age and is showing an interest in objects and activities, the maternal utterances also refer to those objects and activities. As the child's world and interests expand, so do the mother's references.

Snow (1978) has also shown how the ubiquitous category of "interrogative" is used by mothers not only to engage their infants conversationally from as early as three months onward, but how the interactional function of the interrogative changes subtly over time. At three months Snow found "What is it?," "What can you see?," and "Where is it?" were used by both mothers as techniques for establishing joint attention with the infant by following the infant's attention. At 7 and 12 months these same questions were used during games and routines to direct the infant's attention to what the mother was interested in. By 18 months these same questions began to function as informational or tutorial demands for specific responses. Questions, by their very nature, function interactionally to establish a context of turn-taking. By asking questions, Snow argues, mothers create the required conditions for the establishment of effective communication.

1. Children's utterances are made interpretable simply by virtue of the fact that questions are posed. Polyinterpretable utterances and behaviors become specific and meaningful if they can be seen as responses to questions.
2. Questions are posed in early mother-infant interaction to establish joint attention and to confirm that experiences are being shared. Later, question routines are established which enable the child to contribute to complex, high-level discussions of past shared experiences.
3. Expectations as to which aspects of a situation the mother finds important and worthy of comment are created by the use of questions in games and tutorial routines. Frequent repetition of such games and routines enables the child to practice the correct response and eventually to contribute creatively by varying his responses.
4. By asking questions, mothers create situations within which their children can function as effective and informative conversational partners. It is to a large extent the experience of having successfully communicated with a child which convinces one that effective communication is possible. (Snow, 1978, pp. 267–268)

The view of pre- and early language acquisition that emerges from the functional-interactional studies of motherese is that mothers impute intention and meaning to the infant's earliest behaviors, making the infants appear conversationally and interactionally more adept than they in fact are. By interacting with the infant based on this imputation, these imputations eventually lead to meaningful behavior.

Motherese: Research on Group Differences

A significant proportion of the research on motherese has concerned the investigation of group differences, specifically the differences between the motherese addressed to male versus female children, differences between racial and socioeconomic classes, and differences between cultural groups.

Although Phillips (1973) reported no clear sex-based differences on the ten syntactic and lexical dimensions of motherese included in her study, Cherry and Lewis (1978) and Lewis and Freedle (1973) report sex differences. Cherry and Lewis (1978) investigated the verbal-interactional styles of 12 upper-middle-class mothers with their two-year-old children (6 female, 6 male) and found both significant differences as well as nonsignificant "trends." Significant differences were that mothers of girls talked more (i.e., used a greater number of utterances), were more likely to ask questions and use other-repetition, and had greater MLU's. "Trends" were that mothers of girls used more verbal acknowledgement and talked more as measured by number of turns, whereas mothers of boys used more directives; moreover, girls talked more than boys as measured by number of both utterances and turns. Cherry and Lewis (1978) claim these results support the earlier studies of mother-infant (three months) dyads. They suggest that mothers of girls may be placing greater demands on their daughters to become involved in conversational exchanges, while mothers of boys may be encouraging their sons to act in a nonverbal fashion.

Studies of differences in motherese due to socioeconomic status and/or race have yielded mixed findings. Lewis and Freedle (1973) interpret their results from observations of more than 80 pairs of mothers and three-month-old boys and girls from different socioeconomic status at all levels of analysis. It is suggested not only are girls vocally more responsive to maternal behavior, but higher socioeconomic status (SES) infants appear to be more "advanced" in their vocalizations. Pointing to follow-up testing of three infants at two years, it is suggested that these differences are relevant to subsequent formal linguisic skills. However Holzman (1974), in a study comparing two middle and two lower socioeconomic class mothers (children were two boys and two girls ranging in age from 1,3 to 2,3), concluded that except for the presence of nonstandard utterances in the speech of the lower-class mothers, there were no differences in verbal environment related to SES. Similar results were reported by Ringler (1973) in a study of ten lower-class mothers, all speakers of Black English. In the mother's speech to her child, collected when the child was 1,0 and again when the child was 2,0, the same types of syntactic simplifications were found as had been found in the motherese of speakers of standard English.

Studies of motherese in cultures far removed from North America have also yielded mixed, but very interesting, results. Jocic (1978) studied syntactic and morpho-semantic adaptations in the child-directed speech of ten Serbo-Croatian-speaking adults to four individual children (age 0,6 to 4,0) and three pairs of twins (age 1,3 to 3,0). Modifications similar to those reported for English-speaking mothers were found. Blount (1972), in one of the few cross-cultural studies published, analyzed adult-child dialogues in Samoan (a mother and elder sister to one boy aged 2,6) and in Luo (father and research assistant to one boy and one girl, both 2,6). Similar patterns of speech were found in these two quite different cultures. Interrogatives were the most frequent sentence type, followed by imperatives and declaratives (cf. similar findings for English). The suggestion is made that differences between this speech and adult conversation are a result of different social definitions and constraints: In adult-child interaction a hierarchical relationship is established which gives the adult superordinate position and the role of conversation initiator. This may explain differences in the choice of interrogative type between these data and that in an American sample, where children seem to be allocated "conversational peer status." Schieffelin (1979), in her study of the language acquisition of four Kaluli children (ages 22 to 25 months at the beginning of her longitudinal study) in Papua, New Guinea, discusses an interactional routine used by Kaluli mothers to teach their children how to talk and act like Kaluli children. This elicitation routine, and the cultural beliefs of the people behind it, appear quite different from anything familiar in North American culture. She suggests that it would be interesting to further examine Kaluli children's responses to this elicitation routine as to whether they repeat verbatim the input message from the mother, add new information, recode the message, reduce it, or provide no response at all, and how these responses change over time and according to the speech act and speech event. Treating these responses as elicited imitations in a natural context may offer some explanations as to the interactions between the child's level of development, grammatical complexity of input, and motivation to respond (Hood & Lightbown, 1978; Hood & Schieffelin, 1978).

MOTHERESE AND LANGUAGE ACQUISITION: TOWARD AN INTERACTIONAL VIEW OF LANGUAGE ACQUISITION

The only truly experimental studies of the relationship of mothers' speech to the course of the language acquisition have been based on the observation that expansions occurred frequently in adults' speech to children (Brown & Bellugi, 1964). Expansions have been manipulated in the hope of demonstrating that providing expansions speeded up language acquisition. The first two studies designed to show this effect were, however, unsuccessful (Cazden, 1965; Feldman, 1971). No positive effect of providing expansions to children was found.

Another experiment in which an experimental group of children received not only expansions of their incomplete utterances (syntactically correct and complete versions of their telegraphic utterances retaining all the child's content words in their original order) but also recast versions of their complete sentences (repetition of the child's sentence in a new syntactic form) did show an effect on children's language ability after 22 20-minute sessions (Nelson, Carskaddon, & Bonvillian, 1973) as compared to an untreated control group. However a second treatment group of children who received no expansions or recast sentences but did receive the same amount of interaction with an adult was not significantly different from the expansion-recast group. This suggests that interaction with an interested adult may be more crucial to the acquisition of formal patterns than any particular expanding or recasting technique used by the adult.

More recent research examining the relationship between the child's linguistic level and the various formal measures of motherese has failed to show any high degree of correlation between the two (Cross, 1977, 1978; Newport, 1976; Newport et al., 1977). While some measures of the mothers' syntactic adjustments are tailored to the child's capacity (e.g., in Cross, 1977, mothers' MLU, percentage of long utterances, and ratio of propositions per utterance were significantly correlated to child listener variables), others are not (e.g., again in Cross, 1977, preverb complexity, various measures of sentence types, numbers of ungrammatical, run-on, or abbreviated sentences). Similarly Newport et al. (1977) report that certain language-specific aspects of child language acquisition seem to be influenced in their rate of growth by aspects of motherese (e.g., they report significant partial correlations between growth in mean number of elements in the child's verbal auxiliary with the mother's tendency to ask *yes-no* questions and to expand, and a negative partial correlation with the mother's tendency to use imperatives). However several other measures of child language development that are commonly taken to be indices of universal aspects of language structure and content appear to be insensitive to variation in motherese (e.g., the child's growth in the use of complex sentences). Both the Cross (1977, 1978) and Newport (1976, Newport et al., 1977) studies suggest a more profitable look at semantic, discourse, and functional-interactional aspects of motherese.

Cross (1977) reports that the majority of the maternal speech parameters which correlated significantly with child listener variables were those she categorized as "discourse adjustments."

The best evidence that the input may play an important facilitative role in these children's acquisition processes is provided by the finding that, in general, the mothers' discourse adjustments were most closely associated with measures of the children's psycholinguistic, linguistic and communicative abilities (i.e., receptive control, maximum output, mean utterance length and comprehensibility). (Cross, 1977, p. 166)

Most of the discourse adjustments examined in her study (e.g., expansions of various types semantically related to the child's utterances, maternal self-repetitions, references to immediate context) have been argued to provide the child with informal language lessons on the formal means available to express a communicative intent. Expansions of the child's communicative intention have been claimed to directly help him/her see what is lacking in his/her realization (Cazden, 1965; McNeill, 1970a). Maternal redundancy supposedly provides the child with extra opportunities to process and comprehend the original utterance (Broen, 1972; Snow, 1972). Yet Cross observes that the provision of such language lessons is not

the mother's primary motivation for mothers' speech adjustments but is rather an incidental consequence of trying to communicate with a listener with very undeveloped linguistic skills. She suggests that mothers are sensitive to their child's underlying, receptive, cognitive abilities and have the ability to monitor the child's psycholinguistic abilities rather than the characteristic level of his/her spontaneous speech.[3]

The view that emerges from the functional-interactional studies on the relationship between motherese and child language acquisition is that many of the features of speech addressed to children result from the process of carrying on conversations with immature conversational partners—i.e., the nature of the interaction determines semantic simplicity, which in turn determines syntactic complexity (Snow, 1979). The small amount of evidence available on the question of whether language acquisition is facilitated by motherese suggests that semantic interpretability and relevance are the crucial features in facilitating language acquisition. However, semantic simplicity and relevance are determined by the conversational nature of the interaction, and the level at which this interaction takes place is determined to a great extent by the child and his/her existing cognitive and receptive language abilities. Rather than directing the course of language acquisition as was earlier claimed, motherese may be as much determined by the child's receptive cognitive abilities.

Newport et al. (1977) summarize this view as follows:

... Motherese is syntactically complex on most obvious definitions. Whatever constructional simplifications occur in Motherese seem to arise for interactional reasons—as constraints on the kinds of things one talks about to children and gross constraints on psychological complexity in the ways one talks to them. ... We have suggested in outline a position of this kind in which (1) the acquisition of universal aspects of language design proceeds in indifference to the details of varying individual environments, at least within the range of some gross syntactic simplifications (which would appear to occur necessarily in any world where mothers wish to communicate with their children), and (2) individual differences in the linguistic environment, exemplified by the mother, exert their effects only on the acquisition of language-specific aspects of surface structure, and even then only through the *listening biases* of the child [emphasis added]. We have suggested a processing-bias hypothesis as components of such a theory: to the extent that a mother makes syntax perspicuous for the child, underlining constructions by placing them in salient positions in surface structure, or by providing exemplars at the moment the child's attention is drawn to their referents (in the world or in the mind), the child acquires the appropriate formal devices more quickly. (Newport et al., 1977, pp. 145–146)

These recent developments in the research on the interactional relationships between motherese and lan-

---

[3] It should be noted here that most research along these lines has not been able to dismiss the child's age as an equally strong correlate of mothers' discourse adjustments, leaving unresolved whether the cause of the mothers' adjustments are differences in things the child actually does or to a large extent what the mother predicts the child is capable of doing based on his/her age (cf. Cross, 1977, and Newport et al., 1977, for differing views on the role of the child's age).

guage acquisition, and in particular the view that certain aspects of the child's linguistic growth—e.g., acquisition of cognitive-semantic relations—may be accomplished with less close reliance on environmental linguistic support than is the acquisition of some properties of surface stucture (Newport et al., 1977) have contributed to renewed interest in researching the child's early cognitive and semantic development. We review this area of early language development in the next section.

SEMANTIC DEVELOPMENT: COMMUNICATION, COGNITION, FIRST WORDS

Studies of semantic development in infancy are currently exhibiting two changes from the longstanding interest in applying linguistic theories and grammatical intent to infant word use. The first change is reflected in research on prelinguistic communication, communicative acts, and the development of intentional communication. This change in focus is expressed in statements such as this one by Clark (1978).

One ingredient that is all too often omitted in discussions of language acquisition is communication. But the strategies children rely on in production are motivated by communicative concerns. In the early stages of acquisition, children have only a very small vocabulary at their disposal, and, while they freely supplement this with gestures and demonstrations, it is only adequate for talking about a limited number of events. They are often faced, therefore, with wanting to talk about things for which they have no words. . . . Learning a language is not simply a matter of learning a system of rules for linking sounds and meaning: it is learning how to use such a system for communication. (p. 958)

The second change is reflected in research examining the role of basic cognitive structures as precursors of linguistic and communicative development. The focus of this research has been on determining the nature of the basic cognitive structures and their specified relationships to semantics.

Theories of Semantic Development

Several theories applicable to the infancy period are part of the semantic literature. The following theories vary in the extent to which each is part of current research activity, but each certainly has made contributions to the semantic area in the past decade.

Abstraction Theory. Concept formation is assumed to be based on a process involving repeated word-referent pairings through which the common elements are abstracted. Classification of concepts occurs through noting similarities and differences between the abstracted elements.

Relational Concept Theory. Cassirer (1953) proposed that concepts acquire meaning from observing the relationships and functions of objects rather than by common elements. Nelson (1974) describes this theory as "concerned with variability and invariability within things and the relations of things" (p. 273).

Semantic Feature Theory. Basically similar to the abstraction theory, the meaning of words is assumed to develop by gradually adding common components (features). According to Clark (1973) initial meanings are based on perceptual experiences which adults can share. Thus communication is possible based on partial overlap of child and adult word meanings until the adult meaning of the word is achieved. Clark (1978) describes semantic development in infancy as involving two strategies. The first involves the application of a few "general purpose words" (e.g., deictic words, category words, verbs) plus gestures to cover a variety of different objects or actions. Because their language abilities are not adequate for all they want to communicate about, children "stretch" or overgeneralize words as a second communication strategy. Clark (1973) sees overextended words as governed by perceptual similarities among referents which are not compatible with adult perceptions. Overextensions are seen by Clark as providing information about semantic development.

Piagetian Theory. Much attention has been paid to Piaget's descriptions of the relation between thought and language in the young child. Piaget's basic assumption is that the basic categories of thoughts developed during the sensorimotor period are similar to the semantic relations expressed in early language. Reviews of the relationship of Piaget's theory to language development in infancy have been published by Moerk (1975) and Morehead and Morehead (1974).

Functional Core Concepts Theory. This attempts to join aspects of abstraction and relational theories to account for conceptual and semantic development. Nelson (1974) proposes that a concept develops when an object is distinguished as an individual whole in the environment. Through experience with the object, associated relationships and functions become identified and, later, abstracted. Gradually specific defining functions of the object are learned and compose the concepts "core." Thus early concepts have relational and abstract information. Once a concept is formed, new instances of the concept can be identified. Names of concepts become attached after the concept is acquired.

Nelson, Rescorla, Gruendel, and Benedict (1978) provide approximate age ranges of three phases of language learning. The phases are based on data from three studies of children 10 to 19 months. Each study used a different method—naturalistic observation, augmented diary, or videotaping of play sessions. Phase 1 (10 to 13 months): The children comprehended adult words which matched their existing concepts. Generalization is accomplished based on perceptual similarities and differences. Undergeneralization occurs because the concepts may be too limited in associations. Phase 2 (11 to 15 months): When production begins children acquire a small number of words bonded to concepts. These words have constrained usages which are relative to the extent to which the concept is developed. The child must become able to detach the word from the concept in order to use it symbolically in situations out of the context in which it was developed. Phase 3 (16 to 20 months): The child acquires new production words from old concepts, new concepts become matched to new words, and words are used in new contexts. Words can be used to categorize (which produced overgeneralization), propositionalize, and analogize. Volterra, Bates, Benigni, Bretherton, and Camaioni (1979) describe four stages of word production found in children 9 to 13 months which are quite similar to those described by Nelson et al., 1978.

Cognitive Bases Theory. MacNamara's (1972) theory assumes the Piagetian view that cognitive structures are more developed than linguistic structures. Words and concepts become attached when the infant has the capacity to distinguish an object from the rest of the environment. This may arise through the mother directing the infant's attention and naming the object. The infant initially takes the word s/he hears as the name for the whole entity. Gradually names relating to variable states and actions of the object are acquired followed by names for the object's permanent attributes.

Current Research

Two major categories are apparent in current research activities: research on the development of intentional communication and research on the single word phase. Some research overlaps the two categories, but much seems to belong exclusively to one category or the other. The work of researchers interested in the cognitive bases of language are found in both categories.

Intentional Communication. Bates (1979) defines intentional communication as "signaling behavior in which the sender is aware a priori of the effect that a signal will have on his listener, and he persists in that behavior until the effect is obtained or failure is clearly indicated" (p. 36). Bates, Camaioni, and Volterra (1975) have applied Austin's (1962) speech acts theory to the development of intentional communication in infancy. Three phases (perlocutionary, illocutionary, locutionary) are proposed in which the infant progresses from a user of unintentional signals which have meaning only to the listener to a user of meaningful, intentional signals and words. Bates (1979) describes these phases as "social tool use" development, and she sees progression as dependent on achievement of key aspects of Piaget's sensorimotor stages or development of "nonsocial tool use." Object relations, means-ends sequences, and imitation have been identified as influencing the development of intentional communication.

Perlocutionary Phase. During this phase communicative acts produced by the infant have an effect on their listener, but the infant is not aware of the effect. This is a stage of unintentional communication and is hypothesized to occur prior to the development of the causality notion. Case study observations are provided by Bates et al. (1975) and Trevarthen and Hubley (1978), who describe the noncommunicating nature of object and person behaviors during the first six months of life. A variety of infant behaviors have been shown to serve perlocutionary functions.

The cry as an early perlocutionary signal has received much attention. Researchers have postulated that infant cries are meaningful and are an early indicator of individuality. Several studies of cry types and identity of crying infants have been conducted. Wolff (1969) examined the early crying of 12 infants from birth to three months of age and 3 infants from birth to six months of

age for cry patterns (determined spectographically), causes of the cries, and effects of the cries on the mother. Three cry patterns were identified: the basic (or hunger) cry, mad or angry cry, and the pain cry. Wolff found that maternal reaction to crying was more related to maternal style rather than cry type, although response to pain crying was somewhat more consistent across mothers. Other studies by Sherman (1927) and Aldrich, Sung, and Knopp (1945) found that mothers and other adults (college students, nurses, and unidentified "listeners") could not identify the cause of newborn cries. Bruner, Roy, and Ratner (in press) reported that mothers' interpretation of cries changed as a function of the infant's age. Prior to 26 weeks mothers interpreted cries as physically caused and not as intentional requests. After 26 weeks, however, mothers interpreted cries as indicators of psychological states and reflecting intentional requests. Muller, Hollien, and Murry (1974) tested the assumption that infants' cries actually become more differentiated with age. They examined the abilities of mothers to identify the causes of their three- to five-month-old infants' cries. Their identifications were more often wrong than right. Interestingly the mothers tended to identify cries as hungry cries regardless of their true cause. Thus despite the contention of theorists and parents as to the identifiability of cry types, experimental studies have provided little support. The mother's prior information about her child's schedule and cues present in the natural environment may be necessary for disambiguating cries.

Other researchers have sought to determine if the cry serves as a signal of the infant's identity. Murry, Hollien, and Muller (1975) recorded pain, startle, and hunger cries from eight infants aged three to five months. Mothers had to identify whether a cry was produced by their own infant or another infant. Mothers were correct in their identification of their own infant 90 percent of the time. However, experience has an influence on such identifications. Formby (1967) found only one-third of the mothers of newborn infants could identify their infant's cry from that of other infants, and Morsbach and Murphy (1979) found parents of newborn infants were not as good as midwives in making same-different judgments of pairs of newborn cries. Thus while parents and researchers postulate that cries are meaningful and individualized, the response to specific cry types is not generally consistent, and the identification of an infant's cry seems to develop in accuracy over time.

Other behaviors of infants which also seem to serve perlocutionary functions include: smile types (Spitz & Wolf, 1946), early babbling (as discussed by Lewis, 1951), differential responsiveness to facial expressions (Browne, Rosenfeld, & Horowitz, 1975) and to human faces (Bates et al., 1975). A variety of behaviors which have been interpreted as "intentional" have been shown to be elicitable from very young infants—e.g., imitative behaviors in infants 12 to 21 days old (Meltzoff & Moore, 1977), intonational patterns which match those of adults (Tonkova-Yampol'skaya, 1969), interactional mutuality between 3-month-old infants and their mothers (Tronick, Als, & Brazelton, 1977), and nonverbal reciprocity of behavior between infants 2 to 24 weeks and adults (Yogman, Dixon, Tronick, Adamson, Als, and Brazelton, 1976). These behaviors, however, are not spontaneously generated by the infant and do not show evidence that the infant intended the behavior to have a particular effect on others who hear or observe the behaviors. Thus they would not be considered communicative behaviors by the criteria stated previously.

Illocutionary Phase. This is the beginning of the intentional use of signals to convey nonverbal requests and for social interaction. Piagetian Stage 5 and the development of causation are hypothesized to provide the foundation for an understanding of how one's own actions affect others. During this phase Bates et al. (1975) observed the development of three types of communication: protodeclarative schemes in which objects were used to obtain adult attention through showing, giving, showing off, and pointing behaviors; proto-imperative schemes involving the use of adults to obtain objects; and use of an object to obtain other objects. The sequences of nonverbal development observed in the case studies by Bates et al. (1975) were later replicated by Bates, Benigni, Bretherton, Camaioni, and Volterra (1979).

The force responsible for the change in perlocutionary behaviors toward the use of intentional signals is unclear. However Bates (1979) describes three indicators which mark the transition. First, alternating eye contact between the goal (e.g., an object) and the adult while the child produces a signal. Bates takes this as evidence of the child's awareness of the relationship between the signal, the goal, and the adult. Second, the signals undergo sequencing and substitution changes. Changes in signals become dependent on the adult's behavior toward the goal rather than toward the goal itself. Third, changes appear in individual signals. They may become abbreviated, ritualized, and more conventional.

Bruner (1974) has also described three changes in modes of infant-adult interaction during the first year, and these descriptions resemble some of the indicators described before. In the "demand" mode the infant vocalizes expressions of discomfort (e.g., cries, frets). Bruner provides some evidence indicating that the vocalizations in the demand mode must recede in frequency in order for other types of communications to increase. Ainsworth and Bell (1974) found that children slow in developing communication have persisting demand mode vocalizations. The second mode to appear is the "request" mode in which the infant's prior experience with having adults respond to demand vocalizations sets up expectancy that a vocalization will meet with a response. Such a response becomes "requested" by vocalizations which are increasingly stylized. In the third mode, the "exchange" mode, gestures and vocalizations become accompaniments to interactions with adults in "games."

Evidence as to the role of Stage 5 or causal understanding in the development of intentional communication has come from the work of Harding and Golinkoff(1979) and Sugarman (1977). Infants 8 to 14 months were examined by Harding and Golinkoff (1979) for use of intentional vocalizations ("any sequence of infant behavior which included vocalizing while making eye contact with the mother," p. 36) and for evidence of the object concept and the understanding of causality as assessed by tasks from the Uzgiris and Hunt (1975) scale and tasks developed by Piaget (1954). The results were that only infants at Stage 5 used intentional communications, but not all Stage 5 infants used intentional com-

munications. Thus Stage 5 may be necessary for intentional communication but not sufficient. Sugarman (1977) also found support for the role of Stage 5 reasoning in the infant's use of adults for aid in object schemes.

Locutionary Phase. Speech sounds gradually come to be used along with the nonverbal signals, particularly gestures, to convey request and participate in social interactions. Bates et al. (1975) identified three types of early locutionary utterances: word-like signals with no referential value which accompany performatives (e.g., one sound which signals desire or need); use of sound with referential value but only in restricted instances (e.g., an object named as part of an activity but not named in any other context); and names used to depict an object or event in a variety of contexts. One-word utterances begin during this phase.

Several case studies have been published which offer evidence of semantic development which fit Bates et al. (1975) case descriptions of the transitions from illocutionary to locutionary phase. Okamoto (1962) kept a daily record of the vocalizations of a female infant between the ages of six months and two years. Three stages, beginning at around nine to ten months, were identified. The infant progressed from connecting specific sounds with specific objects (age 9 to 10 months), to using sounds to represent objects and overextending the sounds to other objects (10 to 13 months), to using conventional names for objects (13 to 18 months). A case study by Ninio and Bruner (1978) describes the development of labeling in an infant between the ages of 8 and 18 months. The authors examined changes in the nature of the infant's labeling behaviors, changes in the mother's responses toward more exacting behaviors by the infant, and descriptions of the infant's growing awareness of the social function of labels. Bruner et al. (in press) described the development of requests in two children between 8 months and 18 months. Three criteria for requesting were established: The infant had to clearly indicate that something was wanted and what was wanted, signals had to be more than fleeting, and requests had to contain some acknowledgment of another person's assistance. Not until ten months did the requests satisfy the three criteria. With advancing age vocalizations became increasingly part of the requesting behaviors and became more stylized.

Other researchers have sought to establish the connection between communicative development in the locutionary phase and measures of sensorimotor skills (typically assessed by the Uzgiris and Hunt scales, 1975). Some sensorimotor skills have been found to be good predictors of communicative development. Bates et al. (1975) hypothesized, based on data from their case studies, that means-ends relations are necessary for the locutionary phase. This was confirmed in later research (Bates et al., 1979). Snyder (1978) also showed such a relationship in normal (mean age: 14.0 months) and language disabled (mean age: 24.9 months) infants matched for mean length of utterance and social class. These infants were tested for communicative abilities (use of imperative and declarative performatives and the encoding of informative elements in a context) and for cognitive abilities as assessed by the Uzgiris and Hunt scales. The two groups of subjects differed on all communicative abilities, with the differences being attributed to representational deficits. The representational deficit seemed to be particularly reflected in the absence of Stage 6 (means-ends relations) abilities in the language disabled infants. All the normal infants showed Stage 6 reasoning. Assessments of imitative skills by Bates et al. (1979) also were found to be good predictors of development, a finding replicated by Nicholich and Raph (1978). Corrigan (1978) investigating object permanence and Bates et al. (1979) investigating object permanence and spatial relations both found no significant correlation between measures of these skills and language development in normal infants.

Several researchers have examined the relationship between gestures and vocalization in the locutionary infants. DeLaguna (1927) observed that single-word utterances in children are accompanied by overt action but gradually become separated as utterance length increased. Rodgon (Rodgon, 1976; Rodgon, Jankowsky, & Alenskas, 1977) found that the period during which overt action accompanies speech lasted well into the word combination stage. She and her colleagues observed the utterances of three children during the period between 1.4 and 2.2 years. At the start two of the children were in the one-word stage, and one had a mean length of utterance of 1.2 words. Rodgon et al. report that 67 percent to 73 percent of the utterances were made in conjunction with or just after performing an overt action. Carter (1978) also reports on gesture plus vocalization combinations, which she calls "sensorimotor morphemes," of a boy between the ages of 12 and 16 months. She describes eight types of sensorimotor morphemes in which, for example, reaching was always accompanied by one sound and pointing by another. Carter (1978) found that the gesture in some sensorimorphemes seemed to indicate more clearly the intention of the communication than did vocalization. She infers that the cognitive connection between gesture and vocalization which make their co-occurrence predictable is sensorimotor in nature. Bates et al. (1979) also refer to a common underlying capacity. They found the correlation between gestures and vocalizations increased over the five-month period (9 to 13 months) in which they studied 25 infants.

Single-Word Phase. Debates over the function, definition, and meaning of the first words of infants have been popular over the past decade. Several theoretical controversies have arisen over accounts of the function of first words. The most frequent view of the first word is that it represents a holophrase or a one-word sentence. McNeill (1970b), following Chomsky's tranformational theory, postulates that infants have an innate understanding of linguistic structure. However, immaturity of memory and vocal apparatus initially prevent utterances longer than one word. The underlying linguistic knowledge is thought to be reflected in the infant's use of prosodic elements and the infant's ability to understand more complex speech than s/he can produce. Case grammar approaches, proposed by Ingram (1971) and Greenfield, Smith, and Laufer (1976), shift from a syntactic view of one-word utterances to a semantic view but otherwise seem to adhere to the assumptions of the syntactic view of holophrases.

Bloom (1973) and Dore (1975) have both challenged the view of single words as holophrases. Bloom (1973) argued that knowledge of syntax is not innate and that single words, strings of single words, and use of prosodic elements do not provide evidence of syntactic knowledge. Dore (1975) proposed that one word not be considered as a sentence in either form or function but as a "primitive speech act." These speech acts are described as containing two components: "a rudimentary referring expression (e.g., words)" (p. 31) and "a primitive force indicating device (e.g., intonation)" (p. 31). In primitive speech acts, one word can be used for various reasons: labeling, requesting, answering, calling, repeating, greeting, and protesting. Intonation and context provide cues to the listener as to the child's intentions, although the child may not be initially aware of the function of context. The primitive speech acts approach does not assume that one-word utterances represent sentences but that they do express an intention with regard to a concept. The communicative intentions conveyed in primitive speech acts later become grammaticalized.

Other theoretical controversies over first words have concerned their operational definitions—that is, when is an utterance considered a word? Darley and Winitz (1961) reviewed the types of operational definitions used by researchers and found two common, but not universally agreed upon, definitions: "[T]he use of a sound, syllable or word consistently in reference to an object or situation" and "the structure or form of the word which . . . should resemble the adult form" (p. 278). The use of different operational definitions has been responsible for the discrepant findings across studies on the age of onset of first words. Darley and Winitz (1961) found by their literature survey that the average age was 1 year, but the average age of onset across studies ranged from an average of 9 months (Griffith, 1954) to an average of 19 months (Abt, Adler, & Bartelme, 1929). A more recent study by Benedict (1979) used an operational definition of first word in which the word had to be used spontaneously with meaning and meaning could be dependent on context. The word did not have to be in the adult form, but the form did have to be used consistently. Benedict found a range from 9 to 14 months in age of production of the first word. She does not report the average age at which the first word is produced but does report that by 1 year, 1½ months the average infant produced ten words.

There have also been controversies over the classes of first words produced. Gleitman, Gleitman, and Shipley (1972), Huttenlocker (1974), and MacNamara (1972) have found nominals or object words to be most frequent first words. Bloom (1973) and Piaget (1962) argue in favor of action words which Bloom refers to as function words over object or substantive words. Nelson (1973a) found several word classes were used although nominals were the most frequent. Benedict (1979) studied the first words produced and those comprehended by infants 9 to 21 months. The results supported Nelson's (1973a) findings that the first words belonged to several classes. The most frequent classes were object and action classes, with object words produced twice as often as action words. In first comprehended words, however, action words were more frequent than object words. This finding is in contrast with that of Goldin-Meadow, Seligman, and Gelman (1976) who found more nouns were comprehended than verbs. This discrepancy may be due to the broader categories used by Benedict in which object words included specific nominals and general nominals (including pronouns) and action words included social action games (elicitors of specific action responses), event words (elicitors of an action sequence), action inhibitors, locatives and general action words (object-related and non-object-related). Gentner (1978) presented a thorough discussion of the difficulties of acquiring verb meaning compared to noun meaning. Gentner presents theoretical arguments and data to support a contention that verb acquisitions lag behind noun acquisition.

Benedict does agree with Goldin-Meadow et al. (1976) that comprehension of words is earlier and develops faster than production. Subjects in Benedict's study could understand 50 words before they could produce 10 words. The average rate of acquiring comprehended words in children moving from comprehending 10 words to comprehending 50 words is 22.2 words per month while the rate of acquisition for produced words is 9.1 words per month. Benedict's observed rate of produced words is comparable to the 11.1 words per month rate reported by Nelson (1973a).

Several researchers have examined the individual styles by which infants acquire words. Nelson (1973a) examined the first 50 words acquired by a group of 18 infants and found two styles. The "referential" children used language to refer to objects, and their language was oriented toward the cognitive aspects of language. The "expressive" children's language was socially oriented and expressed feelings and needs. Their language was described as more self-oriented in contrast to the referential children who were more object-oriented. Interestingly Nelson found that referential children acquired their language faster and at age two had a larger vocabulary. Starr (1975) examined the relationship between types of single words and word combinations acquired by children 1 to 2.5 years. She also found two language styles (object-oriented and self-oriented) which were similar to those described by Nelson (1973a). In addition she found that the strategy used at the single-word stage was also present at the two-word stage. Finally Dore (1974) described two language styles of infants acquiring words. He called the strategies *message-oriented,* which showed an orientation toward the social role of language, and *code-oriented,* in which words were acquired to identify and describe objects and events. The code-oriented style corresponded to Nelson's referential style, and children with that style also show more rapid acquisition of words.

REFERENCES

ABBS, J., & MINIFIE, F. The effects of acoustic cues in fricatives on perceptual confusions in preschool children. *Journal of the Acoustical Society of America,* 1969, *45,* 1535–1542.

ABT, I., ADLER, H., & BARTELME, P. The relationship between onset of speech and intelligence. *Journal of the American Medical Association,* 1929, *93,* 1351–1355.

ALDRICH, C., SUNG, J., & KNOPP, C. The crying of newly born babies. *Journal of Pediatrics,* 1945, *26,* 313.

ANDERSON, E. S., & JOHNSON, C. E. Modifications in the speech of an eight-year-old to younger children. *Stanford Occasional Papers in Linguistics,* 1973, No. 3, 149–160.

AUSTIN, J. *How to do things with words.* Cambridge, England: Oxford University Press, 1962.

BATES, E. Intentions, conventions, and symbols. In E. Bates (Ed.), *The emergence of symbols: Cognition and communication in infancy.* New York: Academic Press, 1979.

BATES, E., BENIGNI, L., BRETHERTON, I., CAMAIONI, L., & VOLTERRA, V. Cognition and communication from nine to thirteen months: Correlational findings. In E. Bates (Ed.), *The Emergence of symbols: Cognition and communication in infancy.* New York: Academic Press, 1979.

BATES, E., CAMAIONI, L., & VOLTERRA, V. The acquisition of performatives prior to speech. *Merrill-Palmer Quarterly,* 1975, *21,* 205–226.

BENEDICT, H. Early lexical development: Comprehension and production. *Journal of Child Language,* 1979, *6,* 183–200.

BERG, W. Cardiac orienting responses of 6- and 16-week-old infants. *Journal of Experimental Child Psychology,* 1974, *17,* 303–312.

BEVER, T.G., FODOR, J. A., & WEKSEL, W. On the acquisition of syntax: A critique of "context generalisation." *Psychological Review,* 1965, *72,* 467–482.

BLOOM, L. *One word at a time: The use of single word utterance before syntax.* The Hague: Mouton, 1973.

BLOUNT, B.G. Parental speech and language acquisitions: Some Luo and Samoan examples. *Anthropological Linguistics,* 1972, *14,* 119–130.

BLOUNT, B. G., & PADGUG, E. J. Prosodic, paralinguistic, and interactional features in parent-child speech: English and Spanish. *Journal of Child Language,* 1977, *4,* 67–86.

BROEN, P. A. The verbal environment of the language-learning child. *American Speech and Hearing Association Monograph,* No. 17, December 1972.

BROWN, R., & BELLUGI, U. Three processes in the child's acquisition of syntax. *Harvard Educational Review,* 1964, *34,* 133–151.

BROWNE, G., ROSENFELD, H., & HOROWITZ, F. *Discrimination of normative facial expressions by 12-week-old infants.* Paper presented at the Biennial meeting of Society for Research in Child Development, Denver, 1975.

BRUNER, J. From communication to language—A psychological perspective. *Cognition,* 1974/75, *3,* 255–287.

BRUNER, J., ROY, C., & RATNER, N. The beginnings of request. In K. Nelson (Ed.), *Children's language* (Vol. 3). New York: Gardner Press, in press.

CARTER, A. The development of systematic vocalization prior to words: A case study. In N. Waterson & C. Snow (Eds.), *The development of communication: Social and pragmatic factors in language acquisition.* London: John Wiley, 1978.

CASSIRER, E. *Structure and function and Einstein's theory of relativity.* (Trans. by W. C. Swaby and M. C. Swaby). New York: Dover Publications, 1953.

CAZDEN, C. B. *Environmental assistance to the child's acquisition of grammar.* Doctoral dissertation, Harvard University, 1965.

CHEN, H. P. & IRWIN, O. C. Infant speech: Vowel and consonant types. *Journal of Speech Disorders,* 1946, *11,* 27–29.

CHERRY, L., & LEWIS, M. Differential socialization of girls and boys: Implications for sex differences in language development. In N. Waterson & C. Snow (Eds.), *The development of communication.* New York: John Wiley, 1978.

CHOMSKY, N. The formal nature of language. Appendix A in E. H. Lenneberg, *Biological foundations of language.* New York: John Wiley, 1967.

CHOMSKY, N., & HALLE, M. *The sound patterns of English.* New York: Harper & Row, 1968.

CLARK, E. What's in a word? On the child's acquisition of semantics in his first language. In T. Moore (Ed.), *Cognitive development and the acquisition of language.* New York: Academic Press, 1973.

CLARK, E. Strategies for communicating. *Child Development,* 1978, *49,* 953–959.

COHEN, S., & BECKWITH, L. Maternal language in infancy. *Developmental Psychology,* 1976, *12,* 371–372.

CORRIGAN, R. Language development as related to stage 6 object permanence development. *Journal of Child Language,* 1978, *5,* 173–189.

CROSS, T. G. Mothers' speech adjustments: The contributions of selected child listener variables. In C. E. Snow & C. A. Ferguson (Eds.), *Talking to children: Language input and acquisition.* Cambridge, England: Cambridge University Press, 1977.

CROSS, T. G. Mothers' speech and its association with rate of linguistic development in young children. In N. Waterson & C. Snow (Eds.), *The development of communication.* New York: John Wiley, 1978.

CUTTING, J. E., & ROSNER, B. S. Categories and boundaries in speech and music. *Perception & Psychophysics*, 1974, *16*, 564–570.

DARLEY, F., & WINITZ, H. Age of first word: Review of research. *Journal of Speech and Hearing Disorders*, 1961, *26*, 272–290.

DELAGUNA, G. *Speech: Its function and development.* New Haven, Conn.: Yale University Press, 1927.

DORE, J. A pragmatic description of early language development. *Journal of Psycholinguistic Research*, 1974, *4*, 343–351.

DORE, J. Holophrases, speech acts and language universal. *Journal of Child Language*, 1975, *2*, 21–40.

DOTY, D. Infant speech perception: Report of a conference held at the University of Minnesota, June 20–22, 1972. *Human Development*, 1974, *17*, 74–80.

DRACH, K. The language of the parent: A pilot study. In *The structure of linguistic input to children* (Working Paper No. 14). Language Behavior Research Laboratory, University of California, Berkeley, 1969.

EILERS, R. Context-sensitive perception of naturally produced stop and fricative consonants by infants. *Journal of the Acoustical Society of America*, 1977, *61*, 1321–1336.

EILERS, R., GAVIN, W., & WILSON, W. Linguistic experience and phonemic perception in infancy: A cross-linguistic study. *Child Development*, 1979, *50*, 14–18.

EILERS, R., & MINIFIE, F. Fricative discrimination in early infancy. *Journal of Speech and Hearing Research*, 1975, *18*, 158–167.

EILERS, R., & OLLER, D. The role of speech discrimination in developmental sound substitutions. *Journal of Child Language*, 1976, *3*, 319–329.

EILERS, R., WILSON, W., & MOORE, J. Developmental changes in speech discrimination in infants. *Journal of Speech and Hearing Research*, 1977, *20*, 766–780.

EILERS, R., WILSON, W., & MOORE, J. Speech discrimination in the language-innocent and the language-wise: A study in the perception of voice onset time. *Journal of Child Language*, 1979, *6*, 1–18.

EIMAS, P. Auditory and linguistic processing of cues for place of articulation by infants. *Perception and Psychophysics*, 1974a, *16*, 513–521.

EIMAS, P. Linguistic processing of speech by young infants. Pp. 55–73 in R. Schiefelbusch & L. Lloyd (Eds.), *Language perspectives—Acquisition, retardation, and intervention.* Baltimore, Md.: University Park Press, 1974b.

EIMAS, P. Auditory and phonetic coding of the cues for speech: Discrimination of the [r-l] distinction by young infants. *Perception and Psychophysics*, 1975a, *18*, 341–347.

EIMAS, P. Speech perception in early infancy. Pp. 193–231 in L. Cohen & P. Salapatek (Eds.), *Infant perception: From sensation to cognition* (Vol. 2). New York: Academic Press, 1975b.

EIMAS, P. Developmental aspects of speech perception. In R. Held, H. Leibowitz, & H. Teuber (Eds.), *Handbook of sensory physiology: Perception.* New York: Springer-Verlag, 1976.

EIMAS, P., & CORBIT, J. Selective adaptation of linguistic feature detectors. *Cognitive Psychology*, 1973, *4*, 99–109.

EIMAS, P., & MILLER, J. L. Contextual effects in infant speech perception. *Science*, 1980, *209*, 1140–1141.

EIMAS, P., SIQUELAND, E., JUSCZYK, P., & VIGORITO, J. *Speech perception in early infancy.* Paper presented at meetings of Eastern Psychological Association, April 1970.

EIMAS, P., SIQUELAND, E., JUSCZYK, P., & VIGORITO, J. Speech perception in infants. *Science*, 1971, *171*, 303–306.

ENTUS, A. Hemispheric asymmetry in processing of dichotically presented speech and nonspeech stimuli by infants. Pp. 63–73 in S. Segalowitz & F. Gruber (Eds.), *Language development and neurological theory.* New York: Academic Press, 1977.

ERVIN, S. M., and MILLER, W. Language development. *Yearbook of the National Society for the Study of Education*, 1963, *62*, Part 1, 108–143.

FARWELL, C. B. The language spoken to children. *Papers and Reports in Child Language Development*, 1973, No. 5, 31–62.

FELDMAN, C. *The effects of various types of adult responses in the syntactic acquisition of two to three year olds.* Unpublished paper, University of Chicago, 1971.

FERGUSON, C. A. Baby talk in six languages. *American Anthropologist*, 1964, *66*, 103–114.

FERGUSON, C. A. Baby talk as a simplified register. In C. E. Snow & C. A. Ferguson (Eds.), *Talking to children: Language input and acquisition.* Cambridge, England: Cambridge University Press, 1977.

FODOR, J., GARRETT, M., & BRILL, S. Pi ka pu: The perception of speech sounds by prelinguistic infants. *Perception and Psychophysics*, 1975, *18*, 74–78.

FODOR, J. A. How to learn to talk: Some simple ways. In F. Smith & G. A. Miller (Eds.), *The genesis of language.* Cambridge, Mass.: M.I.T. Press, 1966.

FORMBY, D. Maternal recognition of the infant's cry. *Developmental Medicine and Child Neurology*, 1967, *9*, 293–298.

GARNICA, O. K. *Some prosodic characteristics of speech to young children.* Doctoral dissertation, Stanford University, 1975.

GARNICA, O. K. Some prosodic and paralinguistic features of speech directed to young children. In C. E. Snow & C. A. Ferguson (Eds.), *Talking to children: Language input and acquisition.* Cambridge, England: Cambridge University Press, 1977.

GENTNER, D. On relational meaning: The acquisition of verb meaning. *Child Development*, 1978, *49*, 988–998.

GLANVILLE, B., BEST, C., & LEVENSON, R. A cardiac measure of cerebral asymmetries in infant auditory perception. *Developmental Psychology*, 1977, *13*, 54–59.

GLEASON, J. *Fathers and other strangers: Men's speech to young children.* Paper presented at the 26th Georgetown Round Table, Georgetown University, Washington, D.C., 1975.

GLEITMAN, L., GLEITMAN, H., & SHIPLEY, E. The emergence of the child as grammarian. *Cognition*, 1972, *1*, 137–164.

GOLDIN-MEADOW, S., SELIGMAN, M., & GELMAN, R. Language in the two-year-old. *Cognition*, 1976, *4*, 189–202.

GRAHAM, F., LEAVITT, L., STROCK, B., & BROWN, J. Precocious cardiac orienting in a human anencephalic infant. *Science*, 1978, *199*, 322–324.

GREENFIELD, P., SMITH, J., & LAUFER, B. *Communication and the beginning of language: The development of semantic structure in one word speech and beyond.* New York: Academic Press, 1976.

GRIFFITH, R. *The abilities of babies.* New York: McGraw-Hill, 1954.

GRIMSHAW, A. D. A sociologist's point of view. In C. E. Snow & C. A. Ferguson (Eds.), *Talking to children: Language input and acquisition.* Cambridge, England: Cambridge University Press, 1977.

HADDING-KOCH, K., & STUDDERT-KENNEDY, M. An experimental study of some intonation contours. *Phonetics*, 1964, *11*, 175–185.

HARDING, C., & GOLINKOFF, R. The origins of intentional vocalization in prelinguistic infants. *Child Development*, 1979, *50*, 33–40.

HECOX, K. Electrophysiological correlates of human auditory development. Pp. 151–191 in L. Cohen & P. Salapatek (Eds.), *Infant perception: From sensation to cognition* (Vol. 2). New York: Academic Press, 1975.

HILLENBRAND, J., & MINIFIE, F. *Tempo frequency change as a cue in speech-sound discrimination by infants.* Paper presented at the biennial meetings of the Society for Research in Child Development, New Orleans, March 1977.

HOLMBERG, T., MORGAN, K., & KUHL, P. Speech perception in early infancy: Discrimination of fricative consonants. *Journal of the Acoustical Society of America*, 1977, *62*, Suppl. 1, S99 (A).

HOLZMAN, M. The verbal environment provided by mothers for their very young children. *Merrill-Palmer Quarterly*, 1974, *20*, 31–42.

HOOD, L., & LIGHTBOWN, P. M. What children do when asked to "say what I say": Does elicited imitation measure linguistic knowledge? *Allied Health and Behavioral Sciences*, 1978, *1*(No. 1).

HOOD, L., & SCHIEFFELIN, B. B. Elicited imitation in two cultural contexts. *Quarterly Newsletter*, Institute for Comparative Human Development, Rockefeller University, 1978, *2*, 4–12.

HUTTENLOCKER, J. The origins of language comprehension. In R. Solso (Ed.), *Theories of cognitive psychology.* Hillsdale, N.J.: Lawrence Erlbaum Associates, 1974.

INGRAM, D. Transitivity in child language. *Language*, 1971, *47*, 888–910.

IRWIN, O. C. Research on speech sounds for the first six months of life. *Psychological Bulletin*, 1941, *38*, 277–285.

IRWIN, O. C. Reliability of infant speech sound data. *Journal of Speech and Hearing Disorders*, 1945, *10*, 227–235.

IRWIN, O. C. Infant speech: Consonantal sounds according to place of articulation. *Journal of Speech Disorders*, 1946, *312*, 397–401.

IRWIN, O. C. Infant speech: Consonant sounds according to manner of articulation. *Journal of Speech and Hearing Disorders*, 1947, *12*, 402–404.

IRWIN, O. C. Development of vowel sounds. *Journal of Speech and Hearing Disorders*, 1948, *13*, 31–34.

IRWIN, O. C. Infant speech: Consonantal position. *Journal of Speech and Hearing Disorders*, 1951, *16*, 159–161.

IRWIN, O. C., & CHEN, H. P. A reliability study of speech sounds observed in the crying of newborn infants. *Child Development*, 1941, *12*, 351–368.

IRWIN, O. C., & CHEN, H. P. Speech sound elements during the first year of life: A review of the literature. *Journal of Speech Disorders*, 1943, *8*, 109–121.

IRWIN, O. C., & CHEN, H. P. Development of speech during infancy: Curve of phonemic types. *Journal of Experimental Psychology*, 1946, *36*, 431–436.

JAKOBSON, R. *Kindersprache, Aphasie, und Allgemeine Lautgesetze.* Uppsala: Almqvist & Wiksell, 1941.

JAKOBSON, R. *Child language aphasia and phonological universals.* (A. R. Keiler, trans.). The Hague: Mouton, 1968.

JAKOBSON, R., FANT, C.G.M., and HALLE, M. *Preliminaries to speech analysis. The distinctive features and their correlates.* Cambridge, Mass.: M.I.T. Press, 1952.

JAKOBSON, R., & HALLE, M. *Fundamentals of language.* The Hague: Mouton, 1956.

JOCIC, M. Adaptation of adult speech during communication with children. In N. Waterson & C. Snow (Eds.), *The development of communication.* New York: John Wiley, 1978.

JONES, S., & MOSS, H. Age, state and maternal behavior associated with infant vocalizations. *Child Development*, 1971, *42*, 1039–1051.

JUSCZYK, P. Perception of syllable-final stop consonants by 2-month-old infants. *Perception and Psychophysics*, 1977, *21*, 450–454.

JUSCZYK, P., COPAN, H., & THOMPSON, E. Perception by 2 month old infants of glide contrasts in multisyllabic utterances. *Perception and Psychophysics*, 1978, *24*, 515–520.

JUSCZYK, P., PISONI, D., WALLEY, A., & MURRAY, J. Discrimination of relative onset time of two component tones by infants. *Journal of the Acoustical Society of America*, 1980, *67*, 262–270.

JUSCZYK, P., ROSNER, B., CUTTING, J., FOARD, C., & SMITH, L. Categorical perception of nonspeech sounds in 2-month-old infants. *Perception and Psychophysics*, 1977, *2*, 50–54.

JUSCZYK, P., & THOMPSON, E. Perception of a phonetic contrast in multisyllabic utterances by two-month-old infants. *Perception and Psychophysics*, 1978, *23*, 105–109.

KAPLAN, E. *The role of intonation in the acquisition of language.* Unpublished doctoral dissertation, Cornell University, Ithaca, N.Y., 1969.

KEWLEY-PORT, D., & PRESTON, M. Early apical stop production: A voice onset time analysis. *Journal of Phonetics*, 1974, *2*, 195–210.

KHADEM, F., & CORBALLIS, M. *Cerebral asymmetry in infants.* Paper presented at biennial meetings of Society for Research in Child Development, New Orleans, 1977.

KOBASHIGAWA, B. Repetitions in a mother's speech to her child. In *The structure of linguistic input to children.* Working Paper No. 14. Language Behavior Research Laboratory, University of California, Berkeley, 1969.

KUHL, P. Speech perception by the chinchilla: Categorical perception of synthetic alveolar plosive consonants. *Journal of the Acoustical Society of America*, 1976a, *60*, Suppl. S81.

KUHL, P. Speech perception in early infancy: The acquisition of speech-sound categories. Pp. 265–280 in S. Hirsch, D. Eldredge, I. Hirsch, & S. Silverman (Eds.), *Hearing and Davis: Essays honoring Hallowell Davis.* St. Louis, Mo.: Washington University Press, 1976b.

KUHL, P. Speech perception in early infancy: Perceptual constancies for vowel categories. *Journal of the Acoustical Society of America*, 1976c, *60*, Suppl. 1, S90 (A).

KUHL, P. Speech perception in early infancy: Perceptual constancy for the vowel categories /a/ and /ɔ/. *Journal of the Acoustical Society of America*, 1977, *61*, Suppl. 1, S39(A).

KUHL, P. Speech perception in early infancy: Perceptual constancy for spectrally dissimilar vowel categories, *Journal of the Acoustical Society of America*, 1979, *66*, 1668–1679.

KUHL, P., & MILLER, J. Speech perception by the chinchilla: Voiced-voiceless distinction in alveolar plosive consonants. *Science*, 1975, *190*, 69–72.

LASKY, R., SYRDAL-LASKY, A., & KLEIN, D. VOT discrimination by four- to six-month-old infants from Spanish environments.

Journal of Experimental Child Psychology, 1975, *20*, 215–225.

LEAVITT, L., BROWN, J., MORSE, P., & GRAHAM, F. Cardiac orienting and auditory discrimination in 6-week infants. *Developmental Psychology*, 1976, *12*, 514–523.

LEWIS, M., & FREEDLE, R. Mother-infant dyad: The cradle of meaning. In P. Pliner, L. Krames, & T. Alloway (Eds.), *Communication and affect, language and thought.* New York: Academic Press, 1973.

LEWIS, M. M. *Infant speech.* New York: Humanities Press, 1951.

LIBERMAN, A., COOPER, F., SHANKWEILER, D., & STUDDERT-KENNEDY, M. Perception of the speech code. *Psychological Review*, 1967, *74*, 431–461.

LIEVEN, E.V.M. Conversations between mothers and young children: Individual differences and their possible implications for the study of language learning. In N. Waterson & C. Snow (Eds.), *The development of communication.* New York: John Wiley, 1978a.

LIEVEN, E.V.M. Turn-taking and pragmatics: Two issues in early child language. In R.N. Campbell & P. T. Smith (Eds.), *Recent advances in the psychology of language* (Vol. 4a). New York: Plenum, 1978b.

LYNIP, A. W. The use of magnetic devices in the collection and analysis of preverbal utterances of an infant. *Genetic Psychology Monographs*, 1951, *44*, 221–262.

McCAFFREY, A. *Speech perception in infancy.* Unpublished doctoral dissertation, Cornell University, Ithaca, N.Y., 1971.

MacNAMARA, J. Cognitive basis of language learning in infants. *Psychological Review*, 1972, *79*, 1–13.

McNEILL, D. *The acquisition of language.* New York: Harper & Row, Pub., 1970a.

McNEILL, D. The development of language. In P. Mussen (Ed.), *Carmichael's handbook of child psychology.* New York: John Wiley, 1970b.

McNEILL, D. A. The creation of language by children. In J. Lyons & R. J. Wales (Eds.), *Psycholinguistic papers.* Edinburgh: Edinburgh University Press, 1966.

MAYO, C., & LaFRANCE, M. On the acquisition of nonverbal communication *Merrill-Palmer Quarterly*, 1978, *24*, 213–228.

MELTZOFF, A., & MOORE, M. Imitation of facial and manual gestures in human neonates. *Science*, 1977, *198*, 75–78.

MILLER, C., & HANKES-RUZICKA, E. A parametric investigation of the cardiac no-delay discrimination paradigm and voice-onset-time discriminations in infants. *Research Status Report II.* Infant Development Laboratory, University of Wisconsin, 1978.

MILLER, C., & MORSE, P. The "heart" of categorical speech discrimination in young infants. *Journal of Speech and Hearing Research*, 1976, *19*, 578–589.

MILLER, C., & MORSE, P. Selective adaptation effects in infant speech perception paradigms. *Research Status Report III.* Infant Development Laboratory, University of Wisconsin, 1978.

MILLER, C., MORSE, P., & DORMAN, M. Cardiac indices of infant speech perception: Orienting and burst discrimination. *Quarterly Journal of Experimental Psychology*, 1977, *29*, 533–545.

MILLER, G. A., & CHOMSKY, N. Finitary models of language users. In R. Bush, E. Galanter, & R. Luce (Eds.), *Handbook of mathematical psychology* (Vol. 2). New York: John Wiley, 1963.

MILLER, J. *Phonetic determination of infant speech perception.* Unpublished doctoral dissertation, University of Minnesota, Minneapolis, 1974.

MIYAWAKI, K., STRANGE, W., VERBRUGGE, R., LIBERMAN, A., JENKINS, J., & FIJIMURA, O. An effect of linguistic experience: The discrimination of /r/ and /l/ by native speakers of Japanese and English. *Perception and Psychophysics*, 1975, *18*, 331–340.

MOERK, E. Piaget's research as applied to the explanation of language development. *Merrill-Palmer Quarterly*, 1975, *21*, 151–170.

MOFFITT, A. *Speech perception by infants.* Unpublished doctoral dissertation, University of Minnesota, Minneapolis, 1968.

MOFFITT, A. Consonant cue perception by twenty- to twenty-four-week-old infants. *Child Development*, 1971, *42*, 717–731.

MOLFESE, D. L. *Cerebral asymmetry in infants, children and adults: Auditory evoked responses to speech and music stimuli.* Unpublished doctoral dissertation, Pennsylvania State University, 1972.

MOLFESE, D. L. Infant cerebral asymmetry. Pp. 21–35 in S. Segalowitz & F. Gruber (Eds.), *Language development and neurological theory.* New York: Academic Press, 1977.

MOLFESE, D. L. Electrophysiological correlates of categorical speech perception in adults. *Brain and Language*, 1978a, *5*, 25–35.

MOLFESE, D. L. Left and right hemispheric involvement in speech perception: Electrophysiological correlates. *Perception and Psychophysics*, 1978b, *23*, 237–243.

MOLFESE, D. L. Cortical and subcortical involvement in the processing of coarticulated cues. *Brain and Language*, 1979, *7*, 86–100.

MOLFESE, D. L. The phoneme and the engram: Electrophysiological evidence for the acoustic invariant in stop consonants. *Brain and Language*, 1980, *9*, 372–376.

MOLFESE, D. L. Hemispheric specialization for temporal information: Implications for the processing of voicing cues during speech perception. *Brain and Language,* in press.

MOLFESE, D. L., & ERWIN, R. J. Intrahemispheric differentiation of vowels: Principal component analysis of auditory evoked responses to computer synthesized vowel sound. *Brain and Language,* in press.

MOLFESE, D. L., FREEMAN, R., & PALERMO, D. The ontogeny of brain lateralization for speech and nonspeech stimuli. *Brain and Language*, 1975, *2*, 356–368.

MOLFESE, D. L., & HESS, T. Hemispheric specialization for VOT perception in the preschool child. *Journal of Experimental Child Psychology*, 1978, *26*, 71–84.

MOLFESE, D. L., & MOLFESE, V. J. VOT distinctions in infants: Learned or innate? In H. Whitaker (Ed.), *Studies in Neurolinguistics* (Vol. 4). New York: Academic Press, 1979a.

MOLFESE, D. L., & MOLFESE, V. J. Hemisphere and stimulus differences as reflected in the cortical responses of newborn infants to speech stimuli. *Developmental Psychology*, 1979b, *15*, 505–511.

MOLFESE, D. L., & MOLFESE, V. J. Cortical responses of preterm infants to phonetic and nonphonetic speech stimuli. *Developmental Psychology*, 1980, *16*, 574–581.

MOLFESE, D. L., & MOLFESE, V. J. *Electrophysiological evidence for consonant invariance in newborn human infants.* Paper presented at the biennial meeting of the Society for Research in Child Development, Boston, Mass., April 1981.

MOLFESE, D. L., MORSE, P., TAYLOR, J., & ERWIN, R. *Cortical responses of infant rhesus monkeys to consonant invariant cues: Evidence for an innate basis for language development.* Paper presented at the International Neuropsychological Society, February 1981.

MOLFESE, D. L., & SCHMIDT, A. L. Human laterality: Is it unidimensional? *The Behavioral and Brain Sciences*, 1978, *2*, 307–308.

MOREHEAD, D., & MOREHEAD, A. From signal to sign: A Piagetian view of thought and language during the first two years. In R. Schiefelbusch & L. Lloyd (Eds.), *Language perspectives—Acquisition, retardation, and intervention.* Baltimore, Md.: University Park Press, 1974.

MORSBACH, G., & MURPHY, M. Recognition of individual neonate's cries by experienced and inexperienced adults. *Journal of Child Language*, 1979, *6*, 175–179.

MORSE, P. The discrimination of speech and nonspeech in early infancy. *Journal of Experimental Child Psychology*, 1972, *14*, 477–492.

MORSE, P. Infant speech perception: A preliminary model and review of the literature. Pp. 19–53 in R. Schiefelbusch & L. Lloyd (Eds.), *Language perspectives—Acquisition, retardation, and intervention.* Baltimore, Md.: University Park Press, 1974.

MORSE, P. Infant speech perception: Origins, processes, and Alpha Centauri. In F. Minifie & L. Lloyd (Eds.), *Communicative and cognitive abilities—Early behavioral assessment.* Baltimore, Md.: University Park Press, 1978.

MORSE, P., & SNOWDON, C. An investigation of categorical speech discrimination by rhesus monkeys. *Perception and Psychophysics*, 1975, *17*, 9–16.

MULLER, E., HOLLIEN, H., & MURRY, T. Perceptual responses to infant crying: Identification of cry types. *Journal of Child Language*, 1974, *1*, 89–95.

MURRY, T., HOLLIEN, H., & MULLER, E. Perceptual responses to infant crying: Maternal recognition and sex judgments. *Journal of Child Language*, 1975, *2*, 199–204.

NELSON, K. Structure and strategy in learning to talk. *Monographs of Society for Research in Child Development*, 1973a, *38* (Nos. 1–2).

NELSON, K. Some evidence for the cognitive primacy of categorization and its functional basis. *Merrill-Palmer Quarterly*, 1973b, *19*, 21–40.

NELSON, K. Concept, word and sentence: Interrelations in acquisition and development. *Psychological Review*, 1974, *81*, 267–285.

NELSON, K., RESCORLA, L., GRUENDEL, J., & BENEDICT, H. Early lexicons: What do they mean? *Child Development*, 1978, *49*, 960–968.

NELSON, K. E., CARSKADDON, G., & BONVILLIAN, J. Syntax acquisition: Impact of experimental variation in adult verbal interaction with the child. *Child Development*, 1973, *44*, 497–504.

NEWPORT, E. L. Motherese: The speech of mothers to young children. In N. J. Castellan, D. B. Pisoni, & G. R. Potts (Eds.), *Cognitive theory.* Hillsdale, N.J.: Lawrence Erlbaum Associates, 1976.

NEWPORT, E. L., GLEITMAN, L. R., & GLEITMAN, H. A study of mothers' speech and child language acquisition. *Papers and Reports on Child Language Development*, 1975, *10*, 111–116.

NEWPORT, E. L., GLEITMAN, H., & GLEITMAN, L. R. Mother, I'd rather do it myself: Some effects and non-effects of maternal speech style. In C. E. Snow & C. A. Ferguson (Eds.), *Talking to children: Language input and acquisition.* Cambridge, England: Cambridge University Press, 1977.

NICHOLICH, L., & RAPH, J. Imitative language and symbolic maturity in the single word period. *Journal of Psycholinguistic Research*, 1978, *7*, 401–417.

NINIO, A., & BRUNER, J. The achievement and antecedents of labelling. *Journal of Child Language*, 1978, *5*, 1–15.

OKAMOTO, N. Verbalization process in infancy-transpositive use of sounds in development of symbolic activity. *Psychologia*, 1962, *5*, 32–40.

PALERMO, D. S. Language acquisition. In H. Reese & L. Lipsitt (Eds.), *Experimental child psychology.* New York: Academic Press, 1971.

PHILLIPS, J. Syntax and vocabulary of mothers' speech to young children: Age and sex comparisons. *Child Development*, 1973, *44*, 182–185.

PIAGET, J. *The construction of reality in the child.* New York: Ballantine, 1954.

PIAGET, J. *Play, dreams and imitation.* New York: W. W. Norton & Co., Inc., 1962.

REMICK, H. *The maternal environment of language acquisition.* Doctoral dissertation, University of California at Davis, 1971.

REMICK, H. Maternal speech to children during language acquisition. In W. vonRaffler-Engel & Y. Lebrun (Eds.), *Baby talk and infant speech.* Amsterdam: Swets & Zeitlinger, 1976.

RINGLER, N. *Mothers' language to their children and to adults over time.* Doctoral dissertation, Case Western Reserve University, Cleveland, Ohio, 1973.

RINGWALL, E. A., REESE, H. W., & MARKEL, N. N. A distinctive feature analysis of prelinguistic infant vocalizations. Pp. 69–78 in K. F. Riegel (Ed.), *The development of language functions.* Report No. 8. Ann Arbor, Michigan: Center for Human Growth and Development, University of Michigan, 1965.

RINGWALL, E. A., REESE, H. W., & MARKEL, N. N. Behavioral correlates of infant vocalizations. Final Report, United States Public Health Service Grant No. NB 04923-01, 1970.

RODGON, M. Overt action and the semantic expression of action in one-word utterances. In R. Campbell & P. Smith (Eds.), *Recent advances in the psychology of language.* New York: Plenum, 1976.

RODGON, M., JANKOWSKY, W., & ALENSKAS, L. A multi-functional approach to single-word usage. *Journal of Child Language*, 1977, *4*, 23–43.

ROTH, D., & MORSE, P. An investigation of infant VOT discrimination in using the cardiac OR. Pp. 207–218 in *Research Status Report I.* Infant Development Laboratory, University of Wisconsin, 1975.

SACHS, J., BROWN, R., & SALERNO, R. Adults' speech to children. In W. vonRaffler-Engel & Y. Lebrun (Eds.), *Baby talk and infant speech.* Amsterdam: Swets & Zeitlinger, 1976.

SACHS, J., & DEVIN, J. Young children's use of age-appropriate speech styles. *Journal of Child Language*, 1976, *3*, 81–98.

SCHIEFFELIN, B. B. Getting it together: An ethnographic approach to the study of the development of communicative competence. In E. Ochs & B. B. Schieffelin (Eds.), *Developmental pragmatics.* New York: Academic Press, 1979.

SHATZ, M., & GELMAN, R. The development of communication skills: Modifications in the speech of young children as a function of listener. *Monograph of Society for Research in Child Development*, 1973, No. 152.

SHERMAN, M. The differentiation of emotional responses in infants. Ability of observers to judge emotional characteristics of crying of infants and of voice of adults. *Journal of Comparative Psychology,* 1927, *7,* 335–341.

SHUGAR, G. W. Text analysis as an approach to the study of early linguistic operations. In N. Waterson & C. Snow (Eds.), *The development of communication.* New York: John Wiley, 1978.

SINNOT, J., BEECHER, M., MOODY, D., & STEBBINS, W. Speech sound discrimination by humans and monkeys. *Journal of the Acoustical Society of America,* 1976, *60,* 687–695.

SNOW, C. E. Mothers' speech to children learning language. *Child Development,* 1972, *43,* 549–565.

SNOW, C. E. Mothers' speech research: From input to interaction. In C. E. Snow & C. A. Ferguson (Eds.), *Talking to children: Language input and acquisition.* Cambridge, England: Cambridge University Press, 1977a.

SNOW, C. E. The development of conversation between mothers and babies. *Journal of Child Language,* 1977b, *4,* 1–22.

SNOW, C. E. The conversational context of language acquisition. In R. N. Campbell & P. T. Smith (Eds.), *Recent advances in the psychology of language* (Vol. 4a). Language development and mother-child interaction. New York: Plenum, 1978.

SNOW, C. E. Conversations with children. In P. Fletcher & M. Garman (Eds.), *Language acquisition: Studies in first language development.* Cambridge, England: Cambridge University Press, 1979.

SNOW, C. E., ARLMAN-RUPP, A., HASSING, Y., JOBSE, J., JOOSTEN, J., & VORSTER, J. Mothers' speech in three social classes. *Journal of Psycholinguistic Research,* 1976, *5,* 1–20.

SNYDER, L. Communicative and cognitive abilities and disabilities in the sensory motor period. *Merrill-Palmer Quarterly,* 1978, *24,* 161–180.

SPITZ, R., & WOLF, K. The smiling response: A contribution to the ontogenesis of social relations. *Genetic Psychology Monographs,* 1946, *34,* 57–125.

SPRING, D., & DALE, P. The discrimination of linguistic stress in early infancy. *Journal of Speech and Hearing Research,* 1977, *20,* 224–231.

STARR, S. The relationship of single words to two word sentences. *Child Development,* 1975, *46,* 701–708.

STEVENS, K., & KLATT, D. Role of formant transitions in the voiced-voiceless distinction for stops. *Journal of the Acoustical Society of America,* 1974, *55,* 653–659.

STREETER, L. Language perception of 2-month-old infants shows effects of both innate mechanisms and experience. *Nature,* 1976, *259,* 39–41.

SUGARMAN, S. A description of communicative development in the prelanguage child. In I. Markova (Ed.), *The social context of language.* London: John Wiley, 1977.

SWOBODA, P., KASS, J., MORSE, P., & LEAVITT, L. Memory factors in infant vowel discrimination of normal and at-risk infants. *Child Development,* 1978, *49,* 332–339.

SWOBODA, P., MORSE, P., & LEAVITT, L. Continuous vowel discrimination in normal and at risk infants. *Child Development,* 1976, *47,* 459–465.

TILL, J. *Infants' discrimination of speech and nonspeech stimuli.* Unpublished doctoral dissertation, University of Iowa, Iowa City, 1976.

TONKOVA-YAMPOL'SKAYA, R. Development of speech intonation in infants in the first two years of life. *Soviet Psychology,* 1969, *7,* 48–54.

TREHUB, S. Infants' sensitivity to vowel and tonal contrasts. *Developmental Psychology,* 1973, *9,* 81–96.

TREHUB, S. The discrimination of foreign speech contrasts by infants and adults. *Child Development,* 1976, *47,* 466–472.

TREHUB, S., & CHANG, H. W. Speech as reinforcing stimulation for infants. *Developmental Psychology,* 1977, *13,* 170–171.

TREHUB, S., & RABINOVITCH, M. Auditory-linguistic sensitivity in early infancy. *Developmental Psychology,* 1972, *6,* 74–77.

TREVARTHEN, C., & HUBLEY, P. Secondary intersubjectivity: Confidence, confiding and acts of meaning in the first year. In A. Lock (Ed.), *Action, gesture and symbol: The emergence of language.* New York: Academic Press, 1978.

TRONICK, E., ALS, H., & BRAZELTON, T. Mutuality in mother-infant interactions. *Journal of Communication,* 1977, *27,* 74–79.

UZGIRIS, I., & HUNT, J. *Assessment in infancy: Ordinal scales of psychological development.* Urbana: University of Illinois Press, 1975.

VOLTERRA, V., BATES, E., BENIGNI, L., BRETHERTON, I., & CAMAIONI, V. First words in language and action: A qualitative look. In E. Bates (Ed.), *The emergence of symbols: Cognition and communication in infancy.* New York: Academic Press, 1979.

VORSTER, J. Mommy linguist: The case of motherese. *Lingua,* 1975, *37,* 281–312.

WATERS, R., & WILSON, W. Speech perception by rhesus monkeys: The voicing distinction in synthesized labial and velar stop consonants. *Perception and Psychophysics,* 1976, *19,* 285–289.

WILLIAMS, L. *The effects of phonetic environment and stress placement on infant discrimination of the place of stop consonant articulation.* Paper presented at the Second Annual Boston University Conference on Language Development, Boston, October 1977.

WILLIAMS, L., & BUSH, M. Discrimination by young infants of voiced stop consonants with and without release bursts. *Journal of the Acoustical Society of America,* 1978, *63,* 1223–1226.

WILLIAMS, L., & GOLENSKI, J. Infant speech sound discrimination: The effects of contingent versus non-contingent stimulus presentation. *Child Development,* 1978, *49,* 213–217.

WINITZ, H. *Articulatory acquisition and behavior.* Englewood Cliffs, N.J.: Prentice-Hall, 1969.

WINITZ, H., & IRWIN, O. C. Infant speech: Consistency with age. *Journal of Speech and Hearing Research,* 1958, *1,* 245–249.

WINITZ, H., & IRWIN, O. C. Syllabic and phonetic structure of infants' early words. In C. Ferguson & D. Slobin (Eds.), *Studies of child language development.* New York: Holt, Rinehart & Winston, 1973.

WOLFF, P. The natural history of crying and other vocalization in early infancy. In B. M. Foss (Ed.), *Determinants of infant behavior IV.* London: Methuen, 1969.

YOGMAN, M., DIXON, S., TRONICK, E., ADAMSON, L., ALS, H., & BRAZELTON, T. *Development of infant social interaction with fathers.* Paper presented at the meeting of Eastern Psychological Association, New York, 1976.

18

Cognitive Development
in Infancy

GAIL A. PETERSEN

When one speaks of cognition or cognitive activities, one envisions people engaging in thought processes that are strategic, intelligent, and oftentimes conscious. Therefore it is not surprising that we do not think of infants as engaging in cognitive activity due to their relatively limited repertoire of behavior. In this chapter we will explore prevailing theories and research that have significantly altered such notions and have led us toward a more enlightened understanding of how cognitive processes do occur throughout the infant period.

Any review of the literature on infant cognition would be deficient if it did not devote ample space to the stage theory of Piaget (1952, 1954). His writings and reports based upon detailed observations of his own children have stimulated an extensive body of research in the field. Investigators have drawn prominently from Piaget's description of the sensorimotor stage of developments extending from birth to 18 months with the acquisition of symbolic thought. Consequently much of the research reviewed here will revolve around specific Piagetian concepts.

A major premise of Piaget's theory, and of the works of others (Bruner, 1968; Kagan, 1971; Werner, 1948, 1957), is the infant's active role in the acquisition of knowledge. S/he does not act as a passive recipient of information but rather constructs schemes that are transfigurations of what is experienced. The infant accomplishes schema building by integrating new information into preexisting structures (assimilation) coupled with continuing changes in his/her view of the world in order to take into account the specific characteristics of an object, situation, and other novel information (accommodation). The two cognitive processes are balanced in a way so that the infant can maintain a level of equilibrium between no change and constant change (Piaget, 1977). Another assumption of Piagetian theory states

that any given stage in development will act as a foundation for a succeeding stage; thus, there exists a logical necessity for an invariant sequencing of various cognitive structures. Moreover the composition of these structures is not simply additive.

Wherever development occurs it proceeds from a state of relative globality and lack of differentiation to a state of increasing differentiation, articulation and hierarchical integration. (Werner, 1957, p. 126)

By example an infant who can take a toy from his/her mother can do so because over time s/he has managed to coordinate a scheme for looking with a scheme for grasping.

The major accomplishment of the sensorimotor period is the differentiation of the actions of the self and the external world. This chapter will trace this progression with a major emphasis on the infant's mastery of the object concept.

REFLEXIVE STAGE

From birth to about two months the infant is controlled primarily by reflexive acts that are internally monitored. Thus the infant spends the better part of the day remaining in or moving in or out of the physiological states of sleep, hunger, satiation, and comfort. However it would be incorrect to assume that the neonate is incapable of perceiving the surrounding world or learning from it. On the contrary investigations reveal that, even in the first two weeks, the infant can detect alterations in shapes and sounds. A newborn, one week old, will gaze toward a bright light presented at the midline and in the peripheral field (Harris & MacFarlane, 1974). There even exists a small body of research showing that newborns will react to odor. Reiser, Yonas, and Wikner (1976) found that infants as young as three days will turn away from the specific location of an ammonia substance. Likewise Eimas (1975) demonstrated that one-month-old infants are able to detect changes between speech patterns. Also during the first month the infant has a predisposition to attend to changes such as differences in hue or contour. Kessen, Salapatek, and Haith (1972) presented newborn infants with contrasting black and white edges and found that they would dramatically shift their gaze in the direction of vertically presented edges. In addition they will tend to scan across the border of contrasting features; searching the outline of a face is a common example (Salapatek, Note 1). By eight weeks they will also begin to scan internal features of a stimulus, such as the eyes of a human face (Maurer & Salapatek, 1976). Consequently, even as newcomers to the world, infants can attend to stimuli in the different sense modalities and respond in very specific ways. The evidence tends to show that infants have an early preference for stimuli that carry the most information.

The infant's early perceptual ability of selective attention and differential responding sets the stage, so to speak, for developing schemes. Piaget (1952), holding essentially the same view, asserts that, from the beginning, the infant must necessarily accommodate his/her innate reflexes to variations in the environment. As an illustration the infant over the first week shows increasing efficiency in searching for a nipple, thus refining his/her scheme for suckable objects.

OBJECT IDENTITY

In the third month of life there is a distinct sharpening of perceptual cognitive abilities. One of the more significant gains during this period is the enhancement of recognition memory, the ability to detect when objects are familiar. Before two months infants are able to build internal models of an object as evidenced by their gradual habituation to repeated exposure of a stimulus. Now, however, the infant cannot only acquire a schema for an object but can also retrieve that schema from past experience when confronted with an eliciting stimulus. In one study Super (Note 2) exposed 10-week-old infants to an orange ball moving vertically against a black background. The viewing for each infant lasted for a minimum of three minutes. The infants were brought back to the laboratory either one day or two weeks later for a repeated viewing and compared to infants who were seeing the stimulus for the first time. The first two groups habituated to the stimulus more quickly than the latter group, indicating that the stimulus was recognized as familiar. More recent evidence seems to indicate that recognition memory abilities for auditory stimuli may even occur before two months. Ungerer, Brody, and Zelazo (1978), in a longitudinal design, had mothers repeat a specific word to their two- to four-week-old infants 60 times a day for 13 days. One experimental group heard the word *tinder* and the other, *beguile*. During the test session at the end of the training period, the infants in both groups were exposed to both training words and their first name. The experimenters assured that at least 14

hours elapsed between the training sessions and the recognition tests. Additionally a control group of infants who received no training received the same test. The experimental infants exhibited recognition of their specific training word but not the novel training word or their name. Control infants did not recognize any of the three words. As a result the authors suggest that the infant's increasing memory abilities are influenced not just by physical maturity but also by the strength of stimulus exposure. Their view is complemented by Werner and Perlmutter (1979) who argue that the complexity of the stimulus is also a major factor and that even neonates can successfully recognize simple forms (Friedman, 1972). Following their line of reasoning, then, age differences in memory abilities are due to increasing encoding strategies rather than retention capacity per se.

According to Piaget recognitive ability plays a significant role in the infant's beginning adaptations to the external world. Prior to the onset of that ability, any accommodatory behavior (e.g., adapting the shape of the mouth to various size nipples) constitutes a hereditary adaptation with the purpose of sustaining the reflex (e.g., sucking). However as the infant's memory abilities increase, s/he begins to attend to objects for their own features and not merely for the function they serve. This new turn of events is most evident in social smiling. Infants by three to four months will react selectively to a familiar person by smiling—an activity which presupposes that the infant, through experience, sees the person as distinct from others.

This new activity initiates coordination among all the senses. For example a looking scheme will be organized with a grasping scheme, thus allowing the infant to reach for and grasp objects.

Although the five-month-old infant has learned to identify objects as new or old based upon his/her experience and can notice numerous features of objects, s/he still engages in some puzzling behavior. If the infant is holding an object in his/her hand and someone then places a cloth over the object, the infant will simply drop the object and remove his/her hand (Gratch & Landers, 1971). Likewise when a favorite toy is hidden behind a screen in full view of the infant, the infant will not attempt to recover it even though s/he is motorically capable of doing so (Bower & Wisehart, 1972). The saying "out of sight, out of mind" certainly is most pertinent here; the object simply ceases to exist as far as the infant is concerned. How is it possible for the infant to have recognition and therefore a schema for an object, but still not exercise it in this situation? Piaget (1954) believes that, up to this point in development, the infant still sees objects as pictures or interesting sights whose subjective existence is dependent upon the child's own actions. The infant has not yet had sufficient experience to understand that objects remain invariant in spite of temporal location, alterations in form, and so forth.

Bower has argued strongly against Piaget, contending that even very young infants see objects much as children and adults do. To support his claim Bower and colleagues have carried out a series of studies involving, primarily, tracking (Bower, Broughton, & Moore, 1971; Bower & Paterson, 1973) and reaching for objects (Bower, 1972; Bower & Wisehart, 1972). From their findings, Bower et al. purport that infants as young as 20 weeks can perceive objects as three-dimensional and always in existence.

Bower's work, however, has been criticized on methodological grounds. Due to the complexity of the argument and the excellent reviews on the subject published elsewhere (Gratch, 1975, 1977), it will not be discussed in length here. Briefly the major criticism lies with Bower's interpretation of the infant's responses to task demands. It has been argued that the very same behavior used as evidence for object permanence can be construed as merely attention to interesting sights or the repetition of simple action schemes. To date the bulk of the research tends to place the skill for the permanence of objects well into the latter half of the first year.

OBJECT CONCEPT

Many investigators consider the acquisition of the object concept to be the most important milestone in early cognitive development. With this achievement the infant cannot only recognize an object as familiar or novel when viewing it but can also have a mental image of the object when it is not present. S/he sees the object as permanent, no longer as a thing whose existence is contingent on the infant's acting upon it. The importance of this developmental stage is reflected in the plethora of empirical work designed to broaden and clarify the underlying factors determining the transition in skills. The most basic paradigm in the research is the one adopted by Piaget: Present an object to the infant, hide it under a cloth, and watch to see if the infant attempts to retrieve it. Deliberate searching is evidence that the infant believes that the object is enduring despite its occlusion. Piaget found that his own children were able to succeed at this task at approximately nine months of age.

According to Piaget the coordination of action schemes leads toward search and retrieval; in the present case, the infant combines the scheme for looking with the scheme for grasping. However the infant at approximately nine months (at Piaget's Stage 4) is still constrained by his/her own actions upon the object and, as Piaget argues, has still not reached the true level of object permanence as such. This situation is exemplified in the following task Piaget presented to his children. He showed a toy and placed it behind cover A and allowed the infant to retrieve the toy. Subsequently he placed the same toy behind a different cover B while the infant was watching and was amazed to discover that the infant repeated his search at cover A! This $A\bar{B}$ error seems to indicate that the infant is still "locked in" to his motor schemes and prefers to repeat a previously successful grasping pattern. More specifically the object's identity is still determined by its place in the spatial field with the original cover acting as a sign for the object's presence.

Piaget's emphasis on the role of motor behavior has received criticism from other researchers on primarily two grounds: (1) There is insufficient evidence to conclude that the infant's cognitive abilities are so heavily influenced by action, and (2) his descriptions are too ambiguous and do not do justice to the subtle and complex transitions in memory that most likely are occurring (Gratch, 1977; Kagan, 1979). Focusing on the former, Evans (Note 3) attempted to isolate the level at which an

infant's actions were critical in the hiding task. Nine-month-olds were either given the opportunity to search for a hidden toy at point A or were allowed to watch only its disappearance–appearance for varying numbers of trials. When they were presented with a subsequent $A\bar{B}$ trial, Evans found that all infants were as likely to err, indicating that manual search was not a precondition for choosing the incorrect spot.

Although Piaget acknowledges that memory does come into operation during the $A\bar{B}$ task, he tends to downplay its influence, again emphasizing action. In contrast Kagan and associates, through extensive experiments, conclude that developing memory processes explain the progression through the sensorimotor stages more clearly (Kagan, 1979; Kagan, Kearsley, & Zelazo, 1978). In a longitudinal study, Kagan's group presented infants from 3½ to 29 months with two events. In one, infants were shown a visual display in which they saw a hand move a rod toward three light bulbs which lit as they were touched. The episode was repeated 8 to 10 times, followed by 5 episodes in which the hand moved (rod stationary) and touched the lights which went on 3 seconds later. In the next sequence the lights did not go on when touched. Finally they saw 3 episodes of the original display. In the second event the infants listened to a meaningful phrase for 10 to 12 trials, then an altered phrase 5 times, and the original phrase once again for 3 trials. The authors found a u-shaped trend for fixation and search time in the final trials of the visual event and during all 3 episodes of the auditory event. There was high attentiveness at the younger age, a drop at approximately 7½ months, and a rise beginning at about 9 months and continuing through the second year.

Kagan argued that the drop cannot indicate an increased ability to assimilate the event because the older infants exhibited longer fixation times. Although one can reason that the infant had developed a new cognitive stucture for understanding the visual and auditory displays, it seems unlikely that one stucture could account for the highly similar findings for two very different events. Rather Kagan felt that the infant had acquired a new competency in which s/he could compare a new event (a transformation) with the old event which had been retrieved from memory. The infant could continue to make the comparison until the discrepancy—present and visible vs. present and invisible—was detected and acted upon. Thus the seven-month-old is quicker to solve a discrepant event than a four-month-old, and the older infant is better able to hold both internal and external events in short-term memory allowing for more sustained processing of the similarities and dissimilarities.

Kagan's argument here helps us to understand the cognitive processes that are occurring when the infant is trying to retrieve a hidden object, but it is not sufficient to explain the $A\bar{B}$ dilemma. However Kagan has been able to supply supporting evidence for the predominance of memory. He presented infants with the $A\bar{B}$ task, allowing them to search after a three- or seven-second delay. Seven-month-olds were successful with the shorter delay and tended to err with the longer delay; ten-month-olds were successful in both conditions. Similar results have been obtained by Gratch, Appel, Evans, LeCompte, and Wright (1974). Again the findings can be interpreted in terms of increased memory recall.

Others have tried to state more specifically the nature of memory recall and the observed error. Harris (1971) looked at delay time before allowed search and suggested that, even though the infant registers the second cover as the actual retrieval spot, s/he becomes confused the longer s/he must wait to act upon the scheme. As a result the memory traces of the successful search at *A* increasingly become a proactive interference causing the infant to forget the newer information. However more recent findings have tended to undermine such an orientation. Butterworth (1977) presented eight-, nine-, and ten-month-old infants with three hiding conditions: (1) object hidden at *A* and *B*, (2) object covered at *A* and *B* by transparent covers, and (3) object uncovered and visible at both *A* and *B*. Almost none of the infants had any difficulty finding an object at *A* in all three conditions. Yet, interestingly enough, the infants at all ages performed at chance level on the first *B* trial except when the object was visible and uncovered. Over a series of five *AB̄* trials, infants tended to be consistently correct or incorrect reflecting perhaps that performance on the first *B* trial was not random. Butterworth concluded that more complex operations were in play than just proactive interference since many infants failed in the second condition where the object was always in full view. Instead he contended that the infant must confront a dual conflict between a self-centered space and the visual field. When the object is visible and uncovered, the infant can establish a congruency between his/her sitting position (self-center) and the object's position (visual field). As it is moved to *B*, the total visual field is changed, and the infant therefore reestablishes congruency. When the object is covered but visible, its displacement to *B* creates a dilemma since the infant must now resolve the two visual fields, the original cover and the new cover with the object underneath, in relation to his/her own position. Since the two visual displays are almost identical, it is then possible to see why the infants vacillated from correctly to incorrectly consistent responses. The dual code approach for resolving *AB̄* object permanence tasks applies as well to the complete covering position. Since the visual fields are essentially the same, the chance performance indicates that the self-centered code supersedes the visual code oftentimes. With these findings and more recent information (Butterworth, Note 4), Butterworth has challenged Piaget's requirement of the *belief* in object permanence as a prerequisite for successful search. The infant's ability, rather, is guided by his/her perceptions—not incomplete concepts—which take into account the total physical context. Butterworth's view does not actually refute Piaget's overall theory of the object concept, but it does present a more in-depth perspective based upon extensive data.

Bremner and Bryant (1977) argue more strongly in favor of Piaget. They presented nine-month-old infants with a variation of the *AB̄* hiding task by letting infants search successfully at *A* for five trials. For the second hiding phase, two groups (*A* and *B*) of infants were moved to the other end of the table and in front of another hiding spot. Group *A* witnessed the object being hidden in exactly the same spot as before and therefore had to make a new motor response to be successful. Group *B* infants saw the object being hidden in front of them at the new location and needed only to employ the same motor response for success. Groups *C* (similar to *A*) and *D* (similar to *B*) were included to check for the influence of position of the table, and a control group, *E*, received a traditional *AB̄* task. The groups and results are summarized in Table 18–1. The findings, with fewer errors for groups *B* and *D*, strongly favor a motor response hypothesis over a place hypothesis. Yet the authors sense the difficulty in positing why the motor response is predominant. Their reasoning is akin to those who favor the influence of repeated practice through development (a component of Piaget's view) as well as that of proactive interference.

By the time the infant approaches the middle of his/her second year, s/he has graduated to successful retrieval of hidden objects which have gone through numerous visible displacements (Kopp, Sigman, & Parmalee, 1974; Piaget, 1952; Uzgiris & Hunt, 1975). Consequently the infant can continually update his/her knowledge of the object's current location, relying much more on the object's perceptual invariance than his/her own actions. This new facility may be viewed, in part, as an outgrowth of increased recall memory; thus, as Piaget discovered in observing this Stage 5 behavior, it is harder for a child to remember four or five displacements opposed to only a few.

At the present stage, nevertheless, the infant is still bound by some remnants of knowledge through motion. If a toy is hidden first inside a box, then the box placed under a cover and reintroduced to the child with no toy inside, the child will most likely search just the box. Only later will s/he attempt to continue his/her search under the cover. The critical skill still required here is the ability to *infer* the object's location—a mental act that is predicated on combining representations of possible alternatives. To be successful on this task, the child would need to deduce that the toy can remain under the cover even when the box is removed. It is after this point, during the latter part of the second year, that Piaget ac-

Table 18-1 Experimental Design together with Scores on Trial 1 of Stage 2

GROUP	MEAN AGE (DAYS)	ROTATION	STAGE 2 RESPONSE	STAGE 2 TABLE POSITION	STAGE 2 ABSOLUTE POSITION	NUMBER INCORRECT (OUT OF 16) TRIAL 1 STAGE 2
A	281.3	Child rotated	*D*	*S*	*S*	11
B	279.4	Child rotated	*S*	*D*	*D*	4
C	280.8	Table rotated	*D*	*S*	*D*	11
D	278.2	Table rotated	*S*	*D*	*S*	3
E	277.5	None	*D*	*D*	*D*	12

Note: *S*—same as in Stage 1; *D*—different from Stage 1.
Source: Bremner & Bryant (1977).

326

knowledges the infant's "true" acquisition of the object concept (Stage 6).

In effect, by virtue of the very fact that it enters the system of abstract or indirect images and relations, the object acquires in the subject's consciousness, a new and final degree of liberty. (Piaget, 1954, p. 94)

Naturally the object's freedom in this sense is part and parcel of the infant's own flexibility in dealing with novel experiences as illustrated by the following two studies. In the first DeLoache (Note 5) had 20- and 24-month-old children play a "hide-and-seek" game in the home. Both age groups were very successful in retrieving a toy hidden in various locations even after a three- or five-minute waiting period. In a second task the experimenter secretly moved the toy to another hiding place and then noticed some striking differences in the children's behavior. The younger children typically did not attempt any further search, and if they did, it was usually at the previous hiding position. Furthermore their affect was one of puzzlement accompanied by frustration and crying. Conversely the older children proceeded to search for the missing toy in a deliberate fashion, looking in the adjacent area or in an analogous location (e.g., if it was hidden under a pillow, they would look under a nearby pillow). Searching in the previous position was seen as just one of numerous possibilities.

In a second study Zelazo and Kearsley (Note 6) observed the types of play evident among infants ranging from 9½ to 15½ months of age. The four types, ordered hierarchically, were (1) undifferentiated play, (2) stereotypical responding (mouthing, fingering), (3) relational play (association of two or more objects in a nonfunctional manner), and (4) functional play (use of toys according to adult purposes—e.g., brushing doll's hair). The observations revealed some highly significant age differences in the occurrence and order of the four types of play. Type 2 play was dominant at 9½ months and was overshadowed by Type 3 at 13½ months which, in turn, was supplanted by Type 4 by 15½ months.

One overall explanation can be offered for the findings of both studies. The increased ability could not be due simply to locomotor ability and neuromotor coordination since infants under one year have such capacities. Again the changes are due to increased cognitive abilities. More specifically, infants, as they grow older, are better equipped to deal with novel situations. This can only be accomplished when the infant is truly separated from the immediate environment (McCall, 1979). To search successfully for the missing object requires the child to deal with the unexpected in a planful and goal-oriented manner; this is also true for the ability to use toys in an adult-accepted style. Because the child thinks of possibilities, s/he invents wholly new ways to combine objects in some functional manner (see also McQuiston & Wachs, Note 7).

In sum, then, the period from 7 to 18 months is marked by sharp increases, both quantitative and qualitative, in the infant's mental processes and in the way s/he deals with the environment. The highlight of this period is the infant's gradual decentering of self culminating in the attainment of the object concept. Piaget places the infant's initial difficulty in realizing the permanence of objects on egocentric responding which relies on action schemes. Other researchers have tried to identify more precisely the underlying mechanisms and have argued for the preeminence of increased memory (Fox, Kagan, & Weiskopf, 1979; Kagan et al., 1978), interfering memory (Harris, 1971, 1973), or specific orienting responses (Bremner & Bryant, 1977; Butterworth, 1977; Gratch et al., 1974). Such seemingly competing views do not necessarily refute Piaget's claims, nor do they always counter each other (Gratch, 1977). Instead they serve to broaden Piaget's writings and to provide the reader with an overall picture of the complex processes that are involved. Indeed the depth to which this topic has been explored has tended to generate as many questions as solutions.

COGNITIVE INFLUENCES IN DEVELOPMENT

Self-Recognition

The ability to have some concept of self is necessarily dependent on the infant's capability for seeing him/herself separate from his/her surroundings. Thus it is not surprising that a baby will not acquire self-recognition until s/he has attained some semblance of object permanence. Amsterdam (1972), by using mirrors, observed that infants between three and eight months tended to treat a mirror as a spectacle or as an object to be manipulated. After nine months when infants had a dot of red color placed on their foreheads and were placed in front of a mirror, they would touch the dot while looking at themselves. This was followed, at 18 months, by self-naming when looking in a mirror.

Mother-Infant Attachment

By the end of the first year, the infant shows signs of attachment to the mother reflected by wariness of strangers and signs of distress when separated from her (Ainsworth, 1973; Sroufe, 1977). The onset of such behavior typically begins at about seven or eight months. In Kagan's (1979) view the foremost underlying cognitive operation at play here is object, or people, permanence and, more specifically, increased memorial competence. Since the infant is better able to retrieve a past schema (mother), s/he has the opportunity to try and assimilate the present image. The ability to detect discrepancies in this manner is tempered by the child's relative immaturity in resolving the conflict; thus, distress occurs. Kagan cites the infant's gradual decrease in wariness by the second year as evidence for his/her increased ability to interpret and act upon the novel event. Kagan's argument seems quite plausible, and no one would doubt that seeing someone as permanent (i.e., a separate entity) would be integral to attachment; but, it is only part of the picture. There are corollary changes in the infant's and mother's affective bond (Sroufe & Waters, 1977), possibly attributable to the consistency of their continued interaction. Moreover the infant's increased mobility and sophistication in communication make him/her more adept at resolving conflicts in numerous domains. It is more helpful in understanding the attachment phenomenon to take the view that cognitive growth is linked in some basic and inseparable way to all other aspects of the baby's evolution.

Imitation

One of the more complete descriptions of a child's imitative abilities extends from the work of Piaget (1962) and will be briefly summarized here.

The ability to repeat another's actions would logically require that the infant view his/her own actions as separate from those of others which, as we saw earlier, does not occur until after the first half-year. Kaye (1978) has attempted to show that infants six months old can be trained to imitate adult movements. He had adults hold infants on their laps, face to face, while they made open and close movements for three to five seconds. The 40 infants received a median of 20 trials during which the number of infant mouth movements was recorded. There was a significant increase of infant mouthing when compared to base line levels. Kaye suggested that an extensive number of trials is the key factor. Complementary findings have been obtained by Meltzoff and Moore (1977) with newborns. The interpretations are tenuous since the stimulation could have triggered an increase in many movements, including the desired one, attenuating the specificity to certain features—a necessity for true imitation. McCall (1979), in concert with Piaget, prefers to call these instances *social facilitation* and not *social imitation,* stressing that the infants are exhibiting movements well within their repertoire and that the "feedback" from the adults aids in just perpetuating a simple action.

At about seven months the infant shows imitative behavior that is initiated by another; it is not necessary for the adult to respond to a spontaneous behavior of the child. Yet the infant still imitates only that behavior that s/he already possesses and sometimes will generalize the action to another part of his/her body—e.g., s/he may open and close his/her mouth in response to an adult's eyeblinking. By the end of the second year, s/he begins to imitate *new,* but simple, behavior that s/he can check for accuracy (McCall, Parke, & Kavanaugh, 1977). Not surprisingly hand movement games are very popular at this age. Within a short time, around the first birthday, the infant will imitate a model even though s/he cannot see his/her own actions. Finally, after thirteen months, the infant engages in deferred imitation—that is, s/he can repeat a model's actions in the absence of the model and when there has been a significant lapse in time. This period is marked by a jump in the frequency of imitation as discovered by McCall et al. (1977); 12-month-olds imitated 28 percent of the actions modeled by an adult with an increase to 76 percent by 24 months. It appears that the infant by this age focuses heavily on adult behavior and almost feels obligated to imitate. It is interesting to note the affective behavior that accompanies infants at this time. Richman et al. (Note 8) had 18- and 24-month-old infants watch an adult model three different acts; in the results, 43 percent of the infants who imitated exhibited a lower post- than premodeling distress. Conversely 41 percent of the imitative infants showed more distress after the sessions. There were no age differences.

Richman et al. report that 15- and 30-month-olds rarely display such negative affect and reasoned that the non-imitative infants were at a stage when they are not yet very skilled in imitating adults and yet they realize the discrepancy between the adult's standard and their own. Before 18 months the infants seem not to be bothered by any differences in their imitation; when they cross into their third year, they have achieved greater success in exact repetitions presenting fewer opportunities for discrepancies to occur.

In summary, because the child can eventually separate his/her actions from the external world and because of his/her increased memory, s/he can internalize images of actions and use these to guide his/her own behavior. The infant uses his/her imitative facility to engage in more socially appropriate ways such as repeating a dinner scene with a tea set or dressing a doll. By this time these examples of deferred imitation may not be imitative at all; their continued display in the absence of a model would mark them as true assimilations, "in which the world is fitted to what the child already knows" (Bates, 1979). The child will capitalize on his/her mastery by trying variations on a theme (e.g., using a block as a telephone receiver), displaying actions never seen before.

Cognition and Language

Over the past decade the study of language has extended downward through the developmental period to the point where language has not even yet emerged. Primarily researchers have developed strong interests in isolating cognitive prerequisites of emerging language skills (Bates, 1979).

Piaget and others (Bruner, 1974/1975; Nelson, 1973; Sinclair-deZwart, 1969, 1971; Slobin, 1973) stress the infant's dealings with objects and the way s/he organizes them cognitively as some of the central components which foster beginning language. Nelson (1974) and Kessen and Nelson (1978) have proposed three cognitive achievements which are necessary conditions for language: (1) The infant must be able to form schemas that represent whole objects in context, (2) the schemas must maintain themselves in the absence of that which they represent, and (3) the infant must be able to expand the schemas to include new instances (assimilation). The former two conditions become readily apparent as the child moves through the different phases of the object concept. The third case, concept formation, also finds its expression beginning in the latter part of the first year (Starkey, Note 9) and becomes quite evident by 18 months (Riccuiti, 1965).

Initially the child's first utterances reveal that his/her mental representations are tied to some actual feature of the named object. Thus we hear the signs, *woo-woo* for dog and *hot* for stove. When the infant has acquired true object concept skills (i.e., symbolic thought), s/he can employ arbitrary verbalizations that do not depend upon specific characteristics of an object.

In spite of the sensibility of arguing for such cognitive primacy, the actual evidence has been equivocal. Bates, Benigni, Bretherton, Camaioni, and Volterra (1977) were unable to find any significant correlations between object permanence and nine language measures. However they did find correlations with the cognitive measures of means-ends, imitation, and play. Corrigan also failed to find any correlation between object permanence and language level. As Bates et al. (1979) caution, however, such correlational information which relies on sequential onset of developmental abilities is fraught with interpretive difficulties. The lack of clear support for cognitive prerequisites may be due to several reasons. First and foremost the cognitive domains may be, in and of themselves, difficult to integrate. Indeed Uzgiris and Hunt (1975) found a definite lack of correlation among many cognitive measures, so it is not surprising to see that the same would hold for assessment between developmental areas. Second, and on a more discrete level, varying task demands for cognitive performance may preclude the validity of defining what is being measured. Third, as Nelson (1979) has emphasized, correlational studies rely too heavily on language production instead of comprehension which does depend on representational ability and yet precedes expression by approximately six months. If her argument were accepted, naming would tend to occur before object permanence in development.

The problem in understanding the cognition-language interplay lies in the use of the term *prerequisite*. Instead of saying that certain cognitive achievements are necessary for language, it would be more helpful, at the present, to step back and state that there are shared underlying structures with particular features in each domain increasing at varying rates. The problem, then, is to test infants on more subtle changes in their growth and at key points in time in order to achieve a better sense of their connection (Bates et al., 1979).

CONCLUSIONS

An attempt has been made to present an overall picture of some of the major cognitive steppingstones throughout the infancy period. A central thesis of this chapter has been to go beyond mere description and, more importantly, to alert the reader to the differing opinions of researchers in each of the areas. Piaget has done much over the past thirty years to alter completely our ideas about infants. Most significantly he has shown us that their mental processes can be ordered in a hierarchical sequence which assumes progressively greater awareness of outside events with concomitant sophistication in integrating schemas. Through his presentation of sensorimotor stages, Piaget has provided developmental psychologists with concepts that they have strived to refine through larger numbers of children, controlled experimentation, and the latest findings in related areas such as memory and perception. Because of the complexity of the issues, and the relative newness of the field, our understanding stands at a middle level—advanced from where we stood in the 1960s during which infancy was just coming into its own as a legitimate area of study, but far from consolidation.

Ambitious researchers endeavor to give us fresh models and theories of infant cognition that make use of all the information gathered thus far (Fischer, 1980; Kagan, 1976; McCall, 1976, 1979), and they will certainly generate even more advanced research.

Because of the ambiguity in the area, attempts to relate cognitive development to other areas (e.g., social, language) must be viewed as preliminary, although crucial. Unquestionably a detailed examination of an infant's evolving personality, for instance, would be deficient if it did not include some acknowledgement of the infant's or child's ever-changing intellectual capabilities and his/her potential influences. On the other hand, future investigations have much to gain from incorporating the findings of those "soft" areas (e.g., emotional development, parental attitudes) into the understanding of how infants acquire cognitive competence.

REFERENCE NOTES

1. Salapetak, P. *Visual investigation of geometric pattern by the human infant.* Paper presented at the meeting of the Society for Research in Child Development, Philadelphia, 1973.

2. Super, C. M. *Long term memory in infancy.* Doctoral dissertation, Harvard University, 1972.

3. Evans, W. F. *The stage IV error in Piaget's theory of object concept development: An investigation of the role of activity.* Unpublished dissertation, University of Houston, 1973.

4. Butterworth, G. *Logical competence in infancy: Object percept or object concept?* Paper presented at the meeting of the Society for Research in Child Development, San Francisco, 1979.

5. DeLoache, J. S. *A naturalistic study of memory for object location in very young children.* Paper presented at the meeting of the Society for Research in Child Development, San Francisco, 1979.

6. Zelazo, P. R., & Kearsley, R. B. *Functional play: Evidence for a cognitive metamorphosis in the year-old infant.* Paper presented at the meeting of the Society for Research in Child Development, New Orleans, 1977.

7. McQuiston, S., & Wachs, T. D. *Developmental changes in the nature of infants' exploratory behavior.* Paper presented at the meeting of the Society for Research in Child Development, San Francisco, 1979.

8. Adams, K., Mitchell, D., Mount, R., Reznick, D., & Richman, C. L. *The consequences of failing to imitate.* Paper presented at the Society for Research in Child Development, San Francisco, 1979.

9. Starkey, D. *The origins of concept formation: Object sorting and object preference in early infancy.* Paper presented at the Society for Research in Child Development, San Francisco, 1979.

10. Corrigan, R. *The relationship between object permanence and language development: How much and how strong?* Paper presented at the Eighth Annual Stanford Child Language Forum, Stanford, April 1975.

REFERENCES

AINSWORTH, M. D. The development of infant-mother attachment. In B. Caldwell & H. Riccuiti (Eds.), *Review of child development and research* (Vol. 3). Chicago: University of Chicago Press, 1973.

AMSTERDAM, B. Mirror self-image reactions before age two. *Developmental Psychobiology*, 1972, 5, 297–305.

BATES, E. (Ed.). *The emergence of symbols: Cognition and communication in infancy.* New York: Academic Press, 1979.

BATES, E., BENIGNI, L., BRETHERTON, I., CAMAIONI, L., & VOLTERRA, V. From gesture to the first word: On cognitive and social prerequisites. In M. Lewis & L. Rosenblum (Eds.), *Interaction, conversation, and the development of language.* New York: John Wiley, 1977.

BOWER, T.G.R. Object perception in infants. *Perception*, 1972, 2, 411–418.

BOWER, T.G.R., BROUGHTON, J. M., & MOORE, M. K. Development of the object concept as manifested in the tracking behavior of infants between seven and twenty weeks of age. *Journal of Experimental Child Psychology,* 1971, *11,* 182–193.

BOWER, T.G.R., & PATERSON, J. G. The separation of place, movement, and object in the world of the infant. *Journal of Experimental Child Psychology,* 1973, *15,* 161–168.

BOWER, T.G.R., & WISEHART, J. G. The effects of motor skill on object permanence. *Cognition,* 1972, *1,* 165–172.

BREMNER, J. G., & BRYANT, P. E. Place versus response as the basis of spatial errors made by young infants. *Journal of Experimental Child Psychology,* 1977, *23,* 162–171.

BRUNER, J. S. *Processes of cognitive growth: Infancy.* Worcester, Mass.: Clark University Press, 1968.

BRUNER, J. S. From communication to language—A psychological perspective. *Cognition,* 1974/1975, *3,* 255–287.

BUTTERWORTH, G. Object disappearance and error in Piaget's Stage IV task. *Journal of Experimental Child Psychology,* 1977, *23,* 391–401.

EIMAS, P. D. Speech perception in early infancy. In L. B. Cohen & P. Salapatek (Eds.), *Infant perception: From sensation to cognition* (Vol. 2). New York: Academic Press, 1975.

FISCHER, K. W. A theory of cognitive development: The control and construction of hierarchies of skills. *Psychological Review,* 1980, *87,* 477–531.

FOX, N., KAGAN, J., & WEISKOPF, S. The growth of memory during infancy. *Genetic Psychology Monographs,* 1979, *99,* 91–130.

FRIEDMAN, S. Habituation and recovery of visual response in the alert human newborn. *Journal of Experimental Child Psychology,* 1972, *13,* 339–349.

GRATCH, G. Recent studies based on Piaget's view of object concept development. In L. B. Cohen & P. Salapatek (Eds.), *Infant perception: From sensation to cognition* (Vol. 2). New York: Academic Press, 1975.

GRATCH, G. Review of Piagetian infancy research: Object concept development. In W. F. Overton & J. G. Gallagher (Eds.), *Knowledge and development* (Vol. 1). Advances in research and theory. New York: Plenum, 1977.

GRATCH, G., APPEL, K. J., EVANS, W. F., LeCOMPTE, G. K., & WRIGHT, N. A. Piaget's stage IV object concept error: Evidence of forgetting or object conception? *Child Development,* 1974, *45,* 71–77.

GRATCH, G., & LANDERS, W. F. Stage IV of Piaget's theory of infants' object concepts. *Child Development,* 1971, *42,* 359–372.

HARRIS, L. J., & MACFARLANE, A. The growth of the effective visual field from birth to seven weeks. *Journal of Experimental Child Psychology,* 1974, *18,* 340–348.

HARRIS, P. L. Examination and search in infants. *British Journal of Psychology,* 1971, *62,* 469–473.

HARRIS, P. L. Perseverative errors in search by young children. *Child Development,* 1973, *44,* 28–33.

KAGAN, J. *Change and continuity in infancy.* New York: John Wiley, 1971.

KAGAN, J. Emergent themes in human development. *American Scientist,* 1976, *64,* 186–196.

KAGAN, J. Structure and process in the human infant: The ontogeny of mental representation. In M. H. Bornstein & W. Kessen (Eds.), *Psychological development from infancy: Image to intention.* Hillsdale, N.J.: Lawrence Erlbaum Associates, 1979.

KAGAN, J., KEARSLEY, R. B., & ZELAZO, P. R. *Infancy: Its place in human development.* Cambridge, Mass.: Harvard University Press, 1978.

KAYE, K. Imitation over a series of trials without feedback: Age six months. *Infant Behavior and Development,* 1978, *1,* 141–155.

KESSEN, W., & NELSON, K. What the child brings to language. In B. Z. Presseisen, D. Goldstein, & M. H. Appel (Eds.), *Topics in cognitive development* (Vol. 2). Language and operational thought. New York: Plenum, 1978.

KESSEN, W., SALAPATEK, P., & HAITH, M. The visual response of the human newborn to linear contour. *Journal of Experimental Child Psychology,* 1972, *13,* 9–20.

KOPP, C. B., SIGMAN, M., & PARMELEE, A. H. Longitudinal study of sensorimotor development. *Developmental Psychology,* 1974, *10,* 687–695.

McCALL, R. B. Toward an epigenetic conception of mental development in the first three years of life. In M. Lewis (Ed.), *Origins of intelligence.* New York: Plenum, 1976.

McCALL, R. B. Qualitative transitions in behavioral development in the first two years of life. In M. H. Bornstein & W. Kessen (Eds.), *Psychological development from infancy: Image to intention.* Hillsdale, N.J.: Lawrence Erlbaum Associates, 1979.

McCALL, R. B., PARKE, R. D., & KAVANAUGH, R. D. Imitation of live and televised models in the first three years of life. *Monographs of the Society for Research in Child Development,* 1977, *42*(5, Whole No. 173).

MAURER, D., & SALAPATEK, P. Developmental changes in the scanning of faces by infants. *Child Development,* 1976, *47,* 523–527.

MELTZOFF, A. N., & MOORE, M. K. Imitation of facial gestures by human neonates. *Science,* 1977, *198,* 75–78.

NELSON, K. Some evidence for the cognitive primacy of categorization and its functional basis. *Merrill-Palmer Quarterly of Behavior and Development,* 1973, *19,* 21–39.

NELSON, K. Concept, word and sentence: Interrelations in acquisition and development. *Psychological Review,* 1974, *81,* 267–285.

NELSON, K. The role of language in infant development. In M. H. Bornstein & W. Kessen (Eds.), *Psychological development from infancy: Image to intention.* Hillsdale, N.J.: Lawrence Erlbaum Associates, 1979.

PIAGET, J. *The origins of intelligence in children.* New York: W. W. Norton & Co., Inc., 1952.

PIAGET, J. *The construction of reality in the child.* New York: Basic Books, 1954.

PIAGET, J. *Play, dreams, and imitation in childhood.* New York: W. W. Norton & Co., Inc., 1962.

PIAGET, J. Problems of equilibration. In M. H. Appel & L. S. Goldberg (Eds.), *Topics in cognitive development* (Vol. 6). Equilibration: Theory research and application. New York: Plenum, 1977.

REISER, J., YONAS, A., & WIKNER, K. Radial localization of odors by human newborns. *Child Development,* 1976, *47,* 856–859.

RICCUITI, H. N. Object grouping and selective ordering in infants 12 to 24 months. *Merrill-Palmer Quarterly,* 1965, *11,* 129–148.

SINCLAIR-deZWART, H. Developmental psycholinguistics. In D. Elkind & J. Flavell (Eds.), *Studies in cognitive development: Essays in honor of Jean Piaget.* New York: Oxford University Press, 1969.

SINCLAIR-deZWART, H. Sensori-motor action patterns as a condition for the acquisition of syntax. In R. Huxley & E. Ingram (Eds.), *Language acquisition: Models and methods.* New York: Academic Press, 1971.

SLOBIN, D. I. Cognitive prerequisites for the development of grammar. In D. I. Slobin & C. Ferguson (Eds.), *Studies of child language development.* New York: Holt, Rinehart & Winston, 1973.

SROUFE, L. A. Wariness of strangers and the study of infant development. *Child Development,* 1977, *48,* 731–746.

SROUFE, L. A., & WATERS. E. Attachment as an organizational construct. *Child Development,* 1977, *48,* 1184–1199.

UNGERER, J. A., BRODY, L. R., & ZELAZO, P. R. Long-term memory for speech in 2- to 4-week-old infants. *Infant Behavior and Development,* 1978, *1,* 177–186.

UZGIRIS, I. C., & HUNT, J. McV. *Assessment in infancy: Ordinal scale of psychological development.* Urbana: University of Illinois Press, 1975.

WERNER, H. *Comparative psychology of mental development.* Chicago: Follett, 1948.

WERNER, H. The concept of development from a comparative and organismic point of view. In O. B. Harris (Ed.), *The concept of development.* Minneapolis: University of Minnesota Press, 1957.

WERNER, J. S., & PERLMUTTER, M. Development of visual memory in infants. In H. W. Reese & L. P. Lipsitt (Eds.), *Advances in child development and behavior* (Vol. 14). New York: Academic Press, 1979.

Childhood

PART THREE

19

The Development
of Cognitive Skills
during Childhood

SCOTT G. PARIS
BARBARA K. LINDAUER

As children investigate the world around them, they acquire cognitive skills for gathering and organizing new knowledge. We can observe these information-handling skills in many situations where children pay attention, recall, and solve problems strategically. However it would be uncommon to find preschoolers scrutinizing task demands, reflecting on possible solution paths, generating multiple strategies, or monitoring their own progress to achieve particular goals. Yet we would not be surprised to notice such planful activities in a 12-year-old and certainly would expect adults to regulate thinking systematically. The processes involved in learning how to learn, both deliberately and efficiently, have been the focus of considerable research in American psychology and are fundamental to children's cognitive development. In this chapter we shall provide a summary of research on some representative cognitive skills that develop during childhood. Many of these skills reveal common accomplishments with age in expanding repertoires of strategies, increasing selectivity and planfulness, and a growing awareness of the skills themselves. These trends and some potential factors underlying skill development will be described.

AN ILLUSTRATION OF AGE-RELATED CHANGES IN ATTENTIONAL STRATEGIES

As a starting point let us consider the strategies that children acquire for allocating attention selectively and systematically. When presented with an array of pictures and asked to name the items, children between 3 and 11 years of age become progressively better and faster at scanning the pictures exhaustively, focusing on salient

information, and decreasing errors (Day, 1975). A similar developmental pattern is observed when children are asked to compare and judge the identity of two pictures that differ slightly. Vurpillot and Ball (1979) recorded children's eye movements in such paired-comparison tasks and found that four-year-olds did not examine all features of the pictures systematically while six- to nine-year-olds did. Before the age of five salient aspects of the pictures capture children's attention. They seldom differentiate among components (Hale, 1979) or selectively attend to specific features in a strategic fashion.

After age six to seven there is a shift to cognitive control of attention so that children act less precipitously and more reflectively. For example attention can be directed more effectively if relevant stimulus features are noted beforehand. When second- and sixth-graders were asked to match animal pictures on the basis of size, color, or shape, only older children responded faster and more accurately when the comparative dimension was specified before viewing the pictures (Pick & Frankel, 1973, 1974). The poorer performance of young children in directing attention and visual scanning is not simply an inability to understand the stimuli but appears to be a failure in imposing a strategic organization on the task (Day, 1975).

In addition to increasing selectivity there are developmental trends in the dispositions to pick up more useful information from stimulus components and to tailor attention to the task demands (Hale, 1979). Older children adjust their strategies to the task goal more readily than young children and understand not only *how* to attend selectively but also *when* it is advantageous (Hagen & Hale, 1973). Wright and Vliestra (1975) characterized the development of selective attention as a shift from stimulus-bound exploration to internally controlled logical search behavior that includes strategic regulation.

By age 6 or 7, a child still explores novel environments erratically and still executes highly familiar search routines rigidly on many occasions, but he begins to demonstrate a sharper discrimination between occasions for playful exercise of curiosity through exploration and those in which organized search will achieve a more or less recognizable goal. He begins to appreciate the advantages of keeping track of where he has looked and where he has not. He begins to exhaust the logical possibilities by looking everywhere once before he looks anywhere twice. He is at first inept in inventing search routines and applying them to new situations, but in a variety of tasks he seems much more organized and much less distractable. (p. 200)

The acquisition and use of attentional strategies varies among children and is not always indexed clearly by age alone. Low-achieving students in the classroom and impulsive children often fail to maintain visual contact on the task, fail to monitor their own attention, underestimate task demands, and fail to mobilize sufficient effort or strategies (Piontkowski & Calfee, 1979; Zelniker & Jeffrey, 1979). Many of these deficiencies have been traced to self-attributions of failure, low motivation, and the lack of personal relevance of the task. Fortunately children's understanding and use of attentional strategies can often be improved through training.

However, the development of systematic attentional strategies involves more than direct instruction. Children must learn to analyze task dimensions, coordinate special activities with particular goals, and monitor their own performance—all of which may be influenced by their level of conceptual development. Gibson and Rader (1979) summarized several factors that are crucial for skill development in attention and perception as:

(1) the degree of match between the information extracted from ongoing events . . . and its utility for the task of the perceiver; (2) the nature and specificity of the goals, task-sets, and expectations of the perceiver-performer; (3) the alternative means that are available and the strategic quality of choosing an alternative; (4) the extent to which the task of the perceiver is in tune with his needs; that is, the extent to which attention is self-directed and to what extent other-directed; and (5) the extent to which information, alternative modes of action, and the task can be economically organized as a single structure. (p. 20)

OLD PROBLEMS AND NEW INTERPRETATIONS

The development of attention exemplifies an enduring issue in psychology: How do children acquire and use knowledge-building skills? Before the age of five or so, children's attention, problem solving, and reasoning seem captured by characteristics of the stimuli, and they rarely impose organization on the task as an attempt to guide and regulate behavior. Although development is continuous, there is a marked shift in cognitive functioning between five and seven years of age that has been described in several different ways.

The most well-known description of the infamous five-to-seven shift may be the Piagetian transition from preoperational to concrete operational thinking when children overcome the limitations of egocentrism, centration, and irreversibility. More generally the shift has

been characterized as perceptual to conceptual reasoning (Werner, 1961). Kendler and Kendler (1962) hypothesized that preschoolers respond to perceptual similarities and reinforcement probabilities while school-aged children use language to mediate problem solving. Vygotsky (1962) also argued that speech becomes internalized between three and seven years of age and becomes a symbolic tool that is instrumental in representing, planning, and regulating actions. Soviet proposals stress the development of intentional and voluntary cognitive skills in childhood that evolve from social interactions and eventually become internalized and automatic. White (1965) proposed that preschoolers use fast, associative responses while a cognitive level of reasoning develops to inhibit associative responses and to process information more slowly and deliberately after age seven.

These various proposals emphasize a cognitive shift during childhood to self-controlled, intentional, and systematic problem solving and have led to considerable research on children's acquisition of cognitive strategies. As children develop strategies for attending, remembering, and studying, they also show a growing awareness of their own thinking skills, especially after age seven to eight. Metacognitive understanding of how, when, and why to use cognitive strategies accompanies the deliberate regulation of children's cognitive resources (Brown, 1978). In some situations awareness may be the consequence of learning while in others it may stimulate children's construction of general information-processing skills. Although metacognition is not equivalent to, nor responsible for all of, cognitive development, we believe that it is important for children's skill learning, and it is an underlying theme of this chapter.

METACOGNITIVE DEVELOPMENT DURING CHILDHOOD

Metacognition refers to knowledge we have about people's mental states, abilities, and processes of behavioral regulation. It includes our understanding of task goals and the strategies that are useful for accomplishing different purposes. Information of this sort is often conscious and deliberate and would include realizations such as, "I should write that phone number down or else I'll forget it," "I had better reread this paragraph to understand the author's point," and "I don't think that I'll pursue this task because it is too difficult or boring." Unfortunately metacognition has not been defined operationally or conceptually in a uniform manner among researchers but, instead, has been defined by such prototypical examples for particular situations. Flavell's (1978) pioneering work has grouped metacognitive variables according to three categories: knowledge about people, tasks, and strategies. Examples of each variable are realizing that you do not understand or know a bit of information, knowing that it is easier to remember a list of related rather than randomly paired words, and knowing that underlining important sentences helps reading comprehension.

Despite the lack of a rigorous definition, research on children's metacognition appears to be a promising avenue for interpreting, synthesizing, and integrating diverse data on children's learning and cognitive development. Understanding how to use cognitive strategies and how to apply them selectively in the face of various task conditions appears to lead to both self-controlled and generalized use of cognitive skills. For example, the selective and systematic use of attentional strategies in childhood is accompanied by increased understanding of the factors that affect attention. Miller and Bigi (1979) questioned first-, third-, and fifth-grade children about their abilities to pay attention, avoid distractions, conduct visual searches, and so forth. While younger children believed that attention was primarily determined by the noise level of situations, older children attributed attention to internal psychological characteristics such as motivation, mental effort, and resistance to temptation. Thus awareness of how to control and direct attention develops concurrently with selective, systematic strategies.

In the following review of empirical studies, we try to point out the similarities in children's metacognitive understanding of person, task, and strategy variables that accompanies the development of cognitive skills across many domains. We believe that the developmental trends in strategy acquisition, mediation, intentionality, and cognitive control reflect changes in children's metacognitive *evaluation, planning,* and *regulation* of their own thinking skills. Much of the research during the last ten years on children's cognitive development reveals progressive reflectivity and self-control of cognition for memory, reading, attention, and language. Each of these cognitive skills has sometimes been amended with the prefix *meta* in current studies to indicate the investigator's concern for children's awareness and understanding of their own processes. We believe that these similarities reflect more than faddish labels and point to common accomplishments across domains that may characterize cognitive development generally in middle childhood. Our purpose is not to substantiate *meta* labels as viable constructs but rather to synthesize some recurring trends into a coherent developmental characterization. Because of the enormous literature on children's thinking, we have been deliberately selective and have chosen to review only four topics—*memory, reading, communication,* and *social cognition*—where the importance of metacognitive development is readily apparent. The interested reader can find further evidence about the relationship of metacognition and cognitive skills in provocative volumes by Hale and Lewis (1979), Resnick (1976), and Siegler (1978).

MEMORY SKILLS

Preschoolers' Memory Abilities

Although the ability to remember past experience is evident from early infancy onward, some aspects of memory reveal more striking developmental changes than others. Recognition memory, for example, is highly accurate throughout childhood. In general tasks that involve stimulus items of low meaningfulness and do not require special strategies (e.g., judgments of recency) reveal slight performance changes during childhood (Brown, 1975). Even though the basic processing functions and storage capacity of memory seem well established by early childhood (Flavell, 1977; Morrison,

Holmes, & Haith, 1974), research has revealed significant developmental changes in children's memory when (1) the information is new or unfamiliar, (2) the task involves intentional memorization as the goal, (3) encoding and retrieval strategies are required to organize the information, and (4) modification of study or recall behaviors are necessitated by changing task demands. In short one would expect to find poor performance of young children whenever self-guided strategies, plans, and reflection could be used to adjust customary behavior as an aid to memory.

Preschoolers rarely use mnemonic strategies to aid remembering and instead rely on their natural activities and understanding of object-event relations to mediate recall. They may not even realize that the instruction "to remember" is an implicit invitation to be planful and strategic, and even if they do have this intention, they may not know how to fulfill it. Appel, Cooper, McCarrell, Sims-Knight, Yussen, and Flavell (1972) showed pictures to four-, seven-, and eleven-year-olds under two instructional conditions: "to look at the pictures" or "to remember the pictures." The four-year-olds behaved the same way with both instructions while older children employed study strategies when trying to remember. Myers and Perlmutter (1978) concluded from their study of memory development from two to five years that,

There was little evidence of planful, deliberate, strategic deployment of memory processes or age-related increases in strategy utilization in the age range studied. Probably as the naturalistic memory demands on the child become more extensive, he develops deliberate then planful ways that permit him to control and utilize the full gamut of memory operations potentially available. (p. 215)

However there is an important difference between being naive and being ignorant. Preschoolers can use strategies to aid recall but appear to do so only when the strategy requires an external response or aid that is highly familiar to them within the task. Preschoolers will touch, point, and look at a cup concealing a hidden object in order to remember it (Wellman, Ritter, & Flavell, 1975) and will use spatial landmarks in trying to recall where someone lost an object (Acredolo, Pick, & Olsen, 1975). Young children know that writing something on a note, tying a string around your finger, or better yet, having Mommy remind you are memory aids. Wellman (1977) has shown that three- and four-year-olds understand some of the task and strategy variables that affect memory, albeit in a crude and unsophisticated fashion.

The problem seems to be remembering novel information for its own sake when artificial strategies are required or the goal is unclear. Perhaps the most striking example of the effect of "naturalness" on memory in young children was provided by Istomina (1975). She required three- to seven-year-olds to remember a list of five words under two different conditions. In one condition children were playing a game of grocery store and had to remember the items so that they could purchase them. In the other condition children were simply told to learn and remember the items. Children recalled nearly twice as many items in the game-playing situation as in the list-learning condition. Istomina argued that the purposefulness of the child's task must be natural and motivating and that children "must not only know what remembering is by itself, but also be able to see it as an end result, an objective to which activity must be directed, i.e., to grasp it as a goal" (Istomina, 1975, p. 59).

Memory Strategies in Middle Childhood

The most documented aspect of children's memory development is the dramatic increase in the use of mnemonic strategies to aid encoding and retrieval. Since several excellent reviews are available (Brown, 1975; Kail & Hagen, Chap. 20, this volume; Ornstein, 1978), we shall summarize the findings briefly and focus more on possible explanations for the development of strategy use.

Rehearsal Strategies. Flavell, Beach, and Chinsky (1966) presented pictures to five-, seven-, and ten-year-old children and asked them to remember several over a brief delay. During the interval a visor was lowered over the children's eyes, and the experimenter recorded lip movements as indications of labeling and rehearsal. Few of the five-year-olds spontaneously rehearsed the picture names while most of the older children did. In a follow-up study Keeney, Cannizzo, and Flavell (1967) taught strategy nonproducers to rehearse in a similar situation. Recall improved significantly when the children used instructed rehearsal, but on a subsequent trial without instructions, most children failed to generate rehearsal spontaneously. While young children could utilize the strategy to improve recall, they did not internalize and maintain using it without explicit directions.

It is not just the frequency of rehearsal that changes with age. Ornstein and Naus (1978) demonstrated that third-graders tend to rehearse only two or three items together while eighth-graders rehearse four or five items as a unit. There is a shift with age toward cumulative rehearsal that reveals active restructuring of the information to be recalled (Cuvo, 1975). The consequence of rehearsing more items, in larger and more varied units, is better recall. Ornstein and Naus (1978) suggest that active rehearsal generated by children provides organization of the stimuli and thus functions as a "plan" to consolidate information. When stimuli are presented together as blocked category members, when active rehearsal sets are obtained through training, or when stable rehearsal sets are established through practice, recall is comparably high across ages. The crucial developmental change is the planful construction of organized sets of items which are then rehearsed as a means for later retrieval.

Organizational Strategies. When words to be remembered are grouped by category membership or associations or when pictures are presented as a unitized scene, memory is better than when the stimuli are presented as unrelated items. Young children can capitalize on existing stimulus relationships among items to aid memory but often fail to provide or generate such unifying relations spontaneously. Consider a typical task used to test children's organizational strategies. Twenty pictures or words are shown to children (five items in each of four categories) and they are asked to study and remember them. Before the age of nine or ten, children typically display little reorganization of the stimuli into consistent

categories or groups (Neimark, Slotnick, & Ulrich, 1971). When young children are directed to group items or when their sorting patterns are yoked to adult groupings (Liberty & Ornstein, 1973), recall improves dramatically. However they fail to generate and maintain effective organizational strategies on their own.

Elaboration and Inference. Children's memory is also improved when pairs of words are elaborated into sentences or when the words are accompanied by instructions to form interactive or distinctive images. Children can utilize elaborated relationships to remember words and pictures, but they do not employ efficient strategies without prompting. Inferring additional relationships from sentences and stories reveals a similar developmental pattern. When children hear sentences such as, "The workman dug a hole in the ground" or "My brother fell down on the playground," they are unlikely to infer the implied instruments and consequences and are unable to use them as retrieval cues until nine or ten years of age. However when younger children are forced to infer the relations by acting out the sentences or making up stories about the sentences, memory for the sentences improves significantly (Paris & Lindauer, 1976; Paris, Lindauer, & Cox, 1977). In general young children often process information at a literal level and fail to infer elaborated relationships as a strategy to aid comprehension and memory, although they can use elaboration to mediate recall when it is provided.

Pervasive Production Deficiencies

We could continue to catalogue young children's strategy failures, but the point is evident here and in other reviews. Before the age of nine or ten, on many memory tasks, children do not construct effective strategies that transform and reorganize information into consolidated chunks or units. They can profit from such relations when they are inherent in the stimuli or when directed to use appropriate strategies. Flavell (1970) characterized this general problem as a *production deficiency* because it seemed to indicate a failure to produce a relevant activity rather than an inability to use the activity to mediate memory. However *production deficiencies* is only a nominal description, and a sketchy, negative one at that. We have little evidence about how children remember everyday events, the actions they normally use, or how they overcome their deficiencies.

Several hypotheses have been offered for remediating production deficiencies, including knowledge and awareness. Children's increasingly sophisticated knowledge base permits more concepts, rules, and schemata to mediate recall (Piaget & Inhelder, 1973). Chi (1978) has shown that knowledge and expertise drive certain memory strategies. In her study, children who were expert chess players were superior to adults in recalling the arrangements of chess pieces on a board, given that the arrangements represented plausible game moves. A second factor correlated with the development of memory strategies is *metamemory* or awareness of the variables that influence remembering. Between 5 and 12 years of age, children show dramatic changes in their understanding of task parameters and generation of plans for remembering (Flavell & Wellman, 1977). Unfortunately we do not have a clear picture of if, how, or when metamemory stimulates the development of memory strategies, and the issue requires further study. Initial attempts to increase children's memory abilities by increasing awareness have been disappointing, although training awareness has been useful when embedded in other behavioral interventions (Brown, 1978; Meichenbaum & Asarnow, 1978).

While memory capacity, knowledge, task familiarity, practice, and awareness are all correlated with memory development, we still do not have a satisfactory account of why children overcome production deficiencies and learn to use mnemonic strategies effectively. Part of the problem may be that simplified experimental paradigms have made us look for uncomplicated explanations. The overwhelming experimental concentration has been on what children do (or do not) rather than on why they choose some strategies or activities over others. In the typical laboratory experiment, memory is the sole purpose of the task, and the strategies may appear contrived and unnatural to children. The key word here is "natural" since children most often fail to use "unnatural" strategies for "unnatural" purposes. Recall Istomina's demonstration of superior memory in a play situation as opposed to a list-learning task. Rarely do experimenters measure the child's purpose, goal, or perceived value of the strategy used in memory tasks. We would like to mention a few examples of such studies that suggest reasons for young children's production deficiencies in terms of the child's choices and expectations about the purpose of the task and the strategy employed.

Children's Perceptions of Memory Tasks and Strategies

According to the Soviet view of memory development as exemplified by Istomina's study, memory arises as an involuntary action in the service of other goals and, in later childhood, functions as a goal in itself (Smirnov & Zinchenko, 1969). We have, however, virtually no direct information on how children of different ages interpret memory tasks and adopt memory goals. Indirect evidence suggests that young children interpret instructions to remember as directions to reiterate the output in a rote and literal manner (Paris, 1978b). Young children may not perceive the need to use any strategy or choose to use familiar strategies rather than more effective but foreign activities.

One reason that young children may not adopt experimenter-provided strategies after brief training is that they do not completely understand the utility or benefits of the actions. Kennedy and Miller (1976) demonstrated this by providing informative feedback to one group of young children trained to rehearse the names of pictures. In essence the feedback told children that rehearsal was responsible for improving memory and that it was an effective mediator. Children who received this information continued to use rehearsal without prompting on a subsequent trial while a no-feedback group abandoned the instructed strategy.

The key to enhanced durability and internalization of memory strategies is awareness of the strategy benefits and not just awareness of the technique's existence. Borkowski, Levers, and Gruenenfelder (1976) demonstrated

that children four to seven years of age were most likely to learn and generalize a strategy after viewing a model use it successfully. Children were trained in the use of an elaboration strategy for recalling paired associates in a passive observation, active manipulation, or an active condition that involved viewing a filmed model use elaboration while the experimenter commented on the utility of the strategy during the film. The last condition led to the highest levels of transfer after a two-week interval, and the authors interpreted the results as increasing children's awareness about the value of elaboration as a recall aid. Procedures such as feedback and modeling tell the child *why*, and not just *how*, to use a given strategy and thereby provide a rationale for future action. The procedures allow the child to attach personal significance and value to the strategy which may be crucial for internalized, spontaneous generation of the actions.

When the utility of the instructed strategy is not apparent to subjects, they may choose familiar actions that they believe are effective. Cox and Paris (1979) observed that fourth-graders when given a random list of categorically related words reported that saying the words over and over would be the best study technique. They subsequently used rehearsal and rated it more highly than other strategies such as grouping and elaboration. Even those children instructed in the use of categorization strategies rated rehearsal as a more effective strategy and said they would elect to use rehearsal as a future study activity on a similar task. Children choose to use familiar strategies that they believe are effective, and simple exposure to or brief practice with a more sophisticated strategy may not change their beliefs about what mnemonic techniques lead to good recall.

We want to mention cross-cultural investigations of memory because the explanations for developmental and cross-cultural production deficiencies are strikingly similar. As Cole and Scribner (1977) note in their summary of previous research, uneducated people from non-Western cultures do not use or learn mnemonic strategies such as clustering easily. Instead they rely on external or culturally specific memory aids (e.g., poems, songs, knotting, carved sticks) and do not benefit from training on internal mnemonics. Cole and Scribner (1977) suggest that the reason for these production deficiencies in other cultures is the unnaturalness of the tasks and strategies, where the value of the strategy is not apparent and where the goal of remembering for its own sake is unfamiliar.

The kind of cultural experience that promotes better understanding about memory skills seems to be formal schooling. Deliberate memorization is a common activity in schools, and the task demands of schooling may provide the practice and motivation for the development of mnemonic strategies. The overwhelming finding from cross-cultural investigations is that educated subjects remember significantly more information than uneducated subjects when specialized memory strategies are required (Wagner, 1978).

In summary preschool children's memory is usually guided by their world knowledge and natural activities. After five to six years of age, actions can be employed deliberately as memory strategies with social prompting. Yet practice, schooling, and training may be required for the internalization of sophisticated mnemonic techniques. There is a dramatic increase in children's repertoires of available strategies, awareness, and spontaneous access to skills from 5 to 12 years of age. Part of this process involves coordination of special activities with memory goals in academic settings through which children develop an appreciation of the benefits of memory strategies.

READING

Reading as Applied Cognition

Reading is a deliberate cognitive activity that involves perception, attention, memory, and evaluative thinking applied to specific goals in strategic and often conscious manners. It is "thought-getting" (Huey, 1968), "reflective thinking" (Dewey, 1910), a "psycholinguistic guessing-game" (Goodman, 1976), and a stimulus for readers to construct ideas out of their own experience (Horn, 1937). Reading effectively involves awareness and the construction of plans so that the reader recognizes the essential ideas presented, reflects on their significance, evaluates them critically, discovers relationships between them, and clarifies understanding of the text.

Current research on reading development and differences between good and poor readers has concentrated on the use of decoding, comprehension, and study strategies, but many cognitive differences between beginning/poor versus accomplished readers may lead to performance differences on almost any task we present. Observed performance differences on an experimenter-selected task or strategy does not imply that mastery of a single strategy is the only or primary problem for beginning/poor readers nor does it insure that remediation of that deficiency will be a necessary or sufficient condition for reading improvement. With this constraint in mind and with a similar conceptual and methodological orientation observed in memory development research, we shall review studies that have described strategy differences among children of various reading abilities. These strategies involve literal decoding, comprehension monitoring, and planning for study and memory. In general immature readers display less understanding and use of reading strategies than accomplished readers. Although some studies have compared young and older children and others good and poor readers, we shall not distinguish these two developmental indices. The manifestation of strategies may be similar, but the etiologies and interventions can be quite different.

Decoding Strategies

Perhaps the fundamental paradox in reading disabilities is that some children can pronounce words but show little understanding of what they read. Literal decoding (or word calling) is characteristic of both beginning and poor readers, and as Golinkoff (1976) noted in her review, it seems to be the major purpose of reading for these children. Smith (1975) suggested that poor readers adopt decoding goals of word pronunciation and do not seem to expect or care if the material makes sense. Ryan (1979) and others have suggested that poor readers (1) devote all their attention and effort to decoding, (2) do not understand the constructive purposes of reading, and

(3) have few strategies available as deliberate aids for reading. Let's consider some representative problems.

Poor readers often fail to use grammatical structure as an aid for processing and learning sentences. Vogel (1974) compared dyslexic and normal second-graders on nine measures of oral syntax and found that dyslexic children were significantly inferior on tests such as oral cloze, sentence repetition, and morphological rules. When poor readers are compared with good readers on memory tests for meaningful or grammatically related lists of words and phrases, poor readers usually fail to show a memory superiority for the organized list (Weinstein & Rabinovitch, 1971), particularly when subjects are required to read the stimuli (Guthrie & Tyler, 1976). Steiner, Wiener, and Cromer (1971) asked good and poor readers from fifth grade to read aloud sentences as they self-presented words sequentially on a machine and found that only good readers grouped words into grammatical phrases and units. Similarly Clay and Imlach (1971) observed that only the best seven-year-old readers imposed juncture, pitch, and stress at intersentence and phrase levels during oral reading. Thus using grammatical organization as an aid for reading appears to be an infrequent strategy for less skilled readers.

Poor readers' concentration on single words is evident from other research, too. Analyses of eye-voice span during reading indicates that poor readers' span is approximately one word, while good readers have a significantly longer span that implies a scan-for-meaning search across word boundaries. As might be expected poor readers do not use surrounding context strategically as an aid for decoding or meaning construction. Studies by Cromer and Wiener (1966) and Neville and Pugh (1976) demonstrated that poor readers provide fewer correct words in cloze tasks and are not attentive to grammatical and meaning constraints on the missing words. Samuels, Begy, and Chen (1975) found that fourth-grade poor readers were less able to supply missing words from context, and, importantly, they were less aware of when their answer was incorrect. Thus poor readers do not use strategies as aids for organizing, scanning, or interpreting sentence meaning and instead concentrate on pronouncing individual words. These strategy deficiencies are similar to production deficiencies in memory research since rote processing reflects a lack of the inclination to apply strategies rather than the inability to do so (Ryan, 1979).

Comprehension Strategies

A major component of reading is monitoring the meaning of the author's message. Concentration on word decoding alone may interfere with comprehension monitoring, and poor readers should be expected to use monitoring strategies less often. Young children do not monitor meaning while listening very often and frequently believe that they have understood ambiguous or incomplete messages (Karabenick & Miller, 1977), incomprehensible instructions (Markman, 1977), and contradictory information (Markman, 1979). Young children show similar difficulties while reading and do not evaluate their own understanding well (Forrest & Waller, 1979). For example Isakson and Miller (1976) found that fourth-grade poor readers were not disrupted in their oral reading by the substitution of inappropriate words within sentences. Even when given instructions to underline words that did not make sense in a passage, poor readers from fourth grade were significantly worse than good readers at noticing nonsense words and scrambled clauses while they read (Paris & Myers, 1981).

Good readers attend to meaning and have tactics for keeping track of the sense of the message. One good method is to notice and correct one's own errors. Clay (1973) oberved that good readers spontaneously corrected their own grammatical and semantic errors significantly more often than poor readers during oral reading. Furthermore the rate of self-correction was highly predictive of reading progress in early elementary grades. Kavale and Schreiner (1979) compared average and above-average sixth-grade readers and found that average readers often distorted the passage meaning while reading and were less likely to correct their errors.

Beginning and poor readers do not evaluate their own understanding well nor do they spontaneously invoke tactics for regulating their comprehension. Inadequate self-correction is one example and examining the passage context is another. DiVesta, Hayward, and Orlando (1979) found that poor readers from sixth, seventh, and eighth grades were less efficient than good readers at searching story context to identify missing words in a cloze task. Forrest and Waller (1979) reported that young and poor readers (from third or sixth grade) were unable to adjust their reading strategies for different purposes when instructed to read for fun, to make up a title, to skim, or to study. Thus poor or young readers display few flexible strategies for monitoring and regulating comprehension. A similar picture emerges when we examine children's use of strategies for studying text passages.

Study Strategies

While comprehension monitoring and self-correction are strategies for checking one's understanding and mastery during reading, study strategies serve to insure comprehension and memory in the future. Studying affords self-testing of comprehension and a means for recalling important and goal-relevant ideas as well as an opportunity for critical and evaluative thinking about the information. Studying requires attention to the information as well as to the strategies that will produce effective learning (Locke, 1975), and it is not surprising that young readers have difficulty studying effectively.

In order to study text information, one needs to isolate the important material and ignore irrelevant detail, but until 11 to 12 years of age, children usually cannot select the main ideas in text when directed. Brown and Smiley (1977) found that children below seventh grade could not discriminate important from unimportant sentences in a sentence-rating task. Similarly elementary school children have difficulty identifying the central point of stories (Danner, 1976) and the critical sequences of initiating events-actions-consequences in judgments about stories (Yussen, Mathews, Buss, & Kane, 1980). If they cannot identify and select important information to study, they will be constrained in their apportionment of study time and strategies.

Less successful students do not monitor comprehension nor regulate study behavior accordingly. Owings,

Peterson, Bransford, Morris, and Stein (1980) presented sensible and unusual passages to fifth-graders to study and recall. The lowest quartile of students did not discriminate the different difficulty of the passages in ratings or in study behavior. They could distinguish the two types and spend more time studying difficult passages when explicitly prompted, but they failed to notice and regulate learning strategically and spontaneously. In a similar vein children below the fifth or sixth grade do not use summarization rules such as inventing or selecting topic sentences (Baker & Brown, in press), provide elaborative inferences (Paris & Upton, 1976), or generate good retrieval cues from text (Brown & Campione, 1979). Younger children not only do not adjust their apportionment of study time to fit the task, but they also are less inclined to underline, take notes, and ask questions as study aids (Brown & Smiley, 1978; Paris & Myers, 1981). Throughout the early elementary school grades, children have difficulty spontaneously analyzing task parameters, invoking strategies to check comprehension, and regulating study behaviors for future recall. One major hypothesis for the lack of strategic intervention during reading is the lack of awareness and understanding about reading.

Awareness of Reading Variables

As Gibson (1974) said, "There seems to be a consciousness-raising that goes along with many aspects of cognitive development, and it turns out, I think, to be associated with attaining mature reading skills" (p. 25). In one of the first studies of children's understanding of reading processes, Reid (1966) found that four- and five-year-olds are unaware of the function of print, goals of reading, or component skills. Clay (1973) observed that beginning readers often did not realize that the words rather than the pictures conveyed the information and even seven-year-olds were frequently unaware of how to resolve comprehension failures. In structured interviews of children's understanding of reading variables, striking improvements in children's awareness of reading strategies are observed between 8 and 12 years of age. Older children know that meaning-getting is the goal of reading and decipher incomprehensible information (Myers & Paris, 1978), understand skimming strategies (Kobasigawa, Ransom, & Holland, 1979), and adjust reading strategies to meet different goals (Forrest & Waller, 1979).

Evaluating children's implicit theories about reading through interviews includes many problems. First, the data are only correlational, and it is unclear whether metacognitive understanding follows or stimulates the acquisition of reading strategies. Second, the methods are susceptible to distortion in children's beliefs and reports as well as the interpretation of subjective data. Third, children do read without thorough understanding of the cognitive processes of reading, and it is unclear (1) what strategies they choose to follow or discard before using mature strategies and (2) when awareness is sufficient or necessary for strategic reading and studying. Young and poor readers are not oblivious to reading strategies but instead may *choose* to employ decoding strategies to meet decoding goals. Early practice and instruction are usually consistent with this choice, and only in later childhood are the reading comprehension goals geared toward strategies, awareness, and complex self-monitoring skills.

On the positive side a growing body of evidence suggests that reading skills can be improved through direct instruction. Ryan (1979) suggests two kinds of intervention techniques: (1) cognitive functional training in which students are taught to analyze reading tasks and strategies and then given opportunities for practice and generalization and (2) self-instructional training in which students guide their own learning and adopt internal directions for strategy use. Both techniques increase awareness of when, how, and why to use reading strategies similar to metacognitive training in memory (Brown, 1978) and cognitive behavior modification techniques (Meichenbaum & Asarnow, 1978).

It is interesting to note that cognitive developmental research converges here with classroom teaching practices. Stauffer (1969), in his method of "Directing Reading as a Thinking Activity" advocated (1) identifying purposes of reading, (2) sensitivity to task parameters, (3) using strategies such as skimming, scanning, and critical evaluation, (4) monitoring and observing your own reading, (5) checking, generating, and changing hypotheses as you read, and (6) automating component skills. In all these programs,

the essential aim is to make the reader aware of the active nature of reading and the importance of employing problem-solving, trouble-shooting routines to enhance understanding. If the reader can be made aware of (1) basic strategies for reading and remembering, (2) simple rules of text construction, (3) differing demands of a variety of tests to which his knowledge may be put, and (4) the importance of attempting to use any background knowledge he may have, he cannot help but become a more effective reader. Such self-awareness is a prerequisite for self-regulation, the ability to monitor and check one's own cognitive activities while reading. (Baker & Brown, in press)

CHILDREN'S ORAL COMMUNICATION SKILLS

Dimensions of Communication Development

Verbal communication requires knowledge of the language as well as understanding of rules for social interaction. Children learn how to gain the attention of a listener, adjust their messages to situational constraints, and monitor reciprocal interchanges. The development of these social-cognitive skills is reflected in three general trends: increasing internal control, progressive social reciprocity, and the acquisition of cognitive strategies that expand the child's capacity to communicate.

Before the age of three children's speech is often tied to the immediate context and accompanied by gestures. Gradually children's communications become "decontexualized" (Bruner, 1975), and they begin to make novel contributions to conversations. At the same time children rely less and less on others to initiate and regulate conversation and assume equal partnership in exchanges (Keenan & Klein, 1975). Adults initially provide

communicative directions by "scaffolding" conversations (Bruner, 1975) or providing metacognitive regulation (Wertsch, 1979) and gradually decrease their support as children mature. The burden of initiating and modifying communication shifts from the adult to the child and requires internalization of conversational plans and strategies.

The developmental shift from external to internal control of communication is paralleled by a related trend toward social role reciprocity. When adults do not structure and guide conversations, children have responsibility for regulating interchanges and should converse at appropriate junctures, avoid interrupting others, and respond appropriately to the form and content of other speakers. Researchers generally agree that there is a developmental progression in turn-taking from "role rigid" to "role complementary" exchanges (Mueller & Lucas, 1975). This may begin in infancy when children learn give-and-take games with mothers and how to share, offer, and deprive visual perspectives on objects (Lempers, Flavell, & Flavell, 1977). Although social role-taking begins in infancy, turn-taking in verbal interactions may not be firmly established until age five (Garvey, 1974).

Shatz (1978) notes that a major stumbling block for successful communication in young children is the allocation of limited cognitive resources for meeting multiple and simultaneous demands. She has argued that the Piagetian construct of centration is a strategy for deploying limited attention and skills. The child's cognitive capacities for communication are "stretched" by "the acquisition and routinization of new techniques that make efficient use of limited processing capacity" (Shatz, 1978, p. 42).

Internal control, social reciprocity, and capacity-stretching techniques are interwoven throughout communication development. They are exemplified by the strategies that children acquire for controlling and monitoring communication. We shall review some of those findings briefly, but more thorough discussions can be found in Dickson (1981); Schmidt and Paris (1980); and Whitehurst (Chap. 21, this volume).

Strategies and Plans for Communicating

Children learn to secure the attention of the listener and engage in mutual conversation. Although two-year-olds can use vocatives (e.g., "Mommy, Mommy"), tag questions (e.g., O.K.?), and gestures to signal an intended audience (Bloom & Lahey, 1978; Dore, 1975), children use these strategies in peer conversations infrequently before the age of five (Mueller, Bleier, Krakow, Hegedus, & Cournoyer, 1977; Wellman & Lempers, 1977). Another way of gaining listener acknowledgment is the summons-answer routine (e.g., speaker: "Guess what?"; listener: "What?"; speaker: "I got a new bike yesterday."). Garvey and Hogan (1973) observed an increase in the use of this strategy by age five. Five-year-olds also tend to talk more about the listener's activities than "egocentric" topics (Mueller et al., 1977; Schacter, Kirshner, Klips, Friedricks, & Sanders, 1974). Clearly young children learn a variety of means for engaging the listener in communication.

Another important aspect of achieving communication success is the ability to adjust the message to listener characteristics. Perhaps the most well-known example is that four-year-olds can adapt their speech in content and style to the age of the listener (Shatz & Gelman, 1973, 1977). Similarly Sachs and Devin (1976) found that the speech of three- to five-year-olds was less complex when directed to a baby or a doll than to a peer or a child's mother.

Children have difficulty communicating information to a listener whom they cannot see (in the standard referential communication task) until seven to eight years of age (Glucksberg, Krauss, & Higgins, 1975). However Maratsos (1973) found that preschoolers could recode their messages to blindfolded listeners. Subjects were told to specify which of two toy passengers should be given a ride down a hill. Four- and five-year-olds provided more information to blindfolded than to sighted listeners, while three-year-olds simply refrained from pointing. Maratsos (1973) argued that the task was "natural" for young children, the goal was obvious, and the stimuli were readily discriminable. Thus children could achieve effective communication earlier on this task than on referential communication tasks.

In many studies young children have been observed to recode their messages in accordance with the listener's characteristics and task demands. From three to eight years of age, they acquire strategies for adjusting gestures, message content, and syntactic complexity to the situation and are not generally egocentric in their conversations. By age five, children can alternate turns and attend to the form and content of previous utterances. However, the feedback provided by listeners must be explicit to initiate speaker reformulations of messages (Peterson, Danner, & Flavell, 1972; Spilton & Lee, 1977).

One problem that persists beyond age five, though, is the child's ability to be an effective listener. Listening requires a constant monitoring of the speaker's information, and even elementary school children often seem oblivious to incomplete and inadequate messages (Markman, 1977). Karabenick and Miller (1977) administered a referential communication task to kindergartners, first-graders, and second-graders and found that only 57 percent of listeners' questions were directed at inadequate messages and they accepted and acknowledged 60 percent of inadequate messages; however, when children are provided with a "plan" to ask questions, six- to ten-year-olds monitor the messages more often and provide listener feedback to regulate the conversation (Cosgrove & Patterson, 1977; Patterson, Massad, & Cosgrove, 1978). It is particularly interesting to note that the subjects in Karabenick and Miller's (1977) study had the means available for correcting message inadequacies (they could and did ask questions), but they did not know how to coordinate their question-asking behavior with the goal of disambiguating speaker messages. The plans for feedback in the Patterson studies provided information to the children about what they should do as listeners and when to do it. Awareness of how, why, and when to use strategies is an integral part of communication development.

Cognitive Skills underlying Communication Development

By three or four years of age, children can speak about a listener's activity, expect a response from the listener, recode messages according to listener characteristics, adapt utterances to previous listener remarks, believe that a message is not comprehended by the listener, and attend to and understand speaker utterances. By five years children speak differently in social and nonsocial situations and do not always assume that they have understood another's message; the tendencies to speak for themselves, to fail to provide feedback as listeners, and to fail to respond to another's feedback persist beyond age five however (Schmidt & Paris, 1980). These early communication skills contradict Piaget's (1926) claims about the pervasiveness of egocentric speech prior to six or seven years and reveal developmental trends in internal control, social reciprocity, and strategy acquisition. The accomplishments indicate increased understanding about the goals and actions for achieving reciprocal communicative success (Higgins, 1980). Let us briefly consider how social-cognitive goals and strategies are coordinated during communication development.

Conversations include a motive or *goal*, a *plan*, and a *means* for communicating that represent why, what, and how the participants interact. Linking goals, plans, and means together represents the translation of thought to action in communicative interchanges. Communicative goals are the social and cognitive intentions of the participants, and if these goals are not shared to some extent, prolonged dialogue or interaction is unlikely. It is impossible for all goals to be realized simultaneously, and participants must choose to give precedence to some purposes over others and to monitor the interaction so that various goals can be modified or replaced. The limited capacity to regulate conversation impedes successful (and multiple) goal selection by young children. Early communication goals may simply be to "make something common or shared" (Higgins, 1980), and they may be set primarily by adults within the immediate context. New communicative goals are differentiated with age so that proximity, eye contact, common objects and topics are no longer required for successful interaction. Children begin to initiate new grammatical forms and topic content and can fulfill multiple goals. They also can form mutual goals between listener and speaker that insure social reciprocity.

Communicative goals are implemented via plans for speaking and listening that direct attention and regulation. Young children may learn some of these rules quite early in scaffolded interactions, such as maintaining proximity, eye contact, and attention. Being understood and speaking about relevant topics may take precedence over other plans such as being polite, funny, or accurate. Plans require an understanding of the other person's perspectives, goals, and limitations and require internal control when the situation is not rigorously structured by the audience. As the Patterson studies indicated, children often fail to provide their own plans for regulating conversation, but they can profit from instructions generated by others.

As goals and plans become differentiated and reciprocal, children learn a rich variety of means for communicating. Language development allows more sophisticated speech, and children learn to use summons-answer routines, explicit messages, and questions to gain the listener's attention and comprehension. These new skills stretch the limited capacity of the young child (Shatz, 1978) and allow the child to meet more communication goals in diverse ways. Thus the cognitive skills of forming goals and choosing plans and means to insure communicative success underlie the development of internalized control and social reciprocity evident in childhood.

STRATEGY ACQUISITION AND IMPLICATIONS FOR SOCIAL COGNITION

Our brief review of selected cognitive strategies reveals that children between 3 and 12 years of age acquire a variety of sophisticated techniques for attacking and solving problems. At the risk of simplifying the process too much, we can surmise that preschoolers use few deliberate strategies, show little awareness of task parameters, and do not readily adapt their behavior to novel or changing task demands. Their naturally occurring problem-solving activities gradually become deliberate and goal-directed while the demands of peer interaction, parental teaching, and schooling exert increasing pressure to become a problem analyst and solver. While most five-year-olds can remember, communicate, infer, and solve problems with the support of others, spontaneous and self-controlled cognitive strategies often do not appear until 10 to 12 years of age. Development in related domains, such as number skills and scientific reasoning, confirms this trend, and the global characteristics of the learner are strikingly similar in the broad developmental picture. Cognitive strategies have implications for social understanding, and we want to mention some of the parallel findings from social developmental research.

Children's understanding of social events shares many similarities with Piagetian accounts of cognitive development in other domains. From approximately 3 to 12 years, children overcome the limitations of egocentrism and centration and progressively infer other people's perspectives, roles, and psychological characteristics in an accurate fashion. They learn about enduring social qualities and covert traits and display increased reflection about themselves and others (Flavell, 1977). Most research on social cognition has described what children know about social situations and how developmental improvements in inferences, attributions, role taking, and decentration are correlated with advances in social understanding (Shantz, 1975). Although less work has been done on how social cognition influences social behavior, it is clear that understanding the contingencies that control behavior, within the self and others, leads to self-determination of goals (deCharms, 1976), behavior management and self-regulation (Thoreson & Mahoney, 1974), and accurate attributions (Weiner, 1979). Awareness and experience foster metacognitive development of social skills and a sense of personal causation and self-control. We would like to describe some intriguing findings on children's resistance to temptation as an example of how social-cognitive strategies can influence behavior.

Mischel and Patterson (1978) summarized several studies investigating children's use of plans to reduce distraction and promote concentrated work. Children from three to five years of age were asked to copy or put pegs in a board while a talking, flashing Mr. Clown Box periodically asked the child to "come play with me." In the initial study children were given three plans including instructions to not look at Mr. Clown, keep working, and pretend that the clown could not be seen. These plans were effective in promoting resistance to temptation, partly because they were similar to children's spontaneous behavior in the control condition and were readily verbalized. In follow-up studies Mischel and Patterson found that instructions emphasizing temptation inhibition and positive reward for successful resistance were more effective than plans to keep working. The reasons for the plans' effectiveness appear to be children's beliefs in the utility of the plans for completing work and the provisions of a specific regulating response at the critical point of disruption. For example when Mr. Clown Box pleaded with children, they all looked at the distraction, but children with plans for temptation inhibition quickly returned to working. A final result of these studies is that elaborated plans (i.e., highly specific verbal responses and guides) were effective while unelaborated plans were not. Young children could not provide their own actions or words to meet the intended goal of resistance to temptation and needed explicit plans provided by the experimenter in order to regulate their behavior. Thus effective plans for self-control can be taught to preschoolers when the strategies are natural, explicit, operative at critical points in behavior, and believed to be useful by children.

Flavell (1977) characterized the child's developing social cognition according to three factors: existence, need, and inference. Initially infants and preschoolers develop concepts of themselves and other people: their spatial positions, independent actions, feelings, and intentions. There can hardly be any social reciprocity without awareness of the existence of others' social status. *Need* refers to the inclination to consider another person's social position or feelings when acting. It represents the sensitivity to plan to act in nonegocentric ways. "Inference concerns the skill or capacity to carry off a given form of social thinking successfully" (Flavell, 1977, p. 121). Children's inferences about other people appear predicated on the existence and need to consider mutual perspectives and roles and show dramatic changes from five or six years on. In a subsequent paper Flavell (1979) has speculated that these three factors reflect the interaction of children's metacognitive knowledge and experiences (*existence* and *need*) with their goals and strategies (*inference*). There appears to be a dawning awareness of the need to plan, regulate, and monitor social enterprises as school-aged children develop multiple strategies to meet social goals.

Many current views of social behavior and development give renewed emphasis to cognitive and affective mediators. Personal causation, subjective value, and cognitive constructive competencies focus on the person's interpretation of social situations and plans for regulating behavior. The interested reader can chart the implied role of metacognition in social learning theories (e.g., Bandura, 1978) and cognitive behavior modification (e.g., Meichenbaum & Asarnow, 1978). The role of metacognitive self-control in social learning was summarized cogently by Mischel and Mischel (1976).

[A] comprehensive approach to social behavior must take account of the individual's self-regulatory systems. These systems include (1) the rules that specify goals or performance standards in particular situations; (2) the consequences of achieving or failing to achieve those criteria; (3) the self-instruction and cognitive stimulus transformations required to achieve the self-control necessary for goal attainment; and (4) the organizing rules (plans) for the sequencing and termination of complex behavioral patterns in the absence of external supports and in the presence of external hindrances. (p. 94)

METACOGNITIVE DEVELOPMENT

The current concerns in developmental cognition are to describe and explain the common accomplishments across skill domains in order to yield a coherent account of the developing child's abilities instead of a fragmented description of discrete strategies. One approach for analyzing the developmental similarities in skills is children's metacognitive understanding of cognitive processes. Underlying the current focus on metacognition is a rediscovery of purposiveness and consciousness as motivating directives for learning and development since awareness of one's cognition seems to accompany the development of cognitive strategies in childhood. The critical issue concerns understanding of the self (e.g., self-knowledge, self-concept, self-perception) and subsequent behavioral regulation. This idea is a recurrent theme in psychology and can be found in the works of Gesell, Tolman, Lewin, Werner, Piaget, and Vygotsky to name only a few prominent examples. Today, *meta* prefixes are appended to psychological terms to indicate awareness of the cognitive object or process, and researchers refer to this "higher" level of knowledge as *metacognition, metastatements* (Anzai & Simon, 1979), *metastrategies,* or *metacomponents* (Sternberg, 1979). In all of these accounts, the "thing" being characterized is the person's sensitivity to the variables and procedures that influence problem-solving behavior. Flavell (1978) has delineated the variables according to person, task, and strategy categories while Brown (1978) refers to processes of predicting, planning, and checking. Obviously both declarative and procedural knowledge are incorporated into metacognition. We shall try to summarize the burgeoning literature on metacognition according to three common threads that we have emphasized in our review: evaluation, planning, and regulation.

Evaluation

An important component of metacognition is the assessment of one's current knowledge states. For example one could ask, "Do I know my checking account number, would I recognize the first few bars of a song, or did I understand the symbolism in this novel?" Self-evaluation of knowledge states is both the beginning and endpoint for problem solving, and children often have difficulty taking their own "mental temperatures" spontaneously. We have seen that young children often listen to ambiguous instructions, speak with inaccurate references, and read incomprehensible information without pausing to consider if the text or conversation makes sense. Flavell, Friedrichs, and Hoyt (1970) observed that five- to seven-year-olds did not evaluate their own memory states and readiness to recall often. Wellman (1977) observed that five-year-olds did not judge their prescient, tip-of-the-tongue understanding accurately. The problem of not knowing when you do not understand is evident for young learners on a variety of tasks. Holt (1964) described the educational problem succinctly.

Part of being a good student is learning to be aware of one's own mind and the degree of one's understanding. The good student may be one who often says that he does not understand, simply because he keeps a constant check on his understanding. The poor student, who does not, so to speak, watch himself trying to understand, does not know most of the time whether he understands or not. Thus the problem is not to get students to ask us what they don't know; the problem is to make them aware of the difference between what they know and what they don't. (pp. 28–29)

Another important aspect of metacognitive evaluation is the assessment of one's abilities. Young children are notoriously inaccurate and inconsistent in predicting their own memory abilities and, more generally, often believe they have sufficient cognitive skills when they do not. By 10 to 12 years of age, children are more adept at differentiating the causes for their successes and failures and attribute outcomes to effort, ability, and others more accurately (Weiner, 1979). Perhaps more important than accuracy, children develop an appreciation of the broad range of special abilities needed for effective performance and a sensitivity to their deliberate application. They realize that "thinking hard" does not insure memory, and they invoke mnemonic strategies as aids for encoding and retrieval. They begin to restructure messages, ask questions, anticipate outcomes, and consider the other person's point of view deliberately and strategically.

Finally we have seen that young children do not evaluate task goals and parameters spontaneously. We know from a variety of interview studies that young children are not aware of the task dimensions that influence reading and memory (Brown & Smiley, 1977; Kreutzer, Leonard, & Flavell, 1975; Myers & Paris, 1978). Their goals, if conscious or not, are often restricted to rote recall (Paris, 1978a), word decoding while reading (Ryan, 1979), or simply talking without insuring comprehension by the speaker (Schmidt & Paris, 1980). We have abundant evidence that children do not evaluate available strategies and are not sensitive to task requirements for their use, but we have less information on how children form goals and evaluate their purposes in tasks. Piaget's notions of centration and egocentrism capture the young child's obliviousness to task analysis, but we need more detailed examinations of how children overcome these constraints. In summary one must evaluate the problem at hand before attempting solutions. The evaluations include self, others, and the task with attention to the goals and purposes of the task and the range of abilities that are available and required. Many times this kind of evaluation occurs automatically, but when learning a new skill or when normal procedures fail, one may need to consider the goals and means deliberately and consciously. Awareness then needs to be translated into actions which may involve a stage of conscious planning.

Forming Plans

The essence of metacognitive planning is deliberate selection of strategies to fulfill task goals. After the purpose of the task and one's available skills have been determined by evaluation, it is necessary to select and order appropriate actions. Selection is required because of the limitations on using all strategies ideally or simultaneously. Motivation also plays a role since an individual may realize a particular goal or ability but choose not to follow or use it. Thus task dimensions, limited cognitive abilities, and motivation combine to yield decisions or plans for action. Coordinating particular cognitive strategies with goals is a subjective decision based on the personal significance of the task, goal, and the amount of effort required.

When do children begin to form and use plans? Although the best answer is probably that it depends upon the particular task, plan, and child being investigated, some data indicate that effective planning is not often observed until seven or eight years of age. Piaget (1976) observed that trial-and-error reasoning seems to characterize problem solving before the concrete operational period while reflection and planfulness appear in later childhood. Klahr (1978), however, observed that even some five-year-olds anticipate and talk about potential moves on a "Tower of Hanoi" problem (i.e., moving ordered discs from one peg to another under special size constraints). Memory plans can be used by four-year-olds if they are simple and direct actions, such as pointing and looking at hidden objects (Wellman et al., 1975), but generating plans for future encoding or retrieval remains difficult until eight or nine years of age (Kreutzer, Leonard, & Flavell, 1975).

Similarly generating plans for the apportionment of studying in reading and memory improves with age. Masur, McIntyre, and Flavell (1973) found that first-graders did not select forgotten items to study in a multi-trial memory test as often as third-graders or adults. They did not form a plan for concentrating their efforts on the items most in need of additional study. We have observed the same problem in reading where young and poor readers do not know how to formulate plans for remediating comprehension failures or adjusting their study behavior to task goals or the difficulty of the passage. Children's question-asking and communication can be improved by the provision of plans; production deficiencies for mnemonic strategies, self-control, and reading skills can be attenuated by instruction. The lack of planfulness may be due to children's inability to perceive the future benefits of the strategies and to plan to use effective actions and ignore irrelevant or unimportant aspects of the task. When modeling or feedback provide children with information about the utility of strategies, children are more likely to adopt them as future plans. Thus recognizing the benefits of future actions may be a

crucial component of the development of plans on cognitive tasks.

Regulating and Implementing Cognitive Plans

Evaluating the task and one's own knowledge states and abilities, like the planning and selection of strategies, must be put into action. While we usually consider evaluation and planning as precursors to behavior, they are interwoven during efforts to learn, remember, and communicate. *Metacognitive regulation* refers to the constant monitoring of progress toward a goal and to the redirection of one's effort. We have already seen that comprehension monitoring is rare in young children as they read, listen, speak, or prepare for recall. Young and poor readers also do not correct their own errors while reading, nor do young communicators monitor dyadic understanding. Siegler and Liebert (1975) found that only older children sensed the need to keep records of their hypotheses and solution attempts during a problem-solving task.

The failure to check one's own progress or solutions has been characterized by Brown (1978) as blind rule following. She cites a number of examples from mathematics lessons where young children believe their answers are correct even in the face of blatant contradictory evidence. The findings are generalizable to nonconservers on Piagetian tasks and children who blindly follow advice to use particular mnemonic strategies. Rarely do these children check or correct their own errors. Persistence of erroneous learning methods or random changes are both instances of poor metacognitive regulation and reveal little flexibility in strategy use. Belmont and Butterfield (1977) found that young children were slower to abandon rehearsal strategies and slower to reinstate the strategies when the task was changed to require rehearsal or not.

Training children to regulate and monitor their own progress can be effective, though. Brown (1978) summarizes several studies that have shown improvement and generalization in children's (retarded and nonretarded) use of study time apportionment, recall readiness, and estimation abilities. Directions to talk aloud and provide self-guiding verbalizations likewise have been shown to increase performance on motor tasks, reading comprehension, social skills, and behavior management (Meichenbaum & Asarnow, 1978). The remarkable similarity across tasks in young children's inability to regulate their own cognitive strategies and the general improvements with training highlight the pervasive influence of metacognitive regulation on cognitive development.

Meta-Metacognition

There is not space enough to critique the current use of the term *metacognition*, but we would be remiss to extol the virtues of this trend in developmental psychology without mentioning some pitfalls. First, our characterization is general and glosses over subtle changes in the development of cognitive strategies. Detailed analyses are clearly needed (e.g., Siegler, 1978) that relate to both naturalistic and ethnographic analyses (Cole & Scribner,

1977) and to unifying theories (e.g., Fischer, 1980). Second, the reader may erroneously infer that metacognition is adequately indexed by age and is nonexistent at 3 and fully developed at 12. Most researchers deny this simple age correlation and emphasize metacognitive development as a function of expertise, experience, and sociocultural milieu (Brown, 1978, 1980). Age is not a causal variable but happens to be highly correlated with the strategies and tasks presented in experimental assessments and formal schooling. Third, we are well aware of controversies regarding interview data and subjective awareness (e.g., Nisbett & Wilson, 1977; White, 1980). Despite the problems with the veridicality of subjective reports and operational measures of metacognition, the centrality of consciousness in psychology has an enduring history (Mandler, 1975). We believe that the new data afforded by metacognitive inquiries have been valuable for describing children's understanding of cognition and have been an important addition to performance measures.

A fourth critical problem is that metacognition has been reified as a unitary construct. While the term provides a convenient and general label, it does not imply that a single factor underlies development nor that metacognition is necessarily causally related to problem solving throughout development. Flavell (1978) and Brown (1978) have both discussed the epiphenomenal nature of awareness and how metacognition may be expected to vary in its relation to performance. One clear implication of the data reviewed in this chapter is that metacognition and strategy development may vary considerably across tasks, domains, and children. Variability in this sense is not construed as a weakness but rather as a more precise statement of the interactive nature of learning and development that merits examination. Finally, the emphasis on metacognitive development promises new directions for training children to use intellectual skills of evaluation, planning, and regulation that can be internalized and generalized. The training is broader than past paradigms in that executive functioning and generalization are explicitly manipulated. Also the broad conceptual emphasis on motivation, learning, development, and cross-domain similarities may blur traditional boundaries in psychology and yield a more comprehensive picture of the developing child's social and cognitive skills.

STRATEGY ACQUISITION AND SKILL DEVELOPMENT

What Develops?

It makes us uneasy to attempt a simple answer to such an important and bold question, and the reader may find the hypotheses in Siegler (1978) intriguing. The data reviewed in the present chapter suggest that two major factors in cognitive development are the acquisition of strategies and the awareness of cognitive functioning. But what does it mean to "acquire" a strategy? Use of a strategy, particularly with the aid and directions of another, is a minimal criterion for acquisition and does not differentiate "doing" from "knowing." Training young children to use mnemonic strategies and communicative plans may result in transient learning of the barest kind,

similar to pseudoconservation or pseudo-operativity training on Piagetian tasks. To us teaching children cognitive "tricks" on particular tasks is not sufficient for the acquisition of cognitive skills (although such experience may often be necessary) and may often reflect blind rule following or social compliance. Internalization and self-control of the strategy, realization of the benefits and appropriateness of the technique, maintenance and generalization across tasks, and automation of goal-directed efforts are more stringent criteria for measuring dynamic skill development. Meeting successively more rigorous task requirements is part of skill development, and it is clear that strategy acquisition is not a rapid or all-or-none accomplishment.

The flexible and systematic use of strategies (as cognitive tools or skills) reflects developmental trends noted by other theorists. Information-processing accounts (Klahr & Wallace, 1976), Soviet theories (Vygotsky, 1978), and mediational hypotheses (White, 1965) of cognitive development in childhood all emphasize deliberate methods of attending to information and repackaging it in meaningful, economical units. With development these skills become progressively differentiated and integrated. Case (1978) has interpreted Piaget's stage theory of cognitive development according to the acquisition and automation of strategies that permit qualitative and functional advances in learning. A lengthy quote summarizes this neo-Piagetian position.

During each of the major stages of intellectual development, there is a succession of substages. The first postulate of my theory is that this succession of substages stems from a succession of qualitatively distinct control structures or executive strategies. The second postulate is that two sorts of factors explain the succession of strategies with any stage. The first is the child's responsiveness to the strategy-related experiences he encounters. In order of increasing power, one would expect practice, practice with feedback, cue highlighting, and modeling to affect the rate at which a child progresses through a given strategy sequence. The second factor is a gradual increase within each stage in the size of the child's working memory. As working memory increases, it becomes easier to acquire and utilize more complex executive strategies. The third major postulate is that the gradual increase in working memory does not stem from a structural increase in the attentional capacity of the organism but rather from an increase in the automaticity of the basic operations it is capable of executing. As these operations become more automatic, their execution requires a smaller proportion of total attentional capacity. The result is that more capacity is available for "storage" or "working." Exactly how the increase in automaticity occurs is unclear, but it seems likely that, if experiential input plays a role, it is general rather than specific. The fourth major postulate is that the executive strategies of each major stage involve qualitatively distinct underlying operations and that the operation at any given stage must be assembled in working memory from components available at the previous stage. It follows that the transition to any given stage depends on the attainment of a certain degree of automaticity during the previous stage. (Case, 1978, p. 64)

Strategy acquisition, executive control, goal-directed actions, and automatic processes are embedded in metacognitive aspects of evaluation, planning, and regulation. Thus in Soviet, Piagetian, and information-processing accounts of cognitive development, what develops in childhood is a self-controlled system of strategies and operations for learning.

How Do Children Acquire Skills?

An equally formidable question confronting developmental psychologists is to explain how cognitive skills are acquired. As Brown (1980) notes, most theories of learning (such as *S-R* laws, schema theories, and computer metaphors) are silent on the processes of strategy acquisition and dynamic growth. On the other hand developmental theories often include global (and perhaps teleological) mechanisms like assimilation-accommodation or reflection-refraction as explanatory constructs that do not provide detailed or prescriptive guidelines for the development of skills. Current research on metacognitive development may provide the descriptive detail needed to integrate learning and developmental theories, although this is more hopeful than accomplished at this time. However, our confidence is bolstered by current researchers' concern for social, motivational, and conscious factors in skill development. Some current views are directly borrowed from Soviet work, and we would like to mention those briefly as illustrations of the conceptual bridges between Soviet and American research on development and learning.

Vygotsky (1978) related learning and development in the construct "zone of proximal development." In his view children's developmental competencies (i.e., self-controlled skills) lag behind their abilities to solve problems or learn with the help of others. Development is predicted by the ease with which children can perform tasks with the support of others, and thus learning "pulls" cognitive development and reveals a shift from inter- to intrapersonal control of skills. Wertsch (1979) has proposed that the roots of metacognition are found in these social interactions and that children learn gradually to adopt the means and goals provided by others. Analyses of social interactions and learning within children's zones of potential development may provide a powerful methodology for examining how children acquire strategies as well as afford a better method of diagnosing and predicting intellectual development (Brown & French, 1979).

The following quotation on the Soviet view of memory development illustrates the learning-development interaction.

In the first stage they [mnemonic strategies] are formed as a special purposive action and are not yet generalized; the fulfillment of these actions requires especially intensive conscious control. In the second stage, as a result of the transfer of actions to material of varying content, they begin to generalize. In the third stage, through further use they become, to a certain degree, automatized and acquire the form of generalized skills.

The formation of mnemonic operations differs from the formation of cognitive processes in that it is always one stage behind cognitive processes when the latter are used as a means of remembering. . . . The initial use of a cognitive process for mnemonic ends becomes possible only when the individual can exercise a certain degree of freedom in operating with it.

. . . [C]ognitive operations which become the means towards another activity first develop as goal-oriented processes and only later assume the characteristics of a distinctly intellectual skill. (Smirnov & Zinchenko, 1969, p. 469)

The Soviet view of how strategies develop into generalized skills illustrates how natural activities become transformed into deliberate actions and are used as general operations for new goals (Meacham, 1977). The sequence of skill development includes *identification* of an action, *mapping* the means-goals relation, *subordination* of action to new goals, and *coordination* among different means and goals. This sequence is evident in the data reviewed and several conceptual positions. Flavell's sequence of existence, need, and inference mirrors the same increasing complexity. Fischer (1980) discusses skill development according to four recurring trends (on sensorimotor, representational, and abstract tiers) that are also similar. He proposes that skills initially form *simple sets* (like operant procedures), then a set is *mapped* onto another (like a means-goals relation), then sets form a reciprocal and reversible *system,* and finally the sets are interrelated (among similar means and goals) to form a *system of systems.* The reader may find further similarities in other conceptualizations such as Brown's (1980) tetrahedral model of learning, Sternberg's (1979) componential analysis, and Paris's (1978a) means-goals analysis. In all of these conceptual frameworks, skill development is characterized as a progression of task and strategy analysis to deliberate use to generalized, internal, and automatic control. Metacognitive aspects of evaluation, planning, and regulation are intertwined as both processes and products of skill development, and regardless of one's conceptual preferences, current research is providing insight on how children develop functional control of cognitive skills.

One additional aspect of current approaches to cognitive development deserves mention, and that is the renewed emphasis on motivation as a shaping factor in learning and development. Cognitive strategies have assumed a priori importance for researchers but not necessarily for children. Throughout our review we have noted that children use strategies easily and early when the actions are sensible and the strategy-task goal connection is natural. Training children to use and maintain strategies is difficult when children are unaware of the task purposes or strategy benefits. Metacognition focuses on beliefs and understanding as mediators of cognitive skills, and the injection of personal values and significance is an attempt to incorporate motivational factors into cognitive development. This trend appears valuable to us because it forces investigators to consider the subject's perception of themselves and the tasks and the adaptive significance for learning new skills.

Analyses of children's skill adaptation also requires consideration of the environmental constraints/opportunities and individual differences in cognitive development, both healthy additions to traditional descriptions of universal, internal changes in cognitive functioning. The abilities to identify, map, subordinate, and coordinate skills are formed in a crucible of personal motivation, and attention to these variables may provide more complete accounts of development. This trend can be identified in Brown's (1980) plea for a comparative model of cognitive development; Bransford, Stein, Shelton, and Owing's (1980) emphasis on transfer-appropriate training; and Cole, Hood, and McDermott's (1978) emphasis on ethnographic analysis and ecological validity. Quite simply skill development must be related to one's experience, purposes, and motivation within a social-cultural context. By grounding children's acquisition of cognitive strategies in metacognitive skill development, we may be able to achieve the goals of relevancy and relativity in our theories.

REFERENCES

ACREDOLO, L. P., PICK, H. L., & OLSEN, M. G. Environmental differentiation and familiarity as determinants of children's memory for spatial location. *Developmental Psychology*, 1975, *11*, 495–501.

ANZAI, Y., & SIMON, H. A. The theory of learning by doing. *Psychological Review*, 1979, *86*, 124–140.

APPEL, L. F., COOPER, R. G., McCARRELL, N., SIMS-KNIGHT, J., YUSSEN, S. R., & FLAVELL, J. H. The development of the distinction between perceiving and memorizing. *Child Development*, 1972, *43*, 1365–1381.

BAKER, L., & BROWN, A. L. Metacognitive skills of reading. In D. Pearson (Ed.), *Handbook of reading research*, in press.

BANDURA, A. The self system in reciprocal determinism. *American Psychologist*, 1978, *33*, 344–358.

BELMONT, J. M., & BUTTERFIELD, E. C. The instructional approach to developmental cognitive research. In R. V. Kail & J. W. Hagen (Eds.), *Perspectives on the development of memory and cognition*. Hillsdale, N.J.: Lawrence Erlbaum Associates, 1977.

BLOOM, L., & LAHEY, M. *Language development and language disorders*. New York: John Wiley, 1978.

BORKOWSKI, J. G., LEVERS, S. R., & GRUENENFELDER, T. A. Transfer of mediational strategies in children: The role of activity and awareness during strategy acquisition. *Child Development*, 1976, *47*, 779–786.

BRANSFORD, J. D., STEIN, B. S., SHELTON, T. S., & OWINGS, R. A. Cognition and adaptation: The importance of learning to learn. In J. Harvey (Ed.), *Cognition, social behavior, and the environment*. Hillsdale, N.J.: Lawrence Erlbaum Associates, 1980.

BROWN, A. L. The development of memory: Knowing, knowing about knowing, and knowing how to know. In H. W. Reese (Ed.), *Advances in child development and behavior* (Vol. 10). New York: Academic Press, 1975.

BROWN, A. L. Knowing when, where, and how to remember: A problem of metacognition. In R. Glaser (Ed.), *Advances in instructional psychology*. Hillsdale, N.J.: Lawrence Erlbaum Associates, 1978.

BROWN, A. L. Learning and development: The problems of compatibility, access, and induction. *Human Development*, in press.

BROWN, A. L., & CAMPIONE, J. C. The effects of knowledge and experience on the formation of retrieval plans for studying from texts. In M. M. Gruneberg, P. E. Morris, & R. N. Sykes (Eds.), *Practical aspects of memory*. London: Academic Press, 1979.

BROWN, A. L., & FRENCH, L. A. The zone of potential development: Implications for intelligence testing in the year 2000. *Intelligence*, 1979, *3*, 255–273.

BROWN, A. L., & SMILEY, S. S. Rating the importance of structural units of prose passages: A problem of metacognitive development. *Child Development*, 1977, *48*, 1–8.

BROWN, A. L., & SMILEY, S. S. The development of strategies for studying texts. *Child Development*, 1978, *49*, 1076–1088.

BRUNER, J. S. The ontogenesis of speech acts. *Journal of Child Language*, 1975, *2*, 1–19.

CASE, R. Intellectual development from birth to adulthood: A neo-Piagetian interpretation. In R. S. Siegler (Ed.), *Children's thinking: What develops?* Hillsdale, N.J.: Lawrence Erlbaum Associates, 1978.

CHI, M.T.H. Knowledge structures and memory development. In R. Siegler (Ed.), *Children's thinking: What develops?* Hillsdale, N.J.: Lawrence Erlbaum Associates, 1978.

CLAY, M. M. *Reading: The patterning of complex behavior*. Auckland, New Zealand: Heineman Educational Books, 1973.

CLAY, M. M., & IMLACH, R. Juncture, pitch, and stress as reading behavior variables. *Journal of Verbal Learning and Verbal Behavior*, 1971, *10*, 133–139.

COLE, M., HOOD, L., & McDERMOTT, H. Concepts of ecological validity: Their differing implications for comparative cognitive research. *Quarterly Newsletter of the Institute for Comparative Human Development*, 1978, *2*, 34–37.

COLE, M., & SCRIBNER, S. Cross-cultural studies of memory and cognition. In R. V. Kail & J. W. Hagen (Eds.), *Perspectives on the development of memory and cognition*. Hillsdale, N.J.: Lawrence Erlbaum Associates, 1977.

COSGROVE, J. M., & PATTERSON, C. J. Plans and the development of listener skills. *Developmental Psychology*, 1977, *13*, 557–564.

COX, G. L., & PARIS, S. G. *The nature of mnemonic production deficiencies: A lifespan analysis*. Paper presented at the biennial meeting of the Society for Research in Child Development, San Francisco, 1979.

CROMER, W., & WIENER, M. Idiosyncratic response patterns among good and poor readers. *Journal of Consulting Psychology*, 1966, *30*, 1–10.

CUVO, A. J. Developmental differences in rehearsal and free recall. *Journal of Experimental Child Psychology*, 1975, *19*, 265–278.

DANNER, F. W. Children's understanding of intersentence organization in the recall of short descriptive passages. *Journal of Educational Psychology*, 1976, *68*, 174–183.

DAY, M. C. Developmental trends in visual scanning. In H. W. Reese (Ed.), *Advances in child development and behavior* (Vol. 10). New York: Academic Press, 1975.

deCHARMS, R. *Enhancing motivation: Change in the classroom*. New York: Irvington, 1976.

DEWEY, J. *How we think*. Lexington, Mass.: Heath, 1910.

DICKSON, W. P. *Children's oral communication skills*. New York: Academic Press, 1981.

DiVESTA, F. J., HAYWARD, K. G., & ORLANDO, V. P. Developmental trends in monitoring text for comprehension. *Child Development*, 1979, *50*, 97–105.

DORE, J. Holophrases, speech acts, and language universals. *Journal of Child Language*, 1975, *2*, 21–40.

FISCHER, K. W. A theory of cognitive development: The control and construction of hierarchies of skills. *Psychological Review*, 1980, *87*, 477–531.

FLAVELL, J. H. Developmental studies of mediated memory. In H. W. Reese & L. P. Lipsitt (Eds.), *Advances in child development and behavior* (Vol. 5). New York: Academic Press, 1970.

FLAVELL, J. H. *Cognitive development*. Englewood Cliffs, N.J.: Prentice-Hall, 1977.

FLAVELL, J. H. Metacognitive development. In J. M. Scandura & C. J. Brainerd (Eds.), *Structural/process theories of complex human behavior*. The Netherlands: Sijthoff & Noordoff, 1978.

FLAVELL, J. H. *Monitoring social-cognitive enterprises: Something else that may develop in the area of social cognition*. Paper presented at the Social Science Research Council Committee on Social and Affective Development During Childhood, January, 1979.

FLAVELL, J. H., BEACH, D. R., & CHINSKY, J. M. Spontaneous verbal rehearsal in a memory task as a function of age. *Child Development*, 1966, *37*, 283–299.

FLAVELL, J. H., FRIEDRICHS, A. G., & HOYT, J. D. Developmental changes in memorization processes. *Cognitive Psychology*, 1970, *1*, 324–340.

FLAVELL, J. H., & WELLMAN, H. M. Metamemory. In R. V. Kail & J. W. Hagen (Eds.), *Perspectives on the development of memory and cognition*. Hillsdale, N.J.: Lawrence Erlbaum Associates, 1977.

FORREST, D. L., & WALLER, T. G. *Cognitive and metacognitive aspects of reading*. Paper presented at the biennial meeting of the Society for Research in Child Development, San Francisco, 1979.

GARVEY, C. Some properties of social play. *Merrill-Palmer Quarterly*, 1974, *20*, 163–180.

GARVEY, C., & HOGAN, R. Social speech and social interaction: Egocentrism revisited. *Child Development*, 1973, *44*, 562–568.

GIBSON, E., & RADER, N. Attention: The perceiver as performer. In G. Hale & M. Lewis (Eds.), *Attention and cognitive development*. New York: Plenum, 1979.

GIBSON, E. J. Trends in perceptual development. Implications for the reading process. In A. Pick (Ed.), *Minnesota symposia on child psychology*, 1974, *8*, 25–54.

GLUCKSBERG, S., KRAUSS, R., & HIGGINS, E. T. The development of referential communication skills. In F. D. Horowitz (Ed.), *Child development research* (Vol. 4). Chicago: University of Chicago Press, 1975.

GOLINKOFF, R. A comparison of reading comprehension processes in good and poor comprehenders. *Reading Research Quarterly*, 1976, *11*, 623–659.

GOODMAN, K. S. Behind the eye: What happens in reading. In H. Singer & R. B. Ruddell (Eds.), *Theoretical models and processes of reading.* Newark, Del.: International Reading Association, 1976.

GUTHRIE, J. T., & TYLER, S. J. Psycholinguistic processing in reading and listening among good and poor readers. *Journal of Reading Behavior,* 1976, *8,* 415–426.

HAGEN, J. W., & HALE, G. A. The development of attention in children. In A. Pick (Ed.), *Minnesota symposia on child psychology* (Vol. 7). Minneapolis: University of Minnesota Press, 1973.

HALE, G. A. Development of children's attention to stimulus components. In G. Hale & M. Lewis (Eds.), *Attention and cognitive development.* New York: Plenum, 1979.

HALE, G. A., & LEWIS, M. *Attention and cognitive development.* New York: Plenum, 1979.

HIGGINS, E. T. Rules and roles: Speaker-listener processes of the "communication game." In W. P. Dickson (Ed.), *Children's oral communication skills.* New York: Academic Press, 1980.

HOLT, J. H. *How children fail.* New York: Dell Pub. Co., Inc., 1964.

HORN, E. V. *Methods of instruction in the social studies.* New York: Scribner's, 1937.

HUEY, E. B. *The psychology and pedagogy of reading.* Cambridge, Mass.: M.I.T. Press, 1968.

ISAKSON, R. L., & MILLER, J. W. Sensitivity to syntactic and semantic cues in good and poor comprehenders. *Journal of Educational Psychology,* 1976, *68,* 787–792.

ISTOMINA, Z. M. The development of voluntary memory in preschool-age children. *Soviet Psychology,* 1975, *13,* 5–64.

KARABENICK, J. D., & MILLER, S. A. The effects of age, sex, and listener feedback on grade school children's referential communication. *Child Development,* 1977, *48,* 678–683.

KAVALE, K., & SCHREINER, R. The reading processes of above average and average readers: A comparison of the use and reasoning strategies in responding to standardized comprehension measures. *Reading Research Quarterly,* 1979, *15,* 102–128.

KEENAN, E. O., & KLEIN, E. Coherency in children's discourse. *Journal of Psycholinguistic Research,* 1975, *4,* 365–380.

KEENEY, T. J., CANNIZZO, S. R., & FLAVELL, J. H. Spontaneous and induced verbal rehearsal in a recall task. *Child Development,* 1967, *38,* 953–966.

KENDLER, H. H., & KENDLER, T. S. Vertical and horizontal processes in problem solving. *Psychological Review,* 1962, *69,* 1–16.

KENNEDY, B. A., & MILLER, D. J. Persistent use of verbal rehearsal as a function of information about its value. *Child Development,* 1976, *47,* 566–569.

KLAHR, D. Goal formation, planning, and learning by preschool problem solvers or: "My socks are in the dryer." In R. S. Siegler (Ed.), *Children's thinking: What develops?* Hillsdale, N.J.: Lawrence Erlbaum Associates, 1978.

KLAHR, D., & WALLACE, J. G. *Cognitive development: An information processing view.* Hillsdale, N.J.: Lawrence Erlbaum Associates, 1976.

KOBASIGAWA, A., RANSOM, C. C., & HOLLAND, C. J. *Children's knowledge about skimming.* Unpublished paper, University of Windsor, Windsor, Ontario, 1979.

KREUTZER, M. A., LEONARD, C., & FLAVELL, J. H. An interview study of children's knowledge about memory. *Monographs of the Society for Research in Child Development,* 1975, *40*(1, Serial No. 159).

LEMPERS, J. O., FLAVELL, E. H., & FLAVELL, J. H. The development in very young children of tacit knowledge concerning visual perception. *Genetic Psychology Monographs,* 1977, *95,* 3–53.

LIBERTY, C., & ORNSTEIN, P. A. Age differences in organization and recall: The effects of training in categorization. *Journal of Experimental Child Psychology,* 1973, *15,* 169–186.

LOCKE, E. Q. *A guide to effective study.* New York: Springer-Verlag, 1975.

MANDLER, G. Consciousness: Respectable, useful, and probably necessary. In R. Solso (Ed.), *Information processing and cognition: The Loyola symposium.* Hillsdale, N.J.: Lawrence Erlbaum Associates, 1975.

MARATSOS, M. Nonegocentric communication abilities in preschool children. *Child Development,* 1973, *44,* 697–700.

MARKMAN, E. M. Realizing that you don't understand: A preliminary investigation. *Child Development,* 1977, *48,* 986–992.

MARKMAN, E. M. Realizing that you don't understand: Elemen-

tary school children's awareness of inconsistencies. *Child Development,* 1979, *50,* 642–655.

MASUR, E. F., McINTYRE, C. W., & FLAVELL, J. H. Developmental changes in apportionment of study time among items in a multitrial free recall task. *Journal of Experimental Child Psychology,* 1973, *15,* 237–246.

MEACHAM, J. A. Soviet investigations of memory development. In R. V. Kail & J. W. Hagen (Eds.), *Perspectives on the development of memory and cognition.* Hillsdale, N.J.: Lawrence Erlbaum Associates, 1977.

MEICHENBAUM, D., & ASARNOW, J. Cognitive behavior modification and metacognitive development: Implications for the classroom. In P. Kendall & S. Hollon (Eds.), *Cognitive-behavioral interventions: Theory, research, and procedures.* New York: Academic Press, 1978.

MILLER, P. H., & BIGI, L. The development of children's understanding of attention. *Merrill-Palmer Quarterly,* 1979, *25,* 235–250.

MISCHEL, W., & MISCHEL, H. N. A cognitive social-learning approach to morality and self-regulation. In T. Lickona (Ed.), *Moral development and behavior.* New York: Holt, Rinehart & Winston, 1976.

MISCHEL, W., & PATTERSON, C. J. Effective plans for self-control in children. In W. A. Collins (Ed.), *Minnesota symposium on child psychology* (Vol. 11). Hillsdale, N.J.: Lawrence Erlbaum Associates, 1978.

MORRISON, F. J., HOLMES, D. L., & HAITH, M. M. A developmental study of the effect of familiarity on short-term memory. *Journal of Experimental Child Psychology,* 1974, *18,* 412–425.

MUELLER, E., BLEIER, M., KRAKOW, J., HEGEDUS, K., & COURNOYER, P. The development of peer verbal interaction among two-year-old boys. *Child Development,* 1977, *48,* 284–287.

MUELLER, E., & LUCAS, T. A developmental analysis of peer interaction among toddlers. In M. Lewis & L. A. Rosenblum (Eds.), *Friendship and peer relations.* New York: John Wiley, 1975.

MYERS, M., & PARIS, S. G. Children's metacognitive knowledge about reading. *Journal of Educational Psychology,* 1978, *70,* 680–690.

MYERS, N. A., & PERLMUTTER, M. Memory in the years from two to five. In P. Ornstein (Ed.), *Memory development in children.* Hillsdale, N.J.: Lawrence Erlbaum Associates, 1978.

NEIMARK, E., SLOTNICK, N. S., & ULRICH, T. Development of memorization strategies. *Developmental Psychology,* 1971, *5,* 427–432.

NEVILLE, M. H., & PUGH, A. K. Context in reading and listening: Variations in approach to cloze tasks. *Reading Research Quarterly,* 1976, *12,* 13–31.

NISBETT, E. R., & WILSON, T. D. Telling more than we know: Verbal reports on mental processes. *Psychological Review,* 1977, *84,* 231–279.

ORNSTEIN, P. A. *Memory development in children.* Hillsdale, N.J.: Lawrence Erlbaum Associates, 1978.

ORNSTEIN, P. A., & NAUS, M. J. Rehearsal processes in children's memory. In P. Ornstein (Ed.), *Memory development in children.* Hillsdale, N.J.: Lawrence Erlbaum Associates, 1978.

OWINGS, R. A., PETERSON, G. A., BRANSFORD, J. D., MORRIS, C. D., & STEIN, B. S. Spontaneous monitoring and regulation of learning: A comparison of successful and less successful fifth graders. *Journal of Educational Psychology,* 1980, *72,* 250–256.

PARIS, S. G. Coordination of means and goals in the development of mnemonic skills. In P. A. Ornstein (Ed.), *Memory development in children.* Hillsdale, N.J.: Lawrence Erlbaum Associates, 1978a.

PARIS, S. G. The development of inference and transformation as memory operations. In P. Ornstein (Ed.), *Memory development in children.* Hillsdale, N.J.: Lawrence Erlbaum Associates, 1978b.

PARIS, S. G., & LINDAUER, B. K. The role of inference in children's comprehension and memory for sentences. *Cognitive Psychology,* 1976, *8,* 217–227.

PARIS, S. G., LINDAUER, B. K., & COX, G. L. The development of inferential comprehension. *Child Development,* 1977, *48,* 1728–1733.

PARIS, S. G., & MYERS, M. Comprehension monitoring in good and poor readers. *Journal of Reading Behavior,* 1981, in press.

PARIS, S. G., & UPTON, L. R. Children's memory for inferential relationships in prose. *Child Development,* 1976, *47,* 660–668.

PATTERSON, C. J., MASSAD, C. M., & COSGROVE, J. M. Children's referential communication; Components of plans for effective listening. *Developmental Psychology,* 1978, *14,* 401–406.

PETERSON, C. L., DANNER, F. W., & FLAVELL, J. H. Developmental changes in children's response to three indications of communicative failure. *Child Development,* 1972, *43,* 1463–1468.

PIAGET, J. *The language and thought of the child.* New York: Harcourt Brace Jovanovich, Inc., 1926.

PIAGET, J. *The grasp of consciousness.* Cambridge, Mass.: Harvard University Press, 1976.

PIAGET, J., & INHELDER, B. *Memory and intelligence.* New York: Basic Books, 1973.

PICK, A. D., & FRANKEL, G. W. A study of strategies of visual attention in children. *Developmental Psychology,* 1973, *4,* 348–357.

PICK, A. D., & FRANKEL, G. W. A developmental study of strategies of visual selectivity. *Child Development,* 1974, *45,* 1162–1165.

PIONTKOWSKI, D., & CALFEE, R. Attention in the classroom. In G. Hale & M. Lewis (Eds.), *Attention and cognitive development.* New York: Plenum, 1979.

REID, J. Learning to think about reading. *Educational Research,* 1966, *9,* 56–62.

RESNICK, L. B. *The nature of intelligence.* Hillsdale, N.J.: Lawrence Erlbaum Associates, 1976.

RYAN, E. B. Identifying and remediating failures in reading comprehension: Toward an instructional approach for poor comprehenders. In T. G. Waller & G. E. MacKinnon (Eds.), *Advances in reading research.* New York: Academic Press, 1979.

SACHS, J., & DEVIN, J. Young children's use of age-appropriate speech styles. *Journal of Child Language,* 1976, *3,* 81–98.

SAMUELS, S. J., BEGY, G., & CHEN, C. C. Comparison of word recognition speed and strategies of less skilled and more highly skilled readers. *Reading Research Quarterly,* 1975, *11,* 72–86.

SCHACTER, F. F., KIRSHNER, K., KLIPS, B., FRIEDRICKS, M., & SANDERS, K. Everyday preschool interpersonal speech usage: Methodological, developmental, and sociolinguistic studies. *Monographs of the Society for Research in Child Development,* 1974, *39* (Serial No. 156).

SCHMIDT, C. R., & PARIS, S. G. *The development of children's communication skills.* Unpublished manuscript, University of Michigan, 1980.

SHANTZ, C. U. The development of social cognition. In E. M. Hetherington (Ed.), *Review of child development research* (Vol. 5). Chicago: University of Chicago Press, 1975.

SHATZ, M. The relationship between cognitive processes and the development of communication skills. In C. B. Keasey (Ed.), *Nebraska symposium on motivation.* Lincoln: University of Nebraska Press, 1978.

SHATZ, M., & GELMAN, R. The development of communication skills: Modifications in the speech of young children as a function of the listener. *Monographs of the Society for Research in Child Development,* 1973, *38*(5, Serial No. 152).

SHATZ, M., & GELMAN, R. Beyond syntax: The influence of conversational constraints on speech modifications. In C. Snow & C. A. Ferguson (Eds.), *Talking to children.* Cambridge, England: Cambridge University Press, 1977.

SIEGLER, R. S. *Children's thinking: What develops?* Hillsdale, N.J.: Lawrence Erlbaum Associates, 1978.

SIEGLER, R. S., & LIEBERT, R. M. Acquisition of formal scientific reasoning by 10- and 13-year-olds: Designing a factorial experiment. *Developmental Psychology,* 1975, *10,* 401–402.

SMIRNOV, A. A., & ZINCHENKO, P. I. Problems in the psychology of memory. In M. Cole & I. Maltzman (Eds.), *A handbook of contemporary Soviet psychology.* New York: Basic Books, 1969.

SMITH, F. *Comprehension and learning.* New York: Holt, Rinehart & Winston, 1975.

SPILTON, D., & LEE, L. C. Some determinants of effective communication in four years olds. *Child Development,* 1977, *48,* 968–977.

STAUFFER, R. G. *Directing reading maturity as a cognitive process.* New York: Harper & Row, Pub., 1969.

STEINER, R., WIENER, M., & CROMER, W. Comprehension training and identification for poor and good readers. *Journal of Educational Psychology,* 1971, *62,* 506–513.

STERNBERG, R. J. The nature of mental abilities. *American Psychologist,* 1979, *34,* 214–230.

THORESON, C., & MAHONEY, M. J. *Behavioral self-control.* New York: Holt, Rinehart & Winston, 1974.

VOGEL, S. A. Syntactic abilities in normal and dyslexic children. *Journal of Learning Disabilities,* 1974, *7,* 103–109.

VURPILLOT, E., & BALL, W. A. The concept of identity and children's selective attention. In G. Hale & M. Lewis (Eds.), *Attention and cognitive development.* New York: Plenum, 1979.

VYGOTSKY, L. S. *Thought and language.* Cambridge, Mass.: M.I.T. Press, 1962.

VYGOTSKY, L. S. *Mind in society.* Cambridge, Mass.: Harvard University Press, 1978.

WAGNER, D. A. Memories of Morocco: The influence of age, schooling, and environment on memory. *Cognitive Psychology,* 1978, *10,* 1–28.

WEINER, B. A theory of motivation for some classroom experiences. *Journal of Educational Psychology,* 1979, *71,* 3–25.

WEINSTEIN, R., & RABINOVITCH, M. S. Sentence structure and retention in good and poor readers. *Journal of Educational Psychology,* 1971, *62,* 25–30.

WELLMAN, H. M. Preschoolers' understanding of memory-relevant variables. *Child Development,* 1977a, *48,* 1720–1723.

WELLMAN, H. M. Tip of the tongue and feeling of knowing experiences: A developmental study of memory monitoring. *Child Development,* 1977b, *48,* 13–21.

WELLMAN, H. M., & LEMPERS, J. D. The naturalistic communicative abilities of two-year-olds. *Child Development,* 1977, *48,* 1052–1057.

WELLMAN, H. M., RITTER, K., & FLAVELL, J. H. Deliberate memory behavior in the delayed reactions of very young children. *Developmental Psychology,* 1975, *11,* 780–787.

WERNER, H. *Comparative psychology of mental development.* New York: Science Editions, 1961.

WERTSCH, J. V. *The social interactional origins of metacognition.* Paper presented at the biennial meeting of the Society for Research in Child Development, San Francisco, 1979.

WHITE, P. Limitations on verbal reports of internal events: A refutation of Nisbett and Wilson and of Bem. *Psychological Review,* 1980, *87,* 105–112.

WHITE, S. H. Evidence for a hierarchical arrangement of learning processes. In L. P. Lipsitt & C. C. Spiker (Eds.), *Advances in child development and behavior* (Vol. 2). New York: Academic Press, 1965.

WRIGHT, J. C., & VLIESTRA, A. G. The development of selective attention: From perceptual exploration to logical search. In H. W. Reese (Ed.), *Advances in child development and behavior* (Vol. 10). New York: Academic Press, 1975.

YUSSEN, S. R., MATHEWS, S. R., BUSS, R. R., & KANE, P. T. Developmental change in judging important and critical elements of stories. *Developmental Psychology,* 1980, *16,* 213–219.

ZELNIKER, T., & JEFFREY, W. E. Attention and cognitive style in children. In G. Hale & M. Lewis (Eds.), *Attention and cognitive development.* New York: Plenum, 1979.

20

Memory in Childhood

ROBERT KAIL

JOHN WILLIAM HAGEN

As children grow older they remember more effectively. This fact is obvious to anyone who has worked with children and is accepted without qualification by students of developmental psychology. Why, then, has memory been one of the most active areas of research in cognitive development since the late 1960s?

One answer to this question is that to speak of the *development of memory* is to underestimate the complexity of the phenomenon, for memory does not refer to a single process or structure. Instead memory is merely a convenient shorthand for an assortment of cognitive processes. Encoding, retrieval, rehearsal, search, clustering, elaboration, schemas—the list of mnemonic phenomena studied by developmentalists proliferates annually. Here is one source of interest in memory development: Not all components of memory develop at the same rate. Some processes seem to function in essentially the same manner in five-year-olds and adults, while others continue to develop throughout childhood, adolescence, and adulthood.

A second answer to the question stems from the first. When memory is seen as an assortment of intellectual skills and processes, it becomes increasingly difficult to place the line dividing mnemonic processes and cognitive processes. In fact, most memory theorists would agree that

... memory is in good part just *applied cognition*. That is, what we call "memory processes" seems largely to be just the same old, familiar, cognitive processes, but as they are applied to a particular class of problems. In other words, memory seems mostly to be just a matter of the head doing its characteristic "thing" while coping with the specific task of storing or retrieving factual information, ideas, and other cognitive contents. (Flavell, 1971, p. 273 [emphasis added])

As a result of the kinship between memory and cognitive activities, research on memory is now seen as an important means of understanding more general changes in children's cognitive functioning. For example research on children's use of strategies to improve retention (discussed in the next section) provides some important insights into general developmental changes in children's problem-solving skills.

For these and other reasons researchers have shown considerable interest in the development of memory for the past several years, and a large literature exists to document this interest. In this chapter we shall provide an overview of research and theory on the development of memory in children. We begin, in the next section, with an overview of the empirical literature. The section on memory models concerns some of the theoretical frameworks that have been used to organize the literature. We conclude with our assessment of the "state of the art" in research on the development of memory.

OVERVIEW OF THE LITERATURE

Use of Strategies

Children's use of mnemonic strategies has been the subject of extensive investigation over the past 15 years. The initial studies of this topic, conducted in the middle and the late 1960s, revealed that by eight or nine years of age children would use numerous strategies as aids in their efforts to remember. They would rehearse the names of stimuli (i.e., say the names repeatedly, either overtly or covertly) and organize stimuli in terms of various semantic properties. Younger children typically would fail to use either of these or any of a number of other potentially helpful mnemonics. Younger children often seemed to be conspicuously inactive cognitively in response to instructions to remember, a marked contrast to the elaborate memorization schemes of older children.

Later studies were designed to examine the young child's apparent lack of efforts to memorize. It was found that young children are, in fact, often aware that a memorization instruction is an implicit call for cognitive activity. Young children were found to heed this call sometimes, but with simpler strategies than had been examined in the initial studies.

Another line of research concerned developmental change in use of strategies in middle and late childhood and during adolescence. After strategies are first used with some consistency in the early elementary school years, there seems to be a gradual developmental progression in the effectiveness and flexibility with which strategies are implemented.

We will substantiate this general picture by selectively examining the relevant empirical literature. General reviews of the literature on children's use of strategies are available in Brown (1975, 1978), Hagen, Jongeward, and Kail (1975), and Kail (1979a). Reviews of the development of specific strategies are found in Hagen and Stanovich (1977), Kobasigawa (1977), Ornstein and Naus (1978), and Reese (1977).

An Illustrative Example. The developmental course of numerous strategies has been charted. Rehearsal, organization, imagery, and cueing would be prominent examples of mnemonic strategies studied by developmental psychologists. Here we shall examine developmental changes in rehearsal, for converging data lead to a clear pattern of developmental change.

An early study by Flavell, Beach, and Chinsky (1966) is instructive. Seven pictures were shown to five-, seven-, and ten-year-olds, and an experimenter pointed to three of the pictures as the stimuli to be remembered on a given trial. Rehearsal was assessed by observing a child's spontaneous verbalizations—a procedure made feasible because the experimenter was trained as a lip reader and because the names of the stimuli were quite discriminable from one another. Only 10 percent of the five-year-olds showed evidence of verbalization on any of the recall trials. Among the seven-year-olds 60 percent of the children verbalized at least once, but only 25 percent verbalized with some regularity. Finally by age ten, 85 percent of the children verbalized, and 65 percent did so consistently. Recall also improved with development, as predicted.

Variations of Flavell et al.'s procedure have appeared in several studies. One tack is to tell children that if they "think about the stimuli" to do so aloud (e.g., Ornstein & Naus, 1978), a procedure that facilitates accurate measurement but which may also serve to prompt behaviors that might not occur spontaneously. Another approach is to make electromyographical recordings of vocalizations (e.g., Locke & Fehr, 1970) which detect the presence of inaudible verbalizations but do not identify the contents of those verbalizations. Fortunately, however, the use of these various procedures leads to conclusions similar to those reached by Flavell et al. (1966): Rehearsal is not a

common cognitive activity prior to nine or ten years of age.

Studies in which children's verbalizations are measured directly are complemented by experiments in which rehearsal has been measured inferentially. One popular procedure has been to examine children's recall as a function of the serial position in a list in which an item is presented. Adults recall initial stimuli in a list much more accurately than subsequent stimuli. This "primacy effect" is attributable to the use of rehearsal, and thus it is of considerable interest that a distinct primacy effect is rarely seen in recall by children eight years of age and younger (Hagen & Kail, 1973; Hagen & Kingsley, 1968; Hagen, Meacham, & Mesibov, 1970).

Another inferential measure of rehearsal is based on the temporal characteristics of rehearsal. When subjects are allowed to control rate of presentation of stimuli, individuals who rehearse will gradually increase the amount of time between presentation of successive stimuli. This differentiated pattern of study time, necessitated because each additional stimulus increases the total amount of time needed for rehearsal, is not seen in children younger than age ten (Belmont & Butterfield, 1971).

Studies in which rehearsal has been measured inferentially converge with those in which it was measured directly to suggest that not until approximately nine or ten years of age do children routinely rehearse stimuli in a memory task. The principal discrepancy between the studies concerns the activities of younger children. Inferential measures provide no clear evidence of deliberate memory behavior in young children, while studies with direct measures suggest some nominal memorization, such as cursory naming of stimuli during presentation. This difference perhaps reflects the greater sensitivity of the direct measurement techniques.

More generally it should be emphasized that a similar pattern of developmental change could be enumerated for each of the strategies mentioned earlier. Not until 10 or 11 years of age will children try to aid retention by deliberately organizing stimuli in terms of their membership in conceptual categories (Moely, Olson, Halwes, & Flavell, 1969). Similarly 11-year-olds will intentionally use category cues to help them retrieve information while 6-year-olds do so only irregularly (Kobasigawa, 1974). In other words the research described thus far points to a reasonably consistent developmental progression (Flavell, 1977; Kail, 1979a): (1) infrequent use of strategies among five- and six-year-olds; (2) a transitional stage from seven to ten years of age, when strategies may appear depending upon factors related to the strategy itself and to the context in which the strategy is to be used; and (3) the first inkling of mature strategy use at approximately ten years of age.

The Young Child as Strategist—A Closer Look. Thus far our description of young children's strategic efforts has been decidedly negative: Young children do not rehearse, they do not organize stimuli, and they do not use cues to aid retrieval. Efforts to explain the young child's apparent lack of strategic activity have increasingly focused on young children's knowledge of memory phenomena and how such knowledge may guide their memory behavior. Among mature memorizers much memory behavior is generated by a vast, often implicit, knowledge about memory. College students generally prefer multiple-choice exams to essay exams because of the implicit understanding that recognition is usually less demanding than recall. Similarly college students typically prefer unit exams to final exams because of the tacit awareness that a small amount of material is more readily remembered than a large amount. Other examples could be given; the point is that such knowledge of memory—referred to as *metamemory* (Flavell, 1971)—serves to direct much memory behavior.

Much of this knowledge probably is not taught directly but is instead acquired gradually throughout development as children experience new and varied demands on their memory skills (Hagen, 1971). This realization has led to considerable study of the development of metamnemonic knowledge, with special emphasis on ways in which limitations in such knowledge might be a factor underlying young children's infrequent use of strategies (Brown, 1978; Flavell & Wellman, 1977).

Consider, for example, the child's growing awareness with development that there is a need to remember (Flavell & Wellman, 1977). A child must become sensitive to cues that signal the need to remember and realize that such cues have implications for one's behavior. Perhaps five- and six-year-olds simply do not understand that the phrase "Try to remember these" should be associated with a distinct class of mental activities.

Understanding of these phenomena typically has been assessed by testing children on a memory task in two conditions. In one condition they are given explicit instructions to remember the stimuli; in the other, stimuli are introduced with instructions that do not mention retention, either explicitly or implicitly. To the extent that recall in the first condition exceeds that in the second, we have tentative evidence that instructions to remember have some distinct cognitive implications for the child.

This procedure was used by Appel, Cooper, McCarrell, Sims-Knight, Yussen, and Flavell (1972) in a study with 4-, 7-, and 11-year-olds. Two sets of pictures were shown to the children, one with instructions to look at them—on the pretext that it would improve performance on a later task—and one with instructions to remember the pictures. The 11-year-olds were much more likely to engage in mnemonic activity (e.g., rehearsal, categorization) following instructions to remember than instructions to look, and their recall was higher as well. The four-year-olds, in contrast, behaved and recalled similarly in the two conditions. The seven-year-olds were the most interesting group, for while their recall was nearly identical in the two conditions, mnemonic strategies like naming and sequential pointing were much more likely after instructions to remember. Apparently these children ". . . did know that any memory task calls for some special effort and activity . . . but knew less well just what to do, in the way of mnemonically effective activity" (Appel et al., 1972, p. 1380).

These findings suggest that earlier research on the development of strategies may have underestimated young children's strategic competence. By focusing, for the most part, on the development of particular strategies, investigators may have missed other signals of strategic intentions. In fact when tasks are devised in which such simple

behaviors as looking and pointing are the appropriate strategies, even preschoolers show surprising skill. They will recall the activities of an adult more accurately if told beforehand that they will be asked to remember the **activities** than if told that they will be playing a game with the adult (Yussen, 1974). Also preschoolers will recall the location of an object or event more accurately **when** told beforehand that they will be asked to do so (Acredolo, Pick, & Olsen, 1975; Wellman, Ritter, & Flavell, 1975). In each case the increase in recall was associated with increases in pointing and looking at the to-be-remembered information.

These results necessitate a revision of the developmental sequence proposed initially. Even very young children seem to have the intent to behave strategically; whether they will be able to effect that intention will depend on the particular memory problem and the strategies appropriate to its solution. Nonverbal, motor activities like pointing and looking are more likely to be in the strategic repertoire of young children than are such verbal-semantic mnemonics as rehearsal and categorization. However this dichotomy is little more than a first attempt at a framework for understanding young children's strategic behavior. It is a framework that is undeniably simplistic and probably wrong in some important ways. A detailed characterization of the young child's strategic talents is one important target for future research (Brown & DeLoache, 1978; Kail, 1979a).

Later Developments in Strategic Behavior. Whether we mark the onset of strategic activity with looking in the four-year-old or with rehearsal in the nine-year-old, one point remains the same: There is considerable additional development in strategic behavior after this initial appearance. With development children become increasingly flexible in their use of strategies, tailoring them as necessary to fit a memory problem, thereby improving retention maximally. Research in this area has revealed several ways in which children diagnose memory tasks more efficiently as they grow older.

Structure of information to be remembered. By five or six years of age children realize that the number of stimuli affects the difficulty of a memory problem (Kruetzer, Leonard, & Flavell, 1975; Wellman, 1977) and that the spatial arrangement of stimuli typically is irrelevant to task difficulty (Kreutzer et al., 1975). They are much less knowledgeable concerning the beneficial effects of semantic relations among stimuli (Kreutzer et al., 1975; Moynahan, 1973; Yussen, Levin, Berman, & Palm, 1979). Not until early adolescence will children modify their rehearsal to take advantage of the semantic structure of a list of words (Ornstein, Naus, & Liberty, 1975). Similarly only in early adolescence do people allocate additional study time to the important portions of a narrative; prior to this period they often distribute their study time evenly between the essential and nonessential portions of a text (Brown & Smiley, 1978).

Format of a memory problem. Along with the content of a memory problem, the format of a memory problem can be an important determinant of task difficulty. The recognition-recall distinction mentioned earlier is one such structural characteristic. As early as age five, children may have a rudimentary understanding of the relative ease of recognition memory tasks (Speer & Flavell, 1979), but there is discordant evidence (Levin, Yussen, DeRose, & Pressley, 1977). More consistent evidence is available for two other structural characteristics of memory tasks. By eight years of age children have a firm understanding that the length of a retention interval affects task difficulty (Kreutzer et al., 1975) and allocate their study time accordingly, studying more in anticipation of longer retention intervals (Rogoff, Newcombe, & Kagan, 1974). Further by age eight, children also understand that verbatim retention is more difficult than gist retention (Kreutzer et al., 1975) and report that different study strategies should be used for each (Myers & Paris, 1978).

Contents of memory. The ability to analyze the contents of one's memory is a third factor that operates in conjunction with the preceding two factors to determine the ease with which a child learns information. A skilled learner periodically evaluates his/her progress on a learning or memory task in order that subsequent study may be allocated in the most efficacious way. By five or six years of age, children can reliably distinguish what they know from what they do not (Berch & Evans, 1973), although such judgments will become much more accurate throughout the elementary school years (Bisanz, Vesonder, & Voss, 1978; Moynahan, 1976; Wellman, 1977). We know very little about children's spontaneous use of such judgments to guide their mnemonic activity. The lone study in the literature (Masur, McIntyre, & Flavell, 1973) indicates that eight-year-olds' study behavior is influenced by their progress on a memory task, while six-year-olds' behavior is not.

Cultural Prerequisites for the Development of Strategies.
Earlier we suggested that strategies are probably acquired gradually in response to different experiential demands for retention. As Hagen put it,

He [a child] acquires new skills, some of which come about without his intending to learn them, and others which he sets out to attain. At the same time, he begins to realize that he is an actor in his environment as well as a reactor to it. Task demands are made increasingly upon him and more differentiated responses are required. What he is really learning is that *he* himself determines how well he does, and that he can improve his performance if he uses certain of his new skills in certain task situations. (1971, pp. 267–268)

Thus as children grow older, they may detect regularities between their behavior and their success in coping with memory problems.

The intriguing problem, of course, is to identify those experiences that may be critical in the child's emergence as a strategist. Some theorists, notably Cole and Scribner (1977), have argued that experience in formal school settings may be a necessary condition for the development of mnemonic strategies.

Schools represent the major cultural institution in technological societies where remembering as a distinct activity, occurring apart from the application of anything remembered, is engaged in repeatedly with a great variety of stimulus materials.... It is difficult to think of any other generally experienced setting in which members of technological societies engage in deliberate memorizing.... When we turn to societies that lack formal educational institutions, where can we find

such activities? The answer, we believe, is rarely. (Cole & Scribner, 1977, p. 269)

In other words Cole and Scribner (1977) believe that schools are unique in their vigorous emphasis on memorization per se as a behavioral goal and that children apparently acquire "general purpose" mnemonic strategies and attendant metamnemonic knowledge in response to this emphasis.

As might be expected efforts to evaluate this hypothesis have taken the form of cross-cultural research. The findings of this literature are surprisingly consistent: Uneducated persons generally behave in ways akin to young Western children—that is, these individuals rarely use mnemonics on memory tasks when it would be advantageous to do so.[1] A brief sampling of findings documents this conclusion.

1. Stevenson, Parker, Wilkinson, Bonnevaux, and Gonzalez (1978) compared the performance of schooled and unschooled six-year-olds on a battery of seven memory tasks. The schooled children's performance exceeded that of the unschooled children on every task, by margins that ranged from approximately 10 percent to nearly 50 percent. While no effort was made to see if these differences were attributable to the schooled children's use of strategies, the tasks used were ones for which many simple strategies would be appropriate.
2. Wagner (1974) used a serial position task like that described earlier to examine rehearsal by individuals living on the Yucatan peninsula of Mexico. Among educated individuals the developmental changes resembled those found with samples of North American children. In contrast uneducated persons at all ages were unlikely to rehearse.
3. Cole, Gay, Glick, and Sharp (1971), working among the Kpelle of Liberia, found that high school students used the conceptual structure of a list to organize their recall, while uneducated adolescents did not.

Despite the consistency of these findings, one potential problem is that the presence of schools in a culture is often highly correlated with other characteristics, such as urbanization, which might be responsible for the differences between educated and uneducated groups. However when care is taken to include as subjects uneducated urban individuals as well as rural educated persons, the pattern of results does not change noticeably. In the Stevenson et al. (1978) study cited earlier, urban dwelling children had higher retention on four of seven measures, but education and cultural setting interacted statistically for only two of the seven measures. Similar effects were reported by Wagner (1978). Thus it seems that at least some of the memory differences found in these studies are due to differences in education, although other cultural variations may modulate the magnitude of effects associated with schooling.

If we accept the conclusion that differences in strategic behavior are linked to schooling, what can be said of

[1] It is not being claimed that uneducated persons are totally incapable of strategic behavior. Indeed societies lacking formal schools often provide complicated mnemonics for retention of culturally valued events and information (Colby, 1975). However these mnemonics are tied explicitly to specific to-be-remembered information and are not generalized for use in other memory problems where they might be useful (Cole & Scribner, 1977).

these differences? Perhaps unschooled individuals simply fail to use strategies because they are unfamiliar with or are intimidated by the laboratory setting. An alternative is that the failure to use strategies actually reflects a more general memory or cognitive deficiency; inefficient use of strategies is, according to this view, just one instance of deficient cognitive skill in illiterate people.

If either of these suggestions is accurate, then we would expect uneducated individuals to perform poorly on all memory tasks, not just those that require the use of strategies—that is, unfamiliarity, intimidation, or global cognitive limitations all point to pervasive deficits in performance. Relevant data come from a study by Wagner (1978) in which literate and illiterate Moroccan children and adults were tested on two different memory tasks. In a serial position task, developmental changes in rehearsal typical of those found in Western samples were found for groups of educated subjects; rehearsal was uniformly infrequent at all grades in the unschooled groups. All individuals were also tested on a recognition memory task that minimized the need for strategies. A very different pattern of results emerged, with the differences between literate and illiterate people completely eliminated in rural areas and greatly reduced among those living in the city.

Thus the findings cited earlier about cultural differences in strategic activity cannot be explained away in terms of (1) the schoolchild's greater awareness and ease with laboratory-like tasks and settings or (2) an all-encompassing cognitive shift that is provided by education. Schooling fosters the development of a multitude of intellectual skills, with strategic behavior being one important instance.

Two points should be made regarding the role of education in facilitating the growth of strategic behavior. First, our understanding of how schooling fosters a child's acquisition of strategies and associated mnemonic knowledge is essentially nil. Evidence is scant on the specific memory demands that teachers may make and how children respond to these early demands. Second, we have seen that young children are capable of at least some strategic activity long before they enter elementary school. Consequently a search for the experiential antecedents of early strategic behavior will necessarily involve probing the memory demands of the young child's play and home environments.

Knowledge and Memory

The research described in the previous section—like much memory work in experimental psychology—is a part of the Ebbinghaus tradition of memory experimentation. Subjects are asked to remember for brief periods of time information that is not abundant in meaning. The stimuli are likely to be pictures of familiar objects, lists of common words, or series of digits. Investigators often go to great lengths to ensure that older children do not have a mnemonic advantage by virtue of greater familiarity or knowledge of the stimuli.

There is, however, another tradition of memory research, that traced to Bartlett (1932), which has had growing impact on empirical and theoretical efforts in developmental and experimental psychology. From this perspective the growing child's increase in knowledge and understanding is more than a variable subject to experimental control. It is, instead, seen as a valuable mnemonic asset that is probably an important source of developmental change in memory. As Flavell and Wellman put it,

Older individuals presumably store, retain, and retrieve a great many inputs better or differently than younger ones. They will do so simply because developmental advances in the content or structure of their semantic or conceptual systems render these inputs more familiar, meaningful, conceptually interrelated, subject to inference and gap filling, or otherwise more memorable for them. (1977, p. 4)

Interest in these developmental changes is more recent than interest in the strategic aspect of memory. The empirical and theoretical bases are limited by comparison and lack the focus of the research on strategic development. In this section we shall examine three primary lines of inquiry that represent this new tradition of research.

Piagetian Research on Memory. It is hardly surprising that Piaget (1968; Piaget & Inhelder, 1973) was among the first to probe ways in which conceptual development—*operative development* in Piagetian terminology—can have important implications for retention. Piaget (1968) argued that the memory trace for an event changes with development in step with changes in the operative schemes reponsible for interpreting that event. For example preoperational children should be incapable of accurately remembering an ordered series of sticks because they lack the concept of seriation; concrete operational children should be considerably more capable because of their acquisition of the seriation concept.

Piaget's (1968) theory leads to two testable claims about memory change (Liben, 1977). First, as in the example just cited, cross-sectional studies should reveal large differences in performance when the stimuli tap operative schemes that will be developed in older children but not in younger ones. Second, as children acquire new operative schemes, their representations of previously experienced, operatively related stimuli should be updated, and consequently their retention should actually improve. This claim has led to longitudinal experiments in which children's retention is tested soon (e.g., one week) after presentation of an operative stimulus and again after a much longer interval (e.g., several months). The prediction is that retention should be more accurate at the longer interval than the shorter one, due to the intervening operative growth.

Several types of evidence are available for evaluating these claims, and three are considered here.

Cross-sectional evidence. While the original Piagetian work (Piaget, 1968; Piaget & Inhelder, 1973) suggested much agreement between children's operative level and their retention of operatively relevant stimuli, later cross-sectional efforts have not achieved similar high levels of correspondence. Consistent with the Piagetian position Liben (1975) found that drawings of seriated sticks by nine-year-olds were much more accurate than five-year-olds' drawings of these stimuli. Unexpected, however, was the finding that five-year-olds drew the pictures of verticality and seriation concepts with approximately equal ease, despite the fact that the children were operatively much more advanced on the seriation concept than the verticality concept.

Similarly in a study by Furth, Ross, and Youniss (1974), children were shown operatively incorrect pictures and immediately thereafter were asked to draw the stimuli. The percentage of children whose drawings were operatively correct (and hence inaccurate renderings of the picture) increased steadily from kindergarten to grade four. Yet even among the oldest children the modal response was an accurate, operatively incorrect drawing.

Correlational evidence. Cross-sectional studies involve examining retention by children of different ages and, hence, different operative levels (with age often being used to infer operative level). A related strategy has been to examine children at an age where many are likely to be in transition between operative stages. Their operative level is assessed, then is correlated with the extent to which their drawings of stimuli reflect this operative level. The general finding here is that the correlations are positive but of modest size. Maurer, Siegel, Lewis, Kristofferson, Barnes, and Levy (1979) reported a correlation of .42 between seriation ability and children's drawing of a seriated array. Seriation ability was unrelated ($r = -.13$) to retention of a figure that was thought to be unrelated to any operative schemes. Other investigators (e.g., Liben, 1975) have reported similar correlations.

It is also the case that the correlations often vary considerably across experimental conditions, for reasons that are not at all obvious. For example the correlations mentioned earlier from the Maurer et al. (1979) study involved retention as measured by a drawing task. When a recognition task was used to measure retention, seriation ability was unrelated to retention of the operative stimulus but did relate to retention of the nonoperative stimulus ($r = .45$). Similar variations in correlations across conditions or stimuli have been found by Liben (1975) and Murray and Bausell (1970).

Longitudinal evidence. Piaget and Inhelder (1973) reported dramatic changes in retention in their longitudinal data. In retention of seriated arrays, nearly 75 percent of the children drew more accurate pictures after six to eight months had elapsed since initial presentation of a stimulus. Replications of these studies (see Liben, 1977) have never reported improvements of this magnitude. At one extreme Maurer et al. (1979) found that only 15 percent of the six-year-olds in their study had operatively more advanced drawings after a six-month interval. At the other extreme investigators have reported that 40 percent to 45 percent of the children tested had more advanced drawings after an interval of several months (e.g., Altemeyer, Fulton, & Berney, 1969; Dahlem, 1968, 1969).

These findings, while not as dramatic as those of the original work (Piaget, 1968; Piaget & Inhelder, 1973), seem consistent with it. However two related findings should be considered in conjunction with these results. First, in most studies the modal response is for children to produce operatively similar drawings regardless of the time elapsed since a stimulus was last seen—that is, there is no change in the operative level of a child's drawing.

Second, the number of children with improved drawings is generally matched by the number of children whose performance deteriorated over time (i.e., becomes operatively less advanced). In none of the replication studies has the number of improvements significantly surpassed the number of regressions.

Evaluation. The close correspondence between memory and a child's operative level noted by Piaget and Inhelder (1973) is not found in the replication studies. Evidence from the cross-sectional and correlational studies provide the greatest support for the Piagetian view; longitudinal studies provide the least support. Some investigators (e.g., Maurer et al., 1979) seem to view this imperfect correspondence as sounding a death knell for the Genevan description of memory change. A more reasonable approach would be to acknowledge that a perfect correspondence between operativity and retention is highly unlikely. Operative level must interact with other memory processes in order to produce retention, and these latter processes probably serve to reduce the degree of empirical correspondence. Rather than focusing on the absolute magnitude of the relationship—an apparent preoccupation with much of the extant literature—a more useful aim for future research would be to determine those processes that modulate the effect of operative level on retention.

Encoding of Words. One line of investigation represents a blend of the Ebbinghaus and Bartlett traditions of memory research. Investigators in this area have been concerned with ways in which children's increased knowledge—in particular their increased lexical knowledge—may affect the ways in which words or pictures are encoded in memory.

The encoding shift hypothesis. Several theorists have proposed that young children typically encode events in memory in terms of their perceptual features; with development these features are supplanted by conceptually or semantically based characteristics. Bruner (1964) proposed the well-known developmental sequence in which the primary mode of mental representation shifts from enactive (i.e., motorically based) to iconic (i.e., coding in the form of percepts and images) to symbolic. Bruner's formulation stimulated some research on memory in the 1960s (e.g., Corsini, 1969a, 1969b), but there has been little related research since that time, primarily because the various modes of representation were not well defined by Bruner, making evaluation of the framework problematic (see Kosslyn, 1978, for a telling critique of Bruner's representational scheme).

A second notion of developmental change in mnemonic representations has provoked much controversy among researchers of memory development. The hypothesis, proposed by Underwood (1969), is more circumscribed than Bruner's; rather than attempting to account for mental representation of all experience, Underwood's proposal concerned the ways in which individual words might be represented in memory and possible developmental change therein. Underwood, like other theorists (e.g., Bower, 1967), conceptualized the representation of a word in memory as consisting of a list of features characterizing that word. *Dog* for instance might be represented in memory as *animal, four-legged, furry,* and *barks.* Underwood (1969) suggested that the features used to represent a word in memory might change developmentally. "In a very young child, the associative attributes may be subordinate to other attributes, particularly the acoustic and spatial. . . . As a child ages . . . the primary attributes may change, with the associative verbal attributes becoming more and more common" (p. 571).

These claims have been examined in the case of words and pictures using a "false recognition procedure." Bach and Underwood (1970) asked children to remember a list of words. A recognition test followed which included words presented originally plus distractors that either rhymed with or were semantically related to the original words. The seven-year-olds falsely recognized rhyming distractor words much more often than semantically related distractors, results that point to the importance of acoustic characteristics in young children's encoding. It is also important to note that the false recognition of rhyming words was similar at the two ages. The developmental interaction resulted from a large increase in the frequency of false recognitions of semantically related words.

Similar findings have been reported by Felzen and Anisfeld (1970) and Means and Rohwer (1976) which would appear to give strong support to the notion of a "perceptual to conceptual" shift in the development of encoding. However interpretation of these data is not as straightforward as it might seem. A methodological problem in these studies is that false recognition errors occur relatively infrequently (Lindauer & Paris, 1976). Thus the pattern of developmental change reported is often based on errors to a limited group of words. Conclusions from these words about the typical nature of children's encoding are probably hazardous. When other methods are used, such as providing different types of cues for recall (Ghatala & Hurlbut, 1973), examining release from interference (Geis, 1975), or using response latency as a dependent measure (Bisanz, Kail, Pellegrino, & Siegel, 1979), little support is found for the proposed developmental shift in encoding.

A second problem with this literature is that none of the methods used would allow an investigator to determine unequivocally that encoding was the locus of developmental change. Susceptibility to interference (or rate of decay) might decrease rapidly with development for semantic information but remain relatively stable for acoustic information, or perhaps retrieval processes for acoustic and semantic information change differentially with age. Either of these explanations could account for the findings of Bach and Underwood (1970) and other investigators, yet neither assumes that encoding per se changes developmentally (Bisanz et al., 1979).

What, then, is the status of the encoding shift hypothesis? The broadest, most general form of the hypothesis appears to be incorrect: Young children do not rely consistently on perceptual codes. A more limited form of the hypothesis may well survive. In certain contexts young children may be more prone than older ones to use perceptually based codes. The empirical problem is to determine the factor(s) that lead to the formation of perceptual codes and to discover the specific mnemonic processes associated with their use.

More on semantic encoding. Several lines of research which have evolved independently of the encoding shift literature suggest the importance of conceptual encoding from an early age and also indicate an interesting developmental change in this encoding.

Preschoolers' encoding of a word's conceptual category was demonstrated by Esrov, Hall, and LaFaver (1974) using a "release from interference" paradigm (Wickens, 1972). Each trial consisted of (1) presentation of three pictures to be remembered, (2) a distracting task, reading numbers for 15 seconds, and (3) a brief period for recall of the three pictures. On Trials 1–3, three different pictures from the same category (e.g., animals) were shown on each trial. Recall was nearly perfect on Trial 1 but declined on Trials 2 and 3. Words presented on Trial 4 to children in the experimental group were from a different category (e.g., clothing); for children in the control group, additional pictures were selected from the original category. Only recall by children in the experimental group increased between Trials 3 and 4. The increase presumably reflects the fact that children encoded the conceptual category distinguishing the words on Trial 3 and those on Trial 4.

Converging evidence for encoding of conceptual categories by very young children comes from a study by Faulkender, Wright, and Waldron (1974) in which two- and three-year-olds were shown six different pictures, six times each. Then 18 additional pictures were shown, including the familiar ones (i.e., the original six), pictures not seen previously but from the same conceptual categories and pictures from a different category. Children looked longer at both classes of novel pictures than at the familiar pictures. More importantly children looked longer at the novel pictures from a different category than those from the familiar category, suggesting that the children had encoded the conceptual categories of the pictures.

A third relevant line of inquiry concerns children's recall of categorized lists. Here children's recall of related words—usually drawn from several familiar categories—is compared to recall of unrelated words. The typical finding is that recall is greater in the former condition, regardless of the age of the child tested (Moely, 1977). The point is well illustrated in a study by Perlmutter and Myers (1979), who compared children's recall of a related list of words (*bear, cow, pig; boat, car, plane; bowl, cup, plate*) with their recall of an unrelated list (*bell, clock, drum, flag, horse, leaf, pen, star, truck*). For both two- and four-year-olds, recall of the related list exceeded recall of the unrelated list, a common finding with school-age children and adolescents as well (Moely, 1977; Ornstein & Corsale, 1980). However, the mnemonic benefits of the related list increased with age. The four-year-olds recalled approximately 1 to 1½ more words from related lists than from unrelated lists, while the difference was less than one word for two-year-olds.[2]

---

[2] This interaction with age is not always found with school-age children and adolescents (Lange, 1978). Several investigators report comparable mnemonic benefits for related lists throughout the 6- to 14-year-old range (Cole, Frankel, & Sharp, 1971; Jongeward, 1975; Vaughan, 1968) while other experimenters report developmental increases in the additional words recalled to related lists (e.g., Furth & Milgram, 1973). The prevailing explanation of

The findings of Perlmutter and Myers (1979) when combined with those of Esrov et al. (1974) and Faulkender et al. (1974) point to a common conclusion, one that was certainly unanticipated by most memory researchers: Almost as soon as children can speak well (and hence can be tested with the pet paradigms of memory researchers), their mnemonic representations of individual pictures and words seem to be semantically based.

Recall of Prose. When Bartlett (1932) asked adults to recall stories they had heard previously, he found that subjects almost always remembered the general form of the story and recalled the major events in their appropriate order. At the same time they rarely retained individual sentences, tending to paraphrase the text instead. Furthermore they often "recalled" information that had not even been presented; in effect they elaborated the story line by drawing upon their general knowledge about events like those in the story. In sum, recall of stories was seen to be a *constructive* act in which subjects remembered a story framework, then filled in that framework with details from the story as well as information from their general knowledge.

Many of these same phenomena occur when children are asked to recall prose. By six or seven years of age children's recall resembles that of adults in many ways. First, they tend to recall important features of a story and forget the trivial ones (Christie & Schumacher, 1975; Mandler & Johnson, 1977). Second, children at this age forget the syntactic structure of sentences but remember their meanings (Barclay & Reid, 1974; Frasure & Entwisle, 1973; Heras & Nelson, 1972). Finally, they often "recall" information that is semantically consistent with a story but which was not really presented (Brown, Smiley, Day, Townsend, & Lawton, 1977). From the early elementary school years, then, the qualitative structure of children's recall is similar to that of adults in its emphasis on constructive recall of meaning.

Yet there are important developmental advances relating to children's ability to construct an elaborated semantic representation of prose. One noteworthy developmental acquisition is the tendency to integrate semantically similar or redundant material. Hearing "The batter hit the ball. It sailed into left field," a listener is likely to represent the information in memory as "The batter hit the ball into left field." By eight years of age children integrate sentences in this manner, with the consequence that they think the integrated sentence was actually presented earlier, when in fact only its constituents were presented (Liben & Posnansky, 1977; Paris & Carter, 1973). Eight-year-olds will also integrate a series of related pictures, again as indicated by their tendency to "recognize" a composite picture as having been shown earlier when in reality only components had been shown previously (Paris & Mahoney, 1974).

A second important age-related change occurs in children's ability to make inferences from elements within prose and include these inferences as part of their mnemonic representations of the prose. When a passage describes a familiar simple action (e.g., baking), 11- and 12-year-olds automatically infer the agent that performs the activity (e.g., oven) and include the agent as part of their representation of that passage; 6- and 7-year-olds are much less likely to do so (Paris & Lindauer, 1976). Not all inferences show exactly this pattern of change. Adults will often infer the consequences of an action (e.g., turning off the lights—a dark room), while children and adolescents are less likely to make these inferences (Paris, Lindauer, & Cox, 1977). Exactly why inference of instruments occurs developmentally prior to inference of consequences remains unclear. The more general point, however, is that throughout childhood and adolescence children are increasingly likely to use their knowledge of the world to embellish prose, with improved retention the result (Paris & Upton, 1976).

In summary three findings stand out in research on children's retention of prose. One is a finding of developmental invariance in the overall quality of recall: The emphasis on recall as the construction of the gist of a passage is evident by age six or seven years. The second and third findings emphasize complementary developmental changes. On the one hand children's representations of passages are economical in that they retain only the salient semantic features of prose, eliminating redundancies and irrelevant information to pare a text down to its semantic essentials. Yet on the other hand they will often draw upon their relevant knowledge of those semantic essentials to embellish their mnemonic representation of a passage in various meaningful ways, thus providing a multitude of potentially helpful cues for use in trying to recall the passage.

Commentary. The literature reviewed in this section lacks the cohesiveness of the research on strategic development. Important theoretical issues are not yet pinpointed; a comprehensive conceptual framework is not available. Methodological problems abound; useful and insightful paradigms are sought eagerly. In part this state of affairs is attributable to the relative recency of Bartlett's (1932) influence on research in memory development. However this also reflects the complexity of the problem at hand: Unraveling the many intricate relations between conceptual development and memory appears to be a decidedly more complicated problem than charting children's strategic development, and its solution will require considerable empirical ingenuity and theoretical scope.

Developmental Invariance in Memory

A third literature on children's memory is tied together primarily by similar findings—i.e., the absence of age differences in performance. When memory tasks minimize the use of strategies or minimize the potential role of conceptual knowledge, developmental differences in performance are likely to be minimized as well. In this section some of the tasks where the rule is developmental similarity of performance are examined.

---

the discrepancy is Lange's (1973, 1978) who argues that when categorized words are highly related associatively (*cat-dog*) that similar gains in recall will be found throughout childhood and adolescence. However when words from a common category do not share this associative relation (e.g., *cat-ostrich*) only older children should profit from categorical relations.

Recognition Memory. Young children's recognition skills stand in marked contrast to their recall skills. Brown and Campione (1972) showed a series of 80 pictures of people and animals to four-year-olds. A recognition test given later consisted of pairs of pictures. Some pairs included a picture seen previously as well as a new picture depicting the same character in a novel pose. Other pairs of pictures consisted of a new character in two different poses. One week after viewing the stimuli, children discriminated old characters from new ones with approximately 90 percent accuracy. Given that a character was correctly identified as having been seen previously, children recognized the correct pose approximately 85 percent of the time.

Similarly impressive findings emerge with much younger children if nonverbal techniques are used. Daehler and Bukatko (1977) measured the length of time children spent looking at pictures that were shown to them. A picture was shown twice, once alone and a second time with a novel picture. Even when 50 pictures intervened between the two presentations, 18-month-olds looked reliably longer at the novel picture, indicating that they recognized the familiar picture as just that—one seen before.

Of course there are exceptions to these findings. Younger children's performance can be shown to be considerably poorer than that of older children and adults when recognition is made dependent upon conceptual development (e.g., Mandler & Robinson, 1978) or attentional processes (e.g., Hoffman & Dick, 1976). These findings notwithstanding, the preschool child is generally able to recognize large numbers of stimuli with considerable accuracy.

Memory Search. When adults are shown a subspan set of stimuli and immediately thereafter are asked if a particular stimulus was a member of that set, response time is typically a linear increasing function of the number of stimuli in the set (Sternberg, 1966). For adults, response time typically increases about 35 to 40 milliseconds for each additional stimulus, a value thought to reflect the amount of time necessary to search memory for each additional stimulus.

Studies of developmental change in memory search generally find similarities across age in the rate of memory search. From age five years through young adulthood, individuals search memory for sets of two to four familiar pictures at a rate of approximately 40 milliseconds per digit (Baumeister & Maisto, 1977; Hoving, Morin, & Konick, 1970; Maisto & Baumeister, 1975). Similar developmental consistency has been found in three studies in which digits constituted the set to be searched (Harris & Fleer, 1974; Maisto & Baumeister, 1975). In two other studies using digits (Herrmann & Landis, 1977; Naus & Ornstein, 1977), search became faster with age. An explanation for the disparate outcomes is not obvious. Suffice it to say that under certain as yet unknown conditions, developmental differences in the rate of memory search are negligible.

There are some interesting exceptions to the rule of developmental similarity in rate of memory search. Baumeister and Maisto (1977) compared 5- to 11-year-olds' search of familiar pictures with their search of random forms. All age groups searched familiar pictures at com-

parable rates. More important was the finding that all groups scanned the random shapes more slowly than the familiar pictures and that the difference in search rates was particularly large for the five-year-olds. However if these children were given pretraining in which a unique verbal label was associated with each form, forms were searched as rapidly as familiar pictures.

A second exception was reported by Naus and Ornstein (1977). They compared third- and sixth-graders' search rates for sets that consisted of digits, letters, or a mixed set of digits and letters. The result of interest was that sixth-graders, like adults, searched mixed sets approximately 25 percent more rapidly than the unmixed sets, while third-graders searched mixed and unmixed sets at approximately the same rate. Naus and Ornstein (1977) suggest that the sixth-graders' faster rate of search on mixed lists reflects their use of a different, more efficient, algorithm for search. They argued that sixth-graders (1) began their search by randomly selecting one of the two categories and (2) terminated their search when the category of the test stimulus is selected first (on approximately 50 percent of the trials). Only half the set would be searched, resulting in the shallower function obtained.

The findings of Naus and Ornstein (1977) point to the conclusion that the magnitude of developmental differences in memory search may well be linked to the extent to which semantic information can be used to direct search. If semantic influence is minimal (e.g., as in searching through digits), developmental differences will be small or nonexistent. When lexical and other forms of knowledge can be used to make search of memory more efficient, age differences will more likely occur.

Judgments of Recency. In a judgments of recency task, children are shown a series of pictures. Later they are shown a pair of pictures from the series and are asked to judge which of the pair was presented later (i.e., more recently) in the list. An initial experiment by Mathews and Fozard (1970) indicated a developmental improvement in judgments of recency. However, the series used by Mathews and Fozard contained 7 or 12 pictures, thus allowing for the possibility that age differences in performance may have reflected the older children's use of rehearsal or some other mnemonic that preserves information about the order of simuli. In fact when longer series (i.e., 20+) of pictures are used, there is consistent developmental similarity in performance. Brown (1973) found that 7- to 17-year-olds judged recency with near-perfect accuracy if pictures to be judged were separated by 20 intervening pictures in the presentation series; all groups were at chance levels if the pair had been separated by only 5 pictures.

The developmental pattern is very different, however, when cues are provided to aid in making these judgments. If pictures in the first half of a list appear against one background color while those in the second half appear on a second color, older children will spontaneously use these color cues while younger children will not, as would be expected from our earlier review of strategic development (Brown, Campione, & Gilliard, 1974). Thus the pattern of results on judgments of recency tasks depends upon the extent to which strategies are available.

Individual Differences in Children's Memory

There is only a small amount of research in the literature on individual differences in children's memory. It is presented here to demonstrate (1) the range of ways in which persons of the same chronological age may differ in memory processes and (2) the typical experimental designs that have been used to isolate memory processes as loci of individual differences. It is convenient to discuss two types of work in this area. The first concerns interrelations among measures of memory. The second type of research concerns relations between measures of memory and so-called *index variables*, such as sex and socioeconomic status (SES).

Interrelations among Measures of Children's Memory. When a memory test is used in educational or clinical settings, typically the reason is to provide an estimate of a person's "memory ability." Implicit in this use of memory tests is the notion that memory is a unitary skill and that a chosen test provides an accurate estimate of this skill. In fact there is little evidence supporting the notion of a unitary memory skill. Stevenson, Parker, and Wilkinson (1975) tested 255 five-year-olds on 11 different memory tasks, including digit span, recall of stories, and recall of pictures. Less than half of the correlations were significant; the median correlation was .14. Kail (1975) found similar results with eight- and nine-year-olds: The median correlation between eight measures of memory was .18. A simple notion like a "general memory ability" appears insufficient to explain the nature of individual differences in children's memory.

An alternative explanation is that individual differences in children's memory—like developmental change in memory—might be attributable to differences in children's use of mnemonic strategies. Some children may use strategies consistently and execute them well, with the result that they remember accurately. Other children of the same age may use strategies poorly or not at all and remember inaccurately as a consequence. To evaluate this hypothesis Kail (1979b) tested 8- and 11-year-olds on a battery of memory tasks. Included were tasks for which strategies were appropriate (e.g., the serial position task discussed in the previous section on the use of strategies) as well as tasks presumed to be relatively free of strategic influence (e.g., the judgments of recency task described in the section on developmental invariance). Factor analyses of the data revealed the hypothesized strategic factor for 11-year-olds, as all three strategy-based measures loaded heavily on a single factor. In contrast for 8-year-olds the three strategy measures loaded on three separate factors. Thus "general strategic ability" seems to emerge as a source of individual differences in memory between the ages of 8 and 11 years—that is, as children approach adolescence their strategic proficiency becomes more consistent across different memory problems.

Relations between Index Variables and Memory Performance. Individual differences in children's memory have also been studied by examining relations between memory and several "index" variables. Each area will be summarized briefly, then some of the commonalities that can be seen in this general type of research will be considered.

Sex. Two conclusions can be drawn from research on sex differences in memory. First, sex differences are the exception rather than the rule when memory is concerned (Maccoby & Jacklin, 1974). Boys and girls are equally likely to use mnemonic strategies to aid recall. As Maccoby and Jacklin (1974) conclude, ". . . it clearly cannot be said that either sex has a superior memory capacity or a superior set of skills in the storage and retrieval of information. . . ." (p. 59). Second, sex differences, when found, are not unique to memory but instead mirror the pattern of sex differences in overall cognitive functioning. Girls typically score higher than boys on tests of verbal ability, while the reverse is true for tests of spatial ability (Harris, 1978). This finding would lead us to expect that girls would recall verbal stimuli more accurately than boys who would excel when spatial stimuli are to be recalled. Exactly this pattern of results was found in a recent study with third-graders, sixth-graders, and adults (Kail & Siegel, 1977).

Cognitive styles. Several theorists have argued that individuals differ reliably in their approach to or style of problem solving. A partial list of these styles would include field-independence versus field-dependence, leveling versus sharpening, and reflection versus impulsivity. Of these reflection-impulsivity seems to have been the focus of the most research (Kagan & Kogan, 1970). Typically reflection-impulsivity is assessed with the Matching Familiar Figures (MFF) test (Kagan, Rosman, Day, Albert, & Phillips, 1964) in which the child is shown a standard stimulus and is asked to select the one of several highly similar variants that matches the standard exactly. Impulsive children answer quickly and make many mistakes; reflective children answer more slowly but make few errors.

In recent years the use of the MFF as a measure of reflection-impulsivity has been criticized, as has the construct itself (e.g., Block, Block, & Harrington, 1974). These criticisms notwithstanding there are studies of recognition memory in reflective and impulsive children that should be mentioned. Siegel, Babich, and Kirasic (1974) tested picture recognition in fifth-grade reflective and impulsive boys. Subjects first viewed 96 target pictures. Then they were shown 96 picture pairs, each pair consisting of a target and a distractor. The similarity between the target and distractors was varied systematically. Reflective and impulsive boys were equally accurate when targets and distractors were maximally differentiated. As differences between target and distractor became more subtle, reflective subjects' recognition exceeded that of impulsive subjects. This result has been replicated in similar research (e.g., Siegel, Kirasic, & Kilburg, 1973). From these results it appears that impulsive children's encoding of visual stimuli incorporates considerably less detail than is the case for reflective children.

Socioeconomic status (SES) and race. Interest in the effects of SES and race on memory can be traced to Jensen's (1969) distinction between two types of learning abilities—associative and conceptual learning. Associative learning is said to involve ". . . the neural registration and consolidation of stimulus inputs and the formation of associations. There is relatively little transformation of input" (pp. 110–111). In contrast conceptual learning involves ". . . self-initiated elaboration and transformation of the stimulus input before it eventuates in an overt response" (p. 111). Jensen initially argued that these two learning abilities were distributed differentially according to SES. Lower- and middle-class children were thought to have comparable associative learning abilities; middle-class children were thought to have superior conceptual learning skills. In more recent publications (e.g., Jensen & Figueroa, 1975), the theory has been reformulated in terms of race rather than SES differences.

This theory has resulted in research on memory primarily because Jensen (1969) suggested that two memory tasks provided straightforward estimates of the two learning abilities. Digit span was said to tap associative learning, while free recall of categorized lists (and the extent to which recall was organized around those categories) was said to assess conceptual learning. Thus the theory predicts that social class-race differences should not appear on digit span but that middle-class white children should exceed lower-class black children in terms of the number of words recalled from categorized lists.

The first prediction has been supported consistently in the literature (e.g., Jensen & Figueroa, 1975; Jensen & Frederiksen, 1973; Lacher, 1976; McCarver & Ellis, 1972). Evidence regarding the second prediction is inconsistent. Jensen and Frederiksen (1973) compared free recall of 20 words by lower-class black and middle-class white children. The words were either (1) from 20 different categories, (2) from 5 different categories, with words presented in a random order, or (3) from 5 different categories, with words from the same category presented successively. SES-race differences were found in (2) and (3), but not (1), as predicted from Jensen's theory. Also in line with the theory, Jensen and Figueroa (1975) found essentially no race differences in performance on forward digit span tasks but did find race differences in backward digit span, which is considered to involve conceptual learning because of the lack of correspondence between input and output orders.

Three other studies, however, provide conflicting results. Kee and Helfand (1977) found that lower-class black and middle-class white children were equally likely to encode conceptual categories in a memory task. Schultz, Cherness, and Berman (1973) examined free recall in conditions similar to those used by Jensen and Figueroa (1975) and found no differences in either the number of words recalled nor in the extent to which children used conceptual categories to organize their recall. Finally Stein and Mandler (1975) tested black and white kindergarteners and second-graders on a recognition memory task in which children were asked to detect transformations in the orientation and location of objects and pictures. Few differences were found between black and white children, and those that did emerge were not systematic.

Given the mixed pattern of evidence, it is difficult to provide a definitive evaluation of Jensen's (1969) theory. It should be pointed out, however, that there is evidence which questions the distinction between associative and conceptual learning abilities that is at the heart of this position (e.g., Stevenson, Williams, & Coleman, 1971).

Intelligence (IQ). The relation between IQ and memory has been studied extensively. Retarded children typically remember less accurately than their nonretarded peers, a finding that has stimulated attempts to identify the locus of a retardate memory deficit. In 1963 Ellis proposed that memory traces decay more rapidly in retarded than nonretarded individuals. If decay is more rapid in retardates, then recall differences between retarded and nonretarded individuals should become larger as the retention interval increases. After considerable investigation of this hypothesis in the 1960s, it became clear that the predicted pattern of results was not found frequently. Furthermore when it did emerge, it seemed to reflect differences in the extent to which children used effective strategies to learn material initially rather than differences in rate of decay per se (Belmont & Butterfield, 1969).

This latter conclusion, in turn, prompted research designed to show that retarded and nonretarded persons differ in the likelihood and success with which they use mnemonic strategies. It is now accepted that one basis for the memory deficits found in retardates is their failure to use strategies appropriately (Belmont & Butterfield, 1971; Brown, 1974). There is now complementary evidence indicating that structural components of memory, as well, may be implicated in retardate memory deficiencies (Campione & Brown, 1977). Specifically while rate of decay does not appear to differ in retarded and nonretarded populations, speed of memory search does (Dugas & Kellas, 1974; Harris & Fleer, 1974).

Commentary. Two comments are warranted on the research just outlined. First, several different memory processes have been implicated in individual differences, including use of strategies, encoding, and memory search. Second, differences among groups typically tend to be small relative to variability within the separate groups. The differences described here, when expressed in sigma units, rarely exceed 1; the average difference typically is somewhat less than 0.5. In other words the distributions of memory scores for different groups tend to overlap considerably. Stated another way between-group variability is small compared to within-group variability. This result is not surprising, since groups resulting from classification along index variables are usually broad and loose conglomerates. It does, however, suggest the research strategy that is needed for investigating individual differences in memory. Specifically there seems to be little value in isolating index variables that produce group differences in memory. Rather what is necessary is to study differences among individuals *within* groups. For example in a digit span task, what mnemonic processes differentiate those individuals within an age group who recall well from those who recall only moderately well or poorly?

MODELS OF MEMORY

Initial Reliance on the Model of Atkinson and Shiffrin

As we have pointed out earlier, memory is closely interwoven with cognition and, in fact, is viewed as a key component of cognition in current models of information processing (Kail, 1979a). The definition of memory has been refined and broadened drastically in the past 15 years, and various distinctions have been made that allow for the separation of components in mnemonic processing. An early model that has proven especially useful in conceptualizing developmental issues was offered by Atkinson and Shiffrin (1968). They offered a distinction between *structural features,* which refer to limitations imposed by the biology of the organism and provide the boundaries or invariant features of memory, and *control processes,* which are under the control of the individual, such as mnemonic strategies.

The structure consists of three components. The first is a *sensory register,* in which a literal copy of information is stored but can remain only very briefly. The next is a *short-term store,* which is the subject's working memory. Although its capacity is severely limited, information can be maintained by rehearsal so that it can be acted upon and in some cases transferred to the third component, *long-term store.* This component has an unlimited capacity. Control processes are ". . . transient phenomena under the control of the subject; their appearance depends on such factors as instructional set, the experimental task, and the past history of the subject" (Atkinson & Shiffrin, 1968, p. 106). The control processes give the system its flexibility. The developmental phenomena reviewed in the preceding section come primarily under these processes. For example rehearsal comes to be viewed as an activity to prevent loss of information from short-term store.

The view of memory as dynamic and changing with development has been embraced by nearly all investigators. However it should not be concluded that a satisfactory developmental model of memory has emerged. Rather attempts have been made to fit existing data into the framework available. Changes occurring during infancy and early childhood are not usually attributed to control processes but rather to changes occurring in the structure, perhaps in neurological structure. By the preschool level there does seem to be acceptance of the notion that control processes are responsible for at least some of the age-related improvements that are found in memory, and the striking changes during the grade school years fit well with the control processes as defined by Atkinson and Shiffrin (1968).

Depth of Processing

A more recent view that has been embraced by at least some developmentalists is the levels-of-processing model as put forth by Craik and Lockhart (1972). It is really a simpler model than the multistore model reviewed before. Perceptual analyses of incoming stimuli proceed through a number of levels. The more levels that a given memory trace proceeds through, the greater the strength of that trace. At the initial levels, physical or sensory features of the external stimulus are processed. The resultant trace is highly transient. At a deeper level, pattern recognition occurs, and meaning is extracted. As the processing becomes deeper, it is also more cognitive and may involve semantic elaboration and enrichment of the stimulus. The deeper the processing, the more resistant is the memory trace to forgetting.

Rehearsal is described by Craik and Lockhard (1972) as

a key concept and may take one of two forms. Attention to an item to be remembered can be maintained through the use of active rehearsal. Forgetting does not occur, but the memory trace is not strengthened. When attention is not longer given to the item, the probability of its loss from memory is determined by the strength characteristic of that level of analysis. The second form rehearsal may take is more complex and involves elaboration of the material to be remembered. Here increasingly deeper modes of analyses may be invoked. Through this activity the memory trace can be strengthened. Processing is primarily under the control of the individual in this model. The amount and type of processing to be employed is determined by the subject, given the material to be remembered and the demands of the particular situation.

While the depth-of-processing model has influenced research on memory in adults to a considerable degree, relatively little research with children has drawn upon this model. Studies by Murphy and Brown (1975) and Sophian and Hagen (1978) are notable exceptions. Both the models reviewed here stress the active role played by the memorizer in the memory situation, and hence both fit well with the trends in research on the development of mnemonic processing reviewed in the second section of this chapter.

The Constructivists' Model

Another model has been proposed that emphasizes the active role of memory in cognitive processing, a constructivist model (e.g., Norman & Bobrow, 1976). While the essential features of the depth-of-processing model are incorporated here, the emphasis is on the organism as a constructor of information. According to these authors,

Memory is constructed of active units—schemata—that use the data available in a common pool, perform computations on these data, and then both send new results back . . . and/or request specific information from other schemata. (p. 123)

An attempt has been made recently to incorporate the essential features of this model into a developmental framework (Collins & Hagen, 1979). It is argued here that the role of conscious processes must be taken into account in any theory of cognitive development and that these processes can be identified as early as the beginning of the second year. A second major transition, beginning during the early grade school years, involves the automization of perceptual processing, thereby freeing much of the channel capacity of the central processor to perform other activities under conscious control. While the arguments for such a position cannot be given in detail here, the implications are important. The burden of too much information poses a limit on the preschool child's ability to encode, retain, and construct new cognitions. The second transition, which occurs gradually over a period of years, serves to resolve this processing burden. Information in storage (or schemata) and certain categories of newly received information can be handled automatically, thereby allowing attention to be focused on the task at hand. Evidence consonant with this interpretation is presented by Collins and Hagen (1979).

Commentary

Three models have been presented that have influenced research on memory and cognition during the past decade or so. While none of these was proposed originally to take into account developmental findings, each has been found to be compatible with much of the research and thinking that has included comparisons of performance of children at various age levels. In the next section some speculations are offered concerning the influence that these models appear to have on children's memory research.

THE STATE OF THE ART

In reviewing this literature we are impressed with the strides that memory researchers have made since interest in memory was piqued during the late 1960s. The amount of information about children's memory generated since that time is considerable. More important is the fact that research questions are now phrased with greater sophistication and precision than was the case in the "early days" of research on memory development.

At the same time in preparing a chapter such as this, one inevitably notices gaps in our knowledge. Certainly many questions remain unanswered, and some of these have been encountered at various points in this chapter. What we wish to consider here, however, are two general characteristics of existing research on the development of memory.

The Modal Experiment in Research on the Development of Memory

The modal memory experiment (Brown & DeLoache, 1978) in the developmental literature involves children of (at least) two different age groups who are presented a relatively brief list of pictures or words to be recalled or recognized after an interval that is almost always measured in minutes rather than hours, days, or weeks. Two limitations are evident in this characterization. First, the modal memory experiment is restricted in terms of the stimuli used as well as the manner in and time after which retention is assessed. Stimuli typically are presented visually or, less often, auditorily. Children's retention of olfactory, gustatory, or motoric experiences have been ignored for the most part (see Foellinger & Trabasso, 1977, and Paris & Lindauer, 1976, Experiment 3 for interesting exceptions).

A second limitation is the age levels of the children chosen. Typically two ages, usually selected from the two ends of the elementary school grades, are employed. Research of this type often reads like a comparison of the "haves" versus the "have nots." Older children are competent with regard to the memory processes of interest while younger children are incompetent. While such experiments certainly can be useful in highlighting developmental *differences* in a mnemonic phenomenon, they provide few insights into the way in which mnemonic competence develops with age. Competence is not acquired in one giant developmental leap forward from incompetence; children typically progress through states of successively greater skill. Unfortunately the modal memory experiment generally contrasts disparate points along this progression and consequently provides few clues as to the shape of the developmental function (Wohlwill, 1973).

The thrust of this discussion is *not* to denigrate the modal memory experiment—for it has served memory researchers well—but to suggest that additional modes of research are now appropriate. We merely wish to emphasize the need to enlarge the scope of memory experimentation with children. More varied kinds of laboratory investigations are needed, as are naturalistic studies of children's memory (DeLoache & Brown, 1979, provide one example of the way in which such naturalistic research might be conducted). Experimentation that yields more precise developmental data is needed. In the case of memory change that is presumably qualitative in nature—such as the emergence of rehearsal and related strategic skills—the aim should be to identify the nature and sequence of intermediate levels of competence. In the case of quantitative change in memory—rate of memory search is one example—determining the general shape of the developmental function should be the goal.

Models of Memory

Models of memory can range from general ones corresponding to what we might call *world views* of memory (Kuhn, 1962) to quite specific models of highly circumscribed mnemonic domains (Reese, 1973). What has been the role of models in developmental research on memory? The answer varies depending upon the level of generality of the model.

Consider first the most general models of memory. Since the mid-1960s the dominant view of memory has been a cognitive one—that is, most researchers have assumed that the goal of memory research is to identify the processes that intervene between a stimulus and a particular mnemonic response. At a slightly less general level, most models of memory during this period have been information-processing models. Most theorists agree that internal processes of memory consist, in large part, of different ways of coding, manipulating, and retrieving information (Bower, 1975).

Moving from this still quite general level, a series of different comprehensive models of memory have been proposed since the mid-1960s. The model by Atkinson and Shiffrin (1968) was the first one to provide a reasonably detailed description of the major components of memory. There have been two noteworthy theoretical developments since the Atkinson and Shiffrin paper. First, Craik and Lockhart (1972) marshaled evidence which questioned the separate memory stores proposed by Atkinson and Shiffrin. Information processing was conceptualized as a continuum of different levels of processing as pointed out earlier. The levels of processing framework was refined throughout the 1970s (e.g., Cermak & Craik, 1979; Craik & Tulving, 1975) and by the end of that decade had replaced the Atkinson and Shiffrin (1968) model as the dominant memory framework (but see Baddeley, 1978, for a dissenting view).

A second theoretical development was to elaborate a portion of the memory system that Atkinson and Shiffrin (1968) had considered only briefly—namely, the structure and utilization of information in permanent memory. Most children know that "dogs are animals" and that "2 + 5 = 7." To say that children "know" these facts is to say that the information is stored in and can be accessed from permanent memory. Numerous models designed to explain storage and retrieval of such knowledge were proposed, including those of Anderson and Bower, (1973), Collins and Quillian (1972), Kintsch (1972, 1974), and Rumelhart, Lindsay, and Norman (1972), to name a few of the early efforts.

What has been the impact of these general models of memory on developmental research? Certainly one important effect was to legitimize a cognitive approach to the study of memory (Kail & Hagen, 1977). Along with the rediscovery of Piaget in the mid-1960s and with certain developments in linguistics, cognitive models of memory made investigators seek cognitive explanations of children's memory rather than the associative explanations in vogue during this time among scientists studying children's learning (e.g., Stevenson, 1970, 1972).

Beyond the creation of a cognitive, information-processing–oriented world view, direct links between general memory theory and developmental research are difficult to pinpoint. The problem is that most general models of memory have few specific (much less unique) developmental implications (c.f., Brown, 1979). Developmental change in use of mnemonics, for example, is as clearly described as change in control processes in the Atkinson and Shiffrin (1968) model as change toward semantic analysis in the levels of processing framework (Brown, 1975).

This, of course, does not imply that developmentalists have ignored general models of memory. Many authors (e.g., Brown, 1975; Hagen et al., 1975; Kail, 1979a) have used these general models as frameworks to organize the literature on memory development. However, the various general memory models seem to organize the developmental literature in surprisingly similar ways, suggesting that the models do not provide unique developmental insights.

Finally we can turn to precise models of limited mnemonic domains. The surprising finding here is the complete absence of this type of modeling in the developmental literature. When we focus on quantitative comparisons of a model's predicted results with those of actual data, the developmental literature is barren. Instead there is an enormous amount of research that can be characterized as studies of "age-related changes in the effect of variable X on mnemonic process Y." Sometimes this research is simply descriptive, and there is no interest in determining the processes underlying experimental outcomes. More often, however, hypotheses *are* stated regarding expected effects, hypotheses derived from models that are often stated vaguely or perhaps only implicitly. In such cases when the expected results are not obtained, it is difficult to know whether (1) the model was inaccurate, (2) the hypotheses did not follow from the model, or (3) both. We would argue, then, that the developmental literature is in need of research in which multiple models of processes are formulated that yield precise predictions regarding experimental outcomes so that (1) the accuracy of a given model can be evaluated with reference to data and (2) the predictive power of models can be evaluated comparatively.

REFERENCES

ACREDOLO, L. P., PICK, H. L., & OLSEN, M. G. Environmental differentiation and familiarity as determinants of children's memory for spatial location. *Developmental Psychology*, 1975, *11*, 495–501.

ALTEMEYER, R., FULTON, D., & BERNEY, K. Long-term memory improvement: Confirmation of a finding by Piaget. *Child Development*, 1969, *40*, 845–857.

ANDERSON, J. R., & BOWER, G. H. *Human associative memory.* Washington, D.C.: D. H. Winston & Sons, 1973.

APPEL, L. F., COOPER, R. G., McCARRELL, N., SIMS-KNIGHT, J., YUSSEN, S. R., & FLAVELL, J. H. The development of the distinction between perceiving and memorizing. *Child Development*, 1972, *43*, 1365–1381.

ATKINSON, R. C., & SHRIFFRIN, R. M. Human memory: A proposed system and its control processes. In K. W. Spence & J. T. Spence (Eds.), *The psychology of learning and motivation* (Vol. 2). New York: Academic Press, 1968.

BACH, M. J., & UNDERWOOD, B. J. Developmental changes in memory attributes. *Journal of Educational Psychology*, 1970, *61*, 292–296.

BADDELEY, A. D. The trouble with levels: A reexamination of Craik and Lockhart's framework for memory research. *Psychological Review*, 1978, *85*, 139–152.

BARCLAY, J. R., & REID, M. Semantic integration in children's recall of discourse. *Developmental Psychology*, 1974, *10*, 277–281.

BARTLETT, F. C. *Remembering.* Cambridge, England: Cambridge University Press, 1932.

BAUMEISTER, A. A., & MAISTO, A. A. Memory scanning by children: Meaningfulness and mediation. *Journal of Experimental Child Psychology*, 1977, *24*, 97–107.

BELMONT, J. M., & BUTTERFIELD, E. C. The relations of short-term memory to development and intelligence. In L. P. Lipsitt & H. W. Reese (Eds.), *Advances in child development and behavior* (Vol. 4). New York: Academic Press, 1969.

BELMONT, J. M., & BUTTERFIELD, E. C. Learning strategies as determinants of memory deficiencies. *Cognitive Psychology*, 1971, *2*, 411–420.

BERCH, D. B., & EVANS, R. C. Decision processes in children's recognition memory. *Journal of Experimental Child Psychology*, 1973, *16*, 148–164.

BISANZ, G. L., VESONDER, G. T., & VOSS, J. F. Knowledge of one's own responding and the relation of such knowledge to learning: A developmental study. *Journal of Experimental Child Psychology*, 1978, *25*, 116–128.

BISANZ, J., KAIL, R., PELLEGRINO, J. W., & SIEGEL, A. W. Developmental changes in the speed and effects of acoustic and semantic encoding. *Bulletin of the Psychonomic Society*, 1979, *14*, 209–212.

BLOCK, J., BLOCK, J. H., & HARRINGTON, D. M. Some misgivings about the Matching Familiar Figures Test as a measure of reflection-impulsivity. *Developmental Psychology*, 1974, *10*, 611–632.

BOWER, G. H. A multicomponent theory of the memory trace. In K. W. Spence & J. T. Spence (Eds.), *The psychology of learning and motivation* (Vol. 1). New York: Academic Press, 1967.

BOWER, G. H. Cognitive psychology: An introduction. In W. K. Estes (Ed.), *Handbook of learning and cognitive processes* (Vol. 1). Hillsdale, N.J.: Lawrence Erlbaum Associates, 1975.

BROWN, A. L. Judgment of recency for long sequences of pictures: The absence of a developmental trend. *Journal of Experimental Child Psychology*, 1973, *15*, 473–480.

BROWN, A. L. The role of strategic behavior in retardate memory. In N. R. Ellis (Ed.), *International review of research in mental retardation* (Vol. 7). New York: Academic Press, 1974.

BROWN, A. L. The development of memory: Knowing, knowing about knowing, and knowing how to know. In H. W. Reese (Ed.), *Advances in child development and behavior* (Vol. 10). New York: Academic Press, 1975.

BROWN, A. L. Knowing when, where, and how to remember: A problem of metacognition. In R. Glaser (Ed.), *Advances in instructional psychology* (Vol. 1). Hillsdale, N.J.: Lawrence Erlbaum Associates, 1978.

BROWN, A. L. Theories of memory and the problems of development: Activity, growth, and knowledge. In L. S. Cermak & F.I.M. Craik (Eds.), *Levels of processing in human memory.* Hillsdale, N.J.: Lawrence Erlbaum Associates, 1979.

BROWN, A. L., & CAMPIONE, J. C. Recognition memory for perceptually similar pictures in preschool children. *Journal of Experimental Psychology*, 1972, *95*, 55–62.

BROWN, A. L., CAMPIONE, J. C., & GILLIARD, D. M. Recency judgments in children: A production deficiency in the use of redundant background cues. *Developmental Psychology*, 1974, *10*, 404.

BROWN, A. L., & DeLOACHE, J. S. Skills, plans, and self-regulation. In R. Siegler (Ed.), *Children's thinking: What develops?* Hillsdale, N.J.: Lawrence Erlbaum Associates, 1978.

BROWN, A. L., & SMILEY, S. S. The development of strategies for studying texts. *Child Development*, 1978, *49*, 1076–1088.

BROWN, A. L., SMILEY, S. S., DAY, J. D., TOWNSEND, M.A.R., & LAWTON, S. C. Intrusion of a thematic idea in children's comprehension and retention of stories. *Child Development*, 1977, *48*, 1454–1466.

BRUNER, J. S. The course of cognitive growth. *American Psychologist*, 1964, *19*, 1–15.

CAMPIONE, J. C., & BROWN, A. L. Memory and metamemory development in educable retarded children. In R. V. Kail & J. W. Hagen (Eds.), *Perspectives on the development of memory and cognition.* Hillsdale, N.J.: Lawrence Erlbaum Associates, 1977.

CERMAK, L. S., & CRAIK, F.I.M. (Eds.). *Levels of processing in human memory.* Hillsdale, N.J.: Lawrence Erlbaum Associates, 1979.

CHRISTIE, D. J., & SCHUMACHER, G. M. Developmental trends in the abstraction and recall of relevant versus irrelevant thematic information from connected verbal materials. *Child Development*, 1975, *46*, 598–602.

COLBY, B. N. Culture grammars: An anthropological approach to cognition may lead to theoretical models of microcultural processes. *Science*, 1975, *187*, 913–919.

COLE, M., FRANKEL, F., & SHARP, D. Development of free recall learning in children. *Developmental Psychology*, 1971, *4*, 109–123.

COLE, M., GAY, J., GLICK, J., & SHARP, D. *The cultural context of learning and thinking.* New York: Basic Books, 1971.

COLE, M., & SCRIBNER, S. Cross-cultural studies of memory and cognition. In R. V. Kail & J. W. Hagen (Eds.), *Perspectives on the development of memory and cognition.* Hillsdale, N.J.: Lawrence Erlbaum Associates, 1977.

COLLINS, A. M., & QUILLIAN, M. R. How to make a language user. In E. Tulving & W. Donaldson (Eds.), *Organization of memory.* New York: Academic Press, 1972.

COLLINS, J. T., & HAGEN, J. W. A constructivist account of the development of perception, attention, and memory. In G. Hale & M. Lewis (Eds.), *Attention and the development of cognitive skills.* New York: Plenum, 1979.

CORSINI, D. A. Developmental changes in the effect of nonverbal cues on retention. *Developmental Psychology*, 1969a, *1*, 425–435.

CORSINI, D. A. The effect of nonverbal cues on the retention of kindergarten children. *Child Development*, 1969b, *40*, 599–607.

CRAIK, F.I.M., & LOCKHART, R. S. Levels of processing: A framework for memory research. *Journal of Verbal Learning and Verbal Behavior*, 1972, *11*, 671–684.

CRAIK, F.I.M., & TULVING, E. Depth of processing and the retention of words in episodic memory. *Journal of Experimental Psychology: General*, 1975, *104*, 268–294.

DAEHLER, M. W., & BUKATKO, D. Recognition memory for pictures in very young children: Evidence from attentional preferences using a continuous presentation procedure. *Child Development*, 1977, *48*, 693–696.

DAHLEM, N. W. Reconstructive memory in kindergarten children. *Psychonomic Science*, 1968, *13*, 331–332.

DAHLEM, N. W. Reconstructive memory in kindergarten children revisited. *Psychonomic Science*, 1969, *17*, 101–103.

DeLOACHE, J. S., & BROWN, A. L. Looking for Big Bird: Studies of memory in very young children. *Quarterly Newsletter of the Laboratory of Comparative Human Cognition*, 1979, *1*, 53–57.

DUGAS, J., & KELLAS, G. Encoding and retrieval processes in normal children and retarded adolescents. *Journal of Experimental Child Psychology*, 1974, *17*, 177–185.

ELLIS, N. R. The stimulus trace and behavioral inadequacy. In N. R. Ellis (Ed.), *Handbook of mental deficiency.* New York: McGraw-Hill, 1963.

ESROV, L. V., HALL, J. W., & LaFAVER, D. K. Preschoolers' conceptual and acoustic encoding as evidenced by release from PI. *Bulletin of the Psychonomic Society,* 1974, *4*, 89–90.

FAULKENDER, P. J., WRIGHT, J. C., & WALDRON, A. Generalized

habituation of concept stimuli in toddlers. *Child Development*, 1974, *45*, 1002–1010.

FELZEN, E., & ANISFELD, M. Semantic and phonetic relations in the false recognition of words by third- and sixth-grade children. *Developmental Psychology*, 1970, *3*, 103–108.

FLAVELL, J. H. First discussant's comments: What is memory development the development of? *Human Development*, 1971, *14*, 272–278.

FLAVELL, J. H. *Cognitive development.* Englewood Cliffs, N.J.: Prentice-Hall, 1977.

FLAVELL, J. H., BEACH, D. R., & CHINSKY, J. M. Spontaneous verbal rehearsal in a memory task as a function of age. *Child Development*, 1966, *37*, 283–299.

FLAVELL, J. H., & WELLMAN, H. M. Metamemory. In R. V. Kail & J. W. Hagen (Eds.), *Perspectives on the development of memory and cognition.* Hillsdale, N.J.: Lawrence Erlbaum Associates, 1977.

FOELLINGER, D. R., & TRABASSO, T. Seeing, hearing, and doing: A developmental study of memory for actions. *Child Development*, 1977, *48*, 1482–1489.

FRASURE, N. E., & ENTWISLE, D. R. Semantic and syntactic development in children. *Developmental Psychology*, 1973, *9*, 236–245.

FURTH, H. G., & MILGRAM, N. A. Labeling and grouping effects in the recall of pictures by children. *Child Development*, 1973, *44*, 511–518.

FURTH, H. G., ROSS, B., & YOUNISS, J. Operative understanding in children's immediate and long-term reproductions of drawings. *Child Development*, 1974, *45*, 63–70.

GEIS, M. F. Encoding dimensions in memory: Developmental similarities at two grade levels. *Developmental Psychology*, 1975, *11*, 396–397.

GHATALA, E. S., & HURLBUT, N. L. Effectiveness of acoustic and conceptual retrieval cues in memory for words at two grade levels. *Journal of Educational Psychology*, 1973, *64*, 347–352.

HAGEN, J. W. Some thoughts on how children learn to remember. *Human Development*, 1971, *14*, 262–271.

HAGEN, J. W., JONGEWARD, R. H., & KAIL, R. V. Cognitive perspectives on the development of memory. In H. W. Reese (Ed.), *Advances in child development and behavior* (Vol. 10). New York: Academic Press, 1975.

HAGEN, J. W., & KAIL, R. V. Facilitation and distraction in short-term memory. *Child Development*, 1973, *44*, 831–836.

HAGEN, J. W., & KINGSLEY, P. R. Labeling effects in short-term memory. *Child Development*, 1968, *39*, 113–121.

HAGEN, J. W., MEACHAM, J. A., & MESIBOV, G. Verbal labeling, rehearsal, and short-term memory. *Cognitive Psychology*, 1970, *1*, 47–58.

HAGEN, J. W., & STANOVICH, K. G. Memory: Strategies of acquisition. In R. V. Kail & J. W. Hagen (Eds.), *Perspectives on the development of memory and cognition.* Hillsdale, N.J.: Lawrence Erlbaum Associates, 1977.

HARRIS, G. J., & FLEER, R. E. High speed memory scanning in mental retardates: Evidence for a central processing deficit. *Journal of Experimental Child Psychology*, 1974, *17*, 452–459.

HARRIS, L. J. Sex differences in spatial ability: Possible environmental, genetic, and neurological factors. In M. Kinsbourne (Ed.), *Asymmetrical function of the brain.* Cambridge, England: Cambridge University Press, 1978.

HERAS, I., & NELSON, K. E. Retention of semantic, syntactic, and language information by young bilingual children. *Psychonomic Science*, 1972, *29*, 391–393.

HERRMAN, D. J., & LANDIS, T. Y. Differences in the search rate of children and adults in short-term memory. *Journal of Experimental Child Psychology*, 1977, *23*, 151–161.

HOFFMAN, C. D., & DICK, S. A. A developmental investigation of recognition memory. *Child Development*, 1976, *47*, 794–799.

HOVING, K. L., MORIN, R. E., & KONICK, D. S. Recognition reaction time and size of the memory set: A developmental study. *Psychonomic Science*, 1970, *21*, 247–248.

JENSEN, A. R. How much can we boost IQ and scholastic achievement? *Harvard Educational Review*, 1969, *39*, 1–123.

JENSEN, A. R., & FIGUEROA, R. A. Forward and backward digit span interaction with race and IQ: Predictions from Jensen's theory. *Journal of Educational Psychology*, 1975, *67*, 882–893.

JENSEN, A. R., & FREDERIKSEN, J. Free recall of categorized and uncategorized lists: A test of the Jensen hypothesis. *Journal of Educational Psychology*, 1973, *65*, 304–312.

JONGEWARD, R. H. *Developmental changes in children's use of organiza-*

tion in recall. Unpublished doctoral dissertation, University of Michigan, 1975.

KAGAN, J., & KOGAN, N. Individual variation in cognitive processes. In P. H. Mussen (Ed.), *Carmichael's manual of child psychology* (Vol. 1). New York: John Wiley, 1970.

KAGAN, J., ROSMAN, B. L., DAY, D. ALBERT, J., & PHILLIPS, W. Information processing in the child: Significance of analytic and reflective attitudes. *Psychological Monographs,* 1964, *78* (1, Whole No. 578).

KAIL, R. *The development of memory in children.* San Francisco: W. H Freeman & Company Publishers, 1979a.

KAIL, R. Use of strategies and individual differences in children's memory. *Developmental Psychology,* 1979b, *15,* 251–255.

KAIL, R. V. *Interrelations in children's use of mnemonic strategies.* Unpublished doctoral dissertation, University of Michigan, 1975.

KAIL, R. V., & HAGEN, J. W. (Eds.). *Perspectives on the development of memory and cognition.* Hillsdale, N.J.: Lawrence Erlbaum Associates, 1977.

KAIL, R. V., & SIEGEL, A. W. Sex differences in retention of verbal and spatial characteristics of stimuli. *Journal of Experimental Child Psychology,* 1977, *23,* 341–347.

KEE, D. W., & HELFAND, L. Assessment of taxonomic encoding categories in different populations. *Journal of Educational Psychology,* 1977, *69,* 344–348.

KINTSCH, W. Notes on the structure of semantic memory. In E. Tulving & W. Donaldson (Eds.), *Organization of memory.* New York: Academic Press, 1972.

KINTSCH, W. *The representation of meaning in memory.* Hillsdale, N.J.: Lawrence Erlbaum Associates, 1974.

KOBASIGAWA, A. Utilization of retrieval cues by children in recall. *Child Development,* 1974, *45,* 127–134.

KOBASIGAWA, A. Retrieval factors in the development of memory. In R. V. Kail & J. W. Hagen (Eds.), *Perspectives on the development of memory and cognition.* Hillsdale, N.J.: Lawrence Erlbaum Associates, 1977.

KOSSLYN, S. M. The representational-development hypothesis. In P. A. Ornstein (Ed.), *Memory development in children.* Hillsdale, N.J.: Lawrence Erlbaum Associates, 1978.

KREUTZER, M. A., LEONARD, C., & FLAVELL, J. H. An interview study of children's knowledge about memory. *Monographs of the Society for Research in Child Development,* 1975, *40*(1, Whole No. 159).

KUHN, T. S. *The structure of scientific revolutions.* Chicago: University of Chicago Press, 1962.

LACHER, M. R. The relation of serial recall performance to verbal and nonverbal encoding strategies in middle- and lower-class children. *Child Development,* 1976, *47,* 445–451.

LANGE, G. W. The development of conceptual and rote recall skills among school age children. *Journal of Experimental Child Psychology,* 1973, *15,* 394–406.

LANGE, G. W. Organization-related processes in children's recall. In P. A. Ornstein (Ed.), *Memory development in children.* Hillsdale, N.J.: Lawrence Erlbaum Associates, 1978.

LEVIN, J. R., YUSSEN, S. R., DEROSE, T. M., & PRESSLEY, G. M. Developmental changes in assessing recall and recognition memory capacity. *Developmental Psychology,* 1977, *13,* 608–615.

LIBEN, L. S. Long-term memory for pictures related to seriation, horizontality, and verticality concepts. *Developmental Psychology,* 1975, *11,* 795–806.

LIBEN, L. S. Memory in the context of cognitive development: The Piagetian approach. In R. V. Kail & J. W. Hagen (Eds.), *Perspectives on the development of memory and cognition.* Hillsdale, N.J.: Lawrence Erlbaum Associates, 1977.

LIBEN, L. S., & POSNANSKY, C. J. Inferences on inference: The effects of age, transitive ability, memory load, and lexical factors. *Child Development,* 1977, *48,* 1490–1497.

LINDAUER, B. K., & PARIS, S. G. Some methodological problems with a false recognition paradigm in the assessment of developmental changes in memory organization. *Journal of Experimental Child Psychology,* 1976, *22,* 319–330.

LOCKE, J. L., & FEHR, F. S. Young children's use of the speech code in a recall task. *Journal of Experimental Child Psychology,* 1970, *10,* 367–373.

MCCARVER R. B., & ELLIS, N. R. Effect of overt labeling on short-term memory in culturally deprived and nondeprived children. *Developmental Psychology,* 1972, *6,* 38–41.

MACCOBY, E. E., & JACKLIN, C. N. *The psychology of sex differences.* Stanford, Calif.: Stanford University Press, 1974.

MAISTO, A., & BAUMEISTER, A. A. A developmental study of choice reaction time: The effects of two forms of stimulus degradation on encoding. *Journal of Experimental Child Psychology,* 1975, *20,* 454–464.

MANDLER, J. M., & JOHNSON, N. S. Remembrance of things parsed: Story structure and recall. *Cognitive Psychology,* 1977, *9,* 111–151.

MANDLER, J. M., & ROBINSON, C. A. Developmental changes in picture recognition. *Journal of Experimental Child Psychology,* 1978, *26,* 122–136.

MASUR, E. F., McINTYRE, C. W., & FLAVELL, J. H. Developmental changes in apportionment of study time among items in a multitrial free recall task. *Journal of Experimental Child Psychology,* 1973, *15,* 237–246.

MATHEWS, M. E., & FOZARD, J. L. Age differences in judgments of recency for short sequences of pictures. *Developmental Psychology,* 1970, *3,* 208–217.

MAURER, D., SIEGEL, L. S., LEWIS, T. L., KRISTOFFERSON, M. W., BARNES, R. A., & LEVY, B. A. Long-term memory improvement? *Child Development,* 1979, *50,* 106–118.

MEANS, B. M., & ROHWER, W. D. Attribute dominance in memory development. *Developmental Psychology,* 1976, *12,* 411–417.

MOELY, B. E. Organizational factors in the development of memory. In R. V. Kail & J. W. Hagen (Eds.), *Perspectives on the development of memory and cognition.* Hillsdale, N.J.: Lawrence Erlbaum Associates, 1977.

MOELY, B. E., OLSON, F. A., HALWES, T. G., & FLAVELL, J. H. Production deficiency in young children's clustered recall. *Developmental Psychology,* 1969, *1,* 26–34.

MOYNAHAN, E. D. The development of knowledge concerning the effect of categorization upon free recall. *Child Development,* 1973, *44,* 238–246.

MOYNAHAN, E. D. The development of the ability to assess recall performance. *Journal of Experimental Child Psychology,* 1976, *21,* 94–97.

MURPHY, M. D., & BROWN, A. L. Incidental learning in preschool children as a function of level of cognitive analysis. *Journal of Experimental Child Psychology,* 1975, *19,* 509–523.

MURRAY, F., & BAUSELL, R. Memory and conservation. *Psychonomic Science,* 1970, *21,* 334–335.

MYERS, M., & PARIS, S. G. Children's metacognitive knowledge about reading. *Journal of Educational Psychology,* 1978, *70,* 680–690.

NAUS, M. J., & ORNSTEIN, P. A. Developmental differences in the memory search of categorized lists. *Developmental Psychology,* 1977, *13,* 60–68.

NORMAN, D. A., & BOBROW, D. G. On the role of active memory processes in perception and cognition. In C. N. Cofer (Ed.), *The structure of human memory.* San Francisco: W. H. Freeman & Company Publishers, 1976.

ORNSTEIN, P. A., & CORSALE, K. Organizational factors in children's memory. In C. R. Puff (Ed.), *Memory organization and structure.* New York: Academic Press, 1980.

ORNSTEIN, P. A., & NAUS, M. J. Rehearsal processes in children's memory. In P. A. Ornstein (Ed.), *Memory development in children.* Hillsdale, N.J.: Lawrence Erlbaum Associates, 1978.

ORNSTEIN, P. A., NAUS, M. J., & LIBERTY, C. Rehearsal and organization processes in children's memory. *Child Development,* 1975, *26,* 818–830.

PARIS, S. G., & CARTER, A. Y. Semantic and constructive aspects of sentence memory in children. *Developmental Psychology,* 1973, *9,* 109–113.

PARIS, S. G., & LINDAUER, B. K. The role of inference in children's comprehension and memory for sentences. *Cognitive Psychology,* 1976, *8,* 217–227.

PARIS, S. G., LINDAUER, B. K., & COX, G. L. The development of inferential comprehension. *Child Development,* 1977, *48,* 1728–1733.

PARIS, S. G., & MAHONEY, G. J. Cognitive integration in children's memory for sentences and pictures. *Child Development,* 1974, *45,* 633–642.

PARIS, S. G., & UPTON, L. R. Children's memory for inferential relationships in prose. *Child Development,* 1976, *47,* 660–668.

PERLMUTTER, M., & MYERS, N. A. Development of recall in 2- to 4-year-old children. *Developmental Psychology,* 1979, *15,* 73–83.

PIAGET, J. *On the development of memory and identity.* Worcester, Mass.: Clark University Press, 1968.

Piaget, J., & Inhelder, B. *Memory and intelligence.* New York: Basic Books, 1973.

Reese, H. W. Models of memory and models of development. *Human Development,* 1973, *16,* 397–416.

Reese, H. W. Imagery and associative memory. In R. V. Kail & J. W. Hagen (Eds.), *Perspectives on the development of memory and cognition.* Hillsdale, N.J.: Lawrence Erlbaum Associates, 1977.

Rogoff, B., Newcombe, N., & Kagan, J. Planfulness and recognition memory. *Child Development,* 1974, *45,* 972–977.

Rumelhart, D. E., Lindsay, P. H., & Norman, D. A. A process model for long-term memory. In E. Tulving & W. Donaldson (Eds.), *Organization of memory.* New York: Academic Press, 1972.

Schultz, T. R., Cherness, M., & Berman, S. Effects of age, social class and suggestion to cluster on free recall. *Developmental Psychology,* 1973, *8,* 57–61.

Siegel, A. W., Babich, J. M., & Kirasic, K. C. Visual recognition memory in reflective and impulsive children. *Memory & Cognition,* 1974, *2,* 379–384.

Siegel, A. W., Kirasic, K. C., & Kilburg, R. R. Recognition memory in reflective and impulsive preschool children. *Child Development,* 1973, *44,* 651–656.

Sophian, C., & Hagen, J. W. Involuntary memory and the development of retrieval skills in young children. *Journal of Experimental Child Psychology,* 1978, *26,* 458–471.

Speer, J. R., & Flavell, J. H. Young children's knowledge of the relative difficulty of recognition and recall memory tasks. *Developmental Psychology,* 1979, *15,* 214–217.

Stein, N. L., & Mandler, J. M. Development of detection and recognition of orientation of geometric and real figures. *Child Development,* 1975, *46,* 379–388.

Sternberg. S. High-speed scanning in human memory. *Science,* 1966, *153,* 652–654.

Stevenson, H. W. Learning in children. In P. H. Mussen (Ed.), *Carmichael's manual of child psychology* (Vol. 1). New York: John Wiley, 1970.

Stevenson, H. W. *Children's learning.* Englewood Cliffs, N.J.: Prentice-Hall, 1972.

Stevenson, H. W., Parker, T., & Wilkinson, A. *Ratings and measures of memory processes in young children.* Unpublished manuscript, University of Michigan, 1975.

Stevenson, H. W., Parker, T., Wilkinson, A., Bonnevaux, B., & Gonzalez, M. Schooling, environment, and cognitive development: A cross-cultural study. *Monographs of the Society for Research in Child Development,* 1978, *43*(3, Whole No. 175).

Stevenson, H. W., Williams, A. W., & Coleman, E. Interrelations among learning and performance tasks in disadvantaged children. *Journal of Educational Psychology,* 1971, *62,* 179–184.

Underwood, B. J. Attributes of memory. *Psychological Review,* 1969, *76,* 559–573.

Vaughan, M. E. Clustering, age, and incidental learning. *Journal of Experimental Child Psychology,* 1968, *6,* 323–334.

Wagner, D. A. The development of short-term and incidental memory: A cross-cultural study. *Child Development,* 1974, *45,* 389–396.

Wagner, D. A. Memories of Morocco: The influence of age, schooling and environment on memory. *Cognitive Psychology,* 1978, *10,* 1–28.

Wellman, H. M. Preschoolers' understanding of memory-relevant variables. *Child Development,* 1977, *48,* 1720–1723.

Wellman, H. M., Ritter, K., & Flavell, J. H. Deliberate memory behavior in the delayed reactions of very young children. *Developmental Psychology,* 1975, *11,* 780–787.

Wickens, D. D. Characteristics of word encoding. In A. W. Melton & E. Martin (Eds.), *Coding processes in human memory.* Washington, D.C.: D. H. Winston & Sons, 1972.

Wohlwill, J. F. *The study of behavioral development.* New York: Academic Press, 1973.

Yussen, S. R. Determinants of visual attention and recall in observational learning by preschoolers and second graders. *Developmental Psychology,* 1974, *10,* 93–100.

Yussen, S. R., Levin, J. R., Berman, L., & Palm, J. Developmental changes in the awareness of memory benefits associated with different types of picture organization. *Developmental Psychology,* 1979, *15,* 447–449.

21

Language
Development

GROVER J. WHITEHURST

Writing a chapter on language development is like planning a six-week round-the-world tour. There is no way to do it all, so you start by deciding what you will not include and hope you will end up with a manageable list of destinations. Your final list is still much too long, and you know you can't do justice to any single stopover. You are excited, nonetheless, hoping that a series of dalliances will be enlightening in a way that a focused exploration might not.

The reader should be forewarned by this simile. This chapter is not written for experts in language development, but rather for readers who are knowledgeable about psychology or education but who are not familiar with the voluminous literature on psycholinguistics—graduate students, perhaps, or professionals with another specialization. My concern is to select some issues that have general relevance and that may be interesting to readers who are unlikely to care about the intricacies of the development of tense forms or interrogatives. At the same time I want this chapter to be different from the surveys that can be found in any good undergraduate text on child development so I am not providing descriptions of classic investigations or thumbnail sketches of principal theorists. I am going to try to confront the issue of the importance of language development to our understanding of how complex human skills are acquired and, at the same time, try to give the reader a good flavor of the major phenomena and issues in language development. I apologize here to many of the investigators who were kind enough to send me reports of their recent work for possible inclusion in this chapter. At last measure there was a pile nearly three feet high of those reprints and preprints. This testifies to the vitality of the study of language development, but most of this work cannot be surveyed here for obvious reasons.

A SHORT HISTORY

It is traditional to begin surveys of language development with the story of the Egyptian king Psammetichus, who chose to end the long debate about which was the older race, Egyptians or Phrygians, by conducting the first recorded study of language development. Psammetichus had two infants reared in an isolated cabin by a shepherd who was never to speak in their presence. The shepherd's task, in addition to not speaking in the presence of the children (a difficult chore I would imagine), was to report back to the king on the nature of the language that the children eventually used. Legend has it that the shepherd returned to the cabin one day after a longer than usual absence to find both children running towards him saying, "becos," "becos." The children were brought to the king and there repeated the word the shepherd had heard. Psammetichus inquired and learned that *becos* was the Phrygian word for *bread*. Convinced of the validity of his experiment, Psammetichus proclaimed the Phrygians the older race.

The subsequent 3000-odd years of the history of the study of language development indicate that the problem addressed by Psammetichus may have been the last to be decided so cleanly. Not only are critical experiments rare, experiments of any type are the exception rather than the rule. But I am getting ahead of myself.

There is a significant history of the psychological study of language that begins in the 1800s when psychology itself was in its infancy. With commitment to brevity I will not take the reader on a tour of the period from 1850 to 1950, but there is much of interest there for anyone who wishes perspective on current issues in psycholinguistics. In particular there are the philosophical antipodes of rational thought and empirical thought. The former, characterized by the writing of Wilhelm Wundt, relied on innate properties of the mind and internal mental principles. The empirical-functional approach, on the other hand, explained language with associationistic principles external to the mind. This approach came to dominate psycholinguistics up until about 1960, with the leading American linguist, Leonard Bloomfield (1933), stressing descriptive methods which would lead to the induction of behavioral principles of language. Within psychological research on language development, most studies were devoted to determining developmental norms for number of words or sentence length, for example. The results of this tradition are summarized well in McCarthy's review of "Language Development in Children" in the 1954 edition of Carmichael's *Manual of Child Psychology.* An excellent introduction to the history of psycholinguistics during this period may be found in Blumenthal's *Language and Psychology* (1970).

The real fireworks in modern psycholinguistics may be traced to 1957, which saw the publication of two forceful statements on the nature of language that could not have been further apart. Skinner's *Verbal Behavior* was a capstone of the empiricist approach. He argued that language is a type of social behavior no different in principle from any other behavior and that learning principles of reinforcement, discrimination, and generalization could account for the acquisition and maintenance of language skills. Chomsky's *Syntactic Structures* was a reaffirmation of the flickering and nearly dead rationalist approach to language. Chomsky argued that language is a unique human characteristic, based on innate abilities and operating on the basis of a priori mental mechanisms. The conflict between these two approaches was made infinitely more visible by Chomsky's (1959) review of Skinner's *Verbal Behavior.* The review was a savage critique of everything that behaviorism stood for. It was widely read and probably was a critical factor in a general shift in America toward cognitive psychology and away from behaviorism. Skinner never replied to Chomsky's attack, and subsequent rejoinders by other behaviorists (e.g., MacCorquodale, 1970) were too little and too late to have much effect on the general impression that behavioral principles were incapable of explaining language. Because of the importance of this issue, I will devote some space to a consideration of how Skinner and Chomsky explained syntactic abilities.

Skinner (1957) used the device of the *autoclitic* to describe verbal behavior that depends on the relations among more primary verbal units (syntax or grammar).

The responses evoked by a situation are essentially non grammatical until they have been dealt with autoclitically. . . . Suppose a speaker is primarily concerned with the "fact" that "Sam rented a leaky boat." The "raw" responses are *rent, boat, leak,* and *Sam.* The important relations may be carried in broken English by autoclitic ordering and grouping: *Sam rent boat—boat leak.* If we add the tag *-ed* to *rent,* as a minimal tack indicating "past time," and the articles *a* and *the* to serve a subtle function in qualifying *boat*— . . . we get: *Sam rented a boat. The boat leaked.* Other manipulative autoclitics, including punctuation, produce at least seven other versions. (Skinner, 1957, pp. 346–347)

Skinner seems to be making the point that primitive labels are evoked by the primary events in a situation and that those words are then ordered and inflected to signify relations among the events, such as that an event happened in the past or that an event is the agent of action. There is little that is overtly controversial in this; indeed, Segal (1975) has argued that Skinner's terminology on autoclitics can be translated into that of a Chomskian transformational grammar without great difficulty.

The real issue, of course, is how a person is able to do this ordering and inflecting. More particularly how is a child able to learn to do this? It matters not greatly what we call the process unless there is some insight or at least a testable prediction of how the child achieves the function in question.

Skinner moves in the direction of such a specification in his discussion of grammatical frames.

If he has acquired a series of responses such as *the boy's gun, the boy's shoe,* and *the boy's hat,* we may suppose that the partial frame *the boy's _____* is available for recombination with other responses. The first time the boy acquires a bicycle, the speaker can compose a new unit *the boy's bicycle.* This is not simply the emission of two responses separately acquired. . . . The relational aspects of the situation strengthen a frame, and specific features of the situation strengthen the responses fitted into it. (Skinner, 1957, p. 336)

Most of the message of this passage is implicit. To me Skinner is saying that the process of becoming grammatically generative depends on a lot of small inferences, analogies, or generalizations on the part of a child. Experience with a particular pattern of usage—e.g., *the boy's gun, the boy's shoe*—allows the child to make cautious leaps by substituting elements with similar properties. Presumably different devices—some frame-like, some not—would be required for other grammatical constructions. The important point is that the abilities attributed to the child are rather modest: generalization, abstraction, and so forth. It follows that language development must be the result of a patchwork of thousands of separately acquired frames, patterns, responses, rules, and small tricks. The elegance of the final product belies the chaos of its construction.

Chomsky (1959) has a different view.

The child who learns a language has in some sense constructed the grammar for himself . . . this grammar is of an extremely complex and abstract character, and . . . the young child has succeeded in carrying out what from a formal point of view, at least, seems to be a remarkable type of theory construction. Furthermore, this task is accomplished in an astonishingly short time, to a large extent independently of intelligence, and in a comparable way by all children. (p. 57)

In Chomsky's analysis, called *transformational grammar,* classes such as *subject, predicate, object, verb,* and *modifier* are innately given. Applying a Chomskian analysis to language development, NcNeill (1970) has put it this way:

The facts of language acquisition could not be as they are unless the concept of a sentence is the main guiding principle in a child's attempt to organize and interpret the linguistic evidence that fluent speakers make available to him. (p. 2)

The distinction between what Skinner and Chomsky are saying is made easier for me by imagining moving to a new city, say Washington, D.C., and finding my way around. Suppose I knew nothing about the layout of streets. Gradually through many forays, mistakes, instructions from others, I would get my bearings. If I lived in the city long enough, I might even get to a point at which I had a kind of cognitive map. But this cognitive model of Washington's structure would be induced from my experience. In the second case I imagine going to Washington with a street map in my possession and constantly in use. I would check all my experiences against the map, filling in details with time. I would not have to discover, for example, that streets are laid out like spokes and wheels, that being given by the street map. I would have to discover the physical appearance of the various streets, that not being evident from the map. If I imagine that the map is given innately in the second case instead of by Exxon, I have a grasp of the essentially philosophical difference between Chomsky and Skinner.

That is about all I want to make of the Skinner-Chomsky debate. Are grammatical categories innate constructions, or do they emerge gradually with experience? I wish there were more implications for acquisition in the work of either theorist. From Skinner's empirical perspective one would hope to learn the particular experiences that lead to novel and grammatical—i.e., generative—utterances. But with the exception of the proposition that reinforcement and imitation are important, few details on acquisition are present. Chomsky's position has surprisingly similar deficiencies. Even if the child begins with a priori ideas of the structure of language, s/he must learn how that structure is substantiated in his/her parents' language; after all, Swahili is different from Japanese. Some minimal input principles must operate. None are suggested in transformational grammar.

Though we are left with little but the ageless debate between empiricism and nativism, this issue is a useful springboard for the substance of this chapter. My plan is to discuss, in turn, *syntax* and *semantics*. I will consider for each topic when children express major skills, the extent to which those skills seem to reflect universal, biologically given properties, and the environmental processes that affect those skills. Note here that we are really discussing a continuum of openness to environmental influence. As every college sophomore learns, genotypes are never expressed directly, and phenotypes are always a result of gene-environment interaction. Or as William James put it, the innate occurs only once; after that it becomes subject to the effects of experience.

For this chapter the plan is this: Here is what most children seem to do, and this is the age at which they seem to be capable of doing it. What type of environmental support is necessary for these particular abilities to emerge?

SYNTAX

Syntax refers to the organizational principles by which elements of meaning, words and morphemes, are combined. Many syntactic rules are general devices for marking important relationships among events. *John hit Mary* has a different meaning from *Mary hit John:* The agent-recipient relationship is signaled by word position. *John lived in Germany* means something different from

John lives in Germany: The morpheme /ed/ signals past action.

Two characteristics of this type of syntactic rule are important. First, such rules are based on abstract commonalities among words—i.e., the rules apply to open-ended classes of words rather than a discrete list. Any word that has the feature or features that define membership in the class may be combined with other words in the manner specified by the rule. The second important characteristic flows directly from the first: Such rules are generative. If I show a three-year-old a funny puppet and name it *gokem* and another and name it *zumap* and then make gokem strike a blow at zumap, I may ask the child what happened and expect him/her to say, *Gokem hit zumap.* S/he can generate a sentence based on knowing to place the names of agents before the verb and the names of recipients after, even though s/he may never have heard the words *gokem* or *zumap* used that way. How does the child do this?

I will return to this important issue after a diversion to consider another type of syntactic rule, one that is often overlooked. This type of rule is arbitrary and nonfunctional in the sense that one could well imagine a language doing without it with no sacrifice in communicative effectiveness. There are many examples. Irregular morphemes are one: *jumped* from *jump* and *ducks* from *duck* are regular, but *sold* from *sell* and *children* from *child* are irregular. Here is another irregularity: I can say *I hurt my car* and *I hurt myself; I harmed my car* and *I harmed myself;* and *I injured my car* and *I injured myself.* But while I can say *I damaged my car,* I cannot say *I damaged myself. Damage,* while superficially like all these other verbs in that it is transitive, does not ordinarily take a whole living person or animal as an object. *The truck damaged the carcass* is permissible but not *the truck damaged the steer.*

Maratsos and Chalkley (1980) provide an excellent example of nonfunctional syntax. Nouns in German take different pronouns and different articles depending on whether they are categorized as masculine, feminine, or neuter and depending on their case—nominative, accusative, dative, or genitive (see Table 21–1). This makes the German system far more complicated than English. Thus we would say in English, *The knife is here. It is here; The spoon is here. It is here; The fork is here. It is here.* If we were working with German pronouns and adjectives, the following sentences would result because knife, spoon, and fork are neuter, masculine, and feminine, respectively: *Das knife is here. Es is here; Der spoon is here. Er is here; Die fork is here. Sie is here.* The situation becomes more complicated when the effect of case is entered. While we would say, *The spoon is here. It is here; He discussed the spoon; He discussed it;* and *He is speaking about the spoon. He is speaking about it.* German usage would necessitate *Der spoon is here. Er is here; He discussed den spoon. He discussed ihn;* and *He is speaking about dem spoon. He is speaking about ihm.*

While some of these nonfunctional syntactic markers are idiosyncratic and completely irregular (e.g., *child; children*), others are generative, just as syntactic devices that mark more critical distinctions. The German system for pronouns and articles is one example. As evidence MacWhinney (1978) labeled a nonsense object for German preschoolers, *This toy is called X,* then referred to it by a pronoun, *I'm picking es (sie, ihn) up,* then hid the toy

Table 21-1 Gender and Case Effects on German Definite Articles and Personal Pronouns to Be Used with Singular Nouns

	GENDER					
	Masculine		Feminine		Neuter	
CASE	Article	Pronoun	Article	Pronoun	Article	Pronoun
Nominative	*der*	*er*	*die*	*sie*	*das*	*es*
Accusative	*den*	*ihn*	*die*	*sie*	*das*	*es*
Dative	*dem*	*ihm*	*der*	*ihr*	*dem*	*ihm*
Genitive	*des*	—	*der*	—	*des*	—

under the table and asked the children to request its location, *How do you ask? Where is _____?* Depending on the pronoun used in Step 2 (*es, sie,* or *ihn*), the children had the information that could have allowed them to deduce the gender of the novel toy and thereby the correct definite article to use in replying to the experimenter's question, *Where is das X? Where is die X?* or *Where is der X?* The preschoolers who were subjects of this investigation were able to use the German gender-article-case rules to generate correct definite articles after hearing the experimenter use personal pronouns. Of course mistakes were made and ability increased with age, but the point is that the system, however arbitrary and nonfunctional, is acquired and becomes generative for young German children.

What I have been trying to do in a rough way is characterize *syntax.* I hope the examples have indicated at least three generic types of syntactic phenomena: (1) generative rules based on open-ended classes of words signaling important functional information—e.g., *verb + ed = past*—where verb is the open-ended class; (2) generative rules based on open-ended classes of words signaling little or no important functional information—e.g., *der + noun = er*—where noun is the open-ended class; and (3) nongenerative irregularities—e.g., *child + plural = children.*

Children learn all three types of syntactic devices. This is important because an explanation of syntactic skill must address the child's ability to acquire the arbitrary, idiosyncratic, and nonfunctional as well as the regular and generative.

A Developmental Perspective

Before delving further into the nature of syntax and how it is acquired, it is worthwhile to know something about what develops and when. There are so many syntactic characteristics that have been explored that it is hopelessly ambitious to try an authoritative summary. What follows is an attempt to give some flavor of important developmental progressions.

I will use both *chronological age* and *mean length of utterance* (MLU) as organizers for the following summary. I use chronological age with apologies to the researchers whose work is the basis of my summary (Bellugi, 1967; Bloom & Lahey, 1978; Brown, 1973; Brown, Cazden, & Bellugi, 1969; Palermo & Molfese, 1972) and with concern that readers might misinterpret. There is tremendous individual variation in the rate and form of language development. Some children, for instance, do not even begin to talk until well into their third year (McCarthy, 1954); others are producing long sentences at that point. There is little evidence that developmental

variations in productive syntax have implications for adult language skill, given that a child is normal in other respects. It is perhaps for that reason that many investigators have preferred MLU as an organizing device. MLU, roughly correlated with chronological age, is a measure of the average number of independent units of meaning (*morphemes*) in the spontaneous utterances of a child. An *utterance* is defined by pauses and intonation. Usually about a hundred utterances are used for computation of MLU. To illustrate suppose the following were recorded:

Mother	*Child*
What are you doing?	Doggie. Gonna get Doggie.
Don't hurt the doggie.	Don't hurt. Wanna play.
Be gentle.	Here doggie. Doggie come here.

Separate utterances are indicated by sentence punctuation. Our hypothetical child has made six utterances. There is one 1-word utterance, three 2-word, and two 3-word utterances:

$$MLU = \frac{1 + 2 + 2 + 2 + 3 + 3}{6} = 2.17.$$

Note that *don't* is counted as one morpheme for the child while it would be counted as two (*do not*) for an adult. Other rules and conventions apply that are beyond the scope of this presentation (see Brown, 1973). MLU is a good device for making comparisons of form, content, and function across children. Thus instead of asking how two-year-olds are similar and dissimilar in various language capacities, investigators usually ask how children of, say, MLU 2.25 compare in linguistic skills. I have included age along with MLU because it is of value to have in mind the usual nonlinguistic characteristics of a child with a given MLU.

Table 21–2 summarizes major developments in syntax during early childhood. Several characteristics of these phenomena deserve more comment.

Age 1½ to 2½. Much has been made of the universality of the stage of one- and two-word utterances. Virtually all utterances of this type can be categorized as expressing a limited number of semantic relations such as nonexistence (*allgone ball*). Inflections or "little" words are never present, and word order and intonation are the only expressive devices. These characteristics are said to be common to the first stage of first language learning in all cultures (Brown, 1973). Brown and Herrnstein say, "One irresistibly has the impression of a biological process developing in just the same way in the entire human species, though greatly varying in its speed in different individuals" (1975, p. 479).

Table 21-2 The Development of Syntactic Skills

AGE (in years)	MLU	SYNTACTIC SKILLS	EXAMPLES
1½ to 2½	1.5	One-word utterances, called *holophrases,* and two-word utterances, called *duos.* The child can express basic semantic relationships such as:	
		Recurrence	*More ball.*
		Nonexistence	*All gone ball.*
		Attribution	*Big ball.*
		Possession	*My ball.*
		Nominations	*That ball.*
		Agent-Action	*Adam hit.*
		Agent-Action-Object	*Adam hit ball.*
2½ to 3	2.25	Grammatical morphemes are added such as:	
		Present Progressive Inflection	*I walking.*
		Locative Prepositions	*Kitty in basket.*
		Plurals	*Two balls.*
		Possessive	*Adam's ball.*
		Past	*It broke.*
		Verb Inflections	*He walks.*
3 to 3½	2.75	Auxiliary Verbs	*I am walking.*
			I do like you.
		Negative Particles	*I didn't do it.*
			This isn't ice cream.
		Yes-no Questions	*Will I go?*
			Do you want it?
		Wh Questions	*What do you have?*
			Where is the doggie?
3½ to 4	3.25	Sentence Clauses	*You think I can do it.*
			I see what you made.
4 to 5	3.75	Conjunctions of Two Sentences	*You think I can, but I can't.*
			Mary and I are going.
>5	>4	Reversible Passives	*The truck was chased by the car.*
		Connectives	*I am going to go although I don't want to.*
		Indirect Object - Direct Object Constructions	*The man showed the boy the friend.*
		Pronominalization	*He knew that John was going to win the race.*

This is a remarkable assertion if it implies more than the involvement of general biological processes in language acquisition, and it must imply more because all learning and development are mediated biologically. A reasonable interpretation of Brown's view is that the facts of Stage 1 suggest that early human language acquisition has a unique biological substrate which constrains development to a particular form.

Nothing is as frustrating and as much fun as taking sides in a debate over nativism vs. empiricism. It is certainly possible that children are biologically prepared to do just what they do in the one- and two-word stages, but is that conclusion supportable? If not, there is much for psycholinguistics to learn about these developments that will be delayed by the assumption that the determinants are primarily or exclusively biological.

Before examining the facts as Brown (1973) has presented them, it is worth pointing out that universality can arise for environmental as well as biological reasons, and by reason of very general and indirect biological influences as well as specific biological underpinnings. Individuals stand with their feet on the floor all around the world, not because they are biologically unable to stand on the ceiling but because gravity is a universal environmental force. Individuals go through grossly similar steps in learning to ski or learning to play the piano all around the world, not because they have specific genes for skiing or piano playing but because skills have hierarchies of components that lead to natural progressions along dimensions of complexity and relatedness. Thus even if we were to find the facts to be exactly as Brown believes them to be, we would not necessarily need to accept an innate view of Stage 1 language.

The facts, however, seem to be in question. Is it the case that children use standard word order to express a fixed number of semantic relations? Brown (1973) suggests 15 relations that form the basis of syntactic rules: examples are *Possessor + Object, Agent + Action, Attribute + Object* (cf. Table 21-2). But what is the basis for deciding that *my ball* falls into a *Possessor + Object* category and *big ball* into an *Attribute + Object* category? Perhaps there is just one category into which both utterances fit: *Characteristic + Object,* where possession and size are both characteristics of objects. In fact early work on two-word utterances defined just one syntactic pattern, *Pivot + Open* (Braine, 1963).

Alternatively instead of there being fewer than 15 productive patterns, perhaps there are more. Braine (1976) and Bowerman (1976) suggest that early two-word combinations are often based on individual patterns rather than general categories. One very frequent pattern seems to be *More + Object*—the child will say, *more ball, more cookie, more milk.* It may be inappropriate to say that the child is expressing the general pattern *Recurrence + Object* because the word *again*, in one child's vocabulary at the same time as *more*, was not combined with object labels—i.e., there were no utterances like *again ball, again cookie.* When *again* was eventually combined with other words, it was in the pattern *Object + Again*—e.g., *play again.* If we can contract the list of patterns to one or expand it to many more than 15 based on distributional evidence, where are the fixed number of semantic relations expressed universally in Stage 1 of language acquisition?

Similarly word order does not seem to be as regular as Brown suggests. I will simply quote from a recent review by Maratsos and Chalkley, "[T]here is . . . no uniform ordering tendency. Sometimes . . . relational terms take their future subject arguments in initial position in this early speech (*X + sleep, X + write, X + go*). But they also take them in second position as well (*red + X, wet + X, big + X*)" (1980, p. 166).

Finally what of the absence of inflections in Stage 1, even when the language the child is using relies on inflections for marking important relations such as *subject* and *object* (e.g., Japanese)? Brown himself provides one answer to this by noting that inflections are structurally more complex than earlier noninflected utterances. Playing Bach two-part inventions is more complex than playing scales on the piano; it is not surprising that simple precedes complex.

On examining this evidence the universality of Stage 1 syntax seems to fade. Children all around the world begin productive language with one- and two-word utterances that refer to what seem to be important events from the child's perspective. Beyond this similarity children differ in the rate, form, and semantics of early utterances.

Age 2½ to 3. Two characteristics of the acquisition of inflectional morphemes are worthy of note. First, Brown (1973) and de Villiers and de Villiers (1973) have discovered what seems to be an invariant order in the acquisition of morphemes by English-speaking children. The order is *present progressive, in, on, plural, past irregular, possessive inflection, uncontractible copula, articles, past regular, third person regular, third person irregular, uncontractible progressive auxiliary, contractible copula,* and *contractible progressive auxiliary.* Correlations between the order in which these morphemes are acquired by different children are in the + 0.80 to + 0.90 range.

Brown (1973) considers two likely reasons for this order: *grammatical complexity* (how far removed the form is from a simple active declarative base of verbs and nouns) and *semantic complexity* (the difficulty or sophistication of the idea expressed by the form). Ratings of the list of morphemes on these two dimensions are highly correlated so both factors are consistent with the obtained sequence.

Before accepting either grammatical or semantic com-

plexity or some combination of the two as the sole determinants of the sequence of development in Stage 2, we should consider alternatives. MacWhinney (1978) argues that *functionality*—defined as the degree to which a child wishes to express an intention—is actually the major determinant of the sequence of morpheme acquisition. In this argument it is more important to a child—i.e., more functional—to express plurality, locations, and possession than the copula or third person verb inflections.

It is very unlikely that these various hypotheses will be decided on the basis of observational studies of the sort that have provided much of the data base in syntactic development. A decision on the role of functionality, semantic difficulty, or syntactic complexity would seem to require research in which these variables could be manipulated independently. Perhaps a miniature linguistic system approach would be optimal (see Tweney, 1974; Wetherby, 1978)—that is, one could introduce young children to a constructed language in which morphemes and semantic referents could be made independent of each other. Tests of the rules of semantic and syntactic complexity should then be possible.

The second noteworthy characteristic of Stage 2 is the nature of errors made by children. Those morphemes that have irregular forms are almost always acquired before regular forms, but once the child begins to use regular forms, they are often extended inappropriately to the previously correct irregulars (Cazden, 1968; Ervin, 1964). For instance *foot* becomes *feets; went* becomes *goed* or *wented.* This process, called *overregularization,* is important because it is the best evidence that the child has acquired a productive rule system (albeit an incorrect one). For past tense the rule might be characterized as *Verb + ed = past,* where verb is an open class that can have an ever-expanding set of members, including verbs like *to go* that should not be included.

Understanding of the overregularization phenomenon is aided significantly by miniature linguistic system research by Palermo and Eberhart (1968). These investigators have shown that the phenomenon occurs whenever a system is being acquired in which irregular forms are fewer in number but presented more frequently than regular forms. Individuals learn the irregular forms first but overextend the regular system when they first begin to apply it. Since irregular forms in all languages tend to be applied to the most important and thus most used words, this modeling factor could well explain the initial learning of irregular forms in Stage 2. At the same time irregular forms (e.g., *to be*) usually refer to more important semantic concepts so functionality produces the same sequence as modeling frequency. In any case overregularization seems to be a reliable phenomenon in concept learning under certain mixes of regular and irregular instances of a rule. Linguistic overregularization is a result of general processes of concept learning.

Age 3 to 3½. This period is notable for the further development of simple sentences through addition of auxiliary verb forms which allow questions and negatives to become more adult-like. Question forms have received considerable study (Bellugi, 1965; Brown & Hanlon, 1970). Of interest is the fact that when auxiliary verbs are first produced in questions they are not inverted. The child will say, *Why you are thirsty?* or *How he can be a doctor?*

before correctly inverting the auxiliary and the noun phrase, *Why are you thirsty?* This is a particularly vivid demonstration that language acquisition involves more than a simple imitation of adult speech that progresses from a rough to a good approximation. Phenomena such as failure to invert auxiliary verbs show that the child is compromising what s/he hears adults say with the characteristics of the syntactic system s/he has already acquired with his/her own cognitive abilities to produce intermediate forms. These forms are unlike what the child has heard and are not merely degraded copies of what the child has heard. Little, if any, work has been done to illuminate this process.

Ages 3½ and Up. I am collapsing the final three stages of Table 21–2 into one because the general developmental trend is to acquire increasing complex syntactic forms. Conjunctions, other connectives, clauses, passives, indirect objects all represent both increasing syntactic and semantic complexity.

Much has been made of the supposed fact that syntactic development is essentially complete by the age of six: "... by the time children enter school, mistakes in syntax are striking abnormalities" (Gardner, 1978, p. 173). Considerable research suggests otherwise (Palermo & Molfese, 1972) as does my personal experience. I struggle to not split infinitives, I am one of those people who sometimes are unable to get their pronouns and verbs to agree, and the use of case has long been difficult for others as well as I.

Maclay and Osgood (1959) recorded the spontaneous speech of 13 professionals during a conference on psycholinguistics. The following is a sample of that discourse.

As far as I know, no one yet has done the in a way obvious and interesting problem of doing a in a sense a structural frequency study of the alternative syntactical in a given language, say, like English, the alternative possible structures, and how what their hierarchal probability of occurrence is. (p. 25)

Continuing,

For example, a if under I was speaking to you George, the at supper last night, I think. If you find that at each point, say, in English structure you have an alt- several alternatives, some of which are highly probable in ordinary English sentences, syntactical sequences of, for example, adjective, noun, verb vs. a dependent phrase inserted, and so on. But these have . . . (p. 25)

Perhaps there is a *U*-shaped function: Children have perfect control over syntactic rules by the time they are age six, but there is a deterioration thereafter with adult academics being hardest hit. Or perhaps those who have seen syntactic development as essentially complete by school age have defined the child's abilities in such abstract terms that the difficulties and errors of day-to-day syntactic processing do not count. That is like saying that transportation consists of two categories—surface and air—therefore the development of transportation was completed when the first balloon carried passengers. It is difficult to identify a human skill that is not subject to development across the lifespan; syntax is no exception.

The Determinants of Syntactic Development

I have charactertized *syntax* as consisting of nongenerative irregularities as well as generative rules, some of which code important information and some of which do not. The generative rules must consist of operations to be performed on open-ended classes of words and morphemes—that is, when a child produces sentences s/he has not heard others use and when those sentences are grammatically appropriate or at least grammatically regular, the child must be using some cues to organize words into classes so that the words may be appropriately ordered to be meaningful. Two questions arise: What cues does the child use to form syntactic word classes? How does the child learn to use those cues? The first question asks the nature of the rules; the second asks how the child acquires the rules.

What Is Learned?

There are four possible or at least imaginable bases for the formation of syntactic rules.

1. Deep Structures. It is difficult to describe *deep structures* to the uninitiated. The term was invented by Chomsky (1957) as a device to explain the differences existing among what people actually say, the surface structure of sentences, and the underlying meaning of sentences. *The shooting of the hunters was terrible* has two meanings that can be expressed as two different deep structures. Sentences with quite different surface structures, *John is kissing Mary, Mary is being kissed by John,* can be said to have the same meaning because they have the same deep structures. Thus deep structure is a theory of the categories that underlie overt language. Language production starts with deep structures and applies transformation rules to produce surface sentences. Language comprehension works in the opposite direction. The set of rules by which surface structures are mapped onto deep structures could be thought of as what is learned in the course of language acquisition.

There are several problems with the view that children learn deep structures and transformations on those structures. First, there can be as many different deep structures as there are linguists with the ingenuity to devise systems that are consistent with the facts that such systems confront. Chomsky, for example, changed very important details of his 1957 transformational grammar in 1965. There are currently at least four competing transformational grammars (Fodor, 1977). Which of these are children supposed to be learning?

This leads into the question of the psychological reality of such grammars. Presumably if a theory of deep structure is a theory of how people process sentences, one should be able to garner behavioral evidence supportive of the predictions of the theory. Much of the research on this issue has utilized latency data, measuring how long it takes adults to understand sentences that vary on their derivational complexity within a theory of transformational grammar. Sentences that are theoretically more complex should take longer to process—e.g., a passive sentence should take longer to be understood than an active sentence. Early studies seemed to offer support

(Mehler, 1963; Miller & McKean, 1964; Savin & Perchonock, 1965), but this research was flawed in that the derivationally more complex sentences were usually semantically more complex and longer as well. *Was not the ball hit by the boy?* takes longer to process than *The boy hit the ball.* The transformational derivation of the first sentence is more complex than the first, but it also includes three more words as well as the semantic notions of negation and question. When later research was conducted in which length and meaning were not confounded with derivational complexity, no differences emerged in sentence-processing time (Fodor & Garrett, 1966; Fodor, Jenkins, & Saporta, 1966).

Even if there were only one transformational grammar and even if there were evidence for its psychological reality, a serious problem would still remain for a development analysis. As I stated, a *transformational grammar* is a set of rules by which the surface structure of a sentence is mapped onto an underlying set of theoretical categories. Such rules exist for idealized adult speakers who are assumed to know their language perfectly. The method for developing such grammars, if it may be called that, is the intuitions of psycholinguists about what constitutes acceptable and unacceptable, similar and dissimilar sentences in a language. By comparing intuitions this method develops a loose form of consensual validity. There is no such method to be applied to young children who are extremely handicapped in expressing whatever intuitions they might possess about the structure of sentences. Developmental psycholinguistics is left with a set of fragmentary efforts to build child transformational grammars that are based on the intuitions of adults about the intuitions of children. Given that there are no rules for constructing such grammars, it is difficult to see how they can be assessed.

Efforts have been made to assess the validity of the deep structure–surface structure distinction itself, rather than the particulars of any individual grammar. Goldin-Meadow and Feldman (1977) published data on the spontaneous sign system of six deaf children whose parents decided against exposing them to a manual language in order to concentrate on an oral approach. These investigators concluded that the children's spontaneous signing displayed an orderly structure consistent with the distinction between surface and deep structure. These are very important results in that they suggest that the children produced a structured language without being exposed to a structured language.

Goldin-Meadow and Feldman's conclusion is highly questionable. The sign systems produced were very impoverished; most signs were points. For example a child might point at a shoe and then to a table indicating that the shoe should be put on the table. Others were some type of iconic sign for an action—e.g., a flapping motion for a flying bird. The following logic was applied to this data base. (1) Signs were categorized into one of several categories from the case grammar developed by Fillmore (1968). Almost all elements of signing sequences could be broken down into three categories: *patient* (the object or person acted upon), *act* (the action), and *recipient* (the locus or person toward which someone or something moves). (2) Regularities in sequences of signs were tested. The investigators found that some children showed no ordering tendencies at all, but such tendencies as were

found were claimed to be consistent with the following rule:

(Choose any two maintaining order)
Phrase → (patient) (act) (recipient)

(3) The presence of the regularity described by the previous rule was assumed to be evidence that the children produced sign sequences "by following a syntactic rule based on the semantic role of each of the sign units" (Goldin-Meadow & Feldman, 1977, p. 402). In other words a deep structure of the form described was assumed to underlie the surface regularities that were observed to occur.

There are three significant problems with this logic. First, the descriptive adequacy of a rule is a prerequisite to its candidacy for psychological reality but not evidence for reality. Children obey the laws of physics when they ride a bicycle, but we would not say that they move forward "by following physical laws based on force vectors and gravitational fields." We would find such a statement distasteful, not because it is an inappropriate description of what the bicycle rider does but because it is obviously not a statement of how he does it. Goldin-Meadow and Feldman's rule may not be distasteful, but that means it is merely plausible. Without evidence of psychological reality there is no reason to consider the rule in question more than one of a number of possible accounts of the subject's performance.

A second problem is that the evidence is weak that the rule is even consistent with performance. The investigators speak of tendencies toward ordering in some subjects. Actually only three of six subjects showed at least one statistically significant tendency toward regular ordering—e.g., placing patients before recipients. It follows that half the subjects did not. Only one subject, David, ordered all three categories—patients, acts, and recipients—in a manner statistically concordant with the rule. It follows that five of the six subjects did not. Finally, even David often performed in a manner inconsistent with the rule—e.g., placing a sign for an act before a sign for a patient. It appears that all evidence against a structured language system is ignored while any evidence for a structured language system is accepted.

The third and final problem is that there are readily available alternative explanations for the regularities that do exist in the signing data. Consider, for instance, the congruence between the sequence of signs and the sequence of actions referred to by those signs. If a shoe (patient) is to be put on a table (recipient), then a sequence of sign (*shoe*) + sign (*table*) maintains the sequence of action. Research indicates that such sequence-maintaining statements are easier to comprehend (Huttenlocher & Strauss, 1968). This factor would explain any tendency toward (patient) (act) (recipient) order.

At the same time informational variables could explain substantial variations from such a sequence. Children may be expected to notice and describe first those aspects of a situation that carry the most information (Greenfield & Smith, 1976). Imagine a situation in which a mother and her child have been playing with a ball. The mother holds the ball out of the child's reach, and s/he signs *give* (act) *ball* (patient). We may speculate that the ball is a relative given in this situation because both mother and child have been playing with it and are attending to it. The information to be conveyed is that the child wishes the ball given back, so the sign (*give*) is produced first. Now imagine that the child is playing with a ball but the mother, while nearby, is not actively engaged with the child. The ball rolls out of reach, the child fusses, the mother attends, and the child signs *ball* (patient) *give* (act). In this scenario it is the object that is most informationally relevant, so it is signed first.

I am not suggesting that an informational analysis or the congruence between sign sequence and action sequence accounts for the data of Goldin-Meadow and Feldman, only that these are plausible alternatives. When the existence of alternative explanations for the deaf children's performance is joined with the inconsistency between the children's actual performance and the rule formulated by Goldin-Meadow and Feldman, plus the absence of data on the psychological reality of the rule, one wonders what this study demonstrates. Certainly it is weak evidence that children learn a language by acquiring deep structure rules.

Remember the question: What is the basis for the child's ability to order words appropriately? The evidence is minimal for this being a result of the acquisition of deep structures. As discussed one of the supposedly strongest pieces of evidence, the study of deaf children's spontaneous signs, is found wanting in many respects. Indeed it is arguable that the theoretical concept of deep structure has become so shallow when applied to child language that one can barely see a dent in the surface of what children say. Brown (1978) says, "... whenever a parent or a developmental psycholinguist interprets a young primate's 'telegraphic' sentence as meaning more, in full context, than it actually says or signs, a distinction has been made between a richer deep structure and a more impoverished surface structure" (pp. 6–7). I submit that if the distinction between surface structure and deep structure is to mean nothing more than that a child's words are often impoverished with respect to his/her communicative goals, then there is little to debate and little to profit from the issue. There is certainly nothing in this broad conceptualization of deep structure that speaks to how children order words appropriately.

2. Rote. One of the contributions of the linguistic revolution fomented by Chomsky was the awareness it produced of the novel, rule-governed characteristics of language. Our ability to produce and comprehend sentences that we may never have heard points to the existence of a grammatical system that operates on classes of words. Such a rule-based system can be contrasted with a rote system in which routines are acquired directly from parental speech. A grammatical system based entirely on rote would not be capable of generating or comprehending novel sentences.

The existence of a rule-based system does not, however, preclude the simultaneous operation of a rote system. This has been overlooked. As a result there is little research or theoretical consideration of the role of rote in the acquisition of syntax. My previous introductory discussion of syntax included several examples of forms that are likely to be rote acquisitions—irregular plurals for instance (*child-children; foot-feet*). The previously described sequence in which irregular forms are learned before regular forms points to an early stage in which rote predominates. While the existence and early acquisition of irregular forms points logically to the role of rote, there are also many regular forms that may be based on rote even though they are also consistent with rules and word classes. MacWhinney (1975, 1978) has demonstrated how irregular forms such as *feet* as well as regular forms such as *horses* may be attributed to rote learning.

Rote is at work in grammar as well as morphological forms. Braine's (1976) extensive analysis of children's first word combinations identified a frequent pattern called *positional associative*. Here a child learns the position of a fixed word such as *all* and associations between that fixed term and each of the words occurring with it—e.g., *all broke, all day, all shut*. This is not a productive rule because children do not produce combinations they have not heard.

The role of rote beyond the earliest language learning is unexplored. One hypothesis is that all language forms begin in rote and that rote forms maintain an anchoring role in mature language. Theories that overlook rote forms will be incapable of explaining language acquisition.

3. Distributional Classes. When I was a fuzzy-faced undergraduate, I never appreciated my professors' arguments about swinging pendulums and the constant recurrence of themes in psychology. Everything seemed fresh. Now I believe.

One of the most detailed attempts to account for syntactic word classes was generated by Braine and published in 1963. Braine proposed that much grammatical ordering could be explained by word classes being formed on the basis of the sentence positions in which words recur. Hearing the sentence, *People kivil every day,* can lead to the generation of sentences such as *Kiviling is fun* and *I want to kivil,* because the position in which *kivil* appears marks it as a verb. Because we have previously heard and understood sentences such as *People eat everyday, Eating is fun,* and *I want to eat,* we can generalize to other words that appear in the same position. The generalization takes the form of treating the new word (*kivil*) as if it has the grammatical properties of words that have previously appeared in the same sentence position (*eat*).

A remarkably similar account has been offered almost 20 years later by Maratsos and Chalkley (1980). Maratsos and Chalkley propose that word classes are formed on the basis of common combinational-semantic properties. A word is treated as a verb, for instance, because it enters into a common set of grammatical operations. These include being marked directly for tense (*kick-kicked*), appearing with a form of *do* (*He didn't kick*), taking -*ing* forms (*He is kicking*). Maratsos and Chalkley (1980) say, "By hearing a novel term used in one of the contexts, we can predict its occurrence and accordant change of meaning and structure in still others" (p. 133). Braine (1963) says, "... there must exist generalization mechanisms in language learning whereby a word learned in one context generalizes to another context, even though no associations may have previously formed between the word and its new context" (p. 324).

Maratsos and Chalkley's arguments benefit from the 20 years of research that have intervened since Braine's work. Work on the acquisition of the previously discussed

German gender system is strongly supportive of contextual generalization as the basis of grammatical classes (see Table 21-1). Recall that the German gender and case system is largely arbitrary—that is, there is no semantic basis for categorizing a spoon as masculine and a fork as feminine. The only basis for categorizing a new word is distributional; if it occurs with *der* and *er,* it must be masculine. Yet young children are able to use this system productively (MacWhinney, 1978), and they learn it at about the same time as English-speaking children acquire their much simpler determiner system (Stern, 1931/1964).

There seem to be many reasons to accept the proposition that novel words can come to be ordered appropriately because the child can generalize or analogize on the basis of distributional context. If an old word has been learned and used in five different contexts, a new word appearing in one of those contexts can be expected to generalize to other contexts in which the old word appears.

4. Semantic Classes. Both Braine (1963) and Maratsos and Chalkley (1980) have recognized that word classes may benefit from semantic as well as distributional commonalities. Braine (1965) says,

... when items are already similar by virtue of a semantic property or relation of some sort, it would be readily understandable that the overt marker might not be needed.... Proper names provide an obvious example: A speaker hearing an exotic name for the first time presumably does not need to hear it used in noun positions in sentences in order to know its grammatical category. Unfortunately, semantic correlates are rarely so transparent. (p. 488)

Maratsos and Chalkley (1980) say,

We are not, however, attempting a formulation of the child's analysis of form class and other syntactic categories on purely distributional bases. The semantic entailments of such combinations of morphemes also form an essential part of the account. (p. 134)

Both Braine and Maratsos and Chalkley agree that grammatical categories are unlikely to be based entirely on semantic commonalities. While there may be some statistical tendency for nouns to denote concrete referents, adjectives to denote states, and verbs to denote changes of state, this relationship is far from perfect. For instance *aware* (adjective) and *know* (verb) refer to essentially the same thing. Maratsos and Chalkley have developed these notions most. They seem to suggest a type of conditional discrimination in which the semantic referent for a word narrows its possible class membership and distributional evidence is used to complete the analysis *Aware* refers to a state and is often preceded by forms of the verb *to be* (*He was aware*). *Know* refers to the same state but is marked directly for tense (*He knew*). Much grammatical ordering may be based on the joint cues of syntactic distribution and semantic referent. The important role of semantic cues is indicated clearly by research with miniature linguistic systems. It is remarkably easier for subjects to learn the grammar of nonsense syllable languages that have correlated referents than it is to learn those languages on the basis of position alone (Moeser & Bregman, 1972; Moeser & Olson, 1974).

What Is Learned—A Recap

A role for deep structures in the acquisition of grammar is questionable at best. The alternative lies in a combination of the other three bases that have been considered: rote, distributional classes, and semantic classes. Children seem to use everything at their disposal in acquiring their mother tongue. Rather than working from a grand structure, children seem to move forward through bits and pieces—a little rote here and a little generalization there. For the last 20 years we have marveled at the child's accomplishment and have been tempted to attribute the result to miraculous powers. I think of the first Europeans to "discover" the Egyptian pyramids. It seemed impossible that such structures could have been built by a mechanically primitive culture, but in fact very simple techniques were responsible. Likewise language seems to be based on a hodgepodge of simple components that could not possibly result in such a complex whole. Yet they do. The challenge for the next 20 years of developmental psycholinguistics will be to discover how so much is generated by so little.

How Is Syntax Learned?

It is clear from my preceding statement that there will be no detailed answer to the question of how children learn syntax. The acquisition process, however, must depend on these three categories of influences: (1) innate abilities, (2) previously acquired skills and abilities, and (3) environmental input.

Innate Abilities. The previous discussion of deep structures will suggest that my candidates for innate abilities are not of the grandiose sort and are not even primarily linguistic, rather they are the biologically prepared abilities that underlie the acquisition of most complex cognitive skills. A partial list follows.

Sensitivity to the human voice. Condon and Sander (1974) have demonstrated an early propensity for neonates to respond with synchronous movements to human speech sounds compared to other sound sources. A more developed area of inquiry has explored infants' abilities to discriminate among various speech sounds. In reviewing research in this area Jusczyk (1981) concludes, "It appears that infants are innately endowed with mechanisms necessary for making phonetic distinctions in any natural language, at least to a first approximation." This biological pretuning of the human attentional and perceptual apparatus would seem well established and an understandable genetic characteristic given the importance of spoken language in human development.

Language specific processing strategies. Slobin (1973) has hypothesized a number of operating principles that represent genetic predispositions for processing language. Slobin suggests that children are predisposed to pay more attention to suffixes than prefixes. He notes that Hungarian children acquire the ability to express the locative prior to Serbo-Croatian children, presumably because the Hungarian locative is expressed by noun suffixes while the Serbo-Croatian is not. But this, like most descriptive data, is flawed—the Serbo-Croatian form seems more linguistically complex than the Hungarian disregarding position (also see Maratsos, 1979, and Mac-Whinney, 1978). Kuczaj (1979) gathered experimental evidence in favor of Slobin's hypothesis in that children learned novel suffix labels for tense, color, and so on, easier than they learned prefix labels. The English-speaking children in Kuczaj's study already had considerable experience with a language that is heavily weighted toward the use of suffixes so it is unclear whether these results are due to a genetic or learned propensity.

Other supposed language specific operating principles rest on less support than the hypothesis that children are biased to attend to the end of words. More research is needed, and considerable caution is called for in the meantime in attributing extensive language specific operating principles to children.

General learning abilities. It is easy to forget that general learning abilities, what Lorenz (1977) calls *open* programs, are as much a part of an organism's biological heritage as are closed, discrete abilities. The field of psycholinguistics may be moving toward greater recognition of the role of traditional learning processes and general cognitive capacities in the acquisition of syntax (e.g., Maratsos & Chalkley, 1980). Obviously I cannot describe all the learning processes that might be relevant to the acquisition of syntax. I suggest *two* that may be particularly important to the rapid acquisition of syntax by humans: *abstraction* and *analogy.*

Abstraction refers to the ability to discriminate commonalities in otherwise diverse collections of events. This is a characteristic of observational learning that is highly developed in humans and relevant to the learning of many cognitive skills (I. Brown, 1979; Rosenthal & Zimmerman, 1978). Abstraction is the key process in the formation of word classes, and I have already argued that word classes are the entities on which syntactic rules operate. The previous discussion points out that children use every cue at their disposal in abstracting word classes, including semantic commonalities and sentential context.

Analogy is the related action ability to use abstracted cues for class membership in the formation of novel utterances. Thus if a child has learned that names for people and animals fall into the noun class (abstraction) and if s/he has learned to form such sentences as *Give it to me, mommy,* s/he is prepared on being introduced to a new playmate named *Johnny* to produce by analogy the untutored sentence, *Give it to me, Johnny* (cf. Skinner, 1957, on grammatical frames).

Processes such as abstraction and analogy need to be explored in great detail to learn the constraints that apply to them in language learning. How often does a form need to be practiced before it can lead to novel utterances through analogy? How is the abstraction of word classes affected by the number and variety of exemplars in those classes? How is it affected by the form of classes? The whole issue of category or class formation is currently under intense scrutiny in cognitive psychology (e.g., R. Brown, 1979; Rosch & Mervis, 1975). The extension of this work into the acquisition of linguistic classes represents an exciting new frontier for developmental psycholinguistics.

Previously Acquired Abilities. Each developmental acquisition, whether or not linguistic, depends on the sys-

tem of related abilities that has been acquired and sets the stage for the new occurrence. One of the most recently active areas of research in language development is on the role of early social interaction in language acquisition. Bruner (1977) has led the way in showing the relevance of such ritualized infant-mother activities as "give and take" to the child's learning of the need to signal intent, to obtain joint attention, and to mark important segments or junction points in action, all significant precursors to language. Consistent with much of the previous discussion, Bruner's data argue for a system of language acquisition that is a pastiche of principles, processes, and props, with the earliest stages of acquisition heavily dependent on previously acquired social skills.

There are critics of this view. Shatz (1981), for instance, argues that a system of environmental supports and very general learning mechanisms is incapable of explaining the sequence of language development. Shatz presents specific evidence that maternal gestures, as one instance of the type of social precursors to which Bruner has attended, are too ambiguous with regard to particular linguistic forms to be a basis for a child decoding language. But Shatz's conclusion misses the point that no single set of cues to word class membership or syntactic rules will in itself be consistent and reliable. One can imagine a child averaging many cues, a maternal gesture here, a semantic referent there, a sentential context somewhere else, to arrive at a probabilistic basis for class membership and the application of syntactic rules. It is exactly this type of multicue messiness that is explicit in recent models of category formation to which I have referred (e.g., R. Brown, 1979).

Environmental Input. If the models of speech to which young children were exposed were always the lengthy, complicated, and mature sentences that are the subject matter of linguists' debates, one might lean toward a language acquisition system with many specific innate decoding strategies. Evidence suggests, however, that the linguistic environment of early language acquisition is remarkably simplified for the child. Snow and Ferguson (1977) present considerable research on what has come to be called *motherese.* Mothers tend to limit their input to children to simple sentence forms with accentuated stress and other cues that should be of considerable help to the child. Bohannon and Marquis (1977) have shown that this is an active process in which the child's signal of noncomprehension leads the mother to rephrase and simplify. Other teaching techniques that are used spontaneously and frequently by mothers have been catalogued and measured by Moerk (1978).

These demonstrations that the linguistic environment is specifically modified for the child suggest but do not demonstrate that the child needs or even is affected by these informal teaching strategies. Experimental evidence for the role of maternal linguistic input in the acquisition of syntax may be found in the work of I. Brown (1979), K. E. Nelson (1976), and Whitehurst (1977). I. Brown (1979) found that modeling of novel grammatical constructions when accompanied by clear concrete referents for the words in those constructions was a particularly potent instructional strategy.

Summary

I have devoted considerable space to the consideration of syntactic development because many of the most important theoretical issues have been confronted more directly within the domain of syntax than in other areas of language development. I have characterized syntax as consisting of both irregular elements and regular rules that are applied to open-ended classes of words. Four possible bases for the learning of word classes and syntactic rules were considered. Deep structures were eliminated because there are no articulated, testable sets of rules for mapping deep structures onto surface structures in child language. The psychological reality of deep structures is in doubt when tested with adults, and evidence for even the generic distinction between deep and surface structure is weak or nonexistent at the level of child language. Three other factors were considered in combination to be the basis for what is learned in the process of syntactic development. They were rote or imitation, word classes based on distributional evidence, and word classes based on semantic evidence.

The mechanisms of learning these rote and class-based syntactic forms were considered. Innate abilities take the form of putative language specific processing strategies as well as general learning skills and cognitive processes. Among the latter the ability to form abstractions and to analogize seem particularly important. These processes operate on the current linguistic input to the child, which is often simplified, and are aided by precursor skills, sometimes of a social-interactional nature.

The picture that emerges from this survey is of a process of acquisition that is perhaps more mysterious than when one could rely on the miracle of an innate acquisition device requiring little more than an adequate sample of mature language as input. The mystery we face currently is of the type with which psychologists are used to dealing. A sustained attack on the interaction of general cognitive abilities, the linguistic environment of the child, and the supporting social interactions on which language depends is likely to produce the type of cumulative knowledge that will be both interesting and practical.

SEMANTICS

The conclusions of the previous section on syntactic development point out the difficulty of separating semantics from other aspects of language. I defined *syntax* as the organizational principles by which elements of meaning are combined, and I discussed the role of *meaning* in the acquisition of syntax through the formation of semantic classes. All aspects of language depend heavily on semantics.

But what is *meaning* or *semantics?* Philosophers, linguists, and psychologists have tried to answer this question for at least 200 years. It is a depressing history: The same themes and arguments reappear with regularity and with little apparent progress. One begins to expect there is something wrong with the question.

The issue is, and always has been, whether meaning is a thing that has a psychic existence or whether it is an attribution referring to a diverse collection of skills and behaviors that allow someone to use language in socially accepted ways. In the first approach one tries to pin down meaning and identify its molecules. In the second approach meaning is nothing more than a descriptive summary label. It is like the concept of *speed*. An automobile has speed, but there is nothing in particular inside the automobile that is speed.

The most recent incarnation of the approach that reifies meaning is *semantic feature theory* (Bierwisch, 1970; E. Clark, 1973; Katz, 1972; Smith, Shoben, & Rips, 1974; Weinreich, 1966). The meaning of words in feature theories is thought to be based on a set of atomic sense components into which every word decomposes. These atomic features are thought to perform the following functions:

1. Determine if a sentence is semantically ambiguous—e.g., *John was looking for the glasses.*
2. Determine if a sentence is semantically anomalous—e.g., *My sister is a bachelor.*
3. Determine the existence of paraphrase and synonymy—e.g., *Mary is short; Mary is not tall enough.*
4. Distinguish between sentences that are analytically true and those that are synthetically true—e.g., *All dogs are canines; All dogs are friendly.*

The mechanism for achieving these goals is a set of largely binary contrasts. Take as an example the feature analysis of selected animal terms that is represented in Table 21–3. The symbol (+) indicates that a given animal term has that feature—e.g., *ram* is (+) male. The symbol (−) indicates the absence of feature—e.g., *ewe* is (−) male. The symbol (±) means that the term is indefinite on that feature—e.g., *sheep* is (±) male.

The preceding goals of semantic feature theory can be exemplified with the entries in Table 21–3. A sentence can be ambiguous if it includes a word that has two different feature analyses. Thus *He chased the chick* is ambiguous depending on whether the *chick* in question has the feature analysis *chick*[a] (+chicken, ±male, −adult) or *chick*[b] (−chicken, −male, +adult). In other words is the *chick* a chicken or a young woman? Of course the analysis of *chick*[b] as (−chicken, −male, +adult) is seriously deficient in that it includes no indication that the term refers to humans. We could remedy our feature table by including these contrasts, but doing so presents its own problems that will be addressed shortly.

Table 21–3 Feature Analysis of Selected Animal Labels

| LABELS | FEATURES | | | | |
	± sheep	± horse	± chicken	± male	± adult
sheep	+	−	−	±	±
ram	+	−	−	+	+
ewe	+	−	−	−	+
lamb	+	−	−	±	−
horse	−	+	−	±	±
stallion	−	+	−	+	+
mare	−	+	−	−	+
colt	−	+	−	±	−
chicken	−	−	+	±	±
rooster	−	−	+	+	+
hen	−	−	+	−	+
chick[a]	−	−	+	±	−
chick[b]	−	−	−	−	+

A sentence can be anomalous if the grammar of the sentence suggests a relation between two or more words that could not hold given their features—e.g., *A colt is a type of chicken.* Paraphrase exists to the extent that two words have overlapping features—e.g., *I am cooking a chicken* would be a closer paraphrase of *I am cooking a hen* than would *I am cooking a colt.* The distinction between analytic and synthetic truth is captured by not including aspects of meaning that depend on usual experience with referents in the feature analysis of a word unless those aspects are critical for use of the word. Thus (±friendly) would not be part of the feature analysis of the terms in Table 21-3 so that *Colts are friendly* might be true synthetically but not relevant analytically.

The overwhelming internal difficulty with semantic features is that the list of features that is supposed to represent the meaning of a word varies and grows depending on the items with which the word is compared and the sentences in which it is used. Take *chick*[a] and *chick*[b] from Table 21-3, which we have agreed refer to a young chicken and a woman, respectively. Let us say that an initial feature analysis of these terms might be *chick*[a] (+chicken, −human, ±male, −adult), *chick*[b] (−chicken, +human, −male, +adult). What then of the sentence, *Would you take a look at that chick!* To take into account the fact that few people would think this sentence ambiguous with respect to *chick*[a] and *chick*[b], we would have to add the feature (+aesthetically pleasing) to *chick*[b] and (±aesthetically pleasing) to *chick*[a]. To explain the lack of ambiguity in *The chick pecked at the corn*, we would have to add the feature (±pecks) to our analysis. The lack of ambiguity in *The chick flew to San Francisco* would depend on the counter-intuitive but commonly known fact that people can fly and chickens cannot; thus (±flies) would have to be added. Further our analysis would have to take into account the fact that *The chick flew to San Francisco* would have been anomalous 100 years ago though it is not today, and this would require still other features and so forth.

The plain fact is that the ability to recognize ambiguity, anomaly, and paraphrase depends on our encyclopedic knowledge of the linguistic and nonlinguistic world. To represent all the ways that one event may differ from all the other events with which it may be contrasted, to represent all the ways that one event may be similar to all the other events with which it may be compared, to represent all the relations that one event may enter into with all other possible events would require an endlessly proliferating list of features. Semantic features cannot possibly be the psychological basis for meaning if a person must process an infinite or even lengthy list of features to understand the meaning of a word.

Alternatives to an approach that reifies meaning and searches for its components have been articulated by Dewey (1958), Quine (1971), Skinner (1957), Whitehurst (1979), and others. Wittgenstein's dictum that "the meaning of a word is its use in the language" (1953, p. 20) captures this approach well. If meaning is use, then a psychological analysis would explore the experiences and skills that allow a child to use words in ways that are socially acceptable—i.e., that achieve desirable social ends.

Since the appropriate use of words involves every conceivable linguistic and cognitive skill, a full examination of semantics would move out into wider and wider circles of influence. Here we will examine only the very center of the issue: the child's acquisition of early vocabulary.

A Developmental Perspective

One of the most notable changes in children's language as it matures is in the number of words produced and understood. A number of studies have been conducted in which mothers were asked to report when their children uttered their first word. The average age from these reports is about 11 to 12 months, with a range in normal children of from 8 to 18 months (Darley & Winitz, 1961; McCarthy, 1954). If the first word is delayed longer than 18 months, there is reason to search for some abnormality in the child's auditory system or in the psychological interactions between the child and the child's caretakers. Because an adult's vocabulary may include upward of 30,000 words, the child mastering a first utterance obviously has a long way to go. In what is still the most extensive study of vocabulary growth, Smith (1926) tested children at a number of ages with sentences that were understandable only if the child knew a critical word. Computations with Smith's data disclose that between the ages of 1½ and 6½ years, the average child learns approximately 10 new words each week for a rate of nearly 1½ new words per day.

The types of words being acquired also change over the years of early childhood. Early words seem to break into three categories (Bloom & Lahey, 1978; Nelson, 1973, 1974) which I will call *nominals, relationals,* and *expressives.* For those interested these three categories relate in an interesting way to Skinner's (1957) description of *tacts, mands,* and *intraverbals. Nominals* name or describe things. Children in the period from age one to two years frequently use labels for food (*cookie*), body parts (*nose*), clothing (*shoe*), animals (*doggie*), vehicles (*ball*), household items (*cup*), and people (*mommy*). Words like *this, that,* and *it* are also often used as general purpose terms of reference. *Relational* terms include negative words like *no* and *no more,* requests for recurrence such as *more, again, mother,* and indications of disappearance such as *all gone* and *away. Expressives* are social words such a *hi, bye-bye,* and *thanks.*

Later vocabulary development occurs in many directions. Existing words come to be used more precisely; the child comes to talk about people and events that are distant from him/her in time or space; dimensional terms (e.g., *big, tall,* and *wide*), spatial terms (e.g., *in, on,* and *between*), and other modifiers are added; and the child begins to use words that are complex and abstract. Words like *freedom* or *obnubilate* are what Bertrand Russell (1940) called *dictionary words,* implying that we learn their meanings through verbal definitions rather than through correspondences with nonverbal events and object. Perhaps for this reason the language of young children does not include many such words. Knowing this a friend of mine was shocked at the sophistication of his three-year-old daughter when she looked at the overhead clouds and blue sky and said, *When I'm older, I'll be free.* He recovered quickly when she added, *I mean four.*

One of the most frequently studied and most interesting phenomena in early semantic development involves mistakes of overextension and underextension of words

(Anglin, 1977; Bowerman, 1978; Clark, 1978; Nelson, Rescorla, Gruendel, & Benedict, 1978; Smith, 1978; Thomson & Chapman, 1975). An *overextension* involves the child applying a term to a wider collection of events than would an adult—e.g., calling a cat *doggie*. Conversely *underextension* involves applying a term to a smaller collection of events than would an adult—e.g., failing to recognize that a chicken is a *bird*.

A number of studies have demonstrated that overextensions are a far more frequent characteristic of production than of comprehension, where underextensions and appropriate usage are more likely (Anglin, 1977; Huttenlocher & Strauss, 1968; Nelson et al., 1978; Thomson & Chapman, 1975). In the Thomson and Chapman study, one 23-month-old consistently overextended *apple* in production to include many round objects (cherries, balls) while always identifying the correct referent in a comprehension test involving pointing to pictures.

An incomplete meaning account of overextension derives from semantic feature theories as described in a previous section.

> When children acquire the meaning of a word, they construct an entry for it in their mental lexicon. They start off with a very simple entry containing only a few of the components relevant to its use by an adult. And as they learn more about its meaning and how it contrasts with other words, they may add further components and, if necessary, discard irrelevant ones. Eventually their entry comes to coincide with the adult entry. (Clark & Clark, 1977, p. 509)

From this point of view overextension would be due to the child having only a few of the component features of the adult meaning of a word. Thus when we find a child overextending the word *moon* to such diverse elements as a half-grapefruit, lemon slices, a chrome dishwasher dial, and hangnails (Bowerman, 1976, p. 13), we might expect from a semantic feature theory that the meaning of the word for the child might be represented by the simple semantic component (+moon-shaped). This incomplete meaning theory encounters not only the logical difficulties of feature theories that were discussed earlier but also the empirical problem of children overextending words in production that they are responding to correctly or underextending in comprehension. For instance a child who overextended *car* to a wide range of vehicles was able to pick out all the same objects in response to their correct names; these included *motorcycle, bike, truck, plane,* and *helicopter* (Nelson et al., 1978). How can the overextension of words be said to be due to incomplete meaning components when the child comprehends the words appropriately?

A more supportable hypothesis is that overextension is due primarily to *communicative need.* The child might be thought of as a mechanic who needs to use a particular tool to achieve a desirable outcome. If the tool is not available, the mechanic and the child use the most similar substitute. We can predict, then, that overextensions will occur when (1) there is an event that would have a high probability of being described by a child if the child had the appropriate productive vocabulary, (2) the child does not have the appropriate productive vocabulary for that event, (3) the child does have the appropriate productive vocabulary for a perceptually similar event, and (4) the perceptually similar event is outside of the normal

boundaries for the conceptual category of the event that the child needs to label. In other words in overextension the child is saying, *X looks like Y* not *X is Y.*

Interestingly we can use these points to predict the probability of underextension and appropriate usage as well as overextension. Consider Figure 21–1. Each group represents a gradient of perceptual similarity for a number of referential events related respectively to the semantic categories of *moon, animal,* and *book.* The vertical lines on the three graphs represent the analytic boundaries of the categories of events that adults would label as *moon, animal,* and *book.* The polygons represent the perceptual similarity among the members of the categories. The two referential events on the extremes of each graph—e.g., lemon slice and grapefruit—represent events that the child needs to communicate about but for which the child has not acquired labels. The two remaining events on each graph—e.g., quarter moon and full moon—represent events the child has already learned to label appropriately—e.g., *moon.* Graph *A* depicts the situation where overextension is likely. There are events that the child needs to describe that are physically similar to the referents the child can label already but that fall outside of the adult category boundaries. In graph *B* the category boundaries fall outside of the limits of perceptual similarity. Children's use of a word like *animal* is likely to be underextended by adult standards be-

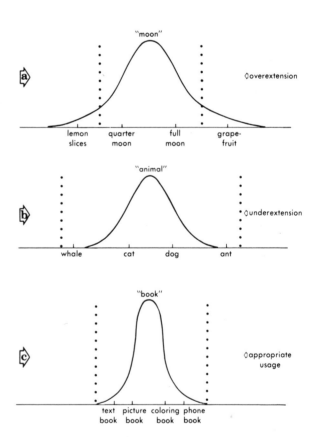

***Figure* 21-1** The relation between a young child's semantic categories based on perceptual similarity (polygons) versus well-bounded, analytic, adult categories (dotted vertical lines). When perceptual boundaries extend beyond analytic boundaries, child will overextend (a); when analytic boundaries fall beyond limits of perceptual boundaries, child will underextend (b); when perceptual and analytic boundaries are coterminous, child will use word correctly (c).

cause it will not be applied to events that are physically dissimilar to those that have served as the basis for original word learning even though such events would be labeled as *animals* by adults. Graph *C* represents a tight category (cf. Rosch & Mervis, 1977) in the sense that all of the instances belonging to it share a high degree of perceptual similarity while noninstances are very dissimilar. The generalizations that occur here will be deemed appropriate by adult standards and hence neither overextensions nor underextensions are likely.

There is support for this analysis in the research of Anglin (1977) who found, for example, that children tend to underextend the word *plant,* not including such instances as trees; they overextend the word *flower,* including such noninstances as cacti, while they use and comprehend the word *dog* in a manner very close to the adult norm. The relation of these results to the analysis in Figure 21–1 should be clear.

In each of the cases in Figure 21–1 and in the examples from Anglin (1977), the child is generalizing based on perceptual similarity in an attempt to describe referents for which labels are unknown. In that sense overextension, underextension, and appropriate labeling of novel instances do not represent different semantic processes on the part of the child, rather, they represent the way that adult category boundaries fit into the child's generalization gradient.

Determinants of Semantic Development

The focus here as it was in the preceding section is on the development of basic labels. What are the factors, biological and environmental, which lead the child to be able to understand and use words according to adult standards?

Parental Labeling. It is generally acknowledged that many of the child's first terms of reference are learned in the context of what Brown (1958) has called the *original word game.* The game is apparently simple.

The tutor names things in accordance with the semantic customs of the community. The player forms hypotheses about the categorical nature of the things named. He tests his hypotheses by trying to name new things correctly. The tutor compares the players' utterances with his own anticipations of such utterances and, in this way, checks the accuracy of fit between his own categories and those of the player. He improves the fit by correction. (p. 194)

The child, in playing the original word game, has two sources of information at his disposal: (1) the tutor's naming of things and (2) feedback for his own utterances. The first operation assures that something is learned; the second assures its validity. The concern here is with the first process, the initial connecting of words and things.

One of the problems with the child's learning of word meanings through parental labeling has been raised by Bruner (1975).

[A]ssociative theories of naming or reference are beleaguered by the presupposition that uttering a sound or making a gesture in the presence of a referent somehow evokes a nascent or innate recognition in the child that the name is associated with some features of something that is at the focus of the child's attention, so that any concatenation of sign and referent is as likely as any other to be learned, and that is plainly not so. (p. 268)

The problem, however, is not with associative theories. Any theory of vocabulary acquisition must confront the issue of why certain words are learned more readily than others. What we know of that process suggests the importance of classic associationistic variables.

Frequency. As related in the previous section on syntactic development, there is substantial evidence that mothers tailor their input to their child's abilities. In the semantic realm this *motherese* could provide one solution to why children learn certain words more easily. In part these should be those labels and words that the mother directs deliberately toward the child.

One among several lines of evidence for the role of input frequency has been presented by Moerk (1980) who reanalyzed Brown's (1973) data. Brown had concluded from his own analysis that ". . . there is no evidence whatever that frequency of any sort is a significant determinant of order of acquisition" (1973, p. 409). The intervals between the time when parental input frequencies were calculated and the time when acquisition data were obtained for Brown's subjects ranged from 6 to 14 months. Moerk makes the point that these are extremely long intervals over which to expect measurable effects of input frequency. Moerk's reanalysis, which focuses on productions occurring within short periods after input is calculated, shows an average correlation of −.65 between input frequency and age of acquisition—that is, words or constructions used more frequently by parents tend to be used at earlier ages by children. The magnitude of this relationship is amazingly high given the nature of the data and the many other variables that might be expected to influence acquisition.

Other evidence, this highly relevant to the previous discussion of underextension, is reported by Whitehurst, Kedesdy, and White (1981). Mothers of preschool children were shown color slides of objects from six different categories. Half of the objects were those that children typically label correctly, and half were those that children often do not recognize or label as members of the adult category. Mothers were more than four times as likely to provide a superordinate label for the typical members of the category than for the atypical. For example mothers were likely to label a picture of a robin as *bird,* while a turkey was called *turkey.* A fern was called a *plant,* but a tree was called *tree.* Shirts and pants were called *clothes,* while mittens were called *mittens.* Meat and peas were called *food,* but candy was labeled *candy.* Children of these mothers made "mistakes" of underextension that were completely consistent with their mothers' labeling practices. Between 70 percent and 80 percent of the three- to five-year-old children answered "no" to the questions, "Is this (picture of a turkey) a bird?" and "Is this (picture of a tree) a plant?"

These studies demonstrate that frequency of exposure in the natural environment is highly correlated with the nature of the child's acquisition. Other research builds a causal link through manipulative-experimental studies (e.g., Hart & Risley, 1968; Hursh & Sherman, 1973; White, 1979). It is important to keep in mind that the parental labeling of interest in all these studies is not the use of words alone but the relation of words to things in such a way that the child learns what goes with what. No one imagines that a child could learn his/her language by listening to radio.

Contiguity. The importance of things to a child's learning of words is further demonstrated in a study by Stewart and Hamilton (1976). Children aged 1½ to 2½ were exposed to adult labeling of novel words. The treatments could be dichotomized into those in which a referent was present along with the adult's use of a word vs. those in which no referent was available. In the referent present conditions, the adult, holding a novel object, might have said to the child, *This is a marteau. Can you say marteau, Mary?* In the referent absent condition, the adult might have said, *Did you see the bateau yesterday? Can you say bateau, John?* The differences among conditions in the ability to repeat the words immediately were not large, but subsequent tests of spontaneous usage indicated very rare production of the referent absent words, with the referent present words occurring seven times more frequently.

This study might be thought of as an extreme test of the role of contiguity between referent and word. In this case there was no contiguity because there were no referents for half the words. Kedesdy (in Whitehurst et al., 1981) extended the Stewart and Hamilton design by utilizing three conditions for labeling of objects. In a present tense condition, label and referent were presented simultaneously. In future tense, ten seconds intervened between label and subsequent referent. This temporal relationship was reversed in the past tense condition. Children only learned to use the new words they were hearing in the present tense condition. The contiguity between referent and label is an important variable in vocabulary development.

Informativeness. Greenfield and Smith (1976) among others have pointed out the role of the information carried by a word in determining whether children will use it. Leonard, Schwartz, Folger, Newhoff, and Wilcox (1979) examined this variable by labeling novel objects on either their first presentation to a child or their fifth presentation. First presentations were assumed to carry more information. Children were much more likely to produce those words that were labeled on the first occurrence of an object than they were those words that occurred on the fifth presentation of an object.

Value. There are many reasons that certain objects might be more interesting and desirable to children than other objects. Nelson (1973) suggests that objects that are manipulable or movable are likely to have their labels learned by young children. Whitehurst et al. (1981) have suggested an empirical metric of the value of an object to a child—the time the child spends interacting with the object (cf. Premack, 1971). The prediction is that children will learn more readily the labels for objects that are more valued, all other variables such as input frequency being equal. This was confirmed in a study with two-year-olds. Children were allowed to play for a brief period with a number of toys. Time allocation to the various toys was measured, and relative value was determined. Then each of the referents was labeled three times for each child—e.g., *Look, Sandy, this is the punch.*

Subsequent measures were taken of each child's ability to produce and comprehend the various referent labels. The mean correlation between referent value scores for children and the comprehension and production scores for the various referent labels was +.69, a very powerful relationship. An association tends to occur when an adult labels an object that a child already values and has interest in.

Feedback. Parental labeling as it interacts with variables of frequency, contiguity, informativeness, and value may still leave the child with word meanings that are not completely congruent with adult practice. One of the variables that might be thought to correct children's semantic errors is parental feedback. Brown and Hanlon's (1970) study of parents' tendency to correct child speech is often viewed as demonstrating that hypothetical feedback mechanisms do not occur in the normal environment of language acquisition. Brown and Hanlon demonstrated that the parents of their subjects seldom corrected the children's errors in grammar, focusing instead on what was called *truth value*. Thus when one child poorly expressed the opinion that her mother was a girl by saying, *He a girl*, her mother answered, *That's right*, apparently rewarding truthfulness. When the child produced the grammatically correct sentence, *There's the animal farmhouse*, the sentence was corrected by the parent because the building was a lighthouse.

Few have recognized that Brown and Hanlon's indictment of the role of parental feedback in grammatical productions stands as strong evidence on the potential role of feedback in semantic development. Truth value can be translated into the accuracy of the child's word referent relations as measured against adult norms. What parents seem to be doing, according to the Brown and Hanlon evidence, is listening to children and responding in positive ways when children use words appropriately and correcting children when they overextend a word beyond adult boundaries. The evidence for this is very strong in the work of Ninio and Bruner (1978) on reading dialogues between mothers and their 1- to 1½-year-old children. All incorrect labels offered by a child for picture book characters were corrected by the mothers, and 81 percent of the children's correct labels were followed by some form of positive feedback from the mother. Consistent with Brown's (1958) description of the original word game, feedback from parents seems to be an extremely important mechanism by which the child's labeling practices come to conform to parents'.

Cognitive and Perceptual Dispositions. Parental labeling and feedback are the immediate input variables for semantic development, but they operate within the context of a child's existing cognitive and perceptual dispositions and skills. The relation between language and thought, for that is what we are discussing, is a topic with a long and not particularly enlightening history. Current wisdom is that thought precedes and sets the stage for language, at least in the early years. Bruner (1979) says, "The child's knowledge of language is deeply dependent upon a prior mastery of concepts about the world to which language will refer" (p. 266). Many others would agree (e.g., Bloom, 1973; Brown, 1973; Greenfield & Smith, 1976; Miller & Johnson-Laird, 1976; Nelson, 1973; Schlesinger, 1974).

I willingly fall in with this splendid company in believing that much of early semantic development is a process of mapping language onto the child's existing knowledge. Unfortunately the evidence for this belief is more inferential than direct. One infers from research with older children and adults that similar cognitive and perceptual dispositions exist in younger children. I will survey some of that research later, though it has its own problems. More important perhaps, one notes the extreme selectivity of early word learning. Parents use a lot of words in the presence of children; children acquire only a few, and there are consistencies across children in what is acquired, as discussed previously. It seemed necessary to infer that some nonlinguistic characteristics of the child's perceptions or concepts are controlling the selection process.

Markedness. The notion of *markedness* derives from the observation that in certain pairs of complementary words one member of the pair is linguistically marked with an appendage while the other member is unmarked—e.g., *host* and *hostess, friendly* and *unfriendly* (Lyons, 1977). This concept has been extended to pairs which have no formal marking but which differ in distribution in that one member of the pair, said to be the marked member, has a less general usage than the unmarked member—e.g., *high* and *low, tall* and *short.* In each of these cases the term for the negative end of the dimension is said to be the marked member. That we refer to dimensions of *height* not *lowness* and ask how *tall* a person is but not how *short* suggests that the marked members have a more limited use.

H. Clark (1973), among others, has argued that humans have a perceptual bias toward the positive ends of many dimensions, that upward and forward, for instance, are likely to be more perceptually salient than downward and backward. If this is true, then the unmarked labels for positive ends of dimensions should be acquired first and applied to both the positive and negative instances with the marked term being acquired later. This hypothesis has generated considerable controversy. There seems to be strong evidence that children have a perceptual preference for object tops, object fronts, and tall objects over object bottoms, object backs, and short objects (Braine, 1972; E. Clark, 1973, 1980; Palermo, 1974). However it does not always follow that children will learn the label for the preferred dimension first or that they will go through a period of believing that the marked label means the same as the unmarked label.

Kuczaj and Maratsos (1975) found that children understand that *front* and *back* are opposites before they acquire a general understanding of either term, which occurs simultaneously. Kuczaj and Lederberg (1977) likewise found that children do equally well or equally poorly with the autonyms *younger* and *older.* Similar results have been obtained by Harris and Strommen (1972) and Johnston and Slobin (1979). These results appear to have resulted in a retreat from the markedness hypothesis. Clark (1980) says, "While these asymmetries could make tops and fronts more salient conceptually, they do not seem to make for any asymmetry in the acquisition of the meanings of relevant orientation terms" (p. 337).

Basic objects. Rosch and Mervis (1975) have argued for a basic level of human abstraction that forms the basis for early semantic concepts. Basic level objects categories are those for which (1) clusters of attributes occur which subjects agree are possessed by category members, (2) common movements are made when using the objects, (3) commonalities in overall look occur, (4) it is possible to recognize an average shape of an object in the category, and (5) it is possible to form a concrete image of a typical class member. In essence basic level concepts consist of instances that look and act alike while abstract level concepts do not. Examples make it easier. *Chair* is a basic level semantic concept; *furniture* is not. *Piano* is a basic level concept; *musical instrument* is not.

Words that apply to basic level concepts should be learned more easily than words that do not. Rosch (1973) had an African tribe, the Dani, learn names for geometric shapes. Some figures were basic level shapes like square and triangle; others were less basic but no more complex. The Dani learned the labels for triangles, squares, and so forth much more easily than they learned the names for the less basic figures.

There is every reason to expect that children will learn to categorize those objects that have strong visual and functional commonalities more easily than objects that are related more subtly and abstractly (cf. Fig. 21-1). It follows that labeling should occur faster and more accurately for basic level concepts. It is well to remember, however, that there are an extremely large number of events in a child's environment that could be organized into classes that fit Rosch and Mervis's criteria for basic level concepts. Most are not learned by the young child. *Ceiling,* for instance, fits the five criteria listed previously, but few young children have such a semantic category. A second important point is that there are many levels of differentiation within a single domain that could fit the basic level criteria. Which is more basic: *money, bills, coins, checks, dimes, dollars,* or *cash*? The point is that basic level categories are not "out there" as physically given entities. What is basic is to a large extent culturally and developmentally relative. Within the large array of objects and events that may have some close perceptual or functional commonalities, the culture picks those that are functional for that culture, and mothers pick and transmit those that are functional for a young child. Anglin (1977) has shown, for example, that an adult will label a dime *dime* for another adult but *money* for a child.

It is unfortunate if one yearns for simplicity, but the attractive notion of basic level concepts being the basis for much early labeling is not going to be very predictive without a careful analysis of what is perceptually and functionally meaningful to a given child at a given age. It will not be sufficient to use an adult's intuitions about what looks alike or has common attributes. If consistent universals emerge from such analyses with children, then the Rosch and Mervis (1975) hypothesis will have considerable power; if the rule is individual variability, then *basic concept* will be a label that can only be applied post hoc.

Despite the theoretical appeal of the notion that early semantic development is a matter of teaching names for concepts the child already knows, there is surprisingly little direct evidence, as this brief review should indicate. Developmental psychologists are going to have to come to grips with the difficulty of this topic if there is to be movement beyond reasonable surmises.

Summary

This survey of semantic development began with a consideration of semantic feature theories of meaning. These approaches were rejected on the basis that meaning depends on one's encyclopedic knowledge of the world and that this cannot be represented by a set of binary features. A functional approach was preferred which examines the many variables that affect a child's ability to use words correctly—i.e., meaningfully.

A brief examination of developmental data indicated that early vocabulary begins in the categories of nominals, relationals, and expressives and expands in both variety of functions and differentiation of individual words. Word learning through observation or ostensive definition makes way for word learning through verbal definitives, what Russell (1940) called dictionary words.

The phenomena of over- and underextensions were examined in some detail. Overextensions were seen to come about when the child needs to describe something that is similar to something for which he has learned a label directly but that falls outside the adult boundary for the category. Underextensions were seen to occur when adult category boundaries extend beyond the gradient of similarity among objects that is perceivable by the child.

Determinants of semantic development were examined in the categories of parental labeling, parental feedback, and cognitive and perceptual dispositions. There is strong evidence that children's semantic development is affected by (1) the frequency of parental labeling, (2) the contiguity of labels and objects in the parents' labeling attempts, (3) the informativeness of parental labeling, and (4) the value to the child of the objects being labeled. Feedback from parents is likely to play an important role in bringing the child's usage into conformity with his/her parents'. While cognitive and perceptual dispositions are likely to be a base on which early language builds, the evidence for this position is weak. Specifically perceptual biases for dimensional directions, such as *up*, do not apparently lead to any more rapid acquisition of unmarked terms, such as *up*, compared with their autonyms, such as *down*. The notion of basic object categories shows much promise for explaining several characteristics of early semantic concepts, but further development awaits methods for directly measuring the basicity of categories to children.

CONCLUSIONS

As any but the most naive reader will have noticed, I have made no attempt at maintaining a neutral stance in this review. Neutrality is not really possible, and what passes for it is usually a transmittal of current wisdom. If anything is clear in a review of the last 20 years of developmental psycholinguistics, it is that today's current wisdom is tomorrow's discarded theory.

The thread that weaves consistently through the fabric of this review is that semantic and syntactic development are heavily dependent on environmental variables and that the child's contributions consist in large part of general learning skills and cognitive processes that are shared in the acquisition of all complex behavior. This is not to say that the human child is not primed in special ways to learn oral language; it is to say that such preparedness accounts for far less of the process than was recently supposed. If the field of developmental psycholinguistics is now ready to shift toward a more social conception of language, we may be close to a point at which the interaction of biological preparation and social learning of language may be addressed productively. Paradoxically it is only a rigorous examination of the role of environmental variables that can clarify the contributions of biology to the acquisition of that most complex and intriguing of skills—human language.

REFERENCES

ANGLIN, J. M. *Word, object and conceptual development.* New York: W. W. Norton & Co., Inc., 1977.

BELLUGI, U. The development of interrogative structures in children's speech. In K. Riegel (Ed.), *The development of language functions.* Ann Arbor, Mich.: Language Development Program, Report No. 8, 1965.

BELLUGI, U. *The acquisition of negation.* Unpublished doctoral dissertation, Harvard University, 1967.

BIERWISCH, M. Semantics. In J. Lyons (Ed.), *New horizons in linguistics.* Baltimore, Md.: Penguin, 1970.

BLOOM, L. *One word at a time: The use of single-word utterances before syntax.* The Hague: Mouton, 1973.

BLOOM, L., & LAHEY, M. *Language development and language disorders.* New York: John Wiley, 1978.

BLOOMFIELD, L. *Language.* New York: Holt, Rinehart & Winston, 1933.

BLUMENTHAL, A. L. *Language and psychology: Historical aspects of psycholinguistics.* New York: John Wiley, 1970.

BOHANNON, J. N., & MARQUIS, A. L. Children's control of adult speech. *Child Development,* 1977, *48,* 1002–1008.

BOWERMAN, M. Semantic factors in the acquisition of rules for word use and sentence construction. In D. M. Morehead & A. E. Morehead (Eds.), *Normal and deficient child language.* Baltimore, Md.: University Park Press, 1976.

BOWERMAN, M. Systematizing semantic knowledge: Changes over time in the child's organization of word meaning. *Child Development,* 1978, *49,* 977–987.

BRAINE, L. G. A developmental analysis of the effect of stimulus orientation on recognition. *American Journal of Psychology,* 1972, *85,* 157–188.

BRAINE, M.D.S. On learning the grammatical order of words. *Psychological Review,* 1963, *70,* 323–348.

BRAINE, M.D.S. On the basis of phrase structure: A reply to Bever, Fodor, and Weksel. *Psychological Review,* 1965, *72,* 483–492.

BRAINE, M.D.S. Children's first word combinations. *Monographs of the Society for Research in Child Development,* 1976, *41* (Serial No. 164).

BROWN, I. Language acquisition: Linguistic structure and rule-governed behavior. In G. J. Whitehurst & B. J. Zimmerman (Eds.), *The functions of language and cognition.* New York: Academic Press, 1979.

BROWN, R. *Words and things.* New York: Free Press, 1958.

BROWN, R. *A first language: The early stages.* Cambridge, Mass.: Harvard University Press, 1973.

BROWN, R. A good book about the human mind. *Contemporary Psychology,* 1979, *24,* 551–553.

BROWN, R. *It may not be phrygian but it is not ergative either.* Unpublished manuscript, Harvard University, 1978.

BROWN, R., CAZDEN, C., & BELLUGI, U. The child's grammar from I to III. In J. P. Hill (Ed.), *Minnesota Symposia on Child Psychology* (Vol. 2). Minneapolis: University of Minnesota Press, 1969.

BROWN, R., & HANLON, C. Derivational complexity and order of acquisition in child speech. In J. R. Hayes (Ed.), *Cognition and the development of language.* New York: John Wiley, 1970.

BROWN, R., & HERRNSTEIN, R. J. *Psychology.* Boston: Little, Brown, 1975.

BRUNER, J. S. From communication to language: A psychological perspective. *Cognition,* 1975, *3,* 255–287.

BRUNER, J. S. Early social interaction and language acquisition. In H. R. Schaffer (Ed.), *Studies in mother-infant interaction.* London: Academic Press, 1977.

BRUNER, J. S. Learning how to do things with words. In D. Aaronson & R. W. Rieber (Eds.), *Psycholinguistic research: Implications and applications.* Hillsdale, N.J.: Lawrence Erlbaum Associates, 1979.

CAZDEN, C. B. The acquisition of noun and verb inflections. *Child Development,* 1968, *39,* 433–448.

CHOMSKY, N. *Syntactic structures.* The Hague: Mouton, 1957.

CHOMSKY, N. Review of B. F. Skinner's *Verbal behavior. Language,* 1959, *35,* 26–57.

CLARK, E. V. What's in a word? On the child's acquisition of semantics in his first language. In T. E. Moore (Ed.), *Cognitive development and the acquisition of language.* New York: Academic Press, 1973.

CLARK, E. V. Strategies for communicating. *Child Development,* 1978, *49,* 953–959.

CLARK, E. V. Here's the *top:* Non-linguistic strategies in the acquisition of orientational terms. *Child Development,* 1980, *51,* 329–338.

CLARK, H. H. Space, time, semantics, and the child. In T. E. Moore (Ed.), *Cognitive development and the acquisition of knowledge.* New York: Academic Press, 1973.

CLARK, H. H., & CLARK, E. V. *Psychology and language. An introduction to psycholinguistics.* New York: Harcourt Brace Jovanovich, 1977.

CONDON, W. S., & SANDER, L. W. Synchrony demonstrated between movements of neonate and adult speech. *Child Development,* 1974, *45,* 456–462.

DARLEY, F. L., & WINITZ, H. Age of the first word: Review of research. *Journal of Speech and Hearing Disorders,* 1961, *26,* 272–290.

deVILLIERS, J. G., & deVILLIERS, P. A. A cross-sectional study of the acquisition of grammatical morphemes in child speech. *Journal of Psycholinguistic Research,* 1973, *2,* 267–278.

DEWEY, J. *Experience and nature.* La Salle, Ill.: Open Court, 1958.

ERVIN, S. M. Imitation and structural change in children's language. In E. Lenneberg (Ed.), *New directions in the study of language.* Cambridge, Mass.: M.I.T. Press, 1964.

FILLMORE, C. J. The case for case. In E. Bach & R. T. Harms (Eds.), *Universals in linguistic theory.* New York: Holt, Rinehart & Winston, 1968.

FODOR, J., & GARRETT, M. Some reflections on competence and performance. In J. Lyons & R. J. Wales (Eds.), *Psycholinguistic papers: The proceedings of the 1966 Edinburgh conference.* Edinburgh: Edinburgh University Press, 1966.

FODOR, J., JENKINS, J., & SAPORTA, S. *Some tests on implications from transformational grammar.* Unpublished manuscript, Palo Alto, Calif.: Center for Advanced Study, 1966.

FODOR, J. D. *Semantics: Theories of meaning in generative grammar.* New York: Thomas Y. Crowell, 1977.

GARDNER, H. *Developmental psychology: An introduction.* Boston: Little, Brown, 1978.

GOLDIN-MEADOW, S., & FELDMAN, H. The development of language-like communication without a language model. *Science,* 1977, *197,* 401–403.

GREENFIELD, P.M., & SMITH, J. H. *The structure of communication in early language development.* New York: Academic Press, 1976.

HARRIS, L. J., & STROMMEN, E. A. The role of front-back features in children's "front," "back," and "beside" placements of objects. *Merrill-Palmer Quarterly,* 1972, *18,* 259–271.

HART, B. M., & RISLEY, T. R. Establishing use of descriptive adjectives in the spontaneous speech of disadvantaged preschool children. *Journal of Applied Behavior Analysis,* 1968, *1,* 109–120.

HURSH, D. E., & SHERMAN, J. A. The effects of parent-presented models and praise on the verbal behavior of their children. *Journal of Experimental Child Psychology,* 1973, *15,* 328–339.

HUTTENLOCHER, J., & STRAUSS, S. Comprehension and a statement's relation to the situation it describes. *Journal of Verbal Learning and Verbal Behavior,* 1968, *7,* 527–530.

JOHNSTON, J. R., & SLOBIN, D. I. The development of locative expressions in English, Italian, Serbo-Croatian, and Turkish. *Journal of Child Language,* 1979, *6,* 529–545.

JUSCZYK, P. W. Infant speech perception: A critical appraisal. In P. D. Eimas & J. L. Miller (Eds.), *Perspectives on the study of speech.* Hillsdale, N.J.: Lawrence Erlbaum Associates, 1981.

KATZ, J. *Semantic theory.* New York: Harper & Row, Pub., 1972.

KUCZAJ, S. A. Evidence for a language learning strategy: On the relative ease of acquisition of prefixes and suffixes. *Child Development,* 1979, *50,* 1–13.

KUCZAJ, S. A., & LEDERBERG, A. R. Height, age, and function: Differing influences on children's comprehension of "younger" and "older." *Journal of Child Language,* 1977, *4,* 395–416.

KUCZAJ, S. A., & MARATSOS, M. On the acquisition of *front, back,* and *side.* Child Development, 1975, *46,* 202–210.

LEONARD, L., SCHWARTZ, R., FOLGER, M., NEWHOFF, M., & WILCOX, M. Children's imitations of lexical items. *Child Development,* 1979, *50,* 19–27.

LORENZ, K. *Behind the mirror: A search for the natural history of human knowledge.* New York: Harcourt Brace Jovanovich, 1977.

LYONS, J. *Semantics* (Vol. 1). Cambridge, England: Cambridge University Press, 1977.

McCARTHY, D. A. Language development in children. In L. Carmichael (Ed.), *Manual of child psychology* (2nd ed.). New York: John Wiley, 1954.

MacCORQUODALE, K. On Chomsky's review of Skinner's *Verbal behavior. Journal of the Experimental Analysis of Behavior,* 1970, *13,* 83–99.

MACLAY, H., & OSGOOD, C. E. Hesitation phenomena in spontaneous English speech. *Word,* 1959, *15,* 19–44.

McNEILL, D. *The acquisition of language.* New York: Harper & Row, Pub., 1970.

MacWHINNEY, B. Rules, rote, and analogy in morphological formations by Hungarian children. *Journal of Child Language,* 1975, *2,* 65–77.

MacWHINNEY, B. The acquisition of morphophonology. *Monographs of the Society for Research in Child Development,* 1978, *43* (Serial No. 174).

MARATSOS, M. P. How to get from words to sentences. In D. Aronson & R. J. Rieber (Eds.), *Psycholinguistic research: Implications and applications.* Hillsdale, N.J.: Lawrence Erlbaum Associates, 1979.

MARATSOS, M. P., & CHALKLEY, M. A. The internal language of children's syntax: The ontogenesis and representation of syntactic categories. In K. Nelson (Ed.), *Children's language* (Vol. 2). New York: Gardner Press, 1980.

MEHLER, J. Some effects of grammatical transformations on the recall of English sentences. *Journal of Verbal Learning and Verbal Behavior,* 1963, *2,* 346–351.

MILLER, G. A., & JOHNSON-LAIRD, P. N. *Language and perception.* Cambridge, Mass.: Harvard University Press, 1976.

MILLER, G. A., & McKEAN, K. O. A chronometric study of some relations between sentences. *Quarterly Journal of Experimental Psychology,* 1964, *16,* 297–308.

MOERK, E. L. Determiners and consequences of verbal behaviors of young children and their mothers. *Developmental Psychology,* 1978, *14,* 537–545.

MOERK, E. L. Does mastery of specific linguistic items proceed according to a gradual learning curve without showing any effects of input frequency? A reanalysis of some of Brown's (1973) data. *Journal of Child Language,* 1980, *7,* 105–118.

MOESER, S. D., & BREGMAN, A. S. Imagery and language acquisition. *Journal of Verbal Learning and Verbal Behavior,* 1972, *12,* 91–98.

MOESER, S. D., & OLSON, J. A. The role of reference in children's acquisition of a miniature artifical language. *Journal of Experimental Child Psychology,* 1974, *17,* 204–218.

NELSON, K. Structure and strategy in learning to talk. *Monographs of the Society for Research in Child Development,* 1973, *38* (Nos. 1–2).

NELSON, K. Concept, word, and sentence: Interrelations in acquisition and development. *Psychological Review,* 1974, *81,* 267–285.

NELSON, K., RESCORLA, L., GRUENDEL, J., & BENEDICT, H. Early lexicons: What do they mean? *Child Development,* 1978, *49,* 960–968.

NELSON, K. E. Facilitating children's syntax. *Developmental Psychology,* 1976, *13,* 101–107.

NINIO, A., & BRUNER, J. The achievement and antecedents of labelling. *Journal of Child Language,* 1978, *5,* 1–15.

PALERMO, D. S. Still more about the comprehension of "less." *Developmental Psychology,* 1974, *10,* 827–829.

PALERMO, D. S., & EBERHART, V. L. On the learning of morphological rules: An experimental analogy. *Journal of Verbal Learning and Verbal Behavior*, 1968, *7*, 337–344.

PALERMO, D. S., & MOLFESE, D. L. Language acquisition from age five onward. *Psychological Bulletin*, 1972, *78*, 409–428.

PREMACK, D. Catching up with common sense or two sides of a generalization: Reinforcement and punishment. In R. Glaser (Ed.), *The nature of reinforcement*. New York: Academic Press, 1971.

QUINE, W. V. The inscrutability of reference. In D. D. Steinberg and L. A. Jakobovits (Eds.), *Semantics: An interdisciplinary reader in philosophy, linguistics, and psychology*. Cambridge, England: Cambridge University Press, 1971.

ROSCH, E. On the internal structure of perceptual and semantic categories. In T. E. Moore (Ed.), *Cognitive development and the acquisition of language*. New York: Academic Press, 1973.

ROSCH, E., & MERVIS, C. B. Family resemblances: Studies in the internal structure of categories. *Cognitive Psychology*, 1975, *7*, 573–605.

ROSCH, E., & MERVIS, C. B. Children's sorting: A reinterpretation based on the nature of abstraction in natural categories. In R. C. Smart & M. S. Smart (Eds.), *Readings in child development and relationships* (2nd ed.). New York: Macmillan, 1977.

ROSENTHAL, T. L., & ZIMMERMAN, B. J. *Social learning and cognition*. New York: Academic Press, 1978.

RUSSELL, B. R. *An inquiry into meaning and truth*. London: Allen & Unwin, 1940.

SAVIN, H. B., & PERCHONOCK, E. Grammatical structure and the immediate recall of English sentences. *Journal of Verbal Learning and Verbal Behavior*, 1965, *4*, 348–353.

SCHLESINGER, I. Relational concepts underlying language. In R. L. Schiefelbusch & L. Lloyd (Eds.), *Language perspectives: Acquisition, retardation, and intervention*. Baltimore, Md.: University Park Press, 1974.

SEGAL, E. F. Psycholinguistics discovers the operant: A review of Roger Brown's *A first language: The early stages. Journal of the Experimental Analysis of Behavior*, 1975, *23*, 149–158.

SHATZ, M. On mechanisms of language acquisition: Can features of the communicative environment account for development? In L. Gleitman & E. Wanner (Eds.), *Language acquisition: The state of the art*. New York: Plenum, 1981.

SKINNER, B. F. *Verbal behavior*. Englewood Cliffs, N.J.: Prentice-Hall, 1957.

SLOBIN, D. I. Cognitive prerequisites for the development of grammar. In C. A. Ferguson & D. I. Slobin (Eds.), *Studies of child language development*. New York: Holt, Rinehart & Winston, 1973.

SMITH, E. E., SHOBEN, E. J., & RIPS, L. J. Structure and process in semantic memory: A featural model for semantic decisions. *Psychological Review*. 1974, *81*, 214–241.

SMITH, M. D. The acquisition of word meaning: An introduction. *Child Development*, 1978, *49*, 950–952.

SMITH, M. E. An investigation of the development of the sentence and the extent of vocabulary in young children. *University of Iowa Studies in Child Welfare*, 1926, *3* (No. 5).

SNOW, C., & FERGUSON, C. (Eds.). *Talking to children*. Cambridge, England: Cambridge University Press, 1977.

STERN, G. *Meaning and change of meaning*. Bloomington: Indiana University Press, 1964. (Originally published in Germany, 1931.)

STEWART, D. M., & HAMILTON, M. L. Imitation as a learning strategy in the acquisition of vocabulary. *Journal of Experimental Child Psychology*, 1976, *21*, 380–392.

THOMSON, J. R., & CHAPMAN, R. S. Who is "Daddy"? The status of two-year-olds over-extended words in use and comprehension. *Papers and Reports on Child Language Development* (Stanford University), 1975, *10*, 59–68.

TWENEY, R. D. Review of E. A. Esper's *Analogy and association in linguistics and psychology. Historiographia Linguistica*, 1974, *1*, 385–398.

WEINREICH, V. Explorations in semantic theory. In T. Sebeok (Ed.), *Current trends in linguistics III*. The Hague: Mouton, 1966.

WETHERBY, B. Miniature languages and the functional analysis of verbal behavior. In R. Schiefelbusch (Ed.), *Bases of language intervention*. Baltimore, Md.: University Park Press, 1978.

WHITE, T. A. *Naming practices, typicality, and underextension in child language*. Unpublished doctoral dissertation, State University of New York at Stony Brook, 1979.

WHITEHURST, G. J. Imitation, response novelty, and language acquisition. In B. C. Etzel, J. M. Le Blanc, & D. M. Baer (Eds.), *New developments in behavioral research: Theory, method, and application*. Hillsdale, N.J.: Lawrence Erlbaum Associates, 1977.

WHITEHURST, G. J. Meaning and semantics. In G. J. Whitehurst & B. J. Zimmerman (Eds.), *The functions of language and cognition*. New York: Academic Press, 1979.

WHITEHURST, G. J., KEDESDY, J., & WHITE, T. A. A functional analysis of meaning. In S. A. Kuczaj (Ed.), *Language development: Syntax and semantics*. Hillsdale, N.J.: Lawrence Erlbaum Associates, 1981.

WITTGENSTEIN, L. *Philosophical investigations*. Oxford: Blackwell, 1953.

22

Social-Cognitive Development

MICHAEL CHANDLER
MICHAEL BOYES

This chapter selectively reviews and interpretively summarizes certain key research findings in the area of social-cognitive development. The emphasis given to the qualifiers "selectively" and "interpretively" in this cautiously worded agenda is intended not only as a hedge against future criticisms regarding possible lack of scope or objectivity but also, more importantly, as a means of signaling to the reader something of the constructivistic orientation which has shaped the approach taken to this review. *Knowing* of any sort, according to the Piagetian framework adopted here, is a relational act which samples and structures the interactions between persons and events by selectively assimilating and organizing experiences in ways which accord them human meaning. This constructivistic interpretation of the knowing process, if it is to be consistently maintained, consequently must be understood to apply not only to the attempts of children to comprehend their worlds but also to efforts, such as our own, to impose meaning upon the knowledge-generating activities of developing children. By this standard, total objectivity and representativeness are not feasible. As if this reflexive twist did not sufficiently complicate matters, the study of social cognition, which deals with knowledge about the knowledge of others, carries this recursive process one step further and concerns the efforts of social scientists to understand something of the knowing process of children as they attempt to understand what is known by others.

The momentary wave of vertigo which accompanies the struggle to disembed nested sentences of the preceding sort is symptomatic of the more chronic sense of disorientation suffered by those whose research interests cause them to spend long hours in this conceptually unstable work environment. What seems required, both as a stabilizing heuristic for organizing this chapter and for achieving a better equilibrium in the field of social-cog-

nitive research as a whole, is some orienting reference frame which permits coherent discussion of cognitions which have as their objects other cognitions. The task of providing such an interpretive framework is seriously complicated, however, by the one-dimensional nature of many of the constructs which populate the field of social cognition.

Historically psychology sought a solution to its organizational problems by neatly subdividing its subject matter into classes of objective stimuli and subjective responses. Over the last half century, however, this convenient packaging principle has fallen into disrepute, as repeated evidence has shown that organisms choose and subjectively deform their own stimulus environments. Especially in the hands of cognitively oriented developmentalists, this evidence has been used to justify selectively focusing attention upon the dramatic and qualitative changes which occur in the ways in which children of various ages process their experience. Persons, according to this standard view, actively impose varying sorts of human order upon what are essentially unordered material events. Such constructive efforts are consequently understood to reveal something about the human mind but not necessarily anything about raw nature, which is viewed as fickle to the point of total untrustworthiness, capable of supporting an infinity of such alternative constructions. This one-sided constructivism has turned order into an exclusively human byproduct and the study of cognition into a monocular science of pure assimilation.

Without necessarily offering a means of resolving this problem more generally, the inherently recursive character of social cognition does appear to offer a local solution to this relativistic dilemma. If individuals, in their role as subjects, are held to think in organized ways which reflect the presence of underlying cognitive structure, there would seem to be no defensible justification for forbidding them these same structures simply because they become the objects of the cognitions of others. In other words, in the special "quarry is the hunter" case of social cognition where the intended objects of cognition are the cognitions of others, both subjects and their possible objects of knowledge may be seen to vary along a common dimension of organized complexity, and any adequate description of the means of knowing must also count as a fair description of that which needs to be understood. One is not excused on these grounds from actively construing his/her own experience, but when what is to be understood is the understanding of others, such targeted forms of knowledge must be recognized to have a premasticated existence, the structure of which is independent of the ways in which they are assimilated.

As a consequence of its inherently reflexive character, the study of social cognition necessarily requires some form of double entry bookkeeping by means of which the changing complexities of children's abilities to understand are coordinated and cross-referenced with counterpart descriptions of the event complexities of the objects of their understanding who are also subjects. The individual cells of such a subject by object matrix would reference the attempts of children of particular levels of cognitive developmental complexity to come to terms with social events of specifiable complexity levels. While the row and column ledgers of such matrices would differ from one subdomain of social cognition to the next, all such accounts would have the common property of dividing the transactions between individuals and social events into one or the other of two distinct classes. One of these classes would consist of a cluster of above-diagonal cells which described the attempts of subjects to cognize events which were structured at a higher level of complexity than themselves. Under these circumstances individuals would be expected to fail in their attempts to understand what is known or understood by others. The second cluster would include all of these residual instances in which the events to be understood are structured at levels at or below the complexity level of the individual seeking to understand them. Here regular success in social-cognitive understanding would be anticipated. Given such a subject by subject-as-object matrix, it should become possible to recast the traditional problems of social-cognition research into a common interpretive framework and to clarify certain persistent confusions in the study of these problems.

In the following pages this transactional mode of subject-by-object analysis will be utilized as a framework within which to discuss the two most heavily researched and intractable problem areas in the social-cognition literature—the areas of social role-taking and moral reasoning.

ROLE-TAKING AND EGOCENTRICITY

The degree to which one is able to achieve an informed understanding of the knowledge base upon which others operate obviously plays a crucial role in determining how successful one will be in attempting to navigate his/her social world. *Social role-taking* is the name most commonly applied to this inference process, and the study of its development has been the subject of almost a half century of research. In view of the position outlined in the preceding pages, it follows that an adequate understanding of this role-taking process is dependent upon a careful cross-referencing of *both* the kinds of knowing of which a particular individual is developmentally capable and the particular sorts of knowledge present in others which s/he is seeking to become knowledgeable about. If, as Piaget (1926) has argued, children evidence qualitatively different modes of knowing at different junctures in their own developmental course, then the level of their cognitive maturity at any particular moment will set obligatory limits upon their ability to appreciate the existence of various kinds of knowledge in others. It follows from these assumptions that various sorts of egocentric errors, or short-falls, in the role-taking process will necessarily arise whenever individuals are required to anticipate a kind of knowledge in others of which they are themselves not yet capable. At least two kinds of information are consequently required to anticipate how children of various developmental levels will fare when required to take the role of others. The first concerns the various sorts of knowledge of which they are capable. The second involves an assessment of the kind of knowledge present in others which they are expected to know about. In the following pages this interactive approach to the problem of social role taking will be elaborated in an attempt to impose some conceptual order upon what has proven to be a confusing and apparently contradictory research literature. Prior to undertaking this review, however, it will be necessary to discuss in greater detail what is implied by the joint claims (1) that in the course of their development children advance through a sequence of qualitatively different modes of knowing and (2) that, by implication, when human knowledge is the target of knowing, the objects, as well as the subjects, of such knowledge must be understood to express one or another of these different epistemic modes. The goal, then, of this preliminary conceptual analysis is to arrive at a descriptive matrix of different subjective modes of knowing by different objective forms of targeted knowledge. The various cells of such a proposed matrix will refer to the circumstance of subjects characterized by developmentally constrained upper limits in their strategies of knowing the world as they attempt to comprehend what is known by various target individuals whose knowledge they must take into account. Such an interpretive framework offers a typology according to which various role-taking studies can be classified, and hopefully, certain of their apparently contradictory findings can be resolved.

MODES OF KNOWLEDGE ACQUISITION

Although the writings of Baldwin (1906), Werner (1948), and others have contributed to the widespread interest among developmental psychologists in the process of role-taking, it is unquestionably the work of Piaget and his co-workers (Inhelder & Piaget, 1958; Piaget, 1926, 1970; Piaget & Inhelder, 1956, 1968) which has prompted the majority of contemporary research studies in this area. Despite the germinal role which his early writings on childhood egocentrism have played, Piaget's theory appears to have functioned more as a springboard to, than a solid theoretical foundation for, much of this subsequent research. In fact the success of the Geneva group in drawing attention to the construct of role-taking appears to have had the paradoxical effect of rendering "egocentrism" a seemingly disembodied "fact" of childhood, capable of being transported out of its original context and studied in theoretically neutral ways. As a consequence of this decontextualization, the literature on childhood egocentrism seems to lack any firm conceptual footing and instead has come to rest much of its weight upon procedural debates and local competitions among various measurement strategies. Without wishing to argue that any one theory is uniquely suited to the task of ordering these findings, some recognition of the fact that egocentrism is a theoretically bounded construct, rather than a raw a-theoretical fact, seems required. On the grounds that some theoretic framework is required, there is at least historical precedent for attempting to use Piaget's own theory for organizing this largely Piagetian-inspired research literature.

The particular aspects of Piaget's wide-ranging theoretical conception which are seen to have the most direct relevance for the study of the role-taking process are his broad conclusions regarding the ontogenetic course of knowledge acquisition in general. The first step toward making better developmental sense of the ways in which children come to know about the knowledge of others would seem to be an attempt to provide a clear formulation of how, within Piaget's broad theoretical account, children of various ages are to be understood to come to know anything at all. While much of Piaget's writings bear more or less directly upon this broad topic, it is possible to isolate from this body of work two radical propositions which set his views apart from those of most of his contemporaries. The first of these is that, in the course of development, knowledge exists prior to, and is not dependent upon, the availability of representational processes. This central assumption differentiates Piaget's views from other more widely held copy theories of knowledge, in which thoughts are understood to be equivalent to the intrapsychic juggling of internal representations of outside events (Furth, 1969). Piaget's second and equally radical assumption is that, in addition to both nonrepresentational knowledge *of* the world and second-order representational or symbolic knowledge *about* the world, there also exists a third order of formal operational understanding which operates upon and takes second-order representational knowledge as its object. These conceptions, along with the more familiar notion of symbolic or representational knowledge which they bracket, form for Piaget an ordered sequence, the levels of which reference qualitatively different modes of knowing.

This proposed sequence begins with a zero-order plane of material things and events and includes (1) a first-order nonsymbolic form of enactive (Bruner, 1964) or sensorimotor knowing which takes material reality as its object; (2) a second-order symbolic mode of knowing which "re-presents" and references that which is already known on the broader, first-order plane of nonsymbolic knowledge; and (3) a third or metarepresentational mode of knowing which involves symbolizing symbols and

which takes as its object second-order representational knowledge. These three modes of knowing refer to, and partially define, Piaget's preoperational, concrete operational, and formal operational stages of cognitive development and, consequently, form an ordered and cumulative developmental sequence which defines the ways children of different levels of cognitive development may be expected to understand anything whatsoever. Depending upon their developmental station, children may either give evidence of knowing things in action, symbolically expressing their concrete knowledge, or knowing that they know.

KNOWLEDGE AS AN OBJECT OF KNOWLEDGE

A long psychological tradition has contributed to the preceding description of alternative modes of knowing. By contrast practically nothing is written about the counterpart problem of defining the various forms which the objects of such knowledge assume.

Outside of certain educational circles, questions concerning event difficulty are rarely asked, and for the great majority of potential objects of knowledge, little or nothing is known about their formal complexity relative to the cognitive complexity of those who seek to understand them. In those special instances where the potential object of knowledge is the knowledge of others, however, this usual short-fall in understanding is avoided; what is known about the process of knowledge acquisition reflexively applies to its own intended object. If Piaget's characterization of various modes of knowing is judged to be descriptively accurate, then whenever what is known by others becomes the target of knowledge, these same modes of knowing also constitute a description of the possible forms which the objects of knowledge may assume. Quite apart from how it might be subjectively construed, the knowledge of others may be said to be either presymbolic, symbolic, or metarepresentational in character. These target characteristics constitute "objective" features of the social stimulus environment, which together represent a typology of free-standing knowledge *forms,* separable from the parallel *modes* of knowing through which they are potentially understood.

Having specified both the available *modes* of understanding through which knowledge can be acquired and the potential *forms* which the possible objects of such knowledge can take, the role-taking process can be represented as a transaction in which subjects, characterized by one or another distinct mode of knowing, attempt to comprehend as an object one or another of these possible forms of knowing in others. The range of such possible interactions can be figuratively represented as a redundant three-by-three matrix listing subjective modes of knowing by objective forms of knowledge (see Table 22–1).

This proposed matrix can be partitioned into two distinct subclasses. The first of these, which includes the diagonal and below-diagonal cells (coded as "+" in Table 22–1), refers to instances in which individuals, characterized by particular developmentally constrained modes of knowing, attempt to comprehend, as targets of understanding, forms of knowledge in others which are no

Table 22–1 A Transactional Matrix of Subjective Modes and "Objective" Forms of Social-Cognitive Knowledge

		TARGETED FORMS OF KNOWLEDGE		
		Presymbolic	Symbolic	Metarepresentational
PSYCHOLOGICAL MODES OF KNOWING	Presymbolic	+	−	−
	Symbolic	+	+	−
	Metarepresentational	+	+	+

more complex than themselves. This would include the efforts of presymbolic individuals to comprehend presymbolic forms of knowledge, the attempts of persons capable of symbolic understanding to comprehend either presymbolic or symbolic knowledge forms, and the efforts of individuals capable of metarepresentational modes of knowing to appreciate knowledge forms of any sort. The second category, of above-diagonal cells—which includes the effort of presymbolic children to comprehend symbolic and metarepresentational forms of knowledge and the attempt of children with only second-order symbolic modes of knowing to grasp metarepresentational forms of understanding in others—defines a different domain of instances in which the subjects in question seek to grasp forms of knowledge in others which exceed in formal complexity their own highest mode of knowing. It is within this second category of subject-object interactions that most instances of egocentric errors in social role taking will be shown to occur.

EGOCENTRISM AS A LOGICAL TYPE CONFUSION OF KNOWLEDGE FORMS

Within the descriptive framework just outlined, failures in social role-taking are best understood as category mistakes or confusions regarding the logical type characteristics of events within the social stimulus world. Each of the three forms of knowledge to which Piaget refers references qualitatively different levels of abstraction and occupy different planes of reality. Nonsymbolic knowledge takes material reality as its object and, by acting as a guide to adaptive action, functions as a nonaspirated comment upon external events. Symbolic knowledge, by contrast, is not simply an alternative mode of understanding the same material world but represents instead a different order of knowing which represents and takes as its object nonsymbolic forms of first-order knowledge. Symbols, in other words, reference our knowledge of events rather than events themselves. Finally metarepresentational knowledge is about, or takes as its object, second-order symbolic understanding. Such operations upon operations consequently occupy a third order of abstraction, one logical type level removed from simpler symbolic modes of knowing. In attempting to understand what is understood by others, the most abstract mode of knowing of which an individual is capable sets necessary limits upon the range of knowledge forms in others which they are capable of processing. Any targeted form of understanding which exceeds in complexity or logical type level the cognitions which are brought to bear upon it will consequently be reconstrued or

misrepresented as an event of a lower order of abstraction than is objectively warranted—that is, persons employing presymbolic modes of understanding will necessarily misconstrue instances of symbolic knowledge in presymbolic ways. Similarly persons capable of symbolic, but not metarepresentational, knowledge will misconstrue such higher-order knowledge forms and will incorrectly reinterpret them as instances of simpler forms of symbolic knowing. Confusions of both of these sorts constitute proper instances of category mistakes in that they express failures in correctly judging the levels of abstraction or logical type characteristics of events and involve unwarranted attempts to bracket together things which legitimately occupy different reality planes. The individual who upon hearing that a lady just arrived in a sedan chair and a flood of tears demands clarification and insists that no one can arrive in two things at one time is guilty of a comparable category mistake (Ryle, 1949). As the empirical work of the Geneva group has shown, such logical type confusions account for many of the difficulties which characterize the thinking of preoperational and concrete operational children. Outside of the social or interpersonal realm, for example, the word realisms and physiognomic perceptions characteristic of preschool children represent clear instances of a logical type confusion between symbolic tokens and their referents. Similarly the difficulties which young adolescents experience in differentiating hypothesis from fact (Elkind, 1967), truth from validity (Elkind, 1968), and language from metalanguage (Osherson & Markman, 1975) also imply a comparable kind of category confusion between symbols and symbols of symbols—i.e., between symbolic and metarepresentational thought.

Inside the social or interpersonal domain where the objects of knowledge are often the knowledge forms of others, parallel logical type confusions operate and produce the familiar array of usual egocentric errors. Preoperational children, because they have not yet firmly differentiated between their own presymbolic cognitive acts and the events to which these thoughts refer, cannot yet appreciate the same distinction in others and, consequently, treat the symbolic meanings which others impose upon events as though they were the direct and inescapable material consequences of physical exposure to concrete material events. Without the benefit of such a categorical distinction, it is impossible to differentiate between *what kinds* of information another person has physical access to and *how* that information is construed or understood. Similarly concrete operational children, who employ symbols but who cannot yet bracket such knowledge and produce metarepresentational comments upon it, must necessarily fail to appreciate such accomplishments in others. Without this ability they are blind to the fact that others not only know things and symbolize about them but also know *that* they know and use this recursive understanding in thinking about themselves and others.

The preceding analysis of the social role-taking process both answers and raises a series of important questions concerning the manner in which persons come to know about the knowledge of others. First, it should be clear that the question of *when*, or at what particular developmental point, children first acquire role-taking abilities is the wrong question to attempt to answer. From a Piagetian perspective children are always capable of behaving adaptively and, from a point in development well before they are able to respond to the simplest form of psychological inquiry, are almost certainly knowledgeable about certain forms of knowledge in others. What seems required instead is a different kind of inquiry concerned with interactions between the various modes of knowledge of which children are capable and the various forms of knowledge in others they are likely to be knowledgeable about. In the following pages such questions will be taken up by considering the kinds of role-taking abilities which characterize children who function in presymbolic, symbolic, and metarepresentational ways.

PRESYMBOLIC MODES OF SOCIAL ROLE-TAKING

Knowledge in any form, according to Piaget (1970), exists as a relationship between a knower and a potential object of understanding. As with any such relational phenomena, knowledge, as a potential *object* of knowledge, consequently has no material status which would permit it to be directly apprehended or responded to as a trigger to sensorimotor functioning. Some kind of summing across past instances or generalization across comparable instances, of the sort which Piaget intends by the concept of object permanence, therefore seems required in order for knowing relationships to be distilled from the flux of particular interactions and emerge as potential elements of thought. This assumption precludes the theoretic possibility of social role-taking in earliest infancy and demands, as a prerequisite for its emergence, the existence of some representational machinery which would allow relational constancies to be encoded and held in mind as potential objects of knowledge. Such representational abilities, which are assumed by the Geneva group to emerge during the second year of life, signal the end of the sensorimotor period and usher in the subperiod of preoperational thought. Unfortunately Piaget and his co-workers have been far from explicit regarding the exact nature of the role-taking potentialities which are presumably opened up by the emergence of such early representational skills, and a great deal of controversy has been generated concerning the kinds of evidence which might support, as opposed to embarrass, the theory.

What has been generally agreed upon, and also emphasized by the Geneva group, is that at a much later point in development—sometime around the period marked by the beginning of formal education—young school-aged children begin behaving in new and qualitatively different ways which reflect a shift in the kinds of ideas they hold about the knowledge of others. This period of transition to concrete operational modes of thought served as the testing ground for many of Piaget's own ideas about childhood egocentrism. This fact has sponsored the widely shared, but unwarranted, assumption that the development of role-taking abilities of any sort is regarded by the Geneva group as an exclusive accomplishment of concrete operational thought. One unfortunate consequence of this rumor has been the frequent presumption that the fallibility or infallibility of Piaget's theory is, in some way, put on trial by evidence suggesting the earlier emergence of role-taking skills. If, as this argument goes, very young children can be proven capable of taking on the role of others and if Piaget can be demonstrated to have said that such early accomplishments are impossible, then a heresy has been committed, and fallibility has been established. While, at the frontiers of science, reputations are still sometimes made by "calling out the top guns" and blazing away with theoretically embarrassing facts, such efforts to beat Piaget to the draw with volleys of evidence of earlier and earlier forms of social role-taking competence have misfired and succeeded only in producing a smoke screen which further beclouds the real issues. While it is unquestionably the case that Piaget placed great emphasis upon the contributions of concrete operational thought to the development of the role-taking process, this fact in no way counts against the theoretic possibility of still earlier, although less mature, forms of role-taking which are consistent with his account of preoperational thought. In fact given the elaborate account which the Geneva group has provided of the preoperational subperiod, little is required to extend this framework to cover the special class of instances in which the objects of knowledge happen to be the knowledge of others.

According to the descriptive framework outlined in the previous sections, the defining and limiting characteristic of preoperational thought is that it is restricted to a mode of knowing which is presymbolic in character. As a consequence of this restriction, symbolic and metarepresentational forms of knowledge in others cannot be adequately processed and are instead necessarily misconstrued as instances of presymbolic understanding. The cumulative effect of such systematic category mistakes is to reduce the functional epistemology of such preoperational children to a kind of "copy theory" of knowledge. In ways reminiscent of certain early psychological theories of perception (Furth, 1969), such children seem to proceed as though they believe objects to transmit, in a direct-line-of-sight fashion, faint copies of themselves, which actively assault and impress themselves upon anyone who happens in the path of such "objective" knowledge.

Within such a view projectile firings from things themselves bombard and actively victimize individuals who function as passive recorders and simply bear the scars of information which has been embossed upon them. Later arriving forms of symbolic knowledge, because of their arbitrary relation to the events which they represent, draw attention to their own subjective origins. By contrast presymbolic forms of representation, because they are more iconic, appear to have their origins in the thing known and not in the persons who know them.

Knowing *that* one knows is possible in this context in ways that knowing *how* or in *what way* one knows is not.

Given this Piagetian interpretation of the toddler's functional epistemology, much of the existing research evidence about early forms of "visual" perspective taking can be anticipated on theoretic grounds. Children who themselves apply, and consequently attribute to others, such a copy theory of knowing should appreciate that information directed to others must be aimed or positioned in such a way that it comes into line-of-sight contact with the sensory apparatus of others. This would account for the observation reported by Lempers, Flavell, and Flavell (1977) that when asked to show someone a picture glued to the bottom of a deep cup children as young as 24 months will aim the open end of the cup, much as one might point a microphone or a gun. Similarly data have been reported by Flavell, Botkin, Fry, Wright, and Jarvis (1968) and later by Masankay, McCluskey, McIntyre, Sims-Knight, Vaughn, and Flavell (1974), which indicate that most three-year-olds appreciate that a display board with a cat and dog painted on its opposing sides presents a different face to persons who view it from opposite sides, is consistent with the application of such a copy theory of knowing. Comparable findings by Lempers et al. (1977) and by Flavell, Everett, Croft, and Flavell (1981) reinforce the point that well before they are capable of genuine symbolic representations preschool children give evidence of knowing who is and who is not strategically well situated in space or time to receive direct hits from incoming rounds of information.

Preschoolers appear to apply this ballistics approach to knowledge acquisition to themselves as well as others. Shantz and Watson (1970) have shown that children as young as three and four react with surprise when, upon arrival at a new viewing position, they find that the same, rather than a different, informational payload is delivered. What such children appear ignorant of, however, and what Piaget's assumptions about presymbolic representational modes of knowledge would necessarily preclude, is any understanding of the fact that information is subjectively organized and that knowledge is actively construed. Facts, from the perspective of preschool children, are the epistemological equivalent of a bullet in the brain and, because information is understood to be oriented with respect to the objects which omit them rather than by the subjects who are struck by this knowledge, the subjective orientation of the knower is judged as irrelevant. Consistent with this view Flavell et al. (1981) have shown that such children do not appreciate that a book which appears right side up to them will be seen as upside down by someone sitting across the table or that a turtle which they view as lying on its back will be seen to be standing on its feet by another person whose viewing position is 180 degrees out of phase with their own. Any adequate appreciation of such orientational phenomena would require a more constructivistic epistemology which views one's own and other's knowledge as the interpretive consequence of an act of subjective knowing.

In this context Piaget's own task of three mountains poses an especially interesting problem. If a three-dimensional display, such as the one employed by Inhelder and Piaget, is treated by preoperational subjects as though it were a unitary perceptual event, it follows that such subjects would proceed as though the same knowledge which is available to them would be similarly available to others. If, however, the display happened to be regarded as more than one thing rather than a single-point source of information, even preschoolers would be expected to appreciate that persons on different sides of this display would be assaulted by and possess different knowledge. On these grounds one might assume that "egocentric" subjects could be made to appear more decentered simply by increasing the size of the stimulus display until, dwarfed by its size, the subjects began treating their own mountain side as a source of information different from that projected by the opposing slope. Research by Masankay et al. (1974) lends support to this assumption. Utilizing a three-dimensional witch head as a stimulus, these authors first demonstrated that children in the 3½- to 4-year age range were essentially unable to adopt the perspective of an opposite-seated experimenter when the witch head was placed on the table between them. When the witch head was literally split down the middle, however, and the resulting halves mounted on opposing sides of a board, all the subjects were able to identify correctly what the experimenter saw on at least five out of six trials. Virtually the same results were obtained when the front and back of a whole witch's head were marked by different colored dots and referenced by these dots for the subjects. Similarly Flavell et al. (1981) have shown that the same children who fail to appreciate that a picture of a turtle may be seen right side up to some and upside down to others do understand when a screen is erected down the middle of the figure that some people see only the turtle's feet while others see only its back.

On the basis of such results certain of the divergent findings which have been obtained with Piaget's task of three mountains may be seen as a consequence of the potentiality of such stimulus materials for being alternatively regarded as either a single-point source of information or as a two or more distinct object of knowledge. Utilizing a display of blocks and a task format similar to Piaget's three-mountain test, Liben (1978) found that three-year-old children not only failed to correctly identify the perspective of others but were also prepared to regard any of the eight photographs available as equally representative of their own point of view. Interestingly more such errors were made when the blocks were arranged in such a way that all were visible than when certain blocks partially or completely masked others. In effect these subjects functioned precisely as would be required by the copy theory of knowledge being attributed to them. Knowledge, for such preoperational subjects, seems to reside entirely within the world of material objects and, as such, is a feature of things rather than of persons and is thus given like a present to all those who are in a position to receive it. So long as one is in a position to accept delivery, the orientation of the perceiver is regarded as a subjective matter and is consequently thought to be irrelevant to the question of who knows what.

Certain findings which, at first, appear to suggest some capacity on the part of preoperational children to appreciate the subjective character of knowledge also seem, on closer inspection, to be consistent with a copy theory interpretation. First Vygotsky (1962), then Flavell et al. (1968), and still later Genesee, Tucker, and Lambert (1975), Marvin, Greenberg, and Mossler (1976), Meissner and Apthorp (1976), Lempers et al. (1977), and Liben (1978) have all shown that preschool children proceed differently when asked to interact with or explain themselves to other children who are unable to hear, or who are blindfolded, or who have their vision colored by tinted glasses. While all of these studies introduced individual differences in the groups of target individuals whose roles subjects were required to assume, they all did so by manipulating the kinds of sensory access which target individuals had to relevant information and not by varying the kinds of constructions which different individuals imposed upon the same information. Similarly the work of Menig-Peterson (1975), which indicates that young children bother to explain events to persons who were not present to experience them firsthand, also makes a comparable point about temporal, as opposed to physical, access to information. Preschoolers obviously appreciate that one must not only be *in* the right place to receive information but must also be *at* the right place at the right time.

The only data which appear to contradict the view that preschoolers are ignorant of the fact that different individuals may actually construe the same "facts" differently are those provided by Shatz and Gelman (1973) and others summarized in Shatz (1977). By demonstrating that even three- and four-year-olds talk in different ways to younger and older persons, these authors claim support for the view that such children appreciate that different age groups construe their worlds in different ways. As Higgins (1976, 1977) points out, however, the existence of such alternative modes of speech may reflect nothing more than a set of well-rehearsed forms of address and need not indicate any understanding of the different ways in which different age groups are likely to understand their worlds.

In summary children, whose own mode of knowing the world is presymbolic in character and who think instead with the assistance of figurative signs or signals, do appear to possess certain real, although limited, forms of role-taking competence. Because of their own restricted mode of knowing the world, knowledge of higher-order symbolic and metarepresentational knowledge is closed to them and is either overlooked or degraded through various kinds of category mistakes. What they are left with is a kind of primitive copy theory of knowledge, according to which they judge knowledge to reside in objective events which telegraph this information to any observer who gets in harm's way. Other people are consequently known to know only those bits of information they happen to be in the right place to receive. Such knowledge, however, is assumed to be free of any orientation markers or subjective-processing considerations. While such capacities are limited in accordance with the knowledge modes which bring it about, they do, nevertheless, stand as legitimate forms of knowledge about the knowledge of others. Far from being a source of potential embarrassment to Piaget's theory, however, the kinds of early role-taking skills so far demonstrated in the litera-

ture appear to be the expectable byproducts of preoperational or presymbolic knowing.

SYMBOLIC MODES OF SOCIAL ROLE-TAKING

As children leave toddlerhood and approach early school age, they begin, according to Piaget (1970; Inhelder & Piaget, 1958), a cognitive transition which, when completed in middle childhood, will permit them to represent symbolically their own knowledge and allow them to appreciate the existence of such knowledge in others. Implied in this transition to concrete operational thought is a shift from an object-centered or copy theory of knowledge to a subject-oriented or constructivistic epistemology within which it becomes possible to make sharp category distinctions between material events and their psychological representations. Unlike younger children who proceed as though their knowledge is imported directly from, and continues to exist upon, the same reality plane as the material objects to which their knowledge refers, older, concrete operational children come to appreciate that material events and knowledge of these events are not things of the same logical or semantical type. As a consequence of this levels distinction, they begin to appreciate that they live simultaneously in two worlds: a world of concrete things and happenings and a symbolic world of meaning within which known events of the first order are psychologically represented as conceptual objects of knowledge of a second order. When such distinctions are firmly in place, such school-age children no longer confuse their dreams with actual events, clearly differentiate physical and psychological causality, and abandon the realisms which earlier caused them to confuse words, ideas, and mental images with their referents. In the area of social role-taking, where the thing to be known is the knowledge of others, such concrete operational children begin to entertain, for the first time, the possibility that their own understanding is not always the proper measure of, and may be different from, the understanding of others. They are now capable of appreciating not only that different persons may have access to different information but also of realizing that even access to the same events may result in different meanings being attached to them. Such newly won symbolic representational abilities do not imply, however, that such children are reflectively aware or know about their own or other's constructivistic efforts. The proper objects of this second-order form of symbolic understanding are limited to instances of one's own first-order or implicit knowledge, and this restriction sets important limits upon the kinds of role-taking activities of which such concrete operational children are capable. What they cannot yet do, according to this Piagetian view, is consider in a metarepresentational sense their own or other's constructivistic styles—i.e., they cannot yet bracket or cluster together a number of such symbolic representational acts and then comment upon or metacommunicate about them as a group. Activities of this metarepresentational sort, which involve representations upon representations or operations upon operations, are held by Inhelder and Piaget (1958) to be defining features of formal operational thought and will be discussed more fully in the following section. For the present, attention will be restricted to a consideration of the emergent role-taking abilities characteristic of the concrete operational child.

Any attempt to summarize available research evidence concerning the role-taking abilities of early school-age children must contend with the fact that the period of transition to, and the period of eventual consolidation of, concrete operational competencies are characterized by importantly different sorts of role-taking skills. During the earlier transitional period such children sometimes give evidence of appreciating that the concepts which they employ are subjectively generated symbolic re-presentations rather than concrete instances of material events. At other times such children collapse this logical type distinction and revert to an earlier presymbolic mode of understanding. During these lapses psychological and material events are again treated interchangeably, and as before, meaning is thought to be literally embossed upon the minds of all those who stumble into its path. Later in their own development, as their facility in manipulating symbols increases and their concrete operational competences become better consolidated, these same children are assumed to become much more reliable in preserving the distinction between material events and their psychological representations and rarely stumble into such simple egocentric errors. As a consequence of these different response patterns, investigators concerned with the measurement of role-taking competence have generally focused their attention upon one or another, but not both, of these groups. The lion's share of such attention has been directed to the study of children who are transitional between preoperational and concrete operational modes of thought. A much smaller contingent of researchers, prompted by interests in the possibility of later occurring forms of egocentric thought, have concerned themselves with the role-taking abilities of children in the late concrete operational period. Each of these areas of research interest will be considered separately under the headings of (1) transitional and (2) consolidated modes of concrete operational thought.

TRANSITIONAL MODES OF CONCRETE OPERATIONAL THOUGHT

As recently as a decade ago it was widely maintained that preoperational thinking was uniformly egocentric in character and that the first appearance of role-taking skills marked a kind of watershed, signaling the onset of concrete operational modes of thought. New evidence of the sort cited in the previous section has produced something of a crisis of conviction in these circles and has obliged investigators working in this area to find a means of reconciling two seemingly contradictory research literatures. The first and oldest of these bodies of evidence consists of numerous studies (see Chandler, 1978, for a review of this literature) which apparently demonstrated that regular failures in role-taking characterized most children well into middle childhood and that egocentricity is a defining feature of preoperational thought. The second and more recent body of evidence, already cited in part in the previous section, raises serious doubts re-

garding the validity of earlier claims that preschool children are entirely ignorant of the thoughts and feelings of others.

Two general kinds of strategies have emerged for dealing with these seemingly contradictory findings. According to the first the concept of role-taking is regarded as a kind of wastebasket category which includes not only matters pertaining to early knowledge about the existence of knowledge in others but also a variety of other performance matters which determine the success or failure of one's role-taking efforts. The continuity position proposed by Higgins (1976, 1977) and the "existence-need-inference-application" model advanced by Flavell (1974) and Flavell et al. (1968) are examples of this information-processing approach. From this perspective, evidence indicating very early role-taking competencies is accepted on its face, and the slow progress which children demonstrate in solving other role-taking problems is seen as a function of various hurdles which they must overcome in uniformly applying this ability. The alternative approach to dealing with this problem has been to propose the existence of two or more distinct types of role-taking. While something of this sort will be the eventual conclusion of the present argument, existing explanations of this type (i.e., Coie, Costanzo, & Farnill, 1973; Flavell, 1977; Flavell et al., 1968; Flavell et al., 1981; Lempers et al., 1977; Masankay et al., 1974; Mossler, Marvin, & Greenberg, 1976; Salatas & Flavell, 1976; Shantz, 1975) have most commonly proposed a distinction between *perceptual* and *conceptual* role-taking.

Both of these explanatory strategies are somewhat curious fall-back positions for investigators working within a general cognitive developmental framework. Central to this tradition has been an insistence upon the notion that cognitive processes are implicated in even the most peripheral of sensory reactions, and consequently, little credence has typically been attached to the traditional perception-cognition dichotomy. The reintroduction of this dichotomy seems regressive in the present developmental context and has potential merit only insofar as those who invoke it also make clear the ways in which such perceptions and cognitions are assumed to be different and to interact. Similarly information-processing accounts, which conceptualize role-taking as a train of interlocking subroutines, also seem to have largely slipped the leash. While recognizing appropriate occasions, or having the motives or means, for applying one's role-taking skills are unquestionably important features in their regular use, the elaborate detailing of these performance conditions often appears to have had the effect of miniaturizing the prior question of their existence and losing this key issue amongst a forest of practical considerations. What seems required in the place of either of these approaches is an alternative which re-embeds the study of role-taking in a broader cognitive context concerning what is known about knowing and what is understood about the understanding of social objects.

From the perspective of the present chapter, the transition from preoperational to concrete operational thought is marked by neither a gradual accumulation of role-taking competence nor a shift from perceptual to conceptual role-taking but involves instead the acquisition of an additional mode of symbolic knowing and the consequent ability to appreciate such knowledge forms

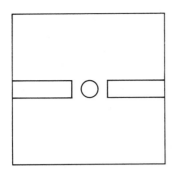

Figure 22-1 Two elephants sniffing a grapefruit

in others. Because such early school-age children have begun to solidify for themselves a new symbolic mode of knowing, they presumably begin to acquire, for the first time, the capacity to recognize such symbolic forms of knowledge in others. With this achievement the locus of knowledge begins to shift from *objects* to *subjects,* and knowing begins to be recognized as a constructive, meaning-generating, human activity. What is known by others ceases to be interpretable exclusively as a question about spacial or temporal access to different potential objects of knowledge and comes to include an appreciation of the fact that different persons can have a different understanding of the same objective fact.

The nature of this qualitative shift to a constructivistic orientation is made explicit by an assessment procedure developed by one of the writers (Chandler & Helm, 1980). This procedure made use of a cartooning technique known as *droodles*. Droodles are a cryptic form of line drawing, popularized by Price (1953), which present a restricted or keyhole view onto some larger, tacitly implied scene. While such drawings are intentionally obscure in that they disallow any reasonable guess as to the subject matter of the larger scene of which they are a fractional part, they are captioned in such a way that their titles contextualize the visible cartoon fragments and prompt the viewer to fill in the expanded scene which the cartoonist intended. One of these drawings consists of a square frame (see Figure 22-1) which contains two dashes and a dot.

The drawing is captioned, "Two elephants smelling a grapefruit." Given the tunnel vision imposed, it is ludi-

crous to imagine that anyone could ever anticipate the larger scene of which the droodle is only a part. Once oriented by the caption, however, the fragments of the original drawing fall into place, and it becomes possible to imagine—even difficult not to imagine—that the drawing is the leading edge of what it is claimed to be.

The assessment procedure which made use of this and other droodles involved the presentation of a set of expanded drawings of the sort implied by the captions of the cartoons. Each of these drawings was outfitted with a cardboard overlay into which a viewing window had been cut. Once in place these overlays masked most of the drawing and exposed, through the window provided, only the droodle portion of the picture (see Figure 22-2).

Subjects of various ages were first shown the completed drawings and asked to describe and caption these pictures. Once this procedure had been completed, the cardboard overlays were put in place exposing only the original droodles. Subjects were then asked to guess how this abridged picture would be interpreted by a second child who they observed examining these partially masked drawings. These manipulations had the effect of installing within the subjects key pieces of privileged information which had to be entirely set aside if they were successfully to take the role of the other children who had access to less information than themselves. While the subjects could see exactly what was seen by the other children, their own constructions of these picture fragments were informed by the broader context of meaning to which they, and not their role-taking partners, had been exposed. Any attribution on the part of such subjects which equates their own understanding of these materials with that of the less broadly informed bystanders constitutes a clear failure to set aside their own point of view and an inability to adopt accurately the roles or perspectives of others. Results from the application of this procedure with several different populations have indicated that five- and six-year-old children regularly fail to appreciate that they construe these materials differently than do others who are less well informed and demonstrate that children do not consistently solve this problem until middle childhood.

While less encumbered by the incidental task requirements than most (Edelstein, Keller, & Wahlen, 1980), the procedure just outlined is formally similar to the major-

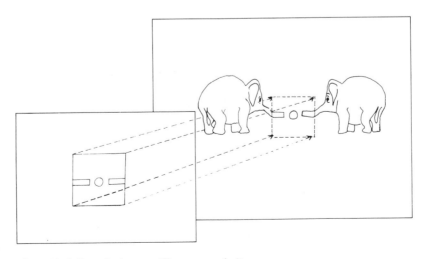

Figure 22-2 Two elephants sniffing a grapefruit

ity of other role-taking measures commonly in use. Like the *apple-dog* procedure of Flavell et al. (1968), the *hidden room technique* of Selman (1971b), and the cartoon sequences employed by Badal, Gerris, and Oppenheimer (1979), Chandler (1972), Urberg and Docherty (1976), and others, the droodles procedure systematically gerrymanders the boundaries of shared and privileged information in such a way that the subject always has an expanded context of meaning in which to embed various pieces of information which they hold in common with those roles they are asked to take. What is only a part for them is the whole for others, and consequently, their construction of the same events is necessarily different. Whether or not a particular child appreciates this fact hinges entirely upon the kinds of knowing of which they are capable. Children whose principal mode of knowing is presymbolic in character, and who are consequently functionally blind to the symbolic acts of others, are obliged to operate in terms of a copy theory of knowledge. By this object-centered standard, knowledge is viewed as the passive byproduct of direct exposure to information-laden events; any understanding of knowing as a subject-centered process, which actively construes and imposes meaning upon material events, is necessarily closed to them. When such presymbolic children view a stimulus object, such as the dot and dashes of Figure 22–1, and know, on the basis of previous experience, that these cryptic lines represent the tips of two elephant trunks and a grapefruit, they have no alternative other than to assume that these same drawing fragments would telegraph an identical understanding to anyone else who was exposed to them. To arrive at any other conclusion would require that they appreciate the subjective nature of the knowing process and recognize the essential distinction between symbols and their referents. Later in the course of their development as such children begin to impose a logical type distinction upon the separate plane of material and symbolic reality, it becomes possible for them to appreciate a lack of identity between sensory experiences and the meanings that are assigned to them. Armed with this category distinction and their newly acquired mode of symbolic knowing, counterpart forms of symbolic knowledge in others become accessible, and a permanent wedge is driven between objective events and the subjective ways in which such events are construed. The fact that an object is construed in one way by a subject is no longer seen as guarantee that it will be construed in identical ways by other individuals who experience the same object in a different context. What one appreciates to be the tips of two elephant trunks and a grapefruit can now be understood to appear quite differently to others who do not share one's own expanded context of understanding.

Knowledge concerning the kinds of information to which others have been exposed and knowledge concerning the fact that others may construe the same stimulus event differently are, according to the view advanced here, importantly different kinds of achievements, necessarily rooted in different modes of knowing. Evidence which indicates that, in the course of development, one of these kinds of role-taking normally precedes the other by three or more years is consequently seen to confirm rather than contradict the theoretic expectations which flow from a general Piagetian account of the knowing process. At the same time this multidimensional analysis of social role-taking challenges the wisdom of several different attempts (Kurdek, 1977a, 1977b; Rubin, 1973; Urberg & Docherty, 1976) to find a unitary factor underlying the full range of available role-taking measures. Procedures such as those introduced by Flavell et al. (1968), Lempers et al. (1977), or Masankay et al. (1974) which measure a child's understanding of the access which others have to various bits of information and other measurement strategies such as the droodle procedure (Chandler & Helm, 1980) which index awareness of how different persons construe the same event should not and, according to the work of Glucksberg, Krauss, and Higgins (1975), Kurdek and Rodgon (1975), Rotenberg (1974), Rothenberg (1970), Rubin (1978), and Zahn-Waxler, Radke-Yarrow, and Brady-Smith (1977), do not correlate.

CONSOLIDATED MODES OF CONCRETE OPERATIONAL THOUGHT

Despite the significant strides made in the role-taking competencies of concrete operational children, these accomplishments still fall importantly short of the kinds of abilities which typically accompany the transition to formal operational thought. The principal short-fall of this second-order, symbolic mode of knowing is that it is restricted in its scope of application to those variations in constructivistic orientation which are in some way situationally determined. Almost without exception the various role-taking measures currently in common use enforce the necessity of an alternative perspective by ensuring that the subject has a broader historical frame of reference than does the target individual whose perspective is in question. While the subjects' more inclusive context of understanding guarantees the uniqueness of their perspectives relative to others who are less broadly informed, the differences which set them apart have to do with the train of external events in question and not the idiosyncratic constructivistic styles of those involved. In Flavell's apple-dog story, the subject sees a full account of a boy being chased into a tree by a vicious dog, whereas the person whose perspective is to be inferred sees only an abridged version which deletes all reference to the fact that the dog is vicious or that the boy arrived in the tree after being chased there. What is meant to be different about the perspectives of the two individuals involved would be similarly different for any two persons who were privy to the same long and short versions of this cartoon sequence. It is, in effect, the different situations to which the subjects and their role-taking targets have been exposed, rather than anything endemic to them as idiosyncratic centers of knowing, which sets them apart.

While in hindsight this pattern of reliance upon situationally induced variations in perspectives appears more a product of preservation than deliberate decision, this choice of measurement strategies appears to have both guaranteed the success and limited the vision of these assessment efforts. As indicated earlier, symbolic modes of knowing take as their object first-order or nonsymbolic forms of knowledge but may not reference themselves. The act of bracketing such symbolic achievements and formulating metarepresentational comments upon them is instead held to constitute a third order of self-reflexive symbolic activity which serves as a defining feature of formal operational thought. As a consequence of this limitation, concrete operational children lack the capacity to look across a range of symbolic activities and distill stylistic commonalities in the way that particular others construe their experience. Because of their newly acquired symbolic skills, they are in a position to appreciate that others construct, rather than receive, meaning directly from the material world, but this realization is necessarily limited to alternative constructs which are determined by variations in situational access.

It follows from all of this that concrete operational children may appreciate that any two individuals who have come to know an event in different situational contexts will interpret it differently but will still fail to understand that even the same event in the same situational context can still be construed differently by persons whose habitual modes of construing the world are stylistically different. In this sense the role-taking abilities of concrete operational thinkers are still somewhat object centered, in that they do not yet appreciate how different patterns of attitudes, beliefs, and values exercise influence over the kinds of constructions which persons impose upon events. This accomplishment is a feature of third-order metarepresentational modes of knowing.

METAREPRESENTATIONAL MODE OF KNOWING

As just indicated in the preceding section, formal operational reasoning, assumed by Piaget to characterize certain aspects of the thought of adolescents and adults, is unique in that it is a mode of cognition capable of reflexively taking itself as its own object or performing operations upon operations. When this third-order mode of metarepresentational knowing takes as its object the knowledge of others, a similarly unique kind of role-taking becomes possible. Individuals whose thinking is characterized by this formal operational mode of knowing are not only capable of recognizing the moment-by-moment shifts in situational context which influence the constructive efforts of others but also possess the ability to bracket a variety of such constructions and formulate metarepresentations about such classes of symbolic events. Overarching metaformulations of this sort are functionally equivalent to ipsative psychological theories which permit predictions as to how a given individual might proceed in the face of a variety of constructivistic tasks. Such metarepresentational acts finally permit the kind of performance which laymen intend when role-taking abilities are discussed—the general ability to appreciate what sorts of meaning a situation would have for another, given the kind of individual that person is understood to be. It is this capacity, rather than any simple appreciation of *what* information a person is exposed to or the special temporal or spatial context of their interpretations, which people seem to have in mind when the claim is laid that someone is able to put themselves in the perspective of another.

Very little is available in the contemporary research literature on social role-taking which attempts to assess directly this kind of metarepresentational knowledge of the knowledge of others. A few preliminary studies of recursive thinking of the sort undertaken by Barenboim (1978) and Miller, Kessel, and Flavell (1970) allude to such reflexive modes of thought. Only the work of Feffer (1959), Feffer and Gourevitch (1960), and Selman (1971a) seems to be directed specifically to this issue. In his discussion of sequential decentering, Feffer (1959) has shown that by adolescence children begin to appreciate that the same thematic sequence may be differently understood by two or more individuals who, because of their own unique characteristics, place objectively identical events into different subjectively determined contexts of meaning. Similarly Selman (1971a) and Selman and Byrne (1974) have shown that, at a point in development consistent with the emergence of formal operational thought, young adolescents begin to understand that other people not only construe their own experience but also bracket and generate metarepresentational conclusions about such constructions. Such individuals, as Selman has shown, not only know that other people know but also appreciate that they and others know that they know and act accordingly.

In summary the presymbolic, symbolic, and metarepresentational modes of knowing differentiated in Piaget's general theory of cognitive development are seen as responsible for alerting children to the possibility of counterpart forms of knowledge in others. Children who function in presymbolic ways do appear partially informed about what is known by others, but this understanding appears to be restricted to an object-centered view of the kinds of "facts" to which others are recognized to have reasonable access. Symbolically oriented, concrete operational children, by contrast, are seen to have accomplished a logical type distinction between symbols and their referents and, consequently, shift the locus of the knowing process from material object to the subjects who construe them. This accomplishment permits them to appreciate that the question of how an event is understood may depend upon the situational context in which it is experienced. Such concrete operational subjects consequently appreciate that two individuals operating out of different contexts of meaning may differently construe the same "objective" event.

Finally, because concrete operational thought may not reflexively take symbolic thought as its own object, children in middle childhood know without knowing that they and others know. With the emergence of formal operational thought, however, a new logical type distinction becomes possible which allows second-order symbolic representations to be bracketed and commented upon by third-order forms of metarepresentational knowing. The existence of this third-order form of knowing allows adolescents and adults to recognize individual stylistic modes of knowledge construction and to employ fully subjectivized forms of social role-taking.

INFERENCE ABOUT MORALLY HAZARDOUS SITUATIONS

The processes of moral development have preoccupied generations of child psychologists and, with the possible exception of social role-taking, more journal space has been devoted to this issue than any other topic in the social-cognition literature. In view of the scope of this complex topic, any brief synoptic comments about the area as a whole would provide little more than a gloss upon an already top-heavy body of abstractions. Instead what seems potentially more useful, and in better keeping with the organizing thrust of this chapter, is to choose from this broad topic some single facet of concern and to examine this candidate issue from the transactional perspective already developed. If such a choice were to be decided by popular vote, the alternative elected would most likely prove to be the nature of the relationship between moral judgment and moral action. Both within and outside of the inner circle of investigators concerned with the moral developmental process, there has been a growing sense of concern over the extent to which cognitive considerations have preoccupied the field, and many have argued that if moral development research is not to become entirely lost in thought a revitalization of interest in the relationship between judgment and action is required. Stated most broadly the question in the minds of both interested professionals and persons more generally is whether individuals will or will not pursue in action what they hold in principle to be the loftier of available moral alternatives. There does exist, of course, some data on this issue (see Bryan, 1975; Emler & Rushton, 1974; Haan, Smith, & Block, 1968; LaVoie, 1974; Nelsen, Grinder, & Biaggio, 1969; Olejnik, 1975; Rubin & Schneider, 1973; Rushton, 1975). The upshot of all this empirical evidence, however, is that, for unspecified reasons and in unpredictable ways, people sometimes do and sometimes do not proceed in ways that they think best (Chandler, Siegal, & Boyes, 1980).

The efficient cause of this unsettled state of affairs lies in the fact that thinking about and acting upon morally relevant alternatives have traditionally been regarded as events of different orders, and separate and seemingly unbridgeable psychologies have arisen to account for each. Here, however, as with the role-taking literature discussed in the previous section, final responsibility for the present schism between moral thought and moral action appears traceable to a studied disregard for the environmental side of such subject-object transactions.

Historically most investigators concerned with the moral development process (i.e., Kohlberg, 1958; Kohlberg & Turiel, 1971; Piaget, 1932, 1970) have restricted their research attention almost exclusively to the role which cognitive structures play in shaping beliefs about morally relevant events. In the context of this active organism-passive environment interpretation (Payne, 1968), persons are viewed as radical constuctivists (Von Glasersfeld, 1974) who so thoroughly assimilate externally imposed events to existing cognitive structures that only limited attention to the stimulus environment is required. In the typical moral judgment study carried out in this tradition, persons of varying ages (Kohlberg, 1958) or cognitive abilities (Selman, 1971a; Selman, Damon, & Gordon, 1973) are shown to construe differently the same moral dilemmas, which are regarded as a kind of infinitely malleable grist, equally suited to any moral reasoning mill. Because in this view any given level of moral reasoning ability can presumably be indexed through responses to the same stimulus materials,

it is assumed that all of the organization worthy of comment belongs to the subjects and not the objects or events upon which they operate (Chandler, in press). Morally relevant action within this essentially closed interpretive system is not understood as the interactive products of both persons and their independently structured environments but represents instead a kind of privatistic response to a self-insulating subjectivity.

From the perspective of the present chapter and its self-assigned role as the champion of the unsung stimulus environment, the difficulty with this now-standard interpretation of the moral judgment process is that it sponsors a lopsided preoccupation with the assimilatory side of the knowing process and an equally unhealthy disregard for the particulars of the morally relevant stimulus environment which must be accommodated. What seems to be the case is that many developmentalists, in attempting to keep faith with their own constructivistic premises, have been led into a kind of self-defeating sophistry, according to which individuals, but not their social stimulus environments, are assumed to be structured in specifiable ways. Since on this rationale the component parts which make up the horns of various moral dilemmas are understood to be assimilated to each individual's current level of cognitive operational competence, the stimulus environment is seen to lose its independent character and reverts to the status of another subject variable. One's social and moral life, by this subjective standard, becomes analogous to a kind of endless projective test where there are no right or wrong answers and where the task of psychology resolves into a search for the characteristic ways in which persons of different developmental ages construct order out of an essentially unordered environment.

From the perspective advanced in this chapter, all of this amounts to a kind of unnecessary and unwarranted constructivistic overkill. If in reacting to various moral dilemmas individuals respond in ways which can be reliably scored as representative of one or another level of moral reasoning, there would seem to be no reason in principle why these or similar prescriptive comments could not be salvaged and given as stimulus materials to other individuals and still be said legitimately to retain their own previously established level of structural complexity. On these grounds the social environment can be understood to bristle with competing, and often contradictory, morally relevant claims which possess an existence and a specifiable structure that is quite independent of those who might construe and arbitrate among them. While individuals will go on transforming such events in ways consistent with their own abilities, it is, nevertheless, a matter of some importance to know something about these moral aliments in their premasticated form. Moral transactions, in this view, take place as interchanges between individuals and particular prescriptive forms of social obligation, both of which are structured separately but to a common design. Moral reasoning, in this sense, involves reasoning about the moral reasoning of others, and the same structural forms which characterize a range of subjects will consequently also characterize the possible range of moral alternatives with which they must deal. What all of this suggests is the need for a more balanced or even-handed orientation toward the study of moral development which requires a binocular splitting of research attention between the structural characteristics of one's subjects and the structural features of the moral event to which they are exposed.

While moral development research carried out within this proposed transactional framework is in short supply, a recently completed study by the authors (Boyes & Chandler, 1980; Chandler et al., 1980) has demonstrated something of the utility of this approach. What is required to accomplish such an interactive study of the sort just outlined is some common language in which to discuss simultaneously both the cognitive competencies of children and the event complexities of the moral situations which they confront. Piaget's descriptive framework was employed in this study as a familiar means of characterizing the qualitative changes characteristic of the course of cognitive development. Much less is known about the formal structure of prescriptive obligations, however, and in order to arrive at an appropriate typology for characterizing various moral dilemma situations, it was necessary to go somewhat further afield.

Drawing upon the work of authors such as Hare (1952) and Taylor (1961), it was argued that prescriptive obligations may be understood to vary considerably in the scope of their intended domain of application. At one end of this dimension are prescriptions such as "open the door" or "keep your mouth shut," which are intended as simple, one-shot commands, not meant to be generalized to all doors or to other occasions upon which "open wide" or "speak up" would be more appropriate. Commands of this sort are intended to apply to particular individuals, in specific situations, for specified periods of time, and are meant to have only the most minimal kind of generality. At the other extreme are obligations of a more unambiguously "moral" sort, involving prescriptions of unlimited generality, meant to apply to all comers, at all times, under all conceivable circumstances. Universal prescriptions of this "golden rule" variety, referred to here as *meta-rules* or *principles*, achieve their special status precisely because no hedge is placed against their unremitting generality. Intermediate between these extremes of particularistic commands and universal principles are *concrete rules* of real, but limited, generality which are meant to apply to certain classes of situations but not others. While concrete rules of this sort are sometimes viewed as drawing their authority from still more general principles, this need not be the case, and their only necessary feature is that they prescribe to classes and relations between classes of events. As such they are component features of interdependent systems of obligations which bear upon one another in such a way that some rules may contradict or make logical impossibilities of others. Without attempting to prejudge the question of whether other intermediate distinctions might be drawn among such commands, rules, and principles, this research proceeded upon the assumption that each of these three brands of prescriptive obligations refer to events of a different logical or semantical type (Tarski, 1956).

Commands, rules, and principles of the sort just outlined were understood as prospective candidates for outfitting the horns of various moral dilemmas. When set in opposition to one another, in all possible combinations, these three different brands of obligation generate an array of six structurally distinct dilemma types (i.e., one command vs. another, a command vs. a rule, a rule vs. a rule, a rule vs. a principle, a principle vs. a principle, a principle vs. a command). This typology, then, stands as the descriptive framework for characterizing the independent social stimulus environment of possible moral dilemma types with which subjects were asked to deal. A series of short, child-oriented story problems were written which pitted prescriptive obligations of each of these various sorts against one another and required that the subjects decide upon and justify which of these competing alternatives they would advocate following.

While the descriptive framework just outlined provides a means of independently type-casting various sorts of moral dilemmas, the number and kind of such dilemma types psychologically available to particular individuals was understood to vary as a function of their cognitive developmental level. According to this view preoperational children, whose thoughts are understood to lack the systemic character required to appreciate either formal rules or universal principles, were expected to reduce all moral conflicts to contests between competing commands. Concrete operational children were assumed to possess the capacity to process both rules and commands and, consequently, expected to interpret accurately contests between two rules or two commands and to appreciate when a single command is pitted against a rule. When confronted with instances of conflicts between rules and principles or between two principles, however, such concrete operational subjects were expected to fail to appreciate such higher-order principles and to reinterpret and consequently misconstrue them as simple rules and regulations. Children possessing formal operational skills, by contrast, were assumed to be able to discriminate and accurately interpret all six of these conflict types.

On the strength of the rationale outlined above, it was possible to detail a testable model for anticipating the outcome of the moral deliberations of children at various levels of cognitive maturity as they attempt to arbitrate moral dilemmas of any one of the six different structural types identified. The model proposes a two-step process of deliberation. The first step involves the application of a transformational rule which specifies the manner in which moral dilemmas of various types are to be interpreted and differently construed by individuals representative of the three cognitive developmental levels under study. This transformational rule states that individuals lack the cognitive means for adequately comprehending prescriptions justified by universality claims more general or abstract than themselves and that persons will consequently reinterpret such obligations as representative of prescriptions of the same logical type as their own current level of operational competence. By this same transformational rule, preoperational children were expected to reinterpret and misconstrue all rules and principles as instances of concrete commands, and concrete operational children were expected to reconstrue universal principles as instances of social rules. The second step in this proposed model of moral deliberation consisted of a single decision rule which states that individuals of all cognitive developmental levels will systematically prefer and advocate whichever of two alternative behavioral courses they judge to express the more universally prescriptive obligation (i.e., principles would be preferred to rules or commands, and rules to commands for all who are in a position to make these distinctions). Conversely the model specified that whenever individuals of any given cognitive developmental level construe both of two available morally relevant behavioral alternatives as being warranted at the same perceived level of prescriptive universality (i.e., as being obligations of the same logical type), their choices will cease to be a predictable function of their current level of competence.

The implication of this proposed model is that, for reasons unique to each different ability level group, the various moral deliberation problems presented would resolve into instances of one of two distinct dilemma types. The first of these types consists of a class of dilemmas for which the subject in question is able to appreciate a levels distinction between the two prescriptive alternatives presented. Dilemmas of the second type consist of those pairs of alternatives for which no such levels distinction is possible. The important point to appreciate is that membership in either of these categories was not understood to be an attribute of the subject alone or the moral dilemma alone but rather a joint function of the interaction between relevant features of both the person in question and the situation which s/he is asked to arbitrate.

Given this set of transformation and decision rules, one of two classes of outcomes automatically results from every act of moral deliberation. In the first instance the available moral alternatives are, or are construed to be, of different logical types, and the loftier of these perceived alternatives is consequently chosen as the preferred course of action. In the second case both horns of the dilemma are, or are understood to be, alternatives of the same logical type, in which case no logical grounds exists for choosing between them, and behavioral choice ceases to be a predictable function of cognitive ability level. The net result of all of this is that the model predicts that persons sometimes will and sometimes will not choose to behave in ways related to their level of moral maturity. The important advance made here over what is otherwise a widely shared, common-sense conclusion, however, lies in the fact that the present model specifies in advance which of these alternatives will hold in any given moral transaction. Given knowledge of both an individual's cognitive developmental level and the particular sort of moral dilemma which is at issue, the outcome will either be predictable or, if not, at least fail to be predictable for known reasons.

The logical test of this transactional model should, and did, involve the presentation of instances of all six of the proposed moral dilemma types to groups ($N = 20$) of individuals characterized by one or the other of the three cognitive ability levels in question. This arrangement resulted in a 3×6 matrix with 18 data points, each of which described a unique subject by situation transaction. For all of these instances one or the other of two predictions was made. In instances in which the individuals in question construed the available alternatives to be prescriptions of the same logical type, no structural grounds were assumed to exist for dictating a strong preference for one alternative over another, and the proportion of subjects electing either alternative was expected to approach 0.5. When, by contrast, the competing alter-

natives were both of different logical types and recognized as such by the subject in question, strong preferences were anticipated, and the expected value for the more universalizable of the two alternatives was anticipated to approach 1.0. The overall descriptive adequacy of this proposal model was tested by means of a *pattern hypothesis* (Steiger, 1979, 1980) which evaluated the degree of match between these expected and obtained proportions. The resulting *chi* square statistic obtained by this procedure lent strong support to the view that the obtained data closely approximate that predicted by the model. The outcomes of moral deliberations are, in fact, directly predictable given a knowledge of both the cognitive ability level of subjects and an awareness of the structural complexity of the moral conflicts which they face.

CONCLUSIONS

As this interpretive summary of the moral deliberation and role-taking literatures has attempted to show, the study of social cognition offers a potential foot in the door in dealing with the problems of cognitive development more generally. Historically the constructivistic orientation featured by most cognitive developmental theories has sacrificed the stimulus environment to the deforming process of pure assimilation and left its subjects objectless and lost in a sea of thought. In large part responsibility for this kind of constructivistic overkill may be laid at the door of the difficulties experienced in attempting to say anything objective about objective reality. Social cognition, because of its inherently reflexive character, partially finesses this difficulty by dint of the fact that, in this limited case, the objects of thought are also subjects. As a consequence of this fact whatever is known about the form or structure of the cognitive process of one's subjects applies with equal legitimacy to the objects' side of such subject-object interactions. In this context the stimulus environment loses its otherwise featureless character and is restored as a potentially equal partner in interactive processes. Provided with an environment which is not all things to all people, the concept of accommodation takes on new meaning, loses some insular qualities, and can again be understood as part of a process of adaptation. While, as the preceding review has attempted to show, research in the areas of role-taking and moral development have only begun to exploit these possibilities, the area of social-cognitive development promises to continue to define a growth edge of developmental theory and research.

REFERENCES

BADAL, C., GERRIS, J., & OPPENHEIMER, L. *Social-cognitive operations and their task-operationalizations: A conceptual analysis.* Internal report 79 ON 05 S.V.O. projekt 0360, Psychologisch Laboratorium, Nijmegen, The Netherlands, 1979.

BALDWIN, J. M. *Social and ethical interpretations of mental development.* New York: Macmillan, 1906.

BARENBOIM, C. Development of recursive and non-recursive thinking about persons. *Developmental Psychology*, 1978, *14*(No. 4), 419–420.

BOYES, M. C., & CHANDLER, M. J. *Situational determinants and cognitive prerequisites of moral deliberations.* Paper presented at the annual convention of the American Psychological Association, Montreal, September 1980.

BRUNER, J. S. The course of cognitive growth. *American Psychologist,* 1964, *19,* 1–15. ·

BRYAN, J. H. You will be well advised to watch what we do instead of what we say. In D. J. DePalma & J. M. Foley (Eds.), *Moral development: Current theory and research.* London: Wiley, 1975.

CHANDLER, M. Egocentrism in normal and pathological childhood development. In W. Hartup & J. DeWitt (Eds.), *Determinants of behavioural development.* New York: Academic Press, 1972.

CHANDLER, M. J. Social cognition: A selected review of current research. In W. Overton & J. Gallagher (Eds.), *Knowledge and development: Yearbook of developmental epistemology.* New York: Plenum, 1978.

CHANDLER, M. J. Social cognition and social structures: Adapting to a social world more complicated than oneself. In F. C. Serafica (Ed.), *Social cognition, social context, and social behaviour,* in press.

CHANDLER, M. J., & HELM, D. *Knowing the sort of help that is really needed.* Paper presented at the International Conference on the Development and Maintenance of Prosocial Behaviour, Warsaw, 29VI–3VII, 1980.

CHANDLER, M. J., SIEGAL, M., & BOYES, M. C. The development of moral behaviour. Continuities and discontinuities. *International Journal of Behavioral Development,* 1980, *3,* 323–332.

COIE, J. D., COSTANZO, P. R., & FARNILL, D. Specific transitions in the development of spacial perspective-taking ability. *Developmental Psychology,* 1973, *9,* 167–177.

EDELSTEIN, W., KELLER, M., & WAHLEN, K. *Structure and content in social cognitions: A logical and empirical analysis.* Paper presented at the Sixth Biennial Southeastern Conference on Human Development, Alexandria, Va., 1980.

ELKIND, D. Egocentrism in adolescence. *Child Development,* 1967, *38,* 1025–1034.

ELKIND, D. Cognitive structure and adolescent experience. *Adolescence,* 1968, *11*(No. 8), 427–434.

EMLER, N. P., & RUSHTON, J. P. Cognitive developmental factors in children's generosity. *British Journal of Social and Clinical Psychology,* 1974, *13,* 277–281.

FEFFER, M. H. The cognitive implications of role-taking behavior. *Journal of Personality,* 1959, *27,* 152–168.

FEFFER, M. H., & GOUREVITCH, V. Cognitive aspects of role-taking in children. *Journal of Personality,* 1960, *28,* 383–396.

FLAVELL, J. H. The development of inferences about others. In T. Mischel (Ed.), *Understanding other persons.* Oxford: Basil Blackwell, 1974.

FLAVELL, J. H. The development of knowledge about visual perception. In H. E. Howe, Jr., & C. B. Keasey (Eds.), *Nebraska symposium on motivation.* Lincoln: University of Nebraska Press, 1977.

FLAVELL, J. H., BOTKIN, P. I., FRY, C. C., WRIGHT, J. W., & JARVIS, P. G. *The development of role-taking and communication skills in children.* New York: John Wiley, 1968.

FLAVELL, J. H., EVERETT, B. A., CROFT, K., & FLAVELL, E. R. Young children's knowledge about visual perception: Further evidence for the level-1–level-2 distinction. *Developmental Psychology,* 1981, *17*(No. 1), 99–103.

FURTH, H. G. Piaget and knowledge: Theoretical foundations. Englewood Cliffs, N.J.: Prentice-Hall, 1969.

GENESEE, F., TUCKER, G. R., & LAMBERT, W. E. Communication skills of bilingual children. *Child Development,* 1975, *46,* 1010–1014.

GLUCKSBERG, S., KRAUSS, R., & HIGGINS, E. T. The development of referential communication skills. In F. D. Horowitz (Ed.), *Review of child development research.* Chicago: University of Chicago Press, 1975.

HAAN, H., SMITH, M. B., & BLOCK, J. Moral reasoning of young adults: Political-social behavior, family background, and personality correlates. *Journal of Personality and Social Psychology,* 1968, *10,* 183–201.

HARE, R. M. *The language of morals.* Oxford: Clarendon Press, 1952.

HIGGINS, E. T. Social class differences in verbal communication accuracy: A question of "which question"? *Psychological Bulletin,* 1976, *83,* 695–714.

HIGGINS, E. T. Communication development as related to channel, incentive, and social class. *Genetic Psychology Monographs,* 1977, *96,* 75–141.

HUDSON, L. On the coherence of role-taking abilities: An alternative to correlational analysis. *Child Development,* 1978, *49,* 223–227.

INHELDER, B., & PIAGET, J. *The growth of logical thinking from childhood to adolescence.* New York: Basic Books, 1958.

KOHLBERG, L. *The development of modes of moral thinking and choice in the years ten to sixteen.* Unpublished doctoral dissertation, University of Chicago, 1958.

KOHLBERG, L., & TURIEL, E. Moral development and moral education. In G. S. Lesser (Ed.), *Psychology and educational practice.* Glenview, Ill.: Scott, Foresman, 1971.

KURDEK, L. Convergent validation of perspective taking: A one year follow-up. *Developmental Psychology,* 1977a, *13,* 172–173.

KURDEK, L. Structural components and intellectual correlates of a cognitive perspective taking in first through fourth grade children. *Child Development,* 1977b, *48,* 1503–1511.

KURDEK, L., & RODGON, M. Perceptual, cognitive, and affective perspective taking in kindergarten through sixth-grade children. *Developmental Psychology,* 1975, *11,* 643–650.

LA VOIE, J. C. Cognitive determinants of resistance to deviation in seven, nine, and eleven year old children of low and high maturity of moral judgement. *Developmental Psychology,* 1974, *10,* 393–403.

LEMPERS, J. D., FLAVELL, E. R., & FLAVELL, J. H. The development in very young children of tacit knowledge concerning visual perception. *Genetic Psychology Monographs,* 1977, *95,* 3–53.

LIBEN, L. S. Perspective-taking skills in young children: Seeing the world through rose colored glasses. *Developmental Psychology,* 1978, *14,* 87–92.

MARVIN, R. S., GREENBERG, M. T., & MOSSLER, D. G. The early development of conceptual perspective taking: Distinguishing among multiple perspectives. *Child Development,* 1976, *47,* 511–514.

MASANKAY, Z. S., McCLUSKEY, K. A., McINTYRE, C. W., SIMS-KNIGHT, J., VAUGHN, B. E., & FLAVELL, J. H. The early development of inferences about the visual percepts of others. *Child Development,* 1974, *45,* 357–366.

MEISSNER, J. A., & APTHORP, H. Nonegocentrism and communication mode switching in black pre-school children. *Developmental Psychology,* 1976, *12,* 245–249.

MENIG-PETERSON, C. The modification of communicative behavior in preschool aged children as a function of the listener's perspective. *Child Development,* 1975, *46,* 1015–1018.

MILLER, P. H., KESSEL, F. S., & FLAVELL, J. H. Thinking about people thinking about people thinking about . . . : A study of social cognitive development. *Child Development,* 1970, *41,* 613–623.

MOSSLER, D. G., MARVIN, R. S., & GREENBERG, M. T. Conceptual perspective taking in 2 to 6 year old children. *Developmental Psychology,* 1976, *12*(No. 1), 85–86.

NELSEN, E. A., GRINDER, R. E., & BIAGGIO, A. B. Relationships among behavioral, cognitive-developmental, and self-support or morality and personality. *Multivariate Behavioral Research,* 1969, *4,* 483–500.

OLEJNIK, A. B. *Developmental changes and interrelationships among role-taking, moral judgements and children's sharing.* Paper presented at the Biennial Meeting of the Society for Research in Child Development, Denver, 1975.

OSHERSON, D., & MARKMAN, E. Language and the ability to evaluate contradictions and tautologies. *Cognition,* 1975, *3,* 213–226.

PAYNE, T. R. *S. L. Rubinstein and the philosophical foundations of Soviet psychology.* New York: Humanities Press, 1968.

PIAGET, J. *The language and thought of the child.* New York: Harcourt Brace Jovanovich, 1926.

PIAGET, J. *The moral judgement of the child.* London: Routledge and Kegan Paul, 1932.

PIAGET, J. Piaget's theory. In P. H. Mussen (Ed.), *Carmichael's manual of child psychology.* New York: John Wiley, 1970.

PIAGET, J., & INHELDER, B. *The child's conception of space.* London: Routledge and Kegan Paul, 1956.

PIAGET, J., & INHELDER, B. *The psychology of the child.* New York: Basic Books, 1968.

PRICE, R. *Droodles.* New York: Simon & Schuster, 1953.

ROTENBERG, M. Conceptual and methodological notes on affective and cognitive role-taking (sympathy and empathy): An illustrative experiment with delinquent and nondelinquent boys. *Journal of Genetic Psychology,* 1974, *125,* 177–185.

ROTHENBERG, B. Children's social sensitivity and the relationship to interpersonal competence, interpersonal comfort, and intellectual level. *Developmental Psychology,* 1970 *2,* 335–350.

RUBIN, K. Egocentrism in childhood: A unitary construct? *Child Development*, 1973, *44,* 102–110.

RUBIN, K. Role-taking in childhood: Some methodological considerations. *Child Development*, 1978, *49,* 428–433.

RUBIN, K. H., & SCHNEIDER, F. W. The relationship between moral judgement, egocentrism and altruistic behavior. *Child Development*, 1973, *44,* 661–665.

RUSHTON, J. P. Generosity in children: Immediate and long-term effects of modelling, preaching and moral judgement. *Journal of Personality and Social Psychology,* 1975, *31,* 459–466.

RYLE, G. *The concept of mind.* London: Hutchinson, 1949.

SALATAS, H., & FLAVELL, J. H. Perspective-taking: The development of two components of knowledge. *Child Development*, 1976, *47,* 103–109.

SELMAN, R. L. The relation of role-taking to the development of moral judgements in children. *Child Development*, 1971a, *42,* 79–91.

SELMAN, R. L. Taking another's perspective: Role-taking development in early childhood. *Child Development*, 1971b, *42,* 1721–1734.

SELMAN, R. L., & BYRNE, D. F. A structural developmental analysis of levels of role-taking in middle childhood. *Child Development*, 1974, *45,* 803–806.

SELMAN, R., DAMON, W., & GORDON, A. *The relation between levels of social role-taking and stages of justice conception in children ages four to ten.* Paper presented at the meeting of the Society for Research in Child Development, Philadelphia, 1973.

SHANTZ, C. The development of social cognition. In E. Hetherington (Ed.), *Review of child development research* (Vol. 5). Chicago: University of Chicago Press, 1975.

SHANTZ, C. V., & WATSON, J. S. Assessment of spacial egocentrism through expectancy violation. *Psychonomic Science,* 1970, *18,* 93–94.

SHATZ, M. The relationship between cognitive processes and the development of communication skills. In H. E. Howe & C. B. Keasey (Ed.), *Nebraska symposium on motivation.* Lincoln: University of Nebraska Press, 1977.

SHATZ, M., & GELMAN, R. The development of communication skills: Modifications in the speech of young children as a function of listener. *Monographs of the Society for Research in Child Development,* 1973, *38*(No. 2, Serial No. 152), 1–37.

STEIGER, J. H. *Testing pattern hypotheses on correlation matrices: Alternative statistics and some empirical results.* Paper presented at the meeting of the Psychometric Society, Monterey, Calif., June 1979.

STEIGER, J. H. Tests for comparing elements of a correlation matrix. *Psychological Bulletin,* 1980, *87*(No. 2), 245–251.

TARSKI, A. *Logic, semantics, and metamathematics.* Oxford: Clarion Press, 1956.

TAYLOR, W. T. *Normative discourse.* Englewood Cliffs, N.J.: Prentice-Hall, 1961.

URBERG, K., & DOCHERTY, E. M. The development of role-taking skills in young children. *Developmental Psychology,* 1976, *12,* 198–203.

VON GLASERSFELD, E. *Assimilation and accommodation in the framework of Piaget's constructivist epistemology.* Paper presented at the Third Biennial Southeastern Conference of the Society for Research in Child Development, Chapel Hill, N.C., March 7–9, 1974.

VYGOTSKY, L. *Thought and language.* Cambridge, Mass.: M.I.T. Press, 1962.

WERNER, H. *Comparative psychology of mental development.* New York: International Universities Press, 1948.

ZAHN-WAXLER, C., RADKE-YARROW, M., & BRADY-SMITH, J. Perspective taking and prosocial behavior. *Developmental Psychology,* 1977, *13,* 87–88.

Sex Differentiation
and the Development
of Sex Roles

DEE L. SHEPHERD-LOOK

Research exploring the differences between the sexes has been reported since the mid-nineteenth century (Shields, 1975). Until recently, however, the data showing sex differences has been inconsistent and has lacked a theoretical framework. Much of the confusion stems from the fact that the majority of research on sex differences has been tangential to other experimental concerns (Maccoby & Jacklin, 1974). Researchers have typically matched their experimental and control groups to allow analyses by sex with the intention of ruling it out in further analyses. If the results were nonsignificant, the researcher was relieved and rarely reported the findings; if positive, the results were regarded as unwanted noise or as spurious individual differences. Sex differences have been reported only as significant interactions in which sex was one of the variables. The result of this approach has been twofold: an emphasis on differences between the sexes rather than similarities and the production of a vast body of literature relating sex at least tangentially to every conceivable aspect of human behavior (Wolman & Money, 1980).

The observed differences between males and females have typically been attributed to an underlying biological mechanism (Unger, 1979). Such assumptions have a profound impact on limiting the range of possible hypotheses to be investigated to those in which there is an implicit unidirectional causality from the biological to the psychological. A finding that shows a significant difference between the sexes is one of the few phenomena in psychology which has been considered explained by the very fact that it occurred. The result has been that the topic of sex differences has been considered the province of disciplines other than the social sciences—physiology, or maybe theology. Biological determinist hypotheses have also obscured the exploration of such issues as how the environment may affect biological mechanisms, the situational determinants of behavior, and the properties sex may have as a stimulus variable. Perhaps it is the belief that biology is immutable destiny that explains why myths about sex differences continue to be tenaciously held even in the face of clear and contradictory evidence.

The political and cultural milieu has also had a subtle but pervasive influence on inquiry into the area of sex differences. The direction of influence in the power structure has been to maintain the status quo. Cultural norms have exerted their influence by implying that "what is" is based on the nature of humankind and, thus, "should always be." Traditional views about the nature of men and women and the roles they should fulfill have been a major factor in determining every facet of research in this area: the prevalent use of male subjects; the tendency to select male subjects for masculine behavior (aggression) and females for feminine behavior (attraction); the greater quantity of research related to male as opposed to female stereotyped behaviors (achievement versus nurturance, aggression versus cooperation, acquisition of mathematical skills versus reading skills); the procedures used for assessment of variables (the measurement of active aggression in males as opposed to the use of paper and pencil tests for females); and the reporting of results. Maccoby and Jacklin (1974) have noted instances of direct pressure to keep findings which do not agree with an accepted view out of the published literature.

I would like to acknowledge Alan J. Mann for his invaluable assistance in the preparation of this manuscript; my sons Launis and Jeremy for allowing Mommy her "space" to write; my mother for her continued support in whatever I pursue, regardless of its "masculine" or "feminine" characteristics.

Since the mid-1960s there has been a burgeoning interest in sex-role psychology as a legitimate scientific concern in its own right. The number of sex-role studies has increased tenfold in the decade from 1965 to 1975, from 50 reported in *Psychological Abstracts* in 1965 to about 500 reported in 1975 (Wesley & Wesley, 1977). Many social scientists are puzzled (and antagonistic) about the growing interest in this field. The current interest for some is in correcting the misconceptions about sex differences which have arisen from the limited nature and questionable validity of previous research and which have led to sex discrimination and sex stereotyping. Others are interested in the findings for their current relevance in making social policy decisions. As Maccoby (1976) has pointed out in her recent presidential address to the Western Psychological Association, "Psychologists are increasingly being asked to comment on what kinds of jobs members of the two sexes should or could hold, and what kinds of life styles are appropriate for men and women" (p. 2). There are an amazing number of current social issues which seem to boil down to certain assumptions about the basic differences between the sexes and how modifiable they are. To name a few: Are women able to function as adequately as men in the armed forces? Should women be drafted? Are men able to function in a role as a single parent? Should men be awarded custody of their children? What about educational policies in the high schools and colleges? Should females be encouraged (or forced) to take courses in higher mathematics or machine shop? Should males be encouraged (or forced) to take courses in the arts or home economics?

In addition to the matter of social importance, there are many scientific issues to which studies of sex differences are relevant: determining the relationship between the psychology of sex differences and the biology of sex differences—how chromosomes and hormones affect the central nervous system; specifying the process by which environmental events have an impact on biological predisposition; understanding how situational determinants interact with various sex differences to determine behavior; determining the effect that sex role expectations and/or self-labeling processes have on such variables as achievement motivation, success, or cognitive functioning. In addition there are the matters of understanding how sex role differences develop and change throughout the life span and of identifying possible sources of variation. Knowing how a phenomenon develops leads to the ability to make more accurate predictions and enables the possibility of developing intervention strategies in order to maximize human potential.

TERMINOLOGY

One of the major obstacles to understanding and interpreting sex-role research is the ambiguous use of terminology. The definition of the term *sex* is by no means clear. In various contexts *sex* can be used to describe the genetic and/or the chromosomal composition of the individual, the reproductive organs and the secondary sex characteristics, intrapsychic characteristics which are associated with being male or female, and, in the case of sex role, any behaviors, traits, attitudes, or expectations thought to differentiate the sexes. To make things more confusing there is strong evidence that the physiological dichotomy between the sexes is not as clear as it was once assumed. In extensive studies on sexually ambiguous humans, Money and Ehrhardt (1972) have found little correlation among chromosomal, hormonal, and morphological indicators of sex in large categories of people. As Unger (1979) points out, however, researchers have been unwilling to accept anything other than a two-category system. The critical demarcation is the presence or absence of anything that closely resembles a penis. If a penis is present, even in the presence of such contradictory evidence as breasts or feminine hips (as in Klinefelter's disease), the individual is categorized a male (Kessler & McKenna, 1978).

Psychologists have tended to use the term *sex* interchangeably as both an independent and dependent variable (Unger & Denmark, 1975). As an independent variable it is implied that sex (and the psychological characteristics of males and females) are biologically determined by the chromosomal, hormonal, and morphological structure of the organism. As a dependent variable it is assumed that sex is derived (except for physical structure) from postnatal experiences as defined by different sociocultural milieus. Unger (1979) has argued quite convincingly for partitioning sex into two categories—sex and gender—on the basis of the various ways it can function biologically and socially.

The term gender may be used to describe those nonphysiological components of sex that are culturally regarded as appropriate to males or to females. Gender may be used for those traits for which sex acts as a stimulus variable, independently of whether those traits have their origin within the subject or not. (p. 1086)

The advantage of this dichotomy is to make biological and psychological mechanisms explicit and separate and to do away with the idea that one necessarily depends on or causes the other. The disadvantage is that researchers will probably find that this distinction distorts reality for some phenomena (perhaps cognitive differences) since the truth is likely to be a result of an interaction between the two. However it is a good first step which may lead to greater clarity in the conceptualization of hypotheses.

Sex-role stereotypes (or *gender-role stereotypes*) are abstractions, crystallized into well-defined expectations, which exert pressure on the members of a particular social category to display behaviors, attitudes, and traits consistent with membership in the social category. In addition to the behavioral consequences, the expectations that sex-role stereotypes generate can have constraining effects on person perception by limiting one's observations. Tunnel vision may have either one of two consequences: perceiving stereotypic behavior with greater frequency than it actually occurs or the tendency to be more likely to perceive behavior which is counter to a stereotype (Meyer & Sobieszek, 1972).

Sex-role stereotypes are widely shared and pervasive concepts that prescribe how each sex ought to perform. Kagan (1964) has suggested that cultural stereotypes which are widely supported generate *sex-role standards* (or *gender-role standards*). Sex-role stereotypes and sex-role standards appear to reinforce one another. The sex-role stereotypes result in judgments that males and females are suited for different roles. When a role becomes sex specific, the demand characteristics of the role become linked with the sex of the person filling the role; the resultant sex-role appropriate behavior, in turn, strengthens the sex-role stereotype. The child's sex-role standards become more definite and more similar to those of an adult with increasing age, through a developmental process termed *sex-role identification*. There is much controversy over whether the term *identification* refers to observable behavior (the degree to which the child behaves like the parent), a motive (the degree to which the child has a disposition to behave like the parent), or the process by which the child acquires behaviors, traits, and attitudes which are similar to those of the parent (for a detailed review see Shepherd-Look, 1977).

Lynn (1959) has defined *sex-role preference* as "the desire to adopt the behavior associated with one sex or the other, or the perception of such behavior as preferable or more desirable" (p. 127). Preference is typically assessed by asking the child or the adult to choose among a set of masculine versus feminine stereotyped stimulus cues (frequently used materials are pictures, toys, activities, behaviors, traits, attitudes). Preference measures are often ambiguous since they confound an assessment of the actual self and the ideal self. *Sex-role orientation* is a measure which is quite similar to sex-role preference except that the former attempts to distinguish between traditional and nontraditional sex-related activities, roles, careers, or life styles. A career-oriented female or a nurturant male would be defined as nontraditional from a role orientation perspective. The underlying premise of both measures is that they are more predictive of actual behavior and judgments than is the individual's gender.

Sex-typed behavior is the degree to which a person has incorporated the behaviors, traits, and attitudes which are appropriate to his/her biological sex or the sex of assignment at birth. Sex typing is the process whereby an individual internalizes a sex-role standard or becomes sex typed, and as such, it is a term that can be used synonymously with sex-role identification. Masculinity and femininity are sex-specific subdivisions of the quantitative phenomenon *sex typed* (i.e., a measure of the number of items from a sex-role standard that an individual has incorporated). A highly masculine male and a highly feminine female are highly sex typed.

Cross-sex typed is used to refer to an individual who has incorporated a sex-role standard which is in the opposite direction from his/her biological sex (i.e., feminine males and masculine females). It is synonymous with the term *androgenized*. An androgenized male or female is cross-sex typed to one degree or another (the degree varies with the researcher). The above concepts are not the same as *androgeny*, a term developed by Bem (1974). Measures of sex typing or cross-sex typing (which includes measures of masculinity and femininity) elicit artificial bipolar characteristics because they have been treated as opposite poles of a single continuum. When masculinity and femininity are measured independently, they are found to be orthogonal (i.e., each dimension is present in varying degrees in both males and females) (Bem, 1974; Spence, Helmreich, & Stapp, 1975). *Androgeny* refers to the incorporation of both masculine and feminine traits within a single individual. Bem (1974, 1975) has found that androgenous individuals are less rigid, more adap-

tive, and more effective in situations which call for the characteristics of both sexes.

Researchers studying sex differences have taken a great deal of latitude in defining concepts. Thus it is not surprising to find weak or zero correlations among the various measures discussed. In addition there are serious problems in reliability and construct validity. Most promising for further research seem to be the distinction between sex and gender (Unger, 1979) and the measurement of sex roles as an orthogonal variable (Bem, 1974).

SEX-ROLE STANDARDS: CONSTANCIES AND VARIATIONS

There is considerable agreement both within and between cultures as to the appropriate sex-role behaviors for males and females. The male is oriented toward controlling and manipulating the environment and is expected to assume achievement-career and protector-provider roles. The female is oriented toward affiliative and nurturant interactions in the environment and is expected to assume domestic and maternal roles. The sex-role standard for males consists generally of being competent, independent, assertive, aggressive, dominant, and competitive in social and sexual relations. The female sex-role standard, on the other hand, is to be passive, affiliative, affectionate, nurturant, intuitive, and supportive, particularly in her familiar role as wife and mother. It is more appropriate for women than for men to express affection in interpersonal relationships, anxiety and/or fear under duress, and to suppress overt aggression and sexuality. Stein and Smithells (1969) have looked at sex-role standards regarding achievement in certain academic areas among children ranging in age from 7 to 19 years. Athletic, spatial, mechanical, and arithmetic skills were considered most masculine, while social, artistic, and reading skills were considered most feminine.

It is customary and fashionable to deplore sex-role stereotypes as archaic and constraining and to attribute them to the impersonal demands of "society." However the fact remains that society is composed of real individuals who continue to behave according to the expectations set forth in the aforementioned stereotypes. There is overwhelming evidence to indicate that sex-role differentiation begins very early in infancy through differential treatment of male and female infants by parents (Ban & Lewis, 1974; Moss, 1967; Rebelsky & Hanks, 1971; Will, Self, & Datan, 1976). Sex-appropriate toy preferences for both males and females are clear and distinct by the age of two (Etaugh, Collins, & Gerson, 1975; Fein, Johnson, Kosson, Stork, & Wasserman, 1975), and by the age of three, girls play about 90 percent of the time at "girlish" activities, and boys play at "boyish" activities 90 percent of the time. Hartley (1960) has found that by elementary school age the majority of both boys and girls have developed stereotypes about sex-appropriate interests, activities, behaviors, traits, and attitudes which closely approximate those of adults.

Cross-cultural studies also find these stereotyped roles widespread in the majority of societies outside the United States (Best, Williams, Cloud, Davis, Robertson, Edwards, Giles, & Fowles, 1977). Using ethnographic reports Barry, Bacon, and Child (1957) studied differential socialization practices for males and females in a number of mostly nonliterate cultures. Stereotypic socialization practices tended to be more restrictive than in the American culture and were associated with an economy which placed a high premium on superior strength and with customs that make for a large family group with high cooperative interaction. In Scandinavia (Haavio-Mannila, 1975; Safilios-Rothschild, 1971) and on the kibbutz (Gerson, 1971; Tiger & Shepher, 1975), societies which profess to hold egalitarian views of sex roles and where protagonists for equality have been vociferous, the traditional division of labor is still maintained. Societies which have made an ideological commitment to the abolition of sexual differentiation, such as the Soviet Union (Scott, 1974; Tikhomirov, Gordon, & Klopov, 1971) and the People's Republic of China (Tavris & Offir, 1977), are particularly interesting since there is considerable disparity between the ideology and the practice.

Amidst a great deal of similarity, there is some variation in culturally accepted sex-role standards within the United States. Sex-role standards tend to be more rigidly defined with less tolerance for deviation among males, the lower social classes, and the less educated. Hetherington (1974) has found that female students and college-educated women between the ages of 18 and 35 are more likely to perceive the feminine role as involving greater independence and achievement striving than do older or less educated females. In comparison to children whose mothers are unemployed, children of working mothers are more likely to regard female educational and professional aspirations and the assumption of housekeeping and childcare tasks by males as appropriate. Males, on the other hand, even young, educated males, maintain more rigid sex-role standards than do women. Fathers are also more likely than mothers to react to their children differentially according to sex and to demand sex-appropriate behavior from them (Fagot, 1974). In the lower (as opposed to the middle and upper) socioeconomic classes, different sex-role proscriptions for males and females appear in a wider variety of behaviors, interests, and attitudes; are learned at earlier ages; and are more rigidly defined (Pope, 1953; Rabban, 1950).

One of the most frequently cited reports of divergence among cultures in sex-role standards and behavior is Mead's (1935) study of three primitive tribes in New Guinea. In the Arapesh tribe both men and women exhibited "feminine" traits, both being passive, cooperative, gentle, and nonaggressive. The opposite behaviors were observed for the Mundugumor tribe, where both men and women were equally hostile, aggressive, and competitive. In the third tribe, the Tchambuli, sex roles were reversed, with the women holding decision-making roles and being independent and aggressive, while the men were socially sensitive, dependent, and engaged in arts and crafts. There are more consistencies than variations in sex-role standards both within and among cultures; however, there is enough variation to indicate a great deal of plasticity in the development of sex-appropriate behaviors. Considerable consistency is often misconstrued as prescriptive and taken to imply biological determinism. Evidence of variation, however, suggests that statements about causes should be interpreted more correctly as statements about probabilities.

SEX DIFFERENCES AND SEX SIMILARITIES

Cultural sex-role stereotypes have been examined. The issue in this section is whether or not these widely held stereotypes reflect actual differences in the behaviors of males and females. In order to find out which generalizations were justified and which were not, Maccoby and Jacklin (1974) compiled, reviewed, and interpreted over 2000 books and articles on sex differences in motivation, social behavior, and intellectual ability. The result of this exhaustive and oustanding work was a determination as to which beliefs about sex differences were supported by evidence, which beliefs had no support, and which beliefs were suggestive but inadequately tested at the present time. In examining these sex differences it is critical to keep in mind that there is considerable overlap in the characteristics of males and females in all of the areas discussed. Some males appear in the upper quartile on measures of "feminine" characteristics, while some females appear in the upper quartile on "masculine" characteristics (see also Wolman & Money, 1980).

Methodological Problems

Before launching into the data on sex differences, several common methodological problems should be discussed since they present some distinct limitations on what can be learned from the published body of research. One of the most basic problems in this area is that it is almost impossible for observers and experimenters to be blind to the sex of the subjects; thus, the research is almost inevitably biased to some extent. There are several instances in which a commonly believed sex difference is confirmed when ratings are used but is not confirmed when simple frequency counts of specific categories of behavior are tallied in the course of direct observation. Since sex is such a powerful stimulus variable, random assignment by sex is probably meaningless. Bias is evident in still another way. There are certain restricted aspects of behavior that have been extensively studied, while other broad areas have received minimal research attention. The problem is particularly evident in areas where the rate of occurrence for a particular behavior is thought to be nearly zero for one sex. Until recently there have been few studies on phenomena such as cyclical variations in males or aggressive criminal acts committed by females such as spouse abuse or rape.

In the majority of research on sex differences, sample selection has been limited to work done with white, middle-class, American children and adults, studied in nursery schools, public schools, or colleges. Most of the subjects have been volunteers which tends to confound an individual's interest in a particular topic with his/her ability. Research on sex differences in mathematical ability may be confounded with a subject's interest if coursetaking is not similar for males and females. Sample selection often compares a heterogeneous sample of one sex with a homogeneous sample of the other sex. A sample of high school students may contain a heterogenous group of females but a homogeneous group of males, since males are more likely to drop out of school. If males and females differ in variability, the usual statistical comparisons of average performance are invalid and must be corrected for unequal variance. This is seldom done.

Sample selection in research on sex differences is further complicated by differences in physical maturation rates between males and females. Thus one cannot compare males and females of the same age. In a few instances sex differences are shown to be a transitional phenomenon. At an early point of measurement, the sexes are similar; at intermediate points, the sexes diverge showing significant differences, after which they closely resemble each other. This pattern generally reflects differences in maturational rates or differences in the process by which the phenomenon is acquired, rather than true sex differences. In cross-sectional designs, selection of subjects on the basis of cohort membership (persons sharing the same birth year) is frequently confounded with cultural changes.

Sex is frequently used as a subject variable, and individuals are randomly assigned to groups. However, many researchers have pointed out that sex can (and probably almost always does) function as a stimulus variable in a situation as well as a subject variable (Maccoby, 1976; Unger, 1979; Wittig, 1979). Thus the assignment of subjects to groups by sex is no more meaningful for purposes of understanding behavior than assigning them at random. The use of sex as an independent variable does not justify concluding that variation in behavior associated with sex has been caused by it. The researcher must randomly assign individuals to interact with one or another stimulus person, such that sex as a stimulus variable can be varied systematically, thus allowing cause-effect conclusions. Even in this case the results may be due to a sex bias on the part of the respondent rather than to any quality inherent in the sex of the stimulus person.

There have been serious problems with comparing measures and methods between studies and across different developmental ages. The construct spatial ability has been defined in a variety of ways (ability to rotate a two-dimensional object in three-dimensional space, auditory spatial location, haptic pattern tracing, body steadiness, perceptual disembedding, and perceptual restructuring, to name a few) and has been measured by an even greater variety of methods (mazes, form boards, block counting, the Differential Aptitudes Space Relations Test (DAT), the Primary Mental Abilities Space Test (PMA), the WISC Block Design, the Embedded Figures Test (EFT), the Rod and Frame Test (RFT), and the Body Adjustment Test (BAT). Spatial ability has even been used synonymously with analytic cognitive style. One has to pay close attention to the way in which a construct is defined and the way in which it is actually measured. There is a great need for reliable and valid measures.

The Wechsler block design is a good example of how the same test can measure qualitatively different cognitive abilities in children at different ages. On the preschool level many of the block design items are already represented in a block-by-block fashion, while those at the adolescent level require the subject to break the design down into its block-by-block components. In the children's version the set-breaking and figure-ground aspects of the test are minimized, requiring much more analytic and part orientation. If females are more field de-

pendent, the test would favor them at the preschool level but would favor males at the adolescent level. Thus an apparent reversal of a sex-related difference in cognitive style may actually reflect a change in the nature of the task demands as complexity increases. There are many other measures which lack comparability across ages.

In their review of the literature on sex differences, Maccoby and Jacklin (1974) have encountered several peculiarities in the interpretation of data. In studies using only male subjects, a within-sex correlation is sometimes interpreted as demonstrating a between-sex difference. For example a positive correlation between testosterone levels and activity rate in males may be reported as evidence that boys have been found to have higher activity rates than girls, even though girls were not studied. In other instances the correlation for one sex may be significantly different from zero, but the correlation for the other sex is not. The results are then interpreted as if there were a significant difference between the correlations. Sometimes different patterns of findings within each sex will be mistaken as sex differences. In a study of preschool children, it was found that verbal aggression was more frequent than physical aggression in girls while the reverse was true for boys (Sears, Rau, & Alpert, 1965). The findings were later quoted as showing that girls were higher than boys in verbal aggression when, in fact, boys showed more of both kinds of aggression than girls.

Lastly there is the question of significance when a large body of data is compiled. What magical number should be chosen to determine what percentage of studies which show positive results is needed to demonstrate that a sex difference exists? Should the research in this area be weighted according to some criterion: quality or sample size or magnitude of difference? When is a sex-related difference a real difference? Large samples can show statistically significant differences at the .001 level, when the absolute difference is quite small relative to the distribution of scores. Maccoby and Jacklin (1974) got around most of these issues by reporting all studies from January 1966 to Spring 1973. They listed a study as showing a sex difference if the statistical test yielded a probability (p) value of .05 or less; the difference was listed as a trend if the p value was between .05 and .10; otherwise, it was listed as no difference.

Biological Differences

Physical Variations. There are several physiological differences apparent at birth and thereafter that interact with the way males and females think, feel, and behave (Wesley & Wesley, 1977). Females mature between 2 and 2½ years faster than males. At birth their skeletal development is four weeks in advance of boys and at adolescence, three years in advance. Height remains equal for both sexes until age 7, when girls become taller than boys; at age 10, boys become taller than girls. By adulthood there is a 6 percent difference in height and a 20 percent difference in weight in favor of males. At puberty, males begin to show an increase in blood pressure, while a higher pulse rate (2 to 6 beats per minute) develops in females. The male blood has about 300,000 more red corpuscles per cubic millimeter; during adolescence the bood pressure after exercise for males begins to increase, while in females it decreases. During puberty, males develop a 20 percent higher metabolic rate and require more food. They produce more physical energy, have slower rates of muscle fatigue, and faster recuperation times. From age 13, their recommended daily allowances for energy and protein are about 25 percent more than for females, except during pregnancy and lactation.

Male Vulnerability. From conception through senescence, males are more vulnerable to most every type of physical disease, developmental difficulty, and environmental insult. Approximately 140 males are conceived for every 100 females, but by the end of the prenatal period, there is a great loss in male concepti as the birth ratio is 105 males to 100 females (Reinisch, Gandelman, & Spiegel, 1979). About 78 percent of the stillborn fetuses delivered before the fourth month are male (Bentzen, 1963). By the end of childhood the ratio of surviving males to females has dropped to one. In general males are more vulnerable to many childhood diseases. Stott (1966) reported that pneumonia occurred significantly more often in males than in females and that eight times as many boys die of the disease. With respect to environmental trauma males are more vulnerable to malnutrition (Stott, 1966). Bayley (1966) has reviewed studies of the effects of the atomic bombing of Hiroshima and Nagasaki and found that boys were more frequently affected than girls in terms of growth retardation and duration of ill effects.

During the elementary school years boys are overrepresented among children who have speech, learning, and behavior disorders. In surveys of speech disorders about twice as many boys as girls show articulatory errors, while stuttering occurs in three times as many boys as girls (Bentzen, 1963). The incidence of reading problems is three to five times more prevalent in boys than girls (Knopf, 1979). Mental deficiency is also higher among males than females: 1.3 to 1 for mild retardation and 2 to 1 for severe retardation (Jensen, 1971). The ratio of boys to girls who are referred for emotional and/or behavior problems is 2 to 1 (Bentzen, 1963). There are more males than females among children who have night terrors, enuresis, hyperactivity, and autism (Knopf, 1979). During adolescence males have a higher rate of schizophrenia, delinquency, academic underachievement, and suicide than females (Weiner, 1970). Until adulthood it is difficult to find a pathological condition in which the incidence among females is higher than among males.

Intellect and Achievement[1]

Verbal Ability. There are probably three distinct phases in the development of verbal skills. In the very early period, before the age of three, recent work has contradicted earlier research in that no sex differences have been found on age of beginning to speak, age of first combining words into sentences, mean length of utterance, or picture vocabulary. After the initial establishment of speech until puberty (ages 3 to 11), research

[1] Unless otherwise noted, the remainder of this section will be based on the work of Maccoby and Jacklin (1974), to date one of the most significant contributions to the field of sex differences.

tends to show that the two sexes perform quite similarly. Differences in favor of girls tend to occur only in underprivileged populations. During early adolescence female superiority on both receptive and productive language begins to emerge and continues to increase through high school and beyond. Girls score higher on both "high level" verbal tasks (comprehension of difficult written material, quick understanding of complex logical relations, verbal creativity) as well as on "lower level" verbal fluency measures (spelling, grammar, punctuation, talkativeness). The magnitude of the difference ranges from .1 to nearly .5 of a standard deviation (SD), averaging about .25 of an SD.

Visual Spatial Ability. Spatial ability has been measured in a great variety of ways and is, therefore, a difficult concept to define. The majority of measures, however, can be placed at either end of two separate continuums: one being visual versus nonvisual spatial ability and the other being analytic versus nonanalytic spatial ability. Nonanalytic spatial ability has been measured using visual stimuli (mazes; form boards; mental rotations of two-dimensional objects in three-dimensional space in a matching task or in a puzzle-type task; estimating the number of blocks in a two-dimensional array, which represents a three-dimensional array from a different perspective; determining what motion in one part of a system of gears would be produced by a given motion in another part of the system); auditory stimuli (auditory localization); and tactual stimuli (tactual recognition of objects as they change orientation in space). In the very few studies that deal with nonvisual, nonanalytic spatial skills, no sex differences have been found. However in visual spatial abilities measured by tasks that do not call for analytic processes, male superiority on this factor has been found to appear in adolescence and to increase through the high school years, at which time male scores exceed those of females by at least .40 standard score units. Until the age of 8, there are no sex differences. From ages 8 to 11, the findings are inconsistent; a few studies show male superiority, most do not.

Visual spatial abilities thought to reflect an analytic component have been measured primarily by the Embedded Figures Test (EFT) and the Rod and Frame Test (RFT). These tests are analytic only in the narrowly defined sense that they require the subject to separate an element from its background, ignoring the latter. Both the EFT and the RFT have been shown to load heavily on a spatial factor when they are included in batteries containing other visual spatial tests (Gardner, Jackson, & Messick, 1960; Goodenough & Karp, 1961). Maccoby and Jacklin have found that analytic visual spatial tasks that involve disembedding (EFT, RFT, and modified children's versions, the CEFT and PEFT) and those that do not, have a similar developmental course—i.e., no sex differences in early childhood, inconsistent findings between the ages 8 to 11, and consistent male superiority from adolescence through adulthood. The marked similarity in developmental trends suggests that the disembedding process does not contribute anything to the sex differences beyond what would be produced by the visual spatial component of the EFT or the RFT. In the small number of studies which involve disembedding in nonvisual modalities (tactual block design, EFT, and matchstick problems; and selective listening in which a subject is asked to listen to one voice and ignore another) no sex differences have been found. Although data are sparse they are supportive of a position taken by Sherman (1967) that the poorer performance of females on analytic visual spatial tasks may simply be a result of their lesser visual spatial ability and have nothing to do with disembedding (or poor analytic abilities).

Quantitative Ability. Except in disadvantaged populations (where girls are superior to boys), the two sexes are similar in their early acquisition of quantitative concepts and their mastery of arithmetic. Between the ages of 9 and 13, the majority of studies show no differences, but when differences are found, they favor males. After this age mathematical skills for males tend to increase faster than for females, although there is great variation in the degree of male advantage reported. Since the publication of the Maccoby and Jacklin review, there has been mounting evidence that male superiority in mathematics may be a function of interest and training effects since males take more math courses (for an excellent review see Fox, Tobin, & Brody, 1979). In addition factor analytic studies of mathematical ability tests indicate that a space factor emerges for males but not for females. Other studies show that sex differences disappear on verbal items and/or when verbal strategies are employed to solve problems but not when spatial items and/or spatial strategies are used (Fox et al., 1979). It is interesting that male superiority in science directly parallels the findings for sex differences in mathematics—i.e., the presence of training effects and the presence of verbal and spatial factors. Further research may find that sex differences in mathematics and science can be attributed to training effects or can be reduced to a visual spatial factor.

Analytic Abilities. The myth that males have a more analytic cognitive style than females is due in large part to an overgeneralization of the sex differences found on measures of field independence-dependence such as the EFT and the RFT. It has already been shown that this difference is most likely due to female inferiority on visual spatial tasks. Nonvisual measures of disembedding frequently involve some aspect of set-breaking or restructuring which is an important dimension of problem-solving ability. Set-breaking and/or restructuring requires the subject to inhibit a dominant (or initially probable) response in order to explore other solutions. There are no significant sex differences on either of the following tasks which measure these abilities: (1) The Stroop Color Word Test (the subject is given a series of color names printed in the wrong color ink; the subject must respond to the color of the ink suppressing a strongly established dominant response to read the printed word); (2) the Matching Familiar Figures Test, a measure of reflectivity-impulsivity (the subject must select a match for a standard figure from a series of similar figures only one of which does not differ in small details from the standard). Male superiority has been found on some types of restructuring tasks (the Luchens jar problems and the Dunker two-string problem) but not on others (anagrams). Thus data on perceptual restructuring or set-breaking does not generalize across tasks.

The term *analytic style* has also been applied to the way a subject groups objects: *relational* (putting objects together that have a functional relationship), *inferential* (putting objects together that belong to the same more inclusive class), and *descriptive-analytic* (putting objects together that are similar with respect to some detail). The latter is considered more analytic because it involves responding to a part of an object rather than the whole and ignoring irrelevant attributes. No sex differences have been found in children ranging in age from 3 to 16 years. Additionally the vast majority of studies show no sex differences on Piagetian tasks such as conservation, concept information, or tests of formal operations (which involve both inductive and deductive reasoning). Commonly used tests of creativity which require the generation of a variety of hypotheses and the production of unique ideas show no sex differences if the methods are nonverbal. Girls show superiority on verbal measures, a reflection of the already documented sex difference on verbal abilities.

Variability. There is evidence for greater variability (more high scorers and more low scorers) among males in mathematical and spatial abilities, but the evidence for verbal abilities is inconsistent. Greater variability at the low end of the distribution is probably due to greater male vulnerability to disease and developmental deviation. In the verbal domain for females, the distribution is simply displaced upward; it is not accompanied by larger standard deviations—i.e., there are more high scorers and fewer lower scorers among females.

Perceptual Sensitivity. The research base with regard to the chemical senses of taste and smell is quite small. There is a trend toward females being both more sensitive and more variable in their responses to taste and smell cues. Data on touch sensitivity and pain thresholds are likewise equivocal. Most studies show no sex differences, but those that do favor greater female sensitivity. Pain tolerance, a different measure than sensitivity to pain, has shown that males are able to tolerate more pain than females. Newborns and children of school age are very similar in the speed and duration of their responses to a variety of auditory and visual cues. Both boys and girls prefer social to nonsocial visual and auditory stimuli. Hence there is no support for the suggestion that females more than males prefer either auditory to visual or social to nonsocial cues. However there do appear to be individual differences in the competent use of information in visual versus auditory stimulus patterns, and these have been related to superiority in arithmetic and reading respectively. As Maccoby and Jacklin conclude, "Hence we do not see differences in sensitivity to these two kinds of stimulation as being the foundation of any sex differences in language acquisition or in processing of visual-spatial materials" (p. 61). With regard to perceptual motor abilities, girls have better finger dexterity (fine motor movements), but there are no sex differences in manual dexterity (large motor movements).

Learning and Memory. There are no sex differences in a wide variety of learning processes: conditioning, paired-associates learning, discrimination learning with either reversal or nonreversal shifts, learning incidental information or inhibiting attention to it when necessary, probability learning, learning through imitation. Likewise neither sex has a superior memory capacity or superior skills in the storage or retrieval of information. There are no differences in *how* the sexes learn or remember; however, *what* they choose to learn and respond to in the environment is a different matter, as indicated by sex differences in interests and curriculum choices.

Achievement Motivation and Self-Concept. If achievement motivation is assessed by academic accomplishments such as grades, females would certainly have greater needs for achievement than males since they get better grades.

When need for achievement is measured projectively with male pictures, females in high school and college show a high level of achievement whether given an "arousal" treatment or not; men show a high level only when aroused by reference to assessment of their intelligence and leadership ability [or competitive conditions]. There may be a clue here to boys' lower grades in school—it appears it takes stronger efforts to motivate them. But the results certainly do not indicate a generally low level of achievement motivation in girls, or that they are motivated only by appeals to their social acceptability. (p. 138)

Neither do females show less task persistence or curiosity than males. There is indication, however, that females have more conflict about succeeding and take less risks.

The research on self-concept indicates that when males and females rate themselves on a series of characteristics, they have equally positive self-images on the whole, at least through the college years. Males, however, expect to do well more often and rate their performance on a task more favorably than do females. In addition males attempt to present themselves more favorably, brag more about their accomplishments, are more defensive about their actual performances, and take in less negative feedback than females, while females are more willing than males to disclose their weaknesses. Males are also more apt to defend their egos by turning against an external frustrating object; females, on the other hand, engage in more self-blame. While females blame themselves for failure, they are more likely than males to attribute success to external factors rather than skill or persistence. This sex difference appears in college but not before; however, during middle childhood, males clearly see themselves as higher on strength, dominance, and power than females see themselves.

Temperament and Social Behavior

Activity Level. During infancy males spend more time awake. However other measures of activity during this age are not correlated with each other, lack reliability, and in general are not predictive of future behavior; they also fail to show sex differences. During the preschool years there is evidence that boys are more active when other boys are around, but this is not true for females playing with other females. Increased activity levels of boys in same-sex peer groups may be the reason that sex differences in activity levels begin to favor males at about the age of two when social play begins. The tendency to

show emotional reactions to frustrations is similar for the two sexes before the age of 18 months; afterward, females show a faster decrease than males in the frequency and intensity of their emotional reactions.

Fear and Anxiety. When direct observations to fearful stimuli have been measured, there are no sex differences in fearful reactions. However, teacher ratings and self-report measures show girls to be more fearful than boys. Females also score higher than males on self-report measures of general anxiety but not on test anxiety where the finding is no sex difference.

Dependency. In preschool-age children there are no sex differences in observational data on proximity, touching, or resistance to separation in relation to the mother or other adults. Neither sex is more likely to choose to be with others rather than alone during stressful situations. Boys are more gregarious than girls in that they play in larger groups, yet there is no evidence to support that the greater exclusiveness of female friendship patterns implies greater hostility to newcomers or greater self-disclosure. There is somewhat limited evidence that males rather than females are more susceptible to peer influence according to self-reports and ratings by other children. No sex differences have been found to indicate greater sensitivity or responsiveness to social cues by females rather than males. Empathic behavior seems to depend more on familiarity with a situation than on sex of the observer. Thus children are more empathic toward other children versus adults and with same-sex peers versus opposite-sex peers.

Nurturance and Altruism. There are very few studies concerning nurturant behavior in children, and there is very little information on the responses of adult men to infants and children. Among American children no sex differences have been observed in play situations, but then there are few opportunities to elicit such behavior as playgroups tend to be composed of children of the same age. Studies of altruistic behavior show no overall sex differences; a person's willingness to help another depends on the person needing help and the kind of help needed.

Aggression. For the present review *aggression* is defined as the intent of one individual to hurt another, either for its own sake or for the desire to control another person. Males are more aggressive than females in a wide variety of situations, using a wide variety of behavioral indexes, in a wide variety of cultures. There have been a number of suggestions in previous research that the two sexes are equally aggressive in their underlying motivations, but that the two sexes demonstrate their aggression in different ways. This position has not been supported by evidence; boys are more aggressive than girls both physically and verbally. The hypothesis that female aggressive impulses are more frequently expressed in displaced, attenuated, or disguised form (due to greater anxieties or inhibitions against displaying aggression) has also not been supported. Males show the displaced and attenuated forms of aggression such as mock fighting or aggressive fantasies more frequently than females. The sex differences in aggression are found with the emergence of social play at about the age of two and continue through the college years (Wolman, 1978).

Competition and Cooperation. Much of the work on competition and cooperation with children has used the *Madsen "marble pull" game.* The game involves a two-piece marble holder which will slide back and forth across a table. Two children, standing on either side of a table, control the marble by pulling strings attached to each side of the holder. If both players pull at once the marble holder splits apart, and the marble drops into a trough and is not won by either player. However if one child pulls the marble holder and the other child releases his/her string, the marble holder can be pulled to one or the other side of the table and is won by that player. The objective of the game is for both players to get as many marbles as possible. In this situation the boy-boy pairs were most competitive, obtaining the fewest marbles. The girl-girl pairs were most cooperative and quickly developed a strategy of taking turns. The mixed-sex pairs were in the middle of the distribution; girls became more competitive, and boys became more cooperative. Other studies reporting cooperative and competitive behavior among children of various ages show inconsistent results. About half of the studies find no sex differences; among those that do, boys are more competitive than girls. The *"prisoner's dilemma" game* is the adult version of the marble game. The studies using this paradigm are remarkably consistent in finding no sex differences. As Maccoby and Jacklin point out, research on competition has almost always involved situations in which competition is maladaptive. Any conclusion at the current time is premature, but it seems clear that the age of the subject and the sex of the opponent are important variables.

Dominance. *Dominance* is defined as a successful effort by one person to control or manipulate the behavior of another. Dominance is a complex phenomenon since it can be manifested directly or indirectly and can serve many motives: to satisfy needs of the ego, as an instrument to achieve one's goals, to assume leadership to organize a group to strive cooperatively for a mutually rewarding goal, counterdominance—a refusal to be controlled, to humiliate another. Thus it is not surprising to find that dominance is quite situation specific, particularly as age increases. Most research relevant to dominance relations has been of leadership in small, adult, same-sex groups. When a group is first formed, leadership tends to go to males with pre-existing status indicators such as education, occupation, and age. With increased acquaintance, influence processes are more equal, and expertise in areas related to the group's objective is an important leadership factor. In analyses of dominance patterns among married couples, the power structure shows great variability, with dominance varying according to task domain and changing with time.

In children's playgroups dominance appears to be associated with "toughness" for both males and females, such that tough boys dominate other boys and dominate girls. Boys make more attempts at dominance in same-sex groups than girls do in same-sex groups, but boys also congregate in larger groups than girls. Boys also make more attempts to dominate adults than girls do. In cross-cultural data there is evidence of sex differences in dominance motivation: Boys show more egotistic dominance, while girls show more attempts to control another

child's behavior in the interest of safety or some social value.

Compliance, Submission, Suggestibility. Young girls (preschool age or younger) tend to comply sooner and more frequently than boys to the requests and demands of adults. However girls are not any more compliant than boys to pressure from age-mates who attempt to dominate them, nor do girls show more spontaneous imitation than boys. In studies of persuasive communication females do not change their mind more often than males, nor do they yield more to group pressure in the Asch-type experiments. Maccoby and Jacklin conclude,

Considering the findings on dominance and compliance jointly, the conclusion seems to be that boys are more dominant than girls, in the sense that they more frequently attempt to dominate others, but their dominance attempts are primarily directed toward one another. Girls are more compliant, but primarily toward adults. It is possible that girls form a coalition with the more dominant adults as a means of coping with the greater aggressiveness of boys, whose dominance they do not accept. (p. 273)

Stability of Sex Typing. The longitudinal Fels Institute Study (Kagan & Moss, 1962) found that sex-typed behavior and interests in preschool children were remarkably predictive of adult behavior when the early behaviors were congruent with culturally accepted sex-role standards. For example childhood sexuality and aggression were predictive of adult sexuality and anger arousal in males but not in females; whereas childhood passivity and dependency were predictive of these adult behaviors in females but not in males. When characteristics conflicted with sex-role standards, some form of more socially acceptable or derivative behavior was substituted in adulthood, such that anger and tantrums in girls were associated with intellectual competitiveness in adult women and passivity in boys was related to social apprehension and noncompetitiveness. Earlier sex typing and greater stability were demonstrated more frequently for boys than girls.

Evaluation. Maccoby and Jacklin summarized their findings by indicating (1) which of the sex differences they considered to be fairly well established: verbal ability, visual spatial ability, quantitative ability, and aggression; (2) which were still open questions based on the lack of sufficient research: tactual sensitivity, activity level, fear, timidity and anxiety, competitiveness, dominance, compliance, and nurturance; and (3) which were unfounded: that girls are more affected by heredity, boys by environment; that girls are more auditory, boys more visual; that girls are better at rote learning and repetitive tasks, boys at analytic ability; that girls are more social and suggestible than boys; and that girls have lower self-esteem than boys and lack achievement motivation. Block (1978) has criticized Maccoby and Jacklin for being too stringent in their compilation of the data. She believes that there are really more areas of differences between the sexes than Maccoby and Jacklin indicate. If this is so, the differences will most likely emerge in the areas that Maccoby and Jacklin refer to as open questions—i.e., the well-established differences and the unfounded beliefs appear to be well documented. It is also probably true that the emergence of sex differences will depend on the specific details of a situation which may change the way it is perceived by males and females—details which have not yet been experimentally manipulated.

FACTORS WHICH INFLUENCE SEX DIFFERENTIATION AND THE DEVELOPMENT OF SEX ROLES

Cognitive and behavioral differences between the sexes that develop during childhood are a result of the interaction among biological, cognitive, and social factors. The traditional view in psychology has been to emphasize the effect of sex-role assignment. The process of differentiation is attributed to the powerful socialization pressures of the family and society through differential reinforcement and the process of identification with the same-sex parent. The most recent developments in the area of sex differences have been a challenging and a rethinking of some of these traditional assumptions. There has been a renewed interest and also a flurry of research activity attempting to determine the ontogeny of the biological mechanisms which underlie sex differences and their interaction with the social environment. Most of the interest in the influence of biological factors on sex differences has centered on three areas: genetic sex linkage, cerebral lateralization, and the effects of hormones. Wittig and Petersen (1979) have edited an excellent and comprehensive source book which reviews the influence of biological factors on cognitive development.

Wittig (1979) clearly points out that studying the biological bases of behavior does not have to get researchers hopelessly entangled in the nature-nurture controversy. There is little evidence to suggest that any biological characteristics act directly on psychological functioning, nor do they operate in a vacuum. The biological system is an open one in which biological state and behavior interact, each in a reciprocal influence relationship with the other. Further the organism develops through a sequence of changes in both structure and function in the direction of greater differentiation and more complex levels of organization such that the definition of environment is different at different stages of development. The question, then, is not one of heredity versus environment, but rather one of explaining the process by which biological characteristics influence behavior.

Biological Factors

X-Linkage Hypothesis. Patterns of transmission of single gene[2] phenotypes depend upon two factors: (1) whether the gene responsible is on an autosome (22 pairs which are alike in males and females) or on the X chromosome[3] (Thompson & Thompson, 1980); (2) whether it

is dominant—i.e., expressed even when present on only one chromosome of a pair—or recessive—i.e., only expressed when present on both chromosomes. Thus there are only four basic patterns: autosomal-dominant, autosomal-recessive, X-linked dominant, and X-linked recessive.

Several recent studies have investigated by observing within family correlations the possibility that a recessive gene on the X chromosome enhances performance on tasks requiring spatial visualization. From the female XX and the male XY combinations, the X-linkage theory predicts that fathers and sons should show a zero correlation on spatial ability since the son does not inherit a Y chromosome from his father. Father-daughter correlations should be higher (.58) than father-son correlations (0) since the daughter inherits one X chromosome from her father. Father-daughter correlations should be higher than mother-daughter correlations (.33) because the father's X-linked trait will always be given to the daughter, while the mother's X-linked trait will only be given to half her daughters since she has two X chromosomes of which only one is transmitted to her offspring.

Vandenberg and Kuse (1979) have carefully reviewed data from five separate studies comparing sample size, populations sampled, test instruments, and methods used to correct for age effects. They conclude that none of the measures displays the unique pattern of correlations effected by a gene on the X chromosome. These reviews conclude that the measures of spatial ability employed in each study were quite comparable and valid measures of spatial ability. No other systematic differences could be found to account for the conflicting sets of patterns of results found in the studies. It appears that the most recent evidence available seriously questions the X-linkage hypothesis for differences between males and females in spatial ability.

Support for an X-linkage hypothesis has been further weakened by investigations of phenotypic females with Turner's syndrome, a condition in which only one sex chromosome is genetically present (XO). If spatial ability is X-linked, Turner's syndrome cases should display the same kind of spatial skills as normal males, since the X chromosome complement is the same in both groups. Polani, Lessof, and Bishop (1956) did not find that spatial ability in Turner's syndrome cases was similar to males and greater than in normal females.

Vandenberg and Kuse (1979) have criticized the traditional genetic linkage analyses because researchers use only dichotomous variables such as the two marker genes, each of which has two alleles. They suggest that the only method which will ultimately prove or disprove the sex-linkage hypothesis is a modified-linkage analysis. This analysis compares the correlations between scores on spatial ability tests of subjects having the same allele at a specific marker locus for markers known to be located on the X chromosome such as the $Xg(a)$ blood group and red-green color blindness with the correlations between subjects having different markers. If linkage were present the first group of subjects would have a significantly higher correlation on measures of spatial abil-

---

[2] Many genetic traits are determined by genes at a single locus on a chromosome. There are 2786 such conditions, among the estimated 30,000 human structural genes. Of the total, 1473 are autosomal dominant, 1108 are autosomal recessive, and 205 (or about 7 percent) are X-linked (McKusick, 1978).
[3] Sex-linked genes may be either X-linked or Y-linked, but for all practical purposes only X-linkage has any significance, since apart from male sex determination, the Y chromosome appears to have few loci at which segregation has been recognized. Thus the

terms *sex-linkage* and *X-linkage* may be used synonymously, since the distribution of X-linked traits follows the course of the X chromosome.

ity than the second group of subjects. Goodenough, Gandini, Olkin, Pizzamiglio, Thayer, and Witkin (1977) administered a battery of seven spatial ability tests and measured two genetic markers known to be located on the X chromosome, the $Xg(a)$ blood group and red-green color blindness, among 67 Italian families with three sons. Results showed a possible linkage with the $Xg(a)$ marker and the Rod and Frame Test and the Embedded Figures Test. Negative results were obtained for all other tests. Since the sample size was small and a large number of correlations were used, the results of this study cannot be taken as significant support for an X-linkage hypothesis. The significance of this study is not in the results but in the methodology employed. If conclusive data on the X-linked hypothesis is to be forthcoming, a modified-linkage analysis such as the one used in this study has promise.

Cerebral Specialization. The existence of a relationship between cognitive functions and hemispheric specialization was recognized over a century ago by Broca (1865) in his work with aphasics who had suffered unilateral brain lesions. More recent work by Sperry (1974) on the performance of patients who have had interhemispheric connections surgically severed has confirmed Broca's finding of hemispheric specialization and has led to an increased realization that behavior is at least partially determined by the way in which the two cerebral hemispheres are organized. *Hemispheric specialization* indicates that one hemisphere or a particular area within the hemisphere is specialized for a certain kind of processing once the stimulation has reached the cortical level. Hemispheric specialization can be inferred with certainty only by observing performance deficits in patients with localized brain damage or by the use of certain clinical techniques such as the chemical anesthetization of one cerebral hemisphere with concomitant monitoring of behavior. *Hemispheric lateralization* is a term which refers to the tendency to process perceptual stimuli on one side more effectively than on the other side. The tendency to lateralize is thought to depend on hemispheric specialization.

Any physical stimulus can be perceived bilaterally by normal individuals, yet one side may perceive it more rapidly and/or more accurately than the other side. Cerebral asymmetries have been assessed in a variety of ways by investigators of individual differences. Left- versus right-sided superiorities have been measured in manual, auditory, visual, tactual, and cortical activity (EEG). Lateralization paradigms usually involve unilateral presentation of a single stimulus (tapping with a stylus, words presented auditorily through earphones to one ear, shape identification presented in either the right or left visual hemifield, sensitivity to pressure) or bilateral presentation of two different competing stimuli. Which side is favored can depend on the nature of the stimulus presented, the type of processing required by the task, or the handedness of the subject. For most subjects the pattern of errors is nonrandom. A right-side advantage indicates a left-hemispheric processing advantage—since information travels first to the contralateral hemisphere before crossing the cerebral commissures, the cortical avenues of interhemispheric communication. Bilateral presentations are thought to induce competition between hemi-

spheres so that the hemisphere most suited to the processing of a particular kind of information will have an advantage. This advantage will result in superior accuracy in reporting information presented to the contralateral side. Investigators such as Bryden (1979) and Waber (1979) point out that hemispheric specialization can only be inferred from these lateralization paradigms since most of these investigations have not controlled for differential effects of memory, deployment of attention, or problem-solving strategies. All of these factors lead to shifts in performance that may have nothing to do with cerebral asymmetry.

Functional lateralization has been found in normal right-handed subjects for verbal material, spatial ability, and styles of processing over a wide range of methods of presentation—auditory, visual, and tactual.[4] The left hemisphere has been found to process items one at a time, to be analytic in style, and to be the locus for speech and verbal activities. The right hemisphere, on the other hand, is more wholistic in style, processing items simultaneously, and is the locus for spatial activities. As an example, in dichotic-listening experiments subjects are able to report a greater number of items more accurately using the right ear (REA) when the presentation consists of lists of numbers, pairs of words, or consonant-vowel (CV) pairs (Kimura, 1961a, 1961b; Lake & Bryden, 1976; McGlone & Davidson, 1978). A left-ear advantage (LEA) is reported for nonverbal stimuli such as musical chords, environmental noises, human emotional sounds, and animal sounds (Carmon & Nachson, 1973; Curry, 1967; Gordon, 1970; Kimura, 1964).

In view of the recent widespread interest among researchers in demonstrating the functional organization of the brain as a mediator of particular abilities, the data on sex differences in this area are disappointing. There are few researchers who report sex differences in their data and fewer yet who systematically use sex as a variable. In studies employing the dichotic-listening paradigm using verbal material, it has been found that males are more lateralized than females. Lake and Bryden (1976) found males were more likely than females to show a right-ear advantage (30 out of 32 males showed an REA, while for females, 22 demonstrated an REA and 11 showed an LEA). Where an REA exists for both sexes, a higher percentage of males demonstrate an REA, and this advantage is also larger than for females. At present there do not appear to be any studies which report sex-related differences for nonverbal dichotic material.

In contrast to the dichotic-listening literature, most of the visual studies use nonverbal stimuli. Bryden (1979) combined data from a series of studies using a unilateral presentation where items were presented randomly in the left visual field (LVF) or the right visual field (RVF). The combined data showed that 65 percent of the males as opposed to 57 percent of the females demonstrated an LVF superiority in dot localization. Though these results were not statistically significant, the evidence is consistent with the auditory material in suggesting that males are more lateralized than females. It should be noted

[4] There is considerable disagreement as to whether left-handed subjects are similar to right-handed subjects in cerebral organization or whether they have mirror imaged representations with verbal abilities on the right side and spatial abilities on the left side.

that results for the nonverbal spatial material do not show as strong a lateralization effect in males as results using verbal material.

Lateralization effects are thought to be indicative of differential cerebral specialization between the sexes which in turn mediates differences in cognitive abilities. Greater degrees of lateralization among males have led some theorists to postulate that a high degree of specialization in the cerebral hemispheres fosters visual spatial abilities. Levy (1969) has argued that verbal and spatial functions are incompatible processes and that hemispheric specialization has evolved to reduce competition and keep them separate. In less lateralized females the right and left hemispheres might share responsibility for certain highly lateralized cognitive functions that in more lateralized subjects were controlled by either the left (verbal) or the right (spatial) hemisphere. For example bilateral representation of speech would intrude on the normally spatial right hemisphere causing competition within that hemisphere between the linguistic functions and the spatial functions usually controlled by that hemisphere. Thus females would show a superiority in linguistic abilities and a deficit in spatial abilities.

There have been several viewpoints as to what extent the functional differences in cerebral organization are the result of maturational factors and to what extent they are genetically determined and present at birth. Lenneberg (1967) has argued that hemispheric specialization develops gradually through childhood and specific functions such as speech are not fully lateralized until puberty. The fact that many of the cognitive ability differences found in adults do not appear reliably and consistently until puberty seems to support this view. On the other hand several authors have taken the view that the cerebral hemispheres become more specialized with age. Anatomical differences in the size of the temporal planum (Witelson & Paille, 1973) and asymmetries in evoked potentials (Molfese, 1976) have been found in infancy. If hemispheric specialization is present from birth, males of all ages should show greater degees of lateralization in both verbal auditory and visual spatial perception. However if the cerebral hemispheres gradually become specialized, the perceptual studies should reflect these changes by corresponding increments in lateralization effects.

As with adults the majority of studies with children have employed a form of the dichotic-listening paradigm using verbal stimuli. An REA is shown for most right-handed children; however, there are no consistently significant results showing developmental or sex differences. There is a slight trend in some studies which show a greater REA for females at some ages (Geffner & Hochberg, 1971; Kimura, 1964). Bryden (1979) has conducted a number of unpublished studies using CV pairs with 316 males and females between the ages of 4 and 14. In these studies, 81.5 percent of females showed an REA, whereas only 71.6 percent of males did so ($X^2 = 3.01; p < .10$). Lateralization effects have also been studied in spatial perception using nonverbal stimuli in both the visual and tactual modes. The results are quite comparable with the auditory system; there is little significant evidence for sex-related differences, although most children show an LVF (Leehey, 1977) or left hand (LH) (Flannery & Balling, 1977) preference for spatial stimuli.

Where trends occur, females show the maturational advantage and exhibit laterality effects earlier (Buffery, 1970).

There is a great deal of speculation as to what type of neuropsychological model could account for the phenomena under discussion. Lateralization studies in adults showing higher degrees of laterality in males are consistent with the assumption that a high degree of specialization between the two cerebral hemispheres fosters visual spatial processes (see Levy's 1969 model). It is not clear why hemispheric specialization does not have the same effect on verbal processes. Why are less lateralized females superior in verbal abilities? Highly differentiated cerebral hemispheres may facilitate some cognitive processes and hinder others. Since the brain is functionally differentiated within hemispheres as well as between hemispheres, it may be that cognitive functions which depend on both hemispheres are facilitated by high degrees of specialization while functions located within a hemisphere are subverted by specialization. Evidence obtained from studying subjects with brain lesions indicates that language abilities are clearly associated with left hemispheric function, but performance on visual spatial abilities cannot be localized to either hemisphere (Waber, 1979). For example Porteus Maze Performance is disrupted by lesions to either the right or left frontal lobe (Porteus, 1965); perceptual disembedding is impaired by a lesion to the right hemisphere but even more impaired by a lesion to the left hemisphere (Russo & Vignolo, 1967). In contrast visual closure is disrupted by a lesion to the right, but not the left, hemisphere (Lansdell, 1968). In this vein it is interesting that lateralization effects are more pronounced in dichotic-listening studies using verbal material than in visual studies using spatial stimuli.

There are also indications of sex-related differences in the involvement of the two hemispheres in the processing of visual spatial information. Waber (1979) asked right-handed children between the ages of 5 and 14 to copy the Rey-Osterrith Complex Figure using different colored pencils in a specified order so that strategies could be analyzed. At age 11 females tended to use a style characteristic of left-hemispheric processing while males employed strategies more characteristic of right-hemispheric processing. It is entirely possible that sex-related differences in visual spatial abilities are a result of attention and strategy factors, which may or may not interact with cerebral specialization.

A neuropsychological theory must also be able to explain the appearance of specific abilities at certain ages as well as changes in these abilities during development. Waber (1977) has been able to show that both spatial ability and degree of lateralization of verbal auditory perception are systematically related to the rate of physical maturation at puberty. She hypothesized that sexual maturation at puberty reduces the rate of lateralization of the two cerebral hemispheres. Since a high degree of lateralization is associated with superior performance on visual spatial tasks, females who mature earlier would have their rate of growth slowed down sooner. Waber studied two groups of females, aged 11 and 13, and two groups of males, aged 13 and 15, each sex of both early and late maturers. Each subject was rated along the Tanner Rating System for bodily sexual maturity and given a battery of three linguistic sequencing and three spatial tasks. A measure of lateralization through the dichotic-listening technique was also administered. The results confirmed the hypothesis: Within each sex at every age, later maturers scored better than early maturers on each of the tests of spatial ability; later maturers had higher degrees of lateralization. It looks as though there are different rates of growth in brain lateralization, that females move through this process faster until puberty at which time males catch up and continue to increase for a longer period of time. Maturation is certainly a plausible explanation for why sex-related differences in visual spatial ability are not found before adolescence and for why females show higher degrees of lateralization before puberty, while males show higher degrees afterward. These findings are also relevant to studies which show that the more "masculine" boys have lower scores in spatial ability measures (Petersen, 1979). Boys with more androgenized bodies have matured sexually earlier. Thus their growth in visual spatial ability hit a ceiling earlier.

The Waber study suggests that performance dips seen at puberty in many cognitive abilities may be due to a reorganization of brain functions characterized by increased sexual differentiation. There are also performance dips seen between the ages of five and seven. Performance dips in visual spatial abilities closely parallel Piaget's documentation of major qualitative changes in children's thinking occurring at times of movement from the preoperational stage to the concrete operational stage and from that stage to formal operations. Most of the neuropsychological theories imply that hemispheric specialization occurs in a linear, additive fashion. However, Waber's approach suggests neuropsychological maturation entails repeated reorganization of functions, a model which more closely mirrors the types of changes seen in cognitive development.

Effects of Hormones: Circulating Levels. The endocrine system consists of structures which regulate and produce hormones (the endocrine glands), the chemical secretions from the glands (the hormones themselves), the intracellular mechanisms that permit receptivity of the cells to the hormones, and axillary tissues which can transform sex hormones into one another (Petersen, 1979). The hypothalamus, the pituitary gland, and the gonads (ovaries and testes) are of central importance in regulating hormone levels in both sexes.

The sex hormones appear to be especially critical during two phases of development: the prenatal and the pubertal phases (Petersen, 1979). During the prenatal period the organism is organized or sensitized such that when hormone levels increase during puberty the potentials set during the prenatal phase are then activated. In the prenatal phase hormones exert this most direct influence in two areas: the differentiation of the gonads and the differentiation of the morphology of the brain.

The gonads of both sexes are undifferentiated at conception; however, the cells contain either *XX* or *XY* sex chromosomes. If the gonads contain the *XY* chromosome complement, testes will form; if *XX* chromosomes are present, ovaries will differentiate from the gonad about six weeks later than the development of testes. In order for a male to develop, the testes must produce large

amounts of androgen by the eighth week postconception. Secretions from the testes stimulate the growth and differentiation of the Wolffian (male) duct and cause the Mullerian (female) duct to atrophy. Androgen also stimulates the development of internal (seminal vesicles, vas deferens, and epididymis) and external (penis and scrotum) sexual structures. Differentiation of a male depends on the presence of androgen, while in the female the ovaries, uterus, and Fallopian tubes, as well as the external structures (clitoris, vagina, and labia), will develop in the absence of estrogen.

It has been demonstrated that exposure to androgen is clearly responsible for the differentiation of the hypothalamus into a male type while the absence of androgen causes a female hypothalamus to develop. There are two types of control systems for the release of gonadotropins from the pituitary—a cyclic control pattern which results in the menstrual cycle in females and a tonic or continual pattern which results in stabilizing hormone levels over time (Dan, 1979). Recent evidence has shown that both types of control exist in both males and females. Tonic regulation is responsible for maintaining the basal level of gonadotropin release (Whalen, 1968). There is also some data indicating that males experience near-monthly rhythms which are hormonal (Curtis, 1974; Doering, Kraemer, Brodie, & Hamburg, 1975; Harkness, 1974) and psychological (Kuhl, Lee, Halberg, Gunther, & Knapp, 1974; Wynn, 1973). Early exposure to androgen also sensitizes the central nervous system (CNS) so that it will be maximally activated by testosterone at puberty, eliciting male characteristics, and will be insensitive to the opposite sex hormones, estrogen and progestin.

Hormone research is fraught with problems of when and how it is best to measure hormone levels, since the levels themselves are cyclic and, additionally, are very sensitive to environmental influences. It is also difficult to determine whether a sex-related characteristic is due to a genetic or hormonal factor since much of hormonal behavior is given in the genetic code. Past research has concentrated on finding instances of covariation between hormonal and psychological events using an implicit assumption of unidirectional influence: Sex hormones cause certain physiological changes. Current research has been more concerned with interactions and contingencies: Behavior can also influence hormone levels in certain types of situations.

An interesting example of the contingency approach to finding linkages between hormones and behavior is a series of studies, initially with rhesus monkeys and later with human males, by Rose and associates (Kreuz & Rose, 1972; Kreuz, Rose, & Jennings, 1972; Rose, Gordon, & Bernstein, 1972; Rose, Holaday, & Bernstein, 1971). These researchers have demonstrated that the relationship between high levels of testosterone and aggression in males is mediated by psychological stress.

They found that being in a lower status position in a dominance hierarchy created stress which in turn lowered testosterone levels in their subjects. The frequently cited relationship between testosterone and aggression has come from studies of animals. Previous research with humans, however, has been contradictory on the existence of such a relationship. Some have found a significant positive relationship between testosterone and aggression (Persky, Smith, & Basu, 1971), while others have found no such relationship (Doering et al., 1975). Researchers are now beginning to hypothesize a contingency relationship in humans where the relationship between testosterone levels and aggression occurs only in provocative situations producing stress. It is also becoming more clear that the hormonal system is an open one since it appears that stress reduces testosterone levels.

Stress may, in fact, be the key to unraveling equivocal data on the relationship between circulating levels of sex hormones and other affective states such as depression and anxiety. There is a great deal of literature which indicates more frequent occurrences of negative affect among females during and immediately prior to menstruation (Dan, 1979). However the source of menstrual cycle mood changes is unclear (Koeske, 1977). In a review of the literature on the menstrual cycle and sex-related differences, Dan suggests the possibility that menstrual cycle changes in affect may only occur in some women in situations of environmental stress. The timing of both ovulation and menstruation are affected by stress. Thus if environmental stress alters the hormonal system, premenstrual and menstrual changes in affect may represent the effects of stress rather than menstrual cycle changes themselves. It is interesting to note that in her review Dan could not find any significant evidence demonstrating an impairment of cognitive functioning during the menstrual cycle.

A group of researchers from Worcester, Mass., has focused on the idea that changes in testosterone levels may influence cognitive functioning through an activating effect on the CNS. They have been studying automatizing as a bipolar factor with simple repetitive tasks defining one pole and perceptual-restructuring tasks defining the other pole. In one study Vogel, Broverman, Klaiber, and Kun (1969) demonstrated that the EEG driving response to photic stimulation was negatively related to automatization, while the next study (Stenn, Klaiber, Vogel, & Broverman, 1972) found a decrease in the EEG driving response after testosterone therapy in hypogonadal males. Thus it appears that testosterone level has a measurable effect on both automatization ability and the EEG driving response.

Effects of Hormones: Prenatal Exposure. Money and colleagues have been studying individuals who have genetic anomalies leading to either marked alterations in hormone levels or to alterations in sensitivity to endogenous hormones. Their research also includes a group of individuals exposed in the prenatal period to exogenous hormones given to their mothers for the maintenance of at-risk pregnancies.

An autosomal recessive gene causes a condition known as *adrenogenital syndrome* (AGS), a metabolic disorder in which the adrenal gland secretes excessive amounts of adrenal androgens rather than the adrenal hormone cortisol in response to ACTH (*adrenocorticotrophic hormone*) from the pituitary. Cortisol normally inhibits the pituitary from releasing excessive amounts of ACTH, which in turn reduces adrenal androgen output. Males with this syndrome will be born with normal external genitalia. However, the excessive amount of androgen results in premature puberty and short adult stature due to an increased rate of muscle growth and premature closure of the epiphysial tissue of the bone. AGS females have varying degrees of masculinization of the external genitalia which range from enlarged clitoris to the presence of a penis and an empty scrotum. If these cases are not treated with cortisone therapy, AGS females will show further masculinization at puberty; the voice deepens and facial hair will appear. There is no development in the breasts; menstruation and ovulation do not occur.

Money and Lewis (1966) administered the Wechsler Intelligence Scale to a group of 70 AGS subjects. There was a significantly higher proportion of superior full-scale IQ scores among the sample than would be predicted from the test norms. However subsequent studies using matched controls (Perlman, 1971) on parents and siblings of AGS subjects (Baker & Ehrhardt, 1974) found that the control groups also received high full-scale IQ scores and did not differ significantly from the controls. Thus it is now believed that the early proposition suggesting prenatal virilization led to an increased IQ was an artifact due to the use of inappropriate control groups. There were also no significant differences between any groups on subtests of verbal abilities in comparison to spatial perceptual abilities.

If excessive prenatal androgen levels affect cognitive abilities in a masculine direction, it is not evident in AGS subjects. However there is some indication that prenatal exposure to excess estrogen may have a negative influence on spatial perceptual skills and a positive influence on verbal skills. Males with an androgen insensitivity syndrome (genetic males who cannot utilize either endogenous or exogenous androgen because its absorption is blocked at the cellular level) and male pseudohermaphrodites (insufficient production of androgen in utero) are born with female external genitalia due to the normal amounts of male estrogen produced by the testes. At puberty they develop female secondary sex characteristics and are usually raised psychosexually as females. In two separate investigations, one using androgen insensitive subjects (Masica, Money, Ehrhardt, & Lewis, 1969) and the other with male pseudohermaphrodites (Perlman, 1971), a superiority on the verbal as compared to the performance IQ was found for these subjects, as well as significantly lower scores on block design. Lack of androgen coupled with excess estrogen during the prenatal period may be directly related to poor spatial ability.

Research with subjects where mothers have been treated with synthetic or naturally occurring estrogens or progestins for the maintenance of at-risk pregnancies provides some confirmation of the effect of estrogen and progestin. Dalton (1968) found that prenatal progesterone exposure was positively correlated with grades in school and to teachers' ratings of academic achievement in verbal reasoning, English, and mathematics. In a follow-up study of these subjects, superior school achievement (particularly in numerical, spatial, and mechanical abilities) continued into adolescence and was positively correlated with early exposure, length of treatment, and high dosage. Yalom, Green, and Fisk (1973) reported a lower performance score on EFT in boys whose mothers had been treated with a combination of synthetic nonsteroidal estrogens, such as diethylstilbestrol (DES), and small amounts of synthetic progestin during pregnancy.

The most consistent results demonstrating a linkage between hormones and sex-related behaviors are obtained from studies of prenatal exposure to excess hormones or from studies using somatic characteristics (androgenized individuals) rather than from endocrine status. There is little evidence to support a theory that circulating hormone levels have a direct effect on sex-related behaviors. Petersen (1979) has proposed a general model for biopsychosocial development applied to those cognitive skills which show sex-related differences. She suggests that some potential, establishing a broad range for skill in these cognitive abilities, is probably inherited via timing and level of hormone release programmed by the genes. At a critical prenatal period, appropriate levels of active unbound hormones set potentials for hemispheric specialization, prefrontal development, and degree of response to activation during puberty. At puberty hormone levels are activated, producing the profile of the mature male who is better at spatial relations and of the female who is better at verbal skills. Thus more mature males and females would be better at spatial abilities than verbal skills, would be more androgenized in physical appearance, and have right-hemispheric dominance. Females and males better at verbal than spatial skills would appear physically to be more feminine or masculine respectively and have left-hemispheric dominance. Socialization influences would probably intensify these biological effects.

It is also possible that hormones exert their influence on discrete systems which only mediate directly observable sex-related differences. Differences between the sexes in cognitive abilities and aggression may be a reflection of differences in activity level, which has been shown to be relatd to testosterone. Researchers at the Oregon Regional Primate Center were the first to observe that female rhesus monkeys whose mothers had been treated with testosterone propionate exhibited frequencies of rough-and-tumble play, chasing play, threat, and play imitation that matched normal male behaviors or were intermediate between male and female patterns (Goy, 1968; Phoenix, 1974). These behaviors occurred at a time when the testes and ovaries were quiescent, indicating a long-term effect of exposure to prenatal androgen rather than a direct influence by circulating hormone levels. Several studies have shown that AGS females had increased activity levels, preferred more vigorous outdoor play, were more athletic and self-assertive, and were more frequently labeled by themselves and others as tomboys (Ehrhardt & Baker, 1974; Money & Ehrhardt, 1972; Perlman, 1971). Supportive evidence comes from exogenous hormone exposure in females whose mothers were treated with androgenic synthetic progestin for high-risk pregnancies. Ehrhardt and Money (1967) report that these females show frequent participation in muscular exercise, recreation, competitive play with boys in sports, interest in boys' toys, less need for sleep, and high levels of self-assertiveness and self-reliance as reported by both themselves and their mothers. Yalom et al. (1973) report prenatal exposure to DES in diabetic mothers resulted in children who were less aggressive, less assertive, and exhibited less ability in athletic skill. Reinisch (1977) and colleagues (Reinisch & Karow, 1977) found a progestin-exposed group to be more independent, individualistic, self-sufficient, and self-assured than their siblings, while estrogen-exposed subjects evidenced more group dependence and group orientation.

In a review of prenatal influences on cognitive abilities, Reinisch et al. (1979) suggest that hormones may exert physiological effects on the system of sensory thresholds, which may in turn cause environmental stimuli to be processed differently for males and females. Changes in sensory acuity have been studied in several modalities—smell, taste, vision, touch, and hearing. LeMagnen (1950, 1952) has reported that females are more sensitive to specific odorants than males; others have indicated that estrogen might be responsible for such acuity since female sensitivity varies across the menstrual cycle. Estrogen therapy was found to increase olfactory acuity in hypogonadal females, whereas acuity decreased in those females who received testosterone (Schneider, Sustiloe, Howard, & Wolf, 1958). Mid-cycle superiority (high estrogen associated with ovulation) has been found in auditory sensitivity (Henkin, 1974; Messent, 1976), visual sensitivity (Diamond, Diamond, & Mast, 1972), skin sensitivity to touch, temperature, and two-point discrimination (Henkin, 1974; Kenshalo, 1970), and perception of pleasantness of taste (Wright & Crow, 1973). Henkin (1974) suggests that estrogen appears to be important for mid-cycle increases in acuity, while progesterone may be instrumental in decreasing sensitivity later in the cycle due to its contribution to a decreased concentration of zinc in the body. Lower testosterone levels are implicated in a decreased ability to detect certain odorants among males with a gonadotropin deficiency (Hamilton, Henkin, Weir, & Kliman, 1973). Although the exact mechanism is unknown, Pfaff and Pfaffman (1969) have shown that testosterone influences the firing rate of neurons in the preoptic areas of the brain in response to odors.

Social Factors: The Influence of the Family

There are several major papers which have presented summaries on the acquisition of sex-typed behavior in children from a social learning point of view (Bandura & Walters, 1963; Kagan, 1964a; Mischel, 1970; Mussen, 1969; Sears et al., 1965). Although treatments and emphases differ, there is considerable agreement as to the central importance of two major processes: differential reinforcement and identification. Kagan (1964a) suggests that a sex-role standard is acquired by three processes: (1) identification with models, (2) expectation of affection and acceptance for possession of sex-appropriate attributes, and (3) expectation that possession of such attributes will prevent social rejection. Once acquired, individuals become less dependent on external sources of reinforcement and rely more on self-monitoring and self-evaluation in relation to sex-role standards.

Parental Tuition of Sex Roles. Differential treatment of boys and girls begins on the first day they are born. Rubin, Provenzano, and Luria (1974) interviewed the mothers and fathers of 15 infant boys and 15 infant girls within 24 hours of birth. Most of the mothers had held and fed their infants, but the fathers had been allowed only to view them through a display window in the hospital nursery. Parents rated their children on an 18-item bipolar adjective scale and were asked to describe their child as they would to a close friend or relative. In actuality the sample of newborn male and female infants did not differ in average length, weight, or Apgar scores, yet they were differentially perceived and labeled. Both mothers and fathers described daughters, in contrast to sons, as softer, finer featured, weaker, smaller, prettier, more inattentive, more awkward, and more delicate. Sons were characterized as firmer, larger featured, better coordinated, more alert, stronger, and hardier. Fathers as compared to mothers were stronger sex typers in that they labeled the two sexes farther apart on the adjective pairs. One measure produced a cross-sex effect: Fathers rated daughters as cuddlier than sons, while mothers rated sons as cuddlier than daughters.

In another innovative study (Will et al., 1976), the same infant, a six-month-old boy, was presented as "Adam," wearing blue pants, to some mothers and as "Beth," wearing a pink dress, to other mothers. Each mother, who had small children of both sexes of her own, was asked to play with the child for a few minutes. The researchers then observed which of three toys—a doll, a train, or a fish—the mothers offered the child. Although each mother claimed she did not perceive any differences between boys and girls at that age, the mothers who thought the child was a girl most often offered her a doll to play with. The women who thought the child was a boy more frequently offered him a train. Mothers also smiled more frequently when they thought they were holding a girl. Further the mothers did not seem to be aware of this differential treatment.

The amount of interaction between parent and infant has been studied by Rebelsky and Hanks (1971) who attached microphones to infants' shirts for 24-hour periods. Fathers interacted vocally with their newly born infants only 37 seconds a day. This vocalization time decreased during the first three months, more so for girls than for boys. Mothers' interaction time was found to increase for both sexes. The majority of other studies which have sampled the amount of time a parent spends with the child have found no differences in time spent between male and female infants (Maccoby & Jacklin, 1974). However of the studies that do find significant differences, they are in the direction of greater amounts of interaction with boy infants rather than girl infants and, as such, support the findings of Rebelsky and Hanks. Most of this research has focused on the mother. When fathers are studied there is a tendency for them to have more interactions with sons than with daughters, particularly as the child gets older (Gewirtz & Gewirtz, 1968; Sears et al., 1965).

Various hypotheses have been proposed to explain sex differences in a mother's amount of interaction, when such differences are found. Moss (1967), who has shown that in the first weeks of life boys tend to be picked up more and cuddled more than girls, suggested that mothers initially respond more to boy infants because they are more active and are awake for longer periods of time. After three months Moss found that mothers begin to talk less to their sons and more to their daughters. After several months mothers may extinguish on talking to their more irritable boys and may find talking to their girls more reinforcing. The hypothesis put forth by Moss follows an interactionist point of view that the differential treatment on the part of mothers is a response to different biological predispositions in the infant. However differential treatment in favor of males may reflect a general, cultural bias toward males rather than an interaction with biological factors. The Petersons (1973) found that 90 percent of men and 92 percent of women wanted a boy as their first child.

In addition to differences in the amount of time mothers spend interacting with male versus female infants, the Moss study found differences in the type and quality of interaction. Some of the research by others has supported the Moss findings. Goldberg and Lewis (1969) have found that at 6 months of age girls received more physical, vocal, and visual contact from their mothers than boys. By the time these same children were 13 months old, the girls clung to, looked at, and talked to their mothers more often than boys. In order to establish a causal relationship, Goldberg and Lewis reclassified the mothers they had observed at 6 months into groups with high and low rates of touching. They found that both boys and girls of mothers with high touching rates at 6 months sought the most maternal contact at 13 months.

It has sometimes been assumed that the greater verbal ability in females may be due to the fact that girls receive more verbal stimulation from their mothers. In their review of the literature, however, Maccoby and Jacklin (1974) point out that the majority of studies show no difference in the amount or kind of parental vocalizations to daughters as compared to sons. When differences are found they show girls are talked to more frequently than boys but only in specific subsamples, such as middle- but not lower-class mothers, more-educated rather than less-educated mothers, or with first-born but not later-born girls.

Rebelsky and Hanks (1971) found differential treatment of boys and girls by fathers. Fathers interacted with girl infants 62 percent during caretaking (diapering and feeding) and 38 percent during noncaretaking. With boy infants their interaction was almost the reverse, with 34 percent during caretaking and 66 percent during noncaretaking. Fathers apparently relate caretaking to mothering and feel that it is worse to mother a boy than a girl. There may be some general differences in the way in which children relate to fathers as opposed to mothers. Ban and Lewis (1974) found that boys and girls spent about twice as much time in the proximity of their mothers, but they looked about twice as often at their fathers as at their mothers.

A consistent trend has been found in what parents respond to in their children. Parents respond more frequently to large muscle movements in boys than in girls (Moss, 1967). Boys are handled more roughly than girls (Yarrow, Rubenstein, & Pedersen, 1971) and are more frequently engaged in rough-and-tumble play (Tasch, 1952). Girls are treated as though they are more fragile than boys, and parents are more apprehensive about their physical well-being than about that of boys' (Minton, Kagan, & Levine, 1971; Pedersen & Robson, 1969).

As far as independence training is concerned, mothers placed similar demands on both boys and girls in areas of practical autonomy, such as dressing and bathing themselves, taking care of their belongings, and keeping their rooms tidy (Nakamura & Rogers, 1969; Sears, Maccoby, & Levin, 1957). At least until the age of five, mothers set similar limits for boys and girls with respect to how far away from home they were allowed to go (Newson & Newson, 1968; Sears et al., 1957). Mothers checked on the child's whereabouts equally often for both sexes, and girls were allowed to make as many decisions as boys about where they wanted to go and what they wanted to do. In studies which show differences between the sexes in the granting of independence, the results show that mothers were more likely to restrict the independent movements of boys rather than girls (Hatfield, Ferguson, & Alpert, 1967). Boys were also more likely to be punished for independence gestures. There is some evidence, however, that things begin to change as children get older. In a longitudinal study done in England, substantial differences between the sexes began to emerge about the age of seven, in an area the authors called *chaperonage*. Girls were more often in the company of an adult than boys at this age, and their whereabouts were more closely monitored (Newson & Newson, 1968). In exploratory or stressful situations girls show more dependency upon their mothers, and in turn, mothers are more protective of daughters than sons (Baumrind & Black, 1967; Hoffman, 1972).

In the small amount of existent literature investigating parental responses to dependency demands from children, the results indicate a cross-sex effect. Mothers are more permissive toward such demands from boys, while fathers are more permissive with girls (Osofsky & Oldfield, 1971; Rothbart & Maccoby, 1966). Overall boys are more frequently punished than girls for dependency bids (Hatfield et al., 1967), and girls are more frequently comforted than boys when they seek help or nurturance (Block, 1972). However the majority of research has found no sex differences in a related variable—parental affection (Allaman, Joyce, & Crandall, 1972; Hatfield et al., 1967; Wolman & Money, 1980)—even though girls at older ages are likely to report retrospectively receiving more affection than males.

It is commonly thought that aggression in boys is more often allowed or reinforced than in girls. Some studies have found no sex differences in permissiveness of parents toward a child's display of aggression, in allowing children to settle their own arguments, or in encouraging a child to hit back when attacked (Newson & Newson, 1968; Sears et al., 1965). Other researchers have found that boys are reprimanded more frequently and more harshly than girls for demonstrating aggressive behavior toward objects or other people, either at home or at school (Lambert, Yackley, & Hein, 1971; Minton et al., 1971; Serbin, O'Leary, Kent, & Tonick, 1973). There is also strong evidence for a cross-sex effect. Mothers were more willing to accept angry behavior toward themselves from sons rather than from daughters, whereas fathers reacted in the reverse manner, being more permissive of aggression from daughters than from sons (Baumrind & Black, 1967; Rothbart & Maccoby, 1966). Fathers were more likely to allow girls to get angry at them (Block, 1972) and to accept insolence from them (Lambert et al., 1971). In general it appears that parents do not want either their sons or daughters to be taken advantage of,

yet aggression is not permissible for either sex as a way of solving problems.

There is consistent evidence to suggest that boys receive more of both positive and negative feedback from parents (Bee, Van Egeren, Streissguth, Nyman, & Leckie, 1969) and teachers (Meyer & Thompson, 1956; Serbin et al., 1973). Boys are more likely than girls to receive forms of direct coercion, negative reinforcement, and physical punishment (Feshbach, 1972; Hoffman & Saltzstein, 1967; Newson & Newson, 1968; Sears et al., 1957). For example mothers of 27-month-old boys were more likely to prohibit an action with a loud "NO," whereas with girls the mothers suggested alternatives (Minton et al., 1971). Block (1972) has also found that mothers are more reluctant to punish their daughters than their sons. It appears that the relationship between adults and boys is more evaluative and controlling than it is for girls. Maybe this is because sex-role stereotypes depict girls as weaker, less able to defend themselves, and more sensitive, or perhaps boys are more attention getting and less obedient. In a sequential analysis Minton et al. (1971) found that boys generally do not obey the first command; the result is that the mother raises her voice or physically forces compliance. Furthermore these episodes had a cumulative effect in that noncompliance on one occasion led to the use of more coercive methods on the next occasion.

In three interview studies on socialization practices directed toward childhood sexuality (Newson & Newson, 1968; Sears et al., 1957; Sears et al., 1965), working-class parents were found to be less permissive toward children's expression of sexuality than middle-class parents, but there were no differences based on the sex of the child. Parents responded to a son or a daughter in a similar manner in their reactions to masturbation, allowing the child to be seen nude, and instances of sex play with other children. Parents were equally likely to give both boys and girls information about sex.

There are many sex-differentiated behaviors which are associated with achievement, particularly in the attitudes of fathers. Mothers stress competent task performance for both sexes, but fathers of girls are less concerned with performance and more concerned with interpersonal interactions with their daughters (Block, Block, & Harrington, 1974). In addition fathers are more likely to reinforce inappropriate dependency bids from daughters but will respond to appropriate task-oriented questions from sons (Cantor, Wood, & Gelfand, 1977; Hetherington, 1978; Osofsky & O'Connell, 1972). The importance of achievement, career, and occupational success is stressed more for boys than for girls, particularly by fathers (Block, 1978; Hoffman, 1975).

Differential parental responses to particular behaviors commonly associated with differences between the sexes have been examined. However, the ability to "shape" a behavior depends upon its prior occurrence—that is, the behavior is already in the child's repertoire. Do parents merely respond to natural preferences in a child, or are parents instrumental in eliciting and developing the child's behaviors? The research on toy and activity preferences may shed some light on this issue.

Early studies at the one-year level found that boys played more vigorously and that girls spent more time with stuffed animals (Bronson, 1971; Goldberg & Lewis,

1969). However several detailed and thorough investigations of toy attributes thought to be responsible for these choices have not confirmed these findings. McCall (1974) presented infants between 8 and 11 months with toys varying in configuration, plasticity, sound quality, and familiarity. He reported no consistent sex differences in selection preferences, nature of play behavior, nor the infant's orientation toward the parent. At the 13- to 15-month level, McCall found small differences such that males played more vigorously with mechanical and manipulative toys and girls more often with stuffed animals, but these differences seemed to depend on specific toys. Other authors have investigated variables such as "faceness," soft tactual quality, and manipulability and have found no consistent sex differences (Jacklin, Maccoby, & Dick, 1973; Kaminski, 1973). Maccoby and Jacklin (1974) conclude,

It would be interesting to be able to find developmental links between the early toy preferences and the choices of more clearly "masculine" and "feminine" toys that may be discerned from age 2 onward, but the elements that differentially attract one-year-old boys and girls are not well enough understood to permit identifying the continuities that exist. The point is of some interest, because it is possible that societies begin to label as "masculine" those toys that differentially attract boys even if there is no relationship of the toy to the masculine role. (p. 278)

Several researchers have shown that toy preferences are formed during the second year of life and are clear and distinct by the age of three (Etaugh et al., 1975; Fein et al., 1975; McCandless & Evans, 1973). Girls are more likely than boys to paint, help the teacher, look at books, listen to stories; boys prefer to hammer or play with transportation toys. Girls contact girl toys and play much of the time with stuffed animals, dolls, and dress-up clothes; boys contact boy toys and play much of the time manipulating objects or building things. Sears et al. (1965) found that four-year-old boys spent more time in the portion of a large nursery school playroom containing blocks, wheel toys, and carpenter tools; girls spent more time in areas having dress-up clothes, cooking equipment, and doll houses. During middle childhood boys prefer physical and athletic activities (Brindley, Clarke, Hutt, Robinson, & Wethli, 1973; Hutt, 1978a), such as games involving strength, body contact, and competition; girls, on the other hand, like play which could be characterized by taking turns, choral activities, and verbalism (Sutton-Smith & Sovasta, 1972).

It is clear that boys and girls show definite sex-typed interests from the early preschool years onward. Are there differences in the degree to which the sexes are sex typed? Does one sex avoid opposite-sex interests and activities more than the other sex? In the toy preference studies discussed before, it was frequently found that girls owned and play with boy toys more frequently than boys owned or played with girl toys. Researchers measuring the degree of sex typing in children commonly use the It test (a projective measure in which an It doll is offered the opportunity to choose among a variety of sex-typed activities). Boys develop sex-typed preferences at an earlier age than girls and adhere to them more rigidly (Best et al., 1977; Brown, 1962; Kohlberg, 1966). Hartup, Moore, and Sager (1963) found boys were more likely than girls to avoid sex-inappropriate toys. The avoidance of the feminine toys was especially marked when an experimenter was present, suggesting that boys expected adult disapproval. Ross (1971) found boys (aged three to five) were more concerned than girls that a same-sex peer choose a sex-appropriate toy when playing the role of shopkeeper in a toy store. Boys continue to play consistently with masculine toys and to prefer male activities through middle childhood (Ferguson & Maccoby, 1966; Pulaski, 1970; Wolf, 1973).

When parents are given the It test and asked to choose activities for their children, they choose more sex-appropriate activities for their sons than for their daughters (Fling & Manosevitz, 1972). Lansky (1967) presented parents of preschool children with hypothetical situations in which boys and girls chose cross-sexed activities. When females chose a masculine activity, the parents were not concerned. However when a boy made a feminine choice, both parents reacted negatively. Fathers were more likely than mothers to show both more intense positive and more intense negative reactions concerning their sons' choices than their daughters' choices. It is clear that there is more social pressure exerted against boys for sex-inappropriate choices than for girls and that the fathers exert more of this pressure than the mothers.

Most researchers have simply assumed that parents have the dominant role in teaching sex-role stereotypes to children. After their thorough review of the literature, however, Maccoby and Jacklin (1974) have questioned this assumption. They conclude, "Our survey of the research on socialization has revealed surprisingly little differentiation in parent behavior according to the sex of the child" (p. 338). The socialization literature certainly does contain many more similarities in sex-role training than differences. With a few exceptions parents do not reward one sex more than the other for most behaviors thought to be relevant to the development of sex typing, such as aggression, dependency, autonomy, and sexual behavior or curiosity.

There are several possible explanations for the lack of positive results in the socialization literature. In a critique of the Maccoby and Jacklin (1974) work, Block (1978) suggests that the published research reviewed by them relies on samples that tend to obscure sex differences. Block notes, for example, that only 9 percent of the studies focused on fathers. Since there is some fairly strong evidence that fathers are more sex differentiating than mothers, the results are most likely biased. Furthermore Block indicates that 77 percent of the samples used children aged five and under. Sex-related differences in socialization are not as likely to occur in small children as in older children. Block's own research on parental training in six different countries has shown sex differentiation in socialization increased with the age of the child and peaked during the teenage years (Block, 1978).

Another interpretation of the Maccoby and Jacklin findings is that past research has not been able to measure the way in which sex-role standards are communicated to children. The existent research has focused on the content of the parental response or *what* the parent does in response to a particular behavior elicited from a child. *How* the parent delivers the message, however, goes unrecorded and unmeasured. How a parent responds to a child probably contains a more important message than what is said. A father may say to his son, "You shouldn't have hit him back," but his tone of voice may indicate, "I'm glad you did." There are many subtle ways in which messages can be communicated. A father may say to his daughter in response to a dependency bid, "I think you can do that by yourself," but the twinkle in his eye says, "I'd like it more, though, if you'd let me do it for you."

There is some indication that parents try to socialize children of both sexes toward the same major goals (Lambert et al., 1971; Levitin & Chananie, 1972; Smith, 1971). Lambert et al. (1971) asked parents to check a series of 40 items (such as "more helpful around the house," "more likely to be rough and boisterous at play," "more likely to act scared") according to whether they believed a boy or a girl would be more likely to engage in the behavior. The parent was also asked how important s/he thought it was for a child to have each of the behavioral characteristics. The findings indicated that parents held fairly stereotyped views of what the typical behavior of a boy or girl was like. However, their values of how boys or girls ought to behave were quite similar. Some of the role expectations of a parent are to treat all children equally and to inculcate in them particular values. However, it appears that the conceptions that parents have about how the two sexes differ tend to sabotage their child-rearing goals. If parents consider certain behaviors natural for one sex or the other, these beliefs will become the basis for expectations by which a particular child will be evaluated. A mother may believe that it is natural for a boy to be active, rough at play, and noisy. When her son behaves according to these expectations, mother doesn't even notice it; by permitting the behaviors, they are reinforced. However, a daughter who is behaving in the same way may be noticed immediately because her behavior runs counter to expectations; she would be punished.

A third possibility is that parental reactions are a consequence, rather than a cause, of sex-typed behaviors. Perhaps boys and girls are born with certain biological predispositions and, because of their different initial behaviors, they elicit different responses from parents. This interaction becomes habitual and a circular pattern is initiated. The Moss hypothesis explaining differential maternal handling is an example of this process. The fact that boys are more active than girls and that adults permit such activity in boys, is another example of the dependency of nature and nurture. Finally the fact that boys make more dominance attempts toward adults and do not comply as readily as girls to adult commands may explain why boys receive more punishment than girls.

The findings of the Maccoby and Jacklin research lend themselves to still another inference. Perhaps the overall socialization influence of parents has been exaggerated. It may well turn out that other influences such as peers and the mass media may have more of an impact than parents on the development of sex typing, or other processes such as imitation or cognitive self-socialization may be more central in learning sex-typed behavior.

Imitation and the Acquisition of Sex Roles. It is widely accepted that children learn sex-typed behavior by imitating same-sex parents and peers. It must be so, argue theorists like Robert Sears.

Gender roles are very broad and very subtle. It would be difficult to imagine that any kind of direct tuition could provide for the learning of such elaborate behavioral, attitudinal and manneristic patterns as are subsumed under the rubrics of masculinity and femininity. Furthermore, these qualities are absorbed quite early and are highly resistant to modification. (Sears et al., 1965, p. 171)

In order to explain the acquisition of sex-typed behavior through imitation, it must be shown that children do, in fact, tend to imitate same-sex models more than opposite-sex models. In a review of the literature concerned with trying to specify both the characteristics of effective models and the type of relationship between the model and the observer, Shepherd-Look (1977) found little confirmation that children tend to prefer same-sex models.

Several researchers have manipulated the sex of the model to investigate the possibility of systematic effects of sex of the model and to control unwanted interactions. In some cases, sex of the model has no effect, while in others the variable enters higher order interactions, of little predictive value. The only trend appears to be that models whose behavior is sex appropriate are more frequently imitated by children of the same sex (e.g., girls are more affected by female nurturance than boys, while boys are more affected by male aggressive behaviors). (p. 491)

A related finding is that observing a same-sex model play with a sex-inappropriate toy can disinhibit the prohibition in the observer. Thus children will play with a sex-inappropriate toy after having watched a same-sex peer play with the same toy (Wolf, 1973).

Children do imitate models, but it appears that they do not consistently imitate a same-sex model. Perhaps children are imitating both parents. Studies which report within-family correlations on particular sex-typed attributes find that children are not similar to their own parents. Children may be like their parents, but they are no more like their parents than they are like a randomly selected group of other children's parents. Further when there is a correlation between parent and child scores, the correlations are not stronger between same-sex parent and child than between opposite-sex parent and child. Hetherington (1965) was unable to find significant correlations between the femininity scores of girls aged three to six and the femininity scores of their mothers. Mussen and Rutherford (1963), using the It test, found that boys' masculinity scores were unrelated to either their fathers' masculinity or their mothers' interests. Boys whose mothers particularly enjoyed highly feminine activities such as cooking and sewing did not choose those activities for the It doll.

Maccoby and Jacklin (1974) suggest that measures of parent-child similarity contain several methodological problems, one of which is that different characteristics may be being measured in adults than in children.

A mother's M-F score reflects interests, activities, and attributes that her daughter may not even perceive, much less be able to copy. Perhaps little girls are learning their sex typed behavior by imitating their mothers, but perhaps they are imitating behaviors that are not normally included in the measures of the mother's femininity. (p. 298)

Adult masculine and feminine behavior is qualitatively different from the same behavior during childhood. Further there are societal prohibitions against young children being "too adult" or "too sex typed." Children should be children (asexual), not miniature adults. Children may be acquiring a relatively large storehouse of sex-typed behavior but simply not performing them because of societal prohibitions or because the eliciting conditions do not arise. As Maccoby and Jacklin (1974) suggest, perhaps children are copying the meaning of an action and reproducing it using a structure more appropriate to the child's age.

If the little girl perceives her mother as being affectionate toward the father, and sets out to copy this behavior, the behavioral output will have to be constrained by the child's already developed behavioral capabilities, at least to a degree, and the result will be childlike affection-showing. (p. 300)

Other investigations of imitation relevant to sex typing have focused on characteristics of the model such as nurturance, power, and punitiveness. Nurturance and warmth in the same-sex parent increase sex-typed learning for both boys and girls (Mussen & Distler, 1959, 1960; Mussen & Rutherford, 1963; Payne & Mussen, 1956). However, nurturance on the part of the father is more important to the sex-role learning of boys than maternal nurturance is to sex-role learning in girls. Thus maternal nurturance (and also paternal nurturance) has some effect on the development of femininity in girls, but highly masculine boys perceive their fathers, but not their mothers, as more nurturant and rewarding than do boys who are lower in masculinity (Hetherington, 1967).

Hetherington (1965, 1967) has carefully investigated the influence of parental power on sex typing in boys. She has found a strong and consistent relationship between the development of masculinity in boys and parental power. Highly masculine boys tend to have fathers who are decisive and dominant in setting limits and dispensing both rewards and punishments. Paternal punishment facilitates sex-role typing in boys only if the father is also dominant and nurturant. Parental power seems to have little effect on the development of femininity in girls. Hetherington has also found that neither the degree of sex typing in the parents nor the encouragement of sex-typed activities by the parents is related to masculinity in boys. She points out that in girls, just as in boys, it is the father who has the critical role in the development of femininity. Femininity in daughters is related to father's masculinity, father's approval of the mother as a model, and father's reinforcement for participation in feminine activities. More feminine mothers do not have more feminine daughters (Hetherington, 1967). Even sexual adjustment and marital relations in adulthood are more influenced by earlier relations with fathers than mothers. This may be a result of the fact that a boy can be masculine independent of anyone else—i.e., he can achieve, compete, and be aggressive by himself. Femininity, on the other hand, is defined by being wanted and accepted by a man. A woman depends on the reactions of a man to validate her femininity.

The idea that nurturance facilitates sex-role learning has led some theorists to postulate that boys have more difficulty learning appropriate sex-role behavior than

girls (Lynn, 1969). Because the mother is highly nurturant and is usually the primary caretaker, boys will form their initial attachment to the mother. Thus the male must shift his identification from his mother to his father in order to develop masculine behaviors. Girls, on the other hand, may continue identification with their initial model; hence, the acquisition of sex-typed behavior for girls is thought to be simpler, more consistent, and capable of consolidation at earlier ages. Lynn (1969) has suggested that anxiety and conflict arise in the male because he must give up his close attachment to the mother and because he must shift his identification to a male with whom he has little direct or continuous exposure. The female, however, is able to observe her mother throughout the day and is able to maintain continuous and intimate contact with her.

Girls are also thought to have more opportunity to practice appropriate behaviors. There are several reasons why this view is somewhat naive. In the first instance, the evidence does not support this position. If the imitation process for girls is much simpler and more consistent, then females should be more fully sex typed at earlier ages than boys. However the opposite is the case. Second, it is not intuitively obvious that the mother is a more visible and consistent role model than the father. Visibility may be hampered for many women because they work full time. Consistency in a role is difficult to assess, but it seems that women play as many different and conflicting roles as do men; consider, for example, the working mother. Third, the role with which females are supposed to identify is held in low esteem and has little power or recognition associated with it. In fact many of the role demands of the traditional female role are often delegated to paid domestics or, at the very least, performed with displeasure. It must be anxiety producing for girls to perceive that they must either assume a role which has such little prestige in society or run counter to the feminine image. The girl also experiences considerable conflict in being asked to assume a role which has brought little recognition to her own mother, whom she loves and identifies with.

In addition to the fact that low prestige is afforded feminine tasks, many girls find boys' activities less confining and more enjoyable. Komarovsky (1953) has reported many instances in which girls have envied the freedom and the activity allowed for boys. It is ironic that many theorists have suggested that boys have a more narrowly defined sex role than girls. It is unclear what is really meant by *narrowly defined* since it seems obvious even to the casual observer that there are a greater number and variety of activities, clubs, interests, and toys that are masculine as opposed to feminine. What could be more *narrowly defined* than being quiet, looking pretty, and playing with dolls? *Narrowly defined* can also be taken to mean the ease with which a child can engage in cross-sex activities and/or how severely a child is punished for deviations. It is acceptable for a girl to be a tomboy, but a boy is harshly reprimanded for being a sissy. This is certainly an accurate observation during the preschool and elementary school years; however, during adolescence the definition of feminine becomes considerably more circumscribed. It has further been hypothesized that boys learn their sex role by vague, negative proscriptions rather than by concrete, positive reinforcement. Girls learn how to be women by being encouraged to imitate their mothers; boys, on the other hand, learn how not to be girls. Thus it is more difficult to learn from punishment particularly when the behaviors to be learned are obscure. Weitzman (1979) has written an excellent counter to these suggestions.

In reviewing the socialization literature I was struck by the fact that the harsh restrictions placed on girls are ignored. In fact, there is no reason to believe that the socialization of boys involves greater restrictiveness, control and protectiveness. Boys may be punished more often, but girls' activities are so limited to begin with that they never have a chance to engage in punishable behavior. It is also possible that the kinds of sanctions used to socialize women may be more subtle, but no less severe: boys are spanked, but girls may be made to feel unworthy, deviant, guilty or queer. (p. 16)

Father-Absence Effects on Sex-Role Development. Since it has been demonstrated that the father has a critical influence on sex-role development, it might be expected that disturbances in sex typing would occur in families where the father is permanently absent or away from home for long periods. Marital disruption and rearrangement is becoming a more frequent occurrence in the lives of many children. In 1978 it was estimated that approximately 20 percent of all U.S. children resided with only one parent (Glick, 1979). The average amount of time spent by the child in a single-parent family is now estimated at six years.

Separation of the father from the home environment, either temporarily or permanently, has definite negative effects upon male children (Drake & McDougall, 1977; Hetherington & Deur, 1971). These sex-role problems are most apparent in preadolescent boys and are most severe if the separation occurred at or before the age of five (Biller & Bahm, 1971). Recent research indicates that boys who were separated from their fathers early in life show a sex-role disruption pattern characterized by high verbal aggression, low physical aggression, more dependent behaviors, and a more feminine self-concept (as measured by an adjective check list of 56 items associated with either masculinity or femininity). Hetherington (1967) determined that boys who were separated from their fathers at the age of six or later showed no differences in sex-role development when compared to boys reared within intact nuclear families. However if the father separation took place before the age of five, the boy was rated as less aggressive and more dependent than boys from two-parent families. These results lend some credence to the assumption made by many researchers concerning a critical or sensitive period for appropriate sex typing in the preschool years (e.g., Biller & Bahm, 1971).

The research findings on older male children are largely inconsistent and form no such clearcut patterns. Barclay and Cusumano (1967) found that, although black, as well as white, father-absent adolescent males were shown to be more passive in their orientation to their environment than father-present males, there was no significant difference in masculinity scores or on indices of cross-sex identity. Moreover it appears that boys deprived of the influence of their fathers develop a form of "compensatory masculinity" which involves both male and female behavioral traits employed in an inconsistent manner.

With increasing age father-absence effects are at least partially mitigated by other sex-role models such as the mother, siblings, the media, teachers, and peers. A number of authors have isolated some of these effects on the child's developing sex-role identity. Brim (1958) reports that the younger child from a two-child family often manifests sex-typed traits similar to those of an older brother or sister. In other words boys with older brothers show more masculine traits than those with older sisters. A similar pattern was evident for younger girls. In addition older girls with younger brothers have more masculine traits than do older girls with younger sisters. Again a similar pattern was found for older boys. In single-parent, mother-dominant households, similar patterns of sex typing were also evident. Children from such families who had older brothers demonstrated more aggressive and less dependent behaviors than children with no older male siblings (Wohlford, Santrock, Berger, & Lieberman, 1971). In a related finding Steimel (1960) has established that early childhood experiences and associations are related to sex-role development. Children who were rated as high in sex-appropriate identity had significantly more same-sex associations in their early development.

The findings of current research indicate that the absence of a father or significant male model may be only a partial cause of the disruption of masculine identity patterns in boys. Father absence may change the nature of the relationship that a mother has with her son. In a longitudinal study of both parents and children from broken homes, Hetherington, Cox, and Cox (1979) found that many mothers who were single parents tended to treat their sons in an overprotective manner characterized by apprehension concerning adventurous behaviors. When the single mother did not exhibit these negative traits and encouraged masculine exploratory behaviors, problems in sex-role development were minimal. These researchers further identified those single mothers who fostered inadequate or inappropriate sex typing in their children as being egocentric and self-fulfilling. This type of mother reported a rapid recovery from the trauma of marital separation due largely to the frenetic pace at which she lived. The rapid recovery was often accomplished at the expense of her children who often manifested frequent, enduring, and intense behavioral problems and emotional disturbances. The single mothers of children with sex-typing difficulties frequently related to them in a hurried, erratic, preoccupied, emotionally detached, and noncommunicative manner. McCord, McCord, and Thurber (1962) found that boys' behavior problems were related to father absence only if the mother was deviant or rejecting. Pedersen's (1966) results also suggested an interaction between maternal pathology and amount of father absence; unavailability of the father was detrimental only when the boy was left to grow up with a disturbed mother. Biller (1969) found that masculine sex-role adoption in father-absent boys was positively related to a measure of maternal encouragement for masculine behavior.

In general research findings indicate that the effects of an absent father on preadolescent girls are minimal. Santrock (1970) found no significant differences in dependency or aggression between father-absent and father-present preschool girls. There was, however, a tendency for father-absent girls with older female siblings to be more dependent and those with older male siblings to be more aggressive. It appears that father absence has no immediate effects upon young females, yet it may affect their sex-role development in later life.

Hetherington (1972) investigated paternal-absence effects upon girls whose parents were divorced or whose father was deceased. There were few significant differences between father-present and father-absent girls in traditional measures of sex typing. The most striking finding of this research concerned the differential patterns of heterosexual development of father-absent girls when compared with those whose fathers still resided in the home. Girls from mother-headed households manifested patterns characterized by either sexual anxiety and discomfort or sexual precociousness and inappropriately aggressive behaviors toward males. The former of these patterns most often characterized girls whose fathers were absent due to death. The latter pattern portrayed those girls whose parents were divorced. Both groups of father-absent girls reported general anxiety in dealings with males, yet each apparently adopted different strategies for coping with this stress.

In a subsequent follow-up study conducted on these same subjects, it was demonstrated that girls from homes disrupted due to divorce tended to marry earlier and were more often pregnant at the time of marriage, and more were separated or divorced at the time of the investigation. Moreover females from single-parent families reported less sexual satisfaction in marriage than females from intact families, although the frequency of marital sexual intercourse was similar. Girls from intact families viewed their fathers and their husbands as being dissimilar. In contrast girls from single-parent homes viewed their fathers and husbands as being very similar to each other. It seems likely that girls from father-absent homes have little or no chance to resolve negative feelings toward their fathers and these may later be projected onto their husbands.

COGNITIVE FACTORS

The processes of differential reinforcement and imitation are certainly involved in the acquisition of sex-typed behavior. However, the strength of the relationship that can be shown with experimental evidence is disappointing. Lack of evidence can be attributed, in part, to serious methodological problems, but that alone is not a sufficient explanation. Another type of psychological process must be involved—one that relies on both cognitive processes and self-socialization mechanisms. These ideas have been most explicitly espoused by Kohlberg (1966).

In contrast to the social learning position that sex typing is a function of direct reinforcement and imitation, Kohlberg argues that the child actively organizes and structures his/her perceptions and experiences around his/her sexual self-categorization. When a male child categorizes himself into "we males" as opposed to "those females" on the basis of physical self, this self-categorization or gender identity becomes the fundamental organizer of sex-role differentiation. It is irreversible and relatively immune to conventional reinforcements. Kohlberg sums up the essential process as follows: "I am a boy,

therefore I want to do boy things, therefore the opportunity to do boy things (and to gain approval for doing them) is rewarding" (p. 89). Self-reinforcement is sustained by maintaining cognitive consistency among physical sex, self-categorization, and sex-appropriate behaviors and values.

The genesis of the child's gender identity stems from organized rules the child has induced from what s/he has observed, been told, and experienced. The rules (all police officers are men) are based upon a limited set of characteristics that are salient to the child at a particular age (all policemen wear uniforms; only men wear uniforms). Thus the child's sex-role conceptions are oversimplified, exaggerated, and stereotyped and do not allow for variations (a girl can be a policeman, too). At any given age a child's sex-role concepts are limited in the same way as any other concepts that have been acquired, by the level of cognitive skills developed.

Kohlberg postulates that all children go through the following stages in gaining an understanding of gender:

1. *Basic gender identity.* The child recognizes that s/he is a boy or a girl.
2. *Gender stability.* The child realizes that his/her own gender is unchangeable. Males remain male and females remain female.
3. *Gender constancy.* The child understands that superficial changes in appearance or behaviors do not alter gender. Sex remains constant across various conditions: long hair, short hair, holding a baby, or playing soccer.

As early as age three, children seem to understand gender labels and also have a clear conception of their own sex identity (Slaby & Frey, 1975; Thompson, 1975). Several researchers have investigated the presence or absence of gender constancy as reflected in experiments employing Piagetian paradigms (DeVries, 1969; Emmerich & Goldman, 1972; Shipman, Barone, Beaton, Emmerich, & Ward, 1971). They have concluded that children between the ages of 3½ and 5 have little gender constancy. Between 5 and 7, gender constancy becomes increasingly evident. Children understand gender constancy earlier when it is applied to themselves than when it is applied to others. After gender constancy has been achieved, the child must then determine which behaviors are sex appropriate and which are not. In the early stages of development a child may not know who shares a sex category with him/her, particularly if the other person is an adult. Kohlberg has stated that it is a cognitively more difficult task to perceive similarity between an adult female and a girl than to perceive similarity between two girls. When a child understands sex groupings, s/he is in a position to identify sex-appropriate behaviors by observing what same-sex persons do and then matching his/her own behavior to the construct s/he has developed (Wolman, 1978; Wolman & Money, 1980).

Experimental support for the Kohlberg position is somewhat ambiguous. On the one hand gender constancy has been related to cognitive level and to performance on Piagetian tasks of physical conservation, which require the recognition of constancy of physical objects despite changes in appearance (LaVoie & Andrews, 1975; Marcus & Overton, 1978). There is also some indication that the development of gender constancy accelerates the process of sex typing. Slaby (in Maccoby &

Jacklin, 1974) has found that kindergarteners who understand gender constancy choose to observe same-sex models as opposed to opposite-sex models, whereas children who have not developed gender constancy have no such preferences. On the other hand, however, sex typing of behavior begins before the child has a stable concept of gender constancy. Gender constancy has been determined by presenting a picture of a male or a female, appropriately labeled, and then making successive changes either verbally or visually which are characteristic of the opposite sex. If the original sex identification was maintained by the child in spite of transformations, constancy of gender identity was revealed—if the child changed the judgment early, s/he was assumed to lack gender constancy. Hutt (1978a) has argued that this conclusion might be fallacious: It is possible that a child who changed judgments early had a stronger (if more rigid) gender identity, thereby making him/her less tolerant of the transformations. Maccoby and Jacklin (1974) point out that *complete* acquisition of gender constancy is not necessary in order for self-socialization into sex roles to begin.

Sex Role as a Mediator of Intellectual Differences

Recently there has been a great deal of interest in examining sex role as a mediator of intellectual differences. For some people sex-role prescriptions regarding appropriate and inappropriate behavior are translated into personal beliefs which can affect intellectual pursuits in sex-typed domains. Nash (1979) has written an excellent review of this literature and has suggested that the findings support a "cognitive-consistency" type of model. There is clear evidence in this literature to support Kohlberg's prediction that the child will strive to act consistently with his/her gender self-categorization. Nash has further traced the development of gender identity and related this development to corresponding changes in sex-role behaviors and intellectual performance. She contends that sex-related differences emerge more strongly during adolescence because sex-role requirements are more rapidly augmented at that time. During childhood a child is relatively asexual and is busy playing and learning about the world. The child is task oriented, and sex-specific behaviors are not demanded in most situations. At adolescence, however, there is a heightened self-awareness, and sex roles become more critical to a child's self-definition because of the salience of sexual maturation, the need for reciprocal role behaviors in heterosexual relationships, and the importance of appropriate traits and behaviors in defining one's acceptability in the peer group.

Several researchers have examined the differential effects on the performance of each sex when cognitive tasks were labeled as masculine or feminine. Simply labeling a task as appropriate for either boys or girls has had the effect of increasing expectancy for success, appeal of the game, task persistence, quality of performance, and achievement level attained (Etaugh & Ropp, 1976; Montemayor, 1974; Stein, Pohly, & Mueller, 1971) when the task was sex appropriate. Moreover using a same-sex examiner increased third-grade students' scores on the WISC (Pedersen, Shinedling, & Johnson, 1975), and

feminizing the content of problems on a measure of spatial ability increased the performance of females (Naditch, 1976). Stein and Bailey (1973) have shown that females consistently demonstrate higher expectations for success and higher standards of performance for sex-appropriate versus sex-inappropriate areas of achievement.

A second research strategy has been to explore within-group differences in cognitive performance as a function of personal strength of sex-role orientation and salience of sex role to their self-definition. Maccoby and Jacklin (1974) have speculated that if researchers had chosen subsamples of the population who had strong beliefs about their sex-role preferences, then it is highly probable that greater and more consistent sex-related differences would have emerged. As Nash (1979) points out, individual differences in defining achievement as sex-role appropriate or inappropriate appear to determine performance levels. Females who defined academic achievement as sex appropriate have been found to get better grades (Houts & Entwisle, 1968), be more successful students (Lesser, Krawitz, & Packard, 1963), and engage in more achievement-related behaviors (Stein, 1971). Alper (1976) has found that females with nontraditional role orientations received higher grade point averages than traditional types. Fear of success has also been shown to be strongest among women with more traditional sex roles (Alper, 1974; Tresemer & Pleck, 1976; Zuckerman & Wheeler, 1975). Condry and Dyer (1976) point out that fear of success is actually the fear of deviating from sex-role standards, and Deaux (1976) concludes that neither sex fears success, but rather both sexes will avoid success if it is clear that the consequences are negative because success conflicts with social norms relating to sex roles.

SOCIAL FACTORS: EXTRAFAMILIAL INFLUENCES

Sex Roles in the Media

Television Programming. It has been estimated that children under the age of five view an average of 25.5 hours of television per week. By the time a child finishes high school, s/he will have spent more than 15,000 hours watching television, or about one year and nine months. This is almost one-ninth of his/her lifetime. During this time the child will have been exposed to 20,000 commercials per year, or a total of 360,000 by the age of 18 (Action for Children's Television, 1978).

A vast body of evidence has been accumulated over the past three decades which describes the portrayal of male and female roles in television programming intended for both children and general audiences. There exists considerable agreement among most of these studies as to the number of male and female characters presented and the range of behaviors of these characters, as well as the accuracy of these roles in reflecting the real world.

In a representative study Sternglanz and Serbin (1974) examined many popular children's shows in much the same manner that Child, Potter, and Levine (1960) analyzed the sex-role content of children's books. The results indicate that children's programs present disproportionate numbers of male and female characters and a severely limited and stereotyped repertoire of sex-typed behaviors. Moreover boys are often shown being rewarded for engaging in interesting behaviors, while girls are frequently shown being ignored.

In other content studies Long and Simon (1974) found only 34 female characters in all the programs studied, and these were presented in very traditional female roles characterized by dependence and overemotionalism. There was not a single instance in which a married woman worked outside the home. Similarly Busby (1974) studied the sex-role content of network children's programming and found significant differences between males and females on 24 of 40 semantic differential items. Male characters in these shows were perceived as more ambitious, violent, aggressive, independent, and competitive than their female counterparts. At the same time they were also seen as less sensitive, less emotional, and less affectionate. Streicher (1974), in a content analysis of cartoons, found that females were less numerous, had fewer lines, played fewer lead roles, and made fewer appearances than their male counterparts. Moreover female characters held fewer positions of responsibility and were portrayed as less active, less noisy, less skillful, and more juvenile in their characterizations.

Content analyses of educational television shows indicate little difference between commercial and public broadcasting networks in their presentations of sex roles. Even *Sesame Street,* the award-winning, progressive educational program, appears to have a sex-ratio problem. Vogal (1970) reported a 2:1 male to female ratio in the roles portrayed. A few years later after considerable protest from parent and feminist groups, the ratio had *risen* to 2.5:1 (Bernabei, 1974). It is interesting to note that neither of these studies included the animated or puppet characters—a fact which would raise the male to female ratio quite significantly.

For the sake of brevity, only the program content of children's shows has been discussed in detail. However the depiction of inaccurate or inappropriate sex-role stereotypes is not solely the province of children's programming. Indeed the patterns discussed above are evident in regular prime-time programming (Kanuiga, Scott, & Gade, 1974; Tedesco, 1974), advertising aimed at children (Courtney & Whipple, 1974; Dominick & Rauch, 1972), and all other types of television programming. The consistency of the results of these content studies is quite striking.

It is difficult to generalize from the large body of evidence as to the effects of television exposure on children because of the difficulty in isolating such effects from those of other socialization agents. For the child television is a diversified form of entertainment which is very active, discontinuous, and largely devoid of parental influence. The child often begins viewing television about the age of two and develops definite preferences by the age of three. That which is viewed on television is perceived by the child as reality, and observed behaviors may be learned without immediate practice or reinforcement. In this way television can affect both the informational and attitudinal systems of the child (Comstock, 1975). It has been assumed that television exposure has definite effects (both positive and negative) upon the

sex-role development of children, yet this assumption is difficult to prove or disprove. However the potential power of television as a socialization agent seems beyond dispute. Ra (1977) has established that television has had a great impact on the social relationships of children. This researcher found that 44 percent of the children questioned stated that they would rather watch television than spend time with their fathers. On the other hand only 20 percent of children preferred watching television to being with their mothers. Boys did not differ significantly from girls in their preferences for parents versus television.

In a study which sought to investigate television effects upon sex-role socialization, Freuh and McGhee (1975) found that children who viewed a great deal of television achieved higher It scale scores (i.e., had more traditional sex-role identities). Furthermore boys had higher scores than girls, and all scores increased with age as the exposure to television increased.

Printed Matter. Many of the sex-role stereotypes observed in the broadcast media are also evident in the various types of printed matter directed at the children's market. In 1971 Nilsen examined all of the Caldecott Award–winning literature published over two decades and found that all had male characters, yet six of the books had no females. Almost 25 percent of these books contained females only in minor roles. In 1972 Weitzman, Eifler, Hokada, and Ross took another look at the literature awarded the Caldecott medal. The most salient fact about the image of females in these books was simply that they were invisible; females were underrepresented in titles, central roles, pictures, and stories. Most of the books were about boys, men, male animals, and male adventures. The ratio of males to females represented in pictures was 11:1. The female characters were portrayed as passive and doll-like; they were engaged primarily in service activities—loving, mothering, helping, watching. The boys, on the other hand, were shown as active and adventuresome; they were engaged in a variety of diverse, interesting, and independent tasks—storekeepers, builders, storytellers, fighters, fishermen, policemen, soldiers, adventurers, preachers, judges, farmers, and, of course, kings and gods. The authors conclude,

Little girls receive attention and praise for their attractiveness, while boys are admired for their achievements and cleverness. For girls, achievement is marriage and becoming a mother. Most of the women in picture books have status by virtue of their relationships to specific men—they are the wives of the kings, judges, adventurers, and explorers, but they themselves are not the rulers, judges, adventurers, and explorers. (p. 1141)

The Influence of the School System

As the child matures and begins to participate in the school system and the peer group, other socialization agents take on more significance in shaping sex-role behaviors. In general the educational system helps to instill and reinforce sex-role stereotypes, particularly those characteristics which are often seen as feminine—quietness, obedience, and passivity. It is not surprising, then, that during the elementary school years, girls like school more than boys do and demonstrate higher achievement scores. Boys, on the other hand, perform generally below their ability levels and have more difficulty adjusting to the school environment.

The Role of the Teacher. A large body of evidence has been accumulated which demonstrates that teachers respond differentially to male and female students. Serbin et al. (1973) recorded and analyzed teacher responses to two types of behavior—disruption and dependency. It was found that teachers were more likely to respond to disruptive behaviors, especially aggressive behaviors, in boys than in girls. The teacher response rate toward boys was three times that for girls. Moreover teachers spoke more loudly when reprimanding boys. Girls, on the other hand, were rewarded for dependency behaviors and received more attention while in close proximity to the teacher. No such proximity effect was demonstrated for boys who received a constant rate of attention.

In an earlier study O'Leary, Kaufman, Kass, and Drabman (1970) showed that loud reprimands by the teachers reinforced and maintained disruptive behaviors at a high rate. Further investigation had demonstrated that when such behaviors are simply ignored, their incidence decreases markedly (Pinkston, Reese, LeBlanc, & Baer, 1979).

Teachers are more likely to respond favorably to boys engaged in task-oriented behaviors (Fagot, 1977; Serbin et al., 1973) and to criticize boys who participate in cross-sex activities such as dress-up and doll play (Fagot, 1977). Research evidence suggests that girls, at least at young ages have more latitude in their play interests.

Dweck and colleagues have studied type of teacher feedback and its relationship to female underachievement (Dweck & Bush, 1976; Dweck, Davidson, Nelson, & Enna, 1978; Dweck & Goetz, 1977). Girls are more likely than boys to exhibit a phenomenon Dweck calls *learned helplessness,* a decreased persistence in response to failure or increased task difficulty. Failure is perceived as insurmountable because it is attributed to stable, uncontrollable factors such as lack of ability; thus, females give up after failure. Boys, on the other hand, tend to externalize failure and view it as bad luck or lack of effort; after failure they tend to increase their persistence and improve performance. Dweck has related these reactions to failure to differential feedback given by teachers. For boys about 45 percent of the teachers' negative criticism was given for conduct or nonintellectual aspects of their work, such as failure to obey the rules of form, lack of neatness, or motivation. For girls almost 90 percent of negative feedback related directly to the accuracy and intellectual quality of their work. Thus girls come to feel that an evaluation is indicative of their level of ability, and they become disrupted by failure. Boys, however, perceive the teacher's evaluations as unrelated to their intellectual performance and begin to discount it or attribute it to external factors; thus, negative feedback has little effect on the estimation of their own ability.

Several recent studies indicate that male teachers are more critical of male students, yet have a positive effect on boys without a disruptive effect on girls. Lee and Wolinsky (1973) found that boys felt closer to, and better liked by, male teachers, perhaps because male teachers are more likely to get involved in male activities and assign leadership roles to boys. Other investigations, more international in scope, have shown that the high incidence of reading problems among boys is significantly reduced by having male teachers who foster the idea that learning is male appropriate. In Japan reading problems are equally distributed between boys and girls (cited by Janis, Mahl, Kagan, & Holt, 1969), while in Germany boys demonstrate significantly higher reading achievement scores than girls (Preston, 1962). Similar results have been shown in England (Brimer, 1969) and in the United States where male students are taught by male teachers (Shinedling & Pederson, 1970).

Textbooks and Tests. The school system facilitates the role learning of sex-appropriate behaviors (i.e., passivity, conformity, and obedience) to the detriment of *both* boys and girls. The system which encourages the early achievement of girls also communicates to them that they are less important than boys, as seen in the content of textbooks at almost all educational levels. Taylor (1973) analyzed all of the California state elementary reading texts and concluded that (1) many failed to portray women in positive roles, (2) most had no females in major roles, and (3) males were most often shown performing important, interesting tasks while females observed them passively. Weitzman and Rizzo (1974) demonstrated that these stereotypes are not restricted to elementary readers but are also found in spelling, mathematics, science, and social science texts. Women are rarely mentioned in important roles in history such as diplomats or scientists. For example only 6 percent of the pictures in science textbooks include adult women.

A number of researchers have found a similar masculine bias in educational achievement tests. Test items contained substantially more male noun and pronoun references. Item content analysis also revealed that all of the professors, doctors, presidents of companies, and members of professional teams were male, while almost all school teachers were female. Moreover most biographies were about men, and some questions implied that certain professions were closed to women (Saario, Jacklin, & Tittle, 1973).

Educational Teaching Systems. Many high schools have had a sex-stereotyped tracking system. In college preparatory courses females are tracked into English and the social sciences while males are tracked into the hard sciences and mathematics. In the more vocational areas girls are encouraged to take typing, bookkeeping, consumer, and homemaking courses; boys are encouraged to take agriculture, mechanics, and various technical courses such as metallurgy, engineering, and police science. As Weitzman (1979) points out, tracking systems have not only channeled the two sexes into two different vocational directions but have also kept boys and girls from learning skills useful in later life. Thus girls do not understand the mechanics of an automobile or how to fix things around the house, and boys are unable to cook and care for young children. In addition to the tracking system, girls have also been excluded from most rigorous sports and school athletic teams, such that boys' participation in sports is 12 times that of girls (Saario et al., 1973).

ANDROGENY

Is androgeny the answer to the confining effects of sex-role standards? Theoretically *androgeny* implies an integration of both high masculine and high feminine traits in a single individual. This person should be maximally effective in a wide range of situations because s/he will not be constrained by either set of sex-role standards. Bem (1975) has reported findings to support this idea. She found that individuals who scored high on her measure of androgeny were more effective than either highly masculine or highly feminine scoring individuals in situations calling for both masculine and feminine stereotyped behaviors. However there are also a few studies which have reported that high general intelligence and creativity are associated with cross-sex typing (a measure indicating neither strong nor weak masculine or feminine traits) (Barron, 1957; Bieri, 1960; Maccoby, 1966; MacKinnon, 1962). Oetzel (1961) and Stein and Bailey (1973) confirmed these findings in children and postulated that such children who were high in achievement and creativity have expanded their behavioral repertoire to include characteristics of both sexes. As Nash (1979) points out, the implicit assumption here is that cross-sex typing is analogous to androgeny. However, at present, because of the problems associated with measuring masculinity and femininity, it is not clear whether the superior performance attributed to the cross-sex typed and androgenous individual is real or whether it is an artifact of measurement. Further it is not clear what effect androgeny would have on the development of the child. Sex typing is related to popularity among peers and is an important part of self-concept development. Would an androgenous child feel as good about him/herself, and would s/he be able to maintain a position of status in the peer group? More research is critically needed. We must understand the effect sex role has on other developing systems and how personal sex-role attributions become central to some individuals and not others. Rather than trying to socialize a child into having an equal number of masculine and feminine traits, it might be more profitable to alter the system of values, such that all sex-typed behaviors would be equally valued whether they were performed by a male or a female. In this way each child could develop his/her full potential without regard for which traits would be more socially acceptable than others.

REFERENCES

Action for Children's Television (ACT). Spring 1978, *7* (No. 3).

ALLAMAN, J. D., JOYCE, C. S., & CRANDALL, V. C. The antecedents of social desirability response tendencies of children and young adults. *Child Development,* 1972, *43,* 1135–1160.

ALPER, T. G. Achievement motivation in college women: A now you see it—now you don't phenomenon. *American Psychologist,* 1974, *29,* 194–203.

ALPER, T. G. The relationship between role orientation and achievement motivation in college women. Pp. 99–121 in F. L. Denmark (Ed.), *Women* (Vol. 1). New York: Psychological Dimensions, 1976.

BAKER, S. W., & EHRHARDT, A. A. Prenatal androgen, intelligence and cognitive sex differences. Pp. 53–84 in R. C. Friedman, R. N. Richart, & R. L. Vande Wiele (Eds.), *Sex differences in behavior.* New York: John Wiley, 1974.

BAN, P. L., & LEWIS, M. Mothers and fathers, girls and boys: Attachment behavior in the one-year-old. *Merrill-Palmer Quarterly,* 1974, *20,* 195–204.

BANDURA, A., & WALTERS, R. W. *Social learning and personality development.* New York: Holt, Rinehart & Winston, 1963.

BARCLAY, A. G., & CUSUMANO, D. Father absence, cross-sex identity and field dependent behavior in male adolescents. *Child Development,* 1967, *38,* 243–250.

BARRON, F. Originality in relation to personality and intellect. *Journal of Personality,* 1957, *25,* 730–742.

BARRY, H., BACON, M., & CHILD, I. L. A cross-cultural survey of some sex differences in socialization. *Journal of Abnormal and Social Psychology,* 1957, *55,* 327–332.

BAUMRIND, D., & BLACK, A. E. Socialization practices associated with dimensions of competence in preschool boys and girls. *Child Development,* 1967, *38,* 291–327.

BAYLEY, N. Developmental problems of the mentally retarded child. Pp. 85–110 in I. Philips (Ed.), *Prevention and treatment of mental retardation.* New York: Basic Books, 1966.

BEE, H. L., VAN EGEREN, L. F., STREISSGUTH, A. P., NYMAN, B. A., & LECKIE, M. S. Social class differences in maternal teaching strategies and speech patterns. *Developmental Psychology,* 1969, *1,* 726–734.

BEM, S. L. The measurement of psychological androgyny. *Journal of Clinical and Consulting Psychology,* 1974, *42,* 155–162.

BEM, S. L. Sex-role adaptability: One consequence of psychological androgyny. *Journal of Personality and Social Psychology,* 1975, *31,* 634–643.

BENTZEN, F. Sex ratios in learning and behavior disorders. *American Journal of Orthopsychiatry,* 1963, *33,* 92–98.

BERNABEI, R. *Can you tell me how to get to Sesame Street?* Columbus: Ohio State University, 1974.

BEST, D. L., WILLIAMS, J. E., CLOUD, J. M., DAVIS, S. W., ROBERTSON, L. S., EDWARDS, J. R., GILES, H., & FOWLES, J. Development of sex-trait stereotypes among young children in the United States, England and Ireland. *Child Development,* 1977, *48,* 1375–1384.

BIERI, J. Parental identification, acceptance of authority, and within-sex differences in cognitive behavior. *Journal of Abnormal and Social Psychology,* 1960, *60,* 76–79.

BILLER, H. B. Father absence, maternal encouragement, and sex role development in kindergarten age boys. *Child Development,* 1969, *40,* 539–546.

BILLER, H. B., & BAHM, R. M. Father absence, perceived maternal behavior and masculinity of self-concept among junior high school boys. *Developmental Psychology,* 1971, *4,* 178–181.

BLOCK, J. H. *Conceptions of sex roles: Some cross-cultural and longitudinal perspectives.* Unpublished manuscript, 1972.

BLOCK, J. H. Another look at sex differentiation in the socialization behaviors of mothers and fathers. In F. Wenmark & J. Sherman (Eds.), *Psychology of women: Future direction of research.* New York: Psychological Dimensions, 1978.

BLOCK, J. H., BLOCK, J., & HARRINGTON, D. M. *The relationship of parental teaching strategies to ego-resilience in pre-school children.* Paper presented at the meeting of the Western Psychological Association, San Francisco, 1974.

BRIM, O. G. Family structure and sex role learning by children: A further analysis of Helen Koch's data. *Sociometry,* 1958, *21,* 1–16.

BRIMER, M. A. Sex differences in listening comprehension. *Journal of Research and Development Education,* 1969, *3,* 72–79.

BRINDLEY, C., CLARKE, P., HUTT, C., ROBINSON, I., & WETHLI, E. Sex differences in the activities and social interactions of nursery school children. In R. P. Michael & J. H. Crook (Eds.), *Comparative ecology and behavior of primates.* New York: Academic Press, 1973.

BROCA, P. Sur la faculté du langage articulé. *Bulleten Societie d'Anthropologie* (Paris), 1865, *6,* 337–393.

BRONFENBRENNER, U. Some familial antecedents of responsibility and leadership in adolescents. In L. Petrullo & B. M. Bass (Eds.), *Studies in leadership.* New York: Holt, Rinehart & Winston, 1960.

BRONSON, W. C. *Exploratory behavior of 15-month-old infants in a novel situation.* Paper presented at the meeting of the Society for Research in Child Development, Minneapolis, 1971.

BROWN, D. G. Sex-role preference in children: Methodological problems. *Psychological Reports,* 1962, *11,* 477–478.

BRYDEN, M. P. Evidence for sex-related differences in cerebral organization. In M. A. Wittig & A. C. Petersen (Eds.), *Sex related differences in cognitive functioning: Developmental issues.* New York: Academic Press, 1979.

BUFFERY, A.W.H. Sex differences in the development of hand preference, cerebral dominance for speech and cognitive skill. *Bulletin of the British Psychological Society,* 1970, *24,* 242–243.

BUSBY, L. J. *Sex roles as presented in commercial network programs directed toward children: Rationale and analysis.* Unpublished doctoral dissertation, University of Michigan, 1974.

CANTOR, N. L., WOOD, D., & GELFAND, D. Effects of responsiveness and sex of children on adult males' behavior. *Child Development,* 1977, *48,* 1426–1430.

CARMON, A., & NACHSON, I. Ear asymmetry in perception of emotional non-verbal stimuli. *Acta Psychologia,* 1973, *37,* 351–357.

CHILD, I., POTTER, E., & LEVINE, E. Children's textbooks and personality development: An exploration in the social psychology of education. Pp. 292–305 in M. L. Haimowitz & N. R. Haimowitz (Eds.), *Human development: Selected readings.* New York: Harper & Row, Pub., 1960.

COMSTOCK, G. The effects of television on children and adolescents. *Journal of Communication,* 1975, *11,* 25–34.

CONDRY, J., & DYER, S. Fear of success: Attribution of cause to the victim. *Journal of Social Issues,* 1976, *32,* 63–83.

COURTNEY, A. E., & WHIPPLE, T. W. Women on TV commercials. *Journal of Communication,* 1974, *24,* 110–118.

CURRY, F.K.W. A comparison of left-handed and right-handed subjects on verbal and non-verbal dichotic listening tasks. *Cortex,* 1967, *3,* 343–352.

CURTIS, G. H. Long-term changes in corticosteroid excretion. In M. Ferin, F. Halberg, R. M. Richart, & R. L. Vande Wiele (Eds.), *Biorhythms and human reproduction.* New York: John Wiley, 1974.

DALTON, K. Ante-natal progesterone and intelligence. *British Journal of Psychiatry,* 1968, *144,* 1377–1382.

DAN, A. J. The menstrual cycle and sex-related differences in cognitive variability. In M. A. Wittig & A. C. Petersen (Eds.), *Sex related differences in cognitive functioning: Developmental issues.* New York: Academic Press, 1979.

DEAUX, K. *The behavior of women and men.* Monterey, Calif.: Brooks/Cole, 1976.

DEVRIES, R. Constancy of generic identity in the years three to six. *Monographs of the Society for Research in Child Development,* 1969, *34* (Whole No. 3).

DIAMOND, M., DIAMOND, A., & MAST, M. Visual sensitivity and sexual arousal levels during the menstrual cycle. *Journal of Nervous Mental Disorders,* 1972, *155,* 170–176.

DOERING, C. H., KRAEMER, H. C., BRODIE, H.K.H., & HAMBURG, D. A. A cycle of plasma testosterone in the human male. *Journal of Clinical Endocrinology and Metabolism,* 1975, *40,* 492–500.

DOMINICK, J. R., & RAUCH, G. E. The image of women in network television commercials. *Journal of Broadcasting,* 1972, *16,* 259–265.

DRAKE, C. T., & McDOUGALL, D. Effects of the absence of a father and other male models on the development of boys' sex roles. *Developmental Psychology,* 1977, *13,* 537–538.

DROPPLEMAN, L. F., & SCHAEFER, E. S. Boys' and girls' reports of maternal and paternal behavior. *Journal of Abnormal and Social Psychology,* 1963, *67,* 648–654.

DWECK, C. S., & BUSH, E. S. Sex differences in learned helplessness: I. Differential debilitation with peer and adult evaluators, *Developmental Psychology,* 1976, *12* (No. 2), 147–156.

DWECK, C. S., DAVIDSON, W., NELSON, S., & ENNA, B. Sex differences in learned helplessness: II. The contingencies of evaluative feedback in the classroom and III. An experimental analysis. *Developmental Psychology,* 1978, *14* (No. 3), 268–276.

DWECK, C. S., & GOETZ, F. E. Attributions and learned helplessness. In J. H. Harvey, W. Ickes, & R. F. Kidd (Eds.), *New directions in attribution research* (Vol. 2). Hillsdale, N.J.: Lawrence Erlbaum Associates, 1977.

EHRHARDT, A. A., & BAKER, S. W. Fetal androgens, human central nervous system differentiation and behavior sex differences. Pp. 33–51 in R. C. Friedman, R. M. Richart, & R. L. Vande Wiele (Eds.), *Sex differences in behavior.* New York: John Wiley, 1974.

EHRHARDT, A. A., & MONEY, J. Progestin-induced hermaphroditism: I.Q. and psychosexual identity in a study of ten girls. *Journal of Sex Research,* 1967, *3,* 63–100.

EMMERICH, W., & GOLDMAN, K. S. Boy-girl identity task (techni-

cal report). In V. Shipman (Ed.), *Disadvantaged children and their first school experiences* (Technical Report PR-72-20). Princeton, N.J.: Educational Testing Service, 1972.

ETAUGH, C., COLLINS, G., & GERSON, A. Reinforcement of sex-typed behaviors of two-year-old children in a nursery school setting. *Developmental Psychology,* 1975, *11,* 255–259.

ETAUGH, C., & ROPP, J. Children's self-evaluation of performance as a function of sex, age, feedback, and sex type task label. *The Journal of Psychology,* 1976, *94,* 115–122.

FAGOT, B. I. Sex differences in toddlers' behavior and parental reaction. *Developmental Psychology,* 1974, *10,* 554–558.

FAGOT, B. I. Consequences of moderate cross-gender behavior in preschool children. *Child Development,* 1977, *48,* 902–907.

FEIN, G., JOHNSON, D., KOSSON, N., STORK, L., & WASSERMAN, L. Sex stereotypes and preferences in toy choices in 20-month-old boys and girls. *Developmental Psychology,* 1975, *11,* 527–528.

FERGUSON, L. R., & MACCOBY, E. E. Interpersonal correlates of differential abilities. *Child Development,* 1966, *37,* 549–571.

FESHBACH, N. D. *Cross-cultural studies of teaching styles in four-year-olds and their mothers: Some educational implications of socialization.* Paper presented at the Minnesota Symposium on Child Psychology, April 1972.

FLANNERY, R., & BALLING, J. D. *Hemispheric specialization of spatial ability in children.* Paper presented to Society for Research in Child Development, New Orleans, March 1977.

FLING, S., & MANOSEVITZ, M. Sex typing in nursery school children's play interests. *Developmental Psychology,* 1972, *7,* 146–152.

FOX, L. H., TOBIN, D., & BRODY, L. Sex role socialization and achievement in mathematics. In M. A. Wittig & A. C. Petersen (Eds.), *Sex related differences in cognitive functioning: Developmental issues.* New York: Academic Press, 1979.

FREUH, T., & McGHEE, P. E. Traditional sex role development and amount of time spent watching television. *Developmental Psychology,* 1975, *11,* 109.

GARDNER, R. W., JACKSON, D. N., & MESSICK, S. J. Personality organization in cognitive controls and intellectual abilities. *Psychological Issues,* 1960, *2* (No. 8).

GEFFNER, D. S., & HOCHBERG, I. Ear laterality performance of children from low and middle socioeconomic levels on a verbal dichotic listening task. *Cortex,* 1971, *7,* 193–203.

GERSON, M. Women in the kibbutz. *American Journal of Orthopsychiatry,* 1971, *41,* 566–573.

GEWIRTZ, H. B., & GEWIRTZ, J. L. Visiting and caretaking patterns for kibbutz infants: Age and sex trends. *American Journal of Orthopsychiatry,* 1968, *38,* 427–443.

GLICK, P. C. *Who are the children in one-parent households?* Paper delivered at Wayne State University, Detroit, 1979.

GOLDBERG, S., & LEWIS, M. Play behavior in the year-old infant: Early sex differences. *Child Development,* 1969, *40,* 21–31.

GOODENOUGH, D. R., GANDINI, E., OLKIN, I., PIZZAMIGLIO, L., THAYER, D., & WITKIN, H. A. A study of chromosome linkage with field dependence and spatial visualization. *Behavior Genetics,* 1977, *24,* 377–388.

GOODENOUGH, D. R., & KARP, S. A. Field dependence and intellectual functioning. *Journal of Abnormal and Social Psychology,* 1961, *63,* 241–246.

GORDON, H. W. Hemispheric asymmetries in the perception of musical chords. *Cortex,* 1970, *6,* 387–398.

GOY, R. W. Organizing effects of androgen on the behavior of rhesus monkeys. Pp. 12–31 in R. P. Michael (Ed.), *Endocrinology and human behavior.* London: Oxford University Press, 1968.

HAAVIO-MANNILA, E. Convergences between East and West: Tradition and modernism in sex-roles in Sweden, Finland and the Soviet Union. In M.T.S. Mednick, S. S. Tangri & L. W. Hoffman (Eds.), *Women and achievement: Social and motivational analyses.* New York: Halsted Press, 1975.

HAMILTON, C. R., HENKIN, R. I., WEIR, G., & KLIMAN, B. Olfactory status and response to clomiphene in male gonadotropin deficiency. *Annals of Internal Medicine,* 1973, *78,* 47–55.

HARKNESS, R. A. Variations in testosterone excretion by man. In M. Ferin, F. Halberg, R. M. Richart, & R. L. Vande Wiele (Eds.), *Biorhythms and human behavior.* New York: John Wiley, 1974.

HARTLEY, R. E. Sex role pressures and the socialization of the male child. *Psychological Reports,* 1959, *5,* 457–468.

HARTLEY, R. E. Children's concepts of male and female roles. *Merrill-Palmer Quarterly,* 1960, *6,* 83–91.

HARTUP, W. W., MOORE, S. G., & SAGER, G. Avoidance of inappropriate sex-typing by young children. *Journal of Consulting Psychology*, 1963, *27*, 467–473.

HATFIELD, J. S., FERGUSON, L. R., & ALPERT, R. Mother-child interaction and the socialization process. *Child Development*, 1967, *38*, 365–414.

HENKIN, R. I. Sensory changes during the menstrual cycle. In M. Ferin, F. Halberg, R. M. Richart, & R. L. Vande Wiele (Eds.), *Biorhythms and human reproduction*. New York: John Wiley, 1974.

HETHERINGTON, E. M. A developmental study of the effects of sex of the dominant parent on sex role preference, identification and imitation in children. *Journal of Personality and Social Psychology*, 1965, *2*, 188–194.

HETHERINGTON, E. M. The effects of familial variables on sex typing, on parent-child similarity and on imitation in children. Pp. 82–107 in J. P. Hill (Ed.), *Minnesota Symposia on Child Psychology* (Vol. 1). Minneapolis: Minnesota University Press, 1967.

HETHERINGTON, E. M. Effects of father-absence on personality development in adolescent daughters. *Developmental Psychology*, 1972, *7*, 313–326.

HETHERINGTON, E. M. *Changing sex-role stereotypes*. Unpublished manuscript, 1974.

HETHERINGTON, E. M. *Mothers' and fathers' responses to appropriate and inappropriate dependency in sons and daughters*. Unpublished manuscript, 1978.

HETHERINGTON, E. M., COX, M., & COX, R. Family interaction and the social, emotional and cognitive development of children following divorce. In V. Vaughn & T. B. Brazelton (Eds.), *The family: Setting priorities*. New York: HBJ Legal & Professional Publications, 1979.

HETHERINGTON, E. M., & DEUR, J. The effects of father absence on child development. *Young Children*, 1971, *26*, 233–248.

HOFFMAN, L. W. Early childhood experiences and women's achievement motives. *Journal of Social Issues*, 1972, *23*, 129–155.

HOFFMAN, L. W. The value of children to parents and the decrease in family size. *Proceedings of the American Philosophical Society*, 1975, *119*, 430–438.

HOFFMAN, M. L., & SALTZSTEIN, H. D. Parent discipline and the child's moral development. *Journal of Personality and Social Psychology*, 1967, *5*, 45–57.

HOUTS, P. S., & ENTWISLE, P. R. Academic achievement effort among females: Achievement attitudes and sex role orientation. *Journal of Consulting Psychology*, 1968, *15*, 284–286.

HUTT, C. Curiosity in young children. *Science Journal*, 1970, *6*, 68–71.

HUTT, C. Sex-role differentiation in social development. In H. McGurk (Ed.), *Issues in childhood social development*. Cambridge, England: Cambridge University Press, 1978a.

HUTT, C. Biological bases of psychological sex differences. *American Journal of Diseases of Children*, 1978b, *132*, 170–177.

JACKLIN, C. N., MACCOBY, E. E., & DICK, A. E. Barrier behavior and toy preference: Sex differences (and their absence) in the year-old child. *Child Development*, 1973, *44*, 196–200.

JANIS, I. L., MAHL, G. F., KAGAN, J., & HOLT, R. R. *Personality: Dynamics, development and assessment*. New York: Harcourt Brace Jovanovich, 1969.

JENSEN, A. R. The race × sex × ability interaction. Pp. 107–161 in R. Cancro (Ed.), *Intelligence: Genetic and environmental influences*. New York: Grune & Stratton, 1971.

KAGAN, J. Acquisition and significance of sex typing and sex role identity. In M. Hoffman & L. Hoffman (Eds.), *Review of child development research* (Vol. 1). New York: Russell Sage Foundation, 1964a.

KAGAN, J. The child's sex-role classification of school objects. *Child Development*, 1964b, *35*, 1051–1056.

KAGAN, J., & MOSS, H. A. *Birth to maturity: A study in psychological development*. New York: John Wiley, 1962.

KAMINSKI, L. R. *Looming effects on stranger anxiety and toy preference in one-year-old infants*. Unpublished master's thesis, Stanford University, 1973.

KANUIGA, N., SCOTT, T., & GADE, E. Working women portrayed on evening television programs. *The Vocational Guidance Quarterly*, 1974, *8*, 134–137.

KENSHALO, D. R. Psychophysical studies of human temperature sensitivity. In W. D. Neff (Ed.), *Contributions to sensory physiology* (Vol. 4). New York: Academic Press, 1970.

KESSLER, S. J., & McKENNA, W. *Gender: An ethnomethodological approach*. New York: John Wiley, 1978.

KIMURA, D. Some effects of temporal lobe damage on auditory perception. *Canadian Journal of Psychology*, 1961a, *15*, 156–165.

KIMURA, D. Cerebral dominance and the perception of verbal stimuli. *Canadian Journal of Psychology*, 1961b, *15*, 166–171.

KIMURA, D. Left-right differences in the perception of melodies. *Quarterly Journal of Psychology*, 1964, *16*, 355–358.

KNOPF, I. J. *Childhood psychopathology*. Englewood Cliffs, N.J.: Prentice-Hall, 1979.

KOESKE, R. K. *Theoretical perspectives of menstrual cycle research: The relevance of attributional approaches for the perception and explanation of premenstrual emotionality*. Paper presented to The Menstrual Cycle: An Interdisciplinary Nursing Research Conference, Chicago, June 1977.

KOHLBERG, L. A cognitive-developmental analysis of children's sex role concepts and attitudes. Pp. 82–173 in E. E. Maccoby (Ed.), *The development of sex differences*. Stanford, Calif.: Stanford University Press, 1966.

KOMAROVSKY, M. *Women in the modern world*. Boston: Little, Brown, 1953.

KREUZ, L. E., & ROSE, R. M. Assessment of aggressive behavior and plasma testosterone in a young criminal population. *Psychosomatic Medicine*, 1972, *34*, 321–332.

KREUZ, L. E., ROSE, R. M., & JENNINGS, J. R. Suppression of plasma testosterone levels and psychological stress. *Archives of General Psychiatry*, 1972, *26*, 479–482.

KUHL, J.F.W., LEE, J. K., HALBERG, F., GUNTHER, R., & KNAPP, E. Circadian and lower frequency rhythms in male grip strength and body weight. In M. Ferin, F. Halberg, R. M. Richart, & R. L. Vande Wiele (Eds.), *Biorhythms and human reproduction*. New York: John Wiley, 1974.

LAKE, D. A., & BRYDEN, M. P. Handedness and sex differences in hemispheric asymmetry. *Brain and Language*, 1976, *3*, 266–282.

LAMBERT, W. E., YACKLEY, A., & HEIN, R. N. Child training values of English Canadian and French Canadian parents. *Canadian Journal of Behavioral Science*, 1971, *3*, 217–236.

LANSDELL, H. Effect of extent of temporal lobe ablations on two lateralized deficits. *Physiology and Behavior*, 1968, *3*, 271–273.

LANSKY, L. M. The family structure also affects the model sex role attitudes in parents of preschool children. *Merrill-Palmer Quarterly*, 1967, *13*, 139–150.

LaVOIE, J. C., & ANDREWS, R. *Cognitive determinants of gender identity and constancy*. Paper presented at the annual meeting of the American Psychological Association, Chicago, 1975.

LECHY, S.C.A. *A developmental change in right hemisphere specialization*. Paper presented at the Society for Research in Child Development, New Orleans, 1977.

LEE, P. C., & WOLINSKY, A. L. Male teachers of young children. *Young Children*, 1973, *28*, 342–353.

LeMAGNEN, J. Nouvelles donneés sur le phénoméne de l'exaltolide. *Comptes Rendus Hebdomadaires es Seances de l'Academie des Sciences; D: Sciences Naturelles* (Paris), 1950, *230*, 1103–1105.

LeMAGNEN, J. Les phénoménes olfacto-sexuels chez phomme. *Archives des Science et Physiologiques* (Paris), 1952, *6*, 125–160.

LENNEBERG, E. *Biological foundations of language*. New York: John Wiley, 1967.

LESSER, G. S., KRAWITZ, R. N., & PACKARD, R. Experimental arousals of achievement motivation in adolescent girls. *Journal of Abnormal and social Psychology*, 1963, *66*, 59–66.

LEVITIN, T. E., & CHANANIE, J. D. Responses of female primary school teachers to sex-typed behaviors in male and female children. *Child Development*, 1972, *13*, 1309–1316.

LEVY, J. Possible basis for the evolution of lateral specialization of the human brain. *Nature*, 1969, *224*, 614–615.

LONG, M. L., & SIMON, R. J. The roles and statuses of women on children's and family TV programs. *Journalism Quarterly*, 1974, *16*, 107–110.

LYNN, D. B. A note on sex differences in the development of masculine and feminine identification. *Psychological Review*, 1959, *66*, 126–135.

LYNN, D. B. *Parental and sex-role identification*. Berkeley, Calif.: McCutchen, 1969.

McCALL, R. B. Exploration manipulation and play in the human infant. *Monographs of the Society for Research in Child Development*, 1974, *39*, 1–12.

McCANDLESS, B. R., & EVANS, E. D. *Children and youth: Psychological development*. Hinsdale, Ill.: Dryden Press, 1973.

MACCOBY, E. E. Sex differences in intellectual functioning. In E.

E. Maccoby (Ed.), *The development of sex differences*. Stanford, Calif.: Stanford University Press, 1966.

MACCOBY, E. E. Sex differentiation during childhood. *Catalog of Selected Documents in Psychology*, 1976, *6*(No. 4), 97.

MACCOBY, E. E., & JACKLIN, C. N. *The psychology of sex differences*. Stanford, Calif.: Stanford University Press, 1974.

MCCORD, J., MCCORD, W., & THURBER, E. Some effects of paternal absence on male children. *Journal of Abnormal and Social Psychology*, 1962, *64*, 361–369.

MCGLONE, J., & DAVIDSON, W. The relationship between cerebral speech laterality and spatial ability with special reference to sex and hand preference. *Neuropsychologia*, 1978, *11*, 105–113.

MACKINNON, D. W. The nature and nurture of creative talent. *American Psychologist*, 1962, *17*, 484–495.

MCKUSICK, V. A. *Mendelian inheritance in man: Catalogs of autosomal dominant, autosomal recessive and X-linked phenotypes* (5th ed.). Baltimore, Md.: Johns Hopkins University Press, 1978.

MARCUS, D. E., & OVERTON, W. F. The development of cognitive gender constancy and sex role preferences. *Child Development*, 1978, *49*, 420–426.

MASICA, D. N., MONEY, J., EHRHARDT, A. A., & LEWIS, V. G. I.Q., fetal sex hormones and cognitive patterns: Studies in the testicular feminizing syndrome of androgen insensitivity. *Johns Hopkins Medical Journal*, 1969, *124*, 34–43.

MEAD, M. Sex and temperament in three primitive societies. New York: Morrow, 1935.

MESSENT, P. R. Female hormones and behavior. In B. Lloyd & J. Archer (Eds.), *Exploring sex differences*. New York: Academic Press, 1976.

MEYER, W. J., & SOBIESZEK, B. J. The effect of a child's sex on adult interpretations of its behavior. *Developmental Psychology*, 1972, *6*, 42–48.

MEYER, W. J., & THOMPSON, G. G. Sex differences in the distribution of teacher approval and disapproval among sixth grade children. *Journal of Educational Psychology*, 1956, *47*, 385–397.

MINTON, C., KAGAN, J., & LEVINE, J. A. Maternal control and obedience in the two year old. *Child Development*, 1971, *42*, 1873–1894.

MISCHEL, W. Sex-typing and socialization. In P. Mussen (Ed.), *Carmichael's manual of child psychology* (Vol. 2). New York: John Wiley, 1970.

MOLFESE, D. *Auditory evoked potentials in left and right hemispheres of infants.* Paper presented at the Fourth Annual Meeting of the International Neuropsychology Society, Toronto, February 1976.

MONEY, J., & EHRHARDT, A. A. *Man and woman, boy and girl.* Baltimore, Md.: Johns Hopkins University Press, 1972.

MONEY, J., & LEWIS, V. Genetics and accelerated growth: Adrenogenital syndrome. *Bulletin of Johns Hopkins Hospital*, 1966, *118*, 365–373.

MONEY, J., LEWIS, V., EHRHARDT, A. A., & DRASH, P. W. I.Q. impairment and elevation in endocrine and related cytogenetic disorders. Pp. 22–27 in *Psychopathology of mental development.* New York: Grune & Stratton, 1967.

MONTEMAYOR, R. Children's performance in a game and their attraction to it as a function of sex-typed labels. *Child Development*, 1974, *45*, 152–156.

MOSS, H. A. Sex, age and state as determinants of mother-infant interaction. *Merrill-Palmer Quarterly*, 1967, *13*, 19–36.

MUSSEN, P. H. Early sex-role development. In D. A. Goslin (Ed.), *Handbook of socialization theory and research.* Skokie, Ill.: Rand McNally, 1969.

MUSSEN, P. H., & DISTLER, L. Masculinity identity and father-son relationships. *Journal of Abnormal and Social Psychology*, 1959, *59*, 350–356.

MUSSEN, P. H., & DISTLER, L. Child-rearing antecedents of masculine identity in kindergarten boys. *Child Development*, 1960, *31*, 89–100.

MUSSEN, P. H., & RUTHERFORD, E. Parent-child relations and parental personality in relation to young children's sex role preferences. *Child Development*, 1963, *34*, 589–607.

NADITCH, S. F. *Sex differences in field dependence: The role of social influence.* Paper presented at Symposium on Determinants of Gender Differences in Cognitive Functioning, meeting of American Psychological Association, Washington, D.C., 1976.

NAKAMURA, C. Y., & ROGERS, M. M. Parents' expectations of autonomous behavior and children's autonomy. *Developmental Psychology*, 1969, *1*, 613–617.

NASH, S. C. Sex role as a mediator of intellectual functioning. In M. A. Wittig & A. C. Petersen (Eds.), *Sex related differences in cognitive functioning: Developmental issues.* New York: Academic Press, 1979.

NEWSON, J., & NEWSON, E. *Four years old in an urban community.* Harmondsworth, England: Pelican Books, 1968.

NILSEN, A. P. Women in children's literature. *College English*, 1971, *29*, 918–926.

OETZEL, R. *The relationship between sex role acceptance and cognitive abilities.* Unpublished master's thesis, Stanford University, 1961.

O'LEARY, K. D., KAUFMAN, K., KASS, R., & DRABMAN, R. The effects of loud and soft reprimands on behavior of disruptive students. *Exceptional Children*, 1970, *37*, 145–155.

OSOFSKY, J. D., & O'CONNELL, E. J. Parent-child interaction: Daughters' effects upon mothers' and fathers' behavior. *Developmental Psychology*, 1972, *7*, 157–168.

OSOFSKY, J. D., & OLDFIELD, S. Children's effects upon parental behavior: Mothers' and fathers' responses to dependent and independent child behavior. *Proceedings of the 79th Annual Convention of the American Psychological Association*, Washington, D.C., 1971.

PARLEE, M. C. The premenstrual syndrome. *Psychological Bulletin*, 1973, *80*, 454–465.

PAYNE, D. E., & MUSSEN, P. H. Parent-child relations and father identification among adolescent boys. *Journal of Abnormal and Social Psychology*, 1956, *52*, 358–362.

PEDERSEN, F. A. Relationships between father absence and emotional disturbance in male military dependents. *Merrill-Palmer Quarterly*, 1966, *12*, 321–337.

PEDERSEN, F. A., & ROBSON, K. S. Father participation in infancy. *American Journal of Orthopsychiatry*, 1969, *39*, 466–472.

PEDERSON, D. M., SHINEDLING, M. M., & JOHNSON, D. L. Effects of examiner and subject on children's quantitative test performance. Pp. 409–416 in R. K. Unger & F. L. Denmark (Eds.), *Woman: Dependent or independent variable.* New York: Psychological Dimensions, 1975.

PERLMAN, S. M. *Cognitive function in children with hormone abnormalities.* Unpublished doctoral dissertation, Northwestern University, 1971.

PERSKY, H., SMITH, K. D., & BASU, G. K. Relation of psychologic measures of aggression and testosterone production in man. *Psychosomatic Medicine*, 1971, *33*, 265–277.

PETERSEN, A. C. Hormones and cognitive functioning in normal development. In M. A. Wittig & A. C. Petersen (Eds.), *Sex related differences in cognitive functioning: Developmental issues.* New York: Academic Press, 1979.

PETERSON, C. C., & PETERSON, J. L. Preference for sex of offspring as a measure of change in sex attitudes. *Psychology*, 1973, *10*, 3–5.

PFAFF, D., & PFAFFMAN, C. Olfactory and hormonal influences on the basal forebrain of the male rat. *Brain Research*, 1969, *15*, 137–156.

PHOENIX, C. H. Prenatal testosterone in the nonhuman primate and its consequences for behavior. Pp. 19–32 in R. C. Friedman, R. M. Richart, & R. L. Vande Wiele (Eds.), *Sex differences in behavior.* New York: John Wiley, 1974.

PINKSTON, E. M., REESE, N. M., LEBLANC, J. M., & BAER, D. M. Independent control of aggression and peer interaction by contingent teacher attention. *Journal of Applied Behavior Analysis*, 1979, *12*, 102–106.

POLANI, P. E., LESSOF, M. H., & BISHOP, P.M.F. Colour-blindness in "ovarian agenisis" (gonadal dysplasia). *The Lancet*, 1956, *2*, 118–119.

POPE, B. Socio-economic contrasts in children's peer culture prestige values. *Genetic Psychology Monographs*, 1953, *48*, 157–220.

PORTEUS, S. D. *Porteus Maze Test: Fifty years application.* Palo Alto, Calif.: Pacific Books, 1965.

PRESTON, R. C. Reading achievement of German and American children. *School and Society*, 1962, *90*, 350–354.

PULASKI, M. Play as a function of toy structure and fantasy predisposition. *Child Development*, 1970, *41*, 531–537.

RA, J. B. A comparison of preschool children's preferences for television and their parents. *Journal of Social Psychology*, 1977, *102*, 163–164.

RABBAN, M. Sex role identity in young children in two diverse social groups. *Genetic Psychology Monographs*, 1950, *42*, 81–158.

RALPH, J. B., GOLDBERG, M. L., & PASSOW, A. H. *Bright underachievers.* New York: Teachers College, 1966.

REBELSKY, F., & HANKS, C. Fathers' verbal interaction with infants in the first three months of life. *Child Development*, 1971, *42*, 63–68.

REINISCH, J. M. Prenatal exposure of human fetuses to synthetic progestin and estrogen affects on personality. *Nature*, 1977, *266*, 561–562.

REINISCH, J. M., GANDELMAN, R., & SPIEGEL, F. S. Prenatal influences on cognitive abilities: Data from experimental animals and human and endocrine syndromes. In M. A. Wittig & A. C. Petersen (Eds.), *Sex related differences in cognitive functioning: Developmental issues*. New York: Academic Press, 1979.

REINISCH, J. M., & KAROW, W. G. Prenatal exposure to synthetic progestins and estrogens: Effects on human development. *Archives of Sexual Behavior*, 1977, *6*, 257–288.

ROSE, R. M., GORDON, T. P., & BERNSTEIN, I. S. Plasma testosterone levels in male rhesus monkeys: Influence of sexual and social stimuli. *Science*, 1972, *178*, 643–645.

ROSE, R. M., HOLADAY, J. W., & BERNSTEIN, I. S. Plasma testosterone, dominance rank and aggressive behavior in male rhesus monkeys. *Nature*, 1971, *231*, 366–368.

ROSS, S. A. A test of generality of the effects of deviant preschool models. *Developmental Psychology*, 1971, *4*, 262–267.

ROTHBART, M. K., & MACCOBY, E. E. Parents' differential reactions to sons and daughters. *Journal of Personality and Social Psychology*, 1966, *4*, 237–243.

RUBIN, J. Z., PROVENZANO, F. J., & LURIA, Z. The eye of the beholder: Parents' views on sex of newborns. *American Journal of Orthopsychiatry*, 1974, *43*, 720–731.

RUSSO, M., & VIGNOLO, L. A. Visual figure-ground discrimination in patients with unilateral cerebral disease. *Cortex*, 1967, *3*, 113–127.

SAARIO, T., JACKLIN, C. N., & TITTLE, C. K. Sex role stereotyping in the public schools. *Harvard Educational Review*, 1973, *43*(No. 3), 386–404.

SAFILIOS-ROTHSCHILD, C. A cross-cultural examination of women's marital, educational and occupational opinions. *Acta Sociologica*, 1971, *14*, 96–113.

SANTROCK, J. W. Paternal absence, sex-typing and identification. *Developmental Psychology*, 1970, *2*, 264–272.

SCHNEIDER, R. A., SUSTILOE, J. P., HOWARD, R. D., & WOLF, S. Olfactory perception thresholds in hypogonadal women: Changes accompanying administration of androgen and estrogen. *Journal of Clinical Endocrinology and Metabolism*, 1958, *18*, 379–390.

SCOTT, H. *Does socialism liberate women: Experiences from Eastern Europe*. Boston: Beacon Press, 1974.

SEARS, R. R., MACCOBY, E. E., & LEVIN, H. *Patterns of child rearing*. Evanston, Ill.: Row, Peterson, 1957.

SEARS, R. R., RAU, L., & ALPERT, R. *Identification and child rearing*. Stanford, Calif.: Stanford University Press, 1965.

SERBIN, L. A., O'LEARY, D. K., KENT, R. N., & TONICK, I. J. A comparison of teacher response to the preacademic and problem behavior of boys and girls. *Child Development*, 1973, *44*, 796–804.

SHEPHERD-LOOK, D. L. Imitation: Theoretical, experimental, and developmental approaches. Pp. 487–493 in B. Wolman (Ed.), *International encyclopedia of psychiatry, psychology, psychoanalysis and neurology*. New York: Aesculapius Pub., 1977.

SHERMAN, J. A. Problems of sex differences in space perception and aspects of intellectual functioning. *Psychological Review*, 1967, *74*, 290–299.

SHIELDS, S. A. Functionalism, Darwinism and the psychology of women: A study of social myth. *American Psychologist*, 1975, *30*, 739–754.

SHINEDLING, M. M., & PEDERSON, D. M. Effects of sex of teacher and student on children's gains in quantitative and verbal performance. *Journal of Psychology*, 1970, *76*, 79–84.

SHIPMAN, V. C., BARONE, J., BEATON, A., EMMERICH, W., & WARD, W. *Disadvantaged children and their first school experiences: Structure and development of cognitive competencies and styles prior to school entry*. (Report No. 71–19) Princeton, N.J.: Educational Testing Service.

SIEGELMAN, M. Evaluation of Bronfenbrenner's questionnaire for children concerning parental behavior. *Child Development*, 1965, *36*, 163–174.

SINGER, G., & MONTGOMERY, R. G. Comment on "Role of activation and inhibition in sex differences in cognitive abilities." *Psychological Review*, 1969, *76*, 326–331.

SLABY, R. G. *Verbal regulation of aggression and altruism in children*. Paper presented at the First International Conference on the "Determinants and Analysis of Aggressive Behavior," Monte Carlo, 1973.

SLABY, R. G., & FREY, K. S. Development of gender constancy and selective attention to same-sex models. *Child Development*, 1975, *46*, 849–856.

SMITH, W. D. *Black parents' differential attitudes toward childhood behaviors and child-rearing practices*. Unpublished first year project, Stanford University, 1971.

SOMMER, B. The effect of menstruation on cognitive and perceptual-motor behavior: A review. *Psychosomatic Medicine*, 1973, *35*, 516–534.

SPENCE, J. T., HELMREICH, R., & STAPP, J. Ratings of self and peers on sex role attributes and their relation to self-esteem and conceptions of masculinity and femininity. *Journal of Personality and Social Psychology*, 1975, *32*, 29–39.

SPERRY, R. W. Lateral specialization in the surgically separated hemispheres. In F. O. Schmidt & F. G. Worden (Eds.), *The neurosciences: Third study program*. Cambridge, Mass.: M.I.T. Press, 1974.

STEIMEL, R. J. Childhood experiences and masculinity-femininity scores. *Journal of Counseling Psychology*, 1960, *7*, 212–217.

STEIN, A. H. The effects of sex-role standards for achievement and sex-role preference on the determinants of achievement motivation. *Developmental Psychology*, 1971, *4*, 219–231.

STEIN, A. H., & BAILEY, M. M. The socialization of achievement orientation in females. *Psychological Bulletin*, 1973, *5*, 345–366.

STEIN, A. H., POHLY, S. R., & MUELLER, E. The influence of masculine, feminine and neutral tasks on children's achievement behavior, expectancies of success and attainment values. *Child Development*, 1971, *42*, 195–207.

STEIN, A. H., & SMITHELLS, J. Age and sex differences in children's sex role standards about achievements. *Developmental Psychology*, 1969, *1*, 252–259.

STENN, P. G., KLAIBER, E. L., VOGEL, W., & BROVERMAN, D. M. Testosterone effects upon photic stimulation of the electroencephalogram (EEG) and mental performance of humans. *Perceptual and Motor Skills*, 1972, *34*, 371–378.

STERNGLANZ, S. H., & SERBIN, L. A. Sex role stereotyping in children's television programs. *Developmental Psychology*, 1974, *10*, 710–715.

STOTT, D. H. *Studies of troublesome children*. London: Tavistock Publications, 1966.

STREICHER, H. W. The girls in cartoons. *Journal of Communication*, 1974, *4*, 125–129.

SUTTON-SMITH, B., & SOVASTA, M. *Sex differences in play and power*. Paper presented at the Eastern Psychological Association, Boston, April 1972.

TASCH, R. J. The role of the father in the family. *Journal of Experimental Education*, 1952, *20*, 319–361.

TAVRIS, C., & OFFIR, C. *The longest war: Sex differences in perspective*. New York: Harcourt Brace Jovanovich, 1977.

TAYLOR, M. E. Sex role stereotypes in children's readers. *Elementary English*, 1973, *50*, 1061–1064.

TEDESCO, N. S. Patterns in prime time. *Journal of Communication*, 1974, *24*, 119–124.

THOMPSON, J. S., & THOMPSON, M. W. *Genetics in medicine*. Philadelphia: Saunders, 1980.

THOMPSON, S. K. Gender labels and early sex-role development. *Child Development*, 1975, *46*, 339–347.

TIGER, L., & SHEPHER, J. *Women in the kibbutz*. Harmondsworth, England: Penguin Books, 1975.

TIKHOMIROV, N., GORDON, L., & KLOPOV, E. A study of the way of life of the workers and questions of social planning. *The Working Class and the Contemporary World*, 1971, *1*, 99–112.

TRESEMER, D., & PLECK, J. Sex-role boundaries and resistance to sex-role change. In F. L. Denmark (Ed.), *Women* (Vol. 1). New York: Psychological Dimensions, 1976.

UNGER, R. K. Toward a redefinition of sex and gender. *American Psychologist*, 1979, *34*, 1085–1094.

UNGER, R. K., & DENMARK, F. L. (Eds.). *Woman: Dependent or independent variable*. New York: Psychological Dimensions, 1975.

VANDENBERG, S. G., & KUSE, A. R. Spatial ability: A critical review of the sex-linked major gene hypothesis. In M. A. Wittig & A. C. Petersen (Eds.), *Sex related differences in cognitive functioning: Developmental issues*. New York: Academic Press, 1979.

VOGAL, S. *Sesame Street and sex role stereotypes.* Pittsburgh, Pa.: KNOW, 1970.

VOGEL, W., BROVERMAN, D. M., KLAIBER, E. L., & KUN, K. J. EEG response to photic stimulation as a function of cognitive style. *Electroencephalography and Clinical Neurophysiology,* 1969, *27,* 186–190.

WABER, D. P. Sex differences in mental abilities: Hemispheric lateralization and rate of physical growth in adolescence. *Developmental Psychology,* 1977, *13,* 29–38.

WABER, D. P. Cognitive abilities and sex related variations in the maturation of cerebral cortical functions. In M. A. Wittig & A. C. Petersen (Eds.), *Sex related differences in cognitive functioning: Developmental issues.* New York: Academic Press, 1979.

WEINER, J. B. *Psychological disturbance in adolescence.* New York: Wiley International, 1970.

WEITZMAN, L. J. *Sex role socialization.* Palo Alto, Calif.: Mayfield Publishing Co., 1979.

WEITZMAN, L. J., EIFLER, D., HOKADA, E., & ROSS, C. Sex role socialization in picture books for pre-school children. *American Journal of Sociology,* 1972, *77,* 1125–1150.

WEITZMAN, L. J., & RIZZO, D. *Images of males and females in elementary school textbooks.* New York: National Organization for Women's Legal Defense and Education Fund, 1974.

WESLEY, F., & WESLEY, C. *Sex-role psychology,* New York: Human Sciences, 1977.

WHALEN, R. E. Differentiation of the neural mechanisms which control gonadotrophin secretion and sexual behavior. In M. Diamond (Ed.), *Reproduction and sexual behavior.* Bloomington: Indiana University Press, 1968.

WILL, J. A., SELF, P. A., & DATAN, N. Maternal behavior and perceived sex of infant. *American Journal of Orthopsychiatry,* 1976, *46*(No. 1), 135–139.

WITELSON, S. F. Sex and the single hemisphere: specialization of the right hemisphere for spatial processing. *Science,* 1976, *193,* 425–426.

WITELSON, S. F., & PAILLE, W. Left hemisphere specialization for language in the newborn: Neuroanatomical evidence of asymmetry. *Brain,* 1973, *96,* 641–646.

WITTIG, M. A. Genetic influences on sex-related differences in intellectual performance: Theoretical and methodological issues. In M. A. Wittig & A. C. Petersen (Eds.), *Sex related differences in cognitive functioning: Developmental issues.* New York: Academic Press, 1979.

WITTIG, M. A., & PETERSEN, A. C. (Eds.). *Sex related differences in cognitive functioning: Developmental issues.* New York: Academic Press, 1979.

WOHLFORD, R., SANTROCK, J. W., BERGER, S. E., & LIEBERMAN, D. Older brothers' influence on sex-typed aggressive and dependent behavior in father absent children. *Developmental Psychology,* 1971, *4,* 124–134.

WOLF, T. M. Influence of sex and age of model on sex-appropriate play. *Psychological Reports,* 1973, *9,* 120–123.

WOLMAN, B. B. (Ed.). *Psychological aspects of gynecology and obstetrics.* Oradell, N.J.: Medical Economics, 1978.

WOLMAN, B. B., & MONEY, J. (Eds.). *Handbook of human sexuality.* Englewood Cliffs, N.J.: Prentice-Hall, 1980.

WRIGHT, P., & CROW, R. A. Menstrual cycle: Effect on sweetness preferences in women. *Hormones and Behavior,* 1973, *4,* 387–391.

WYNN, V. T. Study of rhythms in auditory perception and simple reaction times. *Journal of Interdisciplinary Cycle Research,* 1973, *4,* 252–260.

YALOM, I. D., GREEN, R., & FISK, N. Prenatal exposure to female hormones: Effect on psychosexual development in boys. *Archives of General Psychiatry,* 1973, *28,* 554–561.

YARROW, L. J., RUBENSTEIN, J. L., & PEDERSEN, F. A. *Dimensions of early stimulation: Differential effects of infant development.* Paper presented at the meeting of the Society for Research in Child Development, 1971.

ZUCKERMAN, M., & WHEELER, L. To dispel fantasies about the fantasy-based measure of fear of success. *Psychological Bulletin,* 1975, *82,* 932–946.

24

Moral Development

JAMES L. CARROLL
JAMES R. REST

For many generations, morality was the central category for defining social relationships and development, and the social sciences were termed "the moral sciences." The great theorists of the early twentieth century also considered morality to be the key to understanding social development, as indicated by McDougall's (1908) statement that "the *fundamental problem* of social psychology is the moralization of the individual by the society," or Freud's (1930) statement that "the sense of guilt is the most important problem in the evolution of culture." (Kohlberg, 1964, p. 383)

Recent events have heightened popular concern with morality: Watergate, the civil rights movement, the women's movement, student protests, protests against the Vietnam War, exposures of corruption in big business, inner-city riots when the summers get too hot or when the lights go off. Moreover in recent years we have begun to appreciate the interdependence of world economic, ecological, and political systems—we are fellow travelers who will find better ways of living together or we will not live at all.

A question of morality arises if a person can do something that helps or hurts another person. Humans live in groups, and each person's activities can affect the welfare of others. Moral problems are those that involve deciding what rights and responsibilities each person has in interaction with other people. Ongoing social groups devise practices, norms, and procedures to regulate and coordinate these interactions—this constitutes the institutionalized morality of a group. People have vested interests both in pursuing their own personal goals and in the design and maintenance of the social order. Morality concerns how the benefits and burdens of cooperative living are to be distributed.

Psychologists have depicted moral development in various ways: as increasing capacity for guilt, as conformity to group norms, as the internal regulation of behavior in the absence of external sanctions, as prosocial or helping behavior, and as reasoning about justice. These conceptions of morality have been helpful in guiding research, and each notion has intuitive appeal. But these depictions are not independently adequate. We want to define morality in a way that captures the insights of these conceptions and, additionally, provides a guide for integrating psychological research. Our approach is to identify the major psychological components involved in behaving morally. We propose that a fully developed morality involves

1. *Recognition and sensitivity:* translating and disambiguating a given social situation so as to be aware that a moral problem exists; to be sensitive enough to recognize that someone's welfare is at stake;
2. *Moral judgment:* determining what ideally ought to be done in the situation, what one's moral ideals call for or which moral norms apply in the given circumstances;
3. *Values and influences:* devising a plan of action with one's moral ideal in mind but also taking into account nonmoral values and goals which the situation may activate, as well as the influence of situational pressures;
4. *Execution and implementation of moral action:* behaving in accordance with one's goal despite distractions, impediments, and incidental adjustments; organizing and sustaining behavior to realize one's goals.

People can fail to act morally due to deficiencies in any one of these four processes: (1) If a person is insensitive to the needs of others, s/he may fail to notice that

Preparation of this chapter was supported in part by a faculty grant from Arizona State University to J. L. Carroll. The authors would like to thank Wayne Stutzer for his assistance.

there is a moral problem. Likewise if a person is confused about a social situation and cannot settle on an interpretation of what is happening, s/he may fail to act morally. (2) It may be that a person accurately interprets the situation, but his/her concepts of fairness and moral ideals are simplistic and inadequate. (3) It may be that his/her moral ideas are adequate but they get compromised or preempted by other values (such as personal ambition, chauvinism, need to be liked) or by pressures in the situation (e.g., threats by others, contrary prevailing opinion, physical danger). (4) It may be that a person has addressed all these considerations and has formulated a plan of action but then runs out of energy to carry it out, is sidetracked by some diversion, or loses sight of the goal. The various processes described here are similar to what other writers have described as moral sensitivity, moral judgment, moral value, and moral character; however, our intention is not simply to have a list of virtues but to depict moral development in terms of component processes of moral problem solving. Full moral development, then, is depicted in terms of the adequacy of functioning in all processes; understanding and studying moral development and moral behavior require consideration of interacting processes.

RECOGNITION AND SENSITIVITY

Within the outline of psychological processes involved in moral development and moral behavior there can be little doubt of the primacy of recognition. Whether responses to a situation are immediate or highly reflective, there can be no moral response without recognition of the existence of an event or situation in which a response is possible. Even in the most rushed of circumstances, the decision to act or the response that fits a pattern of behavior based on previous decisions is dependent upon seeing the need for a decision or action. What may at first glance appear to be a failure to act or reason morally may be a failure to perceive a need. The situation as most individuals have at times experienced it is, "By the time I had figured out what was needed, it was too late to be of any assistance." Whether or not there is opportunity to reflect, characteristics of situations and individuals appear to affect whether or not moral problems are recognized.

Situation variables affecting recognition include time of exposure; amount, complexity, and organization of essential information; and salience of information concerning the moral problem. First, many situations arise quickly and pass quickly. In our surprise or shock, we may fail to perceive the situation accurately. When the event and opportunity have passed beyond our influence and we have had time to review what occurred, then, and only then, do we recognize the moral problem. We are unaware, of course, of the many moral problems or issues that pass within our view and depart unrecognized. Second, in other instances we may be vaguely aware of a problem but be unable to compute the total situation. One of the most striking findings coming from research on bystander reactions to emergencies is that people often fail to help others, but the reason they fail to help is not usually general apathy or evil intent but confusion. In emergencies people are often unable to define and appraise the situation (Huston & Korte, 1976). La-

tané and Darley (1970) indicate in their monograph on bystander intervention that the event must first be noticed and, second, be interpreted as an emergency.

Lack of information and complexity of information can each serve to block recognition of situations where a moral response is called for. When situations are most ambiguous, the frequency of offers to help is lowest. As more information is made available, help is more often offered (Staub, 1978), and when needs are clear, solitary bystanders are highly likely to help (Hoffman, 1976). When a person is in need of assistance, bystanders are more likely to help when they can see the cause of discomfort, are clearly in a position to help, and most powerfully, hear the need stated.

Situations characterized by vagueness and/or strangeness are often misperceived or misinterpreted. In the Texas Tower shooting incident, many individuals within range of the sniper at the top of the tower walked on. The sound of shooting, the sight of bodies lying on the sidewalk, and motivation for self-preservation did not stop some individuals from walking directly into the area of danger.

Of those who were only wounded, or who were lucky not to be hit, several described their reactions at the time in terms of confusion about what was going on. . . . One wounded student described his confusions about what was going on and his feeling that he would look foolish if he altered his plans and stopped walking toward the student union where he intended to eat lunch. (Baron & Byrne, 1976, quoted in Staub, 1978, pp. 86–87)

Careful preparation and unannounced simulation exercises are common elements of training and continuing education for the crisis counselors, hospital personnel, and police and fire personnel on whose clear perception and integration we depend in emergencies and disasters. Moral responses may not be forthcoming in our encounter with situations where we have inadequate information or situations where the information is available but is too complex or disorganized. In many situations we either fail to compute the array of information or do not have enough information on which to operate. Given time enough and the persistent pointing of others to the relevant aspects of a situation, most individuals can recognize the moral problem.

Experimental studies of bystander responses indicate that the particular characteristics of situations strongly affect helping behavior. Darley and Batson (1973) examined the character of the religious views of 40 Princeton seminarians and divided the group into three types of religious commitment. Seminarians, who were paid volunteers for the study, were then assigned to prepare a lecture on (1) the parable of the Good Samaritan or (2) job opportunities for seminarians. Then under (1) hurried or (2) more leisurely time constraints, they were instructed to go to another building to deliver the lecture. In order to get to their destination, each seminarian walked by an individual (actor) who lay in an entryway coughing with eyes shut. Sixteen of the 40 subjects stopped to help the victim. Greenwald's (1975) reanalysis of this study indicated that those who prepared to lecture about the Good Samaritan helped more frequently than the employment lecture group. Religious classification was unrelated to helping. No doubt the lectures on the Good Samaritan were quite adequate in their ethical reasoning. However the majority of seminarians in both lecture conditions were lacking either sensitivity to, or recognition of, the individual in need. Darley and Batson (1973) observe that more than one Good Samaritan lecturer "literally stepped over the victim as he hurried on his way" (p. 100). Other possible influences that may have affected the seminarians are included in our discussion of values. Huston and Korte (1976) have described individual characteristics associated with or affecting helping behavior but conclude that little work has been done that concurrently examines both situational and personality variables affecting bystander responses.

Even when all the information is present for all participants, individuals may perceive a situation in different ways. Developmental differences in role-taking and differences in empathy appear to affect recognition of others' needs. Moral behavior in the sense of intentionally helping another person is inconceivable before the child differentiates perspectives of self and others. Once this differentation can be made, there is still likely to be a high frequency of inappropriate or unsuccessful attempts to respond to others' needs—that is, the ability to take the perspective of another accurately is a step beyond recognition that others have different perspectives (Selman & Damon, 1975; Shantz, 1975). Flavell (1970, 1977) has defined the preconditions for executing specific acts of social cognition as including at least *existence, need,* and *inference. Existence* refers to the young child's awareness that certain social cognitive phenomena even exist—e.g., an awareness that it is even possible for another person to have a different point of view. *Need* refers to a disposition to attempt to think about events when the existence of such events is clearly known. "He may not think to, may not want to, or may not see any point to making such an effort" (Flavell, 1977, p. 121). *Inference* is the capacity to perform the social cognition adequately.

I may know of the existence of the type of thought or feeling you are currently having (Existence) and I may badly want to figure out what you are presently experiencing (Need), and yet I may simply not have the ability to identify it on the basis of the evidence provided (Inference). (Flavell, 1977, p. 121)

Barrett and Yarrow (1977) found social inferential ability to be a significant mediating variable in a study of prosocial behavior, social inferential ability, and assertiveness in children. Interpersonal assertiveness was most highly predictive of prosocial behavior within the group of children who were most successful in the social inference interviews. The prosocial behavior measure in this study was collected in eight 15-minute naturalistic observations over a six-week period and is not subject to the demand characteristic criticisms frequently directed at prosocial behavior measures in experimental studies. It was concluded, "For children who are unable to utilize information from earlier events in a behavior sequence to interpret subsequent behaviors, assertiveness appears to be unrelated to prosocial behavior" (p. 479). Barrett and Yarrow also suggest, however, "The processes by which sensitivity to others may influence the likelihood of prosocial responding are not readily apparent and need to

be explored" (p. 480). When we later discuss follow-through on action plans, we return to the Barrett and Yarrow study to examine the effects of assertiveness on prosocial behavior.

Not being able to take the role of the other accurately does not mean there is no response to signs of need from others. Empathic responses are evident even in infancy. Frequently young children, even infants, cry when they hear the crying of others, feel badly when parents appear upset or sad, and become excited or fearful when adults are angry (whether or not the anger is directed at the child). In a sense these reactions may be a precursor of affective recognition of others' needs (Sagi & Hoffman, 1976). There are several questions, however, about the relationship of this affective empathic responding to moral development. First, the data are mixed regarding the relationship of empathic responding to helping or sharing (Hoffman, 1977). Hoffman defines empathy as "the vicarious affective response to another person's feelings" (p. 712). His reanalysis of 30 studies indicated that only 6 of the 30 studies fit his definition of empathy, and mixed results and moderate relationships can be expected when varying theoretical and operational definitions have been used. Second, it is difficult to know what empathic responding means. Mood, Johnson, and Shantz (1974) found that some preschoolers understood others' feelings (40 percent) but infrequently both felt the same emotion and correctly understood the others' feeling (17 percent). Shantz (1974) interpreted these results as indicating that "with young children affective empathy is much less frequent than a correct understanding of another's feelings, and understanding is typically not accompanied by the same felt emotion" (p. 2). In some instances even physiological arousal has been used as a measure of empathic responding, but physiological measures have provided little information on the nature of human responding to the needs of others.

Some people need minimal cues to recognize a moral problem, whereas others require blatant signs of human suffering before recognizing a moral issue. The relationship of sensitivity to levels of moral reasoning or to acting on the dilemmas one recognizes has received limited attention. In a later section we will again consider empathy, but we will focus on its motivational influence rather than its role in interpersonal perception and sensitivity.

MORAL JUDGMENT

Once a person has a clear perception of what the desires, needs, and intentions of people are in a given situation, the problem remains to determine what rights and responsibilities one has. Sometimes the situation is relatively simple, as when one person obviously needs and wants help and another person can render help with little inconvenience; but frequently there is a complex conflict of interests involved, as when a college is determining an "affirmative action" policy for recruiting minority candidates. Moral ideals and moral standards provide guidelines for identifying the considerations relevant to a judgment, for prioritizing these concerns, and for organizing a course of action.

Piaget's General Approach

Piaget's 1932 book on the development of moral judgment remains one of the most influential and seminal works. Piaget's conceptualization of moral development and his general research direction are more important than the specifics of his research procedures and particular findings. His major directions might be summarized under four points. First, Piaget portrayed a subject's reaction to a moral situation as involving an underlying interpretive framework by which the specific stimuli are organized into basic patterns, concepts, and categories. Piaget emphasized the active, interpretive activity of the subject in constructing meaning and assimilating social experience into patterns. As in other of Piaget's books on other topics, he talks about "the world of the child" as a unified perspective and as involving a system of categorizing and organizing experience. Furthermore Piaget claims that the organizing principles of the child's world are different from those of the adult world—not only is it possible for there to be more than one view of the world, different views are inevitable. Accordingly the starting point of a psychology of morality is to discover the inner cognitive structures of the subject, for we cannot assume that social situations are perceived in the same way by all subjects, nor can we assume that a particular observable act is intended in the same way by all subjects. Piaget's approach contrasts with the behavioral approach which seeks to discover empirical covariance between situations (defined from the external point of view of the experimenter) and behavior (also defined externally).

Second, Piaget is concerned with presenting an alternative to Durkheim's (1925/1961) view of moral development. On the first page of Piaget's book, Durkheim is mentioned, and throughout the book Durkheim is constantly referred to, more so than any other person. Interestingly the controversy between Piaget and Durkheim parallels the controversy today between cognitive developmental theorists and social learning theorists over what determines respect for moral standards. Durkheim's view essentially is that moral development is a process of *socialization:* Moral standards originate external to the subject, are pressed upon the individual through social pressure, and eventually are "internalized" by the subject.

Piaget does not dispute that the child's *first* experience of social rules is that of commands handed down by authorities recognized as deserving of respect. At first the respect for rules is based on this unilateral respect for authority, a *heteronomous morality.* At first social rules seem to be fixed in the nature of things, like natural laws. The child attends to the letter of the law rather than the spirit of the law; the child does not understand social rules as instruments for structuring social cooperation. S/he judges an act on the basis of its exact conformity to established rules, on the amount of objective damage it causes, and on whether it was punished or not. In contrast to Durkheim, Piaget claims that the basis of respect for rules shifts with development in social awareness. With the experience of making cooperative agreements with peers, the child comes to recognize that the binding force which keeps people to the terms of an agreement is mutual respect and the reciprocal benefit that each de-

rives from fulfilling the terms of the agreement. Social rules need not be one-sided arrangements whereby an inferior obeys the commands of a superior, but social rules come to be seen as instruments for structuring cooperation. So only at first, in young children, is respect for rules based on "heteronomous" respect; later, it is based on "autonomous" respect. For Durkheim the crux of moral development is acceptance of group discipline and the superior authority of society. For Durkheim understanding the rationale behind rules may come later but is not a prerequisite for respect for rules. For Piaget understanding the rationale behind rules is the basis for "autonomous" morality. Piaget therefore pays attention to cognitive development in understanding the nature of cooperation, the child's give-and-take with peers, and his/her experiences in taking various roles. In contrast Durkheim and social learning theorists pay attention to strengthening a child's motives to serve and abide by group norms and to the socializing agent's reinforcements, didactic teaching, and modeling.

A third important point in Piaget's approach is that *justice* is the key concept in the development of moral standards. This follows from Piaget's view that moral development is based on experiences of reciprocity among equals. The concept of *justice* is used to portray how social systems of cooperation attempt to balance the interests of the individuals who are participating (to give each his/her fair share). Just social systems are "equilibrated" social systems in that the governing rules are not coercive demands of "superior" people upon "inferior" people but rather represent a set of mutually agreed-upon arrangements for mutual benefit. Thus in his moral judgment work Piaget continues a theme from his other work in describing how human thought tends to construct equilibrated systems, in this case an equilibrated social system. A social system can be said to be equilibrated if its rules adjudicate conflicts of interest and coordinate individual effort in ways that win compliance and support from its participants who appreciate the balance and logic of the prescriptions. Other writers have stressed concepts other than justice and social equilibrium in their accounts of moral development—e.g., the concept of *benevolence* (altruism, caring) or of *group loyalty.* However no other developmental accounts have as yet been elaborated in as much theoretical detail or with as much empirical investigation as those keying on the concept of *justice.*

A fourth major characteristic of Piaget's approach to morality is his notion that development involves a fundamental reorganization of the person's behavior and thinking, starting with *heteronomous morality* (the morality of constraint) and culminating in *autonomous morality* (the morality of cooperation). Instead of viewing moral development as the progressive "socialization" of the child (whereby socializing influences cause more and more behavior to conform to social standards), Piaget sees the two moralities as involving different organizational principles, different rationales, and different dynamics. Development involves transformation of organization principles, not just successive refinements and additions to one kind of organizing principle. Piaget spoke of the two moralities as two different stages, although he explicitly denied that moral judgment stages were very clearcut or tightly unified stages (e.g., 1932/1965, pp. 84–85, 124, 133); rather, the two moralities are end points on a developmental course, one shading into the other. For the purpose of arguing with Durkheim, it was not necessary for Piaget to give a very detailed or complete description of the entire course of moral development nor to define a series of tightly unified stages; it was only necessary for Piaget to document the claim that all morality is not "imposed by the group upon the individual and by the adult upon the child" (p. 341), but that there are *different* moralities, each organized by fundamentally different principles. As empirical support for his claim, Piaget contrasted the behavior and verbalizations of younger and older children on several dimensions. However incomplete, loose, or methodologically flawed we may regard Piaget's data in these analyses today, it is important to see the general argument Piaget is making: A "socialization" view of morality presupposes a single process of acquiring and organizing moral standards (i.e., heteronomous morality). If, on the other hand, we find a succession of different organizing principles, a theory of moral development must attend to the active role of human interpretation and cognitive organization.

These four major aspects of Piaget's theory have provided the direction for extensive elaborations and are the focal point of major controversies about the fundamental nature of moral development today.

Research on Piaget's Dimensions. Piaget's specific research methods and findings involve both observations of children's behavior (playing marbles) and verbalizations about hypothetical stories, but the latter have received most attention. Reviews of this research are given in Hoffman (1970), Karniol (1978), Keasey (1978), and Lickona (1976). Lickona (1976, p. 220) lists nine dimensions on which Piaget and his followers have contrasted heteronomous morality with autonomous morality. One of the most investigated dimensions is called *objective responsibility* by Piaget. His method was to present subjects with a pair of hypothetical stories, one depicting a boy who knocks over 15 cups while coming to dinner, the other story depicting a boy who breaks one cup while attempting to sneak some jam out of a cupboard. Piaget then asked subjects whether the two boys in the stories were equally naughty and whether they should be punished the same. Up to the age of ten, children often based their judgments on the objective, obvious, material consequences (i.e., the boy in the first story is naughtier because he broke 15 cups and the second boy only broke one), whereas older children consistently took the more subtle, subjective aspects of the stories into account (the boy who was trying to sneak some jam was naughtier). Piaget interprets this age difference as supporting the general view that younger children have a literal and reified view of morality—rules that are handed down by external authorities. The older children have a more subtle appreciation of rules and take into account the subjective states of actors. Many other investigators also have found cross-sectional age trends on this dimension in a variety of countries. Some of the other dimensions investigated by Piaget include the young child's belief that physical misfortunes and accidents are moral punishments (*immanent justice*) and the young child's unresponsiveness to reciprocity.

Since 1970 dozens of studies have reexamined how children make judgments of responsibility, using "objective" and "subjective" information in stories. These studies have modified Piaget's stories and procedures in many ways in order to determine more precisely what story information is used in making judgments, how information is extracted, how changes in the stimuli array affect judgments, and what decision rules are used. These studies are not oriented to explaining moral judgment with reference to two global moral stages, but rather their focus is on a fine-grained analysis of information processing. All of these researchers agree that Piaget's stories confounded many variables. Recent modifications of Piaget's stories include use of single stories rather than story pairs, disconfounding of consequent information from motive and intent information, systematic variation of types of consequences, varying story order and mode of presentation (see Keasey, 1978). Some investigators have introduced information-processing models of story grammar (e.g., Grueneich & Trabasso, 1981); others introduce *information integration theory* (Anderson & Butzin, 1978). Research to date has shown what complex processes are involved in making responsibility judgments and how variations in story characteristics and presentation affect moral judgment.

Extensions of Piaget: Kohlberg and Associates

Kohlberg and associates have elaborated the major points of Piaget's general approach (Colby, Gibbs, & Kohlberg, 1980; Kohlberg, 1969, 1971, 1976). "Kohlbergian" theory and research is not really a single theory and research paradigm but a collection of theories and methods which bear a family resemblance to each other, although some are distant cousins. All have in common, however, these basic points: (1) A focus on the underlying interpretive frameworks of a subject in perceiving social-moral situations and organizing a judgment about what ought to be done; furthermore, these interpretive frameworks are presumed to be unified, global systems of thinking. (2) The assumption that these basic cognitive structures are not rules taught by direct tuition, modeling, or reinforcement of socializing agents but are schemas of social understanding developed by the person in interaction with others. (3) Concepts of *justice* are the key to development in moral understanding. Subjects come to understand successively more complicated and encompassing systems of reciprocal cooperation. (4) Development involves the successive transformations of basic organizing principles—although instead of Piaget's two stages, six stages are proposed. Kohlberg goes beyond Piaget's 1932 work in proposing a more elaborate set of stage descriptions, in taking a more "hard-line" position on the stage concept in moral judgment development than Piaget did, in introducing new assessment techniques, in carrying out immensely more complete and intricate empirical studies, and in becoming involved in moral education programs.

Instead of using story pairs as Piaget did to elicit samples of subjects' thinking about moral problems, Kohlberg presented more complicated moral dilemmas to subjects and asked them to describe what the actor in that situation ought to do and to justify that course of action. One of the most familiar dilemmas is about a man, Heinz, who can only obtain a drug that might save his wife by stealing it.

In examining subjects' responses to this and other dilemmas, Kohlberg discovered a greater variety of patterns of thinking than Piaget had described. Work was begun in the mid-1950s to construct a taxonomy of these response types and has continued for over 20 years—only recently have Kohlberg and his colleagues at Harvard come to regard their scoring system as near completion (Colby et al., 1980). This scoring system identifies hundreds of features (in contrast to Piaget's nine dimensions) and is over 800 pages long. The following are examples of responses to the Heinz dilemma and their scoring with the current manual: "Yes, he should steal. If you had a wife that had cancer and you only had half of the money, and you had to break into a store for a good reason, if your wife is dying, you'd do it" (p. 14). "Obeying the law, in general, is essential if society is to survive and operate smoothly. The law ought to be obeyed not out of fear of punishment but out of respect for the principles embodied in it" (p. 108). The first example is scored a Stage 2 response because it is based on a concrete projection of the actor's immediate needs and wants; the second example is scored Stage 4 because it takes into account the social system in which this particular episode is taking place.

Kohlberg's new scoring system is impressive (1) in providing an analytical scheme for classifying even the thinking of professional moral philosophers, (2) for using longitudinal data in its derivation and not just cross-sectional data, and (3) for devising ways to deal with the many methodological problems in free-response interview material. Inter-judge agreement among trained judges is very high, although the system is very difficult to learn. Studies of the validity and reliability on the newest version are just beginning to accumulate, and first reports are impressive (Kohlberg, 1979).

Another method of assessment, called the Defining Issues Test, was developed at the University of Minnesota (Rest, 1979). While it is derived from Kohlberg's six-stage theory, it uses a multiple-choice format and can be objectively scored (instead of scoring by trained judges). The DIT assumes that people at different developmental stages perceive moral dilemmas differently. Presumably if presented with different ways of stating the crucial issue of a moral dilemma, people at different developmental stages will choose different issues as the most important ones. The way that a subject rates and ranks these statements can be used to derive a developmental score for the subject. Several reliability checks are built into the questionnaire as a test of a subject's random checking or checking items on the basis of verbal complexity rather than of meaning. Extensive research has been done on the reliability and validity of the DIT and currently represents the largest data base accumulated on a single measure of moral judgment (treating the different versions of Kohlberg's tests as separate instruments).

The DIT is not simply a multiple-choice version of Kohlberg's test since the two tests diverge on several theoretical points and the empirical correlations are at best only in the .60s and .70s in heterogeneous samples. The DIT is a recognition task (various ways of thinking are presented to the subject) whereas Kohlberg's test is a production task (subjects generate a line of reasoning on their own), and subjects are credited with higher stages of thinking on the DIT than on the Kohlberg. Furthermore the DIT presupposes at least a 12-year-old reading level whereas the Kohlberg test can be given to younger subjects. Nevertheless the DIT correlates higher with the current Kohlberg test than the 1958 Kohlberg test correlates with the current Kohlberg test ($r = .39$), and since it derives from the 6-stage model, research from the various Kohlberg tests and the DIT will be treated together.

Over the years a variety of characterizations of the six stages has been presented (Kohlberg, 1976; Rest, 1979). The crux of the six-stage model is the conception of *justice*—coming to understand the possibilities and conditions for structuring cooperation. The "higher" stages are more encompassing of varieties of human situations and less affected by arbitrary factors than "lower" stages. At every stage there is an intuitive sense of what is right and fair. This moral sense changes as more complexities of social life are taken into account. Stage 1 provides a normative structure (the caretaker's demands) for the regulation of human interaction; however, in this system of cooperation, there is great inequality between parties and hardly any reciprocity. The system comes into being because of the accidents of birth—i.e., who was born first, who is bigger and more powerful. Stage 2 makes significant progress toward establishing equality among participants through the notion of relative individual interests and simple exchange. Stage 2, however, provides only a very temporary and fragmentary system of social cooperation and is arbitrarily bound by the particular circumstances of parties getting together and having favors that each one wants. Stage 3 provides for a more enduring system of cooperation through relationships of mutual caring and affection, each party being committed to the other's welfare; however, Stage 3 arbitrarily limits cooperation to whatever friendships have been established at a given time. Stage 4 establishes a societywide system of cooperation in which all participants equally are under the law and in which all are reciprocating by each carrying out his/her own role. Stage 4, however, can allow gross inequalities and arbitrary distribution of the benefits and burdens of cooperation, because the social order itself may be set up legally to give advantage to some at the expense of others (e.g., a slave society). Stage 5 attempts to eliminate arbitrary rules by providing procedures for making rules that reflect the will of the people, giving each person an equal voice in determining the arrangements of society. Stage 5, therefore, has gone a long way in neutralizing inequities and lopsided reciprocity due to accidents of birth, historical accidents, and other arbitrary circumstances while at the same time providing for enduring social structures which can win the support of the participants. Stage 5, however, has not completely insured that the outcomes of duly enacted laws produce a nonarbitrary balancing of people's interests; the collective judgment of the people at one time may be unfair as viewed by the people at a later time (e.g., the acceptance of slavery in early America). Stage 6 maintains, therefore, that although a majority of people may want a law (or social policy), that still does not necessarily make it moral, for there is a more ultimate test of morality than social consensus. The defining feature of Stage 6 is its appeal to ideal principles of justice (e.g., Rawl's two principles of justice, Brandt's extended rule utilitarianism, Kant's categorical imperative) which are presented such that rational, equal, and impartial people could choose them as the governing terms of their cooperative interaction. According to this characterization of Stage 6, virtually all modern moral philosophers would be scored at Stage 6 insofar as their conceptions of fairness were principles of social organization that balance competing claims of individuals and which attempt to optimize everyone's stake in that social order while eliminating or neutralizing arbitrary factors.

RESEARCH ON THE SIX-STAGE MODEL OF MORAL JUDGMENT

The six-stage model has been the basis for an enormous amount of research. Kohlberg's own studies and those of his colleagues, critics, revisionists, and reviewers have now generated hundreds of studies, by far the most extensively researched and discussed account of moral judgment. The kinds of ideas, issues, and research strategies in the field can best be illustrated by research on the six-stage model.

Age Trends. One of the most obvious empirical implications of a stage model is that of age-related sequential changes—that is, do people change over time in their moral orientation in the ways postulated by the theory? A large number of studies using one or another form of Kohlberg's test or the DIT have tested subjects of various ages (the same cross-sectional strategy used by Piaget) and have consistently found differences in moral judgment scores across student groups (see Kohlberg, 1969, 1979; Rest, 1979). Age trends are found in both sexes and in samples from various socioeconomic groups and geographical areas. In some studies almost 50 percent of the variance in moral judgment scores was attributable to the age factor. Shifts in the lower stages are most dramatic in the Kohlberg measure, shifts in the higher stages are most dramatic in the DIT (testing older subjects). Among (nonstudent) adults, however, moral judgment scores seem to increase as long as subjects remain in formal schooling, then seem to plateau after leaving school even though many years may pass. Moral philosophers and political scientists have the highest scores as a group, although other individuals without that special training occasionally have scores as high.

About 12 longitudinal studies which test the same subjects repeatedly, at one- to four-year intervals, provide stronger evidence on age trends, and the trends largely confirm the cross-sectional trends of upward movement. This is not to say that all subjects always move upward: Many subjects show no change between two testings; adult subjects who are not in school tend to stay about the same; a small portion of subjects (about 7 percent) actually move downward; developmental change is more dramatic over longer intervals of time (four years) than over shorter intervals (one year or less); and, in general, change appears to be slow. Nevertheless the ratio of upward movement to downward movement is about ten to one in the largest studies using either Kohlberg's test or the DIT. Kohlberg and the group at Harvard have recently completed a 20-year longitudinal

study which finds gradual change in *all* subjects with *no* subjects skipping a stage (Kohlberg, 1979). DIT studies have included time-sequential and cohort-sequential analyses which indicate that the age trends are not attributable to cohort or generation effects; also sample bias and retesting effects do not seem to explain the age trends (Rest, 1979, chap. 5).

The Cognitive Component in Moral Judgment. What evidence is there that higher stages of moral judgment are *cognitively* more advanced? Aside from the logical analysis of the stages which describes theoretically how a higher stage is more complicated but more adequate, the empirical evidence is correlational, longitudinal, and experimental. One line of research has approached this issue by devising a test of the ability to understand arguments at each stage (see Rest, 1979, chap. 6). A test of moral comprehension differs from a test of moral judgment in that a test of comprehension does not ask subjects which concepts they use in making a moral decision but rather inventories which concepts a subject understands. Comprehension tests either ask a subject to paraphrase and discuss statements exemplifying the various stages (so as to show that the subject understands the main idea of the statement) or ask a subject to match one statement with the best equivalent among a list of alternatives (where presumably a correct match indicates comprehension of the stage distinctive idea). The major conclusions of the comprehension studies are as follows: (1) Comprehension of the stages is cumulative—that is, Stage 1 concepts are easiest to understand, then Stage 2, Stage 3, etc. A person who shows high comprehension of Stage 4, for instance, also shows high comprehension of Stages 1, 2, and 3. (2) Subjects who comprehend high stage concepts tend to use those concepts as critical elements in their judgments about what ought to be done. Subjects who show low comprehension tend to have low moral judgment scores. Comprehension, therefore, seems to place an upper limit on the way that subjects make moral judgments. (3) Longitudinal studies indicate that as subjects increase in comprehending high stage concepts, they also increase in moral judgment scores. Although there are problems in the reliability of the comprehension measures, these data support the idea that cognitive advancement is a major determinant in moral judgment advancement.

Experimental studies support the conclusions of the comprehension studies (see review in Rest, 1979, chap. 7). Manipulating test instructions, in one condition subjects are asked to "fake high," in another condition to "fake low," and in a third condition to take the DIT under the usual instructions. Subjects dramatically lower their scores under the "fake low" condition (which agrees with the findings about the cumulative nature of moral comprehension) and do not increase their scores under the "fake high" condition (which agrees with the findings about the upper limit that comprehension places on the concepts used in making moral judgments).

Another line of evidence regarding the cognitive basis of moral judgment comes from studies aimed at identifying the basic cognitive building blocks of moral judgment. Kohlberg (1976) and others have claimed that development in Piagetian logical operations and in role-taking are necessary but not sufficient prerequisites of moral thinking—that is, moral thinking is not reducible or equivalent to Piaget's stages of logico-cognitive development nor to stages of role-taking; however, a person cannot reach higher stages of moral judgment without being able to perform certain Piagetian logical operations and certain role-taking operations. For instance basic Formal Operations are said to be prerequisite to Stage 4 moral thinking. Three types of studies have been proposed to test this sort of prerequisite relationship. First, if a subject shows Stage 4 moral thinking, s/he is expected also to show basic Formal Operations on the Piagetian task, although the reverse is not necessarily expected (referred to as *contemporaneous contingent association*). Second, in a longitudinal study if a subject previously scored at Stage 3 moves into Stage 4 moral thinking, s/he is also expected to have moved into basic Formal Operations, although if a subject moves into basic Formal Operations, s/he is not necessarily expected to show Stage 4 moral thinking (*longitudinal prerequisite movement*). Third, in an intervention study subjects at Stage 3 who already have basic Formal Operations are expected to be more susceptible to intervention to Stage 4 than Stage 3 subjects without basic Formal Operations (*intervention readiness*). Studies of these three types have been conducted to examine Piagetian logical operations and role-taking operations as prerequisites of moral thinking (reviews in Colby & Kohlberg, 1975; Kurdek, 1978; Selman, 1976; Walker, 1978). These studies generally indicate a relation between Piagetian logical operations, role-taking capacities and moral judgment, although the results are mixed depending on what measures are used. Recent experimental studies by Walker are particularly impressive (Walker, 1978; Walker & Richards, 1979). The generality is unclear, however, because the developmental measures used always employ particular scoring criteria, particular test content, and particular forms of subject response; research shows that changes in these particulars affect the developmental assessment, and therefore the specific correspondences between measures will be affected by whatever particular instruments have been used.

A third line of evidence for the cognitive nature of moral judgment comes from its consistently significant correlations with IQ, achievement test, and aptitude test measures. Generally the correlations are in the .20s to .50s range (Kohlberg, 1969; Rest, 1979, chap. 6). Moreover this general trend contrasts to the generally low or inconsistent correlations of moral judgment with personality and "affective" measures (Rest, 1979). Moral judgment, then, seems to have more in common with cognitive measures than with affective measures.

Given the evidence linking moral judgment measures with cognitive measures, what evidence is there that moral judgment is really distinct from general cognitive development or verbal facility? Several lines of evidence speak to the distinctiveness (but not total independence) of moral judgment from general cognitive development (Rest, 1979). For one, measures of moral thinking are more highly correlated among themselves than with measures of general cognitive ability. Second, when IQ or general ability measures are controlled or statistically partialled out of the correlation between moral judgment and some predictor variables (e.g., delinquency, voting behavior), moral judgment often has unique predictability beyond that shared in common with IQ or general

ability. Third, experimental interventions focused on the stimulation of *moral* thinking and *moral* reflection have a greater impact on the facilitation of moral judgment than interventions focused on the stimulation of *general logical* development. Fourth, subjects who score very high on Piagetian measures or on general ability measures do not always score high on moral judgment measures (Colby & Kohlberg, 1975)—i.e., there are Dr. Strangeloves in the world.

The "Stage Concept." A "strong" interpretation of the stage concept contends (1) that the notion of stages as "structured wholes" entails stage consistency across situations and testing conditions; (2) that development is to be conceived as invariant movement through the stage, step by step, one at a time, without skipping any stages; and (3) that the six-stage model describes development cross-culturally.

With regard to the "structured whole" notion, research has shown great stage mixture in subjects rather than subjects who are 100 percent at one stage. Furthermore differences in dilemma content, in the type of response used (i.e., in spontaneously generated justifications versus preference for prototypic statements), and in conditions of testing (a first or second testing, which alternative form is used) all seem to influence somewhat the assessment of a subject's underlying structure (see Rest, 1979, chap. 3, for extended discusssion). While there is certainly a great deal of consistency in the way a subject organizes his/her judgments, it is misrepresentative of the data to talk about a subject being "in" this or that stage. Rather we should regard the stages as different organizations of thought; a given subject may show two or more organizations to some degree, depending on the situation. The "structured whole" notion is best applied to the *logical* interrelationships of the subconcepts with a particular system of thinking; it is misleading if it suggests near perfect *empirical* consistency in applying a system of thinking to diverse situations.

Since subjects are not 100 percent "in" one or another stage, it is misleading to describe the course of development as step by step, moving through each stage one at a time. Development is more a matter of gradual shifts in percent usage of stages, the lower stages diminishing as the higher increase. Stages are ordered in the sense that their onset, maximum usage, and decline are staggered over the course of development; but the stages overlap to a considerable degree. Subjects seem to become aware of aspects of new perspectives while they are using a less advanced perspective and at the same time occasionally resorting to a really primitive perspective.

A review by Edwards (1977) reports cross-cultural research on Kohlberg's test in Mexico, Taiwan, Kenya, the Bahamas, Honduran Carib, India, Nigeria, Israel, Thailand, Turkey, Britain, Canada, New Zealand, and the Yucatan. Two studies (one in Turkey, the other in the Bahamas) report longitudinal age trends, and numerous studies report age trends using cross-sectional comparisons. The Kohlberg scoring system seems to be usable in other countries, and the older subjects tend to score at higher stages. Thus there is some support for the claim for universality. However only Stages 1 through 4 appear in the non-Western traditional cultures. At this time several interpretations are possible: (1) Kohlberg stages are universal and the testing procedures are valid, but some cultures do not foster development beyond Stage 4; (2) the testing procedures are not conducive to eliciting the highest stages possible in certain non-Western cultures; or (3) Kohlbergian definitions of moral maturity are not applicable to non-Western cultures; there is no single set of stages which captures development in moral thinking all over the world. Arguments can be made pro and con for each of these positions. Even if the third position were true, a modified stage model might claim that the six stages still depict basic structural changes in Western thinking.

Determinants and Mechanisms of Change. From Piaget come two suggestions for what promotes structural change in moral judgment: cognitive disequilibrium and cooperation with peers. The first follows from Piaget's general discussions of assimilation and accommodation and his view that all cognitive structures are forms of organizing experience and action, hence are forms of equilibration. When new experience cannot be assimilated into existing cognitive structures, the person is in a state of disequilibration and searches for new cognitive structures to reestablish cognitive equilibrium. Turiel (1972) most notably has elaborated this notion as the mechanism of change in moral judgment. He introduced an experimental paradigm for studying change (inducing cognitive conflict) and has influenced a major feature of Kohlbergian moral education programs (discussion of controversial moral problems and "+1 modeling"). In a short-term experimental intervention, Turiel exposed one group of subjects to arguments one stage above their own stage (the "+1" condition), another group to two stages above their own ("+2"), and a third group to arguments one stage below their own ("−1"). Turiel predicted that the group exposed to arguments one stage above their own would show the greatest change on a posttest because, in such a condition, subjects could grasp the significance of the argument and would experience disequilibrium, hence supplying the crucial condition for the transformation of cognitive structures. In the "−1" condition subjects would be unimpressed with arguments less adequate than their own. In the "+2" condition the arguments would be too far advanced for the subjects to understand and hence would be less effective. A number of short-term experimental studies have utilized this basic paradigm, and at this point, the findings are confusing and contradictory. A major difficulty is that short-term studies are attempting to promote change which in naturalistic longitudinal studies takes years to show. Longer-term educational studies of several months' duration have been undertaken, employing peer discussion (which presumably also furnishes disequilibrating experiences). However these educational interventions are so complex that it is difficult to separate out the various influences that are operating. Furthermore no study as yet has devised an adequate way of determining if "disequilibration" is taking place (to what subjects, to what degree, and over what issue?). Therefore it is difficult to attribute the effects of educational programs solely to cognitive conflict. Nevertheless one reviewer of Kohlbergian moral education programs (Lockwood, 1978) concludes that programs employing peer discussion of controversial issues do fairly consistently show significant treatment effects. The most outstanding study in terms of design and effects is by Blatt and Kohlberg (1975).

Piaget's other suggestion for what produces structural change in moral judgment was the social interaction of peers who negotiate and bargain with each other for arranging mutually benefiting agreements. This give-and-take among peers fosters a recognition of the *reciprocity* of cooperation, of the basic *equality* among peers (each is free to enter into cooperative agreements, and each must be satisfied with the arrangement in order for it to work); and it also fosters *role-taking* opportunities—that is, trying to figure out what the situation must look like from the other person's point of view. In addition experiences in coordinating, reconciling, and balancing the various points of view of individuals would also seem to be an important ingredient in development. Some correlational research supports these speculations (see Edwards, 1977, and Kohlberg, 1969, for reviews). Children who are more socially active, more popular, more in leadership positions, and who live in more democratic families score higher on moral judgment. Furthermore some intervention studies (experimental and educational) which stress role-playing procedures have been effective in fostering moral judgment development.

The classic cognitive developmental explanations of the mechanisms of change stress *self-discovery,* as if the basic rationale for social institutions and morality has to be rediscovered spontaneously by each individual. This position stems from the insistence of cognitive developmentalists that systems of meaning (schemas, interpretive frameworks, basic categories of thinking) are constructions and *active* integrations of experience rather than passive reflections of external environmental patterns or of direct teaching. Yet one of the most powerful determinants of moral judgment development seems to be formal education. Cross-sectional studies of adults show education is powerfully correlated with moral judgment; longitudinal studies of high school graduates show that those who go on to college become increasingly divergent from those who do not; certain educational interventions which have a heavy emphasis on moral reasoning and philosophical analysis show significant effects (Lawrence, 1980); cross-cultural studies indicate that the "higher" stages of moral thinking are missing from many traditional, non-Western societies (Edwards, 1977); and "social learning" studies show that modeling can influence moral judgment (Rosenthal & Zimmerman, 1978). The effects of exposure to formal education in these studies is too striking to attribute the acquisition of moral judgment development solely to spontaneous self-discovery of people reflecting upon general social experience. On the other hand the mechanisms by which formal education has its influence need not be viewed as mindless indoctrination or the shaping of verbal responses in a passive organism by an intrusive environment in control of the reinforcers, as recent social learning theorists point out (Bandura, 1977; Mischel & Mischel, 1976). A particular intellectual milieu may call attention to certain features of the social environment, may highlight certain problems, may reinforce certain conceptualizations, and may call for justifications. Such a milieu would likely influence people's thinking, not necessarily by mindless indoctrination.

Moral Judgment and Moral Behavior. The position taken in this chapter is that *moral* behavior cannot be defined externally in terms of its consequences for others or its conformity to normative patterns of group behavior. Intestinal bacteria help humans, but we do not regard the bacteria as behaving morally. Ants and bees behave in ways that conform to normative patterns of their societies, but also we do not regard that as moral behavior. Moral behavior is that regulated by moral standards, behavior in the service of a moral ideal. Consequently the way that moral standards are derived, constructed, and applied to situations should have a great deal to do with moral behavior. In considering the relation of the six-stage model of moral judgment to behavior, three points should be kept in mind: (1) The other psychological components of moral development (moral sensitivity, moral values, moral character) mediate and complicate the relationship; (2) the six-stage model at best gives only highly abstract information about basic moral perspectives, it does not describe more specific moral ideals and standards; (3) our current ways of assessing basic moral perspectives are heavily tied to the ability (and willingness) of a subject to express his/her thinking through language. The operative structures which actually influence decision making in a specific real world context may be the same or different from those given on moral judgment tests.

Regarding the second point the abstractness of a moral judgment stage characterization may be illustrated by the fact that diverse people may all exhibit thinking at Stage 4: a Catholic nun, a Nazi stormtrooper, a Russian Bolshevik, an Indian peasant, a Mississippi Boy Scout, an Israeli kibbutznik, an Iranian Muslim. Even though all these people may be said to be similar in that they define justice in terms of preserving the established social institutions and practices, nevertheless their ideologies and specific moral standards obviously are very different. Whereas a stage analysis might be viewed as an attempt to assess moral thinking at a very abstract level, many attitude tests assess moral thinking at a more particular level—e.g., Kohlberg and Elfenbein (1975) related moral judgment to the specific issue of capital punishment, and Candee (1976) related moral judgment to issues concerning the Watergate scandal of the Nixon administration. A number of studies report significant relationships between moral judgment scores and particular attitudes toward issues such as the right to free speech, due process protections of people accused of crimes, civil rights demonstrators, the My Lai massacre, and various stances of political parties (see Rest, 1979, pp. 158–169). Only when different basic moral perspectives (e.g., an orientation toward interpersonal concordance versus an orientation toward "law and order") have a direct bearing on how a particular issue is to be construed would there be grounds for predicting a relation between moral judgment and particular attitudes. Many studies have mindlessly correlated attitude measures with moral judgment measures without first logically deriving how different basic moral perspectives should relate to the particular issue at hand.

Blasi (1980) has reviewed over 70 studies relating measures of moral judgment to various behavioral measures—e.g., delinquency-nondelinquency, participation in civil rights demonstrations, teacher ratings of fair-mindedness, cheating in games or on school tests, sharing, keeping a promise, helping a person in distress, distribution of rewards, and resistance to conformity pressure. Blasi is critical of many studies for not having a clear theoretical basis for relating the particular moral judgment instrument to the particular behavioral options in the situation, for not taking into account many of the mediating and complicating variables, and in some cases for using very questionable measures. Yet after discussing many flaws and shortcomings in these studies, Blasi's tables reveal that 78 percent of the studies (58 out of 74) report at least some significant relationship of moral judgment with behavior. He concludes, "There seems to be overall support for the hypothesis that moral reasoning and moral action are related," but insists that more complicated formulations on the nature of this relationship be advanced (Blasi, 1980, p. 60; see also Rest, 1979, pp. 169–195).

Earlier in the discussion a third point was raised which distinguished between verbalized moral judgment versus operative moral judgment, a distinction Piaget (1932/1965) made long ago. The main thrust of moral judgment research to date has been to study what kinds of integrations and organizations of thought are evident in people's verbal discussions and to study this development. Having now some descriptions of these structures, researchers are only beginning to address the question of whether assessment through verbal means gives an accurate picture of moral decision making in actual operation. The problem is not unique to morality but applies as well to the attitude-behavior problem and to relating cognitive tests such as Formal Operations or IQ tests to naturalistic, intelligent behavior and to many other areas of psychology.

Nevertheless there is evidence for a link between verbalized moral judgment and behavior. The hope for more powerful predictability must come from more complicated multivariate studies. Yet comparing Blasi's review with Hoffman's (1970) review of the association of parental discipling styles with moral development, there is stronger evidence for the connection of morality with understanding justice than with parental disciplining styles; still, most American psychologists would probably be comfortable in affirming the linkage of morality with parental discipline and remain skeptical about a linkage with moral understanding.

Research on Moral Standards outside the Kohlberg Tradition

There is roughly as much research on moral standards outside the Kohlberg tradition as within it; however, this research is divided among dozens of approaches, and none of them has, as yet, the sustained or extensive research base of the six-stage model (Rest, in press). In this brief review only a few comments are possible about the main directions of the other approaches: (1) One direction is to construe moral standards as developing in terms of the concept of *benevolence* (altruism, empathy, caring) instead of *justice* (e.g., Eisenberg-Berg, 1979; Hoffman, 1979). (2) Another direction is to assume that people do not necessarily have global world views or such large encompassing perspectives as the *stage* concept implies but that moral standards and other moral decision-making strategies are best described at a more molecular level and elicited in certain kinds of social situations. Drawing from the social psychology literature some researchers are investigating the development of norms of *equity, social responsibility, reciprocity,* and *justice* (e.g., Berndt, 1977; Hook & Cook, 1979; Lerner, 1977; Peterson, Hartmann, & Gelfand, 1977). This approach is especially concerned with how varying the features of situations affects the decision-making process, whereas the Piagetian and Kohlberg traditions deemphasize situational variables and emphasize the individual's global social-moral perspective. (3) Another large but highly diverse area is inquiry into legal and political beliefs, attitudes, and concepts (see reviews by Gallatin, 1979; Renshon, 1977).

Values and Influences

Goals, decisions, and action directions can be chosen with or without judgments of fairness and justice. A moral response to a problem implies by definition judgment of the moral ideal, but one's action choice or direction can also be affected by influences arising from the nature of the animal, other nonmoral values, and environmental influences.

Various natural, biologically derived influences affect the course of action. There is a primitive form of self-interest by which pain is avoided and pleasure is sought—innate pain responses to hunger, cold, and physical insult and pleasure responses to satisfaction of hunger, adequate warmth, and gentle human contact. Empathy also has been proposed as an innate motivational system. In Hoffman's (1976) view people are born with both self-interest and empathy. Research with 34-hour-old infants (Sagi & Hoffman, 1976) and with 2-day-old infants (Simner, 1971) indicated that newborns respond more intensely to the crying of other infants than they do to other sounds of equal pitch and volume. Other genetic and evolutionary bases for social functions and behavior have been suggested by Wilson (1975) and Campbell (1975). Hogan, Johnson, and Emler (1978), in their presentation of a socioanalytic theory of moral development, also claim ties to evolutionary theory and evolutionary ethics. The genetic base they describe includes a human disposition to rule-governing behavior. This perspective is relatively untested, and Hogan's starting point, *relative absolutism,* leaves one uncertain about what is meant by *moral.*

For other theorists the crucial influences or motives affecting moral behavior arise from increased cognitive understanding. From Piaget's epigenetic perspective, as individuals come to comprehend the equilibrium of social systems, they define themselves more expansively and appreciate their stake in the social system. Kohlberg (1969) shares with Piaget this implicit assumption that understanding is a motivating force that develops as one comes to see oneself as a participant in a social system. Understanding leads to social commitment and responsibility. The liberal tradition which advocates universal education as necessary in a democracy also assumes that understanding leads to social concern and responsibility. Many liberal arts colleges have espoused the view that education "liberated" one from prejudice, pettiness, and provincialism.

From another cognitive point of view Dienstbier, Hillman, Lehnhoff, Hillman, and Valkenaar (1975) point out that when people are fearful and highly aroused, it is the way that the situation is coded that determines the situation's moral or immoral characterization—that is, the cognitive coding of a situation affects how arousal is perceived and, therefore, also determines the course of behavior.

Environmental and, in particular, social influences on moral decisions and actions have been the focus of numerous recent studies of prosocial behavior, resistance to deviation, and delay of gratification. It is the nature of social influences to be relative—that is, sometimes social influence works for good, sometimes for bad. Milgram's (1963, 1964) studies of obedience provide powerful evidence that the demands of an authority figure can influence many individuals to harm others. Milgram (1963) asked subjects to help him study the effects of punishment (electric shock) on students' learning of paired associates. The subjects were instructed to administer shocks of ever-increasing voltage whenever a student made an error. Although all subjects were upset by their task, the vast majority (almost 70 percent) obeyed the experimenter even when the instructions called for allegedly 450-volt shocks as actors playing the student role groaned and screamed for release from the pain. Even those who eventually refused to continue and thus resisted authority followed directions to the 300-volt level of punishment. Milgram's study is strong evidence for the power of situational influences in getting people to perform acts they would under most circumstances abhor. Derogation and devaluation of those who are to be judged or punished also affects the likelihood and intensity of subjects' administration of punishment (Bandura, Underwood, & Fromson, 1975). The Bandura et al. study also showed effects for individual versus diffused responsibility for the level of shock to be administered.

The nature of social influences on moral behavior has been described by operant and social-learning theorists as well as by those who have focused on identification. Operant theorists focus on the response rather than on internal processes. Antecedent and consequent conditions are assumed to control the rate of response. In this view prosocial behavior or any other nonreflexive response increases in rate when positively or negatively reinforced and decreases in rate when punished. Situational cues, then, are not regarded as the information base of moral judgments and problem solving; rather, such cues indicate that reinforcement is likely for responses previously reinforced when similar stimuli were present.

A study by Warren, Rogers-Warren, and Baer (1976) illustrates the operant perspective on prosocial or "moral" behavior. Small groups of preschool children were brought to an experimental room and seated around a play area on which the experimenters placed play materials. In the first of two experiments, the children were told before playing that sharing might result in their receiving "something." After five-minute play sessions, food and praise were given to children who had offered to share play materials one or more times. The effect of this extrinsic reinforcement for a social behavior was a rapid increase in offers to share in the classroom and, interestingly, a rapid increase in the proportion of share offers rejected. In a second experiment the children were given an explanation of better ways to share the toys, and the experimenter gave descriptive verbal reinforcement for appropriate sharing during each five-minute session in addition to the food and praise reinforcement at the end of each session. In separate sessions children were told, "If you make less than six share offers but at least one, then you might get something." In the sessions where children were reinforced for making one or two share offers, the proportion of offers accepted increased 24 to 55 percentile points over the rates of acceptance during the first experiment. Thus while reinforcement could be used to increase the rate of share offers even when the offers were most often rejected, modification of the instructions and of the share-offer rates reinforced resulted in a more appropriate number of offers to share and a higher proportion of acceptances. Warren et al. concluded,

Controlling a social behavior's rate sometimes may significantly alter the manner in which other persons in the environment respond to the behavior. Further research into the functional relationships of different behavior rates and their consequences may provide behavior analysts with important information relative to the successful, durable programming of complex social behaviors in the natural environment. (1976, p. 497)

From this perspective, then, the appropriateness of share offers is not based on recognition of others' needs in relationship to one's own responsibilities and the welfare of the larger "other." Rather *appropriateness* is defined as a balance between rate of share offer and share-offer acceptance. With the exception of some unspecified explanation and description of *appropriateness* in the directions for the second experiment, there is little room in this paradigm for the child to be a reasoning, deciding organism. Reinforcing or aversive consequences are viewed as controlling children's prosocial responding and other nonreflexive behaviors. Socialization, then, is training the child to perform prosocial behavior in such a way and at such a rate that it will be maintained by consequences in the natural environment. While the operant experiments contain the minimum amount of inference about mediating events or processes, considerable inference and speculation is often included in discussions of results. As Gelfand and Hartmann (1980) note, "the existence of various subtle interpersonal reinforcers are [sic] postulated on a post hoc basis," and "typically neither these mechanisms nor their absence are [sic] demonstrable in everyday examples of prosocial behavior" (p. 40).

All views of moral development have an interest in moral behavior whether the focus is on recognition, moral reasoning, decision making and action planning, or performance. In isolation the operant research demonstrates immediate performance effects on narrowly defined behaviors and, in some cases, maintenance of those behaviors over days or weeks. Operant research on generalization across responses and settings has been quite limited (Stokes & Baer, 1977) although there are recent exceptions (Peterson et al., 1977). The effects of development on moral or prosocial behaviors have also received scant attention from operant researchers. At present the most that can be confidently asserted is that the mechanisms of operant learning have been shown to affect pro-

social and resistance to deviation behavior in experimental situations although such behaviors are also present where there are no observable reinforcing consequences.

Identification theory also addresses the acquisition of values, standards, and action tendencies. Parental identification has been hypothesized to be one of the sources of values, standards, and action decisions. Identification with the parent(s) affects decisions in that the child is motivated to establish goals and to perform in accordance with values that maintain the child's view of him/herself as being similar to the parent. In this view, then, it is not necessary that a specific response be externally reinforced or punished. Rather the desire to maintain similarity to the parent is broad in scope and does not require that the parent model the specific behavior or be present in the situation when the child is making a decision. Congruence with the parental pattern of values, goals, and actions is rewarding in and of itself.

The two types of identification most often cited are (1) anaclitic identification in which the child in the parents' absence attempts to acquire the nurturance usually provided by the parent by acting as the parent might act and (2) identification with the aggressor or defensive identification in which the child imitates the action of the individual who controls resources the child desires (Brown, 1965; Freud, 1938). Hoffman (1970) has examined children's responses to questions about the extent to which they admired a parent or saw themselves as similar to each parent and the relationship of these responses to measures of moral behavior and moral reasoning. Although there were some relationships between the identification measure and moral values, Hoffman did not find identification to be a unique or particularly powerful predictor of moral development.

Moral internalization, which subsumes identification with parental moral standards and values, is based on the premise that "most people do not go through life viewing society's moral norms (e.g., honesty, justice, fair play) as external, coercively imposed pressures" (Hoffman, 1979, p. 958)—that is, the standards that are imposed in early childhood through parental discipline and rewards become the child's own standards. These standards no longer require the presence of the parent or socializing agent for their consideration or influence. Research on identification and internalization, as well as much of the rest of the early childhood socialization literature, has focused on parenting practices. Although it has been shown that parenting practices and the results of parenting practices interact with the behavioral disposition of the child (Inhoff & Halverson, 1977), there is increasing evidence that parental nurturance and control are significantly related to and precede high levels of social responsibility and prosocial behavior (Baumrind, 1975; Yarrow, Scott, & Waxler, 1973). In related research the effects of parental correction and punishment on standards, values, and resistance to temptation were discussed by Aronfreed (1968) and thoroughly reviewed by Walters and Grusec (1977). The generalization effect of the factors involved in punishment have also received attention (LaVoie, 1974).

Evidence of internalization has been gathered in completion responses to projective stories, confession, and resistance to temptation responses. The projective story completions have been shown to be related to how parents handle the teaching of standards and how they deal with transgression. In the moral internalization research the standards being examined are moral standards only in that they are socially approved or disapproved. On this point Staub (1979) in his review of the internalization approach to development concluded, "In general, no serious attempts have been made by the psychologists who studied internalization to define which societal values and norms are morally relevant" (p. 30).

The question of internalization of standards versus the imitation of models has been examined in the context of resistance to deviation. In 1970 Hoffman concluded in a review of resistance to temptation modeling studies that there was much greater evidence that models of yielding to temptation or deviation could overcome the previous training of the child than that models of resistance to deviation or temptation could facilitate the development of such resistance in children. A recent summary of moral development theory reiterates that view (Hoffman, 1979). Although earlier modeling studies might have supported rejection of modeling as a factor in learning resistance to temptation, recent experiments provide evidence that under some conditions modeled resistance to temptation may have effects greater than modeled yielding (Bussey & Perry, 1977; Grusec, Kuczynski, Rushton, & Simutis, 1978; Perry, Bussey, & Perry, 1975).

In the Grusec et al. study four- and five-year-old boys and girls were asked to sort different colored cards into piles of the same colors. The child and a model were distracted and tempted to leave their work and to play with a variety of attractive toys by Charlie, a colorful, toy-loaded, talking table. In the resisting condition the model talked back to Charlie and said "s/he would like to play but could not because s/he was working." The yielding model said, ". . . the toys were more fun" and went over to play with them for 30 seconds and later for one minute. In the control condition an adult drew with the child for five minutes while Charlie, the talking table, made no comments. The child was then left alone to sort cards for ten minutes, and Charlie periodically enticed the child to leave the task and play with toys. The experimenters also collected a generalization test—resisting temptation to play with a forbidden toy in a bag while being allowed to play with the rest of the toys in the room—and a two- to four-week delayed test of the card-sorting experiment. On the immediate and delayed tests of resistance to deviation, the mean latency to deviation was longer for children in the resisting-model condition than for control-condition children, and yielding-model children yielded sooner than did control-condition children. Children in the resisting-model condition also spent more time on the sorting task than did those in the control or yielding-model conditions (all p's < .01). More children in the yielding-model and control conditions examined the prohibited toy in the generalization condition than did children in the resisting-model condition (p = .058). Although this description abbreviates the study (the authors might say amputates), it is presented only to provide a sample of recent evidence that resisting models can have an effect on children's resistance to deviation.

The study also provides an illustration of the social-learning approach to moral decision making and moral behavior. The child is made to recognize the issue—that is, there can be no doubt that the child is aware of the di-

rections and the prohibition, and as little doubt as possible is left regarding the attractiveness of the deviating alternative. No interest is shown in the child's reasoning about why s/he should keep working or should not play with the toys, and the decision to deviate and the action are not differentiated. One cannot tell from these results whether the model thinks about the situation and makes a decision based on a different set of circumstances or whether all children made the same decision based on similar or different circumstances and the models served only to inhibit or release the chosen response.

The acquisition of observed behaviors has been clearly demonstrated in social-learning research (Bandura & Walters, 1963; Mischel, 1971). Recently, however, it has been hypothesized that observed patterns of behavior and the standards inferred from such observations may yield broad patterns of preference and performance (Bandura, 1977). Numerous studies have been performed to examine the effects of models on specific instances of sharing, helping, and resistance to deviation (Mussen & Eisenberg-Berg, 1977; Staub, 1978, 1979). With several recent exceptions little research has been conducted on the generalization of observational learning of sharing, helping, and resistance to temptation (Rushton, 1976; Yarrow et al., 1973). The social-learning studies of direct imitation have examined the characteristics of models, the consequences of the behavior for the model (vicarious reinforcement) or of imitation of the behavior (reinforcement), and the characteristics of the observers (Bandura, 1977). Given that general guidelines based on past modeling studies are followed, observation of behavioral models can increase immediate imitation of prosocial responses and of resistance to deviation. There is also some evidence that both direct observation and film-mediated presentation of helping and sharing models produce effects that generalize to natural settings (Coates, Pusser, & Goodman, 1976; Friedrich & Stein, 1973; Yarrow et al., 1973).

The complexity of applying these basic findings to the acquisition of standards or values is well illustrated in a study of donation and sharing in which seven- to ten-year-old children were exposed to (1) models of donation to a charity, (2) direct instruction to donate, or (3) both modeling and direct instruction to donate (Grusec et al., 1978). Each instructional condition was also divided into three attribution groups: one told they donated because they enjoyed helping others (self-attribution), one told they donated because that was the expected behavior (external-attribution), and a third group in which no reasons for their behavior were given. A two-week delayed test and a test of generalization (donation of pencils to children who could not participate) were included in the study. The data indicated that children given self-attribution reasons did, indeed, share more after a delay and donate more in a test of generalization than did children given external attributions or no reasons. Thus a single sentence about the nature of the sharing responses was powerful over a two-week delay and across responses. In the immediate test of sharing, there were no main effects for type of training, attribution, or sex. There was, however, a significant simple effect for attribution within the modeling condition in the immediate test. More powerful self-perception or attribution effects would be expected if long-term, consistent self-attributions were examined rather than experimental results of brief statements (Bem, 1972). As did Lepper, Sagotsky, and Mailer (1975) and White (1972), Grusec et al. found,

One surprising feature of the data reported in this article was the substantial amount of donation that occurred in the direct-instruction conditions, even in the delayed tests. We expected that modeling would be better, on the whole, than direct instruction, but it was not. (1978, p. 56)

Findings like these have directed social-learning theorists and researchers away from a focus on the immediate situation and observable consequences. The questions that demanded broader considerations include:

Why does a child refrain from attractive pleasures even in the absence of external constraints? Why does one berate oneself for enacting, or even fantasizing, behaviors that others cannot detect? Why does one aid another even when doing so is painful and costly to oneself? Why does one share one's bounty with others even when not pressured to be so generous? These are the kinds of questions that have led to the construction of mediating systems as explanations. (Mischel & Mischel, 1976, p. 97)

The responding individual is, then, a social decision maker rather than simply a passive but learning observer who performs the learned response when there has been adequate reinforcement. "The moral situations encountered in everyday life contain many decisional ingredients that vary in relative importance, depending upon the particular configuration of events" (Bandura, 1977, p. 46). Thus the observer may never imitate the particular behavior observed. Rather s/he infers rules, standards, and principles from multiple observations of responses based upon or relevant to those formulations.

There can be little doubt that response choices can be influenced by observation of others in similar circumstances and by experienced or observed consequences. Evidence for observational learning of rule-governed behavior is presented in Zimmerman and Rosenthal (1974). Operant and observational learning alone, however, cannot account for all standards or patterns of preference.

It has been customary in psychological theorizing to construct entire explanatory schemes around a single regulatory system, to the relative neglect of other influential determinants and processes. . . . Strong allegiances to part processes encourage investigations of subfunctions, but considered independently they do not provide a complete understanding of human behavior. (Bandura, 1977, p. 191)

With the exception of acknowledgment of cognitive developmental sequences and regularities, social-learning theorists appear now to be turning their attention toward the rule and standard construction processes that influence decision making and action choices and toward the mediated effects, expectancies, resulting from reinforcement histories and vicarious reinforcement.

Action choices often take into account values other than justice or fairness. In a study of distribution of rewards by preschool and elementary school children, Damon (1977) found striking developmental differences in the children's discussions about how they thought rewards ought to be distributed ideally. But even the most

developmentally advanced children tended to reward themselves to a greater extent than their stated judgments allowed. Actual distributive decisions tended to be influenced by, "What's in it for me?" The concerns for justice expressed in their verbal judgments proved quite transient when they were personally involved in the outcome of the decision. The moral judgment itself of what was most fair for all parties was not shown to be transient, but the inclination to act in self-interest overwhelmed the judgment of fairness. Damon (1977) indicated that "predicting a child's social conduct from his or her reasoning remains a complex and risky task" (p. 116).

Self-interest comes in many forms. For some it is not an increase in chocolate bars or other hedonistic pursuits, rather it appears as increased control or power, star status, or artistic excellence. In some instances these other values are in direct conflict with the self-defined moral ideal. Sometimes moral values are completely set aside. For instance John Dean in his book *Blind Ambition* recounts that his nefarious activities as Special Council to President Nixon were motivated by unquestioning loyalty to that administration and by his own ambitions within it. Dean says that he constantly put aside the larger question of morality—such thinking was completely preempted by more pressing practical concerns. Dean's actions, then, are not necessarily a reflection of inadequate moral reasoning. A measure of moral reasoning would not have predicted his behavior unless his values context was also tapped. The decisions that precede action involve more than consideration of the justice ideal; other values or motives must be included in any equation that hopes to predict behavior.

Self-interest need not, however, be regarded as the enemy of justice—that is, what is good for the welfare of others, what is fair or right, often is in the interest of one's self as well. There are individual benefits to cooperative living arrangements, protection of civil rights, and aid for those in greatest need. In all but the shortest view, concern for paying the costs and fulfilling the responsibilities of support for social justice and human welfare are in the self-interest of all who recognize their interdependence in an often precarious existence.

ORGANIZATION AND EXECUTION OF MORAL ACTION

The nonswimmer who fails to save a drowning person may not lack sensitivity, may not be deficient in judging the moral ideal, and may not be compromised by competing values. The failure may come from an inability to execute an adequate response. Sometimes we are not even aware of our inabilities. Furthermore sometimes we have decided upon some distant goal but are uncertain how to achieve it. Some of the most energetic debates concern alternative means of reaching an agreed-upon "ought." The records of most deliberative bodies contain not only blatant self-interest but also vehement disagreements about action choices once the group has decided that it will act in the interests of justice. While some problems may require additional knowledge or technical skills and abilities, some aspects of problem solving apply across a wide range of problem situations. Spivak, Platt, and Shure (1976) suggest that interpersonal problem solving involves divergent thinking, generating alternative solutions to problems, devising the sequential means to a chosen end with recognition of potential barriers or hazards, and consideration of all possible consequences of the problem solutions being considered.

Ego strength, the cluster of constructs most often examined in the study of *moral character,* includes variables closely linked to decision making and problem solving—e.g., intelligence, attention, achievement motivation, reflectivity. These measures of ego strength relate to ability to delay gratification and to resist distractions. Mischel (1974) found the following characteristics correlated with delay of gratification: future orientation, high ego control, high achievement motivation, high social responsibility, and lower impulsivity. His findings were in agreement with those of Grim, Kohlberg, and White (1968) regarding positive correlations between delay of gratification and both higher intellectual ability and greater ability to attend. The relationship between resistance to deviation and ego strength variables was examined by Krebs (1967) in a study of resistance to cheating behavior. For the sixth-graders at conventional or principled stages of moral judgment, Krebs found ego controls (IQ and attention) contributed to the prediction of resistance to cheating—i.e., subjects with high ego strength were able to follow through on their convictions.

The Barrett and Yarrow (1977) study of prosocial behavior, social inferential ability, and assertiveness was described earlier in the section on recognition of situations involving moral issues. The study shows that, of the children aware of the needs of others, the amount of prosocial behavior observed was a function of the child's assertiveness. In other words prosocial behavior not only requires empathic role-taking but also some assertiveness for it to be carried out. Studies which look only at role-taking or at social assertiveness are less likely to find significant correlates with prosocial behavior.

It may be possible to identify some of the antecedents and correlates of tenacious follow-through on moral actions. Some parental characteristics have been examined with a specific focus on acting on one's judgments. Cowdry, Keniston, and Cabin (1970) examined relationships between students' pro- or anti-war beliefs and actions (petition signing) and their perception of their relationships with their parents. Those who acted in accordance with their beliefs, regardless of the belief, indicated greater affection in their family relationships, greater happiness and greater similarity of values between their father and mother, greater acceptance by the father, and greater respect for parents. Nurturance and child-rearing attitudes and practices may then affect not only formation of attitudes and standards but also action congruent with belief (see also Hoffman, 1970).

Increases in ego strength may also be attainable through increased understanding and application of self-regulatory strategies. Mobilizing self-statements have been shown to increase persistence (Masters & Mokros, 1974). One could list other possible measures of ego strength or self-control mechanisms (Mischel & Mischel, 1976). Note, however, that the carrying out of actions in support of one's moral judgments requires ego strength, but ego strength in and of itself is nonmoral. As regards

attention, intelligence, perseverance, and delay of gratification, it seems reasonable to assume that efficient genocide, too, has required such characteristics. Endless hours of practice and self-discipline are essential to all great artistic performance, but they are not a satisfactory definition of aesthetics; no more so is ego strength a satisfactory definition of ethical or moral development.

GENERALITY AND SPECIFICITY

It has not been our goal to describe a linear decision-making sequence of the processes involved in moral behavior; rather, the component processes or functions have been isolated to illustrate the interdependence of and interactions between part processes. Most research on morality has not attended to more than one or two of these components at a time. Studies of moral character have often related some single person variable to moral behavior in a specific situation or examined the consistency of subjects' responding across situations.

Hartshorne and May's (1928) analysis of the generality or specificity of moral tendencies and responses led many to the perhaps premature conclusion that moral responding was situation specific and that there was little support for general dispositions such as honesty. Two recent studies provide a different perspective on Hartshorne and May's analyses and conclusions. Burton (1963) factor analyzed the data gathered by Hartshorne and May and found that for a selected matrix of intercorrelations a first principal component accounted for at least 40 percent of the common variance. He concluded, "There is an underlying trait of honesty which a person brings with him to a resistance to temptation situation. However, the results strongly agree with Hartshorne and May's rejection of an 'all or none' formulation regarding a person's character" (p. 492). Nelsen, Grinder, and Mutterer (1969) replicated and extended the Hartshorne and May (1928) and Burton (1963) studies. Their results were in substantial agreement with Burton's and indicated that for their measures situation accounted for a modest proportion (13 percent to 15 percent) of the total variance in comparison to personality variance (35 percent to 40 percent).

Until quite recently the issue of the generality or specificity of individual responses and/or person characteristics in the moral domain has been addressed at a quite global level—e.g., honesty, altruism, empathy—and has most often reflected a unitary view of morality (cf., Hoffman, 1970). Far from being unitary, moral development appears to involve interrelated processes between which there may at times be considerable tension. For example consider again the seminarians in the Good Samaritan study (Darley & Batson, 1973). A seminarian stepping over the victim in an attempt to get to the specified room to deliver the project on which he had worked so diligently cannot be accused of lack of resolution or follow through (he would be high on our fourth component, *execution*). Some of the most resolute seminarians, however, appear to have been momentarily, or perhaps chronically, deficient in recognition or sensitivity (low on the first component, *recognition*). At the other extreme are individuals who are supersensitive, who may be so aroused as to think poorly or to be so often and powerfully swayed by events as to be ineffective at sorting out what to do or in acting to effect change (high on the first component, low on the fourth).

The affect-cognition and person-situation dichotomies stand in the way of understanding moral development. Often the predictions tested have been simplistic and yield unsurprisingly nonsignificant or modest relationships (cf. Rushton, 1976, regarding altruism and the traditional correlation of about .30). While recent reviews indicate that the limitation of person variables for the prediction of moral action may have been overstated by some recent critics, the integration and interdependence of processes in moral development are only beginning to receive attention (Barrett & Yarrow, 1977; Krebs, 1967; Staub, 1974, 1979). Thus within the processes outlined in this chapter, an attempt to predict moral behavior on the basis of only one of the processes described is likely to have modest success at best. This may reflect a need to attend simultaneously to the other processes more than it reflects a lack of meaningful relationship between action and sensitivity, or judgments, or values.

REFERENCES

ANDERSON, N. H., & BUTZIN, C. A. Integration theory applied to children's judgments of equity. *Developmental Psychology,* 1978, *14,* 593–606.

ARONFREED, J. *Conduct and conscience.* New York: Academic Press, 1968.

BANDURA, A. *Social learning theory.* Englewood Cliffs, N.J.: Prentice-Hall, 1977.

BANDURA, A., UNDERWOOD, B., & FROMSON, M. E. Disinhibition of aggression through diffusion of responsibility and dehumanization of victims. *Journal of Research in Personality,* 1975, *9,* 253–269.

BANDURA, A., & WALTERS, R. *Social learning and personality development.* New York: Holt, Rinehart & Winston, 1963.

BARRETT, D. E., & YARROW, M. R. Prosocial behavior, social inferential ability, and assertiveness in children. *Child Development,* 1977, *48,* 475–481.

BAUMRIND, D. *Early socialization and the discipline controversy.* Morristown, N.J.: General Learning Press, 1975.

BEM, D. J. Self-perception theory. In L. Berkowitz (Ed.), *Advances in experimental social psychology* (Vol. 6). New York: Academic Press, 1972.

BERNDT, T. J. The effect of reciprocity norms on moral judgment and causal attribution. *Child Development,* 1977, *48,* 1322–1330.

BLASI, A. Bridging moral cognition and moral action: A critical review of the literature. *Psychological Bulletin,* 1980, *88*(No. 1), 1–45.

BLATT, M., & KOHLBERG, L. The effects of classroom moral discussion upon children's level of moral judgment. *Journal of Moral Education,* 1975, *4,* 129–161.

BROWN, R. W. *Social psychology.* New York: Free Press, 1965.

BURTON, R. V. Generality of honesty reconsidered. *Psychological Review,* 1963, *70,* 481–499.

BUSSEY, K., & PERRY, D. G. The imitation of resistance to deviation: Conclusive evidence for an elusive effect. *Developmental Psychology,* 1977, *13,* 438–443.

CAMPBELL, D. T. On the conflicts between biological and social evolution and between psychology and moral tradition. *American Psychologist,* 1975, *30,* 1103–1126.

CANDEE, D. Structure and choice in moral reasoning. *Journal of Personality and Social Psychology,* 1976, *34,* 1293–1301.

COATES, B., PUSSER, H. E., & GOODMAN, I. The influence of "Sesame Street" and "Mister Rogers' Neighborhood" on children's social behavior in the preschool. *Child Development,* 1976, *47,* 138–144.

COLBY, A., GIBBS, J., & KOHLBERG, L. *Standard form scoring manual.* Cambridge, Mass.: Center for Moral Education, 1980.

COLBY, A., & KOHLBERG, L. *The relation between logical and moral development.* Unpublished manuscript, Harvard University, 1975.

COWDRY, R. W., KENISTON, K., & CABIN, S. The war and military obligations: Private attitudes and public actions. *Journal of Personality,* 1970, *38,* 525–549.

DAMON, W. *The social world of the child.* San Fransicso: Jossey-Bass, 1977.

DARLEY, J., & BATSON, C. "From Jerusalem to Jericho": A study of situational and dispositional variables in helping behavior. *Journal of Personality and Social Psychology,* 1973, *27,* 100–108.

DIENSTBIER, R. A., HILLMAN, D., LEHNHOFF, J., HILLMAN, J., & VALKENAAR, M. C. An emotion-attribution approach to moral behavior: Interfacing cognitive and avoidance theories of moral development. *Psychological Review,* 1975, *82,* 299–315.

DURKHEIM, E. *Moral education.* New York: Free Press, 1961. (Originally published, 1925.)

EDWARDS, C. P. The comparative study of the development of moral judgment and reasoning. In R. Monroe, R. Monroe, & B. B. Whiting (Eds.), *Handbook of cross-cultural human development.* New York: Garland, 1977.

EISENBERG-BERG, N. Development of children's prosocial moral judgment. *Developmental Psychology,* 1979, *15,* 128–137.

FLAVELL, J. H. Concept development. In P. H. Mussen (Ed.), *Carmichael's manual of child psychology.* New York: John Wiley, 1970.

FLAVELL, J. H. *Cognitive development.* Englewood Cliffs, N.J.: Prentice-Hall, 1977.

FREUD, S. *Civilization and its discontents.* London: Hogarth Press, 1955. (Originally published, 1932.)

FREUD, S. *The basic writings of Sigmund Freud.* New York: Modern Library, 1938.

FRIEDRICH, L. K., & STEIN, A. H. Aggressive and prosocial television programs and the natural behavior of preschool children. *Monographs of the Society for Research in Child Development,* 1973, *38*(4, Serial No. 151).

GALLATIN, J. The adolescent in political socialization research: Contradiction and consistency. In J. Adelson (Ed.), *Handbook of adolescent psychology.* New York: John Wiley, 1979.

GELFAND, D. M., & HARTMANN, D. P. The development of prosocial behavior and moral judgment. In R. Ault (Ed.), *Selected topics in child development.* Pacific Palisades, Calif.: Goodyear, 1980.

GREENWALD, A. Does the Good Samaritan parable increase helping? A comment on Darley and Batson's no effect conclusion. *Journal of Personality and Social Psychology,* 1975, *32,* 578–583.

GRIM, P. F., KOHLBERG, L., & WHITE, S. H. Some relationships between conscience and attentional processes. *Journal of Personality and Social Psychology,* 1968, *8,* 239–252.

GRUENEICH, R., & TRABASSO, T. The story as a social environment: Children's comprehension and evaluation of intentions and consequences. In J. Harvey (Ed.), *Cognition, social behavior and the environment.* Hillsdale, N.J.: Lawrence Erlbaum Associates, 1981.

GRUSEC, J. E., KUCZYNSKI, J., RUSHTON, P., & SIMUTIS, Z. M. Modeling, direct instruction, and attributions: Effects on altruism. *Developmental Psychology,* 1978, *14,* 51–57.

HARTSHORNE, H., & MAY, M. A. *Studies in the nature of character* (Vol. 1). Studies in deceit. New York: Macmillan, 1928.

HOFFMAN, M. L. Moral development. In P. H. Mussen (Ed.), *Carmichael's manual of child development.* New York: John Wiley, 1970.

HOFFMAN, M. L. Empathy, role-taking, guilt, and development of altruistic motives. In T. Lickona (Ed.), *Moral development and behavior: Theory, research and social issues.* New York: Holt, Rinehart & Winston, 1976.

HOFFMAN, M. L. Sex differences in empathy and related behaviors. *Psychological Bulletin,* 1977, *84,* 712–720.

HOFFMAN, M. L. Development of moral thought, feeling, and behavior. *American Psychologist,* 1979, *34,* 958–979.

HOGAN, R., JOHNSON, J. A., & EMLER, N. P. A socioanalytic theory of moral development. In W. Damon (Ed.), *Moral development: New directions for child development.* San Francisco: Jossey-Bass, 1978.

HOOK, J. G., & COOK, T. D. Equity theory and the cognitive ability of children. *Psychological Bulletin,* 1979, *86,* 429–445.

HUSTON, T. L., & KORTE, C. The responsive bystander: Why he

helps. In T. Lickona (Ed.), *Moral development and behavior*. New York: Holt, Rinehart & Winston, 1976.

INHOFF, G. E., & HALVERSON, C. F., JR. Behavioral disposition of child and caretaker-child interaction. *Developmental Psychology*, 1977, *13*, 274–281.

KARNIOL, R. Children's use of intention cues in evaluating behavior. *Psychological Bulletin*, 1978, *85*, 76–85.

KEASEY, C. B. Children's developing awareness and usage of intentionality and motives. In C. B. Keasey & H. E. Howe (Eds.), *Nebraska Symposium on Motivation* (Vol. 25). Lincoln: University of Nebraska Press, 1978.

KOHLBERG, L. Development of moral character and moral ideology. In M. L. Hoffman & L. W. Hoffman (Eds.), *Review of child development research* (Vol. 1). New York: Russell Sage Foundation, 1964.

KOHLBERG, L. Stage and sequence: The cognitive-developmental approach to socialization. In D. Goslin (Ed.), *Handbook of socialization theory and research*. Skokie, Ill.: Rand McNally, 1969.

KOHLBERG, L. From is to ought: How to commit the naturalistic fallacy and get away with it in the study of moral development. In T. Mischel (Ed.), *Cognitive development and epistemology*. New York: Academic Press, 1971.

KOHLBERG, L. Moral stages and moralization: The cognitive-developmental approach. In T. Lickona (Ed.), *Moral development and behavior*. New York: Holt, Rinehart & Winston, 1976.

KOHLBERG, L. *The meaning and measurement of moral development*. Clark Lectures, Clark University, 1979.

KOHLBERG, L., & ELFENBEIN, D. The development of moral judgments concerning capital punishments. *American Journal of Orthopsychiatry*, 1975, *45*, 614–640.

KREBS, R. L. *Some relations between moral judgment, attention, and resistance to temptation*. Unpublished doctoral dissertation, University of Chicago, 1967.

KURDEK, L. A. Perspective taking as the cognitive basis of children's moral development: A review of the literature. *Merrill-Palmer Quarterly*, 1978, *24*, 3–28.

LATANÉ, B., & DARLEY, J. *The unresponsive bystander: Why doesn't he help?* Englewood Cliffs, N.J.: Prentice-Hall, 1970.

LAVOIE, J. C. Aversive, cognitive, and parental determinants of punishment generalization in adolescent males. *Journal of Genetic Psychology*, 1974, *124*, 29–39.

LAWRENCE, J. A. Moral judgment intervention studies using the Defining Issues Test. *Journal of Moral Education*, 1980, *9*, 178–191.

LEPPER, M. R., SAGOTSKY, G., & MAILER, J. Generalization and persistence of effects of exposure to self-reinforcement models. *Child Development*, 1975, *46*, 618–630.

LERNER, M. J. The justice motive: Some hypotheses as to its origins and forms. *Journal of Personality*, 1977, *45*, 1–53.

LICKONA, T. Research on Piaget's theory of moral development. In T. Lickona (Ed.), *Moral development and behavior: Theory, research, and social issues*. New York: Holt, Rinehart & Winston, 1976.

LOCKWOOD, A. L. The effects of values clarification and moral development curriculum on school-age subjects: A critical review of recent research. *Review of Educational Research*, 1978, *48*, 325–364.

McDOUGALL, W. *An introduction to social psychology*. London: Methuen, 1908.

MASTERS, J. C., & MOKROS, J. R. Self-reinforcement processes in children. In H. Reese (Ed.), *Advances in child development and behavior* (Vol. 9). New York: Academic Press, 1974.

MILGRAM, S. Behavioral study of obedience. *Journal of Abnormal and Social Psychology*, 1963, *67*, 371–378.

MILGRAM, S. Group pressure and action against a person. *Journal of Abnormal and Social Psychology*, 1964, *69*, 137–143.

MISCHEL, W. *Introduction to personality*. New York: Holt, Rinehart & Winston, 1971.

MISCHEL, W. Processes in delay of gratification. In L. Berkowitz (Ed.), *Advances in social psychology* (Vol. 7). New York: Academic Press, 1974.

MISCHEL, W., & MISCHEL, H. N. A cognitive social learning approach to morality and self-regulation. In T. Lickona (Ed.), *Moral development and behavior*. New York: Holt, Rinehart & Winston, 1976.

MOOD, D., JOHNSON, J., & SHANTZ, C. U. *Affective and cognitive components of empathy in young children*. Paper presented at the South-

east Regional Meeting of the Society for Research in Child Development, Chapel Hill, N.C., 1974.

MUSSEN, P. H., & EISENBERG-BERG, N. *Roots of caring, sharing and helping*. San Francisco: W. H. Freeman & Company Publishers, 1977.

NELSEN, E. A., GRINDER, R. E., & MUTTERER, M. L. Sources of variance in behavioral measures of honesty in temptation situations: Methodological analyses. *Developmental Psychology*, 1969, *1*, 265–279.

PERRY, D. G., BUSSEY, K., & PERRY, L. C. Factors influencing the imitation of resistance to deviation. *Developmental Psychology*, 1975, *11*, 724–731.

PETERSON, L., HARTMANN, D. P., & GELFAND, D. M. Developmental changes in the effects of dependency and reciprocity cues on children's moral judgments and donation rates. *Child Development*, 1977, *48*, 1331–1339.

PIAGET, J. *The moral judgment of the child* (M. Gabain, trans.). New York: Free Press, 1965. (Originally published, 1932.)

RENSHON, S. A. *Handbook of political socialization: Theory and research*. New York: Free Press, 1977.

REST, J. R. *Development in judging moral issues*. Minneapolis: University of Minnesota Press, 1979.

REST, J. R. Morality. In J. Flavell & E. Markman (Eds.), *Cognitive development*. A volume in P. Mussen (Ed.), *Carmichael's manual of child psychology* (4th ed.). New York: John Wiley, in press.

ROSENTHAL, T. L., & ZIMMERMAN, B. J. *Social learning and cognition*. New York: Academic Press, 1978.

RUSHTON, J. P. Socialization and the altruistic behavior of children. *Psychological Bulletin*, 1976, *83*, 898–913.

SAGI, A., & HOFFMAN, M. L. Empathic distress in the newborn. *Developmental Psychology*, 1976, *12*, 175–176.

SELMAN, R. Toward a structural analysis of developing interpersonal relationship concepts: Research with normal and disturbed preadolescent boys. In A. Pick (Ed.), *Tenth Annual Minnesota Symposia on Child Psychology*. Minneapolis: University of Minnesota Press, 1976.

SELMAN, R., & DAMON, W. The necessity (but insufficiency) of social perspective taking for conceptions of justice at three early levels. In D. J. DePalma & J. M. Foley (Eds.), *Moral development: Current theory and research*. Hillsdale, N.J.: Lawrence Erlbaum Associates, 1975.

SHANTZ, C. U. *Empathy in relation to social cognitive development*. Paper presented at the convention of the American Psychological Association, New Orleans, September 1974.

SHANTZ, C. U. The development of social cognition. In E. M. Hetherington (Ed.), *Review of child development research* (Vol. 5). Chicago: University of Chicago Press, 1975.

SIMNER, M. L. Newborn's response to the cry of another infant. *Developmental Psychology*, 1971, *5*, 136–150.

SPIVAK, G., PLATT, J. J., & SHURE, M. B. *The problem-solving approach to adjustment*. San Francisco: Jossey-Bass, 1976.

STAUB, E. Helping a distressed person: Social, personality, and stimulus determinants. In L. Berkowitz (Ed.), *Advances in experimental social psychology* (Vol. 7). New York: Academic Press, 1974.

STAUB, E. *Positive social behavior and morality: Social and personal influences* (Vol. 1). New York: Academic Press, 1978.

STAUB, E. *Positive social behavior and morality: Socialization and development* (Vol. 2). New York: Academic Press, 1979.

STOKES, T. F., & BAER, D. M. An implicit technology of generalization. *Journal of Applied Behavior Analysis*, 1977, *10*, 349–367.

TURIEL, E. Stage transition in moral development. In R. M. Travers (Ed.), *Second handbook of research on teaching*. Skokie, Ill.: Rand McNally, 1972.

WALKER, L. J. *Cognitive and perspective-taking prerequisites for the development of moral reasoning*. Unpublished doctoral dissertation, University of Toronto, 1978.

WALKER, L. J., & RICHARDS, B. S. Stimulating transitions in moral reasoning as a function of stage of cognitive development. *Developmental Psychology*, 1979, *15*, 95–103.

WALTERS, G. C., & GRUSEC, J. E. *Punishment*. San Francisco: W. H. Freeman & Company Publishers, 1977.

WARREN, S. F., ROGERS-WARREN, A., & BAER, D. M. The role of offer rates in controlling sharing by young children. *Journal of Applied Behavior Analysis*, 1976, *9*, 491–497.

WHITE, G. M. Immediate and deferred effects of model observation and guided and unguided rehearsal on donating and stealing. *Journal of Personality and Social Psychology,* 1972, *21,* 139–148.

WILSON, E. O. *Sociobiology: The new synthesis.* Cambridge, Mass.: Harvard University Press, 1975.

YARROW, M. R., SCOTT, P. M., & WAXLER, C. Z. Learning concern for others. *Developmental Psychology,* 1973, *8,* 240–261.

ZIMMERMAN, B. J., & ROSENTHAL, T. L. Observational learning of rule-governed behavior by children. *Psychological Bulletin,* 1974, *81,* 29–42.

25

The Impact of the Schools on Social and Emotional Development

NANCY A. BUSCH-ROSSNAGEL

ANNETTE K. VANCE

At the age of five or six years, the world of the child broadens to encompass a new influence on the development of children. This new force is, of course, the educational system. Although children may have been exposed to teachers and peers in daycare or nursery school, the size and organization of the school as a system are new to most children. For the first five years of life, the family was the child's main environment. During the years to come, the family will continue to influence the child, but the schools, including teachers, peers, and "the system," will be the center of the child's extrafamilial existence for a decade or more. Schools can complement the child's family by reinforcing the values, traditions, and expectations which the family and child hold. Schools can also supplement the family by teaching skills and introducing ideas that are not a part of the family's background. Schools and families may also contradict each other, as is the case when the middle-class orientation of the school conflicts with the values of a lower-class family.

Concern with the impact of schools is justified because of the scale of the influence. By the time a child graduates from high school s/he will have spent 10,000 hours in the classroom (Kazalunas, 1978). The number of individuals involved is also staggering. As the result of compulsory education, elementary schools touch the lives of all the children in Western cultures. The schools influence even those children who are not in the educational system because of the implications of being excluded. According to the Bureau of the Census (1978), in the United States the number of children in elementary school (kindergarten and grades one through eight) in 1977 was 32.4 million. Add to this 15.8 million children

in high school, and the number is immense. These numbers—and the breadth of the schools' influence—are of greater importance today than in past generations because more individuals are in school longer. In 1900, 11.4 percent of 14- to 17-year-olds were in school, while today 94 percent of the same age group are in school (Smith & Orlosky, 1975). Any impact of schools on individuals will be more widespread simply as a function of the number of individuals involved.

In addition to the greater number of individuals, the effect of schools on society is also enlarging because the functions of schooling are changing to increase the depth of the impact. Three major functions of schools can be defined. The first function focuses on literacy for all children, not just the privileged. Schools are not an inherent feature of societies. At least until the Industrial Revolution, the function of the schools was to prepare a select few for certain professions. For most persons training in skills occurred on an informal basis in much the same way that a child is taught to walk or talk—through observation and imitation. With the emergence of modern industrial societies, the skills of the adult were often rendered obsolete by rapid social change. This trend, as evidenced by the increasing need for skilled labor, gradually led to compulsory education between the ages of 8 and 16 (Bakan, 1971). The primary function of the schools was defined as teaching the basic skills of reading, writing, and arithmetic that were required by the urban-industrial society, and this function continues to this day.

Compulsory education also reflected a feeling that in a democratic society parents could no longer be trusted with the socialization of their children, *socialization* being defined as enculturation or indoctrination of the children into the dominant culture. Thus the stage was set for the second function of schooling: teaching societal values. Within this function the public schools teach general

We wish to thank Janet Fritz, Don Peters, and Dan Weigel for their comments on an earlier version of this chapter.

skills in addition to the basic skills. "The school can foster, among other things, self-discipline, growth in personal interactions and acceptance of group norms" (Smith & Orlosky, 1975, p. 29). In teaching general skills the impact of the schools may be perceived as negative. Personality traits such as passivity, conformity, and dependency may be emphasized (Saario, Jacklin, & Tittle, 1973). In addition since the prevailing mores of the society are taught, the schools have a decidedly middle-class bias. The teaching of general skills may be seen as preparing students to function in their future occupation. As a reflection of this future orientation, the structure and competition of the schools mirror the hierarchy of the workplace (Bowles & Gintis, 1976). In line with this function of socialization, some writers have suggested that the school should become a substitute home and the teachers should become more "deliberate" in their socialization of the next generation (Kay, 1975, p. 181).

The second function of schools represents an attempt to preserve the status quo, while the third function is an attempt to change the status quo by improving society. In part the introduction of compulsory education was an attempt to cure some of society's ills, such as the "immorality" of the growing cities, the "un-American" ideas of the immigrants, and the crimes against property by juveniles (Bakan, 1971). In more recent years the use of the schools to reform society has reached even greater proportions. Schools are asked to correct racial and economic inequalities and to compensate for poor parenting and malnutrition (Sawhill, 1979). In effect society has adopted the principle of residual functions in regard to the schools; whatever needs of children and society are "not satisfied by other agencies are the schools' responsibility" (Smith & Orlosky, 1975, p. 33).

In considering any function or effect of the schools, one basic caution must be noted. Schools are not the only agent for education, socialization, or social reform. Agents such as the family, religion, and occupation also have responsibilities in these areas, and evaluations of the success of schools are difficult because they may be helped or hindered by these agencies (Smith & Orlosky, 1975).

The focus of this chapter is the impact of the schools on children as individuals. Hence we are more concerned with the functions of teaching basic skills and socialization. The body of literature that deals with acquisition of basic skills, as evidenced by academic achievement and other cognitive outcomes, could appropriately be included in this chapter. The impact of the school's second function of socialization implies examination of affective outcomes. Obviously consideration of both cognitive and affective outcomes would require that volumes, rather than a chapter, be devoted to the topic. Thus we have further limited the focus of the chapter to be nonacademic outcomes with an associated concern with the school as a socializing agent. Cognitive outcomes, academic achievement, and skill acquisition will be noted when they influence affective outcomes. This reflects the trend in society to be increasingly concerned with the effects of schooling on the "whole" child, rather than just the child's intellectual achievements. Although there may be a trend back toward emphasizing the three R's and a need for minimum competency requirements for high school diplomas, we still need to explore the result of our attempts at affective education. Any separation of academic and nonacademic outcomes is, of course, artificial but deemed necessary.

The exploration of findings in the area of social-emotional development is limited by certain problems with the literature itself. While there is a great deal of research on the educational system, the designs of most studies incorporate achievement, acquisition of basic skills, and other intellectual tasks as the dependent variables. When affective factors are included, they are usually portrayed as influencing the intellectual gains and not as being influenced themselves. Social-emotional development is often discussed in "how-to" articles, those that advocate a specific approach for fostering the child's development. However, these approaches are seldom evaluated, and in general, examinations of nonacademic factors as the dependent variables are scarce.

In part this paucity of research may reflect a difficulty in measuring affective outcomes especially in young children except through observational studies. An exception to this is the research done in Head Start and follow-through programs. In order to show the effectiveness of these programs, these researchers emphasized the affective domain as well as the cognitive, usually using observational measures (cf. Miller & Dyer, 1975; Stallings, 1975). Evaluation research, by its nature, is plagued by other methodological problems as well, such as difficulty in controlling other variables beside schooling, the improbability of randomization, and the representativeness of the sample.

A final limitation of the research in this area is its nondevelopmental and atheoretical nature. "No theory guides the selection of traits which are measured in assessments of nonacademic outcomes" (Greenberger & Sorenson, 1974, p. 335). In addition few studies are longitudinal, so it is difficult to delineate the changes that occur in order to examine how social-emotional development is affected by schooling. Because the nature of schooling has itself changed, there are probably cohort effects in the impact of schools. Thus longitudinal-sequential designs are appropriate so that researchers can deal with both changes in children and changes in schooling. These shortcomings have defined the nature of the review in this chapter. We have concentrated on empirical research with aspects of schooling as independent variables and social-emotional development as the dependent measure. However the paucity of empirical research requires that we also refer to the "how-to" articles. We have organized both the schooling variables and the child variables in a framework that will hopefully delineate needed developmental research and foster future theorizing in this area.

ORGANIZATION OF THIS REVIEW

This chapter has two major sections. The first half deals with social-emotional variables as the dependent measures in schooling studies. In considering the universe of possible affective outcomes of the educational process, three major categories are more thoroughly researched than other areas and show the developmental nature of the impact of the schools. These are (1) the child's sense of self, (2) the child's personal adjustment to school, and (3) the child's social relationships. Discussion of these dependent variables is organized by looking at three characteristics of schooling: pre- and early school experience, classroom practices, and the school environment. Each of the categories contains a number of specific independent variables, and the discussion of these provides continuity across the three areas of social-emotional development. The second half of the chapter analyzes the outcome of schooling in two areas in which there has been increasing societal interest: morality and sex roles. The first half is thus a general look at what we know about the effects of schooling on the social-emotional development of children, while the second half is an application of teaching methods to influence two specific areas. The conclusions of the chapter are tempered with a plea for subsequent research which overcomes some of the limitations described previously.

THE SENSE OF SELF

Within the sphere of social-emotional development, possibly no other construct receives the attention that is paid to the sense of self. As schools have increased their socialization functions, there has been a concomitant concern with self-concept, self-esteem, self-image, identity, ego, or whatever one operationally defines as the *sense of self*. A variety of measures, such as teacher-rating forms, self-ratings, and behavioral observations, have been used to assess this construct. In this chapter these different operational definitions are clustered together to indicate that they probably relate to the same construct. Associated with this concern is a growing body of literature which prescribes practices for developing the child's positive sense of self. However very little empirical research has been done on the features of schooling which contribute to the optimal development of the sense of self (Goebes & Shore, 1978). The research which is available can be categorized and examined using three major classes of independent variables in relation to the child's sense of self: (1) pre- and early school experiences, (2) classroom practices, and (3) the school environment.

Pre- and Early School Experiences

Several interrelated trends in our society, such as feminism, inflation, and the increased number of working mothers, are changing the nature of childcare in the preschool years. As a result the child who is entering the public school system at age five or six is likely to have had previous experiences with "school" in the form of nursery school, daycare, or early interventions, such as Head Start. What are the effects of these programs on the child's sense of self? Interestingly the research focus has varied depending on the type of program. Daycare research has been examining whether or not there are harmful effects of separating children from their mothers before school (Belsky & Steinberg, 1978). Intervention research has been hunting for cognitive gains. In recent years nursery school evaluation has been limited as educators became more concerned with Head Start and daycare. The earlier research often focused on global variables, such as "improved social skills" or "healthy emotional adjustment." When these studies using current standards are reviewed, the studies have a criterion problem for their dependent measures which renders the studies inconclusive (Sears & Dowley, 1963; Swift, 1964).

Fifteen years after the birth of Head Start, there is a renewed interest in the long-term effects of this before-school intervention. While earlier reports supposedly documented the lack of long-term cognitive gains (Cicirelli, 1969), the recent evaluations have been more concerned with long-term social-emotional development than was the original work. When the dependent variable is a sense of self (usually defined as *self-concept*), the research conclusions on the effect of early intervention are conflicting (Mann, Harrell, & Hurt, 1978). According to the Mann et al. review, if there is a high degree of parental participation in the program, the children are likely to show gains in self-concept. Without parental involvement the gains are nonsignificant or short-term. In a study on the effect of daycare on self-concept, Harper (1978) found no meaningful differences between daycare and nondaycare children (which in the daycare literature is interpreted positively). However Harper and Mann et al. did find differences in personal adjustment to school and in social relationships (as discussed later).

Even without preschool experience the child comes to school with a history of interactions with family members, others in the social environment, and the physical environment which contributes strongly to his/her sense of self. Indeed some researchers suggest that the self-concept is well formed at school entry (Brandes, 1978; Calhoun & Morse, 1977). As part of this sense of self, children start school with expectations about school and about their school performance. In a lengthy study Entwisle and Hayduk (1978) explored the development and effect of first- and second-graders' early expectations about school. Although initially the effect of evaluations upon the children's own expectations was examined, the authors suggest that one first study the development of those expectations. Based on what a child is told s/he is good at, the child develops self-expectations consistent with these evaluations. These expectations lead the child to behave in ways that make the evaluations come true. Further scrutiny should investigate what day-to-day happenings in school over the years shape a child's self-expectations. "The early days of school plunge children into a confusing new environment of social comparison. The net residue of these comparisons . . . shapes the child's evaluation of himself" (Entwisle & Hayduk, 1978, p. 3). A child is the receiver of much obscure feedback from teachers, peers, and principals. Early school events influence the child's self-image and subsequently determine his/her experiences. According to Entwisle and Hayduk, how well the child is doing after the first few school years is a good long-term indicator of future school performance. Thus the self-expectations and evaluations are an example of a self-fulfilling prophecy. However, the ultimate effect of the child's early experiences is tempered by subsequent classroom practices.

Classroom Practices

When considering the impact of school on affective development, the cluster of independent variables related to classroom practices includes teacher characteristics, methods of instruction and evaluation, and classroom atmosphere. Teacher characteristics have more often been examined in relation to achievement than to the student's sense of self. However there are some data which point to the teacher's contribution to this aspect of the child's personality. Edeburn and Landry (1974) showed that teachers' self-acceptance was related to the development of a good self-concept in children in grades three, four, and five. Similarly when Peck, Fox, and Marston (1977) studied teacher-student interaction effects on self-esteem, they found that teachers who rated themselves high on "efficiency" produced greater gains in the self-esteem of their sixth-graders than teachers who rated themselves medium or low on these two characteristics.

In a review of the effect of social structure in the classroom, Glidewell, Kantor, Smith, and Stringer (1966) concluded that a democratic atmosphere increased mutual esteem, rapport, and self-esteem. A study by Blaney, Stephan, Rosenfield, Aronson, and Sikes (1977) has demonstrated how a specific technique reflecting democratic practice may influence self-esteem. In an experimental condition fifth-grade students were divided into groups with four to seven members. For social studies or mathematics the students each learned a part of the material and were responsible for teaching it to the others in the group. Each student was required to learn all of the material, so interdependency within the group was created. A group of control students was taught in a traditional manner. Even though the students were in the experimental groups for less than three hours per week for six weeks, the self-esteem of the experimental group members increased. Other approaches may also positively influence the sense of self. A project in Great Britain has shown that *confluent education,* which combines cognitive and affective learning, has a direct influence on self-concept (Brandes, 1978).

Democratic practices may also be reflected in the success and failure of the students. Kifer (1975) suggested that the history of success in academic tasks leads to positive personality characteristics, while failure results in lower levels of regard for the self and personal abilities. In the early school years home factors are highly salient for personality characteristics. However the relationship between history of success and failure and self-regard becomes more important in the later elementary years, as the result of the duration and consistency of the pattern of success and failure.

In his quasi-longitudinal study Kifer (1975) tested this conceptual model. Students were included if they were in the top (successful) or bottom (unsuccessful) 20 percent of their class in academic marks. Two dependent measures were self-esteem and self-concept of ability. With a few exceptions the self-esteem of the students conformed to the hypothesized pattern. There were increasing differences in self-esteem between the successful and unsuccessful students for grades four through seven. The differences were the result of decreasing self-esteem in the unsuccessful group since the scores for the successful students were stable. The more specific measure, self-concept of ability, was more highly related to achievement than self-esteem, but the pattern of decreasing scores for the unsuccessful students and stable scores for successful subjects was the same. In a similar study the procedure of cross-lagged panel correlations was used by Calsyn and Kenny (1977) to investigate the association between grade point average and self-concept of ability. This analysis allows cause-effect relationships to be determined because the variables are time-ordered. Their reanalysis of earlier data supported the findings of Kifer by showing that grade point average is causally predominant over self-concept of ability, with the pattern being much stronger for females.

The duration and consistency of success were examined by Calhoun and Morse (1977). They suggest that failure in the school setting may have only a temporary negative effect on self-esteem if the initial self-concept was generally positive. However if the self-concept was originally negative, the child "may not have the balancing condition to mitigate the failure" (p. 321).

Bloom (1976) has translated the implications of these studies on the effect of success and failure on the sense of self into a theory of teaching for mastery learning. He suggested that a student's perception of his/her competence in school learning is a major factor influencing affect. Various short-term studies by Bloom and colleagues (including Kifer, 1975) have shown the correlation between success and positive attitudes about school subjects to range between +.20 and +.40. Bloom concludes that the child's school success or failure ultimately influences not only attitudes toward school but also the child's basic view of him/herself. To confirm these effects, longitudinal, empirical studies are required, and they must encompass longer time periods than a few months.

The judgment of student success or failure—evaluation of students—also has an impact on the child's sense of self. Although the schools do influence the child's self-concept, Silberman (1978) in her study of 271 report cards from all parts of the country found that few schools included any evaluation of this characteristic.

Self-worth, self-confidence, self-esteem, self-regard—call it what you will—was almost never included in the items. "Follows directions," on the other hand, was included in 98 percent of the kindergarten and elementary school report cards. Self-reliance, self-direction, self-discovery, self-awareness were all conspicuously missing, but "practices self-control" appeared on 97 percent of the cards. (p. 24)

Although schools do not explicitly evaluate the child's sense of self, school practices do affect this construct. Ability grouping often leads to children believing their assigned labels and in effect becoming "smart" or "dumb" (Silberman, 1978).

In order to understand better how classroom practices affect children, one should look at children's school experiences from their point of view. In the first national survey of children (Foundation for Child Development, Note 1), researchers scrutinized the accuracy of children's self-appraisals and their feelings about school. Of the over 2000 children ages 7 to 11 in the survey, 30 percent felt they were "one of the best" in class, while 4 percent felt they were "near the bottom" of the class in response to a question about how well they were doing in school. Assessment by teachers showed only 19 percent of the children to be considered "one of the best" and 13 percent to be "near the bottom." This suggests that teachers' evaluations do not match the children's self-appraisals. Entwisle and Hayduk (1978) had similar findings in regard to children's expectations of achievement in math and reading. Children consistently expected to do better in one subject or the other, while teachers' marking practices indicated that they performed well in both or poorly in both.

More than two-thirds of the children in the national survey worried about tests. These children also felt they just could not learn and felt angry about that. Woyshner (1979) claims that these feelings have a strong relationship with the child's perception of him/herself as a student. "The lower his self-appraisal, the more likely he is to feel worried, shamed and angry about his performance in school, or to feel frustrated about his ability to learn" (p. 45). Entwisle and Hayduk (1978) concluded that worries over evaluations ultimately affect a child's expectations and his/her sense of self. They found that the grades a child receives on his/her first report card may have enormous importance because they are the marks s/he will tend to get repeatedly. These marks may be accurate or erroneous feedback. Nonetheless they will affect children's expectations and sense of self. "As time passes, unrealistically high expectations, if they persist, may become severely dysfunctional. . . . A child whose initial level of expectations is too low, on the other hand, may suffer relatively benign consequences" (p. 167). However the work of Calhoun and Morse (1977) provides a cautionary note to these ideas. A lack of success on a one-time evaluation is not likely to damage irreparably the child's sense of self. The consistency and duration of negative evaluations are the critical components.

The School Environment

There are additional independent variables outside the realm of the classroom which impact on the child's sense of self. These variables may be categorized as dealing with the school environment and include the effect of open versus traditional approaches, bicultural education, and the middle-class orientation of the school. In a review paper Hetherington (1971) suggested that most teachers have a middle-class orientation, and this has a negative influence on the personality development of lower-class children. Specifically lower-class children have low self-evaluations and low achievement motivation. These variables are, in turn, associated with school failure and high dropout rates. The work of Entwisle and Hayduk (1978) contradicts the assumption that lower-class children have low self-evaluation. Originally their expectations may be extremely high. However, these high expectations may be dysfunctional, and the end result is still school failure.

One way to overcome the middle-class orientation of the schools is to establish bicultural school environments. *Bicultural environments* are defined as those in which both cultures are officially recognized in all aspects of school functioning and are an integral part of the setting (Goebes & Shore, 1978). Goebes and Shore investigated the influence of such a program on the sense of self. After comparing girls from bicultural and monocultural schools, they found that preadolescent Anglo and Latino girls (ages 10½ to 12½ years) in the bicultural environment had better self-images than the girls in the monocultural programs. There were no differences for the younger girls (ages 8½ to 10½ years). Apparently positive self-image decreases as students spend more time in the monocultural school.

Court-mandated desegregation appears to offer a bicultural environment, but studies on the effects of desegregation on self-esteem yield conflicting results. Stephan and Rosenfield (1978) found a slight increase in self-esteem for blacks after desegregation. However Stephan (1978) concludes that the self-esteem of blacks rarely increases after desegregation. Considering the success of Goebes and Shore's bicultural program in raising self-esteem, why does desegregation have little or no effect? The age at onset of bicultural schooling appears to be one significant factor. Desegregation has usually occurred during the preadolescent years for students (grade six in Stephan and Rosenberg's study), while Goebes and Shore studied elementary school-age children. The length of such programs is also crucial. Stephan (1978) suggested that we need long-term studies to see the effect of desegregation truly. Another factor is the type of program offered in the environment. Desegregation does not ensure integration or that bicultural approaches are used. If the school maintains a white cultural orientation after desegregation, it is not logical to expect gains in self-esteem. However if both cultures are stressed and respected, as in Goebes and Shore's (1978) program, increases in self-esteem may be anticipated. Classroom practices which use mixed racial groups and require interdependence (Blaney et al., 1977) can also be a part of turning desegregation into integration.

As mentioned before, a democratic class structure increases mutual esteem, rapport, and self-esteem. However a democratic environment is probably a cluster of variables which need further specification. This specification might start with a contrast of open- and traditional-classroom structures. Open approaches may be reflected in architectural design, time scheduling, or teacher philosophy but generally may be characterized as child-directed as opposed to teacher-directed (Silberman, 1973). Because the open approaches center on the child, these approaches to education have been espoused as having a beneficial effect on the child's sense of self when compared to traditional approaches. However empirical studies have not produced evidence of the advantages of open classrooms. Allen (1974) found no differences in attitudes or self-esteem between students in open-area and self-contained classrooms. When Klass and Hodge (1978) measured the self-esteem of 350 seventh-graders in classrooms differing in philosophy and practice, they also found no differences in self-esteem. Perhaps the promise of the open classroom lies more in changes in teacher self-acceptance, a sharing of authority, positive evaluation, and other variables which have been associated with students' self-esteem, rather than in a direct relationship between the sense of self and open versus traditional approaches. Alternatively there are possible benefits of open education environments other than increases in self-esteem, such as positive peer interaction (see following section).

The research thus shows that schooling does influence the child's sense of self. While the specific procedures that should be used to enhance the child's self-concept have not been investigated, we can start to outline the interrelated variables which do have an effect. A democratic atmosphere in the school and classroom has a positive influence on the child's self-esteem, but atmosphere is probably a cluster of other variables including administration procedures, teacher characteristics, teaching approaches, and evaluation methods. Taking a developmental perspective, evaluations and the child's history of, and expectations for, success and failure have a long-term effect on the child's sense of self and on the child's adjustment to school.

PERSONAL ADJUSTMENT TO SCHOOL

In considering the schools' impact on social-emotional development of the child, one can see the intimate relationship between schooling and the child's personal adjustment to the school experience. This relationship is represented by the following variables: attitudes toward school including motivation; personal-social behaviors acceptable in the classroom such as self-initiated work and conformity; school anxiety; and school phobia. The importance of these variables is best considered in relation to the child's long-term development by noting the importance of school success in Western culture. When a child has a healthy adjustment to school (as evidenced by these variables), success in school—measured either by achievement or just staying in school as opposed to dropping out—is a likely result. The dependent variables of the child's personal adjustment may, in turn, act as independent variables which influence the child's sense of self. The reciprocal functions of the child's sense of self, personal adjustment, and success in school highlight the importance of models in order to understand better the complexity and reciprocity inherent in the impact of the schools upon the developing child. However since the research in this area is atheoretical, this review indicates which variables may be appropriate for inclusion in such a model.

As an introduction to the impact of school on the child's personal adjustment to schooling, consider some descriptive data on children's attitudes toward school. When exploring sex differences in children's attitudes toward school in kindergarten and grades one and two, Fink and Kosecoff (1977) found that girls and boys have similar attitudes in kindergarten; girls' attitudes remained stable while boys' attitudes improved from kindergarten to second grade. May (1975) also found that a majority of kindergarten children expressed happy feelings for school work. However as children stay in school after the early years, their feelings about school shift from happy to sad. By sixth grade only 12.8 percent of the children are happy to be in school, and by eighth grade this number has dwindled to 5 percent.

What is the cause of these changes? Are there specific variables within the schooling process which can be modified to influence the child's attitudes toward school? While there is not a great deal of empirical research on the specific factors which influence personal adjustment to school, there are studies which do suggest that critical agents lie in all three areas of independent variables: the child's early and preschool experience, classroom practices, and the school environment and structure.

Preschool Experiences

While the evaluations of early intervention programs designed to foster development of the lower-income child (such as Head Start) may indicate less than encouraging gains in IQ, they may realistically be labeled a success when considering the child's later adjustment to school. If the intervention programs are not producing long-lasting gains in cognitive skills, why are these children showing later success in school? Thompson (1975) suggested that preschool experience makes the initial adjustment easier and, therefore, is related to later school success. "The child who is ready for school and hence makes a satisfactory initial adjustment to it is more likely to be successful in the rest of his educational career than the child who, because he is not ready, finds difficulty in coping with the school situation" (p. 128). Apparently the intervention programs help the low-income children learn the personal social behaviors that lead to the success of middle-class children in school (Mann et al., 1978). These behaviors have been specified in several reviews and studies. In one review (Brown, 1978), the low-income children who had had preschool experience were compared to children without such experience and were described as more involved, purposeful, independent, and energetic. Similarly Stallings (1975) found that children in child-centered, discovery follow-through programs had high levels of problem solving and took responsibility for their successes and failures. These children also had high levels of inventiveness and curiosity (Miller & Dyer, 1975) and were better able to monitor their own behavior (Bissell, 1971).

The initial adjustment and the acquisition of self-confidence, involvement with school work, and other healthy personal social behaviors may produce a "sleeper" effect, at least for girls (Seitz, Apfel, & Efron, 1978). The girls who were in intervention programs showed increasingly greater differences when compared to controls, even after the intervention had ceased. The findings from the reviews of early intervention research support the conclusions of Entwisle and Hayduk (1978) regarding the pervasive influence of the child's first experiences in the school environment. When considered as a whole the research suggests that intervention programs should concentrate on personal-social development, as well as cognitive skills, in order to foster the school success of low-income children effectively.

Classroom Practices

Once a child has entered school, what are the variables that influence his/her adjustment? One cluster may be identified as defining the teaching method including the use of grades. Hicks, Edwards, and Sgan (1973) found that grading and intelligence interacted to influence attitudes about school. In general more intelligent children liked school better. However, nongraded classroom practices created more favorable attitudes in the less intelligent. The effect of grades was also examined by Maehr (1976) in a consideration of students' continuing motivation as an educational outcome. He suggested that school should be considered a place where learning and interest in learning are fostered rather than considering schools to be the only place where learning occurs. With this perspective Maehr concludes that extrinsic motivators seem to decrease students' continuing motivation. However grades may be either extrinsic or intrinsic, depending on the students' perception. Coupling Maehr's ideas with the work of Hicks et al. leads to the implication that less intelligent children may define grades as extrinsic rewards and have less favorable attitudes and motivation. More intelligent children may define grades intrinsically, and this is correlated with their continuing interest in school. In a study on school anxiety Phillips (1978) found that anxiety was higher in the later elementary school years than in grades one, two, and three. There was a greater increase in anxiety in graded classrooms than in nongraded. In addition subject matter marks in grades two and three were predictive of anxiety in grade four.

These findings on the relationship of grading practices and school attitudes and anxiety support the teaching method of mastery learning as proposed by Bloom (1976). In a number of short-term studies compiled in his book, he shows the positive effect of mastery learning on the child's interest in subjects. According to Bloom this is because children's perception of themselves as adequate or inadequate in school affects their views of school and ultimately their sense of self. Bloom's work has been supported by other research, such as the study of Kifer (1975) discussed before in relation to the sense of self. In addition to relating the history of successful academic achievement to the child's self-esteem and self-concept of ability, Kifer related academic achievement to responsibility for school achievement. A measure of intellectual achievement responsibility was more highly related to the history of academic achievement than self-esteem was. The difference in responsibility between successful and unsuccessful students was due to the increased scores of the successful students. These findings imply that mastery learning and its goal of high achievement for all would have a positive impact on personality characteristics as well as on achievement.

The teaching method of mastery learning might logically be related to the atmosphere in the classroom. Since the goal of mastery learning is high achievement for all, the atmosphere might be considered democratic. In their review of the effects of classroom atmosphere, Glidewell et al. (1966) found that a democratic atmosphere was related to self-initiated work and independence of opinion in children.

Class size and teacher characteristics also influence school attitudes and adjustment. Glass and Down (1979) express opposing viewpoints on the effects of class size on personality development. Glass suggests that the relationship between class size and affective characteristics is stronger than the relationship between class size and achievement. Students in very small classes (10 to 15 pupils) had more positive attitudes about school. Down refutes this argument by stating that it is inappropriate to cite figures from such small classes when arguing about reducing class size from 28 to 25 pupils.

What are the teacher characteristics which relate to personal adjustment to school? Denno (1977) states that elementary school teachers are politically conservative, moralistic, conforming, submissive, and sex discriminating. As a result there is a tendency to reward students who conform and to squelch individual creativity and constructive deviation. In Denno's view success in personal adjustment to elementary school required the acquisition of less than positive personality traits.

For some of those children who do not conform, the end result may be *school phobia*, "an irrational fear of going to school" (Lall & Lall, 1979, p. 96). Girls are affected more than boys, it is more common in the higher socioeconomic status (SES) levels, and the peak of incidence is between third and fifth grade. Many of the hypothesized causes of school phobia are related to the home, rather than to the school. However "sometimes, an aspect of school itself may cause the phobia" (p. 98). Lall and Lall suggest that a harsh, restrictive teacher, school failure, or difficulties with peer relationships may trigger the phobia. As a cure the school-phobic child needs recognition of both his/her successes and his/her efforts. These procedures are appropriate for all children, not just those with school phobia, and they may be considered specific examples of a democratic atmosphere. Thus the child's personal adjustment to school is influenced by the same classroom variables which affect the child's sense of self.

The School Environment

The total school environment may also contribute to the development of negative personality traits. In a study on docility in primary school children, Punch and Rennie (1978) admit that a certain degree of conformity and docility is necessary for efficient schooling. However when the behavior extends beyond school time, it should be considered a negative consequence of schooling. Contrary to popular opinion Punch and Rennie found that children in small schools are more docile than children in larger, "more institutional" schools. According to Seeley (1977), docility in the school system is an inherent, historical feature. Bureaucratic school systems were created to provide skilled, yet docile, labor for the growing industries.

More recent practices of the school system as a whole also have an impact on the developing child's personality; one of the major influences is integration. In his study of school anxiety Phillips (1978) examined the effects of integration. Integration of blacks, Mexican-Americans, and Anglos was achieved by means of an innovative learning center for sixth-graders. After establishment of the learning center, anxiety decreased over the year for Anglo and Mexican-American, but not for black, students. To complete the picture Phillips also studied the relationship of anxiety and achievement. School anxiety was the best predictor of reading and math achievement for Mexican-American girls—i.e., it predicted achievement better than intelligence. Anxiety was the best noncognitive predictor for Anglo males, and it made significant contributions for the other subgroups. Except for black children there was a substantial negative relationship between anxiety and academic achievement. From his review of previous studies and his own research, Phillips (1978) found evidence that anxiety is a causal agent in the relationship with achievement.

In conclusion the child's personal adjustment to and in school has implications for his/her later success in life. This relationship is the logical result of the school's socializing function. According to Greenberger and Sorenson (1974), the goal of socialization is psychosocial maturity which has three relevant dimensions: (1) the capacity to function adequately on one's own, (2) the capacity to interact adequately with others, and (3) the capacity to contribute to social cohesion. Even though schools are preoccupied with cognitive skills, they also function to enhance or disrupt social-emotional development. However the socializing effects of schools "are largely unrecognized and unmeasured" (Greenberger & Sorenson, 1974, p. 355). Greenberger and colleagues are making progress toward measuring psychosocial maturity, the first step in examining the effects of schools (Josselson, Greenberger, & McConochie, 1977a, 1977b). However, the measure has not yet been applied to school effects.

SOCIAL RELATIONSHIPS AND DEVELOPMENT

Another cluster of dependent variables appropriate for examination in relation to schooling lies in the area of social relationships. What is the impact of schooling on children's relationships with peers and teachers, and how does schooling contribute to the development of social skills? Examination of the research in this area is plagued by the same difficulty as reviews in the areas of personal adjustment and self-concept because social relationships are both independent and dependent variables. Since this chapter is focusing on the impact of schools on personality development, this review considers social relationships as the dependent variable. However caution will be noted in several places since much of the research does not allow us to specify cause-effect relationships clearly. The independent variables discussed in relation to social relationships once again fall into the categories of pre- and early school experience, classroom practices, and the school system environment.

Pre- and Early School Experience

The effects of preschool experience on social relationships show a sharp contrast to the muddy findings on cognitive and achievement outcomes. According to the review by Belsky and Steinberg (1978), children with daycare experience interact more with their peers and at earlier ages than children without daycare. There is some indication that daycare may "predispose children toward greater aggressiveness, impulsivity, and egocentrism" (p. 942), but these traits may be more reflections of values of the programs and American society than effects of daycare per se. Since most daycare research has used samples from high-quality centers, Harper (1978) included not only the traditional subjects from experimental or university laboratory daycare but also children from the wide variety of daycare programs which exist. He concluded that daycare experience enhances the social development of the child.

Reviews of the effect of early intervention programs have also found a positive impact on social relationships. After five years in an intervention program, children were more social, affectionate, flexible, and friendly (Brown, 1978). In a review of Head Start research, Mann et al. (1978) concluded that early intervention has a positive impact on the child's socialization and social behav-

ior. Specifically the children with early intervention showed positive increases in interpersonal skills, social-emotional development, and social maturity. In addition the organization of the personal-social behaviors of these children was comparable to the organization in middle-class children. The differential influence of the variations in Head Start has also been noted. Miller and Dyer (1975) conclude that children in child-directed, individualized programs show higher levels of social interaction than children in teacher-directed programs. According to Stallings (1975), these teacher-directed programs may interfere with the development of independence and cooperation, while the child-centered programs foster these characteristics. In general parent participation, continuing intervention, and a curricular emphasis on social skills appear to be salient factors.

The study by Entwisle and Hayduk (1978) showed the effects of initial school experience on the child's sense of self. A report by Rist (1970) also documented the effects of the child's initial experiences and the class bias of the school system. He observed one class of children from their first days in kindergarten through second grade in order to examine teacher behavior and its influence on children. The main thrust of his study was to relate teachers' expectations and behavior to children's achievement, but his observations also showed the effects on the children's social relationships. At the beginning of kindergarten, the children were assigned seats at three different tables. The children at the first table were characterized by the teacher as "fast learners," while she saw those at the other two tables as having "no idea of what was going on in the classroom" (Rist, 1970, p. 422). Since there had been no formal testing of the children and the seating assignments were made after only eight days of school, Rist believed that the seating assignments reflected the teacher's bias. Children who sat at table 1 closely fit the teacher's stereotype of the ideal child, while those at table 3 were least like her ideal type. What was the effect of these seating assignments on the children's social relationships? First, the children at tables 2 and 3 were ridiculed and belittled by the children at table 1 and by themselves, while the children at table 1 saw themselves as better than the others. A second effect was that the children at table 1 sought the attention of the teacher and modeled her behavior. In further observations of these children, the children from table 1 were placed in the first groups for reading in first and second grade. Although observations on the social relationships in first and second grade were not reported, Rist concluded that the initial experience preordained the children's experience through the early school years.

Classroom Practices

When the child is in the public school system, some specific practices within the classroom have been shown to influence the child's social relationships and development. Class size is one such variable. While intimate relationships (presumably found in smaller classes) promote maximum personality development, small class size has some negative side effects. "Studies have also shown that students in small classes tend to be more rude and discourteous and that students in large classes tend to share information with their peers more readily than do those in small classes" (Reisert, 1971, p. 159). The effect of class size is thus complex. Individual personality development may be optimal in smaller classes, but greater social development is found in larger classes. This research also exemplifies the consideration of relationships as an independent variable, since it is the relationships in small classes which promote personality development. Is it the relationships in large classes which positively affect social development? An affirmative answer would suggest a circular function between social relationships and development, an idea which is supported in theoretical proposals, but not yet by empirical research (Lerner & Busch-Rossnagel, 1981).

The democratic atmosphere which is positively related to self-concept development and personal adjustment to school is also positively related to social relationships (Glidewell et al., 1966). In democratic classrooms there is more pupil-to-pupil interaction, greater rapport, and a wider dispersion and flexibility of peer social power. The democratic atmosphere also reduces interpersonal conflicts between peers. A specific example of the democratic approach is the variable of teacher approval. Investigations by Herrmann (1972), Lippitt and Gold (1959), and Retish (1973) have related teacher support and peer status. Lippitt and Gold analyzed teacher-pupil interaction combined with sociometry and found that teachers gave a higher number of supportive statements to the higher-status students. Retish found that teacher reinforcements could change the status of peers. In Herrmann's study the correlation between student acceptance and teacher approval was positive and highly significant. Again caution should be noted in interpreting teacher support as the causal agent since the research has not always sorted out the cause-effect relationship. In a study by Foley (1979), there was greater peer approval when the teacher reacted positively to the child than when the reaction was negative. In this study teacher acceptance is clearly the causal agent, but the external validity of the study may be questioned since the children were responding to videotapes and not to interaction with the child.

The Environment of the School

Variables influencing the child's social relationships and development which are characteristic of the entire school rather than just the single classroom are open- versus traditional-space schools, bicultural approaches, and racial integration. Downing and Bothwell (1979) investigated expectations of peer interaction and cooperation in students from open-space and closed-space (traditional) schools. According to the research the traditional school is designed for parallel activities, without interaction among peers. This was defined as co-action and was contrasted with interaction, which was seen as the sharing of activities. Thus Downing and Bothwell hypothesized that students from the traditional school would anticipate co-action with peers while students from open-space would indicate (by seat selection) that they expected social interaction. These hypotheses were supported. In addition the rate of cooperation in a game situation was higher for open-space students than for closed-space students. Apparently open-space schools enhance social de-

velopment, although the exact characteristics which facilitate relationships are not yet specified. It is quite possible that differences in teaching style, although not mandated, exist between the two school systems.

Federal courts have mandated changes in cultural-racial composition of schools. What is the effect of these interventions in schooling on the social relationships of students? Slavin and Madden (1978) identified four categories of interventions: (1) workshops for teachers and principals; (2) positive portrayal of minorities in textbooks, history classes, and school positions; (3) heterogeneous grouping; and (4) work and play in interracial groups. Only the fourth—actual interaction among students—has been shown to influence students' interracial attitudes and behaviors positively. The application of the fourth category may result in what Goebes and Shore (1978) term *bicultural education*. In their study the preadolescent girls (10.5 to 12.5 years) in a bicultural school showed more heterocultural peer-group organization and greater acceptance of unknown cultural groups.

Teaching methods which create interdependence among group members can also enhance peer relationships. In the Blaney et al. (1977) study, the experimental subjects showed a greater liking for groupmates than did the control subjects. In a similar study Johnson, Johnson, Johnson, and Anderson (1976) examined the effects of cooperative and individualized instruction on students' prosocial behaviors. The subjects were 30 fifth-graders in a single classroom. Half of the subjects were taught language arts for approximately one hour a day for 17 days in a cooperative manner. They were instructed to study together as a group, complete one assignment sheet per group, and to seek help from the group rather than from the teacher. The other students continued to work on their own. The cooperative group subjects were higher than the individualized subjects in prosocial behaviors such as altruism and recognition of others' feelings. The cooperative group subjects also thought that both teachers and peers liked them more.

The review by Glidewell et al. (1966) on classroom socialization provides a vantage point to draw some conclusions for this section. Their review documents the existence of different social structures in the classroom; other researchers have termed this the *hidden curriculum* (Cartledge & Milburn, 1978). Most of the empirical studies in the review examined the effects of individual characteristics on the structure and not the effects of the structure on the individual. Although Glidewell et al. propose a circular function between these variables, they state that there is a lack of research to validate the idea. Since that review there have been more studies on the effects of schooling on the socialization of students, but there are still few studies which scrutinize the possibility of a circular effect. There is research on teaching social skills in schools, but it has usually dealt with handicapped children (Cartledge & Milburn, 1978). In total we have two bodies of literature which look at schooling variables and child variables as both independent and dependent measures. However we do not have the research to examine the interaction of the two sets of variables.

While the research reviewed above does have many limitations, it is still appropriate to conclude that schooling does influence a child's sense of self, personal adjustment to school, and relationships with peers and teachers. In each of the above areas we have been concerned, for the most part, with the impact of "typical" schooling. In other words we focused on the general characteristics of schools which may be found in a variety of situations, but we did not examine the effects when schools make deliberate efforts to focus on a specific aspect of social-emotional development. A variety of forces determines what will be taught in the public schools: government policies, community values, perceived wants and needs of pupils and parents, and professional interest (Schwab, 1976). As a result of these forces, there has been a great deal of interest in two affective outcomes of schooling: moral development and sex-role learning. It is to the schools' efforts in these areas that we now turn.

MORAL DEVELOPMENT

One of the functions of schooling in a publicly controlled system is to teach the dominant value system of the society to its students. Thus public schooling in the United States is associated with American morals, while private schooling or no schooling at all is seen as promoting un-American ideals (Bakan, 1971). In spite of this tie between morality and public education, there is little explicit provision made for moral education in our schools, and this has been true throughout this century. "Hardly anywhere in this country is provision made for careful, systematic, graded moral training in the schooling. We get along with what at best can be called incidental instruction" (Sneath & Hodges, 1914, p. 2).

However the development of morals, values, or ethics is of increasing concern in the American educational system. Many reasons for this may be proposed. Watergate and the resulting lack of trust in public officials, the epidemic of teenage pregnancies, and the use of drugs (including alcohol and tobacco) by younger and younger children are a few trends that may lead to a preoccupation with the development of morality in American schoolchildren. While it is impossible to identify a single cause for the concern, it is possible to document the scholarly interest in moral education. "Current educational and psychological journals are focusing attention on controversial aspects of moral and value education" (Fedorko, 1978, p. 77).

The attention given to moral education must be understood within the context of two forces with a mutually reciprocal effect: the home and the school. Certainly the suggestions of parents that occur in the early years have priority over the ideas of schools (Fedorko, 1978). Once the child enters school the role of teachers and school has been characterized in a variety of ways: as a substitute home (Kay, 1975) or as a rescue operation and replacement for the home (Musgrave, 1968). Empirical research affirms that both the home and the school mold a child's morality, and the complex interaction between them makes cooperation essential in order to enhance value development (Kay, 1975). However by examining the different approaches to morality in the schools, we can start to sort out the effects of schooling on the child's moral development.

Approaches to Moral Education

Weaver (1978) defines moral education as the "assistance given to individuals so they can choose the right, or the wrong, or the best of suggested alternatives in their interpersonal relations" (p. 59). The traditional approach to moral education has been termed *character education* or *conduct development*. This approach made the school into a community in which the students anticipated and accepted some of the responsibilities which they would have as adults. Thus character education led to student government and student control of some activities. However, the results of 50 years of character development have yielded questionable results, though we do know that student participation is more effective than punishment in training moral decision making (Riles, 1975).

In taking the approach of conduct development, the schools have also been upholding and reinforcing middle-class values (Kazalunas, 1978). Students from lower-class homes are thus faced with a conflict in learning the (middle-class) values of the schools (Kay, 1975). If the lower-class child resolved the conflict by accepting middle-class values, society considered this approach to moral education to be successful. If the child did not accept the middle-class values, the schools had failed in their task of socialization.

Current approaches to moral education fall into two groups and are continuations of the earlier approaches. To modernize the character education approach, Riles (1975) states that schools must take the responsibility for developing both individual values and the moral personality. Riles does not envision moral education being a separate course but suggests instead that moral examples may occur in a variety of teaching situations. In addition "positive reinforcement should be practiced by teachers and administrators as the basic way of encouraging moral behavior among youngsters" (Riles, 1975, p. 76).

The presentation of conflicts as a teaching technique has been systematized into the approach termed *values clarification*. In values clarification the students are presented with a value-laden situation. Through a cognitive process and with techniques such as role-playing, the student is taught to think through the issues as a prelude to developing his/her own value system (Boyer, 1978; Galbraith, 1979). Values clarification is the application of Piaget's and Kohlberg's theory to moral education. Adler (1979) suggests that we need such approaches because when our schools are value-less: "We may be producing mechanical people who do not consider the moral implications of their actions" (p. 325).

The two approaches of using moral examples and values clarification may easily be combined into one teaching technique. By using moral conflicts from history or literature, the teacher can encourage the students to examine alternate points of view. This combined approach would appear to foster the moral reasoning of the students (Weaver, 1978).

Effects of Schooling on Morality

What is the effect of the practices implied by the above approaches on a child's moral development? Empirical studies have been plagued by major problems. First, the relationship between moral reasoning and moral behavior has not been well researched (Weaver, 1978). Thus researchers have a problem in translating the results in one area to effects in other areas. In addition there are few evaluative studies on the impact of moral education (Kay, 1975). This is related in part to the first problem and also to the larger problem of measuring affective outcomes.

There is some research that, while not specifically defined as examining morality, has implications for moral behavior. Kay (1975) concludes that children respond to the structure of the school situation. When the teacher was authoritarian, children withdrew into submission. In a laissez-faire situation children became indifferent and irresponsible, whereas the democratic atmosphere had a more positive effect. Here the children cooperated, developed responsibility, and emerged as individuals. With the dispersion of social power in democratic classrooms, the children held adult-oriented values. In the more traditional, authoritarian classrooms, the values were peer-oriented (Glidewell et al., 1966). The findings of a more recent review by Bushway and Nash (1977) support the conclusions of Kay and Glidewell et al. According to Bushway and Nash the totalitarian teacher was more likely to have students who cheated. When students were free to voice their opinions, as in a democratic classroom, there was less tendency to cheat.

The eventual effect of moral training on the child's personality is debatable. Kay (1975) suggests that the personality patterns of teachers are eventually replicated in the student. By changing the child's self-picture, the teacher ultimately affects the child's moral attitudes. However any effect is the product of an interaction among the child's personality, the teacher's personality, and classroom practices; thus, it is difficult to identify the impact of single variables.

Using developmental ideas the ultimate effect of schooling may best be assessed by looking not at the moral behavior of students, but at the morality of society as a whole. As Riles (1975) states, "The present moral tone of America was set in the classrooms of our local schools over the past decades and there it will continue to be set in the years to come" (p. 69).

SEX-ROLE DEVELOPMENT

Of increasing concern to many psychologists, educators, and parents today is the impact of schools on the development of sex roles in children. In a time of changing mores regarding the appropriateness of sex roles, what is the role of the school in sex-role development? Although many researchers agree that both the family and the schools have great impact, there are two viewpoints in assessing the effect of the schools on sex-role development. One is that the schools actually teach sex roles. The other is that the schools "liberate" the child from the sex roles of the home (Parsons, 1959). In either case the influences of home and school interact so that it is difficult to sort out the differential effects of each.

The structure of most school systems reflects the sex differentiation of the larger society with its male-dominated social patterns. Elementary school teachers are predominantly female (87 percent), while 85 percent of the principals are males (Kazalunas, 1978). In mirroring the discrimination of society, schools uphold and reinforce society's values through teaching and guidance practices (Kazalunas, 1978). The sex roles of children's authority figures (teachers and principals) are "somewhat idealized, rigid, and non-overlapping" (Saario et al., 1973, p. 387).

The sex-role attitudes of the system are also present in the classroom. In their review Lee and Gropper (1974) conclude that teachers have well-defined sex-role expectations, and their idealized pupil role is a student who is orderly, conforming, and dependent. This role conflicts with a traditional male sex role. Guttentag and Bray (1976) also suggest that teachers have different expectations for boys and girls although these expectations may not be consciously held. Pottker and Fishel (1977) agree that the sexism in the schools is subtle and may not be perceived by the educators themselves, although they do categorize sex-typed behaviors for discipline purposes, thereby unconsciously teaching appropriate sex-role behavior. Joffe (1977) argues that a considerable amount of sex stereotyping by teachers exists, even in schools that stress nonsexist approaches. Panko (1979) found that future teachers held beliefs about women's rights and roles that were similar to other college students. Because these attitudes were sexist, Panko suggested that future teachers should receive training to modify their acceptance of sex stereotypes.

In order to examine the effect of schools on sex-role development, we must first consider whether or not classroom practices reflect the sex-role attitudes of the school system. Does sex-role stereotyping actually occur in the classroom? Once we understand the classroom practices, then we can assess the effects of these practices on sex-role learning.

Classroom Practices

Classroom practices may be looked at from both material and behavioral points of view. A number of studies have shown that the books used in schools have sex-stereotyped contents. When the Princeton Chapter of the National Organization of Women (NOW) (reported in Kazalunas, 1978) attempted to find a series of books portraying men and women as equal in ability and aspirations, they found no such representations in 2760 stories from 134 books published by 12 companies. In these stories boys were depicted as creators and builders, as well as more competitive and more independent than girls. Girls were often dependent upon boys to extricate themselves from trouble, while boys used their own wits to get themselves out of trouble. Boys could master all types of tasks, while the skills of girls were associated with the home.

Different curricula for boys and girls are also relatively easy to document (Saario et al., 1973). In vocational education girls still take home economics while boys take industrial arts. The financial support and facilities are usually better for boys' physical education and athletic programs than for girls' programs. Although recent federal rulings may have changed policy in this area, there is still much to be changed in practice. The U.S. Office of Education recently sponsored a study

(Harrison, Dahl, Appleby, & Park, 1979) to determine how much sex discrimination and stereotyping has been eliminated in vocational education programs since 1972. Female students are still being discouraged from vocational programs which lead to high-paying jobs. The project report further reveals that 60 percent of staffs (both state and local) reported that practices continue to discourage male and female students from entering nontraditional areas. There is still a preference for auto mechanics for boys and home economics for girls. Little corrective action has been taken by state agencies to overcome inequities. The report also claims that schools which put the most effort into activities to enhance sex equity also have the greatest number of students enrolled in nontraditional courses.

The materials and curricula of the classroom are thus sex stereotyped. The behavior of teachers also shows differential treatment. Boys receive more punishment but also more praise and attention than girls (Etaugh, 1977; Guttentag & Bray, 1976). Teachers tend to reinforce any sex-typed behaviors in boys but only feminine behaviors in girls (Fagot & Patterson, 1969). Information about students' sex-role behavior influences teachers' evaluations of students' written performance (Bernard, 1979).

The conclusion which can be drawn from studies of classroom practices is that the boys and girls in the same class are receiving different school experiences. In the past this difference has been portrayed as a negative experience for boys, since the teachers have reinforced feminine behaviors and are usually females themselves. More recently the idea has been proposed that the negative effect may be greater for girls since schools are where they are socialized into feminine behaviors (Lightfoot, 1976). Feminine behaviors include dependency, submission, obedience, and conformity; these negatively correlate with later academic success (Guttentag & Bray, 1976). Therefore the effect of sex-stereotyped classroom practices should be examined for both boys and girls (Watson, 1977).

Effect on Sex-Role Learning

Just because there are differences in the classroom experiences of boys and girls does not mean that the differences have any effect. However, research suggests that differential treatment by sex is associated with sex differences in achievement and personality. There are sex differences in elementary school children's achievement—e.g., girls perform better in reading, while boys do better in math. A study by Leinhardt, Seewald, and Engel (1979) demonstrates that these differences in achievement may be the result of difference in instruction. Observations in second-grade classrooms showed that teachers had more contact with boys in math and with girls in reading. There were no sex differences in initial ability, but by the end of the year, girls were higher in reading achievement than boys. Gold, Reis, and Berger (1977) found that the sex of the teacher also influenced achievement in boys. Boys had higher mathematical achievement when taught by a male-female team.

The sex-differentiated treatment may also lead to sex differences in personality. In the school setting girls become acquiescent, conforming, and dependent, while boys become self-motivated and independent (Guttentag

& Bray, 1976; Pottker & Fishel, 1977). The emphasis-requirement-preference for docility, which is an inherent feature of most elementary schools (Punch & Rennie, 1978; Seeley, 1977), reinforces a societal message to girls, while it creates a conflict in boys between their masculine-oriented socialization at home and the socialization for docility at school (Joffe, 1977).

A 1971–1972 study (Iglitzen, cited in Kazalunas, 1978) reports that fifth-grade children themselves learned to sex-type personality traits and abilities. A majority of girls saw themselves as kinder, more serious, and better behaved than boys. Both sexes saw personality traits as being sex linked. Girls saw boys as better in science, but themselves as better in math (contrary to achievement results!). Although girls may ascribe to themselves positive personality traits, they may not perceive being female as positive.

It has been found that grade school boys are more certain that it's great to be male, they are more confident and assertive. In contrast grade school girls are not enthusiastic about having been born female. They are less confident about their accomplishments, their popularity, and their adequacy in general. (Sadker & Sadker, 1974, p. 61)

In addition there is speculation that sex differences and self-concept are correlated. According to Pottker and Fishel (1977), teacher and administration emphasis on sex-appropriate behavior results in impaired self-esteem and self-actualization, especially in girls. However many studies have failed to find differences in self-concept between girls and boys when self-ratings are used (Lekarczyk & Hill, 1969). Sears (1970) found that femininity in both boys and girls was related to poor self-concept; however, there were no sex differences in self-concept. Reed, Felker, Kay, and Stanwyck (1977) found no sex differences in total self-concept scores but suggest that it is more profitable to look at differences in factor or item scores. Using this method girls rate themselves more positively on the behavior items, while boys are superior on the factors of achievement and school status, appearance and attributes, low anxiety, popularity, and happiness and satisfaction. According to Reed et al., this may be the source of teacher's stereotypes about sex differences in self-concept. Because good behavior is important to a girl's self-concept, girls tend to be more conforming and do what the teacher tells them. However "since conformity or good behavior are [sic] not important to a boy's self-concept, boys are freer to develop creativity than girls" (Barwick, cited in Reed et al., 1977, p. 56). Differentiation of self-concept into factors thus results in data which imply that schools should change their practices in order to enhance the self-actualization of the pupils.

Approaches to Sex-Role Learning

Unlike the area of moral development, the concern with sex stereotyping has not been translated into widely adopted teaching methods for sex-role learning. However a number of authors have made suggestions about combating sexism in the classroom. Watson (1977) argued that schools should concentrate on "developing the person rather than the role" (p. 41). Pottker and Fishel

(1977) listed five pursuits to eradicate sex-role stereotyping in the schools: (1) consciousness-raising sessions with teachers and administrators to reverse stereotyping; (2) workshops on sexism; (3) reviewing numbers of boys and girls in specific school functions—i.e., street-crossing guards, audio-visual aides; (4) role-playing in classes and discussions about being male or female; and (5) increased sensitivity to needs of non–middle-class kids. The steps which are taken to erase sex stereotyping may be generalized to approaches which enhance the child's self-concept. Felker, Stanwyck, and Kay (1973) generated five principles for cultivating positive self-concept in school settings, and they may also reverse limitations from sex stereotyping. Adults should (1) praise themselves, (2) help children evaluate realistically, (3) teach children to set reasonable goals, (4) teach them to praise themselves, and (5) teach children to praise others.

In addition to evaluation of the preceding methods, there are still many omissions from the research on the impact of schools on sex-role development. First, classroom practices are usually studied at the classroom level, but the effect is on the individual child. There is little child-level research (Lightfoot, 1976). Second, the research has primarily focused on feminine traits in both boys and girls, so there is ignorance about the influence of schooling on masculine traits (Lee & Gropper, 1974). Finally, although the teacher is an important role model, the effect of the teachers' attitudes as opposed to behaviors is unclear (Pottker & Fishel, 1977).

We also need to examine the correlation between teacher's sex-stereotyping attitudes and other attitudes and classroom practices. Rees and Grogan (1978) found that teachers who are authoritarian exhibit a higher degree of sexism than do teachers who are less authoritarian. Other research suggests that authoritarian teachers have a negative impact on self-concept and that democratic classroom practices (which presumably are less authoritarian) positively influence the child's sense of self, adjustment to school, and relationships with peers and teachers (Glidewell et al., 1966; Herrmann, 1972; Lippitt & Gold, 1959; Retish, 1973). Taken together the findings imply that sexist attitudes on the part of the teachers will be negatively related to the child's social-emotional development. However authoritarian and democratic classroom practices are probably clusters of variables which need further scrutiny. It may be that sexist attitudes are simply one variable within this cluster and not directly related to the child's development in a cause-effect relationship.

CONCLUSIONS

This chapter has focused on the literature which examines the influence of schools on the social-emotional development of children. Concern with the impact of schooling is justified because this institution is a fact of life for almost every child in Western culture. Since the research on both academic and nonacademic effects could not be reviewed in one chapter, the review emphasized affective outcomes which are the result of the school's role as a socialization agent, one of three functions which schooling currently fulfills in society.

Within this focus what can we conclude about the impact of schooling on the individual child's social-emotional development? One aspect of schooling that has been related to the child's sense of self, personal adjustment to school, and social relationships, as well as to moral development and sex-role learning, is the atmosphere of the classroom. A democratic atmosphere positively influences the child's affective development. Specifically democratic practices increase self-esteem, independence, and social relationships (Glidewell et al., 1966). Under authoritarian structures children tend to cheat more and withdraw into submission (Bushway & Nash, 1977; Kay, 1975). However classroom atmosphere is probably a cluster of variables which needs further examination itself. What are the characteristics of a democratic classroom atmosphere? Several of the variables which have been reviewed in this chapter logically may be expected to be an aspect of classroom atmosphere. Teacher self-acceptance and efficiency are related to good self-concept in children (Edeburn & Landry, 1974; Peck et al., 1977). Are these and other teacher characteristics part of the classroom atmosphere? Specific instructional methods, such as interdependency within groups, teaching for mastery learning, and nongraded approaches, are also positively related to the child's social-emotional development (Blaney et al., 1977; Bloom, 1976; Phillips, 1978). Student government is an attempt to enhance moral development (Riles, 1975). Do these methods define a democratic atmosphere? It is appropriate to conclude that a democratic structure within the classroom and school fosters positive affective outcomes in children, but the research does not clarify exactly what is included within this variable of atmosphere.

It is more difficult to draw conclusions regarding the effects of early school experience and school environment. We can say that early intervention can foster the development of positive social behavior, especially when the curricula have an objective of enhancing social development (Brown, 1978; Mann et al., 1978; Miller & Dyer, 1975). In addition the child's initial experiences in school (especially the evaluations) shape the childs' view of him/herself (Entwisle & Hayduk, 1978). The school environment reflects the concerns of the larger society—e.g., desegregation and bicultural approaches (Goebes & Shore, 1978; Stephan, 1978). In total the bureaucracy of the school environment mirrors the organization of the larger society (Bowles & Gintis, 1976; Punch & Rennie, 1978; Seeley, 1977).

Any review is necessarily limited by the nature of the research in the area, and this chapter is no exception. The primary limitation is the predominance of concern with cognitive measures as dependent variables and the inclusion of social-emotional variables only as independent variables. Research that allows for a possible circular relationship between academic and nonacademic effects is necessary to understand the impact of schools on children. In addition paradigms including interactions between teaching methods and other schooling variables and cognitive and affective outcomes (e.g., an aptitude-treatment-interaction) are necessary (Barclay, 1978). More specific limitations are already being overcome. In 1971 Averch, Carroll, Donaldson, Kiesling, and Pincus completed a review of the effects on school in the cognitive sphere but highlighted the need for more objectively based empirical research into noncognitive outcomes.

Some progress is being made. The difficulties of constructing valid, reliable instruments to measure affective outcomes have been attacked by Kifer (1977) and others. Greenberger and colleagues are using an approach to the effects of schooling on psychosocial maturity that has a theoretical basis (Greenberger & Sorenson, 1974). However we still are lacking research which includes the uniqueness of each classroom in the analyses and does not simply include it in the error variance (Carew & Lightfoot, 1977). We also need research that examines the teaching practices for individual children. When research is conducted with the entire classroom as the unit of analysis, we may mistakenly assume that every child is receiving an identical treatment (Lightfoot, 1976). Most importantly the effect of schooling on the development of children can best be assessed by using longitudinal designs. The possible cohort effects associated with changes in schools require examination by longitudinal-sequential designs.

In spite of the limitations of the research reviewed, there are several implications for professionals which can be drawn. Schools do have an impact on the social-emotional development of children. However because the primary function of schools is more closely related to cognitive outcomes, this influence is not always acknowledged. The obtuse influence of schools is exemplified by the unconsciously held, sex-stereotyped attitudes of teachers (Guttentag & Bray, 1976; Panko, 1979; Pottker & Fishel, 1977). The research also makes a strong case for a tie between societal values and schooling (Riles, 1975). What is wanted by the public will eventually be a part of the educational process (Schwab, 1976). Coupled with the ignorance about nonacademic effects of schooling, the importance of public attitudes should lead us to examine what we preach and what we practice. If we say we are trying to foster the development of the whole child, we should question whether or not as professionals we are taking the steps to do that.

REFERENCE NOTES

1. Foundation for Child Development. *Summary of preliminary results: National survey of children.* New York: Author.

REFERENCES

ADLER, G. Dealing with controversial issues: A response. *Social Education*, 1979, *43*(No. 4), 325, 327.

ALLEN, D. I. Student performance, attitude, and self-esteem in open-area and self-contained classrooms. *Alberta Journal of Education Research*, 1974, *20*, 1–7.

AVERCH, H. A., CARROLL, J. J., DONALDSON, T. S., KIESLING, H. J., & PINCUS, J. *How effective is schooling? A critical review and synthesis of research findings.* Santa Monica, Calif.: Rand Corporation, 1971.

BAKAN, D. Adolescence in America: From idea to social fact. *Daedalus*, 1971, *100*(No. 4), 979–995.

BARCLAY, J. R. Temperament clusters and individual differences in the elementary classroom: A summary. 1978 (ED 157600).

BELSKY, J., & STEINBERG, L. D. The effects of day care: A critical review. *Child Development*, 1978, *49*, 929–949.

BERNARD, M. E. Does sex role behavior influence the way teachers evaluate students? *Journal of Educational Psychology*, 1979, *71*(No. 4), 553–562.

BISSELL, J. S. *Implementation of planned variation in Head Start.* Washington, D.C.: Office of Child Development, 1971.

BLANEY, N. T., STEPHAN, C., ROSENFIELD, D., ARONSON, E., & SIKES, J. Interdependence in the classroom: A field study. *Journal of Education*, 1977, *69*, 121–128.

BLOOM, B. S. *Human characterstics and school learning.* New York: McGraw-Hill, 1976.

BOWLES, S., & GINTIS, H. *Schooling in capitalist America: Educational reform and the contradictions of economic life.* New York: Basic Books, 1976.

BOYER, E. P. Value-clarification as an approach to moral development. *Educational Horizons*, 1977–1978, *56*(No. 2), 101–106.

BRANDES, D. Enhancing self-concept in the classroom. *British Journal of Educational Psychology*, 1978, *48*, 355–356.

BROWN, B. Long-term gains from early intervention. In B. Brown (Ed.), *Found: Long-term gains from early intervention.* Washington, D.C.: American Association for the Advancement of Science, 1978.

BUSHWAY, A., & NASH, W. R. School cheating behavior. *Review of Education Research*, 1977, *47*, 623–632.

CALHOUN, G., JR., & MORSE, W. C. Self-concept and self-esteem: Another perspective. *Psychology in the Schools*, 1977, *14*, 318–322.

CALSYN, R. J., & KENNY, D. A. Self-concept of ability and perceived evaluations of others: Cause or effect of academic achievement? *Journal of Educational Psychology*, 1977, *69*, 136–145.

CAREW, J. V., & LIGHTFOOT, S. L. *First grade: A multi-faceted view of teachers and children.* Final report. Washington, D.C.: Office of Child Development, 1977. (ERIC Document Reproduction Service No. ED 148 495)

CARTLEDGE, G., & MILBURN, J. F. The case for teaching social skills in the classroom: A review. *Review of Educational Research*, 1978, *1*, 133–156.

CICIRELLI, V. G. *The impact of Head Start.* (Under Office of Economic Opportunity contract B89-4536). Ohio University: Westinghouse Learning Corporation, 1969.

DENNO, D. The elementary school teacher: Conformity and maladjustment is a prefabricated role. *Adolescence*, 1977, *12*(No. 46), 247–259.

DOWNING, L. L., & BOTHWELL, K. H. Open-space schools: Anticipation of peer interaction and development of cooperative independence. *Journal of Educational Psychology*, 1979, *71*, 478–484.

EDEBURN, C. E., & LANDRY, R. G. Self-concepts of students and a significant other, the teacher. *Psychological Reports*, 1974, *35*, 505–506.

ENTWISLE, D. R., & HAYDUK, L. A. *Too great expectations: The academic outlook of young children.* Baltimore, Md.: Johns Hopkins University Press, 1978.

ETAUGH, C. *Development of sex-role attitudes.* Paper presented at the Annual Meeting of the Midwestern Psychological Association, Chicago, May 1977. (ERIC Document Reproduction Service No. ED 146 514)

FAGOT, B. I., & PATTERSON, G. R. An in vivo analysis of reinforcing contingencies for sex-role behaviors in the preschool child. *Developmental Psychology*, 1969, *1*, 563–568.

FEDORKO, R. A. Effects of parent training on the moral development of five-, six- and seven-year-olds. *Educational Horizons*, 1977–1978, *56*(No. 2), 77–83.

FELKER, D. W., STANWYCK, D. J., & KAY, R. S. The effects of a teacher program in self-concept enhancement on pupils' self-concept, anxiety, and intellectual achievement responsibility. *Journal of Educational Research*, 1973, *66*, 443–445.

FINK, A., & KOSECOFF, J. Girls' and boys' changing attitudes toward school. *Psychology of Women Quarterly*, 1977, *2*, 44–49.

FOLEY, J. M. Effect of labeling and teacher behavior on children's attitudes. *American Journal of Mental Deficiency*, 1979, *83*(No. 4), 380–384.

GALBRAITH, R. E. Teaching for moral development in the schools: Reason for caution but reason to proceed: An editor's perspective. *Social Education*, 1979, *43*(No. 3), 233, 241–249.

GLASS, G. V., & DOWN, A. G. Does class size make a difference? *Instructor*, 1979, *89*(No. 4), 22.

GLIDEWELL, J. C., KANTOR, M. C., SMITH, L. M., & STRINGER, L. A. Socialization and social structure in the classroom. In M. L. Hoffman & L. W. Hoffman (Eds.), *Review of child development research* (Vol. 2). New York: Russell Sage Foundation, 1966.

GOEBES, D. D., & SHORE, M. F. Some effects of bicultural and monocultural school environments on personality development. *American Journal of Orthopsychiatry*, 1978, *48*, 407–498.

GOLD, D., REIS, M., & BERGER, C. Male teachers and the development of nursery-school children. 1977 (ED 145965).

GREENBERGER, E., & SORENSEN, A. B. Toward a concept of psychosocial maturity. *Journal of Youth and Adolescence,* 1974, *3,* 329–358.

GUTTENTAG, M., & BRAY, H. *Undoing sex stereotypes.* New York: McGraw-Hill, 1976.

HARRISON, L., DAHL, P., APPLEBY, J., & PARK, B. *Vocational education equity study.* Palo Alto, Calif.: American Institutes for Research, 1979.

HARPER, C. L. New evidence of impact of day care centers on children's social-psychological development. *Child Welfare,* 1978, *57,* 527–533.

HERRMANN, R. Classroom status and teacher approval and disapproval: A study of children's perceptions. *Journal of Experimental Education,* 1972, *41*(No. 2), 32–39.

HETHERINGTON, E. M. Personality development. In L. C. Deighton (Ed.), *The encyclopedia of education* (Vol. 7). New York: Macmillan, 1971.

HICKS, J. M., EDWARDS, K. T., & SGAN, A. D. Attitudes toward school as related to nongrading and intelligence. *Psychological Reports,* 1973, *33,* 739–742.

JOFFE, C. Sex role socialization and the nursery school: As the twig is bent. In J. Pottker & A. Fishel (Eds.), *Sex bias in the schools.* Cranbury, N.J.: Associated University Presses, Inc., 1977.

JOHNSON, D. W., JOHNSON, R. T., JOHNSON, J., & ANDERSON, D. Effects of cooperative versus individualized instruction on student prosocial behavior, attitudes toward learning, and achievement. *Journal of Educational Psychology,* 1976, *68,* 446–452.

JOSSELSON, R. GREENBERGER, E., & McCONOCHIE, D. Phenomenological aspects of psychosocial maturity in adolescence. Part 2. Girls. *Journal of Youth and Adolescence,* 1977a, *6,* 25–55.

JOSSELSON, R., GREENBERGER, E., & McCONOCHIE, D. Phenomenological aspects of psychosocial maturity in adolescence. Part 1. Boys. *Journal of Youth and Adolescence,* 1977b, *6,* 25–55.

KAY, W. *Moral education: A sociological study of the influence of society, home and school.* Hamden, Conn.: Linnet Books, 1975.

KAZALUNAS, J. R. Sexism in education. *Clearing House,* 1978, *51,* 388–391.

KIFER, E. Relationships between academic achievement and personality characteristics: A quasi-longitudinal study. *American Educational Research Journal,* 1975, *12,* 191–210.

KIFER, E. An approach to the construction of affective evaluation instruments. *Journal of Youth and Adolescence,* 1977, *6,* 205–214.

KLASS, W. H., & HODGE, S. E. Self-esteem in open and traditional classrooms. *Journal of Educational Psychology,* 1978, *70,* 701–705.

LALL, G. R., & LALL, B. M. School phobia. *Instructor,* 1979, *89*(No. 2), 96, 98.

LEE, P. C., & GROPPER, N. B. Sex-role culture and educational practice. *Harvard Educational Review.* 1974, *42*(No. 3), 369–410.

LEINHARDT, G., SEEWALD, A. M., & ENGEL, M. Learning what's taught: Sex differences in instruction. *Journal of Educational Psychology,* 1979, *71*(No. 4), 432–439.

LEKARCZYK, D. T., & HILL, K. T. Self-esteem, test-anxiety, stress and verbal learning. *Developmental Psychology,* 1969, *1,* 147–154.

LERNER, R. M., & BUSCH-ROSSNAGEL, N. A. (Eds.). *Individuals as producers of their development.* New York: Academic Press, 1981.

LIGHTFOOT, S. L. Socialization and education of young black girls in school. *Teachers College Record,* 1976, *78,* 239–262.

LIPPITT, R., & GOLD, M. Classroom structure as a mental health problem. *Journal of Social Issues,* 1959, *15*(No. 1), 40–49.

MAEHR, M. L. Continuing motivation: An analysis of a seldom considered educational outcome. *Review of Educational Research,* 1976, *46,* 443–462.

MANN, A. J., HARRELL, A. V., & HURT, M., JR. A review of Head Start research since 1969. In B. Brown (Ed.), *Found: Long-term gains from early intervention.* Washington, D.C.: American Association for the Advancement of Science, 1978.

MAY, R. D. Students turned-off by school. Harrisburg: Pennsylvania State Department of Education, 1975. (ERIC Document Reproduction Service No. ED 145 314)

MILLER, L. B., & DYER, J. L. Four preschool programs: Their dimensions and effects. *Monographs of the Society for Research in Child Development,* 1975, *40*(Nos. 5–6, Serial No. 162).

MUSGRAVE, P. W. *The sociology of education.* New York: Metheun, 1968.

PANKO, J. S. *Sexism in education? A study of future teachers' attitudes toward women.* Paper presented at National Meeting of the Association of Teacher Educators, Orlando, Florida, February 1979. (ERIC Document Reproduction Service No. ED 167 513)

PARSONS, R. The school class as a social system: Some of its functions in American society. *Harvard Educational Review,* 1959, *29* (No. 4), 300–301.

PECK, R. F., FOX, F. B., & MARSTON, P. T. Teacher effects on student achievement and self-esteem. Washington, D.C.: National Institute of Education, 1977. (ERIC Document Reproduction Service No. ED 141 723)

PHILLIPS, B. *School stress and anxiety: Theory, research and intervention.* New York: Human Sciences, 1978.

POTTKER, J., & FISHEL, A. (Eds.). *Sex bias in the school.* Cranbury, N.J.: Associated University Presses, Inc., 1977.

PUNCH, K. F., & RENNIE, L. Some factors effecting docility in primary school children. *British Journal of Educational Psychology,* 1978, *48,* 168–175.

REED, C. L., FELKER, D. W., KAY, R. S., & STANWYCK, D. J. Sex differences in the self-concepts of elementary-school children. In J. Pottker & A. Fishel (Eds.), *Sex bias in the schools.* Cranbury, N.J.: Associated University Presses, Inc., 1977.

REES, R. T., & GROGAN, J. The relation of sexism and authoritarianism in teacher attitudes. *Phi Delta Kappa,* 1978, *59*(No. 8), 564.

REISERT, J. E. Class size. In L. C. Deighton (Ed.), *The encyclopedia of education* (Vol. 2). New York: Macmillan, 1971.

RETISH, P. Changing the status of poorly esteemed students through teacher reinforcement. *Journal of Applied Behavioral Science,* 1973, *9*(No. 1), 44–50.

RIEGEL, K. F. The dialectics of human development. *American Psychologist,* 1976, *31,* 689–700.

RILES, W. The role of the school in moral development. In *Moral Development, Proceedings of the Educational Testing Service 35th Invitational Conference.* Princeton, N.J.: Educational Testing Service, 1975. (ERIC Document Reproduction Service No. ED 150 190)

RIST, R. C. Student social class and teacher expectations: The self-fulfilling prophecy in ghetto education. *Harvard Educational Review,* 1970, *40,* 411–451.

SAARIO, T. N., JACKLIN, C. N., & TITTLE, C. K. Sex role stereotyping in the public schools. *Harvard Educational Review,* 1973, *43,* 386–416.

SADKER, M., & SADKER, D. Sexism in schools: An issue for the 70s. *The Educational Digest,* 1974, *34,* 59.

SAWHILL, J. C. Why our public schools don't work. *Reader's Digest,* 1979, *115*(No. 691), 7–12.

SCHWAB, J. J. *What "drives" the schools?* Paper prepared for the NIE Curriculum Development Task Force, 1976. (ERIC Document Reproduction Service No. ED 170 263)

SEARS, P. S., & DOWLEY, E. M. Research on teaching in the nursery school. In N. L. Gage (Ed.), *Handbook of research on teaching.* Skokie, Ill.: Rand McNally, 1963.

SEARS, R. R. Relation of early socialization experiences to self-concepts and gender role in middle childhood. *Child Development,* 1970, *41,* 267–289.

SEELEY, D. *Bureaucracy and the schools.* New York: Public Education Association, 1977. (ERIC Document Reproduction Service No. ED 143 745)

SEITZ, V., APFEL, N. H., & EFRON, C. Long-term effects of early intervention. In B. Brown (Ed.), *Found: Long-term gains from early intervention.* Washington, D.C.: American Association for the Advancement of Science, 1978.

SILBERMAN, A. Do you enhance a sense of self? *Instructor,* 1978, *87,* 24.

SILBERMAN, C. E. (Ed.). *The open classroom reader.* New York: Vintage Books, 1973.

SLAVIN, R. E., & MADDEN, N. C. *School practices that improve race relations: A reanalysis* (Report No. 264). Baltimore, Md.: Johns Hopkins University, Center for Social Organization of Schools, 1978. (ERIC Document Reproduction Service No. ED 170 437)

SMITH, B. O., & ORLOSKY, D. E. *Socialization and schooling* (*Basics of reform*). Bloomington, Ind.: Phi Delta Kappa, 1975.

SNEATH, E. H., & HODGES, G. *Moral training in the school and home.* New York: Macmillan, 1914.

STALLINGS, J. Implementation and child effects of teaching practices in follow through classrooms. *Monographs of the Society for Research in Child Development,* 1975, *40*(Nos. 7–8, Serial No. 163).

STEPHAN, W. G. School desegregation: An evaluation of predictions made in *Brown* v. *Board of Education. Psychological Bulletin,* 1978, *85,* 217–238.

STEPHAN, W. G., & ROSENFIELD, D. Effects of desegregation on race relations and self-esteem. *Journal of Educational Psychology,* 1978, *70,* 670–679.

SWIFT, J. Effects of early group experience: The nursery school and day nursery. In M. L. Hoffman & L. Hoffman (Eds.), *Review of child development research* (Vol. 1). New York: Russell Sage Foundation, 1964.

THOMPSON, B. Adjustment to school. *Educational Research,* 1975, *17,* 128–136.

U.S. Bureau of the Census. *Statistical abstract of the United States: 1978* (99th ed.). Washington, D.C.: Author, 1978.

WATSON, J. Sex role stereotypes: Dispelling the myth in the schools. *Integrated Education,* 1977, *15,* 40–41.

WEAVER, C. G. Schools and moral development: Symposium. *Educational Horizons,* 1977–1978, *56*(No. 2), 58–106.

WOYSHNER, K. At last, a survey of children. *Learning,* 1979, *7,* 43–45.

Adolescence

PART FOUR

26

Physical Growth in Adolescence

WM. CAMERON CHUMLEA

Adolescence is not an easily defined period in a child's physical development. First, one must distinguish between adolescence and puberty, two words that are unfortunately used synonymously. Puberty is an event, the age when the reproductive system becomes mature and sexual reproduction possible. This age is easily identified in girls by the onset of menstruation, menarche. In boys, however, a similar event, the ability to ejaculate mobile sperm, is not obvious. Adolescence is a period of time, the years of life following puberty, which ends with the completion of general physical growth and maturation (Malina, 1978a; Roche, 1976). However, the growth processes occurring during adolescence start before puberty. In order to discuss growth during adolescence, one must start with the physical changes that precede puberty.

A distinct difference exists between normal boys and girls in their age at the onset of puberty; girls start to mature about two years earlier than boys. Within a sex there is a range of variation in the ages when children reach puberty. Normal girls may begin to mature physically as early as 7.25 years and boys at 9.5 years; however, the prolongation of childhood can last until 13.5 years for girls and 14 years for boys (Stuart, 1946). The time necessary for completion of physical and sexual maturity—i.e., attainment of adult status—varies also. In general children who start their pubescent development early reach maturity quickly; children starting at older ages may take a longer period of time to reach maturity (Tanner, 1962).

Many changes occur in the transformation of a child's body into that of an adult. The most obvious are physical alterations, an increase in size, changes in body proportions, and the development of secondary sex characteristics. Changes in size and proportion are due to skeletal and muscular growth and to differences in the amount and patterning of body fat. Development of secondary sex characteristics (growth of the penis and testicles in boys, breast development in girls, and pubic hair for both) coincides with sexual maturation. Along with all these changes is an increase in physical ability and performance (Malina, 1978a). This progression toward adulthood is controlled, integrated, and orchestrated by the central nervous system and endocrine glands. Changes in the sensitivity of neuroreceptors and an increase in hormone production from the pituitary, gonads, and adrenal cortex initiate and guide the differentiation of a child's body into its adult form and functions.

SEXUAL DEVELOPMENT

Maturation of the sex organs and development of secondary sex characteristics is a dramatic change to a child's body. In boys the first indication of approaching puberty is enlargement of the testes and scrotum; the increase in testicular size is due to growth of the seminal tubules (Tanner, 1962). At the same time Leydig cells appear in the testicles which produce increasing amounts of the male hormone, testosterone (Bloom & Fawcett, 1968). The age when boys start to produce sperm is unknown, but a recent study (Richardson & Short, 1978) reports that sperm production is present in approxi-

My gratitude is extended to Kathy Frasure for her help with the manuscript and Nancy Harvey for the illustrations. This work was supported by the National Institutes of Health, Bethesda, through grant HD-10246.

mately 50 percent of a select group of boys after 14.9 years of age. The penis starts to grow in length about a year or more after the testes and scrotum, just after the commencement of an increased rate of growth in stature (Tanner, 1962). Pubic hair appears at the base of the penis shortly after the start of testicular development. This initial pubic hair is straight, pigmented, and sparse (Reynolds & Wines, 1951). Pubic hair changes from this early appearance to become slightly curly and encircling the penis and scrotum; finally, this hair becomes curly and darkly pigmented and reaches the adult pattern of an inverse pyramid, extending from the genitalia onto the thighs (Greulich, Dorfman, Catchpole, Solomon, & Culotta, 1942; Reynolds & Wines, 1951). About two years later pigmented and coarse hair appears on the face, and axillary hair develops in the armpits. Facial hair appears first on the upper lip, then upper cheeks and lower lip; finally, the beard covers the cheeks, chin, and under the jaw to the neck (Tanner, 1962). The amount and distribution of body hair in males is influenced greatly by heredity (Reynolds, 1951). In some boys the breasts may enlarge during the course of sexual maturation. This process, called gynecomastia, is reversible and of short duration in normal boys; the incidence is rather low, 1.6 percent to 8 percent (Harlan, Grillo, Coroni-Huntley, & Leaverton, 1979; Reynolds & Wines, 1951).

Budding of the breast is the first indication of approaching puberty in young girls. At about the time breast development begins, rapid growth starts in the uterus and vagina. Vaginal length increases; the epithelium thickens and the mucosa becomes more acidic (Stuart, 1946). In the uterus the fundus has a greater amount of growth than the cervix, and the endometrium thickens (Tanner, 1962).

Menstruation starts about two years after commencement of breast and uterine pubescent growth. Exactly when and why menstruation begins in a girl is unknown. Several of the body's dimensions and functions which change during adolescence may affect the onset of menarche. Body weight or total body fat has been hypothesized as a possible cause or indicator of the physiological readiness for a girl's first menstruation (Frisch & Revelle, 1970, 1971; Frisch, Revelle, & Cook, 1973). However, these ideas have been criticized primarily because they made use of derived data and statistical artifacts and ignored reduction in the variability of parameters—all of which do not support the hypotheses (Billewicz, Fellows, & Hytten, 1976; Cameron, 1976; Chumlea & Malina, 1979; Johnston, Malina, & Galbraith, 1971; Johnston, Roche, Schell, & Wettenhall, 1975; Trussell, 1978).

Coincident with breast development is the appearance of pubic hair, but pubic hair may develop before the breasts begin to mature (Tanner, 1962). Girls' pubic hair has the same changes in texture and appearance as does boys', but distribution on the body is different. A girl's axillary hair also becomes visible about two years after her pubic hair has appeared.

ASSESSMENT OF SEXUAL MATURITY

Sexual maturation and development of secondary sex characteristics are continuous processes. However, children at the same or various chronological ages may differ considerably in the degree or level of their sexual maturity—i.e., their biological age. Two children of the same chronological age may have different biological ages—e.g., an early maturing child and a late maturing one differ in their biological ages at the same chronological age. Several very similar rating systems have been developed to group children into levels of sexual maturity (Nicolson & Hanley, 1953; Reynolds & Wines, 1951; Tanner, 1962; Van Wieringen, Wafelbakker, Verbrugge, & DeHaas, 1971). Basically maturation of the genitalia, pubic hair development in boys, and breast and pubic hair development in girls are divided into five grades. Grade 1 is the pre-adolescent stage—i.e., the absence of any sexual development. Grade 5 is given to an individual when adult development for a characteristic is attained. The criterion for grade 2 is the first appearance of a characteristic and for grades 3 and 4, more mature stages of that characteristic. An individual's level of sexual maturity can be assessed visually during a clinical examination or from a standardized photograph. Presently the maturity system of Tanner (1962) is the most commonly used method.

VARIABILITY OF SEXUAL MATURATION

Ages at the onset of stages of sexual development are highly variable (Marshall & Tanner, 1969, 1970; Roche, 1976; Tanner, 1962). This is obvious if one observes boys in a seventh- or eighth-grade gym class. Some boys are physically and sexually children; others are fully mature, while the rest are in transition. The percentage of boys in various stages of pubescence depends upon the ages observed. In Table 26–1 the percentage of boys in genital stage 3 ranges from 9 to 42 percent between the ages of 12 and 12.5 years; the percentage of boys in stage 4 ranges from 5 to 7 percent over the same time period (Reynolds & Wines, 1951). The age range for the onset of a pubertal stage in boys or girls can span several years (Figure 26–1). Growth of the testes occurs during about a four-year period starting as early as 9.5 years (Harlan et al., 1979; Marshall & Tanner, 1970; Reynolds & Wines, 1951; Tanner, 1962). Similarly breast development occurs as early as 8 years or as late as 13.5 years (Marshall & Tanner, 1969; Tanner, 1962).

Generally girls mature earlier than boys, by about two years. For some adolescent events, such as peak height velocity (age at most rapid growth in stature), this is true. For other events the time difference between mean ages of maturity stages is as short as four-tenths of a year (Figure 26–1). In fact boys, on the average, attain grade 5 genital development (G5) before girls reach the average age of grade 5 breast development (B5) (Figure 26–1).

Variability in the sequence of pubertal events is not as great as variation in the ages at onset (Tanner, 1962). Roche (1976) notes that stages of puberty differ in their order of appearance, and variation in the sequence of stages is as large between the sexes as within a sex. The age range at the onset of events (± 2 standard deviations) is large enough that a child may progress, for example, from genital stage 3 to stage 4 and still be in pubic hair stage 3 (Figure 26–1). The length of time required for the secondary sex characteristics of a child to pass from one prepubescent stage to another may be

Table 26-1 Percentage of Boys in Genital Stages of Puberty

AGE IN YEARS	GENITAL STAGES				
	1	2	3	4	5
9	100				
9.5	97	3			
10	95	5			
10.5	83	17			
11	65	33	2		
11.5	36	55	4	4	
12	23	63	9	5	
12.5	9	42	7		
13	3	18	41	38	
13.5		13	23	64	
14		8	5	87	
14.5		3	3	94	
15			3	97	
15.5				97	3
16				96	4
16.5				88	12
17				77	23
17.5				56	44
18				25	75
18.5					100

Source: Selected from Table 1, p. 533 in E. L. Reynolds & J. V. Vines, Physical changes associated with adolescence in boys. *American Journal of Diseases of Children,* 1951, *82,* 529–547. Copyright 1951, American Medical Association.

rather short in one child but much longer in another. However the ages of occurrence of pubertal events are not influenced by the length of time between them, but there is some degree of association (Marshall & Tanner, 1969). Correlations between ages at peak height velocity and ages at breast stage 2 in females vary from 0.76 to 0.82 (Table 26–2). Similar, but smaller, correlations (peak height velocity versus genital stage 2) are reported

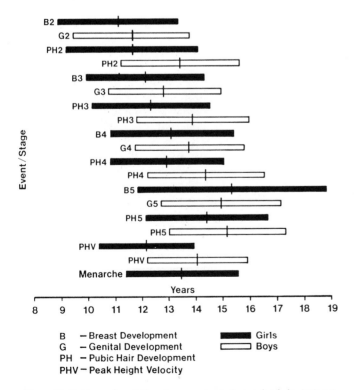

Figure 26-1 Normal variation (mean age ± 2 standard deviations) for events and stages of sexual development. (Source: Adapted from Marshall & Tanner, 1969, 1970.)

Table 26-2 Correlation Coefficients between Ages of Selected Maturity Events during Adolescence

REFERENCE	EVENTS[a]	
	PHV-B2 Girls	PHV-G2 Boys
Nicolson & Hanley (1953)	0.80	0.67
Marshall & Tanner (1969)	0.82	—
Bielicki (1975)	0.76	—
Taranger et al. (1976)	0.80	0.78

[a] PHV = peak height velocity; B2 = breast development, stage 2; G2 = genital development, stage 2

for boys (Table 26–2). The high degree of correlation between ages of occurrence of maturity levels allows the accurate prediction of the age of occurrence of one event during pubescence from another (Marshall & Tanner, 1969). Age at menarche is predicted more frequently than the ages of other pubertal events.

SKELETAL GROWTH

Basically there are three types of bones: long bones, round or irregular bones, and flat bones. Long bones, such as the humerus or femur, are located in the arms and legs. Round or irregular bones are present as carpals in the wrist, tarsals in the ankle, and the vertebrae. Flat bones are found in the vault of the skull and the pelvis. Long bones of the legs and the vertebrae are major locations of rapid growth in stature during adolescence.

Bones of the appendicular skeleton and the vertebrae grow in length and size, but their shapes must remain fairly constant. Long bones have one or more growth plates of cartilage which separate the metaphysis and disphysis (shaft of a bone) from the epiphysis (end of a bone) (Figure 26–2). During adolescence there is a rapid proliferation of cartilage cells in these growth plates. The morphology of the cartilage cells changes; they are converted into bone and deposited upon the metaphysis, which increases the length of a bone. As new bone tissue is being deposited at both ends of a bone, bone tissue is being removed or added in other locations along the shaft, on the inside and outside, so that the shape of the bone remains essentially the same. This type of growth is typical of long bones in the arms, legs, and hands. Later in adolescence growth slows, and the thickness of the epiphyseal cartilage is reduced. After approximately 18 years of age for girls and 20 years of age for boys, epiphyses of most long bones are closed; the cartilage has been replaced by bone, which prevents any further growth.

The epiphysis of a long bone is initially a cartilage model which becomes ossified from the inside out; this is true also for round bones of the wrist and ankle. These cartilage models grow in size in order to keep up with the growth in length of long bones. Inside the cartilage model, ossification is more rapid than production of new cartilage at the surface. Thus with maturation the cartilage of a carpal bone or an epiphysis is replaced by bone, except for the articular surface (Roche, Wainer, & Thissen, 1975a).

Many bones of the skull do not experience a rapid period of growth during adolescence. Growth of the vault of the skull is a function of growth of the brain (Sinclair,

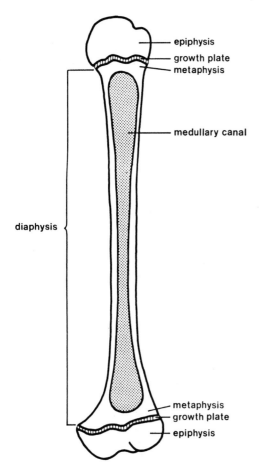

Figure 26-2 Location of epiphyseal growth plates on a typical long bone

with an epiphysis at each end; the epiphysis at the distal end of the tibia matures before its proximal epiphysis (Eveleth & Tanner, 1976).

Bones of the skeleton vary in their age at maximum growth. Among children of the Fels and Denver Longitudinal Studies, differences within a sex between mean ages of maximum growth for a bone or bones are small, but standard deviations are generally about a year. This is similar to reports for stature or menarche (Roche, 1974). The sequence of mean ages of maximum bone growth is the same for boys and girls, but the ages of onset and maximum growth occur about two years later in boys. This delay of two years accounts for the larger skeleton of the male body. Very simply stated boys grow for a longer length of time. Between the ages of 11 and 14 years, most girls are taller than their male age-mates, but these same girls also stop growing earlier than boys. When boys enter their pubescent growth spurts, their two-year advantage in prepubertal growth in stature is primarily located in the legs which have been growing at a greater rate than the trunk (Tanner, 1962). The adolescent growth spurt lasts for a longer time in boys than girls, and the intensity or amount of growth is greater. Average peak height velocities in boys range from 9.5 cm to 10.3 cm per year; in girls the maximum velocity is from 8.4 cm to 9.0 cm per year (Marshall, 1978).

ASSESSMENT OF SKELETAL MATURITY

Aspects of the growing skeleton provide investigators with accurate estimates of a child's biological or skeletal age that are highly correlated with other aspects of physical and sexual maturation. By careful study of certain characteristics of a bone or groups of bones, one can assess the level of an individual's skeletal maturity or skeletal age. Estimates of skeletal age are made from radiographs of selected portions of the body. The most commonly used areas are the hand-wrist and knee. Selection of these sites is, in part, due to the ease of irradiating these areas of the body and at the same time to the ability to limit radiation exposure to the rest of the body. Other parts of the skeleton can and have been utilized, such as the foot-ankle, elbow, shoulder, and hip (Hansman & Maresh, 1961; Hoer, Pyle, & Francis, 1962; Pyle, Stuart, Cornoni, & Reed, 1961). However the hand-wrist has a long history in the study of skeletal maturation (Bardeen, 1921; Flory, 1936; Greulich & Pyle, 1959; Pryor, 1906, 1925; Tanner, Whitehouse, Marshall, Healy, & Goldstein, 1975; Taranger, Bruning, Claesson, Karlberg, Lindstrom, & Lindstrom, 1976; Todd, 1937), but the use of the knee in assessing skeletal maturity is relatively new (Pyle & Hoer, 1969; Roche et al., 1975a). The knee is an important area to measure skeletal age because it is a major site for growth in stature. This is clinically important if one is attempting to control or treat a child's growth or estimate adult stature (Roche, Wainer, & Thissen, 1975b).

Skeletal age can be estimated from a radiograph by recognition of maturity indicators. A maturity indicator is a radiographic calcified or ossified feature of a bone (Roche, 1978)—for example a line or zone of ossifying cartilage, shape of one epiphysis, spatial or metric rela-

1978), and it reaches approximately 96 percent of its adult size by ten years of age (Tanner, 1962). The base of the skull and the mandible, however, do have a growth spurt during the adolescent period. With the onset of puberty, directional changes and increases in the growth rate are noted in the ramus of the mandible (Graber, 1966). At the same time the body of the jaw increases in length and vertical height (Sinclair, 1978). Normal sex differences are reported in the timing and intensity of growth spurts for the base of the skull; girls start and finish first, but boys have larger growth increments (Roche & Lewis, 1974; Roche, Lewis, Wainer, & McCartin, 1977).

Rapid growth of the skeleton during adolescence is not simultaneous but is coordinated. However, differential growth of the skeleton produces changes in the size of body segments between the sexes—e.g., longer arms and broader shoulders in males than in females. A bone's growth depends upon its type, but bones of the same type grow at different rates and start or stop growing at different times depending upon their location (Davenport, 1944; Hellman, 1928; Hewitt, 1963; Ikeda, Higurashi, Harayama, Ishakawa, & Hoshima, 1977; Kimura, 1973; Roche & Hermann, 1970). The long bones in the arms and legs have a distal-proximal gradient in their rate of growth (Roche, 1974); the hand is nearer its adult length at a given age than the upper arm. This distal-proximal gradient is also noted in the rate of maturation for bones

tionships of bones or metaphyses with epiphyses or stages of epiphyseal fusion (Greulich & Pyle, 1959; Roche et al., 1975a; Tanner et al., 1975). An indicator is useful in assessment of skeletal maturity if it satisfies four criteria: discrimination, the indicator differentiates children of the same chronological age; universality, the indicator progresses through recognizable changes from complete immaturity to complete maturity in all individuals; reliability, the indicator can be distinguished with little intra- or interobserver error; validity, the indicator shows orderly recognizable changes in appearance indicating maturation—i.e., there are no reversals in the levels of maturation (Roche et al., 1975a).

At present there are three acceptable methods of measuring skeletal maturity: two for the hand (Greulich & Pyle, 1959; Tanner et al., 1975) and one for the knee (Roche et al., 1975a). Greulich and Pyle (1959) extended the work of Todd (1937) at the Brush Foundation in Cleveland, Ohio. They used data from upper-class, white children to develop an atlas of standard hand-wrist radiographs from birth to 18 years for boys and girls. The skeletal age of a child is determined by separately comparing each of the 29 bones or epiphyseal centers in a hand-wrist radiograph with the standards, locating the most similar comparison (interpolating when necessary) and recording the age of that particular bone. The skeletal age of the child in question is the mean of these bone-specific ages.

The Tanner-Whitehouse method (Tanner et al., 1975) of assessing skeletal age from the hand-wrist is similar to that of Greulich and Pyle (1959) except there is less reliance on pictures and more on a written description of the indicators. An age is not assigned to each bone or epiphysis; instead, a numerical score is given representing the level of maturity (Tanner et al., 1975). The numerical scores are added, and the appropriate skeletal age is estimated from tables in the back of the book. This method is more objective because an individual's chronological age cannot influence the assessment of skeletal maturity. The Tanner-Whitehouse method is based upon data from British children who were less mature skeletally at each age than the Brush Foundation children.

The Roche et al. (1975a) estimate of skeletal age from the knee compares a radiograph to a visual and written description of several indicators. A grade is assigned to each indicator depending upon its definition and presence. The number of indicators assessed depends upon the chronological age of the child, but only 3 bones are used instead of the 29 in the hand-wrist. Once a radiograph is assessed the results are analyzed statistically by an inexpensive desktop computer which provides the skeletal age and standard error of the individual estimate. A corresponding method is being developed for the hand-wrist.

Each of these three methods of estimating skeletal age requires considerable training for suitable accuracy. Depending upon the chronological age and population from which a child is drawn, each method will provide a relatively different skeletal age due to inherent differences in the rates of skeletal maturity of the children upon which the methods are based (Roche, Davila, & Eyman, 1971).

BODY COMPOSITION

The amount of muscle and fat in the body can be estimated by several methods: total body potassium (K^{40}), total body water (D_2O), creatinine excretion, gas dilution, neutron activation, and measures of body density. These methods do not measure or estimate exactly the same thing. Creatinine is a muscle metabolite, and the amount voided in the urine per 24 hours is an indirect measure of muscle mass (Timiras, 1972). Total body water measures the amount of water in the body, and about 72 percent of this water is found in muscle tissue. Estimates of body density actually measure body volume by employing variations of Archimedes' principle of fluid displacement; density is derived by dividing weight by volume. The percentages of the body's weight as fat can be calculated from body density using the formula of Siri (1961), then multiplying percent fat and body weight to yield total body fat (TBF). TBF is subtracted from body weight, providing an estimate of lean tissue weight.

The methods of estimating body composition have spawned some terms that need to be defined clearly: lean body mass (LBM), fat-free weight (FFW), structural fat, storage fat, and total body fat (TBF). LBM is the remainder of total body weight less total body fat. LBM contains 3 percent to 5 percent structural fat (Behnke & Wilmore, 1974) and is the active, potassium-rich, protoplasmic portion of the body, primarily muscle (Behnke, 1963). FFW is body weight less all fat, structural and storage. FFW can be measured only by extracting fat from the body in ether, and this is only possible in an analysis of a cadaver.

Two important functions of body fat are to store energy and to act as a structural component. Storage fat is primarily subcutaneous and comprises the majority of TBF. Structural fat is an integral part of a cell or cellular edifice. Estimates of LBM must include the weight of the internal organs and skeleton because both are very difficult to estimate accurately in the living. Although many errors are present, significant changes and sex differences in estimates of LBM and TBF can be distinguished during adolescence.

GROWTH OF LEAN BODY MASS

During childhood there is little difference in the LBM of boys and girls (Figure 26-3; Forbes, 1972, 1974; Malina, 1978a); however, girls have an increase in LBM at younger ages than boys (Figure 26-3; Cheek, 1974; Forbes, 1972, 1974) due to their earlier maturation. This growth in LBM is relatively small and short-lived (Clark, Thompson, Beck, & Jacobson, 1951). After 15 years of age there is little change in the LBM of girls until later in life (Forbes, 1975). In boys LBM increases very rapidly after 13 years of age (Figure 26-3) and peaks late in adolescence or early adulthood. This sex difference in LBM can also be judged from changes in levels of creatinine excretion (Figure 26-4). Mean statures for the same subjects are presented to indicate similar changes in these two variables for both sexes (Clark et al., 1951) and because LBM is positively related to stature (Forbes, 1974). Tall boys and girls have greater LBM than shorter chil-

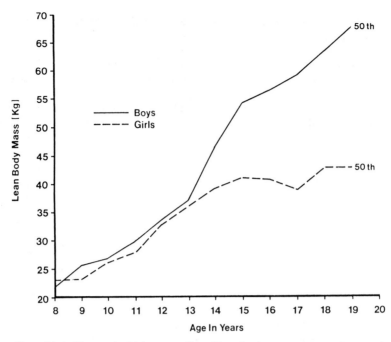

Figure 26–3 Changes in 50th percentiles of lean body mass (LBM) in boys and girls. (Source: Adapted from Forbes, 1972.)

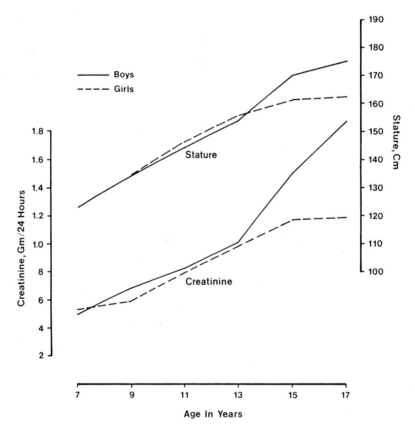

Figure 26–4 Changes in creatine excretion and growth in stature for boys and girls. (Source: Based on data from Tables 1 and 2, p. 776, in Excretion of creatine and creatinine of children by L. C. Clark, H. L. Thompson, E. I. Beck, & W. Jacobson in *American Journal of Diseases of Children,* 1951, *81,* 774–783. Copyright 1951, American Medical Association.

dren at the same level of maturity, but after puberty boys have greater absolute amounts of LBM than girls, irrespective of stature. During adolescence LBM in boys increases from parity with girls to become three to five times greater.

Growth in LBM during adolescence is due to an increase in muscle mass. Muscle grows by an increase in fiber size. The number of muscle fibers is fixed in postnatal life (Goldspink, 1972; Malina, 1978b; Montgomery, 1962), and any further change in a muscle fiber is an increase in length and diameter. There is the possibility that muscle fibers may increase in number until middle age (Adams & DeReuch, 1973), but few data are available to support this view. Muscle fibers are the cellular units of muscle tissue. They are multinucleated, and the number of muscle fiber nuclei increases with age. Cheek and Hill (1970) report a 14-fold increase in muscle nuclear numbers for males from 2 through 16 years of age; this is not a slow steady rise. Between the ages of 5 and 10 years, nuclear number increases by 30 percent, but from 10 to 16 years of age, the number of nuclei almost triples (Brasel & Gruen, 1978). Nuclear number in the muscles of girls increases only 10-fold between 2 and 16 years of age (Malina, 1978b). However all estimates of muscle cell size and number are, for the most part, made from gluteal biopsies, and one is cautioned about generalizing from one muscle to the body's muscle mass as a whole.

MOTOR PERFORMANCE

Muscle growth during adolescence produces differences between and within the sexes in strength and motor performance. There is an interrelationship between strength and motor performance and among their constituents. Strength of the average girl increases linearly through adolescence and levels off between 16 and 18 years of age; a small adolescent spurt occurs between 10 and 13 years (Malina, 1974, 1979). On the average boys possess greater strength than girls throughout childhood (Figure 26–5; Malina, 1978b). A normal boy's increase in strength is similar to that of girls until about 13 years of age, when there is a marked rise in his strength (Figure 26–5) continuing through 18 years of age (Malina, 1974, 1979; Montpetit, Montoye, & Laeding, 1967). Changes in strength in boys occur at about the same age that LBM increases. Figures 26–3 and 26–4 show that LBM starts to increase, particularly in boys, at approximately 12 to 13 years of age, which is similar to the timing of the increase in grip strength at 12 years of age (Figure 26–5). A muscle's strength, its force of contraction, is directly proportional to its cross-sectional area. Increases in muscle fiber diameter are a linear function of age and body size (Aherne, Ayyar, Clarke, & Walton, 1971; Bowden & Goyer, 1960). Thus larger muscles in boys account for their greater strength.

During adolescence the bones and muscles of the shoulders, arms, and trunk become considerably larger in boys than girls, and boys possess greater strength in these areas (Asmussen, 1962; Carron & Bailey, 1974; Malina, 1978b). Similar results are reported for the legs, but if one adjusts for stature, little difference in strength of the legs is noted between boys and girls. Greater strength in the upper extremities and torso of boys remains, irrespective of stature (Asmussen, 1962; Malina, 1978b). A large part of the changes in strength during adolescence are muscle-specific and depend on the muscle's workload. Moreover maximum increase in muscle mass exceeds peak strength development, which implies the need for maturation of neuromuscular interactions before maximum additional strength can be developed (Malina, 1978b).

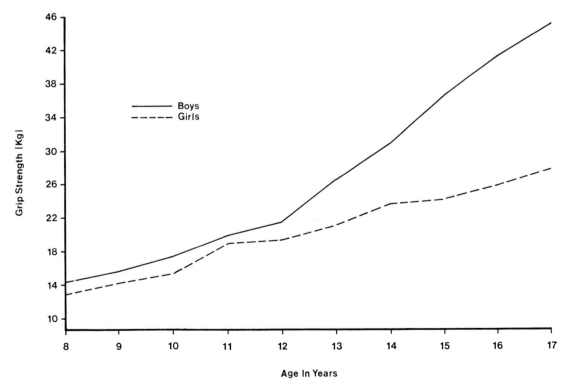

Figure 26–5 Changes in mean grip strength with age in boys and girls. (Source: Adapted from Montpetit et al., 1967.)

A girl's performance on a motor task of speed, agility, and balance peaks at about 14 years of age (Malina, 1974), while the motor performance of boys on similar tasks improves steadily and markedly during adolescence (Espenschade, 1940; Malina, 1974). Girls have a brief increase in their levels of motor performance over that of boys due to their early maturation; however, after puberty in boys, sex differences in motor performance are reversed and enlarged. A few girls will perform as well as the average boy after 16 years of age, but only a few boys will perform as low as the average girl (Jones, 1949).

ADIPOSE TISSUE

There are quanitifiable alterations in the body's amount of adipose tissue during adolescence. Changes occur primarily in the subcutaneous or storage fat of the body. Adipose tissue is found in association with internal organs and in visceral parts of the body, but this structural fat cannot be measured in free living subjects. Most of the body's storage fat is subcutaneous, and distribution is sex-specific, environmentally labile, and readily accessible for measurement.

Girls have more subcutaneous fat than boys at puberty, although boy-girl differences in amounts and percentages of body fat are significant at 6 years of age (Johnston, Hamill, & Lemeshow, 1972, 1974; Reynolds, 1951). In adolescent boys mean percent body fat decreases from 17–20 percent to 10–12 percent; in girls percent body fat increases from 19–23 percent to 25–28 percent during the same time period (Figure 26–6; Forbes, 1972; Widdowson, 1974). The greater subcutaneous fat of girls is not an artifact of their earlier maturation. Sex differences in total body fat are present when body size is held constant; this variation in fat reflects an actual difference in body composition (Johnston et al., 1972, 1974).

In addition to their absolute differences in body fat, boys and girls also have a great variability in the deposition and patterning of subcutaneous fat on their arms, legs, and trunk during adolescence than at other periods (Malina, 1974; Maresh, 1966). These local amounts of subcutaneous fat can be measured by skinfold calipers. A skinfold measurement is possible wherever a fold of skin and subcutaneous fat can be picked up. Both sexes deposit subcutaneous fat on the torso through adolescence (Figure 26–7). In girls additional subcutaneous fat is added to breast, buttocks, lateral and medial thighs, and across the back of the arms (Sinclair, 1978). This additional fat accentuates sexual dimorphism (sex differences in body form).

Subcutaneous fat thickness on the arms and legs of boys decreases during adolescence; similar measures on girls increase continuously during the same time period (Malina & Johnston, 1967; Maresh, 1966; McCammon, 1970; Reynolds, 1951). These measures of subcutaneous fat thickness on the extremities (skinfolds) are estimates of the ring of fat surrounding muscle and bone in the arm or leg. One must keep in mind that a skinfold measurement is roughly double the actual thickness of subcutaneous fat. Decrease in fat on the extremities of boys may not indicate a loss of body fat. During adolescence a boy's muscle and bone grow more rapidly than his fat, which accounts for the fall in percentage of body fat (Tanner, 1962; Widdowson, 1974). Greater growth of bone and muscle on the extremities causes local subcutaneous fat to be stretched thinner. Thus a boy's subcutaneous fat thickness on the arm or leg decreases during adolescence. For girls body fat grows as rapidly as muscle and bone, if not more so (Malina, 1969); this causes an increase in the subcutaneous fat on the arm or leg.

Sex differences in body fat also occur at the cellular level during adolescence. The fat cell size of a normal individual at an age depends, to a great extent, on his/her amount of body fat. If a normal person is carrying a lot

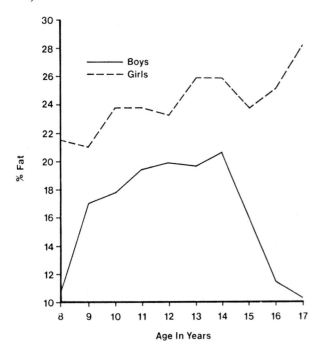

Figure 26–6 Changes in mean percent body fat of boys and girls with age. (Source: Adapted from Forbes, 1972.)

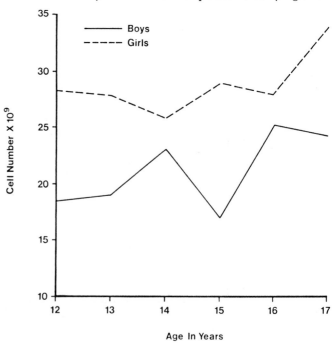

Figure 26–7 Changes in mean fat cell number with age in boys and girls. (Source: Data from Chumlea & Knittle, 1980.)

of fat, the cells will be large and vice versa. Fat cell number is not so easily regulated. There are few differences between normal boys and girls before puberty in the number or size of their fat cells (Häger, Sjörnström, Arvidsson, Björntörp, & Smith, 1977; Knittle, Ginsberg-Fellner, & Brown, 1977). By the age of puberty fat cell number in girls exceeds that of boys and continues to do so throughout adolescence (Figure 26-7; Björntörp, 1974; Chumlea, Knittle, Roche, Siervogel, & Webb, in press; Greenwood, Greun, & Cleary, 1978). During the same time period fat cell size in boys decreases slightly but only until the early 20s. In girls fat cell size changes little during adolescence (Figure 26-8; Björntörp, 1974; Chumlea et al., in press). These differences in fat cell size and number account, in part, for changes reported in percent fat and total body fat of adolescent boys and girls. Girls add fat which is reflected in their increased number of fat cells, but boys, although not losing total body fat, experience a reduction in percent body fat and a small decrease in fat cell size (Chumlea et al., in press).

NEUROENDOCRINE REGULATION

The central nervous system controls the endocrine glands which regulate the physical changes that occur during adolescence. The integration of these two systems is found in the association between the hypothalamus of the brain and the anterior pituitary gland. Before puberty hormone levels are low due to the inhibition of the central nervous system (Donovan & van der Werff ten Bosch, 1965) through the interaction of the hypothalamus and anterior pituitary. As puberty approaches, the central nervous system matures, causing a progressive decrease in the sensitivity of the nervous system to hormone levels (Grumbach, 1978). Therefore hormones appear in the blood in greater concentrations.

The hypothalamus produces hormone-specific releasing factors that are transported by the blood to the anterior pituitary at the base of the brain, where, in turn, specific hormones and specific stimulating hormones are produced. Stimulating hormones are released into the blood to affect their target organs (adrenals, gonads, thyroid) in the final production of particular hormones (testosterone, estrogen, thyroxin). As this production proceeds blood levels of the hormones rise, and this rise is monitored by neuroreceptors. When the concentration of a hormone in the blood reaches a preset limit, a neuroreceptor inhibits its production by limiting the release of the appropriate stimulating hormone by the hypothalamus. As the blood concentration of the hormone falls and when a preset lower concentration limit is reached, a neuroreceptor reactivates stimulating hormone production. Set points of the neuroreceptors control the level of hormones in the blood. These set points are low before puberty, but at puberty they have reached their higher adult settings, and sex hormones are many times their prepubescent levels. The age at which the change in the setting of these neuroreceptors occurs is affected by genetic and environmental factors (Grumbach, 1978). Puberty is a result of the effects of increased levels of sex hormones.

GROWTH HORMONE AND SOMATOMEDIN

Growth hormone is produced directly by the anterior pituitary. The concentration of growth hormone is approximately the same in the serum of children and adults (Bryson & Reichlin, 1966; Winter, 1978); moreover, serum levels of growth hormone do not increase before the accelerated growth of pubescence.

The anterior pituitary secretes growth hormone in

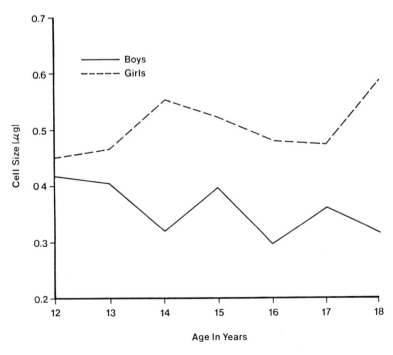

Figure **26-8** Changes in mean fat cell size with age in boys and girls. (Source: Data from Chumlea & Knittle, 1980.)

cyclic bursts, and concentration in the serum rises and falls during the day. However, external stimuli such as stress, exercise, and sleep can also produce a rise in blood growth hormone levels (Tanner, 1972; Winter, 1978). Growth hormone affects metabolic activities, and its release can also be stimulated by changes in blood glucose, amino acid, or fatty acid levels (Villee, 1975).

Growth is an acyclic continuous process, unlike the secretion of growth hormone. In fact growth can occur in the absence of growth hormone as demonstrated in anencephalic fetuses. Growth hormone alone does not directly stimulate growth because it requires the action of somatomedin, which is produced in the liver and kidney (Daughaday, Herington, & Phillips, 1975; Kostyo & Isaksson, 1977; Tanner, 1972; Van Wyk & Underwood, 1975; Van Wyk, Underwood, Lister, & Marshall, 1973). Exact functions and effects of somatomedin are not yet clear, and there appear to be several closely related compounds with somatomedin-like activities (The Somatomedins: Growth, 1975). Somatomedin stimulates skeletal growth (Daughaday, 1971), and its absence inhibits normal somatic growth. This latter fact was demonstrated in children who are pseudohypopituitary dwarfs (Laron-type dwarfism). Hypopituitary dwarfs generally have very low levels of serum growth hormone, but these pseudohypopituitary dwarfs have more than adequate levels of growth hormone but very low levels of serum somatomedin (Laron, Pertjelan, & Mamnheimer, 1966). In these few children adequate somatomedin production is blocked, and the results are basically the same as in the absence of growth hormone.

SEX HORMONES

Production of the primary sex hormones, estrogen and testosterone, is controlled by two stimulating hormones, follicle-stimulating hormone (FSH) and luteinizing hormone (LH), produced by the anterior pituitary. Increased levels of these stimulating hormones in the blood stimulate the gonads to mature which, in turn, increases production of testosterone in males and estrogen in females.

Males produce sperm cells on a continual basis due to the stimulation of testosterone. In females, however, only one ovum matures approximately every 28 days, due to cyclic changes in FSH and LH which also prepare the uterus for a possible pregnancy. FSH levels rise at the beginning of each menstrual cycle producing an increase in estrogen secretion. This rise in estrogen concentration causes follicles on the ovaries to start to mature, but only one follicle reaches maturity each month. The preovulatory increase in estrogen stimulates the endometrium of the uterus to thicken and become more vascular. The high concentration of estrogen inhibits FSH production but stimulates LH production. As LH levels rise estrogen concentration decreases, and once more there is an increase in serum FSH. LH and FSH concentrations are at their peak about the time of ovulation, and the high concentration of LH causes a follicle to rupture, releasing its ovum into the Fallopian tube. After ovulation the follicle forms a corpus luteum which produces progesterone and estrogen. Progesterone promotes development of milk-secreting cells in the breast and further

prepares the uterus for reception of the ovum (Villee, 1975). If conception occurs the ovum implants in the wall of the uterus, and the corpus luteum continues to produce progesterone and estrogen. If the ovum is not fertilized, estrogen and progesterone levels fall to their basal levels, and the thickened endometrium of the uterus is sloughed off in menstruation (Villee, 1975).

Testosterone and estrogen also affect general body growth and maturation. Both boys and girls produce testosterone and estrogen but in significantly different amounts. Changes with age in blood levels of testosterone and estradiol (the major estrogen compound in adult women) are presented in Figures 26–9 and 26–10, respectively. Increases in these two sex hormones follow a pattern coincident with those of FSH and LH. These curves are also very similar to those for growth in LBM, stature, and body fat (Figures 26–3, 26–4, 26–5, 26–9, and 26–10). The anabolic effects of testosterone stimulate muscle growth, and because of the higher levels in boys, more muscle is deposited (Cheek, 1974; Villee, 1975). Estrogen stimulates epiphyseal maturation (closure of epiphyseal growth plates) in bones and deposition of fat (Bryson & Reichlin, 1966; Villee, 1975). These two hormones together with several androgenic hormones (produced by the adrenal gland) are responsible for development of secondary sex characteristics (Villee, 1975).

Production of several other hormones, such as parathormone, calcitonin, and thyroxin, is controlled by the anterior pituitary during adolescence. Parathormone and calcitonin produced by the parathyroid gland, together with vitamin D, regulate calcium concentration in the blood. This is accomplished by controlling the absorption of calcium from the intestine and the deposition or resorption of calcium in the skeleton. Thyroxin and other hormones of the thyroid gland affect the body's rate of metabolism which increases during adolescence (Villee, 1975). These hormones do not act independently. An isolated hormone produces only one or more specific effects upon the body. However, under the control of the central nervous system, the hormones of the body operate together to ensure an orderly, coordinated growth in the skeleton, muscles, and internal organs during adolescence.

SECULAR TREND

Today boys and girls in the United States, Western Europe, and Japan are taller, heavier, and more mature than were their parents, grandparents, and particularly their great-grandparents during adolescence. These differences are known as the "secular trend," and it is not reported in all countries of the world (Malina, 1979; Roche, 1979). However in some of those countries where the trend has been very evident, it may have stopped (Damon, 1974; Greulich, 1976; Malina, 1979; Roche, 1979).

The secular trend is not unique to adolescence except for its effects upon sexual maturation. Among European populations, age at menarche has decreased over the past 100 or so years from a range of 15 to 17 years to between 12 and 14 years of age (Malina, 1979; Roche, 1979; Tanner, 1962). However, in less developed parts of the world menarche still occurs very late, for example, between the

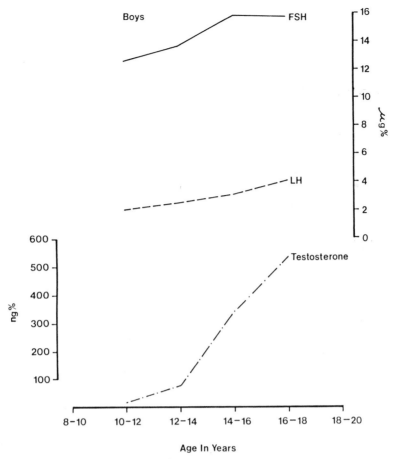

***Figure* 26-9** Changes in mean serum concentrations of testosterone, follicle-stimulating hormone (FSH), and luteinizing hormone (LH) in boys. (Source: Adapted from Winter, in Falkner & Tanner, 1978.)

ages of 15.5 and 18.4 years in New Guinea (Eveleth & Tanner, 1976). Earlier rates of maturation in boys are more difficult to detect; however, the age when a boy's voice changes is reported to have decreased from 18 years to 13 or 14 years of age (Daw, 1970). The reasons for the secular trend are unknown, but since its occurrence is limited to the past 150 to 200 years possible causes could include, in part, improved health care as reflected in reduced infant and childhood mortality, improved living conditions, urbanization, and improvement in nutrition.

POPULATION DIFFERENCES

The events of puberty and adolescence are constants, but there are differences between groups of people in the ages at which an event occurs or its duration. Genetics explains some of this dissimilarity, but many population differences in the events of adolescence are also due, in part, to socioeconomic status, disease, nutrition, or the amount and quality of health care. Each of these factors affects human growth before puberty so they and others can be expected to affect growth and maturation during adolescence.

Mean ages at menarche and genital, breast, or pubic hair development are similar among samples of Western European adolescents and their counterparts in the

United States. Age at menarche of European girls ranges from 13.4 years in England (Roberts, Rozner, & Swan, 1971) to 12.5 years in Naples (Carfagna, Figurelli, Matarese, & Matarese, 1972). The median age of menarche in the United States is 13.1 years and 12.9 years for white and black girls respectively (MacMahon, 1973). Among the young girls of developing countries, however, age at menarche may be delayed because of their low socioeconomic status or poor nutrition (Eveleth & Tanner, 1976). For example, the median age at menarche for several groups of rural Mexican girls varies from 13.8 to 14.2 years of age (Malina, Chumlea, Stepick, & Lopez, 1977). The same is true for the ages at onset of other pubertal stages in populations living under less than adequate health or socioeconomic conditions (Eveleth & Tanner, 1976). However within a developing country, upper-class adolescents have a rate of sexual development that is similar to adolescents of Western Europe and the United States (Eveleth & Tanner, 1976). For example Chinese girls in Hong Kong attain breast stage 2 before European girls but not pubic hair stage 2, while age at menarche is the same in both (Lee, Chang, & Chan, 1963).

A population's delay in sexual maturity does not imply that its skeletal maturity will be delayed also. Small differences in the rate of skeletal maturity occur between populations having a high socioeconomic status, but these variations in skeletal age are rarely greater than a year (Eveleth & Tanner, 1976). However, poor living

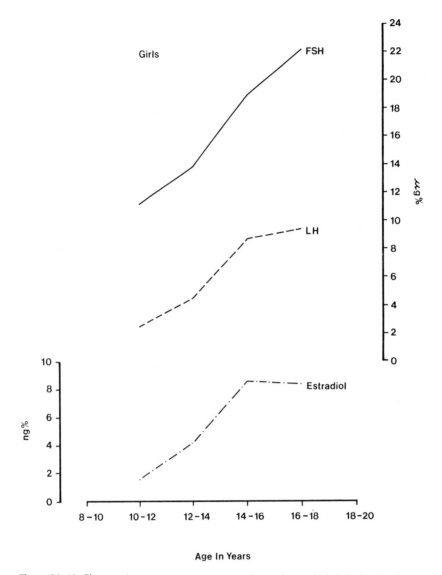

Figure 26-10 Changes in mean serum concentrations of estradiol, follicle-stimulating hormone (FSH), and luteinizing hormone (LH) in girls. (Source: Adapted from Winter, in Falkner & Tanner, 1978.)

conditions accentuate or reverse trends in skeletal maturity. Levine (1972) reports that when the socioeconomic status of blacks is low the skeletal ages of black African children are delayed compared to those of Europeans at the same chronological age.

Differences between racial groups in body size and shape influence the growth of bone muscle and fat during adolescence. The adult body results from a complex interaction of genetic composition and the environment. No two adolescents grow or mature under identical conditions, and environmental differences magnify normal variation observed between groups and populations. If living conditions are optimal, blacks are taller and heavier than whites during adolescence, while Asiatics are smaller and lighter than whites and blacks. These very elemental differences in body size are reflected in adults of these three racial groups (Eveleth & Tanner, 1976). However, adverse environmental or socioeconomic conditions can delay sexual or skeletal maturity and thus permanently reduce the adult stature and body size of those adolescents lucky enough to survive that long.

CONCLUSIONS

Growth of the body is a very complex process. For some tissues it is simply cell division, but for others the tissue changes as it assumes new importance or functions in the body. Many changes occur during prenatal development, but some are only partially completed at birth and must await full development during adolescence. An adolescent watches and tries to cope with family, friends, and society as his/her body grows, enlarges, and protrudes from what s/he has grown accustomed to as a child. The new body is familiar but with different and exciting capabilities and functions. Unfortunately these changes may not be readily accepted in some societies as fact for several years. The trauma of puberty and adolescence on an individual, his/her family, and society might be spared if maturation occurred over a longer period of time. However, the ability to procreate requires the ability to carry the fetus to term and then provide child care afterward. Thus the adult body must follow shortly on the heels of sexual maturity.

Growth and maturation during adolescence have been briefly illustrated. If a more detailed or thorough description is desired, one of the references should be consulted. Reference articles and books have generally been selected for their accessibility and should provide an avenue to in-depth study of a particular topic.

REFERENCES

ADAMS, R. D., & DeRUECH, J. Metrics of muscle in basic research in myology. Proceedings of the II International Congress on Muscle Diseases, Part I. *Exerpta Medica,* 1973, *Series 294,* Amsterdam.

AHERNE, W., AYYAR, D. R., CLARK, P. A., & WALTON, J. N. Muscle fiber size in normal infants, children and adolescents: An autopsy study. *Journal of the Neurological Sciences,* 1971, *14,* 171.

ASMUSSEN, E. *Muscular performance in muscle as a tissue.* K. Rodahl & S. M. Horvath (Eds). New York: McGraw-Hill, 1962.

BARDEEN, C. R. The relation of ossification to physiological development. *Journal of Radiology,* 1921, *2,* 1–8.

BEHNKE, A. Anthropometric evaluation of body composition throughout life. *Annals of the New York Academy of Sciences,* 1963, *110,* 450–464.

BEHNKE, A. R., & WILMORE, J. H. *Evaluation and regulation of body build and composition.* Englewood Cliffs, N.J.: Prentice-Hall, 1974.

BIELICKI, T. Interrelationships between various measures of maturation rate in girls during adolescence. *Studies of Physical Anthropology,* 1975, *1,* 51–64.

BILLEWICZ, W. Z., FELLOWS, H. M., & HYTTEN, C. A. Comments on the critical metabolic mass and the age at menarche. *Annals of Human Biology,* 1976, *3,* 51–59.

BJORK, A., & HELM, S. Prediction of the age of maximum pubertal growth in body height. *Angle Orthodontist,* 1967, *37,* 134–143.

BJÖRNTÖRP, P. Effects of age, sex and clinical conditions on adipose tissue cellularity in man. *Metabolism,* 1974, *23,* 1091–1102.

BLOOM, W., & FAWCETT, D. W. *A textbook of histology.* Philadelphia: Saunders, 1968.

BOWDEN, D. H., & GOYER, R. A. The size of muscle fibers in infants and children. *Archives of Pathology,* 1960, *69,* 188–189.

BRASEL, J. A., & GRUEN, R. K. Cellular growth: Brain, liver, muscle and lung. In F. Falkner & J. M. Tanner (Eds.), *Human growth* (Vol. 2). Postnatal growth. New York: Plenum, 1978.

BRYSON, M. F., & REICHLIN, S. Neuroendocrine regulation of sexual function and growth. *Pediatric Clinics of North America,* 1966, *13,* 423–436.

CAMERON, N. Weight and skinfold variation at menarche and the critical body weight hypothesis. *Annals of Human Biology,* 1976, *3,* 279–282.

CARFAGNA, M., FIGURELLI, E., MATARESE, G., & MATARESE, S. Menarcheal age of school girls in the District of Naples, Italy, in 1969–70. *Human Biology,* 1972, *44,* 117–125.

CARRON, A. V., & BAILEY, D. A. Strength developments in boys from 10 through 16 years. *Monographs of the Society for Research in Child Development,* 1974, *39,* 1–37.

CHEEK, D. B. *Human growth.* Philadelphia: Lea and Febiger, 1968.

CHEEK, D. B. Body composition, hormones, nutrition and growth. In M. M. Grumbach, G. D. Grave, & F. E. Mayer (Eds.), *Control of the onset of puberty.* New York: John Wiley, 1974.

CHEEK, D. B., & HILL, D. E. Muscle and liver cell growth: Role of hormones and nutritional factors. *Federation Proceedings,* 1970, *29,* 1503–1509.

CHUMLEA, W. C., & KNITTLE, J. L. *Associations between fat cellularity and total body fatness in adolescence and adulthood.* Paper presented at the 49th annual meeting of the American Association of Physical Anthropologists, Niagara Falls, New York, 1980.

CHUMLEA, W. C., KNITTLE, J. L., ROCHE, A. F., SIERVOGEL, R. M., & WEBB, P. Size and number of adipocytes and measures of body fat in boys and girls 10 to 18 years of age. *American Journal of Clinical Nutrition,* in press.

CHUMLEA, W. C., & MALINA, R. M. Weight at menarche in deaf girls. *Annals of Human Biology,* 1979, *6,* 477–479.

CLARK, L. C., THOMPSON, H. L., BECK, E. I., & JACOBSON, W. Excretion of creatine and creatinine of children. *American Journal of Diseases of Children,* 1951, *81,* 774–783.

DAMON, A. Larger body size and earlier menarche: The end in sight. *Social Biology,* 1974, *21,* 8–11.

DAUGHADAY, W. H. Sulfation factor regulation of skeletal growth. A stable mechanism dependent of intermittent growth hormone secretion. *The American Journal of Medicine,* 1971, *50,* 277–280.

DAUGHADAY, W. H., HERINGTON, A. C., & PHILLIPS, L. S. The regulation of growth of endocrines. *Annual Review of Physiology,* 1975, *26,* 211–244.

DAVENPORT, C. B. Postnatal development of the human extremities. *Proceedings of the American Philosophical Society,* 1944, *88,* 375–455.

DAW, S. F. Age of boys' puberty in Leipzig 1727–49 as indicated by voice breaking in J. S. Bach's choir members. *Human Biology,* 1970, *42,* 87–89.

DONOVAN, B. T., & VAN DER WERFF TEN BOSCH, J. J. *Physiology of puberty.* Baltimore, Md.: Williams & Wilkins, 1965.

ESPENSCHADE, A. Motor performance in adolescence. *Monographs of the Society for Research in Child Development,* 1940, *5,* 1–126.

EVELETH, P. B., & TANNER, J. M. *Worldwide variation in human growth.* Cambridge, England: Cambridge University Press, 1976.

FLORY, C. D. Osseous development in the hand as an index of skeletal development. *Monographs of the Society for Research in Child Development,* 1936, *1,* 1–126.

FORBES, G. B. Growth of the lean body mass in man. *Growth,* 1972, *36,* 325–338.

FORBES, G. B. Stature and lean body mass. *American Journal of Clinical Nutrition,* 1974, *27,* 595–602.

FORBES, G. B. Mathematical modes for the analysis of human growth. In *Proceedings of the 9th International Congress of Nutrition (Mexico)* (Vol. 2). Basel: Karger, 1975.

FRISCH, R. E., & REVELLE, R. Height and weight at menarche and a hypothesis of critical body weight and adolescent events. *Science,* 1970, *169,* 379–399.

FRISCH, R. E., & REVELLE, R. Height and weight at menarche and a hypothesis of menarche. *Archives of Diseases in Childhood,* 1971, *46,* 695–701.

FRISCH, R. E., REVELLE, R., & COOK, S. Components of weight at menarche and the initiation of the adolescent growth spurt in girls: Estimated total water, lean body weight and fat. *Human Biology,* 1973, *45,* 469–483.

GOLDSPINK, G. Postembryonic growth and differentiation of striated muscle. In G. H. Bourne (Ed.), *The structure and function of muscle* (Vol. 1, 2nd ed.). New York: Academic Press, 1972.

GRABER, T. M. Craniofacial and dentitional development. In F. Falkner (Ed.), *Human development.* Philadelphia: Saunders, 1966.

GREENWOOD, M. R. C., GRUEN, R., & CLEARY, M. P. Adipose tissue growth and the development of fat cells. In G. Brag (Ed.), *Recent advances in obesity research.* London: Neuman, 1978.

GREULICH, W. W. Some secular changes in the growth of American-born and native Japanese children. *American Journal of Physical Anthropology,* 1976, *45,* 553–568.

GREULICH, W. W., DORFMAN, R. I., CATCHPOLE, H. R., SOLOMON, C. I., & CULOLTTA, C. S. Somatic and endocrine studies of pubertal and adolescent boys. *Monographs of the Society for Research in Child Development,* 1942, *7,* 1–85.

GREULICH, W. W., & PYLE, S. J. *Radiographic atlas of skeletal development of the hand and wrist* (2nd ed.). Stanford, Calif.: Stanford University Press, 1959.

GRUMBACH, M. M. The central nervous system and the onset of puberty. In F. Falkner & J. M. Tanner (Eds.), *Human growth* (Vol. 2). Postnatal growth. New York: Plenum, 1978.

HÄGER, A., SJÖRNSTRÖM, L., ARVIDSSON, B., BJÖRNTÖRP, P., & SMITH, U. Body fat and adipose tissue cellularity in infants: A longitudinal study. *Metabolism,* 1977, *26,* 607–614.

HANSMAN, C. F., & MARESH, M. M. A longitudinal study of skeletal maturation. *American Journal of Diseases of Children,* 1961, *101,* 305–321.

HARLAN, W. R., GRILLO, G. P., CORONI-HUNTLEY, J., & LEAVERTON, P. E. Secondary sex characteristics of boys 12 to 17 years of age—The U.S. Health Examination Survey. *Journal of Pediatrics,* 1979, *95,* 292–297.

HELLMAN, M. Ossification of the epiphyseal cartilage in the hand. *American Journal of Physical Anthropologists,* 1928, *11,* 223–243.

HEWITT, D. Pattern of correlations in the skeleton of the growing hand. *Annals of Human Genetics,* 1963, *27,* 157–168.

HOER, N. L., PYLE, S. I., & FRANCIS, C. C. *Radiographic atlas of skeletal development of the foot and ankle. A standard reference.* Springfield, Ill.: Chas. C Thomas, 1962.

IKEDA, Y., HIGURASHI, M., HARAYAMA, M., ISHAKAWA, N., & HOSHIMA, H. A longitudinal study on the growth of stature, lower limb and upper limb length in Japanese children with Down's syndrome. *Journal of Mental Deficiency Research,* 1977, *21,* 139–151.

JOHNSTON, F. E., HAMILL, P.V.V., & LEMESHOW, S. *Skinfold thickness of children 6–11 years* (Vital Health Statistics No. 120, U.S. Public Health Service Publications No. 120). Washington, D.C.: U.S. Government Printing Office, 1972.

JOHNSTON, F. E., HAMILL, P.V.V., & LEMESHOW, S. *Skinfold thickness of youths 12–17 years* (Vital Health Statistics No. 132, U.S. Public Health Service Publication No. 132). Washington, D.C.: U.S. Government Printing Office, 1974.

JOHNSTON, F. E., MALINA, R. M., & GALBRAITH, M. A. Height, weight and age at menarche and the critical weight hypothesis. *Science,* 1971, *174,* 1148.

JOHNSTON, F. E., ROCHE, A. F., SCHELL, L., & WETTENHALL, N. B. Critical weight at menarche. *American Journal of Diseases of Children,* 1975, *129,* 19–23.

JONES, H. E. *Motorperformance and growth.* Berkeley: University of California Press, 1949.

KIMURA, K. On the variability and correlation of the lengths of phalanges and metacarpals. *Journal of the Anthropological Society of Nippon,* 1973, *81,* 174–184.

KNITTLE, J. L., GINSBERG-FELLNER, J., & BROWN, R. E. Adipose tissue development in man. *American Journal of Clinical Nutrition,* 1977, *30,* 762–766.

KOSTYO, J. L., & ISAKSSON, O. Growth hormone and the regulation of somatic growth. *International Review of Physiology,* 1977, *13,* 255–274.

LARON, Z., PERTJELAN, A., & MAMNHEIMER, S. Genetic pituitary dwarfism with high serum concentration of growth hormone. A new inborn error of metabolism? *Israel Journal of Medical Science,* 1966, *2,* 152–155.

LEE, M.M.C., CHANG, K.S.F., & CHAN, M.M.C. Sexual maturation of Chinese girls in Hong Kong. *Pediatrics,* 1963, *32,* 389–398.

LEVINE, E. The skeletal development of children of four South African populations. *Human Biology,* 1972, *44,* 399–412.

MACCAMMON, R. S. *Human growth and development.* Springfield, Ill.: Chas. C Thomas, 1970.

MACMAHON, B. *Age at menarche* (Vital Health Statistics No. 133, U.S. Public Health Service Publication No. 133). Washington, D.C.: U.S. Government Printing Office, 1973.

MALINA, R. M. Quantification of fat, muscle and bone in man. *Clinical Orthopaedics and Related Research,* 1969, *65,* 9–38.

MALINA, R. M. Adolescent changes in size, build, composition and performance. *Human Biology,* 1974, *46,* 117–131.

MALINA, R. M. Adolescent growth and maturation: Selected aspects of current research. *Yearbook of Physical Anthropology,* 1978a, *21,* 63–94.

MALINA, R. M. Growth of muscle tissue and muscle mass. In F. Falkner & J. M. Tanner (Eds.), *Human growth* (Vol. 2). Postnatal growth. New York: Plenum, 1978b.

MALINA, R. M. Secular changes in growth, maturation and physical performance. *Exercise and Sport Science Reviews,* 1979, *6,* 203–255.

MALINA, R. M., CHUMLEA, W. C., STEPICK, C. D., & LOPEZ, F. G. Age of menarche in Oaxaca, Mexico, school girls with comparative data for other areas of Mexico. *Human Biology,* 1977, *4,* 551–558.

MALINA, R. M., & JOHNSTON, F. E. Relations between bone, muscle and fat widths in the upper arm and calfs of boys and girls studied cross-sectionally at ages 6 to 16 years. *Human Biology,* 1967, *39,* 211–223.

MARESH, M. Changes in tissue widths during growth. *American Journal of Diseases of Children,* 1966, *111,* 142–155.

MARSHALL, W. A. Puberty. In F. Falkner & J. M. Tanner (Eds.), *Human growth* (Vol. 2). Postnatal growth. New York: Plenum, 1978.

MARSHALL, W. A., & TANNER, J. M. Variations in the pattern of pubertal changes in girls. *Archives of Disease in Childhood,* 1969, *44,* 291–303.

MARSHALL, W. A., & TANNER, J. M. Variations in the pattern of pubertal changes in boys. *Archives of Disease in Childhood,* 1970, *45,* 13–23.

MONTGOMERY, R. D. Growth of human striated muscle. *Nature,* 1962, *195,* 194–195.

MONTPETIT, R. R., MONTOYE, H. J., & LAEDING, L. Grip strength of school children, Saginaw, Michigan: 1899–1964. *Research Quarterly,* 1967, *38,* 231–240.

MOSS, F. P., & LEBLOND, C. P. Nature of dividing nuclei in skeletal muscle of growing rats. *Journal of Cell Biology,* 1970, *44,* 459.

NICOLSON, A. B., & HANLEY, C. Indices of physiological maturity: Derivation and interrelationships. *Child Development,* 1953, *24,* 3–38.

PRYOR, J. W. *Ossification of the epiphyses of the hand.* Lexington, Ky.: Press of Transylvania Co., 1906.

PRYOR, J. W. Time of ossification of the bones of the hand of males and females and union of epiphyses with the diaphyses. *American Journal of Physical Anthropology,* 1925, *8,* 401–410.

PYLE, S. I., & HOER, N. L. *A radiographic standard of reference for the growing knee.* Springfield, Ill.: Chas. C Thomas, 1969.

PYLE, S. I., STUART, H. C., CORNONI, J., & REED, R. B. Onsets, completions and spans of the osseous stage of development in representative bone growth centers of the extremities. *Monographs of the Society for Research in Child Development,* 1961, *26,* 1–126.

REYNOLDS, E. L. The distribution of subcutaneous fat in childhood and adolescence. *Monographs of the Society for Research in Child Development,* 1951, *15,* 1–189.

REYNOLDS, E. L., & WINES, J. V. Individual differences in physical changes associated with adolescence in girls. *American Journal of Diseases of Children,* 1948, *75,* 329–350.

REYNOLDS, E. L., & WINES, J. F. Physical changes associated with adolescence in boys. *American Journal of Diseases of Children,* 1951, *82,* 529–547.

RICHARDSON, D. W., & SHORT, R. V. Time of onset of sperm production in boys. *Journal of Biosocial Science,* 1978, *5,* 15–25.

ROBERTS, D. F., ROZNER, L. M., & SWAN, A. V. Age at menarche physique and environment in industrial North East England. *Acta Paediatrica Scandinavica,* 1971, *60,* 158–164.

ROCHE, A. F. Differential timing of maximum length increments among bones within individuals. *Human Biology,* 1974, *46,* 145–157.

ROCHE, A. F. Growth after puberty. In E. Fuchs (Ed.), *Youth in a changing world, cross-cultural perspectives on adolescence.* The Hague: Mouton Publishers, 1976.

ROCHE, A. F. Bone growth and maturation. In F. Falkner & J. M. Tanner (Eds.), *Human growth* (Vol. 2). Postnatal growth. New York: Plenum, 1978.

ROCHE, A. F. Secular trends in stature, weight and maturation. In A. F. Roche (Ed.), *Secular trends in growth, maturation and development of children.* Monographs of the Society for Research in Child Development, 1979, *44,* 3–27.

ROCHE, A. F., DAVILA, G. H., & EYMAN, S. L. A comparison between Greulich-Pyle and Tanner-Whitehouse assessments of skeletal maturity. *Radiology,* 1971, *98,* 273–280.

ROCHE, A. F., & HERMANN, R. F. Rates of change in width and length-width ratios of the diaphyses of the hand. *American Journal of Physical Anthropology,* 1970, *32,* 89–96.

ROCHE, A. F., & LEWIS, A. B. Sex differences in the elongation of the cranial base during pubescence. *Angle Orthodontist,* 1974, *44,* 279–284.

ROCHE, A. F., LEWIS, A. B., WAINER, H., & McCARTIN, R. Late elongation of the cranial base. *Journal of Dental Research,* 1977, *56,* 802–808.

ROCHE, A. F., WAINER, H., & THISSEN, D. *Skeletal maturity, the knee joint as a biological indicator.* New York: Plenum, 1975a.

ROCHE, A. F., WAINER, H., & THISSEN, D. The RWT method for the prediction of adult stature. *Pediatrics,* 1975b, *56,* 1026–1033.

SINCLAIR, D. *Human growth after birth.* London: Oxford University Press, 1978.

SIRI, W. K. Body composition from fluid spaces and density. In J. Brozek & A. Henschel (Eds.), *Analysis of methods in techniques for measuring body composition.* Washington, D.C.: National Academy of Sciences, 1961.

The Somatomedins: Growth. *Nutrition Reviews,* 1975, *33,* 262–265.

STUART, H. C. Normal growth and development during adolescence. *New England Journal of Medicine,* 1946, *234,* 666–672, 693–700, 732–738.

TANNER, J. M. *Growth at adolescence.* Oxford: Blackwell Scientific Publications, 1962.

TANNER, J. M. Human growth hormone. *Nature,* 1972, *237,* 433–440.

TANNER, J. M., WHITEHOUSE, R. H., MARSHALL, W. A., HEALY, M. J. R., & GOLDSTEIN, H. *Assessment of skeletal maturity and prediction of adult height: TW2 method.* New York: Academic Press, 1975.

TARANGER, J., BRUNING, B., CLAESSON, I., KARLBERG, D., LINDSTROM, T., & LINDSTROM, B. A new method for the assessment of skeletal maturity—the MAT method (mean appearance time of bone stages). *Acta Paediatrica Scandinavica,* 1976, *258,* 109–120.

TIMIRAS, P. S. *Developmental physiology and aging.* New York: Macmillan, 1972.

TODD, T. W. *Atlas of skeletal maturation.* St. Louis, Mo.: C. V. Mosby, 1937.

TRUSSELL, J. R. Menarche and fatness reexamination of the critical body composition hypothesis. *Science,* 1978, *200,* 1506–1509.

VAN WIERINGEN, J. C., WAFELBAKKER, F., VERBRUGGE, H. P., & DE HASS, J. H. *Growth diagrams, 1965 Netherlands: 2nd national survey on 0–24 year olds.* Leiden: Groeningen Walters-Noordhoff, 1971.

VAN WYK, J. J., & UNDERWOOD, L. E. Relation between growth hormone and somatomedin. *Annual Review of Medicine,* 1975, *26,* 427–441.

VAN WYK, J. J., UNDERWOOD, L. E., LISTER, R. C., & MARSHALL, R. N. The somatomedins. *American Journal of Diseases of Children,* 1973, *126,* 705–711.

VILLEE, M. S. *Human endocrinology, a developmental approach.* Springfield, Ill.: Chas. C Thomas, 1975.

WIDDOWSON, E. M. Changes in body proportions and composition during growth. In J. A. Davis & J. Dobbing (Eds.), *Scientific foundations of pediatrics.* Philadelphia: Saunders, 1974.

WINTER, J.S.D. Prepubertal and pubertal endocrinology. In F. Falkner & J. M. Tanner (Eds.), *Human growth* (Vol. 2). Postnatal growth. New York: Plenum, 1978.

27

Adolescent Thought:
Transition
to Formal Operations

EDITH D. NEIMARK

This is not the right time for a review of adolescent thought. For almost a decade following the 1958 publication of its English translation, Inhelder and Piaget's *The Growth of Logical Thinking* was largely ignored by the psychological community. Thereafter interest and experimental activity swelled in volume, issues emerged, and theoretical battlelines were drawn. Many pointless experiments were run, many meaningless arguments were waged with great heat, many obvious applications were tried and failed. We are not yet out of the period of great effort for tiny advance and may not be for some time, although I discern some propitious omens that investigators of adolescent thought are abandoning their concrete operational approaches to the subject and starting the transition to a formal operational level of investigation and discussion. The route I propose to follow toward the tentative conclusions of the final section will proceed through a thicket of contending theoretical orientations, over the desert of methodology and data to a delineation of the current resting place: a forest of questions. The journey begins with a brief summary of Piaget's theory—the proper starting point—and concludes with renewed admiration for that theory, albeit tempered by appreciation of the complexities of properly relating it to the world of data and of empirical test.

THE THEORETICAL BACKGROUND

Piaget's Theory of Formal Operations

Piaget's treatment of adolescent thought is sufficiently well known so no extended summary is needed here. *The*

Critical comments from Carol Tomlinson-Keasey, David Moshman, and Michael Shayer on a draft chapter are gratefully acknowledged.

Growth of Logical Thinking is still the official summary of the theory and of the research upon which it is based, although Piaget, in view of some of the later evidence, did offer some qualifications and possible alternative interpretations in 1972. Accurate summaries of the theory are available in a number of sources: Brainerd (1978), Flavell (1963, 1977), Ginsburg and Opper (1979), Neimark (1975a).

One central aspect of the theory which must be emphasized at the outset is that it is part of a much larger system of genetic epistemology—a view of how knowledge unfolds over the course of development from birth to maturity. Individuals differ with respect to their native endowments and the environments and experiences in which they develop. The theory does not attempt to deal with either these details of individual development or with their effects upon observed performance; rather, the theory offers a very general idealized characterization of the nature of the processes which should be available at the onset of adulthood and of the means of their organization into a unified structure. Because of the formalization of the theory in this manner, it should not be expected to provide an accurate detailed description of the behavior of any individual or group of individuals in a specific context. A general lack of awareness of the status of the theory and of the implications of that status for testing and application underlies most of the controversy and confusion in the area. To avoid repeating that error the reader should not interpret the theory as a description of behavior nor its central constructs as existential entities.

The theory of formal operations treats adolescent thought as characterized by the following: (1) The theory consists of a new category of mental transformations, *formal operations*, (2) which operate upon more abstractly structured content units, *propositions*. (3) These operations are organized into a powerful and flexible structure characterized in terms of two organizing principles borrowed from outside psychology proper: the lattice of 16 propositional combinations and the INRC (Identity, Negation, Reciprocal, Correlative) group of transformations, both of which are so named to indicate their similarity to mathematical structures having group and lattice properties. Finally, (4) this higher level of thinking, while described as qualitatively different from the level of concrete operations which preceded it, is nevertheless derived from that antecedent level through the operation of the universal process of adaptation which, in turn, is characterized by equilibration of the functional invariants of assimilation and accommodation. Whereas during earlier developmental stages the course of adaptation proceeded largely through direct interaction with the environment, at the formal level the process of interaction increasingly assumes a more symbolic form, reflexive abstraction. The course of the process of adaptation is best analogized as an ever-widening spiral (Gallagher, 1978a) rather than as a linear process of incorporating additional elements into an existing structure. The attainment of formal operations does not simply mean that more kinds of things can be thought about, or that they are dealt with more efficiently, but that both of these conditions result because the thinking process now operates differently than it did before.

As its name implies the defining property of formal operational thought is a focus upon the form or structure of a chain of reasoning—i.e., whether its conclusion is logically necessary—rather than upon the correspondence of its content to states of reality. This detachment of thought processes from dependence upon direct experience enables the adolescent to advance suppositions and to explore their consequences in a process analogous to the hypothetico-deductive reasoning employed in science and mathematics. The obviousness of this analogy was doubtless influential in Inhelder's devising of the original experimental procedures for assessing the adolescent's ability to conduct experiments and to derive explanations for simple physical phenomena such as balance beams and projected shadows. Tasks embodying less specialized content and apparatus derive from the eight formal operations concepts, or schemes, e.g., proportions, combinations, correlations, probabilities, equilibrium, and coordination of frames of reference. The examples chosen tend to be physical in content although, in principle, a great variety of contents could be employed to embody the general scheme. The cognitive feature to be sought is sufficient detachment from context to proceed from the possible to the actual, rather than, as in concrete operations, in the reverse direction. The problem of measurement will be discussed in more detail later. It is raised at this point simply to note that the original choice of experimental task may have had some unfortunate consequences such as (1) unduly limiting the interpretation of the theory and (2) giving rise to controversy deriving from problems associated with the tasks themselves rather than with the theory underlying them.

The Competition

In my opinion there is not yet any serious competition to Piaget's theory of formal operations. Nevertheless there are fundamental issues which must be confronted in the choice of guiding assumptions to direct the investigation of adolescent thought. My evaluation is not intended to deny their importance, to evade their consideration, or to denigrate the value of disagreement but rather to direct the reader to sources, noted earlier, which deal with them in greater depth. As has already been observed Piaget describes optimal processes characterized in terms of a logico-mathematical formalism which has not yet been explicitly coordinated to experimental procedures for their detailed examination. It is, in terms of contemporary parlance (e.g., Flavell & Wohlwill, 1969), a competence rather than a performance model. To the extent that the ultimate goal of any theory is explanation of observed behavior, there must eventually be some explicit relating of theory to observation. There are, however, in principle, many alternative routes to that goal. One can start from direct observation of behavior and proceed inductively to a more abstract set of explanatory principles; one can reverse the direction and attempt to coordinate a formal general model to observables; or one can work with some combination of these a priori extremes in a shuttling back and forth from theory to data. The third route, or class of routes, is probably a more accurate description of actual practice. For expository purposes I shall describe alternative views which do purport to deal with performance under the rubrics of component and structural models while acknowledging that my classification scheme is a gross oversimplification of the issues.

Component Models. Under the heading of *component models* can be included a variety of theories which assume an underlying continuum of development—i.e., that adolescent thought represents a genuine advance in terms of the component skills comprised rather than a qualitative change in the nature of their organization. Included in this category are a variety of views largely deriving from the information-processing computer analogy best exemplified by the work of Newell and Simon (1972). The guiding purpose of such approaches is to design a mechanism—i.e., an information-processing system—which will exhibit the essential properties of a human thinker. The mechanism is characterized in terms of its "hardware"—inherent structures such as rates and capacities—and its "software"—content and organization of processes and data structures. The description of the information-processing system takes the form of a set of rules for processing information, generally cast in the form of a computer program which may be run to generate a predicted sequence which can then be compared with observed behavior. Although the specificity of the program depends upon the level at which the model is expressed (the lowest level being for a specific task; the highest, the metaphorical level; and the intermediate level comprising a class of tasks), the program takes the form of a collection of ordered condition-action links, called *productions,* which comprise the *production system.* The *condition side* of the link refers to symbols in short-term memory that represent goals and knowledge in the system's momentary *knowledge state;* the *action side* of the link refers to a variety of transformations performed on the contents of short-term memory. The course of cognitive development within this type of model is described in terms of advances in (1) knowledge states and their encoding, (2) operations upon knowledge states, and (3) increasing scope and power of executive strategies which direct the selection of operations and knowledge states to which they are applied. Thus in terms of the explanatory constructs themselves, there would seem to be some direct parallels to Piagetian constructs. Specifically there is a rough correspondence of (1) knowledge states to figurative aspects of knowledge, (2) operations to operative aspects, and (3) executive strategies to organizing structures and schemes. The difference, however, lies in the emphasis placed in their application upon the continuity of the principles of integration. In practice the research tends to describe task behavior in more specific detail. As a consequence the resulting descriptions seem to be much more task-specific than do comparable Piagetian descriptions, (for some specific examples see Case, 1978; Klahr & Siegler, 1978; Klahr & Wallace, 1976).

Another class of componential models which places less reliance upon computer analogues and more upon traditional psychometric methods, as for example those used in the assessment of intelligence, is exemplified in the work of Keating and associates (e.g., Keating, 1979a, 1979b). They treat the cognitive accomplishments associated with different age levels as sources of variance to be subjected to multivariate analysis in order to determine the relative weighting of component skills in determination of specific task performance. Some preliminary research has substantiated age changes in such component sources of variance as basic processing efficiency, acquisition of basic content knowledge and problem-solving strategies, and frequency of generalization across content areas. Another instance of this general type of approach is exemplified by the work of Sternberg (1979a) whose components are more closely aligned to those employed generally by information-processing theorists (e.g., encoding, mapping) and who has already proceeded to detailed analysis of the kinds of behavior generally construed as formal operational (e.g., analogical reasoning, Sternberg & Rifkin, 1979; and interpretation of logical connectives, Sternberg, 1979b).

Structural Models. Among the models which attempt to account for performance and the variables affecting it while still retaining the central structural feature of Piaget's theory, by far the best-elaborated is that of Pascual-Leone. Pascual-Leone (1970, 1980) and his students (e.g., Case, 1974, 1978) describe performance in terms of the momentary state of a system of habitual schemes, *H.* The schemes in this repertoire serve three functions: figurative, transformational, and executive. The availability of schemes in the repertoire is moderated by a number of "silent operators"—*M, C, L, F, A, B, I*—each of which is described as follows.

The *M* operator refers to attentional capacity: the maximum number of schemes that can be activated in support of an executive scheme. It is a capacity factor,

somewhat analogous to general intelligence, assumed to increase linearly with age.

The *C* operator has to do with specific content knowledge and is affected by individual differences in experience and prior learning.

A structural learning operator, *L* refers to schemes for the organization and augmentation of content knowledge—e.g., knowing how to prove theorems or present legal arguments.

Specific features of the immediate stimulus situation are reflected in the *F* (field) factor dealing with features salient for the individual that may facilitate or impede optimal performance.

There are two individual difference factors associated with the personality and style of a given individual: *A* refers to affective and motivational factors; *B* refers to biases and beliefs, chief among which are field dependence or independence, which, in turn, affects susceptibility to field factors and readiness for utilization of *M* power.

The last, and least elaborated, operator, *I,* is associated with inhibitory factors.

There are a number of views, which might be characterized as performance-oriented structuralisms, sharing a common property of accepting a qualitative change in organizing structure but questioning the need for Piaget's particular formalization of it. Strauss and Kroy (1977), proceeding by analogy to distinctions made in language theory, suggest that quantified modal logic would provide a more appropriate description of formal operations than does propositional logic. Neimark (1970) proposes a looser characterization of the organizing structure in terms of deliberate and conscious imposition of order upon knowledge—in a sense, the construction of theory for everyday experience (see also Karmiloff-Smith & Inhelder, 1974–1975; Moshman, 1979a).

The increasing detachment of knowledge from its context of experience is a generally accepted universal property of intellectual development. Concomitant with this process of abstraction is an increasing detachment of knowledge from the transformations in thought of which it is a product—i.e., the individual's awareness of his/her means of encoding and organizing knowledge (what Piaget, 1976, calls *grasp of consciousness,* and Flavell, 1979, calls *metacognition*) and his/her deliberate intent to apply them (*executive strategies*). Recently Lunzer (1978) and Collis (1978) have characterized adolescent thought in terms of acceptance of lack of closure (which has some features of cognitive style in the emphasis upon search for structure prior to response) and multiple interacting systems (a broadening of capacity sharing some features of Pascual-Leone's *M* space).

Summary

In introducing this review of recent theoretical descriptions of adolescent thought, it was pointed out that much current confusion arises from differing metatheoretic assumptions concerning the development and interpretation of theory. After a brief summary of the central assumptions of Piaget's theory of formal operations, it was emphasized that this position is part of a larger view of the origin of knowledge. It offers a logico-mathematical analogue for the structure integrating the operations of adult thought and, in so doing, highlights qualitative changes in the level of competence. Other views tend to focus more directly upon various aspects of observable performance. These views were discussed under the rubrics of component and structural theories. Under the first heading are included information-processing and computer analogue models as exemplified by the work of Case (1978), Keats, Collis, and Halford (1978), and Klahr and Siegler (1978) and more psychometrically oriented approaches such as those of Keating (1979b) and Sternberg (1979a). Among the structural models the theory proposed by Pascual-Leone was described as the best-elaborated example.

HOW SHOULD ADOLESCENT THOUGHT BE MEASURED?

In posing that question I do not mean to imply that an adequate answer will be forthcoming at the end of this section but, rather, to suggest that measurement questions are at least as important as theoretical ones and can not be overlooked. Just as theoretical assumptions direct the choice of observations to be made and the means of their measurement and interpretation, so, too, does the nature of available evidence which results determine evaluation and modification of theory. At present the physical experiments devised by Inhelder are widely construed as constituting *the* operational definition of formal operational thought. As I shall try to show in an examination of some of the problems associated with these tasks, (1) they probably provide an underestimate of adolescent competence and (2) evidence from them concerning the hypothesized underlying structure is not very compelling. Moreover there has been a tendency to overgeneralize from the use of hypothetico-deductive thought as *a* model of adolescent reasoning to the conclusion that it is *the* paradigm of all mature reasoning. This, in turn, has lead to a number of criticisms which are not altogether justified, such as (1) Piaget's theory is incomplete because it does not deal with social or moral reasoning (Broughton, 1977; Keating, 1979b); (2) since scientific reasoning is dependent upon formal schooling and instruction in specific content, formal operational thought must similarly be dependent upon such training; (3) failure of reasoning to follow the rules of formal logic—whatever that is construed to mean (Ennis, 1976; Osherson, 1975)—should be construed as disconfirmation of formal operations (Shaklee, 1979; Wason & Johnson-Laird, 1972). Similarly the widespread evidence of poor performance on these tasks has been interpreted to mean either that the final stage of development is not universally attained or that Piaget's theory is disconfirmed because of this evidence (Blasi & Hoeffel, 1974; Dulit, 1972).

The Inhelder Experiment Tasks

Inhelder and Piaget (1958) base their discussion of formal operations upon evidence obtained from 15 tasks. The first six are designed to illustrate the development of

propositional logic and include equality of angles of incidence and reflection and the operation of reciprocal implication; law of floating bodies and the elimination of contradictions; flexibility and the operations mediating separation of variables (bending of rods); oscillation of a pendulum and the operations of exclusion; falling bodies on an inclined plane and the operation of disjunction; and the role of invisible magnetization and the 16 binary propositional operations. The second group contains tasks requiring more advanced reasoning in the sense that their structuring presupposes formal reasoning and, in addition, entails the operational schemes of the formal operations concepts. These tasks include combinations of chemicals, conservation of motion on a horizontal plane, and communicating vessels (which deals with equilibrium and coordination of inversion and reciprocity). Equilibrium is further explored in the hydraulic press, the balance, and hauling weight on an inclined plane; proportion is required for the projection of shadows and centrifugal force (which examines the relation of proportions and the notion of compensation). The final section explores understanding of random variation and correlation. Earlier work utilizing these tasks has been described in Modgil and Modgil (1976) and Neimark (1975a) and will not be further detailed here. Since the publication of these summaries, the volume of reported research which has appeared using these tasks has become too large and too heterogeneous to permit useful updating. The present discussion will focus upon a number of methodological issues which have emerged in the course of recent research. These issues have to do with (1) lack of standardization and resulting difficulty in attaining comparability among studies as well as some question concerning whether observed performance provides adequate basis for inferring competence and (2) questions concerning possible ordering among tasks and the presence of a common factor.

Questions of Standardization and Optimal Performance. The tasks designed to assess development of a scheme for the control of variables have served to focus attention upon uncertainty as to what is being measured in these tasks. In the pendulum task Kerst and Youniss (1977) question the precise referent for "period of the pendulum" and note variation among procedures employed. Pulos and Linn (1978) used Tuddenham's (1970) version of this task with 244 thirteen-year-olds and analyzed performance with respect to three different measures: a score for answers to the control-of-variables question, a score for controlled experiments produced in response to additional prodding by the experimenter, and a score for interpretation of experimental results. Twice as many subjects (56 percent) passed at a formal level with the second measure as with the first (28 percent); intercorrelations among the three measures were distressingly low.

Even more compelling evidence as to sources of performance variability in the control of variables tasks is provided by Danner and Day (1977) who administered three tasks to each of three age groups: 10–11-year-olds, 13–14-year-olds, and 17–18-year-olds. A graded series of up to five increasingly more explicit prompts (the last being demonstration of unconfounded tests for each of the four variables associated with that task) was given following the second task. As a result performance on the third task, which was given without any prompting, substantially improved for the two older groups. These findings were later replicated in subsequent experiments (Stone & Day, 1978) which demonstrated that (1) performance on the transfer test of subjects who improved after explicit prompting did not differ significantly from that of subjects who spontaneously performed at a formal level and (2) improvement was not directly related to details of the prompting procedures. Thus, it appears that competence in devising adequate tests for control of variables may be substantially underestimated with "traditionally administered" tests of this skill. Additional evidence for this conclusion is provided by a report of Kuhn, Ho, and Adams (1979).

In striking contrast to the noisy variability resulting from adherence to the clinical method is the pattern of findings reported by Siegler (1976) with his revision of the balance task. He identified four hierarchically nested rules (which closely correspond to the Inhelder and Piaget criteria for assessment of level) and devised a series of specific problems designed to reflect uniquely which of the rules was being used by the subject. By means of this procedure he was able to assess not only initial level of understanding but also the ability to profit from instruction of children as young as five years old. More task refinement of this sort is sorely needed. The effort of detailed task analysis, as advocated by information-processing theorists, promises to be richly repaid by a clearer understanding of performance determinants.

The individual administration necessitated by Inhelder's application of the clinical method imposes heavy demands upon the time and skill of the experimenter which, in turn, effectively constrains the size of groups that can be tested. In an attempt to eliminate these constraints, a number of investigators have developed group-tests, most of which are closely modeled upon the original Inhelder tasks (Lawson, 1978; Longeot, 1965; Raven, 1973; Shayer, 1979; Tisher & Dale, 1975; Tomlinson-Keasey, 1975). Although, by virtue of the means of their derivation, all of these tests would seem to have a certain amount of "face-validity," only the Shayer and Lawson tests have been subjected to the kind of rigorous standardization normally expected of a group test. Other group tests which have been developed include a control-of-variables task, the plant problem (Kuhn & Brannock, 1977), and an attempt to embody directly the lattice of 16 propositional combinations, the saga of Butch and Slim (Ward, 1972). Although both were at least partially motivated by an assumption that more "natural" and familiar content would lead to more accurate reflection of competence, the results do not support that assumption, nor does either test have any other superior psychometric properties to recommend it.

As suggested by the foregoing discussion, the existing procedures for measurement of formal operations are long overdue for searching scrutiny of their psychometric properties. As a first step toward that goal, there is need for good age norms in the form of frequency distributions for the most widely used tasks. Such data would provide unique evidence on the course of development and rate of transitions (Wohlwill, 1973). Lovell (1961) made an

early start at providing distribution data; Shayer and associates appear to be continuing it (Shayer, Kücheman, & Wylam, 1976; Shayer & Wylam, 1978). Their task 3, which consists of 14 items based on Somerville's (1974) version of the pendulum problem, is most directly concerned with formal operations (part of task 2 dealing with displacement and density is also relevant). Their data for over one thousand children at each age at ages 12, 13, 14 on task 3 show only 14 percent, 18 percent, and 22 percent of the population of normal English schoolchildren at each age respectively to be formal operational. Among over one hundred children at each age level selected from good grammar schools with students at the top 20 percent of the ability range, the percentage at each age at the level of formal operations are 40, 43, and 64. For the most selective schools whose students are drawn from the top 8 percent of the ability range, the corresponding figures are 61 percent, 80 percent, and 85 percent. Other data collected by Shayer (1979) from a large group of 14-year-olds (about two-thirds of whom were boys) on his group test showed the majority of the group to be formal operational with some suggestion of differences among the five tasks comprising the battery. On the basis of these data it would appear that the course of development is in accord with Piaget's theory, but the role of ability, as defined by traditional measures, is clearly highlighted. Although the narrow age range employed in these studies seems to encompass the assumed transitional period adequately, it would be highly desirable to extend the age range in either direction for a clearer answer to at least two questions: Does attainment of formal operations continue with age but at a slower rate, at lower ability levels? and What is the earliest age at which formal operations begin to be manifest at the higher ability levels? On the basis of existing evidence, it would appear that over the range of ability level there is very wide variation in modal age of attainment. In light of data reported by Hunt (1977) showing a two-year range in modal age of attainment of object concept (with considerable within-group variation as well), this is exactly what one would expect. The widespread naive interpretation which assumes that between the ages of 11 to 15 the adolescent is suddenly and totally transformed from a concrete to a formal thinker is clearly totally unwarranted.

Questions of Ordering and Coherence. A second set of primarily psychometric questions concerns the coherence among tasks designed to measure formal operations. A naive interpretation of the theory of formal operations assumes that since formal operations are, by their very nature, more powerful and more abstract this final level should be rapidly consolidated and broadly generalized to a wide range of tasks. Tomlinson-Keasey (1981) has noted that there is no necessary implication of discontinuity in the transition. Pascual-Leone (de Ribaupierre & Pascual-Leone, 1979) reasons that since a tool (in this case, of reasoning) must be adapted to the constraints of the tasks to which it applies and the more general the tool the more complex the interface connecting it to a variety of tasks, it follows that horizontal decalages should be more common and more extreme at the level of formal operations that at earlier developmental stages. At present, the data with respect to these issues are largely ambiguous, in part because of the impossibility of determining whether observed performance differences are attributable to (1) differential difficulty of the items themselves (i.e., purely performance moderators), (2) differential demands upon the skill assumed to be tapped by the item (i.e., levels of competence), or (3) differential accessibility of the skills themselves (i.e., strength or generality of competence). Since I do not see any evidence that these deep and difficult methodological problems will be resolved in the near future, the discussion of the question of coherence will be brief and, of necessity, inconclusive.

The unreliability of using any single task as a comprehensive test of formal operations is almost universally appreciated. Most investigators use a battery of three or four tasks; of this group a fair number also report intercorrelations among tasks (usually without partialling out the effects of age and ability). For the most part the reported correlations tend to be statistically significant and of meaningful magnitude—e.g., .5 to .8 or more (see Neimark, 1975a, or Shayer, 1979, for citation of some reported values). Admittedly this is very weak evidence for the existence of a unifying structure, but on the other hand, the absence of any consistent disconfirming evidence is surely compatible with that assumption. A more stringent test for coherence among tasks looks for within-individual consistency across tasks. Jackson (1965) was the first to report evidence of this sort; while only 10 percent of his subjects were at a uniform level, 60 percent spanned only two substages. Martorano (1977) who used one of the largest batteries to date (two versions of each of five schemes) on four groups of girls from grades 6 to 12 found only two girls to be fully formal on all tasks; 33 percent of the group varied by two substages and 61 percent by three. This lack of consistency, however, is undoubtedly partly attributable to wide variation in task difficulty. Among Martorano's twelfth graders the combinations and correlations tasks were passed by 90 percent and 95 percent of the group respectively, whereas only 15 percent passed the hydraulic press. Although the ordering of tasks with respect to the proportion passing at a given age is generally in line with comparable data reported earlier (see Neimark, 1975a), there are some inconsistencies in the data—e.g., for correlations—which seem to be a function of stringency of criteria for passing. The data are not adequate for inferring the existence of a horizontal decalage. The only study which purports to assess ordering among tasks (Bart & Airasian, 1974) used only three concrete and four formal tasks and a procedure for assessing order which is not particularly compelling. The most convincing procedure for identification of a hierarchical ordering among schemes seems to be a cross-lagged panel analysis of longitudinal data (Tomlinson-Keasey, Eisert, Kahle, Hardy-Brown, & Keasey, 1979, report such an analysis for concrete operations, but appropriate longitudinal data for formal operations are not yet available).

The most common method for assessing task communality seems to be factor analysis; in most cases, of a small task battery administered to small groups of subjects and usually without inclusion of items which should not load on a common factor or control for age and ability. Some of these analyses report a common factor (e.g., Bart, 1971; Lawson, 1977, 1979), whereas others do not (Roberge & Flexer, 1979). Shayer (1979) found a single common factor in one analysis with age constant of data from his group test, whereas Lawson (1978) with a range of ages and a more heterogeneous battery found evidence for two (with conservation of volume defining the second factor). Humphreys and Parsons (1979) in a reanalysis of Stephens and McLaughlin's (1974) longitudinal data for a normal and a retarded group tested with 27 Piagetian tasks (only 3 at the level of formal operations), 11 WAIS items, and 3 academic achievement tests found one general factor, which they label *general intelligence,* and four first-order group factors: *academic achievement, operational thought, classificatory thought,* and a Piagetian factor which is not identified. All of the items which load heavily on this last factor (conservation of volume, dissociation of weight and volume, rotation of squares, dissolution of sugar, changing perspectives) seem to bear some relation to formal operations or to broader *M* space. All of the items in the battery loaded on the general intelligence factor.

Work with the Formal Operations Concepts

Examination of the level of understanding of one or more of the eight formal operations concepts, or schemes, would seem to provide another, less content-specific, medium of assessment of formal operations. Although some of the concepts, especially conservation of volume, have been used for this purpose, others—e.g., coordination of schemes of reference—seem never to be used. This section will briefly review some of the work which has been done using these concepts, primarily for the purpose of showing how understanding of formal operations is broadened and suggesting the potential value of some of the neglected concepts.

Conservation of volume has been widely employed in work with the retarded (Wilton & Boersma, 1974), the aged (Papalia, 1972), the less educated (Graves, 1972), and members of other cultures (Dasen, 1977)—usually in conjunction with the concrete operations conservations such as number, weight, and quantity. In her early work with the retarded, Inhelder (1968) suggested that maximum cognitive level attained provided a means for characterizing degree of retardation: The most profoundly retarded should not get beyond the sensorimotor level, whereas the least handicapped should attain the level of concrete, but not formal, operations. Weitz and Zigler (1979), in their review of the literature, conclude that evidence generally supports this "similar sequence" hypothesis. One intriguing aspect of the data which has occasioned very little comment is the extraordinary variability reported. In her series of training studies, Lister (1969, 1970, 1972) reports results of pretesting on the entire available population of 8- to 16-year-old retarded children (with an IQ range of 46 to 81) whose equivalent mental age should be below the level of formal operations. Nevertheless out of one group (1970) of 104 children, 34 conserved on all tasks including volume (the lowest chronological age [CA] among this group was 10 years, the lowest mental age [MA] was 5.7 years; in either case below the level at which normal children usually display conservation of interior and occupied volume); in the second (1972) similar group of 115 children, only 7 conserved on all tests. Although her testing procedures were extensive and seemingly concerned with artifacts, there may well have been some inadequacies in the scoring criteria. That suspicion is strengthened by the fact that in three replications she succeeded in training all the members of a group of total nonconservers to a level of complete conservation, including volume, which was retained over an interval of several months. Her dramatic success has not been duplicated by later investigators (Field, 1977; Kahn, 1974).

As will be considered in more detail in the next section, there is some question as to what constitutes "training" of schemes. For example Hornblum and Overton (1976) found that although only 33 percent of a group of 65- to 75-year-olds of varied educational background (6–18 years) displayed conservation according to a strict criterion, when a small group of total nonconservers were subjected to a series of trials with correction following initial judgment, they made many fewer errors on the rest of the training series than the control group and showed both near and, to a lesser extent, far transfer. The authors conclude that the effect of "training" was to activate existing structures, a conclusion also proposed in the Danner and Day study reviewed earlier.

The proportionality scheme has also been widely used, especially among investigators who assume that performance will improve if familiar content is used: Sinnott (1975) used modification of a recipe and reassignment of factory workers as content; Kuhn and Capon (1979) used comparison pricing of grocery items. Neither found much evidence of proportional reasoning among adult subjects. Since the proportion scheme is so central to a great deal of mathematics from fractions on, as well as much of physics instruction, it has served as a focus for most investigators of educational applications. The work of Karplus (1978b, 1980) and associates, as well as Siegler's (1976) analysis of proportionality in the balance beam and in judgment of relative fullness (Siegler & Vago, 1978), clearly demonstrates that many kinds of proportionality problems can be solved by concrete means, such as multiplication or division by two. To state the conclusion in another way, the development of a proportionality scheme proceeds through progressively more general levels of understanding of which only the final one is interpreted by Piagetians as fully formal operational (see pp. 493-494). Information-processing theorists like Siegler, on the other hand, emphasize that the roots of the concept's development appear earlier in childhood and that growth of understanding proceeds more or less continuously from there. Similar polarities in interpretation arise in examination of some of the other schemes closely related to proportionality—e.g., correlations and probability. Although some early research suggests that children as young as five or six are able to deal with notions of probability (Yost, Siegel, & Andrews, 1962), later work (e.g., Chapman, 1975) clearly demonstrates that probability judgments requiring a proportionality scheme do not appear until about the age of formal operations. This issue of where one assigns capacity for a process which undergoes development is a major one to be considered directly in the next section. Piagetians

generally consider a capacity attained when it is consolidated into a structure; their critics tend to use less stringent criteria, such as first manifestation of an operation.

The formal operational scheme required for coordinating different frames of reference has been totally ignored as a research focus. To the extent that most examples of formal operations in everyday life of nonindustrialized or even preliterate peoples can be described under this rubric, it is a very serious omission. The rules of jurisprudence, for example, may be treated as means for comparing views of two contending sides to achieve an equitable solution. Strategy games also fall within this heading, and as Spitz (1978) has observed, they provide compelling evidence for the universal nature of human intelligence. Early systems of navigation (Oatley, 1977) and the independent invention in widely separated cultures of devices for measuring the changing position of the sun in relation of the earth (e.g., Stonehenge and Fajada Butte) provide still other examples of this important scheme.

Other Tasks

This is obviously a wastebasket which serves as a convenient handle for introducing a variety of work aimed at broadening the focus and generality of formal operations beyond the confines of physico-mathematical sorts of reasoning tasks. This enterprise has generally taken the form of varying the content of reasoning and judgment tasks or of looking at other embodiments of formal operations structure. Under the first heading, *change of content*, perhaps the most extensive example is offered by Peel (1971) who presents a number of studies of adolescent reasoning with a variety of course content. His data are compatible with a conclusion that adolescent thought changes qualitatively in terms of increased abstraction and broader generalization (a process which he attempts to measure separately, 1975). Recently a number of investigators have taken up the study of interpretation of art (Kenney & Nodine, 1979; Seefeldt, 1979), poetry (Hardy-Brown, 1979), and metaphor (Cometa & Eson, 1978; Gallagher, 1978b). All report a shift with advancing adolescence away from literal, content-oriented responding toward a focus on form and on the artists' intent. This sort of finding is certainly what would be expected in a shift from concrete to formal operational reasoning.

Although the 1970s were marked by a deluge of papers on developmental changes in memory (see Kail & Hagen, 1977, for a recent compendium) and the appearance of organizing strategies, most of this work was confined to grade school children. Examinations of strategy development over a broader age range or which attempted to relate mnemonic strategy to operational status were almost nonexistent. Among the former the most extensive examination is a report by Neimark (1976) of the development of spontaneous mnemonic strategies for free recall of words and of pictures among students stratified with respect to three levels of intellectual ability over the age range of 10 to 19 years. She found a change not only in degree of organization but also in the nature of the organizing principle employed which developed over the high school age period and which was interpreted as indicating the effect of a shift to formal operations. There were also clearcut effects of intellectual ability level. A direct relationship between performance on a memory task and operational status is reported by Tomlinson-Keasey, Crawford, and Eisert (1979) for concrete operations and by Arlin (1977), Neimark (1971), and Wyatt and Geis (1978) for formal operations.

Most of the research reported in this section reflects a central defining property of formal operational thought: the shift from content to form. This is a very general characteristic which could be embodied in any task in which the subject can proceed by trial and error or by induction of a structural rule at progressively higher levels of abstraction. All the Piagetian tasks can be so described but so can a variety of tasks specifically designed to study induction of structural principles (e.g., Neimark, 1975b; Scandura, 1974; Simon, 1975). Both the diagnostic problem-solving task (Neimark, 1975b) and the Tower of Hanoi task (Byrnes & Spitz, 1979) have now been shown to have clear, concrete, and formal levels and are, therefore, especially useful for examining transition. Another interesting possibility is a task devised by Dienes and Jeeves (1965), employed by Somerville and Wellman (1979), which directly embodies the INRC group.

Another promising task format is the analogy which was proposed early (Lunzer, 1965) and is once again becoming a focus for systematic investigation (Gallagher, 1978b; Sternberg & Rifkin, 1979). Achenbach (1975) has provided interesting evidence on style factors which affect performance in this task. Categories of traditional logic have also been used as a format for much research on logical reasoning, which is generally and wrongly construed to be synonymous with formal operations reasoning. Although this research tends to be of generally high quality, there is now too much of it to be summarized here; it has become an active area of investigation in its own right (for representative books see Falmagne, 1975; Osherson, 1975; Wason & Johnson-Laird, 1972). The evidence from syllogistic reasoning, conditional reasoning, and the interpretation of logical connectives yields a clear growth function in showing marked improvement during adolescence (starting around 15 years) but with a below-optimum asymptote even for adults.

Summary

Three classes of experimental procedure—the Inhelder experiments, the formal operations concepts, and other tasks (embodying induction of a formal principle)—were used as a rather arbitrary organizing framework in which to introduce a sampling of some of the recent relevant research on formal operations in theoretically neutral terms. Practically all of the available research, regardless of task employed or theoretical persuasion of the investigator, shows a clear change in the quality and power of thought during the 11- to 15-year age range. Assessment of formal operations with other types of tasks or with more humanistic material is in accord with this generalization. Although the general form of the growth function relating age and relative frequency of attainment has been replicated with awesome reliability, there is distressing variation with respect to

attainment frequency, with most evidence suggesting asymptotes well below 100 percent. In the past the low asymptotic level was interpreted as indicative that formal operations are not universally attained (Blasi & Hoeffel, 1974; Dulit, 1972). More recent research (e.g., Danner & Day, 1977) suggests that competence is underestimated by traditional procedures; procedural modifications lead to prompt improvement in practically all children in the appropriate age ranges. Results showing precocious formal operational performance in some subjects, on the other hand, has occasioned less comment. At the same time an increasing number of investigators are attempting to demonstrate that operational thought is present at preoperational age levels (e.g., Gelman & Galistel, 1979; Trabasso, 1977).

Some persistent concerns in recent research have to do with the appropriateness, convenience, and coherence among measures. Factor analyses and correlation matrices from task batteries provide weak, but generally positive, evidence of communality across a great variety of tasks. Although this could be interpreted as evidence of a structure, it is also compatible with a variety of other interpretations. Most investigators seem to have focused on a limited subset of tasks without adequate assessment of their psychometric properties. Recent research, primarily directed by information-processing analyses, has tended to focus upon careful analysis of a particular class of reasoning (e.g., Siegler's [1976] analysis of the balance beam or Scardamalia's [1977] analysis of combinations) and has led to the development of more illuminating procedures for assessing underlying processes and the variables which affect them.

ADOLESCENT THOUGHT FROM THE STANDPOINT OF CENTRAL ISSUES

As suggested in the preceding section, an enormous amount of evidence from an assortment of tasks shows that adolescents and adults are capable of feats of reasoning not attained under normal circumstances by older children and that these abilities develop fairly rapidly during the ages of about 11 to 15. In describing this development investigators of a variety of persuasions distinguish four identifiable levels. Piagetians characterize them as 2-A, 2-B, early and late concrete; 3-A, 3-B, early and late formal. My own work is described in terms of generality and degree of elaboration of an induced principle: 0, no rule; 1, limited rule; 2, collection of rules or unelaborated principle; 3, general principle. In his work with the balance beam, Siegler finds these levels: 1, focus on a single variable; 2, focus on a second variable given equality with respect to the first; 3, two variables considered but without a structure for their coordination; 4, a coordination rule, the scheme of proportions. Karplus (1981) characterizes the observed levels of proportional reasoning as intuitive, additive, transitional, and ratio. Somerville and Wellman (1979) also report four levels. I interpret these reliable consistencies as indication that the development of adolescent thought is an orderly and lawful phenomenon established beyond any reasonable doubt. The questions to be addressed in this final section concern a more detailed description of the course of that development, not only in the adolescent as an abstract generalization but also as a specific individual, and how best to account for it.

Is There Evidence for an Organizing Structure? Do We Need the Concept?

The short history of psychology can be recounted as a series of heated controversies which turn out to be impervious to empirical resolution. An instructive and representative example is provided by the controversy over the nature of the associative bond in verbal learning (Neimark & Estes, 1967): Does it develop through accumulation of increments or in an all-or-none fashion? As it turned out, models based upon either of these idealizations described the data equally well. Thus choice between them was largely a matter of personal preference. This may be the ultimate resolution of the clash between structural and component accounts of the development of adolescent thought. Since the notion of an organizing structure is central to the theory, I shall begin by examining evidence for it.

As noted in the preceding section the plethora of generally positive evidence from intercorrelations and factor analyses provide weak evidence at best (methodological "mushiness" in the composition of the test batteries further weakens its utility) and is probably not a fruitful direction to pursue in the first place. A more promising approach is to start from the properties of a structure (Bart, 1974). A structure produces not only coherence but also hierarchical organization and stability of organization. The Genevans have long used counter-suggestion as a feature of the clinical method; Smedslund (1961) invented a more forceful version of this test for stability in which the subject, through deception, is presented visible evidence counter to his/her belief. Strauss, Danziger, and Ramati (1977) presented college students with counterevidence for conservation of weight. Nine rejected the evidence as artifact or trick; the 21 who accepted it tried to account for it by invocation of physical principles. The 11 members of the latter group who "gave up conservation" on the posttest justified their doing so with sensible physical principles. In other words the apparent abandonment of operational reasoning was clearly not a regression to preoperational thought; rather, the perplexing data were dealt with in a formal operational manner. We are, of course, still faced with the problem of determining why the 11 students abandoned what they should have seen as logical necessity.

Evidence of this sort suggests the presence of an organizing structure, but evidence for an organizing structure having the properties of the lattice of propositional combinations and the INRC group is what is needed. Demonstration of that structural form was the purpose of the Inhelder and Piaget work; subsequent work seems not to have addressed that goal. Recent work on conditional reasoning seems to fit within that framework. Conditional reasoning is of the form: if A then B (or A implies B), followed by the assertion or denial of A or B and a conclusion (assertion or denial of B or A). Interpretation of conditional sentences has generally been found to show a broadening with age from an initial interpretation, characteristic of young children, in which only AB is treated as true (a conjunctive interpretation)

(Staudenmayer & Bourne, 1977; Taplin & Staudenmayer, 1973; Taplin, Staudenmayer, & Taddonio, 1974). Later understanding is broadened to encompass $A\overline{B}$ (a biconditional interpretation). Full correct interpretation of the conditional (which includes AB, $\overline{AB}$, and $\overline{A}B$ as true) seems to be attained at adolescence, if at all. A similar pattern of broadened interpretation has been found for other logical connectives (Paris, 1973; Sternberg, 1979b) and quantifiers (Neimark & Chapman, 1975). These findings with respect to development of comprehension of logical terms are certainly compatible with assumptions following from development of the lattice of 16 propositional combinations. An addition suggesting the relation of an INRC group-like structure to the lattice is Moshman's (1979b) demonstration of the concomitant development of what he calls *falsification strategy* and *nonverification insight*—i.e., understanding that test of theory proceeds through attempt at disproof, rather than accumulation of evidence. In terms of the previous example this would mean that to test "*A* implies *B*" one looks for instances of the one sort of observation which would disprove it, $A\overline{B}$, and shows it to be false (in other words, adopts an indirect approach implying coordination among operations to get from negation to identity). Earlier research by Wason and associates (Wason & Johnson-Laird, 1972) showed this type of reasoning to be difficult even for adults, partly because of features of task presentation.

Some of the most tantalizing, but also most confusing, evidence for the existence of structures comes from the evidence of training studies. At first there were few training studies with limited evidence of behavioral change, but reports of effective training are beginning to appear (probably as the result of such work as Beilin, 1976, and Inhelder, Sinclair, & Bovet, 1974). Although the reported data differ widely with respect to the age range of subjects, type of task used, nature and amount of training, and presence of test for retention and generalization, one factor which clearly emerges from all the evidence is the role of the subject's age in determining training effectiveness. Precisely the same procedures will have a negligible effect upon the youngest subjects while producing a significant change for the older ones (Barclay, 1979; Barratt, 1975; Case, 1974; Siegler & Liebert, 1975). In fact the improvement among the older subjects appears with such speed and ease (Danner & Day, 1977; Kuhn, Ho, & Adams, 1979) and such independence of details of training procedure (Stone & Day, 1978) as to raise the question whether it is even appropriate to speak of training rather than evocation of an existing competence not spontaneously evoked earlier. The question of why some subjects spontaneously apply their skills whereas others do not is an important and persistent one to which more detailed consideration will be given in the final section. A training study by Case (1974) in which the control-of-variables scheme was developed in very bright eight-year-olds (in the control as well as experimental groups) suggests that factors of age, intelligence, and cognitive style are involved, probably in a complex interaction. The marked difference in ease of "training," however, would seem to be most readily accounted for in terms of existence of a structure (in which case material is readily assimilated to it and generalized) versus absence of structure (in which case component skills must first be extensively drilled prior to attempts at their integration).

A final question with respect to the concept of structure concerns its utility. As Larsen (1977) suggested, anti-structuralists provide much more detailed data with respect to development of a given skill, but there is no basis for integrating their lapidary descriptions into a comprehensive picture of cognitive development. The comprehensive structural view, on the other hand, has been highly influential in directing the vast bulk of existing research.

Tracing the Development of Formal Operations: The Generic Case

Where Does Development Begin? The obvious first question to be raised is at what point should one begin in tracing the course of development? There seems to be a prevalent view that the development of a stage starts late in the course of structuring of the preceding stage and develops relatively rapidly over the course of a brief transition period. The early appearance of some components of the final stage is, therefore, assumed to show that a stage view is incorrect. It should be emphasized at the outset that Piaget's theory of formal operations in no way necessitates an assumption of rapid or discontinuous transitions; in fact, such an assumption runs counter both to theory and to common sense. What characterizes formal operations is not the development of higher order operations per se but their organization into a new structure. While the consolidation of a new structure should be relatively rapid, the attainment of component operational skills might very well take a long time simply by virtue of the self-regulating nature of the acquisition process—that is, skill development must start from an existing repertoire and structure to which it is assimilated. Subsequent refinement and enrichment might then continue in a more or less continuous fashion for a long period of time. Consider, for example, the INRC group of transformations hypothesized to characterize formal operations structure. The component transformations were acquired and practiced years earlier. Reversibility through negation or through reciprocity is a defining feature of concrete operations, while identity undoubtedly precedes both by many years. The new creation of the formal operations level concerns not the transformations themselves but rather their integration into a functional unit which permits application of the transformations to each other for great representational flexibility. Evidence that some counting skills (Gelman & Gallistel, 1979) or some reasoning skills (O'Brien & Shapiro, 1968) appear early is similarly dealt with. The common defining ingredient of all such precocious components is that they are simple and isolated at first appearance. Their incorporation into the structure of a later stage, however, transforms their later deployment—e.g., simple early acquired words like *love, country, parent* change their meaning with age, not simply through the linear accretion of associations but through restructuring of concept systems.

The Course of Transition. Whereas the choice of a starting point for description is relatively arbitrary, de-

scription of later development, and especially of the course of transition, certainly should not be. Development might more accurately be called *ontogeny* to emphasize the intraindividual nature of the process. Relevant evidence concerning it should, therefore, be longitudinal evidence. Unfortunately there is still only one longitudinal study of the development of formal operations (Neimark, 1975b) published in any detail. Results of that study provide quite consistently uniform evidence that transitional states are unstable and transitory. The evidence comes primarily from two sources: A plot of problem-solving strategy levels over repeated sessions shows that the transition from no rule to a collection of rules or to a general principle takes place quite rapidly when it finally starts to occur. A similar picture emerges from examination of transition matrices for a variety of tasks which, again, show the extremes of no rule and general rule to be stable states, whereas the intervening transition states are not. Instances of regression are almost nonexistent. A cross-sectional examination of the nature of transition based upon the Flavell and Wohlwill (1969) model is offered by Moshman (1977) who used data for understanding the logical connectives of disjunction and implication among tenth-grade boys. In the early stages comprehension of disjunction (*or*) precedes understanding of implication (*if then*), but at the final stage (where the two are presumably organized as part of a larger structure), differences in difficulty largely disappear.

Where Does It End? Does the process of development end? And if so, where? Extensive evidence of the persistence of concrete operational reasoning even in mature adults was generally interpreted to show that not all normal adults attain the final level. Of course the fact that individuals do not perform at a higher level does not mean that they are incapable of doing so. Recent evidence from a number of laboratories reliably demonstrates marked improvement following relatively simple and brief task structuring (Danner & Day, 1977; Stone & Day, 1978) or following continued familiarization (Kuhn et al., 1979). This evidence suggests that improved tasks administered under better-structured conditions are likely to yield a more optimistic picture of the presence of formal operations among a majority of adolescents and adults in future research. It also indicates that continued use of traditional instructions (e.g., "what makes it work?") is no longer defensible.

At the same time that many critics fault the theory of formal operations because the stage does not seem to be universally attained, still others complain that the final stage is too narrowly conceived (Broughton, 1977; Gruber & Vonèche, 1976) or the ceiling is too limiting (Arlin, 1975; Riegel, 1973). To the extent that these criticisms are directed to the physics laboratory aspect of many of the Inhelder tasks, the point is not well taken. As noted earlier there is nothing in the theory which demands use of this type of material; in fact, recent work using poetry, metaphor, art appreciation, and a variety of subject matter areas consistently provides evidence of an early adolescent shift from a concrete, content-oriented approach to a formal, more abstract one. To the extent that the criticism demands an account for levels of especial creativity or genius, it betrays a lack of understanding: first, that general theories do not usually describe the atypical case and, second, that creativity plays a fundamental role throughout *all* the stages of intellectual development. It is a central tenet of Piaget's theory that the child creates his/her world through a process of acting upon it. Some of these inventions (e.g., object constancy) are discovered anew by every member of the human race; others may be unique accomplishments. The proponents of a higher level present no compelling reason to believe that a different process underlies the two. An alternative explanation invokes a number of variables to account for observed variability in the rate and extent of development of specific individuals.

Tracing the Development of Formal Operations: Moderating Variables and Individual Differences

Throughout this long discussion we have encountered evidence of wide interindividual variation as well as conceptual problems of relating a competence theory to observed performance. It is now time to deal directly with those issues. With respect to the second, Pascual-Leone and his neo-Piagetians incorporate performance factors into their functional model at the outset. Although their classification of variables (see Case, 1974, for a clear description of them) has been validated by evidence, the description to follow will use an arbitrary, but theoretically neutral, taxonomy to introduce variables demonstrated to affect the course of development.

Stimulus Factors. We begin with stimulus conditions whose role is considered with respect to effects upon (1) evoking available skills in a given context and (2) influencing the course of behavioral modification. With respect to the first aspect it seemed intuitively obvious to many investigators that performance should be affected by variation of the content of experimental tasks: Familiar content should be easier to deal with and to lead to better performance. Available evidence shows intuition to be wrong on several counts. First, as noted earlier, use of "homey" instances such as recipes and grocery prices does not evoke formal operations (Kuhn & Capon, 1979; Sinnott, 1975). Second, use of familiar content might even bias toward use of accustomed but inferior approaches and so interfere with optimal performance (Karplus, 1981; Kuhn & Phelps, 1979). There is an extensive literature concerning the effect of variation of meaningfulness and level of abstraction of its content upon a variety of reasoning processes, but no consistent generalizations emerge. In some instances (e.g., Wason's four-card problem), familiar meaningful material appears to simplify the problem.

In other instances (Karplus, 1981), abstract material helps to evoke a more serious abstract approach. For example the distracting effect of emotionally toned material upon syllogistic reasoning has been reported early and often. All these data suggest that the major feature of stimulus material which determines its role in evoking optimum performance is its salience rather than its familiarity. It is not adequate for the stimulus feature to be present in the situation; it must also be noted by the sub-

ject in an appropriate manner, or to all intents and purposes, it does not exist (Duckworth, 1978).

With respect to the role of stimulus factors in modification of performance, effective investigation of that area is just beginning, and conclusions seem unwarranted now. Case's (1978) classification of relevant stimulus conditions for producing learning seems as promising as any: (1) exposure to relevant situations, (2) exposure to situations where the current basis of responding is inadequate, (3) making the unattended feature salient, and (4) modeling appropriate means of incorporating the feature.

Interindividual factors associated with culture, class, and aspects of schooling have been widely demonstrated to affect rate and level of development, but interpretation of the focus (i.e., on performance or competence) or mechanisms of their effect is by no means clear. There have been almost no cross-cultural tests at the level of formal operations undoubtedly, as Dasen (1977) notes, because the traditional assessment techniques are so obviously inappropriate for unschooled adults. Feldman and associates (1974) tried to develop a more culture-fair test for the purpose; problems with the test limit the interpretation of their Eskimo data. Recent research on cross-cultural comparisons of personality development in Mexicans and Americans (Diaz-Guerrero, 1979; Holtzman, 1979) may shed light on the role of social-cultural premises, value orientations, and environment on shaping cognitive growth through the mediation of their influence on personality development.

Some idea of the complexity of interactive effects likely to be operating is conveyed by results of a cross-national study of proportional reasoning and control of variables in eighth-grade children (Karplus, 1981) at all socioeconomic levels and in a variety of school systems in seven countries. The finding that 7 percent of the total sample were fully formal on both measures, 14 percent on neither, validates the original intention of examining these reasoning processes during the course of their formation. Differential difficulty of the two types of tasks varied with country and, presumably, with type of school. Germans and Austrians had difficulty with control-of-variables tasks, whereas for American children these were easier than proportional reasoning. There were class differences in all countries but sex differences (in favor of boys) only in some. Similarly the type of school system seemed to play a role. The fortuitous inclusion of an Italian group who had the same outstanding teacher for three years indicated that the quality of teaching also plays a role. The kind of mathematics training (Karplus, 1978b) is also relevant for proportional reasoning. Children who had trigonometry or geometry did much better than children who had algebra.

The only available attempt at clarifying the mechanism by means of which intraindividual differences of this sort arise is Case's (1975) neo-Piagetian analysis of four areas of developmental differentiation: (1) the repertoire of strategies and content knowledge, (2) the repertoire of executive strategies (general orientations), (3) M space (the Pascual-Leone concept of maximum number of transformations that can be dealt with at one time), and (4) style factors. The first two should be affected by experience, the third by maturational factors, while the fourth is assumed to be stable within an individual but to differentiate among individuals. In two studies he found no performance differences between 10- to 12-year-old upper-middle and working-class children on either a measure of M space or of field independence. In both cases there were consistent differences with respect to executive strategies: Upper-class children were far more likely to adopt an optimal strategy and to perform better as a result of it.

Individual Differences. Throughout this chapter there has been occasion to note what might be characterized as style differences in task performance—e.g., the latent versus spontaneous formal operations performers of Stone and Day (1978) or the acceptors and rejectors of nonconservation of weight (Strauss et al., 1977). There have also been several occasions to note the neglected end of the distribution—i.e., subjects who attain formal operations early as well as the oft-noted other extreme who never seem to arrive at all. It is natural to assume that some factor or factors differentiate these dichotomies and to attempt to identify them. One obvious candidate is intelligence—whatever that is taken to mean. The slippery status of this proposed differentiating factor becomes more evident when one recalls that much of the interest in Piaget in America was inspired by the hope that the stage sequence described by him would provide a meaningful universal developmental basis for assessment of intelligence. Using one aspect of intelligence to explain another is an obviously circular enterprise.

The handful of experimenters who stratify their subjects with respect to ability level as assessed by traditional intelligence tests (e.g., Neimark, 1976; Shayer, 1979) find clear separation of developmental trends with the brightest being at least two years ahead of their normal age-mates. Development appears to be more readily described as a continuous process when cross-sectional performance data are plotted as a function of mental age (e.g., Neimark, 1975b), but a suggestion remains of continuing separation of the extremes of the distribution. Inhelder (1968) speculated that the retarded never attain formal operations, and data reviewed earlier in the chapter tend to support that view. The best picture of the limitations of thought in the retarded, however, is provided by a series of studies by Spitz and associates (see Spitz, 1981) which raises questions whether even concrete operations are attained. In comparing retarded adolescents and young adults to grade school children younger and of equivalent mental age on a great variety of tasks (diagnostic problem solving, Tower of Hanoi, series completions), they consistently found retardate performance to be below that of children of equivalent mental age (9 to 10 years); it was more comparable to that of 6- to 7-year-olds. The retardates seemed to approach each task in a mechanical trial-and-error fashion with little evidence of ability to derive and apply a structural rule. In terms of the Case (1975) analysis presented earlier, retarded adolescents lack executive strategies.

At the opposite extreme data on the gifted are more sparse and less consistent. Lovell and Shields (1967) and Webb (1974) do not find precocious attainment of formal operations in gifted children whereas Keating (1975) does. There is some suggestion that additional factors

may moderate precocious development. Keating and Schaefer (1975) find boys more advanced than girls prior to age ten; Case (1974) finds field-independent, gifted boys superior to their field-dependent counterparts. The one feature of thought among the gifted which consistently emerges in all reports (e.g., Krutetski, 1976; Spitz, 1981) is their delight in intellectual activity, their readiness to create and solve problems, and the amount of affect associated with these activities. One could characterize this quality of gifted thought as precocious creation of executive strategies, but that characterization captures none of the motivational features of their intellectual verve.

There have been many attempts to capture the elusive nonintellective feature, or features, which must account for individual variation in rate and level of intellectual growth; none to date has met with notable success. Cloutier and Goldschmid (1976; see Bereiter, 1978) tried direct attack with a battery of formal operations, intelligence, and personality ratings administered to 117 Montreal 10- to 12-year olds. The data were subjected to a multiple-regression analysis in which the best predictors of formal operations status were level of activity (the advanced child is active and quick to respond); systematic strategies on the Raven Progressive Matrices, creativity, discipline (i.e., class deportment), self-confidence, and initiative, in that order. Some other empirically identified factors include preferred form of information encoding (Tamir, 1976) and cognitive complexity (Eisert & Tomlinson-Keasey, 1978).

Although the interpretation of individual difference factors specifically incorporated in the neo-Piagetian theory of Pascual-Leone (1970, 1976a, 1976b, 1980) has changed somewhat with the evolution of his theory— e.g., readiness to use available M space fully is an early characterization (Case, 1974)—Witkin's (Witkin, Dyk, Paterson, Goodenough, & Karo, 1962) concept of field-dependence/independence has always been the central index of it. Evidence that field-independence is positively correlated with superior performance on formal operations tasks is now fairly abundant (Lawson, 1976; Lawson & Wollman, 1977; Neimark, 1975b). It is generally assumed (Case, 1974; Neimark, 1981) that in situations where the relevant cues or task features are not salient or where they are obscured by conflicting perceptual cues (as is always the case in conservation tasks) that field-dependent individuals should be disadvantaged relative to field-independent individuals of equivalent ability. We have already reviewed evidence showing that some individuals spontaneously respond at a formal level or resist counter-suggestion for a lower level, whereas others need some additional restructuring to do so. It is assumed that this differential responding is a stable individual characteristic and that it is correlated to field-dependence/independence. While there is little direct evidence of this to date (Stone & Day, 1978), there is accumulating evidence of an interaction of style and stimulus condition: Field-independents perform better where relevant features are not salient (Linn, 1978), but field-dependents do better where social nuances are involved (Pascual-Leone & Goodman, 1974).

Although the factor of differentiation (Witkin, Moore, Goodenough, & Cox, 1977) has now been clearly shown to affect performance on formal operations tasks, it is by no means clear that this is the exclusive, or even major, component of the individual difference involved; rather, it was chosen because there is a theoretical rationale for it and because existing tests (rod and frame, embedded figures, WISC and WAIS block test) have been widely used with an awesome variety of ages and cultures. A great deal of research is still needed, however, to answer three questions: What sorts of behavior should be included in the wastebasket category of individual differences? How should they be measured? What is the mechanism of their operation? With respect to the relevant style components, Pascual-Leone (1980) emphasizes resistance to salient perceptual features and readiness to use full mental capacity. Quite possibly a broad range of ingredients must be included ranging from broad aspects of motivation (the delight in intellectual activity of the gifted) and task orientation (predilection for reflection prior to action) to details of method of exploration of the stimulus field as indexed by eye movements (Wilton & Boersma, 1974) or haptic scanning (Kleinman, 1979). This preliminary speculation might seem to suggest that a large test battery must be administered, but existing evidence shows many of the candidates for inclusion to be intercorrelated with each other. Two of the better examples of relevant research are, unfortunately, in unpublished doctoral dissertations (Kleinman, 1977; Pascual-Leone, 1969). Neimark (1975b) showed reflection-impulsivity and field-dependence/independence, singly and in combination, to be related to formal operational status. The most pressing question of the trio raised earlier concerns the means by which the melange of cognitive style aspects affect operational development. Evidence for effect upon performance in interaction with stimulus conditions of task has already been noted. However, rational considerations suggest, to me at any rate, that the effect of style factors is not confined to performance but must influence the development of competence as well.

Evidence is not now available to support any speculative scenario as to when and how cognitive style factors influence the course of cognitive development, nor does space permit an extended tangent from formal operations to cognitive development in a life-span perspective. Rather than abandon the topic, I close with some sketchy observations which will not be documented in detail. First, there is evidence that the course of cognitive development is not smooth and continuous. There may be some brain growth basis (Epstein, 1974) for the observed pattern of periods of consolidation and transitions—i.e., rate changes. Moreover poor prediction from relative status at one stage, especially infancy, to later status is widely reported. To the extent that each stage has its own distinctive properties, conditions which enhance those properties should be favorable for the development of that stage but not necessarily of the next stage. Thus freedom for exploration in an environment rich with potential for discovery should promote rapid sensorimotor development. The same environment, however, may be much less conducive, and perhaps even inimical, to fostering of formal operations if exploration is conducted at a purely manipulative level. Formal operational thought involves exploration at a symbolic level; therefore, conditions which foster reflection and discourage immediate direct response probably become increas-

ingly more conducive to its development—an implication which does not seem to be evident to many educators attempting to apply Piagetian theory to curriculum development. Similarly some stable characteristic response styles such as systematic exploration of stimuli, assessing alternate interpretations, and encodings prior to response, while of limited import in many situations—e.g., in nursery school where social responsiveness is a primary concern—may become more important at later stages and may well pave the way for precocious appearance of components of formal operations. Early development of components combined with increasingly more complex demands upon them should, in turn, facilitate development of a consolidating structure. Most past theoretical speculation has not taken these sorts of variables into account, nor have most models of development allowed for interactive effects of the sort suggested. I suspect that future research will be forced to confront such complexities of development and hope that a similar review five years from now will provide more detail concerning them.

Summary

This section started with the premise that a level of formal operations which differs qualitatively from the preceding stage of concrete operations has been convincingly demonstrated and raised three questions with respect to it: Is there evidence of an organizing structure? What is the general course of transition from concrete to formal thought? What factors determine individual differences in performance? In answer to the first question, it was noted that correlational and factor analysis, while compatible with the notion of an organizing structure, cannot provide compelling evidence for it. The results of training studies provide the strongest evidence for a structure currently available because (1) at concrete operational age levels training is rarely effective; (2) at formal operational age levels improvement is so rapid and pervasive as to raise the question whether it was trained or simply evoked; and (3) at transitional ages effects are intermediate. Whether this structure is uniquely describable in terms of the propositional lattice and the INRC group, however, is a question remaining to be answered.

In tracing the general course of transition from concrete to formal operations, it was noted that component operational skills may originate fairly early in the period of concrete operations. At that level they are isolated, whereas at the formal level they attain greater power and generality through coordination with other formal operational skills. At the opposite end of the continuum, the question of universal attainment of formal operations is still open, although there is mounting evidence that prior data which gave rise to it may reflect the operation of procedural artifacts, possibly interacting with individual differences. As to the course of the transition itself, only longitudinal data can provide a direct picture of it. Data from the one relevant study currently available show transitional levels of performance to be unstable and transitory.

A number of factors contributing to individual differences in performance were identified. For comparison across groups they include culture, class, and educational experience. Factors operating within groups include intelligence and a melange of features characterized, for want of a better term, as *cognitive style*. It was suggested that these factors probably influence not only immediate performance but also the rate and course of cognitive development from early childhood on.

REFERENCES

ACHENBACH, T. M. A longitudinal study of relations between associative responding, IQ changes, and school performance from grades 3–12. *Developmental Psychology,* 1975, *11,* 653–654.

ARLIN, P. K. Cognitive development in adulthood: A fifth stage? *Developmental Psychology,* 1975, *11,* 602–606.

ARLIN, P. K. The modification of mnemonic code by the construction of formal operational schemes. *Journal of Genetic Psychology,* 1977, *13,* 59–64.

BARCLAY, O. R. The executive control of mnemonic activity. *Journal of Experimental Child Psychology,* 1979, *27,* 262–276.

BARRATT, B. B. Training and transfer in combinatorial problem solving: The development of formal reasoning during adolescence. *Developmental Psychology,* 1975, *11,* 700–704.

BART, W. M. The factor structure of formal operations. *British Journal of Educational Psychology,* 1971, *41,* 70–77.

BART, W. M., & AIRASIAN, P. W. Determination of the ordering among seven Piagetian tasks by an ordering theoretic method. *Journal of Educational Psychology,* 1974, *66,* 277–284.

BART, W. M., & SMITH, B. An interpretative framework of cognitive structures. *Human Development,* 1974, *17,* 161–175.

BEILIN, H. Constructing cognitive operations linguistically. Pp. 67–106 in H. Reese (Ed.), *Advances in child development and behavior.* New York: Academic Press, 1976.

BEREITER, C. An error of interpretation in Cloutier and Goldschmid's "Individual differences in the development of formal reasoning." *Child Development,* 1978, *49,* 251–252.

BLASI, A., & HOEFFEL, E. C. Adolescence and formal operations. *Human Development,* 1974, *17,* 344–363.

BRAINERD, C. J. *Piaget's theory of intelligence.* Englewood Cliffs, N.J.: Prentice-Hall, 1978a, 202–240.

BRAINERD, C. J. The stage question in cognitive-developmental theory. *Behavioral and Brain Science,* 1978b, *2,* 173–213.

BROUGHTON, J. Beyond formal operations: Theoretical thought in adolescence. *Teachers College Record,* 1977, *79,* 87–97.

BYRNES, M. M., & SPITZ, H. H. Developmental progression of performance on the Tower of Hanoi problem. *Bulletin of the Psychonomic Society,* 1979, *15,* 379–381.

CASE, R. Structures & strictures: Some functional limitations on the course of cognitive growth. *Cognitive Psychology,* 1974, *6,* 544–573.

CASE. R. Social class differences in intellectual development: A neo-Piagetian investigation. *Canadian Journal of Behavioral Science,* 1975, *7,* 244–261.

CASE, R. Intellectual development from birth to adulthood: A neo-Piagetian interpretation. Pp. 37–72 in R. S. Siegler (Ed.), *Children's thinking: What develops?* Hillsdale, N.J.: Lawrence Erlbaum Associates, 1978.

CHAPMAN, R. H. The development of children's understanding of proportions. *Child Development,* 1975, *46,* 141–148.

CLOUTIER, R., & GOLDSCHMID, M. L. Individual differences in the development of formal reasoning. *Child Development,* 1976, *47,* 1097–1102.

COLLIS, K. F. Operational thinking in elementary mathematics. Pp. 221–283 in J. A. Keats, K. F. Collis, & G. S. Halford (Eds.), *Cognitive development research based on a neo-Piagetian approach.* New York: John Wiley, 1978.

COMETA, N. S., & ESON, M. E. Logical operations and metaphor interpretation: A Piagetian model. *Developmental Psychology,* 1978, *49,* 649–659.

DANNER, F. W., & DAY, M. C. Eliciting formal operations. *Child Development,* 1977, *48,* 1600–1606.

DASEN, P. R. Are cognitive processes universal? A contribution to cross-cultural Piagetian psychology. Pp. 155–201 in N. Warren (Ed.), *Studies in cross-cultural psychology* (Vol. 3). New York: Academic Press, 1977.

DE RIBAUPIERRE, A., & PASCUAL-LEONE, J. Formal operation and

M power: A neo-Piagetian investigation. In D. Kuhn (Ed.), *Intellectual development beyond childhood. New Directions for Child Development,* 1979, *5,* 1–43.

DIAZ-GUERRERO, R. The development of coping style. *Human Development,* 1979, *22,* 320–331.

DIENES, R., & JEEVES, M. A. *Thinking in structures.* London: Hutchinson, 1965.

DUCKWORTH, E. Either we're too early and they can't learn it, or we're too late and they know it already: The dilemma of "applying Piaget," II. *Genetic Epistemologist,* 1978, *7,* 3–7.

DULIT, E. Adolescent thinking à la Piaget: The formal stage. *Journal of Youth and Adolescence,* 1972, *1,* 281–301.

EISERT, D. C., & TOMLINSON-KEASEY, C. Cognitive interpersonal growth during the college freshman year: A structural analysis. *Perceptual and Motor Skills,* 1978, *46,* 995–1005.

ENNIS, R. H. An alternative to Piaget's conceptualization of logical competence. *Child Development,* 1976, *47,* 903–919.

EPSTEIN, H. Phrenoblysis: Special brain and mind growth periods: I. Human brain and skull development. *Developmental Psychobiology,* 1974, *7,* 207–216.

FALMAGNE, R. J. (Ed.). *Reasoning: Representation and process.* Hillsdale, N.J.: Lawrence Erlbaum Associates, 1975.

FELDMAN, C. F. *The development of adaptive intelligence.* San Francisco: Jossey-Bass, 1974.

FELDMAN, C. F., & TOULMIN, S. Logic and the theory of mind. Pp. 409–476 in J. K. Cole (Ed.), *Nebraska Symposium on Motivation.* Lincoln: University of Nebraska Press, 1975.

FIELD, D. The importance of verbal content in the training of Piagetian conservation skills. *Child Development,* 1977, *48,* 1583–1592.

FLAVELL, J. H. *The developmental psychology of Jean Piaget.* Princeton, N.J.: Van Nostrand, 1963.

FLAVELL, J. H. *Cognitive development.* Englewood Cliffs, N.J.: Prentice-Hall, 1977.

FLAVELL, J. H. Metacognition and cognitive monitoring: A new area of cognitive developmental inquiry. *American Psychologist,* 1979, *34,* 906–911.

FLAVELL, J. H., & WOHLWILL, J. F. Formal and functional aspects of cognitive development. Pp. 67–120 in D. Elkind & J. H. Flavell (Eds.), *Studies in cognitive development.* New York: Oxford University Press, 1969.

GALLAGHER, J. M. Reflexive abstraction and education. In J. M. Gallagher & J. Easley (Eds.), *Knowledge and development* (Vol. 2). Piaget and education. New York: Plenum, 1978a.

GALLAGHER, J. M. The future of formal thought: A study of analogy and metaphors. Pp. 77–97 in B. Presseisen, D. Goldstein, & M. Appell (Eds.), *Topics in cognitive development* (Vol. 2). Language and operational thought. New York: Plenum, 1978b.

GELMAN, R., & GALLISTEL, R. *The young child's understanding of number.* Cambridge, Mass.: Harvard University Press, 1979.

GINSBURG, H., & OPPER, S. *Piaget's theory of intellectual development* (2nd ed.). Englewood Cliffs, N.J.: Prentice-Hall, 1979.

GRAVES, A. J. Attainment of conservation of mass, weight and volume in minimally educated adults. *Developmental Psychology,* 1972, *7,* 223.

GRUBER, H., & VONÈCHE, J. Reflexions sur les operations formelles de la pensee. *Archives de Psychologie,* 1976, *44,* 45–55.

HARDY-BROWN, K. Formal operations and the issue of generality: The analysis of poetry by college students. *Human Development,* 1979, *22,* 127–136.

HOLTZMAN, W. Conceptual methods in the cross-cultural study of personality development. *Human Development,* 1979, *22,* 281–295.

HORNBLUM, J., & OVERTON, W. F. Area and volume conservation among the elderly: Assessment and training. *Developmental Psychology,* 1976, *12,* 68–74.

HUMPHREYS, L. G., & PARSONS, C. K. Piagetian tasks measure intelligence and intelligence tests assess cognitive development: A reanalysis. *Intelligence,* 1979, *3,* 369–382.

HUNT, J. McV. Sequential order and plasticity in early psychological development. Pp. 33–49 in M. H. Appell & L. Goldberg (Eds.), *Topics in cognitive development* (Vol. 1). New York: Plenum, 1977.

INHELDER, B. *The diagnosis of reasoning in the mentally retarded.* New York: Harper & Row, Pub., 1968.

INHELDER, B., & PIAGET, J. *The growth of logical thinking.* New York: Basic Books, 1958.

INHELDER, B., SINCLAIR, H., & BOVET, M. *Learning and the develop-*

ment of cognition. Cambridge, Mass.: Harvard University Press, 1974.

JACKSON, S. The growth of logical thinking in normal and subnormal children. *British Journal of Educational Psychology,* 1965, *35,* 255–258.

KAHN, J. V. Training EMR and intellectually average adolescents of low and middle SES for formal thought. *American Journal of Mental Deficiency,* 1974, *79,* 397–403.

KAIL, R. V., & HAGAN, J. W. (Eds.). *Perspectives in the development of memory and cognition.* Hillsdale, N.J.: Lawrence Erlbaum Associates, 1977.

KARMILLOFF-SMITH, A., & INHELDER, B. If you want to get ahead, get a theory. *Cognition,* 1974–1975, *3,* 195–212.

KARPLUS, R. Opportunities for concrete and formal thinking on science tasks. Pp. 183–195 in B. Z. Presseisen, D. Goldstein, & M. H. Appel (Eds.), *Topics in cognitive development* (Vol. 2). New York: Plenum, 1978a.

KARPLUS, R. *Intellectual development beyond elementary school.* Berkeley, Calif.: AESOP ID-51, 1978b.

KARPLUS, R. Education and formal thought—a modest proposal. In I. Siegel, D. Brodzinsky, & R. Golinkoff (Eds.), *Piagetian theory and research: New directions and applications.* Hillsdale, N.J.: Lawrence Erlbaum Associates, 1981.

KEATING, D. P. Precocious cognitive development at the level of formal operations. *Child Development,* 1975, *46,* 276–280.

KEATING, D. P. Adolescent thinking. In J. P. Adelson (Ed.), *Handbook of adolescence.* New York: John Wiley, 1979a.

KEATING, D. P. Toward a multivariate life span theory of intelligence. *New Directions for Child Development,* 1979b, *5,* 69–84.

KEATING, D. P., & SCHAEFER, R. A. Ability and sex differences in the acquisition of formal operations. *Developmental Psychology,* 1975, *11,* 531–532.

KEATS, J. A., COLLIS, K. F., & HALFORD, G. S. *Cognitive development.* New York: John Wiley, 1978.

KENNEY, J. L., & NODINE, C. F. Developmental changes in sensitivity to the content, formal and affective dimensions of painting. *Bulletin of the Psychonomic Society,* 1979, *14,* 463–466.

KERST, S. M., & YOUNISS, J. Complexities of the pendulum problem. *Formal Operator,* 1977, *1*(No. 1), 6–9.

KLAHR, D., & SIEGLER, R. S. The representation of children's knowledge. Pp. 62–116 in H. W. Reese & L. L. Lippitt (Eds.), *Advances in child development and behavior* (Vol. 12). New York: Academic Press, 1978.

KLAHR, D. , & WALLACE, J. G. *Cognitive development: An information processing view.* Hillsdale, N.J.: Lawrence Erlbaum Associates, 1976.

KLEINMAN, J. M. *Haptic perceptual search: The effects of conservation status, reflection-impulsivity, and systematic search training.* Unpublished doctoral dissertation, Rutgers University, 1977.

KLEINMAN, J. M. Developmental changes in haptic exploration and matching accuracy. *Developmental Psychology,* 1979, *15,* 480–481.

KRUTETSKI, V. A. *The psychology of mathematical abilities in school children.* Chicago: University of Chicago Press, 1976.

KUHN, D., & BRANNOCK, J. Development of the isolation of variables scheme in experimental and "natural experiment" contexts. *Developmental Psychology,* 1977, *13,* 9–14.

KUHN, D., & CAPON, N. Logical reasoning in the supermarket: Adult females' use of a proportional reasoning strategy in an everyday context. *Developmental Psychology,* 1979, *15,* 450–452.

KUHN, D., HO, V., & ADAMS, C. Formal reasoning among pre- and late-adolescents. *Child Development,* 1979, *50,* 1128–1135.

KUHN, D., & PHELPS, E. A methodology for observing development of a formal reasoning strategy. *New Direction for Child Development,* 1979, *5,* 45–57.

LARSEN, G. Y. Methodology in developmental psychology: An examination of research on Piagetian theory. *Child Development,* 1977, *48,* 1160–1166.

LAWSON, A. E. Formal operations and field independence in a heterogeneous sample. *Perceptual and Motor Skills,* 1976, *42,* 981–982.

LAWSON, A. E. Relationship among performance on three formal operations tasks. *Journal of Psychology,* 1977, *96,* 235–241.

LAWSON, A. E. The development and validation of a classroom test of formal reasoning. *Journal of Research in Science Teaching,* 1978, *15,* 11–24.

LAWSON, A. E. Relationships among performance of group administered items of formal reasoning. *Perceptual and Motor Skills,* 1979, *48,* 71–78.

LAWSON, A. E., & WOLLMAN, W. T. Cognitive level, cognitive style, and value judgment. *Science Education,* 1977, *61,* 397–407.

LEGRENZI, P. Discovery as a means to understanding. *Quarterly Journal of Experimental Psychology,* 1971, *23,* 417–422.

LINN, M. C. Influence of cognitive style and training on tasks requiring the separation of variables schema. *Child Development,* 1978, *48,* 874–877.

LISTER, C. M. The development of a concept of weight conservation in E. S. N. children. *British Journal of Educational Psychology,* 1969, *39,* 245–252.

LISTER, C. M. The development of a concept of volume conservation in E. S. N. children. *British Journal of Educational Psychology,* 1970, *40,* 55–64.

LISTER, C. M. The development of E. S. N. children's understanding of conservation in a range of attribute situations. *British Journal of Educational Psychology,* 1972, *42,* 14–22.

LONGEOT, F. Analyze statistique de trois tests genetiques colletifs. *Bulletin de l'Institut National d'Étude.* 1965, *20*(No. 4), 219–237.

LOVELL, K. A follow-up study of Inhelder and Piaget, "The growth of logical thinking." *British Journal of Psychology,* 1961, *52,* 143–153.

LOVELL, K., & SHIELDS, J. B. Some aspects of a study of the gifted child. *British Journal of Educational Psychology,* 1967, *37,* 201–208.

LUNZER, E. A. Problems of formal reasoning in test situations. *Monographs of the Society for Research in Child Development,* 1965, *30*(Serial No. 100), 19–46.

LUNZER, E. A. Formal reasoning: A reappraisal. Pp. 47–76 in B. Z. Presseisen, D. Goldstein, & M. H. Appel (Eds.), *Topics in cognitive development* (Vol. 2). New York: Plenum, 1978.

MARTORANO, C. S. A developmental analysis of performance on Piaget's formal operations tasks. *Developmental Psychology,* 1977, *13,* 666–672.

MODGIL, S., & MODGIL, C. *Piagetian research* (Vol. 3). The growth of logic—concrete and formal operations. Atlantic Highlands, N.J.: Humanities Press, 1976.

MOSHMAN, D. Consolidation and stage formation in the emergence of formal operations. *Developmental Psychology,* 1977, *13,* 95–100.

MOSHMAN, D. Logical reasoning in young children: Case study of a paradigm clash. *Formal Operator,* 1978, *1*(No. 4), 9–10.

MOSHMAN, D. To really get ahead get a metatheory. *New Directions for Child Development,* 1979a, *5,* 15–24.

MOSHMAN, D. Development of formal hypothesis-testing ability. *Developmental Psychology,* 1979b, *15,* 104–112.

NEIMARK, E. D. Model for a thinking machine: An information processing framework for the study of cognitive development. *Merrill-Palmer Quarterly,* 1970, *16,* 345–368.

NEIMARK, E. D. An information processing approach to cognitive development. *Transactions New York Academy of Sciences,* 1971, *33,* 516–528.

NEIMARK, E. D. Intellectual development during adolescence. In F. D. Horowitz (Ed.), *Review of child development research* (Vol. 4). Chicago: University of Chicago Press, 1975a.

NEIMARK, E. D. Longitudinal development of formal operations thought. *Genetic Psychology Monographs,* 1975b, *91,* 171–225.

NEIMARK, E. D. The natural history of spontaneous mnemonic activities under conditions of minimal experimental constraint. In A. Pick (Ed.), *Minnesota Symposium* (Vol. 10). Minneapolis: University of Minnesota Press, 1976.

NEIMARK, E. D. Current status of formal operations research. *Human Development,* 1979, *22,* 60–67.

NEIMARK, E. D. Toward the disembedding of formal operations from confounding with cognitive style. In I. Sigel, D. Brodzinsky, & R. Golinkoff (Eds.), *Piagetian theory and research: New directions and applications.* Hillsdale, N.J.: Lawrence Erlbaum Associates, 1981.

NEIMARK, E. D., & CHAPMAN, R. H. Development of the comprehension of logical quantifiers. Pp. 135–152 in R. J. Falmagne (Ed.), *Reasoning: Representation and process.* Hillsdale, N.J.: Lawrence Erlbaum Associates, 1975.

NEIMARK, E. D., & ESTES, W. K. *Stimulus sampling theory.* San Francisco: Holden-Day, 1967.

NEWELL, A., & SIMON, H. A. *Human problem solving.* Englewood Cliffs, N.J.: Prentice-Hall, 1972.

OATLEY, K. G. Inference, navigation and cognitive maps. Pp.

537–547 in P. N. Johnson-Laird & P. C. Wason (Eds.), *Thinking.* Cambridge, England: Cambridge University Press, 1977.

O'BRIEN, T. C., & SHAPIRO, B. J. The development of logical thinking in children. *American Educational Research Journal,* 1968, *5,* 531–542.

OSHERSON, D. N. *Logical abilities in children* (Vol. 3). Reasoning in adolescence: Deductive inference. Hillsdale, N.J.: Lawrence Erlbaum Associates, 1975.

OVERTON, W. F. General systems, structure and development. Pp. 61–81 in K. F. Riegel & G. C. Rosenwald (Eds.), *Structure and transformation.* New York: John Wiley, 1975.

OVERTON, W. F., & REESE, H. W. Conceptual prerequisites for an understanding of stability-change and continuity-discontinuity. *International Journal of Behavioral Development,* 1981, *4,* 99–123.

PAPALIA, D. E. The status of several conservation abilities across the life span. *Human Development,* 1972, *15,* 229–243.

PARIS, S. G. Comprehension of language connectives and propositional logical relationships. *Journal of Experimental Child Psychology,* 1973, *16,* 278–291.

PASCUAL-LEONE, J. *Cognitive development and cognitive style: A general psychological integration.* Unpublished doctoral dissertation, University of Geneva, 1969.

PASCUAL-LEONE, J. A mathematical model for the transition rule in Piaget's developmental stages. *Acta Psychologica,* 1970, *32,* 301–345.

PASCUAL-LEONE, J. Metasubjective problems of construction: Forms of knowing and their psychological mechanism. *Canadian Psychological Review,* 1976a, *17,* 110–125.

PASCUAL-LEONE, J. On learning and development, Piagetian style: II. A critical historical analysis of Geneva's research programme. *Canadian Psychological Review,* 1976b, *17,* 289–297.

PASCUAL-LEONE, J. Constructive problems for constructive theories: The current relevance of Piaget's work and a critique of information processing simulation psychology. In H. Spada & R. Kluwe (Eds.), *Developmental models of thinking.* New York: Academic Press, 1980.

PASCUAL-LEONE, J., & GOODMAN, D. *Cognitive style factors in linguistic performance.* Paper presented at Canadian Psychological Association, Windsor, 1974.

PEEL, E. A. *The nature of adolescent judgment.* New York: Wiley-Interscience, 1971.

PEEL, E. A. Predilection for generalizing and abstracting. *British Journal of Educational Psychology,* 1975, *45,* 177–188.

PIAGET, J. Intellectual evolution from adolescence to adulthood. *Human Development,* 1972, *15,* 1–12.

PIAGET, J. *The grasp of consciousness.* Cambridge, Mass.: Harvard University Press, 1976.

PULOS, S. M., & LINN, M. C. Pitfalls and pendulums. *Formal Operator,* 1978, *1*(No. 2), 9–11.

RAVEN, R. J. The development of a test of Piaget's logical operations. *Science Education,* 1973, *57*(No. 3), 33–40.

RIEGEL, K. F. Dialectic operations: The final period of cognitive development. *Human Development,* 1973, *16,* 346–370.

ROBERGE, J. R., & FLEXER, B. K. Further examination of formal operational reasoning abilities. *Child Development,* 1979, *50,* 478–484.

SCANDURA, J. Role of higher-order rules in problem solving. *Journal of Experimental Psychology,* 1974, *102*(No. 6), 984–991.

SCARDAMALIA, M. Information processing capacity and the problem of horizontal decalage: A demonstration using combinatorial reasoning tasks. *Child Development,* 1977, *48,* 28–37.

SEEFELDT, F. M. Formal operations and adolescent painting. *Genetic Epistemologist,* 1979, *5*(No. 3), 5–6.

SHAKLEE, H. Bounded rationality and cognitive development: Upper limits on growth? *Cognitive Psychology,* 1979, *11,* 327–345.

SHAYER, M. Has Piaget's construct of formal operational thinking any utility? *British Journal of Educational Psychology,* 1979, *49*(No. 3), 265–276.

SHAYER, M., KÜCHEMAN, D. E., & WYLAM, H. The distribution of Piagetian stages of thinking in British middle and secondary school children. *British Journal of Educational Psychology,* 1976, *46,* 164–173.

SHAYER, M., & WYLAM, H. The distribution of Piagetian stages of thinking in British middle and secondary school children, II: 14 to 16 year old and sex differentials. *British Journal of Educational Psychology,* 1978, *48,* 62–70.

SIEGLER, R. S. Three aspects of cognitive development. *Cognitive Psychology,* 1976, *8,* 481–520.

SIEGLER, R. S., & LIEBERT, R. M. Acquisition of formal scientific reasoning by 10 to 13 year olds. Designing a factorial experiment. *Developmental Psychology,* 1975, *11,* 401–402.

SIEGLER, R. S., & VAGO, S. The development of a proportionality concept: Judging relative fullness. *Journal of Experimental Child Psychology,* 1978, *25,* 371–395.

SIMON, H. A. The functional equivalence of problem solving skills. *Cognitive Psychology,* 1975, *7,* 268–288.

SINNOTT, J. D. Everyday thinking and Piagetian operativity in adults. *Human Development,* 1975, *18,* 430–443.

SMEDSLUND, J. The acquisition of conservation of substance and weight in children III. *Scandinavian Journal of Psychology,* 1961, *2,* 85–87.

SOMERVILLE, S. C. The pendulum problem. *British Journal of Educational Psychology,* 1974, *44,* 266–281.

SOMERVILLE, S. C., & WELLMAN, H. M. The development of understanding as an indirect memory strategy. *Journal of Experimental Child Psychology,* 1979, *27,* 71–86.

SPITZ, H. H. The universal nature of human intelligence: Evidence from games. *Intelligence,* 1978, *2,* 371–379.

SPITZ, H. H. Intellectual extremes, mental age, and the nature of human intelligence. Unpublished manuscript, 1981.

STAUDENMAYER, H., & BOURNE, L. E. Learning to interpret conditional sentences: A developmental study. *Developmental Psychology,* 1977, *13,* 616–623.

STEPHENS, B., & MCLAUGHLIN, J. A. Two-year gains on reasoning by retarded and non-retarded persons. *American Journal of Mental Deficiency,* 1974, *79,* 116–126.

STERNBERG, R. J. The nature of mental abilities. *American Psychologist,* 1979a, *34*(No. 3), 214–230.

STERNBERG, R. J. Developmental patterns in the encoding and combination of logical connectives. *Journal of Experimental Child Psychology,* 1979b, *28,* 469–498.

STERNBERG, R. J., & RIFKIN, B. The development of analogical reasoning processes. *Journal of Experimental Child Psychology,* 1979, *27,* 195–232.

STONE, C. A., & DAY, M. C. Levels of availability of a formal operational strategy. *Child Development,,* 1978, *49,* 1054–1065.

STONE, C. A., & DAY, M. C. Competence and performance models and the characterization of formal operational skills. *Human Development,* 1980, *23,* 323–353.

STRAUSS, S., DANZIGER, J., & RAMATI, T. University students' understanding of nonconservation: Implications for structural reversions. *Developmental Psychology,* 1977, *13,* 359–363.

STRAUSS, S., & KROY, M. The child as logician or methodologist? A critique of formal operations. *Human Development,* 1977, *20,* 102–117.

TAMIR, P. The relationship between achievement in biology and cognitive preference styles in high school students. *British Journal of Educational Psychology,* 1976, *46,* 57–67.

TAPLIN, J. E., & STAUDENMAYER, H. Interpretation of abstract conditional sentences in deductive reasoning. *Journal of Verbal Learning and Verbal Behavior,* 1973, *12,* 530–542.

TAPLIN, J. E., STAUDENMAYER, H., & TADDONIO, J. L. Developmental changes in conditional reasoning: Linguistic or logical? *Journal of Experimental Child Psychology,* 1974, *17,* 360–373.

TISHER, R. P., & DALE, L. G. *Understanding in science test.* Victoria: Australian Council for Educational Research, 1975.

TOMLINSON-KEASEY, C. *Introduction to formal operations task.* Unpublished manuscript, University of Nebraska, 1975.

TOMLINSON-KEASEY, C. Structures, functions, and stages: A trio of unsolved issues in formal operations. In S. Modgil & C. Modgil (Eds.), *The taming of Piaget: Crossfire and crosscurrents.* London: National Foundation for Educational Research, 1981.

TOMLINSON-KEASEY, C., CRAWFORD, D. G., & EISERT, D. C. Organization facilitates memory—if you have the appropriate classification skills. *Journal of Genetic Psychology,* 1979, *134,* 3–13.

TOMLINSON-KEASEY, C., EISERT, D. C., KAHLE, L. R., HARDY-BROWN, K., & KEASEY, B. The structure of concrete operational thought. *Child Development,* 1979, *50,* 115–116.

TRABASSO, T. Memory processes in logical thought. In R. V. Kail & J. W. Hagen (Eds.), *Perspective on the development of memory and cognition.* Hillsdale, N.J.: Lawrence Erlbaum Associates, 1977.

TUDDENHAM, R. D. A Piagetian scale of cognitive development. In W. B. Dockrell (Ed.), *On intelligence: The Toronto Symposium, 1969.* London: Methuen, 1970.

WARD, J. The saga of Butch and Slim. *British Journal of Educational Psychology*, 1972, *42*, 267–289.

WASON, P. C., & JOHNSON-LAIRD, P. N. *Psychology of reasoning.* Cambridge, Mass.: Harvard University Press, 1972.

WEBB, R. A. Concrete and formal operations in very bright 6–11 year olds. *Human Development*, 1974, *17*, 292–300.

WEITZ, J. R., & ZIGLER, E. Cognitive development in retarded and nonretarded persons: Piagetian tests of the similar sequence hypothesis. *Psychological Bulletin*, 1979, *86*, 831–851.

WILTON, K. M., & BOERSMA, F. J. Conservation research with the mentally retarded. In N. R. Ellis (Ed.), *International review of research in mental retardation* (Vol. 7). New York: Academic Press, 1974.

WITKIN, H. A., DYK, R. B., PATERSON, H. F., GOODENOUGH, D. R., & KARP, S. A. *Psychological differentiation.* New York: John Wiley, 1962.

WITKIN, H. A., MOORE, C. A., GOODENOUGH, D. R., & COX, P. W. Field-dependent and field-independent cognitive styles and their educational implications. *Review of Educational Research*, 1977, *47*, 1–64.

WOHLWILL, J. F. *The study of behavioral development.* New York: Academic Press, 1973.

WOLLMAN, W., EYLON, B. S., & LAWSON, A. E. Acceptance of lack of closure: Is it an index of advanced reasoning? *Child Development*, 1979, *50*, 656–665.

WYATT, K. B., & GEIS, M. F. Level of formal thought and organizational memory strategies. *Developmental Psychology*, 1978, *14*, 433–444.

YOST, P. A., SIEGEL, A. E., & ANDREWS, J. M. Non-verbal probability judgments by young children. *Child Development*, 1962, *33*, 769–780.

28

Social Behavior
in Adolescence

RICHARD M. LERNER

JUDY A. SHEA

Human behavior is basically social. Biological adaptation requires meeting the demands of the environment, and ecologically prototypic milieus contain other conspecifics. Adjustment to these other organisms becomes a requisite of survival (Lerner, 1979; Lerner & Busch-Rossnagel, 1981); hence, biological adaptation is, in essence, social behavior. Anthropological information (e.g., Washburn, 1961) indicates that the relative defenselessness of early humans, coupled with the dangers of living on the open African savannah, made group living essential for survival. The content of evolution was such that it was more adaptive to act in concert with the group than in isolation. Accordingly processes facilitating social relatedness were selected over the course of human evolution (Hogan, Johnson, & Emler, 1978; Sahlins, 1978).

No form of life, as we know it, comes into existence independent of other life, and no animal lives in total isolation from its conspecifics across its entire life span (Tobach & Schneirla, 1968). Humans at all portions of their life span may be seen as embedded in a social context within which they interact. The social context is composed of other humans as well as social institutions. Given that all humans within the social context have some evolutionary and ontogenetic bases of social behavior, humans do not merely exist within a social context; they interact within it. In other words there is reason to believe that a specific type of relation exists between

people and their contexts: a multidirectional one. Adaption to one's context involves bidirectional influences involving changes in the context to fit individual "needs" and changes in the individual to meet contextual "demands" (Dobzhansky, 1973; Harris, 1957; Lerner, 1978; Piaget, 1970)—that is, such interactions may involve one or multiple components of the context and one or more individual-psychological processes (Riegel, 1975, 1976a, 1976b). The individual behavioral processes of the developing person should be moderated by variables in the social context, and the character of the social context should be altered in relation to the individuality of the people interacting within it (Lerner, 1979; Lerner & Busch-Rossnagel, 1981; Lewis & Lee-Painter, 1974; Sameroff, 1975).

Such complex multilevel and multidirectional relations between an individual and his/her context have been labeled *dynamic interactions* (Lerner, 1978, 1979; Lerner & Busch-Rossnagel, 1981; Lerner & Spanier, 1978, 1980). A synopsis of this view is that there are several sources of development and that each source is influenced by and influences all other sources. As such, changes in one source (e.g., the social context or the individual) will promote changes in all others. From this view then the potential for change is continual across the life span; this suggests that there are no totally fixed characteristics of development.

The study of interactions between individuals and their social contexts has been undertaken at several portions of the life span. Data supportive of the presence of such relations exist in infancy (Lewis & Rosenblum, 1974), childhood (Burgess & Conger, 1978), and adolescence (Bengtson & Troll, 1978). Despite this support, at this writing most of the empirical literature pertaining to a particular portion of the life span has not been derived on the basis of a conceptual framework emphasizing dy-

The authors thank Nora Newcombe and Jacqueline V. Lerner for critical readings of the manuscript and Graham B. Spanier for contributing to many of the ideas expressed in this chapter. Work on this chapter was completed while the first author was a Fellow at the Center for Advanced Study in the Behavioral Sciences, and he appreciates the assistance of the center's staff. He is also grateful for the financial support provided by National Institute of Mental Health Grant 5-T32-MH14581-05 and by the John D. and Catherine T. MacArthur Foundation.

namic interactions. In fact the theoretical themes running through most existing research on social behavior emphasize either personological variables as providing the primary impetus for social engagement or disengagement (e.g., Cumming & Henry, 1961; Erikson, 1959, 1968) or the unidirectional molding of social behavior by the external socializing environment (Hartup, 1978). Dynamic person-context interactions have thus received relatively little empirical attention.

Such omission may be unfortunate not only because of the multidisciplinary data suggesting that such interactions serve important evolutionary and ontogenetic functions but also because there may be several portions of the life span that may be particularly informed by such a conceptual orientation. In our view adolescence is one such developmental period. Despite the generally personological—or "social mold" (Hartup, 1978)—theoretical stance guiding research, the empirical literature in adolescence often supports the view that major, often qualitative, changes occur in the linkages people show to their social context. Alterations in social behavior involving the institution of the family, educational and political institutions, and the roles played in one's society are some of the well-documented changes in adolescent social behavior (Lerner & Spanier, 1980). In turn there is increasing evidence that different intraindividual psychological changes at this time of life are associated with different contextual (e.g., familial, college vs. noncollege) milieus (e.g., Haan, Smith, & Block, 1968; Hoffman, 1975) and with historical changes in the context (Nesselroade & Baltes, 1974). The literature on social behavior in adolescence may be usefully integrated by employing a dynamic interactional model of social functioning.

Such a demonstration is the goal of this chapter. We will review literature pertinent to selected aspects of the adolescent's social context (e.g., the institution of the family) and appraise whether ideas pertinent to dynamic interactions between the person and his/her context are useful in ordering, integrating, and extending these data. We will focus on a major aspect of individual development in adolescence, one having a clear import for social functioning—that is, moral development—in order to assess the use of such interaction notions for understanding the literature pertinent to this component of ontogenetic progression. Our goal is to be illustrative and not exhaustive. Much of the burden of reviewing literature relevant to adolescent social behavior has been given to other chapters in this volume (e.g., those pertaining to sexuality, peer group, and popular culture in adolescence). On the other hand there will be instances where topics discussed in other chapters (e.g., morality) will be dealt with here. However, our treatment—focusing exclusively on the adolescent period through use of the dynamic interactional notion—will largely obviate repetition. We will begin by focusing on the roles of major institutions in adolescent social behavior.

THE ROLES OF SOCIAL INSTITUTIONS IN ADOLESCENT SOCIAL BEHAVIOR

Dynamic interactional changes in adolescence would involve reciprocal, multidirectional exchanges between the adolescent and his/her environment. The environment includes both other people and numerous societal institutions such as religion, education, and politics. Additional contextual variables such as the mass media, economic factors, and contemporary cultural and subcultural issues also undoubtedly influence and are influenced by adolescent development. The following section will only illustrate the use of the dynamic interactionist view by discussing both basic and general components of the social context: familial and peer influences and social roles, respectively.

The Influences of Parents and Peers

Adolescents interact with both family and peer groups, and one may ask how such dual commitments influence the adolescent's behavior and socialization. Do the family and peer relationships that adolescents have contribute in similar ways to their development? Is one set of relationships more influential, or are the influences so different they cannot be compared? There are data to suggest that both parents and peers are important. Depending on the context and meaning of the social relationship, either parents or peers may be shown to be more influential.

Douvan and Adelson (1966) indicate that among 14- to 18-year-old male and female adolescents there are few, if any, serious disagreements with parents. They report that in choosing their peers adolescents are oriented toward those who have attitudes and values consistent with those maintained by the parents. Similarly Smith (1976), in a study of over 1000 sixth- through twelfth-grade, urban and suburban, black and white adolescents, found that adolescents sought the advice and considered the opinions of parents, more than those of peers. Similar findings have been reported by Kandel and Lesser (1972).

Although there are data indicating that in adolescence the person spends more time with peers than with parents (Bandura, 1964; Douvan & Adelson, 1966), this shift in time commitments does not necessarily indicate a corresponding alteration from parental to peer influence. Costanzo and Shaw (1966) found that conformity to peer group norms increased between 7 and 12 years of age for males and females, but it declined thereafter. Floyd and South (1972) studied sixth-, eighth-, tenth-, and twelfth-grade males' and females' orientation to parents and peers. They found less orientation to parents and more orientation to peers, primarily at higher grade levels. Nevertheless there was a mixed orientation to both parents and peers in older age groups. Not only are the influences of parents and peers compatible in the values and behavioral orientations they direct to adolescents (Douvan & Adelson, 1966), but also at older ages adolescents show an orientation to be influenced simultaneously by both generational groups (Floyd & South, 1972).

Which generational group is more influential at any particular time is dependent on the issue adolescents are confronting. Floyd and South (1972) found that when parents were seen as the better source about a particular issue adolescents were more parent- than peer-oriented. Larson (1972) also found that the demands of the particular choice situation (e.g., those associated with school or with dating) determined adolescents' choices, regardless of the direction of parent or peer pressures. This was true despite the fact that the fourth-, ninth-, and twelfth-graders Larson (1972) studied more often complied with parental than with peer desires. Similarly Brittain (1963, 1969) found that both parents and peers influence adolescents, depending on the issue at hand; adolescent females were more likely to accept the advice of parents concerning the future and the advice of peers concerning school-related issues. Consistent with Brittain's data Kandel and Lesser (1969) reported that 85 percent of the middle-class adolescents and 82 percent of the lower-class adolescents they sampled were influenced directly by parents in formulating future goals (in this case concerning educational plans).

Other studies also show an orientation to both parents and peers, depending on the issue of concern. Chand, Crider, and Willets (1975) found agreement between adolescents and parents on issues related to religion and marriage but not on issues related to sex and drugs. Similarly Kelley (1972) found high parent-adolescent similarity on moral issues but not on issues pertinent to style of dress, hair length, and hours of sleep. Several studies indicate that although groups of adolescents and parents have somewhat different attitudes about issues of contemporary social concern (e.g., war, drug use, and sexuality), most of these differences reflect contrasts in attitude intensity rather than attitude direction (Lerner, Karson, Meisels, & Knapp, 1975; Lerner & Knapp, 1975; Lerner, Schroeder, Rewitzer, & Weinstock, 1972; Weinstock & Lerner, 1972).

Consistent with the preceding data indicating influences by both peers and parents, there are data suggesting that adolescents perceive their own attitudes as lying between these two generational groups. In one study (Lerner et al., 1975), adolescents were asked to rate their own attitudes toward a list of 36 statements pertaining to the issues of contemporary social concern noted before; they rated these same statements in terms of how they thought their peers would respond to them, and they responded in terms of how they thought their parents would answer. The adolescents tended to see their own attitudes as lying *between* those of others of their own generation and those of their parents' generation (with 75 percent of the items). Adolescents tended to place their own positions between the "conservative" end of the continuum, where they tended to put parents, and the "liberal" end, where they tended to place peers. Thus adolescents think their peers are more liberal than they actually are since the average of their groups' "own" attitudes *is* their peers' attitudes.

The preceding data suggest that adolescents and their parents do not have many major differences in attitudes and values. Apparently the impact of the intra- and intergenerational social contexts is often compatible. Indeed adolescents tend to perceive that their values lie between those of their parents and peers. Despite the character of the influences of parents and peers that actually exist for the adolescent, there are recurring reports in the media and elsewhere that suggest significant disparities between adolescents and their parents. Often this impression is based on the belief that adolescence is necessarily a period of developmental turmoil—that is, a pe-

riod involving a disruption in previously established person-social context relations (e.g., as would be involved in a "gap" in attitudes, behaviors, or values appearing between youth and their parents, cf. Bandura, 1964; Gallatin, 1975). In the next sections we evaluate evidence bearing on the presence of such social relations in adolescence.

Types of Intergenerational Relations. There can be different types of intergenerational relations characteristic of society at any time in history. Bengtson (1970) describes several such types, defining each in relation to the extent to which the behaviors, values, and attitudes of one generation are consistent with those of another. If there is great consistency between adolescents and their parents and other adults, there is likely to be little social change. When there is little consistency between these generational groups, a greater degree of social change would be likely. Thus to Bengtson (1970) alternative types of intergenerational relations constitute contrasting modes of social change. It is possible to find historical times and/or societies where any of several types of social relationships were prominent. However in this chapter it is useful to consider the type of intergenerational relationship most characteristic of adolescents in contemporary society.

Studies of Intergenerational Relations. The data reviewed before suggest that when the *actual* attitudes of adolescents and their parents are compared, few major differences in attitudes can be found, although intensity differences often do exist. Most studies find even this type of intergenerational disparity to occur in only a minority of attitude comparisons between the generations (Lerner et al., 1975; Lerner & Knapp, 1975; Lerner et al., 1972). These data suggest that the purported generation gap may not be real (Adelson, 1970).

Nevertheless there are both empirical and theoretical reasons to expect that a generation gap might exist to some degree. There are data showing that adolescents and parents do not perceive the influence of social relationships accurately. Adolescents perceive their parents to be less influential than they actually are, while parents perceive themselves to be more influential than they actually are (Bengtson & Troll, 1978; Lerner, 1975; Lerner & Knapp, 1975). For example, two studies compared the actual and the perceived attitudes of adolescents and parents (Lerner et al., 1975; Lerner & Knapp, 1975). Actual intergenerational differences in attitudes about issues of contemporary societal concern occurred with fewer than 30 percent of the comparisons made in either study by Lerner and colleagues. However in both investigations adolescents *overestimated* the magnitude of the differences that existed between themselves and their parents; they saw their parents as having attitudes less congruent with their own than was actually the case. In both studies parents *underestimated* the extent of the differences between themselves and their children; they saw their children as having attitudes very consistent with their own. Thus although only a small and selective generation gap can be said to actually exist, parents underestimate this division, while adolescents overestimate it.

Both psychological and sociological theorists have

suggested reasons for the existence of these different perceptions regarding the generation gap. Erikson (1959, 1963) believes adolescence is a period in life which involves the establishment of a sense of personal identity, of self-definition. Other theorists (e.g., Elkind, 1967; Piaget, 1950, 1970) believe that adolescence is a period involving the development of new thought capabilities; these capabilities lead adolescents to believe their ideas are not only new in their own lives, but in general as well. Adolescents need to establish their own identities, and their beliefs in the uniqueness of their thoughts facilitate this. These beliefs may lead them to think they are quite different from those around them, especially their parents. This might result in their overemphasizing and magnifying whatever differences actually exist (Lerner, 1975).

A sociological approach suggests why parents might minimize differences between themselves and their children. Bengtson and Kuypers (1971) suggest that members of the parental generational group have a stake in maximizing consistency between themselves and members of their children's generation. The parents have "invested" in society, for example, by pursuing their careers and accumulating society's resources. Because they want to protect their investment, they want to rear their children—the new members of society—in ways that will maintain the society in which they have invested. It may be that as a consequence of such a "generational stake" (Bengtson & Kuypers, 1971; Bengtson & Troll, 1978) parents are oriented to believing they have produced children who—because they agree with parental attitudes—will protect their investment. This orientation is consistent with one Erikson (1959, 1963) describes; he believes that adults have a psychosocial need to feel they have generated children who will perpetuate society. This idea, as well as the generational stake, suggests that parents may be oriented to minimizing whatever differences exist between themselves and their adolescent children.

In summary both theory and research combine to suggest that the adolescent's social context is composed of not one, but several, generation gaps. First, there exists a relatively minor and selective set of differences between adolescents and their parents. However in addition to this actual gap, there exist two perceived gaps: the overestimated one of the adolescents and the underestimated one of the parents. The simultaneous presence of these gaps, at the very least, makes the social context of the adolescent a complex, diverse setting. Nevertheless it is not necessary that the presence of such phenomena in adolescence requires the period to be a stormy, stressful one insofar as adolescent-parent relations are concerned. Indeed the following evidence suggests that disruptive adolescent-parent relations are not emblematic of adolescence.

Adolescent Storm and Stress: Fact or Fiction? G. Stanley Hall, who proposed the first scientific theory of adolescent development, depicted adolescence as a recapitulationist transition period between an uncivilized, beast-like state and a civilized, human-like one. Such a transition, he argued, gave an emotional and behavioral texture to the period that inevitably involved storm and stress (Gallatin, 1975; Hall, 1904). Like the recapitulationist theory from which it was derived, this conception is inconsistent with a wealth of data derived from diverse sources (Lerner & Spanier, 1980; Thorndike, 1904).

As early as the 1920s and 1930s data were available from cross-cultural studies of adolescence that spoke against the universality of storm and stress. These cultural anthropological studies (e.g., Mead, 1928, 1930) demonstrated that in some societies adolescence is a quiescent, stable period of personal and social development. Additionally these studies showed that in some other societies there is no period of life corresponding to what Western civilization labels *adolescence.* As a consequence of a puberty or a fertility rite, there is a rapid, abrupt transition from child to adult status (Mead, 1930) with no time for any prolonged turmoil.

It is possible that nature theorists such as Hall, who believe that effects of inherited characteristics are more pervasive than are socialization influences, would argue that using events from non-Western societies to evaluate the character of adolescence in Western societies is not appropriate because of the possibly different genetic background of the two groups. There is as much genotypic diversity within any one group as between any two groups (Hirsch, 1970; Lewontin, 1976), and thus such a view would not be a tenable one. Nevertheless one may look at studies done within Western civilization and still find evidence inconsistent with a notion of universal storm and stress (Wolman, 1973).

Bandura (1964; Bandura & Walters, 1959) interviewed middle-class families with adolescent boys. The findings of this research run counter to the idea that adolescence is a typically stressful period. Although it is stereotypically held that parents of adolescents become more controlling and prohibitive of their children, Bandura (1964) reports that by the time of adolescence the males had adopted parental values and standards to such an extent that parental restrictions were actually reduced. Similarly Bandura notes that, although the storm-and-stress notion of adolescence suggests a struggle by youth to free themselves of dependence on parents, independence training had begun during childhood for the males in his sample. As such, independence was largely accomplished by adolescence. Although adolescence is a time when people begin to move from having primary ties with parents to having primary ties with peers, Bandura did not find that choosing friends was a major source of friction between parents and adolescents. He found that adolescents tended to form friendships with those who shared similar values, and as such, the peers tended to support those standards of the parents that the boys had already adopted.

Bandura points out, however, that these data cannot be construed to mean that adolescence is a stressless, problem-free period of life. He is careful to note that *no* period of life is free of crisis or adjustment problems, and any period of life may present particular adjustment problems for some people and not for others. Indeed Bandura (1964) notes that in the portion of his study that assessed a sample of antisocial boys whose excessive aggression did lead to their adolescence being associated with storm and stress one could not appropriately view their problems as being derived from their adolescence per se. Bandura found that their problem behaviors were present through their childhood as well. However when the boys were physically smaller, the parents were able to control their aggressive behavior better than they could during adolescence. Thus while adolescence seemed to be a stormy period for some boys, it was more a function of the boys' previous history than of the adolescent portion of life.

Offer (1969), also studying adolescent boys, found three major routes through the adolescent period. He notes that there is a *continuous growth* type of development involving smooth and nonabrupt changes in behavior. Subjects here were not in any major conflict with their parents and did not feel parental rearing practices were inappropriate or parental values were different from their own. Most adolescents fell into this category, and such a pattern is like the one we have seen Bandura (1964) describe. A second type of pattern is *surgent growth;* development involves an abrupt spurt, analogous to transitions in cultures having puberty or fertility rites. Such rapid progression does not necessarily involve the turmoil associated with storm and stress. However, Offer (1969) did identify a *tumultuous growth* type of adolescent development; crisis, stress, and problems characterize the period. For such adolescents "storm and stress" aptly characterizes the nature of their change.

Thus the adolescent period is one of storm and stress only for some people. Indeed, based on the Bandura (1964) and Offer (1969) data, it may be assumed that such a tumultuous period involves only a minority of adolescents. Moreover although this conclusion is derived from these two studies of male adolescents, it is bolstered by the data of Douvan and Adelson (1966) who studied both male and female adolescents. As in the previously noted studies, most males and females shared the basic values of their parents and were satisfied with their family life and their parents' treatment of them. Indeed girls exemplified this pattern even more than boys did. Douvan and Adelson found only a few signs of rebellion or conflict, and most girls regarded parental rules as fair and appropriate. Only 25 percent of the females had *any* reservation at all about parental rules, and only 5 percent considered these rules unjust or severe. Moreover about 50 percent of the girls studied took part in setting their own rules, although whether they participated did not relate to their degree of satisfaction with their parents.

In summary, available data indicate that adolescence is not universally a stressful period. More often than not it seems adolescent experiences do not involve major upheavals, maladaptive developments, or angry, antagonistic interpersonal relations with parents. Yet there are some adolescents who do experience some of these negative events, and others who experience all of them. Accordingly there is a range of potential developments that can characterize adolescence within even the same cultural or familial setting. Particular developmental outcomes appear to derive from the specific combination of peer group pressures, family orientations, contextual issues being confronted (e.g., education versus sexuality), and personological statuses (e.g., regarding ego and cognitive development) that pertain to a given adolescent existing within a specific sociocultural-historical milieu.

We will continue to see the role of such complex interactions as we consider the topic of social roles and social institutions in adolescent social behavior.

Roles and Social Behavior in Adolescence

Society would not have evolved if humans could have survived in complete social isolation. Hominid evolution on the African savannah involved selection for social cooperation and interdependency since humans as independent units were characterized by relative defenselessness—e.g., lack of claws and sharp teeth (Sahlins, 1978; Washburn, 1961). Thus social behaviors appear to have provided a means for the perpetuation and maintenance of humanity. Social interrelations probably began because all behaviors needed for an individual's survival could not efficiently be emitted by that single person; different people came to emit different behaviors—that is, social roles emerged. A division of labor according to sex probably came about since men, as the physically stronger members of the social unit, were needed to do the hunting, fishing, gathering, and physically demanding agricultural tasks requisite for survival on the savannah, while females, as a result of pregnancy, childbirth, and breast-feeding, were given tasks associated with childbearing and rearing (Block, 1973).

As the settings within which humans lived changed and became more differentiated and complex, new adaptational demands were placed on people in order for them to maintain and perpetuate themselves. One social unit could not, for example, produce all the resources necessary for survival. Different units took on different roles, and role structure became more complex, more specialized, and more interdependent as society evolved.

We must reemphasize that because individuals needed the group for their survival at the same time that the group needed individuals (to populate it and to perpetuate it) children born into a society were always instructed in the rules and tasks of that society (i.e., they were socialized) in order to ensure their eventual contribution to society's maintenance. Society, the roles it evolves, and the process of socialization within society are all components of adaptive individual and social functioning.

Various theorists have described this adaptive linkage between the person and his/her social context (Brent, 1978; Hogan et al., 1978). In the study of adolescence Erikson's (1959, 1963) ideas about this function of social roles have been the most prominent. To Erikson the aspect of the person attaining the competency to perform these individual-social linkages is the ego. Independent of whether or not one chooses to talk of an *ego* as being involved, all theorists agree that the person must attain those skills requisite for survival in his/her society. Yet it is clear that the demands placed on the person are not constant across life. Although society may expect certain behaviors of its adult members, similar expectations are not maintained for infants, children, and in some societies, adolescents. In other words the adaptive demands on an adolescent may not be the same as those on any other age group.

The Nature of Roles in Adolescence

The adolescent period, involving so many changes, may produce special adaptational demands on the person. The body looks and feels different. The adolescent thinks differently, may judge right and wrong differently, engages in different types of social relationships, and acquires a new genital capacity. The combination of all these transitions has a dramatic effect. Prior to adolescence the person's characteristics changed in less rapid ways (e.g., the quantitative changes involved in height and weight) and, if cognized by the person, were thought of in relatively concrete, nonabstract terms—that is, while going through such changes gradually, the person's definition of self was based on relatively continuous, concrete cues.

With adolescence, not only are there discontinuities, but their potential impact for the future is also uncertain. The attributes defining the person are in a stage of change, and their eventual developmental endpoint is far from certain for the person. Yet the adolescent must integrate all these changing cues by reestablishing a definition of self in order to interact adaptively with his/her social context.

Defining or identifying oneself becomes a central task in adolescence. Who they are, their identity, gives adolescents an integrated specification of what they will do with their bodies, with their sexuality, with their minds, with their relationships, and with their morality. In turn society wants to know what socially prescribed set of behaviors will be adopted. Such a set of behaviors is a role, and thus the key aspect of this adolescent dilemma is one of finding a role. This need is termed by Erikson (1959) the *identity crisis*. To resolve this crisis and achieve a sense of identity, Erikson (1959) sees the necessity for attaining a complex synthesis between psychological processes and societal goals and directives.

At one time, it will appear to refer to a conscious sense of individual identity; at another to an unconscious striving for a continuity of personal character; at a third, as a criterion for the silent doings of ego synthesis; and finally, as a maintenance of an inner solidarity with a group's ideals and identity. (Erikson, 1959, p. 57)

To achieve identity, then, the adolescent must find an orientation to life that both fulfills the attributes of the self and at the same time is consistent with what society expects of a person. As such this orientation must be both individually and socially adaptive. Most research on adolescent role behavior has been influenced to some extent by Erikson's ideas about the identity crisis and about ego development. The contribution of his work is apparent in the succeeding sections.

Identity Development in Adolescence: Research Directions

Research about adolescent identity processes has fallen into three interrelated catagories. First, there has been research assessing whether ego identity occurs in a stage-like progression as theorists such as Erikson (1959) specify. Do issues of industry versus inferiority invariably precede those of identity versus role confusion, and in turn, do these issues always become of concern prior to problems of intimacy versus isolation? If such universality of sequencing were to be found, Erikson's (1959) ideas about the critical importance of successful development in a prior stage for subsequent stage functioning would be supported. If such universality were not found, a search would be appropriate for those variables which provide a basis of the various sequences of ego development that could occur.

A second direction that research about adolescent identity processes has taken has been to focus on what changes, if any, occur in a person's identity status over time. Erikson describes the identity crisis as a bipolar continuum ranging from identity to role confusion. A person may have a location along this continuum close to the identity end, close to the confusion or diffusion end, or at any one of several points in between. Researchers (e.g., Marcia, 1964, 1966) have tried to describe the array of different statuses a person may have along this dimension and how, across life, these statuses may change.

Because Erikson's sequences have not been found to be universal and because one's identity status within the adolescent stage of life has also been found to change, a third area of research pertinent to ego identity has arisen. People have been concerned with what variables are related to ego development and identity status changes. Of particular relevance in this chapter are the social dimensions of identity development. Although such work has been largely descriptive, it can provide ideas about the explanation of identity changes.

Sequences in Ego Development. Does the emergence of an identity crisis in adolescence occur in a stage-like manner? Is the adolescent crisis, as Erikson (1959, 1963) described it, inevitably preceded by the specified childhood crises and followed by the hypothesized adult ones? Although much research supports the idea of adolescence as a time of crisis in self-definition, the universal, stage-like characteristics of this challenge are in doubt.

Several studies, independent of Erikson's framework, do show adolescence to be a period of change in self-definition. Montemayor and Eisen (1977) found that self-concept development from childhood to adolescence followed a sequence from concrete to abstract. Significant increases from grades 4 through 12 were seen in self-definitions relating to occupational role, individuality of one's existence, and ideology. Additional support for the view that adolescence is a time of personal reorganization was found by Haan (1974) and by Martin and Redmore (1978). In the former study involving a longitudinal assessment of 99 adolescents, it was found that being able to cope with adaptive demands in adulthood was apparently preceded by progressive reorganization of personality characteristics during adolescence. In the latter study of 32 black children studied longitudinally from the sixth to the twelfth grade, 30 showed an increase in level of ego development, and these increases showed intraindividual stability (the correlation in ego scores between the two grades was +.5).

Thus people's egos do develop, their personalities reorganize, and their self-definitions come to include occupational and ideological concerns, but such alterations do not necessarily correspond to stage-like progression.

Research aimed directly at assessing such a conception has not provided complete support for Erikson's ideas. In the largest study involving an assessment of the presence of stage-like qualities in adolescent development, Constantinople (1969) tested more than 900 male and female college students from the University of Rochester. In 1965 she tested members of the freshman through senior classes; in 1966 and again in 1967 she retested portions of these original groups. Because our concern is adolescence, we focus on Constantinople's (1969) findings regarding the crises of industry versus inferiority, identity versus identity diffusion, and intimacy versus isolation.

Insofar as scores for measures of these crises are concerned, it appeared that, in general, scores on the positive continuum ends increased, while those for the negative ends decreased across groups. There was increasingly more successful stage resolution among males and females having higher college standing. Since between-cohort differences (people studied at different times but in the same college level) did not appear great, it seems that the age group differences may reflect true age changes. Another characteristic of the cross-sectional data was a trend involving stage resolution being less evident for the intimacy versus isolation crisis, a finding consistent with Erikson's idea that identity issues must be solved first before intimacy ones can be dealt with. These college students may have just resolved their identities, made career plans for the senior years, and just begun to focus on intimacy. Although seniors scored higher than freshmen on the positive industry and identity crisis ends and lower on the negative inferiority end, there were *no* college level differences for diffusion, or isolation—negative crisis ends that should have been lowered if successful development in accordance with Erikson's stage theory had occurred. This failure to show the expected developmental trend was particularly evident for females (Constantinople, 1969).

Constantinople (1969) undertook longitudinal followups of the subjects in order to provide further information about the differences in successful resolution of stages found in the cross-sectional data. The three-year repeated measurements provided some support for the suggestion of developmental changes in the cross-sectional data insofar as alterations in identity and identity diffusion were concerned. There were consistent increases in the successful resolution of identity from the freshman to the senior year across subjects *and* from one year to the next within subject groups. Even here, however, there are problems for Erikson's theory. Only males showed consistent decreases in the scores for identity diffusion. Changes in scores for the other crises did not always decrease or increase in accordance with Erikson's theory, and furthermore the changes that did occur were often accounted for by time and cohort effects.

Recently Whitbourne and Waterman (1979) completed a ten-year follow-up of a portion of the subjects in the original Constantinople (1969) study, and data from current undergraduates were also collected. The results provide some support for Erikson's theory in regard to the crises of industry versus inferiority, identity versus identity diffusion, and intimacy versus isolation, but essentially for males. While the change patterns of males

were consistent with an Eriksonian ontogenetic sequence formulation, for females the results were indicative of individual change in relation to historical variation in the cultural context.

Similarly LaVoie (1976) used Constantinople's (1969) measure and classified sophomore, junior, and senior, male and female, high school students on the basis of their degree of successful stage 5 crisis resolution (identity achievement). He found that, although those who were high on identity scored higher on the positive crisis ends for stages 1 and 4, there were no differences between high and low identity achievers for the positive scores for stages 2, 3, and 6. Although LaVoie and Adams (in press) found that positive resolution of industry, identity, and intimacy crisis, as measured by Constantinople's (1969) test, is related to adult attachment (i.e., liking and love) scores, negative crisis scores were not so related.

In summary it appears that ego development does not proceed in the stage-like manner that Erikson suggests, at least when the Constantinople (1969) measure is used. The ego identity crisis may not necessarily arise after the crises typically associated with earlier portions of life or precede those typically associated with later portions. Instead a more plastic ordering of crises seems to exist between individuals (Douvan & Adelson, 1966; Gallatin, 1975). However there seems to be a progressive increment in resolution of issues dealing with identity. For instance the major consistency between cross-sectional and longitudinal data that Constantinople (1969) reported was the general movement across life toward a change in location along the identity-identity diffusion continuum. Most students changed in the direction of increased identity and decreased diffusion scores. Hence there do seem to be developmental progressions involved in the resolution of the identity crisis of adolescence. Adolescents' changing statuses along the crisis continuum have thus become the second major focus of research on adolescent identity development.

The Differentiation of Identity Status. What are the major types of ego changes adolescents go through in meeting the challenge of the identity crisis? Are there adolescents who occupy locations along the identity-identity diffusion continuum other than at or near these two extremes? If so, what is their location or status? These were the major issues Marcia (1964, 1966) confronted in a series of studies of identity development in adolescence. Rather than viewing identity as a global phenomenon, Marcia (1964, 1966) hypothesized that more differentiation existed.

Erikson noted that the adolescent period involves a *crisis* in self-definition, and in order to resolve this crisis, one must *commit* oneself to a role. Such commitment means adoption of an ideology (attitudes, values, beliefs) that coincides with the behavioral prescriptions for one's adopted role or occupation.

With a semi-structured, open-ended interview, Marcia (1966) evaluated adolescents' levels of crisis and commitment insofar as issues of occupational choice, religion, and political ideology were concerned. Using 86 male college students as subjects, Marcia (1966) found evidence for four identity statuses. Two of these statuses were those adolescents who had achieved identity: *Iden-*

tity achievers had experienced crises, whereas *foreclosure* subjects were committed without any apparent crisis. The third group, *identity diffusion,* may or may not have had a crisis; their defining characteristic was their lack of commitment. Moreover they were not concerned about this lack of commitment. The final status Marcia identified as *moratorium.* Students here were in a crisis and had, at best, vague commitments to an occupation or to an ideology. However, moratorium status adolescents were actively trying to make commitments; they were in a state of search.

Marcia (1966) found some evidence that there were differences among these four groups that were consistent with Erikson's theory. Identity achievers had the highest scores on an independent test of ego identity and did not follow authoritarian values (e.g., the belief that one should conform, a stress on obedience to authority) as much as members of some other statuses (e.g., foreclosure adolescents). The achievers maintained their feelings of self-esteem (i.e., positive self-regard) more than did members of other groups in the face of experimental manipulations having negative information about them. Foreclosure adolescents endorsed authoritarian values more than did other groups and had a self-esteem more vulnerable to negative information than had the identity achievers.

Evidence regarding the validity of the other two statuses was not as compelling. In a concept attainment task involving experimentally induced stress, the moratorium subjects showed more variability than others but were otherwise not distinguishable from the identity achievers. Furthermore the identity diffusion subjects performed lower than did the identity achievement subjects on the stress task, but in no other way did their behavior conform to theoretical expectations (Marcia, 1966).

Other studies provide more evidence that these four identity statuses exist. Schacter (1968) found that even among emotionally disturbed adolescent males, resolution of the identity crisis was positively related to attainment of occupational commitment. Marcia (1967) found that identity achieving and moratorium adolescent males were less vulnerable to attempts to manipulate their self-esteem than were foreclosed or diffusion males. Marcia and Friedman (1970) found that identity achievement adolescent females chose more difficult college majors than did identity diffusion females. In addition foreclosure females, although like identity achievers in many respects, were higher in authoritarianism. They also had higher self-esteem and lower anxiety than did the achievers, a finding not seemingly consistent with data from males.

Partial support for the fourfold differentiation of identity status comes from studies by Adams, Shea, and Fitch (1979) and Toder and Marcia (1973). In the Toder and Marcia study attempts were made to induce conformity to group demands experimentally among 64 college females. While identity achievers conformed less than those having unstable statuses (the moratorium and diffusion subjects), the foreclosure subjects also conformed less than those in the other two groups. Although this lack of conformity to group pressure would be expected on the basis of the foreclosure subjects' stable identity status, it would not be expected by virtue of their author-

itarian, and hence conforming and obedient, values. In a series of studies to validate an objective assessment of identity status, Adams et al. (1979) found foreclosure students to show the highest levels of rigidity and authoritarianism, while identity achievers exhibited the most self-acceptance.

These data are far from unequivocal in showing distinctions among the four different statuses. Other data, however, provide more compelling support. Several studies have shown that when adolescents are studied longitudinally, they progress through the four identity statuses in ways consistent with theoretical expectations. Waterman and Waterman (1971) longitudinally studied 92 male college adolescents through the course of their freshman year. Using Marcia's (1966) interview, changes in occupational and ideological status were assessed. In regard to occupational commitment there was a significant increase in the number of moratorium subjects and a significant decrease in the number of identity diffusion subjects. Insofar as ideology was concerned there was a significant increase in the number of identity diffusion subjects. About 44 percent of the subjects changed identity status for occupation over the course of the freshman year, and about 51 percent did so in regard to ideology; *but* people who had an identity achiever status at the beginning of the freshman period were just as likely to change as those who initially had other statuses.

These one-year longitudinal data do not provide compelling support for general progression toward more adaptive identity statuses in adolescence. The freshman year of college may involve demands on the person that produce instability in identity. Progressively more stability in identity achievement might be found if adolescents were followed beyond the freshman year. Longer-term longitudinal assessments support this expectation.

Waterman, Geary, and Waterman (1974) studied 53 male college seniors, all of whom had been subjects in the Waterman and Waterman (1971) study of identity development in the freshman college year. Over this longer time period there were significant increases in the frequency of subjects falling in the achievement status for *both* occupation and ideology ratings. Although about 50 percent of these subjects stayed in the same status from the freshman to the senior year, the achiever status was the most stable across this period. The moratorium status was the least stable. Similarly Marcia (1976), in a reinterview of 50 males who were given identity status interviews six to seven years earlier, found the moratorium status to show a 100 percent rate of change. Waterman and Goldman (1976), reinterviewing 18 seniors first studied as freshmen in 1970 and 41 seniors first studied as freshmen in 1971, found with both cohorts that there were significant increases in the frequency of identity achievement and decreases in moratorium and diffusion statuses. In summary there was a very high probability for resolution of the identity crisis. About 74 percent of those youth studied over the entire period of their college experience reached a status of identity achievement.

In summary there is some evidence for differentiation among ego identity statuses within adolescence. Most people move adaptively from other statuses toward identity achievement, and hence crisis resolution, by virtue of occupational and ideological role commitment. However it is clear that there is variability in this pattern. Not all people go through this sequence. Some begin and end adolescence as foreclosure youth. People differ in their rates of development, and some never seem to attain an identity of either achievement or foreclosure. Waterman et al. (1974) found that a substantial proportion of subjects completed their college years in the identity diffusion status. In their study 13 percent of seniors were diffuse on both occupational and ideology ratings, and an additional 33 percent were diffuse in one or the other of these areas.

Thus not only is there considerable plasticity of when in the sequence of other psychosocial crises the identity crisis occurs, but there also is plasticity in developments within this adolescent crisis. Because of this variability the third area of research pertaining to adolescent identity has arisen. Researchers have become concerned with what variables may interrelate with those pertaining to identity processes. Through describing how identity may be moderated by those other variables to which it is related, this research provides an explanation of the basis of adolescent identity and, as such, its changing character.

Identity: Psychological Dimensions. Processes of cognitive and moral development are intertwined with those of identity. Podd (1972) found that principled moral reasoning, formal operational thought, and identity achievement were positively related. Those whose identity status was diffuse tended to show preconventional moral thought (Podd, 1972). Furthermore independent data show the interrelation between advances in identity development and other, theoretically relevant, psychological functions.

Advances in formal operations involve progressions in dealing with abstract thought. If such development is indeed related to identity formation, one should expect to see those who engage in abstraction processes tending to have the identity achievement status. If one construes engaging in poetry writing as an activity at least in part based on abstract thought, then support for this relation is found in a report by Waterman, Kohutis, and Pulone (1977). In two studies of college students, these investigators found that those people who wrote poetry were more likely to be in the achievement status than those who did not write poetry. Moreover poetry writers were less frequently found in the foreclosure and diffusion statuses than people who did not write poetry. Yet writing per se was not related to identity status since there were no identity differences among students who did or who did not keep a personal journal or diary. Similarly Waterman and Goldman (1976) found that among the two cohorts they studied longitudinally from the freshman to the senior college year, an interest in literary and art forms was predictive of becoming an identity achiever by the end of college for those who were not in this status as freshmen. Moreover Jones and Strowig (1968) report that identity status is positively related to intellectual achievement as well as to abstract cognitive functions.

Advanced cognitive performance is associated with an advanced identity status, and this relation suggests that a generally greater level of adaptive functioning is associated with identity attainment. Data reported by La-Voie (1976) support this idea. High school male and female students who were measured as having high identity had lower scores on measures of defensiveness, general maladjustment, and neurosis than did students measured as low in identity. Moreover the self-concepts of the high identity scorers were more positive than those of the low identity scorers. Matteson (1977) found that among 99 Danish 17- to 18-year-olds more advanced identity status was related to the ability to control the expression of impulses among males and to rejection of compliance to authority among both sex groups. It may be that in rejecting authority high identity youth see themselves as more capable of controlling their own lives.

Three studies support these interpretations. Waterman, Beubel, and Waterman (1970) found that identity achievers (and also moratorium subjects) had higher internal locus of control scores. The reverse ideas about the locus of control for one's behavior were held by subjects in the foreclosure and diffusion statuses. Adams and Shea (1979) found that identity achievers were more internally controlled than were students in the other statuses. Schenkel (1975) found that identity achievers were least dependent on extraneous cues from the environment in performing a perceptual task, while the reverse was the case with identity diffusion adolescents.

Thus the development of identity is associated with cognitive, adjustment, perceptual, and other psychological processes. However, the character of these psychological interactions may be moderated by the reciprocal relations they bear to interindividual social processes.

Identity: Social Dimensions. We have argued that since achieving an identity denotes finding a role meeting society's demands identity processes are basically interpersonal. In other words they link the person to society in a way that facilitates both individual and social maintenance and survival. One might expect that people who have achieved identity should engage in interpersonal relationships useful in advancing this individual and social functioning—i.e., intimate relations. Orlofsky, Marcia, and Lesser (1973) found evidence of just such a relation. In a study of 53 college males, they found that those subjects who were in the identity achievement status were among those who had the greatest capacity for intimate interpersonal relationships. The interpersonal relationships of foreclosed and diffusion students were stereotyped, superficial, and hence not very intimate. The searching moratorium students showed the most variability between these two extremes. Similarly Kacerguis and Adams (1980) studied 44 male and 44 female college students and found that those people of either sex who were in the identity achievement category were more likely to be engaged in intimate relationships than were males or females in the foreclosure, moratorium, and diffusion categories. People in these latter three groups were much more variable in their level of intimacy.

Because identity links the adolescent to his/her social world, a basis of the different interpersonal styles of adolescents differing in identity status may lie in their social interaction history; perhaps this involves the family, since it is the major social institution delivering those societal demands to which the person must adapt. Erikson (1959) conceives of identity as being in part composed of self-esteem. O'Donnell's (1976) finding that in eighth- and eleventh-grade adolescents the degree of positive feelings toward parents was generally more closely related to self-esteem than were positive feelings for friends may be taken as support for the saliency of family interaction in identity development. Other studies show that different family structures—e.g., presence of a working or nonworking mother (Nelson, 1971) or father absence (Santrock, 1970)—are associated with contrasts in levels of adjustment in adolescence or in ego development prior to adolescence, respectively. However neither these reports nor that of O'Donnell suggest what sort of parental or familial functions may facilitate ego identity development.

Several studies suggest that parental personal and interpersonal characteristics may be transmitted to their offspring in the context of the family milieu. LaVoie (1976) reports that male high school students high in identity reported less regulation and control by their mothers and fathers and more frequent praise by their fathers than did males low in identity. Similarly LaVoie found that high identity high school females reported less maternal restrictiveness and greater freedom to discuss problems with their mothers and fathers than did low identity females. Thus high identity adolescents appear to be characterized by a family milieu involving less parental restrictiveness and better child-parent communication than do low identity adolescents. Waterman and Waterman (1971) and Matteson (1974) provide further· data to support this conclusion.

In their longitudinal study of college freshmen, Waterman and Waterman (1971) found that those students who showed stable identity achievement status for the entire year—and many did not—scored significantly higher on a measure of family independence than did those students who changed out of the achievement status. In addition those students who initially were foreclosed and then left this status by the end of the freshman year were also significantly higher scorers on a measure of family independence than those students who did not change out of this status.

In Matteson's (1974) study involving ninth-grade students, a measure of adolescent self-esteem and of communication with parents was taken. In addition the parents of the adolescents completed questionnaires about parent-adolescent communication and their own marital communication. Matteson reported that adolescents with low self-esteem viewed communication with their parents as less facilitative than did adolescents with high self-esteem. Moreover parents of low self-esteem adolescents perceived their communication with their spouses as less facilitative and rated their marriages as less satisfying than did parents of adolescents with high self-esteem.

Thus family milieu variables relating to communication quality among *all* family members and to patterns of parental control appear to relate to identity development. A family milieu having open communication and low restrictions on the individual seems to be most facilitative in providing a context for successful resolution of role search. Of course milieus having such characteristics need not be just conventional American familial ones. Although there have been few studies, other types of family structures, on the one hand, or other types of social milieus, on the other, can promote such development.

Long, Henderson, and Platt (1973) studied 51 Israeli male and female adolescents, aged 11 to 13 years, reared in a kibbutzim, and compared them to two groups of same-aged youth reared in more traditional family settings. The adolescents reared in the kibbutzim showed more social interest and higher self-esteem than those adolescents reared in the other settings.

Moreover the college environment may be seen as a nonfamilial social milieu where open communication of ideas and minimal restrictiveness of search for roles are involved. Sanford (1962) has speculated that because of these properties the college experience promotes movement toward identity achievement. The longitudinal data of Waterman and Waterman (1971), Waterman et al. (1974), and Waterman and Goldman (1976) support this view. Most college students experience an identity crisis during their college years, and of these about three-fourths reach the achievement status.

Although future research is needed to evaluate the appropriateness of these interpretations, it does appear that if an adolescent is placed in a social setting involving openness of social communication and minimal restrictiveness on role search an adaptive coordination between self and society will be attained. An identity will be achieved.

Sex-Role Stereotypes

Social institutions, such as the family, play a part in adolescent identity formation—that is, they aid the adolescent in answering the question, "Who am I?" In a very general sense the final answer is left to the individual even though there may be forceful social influences to respond in a particular manner. One part of a person's identity or role that has been relatively stereotypically bound to general societal influences and expectations is the role associated with one's gender. However, perhaps unlike the past a currently greater societal permissiveness may allow one to alter traditional orientations (e.g., Huston-Stein & Higgins-Trenk, 1978) toward selecting a role and exhibiting behaviors that are stereotyped as consistent with one's gender. The dynamic interactionist perspective aids in understanding how the reciprocal interchange between an individual and the social context results in selecting an orientation that may or may not fit with sex-role stereotypes. Since the behaviors that result from the selection of a particular orientation have important implications for social behavior, the next sections present data concerning sex-role stereotypes, sex roles, and sex differences in role behavior.

Sex-Role Stereotype Research. A *sex role* may be defined as a socially defined set of prescriptions for behavior for people of a particular sex group; *sex-role behavior* may be defined as behavioral functioning in accordance with the prescriptions; *sex-role stereotypes* are the generalized beliefs that particular behaviors are characteristic of one sex group as opposed to the other (Worell, 1978). Broverman, Vogel, Broverman, Clarkson, and Rosenkrantz (1972) report a series of studies they conducted using a questionnaire that assessed perceptions of "typical masculine and feminine behavior." In order to study sex-role stereotypes, Broverman et al. gave a group of college males and females a list of traits, with each trait presented in a bipolar manner (e.g., "not at all aggressive" to "very aggressive"). They conceptualized sex roles as "the degree to which men and women are perceived to possess any particular trait" (Broverman et al., 1972).

Those item-ends associated with males, as judged by *both* males and females, were markedly consistent with social expectations. Males were described as very aggressive, very independent, very dominant, very active, very skilled in business, and not at all dependent. These items form what Broverman et al. (1972) term a *competency cluster*.

Not only are females judged by both males and females to be at the opposite (low) ends of these competency-effectiveness dimensions, but also they are judged to be high on warmth-expressiveness items. They were seen to be very gentle, very aware of feelings of others, very interested in appearance, and having a very strong need for security.

For competency items the masculine end of the trait dimension was more desirable, and for the warmth-expressiveness cluster, the feminine end was more desirable. There are more competency items than warmth-expressiveness items. Thus there are more positively evaluated traits stereotypically associated with males than with females. Broverman et al. (1972) found evidence that these attitudes are quite pervasive in society. They report that their questionnaire has been given to 599 men and 383 women, who vary in age (from 17 to 60 years), educational level (from elementary school completed to an advanced graduate degree), religious orientation, and marital status. Among all of the respondents there was considerable consensus about the different characteristics of males and females; the degree of consensus was not dependent on one's age, sex, religion, educational level, or marital status (Broverman et al., 1972).

Overall then it can be said that sex-role stereotypes operate in a variety of situations. However, Stricker (1977) argues that there are two major reasons that one must exert caution in interpreting and generalizing these data. First he notes that the bipolar continuum was formed by the researchers, *not* the subjects, and that the Broverman et al. (1972) methodology may have exaggerated the distinctions between the sexes. Perhaps more importantly a second caution is concerned with generalizing the findings of a research study of this sort to real-life occurrences—that is, when subjects are asked to respond globally to items as characteristic of males in general or females in general evidence for sex-role stereotypes may be compelling. However such findings do not mean that the stereotypes are reflected in behaviors directed toward specific individuals in specific contexts or that the stereotypes are actually used in moderating actual, ecologically prototypic, behavioral interactions. Stricker (1977) contends that unwarranted extensions of data, such as these, occur often. Stricker's cautions are quite appropriate in our view; they provide an interpretative backdrop for us in the remainder of this section wherein we explore the implications of these stereotypes for social behavior.

Not only is there evidence that sex-role stereotypes are fairly consistent across the sex, age, and educational levels within society, but there is also evidence for considerable cross-cultural consistency in sex-role stereotypes.

Block (1973), in a study of six different countries (Norway, Sweden, Denmark, Finland, England, and the United States), not only found marked cross-cultural congruence but also found empirical verification of the differential emphases on competence-effectiveness and warmth-expressiveness for the two sexes that Broverman et al. (1972) found people to *believe* to exist.

Block's (1973) term for the type of behaviors we have labeled competence-effectiveness is *agency*. The items she sees as characteristic of agency (e.g., assertive, dominating, competitive, and independent) correspond to those in the Broverman et al. (1972) competency cluster. Block's (1973) term for the type of behaviors we label warmth-expressiveness is *communion*. The items she sees as comprising communion (e.g., loving, affectionate, sympathetic, and considerate) correspond to those in the Broverman et al. warmth-expressiveness cluster.

Among the university students in the samples, there were 16 items on which males were more stereotypically associated than were females. In this group *all* items receiving a classification were agency (competence) items. Although there were cross-cultural differences (the implications of which will be discussed below) in at least four of the six cultural groups, both males and females within and across cultures agreed that males are higher than females in regard to being practical, shrewd, assertive, dominating, competitive, critical, and self-controlled. In at least four of the six cultural groups, males and females within and across cultures agreed that females are higher than males in regard to being loving, affectionate, impulsive, sympathetic, and generous.

In summary, across groups in American society and in comparisons among samples from different societies, there is clear evidence that stereotypes exist which specify that different sets of behaviors are expected from males and females. This evidence shows that the male role is associated with individual effectiveness, independent competence, or agency. On the other hand the evidence shows that the female role is associated with interpersonal warmth and expressiveness, or communion. Although the existence of these stereotypes means that people believe males and females differ in these ways, the existence of the stereotype does not *necessarily* mean that males and females actually behave differently along these dimensions. Thus although people's stereotypic beliefs do correspond to the theoretical expectations of social scientists such as Erikson (1968) and McCandless (1970), this correspondence does not necessarily confirm such views because, as noted, stereotypic differences need not correspond to behavior differences. Other processes, to be discussed, could be involved in shaping behavior. Before we evaluate data pertinent to the relations between sex-role stereotypes and sex differences in adolescent social behavior, we discuss these alternative processes by considering some implications of the character of existing sex-role stereotypes.

Implications of Sex-Role Stereotypes for Socialization. In order to understand social development in adolescence, it is crucial to present some ideas about the potential role that stereotypes could have for behavioral and social development. On the basis of initial stereotypic appraisals of people categorized in a particular group (e.g., "adolescents," "endomorphs," "blacks," "women"), behavior is channeled in directions congruent with the stereotype. As a consequence stereotype-consistent behavior often is developed. Once this self-fulfilling prophecy is created, behavior maintains the stereotype, and a circular function is thus perpetuated.

The socialization experiences of males and females differ in ways consistent with traditional sex-role stereotypes and hence with the existence of a self-fulfilling prophecy process. Miller and Swanson (1958) found that a majority of urban, midwestern mothers who were studied channeled the behaviors of their children in ways congruent with traditional notions about divisions of labor (e.g., regarding "women's work" such as dishwashing). Brun-Gulbrandsen (1958) found in Norway results similar to those of Miller and Swanson (1958) and, in addition, found that mothers put more pressure on girls than on boys to conform to societal norms.

In a series of investigations involving the mothers and fathers of boys and girls ranging in age levels from early childhood through late adolescence, Block (1973) found further evidence pertaining to stereotype-related differences in the ways males and females are socialized. The parents were asked to describe their child-rearing attitudes and behaviors regarding one of their own children. Block assumed that parents of boys are not (at least beforehand) intrinsically different from parents of girls. Therefore differences in the way parents socialize males or females should reflect sex-role stereotyping imposed by parents on the children.

In comparing the parents of boys with the parents of girls, Block (1973) reports that the socialization practices for boys across the age range studied reflected an emphasis on achievement, competition, an insistence on control of feelings, and a concern for rule conformity (e.g., to parental authority). However for girls of the age range studied, the socialization emphasis was placed—particularly by their fathers—on developing and maintaining close interpersonal relationships; the girls were encouraged to talk about their problems and were given comfort, reassurance, protection, and support (Block, 1973).

Thus there appears to be evidence that parents strive to socialize their children in accordance with sex-role stereotypes. At least the attempt by parents to channel behavior, in a manner consistent with a self-fulfilling prophecy process, is apparent. Data are reviewed later pertaining to whether adolescents conform to these attempts; here, however, we must address the more basic issue of what is the source of behaviors that comprise the definition of the role for each sex.

The Adaptive Basis of Sex Differences in Roles.
Why are there traditional, stereotypic sex-role prescriptions, and why does their content exist as it does? Earlier we briefly discussed the adaptive significance of roles. The function of roles is to allow society to maintain and perpetuate itself. Although there is no easy way to test this idea directly, sex roles, like all other social roles, should have some basis in the functions of people and their society. Accordingly from this reasoning it follows that sex differences in role behavior, at least initially, arose from the different tasks males and females performed for survival, including reproduction.

Although maintaining these sex differences—that is to say, making them traditional—could continue to serve this survival function (if the survival demands on people remained the same), it is also possible that sex roles could become traditionalized despite a change in the adaptive demands facing society. Not only is there cross-cultural empirical evidence consistent with our speculations about the basis of sex differences in roles, but there also is at least some indirect support for the possibility that sex roles may not be evolving apace with social changes promoting new adaptive demands.

Barry, Bacon, and Child (1957) reviewed anthropological (ethnographic) material which described patterns of socialization in mostly nonliterate cultures. They reported a general trend of greater socialization pressures toward nurturance, responsibility, and obedience for females and greater socialization pressures toward self-reliance and achievement behaviors for males. In these relatively primitive societies, these different socialization pressures were seen to be associated with the contrasting biological and socioeconomic functions each sex had to assume when adult. Accordingly, as argued by Block (1973), such findings suggest that

when hunting or conquest is required for societal survival, the task naturally and functionally falls upon the male because of his intrinsically superior physical strength. So, boys more than girls receive training in self-reliance, achievement, and the agentic corollaries. Child-bearing is biologically assigned to women, and because, in marginally surviving societies, men must be out foraging for food, child rearing, with its requirement of continuous responsibility, is assigned to women. Thus, girls more than boys are socialized toward nurturance responsibility, and other qualities of communion. (p. 518)

Cultural-Historical Change and Sex-Role Evolution.
In modern countries the demands of day-to-day life are considerably different from those of primitive, marginally surviving societies. Accordingly the meaning and function of these traditional sex roles may be different. As Block (1973) states the issue,

The heritage and functional requiredness of sex typing in early or marginal cultures seem clear. The question for our times, however, is to what extent past socialization requirements must or should control current socialization emphases in our complex, technological, affluent society where, for example, physical strength is no longer especially important and where procreation is under control. Under present conditions, and for the future, we might ask: What is necessary? What is "natural" in regard to sex typing? (p. 519)

One way of addressing this issue is to reconsider the data on cross-cultural analyses of sex-role stereotypes presented earlier. If sex roles do reflect to some extent the requirements placed on men and women in their particular societal setting, differences in these settings should, to some extent, relate to differences in sex-role prescriptions in the different cultures. Despite the fact that we have seen general trends in all culture toward agency stereotypes for males and communion stereotypes for females, there are nevertheless differences in the socioeconomic, political, and physical environmental pressures of people in the respective societal settings.

Bakan (1966) found a relationship to exist between socialization pressures for agency (competence-effectiveness) and the presence of a capitalistic social and economic system, which he believed required an intensification of the agentic orientation. Consistent with this view Block (1973) reported that in the two countries in her research that had long and widespread commitments to social welfare—Sweden and Denmark—there were fewer sex differences and less emphasis on agency than in the United States. In fact Block (1973) found that American males were significantly different from the males of the other countries studied; they placed greater emphasis in their ratings on depictions of the male role as being adventurous, self-confident, assertive, restless, ambitious, self-centered, shrewd, and competitive. Their emphasis on these characteristics reflects their greater orientation to agency.

Block's findings regarding the females are also consistent with Bakan's (1966) idea of a relation between capitalism and agency, and our more general notion that behaviors associated with the roles of each sex necessarily reflect the sociocultural (e.g., economic, political, and environmental) demands placed on people at a particular time in their society's history. Despite being more oriented to communion than to agency, American women nevertheless placed greater emphasis in their ratings on agency terms than did women in the other countries studied (Block, 1973). To a significantly greater extent than did the women from the other cultural settings, the American women gave higher ratings to traits such as practical, adventurous, assertive, ambitious, self-centered, shrewd, and self-confident in their responses about a woman's role (Block, 1973). These characteristics are also all agency ones.

The United States is the most capitalistic of the countries studied by Block (1973); if we can assume that this characteristic is a salient one differentiating the countries, the differences between the sex-role stereotypes of males and females in the United States and those of the other countries may be understood better. Thus differences in the behavior expected from males and females of a particular society are understandable on the basis of the sociocultural forces acting over time on the people. Not only should these different sociocultural-historical pressures influence behavioral expectations, but they should also influence child-rearing (socialization) practices. If the adaptive demands placed on people in a society are different, the socialization of people to meet these demands should be different.

In support of this idea Block (1973) reported that student's ratings of parental child-rearing practices differed between the United States sample, on the one hand, and those of the five other countries, on the other. In the United States it was found that significantly greater emphasis was placed on early and clear sex typing and on competitive achievement, and less importance was placed on the control of aggression in males (Block, 1973).

These differences between American and European child-rearing orientations and sex-role stereotypes not only show that there can be and are contrasts between different cultures (Block, 1973)—although they are highly similar, Western ones—but also that these contrasts are related to familial, sociocultural, and historical differences. Moreover the character of the sex differences in some cultural settings shows that because of its long-term nature a presumably adaptive narrowing of some of the agency-communion differences found traditionally in other cultural settings (e.g., American ones) can occur. This suggests that humans can, insofar as sex-role stereotypes and socialization practices are concerned, overcome the divisions between the sexes that remain as perhaps less than optimal remnants from earlier times (Block, 1973).

Conclusions. The preceding evidence and arguments suggest that any biological notion, which stresses that anatomy is destiny (e.g., Erikson, 1968), or any nurture notion, which emphasizes only social rewards and punishments (e.g., McCandless, 1970), are limited views. Biology certainly does exert pressures on psychosocial development. However, this influence does not occur independently of the demands of the cultural and historical milieu. The biological basis of one's psychosocial functioning relates to the adaptive orientation for survival. Although it may be adaptive at some time in a given society to perform roles highly associated with anatomical and physiological differences, these same roles may not be adaptive in other societies or at other times in history. The agency-communion differences that were previously functional in primitive times may no longer be so in a modern society having greater leisure time, nearly equal opportunity for employment, and almost universal formal education.

In fact Block (1973) shows that at least one measure of more developed psychosocial functioning—the presence of a principled level of moral reasoning—is associated with American college-aged males and females who have less traditional sex-role definitions of themselves. In a series of studies by Bem (1974, 1975, 1977) it has been found that among men and women who have an orientation to both traditional male and female behaviors, there is evidence for adaptive psychosocial functioning. Bem (1974, 1975) argued that internalization of the culturally stereotypic sex role inhibits the development of a fully adaptive and maximally satisfying behavioral repertoire. Instead a male or female who identifies with both desirable masculine and desirable feminine characteristics—an androgynous person—is not only free from the limitations of unidimensionally stereotyped sex roles but should also be able to engage more effectively in both traditional male and traditional female behaviors across a variety of social situations, presumably because of his/her flexibility, than should a nonandrogynous person (Jones, Chernovetz, & Hansson, 1978). Several studies (Bem, 1974, 1975, 1977; Spence & Helmreich, 1978; Worell, 1978) have provided data validating this general idea—i.e., that the greater vocational and sex-role flexibility which defines androgynous men and women is associated with greater social competence and psychological health than is the case with males and females oriented to traditional sex-role adoption.

If one views individual development as reciprocally related to sociocultural change, one may be led to predict that the current historical context presses males and females to forego the traditional vocational roles, perhaps adaptive in earlier epochs. Instead today's cohorts of males and females may be encouraged to adopt role orientations showing flexibility and independence from traditional sex-role prescriptions in order to be adaptive in the current social context. Thus anatomy is not destiny; rather, it is just one component of biology that *may be* of relevance for the adaptive roles in a particular sociocultural-historical milieu.

A person's behavior in his/her cultural setting appears to involve much more than obtaining rewards for emitting behaviors that are drive reducing. At any point in history such behaviors involve (1) a coordination of the cultural, political, and economic values of one's society as (2) that society exists in a physical environmental setting placing changing survival demands on the people embedded within it, and (3) in the context of familial rearing pressures and psychological (e.g., moral) development. Given a shared understanding of the societal bases of sex-role stereotypes from a dynamic interactionist perspective, we can now examine sex differences in social behavior.

Sex Differences in Agency-Related and Communion-Related Behaviors

The first issue to address is whether the existing research literature indicates that males and females differ in agency-related and communion-related behaviors. If so, to what extent are these differences consistent with theoretical views? Although there are literally hundreds of studies that may be considered in order to address this issue, there have been several attempts to integrate these studies (Block, 1976; Maccoby & Jacklin, 1974; O'Leary, 1977). One of these (Maccoby & Jacklin, 1974) was sufficiently encompassing that it may serve as a basis for our presentation.

Maccoby and Jacklin (1974) evaluated the results of about 1600 research reports, published for the most part between 1966 and 1973. Maccoby and Jacklin derived these studies from those professional research journals that frequently include information about psychological sex differences, as well as from other sources (e.g., review chapters and theoretical papers). The studies they reviewed were classified into eight major topical areas (e.g., perceptual abilities, intellectual abilities, and achievement motivation). Within each of these areas studies were sorted on the basis of their relevance to particular behaviors or constructs (e.g., aggression, dependency, helping, or anxiety). Although the number of studies dealing with the more than 80 behaviors or constructs evaluated by Maccoby and Jacklin differed from topic to topic, tables were formed for each of these behaviors or constructs. These tables included information about the authors of the study, the ages and numbers of the people studied, and whether or not statistically significant differences between males and females had been found. Depending on the proportion of studies done on a topic for which significant sex differences occurred, Maccoby and Jacklin drew conclusions about whether sex differences were or were not well established.

However there are some problems with the conclusions they drew. First, the proportion of findings used to decide whether a sex difference was well established varied for different domains of behavior. In addition not all studies pertinent to a particular behavior were of the same quality—e.g., some studies assessed very small samples, and thus the statistics lacked power.

Another problem with the conclusions that Maccoby and Jacklin (1974) drew was an unevenness in the representation of various age groups in the research they reviewed. Of the studies on which Maccoby and Jacklin based their conclusions, 75 percent involved people 12 years of age or younger, and about 40 percent studied preschool children (Block 1976). This differential representation of age is important because there is some evidence (Terman & Tyler, 1954) that sex differences increase in frequency during adolescence. Thus Maccoby and Jacklin (1974) may have underestimated the proportion of sex differences that actually exist for a particular behavior by their review of studies of preadolescent samples.

Because of such problems with the conclusions that Maccoby and Jacklin reached, Block (1976) attempted to draw her own conclusions by tallying the number of studies reviewed by Maccoby and Jacklin which pertained to various domains of behavior. In other words Block took those studies reviewed by Maccoby and Jacklin for each of several behaviors and calculated the ratio of significant differences favoring one or the other sex in each set of studies. Table 28–1 is an adaptation of Block's (1976) tally. For each behavior the number of studies in which females were significantly higher is reported in terms of both the ratio and the proportion of studies showing such a difference. The corresponding information for males is presented also. Finally Lerner and Spanier (1980) classified each of the behaviors listed in the exhibit into either an agency or a communion category, based on the criteria for such behavior presented by Bakan (1966), Block (1973), and Broverman et al. (1972).

On 8 of the 11 behaviors classified into the communion category in Table 28–1, females scored significantly higher than males in more studies. Moreover on all five of the behaviors classified into the agency category, males scored significantly higher than females in more studies. This contrast shows that *when* sex differences are found in communion behavior the differences most often "favor" females and, in turn, *when* sex differences are found in agency behaviors the differences most often favor males. However just how often are these differences actually seen?

To answer this we must evaluate the magnitude of the proportion of studies showing sex differences for each of the behaviors listed. For communion behaviors the total proportion of studies showing sex differences in either direction was greater than .50 for only 4 of the 11 behaviors. Thus in most studies of communion behaviors, females and males do not differ. For agency behaviors the total proportion of studies showing sex differences in either direction was greater than .50 for only 2 of the 5 behaviors. Thus in most studies of most agency behaviors, males and females do not differ.

It can be concluded that *most* studies of either agency or communion behaviors *do not* show that the sexes differ. However when they do differ, females tend to score higher on communion behaviors, such as dependency, social desirability, compliance, general anxiety, and staying in the proximity of friends (Block, 1976), and males tend to score higher on agency behaviors, such as aggression, confidence in task performance, dominance, and activity level (Block, 1976). Thus only a minority of

Table 28-1 A Summary of Block's (1976) Tally of Studies Reviewed by Maccoby and Jacklin (1974) Showing Significant Sex Differences

		RATIO OF SIGNIFICANT COMPARISONS TO TOTAL NUMBER OF COMPARISONS[a]			
	CLASSIFICATION OF THE BEHAVIOR INTO AGENCY OR COMMUNION CATEGORY[b]	Number of Studies in Which Girls and Women Were Significantly Higher		Number of Studies in Which Boys and Men Were Significantly Higher	
BEHAVIOR ASSESSED		Ratio	Proportion	Ratio	Proportion
Dependency, on other than parent	Communion	13/13	1.00	0/13	.00
Social Desirability	Communion	7/9	.78	0/9	.00
Compliance	Communion	13/24	.54	1/24	.04
Proximity to friends	Communion	10/23	.52	2/23	.09
Conformity, Compliance with peers	Communion	19/59	.32	4/59	.07
Proximity to non-family adult	Communion	5/21	.24	2/21	.10
Empathy; sensitivity to social cues	Communion	7/31	.23	3/31	.10
Dependency (proximity to parent)	Communion	8/48	.17	7/48	.15
Helping	Communion	4/29	.14	4/29	.14
Positive sociability—peers	Communion	4/30	.13	10/30	.33
Positive sociability—adults	Communion	3/25	.12	3/25	.12
Competitiveness	Agency	3/26	.11	8/26	.31
Aggressiveness	Agency	5/94	.05	52/94	.55
Activity Level	Agency	3/59	.05	24/59	.41
Dominance	Agency	2/47	.04	20/47	.42
Confidence in task performance	Agency	0/18	.00	14/18	.78

[a]When the number of studies showing a sex difference does not correspond to the total number of studies involved in a comparison, this means that in the remaining studies no sex difference occurred.

[b]Classifications by Lerner & Spanier (1980).

Source: Adapted from Block (1976, pp. 305–306) and Lerner & Spanier (1980, p. 383).

the studies are consistent with male and female agency and communion differences. As such, researchers must search for those biological-through-historical processes that produce such plasticity in the presence and quality of communion and agency behaviors in *both* males and females. In the final part of this section we thus change our focus from looking at differences between the sexes to examining the bases of differences between individuals. As before, the discussion of individuality will be embedded in the dynamic interaction framework.

Interactive Bases of the Development of Individuality. Because of the particular combination of forces acting on a person, the individual character of development stands out. Block (1973) notes that one's characterization of the attributes of the sexes "represents a synthesis of biological and cultural forces" (p. 513). We have noted that variables associated with many processes play a role in the social development of males and females, and one may conclude that few sex differences must necessarily apply across time, context, and age. Indeed the major implication of the analysis in this chapter is that individual differences are dependent on the person's developmental context. One component of this context is composed of phenomena associated with time of testing. In support of this view, results of a sequential longitudinal study by Nesselroade and Baltes (1974) indicate that

the basis of personality changes in adolescence was most related to the type of social change patterns which comprised the environmental milieu for *all* adolescents over time.

Perhaps the best example of how the changing social context provides a basis of individual development is derived from a study by Elder (1974) who presents longitudinal data about the development of people who were children and adolescents during the great economic depression in the United States (from 1929 to late 1941). Elder reports that among a group of 84 males and 83 females born in 1920 and 1921, characteristics of the historical era produced alterations in the influence that education had on achievement, affected later adult health for youth from working-class families suffering deprivation during this era, and enhanced the importance of children in later adult marriages for youth who suffered hardships during the depression.

Other components of an adolescent's context are the physical and social characteristics of his/her school environment. Simmons, Rosenberg, and Rosenberg (1973) found that changes in the school context may influence adolescent functioning. In a study of about 2000 children and adolescents, they found that in comparison to 8- to 11-year-old children, early adolescents—and particularly those 12 to 13 years of age—showed more self-consciousness, greater instability of self-image, and slightly lower self-esteem. However, they discovered that contextual, rather than age-associated effects, seemed to account for these findings. Upon completion of the sixth grade, one portion of the early adolescent group had moved to a new school—i.e., a local junior high school—while the remaining portion of the early adolescents stayed in the same schools (which offered seventh- and eighth-grade classes). The group of early adolescents who changed their school setting showed a much greater incidence of change than did the group who remained in elementary school. Thus variables related to the school context seem to influence the individual functioning of young adolescents. This idea finds further support in a study of 184 male and female black early adolescents (Eato, 1979). It was found that perceptions of the social environment of the school were a significant influence on the females' self-esteem and that perceptions of both the physical and social environments of the school setting significantly influenced the males' self-esteem.

Still another component of an adolescent's context is provided by his/her family setting. Matteson (1974) found that adolescents with low self-esteem viewed communication with their parents as less facilitative than did adolescents with high self-esteem. Moreover parents of low self-esteem adolescents perceived their communication with spouses as less facilitative and rated their marriages as less satisfactory than did parents of high self-esteem youth. Similarly Scheck, Emerick, and El-Assal (1974) found that feelings of internal (personal) control over one's life, as opposed to believing that fate or luck was in control, were associated with adolescent males who perceived parental support for their actions. Furthermore interactive differences associated with different types of families promote individual differences in development. Long et al. (1973) found that among 11- to 13-year-old Israeli adolescents of both sexes rearing in a kibbutz, as compared to more traditional familial rearing situations, was associated with higher self-esteem and social interest among both sexes.

The cultural context can also be influential. Evidence suggests that development in different cultures is differentially related to the presence of sex differences. Offer and colleagues (Offer & Howard, 1972; Offer, Ostrov, & Howard, 1977) report variation in sex differences from culture to culture. For example the differences between the sexes in the United States are not as great as they are in Israeli and Irish cultural settings. However there seem to be no differences in the types of sex differences found between American and Australian adolescent samples (Offer & Howard, 1972). Similarly cultural context is related to the absence or presence of sex differences. Ramos (1974) found that among Brazilian adolescents of Japanese origin there are no sex differences in self-esteem.

In summary it is our view that the nature of individual differences between the sexes is dependent on interactions among biological, psychological, sociocultural, and historical influences. In other words we stress the implications of all aspects of the adolescent's context in attempts to understand his/her individual social development. This argument, although finding support in the preceding sections, may be further advanced by reference to a key feature of adolescent social behavior—moral functioning.

MORAL DEVELOPMENT

There are both practical and scientific reasons to question whether and how the adolescent will come to obey laws, conform to established social institutions, and think in a manner that others might judge as "correct," "good," "ethical," or "moral." In regard to the scientific reasons for focusing on moral behavior and thought, most developmental theorists see morality as a core dimension of the person's adaptation to his/her world. Although different theorists define moral behavior and development in markedly distinct ways, all ideas about moral functioning suggest an adjustment of the person to the social world, an adjustment which serves the dual purpose of fitting the person to his/her society, and at the same time, contributing to the maintenance and perpetuation of that society.

Thus moral development appears to be a core component of human adaptation and societal survival. This view is reflected in the position taken by Hogan and Emler.

... the capacity of human groups to survive and to extend their domination over the environment is a direct reflection of their ability to solve the problems of social organization and cultural transmission.

Most scholars who have thought seriously about these problems have concluded that they are rooted largely, if not mainly, in the moral socialization of the group. The great social philosophers of recent times—Emile Durkheim, Karl Marx, Max Weber, L. T. Hobhouse, and Sigmund Freud— have all taken the view that human societies are at their core, embodiments of moral orders. If we wish to understand that uniquely human invention, culture, and more specifically, the adolescent, we must analyze the relation of the individual to this moral issue. (1978, p. 200)

Although there are several possible ways to examine the nature of adolescent moral functioning, we focus first on the theoretical and research literature to discover what variables are related to moral functioning.

Variables Relating to Moral Development

In indicating that moral development involves an orientation of the person toward others in his/her world, the social relational character of morality is suggested. As we have been emphasizing, one central phenomenon of adolescence involves the person's attempt to find a role in society, and indeed it might be expected that such role search requires the ability to try to see the world from the perspective of alternative roles. Thus perspective taking would seem to be as much involved in the search for adolescent identity as it is in overcoming egocentrism (Neimark, 1975) and hence moving to higher levels of formal thinking (Inhelder & Piaget, 1958) and of principled morality (Kohlberg, 1958, 1963).

Personality-Moral Reasoning Relations

This interaction among processes relating to identity, formal operations, and morality has found theoretical and empirical support. In regard to theory Piaget believes that the transition from earlier to later formal operational thought involves attainment of a role (Inhelder & Piaget, 1958). Piaget believes that a person becomes an adult cognitively when s/he has attained a firm role to play in society. In Erikson's (1959, 1963) terms the person has found an identity; Erikson (1959) believes that transition to a stage beyond adolescence also involves such identity achievement. Kohlberg (1973) also has posited that identity achievement is a prerequisite for principled morality (see Rest, Chapter 24, this volume, for a presentation of Kohlberg's theory of moral development).

Empirical support for these hypothesized interrelations among individual-psychological processes is provided by Tomlinson-Keasey and Keasey (1974). They found that older adolescents who should be more practiced in formal operational thought (i.e., female college students) showed more advanced moral judgments than younger adolescents who had just begun to acquire formal operations (i.e., sixth-grade females). The findings were interpreted as suggesting that, although formal thought may be a prerequisite of higher levels of moral reasoning, there may be a time lag between the acquisition of formal thought and its use in moral reasoning.

Evidence also exists about relations between ego functioning and moral reasoning level. Podd (1972) studied a group of about 100 white, middle-class, male college students. Subjects who had achieved an ego identity were generally characterized by the higher levels of moral judgment, while those with a relative lack of ego identity were generally characterized by either the least advanced level of moral reasoning or a transitionary level between intermediate and high levels of reasoning. Moreover those who were in a crisis over their identity were inconsistent in their reasoning levels. Similarly Sullivan, McCullough, and Stager (1970) found low to moderate correlations among ego, conceptual, and moral development measures.

While Podd's data and those of Sullivan et al. are consistent with the ideas of Piaget, Kohlberg, and Erikson, there are some studies in the literature which provide either no support (Cauble, 1976) or only indirect support for the interrelations between identity and morality (Bachrach, Huesmann, & Peterson, 1977). In the latter study, for instance, if it can be assumed that feeling one's destiny is controlled by oneself is an emotion consistent with feeling a sense of self-knowledge (identity), then the relation between this feeling and intentionally based moral reasoning is consistent with an identity-morality relation.

Behavior-Moral Reasoning Interrelations

There is theoretical justification and some empirical support for an interrelation among those individual processes that pertain to the person's role search and attainment; yet, none of the preceding information involves measures of the *behavior* implications of these psychological orientations. Data pertinent to these implications do exist however. Harris, Mussen, and Rutherford (1976) administered Kohlberg's interview and a measure of psychometric intelligence to 33 fifth-grade boys. In addition the peers of these boys rated their moral conduct, and the boys' honesty was evaluated in a structured test. Higher levels of moral reasoning were associated with better cognitive ability. On a behavioral level higher reasoners showed greater resistance to temptation and were rated by their peers as behaving in a prosocial manner (e.g., as being concerned with the welfare of others).

Moral reasoning differences associated with behavioral differences exist among adolescents and adults as well. Krebs and Rosenwald (1977) found that adults at higher moral levels were more helpful to a researcher in need of their cooperation. In a large project conducted by Haan et al. (1968), a study was made of about 500 University of California and San Francisco State College students and Peace Corps volunteers-in-training, divided into male and female groups. Because of the study's prominent empirical and theoretical implications, we shall consider its details quite carefully. All subjects in the study had responded to Kohlberg's interview, and insofar as the college students were concerned, they had a diverse array of behavioral and social involvement in various campus activities and groups. Some students had been arrested as a consequence of their participation in a protest advocating free speech. Others were members of such groups as Young Democrats, Young Republicans, California Conservatives for Political Action, a student-body–sponsored Community Involvement Program, or a tutorial group. On the basis of answers to Kohlberg's interview, the subjects were divided into one of five "pure" moral type groups, basically one for each of the stages from two through six.

Haan et al. (1968) obtained several biographical, behavioral, and cognitive-personality test measures on the subjects. Together the data serve to provide a profile of the behavioral as well as the personality characteristics of members of each moral reasoning group. In addition the data provide clues about the bases of differences among these groups.

Characteristics of Principled Reasoners. The members of the principled reasoning groups were more likely to have interrupted their college careers, to live in apartments or houses on their own, to be politically more radical, and to have been in strong support of the protest movement. Indeed the political-social activity of these people was the highest of all groups studied. They affiliated with more organizations—and thus played more roles as members of different groups—and were more involved with them. They were active participants in a lot of groups and were not just passive joiners.

In addition to these behavioral characteristics, male members of this principled group described their own personalities as being "idealistic" and conceived of the ideal good man in society as being perceptive, empathic, and altruistic. These ideas emphasize their commitment to taking the roles of others (Haan et al., 1968). The principled women saw themselves as guilty, doubting, restless, and altruistic. Their idea of the ideal woman was one who is rebellious and free.

Characteristics of Conventional Reasoners. The members of the conventionally reasoning moral groups were the least likely to interrupt their college careers; lived predominantly in institutional, adult-approved arrangements; were politically more conservative; and were the groups least in support of (although still approving) the protest movement. Members of these groups affiliated with few political-social organizations and were relatively inactive.

The self-descriptions that coincided with these behaviors for the males in these groups reflect traditional social values: conventional, ambitious, sociable, practical, orderly, and not curious, individualistic, or rebellious. The women saw themselves as ambitious and foresightful, and not as guilty, restless, or rebellious. Both sexes shared an idea of the good person in society as one who had efficient control of the self and had social skillfulness.

Characteristics of Preconventional Reasoners. With those people who reasoned predominantly at a preconventional, naive, egoistic moral level, Haan et al. found a high likelihood of college career interruption. Although the men in this group were more likely than the women to live on their own, both men and women strongly supported the protest movement. The men in this group belonged to only a moderate number of organizations, but they participated intensely. On the other hand the women in this group joined the most organizations but were the most inactive.

The personal descriptions of these behavioral orientations showed that both men and women saw themselves as rebellious. The men's self-descriptions reflected a lack of involvement with others, and their ideal person was someone who is aloof, stubborn, uncompromising, playful, and free. Similarly women also rejected interpersonal obligations, saw themselves as stubborn and aloof, and idealized such characteristics as practicality and stubborness.

Conclusions

To summarize the Haan et al. (1968) findings, it seems that differences in moral reasoning level indeed relate to contrasts in attitudes, personality, and behavior. Principled thinkers are actively involved in the role orientations of others and see themselves as altruistic and idealistic. Their principled view of the person's relation to his/her social world permeates their own self-conceptions and provides a basis for their active involvement in their world. Alternatively preconventional thinkers, although showing *some* behavioral similarities to principled thinkers (e.g., living alone, engagement in protests), do so for entirely different reasons (ones consistent with their naive, egoistic orientation). They are unconcerned with the welfare of others, show little concern for interpersonal obligation, and engage in protest behaviors to abet their individual rights or goals. In contrast the conventional thinkers are not actively involved in many organizations, tend to live in situations and behave in accordance with traditional and adult-approved values, and show additional ideas and values that are consistent also with their conventional reasoning and behavior.

As a final instance of the moral reasoning and behavioral differences among these groups, consider the percentage of men and women in the Haan et al. sample from each moral reasoning group who were arrested in a protest demonstration regarding the free speech movement. As expected the conventional thinkers (stages 3 and 4) were by far the group having the lowest proportion of arrests. Similarly the postconventional group (stages 5 and 6) had the highest percentage. While the preconventional thinkers (stage 2) also had a high arrest

proportion, their involvement was for reasons qualitatively different from those used in the principled groups. Consistent with their egotistic, nonsocially concerned orientation, the stage 2 thinkers were mostly concerned with their individual rights in a power conflict. The principled thinkers apparently used their perspective-taking abilities behaviorally and based their involvement on concerns with basic issues of civil liberties and rights and on the relation of students as citizens within a university community. These data show that there are behavioral consequences of moral thought; but as stressed by Kohlberg (1958, 1963), Piaget (1965), and Turiel (1969), it is necessary to focus on the thought because the same behavior (e.g., protest) can be based on qualitatively and developmentally different individual-psychological levels of functioning.

These conclusions indicate that adolescents and youth who may be described as differing in their levels of moral reasoning may be also described as differing on their personal (e.g., identity, attitudes, values) and behavioral attributes. However these descriptions do not suggest an explanation for these differences. Some of the elements for a potential explanation lie in some of our previous discussion as well as in the data from the Haan et al. (1968) study presented later.

Social Interactive Bases of Moral Development

Rest (1975) has shown that college youth show greater increases in principled reasoning than do their noncollege age peers. However if one brings certain characteristics to a social situation (such as the college one) having apparently facilitative characteristics, moral development would be further enhanced. Interacting in a milieu that fosters social perspective taking may foster moral development among those adolescents who have certain levels of formal operational egocentrism, IQ, and identity. The time of testing effects found (White, Bushnell, & Regnemer, 1978) or implicated (Holstein, 1976; Kuhn, 1976) in moral development research may in fact represent the outcome of a time-specific interaction between individuals having such predispositions and the facilitative presses in the milieu promoting such change.

A question remains as to what brings an adolescent into a facilitative milieu, such as college, with a predisposition amenable to influence. Why do some adolescents show principled morality as a consequence of their college experience, while others remain at levels not as high? Indeed why do people enter into their college years with different levels of morality? One suggestion we may make is that adolescents show such differences because of differences in their history of social interactions. It may be that if adolescents experience different interactional histories, they will develop at different rates after entering potentially facilitative milieus.

Although the sequential research needed to test this idea has not been done, there are data that suggest, at the very least, that adolescents and youth who do have different levels of moral reasoning also have different types of social interactional experiences. Most of these data relate to interactions with family members or with peers.

Family Interactions

Mussen, Harris, Rutherford, and Keasey (1970) studied honesty and altruism among preadolescents, ranging in age from 11.6 to 12.6 years. Girls who showed high levels of honesty and altruism were found to have warm, intimate interactions with their mothers and high self-esteem. However for boys honesty was negatively related to gratifying relationships with parents and peers and with self-esteem, but altruism was associated with good personal ego strength.

Haan et al. (1968) found that the preconventional, conventional, and postconventional subjects they studied all reported different types of familial interaction patterns. Subjects were evaluated on how discrepant their own political views were from each of their parents (e.g., in regard to commitment to various issues), how different their views were from those of their parents on various social issues pertinent to the two generational groups, and how much conflict they had with their parents. These measures were combined to form one index of conflict and disagreement.

There is a curvilinear relation between conflict and moral reasoning for the men. Intense family conflict, especially with the father, is associated with preconventional thinking. Alternatively and as expected on the basis of their moral orientation, there is least conflict found with the conventional thinkers. A moderate level of conflict exists for those with principled reasoning. For the women there is a trend toward increased conflict with the mother being associated with higher moral reasoning. Although this trend is not as evident with the father, it seems that for both males and females conflict with the parent of the same sex is most related to moral reasoning.

Thus among students measured at one point in time, there is a relation between differing reports of conflict in familial interactions and contrasts in moral reasoning. From such data we do not know if differing levels of conflict produced moral development or the reverse. However from the dynamic interactional perspective, we could expect both. Hoffman (1975), in a study of fifth- and seventh-grade, white, middle-class children and their parents, concluded that differences in the moral orientation of children (e.g., in their consideration for others, feelings of fear or guilt upon transgression) are at least in part due to different discipline and affection patterns of parents.

Data reported by Santrock (1975) provide direct support for this notion. Subjects were 120 six- to ten-year-old, predominantly lower-class boys from either an intact home environment or a family where the father was absent (due to separation, divorce, or death). Based on reports by the subjects, the sons of divorced women experienced more power-assertiveness disciplinary action (as opposed, for instance, to love-withdrawal discipline) than did the sons of widows. Such interaction differences influence moral behavior. According to teachers' ratings the sons of divorced women have more social deviation, but more advanced moral judgment, than do the sons of widows. In relation to interaction differences associated with being in a father-absent or a father-present home, there were also differences in moral functioning. Teachers rated the former group of boys as less advanced in moral development than the latter group.

Social interactions involving parents and children do seem to provide a basis of moral development differences. Yet such familial social interactions are not the only ones that an adolescent experiences. Not only do adolescents show development toward more social interactions with peers, but even insofar as their interactions with parents are influential, they also do not seem to replicate the moral reasoning orientations of their parents. Haan, Langer, and Kohlberg (1976) found that in a large sample of children ranging in age from 10 to 30 years and their parents there was little relation between moral stages among family members. Although husbands' and wives' moral stages were correlated at a low level, there was no relation among siblings' moral levels. Parents' and daughters' stages were also unrelated, and parents' and sons' stages were related only among younger sons. Although family interactions do contribute to moral functioning, they do not seem to shape it totally.

Peer Interactions

Social interactions outside the family may be more likely to advance moral development because, by avoiding the inevitable power differences between parents and children, they may more readily promote the reciprocal and mutual interactions involved in decentered, morally principled thinking. It may be that children's and adolescents' greater interaction with their peers, who by definition are equal to them, provides them with the precise context necessary to facilitate moral development.

Findings reported by Gerson and Damon (1978) and by Haan (1978) support this position. Gerson and Damon studied children aged 4 to 10 years old. The longer the children took part with their peers in a group discussion of how to distribute candy, the more likely they were to agree to an equal distribution of candy. This was true at all ages but most markedly among the older children—that is, 77 percent of all children in the study made an equal distribution by their final choice, but 100 percent of the 8- to 10-year-olds did so.

In the study reported by Haan (1978), six adolescent friendship groups (sexually mixed, but either all black or all white) participated in a series of moral "games" to see if moral behavior was accounted for better by Kohlberg's formal, abstract reasoning ideas or by an interpersonal formulation stressing that "moral solutions are achieved through dialogues that strive for balanced agreements among participants" (Haan, 1978, p. 286). The games presented to subjects, aged 13 to 17 years, included having to role-play life in two cultures, competing or cooperating as teams in a game having only one winner, constructing a society, and role-playing being the last survivors on earth and deciding what to do.

Haan scored the subjects on *Kohlberg* and *interpersonal* measures of morality across games. Although these scores fluctuated between games, the interpersonal scores were more stable than the Kohlberg scores, particularly in games involving stress (e.g., the competition one). In all situations requiring action, all subjects used interpersonal morality—which required a balance of positions among all those who were interacting—more than the measures of moral reasoning associated with Kohlberg's theory. Insofar as moral behavior was concerned, moral reasoning involved establishment of social interaction agreements among the adolescents and was not primarily based on principled thought independent of the group consensus.

The use of such interaction-based, social reciprocity morality facilitated development of both the interpersonal- and Kohlberg-related measures of morality. After the games the levels of scores for both these assessments of morality increased for all six adolescent groups, as compared to a control group that did not play any moral games. This suggests that any explanation of moral development is enhanced by considering the interaction between abstract reasoning and the demands of the particular social situation.

CONCLUSIONS

We have argued that human behavior develops as a consequence of multidimensional, multidirectional relations between the person and his/her context. Our review of the literature on adolescent social behavior, albeit selective, shows the use of this dynamic interactional perspective in integrating existing data sets. It must be emphasized that, to date, most studies (1) have not been theoretically based on an interactional conception such as this; (2) have not included measures of more than one level of analysis (e.g., individual *and* cultural phenomena) and/or more than one dimension within one level (e.g., simultaneously looked at cognition, morality, *and* identity) involved in adolescent development; and (3) have not therefore provided data directly relevant to our interactional perspective. Consequently in indicating that such interactions are involved in adolescent development, our review suggests that important extensions of research would involve exploration of the components of adolescent–social context interdependencies.

In summary adolescents may be seen as inevitably embedded in a social context and as invariably being both products and producers of this context as a consequence of this embeddedness. Such a perspective offers challenges for intervention (as well as for research and theory). In light of the status of the existing literature, we suggest that development-specific methodologies must be used to meet the conceptual challenge of studying changing people in a changing world (Baltes, Reese, & Nesselroade, 1977; Lerner, Skinner, & Sorrell, 1980) and that these theoretical and methodological revisions need to be coupled with alternative foci for intervention. If attempts to optimize human development are to capitalize on the insights that may be gained from a dynamic interactional perspective, the targets of interventions in adolescence should be neither the adolescent nor the context per se; rather, a focus on the *relations* that exist between the two domains—at particular times of measurement and for people of cohorts having a particular array of ideographic and nomothetic characteristics—must be adopted. Such a focus requires interventionists to individualize their mechanisms of modification and to be oriented to a multidisciplinary array of strategies. It is our view that such an approach will be most useful for scientifically and professionally confronting issues raised by studying developing adolescents in their changing world.

REFERENCES

Adams, G. R., & Shea, J. The relationship between identity status, locus of control, and ego development. *Journal of Youth and Adolescence*, 1979, *8*, 81–89.

Adams, G. R., Shea, J. A., & Fitch, S. A. An objective assessment of ego-identity status. *Journal of Youth and Adolescence*, 1979, *8*, 223–237.

Adelson, J. What generation gap? *New York Times Magazine*, January 18, 1970, Section 6, pp. 10–45.

Bachrach, R., Huesmann, L. R., & Peterson, R. A. The relation between locus of control and the development of moral judgment. *Child Development*, 1977, *48*, 1340–1352.

Bakan, D. *The duality of human existence.* Skokie, Ill.: Rand McNally, 1966.

Baltes, P. B., Reese, H. W., & Nesselroade, J. R. *Life-span developmental psychology: Introduction to research methods.* Monterey, Calif.: Brooks/Cole, 1977.

Bandura, A. The stormy decade: Fact or fiction? *Psychology in the Schools*, 1964, *1*, 224–231.

Bandura, A., & Walters, R. H. *Adolescent aggression.* New York: Ronald Press, 1959.

Barry, H., Bacon, M. K., & Child, I. L. A cross-cultural survey of some sex differences in socialization. *Journal of Abnormal and Social Psychology*, 1957, *55*, 527–534.

Bem, S. L. The measurement of psychological androgyny. *Journal of Consulting and Clinical Psychology*, 1974, *47*, 155–162.

Bem, S. L. Sex-role adaptability: One consequence of psychological androgyny. *Journal of Personality and Social Psychology*, 1975, *31*, 634–643.

Bem, S. L. On the utility of alternative procedures for assessing psychological androgyny. *Journal of Consulting and Clinical Psychology*, 1977, *45*, 196–205.

Bengtson, V. L. The generation gap: A review and typology of social-psychological perspectives. *Youth and Society*, 1970, *2*, 7–32.

Bengtson, V. L., & Kuypers, J. A. Generational differences and the developmental stake. *Aging and Human Development*, 1971, *2*, 249–260.

Bengtson, V. L., & Troll, L. Youth and their parents: Feedback and intergenerational influence in socialization. In R. M. Lerner & G. B. Spanier (Eds.), *Child influences on marital and family interaction: A life-span perspective.* New York: Academic Press, 1978.

Block, J. H. Conceptions of sex roles: Some cross-cultural and longitudinal perspectives. *American Psychologist*, 1973, *28*, 512–526.

Block, J. H. Issues, problems, and pitfalls in assessing sex differences: A critical review of *The psychology of sex differences. Merrill-Palmer Quarterly*, 1976, *22*, 283–308.

Brent, S. B. Individual specialization, collective adaptation and rate of environment change. *Human Development*, 1978, *21*, 21–33.

Brittain, C. V. Adolescent choices and parent-peer cross pressures. *American Sociological Review*, 1963, *28*, 385–391.

Brittain, C. V. A comparison of urban and rural adolescence with respect to peer versus parent compliance. *Adolescence*, 1969, *4*, 59–68.

Broverman, I. K., Vogel, S. R., Broverman, D. M., Clarkson, F. E., & Rosenkrantz, P. S. Sex-role stereotypes: A current appraisal. *Journal of Social Issues*, 1972, *28*, 59–78.

Brun-Gulbrandsen, S. *Kjønnsrolle og ungdomskviminalitet.* Oslo: Institute of Social Research, 1958. (Mimeo)

Burgess, R. L., & Conger, R. D. Family interaction in abusive, neglectful, and normal families. *Child Development*, 1978, *49*, 1163–1173.

Cauble, M. A. Formal operations, ego identity, and principled morality: Are they related? *Developmental Psychology*, 1976, *12*, 363–364.

Chand, I. P., Crider, D. M., & Willets, F. K. Parent-youth disagreement as perceived by youth: A longitudinal study. *Youth and Society*, 1975, *6*, 365–375.

Constantinople, A. An Eriksonian measure of personality development in college students. *Developmental Psychology*, 1969, *1*, 357–372.

Costanzo, P. R., & Shaw, M. E. Conformity as a function of age level. *Child Development*, 1966, *37*, 967–975.

CUMMING, E., & HENRY, W. E. *Growing old: The process of disengagement.* New York: Basic Books, 1961.

DOBZHANSKY, T. Ethics and values in biology and cultural evolution. *Zygon,* 1973, *8,* 261–281.

DOUVAN, E., & ADELSON, J. *The adolescent experience.* New York: John Wiley, 1966.

EATO, L. E. *Perceptions of the physical and social environment in relation to self-esteem among male and female black adolescents.* Unpublished master's thesis, Pennsylvania State University, 1979.

ELDER, G. H. *Children of the great depression.* Chicago: University of Chicago Press, 1974.

ELKIND, D. Egocentrism in adolescence. *Child Development,* 1967, *38,* 1025–1034.

ERIKSON, E. H. Identity and the life cycle. *Psychological Issues,* 1959, *1,* 18–164.

ERIKSON, E. H. *Childhood and society* (2nd ed.). New York: W. W. Norton & Co., Inc., 1963.

ERIKSON, E. H. *Identity, youth and crisis.* New York: W. W. Norton & Co., Inc., 1968.

FLOYD, H. H., JR., & SOUTH, D. R. Dilemma of youth: The choice of parents or peers as a frame of reference for behavior. *Journal of Marriage and the Family,* 1972, *34,* 627–634.

GALLATIN, J. E. *Adolescence and individuality.* New York: Harper & Row, Pub., 1975.

GERSON, R. P., & DAMON, W. Moral understanding and children's conduct. *New Directions for Child Development,* 1978, *2,* 41–59.

HAAN, N. The adolescent antecedents of an ego model of coping and defense and comparisons with Q-sorted ideal personalities. *Genetic Psychology Monographs,* 1974, *89,* 273–306.

HAAN, N. Two moralities in action contexts: Relationships to thought, ego regulation and development. *Journal of Personality and Social Psychology,* 1978, *36,* 286–305.

HAAN, N., LANGER, J., & KOHLBERG, L. Family patterns in moral reasoning. *Child Development,* 1976, *47,* 1204–1206.

HAAN, N., SMITH, M. B., & BLOCK, J. Moral reasoning of young adults: Political-social behavior, family background and personality correlates. *Journal of Personality and Social Psychology,* 1968, *10,* 183–201.

HALL, G. S. *Adolescence.* New York: Appleton, 1904.

HARRIS, D. B. (Ed.). *The concept of development.* Minneapolis: University of Minnesota Press, 1957.

HARRIS, S., MUSSEN, P., & RUTHERFORD, E. Some cognitive, behavioral, and personality correlates of maturity of moral judgment. *Journal of Genetic Psychology,* 1976, *128,* 123–135.

HARTUP, W. W. Perspectives on child and family interaction: Past, present, and future. In R. M. Lerner & G. B. Spanier (Eds.), *Child influences on marital and family interaction: A life-span perspective.* New York: Academic Press, 1978.

HIRSCH, J. Behavior-genetic analysis and its biosocial consequences. *Seminars in Psychiatry,* 1970, *2,* 89–105.

HOFFMAN, M. L. Sex differences in oral internalization and values. *Journal of Personality and Social Psychology,* 1975, *32,* 720–729.

HOGAN, R., & EMLER, R. H. Moral development. In M. E. Lamb (Ed.), *Social and personality development.* New York: Holt, Rinehart & Winston, 1978.

HOGAN, R., JOHNSON, J. A., & EMLER, N. P. A socioanalytic theory of moral development. *New Directions for Child Development,* 1978, *2,* 1–18.

HOLSTEIN, C. B. Irreversible, stepwise sequence in the development of moral judgement: A longitudinal study of males and females. *Child Development,* 1976, *47,* 51–61.

HUSTON-STEIN, A., & HIGGINS-TRENK, A. Development of females from childhood through adulthood: Career and feminine orientations. In P. B. Baltes (Ed.), *Life-span development and behavior* (Vol. 1). New York: Academic Press, 1978.

INHELDER, P., & PIAGET, J. *The growth of logical thinking from childhood to adolescence.* New York: Basic Books, 1958.

JONES, J. G., & STROWIG, R. W. Adolescent identity and self-perception as predictors of scholastic achievement. *Journal of Educational Research,* 1968, *62,* 78–82.

JONES, W. H., CHERNOVETZ, M. E. O'C., & HANSSON, R. O. The enigma of androgyny: Differential implications for males and females. *Journal of Consulting and Clinical Psychology,* 1978, *46,* 298–313.

KACERGUIS, M. A., & ADAMS, G. R. Erikson stage resolution: The relationship between identity and intimacy. *Journal of Youth and Adolescence,* 1980, *9,* 117–126.

KANDEL, D. B., & LESSER, G. S. Parental and peer influences on educational plans of adolescents. *American Sociological Review,* 1969, *34,* 213–223.

KANDEL, D. B., & LESSER, G. S. *Youth in two worlds.* San Francisco: Jossey-Bass, 1972.

KELLEY, R. K. The premarital sexual revolution: Comments on research. *Family Coordinator,* 1972, *21,* 334–336.

KOHLBERG, L. *The development of modes of moral thinking and choice in the years ten to sixteen.* Unpublished doctoral dissertation, University of Chicago, 1958.

KOHLBERG, L. The development of children's orientations toward a moral order: 1. Sequence in the development of moral thought. *Vita Humana,* 1963, *6,* 11–33.

KOHLBERG, L. Continuities in childhood and adult moral development revisited. In P. B. Baltes & K. W. Schaie (Eds.), *Life-span developmental psychology: Personality and socialization.* New York: Academic Press, 1973.

KREBS, D., & ROSENWALD, A. Moral reasoning and moral behavior in conventional adults. *Merrill-Palmer Quarterly,* 1977, *23,* 77–80.

KUHN, D. Short-term longitudinal evidence for the sequentiality of Kohlberg's early stages of moral development. *Developmental Psychology,* 1976, *12,* 162–166.

LARSON, L. E. The influence of parents and peers during adolescence: The situation hypothesis revisited. *Journal of Marriage and the Family,* 1972, *34,* 67–74.

LAVOIE, J. C. Ego identity formation in middle adolescence. *Journal of Youth and Adolescence,* 1976, *5,* 371–385.

LAVOIE, J. C., & ADAMS, G. R. Erikson developmental stage resolution and attachment behavior in young adulthood. *Adolescence,* in press.

LERNER, R. M. Showdown at generation gap: Attitudes of adolescents and their parents toward contemporary issues. In H. D. Thornburg (Ed.), *Contemporary adolescence* (2nd ed.). Monterey, Calif.: Brooks/Cole, 1975.

LERNER, R. M. Nature, nurture, and dynamic interactionism. *Human Development,* 1978, *21,* 1–20.

LERNER, R. M. A dynamic interactional concept of individual and social relationship development. In R. L. Burgess & T. L. Huston (Eds.), *Social exchange in developing relationships.* New York: Academic Press, 1979.

LERNER, R. M., & BUSCH-ROSSNAGEL, N. A. Individuals as producers of their development: Conceptual and empirical bases. In R. M. Lerner & N. A. Busch-Rossnagel (Eds.), *Individuals as producers of their development: A life-span perspective.* New York: Academic Press, 1981.

LERNER, R. M., KARSON, M., MEISELS, M., & KNAPP, J. R. Actual and perceived attitudes of late adolescents and their parents: The phenomenon of the generation gaps. *Journal of Genetic Psychology,* 1975, *126,* 195–207.

LERNER, R. M., & KNAPP, J. R. Actual and perceived intrafamilial attitudes of late adolescents and their parents. *Journal of Youth and Adolescence,* 1975, *4*(No. 1), 17–36.

LERNER, R. M., SCHROEDER, C., REWITZER, M., & WEINSTOCK, A. Attitudes of high school students and their parents toward contemporary issues. *Psychological Reports,* 1972, *31,* 255–258.

LERNER, R. M., SKINNER, E. A., & SORELL, G. T. Methodological implications of contextual/dialectical theories of development. *Human Development,* 1980, *23,* 225–235.

LERNER, R. M., & SPANIER, G. B. A dynamic interactional view of child and family development. In R. M. Lerner & G. B. Spanier (Eds.), *Child influences on marital and family interaction: A life-span perspective.* New York: Academic Press, 1978.

LERNER, R. M., & SPANIER, G. B. *Adolescent development: A life-span perspective.* New York: McGraw-Hill, 1980.

LEWIS, M., & LEE-PAINTER, S. An interactional approach to the mother-infant dyad. In M. Lewis & L. A. Rosenblum (Eds.), *The effect of the infant on its caregiver.* New York: John Wiley, 1974.

LEWIS, M., & ROSENBLUM, L. A. *The effect of the infant on its caregiver.* New York: John Wiley, 1974.

LEWONTIN, R. C. The fallacy of biological determinism. *The Sciences,* 1976, *16,* 6–10.

LONG, B. H., HENDERSON, E. H., & PLATT, L. Self-other orientations of Israeli adolescents reared in kibbutzim and moshavim. *Developmental Psychology,* 1973, *8,* 300–308.

McCANDLESS, B. R. *Adolescents.* Hinsdale, Ill.: Dryden Press, 1970.

MACCOBY, E. E., & JACKLIN, C. N. *The psychology of sex differences.* Stanford, Calif.: Stanford University Press, 1974.

MARCIA, J. E. *Determination and construct validity of ego identity status.* Unpublished doctoral dissertation, Ohio State University, 1964.

MARCIA, J. E. Development and validation of ego-identity status. *Journal of Personality and Social Psychology,* 1966, *3,* 551–558.

MARCIA, J. E. Ego identity status: Relationship to change in self-esteem, "general maladjustment," and authoritarianism. *Journal of Personality,* 1967, *1,* 118–133.

MARCIA, J. E. Identity six years after: A follow-up study. *Journal of Youth and Adolescence,* 1976, *5,* 145–160.

MARCIA, J. E., & FRIEDMAN, M. L. Ego identity status in college women. *Journal of Personality,* 1970, *38,* 249–263.

MARTIN, J., & REDMORE, C. A longitudinal study of ego development. *Developmental Psychology,* 1978, *14,* 189–190.

MATTESON, D. R. Adolescent self-esteem, family communication, and marital satisfaction. *Journal of Psychology,* 1974, *86,* 35–47.

MATTESON, D. R. Exploration and commitment: Sex differences and methodological problems in the use of identity status categories. *Journal of Youth and Adolescence,* 1977, *6,* 353–374.

MEAD, M. *Coming of age in Samoa: A psychological study of primitive youth for Western civilization.* New York: Morrow, 1928.

MEAD, M. *Growing up in New Guinea.* New York: Morrow, 1930.

MILLER, D. R., & SWANSON, G. E. *The changing American parent.* New York: John Wiley, 1958.

MONTEMAYOR, R., & EISEN, M. The development of self-conceptions from childhood to adolescence. *Developmental Psychology,* 1977, *13,* 314–319.

MUSSEN, P. H., HARRIS, S., RUTHERFORD, E., & KEASEY, C. B. Honesty and altruism among preadolescents. *Developmental Psychology,* 1970, *3,* 169–194.

NEIMARK, E. D. Intellectual development during adolescence. In F. D. Horowitz (Ed.), *Review of child development research* (Vol. 4). Chicago: University of Chicago Press, 1975.

NELSON, D. D. A study of personality adjustment among adolescent children with working and non-working mothers. *Journal of Educational Research,* 1971, *64,* 328–330.

NESSELROADE, J. R., & BALTES, P. B. Adolescent personality development and historical change: 1970–1972. *Monographs of the Society for Research in Child Development,* 1974, *39,* 1–80.

O'DONNELL, W. J. Adolescent self-esteem related to feelings toward parents and friends. *Journal of Youth and Adolescence,* 1976, *5,* 179–185.

OFFER, D. *The psychological world of the teen-ager.* New York: Basic Books, 1969.

OFFER, D., & HOWARD, K. I. An empirical analysis of the Offer self-image questionnaire for adolescents. *Archives of General Psychiatry,* 1972, *27,* 529–533.

OFFER, D., OSTROV, E., & HOWARD, K. I. The self-image of adolescents: A study of four cultures. *Journal of Youth and Adolescence,* 1977, *6,* 265–280.

O'LEARY, V. E. *Toward understanding women.* Monterey, Calif.: Brooks/Cole, 1977.

ORLOFSKY, J. L., MARCIA, J. E., & LESSER, I. M. Ego identity status and the intimacy versus isolation crisis of young adulthood. *Journal of Personality and Social Psychology,* 1973, *27,* 211–219.

PIAGET, J. *The psychology of intelligence.* London: Routledge and Kegan Paul, 1950.

PIAGET, J. *The child's conceptions of numbers.* New York: W. W. Norton & Co., Inc., 1965.

PIAGET, J. Piaget's theory. In P. H. Mussen (Ed.), *Carmichael's manual of child psychology* (Vol. 1). New York: John Wiley, 1970.

PODD, M. H. Ego identity status and morality: The relationship between two developmental constructs. *Developmental Psychology,* 1972, *6,* 497–507.

RAMOS, E. Imagen personal del adolescente Nisei. *Revista Latinoamericana de Psicologia,* 1974, *6,* 229–234.

REST, J. R. Longitudinal study of the defining issues test of moral judgment: A strategy for analyzing developmental change. *Developmental Psychology,* 1975, *11,* 738–748.

RIEGEL, K. F. Toward a dialectical theory of development. *Human Development,* 1975, *18,* 50–64.

RIEGEL, K. F. The dialectics of human development. *American Psychologist,* 1976a, *31,* 689–700.

RIEGEL, K. F. From traits and equilibrium toward developmental dialectics. In W. J. Arnold & J. K. Cole (Eds.), *Nebraska symposium on motivation.* Lincoln: University of Nebraska Press, 1976b.

SAHLINS, M. D. The use and abuse of biology. In A. L. Caplan (Ed.), *The sociobiology debate.* New York: Harper & Row, Pub., 1978.

SAMEROFF, A. Transactional models in early social relations. *Human Development,* 1975, *18,* 65–79.

SANFORD, N. Developmental status of the entering freshman. In N. Sanford (Ed.), *The American college.* New York: John Wiley, 1962.

SANTROCK, J. W. Influence of onset and type of paternal absence on the first four Eriksonian developmental crises. *Developmental Psychology,* 1970, *3,* 273–274.

SANTROCK, J. W. Father absence, perceived maternal behavior, and moral development in boys. *Child Development,* 1975, *46,* 753–757.

SCHACTER, B. Identity crisis and occupational processes: An intensive exploratory study of emotionally disturbed male adolescents. *Child Welfare,* 1968, *47,* 26–37.

SCHECK, D. C., EMERICK, R., & EL-ASSAL, M. M. Adolescents' perceptions of parent-child external control orientation. *Journal of Marriage and the Family,* 1974, *35,* 643–654.

SCHENKEL, S. Relationship among ego identity status, field-independence, and traditional femininity. *Journal of Youth and Adolescence,* 1975, *4,* 73–82.

SIMMONS, R. G., ROSENBERG, F. R., & ROSENBERG, M. Disturbances in the self-image in adolescence. *American Sociological Review,* 1973, *38,* 553–568.

SMITH, T. E. Push versus pull: Intra-family versus peer-group variables as possible determinants of adolescent orientations toward parents. *Youth and Society,* 1976, *8,* 5–26.

SPENCE, J. T., & HELMREICH, R. *Masculinity and femininity: The psychological dimensions, correlates, and antecedents.* Austin: University of Texas Press, 1978.

STRICKER, G. Implications of research for psychotherapeutic treatment of women. *American Psychologist,* 1977, *32,* 14–22.

SULLIVAN, E. V., McCULLOUGH, G., & STAGER, M. A developmental study of the relationship between conceptual, ego, and moral development. *Child Development,* 1970, *41,* 399–411.

TERMAN, L. M., & TYLER, L. E. Psychological sex differences. In L. Carmichael (Ed.), *Manual of child psychology.* New York: John Wiley, 1954.

THORNDIKE, E. L. The newest psychology. *Educational Review,* 1904, *28,* 217–227.

TOBACH, E., & SCHNEIRLA, T. C. The biopsychology of social behavior of animals. In R. E. Cooke & S. Levin (Eds.), *Biologic basis of pediatric practice.* New York: McGraw-Hill, 1968.

TODER, N. L., & MARCIA, J. E. Ego identity status and response to conformity pressure in college women. *Journal of Personality and Social Psychology,* 1973, *26,* 287–294.

TOMLINSON-KEASEY, C., & KEASEY, C. B. The mediating role of cognitive development in moral judgment. *Child Development,* 1974, *45,* 291–298.

TURIEL, E. Developmental processes in the child's moral thinking. In P. H. Mussen, J. Langer, & M. Covington (Eds.), *Trends and issues in developmental psychology.* New York: Holt, Rinehart & Winston, 1969.

WASHBURN, S. L. (Ed.). *Social life of early men.* New York: Wenner-Gren Foundation for Anthropological Research, 1961.

WATERMAN, A. S., GEARY, P., & WATERMAN, C. Longitudinal study of changes in ego identity status from the freshman to the senior year at college. *Developmental Psychology,* 1974, *10,* 387–392.

WATERMAN, A. S., & GOLDMAN, J. A. A longitudinal study of ego identity development at a liberal arts college. *Journal of Youth and Adolescence,* 1976, *5,* 361–370.

WATERMAN, A. S., KOHUTIS, E., & PULONE, J. The role of expressive writing in ego identity formation. *Developmental Psychology,* 1977, *13,* 286–287.

WATERMAN, A. S., & WATERMAN, C. K. A longitudinal study of changes in ego identity status during the freshman year at college. *Developmental Psychology,* 1971, *5,* 167–173.

WATERMAN, C. K., BEUBEL, M. E., & WATERMAN, A. S. Relationship between resolution of the identity crisis and outcomes of previous psychosocial crises. *Proceedings of the 78th Annual Convention of the American Psychological Association,* 1970, *5,* 467–468.

WEINSTOCK, A., & LERNER, R. M. Attitudes of late adolescents and their parents toward contemporary issues. *Psychological Reports,* 1972, *30,* 239–244.

WHITBOURNE, S. K., & WATERMAN, A. S. Psychosocial development during the adult years: Age and cohort comparisons. *Developmental Psychology*, 1979, *15*, 373–378.

WHITE, C. B., BUSHNELL, N., & REGNEMER, J. L. Moral development in Bahamian school children: A 3-year examination of Kohlberg's stages of moral development. *Developmental Psychology*, 1978, *14*, 58–65.

WOLMAN, B. B. The rebellion of youth. *International Journal of Social Psychiatry*, 1973, *18*, 11–19.

WORELL, J. Sex roles and psychological well-being. Perspectives on methodology. *Journal of Consulting and Clinical Psychology*, 1978, *46*, 777–791.

29

The Peer Group

PHILIP R. NEWMAN

DEFINITION

During early adolescence we expect young people to be involved in an increasingly differentiated, active, and complex peer group. Broadly defined, *peers* are age-mates. The concept of *peer group* refers more specifically to the cluster of associates who know each other and who serve as a source of reference or comparison for one another. In adolescence the peer group consists of the age-mates in a neighborhood or school. Even though an adolescent may have friends in another neighborhood or town, the peer group that has direct impact is the one that dominates the adolescent's daily life settings.

The potential functions of peer group participation are varied. First, we expect the peer group to be a supportive setting that permits adolescents to establish increased autonomy from parents and older siblings. Second, the peer group offers avenues for experimentation with cultural values and for a restatement of one's own commitment or resistance to family or cultural ways. Third, peers are a nonfamily group that invites adolescents to feel a sense of bondedness or affection for a larger, more diverse segment of the society beyond the nuclear and extended family. Finally, peers operate to regulate and direct the behavior of individuals. In some cases this control function is a press toward deviance and impulsiveness. In other cases peer pressures toward conformity are socially desirable forces that reduce egocentrism and tendencies to act in self-centered, antisocial ways.

The Peer Group Structure

Characteristics of the adolescent peer group structure have been described by Dunphy (1963). He based his analysis on naturalistic observation of peer interactions in Sydney, Australia, in the period 1958–1960. His observations "on street-corners, in milkbars and homes, at parties and on Sydney beaches" were complemented by questionnaires, diaries, and interviews that provided a conceptual map of the evolving peer group structure. Two areas of group structure emerge from his work: group boundaries and group roles. The group boundaries outlined two types of groups: cliques and crowds. The cliques were small, with an average of six members in each (range 3–9). The crowds were associations of two, three, or four cliques. There were 15 to 30 members. The feeling of intimacy and closeness extended to the clique, but the crowd created larger social events, especially parties and dances. Dunphy observed that clique membership seemed to be a prerequisite for crowd membership. Not every clique was included in a crowd, but no one claimed to be a member of a crowd and not a member of a clique. There were very few isolates.

The formation of the crowd appeared to take a developmental trend. Adolescents began their group experience in same-sex cliques. The next stage was the interaction of a girl's clique and a boy's clique in some kind of group activity, such as a bike trip or a volleyball game. The third stage involved individual meetings between leaders of the two cliques and the beginning of dating. After these early heterosexual interactions, the cliques themselves began to be heterosexual and to join with other cliques to form a heterosexual crowd. At this stage most peer contacts, including friendships, dates, and larger group activities, were confined to other members of the crowd. In the last stage the crowd began to disintegrate as couples who were going steady had less need for the crowd.

Dunphy described two central group roles: the leader

and the sociocenter. There were two kinds of leaders: the clique leader and the crowd leader. Cliques were often described by referring to the leader's name. Clique leaders were notable for participating in more advanced heterosexual activities, for being in touch with other cliques, and for serving as advisers or counselors in matters of dating and love. Clique leaders of a crowd formed a special group which planned, executed, and promoted social activities.

The sociocenter was the crowd joker. That person was usually popular and outgoing. The function of the sociocenter was to maintain good feelings within the group and to provide the group with a playful, affiliative atmosphere. The more dominant and assertive the group leader is, the more clearly articulated is the role of the sociocenter.

Sources of Pressure to Join Groups

At the ages of 13 and 14 adolescents begin to spend increasingly long periods of time away from home. When they enter high school they no longer come home for lunch, and they may spend time after school with friends, in school activities, or at a job. On weekends and in the evening they may also spend time with friends, go out on dates, or attend school functions. Once adolescents have a car or the use of a car, they may be away still more and at greater distances from home. Parents may notice that it is difficult to plan meals and other family events for the entire family once the children have reached adolescence. The children's increased mobility and involvement away from the family make it obvious that the parents have fewer opportunities than previously to guide or influence their children directly.

At this stage parents become concerned about the other adolescents with whom their children are spending time and the kinds of activities in which their children are participating. They may ask what to an adolescent appears to be intrusive questions about their friends regarding the social status, religious affiliation, race, or character of these friends and their families. Parents may try to discourage or forbid associations that they deem inappropriate or harmful for their children and to encourage certain relationships that they consider favorable or advantageous.

The following example illustrates an extreme case of parental resistance to an adolescent's choice of peer involvement. It was shared by a black adolescent who attended an integrated school in Kansas. "This boy I used to date went with a white girl once. She went through hell with her parents and everyone else to go out with him. But he didn't really care. He was just showing off. Her father even spit in her face. Her parents attacked her; they beat her and called her a slut" (Petroni, 1971, p. 58).

To the extent that the adolescent's peer associations reflect the parents' values and goals, there will be minimal conflict about friendships, but there may still be considerable pressure for the child to take an active part in social activities. If the adolescent's friendship choices do not reflect parents' values, conflict between the adolescent and parents over this issue is to be expected. In either case there is perceptible influence from the parents concerning peer group membership.

Even if adolescents resist or reject parental pressure to affiliate with a specific group of peers, they are unlikely to be able to withstand the demands from their age-mates to make some kind of peer group commitment. Adolescents' circles of friends, their interests, and their style of dress quickly link them to a subgroup that has continuity and meaning within the context of their neighborhood or school. There are demands from within this group to conform to the norms of the group and to demonstrate commitment and loyalty to the other group members. There are also expectations from those outside the group that reinforce the individual's connection to a specific peer group and prohibit movement to other peer groups. The peer group social structure is usually well established in most high school settings, and members of that structure exert considerable pressure on newcomers to join one peer group or another. The individual who becomes a member of any group is more acceptable to the social system as a whole than one who tries to remain unaffiliated and aloof.

Another source of pressure for peer group identification emanates from the school itself. School adults both passively accept and actively encourage the organization of students into peer groupings. In the passive mode they accept the friendship groups as they exist in the school and do little, if anything, to bring members of different peer groups into a working relationship with one another. They allow students to establish the boundaries, the rivalries, and the areas of cooperation in their relationships. In the active mode they reinforce some characteristics of the peer group by selecting certain students for certain kinds of tasks. In most schools, for example, members of one peer group monitor the halls and assist in record-keeping functions, while members of another peer group fix the teachers' cars and operate equipment.

There is an implicit acceptance by school adults of the peer group structure as it exists. They make almost no effort to alter the structure, which they may remember from their own high school days. The evolution of a new group (e.g., "freaks," "hippies," or "burn-outs") may, however, meet some strong resistance from school adults. Explicitly they rely on members of certain peer groups to perform certain functions and to act along certain expected lines. Expectations emanate from teachers as well as students that individuals who dress in a particular way will be members of one peer group or that students who have a particular level of intellectual skill will be members of a particular peer group. School adults often rely on the leaders of the various groups to convey and enforce school norms for acceptable behavior within their own groups. The peer group structure, then, is an important vehicle for the maintenance of order and predictability within the school. Far from challenging this arrangement, school adults count on it to facilitate their jobs.

Thus there is strong pressure from three highly influential sources for the adolescent to make an identification with a specific peer group: pressure from parents, peers, and school adults. The need for peer acceptance and approval comes not only from the adolescent but also from at least these three other groups in the environment.

INDIVIDUAL PSYCHOLOGY AND THE PEER GROUP

Early adolescents experience a search for membership, an internal questioning about the group of which they are most naturally a part. They ask themselves, "Who am I, and with whom do I belong?" While membership in a peer group may be the most pressing concern, questions about other group identifications also arise. Adolescents may seek commitment to a religious organization, they may evaluate the nature of their ties to immediate or extended family members, and they may begin to understand the unique characteristics of their neighborhood or community. In the process of seeking group affiliation, the adolescent is confronted with the fit or lack of fit between personal needs and values and the values held by relevant social groups in the environment. The process of self-evaluation takes place within the context of the meaningful groups that are available for identification. Individual needs for social approval or affiliation, for leadership or power, and for status or reputation are expressed in the kinds of group identifications that are made and rejected during early adolescence.

Most adolescents perceive an existing group that meets their social needs and provides them with a sense of group belonging. It is this sense of group belonging that facilitates the psychological growth of the individual and serves as an integrating force in efforts to succeed in the developmental tasks of early adolescence.

Some adolescents develop a pervasive sense of alienation from peers. The person does not experience a sense of belonging to a group but rather is continually uneasy in the presence of peers. One way this may be brought about is that parents may press the adolescent to restrict associations to a particular peer group, but that group may not offer the adolescent membership. Another possibility is the situation in which the individual looks over the existing groups and does not find one that would really meet personal needs. In this case the adolescent may never become a member of a peer group. A third possibility is that no peer group may offer acceptance or friendship to an individual, and the person will gradually be shut out of all the existing groups in the social environment. A fourth possibility is that isolation has genetic roots.

It is not uncommon for young people to become preoccupied with their own feelings and thoughts. They may withdraw from social interactions, feeling unwilling to share the areas of vulnerability and confusion that accompany physical, intellectual, and social growth. Most adolescents feel some of the loneliness and isolation that is implied in the term *alienation*. Even with peers there is a need to exercise caution about sharing one's most troublesome concerns for fear of rejection or ridicule from others for weaknesses or fears. The maintenance of an interpersonal "cool," a desire to be perceived as someone who is "together" rather than vulnerable, may stand in the way of building strong bonds of commitment to social groups.

There is a tension between expectations for group affiliation and barriers to group commitment that are a product of the self-consciousness and egocentrism of this life stage and of the potential for rejection from existing groups. For most adolescents the negative resolution of this conflict is far less likely than the positive one. In this case, however, the emergence of personal choice in the resolution of the psychosocial conflict can be seen. Also for the first time a resolution of the psychosocial crisis depends not on the relationship of an individual to an adult in the environment but on the interaction of an adolescent and peers.

Social Status and Reputation

There is considerable evidence to show that a dynamic peer group structure operates as a system of status ranking (Coleman, 1961; Jones, 1976; Trickett, Kelly, & Todd, 1972). The precise impact of this peer status system on social development is not clear. Several kinds of learning are going on at the same time as one confronts an existing status structure. First, students learn to identify the existing status system. They know what each group wears, where its members hang out, what their reputation is in the school, and what kinds of activities they are likely to engage in. One might call this the ability to read the status system. This kind of social skill is essential to the adaptive efforts of the student at the school and also contributes to later participation in the adult community.

Among the paths to status are physical appearance, including early maturation for boys; good looks and good grooming; athletic ability; leadership in school activities; and popularity (Coleman, 1961; Jones, 1958). In his analysis of ten midwestern high schools, Coleman (1961) was discouraged to find that the adolescent culture gave little emphasis to academic achievement as a prerequisite for status or popularity. Two more recent analyses of this problem suggest that adolescents may be developing their status system in response to patterns of reinforcement from the community and the school. Friesen (1968) analyzed the responses of Canadian students about characteristics that were descriptive of the leading crowd, characteristics that they perceived to be important for success in life, and characteristics that they perceived as important to their own future. Only 2.5 percent of the samples saw academic excellence as important for membership in the leading crowd, and only 15.6 percent viewed academic excellence as important to success in life. However, 80 percent saw academic excellence as important for their own future. Thus although adolescents perceive the immediate and even the long-term rewards of academic excellence to be less important than friendliness, good looks, or personality, they recognize the importance of the sequential chain of life events that are tied to academic achievement in their culture.

Eitzen (1975, p. 268) asked high school males the same question that Coleman used in his study from the 1950s: If you could be remembered here at school for one of the three things below, which would you want it to be?

Athletic star
Brilliant student
Most popular

Table 29-1 Percent of High School Boys Who Would Rather Be Remembered as . . . in 1950 and 1970

	COLEMAN	EITZEN
Athletic star	44%	47%
Brilliant student	31	23
Most popular	25	30

Table 29-1 compares the responses of Coleman's and Eitzen's samples to these choices. *Athletic star* continues to be viewed as a desirable characteristic for status in the high school and as an "unusual achievement." In the more recent sample the importance of the *brilliant student* has dropped somewhat as a valued source of status.

Eitzen suggests that the importance of athletics for high school boys varies depending on characteristics of the school, the boy, and the community. The role of athletic star is less important to seniors than to sophomores. It is more important to students who are highly involved in school activities than to those who are uninvolved. Athletics is seen as a greater source of status in small rather than in large schools and in highly structured, authoritarian schools rather than in permissive schools. Finally athletics is less important in large communities with a high percentage of professionals and with comparatively few (less than 5 percent) very poor families. Although sports continues to be a highly visible area for success in high school, variations in student responses suggest that aspects of the school organization and the opportunity structure of the larger community clearly feed into the status characteristics of high school athletics.

In addition to learning to read the status system, adolescents eventually identify with a peer clique. Involvement with the peer group and commitment to a particular group of friends provide the adolescent with a sense of peer understanding and support. They also carry pressures for peer conformity. Peer group identification is of central importance for the formation of social skills that continue to be a vital part of adult life.

Finally there is the reputational consequence of joining a particular peer group. Once one is associated with the "elites" or the "greasers" or the "jocks" or the "hippies," certain school and community resources may open and others may close. Expectations that peers and adults hold for your behavior as a member of a group will influence their reactions and responses.

One senior who was involved in a small, low-status group whose members were identified by their use of drugs described the consequences for his reputation at school.

I have a hard time being myself around people in general, 'cause like, I play a part, and as time progresses, you get tired of the part you're playing, and you try to change, and people act as if they expect you to be your old self . . . the drug-crazed hippy, which I play pretty good. (Gottlieb, 1975, p. 216)

Over time participation in the social status system of the peer culture sensitizes adolescents to the costs and benefits of certain kinds of reputations. In some smaller communities one's reputation during high school can follow well into adult life, providing a positive "halo" effect on adult activities for some and isolating others

(Jones, 1958). To some extent once the status hierarchy of the peer culture is established, it continues to have self-perpetuating reputational features. Perhaps the early-maturing boys and the good-looking girls did show some social maturity as they entered the high school scene. By the senior year, however, physical maturation and social competence are well distributed among the student population. Yet this early "elite" group continues to benefit during its high school career from the status that it achieved during the first months of high school. In this sense adolescents learn about the power of reputation, and they begin to evaluate reputational claims in a more critical light.

PEER PRESSURE AND CONFORMITY

The process of affiliating with a peer group involves opening oneself up to the pressure and social influence of that group. Adolescents are at a point in their intellectual development at which they are able to conceptualize themselves as objects of expectations. These expectations may be perceived by adolescents as a force drawing them to be more than they think they are—that is, to be braver, more outgoing, more confident. In these cases peer pressure may have a positive effect on the adolescent's self-image and serves as a motive for group identification.

As members of a peer group adolescents have more influence than they would as single individuals. They begin to understand the value of collective enterprise. In offering membership the peer group enhances adolescents' feelings of self-worth and protects them from loneliness. When conflicts develop in the family, the adolescent can seek comfort and intimacy among peers. In order to benefit in these ways from the peer group affiliation, adolescents must be willing to suppress some of their individuality and to find pleasure in focusing on those attributes that they share with peers. Total conformity is not demanded within the peer group. In fact most peer groups depend on the unique characteristics of their members to lend definition and vigor to the roles that emerge within the group. However, the peer group places considerable importance on some maximally adaptive level of conformity in order to bolster the structure of the group and to strengthen its effectiveness in satisfying members' needs. Most adolescents find some security in peer group demands to conform. The few well-defined characteristics of the group lend stability and substance to the adolescent's self-concept. In complying with group pressure, each adolescent has an opportunity to state, unambiguously, that s/he is someone and that s/he belongs somewhere.

The Strength of the Tendency to Conform

Several studies have tried to provide evidence about the strength of the tendency to conform to peer pressure during early adolescence. Costanzo (1970) asked male subjects in four age groups—7–8, 12–13, 16–17, and 19–21—to make judgments of the length of a line and to give their answers by lighting a button on a response panel. Each subject saw his own answer as well as what

Figure 29-1 Percentage of conformity as a function of age level (n = 36 per age level). (Source: Costanzo, P. R. Conformity development as a function of self-blame. *Journal of Personality and Social Psychology,* 1970, *14,* 372. Copyright [1970] by the American Psychological Association. Reprinted by permission.)

he thought were the answers of three other subjects. Figure 29-1 shows the percentage of subjects in each age group who made errors in the direction of the peer judgments. The pattern of peer conformity appears to peak at the 12- to 13-year age range and to decrease slowly during the high school years. Other comparisons of early and later adolescence confirm the tendency for early adolescence to be a peak period for peer conformity, especially when conformity is measured by the readiness to change one's judgment in the direction of peers' perceptions even when those perceptions are in error (Brownston & Willis, 1971).

A somewhat disturbing fact is that pressures toward peer conformity appear to increase young adolescents' willingness to be involved in pranks or behavior of which adults would disapprove. Children at three grade levels (grades three, six, and eight) were asked whether they would go along with peers in certain hypothetical situations involving misbehavior. At each higher grade level children saw the pranks as less serious and said that they would be more likely to get involved with their peers in the misbehavior (Bixenstine, DeCorte, & Bixenstine, 1976). Bronfenbrenner (1966; Rodgers, Bronfenbrenner, & Devereux, 1968) compared the willingness of American and Russian children to engage in misbehavior, including cheating on a test or denying responsibility for damage that one had done. The Russian children were equally unlikely to engage in such behavior if parents, peers, or school adults might learn of the act. The American children were more likely to participate in misbehavior if they thought that their peers might find out about it. In general Soviet children are trained to use peer pressure and social criticism to enforce moral behavior. Soviet peers come through a consistent program of moral education in which they learn to correct one another, to help one another to succeed, and to feel shamed if they are the object of peer disapproval (Bronfenbrenner, 1970). In American society there is no such clear picture of one correct way to behave. Peers have not generally been taught to feel responsible for one another. More than likely they have experienced peer competition

in the school setting. Children come to learn that adults in the school are responsible for monitoring and punishing misconduct. Norms against "tattling" become very strong in the elementary grades. One way to begin to demonstrate autonomy from adult authorities is to participate in behavior of which adults might disapprove. Although this misconduct may be minimal and may never result in any form of discipline or police intervention, a large number of adolescents do perform delinquent acts in the company of their peers (Reynolds, 1976; Schimel, 1974; Weiner, 1970).

Value Areas Which Are Influenced by Peers

Two rather different questions have been raised about the impact of the peer group on values. First, how do peer groups influence acceptance? Second, do peer group values dominate or conflict with parental values?

Coleman (1961) has addressed the first question in his description of a system of cliques within the American high school. The cliques generate a value profile for the school that determines the status or importance of individual students. In most schools the hierarchy of the peer group structure is determined by success in the primary areas that are valued by the cliques. These tend to include athletic skills, student activities, and social leadership, but not academic excellence. Thus peer group values determine the acceptance of students, the boundaries around clique groupings, and the kinds of behaviors that are likely to be approved, rejected, or ignored among clique members.

The impact of friendship groups can be seen in the kinds of behaviors that friends engage in together and in their orientation toward school. Kandel (1978) found that high school friends tend to be in the same grade in school and of the same sex and race. Of all the many activities and attitudes that friends were asked about, the highest degrees of similarity were in drug use, educational expectations, and involvement with peer activities. In general friends, even friends who had liked each other for more than three years, did not hold similar attitudes about such things as politics, materialism, career aspirations, closeness with parents, or evaluation of teachers. This picture of peer friendships suggests that peer groups tend to be structured around several rather obvious characteristics—age, race, and sex—and that they are probably fostered by frequent interactions or physical proximity within the school. Similarities in behavior may eventually produce similarity in attitudes, but attitudes do not tend to be the force that binds most adolescent peers together.

Peer Values and Parent Values

The second question about the impact of peer groups on values focuses on the extent to which parents' values and peers' values are in harmony or conflict and, if in conflict, on whether peers have more influence over adolescents than their parents do. One approach to this question has been to survey the attitudes of adolescents and their parents on a range of issues, including sex, drugs, religion, war, law and law enforcement, racism, and politics. In surveys of this kind attitudes of the two groups tend to be similar in most areas (Lerner & Weinstock, 1972; Weinstock & Lerner, 1972).

Another approach has been to pose hypothetical situations in which parents and peers offer opposing views of how to behave. The subjects are then asked whether they would follow the advice of parents or peers. Early studies of this type suggested that adolescents turned to peers when the situation involved a current question about popularity or membership in a club but that they turned to parents in deciding about future plans or moral decisions with consequences for the future (Brittain, 1963, 1967–1968, 1969).

Later studies modified the method somewhat and came out with a rather different picture. In these studies (Larson, 1972a, 1972b), the subject was asked to tell what s/he would do in a given situation. The situation was described in two different ways: once so that the parents urged against some behavior that friends supported, and again so that friends urged against the behavior and the parents supported it. The majority of subjects (73.6 percent) were neither parent-oriented nor peer-oriented. They made their decision about the situation and did not modify it, regardless of who approved or disapproved. The next largest group (15.7 percent) were parent-compliant. They went along with their parents' decisions in at least four of the six situations. In general the group of adolescents tested in this situation were strongly parent-oriented. In other words they felt that their parents understood them, supported them, and generally had good advice. Nonetheless when the decision about how to behave in a particular situation had to be made, the adolescents made their judgments independent of their parents' wishes.

A third approach to the question of the respective impact of parents and peers on the values of adolescents is simply to ask adolescents directly how highly they regard parental advice. Curtis (1975) described the responses of over 18,000 adolescents in grades 7 to 12 to questions about the degree to which they valued fathers', mothers', and friends' opinions. At every age parents were more valued sources of advice and opinions than friends. However, the number of students who gave a high rating to parents declined rather steadily from seventh through tenth grade. At grade 11 the middle-class and the working-class boys seemed to show an increased valuation of fathers. The value of friends' opinions and advice remained much more stable across ages. About 28 percent of boys and 50 percent of girls placed high value on their friends' opinions at every age. Although friends do not become more important, parents become somewhat less important, suggesting a gradual process of individuation and a strengthening of the individual's own value system.

An interesting comparison is provided in a survey of friendship relations among Soviet students aged 14 to 17 (Kon & Losenkov, 1978). The students felt that their friends understood them better than either their mothers or fathers. They also felt more comfortable sharing confidential problems with their friends rather than with their parents. On the other hand in response to the question "With whom would you consult in a complicated life situation?" boys and girls both chose their mothers.

We see a picture of adolescent friendship as providing companionship in activities, emotional support, and understanding. However, adolescents appear to realize that on some matters parental opinions are likely to be sounder, perhaps more protective of their well-being, and more likely to result in a positive outcome than the opinion of peers. In addition personal judgment is emerging to provide a more autonomous basis for value decisions. Individual adolescents become increasingly capable of evaluating situations and making their own choices without guidance from parents or peers.

PEER GROUP RELATIONS DURING THE COLLEGE YEARS

There can be no question that friendships made during the college years have the potential for providing deep and lasting relationships. As adolescents free themselves from the intense peer pressures of the high school peer group, friendships begin to reflect a growing sense of personal identity. A desire and an expectation for intimacy and understanding brings later adolescents together. Of course this need to be understood may result in disappointments if friendships fail to provide the sense of closeness that is hoped for.

Developmental Changes in Adolescent Friendships

The more work adolescents do on the resolution of their own identity, the more important it is for them to find friends who share their values and understand their questions. During later adolescence young people continue to become less conforming and more independent in their judgments (Boyd, 1975; Costanzo & Shaw, 1966; Lehman, 1963). They are less likely to seek peer friendships in order to be accepted by a clique or crowd and are more interested in honesty and commitment in a friendship. In a survey of Soviet adolescents, two characteristics were predominant in the definition of friendship: "(1) the requirement of mutual aid and loyalty; and (2) the expectation of empathetic understanding" (Kon & Losenkov, 1978, p. 196). The former became less important with age, and the latter became more important. At every age loyalty was more important to males, and understanding was more important to females.

Increased emphasis on friendships that facilitate work on identity can be inferred from several studies of college-age adolescents. Newcomb (1962) described the process of peer group friendship formation in a student rooming house. At first friendships were based on proximity. Men who lived on the same floor or who shared a room became friends. After four months it was a commonality of values that drew friends together. Newcomb's subjects felt closest to others who were struggling with the same problems and who were committed to similar values.

Tangri (1972) asked women whom she had typed as *role innovators* to discuss their friendship relations. The role innovators were college women who had selected male-dominated careers. They tended to have more males among their ten closest friends than did traditional women (women who had chosen occupations with 50 percent or more women). These males were likely to support the idea of having a wife pursue a career and to encourage this career orientation for the benefits or satisfactions that it would give her. Role innovators were also likely to find female friends who supported their career aspirations. Thus the female students who have made what might be described as a high-risk or a potentially conflict-laden career choice have managed to find encouragement and support from both male and female friends who share their values.

A student at a small New England liberal arts college described the quality of her closest college friendship. In this description we begin to understand how opening oneself up to the vulnerability of intimacy can help foster real progress in self-awareness and personal growth.

Junior year I formed the closest relationship to anyone I've ever had, not only at Berkshire but anywhere. Lisa and I became extremely close. She cared about what I thought, and many times, even though she had reservations about what I was feeling, she never attacked but asked questions, her questions making me question in turn and generally causing me to at least reevaluate those feelings. We talked hours on end about Berkshire and what was happening to us and everyone else here. I didn't like Berkshire because it placed me in a state of, I guess, being nowhere. The academics of Berkshire seemed so unreal, the people seemed unreal, and increasingly it became harder to identify with other black students since it seemed the college was doing some grand experiment in coming up with the perfect black Berkshire student. I didn't identify with any black student who felt comfortable here because it implied being comfortable in other places also. I can't be comfortable because I know where I came from and am going back to, and the black people in the world out there, the real world, are terribly uncomfortable. (Goethals & Klos, 1976, p. 234)

Friendships between Males and Females

Individuals differ in the patterns of friendships they desire. Some adolescents have both male and female friends, some have friends of only the same sex, some have friends of only the opposite sex, and some have only one intimate friendship that combines sexuality and understanding. In the sample of Soviet adolescents discussed before, 75 percent agreed that it would be possible to have a friendship with someone of the opposite sex without being in love. However among the oldest males (age 20), more than half doubted that this would be possible. In general among all age groups in the Soviet sample, more males preferred same-sex friendships, and more females preferred opposite-sex friendships. If this pattern was reflected in real friendship choices, one could expect that more females would feel disappointed in not being able to have the close friendships they desired. This was in fact the case. At every age the Soviet girls were less optimistic about the possibility of finding a "genuine friendship."

Opposite-sex friendships are viewed as both desirable and problematic in the United States. In a study of black college students, friendships across sex were more intimate than friendships between members of the same sex (Peretti, 1976). Opposite-sex friendships were characterized by more sharing of information about the self, more participation in shared activities, and greater feelings of reciprocity than same-sex friendships. We know from Tangri's (1972) study of role innovators that male friends

can be very important in supporting women's untraditional aspirations. We also expect adolescent males to benefit from close friendships with females. In these friendships it is possible for males to share some of their doubts and weaknesses—that is, to disclose more of their personal thoughts without being viewed as overly dependent or incompetent. Usually women are more comfortable than men about sharing intimate aspects of themselves. Since this makes them more vulnerable to exploitation or rejection, they are likely to encourage their male friends to do the same. If a male friend is able to collaborate with a female friend in the process, it is possible that the male will benefit by increasing his feelings of being understood (Cozby, 1973; Derlega & Chaiken, 1977).

Although friendships between males and females may have beneficial and satisfying consequences, there are some serious barriers to opposite-sex friendships. If we think of one of the goals of friendship as the facilitation of identity formation and value clarification, relationships that interfere with a developing sense of competence and personal values would be counterproductive. It is from this standpoint that male-female friendships are most likely to run into difficulties.

Studies of attitudes toward the female sex role suggest a gap between males and females in their acceptance of feminism. Male and female peers do not share the same commitment to the equal participation of women in all spheres of cultural life (Roper & Labeff, 1977; Zey-Ferrell, Tolone, & Walsh, 1978). Furthermore males and females tend to agree with a stereotyped image of women as less competent, more submissive, and less independent than men (Broverman, Vogel, Broverman, Clarkson, & Rosenkrantz, 1972). Women who reject the traditional female sex role and strive for academic competence or innovative careers will find it difficult to find male friends who really share those values.

Both males and females bring stereotypes about the opposite sex that may interfere with the development of a friendship. Females tend to expect that males will have fewer "feminine" characteristics than they actually have (Nicol & Bryson, 1977). Thus females will expect males to be less supportive, empathic, dependent, or nurturant than the males feel they are. In this sense females may not be ready to accept or support the interpersonal or emotional qualities that are part of a male friend's personality. In contrast males have trouble accepting the intellectual challenge of a bright female friend. Despite the growing value in finding a life partner who will provide intellectual companionship, many males have difficulty with heterosexual relationships in which they do not feel superior (Komarovsky, 1973). Such males either avoid heterosexual relationships that might threaten their feelings of intellectual competence or try to turn their female companions into "good listeners." For their part some women play into the male superiority stereotype by pretending to be less competent or by disguising their abilities. Although this kind of charade is becoming less acceptable among college women, it continues to be an expectation that females identify in the college environment. Obviously a productive friendship would not be easy to achieve in a relationship in which one partner had to disguise her intellectual abilities.

As adolescents work toward their own solutions to the

challenges of political, occupational, family, and moral ideologies, they can ill afford friendships with either males or females that do not support the expression of their fullest potential. If understanding, support, and empathy are the goals of friendship, then self-doubt, competition, and shame are its pitfalls. It is important that a friendship begin on a foundation of respect and acceptance. Otherwise the price of companionship is likely to be the abandonment of personal growth.

CROSS-CULTURAL EVIDENCE AND THE PEER EXPERIENCE

Peer relations in adolescence have been studied in a variety of cultures. A look at the experiences of adolescents across cultures reveals the answers to some important questions about the functions of the peer group. First, can peer groups be used to support and maintain the values of a culture? Second, is it possible to develop longlasting bonds of affection between people outside of one's family? Third, can the peer group serve as a supportive structure for the development of skills and competence?

As one looks across cultures at the experiences adolescents share with their peers, it becomes clear that many societies make deliberate use of the adolescent peer group as an agent of socialization. In contrast to the sentiment often expressed in American society that adolescent peers challenge, deviate from, or ignore cultural values, many societies create peer cultures that actively support and encourage individual allegiance to the societal norms. In the following material an attempt will be made to answer the questions raised earlier. Answering these questions will open the way to an understanding that the *peer group* is really a variable entity in the life of an individual and in the role it plays in a social structure. While we may sense a oneness with each other when the term is mentioned, it is important to remember that our experiences may be rather different.

Supporting and Maintaining Cultural Values

The pattern of Soviet character education and "upbringing" is an example of how a culture can encourage peers to feel responsible for maintaining cultural values (Bronfenbrenner, 1970). Soviet society uses both the family and the school as socialization agents. The family emphasis includes open expression of affection and clear expectations for obedience and self-control. Parents have access to a variety of media which communicate the findings and views of child-rearing experts about how to function effectively in the parent role. Parents are told that obedience is to be encouraged through explanations of how to behave, praising when correcting faults, and punishing when disobedience occurs.

When children begin school at age seven, character education is continued through the school. A manual outlining specific goals for socialization guides the expectations, the activities, and the responsibilities that children encounter at each grade level. Within each classroom children are organized into cells. At first teachers identify the goals for the class and reward the cells

that perform the best. Eventually student monitors take over this function, evaluating each cell's achievements.

The principle of social criticism is used to foster peer responsibility for group behavior. If a child is disobedient the other children try to decide on a fitting plan to improve the child's behavior. Children compete with the class monitors, criticizing their performance. Within cells children are encouraged to point out one another's errors and to figure out how to improve one another's performance so that they can compete more successfully with other cells. Even parents are asked to submit critical reports of the ways in which their children are achieving the goals of character education at home.

Research on moral behavior and on response to the peer group illustrates some of the consequences of this consistent and well-defined program. A comparison of 12-year-old American and Soviet schoolchildren showed that the Soviet schoolchildren were less willing to participate in a wide variety of behaviors if these were disapproved by adults (Bronfenbrenner, 1966). A number of situations, including cheating on a quiz, neglecting homework, and taking fruit from someone's orchard, were presented to the children. They were asked to tell whether they would go along with friends or refuse to go along with friends in each situation. The children had to evaluate the situation under one of three conditions: (1) a condition in which they were told that no one except the experimenter would see their responses; (2) a condition in which they were told that parents and teachers would see their responses; or (3) a condition in which they were told that their classmates would see their responses. Among the Russian children the knowledge that peers would see their responses increased the extent of their resistance temptation. Among the American children the knowledge that peers would see their responses increased their willingness to participate in deviant behavior.

In a comparison of Soviet and Swiss children, the same pattern was observed (Bronfenbrenner, 1970). Children were asked how they would handle 21 examples of peer misconduct. The children had four choices: telling a grown-up, telling the other children, handling it by themselves, or doing nothing. Of the Soviet children 75 percent said that they would speak to the child themselves, whereas only 33 percent of the Swiss children chose that strategy. Twenty percent of the Swiss children, but less than one percent of the Soviet children, said that they would do nothing. Clearly the Soviet strategy of gradually increasing the peer group's obligation for the maintenance of standards of excellence serves to create a sense that peers are responsible for one another's behavior.

We see, then, that a government with extensive control over the lives of its citizens can train its people to keep an eye on each other. Responsiveness to peers is used to enhance the individual's internalized allegiance to a set of values to guide their behavior. The United States is a different case. No one has the power to dictate to one's family and friends specific procedures for telling people how to do better. The emphasis in the United States is on individual development. Argument, conflict, and disagreement are what we agree to do. Strong self-concepts and rugged individualists are valued. People succeed by taking the road not taken. No one controls how people, family, and friends treat a person; that is more or less left to the individual social unit. Peer groups and families can agree or disagree. Most likely it is some of each. There is no uniform code for expected or accepted behavior in American peer groups. In fact the American data suggest that American adolescents see peers as valuing risky, unpredictable behavior. Within U.S. families and peer groups one can imagine a variety of patterns of influence. The Russian experience indicates that it is possible for the peer group to be used to control individual behavior.

The Development of Bonds of Affection beyond Kinship Lines

The peer group represents a potential source of lifelong friendships and emotional commitments that range far beyond the kinship structure. There are several examples of life patterns that appear to foster strong peer bonds.

In the Israeli kibbutz strong peer bonds are created as a result of communal child rearing. Children in the same age group go through a number of transitions from one children's house to another, from one caregiver to another, and from one set of school and work experiences to another. By the time they reach adolescence, they have developed a sense of one another as members of a large family (Barnouw, 1975; Spiro, 1954, 1965). In Spiro's observations of kibbutz life, he noted, for example, that those adolescents who were born and raised in the kibbutz married individuals from outside the kibbutz. Although there were no rules to enforce this practice, it appeared to be a reflection of the sentiment that it would be inappropriate to marry someone who was so much like a sibling. The consequences of this intimate experience among peers are difficult to evaluate. On the one hand kibbutz-reared children tend to see peers as exerting more of a controlling function in their lives than do urban, family-reared Israelis (Devereux, Shouval, Bronfenbrenner, Rodgers, Kav-Venaki, Keely, & Karson, 1974). Bettelheim (1969) points out that there is strong pressure toward conformity among adolescent peers. A child who is rejected by the kibbutz peer group experiences intense alienation and isolation. On the other hand one of the strongest motives for continuing one's commitment to the kibbutz community is a sense of obligation and love for one's peers. Peers coax one another into the decision to reject the diversity and potential luxury of noncommunal life for the security, warmth, and moral virtue of kibbutz existence (Spiro, 1965, 1968, 1970).

Samoan society of 50 years ago offers another pattern of positive adolescent peer commitment (Mead, 1928). Boys and girls joined same-sex peer groups when they were about seven years old. The children played together often and developed some antagonism toward groups from other villages or neighborhoods. There was strong avoidance of opposite-sex peers. For girls the intensity of these friendships was limited by the girls' responsibility to care for younger siblings during this time. As soon as a girl reached puberty, her family involved her in new and more difficult household tasks which left her few hours for peer play. As girls became interested in love affairs and seriously involved in courtship, the need for secrecy made any close friendship hazardous.

For Samoan boys the pattern was different. They did not have the responsibility of caring for younger siblings, nor were they expected to assume heavy household tasks at puberty. Therefore the male peer groups were freer to retain their camaraderie for a longer time. Peer cooperation was required in many of the tasks that adolescent and young adult males were expected to perform. These tasks included manning the canoes, fishing for eels, and laboring in the taro plantations. Finally young men became members of the Aumaga, an organization of males who performed central work tasks and organized important social events for the village. While Samoan females were more likely to find friendship among the wives of one another's husbands, the peer group bonds of Samoan males were fostered and maintained throughout adult life.

This information ensures us of a choice of life patterns which may be personally satisfying. Lives which emerge from families of related kin may be meaningful and satisfying. Lives which emerge from peer groups of biologically unrelated people may also be meaningful and productive. Finally it must be noted that patterns of peer relations that occur in adolescence may be socialization systems for the adult forms of peer relations in a culture.

THE PEER GROUP AS AN ENVIRONMENT FOR BUILDING AUTONOMY AND COMPETENCE

The third function of the adolescent peer group is to provide new opportunities for adolescents to rely on their own skills and problem-solving capacities rather than on the competences of adults. In order to achieve this goal, some societies create youth dormitories or age-graded communities where young people are expected to perform many of the tasks of daily survival. Among the Muria of eastern India, male and female children live in a dormitory from the time they are six until marriage (Barnouw, 1975; Elwin, 1947). The dormitory, or *ghotul*, is viewed as a religious sanctuary where members are dedicated to work and spiritual harmony. Children work for their parents and other villagers. They also perform ceremonial dances for the village. Marriage is arranged by a child's parents, and once children are married they must leave the ghotul.

The training for autonomy is even more pronounced among the Nyakyusa of East Africa (Barnouw, 1975; Wilson, 1951). Children leave their fathers' houses and begin a new village of reed huts when they are ten years old. As they get older the boys build stronger huts to which they bring their wives when they marry. Before marriage the boys continue to eat in their fathers' homes. After marriage each young couple and their children begin to cultivate their own land and prepare their own fields. About ten years after most of the young people have been married and are functioning autonomously, their fathers transfer the responsibilities of government to the young people's village. Among the Muria and the Nyakyusa, adolescents have the opportunity to exercise their new skills and to experience many of the responsibilities of adult life before achieving adult status.

While it is not always true, it is clear that peer groups may be organized to enhance skill learning. Through the peer experiences adolescent members of a culture may engage in meaningful adult-like behaviors in order to become familiar with jobs and roles. During this period adolescents acquire skills and a sense of competence (a related outcome of new learning).

CONCLUSIONS

The *peer group* is a phrase which is almost immediately associated in most people's minds with the adolescent. *Peer group* and *teenager* go together like the horse and carriage. In this chapter the concept of the peer group has been limited to individual psychology. Individuals' social skills become increasingly complex as they grow up. Pubertal maturation readies the person for social interactions that are quantitatively and qualitatively different from the social interactions of middle childhood. The social structures of high school and college are usually more complex than the corresponding systems of the elementary, junior high, or middle school from which the student has come. These new needs and capabilities, along with new demands, are blended by individuals into their own patterns of social behavior. The person's relationships with 6 (± 3) people provide the experiences which help the person to create his/her social style; this is the individual's *friendship group*. During the high school years the friendship group is so important that it becomes an identifiable social structure as Coleman (1961), Dunphy (1963), and others have found. During college the friendship groups develop more intense relations. The *crowd* is another part of the peer group. It is composed of a large number of people and provides opportunities for more complicated social functions such as parties and dances. Most people are part of a friendship group; fewer are members of crowds. Perhaps the level of activity of the crowd is beyond the reach of many adolescents. Complicated dances, dinners, and meetings are part of the social experiences of most adults. However it may be harder for adolescents to engage in and find value in larger, less personal, social occasions.

The group composed of all students in a school or community is the final component of the peer group. As we have seen this group is ordered by age in the United States. It is important because it provides the standards and status hierarchies which people use to define themselves. It may not be possible for all adolescents to relate cognitively to this nebulous entity. For those who do, however, it provides a social map to clusters of people in a complex community. It also sets the moral standards and situational ethics which pose challenges to the developing social intellect.

The peer group is not the same from community to community or nation to nation. In some societies the peer group is complex; in others, it is simple. In Russia the peer group is actively developed by the state as a mechanism for the transmission and maintenance of rules of allegiance and conduct. In Yoredale, England, as Baker and Schoggen (1973) discovered, it provides a mechanism for learning about interaction for the class structure. In Israeli kibbutzim it provides a strong friendship group to serve many of the functions that the family serves in other cultures. In the United States peer groups are diverse. They reflect the basic principle that social life is independent from the state. American ado-

lescents have access to most settings in their communities. The peer group provides a mixing of the various groups which make up the United States melting pot. Whether these groups choose to associate with one another in adulthood is up to them. All friendship groups and crowds are not homogeneous in their composition and associations even during adolescence. However, the peer group includes all of the adolescents who live in the same place at the same time. The social structure, the values, the pressures and the rewards are open to everyone. Even if the structure is not equally open to all, it is visible to everyone. The peer group in American life provides adolescents with the opportunities and the challenges to define themselves as group members. An understanding of close relationships, including intense friendships and love, begins to develop. A cognitive map of social groups and their relationships to one another develops. The person develops a style of interacting with equals. Finally individuals learn to see themselves as important members of social groups providing important evidence of their value as people.

REFERENCES

BARKER, R. G., & SCHOGGEN, P. *Qualities of community life: Methods of measuring environment and behavior applied to an American and an English town.* San Francisco: Jossey-Bass, 1973.

BARNOUW, V. *An introduction to anthropology* (Rev. ed.) (Vol. 2). Ethnology. Homewood, Ill.: Dorsey Press, 1975.

BETTELHEIM, B. *The children of the dream.* New York: Macmillan, 1969.

BIXENSTINE, V. E., DeCORTE, M. S., & BIXENSTINE, B. A. Conformity to peer-sponsored misconduct at four grade levels. *Developmental Psychology*, 1976, *12*, 226–236.

BOYD, R. E. Conformity reduction in adolescence. *Adolescence*, 1975, *10*, 297–300.

BRITTAIN, C. V. Adolescent choices and parent-peer cross pressures. *American Sociological Review*, 1963, *28*, 385–391.

BRITTAIN, C. V. An exploration of the bases of peer-compliance and parent-compliance in adolescence. *Adolescence*, 1967–1968, *2*, 445–458.

BRITTAIN, C. V. A comparison of rural and urban adolescents with respect to peer vs. parent compliance. *Adolescence*, 1969, *3*, 59–68.

BRONFENBRENNER, U. Response to pressure from peers versus adults among Soviet and American school children. Pp. 7–18 in U. Bronfenbrenner (Chair), *Social factors in the development of personality.* Symposium 35 presented at the 18th International Congress of Psychology, Moscow, August 1966.

BRONFENBRENNER, U. *Two worlds of childhood: U.S. and U.S.S.R.* New York: Russell Sage Foundation, 1970.

BROVERMAN, I. K., VOGEL, S. R., BROVERMAN, D. M., CLARKSON, F. E., & ROSENKRANTZ, P. S. Sex-role stereotypes: A current appraisal. *Journal of Social Issues*, 1972, *28*(No. 2), 59–78.

BROWNSTON, J. E., and WILLIS, R. H. Conformity in early and late adolescence. *Developmental Psychology*, 1971, *4*, 334–337.

COLEMAN, J. S. *The adolescent society.* New York: Free Press, 1961.

COSTANZO, P. R. Conformity development as a function of self-blame. *Journal of Personality and Social Psychology*, 1970, *14*, 366–374.

COSTANZO, P. R., & SHAW, M. E. Conformity as a function of age. *Child Development*, 1966, *37*, 967–975.

COZBY, P. C. Self-disclosure: A literature review. *Psychological Bulletin*, 1973, *79*, 73–91.

CURTIS, R. L. Adolescent orientations toward parents and peers: Variations by sex, age, and socioeconomic status. *Adolescence*, 1975, *10*, 483–494.

DERLEGA, V. J., & CHAIKEN, A. L. *Privacy and self-disclosure in social relationships.* Paper presented at American Psychological Association meetings, San Francisco, 1977.

DEVEREUX, E. C., SHOUVAL, R., BRONFENBRENNER, U., ROD-

GERS, R. R., KAV-VENAKI, S., KEELY, E., & KARSON, E. Socialization practices of parents, teachers, and peers in Israel: The kibbutz versus the city. *Child Development*, 1974, *45*, 269–281.

DUNPHY, D. C. The social structure of urban adolescent peer groups. *Sociometry*, 1963, *26*, 230–246.

EITZEN, D. S. Athletics in the status system of male adolescents: A replication of Coleman's *The adolescent society*. *Adolescence*, 1975, *10*, 267–276.

ELWIN, V. *The Muria and their ghotul*. Bombay: Oxford University Press, 1947.

FRIESEN, D. Academic-athletic-popularity syndrome in the Canadian high school society. *Adolescence*, 1968, *3*, 39–52.

GOETHALS, G. W., & KLOS, D. S. *Experiencing youth: First person accounts* (2nd ed.). Boston: Little, Brown, 1976.

GOTTLIEB, B. H. The contribution of natural support systems to primary prevention among four social subgroups of adolescent males. *Adolescence*, 1975, *10*, 207–220.

JONES, M. C. A study of socialization patterns at the high school level. *Journal of Genetic Psychology*, 1958, *93*, 87–111.

JONES, S. S. High school social status as a historical process. *Adolescence*, 1976, *11*, 327–333.

KANDEL, D. B. Similarity in real-life adolescent friendship pairs. *Journal of Personality and Social Psychology*, 1978, *36*, 306–312.

KOMAROVSKY, M. Cultural contradictions and sex role: The masculine case. *American Journal of Sociology*, 1973, *78*, 873–884.

KON, I. S., & LOSENKOV, V. A. Friendship in adolescence: Values and behavior. *Journal of Marriage and the Family*, 1978, *40*, 143–155.

LARSON, L. E. The influence of parents and peers during adolescence: The situation hypothesis revisited. *Journal of Marriage and the Family*, 1972a, *34*, 67–74.

LARSON, L. E. The relative influence of parent-adolescent affect in predicting the salience hierarchy among youth. *Pacific Sociological Review*, 1972b, *15*, 83–102.

LEHMANN, I. J. Conformity in critical thinking, attitudes, and values from freshman to senior years. *Journal of Educational Psychology*, 1963, *54*, 305–315.

LERNER, R. M., & WEINSTOCK, A. Note on the generation gap. *Psychological Reports*, 1972, *31*, 457–458.

MEAD, M. *Coming of age in Samoa*. New York: Morrow, 1928.

NEWCOMB, T. M. Student peer group influence. Pp. 469–488 in N. Sanford (Ed.), *The American college*. New York: John Wiley, 1962.

NICOL, T. L., & BRYSON, J. B. *Intersex and intrasex stereotyping on the Bem sex role inventory*. Paper presented at American Psychological Association meetings, San Francisco, 1977.

PERETTI, P. O. Closest friendships of black college students: Social intimacy. *Adolescence*, 1976, *11*, 395–403.

PETRONI, F. A. Teenage interracial dating. *Trans-action*, 1971, *8*(No. 11), 54–59.

REYNOLDS, D. J. Adjustment and maladjustment. Pp. 334–368 in J. F. Adams (Ed.), *Understanding adolescence: Current developments in adolescent psychology* (3rd ed.). Boston: Allyn & Bacon, 1976.

RODGERS, R. R., BRONFENBRENNER, U., & DEVEREUX, E. C., JR. Standards of social behavior among children in four cultures. *International Journal of Psychology*, 1968, *3*(No. 1), 31–41.

ROPER, B. S., & LABEFF, E. Sex roles and feminism revisited: An intergenerational attitude comparison. *Journal of Marriage and the Family*, 1977, *39*, 113–119.

SCHIMEL, J. L. Problems of delinquency and their treatment. Pp. 264–274 in G. Caplan (Ed.), *American handbook of psychiatry* (2nd ed.) (Vol. 2). Child and adolescent psychiatry, socio-cultural and community psychiatry. New York: Basic Books, 1974.

SPIRO, M. E. Is the family universal? *American Anthropologists*, 1954, *56*, 840–846.

SPIRO, M. E. *Children of the kibbutz*. New York: Schocken Books, 1965.

SPIRO, M. E. Is the family universal?—The Israeli case (Addendum, 1958). In N. Bell & E. Vogel (Eds.), *A modern introduction to the family*. New York: Free Press, 1968.

SPIRO, M. E. *Kibbutz: Venture in Utopia*. New York: Schocken Books, 1970.

TANGRI, S. S. Determinants of occupational role innovation among college women. *Journal of Social Issues*, 1972, *28*(No. 2), 177–199.

TRICKETT, E. J., KELLY, J. G., & TODD, D. M. The social environment of the high school: Guidelines for individual change and organizational redevelopment. In S. Golann & C. Eisdorfer (Eds.), *Handbook of community psychology*. New York: Appleton-Century-Crofts, 1972.

WEINER, I. B. *Psychological disturbances in adolescence*. New York: Wiley-Interscience, 1970.

WEINSTOCK, A., & LERNER, R. M. Attitudes of late adolescents and their parents toward contemporary issues. *Psychological Reports*, 1972, *30*, 239–244.

WILSON, M. *Good company: A study of Nyakyusa age-villages*. London: Oxford University Press, 1951.

ZEY-FERRELL, M., TOLONE, W. L., & WALSH, R. H. The intergenerational socialization of sex-role attitudes: A gender or generation gap? *Adolescence*, 1978, *13*, 95–108.

30

Personality Development
in Adolescence

OZZIE SIEGEL

It has been said that adolescence is a cultural artifact. While certain features of adolescence may, indeed, be cultural creations, there is ample evidence to indicate that adolescence is a separate stage of development. Despite wide variations all cultures and societies recognize a division of labor and assignment of roles based on age; distinguish among childhood, youth, and adulthood; and more specifically, offer some type of social recognition of adolescence (Kagan, 1971; Muuss, 1970). Kiell (1964), for example, has presented evidence from a variety of cultural contexts and historical periods to demonstrate that adolescence is a universal phenomenon. Beyond this it is possible to identify certain universal tasks associated with adolescence: the incest taboo; the movement from family of origin to family of procreation; the change from being nurtured to providing nurture; and the ability to work and to love (Group for the Advancement of Psychiatry, 1968).

Adolescence is, then, a cultural and social time period, and the problems associated with adolescence have broad social consequences. Our interests, however, are more specifically related to the fact that adolescence is also a new period of personality development. It is a period during which changes in personality will transform the child into an adult. Adolescence, after all, literally means "to grow into maturity" or "to become an adult." It is a period ushered in by enormous physiological and anatomical changes which, in turn, produce new feelings and experiences. In this regard there is another universal associated with adolescence: that personality proceeds along lines of increasing responsibility, morality, and independence (Ausubel, Montemayor, & Svajian, 1977). Adolescence may thus be thought of as a process of separation-individuation (Blos, 1967; Mahler, Pine, & Bergman, 1975), involving a variety of adjustments to the bodily changes of puberty and the shedding of family ties

on the way to developing a relatively stable set of definable individual characteristics.

It is useful, in this context, to distinguish between two major phases of adolescent development: early and late. Although personality development is a continuous process, the distinction between early and late adolescence seems warranted on the basis of the differences in central developmental tasks associated with each phase. Puberty and its attendant physiological and bodily changes are the major contexts for understanding the psychology of early adolescence. As the early adolescent adjusts to these changes and as the changes themselves recede into the background, the adolescent can and must contend with the critical developmental task of late adolescence: the consolidation of identity. It is nevertheless important to bear in mind that there are no hard lines in this matter and that identity formation is an ongoing process. It is rather a matter of shifting emphasis over time. The early adolescent is beginning to experience the "self" in ways vastly different from the childhood years. Blos (1979) refers to adolescence as witnessing "the ascent of self-conscious man" (p. 415). It is, however, in the latter part of adolescence that issues specifically related to finding oneself—morally, politically, occupationally, sexually, and personally—become the focal point of experience.

In the first part of this chapter, we will focus our attention primarily on phenomena associated with early adolescence, with particular emphasis on the psychological adaptations to, and consequences of, puberty. Bearing in mind that the early adolescent is also beginning to separate from childhood ties and thus beginning the process of defining a unique identity, we will examine issues related to the "self" in early adolescence as well as the somewhat controversial matter of "adolescent turmoil." The separation-individuation process, as it proceeds toward the establishment of identity in late adolescence, will be the focus of the second part of the chapter. Along the way we will examine selected aspects of the parent-child relationship, the role of peers in adolescence, and adolescent interests, activities, moods, and sexuality. Although the purpose here is to provide an exposition of normal personality development in adolescence, there will be inevitable occasional forays into oft-encountered developmental disruptions and deviations as a way of sharpening the focus on normative processes. I will try to offer throughout a contextual basis for understanding the behaviors, experiences, and psychological phenomena of adolescence. It is my hope to be able, where possible, to anchor theoretical issues and clinically derived speculations, observations, and hypotheses in empirical evidence and in this way perhaps to approach an accurate understanding of the psychology of adolescence.

PSYCHOLOGICAL IMPACT OF PUBERTY

Puberty refers to the numerous, significant, and rapid bodily changes which initiate the psychological process of adolescence. These physical changes are enormous and occur at a faster rate than at any other period with the exception of the fetal and infantile periods. Over the approximately two years of the pubertal growth spurt, reproductive functions and primary sex organs mature, the secondary sexual characteristics appear, height and weight increase, and bodily proportions change.

For boys the size of the penis and testes increases; the skin of the scrotum reddens; pubic, axillary, and facial hair develop; the voice deepens; bone and muscle growth increases; sweat and sebaceous glands enlarge. There are other important changes as well: Nocturnal emissions, stronger body odors, and skin changes (e.g., acne) are among those of particular importance.

For girls the primary sexual characteristics, the ovaries and the uterus, develop. The vagina and clitoris are developing during this period, as are a number of secondary sexual characteristics: breast growth, pelvic and hip changes, pubic and axillary hair, and the onset of menses. The pubescent girl also experiences skin changes, voice changes, and stronger body odors.

From this admittedly highly condensed survey of the physiological changes of puberty, it is nevertheless apparent that the maturational changes during this period are impressive indeed. The early adolescent thus contends with a host of bodily changes which, not surprisingly, have important psychological consequences. Body image is, after all, at the very core of the overall self-image. Among the many adjustments the adolescent must make, perhaps most outstanding is learning about a "new" body. Until puberty growth proceeds at a rather even pace and, under ordinary circumstances, remains a relatively silent background factor in the younger child's life. While physical size, appearance, and abilities are standards by which people evaluate themselves and others from early childhood on, it is with the onset of puberty in particular that feelings, questions, and concerns about bodily appearance begin to occupy a central place in the experience of the individual. Virtually any and all physical characteristics receive extraordinary attention and examination during this phase. This is a time when

being different is to be avoided at almost any cost and when undesirable physical characteristics put the adolescent at risk for teasing, ridicule, or exclusion (Berscheid, Walster, & Bohrnstedt, 1973).

In addition to personal testimony or clinical experience, the research evidence is clear in documenting the important psychological consequences of physical appearance in early adolescence. Numerous studies over many years all point to the same conclusions: (1) There is an increased awareness of and interest in matters relating to the body (Clifford, 1971); (2) most early adolescents are more concerned about their physical appearance than about any other aspect of themselves (Jersild, 1952; Simmons & Rosenberg, 1975; Simmons, Rosenberg, & Rosenberg, 1973; Stolz & Stolz, 1944); (3) girls report greater dissatisfaction with their bodies and appearance than do boys of the same age. Approximately one-third of early adolescent boys and one-half of early adolescent girls report distress and dissatisfaction with some aspect of their physical development or appearance (Jersild, 1952; Rosenbaum, 1979; Simmons & Rosenberg, 1975; Stolz & Stolz, 1944); and (4) there is a positive relationship between physical attractiveness and social acceptance during adolescence (Kleck, Richardson, & Ronald, 1974; Walster, Aronson, Abrahams, & Rottman, 1966). There is evidence as well that socially desirable personality traits tend to be attributed more often to the physically attractive than to the physically unattractive (Dion, Berscheid, & Walster, 1972), again underscoring the very powerful impact of physical appearance on how the early adolescent is viewed by others.

Psychological Effects of Early and Late Maturation

In light of these findings it would seem to follow that the timing of pubertal onset has significant psychological consequences. The early and late maturer face different types of problems. The early maturing adolescent must contend with the discrepancy between a grown-up physical appearance on the one hand and the continued perception and treatment as a child on the other. There are, however, not only different kinds of issues confronting the early and late maturer of both sexes but important sex differences regarding the timing of maturation as well. In the following sections we will explore in some detail the effects of the differential timing of maturation on both boys and girls.

Males. The early maturing boy is at an advantage physically, athletically, and socially. The late maturing boy, on the other hand, is smaller than both boys and girls his age and thus at a disadvantage in many ways. Indeed at first glance we might be hard pressed to find any advantages in delayed onset of puberty for boys. Numerous studies indicate that early pubertal onset carries distinct advantages. Ratings of adults and peers as well as self-ratings suggest a similar pattern of the early maturing boy as more poised, relaxed, good-natured, and unaffected. The early maturing boy seems to be more popular with peers and more likely to be a school leader. He is portrayed as being more concerned with making a good impression as well as having a higher degree of social responsibility. In addition the early maturing boy is described as less impulsive and more concerned with self-control (Jones, 1957, 1965; Jones & Bayley, 1950; Mussen & Jones, 1957). These findings have led to the conclusion that the early maturing boy is psychologically healthier than is the late maturer. It is also worth noting that the profile of the early maturer is colored by a certain conformity accompanying his apparently better adjustment. In other words as the data are scrutinized more carefully, the early maturing boy begins to appear as somewhat less flexible and perhaps overcontrolled. This point will be covered later.

As for the late maturing boy he is generally regarded as faring less well than his early maturing counterpart. He is described as more tense, restless, talkative, attention-seeking, and less popular (Jones, 1957; Jones & Bayley, 1950). The late maturing boy seems to have a more negative self-concept and expresses more feelings of inadequacy, rejection, and parental domination. He is also less dominant, less likely to lead, and more inclined to seek encouragement from others (Weatherly, 1964). Late onset of puberty is, then, seen for the most part as a handicap for the adolescent boy. In contrast to the picture of the early maturer, the late maturing boy is portrayed as lacking in self-confidence, anxious, and tense. He has a prolonged dependence on his parents and concomitant rebellious attitudes toward them. He is apparently not highly regarded by peers, nor does he hold himself in very high esteem.

The implication is that, while early maturation confers certain psychological advantages, late maturation interferes with optimal personality development. As Weatherly (1964) and others have suggested, it makes good sense (i.e., it matches our observations and expectations) that for an adolescent boy to be short, beardless, and generally immature in his physical appearance is a social and psychological liability. Conversely it seems perfectly sensible that the early adolescent boy who is tall and broad-shouldered, who possesses the physical attributes generally associated with masculinity, has distinct advantages.

Yet there is more to be said about the matter. The timing of maturation has more diversified psychological implications than what at first seems to be the case. As we look more closely at the literature, we begin to see that the early maturer pays a certain price and that the late maturer seems to gain some important compensation along the way.

Longitudinal studies that have followed early and late maturing boys into adulthood, as well as studies that have focused on the psychological rather than social correlates of maturational timing, suggest important modifications in our understanding of the psychological consequences of pubertal timing. The longitudinal studies that have followed early and late maturers into adulthood suggest for the most part an attenuation of the differences found during adolescence itself. Jones (1957) reports that most of the differences found between early and late maturing boys during adolescence disappeared at follow-up at age 33. A subsequent study confirmed these findings five years later when the same subjects were age 38 (Jones, 1965).

However, some psychological differences still remained long after the physical differences had vanished. The early maturers, for example, showed earlier patterns of success in their chosen careers and were more concerned with making a good impression. At the same time the earlier success and more secure vocational status of the early maturer seemed to be tempered by his greater emotional constriction and his relative inflexibility. On the other hand the late maturer in adulthood, while seen as more tense, is also described as more tolerant of ambiguity and as having a more flexible personality (Jones, 1957, 1965). Studies by Peskin (1967, 1973), focusing more particularly on psychological as opposed to social adjustment, portray the early maturer at puberty as more cautious, rigid, bound by rules and routines, and more anxious and worried (e.g., over not doing well, not being liked). The late maturing boy, however, while generally found to be more active (in some studies, "impulsive"), is also noted by Peskin to be more expressive, curious, and uninhibited.

It begins to appear, then, that to view the early maturing boy as psychologically healthier than the late maturer is an oversimplification based upon an equation of social with psychological adjustment. The early maturer seems to pay a certain price for his social advantages—and it is substantial—in terms of his emotional constraint, while the late maturer seems somewhat freer and more tolerant of his own impulses and inner life.

In this regard Peskin has proposed the interesting hypothesis that the shortened latency period of the early maturer affords less opportunity to prepare for the sudden intensification of drives in adolescence. The relatively protracted latency of the late maturer, on the other hand, provides a preparatory period and makes his drives less threatening and easier to adjust to and integrate into the personality (Group for the Advancement of Psychiatry, 1978; Peskin, 1967). As we shall see later the intensification of sexual and aggressive urges, drives, and fantasies in adolescence is one of the critical developmental issues and motivating forces in the separation process of adolescence. Coming to terms with what are, in a sense, newly and intensely experienced inner feelings is a major task confronting the adolescent. A longer latency period provides the opportunity for developing, practicing, and expanding motor and intellectual skills in a relatively conflict-free setting, which thus "equip the normal child with a rich diversity of ego mechanisms with which to regulate past and future instinctual crises adaptively" (Peskin, 1973, p. 275).

Females. The psychological consequences of maturational timing are less clearcut for girls. In general psychological differences between early and late maturing girls are less striking than for their male counterparts (Faust, 1960; Jones & Mussen, 1958; Weatherly, 1964). Furthermore the literature suggests that, in contrast to boys, early pubertal onset may be both a social and psychological disadvantage for girls (cf. Peterson, 1979). Jones (1958) found that the earlier maturing girl is rated lower on a number of socially desirable traits such as sociability, poise, and expressiveness and tends to play a less prominent role in school activities than is the late maturing girl. Jones and Mussen (1958) found that while early maturing girls tended to have more favorable self-concepts than late maturing girls when this was assessed at age 17, peer and adult ratings made over preceding years (i.e., in early adolescence) tended to favor the late maturer.

Since on the average girls mature earlier than do boys, the early maturing girl is likely to be big and physically conspicuous, and this may present problems in relationships with both girls and boys in early adolescence (Jersild, Brook, & Brook, 1978). Along these lines Peskin (1973) found the early maturing girl to have a more difficult time of it psychologically as well. The early maturing girl is described as more introverted and shy and as generally experiencing greater stress. Interestingly this seems to change over the years. Both Jones and Mussen (1958) and Peskin (1973) provide data to suggest that the differences diminish over time and that as adults early maturing girls seem to make better adjustments. As Peskin (1973) observes, "The early maturer has developed from a quite unpromising adolescent to a quite integrated woman" (p. 282).

These findings coincide with the hypothesis that adolescence is a more difficult transition for girls (Blos, 1958). The social structure and sex-role stereotypes, among other things, offer the early maturing boy an accepted and even admired status. Parents and society expect and encourage competence in other-than-sexual and athletic activities. The early maturing girl is less likely, however, to meet with the same kind of approval. She is more likely to experience social and interpersonal difficulties because of her outstanding physical appearance. A most important consideration in this context is the relative absence for the early maturing girl of built-in safeguards from her intensifying drives. This phase of development may thus present the early maturing girl with special difficulties in the area of intensified sexual feelings, and she may thus require a longer period of adjustment. We will comment on other dimensions of this issue in the following section and later as we consider some aspects of parental identification.

The Self in Early Adolescence

As part of the long and complex process of establishing a separate identity, early adolescents begin to evaluate their own thoughts and perceptions of themselves as well as those of others—that is, the "self" becomes the object of examination as well as of anxiety and concern. The term *self* will be used to refer to the whole person of an individual—that is, to the ideas and feelings one has about one's thoughts, body, appearance, and personal characteristics.

The shift to formal operational thinking (Inhelder & Piaget, 1958) is a critical cognitive development of adolescence and enables the adolescent to "discover the privateness of his thoughts and the social isolation of his reflective self" (Elkind, 1975, p. 55). Together with the bodily changes associated with puberty, the intensification of sexual and aggressive drives, the influences of parental and peer evaluations and approval, and eventually the need to make decisions about the future, these cognitive changes contribute to the self becoming a crucial focus of awareness. Daydreaming, diaries, and preoccupation with physical appearance during adolescence all speak to the heightened egocentrism and narcissism of

the early adolescent period. The adolescent is typically self-conscious, self-critical, self-admiring—in other words, in many ways preoccupied with various aspects of this self.

Elkind (1967) has addressed the heightened egocentrism of early adolescence from a cognitive perspective. He relates the adolescent's concern over physical appearance and behavior to the failure to differentiate thoughts belonging to the self from the thoughts of others. Early adolescents believe that others are as preoccupied with the adolescents' concerns as they are. Elkind (1967) tells us that early adolescents construct an "imaginary audience" accompanied by "a personal fable" that their thoughts, beliefs, and feelings are unique and that they are immortal.

These same phenomena can be understood, integrated, and enriched within the more comprehensive psychoanalytic framework. The "imaginary audience" and "personal fable" may be viewed as more than mental constructs based on the attainment of formal operational thought. They are, after all, fantasies which have conscious and unconscious aspects and determinants and which imply important affective, in addition to cognitive, considerations. The impelling forces of the need to establish independence and to be free of attachment to the parents provide a context for understanding these as well as other narcissistic phenomena which are so much a part of the adolescent experience (Group for the Advancement of Psychiatry, 1968). The adolescents' overevaluation of the self is at least partially determined by the efforts made to gain emotional independence (Aarons, 1970) and represents an adaptation to the disengagement from the parents. We will explore this more thoroughly in a later section as part of a consideration of adolescent moods, but we can note here that the investment in the self occurring during adolescence is unmatched by childhood experiences. Never before has it been possible to conceive of oneself in terms of a past, present, and future—to view one's life in terms of larger, existential issues.

In this context we might inquire into the developmental course and stability of the adolescent's self-concept (i.e., self-image, self-esteem). Two longitudinal studies, one by Engel (1959) and the other by Carlson (1965), have reported consistency, continuity, and stability in the self-concepts of adolescents. Interestingly, however, while the self-concept seems to be relatively stable, there is evidence from several sources that a disturbance in self-image occurs in early adolescence. Simmons et al. (1973), in a cross-sectional study of third- to twelfth-grade students, found that 12- to 14-year olds were more self-conscious, had less positive attitudes toward themselves, and also felt that parents, peers, and teachers viewed them more unfavorably. There is reason to think, furthermore, that this apparently transient disturbance in self-esteem reflects the social pressures and anxieties of entering junior high school, in addition to the anxieties associated with puberty itself. Simmons et al. (1973) found that 12-year-olds in junior high school seemed especially vulnerable compared to those who remained in elementary school.

It seems, too, that girls have even more difficulty in maintaining self-esteem during early adolescence (Simmons & Rosenberg, 1975). This is consistent with the findings that girls are generally more dissatisfied with their bodies and with their physical appearance.

Data from studies comparing early and late adolescents provide another source of evidence that the early adolescent period is associated with a disturbance of self-esteem. Offer and Howard (1972) found that older adolescents of both sexes have better self-images than do younger adolescents. In a similar vein Protinsky (1975) found that older adolescents were less anxious and confused and more secure and comfortable with themselves than were younger adolescents.

It seems fair, then, to conclude on both theoretical and evidential grounds that (1) the sense of self (i.e., self-concept, self-image, self-esteem) is relatively stable over the long haul; (2) a temporary disturbance in self-esteem occurs during early adolescence; and (3) the early adolescent female has a more difficult transition in a number of ways, including disturbance in self-image, than does her male counterpart.

Adolescent Turmoil

From the issues and literature we have reviewed up to this point, it begins to appear that under ordinary circumstances the early adolescent period is difficult and unsteady. It certainly is a period of impressive transitions; the physiological-anatomical as well as the social-psychological changes are vast and occur very rapidly. Are we, then, justified in thinking of adolescence, and early adolescence in particular, as a period of disequilibrium?

The issue of "adolescent turmoil" has received a great deal of attention over the years from various quarters. Indeed Hall's (1904) classic work on adolescence described adolescence as a period of storm and stress (*sturm und drang*). Numerous clinicians since have argued that adolescence is a time of great upheaval and is by definition a disturbed state (Blos, 1979; Freud, 1958; Geleerd, 1961; Josselyn, 1954). Erikson's (1968) view of adolescence as a "normative crisis" is similarly consistent with the notion of adolescent turmoil. On the other hand there is a group of clinicians and researchers who contend that there is little, if any, evidence that adolescence is a time of turbulence. It is their contention that disturbance is not modal among adolescents and that the normative course of adolescent development is relatively continuous (cf. Douvan & Adelson, 1966; Offer, 1969).

It has been argued that psychoanalytic writers see adolescents as disturbed because they are working within a clinical context (i.e., with patients). It might be suggested, too, that these are clinical impressions which, although conforming to certain psychoanalytic theoretical expectations, are nevertheless without empirical basis. The possibility has also been raised that turmoil is a natural concomitant of early adolescence but cannot be detected by questionnaires and the like (Rutter, Graham, Chadwick, & Yule, 1976). Offer (1969), too, raises the possibility that turmoil may be present but detectable only by in-depth individual investigations. He concludes, however, that such is not the case, but rather that adolescent turmoil is a concept of questionable validity.

It is true that psychoanalytic observations of adolescent turmoil derive from clinical experience. The psychoanalytic writer is essentially addressing the world of inner experience as opposed to overt behavioral patterns. Blos (1971) emphasizes the difference between what he calls the "public noise" and the inner psychic changes and experiences of adolescence. Muslin (1979) also comments on the difficulty in finding a match between such obviously different levels of experience. Nevertheless it is my contention that there is ample evidence at all levels to suggest that turmoil in early adolescence is a fact and not simply a fiction of depth psychology. Indeed as I hope to demonstrate, the work of Offer and colleagues is to a considerable extent itself surprisingly consistent with this view. In other words "inner versus outer" and "surface versus depth" are not the critical dimensions. Looked at more thoroughly the data from numerous studies and sources support the view that early adolescence is normatively a turbulent period. We have already seen that a number of survey-questionnaire–type studies have demonstrated a transient disturbance of self-esteem in early adolescence. The studies reviewed earlier in the area of body image also point to substantial distress and dissatisfaction among early adolescents.

The results of studies in other areas as well converge on these findings, and the evidence builds that early adolescence is an unsteady time. The expectations derived from our conceptualization of adolescence as a time of inner psychic change, as a process entailing separation and increasing independence and autonomy, as well as the coming to terms with major bodily changes, seem to be borne out in studies, for example, which consistently find that sizable percentages of "normal" adolescents experience anxieties and worries.

Masterson (1967), for one, found anxiety symptoms in approximately 65 percent of a group of normal adolescents between 12 and 18 years of age. Depression was found in 41 percent of this nonpatient group. A study of high school students in Indiana found nearly half of the students reporting worries about inadequacy and lack of self-confidence. One-third reported feeling overwhelmed by their many worries (Husni-Palacios & Scheur, 1972). While these percentages of what may be viewed as subclinical symptoms are consistent with those found in adult populations (cf. Srole, Langner, Michael, Opler, & Rennie, 1962), they nevertheless provide a backdrop for viewing the intensification of these affects in the opening phase of adolescent development.

In this regard two recent studies are relevant. Rutter et al. (1976) have recently addressed the question of adolescent turmoil. Working with the data of the well-known "Isle of Wight" study of normal 14- to 15-year-olds (cf. Rutter, Tizard, & Whitmore, 1970), they report "some appreciable misery or depression" in nearly half the adolescents studied. They conclude that "there can be no doubt from these findings that many 14–15 year olds experience quite marked feelings of affective disturbance which could well be described as 'inner turmoil' " (p. 42). More recently a study of normal twins found that self-doubt, avoidance of responsibility, resentment of parents, and anxiety about social relationships peaked in early puberty, and emotional upset peaked in early to mid-puberty. The authors of this study conclude that transiently upset feelings are normal at ages 11 to 14 (Frank & Cohen, 1979).

How, then, do we account for the apparently contradictory findings of Offer and associates (e.g., Offer, 1969;

Offer & Howard, 1972; Offer & Offer, 1975)? There are a number of reasons for thinking that Offer's findings are not representative. The adolescent boys studied by Offer and colleagues were selected as a "modal" group. They were heavily middle and upper middle class. Of this population 84 percent went on to college. Furthermore the subjects selected were screened for indications of behavioral problems.

Nevertheless even with a population intentionally selected for its apparent normality, it is interesting to note that 21 percent were classified as experiencing adolescent turmoil. Offer and co-workers identified three developmental routes through adolescence. In addition to the *tumultuous growth* group, they found approximately 23 percent of the adolescents studied belong to what they refer to as a *continuous growth* group characterized by smooth and steady development and 35 percent were identified as following a course of *surgent growth*—that is, developmental spurts alternating with periods of conflict and turmoil. The remaining 21 percent could not be classified although they apparently fell mostly within the *continuous* and *surgent* groups. Thus even in this group of adolescents selected for its presumed psychological health, we find 56 percent of the adolescents experiencing anxiety, depression, and worry of some measure.

While maintaining and underscoring the importance of distinguishing between adolescent turmoil on the one hand and psychopathology on the other, it seems a reasonable conclusion that the adolescent process is an interruption of peaceful growth and is normatively attended by anxiety, worry, and concerns regarding self-esteem, physical appearance, and body image. In this context it seems worthwhile to turn for a moment to a consideration of the psychological mechanisms of defense, perhaps distinctive of adolescence, which are set into motion by this to-be-expected inner turmoil.

Josselyn (1954) described adolescence as a phase ordinarily characterized by *ego exhaustion.* She maintains that the rapid physical changes undermine familiarity with the body, that the surge toward independence exposes the adolescent to new situations which threaten self-esteem, and that sexual feelings are so powerfully experienced as to create considerable anxiety.

Anna Freud (1958) similarly portrays the adolescent as being in the midst of inner upheaval. She emphasizes adolescence as a time of revived and intensified sexual and aggressive drives, feelings, and fantasies which are, furthermore, now realizable and which in important ways reinforce the need to separate from the parents (i.e., the redirection of sexual strivings outside of the family). The intensification of drives and the attendant anxieties lead to certain defensive efforts. We are familiar, for instance, with the so-called "ascetic" adolescent who, as Freud suggests, fights all impulses, renounces all inner desires, and even avoids socializing with friends—in other words, becomes moral, joyless, and ascetic as a way of contending with the intensification of inner drives. Intellectualization is also frequently observed in adolescents, often taking the form of preoccupation with abstract interests and philosophical problems; this may, in large part, be understood as a means of coping with powerful feelings and in its own way of telling us something

of the psychological climate of the early adolescent phase of development.

SEPARATION-INDIVIDUATION AND IDENTITY FORMATION

While we have examined certain facets of the separation-individuation process, at this point we will tune in more selectively on the process of identity formation and the establishment of what Erikson (1968) labels *ego identity.* As indicated earlier the duration of adolescence may be specified according to any number of criteria. The popular notion is that adolescence is synonymous with the teenage years. In addition to this chronological standard, however, there are a number of other delimiting criteria for the duration of adolescence. Education is one, and the completion of high school or college is often used as an indicator of the end of adolescence. Legal criteria, such as the attainment of legal maturity, are also frequently used to define the end of adolescence. Each of these criteria, however, has major shortcomings and, for our purposes, seems unduly arbitrary and narrow. It is the more widely held view that adolescence can most meaningfully be defined as a psychological process and that the criteria for closure similarly involve certain psychological and developmental tasks such as the resolution of the parent-child relationship and the establishment of a personal and sexual identity (Blos, 1976; Coons, 1971; Josselyn, 1952; Weiner, 1970).

In addressing this issue and emphasizing the importance of viewing adolescence as a process, Erikson (1968) refers to the following tasks of "adolescing": maintaining ego defenses against intensifying impulses; consolidating conflict-free achievements in line with work opportunities (i.e., applying one's academic knowledge and intellectual resources toward the development of an occupational choice); and resynthesizing childhood identifications in a manner unique to the individual yet in agreement with the roles sanctioned by society. We will be returning to these developmental tasks in what follows, but for the moment I would suggest that what is important to understand about this process of "adolescing" is that just as the infant "hatches" from a symbiotic union from the mother to become an individuated toddler, so in a parallel way does the adolescent shed family dependencies to become an adult (Blos, 1967). With these conceptual issues in the background, let us now turn our attention more specifically to the form and substance of the adolescent transition.

The Parent-Child Relationship

The adolescent faces the seemingly impossible challenge of relinquishing parental ties and childhood identifications in order to establish a separate identity outside of the family while still maintaining the continuity of parental and familial relationships. Major adjustments, at times painful, are required of both parent and adolescent in order for the child to become an autonomous individual (Anthony, 1969; Lidz, 1969). As Freud emphasized, detachment from parental authority is "one of the most significant, but also one of the most painful, psychical achievements" of adolescence (1905/1962, p. 62). It is this process of disengagement that provides the setting for the popular lore regarding adolescent rebelliousness and the so-called generation gap. Youth is so often portrayed in literature and movies as alienated and troubled, and indeed, this picture does seem to have face validity. What we have reviewed up to this point regarding the adolescent's adjustments to puberty, the evidence for a certain degree of turmoil, and difficulties in the area of self-image all lead us to expect to find evidence of parent-child conflicts.

Nevertheless there is generally good agreement across a number of studies that whatever parent-child conflict exists should not be equated with what is implied by the idea of a generation gap. By and large the research suggests a relative compatibility of views and values held by parents and adolescents (Douvan & Adelson, 1966; LoSciuto & Karlin, 1972; Meissner, 1965; Rutter et al., 1976; Yankelovich, 1969).

Strong parental identification is generally associated with good adjustment. For girls, however, strong identifications with the mother are negatively related to autonomy, adjustment, and self-esteem while identification with masculine traits is associated with high self-esteem (Baruch & Barnett, 1975). This is in itself a complicated matter and undoubtedly reflects changes in the social structure and touches as well on the vast literature in the area of sex-role stereotypes (e.g., Broverman, Vogel, Broverman, Clarkson, & Rosenkrantz, 1972). In addition these findings blend with those referred to earlier regarding the difficulties confronting the early adolescent girl. Together they lend support as well to the psychoanalytic hypothesis that the early adolescent girl faces special difficulties in the area of the mother-daughter relationship. The severing of childhood attachments to the mother may be particularly problematic for the adolescent girl (cf. Blos, 1958; Deutsch, 1944).

The important point for our purposes, however, is that strong identifications with one or both parents are normative in adolescence. It is of interest in this regard to consider briefly Erikson's conceptualization of *negative identity choice* in adolescence. Underscoring the importance of identity formation in adolescence and the parental identifications which are its building blocks, Erikson (1968) describes the negative identity as one "perversely based on all those identifications and roles which, at critical stages of development, had been presented . . . as most undesirable or dangerous" (p. 174). This too-often-encountered deviation in identity development serves to remind us of the importance of parental identifications in adolescence.

The fact that over recent years the family structure has undergone major changes would seem to have important implications for perceptions of and identifications with parents. The dramatic rise in the divorce rate and the financial need for both parents to work have had consequences for children and their developing personalities. In this regard there is evidence to suggest that sons of working mothers express disapproval of their fathers more often than do sons of nonworking mothers (Hoffman, 1974). The single-parent family is now more prevalent, and for the most part, this means that the children live with the mother. Absence of the father in the family

has been the focus of much recent research. While certainly beyond the scope of this chapter, it is nevertheless pertinent to note that girls who lose their fathers through death or divorce experience more anxiety when they are with males. They also exhibit more attention-seeking behavior with boys and exhibit earlier heterosexual behavior than do girls from intact families (Hetherington, 1972). The effects of father absence on boys are seen in an impairment of the masculine identification process, to cite but one consequence (Biller & Bahm, 1971). It would seem that there is no escaping the reality that ultimately large-scale, sweeping changes in societal norms, values, and practices have their telling effects on the individual psyche.

Under ordinary circumstances the adolescent is typically at neither the extreme of compliance and conformity on one end nor of alienation and rejection of parents on the other. The separation process normally occurs within the context of an enduring parent-child relationship. The studies noted earlier argue against the idea that adolescents and parents are constantly at odds. Yet these same studies take note of the areas of contention, complaint, and dissatisfaction which are also normatively experienced—e.g., disagreements between parents and adolescents regarding clothes, hair style, curfew, friends. While perhaps transient and seemingly less important than the religious, moral, and ethical values which are shared by parents and adolescents, it is worth bearing in mind that these are issues about which disagreements are often heated and, in large part, for the reason that they represent and concretize struggles over emancipation and autonomy. Furthermore it is important to be aware that we are, of necessity, addressing what is normative. Yet in the process we ought not to lose sight of the fact that substantial minorities of adolescents experience significant dissidence in their relationships with their parents (LoSciuto & Karlin, 1972; Meissner, 1965).

Normatively then it is within the framework of an ongoing sustaining parental relationship that we view the adolescent's inner turmoil, transient self-esteem problems, and conflicts with parents. This brings us to a crucial issue and one which perhaps helps place in perspective some of the divergent views regarding issues such as adolescent turmoil and the generation gap—namely, that conflict is a necessary condition for growth. Within certain limits it is to be expected and ought not to be denied. There is a crucial distinction between the idea of a generation gap on the one hand and intergenerational conflict on the other. It is, after all, conflict which allows for continued development. This does not necessarily imply pathology. A generation gap implies a distance between adolescent and parents and to that extent suggests conflict avoidance as opposed to conflict resolution. As Blos (1971) so cogently observes, "Generational conflict is essential for the growth of the self and of civilization" (p. 7).

The Peer Group

It is, of course, commonly observed that peers take on added importance as the child enters adolescence. This, too, is a phenomenon often dramatized in the press, on the screen, and in novels. The adolescent's friends are at times a source of parental concern or perhaps a target of blame and anger. The increased importance of the peer group in the life of the adolescent is itself a major indicator of the adolescent's disengagement from the family. However, parents and peers are not necessarily nor normatively at odds. Much depends on the areas and issues involved. We have seen that this is the case in the parent-child relationship as well (cf. Bengtson, 1970). Insofar as larger issues regarding basic values are concerned, parental influences continue to be powerful in adolescence. Kandel and Lesser (1969) found that when it comes to issues regarding the adolescent's educational aspirations and future life goals, parents have a stronger influence by far than do peers. Nevertheless in many other areas such as fashion, music, and other leisure-time activities, the peer group may be more influential.

Beyond this, however, the peer group serves the critical functions of providing a vehicle for adolescent's separation while at the same time helping to maintain a certain continuity with parental values. Caste and class lines are drawn quite sharply during adolescence, and adolescents tend to choose friends of similar race, religion, and economic status (Ausubel et al., 1977; Campbell, 1969). As a byproduct the peer group serves to reinforce basic identification patterns. In contrast to something often perceived as a threat to the integrity of the family and society, the peer group may be more accurately viewed as necessary for the successful negotiation of the developmental tasks of adolescence as well as for the transmission of the attitudes, beliefs, and practices of the family and the culture.

The peer group assists the adolescent in the journey from childhood to adulthood by providing a sense of derived status. Peers provide security and a sense of belonging at a time when familial ties are loosening. The peer group thus provides a setting within which the adolescent may practice and experiment with new interests and skills. Another important consideration is that the peer group belongs to the adolescent just as the adolescent belongs to it. The peer group represents a stabilizing force during this transitional period and provides a backdrop of support in the ongoing self-evaluations of adolescence and the attendant uncertainty, guilt, and anxiety.

Action and Adolescence

At this juncture we might reflect upon the importance of action and activity in adolescence. The adolescent's proclivity to action may be viewed as a phase-specific concretization of the inner psychological changes of this period of development. More specifically this disposition is determined primarily by several important psychological events: the intensification of the drives in early adolescence, the loosening of parental ties, and the increase in narcissism that accompanies early adolescence.

Efforts to grow up and out of the parental fold are accompanied by regressive forces which threaten to pull the adolescent back into childhood positions. While the adolescent boy can avoid the regressive pull toward the mother of childhood through his masculine identifications, the adolescent girl faces a more complicated task and, at least temporarily, may need to reject maternal

identifications. Action and activity thus reflect the phase-specific need to continue to move forward and to defend against passive longings. In addition activity (i.e., acting and doing) represents the adolescents' efforts to anchor themselves in reality as a means of warding off the anxieties accompanying the movement away from the parents. As Blos (1979) notes, "The adolescent turns so frantically toward reality because he is in constant danger of losing it" (p. 262). Action provides the adolescent with a measure of control over reality or at least the temporarily reassuring belief that external reality can be controlled.

It is essential to be mindful of the central role narcissism plays in the adolescent's turning to action and reality. It is seen in the efforts to control reality (and at times in the belief that this is quite possible) as well as in the adolescent's use of the external world for the gratification of narcissistic needs. I might note, too, that the adolescent sense of entitlement as well as the belief in their invulnerability and magical protection from harm speak to the heightened narcissism of the adolescent period and its translation into action as a preferred mode of behavior and expression.

On the pathological side we see this manifested in adolescent delinquency where both the sense of narcissistic entitlement and the high degree of inner arousal during adolescence seem to be involved. Delinquent acts are not uncommon even in normal adolescents. Offer (1969) found 25 percent of his "modal" group of adolescent boys to have been involved in delinquent activities. The relative prevalence of delinquent acts in adolescence is a reminder of the phase-specific demands and problems confronting the adolescent.

To put this in perspective let us be aware that violent deaths (i.e., accidents, homicide, and suicide in that order) are the leading cause of death in adolescence (cf. Holinger, 1979). To choose but one glaring example, the adolescent preference for driving automobiles fast and recklessly is a factor in the high rate of accidental deaths in adolescence. Together with the relatively high incidence in adolescence of violence and self-destructive behaviors, these are painful reminders indeed that adolescence is a time of major inner changes, of the activation of powerful drives, and of intensified narcissistic interests and concerns.

More typical, however, are the adolescent interests (at times, preoccupations) in such activities as telephoning, dancing, and "hanging out." Driving is also a favored adolescent activity and, of course, not always or necessarily recklessly or dangerously done. Each of these adolescent activities has in common several important elements. First, the activity is a vehicle for separation. The telephone is a bridge between the adolescent and the world outside the family. It allows the adolescent to begin to establish relationships apart from the family and an identity other than that of a child. "Hanging out" is a well-known favored pastime of adolescents—not in the local teen community center established by adults but in places they discover and can claim as their own. Second, the activity allows for a phase-appropriate channeling of the now-intensified sexual and aggressive drives. Telephoning, dancing, and driving provide a means of discharging sexual and aggressive feelings and tensions in a rather safe setting. Third, the activity serves important self-esteem regulating functions. It provides a socially accepted means of obtaining narcissistic gratification, of feeling important, and of being the master of inner drives as well as of external reality.

Adolescent Moods

The loss of anchorage in childhood identifications is one of the important factors responsible for the self-esteem disturbances of adolescence. We touched on an aspect of this issue earlier in the context of the psychological impact of puberty when we noted the evidence for a transient disturbance in the self-image during early adolescence. We turn our attention now to the impact of the loss of the parents as regulators of self-esteem. The consequences are apparent not only in the transient self-image disturbance of early adolescence but also in the moods, idealizations, and devaluations so characteristic of adolescence. Blos (1979) puts this in perspective when he notes that "the mood swings of adolescence represent the corollary of the second individuation process" (p. 413).

The peer group is supportive in this regard and plays an important role as a continuous source of self-esteem. A study by Costanzo and Shaw (1966) provides some empirical support for this. These investigators found an inverted U pattern for peer conformity between ages 7 and 12 which began to decline thereafter. The authors attribute this pattern to a variety of factors including the adolescent's uncertainty about pubescent changes, the recent onset of sexual maturation in early adolescence, and the marginal status of the early adolescent as a consequence of which peers are sought as models for correct and appropriate behavior. Peer conformity was found to decline over the course of adolescence, suggesting again the role of the peer group in regulating self-esteem in early adolescence. The declining importance of the peer group during adolescence is similarly consistent with the separation process and the fact that identity development is more firmly established in later adolescent years.

Although peers function as a kind of external self-esteem regulating agency, it is important to bear in mind that to the extent that the standards and expectations of peers are at variance with the older, now-internalized, parental ideals, the stability of the adolescent's self-esteem is at risk. As Laufer (1964) puts it,

It is as if the adolescent were saying, "to feel wanted by my contemporaries, and to avoid ostracism, I must perform in a prescribed way, and I must be interested in certain accepted things. But at the same time there are things I do and think which are contrary to this picture. I must fight against these manifestations." (p. 203)

As the disengagement process unfolds, the adolescent is faced not only with peer group values which may differ from and compete with parental values but also with a necessary reassessment of the parents. What happens, then, when the parents fall from perfection? Among the consequences of parental disillusionment are the variable mood states of adolescence and the complementary phenomena of self-aggrandizement and idealization on one side and self-devaluation and disappointment in adults and society on the other. Glorified images of the self and others (e.g., movie and rock music stars, sports heroes)

serve to regulate the adolescents' narcissistic balance—just as the idealized parents of childhood did in earlier years.

This finds behavioral expression in any number of different ways. Fads of dress, hair style, and language point to the self-centeredness of adolescence. The sense of invulnerability and perfection finds more serious expression in the frequency of accidents during the adolescent period. Bedrooms filled with posters and the barely containable excitement stirred by one or another adolescent idol are common adolescent phenomena which also develop in this psychological setting. Rarely, however, does all this occur without the counterparts of a sense of nothingness and helplessness.

Jacobson (1961) portrayed the state of the adolescent exquisitely when she described the

tensions between images of the grown-up, powerful, glamorous, brilliant, or sophisticated person he wants to be, and sometimes believes himself to be, and the undeniable aspect of the physically and mentally immature, half-baked creature between two worlds which he actually is. (p. 174)

In describing *identity-consciousness* in adolescence, Erikson (1968) also refers to the "painful self-consciousness which dwells on discrepancies between one's self-esteem, the aggrandized self-image as an autonomous person, and one's appearance in the eyes of others" (p. 183). I would point out here again that these ideas complement and enrich the observations of cognitive theorists such as Elkind who, as mentioned earlier, has discussed the adolescent phenomenon of the "personal fable." The sensitivity to shame and humiliation in adolescence is remarkable and of considerable importance in understanding the tendency toward depressive moods and moodiness which accompany the adolescent years.

The narcissistic grandeur and the idols of early and middle adolescence, having fulfilled their developmental purposes, eventually give way to more realistic self-appraisals and relationships which have substance, meaning, and the potential for intimacy. We will consider these developments now as they occur within and exert their influence upon adolescent relationships, with particular emphasis on the patterns of sexuality and identification in adolescence.

Sexual Attitudes, Behaviors, and Relationships

Development in the realm of adolescent sexuality normatively proceeds from self-centered sexual preoccupations which characterize early adolescence to sexual relationships based on mutuality in late adolescence. Feinstein and Ardon (1973) have proposed an interesting model of adolescent sexual development which suggests that there is a sequential course of increasing separation-individuation in this sphere, beginning with a stage of sexual awakening in early adolescence and moving toward the acceptance of a sexual role and the capacity for a mature and lasting relationship.

Sexuality is a cornerstone of identity, and adolescent sexual explorations are a means by which this aspect of identity develops and crystallizes. The early adolescent is typically absorbed with the bodily changes of puberty and the accompanying sexual excitement and curiosity. In early adolescence sexuality tends to be relatively self-centered, although the sexual investigations of early adolescence take many forms including the exploration of books and magazines, sexually explicit and exciting conversations with peers, masturbation, mutual masturbation with a friend of the same sex, and heterosexual experimentation as well. We can take note here that masturbation is indeed a rather common early adolescent practice, with estimates suggesting that among boys anywhere from 50 percent to 80 percent have masturbated by age 15, while among girls the figure is about 33 percent (Chilman, 1978; Diepold & Young, 1979).

Much has been written about the "sexual revolution," and there does seem to be a popular mythology developed around the adolescent as a sexually uninhibited, hedonistic creature. This may reflect adult fantasies (and anxieties) more accurately than it does in any way the actual sexual behaviors of adolescents. Flamboyant and sexually provocative styles of dress and fashion are part of the practicing of sexual roles so necessary for the eventual establishment of gender identity and ought not to be taken as evidence of unrestrained sexuality. Indeed the evidence suggests something on the order of evolutionary rather than revolutionary changes in adolescent sexual behaviors over recent decades (Diepold & Young, 1979; Simon, Berger, & Gagnon, 1972). Moreover it seems that changes in sexual attitudes have been far greater than changes in actual sexual behaviors (Starr, 1974).

There still seems to be a more or less orderly sequence of sexual practicing behaviors leading up to the first coital experience (i.e., "necking," "petting," "heavy petting"). At the same time some significant changes in adolescent sexual activities have occurred over the past several decades. Perhaps most impressive in this regard has been the trend in the direction of earlier sexual experiences for both males and females and the increase in premarital sexual intimacies, including intercourse, for females. Looking at the Kinsey (1948, 1953) data, it is interesting to note that fewer than 5 percent of the females had their first intercourse by age 15. More recent studies suggest that roughly 25 percent of females are sexually active by age 15. The percentages for males have generally been higher and have remained so over the years (i.e., about 40 percent of males have had their first intercourse by age 15). These are approximate percentages, and it should be noted that there are geographic, religious, educational, psychological, familial, socioeconomic, and racial factors among others which are associated with premarital sexual patterns. Black adolescents of both sexes, for example, tend to be more sexually active at earlier ages than are their white counterparts. White adolescents, however, tend to have more sex partners and have sex more frequently than do black adolescents (Kantner & Zelnick, 1972). The explanations for these findings are well beyond the scope of this chapter but are noted as a reminder that we are of necessity here describing prototypical patterns.

These changes in adolescent sexual behaviors reflect and have accompanied perhaps more impressive changes in adolescent attitudes toward premarital sexual behaviors. The changes in sexual attitude, in turn, reflect enormous changes in American society over the decades of the 1950s, 1960s, and 1970s—a subject that would lead

us too far afield but which should nevertheless be kept in mind as a context. Sexual standards have become more liberal, and there is greater acceptance of premarital sexual activity, especially for women (Chilman, 1978). Nevertheless the extent to which certain traditional values and practices persist in the face of vast cultural changes is impressive. Thus while greater numbers of younger adolescents are sexually active, intercourse is still not normative in early adolescence. Furthermore even among sexually active adolescents, intercourse is relatively infrequent and generally confined to a single partner—that is, a pattern of serial monogamy seems to prevail.

In the long run behavior is determined by its phase appropriateness—the degree to which the activity is consistent with the developmental tasks which must be negotiated in order for growth to occur. From what we have seen it is apparent that the early adolescent, burdened by all that enters into the turmoil of these years, may be biologically ready but is as yet psychologically unprepared for intercourse. To some extent this is borne out in the relative infrequency of coitus following early initial heterosexual experimentation. Beyond this we must consider as well that anxiety and guilt tend to underlie the new and as yet unfamiliar sexual investigations of adolescence despite surface statements of comfort and ease (Call, 1979; Chilman, 1978). Erikson (1968) tells us that in seeking intimacy—whether in friendships, competition, sex play, arguments, or gossip—the adolescent experiences a strain. Intimacy poses a threat to the adolescent, whose own identity is not yet firm but rather only in the process of consolidating. The emotional demands for intimacy, mutuality, and love in a sustaining relationship remain for the most part the developmental tasks to be tackled in the later adolescent years, and perhaps even beyond.

The Resolution of Adolescence

As I indicated earlier there are any number of criteria available for defining the closure of adolescence. Up to this point we have given some consideration to two of the most important psychological criteria, the completion of the separation-individuation process of adolescence and the development and formation of a sexual identity. Blos (1976) suggests two other tasks or challenges which the late adolescent must meet. One he labels *ego continuity*, which refers to the capacity to view oneself and one's life in the context of the realities of the past and thus to be able to form a view of the present and future. It involves a critical reevaluation of parents and the correction of distorted childhood perceptions. The other challenge or task in Blos's scheme is *residual trauma*, which refers to the necessity of coming to terms with one's shortcomings, vulnerabilities, and childhood disappointments.

This touches on one of the truly delicate and difficult issues in adolescent identity formation: disengaging from the parents while maintaining basic and lasting identifications with them. If conflict and detachment from parental ties on the one hand seem inconsistent with identifications with the parents on the other, this is but a small measure of the enormous adjustments, reappraisals, and reorganizations, at both conscious and unconscious levels, confronting the adolescent. In normal development separation occurs without the eradication of the identifications of the past. The identifications with the parents are instead modified in adolescence. Idealized and otherwise exaggerated images of the parents must undergo a corrective process so that a more realistic appraisal of the parents can be developed (Jacobson, 1961). As Erikson (1968) suggests, "Identity formation begins where the usefulness of identification ends. It arises from the selective repudiation and mutual assimilation of childhood identifications and their absorption in a new configuration" (p. 159).

Coons (1971) has proposed a set of criteria for defining the closure of adolescence, among which he includes the selection of an occupation and the formation of a personal value system. Erikson (1968) emphasizes the importance of what he refers to as *ideological commitment*, without which the adolescent experiences a *confusion of values*. There is some empirical support for this aspect of Erikson's concept of ego identity in studies by Marcia (1966, 1967) and Marcia and Friedman (1970) who found that those late adolescents who had experienced and resolved an identity crisis by developing a personal value system were the best adjusted.

There are, then, a number of criteria for determining the end of adolescence: the resolution of the parent-child relationship, the establishment of a sexual identity, the formation of a personal value system, the development of a sense of continuity of life experiences, and the coming to terms with residual trauma. These are, nevertheless, ideals which are often not attained. For many the difficulties of adolescence remain unresolved well beyond the teenage years. Blos (1954) has described this difficulty in coming to terms with issues relating to commitment and decisions—in other words, the fear of leaving adolescence—as *prolonged adolescence*. At the same time a frequently observed effort at resolving these matters is seen in a premature closure of adolescence, for example, through the choice of a negative identity. As Erikson (1968) notes, for some adolescents to be "nobody" or to be totally bad or even dead, as long as the decision is felt to be one's own, is preferable than to have no identity at all—to be "not quite somebody."

Even under the best of circumstances, there is no single point at which identity is established. The criteria we are considering are dynamic rather than static. Personal growth and development do not end with adolescence, and issues pertaining to parental relationships and sexual identity, for example, are continually reexperienced in different ways throughout the life span. At most we can hope that by the end of adolescence there is a relatively solid foundation in these areas, that the person entering adulthood is more mature than the person who entered adolescence, that there is a relatively firm sense of purpose and direction, and that life choices derive from within and are based on a set of values and ideals which are experienced as belonging to the self.

REFERENCES

AARONS, Z. A. Normality and abnormality in adolescence: With a digression on Prince Hal—"the sowing of wild oats." *The Psychoanalytic Study of the Child,* 1970, *13,* 255–278.

ANTHONY, J. The reactions of adults to adolescents and their behavior. In G. Kaplan & S. Lebovici (Eds.), *Adolescence: Psychosocial perspectives.* New York: Basic Books, 1969.

AUSUBEL, D. P., MONTEMAYOR, R., & SVAJIAN, P. *Theory and problems of adolescent development* (2nd ed.). New York: Grune & Stratton, 1977.

BARUCH, G. K., & BARNETT, R. C. Implications and applications of recent research on feminine development. *Psychiatry,* 1975, *38,* 318–327.

BENGTSON, V. L. The generation gap: A review and typology of social-psychological perspectives. *Youth and Society,* 1970, *2,* 7–32.

BERSCHEID, E., WALSTER, E., & BOHRNSTEDT, G. The happy American body: A survey report. *Psychology Today,* 1973, *7*(No. 6), 119–131.

BILLER, H. B., & BAHM, R. M. Father-absence, perceived maternal behavior, and masculinity of self-concept among junior high school boys. *Developmental Psychology,* 1971, *4,* 178–181.

BLOS, P. Prolonged adolescence: The formulation of a syndrome and its therapeutic implication. *American Journal of Orthopsychiatry,* 1954, *24,* 733–742.

BLOS, P. Preadolescent drive organization. *Journal of the American Psychoanalytic Association,* 1958, *6,* 47–56.

BLOS, P. The concept of acting out in relation to the adolescent process. *Journal of the American Academy of Child Psychiatry,* 1963, *2,* 118–136.

BLOS, P. The initial stage of male adolescence. *The Psychoanalytic Study of the Child,* 1965, *20,* 145–164.

BLOS, P. The second individuation process of adolescence. *The Psychoanalytic Study of the Child,* 1967, *22,* 162–186.

BLOS, P. The generation gap: Fact and fiction. In S. C. Feinstein, P. Giovacchini, & A. A. Miller (Eds.), *Adolescent psychiatry* (Vol. 1). New York: Basic Books, 1971.

BLOS, P. When and how does adolescence end? In S. C. Feinstein & P. Giovacchini (Eds.), *Adolescent Psychiatry* (Vol. 5). New York: Jason Aronson, 1976.

BLOS, P. *The adolescent passage.* New York: International Universities Press, 1979.

BROVERMAN, I. K., VOGEL, S. R., BROVERMAN, D. M., CLARKSON, F. E., & ROSENKRANTZ, P. S. Sex role stereotypes: A current appraisal. *Journal of Social Issues,* 1972, *28,* 59–78.

CALL, J. D. Sources of anxiety and intrapsychic change during adolescence. In J. D. Noshpitz (Ed.), *Basic handbook of child psychiatry* (Vol. 1). New York: Basic Books, 1979.

CAMPBELL, E. Q. Adolescent socialization. In D. A. Goslin (Ed.), *Handbook of socialization theory and research.* Skokie, Ill.: Rand McNally, 1969.

CARLSON, R. Stability and change in the adolescent's self-image. *Child Psychology,* 1965, *36,* 659–666.

CHILMAN, C. S. *Adolescent sexuality in a changing American society.* Washington, D.C.: U.S. Government Printing Office, 1978.

CLIFFORD, E. Body ratification in adolescence. *Perceptual and Motor Skills,* 1971, *33,* 119–125.

COONS, F. W. The developmental tasks of the college student. In S. C. Feinstein, P. Giovacchini, & A. A. Miller (Eds.), *Adolescent psychiatry* (Vol. 1). New York: Basic Books, 1971.

COSTANZO, P. R., & SHAW, M. E. Conformity as a function of age level. *Child Development,* 1966, *37,* 967–975.

DEUTSCH, H. *The psychology of women* (Vol. 1). New York: Grune & Stratton, 1944.

DIEPOLD, J., & YOUNG, R. D. Empirical studies of adolescent sexual behavior: A critical review. *Adolescence,* 1979, *14,* 45–64.

DION, K., BERSCHEID, E., & WALSTER, E. What is beautiful is good. *Journal of Personality and Social Psychology,* 1972, *24,* 285–290.

DOUVAN, E., & ADELSON, J. *The adolescent experience.* New York: John Wiley, 1966.

ELKIND, D. Egocentrism in adolescence. *Child Development,* 1967, *38,* 1025–1034.

ELKIND, D. Recent research on cognitive development in adolescence. In S. E. Dragastin & G. H. Elder, Jr. (Eds.), *Adolescence in the life cycle: Psychological change and social context.* New York: John Wiley, 1975.

ENGEL, N. The stability of the self-concept in adolescence. *Journal of Abnormal and Social Psychology,* 1959, *58,* 211–215.

ERIKSON, E. H. *Identity: Youth and crisis.* New York: W. W. Norton & Co., Inc., 1968.

FAUST, N. S. Developmental maturity as a determinant in prestige of adolescent girls. *Child Development,* 1960, *31,* 173–184.

FEINSTEIN, S. C., & ARDON, M. D. Trends in dating patterns and adolescent development. *Journal of Youth and Adolescence,* 1973, *2,* 157–166.

FRANK, R. A., & COHEN, D. J. Psychosocial concomitants of biological maturation in preadolescence. *American Journal of Psychiatry,* 1979, *136,* 1518–1524.

FREUD, A. Adolescence. *The Psychoanalytic Study of the Child,* 1958, *13,* 255–278.

FREUD, S. [*Three essays on the theory of sexuality*] (J. Strachey, Ed. and trans.). New York: Basic Books, 1962. (Originally published, 1905.)

GELEERD, E. R. Some aspects of ego vicissitudes in adolescence. *Journal of the American Psychoanalytic Association,* 1961, *9,* 394–405.

Group for the Advancement of Psychiatry. *Normal adolescence: Its dynamics and impact.* New York: Scribner's, 1968.

Group for the Advancement of Psychiatry. *Power and authority in adolescence: The origins and resolutions of intergenerational conflict.* New York: Author, 1978.

HALL, G. S. *Adolescence: Its psychology and its relations to physiology, anthropology, sociology, sex, crime, religion, and education* (2 vols.). New York: Appleton, 1904.

HETHERINGTON, E. M. Effects of father-absence on personality development in adolescent daughters. *Developmental Psychology,* 1972, *7,* 313–326.

HOFFMAN, L. W. Effects of maternal employment on the child: A review of the research. *Developmental Psychology,* 1974, *10,* 204–228.

HOLINGER, P. C. Violent deaths among the youth: Recent trends in suicide, homicide, and accidents. *American Journal of Psychiatry,* 1979, *136,* 1144–1147.

HUSNI-PALACIOS, M., & SCHEUR, P. The high school student: A personality profile. *Proceedings of the 80th Annual Convention of the American Psychological Association,* 1972, *7,* 562–566.

INHELDER, B., & PIAGET, J. *The growth of logical thinking from childhood to adolescence.* New York: Basic Books, 1958.

JACOBSON, E. Adolescent moods and the remodeling of psychic structures in adolescence. *The Psychoanalytic Study of the Child,* 1961, *16,* 164–183.

JERSILD, A. T. *In search of self.* New York: Bureau of Publications, Teachers College, Columbia University, 1952.

JERSILD, A. T., BROOK, J. S., & BROOK, D. W. *The psychology of adolescence* (3rd ed.). New York: Macmillan, 1978.

JONES, M. C. The later careers of boys who were early-or-late-maturing. *Child Development,* 1957, *28,* 115–128.

JONES, M. C. A study of socialization patterns at the high school level. *Journal of Genetic Psychology,* 1958, *93,* 87–111.

JONES, M. C. Psychological correlates of somatic development. *Child Development,* 1965, *36,* 899–911.

JONES, M. C., & BAYLEY, N. Physical maturing among boys as related to behavior. *Journal of Educational Psychology,* 1950, *41,* 129–148.

JONES, M. C., & MUSSEN, P. H. Self-conceptions, motivations and interpersonal attitudes of early-and-late-maturing girls. *Child Development,* 1958, *29,* 491–501.

JOSSELYN, I. M. *The adolescent and his world.* New York: Family Service Association of America, 1952.

JOSSELYN, I. M. The ego in adolescence. *American Journal of Orthopsychiatry,* 1954, *24,* 223–237.

KAGAN, J. A conception of early adolescence. *Daedalus,* 1971, *100,* 997–1012.

KANDEL, D., & LESSER, G. S. Parent-adolescent relationships and adolescent independence in the United States and Denmark. *Journal of Marriage and the Family,* 1969, *31,* 348–358.

KANTNER, J., & ZELNIK, M. Sexual experiences of young unmarried women in the U.S. *Family Planning Prospectives,* 1972, *4*(No. 4), 9–17.

KIELL, N. *The universal experience of adolescence.* New York: International Universities Press, 1964.

KINSEY, A. C., POMEROY, W. B., & MARTIN, C. E. *Sexual behavior in the human male.* Philadelphia: Saunders, 1948.

KINSEY, A. C., POMEROY, W. B., MARTIN, C. E., & GEBHARD, P. H. *Sexual behavior in the human female.* Philadelphia: Saunders, 1953.

KLECK, R. E., RICHARDSON, S. A., & RONALD, L. Physical appearance cues and interpersonal attraction in children. *Child Development,* 1974, *45,* 305–310.

LAUFER, M. Ego ideal and pseudo ego ideal in adolescence. *The Psychoanalytic Study of the Child,* 1964, *19,* 196–221.

LIDZ, T. The adolescent and his family. In J. Kaplan & S. Lebovici (Eds.), *Adolescence: Psychosocial perspectives.* New York: Basic Books, 1969.

LOSCIUTO, L. A., & KARLIN, R. M. Correlates of the generation gap. *Journal of Psychology,* 1972, *81,* 253–262.

MAHLER, M. S., PINE, F., & BERGMAN, A. *The psychological birth of the human infant.* New York: Basic Books, 1975.

MARCIA, J. E. Development and validation of ego identity status. *Journal of Personality and Social Psychology,* 1966, *3,* 551–558.

MARCIA, J. E. Ego identity status: Relationship to change in self-esteem, "general maladjustment," and authoritarianism. *Journal of Personality,* 1967, *35,* 119–133.

MARCIA, J. E., & FRIEDMAN, M. L. Ego identity status in college women. *Journal of Personality,* 1970, *38,* 249–263.

MASTERSON, J. F. *The psychiatric dilemma of adolescence.* Boston: Little, Brown, 1967.

MEISSNER, W. W. Parental interaction of the adolescent boy. *Journal of Genetic Psychology,* 1965, *107,* 225–233.

MUSLIN, H. L. The superego in the adolescent female. In M. Sugar (Ed.), *Female adolescent development.* New York: Brunner/Mazel, 1979.

MUSSEN, P. H., & JONES, M. C. Self-conceptions, motivations and interpersonal attitudes of late-and-early-maturing boys. *Child Development,* 1957, *28,* 243–256.

MUUSS, R. E. Puberty rights in primitive and modern societies. *Adolescence,* 1970, *5,* 109–128.

OFFER, D. *The psychological world of the teen-ager: A study of normal adolescence.* New York: Basic Books, 1969.

OFFER, D., & HOWARD, K. I. An empirical analysis of the Offer self-image questionnaire for adolescents. *Archives of General Psychiatry,* 1972, *27,* 529–537.

OFFER, D. & OFFER, J. B. *From teenage to young manhood: A psychological study.* New York: Basic Books, 1975.

PESKIN, H. Pubertal onset and ego functioning. *Journal of Abnormal Psychology,* 1967, *72,* 1–15.

PESKIN, H. Influence of the developmental schedule of puberty on learning and ego functioning. *Journal of Youth and Adolescence,* 1973, *2,* 273–290.

PETERSON, A. C. Female pubertal development. In M. Sugar (Ed.), *Female adolescent development.* New York: Brunner/Mazel, 1979.

PROTINSKY, H. O., JR. Eriksonian ego identity in adolescents. *Adolescence,* 1975, *10,* 428–432.

ROSENBAUM, M-B. The changing body image of the adolescent girl. In M. Sugar (Ed.), *Female adolescent development.* New York: Brunner/Mazel, 1979.

RUTTER, M., GRAHAM, P., CHADWICK, O.F.D., & YULE, W. Adolescent turmoil: Fact or fiction? *Journal of Child Psychology and Psychiatry,* 1976, *17,* 35–56.

RUTTER, M., TIZAID, J., & WHITMORE, K. (Eds.). *Education, health and behavior.* London: Longmans, 1970.

SIMMONS, R. G., & ROSENBERG, F. Sex, sex roles and self-image. *Journal of Youth and Adolescence,* 1975, *4,* 225–258.

SIMMONS, R. G., ROSENBERG, F., & ROSENBERG, M. Disturbance in the self-image at adolescence. *American Sociological Review,* 1973, *38,* 553–568.

SIMON, W., BERGER, A. C., & GAGNON, J. H. Beyond anxiety and fantasy: The coital experiences of college youth. *Journal of Youth and Adolescence,* 1972, *1,* 203–225.

SROLE, L., LANGNER, T. S., MICHAEL, S. T., OPLER, M. K., & RENNIE, T.A.C. *Mental health in the metropolis: The midtown Manhattan study* (Vol. 1). New York: McGraw-Hill, 1962.

STARR, J. M. The peace and love generation: Changing attitudes toward sex and violence among college youth. *Journal of Social Issues,* 1974, *30,* 73–106.

STOLZ, H. R., & STOLZ, L. M. Adolescent problems related to somatic variations. In N. B. Henry (Ed.), *43rd Yearbook of the National Society for the Study of Education* (P. 1), Adolescence. Chicago: University of Chicago, 1944.

WALSTER, E., ARONSON, V., ABRAHAMS, D., & ROTTMAN, L. Importance of physical attractiveness in dating behavior. *Journal of Personality and Social Psychology,* 1966, *4,* 508–516.

WEATHERLEY, D. Self-perceived rate of physical maturation and personality in late adolescence. *Child Development,* 1964, *35,* 1197–1210.

WEINER, I. B. *Psychological disturbance in adolescence.* New York: John Wiley, 1970.

YANKELOVICH, D. *Generations apart.* New York: Columbia Broadcasting System, 1969.

31

Attitudes and Values during Adolescence

JOHN PAUL MCKINNEY
DEWAYNE MOORE

THE CONCEPTS OF ATTITUDES AND VALUES

Attitudes and values are hypothetical constructs which serve as internal guides for the behaving individual. While values are more global than attitudes, both function to make behavioral choices more parsimonious—that is, less random or purely situation-specific. As a result behavior tends to be more object-consistent and therefore more predictable when under the direction of attitudes and values. Not surprisingly therefore this area of social psychology takes on added importance during the developmental period of adolescence. Along with a dramatic change in cognitive functioning, adolescents experience an increase in the rate of developmental change, physically, emotionally, sexually, and socially. While values and attitudes also change, they play an important role in the maintenance of identity and continuity for the adolescent.

The History of the Attitude and Value Concepts in Psychology

The study of attitudes and values is as old as social psychology itself. Although a good deal of research in a wide variety of fields had centered on the attitude concept in the early years of this century, Ostrom (1968) cites Allport's classic chapter in the 1935 Murchison *Handbook of Social Psychology* as the major integrative paper which synthesized and organized the diverse prior uses of the attitude concept and which was primarily responsible for the emergence of attitude as a fundamental area of study in social psychology. Since that time volumes of research and theory have attested to the importance which psychologists have placed on this concept.

While Thurstone (1928) had already demonstrated that attitudes could be measured, Allport (1935) carefully distinguished attitude from a host of interrelated concepts. Lewin's (1935, 1951) construct of *valence* was a related contribution from cognitive field theory; Newcomb's (1943) emphasis on the interpersonal context in which attitudes are embedded led to the famous Bennington study (Newcomb, 1943) demonstrating the importance of friendships and social relations in attitude change. Sherif and Cantril (1945, 1946, 1947) placed perception as the most important component of attitude acquisition. They argued that the same processes at work in forming psychophysical judgments function in arriving at social judgments. Doob's (1947) paper on the behavior of attitudes distinguished between these perceptual components on the one hand and the relationship between attitudes and behavior on the other. Doob labeled these two components, respectively, the *afferent* and the *efferent* drive strengths of attitudes.

Asch's (1948) emphasis on the importance of communicator credibility and prestige, Heider's (1946, 1958) principle of cognitive balance, and Hovland's (1948a, 1948b, 1949) research on the communication process elaborated the concept of attitudes even further.

Since 1950 there has been a burgeoning in the development of theories about attitude formation and change. In fact one author (Ostrom, 1968) was able to list 34 separate significant contributions to the development of attitude theory between 1953 and 1968. Learning theory contributions include the work of Lott (1955) and Osgood, Suci, and Tannenbaum (1957) on mediated generalization, Fishbein (1967) on concept formation, and McGuire (1964) on inoculation. The cognitive consistency theories of Brehm and Cohen (1962), Festinger (1957), Newcomb (1953, 1961), Rokeach (1960) as well as a variety of other cognitive integration theories are included by Ostrom (1968) as discrete contributions since 1950.

Compared with attitude theory, value theory has had a significantly less elaborated treatment historically. Rokeach (1973) observed that between 1961 and 1965 there were roughly five or six times as many attitude studies as value studies cited in the *Psychological Abstracts*. Once again Allport's work is seminal (Allport & Vernon, 1931; Allport, Vernon, & Lindzey, 1951). One of the earliest measures of values was developed by Allport and Vernon (1931) and was designed to assess the strength of the respondent's values in six areas: aesthetic, economic, political, religious, social, and theoretical. The recent work of Rokeach (1968, 1973) represents a modern attempt to measure values by having respondents rank order, in the order of importance, 18 *terminal* (or end-state) values, as well as 18 *instrumental* (or means) values.

While the term *value* has been used in a wide variety of contexts in economics, aesthetics, and philosophy, psychologists have meant one of two things by the term: *behavioral values* or *object values*. Behavioral values are the prescriptive guides of an "ought to" nature which serve to direct behavior. Objects can also be invested with value. Rescher (1969), a philosopher, distinguishes such value objects from the locus of value and from the underlying values themselves which he says are abstract and ideological (e.g., "wealth," "financial security") and far fewer in number than value objects ("money," "cars," "clothes").

Rokeach (1973) makes a similar point.

The value concept has been employed in two distinctly different ways in human discourse. We will often say that a person "has a value" but also that an object "has value." These two usages, which have been explicitly recognized by writers from various disciplines—writers, such as Charles Morris in philosophy (1956), Brewster Smith in psychology (1969), and Robin Williams in sociology (1968)—require from us at the onset, a decision whether a systematic study of values will turn out to be more fruitful if it focuses on the values that people are said to have or on the values that objects are said to have. (p. 4)

After citing those who fall in the "object camp" (e.g., Hilliard, 1950; Jones & Gerard, 1967; Lewis, 1962; Perry, 1954) and those who study values as "person" variables (e.g., Allport et al., 1951; Kluckhohn & Strodtbeck, 1961; Maslow, 1959, 1964; Morris, 1956; Smith, 1969; Williams, 1968), Rokeach sides with the "person camp": "It seems, therefore, that there are compelling theoretical reasons for assuming that the study of a person's values is likely to be much more useful for social analyses than a study of the values that objects are said to have" (Rokeach, 1973, p. 5).

It may not be necessary, however, to take sides in this debate. Since this chapter deals with both the behavioral and object values of adolescents, we are more inclined to adhere to the view which was expressed in an earlier paper: "In other words, 'value' for an individual is neither entirely objective nor entirely subjective but, like perception, lies on the interface between external reality and internal commitment" (McKinney, 1975, p. 806).

A Theory of Attitudes and Values

The Relationship between Cognitive Variables and Behavior. An implicit assumption among those who study cognitive concepts, such as beliefs, attitudes, and values, is that there is some correspondence between behavior and these cognitions. Widely cited papers of the late 1960s emphasized the poor relationships between behavior and cognition (e.g., Wicker, 1969), and by the early 1970s many regarded cognitive concepts as nearly useless (e.g., Abelson, 1972). Based on a recognition that the relationship between behavior and cognition is exceedingly complex, recent research has demonstrated adequate predictability by employing methods based on an understanding of underlying theoretical and methodological issues. More recent reviews of the literature are thus more optimistic (Ajzen & Fishbein, 1977; Calder & Ross, 1973; Kelman, 1974; Schuman & Johnson, 1976).

Fishbein and Ajzen have argued (e.g., Ajzen & Fishbein, 1977; Fishbein, 1967a, 1973; Fishbein & Ajzen, 1974) that a major reason for the weak relationship between attitude and behavior is the lack of correspondence between attitudinal predictors and behavior criteria. Fishbein (1973) notes that although a relationship is frequently assumed between attitude and whatever behavior the researcher happens to be interested in, there is no necessary relationship between a general attitude toward an object and the performance of a specific behavior with respect to that object. However, a general attitude toward an object should be predictive of the overall patterns of behavior engaged in with respect to that object. Ajzen and Fishbein (1977) maintain that "the strength of an attitude-behavior relationship depends in large part on the degree of correspondence between attitudinal and behavioral entities" (p. 891). When correspondence is high the strength of the relationship between attitude and behavior should also be high. They suggest that attitudinal and behavioral entities may be considered in terms of four different elements: an action element, a target toward which the action is directed, a context in which the action is performed, and a time when the action is performed. Thus an attitude toward a specific act to be engaged in at a given time in a specific context will be predictive of the actual performance of that act in that time and situation. By assessing variables at corresponding levels of specificity—that is, measuring an attitude toward the act for the prediction of a specific behavior or measuring a global attitude toward an object for the prediction of a multiple-act behavioral criterion—a reasonable degree of predictive accuracy can be obtained (Ajzen & Fishbein, 1973, 1977; Davidson & Jaccard, 1975; Fishbein & Ajzen, 1974; Heberlein & Black, 1976; Weigel & Newman, 1976).

Another approach, encouraged by Kelman (1974), to studying the cognition-behavior relationship is to consider personal and situational variables which may influence the extent to which people act in accord with their stated attitudes and beliefs. Individual difference variables that have been found to moderate the attitude-behavior relationship among adults include the degree of affective-cognitive consistency (Norman, 1975), the tendency to ascribe responsibility to the self (Schwartz, 1977), and the degree of self-monitoring (Snyder &

Tanke, 1976). Self-monitoring may be particularly useful in studying the attitude-behavior relationship among adolescents. In addition identity status (Marcia, 1980) may be an important individual difference variable moderating the attitude-behavior relationship in adolescence.

Similarly a number of situational variables appear to moderate the attitude-behavior relation. For example the public versus private nature of the behavior situations (Warner & DeFleur, 1969) that increase the relevance of salient attitudes (Snyder & Swann, 1976) direct behavioral experience with the attitude object (Fazio & Zanna, 1976) and the events in the behavioral sequence (Davidson & Jaccard, 1975).

This work suggests that theories that take into account individual difference variables and the important role of the situation in which the behavior occurs may prove valuable for improving attitude-behavior predictions. Sociologists have made similar points when discussing values (Parsons, 1960; Williams, 1971).

Rather than considering the conditions under which cognitions of various kinds lead to behavior, one can consider the effects of behavior on cognitions. We will discuss two theoretical positions which emphasize the effects of behavior on cognitions: dissonance theory (Festinger, 1957) and the perceptual model proposed by McKinney (1973, 1975).

Several articles have summarized the relevant literature on dissonance theory (Bem, 1972; Eagly & Himmelfarb, 1978; Wicklund & Brehm, 1976; Zanna & Cooper, 1976), and we will not attempt to review this literature again. Briefly the basic assumption of the theory is that a state of dissonance motivates the person to reduce or eliminate the dissonance. Dissonance exists, for example, when persons behave in a way contrary to their beliefs. Persons will then be motivated to reduce dissonance by changing their beliefs to be consonant with their behaviors.

A Perceptual Interpretation of Values. In a recent interpretation of value development, McKinney (1975) emphasized the importance of action and one's freedom of choice in the selection of behavior. The person is seen as an active agent whose values are influenced by the feedback from his/her self-initiated behavior. McKinney assumes that values are the result of experience in the same manner that perceptual schemata are. McKinney (1975) defined a value as a "schematic representation of earlier behavior which serves as a guide in the execution of new behavior" (p. 801). The analogy comes from perceptual adaptation and the importance of *reafference,* or feedback from self-produced movement.

Research by Caro (1966) and Thompson and Gardner (1969) can be interpreted as support for the perceptual analogy, and in two studies McKinney (1975) found direct support for the perceptual hypothesis. Translating this theory into the social psychology of values, McKinney suggests that values are influenced by behavior when the behavior is freely chosen (self-produced movement) and when stimulus changes are seen as contingent on behavior (reafference).

In support of that theory McKinney (1975) demonstrated that college students who had a high internal locus of control according to Rotter's (1966) measure and were therefore seen as choosing freely (and perceiving stimulus changes contingent on their own behavior) developed values which were stronger than externally controlled subjects. Three values were assessed which in an earlier factor-analysis study (McKinney, 1973) had been found to be the most relevant for a group of late adolescent subjects. The three values—academic achievement, interpersonal morality, and general competence—were defined by the two behaviors which had loaded highest and lowest on each factor in the earlier study: "Getting a good grade" and "flunking a test" defined academic achievement; "helping someone out" and "doing something deceitful" defined interpersonal morality; and "accomplishing something" and "letting myself down" defined general competence. When high internals rated these items on three purely evaluative semantic differential scales (e.g., good . . . bad), the *difference* scores—i.e., between the two extreme behavior items—were significantly higher than those of the external subjects. When subjects rated the behaviors on activity-evaluative scales (e.g., intentional-unintentional), the *summated* scores for the two extreme items were significantly higher for the internal subjects. These results were seen as supporting the perceptual model of values, as well as a distinction between two components of the valuing process, a motor-affective dimension and a perceptual dimension.

Measurement of Attitudes and Values

Allport observed in 1935 that attitudes are more difficult to define than they are to measure. In a strict sense this statement is still true of both attitudes and values. However in a more general sense we believe measurement and theory are closely interrelated. Measurement reflects the definitional and theoretical assumptions of the researcher. Furthermore theoretical advances, in part, depend on the development of more sophisticated measurement techniques and vice versa. We hope to make explicit some of the theoretical assumptions of various measurement techniques in this section on measurement.

Attitudes and values have been measured in diverse ways as can be seen in recent compendia of tests (Bonjean, Hill, & McLemore, 1967; Johnson, 1976; Johnson & Bonmorito, 1971; Robinson & Shaver, 1969). One of the early measures of values was the Allport-Vernon-Lindzey Scale of Values (1931, 1951, 1960). This scale enables one to measure the relative order of importance of six classes of values suggested by Spranger (1928): theoretical, social, political, religious, aesthetic, and economic. Clearly Rokeach's Value Survey (1973, 1979) is the most popular measure of values (Beech & Schoeppe, 1974; Feather, 1975, 1980; Rokeach, 1979). The Value Survey involves a set of 18 terminal values and a set of 18 instrumental values, each accompanied by a short descriptive phrase.

The usual instruction to the respondent is to "arrange them in order of importance to you, as guiding principles in your life." The ranking method assumes that it is the relative ordering of values that is of interest and not their absolute presence or absence.

As Rokeach (1973) notes, the procedure employed in selecting the instrumental and terminal values was intuitive, and "there is no reason to think that others working independently would have come up with precisely the same list of 18 terminal and 18 instrumental values" (p. 30). Such value selection procedures appear to be the rule rather than the exception (Bengtson, 1975; Kluckhohn & Strodtbeck, 1961; Kohn, 1977; Morris, 1956). These measures necessarily constrain subjects' responses in unknown ways.

Survey researchers have used questionnaire items to monitor value change among youth (Yankelovich, 1973, 1974). The American Council on Education annually surveys first-year college students. Astin and his colleagues at UCLA are the directors of the project (Astin, 1977a, 1977b). Specially tailored items have been developed to assess values concerned with work (Feather, 1979; Mirels & Garrett, 1971; Orpen, 1978; Wollack, Goodale, Whiting, & Smith, 1971); politics (Caplow & Bahr, 1979; Jennings & Niemi, 1974; Klineberg, Zavalloni, Louis-Guérinc, & Ben Brika, 1979); morality (Eppel & Eppel, 1966; Klineberg et al., 1979; Kohlberg, 1976; Wright & Cox, 1971); sex (Astin, 1977a; Bell, 1966; Chilman, 1979; Sorenson, 1973); religion (Caplow & Bahr, 1979; Hastings & Hoge, 1972; Pilkington, Poppleton, Gould, & McCourt, 1976; Wright & Cox, 1971); sex roles (Bem, 1974; Spence & Helmreich, 1978); and achievement (McClellan, 1961; Salili, Maehr, & Gillmore, 1976; Weiner & Peter, 1973). Others are summarized by Feather (1980) and Triandis (1972).

Recently McKinney (1973) suggested an open-ended, inductive approach to the assessment of values. In contrast to the deductive, nomothetic approaches described before which impose an a priori theoretical framework on responses, inductive procedures allow the structure to be determined by the data. Early examples of inductive approaches to value assessment are Gillespie and Allport (1955) and Goodman (1957). The early works of Gillespie and Allport (1955), Goodman (1957), and White (1951) are examples of inductive approaches in which content analysis (Holsti, 1969) of personal and cultural products was used to assess values. In the past phenomenological and inductive approaches to measurement have been criticized for lack of clarity and rigor. However, recent advances in measurement and computer technology have resulted in sophisticated techniques which overcome some of these difficulties. We will briefly consider three related techniques: factor analyses, cluster analysis, and multidimensional scaling.

The factor-analytic approach of the study of values has a long history. Rettig and Pasamanick (1959) factor analyzed the moral judgment ratings of a group of college students in 1958 on a list of items that had also been given to similar groups in 1929, 1939, and 1949. Another factor-analytic approach was used by Brim (1965) and Goodman (1969) in the analysis of a set of prescriptive behavioral statements designed to discover the value structure of a group of high school students.

In each of these studies the items used for the factor analysis were selected by the researcher. An alternative approach by McKinney (1973) was an open-ended procedure in which the items were produced by the respondents themselves. This purely empirical approach allows the researcher to use the universe of value statements given by a sample of subjects. Such a procedure allows one to study the subjective organization of values as given by subjects, rather than as based on a predetermined questionnaire which is necessarily limited in unknown ways by the researcher.

The application of scaling and clustering to free-response data is a recent development (Moore, 1979; Passer, Kelley, & Michela, 1978; Rosenberg & Sedlak, 1972). The most extensive applications of multidimensional scaling (MDS) and cluster analysis have been to studies of attitudes toward the self and others (Rosenberg & Sedlak, 1972). Briefly the application of MDS starts with the selection of a set of entities. The basic input required is a measure for each pair of entities in the set reflecting how closely the two entities are related. What MDS then does is yield the smallest set of dimensions that can best account for the variance in a measure of relatedness or similarity. MDS thus allows one to determine empirically the most important attributes and the interrelationships among them (for reviews of the technique, see Carroll & Arabie, 1980; Kruskal & Wish, 1978).

MDS and cluster analysis may be particularly useful for identifying the presence and nature of stereotypes in different groups of individuals—i.e., how individuals differ in their attitudes toward men, women, the handicapped, homosexuals, parents, teachers. The advantage of these techniques is that they minimally constrain subject responses while providing a mathematical structure to the data.

VALUES DURING ADOLESCENCE

Stated Values of Adolescents

The content of adolescent values can be measured in the variety of ways described before. Examples of two very different approaches will be considered here. First of all, it is possible simply to ask the subjects to rank order a list of values in the order of their importance to the respondent. This was done by Beech and Schoeppe (1974) with groups of fifth-, seventh-, ninth-, and eleventh-graders. Using the Rokeach Value Survey (Rokeach, 1968), the investigators were able to assess both the instrumental ("means") values as well as the terminal ("end-state") values of their subjects. The authors were able, by testing subjects from the fifth to the twelfth grade, to examine the extent to which values held in common by adolescents tend to remain stable, or to change, over the adolescent years. By and large there is a good deal of similarity across the ages and sexes. Such values as *a world at peace, freedom, honest,* and *loving* tend to be given consistently high priority by both boys and girls at all grades, while other values such as *salvation, logical,* and *imaginative* tend to be given lower rankings by both sexes in all grades. Not surprisingly the value of *family security* tends to be ranked higher by young children than by older children, while *equality* and *social recognition* are seen as more important values to the older adolescents. Again not surprisingly the instrumental values *cheerful, helpful,* and *obedient* tend to decline in importance by the eleventh grade, undoubtedly reflecting an increase in autonomy and self-direction. Two terminal values also declined steadily for both sexes—namely, a *world of beauty* and *true friendship.*

Given the limitations of cross-sectional methods (Nesselroade & Baltes, 1974), it is not possible to know whether these changes are a truly developmental trend. They may occur as a result of the social history of the particular cohort. Since few cohorts were tested, it could be that some of the changes reflect not age so much as cohort.

In another study using the Rokeach measure with high school students (Günther, 1975), 400 German boys and girls were given a German translation of the measure. Neither age nor sex differences are given, but differences across religious affiliation and political persuasion are reported. Significant differences among Catholic, Protestant, and agnostic adolescents occurred on five terminal and three instrumental values. Catholics gave higher ranking and agnostics lower (with Protestants in between) to the values *a world at peace* and *salvation* while agnostics gave a higher ranking (and Catholics lower) to *an exciting life* and *pleasure*. Both groups gave a higher ranking to *social recognition* compared to Protestants. Three instrumental values distinguished the groups: *helpful* which Catholics rated higher, Protestants lower, and agnostics still lower; and *logical* and *independent* which showed the opposite trend—i.e., agnostics rating these higher than Protestants, who rated them higher than Catholics.

Keeping in mind the limitations of ordinal scales, it is difficult to know whether those values rated high and low on the hierarchy have greater salience and, therefore, higher reliability than those coming somewhere in the middle of a respondent's ranking. Also there is no assurance that the distance between ranks is equal from top to bottom. An individual may feel very strongly about a few values and very little about the others. Finally it should be recalled that the 18 terminal and 18 instrumental values are a preset list derived from research with college students. Their salience for high school students or for other national groups may be less, although Günther (1975) found the German translation to be reasonably reliable.

Value Orientations of Youth

As mentioned earlier my own work (McKinney, 1971, 1973) demonstrates a very different approach in measuring the values of college students. Initially I was interested not so much in the categories or content of values, but rather in the ascriptive orientation of values. While some individuals maintain prescriptive ("Thou shalt") values, others are oriented in a proscriptive ("Thou shalt not") value direction. Seven of the ten commandments are stated in this proscriptive fashion, and although such religious exhortations as the "Sermon on the Mount" are prescriptively stated, still much religious training and character education has been geared toward proscriptive values.

My first goal (McKinney, 1971) was to see if such a value orientation could be measured reliably as a personality variable and if it related to earlier child-rearing practices. A sentence completion measure was used. This open-ended approach, unlike lists of values, allows the respondent to state his/her own values. The 14 relevant sentence stems were divided into two groups. Seven "reward" stems included a positive social reinforcement,

such as "My parents would be pleased with me if . . . ," or "My teacher trusts me when . . ." The other seven were "punishment" stems: "My father gets angry with me when . . . ." Both sorts could be answered either prescriptively or proscriptively:

"My parents would be pleased with me if . . . I did well at school."
"My father gets angry with me when . . . I don't pay attention."

Both cases illustrate a prescriptive, or "Thou shalt," orientation by emphasizing what ought to be done: doing well and paying attention. The same stems could elicit proscriptive endings which would emphasize what ought not be done:

"My parents would be pleased with me if . . . I didn't smoke so much."
"My father gets angry with me when . . . I bother my sister."

This approach overall reveals the orientation (prescriptive versus proscriptive) rather than the specific content of values. The statements themselves, being highly specific, are more properly behavioral attitudes. The measure proved acceptably reliable; the split-half reliability was 64 percent, and interscorer agreement was 98 percent. This suggests an individual difference variable which is separate from the reward versus punishment, or discipline-emphasis, dimension.

Secondly, it was demonstrated that prescriptively oriented college students perceived their parents as having been more rewarding and less punitive in their formative years. Subjects were given the Parent-Child Relations Questionnaire (Roe & Siegelman, 1963). Direct-object reward and punishment scores differentiated significantly between pre- and proscriptive subjects.

The research demonstrated an important value dimension which had not been examined previously and suggested child-rearing correlates of the variable. This work was initiated in the late 1960s when it appeared that in a number of areas adolescents and youth were beginning to express a more affirmative morality (Wharton, 1969). Students were speaking out and acting on such issues as national policy and sexual morality, in contrast to the passive response to prohibitions which appeared to have marked the previous decade. Research directed at this question (McKinney, Connolly, & Clark, 1973) confirmed the hypothesis that college students had gradually from 1929 to the late 1950s become more severe in their prescriptive moral judgments, but not proscriptive. These data, coupled with the previously reported relationship between value orientation and parent-child relations, fit nicely with Bronfenbrenner's observation that parents over those years had become progressively more love-oriented and less punishment-oriented in their discipline practices (Bronfenbrenner, 1958, 1961). It is not surprising that their children became more prescriptive.

While these studies dealt with value orientation and its relationship to behavior (Olejnik & McKinney, 1973, 1975), it was possible from the results of the sentence completion research to construct an experiment which would yield the structure of the content of college students' values. The universe of responses given to two stems by the 67 subjects of the original study became the basis for a factor-analytic study of the structure of values (McKinney, 1973). A questionnaire using 95 responses to the stems, "I am proud of myself when . . ." and "I would be ashamed of myself if . . . ," was given to 744 students who were asked to rate the 95 items on a five-point scale from *desirable* to *undesirable* (a second study using the terms *important . . . unimportant* yielded an essentially identical factor structure).

The ratings were then factor analyzed revealing nine value dimensions, the first three of which were academic achievement, interpersonal morality, and general competence. These broad "values" were based on the clustering of specific attitude statements and are felt to underlie the large bulk of attitudes of college students. These first three values are differentiated from one another in two important ways. First, two of them were concerned with personal, or private, attitudes dealing with achievement, while the other factor was based on interpersonal, or social, attitudes involved with ethics and morality. This distinction between competence values, which are personal, and social-moral values, which are interpersonal, had been made by philosophers (Rescher, 1969). In this study it was demonstrated empirically. Second, the two achievement values were the clustering of prescriptive statements, while the social-moral factor was stated proscriptively. In a recent study we have found similar results, analyzing the data from the sexes separately (Truhon, McKinney, & Hotch, 1980).

The distinction between achievement values and interpersonal moral values formed the basis for a subsequent study (McKinney, Hotch, & Truhon, 1977) in which we examined the change between the values of late adolescents of the 1960s and a decade later. Based on informal observations of the changes in student values from the 1960s to the 1970s, we predicted, and found, a change in the relative frequency with which students' sentence completions in the two eras stressed interpersonal morality over achievement. We compared the 1969 responses of 67 students to the stems, "I am proud of myself when . . ." and "I would be ashamed of myself if . . . ," to similar data gathered from students in 1975. As predicted the earlier group gave significantly more responses of the social interpersonal morality sort, while the 1975 sample responded with more private achievement-oriented sentences. Once again, however, just as in the Beech and Schoeppe (1974) study where the students' age and cohort were confounded, the times of testing and cohort are confounded. However, the most logical explanation for these results, and the basis of our hypothesis, was that the social climate of the 1970s was changing once again in the direction of private, personal achievement-oriented values.

It would be a mistake, however, to suggest that U.S. youths' values in the 1970s had returned to the "privatistic" level described by Gillespie and Allport (1955) in the 1950s. Instead the answer is more complicated. Kleiber and Manaster (1972) compared the two cohorts, Gillespie and Allport's 1950 college student sample and a new comparable sample twenty years later, on the original values questionnaire used by Gillespie and Allport. In addition the researchers divided their 1970 sample into

activists (who had participated in demonstrations) and nonactivists and gave all of their subjects such additional measures as *Rotter's* (1966) *locus of control measure* and measures of dogmatism and conservatism (Rokeach, 1956; Wilson & Patterson, 1968). Overall there were several differences between the cohorts: "The 1971 students expect and desire fewer children, are more approving of women working, are in better physical condition, desire and expect more racial equality, and are apparently more enthusiastic and self-confident with respect to their futures" compared with the 1950 sample (Kleiber & Manaster, 1972, p. 231). This description did not characterize all of their sample, however, as there were differences between the activists and nonactivists.

In general, activists were more liberal, less dogmatic, less nationalistic, more pessimistic, less oriented to economic success, and more oriented to the present than nonactivists. The greater orientation to the present is an important difference. They are dealing with the value-laden issues of the day in a serious and aggressive manner. They concern themselves more with social problems than do nonactivists, who are probably more content in most cases to remain aloof from such problems with the intention of focusing more on the development of their personal futures. In this regard, the nonactivists are more aligned with the 1950 sample which Gillespie and Allport characterized as having a "strong flavor of privatism." (Kleiber & Manaster, 1972, p. 232)

Adolescent Values versus Parents' and Teachers' Values: An Adolescent Subculture

It has been argued that the high school provides a medium for the development of an adolescent subculture. When American society was mainly postfigurative, to use Mead's (1970) term, the function of the school was primarily to educate children in the ways of the adult world and to impart the skills necessary for youngsters to become responsible members of the adult society. In a cofigurative, and still more in a prefigurative society, in which children learn from one another as well as from their elders, the school itself may become a subculture with its own norms. Whether or not these norms are consonant with the norms of the society at large, they are highly important in determining the direction of the students' behavior. A study by Coleman (1961) bears directly on this proposition.

Coleman's research suggests that the subculture of the high school may be based on a set of values which are not entirely consonant with the values of the larger society or with the traditional conception of the school. Coleman's subjects were students in ten midwestern high schools which were mainly public, mostly coeducational, and drawn from urban, rural, and suburban areas.

In studying the values of these students, Coleman asked the following question: "If you could be remembered here at school for one of the three things below, which one would you want it to be? Boys: Bright student, athletic star, most popular; girls: brilliant student, leader in athletics, most popular." The results demonstrated that athletics are far more important to the students than scholarship or popularity. In fact scholarship came out a losing third. Coleman gave a similar questionnaire to the parents of his subjects. Notice the difference in the parents' responses. They were more concerned with scholarship, at least so they say, than with the other values represented in the school.

While the values of the parents and the values of their children are clearly at odds, the basis of this discrepancy is not entirely clear. One aspect of Coleman's data suggests that the discrepancy should not be so large. For example when the boys and girls were asked under what conditions their parents might be proud of them, more said their parents would be proud of them for making the basketball team or the cheerleading squad than for becoming an assistant to the instructor of the biology class. It would appear that while the parents' values are in reality more academic, the youngsters are perceiving them to be social. The reason for this discrepancy is not clear, although a number of hypotheses could be presented. Perhaps the students simply perceive the values of their parents differently from what they actually are. Perhaps one of the two groups is not being completely honest. Coleman suggested, however, the parents undoubtedly do want their children to be scholarly and do place a higher priority on scholarship than on social or athletic skills. They may want, however, whatever is best for their children. They assume what is best for their children is what would make their children happy in a setting in which they must survive. The children, *knowing what it takes to be successful* in their own subculture, may rightfully assume that their parents would be proud of them if they were recognized according to its values. In other words parents may unwittingly be reinforcing values which are generated in the adolescent subculture.

In a massive study conducted in high schools in upstate New York and in central Ohio, Gardner and Thompson (1963) developed 12 different instruments for the study of adolescent values and tested these instruments on thousands of high school students. Among the authors' measures of values, two tests measured the broad prescription or "ought to" values perceived as desirable and necessary for the "good life." These were the Ways of Living instrument and the Telenomic Trends instrument. The Ways of Living instrument was adapted from Morris's "Ways to Live" (Morris, 1942, 1956) and included measures of 16 different values that define the "good life." Five of these "ways" define self-indulgence versus self-control; six "ways" are used to define an active-aggressive versus sedentary-passive-receptive life; and four "ways" define a self-sufficient versus sociable-socially sensitive life. Finally one "way" combines the preceding three conceptions.

The VEMS (values, ethical-moral-social) Test is a measure of the values of loyalty, honesty, truthfulness, and kindness-generosity. On this test the subject is asked to respond to hypothetical situations according to what s/he thinks ought to be done given the ethical-moral-social dilemmas presented.

When Gardner and Thompson compared the scores of ninth-, tenth-, eleventh-, and twelfth-grade boys and girls with the scores of their teachers on the Ways of Living instrument and the VEMS Test, the following results were obtained. Adolescent boys placed greater emphasis than their teachers on self-indulgence and enjoyment of personal pleasures, on adventure and fighting for the things one wants, on waiting for good things to happen, and on working as part of a group. They tended to place less emphasis than their teachers on sedentary activities and sympathetic concerns for other people. Females were not so different from their teachers as males but gave greater emphasis to self-indulgence, to waiting for good things to happen rather than working hard, to working as part of a group rather than doing things by oneself, and surprisingly to sympathetic concern for other people.

When Gardner and Thompson compared the social, ethical, and moral values of public high school teachers and their pupils, the following results emerged: Boys placed more emphasis on loyalty, impunitiveness, and conformity to the peer group and less emphasis on honesty and truthfulness than their teachers. Public high school girls were more concerned with kindness and generosity and impunitiveness and less concerned with honesty and truthfulness than their teachers. When pupils from Catholic high schools were compared on the VEMS Test with their teachers (who were nuns), the pupils showed more concern with conformity, impunity, kindness, and generosity and placed less emphasis on honesty and truthfulness than did the nuns. Once again the significance of these differences suggests a subculture within the school which is based on a set of values shared by the students but not always consistent with the values of their superiors.

The values of the adolescents were then compared with the values of their parents on the VEMS Test. The results were somewhat surprising. The subjects were a group of twelfth-grade boys and girls who were asked to take the test under two different conditions: once according to their own beliefs, and once according to their perception of the way their parents would take the test. Finally the experimenters asked the parents to take the test as well. Surprisingly the boys' scores correlated more closely with their guesses at the parents' scores than with the parents' actual scores. In other words the boys perceived their values to be more similar to their parents' values than was actually the case. While the same was true for the girls, the results were not nearly so significant. What all this suggests is that adolescents have a set of values which have more in common with the values of their age-mates than with the values of their parents. To the extent that a subculture can be defined in terms of a discrete set of values and to the extent that the values of adolescents differ from those of their parents, adolescence can be considered a separate subculture.

Value Clarification: A Practical Application

A practical application of the recent research in development of values has been the teaching of the valuing process to students. The practice has gone under the various labels of *value clarification, value analysis* and *values education.* Each approach, though differing to some extent from the others, has as its primary goal the analysis and consideration of controversial value issues. Typically the activity takes place in a social studies class and is defended on the basis that it serves one or more of the following objectives: "(1) Helping students make the most rational decisions they can make about the value issue under consideration, (2) helping students develop the capabilities and dispositions required for making rational value decisions, and (3) teaching students how to resolve value conflict between themselves and other members of a group" (Coombs & Meux, 1971, p. 29). Once again in this context as in other value areas, it is not always clear whether "value" refers to the object being valued (e.g., *"Minneapolis* is a beautiful city") or the internal standard by which the object is being judged (e.g., *"Beauty* is one important urban value"). Generally students are taught how to make value judgments and how to resolve conflicts when value judgments are in opposition to one another. A number of situational tasks or practical strategies have been outlined for the teacher (Metcalf, 1971; Raths, Harmin, & Simon, 1966; Simon, Howe, & Kirschenbaum, 1972). These often consist of game-like situations which involve the student with the purpose of helping the individual to clarify his/her own values and to deal effectively with value conflicts.

CONCLUSIONS

In this chapter we have outlined the history of attitudes and values in social psychology and their special place in the psychology of adolescent development. A theory of value development (McKinney, 1975), based on a perceptual analogy, has been proposed. A variety of techniques and measures of attitudes and values were discussed.

The attitudes and values of adolescents are reviewed around two central issues: the content of adolescent attitudes and values and the process of valuing. We have pointed to the relationship between adolescents' values and the values of their parents and teachers. Finally we have discussed briefly the topic of value clarification.

REFERENCES

ABELSON, R. P. Are attitudes necessary? In B. T. King & E. McGinnies (Eds.), *Attitudes, conflict, and social change.* New York: Academic Press, 1972.

AJZEN, I., & FISHBEIN, M. Attitudinal and normative variables as predictors of specific behaviors. *Journal of Personality and Social Psychology,* 1973, *27,* 41–57.

AJZEN, I., & FISHBEIN, M. Attitude-behavior relations: A theoretical analysis and review of empirical research. *Psychological Bulletin,* 1977, *84,* 888–918.

ALLPORT, G. Attitudes. In C. Murchison (Ed.), *Handbook of social psychology.* Worcester, Mass.: Clark University Press, 1935.

ALLPORT, G. W., & VERNON, P. E. *A study of values: Manual of directions.* Boston: Houghton Mifflin, 1931.

ALLPORT, G. W., VERNON, P. E., & LINDZEY, G. *A study of values: A scale for measuring the dominant interests in personality* (Rev. ed.). Boston: Houghton Mifflin, 1951.

ALLPORT, G. W., VERNON, P. E., & LINDZEY, G. *A study of values: Manual of directions* (Rev. ed.). Boston: Houghton Mifflin, 1960.

ASCH, S. E. The doctrine of suggestion, prestige and imitation in social psychology. *Psychological Review,* 1948, *55,* 250–276.

ASTIN, A. *Four critical years.* San Francisco: Jossey-Bass, 1977a.

ASTIN, A. The new realists. *Psychology Today,* September 1977b, pp. 50–53; 105–107.

BEECH, R. P., & SCHOEPPE, A. Development of value systems in adolescents. *Developmental Psychology,* 1974, *10,* 644–656.

BELL, R. R. *Premarital sex in a changing society.* Englewood Cliffs, N.J.: Prentice-Hall, 1966.

BEM, D. J. Self-perception theory. *Advances in Experimental Social Psychology,* 1972, *6,* 1–62.

BEM, S. L. The measurement of psychological androgyny. *Journal of Consulting and Clinical Psychology,* 1974, *42,* 155–162.

BENGTSON, V. L. Generation and family effects in value socialization. *American Sociological Review,* 1975, *40,* 358–371.

BONJEAN, C. N., HILL, R. J., & McLEMORE, S. D. *Sociological measurement: An inventory of scales and indices.* San Francisco: Chandler, 1967.

BREHM, J. W., & COHEN, A. R. *Explorations in cognitive dissonance.* New York: John Wiley, 1962.

BRIM, O. G., JR. Adolescent personality as self-other systems. *Journal of Marriage and the Family,* 1965, *27,* 156–162.

BRONFENBRENNER, U. Socialization and social class through time and space. In E. E. Maccoby, T. M. Newcomb, & E. I. Hartley (Eds.), *Readings in social psychology.* New York: Holt, Rinehart & Winston, 1958.

BRONFENBRENNER, U. The changing American child—a speculative analysis. *Merrill-Palmer Quarterly,* 1961, *7,* 73–84.

CALDER, B. J., & ROSS, M. *Attitudes and behavior.* Morristown, N.J.: General Learning Press, 1973.

CAPLOW, T., & BAHR, H. M. Half a century of change in adolescent attitudes: Replication of a Middletown survey by the Lynds. *Public Opinion Quarterly,* 1979, *43,* 1–17.

CARO, F. G. Social class and attitudes of youth relevant for the realization of adult goals. *Social Forces,* 1966, *44,* 492–498.

CARROLL, J. D., & ARABIE, P. Multidimensional scaling. *Annual Review of Psychology,* 1980, *31,* 607–649.

CHILMAN, C. S. *Adolescent sexuality in a changing American society: Social and psychological perspectives.* DHEW Publication No. (NIH) 79-1426. Washington, D.C.: U.S. Government Printing Office, 1979.

COLEMAN, J. S. Social climates in high schools. *Cooperative Research Monograph Series.* Washington, D.C.: U.S. Government Printing Office, 1961.

COOMBS, J. R., & MEUX, M. Teaching strategies for value analysis. In L. E. Metcalf (Ed.), *Values education: rationale, strategies, and procedures* (Forty-first yearbook, National Council for the Social Studies). Washington, D.C.: National Council for the Social Studies, 1971.

DAVIDSON, A. R., & JACCARD, J. J. Population psychology: A new look at an old problem. *Journal of Personality and Social Psychology,* 1975, *6,* 1073–1082.

DOOB, L. The behavior of attitudes. *Psychological Review,* 1947, *54,* 135–156.

EAGLY, A. H., & HIMMELFARB, S. Attitudes and opinions. *Annual Review of Psychology,* 1978, *29,* 517–574.

EPPEL, E. M., & EPPEL, M. *Adolescents and morality: A study of some moral values of working adolescents in the context of a changing climate of opinion.* London: Routledge & Kegan Paul, 1966.

FAZIO, R. H., & ZANNA, M. P. *Attitude-behavior consistency as a function of the salience of past behavior.* Paper presented at the meeting of the Eastern Psychological Association, New York, 1976.

FEATHER, N. T. *Values in education and society.* New York: Free Press, 1975.

FEATHER, N. T. Human values and the work situation. *Australian Psychologist,* 1979, *14,* 131–141.

FEATHER, N. T. Values in adolescence. In J. Adelson (Ed.), *Handbook of adolescent psychology.* New York: John Wiley, 1980.

FESTINGER, L. *A theory of cognitive dissonance.* Stanford, Calif.: Stanford University Press, 1957.

FISHBEIN, M. Attitude and the prediction of behavior. In M. Fishbein (Ed.), *Readings in attitude theory and measurement.* New York: John Wiley, 1967a.

FISHBEIN, M. A behavior theory approach to the relations between beliefs about an object and the attitude toward the object. In M. Fishbein (Ed.), *Readings in attitude theory and measurement.* New York: John Wiley, 1967b.

FISHBEIN, M. The prediction of behaviors from attitudinal variables. In C. D. Mortensen & K. K. Sereno (Eds.), *Advances in communication research.* New York: Harper & Row, Pub., 1973.

FISHBEIN, M., & AJZEN, I. Attitudes toward objects as predictors of single and multiple behavioral criteria. *Psychological Review,* 1974, *81,* 59–74.

GARDNER, E. F., & THOMPSON, G. G. *Investigation and measurement of the social values governing interpersonal relations among adolescent youth and their teachers.* Cooperative Research Project. No. 259A (8418) SU and 259B (8418) OSU. Washington, D.C.: U.S. Office of Education, 1963.

GILLESPIE, J. M., & ALLPORT, G. W. *Youth's outlook on the future.* New York: Random House, 1955.

GOODMAN, M. E. Values, attitudes and social concepts of Japanese and American children. *American Anthropologist*, 1957, *59*, 979–999.

GOODMAN, N. Adolescent norms and behavior. *Merrill-Palmer Quarterly*, 1969, *15*, 200–211.

GREENWALD, A. G., BROCK, T. C., & OSTROM, T. M. (Eds.), *Psychological foundations of attitudes*. New York: Academic Press, 1968.

GÜNTHER, H. Ein Versuch der Anwendung der Rokeach Value Scale in der Bestimmung von Werthaltungen deutscher Austauschschuler. *Psychologische Beiträge*, 1975, *17*, 304–320.

HASTINGS, P. K., & HOGE, D. R. Religious change among college students over two decades. In P. K. Manning & M. Truzzi (Eds.), *Youth and sociology*. Englewood Cliffs, N.J.: Prentice-Hall, 1972.

HEBERLEIN, T. A., & BLACK, J. S. Attitudinal specificity and the prediction of behavior in a field setting. *Journal of Personality and Social Psychology*, 1976, *33*, 474–479.

HEIDER, F. Attitudes and cognitive organization. *Journal of Psychology*, 1946, *21*, 107–112.

HEIDER, F. *The psychology of interpersonal relations*. New York: John Wiley, 1958.

HILLIARD, A. L. *The forms of value: The extension of a hedonistic axiology*. New York: Columbia University Press, 1950.

HOLSTI, O. R. Content analysis. In G. Lindzey & E. Aronson (Eds.), *The handbook of social psychology* (2nd ed.). Reading, Mass.: Addison-Wesley, 1969.

HOVLAND, C. I. Social communication. *Proceedings of the American Philosophical Society*, 1948a, *92*, 371–375.

HOVLAND, C. I. Psychology of the communication process. In W. Schramm (Ed.), *Communication in modern society*. Urbana, Ill.: University Press, 1948b.

HOVLAND, C. I., LUMSDAINE, A., & SHEFFIELD, F. *Experiments on mass communication*. Princeton, N.J.: Princeton University Press, 1949.

JENNINGS, M. K., & NIEMI, R. G. *The political character of adolescence*. Princeton, N.J.: Princeton University Press, 1974.

JOHNSON, O. G. *Tests and measures in child development* (Handbook 2). San Francisco: Jossey-Bass, 1976.

JOHNSON, O. G., & BONMORITO, J. W. *Tests and measures in child development* (Handbook 1). San Francisco: Jossey-Bass, 1971.

JOHNSON, S. C. Hierarchical clustering schemes. *Psychometrika*, 1967, *32*, 241–254.

JONES, E. E., & GERARD, H. B. *Foundations of social psychology*. New York: John Wiley, 1967.

KELMAN, H. C. Attitudes are alive and well and gainfully employed in the sphere of action. *American Psychologist*, 1974, *29*, 310–325.

KLEIBER, D. A., & MANASTER, G. J. Youth's outlook on the future: A past-present comparison. *Journal of Youth and Adolescence*, 1972, *3*, 223–232.

KLINEBERG, O., ZAVALLONI, M., LOUIS-GUÉRINC, C., & BEN BRIKA, J. *Students, values, and politics: A crosscultural comparison*. New York: Free Press, 1979.

KLUCKHOHN, R., & STRODTBECK, F. L. *Variations in value orientation*. Evanston, Ill.: Row, Peterson, 1961.

KOHLBERG, L. Moral stages and moralization: The cognitive-developmental approach. In T. Lickona (Ed.), *Moral development and behavior: Theory, research, and social issues*. New York: Holt, Rinehart & Winston, 1976.

KOHN, M. L. *Class and conformity: A study in values* (2nd ed.). Chicago: University of Chicago Press, 1977.

KRUSKAL, J. B., & WISH, M. *Multidimensional scaling*. Beverly Hills, Calif.: Sage Publications, Inc., 1978.

LEWIN, K. *Dynamic theory of personality*. New York: McGraw-Hill, 1935.

LEWIN, K. *Field theory in the social sciences*. New York: Harper & Row, Pub., 1951.

LEWIS, C. I. *An analysis of knowledge and valuation*. LaSalle, Ill.: Open Court, 1962.

LOTT, B. E. Attitude formation: The development of a color-preference response through mediated generalization. *Journal of Abnormal and Social Psychology*, 1955, *50*, 321–326.

McCLELLAND, D. C. *The achieving society*. Princeton, N.J.: D. Van Nostrand, 1961.

McGUIRE, W. J. Inducing resistance to persuasion. In L. Berkowitz (Ed.), *Advances in experimental social psychology* (Vol. 1). New York: Academic Press, 1964.

McKINNEY, J. P. The development of values—prescriptive or proscriptive? *Human Development*, 1971, *14*, 71–80.

McKINNEY, J. P. The structure of behavioral values of college students. *Journal of Psychology*, 1973, *85*, 235–244.

McKINNEY, J. P. The development of values: A perceptual interpretation. *Journal of Personality and Social Psychology*, 1975, *31*, 801–807.

McKINNEY, J. P., CONNOLLY, M., & CLARK, J. Development of a prescriptive morality: An historical observation. *Journal of Genetic Psychology*, 1973, *122*, 105–110.

McKINNEY, J. P., HOTCH, D. F., & TRUHON, S. A. The organization of behavioral values during late adolescence: Change and stability across two eras. *Developmental Psychology*, 1977, *13*, 83–84.

MARCIA, J. Identity in adolescence. In J. Adelson (Ed.), *Handbook of adolescent psychology*. New York: John Wiley, 1980.

MASLOW, A. H. (Ed.). *New knowledge in human values*. New York: Harper & Row, Pub., 1959.

MASLOW, A. H. *Religions, values, and peak-experiences*. Columbus: Ohio State University Press, 1964.

MEAD, M. *Culture and commitment: A study of the generation gap*. Garden City, N.Y.: Doubleday, 1970.

METCALF, L. E. (Ed.). *Values education: Rationale, strategies, and procedures* (Forty-first yearbook, National Council for the Social Studies). Washington, D.C.: National Council for the Social Studies, 1971.

MIRELS, H. L., & GARRETT, J. B. The Protestant ethic as a personality variable. *Journal of Consulting and Clinical Psychology*, 1971, *36*, 40–44.

MOORE, D. The structure of motives for not helping. In J. D. Fisher (Chair), *Factors affecting helping*. Symposium presented at the meeting of the American Psychological Association, New York, 1979.

MORRIS, C. *Paths of life*. New York: Harper & Row, Pub., 1942.

MORRIS, C. *Varieties of human value*. Chicago: University of Chicago Press, 1956.

NESSELROADE, J. R., & BALTES, P. B. Adolescent personality development and historical change: 1970–1972. *Monographs of the Society for Research in Child Development*, 1974, *39*(1, Whole No. 154).

NEWCOMB, T. M. *Personality and social change*. New York: Holt, Rinehart & Winston, 1943.

NEWCOMB, T. M. An approach to the study of communicative acts. *Psychological Review*, 1953, *60*, 393–404.

NEWCOMB, T. M. *The acquaintance process*. New York: Holt, Rinehart & Winston, 1961.

NORMAN. R. Affective-cognitive consistency, attitudes, conformity, and behavior. *Journal of Personality and Social Psychology*, 1975, *32*, 83–91.

OLEJNIK, A. B., & McKINNEY, J. P. Parental value orientation and generosity in children. *Developmental Psychology*, 1973, *8*, 311.

OLEJNIK, A. B., & McKINNEY, J. P. Parental value orientation and generosity in children—An extended version. In H. C. Lindgren (Ed.), *Children's behavior*. Palo Alto, Calif.: Mayfield, 1975.

ORPEN, C. The work values of Western and tribal black employees. *Journal of Cross-Cultural Psychology*, 1978, *9*, 99–112.

OSGOOD, C. E., SUCI, G., & TANNENBAUM, P. H. *The measurement of meaning*. Urbana: University of Illinois Press, 1957.

OSTROM, T. M. The emergence of attitude theory: 1930–1950. In A. G. Greenwald, T. C. Brock, & T. M. Ostrom (Eds.), *Psychological foundations of attitudes*. New York: Academic Press, 1968.

PARSONS, T. M. Pattern variables revisited. *American Sociological Review*, 1960, *25*, 467–483.

PASSER, M. W., KELLEY, H. H., & MICHELA, J. L. Mulitidimensional scaling of the causes for negative interpersonal behavior. *Journal of Personality and Social Psychology*, 1978, *36*, 951–962.

PERRY, R. B. *Realms of value: A critique of human civilization*. Cambridge, Mass.: Harvard University Press, 1954.

PILKINGTON, G. W., POPPLETON, P. K., GOULD, J. B., & McCOURT, M. M. Changes in religious beliefs, practices, and attitudes among university students over an eleven-year period in relation to sex differences, denominational differences, and differences between faculties and years of study. *British Journal of Social and Clinical Psychology*, 1976, *15*, 1–9.

RATHS, L. E., HARMIN, M., & SIMON, S. B. *Values and teaching*. Columbus, Ohio: Chas. E. Merrill, 1966.

RESCHER, N. *Introduction to value theory.* Englewood Cliffs, N.J.: Prentice-Hall, 1969.

RETTIG, S., & PASAMANICK, B. Changes in moral values among college students: A factorial study. *American Sociological Review,* 1959, *24,* 856–863.

ROBINSON, J. P., & SHAVER, P. R. *Measures of social psychological attitudes.* Ann Arbor, Mich.: Institute for Social Research, 1969.

ROE, A., & SIEGELMAN, M. A parent-child relations questionnaire. *Child Development,* 1963, *34,* 355–369.

ROKEACH, M. Political and religious dogmatism: An alternative to the authoritarian personality. *Psychological Monographs,* 1956, *70*(18, Whole No. 425).

ROKEACH, M. (Ed.). *The open and closed mind.* New York: Basic Books, 1960.

ROKEACH, M. *Beliefs, attitudes, and values.* San Francisco: Jossey-Bass, 1968.

ROKEACH, M. *The nature of human values.* New York: Free Press, 1973.

ROKEACH, M. (Ed.). *Understanding human values.* New York: Free Press, 1979.

ROSENBERG, S., & SEDLAK, A. Structural representations of implicit personality theory. Pp. 235–279 in L. Berkowitz (Ed.), *Advances in experimental social psychology* (Vol. 6). New York: Academic Press, 1972.

ROTTER, J. B. Generalized expectancies for internal vs. external control of reinforcement. *Psychological Monographs,* 1966, *80*(1, Whole No. 609).

SALILI, F., MAEHR, M. L., & GILLMORE, G. Achievement and morality: A cross-cultural analysis of causal attribution and evaluation. *Journal of Personality and Social Psychology,* 1976, *33,* 327–337.

SCHUMAN, H., & JOHNSON, M. P. Attitudes and behavior. *Annual Review of Sociology,* 1976, *2,* 161–207.

SCHWARTZ, S. Normative influences in altruism. Pp. 221–279 in L. Berkowitz (Ed.), *Advances in experimental social psychology* (Vol. 10). New York: Academic Press, 1977.

SHERIF, M., & CANTRIL, H. The psychology of attitudes: I. *Psychological Review,* 1945, *52,* 295–319.

SHERIF, M., & CANTRIL, H. The psychology of attitudes: II. *Psychological Review,* 1946, *53,* 1–24.

SHERIF, M., & CANTRIL, H. *The psychology of ego-involvements.* New York: John Wiley, 1947.

SIMON, S. B., HOWE, L. W., & KIRSCHENBAUM, H. *Values clarification: A handbook of practical strategies for teachers and students.* New York: Hart Publishing, 1972.

SMITH, M. B. *Social psychology and human values.* Chicago: Aldine, 1969.

SNYDER, M., & SWANN, W. B., JR. When actions reflect attitudes: The politics of impression management. *Journal of Personality and Social Psychology,* 1976, *34,* 1034–1042.

SNYDER, M., & TANKE, E. D. Behavior and attitude: Some people are more consistent than others. *Journal of Personality,* 1976, *44,* 501–517.

SORENSON, R. C. *Adolescent sexuality in contemporary America.* New York: William Collins Publishers, Inc., 1973.

SPENCE, J. T., & HELMREICH, R. L. *Masculinity and femininity: Their psychological dimensions, correlates, and antecedents.* Austin: University of Texas Press, 1978.

SPRANGER, E. *Types of men.* Halle, Germany: Niemeyer, 1928.

THOMPSON, G. G., & GARDNER, E. F. Adolescents' perceptions of happy successful living. *Journal of Genetic Psychology,* 1969, *115,* 107–120.

THURSTONE, L. L. Attitudes can be measured. *American Journal of Sociology,* 1928, *33,* 529–554.

TRIANDIS, H. (Ed.). *The analysis of subjective culture.* New York: John Wiley, 1972.

TRUHON, S. A., MCKINNEY, J. P., & HOTCH, D. F. The structure of values among college students: An examination of sex differences. *Journal of Youth and Adolescence,* 1980, *9,* 289–297.

WARNER, L. G., & DEFLEUR, M. L. Attitude as an interactional concept: Social constraint and social distance as intervening variables between attitudes and action. *American Sociological Review,* 1969, *34,* 153–169.

WEIGEL, R. H., & NEWMAN, L. S. Increasing attitude-behavior correspondence by broadening the scope of the behavioral measure. *Journal of Personality and Social Psychology,* 1976, *33,* 793–802.

WEINER, B., & PETER, N. A cognitive-developmental analysis of achievement and moral judgments. *Developmental Psychology,* 1973, *9,* 290–309.

WHARTON, J. F. Toward an affirmative morality. *Saturday Review,* July 12, 1969, pp. 11–46.

WHITE, R. K. *Value analysis: The nature and use of the method.* Glen Gardner, N.J.: Society for the Psychological Study of Social Issues, 1951.

WICKER, H. W. Attitudes vs. actions: The relationship of verbal and overt behavioral responses to attitude objects. *Journal of Social Issues,* 1969, *25,* 41–78.

WICKLUND, R. A., & BREHM, J. W. *Perspectives on cognitive dissonance.* Hillsdale, N.J.: Lawrence Erlbaum Associates, 1976.

WILLIAMS, R. M. Values. In E. Sills (Ed.), *International encyclopedia of the social sciences.* New York: Macmillan, 1968.

WILLIAMS, R. M. Change and stability in values and value systems. In B. Barber & A. Inkeles (Eds.), *Stability and social change.* Boston: Little, Brown, 1971.

WILSON, G. D., & PATTERSON, J. R. A new measure of conservatism. *British Journal of Social and Clinical Psychology,* 1968, *7,* 264–269.

WOLLACK, S., GOODALE, J. G., WHITING, J. P., & SMITH, P. C. The measurement of work values. *Journal of Applied Psychology,* 1971, *55,* 331–338.

WRIGHT, D., & COX, E. Changes in moral belief among sixth-form boys and girls over a seven-year period in relation to religious belief, age, and sex differences. *British Journal of Social and Clinical Psychology,* 1971, *10,* 332–341.

YANKELOVICH, D. *The changing values on campus.* New York: Pocket Books, 1973.

YANKELOVICH, D. *The new morality: A profile of American youth in the 70's.* New York: McGraw-Hill, 1974.

ZANNA, M. P., & COOPER, J. Dissonance and the attribution process. In J. H. Harvey, W. J. Ickes, & R. F. Kidd (Eds.), *New directions in attribution research* (Vol. 1). Hillsdale, N.J.: Lawrence Erlbaum Associates, 1976.

32

Sexuality
during Adolescence

PHILIP H. DREYER

Adolescence is a period marked by rapid physical growth and sexual maturation. The capacity of the adolescent's body to reproduce itself is thus the single most important developmental event of this period in the life cycle and the one which sets the stage for all other intellectual and social changes so often described during this period. This chapter will review the literature dealing with physiological bases for adolescent sexual behavior, methodological problems in sex research, changes in sexual attitudes, and sexual behaviors and their consequences for adolescents.

PHYSIOLOGICAL DEVELOPMENT OF THE REPRODUCTIVE SYSTEM

While there has been extensive study of physiological changes of the human body during adolescence in terms of body size and mass, skeletal structure, skin, dentition, hematology, cardiovascular function, and brain weight (Epstein, 1978; Greulich, Day, Lachman, Wolfe, & Shuttleworth, 1938; Grumbach, Grave, & Mayer, 1974; Jones, 1944; Meredith, 1967; Tanner, 1962, 1972), there has been much less study of the physiological changes in the endocrine system which cause these somatic changes and bring about sexual maturity during adolescence.

For many years it has been known that the basic predisposition of the human fetus to develop into either a female or male body type is programmed by the chromosomes. The tendency of nature seems to be to produce a fertilized egg with the chromosomal structure 46 *XX* which will normally result in a female infant. The fertilized egg which is made up of an added *Y* chromosome, so that it has the chromosomal structure 46 *XY,* will normally develop into a male child. Thus human sexual dimorphism begins from the moment of conception; how-

ever, the extent to which the fetus develops into a normal female or male child depends upon a complex interaction of fetal hormones with the developing genital organs and the nervous system pathways of the hypothalamus of the brain (Money & Ehrhardt, 1972). The exact nature of this interaction is still not fully understood; however, a major role in the sexual dimorphic development of the fetus seems to be played by the male hormone testosterone which appears either to inhibit the development of the Müllerian ducts into ovaries and vagina or to promote the development of the Wolffian ducts into testes and penis, in both cases producing a male genital configuration. The dimorphic development of the brain is also not fully understood; however, research by Young (1961, 1964) has indicated that the nervous pathways of the hypothalamus of the brain appear to develop differently in males and females and that such development seems to occur during a critical period of the growth of the embryo (Money & Ehrhardt, 1972), most likely as a result of fetal hormone influence which may also be produced by the primitive gonads.

While much of fetal development is still a mystery and involves an extremely complex biochemical system, a few tentative facts do seem to emerge at this time. First, basic sexuality depends upon the chromosomal makeup of the fertilized egg. Second, whether the primitive fetus develops into a normal female or male depends upon the ratio of the amounts of feminizing hormones (estrogens) to masculinizing hormones (androgens), both of which are present in the human fetus. Third, sexual dimorphism involves not only the genitals themselves but also the nervous pathways of the hypothalamus of the brain, so that the female is born with ovaries which produce increased amounts of estrogens and a nervous system in the brain which will send cyclic impulses to the pituitary and ovaries at puberty, while the male is born with testes which produce increased amounts of androgens and a nervous system in the brain which will send noncyclic impulses to the pituitary and testes at puberty. Finally, if Money and Ehrhardt are correct, the sexual identity or gender identity of the young child, which is the psychological sense of identifying oneself as a girl or boy and acting out sex-appropriate behaviors in childhood, depends not so much on these biochemical and morphological facts as it does upon the constancy of the child's psychosexual environment, particularly the ways in which s/he is responded to by parents, siblings, and nonfamily significant others. In summary the child's sexuality which s/he brings into adolescence involves a series of complex interactions involving chromosomes, hormones, sexually dimorphic characteristics, and experiences in the psychosexual environment.

The physiological changes which occur at adolescence represent a truly developmental event, whether one chooses to define *developmental* as age-related quantitative changes in the organism's size and capacity or as age-related qualitative changes in the organism's structure and function. As such, puberty represents one of the few events in the life cycle which is indisputably "developmental," no matter how one defines the term.

Primary and Secondary Sex Characteristics

The tradition among students of adolescence has been to distinguish those physiological changes which involve only the genitalia and the physical equipment necessary for biological reproduction as *primary sex characteristics* from those physiological changes involving the rest of the body as *secondary sex characteristics*. Both primary and secondary sex characteristics are under the influence of gonadotropic hormones; however, only those parts of the body which are indispensable for reproduction—the ovaries, uterus, and vagina of the female and the testes and penis of the male, along with the tissue and ducts which accompany them—are considered primary sex characteristics. All other body changes—breasts, pubic hair, lowered voice pitch, facial and axillary hair, widened hips, broad shoulders, and rapid skeletal growth—while under the control of the sex hormones, are deemed secondary sex characteristics.

From a psychosocial point of view, the adolescent's development of primary sex characteristics, particularly the onset of menstruation in females and nocturnal emission in males, has traditionally been viewed as less important in Western societies than the development of the secondary sex characteristics because it was felt that it was the outward appearance of the adolescent's body which most influenced social interactions, the development of self-concept, and psychosocial identity. Secondary sex characteristics, such as rapid growth in height and strength, development of breasts and facial hair, and lowering of voice pitch, are public events, while primary sex characteristics have traditionally been private events, often dealt with in greater secrecy and confidentiality in Western societies. Furthermore until very recently it was expected that young people would delay reproductive behavior and adult sex activity until they were adults in the sense of being economically independent and married, which meant that personality and social psychological development during adolescence was almost exclusively the result of secondary sex characteristics and their development. Consistent with this set of assumptions have been studies of the influence of early versus late physical maturation upon personality development (Broverman, Broverman, Vogel, Palmer, & Klaiber, 1964; Cortes & Gatti, 1966; Eichorn, 1963; Frisch, 1974; Frisch & Revelle, 1969, 1970; Jones & Mussen, 1958; Mussen & Jones, 1957, 1958) with the consistent finding that early physical maturation has numerous positive effects for the personality, self-concept, and social behavior development of the adolescent. More recently there have been studies which have looked at the development of primary sex characteristics in women, particularly the age of menarche or first menstruation, and their relationship to personality and social attitudes (Bardwick, 1972; Faust, 1977; Maccoby & Jacklin, 1975; Parlee, 1973); however, a consistent relationship between the development of primary sex characteristics and personality has not yet been clearly described.

The Role of Sex Hormones in Adolescent Development

The normal child brings into adolescence a fixed chromosomal structure (46 *XX* in the female and 46 *XY* in the male), a sexually dimorphic brain structure, sexually dimorphic genitalia, and a sense of self as either a girl or a boy with accompanying sex-appropriate attitudes and behaviors or a gender identity which is consistent with both the child's body and his/her psychosexual experiences. At puberty these structures grow and change as a result of increasing amounts of sex hormones produced by the ovaries and testes under the direction of gonadotropic hormones sent out by the pituitary gland which is triggered by nervous impulses from the hypothalamus of the brain. Puberty begins, therefore, in the brain, which sends out nervous impulses to the pituitary, the timing of which seems to be regulated by a little-understood biological clock mechanism. The timing of puberty seems to vary according to a number of environmental conditions, such as nutritional status, climate, and socioeconomic status (Tanner, 1972), as well as according to certain pathological conditions, such as brain lesions and removal of the ovaries or testes (Money & Ehrhardt, 1972). However under normal conditions girls begin puberty with the growth of the bony pelvis and budding of the breasts at an average age of 11 years and end with the arrest of the skeletal growth at an average age of 17, while boys begin puberty with the enlargement of the scrotum and testes at an average age of 13 and end puberty with the arrest of skeletal growth at an average age of 21. As with most developmental norms there is a wide range of normal development of at least two years on either side of the beginning ages and as much as four years around the ending norms, so that it is not uncommon to find some girls who begin puberty at age 8 or 9, while others do not begin until age 13.

Once the hypothalamus of the brain begins to send impulses to the pituitary, the anterior lobe of the pituitary responds by secreting the gonadotropic hormones called FSH (follicle-stimulating hormone), LH (luteinizing hormone, also known as ICSH or interstitial-cell-stimulating hormone), and LTH (luteotropic hormone,

Table 32–1 Average Approximate Age and Sequence of Development of Sexual Characteristics in Boys and Girls

AGE (YEARS)	BOYS	GIRLS
9–10		Growth of bony pelvis Budding of nipples
10–11	First growth of testes and penis	Budding of breasts Growth of pubic hair
11–12	Prostatic activity	Change in vaginal epithelium
12–13	Growth of pubic hair	Pigmentation of nipples
13–14	Rapid growth of testes and penis Subareolar node of breast tissue	Mammae filling in Growth of axillary hair Menarche (average = 13½ years; range = 9–17 years)
14–15	Growth of axillary hair and hair on upper lip Lowering of voice pitch	Earliest normal pregnancies (one year after menarche)
15–16	Mature spermatozoa (average = 15 years; range = 11–17 years)	Acne Deepening of voice pitch
16–17	Growth of facial and body hair Acne	Arrest of skeletal growth
21	Arrest of skeletal growth	

Source: From Wilkins, L. Diagnosis and Treatment of Endocrine Disorders in Childhood and Adolescence, 2/e, 1957. Courtesy of Charles C Thomas, Publisher, Springfield, Illinois.

also known as prolactin or lactogenic hormone). In the female FSH stimulates the development of the ovarian follicles and then interacts with LH to regulate the final stages of follicular development, ovulation, and the secretion of estrogen. LTH is released by the pituitary if and when the female egg is fertilized, at which time it regulates the development of the placenta to support the fertilized egg and the secretion of milk by the breasts. In the male FSH stimulates the seminiferous tubules of the testes, while LH (or ISCH) stimulates other cells of the testes, resulting in the production of sperm and the secretion of androgen. There seems to be no known function of LTH in the male.

In addition to these gonadotropic hormones, the pituitary also secretes three other major hormonal substances: adrenotrophin, which regulates the adrenal gland; thyrotrophin, which regulates the thyroid gland; and somatotrophin, which regulates the growth of bones and tissues (Grossman, 1967). Thus growth and development during puberty involve the complex interaction of no less than six hormones in the female and five in the male, all of which together regulate the form and function of the endocrine system, basal metabolism, skeletal growth, and both primary and secondary sex characteristics.

For this discussion of the hormonal bases for sexual behavior, however, the most important fact is that while the gonadotropic hormones FSH, LH (ISCH), and LTH serve to begin the development of the primary sex characteristics it is the estrogen produced by the newly matured ovary and the androgen produced by the newly matured testes which have the greatest influence on the ultimate development of secondary sex characteristics. Both estrogen and androgen appear to be present in the prepubescent child, and both can be found in most adolescents and adults. What occurs at puberty, therefore, is that in females the presence of ovaries and their production of estrogen increases the ratio of estrogen to androgen so that the normal female develops a feminized body, while in the male the presence of testes and their output of androgen increases the ratio of androgen to es-

trogen so that a masculinized body results. The function of the ovaries and the testes at puberty is therefore critical because the hormones which they secrete determine whether or not the ratio of estrogen to androgen will exceed the necessary threshold value necessary for the appropriate secondary sex characteristics to develop.

While the timing of the onset of puberty begins about two years earlier for girls than for boys and may vary in any two individuals by as much as four years, once puberty begins the sequence of development tends to be invariant. The body develops in a predetermined order, as described in Table 32–1, with individual variation in the relative speed of development but not in the sequence of events.

Secular Trend

Historical studies of the development of adolescents in a variety of countries reveal that during the last 150 years, at least, there has been a tendency for children to reach physiological maturity at earlier and earlier ages. Data from Europe and the United States indicate, for example, that children from average socioeconomic homes increased in height from ages 5 to 7 by about 1 cm to 2 cm each decade and at ages 10 to 14 by 2 to 3 cm each decade. One hundred years ago full adult height was not reached until age 25, whereas by 1970 the average boy achieved full height by age 18 or 19. For the most part these data indicate that full height did not increase very much overall but that children and adolescents achieved full height at earlier ages. Tanner (1972) has termed this acceleration in growth rate the *secular trend* and attributes the change to improved nutrition and health conditions in industrialized societies.

The best data supporting this secular trend comes from historical studies of the average age at which girls reach menarche. Tanner's graphic presentation of these data is presented in Figure 32–1, which shows the steady decline in average age of menarche for girls in several northern European countries, Great Britain, and the United States. In Norway, where records go back to

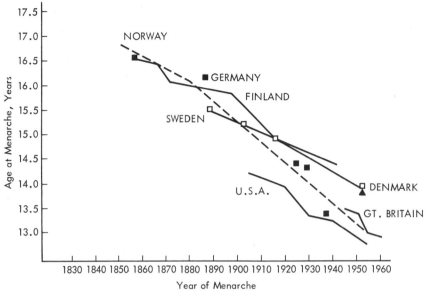

Figure 32-1 Secular trend in age at menarche, 1830–1960. (Source: Sources of data and method of plotting detailed in Tanner, 1962.)

1840, the average age of menarche in 1840 was 17.0 years, after which time it decreased steadily to 15.5 years in 1900 and 13.2 years in 1950. Figures for the United States indicate that in 1900 girls reached menarche at an average age of 14.0 years and in 1950 the average age was slightly under 13.0 years, a decrease of about three months each decade. Tanner argues convincingly that these declines are related to nutritional status, citing data from Asia and Africa which consistently show that well-nourished children in each society reach menarche earlier than do their peers who are less well-fed.

One question which the secular trend data raises is to what extent will this accelerated growth rate continue over time? Will girls become physically mature at earlier and earlier ages until we have a situation where five- and six-year-olds are capable of bearing children? The data to answer these questions are still being gathered; however, a tentative answer to both questions seems to be negative. The average age at which boys achieve full height has not decreased appreciably since 1950 in the United States, and the average age of menarche for girls in America has also not decreased noticeably since 1950. It appears, therefore, that development has reached its maximum potential, especially among the well-nourished segments of American society, and it is unlikely that full height and menarche will be reached at still earlier average ages in the future.

The implications of the secular trend for social-psychological behavior among adolescents are not clear. Since rates of premarital sexual intercourse, veneral disease, and illegitimacy have all increased sharply in the last 30 years, it is tempting to conclude that these changes have been caused by the earlier maturation of adolescents. Cutright (1972) has argued that increases in teenage fecundity since 1945, coupled with decreasing rates of infant mortality, largely account for the rise in the number of children born out of wedlock to teenagers, particularly blacks. Whether there is such a cause-and-effect relationship between earlier physical maturation and increasing sexual activity among teenagers, however, remains to be demonstrated.

In summary physiological development at adolescence begins with nervous impulses from the hypothalamus of the brain which stimulate the pituitary gland to secrete gonadotropic hormones which act on the ovaries in the female to produce estrogen and on the testes of the male to produce androgen. These two hormones, estrogen and androgen, then promote the sequential development of both primary and secondary sex characteristics which typify the normal sexual dimorphism of adults. There has been a secular trend over the last hundred years for adolescents to achieve full adult growth and reproductive capacity at earlier and earlier ages, apparently as a result of improvements in nutrition; however, it now appears that this accelerated growth rate has reached its maximum potential, so that it is unlikely that youth will continue to mature at earlier average ages in the future.

SEX RESEARCH AND ITS METHODOLOGICAL PROBLEMS

The systematic study of sexual behaviors by social scientists is a relatively recent phenomenon, dating primarily from the pioneering work of Kinsey and associates at Indiana University in the 1930s and 1940s (Gebhard, Pomeroy, Martin, & Christenson, 1958; Kinsey, Pomeroy, & Martin, 1948; Kinsey, Pomeroy, Martin, & Gebhard, 1953). Since the time of these publications, there have been at least 25 major studies of adolescent sex behaviors and several hundred smaller studies and reviews of the literature.

All of these studies can be described in three broad categories according to their focus and methodology. The first of these, and the most common, have been descriptive studies of the type and number of physical sex behaviors practiced by different groups of people, usually described according to such parameters as age, sex, socioeconomic status, and educational level. The second of these have been sociological studies of factors which are correlated with certain types of sex behaviors, such as studies of different rates of premarital sexual behavior by different age and ethnic groups or the relationship of education to contraceptive use. The third of these, and the least common, have been studies of psychological factors, such as attitudes, knowledge, intelligence, and personality traits, and their relationship to sexual behaviors. In most of these studies of sex behavior, there has been a dearth of theory and a deluge of elementary statistics, so that it seems fair to say that at this point we have begun to understand a few of the major characteristics of sex behavior and its relationship to some sociological and psychological measures but that we are a long way from understanding the full complexity or meaning of sex behaviors for any age group, particularly adolescents.

Research dealing with adolescent sexuality is prone to all of the most common methodological problems, and it is important to judge each study according to the representative nature of the sample studied, the reliability and validity of the measures used to collect data, the type of analyses presented and the conclusions drawn from analyses, and the types of generalizations which are made about the studies. Among these larger methodological problems some specific difficulties in adolescent sex research include the following:

1. *Lack of theory and testable hypotheses*—Most adolescent sex behavior studies are descriptive and impressionistic and lack even the simplest of theoretical orientations. This is particularly glaring in that adolescence has traditionally been rich in developmental person-situation interaction, social learning, and sociological theories and in that sex behavior itself represents discrete behavioral events which would appear to lend themselves to rigorous study.

2. *Misrepresentative and biased samples*—Probably the single most serious deficiency in this research is that samples are too often drawn by "convenience" without enough care being given to sampling techniques which would produce representative samples. Seldom are control or comparison groups included, and researchers conclude by implying that their results can be generalized to larger populations. A favorite source of subjects, for instance, is college students; yet college students comprise only a small portion of the age group in question. A study which includes only women omits nearly half of the adolescent age group.

3. *Sample attrition due to ethical concerns of parents*—Despite the best attempts of some researchers to draw representative samples, current guidelines for human subject research require the informed consent of the adolescent's parents before a subject can be included in the study. Not surprisingly many parents refuse to give their consent, so many potentially willing subjects are lost. In some studies this has resulted in up to 50 percent attrition in subjects.

4. *Incomplete and conflicting definition of constructs*—Surprisingly there is no commonly agreed upon definition of sex behaviors. In some studies, *kissing, fondling,* and *petting* are defined as sex behaviors; in other studies only *sexual intercourse* is included. *Masturbation* is sometimes defined simply as "self-stimulation," while in others it is defined as "autoerotic behavior resulting in orgasm." *Homosexuality* is variously defined but most often is used to describe almost any type of physical contact between two people of the same sex. Poor definition of sex behaviors is not the only problem. Many studies, for instance, include *socioeconomic*

status as a significant marker variable; yet, few studies define the construct at all, relying upon often outdated conceptions of what social class is or might mean. Particularly difficult in this regard is the fact that the socioeconomic status of an adolescent may no longer be based upon the parents' income or occupation but may reflect his/her own earnings or participation in what some have called the *youth culture.*

5. *Unreliable and invalid measurements*—The most common type of data collection instrument in this type of research involves the subject's retrospective self-report of his/her own behavior and attitudes, which is recorded either on a paper and pencil questionnaire or taken down by an interviewer. Many researchers do report attempts to establish the reliability of questionnaire items and rating systems used by coders, but the fundamental issue of whether the subject is providing accurate information is seldom discussed. Given the sensitivity of sex behavior in our society and the frequently noted anxiety and guilt which often surround sex behavior, the failure to deal with the question of a subject's accuracy of self-report is especially regrettable. Almost no study of adolescent sex behavior done in the United States has utilized direct observational methods, and this will most likely remain the case so long as the social norms regarding such behavior emphasize adolescent virginity. The only exception to this have been a few studies of contraceptive use in which the criterion for contraception failure is the fact of pregnancy.

6. *Insufficient use of longitudinal research designs*—Very few studies follow subjects over a period of time to describe changes in sex behavior or to investigate antecedent-consequent relationships. Currently major attention is being given to this problem, particularly by policy studies researchers who are interested in the long-term consequences of such events as repeated abortions, use of specific contraception devices, and early pregnancy.

7. *Insufficient use of multivariate research designs and data analysis techniques*—While most researchers agree that sex behaviors occur within a complex set of biological, psychological, sociological, and historical forces, few studies have attempted to discuss how these factors interact or to analyze data to arrive at tentative conclusions about how measures of these factors actually appear in multivariate statistical analyses. What is reported instead are usually nonparametric analyses, such as percentages or chi-square statistics, or mean scores for various groups. The difficulty here seems to be not so much in the construction of more sophisticated measurement scales nor in the application of advanced computer methods but in the conceptualization of sex behaviors as part of a larger behavioral or ecological system which is developmental. Until such attempts at understanding the entire behavioral system are attempted, the role of any molar behavior such as sex behavior will most likely remain incompletely understood. Clearly a great deal of work at all levels is still left to be done.

To some extent the subject of adolescent sexuality, particularly adolescent sex behavior, represents a contradiction of terms in our society. Adolescents are usually defined as being in transition from the social status of childhood, which connotes impotence, dependence, irresponsibility, and playfulness, to the social status of adulthood, which connotes power, independence, responsibility, and seriousness. Adolescents are not quite children and not quite adults, particularly in that they are not commited to adult work roles, marriage, and full citizenship. In our society the norms for sex behavior have traditionally supported the idea that sex behavior should take place only within the marriage relationship with its emphasis upon procreational sex. If a young person were married, s/he was automatically an adult and was expected to assume other adult roles and responsibilities, which included the acceptance of sexual expression, but if a young person were not married, s/he maintained his/her status as an adolescent, which did not include sexual behavior. Freud, among others, pointed out that sexual impulses and gratifications were important in every phase of the life cycle, but traditionally adolescents were expected to postpone sex behavior until marriage. Thus to be adolescent meant to be a virgin whose sexuality was not fully expressed.

Today researchers find themselves participants in a remarkable process of social change, the causes of which involve a wide range of medical, political, economic, educational, sociological, and psychological forces. Briefly stated the social norm which required marriage before full sexual behavior is changing very rapidly so that today adolescents engage in every type of sexual behavior possible. Whereas before, sex behavior among adolescents was deviant and was met with conspicuous negative sanctions, today it is not deviant and is regarded as expectable, even though not quite normative.

While a more complete discussion of this changing normative structure for adolescent sex behaviors will be presented later, two aspects of it are particularly important for evaluating sex research. The first is that in many instances the more recent the study, the more accepting are attitudes about sex and the higher the reported rates of sex behaviors. Thus it is impossible to establish clearly just what attitudes or behaviors are for the adolescent group as a whole because studies reflect the rapidly changing norms. It is also impossible to estimate the effects which these studies have had upon influencing norms for sex behavior, but it seems reasonable to guess that adolescent sex research and the behavior it attempts to study are interdependent in a chicken-and-egg fashion. As more studies are published and sex is stripped of traditional taboos, more youth feel free to express their sexuality which in turn leads to changing norms which are the subject of future studies. It is therefore particularly interesting to look at which sex behaviors have *not* changed over the last 30 years as possible indicators of what the potential for adolescent sex behavior actually might be.

The second aspect of this changing normative structure which affects research has to do with research ethics and the protection of the rights of human subjects. Despite the researcher's most objective and scientific intentions, adolescent sex behavior research involves subjects who are legally minors and who are encouraged in this type of research to reveal aspects of their behavior, self-concept, and attitudes which have traditionally been regarded as inappropriate and immoral, if not illegal and sinful. Furthermore sex behavior has always been the exclusive domain of the family unit, with parents being given complete authority over their children's sex education and conduct. The researcher in this situation faces a number of dilemmas. First, s/he must secure the "informed consent" of the adolescent's parents in order to include a person in the study. If the parent refuses such consent, the researcher has no appeal. Second, and more

important, even with the parents' consent the researcher must confront the possibility that participation in the research will harm the subject, particularly by encouraging discussion of subjects which the adolescent may find embarrassing, frightening, confusing, or threatening and which may cause lowered self-esteem, feelings of guilt and anxiety, or serious self-doubt. Whether the researcher agrees with the psychoanalytical point of view or not, the subject of sexuality and sex behavior in our society is often difficult and particularly so for adolescents who are making the transition from childhood to adulthood. For these reasons it is imperative that researchers consider their responsibilities to subjects and not allow their self-acclaimed professionalism to take precedence over the well-being of the young persons they hope to understand.

NONHETEROSEXUAL ATTITUDES AND BEHAVIORS

Masturbation

One of the areas of adolescent sex behavior which has been inadequately studied is masturbation. There are few studies of this subject, and those which exist lack adequate samples and theoretical bases. By and large these studies indicate there has been a lessening of traditional prohibitions against masturbation and that the percentages of teenagers who both accept masturbation as normal for people their age and who practice masturbation have been increasing over the last 20 years. Studies in the early 1970s (Abramson, 1973; Arafat & Cotton, 1974; Hunt, 1974; Sorenson, 1973) generally reported that about 50 percent of boys and 30 percent of girls under age 15 masturbated, while these figures for 16- to 19-year-olds were 85 percent for boys and 60 percent for girls. More recent studies (Hass, 1979; "What's Really Happening on Campus," 1976) indicate that about 70 percent of the boys and 45 percent of the girls masturbate by age 15 and that among 16- to 19-year-olds more than two-thirds of the boys and half of the girls masturbate once a week or more often (Hass, 1979). Sexually active adolescents tend to masturbate more than the less sexually active; however, boys involved in an ongoing sexual relationship tend to forego masturbation, while girls involved in an ongoing sexual relationship increase their rate of masturbation, apparently to release sexual tensions built up as a result of sexual activities which do not result in orgasm (Hass, 1979).

Homosexuality

While there are few good studies of homosexual behavior among adolescents, those which exist reveal three consistent findings. First, homosexual contacts are most frequent before age 15 and are more likely to be experienced by boys than by girls (Hass, 1979; Hunt, 1974; Kinsey et al., 1948; Kinsey et al., 1953; Sorensen, 1973; "What's Really Happening on Campus," 1976). Second, acceptance of homosexual relationships as measured by responses to attitudinal questionnaires by adolescents is widespread, with nearly 70 percent of 16- to 19-year-olds accepting sexual relationships between two girls and only slightly less than that accepting such contacts between two boys. In general boys are more accepting of female homosexuality than they are of male homosexuality, while girls accept both about equally (Hass, 1979). Third, despite liberal attitudes about homosexuality, less than 15 percent of boys and 10 percent of girls report ever having had even one homosexual contact during adolescence, and only 3 percent of the boys and 2 percent of the girls report participating in an ongoing homosexual relationship (Chilman, 1979; Hass, 1979; "What's Really Happening on Campus," 1976). Interestingly while many other types of sexual behaviors show an increase during the last 30 years, participation in homosexual relationships by adolescents appears to have remained the same or even decreased (Chilman, 1979; Freedman, 1971; Hunt, 1974; Karlen, 1971; Komarovsky, 1976).

The developmental conditions which seem to be related to homosexuality in adolescents have been inadequately studied. The most widely discussed set of ideas are the psychoanalytic theories of Freud for whom homosexuality represented a type of perverse activity which reflected the inability of the adolescent to resolve his/her Oedipal dilemma by breaking his/her cathexis to the opposite-sex parent in favor of a satisfying identification with the same-sex parent. In this view boys became homosexuals because they were dominated by their mothers and could not assume the full male role by identifying with the father. Girls presumably were too closely attached to their fathers to identify with their mothers or, on the contrary, could not develop a normal female sex identity with its attraction to men because they had been mistreated by fathers who were brutal, alcoholic, abusive or in other ways inadequate father figures. The research evidence to support this psychoanalytic view is not strong. At least two studies (Bieber et al., 1962; Evans, 1971) of adult male homosexuals found that homosexuals reported family histories in which the mother was domineering, overprotective, seductive, puritanical, frigid, favoring the son over the father, encouraging of "feminine" interests in the son while discouraging or interfering with the son's contacts with other girls, and manipulating the son by a close, confidential relationship with the son. These same men reported poor relationships with their fathers and were conspicuous in their pattern of passive, dependent response and lack of rebelliousness to both parents. Homosexual men also tended to describe themselves as children as awkward, clumsy, frail, nonathletic, nonaggressive, playing with girls, and loners. Studies of the family histories of female homosexuals are virtually nonexistent. Besides the lack of data to support and clarify the psychoanalytic point of view, a more serious issue is that many heterosexuals have patterns of family disturbance similar to those described for homosexuals, so that it seems inaccurate and simplistic to assume that homosexuality is somehow "caused" by particular patterns of family interaction.

There have been numerous studies of sex behaviors in animals showing that hormones, both fetal hormones and sex hormones administered after birth, have effects upon sexual development, sex play, and reproductive behaviors; however, there have been few studies of the role of hormones in the gender identity and sexual preferences of humans. In the best and most complete discussion of this issue, Money (1968; Money & Ehrhardt, 1972) argues that, while hormones play crucial parts in the physiological development of the individual, social and psychological factors during childhood and adolescence are probably more important in determining such behavioral outcomes as homosexual preference.

Another approach to the subject of homosexuality has been the social learning point of view which argues that homosexuality simply reflects sexual experiences between two people of the same sex which have been particularly rewarding and satisfying so that the preference for sex partners of the same sex becomes a conditioned behavior. While this approach has the advantage of not labeling homosexuals as "perverts" or "neurotics," which the psychoanalytical school tends to do, there is almost no evidence to support this social learning understanding of homosexuality.

In her review of adolescent sexuality Chilman (1979) raises a fourth possible explanation for homosexuality. Citing her own observations of girls' summer camps, Chilman argues that same-sex preference in such segregated environments seems to result from homesickness and general loneliness which leads girls to seek warmth and affection from older counselors and leaders. In such situations the extent of the homosexual nature of the camp seems to be dependent upon the overt homosexuality of the leaders; however, Chilman notes that most of the girls quickly revert back to heterosexual preferences when they leave the camp and return home.

In summary while attitudes of young people seem to be quite permissive with regard to homosexuality, only 15 percent of boys and 10 percent of girls report ever having had a homosexual experience, and only 3 percent of boys and 2 percent of girls report an ongoing homosexual preference. These figures have not changed in the last 30 years. While there are many theories of which conditions relate to homosexuality (e.g., the psychoanalytic view of disturbed family relationships, the biological view of hormone influence, social learning ideas about conditioned behaviors, and social environment views about the effects of one-sex living arrangements), there is a dearth of good studies to support or clarify any of these theoretical speculations. Given the current controversy over the civil rights of homosexual adults in the United States and the apparent acceptance of homosexuality as an alternative life style by a wide segment of our society, this lack of substantial research in this area is regrettable.

ATTITUDES ABOUT HETEROSEXUAL BEHAVIORS AND RELATIONSHIPS

Attitudes about sexual behavior between unmarried young people have been changing steadily toward greater acceptance of sexual expression for both men and women since the early 1920s when the earliest studies were published (Bromley & Britten, 1938; Davis, 1929; Hamilton, 1929). To understand the complexity of these changes, it is helpful to review the literature about sexual attitudes from the point of view of changes in courtship behavior factors which seem to be associated with permissive sexual attitudes, and relationship of attitudes to behavior in a time of changing normative expectations.

Changes in Courtship Behaviors

For American young people prior to World War I, there was a clear normative expectation that sexual activity was only acceptable and permissible after marriage. Thus sex and marriage were considered inseparable, and adolescents who violated this norm were strongly sanctioned by both family and peers. Seldom were unmarried couples allowed to be alone together, and whatever contact they had with each other usually took place under the watchful eyes of a chaperone.

One aspect of this early twentieth-century normative structure was that a double standard was set for men and women. Women were required to remain chaste and virginal until marriage, and any woman who violated this norm was subject to strong social rejection, familial anger, and religious condemnation. Men, on the other hand, were given more freedom to engage in sexual activities, as long as they were discreet, and sexual intercourse between a young man and a prostitute or experienced older woman was tolerated to a limited extent. In keeping with this double standard, two different attitudes about sexual behavior developed. For women sex was only acceptable within the context of a loving relationship, preferably within marriage, while for men sex was acceptable in loving relationships but also in casual relationships where there was neither affection nor commitment.

To a very great extent the changes in sexual attitudes in America over the last 70 years have involved the erosion of both of these norms which sanctioned sex only within the context of marriage and the norms which set a double standard for women's and men's physical behavior. It would be incorrect, however, to assume that this change has taken place suddenly; it is more accurate to understand that norms regarding sexual activity for adolescents have been shifting gradually for at least a half-century.

After World War I courtship behavior changed dramatically as chaperones became less prevalent and "dating" by unmarried young men and women increased in popularity. "Dating" at that time stressed enjoying the company of as many different partners as possible as a demonstration of one's popularity and peer acceptance. Despite common jokes about what went on in the back seats of the new Model T cars during that era, the most common sexual activity which was accepted widely was holding hands and occasional kissing.

After World War II dating behavior emphasized longer-term relationships between fewer partners in what became known as "going steady." These changing patterns of courtship were accompanied by increasing acceptance of both light petting (touching of breasts) and heavy petting (touching of genitals with or without orgasm). Studies published from the 1930s through the early 1960s (Burgess & Wallin, 1953; Ehrmann, 1959; Kinsey et al., 1953; Reiss, 1967; Terman, 1938) commonly reported the double standard about attitudes toward sex. In general men tended to feel that sexual "permissiveness" was acceptable in both loving and casual relationships, while women tended to feel that sex was only acceptable within the context of a loving relationship. By the late 1960s and throughout the 1970s, however, there was a lessening of this double standard with both men and women tending to feel that sex was most acceptable within the context of a loving and affectionate, if not committed, relationship (Croake & James, 1973; Hass, 1979; Hunt, 1974; Packard, 1968; Reiss, 1976; Sorenson, 1973; Yankelovich, 1974).

Perhaps the best data supporting the relationship between approval for sexual relations and level of interpersonal involvement have been provided by Reiss (1967, p. 29), shown in Table 32–2.

While the overwhelming majority of both adolescent men and women today approve of premarital sexual intercourse, their permissiveness is not indiscriminate. The new norm is clearly that sex is only acceptable within a loving and affectionate relationship; promiscuity, exploitation, and unprotected sexual intercourse are considered unacceptable and are usually negatively sanctioned by youth.

Factors Associated with Permissive Sexual Attitudes

Studies of factors associated with sexual attitudes have primarily focused upon sociological variables, such as nationality, region within the United States, educational level, race, age, religion, sex, level of sexual experience, and date of the study. There have been relatively

Table 32–2 Approval of Petting and Full Sexual Relations by Stage of Relationship

| | ADULTS | | STUDENTS | |
| | Percent | | Percent | |
	For men	For women	For men	For women
Petting:				
When engaged	60.8	56.1	85.0	81.8
In love	59.4	52.6	80.4	75.2
Strong affection	54.3	45.6	67.0	56.7
No affection	28.6	20.3	34.3	18.0
Full Sex Relations:				
When engaged	19.5	16.9	52.2	44.0
In love	17.6	14.2	47.6	38.7
Strong affection	16.3	12.5	36.9	27.2
No affection	11.9	7.4	20.8	10.8
N	1390	1411	811	806

Source: Data from Reiss, 1967.

few studies relating sexual attitudes to other psychological characteristics, although there have been studies relating sexual attitudes to moral development (Jurich & Jurich, 1974), ego strength (Cvetkovich & Grote, 1976), and proneness to deviant or problem behavior (Jessor & Jessor, 1975, 1977).

Unfortunately it is difficult to generalize about factors related to sexual attitudes because in many instances they confound each other. For instance whites who attend church tend to have more conservative sexual attitudes than whites who do not attend church; however, a similar association between sexual conservatism and religiosity does not hold for blacks (Broderick & Bernard, 1969; Reiss, 1967). Regional differences within the United States, as another example, confuse sex and racial differences in attitudes. In general men have more permissive attitudes than women and blacks tend to have more permissive attitudes than whites; however, Reiss (1967) found that white men in New York were more permissive than black men in Virginia. Christensen and Gregg (1970) found that while men were more permissive than women in both the intermountain (Utah) and midwestern regions, intermountain men were not more permissive than midwesten women. Another complication involves the fact that many factors which traditionally showed a strong relationship with sexual attitudes appear to be becoming less pronounced in recent years. For instance permissiveness was traditionally associated with higher educational levels, lower socioeconomic levels, greater age, greater sexual experience, being male, and being black. Studies in the 1970s, however, tend to indicate that none of these associations is as strong as in the past. Men are not much more permissive than women today, and better-educated people now tend to have the same attitudes as people without advanced educations.

In summary over the last 20 years in the United States, the general increase in attitudinal acceptance of sex behavior for adolescents has superseded the traditional sociological characteristics which explained differences in attitudes about sex, so that knowing a person's race, educational level, or even age and sex, is little help in predicting his/her sexual attitudes. Some recent writers (Oskamp & Mindick, 1981) have called for more studies of psychological characteristics and sexual attitudes, and it seems likely that in future years psychological studies will become more prevalent than they have been.

Sexual Attitudes and Sex Behavior—The Question of Norms

One of the most interesting aspects of the study of attitudes about sex behaviors is the relationship of these attitudes to the practice of sex behaviors. First, there has been a reversal in the relationship of permissive attitudes and sexual behaviors in the last 25 years, which is clearly illustrated in Christensen and Gregg's (1970) study of approval of premarital coitus and experience of such behavior in two regions of the United States. Their data for 1958 indicated that for both men and women in intermountain and midwestern states the percentage of those who had experienced premarital intercourse was greater than the percentage of those who said they approved of

premarital intercourse. In a follow-up study in 1968, they found that the reverse was true; more subjects said they approved of premarital coitus than had actually experienced it. This trend for attitudinal acceptance to exceed participation in sexual behavior has continued throughout the 1970s with almost all studies reporting much higher rates of acceptance for sexual behaviors than participation in such behaviors. In one of the most recent studies of 15- to 19-year-old boys and girls (Hass, 1979), 95 percent of the boys and 83 percent of the girls approved of genital touching, but only 55 percent of the boys and 43 percent of the girls had experienced such heavy petting. The same held for oral sex, where 90 percent of boys and 70 percent of girls approved but only 35 percent of each sex had participated, and for sexual intercourse, where the approval rate was 83 percent for boys and 64 percent for girls while the participation rates were 56 percent and 44 percent respectively. Second, the relatively greater increase in permissive attitudes over permissive behaviors raises several interesting questions about changes in norms about sex generally and specifically what normative behaviors are with regard to sex for adolescents.

A *norm* is usually defined as a standard for behavior which is arrived at by informal processes of social agreement or consensus. Given a range of possible behaviors, the norm defines which are acceptable and likely to be rewarded (positively sanctioned) and which are unacceptable and likely to be punished (negatively sanctioned). There is disagreement among sociologists about whether there has to be enforcement of these standards in order for a norm to be said to exist. For instance if public opinion polls show that people prefer men to be cleanshaven rather than to have beards but no man who wears a beard is negatively sanctioned in any way, can it be said that a norm about facial hair really exists? If there are no sanctions or enforcements for norms, it is probably more useful to say that the social group or society is "normless" with regard to that behavior, rather than to say that it has a norm of permissiveness. In the case of changing attitudes about sex behavior, it is also useful to distinguish among behaviors which are valued, behaviors which are accepted without sanctions, and behaviors which are sanctioned. If it is possible to generalize about American society, it appears that the society as a whole values chastity and virginity in adolescents but that it no longer negatively sanctions premarital sexual intercourse, preferring instead to accept such behavior as part of a caring relationship between two young people who are "in love" without either positive or negative sanctions. In contrast the society has very strong negative sanctions against abusive and exploitative sex, as demonstrated in laws regarding child molestation, rape, and child pornography.

This general view of American society as being normless, valuing virginity but not enforcing it with sanctions, disguises the fact that specific subgroups in the society, defined by such factors as ethnicity, age, education, income, and religiosity, hold very strong values about appropriate sexual behavior for the young and have clear norms which are enforced. Unfortunately for the adolescent, however, these values and norms are not always in agreement from one group to another, so that the individual adolescent who confronts several such reference groups often encounters conflicting values and norms which make the individual's problem of deciding upon a set of personal values and behaviors very difficult. A youth from a highly religious and sexually conservative home joining a peer group at a college where sexual activity is accepted and approved within the norm of "sex with affection" may experience considerable personal stress and value conflict. A youth from a poor urban neighborhood where sexual activity is positively sanctioned by peers as a badge of adulthood and as confirmation of one's masculinity or femininity may experience conflict when dealing with school and public agency workers who do not value such behavior and negatively sanction it. Thus the issue for adolescents appears to be not so much that they are "marginal people" attempting to find a place in an adult society which is normless, but that they are "marginal people" attempting to deal with a variety of adult reference groups which offer conflicting norms. The result of these conflicting subgroup norms is that youth are given very little consistent guidance for their sexual attitudes and behaviors which appears to result in adolescents being highly ambivalent about their own sexual attitudes and behaviors.

Several sets of data illustrate this inconsistency and ambivalence which adolescents experience. The first are the findings that adolescents express highly tolerant attitudes about other people's sexual behavior but seem to be much more conservative about their own behavior, as Hass's (1979) data presented earlier indicate. The second are that studies of contraceptive usage among adolescents, such as Oskamp and Mindick (1981; Oskamp, Mindick, Berger, & Motta, 1978), indicate that one of the chief reasons for poor contraceptive usage among adolescents is their inability or unwillingness to accept themselves as being sexually active. In other words many sexually active teenagers tend to deny their own behavior by failing to protect themselves adequately against pregnancy. A third involves the relative importance which adolescents in Hass's study gave to "having sex with someone," which they ranked as one of the least important issues in their lives, well behind doing well in school, having same-sex friends, having opposite-sex friends, being romantically involved with someone, and athletics.

In summary the data indicating that sexual attitudes among adolescents have become much more permissive probably reflects the conflicting subgroup norms which adolescents encounter in the larger society which is largely normless with regard to sex and do not provide very useful information about what the sexual attitudes of any individual are likely to be nor how that individual is likely to behave sexually. For most adolescents sexual feelings and behaviors remain a subject of personal ambivalence and conflict, and very little consistent guidance is found among the various reference groups with which the adolescent interacts.

HETEROSEXUAL BEHAVIORS AND THEIR CONSEQUENCES

The research on adolescent sex behaviors has traditionally been dominated by studies of older youth who attended college. During the last ten years, however, several studies have provided much-needed insight into the sex behaviors of noncollege youth, women, and younger adolescents (Chilman, 1979; Cvetkovich & Grote, 1975; Hass, 1979; Kantner & Zelnick, 1973; Sorenson, 1973; Vener & Stewart, 1974; Zelnick & Kantner, 1972a, 1972b, 1972c, 1974, 1975, 1978a, 1978b). In general these studies indicate that adolescents are practicing more different types of sexual behaviors at younger ages and that, while boys tend to begin practicing sex behaviors at younger ages than girls, the differences between boys' and girls' sexual experiences are steadily narrowing. The data also indicate that knowledge of teenagers about contraception and the realities of sexual functioning is woefully inadequate, so that, while the birthrate among women over 20 has been declining since 1960, the birthrate among young teenagers, particularly girls aged 13 to 15, has been rising precipitously. In 1979 there were one million pregnancies among teenage American girls; approximately 400,000 were terminated by abortions; of the 600,000 live births, 233,000 were born out of wedlock, and another 100,000 were born to mothers who had hurriedly gotten married to legitimize their babies (Baldwin, 1976; Chilman, 1979). The evidence seems to indicate clearly that increased sexual activity among adolescents is not without serious consequences, both for the individuals involved and for the larger society.

Sex Behaviors preceding Coitus

Adolescents begin sexual behaviors with the simple act of hand-holding and progress through a sequence of activities which end in sexual intercourse. The regularity of this sequence of precoital behaviors is clearly shown in data from Vener and Stewart's study of white middle- and working-class adolescents in a nonmetropolitan town in Michigan in 1970 and 1973 (Vener & Stewart, 1974) which is given in Table 32–3. As these data show, boys at every age are more experienced than girls, and degree of experience for both boys and girls is directly related to age.

Whether a boy or girl is involved in intimate sexual activities, such as petting, seems to depend upon a number of factors, including the person's rate of physical maturation, need for independence from parents, and type of peer group influence (Sorenson, 1973). A number of studies have indicated that lack of sexual experience is related to "religiosity," as measured by reported attendance at religious services (Chilman, 1979; Kinsey, et al., 1948; Kinsey et al., 1953; Reiss, 1967; Robinson, King, & Balswick, 1972; Sorenson, 1973).

Premarital Sexual Intercourse

Studies of premarital sexual intercourse among adolescents indicate clearly that over the last 50 years there has been a dramatic increase in adolescent sexual activity. These studies of youth aged 12 to 19 are reviewed in Table 32–4, while studies dealing specifically with college youth are reviewed in Table 32–5. Table 32–6 provides a summary of the rates of premarital sexual intercourse for high school and college age males and females for three different historical periods. As this summary illustrates, the greatest increases have been experienced by females, as reported by studies between 1925 and 1973, when the percentage of high school girls who had re-

Table 32-3 Levels of Heterosexual Activity of Boys and Girls in One Community in 1970 and 1973

| | PERCENTAGE OF BOYS WHO HAVE PARTICIPATED IN AN ACTIVITY AT LEAST ONCE | | | | | | | | | |
| | 13 and younger | | 14 | | 15 | | 16 | | 17 and older | |
LEVELS OF SEXUAL ACTIVITY	1970	1973	1970	1973	1970	1973	1970	1973	1970	1973
I. Held hands	79	80	83	87	92	93	90	90	93	92
II. Held arm around or been held	60	67	79	78	83	87	90	87	90	90
III. Kissed or been kissed	63	65	72	78	76	84	86	85	86	87
IV. Necked (prolonged hugging and kissing)	46	48	54	56	64	70	76	69	77	78
V. Light petting (feeling above the waist)	37	40	49	55	59	66	70	65	71	71
VI. Heavy petting (feeling below the waist)	32	34	36	42	44	56	53	55	62	62
VII. Gone all the way (coitus)	24	28	21	32	26	38	31	38	38	34
VIII. Coitus with two or more partners	14	17	14	15	11	21	16	23	17	23
Number in sample	192	180	208	220	193	191	217	176	179	173

| | PERCENTAGE OF GIRLS WHO HAVE PARTICIPATED IN AN ACTIVITY AT LEAST ONCE | | | | | | | | | |
| | 13 and younger | | 14 | | 15 | | 16 | | 17 and older | |
LEVELS OF SEXUAL ACTIVITY	1970	1973	1970	1973	1970	1973	1970	1973	1970	1973
I. Held hands	78	84	91	87	92	89	95	91	95	97
II. Held arm around or been held	68	72	85	81	88	87	94	90	92	96
III. Kissed or been kissed	66	68	80	75	82	82	92	89	90	96
IV. Necked (prolonged hugging and kissing)	46	43	64	56	69	65	81	77	82	84
V. Light petting (feeling above the waist)	27	31	41	40	49	55	66	65	71	71
VI. Heavy petting (feeling below the waist)	21	17	20	28	28	40	47	49	57	59
VII. Gone all the way (coitus)	10	10	10	17	13	24	23	31	27	35
VIII. Coitus with two or more partners	7	4	4	5	4	10	8	13	8	14
Number in sample	191	222	197	218	195	220	200	190	142	185

Source: Data from Vener & Stewart, 1974.

ported premarital coitus more than tripled from 10 percent in 1925 to 35 percent in 1973 and the rates for college women nearly tripled from 25 percent in 1925 to 65 percent in 1973. Most recent studies indicate that the rates for females have continued to rise during the 1970s, so that in 1979 approximately 44 percent of high school girls and 74 percent of college women reported premarital coitus. Rates for males have also increased since the 1920s; however these increases have been less dramatic for males than for females because rates for males have always been much higher than for females until very recently. In 1925 there were 25 percent of high school boys and 55 percent of college men reporting premarital coitus. These figures indicate that the rate for high school boys has continued to rise to 56 percent, while the rate for college men has declined to 74 percent. The most recent studies seem to indicate that at the current time (Chilman, 1979; Hass, 1979; "What's Really Happening on Campus," 1976) high school boys are slightly more likely to be sexually active than girls (56 percent vs. 44 percent) but that college men and women are virtually the same in terms of percentage who are nonvirgins (74 percent vs. 74 percent).

Studies of black adolescents are fewer in number than those of whites but seem to indicate that blacks begin sexual activity earlier than whites. While about 25 percent of white boys and girls are sexually active by age 15–16, 90 percent of black boys and 50 percent of black girls have experienced coitus by that age (Chilman, 1979; Finkel & Finkel, 1975; Jessor & Jessor, 1979; Kantner & Zelnick, 1972; Sorenson, 1973; Vener & Stewart, 1974; Vener, Stewart, & Hager, 1972).

While it is difficult to determine the complete meaning of this rise in sexual activity for teenagers and college age youth, it appears that it is more a reflection of an attempt to achieve greater personal identity and fulfillment through physical intimacy than a sort of uncontrolled impulse gratification or wanton promiscuity. As was discussed earlier the current attitude is that sex is an acceptable part of a caring, affectionate, and loving relationship, whether the couple intend to marry or not. Casual or uncaring sex is considered to be undesirable, and exploitative or forced sex is considered to be intolerable. The importance of a caring and romantic relationship is greater for girls than for boys, as is reflected in response to a question in Hass's (1979) study which asked at what time in a dating relationship a subject would consider it permissible to have sex. For the 15- to 19-year-old boys, 50 percent said, "After we had gone out a month or less"; 29 percent said, "Only if I was in love with her"; and 11 percent said, "Only if we were married." For girls in the same age range, only 13 percent said, "After we had gone out a month or less," while 53 percent said, "Only if I were in love with him," and 23 percent said, "Only if we were married" (p. 65). Among that portion of the teenage population who are sexually active, it is quite common for a young person to have had several sex partners in the context of a series of romantic relationships over several years. Studies in the early 1970s indicated that most sexually active teenage girls had intercourse once or twice a month or less, and that over half reported that they had had only one sex partner (Kantner & Zelnick, 1972; Sorenson, 1973). In Hass's recent study (1979), 20 percent of the sexually active boys and 45 percent of the

(*Text continues on p. 575.*)

Table 32–4 Studies of Premarital Sexual Intercourse among Adolescent Females and Males

INVESTIGATIONS, DATES OF STUDIES, AND DESCRIPTION OF SAMPLES	FINDINGS

Kinsey, Pomeroy, Martin, & Gebhard, 1938–1950—Nonrandom sample, mainly northeast and north-central urban white females and males

Age at first intercourse by years of education

	Females					Males			
Age	0–8	9–12	13–16	17	Total	0–8	9–12	13	Total
13	9	1	—	—	1	14.5	16.2	3.1	14.8
14						28.0	33.4	6.0	27.8
15	18	5	2	1	3	42.2	44.7	9.5	38.8
16						56.9	58.1	15.5	51.6
17						66.8	68.3	23.1	61.3
18						76.1	73.7	30.8	68.2
19						80.0	75.6	38.0	71.5
20	25	26	20	15	20	82.9	75.1	44.4	73.1

Gebhard, Pomeroy, Martin, & Christensen, 1938–1955—Nonrandom sample, northern urban black females

Age at first intercourse by education

Age	8th Grade	High School	College	
<15	62	48	8	No males included in study
<20	82	82	49	

Lake, 1966–1967—Nonrandom national sample of 1500 females ages 15–19 (only 15% in college)

Age at first intercourse

Age		
15	6	No males included in study
16–17	13	
18–19	25	

Simon, Berger, & Gagnon, 1972—Random sample, females and males in Illinois

Age at first intercourse by education

Age	College-Bound	Not College-Bound	Total	Education	
15	4	11	10	College-bound	16
17	12	40	27	Not college-bound	31
18	23	40	38	Total	21

Udry, Bauman, & Morris, 1969–1970—Low income-area probability sample of 16 cities. Retrospective interviews with black and white females in birth cohorts by decades and by occupational status of man who was head of household when subjects were ages 10–14

First intercourse by age 17 and occupational status of head of household

Year of Birth	Low Occupational Status		High Occupational Status		
	Black	White	Black	White	
1920–29	41.6	2.5	34.6	3.6	No males included in study
1930–39	47.6	13.1	40.7	7.8	
1940–49	51.9	13.3	52.2	13.6	
1950–59	65.5	33.3	65.5	26.2	

Jessor & Jessor, 1972—Random sample of high school students in a small Rocky Mountain city (52% of original sample responded)

First intercourse by grade

Grade		
10	26	21
11	40	28
12	55	33

Table 32-4 (*cont.*)

INVESTIGATIONS, DATES OF STUDIES, AND DESCRIPTION OF SAMPLES	FINDINGS						

FINDINGS

	Females	Males

First intercourse by SES

	SES		
Miller, 1972—Junior and senior students in two San Francisco high schools, by socioeconomic status (SES); ages about 16–18	Middle	58 (mostly white)	No males included in study
	Lower	48 (races mixed)	

Age at first intercourse

	Age		
Hunt, 1972—Retrospective data, national probability sample, with considerable sample loss	17	25	50

Age at first intercourse

	Age		
Sorensen, 1972—Partial national sample, with many unknown biases, of females and males of both races (white majority)	12	3.2	9.7
	13	8.5	20.0
	14	14.5	30.0
	15	26.0	40.0
	16	35.0	49.0
	17	37.0	55.0
	18–19	45.0	57.0

Age at first intercourse by poverty level and race

	Age	Below Poverty			Above Poverty			Total Both Races and Levels	
		Black	White	Total	Black	White	Total		
Kantner & Zelnik, 1972 (study in 1971)—National probability sample of 4240 white and black females, ages 14–19; almost entire sample reached and interviewed	15	34.1	12.6	32.2	30.2	10.7	10.8	13.8	No males included in study
	16	53.9	18.3	46.4	37.2	17.0	17.5	21.2	
	17	60.0	22.2	57.0	48.7	22.4	21.7	26.6	
	18	64.4	26.4	80.8	81.2	36.1	35.5	37.1	
	19	82.4	38.6	80.8	81.2	41.5	40.4	46.1	

Age at first intercourse by race

	Age	White	Black	Hispanic
Finkel & Finkel, 1974—Sample of males in three high schools in large north-eastern city. No females included in study	12	6.0	45.9	23.3
	13	12.4	60.7	32.8
	14	23.7	74.0	49.8
	15	35.7	78.7	68.7
	16–17	48.0	84.0	75.0

First intercourse by race

	Race	Females	Males
Cvetkovich & Grote, 1974–1975—Nonrandom sample of black and white females and males, ages 16–17, in two cities and one town	Black	63	92
	White	36	51

571

Table 32–4 *(cont.)*

INVESTIGATIONS, DATES OF
STUDIES, AND DESCRIPTION OF
SAMPLES

FINDINGS

		Females				Males			
		Age at first intercourse by type of school							
	Age	1970			1973	1970			1973
		School A	School B	School C	School B	School A	School B	School C	School B
Vener, Stewart, & Hager, 1972— Replication studies with large, similar populations and same instruments, 1970 and 1973. Large sample, nonmetropolitan Michigan area: three high schools in 1970; one in 1973. Probably white majority. School *A*—professional–managerial community; *B*—lower middle- and upper-working-class community; *C*—semirural, working-class community.	13 or less	7	10	7	10	8	24	24	28
	14	7	10	8	17	7	21	23	32
	15	12	13	13	24	19	26	15	38
	16	18	23	21	31	21	31	31	38
	17 or more	26	27	40	35	31	38	38	34

		Females		Males	
		Age at first intercourse by age group			
	Age Group	15–16	17–18	15–16	17–18
Hass, 1979—nonrandom sample of 625 teenagers, 15 to 19 years old (307 boys, 318 girls); 90% from high schools in southern California, 10% from schools in Michigan, New York, New Jersey, and Texas; 12% minority (black, Hispanic, Asian-American); no data reported as to socioeconomic level of subjects. Self-administered paper and pencil questionnaires; 10% of subjects interviewed by same sex interviewer. Data reported as percentages responding to various statements and categories.	*Age of first intercourse*				
	13	7	3	18	7
	16	31	41	43	42

Source: Adapted from Chilman, 1979.

Table 32-5 Studies of College Level Men and Women Reporting Premarital Sexual Intercourse

STUDY	SAMPLE	PERCENTAGE OF GROUP	
		Females	Males
Davis, 1920	1200 college level women; single; mean age 37 at time of study	11	NA
Hamilton, 1929	100 college students married at time of study (retrospective study)	35	54
Bromley & Britten, 1938	618 single females and 470 single males; college or high school education; ages 16–23 at time of study	25	51
Peterson, 1938	419 male college students	NA	55
Porterfield & Ellison, 1946	328 single female and 285 single male college students	9	32
Finger, 1947	111 single male college students, ages 17–23 at time of study	NA	45
Kinsey et al., 1940s and 1950s	5000(+) college level females and 3000(+) males (retrospective study)	20–27	49
Ross, 1950	95 single male college students, age 21	NA	51
Gilbert Youth Research, 1951	National sample of college students; single; ages 17–22 at time of study	25	56
Landis & Landis, 1953	1000 college female students and 610 college male students, single and married	9	41
Ehrmann, 1953	315 single females, ages 18–21 (interviews and questionnaires); 274 single males, ages 18–21 (questionnaires); 50 single males, ages 19–24 (interviews); in a southern university	$\frac{18\text{-}21}{14}$	$\frac{18\text{-}21}{57}$ $\frac{19\text{-}24}{68}$

STUDY	SAMPLE	PERCENTAGE OF GROUP			
		Single	Married	Single	Married
Chilman, 1961	Random sample of 50 single females and males and 40 married females and males, ages 18–21, in a northeastern university	9	46	46	72
Mirande, 1966	Single undergraduate sociology students in a midwestern university	23	—	63	—
Freedman, 1965	Random sample of Stanford University senior female students; white; mostly upper-middle-class	22	—	NA	NA
		1965	*1970*	*1965*	*1970*
Robinson, King, & Balswick, 1965, 1970	Representative samples from undergraduate social science class in a large southern university: 115 females and 129 males in 1965; 158 females and 137 males in 1970	29	37	65	65
Kaats & Davis, 1967	Survey in two introductory psychology courses	41–44		60	
Carns, 1967	Probability sample of 1177 students in nation's nonreligiously based colleges and universities; interview study; adequate reliability stated	32.2		57.4	
		1958	*1968*	*1958*	*1968*
Bell & Chaskes, 1958, 1968	Matched samples at an urban Pennsylvania university:				
	Dating	10	23	NA	NA
	Steady	15	28		
Luckey & Naas, 1967	Survey of 21 nationally representative colleges and universities	43.2		59.2	

Table 32–5 (*cont.*)

STUDY	SAMPLE	PERCENTAGE OF GROUP Females		Males	
		1958	*1968*	*1958*	*1968*
Christensen & Gregg, 1970	Studies in 1958 and 1968 (same instrument and similar samples); three samples of college students—Mormon (Utah), Midwest, and Danish (omitted here); mostly white				
	Mormon	10	32	39	37
	Midwest	21	34	51	50
Playboy, 1970 Survey 1	Survey of 7300 students from 200 colleges		51		81
Playboy, 1971 Survey 2	Random sample of nationally representative colleges		56		77
		1968	*1972*	*1968*	*1972*
Bauman & Wilson, 1968–72	Random sample of University of North Carolina undergraduates; single; white; native-born	46	73	56	73
Jackson & Potkay, 1972	Random sample of females in college dorms		43		NA
Simon & Gagnon, 1972	1967 national sample of 584 female and 593 male college students				
	Freshmen		19		36
	Sophomores		30		63
	Juniors		37		60
	Seniors		44		68
	TOTAL		32		56
Jessor & Jessor, 1973	Random sample of college seniors in a Rocky Mountain community; over 50 percent sample loss[a]		85		82
Sarrel & Sarrel, 1974	Study of 1200 entering freshmen, sophomores, juniors, and seniors at Yale University done in 1968 and 1972	25	75	33	62
Chilman, 1974	Random sample of white freshmen in a large, urban midwest university (majority age 18)		39		50
Playboy, 1976	Random sample of 3700 students from 20 colleges and universities across the country		76		76

[a]When these students were freshmen in 1970, 51 percent of the females and 46 percent of the males were self-reported nonvirgins. By their sophomore year this was true for 70 percent of the females and 65 percent of the males; and by their junior year (1972) these figures were 80 percent and 74 percent, respectively. Thus rates increased by 50 percent from the freshman year to the senior year.

These data, interesting in themselves as descriptive of change for groups of college students over time, also indicate the importance in such studies of delineating the age and college years of the group under consideration and the difficulty of comparing one study to another when these facts are unknown.

Table 32-6 Percentage of White High School and College Students Reporting Premarital Sexual Intercourse at Three Historical Periods

PERIOD	HIGH SCHOOL		COLLEGE	
	Boys	Girls	Boys	Girls
1925–1965[a]	25	10	55	25
1966–1973[b]	35	35	85	65
1974–1979[c]	56	44	74	74

[a] Bromley & Britten, 1938; Chilman, 1961; Davis, 1929; Ehrmann, 1959; Kinsey et al., 1953; Peterson, 1938.

[b] Carns, 1973; Christensen & Gregg, 1970; Hunt, 1974; Jessor & Jessor, 1975; Kaats & Davis, 1970; Lake, 1967; Luckey & Nass, 1969; Robinson et al., 1972; Vener & Stewart, 1974; Vener et al., 1972.

[c] Chilman, 1979; Hass, 1979; "What's Really Happening on Campus," 1976.

sexually active girls aged 15 to 19 reported having had one sex partner, while 56 percent of the boys and 38 percent of the girls reported having had two to five sex partners, and 24 percent of the boys and 6 percent of the girls reported having had more than ten sex partners.

Factors Associated with Premarital Coitus

Studies that describe factors associated with premarital sexual intercourse are reviewed in Table 32–7. As indicated in this review a number of sociological and psychological factors have been studied and been found to relate to sexual activity. While it is difficult to state causal relationships, there are data to support the association of the following sociological factors with premarital sexual behavior for both boys and girls: exposure to permissive sex norms of the larger society, association with peers who are sexually active, being a member of a lower socioeconomic status group, being a member of a racial minority, being poor, and having friends who have sexually permissive attitudes. Psychological factors which appear to be related to premarital sexual activity include the following: use of drugs and alcohol, low educational aspirations and achievement, deviant attitudes, poor relationships with parents, going steady and being in love, and having risk-taking attitudes. There have been few studies of biological factors associated with sexual activity in adolescents; however, it does appear that adolescents who mature early are more likely to become sexually active earlier than their later maturing peers.

In general the profile of the sexually active young adolescent boy which can be drawn from these studies of large groups of young people is quite different from that of the sexually active young adolescent girl. For boys sexual activity is often part of a larger pattern of adolescent rebellion, rejection of parental controls, aggressive acting out, alienation from school, and association with older peers who flaunt their sexual experience as a badge of masculinity. For young adolescent girls, on the other hand, sexual activity is often part of a larger pattern of low self-esteem, feeling rejected and not loved at home, passive dependent longing for nurturance, disinterest in school, and association with an older boyfriend who provides the assurance and affection which the girl lacks. This in part explains the often puzzling finding that girls who espouse a traditionally "feminine" set of sex-role

preferences are often just as sexually active as girls who claim to be more "modern" or "liberated" in their sex-role preferences. Traditionally "feminine" girls sometimes seek their self-identification through a man who will ideally be their husband, and they tend to give in to men whom they feel affection for on the grounds that they seek to please the man and reciprocate his care for her. A "modern" or "liberated" sex-role preference female, on the other hand, who sees her identity and life satisfaction as coming from her own efforts rather than from those of her future husband, will be less likely to give in to an ardent suitor simply because he is an affectionate man, but she may participate in sexual intercourse with him because it satisfies her own sexual needs or because she feels that sexual intimacy is an acceptable part of a close relationship with a mutually caring partner.

These profiles which emerge from the literature on factors associated with premarital sexual activity must be understood as both reflecting large group trends in data and as being somewhat dated since there are few studies that have been done in the last seven years. As sexual activity becomes increasingly popular among teenagers, these large group images of the rebellious, aggressive boy and the passive, insecure girl, both of which perpetuate the old notion that sex is not part of the well-adjusted, happy teenager's life, are increasingly inaccurate and misleading. To a greater and greater extent, as the percentages of sexually active youth indicate, sexual activity is becoming part of the teenage experience and is being experienced by all types of young people, not just those who use sex as a way to express personal frustrations or to meet dependency and security needs.

Contraception

Knowledge about contraception and the use of contraceptives has not kept up with the rate of activity among American youth, especially those aged 15 to 19. While studies of contraceptive use are not numerous and often provide incomplete information, there are enough studies available (Bauman & Udry, 1972; Bauman & Wilson, 1974; Brown, Lieberman, & Miller, 1975; Cvetkovich & Grote, 1976; Finkel & Finkel, 1975; Fox, 1975; Fujita, Wagner, & Pion, 1971; Kantner & Zelnick, 1972; Miller, 1976; Oskamp et al., 1978; Presser, 1974; Settlage, Baroff, & Cooper, 1973; Sorenson, 1973) to indicate that inadequate birth control knowledge and failure to use adequate contraceptive techniques are major problems which have widespread impact on youth and their families.

The data from four separate studies (Bauman & Wilson, 1974; Fox, 1975; Presser, 1974; Sorenson, 1973) indicate that only 45 percent of sexually active teenagers used any type of contraceptive technique at the time of their first intercourse and that only 50 percent of college students and 20 percent of high school students (31 percent of whites and 17 percent of blacks) reported using any sort of birth control consistently (Fujita et al., 1971; Kantner & Zelnick, 1972). Studies of teenage boys indicate that 89 percent of the blacks and 69 percent of the whites who were sexually active in high school reported having had unprotected sexual intercourse at least once. This apparent lack of contraceptive use by young black males is particularly striking, since some data indicate

(Text continues on p. 579.)

Table 32-7 Studies of Factors Associated with Premarital Sexual Intercourse

FACTOR AND STUDY	SAMPLE	METHODS	FINDINGS
Frequency of Dating:			
Kaats & Davis, 1967	Students in college psychology class	Questionnaires	Sexually experienced girls dated more frequently than others.
Simon & Gagnon, 1972	Large sample of Illinois high school students	Interviews	Sexually experienced girls dated more frequently than others.
Ladner, 1971	Anthropological study in St. Louis black ghetto	Interviews and observation	Those who did not have premarital intercourse dated infrequently.
Presser, 1976b	Probability sample of N.Y. females who had had first child (both races)	Interviews, reinterview study	Those who had premarital intercourse dated either infrequently or extensively.
Furstenberg, 1976	Predominantly black, low-income group of adolescent Baltimore females	Longitudinal interview study over a 5–year period	Those who did not have intercourse during teens did not date as young adolescents.
Kinsey, Pomeroy, Martin, & Gebhard, 1948, 1953	Large sample that includes many blacks	Interviews	Premarital intercourse was associated with plans for marriage for females
Ehrmann, 1959	Large sample of students in a southern university	Questionnaires and interviews	Premarital intercourse for both sexes was associated with going steady.
Bell & Chaskes, 1970	Studies in 1958 and 1968 of 200 female students at an urban university	Questionnaires	Premarital intercourse was associated with going steady and engagement in 1958 but not in 1968.
Spanier, 1975	Used data from 1967 Institute of Sex Research study (see Carns, under Effects of Social Reference Groups factor)		Age at first intercourse was associated with age and frequency of dating, going steady, falling in love.
Age:			
Kinsey, Pomeroy, Martin, & Gebhard, 1948, 1953	Large sample (many blacks) of females	Interviews	A rise in age of sexually experienced was noted from 3 percent at age 15 to 20 percent at age 20 (females).
Kantner & Zelnik, 1972	Large national probability sample of females, ages 15–19; races considered separately	Interviews	A rise in age of sexually experienced was noted with 10 percent of white girls having premarital coitus by age 15 and 32 percent of black girls; 20 percent of white girls by age 17 and 57 percent of black girls; 40 percent of white girls by age 19 and 80 percent of black girls.
Sorensen, 1973	National sample of both races but with 46 percent sample loss	Questionnaires	9 percent of girls had premarital intercourse by age 13; 25 percent by age 15.
Jessor & Jessor, 1975	Local sample of white students in Boulder, Colo. (50 percent sample loss)	Interviews and tests	The rates of intercourse doubled between ages 15 and 17; 26 percent for females and 21 percent for males by age 15.
Vener & Stewart, 1974	Large sample from three Michigan high schools, 1970 and 1973	Questionnaires	A 33 percent increase in rates was noted between ages 15 and 17 for females; 20 percent for males.
Age at Puberty:			
Kinsey, Pomeroy, Martin, & Gebhard, 1948, 1953	Large sample (many blacks)	Interviews	Early maturing males, but not females, were sexually experienced at very young age.
Chilman, 1963	Random sample of Syracuse University students	Interviews and questionnaires	Early maturing males, but not females, were sexually experienced at very young age.
Religiosity:			
Kinsey, Pomeroy, Martin, & Gebhard, 1948, 1953	Large sample (many blacks)	Interviews	Females high in religiosity were less likely to have premarital intercourse.
Clayton, 1969	Sample of female and male undergraduates at a private Southern Baptist college	Questionnaires	Students high in religiosity were more apt to be virgins; tendency reduced for fraternity members.

Table 32-7   (cont.)

FACTOR AND STUDY	SAMPLE	METHODS	FINDINGS
Kantner & Zelnik, 1972	Large national probability sample of females, ages 15–19; races considered separately	Questionnaires	Females who do not attend church have highest rates of premarital intercourse. Those who attend church and are least likely to have premarital intercourse are white, fundamentalist, and Protestant.
Jackson & Potkay, 1973	Random sample of 330 white college females living in dormitories at a midwest university	Questionnaires	Religiosity is associated with virginity only when students attend church voluntarily.
Jessor & Jessor, 1975	Local sample of white students in Boulder, Colo. (50 percent sample loss)	Interviews and tests	Nonvirginal girls were unlikely to see themselves as devoutly religious.
Cvetkovich & Grote, 1976	Sample of "convenience" of high school age females and males in three localities	Questionnaires and interviews	Virginity and religiosity are linked, except for black males.
Effects of Social Reference Groups:			
Mirande, 1968	Sample of 93 female and male students at a midwest university	Questionnaires	Sexually experienced females were more likely to associate with similar peers. Males, but not females, received peer pressure to have premarital intercourse.
Clayton, 1969	Sample of female and male undergraduate students at a private Southern Baptist college	Questionnaires	Fraternity members were more likely than nonfraternity members to be nonvirgins. Opposite found for females.
Carns, 1973	Large sample from large nonreligiously based universities	Interviews by the National Opinion Research Center under direction of the Institute of Sex Research	Males were more likely to discuss sex experiences with their peers than females; greater peer approval for males than females.
Social-Psychological:			
Freedman, 1965	Small sample of Stanford University females studied over a four-year period	Interviews and testing	Senior nonvirgins were more apt to have high impulse expression scores (Minnesota Multiphasic Personality Inventory) than virgins. Freshmen nonvirgins had significantly higher scores for "mania."
Kanin, 1967	Small sample of sexually aggressive college males	Interviews and questionnaires	Subjects were seductive, exploitative, sensitive to peer group pressure, and lacked sexual satisfaction.
Vener & Stewart, 1974	Large sample from three Michigan high schools, 1970 and 1973	Questionnaires	Nonvirgin females and males were more likely to engage in delinquent-behavior-use of alcohol and drugs and were less committed to traditional values.
Sorensen, 1973	National sample of both races (46 percent sample loss)	Questionnaires	"Sexual adventurers" were characterized by low school grades, low religiosity, manipulative, early involvement in sex, conflict with parents, oriented to techniques rather than relationships.
Jessor & Jessor, 1975	Four-year longitudinal study of college and high school males and females. High school group had 432 respondents, 50 percent sample loss	Questionnaires and tests	Nonvirgin males were significantly more likely to have higher scores for independence, self-esteem, low achievement expectations, low parental acceptance of deviance, friends approving and modeling deviance, general deviant behavior (including use of alcohol and marijuana), low grade point average. Nonvirgin females had similar scores except self-esteem was low, and they had higher scores than virgin females for social criticism, positive view of sex, low religiosity, high value on affection, high alienation, and parent conflicts.

Table 32-7 *(cont.)*

FACTOR AND STUDY	SAMPLE	METHODS	FINDINGS
Miller, 1975	Small sample of single, white, sexually active females, ages 17–26	Unstructured interviews	Engaging in premarital coitus was associated with going steady, feelings of being in love, increasing levels of intimacy, pressures from partners and peers, growing independence from parents, opportunities for privacy, effects of drugs and alcohol.
Cvetkovich & Grote, 1976	Sample of "convenience" of high school age males and females in three localities	Questionnaires and interviews	Nonvirgin females seemed to be more passive in relation to males, perhaps lower ego strength, risk-taking attitude (similar findings in other studies). Nonvirgin males seemed to be skilled and manipulative in interpersonal relationships, risk-taking, and somewhat irresponsible.
Parent-Child Relationships:			
Ehrmann, 1959	Large sample of students in a southern university	Questionnaires and interviews	Nonvirgin females said home discipline was inconsistent (also found by Terman, 1938, and by Cvetkovich & Grote, 1975).
Bowerman, Irish, & Pope, 1963	Large sample of predominantly black women in North Carolina	Interviews	Women who did not have premarital intercourse were more apt to come from two-parent homes of higher socioeconomic status in which mothers had considerable formal education and verbalized restrictive values.
Kantner & Zelnik, 1972	Large national probability sample of females, ages 15–19; races considered separately	Interviews	Nonvirgin females were more apt to be in one-parent families and in a variety of home situations (such as substitute parents) and in poor communication with parents.
Ladner, 1971	Anthropological study in St. Louis black ghetto	Interviews and observations	Virgin females were more apt to have mothers who were firm, involved with their children, had high educational-vocational goals.
Sorensen, 1973	National sample, both races (46 percent sample loss)	Questionnaires	Sexual "adventurers" were high school students who had a number of sex partners and communicated poorly with parents.
Miller & Simon, 1974	Large sample of high school students in Illinois	Interviews	Nonvirgin females, having many partners, were high on peer involvement and low on parent involvement.
Chilman, 1974	Random sample of urban university freshmen	Questionnaires	Nonvirgin girls were more likely to be in poor communication with parents.
Jessor & Jessor, 1975	A four-year longitudinal study of males and females in college and high school; high school group had 432 respondents (50 percent sample loss)	Questionnaires and tests	Virgins were more apt to have mothers with conventional ideology, firm discipline, and affectionate behavior.
Socioeconomic Factors:			
Kantner & Zelnik, 1972	Large national probability	Interviews	Black females whose fathers had a college education had much lower rates of premarital coitus than other black females; this also was true for those who came from higher income families, especially for younger females. Rates were higher for rural-urban migrants.
Vener, Stewart, & Hager, 1972; Vener & Stewart, 1974	Large sample from three Michigan high schools (study in 1970 and 1973)	Questionnaires	Lower rates of premarital coitus were found for young males (under age 15) in professional-managerial community. For girls influence was most marked at all ages.

Table 32–7 (cont.)

FACTOR AND STUDY	SAMPLE	METHODS	FINDINGS
Udry, Bauman, & Morris, 1975	Urban, low-income sample in 16 cities, with differing age cohorts compared (females only)	Interviews	No difference in rates by socioeconomic status of father (among five graduations of a lower income group).
Educational Levels and Aspirations:			
Kinsey, Pomeroy, Martin, & Gebhard, 1948, 1953	Large sample, many blacks	Interviews	Males with little education were more apt to be nonvirgins.
Pomeroy, Martin, & Christensen, 1958	Analysis of Kinsey data		Women with high levels of education were less likely to have had premarital coitus (especially true for blacks).
Miller & Simon, 1974	Large sample of high school students in Illinois	Interviews	College-bound males were more apt to be virgins.
Udry, Bauman, & Morris, 1975	Urban, low-income sample in 16 cities with differing age cohorts compared (females only)	Interviews	Strong association was found for females between virginity and highly achieved educational level. This was true for both black and white women.

that 90 percent of them experience sexual intercourse by the age of 16 (Cvetkovich & Grote, 1976; Finkel & Finkel, 1975).

Despite the fame of oral contraceptives and the impact they have had upon attitudes about premarital sexual intercourse, their use by teenage girls is limited. Kantner and Zelnick (1972) surveyed a national probability sample of 1300 sexually active white and black girls between the ages of 15 and 19 to report that 50 percent of the whites and 20 percent of the blacks used the "pill," while over 50 percent of the total sample indicated that they relied primarily upon such male-controlled contraceptive methods as the condom and withdrawal. They also reported, however, that in terms of frequency of use highly effective methods, such as the pill, diaphragm, and intrauterine device, were four times more likely to be used than other methods and that among younger girls, aged 15 to 17, blacks were more likely to use an effective contraceptive method than were whites. Other studies of single college campuses reveal that use of the pill varies from 14 percent (Bauman & Wilson, 1974) to 59 percent (Bauman & Udry, 1972) and that in almost all studies the most frequently reported contraceptive methods are the condom (70 percent) and withdrawal (50 percent to 60 percent).

It is unfortunate that there do not appear to be more recent studies of contraceptive use by teenagers because it is important to know if contraceptive use has increased in the late 1970s along with the increased acceptability of sexual activity among teenagers, as reflected in the expansion of planned parenthood clinics, sex education programs in schools, and wider discussion in the public media and governmental agencies which have been debating children's rights and abortion legislation.

Teenagers' knowledge of sex and reproduction is generally inadequate. Only 40 percent of Kantner and Zelnick's sample of sexually active teenage girls had a generally correct notion of the period of greatest risk of pregnancy in their monthly cycle; the majority thought that it was during their menstrual period. Among these same girls 28 percent of the whites and 55 percent of the blacks thought they could not become pregnant easily,

even when they had unprotected intercourse. It seems clear that, given these data and the fact that the most popular contraceptive techniques are those which are male-controlled, there is a pressing need for greater sex education among youth with an emphasis upon the facts of reproduction and the use of contraceptives by both boys and girls.

Factors Related to Contraceptive Usage

There appears to be no simple answer as to why sexually active teenagers do not make more use of contraceptives, even when they are readily available. Studies which have looked at factors related to contraceptive usage are reviewed in Table 32–8. Unfortunately many of these studies are flawed by one or more methodological problems. Probably the most serious of these is that there are very few longitudinal studies which begin by surveying adolescent behaviors and then follow subjects over a period of time to see which ones are successful contraceptors and which are failures. Many studies survey groups, such as college students who report using contraceptives; however, most of these studies do not follow up subjects to determine if their usage is effective. The converse of this problem involves the study of abortion clinic patients who are asked to report retrospectively on their contraceptive practices before their pregnancies. In this case there is clear evidence of contraceptive failure, but retrospective memory is being tested at a time of great stress for the subject. As is common in so much sex research, there are virtually no studies of contraceptive usage by men, despite the fact that the data already reported indicate clearly that adolescent women rely primarily upon men for contraception. When contraception fails studies report the factors related to the woman's poor contraceptive behaviors, when in most cases the adolescent female's pregnancy is the result of her male partner's contraceptive failure. The implicit assumption in most of this research is that contraception is the sole responsibility of the young woman.

While there are a variety of sociological and psycho-

(*Text continues on p. 582.*)

Table 32-8 Studies of Factors Associated with Contraceptive Use

FACTOR AND STUDY	SAMPLE	METHODS	FINDINGS
Age:			
Kantner & Zelnik, 1972	Large national sample of females, ages 15–19	Interviews	Contraceptive use increases with age. Use of medically prescribed methods was more characteristic of females, ages 18 or 19. Younger adolescents were more apt to rely on male methods.
Socioeconomic Status of Parents:			
Kantner & Zelnik, 1972	Large national sample of females, ages 15–19	Interviews	Black females with parent income of less than $10,000 a year and whose fathers were not college graduates were more apt to use orals or intrauterine devices (IUD's). Both white and black females whose fathers were college graduates were more likely to use some form of contraceptives. Black females were more apt to use orals if living in mother-headed home. Respondents from higher income families and those whose parents were college graduates had most accurate knowledge about time of ovulation and pregnancy risk.
Educational Level:			
Kantner & Zelnik, 1972	Large national sample of females, ages 15–19	Interviews	White but not black females in college dormitories or living alone were more apt to use orals; and college students were more apt to have accurate knowledge about ovulation and pregnancy risk.
Frequency of Intercourse:			
Kantner & Zelnik, 1972	Large national sample of females, ages 15–19	Interviews	Use of orals increases with frequency of intercourse, in steady relationships, and with marriage.
Luker, 1975	Sample of over 1000 women in abortion clinic	In-depth interviews	Use of orals increases with frequency of intercourse, in steady relationships, and with marriage.
Availability of Services:			
Bauman and Wilson, 1974a	Surveys of random samples of students at a southeastern university, 1968 and 1972	Self-administered anonymous questionnaires	Contraceptive use increased and methods improved between 1968 and 1972 in one university following an educational campaign and development of university-based clinic.
Kantner & Zelnik, 1972	Large national sample of females, ages 15–19	Interviews	Services were not easily available.
Luker, 1975	Sample of over 1000 women in abortion clinic.	In-depth interviews	Services were not available when needed; intercourse often not predictable; psychic costs of preplanning and of letting others know contraceptives are needed.
Presser, 1974	Sample of women with first-born children, New York City	Interviews, reinterviews	Contraceptives were not available when needed.
Psychological:			
MacDonald, 1970	Sample of 212 women at a state university	Tests of attitudes toward *locus of control* (Rotter's theory)	Nonusers of contraceptives were significantly more apt to think their lives are externally controlled.
Goldsmith, Gabrielson, & Gabrielson, 1972	Sample of 377 sexually active girls at a California family planning clinic	Questionnaire	Contraceptive-using nonpregnant girls were more apt to say they enjoyed sex than girls who were premaritally pregnant and not contraceptive users. Contraceptors also were more apt to be white, middle-class, college-bound.

Table 32–8 *(cont.)*

FACTOR AND STUDY	SAMPLE	METHODS	FINDINGS
Kantner & Zelnik, 1972; Shah, Zelnik, & Kantner, 1975	Large national sample of females, ages 15–19	Interviews	Major reasons given were believe can't get pregnant easily or won't get pregnant this time; will be lucky. Lesser reasons given were contraceptives interfere with sex pleasure and spontaneity; contraceptives are wrong or dangerous; pregnancy wanted.
Monsour & Stewart, 1973	Small group of female college students	Interviews	Guilt over own sex behavior inhibits contraceptive use.
Lindemann, 1974	Nonrandom sample of 2500 females, ages 13–16	Self-administered questionnaires	Girls must come to terms with own sex behavior gradually and realize possibility of a pregnancy. Three stages of contraceptive use are (1) trust to luck; (2) peer prescription—foam, condom, douche, rhythm, withdrawal; (3) medically prescribed methods.
Presser, 1974	Probability sample of wed and unwed women with firstborn children, New York City	Interviews and reinterviews	Major reasons given were believe won't get pregnant, pregnancy wanted. Other reasons given were side effects of orals and IUD's not liked; contraceptives interfere with pleasure.
Cvetkovich & Grote, 1975	Large nonrandom sample	Interviews and questionnaires	Males who were poor users of contraceptives seemed to be more apt to be socially irresponsible and oriented toward risk-taking; also said contraceptives were hard to get and to use. Males who were "good" contraceptive users were more apt to be concerned about sexual pleasure of partner as well as themselves, thought birth control was easily available, were not risk-takers. Females were more risk-taking, more passive dependent, less likely to use contraceptives. Contraceptive-using females were more apt to be trusting in interpersonal relationships, including relying on their partners to use contraceptives.
Fox, 1975	Random sample of 684 male and female undergraduates at one university	Self-administered questionnaires	Females high on Rotter's self-sufficiency scale and who hold equal sex-role attitudes were significantly more apt to use effective contraceptives. Opposite findings for males.
Luker, 1975	Sample of over 1000 women in abortion clinic	In-depth interviews	Major reasons given were believe won't get pregnant; fear might not be able to get pregnant if continue using orals or perhaps not fertile; fear of possible side effects; not in a steady secure love relationship. Men demand coitus even when contraceptives are not available. Benefits of pregnancy can outweigh contraceptive cost.
Miller, 1976	Small clinic sample of sexually active women, ages 17–30 (predominantly white group)	In-depth interviews	Contraceptives were used when fear of pregnancy was high. Use increases as women become more involved with partner, more accepting of own sexuality, more independent of parents. High anxiety and low ego strength often inhibit contraceptive use.

Table 32-8 (cont.)

FACTOR AND STUDY	SAMPLE	METHODS	FINDINGS
Reichelt, 1976	Sample of 500 adolescent girls at a Detroit family planning clinic	Counselor interviews	Major reasons given were not wanting sex to seem planned, fear of side effects; not wanting contraceptives to interfere with sex pleasure.
Rosen, Martindale, & Grisdela, 1976	Sample of over 2000 women with problem pregnancies known to Michigan agencies	Self-administered questionnaires	Contraceptive users significantly more likely to score high on items measuring self-evaluation of personal competence and low on items revealing traditional female role attitudes.
Steinhoff, 1976	Sample of 200 abortion and maternity patients in a Hawaiian maternity hospital	Interviews	Passive orientation and little understanding of cause of pregnancy lead to inadequate contraceptive use. Other reasons were youth, lack of sex enjoyment, not going steady.
Oskamp, Mindick, Berger, & Notta, 1978; Oskamp & Mindick, 1981	Random sample of 283 teenage women at birth control centers in southern California followed longitudinally for three years, beginning in 1973–1974	Measured 11 personality and social variables with battery of tests, questionnaires and interviews. Multivariate data analysis to study successful versus unsuccessful contraceptors	Successful contraceptors were high in sexual knowledge and planfulness and had little sexual activity. They also tended to be higher in measures of socialization, feelings of personal efficacy, positive attitude about contraception, level of adjustment, and past contraceptive success, although results in these areas were not consistently strong.
Race:			
Ladner, 1971	Anthropological study in black urban ghetto	Interviews and observations	Fear of contraceptives was widespread in community, especially among older women. Contraceptives viewed as cause of infertility, harm to baby; fertility was highly valued.
Kantner & Zelnik, 1972	Large national sample of females, ages 15–19	Interviews	Fewer black females showed accurate knowledge about "safe" periods during the month. Three-fourths of total sample thought pregnancy could occur immediately after menarche; fewer black females thought this. Accuracy of knowledge increased with age and college attendance.
Population Reference Bureau, 1975	Not applicable	Review of research and of other materials, including historical documents	Some of the "black power" organizations have expressed opposition to contraceptives as a form of genocide; males tend to be more opposed than females.
Shah, Zelnik, & Kantner, 1975	Large national sample of females, ages 15–19	Interviews	Thirty-one percent of sexually active white females and 17 percent of sexually active black females said they used contraceptives consistently. The white respondents were twice as likely to cite safe time of month, and black respondents were twice as likely to cite low risk and desire for pregnancy as reasons for inconsistent use or nonuse of contraceptives.

Source: Adapted from Chilman, 1979.

logical factors which appear to be related to failure to use contraceptives, the most prominent one is probably the failure of the adolescent woman or man to accept the fact that s/he is sexually active. For many adolescents being sexually active involves a major revision of one's self-concept and an awareness of one's maturity and responsibility which many young people are not prepared to accept. The first sexual encounter, therefore, is often rationalized as an accident, a moment of passion or weakness, an experiment, or a chance to find out what all the talk is about. Having lost his/her virginity the adolescent does not expect to experience sexual intercourse again for some time, and as Kantner and Zelnik's data (1972) showed, most do not, so that it is relatively easy for the adolescent to continue the notion that s/he is not really sexually active.

As sexual activity continues over time, many young women engage in what Luker (1975) described as a rational decision-making process to justify their continued contraceptive risk taking. The young women in Luker's study balanced the benefits of using contraceptives against what they perceived to be the costs. These included the psychic costs of acknowledging that one was sexually active, the costs of planning ahead for intercourse, the costs of continuing use of contraceptives even if one was not expecting intercourse, the costs of obtaining contraceptives at the time they were needed, the costs of possibly losing a man who asks for intercourse when the woman was not protected, the costs of possible negative side effects from the pill or other birth control devices, and the fear of infertility which prevented women from taking the pill. There is now evidence (Lindemann, 1974; Miller, 1976; Steinhoff, 1976) that, as participation in sexual activities continues over time, adolescents become much more proficient in their use of birth control techniques and move through the stages described by Lindemann (1974) as (1) the "natural," (2) "peer prescription," and (3) "expert." The longer a young woman has a relationship with a man, the more likely she is to use contraceptives and the more effective these techniques are likely to be, apparently because in an involved relationship she accepts her sexual behavior and plans ahead adequately. On the other hand a wide variety of life-disrupting events, such as separation from boyfriend, death of a parent, graduation from school, or job loss, can disrupt use of contraceptives and increase risk taking (Miller, 1976).

A second important factor in adolescents' poor use of contraceptives apparently has to do with the fact that many adolescents are ambivalent about getting pregnant and do not fear pregnancy as much as might be expected (Goldsmith, Gabrielson, & Gabrielson, 1972; Luker, 1975; Sorenson, 1973). For this group of adolescents pregnancy is perceived to offer a number of advantages and desirable outcomes, including confirmation of the girl's status and identity as a woman, elevation to the status of being a mother and being equal with one's own parents, providing a dependent child to love, testing the commitment of the father, proving one's fertility, pleasing a lover by presenting him with a baby, getting attention from parents and other adults, and in some cases, providing the woman with eligibility for receipt of welfare funds and her own independent income (Chilman, 1979).

Sociological studies of group characteristics which show a statistical relationship to contraceptive failure and risk taking have been well described by Chilman (1979). According to her review, poor, inconsistent, or nonuse of contraceptives by sexually active adolescent women is related to the following social characteristics:

1. Being younger than age 18—Young women are less likely to accept their sexual activity and to prepare for it than are older women.
2. Being single—Married women are much more likely to use contraceptives than are single women.
3. Not being in a steady, committed, dating relationship—Women who are involved with a man over time are

much more likely to use contraceptives than are women who are not involved.
4. Having intercourse sporadically—Regular intercourse leads one to expect and plan for such activity.
5. Being a fundamentalist Protestant in religious belief—Women who espouse fundamentalist beliefs tend to deny that they are involved in sexual activity and are unlikely to admit such behavior to themselves by using contraceptives.
6. Being from a lower socioeconomic status family.
7. Desiring a pregnancy.
8. Being black or Hispanic.
9. Not being a college student.
10. Not having had a pregancy experience—Women who have had an abortion or a baby are much more likely to use contraceptives than are women who have never been pregnant.

A similar review of the personality and attitudinal factors associated with contraceptive use has been provided by Oskamp and Mindick (1981). In their review contraceptive failure or nonuse is related to the following personality and attitudinal characteristics:

1. Viewing oneself as not sexually active—The failure to accept one's sexuality and the adult responsibility which sexual activity connotes.
2. Being poorly socialized—Having incomplete learning or acceptance of the norms of society, being deviant and irresponsible.
3. Having a poor sense of personal efficacy—Feeling incompetent, having an external locus of control of reinforcement, being passive, and expressing learned helplessness.
4. Having poor cognitive skills—Poor coping skills, being unable to solve problems, being slow to acquire useful knowledge, not having enough knowledge of birth control and reproduction.
5. Not having a future orientation—Not being planful and reflective about one's life and actions, not being in control of one's impulses.
6. Being neurotic, anxious, and having poor social adjustment—Having a high level of sex guilt, not being able to express oneself well or to communicate well with one's partner.
7. Having negative attitudes and intentions about contraception—Being fearful, mistrustful, or ignorant about contraceptives and not intending to use them for whatever reasons.

Oskamp and Mindick's own careful study of adolescent women at family planning clinics in southern California over a five-year period clearly illustrates the complexities of this type of research. Testing a variety of personality and attitudinal measures in a multivariate analysis of the longitudinal scores of successful and unsuccessful contraceptors, they found that the data best supported the factors of sexual knowledge and planfulness with the data being mixed with regard to level of socialization, personal efficacy, attitudes and intentions, and level of past sexual activity. One interesting note in their discussion is that, while a number of cognitive and attitudinal variables seem to interact in the relationship to contraceptive behavior, intelligence, as measured by IQ tests, does not seem to be related in any significant way.

Sexually Transmitted Diseases

One of the most serious consequences of the rise in rates of premarital sexual intercourse among adolescents is that sexually transmitted diseases—gonorrhea and both primary and secondary syphilis—have become serious health hazards for the young. The rate of syphilis among adolescents has not risen in the last 25 years; however, gonorrhea rates have tripled since 1956 with the greatest increase being among young women. Statistics from the Center for Disease Control for 1978 (Center for Disease Control, 1979) provide a breakdown in rates according to age. For both primary and secondary syphilis in 1978, the rate per 100,000 in the population for the age group 0 to 9 was 0.0; for ages 10 to 14 the rate was 0.8 (0.6 for males, 1.0 for females); for ages 15 to 19 the rate was 14.6 (16.5 for males, 12.7 for females); and for ages 20 to 24 the rate was 30.8 (46.0 for males, 16.4 for females). For gonorrhea in 1978 the rate per 100,000 in the population for ages 0 to 9 was 8.7 (4.4 for males, 13.1 for females); for ages 10 to 14 the rate was 49.3 (22.8 for males, 76.8 for females); for ages 15 to 19 the rate was 1228.9 (977.6 for males, 1481.7 for females); and for ages 20 to 24 the rate was 1977.6 (2409.9 for males, 1568.7 for females). As a point of comparison the gonorrhea rate among 20- to 24-year-olds is the highest in the United States among all age groups with the rate for 15- to 19-year-olds being second highest.

Abortion

Abortion has only become a subject of systematic study in the last decade, particularly since 1973 when the U.S. Supreme Court declared unconstitutional all state laws which prohibited abortion during the first three months of a pregnancy. In the last several years the tendency has been for the courts to support right of free choice by pregnant women to decide whether or not to have an abortion, so that at the present time there is no legal prohibition against abortion during the first trimester, and in many instances an adolescent can obtain an abortion at a clinic where the fees will be paid by the federal government.

Until these changes in the law, abortion was a secretive and expensive procedure which was generally only available to girls who were relatively well off. For this reason abortion rates were highest among middle- and upper-class white women until recently. According to Baldwin (1976) the abortion rate for teenagers rose by more than 60 percent between 1972 and 1975, while the rate for women under age 15 doubled during the same time. In a study of abortion among white, black, and Hispanic teenagers in New York City, Pakter, Nelson, and Svigir (1975) found that abortion rates rose steadily between 1970 and 1975 with the greatest increase occurring among Puerto Rican teenagers. As of 1975 in New York City, the rate of abortion per 1000 live births for women under age 19 was 543 for whites, 828 for Puerto Ricans, and 1130 for blacks. These rates are supported by data from the Center for Disease Control reported by Chilman (1979), which showed the national abortion rate was 326 abortions per 1000 live births among white women of all ages and 420 for black women. Overall abortion rates vary greatly from one region of the United

States to another, from rural to urban areas, and according to ethnicity; however, there has been a reversal in rates among white and black women with the rate of abortions among black women now exceeding that for white women by a sizable margin.

Public acceptance of abortion has increased markedly since 1965. As of 1972 more than three-quarters of the people interviewed in a National Opinion Research Center Poll approved of abortions when the mother's health was endangered (83 percent), when the pregnancy resulted from rape (74 percent), or when there was a good chance the child would be deformed (74 percent). Rates of approval for abortions resulting from what are sometimes called "soft reasons" were considerably lower but still were twice as great as polls taken seven years before (mother not married, 40 percent; mother can't afford child, 45 percent; married mother doesn't want more children, 38 percent). People who tend to be the most accepting of abortions tend to be white, Protestant, and from high educational and income levels (American Council on Education, 1970; Gallup, 1974; McCormick, 1975; Sorenson, 1973; Yankelovich, 1974; Zelnick & Kantner, 1975).

Studies of the characteristics of women who seek abortions are reviewed in Table 32–9. The profile which emerges from these studies is one of a woman who tends to be a contraceptive user, who is single, who has high educational and occupational aspirations, who comes from a stable middle-class or higher socioeconomic background, who feels that she has control over her life, and who sees herself as a competent person.

There have been relatively few studies of the psychological effects of abortions upon women who have them, and a review of these is presented in Table 32–10. There is very little evidence that abortion has any serious harmful effects on adolescents who experience them. The majority of women who abort report feelings of relief and happiness at being able to continue their lives without the changes which a baby would bring. The most frequently reported negative effects are feelings of mournfulness and feelings of guilt, both of which tend to be felt more by women who are Roman Catholic, young, of lower socioeconomic background, and who feel that abortion is being forced upon them (Evans, Selstad, & Welcher, 1976). About 15 percent of women who have abortions experience emotional problems which require treatment; in most cases, these women have had a history of psychosocial difficulties or experienced physical complications as a result of the abortion. There is little evidence that having an abortion once leads women to have a second, although there is at least one study (Robbins & Lynn, 1973) indicating that the rate of repeat abortions is increasing, with the rate being 33 percent in one New York State clinic.

Out-of-Wedlock Births to Adolescents

The combined effects of increasing rates of premarital sexual intercourse, insufficient use of contraceptives, and declining rates of teenage marriage have resulted in a sharp increase in the rate of illegitimate births to girls aged 15 to 19 over the last forty years. From 1940 to 1975 the rate of illegitimate births per 1000 unmarried girls aged 15 to 19 in the United States tripled, rising from

(Text continues on p. 587.)

Table 32-9 Major Studies of Characteristics of Women Who Choose Abortion

STUDY AND DATE	SAMPLE	METHODS	FINDINGS
Gebhard, Pomeroy, Martin, & Christensen, 1958	Used data obtained in the Kinsey survey; large but inadequate sample	Interviews with many subjects concerning sex behavior, including pregnancy, birth, and abortion	Abortion rates were higher in the better educated of both races
Gabrielson, Goldsmith, Potts, Matthews, & Gabrielson, 1971	Sexually active adolescent females known at family planning clinics in the San Francisco Bay area	Questionnaires	Abortion patients, pregnant nonaborters, and nonpregnant contraceptors were compared. Black abortion choosers were of higher socioeconomic status (SES) origins than black nonabortion patients. Contraceptive users were more apt to favor abortion. Whites and older girls had more favorable attitudes. All respondents had conflicting attitudes toward abortion.
Bracken & Suigar, 1972	Sample of 443 patients at the abortion service of the Yale-New Haven Hospital	Clinic records	Early aborters were more likely to be between ages 20 and 35, single, childless, white, and contraceptive users.
Diamond, Steinhoff, Palmore, & Smith, 1973	Ongoing studies in Hawaii of abortion, birth control and pregnancy of all clinic and hospital patients (about 50 percent sample loss)	Questionnaires and hospital charts	Aborters were more likely to be single, contraceptive users, and older.
Oppel, Athanasiou, Cushner, Sasaki, Unger, & Wolf, 1972	Early and late aborters known to Johns Hopkins University Hospital, Baltimore, Md.	Questionnaires	Early aborters were more likely to have used diaphragm or intrauterine device and more than one contraceptive method; to have shared information about their pregnancy with the putative father; to be between ages 20 and 35, of higher SES, and nontraditional in attitudes.
Kane & Lachenbruch, 1973	Small biased sample of 99 white adolescents who sought an abortion compared with 33 residents of a maternity home	Neuroticism scale	Higher scores were obtained by nonabortion group for measures of anxiety, impulsivity, and "total" neuroticism; a methodologically weak study.
Butts & Sporakowski, 1974	Similar to Kane sample	Questionnaires	Nonaborters tended to be older, sexually permissive, low in religiosity.
Evans, Selstad, & Welcher, 1976	Sample of 333 Anglo and Mexican-American single adolescents known to pregnancy clinics in Ventura County, Calif.	Interviews and six-month follow-up comparing abortion patients, patients who bore child outside of marriage, patients who married and bore child	Abortion patients were more likely to have been doing well in school before pregnancy and returned to school later. Other respondents were poor students who dropped out of school for the most part. Those on welfare before pregnancy were less likely to marry or choose abortion. Eighty percent of young, unwed mothers and 20 percent of those who married received welfare aid. Nonaborters were more likely to be ages 16–17, Chicano, Catholic; to come from low-income families; and to have divorced parents. Aborters who later regretted decision were more likely to be Catholic, Chicano; of low SES origins; to do poor work in school; to have conservative attitudes toward abortion; to feel abortion was forced on them by parents or sex partners.

Table 32-9 (*cont.*)

STUDY AND DATE	SAMPLE	METHODS	FINDINGS
Rosen, Hudson, & Martindale, 1976	Sample of 2000 women in Michigan known to human services agencies because they sought help with a problem pregnancy; compared aborters with nonaborters	Questionnaires and testing	Aborters significantly were more likely to have used contraceptives in the past. Aborters obtained significantly higher scores on tests that measured feelings of self-competence. Aborters who obtained abortion in first trimester had significantly lower scores with respect to traditional sex-role attitudes.
Steinhoff, 1976	Subset of a sample from the ongoing, large Hawaii study; compared aborters with non-aborters	Interviews	Abortion choosers were more apt to have strong future orientation; high educational-vocational goals; to value control over their lives; to be Caucasian or Japanese and of skilled working-class or higher SES origins; to reject the concept of welfare dependency. Young adolescent aborters usually had decision made for them by parents.

Source: Chilman, 1979.

Table 32-10 Major Studies on Psychological Effects of Abortion

STUDY AND DATE	SAMPLE	METHODS	FINDINGS
Bracken & Suigar, 1972	Sample of 489 succecssive abortion patients in a New York City hospital	Two self-administered questionnaires; data on reactions taken in a recovery room	Self-reported negative reactions were associated with being single, young, lacking support from partner or parents.
Osofsky & Osofsky, 1972	Sample of 380 abortion patients in a Syracuse hospital; many between ages 16 and 20	Interviews shortly after abortion performed	Majority of patients expressed happiness and relief. About 16 percent of patients were judged unhappy, and one-fourth expressed guilt. Catholics were the most apt to express guilt.
Barglow & Weinstein, 1973	Sample of 25 adolescent girls undergoing abortion in first trimester	Interviews soon after abortion	Impression was that many had a mourning experience after abortion. Difficulties arose when the decision to abort was heavily influenced by parents, peers, partners.
Martin, 1973	Nonrandom sample of adolescents who had had an abortion and volunteered to be interviewed	Taped interviews and judgments of psychological traits by three judges (methods questionable); unspecified correlation techniques to assess relationship of many traits to self-reported, postabortion adjustment	Findings need to be viewed with caution. Girls who had difficult post-abortion adjustments appeared to be emotionally involved with their pregnancies, lack of friends, have poor relations with their parents, be unhappy about choosing an abortion, have received no support from sex partner. The situations of the girls who had favorable postabortion adjustments tended to be opposite.
Monsour & Stewart, 1973	Sample of 20 young single college students who had had an abortion	Interviews 6 months after abortion	All continued in college; only one reported postabortion adjustment problems.
Perez-Reyes & Falk, 1973	Sample of 41 girls under age 16 who had hospital abortions	Interviews and testing before and soon after procedure	About two-thirds said they were happy that they had had abortion; about 15 percent had adverse feelings of depression, guilt, anger, and anxiety. The physical and mental health of the patients appeared to be better after abortion than immediately before.

Table 32–10 *(cont.)*

STUDY AND DATE	SAMPLE	METHODS	FINDINGS
Evans, Selstad, & Welcher, 1976	Sample of 333 Anglo and Mexican-American single adolescent girls known to pregnancy health services in Ventura County, Calif.	Interviews and reinterviews following abortion (six months later)	About 20 percent regretted the abortion. They were more likely to be Catholic, Chicano, young; of low socioeconomic status origins; poor students; to have conservative abortion attitudes; and to feel abortion was forced upon them.

Source: Chilman, 1979.

about 7.4 in 1940 to 24.2 in 1975. Since 1955 the illegitimacy rate of nonwhite teenagers has been 7 to 13 times higher than that for white teenagers (Chilman, 1979; Sklar & Berkov, 1974). As of 1975 the illegitimacy rate for women in their twenties was higher than that for teenagers; however, rates for teenagers, particularly girls under 15, have been rising rapidly while rates for older women have been declining. It is particularly interesting that the illegitimacy rate among teenagers has risen despite the increased availability and acceptance of abortions.

Increasingly teenagers who have children premaritally are raising their babies themselves, rather than placing the children with an agency for adoption. This is particularly true for white women, while black women have always tended to keep their babies born out of wedlock (Baldwin, 1976). There is also less likelihood that an unmarried mother will marry either to legitimate an unborn child or to provide a father for children after birth. This trend is reflected in the marriage rate for teenage girls which declined from 80.9 marriages per 1000 single girls aged 14 to 19 in 1960 to 67.7 in 1970. As a result of this set of factors, there has been an increasing number of girls under 20 who have more than one child which they are raising without being married. The consequences of this are not clearly known at this time; however, the fact that there is an increasing number of unmarried teenage mothers who are raising their young children before they themselves are fully mature indicates a change in child-rearing patterns which needs a great deal more study.

Studies of the major sociological factors which appear to be related to adolescent illegitimate births are reviewed in Table 32–11. For the most part these studies reveal that the relationships between illegitimacy and such common factors as race, socioeconomic status, employment status, and poverty level are very complex. For example while being poor is statistically associated with increased rates of illegitimacy, it is unclear whether poverty makes marriage impossible which leads to illegitimacy or whether having a baby and not being married leads one to be poor. A particularly complex issue is the relationship of race to having a baby out of wedlock. While black teenagers are less likely to use contraceptives and are more likely to have babies born out of wedlock than whites, the reasons for this are not so easy to explain as might be assumed. Certainly racial discrimination and the lack of opportunity for blacks has held them in lower socioeconomic positions with the attendant lack of education and economic resources; however, there is considerable discussion about the fact that marriage is often perceived to be undesirable for a lower-class black woman and that the variety of forms of the family among blacks, including the presence of many extended families where grandparents can help care for babies, make marriage for the pregnant young black woman less important than it might be if such help from relatives were not available (Billingsley, 1970; Moore & Caldwell, 1977; Ross & Sawhill, 1975; Stack, 1974). Furstenberg's (1976) longitudinal study of mostly black, low-income, urban adolescents who had babies found that pregnancy was felt by 60 percent of the subjects to be an undesirable event, while 20 percent had mixed feelings and 20 percent said that they were happy to be pregnant. These findings, while representing a small sample, are particularly interesting in that there is some thought that pregnancy might be desired by low-income adolescent girls as a source of personal gratification and identity. This does not appear to be the case (Ladner, 1971; Rains, 1971; Rainwater, 1970; Schulz, 1969; Stack, 1974). At best an unmarried black teenager's pregnancy is considered undesirable but is accepted as an unfortunate and almost inevitable event by most low-income black families.

A subject of considerable controversy has been the relationship between welfare status and illegitimacy. Since Aid to Families with Dependent Children (AFDC) is available to unmarried teenage mothers and since almost half of the beneficiaries of this program are single mothers, it has been suggested that such welfare payments actually encourage, or cause, illegitimacy. The few studies which provide data with which to investigate this issue seem to indicate that the availability of welfare funds does not affect whether a young woman becomes pregnant but may act as an inducement for her to keep her baby, rather than to have an abortion or place the child for adoption, and to remain single if the prospect for marriage is not good (Moore & Caldwell, 1977; Ross & Sawhill, 1975). A study by Presser (1974) found that there were no differences in the fertility attitudes or behaviors of women receiving welfare payments and those who were not. Furstenberg (1976) also found that teenage girls did not get pregnant in order to receive welfare funds but that adolescent girls raised in female-headed households where there was a long history of social and psychological deprivation were more likely to become pregnant and to have the baby without marrying the father who was unable to support a family.

There have been too few studies of psychological factors which are related to illegitimacy; however, there are data indicating that unmarried teenage mothers do not differ from their married peers in any significant ways (Hatcher, 1973; Meyerowitz & Malev, 1973; Parker, cited by Moore & Caldwell, 1977; Pope, 1967; Vincent, 1961). This finding is interesting in light of widely believed stereotypes among professionals in psychology,

(Text continues on p. 590.)

Table 32-11 Factors Studied as Causes of Illegitimacy among Adolescents

FACTOR AND STUDY	SAMPLE	METHODS	FINDINGS
Social:			
Christensen, 1958	Comparison of illegitimacy rates of three cultures	Analysis of secondary data	Concludes that higher illegitimacy rates in a permissive culture (Denmark) than in more conservative ones (Indiana and Utah—most conservative) are a result, in part, of variations in social norms.
Cutright, 1968	Large amounts of secondary data from many countries	Complex statistical analysis	Among the many conclusions drawn by Cutright are countries with restrictive norms concerning illegitimacy do not consistently have lower rates of illegitimacy than countries with permissive norms. No consistent pattern of causes is found from country to country.
Presser, 1976a	New York City sample of mothers with firstborn children	Interviews and reinterviews	Hypothesis that type of socialization for female role affects early childbearing was not confirmed.
Welfare Programs:			
Cutright, 1971	Large amounts of secondary data from many countries	Complex statistical analysis	There is no evidence across cultures that the availability of welfare benefits, regardless of size of benefit, increases illegitimacy rates.
Presser, 1974	New York City sample of mothers with firstborn children	Interviews and reinterviews	No significant differences were found in fertility attitudes and behaviors between welfare recipients and nonrecipients. Nonwelfare mothers were more likely to urge their daughters to keep their babies.
Ross & Sawhill, 1975	Large bodies of secondary data and review of related research	Complex statistical data analysis	Aid to Families with Dependent Children (AFDC) policies make it difficult for families headed by both natural parents to receive public assistance, thus encouraging nonmarriage of these parents. Welfare reform needed. Availability of welfare benefits for mother and children makes it possible for mothers to avoid marriages lacking a sound financial, social and psychological base. Welfare benefits are often large enough to exceed what many husbands would be able to earn, even though benefits are budgeted to meet only a minimum standard of living. Implies improvement of employment and wage opportunities for both sexes.
Moore & Caldwell, 1976	Analysis of large bodies of secondary data plus review of related research	Complex data analysis	Concludes there is no evidence that AFDC benefits, regardless of size, serve as an economic incentive to childbearing outside of marriage. Availability of benefits may influence some women not to have an abortion or not to place the child for adoption.
Poverty and Socioeconomic Status:			
Vincent, Haney, & Cochrane, 1969	Large sample of females in North Carolina	Interviews	Poverty and illegitimacy were found to be more highly associated in the 1940s than in the late 1950s and early 1960s. Early childbearing was associated with later poverty, unemployment, and female-headed households. It was impossible to untangle causes and consequences of teenage childbearing.

Table 32–11 (*cont.*)

FACTOR AND STUDY	SAMPLE	METHODS	FINDINGS
"Selected Vital and Health Statistics in Poverty and Nonpoverty Areas of 19 Large Cities: U.S., 1969–1971," U.S. Department of Health, Education, & Welfare, 1975	Analysis of census data	Comparison of illegitimacy rates in so-called poverty census tracts in 19 cities	Illegitimacy rates were higher in "poverty" census tracts. This does not prove, however, that poverty is a major cause of illegitimacy. Illegitimacy may cause reduced family income and lead more unwed mothers to move into low-income neighborhoods.
Moore & Caldwell, 1977	Analysis of large bodies of secondary data and review of related research	Complex data analysis	Highest rates of adolescent illegitimacy were found among older black teenagers and those young women with poverty origins whose mothers and fathers had less than a college education.
Psychological[a]:			
Vincent, 1961	Sample of unmarried mothers and matching sample of young women who were not unmarried mothers	Interviews and psychological tests	No significant differences were found between the two groups.
Pope, 1967	Large sample of females in North Carolina	Interviews	Differences betweeen married and unmarried mothers were not found in their social lives and with respect to earlier courtship behavior. The only difference between the two groups was observed to be that the unwed group was "unlucky" in getting pregnant.
Hatcher, 1973	Small group of adolescent girls in an abortion clinic	Interviews	Findings show that youngest girls lacked knowledge about conception and contraception and tended to deny that they were pregnant. An older group had better knowledge but blamed pregnancy on authority figures; oldest group was more realistic and independent in seeking a solution. Study concludes that adolescent behaviors concerning premarital pregnancy are strongly affected by stages of cognitive development.
Meyerowitz & Malev, 1973	Used attitude test data and census data in large community	Analyzed data in terms of neighborhoods with high and low illegitimacy rates	Neighborhoods with high illegitimacy rates had school populations that tested higher on attitudes of powerlessness and social rejection. It appears that such attitudes would be correlated with numerous other features of these neighborhoods (such as low socioeconomic status and social disorganization). The relationship of illegitimacy per se to these attitudes seems unwarranted from this study.
Parker, cited by Moore & Caldwell, 1977	All Minnesota school children in ninth grade; a subsample selected	Subsample of 117 girls who later became premaritally pregnant matched to a subsample of those who did not. Minnesota Multiphasic Personality Inventory scores compared	No significant differences were found in measured personality characteristics. The scores of later premaritally pregnant were observed to be somewhat higher with respect to being somewhat more energetic, nonconformist, more outgoing, and socially active. Intelligence test scores of later premaritally pregnant were also somewhat lower.
Race[b]:			
Cutright, 1972	Analysis of large bodies of secondary data	Complex data analysis	Cutright concludes that much of the rise in adolescent illegitimacy since 1940 is due to an earlier age at menarche and reduced fetal loss through improved health care; this particularly applies to black families.

Table 32–11 *(cont.)*

FACTOR AND STUDY	SAMPLE	METHODS	FINDINGS
Kantner & Zelnik, 1972	Large national sample of 15- to 19-year-old females	Interviews	Black adolescent females are less likely than white teenagers are to have an abortion or marry to legitimate an unborn child. (Also on the average black females start intercourse at earlier ages and are less likely to use contraceptives consistently.)

[a] There are a large number of seriously inadequate studies of unmarried mothers and two equally inadequate ones of unmarried fathers. So little confidence can be placed in the results that they are not cited here.

[b] A number of small anthropological studies in urban black ghettos provide evidence to indicate that marriage simply to legitimate a child is considered neither practical nor moral. Illegitimacy is not accepted as desirable, but it is not viewed, generally, as being highly reprehensible. The extended black family, which puts a high value on children, usually helps with childcare. Although a couple may not marry, black fathers often continue an interest in the child and his/her mother and lend financial support within their means (Billingsley, 1970; Liebow, 1967; Ladner, 1971; Rainwater, 1970; Schulz, 1969; Stack, 1974). These attitudes are not found among upwardly mobile or middle-class black families.

Source: Chilman, 1979.

medicine, education, and social work that unwed teenage mothers have deep-seated personality weaknesses which compel them to become pregnant in order to fulfill themselves or to act out some Oedipal impulse. To the contrary while many unwed teenage mothers can be characterized by the same set of psychological descriptors which Oskamp and Mindick found held for contraceptive failures, as described earlier, perhaps the greatest distinction between the unwed mothers and their unwed sisters who are not mothers is that the young mothers were not so lucky with their unprotected sexual behavior.

In summary while the causes of illegitimacy among teenagers are best understood in the larger sense of the causes of increased sexual activity, poor use of contraception, decreasing marriage rates, and differential response to abortion opportunities, there seems to be no clear way to separate teenage illegitimacy from the host of factors which are bound together in the concept of a "culture of poverty." Being poor does not mean, as it did 20 years ago, that one is necessarily more sexually active, nor that one is less sexually informed, nor that one is necessarily less likely to use contraception and to have an abortion, but it does seem to mean that one is more likely to keep a baby, rather than to place it for adoption, and that one is less likely to get married simply to legitimize the baby's birth.

The consequence of illegitimacy for teenagers and their children are reviewed in Table 32–12. Once again the findings of these studies do not support the widely held stereotype that teenagers who have babies out of wedlock make poor parents or that being an unmarried parent necessarily hinders one's educational or occupational outcomes. As with so much of this research, associations between factors and unmarried-parent status reveal little about what the results of having a baby out of wedlock are likely to be. For instance unmarried teenage mothers are less likely to finish high school than are unmarried teenagers who are not mothers; however, it is just as reasonable to say that falling behind in school and having low educational aspirations causes one to have an illegitimate child as it is to say that having an illegitimate child causes one to leave school. Similar reasoning can be applied to findings that unmarried teenage mothers have lower incomes and poorer records of successful employment than other teenagers who are not mothers.

It does seem to be true that children born to mothers younger than age 18 have a higher incidence of mental retardation, low birthweight, learning disabilities, and physical complications than do babies born to mothers between the ages of 19 and 39. Infant mortality rates for babies born to mothers under age 15 are substantially higher than for the rest of the population, with 6 percent of the babies of these very young mothers dying in the first year (Chase, 1970; Jekel, 1975; Kovar, 1968; Menken, 1975).

The few studies of parenting behavior of adolescent mothers with babies born out of wedlock (Chilman, 1979; Furstenberg, 1976) indicate that 85 percent of these young mothers are committed to their children and seem to be very adequate parents. Furthermore there were no significant differences according to age or marital status of mothers in their mid-teens and those in their early twenties on measures of education, income, or employment.

In summary illegitimacy rates for teenagers have risen sharply in the last 20 years, despite increasing acceptance and availability of contraception and abortion. In 1979 it is estimated by the U.S. Department of Health, Education and Welfare that about one-third of all babies born to teenage mothers were born out of wedlock and that one-half of all such children were born to teenage mothers. Sociological factors that are associated with illegitimacy are race, ethnicity, low socioeconomic status, poverty, and low educational attainment. Studies of psychological factors associated with illegitimacy appear to be less clear but are similar to those found for poor use of contraception and abortion refusal, such as low sexual knowledge, poor sense of personal competence, and lack of future orientation and planfulness. Despite these associations the available research seems to indicate that unmarried teenage mothers do not suffer serious adverse effects from illegitimacy and are not significantly different in terms of their income, employment, and educational outcomes from their sisters who live in similar circumstances without a baby. Furthermore the research tends to support the notion that teenagers with babies born out of wedlock are adequate parents and have a serious commitment to the care and well-being of their offspring. There is little support in the literature for the idea that obtaining welfare funds through Aid to Families with Dependent Children acts as an incentive for young women to become pregnant, although such financial

(Text continues on p. 595.)

Table 32-12 Studies of the Consequences of Illegitimacy for Adolescents and Their Children

FACTOR AND STUDY	SAMPLE	METHODS	FINDINGS
Health:			
Vandenberg, 1976	Secondary data of a large sample of families known to a major health service in California	Complex data analysis	There was a higher incidence of premature delivery of infants of young mothers; this also was true of their subsequent deliveries. There was a lower use of early prenatal care and of pediatric prevention services following child's birth, higher use of emergency and hospital care. Children, at age five, were shorter in stature and had a greater tendency to poor hearing.
Education:			
Bowerman, Irish, & Pope, 1966	Large sample of predominantly black, low-income women in North Carolina	Interviews	Many respondents said, retrospectively that they dropped out of high school because they were pregnant; yet just as many left for other reasons.
Coombs & Freedman, 1970	Data from Detroit area survey; large sample	Complex data analysis of interview findings	Men whose wives had been premaritally pregnant were less likely to have finished high school at the time of marriage, regardless of their age at marriage.
Cutright, 1973	Data from 1967 Economic Opportunity National Survey	Complex data analysis	Forty-one percent of white women and 24 percent of black women who had an illegitimate birth were high school graduates, compared with 59 percent of whites and 40 percent of blacks whose first births were within marriage.
Presser, 1976	A random sample of New York City mothers with firstborn children	Interviews and reinterviews	Adolescent mothers were less likely to be high school graduates than older mothers; welfare benefits helped a number of teenagers continue their schooling.
Furstenberg, 1976	Longitudinal study of a select sample of low-income, predominantly black, adolescent females	Interviews, tests, observations	Adolescent mothers who were most apt to continue schooling were those with high educational ambition. Marriage interfered with schooling unless husband also educationally ambitious and supported wife's goals. A second pregnancy usually prevented further education. Special schools for teenage pregnant girls did not seem more effective in holding students through graduation than other schools. Majority of young mothers did finish high school.
Employment and Income:			
Bowerman, Irish, & Pope, 1966	Large sample of predominantly black, low-income women in North Carolina	Interviews	Unmarried mothers, compared with married ones, were not significantly different in employment and income. However data from this study, analyzed by Vincent, Haney, and Cochrane (1969), showed early childbearing made a difference.
Sauber & Corrigan, 1970	A six-year follow-up study of a sample of unwed mothers in New York City	Interviews	No single pattern of economic adjustment was found, but by end of six years a larger proportion had sought public assistance. One-half were self-sufficient.

Table 32–12 (*cont.*)

FACTOR AND STUDY	SAMPLE	METHODS	FINDINGS
Furstenberg, 1976	Longitudinal study of a select sample of low-income, predominantly black, adolescent females	Interviews, tests, observations	Over a five-year period a number of income patterns prevail. Most common income sources were personal earnings, public assistance, husband's earnings. Adolescents who had not had a premarital pregnancy were in best economic condition, but this group had a higher level of ambition. Respondents went on and off welfare in response to changes in job market. Those who married and then separated were in worse condition than those who remained single. Adolescent mothers whose families had been on welfare were most apt to go on welfare themselves. Income was not related to age at first pregnancy. Having more than one child often caused mother to need public assistance. Employment of young mothers was dependent on job market, childcare resources, high levels of educational ambition, high school graduation, and being at least age 20.
Presser, 1975	A large sample of New York City mothers with firstborn children	Interviews and reinterviews	Employment of mothers was mostly related to whether they had held jobs before the child was born, more or less regardless of the mother's age. Teenage mothers were more apt to be on welfare (50 percent of them). Three-fourths of the welfare group were in high school.
Steinhoff, 1976	Sample of young women in a Hawaiian maternity hospital	Questionnaires and interviews	Older mothers were more apt to be married to partners with adequate jobs. Younger mothers were more apt to be single, of lower socioeconomic origins, and to express values that were accepting of dependence and welfare status.
Effects on Marriage:			
Bowerman, Irish, & Pope, 1966	Large sample of predominantly black, low-income women in North Carolina	Interviews	Unwed black mothers were less likely to marry than whites even when fathers of children were willing. Black fathers were likely to continue support anyway (findings similar to those of Ladner, 1971; Liebow, 1967; Rainwater, 1970).
Sauber & Corrigan, 1970	A six-year follow-up study of a sample of unwed New York City mothers	Interviews	Marriage was most durable if mother married father of child (also found by Furstenberg). Least stable marriages were among girls less than 17. Couples with higher incomes were most apt to stay married. Women who had married, then separated, were in the worst economic condition.
Cutright, 1973	Secondary data from 1967	Complex data analysis	Little economic effect found for women who had had an illegitimate birth 15 to 20 years earlier, especially in case of black women.
Haney & Michielutte, 1974	Large sample of predominantly black, low-income women in North Carolina	Interviews	The attitude of respondents toward marriage, sex, and pregnancy was not affected by whether they bore an illegitimate child. Their current marital status was the determining factor.

Table 32-12 *(cont.)*

FACTOR AND STUDY	SAMPLE	METHODS	FINDINGS
Furstenberg, 1976	Longitudinal study of a select sample of low-income, predominantly black, adolescent females	Interviews, tests, observations	Young mothers were rarely married before birth of first child. Marriage was deferred until father had a job; black women were very cautious about getting married, especially when age 18 or less. Girls with highest educational-vocational goals were least likely to marry. Not marrying father did not prevent marriage; marriage was more apt to occur if parents of girl were sexually conservative. Marriages most likely to last were those based on long prior acquaintances and mutually exclusive commitments, plus higher educational-occupational status of husband. Adolescent unwed mothers who married were apt to be in a worse situation than those who did not. Half of these marriages ended in separation in a few years.
Effects on Later Fertility:			
Cutright, 1973	Secondary data from 1967 National Survey of Economic Opportunity	Complex data analysis	Unwed mothers who never married had the smallest number of children. Whites who had been unwed mothers and married later had more children than white women who had not had an illegitimate child. This was not true for black women.
Furstenberg, 1976	Longitudinal study of a select sample of low-income, predominantly black, adolescent females	Interviews, tests, observations	Both married and unmarried mothers had unplanned pregnancies and more children than they wanted. Both groups rapidly increased family size. Aside from the first child born to young mothers, family size was not larger for the young unwed group (over a five-year period). Women with high educational goals were less likely to have more than one child. Fertility rates did not differ between employed and unemployed respondents. Even though family planning services were not used consistently.
Social Consequences:			
Bowerman, Irish, & Pope, 1966	Large sample of predominantly black, low-income women in North Carolina	Interviews	Seventy percent of white unmarried mothers and 40 percent of black unmarried mothers said they had tried to keep their pregnancy secret, but few women of either race said they had lost the respect of their friends because of the pregnancy.
Ladner, 1971; Schulz, 1969	Anthropological studies in urban black ghettos	Interviews and observations	Adolescent girls tended to gain status as women as a result of having children. It usually allowed them a freer social life with fewer parental controls.
Rubin, 1976	A small group of urban white blue-collar families in California; most families in their late twenties and thirties	Series of intensive interviews with both husbands and wives	Participants thought that it was a social requirement to marry to legitimate a premarital pregnancy. Other options were considered unacceptable.

593

Table 32-12   *(cont.)*

FACTOR AND STUDY	SAMPLE	METHODS	FINDINGS
Effects on Mothering Behaviors:			
Furstenberg, 1976	Longitudinal study of a select sample of low-income, predominantly black, adolescent females	Interviews, tests, observations	Only four percent of young mothers gave up child for adoption, and seven percent of the children lived apart from mothers. About half of mothers shared parenthood with another adult, most often a nearby relative. Almost none used formal daycare facilities. No differences in mothering behaviors were asociated with age or marital status. The type of employment (full- or part-time) determined the amount of time the mothers spent taking care of their children. No differences were found in measured parent attitudes and behavior between mothers who had first child at 15 and those who had first child at 17, nor those who had first child at 19 or 20. Those mothers who were unhappy and rejecting of child during the first year of his/her life (about 15 percent of mothers) were likely to have problems with child's adjustment over next four years. Most mothers were seen as responsible and competent. No differences were found between welfare and nonwelfare mothers, between high school graduates and dropouts, married and single mothers. Two-thirds of fathers maintained contact with children and their mothers over study's five-year-period. Most of these fathers also provided financial assistance.
Effects of Children:			
Furstenberg, 1976	Longitudinal study of a select sample of low-income, predominantly black, adolescent females	Interviews, tests, observations	By age 3, no differences had been found in scores on Preschool Inventory among children whose mothers had been age 15 at their birth and those who had been age 17 or 18. No differences had been found by marital or educational status of mothers. Higher scores were found for those children who were cared for by more than one adult. Children whose parents married early and stayed married had the highest scores in the group. Children of young mothers were compared with children of other parents who had their youngsters in preschool programs. The latter group had higher test scores, but investigator thinks this is partly because these children came from families of higher SES and partly because they were all in preschool.
Vandenberg, 1976	Secondary data of a large sample of families known to a major health service in California	Complex data analysis	By age 5, children of teenage mothers scored lower on vocabulary tests than children of older mothers. By ages 9–11 children of adolescent mothers were more apt to have reading problems and receive lower test scores on vocabulary. However the lower SES of parents may have been the major source of these difficulties rather than their age at child's birth.

Source: Chilman, 1979.

support may encourage them to keep their babies and not to marry the baby's father. Perhaps the most important outcome of illegitimate births to teenagers is the fact that such situations create what has been referred to as "two-children" families, where the immature mother attempts to care and raise the immature infant. At this time there has been very little study of this issue; however, the larger implications of increasing numbers of infants and young children being raised by immature mothers deserves a great deal more attention.

Marriage among Adolescents

As has already been noted marriage rates among adolescents have been dropping steadily since 1960, and the average age of first marriage of American youth has been rising for both men and women since 1960, a reversal of a decreasing trend which had held for most of the twentieth century. In 1970, for instance, 12 percent of women aged 15 to 19 were married, compared with 16 percent in 1960. It is generally believed that the primary cause of adolescent marriage is premarital pregnancy; however, this appears to be only one of several factors, including dating, "going steady," "falling in love," having premarital sexual intercourse at an early age for girls, coming from a low socioeconomic status family, having domestic interests and a traditional female sex-role preference, having low educational and occupational aspirations, and coming from either a very happy or a very unhappy home (Chilman, 1979). Separation and divorce rates among married teenagers are two to four times greater than for couples who marry in their twenties (Burchinal, 1965); however, these high rates may not be due so much to the age of the couple as to their tendency to be from low socioeconomic status homes and to have low levels of education (Glick & Mills, 1974). Married teenagers from affluent homes tend to have relatively stable and longer lasting marriages.

While couples who marry in their teens tend to have larger families than those who marry at later ages, there is little evidence that age alone plays any more important role in this finding than do other factors, such as low socioeconomic status. There are also very little data dealing with the issue of whether teenage couples make any worse parents than do older people, although it could be assumed that being immature and having little money place unusual strains upon young parents who are attempting to meet the needs of young children.

Perhaps the greatest change in our society which is reflected by the increases in adolescent sexual behavior of all types is that marriage is no longer considered necessary in order for young people to engage in full sex relations. Thus one of the primary social functions of marriage, to regulate sexual behavior and provide a stable socialization unit for offspring, seems to be declining in importance. Given this shift it might follow that marriage itself is less popular and preceived by the young to be an optional life style at best, a conclusion which is supported by the decreasing marriage rates of adolescents and the rising average ages of first marriages among young adults. As this author has argued elsewhere (Dreyer, 1975), however, the institution of marriage seems to be as popular as ever, with a greater proportion of the adult age group being married than at any time in this century. The important issue seems to be that marriage does not serve the same social functions as before, in that youth do not seek marriage as a goal in order to attain adult social and sexual status but that marriage increasingly serves a psychological function as a means by which young people achieve personal identity through intimacy and commitment to another person. In this way adolescent sexual behavior represents what psychosocial theorists would call "early intimacy" as part of the ongoing search for identity, while marriage represents "commitment" and "adult intimacy" as aspects of identity resolution. For adolescents a central issue in development is not sex or marriage but the saliency which these have for the individual who is struggling with the meaning of intimacy and commitment.

CONCLUSIONS

While research dealing with adolescent sexuality is too often incomplete and marred by methodological problems, the most obvious point to be drawn from this review is that the role and meaning of sex in the development of adolescents has undergone a dramatic shift in the last 30 years. Whereas in the past genital sex and sexual intercourse were considered taboo for unmarried adolescents and developmental theories focused on how adolescents suppressed and sublimated sexual impulses while forming an identity around educational achievement and occupational decisions before marriage, the current evidence indicates that sex for unmarried adolescents is no longer taboo and that sexual intimacy is an important part of the identity formation process.

The reasons for this change are not clear but seem to involve a combination of factors. First, the data regarding the declining age of sexual maturity, the "secular trend," indicate that teenagers today are physiologically ready for sexual intercourse at earlier ages than were their parents or grandparents. There are little recent data indicating that this trend has continued past 1950, however, and it seems unlikely that such a purely physiological trend can account for the rapid increase in sexual activity among teenagers during the past 15 years. Second, advances in contraception technology, particularly the invention of the birth control pill and the widespread publicity it has received, seem to have removed much of the fear that sexual intercourse necessarily leads to pregnancy and have opened the possibility that adolescents may engage in premarital sex without becoming pregnant. The difficulty with this point, however, is that the data clearly indicate that adolescents are poor contraceptors and are much more ignorant about reproduction and contraception than might be expected in light of the attention which schools have given to sex education and the widespread availability of contraceptives and family planning information. Third, adult society in America seems to be undergoing a change in norms about sexual behaviors of all types. Overall adults seem to be more accepting of premarital sexual intercourse and have in general reduced the negative sanctions and punishments for such behavior, creating a more or less normless environment where sex is neither encouraged nor discouraged. At the same time, however, specific subgroups of adult society, such as groups of different ethnicity, educational level, income, age, and religiosity, present very strong values and norms for the young with regard to sex, so that the adolescent, whose social position is still that of the "marginal person," is confronted with not so much a confusion of norms or lack of norms but a conflict of norms among the various reference groups s/he interacts with. Thus the meaning of sexual activity for any specific adolescent depends upon the ways in which subgroup values and norms are perceived and experienced by that person. Fourth, the formation of an "adolescent society" or "youth culture" seems to have led to a normative structure where full sexual relations between a boy and girl who feel affection for each other or who are "in love" are acceptable if not encouraged by the peer group. The norm in this case is that sex should be part of a caring and affectionate relationship; casual sex and exploitative or abusive sex are considered unacceptable. The general contradictory nature of norms in the larger society and the "sex with affection" norm of the adolescent society tends to leave adolescents with little in the way of effective guidance for dealing with their own sexual feelings and their fundamental need to understand themselves and their place in society better. The result, therefore, is that most adolescents seem to be highly ambivalent about their sexual activity, going along with the generally permissive culture while feeling quite uncertain about the appropriateness or meaning of their own sexual activity.

The consequences of this change in adolescent sexual behavior have been adverse in that sexually transmitted diseases, particularly gonorrhea, have become much more prevalent and the rates of teenage pregnancy, abortion, and illegitimacy have risen sharply, especially among young teenagers in the 13 to 17 age group. Beyond these serious health and social problems, however, there is very little evidence to support the notion that engaging in sexual intercourse presents serious personal or emotional problems for unmarried teenagers who use contraceptives consistently and correctly. This seems to be particularly important in light of theories of adolescent ego development which tend to view sexual intercourse as potentially damaging to an immature ego. For an individual who is psychologically immature and unable to cope with the emotions and commitments which sexual intimacy involve, such intimacy can be overwhelming and potentially dangerous; however, the data available now seem to indicate that for the average adolescent sexual activity which is part of the ongoing attempt to relate to caring and supportive peers does not necessarily lead to maladjustment and problem behavior. What does appear to be important in this process, however, is that the sexually active adolescent accepts his/her sexuality and takes the appropriate contraceptive measures to avoid venereal disease and pregnancy. Denial of one's self as a sexually active person appears to be a serious problem for many sexually active adolescents and points up the ambivalence which many adolescents feel about such activity.

Finally, it is important to repeat that most of the research about adolescent sexuality deals with young women, and it is the sexual behavior of adolescent women which has changed the most in the last 30 years. Yet the fact remains that sexuality lies at the foundation of the adolescent's attempt to break away from the family and to make long-term commitments to nonfamily peers. Our knowledge base, therefore, is now severely limited by the lack of good research about men's sexuality and adolescent men's sexual attitudes and behavior. While the "double standard" may be less important today than in earlier times, it is still true that young men have more permissive attitudes and begin sexual activity earlier than women, and it is they who seem to bear most of the responsibility for initiating sex and for contraception. Until we have more information about men's sexuality and the role it plays in the development of young men, we will not be able to deal successfully with the full implications of this complex subject.

REFERENCES

ABRAMSON, P. The relationship of the frequency of masturbation to several aspects of personality and behavior. *Journal of Sex Research,* 1973, *9,* 132–142.

ADLER, N. E. *Factors affecting contraceptive use.* Paper presented at the American Psychological Association meeting, New Orleans, August 1974.

AGER, J. *Comparison of participants and dropouts from a contraceptive teen program.* Paper presented at the American Psychological Association meeting, Washington, D.C., September 1976.

AGER, J., WERLEY, H. H., & SHEA, F. P. Correlates of continuance in a family planning program. *Journal of Obstetric, Gynecologic, and Neonatal Nursing,* 1973, *2,* 15–23.

American Council on Education. National norms for entering college freshmen—Fall 1970. *ACE Research Reports,* 1970, *5*(No. 6), 1–100.

ARAFAT, I., & COTTON, W. Masturbation practices of males and females. *Journal of Sex Research,* 1974, *10,* 293–307.

ARGYRIS, C. Dangers in applying results from experimental social psychology. *American Psychologist,* 1975, *30,* 469–485.

BALDWIN, W. H. Adolescent pregnancy and childbearing—Growing concerns for Americans. *Population Bulletin,* 1976, *31,* 1–34.

BALL, G. W. *A method of identifying the potential unwed adolescent.* Unpublished doctoral dissertation, University of California at Los Angeles, 1973.

BANDURA, A. Self-efficacy: Toward a unifying theory of behavioral change. *Psychological Review,* 1977, *84,* 191–215.

BARDWICK, J. *Readings on the psychology of women.* New York: Harper & Row, Pub., 1972.

BARDWICK, J. Psychological factors in the acceptance and use of oral contraceptives. In J. T. Fawcett (Ed.), *Psychological perspectives on population.* New York: Basic Books, 1973.

BARGLOW, P., & WEINSTEIN, S. Therapeutic abortions during adolescence: Psychiatric observations. *Journal of Youth and Adolescence,* 1973, *2,* 331–342.

BAUMAN, K. E., & UDRY, J. R. Powerlessness and regularity of contraception in an urban Negro male sample. *Journal of Marriage and the Family,* 1972, *34,* 112–114.

BAUMAN, K. E., & WILSON, R. Contraceptive practices of white unmarried university students: The significance of four years at one university. *American Journal of Obstetrics and Gynecology,* 1974a, *118,* 190–194.

BAUMAN, K. E., & WILSON, R. Sexual behaviors of unmarried university students in 1968 and 1972. *Journal of Sex Research,* 1974b, *10,* 327–333.

BELL, R., & CHASKES, J. Premarital sexual experience among coeds, 1958 and 1968. *Journal of Marriage and the Family,* 1970, *32,* 81–84.

BENDIG, A. W. The development of a short form of the manifest anxiety scale. *Journal of Consulting Psychology,* 1956, *20,* 384.

BIEBER, I., DAIN, H., DINCE, P., DRELLICH, M., GRAND, H., GUNDLACH, R., KREMER, M., RIFKIN, A., WILBUR, C., & BIEBER, T. *Homosexuality: A psychoanalytic study.* New York: Basic Books, 1962.

BILLINGSLEY, A. Illegitimacy and the black community. Pp. 70–85 in *Illegitimacy: Changing services for changing times.* New York: National Council on Illegitimacy, 1970.

BOWERMAN, C., IRISH, D., & POPE, H. *Unwed motherhood: Personal* and social consequences. Institute for Research in Social Science, University of North Carolina, Chapel Hill, N.C., 1966.

BRACKEN, M. & SUIGAR, M. Factors associated with delay in seeking induced abortions. *American Journal of Obstetrics and Gynecology*, 1972, *113*, 301–309.

BRODERICK, C., & BERNARD, J. *The individual, sex and society.* Baltimore, Md.: Johns Hopkins University Press, 1969.

BROMLEY, D., & BRITTEN, F. *Youth and sex.* New York: Harper and Bros., 1938.

BROOKS, G. G., & BUTCALIS, M. R. Psychometric testing as a basis for counseling patients choosing a method of contraception. *American Journal of Obstetrics and Gynecology*, 1976, *124*, 85–87.

BROVERMAN, D. M., BROVERMAN, I. K., VOGEL, W., PALMER, R. D., & KLAIBER, E. L. The automatization cognitive style and physical development. *Child Development*, 1964, *35*, 1343–1359.

BROWN, L. S. *Do users have more fun: A study of the relationship between contraceptive behavior, sexual assertiveness, and patterns of causal attribution.* Unpublished doctoral dissertation, Southern Illinois University at Carbondale, 1977.

BROWN, S., LIEBERMAN, J., & MILLER, W. *Young adults as partners and planners: A preliminary report on the antecedents of responsible family formation.* Paper presented at the 103rd Annual Meeting of the American Public Health Association, Chicago, 1975.

BURCHINAL, L. Trends and prospects for young marriages in the U.S. *Journal of Marriage and the Family*, 1965, *27*, 243–254.

BURGESS, E., & WALLIN, P. *Engagement and marriage.* Philadelphia: Lippincott, 1953.

BUROS, O. K. (Ed.). *The seventh mental measurements yearbook.* Highland Park, N.J.: Gryphon Press, 1972.

BUTTS, R., & SPORAKOWSKI, M. Unwed pregnancy decisions: Some background factors. *Journal of Sex Research*, 1974, *10*, 110–117.

BYRNE, D. A pregnant pause in the sexual revolution. *Psychology Today*, 1977, *11*, 67–68.

CAMPBELL, B. K., & BARNLUND, D. C. Communication style: A clue to unplanned pregnancy. *Medical Care*, 1977, *15*, 181–186.

CARNS, D. Talking about sex: Notes on first coitus and the double standard. *Journal of Marriage and the Family*, 1973, 35, 4, 677–688.

Center for Disease Control. Basic statistics on the sexually transmitted disease problem in the United States. *Sexually transmitted disease fact sheet, 34th edition.* Atlanta, GA: Center for Disease Control, U.S. Department of Health, Education and Welfare (HEW Publication No. (CDC) 79-8195), 1979, 1–37.

CERNADA, G. P., & CRAWFORD, T. J. Some practical applications of social psychology to family-planning programs. In J. T. Fawcett (Ed.), *Psychological perspectives on population.* New York: Basic Books, 1973.

CHASE, H. Trends in prematurity: U.S., 1950–1967. *American Journal of Public Health*, 1970, *60*, 117–181.

CHILMAN, C. *A study of married and single undergraduates at Syracuse University.* Unpublished report to Office of Education, U.S. Department of Health, Education and Welfare, Washington, D.C., 1961.

CHILMAN, C. *Adolescent sexuality in a changing American society: Social and psychological perspectives.* Washington, D.C.: U.S. Government Printing Office, 1979.

CHRISTENSEN, H. Value variables in pregnancy timing: Some intercultural comparisons. Pp. 29–45 in N. Anderson (Ed.), *Studies of the family* (Vol. 3). Gottingen, Germany: Vandenhoek & Ruprecht, 1958, 29–45.

CHRISTENSEN, H., & GREGG, C. Changing sex norms in America and Scandinavia. *Journal of Marriage and the Family*, 1970, *32*, 616–627.

CLARK, A. E., & RUBLE, D. N. Young adolescents' beliefs concerning menstruation. *Child Development*, 1978, *49*, 231–234.

CLAYTON, R. R. Religious orthodoxy and premarital sex. *Social Forces*, 1969, *47*, 469–474.

COBLINER, W. G. Teen-age out-of-wedlock pregnancy: A phenomenon of many dimensions. *Bulletin of the New York Academy of Medicine*, 1970, *46*, 438–447.

COBLINER, W. G., SCHULMAN, H., & ROMNEY, S. L. The termination of adolescent out-of-wedlock pregnancies and the prospects for their primary prevention. *American Journal of Obstetrics and Gynecology*, 1973, *115*, 432–444.

COBLINER, W. G., SCHULMAN, H., & SMITH, V. Patterns of contraceptive failures: The role of motivation re-examined. *Journal of Biosocial Science*, 1975, *7*, 307–318.

COLE, S. G. *Critical factors in family planning participation.* Final

Progress Report for NICHD Grant, Texas Christian University, 1975.

COOMBS, L., & FREEDMAN, R. Premarital pregnancy and status before and after marriage. *American Journal of Sociology*, 1970, *75*, 800–820.

CORTES, J. B., & GATTI, F. M. Physique and motivation. *Journal of Consulting Psychology*, 1966, *30*, 408–414.

CRAIK, K. H. *Social and asocial patterns of temporal behavior.* Unpublished doctoral dissertation, University of California, Berkeley, 1964.

CROAKE, J., JAMES, B. A four year comparison of premarital sexual attitudes. *Journal of Sex Research*, 1973, *9* (No. 2), 91–96.

CRONBACH, L. J. Beyond the two disciplines of scientific psychology. *American Psychologist*, 1975, *30*, 116–127.

CUTRIGHT, P. Illegitimacy: Myths, causes and cures. *Family Planning Perspectives*, 1971, *3*, 26–48.

CUTRIGHT, P. The teenage sexual revolution and the myth of an abstinent past. *Family Planning Perspectives*, 1972, *4*, 24–31.

CUTRIGHT, P. Illegitimacy: The prospect for change. *American Journal of Public Health*, 1973, *63*, 765–766.

CVETKOVICH, G., & GROTE, B. *Antecedents of responsible family formation.* Progress report paper presented at a conference sponsored by the Population Division, National Institute of Child Health and Human Development, Bethesda, Md., 1975.

CVETKOVICH, G., & GROTE, B. *Psychological factors associated with adolescent premarital coitus.* Paper presented at the National Institute of Child Health and Human Development, Bethesda, Md., May 1976.

CVETKOVICH, G., GROTE, B., BJORSETH, A., & SARKISSIAN, J. On the psychology of adolescents; use of contraceptives. *Journal of Sex Research*, 1975, *11*, 256–270.

DAVIDSON, A. R., & JACCARD, J. J. *Application of the Fishbein behavioral-intentions model to fertility behavior.* Paper presented at the American Psychological Association meeting, Washington, D.C., September 1976.

DAVIS, K. *Factors in the sex life of twenty-two hundred women.* New York: Harper and Bros., 1929.

DIAMOND, M., STEINHOFF, P., PALMORE, J., & SMITH, R. Sexuality, birth control, and abortion: A decision-making sequence. *Journal of Biosocial Science*, 1973, *5*, 347–361.

DOWNS, P. E. *Examining the intrafamily decision-making process with respect to contraceptive behavior.* Unpublished doctoral dissertation, University of North Carolina at Chapel Hill, 1976.

DREYER, P. H. Sex, sex roles, and marriage among youth in the 1970's. In R. J. Havighurst & P. H. Dreyer (Eds.), *Youth: Part I of the 74th yearbook of the national society for the study of education.* Chicago: University of Chicago Press, 1975.

DRUCKER, C. A. *The psychological aspects of contraceptive choice among single women.* Unpublished doctoral dissertation, Garden City, N.Y., 1975.

EHRMANN, W. *Premarital dating behavior.* New York: Holt, Rinehart & Winston, 1959.

EICHORN, D. H. Geographical correlates of behavior. Pp. 4–66 in H. W. Stevenson (Ed.), *Child psychology: 62nd yearbook of the national society for the study of education.* Chicago: University of Chicago Press, 1963.

EPSTEIN, H. T. Growth spurts during brain development: Implications for educational policy and practice. Pp. 343–370 in J. S. Chall & A. F. Mirsky (Eds.), *Education and the brain: Part II of the 77th yearbook of the national society for the study of education.* Chicago: University of Chicago Press, 1978.

EVANS, J., SELSTAD, G., & WELCHER, W. Teenagers: Fertility control behavior and attitudes before and after abortion, childbearing or negative pregnancy test. *Family Planning Perspectives*, 1976, *8*, 192–200.

EVANS, R. B. Parental relationships and homosexuality. *Medical Aspects of Human Sexuality*, 1971, *5*, 164–177.

FAUST, M. S. Somatic development of adolescent girls. *Monographs of the Society for Research in Child Development*, 1977, *42*(No. 1).

FAWCETT, J. T., & BORNSTEIN, M. H. Modernization, individual modernity, and fertility. In J. T. Fawcett (Ed.), *Psychological perspectives on population.* New York: Basic Books, 1973.

FINGER, F. Sex beliefs and practices among male college students. *Journal of Abnormal and Social Psychology*, 1947, *42*, 57–67.

FINKEL, M., & FINKEL, D. Sexual and contraceptive knowledge, attitudes and behaviors of male adolescents. *Family Planning Perspectives*, 1975, *7*, 256–260.

FISHBEIN, M., & AJZEN, I. *Belief, attitude, intention and behavior: An in-*

troduction to theory and research. Reading, Mass.: Addison-Wesley, 1975.

Fox, G. Sex role attitudes as predictors of contraceptive use. Paper presented at the Annual Meeting of the National Council on Family Relations, Salt Lake City, August 20–23, 1975.

Freedman, M. The sexual behavior of American college women: An empirical study and a historical survey. Merrill-Palmer Quarterly, 1965, 11, 33–47.

Freedman, M. Homosexuality and psychological functioning. Monterey, Calif.: Brooks/Cole, 1971.

Freud, S. Formulations regarding the two principles in mental functioning. In Collected papers (Vol. 4). London: Hogarth, 1953.

Frisch, R. E. Critical weight at menarche, initiation of the adolescent growth spurt, and control of puberty. Pp. 403–423 in M. M. Grumbach, G. D. Grave, & F. E. Mayer (Eds.), Control of the onset of puberty. New York: John Wiley, 1974.

Frisch, R. E., & Revelle, R. Variation in body weights and the age of the adolescent growth spurt among Latin American and Asian populations, in relation to calorie supplies. Human Biology, 1969, 41, 185–212.

Frisch, R. E., & Revelle, R. Height and weight at menarche and a hypothesis of critical body weights and adolescent events. Science, 1970, 169, 397–398.

Fujita, B., Wagner, N., & Pion, R. Contraceptive use among single college students: A preliminary report. American Journal of Obstetrics and Gynecology, 1971, 109, 787–793.

Furstenberg, F., Jr. Unplanned parenthood: The social consequences of teenage childbearing. New York: Free Press, 1976.

Furstenberg, F., Jr., Gordis, L., & Markowitz, M. Birth control knowledge and attitudes among unmarried pregnant adolescents: A preliminary report. Journal of Marriage and the Family, 1969, 31, 34–42.

Gabrielson, I., Goldsmith, S., Potts, L., Matthews, N., & Gabrielson, M. Adolescent attitudes towards abortion: Effects on contraceptive practice. American Journal of Public Health, 1971, 61, 730–738.

Gallup, G. Attitudes of Americans on sex seen undergoing profound change. Family Planning Digest, 1974, 3, 1, 3.

Gebhard, P., Pomeroy, W., Martin, C. E., & Christenson, C. V. Pregnancy, birth and abortion. New York: Harper & Row, Pub., 1958.

Gerrard, M. Sex built in abortion patients. Journal of Consulting and Clinical Psychology, 1977, 45, 708.

Gilbert Youth Research. How wild are college students? Pageant, 1951, 7, 10–21.

Glick, P., & Mills, K. Black families: Marriage patterns and living arrangements. Paper presented at the W.E.B. DuBois Conference on American Blacks, Atlanta, October 1974.

Goldsmith, S., Gabrielson, M., & Gabrielson, I. Teenagers, sex and contraception. Family Planning Perspectives, 1972, 4, 32–38.

Gough, H. G. Theory and measurement of socialization. Journal of Consulting Psychology, 1960, 24, 23–30.

Gough, H. G. Manual for the personal values abstract. Palo Alto, Calif.: Consulting Psychologists Press, 1972.

Gough, H. G. A factor analysis of contraceptive preferences. Journal of Psychology, 1973a, 34, 199–210.

Gough, H. G. Personality assessment in the study of population. In J. R. Fawcett (Ed.), Psychological perspectives on population. New York: Basic Books, 1973b.

Greulich, W. W., Day, H., Lachman, S. E., Wolfe, J. B., & Shuttleworth, F. K. A handbook of methods for the study of adolescent children. Monographs of the Society for Research in Child Development, 1938, 3(No. 2).

Groat, H. T., & Neal, A. G. Social psychological correlates of urban fertility. American Sociological Review, 1967, 32, 945–959.

Grossman, S. P. A textbook of physiological psychology. New York: John Wiley, 1967.

Grumbach, M. M., Grave, G. D., & Mayer, F. E. (Eds.). Control of the onset of puberty. New York: John Wiley, 1974.

Grunebaum, H., & Abernethy, V. Marital decision making as applied to family planning. Journal of Sex and Marital Therapy, 1974, 1, 63–74.

Hagelis, J. P. Unwed adolescent pregnancy and contraceptive practice. Unpublished doctoral dissertation, California School of Professional Psychology, Los Angeles, 1973.

Hamilton, G. A research in marriage. New York: A. & C. Boni, 1929.

Haney, A., & Michielutte, R. Social and psychological factors affecting fertility, family planning and clinic utilization. A report by Behavioral Sciences Center of the Bowman Gray School of Medicine, Wake Forest University, Winston-Salem, N.C., 1974.

Hass, A. Teenage sexuality, a survey of teenage sexual behavior. New York: Macmillan, 1979.

Hatcher, S.L.M. The adolescent experience of pregnancy and abortion: A developmental analysis. Journal of Youth and Adolescence, 1973, 2, 53–102.

Havighurst, R. J., & Dreyer, P. H. (Eds.). Youth: Part I of the 74th yearbook of the national society for the study of education. Chicago: University of Chicago Press, 1975.

Hunt, M. Sexual behavior in the 1970's. Chicago: Playboy Press, 1974.

Jaccard, J. J., & Davidson, A. R. Toward an understanding of family planning behaviors: An initial investigation. Journal of Applied Social Psychology, 1972, 2, 228–235.

Jackson, E., & Potkay, C. Pre-college influences on sexual experience of coeds. Journal of Sex Research, 1973, 9, 143–149.

Jekel, J. The past decade of special programs for school-age parents. National Alliance Concerned with School-Age Parents Newsletter, 1975, 3, 1. Consortium on Early Childbearing and Childrearing, 1145 19th St., N.W., Washington, D.C., 20036.

Jessor, R., & Jessor, S. Problem behavior and psychosocial development. New York: Academic Press, 1977.

Jessor, S., & Jessor, R. Transition from virginity to nonvirginity among youth: A social-psychological study over time. Developmental Psychology, 1975, 11, 473–484

Jones, H. E. Adolescence: Part I of the 43rd yearbook of the National Society for the Study of Education. Chicago: University of Chicago Press, 1944.

Jones, M. C., & Mussen, P. H. Self-conceptions, motivations, and interpersonal attitudes of early-and-late maturing girls. Child Development, 1958, 29, 429–500.

Jurich, A., & Jurich, J. The effects of cognitive moral development upon the selection of premarital sexual standards. Journal of Marriage and the Family, 1974, 36, 736–41.

Kaats, G., & Davis, K. The dynamics of sexual behavior of college students. Journal of Marriage and the Family, 1970, 32, 390–399.

Kane, F. J., Jr., & Lachenbruch, P. A. Adolescent pregnancy: A study of aborters and non-aborters. American Journal of Orthopsychiatry, 1973, 43, 796–803.

Kanin, E. An examination of sexual aggression as a response to sexual frustration. Journal of Marriage and the Family, 1967, 3, 428–433.

Kantner, J., & Zelnick, M. Sexual experiences of young unmarried women in the U.S. Family Planning Perspectives, 1972, 4, 9–17.

Kantner, J., & Zelnick, M. Contraception and pregnancy: Experience of young unmarried women in the United States. Family Planning Perspectives, 1973, 5, 21–35.

Kar, S. B. Individual aspirations as related to early and late acceptance of contraception. The Journal of Social Psychology, 1971, 83, 235–245.

Kar, S. B. Consistency between fertility attitudes and behavior: A conceptual model. Paper presented at American Psychological Association meeting, Washington, D.C., September 1976.

Karlen, A. Sexuality and homosexuality. New York: W. W. Norton & Co., Inc., 1971.

Katz, J., & Cronin, D. Sexuality and college life. Change, 1980, 12(No. 2)., 44–49.

Keller, A. B., Sims, J. H., Henry, W. E., & Crawford, T. J. Psychological sources of "resistance" to family planning. Merrill-Palmer Quarterly of Behavior and Development, 1970, 16, 286–302.

Kinsey, A. C., Pomeroy, W., & Martin, C. E. Sexual behavior in the human male. Philadelphia: W. B. Saunders Company, 1948.

Kinsey, A. C., Pomeroy, W., Martin, C. E., & Gebhard, P. H. Sexual behavior in the human female. Philadelphia: W. B. Saunders, 1953.

Komarovsky, M. Dilemmas of masculinity: A study of college youth. New York: W. W. Norton & Co., Inc., 1976.

Kothandapani, V. A psychological approach to the prediction of contraceptive behavior. Chapel Hill, N.C.: Carolina Population Center, 1971.

Kovar, M. G. Variations in birth weight, legitimate live births, U.S. 1963. Vital and health statistics, Series 22, No. 8. National Center for Health Statistics, U.S Department of Health, Education and Welfare. Washington, D.C.: U.S. Government Printing Office, 1968.

LADNER, J. A. *Tomorrow's tomorrow: The black women.* Garden City, N.Y.: Doubleday, 1971.

LAKE, A. Teenagers and sex: A student report. *Seventeen,* 1967, *26,* 88–131.

LANDIS, J., & LANDIS, M. *Building a successful marriage.* Englewood Cliffs, N.J.: Prentice-Hall, 1977.

LEHFELDT, H. Psychology of contraceptive failure. *Medical Aspects of Human Sexuality,* 1971, *5,* 68–77.

LEWIN, K. Behavior and development as a function of the total situation. In L. Carmichael (Ed.), *Manual of child psychology.* New York: John Wiley, 1946.

LIEBOW, E. *Tally's corner.* Boston: Little, Brown, 1967.

LINDEMANN, C. *Birth control and unmarried young women.* New York: Springer, 1974.

LIPSITZ, J. *Growing up forgotten.* Lexington, Mass.: Heath, 1977.

LUCKEY, E., & NASS, G. A comparison of sexual attitudes and behavior of an international sample. *Journal of Marriage and the Family,* 1969, *31,* 346–379.

LUKER, K. C. *Taking chances: Abortion and the decision not to contracept.* Berkeley: University of California Press, 1975.

LUNDY, J. R. Some personality correlates of contraceptive use among unmarried female college students. *The Journal of Psychology,* 1972, *80,* 9–14.

MACCOBY, E., & JACKLIN, C. *The psychology of sex differences.* Stanford, Calif.: Stanford University Press, 1975.

McCORMICK, E. P. *Attitudes toward abortion.* Lexington, Mass.: Lexington Books, 1975.

MacDONALD, A. P., JR. Internal-external locus of control and the practice of birth control. *Psychological Reports,* 1970, *27,* 206.

McGUIRE, W. J. The ying and yang of progress in social psychology: Seven Koan. *Journal of Personality and Social Psychology,* 1973, *26,* 446–456.

MARTIN, C. Psychological problems of abortion for the unwed teen-age girl. *Genetic Psychiatric Monograph,* 1973, *88,* 23–110.

MENKEN, J. *Health consequences of early childbearing.* Paper given at the Conference on Consequences of Adolescent Pregnancy, Washington, D.C., October 1975.

MEREDITH, H. V. A synopsis of pubertal changes in youth. *Journal of School Health,* 1967, *37,* 171–176.

MEYEROWITZ, J., & MALEV, J. Pubescent attitudinal correlates antecedent to adolescent illegitimate pregnancy. *Journal of Youth and Adolescence,* 1973, *2,* 251–258.

MILLER, P., & SIMON, W. Adolescent sexual behavior: Context and change. *Social Problems,* 1974, *22,* 1.

MILLER, W. B. Psychological vulnerability to unwanted pregnancy. *Family Planning Perspectives,* 1973a, *5,* 199–201.

MILLER, W. B. *The personal style inventory.* Unpublished manuscript, Stanford University, 1973b.

MILLER, W. B. Psychological antecedents to conception among abortion seekers. *Western Journal of Medicine,* 1975, *122,* 12–19.

MILLER, W. B. *Some psychological factors predictive of undergraduate sexual and contraceptive behavior.* Paper presented at the American Psychological Association meeting, Washington, D.C., September 1976.

MILLER, W. B. *Sexual and contraceptive knowledge questionnaire.* Unpublished manuscript, Stanford University, no date.

MINDICK, B. Attitudes toward population issues. In S. Oskamp, *Attitudes and opinions.* Englewood Cliffs, N.J.: Prentice-Hall, 1977.

MINDICK, B. *Personality and social psychological correlates of success or failure in contraception: A longitudinal predictive view.* Unpublished doctoral dissertation, Claremont Graduate School, Claremont, Calif., 1978.

MINDICK, B., & OSKAMP, S. Longitudinal predictive research: An approach to methodological problems in studying contraception. *Journal of Population,* 1979, *2,* 259–276.

MINDICK, B., OSKAMP, S., & BERGER, D. E. Prediction of success or failure in birth planning: An approach to prevention of individual and family stress. *American Journal of Community Psychology,* 1977, *5,* 477–479.

MIRANDE, A. Reference group theory and adolescent sexual behavior. *Journal of Marriage and the Family,* 1968, *30,* 572–577.

MISCHEL, W. *Personality and assessment.* New York: John Wiley, 1968.

MONEY, J. *Sex errors of the body: Dilemmas, education, counseling.* Baltimore, Md.: Johns Hopkins University Press, 1968.

MONEY, J., & EHRHARDT, A. *Man and woman, boy and girl.* Baltimore, Md.: Johns Hopkins University Press, 1972.

MONSOUR, K., & STEWART, B. Abortion and sexual behavior in college women. *American Journal of Orthopsychiatry,* 1973, *43,* 804–814.

MOORE, K., & CALDWELL, S. B. *Out of wedlock childbearing.* Washington, D.C.: The Urban Institute, 1977.

MUSSEN, P. H., & JONES, M. C. Self-conceptions, motivations, and interpersonal attitudes of late- and early-maturing boys. *Child Development,* 1957, *28,* 243–256.

MUSSEN, P. H., & JONES, M. C. The behavior-inferred motivations of late- and early-maturing boys. *Child Development,* 1958, *29,* 61–67.

NOBLE, L. D. *Personality characteristics associated with contraceptive behavior in women seeking abortion under liberalized California law.* Unpublished doctoral dissertation, California School of Professional Psychology, San Francisco, 1972.

OPPEL, W., ATHANASIOU, R., CUSHNER, I., SASAKI, T., UNGER, T., & WOLF, S. Contraceptive antecedents to early and late therapeutic abortions. *American Journal of Public Health,* 1972, *62,* 824–827.

OSKAMP, S. Public opinion. In E. Donnerstein, M. Donnerstein, & A. Kahn, *Social psychology.* Dubuque, Iowa: Wm. C. Brown, 1981.

OSKAMP, S., & MINDICK, B. Personality and attitudinal barriers to contraception. In D. Byrne & W. A. Fisher (Eds.), *Adolescents, sex, and contraception.* New York: McGraw-Hill, 1981.

OSKAMP, S., MINDICK, B., BERGER, D., & MOTTA, E. A. Longitudinal study of success versus failure in contraceptive planning. *Journal of Population,* 1978, *1,* 69–83.

OSOFSKY, J., & OSOFSKY, H. The psychological reaction of patients to legalized abortions. *American Journal of Orthopsychiatry,* 1972, *42,* 48–60.

PACKARD, V. *The sexual wilderness.* New York: D. McKay, 1968.

PAKTER, J., NELSON, F., & SVIGIR, M. Legal abortion: A half decade of experience. *Family Planning Perspectives,* 1975, *7,* 248–255.

PARCEL, G. S. *A study of the relationship between contraceptive attitudes and behavior in a group of unmarried university students.* Unpublished doctoral dissertation, Pennsylvania State University, 1974.

PARLEE, M. B. The premenstrual syndrome. *Psychological Bulletin,* 1973, *80,* 454–465.

PEREZ-REYES, M., & FALK, R. Follow-up after therapeutic abortion in early adolescence. *Archives of General Psychiatry,* 1973, *28,* 120–126.

PETERSON, R. *Early sex information and its influence on later sex concepts.* Unpublished master's thesis in Library of College of Education, University of Colorado, 1938.

Playboy's student survey. *Playboy,* September, 1970, pp. 182–240.

Playboy's student survey, 1971. *Playboy,* September, 1971, pp. 118–216.

POPE, H. Unwed mothers and their sex partners. *Journal of Marriage and the Family,* 1967, *29,* 555–567.

PORTERFIELD, A., & ELLISON, S. Current folkways of sexual behavior. *American Journal of Sociology,* 1946, *52,* 209–216.

PRESSER, H. Early motherhood: Ignorance or bliss? *Family Planning Perspectives,* 1974, *6,* 2.

PRESSER, H. *Some consequences of adolescent pregnancies.* Paper presented at the National Institutes of Child Health and Human Development Conference, Bethesda, Md., 1975.

PRESSER, H. *Role and fertility pattern of urban mothers.* Final Report presented at the National Institute of Health, U.S. Department of Health, Education and Welfare, Bethesda, Md., 1976a. (Contract No. a-HD-2038)

PRESSER, H. *Social factors affecting the timing of the first child.* Paper presented at the Conference on the First Child and Family Formation, Pacific Grove, Calif., March 1976b.

RADER, G. E., BEKKER, L. D., BROWN, L., & RICHARDT, C. Psychological correlates of unwanted pregnancy. *Journal of Abnormal Psychology,* 1978, *87,* 373–376.

RAINS, P. *Becoming an unwed mother.* Chicago: Aldine, 1971.

RAINWATER, L. *Behind ghetto walls: Black families in a federal slum.* Chicago: Aldine, 1970.

REICHELT, P. *Psychosexual background of female adolescents seeking contraceptive assistance.* Paper presented at the Annual Convention of the American Psychological Association, Washington, D.C., 1976.

REISS, I. *The social context of sexual permissiveness.* New York: Holt, Rinehart & Winston, 1967.

REISS, I. *Family systems in America* (2nd ed.). Hinsdale, Ill.: Dryden Press, 1976.

ROBBINS, M., & LYNN, D. The unwed fathers: Generation recidivism and attitudes about intercourse in California youth authority wards. *Journal of Sex Research*, 1973, *9*, 334–341.

ROBINSON, I., KING, K., & BALSWICK, J. The premarital sexual revolution among college females. *Family Coordinator*, 1972, *21*, 189–194.

ROSEN, R., HUDSON, A., & MARTINDALE, L. *Contraception, abortion and self-concept*. Paper presented at the American Sociological Association, Washington, D.C., 1976.

ROSEN, R., MARTINDALE, L., & GRISELDA, M. *Pregnancy study report*. Wayne State University, Detroit, Mich., March 1976.

ROSS, H., & SAWHILL, I. *Time of transition: The growth of families headed by women*. Washington, D.C.: The Urban Institute, 1975.

ROSS, R. Measures of the sex behaviors of college males compared with Kinsey's results. *Journal of Abnormal and Social Psychology*, 1950, *45*, 753–755.

ROVINSKY, J. J. Abortion recidivism: A problem in preventive medicine. *American Journal of Obstetrics and Gynecology*, 1972, *39*, 649–659.

RUBIN, L. B. *Worlds of pain*. New York: Basic Books, 1976.

SARREL, L., & SARREL, P. The college subculture. Pp. 71–84 in M. S. Calderone (Ed.), *Sexuality and human values*. New York: Association Press, 1974.

SAUBER, M., & CORRIGAN, E. *The six year experience of unwed mothers as parents*. New York: Community Council of Greater New York, 1970.

SCHULZ, D. *Coming up black*. Englewood Cliffs, N.J.: Prentice-Hall, 1969.

SCHWARTZ, S. Effects of sex guilt and sexual arousal on the retention of birth control information. *Journal of Consulting and Clinical Psychology*, 1973, *41*, 61–64.

SCOTT, W. A., & WERTHEIMER, M. Introduction to psychological research. New York: John Wiley, 1962.

SEELEY, O. F. Field dependence-independence, internal-external locus of control, and implementation of family-planning goals, *Psychological Reports*, 1976, *38*, 1216–1218.

SELIGMAN, M.E.P. *Helplessness: On depression, development, and death*, San Francisco, Calif.: W. H. Freeman & Company Publishers, 1975.

SETTLAGE, D., BAROFF, S., & COOPER, D. Sexual experience of younger teen-age girls seeking contraceptive assistance for the first time. *Family Planning Perspectives*, 1973, *5*, 233.

SHAH, F., ZELNICK, M., & KANTNER, J. Unprotected intercourse among unwed teen-agers. *Family Planning Perspectives*, 1975, *7*, 39.

SHIPLEY, R. R. *Changes in contraceptive knowledge, attitudes, and behavior in a college current health problems class*. Unpublished doctoral dissertation, Temple University, 1974.

SHUTTLEWORTH, F. K. The adolescent period: A graphic atlas. *Monographs of the Society for the Research in Child Development*, 1951, *14*(1).

SIMON, W., BERGER, A., & GAGNON, J. Beyond anxiety and fantasy: The coital experiences of college youths. *Journal of Youth and Adolescence*, 1972, 1, 3, 203–222.

SKLAR, J., & BERKOV, B. Teenage family formation in postwar America. *Family Planning Perspectives*, 1974, *6*, 80–90.

SLAGLE, S. J., ARNOLD, C. B., & GLASCOCK, E. *A measure of relative risk of unwanted pregnancy*. Paper presented at the American Psychological Association meeting, New Orleans, 1974.

SLAVIN, M. E. *Ego functioning in women who use birth control effectively and ineffectively*. Unpublished doctoral dissertation, Boston University School of Education, 1975.

SORENSON, ROBERT. *Adolescent sexuality in contemporary America*. New York: William Collins Publishers, Inc., 1973.

SPANIER, G. Sexualization and premarital sexual behavior. *Family Coordinator*, 1975, *24*, 33–41.

STACK, C. *All our kin: Strategies for survival in a black community*. New York: Harper & Row, Pub., 1974.

STEIN, K. B., SARBIN, T. R., & KULIK, J. A. Future time perspective. *Journal of Consulting and Clinical Psychology*, 1968, *32*, 257–264.

STEINHOFF, P. *Premarital pregnancy and the first birth*. Paper presented at the Conference on Birth of the First Child and Family Formation, Pacific Grove, Calif., March 1976. Report on part of a larger study, "Hawaii Pregnancy, Birth Control and Abortion Study, University of Hawaii."

STEINLAUF, B. *Attitudes and cognitive factors associated with the contraceptive behavior of young women*. Unpublished doctoral dissertation, Wayne State University, 1977.

SWEET, J. A. Differentials in the rate of fertility decline: 1960–1970. *Family Planning Perspectives*, 1974, *6*, 103–107.

TANNER, J. M. *Education and physical growth*. London: University of London Press, 1961.

TANNER, J. M. *Growth at adolescence* (2nd ed.). Oxford, England: Blackwell Scientific Publications, 1962.

TANNER, J. M. The regulation of human growth. *Child Development*, 1963, *34*, 817–847.

TANNER, J. M. Sequence, tempo, and individual variation in growth and development of boys and girls aged twelve to sixteen. *Daedalus*, 1971, *100*, 907–930. Reprinted in J. Kagan & R. Coles (Eds.), *12 to 16 early adolescence*. New York: W. W. Norton & Co., Inc., 1972, 1–24.

TANNER, J. M. Sequence and tempo in the somatic changes in puberty. Pp. 448–470 in M. M. Grumbach, G. D. Grave, & F. E. Mayer (Eds.), *Control of the onset of puberty*. New York: John Wiley, 1974.

TERMAN, L. M. *Psychological factors in marital happiness*. New York: McGraw-Hill, 1938.

TOWNES, B. D., BEACH, L. R., CAMPBELL, F. L., & WOOD, R. J. *Values, behavioral intentions and fertility behavior*. Paper presented at the American Psychological Association meeting, Washington, D.C., September 1976.

UDRY, J., BAUMAN, K., & MORRIS, N. Changes in premarital coital experience of recent decade of birth cohorts of urban America. *Journal of Marriage and the Family*, 1975, *37*, 783–787.

UDRY, J. R. Differential fertility by intelligence: The role of birth planning. *Social Biology*, 1978, *25*, 10–14.

U.S. Department of Health, Education & Welfare. *Selected vital and health statistics in poverty and non-poverty areas of nineteen large cities: U.S., 1969–71*. Washington, D.C.: U.S. Government Printing Office, 1975.

U.S. Government, House of Representatives Committee on Education and Labor. *Adolescent pregnancy*. Hearing Before the Subcommittee on Select Education, July 24, 1978. Washington, D.C.: U.S. Government Printing Office, 1978.

VANDENBERG, B. Personal communication to Katherine Chilman, 1976. In K. Chilman, *Adolescent sexuality in a changing American society*. (NIH No. 79-1426). Washington, D.C.: U.S. Department of Health, Education and Welfare, 1979.

VENER, A., & STEWART, C. Adolescent sexual behavior in middle America revisited: 1970–1973. *Journal of Marriage and the Family*, 1974, *36*, 728–735.

VENER, A., STEWART, C., & HAGER, D. The sexual behavior of adolescents in middle America: Generation and American-British comparisons. *Journal of Marriage and the Family*, 1972, *34*, 696–705.

VINCENT, C. *Unmarried mothers*. London: Free Press, 1961.

VINCENT, C., HANEY, A., & COCHRANE, C. Familial and generational patterns of illegitimacy. *Journal of Marriage and the Family*, 1969, *31*, 659–667.

WARNER, W. L., MEEKER, M., & EELLS, K. *Social class in America*. Chicago: Science Research Associates, 1949.

WEINSTOCK, E., TIETZE, C., JAFFE, F., & DRYFOOS, J. Legal abortions in the United States since the 1973 Supreme Court decision. *Family Planning Perspectives*, 1975, *7*, 23–31.

WERNER, P. D. Implications of attitude-behavior studies for population research and action. *Studies in Family Planning*, 1977, *8*, 294–299.

What's really happening on campus. *Playboy*, October 1976, pp. 128–169.

WHITE, R. W. Motivation reconsidered: The concept of competence. *Psychological Review*, 1959, *66*, 297–333.

WILKINS, L. *Diagnosis and treatment of endocrine disorders in childhood and adolescence* (2nd ed.). Springfield, Ill.: Chas. C. Thomas, 1957.

YANKELOVICH, D. *The new morality: A profile of American youth in the 1970's*. New York: McGraw-Hill, 1974.

YOUNG, W. C. The hormones and mating behavior. In W. C. Young (Ed.), *Sex and internal secretions* (3rd ed.). Baltimore, Md.: Williams & Wilkins, 1961.

YOUNG, W. C., GOY, R. W., & PHOENIX, C. H. Hormones and sexual behavior. *Science*, 1964, *143*, 212–218.

ZELNICK, M., & KANTNER, J. The probability of premarital intercourse. *Social Science Research*, 1972a, *1*, 335–341.

ZELNICK, M., & KANTNER, J. Some preliminary observations on pre-adult fertility and family formation. *Studies in Family Planning*, 1972b, *3*, 59–65.

ZELNICK, M., & KANTNER, J. Sexuality, contraception, and pregnancy among young unwed females in the U.S. In C. F. Westoff & R. Parke, Jr. (Eds.), *Demographic and social aspects of population growth and American future research report* (No. 1). Washington, D.C.: U.S. Government Printing Office, 1972c.

ZELNICK, M., & KANTNER, J. The resolution of teen-age pregnancies. *Family Planning Perspectives,* 1974, *6,* 74–80.

ZELNICK, M., & KANTNER, J. Attitudes of American teen-agers towards abortion. *Family Planning Perspectives,* 1975, *7,* 89–91.

ZELNICK, M., & KANTNER, J. First pregnancies to women aged 15–19: 1976 and 1971. *Family Planning Perspectives,* 1978a, *10,* 11–20.

ZELNICK, M., & KANTNER, J. Contraceptive patterns and premarital pregnancy among women aged 15–19 in 1976. *Family Planning Perspectives,* 1978b, *10,* 135–142.

33

Vocational Role Development in Adolescence

FRED W. VONDRACEK
RICHARD M. LERNER

The focal point of the decentering process is the entrance into the occupational world or the beginning of serious professional training. The adolescent becomes an adult when he undertakes a real job. (Inhelder & Piaget, 1958, p. 346)

Most psychological theories of adolescent development focus on only one intraindividual change process—e.g., cognition, affect, or maturation (Erikson, 1959; McCandless, 1970; Piaget, 1970). Nevertheless as evidenced by the quote from Inhelder and Piaget (1958), most theorists eventually stress that the adaptive development of any process involves a link between the person and his/her society (cf. Lerner & Shea, Chap. 28, this volume; Lerner & Spanier, 1980). In particular many theorists emphasize that it is the attainment of a vocation, the "launching of a career" (Levinson, 1978), that represents the point in the life span when adolescent development of a target process is completed successfully.

Piaget (1967), explains that

With the advent of formal intelligence, thinking takes wings and it is not surprising that at first this unexpected power is both used and abused . . . each new mental ability starts off by incorporating the world in a process of egocentric assimilation. Adolescent egocentricity is manifested by a belief in the omnipotence of reflection, as though the world should submit itself to idealistic schemes rather than to systems of reality. (pp. 63–64)

But he goes on to note that

True adaptation to society comes automatically when the adolescent reformer attempts to put his ideas to work. Just as experience reconciles formal thought with the reality of things, so does effective and enduring work, undertaken in concrete and well-defined situations, cure dreams. (Ibid., pp. 68–69)

Similar examples of the role of vocational role development in the attainment of theoretically requisite developments in adolescence can, of course, be found in Erikson's (1959, 1963, 1968) ideas, as well as in mechanistically oriented formulations (e.g., McCandless, 1970) and contextually oriented formulations (e.g., Lerner & Shea Chap. 28; Lerner & Spanier, 1980).

Thus there is some unanimity in the view that the development of a vocational role or career choice is a key antecedent of optimal development beyond adolescence. Nevertheless many psychological theorists have not considered the nature of the societal context to which vocational roles provide a link. Rather they have focused on the organismic change processes covarying with role development. Such a "personological" focus has been associated with a lack of attention to the implications for individual development of social change and of societal differences. As a consequence descriptions of adolescent vocational role development have been historically and culturally limited. In our view such omissions preclude an adequate understanding of adolescent vocational role development.

The 1970s, however, bore witness to an increasing stress on "dynamic interactions" (Hartup, 1978, 1979; Lerner, 1978, 1979a; Lerner & Shea, Chap. 28; Lerner & Spanier, 1978, 1980) between developing individuals and their changing worlds, a stress commensurate with the status given to vocational role development by theorists of adolescent development. Piaget (1971) indicated that "society is the supreme unit, and the individual can only achieve his inventions and intellectual constructions insofar as he is the seat of collective interactions that are naturally dependent, in level and value, on society as a whole" (p. 368). Similarly Brent (1978), a contextually oriented theorist, maintains that

A dialectical relationship exists between the tendency toward specialization of each individual member of an organismic collective during the course of individual development (e.g., ontogenesis) and the tendency toward adaptation of the organismic collective-as-a-whole to a shifting set of environmental opportunities and constraints during the course of its development (e.g., phylogenesis). The general principle is this: As each individual within an organismic collective becomes increasingly more specialized in the unique niche which he/she occupies in the collective, the collective-as-a-whole becomes increasingly more flexible in its ability to adapt to its changing environment. Put in other terms: *The specialization of individuals within an organismic collective is the concrete realization at the micro-structural level of differentiation of the organismic collective-as-a-whole at the macro-structural level.* (p. 23)

Yet despite such emphases on the role of the social context in individual development, there have been few attempts to review the literature on vocational role development from a dynamic interactional perspective.

This omission appears problematic. There are data that we see as indicating that social change and cultural differences play important roles in shaping the content of role adoptions and, more importantly, in determining what adaptive role development will be. More generally we see a convergence among data sets from several disciplines—e.g., evolutionary biology, cultural anthropology, family sociology, and developmental psychology—which indicates that a dynamic interactional perspective may be particularly useful for understanding adolescent vocational-role development (Lerner & Busch-Rossnagel, 1981; Lerner & Shea, Chap. 28; Lerner, Spanier, & Belsky, in press). Accordingly our goal in this chapter is to discuss the nature of adolescent vocational role development from this interactional perspective. This presentation will involve our presenting a general prescription for the study of vocational role development in adolescence. We will use this prescription as a template against which to describe and critique the nature of the extant literature and to indicate future needs in theory, in research, and in the devising of intervention strategies for making the links between adolescents and their social contexts as optimal as possible. To reach these goals it will be useful to discuss briefly our conceptualization of the nature of person-social context interactions, particularly in adolescence.

Dynamic Interactions in Development

Complex, multidirectional relations between an individual and his/her context have been labeled *dynamic interactions* (Lerner, 1978, 1979a; Lerner & Busch-Rossnagel, 1981; Lerner & Spanier, 1978, 1980; Lerner et al., in press). In essence this view is that there are several sources of development and that changes in one source (e.g., the social network or the individual) will influence changes in all others. From this view human evolution, too, is based on a synthesis of biological and social functioning. Indeed society would not have evolved if humans could have survived in complete social isolation. Hominid evolution on the African savannah involved selection for social cooperation and interdependency since humans, as independent units, were characterized by relative defenselessness—e.g., lack of claws and sharp teeth (Sahlins, 1978; Washburn, 1961). The individual de-

fenselessness of early humans, coupled with the dangers of living on the open African savannah, made group living essential for survival (Masters, 1978; Washburn, 1961). Therefore the content of evolution was such that it was more adaptive to act in concert with the group than in isolation. Accordingly processes supporting social relations (e.g., attachment, empathy) were selected over the course of human evolution (Hoffman, 1978; Hogan, Johnson, & Emler, 1978; Sahlins, 1978). In this regard Lancaster and Whitten (1980) have noted that humans "can, then, accurately be described as cultural animals whose outstanding characteristics are sharing and reciprocity. The archaeological record, the study of modern primates, and the behavior of present-day hunter-gatherers all attest to the significance of those traits in human evolution" (p. 15).

Social behaviors appear to have provided a means for the perpetuation and maintenance of humanity. Accordingly since a basis of social interactions was probably that all behaviors needed for an individual's survival could not efficiently be emitted by a single person, different people came to emit different behavior—that is, social roles emerged. As the settings within which humans lived changed and became more complex and differentiated, new adaptational demands were placed on people in order for them to maintain and perpetuate themselves. One social unit could not, for example, produce all the resources necessary for survival. Different units took on different roles, and role structure became more complex, more specialized, and more interdependent as society evolved. Brent (1978) has explained this relation between individual specialization and collective (i.e., societal) adaptation.

The Role of Vocational Role Development and Career Choice in Adolescence. Survival at any point in the life span obviously depends on adaptive links between the individual and his/her context. Many developmental theorists (e.g., Erikson, 1959, 1963; Havighurst, 1951, 1953) note that the tasks required for successful linkage are at least in part age-graded by society. In adolescence the key developmental task is attaining a vocational role or making a career choice.

Several reasons for this emphasis have been suggested. Erikson (1959, 1963) sees this task as a key phenomenon of adolescence because of the intrinsic, preprogrammed character of ego development, represented by the meaning he attaches to his "epigenetic principle." Piaget (1971; Inhelder & Piaget, 1958), although not a weak interactionist, critical period theorist like Erikson (Lerner & Spanier, 1978; Overton, 1973), suggests that adaptive (i.e., societally useful) vocational or career choice is an adolescent phenomenon; however, he stresses the cognitive developments requisite for such choice.

Our own view is one which recognizes both the cognitive and ego changes that are, in current cohorts, modally representative of adolescence. However rather than say that the coincidence of adolescence and the developmental task of vocational choice is a biological given, we stress the *relation* between the character of the person's changes and the needs of the social collective. Clearly for its continued survival, society needs individuals to engage in those specific behaviors requisite for the maintenance and perpetuation of the social context

(Brent, 1978; Lerner & Shea, Chap. 28; Lerner & Spanier, 1980). The adolescent period is an optimal one for the "assignment" of this task. Individualization in self-definition is involved in this acquisition, as the person must integrate knowledge of his/her specific personal attributes with the needs and demands of society. Adolescence is a period of change in these personal dimensions of the person (Lerner & Spanier, 1980) and thus placing the task of self-definition on the person at this point in the life span may be seen as an adaptive societal strategy. The adolescent is already moving toward reorganization as a consequence of his/her changes and for the first time in the life span possessing the physical and cognitive attributes needed for choosing and playing an adult role and for making vocational role or career choices; therefore, the essential developmental task of adolescence may be a cost-efficient, appropriately timed societal "demand" (cf. Lerner & Shea, Chap. 28).

From this perspective the character of the individual's development and the requirements of the social context are jointly considered in attempting to understand the presence and nature of the demands placed on adolescents in making vocational or career decisions. Given this multilevel change perspective, we can suggest that evolutionary changes, either in the character of individual development or in the needs of the social context, can alter the presence and/or the nature of these demands in adolescence. For example the secular trend in adolescent puberty (Katchadourian, 1977; Muuss, 1975), the lowered mean age of fertility that has therefore resulted, and the increasing evidence of early adolescent pregnancy and unwed motherhood (Lerner & Spanier, 1980) may require society to impose demands on the developing person before or during his/her adolescence that have limiting implications for later career choices—e.g., earlier childhood marriages are possible (they are not unknown in some cultures) or the adult mothers of the unwed adolescent mothers may be charged with the responsibility of caring for their illegitimate grandchildren, affecting their own vocational plans or activities.

Vocational or career choice can be delayed to a life period beyond adolescence if demands of the society can be served. Foner and Kertzer (1979) have reviewed data about transition to succeeding age grades (e.g., youth or elder) in highly age-stratified African societies. The age set of people who together make the transition from one age grade (e.g., a child or a youth grade) to another (e.g., a warrior or an elder grade) do not do so on the basis of chronological age—as might be expected in highly age-stratified, or age-set, societies—rather, extrinsic, often nonnormative, life event experiences influence transition. Foner and Kertzer (1979) note that "any events, such as an epidemic or a natural disaster, that affect the relative sizes of the age set in power and that seeking power will influence the timing and transitions and the relations among age sets" (p. 130).

In summary we conceptualize the coincidence of adolescent developments and societal demands for vocational development as involving an adaptive synthesis of what are individual and social changes currently prototypic of American society. From this conceptualization we may derive a set of prescriptions for the study of adolescent vocational role development.

Prescriptions for the Study of Adolescent Vocational Role Development

Our dynamic interactional perspective provides a basis for specifying what should be key factors of studies of adolescent vocational role development. These prescriptions provide a means to evaluate the current adolescent vocational role development literature and to illustrate the use of our model for furthering research and intervention. After we detail our recommendations we will evaluate the extent to which the current literature coincides with these suggested research foci. We will then illustrate the use of our perspective by appraising the implications of changes in the American family—e.g., regarding maternal employment—for adolescent vocational role development.

In our view there should be three key foci in the study of adolescent vocational role development.

A Developmental Perspective. Research should have a developmental focus. Events prior to adolescence need to be considered as possible antecedents of vocational development; in turn, adolescent developments provide key antecedents of development in later life (Lerner & Spanier, 1980). As such, an ontogenetic historical focus, which sees adolescent vocational role development as a lifespan process, is necessary. In addition the need to consider the developing interrelation among intraindividual change processes is promoted by this view.

Research methods useful for the study of such intraindividual changes are promoted by this perspective—that is, to identify correctly contributions to the variance in developmental change functions that are attributable to ontogenetic patterns, research designs are needed which are suitable for separating this variance from that related to, for example, birth cohort or time of measurement-related variance. The primary basis of this methodological requirement is conceptual and is presented in the next prescription we suggest.

A Contextual Perspective. Research must consider the nature of the social (including political and economic), physical, and cultural milieu of adolescent vocational role development. This contextual focus also needs to be developmental in focus in order to discern the altering character of the context in regard to (1) the extant array of vocations available for people in general and (2) the array specifically open to adolescents with particular characteristics of individuality (e.g., adolescents of particular cognitive, attitudinal, skill, and sex statuses). Thus the individual characteristics of the developing adolescent must be considered in relation to the particular features of the context within which the person is developing. This raises our last prescription for research.

A Relational Perspective. Research must consider the "goodness of fit" between adolescent and contextual developments. An appraisal must be made of whether the vocational role development of an adolescent is optimal for the person—e.g., in maximizing the probability of adaptive functioning given the nature of the person's characteristics of individuality. An appraisal must also be made of whether the development of the adolescent is congruent with the adaptive functioning of the society—

e.g., one must consider whether the person's development contributes to collective adaptation (Brent, 1978) and whether it serves to maintain and/or perpetuate the society (Lerner & Spanier, 1980).

This view raises other methodological requirements. Variables from at least two domains or levels of analysis—that of the person and that of the social context—must be sampled to achieve a relational perspective. As such, adolescent vocational role development research must be multidimensional and multivariate.

In summary we suggest that developmental, contextual, and relational research is needed to study adolescent vocational role development best. Moreover the theoretical framework which has led us to forward these prescriptions has also allowed us to derive recommendations for the methodological features of such research. We will now discuss the key features of the extant literature, using our prescriptions as a template for evaluation. We will indicate that most of the features we suggest as important are not well represented in the current literature. However we will also indicate how they could be usefully incorporated into the literature by discussing the impact of family changes and maternal employment as a sample case of our position.

THE CURRENT CHARACTER OF THE ADOLESCENT VOCATIONAL ROLE DEVELOPMENT LITERATURE

We have argued against a traditional psychological or "personological" approach to the study of adolescent vocational role development. Instead on the basis of a theoretical perspective stressing the role of a life-span, multidisciplinary perspective, we have recommended that such study be approached with developmental, contextual, and relational foci. However, the most salient perspective represented in the current literature is a personological one. As such there is little literature pertinent to our suggested contextual, and therefore relational, prescriptions. However at least at the level of an acknowledged need, our first perspective—that of a developmental perspective—is a feature of this literature.

The Status of a Developmental Perspective in the Adolescent Vocational Role Development Literature

Since Super (1953, 1957) and Ginzberg, Ginsburg, Axelrod, and Herma (1951), numerous authors have stressed the "developmental" nature of vocational behavior and career development in adolescence. Furthermore although adolescence has typically been viewed as the critical period in vocational development (e.g., Erikson, 1959), several authors have stressed the need to view vocational development as a lifelong process. Super and Hall (1978) point out that the life-span focus on career development has been well accepted since about the mid-1950s. Yet more than 20 years after Super's initial calls for a developmental perspective, Zytowski (1978) stated that "regrettably, while career education endorses a developmental model, there remains little empirical confirmation for it" (p. 144).

Walsh (1979), in reviewing life-span aspects of careers, concluded that there is much to be learned about the life-span aspects of vocational development. One reason for this lack of knowledge is that researchers have not combined their acknowledgment of the need to assess life-span intraindividual change processes with the methodology requisite for such a concern. Indeed only a handful of longitudinally designed studies have been carried out, most notably the *Career Pattern Study* (Super, Crites, Hummel, Moser, Overstreet, & Warnath, 1957), *Project Talent* (Flanagan, Dailey, Shaycroft, Gorhom, Orr, & Goldberg, 1962; Flanagan, Shaycroft, Richards, & Claudy, 1971), the *Career Development Study* (Gribbons & Lohnes, 1968, 1969), and the *Youth in Transition Study* (Bachman, Kahn, Mednick, Davidson, & Johnston, 1967, 1970). While many issues have been raised by these pioneering efforts, reviews have indicated that much more well-designed longitudinal research is needed (Jordaan, 1977); however, as yet no historical (e.g., sequential) design suitable for appraisinig age-, cohort-, and time-related variance has been employed.

The relative absence of appropriately designed longitudinal research in vocational development is only part of a general paucity of such research in the entire area of psychosocial behavior during adolescence and youth (Jessor & Jessor, 1977, p. 5). Part of the reason for the relative lack of longitudinal research dealing with phenomena such as vocational role development in adolescence is the great expense and long-term commitment usually required for appropriate—e.g., repeated measurement (longitudinal)—research. Yet the case for the application of longitudinal methodology in the study of developmental phenomena is becoming increasingly persuasive. McCall (1977) recently stated a widely-accepted position on this issue, "If a primary mission is to discern ontogenetic change within individuals, the sequence and timing of developmental transitions, and the changing social and environmental factors that permit development to occur, then we must use longitudinal approaches to our subject matter" (p. 337).

Admittedly the methodological issues involved in the analysis of change are among the most complex in the entire field of behavioral sciences (e.g., Baltes, 1968; Campbell & Stanely, 1963; Nesselroade, 1970; Schaie, 1965; Wohlwill, 1970). The use of multivariate sequential strategies (Baltes & Nesselroade, 1970, 1972; Nesselroade & Baltes, 1974, 1979) to examine vocational development and historical change appears to be a powerful methodological innovation to be heeded by researchers in this area. Jessor and Jessor (1977) have recently stated that "such designs, especially when applied to those stages in the life trajectory when rapid change is characteristic, appear to have great promise of revealing both the contour and the process of growth and development" (p. 8).

Theories of Vocational Development. In spite of the relative paucity of sophisticated longitudinal research in the area of vocational development, a number of authors have proposed rather elaborate developmental or life-stage theories of vocational development. However as noted earlier these theories remain largely personological in focus. Thus they tend to ignore or minimize the issues raised by contextual and relational perspectives. They tend to see the stages as maturationally, idealistically, or organismically unfolding. With little of the developmental evidence that documents other organismic stage progressions, such as cognitive developmental ones (e.g., Piaget, 1970), these descriptive formulations have relatively little known generalizability. In turn since they fail to specify the contextual variables that may provide antecedents of the stages, these theories do not provide a good basis for explanatory developmental research (Lerner, 1979b).

Ginzberg et al. (1951) proposed three periods of vocational development: the *fantasy period,* which is described as generally occurring before the age of 11, the *tentative-choice period,* which is thought to occur between the ages of 11 and 17, and the *realistic-choice period,* which occurs after age 17 when a more crystallized career choice is made. According to Ginzberg et al. the tentative-choice period is broken down into four stages in which the individual moves from making vocational choices almost exclusively on the basis of interests to increasingly making choices that also consider his/her own capacity and values, resulting in a transition stage when the individual looks forward to college or job. The realistic-choice period breaks down into three stages during which the individual successively explores alternatives, crystallizes his/her choice, and finally delimits his/her choice in the specification stage.

Super's (1953) career theory is consistent in many respects with the theory articulated by Ginzberg and colleagues. However Super is much more explicit about the life-span aspects of his theory. He lists five major stages including the *growth stage* from birth to age 14 during which self-concept develops through identification with key figures in the person's environment. The second stage is called an *exploration stage.* It is envisioned to cover ages 15 through 24. During this stage, which is viewed as that of self-examination, role tryouts and occupational explorations take place in the individual's activities. The *establishment stage* follows and is thought to continue from age 25 through age 44. During the establishment stage the individual is thought to place most of his/her efforts toward the enhancement of his/her position in a chosen occupation. The *maintenance stage,* which occurs from age 45 to 64, is viewed as a period during which the individual maintains and consolidates the occupational position previously achieved. Finally in the *decline stage* from age 65 on, work activity is assumed to decline and gradually cease.

In the vocational development theories of Ginzberg and associates as well as that of Super and colleagues, two constructs appear to have particular salience during adolescence: *vocational maturity* and *vocational exploration.* The following sections summarize the present status of these constructs in the vocational development literature.

Vocational Maturity

The concept of vocational maturity, readiness to make the career decisions required by age and by the social system, has stimulated much productive research and development clarifying concepts which have been welcomed by counseling and personnel psychologists, by career education specialists, and by counselors, even though they have gone unnoticed by de-

velopmental, personality, metric, and social psychologists. (Super & Hall, 1978, pp. 348–349)

There are at least two potential reasons for this omission of concern. One reason is that much of the research on this construct has not been developmental in focus and/or has attempted to appraise development in less than optimal ways (e.g., by assessing age changes through the use of retrospective accounts or by only appraising age group differences).

We will return to a discussion of these problems later. Here we may note that a second reason for the relative lack of attention to the concept of vocational maturity outside of the vocational or career development field may be difficulties in measurement. Super and colleagues (Super, Crites, Hummel, Moser, Overstreet, & Warnath, 1957) in the Career Pattern Study were the first to attempt the measurement of vocational maturity; a detailed scoring manual for the structured interview procedure developed by the Career Pattern Study is available, but it is fairly difficult to use (Westbrook & Cunningham, 1970). Perhaps the most widely used instrument for the measurement of vocational maturity is that developed by Crites (1965). This instrument, initially named the Vocational Development Inventory, is now called the Career Maturity Inventory. Crites, who initially proposed his model of vocational maturity in 1961, postulated a general vocational maturity factor and four group factors consisting of career choice (occupational preferences), career choice attitudes, career choice competencies, and realism of career choices.

Although the Crites inventory appears to be the most widely used, other inventories have been developed. Westbrook (1973) determined that there are three general factors that appear to be measured by all of them: (1) a cognitive domain, (2) a psychomotor domain, and (3) an affective domain. In spite of this general agreement on the major factors making up the vocational maturity construct, Herr and Cramer (1979) have concluded that empirical studies have produced conflicting findings including the disturbing discovery that correlations between aspects of certain instruments which purport to measure the same variable in the construct are low. Another problem, as pointed out by Super and Hall (1978), is the theoretical requirement that vocational maturity must rise monotonically from grade to grade, a requirement that may be unwarranted and untenable in practice. Indeed placing such an organismic requirement on such development means that to a great extent one is ignoring how the person's relation to his/her changing context may place adaptive demands on him/her which, if met, might not be adequately depicted by a monotonic growth curve.

Research on Vocational Maturity

Perhaps the most comprehensive report of research on vocational maturity is the updated Career Pattern Study, one of the few longitudinal studies in the field which focuses on the vocational maturity of the Career Pattern Study subjects during their high school years (Jordaan & Heyde, 1979). The Career Pattern Study used a rather elaborate interview procedure designed to tap the various components of vocational maturity.

Crystallization of Interests. This refers to the organismic assumption that adolescent preferences and interests should become more differentiated, more consistent, and more focused as well as more like those of adults as they become older and gain experience. Several indices, such as the number of fields under consideration, the consistency of vocational preferences within fields or families of occupations, and the presence of a primary interest pattern on interest tests, have been used.

Appropriateness or Wisdom of Preferences. This particular area of inquiry regarding vocational maturity attempts to ascertain whether the vocational choice made by the student is in accordance with his/her level of ability, with his/her interests as measured by a standard interest test, and with his/her socioeconomic and financial circumstances. In our view this area is a promising one in that it, first, assesses one individual process (vocational maturity) in the context of others (abilities, interests) and, second, makes an initial attempt to appraise the "goodness of fit" between the person's maturity and his/her contextual situation.

Nature of Work Experience. This component of the vocational maturity measurement procedure examines the nature of the individual's summer and vacation work experience, the kind of responsibility the student took for securing such employment, and the relationship of such employment to his/her stated vocational goals.

Occupational Information. This measure was based on the assessment of the extent, accuracy, and specificity of the occupational information possessed by the subjects.

Acceptance of Responsibility. To assess this variable, interviews were conducted to assess the extent to which the students were willing to assume responsibility for making decisions, in choosing an occupation, and in taking steps to be trained and admitted to such an occupation.

Planning. Assessment of this area required examination of the specificity of planning, the range of planning, the students' awareness of various contingency factors that might necessitate changes in his/her goals or plans, and the weighing of alternatives.

Implementation. This final variable in the assessment of vocational maturity examined what steps subjects had taken to realize their vocational goals.

Jordaan and Heyde factor analyzed the 62 vocational maturity measures derived in the course of assessing the preceding variables. They obtained 19 vocational maturity factors. The overall findings from the study suggest that those students who are consistently mature (from the ninth through the twelfth grade) are generally brighter, better students who are associated with higher socioeconomic positions. They also found that the consistently mature student held a fairly well-balanced self-concept. On the other hand the authors found that those students who either moved up or down in terms of their overall vocational maturity between the ninth and twelfth grades were difficult to differentiate from one another on the basis of the vocational maturity measures.

In a retrospective analysis of the childhood experience antecedents of career or vocational maturity in college students, Miller (1978) found that facilitative, positive parental behavior tended to be associated with career maturity in the children by college age. Conversely Miller found that parental attitudes and behaviors that could be construed as impeding general well-being and healthy psychological development were associated with attitudes indicative of career immaturity. Miller suggests that, in line with Erikson's formulations, a harsh parental environment would thus interfere with the developmental stage of industry versus inferiority and subsequently produce difficulties in negotiating the stage of identity. Miller's reconstruction through retrospection methodology is, in our view, an inappropriate means to appraise antecedent-consequent relations. However, his work represents one of the few instances of research in this literature showing an appreciation of the need to appraise whether antecedent adolescent interactions with their social (here familial) context provide a basis of current vocational functioning.

Summarizing recent research on vocational maturity is difficult because of the diverse definitions of this construct. The operational definition of the concept via measuring instruments is also cumbersome because of the complexities of some instruments (Jordaan & Heyde, 1979) or the various shortcomings of others (e.g., Katz, Norris, & Pears, 1978). Albeit limited by a largely personological focus and by less than optimal methodologies, it should suffice, for our purposes, to observe that the concept of career maturity has generated a great deal of research. A few illustrations may suggest the variety of variables examined in relation to vocational maturity: Pound (1978) used self-concept subscales in predicting career maturity for different race and sex subgroups; Lunneborg (1978) examined sex differences and vocational maturity, finding that females have generally higher levels of career maturity when compared to same-age male counterparts; Meir and Shiran (1979) found that vocational maturity of eleventh- and twelfth-graders was significantly influenced by their understanding of the structure of occupations, and Young (1979) showed that internal versus external locus of control played a role in the modification of frequency of information-seeking but not in increasing the maturity level of career development attitudes.

In summary we have in today's literature on vocational maturity an array of patterns of covariation among variables that were often not collected for theoretical reasons and/or remain theoretically unintegrated. These data offer a rather static, nondevelopmental view of vocational maturity and one that does not inform us about the extent to which vocational role development supports the adaptive functioning of adolescents or their societies. Similar problems exist in the research pertinent to variables other than vocational maturity.

Exploration

The concept of exploration has been somewhat neglected in recent research on vocational development, but it was postulated as early as 1951 by Ginzberg and colleagues as occurring in the realistic-choice period when the individual engages in a final stage of seeking for alternatives. Super and colleagues in the Career Pattern Study (Super, Starishevsky, Matlin, & Jordaan, 1963) ascribed primary importance to exploratory behavior in the period from 15 to 24 years of age. They postulated that during this period self-examination occurs, role tryouts are made, and occupational exploration is carried out in connection with leisure activities, part-time work, and in school. Super (1953) elaborated this exploration stage and proposed three substages, the first one being the *tentative* stage, occurring between the ages of 15 and 17. During this period tentative choices are made by the individual and tried out in fantasy, in work, in interactions with peers, and with adults. The second substage is titled *transition*. It is thought to occur between the ages of 18 and 21 when reality constraints lead the individual to implement his/her self-concept in the labor market or in some form of professional training. The final substage during exploration is the *trial* substage, which occurs between the ages of 22 and 24. This trial substage usually results in the individual trying out a seemingly appropriate field of work. If the appropriateness of the choice is confirmed by subsequent experience, the individual then moves into the following major stage in the Super model, which is the *establishment* stage that occurs from early adulthood through mid-life.

The concept of exploration or exploratory behavior in relation to vocational development, although postulated and developed in some detail by the vocational development theories of the early 1950s, has not led to a great deal of research subsequently, in spite of the fact that, as Jordaan (1963) has observed, the concept could easily serve as a bridge between vocational and counseling psychologists on the one hand and developmental psychologists concerned with exploratory behavior on the other. Indeed in our view such a construct could be a useful bridge between the changing adolescent and his/her attempts to fit into his/her changing world. In fact Jordaan reviewed the work of developmental psychologists, in particular Berlyne's (1960), and noted that most of that work had been carried out with animals or infants and very young children. At the same time Jordaan pointed out similarities in the conditions postulated to precipitate exploratory behavior in animals and infants and in exploratory behavior postulated to occur in adolescents when searching for a vocational role or life career.

Super and Hall (1978) make a particular point of decrying the neglect of the concept of exploration in vocational development in general and the lack of attention to Jordaan's work in particular. They urge a revival of Jordaan's theoretical analysis of the dimensions of vocational exploration (intended or fortuitous; systematic or random; recognized or not recognized as exploration, self- or environment-oriented, self- or other-initiated, contemporaneous or retrospective; motor or mental; intrinsic or extrinsic; behavior modifying or fruitless; vocationally relevant or irrelevant). To reiterate, however, there is as yet little evidence of empirical interest in this concept, one which basically pertains to reciprocal person-environment interactions (see Berlyne, 1960; Fein, 1981).

The operationalization and measurement of exploratory vocational behavior in adolescents is a critical issue which might have prevented researchers from embracing this particular area. The lack of clear operational defini-

tions also makes it difficult to present research findings in the area of exploration since most studies dealing with exploratory behavior have simply not been conceptualized and/or labeled that way. Increased cross-fertilization between vocational psychologists and developmental psychologists may be important in overcoming those problems. Problems in developing a coherent review of research in this area of vocational exploration may well be symptomatic of the general lack of coherence in the field as a whole (Zytowski, 1978). Significantly Zytwoski also singled out the areas of "developmental tasks and stages of vocational behavior" and "interventions in career development" as requiring "better efforts"—that is, problems of theory and research in the study of adolescent vocational role development also present problems for formulating useful strategies for optimizing vocational development. We address some of these issues of translation from theory and research to intervention in the next section.

Intervention in Vocational Development

In the preceding sections we have appraised the degree to which various developmental perspectives about vocational development have been translated into research. In this section we will briefly summarize the status of intervention in "vocationalization" from a developmental perspective.

As was the case with theory, relatively recent trends in vocational and career guidance have emphasized a developmental perspective. The title of a recent book by Herr and Cramer (1979), *Career Guidance through the Life Span*, signifies this recognition that vocational development starts in early childhood and does not end until the disengagement period following retirement. This life-span developmental emphasis is complemented by an approach to intervention that is typically described as "developmental" rather than "remedial" (Herr & Cramer, 1979).

Current vocational guidance programs in the public school systems emphasize self-knowledge and learning the basics of decision making in elementary school, exploration of vocational options and preliminary planning in the junior high school, and specific planning and initial implementation of vocational decisions in the senior high school. Unfortunately these specific career guidance activities are not clearly linked to the developmental tasks and processes postulated by the various theorists discussed earlier. There are nevertheless some positive trends in the career and vocational intervention literature. First, rather than using a strictly empirical and actuarial approach to assessing the career development needs of individuals, more and more researchers are beginning to ask basic questions about the underlying developmental processes. Osipow (1979) has recently observed that the concept of interests is central to vocational psychology but that very little effort has been made to understand its underlying structure. Considering the important role of vocational interest measurement in vocational guidance, it is clear that understanding the relationship between interests and preferences is not enough. To relate interests to the developmental tasks faced by individuals seeking to establish themselves in the world of work requires a far better understanding of the development of vocational interests. The same is true of other key aspects of vocational development important in the intervention process such as decision making, information acquisition, and problem solving. The recognition that developmental research will pose new and different questions and thus lead to new and different understandings of these processes is an emerging trend that bodes well for the future of intervention in vocational development.

A second area of considerable promise for vocational intervention consists of the rapidly improving understanding of the impact of sex roles on career development and the recognition of sex biases in intervention. As we will discuss in greater detail later, much of the research on sex roles has been stimulated by the changing employment patterns of women and the fact that 50 percent of all American women now hold jobs outside of the home. McLure and Piel (1978) found that relatively few women chose careers in science and technology because of their concerns about combining family life with a career in the sciences. The authors postulated that such choices were also based on a lack of information because they saw few female role models in science and technology fields and because they simply believed influential adults who told them that such roles would not be suitable for them. Stake (1978) found important differences between the occupational motives of male and female college students, with the females expressing greater expectations of intrinsic work enjoyment and fewer future financial responsibilities than the males did. In general studies which appraise individuals' development in relation to such contextual changes have led to a better understanding of the factors which predispose men and women to choose different occupations. As we have been emphasizing, however, what is needed is a greater emphasis on developmental, contextual, and relational research that could, perhaps, illuminate the antecedents of such differences and, in the process, lead to prescriptions for child-rearing that could potentially optimize career choices later in life.

The recognition of subtle biases in intervention in vocational development should also have a salutary effect on the entire field. Donahue and Costar (1977) found biases against girls by high school counselors, with the counselors advising females to choose occupations that involved more supervision and less pay. Interestingly that tendency was strongest among older women counselors.

The foregoing is not intended to suggest that current vocational development intervention is completely ineffective. As a matter of fact the literature is replete with studies that demonstrate at least partial success in career intervention with specific groups and specific procedures. Among such studies Egner and Jackson (1978), in testing the effectiveness of a counseling intervention program for teaching career–decision-making skills, found that it was effective in improving such skills and in raising the subjects' career maturity scores in the process. In another study Omvig-Clayton and Thomas (1977) found that career education increased the level of career maturity in sixth- and eighth-graders. Another example is McGowan's (1977) study that showed Holland's Self-Directed Search for Career Planning (SDS) was effec-

tive in reducing career indecision and increasing career maturity. In a rather ambitious intervention study, Hamdani (1977) exposed disadvantaged inner-city high school students to a semester-long career and self-exploration class. The author found increases in career maturity, in attendance and punctuality, and in the number of vocational preferences stated by the subject.

While the preceding examples provide evidence to support the notion that various career guidance efforts at different levels have some utility, they fall short in that they fail to link career and vocational guidance efforts effectively to the mainstream of developmental research in such areas as the development of social behavior, the acquisition of work values, the development of problem-solving and decision-making skills and others. Similarly they do not adequately link any of these changes to concomitant change in the societal context. However it must be pointed out that developmental psychologists have placed relatively little emphasis on research related to the development of vocational roles. Greatly increased cross-fertilization between vocational psychologists and developmental psychologists would seem to be appropriate.

In summary although the current research literature reflects a growing emphasis on a developmental perspective and an acknowledgement of the use of a life-span perspective, there are still major shortcomings in the implementation of these orientations. These shortcomings involve problems of research design as well as problems of conceptualization—that is, a commitment to a life-span developmental perspective cannot be best actualized, in our view, through reliance on personological, organismic conceptions of vocational-role development. Instead an appreciation of mutually adaptive interchanges between adolescents and their contexts must be attained. Such a focus could best lead to intervention strategies successful in enhancing not only adolescent development but also human development across the life span. We illustrate these contentions in the following section.

SOCIAL CHANGE AND VOCATIONAL ROLE DEVELOPMENT: THE SAMPLE CASES OF FAMILY CHANGES AND MATERNAL EMPLOYMENT

Our dynamic interactional perspective suggests that adaptive vocational and career developments in adolescence will be those congruent with the demands of the social context extant at this time of the person's life. Historical changes in the nature of the context may thus alter the adaptive significance of particular role adoptions. Not all theorists share our views, however.

Erikson (1964, 1968) believes that healthy personality development in adolescence rests on a role adoption which is consonant with one's biological, psychological, and social orientations. We do not dispute such a broad claim; however, in the specifics of Erikson's (1964, 1968) formulation, which stresses that because of nature-based preformations anatomy is destiny, we do take issue. To Erikson healthy personality development involves adoption of roles which allow the person to meet the needs of society but yet, at the same time, are consistent with one's biological (i.e., reproductive) status. Because of their genital structure women are oriented to "inner space," to incorporating others, and thus to playing roles which are dependent on others (cf. Lerner & Brackney, 1978). These roles are the sex-role traditional ones in our society (Broverman, Vogel, Broverman, Clarkson, & Rosenkrantz, 1972). Men, in turn, are oriented to "outer space" because of their genital structure, and this leads to an intrusive mode of dealing with the world, to independence, and to the adoption of stereotypically traditional male roles (Erikson, 1964; Lerner & Brackney, 1978). Thus only those roles consistent with the inner (for women) and outer (for men) orientations would be adaptive in Erikson's (1964, 1968) view. Biocultural (evolutionary) changes and/or cultural differences that were associated with the reversal of these role orientations among either sex, or with a synthesis among them for both sexes, would not be seen as being as adaptive as traditional role orientations.

Another view discrepant from our own has been proposed by McCandless (1970). He has formulated a social learning view of adolescent personality development which involves societal rewards for males showing an instrumental effectance-competence cluster of behaviors and punishment for them having a warmth-expressiveness cluster of behaviors; in turn, the reverse system of contingencies is held to exist for females (see also Broverman et al., 1972). Accordingly independent, manipulative, assertive behaviors of males are established, and males become oriented to traditional male roles in society; the reverse of this process leads females to become oriented to those roles traditional for their sex (McCandless, 1970).

Consistent with this line of reasoning, although based on nurture mechanisms instead of nature ones, the ideas of McCandless lead to the view that adaptive functioning—i.e., in this case behavior associated with the highest probability of reward—is isomorphic with behaviors that are consistent with traditional sex-role prescriptions. Thus as with the ideas of Erikson, the views of McCandless lead to ideas discrepant from those of our contextual model.

Although McCandless focused on socially mediated rewards and punishments, he did not extend his ideas to consider that this social context itself is a dynamically developing level of organization and that as such, as the society changes its adaptive demands pertaining to appropriate male and female career behavior, the implications of vocational role adoption consistent or inconsistent with traditional expectations should similarly alter. As a consequence of this omission, the views of McCandless share with those of Erikson an exclusion of concern with how the historically changed social context of today's adolescents may provide an altered interactive milieu for different adaptive personal and functional vocational role developments.

In our view there are significant changes in the social context of today's adolescents. These changes provide historically altered demands on them, demands which require variation from strictly traditional vocational role developments and career choices for adaptive functioning. We illustrate our position by focusing on the changing family context of adolescent development, the alterations in maternal employment involved therein, and the

consequences of these changes for vocational role development and career choice in adolescence.

The Changing Demography of the American Family

Perhaps as a consequence of new methods of birth control, of changing economic pressures (e.g., a median-sized family with a single working adult earning the median income level could not easily afford a median priced home in 1979), and of changing political, educational, and career aspirations of women, the 1970s were characterized by a marked drop in the birthrate. Compared to the 1957 birthrate, the rate in 1977 dropped by almost 50 percent to 67.8 births per 1000 women, aged 15–55 (David & Baldwin, 1979). By 1978 the total number of births had dropped to 3.3 million. Through the 1970s the birthrate has remained at a relatively low level. Although it is possible that the birthrate might increase slightly in coming years, there is no evidence to suggest that it will increase to a level even approaching that which was seen during the high rates of the 1950s. Thus it is likely that the American family of the future will be relatively small, with two children being the norm (U.S. Bureau of the Census, 1979).

These projections are confirmed by data on birth expectations of recently married young women. Although individuals do change their minds and although there are occasional contraceptive failures, the reports of these young women may be taken as rough indications of what families might look like in the next decade or two. The average number of births a woman expects to have is composed of the number of children already born and the number of additional births expected over her entire reproductive career. Birth expectations are not subject to as rapid fluctuations as annual fertility rates are (U.S. Bureau of the Census, 1978). Thus one potential implication of these changes is that women in intact marriages will not *need* to spend as much of their time, as was previously the case, in within-home caregiving activities. In turn given the increasing number of single-parent families (e.g., occurring as a consequence of divorce) and the fact that in most of these families mothers maintain primary custody of their children (Hetherington, 1979), women in such settings may *have* to spend more of their time outside of the home (in remunerative activities). These ideas are consistent with a second critical change in the American family.

There has been a major impact on the family due to the significant increase in the number of women in the labor force. Considering all married women—not just those with young children—51 percent of those aged 18 to 34 were in the labor force in 1978. The proportion was 43 percent for those with at least one child. Moreover in 1978 one-third of the married women who had given birth within the past year were currently in the labor force (U.S. Bureau of the Census, 1979). In addition more than 40 percent of married mothers with a preschool child (two to four years old) are employed (U.S. Bureau of the Census, 1979), and throughout the last decade over 50 percent of married mothers with school-age children have been employed (Hoffman, 1979). All these rates are higher for mothers in single-parent families. Therefore employment outside the home is now, and is likely to continue to be, a part of a woman's role for a majority of American mothers. Such a trend requires some rethinking of the idea that most women quit work following the birth of their first child.

The increase in working mothers is indicative of the desire of many women to establish careers early in life. It may also indicate a willingness on the part of men and women to enhance a family's standard of living by having two incomes. Apparently many couples see this as a worthwhile sacrifice. However, many women value work because of the rewards it brings. A 1976 national sample of working women revealed that 76 percent would continue to work even if they did not have to (Dubnoff, Veroff, & Kulka, 1978). This percentage represents a considerable increase over the percentage of working women responding similarly to the same question asked in a 1957 survey (Hoffman, 1979). What are the effects of changing maternal employment patterns on adolescent vocational role development and career choice?

Effects of Maternal Employment

As noted earlier more women than ever before are now combining jobs inside the home (wife and mother) with simultaneous careers outside the home, and this trend is likely to continue. We focus on this trend in order to illustrate the role of change in the social context on adolescent vocational role development. What will the effect be on the adolescent of developing in a family where the mother has outside employment?

Effects of maternal employment on the adolescent have been documented best in regard to the person's own vocational aspirations and expectations, and these effects are most pronounced in regard to the daughters of "working mothers." As summarized by Huston-Stein and Higgins-Trenk (1978),

The most consistent and well-documented correlate of career orientation and departure from traditional feminine roles is maternal employment during childhood and adolescence. Daughters of employed mothers (i.e., mothers who were employed during some period of the daughter's childhood or adolescence) more often aspire to a career outside the home (Almquist & Angrist, 1971; Hoffman, 1974; Stein, 1973), get better grades in college (Nichols & Schauffer, 1975), and aspire to more advanced education (Hoffman, 1974; Stein, 1973). College women who have chosen a traditionally masculine occupation more often had employed mothers than those preparing for feminine occupations (Almquist, 1974; Tangri, 1972). (pp. 279–280)

Moreover when females are raised within a family in which their mother is employed, it has also been shown that (1) they have less stereotyped views of females' roles than do daughters of nonworking mothers; (2) they have a broader definition of the female role, often including attributes that are traditionally male ones; and (3) they are more likely to emulate their mothers—that is, they more often name their mother as the person they aspire to be like than is the case with daughters of nonworking mothers (Huston-Stein & Higgins-Trenk, 1978).

These effects of developing in a family in which the mother is employed outside the home can be identified in the childhood and early adolescent years. Bacon and Lerner (1975) found that second-, fourth-, and sixth-grade females whose mothers were employed outside the home had societal vocational role perceptions that were more egalitarian than were the perceptions of grade-mate daughters of nonworking mothers. Gold and Andres (1978b) found that the sex-role concepts of both female *and* male nursery school children were more egalitarian if their mothers were employed. These children's perceptions of their mothers, along a negative-positive dimension, were not related to maternal employment status. However, fathers were perceived more negatively by their sons if the mother was employed.

Thus maternal employment may relate to more than the child's vocational orientation. Gold and Andres (1978a) document this idea further. They assessed the sex-role concepts, personality adjustment, and academic achievement of 223 ten-year-old boys and girls, with either full-time employed or nonemployed mothers from working-class or middle-class families. Children with employed mothers had the most egalitarian sex-role concepts. However this relation was primarily dependent not on maternal employment per se, but rather on their mothers' greater satisfaction with their roles. There was also some relation between maternal employment status and the children's achievement. Middle-class boys with employed mothers had lower scores on language and mathematics achievement tests than did the other middle-class children.

The data of Gold and Andres (1978a) suggest also that the effects of developing in a family in which the mother is employed outside the home may involve family relations that differ from those found in families where the mother is not employed outside the home. They report that employed mothers and their husbands had more similar behavior patterns within the home and more similar childcare attitudes than did nonemployed mothers and their husbands. Moreover there are some data to suggest that mothers of achievement-oriented females take steps to promote independence rather than dependency in their daughters (Stein & Bailey, 1973). Since achievement orientations exist among daughters of working mothers, it may be that such interactions exist in these settings. Moreover the father can promote the nontraditional vocational development of the daughter. Fathers having high occupational status more often promote such achievement in their daughters, especially when the daughter is the oldest child or when there are no sons (Huston-Stein & Higgins-Trenk, 1978). In summary there are data to suggest that a variety of factors may interact in certain families to promote the development of vocational role orientations and behaviors that are nontraditional. However, are such developments adaptive for the individual?

We have argued that any nature-based notion, which stresses that anatomy is destiny (e.g., Erikson, 1968), or a nurture notion, which emphasizes only social rewards and punishments (e.g., McCandless, 1970), are limited views. Biology certainly does exert pressures on psychosocial development. However, this influence does not occur independent of the demands of the cultural and historical milieu. The biological basis of one's psychosocial functioning relates to the adaptive orientation for survival. Hence although it may be adaptive at some time in a given society to perform roles highly associated with anatomical and physiological differences, these same roles may not be adaptive in other societies or at other times in history. The behavioral differences that were functional in primitive times may no longer be so in a modern society which permits greater leisure time, nearly equal opportunity for employment, almost universal formal education, and economic and political presses for members of both sexes, whether married or single, to be employed outside the home. If adolescents are to attain *adaptive development in relation to this changing context,* they should adopt vocational roles that transcend the traditionally sex-role stereotyped vocational distinctions extant in earlier historical eras. Adaptive development should be associated with more egalitarian development.

Block (1973) shows that at least one measure of more developed psychosocial functioning—the presence of a principled level of moral reasoning—is associated with American college-aged males and females who have less traditional sex-role definitions of themselves. Bem (1974, 1975, 1977) found that among men and women who have a simultaneous orientation to both traditional male and traditional female behaviors there is evidence for adaptive psychosocial functioning. Sorell (1979) reports similar results. Bem (1974, 1975) argued that internalization of culturally stereotypic sex roles inhibits the development of a fully adaptive and maximally satisfying behavioral repertoire. A male or female who identifies with both desirable masculine and desirable feminine characteristics—an androgynous person—is not only free from the limitations of unidimensionally stereotyped sex roles but should also be able to engage more effectively in both traditional male and traditional female behaviors across a variety of social situations, presumably because of his/her flexibility, than should a nonandrogynous person (Jones, Chernovetz, & Hansson, 1978). Several studies (Bem, 1974, 1975, 1977; Spence & Helmreich, 1978; Worell, 1978, 1981) have provided data validating this general idea—i.e., that the greater vocational- and sex-role flexibility which defines androgynous men and women is associated with greater social competence and psychological health than is the case with males and females oriented to traditional sex-role adoption.

In summary vocational orientations that are not canalized by sex-traditional perspectives and an orientation to one's career activities which incorporates flexibility may be requisites for adaptive functioning in the current social context. Given the dynamic interactional bases that we see as underlying these adaptive presses, we may now discuss what we see as the key implications for human development intervention.

CONCLUSIONS: OPTIMIZING ADOLESCENT VOCATIONAL ROLE DEVELOPMENT

The prescriptions we have forwarded for advancing research about adolescent vocational role development may be recast as components of a view about optimizing such development. As indicated in our illustration of the effects of family change and maternal employment, adolescents' vocational role developments change in relation to their family context. In turn this context itself changes in relation to other sociocultural alterations. As such the themes of development, context, and relationism are raised in strategies for intervention.

For most children the familial context within which they develop exists prior to their birth. In all cases children come into contact with an array of previously established social institutions from the moment of their birth. Since the nature and developmental trajectory of these elements of the social context have been seen to influence adolescent vocational role development, interventions aimed at enhancing such development may be directed to levels of analysis other than the personological one. Moreover these interventions not only can begin prior to the person's becoming an adolescent but also given the preexistence of these institutions, may commence prior to the birth (or conception) of the child. Interventions aimed at spousal interaction, for example, designed to facilitate the development of egalitarian social exchanges in marriage could begin before the birth of a child. Through fostering the development of spouses who act in egalitarian manners, such intervening could increase the likelihood of such people becoming parental models of egalitarianism.

Of course such interventions need not be historical in character. More immediate interventions with adults as models during the child's adolescence are possible. Here one may capitalize on the relation of the adolescent and the family to the broader social context. Community interventions, involving summer or vacation jobs or apprentice programs, can enhance the vocational development of youth. Federal programs providing incentives to employers to hire youth for jobs fostering desired vocational role developments could facilitate such community programs. Indeed in an era of inflation, rising unemployment, and lowered productivity, such programs would have the benefit of increasing the income level of the family and of fostering intergenerational cooperation within the family.

These examples are only illustrative of the targets, timing, and mechanisms one may suggest in interventions derived from a dynamic interactional perspective which promotes developmental, contextual, and relational perspectives. We believe they suffice in indicating that a theoretically based, life-span, multidisciplinary-oriented study of adolescent vocational role development is appropriate and useful for science, intervention, and social policy.

Traditional interventions in vocational development need to be broadened to incorporate interventions targeted to the individual, the family, the community and its institutions, and finally, social policy. The framework suggested here is more far-reaching and comprehensive than current approaches to vocational development. While the system of secondary education is, and should continue to be, in a leadership position with regard to the implementation of vocational and career development programs, the question needs to be raised whether other segments of society—e.g., industry and business—should be mobilized to participate in specific, targeted ways to optimize vocational development. To simply offer more traditional vocational guidance is certainly not the answer. To reach out into the community (Tillery & Kildegaard, 1973, p. 192) to promote sound (healthy) development and to engage in diagnostic activities prior to intervention (Jordaan & Heyde, 1979, pp. 173–180) are certainly steps in the right direction.

REFERENCES

ALMQUIST, E. M. Sex stereotype in occupational choice: The case for college women. *Journal of Vocational Behavior,* 1974, *5,* 13–21.

ALMQUIST, E. M., & ANGRIST, S. S. Role model influences on college women's career aspirations. *Merrill-Palmer Quarterly,* 1971, *17,* 263–279.

BACHMAN, J. G., KAHN, R. L., MEDNICK, M., DAVIDSON, T. N., & JOHNSTON, L. D. *Youth in transition* (Vol. 2). Ann Arbor: University of Michigan Institute for Social Research, 1970.

BACON, C., & LERNER, R. M. Effects of maternal employment status on the development of vocational-role perception in females. *Journal of Genetic Psychology,* 1975, *126,* 193–197.

BALTES, P. B. Longitudinal and cross-sectional sequences in the study of age and generation effects. *Human Development,* 1968, *11,* 145–171.

BALTES, P. B., & NESSELROADE, J. R. Multivariate longitudinal and cross-sectional sequences for analyzing ontogenetic and generational change: A methodological note. *Developmental Psychology,* 1970, *2,* 2.

BALTES, P. B., & NESSELROADE, J. R. Cultural change and adolescent personality development: An application of longitudinal sequences. *Developmental Psychology,* 1972, *7,* 244–256.

BEM, S. L. The measurement of psychological androgyny. *Journal of Consulting and Clinical Psychology,* 1974, *47,* 155–162.

BEM, S. L. Sex role adaptability: One consequence of psychological androgyny. *Journal of Personality and Social Psychology,* 1975, *31,* 634–643.

BEM, S. L. On the utility of alternative procedures for assessing psychological androgyny. *Journal of Consulting and Clinical Psychology,* 1977, *45,* 196–205.

BERLYNE, D. E. *Conflict, arousal, and curiosity.* New York: McGraw-Hill, 1960.

BLOCK, J. H. Conceptions of sex roles: Some cross-cultural and longitudinal perspectives. *American Psychologist,* 1973, *28,* 512–526.

BRENT, S. B. Individual specialization, collective adaptation and rate of environment change. *Human Development,* 1978, *21,* 21–33.

BROVERMAN, I. K., VOGEL, S. R., BROVERMAN, D. M., CLARKSON, F. E., & ROSENKRANTZ, P. S. Sex-role stereotypes: A current appraisal. *Journal of Social Issues,* 1972, *28,* 59–78.

CAMPBELL, D. T., & STANLEY, J. C. *Experimental and quasi-experimental designs for research.* Skokie, Ill.: Rand McNally, 1963.

CRITES, J. O. Measurement of vocational maturity in adolescence: Attitude test of the vocational development inventory. *Psychological Monographs,* 1965, *79*(2, Whole No. 595).

DAVID, H. P., & BALDWIN, W. P. Childbearing and child development: Demographic and psychosocial trends. *American Psychologist,* 1979, *34,* 866–871.

DONAHUE, T. J., & COSTAR, J. W. Counselor discrimination against young women in career selection. *Journal of Counseling Psychology,* 1977, *24,* 481–486.

DUBNOFF, S. J., VEROFF, J., & KULKA, R. A. *Adjustment to work: 1957–1976.* Paper presented at the meeting of the American Psychological Association, Toronto, August 1978.

EGNER, J. R., & JACKSON, D. J. Effectiveness of a counseling intervention program for teaching career decision-making skills. *Journal of Counseling Psychology,* 1978, *25*(No. 1), 45–52.

ERIKSON, E. H. Identity and the life cycle. *Psychological Issues,* 1959, *1,* 18–164.

ERIKSON, E. H. *Childhood and society* (2nd ed.). New York: W. W. Norton & Co., Inc., 1963.

ERIKSON, E. H. Inner and outer space: Reflections on womanhood. In R. J. Lifton (Ed.), *The woman in America.* Boston: Beacon, 1964.

ERIKSON, E. H. *Identity, youth and crisis.* New York: W. W. Norton & Co., Inc., 1968.

FEIN, G. G. The physical environment: Stimulation or evocation. In R. M. Lerner & N. A. Busch-Rossnagel (Eds.), *Individuals as producers of their development: A life-span perspective.* New York: Academic Press, 1981.

FLANAGAN, J. C., DAILEY, J. T., SHAYCROFT, M. F., GORHOM, W. A., ORR, D. B., & GOLDBERG, I. *Design for a study of American youth.* Boston: Houghton Mifflin, 1962.

FLANAGAN, J. C., SHAYCROFT, J. F., RICHARDS, J. R., JR., & CLAUDY, J. G. *Project talent, five years after high school.* Pittsburgh: American Institutes for Research, 1971.

FONER, A., & KERTZER, D. I. Intrinsic and extrinsic sources of change in life-course transitions. In M. W. Riley (Ed.), *Aging from birth to death: Interdisciplinary perspectives.* Boulder, Colo.: Westview Press, 1979.

GINZBERG, E., GINSBURG, S. W., AXELROD, S., & HERMA, J. L. *Occupational choice: An approach to a general theory.* New York: Columbia University Press, 1951.

GOLD, D., & ANDRES, D. Developmental comparisons between 10-year-old children with employed and non-employed mothers. *Child Development,* 1978a, *49,* 75–84.

GOLD, D., & ANDRES, D. Relations between maternal employment and development of nursery school children. *Canadian Journal of Behavioral Science,* 1978b, *10,* 116–129.

GRIBBONS, W. D., & LOHNES, P. R. *Emerging careers.* New York: Teachers College Press, 1968.

GRIBBONS, W. D., & LOHNES, P. R. *Career development from age 13 to 25.* Final Report, Project No. 6-2151. Washington, D.C.: U.S. Department of Health, Education and Welfare, 1969.

HAMDANI, A. Facilitating vocational development among disadvantaged inner-city adolescents. *Vocational Guidance Quarterly,* 1977, *26*(No. 1), 60–68.

HARTUP, W. W. Perspectives on child and family interaction: Past, present and future. In R. M. Lerner & G. B. Spanier (Eds.), *Child influences on marital and family interaction: A lifespan perspective.* New York: Academic Press, 1978.

HARTUP, W. W. The social worlds of childhood. *American Psychologist,* 1979, *34,* 944–950.

HAVIGHURST, R. J. *Developmental tasks and education.* New York: Longman, 1951.

HAVIGHURST, R. J. *Human development and education.* London: Longman, 1953.

HERR, E. L., & CRAMER, S. H. *Career guidance through the life span: Systematic approaches.* Boston: Little, Brown, 1979.

HETHERINGTON, E. M. Divorce: A child's perspective. *American Psychologist,* 1979, *34,* 851–858.

HOFFMAN, L. W. The employment of women, education, and fertility. *Merrill-Palmer Quarterly,* 1974, *20,* 99–119.

HOFFMAN, L. W. Maternal employment: 1979. *American Psychologist,* 1979, *34,* 859–865.

HOFFMAN, M. L. Empathy, its development and prosocial implications. In H. E. Howe, Jr. (Ed.), *Nebraska Symposium on Motivation, 1978.* Lincoln: University of Nebraska Press, 1978.

HOGAN, R., JOHNSON, J. A., & EMLER, N. P. A socioanalytic theory of moral development. *New Directions for Child Development,* 1978, *2,* 1–18.

HUSTON-STEIN, A., & HIGGINS-TRENK, A. Development of females from childhood through adulthood: Career and feminine orientations. In P. B. Baltes (Ed.), *Life-span development and behavior* (Vol. 1). New York: Academic Press, 1978.

INHELDER, B., & PIAGET, J. *The growth of logical thinking from childhood to adolescence.* New York: Basic Books, 1958.

JESSOR, R., & JESSOR, S. L. *Problem behavior and psychosocial development: A longitudinal study of youth.* New York: Academic Press, 1977.

JONES, W. H., CHERNOVETZ, M. E. O'C., & HANSSON, R. O. The enigma of androgyny: Differential implications for males and females. *Journal of Consulting and Clinical Psychology,* 1978, *46,* 298–313.

JORDAAN, J. P. Exploratory behavior: The formation of self and occupational concepts. In D. E. Super, R. Starishevsky, N. Matlin, & J. P. Jordaan (Eds.), *Career development: Self-concept theory.* New York: College Entrance Examination Board, 1963.

JORDAAN, J. P. Career development theory. *International Review of Applied Psychology,* 1977, *26*(No. 2), 107–114.

JORDAAN, J. P., & HEYDE, M. B. *Vocational maturity during the high school years.* New York: Teacher's College Press, 1979.

KATCHADOURIAN, H. *The biology of adolescence.* San Francisco: W. H. Freeman & Company Publishers, 1977.

KATZ, M., NORRIS, L., & PEARS, L. Simulated occupational

choice: A diagnostic measure of competencies in career decision making. *Measurement and Evaluation in Guidance,* 1978, *10,* 222–232.

LANCASTER, J. B., & WHITTEN, P. Family matters. *The Sciences,* 1980, *20,* 10–15.

LERNER, R. M. Nature, nurture, and dynamic interactionism. *Human Development,* 1978, *21,* 1–20.

LERNER, R. M. A dynamic interactional concept of individual and social relationship development. In R. L. Burgess & T. L. Huston (Eds.), *Social exchange in developing relationships.* New York: Academic Press, 1979a.

LERNER, R. M. The stage concept in developmental theory: A dialectic alternative. *The Behavioral and Brain Sciences,* 1979b, *2,* 144–145.

LERNER, R. M., & BRACKNEY, B. E. The importance of inner and outer body parts attitudes in the self concept of late adolescents. *Sex Roles,* 1978, *4,* 225–228.

LERNER, R. M., & BUSCH-ROSSNAGEL, N. A. Individuals as producers of their development: Conceptual and empirical bases. In R. M. Lerner & N. A. Busch-Rossnagel (Eds.), *Individuals as producers of their development: A life-span perspective.* New York: Academic Press, 1981.

LERNER, R. M., & SPANIER, G. B. A dynamic interactional view of child and family development. In R. M. Lerner & G. B. Spanier (Eds.), *Child influences on marital and family interaction: A life-span perspective.* New York: Academic Press, 1978.

LERNER, R. M., & SPANIER, G. B. *Adolescent development: A life-span perspective.* New York: McGraw-Hill, 1980.

LERNER, R. M., SPANIER, G. B., & BELSKY, J. The child in the family. In C. B. Kopp & J. Krakow (Eds.), *The child: Development in a social context.* Reading, Mass.: Addison-Wesley, in press.

LEVINSON, D. J. *The seasons of a man's life.* New York: Knopf, 1978.

LUNNEBORG, P. W. Sex and career decision-making styles. *Journal of Counseling Psychology,* 1978, *25,* 299–305.

McCALL, R. B. Challenges to a science of developmental psychology. *Child Development,* 1977, *48,* 333–344.

McCANDLESS, B. R. *Adolescents.* Hinsdale, Ill.: Dryden Press, 1970.

McGOWAN, A. S. Vocational maturity and anxiety among vocationally undecided and indecisive students: The effectiveness of Holland's self-directed search. *Journal of Vocational Behavior,* 1977, *10*(2), 196–204.

McLURE, G. T., & PIEL, E. College bound girls and science careers: Perceptions of barriers and facilitating factors. *Journal of Vocational Behavior,* 1978, *12,* 172–183.

MASTERS, R. D. Jean-Jacques is alive and well: Rousseau and contemporary sociobiology. *Daedalus,* 1978, *107,* 93–105.

MEIR, E. I., & SHIRAN, D. The occupational cylinder as a means for vocational maturity enhancement. *Journal of Vocational Behavior,* 1979, *14,* 279–283.

MILLER, M. I. Childhood experience antecedents of career maturity attitudes. *The Vocational Guidance Quarterly,* 1978, *27*(No. 1), 137–143.

MUUSS, R. E. (Ed.). *Adolescent behavior and society: A book of readings* (2nd ed.). New York: Random House, 1975.

NESSELROADE, J. R. Application of multivariate strategies to problems of measuring and structuring long-term change. In L. R. Goulet & P. B. Baltes (Eds.), *Life-span developmental psychology: Research and theory.* New York: Academic Press, 1970.

NESSELROADE, J. R., & BALTES, P. B. Adolescent personality development and historical change: 1970–1972. *Monographs of the Society for Research in Child Development,* 1974, *39*(1, Serial No. 154).

NESSELROADE, J. R., & BALTES, P. B. *Longitudinal research in the study of behavior and development.* New York: Academic Press, 1979.

NICHOLS, I. A., & SCHAUFFER, C. B. *Self-concept as a predictor of performance in college women.* Paper presented at the 83rd Annual Convention of the American Psychological Association, Chicago, September 1975.

OMVIG-CLAYTON, P., & THOMAS, E. G. Relationship between career education, sex, and career maturity of sixth and eighth grade pupils. *Journal of Vocational Behavior,* 1977, *11*(No. 3), 322–331.

OSIPOW, S. H. Career choices: Learning about interests and intervening in their development. In A. M. Mitchell, G. B. Jones, & J. D. Krumboltz (Eds.), *Social learning and career decision making.* Cranston, R. I.: Carroll Press, 1979.

OVERTON, W. F. On the assumptive basis of the nature-nurture controversy: Additive versus interactive conceptions. *Human Development,* 1973, *16,* 74–89.

PIAGET, J. *Six psychological studies.* New York: Random House, 1967.

PIAGET, J. Piaget's theory. In P. H. Mussen (Ed.), *Carmichael's manual of child psychology* (Vol. 1). New York: John Wiley, 1970.

PIAGET, J. *Biology and knowledge.* Chicago: University of Chicago Press, 1971.

POUND, R. E. Using self-concept subscales in predicting career maturity for different race and sex subgroups. *The Vocational Guidance Quarterly,* 1978, *27,* 61–70.

SAHLINS, M. D. The use and abuse of biology. In A. L. Caplan (Ed.), *The sociobiology debate.* New York: Harper & Row, Pub., 1978.

SCHAIE, K. W. A general model for the study of developmental problems. *Psychological Bulletin,* 1965, *64,* 94–107.

SORRELL, G. T. *Adaptive implications of sex-related attitudes and behaviors.* Unpublished master's thesis, Pennsylvania State University, 1979.

SPENCE, J. T., & HELMREICH, R. *Masculinity and femininity: The psychological dimensions, correlates, and antecedents.* Austin: University of Texas Press, 1978.

STAKE, J. E. Motive for occupational goal setting among male and female college students. *Journal of Applied Psychology,* 1978, *63,* 617–622.

STEIN, A. H. The effects of maternal employment and educational attainment on the sex-typed attributes of college females. *Social Behavior and Personality,* 1973, *1,* 111–114.

STEIN, A. H., & BAILEY, M. M. The socialization of achievement orientation in females. *Psychological Bulletin,* 1973, *80,* 345–366.

SUPER, D. E. A theory of vocational development. *American Psychologist,* 1953, *8,* 185–190.

SUPER, D. E. *The psychology of careers.* New York: Harper & Row, Pub., 1957.

SUPER, D. E., CRITES, J. O., HUMMEL, R. C., MOSER, H. P., OVERSTREET, P. L., & WARNATH, C. F. *Vocational development: A framework for research.* New York: Teacher's College, Columbia University, 1957.

SUPER, D. E., & HALL, D. T. Career development: Exploration and planning. *Annual Review of Psychology,* 1978, *29,* 333–372.

SUPER, D. E., STARISHEVSKY, R., MATLIN, N., & JORDAAN, J. P. *Career development: Self-concept theory.* New York: College Entrance Examination Board, 1963.

TANGRI, S. S. Determinants of occupational role innovation in college women. *The Journal of Social Issues,* 1972, *28,* 117–199.

TILLERY, D., & KILDEGAARD, T. *Educational goals, attributes and behaviors: A comparative study of high school seniors.* Cambridge, Mass.: Ballinger Publishing Co., 1973.

U.S. Bureau of the Census. *Perspectives on American fertility* (Current Population Reports, Series P–23, No. 70). Washington, D.C.: U.S. Government Printing Office, 1978.

U.S. Bureau of the Census. *Fertility of American women: June 1978* (Current Population Reports, Series P–20, No. 341, October 1979). Washington, D.C.: U.S. Government Printing Office, 1979.

WALSH, W. B. Vocational behavior and career development, 1978: A review. *Journal of Vocational Behavior,* 1979, *15,* 119–154.

WASHBURN, S. L. (Ed.). *Social life of early men.* New York: Wenner-Gren Foundation for Anthropological Research, 1961.

WESTBROOK, B. W. Content analysis of six career development tests. *Measurement and Evaluation in Guidance,* 1973, *6,* 8–16.

WESTBROOK, B. W., & CUNNINGHAM, J. W. The development and application of vocational maturity. *Vocational Guidance Quarterly,* 1970, *18,* 171–175.

WOHLWILL, J. F. The age variable in psychological research. *Psychological Review,* 1970, *77,* 49–64.

WORELL, J. Sex roles and psychological well-being. Perspectives on methodology. *Journal of Consulting and Clinical Psychology,* 1978, *46,* 777–791.

WORELL, J. Life-span sex roles: Development, continuity, and change. In R. M. Lerner & N. A. Busch-Rossnagel (Eds.), *Individuals as producers of their development: A life-span perspective.* New York: Academic Press, 1981.

YOUNG, R. The effects of value confrontation and reinforcement counselling on the career planning attitudes and behavior of adolescent males. *Journal of Vocational Behavior,* 1979, *15,* 1–11.

ZYTOWSKI, D. G. Vocational behavior and career development, 1977: A review. *Journal of Vocational Behavior,* 1978, *13,* 141–162.

Adulthood

PART FIVE

34

Mid-Life Development

BARBARA M. NEWMAN

MIDDLE ADULTHOOD

When Is Mid-Life?

The concept of *middle adulthood* is based on the current expectation of a life span of about 75 years. The middle third of this life span, from about age 25 through age 50, would then be considered the middle adult years. In 1900 a female who was born in the United States could expect to live to the age of 51 (U.S. Bureau of the Census, 1979). That means that many adults in the past never lived much beyond what we now call middle adulthood. Whether that means that past generations never encountered the growth that is associated with the later adult years or whether they simply condensed the development from middle and later adulthood into a briefer period has not yet been clearly established.

The middle adult period includes major life transitions into the worlds of work, marriage, childbearing and rearing, and community participation. Middle adults are the primary labor force. They are in a period of increasing economic resources, increasing decision-making responsibility, and increasing political power.

The middle adult period ends with the waning of daily responsibilities in the parent role, although the parent role continues as long as one's children are alive. The end of middle adulthood brings a transition toward greater leadership, seniority, or administrative responsibilities in the world of work; opportunities for community leadership; increased leisure time; and grandparenthood. It brings the anticipation of chronic illness, the possibility of widowhood, the promise of retirement, and the challenge of redirecting energy and skills to new roles in family, work, and intimate relationships.

What Are the Significant Events of Middle Adulthood?

The unique aspects of growth during adulthood are complex. They are less tied to biological changes than are the events of infancy, childhood, and adolescence or, for that matter, later adulthood. The diversity of experiences of adult life, especially in our own society, makes the patterns of growth across individuals more difficult to identify. Also the freedom of choice to determine one's involvement in adult life activities means that adults will make significant contributions to the definition of their own adult experiences. In this way the outcomes of person-environment interactions are heavily influenced by the talents and aspirations of the person who chooses to engage in or retreat from specific environments.

The fabric of adulthood is marked by a complex configuration of life events. These life events have the effect of moving the person toward greater responsibilities, expanded self-awareness, and an appreciation of the interdependence of lives, resources, and settings. The events of adulthood may be linked to one or more of five domains: the *biological,* the *psychological,* the *social,* the *cultural,* or the *historical.* Each of these areas provide specific content for experience. For this reason, while there may be some similarities across individuals in adapting to the challenges of adulthood, each generation and each person within a generation experiences adulthood as a unique blend of relevant events.

Let us consider each of the five domains briefly. In subsequent sections, physical, cognitive, and personality development will be discussed in greater detail. Biological events refer to physical changes, illness, and consequences of biological aging. Some of the very obvious biological events of adulthood that require unique adaptation include pregnancy, menopause, sensory deficits including loss of hearing or impaired vision, and some of the dramatic illnesses common in adulthood, especially heart disease, arthritis, and diabetes. Each of these biological events may require changes in the self-image, some redefinition of life activities, and the acquisition of new information about how best to incorporate these events into a satisfying life style.

Psychological events are less readily identifiable than are biological events but perhaps more powerful in the shaping of adult development. By psychological events we refer mainly to changes in self-perception and/or changes in the perception of the environment. They include an achievement of intimacy and deep emotional commitment to another adult; recognizing oneself as an adult rather than a child or an adolescent; perceiving oneself as an effective agent for change; or recognizing that the norms of a particular setting are inappropriate and need to be altered. Perhaps the most powerful psychological insight of adulthood is the realization that each life is limited to a finite number of years. The implicit message in this realization is that each person must generate that configuration of relationships and experiences that will give life depth and meaning.

Social events are those that engage the person in a new group, a new role, or a new set of relationships. Through marriage one assumes the new role of spouse, a new set of kinship relations, and a new array of friendships. The role of worker takes one to a variety of work settings with different norms for performance and for interpersonal behavior. Moving along the career time-line there are potential changes in leadership, in administrative responsibility, or in status that can be viewed as social events. Social events can also be a powerful source of stress. Rejection or isolation by community members, being fired from a job, or experiencing divorce are examples of abrupt changes in roles or alignment with social groups that require especially intense coping efforts.

The cultural events of adulthood may be so pervasive as to go unnoticed, or they may be highly articulated cultural rituals. Cultural expectations to hold a job, to retire, or to socialize one's children may be taken for granted as patterned experiences of adult life. Some of the elaborated rituals, including the marriage ceremony, anniversaries, preparing for your children's graduation, or funerals, are events that have both personal and social meaning. These rituals mark significant transitions to new phases of adulthood. They are programmed rites of passage that are observed from afar during childhood. They are filled with a deep personal meaning in spite of the almost universal participation of cultural members.

Cultural events are especially significant in that they provide the rhythm or timing for adult development. The *social clock,* as Neugarten (1968) describes it, is a set of norms for movement through the phases of adulthood. Age-graded expectations for the "right" age to marry, to bear children, to be financially self-sufficient, or to achieve certain occupational goals provide a background for assessing personal progress.

The fifth dimension, so to speak, is history. Historical events, including wars, revolutions, famines, economic crises, or political scandals, become focal points for adult development. These events are imposed on a background of psychosocial development and cultural patterning. They may dramatically alter the availability of resources, the value orientation, or the daily life activities for adults. Adaptations that are made in response to these historical events can persist well beyond the crisis itself. Particularly when historical events occur at critical life points, they may set the tone for a life course. Historical events may alter the job market, disrupt family groups, destroy buildings or farmlands, or introduce dramatic new technologies. One of the very interesting historical events of the recent past was the postwar baby boom. The so-called boom generation encountered certain deficiencies as they moved through each phase of development. Social settings, such as elementary schools, parks, colleges, jobs, or family housing, had not been prepared to absorb the great numbers of this generation. The boom generation has served as a wedge, opening up opportunities for itself, demanding new resources, and setting new rules for the "games" of adult life including marriage, childbearing, work, and sex-role definition (Glick, 1977). Members of the boom generation, as well as older adults who have had to modify their settings to make room for this group, have all had to cope with the stresses and demands of this particular historical event.

Central Concepts for the Study of Adult Development

In the following section five concepts are introduced that are central to our analysis of adult development. These concepts will be embedded in much of the discussion that follows. They highlight the need to consider both the person and the environment as they contribute to the structure of adult experience.

Individuality. We are impressed by the extent of variability that characterizes human experience. The mechanisms of genetics insure a wide range of variation in the biological endowment of human beings. Genetic differences contribute to the expression of differences in body build, intelligence, temperament, vulnerability, and the tempo of aging, to name a few. Add to these biological sources of variability the enormous range of experiences and settings that influence growth, and the notion of individuality is even more impressive. Finally as people grow older in American society, the degree of choice in all areas of life, including work, marriage, parenting, leisure-time activities, and location, open up even more avenues for the development of individual life styles, personal philosophies, and unique talents. As different as newborn infants are from one another, they are more alike as a cohort in size, in competences, and in experience than they will ever be again.

As we move to the discussion of the central domains of adult development, it is important to keep in mind that the normative patterns that are described are always global, summary statements derived from blending observations from many individuals. The richness of individual life stories must always be superimposed on the more general normative patterns of adult development.

Reciprocity of Relationships. Development at every life stage includes participation in social relationships. Not only are human beings members of social groups, but also they are usually members of groups whose participants are at different developmental stages. Rarely do we find infants alone, unattended by older siblings, parents, grandparents, or other adult caregivers. Families are composed of members at many different stages of life. Work settings, educational settings, and play settings are all populated by participants at different developmental levels. Life provides many opportunities for interaction with people who are not at one's own stage of development. Even though we tend to emphasize the impact of older people on younger people as teachers, parents, and culture bearers, the notion of reciprocity reminds us that younger people also contribute to the life experiences of their elders. Very simply one cannot enact the role of parent without children or the role of teacher without students. At a more complex level the needs, special skills, and quality of thought that characterize infants, young children, or adolescents bring new and changing stimuli to the lives of the older children and adults with whom they interact. At every developmental stage the context of experience may include profound contributions by persons younger or older who help individuals to redefine their own situation or to achieve new skills for coping with contemporary challenges.

Normative Crises. In psychosocial theory the concept of *crisis* refers to the person's psychological efforts to adjust to the demands of the social environment at each stage of development (Erikson, 1959). The word *crisis* in this context refers to a normal set of stresses and strains rather than to an extraordinary set of events. The theory postulates that at each stage of development the society within which one lives makes certain psychic demands upon the individual. These demands are experienced by the individual as mild but persistent guidelines and expectations for behavior. As individuals near the end of a particular stage of development, they are forced to make some type of resolution, adjusting themselves to the demands of society while simultaneously translating the societal demands into personal terms.

The concept of *normative life crises* has important implications for the study of adult development. First, it emphasizes the principle that growth involves psychological tension. As one makes the transition from stage to stage, there will be periods of increased uncertainty about one's capacity to meet coming demands and, perhaps, some resistance to leaving the stability of an earlier stage. This combination of uncertainty and resistance generates anxiety. In fact the idea of normative crisis would suggest that developmental anxiety—that is, anxiety about one's ability to succeed at developmental tasks of each life stage—may be a continuous part of life, waxing and waning during one's movement through each developmental stage. If one can learn to recognize this anxiety as a signal of growth, movement, and transition, one can begin to focus attention on those aspects of life experience that appear to be changing. We often tend to interpret anxiety as a negative sign, a sign of danger or threat. One implication of the notion of normative crisis is that anxiety can serve as a signal and even as a motivational force for work which is necessary in order for growth to continue.

A second implication of the notion of normative crisis is, of course, that the resolution of each life stage involves some balance between the positive and negative poles of the crisis. Just like the moon every person has a "dark" side, an array of life experiences, feelings, and wishes that are perceived by the self as unacceptable. We all have a negative identity, a part of ourselves that we devalue, that we may even deny as representing anything significant in our personality. The experiences of role diffusion, isolation, stagnation, and despair are powerful forces in the psychology of adulthood. People who are functioning well and who feel a great sense of personal fulfillment in their daily lives still encounter moments of discouragement. They may see a discrepancy between the intimacy they desire and the feeling of separateness they actually experience or a sense of futility in the face of efforts to make a meaningful contribution to their social group. Rather than trying to deny or ignore these experiences, we must begin to understand their contribution to personal growth. To what extent is the feeling of isolation a necessary outcome of a well-defined personal identity? To what extent does stagnation represent a resistance to the threat of mortality? How might feelings of despair reflect a person's inability to accept the end of change and growth after a lifetime of seeking to grow? These thoughts suggest a need for further research on the crises of adulthood and a new conceptual orientation toward the role of the negative poles of the life crises in the healthy development of the person.

A third point to be made about normative crises is that positive resolutions of earlier crises may make the later crises easier to resolve, but that is not necessarily the case. At each stage the challenges of development are very great. Because of the characteristics of one's spouse or the personalities of one's children or the particular stresses and demands of the work setting, adults may discover that they are unable to make a fulfilling adaptation during middle adulthood even though they had made successful resolutions of earlier crises. In fact it appears that the adult crises tend to pit the integrity of the individual's personal development against the social, economic, and political fluctuations of the historical period. It is a great challenge to be able to provide those adults who are experiencing tension in their efforts to resolve the crises of intimacy, generativity, and integrity with both the historical perspective and the personal skills that will permit them to evolve a life pattern that is personally fulfilling.

Self-Concept. Throughout our lives we construct a complex, multidimensional understanding of ourselves and our personal reality. The *self-concept* emerges as an integration of seven dimensions: the bodily self, self-recognition, extensions of the self, the reflected self, personal competences, aspirations and goals, and self-esteem (Allport, 1955). At every developmental stage changing competences, new social roles, a history of past successes and failures, and new cognitive capacities to differentiate and integrate ideas will alter the exact nature of the self-concept.

The importance of the self-concept to the process of adaptation cannot be underestimated. The self-concept imposes meaning and goals, even under conditions that might appear meaningless or hopeless. As concentration camp inmates, as slaves, as prisoners of war, or as victims of earthquakes and floods, people remain committed to preserving an integrated, purposeful conception of their own reality. The self-concept acts as a guide, selecting certain experiences as important and ignoring others. Among the enormous array of life experiences, the self-concept serves as a point of focus, identifying the characteristics that make the person unique, comparing the self to others, and pointing the person toward a vision of the self in the future.

Person-Environment Interaction. The final concept, *person-environment interaction,* highlights the dynamic quality of adult life. Persons do not hunt and pick until they have selected the ideal environment. In fact one of the lessons of adulthood is that reality falls short of perfection. Adults discover that the real world satisfactions are distinct from mythical satisfactions. Environments do not totally shape and modify people. There remain areas of choice, direction, and preference that people impose on their settings. The concept of *person-environment interaction* suggests an interdependence between people and their settings (Wright, 1978).

Individuals have some degree of choice in the selection of their social environment. They can decide whom they will marry, whether to have children, which occupation they will follow, and where they will live. To the degree that they have a choice in these matters, they will be able to influence the complementarity between their personality and their social milieu. This requires that they understand themselves and also that they are able to conceptualize the nature of the other people and social institutions that are involved in their choice. This type of thinking is rather difficult for most people. It involves a complex understanding of social settings and the ability to speculate about the future.

Although some settings are a matter of choice, many others are the result of chance. Some settings can be abandoned or altered if they do not meet the individual's needs. Many other settings are permanent and difficult to alter. If one is in an unsuitable setting, one must be willing to leave it, if that is possible, or to discover some way to influence the setting so that it meets one's needs more adequately. Many people, however, find themselves in social settings that can neither be abandoned or altered. In this circumstance adult development requires an adjustment of one's personal needs or expectations in order to reduce continual feelings of frustration and anger. When one is forced to remain in a number of social settings that are contrary to personal needs, the possibility of continued psychosocial development is seriously diminished. If one is unable to experience a personal sense of effectiveness in home, work, or community, one is unlikely to be able to feel capable of contributing to future growth in these spheres.

PHYSICAL DEVELOPMENT

How can you tell how old someone is? For most people the standards by which they judge another person's age are the physical signs of aging. Graying hair, wrinkled skin, flabby muscles, sagging breasts, or stooped shoulders are common physical characteristics that identify a person as elderly. These outward signs are signals to the person, as well as to others, that the life course is moving along. Depending on the person's attitudes about getting older and the culture's attitudes toward older members, these signs may be met with discouragement, acceptance, or even pride.

Sexual Maturation as a Guide to Adulthood

Biologically adulthood begins with puberty. Physical maturation at puberty includes the growth spurt, the maturation of the reproductive system, and the accompanying hormone production that stimulates the onset of secondary sex characteristics. All of these changes modify not only the physical appearance and physical competence of the person but also the potential of the person for reproductive activity.

If we think about puberty as the biological beginning of adulthood, we are immediately struck by the discrepancy between that beginning and the psychosocial onset of adulthood in our society. The height spurt, which is an early sign of puberty for females and an event about one year into the normal maturational sequence for boys, begins at a mean age of 10.12 years for females and 12.76 years for males (Faust, 1977). Menarche begins at about 12.75 years. Male fertility begins in the age range from 16 to 18 years. Taking very gross indexes of adult status, there is a period of 5 years for males and 8 years for females between the onset of puberty and the attainment of the voting age. If we look at vital statistics on marriage patterns, the median age for females to marry is 21.1 years and for males it is 23.5 years (U.S. Census Bureau, 1975). While these data continue to reflect the age difference in the onset of puberty, they suggest at least a full decade when biologically mature persons do not usually assume one of the central roles of adult life, a role that has in the past been most directly tied to the enactment of the reproductive function.

If the biological onset of adult life is comparatively easy to identify, any subsequent stages of adulthood become increasingly difficult to mark. For females we might use the climacteric as a second signpost. Adulthood then would be divided into a reproductive and postreproductive phase. For the male, however, there is no clearcut end to the reproductive potential; rather, there is a gradual reduction in testicular activity with a resulting decline in the production of sperm and the production of testosterone. The reproductive career, despite its importance as a significant biological and psychosocial component of adult life, does not lend itself as a satisfactory marker for discrete phases of biological change during adulthood.

Human sexuality is a multifaceted configuration of biological, psychological, and cultural factors. In order to appreciate the sexual experiences and changes of adult life, it is necessary to tell the story from its beginning in the prenatal period of development. We do not arrive at our capacity for adult sexual behavior from a blank past. The sexual aspect of our nature is fostered, inhibited, and continuously socialized from the moment of birth.

Sexuality in Childhood. Sexuality begins at a genetic level with the presence of the *XX* or *XY* chromosome combination in the fertilized zygote. Fetal development during the third month of gestation includes a differentiation of the sex organs. In the presence of the *Y* chromosome, sperm ducts, testes, penis, and scrotum emerge. In the absence of the Y chromosome, ovaries, Fallopian tubes, uterus, and vagina develop. If chromosomal material is deleted or if chromosomes fail to separate during cell division, the sexual fate of the fetus is put into jeopardy. It is assumed that the vital function of the X and Y chromosomes is to direct the production of the sex organs and hormones that influence the emergence of secondary sex characteristics.

Freud pointed out that from infancy children are sexual beings (Freud, 1905, 1953). In addition he argued that all infants are bisexual in interests, responses, and selection of objects. Today we might state that observation differently, suggesting that infants are sexual without reference to the sex of the object or their own sex. They experience sexual stimulation as pleasurable. In infancy the process of sexual socialization also gets underway. Parents respond to boy and girl babies with varied degrees of physical contact, close fondling, tickling, and gentle rocking. Parents are likely to place boy babies at a greater distance from them at an earlier age than they will girl babies (Lewis, 1972). The history of each person's sexuality begins with the kind of caregiving, handling, and comforting techniques used by important caregivers. If these caregivers made systematic distinctions between the way one handles boys and girls, the results would probably be different personal histories for those males and females.

In childhood, sexuality takes several new turns. First, there is more deliberate masturbation through which children discover the specific sensations associated with genital manipulation. Second, there is peer play during which children may explore each other's bodies, compare sex organs, and even stimulate each other. Third, socialization about sexuality becomes more explicit. In some cultures sexual play between children is quite open and direct. Adults may use genital stimulation as a way of soothing their toddlers. In our society children are generally admonished not to masturbate in public and not to explore or touch the sex organs of their playmates. People who are adults today, let us say those who were born 25 years ago or more, were reared during a time when restrictions on sexual exploration during childhood were even more severely limiting than they are today. Finally, children have more active thoughts about sexuality. They ask questions about babies and birth, about love, about why boys have penises and girls don't, and they may wonder exactly what girls do have. The responses to these questions from parents, grandparents, or other adults set the tone for the legitimacy of thinking about sexuality.

The question of who thinks about sexuality and how often they think about it was addressed directly in a study by Cameron and Biber (1973). They surveyed over 4000 people across the age range from 8 to 99 years in a variety of settings, including home, work, school, church, shopping centers, and parks. In the interview the following questions were included:

"What were you thinking about over the past five minutes?"

"Did you think about sex or were your thoughts sexually colored—even for a moment (perhaps it crossed your mind)?"

"What was the central focus of your thought over the past five minutes?"

(Among the 14 possible responses was "about a personal problem—topic concerning sex.")

Table 34–1 shows the percentage of males and females in each age range who had been focusing their thoughts on sex and those for whom sex had been a "fleeting thought." Sex appears to be a common fleeting thought across the life span, but especially during adolescence and young adulthood. It is less likely to be a primary focus of concentration, at least so far as people will admit to it. The responses also provide evidence that sexuality is somewhat less prevalent as a focus of thought for females than for males, especially after the age of 11. The similarity of percentages for males and females in the 7- to 11-year range suggests that this later difference may be a product more of socialization than of biology.

Puberty brings not only the adult capacity for reproduction but also the secondary sex characteristics associated with adult appearance. For boys the height spurt, increased muscle mass, growth of pubic, facial, and body hair, and voice change are all important signs of masculinity. For girls breast development, the relative broadening of hips in relation to shoulder width, and the redistribution of body fat all converge to produce the more shapely adult female body. These events occur simultaneously with heightened levels of arousal and sensitivity to sexual stimulation. Pictures and thoughts, as well as physical stimulation, can all be more arousing than they were in childhood. For males ejaculation brings a new component to sexual stimulation that separates adolescent sexual experiences from earlier childhood sexual play.

Sullivan (1949) identifies one of the conflicts of adolescence as the struggle to integrate sexual impulse (he calls it the *lust dynamism*) with needs for closeness and emotional support (he calls it the *intimacy dynamism*). That particular conflict and the desire to resolve it provide the basis for much of adolescent sexual experimentation.

Table 34–1 Thoughts about Sex

AGE RANGE	% SEX CROSSED THEIR MINDS		% SEX WAS A FOCUS OF THOUGHT		
	Male	Female	Male	Female	
8–11	25	27	4	4	N = 116 F 119 M
12–13	50	39	16	11	N = 177 F 146 M
14–15	57	42	10	11	N = 137 F 130 M
16–17	51	42	14	6	N = 207 F 104 M
18–25	48	33	10	6	N = 629 F 541 M
26–39	33	19	8	2	N = 493 F 472 M
40–55	20	9	4	2	N = 366 F 379 M
56–64	19	12	3	0	N = 95 F 97 M
65 and over	9	6	0	0	N = 80 F 82 M

Source: Adapted from Cameron P., & Biber, H. Sexual thought throughout the life-span. *The Gerontologist*, 1973, *13*, 144–147.

There is a search for a partner who can gratify sexual needs and at the same time be a good friend.

The sexual experiences encountered during this period of experimentation have important implications for adult sexuality. They can contribute to feelings of being vulnerable or strong, exploited or in control, attractive or ugly, potent or powerless. The significance of what in women might be called *defloration* or loss of virginity is poorly understood for its contribution to adult sexuality. Clearly sometime during adolescence or young adulthood, we pass across the threshold of sexual experience moving from the state of novice to the state of new initiate. From that point on there is continuous learning, adaptation, and some degree of frustration associated with the pursuit of sexual intimacy.

Menstruation and the Hormone Cycle. With puberty the increased production of sex hormones has a direct impact on the reproductive cycle. The impact on the desire for sexual activity is less obvious. Research with nonhuman primates has shown that sex hormones act in an on/off fashion to prompt sexual receptivity in the female (Gagnon, 1977). Female monkeys are only receptive to sexual activity at one phase of the hormonal cycle, generally a phase that coincides with ovulation. In humans sexuality and sexual activity is directly influenced more by social and psychological factors than by hormone levels. Females can be sexually receptive whenever they wish to be.

The hormone cycle does, however, play a part in the pattern of tension, confidence, and sociability generally experienced by women. The menstrual cycle involves an average of 28 days. There is some evidence that the period from about three days before menstruation begins through the first three or four days of the menstrual flow is a time of irritability and tension for many women. The following data support this notion of a disruptive menstrual phase.

During this 25 percent of each month, to cite but a few examples, occur 49 percent of all crimes committed by female prisoners, 45 percent of punishment meted out to school girls, 53 percent of [female] suicides, and 46 percent of [women's] admissions to mental hospitals. In advanced examinations, the pass rate of female students was 13 percent lower [during the menstrual period]. The British Road Research Laboratory reports that 60 percent of women's traffic accidents also occur during the same phase. (Gadpaille, 1975, p. 351)

According to Bardwick (1971) changes in the level of estrogen and progesterone are correlated with emotional changes at various phases of the menstrual cycle. The periods of high estrogen production at the beginning of the menstrual cycle when there has been a relative absence of estrogen and at ovulation when estrogen is at a peak are associated with feelings of self-acceptance, alertness, and well-being. Periods of low estrogen and low progesterone are associated with anxiety, shame, and fears of mutilation.

Even though males do not have such a readily observable reproductive cycle, there is some evidence of a male hormonal cycle. Ramey (1972) reported on the results of a 16-year study of Danish males. Males showed a rhythmic change in hormone levels in a 30-day cycle. This cycle was associated with changes in irritability, effi-

ciency, and reaction to stress. Males did not perceive their behavior as subject to cyclical patterns, but their responses to psychological tests revealed patterned shifts in mood, sociability, and response to stress.

The hormone cycle provides a background biological rhythm of adult life. It is significant in that it influences social interactions, mood, and alertness. Adults come to read these shifts, recognizing some days as "good days" and others as days when they should "hang back." The hormonal cycle is also significant in that it provides patterned regularity. It is against the context of this pattern that the changes of the climacteric are notably disruptive.

The Climacteric. The climacteric or involution and atrophy of the reproductive organs occurs gradually for the female during the years between the mid-thirties and the mid-fifties. There are many physiological changes that accompany this loss of fertility, including the cessation of menstruation (menopause), gradual diminution in the production of estrogen, atrophy of the breasts and genital tissues, and shrinking of the uterus (Sherman, 1971). There is some controversy about whether the menopause affects women on a psychological level, either because of its symbolic meaning or because of physiological changes.

Neugarten and Kraines (1965) administered a symptom checklist to 460 women in six age groups: 13 to 18, 20 to 29, 30 to 44, 45 to 54 (pre- or postmenopausal), 45 to 54 (menopausal), and 55 to 64. The two highest symptom groups were the adolescents and the menopausal subjects. The women in the 45- to 54-year nonmenopausal group had lower symptom incidence than did same-age women who were menopausal. These data suggest that dramatic endocrine changes, either increased production or decreased production of hormones, are likely to result in a high incidence of psychological and somatic symptoms. Neugarten and Kraines note that the younger group was more likely to report psychological symptoms, like crying and irritability, while the menopausal group was more likely to report somatic symptoms, like hot flashes, pelvic or breast pain, and feelings of suffocation or shortness of breath.

The findings of this study of symptoms are in contradiction with the view that only neurotic women experience symptoms during menopause (Weiss & English, 1957). There is considerable agreement that most women experience hot flashes and night sweats as menopause begins. These symptoms can continue for as long as five to six years (McKinley & Jefferys, 1974). The symptoms appear to be closely related to the drastic drop in the production of estrogen. Postmenopausal women produce only one-sixth the amount of estrogen that regularly menstruating women do (Wilson & Wilson, 1963). Several studies on the use of estrogen treatment find that the administration of estrogen to menopausal women alleviates or even avoids menopausal symptoms (Bardwick, 1971).

It is fairly well established, then, that menopause brings about recognizable physical changes. These changes may or may not be viewed by the adult women as unpleasant. The severity of these changes may be determined in part by the attitude of the culture toward the infertile older woman. Flint (1976) has suggested that in cultures where women are rewarded for reaching the end of the fertile period menopause is associated with few physiological symptoms. Similarly a woman's own attitudes toward aging and her involvement in adult roles will influence the ease or difficulty with which menopause is encountered.

Neugarten and associates (Neugarten, Wood, Kraines, & Loomis, 1963) sampled attitudes toward menopause from 100 women between the ages of 45 and 55. A variety of attitudes was revealed. Some women were fearful, particularly of having mental breakdowns or of losing their sexual attractiveness. Some women appeared to be anxious about menopause but were actively defending against their anxiety. They would repeat advice like: "If you keep busy, you won't think about it, and you'll be all right ..." (p. 141). A third group, particularly at the upper-middle-class level, felt that menopause had no social or psychological significance for them.

The degree of anxiety about menopause depends on the individual woman's feelings about no longer being able to bear children, the amount of information she has about the nature of symptoms accompanying menopause, and the degree of anxiety she has about growing old. Neugarten et al. (1963) found that attitudes toward menopause were more positive among their sample of women over 45 years old who were postmenopausal than among younger women. The older group realized that the symptoms were temporary and that after menopause there was the potential for some gains in feelings of well-being and vigor. In contrast to the younger group they were aware that menopause may bring an upsurge in sexual impulses and activity.

It appears that as a young woman views menopause she confuses the physiological phenomena with all the negative connotations of growing old. The importance of physical beauty may be heavily weighted in a woman's definition of femininity. Further the younger woman may be still quite invested in her role as mother and fearful of a potential end to her years of childbearing. The older woman, on the other hand, is likely to be glad to have reached the end of the years of childbearing. She may be eagerly awaiting a future of new roles and new freedoms. In a paper on the awareness of middle age, Neugarten (1968) points out that women who are in the middle adulthood years feel a sense of new opportunities opening to them as they redirect energy from child-rearing into other areas of skill development. This study of attitudes toward menopause is good evidence for the difference in psychosocial growth between the premenopausal and postmenopausal groups. The younger women, still working on the task of generativity and still heavily involved in developing the skills necessary to make a creative contribution to society, fear menopause as a symbol of the termination of this creative period. The older women, having gone through the experience and having developed a sense of personal competence in their maternal role, are less threatened by this event. In fact to some menopause may symbolize a new beginning—a release from obligations of motherhood and an overture to the years of contribution beyond the family circle.

Neugarten and Kraines (1965) suggested that in evolving a model for the understanding of adult development care should be taken in using physiological changes as explanatory concepts. They report that menopausal status and severity of menopausal symptoms of 100 normal women between the ages of 43 and 53 were unrelated to an array of personality measures. They found that other events, such as serious illness or widowhood, were more significantly linked to personality changes. This finding is supported by a paper on depression in middle-aged women by Bart (1971), who identified the source of depression among a sample of women between the ages of 40 and 49 as a result of overinvolvement with their children and overidentification with the role of mother.

Thus the hormonal events of menopause are not as significant as the woman's interpretation of her role and her degree of dependence on her children to fulfill that role. For overinvolved women menopause may merely symbolize the finality of the end of motherhood and, in that way, may generate extended feelings of depression. Women who are already confused and depressed by the disintegration of a critical life role will be likely to find the decline in estrogen production an aggravation to their condition. Here is an example of the interaction between a psychological condition and a physiological change. The reduced production of estrogen, which has been demonstrated to be associated with negative emotions (Bardwick, 1971) combined with a tendency toward depression due to loss of role meaning leads to a more serious psychological depression. The woman may, in fact, be unable to regain her earlier stage of positive affect because of both the reduced hormonal production and the altered role relationship.

It would appear then that menopause may serve as a significant symbolic event for women at the end of the middle adulthood stage. For those who have been successful in developing a sense of personal achievement in child-rearing or in other work, menopause signifies the end of the child-rearing years and the beginning of a period in which new energy can be directed to broader, community-oriented tasks. For the woman who has failed to develop a sense of generativity, who continues to view her children as a path of self-fulfillment, or who is frightened by the prospect of growing old, menopause may indeed highlight a sense of stagnation. Low mood, physical symptoms, and reduced muscle tone are likely to create a strong feeling of uselessness, emptiness, and unattractiveness which permeate the woman's self-attitude as she enters later adulthood.

What about a climacteric for males? Is there any comparable decrease in reproductive capacity for adult men? There is no biological change comparable to the total involution of organs involved in menopause. Most adult males have the potential to fertilize ova throughout life. However there is a gradual decline in the production of testosterone resulting in a variety of changes in the sex organs and sexual activity. Sperm production is decreased. The testicular tubes become narrower, and there is less seminal fluid. Ejaculation therefore occurs with less force. Older males take longer to achieve an erection and require a longer rest interval before erection is possible again. Once the penis is erect it can be maintained for quite a while, but orgasm itself is shorter (Weg, 1978).

For both males and females some version of a climacteric alters the adult's hormone levels and modifies the physiology. It also has implications for sexual activity.

What do we know about the sexual behavior of aging adults? Returning to Table 34–1 there appears to be a decline in thoughts about sex beginning with the 18 to 25 age group that reaches a lifelong low among the oldest group sampled. If thoughts about sex decrease with age, what about sexual activity? The early Kinsey reports (Kinsey, Pomeroy, & Martin, 1948) reported the incidence of impotence for males as 2 percent at 35 years, 10 percent at 55 years, and 50 percent at 75 years. Viewed from the other perspective, studies report that 60 percent of men 75 or older have involuntary morning erections, 75 percent of a sample whose average age was 71 still felt sexual desire, and in this older group frequency of coital activity was as high as three times per week for some subjects (Kinsey et al., 1948; Rubin, 1963, 1965). Sexual activity for older males appears to be closely related to the level of activity they sought as younger adults.

Women experience continued sexual desire at the same level to the age of 60 or even older. This continued sexual interest depends heavily on whether she has the opportunity to remain sexually active. There is no evidence, however, that physiological changes of menopause or even those brought about by hysterectomy diminish the female's sexual drive.

The key factor for continued sexual satisfaction for both males and females is the presence of a cooperative sex partner. In a comparison of adults in four age groups—60 to 64, 65 to 69, 70 to 74, and over 75—60 percent of the married subjects in these groups were sexually active. Among subjects who did not have a partner, only 7 percent remained active (Newman & Nichols, 1960). Since women are likely to live longer than men are and, therefore, to experience a prolonged period without a partner, they are more likely than men are to experience a cessation of sexual activity in later adulthood. Paradoxically even though women may be physiologically more capable of experiencing sexual satisfaction in the later years, because of the norms for men to marry younger women and for women to refrain from making sexual overtures to males, women are most likely to be deprived of a heterosexual outlet for this drive.

Biochemical Changes as a Guide to Adulthood

Another approach to an overview of physical change in adulthood is the search for normative patterns of cellular, enzyme, hormonal, or system change with age. The following generalizations about biological aging are taken from reviews by Jarvik and Cohen (1973) and Diamond (1978). These generalizations are some of the biological "best guesses" about what factors might be associated with aging. Without exception every age-related change is subject to individual variation depending on environmental conditions, physical activity, health, and an unknown contribution of genetic resilience—all of which contribute to longevity.

Cellular errors. With age there is an accumulation of errors in the production of DNA, RNA, and protein synthesis. Over time these errors influence metabolism, enzyme activity at the synapse, and the homeostatic balance of the central nervous system.

The process of producing, placing, and maintaining proteins within the cells involves a series of steps including "DNA replication, translation (protein assembly with RNA), and the active process of positioning and maintaining the protein in the cell" (Jarvik & Cohen, 1973). At any or many points in this chain, errors might occur. Woolhouse (cited in Jarvik & Cohen, 1973) has argued that with age there are "creeping errors" that disrupt the cell system.

In opposition to this argument several criticisms might be raised. First, cells have mechanisms for eliminating error. Molecules only persist for a limited time; then they are broken down and resynthesized. Molecules produced in error might not endure long enough to be included in cell division. Second, tissues age differently with specific enzymes showing different patterns of activity. Without knowing the specific course of each enzyme within each tissue, it is difficult to determine whether errors have occurred. Third, and most important, we do not yet know the exact relation between changes at the cellular level and changes in learning and memory. While we can link cellular errors to changes in protein synthesis, metabolism, and the transmission of impulses at the synaptic membrane, the connection between these changes and the complex mental configurations necessary for learning and remembering has not been demonstrated.

Cell loss. With age there is a gradual loss of cells. This loss differs with different tissues. There is an assumed relationship between cell loss and decreased muscle strength, disturbed eating and sleeping patterns, and impaired mental functioning. This argument is supported by the common observation of decreased brain weight during the eighth decade of life. Certainly if cell loss were to result in specific brain or tissue lesions, this would have a disruptive influence on behavior.

The theory of cell loss is still a controversial issue. Some investigators have not observed cell loss with aging, others have, and still others have observed cell loss during an early or mid-life period rather than in the later phase of development. Diamond (1978) described the change in cell counts of young, adult, and aging rats. Cells in the occipital cortex were counted in rats who were 26, 41, 108, and 650 days old. Neuron density increased during the period from 26 to 41 days. Neuron density decreased markedly, especially in the lower layers of the occipital cortex, from 41 to 108 days. After that time cell decrease was not significant. Diamond offers the hypothesis that cortical nerve cells are overabundant because they do not divide. The number of cells is greater than necessary for survival but provides a potential for adaptation to the variety of environmental conditions in which the organism may find itself. When the environment does not stimulate these cells and relevant behavior patterns are not developed, the cells die.

Cell loss itself can be endured without serious impairment. Humans can lose whole organs and still not show the signs of impaired mental or muscular functioning that have been attributed to cell loss. Finally, Franks (1974) has argued that cell loss is usually counterbalanced by physiological reserves, such as compensation of other tissues, or in the case of the brain, the formation of new neural pathways. These forms of adjustment continue during adulthood and in fact could be viewed as increasing the vigor or the efficiency of functioning (Shelldrake, 1974).

Susceptibility to disease. With age there is increased susceptibility to disease. The reasons for this increased susceptibility are not fully understood. In very general terms the level of immune activity tends to decrease with age. "Antibody response decreases gradually after adolescence and natural antibody fiber decreases. Older individuals are not as responsive to antigens contacted early in life" (Jarvik & Cohen, 1973). Some hypotheses about the cause of this change include the buildup of "senile plaques," the accumulation of dipofuscin pigment (known as the aging pigment—a pigment that is one of the major ways of distinguishing between the cells of young and old animals), and less efficient response or prolonged disequilibrium when exposed to stress.

Neural modifications. A last category of biological age-related changes include a variety of modifications in the neural structure. Many investigators report an increased number of glial cells, a phenomenon that has been associated with exposure to an "enriched environment" for rats. Some studies have shown changes in the synaptic junction, especially reduced dendritic spines, decreases in synaptic contacts, and slowing in the conduction of the neural impulse (Hyden, 1973). Among normal human cells there is a limit to the capacity for reproduction that places the absolute life span at about 90 or 100 years (Hayflick, 1980). Any or all of these changes might account for the slowing of reaction time and general slowing of behavior that has consistently been identified as a correlate of advanced age.

Physical Fitness

Physical well-being can be viewed along a continuum from a state of fitness and smooth, integrated functioning to serious illness and death. This continuum will be experienced differently by different people, each of whom has a potential for certain kinds of optimal states, certain vulnerabilities, and a certain timetable for maturation, aging, and longevity. In addition the quality of health and the optimum level of performance will depend on developmental age. The muscle strength that might be viewed as optimal for a 10-year-old would more than likely be rated as average or even inadequate for an 18-year-old. Failure to menstruate would be viewed as a symptom for a 20-year-old but not for a 65-year-old. Among people with the same illness like diabetes or arthritis, there are differences in the severity of the disease, differences in responsiveness to medication, and differences in the pattern of influence of that disease on other areas of functioning. Even a very ill person can create his/her own scale of well-being—that is, the concepts of health and illness are relative concepts and are best appreciated in the context of the person's own history of well-being or illness, in the context of other people at that life stage, as well as in the context of normative data about the population as a whole.

Aging does, however, place obstacles in the way of fitness. The gradual degeneration of tissues limits the speed, endurance, and resilience of adults. In the following discussion we trace the capacities related to fitness from the period between ages 18 and 30 to the period of age 60 and beyond. This description draws primarily from essays by Marshall (1973).

Eighteen through Thirty. During this period the peak in speed and agility is achieved. This is the age of most Olympic athletes. It is a time when muscle strength is still increasing for males but not for females. Under conditions of prolonged, vigorous exercise, the muscles can produce lactic acid and thereby continue functioning even without the adequate supply of oxygen taken in through the lungs. One of the factors that interferes with fitness is the decrease in physical activity that often comes with a full-time job. During this period the high-calorie diet necessary for adolescent growth is no longer needed. There is a tendency to gain weight during these years if one continues an eating pattern established in adolescence and participates in less physical activity.

Thirty through Forty. During this decade there is some loss of speed. The cartilage of the joints begin to degenerate leading to some decrease in agility; otherwise, oxygen capacity, efficiency of the lungs, strength, and endurance remain strong. There is a gradual decrease in the elasticity of the aorta and smaller arteries, leading to higher blood pressure. Being overweight increases the likelihood that this normal rise in blood pressure can develop into a health problem.

Forty through Sixty. The decline in fitness becomes more marked during these years. Muscle strength decreases, and it is difficult to maintain maximum strength. Movements take longer to initiate and accomplish. Vigorous physical exertion is more taxing as the passage of oxygen from the lungs to the blood and from the blood to the muscles becomes less efficient.

Men in their late fifties can only do hard physical work at about 60 percent of the rate achieved by men of 40. Several different aspects of the aging process account for this change. As a man gets older, thickening of the walls of the minute air sacks in his lungs hinders the diffusion of gases, and he has to increase the amount of air which he breathes in order to pass the same amount of oxygen to his blood. When he is breathing as rapidly and as deeply as he can, he does not oxygenate his blood as well as he did by similar effort when he was younger. (Marshall, 1973, p. 100)

The increased difficulty in doing strenuous activity leads to a more sedentary life. Once life becomes less active, the person is likely to perceive him/herself as heavier and less agile, leading to even greater reluctance to engage in physical activity. The lack of physical activity itself does contribute to the gradual loss of muscle tone and strength (Kreitler & Kreitler, 1970).

After Sixty. There is enormous variability in fitness after age 60 as a life of activity or inactivity, endurance or frailty, illness or health, takes its toll. Strength and capacity for moderate effort are about the same at age 70 as they were at age 40 (Marshall, 1973). However, the older person is less resilient in the face of exertion and simply less able to carry out prolonged intense activity. Continued degeneration of the respiratory and circulatory systems make them less able to provide the heart and the muscle with the needed supply of oxygenated blood. Quick changes in posture may leave an older person feeling "lightheaded." A slowed metabolism reduces the need for calories, but there is a new risk that essential vitamins and minerals will be missing from the older person's diet. Malnutrition can contribute to the feelings of weakness and lack of resilience that might be mistakenly attributed to aging.

The picture is one of increasing factors working against maintaining a high level of physical fitness. Yet the consequences of an inactive life, especially obesity and degeneration of muscle strength, will contribute to an even greater decline in physical capacity, especially after age 60. This is simply to say that the value of fitness is something to which adults have to be consciously committed. In order to remain in good physical condition, adults must make deliberate efforts to compensate for the sedentary nature of their lives and the increasing reluctance of their bodies.

Fitness is not only important for continued efficiency of the circulatory, respiratory, and muscle systems. It contributes to a psychological feeling of well-being. As the saying "You're as young as you feel" suggests, we take important cues from our bodies that influence morale. In 1972 *Psychology Today* conducted a survey of its readers about body image (Berscheid, Walster, & Bohrnstedt, 1973). Respondents were divided into three age groups, under 25, 25 to 44, and over 45. Table 34–2 shows the percentage at each age who rated their body image as above average, average, or below average. The patterns are quite consistent with age. Either subjects at each age are adjusting their ratings to new, age-appropriate criteria, or perhaps body image once formed remains stable despite physical changes associated with aging. At every age body image was rated as less attractive by females than by males. Body image was associated with a number of other indexes of well-being. A positive or above-average rating of body image was linked with higher self-esteem. A greater number of people who viewed their body image as above average also felt likeable, rated themselves as intelligent, and described themselves as assertive.

The body-image survey captures a glimpse of the reactions of early and middle adults to the importance of this concrete component of the self. The group agreed by and large that body image was very important and that it was especially important to have an attractive face. Body image was seen as important to the way others respond, to desirability as a sexual partner, and indeed to the experience of sexual satisfaction. The question of whether the body image remains central to social processes in later adulthood or if it becomes less important in interpersonal relations among the elderly remains to be answered. If this survey is any indication, one would predict that body image and physical attractiveness continue to be meaningful dimensions associated with morale and with satisfying social interactions in the later years.

Sensory Competence

It is not only the difficulty in retaining a high level of physical fitness that poses a challenge to adult functioning. Each adult is also struggling against a gradual decline in sensory acuity and speed of reaction time. One adult, age 56, describes it as follows,

So far I have been able to enjoy a robust health, a strong heart, a good stomach and a healthy back. But I notice my age. My hair gets thinner and grayer. The veins swell. Recently I changed to stronger eyeglasses. The sensory impressions get duller. It is as if some taste buds have dried up and part of an octave is broken. Or rather as if perceptions don't make the same impact on my consciousness. Just now the street lights were lit; the window is open a crack; it is a blue and cold spring evening. I don't feel the same happiness and melancholy about this as before. Then there lay a young light upon the world, as well as upon griefs and sorrows. Now I only remember how it felt. Maybe it is unavoidable, and I accept it with composure. I feel there are profits to be gained from a moderate aging, too. (Ulverstam, 1977, p. 2)

Speed and Reaction Time. One of the most frequently cited changes of adult functioning is reduced speed in responding to stimuli. In experimental studies the amount of time it takes a person to respond after a signal to respond is given is referred to as the *reaction time.* Reaction time might be measured in response to a verbal signal like "Push" or "Now," to a visual signal such as a green light, or to an auditory signal such as a buzzer or tone. Usually the response required is a simple one—e.g., pushing a button or tapping a pointed stick. Sometimes the reaction-time tasks involve making a choice—that is, pushing the red and not the green button. Usually, experimental studies of reaction time do not involve complex decisions like choosing what to wear or deciding how to put out a fire in the kitchen.

There are a variety of hypotheses about why reaction time slows. Some attribute it to changes in the central nervous system, especially to problems in synaptic transmission or decreased autonomic activity (Jarvik & Cohen, 1973). Others point to the changes in heartrate and blood pressure during periods of focused attention (Thompson & Marsh, 1973). Still others suggest that slowed reaction time is a result of the accumulation of many interfering experiences (Anderson, 1958).

Botwinick and Thompson (1968) compared the reaction time of older men (mean age = 74.1) and younger men (mean age = 19.5). The younger subjects were divided into two groups: athletes and nonathletes. The elderly subjects as a group showed slower reaction time than did the young athletes, but they were not significantly slower than were the nonathletes. In fact 30 percent of the younger subjects were slower in reaction time than were the fastest 30 percent of the older sample. The reaction time of the young nonathletes was highly varied, some responding similarly to the fastest athletes and some responding more slowly than did the slowest older subject. This study suggests that speed of reaction time may be better understood as an individual characteristic with the process of slowing being accounted for as much

Table 34–2 Ratings of Body Image

	AGE GROUP		
	Under 25	25 to 44	Over 45
Body image:			
above average	26	28	30
average	51	47	46
below average	24	26	25

Source: Data from Berscheid et al., 1973, p. 122. Reprinted from *Psychology Today* magazine. Copyright © 1973 Ziff Davis Publishing Co.

by the person's level of physical fitness as by the person's chronological age.

There are several questions about reaction-time studies that leave us in some doubt as to its implications for adult behavior. The conditions under which reaction time is studied may be so mechanical as to fail to arouse the older subject's interest. We do not know whether the highly sensitive measures of reaction time obtained in the laboratory would be associated with meaningful differences in behavior in a real-life situation. Does it matter if it takes a few one hundredths of a second longer for a person to respond to a ringing telephone or a doorbell or an assembly line signal? Are there many of life's demands in which these differences in tenths or hundredths of a second would seriously impair performance? Finally, is the decline in speed of reaction time accompanied by a decrease in errors? Do older adults take more care in their responses or are they both slower and less accurate? These kinds of questions need to be considered in drawing inferences from reaction-time research about decisions related to employment, the design of housing for the elderly, or the development of special technology for elderly consumers.

Sensory Modalities. Every sense modality, including hearing, vision, taste, touch, and smell, is vulnerable to age-related changes. In general with age a higher level of stimulation is needed in order to make an impact on the system. We see this in the reactions of older adults who appear to have "tuned out" to an ongoing conversation or who are annoyed by low levels of illumination in a restaurant. What a younger couple might appreciate as "atmosphere," an older couple might find uncomfortable to the point of interfering with their ability to read the menu or to enjoy the meal. The fact that the threshold for stimulation is raised means that older people do not react to the full range of stimuli occurring in the environment. To some extent this reduced sensitivity may result in a degree of sensory deprivation. In another sense the reduction in environmental stimulation opens up more time for private reflection.

Vision. The hardening of the lens of the eye begins at age ten. There is a gradual loss in elasticity over time that makes it more difficult to focus on near objects (Marshall, 1973). As early as the decade of the thirties, this may result in increased difficulty in reading small print. Benjamin Franklin's famous bifocals are a symbol of the human being's determination to compensate for the sensory losses of aging. Dark adaptation becomes less efficient with age. There is a need for greater intensity in illumination in order to stimulate the retina. In a dark room or at night, acuity is reduced. Several physiological conditions may seriously impair vision and result in partial or total blindness in later adulthood. These include cataracts, which are films covering the lens making them less penetrable by the light; deterioration or detachment of the retina; and glaucoma, which is an increase in pressure from the fluid in the eyeball (Smith, 1976).

Hearing. Hearing loss increases with age. This may be due to the accumulated effect of exposure to noise, infection, injury to the bones in the ear, damage to the auditory nerve, or changes in the auditory center of the brain where stimuli are translated into meaningful speech units. The most common effects of hearing loss are reduced sensitivity to high frequency sounds, reduced sensitivity to low intensity (quiet) sounds, and some inability to understand spoken messages.

Losses in vision and hearing pose serious challenges to adult adaptation. There are mechanical devices designed to help compensate for these losses. However these devices are never as adequate as the healthy function they are intended to replace. Also vision and hearing loss have the effect of separating adults from contact with their world. Loss of vision is especially linked with feelings of helplessness. Most older adults are not ready to cope with the challenge of learning to function in their daily world without vision. Loss of vision ends up reducing activity level, autonomy, and the willingness to explore. Loss of hearing interferes with that basic mode of human connectedness—conversation. Hearing impairment may be linked to increased feelings of isolation and suspiciousness. Hearing things imperfectly or perceiving conversations as whispers rather than in regular tones may feed in to feelings of being excluded or ridiculed.

COGNITIVE DEVELOPMENT

Adult thought has many dimensions to it. Thought can vary in how fanciful it is, how much the person actually directs the train of thought, and how much the thought is related to objects or events in the immediate environment (Klinger, 1978). We can experience thought as playful imagining, in which we do not deliberately focus on a particular reality-bound problem or task. Of course sometimes these thoughts can be useful for problem solving without having been intended for that purpose. We can experience thought as a product of our own attention and will, as in specific problem solving. Thought may also be experienced as a random association of images, as it often is during the period before we fall asleep. Finally, thought can be focused on the content of our immediate environment or thought can be about memories, about the relationship among concepts, or about the process of thought itself. The quality of adult thought depends on the frequency and interplay among three kinds of thought: imagery and fantasy; reasoning and problem solving; and monitoring one's thoughts or metacognition. Each of these three kinds of thought is discussed briefly.

The Nature of Adult Cognition

Imagery and Fantasy. Mental images are central to the process of thinking. Mental images are mental representations that people often describe as *pictures in the mind.* Some people have more vivid mental images than others, but we can all produce them if we are prompted. For example if you are asked to draw a picture of your bedroom, you will most likely proceed by trying to match the mental image you hold of that room with a drawn map on which the size, shape, and contents of the room as they are encoded in your mental image are represented by symbols or actual replication. If you drew the map while you were in the room, you would not need the mental image, but if you drew the map while you were someplace else, the mental image would be your primary guide.

Mental images are most often associated with fantasy thought. Dreams, daydreams, and mind-wandering are usually composed of sequences of images accompanied by feelings and sometimes by voices or other sense experiences. In adulthood, however, we have examples of mental images being used as a deliberate tool for problem solving (Shepard, 1978). Perhaps the most famous of the problem solvers who used mental images was Einstein. Einstein depended on visualization of relationships as a primary means of experimenting with abstract variables. One of the most significant events in the history of physics took place during one of Einstein's "thinking" experiments. As he visualized himself traveling alongside a light beam at a speed of 186,000 miles per second, a mental image occurred which identified to Einstein a characteristic of the physical universe which had previously been unknown. This vision of an undiscovered quality of nature led to a reformulation of electromagnetic theory (Einstein, 1949).

Another example of the contribution of mental imagery to problem solving is Kekule's work on chemical bonds and molecular structure. Kekule deliberately generated fantasies about the problems that he was studying. He frequently found that visualization helped him to understand the nature of the bonding of atoms in specific compounds. In one important visual experience Kekule "saw" a snakelike chain of molecules turn on itself as if biting its own tail. This image became the solution to the puzzle about the molecular structure of benzene and unlocked the door to modern organic chemistry (Findlay, 1948).

Mental images have special qualities that make them valuable for certain types of problem solving (Shepard, 1978). Mental images permit the simultaneous integration of several variables. They can preserve three-dimensional space in a way that the written word or the drawn representation may not. Even though the mental image is usually based on dimensions of reality, it is not constrained by those dimensions. One can begin with an image of an animal, let us say a cow, and systematically alter aspects of the animal by giving it another body shape, a different kind of coloration or coat, or even a different size. Mental images can permit movement through space, the unification of several characters or factors into one image, and the simultaneous existence of opposing or contradictory forces. One can, for example, imagine watching one's own funeral. One value of mental imagery then is its modifiability, permitting the systematic modification of objects or relationships without being limited by the constraints of the immediate environment. For these reasons mental imagery may be especially useful in the solution to problems involving social relationships.

Mental images can also be used as a method for coping with stress. One can anticipate a stressful event—e.g., surgery or separation—by imagining the event beforehand. Through imagination one can cull up various scenarios, from the most painful, vulnerable, and helpless state to the most resilient and composed. These images can help to reduce anxiety associated with stress by learning to retain a confident, calm, emotional state even under the most stressful imagined conditions (Wolpe, 1969). This technique, which is sometimes referred to as *desensitization,* does in fact help adults gain greater control over areas of intense fear. In real life part of the difficulty of stressful events is the fact that we have so little chance to prepare or to develop skilled responses. Desensitization makes use of the vividness of mental imagery and its similarity to real experience to help provide practice in encountering stress. With each imagined encounter the person learns to approach the feared event with an attitude of confidence.

As in childhood the amount of mental imagery and fantasy thought people are likely to use will vary from person to person. People have different degrees of a predisposition to fantasy (Singer, 1973). In addition to this individual factor, settings differ in the extent to which they encourage fantasy, and cultures differ in the extent to which they value or place credence in fantasy.

Reasoning and Problem Solving. The events of adult life pose continuous challenges to our capacities for reasoning and problem solving. In every sphere of adult experience, including management of a household, parenting, maintaining meaningful interpersonal relationships, and work, uncertainties and conflicts call for decision making, careful reasoning, and effective problem solving. These challenges of adulthood are not quite the same as the problems we were asked to solve in school. The problems we face are not usually defined by someone else; rather, it is up to each adult to recognize problems as they arise and to identify the essential components of those problems. Adults also have to determine for themselves what the goals or desired outcomes of a conflict or problem might be.

Many problems of adult life do not have a single correct solution. In fact for some problems of adult life, such as the decision to choose a particular career, to end a marriage relationship, or to move to a new town, it is hard to say in advance that one choice is correct and another is wrong. One can imagine successful adaptation or maladaptation resulting from any choice. A great deal depends on the adult's capacity to assess his/her own resources as well as on the adult's attitude toward the problem being faced.

Problems of adult life tend to be more complex and long term than are the problems of earlier states. This calls for a new time perspective on problem solving. One may be asked to project toward the adolescence or adulthood of your own children. One may have a five- or ten-year plan for one's organization. One may in fact be trying to solve problems about retirement when it is 40 years away. Realizing the complex and repeated nature of these challenges, individuals are drawn toward the need for a guiding philosophy or life plan that gives direction, emphasis, and style to the problem-solving orientation. Problems become more than discrete disruptions, inconveniences, or stumbling blocks. They become the patterned, propelling energy source for continued life growth.

When a life problem is confronted in an active, directed way, cognitive growth is stimulated in several ways. First, in recognizing the problem the person experiences some discrepancy between what one wishes were true of reality and what one assesses to be true. This discrepancy itself is energizing, stimulating the person to a new level of arousal and attention. Alert and attentive, the whole mental system is roused from a more "automatic" level of functioning. In this state there is the opportunity to benefit from heightened sensitivity to sensation, increased vividness of imagery, a more lively sense of humor, or greater levels of concentration. Being in a problem-solving state can be mentally stimulating.

Second, the search for a solution can be stimulating. When problems are complex the problem-solving search usually involves generating many solutions and pursuing the consequences of each solution mentally. This is similar to Einstein's *Gedanken* (thinking) experiments. In the mental pursuit of solutions, there is the opportunity to play with reality, modifying conditions so that they suit one's goals more satisfactorily. During this process there is the possibility of stumbling across refreshing new conceptualizations. One can discover solutions to the problem that evoked the search, but one can also identify solutions to unrelated problems. For example, in trying to decide how to lose some weight, Jennifer reviewed the reasons she was likely to gain weight. She thought about various aspects of her life, including time she spent alone, time she spent preparing and eating meals, and people who influenced the kinds of food she was likely to eat. In thinking about her eating habits, she realized that many of her life choices were determined by her husband's preferences. The solution to losing weight led to a new analysis of her marital relationship.

The third phase of problem solving is the implementation of a solution. In this phase a person has a chance to learn how closely his/her problem-solving skills anticipated reality. Having tried to identify relevant variables, to plan for a reasonable time period, and to anticipate consequences of the choices involved, the voice of reality provides new opportunities to improve one's problem solving. In each implementation aspects of the solution that succeed confirm the strategy and the logic employed. Aspects of the solution that do not succeed generate new discrepancies, new uncertainties, and the need for new conceptualizations. It is possible to become aware of new aspects of reality or to reevaluate one's resources in light of the consequences that any particular problem-solving strategy produces.

By young adulthood we expect the development of cognition to have reached the point where abstractions, hypothesis testing, logic, and a capacity for the manipulation of several variables simultaneously have all had a full opportunity to emerge. Yet there is some evidence that the quality of reasoning and problem solving changes during adult life. Two examples serve to illustrate possible variations in thinking through adulthood. Kastenbaum (1966) has described changes in time perspective. In adolescence young people become increasingly aware of the uncertainty of the future as well as the reality of future events. Adolescents tend to have rich and complex expectations for the immediate future but give almost no thought to life after about age 25. Older adults are able to consider both past and future in an integrated time perspective when the situation is not related to their own personal life events. In relation to a personal history, however, the elderly are unwilling to consider future life events. It is as if the cognitive skills are subordinated by the uncertainty and unpreparedness they experience about their personal futures.

A number of studies have reported that the elderly perform a variety of cognitive tasks at a less complex level than do middle-aged subjects (Denney & Wright, 1978). An example is the game of "20 questions." Adolescents and middle adults generally approach that game by asking questions that eliminate large groups of possibilities (Is it alive?). The elderly, like young children, ask specific questions to test specific hypotheses (Is it my shoe?). The supposition is that the elderly are still capable of using the abstract problem-solving strategy, but they are not inclined to approach tasks from that orientation. One might hypothesize that as adults narrow the focus of their attention more and more to immediate needs and immediate obstacles to the gratification of needs they stop using the multifaceted, flexible problem-solving strategies that were called forth by the continuous uncertainties of early adult challenges.

Monitoring One's Thoughts. Not only do adults think and direct their thinking toward the solution of problems, but they also direct their thinking toward thought itself. At a personal level this kind of monitoring of thought includes a variety of administrative activities that psychologists refer to as *metacognition* (Flavell, 1978). For example we review a set of concepts that has recently been learned and make an assessment about how well we know the new material. Based on this assessment we might reread some sections, try to find additional information, or feeling confident, move on to something new.

Monitoring one's thoughts provides a means of detecting errors in logic or misunderstandings. When a decision has been reached, it is possible to stop and check the lines of reasoning that have led to a particular decision. Adults often enroll in seminars and workshops that provide training in just this kind of decision analysis. Adults are capable of imposing or removing constraints on their thoughts, thereby solving the same problem under varied conditions. The technique of *blockbusting* is designed to stimulate creative thought by encouraging the problem solver to relinquish certain "sets" or orientations that might interfere with the generation of new solutions. Under these "no-holds-barred" conditions, the mind operates at two levels simultaneously, at one level generating ideas and at another level keeping the usual constraints from interfering. In adult life many levels of consciousness can exist simultaneously, each offering a unique contribution to knowing.

Metacognition includes one of the early tools of psychological study—introspection. In Wundt's early experiments subjects were trained through 10,000 trials of introspection before they were asked to participate in an experiment (Lieberman, 1979). All this training led to the development of a capacity for detailed, systematic observation of one's mental activities. At a more casual level introspection is focused attention on one's personal thoughts. It might include evaluating the logic used in the solution of a problem, searching for the explanation of a strong emotional reaction, or comparing your perspective with the perspective of another person.

During adulthood the realm of thought devoted to metacognition expands. Greater amounts of time are spent in planning, evaluating, reminiscing, and predicting. Having encountered a variety of people and a variety of situations during adult life, it becomes increasingly obvious that successful adaptation depends heavily upon the accuracy of two kinds of information: information about the environment and information about the self. The metacognitive functions are not those involved in the direct experience of the environment or in determining a response to an experience; rather, they are the functions of analysis, interpretation, and integration that bring a broader perspective to life's experiences. Insofar as the challenges of adulthood become more philosophical, these functions become the cornerstones of adaptation. They permit the formulation of a philosophy of life and provide a basis for determining one's personal meaning. As the reality of one's mortality becomes evident, adults spend energy evaluating their beliefs, assessing their life choices, and searching for the obstacles in their life that may explain their current feelings of despair. The more physical activity, meaningful work, and intimate relationships diminish in the life of the aging adult, the more introspection and reminiscence serve as a central context for continued psychosocial growth. Here we think of the importance of the life review as a vehicle for selecting and reinterpreting the past so that one can face death with a sense of completion (Butler, 1963).

Cognition and Social Life

Much of adult thought focuses on social relationships and social situations. Adults are frequently involved in solving problems that center around the interpersonal rather than the physical demands of their surroundings. While the child struggles to reach a doorknob or ride a two-wheeled bicycle, the adult struggles to achieve intimacy with a marriage partner or to have a productive collaboration with a colleague.

As Simon (1975) argues, many of the same principles of thought that apply to solving mathematical or scientific problems apply to understanding social relationships.

Information is extracted from a complex stimulus situation; it is subjected to the kinds of information processes we call "thinking," "judging," "problem solving," or "inferring"; during the course of that processing, there is brought to bear upon it a wide range and variety of information already stored in memory. We neither need nor want separate theories of social thinking and other (anti-social?) thinking. We simply need a theory of thinking. (p. 3)

The Individual in Face-to-Face Relations. Most people have the following six categories of face-to-face relations:

Single encounters. Over the course of a year, people have a certain number of first-impression relations. A salesperson may have many of these, including potential customers, hotel clerks, seatmates on airplanes, and waitresses in restaurants. An academic recluse will have comparatively few. Every person has some new encounters that do not go beyond a single interaction.

Associational relations. Because of group membership, residence in a particular apartment building or neighborhood, or regular attendance at particular settings, people have repeated encounters with certain people over the course of time. These associational relations

generally do not lead to a high degree of intimacy, although it is possible for one of these associational relations to take on greater intensity. One's public image is known through these relationships, and in that sense they can be very important for establishing an adult's reputation in a community.

Business or colleague relations. All workers have interactions with others because of their work. These relations may involve long hours, close quarters, a high degree of interdependence, and in some cases, intense emotional involvement. Work relations are usually defined by norms that govern the quality of interaction and limit the degree of personal investment. We know that these relations can be terminated because of promotion to a new position, transfers, firings, or a decision to look for a new job. In this sense work relations have the peculiar quality of calling forth distancing mechanisms and engagement simultaneously.

Friendship relations. For most people a small number of others are categorized as *friends*. These people like each other, feel warmly toward each other, and provide an important source of personal support.

Family relations. Family bonds encompass a whole network of relationships from parents, spouse, and children to aunts, uncles, cousins, and in-laws. Even though some of these associations provide only occasional interactions, people usually feel a special way toward family members that distinguishes these relations from those of any other type. The concept of *family,* in other words, frequently overrides other dimensions that govern relationships, including frequency of interaction, similarity of interests and values, physical attractiveness, or likeability. Some people have frequent and involving interactions with family members, while others have few family encounters.

Intimate relations. A special subset of relations can be categorized as *intimate.* These relations, which may exist between husband and wife, between parent and child, or between lovers, are characterized by deep understanding and intense emotional commitment to the well-being and continued development of the other.

A good part of daily thought is devoted to these daily personal relationships. Depending on the pattern of emphasis, adults will be preoccupied with problems of a particular type. For example the business relations will impose certain limits on interaction, certain demands for leadership or collaboration, or certain problems in managing the performance of others. If a large part of thought is devoted to these problems, the direction of thought about self-other social systems will evolve in a different direction than if the majority of thoughts is focused on family, associational, or intimate relations.

The demands of each of these interpersonal systems for thinking is considerable. It may be that these relations are the most compelling life stimuli for thought. Each system requires an analysis of the demands of that system, an evaluation of one's effectiveness in each sphere, monitoring any single person's movement from one kind of relationship to another, and maintaining continuity even when relations place contradictory demands.

The challenge in adulthood is to impose some integration on one's involvement at these various levels. Priorities must be set, a sense of self-awareness must be established, and conflicts among levels for allegiance or truth must be resolved.

The complexity of social thought and the demands placed by others makes the process responsive as well as initiatory. In order to limit the potential vastness of demands of others, individuals create strategies to permit themselves to be most effective. The predominant arena for intellectual activity for adults is devising plans for social interaction that meet personal needs and at the same time conform to the perceived societal norms for responsive, ethical relationships.

Thought Systems for Behavioral Guidance. In order to cope with the levels of social relations and the various kinds of responsibility involved at each level, people develop systematic rules to govern social behavior. These rules, which we refer to as *morality, political ideology,* and *personal philosophy,* impose organization, limits, and meaning on interpersonal experience.

Moral thought. Several theorists have offered analyses of morality in adulthood. Freud (1905/1953) identified morality as a mental structure that first emerged as a result of the resolution of the Oedipal or Electra complex at about age seven. At this age the conscience, or superego, was strict, punitive, and dominated by a fear of retribution. Because the superego developed during a time of limited ego development, its contents focused on a narrow range of concerns, and its organization was highly authoritarian. In adulthood, Freud argued, the superego matures. The strength of impulse weakens, people have more highly developed avenues for sublimation, and there are acceptable outlets for direct expression through love and work. Moral life, then, had its origin in sexual and aggressive impulses, especially impulses toward one's parents. Out of a need to maintain parental love and a fear of parental anger, the child restrains these impulses and incorporates the moral values of the parents. Morality, from generation to generation, is viewed as emerging from the inborn conflict between parental hate and parental love. The child's superego is formed as a product of efforts to resolve that conflict in a context of parental support or parental punitiveness.

The cognitive theorists, especially Piaget (1932/1948) and Kohlberg (1964; Kohlberg & Kramer, 1969) emphasize changing cognitive capacities that underlie changes in moral thought. In early childhood moral judgments are based on observable consequences of actions. Intentions, principles, and motives are less relevant than the actual outcome of an act. Breaking ten cups by accident is viewed as worse than breaking one cup as part of an intentional violation. At the intermediate level moral judgments reflect the desire to maintain the status quo. Rules are respected because they reflect the views of respected authorities. At the highest level, moral judgments reflect one of two positions: (1) The culture establishes moral contracts among individuals—i.e., we maintain certain moral commitments in order to insure that others will maintain their commitments to us; and (2) In adulthood it is possible to take an overview of the moral code and appreciate it in relation to moral systems in other societies. Under these conditions of awareness the adult imposes moral judgments that reflect their own internal code regardless of the norms of the culture.

It is these last two stages of moral thought that are most likely to emerge during the adult years. Of course many adults continue to function at an intermediate level. Some may believe that the cultural code is really an expression of their own moral position. In these cases socialization has worked to create a highly responsive, norm-sensitive adult. However it is possible to recognize morality as a human construction. The compelling nature of a moral precept is its shared acceptance by many other adults. Only by encountering diverse moral systems can the relativity of morality be fully appreciated. Once adults recognize that it is up to them to determine the content of their own morality, the opportunity for generating new and creative systems for guiding moral behavior becomes possible.

Political thought. Political thought is that system that governs a person's relationship with community, county, state, or federal levels of organization. For many adults political thought is not highly developed. At some point, perhaps in early adolescence, these adults make an allegiance to the general orientation of the government. After that point they do their part by paying their taxes but do not become actively involved in political decision making. This approach is an acceptable adult stance in the United States insofar as the government functions through a system of representation. Those who are elected as representatives can assume the active role in the political process, while those who elected the representatives are free to devote their time and energy to work, family, or personal development. The generally low percentage of voters who participate in state and local elections suggests that the vast majority of adults do not feel compelled to exercise their political conceptualizations by trying to change the direction of government.

For these politically inactive adults we assume that they are aware of the nature and organization of the political system that operates in this country. Based on what they learned about American government and American history in elementary school, high school, and/or college, these adults take the stance that they are satisfied with the overall pattern of government. They cannot be viewed as lacking a political conceptualization; rather, they can be seen as living a life that is in harmony with the system. Successful political socialization has created a pool of adults who feel highly identified with the United States, who support its government, and who do not feel the need to influence the political system actively.

Of course some adults have a much more active, highly compelling conceptualization of the political system. Political scientists, politicians, political activists, community change agents, and federal, state, county, or city employees are examples of groups of people who are likely to be more aware of political controversies and who experience more demands to clarify their own political conceptualization. We would expect these groups to be more aware of the process of political decision making, more sensitive to the origins of social policy and legislation, and more realistic about the range of influence of the political system on individual lives. These adults may in fact have a political ideology that actively directs their decision making. Concepts about the public good, individual rights, the system of checks and balances, executive power, and the relationship between state and federal levels of decision making are all examples of political conceptualizations that may be directly translated into action.

With the widespread use of television, it is becoming increasingly difficult to avoid the influence of the political system in daily thought. Political events of all kinds—from gasoline shortages to riverboat cruises, from papal visits to terrorist kidnappings—are part of the public awareness. Given the publicity that the political arena receives, today's adults are continuously challenged to adapt their political ideology to the reality of political life. One might argue that we have an adult population that is more fully informed about political events than was any other generation. Unfortunately many adults do not have a conceptualization that is adequate to integrate the information that is continuously presented. In today's society there is some uneasiness among many adults who realize the gap between the enormity of the political system and their own capacity to understand, interpret, or predict the pattern of political events.

Personal philosophy. Moral thought governs the quality of relationships among individuals. Political thought governs the quality of relationships between people and political units. Personal philosophy governs the quality of relations between individuals and their experience. One's philosophy is a guide to the meaning and purpose in experience.

A personal philosophy is the creation of a mature mind. Generally the philosophy is forged from the analysis of past experiences and anticipation of future possibilities. The philosophy is based on interactions at every level of relationship. It includes some content from one's political, moral, and/or religious orientation, but generally it is a broader and more abstract formulation than any of these. It includes the answers to basic questions that are first asked in the childhood years. These questions include the following: How did the world begin? Why was I born? Why do I have to die? What makes me happy? Will I always be loved? Why do I experience pain? In adulthood the answers to these questions are gradually formulated. Important factors in the maturation of a personal philosophy include one's work, one's relationship with a loving companion, parenting, and one's encounters with political and/or historical events. In addition to the contribution of real-life events and real relationships, adults bring insight, a sense of esthetics, and creativity to bear in order to find meaning in what is bound to be an accumulation of contradictions, accidents, irrelevancies, and redundancies, as well as planned or predictable events. In this respect a personal philosophy is a creative reduction of enormous amounts of data into a few convincing principles. Although it is possible for this personal philosophy to change, once established it is more likely to be the lens through which events are interpreted than to be the object of interpretation itself.

PERSONALITY DEVELOPMENT

Personality is that relatively consistent set of thoughts, feelings, and behavior patterns that guide the organization of experience and the direction of new growth. The word *personality* is a general term that represents the integration of four major factors: traits and talents, motives, roles, and coping style. Taken together they contribute to a configuration that is recognizable to the self from within and to others as observers. Our definition includes a commitment to growth and development against a background of continuity. Change may occur as new talents are discovered or developed; as new motives emerge to direct behavior; as role relationships begin, end, or are redefined; or when the effectiveness of a particular coping style is found wanting and must be modified. Perhaps the most pressing question about personality during middle adulthood is how much change to expect. The second question is what prompts change.

Directions of Change in Adult Personality Development

The fact that there is change in personality during adulthood is evidenced by the attempts of social scientists to study it. If adults were totally consistent from one life period to another, there would be no need to study adult personality.

Expectations for change have been described in a number of theories but most notably by Erikson (1950, 1978) and Jung (1939/1959, 1931/1960). Erikson offers a stage approach including three significant and qualitatively different stages of adult life. Young adulthood is characterized by the crisis of intimacy versus isolation. The central process for resolving the crisis is the establishment of mutuality with an age-mate, and the positive consequences are feelings of loving and reciprocity. Middle adulthood is characterized by the crisis of generativity versus stagnation. The central process requires a creative solution to the incongruence between individual needs and environmental demands. The positive consequences are a sense of caring and a commitment to the quality of life for future generations. The crisis of later adulthood is integrity versus despair. The central process for resolving the crisis is introspection. The positive consequences are a sense of wisdom and acceptance of one's life as it has been lived. In Erikson's theory change is brought about by the discrepancy between personal competences and cultural demands. The psychological context for development, including the period of history, economic factors, family and work roles, and the attitudes held in one's society about one's age group, contribute to the pattern of adult growth. Personal talents, intelligence, motives, and aspirations also contribute to the pattern of adult growth.

Jung described the person as a collection of conflicting forces. The ego or conscious mind is in conflict with the personal and the collective unconscious. The personal unconscious is populated by complexes or patterns of thoughts, feelings, and memories around a specific object. The collective unconscious stores memories and images from the history of human experience. Longings, fears, and hopes can be energized by the content of the collective unconscious. Among the structures of the unconscious are archetypes that provide the content for personality. The major archetypes are the *persona* or mask the person assumes in playing out life roles; the *anima* (the feminine archetype in man) and the *animus* (the masculine archetype in woman); and the *shadow* or animal instincts of the person. At the center of these archetypes is the *self,* an integrating unifying force that moves toward fuller expression at each life stage. Maturity, which Jung sees as an achievement of middle adulthood, requires the full expression and recognition of the diverse elements of the person. When the personality is fully differentiated, a unifying process begins in which opposing forces are brought together. When aspects of the personality are barred from consciousness, essential energy is lost. In middle adulthood the delicate process of unification takes place. When successful there is greater dominance of the self. The person becomes wiser, more spiritual, and more integrated with cultural values. When the transcendence of self is not successful, energy may be directed to one archetype to the loss of the others. Adults may continue to repress the unacceptable instincts and thereby upset the balance of psychological energy.

The two theories emphasize different patterns of adult development. They also emphasize rather different dimensions of growth. Erikson's work suggests that the crystallization of identity during later adolescence sets the tone for many of the life choices of adult life. Growth in adulthood in his view is understood in relation to expanding meaningful relationships with others through love, parenting, work efforts, and community commitment. A full integration and emergence of wisdom is not expected until the later part of life. Jung paints a picture of the middle adult years as the time when a full integration is first possible. Work on identity before that time is really clarification of the many elements that make up the person. No integrating conceptualization is considered possible until adults have had many opportunities to encounter and explore the complexity of their own nature. Jung's model offers a possibility of integration and full expression of the self during the middle years that can serve to guide and energize the later adult years.

Two of the studies of growth during adult life clarify the difference in emphasis of these two approaches. Gould (1978), whose work is more Jungian, describes a process of gradual release from the unnecessary restraints of childhood. At each phase of adulthood there is an examination of what Gould calls *false assumptions* about relationships and experience. Gould describes adulthood as an uneasy confrontation with the many dimensions of the person that have been defined, mythologized, or repressed through childhood socialization. Only when all the skeletons of childhood have been swept from their respective closets can the adult claim a full sense of control over life choices. This achievement is not commonly attained before the age of 50.

Levinson (1978) has based his observations on the intensive study of 40 men who represented four occupations: hourly workers in industry, executives, biologists, and novelists. His description of adult development is more Eriksonian in tone. He describes a stepwise progression through four eras, each separated by a major transition time. The eras are childhood and adolescence (13 to 17), early adulthood (22 to 40), middle adulthood (45 to 60), and late adulthood (65 and over). Each era is influenced by biological changes, relations with older and younger generations, and the unfolding of major careers or life roles, especially the work role. Levinson is interested in the formation of life structures and the revision of these structures throughout adulthood. He describes a process whereby adults construct a guiding framework that reflects (1) the society in which the person lives; (2) the self with its accompanying motives, talents, roles, and coping style; and (3) the meaningful relationships in which the person is involved. Life structures are built, revised, and periodically abandoned as the intrinsic conflicts and changes in the life pattern make a particular structure ineffective.

Both treatments emphasize the potential for growth against a background of risk, infantile wishes, and cultural barriers to change. Even though both projects attempt to paint a picture of change across time, neither is truly a longitudinal study. Gould's work is based on responses of 524 people in the age range from 16 to 50 to a questionnaire about the salience of life issues. His model also draws heavily on his own clinical practice. Levinson worked with his subjects for 10 to 20 hours in a two-month period followed by a two-year return interview. The subjects' biographies were reconstructed from these intensive interviews with added information from spouses, children, close friends, relatives, and co-workers.

Stability and Change in Adult Personality

The picture of stability and change in adult personality is complex. There is some evidence for the stability of personal qualities across life stages. The indexes of stability grow weaker, however, the more time lapses between observations. Measures of personality from early adolescence are better predictors of personality in high school than they are for adulthood (Block, 1971). The most consistent dimensions are those temperamental characteristics that have a clear biological basis. Activity level, heartrate, sensitivity to stimulation, or irritability are examples of qualities that tend to persist from observations made during childhood to those made in adulthood. Haan (1976) was able to show that certain patterns of personality traits remained stable from adolescence through middle adulthood. This does not mean that there is no reorganization of dimensions or emphasis. She described older adults as more tender and intimate and younger adults as more assertive and more involved in problem solving and decision making.

Some studies suggest that stability or variability of personality may itself be a dimension of personality. Vaillant (1977) reported on the maturation of adaptive styles of men who were studied from their college years through their fifties. Some men remained "perpetual boys." They seemed quite mature as adolescents but failed to take the risks or make the commitments that accompanied maturity in adulthood. Those men who achieved a sense of adult generativity were able to develop a more productive career, satisfying love relationships, and a less guilt-ridden relation with their parents.

In Block's (1971) report of the process of personality change from adolescence to adulthood, much the same theme emerges. People differ in when they experience the greatest revisions in personality. Different consequences emerge from change in one period of life rather than another. Block found that for females personality changes during the age period of 11 to 16 were related to stable, traditional, feminine qualities in adulthood. Women who showed personality revisions continuing in later adolescence proved to be more unconventional and rebellious. For men in this study stability in personality during adolescence was predictive of greater maturity, stability, and interpersonal warmth than of change in either early or later adolescence.

Another set of observations suggests a third dimension for consideration in understanding personality development. Livson (1976) described two groups of women: the independents whose health improved from age 40 to age 50 and the traditionals who were healthy at both ages. The independent women were more intellectual and ambitious. They found the release from traditional female role expectations that took place during the late forties and early fifties quite enhancing for their other ambitions. The traditionals were interpersonally gregarious and nurturant. During their middle adulthood they showed steady growth that reflected the good fit between their roles as wife and mother and their personality. Sears (1977) has reported a similar pattern for the middle adult development of Terman's (Terman & Oden, 1959) gifted sample. The period of the thirties and forties was especially constraining because of the limits placed on personal functioning by sex-role expectations. During the fifties these adults felt greater confidence in their own personal styles.

CONCLUSIONS

Middle adulthood holds the potential for significant personality development. This development is prompted by changing physical capacities; new conceptualizations of self, time, and purpose; and the enactment of major life commitments, including marriage, work, and parenting. Whether growth takes place during this period may depend on the individual's capacity for further development. Openness to new ideas, willingness to take risks, and interpersonal responsiveness are all qualities that predispose the person toward continued adult development. Those adolescents who strive to achieve stability by closing out discrepant or disruptive feelings, thoughts, or sensations may strike a premature integration that does not readily permit continued growth. We would suggest that the dramatic crises of middle adulthood are in fact a result of this early foreclosure and a failure to mature during the challenging periods of later adolescence and young adulthood. They represent a sudden collapse of a life structure built on false assumptions, minimal self-insight, and constricted relationships with others.

REFERENCES

ALLPORT, G. W. *Becoming: Basic considerations for a psychology of personality.* New Haven, Conn.: Yale University Press, 1955.

ANDERSON, J. E. A developmental model for aging. *Vita Humana,* 1958, *1,* 5–18.

BARDWICK, J. M. *Psychology of women.* New York: Harper & Row, Pub., 1971.

BART, P. B. Depression in middle-aged women. In V. Gornick & B. K. Moran (Eds.), *Woman in sexist society.* New York: Basic Books, 1971.

BERSCHEID, E., WALSTER, E., & BOHRNSTEDT, G. The happy American body: A survey report. *Psychology Today,* November 1973, pp. 119–131.

BLOCK, J. *Lives through time.* Berkeley, Calif.: Bancroft Books, 1971.

BOTWINICK, J., & THOMPSON, L. W. Individual differences in reaction time in relation to age. *Journal of Genetic Psychology,* 1968, *112,* 73–75.

BUTLER, R. N. The life review: An interpretation of reminiscence in the aged. *Psychiatry,* February 1963, pp. 65–76.

CAMERON, P., & BIBER, H. Sexual thought throughout the life span. *The Gerontologist,* 1973, *13,* 144–147.

DENNEY, N. W., & WRIGHT, J. C. *Cognitive changes during the adult years: Implications for developmental theory and research.* Paper presented at the American Psychological Association meetings, Toronto, 1978.

DIAMOND, M. C. The aging brain: Some enlightening and optimistic results. *American Scientist,* 1978, *66,* 66–71.

EINSTEIN, A. Autobiographical notes. In P. A. Schlipp (Ed.), *Albert Einstein: Philosopher-scientist.* Evanston, Ill.: Library of Living Philosophers, 1949.

ERIKSON, E. H. *Childhood and society.* New York: W. W. Norton & Co., Inc., 1950.

ERIKSON, E. H. *Identity and the life cycle: Selected papers by Erik H. Erikson.* New York: International Universities Press, 1959.

ERIKSON, E. H. *Adulthood.* New York: W. W. Norton & Co., Inc. 1978.

FAUST, M. S. Somatic development of adolescent girls. *Monographs of the Society for Research in Child Development,* 1977, *42*(1, Serial No. 169).

FINDLAY, A. *A hundred years of chemistry* (2nd ed.). London: Duckworth, 1948.

FLAVELL, J. H. *Metacognition.* Paper presented at the American Psychological Association meetings, Toronto, 1978.

FLINT, M. Cross-cultural factors that affect age of menopause. In P. A. Van Keep, R. B. Greenblatt, & M. Albeaux-Fernet (Eds.), *Consensus on menopause research.* Baltimore, Md.: University Park Press, 1976.

FRANKS, L. M. Aging in differentiated cells. *The Gerontologist,* 1974, *60,* 51–62.

FREUD, S. Three essays on the theory of sexuality. In J. Strachey (Ed.), *The standard edition of the complete psychological works of Sigmund Freud* (Vol. 7). London: Hogarth Press, 1953. (Originally published, 1905.)

GADPAILLE, W. J. *The cycles of sex* (Lucy Freeman, Ed.). New York: Scribners, 1975.

GAGNON, J. H. *Human sexualities.* Glenview, Ill.: Scott, Foresman, 1977.

GLICK, P. C. Updating the life cycle of the family. *Journal of Marriage and the Family,* 1977, *39,* 5–13.

GOULD, R. L. *Transformations: Growth and change in adult life.* New York: Simon & Schuster, 1978.

HAAN, N. Personality organizations of well-functioning younger people and older adults. *International Journal of Aging and Human Development,* 1976, *7,* 117–127.

HAYFLICK, L. The cell biology of human aging. *Scientific American,* 1980, *242,* 58–65.

HORN, J. L. Human ability systems. Pp. 212–257 in P. B. Baltes (Ed.), *Life-span development and behavior* (Vol. 1). New York: Academic Press, 1978.

HORN, J. L. The rise and fall of human abilities. *Journal of Research and Development in Education,* 1979, *12,* 59–78.

HYDEN, H. RNA changes in brain cells during changes in behavior function. In G. B. Ansell & P. B. Bradley (Eds.), *Macromolecules and behavior.* Baltimore, Md.: University Park Press, 1973.

JARVIK, L. F., & COHEN, D. A biobehavioral approach to intellectual changes with aging. Pp. 220–280 in C. Eisdorfer & M. P. Lawton (Eds.), *The psychology of adult development and aging.* Washington, D.C.: American Psychological Association, 1973.

JUNG, C. G. Conscious, unconscious, and individuation. In *Collected works* (Vol. 9, P. 1). Princeton, N.J.: Princeton University Press, 1959. (Originally published in English, 1939.)

JUNG, C. G. The stages of life. In *Collected works* (Vol. 8). Princeton, N.J.: Princeton University Press, 1960. (Originally published in German, 1931.)

KASTENBAUM, R. On the meaning of time in later life. *Journal of Genetic Psychology,* 1966, *109,* 9–25.

KINSEY, A. C., POMEROY, W. B., & MARTIN, C. E. *Sexual behavior in the human male.* Philadelphia: Saunders, 1948.

KLINGER, E. Dimensions of thought and imagery in normal waking states. *Journal of Altered States of Consciousness,* 1978, *4,* 97–114.

KOHLBERG, L. Development of moral character and moral ideology. In M. L. Hoffman & L. W. Hoffman (Eds.), *Review of child development research* (Vol. 1). New York: Russell Sage Foundation, 1964.

KOHLBERG, L., & KRAMER, R. Continuities and discontinuities in childhood and adult moral development. *Human Development,* 1969, *12,* 93–118.

KREITLER, H., & KREITLER, S. Movement and aging: A psychological approach. *Medicine and Sport,* 1970, *4,* 302–306.

LEVINSON, D. J. *The season's of a man's life.* New York: Knopf, 1978.

LEWIS, M. State as an infant-environment interaction: An analysis of mother-infant interaction as a function of sex. *Merrill-Palmer Quarterly,* 1972, *18,* 95–121.

LIEBERMAN, D. A. Behaviorism and the mind: A (limited) call for a return to introspection. *American Psychologist,* 1979, *34*(No. 4), 319–333.

LIVSON, F. B. Patterns of personality development in middle-aged women: A longitudinal study. *International Journal of Aging and Human Development,* 1976, *7,* 107–115.

McKINLEY, S. M., & JEFFERYS, M. The menopausal syndrome. *British Journal of Preventive and Social Medicine,* 1974, *28,* 108–115.

MARSHALL, W. A. The body (Chaps. 1, 4, 7, 10, 13, 16, 19). In R. R. Seas & S. S. Feldman (Eds.), *The seven ages of man.* Los Altos, Calif.: William Kaufmann, 1973.

NEUGARTEN, B. Adult personality: Toward a psychology of the life cycle. In B. Neugarten (Ed.), *Middle age and aging.* Chicago: University of Chicago Press, 1968.

NEUGARTEN, B. L., & KRAINES, R. J. Menopausal symptoms in women of various ages. *Psychosomatic Medicine,* 1965, *27,* 266–273.

NEUGARTEN, B. L., WOOD, V., KRAINES, R. J., & LOOMIS, B. Women's attitudes toward the menopause. *Vita Humana,* 1963, *6,* 140–151.

NEWMAN, G., & NICHOLS, C. R. Sexual activities and attitudes in older persons. *Journal of the American Medical Association,* 1960, *173,* 33–35.

PIAGET, J. The moral judgment of the child. Glencoe, Ill.: Free Press, 1948. (Originally published, 1932.)

RAMEY, E. Men's cycles (They have them too, you know). *Ms.,* Spring 1972, pp. 8–14.

RUBIN, I. Sex over 65. In H. G. Beigel (Ed.), *Advances in sex research.* New York: Harper & Row, Pub., 1963.

RUBIN, I. *Sexual life after sixty.* New York: Basic Books, 1965.

SEARS, R. R. Sources of life satisfactions of the Terman gifted men. *American Psychologist,* 1977, *32,* 119–128.

SHELLDRAKE, A. R. The aging, growth and death of cells. *Nature,* 1974, *250,* 381–384.

SHEPARD, R. N. The mental image. *American Psychologist,* 1978, *33,* 125–137.

SHERMAN, J. A. *On the psychology of women: A survey of empirical studies.* Springfield, Ill.: Chas. C Thomas, 1971.

SIMON, H. A. Discussion: Cognition and social behavior. Working Paper No. 298, 1975. (Mimeo)

SINGER, J. L. *The child's world of make believe: Experimental studies of imaginative play.* New York: Academic Press, 1973.

SMITH, M. E. Ophthalmic aspects. In F. U. Steinberg (Ed.), *Cowdry's The care of the geriatric patient.* St. Louis, Mo.: C. V. Mosby, 1976.

SULLIVAN, H. S. *The collected works of Harry Stack Sullivan* (Vols. 1 & 2). New York: W. W. Norton & Co., Inc., 1949.

TERMAN, L. M., & ODEN, M. H. *Genetic studies of genius.* Vol. 5: The gifted group at mid-life: Thirty-five years' follow-up of the superior child. Stanford, Calif.: Stanford University Press, 1959.

THOMPSON, L. W., & MARSH, G. R. Psychophysiological studies of aging. Pp. 112–148, in C. Eisdorfer & M. P. Lawton (Eds.), *The psychology of adult development.* Washington, D.C.: American Psychological Association, 1973.

ULVERSTAM, L. Aging meaningfully. *Social Change in Sweden.* New York: Swedish Information Service, 1977, 3.

U.S. Bureau of the Census. *Marital status and living arrangements: March 1975* (Current Population Reports, Series P. 20, No. 287). Washington, D.C.: U.S. Government Printing Office, 1975.

U.S. Bureau of the Census. *Prospective trends in the size and structure of the elderly population.* (Current Population Reports, Series P-23, No. 78, Table 5). Washington, D.C.: U.S. Government Printing Office, 1979.

VAILLANT, G. E. *Adaptation to life.* Boston: Little, Brown, 1977.

WEG, R. B. The physiology of sexuality in aging. Pp. 48–65 in R. L. Solnick (Ed.), *Sexuality and aging* (Rev. ed.). Los Angeles: The Ethel Percy Andrews Gerontology Center/University of Southern California Press, 1978.

WEISS, E., & ENGLISH, O. S. *Psychomatic medicine.* Philadelphia: Saunders, 1957.

WILSON, R., & WILSON, T. The non-treated postmenopausal woman. *American Geriatrics Society,* 1963, *11,* 347.

WOLPE, J. *The practice of behavior therapy.* Elmsford, N.Y.: Pergamon Press, 1969.

WRIGHT, H. F. Psychological habitat. In R. G. Barker, L. S. Barker, C. L. Fawl, P. V. Gump, L. S. Halstead, A. Johnson, D.D.M. Ragle, M. F. Schoggen, P. Schoggen, A. W. Wicker, E. P. Willems, & H. F. Wright (Eds.), *Habitats, environments, and human behavior.* San Francisco: Jossey-Bass, 1978.

35

The Life-Cycle Approach
to Family Analysis

STEVEN L. NOCK

An accurate appreciation of the processes important to individuals in families recognizes the importance of psychological, historical, and sociological forces. Much of the life span of an individual may be seen as the consequences of the meshing of family history, societal forces, and individual developmental processes. The approach discussed in this chapter, referred to as the *developmental* or *family life-cycle approach,* explicitly recognizes all of these. The focus of the approach is specifically on the longitudinal career of families and the internal dynamics of families as these are changed or directed by events peculiar to the individual, unique to the family, or crosscutting the family and society.

Sociologists have traditionally relied on the concept of *social role* to explain behavior. For example the behavior of a father can be explained, sociologically, by studying the normative expectations surrounding his role as father within the social structure of the family. There are wide variations in behaviors resulting from normative expectations, and variations in "role performance" (Turner, 1970) are understood to arise from idiosyncratic abilities, propensities, resources, and personality and from unique variations associated with time and space locations. We all recognize that to be a father of an infant is quite different from being a father to that child as a teenager. Such a difference derives in part from the many changes associated with the development of each individual involved (father and offspring). However there are other sources of change involved in this interaction. The societal expectations associated with the role of father, for example, are age-graded (cf. Riley, Johnson, & Foner, 1972) so that we may expect the interaction between a father and his son or daughter to reflect the influence of processes within the family as well as those external to the family. In the simplest terms what is seen as "appropriate" behavior for a father interacting with his infant is

considerably different from that which is seen as appropriate when the infant becomes a young adult. What is, and is not, appropriate at each point is partially a result of societal normative standards.

Pursuing this example, over time there are several dimensions of change involved. First, each individual has aged and has experienced developmental growth. In addition to the *individual* changes, there has been considerable change in the structure of the family in terms of role relationships (and possibly the addition or deletion of family members). It is the specific recognition of this constellation of processes which marks the family life-cycle approach to the study of the family as a unique departure from more traditional sociological or psychological formulations of family process.

The timing of events in the family has very important consequences for the development of individuals within it. The length of time between births, for example, will affect the interaction among siblings and parents. We recognize that each member of the family has a timetable unique to him/her that conditions growth and development. The family also has its own timetable including such events as the birth or death of members, the changing relations among members resulting from such structural changes, and the resultant consequences owing to such changes (e.g., geographic migration or job shifts). It is also true that the timing of events within the family is strongly affected by normative (societal) expectations concerning the appropriate age for certain events. If law and custom define the age period 6 to 18 as school age, this will influence the relationship of each child to his/her parents. Normative expectations are not the only things that impinge on the timing of family events. Also important in this regard are certain very basic demographic forces which may result from the application of technology. Lengthened life expectancy and fertility control are among the most important of such factors. When the family can limit fertility, the length of child-bearing age will usually be shortened (cf. Hareven, 1978). Also when life expectancy is extended, the possibility of parents living to enjoy time together after all offspring have left home becomes a reality. The consequences of such changes within the family, as well as within society, are important in attempting to understand the dynamics and nature of interactions within the family. One may view much of the internal workings of families as coping with a number of "clocks" (individual developmental, social, and family) which are often at odds with each other (Hareven, 1977).

A BRIEF HISTORY OF THE LIFE-CYCLE APPROACH

The history of this approach reflects its cross-disciplinary focus. Rowntree (1906), in his analysis of poverty in York, England, at the turn of the century, proposed that families progress through a life cycle which begins with poverty in the early years when children are young, followed by relative prosperity when the children grow up and join the labor force, followed finally by a period when children leave home to establish their own homes during which parents once again are poor. Such an analysis finds its contemporary expression in the works of Wilensky who posits a "life-cycle squeeze"—a situation in which the needs of the family for goods and services are stretched by the presence of children (Wilensky, 1961a, 1961b; see also Gove, Grimm, Motz, & Thompson, 1973). Rural sociologists used a life-cycle approach during the 1930s and 1940s to analyze the economic life history of rural families (cf. Sorokin, Zimmerman, & Galpin, 1931), and economists employed the framework to explain the fluctuations in economic resources within the family associated with expansion and contraction of the unit. In 1948 Havinghurst was the first to formulate developmental tasks for each stage in the life cycle of the individual from birth to old age (Havighurst, 1953). The specification of developmental tasks for parents and children arose as the result of the work of the Committee on the Dynamics of Family Interaction at the 1948 National Conference on Family Life (Duvall & Hill, 1948). It was the work of Hill and Duvall, more than any others, that set the stage for the further elaboration and specification of the entire approach. Following an interdisciplinary workshop held at the University of Chicago in the summer of 1950 directed by Duvall, developmental tasks for the family as a whole were introduced (Duvall, 1957).

Beginning in 1947 Glick, a demographer, applied life-cycle stages to census material by computing median ages of husbands and wives at first marriage, birth of last child, marriage of last child, death of one spouse, and death of remaining spouse. By reporting such ages for decades since 1890, Glick was able to demonstrate significant trends in child spacing, age at first marriage, and length of the "empty nest" that had important consequences for family interaction (Glick, 1947, 1977; Glick & Parke, 1965). In a similar way Rossi was able to explain why families move from one house to another by employing a family life-cycle conceptualization that took specific notice of the addition of new members (Rossi, 1955).

In addition to specific applications that pioneered research in the life-cycle tradition, several paradigms within sociology and social psychology provided necessary concepts and theoretical underpinnings. Particularly noteworthy in this regard were the contributions of functionalists (Parsons, 1951) and symbolic interactionists (Burgess, 1926). From functionalism came the assumption that the family constitutes a social system with interrelated parts striving for some sort of homeostatic equilibrium. Furthermore it is presumed that the family performs certain vital functions for the maintenance and integrity of the entire social system (society). By virtue of its integral part in the structure of society, therefore, the family's structure of roles and positions is shaped as it performs vital tasks for society (e.g., socialization). The family is thus seen as a subsystem of the larger social system serving the individual needs of its members while at the same time serving the "needs" of the society.

From symbolic interaction and the early works of the sociologists Cooley (1922) and Mead (1934) and some social psychologists came the very important assumptions concerning personality and social action. Personality is viewed as an emergent property which arises from interaction with both physical and social environments. In the same way that the "self" or personality emerges as it acquires meaning through interaction, so all human action is directed by the meanings derived from past and present interactions with all environmental elements possessing phenomenological reality for the individual. Hence the individual is seen as *creating* and *reacting* to his/her world. Burgess (1926) and Hill (1971) have applied these symbolic interactionist conceptions to their view of the family as a semiclosed system of actors or a system of interacting personalities. Hence our attention is drawn to the importance of the family to the individual as it develops through interaction among its members. The combination of symbolic interactionists' definitions and assumptions with functionalist formulations provides an image of the family unique in sociological analysis. The structure of the family is seen as influenced by the functional requisites of society as are interactions within the family. At the same time from the individual perspective, the family derives its primary significance through a process of interpersonal interactions and constructed meanings. It is this ingenious combination of orientations that allows the developmental approach to find society at large significant in determining the structure of positions and roles within the family while at the same time allowing analysis of intrafamily processes on the level of social psychological factors. In this way the family is seen as a fundamental bridge linking the overarching structure of society to the interpersonal interactions and development of individuals.

It is also important to acknowledge the contributions of life-span developmental psychology to the formulation of this approach (cf. Baltes & Schaie, 1973), as well as the work of sociologists studying age norms and age stratification (Riley, 1971; Riley et al., 1972). The latter have been particularly important in establishing a view of individual experiences as limited within a range of experience due to the historical period in which people were born and grew up. Finally, social historians (Aries, 1962;

Hareven, 1977, 1978) have demonstrated the historically specific nature of the timing of life events and the social awareness of various age periods.

Given such diverse roots and a relatively recent origin, it is not particularly surprising to find that the developmental approach lacks a clear unambiguous theoretical structure; rather, it is more accurate to describe the approach as a "conceptual framework" (Hill & Rodgers, 1964, p. 202). Researchers employing the approach draw from a number of rather loosely defined concepts which are, as yet, not clearly related through systematic propositions. Further the assumptions underlying these concepts have not been adequately presented. However, the research stimulated by the approach attests to its potential in organizing and integrating diverse disciplinary interests and substantive issues. A clearer understanding will be gained by a very brief review of the more important concepts involved.

CONCEPTUAL FOUNDATION OF LIFE-CYCLE RESEARCH

Family

The conceptualization of the family reveals the blending of functionalist and symbolic interactionist orientations mentioned earlier. The definition presented here is taken from Rodgers.

The family is a semiclosed system of actors occupying interrelated positions defined by the society of which the family system is a part as unique to that system with respect to the role content of the positions and to ideas of kinship relatedness. The definitions of positional role content change over the history of the group. (Rodgers, 1973, p. 15)

Defining the family as a semiclosed system of interrelated positions implies that change in *one* position is extremely unlikely; rather, as any one position changes, all others within the system must adjust. To be semiclosed implies that there is a meaningful distinction between those things "internal" and "external" to the family. Note finally that it is society that is responsible for the organization of the family (*structure* of role relationships) although the *content* of roles is unique to each family.

Role

Normative expectations concerning what is appropriate behavior in social situations tend to cluster around certain positions which we call *roles* (cf. Turner, 1970, p. 185). Positions within families consist of roles which are performed by family members. Each individual may occupy countless roles simultaneously. One may at the same time be mother, daughter, sister, wife, and granddaughter. Each role is accompanied by societal expectations concerning what is appropriate behavior. Hence it will occasionally be found that individuals must emphasize one role over another—that is, they will make one role dominant. For example in the American family the expected role behaviors associated with the roles of wife and mother are generally well known and understood as society specifies the broadest outline of their content (al-

though the actual role behaviors will reflect considerable negotiation within the role with other members of the family). However as a result of changes in the family (such as the arrival of a child), it will be necessary for one role to take precedence over the other. In a similar way the illness of an aged parent may result in placing one's role of son or daughter before that of wife or husband. Such changes obviously have important consequences for interaction within the family.

Not only will roles change in their relative importance, but they will change in their content as well. This amounts to saying that all roles exist only in relationship to some other role. There is no role of husband without its complement of wife nor that of son without its complement of father. Further, owing to the definition of the family as consisting of interrelated positions, a change in any one position will affect all others. Over the life cycle of the family, normal growth and change in personnel will thus alter the expectations associated with positional roles. Hence roles may be said to have careers.

Developmental Task

This concept is quite central to the approach being described. The conceptual, if not the operational, ancestor of the developmental task concept is Havighurst (1953) who defined developmental tasks as follows:

A developmental task is a task which arises at or about a certain period in the life of an individual, the successful achievement of which leads to his happiness and to success with later tasks, while failure leads to unhappiness in the individual, disapproval by the society, and difficulty with later tasks. (p. 2)

Several researchers within the family life-cycle tradition have followed quite closely this classic definition which stresses the individualistic nature of certain periods in an individual's growth when others expect specific performance of him/her (Duvall, 1971, p. 140). However from a purely social-psychological standpoint, Rodgers (1973) has noted that the developmental task is but a special case of the incorporation of a given role into the repertoire of a position at some point in the normal sequence of a family career. Thus Rodgers defines the developmental task in a more imaginative way from the perspective of family life-cycle analysis.

A developmental task is a set of norms arising at a particular point in the career of a position in a social system which if incorporated by the occupant of the position as a role or part of a role cluster, brings about integration and temporary equilibrium in the system with regard to a role complex or set of role complexes; failure to incorporate the norms leads to lack of integration, application of additional normative pressures in the form of sanctions, and difficulty in incorporating later norms into the role cluster of the position. (Rodgers, 1973, p. 51)

This definition alerts us to the fact that over the course of a lifetime an individual in a family will occupy many different roles. The sum of these roles over time constitutes a career of the position, while the sum at any one point constitutes the role cluster of a position.

Thus a developmental task seen from the vantage point of the individual represents a time when others press for the acquisition of new roles. One example might be the situation of the new mother, pressed by structural considerations to assume the new role. Seen this way developmental tasks are the essence of socialization; they represent the forces pushing for the gradual changes in roles which occur over the life history of a family. Such pressure is continuous throughout life, and as such there is no definable set of developmental tasks that will apply to all individuals.

There is yet another way that the concept of developmental task has been applied. Duvall has suggested that the family itself must successfully meet the demands of developmental tasks. For Duvall these tasks are what Parsons (1949) called functional prerequisites—necessary for the survival of the family. She defines them as (1) physical maintenance, (2) allocation of resources, (3) division of labor, (4) socialization of family members, (5) reproduction, recruitment, and release of family members, (6) maintenance of order, (7) placement of members in the larger society, and (8) maintenance of motivation and morale (Duvall, 1971, p. 150). Duvall claims that just as developmental tasks for individuals reflect normative pressures for the acquisition of roles, so those for the family reflect *societal* pressure for the adequate performance of those tasks essential to the continued functioning of the family (and hence of society). Such a formulation of tasks is entirely consistent with a view of the family as the primary unit of analysis (as compared with the individual). The growth responsibilities outlined before prompt major role adjustments which are responsible for complete reorientations of a family in its interactional experience (cf. Rodgers, 1973, p. 52). Despite the appeal of family developmental tasks as analytical devices, they have not received wide use.

At base the concept of developmental tasks as utilized in family life-cycle research amounts to specifying certain behaviors that must be learned at various points in the family life cycle. Reflecting the functionalist view of the family system as a goal-seeking unit, these changes are believed to carry with them cumulative implications for future development of individuals within the family. This is easily seen in the case of the addition of new members to the unit. The new roles associated with parenthood must be learned and enacted adequately to insure the stability and future integrity of the system. Researchers point out that the accomplishment of developmental tasks at different stages of the family life cycle is typically a process of gradual learning. As Kenkel states, "Indeed, there would be some merit in speaking of developmental striving instead of developmental tasks, for the former expression conveys the idea of aiming toward and approaching a goal rather than fully achieving it" (Kenkel, 1977, p. 455). This assertion highlights the problem of circularity involved in employing the concept of developmental tasks. If the family is "successful" it has *ipso facto* met its developmental tasks adequately while families that are not "successful" have obviously not done so. The main problem, of course, is that there are no clearly defined measures of success (see Zimmerman & Cervantes, 1960). When is a family successful, and

when is it not? By what standards do we make such judgments? We know that not all new parents accept their role of mother or father and that some situations involving "poor parenting" are the obvious result. Whether such situations constitute failure or lack of success is a matter of subjective evaluation. When a juvenile court judge removes a child from his/her home and terminates parental rights, this is a formal recognition that parental roles are not being adequately performed. One might then be tempted to say that the parents did not satisfactorily accomplish certain developmental tasks. Seen from another perspective, however (that of the child or the parent), this situation may be a very successful resolution of a developmental task. While the successful resolution of developmental tasks is defined as *assumption* of role behaviors, it may be just as possible to define successful resolution of developmental tasks as *rejection* (or accommodation) of certain role obligations. The difference obviously depends on one's perspective. The nature of developmental tasks is such that virtually any role shifts can be attributed to them.

There has been some effort to refine what is meant by *developmental tasks* by specifying broad groupings of activities included in role behaviors, although attempts have not been particularly fruitful. For example Kenkel outlines physical abilities, mental skills, and attitudes as categorical types of behaviors involved in developmental tasks (1977, pp. 453–454). The vague status of this important concept reflects the lack of agreement concerning what is meant by the term *development*. Developmental psychologists have not even agreed on what development implies in terms of such things as the direction of change or the importance of chronological age. There is further lack of agreement on such important aspects of development as the nature of the change over time: Are developmental changes qualitative or quantitative changes? To find diversity in the views concerning individual development is not particularly surprising owing to the diverse origins of theoretical positions (Looft, 1973).

When we turn to the family level of analysis, we find even less agreement over what is meant by development. Unless one is willing to make the fundamentally reductionist assumption that the family is nothing more than the individual members within it, it is clear that family development should mean changes in the structure and dynamics of the system. Hence changes in structural arrangements owing to the incorporation of new members may imply more than what is captured by examining the individual developmental changes associated with them. Over the life span of families one will typically observe numerous changes in structure and function. The configurations of individual role relationships over time which result from structural changes within the family, changes in the society, and interactions between the two (e.g., through employment) show some regularity. Despite a certain regularity, however, the specific course of family development depends on many things which make regularity in patterning observable only for the most obvious changes (such as the addition of new members). Particularly noteworthy in studying the life course of the family is the element of accident or luck. Accidental deaths, societal crises, or injuries all mark critical points of role transitions. The developmental history of families thus cannot be expected to follow easily anticipated courses.

Family Career

The cornerstone of developmental research in the family is the acknowledgment that chronological time, per se, is meaningless. Time and its passage are important only as they capture process and change. Hence it is not possible to mark off points in developmental growth of families by reference to chronological time; rather, time and change are marked off by processual time. The family career is composed of *meaningful* periods of time in the lives of the family members. Thus a fundamental problem for life-cycle analysts has been the determination of what constitutes a time unit. These units are usually referred to as *stages* of the family life cycle. Typical stages include the early married childless stage, the childbearing stage, and so forth. While there is some overall agreement on what may serve as a stage, there is no clear definition. This is logical because stages (or *categories* in Rodgers's [1962, pp. 23–25] terminology) are nothing more than convenient markers for *presumptively* meaningful periods over the family career. As such, stages of the family life cycle represent *methodological* decisions on the part of the researcher; they operationalize the concept of *family development*. One thus does not expect, nor does one find, regularity in the formulation of family life-cycle stages. Such regularity would be observed only should all researchers investigate similar issues.

Consider an issue such as the decision to move to another house. Were a researcher interested in studying this phenomenon by hypothesizing that stages in the family life cycle act as important predictors of moving, it would make little sense to study families (or individuals) in the engagement period. What would be important would be the specification of stages which describe growth in family size or its obverse (cf. Foote, 1960). Similar comments might be made concerning studies of adjustment to widowhood. In other words the markers used by one researcher will reflect his/her substantive interests for these stages as an operationalization. Economists studying family economics (consumption and income) mark stages in the family life cycle according to the entry and exit of members into and from the labor force as well as the age of children (Lansing & Kish, 1957; Morgan, Dickenson, Dickenson, Benus, & Duncan, 1974). Regardless of the specific formulation used, whenever a researcher specifies stages in the family career, s/he is asserting that the phenomenon under study varies depending on the criteria used to delineate stages.

The career categories used most often today must betray a strong normative assumption that families will assume "typical" patterns. It is assumed that marriage will occur *before* the birth of the first child so that the young couple will spend some time together without children early in their lives. Further it is usually assumed that couples will not dissolve their marriages prior to the death of one spouse. Although such patterns may be more common statistically than any others, some are only slightly so. It is important to recognize that those using such formulations explicitly acknowledge that their work relates only to "typical families" experiencing

statistically typical careers (Duvall, 1971; Glick, 1947, 1955, 1957, 1977; Glick & Parke, 1965). Formulating family life-cycle stages according to statistically typical family life careers is precisely what is demanded given the stated task of describing statistically typical families. Should a researcher be interested in atypical families— families composed of previously married individuals, families disrupted by death or divorce, families with severely handicapped children—the formulation of life-cycle stages will be quite different and will reflect the interests of the particular researcher. As Rodgers (1973) notes, "Any change in the normative content of a role constitutes a new role and, thus, a new period in a role sequence and in a positional career. A change also means that the role complex of which that role is a part is modified, thus modifying the family career" (p. 79). This means that the researcher is responsible for deciding which normative changes should be considered important enough to indicate a new family life-cycle stage.

Hill and Rodgers noted that, for many purposes, three criteria may serve well for marking stages of development: (1) changes in the number of positions in the family (family size), (2) changes in age composition, and (3) changes in occupational status of the breadwinner(s) (1964, p. 189). Duvall (1957) has suggested that, for general purposes, recognition of the presence of children, their age, and school placement may serve as criteria of family cycle stage. Rodgers (1962) elaborated on this scheme by indicating stages that correspond to changes in age categories of the oldest child as well as similar changes for the youngest child. Once again we note that such life-cycle categories represent only rough classification schemes for marking stages of the family career.

Using the criteria of family size, the usual life-cycle categories will resemble the following (taken from Hill & Rodgers, 1964):

1. Childless Young Marrieds
2. Expanding Stages (addition of first child to closing of family)
3. Stable Stage (period of child-rearing until first child leaves home)
4. Contracting Stage (period of launching of children until last child has left)
5. Postparental Childless Stage.

Aldous (1978) provides an example of stages based on the age and school placement of the oldest child as follows:

1. Family with infant, 0 to 2 years of age
2. Family with preschool child, 3 to 5 years of age
3. Family with school-aged child, 6 to 12 years of age
4. Family with adolescent, 13 to 20 years of age
5. Family with young adult, 21 years of age to the leaving of this child.

It is clearly not correct to compare different life-cycle stage formulations except as they illuminate a specific research issue. This is the only standard of evaluation for the schemes.

It may be said that the developmental approach to the study of the family simultaneously applies the two concepts: developmental task and family life cycle. In other words the task of the researcher is to examine the internal structure and dynamics of a family (or families) at different stages in the family career. Such an approach serves two purposes: First, it allows for a thorough examination of the coping mechanisms of family units as they confront various situations over the career of the family, in a sense allowing one to study the consequences of certain life events for the family; and second, it allows predictions of family functioning and adjustment based on knowledge about necessary role relations and changes in them. Research done within this framework necessarily focuses on several dimensions of family life and several levels of influence. As already noted one must acknowledge the crucial importance of the events within the family itself. One must also be aware of the consequences of events external to the family. Finally, one must recognize that there are subtle mechanisms which bridge these two extremes: forces which can be described as neither internal nor external to the family. In the following sections family life-cycle research from each perspective is presented, first focusing on changes within the family and their consequences, then on those events external to the family, and finally on those which bridge family and society. This organization is not meant to imply substantive divisions or methodological differences but only represents one way of describing the approach as it has been used.

FOCUS ON INTERNAL FORCES

It is not surprising to find that a primary focus in family developmental research has been on changes which are associated with the growth or diminution of families. Such an interest traces back to very early studies which sought the implications of group size on interpersonal interactions (cf. Gamson, 1961; Simmel, 1955; Strodtbeck, 1954). There is obviously a qualitative difference between the two-person group and the three-person group, if for no other reason than that with three persons there may arise coalitions (Caplow, 1968; Gamson, 1961). In a much more basic way, however, we note that, while families most often increase by arithmetical progression, the role structure complexity within the family increases geometrically. With only two persons there is but one role relationship; with three persons there are three; with four there are six, and so on. The growth of interpersonal relationships obviously follows the formula for determining pairs from among a larger group—i.e., $N(N - 1)/2$ where N = number in the group (see Bossard, 1945). Hence with the addition of each new member or the loss of a family member, numerous role relationships must be formed, abandoned, or altered.

Focus on size implies much more than the *number* of role relationships. Noteworthy in this regard are issues of excess and deficit structures of families. Within each social system there exists a normative and cultural definition of family structure. While it is true that much research devoted to studying *changing* family structure incorrectly presumes some family structure to predominate (extended, nuclear), it is true that each society defines what is and is not the desired family structure. We know now, owing to the work of several social historians (Laslett & Wall, 1972; Shorter, 1975), that our family structure has *always* been nuclear and that extended families were never either defined as desirable or prevalent. Such a cultural regularity imposes regularly defined role relationships. When a family is aberrant due to the exclusion of some role associated with normality, the consequences are that roles assigned to this member will either be played out by some other family member or some nonfamily member or will be absent. Such an arrangement will alter all other roles within the existing family, often rendering them unworkable. The divorced mother is a good example. Lacking the male in the family, the unit must seek viable substitutes for those activities normally performed by this person. In attempting to assume some of these, the mother may render her normal role performances unworkable. The prior role of comforter and nurturance-giver may not be compatible with her new role of disciplinarian and rule-giver.

Excess structure is just as likely in our society. The incorporation of illegitimate children, offspring of incest, aged parents (grandparents), or other relatives poses its own problems. Here the issue is more likely to be one of a *lack* of clearly defined roles. Very little research has been done by sociologists concerning how such individuals are incorporated into the family or the resulting changes in role relationships they occasion.

With reference to children one should also note the important consequences of spacing. Here we are interested in the length of time from marriage to the birth of the first child and the length of time between births. A later section deals with historical variations in this regard as they have led to different family structures. For the moment, however, it is sufficient to note that the rational application of fertility control and other social forces related to fertility have dramatic consequences for the internal workings of families. While it is clear that the number of children in families will affect the internal dynamics, it is equally clear that different patterns of child spacing will determine what kind of family exists. High fertility without regard to spacing will result in a situation in which adult couples spend the majority of their lives as parents, whereas the typical Western pattern results in parenthood early in life followed rather quickly by an extended period of childlessness (after children leave home). It is becoming increasingly clear that the arrival of children brings a decrease in the level of marital satisfaction (Feldman, 1971; Nock, 1979). The loss of time together and the poorer sexual relations brought about by the arrival of the first child lower satisfaction with marriage, and successive births appear to have similar (and more pronounced) effects (Ryder, 1973, p. 605). Such findings point to the most obvious effects associated with childbirth. Children necessarily move the relationship between husband and wife to that between mother and father. These latter roles are generally associated with less overall satisfaction in our society. Childlessness, like virginity, cannot be recaptured, but the satisfactions associated with adult roles when children are not present apparently can.

There does not appear to be any reliable information concerning the interaction of parents' ages and those of children; however, it is worth considering the long-term implications of a birth midway through the life course. Research on this issue will undoubtedly increase as more and more individuals postpone marriage and more couples postpone childbearing until well into their twenties or even thirties (U.S. Census, 1978, pp. 14–15). What little we know about this issue comes mainly from studies of the effects of birth order. The age of parents is but one factor when considering such effects, and hence we know little about this structural property of families.

Some appreciation for the effects of internal structural changes may be gained by briefly reviewing some of the more important findings done by researchers who employed variations of the family life-cycle categories outlined earlier. The several stages in the life cycle of the typical ("statistically normal") family will be discussed as they illustrate some of the more important consequences of the structural changes which demarcate them.

Childless Stage

Recall that the first stage in most formulations of typical family life cycles is the childless, young-married stage. Hence according to most theorists the first stage is initiated by marriage. As such, family formation may be considered part of family development. Discussions of family change and development as a consequence of marriage, however, imply a history that usually has not been realized. Clearly the most important task facing newly married couples is the establishment of a workable pattern of interaction. From the perspective of role changes, the role transitions involved are mainly those of going from being single individuals to being husband and wife.

It is interesting to note that most literature which discusses the problems and issues surrounding this process presume very little has gone on before the establishment of the married unit. We find very little discussion (by developmentalists) of the very large number of families that are formed as a result of pregnancy or childbirth and relatively little on families formed from couples who have lived together for some extended period of time. Recall, however, that the stated objective in much family development research is to explore the "typical family." Much of what couples come into marriage with amounts to traditional definitions of the roles they must learn. Such normative definitions naturally are archetypical patterns in that they reflect nothing about the unique combination of the partners. The initial adjustment of married mates thus necessarily involves considerable negotiation for the *definitions* of role content (cf. Bernard, 1964). Such negotiations are complicated by the fact that the two individuals will usually hold differing understandings of marital roles. We know that the different social classes define marriage in different ways (Rainwater, 1960). Further the foundation upon which many marriages are presumed to be built (i.e., romantic love) has been analyzed and discussed for its volatility and unreality. Marital roles convey certain notions about maturity, sexuality, fidelity, and a division of labor. In analyzing the newly married couple and their adjustment, it must be kept in mind that marriage implies as much about the individual as about the couple. Such implications, again, derive from societal definitions and assumptions concerning the married status. Turner (1970) notes that marriage conveys a certain amount of prestige. Society values it as do creditors. In addition there is a moral implication involved in the negative value placed on bachelorhood or its equivalent. Finally there is an implication of personal competence and normality associated with being married. As Turner notes, "The attractive man or woman with no discoverable personal deficiencies who fails to marry represents a continuing puzzle to those about him and is likely to be plagued constantly with questions or insinuations about why he or she has not married" (Turner, 1970, p. 50). Newly married couples negotiating the meaning of their marriage will often find that such notions are contradicted by the facts of their marriage. Social definitions of "manly" behavior may be unrealistic as may be the definitions of the role of the "nurturant wife." The individual methods of adjusting to such discrepancies are varied and complex. What is important in this context is to note that such tactics as are employed are in response to a structural implementation of the marriage and the social definitions attached to it. It was once common to describe the result of the realization of the discrepancy between normative definition and actual role behavior as "disillusionment" or "disenchantment" (cf. Burgess & Wallin, 1953). This may account, in part, for the very high divorce rates characteristic of marriages in the early years. The stranger in the marriage of newly married couples is society at large.

It would be difficult to describe the host of issues involved in an analysis of newly married couples, but certainly this period presents rich opportunities for studying such things as sexual adjustment, decision making, defining a workable division of labor, and acquisition and management of family finances. In addition considerable efforts are often involved in integrating two previously unrelated families. Couples will essentially define *who is* and *is not* family. Which family members are to be incorporated into the new family? In-laws extend well beyond the parental generation, and only some will be defined as family members by the couple.

Finally we should note that marriage involves arriving at a common definition of reality. Perception of the present is interpreted through experiences both in the present and definitions of the past. Each partner to a marriage must come to an understanding of events that is compatible to both. Not only must the newly married couple deal jointly with present experiences, they must also redefine their individual pasts in a way that is compatible with each person's own identity and that of the other. The construction of reality in the present is an analogue to that which takes place for past events. Berger reminds us of the common situation in which one partner "remembers" more clearly what happened in the other's past than the other does—and corrects him/her accordingly (Berger & Kellner, 1970, p. 63).

Expanding Stage

The next typical stage in family life cycles corresponds to the birth of the first child. We have noted that this increasingly occurs *before* marriage, but in the usual case, it occurs somewhere between two and five years after the marriage. The transition to parenthood is one of the most significant changes in role structures in the family system, and hence one of the most frequently studied. The stage called *expanding families* includes families defined by the birth of the first child until the birth of the last. Obviously this period of family development is overly broad to allow precise observations. On the other hand it is cumbersome to delineate as many stages as there are meaningful age periods for each child. Since the point is to illustrate the basic nature of life-cycle research, I will employ the descriptive term *expanding families,* although most of the comments will be restricted to families in the earliest stages of childbearing.

It is obvious that different perspectives will yield different pictures of the family during this period. Childbirth suggests a focus on the child and his/her development. Such an approach allows for a consideration of the way the family organization affects the normal course of development of the young child. From another perspective, however, the arrival (or anticipation) of the first child may be seen to affect the marital relationship. This latter approach is more common among family researchers studying the early period of childbearing families.

One of the most obvious consequences of a birth for the family is the addition of a consumer and hence greater demand on family resources. It has been shown that childless couples have as high a median income as occurs at any time in the family life cycle (see Gove et al., 1973). The arrival of a child will often reduce the wife's income (as she drops out of the labor force) while it also increases the demand on family resources. Both lead to changes within the family. While incorporating a number of new role relationships into the constellation of the family (father, mother, son, or daughter), the family will often have to deal with equally important changes in the work life of the wife (and of the husband).

Such very obvious consequences of childbirth are not the most important. From the viewpoint of family interactions, we know that pregnancy and childbirth represent competition for time previously spent in other ways. Parental roles are very demanding and take their toll on many components of the marriage. The consequences of pregnancy and childbirth for sexual relations (see Masters & Johnson, 1966) are well known, and such findings follow a long tradition which views parenthood as a family crisis. Such a view may be traced to an important article by LeMasters entitled "Parenthood as Crisis" (1957). LeMasters noted that, while there are romantic and unrealistic ideas surrounding the notion of marriage, those surrounding parenthood are even stronger and perhaps even more unrealistic. Particularly troublesome is the romantic assumption that children improve marital relationships. Waller and Hill (1951) note that the arrival of the first child changes the household from husband-centered to child-centered.

Rossi (1968) notes that the transition to parenthood carries with it the potential for long-term deterioration of the marriage. Particularly stressful for the woman is the fact that the transition to parenthood is abrupt, allowing very little time for preparation or anticipatory socialization. Her first day of motherhood lasts 24 hours and carries full responsibility for the child. Further, unlike other roles in the life of an adult, motherhood is irrevocable; there are no commonly accepted societal mechanisms for divorcing a child.

It is important to note here that the analysis of childbearing families considers the strains and troubles involved as largely a function of the structural arrangement of our family system and the role relationships within it. Our society defines the role of parent as having almost complete responsibility for the well-being of the child. Parental roles are ordinarily not shared with outside agencies in our system. Provision for support, care, and nurturance are left to the parents. Hence it is not solely the acquisition of the roles of mother and father and the implications of this for internal family dynamics which is of interest; rather, it is the set of expectations and demands that are placed on parents in our system that produce understandable strains.

We also know that a large minority of our population considers early childhood experience and socialization events as important determinants of adult functioning. Middle-class parents state that child-rearing is important because it will have long-term implications for the adult life of their children (Kohn, 1969). For many therefore the role of parent in our society extends well beyond the physical responsibility for the child to include the psychological well-being and adjustment. This century has seen the popularization of child development theories that have resulted in many parents accepting responsibility for the "success" or "failure" of their children. While such a belief is clearly not universal in our society, it is prominent among better-educated members. Middle-class parents reflect the prevailing notions concerning proper child-rearing in their actual child-rearing practices (Broffenbrenner, 1958). A view of parenthood which includes such notions and responsibilities may conflict with a more traditional normative definition of the roles which describes parenthood as enjoyable and rewarding. Particularly troublesome is the situation of parents who expect such enjoyment and instead find the entire process strain-producing. Parenthood in a society which promotes a belief in individual achievement and success resulting from skills developed early in life represents a status of understandable tension and anxiety. Hence it is not surprising to find consistent reference to the decreased marital satisfaction associated with the acquisition of these roles (Blood & Wolfe, 1960; Feldman, 1971). As noted earlier the effects associated with parenthood do not appear to be attached to the first child only; rather, each successive child has similar effects, only somewhat greater than those of the first.

Stable Families

The distinction between families that are expanding and thus experiencing childbirth and those that are "stable" is more apparent than real. After the birth of the first child, all families are rearing at least one child. Still the distinction is helpful for analytical purposes. The third stage typically corresponds to middle age for parents and adolescence and teenage years for children. The developmental tasks and family dynamics of this period can legitimately be considered separately from those of any other stage definition.

This is particularly true because it is during this stage that children begin to interact with major components of the social system beyond their immediate family. Most notable, of course, is the involvement of children and parents in schooling. In addition during adolescence a major change takes place in the orientation of the individual vis-à-vis his/her family. Interactions within the family are considerably altered by the adolescents' participation in outside agencies, and role relationships within the family change accordingly. Hence one's focus during this stage is directed more to those things external to the family than those internal. Rodgers (1973) refers to this as *transaction* with the external society. Transactional forces are most pronounced during this period of the family life cycle. Not only do the *children* expose all family members to new and stressful societal forces (educational and otherwise), but also adult occupations do much the same.

Contracting Families

Once children have reached the age of physical independence and begin to leave the home, the family faces new and challenging problems. This period was once called the *contracting* stage of the family, or alternatively the *launching* stage. The internal changes in the family are most noticeable now as members leave. For the first time in 20 or 30 years, the adult couple faces the prospect of returning to principal roles of husband and wife. In addition there may be new roles of grandparent which emerge during this time. Further younger members of the family typically must acquire roles of uncle or aunt. In short the launching period represents both a release of family members as well as the recruitment of new members by marriage.

One particularly interesting aspect of these changes is the complexity which is introduced by factors associated with social class position. As children begin to establish families and careers of their own, there is often social mobility (change in social status). Children will often attain higher social positions than did their parents. This poses interesting problems for parents who must now accommodate different world views and values. The internal nature of the family will thus often be anchored in two different classes. Success by parents (or by children depending upon one's orientation) in achieving upward social mobility very likely results in difficult disjunctures, for upward mobility requires a certain amount of rejection of those values and orientations that were appropriate in one's family of origin. Such disjuncture is particularly common following marriage of upwardly mobile children. Parental role relationships which include children's spouses are difficult when the new member represents a vastly different social class (and its associated "strange" ideas and values). A tragic accounting by Sennett and Cobb (1972) of the estrangement of parents from their children following upward social mobility notes, "Working class fathers . . . see the whole point of sacrificing for their children to be that the children *will* become unlike themselves, through education and the right kind of peer associations. . . . Indeed, if a father's sacrifices do succeed in transforming his children's lives, he then becomes a burden to them, an embarrassment" (pp. 128, 133).

This stage represents the peak load of family expenses. It is during this time that children need financial help for college or other educational training. As children leave financial aid is required to help them get through the early periods of low incomes, to pay medical costs, or to finance new households. It is also the time during which the main earner is at peak income, but supplementing this income often requires additional sources of revenue such as a second job or overtime. It is also a time during which parental roles must be modified to allow greater independence for children. Hence parents will be called upon to provide greater support while disengaging themselves from the decision-making process of their children.

Released of many childbearing duties, women who had dropped out of the labor force to raise children will often once again seek employment. Not only are children less demanding of time, but also husbands are usually very involved with careers or jobs. Homemaking requires less energy now, and disposable energy for the wife is greater. However, the skills that were once required in the wife's occupation are now several decades out of date. Women face a difficult task in securing rewarding employment in such a situation. Both husband and wife face frustrations with their occupational lives now. For the husband realistic assessment of attainments may lead to a debilitating and disappointing crisis.

Complicating this situation is the fact that at this stage there are explosive expansions in the number of individuals included as "family." Marriage of children results in dramatic increases in the number of adults to be reckoned with. The successful integration of in-laws is a task of considerable complexity. From the perspective of the newly married, loyalties must be realigned to place the new unit ahead of either family of origin. From the perspective of the families of origin, parental roles must be modified to allow for such realignments while integrating new members into the total constellation of family members (see Duvall, 1954). Duvall's depiction of this time as the "accordian" years seems appropriate. The family shrinks rapidly as members leave, swells as they marry.

Childless Families

The final life-cycle stage is the longest, lasting from the time the last child leaves the home until the death of one of the spouses (Glick, 1977). Not only will this stage last for more years than any other, but also the members of the original family will occupy more positions simultaneously than at any other point: spouse, parent, parent-in-law, grandparent, and (often) child (of aging parents). It is also a time of diminished energy, physical health, and productivity. MacIver described this period of family life as "the stage of the empty nest" (1937, p. 199). Most research on this stage has focused on the depression, feelings of abandonment, uselessness, and estrangement which are often found to characterize this life period.

Empirical evidence points to the postparental period as one of initial lowered adjustment and marital satisfaction immediately following the parting of the last child (Blood & Wolfe, 1960, p. 192). When the last child leaves home, many couples confront each other alone for the first time in years, only to discover how much they have changed and drifted apart (Cuber & Harroff, 1965). This period has been described as one of *disengagement* during which adults participate less in community activities. However, recent studies looking at couples *throughout* this period, rather than just immediately after children have left, and which consider such factors as retirement from work and overall physical health suggest that there is a general increase in marital satisfaction once the couple is free of children for some time (Nock, 1979; Spanier, Lewis, & Cole, 1974). In short it would appear that the empty nest poses new problems of adjustment for the adult couple which lead initially to some increased dissatisfaction and loneliness, although the net effects are positive. The negative aspects of the leaving of children have clearly been overemphasized. As Aldous notes, ". . . by the time children leave, a sense of mutual understanding can compensate for a lack of shared activities" (Aldous, 1978, p. 188). Further, couples are less inclined to complaints about each other at this point in their lives (Rollins & Cannon, 1974; Spanier et al., 1974).

The absence of children has been noted as contributing to improved sexual relations among couples (Masters & Johnson, 1966, p. 245). Also important in this regard is the financial advantage of the smaller family unit and associated tensions and anxieties which are no longer present.

It must be remembered that the changes during this period of the life cycle are quite different from those of the previous stage. Unlike the sudden changes associated with the launching period, events such as retirement, though stressful, are anticipated for many years, are experienced rather gradually, and appear to have fewer negative consequences.

The structural changes which define the stages just discussed are those most often associated with family life-cycle analysis. However, other internal forces operate which serve as sources for change within the family. Noteworthy in this regard are those processes associated with aging, physical maturation, illness, death, and idiosyncratic personality factors. A considerable body of literature which focuses upon interaction patterns, conflict resolution, interpersonal communication, and other interactive processes examines the nature of family dynamics as they are affected by internal forces.

We turn now to a consideration of forces operating to influence family life which are more properly considered external to the family. These include such things as technological innovations, occupational demands, legal processes, and specific historical events.

FOCUS ON EXTERNAL FORCES

Returning to the notion that the family is a semiclosed system, it is apparent that family members occupy positions in extrafamilial societal systems. Through participation in such systems interactions within the family are often affected. A focus on such forces alerts the researcher to the interaction of social and family processes. Beyond such forces, however, there are events and processes which are almost entirely external to the family which are important to an understanding of family processes, as outlined in the following section.

Foremost in importance as external forces are those owing to technology—medical advances which account for lengthened life expectancy and those which permit rational fertility control. These social forces, while external to the family in their origins, have dramatic implications for family dynamics because of their influence on the timing of family events. Whether the first child arrives in the first year of marriage, or the fifth, is very important in terms of the nature of family life. Historical evidence is clear in revealing that "patterns of family timing in the past were often more complex, more diverse, and less orderly than they are today . . . demographic changes that have come about since the late nineteenth century have paradoxically resulted in greater uniformity in the timing of transitions along the life course" (Hareven, 1978, p. 61). The technological advances we have seen have resulted in the *voluntary* timing of family events (Uhlenberg, 1974). Between 1810 and 1970 the birthrate declined from an average of eight children per mother to fewer than three (U.S. Census, 1978, p. 22). Much of this decline may be due to social pressures and changing definitions of the role of women, as well as to the ability to limit fertility voluntarily. A corollary consequence is seen in the *timing* of births. Women born in the 1880s bore their last child at the age of 33. For those women born in the 1950s the last child is typically born at age 30 (U.S. Census, 1978, p. 20). Most importantly the average life expectancy for individuals has increased noticeably. A woman born in the 1930s can expect to be 65 years old before death claims her or her husband. Projections by the Census Bureau indicate that women born as recently as 1950 can expect over ten more years of living together after their children have left home than could their grandparents of the 1880s (U.S. Census, 1978, p. 16). Such demographic changes are responsible for the creation of the empty-nest period noted earlier. Prior to the twentieth century considerably less than half the adult population lived long enough to experience this stage of the family life cycle.

The implications of these broad changes for the internal dynamics of the family have only recently been studied, and it is the work of demographers and social historians rather than sociologists which has been most productive. Child spacing is responsible for the associational network and peer relations of children. When children are spread over a wide age range within the family, family interactions are much less age-graded (cf. Aries, 1962). The relationship among children within the family is similarly changed by such forces. Older children will often assume responsibility for younger children when the age difference between them is great. Hence parental responsibility is shared more equally among family members.

The compressed period of childbearing and rearing characteristic of families today results in considerable change in family life at each stage of transition. Since parents will live to see their children reach adulthood outside the family of origin and will live a significant part of their lives alone, the leaving of children will often result in changes of residence and occupation. There is also the very real possibility of institutionalization for aging parents in nursing homes or comparable situations.

Transitions *out* of the family are also rapid and abrupt. Children who have left the family are quickly disengaged as they assume responsibility for their own well-being. Such a situation is fostered by, among other things, the assumption on the part of the state for the welfare of the aged. The social, educational, and occupational independence of individuals within our modern society means that most family and career decisions are made by the individuals involved.

Until recently these . . . individual transitions were treated as *family* moves and were therefore synchronized with other family needs and strategies. The decision to marry, the choice of spouse, and the timing of the event all depended on calculations relating to the transmission of property, the finding of a job and housing, the support of aging parents, and a wide variety of other family needs. (Hareven, 1978, p. 64)

The hallmark of our society is *individual* self-sufficiency rather than familial self-sufficiency. Much has been written on the gradual assumption by the state of important functions once performed by the family. As the welfare state assumes responsibility for occupational training, economic security, and medical care, familial obligations become less important and interaction over the course of the life cycle less continuous. Marriage and parenthood similarly are more individualistic experiences for the young family and hence produce abrupt transitions for the family of origin.

The technological growth of our industrial society which has resulted in great affluence has also lessened the importance of the family unit as a provider of security. The entire set of social changes associated with modernization has been studied intensively, particularly as it relates to our notions concerning childhood and the spacing of events related to childhood. Taking as their point of departure historical evidence which shows the life span divided into very different segments from what it is today, social historians, psychologists, and sociologists point to the influence of modernization and industrialization on our notions concerning age grading both within and outside the family. Skolnick notes,

We see life as dividing naturally into infancy, childhood, adolescence, adulthood, middle age, old age. There are further subdivisions; for example, we put an infant into one of the following categories: the baby in arms, the knee baby, the toddler, and the preschooler. In earlier times, however, the lifespan was segmented differently: infancy, which lasted until five to seven; a period of childhood which was only vaguely differentiated from adolescence; adulthood, which evidently lasted until about age fifty; and old age. (1973, p. 336)

Medieval society imposed few, if any, age restrictions. The very young participated fully in activities shared with adults, and other individuals engaged in much play and game (Aries, 1962, pp. 72–73). With modernization the child assumed a distinct status in European society. Age grading in schools emerged, and one no longer observed young children participating in adult life as free adults, bearing weapons, or being apprenticed (Plumb, 1972, p. 83).

As an urban life based in the main on trade and manufacture developed, the division of labor grew and social structures became progressively more complex. The needs for literacy and literate persons became obvious. Growth of an urban society and growth of schools and literacy were closely related phenomena. The areas that experienced higher rates of economic expansion and more revolutionary social change were also the areas in which schools and teachers were relatively more numerous. (Cipolla, 1969, pp. 41–45)

In short the social changes associated with growing modernity saw concomitant changes in the definition of age

particularly in relation to young persons. Children, separated from the world of adults, came to be seen as innocents who needed protection from the vulgar world of adults. The changes brought about by such societal definitions are reflected in things as concrete as the structure of housing units—separate areas became designated as bedrooms—and as abstract as notions concerning precocity—*age* defined readiness for participation in activities, education, and careers (Aries, 1962, p. 238).

Technology of more modest scope also has had rather drastic implications for the structure and interactions within families. While our family system may have always been nuclear and small, it has not always been characterized by the degree of privacy and sanctuary that it now is. The timing of events (marriages, divorces) within the family are treated as intimately private matters in our time. This is a situation unique in history. Today's home, due to its technological self-sufficiency, allows for a great deal of insulation and protection from others (and hence social control). Telephones, washers, televisions, and a host of other modern amenities have created the "private" household where others are not expected except at certain times or when they have announced that they will arrive.

Most obvious in affecting the internal workings of families today is an external force which only recently took place *within* the family: work life. The timing of work-life events has important consequences for the dynamics of the family. In American society work life makes demands on time and energy that are granted legitimate priority over demands from other institutional spheres. As Turner notes,

That a man's job requires him to work late or to be out of town on a business trip is sufficient excuse for declining or canceling almost any other form of engagement. Job transfer or an opportunity to better himself professionally is sufficient justification for leaving friends, disrupting children's schooling, and abandoning community responsibilities to move the household to another community. The schedule determined by work determines the life schedule and the schedule into which other relationships must fit. (1970, p. 257)

Few members of society would seriously challenge the legitimacy of work demands over family life when it comes to such things as holidays, overtime, or business trips. The external occupation is the source of such influence, although it is normally the male head of the household who presents such demands. In many instances of decision making, the superordinate authority of the husband in families is anchored in his role as passive agent for a larger unit—the economic element upon which family life depends. The husband's dominance hence may be seen by him as an imposition of a higher authority upon him and his family members. From the perspective of the family members, such dominance typically comes to be seen as power rather than authority.

That work life should influence the timing of family events is seen as almost natural in our society. Although wide variations are found in how much influence work has on the internal timing of family events according to social class, ethnicity, or race, it is unquestionably true that such transitions as those due to geographic migration, entry into the labor force, and birth of children are affected by considerations of job and career positions.

Social historians analyzing life histories of workers at the turn of the century have noted, "The decisions as to when people were leaving home, marrying, giving birth to their first child, spacing of births of their subsequent children, or sending their children to work or to school were timed by the internal clock of family traditions as well as by the external pressures of the factory system and by economic needs" (Hareven, 1977, p. 197). During times of economic hardship it was common to find adult children living at home, working outside, and committing the majority of their wages to their parents. Similarly wives typically enter the labor force during those years when the family is in most noticeable economic need, leaving with the birth of children, and reentering with the departure of children or with the arrival of school age.

Demographers have invoked explanations of generational fertility trends which depend upon economic-occupational forces. That generations differ considerably in terms of completed fertility has been noted earlier. A leading theory that attempts to explain such differences relies on the economic consequences of the relative size of birth cohorts (births to women of a certain historical period). Small birth cohorts result in a scarcity of workers, and hence members of these cohorts possess economic advantages in terms of jobs and incomes. They then become more prosperous parents with higher fertility (Easterlin & Condran, 1976, pp. 139–151).

The family *participates* in the economy of the society, but the family is *regulated* by the legal system. Thus one should expect to discover strong influences within the family which are due to legal demands and statutory responsibilities. A full accounting of the legal aspects important to the family life cycle would require considerably more attention than is possible here. Such laws as those relating to requirements for marriage (e.g., minimum age), property rights, responsibility for children, divorce, inheritance, and residence will have significant impacts on the structure of family relationships and the timing of family events. Also the tax structure of our system has been studied as it promotes or inhibits marriage and childbearing. In a similarly obverse way the lack of legal responsibility for care and provision for aged parents and relatives can be seen as a disincentive for integrating parents into the nuclear couple in their later years. In societies that provide great tax advantages to individuals who provide care for retired and/or disabled parents, the structure of families very often includes the parental generation. A very interesting case where lifespan timing, family life-cycle timing, and social and legal timing conflict is that of mandatory retirement age. Chronological age is often asynchronous with other aspects of life time. For some purposes retirement might come significantly earlier in life, for others significantly later. Rarely will retirement at age 65 coincide with other transitions which are logical correlates (e.g., leaving of children).

Recall that Duvall (1971) divided the family life span into stages corresponding to the school experience of the oldest child. The emphasis on schooling is obvious in much family life-cycle literature. I have already commented on the way schooling molds our notions about childhood. Here I would like to mention the mandatory school attendance laws and associated age-grading char-

acteristic of our educational system. While the *educational experiences* of children may influence family life, it is usually the mandatory attendance and regular progression of children through the system that takes the heaviest toll. Similar to the way in which occupational demands are translated through an agent of the family as individual requirements, educational requirements (five-day weeks, summer recess, six- to eight-hour days) also translate as imperatives for families. Were family events geared to the developmental growth of children, we would witness considerably greater fluctuations among families. However, development and progress in the system are independent scheduling phenomena. The family adjusts to the educational system and the bureaucratic requirements of it.

There are numerous systemic relationships which tie the family to external forces beyond the law, technology, and education. However I would like to conclude this section by briefly discussing some research which has attempted to assess the impact on family development of *specific* historical events.

The most common form of such research has investigated the response of families to stressful situations. Since the family is viewed as a system, stress represents a threat to the equilibrium of the system, and research should attempt to describe the response of the system to this threat. Hansen and Hill (1964) have made the fullest statement of the approach in the *Handbook of Marriage and the Family*. Stress is seen as it requires both internal and external resources in the process of disorganization and (possibly) reorganization. It is important to recognize that a developmental study of stressful events may include events entirely internal to the family, as well as those which derive from society or nature.

Consider the occasion of a natural disaster (hurricane, flood). A thorough understanding of the response to such an event will demand an understanding of the organization of the family prior to the disaster. Actual property loss will be less informative than knowing the relative loss suffered by families. The network of extended kin and helping relatives will also explain the immediate reaction to such things as the loss of living quarters. Similarly an event such as the Depression may be understood as it affects the organization of roles within the family. The breadwinner deprived of occupational anchorages is faced with a very difficult role transition. In fact such a transition may present a greater problem than the financial deprivations suffered as a result of the job loss. It is clear that at different points throughout the life cycle of a family the unit will be more or less vulnerable to crisis events—e.g., economic deprivations may be much less threatening in middle years than early in the marriage.

FOCUS ON INTERACTION BETWEEN FAMILY AND SOCIETY

While it is tempting to attribute all sorts of consequences to societal events in studying families, the temptation lures one into the trap of attributing effects to causes and vice versa. Society is, after all, an abstract aggregation of families and individuals. For many important social processes, it is impossible to determine cause. That is particularly true when it comes to studying normative forces for families for they are both initiators of change as well as reactors to change.

Demographic analyses of family life-cycle changes over time document the gradual lengthening or shortening of various stages while leaving the cause of such changes unspecified. To know that the age at first marriage has gradually declined during the twentieth century does not tell us the reason for such a change. Such global processes have diverse origins and consequences. From the perspective of family development it is important to acknowledge that families and individuals within them are responsible for implementing the processes which are revealed in such studies.

Let us take a very simple example. In an analysis of "typical" families, divorce represents an "abnormal" transition or termination of a family career. We know that divorces have increased (in proportion) for at least eight decades. Some have interpreted such information to mean that families are less stable today than in the past. However when "abnormal" termination of marriage due to the premature death of one spouse is considered (which has dropped since 1900), we find that for specific age groups there are no differences in the percentages of women living with their first husbands in 1970 than was the case in 1910. What has happened is that more marriages are terminated by divorce, fewer by death for every age group. What we do not know is the cause of the rising divorce rate (although we know the reason for the declining mortality rates). It has been shown that divorce rates are slightly higher in states with liberal divorce laws (Wright & Stetson, 1978); however, such laws may be a consequence rather than a cause of changing societal attitudes toward divorce. In fact it makes very little sense to isolate certain events or structures as causes of increasing divorces, for there is clearly an interplay on this issue. Norms, like laws, codify existing social opinions.

There are noticeable changes in the societal definition of familial roles which are nonetheless important for an understanding of family processes. Particularly noteworthy in this regard are the changing definitions of sex roles. The institutional anchorages of traditional sex roles are slowly eroding. Barriers based on gender are being removed as more families are composed of two spouses actively engaged in lifelong careers. The growing number of one-parent families similarly contributes to the removal of these barriers. Associated with this change is the necessary acceptance and reliance by parents on alternative childcare and child-rearing arrangements. As more and more couples find satisfaction from careers, it may be that childlessness will assume a much more prominent place in our society as an alternative family life style (cf. Veevers, 1974).

Very little exists in the way of empirical research on normative age assumptions in our society. As such notions change or remain stable, so will the typical life cycle of families. Certainly the assumption of economic responsibility for a family comes later today than in the past as more and more young people postpone marriages until the end of college training. Given the explosive growth in the population of those aged 65 and older that we will witness within the next three decades, is it not reasonable to expect that there will be associated changes in our definitions of age and age-related activities?

There exists some empirical evidence which indicates that the American population places a high value on what is regarded as the "typical" nuclear family consisting of husband, wife, and two or three offspring. That remaining single is unpopular is similarly revealed by the same research (Nock & Rossi, 1978). Americans are clearly not moving toward radically new family forms in significant numbers; rather, there is a stable appreciation for what has always been our dominant family structure and typical sequence of family life-cycle events (cf. Alves & Rossi, 1978). Notions concerning equity and fairness related to incomes are closely tied to family life-cycle stages, and there is little evidence to suggest major changes in our family structure in the near future (Polit, 1978).

A consideration of normative beliefs inevitably leads to speculation on possible changes in the structuring of family events. This is perhaps the best point at which to reconsider the implications of studying "typical" families. If changes are to occur they will be seen as departures from what has been considered "normal." Although there is no reason to expect radical shifts in the orientations of individuals in our society to the basic institutions of marriage and the family, what is typical today will undoubtedly differ from what will be typical in the future. I have already mentioned the changing definitions of sex roles. While only half of all married women now work outside the home, this figure will soon approach two-thirds. The wife-mother who stays home to care for children will soon represent a deviant life style. The implications of this for the timing of events in the family are obvious. Work life intrudes on the internal dynamics of the family by introducing the interests of a third party. When two such "third parties" are involved, the power and authority relations within the family are necessarily altered. Dominance in decision making will no longer remain the prerogative of the male head but rather will be shared more equally. Males and females will participate more evenly in those activities located within the household.

The increasing participation of women in the paid labor force also changes the dependency relationships characteristic of traditional families. It has long been known that economic independence and social independence go hand in hand. As women achieve greater social independence, alternatives to marriage assume greater importance.

Divorce rates will probably continue to climb in the future as they have in the past. While I have not considered this important trend in detail, it must be noted that the "typical" life cycle may soon involve several families: first and second marriages and the children and parents involved in each. For children it may be that transitions to new families (as a result of divorce) become as common as continuous socialization in one's family of origin (Bumpass & Rindfuss, 1979). And we cannot expect that all new families produced by remarriage or by first marriage will follow patterns typical of family life today. Considerable latitude in living arrangements exists today and will become more common in the future. Such latitude does not depart significantly from our basic family system (monogamy, neolocality) but suggests greater freedom in the choice of family life-cycle options. Some such options *are* more unusual (statistically), although certainly not new. Living together, single parenthood, marriages based on contracts, or communal living arrangements are more acceptable, although still not preferred, life styles. The life cycles of families that consist of single parents, reconstituted families, dual-career couples, childless couples, or those in communal arrangements will obviously depart from those of the implicit model used in this chapter.

CONCLUSIONS

The developmental approach to the family cannot be described as a theory for it lacks a logical structure of clearly stated propositions; rather, this conceptual framework is to be seen as an orienting strategy for those who wish to understand events which take place within the family or who wish to study the forces which act upon families and individuals within them. The strengths and weaknesses of the approach can be measured only by how it contributes to the solution of substantively important practical and theoretical questions. More specifically one must question what is gained by employing a family life-cycle approach over one based on chronological time.

The empirical evidence relating to the utility of considering processual time in family careers is ambiguous. Studies cited in this chapter demonstrate the variety of issues which have been found to vary across stages of the family life cycle. Certainly there is no question that noticeable changes in the family correspond with life-cycle stages. Furthermore several problems may best be explained by reference to changes in the family life cycle (e.g., geographic mobility, housing shifts, entry and exit into and from the labor force). However, other changes which have been studied over the life cycle of the family (e.g., family consumption) depend upon simple processes such as the presence or absence of children or the length of marriage.

When seeking to explain some complex family phenomenon such as divorce or violence, one is faced immediately by an equally complex array of causal forces. The ultimate question asked of this approach is what it captures when it explains such complex events. What are the forces and processes tapped by processual time? Few would argue that the primary underlying mechanism involved in the family life cycle is chronological time, although this is clearly involved. Nor would many assert that the presence or absence of children fully accounts for whatever explanatory power there may be; rather, the mechanisms represented by changes in family life-cycle periods are numerous, subtle, and perhaps unmeasurable individually. All of the myriad forces associated with *individual* emotional, physical, and cognitive growth combine in complex ways through intimate interactions within the family to produce changes which may or may not appear continuous when viewed chronologically. Failing to observe regular patterns of change over time may imply little more than an improper assumption about the passage of processual time. Years may go by without there being any growth, while at another period days may produce drastic changes. The markers used to classify families are arbitrary and reflect little more than convenience on the part of the researcher. Whether empirically meaningful changes correspond with these conveniences depends upon what they mean to *families,* not to researchers.

Those who use this approach seek to study process. Unfortunately process cannot be studied except as change, and change implies temporality. Hence one cannot attempt to study process without some measure of time. Acknowledging that processual time is what is important will not make processual time observable; rather, marking points in the career of families must be presumed to provide clues to the experience of time. Still we impose chronological time by presuming that changes associated with process will become obvious at convenient points.

It is very unlikely that we shall ever be able to document the orderly development of families as developmental theorists have sought to do with individuals, and there is no reason to seek such documentation. The developmental approach focuses our attention upon interactions: interactions among family members, between families and other societal structures, between family members and nonfamily members. It alerts us to the importance of the psychological component to interactions and reactions. It suggests entirely new explanations for problems by drawing our attention to structural properties of intimate groups. It allows us to trace the impact of society on the very smallest group. Individual processes take on new meanings when viewed against the variability they display in different historical and social settings.

Individual growth and development reveal the important effects of social and historical definitions of what is "normal." Family group processes, in a similar way, are clearly shaped by the unique personalities involved. Hence the dynamics of family life involve the mutual interdependence of these two sets of forces. The fruitful application of the family developmental approach recognizes this. To apply the approach one must consider interaction within the family and between family and nonfamily members. Family development will be described as changes in interaction patterns.

One of the very important issues still unresolved relates to the methodological implications of the approach. While the focus is explicitly longitudinal, few studies have been produced which are based on longitudinal observations. Attempts to correct for the biases inherent in cross-sectional designs (e.g., through cohort techniques, trend studies, simulated panel designs) are more common today than in the past. Particularly fruitful in this regard have been the applications of life-cycle concepts to historical demographic questions. Much remains to be done, however, and the researcher seeking to employ the approach must become familiar with the tools and techniques appropriate for longitudinal and comparative research.

This chapter is intended to call attention to an approach that spans disciplinary boundaries, substantive areas of interest, and methodological peculiarities. To understand a complex social structure such as the family, one must acknowledge forces which are diverse and often foreign to one discipline. The blending of psychology, sociology, history, and economics is clearly more than desirable; it is necessary for a complete accounting of events and processes which derive from subtle and complex interactions of diverse forces. Our desire to understand family functioning requires that we place the family within the historical and social context which affects it.

REFERENCES

ALDOUS, J. *Family careers: Developmental change in families.* New York: John Wiley, 1978.

ALVES, W. M., & ROSSI, P. H. Who should get what? Fairness judgments of the distribution of earnings. *American Journal of Sociology,* 1978, *84,* 541–564.

ARIES, P. *Centuries of childhood.* New York: Random House, 1962.

BALTES, P. B., & SCHAIE, K. W. (Eds.). *Life-span developmental psychology: Personality and socialization.* New York: Academic Press, 1973.

BERGER, P. L., & KELLNER, H. Marriage and the construction of reality. Pp. 49–72 in H. P. Dreitzel (Ed.), *Recent sociology* (No. 2). New York: Macmillan, 1970.

BERNARD, J. The adjustments of married mates. Pp. 675–739 in H. Christensen (Ed.), *Handbook of marriage and the family.* Skokie, Ill.: Rand McNally, 1964.

BLOOD, R. O., JR., & WOLFE, D. M. *Husbands and wives: The dynamics of married living.* New York: Free Press, 1960.

BOSSARD, J.H.S. The law of family interaction. *American Journal of Sociology,* 1945, *50,* 292.

BROFFENBRENNER, U. Socialization and social class through time and space. Pp. 400–425 in E. E. Maccoby, T. M. Newcomb, & E. L. Hartley (Eds.), *Readings in social psychology.* New York: Holt, Rinehart & Winston, 1958.

BUMPASS, L., & RINDFUSS, R. R. Children's experience of mental disruption. *American Journal of Sociology,* 1979, *85,* 49–65.

BURGESS, E. W. The family as a unity of interacting personalities. *The Family,* 1926, *7,* 3–9.

BURGESS, E. W., & WALLIN, P. *Engagement and marriage.* Philadelphia: Lippincott, 1953.

CAPLOW, T. *Two against one: Coalitions in triads.* Englewood Cliffs, N.J.: Prentice-Hall, 1968.

CIPOLLA, C. M. *Literacy and development in the West.* Baltimore, Md.: Penguin, 1969.

COOLEY, C. H. *Human nature and the social order.* New York: Scribner's, 1922.

CUBER, J. F., & HARROFF, P. *Sex and the significant Americans.* Baltimore, Md.: Penguin, 1965.

DUVALL, E. M. *In-laws: Pro and con.* New York: Association Press, 1954.

DUVALL, E. M. *Family development.* Philadelphia: Lippincott, 1957.

DUVALL, E. M. *Family development* (5th ed.). Philadelphia: Lippincott, 1971.

DUVALL, E. M., & HILL, R. *Report on the committee on the dynamics of family interaction.* Washington, D.C.: National Conference on Family Life, 1948. (mimeo)

EASTERLIN, R. A., & CONDRAN, G. A. A note on the recent fertility swing in Australia, Canada, England and Wales and the United States. Pp. 139–151 in H. Richards (Ed.), *Population, factor movements and economic development: Studies presented to Bainley Thomas.* Cardiff: University of Wales Press, 1976.

FELDMAN, H. The effects of children on the family. Pp. 107–125 in A. Michel (Ed.), *Family issues of employed women in Europe and America.* London: E. G. Brill, 1971.

FOOTE, N. N. *Housing choices and housing constraints.* New York: McGraw-Hill, 1960.

GAMSON, W. A. A theory of coalition formation. *American Sociological Review,* 1961, *26,* 374.

GLICK, P. C. The family life cycle. *American Sociological Review,* 1947, *14,* 164–174.

GLICK, P. C. The life cycle of the family. *Marriage and Family Living,* 1955, *17,* 3–9.

GLICK, P. C. *American families.* New York: John Wiley, 1957.

GLICK, P. C. Updating the life cycle of the family. *Journal of Marriage and the Family,* 1977, *39*(No. 1), 5–13.

GLICK, P. C., & PARKE, R., JR. New approaches in studying the life cycle of the family. *Demography* 1965, *2,* 187–202.

GOVE, W. R., GRIMM, J. W., MOTZ, S. C., & THOMPSON, J. D. The family life cycle: Internal dynamics and social consequences. *Sociology and Social Research,* 1973, *57*(No. 2), 182–195.

HANSEN, D. A., & HILL, R. Families under stress. Pp. 782–821 in H. T. Christensen (Ed.), *Handbook of marriage and the family.* Skokie, Ill.: Rand McNally, 1964.

HAREVEN, T. K. Family time and industrial time: Family and work in a planned corporation town, 1900–1924. Pp. 187–208 in T. K. Hareven (Ed.), *Family and kin in urban communities, 1700–1930.* New York: New Viewpoints, 1977.

HAREVEN, T. K. Family time and historical time. Pp. 57–70 in A. Rossi, J. Kagan, & T. K. Hareven (Eds.), *The family.* New York: W. W. Norton & Co., Inc., 1978.

HAVIGHURST, R. J. *Human development and education.* New York: Longman, 1953.

HILL, R. L. Modern systems theory and the family. *Social Science Information,* 1971, *10,* 299–311.

HILL, R., & RODGERS, R. H. The developmental approach. Pp. 171–211 in H. T. Christensen (Ed.), *Handbook of marriage and the family.* Skokie, Ill.: Rand McNally, 1964.

KENKEL, W. F. *The family in perspective* (4th ed.). Santa Monica, Calif.: Goodyear, 1977.

KOHN, M. L. *Class and conformity: A study in values.* Homewood, Ill.: Dorsey, 1969.

LANSING, J. B., & KISH, L. Family life cycle as an independent variable. *American Sociological Review,* 1957, *22,* 512–519.

LASLETT, P., & WALL, R. *Household and family in post time.* Cambridge, England: Cambridge University Press, 1972.

LEMASTERS, E. E. Parenthood as crisis. *Marriage and Family Living,* 1957, *19,* 325–355.

LOOFT, W. Socialization and personality throughout the life span: An examination of contemporary psychological approaches. Pp. 26–47 in P. B. Baltes & K. W. Schaie (Eds.), *Life-span developmental psychology.* New York: Academic Press, 1973.

MACIVER, R. M. *Society: A textbook for sociology.* New York: Holt, Rinehart & Winston, 1937.

MASTERS, W. H., & JOHNSON, V. E. *Human sexual response.* Boston: Little, Brown, 1966.

MEAD, G. H. *Mind, self, and society.* Chicago: University of Chicago Press, 1934.

MORGAN, J. N., DICKENSON, K., DICKENSON, J., BENUS, J., & DUNCAN, G. *Five thousand American families: Patterns of economic progress* (Vol. 1). Ann Arbor, Mich.: Survey Research Center, Institute for Social Research, 1974.

NOCK, S. L. The family life cycle: Empirical or conceptual tool? *Journal of Marriage and the Family,* 1979, *41,* 15–26.

NOCK, S. L., & ROSSI, P. H. Ascription versus achievement in the attribution of family social status. *American Journal of Sociology,* 1978, *84,* 565–590.

PARSONS, T. *The structure of social action.* Glencoe, Ill.: Free Press, 1949.

PARSONS, T. *The social system.* New York: Free Press, 1951.

PLUMB, J. H. The great change in children. *Intellectual Digest,* 1972, *2,* 82–84.

POLIT, D. F. Stereotypes relating to family size status. *Journal of Marriage and the Family,* 1978, *40,* 105–116.

RAINWATER, L. *And the poor get children.* Chicago: Quadrangle/The New York Times Book Co., 1960.

RILEY, M. W. Social gerontology and the age stratification of society. *Gerontologist,* 1971, *11,* 79–87.

RILEY, M. W., JOHNSON, M. G., & FONER, A. (Eds.). *Aging and society: A sociology of age stratification* (Vol. 3). New York: Russell Sage Foundation, 1972.

RODGERS, R. H. *Improvements in the construction and analysis of family life cycle categories.* Doctoral dissertation, Western Michigan University, 1962.

RODGERS, R. H. *Family interaction and transaction: The developmental approach.* Englewood Cliffs, N.J.: Prentice-Hall, 1973.

ROLLINS, B. C., & CANNON, K. L. Marital satisfaction over the family life cycle: A reevaluation. *Journal of Marriage and the Family,* 1974, *36,* 271–283.

ROSSI, A. S. Transition to parenthood. *Journal of Marriage and the Family,* 1968, *30,* 26–39.

ROSSI, P. H. *Why families move.* Glencoe, Ill.: Free Press, 1955.

ROWNTREE, B. S. *Poverty: A study of town life.* London: Macmillan, 1906.

RYDER, R. G. Longitudinal data relating marriage satisfaction and having a child. *Journal of Marriage and the Family,* 1973, *35,* 604–608.

SENNETT, R., & COBB, J. *The hidden injuries of class.* New York: Vintage, 1972.

SHORTER, E. *The making of the modern family.* New York: Basic Books, 1975.

SIMMEL, G. *Conflict.* (R. Bendix, trans.). Glencoe, Ill.: Free Press, 1955.

SKOLNICK, A. *The intimate environment: Exploring marriage and the family.* Boston: Little, Brown, 1973.

SOROKIN, P. A., ZIMMERMAN, C. C., & GALPIN, C. J. *A systematic sourcebook in rural sociology* (Vol. 2). Minneapolis: University of Minnesota Press, 1931.

SPANIER, G. B., LEWIS, R. A., & COLE, C. L. Marital adjustment over the family life cycle: The issue of curvilinearity. *Journal of Marriage and the Family,* 1974, *37,* 263–275.

STRODTBECK, F. L. The family as a three person group. *American Sociological Review,* 1954, *19,* 23–29.

TURNER, R. *Family interaction.* New York: John Wiley, 1970.

UHLENBERG, P. Cohort variations in family life cycle experiences of U.S. females. *Journal of Marriage and the Family,* 1974, *36,* 284–293.

U.S. Bureau of the Census. *Perspectives on American fertility.* Special Studies Series P-23, No. 70. U.S. Department of Commerce. Washington, D.C.: U.S. Government Printing Office, 1978.

VEEVERS, J. Factors in the incidence of childlessness in Canada: An analysis of census data. *Social Biology,* 1974, *19,* 266–274.

WALLER, W. W., & HILL, R. *The family: A dynamic interpretation* (Rev. ed.). New York: Holt, Rinehart & Winston, 1951.

WILENSKY, H. C. Orderly careers and social participation: The impact of work history on social interpretation in the middle class. *American Sociological Review,* 1961a, *26,* 521–539.

WILENSKY, H. C. Life cycle, work situation and participation in formal organizations. In R. W. Kleemeier (Ed.), *Aging and leisure.* New York: Oxford, 1961b.

WRIGHT, G. C., JR., & STETSON, D. M. The impact of no-fault divorce law reform on divorce in American states. *Journal of Marriage and the Family,* 1978, *40,* 575–580.

ZIMMERMAN, C. C., & CERVANTES, L. F. *Successful American families.* New York: Pageant Press, 1960.

36

Marital Choice

BERNARD I. MURSTEIN

To paraphrase a well-known saying about the weather, it can be said that nearly everybody marries, but few know how it happens. In the present chapter I shall consider a number of theories attempting to account for this phenomenon. The theories considered—Freudian, Complementary Needs, Instrumental, Stimulus-Value-Role—do not represent all the possible theories, but I have elected to mention those that have either influenced marriage researchers or give promise of being amenable to research. Restricting myself to these few theories permits relatively extensive discussion of the main levels of the theories and the results of research efforts to test them.

Before starting, however, a few words need to be said about the omission of the concept of *homogamy* in marital choice. There has been a vast amount of research indicating that "birds of a feather flock together." Individuals tend to marry those of similar race, religion, education, age, socioeconomic status, IQ, and values, among a host of many other variables. Yet I have not dealt with this approach as a theory for a number of reasons. First, little rationale has been developed as to why similarity is so rewarding. Is the similarity itself rewarding, or do similar people tend to group together or be grouped by others (ghetto) and thus marry their neighbors on the basis of propinquity as much as similarity?

Almost everyone agrees that similarity influences marital choice, but the majority of researchers today think of it as limiting the pool of marital eligibles rather than pushing the individual to marry anyone who has a similar cultural-social heritage. Last, an increasing number of people seem to be violating these homogamous influences. Interracial marriages and interreligious marriages, for example, are constantly increasing. The homogamous approach cannot explain these "aberrations" but must treat them as errata. This total inability to deal with these exceptions warrants considering ho-

mogamy as a screening device rather than as accounting for the particular choice pattern.

FREUD'S PSYCHOANALYTIC THEORY

Freud saw human beings as hedonistic but at the mercy of instinctual drives that are irrational in nature. These biologically based drives release emotional or psychic energy: The energy relating to the sexual instinct is called *libido*. The libido is the raw material out of which complex emotional states such as love can develop.

The determinants of marital choice are largely shaped by the success with which the individual navigates the shoals of the stages of psychosexual development: oral, anal, phallic, genital. The result of passing through the various stages successfully is an adult whose principal source of sexual gratification is found in the genitals and whose nonneurotic character enables him/her to pair with a partner in marriage and to reproduce the species.

Of primary importance is the third, or phallic, stage which draws its inspiration from Oedipus who, in Sophocles' tragedy, unwittingly kills his father and marries his mother. Development during this stage becomes a primary factor influencing marital choice, although its inception occurs between the ages of three and six. The principal erogenous zone involves the genitals, but not in the sense that adult sexual tensions are generated; rather, the little boy develops a more demanding and possessive kind of love for his mother than heretofore. He may announce boldly that he will marry his mother when he grows up. However there is a rival in the house—his father. Worse luck yet, his mother seems to prefer his father to him. She sleeps with the father, goes with him on trips, and in numerous ways shows evidence of preference for him over the son. Why? The young male child is unable to conceive of abstract concepts, such as interpersonal needs and companionship. In all probability he also has a distorted understanding of sexual relationships. He thinks concretely, and in a simple fashion he imagines that his mother prefers the father because he is big and strong, whereas her son is small and weak.

The son loves his father, according to Freud, but he also may hate him as a rival for his mother's affection. The boy thinks if he could weaken the father physically perhaps the mother would take the boy as her husband. But if the son can fantasize about destroying the father's masculinity, cannot the father destroy the son's masculinity? He has seen girls, who have no penis. He may assume that they have been bad and had theirs cut off. If the son's hostile wishes were correctly diagnosed, the father might, in anger, cut off the boy's penis, too; thus is born castration anxiety.

The normal boy is able to work his way through these difficulties. Because he loves his father, he begins increasingly to identify with him. He interjects many of the father's characteristics into his own personality, and he represses his interest in the mother into the unconscious. He may become more distant from her, he may fuse his love for both parents into a love for the family, or he may go outside the family for friendships (Kenkel, 1966).

The girl's situation is somewhat different from that of the boy. At around the age of five or so, like the boy, she becomes ambivalent about the parent of the same sex and sexually attracted to the opposite-sex parent, but obviously she cannot have castration anxiety. According to Freudian orthodoxy she regards the clitoris as a poor substitute for the penis and feels herself already castrated. She blames and rejects the mother for her lack of penis, and manifesting penis envy, she turns to the father in the hope that he can supply her with a symbolic penis, a child.

Similarly to the boy, she gradually gives up the father and begins to identify with the mother. However, the lack of castration anxiety makes the psychological weaning process more gradual and incomplete than it is for the boy. Because her *envy* was not *anxiety,* there is much less compunction to renounce the father, give up the search for the penis, and identify strongly with the mother. Penis envy is not really sublimated, therefore, and it plays a major motivating role throughout feminine development.

The woman does not need to repress her desire for her father in a comparable fashion to that of the boy for his mother; consequently, her superego, which is, in part, a sublimated result of the necessity of repression of desire for the parent, is not as strong as that of the man. It remains more dependent on the external world for support compared to the more independently functioning superego of the man. Women, thus, are more dependent on the love of others than are men. Women are also more narcissistic than men "because the sexual, reproductive, and personal demands made upon them are greater than those made upon men, and narcissism serves as a kind of defense in which integrity of the self does not dissolve in the face of agreeing to other people's demands" (Bardwick, 1971, pp. 14–15). The woman is now free to follow the passive, masochistic role she plays in the family— that of serving others.

Between the phallic and genital stages of psychologi-

cal development occurs the latency period, in which the individual's rate of psychological growth diminishes considerably. However at the final development at puberty, the rush of sexual energy reawakens the old Oedipal triangle. The inhibitions against incestuous love nevertheless remain in force for the normal personality, and the adolescent transfers the focus of the insistent sex drive onto another, more socially acceptable, object: the boyfriend or girlfriend.

To understand the influences behind the selection of a spouse for marriage, we must return to the infant's earliest days of life—the time when s/he existed in a state of primary bliss or narcissism and all of his/her needs were met. Initially s/he is unable to distinguish between him/herself and the breast that feeds him/her—ego boundaries are very diffuse and vague. Soon enough, however, s/he learns that his/her needs are not always immediately met—that is, the feeding and diapering apparatus may not immediately sense his/her discomfort; his/her mother may be out of the room. This new ability to differentiate between him/herself and the other leaves him/her the choice of two love-objects. The first is affection for those on whom the infant is dependent for feeding, care, and protection. Freud calls this kind of love *anaclitic* (literally "leaning up against"); the other is to take him/herself as love-object, which Freud calls *narcissistic.*

Object-love of the anaclitic type, according to Freud (1949), is generally characteristic of the man, whereas the narcissistic type is characteristic of the woman. Freud acknowledges that these are general tendencies—there are numerous exceptions in which each sex adopts the other kind of love. No rationale is explicitly given as to why each sex generally follows a different model. It was noted earlier, however, that narcissism is more apt to characterize women than men in accordance with nature's compensation for the demands made on women. Perhaps, therefore, men are more drawn to the anaclitic type of woman because their mothers were more affectionate to them, generally preferring boys to girls.

Another troublesome item not explained by Freud is the seeming contradiction in love types represented by men and women, which ought to preclude their attraction to each other. For example if the typical man follows the anaclitic model, he ought to be drawn toward a nurturant mother type (anaclitic), but the typical woman (narcissistic type) would be taking herself as a love-object and, therefore, ought to exhibit little interest in a nurturant role vis-à-vis the man.

I think the confusion arises because Freud was so focused on unconscious drives that he failed to recognize that a resolution of the paradox depends on realizing that societal roles may be independent of, or contradictory to, unconscious drives. Thus the late Victorian society of which he was a part would have prescribed that the man actively pursue the woman's hand in marriage. Once married, however, her *role* was to focus on her home, children, and husband. Her narcissism would not be allowed to interfere with her societal role but might focus itself in endless primping and concern about her toilette and dress.

However, narcissism does not have to be expressed directly through overconcern with the self. An older individual may love a younger person who seems to represent the qualities that the former possessed in his/her youth. A person may love another who represents what s/he would like to be, and a woman may love a child who was once part of herself. To summarize the paths leading to object-choice, a person may love

1. According to the narcissistic type:
   a. what he is himself (actually himself);
   b. what he once was;
   c. what he would like to be;
   d. someone who was once part of himself;
2. According to the anaclitic type:
   a. the woman who tends;
   b. the man who protects. (Freud, 1949, p. 47)

THE PROCESS OF LOVING

In growing up the individual develops ideals of what s/he would like to be and what s/he wants in a spouse. These generally follow a path of social desirability. They represent what is commonly thought of by society as desirable traits for young people to have—kindness, courtesy, honesty, and sensitivity.

There are also characteristics that are attractive but which the individual cannot accept in his/her self-concept. These are dissociated from the self, but when perceived in a love-object, they may draw the dissociator like a magnet. A man may be attracted to a very narcissistic woman because the narcissism which his conscious idealization forces him to renounce continues to pull him unconsciously. A woman may be drawn to a man for the boyish qualities she herself possessed before she had to abandon them for "girl's" behavior.

The individual is also drawn to the person who can aid him/her to become the person s/he must be, unconsciously speaking. A masochist, for example, would need a sadist as a marital partner. Within less extreme conditions a nurturant person would need a receptive individual who could accept nurturance.

Quite often, however, the members of a premarital couple do not at first know each other well enough to be able to tell, consciously or unconsciously, whether the other will be able to satisfy his/her needs or to fulfill his/her ideals. Consequently in the absence of knowledge, the individual projects qualities of his/her ego-ideal onto the other. According to Freud the sweetheart or fiancé(e) makes a superbly suitable object for projection. Lovers possess strong sexual desires for each other, but the aim (sexual intercourse) is deflected by societal mores or by the personal belief that to engage in sex before marriage is wrong. Indeed the depth of love is often measured by the renouncing of sex in the face of opportunity—a fact undoubtedly more true in Freud's time (1856–1939) than it is today.

The libidinal impulse of the individual that is not expressed in intercourse is repressed and projected as idealization onto the beloved. The individual sexually overestimates the beloved—that is, s/he endows the beloved with characteristics above and beyond what objective assessment would warrant.

The effect of this flow of libido from the self to the beloved is to weaken the self-regard. The individual's original superabundance of narcissism has, through socialization and identification, been considerably forfeited to idealization in the process of growing up. Now through idealization of the beloved, the ego of the projector is virtually impoverished. The lover generally thinks of him/herself in very humble terms. S/he is worthless; the beloved is extolled. S/he is full of longing, s/he is deprived, s/he is empty! What is unconsciously needed is a return of libido from the beloved. The lover consciously experiences this as a desperate need to be loved in return, or at least to be accepted by the beloved. The lover's ego can only be re-enriched by the flow of some libido from the beloved.

Since all love, according to Freud, is narcissistic at the core, the return of libido represents a happy fusion of ego-libido (pertaining to the self) and object-libido (fixed on the beloved). This happy love corresponds to the primal condition of infancy when ego-libido and object-libido also were impossible to differentiate.

This is the overall picture, but the paths are accented differently for each sex. Since men generally follow the anaclitic path, they are more apt to experience a flow of libido from themselves to the woman, and they are more apt than are women to overestimate the partner sexually. They are also more likely to experience an impoverished ego and to idolize the woman. Men therefore are the pursuers who need to love the woman.

Women are depicted as being more narcissistic than men. Since they more often take the self as the love-object, they are less likely to overestimate the man sexually. Their "love" is cooler, more detached. A textbook case of woman's narcissistic love is found in the book *The Magic Mountain,* by Thomas Mann, in which one character says of woman, "You ask her if she loves him, and she answers, 'He loves me very much.'" Even for such a woman, according to Freud, there remains the possibility of object-love. In giving birth to a child, for example, a part of herself becomes a suitable object on which to lavish love. This example also points out clearly that, at the base, anaclitic and narcissistic love are essentially narcissistic in origin.

RESEARCH ON OEDIPAL COMPLEX

Attempts have been made to show a physical resemblance between the choice of partner and the opposite-sex parent (Commins, 1932; Hamilton & MacGowan, 1929; Kirkpatrick, 1937; Strauss, 1946a). The results have either failed outright or been highly equivocal.

Other researchers have attempted to show the influence of the Oedipal complex in the nature of the parent-child relationship rather than by physical semblance. Would parents be more negative to dating by opposite-sex children as opposed to same-sex children? Kirkpatrick and Caplow (1945) asked college students whether their parents prohibited or disapproved, encouraged, or were indifferent to their dating. They reported a possibility of an Oedipal situation in the fathers' greater disapproval of dating for daughters than for sons and the greater encouragement of dating by sons, as shown in Tables 36–1 and 36–2. Inspection of these tables, nevertheless, reveals other possibilities for explanation. Mothers encouraged dating by *both* offspring more than did fathers. It is possible to argue, therefore, that they were

Table 36-1 Attitudes of Fathers toward First Dating as Reported by Students

	MALE		FEMALE	
	N	Percent	N	Percent
Prohibited or disapproved		8.5		18.0
Indifferent		70.7		62.3
Encouraged		20.8		19.7
Replying	130		239	
Blank	11		19	
TOTAL	141	100.0	258	100.0

Source: Reprinted from Courtship in a group of Minnesota students by C. Kirkpatrick & T. Caplow, *American Journal of Sociology,* 1945, *51,* 115. © by the University of Chicago.

more concerned about the courtship of their children than were fathers and that the greater interest in daughters' dating was due to identification with a same-sex younger model of themselves rather than an interest in getting rid of a rival.

Attempts to show that courtship progress was associated with conflict with opposite-sex parents (Hobart, 1958a; Winch, 1943, 1946, 1947, 1949a, 1949b, 1950, 1951) have shown mixed and faint support for men and no support for women. Winch took the converse position and reasoned that successful resolution of the Oedipal situation is achieved by identification with the same-sex parent.

If, however, the parent is absent from the home by reason of divorce or death and the opposite-sex parent has not remarried, identification is impossible, and retarded courtship progress should result. Winch found support for this hypothesis for men but not for women. Unfortunately for his thesis a replication of his study by Andrews and Christensen (1951) revealed no relationship between missing parents and courtship progress for either men or women.

Attempts to show a psychological resemblance between the opposite-sex parent and the spouse have also been largely unsuccessful (Hamilton & MacGowan, 1929; Kent, 1951; Mangus, 1936; Prince & Baggaley, 1963; Strauss, 1946b).

Kent (1951) found considerable similarity in traits of male college students applied to their mothers and to their ideal wives. Since no control group was used, however, it could well have been that similarity existed between the stereotype of mothers (anyone's mother) and

Table 36-2 Attitudes of Mothers toward First Dating as Reported by Students

	MALE		FEMALE	
	N	Percent	N	Percent
Prohibited or disapproved		7.3		9.5
Indifferent		57.6		39.6
Encouraged		35.1		50.9
Replying	137		240	
Blank	4		18	
TOTAL	141	100.0	258	100.0

Source: Reprinted from Courtship in a group of Minnesota students by C. Kirkpatrick & T. Caplow, *American Journal of Sociology,* 1945, *51,* 115. © by the University of Chicago.

ideal mate rather than pertaining to the subject's specific mother and his ideal mate.

Conclusions on Research on Oedipal Situation

A review of the literature does not indicate much support for the Oedipal situation, but no testing of a vaguely formulated theory can be more than suggestive. In addition some of the researchers have made a difficult situation more difficult by ignoring the basic tenets of the Oedipal theory. For example the influence of parental personality ought to be greatest in an unresolved Oedipal situation, but no researchers have tried to determine whether the Oedipal situation had been resolved. The Oedipal *image* of the parent by the child (possibly unconscious) is of utmost importance, but some researchers have unjustifiably accepted the perceived personality of the middle-aged parent by the adult college student as an adequate representation of the earlier Oedipal image. Admittedly it would be next to impossible to test a past image, but in that case perhaps it would be better to conclude that the Oedipal situation is untestable than to introduce spurious tests of it. Whether the physique of a middle-aged parent has any relationship to the Oedipal situation is highly questionable. Even had the researchers been able to determine whether the subject had resolved his Oedipal situation, it might be impossible to test the theory. An unresolved Oedipal situation might lead one to marry a whore or a virgin. With a wide range like that, it is difficult to make predictions.

In summary, research on Freudian theory as it might apply to attraction and to marital choice has either been inadequate or, when adequate, has not substantiated it. Perhaps the most egregious fault of Freud was his categorization of *normal* women as essentially passive, masochistic, and narcissistic. His observations of his female clients were doubtlessly valid, but he failed to grasp that these women were molded into their roles by a male-oriented, patriarchal, Viennese society which seized most of the pleasures of life for men and then rationalized that it was nature, not they, who had so formed women.

WINCH'S COMPLEMENTARY-NEEDS THEORY

Winch (1958) accepts the generally held sociological position that homogamy is a very potent factor in marital choice but only as a preliminary screening to determine a "field of eligibles"—the actual selection of a spouse occurs on psychological grounds, and the basis of selection is from complementary needs.

Murray defines *need* as "... a construct ... which stands for a force ... which organizes perception, apperception, intellection, conation, and action in such a way as to transform in a certain direction an existing, unsatisfying situation" (1938, pp. 123–124).

Two needs are complementary "when A's need X is gratifying to B's need Y and B's behavior in acting out B's need Y is gratifying to A's need X" (Winch, 1958, p. 93). It is not necessary that A's need X be a different one from B's need Y. If the same need is gratified in both A and B but at very different levels of intensity, then it should follow that the couple should be negatively correlated for that need. If, for example, the man is very high on dominance, it should follow that the woman should be very low on dominance. Winch calls this Type 1 complementarity.

If different needs are gratified in *A* and *B,* the interspousal correlation is hypothesized to be positive or negative depending on the particular pair of needs chosen. If a man is high on the need for nurturance, Winch postulates that he would be drawn to a woman who was high on the need for succoring. Similarly if one member of the pair is high on hostility, the other ought to be high on abasement.

The situation involving two different needs is called Type 2 complementarity by Winch. Although theoretically the correlation between the two different needs might be either positive or negative depending on the particular pair chosen, in practice Winch has predicted only positive correlations between pairs of different needs.

Are the couple conscious of their needs? Winch concludes that some individuals are conscious of the needs that had drawn them to their spouse and others are not. The degree of consciousness may vary from individual to individual. Where the pattern of complementarity is contrary to traditional male and female roles, the probability is increased that the couple will not acknowledge the complementary bond between them. An example of such a case would be where the woman is dominant and the man is not.

Another problem was deciding which needs should be chosen for study. After much deliberation Winch selected 12 needs from Murray's list of needs and 3 general traits that would be quantifiable and unidimensional. For the sake of simplicity we shall refer to the list as 15 needs.

Testing the Theory

Population. Winch (1958) studied a small sample of 25 married couples in which one member of each couple was an undergraduate at Northwestern University. The study was conducted in 1950, and each couple was paid $7.50 for participating. Desiring a homogeneous sample he excluded upper-class subjects, Jews, and blacks.

Testing Procedure. Some of the 15 needs were scored for presence within the marriage and some outside of the marriage, some were scored as overt needs and some as covert, resulting in 44 different need scores in all.

Research Findings. Using the normalized ratings for the 44 variables from the need interview, it is possible, by correlating every variable with every other variable, to obtain 1936 interspousal correlations. Winch and colleagues selected 388 for which they hypothesized the signs of the correlations on the basis of the theory of complementary needs. They hypothesized that the 44 variables would be negatively intercorrelated for spouses (Type 1 complementarity, such as nurturance-nurturance). The remaining 344 correlations were selected so as to be positive correlations for different needs or traits (Type 2 complementarity, such as dominance-abasement). The results showed statistical support for the complementary-need hypothesis, though the degree of support was far from overwhelming.

Of the 388 correlations predicted, only 12 proved to be significant. However chance would have dictated only 3.88 as significant. Thus the finding was feeble in terms of magnitude of support, but our confidence that this was not a chance finding is considerable ($p < .01$).

In another analysis of the ratings of the subjects (Winch, 1955), attention focused solely on the Type 1 correlations. In this case each subject's 44 ratings were correlated with those of the spouse, and a mean correlation was obtained. A control group consisted of the mean of all the scores of all the subjects randomly paired so that a given man would be most probably correlated with someone else's wife. It was predicted, in accordance with the complementary theory, that the interspousal correlations of the actual couples would be significantly lower than those of the randomly paired couples. This prediction was supported with the mean correlation for actual husbands' and wives' ratings being .10—that of the randomly paired husbands and wives was .23. The difference in the size of the means was significant ($p < .05$).

Despite this seemingly statistical, if miniscule, support, Winch's work has come under considerable criticism. The full range of criticism is discussed elsewhere (Murstein, 1976), and only a few problems can be noted here.

Pick the needs that look the most promising. Winch's theory implies that all needs are complementary, yet he chose 15 needs to test the theory. He does not tell us why he chose them. Conceivably he might have chosen those needs (perhaps unconsciously) that would fit complementary roles in our society—e.g., a dominant husband and a deferential wife—while ignoring those needs that might contradict complementarity. He tells us that he omitted sex from the list of needs because it did not appear to be unidimensional. Yet it seems unlikely that an individual with a high need for sex would be drawn to one with a low need for it.

The factor of bias in the selection of needs goes beyond the choice of 15 for study out of a far greater number; from these 15 needs he derived 44 variables. Considering all possible pairings we arrive at a total of 1936 possible pairings of needs. Only 388 were actually selected (44 Type 1, 344 Type 2). The selection of the 44 Type 1 needs is entirely consistent with the theory of negative interspousal correlation, but why did he choose the particular 344 out of the remaining 1892 possible pairings? It seems logical to assume that he chose them because they seemed most likely to be complementary, whereas he rejected 1548 pairings because they were more risky in this regard. Considering the operation of this selective bias and the minimal nature of support for the theory, confidence in the theory is somewhat weakened.

When is homogamy complementary? In his test of Type 1 complementarity with the need interview data, Winch found an average correlation of .10 between husband and wife and an average correlation of .23 for the randomly paired couples. The significant difference between the correlations is taken as support for his theory. Strictly speaking, however, the only conclusion that would seem warranted is that the actual couples were less *homogamous* than the control couples. But being less homogamous is not the same as being complementary. Complementarity ought to involve a negative interspousal correlation—as Winch posits in the theory—not a smaller positive correlation.

The vast majority of research attempting to replicate Winch's work has shown no support for complementarity.

Is behavior a direct function of need? By the 1950s psychoanalysis had moved away from an *id* psychology, which suggested a direct one-to-one translation of needs into behavior, apart from the traditional psychoanalytic exception such as sublimation and reaction formation, to an *ego* psychology, which stressed that needs can only be understood as subservient to the ego. Personality is not a collection of needs, but an organized system for adjustment to the environment. Some systems are set up to translate needs directly into behavior; such individuals are termed *impulsive*. Others can only express some of their needs, and these only infrequently and only in specific situations.

It is incumbent, therefore, in understanding an individual's behavior to understand his/her acceptance of his/her needs and also the possible conflict in two simultaneously aroused needs. If a dominant woman sees a passive but eligible bachelor, shall her desire for status-striving (marriage) win out, thereby directing her to play the traditional submissive female? Or shall she respond to her dominance needs when confronted with an indecisive male but thus risk wounding his male ego and threatening her status-striving? Trying to evaluate needs without reference to the goals of the individual seems a little like saying that the tail wags the dog.

To need is not to get, unless you have assets. Winch's theory makes it appear as if once one has passed the criteria for race, religion, social class, occupational grouping, location of residence, income, age, level of education, intelligence, and interests and values, the remaining consideration is need complementarity. This suggests that a balanced consideration of the assets and liabilities that each member of the couple possesses is not important. Other research, however, has suggested that equity of net marital worth (assets minus liabilities) is of some importance (Murstein, 1970). For example two individuals might have perfect Winchian complementarity, but one might be physically attractive, highly sexed, high in self-esteem, and moving to a new out-of-town job next Tuesday. The partner may be fat, relatively low in sex-interest, low in self-esteem, and without plans to leave town in the foreseeable future. Despite need complementarity the interspousal characteristics of the first individual are more highly valued by society and/or at least different from those of the second individual; consequently, in choosing a marriage partner, each might be apt to search out a person with assets more comparable to his/her own.

Our sixth point that Type 1 complementarity is illogical is so well made by Centers (1975) that we can do no better than to cite him.

Winch's "Type I complementarity" as a mechanism of reciprocal need gratification is quite unacceptable.... To show

why this would be so let us take his own favorite example. Say A is high in dominance and B is low, and there is interaction between them. A, activated by n dom, behaves in a dominating way. B, having a weak n dom, is instigated only weakly to counteractive effort to dominate A, or, in other words, puts up little or no struggle for the position of dominance, which is the goal of gratifying state of affairs for both his and A's need. A is able to dominate, and is gratified in doing so. But what about B? What's he getting out of it? In order to be gratified in this interchange he would have to be motivated by *some* need, and if it is assumed, as implied in the concept of Type I complementarity that his need was also n dom, that need is not gratified, for he doesn't accomplish the dominance he is motivated, however weakly, to seek. Since his n dom was weak in the first place, he is not punified too much by losing to A the prize of dominance, but how is he gratified? The mechanism for his gratification is absent. To supply it requires positing a need to be dominated or a need for submission, but that forthwith changes so-called Type I complementarity into Type II. The Type I will simply not work. There is no complementarity in it. That serious students of intersexual attraction could have apparently accepted such fallacious reasoning for nearly two decades is, to say the least, puzzling. (Centers, 1975, pp. 117–118. Courtesy of Charles C Thomas, Publisher, Springfield, Illinois.)

Against a barrage of criticism, Winch in time modified his theory somewhat. His revision was influenced by Bermann's (1966) study of roommate stability in student nurses. Bermann was able to determine normative behavior for the "good nurse" and investigated whether adherence by both roommates to the norm was more predictive of roommate stability than was complementary-need fulfillment. He found that norm adherence predicted stability best and that complementarity predicted it less well, but significantly. Combining both principles provided the best predictor of stability.

Winch now revised his thinking and noted, "A pair of spouses who are attracted to each other on the basis of complementary need will be less stable if the complementariness is counter to role specification than if it is consistent with role specification" (Winch, 1974, p. 406).

Despite this revision Winch did no further work on the theory, and it seems to have passed its apogee of influence on the field. Nevertheless he was the first to propose a theory of marital choice and simultaneously embark on a research program to test it. His work strongly stimulated research on marital choice and resulted in new interest in the field.

INSTRUMENTAL THEORY

The author of this theory, Centers, states, "In intersexual dyad formation each person seeks, among his circle of acquaintances, within the compass of his self-acknowledged compeers, to form a relationship with that person or those persons whose behavioral and other resources provide (or are perceived to provide) maximum gratification and minimum punification for his needs" (1975, p. 63).

Centers proceeded to test the theory with 71 college students who were committed to marriage. Because his theory is need-centered, he chose to administer a revised form of the Edwards Personal Preference Schedule to his participants in which each need was measured through the use of several specific items, rather than as Edwards intended by choosing among a pair of items in which each item depicted a different need. The explanation for the revision is that the paired approach forces individuals to make choices where often neither choice is satisfactory to them.

His theory departs from that of Winch in stating that some needs are generally more important than others. Sex and affiliation are more important than succorance and abasement for both sexes when "in love," and couples should show a significant positive correlation for both needs.

Some needs are more important for one sex than for another.

Male dominance has high *attractiveness value* for females, but female dominance has *less* attractiveness value for males. Again, *female nurturance* has high attractiveness value for males, but male's nurturance has less attractiveness value for females. (Centers, 1975, p. 75)

In contrast Winch's theory of complementarity does not state that certain needs are more appropriate for one sex than for another. Winch's Type 1 complementarity (that partners should be negatively correlated on the same need) is thus rejected. "Only different needs gratifying to each other can be complementary.... For needs to be complementary, they must be *different in quality or kind* and productive of *different kinds of behavior*" (Centers, 1975, pp. 119–120).

By the principle of *genderic congruency*, those needs most typical of men (the mean score for men on a normative group was much higher than the mean score for women) should be most correlated with the needs most typical of women (their mean scores were much higher for women than for men). The biggest need differential was for affiliation. Thus Centers predicted that these two needs should be most highly correlated for premarital couples.

Several needs are somewhat male-linked, rather assertive, and sometimes threatening: achievement, aggression, autonomy, dominance, and exhibitionism. However when men do not suffer from inferiority feelings, it should be possible to tolerate, and even benefit from, the presence of those needs in women. Particularly this should be the case for achievement. Some of these benefits include the gratification in being associated with an achieving person (He must be OK to merit such a "catch"), consensual validation if one is also high in need for achievement, and vicarious gratification. Thus Centers predicts that if men are low in need for abasement (the closest measure of inferiority feelings since he administered no self-esteem tests) their correlation with their girlfriends for need achievement will be significantly higher than will be the case for those men high in need for abasement.

These are but a smattering of a total of 239 hypotheses. Most of these other hypotheses are derived from complex, often torturous, analyses of the interaction of the various needs. For many of these hypotheses Centers predicts the emergence of small correlations, and sure enough the data abound in "Irish" correlations (O'One, O'Two, O'Three). A few of these correlations go into the teens, with only a quite small number reaching a magnitude of .20 or above. Unfortunately these small and insignificant correlations could have arisen from other sources than Centers' predictions. They might also result from inaccurate predictions (no validity) or test unreliability. Thus these findings are ambiguous at best.

Centers used a sign test to list all of his 239 predictions and reported that in well over 90 percent of his predictions that the correlations would be positive or negative were verified. Given the huge number of nonsignificant correlations, I find it very difficult to understand this high rate of accuracy. His case would have been strengthened enormously had he tested a fresh group of couples for the purpose of cross-validation.

Some of the major hypotheses, such as those listed earlier, were supported. Couples correlated very significantly on need for sex (.64) and affiliation (.56). Also, as predicted, when the most masculine need (dominance) was correlated with the most feminine need (affiliation), the highest cross-need correlation resulted ($r = .50$). Last, as predicted, the correlation for couples for achievement was significantly higher where the man was low in need for abasement (.44) than where he was high in abasement (−.01).

Despite this support the theory as such does not allow one to deduce the various hypotheses formulated. The major hypotheses that we have discussed seem reasonable and have evinced some support, but these hypotheses do not bear any special relationship to the simple hedonistic theory stated by Centers. They would make sense without reference to his theory whatsoever.

Some of the analyses are statistically inaccurate. For example Centers compares his correlation matrix of actual couple correlations with the matrix of need correlations for randomly paired men and women. This leads in several cases to erroneous conclusions because the correlation of randomly paired scores will by definition be zero, and any departure from zero should be treated as a chance occurrence rather than a bona fide correlation. Centers found a correlation of .32 between men's sex scores and women's nurturance scores ($N = 71$). The correlation of randomly paired men and women which he used as a control group was .14. When he compared the two correlations for differences, he found no significant difference and concluded that the actual group's correlation was therefore not significant. Had he more properly compared the actual group's correlation of .32 against the null group hypothesis value of .00, he would have found the actual group's correlation to be significant ($p<.01$).

Centers generally advances the idea that individuals high on a given need (e.g., affiliation) will be drawn to members of the opposite sex who are also high on the need. He reports a correlation of .56 as substantiation. However the theory does not really account for the high correlation because a positive correlation also depends on covariation—that is, that men low on affiliation will also match up with low-affiliation women as well as high-affiliation men being drawn to high-affiliation women. Centers offers no explanation as to why a low-affiliation person would need another low-affiliation person. However, the notion of equity of exchange, which Centers does not deal with, can handle this possibility. Some people, in other words, may not *choose* each other so much as *settle* for each other, especially those who do not have many desirable characteristics to offer in the marital market. We will develop this thesis a bit later on.

Last, the theory reeks of Victorian patriarchy. Women are said to fulfill their own identity by finding a male with stronger drives than their own. The female is "submissive, dependent, affectionate." She is "markedly weak and dependent in important respects but tempered with certain kinds of strength as well" (Centers, 1975, p. 69). In Centers' opinion, "Females of the college type tend to see sexual activity more often than not . . . as *only* moral and legitimate within the context of marriage" (Centers, 1975, p. 239). That may be true of some college campuses, somewhere, but none that I have seen lately.

In summary Instrumental Theory is very sketchy, and the data Centers reports are sometimes incorrectly analyzed. Some of the predictions for small, nonsignificant correlations essentially become a defense of the null hypothesis. Although such hypotheses may be justified under special conditions, results in accordance with the null hypothesis of no difference are often difficult to differentiate from a theory's absence of validity or reliability. Nevertheless his thinking, if it does not provide a formal place for role testing and role fulfillment, does represent an advancement over the monolithic complementary-need theory of Winch.

AN EARLY FILTER APPROACH

The first *filter* theory to emerge was that of Kerckhoff and Davis (1962) who hypothesized that after an initial screening for homogamously cultural variables a further screening takes place on the basis of values and, finally, need compatibility. With a Duke University population they found that value similarity, but not need compatibility, was effective in determining courtship progress for couples courting less than 18 months. For longer-term relationships need compatibility was effective but not value similarity. A replication of the study seven years later, however, did not support their findings (Levinger, Senn, & Jorgensen, 1970). However, the theory has been greatly elaborated and extended to a three-stage exchange theory which I shall now discuss in some detail.

THE STIMULUS-VALUE-ROLE THEORY OF DYADIC RELATIONSHIPS

Stimulus-Value-Role Theory (SVR) is a general theory of the development of dyadic relationships. Designed initially to account for courtship, it has been extended with slight modification to account for friendship and husband-wife relationships as well (Murstein, 1971a, 1976).

It is an exchange theory, positing that in a relatively free choice situation attraction and interaction depend on the exchange value of the assets and liabilities that each of the parties brings to the situation. The kinds of variables that influence the course of development of the relationship can be classified under three categories: stimulus, value comparison, and role. These variables are operative during the entire course of courtship, but they are posited to be maximally influential at different stages of the courtship. Each of the three stages reflects by its name the kind of variables most influential during that period.

The chief concern here will be the theory's ability to explain marital choice. However, a theory of attraction to a dyadic relationship cannot aspire to perfect accuracy in predicting marital choice for a number of reasons. First, the search for a marital partner is often highly competitive. Individuals with a large number of interpersonal assets generally have many potentially marriageable partners. It is possible, therefore, that any given relationship in which they are involved may be highly successful, but their other relationships, not examined, may be even more successful.

Second, individuals differ in their desire to marry. An individual who values marriage as a status very highly may be less stringent in his/her requirements for dyadic compatibility than an individual who is not eager to rush into matrimony.

Thus although society has traditionally educated its youth to expect that close heterosexual dyadic relationships between unmarried youths will terminate in marriage, it is evident that more individuals than previously are courting longer and cohabiting without the benefit of matrimony. This factor also contributes to the imperfectness of dyadic closeness as a prognosticator of marriage.

Other factors influencing the incidence of marriage are timing, critical incidents, and the social network. "The right person at the wrong time" is a plaint often mentioned by individuals who met highly compatible individuals at a time when they were not ready for marriage. Critical incidents, such as a job transfer of one member of the couple to another city, may precipitate marriage in some courtship couples but terminate it in others. Last, the social network—relatives, friends, business associates of the couples—may influence courtship by their tendency to treat the pair as a "couple" rather than as individuals.

Courtship may be likened to a slowly accelerating conveyor belt whose destination is matrimony. An individual may jump off relatively easily in the early stages of courtship, but as the destination is approached, it becomes rather hazardous, interpersonally speaking, to jump off—there would be a great deal of disappointment and embarrassment in explaining the circumstances to everybody. Depending on the pressure applied by the particular network and the courage of the individual, some individuals may be "conveyed" into marriage despite a late discovery of less-than-desirable compatibility. These various factors contribute to the conclusion that dyadic compatibility and marital choice are not synonymous. Nevertheless they are sufficiently correlated so that an understanding of heterosexual dyad formation can lead to an understanding of marital choice.

The remaining portion of the section will consist of a discussion of the exchange aspects of SVR theory, followed by an elaboration of the kinds of variables which influence both dyad formation and the various stages of courtship.

Exchange in Courtship

Essentially an exchange approach maintains that each person tries to make social interaction as profitable as possible, *profit* being defined as the rewards s/he gains from the interaction minus the costs s/he must pay. By *rewards* are meant the pleasures, benefits, and gratifications an individual gains from a relationship. *Costs* are factors which inhibit or deter the performance of more preferred behaviors. A young man living in the Bronx, for example, might like a young lady from Brooklyn whom he met while both were at a resort. Back in the city, however, he may doubt that the rewards he might gain from the relationship would be worth the costs in time and fatigue of two-hour subway rides to Brooklyn.

Closely allied to rewards and costs are assets and liabilities. *Assets* are the commodities (behaviors or qualities) that the individual possesses which are capable of rewarding the individual. *Liabilities* are behaviors or qualities associated with an individual which are costly to others.

A man who is physically unattractive (liability), for example, might desire a woman who has the asset of beauty. Assuming, however, that his nonphysical qualities are no more rewarding than hers, she gains less profit than he does from the relationship, and thus his suit is likely to be rejected. Rejection is a cost to him because it may lower his self-esteem and increase his fear of failure in future encounters; hence, he may decide to avoid attempting to court women whom he perceives as much above him in attractiveness.

Contrariwise a man is likely to feel highly confident of success if he tries to date a woman even less attractive than himself where he risks little chance of rejection (low cost). However, the reward value of such a conquest is quite low, so that the profitability of such a move is also low. As a consequence an experienced individual is likely to express a maximum degree of effort and also obtain the greatest reward at the least cost when he directs his efforts at someone of approximately equal physical attractiveness, assuming all other variables are constant.

Couples Need Not Be Matched on the Same Variable. It is not necessary, however, for equity of physical attractiveness to be present in order for a viable relationship to occur. Given that a man and woman are sufficiently acquainted with each other's respective assets and liabilities, it becomes possible for the less attractive member to compensate for his/her "weakness" in a number of ways. Suppose, for example, that the man is unattractive and the woman is attractive. He might render services to his partner far above what she gives him, waiting on her hand and foot. Consistent with this thesis is a study by Dermer (1973) which reports that the greater a woman's attractiveness, the longer the vacations she expected to take when she married, and the fewer hours she expected to work to supplement her husband's income.

The attractive woman "pays" the man back through the status she confers on him by being with him, a cost (loss of status) she incurs in being seen with an unattractive man. Berscheid and Walster (1974), reviewing the literature, have indicated that individuals perceived to associate with physically attractive persons gain in the esteem in which they are held by others, whereas those persons consorting with unattractive partners lose status. The outsider looking only at the physical attractiveness of the couple may find them terribly unbalanced with regard to their exchange value and wonder what she possibly sees in him. The people who know the couple well, however, know that she exploits him miserably and wonder why he puts up with it. Yet the situation is balanced if all of the variables are taken into consideration.

No mention has been made thus far of the status accruing to an individual solely on the basis of his/her sex, but men in our society have traditionally enjoyed a greater social, economic, and political status than have women (Murstein, 1974a). These advantages may be eroding, but they have not disappeared altogether. It follows, therefore, that men should be able to utilize this greater status to extract benefits prior to and during marriage. A physically unattractive man should find it somewhat easier to marry than a physically unattractive woman should, and the United States statistics for 1978 indicated that for every 1000 men and 1000 women aged 14 years and older 64.9 men were married as compared to 53.3 women (Monthly Vital Statistics Report, 1980).

The Stimulus, Value, and Role Stages of Courtship

To understand the second basic concern of SVR theory—the development of the stages of courtship—a few words must be said about the locus in which the relationship unfolds. This context may be categorized into "open" and "closed" fields.

An *"open field"* encounter refers to a situation in which the man and woman do not as yet know each other or have only a nodding acquaintance. Examples of such open field situations are "mixers," a large school class at the beginning of the semester, and brief contacts in the office. The fact that the field is "open" indicates that either the man or woman is free to start the relationship or abstain from initiating it, as they wish. The contrary concept is the *"closed field"* situation in which both the man and woman are forced to relate in some manner by reason of the roles assigned to them by the environmental setting in which they find themselves. Examples of closed field situations might be those of students in a small seminar in a college, members of a Peace Corps unit, and workers in a political campaign. This interaction generally enables the individual to become acquainted with behavior of the "other," which is then evaluated according to the individual's own system of values. This system is a compendium of values acquired in the process of acculturalization to the traditional or current tastes of society, values acquired from one's peers and parents, values derived from experience, and values resulting from genetically based predispositions, which may be labeled *temperament.*

Individuals, of course, may be attracted to members of the opposite sex without necessarily contemplating marriage. The fact that almost all persons in the United States eventually marry, however, suggests that many of the heterosexual social encounters of young adults contain at least the possibility of eventual marriage; consequently, the general heterosexual encounter has been treated as the first step toward possible marriage.

Stimulus Stage. When two members of the opposite sex are in an open field (e.g., a "mixer" dance), there generally has been a considerable amount of incidental screening which has eliminated many of the maritally noneligible persons. If the mixer is held on a college campus, for example, attendance may be restricted to college students. Such students not only reflect educational homogeneity, but they are apt to show greater-than-chance similarity on variables which are correlated with education: socioeconomic status, age, intelligence, and to some extent, values.

There remains, nevertheless, sufficient variability with respect to some other variables for an active selective process. Variables such as physical attractiveness, temperament, and sex drive have undergone very little selectivity through the factors which bring individuals to college, and so interpersonal encounters between the sexes may continue to result in widely varying responses from joy to repulsion.

There is ample evidence that the initial impact in a dating situation depends largely on physical attractiveness (Berscheid & Walster, 1974). The importance of physical attractiveness resides not only in its being highly valued by society as a status-conferring asset and in the fact that it is the only evidence of potential viability of the relationship prior to interaction. One must consider also that all kinds of desirable personality and intellectual attributes are ascribed to the beautiful. They are viewed as "more sensitive, kind, interesting, strong, poised, modest, sociable, outgoing, and exciting—more sexual, warm, and responsive than unattractive persons" (Berscheid & Walster, 1972, pp. 46, 74).

Initial impressions are not wholly dependent on the senses however. An individual's stimulus value may also include information about his/her reputation or professional aspirations, which precede him/her into the initial contact. That Ronald Rabbitfoot is a star running back for Podunk University may compensate for his less-than-classic Greek profile.

In summary initial judgments are formed on the basis of perceptions of the other and/or information about him/her. These may be obtained without any interpersonal contact whatsoever or on the basis of brief introductions.

It is questionable how much such initial impressions correlate with subsequent marital happiness. Nevertheless the stimulus stage is of crucial importance in the open field, for if the other person does not possess sufficient stimulus impact to attract the individual, further contact is not sought. The "prospect" in question might make a potentially exemplary, compatible spouse, s/he might manifest value consensus and superb role compatibility with the perceiver, but the perceiver, foregoing opportunities for further contact, may never find this out. Consequently persons with low stimulus attractiveness (especially those who are physically unattractive) are at a considerable handicap in an open field.

Because physical attractiveness is highly valued, it would seem logical that each individual would seek the most attractive partner available when information about other characteristics is not available. Enjoyment of a date when interaction has been relatively brief also would probably be mainly contingent on the attractiveness of one's partner.

There is evidence that this is the case when either of two conditions exist: (1) The individuals have relatively little experience in dating and have not undergone the costs of rejection and (2) an experimental paradigm is constructed in which the individual is more or less guaranteed a date (Berscheid & Walster, 1974; Huston, 1973). However it is estimated that over 90 percent of the current population will eventually marry, and it is evident that they are not all physically attractive. There is obviously a net decrement in beauty from ideal preference to actual choice. This change, it is postulated, follows the equity of exchange principle. Experienced individuals of equal attractiveness would possess equal rewarding power, in the absence of other information, and would tend to be drawn to each other pending further information about the other.

Value-Comparison Stage. If a couple approximates equality in their stimulus variables—that is, the weighted amalgam of each individual's perceived stimulus attributes (physical attractiveness, status, poise, voice) is approximately equal—they may progress to the second (value-comparison) stage of courtship. It is impossible to fix a specific time limit for passage from one stage to another because the importance of each stage and kinds and rate of interaction between individuals will vary from couple to couple.

Figure 36–1 presents a series of theoretical average curves for the importance and duration of the three variables. The curves in Figure 36–1, strictly speaking, apply separately to each member of the couple. It is possible for one member of the couple to be in the stimulus stage, whereas his/her partner is in the value stage. For example a man may be reacting primarily to a woman's physical attractiveness, and she may have queried him on what he thought about women's liberation, equal careers, and childless marriage. He may not have found out much about her values, so that a disparity exists not only with regard to what each considers important in the relationship but also with regard to the stage of courtship each is in. This disparity is not necessarily inimical to the relationship as long as each is highly rewarded by the relationship.

The termination of the stimulus stage may be defined as occurring at the point in the relationship when the stimulus variables, as a group, become less important to the relationship than the value-comparison variables. Passage from the stimulus to the value-comparison stage might occur in a matter of hours, or it might take weeks. It is also conceivable that such passage might not occur, but we shall deal with this eventuality when we have completed our description of the three stages of courtship.

The label *value comparison* has been used for want of a better name. I infer under this term interests, attitudes, beliefs, and even needs when they are seen as emanating from beliefs. The primary focus of the value-comparison stage, in short, is the gathering of information by verbal interaction with the other.

Verbal interaction will surely be an important feature of the role stage which succeeds the value-comparison stage. In the role stage the emphasis will be more on the dyadic relationship and will include commitment positions regarding depth of feeling for the other and desire for permanency, confirmation of the self-image, and accuracy in predicting the feelings and perceptions of the other.

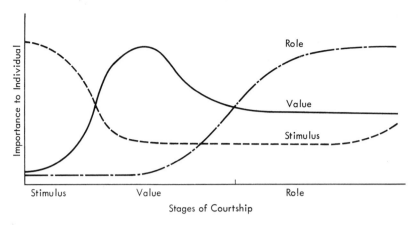

Figure **36–1** Stages of courtship in SVR theory. (Source: Murstein, 1976, p. 123. Reprinted by permission of Springer Publishing Company.)

The value-comparison stage occurs when the couple has not as yet developed sufficient intimacy to learn and confess the innermost percepts, fears, aspirations, and concerns that each has. Nevertheless there is much public and private information that each learns about the other in this period. Information is gleaned about religious orientation; political beliefs; attitudes toward people, parents, and friends; and interest in sports, the arts, dancing, and the like.

The rate of progress through the value-comparison stage depends on the rate of social penetration (Altman & Taylor, 1973). The couple exhibits increasingly larger areas of what they think and feel. They evaluate their comfortableness, the acceptance of what they reveal, and the effect of their disclosure on their partner's behavior. In a successful relationship the partner evinces acceptance of the values of the individual and discloses his/her own values. Self-disclosure among individuals promotes reciprocal self-disclosure, and the relationship may proceed to increasingly deeper levels of personality (Cozby, 1973).

In the most successful relationships consensus on the important values intrinsic to the relationship is generally reached. Consensus is important for a variety of reasons. For one thing it reinforces our perception of the world as correct (Byrne & Clore, 1967). The satisfaction goes beyond simply being "right," because values are introjected into the self and help to define the self-image; hence, the person who rejects our self-image is often perceived as rejecting us. Moreover persons with similar values are likely to engage in similar activities, thus further rewarding each other.

During the value-comparison stage, though the stimulus and role variables are also operative, the importance of the stimulus variables has already waned somewhat. The majority of persons of disparate stimulus attractiveness who have met probably never developed a relationship. Many who started a relationship have broken up. The relatively few couples of disparate stimulus attractiveness who continue their relationship presumably have unusual compensating value consensus or role compatibility.

The testing of role compatibility involves not only intimate verbal communication but also getting to know how to behave vis-à-vis the partner, as well as knowing what roles the partner can play in satisfying one's own needs: friend, teacher, lover, critic. These roles not only involve the greatest intimacies, but they also necessitate a great deal of time to master; hence, the growth rate of role compatibility is slower than that of value comparison, which involves only verbal interaction. There does come a time, however, when role compatibility supersedes value comparison in importance, marking the onset of the role stage, as shown in Figure 36–1.

Role Stage. When a couple has survived the stimulus and value stages, they have established a reasonably good relationship. Some individuals may decide to marry at this point. However for most persons these are necessary, but insufficient, grounds for marriage. It is also important for the couple to be able to *function* in compatible roles.

A primary feature of the role stage is the evaluation of the perceived functioning of oneself in a dyadic relationship in comparison with the role one envisages for oneself and the perceived role functioning of the partner with respect to the roles one has envisaged for him/her. Personal, intimate behaviors are revealed much more slowly than are values, which can be expressed in more abstract, less intimate fashion. Also an overall evaluation of role compatibility may include many roles and may be difficult to make, whereas values are generally simpler to understand.

We can measure role compatibility by comparing expectations and perceptions of the fulfillment of expectations over a wide range of behaviors. Some culturally esteemed behaviors probably may not require measurement of expectations because they are almost universally perceived as rewarding. Individuals with both high social status and high nurturance needs, for example, are generally sought after because such individuals are easy to relate to, are rarely self-centered, and are sensitive and giving toward others. On the other hand neurotics are high-cost persons who are difficult to relate to and often offer few rewards through interaction. Role compatibility is probably the most complex of all the stages and is probably never completely traversed, since individuals seem to be constantly adding new roles or modifying existing ones.

Types of Courtship and Cross-Cultural Influences

Figure 36–1 describes what I conjecture to be the typical path of courtship for most middle-class couples in the United States. Variations due to personality, economic, and cultural differences, however, would alter the graph somewhat. "Stimulus" types would hold stimulus variables to be most important over the course of the courtship. For such persons marrying in the right class or profession would be paramount, and role interaction secondary.

The same would probably be true for other societies in which social change was relatively slight and class structure was stable. A Greek peasant might be most influenced by stimulus variables because almost everyone in the village held similar values. Role stratification also might be rigid, a man's role and a woman's role being clearly defined and differentiated. In that case the role stage along with the value stage might be of relatively small import.

In our own society value consensus seems to be of greatest importance within professional and upper-middle-class couples and of least importance in the lower class (Kerckhoff, 1972, 1974). In the lower class we may presume that the narrowed range of class variability for values and the structuring of roles makes individual selectivity with respect to these dimensions of lesser importance.

Distinguishing between Similarity and Equity

Similarity and equity are often bandied about as if they were equivalent terms. It is necessary, however, to distinguish between them because equity plays an important role in SVR theory, whereas similarity is of lesser importance. *Similarity* within the context of our discussion refers to the number of common components or the degree of similar structure two objects may have. If we say two individuals have similar values, we mean that if we ranked the values of each in order of preference a high rank order correlation would result.

Equity as used here refers to equal rewarding power; hence, two equitable persons might be totally dissimilar. The beautiful but poor woman who marries the ugly but wealthy bachelor represents an equitable balance of beauty and wealth.

The problem arises when members of a couple are equally represented on a variable so that they are similar and equitable with respect to it. Generally similarity functions as an antecedent variable. Individuals possessing similar values are drawn to each other because they receive consensual validation that their views are correct. In some cases, however, logic tells us that two people who share a socially undesirable characteristic may not necessarily be drawn to each other. They may, in fact, *settle* for each other because it is the best they can do. It is doubtful that two physically unattractive individuals are drawn to each other because they admire unattractiveness; rather, they may have learned through experience that if they do not possess outstanding compensating attributes for their unattractiveness they are apt to be rejected by more attractive persons whom

they attempt to court. It is the presence of similars at the bottom of the totem pole which enables us to differentiate similarity as a socially desirable attracting agent from similarity as an equity or exchange factor.

Similarity can be nonrewarding even when the traits involved are socially desirable. Unless similarity leads to a rewarding experience, it may lead to competition and dissatisfaction. When both members of a couple possess strong needs to dominate each other, the couple may function less harmoniously than a tandem of a dominant and submissive member. The strongest interpersonal relationship, therefore, does not necessarily occur between the most similar types but between those with equal rewarding power (equity), even where the variables contributing to these rewards are different for the partners.

A Synopsis of Research on SVR Theory

In the more extensive treatment of SVR and other theories of marital choice (Murstein, 1976), 39 hypotheses relating to SVR theory were tested. Strong, moderate, or modest support was found for 33 of these hypotheses, with 6 being unsubstantiated, sometimes despite strong positive trends. Almost all of the research has tended to focus on the exchange portion of the theory, primarily because the financial resources were not available to study the developmental stages longitudinally. There is, however, some slight indirect support of these stages which in the interests of space cannot be discussed here. Instead several of the more important hypotheses have been selected to give the reader the flavor of the research. First, however, a brief sketch of the subjects and the tests used will be given.

Population and Tests. The subjects were tested in three samples in the late 1960s. They were predominantly college students from Connecticut universities and colleges from middle- and upper-middle-class backgrounds. Couples generally knew each other fairly well (somewhat less than two years on the average) before volunteering for a study on "interpersonal relationships." The first group consisted of 99 couples who took the Minnesota Multiphasic Personality Inventory and the Revised Edwards Personal Preference Schedule, among other tests. A year later, 19 new couples received more intensive testing including such "depth" measures as a lengthy interview, ink blot test, a thematic apperception test, and other tests. A year following, a third group consisting of 98 couples took another series of tests, including the Marriage Expectation Test, specially designed to measure the physical, value, and role characteristics desired in a spouse. This test was taken under eight different perceptual "sets," including such perceptions as boyfriend (girlfriend), self, ideal self, ideal spouse, how boyfriend (girlfriend) sees me, how boyfriend (girlfriend) sees his (her) ideal spouse. Six months after the initial testing, each subject received a follow-up questionnaire which asked how well the couple was currently doing together. Based on a rating sheet the couple could be classified as having made good or poor courtship progress.

Research Findings. One of the most important assertions of SVR theory is that both the need complementarity and homogamy theories are inadequate in accounting for marital choice because individuals seeking a marriage partner are concerned with neither similarity nor complementarity of needs. Rather they seek a partner who represents a fusion of their ideal self and ideal spouse, although, as we shall see shortly, they may be prepared to lower their aspirations somewhat if they perceive themselves as not possessing high marital assets in their own right.

In general, however, when one is about to marry, one does tend to idealize one's partner and to see him/her as close to one's ideal-self and ideal-spouse concepts. This being the case the tendency of an individual to marry someone s/he perceives as being similar or different depends largely on how closely his/her self-concept is to that trinity of desiderata—his/her ideal spouse, his/her ideal self, and his/her perceived partner (Figure 36–2).

This figure shows that individual B, who is high self-accepting, is thus likely to perceive him/herself as very similar to his/her partner. Individual A, who is not highly self-accepting (i.e., there is a greater distance between his/her self-concept and his/her ideal-self concept), tends to view him/herself as relatively dissimilar to his/her partner.

This model was validated in research by Murstein (1971b) and explains the contradictory nature of earlier studies, which sometimes supported the "opposites attract" theory and sometimes the homogamy theory. It suggests that a person who is dissatisfied with him/herself will have complementary perceptions of his/her partner, whereas a highly self-accepting person will perceive his/her partner as similar to him/herself.

Another aspect of SVR theory is that men occupy a higher status than do women in contemporary American society; consequently, the confirmation of the man's self and ideal-self concepts by his partner should be more important to progress in courtship than is confirmation of the woman's concepts.

It was noted earlier that role compatibility in the role stage was essential for smooth courtship progress. Accordingly it was predicted that couples *confirming* the self and ideal-self percepts of their partners on the multi-itemed Marriage Expectation Test (perceiving their partners similar to the way their partners described themselves and their ideal selves) would have made better courtship progress when checked six months later than couples who did not strongly confirm their partners' perceptions of themselves. It was likewise predicted that accuracy of predicting the partner's self and ideal-self

perceptions on the same test would likewise be associated with good courtship progress. Both hypotheses were significantly supported.

It was further argued that, in accordance with equity, individuals of lower status should have to render more services to individuals of higher status in order to attract and hold them. Women have historically occupied a lower status in society than men have and even do so currently, though the gap in status appears to be narrowing (Murstein, 1974a). One way individuals of lower status can attract upper-status individuals is by paying greater attention to them than vice versa and by confirming their images of themselves. Accordingly it was predicted that women who made good courtship progress would have been more likely to confirm their boyfriends' self and ideal-self concepts six months earlier and would also have been more likely to be able to have predicted accurately these concepts as compared to women who did not make good courtship progress. These predictions were also confirmed. It was further predicted that men's tendency to confirm and to predict accurately their partners' self and ideal-self concepts would be less strongly associated with courtship progress if the men possessed greater power in determining courtship progress, since they would have less need to pay attention to and confirm their partners' self-perceptions. The data generally also supported this hypothesis.

In like vein it was predicted and confirmed that the man's proneness to neuroticism would have poorer implications for advancement in courtship than the woman's neurotic tendencies. Further, in accordance with equity, it was predicted that there would be a greater-than-chance similarity between members of couples for physical attractiveness, satisfaction with partner, neuroticism, and self-esteem. All of these hypotheses were supported.

The theory has also been extended to marriages, both intraracial (Murstein & Beck, 1972) and interracial (Murstein, 1973), and to friendship (Murstein, 1971a, 1976), with results strongly supporting those found for premarital couples.

The author of a theory is hardly the most unbiased judge of a theory's worth. However, the data seem to offer support for the exchange portion of the theory. The sequential aspects have been tested only indirectly, and although these data support it, the crucial test of this phase would necessitate a longitudinal study which regrettably has not as yet been undertaken, a point noted by Murstein (1974b) and others (Rubin & Levinger, 1974).

CONCLUSIONS

Several trends are apparent if we consider the theories reviewed in rough chronological order. These include

1. Movement from monolithic theories to complex ones
2. Growing emphasis on the importance of situational events rather than sole reliance on psychodynamic processes
3. Growing focus on the role of extra-dyadic relationships in furthering or retarding the courtship
4. Some emphasis on sex differences in needs and status.

We shall consider each of these trends briefly.

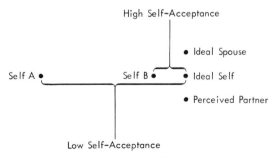

Figure 36–2 A, whose self and ideal-self concepts are far apart (low self-acceptance), will also see partner as unlike him/her, whereas B, whose self and ideal-self concepts are close together (high self-acceptance), will also see partner as highly similar to the self. (Source: Murstein, 1976, p. 189. Reprinted by permission of Springer Publishing Company.)

Movement from Monolithic Theories. Psychoanalysis represented an attempt to explain marital choice by unconscious processes, the Complementary-Needs Theory posited an "opposites attract" thesis, and the homogamy approach favored a "birds of a feather flock together" position. More recent thinking considers that the attempt to explain marital choice on the basis of a single principle is simplistic. Currently the focus is on the process of developing a relationship and the tasks or stages which serve to push the relationship forward. Finally, SVR theory has introduced the idea that in a free-choice situation selection of a marriage partner is competitive and motivated by each participant trying to get the best possible bargain.

More Emphasis on Situational Events in Addition to Psychodynamic Processes. Compatibility and the decision to marry are not necessarily cause and effect. A compatible relationship may show no movement toward permanency until an interpersonal crisis occurs which threatens the relationship. The crisis may either cause the relationship to emerge stronger, ultimately leading to marriage, or else cause it to disintegrate, often rapidly. The crisis may come in the form of a lover's quarrel which tests the strength of commitment. Pregnancy is a crisis which forces action toward marriage or toward abortion, with often a weakening of the relationship following shortly. Graduation or a change in locale of work obliges the members of the dyad to confess a commitment leading to marriage or effectively to sever the relationship.

Increasing Awareness of the Influence of Extra-Dyadic Relationships. Friends and relatives of the members of the couple play an active role in encouraging, retarding, and once again encouraging the relationship (Ryder, Kafka, & Olson, 1971). The attitudes of third parties generally influence the relationship of the couple enormously, even if the couple overtly resist pressures of these outside forces.

Emphasis on Sex Differences and Influence on Needs and Status. Centers (1978) has shown that predictability and compatibility increase if one can assign certain needs by gender, presumably influenced by biology, society, or both. My own work has shown that differences between the sexes in status will influence the needs and behaviors of the couple. The ability to predict progress in courtship is thus improved by abandoning a monolithic model which assumes that needs operate equally on both sexes.

In summary the evidence points conclusively to the fact that marital choice is a complex, multidetermined event beyond the ken of any simple theory. It is likely, therefore, that future theorists of marital choice will concern themselves with selecting and weighing the influence of a considerable number of variables rather than with researching for a simple "alchemist's stone" which will magically explain all.

REFERENCES

ALTMAN, I., & TAYLOR, D. A. *Social penetration.* New York: Holt, Rinehart & Winston, 1973.

ANDREWS, R. O., & CHRISTENSEN, H. T. Relationship of absence of a parent to courtship status: Repeat study. *American Sociological Review,* 1951, *16,* 541–544.

BARDWICK, J. *The psychology of women: A study of bio-cultural conflicts.* New York: Harper & Row, Pub., 1971.

BERMANN, E. A. *Compatibility and stability in the dyad.* Paper presented before the American Psychological Association, New York, September 1966.

BERSCHEID, E., & WALSTER, E. H. Beauty and the best. *Psychology Today,* 1972, *5,* 41–46, 74.

BERSCHEID, E., & WALSTER, E. H. Physical attractiveness. Pp. 157–215 in L. Berkowitz (Ed.), *Advances in experimental social psychology* (Vol. 7). New York: Academic Press, 1974.

BYRNE, D., & CLORE, G. L. Effective arousal and attraction. *Journal of Personality and Social Psychology,* 1967, *6* (4, Whole No. 638).

CENTERS, R. *Sexual attraction and love: An instrumental theory.* Springfield, Ill.: Chas. C Thomas, 1975.

COMMINS, W. D. Marriage age of oldest sons. *Journal of Social Psychology,* 1932, *3,* 487–490.

COZBY, I. Self-disclosure in human relationships. *Psychological Bulletin,* 1973, *79,* 73–91.

DERMER, M. *When beauty fails.* Unpublished doctoral dissertation, University of Minnesota, 1973.

FREUD, S. On narcissism. Pp. 44–50 in *Collected papers* (Vol. 4). London: Hogarth Press, 1949.

HAMILTON, G. V., & MACGOWAN, K. *What is wrong with marriage.* New York: Albert & Charles Boni, 1929.

HOBART, C. W. Emancipation from parents and courtship in adolescents. *Pacific Sociological Review,* Spring 1958, *1,* 25–29.

HUSTON, R. L. Ambiguity of acceptance, social desirability, and dating choice. *Journal of Experimental Social Psychology,* 1973, *9,* 32–42.

KENKEL, W. F. *The family in perspective* (2nd ed.). New York: Appleton-Century-Crofts, 1966.

KENT, D. P. Subjective factors in mate selection: An exploratory study. *Sociology and Social Research,* 1951, *35,* 391–398.

KERCKHOFF, A. C. Status-related value patterns among married couples. *Journal of Marriage and the Family,* 1972, *34,* 105–110.

KERCKHOFF, A. C. *The social context of interpersonal attraction.* New York: Academic Press, 1974.

KERCKHOFF, A. C., & DAVIS, K. E. Value consensus and need complementarity in mate selection. *American Sociological Review,* 1962, *27,* 295–303.

KIRKPATRICK, C. A statistical investigation of the psychoanalytic theory of mate selection. *Journal of Abnormal and Social Psychology,* 1937, *32,* 427–430.

KIRKPATRICK, C., & CAPLOW, T. Courtship in a group of Minnesota students. *American Journal of Sociology,* 1945, *51,* 114–125.

LEVINGER, G., SENN, D. J., & JORGENSEN, B. W. Progress toward permanence in courtship: A test of the Kerckhoff-Davis hypothesis. *Sociometry,* 1970, *33,* 427–443.

MANGUS, A. H. Relationships between young women's conceptions of intimate male associates and of their ideal husbands. *Journal of Social Psychology,* 1936, *7,* 403–420.

Monthly Vital Statistics Reports: Advance Report Final Marriage Statistics, 1978. Vol. 29, No. 6, Supplement 1, September 12, 1980.

MURRAY, H. A. *Explorations in personality.* New York: Oxford University Press, 1938.

MURSTEIN, B. I. Stimulus-value-role: A theory of marital choice. *Journal of Marriage and the Family,* 1970, *32,* 465–481.

MURSTEIN, B. I. A theory of marital choice and its applicability to marriage adjustment and friendship. Pp. 100–151 in B. I. Murstein (Ed.), *Theories of attraction and love.* New York: Springer Publishing Company, 1971a.

MURSTEIN, B. I. Self-ideal–self-discrepancy and the choice of marital partner. *Journal of Consulting and Clinical Psychology,* 1971b, *37,* 47–52.

MURSTEIN, B. I. A theory of marital choice applied to interracial marriage. Pp. 17–35 in L. E. Abt & I. R. Stuart (Eds.), *Interracial marriage.* New York: Grossman, 1973.

MURSTEIN, B. I. *Love, sex, and marriage through the ages.* New York: Springer Publishing Company, 1974a.

MURSTEIN, B. I. Clarification of obfuscation on conjugation: A reply to criticism of the SVR theory of marital choice. *Journal of Marriage and the Family,* 1974b, *36,* 231–234.

MURSTEIN, B. I. *Who will marry whom? Theories and research in marital choice.* New York: Springer Publishing Company, 1976.

MURSTEIN, B. I., & BECK, G. D. Person perception, marriage adjustment, and social desirability. *Journal of Consulting and Clinical Psychology,* 1972, *39,* 396–403.

PRINCE, A. J., & BAGGALEY, A. C. Personality variables and the ideal mate. *Family Life Coordinator,* 1963, *3,* 93–96.

RUBIN, Z., & LEVINGER, G. Theory and data badly mated: A critique of Murstein's SVR and Lewis' PDF models of mate selection. *Journal of Marriage and the Family,* 1974, *36,* 226–231.

RYDER, R. G., KAFKA, J. S., & OLSON, D. H. Separating and joining influences in courtship and early marriage. *American Journal of Orthopsychiatry,* 1971, *4,* 450–464.

STRAUSS, A. The ideal and the chosen mate. *American Journal of Sociology,* 1946a, *52,* 204–208.

STRAUSS, A. The influence of parent-images upon marital choice. *American Sociological Review,* 1946b, *11,* 554–559.

WINCH, R. F. The relation between courtship behavior and attitudes toward parents among college men. *American Sociological Review,* 1943, *8,* 167–174.

WINCH, R. F. Interrelations between certain social background and parent-son factors in a study of courtship among college men. *American Sociological Review,* 1946, *11,* 333–341.

WINCH, R. F. Primary factors in a study of courtship. *American Sociological Review,* 1947, *12,* 658–666.

WINCH, R. F. The relation between loss of a parent and progress in courtship. *Journal of Social Psychology,* 1949a, *29,* 51–56.

WINCH, R. F. Courtship in college women. *The American Journal of Sociology,* 1949b, *55,* 269–278.

WINCH, R. F. Some data bearing on the Oedipus hypothesis. *Journal of Abnormal and Social Psychology,* 1950, *45,* 481–489.

WINCH, R. F. Further data and observation on the Oedipus hypothesis: The consequence of an inadequate hypothesis. *American Sociological Review,* 1951, *16,* 784–795.

WINCH, R. F. The theory of complementary needs in mate-selection: A test of one kind of complementariness. *American Sociological Review,* 1955, *20,* 52–56.

WINCH, R. F. *Mate selection.* New York: Harper & Bros., 1958.

WINCH, R. F. Complementary needs and related notions about voluntary mate-selection. Pp. 399–410 in R. F. Winch & G. Spanier (Eds.), *Selected studies in marriage and the family.* New York: Holt, Rinehart & Winston, 1974.

37

Marriage
and the Family

WILLIAM J. DOHERTY
NEIL S. JACOBSON

For most individuals in all societies, marriage and parenthood are the primary social roles of adult life. In the American culture there is abundant evidence for the salience of family roles in the lives of most adults. A national survey of the "quality of American life" conducted in the early 1970s found, for example, that Americans rate marriage as the most important life domain, ahead of such areas as health and income (Campbell, Converse, & Rodgers, 1976). Even Terman's gifted men, with impressive accomplishments already behind them as they entered late adulthood, retrospectively rated a happy family as the most important goal they set for themselves as young men (Sears, 1977).

Despite this overarching importance of family life in adulthood, researchers have not systematically examined the issue of whether and how family experiences change the adult's personality, values, cognitive structures, and mental health. Responsibility for this scientific inadvertence can be attributed in part to professional territoriality. Developmental psychologists historically have studied childhood and the influence of parents on child development. Life-span developmental psychologists have broadened this perspective to include the individual change in adulthood, but as Lowenthal (1977) has observed, this life-span approach has not adequately dealt with the points of articulation between the individual and his/her social systems. Parallel to and apparently uninfluenced by developmental psychology, a number of social and clinical psychologists have conducted research on the marriage relationship.[1] Most of

this psychological research, however, has focused on some aspect of the marriage relationship (e.g., stability, satisfaction, conflict resolution) rather than on the development or mental health of the individual adult. Indeed the only established psychological theories on adult development in marriage and family derive from the psychoanalytic tradition (Benedek, 1959; Blanck & Blanck, 1968).

The bulk of research on marriage and the family (outside of the parent-child socialization literature) has been conducted by family sociologists. This 50-year research tradition is most accessible to the newcomer in the two-volume *Contemporary Theories about the Family* (Burr, Hill, Reiss, & Nye, 1979). Family sociologists have concentrated on the issues of marital stability and adjustment, mate selection, kinship networks, family power and conflict, intergenerational relationships, the family's relationship with other institutions, the family life cycle, and parent-child socialization.

Just as psychology has tended to ignore the family in the development of adults, family sociology has neglected the developing individual in the family. Hartup (1978), on this point, has forcefully criticized family sociology for ignoring the ontogenetic, individual-development aspect of socialization. He suggests that marital satisfaction should be studied not only in terms of changing marital roles but also from the perspective of the cognitive and social development of the individual spouses. Hartup (1978) maintains that "the lack of such a [individual development] perspective has been the

---

[1] Terman (1938) pioneered research on the psychological factors in marital happiness; later scholars included Levinger (1966) on divorce, Luckey (1960) on interpersonal perception and marital satisfaction, Murstein (1970) on mate selection, Ryder (1970) and Raush and colleagues (1963) on early marriage. More recently there has been an upturn in psychologically oriented research on

marriage—e.g., in behavioral marital therapy (Jacobson & Margolin, 1979; Weiss, 1978); in personality and marriage (Doherty, 1980, 1981a; Doherty & Ryder, 1979); and in the areas of social cognition, social exchange, and the marital relationship (Doherty, 1981b; Kelley, 1979).

most serious deficiency in family social science of the past 25 years" (p. 29).

This chapter, then, is concerned with an area that has not received systematic treatment in the research literature, since individual development and family phenomena have been studied by different social scientists. The late 1970s, however, have witnessed a growing realization of this unfortunate lacuna by scholars who are attempting to communicate across disciplines (Hill & Mattessich, 1979; Lerner & Spanier, 1978).

In line with this interdisciplinary trend, this chapter will cover both sociological and psychological theories and research. The focus will be on how experiences in marriage and parenthood influence adult development and mental health. The plan of the chapter is, first, to review contemporary trends in marriage and parenthood; second, to outline theories that have dealt explicitly with the influence of marriage and parenthood on adult development and adult mental health; third, to review empirical research at the interface between the individual and the roles of marriage and parenthood; and fourth, in light of the salience of marriage for most adults, to discuss marital satisfaction and marital distress.

TRENDS IN MARRIAGE AND THE FAMILY

Burgess and colleagues captured perhaps the fundamental change in modern family life in the title of their classic textbook *The Family: From Institution to Companionship* (Burgess, Locke, & Thomes, 1963). Their thesis was that the contemporary family is characterized by a greater emphasis on intimacy and emotional support than was the traditional family. In the authors' words,

The central theme of this book is that in the last few decades the family has been in transition from an institutional to a companionship form. This transition is in part the result of major social changes which have placed families in a radically different environment from that of the past. Important changes are the shift from a rural to an urban society, from stability of residence to mobility, from familism to individualism, and from a relatively short family life cycle to one which continues for years after the children have established homes of their own. All of these changes have occurred in the United States, and most of them have taken place in other countries. Most of the changes result in situations in which impersonal, secondary associations predominate, and the small-family unit becomes the major area of intimate, affectional association. This has resulted in the growth of the companionship family, characterized by the mutual affection, sympathetic understanding, and comradeship of its members. (1963, p. vii)

In light of Burgess et al.'s thesis it may be argued that contemporary marital and parental roles make historically unprecedented demands on the adult's personal resources. A case in point is what Gadlin (1977) calls "the burden of self-fulfillment" placed on marital relationships. Gadlin contends that until about 1930 the goal of a stable marriage was accepted culturally as the legiti-

mate endpoint of adult development. The last 50 years have witnessed the emergence of personal fulfillment both inside and outside of marriage as a counterbalancing value to that of marital stability. Furthermore the emergent norm of male-female equality in marriage has democratized this expectation of personal growth, the burden of which is borne by the erotic and companionship aspects of marriage. As the Skolnicks (1977) have observed, contemporary marriage is both more intense and more fragile than traditional marriage.

Turning from theories about broad cultural changes to the analysis of specific demographic trends in marriage and parenthood, one can find evidence of both stability and drastic change. Stability is indicated in the continuing predilection of Americans for marrying and bearing children. Paul Glick, senior demographer with the Population Division of the U.S. Census Bureau, calculates that the proportion of women who never marry has averaged about 7 percent over the last 80 years (Glick, 1977). Thus over 90 percent of American adults marry at some point in their lives.

More adults were remaining single longer in the late 1970s, however, than in the historically early marrying period of the 1950s and early 1960s. Between 1960 and 1978 the median age at first marriage rose from 22.8 to 24.2 for males and from 20.3 to 21.8 for females. The proportion of never-married 29-year-old women grew by 51 percent between 1960 and 1978, although even in 1978, 87 percent of women were married by age 29 (U.S. Bureau of the Census, 1979a). Glick (1979) believes that the longer this pattern of marriage postponement continues, the more likely that lifelong singleness among adults will increase, but that the marriage rate will still be over 90 percent.

Although most young adults continue to marry as their parents did, many are breaking with tradition by living with someone of the opposite sex outside of marriage. In 1978 there were an estimated 1.1 million "unmarried-couple" households, a 117 percent increase since 1970 (U.S. Bureau of the Census, 1979a). Cohabitation, while constituting a significant social innovation, does not seem to represent a permanent alternative to marriage for most young adults. Research on cohabitation suggests that cohabitation typically serves as a temporary arrangement, ending within a couple of years either in marriage or a breakup (see review by Macklin, 1978).

Just as in the case of marriage, contemporary parenthood demonstrates both continuity and change from the perspective of historical experience. Two noteworthy demographic trends in the twentieth century related to parenthood are the increased proportion of couples who have children and the decreased number of children they bear. On the first point Glick (1977) reports a decrease in the proportion of childless couples from 21.7 percent in the early 1900s to only 10.4 percent in the 1970s. Perhaps because of improved fertility treatments and lower incidence of maternal deaths, a historically high number of married couples now bear children. Although there is some evidence of an increase in the proportion of couples opting for a child-free life style, it is too early to judge the significance of the trend. For example when surveyed by the Census Bureau about lifetime births expected, 5.4

percent of wives ages 18 to 39 answered "none" in 1976 as compared to 3.1 percent in 1967 (U.S. Bureau of the Census, 1978). These figures suggest an upward trend in childlessness but not a widespread rejection of parenthood; rather, the most impressive change in contemporary parenthood has been the trend toward fewer children rather than no children. Young adults marrying in the late 1970s expect to have an average of only two children, down from an average of three to four from the early twentieth century through the 1950s (Glick, 1979). Finally, couples are waiting longer after marriage to have their first child: an average of 24 months during the 1975–1978 period, up from 18 months in the 1970–1974 period and 14 months in the 1960–1964 period (U.S. Bureau of the Census, 1979b).

This lower fertility rate coupled with higher life expectancy has created a major change in the family life cycle: Married couples spend a much longer period as a couple without children at home. As calculated by Glick (1977, 1979), 14 years of child-free living have been added to the family life cycle since the early 1900s. Most of this increase comes in middle age and later, during the empty-nest phase when the couple return to the privacy of their newlywed years.

If marriage and parenthood continue with some modifications to be nearly universal adult roles in American society, the most striking change in the 1970s has been the upsurge of the divorce rate. After a slow historical incline and a post–World War II peak, the divorce rate in the United States became relatively stable until the late 1960s. In 1970 there were 708,000 divorces, a rate of 15 divorces for every 1000 married couples. This means that 1.5 percent of existing marriages ended in divorce during 1970. In 1978 divorces numbered 1,122,000, a rate of 22 divorces per 1000 married couples, indicating that 2.2 percent of marriages ended in divorce (U.S. Bureau of the Census, 1979c). Thus the divorce rate increased 48 percent from 1970 to 1978. Provisional data for 1979 and 1980 indicate that the rate of divorces is continuing to climb (U.S. Dept. of HEW, 1980), although the rate of increase generally has lessened since 1975. The greatest upturn during the 1970s was in the age group 25 to 39 years and not, as some have speculated, in the middle-years group (Glick, 1979). If current divorce rates persist, some demographers estimate that future generations of married couples will experience a greater than 50 percent probability of divorce (Preston & McDonald, 1979).

These divorce figures imply that a considerable proportion of American adults will experience marital distress sufficient to cause a complete breakdown of their marriage. These adults will then spend a period of time in the divorced role (an average of three years) before remarrying (Glick, 1977). Along with this increase in marital disruption, of course, is the increase in single parenthood. Single-parent families headed by the mother increased 55 percent during the 1960s and another 78 percent from 1970 to 1978 (U.S. Bureau of the Census, 1979c). Thus single parenthood is an increasingly common life role for female adults in our society. The single-parent experience is still relatively rare for males, remaining at the level of one-tenth that of women among the divorced population (U.S. Bureau of the Census, 1979a).

A final important change in contemporary marriage and parenthood is the increased participation of wives in the labor force. In 1978 there were more dual-earner couples than couples in which only the husband was employed (U.S. Department of Labor, 1979). This included 51 percent of all wives ages 18 to 34, 43 percent of all mothers, and 41 percent of mothers with a child aged 2 years or younger (U.S. Bureau of the Census, 1979b).

This section on trends in adult roles in marriage and the family may be summarized as follows:

1. Contemporary family roles place a historically unprecedented emphasis on emotional support, companionship, and personal satisfaction.

2. Despite an increase in unmarried cohabitation and the postponement of marriage, marriage continues to be a nearly universal adult role.

3. Over 90 percent of married couples bear children, although there are signs of a small increase in voluntary childlessness.

4. Married couples are living longer and having fewer children, thus extending the "couple alone" period of the family life cycle.

5. Divorce rates reached historically high levels in the late 1970s, dramatically altering the contemporary experience of adulthood.

6. The dual-earner couple is becoming an increasingly normative marital pattern.

CONCEPTUAL FRAMEWORKS

Only two social science theories have devoted more than passing attention to adult development in the context of marital and family relationships. Unfortunately neither approach has spawned systematic empirical research.

Role Theory

Brim (1966, 1968) is a prominent spokesman for the role-theory viewpoint that important adult personality changes occur as a consequence of changes in the adult's social roles. Socialization after childhood, in this view, consists of learning the skills, attitudes, and knowledge required to perform the major roles of adult life successfully, including spouse and parental roles. Socialization may take the form of learning a new role (e.g., getting married) or of adjusting to the alteration of an already existing role (e.g., entering the empty-nest period).

The prime agents of adult socialization, according to role theory, are the various role partners one encounters during adulthood—e.g., wife, employer, child, physician. Each of these partners has a stake in the adult's personality and behavior. Each seeks to mold the adult through rewards and punishments into an attractive or satisfying partner (Brim, 1968). Socialization agents exercising the strongest influence are those engaging in the highest frequency of controlling behavior, those who are most primary or important to the adult, and those who hold the most control over rewards and punishments (Brim, 1966). It should be noted that Brim also discusses self-initiated socialization in adulthood: people changing themselves in social roles in order to be more consistent with internalized, symbolic standards.

In this perspective personality is viewed fundamentally as a system of learned interpersonal relationships.

The obvious deduction is that as these relationships change adult personality changes. In the words of Clausen (1972), a role theorist, "To a very considerable degree personality is anchored in the primary group membership and major role commitments of the individual. Let these change significantly and the person will change" (p. 502).

Within this general theory of socialization, Brim (1968) speculates about the socialization of adults in families under three headings: marriage, parenthood, and changes within family roles. First, the adjustment to marriage requires significant (but unspecified) changes in young adults: "The relationship between husband and wife is probably the most influential relationship of adult life and the major source of demands for socialization upon the young adult" (Brim, 1968, p. 206). The greater the social class or cultural differences between the partners, presumably the greater the socialization and adjustment required. However despite the intuitive appeal of these speculations about socialization in marriage, little theoretical or empirical work has examined this issue from a role-theory perspective.

Second, the adjustment to parenthood, according to Brim, places the adult under the socializing influences of the infant, of other family members such as grandparents, and of society's representatives such as physicians. On this point researchers have found that adults generally agree with Brim that parenthood changes adult character. In interviews with a national probability sample of adults, Hoffman and Manis (1978) found that most adults believe that becoming a parent has far-reaching effects on men's and women's values and characters, in particular, that parenthood makes one a true adult and a more responsible person. From a cross-cultural perspective Gutmann (1975) proposes that parenthood provides for most adults the ultimate source of the sense of meaning in life; men in three cultures said that their characters changed toward greater responsibility, selflessness, and moderation. It has been difficult, however, for scholars to move beyond such general statements to more specific theoretical propositions and testable hypotheses. Just as for marriage the reasonableness of role theory in proposing adult developmental changes in response to parenthood far outstrips the evidence, although a number of studies to be reviewed later suggest that the period of early parenthood is particularly important for adults. A role-theory explanation will stress the burdens involved in the competing role obligations of marriage and parenthood, as well as the socialization into adult responsibilities.

Third, in addition to adjustment to getting married and bearing a child, Brim believes that evolving family roles over the life cycle lead to continued change in the adult. Socialization does not stop at some mythical point of "adjustment." Family relationships are continually changing as members age, are added, and leave and as external forces work their pervasive impact on family members. Role theory assumes that these changes in family relationships influence personality structure and adult mental health.

In summary, role theory offers a framework for beginning the exploration of the impact of marital and family relationships on adult development and adult mental health. The emphasis is on the reaction of the adult to the new and ever-changing demands of marriage and family life. The chief conceptual challenge facing role theorists is to explicate the *processes* by which family events influence adults as well as the *outcomes* of such influence. An even more ambitious task, proposed by Lerner and Spanier (1978), would be to articulate the circular influences of the family on the individual and the individual on the family. These conceptual hurdles involved in applying role theory to adult development are rendered even more difficult by the fact that individuals and families are embedded in cultures and particular historical time periods. Hill and Mattessich (1979) discuss how these contextual issues complicate the building of an integrated model of individual development and family development:

If societal norms and expectations were "frozen," so to speak, the task of building such a model would be straightforward. We could observe the movement of individuals and families from one rung to the next along each of several ladders of development. In reality, however, such movement along easily identifiable ladders does not occur for two reasons. First, society changes the "rules" of development by altering the sets of expectations and roles assigned to individuals of certain ages. Second, historical events occur; so that even if the rules remain constant, different cohorts have dissimilar opportunities for attaining goals. Since social and historical contexts do influence individual and family developmental sequences, and since no two cohorts of individuals or families ever pass through exactly the same series of contexts, much of what we would like to call a universal pattern of development may, in fact, be situationally determined. This presents a problem which scholars of both family development and life-span development have recognized. (1979, pp. 189–190)

One important notion deriving from the study of cohort and historical effects is that of the timing of events during the life course. Elder (1978) maintains that the timing of an event (such as marriage or parenthood) may be as consequential for the individual as whether the event occurs at all. An important reason why timing is crucial is that individuals face age-related norms in every society (Neugarten & Hagestad, 1976; Riley, Johnson, & Foner, 1972). These norms, which are themselves molded by historical trends or events, are thought to constitute a prescriptive timetable for life events.

The impact of marriage and parenthood on adult development may be created not only by socialization processes within the family but also by such factors as the ages at which the marriage and parenthood occur, society's norms for marital and family role behavior, and historical events impinging on the family. At a further level of complexity it should be remembered that adults are engaged in multiple role careers (education, work, civic involvement, as well as family), each of which has its own socialization requirements and timetable. Marriage from this perspective may be viewed as the blending of two complex interdependent life-course careers with the attendant problems of management and synchronization (Elder, 1978). Empirical literature on marital timing, to be discussed later, may be interpreted from this perspective of age-status and life-course analysis.

Psychoanalytic Theory

Although classical psychoanalytic theory tends to view individual psychological development as virtually complete with the achievement of genital maturity, some theorists have proposed that developmental processes extend into adulthood. The most famous discussion of these issues is Erikson's (1963) work on the eight ages of man, with each age or stage involving a core developmental issue. Erikson, however, did not relate his adult stages explicitly to marital or parental events. The "intimacy versus isolation" developmental task, for example, may be resolved in a variety of close friendships as well as in marriage. Likewise "generativity versus stagnation," the issue for the middle years, refers as much to productivity as to parenthood.

For more explicit treatments of the developmental implications of marriage and parenthood, one must turn to Blanck and Blanck (1968) and Benedek (1959). The discussion will begin with marriage. Operating from object-relations theory Blanck and Blanck (1968) propose five major areas of personality growth which may be stimulated by marriage.

1. The final resolution of sexual prohibitions and inhibitions carried over from childhood;
2. The establishment of a new level of object relations, involving the ability to value another person for him/herself independent of one's own state of need;
3. Completion of another cycle of psychological separation from parents;
4. Increased opportunity for exercising personal autonomy within the context of a close relationship;
5. The opening up of new opportunities for positive identifications with features of another person's personality.

In addition to describing these specific developmental opportunities, Blanck and Blanck (1968) speculate that marriage, as a transitional link between adolescence and parenthood, provides the opportunity for the integration of the earlier developmental stages of childhood and adolescence with the emergent stage of young adulthood. The possibilities, on the other hand, are not all sanguine: Failure to complete the developmental tasks of earlier life undermines growth in marriage, just as inadequate marital growth is thought to inhibit effective parenthood. Blanck and Blanck, however, do not extend their analysis into parenthood.

On the subject of developmental implications of parenthood, Benedek (1959) proposes that adults develop in a parallel manner to their children. Briefly she theorizes that reciprocal interaction between parent and child creates structural change in each of the participants. The key processes involved in this change are identification and introjection. Through identification processes the parent internalizes not only an image of the child but also the child's attitude toward the parent (e.g., good parent). Furthermore the parent introjects the gratifying experience of successful mothering or fathering as follows: good-thriving-infant = good-parent-self. Through a combination of these processes, the parent may achieve a new integration of his/her personality, especially the greater resolution of intrapsychic conflicts related to the same-sex parent. Benedek also observes that these processes can work in the opposite direction: bad-frustrating-infant = bad-parent-self, an introjection which interferes with personal integration. Finally, Benedek proposes that each critical period of the child's development re-

vives in the parent related unresolved developmental conflicts (e.g., Oedipal conflicts), with accompanying opportunities for further resolution of these conflicts. Thus the experience of parenthood offers continuing opportunities for achieving higher levels of personal integration for the adult.

In conclusion psychoanalytic theories of individual development in marriage and parenthood offer a rich diet of speculations and insights. More empirically oriented scholars, however, are apt to find these theories vague, difficult to test, and insufficiently sensitive to how historical-cultural changes may influence the relationship between family events and personal development.

EMPIRICAL RESEARCH

As the previous discussion repeatedly emphasized, there is no systematically conducted body of research on the influence of marriage and parenthood on adult development and adult mental health. Much of the relevant research has focused on broad social categories such as marital status and sex, which leave many causal questions unanswered. Especially lacking is psychologically oriented research using cognitive, personality, or behavioral measures in longitudinal designs. Within these limitations there are several content areas in marriage and family studies that shed light on the importance of marriage and parenthood in adulthood. To be discussed in this section are (1) the consequences of marital timing, (2) personality development in marriage and parenthood, (3) marital status and physical and mental health, and (4) the marital life cycle and mental health. The third topic will focus on health differences between married people and the nonmarried, while the fourth topic will emphasize the impact of children on the mental health of married persons.

The Consequences of Marital Timing

The empirical literature on this issue suggests that the decision on when to marry has a pervasive and long-term impact on an adult's life. Most of this research has focused on the consequences of early marriage on future educational attainment, fertility, occupational attainment, income, and marital stability. In his review of this extensive literature, Otto (1979) concludes that early marriage is causally associated with (1) bearing more children and more closely spacing children, (2) attenuated educational attainment, (3) lessened occupational attainment, (4) lower income, and (5) higher marital instability. While the preceding pattern of correlations is clear in both cross-sectional and longitudinal studies, it is less clear in many of the studies whether marital timing exercises an independent effect on these future life events or whether social class, individual differences, or self-selection variables can explain the adult outcomes of early marriage.

Several studies published after Otto's review was completed have employed statistical controls for some of these possibly confounding variables. Using a national probability sample of high school males followed over a four-year period and controlling for social class, initial educational attainment, initial educational aspirations, and IQ, Kerkhoff and Parrow (1979) found that high school marriage had a depressing effect on educational attainment and educational aspirations. Similarly Call and Otto (1977), in a 15-year longitudinal study of about 300 high school males, found that age at marriage had an independent and negative effect on future income, even after a wide range of statistical controls for background variables. However when high school academic performance was controlled for, marital timing did not have an independent effect on educational attainment.

Most of the longitudinal studies of the consequences of marital timing on the individual adult have used male samples. A notable exception is Marini's (1978) 15-year follow-up study of the high school students involved in Coleman's 1961 study of adolescence. After controlling for socioeconomic background, IQ, parental encouragement, educational expectations, and other variables, Marini found that age at first marriage had a powerful negative effect on educational attainment for women, but no independent effect for men.

Finally, two important cross-sectional studies on the impact of marital timing will be described. Hogan (1978) speculated, from a life-course-analysis framework, that each cohort faces a normative timetable for the ordering and timing of the events of early adulthood. In American society the expected *ages* may vary for the tasks of finishing school, getting a job, and marrying, but the *sequence* of these events is normatively fixed. An adult male, for example, is expected first to finish school, then take a job, and then marry. Hogan reasoned that social structures and social supports are geared to assist adults who are following the "natural" sequence. Hence he hypothesized that the normative ordering of school, job, and marriage would reduce substantially the likelihood of a man's first marriage ending in divorce or separation. Analyzing 1973 data gathered by the U.S. Bureau of the Census on 33,500 men aged 20 to 65, Hogan found strong support for this hypothesis. The lowest divorce rate applied to men who followed the normative sequence. At the other extreme were men who married before finishing school; their divorce rate was 29 percent higher than that of the normative group. Men whose pattern was school-marriage-job fell in between these extremes. This analysis, it should be noted, controlled for age at marriage, level of education completed, and marriage cohort.

Finally, Elder and Rockwell (1976) examined the impact of marital timing on the life course of white women who were born shortly before the Great Depression (1925–1929). For this purpose the authors used data from the 1965 and 1970 National Fertility Studies. Based on the 1925–1929 cohort's statistically normative timing of first marriage, the authors divided their sample into three groups based on marital timing: early (under 19), on time or average (19–22), and later (over 22). Elder and Rockwell's findings indicated that early marriage was associated with a life course of relative deprivation: restricted education, inadequate material resources, and a heavy childcare burden. On the other hand women who delayed marriage until their late twenties were more likely to enhance their social-class standing over that of their origin. This was true not only for women who delayed marriage to advance their education and who therefore would be expected to enhance their social

standing but also for women who completed their education with high school. Elder and Rockwell concluded from their data that the timing of marriage was a prime source of differentiation in the life course for pre-Depression women.

In summary while the causal processes are not fully clear and the effects may be stronger for women, the research on the effects of marital timing attests to the potent influence on the adult life course of both age at first marriage and the sequencing of marriage with other events of young adulthood. While the correlates of early marriage are consistently negative in the preceding literature, two studies cited in the next session found positive personality changes occurring after early marriage.

THE INFLUENCE OF MARRIAGE AND PARENTHOOD ON ADULT PERSONALITY DEVELOPMENT

Textbooks on life-span human development typically espouse the idea that the marital and parental roles are important influences on the personalities of adults. Hunt and Hilton (1975) write, "The achievement of sexual and marital relationships constitutes an important landmark in the lives of most individuals. The quality of such relationships has implications for the development of adults" (p. 183). Unfortunately the data to support this commonsense viewpoint are very scanty. Three longitudinal studies, however, can be interpreted as indication that marriage may influence personality changes in early adulthood. It should be kept in mind, however, that causal inferences are not clear in any of these studies and that the first two studies have severe methodological shortcomings.

Dentler and Pineo (1960) examined the relationship between marital adjustment and an indirect measure of personality growth over a ten-year interval. Using the Burgess and Wallin longitudinal pool of 1000 engaged couples, first tested in 1937–1938, they analyzed husbands' data from the fifth year of marriage and the fifteenth year of marriage. Only 40 percent of the original sample were available at the 15-year follow-up. Dentler and Pineo examined the association over time between self-reported marital adjustment and a measure of the personal growth which the respondent felt had accrued to him because of his marriage (e.g., made me happier, made me do better work). This latter scale, of course, is a fairly indirect measure of personality development and is confounded with marital adjustment, but the results are worth summarizing anyway. The authors found that marital adjustment at the fifth year of marriage was a better predictor of later levels of personal growth ($Q = .44$) than initial personal growth was of later marital adjustment ($Q = .25$). When husbands had initially low personal growth scores but high marital adjustment scores at 15 years, over 78 percent moved in the direction of greater personal growth. In contrast initially low marital adjustment was less apt to climb to match high personal adjustment at the fifteenth year. The authors speculate that improved marital adjustment may be an important stimulant for increased personal growth in adult males. Methodological limitations, however, diminish the contribution of this study.

The second study of the influence of marriage on personality was reported by Vincent (1964), who presented his data in percentage form without statistical tests. His sample began in 1954 with 517 male and female high school seniors from suburban San Francisco who completed the California Psychological Inventory (CPI) as part of a larger questionnaire. In 1959, 110 of these young people completed a follow-up questionnaire containing the CPI. Vincent compared the CPI scores of those who had married young (ages 18 to 20 for males, 17 to 18 for females) with the older marriers and the never-marrieds. Results were as follows: (1) The young marrieds had the lowest (least favorable) CPI scores in 1954—e.g., on dominance, sociability and self-acceptance; (2) however, the young marrieds showed the greatest increases in CPI scores over the five-year period, in fact pulling even with the rest of the sample. Vincent concludes that marriage may be a vehicle used by some young people to gain personal maturity in adult society. The absence of statistical tests unfortunately makes this conclusion difficult to support, as does the nearly 80 percent attrition rate and the exclusion of some low CPI subjects from the analysis.

The Vincent data could be easily dismissed on methodological grounds were it not for their striking parallel to the findings of a very sophisticated study by the Youth in Transition Project of the Institute for Social Research (Bachman, O'Malley, & Johnston, 1978). Between 1966 and 1974 these researchers followed a nationally representative group of over 2000 boys from the beginning of tenth grade through five years beyond high school. Though not primarily concerned with personality changes, the study did employ a ten-item measure of self-esteem administered five times to the subjects, as well as measures of interpersonal aggression and drug use. The authors report a self-esteem pattern similar to Vincent's CPI findings among young men who married and became fathers during the course of the study—that is, this group was significantly (though not substantially) lower in self-esteem than nonparents in 1966 but had caught up to the others in self-esteem by 1974.

A similar pattern was found for delinquent behavior and drug use, except that childless marriers and parents were identical in these analyses. Specifically those young men who married and those who became parents before age 23 had shown, during their high school years, higher interpersonal aggression and drug use than those who did not marry or become parents. But at age 23 they were no more aggressive than their peers and showed less increase in alcohol and drug use than single students. Finally, Bachman et al. (1978) report that those who married, and especially those who had children, showed stronger increases in job ambition between 1966 and 1974 than those who remained single. This finding held when relevant statistical controls were applied for earlier job attitudes, educational attainment, and occupational attainment. The married group also had a lower unemployment rate than the singles. While acknowledging that other interpretations are possible for the job-related findings, the authors concluded the "marriage has a positive effect on ambitious job attitudes" (p. 167).

Bachman et al. (1978) found a number of the preceding results surprising, especially the switch of marrieds from maladjusted behavior patterns in high school to more "model citizen" attitudes and behaviors at age 23. Following is the authors' summary statement:

Does marriage tend to "reform" some overly aggressive individuals, and does it decrease the likelihood of drug use? Our findings in this area are suggestive, but not definitive. In each case an alternative path of causation is also plausible. Increases in aggression and drug use in the years following high school may contribute to unemployment and decrease the likelihood of marriage. But the fact that we are dealing with different patterns of change in behaviors, rather than stable differences in behaviors, leads us to favor an explanation in terms of environmental/experiential impact [of marriage and parenthood]. (p. 200)

To conclude this section on personality changes in marriage and parenthood, it should be noted that the most reliable findings (from the Bachman et al. study) pertain only to changes in early marriers and only during the period of young adulthood. However, the findings of higher self-esteem and more prosocial behavior suggest that marriage and parenthood may offer a positive socialization experience into adult roles for previously maladjusted young adults. Much other research discussed previously, however, indicates a variety of longer-term negative consequences of early marriage. Finally, little is known about personality changes for "on time" or "late" marriers, as well as changes that may occur over the marital life cycle.

MARITAL STATUS, PHYSICAL HEALTH, AND MENTAL HEALTH

Campbell et al. (1976) have noted that the strongest correlate of self-reported happiness among American adults—a finding demonstrated across a variety of studies—is simply the individual's marital status. Married people report the highest levels of happiness, followed by the widowed, the separated-divorced, and the never-married or single. Sex differences show up primarily in the never-married group, with males expressing less life satisfaction than do females.

Moving from studies of global happiness to "harder" indices of well-being—namely, physical and mental health—one finds a similar marital status pattern, except that single people tend to fare better than do the separated and divorced. The evidence here is quite persuasive (see reviews by Bachrach, 1975; Bloom, Asher, & White, 1978; Gove, 1973; and Vernbrugge, 1979). Briefly, married people have the lowest rates of (1) mortality; (2) physical illness (including low rates of acute conditions and the lowest rates of limiting chronic ailments and work-limiting conditions); (3) mental disorders, as measured both in patient studies and in population studies; and (4) institutionalization. On most indices when age-standardized data are used (Vernbrugge, 1979), widowed people rank second for physical and mental illness, followed by single people. Separated and divorced people have the lowest health status: highest mortality, including rates of suicide, homicide, and accidental death (Gove, 1973); highest rates of acute conditions, of chronic conditions that limit social activity, and of health-related disability (Vernbrugge, 1979); and the highest admission rates to both outpatient and inpatient psychiatric facilities (Bloom et al., 1978). The only negative health indicator on which the separated-divorced group is not highest is institutionalization, where single people have the highest rates. Finally, Vernbrugge (1979) notes that this same pattern of marital status differentials is sustained when statistical controls are applied for race and income, as well as age.

This mountain of evidence on the health advantages of being married and disadvantages of being divorced cries out for interpretation. Unfortunately there is no single comprehensive explanation that is universally accepted by scholars in this area. As Bachrach (1975) has observed in her discussion of marital status and mental disorders, "There is far less certainty about the reasons for the statistical relationship between marital status and mental disorder than there is about the fact of such relationships" (p. 5).

The central theoretical issue here for the present discussion is whether the marital role confers health benefits on adults or whether already healthy and well-adjusted people tend to both marry and stay married. Logically, of course, either or both alternatives are possible. Since hard experimental evidence is not likely to be forthcoming—short of the social scientist's totalitarian fantasy of random assignment of individuals to marry, stay single, or divorce—the most conservative approach would involve a combination of both a self-selection explanation and a marital-role explanation.

Borrowing on Bachrach's (1975) review of the relevant hypotheses, Bloom et al. (1978) propose such an integrated view of the relationship between marital status and mental disorder. Similar arguments can be made for physical health as well. These authors propose that the selectivity hypothesis can help to explain the relative advantage of the marrieds over the single since health-disadvantaged individuals may have less access to marriage than healthy people. The role-theory hypothesis, on the other hand, asserts that being married carries with it certain social supports which decrease a person's vulnerability to physical and mental disorder. Disruption of the marital role by separation, divorce, or death would cause a loss of this support and impose other difficult adjustments which make a person vulnerable to physical or mental disabilities. This role-theory approach can help to account for the finding that married persons have a more positive health status than previously married persons. Role theory also supplements the self-selection explanation in accounting for the better health status of marrieds vis-à-vis singles.

In the foregoing discussion social support was viewed as the primary vehicle by which marriage conveys health benefits to individuals. While plausible this argument has not received systematic investigation. An interesting review paper by Cobb (1976) may be a start in this direction. Cobb proposed a definition of social support as "information leading the subject to believe that he is cared for and loved, esteemed, and a member of a network of mutual obligations" (p. 300). After reviewing the relevant empirical studies, many of which were not directly testing a social-support hypothesis, Cobb concluded that social support tends to prevent disorders of various kinds as well as enhance recovery from already existing disorders. In Cobb's (1976) summary,

It appears that social support can protect people in crisis from a wide variety of pathological states: from low birth weight to death, from arthritis through tuberculosis to depression, alcoholism, and the social breakdown syndrome. Furthermore, social support may reduce the amount of medication required, accelerate recovery, and facilitate compliance with prescribed medical regimens. (p. 300)

Before a marriage-as-social-support explanation is accepted too readily, it should be noted that there is little clarity about the mechanisms whereby social support protects individuals from illness and disorders. For instance is a married person less exposed to stressors, or is s/he better prepared to cope with already present stressors? Surely the quality of the marital relationship mediates the relationship between marital status and health, although this issue has seldom been explored empirically. Two studies, however, have reported a positive correlational link between measures of marital satisfaction and self-reported physical health status (Renne, 1970; Weiss & Aved, 1978).

Two kinds of research directions may help to elucidate the influence of marriage on physical and mental health. First, longitudinal studies could examine changes in health status that accompany (1) entrance into marriage, (2) marital life-cycle stages (see next section), (3) changes in marital satisfaction during marriage, (4) exit from marriage, and (5) remarriage. Of special importance would be health improvements that occur *after* a person marries or remarries, since this would be the best correlational evidence for the health benefits of the marital role. Second, as suggested by Weiss and Aved (1978), experimental evidence could be gathered by testing whether a successful marital therapy intervention enhances an individual's health status, especially his/her physical health, the measurement for which is not as readily confounded with marital satisfaction as is the measurement of mental health. These issues lead us to the next section's discussion of the impact of different marital life-cycle stages on adult mental health.

The Marital Life Cycle and Mental Health

This section will review some important findings in the area of the marital life cycle and mental health. The discussion will sidestep the controversial issue of whether married women have poorer mental health than do married men. In this regard Gove (1972, 1973, 1979) has mustered evidence that married women tend to have poorer mental health than do married men in modern industrial nations. Gove explains his findings in terms of role differences—i.e., that the wife-mother role, at least since World War II, has become more burdensome and less gratifying, with no comparable change occurring for the husband-father role. Gove's position has stimulated retorts from Bloom et al. (1978), Dohrenwend and Dohrenwend (1976), and others, who criticize Gove for excluding organic and personality disorders from his data and for ignoring other important evidence. In addition Bloom et al. (1978) have observed that the husband-wife differences reported in the literature are quite small in comparison with the mental health differences across marital status groups—e.g., between the married and the divorced. A recent reanalysis of the Dohrenwends' epidemiological data conducted by Rosenfield (1980), however, has bolstered Gove's sex-role argument. Rosenfield found that when wives were not working outside the home they tended to have higher levels of depressive symptoms than did their husbands (the typical pattern). The reverse was true when wives held jobs outside the home: Working women had lower depression scores than did their husbands.

If his overall picture is cloudy, there is some interesting evidence for an interaction of marital life cycle and sex in accounting for the mental health status of married people. Once again there are problems of causal inference with these studies, but in some cases longitudinal data and statistical controls shed light on causal directions.

The marital life-cycle stage that has been most consistently related to mental health and related indices is that of the couple with young children. To begin with there is extensive evidence that the coming of the first child tends to reduce the level of marital satisfaction for many couples. This pattern has been found across a variety of both cross-sectional and longitudinal studies, some of which (e.g., Ryder, 1973) used comparison groups of couples without children (see review by Rollins & Galligan, 1978). In the only study based on interviews with a national probability sample of parents, Hoffman and Manis (1978) reported evidence that marriage and parenthood are particularly stressful during the preschool-children stage. Parents' specific complaints centered around issues of blocked freedom and the wife's overinvolvement in mothering, to the neglect of her wife role.

Although not directly measuring individual mental health, these marital satisfaction studies do suggest that the presence of young children creates important stresses for parents. Research dealing with psychological stress and psychiatric symptoms generally supports this pattern, especially for women. Campbell et al. (1976) reported that married individuals with a child under age six had the highest psychological stress scores of any of the marital status and family life-cycle groups, with the exception of divorced women. For example 19 percent of mothers with a child under six admitted that they worried about having a nervous breakdown.

Drawing from a household survey in Chicago, Gove and Geerken (1977) studied self-reported psychiatric symptoms (anxiety, depression, psychosis) among employed husbands, employed wives, and unemployed wives (housewives). For present purposes the advantage of this study is its breakdown of psychiatric symptoms by age of youngest child. Results indicated that wives with a child under age five had the highest average psychiatric symptoms scores, with housewives scoring slightly higher than employed wives. Housewives with a child under five also scored highest on (1) the experience of incessant demands, (2) the desire to be alone, and (3) the degree of loneliness. Husbands with children under five did not show elevated psychiatric symptoms. All of these data were age adjusted.

The most provocative evidence relating the early parental stage to poorer mental health comes from Brown and Harris's (1978) study of the social origins of depression in women. Brown and Harris conducted intensive clinical interviews with a random sample of 458 women ages 18 to 65 in a borough of London. The authors analyzed how social class, life stages, threatening life change, and vulnerability factors (especially the presence of a confidant) affected the likelihood that a woman would become clinically depressed. Depression was assessed by the traditional Feighner criteria (low mood, sleep disturbances, appetite changes, suicidal ideation) with reliability checks made by consulting psychiatrists. For present purposes the most important findings of this study were related to the life-stage analysis. To begin with, working-class women with a child under age six had the highest prevalence of depression among five life-cycle groups. Specifically among working-class mothers with a child under six, 31 percent were found to have experienced a psychiatric disturbance (mostly depression) during the three months prior to the interview. The lowest rate was for younger women without children, while the other three life-stage categories (youngest child from 6 to 14 years, youngest child 15+ years, and older women without children at home) each showed a disorder rate of about 20 percent. Middle-class women showed no variation across the life-stage categories and were far less apt to have experienced a depression than were working-class women. However further analyses demonstrated that the presence of three or more children under age 14 at home (especially if one of them was under age 6) was associated with greater likelihood of depressive disorder for middle-class as well as for working-class women.

These findings for the presence of young children were so powerful that Brown and Harris labeled the presence of three or more young children at home (especially if one was under age six) a vulnerability factor in the development of depression. Offsetting vulnerability factors were (1) having a husband or male friend who was regarded as a confidant and (2) employment outside the home. On the other hand the absence of a male confidant, the lack of employment, and the presence of three or more children under age 14 at home substantially increased the likelihood of depression when the women had experienced a threatening life event in the past year. It should be noted that the young-children vulnerability factor was not associated with depression in the absence of precipitating life events or difficulties.

Brown and Harris's impressive study supports other research on the unique stresses of the early parental stage. Furthermore this study raises the issue of whether social class mediates the impact of a child under age six. The authors interpret the social-class difference in terms of fewer resources and more problems in the lives of working-class women, who were found to experience a higher rate of severe life events and ongoing major difficulties. Working-class women in the first stage of child-rearing were also much less likely than were middle-class women to report that their husbands served as confidants. In fact Brown and Harris found that the entire class difference in depression was explained statistically by the twin factors of (1) rate of threatening events and difficulties and (2) the presence of a male confidant. It should be kept in mind, however, that the presence of three or more children under age 14 was a vulnerability factor for depression among both middle-class and working-class women, especially if one child was under six. Perhaps the "protections" of middle-class life are not as effective when a mother must cope with several young children, particularly when this mother is a housewife.

(Parenthetically a more recent study of physical symptoms reported by married women found that having three or more children was associated with higher levels of physical health problems [Woods & Hulka, 1979].)

In summary the evidence reviewed here suggests that parenting young children is a uniquely stressful role for married adults in our society, with a negative impact on both marital satisfaction and, at least for women, on individual mental health. Furthermore the negative mental health impact may be particularly strong for housewives.

This evidence must be interpreted somewhat cautiously since there is a self-selection factor involved in becoming a parent and in seeking employment. However it is unlikely that self-selection accounts for all of the findings related to parenting young children, especially since parenthood is a nearly universal experience for married people; rather, it is likely that the demands associated with raising young children create significant stress for parents, especially for mothers. Whether this is a new phenomenon historically is difficult to determine.

Rollins and Galligan's (1978) discussion of role strain offers a plausible role-theory explanation of the stresses on parents when children are young. *Role strain* refers to "stress within a person who perceives that he or she either cannot measure up or has difficulty measuring up to their expectations for their roles" (Rollins & Galligan, 1978, pp. 87–88). In this case the stress derives from the incompatible demands of being spouse and parent, complicated by the needs of dependent young children and by the cultural expectation of personal fulfillment in family relationships. This discrepancy between expectations and actual experience presumably leads to more negative evaluations of self, partner, and marriage, as well as to a greater likelihood of experiencing depression and anxiety. Rollins and Galligan additionally propose that the degree of role strain and marital distress is mediated by personal and family resources, family social status, and a variety of other factors.

Much more empirical work is needed on the issues covered in this section. In particular longitudinal investigations are needed to follow married couples (1) from the transition to parenthood through the years with young children at home and (2) through the transition from the preschool years to the school-age years when cross-sectional studies suggest that the mental health of mothers should improve. Further empirical research is needed to clarify the relationship between maternal employment and mental and physical health. Also meriting attention is the transition to the empty-nest period, which Lowenthal and colleagues (1976) have found to be stressful for women.

MARITAL SATISFACTION AND DISTRESS

In a previous section evidence was cited that a satisfying marital relationship may be the most important determinant of overall life satisfaction. The critical importance of a successful marriage is also supported by the correlational studies establishing the debilitating effects of marital disruption on both physical and mental health (cf. Bloom et al., 1978). Given the seminal importance of marital satisfaction and stability to a generally happy life, we have decided to close this chapter with a selective review of the psychological literature on the determinants of marital satisfaction. A comprehensive review of this issue from a sociological perspective may be found in Lewis and Spanier (1979).

Unfortunately, as has been the case in previous sections, the psychological literature on marital satisfaction is as modest in methodologically sound studies as it is replete with theoretical speculation. Two traditions can be sharply differentiated: (1) the *psychodynamic tradition,* characterized by theoretical comprehensiveness and richness but virtually devoid of supportive research; and (2) the *behavioral or social-learning tradition,* newer and more parsimonious than the psychoanalytic tradition and characterized by a more cautious, but in many ways unsatisfying, series of theoretical postulates and an emphasis on empirical documentation and controlled investigation. As will become apparent in the following paragraphs, the psychoanalytic tradition can be criticized for the lack of rigor in its model, while the behavioral tradition is guilty of a lack of vigor in the pursuit of a complete model of marital satisfaction and distress.

The Psychoanalytic Tradition

To a psychoanalytic theorist the association of marital distress with debilitated physical and mental health would hardly be surprising. Most psychoanalytic theorists, however, would dispute any inferences which attributed causal importance to marital disruption—that is, psychoanalytic theorists are consistent in their attribution of marital distress to neuroticism on the part of the individual spouses (Dicks, 1967; Gurman, 1978; Martin, 1976; Meissner, 1978). Therefore it would follow that marital disruption would be associated with debilitated physical and mental health but not primarily as the *result* of the disruption per se; rather, two psychologically impaired individuals enter into a marital relationship which cannot succeed, and the individuals remain impaired subsequent to the disruption rather than as a function of the disruption.

In order to understand this process from an analytic perspective, it is necessary to begin by examining the process of mate selection. From the literature of dynamically oriented social psychologists (e.g., Winch, 1958) to the more current writings of psychoanalytic clinicians (Dicks, 1967; Meissner, 1978), the process of mate selection is an extension of each individual's intrapsychic struggles begun in their interactions with their families of origin. Each spouse attempts, through the choice of a mate, to find a partner who will be most compatible with his/her unconscious needs. The "need-complementarity" hypothesis (Winch, 1958) states that individuals choose partners who will aid them in the satisfaction or gratification of needs that would otherwise be frustrated or remain ungratified. For example an individual who emerges from his family of origin with an insufficiently gratified need for nurturance may choose an individual who has more adequately resolved this need, or the former individual may select someone with an unresolved need to nurture. The need-complementarity hypothesis has been widely criticized in recent years (Gurman, 1978; Murstein, 1970). These criticisms fall into four basic categories. First, the hypothesis is very inexplicit, which leaves a great many questions regarding the process of mate selection unanswered. There are a great many plausible interpretations for choices which are apparently based on need complementarity, some of which reflect the degree of complexity inherent in any attempt to explain mate selection on the basis of unconscious processes. Meissner (1978) has suggested that apparently complementary needs may obfuscate an underlying similarity of needs, which manifest themselves differently on a behavioral level.

Second, the need-complementarity hypothesis fails to address the possibility that the process of mate selection may differ in successful and unsuccessful relationships. In fact Murstein (1970) has suggested that distressed couples tend to base their choosing of one another on complementarity of needs, whereas happy couples tend to base their choice on similarity of needs.

Third, empirical research designed to test the need-complementarity hypothesis has been inconsistent in its findings and plagued by a variety of methodological problems.

Fourth, as Gurman (1978) has argued, need complementarity is a static construct, which focuses on the process by which one individual chooses another, but fails to address the collaborative nature of this choice, which involves two people simultaneously choosing one another.

In regard to this last point dynamically oriented clinicians have described the process of mate selection as a dyadic one, in which two people simultaneously choose one another. Implicit in this mutual choice is a *contract* (Sager, 1976), in which each agrees to help maintain the other's self-perception and self-esteem and, more importantly, protect the other from the anxiety inherent in the emerging awareness of unresolved, intrapsychic conflicts. This joint venture has been labeled *collusion* by Dicks (1967). It is important to note that not only is the basis for mate selection unconscious in this model but also the collusive bargain is itself unconscious.

Collusion can be adaptive and, indeed, is normally an adaptive process in the case of nondistressed relationships. Marital conflict results when a spouse cannot tolerate the emerging awareness of the partner's actual qualities. Collusion results in idealization, so that in the early stage of marital relationships spouses see each other as their unconscious need structures require that they be seen. As the relationship progresses these unconscious distortions become less tenable as they are repudiated by the conflicting evidence which each spouse provides as a real person. Whether couples will survive the demystification process without severe conflict depends on how important it is to each partner that the idealization be maintained. The *intensity* of each spouse's need to maintain the other as an idealized object will in turn depend on (be inversely proportional to) his/her degree of neuroticism, the developmental sophistication of their intrapsychic conflict, the extent to which each individual is differentiated from his/her family of origin (Bowen, 1976), and the rigidity of their object-relations schemata (Raush, Barry, Hertel, & Swain, 1974).

This model of marital conflict attributed primary importance to spouses' unwillingness to accept the partner as a real person. As a model of marital distress it can be criticized on both empirical and logical grounds. Not only has supportive research evidence not been forthcoming, but it is also difficult to imagine how the major hypotheses from this model could be adequately tested. As is the case with other psychoanalytic formulations, the major concepts are vague, poorly defined, and exceedingly difficult to operationalize. Moreover, on an intuitive level, the position that marital conflict stems from neuroticism on the part of individual spouses is hard to defend in an era when soon one of every two marriages will terminate in divorce. An increasing number of marital therapists are convinced that even well-adjusted individuals can fail in their attempts to maintain a marital relationship (Gurman, 1978).

The Behavioral Tradition

Behavioristic conceptions of marital distress have generally been subsumed under the rubric *behavior exchange theory* (BET) (cf. Jacobson & Moore, in press). In contrast to the psychoanalytic model, BET emphasizes the interactional antecedents of marital conflict rather than the personality characteristics which partners bring with them when they enter into a marital relationship. It is a model which is both hedonistic (cf. Thibaut & Kelley, 1959) and competency-based. Hedonism is reflected in the straightforward proposition that the quality of spouses' outcomes (their reinforcement value for one another) determines their degree of marital satisfaction (Gottman, 1979; Jacobson & Margolin, 1979; Jacobson & Moore, in press; Stuart, 1969; Weiss, 1978). Competency is reflected in the view that successful relationships require the mastery of specific relationship skills and that skill deficiencies in one or more areas can produce marital distress (Gottman, 1979; Jacobson & Margolin, 1979; Weiss, 1978).

The emphasis on the quality of reinforcement as a determinant of relationship satisfaction represents a straightforward application of operant psychology to the analysis of marital dyads, but BET has also incorporated social-psychological exchange theories (Homans, 1961; Kelley & Thibaut, 1978; Thibaut & Kelley, 1959). This essentially *functional* approach to the study of marital conflict has a distinctly ideographic flavor since it emphasizes the rate of reinforcing and punishing exchange without specifying the content or topography of marital reinforcers and punishers. Let us examine the major premises of this model.

Marital distress is primarily a function of the ratio of rewards to punishments produced by behavior exchanges between spouses. This hypothesized functional relationship between overt behavioral exchanges in the relationship and subjective satisfaction comprises the model's essential distinction from the psychoanalytic model. Whereas dynamic models attribute primary causal importance to intrapersonal factors which spouses bring into relationships, BET asserts that characteristics of the relationship itself are the primary determinants of marital satisfaction. The reward-punishment ratio is alleged to determine not only subjective satisfaction but also the tendency to reciprocate positive and negative behavior (Jacobson & Martin, 1976; Patterson & Reid, 1970)—that is, one partner's tendency to direct rewarding (and punishing) behavior toward the other partner can be predicted from the reward-punishment ratio that s/he receives from that partner.

Numerous studies have been conducted to test this hypothesis; the vast majority of them have produced findings which are consistent with the hypothesis (Barnett & Nietzel, 1979; Birchler, Weiss, & Vincent, 1975; Gottman, 1979; Haynes, Follingstad, & Sullivan, 1979; Robinson & Price, 1980; Vincent, Friedman, Nugent, & Messerly, 1979; Vincent, Weiss, & Birchler, 1975; Wills, Weiss, & Patterson, 1974). All of these studies demonstrate, in one form or another, that subjective marital distress can be predicted by the ratio of rewarding-punishing exchanges. Unfortunately while these studies are consistent with prediction derived from BET, none of them are definitely supportive of the behavioral hypothesis (cf. Jacobson, 1979; Jacobson & Moore, in press). The studies are both correlational and cross-sectional, examining already distressed and nondistressed couples; therefore, the causal relationship between rewarding and punishing exchanges, on the one hand, and marital satisfaction, on the other hand, predicted by BET cannot be confirmed. Only one study (Markman, 1979) investigated this relationship longitudinally beginning with couples who were planning to marry and following them for 2½ years. This study produced data which strongly support the behavioral hypothesis since the overall positiveness of couple communication, as rated by the partners themselves, was highly predictive of marital satisfaction 2½ years later.

Marital distress is, in part, the result of deficits in requisite relationship skills, especially conflict resolution or behavior change skills. This competency-based model of marital satisfaction can be credited to the seminal work of Weiss, Patterson, and their associates (Patterson & Hops, 1972; Weiss, 1978; Weiss & Birchler, 1978; Weiss, Hops, & Patterson, 1973). From the beginning BET has focused on deficits in conflict resolution. The basic notion is that in all marital relationships, behavior changes are necessary at various times. When one spouse desires to bring about some behavior change in the partner, the question is, how will s/he go about eliciting that change? Distressed couples are alleged to rely on *aversive control* tactics to bring about changes—using punishment and negative reinforcement. Although research has not been conducted to test this hypothesis directly, Gottman (1979) has reported findings which demonstrate rather consistent deficits in the problem-solving behavior of distressed couples.

Jacobson and Margolin (1979) and Weiss (1978) have elaborated on a variety of additional relationship skills which are required for a successful relationship. Both emphasize general communication skills, such as the provision of support and understanding. Jacobson and Margolin (1979) also discuss the importance of skills in the effective use of leisure time, sexual relations, and the performance of instrumental tasks. As yet there is no direct evidence as to the importance of any of these areas in the development of marital distress.

Distressed spouses are more reactive to, and more likely to reciprocate, their partner's negative behavior than their nondistressed counterparts. In addition to engaging in higher frequencies of punishing behavior than their nondistressed

counterparts, distressed couples seem to emit negative behavior in chains (Gottman, 1979); moreover, on a subjective level negative behavior takes a greater toll on their satisfaction with the relationship than is the case with nondistressed couples (Jacobson, Waldron, & Moore, 1980). Happy couples generally avoid the destructive effects of stringing together long chains of negative behavior and seem to have developed a mechanism for neutralizing its impact (cf. Jacobson & Moore, in press).

Antecedents of Marital Distress

There has been a scarcity of longitudinal research on the determinants of marital distress in the behavioral literature, with the exception of Markman's (1979) study. However Jacobson and Margolin (1979) have speculated on the antecedents of marital conflict. In addition to various relationship skill deficits, especially deficits in conflict-resolution skills which have been suggested by others as important sources of subsequent marital distress (cf. Weiss, 1978), Jacobson and Margolin (1979) have drawn attention to the phenomenon of *reinforcement erosion*, the tendency for spouses to lose their reinforcing potency for one another gradually over time due to habituation. They have also pointed to inflexible and, in other ways, inadequate *rules* as important developmental precursors. Finally, consistent with a social-psychological exchange theory perspective (Thibaut & Kelley, 1959), they argued that factors external to the relationship can create distress, usually by making alternatives to the current marital relationship more attractive.

Other than Markman's (1979) finding that negative communication is predictive of subsequent marital distress, behavioral hypotheses regarding the antecedents of marital distress remain speculative in the absence of supporting research.

Overview and Conclusions

The behavioral perspective has been more ambitious than has been the psychodynamic perspective in subjecting its basic premises to controlled research. However the research has begun to address the fundamental issues in regard to this theoretical perspective, and much of it can be criticized for not really testing the behavioral hypotheses in a definitive way (Jacobson, 1979; Jacobson & Moore, in press). Moreover as we mentioned at the beginning of this section, the model is incomplete in that it fails to address a number of important questions regarding the etiology of marital distress. First, in its present form it is relatively content-free—that is, above and beyond the utility of conceptualizing marital satisfaction in reinforcement terms, the content of topography of effective reinforcers and punishers in marriage remains largely unexplored. Second, the role of cognitive processes in relationship distress needs to be examined since there has been a growing recognition that spouses are not simply passive recipients of stimuli from one another, but rather impose a cognitive structure onto their experience and actively transform the impact of the behaviors delivered to them (Doherty, 1981b; Jacobson & Margolin, 1979; Jacobson & Moore, in press). An understanding of how cognitive processes moderate the effects of behavior exchanges seems essential to a comprehensive model of marital distress, even one which emphasizes overt behavior exchanges.

This concludes the section surveying the literature on the two predominant psychological models of marital distress. It should be clear that in many ways this literature is only beginning to emerge from the prescientific stage. Although there are some promising beginnings, like other areas of research reviewed in this chapter, future contributions are needed before one can claim a definitive body of knowledge on the determinants of a satisfying marital relationship.

REFERENCES

BACHMAN, J. G, O'MALLEY, P. M., & JOHNSTON, J. *Youth in transition* (Vol. 6). Ann Arbor, Mich.: Institute for Social Research, 1978.

BACHRACH, L. L. *Marital status and mental disorders: An analytic review* (DHEW Pub. No. ADM 75-217). Washington, D.C.: U.S. Government Printing Office, 1975.

BARNETT, L. R., & NIETZEL, M. T. Relationship of instrumental and affection behaviors and self-esteem to marital satisfaction in distressed and nondistressed couples. *Journal of Consulting and Clinical Psychology*, 1979, *47*, 946–954.

BENEDEK, T. Parenthood as a developmental phase. *Journal of the American Psychoanalytic Association*, 1959, *7*, 389–417.

BIRCHLER, G. R., WEISS, R. L., & VINCENT, J. P. A multimethod analysis of social reinforcement exchange between maritally distressed and nondistressed spouse and stranger dyads. *Journal of Personality and Social Psychology*, 1975, *31*, 349–360.

BLANCK, W., & BLANCK, G. *Marriage and personal develoment.* New York: Columbia University Press, 1968.

BLOOM, B. L., ASHER, S. J., & WHITE, S. W. Marital disruption as a stressor: A review and analysis. *Psychological Bulletin*, 1978, *85*, 867–894.

BOWEN, M. Family therapy and family group therapy. In D.H.L. Olson (Ed.), *Treating relationships.* Lake Mills, La.: Graphic Press, 1976.

BRIM, O. G. Socialization after childhood. In O. G. Brim & S. Wheeler (Eds.), *Socialization after childhood.* New York: John Wiley, 1966.

BRIM, O. G. Adult socialization. In J. A. Clausen (Ed.), *Socialization and society.* Boston: Little, Brown, 1968.

BROWN, G. W., & HARRIS, T. *Social origins of depression: A study of psychiatric disorders in women.* New York: Free Press, 1978.

BURGESS, E. W., LOCKE, H. J., & THOMES, M. M. *The family: From institution to companionship* (3rd ed.). New York: American Book, 1963.

BURR, W. R., HILL, R., REISS, I. R., & NYE, F. I. (Eds.). *Contemporary theories about the family* (Vols. 1 & 2). New York: Free Press, 1979.

CALL, V. R., & OTTO, L. B. Age at marriage as a mobility contingency: Estimates for the Nye-Berardo model. *Journal of Marriage and the Family*, 1977, *39*, 67–79.

CAMPBELL, A., CONVERSE, P. E., & RODGERS, W. L. *The quality of American life.* New York: Russell Sage Foundation, 1976.

CLAUSEN, J. A. The life course of individuals. In M. W. Riley, M. Johnson, & A. Foner (Eds.), *Aging and society* (Vol. 3). New York: Russell Sage Foundation, 1972.

COBB, S. Social support as a moderator of life stress. *Psychosomatic Medicine*, 1976, *38*, 300–314.

DENTLER, R. A., PINEO, P. Sexual adjustment, marital adjustment and personal growth of husbands: A panel analysis. *Journal of Marriage and the Family*, 1960, *22*, 45–48.

DICKS, H. V. *Marital tensions.* New York: Basic Books, 1967.

DOHERTY, W. J. *Personality and marriage: Toward a theoretical linkage.* Paper presented at the Theory and Methods Workshop, National Council on Family Relations, Portland, Ore., October 1980.

DOHERTY, W. J. Locus of control differences and marital dissatisfaction. *Journal of Marriage and the Family*, 1981a, *43*, 369–377.

DOHERTY, W. J. Cognitive processes in intimate conflict: I. Extending attribution theory. *American Journal of Family Therapy*, 1981b, *9*, 3–13.

DOHERTY, W. J., & RYDER, R. G. Locus of control, interpersonal trust and assertive behavior among newlyweds. *Journal of Personality and Social Psychology*, 1979, *37*, 2212–2220.

DOHRENWEND, B. P., & DOHRENWEND, B. S. Sex differences and psychiatric disorders. *American Journal of Sociology*, 1976, *81*, 1447–1454.

ELDER, G. H. Family history and the life course. In T. K. Hareven (Ed.), *Transitions: The family and the life course in historical perspective.* New York: Academic Press, 1978.

ELDER, G. H., & ROCKWELL, R. C. Marital timing in women's life patterns. *Journal of Family History*, 1976, *1*, 34–53.

ERIKSON, E. H. *Childhood and society.* New York: W. W. Norton & Co., Inc., 1963.

GADLIN, H. Private lives and public order: A critical view of the history of intimate relations in the U.S. In G. Levinger & H. Raush (Eds.), *Close relationships.* Amherst: University of Massachusetts Press, 1977.

GLICK, P. C. Updating the life cycle of the family. *Journal of Marriage and the Family*, 1977, *39*, 5–13.

GLICK, P. C. The future of the American family. *Current Population Reports* (Special Studies Series P-23, No. 78). Washington, D.C.: U.S. Government Printing Office, 1979.

GOTTMAN, J. M. *Marital interaction: Experimental investigations.* New York: Academic Press, 1979.

GOVE, W. R. Sex roles, marital roles, and mental illness. *Social Forces*, 1972, *51*, 34–44.

GOVE, W. R. Marital status and mortality. *American Journal of Sociology*, 1973, *29*, 45–67.

GOVE, W. R. Sex, marital status, and psychiatric treatment: A research note. *Social Forces*, 1979, *58*, 89–93.

GOVE, W. R., & GEERKEN, M. R. The effect of children and employment on the mental health of married men and women. *Social Forces*, 1977, *56*, 66–76.

GURMAN, A. S. Contemporary marital therapies: A critique and comparative analysis of psychodynamic, systems, and behavioral approaches. In T. J. Paolino, Jr., & B. S. McCrady (Eds.), *Marriage and marital therapy from three perspectives.* New York: Brunner/Mazel, 1978.

GUTMANN, D. Parenthood: A key to the comparative study of the life cycle. In N. Datan & L. H. Ginsberg (Eds.), *Life-span developmental psychology: Normative crises.* New York: Academic Press, 1975.

HARTUP, W. W. Perspectives on child and family interaction: Past, present, and future. In R. L. Lerner & G. B. Spanier (Eds.), *Child influences on marital and family interaction.* New York: Academic Press, 1978.

HAYNES, S. W., FOLLINGSTAD, D. R., & SULLIVAN, J. C. Assessment of marital satisfaction and interaction. *Journal of Consulting and Clinical Psychology*, 1979, *47*, 789–790.

HILL, R., & MATTESSICH, P. Family development theory and life-span development. In P. B. Baltes & O. G. Brim (Eds.), *Life-span development and behavior* (Vol. 2). New York: Academic Press, 1979.

HOFFMAN, L. W., & MANIS, J. D. Influences of children on marital interaction and parental satisfaction and dissatisfaction. In R. M. Lerner & G. B. Spanier (Eds.), *Child influences on marital and family interaction.* New York: Academic Press, 1978.

HOGAN, D. P. The variable order of events in the life course. *American Sociological Review*, 1978, *43*, 573–586.

HOMANS, G. C. *Social behavior: Its elementary forms.* New York: Harcourt Brace Jovanovich, 1961.

HUNT, S., & HILTON, J. *Individual development and social experience.* London: George Allen & Unwin, 1975.

JACOBSON, N. S. Behavioral treatments for marital discord: A critical appraisal. In M. Hersen, R. M. Eisler, & P. M. Miller (Eds.), *Progress in behavior modification.* New York: Academic Press, 1979.

JACOBSON, N. S., & MARGOLIN, G. *Marital therapy.* New York: Brunner/Mazel, 1979.

JACOBSON, N. S., & MARTIN, B. Behavioral marriage therapy: Current status. *Psychological Bulletin*, 1976, *83*, 540–566.

JACOBSON, N. S., & MOORE, D. Behavior exchange theory of marriage: Reconnaissance and reconsideration. In J. P. Vincent (Ed.), *Annual review of family theory* (Vol. 2). Assessment and therapy. Greenwich, Conn.: J.A.I. Press, in press.

JACOBSON, N. S., WALDRON, H., & MOORE, D. Toward a behavioral profile of marital distress. *Journal of Consulting and Clinical Psychology,* 1980, *48,* 696–703.

KELLEY, H. H. *Personal relationships.* Hillsdale, N.J.: Lawrence Erlbaum Associates, 1979.

KELLEY, H. H., & THIBAUT, J. W. *Interpersonal relations: A theory of interdependence.* New York: John Wiley, 1978.

KERKHOFF, A. C., & PARROW, A. A. The effect of early marriage on the educational attainment of young men. *Journal of Marriage and the Family,* 1979, *41,* 97–107.

LERNER, R. M. & SPANIER, G. B. A dynamic interactional view of child and family development. In R. M. Lerner & G. B. Spanier (Eds.), *Child influences on marital and family interaction.* New York: Academic Press, 1978.

LEVINGER, G. Sources of marital dissatisfaction among applicants for divorce. *American Journal of Orthopsychiatry,* 1966, *36,* 803–807.

LEWIS, R. A., & SPANIER, G. B. Theorizing about the quality and stability of marriage. In W. R. Burr, R. Hill, F. I. Nye, & I. Reiss (Eds.), *Contemporary theories about the family* (Vol. 1). New York: Free Press, 1979.

LOWENTHAL, M. F. Toward a sociopsychological theory of change in adulthood and old age. In J. E. Birren & K. W. Schaie (Eds.), *Handbook of the psychology of aging.* New York: Van Nostrand Reinhold, 1977.

LOWENTHAL, M. F., THURNHER, M., CHIRIBOGA, D., & Associates. *Four stages of life.* San Francisco: Jossey-Bass, 1976.

LUCKEY, E. B. Marital satisfaction and its association with congruence of perception. *Marriage and Family Living.* 1960, *22,* 49–54.

MACKLIN, E. D. Review of research on nonmarital cohabitation in the United States. In B. I. Murstein (Ed.), *Exploring intimate life styles.* New York: Springer Publishing Company, 1978.

MARINI, M. M. The transition to adulthood: Sex differences in educational attainment and age at marriage. *American Sociological Review,* 1978, *43,* 483–507.

MARKMAN, H. J. Application of a behavioral model of marriage in predicting relationship satisfaction of couples planning marriage. *Journal of Consulting and Clinical Psychology,* 1979, *47,* 743–749.

MARTIN, P. *A marital therapy manual.* New York: Brunner/Mazel, 1976.

MEISSNER, W. J. The conceptualization of marriage and marital disorders from a psychoanalytic perspective. In T. J. Paolino, Jr., & B. S. McCrady (Eds.), *Marriage and marital therapy: Psychoanalytic, behavioral, and systems theory perspectives.* New York: Brunner/Boyd, 1978.

MURSTEIN, B. I. Stimulus, value, role: A theory of marital choice. *Journal of Marriage and the Family,* 1970, *32,* 465–481.

NEUGARTEN, B. L., & HAGESTAD, G. O. Age and the life course. In R. H. Binstock & E. Shanas (Eds.), *Handbook of aging and the social sciences.* New York: Van Nostrand Reinhold, 1976.

OTTO, L. B. Antecedents and consequences of marital timing. In W. R. Burr, R. Hill, F. I. Nye, & I. L. Reiss (Eds.), *Contemporary theories about the family* (Vol. 1). New York: Free Press, 1979.

PATTERSON, G. R., & HOPS, H. Coercion, a game for two: Intervention techniques for marital conflict. In R. E. Ulrich & P. Mounjoy (Eds.), *The experimental analysis of social behavior.* New York: Appleton-Century-Crofts, 1972.

PATTERSON, G. R., & REID, J. B. Reciprocity and coercion: Two facets of social systems. In C. Neuringer & J. L. Michael (Eds.), *Behavior modification in clinical psychology.* New York: Appleton-Century-Crofts, 1970.

PRESTON, S. H., & MCDONALD, J. The incidence of divorce within cohorts of American marriages contracted since the Civil War. *Demography,* 1979, *16,* 1–25.

RAUSH, H. L., BARRY, W. A., HERTEL, R. K., & SWAIN, M. A. *Communication, conflict and marriage.* San Francisco: Jossey-Bass, 1974.

RAUSH, H. L., GOODRICH, W., & CAMPBELL, J. D. Adaptation to the first years of marriage. *Psychiatry,* 1963, *26,* 368–380.

RENNE, K. S. Correlates of dissatisfaction in marriage. *Journal of Marriage and the Family,* 1970, *22,* 54–67.

RILEY, M. W., JOHNSON, M., & FONER, A. (Eds.). *Aging and society* (Vol. 3). New York: Russell Sage Foundation, 1972.

ROBINSON, E. A., & PRICE, M. G. Pleasurable behavior in marital interaction: An observational study. *Journal of Consulting and Clinical Psychology,* 1980, *48,* 117–118.

ROLLINS, B. C., & GALLIGAN, R. The developing child and marital

satisfaction of parents. In R. M. Lerner & G. B. Spanier (Eds.), *Child influences on marital and family interaction.* New York: Academic Press, 1978.

ROSENFIELD, S. Sex differences in depression: Do women always have higher rates? *Journal of Health and Social Behavior,* 1980, *21,* 33–42.

RYDER, R. G. Dimensions of early marriage. *Family Process,* 1970, *9,* 51–68.

RYDER, R. G. Longitudinal data relating marriage satisfaction and having a child. *Journal of Marriage and the Family,* 1973, *35,* 604–608.

SAGER, C. *Marriage contracts and couple therapy.* New York: Brunner/Mazel, 1976.

SEARS, R. R. Sources of life satisfactions of the Terman gifted men. *American Psychologist,* 1977, *32,* 119–128.

SKOLNICK, A. S., & SKOLNICK, J. H. *Family in transition* (2nd ed.). Boston: Little, Brown, 1977.

STUART, R. B. Operant-interpersonal treatment for marital discord. *Journal of Consulting and Clinical Psychology,* 1969, *33,* 675–682.

TERMAN, L. W. *Psychological factors in marital happiness.* New York: McGraw-Hill, 1938.

THIBAUT, J. W., & KELLEY, H. H. *The social psychology of groups.* New York: John Wiley, 1959.

U.S. Bureau of the Census. Characteristics of children and youth. *Current Population Reports* (Special Studies Series P-23, No. 66). Washington, D.C.: U.S. Government Printing Office, 1978.

U.S. Bureau of the Census. Marital status and living arrangements: March, 1978. *Current Population Reports* (Series P-20, No. 388). Washington, D.C.: U.S. Government Printing Office, 1979a.

U.S. Bureau of the Census. Population characteristics. *Current Population Reports* (Series P-20, No. 341). Washington, D.C.: U.S. Government Printing Office, 1979b.

U.S. Bureau of the Census. Divorce, child custody and child support. *Current Population Reports* (Special Studies Series P-23, No. 84). Washington, D.C.: U.S. Government Printing Office, 1979c.

U.S. Department of Health, Education and Welfare. *Monthly Vital Statistics Report,* May 1980, *29*(No. 2).

U.S. Department of Labor, Bureau of Labor Statistics. *Employment in perspective: Working women* (Report No. 555). Washington, D.C.: U.S. Government Printing Office, 1979.

VERNBRUGGE, L. M. Marital status and health. *Journal of Marriage and the Family,* 1979, *41,* 267–285.

VINCENT, C. E. Socialization data in research on young marriers. *Acta Sociologica,* 1964, *8,* 118–127.

VINCENT, J. P., FRIEDMAN, L. L., NUGENT, J., & MESSERLY, L. Demand characteristics in observations of marital interaction. *Journal of Consulting and Clinical Psychology,* 1979, *47,* 557–566.

VINCENT, J. P., WEISS, R. L., & BIRCHLER, G. R. A behavioral analysis of problem-solving in distressed and nondistressed married and stranger dyads. *Behavior Therapy,* 1975, *6,* 475–487.

WEISS, R. L. The conceptualization of marriage from a behavioral perspective. In T. J. Paolino & B. S. McGrady (Eds.), *Marriage and marital therapy: Psychoanalytic behavioral and systems perspectives.* New York: Brunner/Mazel, 1978.

WEISS, R. L., & AVED, B. M. Marital satisfaction and depression as predictors of physical health status. *Journal of Consulting and Clinical Psychology,* 1978, *46,* 1379–1384.

WEISS, R. L., & BIRCHLER, G. R. Adults with marital dysfunction. In M. Hersen & A. S. Bellack (Eds.), *Behavior therapy in the psychiatric setting.* Baltimore, Md.: Williams & Wilkins, 1978.

WEISS, R. L., HOPS, H., & PATTERSON, G. R. A framework for conceptualizing marital conflict, technology for altering it, some data for evaluating it. In L. A. Hamerlynck, L. C. Handy, & E. J. Mash (Eds.), *Behavior change: Methodology, concepts, and practice.* Champaign, Ill.: Research Press, 1973.

WILLS, T. A., & WEISS, R. L., & PATTERSON, G. R. A behavioral analysis of the determinants of marital satisfaction. *Journal of Consulting and Clinical Psychology,* 1974, *42,* 802–811.

WINCH, R. F. Mate selection: A study of complementary needs. New York: Harper & Row, Pub., 1958.

WOODS, N. F., & HULKA, B. S. Symptom reports and illness behavior among employed women and homemakers. *Journal of Community Health,* 1975, *5,* 36–45.

38

Motherhood

TIFFANY MARTINI FIELD
SUSAN M. WIDMAYER

Is any one of us mature enough for children before the children are born? The value of motherhood is not that mothers produce children but that children produce mothers. (Paraphrased from Peter DeVries, *Through the Valley of Clover*)

Bowlby wrote in 1953 that "what is believed to be essential for mental health is that an infant and young child should experience a warm, intimate, and continuous relationship with his mother . . . in which both find satisfaction and enjoyment" (p. 13). Bowlby referred to this relationship as *attachment* and to its absence as *separation.* Two decades later Toffler (1970) stated that the "mystique of motherhood" was about to be "killed off" and suggested that woman's importance would no longer reside in her ability to bear children. According to Toffler biological parenthood, the "greatest single preserve of the amateur," must soon give way to parenthood by professionals, perhaps in an extended-family setting, as the so-called nuclear family is "racing toward oblivion" (Toffler, 1970).

The significance of this apparent ideological dichotomy has been reevaluated time and again in the last decade, particularly in light of the personal and economic imperatives which have resulted in ever-increasing numbers of working mothers. Contemporary technological insights which have made artificial insemination and in vitro embryonic development commonplace on the dairy farm are increasingly seen to have application in human society. Reproductive engineering, economic pressures, and changing self-concepts of women may combine to make the role of "motherhood" unrecognizable to us within the next two decades and Toffler's predictions the substance of a new society.

A consideration of prime importance, of course, is the nature of motherhood. Is "mothering" instinctual? What is the impact of hormones on psychophysiology in pregnancy and in the postpartum period? If mothering is primarily learned behavior, what are the societal pressures which reinforce the behaviors of mothers and their offspring?

This chapter will attempt to deal with some of these issues from a comparative and ethological perspective. It will also trace some of the life-span experiences of motherhood from pregnancy through the development of the child into adulthood. Insofar as possible problematic patterns of mothering will be considered as well so that we may be advised that even in the "Brave New World" of the 2000s the well-being of the child must be a primary goal of society.

MOTHERHOOD AS INSTINCTUAL BEHAVIOR

It has been suggested that the positive orientation of a mother toward her offspring is instinctive in nature. "The pattern of parental care, being a biological trait like any other, is genetically programmed and varies from one species to the next" (Wilson, 1975, p. 336). Diversity in degree of maternal involvement has been attributed to levels of social complexity which, in turn, is loosely related to brain size and intellect. In many insect societies, however, there appears to be little or no relationship between the complexity of social organization and the degree of attention paid to the young.

The preparation of this chapter was aided by a social and behavioral sciences research grant from the National Foundation-March of Dimes and by grants from the Administration of Children, Youth and Families HEW, OHD 009CI-764-01 and 90-C-1964(2).

681

Insect Societies

The burying beetles of the genus *Necrophorus,* for example, display an advanced form of parental care among insects, despite their comparatively simple social structure. Both male and female work together to excavate the soil beneath the body of a dead vertebrate where the female lays her eggs. Both female and male subsequently work together to feed the young. The honey bee, *Apis mellifera,* on the other hand, who appears to have attained one of the summits of social evolution among insects, has no contact whatsoever with her young. The worker bees fully provision each brood cell with nectar and pollen at the onset. The nurse worker then visits the larval cells repeatedly, cleaning them and placing fresh food nearby. When the larva hatches it feeds on the provisions stored around it, grows through each molt, and pupates all entirely on its own. Larvae of some species of ants, *Monomorium Pharaonis,* and wasps, *Vespula Vulgaris,* have been noted to provide food to the workers of the colony through their salivary secretions. The lives of these workers are thus prolonged until such time as the larvae reach maturity. Such relationships, even among the most primitive of insects, suggests a fundamental instinctual urge to preserve the young among the members of the society, regardless of whether the true parents are active participants.

Animal Societies

Among species more highly placed on the phylogenetic scale, there appears to be less influence of pure economics. The tree shrews, for example, have the most primitive form of parental care among vertebrates. Their parenting is characterized by absenteeism on the part of the mother who visits her young every 48 hours when she permits them to suckle her milk in a most unsystematic way. The odor of the infant's urine is so repulsive to the adults of the community that parents forced to remain too close to their young often kill and eat them.

Among more advanced primate societies there appears to be a more direct relation between social complexity and involvement with the young. Wilson (1975) suggests that the profile of parental investment is determined by what he designates as *environmental prime movers,* as well as by the personal contribution of the mother to her offspring. The environmental prime movers include seasonal availability of food, temperature variation, and predator pressure, while the mother's personal contribution is measured by the length of the gestation period, the larger the size of offspring at birth, and the greater the period of dependency of the offspring. The offspring of certain mammals, such as baboons and deer, are extremely dependent on the adult, most often the mother, for the acquisition and perfection of social acts. In general the female and her young make up the most elementary social unit among mammals. If necessary for defense against predators, the mother and her offspring may aggregate into larger groups. On occasion there may exist a male-female pair which together work for the provision of food for the young. This is frequently the case among wolves, for example.

The most important element binding the baboon troop together is the newborn infant, who at once becomes the center of interest and may absorb the attention of the entire community. Among the baboons child-rearing is essentially a group activity, and after the first week or two the mother will allow juvenile females, dominant males, and others to carry and play with the infant. In fact adult males will protect a young baboon long after its mother has become involved with her next offspring. Any adult with an infant in his arms is immune from attack by others.

During its first few weeks of life, the infant baboon clings to its mother's belly upside down as she moves with the troop. As time passes it becomes progressively more independent and spends more and more time feeding and playing at a distance. By the age of two or three, the baboon is a juvenile and spends all its waking hours fighting and playing within the protective circle of the troop, receiving the most attention from its peers while male and female adults become more involved with its younger siblings. If a baboon dies in infancy, its mother will carry it for several days and finally simply drop it as she moves with the troop. It could be said that among the African baboons of Kenya the entire social organization revolves around the well-being of the infant with every member of the troop acting to protect the mother and infant from predators.

The chimpanzee is considered to be man's closest "relative" and, as such, to portray the most complex level of social organization among the primates. The chimpanzee's brain is approximately twice the size of a baboon's, though considerably smaller than that of humans. Its period of gestation is 225 days compared with approximately 280 days for the human fetus, but the infant chimpanzee is considerably more precocious than is the human infant, reaching childhood at approximately three years of age compared to six years in humans. The newborn chimp has very poorly developed vision and is continually held and nursed by its mother for the first few days of life. The chimpanzee mother spends much time playing with her infant, and at about five months of age, the chimp takes its first quadrupedal steps, climbs on small branches, and begins to eat solid foods. As it perfects its walking, the chimp's social milieu continually expands as it leaves its mother to be patted and groomed by other adults and to play with older infants, juveniles, and adolescents. By three years the chimp is weaned, and with increasing frequency the mother rejects the infant's attempts to nurse, though she continues to protect it from other chimps. During the juvenile stage of about seven years, the chimp makes its own nest but continues to move about with its mother, without attempting to suckle or ride on her back. With adolescence the chimp attains sexual maturity and begins its long initiation into adult society.

In the absence of any troop structure, it appears that the mother-infant bond among the chimpanzees is more enduring and perhaps more intense than among the baboons. A mother, alone and independent of ties with other adults, takes on more individual responsibility for her infant. If she is killed or loses the infant, there is no permanent cluster of individuals to protect it from predators or to help it to find food.

Both the baboon and the chimpanzee appear to give birth at the most optimal season for gathering so that there is little competition for food, which is found in abundance. Among societies of animals which reside in areas of few resources, there appear to be fewer positive feelings toward the newborn infant. The social structure itself may also mitigate against the survival of even healthy infants. Hrdy (1978) has studied the behaviors of India's sacred monkey, the hanuman langur, and has reported the regular practice of infanticide by males struggling for dominance. The mother resists initially and then appears to become quite passive as her young are systematically destroyed. The mother herself will routinely abandon a wounded or malformed infant, leaving it to starve and to be prey for predators. Consequently only about half of the langurs survive infancy.

Among insects and even among man's closest "relatives," the primates, there appear to be multifarious economic, social, and personal imperatives contributing to the survival of the individual infant. The mother acts in unison with the genetic altruism of the society of which she is a member, even when it demands that she abandon or slay her own infant.

The predominance of the so-called instinct of motherhood, thought to include even self-ablation for the survival of the offspring, may be questioned, therefore, among the least organized societies of insects where there are few social pressures, as well as among the highly organized primates where there are many. The survival of the infant depends, rather, on the probabilities of the most optimal replication of the gene pool of each community. The "instincts" of the mother to deliver, shelter, and nurse her young appear to be secondary to the concerns of the community as a whole.

Human Societies

An explication of the instinctive nature of mothering in human communities is far more complex than are profiles of this phenomenon among insect societies or even among the primate groups cited above. The level of social complexity attained in technologically advanced human communities, while so closely linked to economic subsistence patterns, is also strongly influenced by societal pressures unknown in less intelligent species. For example it has been found necessary in some societies in more recent decades to formulate laws in order to protect offspring from physical, and even psychological, abuse.

One of the first recorded references to human motherhood is that found in Genesis, "The man named his wife 'Eve' because she was the mother of all those who live" (Genesis 3:20). This description occurred immediately after the Fall in which the woman was cursed, "I will multiply your pains in childbearing, you shall give birth to your children in pain" (Genesis 3:16), an unfortunate beginning, perhaps, to this relationship which Freud was later to hold primarily responsible for the development of the personality and the prototype of all later love relationships.

History presents myriad accounts of the dangers which surrounded infants and children of every era, many of which occurred in the child's family. Infanticide, mutilation, and abandonment were common throughout the world through the late nineteenth century, particularly in areas where severe environmental pressures made it socially or economically unfeasible to sustain the lives of unproductive members of the commu-

nity for long periods of time. With the Industrial Revolution in Europe, few mothers appear to have objected when their four-year-olds worked 18 hours a day in sweatshops or coal mines. Societal considerations took precedence over any residual mothering "instinct." This also appears to have been the case among the wealthier classes who farmed their infants out to wet nurses for the first eight to ten years of their lives. Fewer than 50 percent of these children survived childhood.

In more recent times among so-called primitive human societies, attitudes toward children are no less hostile and, in some communities, only a fraction of the children survive to the age of five or six. A glaring example are the Ik of Northern Uganda who were required to change their economy from one based on hunting and gathering to agriculture (Turnbull, 1973). The reservation on which they were forced to live was so barren that most of the people were malnourished and some were starving. The acquisition of food became the predominant value in the lives of these people, and the existence of children was a threat to the survival of their parents. Consequently the children of the Ik were not recipients of parental solicitude even as they were dying. The Mundugumor people of New Guinea, the Yanomamö tribe of the Orinoco River region of South America, the Rajputs of India, and other primitive peoples of contemporary times routinely practice infanticide, particularly with female offspring.

A matter of considerable concern in contemporary Western society is the prevalence of child abuse. In the United States today approximately 550,000 children a year suffer from parental abuse and neglect. The largest killer of children is childhood accidents, a relatively unstudied phenomenon but one which is thought to relate to neglect or at least failure to protect. A large proportion of these infants and children are sickly and demand more than the usual amount of care from their parents. In other instances the parents found the children to be too much of an economic burden.

In summary it is a misconception to view motherhood as an "instinctive" behavior, particularly in more complex societies. It is more likely learned behavior which is subject to numerous environmental pressures.

MOTHERHOOD: SYNCHRONY TOWARD INDEPENDENCE

Cultural Imperatives

Motherhood among middle-class people in the United States is rarely researched. Most public school systems have no curricula on the physiology and psychology of pregnancy and motherhood, much less on childcare. The assumption is, perhaps, that the parents will prepare the young woman or young man for parenthood or that experience with younger brothers or sisters will provide the needed background. These are unfortunate assumptions since most young adults in the United States become totally responsible for another human being knowing less about it than they do about the latest disco group or the most recent issue of the *Rolling Stone* magazine.

At one time couples had babies because it was expected, and not to do so suggested some physiological impediment or excessive self-centeredness. The trend away from mindless childbearing appears to be growing in strength, and more and more middle-class Americans choose not to have children or to have only one or two. Nevertheless the numbers of unmarried teenage mothers from many socioeconomic strata remain high, perhaps due to the failure of the parents and the community to impress upon adolescents the awesomeness of the responsibilities which they undertake as parents and also perhaps due to a culture which values conspicuous consumerism above all, even in interpersonal relationships. For the southern black teenage mother, for example, pregnancy is a sign of fulfillment, no more and no less meaningful than her middle-class counterpart's first car.

Single-parenting and co-custody have become increasingly popular as the number of divorces increases as has the adoption of children by unmarried persons as the number of refugees from southeast Asia and other areas continues to mount. All of these ways of becoming responsible for children are types of "mothering," but it may be that comparatively few individuals can be successful at it.

The following short illustration of "motherhood" may be helpful in demonstrating the unique physical and emotional demands which are inherent in mothering. The characters represented are modal Americans of the mid-twentieth century with no training and little experience in child-rearing but whose prognosis for success is good due to the support provided by the society whose future depends upon the development of intelligent and adaptable offspring.

An Experience in Mothering

In any daily newspaper a reader may find a short account like the following:

Died. Mrs. June Arthur, 68, on Saturday evening after a short illness. Mrs. Arthur was a fifth-grade teacher at Springdale Elementary from 1948 to 1976. She is survived by her husband, Charles, her daughters, Sara and Grace, and her sons, Richard and Charles, Jr. Mrs. Arthur also leaves three grandchildren. Services will be held on Thursday, November 8, at 10 A.M. at St. John's Episcopal Church.

This short paragraph is rich in meaning for Mrs. Arthur's family and friends, though passed over with little thought by contemporaries who never knew her. Social historians of the next century would use such an account for their data bank and may even wonder how their ancestors attempted to complete such a life-consuming task so frequently. Forty-five years before this paragraph was written, June Arthur was a newlywed in the suburbs of a large east coast city. Her husband was an accountant who had not yet passed the CPA exam but who had much hope that the world would survive the Depression and that he would be able to provide "the good life" for his wife and family.

Pregnancy was largely unknown to June. She and her husband had decided prior to their engagement that they wanted children after they were married. In the early days after the realization that this decision was to become a reality, June could think of no substantial reason why she had wanted a child. It simply appeared to be the "appropriate thing to do." June had not worked in the year since her marriage, there was little to keep her

occupied, and sometimes she felt that the child might provide a stronger bond between Charles and herself.

June's ambivalence was dissipated somewhat in seeing Charles's excitement and solicitude for her and in the encouragement expressed by family and friends. During the first trimester, however, June's thoughts became increasingly anxious, alternately worrying about the medical bills, whether she and her husband could maintain the closeness of their relationship, and whether she was really ready to take on the responsibility of motherhood. June carried saltines everywhere both to relieve the nausea and to assuage her ever-increasing hunger, gained weight too quickly, and was soundly berated by her doctor for her lack of self-control. During these days June became increasingly sensitive to her physical appearance and to Charles's slightest omissions of attention, alternating between periods of much elation and "the blues."

Around the fourth month June felt the baby move or "quicken," and her thoughts began to transcend the anxieties of the first three months. For the first time she recognized this infant as a separate entity, independent in some way from herself. June no longer fought the idea of being pregnant but accepted the inevitable and consequently appeared to be much happier during the second and third trimesters. Her thoughts began to center about the experience of childbirth itself, worrying about whether she would be able to cope with the long labor and the extreme pain, and whether the baby would be "all right."

By the beginning of the ninth month, June was having restless nights, was visiting the obstetrician every week, and was very anxious to have the whole ordeal over. In general the pregnancy had gone well. June had gained 22 pounds, had edema in her ankles and hands, and her blood pressure was consistently higher than it had been prior to pregnancy, but there was nothing to worry about according to the doctor. Nevertheless June was physically and emotionally exhausted when the baby was born, a week later than anticipated.

Despite the unspoken stresses the baby arrived, and June, anesthetized and asleep, missed her baby's first cry. Exhaustion, postpartum depression, and hospital routines found her alone (and her pacing husband alone) several hours before finally seeing their baby.

The next nine months were more crowded than the first with hurdles or milestones of development for her infant and herself. Trials and tribulations of feedings were accompanied by pleasantries of first smiles and horrific episodes of colic attended by endless pacing and sleepless nights. Her days were punctuated by signs of the baby's emerging independence—crawling, the first steps—and by efforts to baby proof the house for the persistent, perseverant preambulator.

The first words, *da da* (easier to pronounce than *ma ma*), were followed shortly by pointing commands and demands for everything in sight, a stream of chatter and finally the terrible two's, the arrival of a second child, and a painful case of sibling rivalry. Ear infections and hospitalization for the first-born followed closely on the heels of the birth of the second-born, a first and second affliction of separation anxiety for the first-born child.

The ultimate in separation came soon after with nursery school. The child, the mother's fast friend and companion, was suddenly leaving. There were tears, a clinging child, and a mother who wanted to remain but who had another at home who needed her. The child was no longer hers alone. He belonged to his teacher, his peers, his 3 *R*'s, his homework, his sports, and his daydreams; she was now his driver, his helper, his tutor, and his facilitator.

There followed years of joy for little successes, of sorrow for small failures, of anger for petty feuds, of seesawing between dependency and autonomy like a love affair. The child soon moved into adolescence and flirtation with adult ways, ideas, and desires, while the parent prematurely attempted to befriend and to relate. The adolescent had left for a world of his own, first psychologically and then physically. Marriage marked the ultimate leave-taking, and then there were grandchildren, similar but different from her own. Two decades of motherhood passed slowly and quickly, two decades of a life span about which we know very little.

Four decades later motherhood remains, perhaps more complex, perhaps more simple. Some titles of articles in *The Working Mother*, 1979, read like titles of *Good Housekeeping*, 1939; some do not: "Does working wreck some marriages? Sometimes the job is just the last straw"; "Who's doing the driving today? Suzie needs a ride to Girl Scouts, Eddie has a football game . . ."; "The trouble at school"; "I chose the night shift"; "Guess who's coming to dinner, Mom?"; "Does it pay to work part time?"; "How to hire household help"; "The truth about sick days: Why women stay home"; "Helping with homework"; and "Take care of yourself." Popular magazines seem to have a finger on the pulse of motherhood, but where is the research that can legitimize the words they print?

Motherhood—An Unexplored Phenomenon or a Poor Stepsister to Childhood

Developmental psychologists have viewed and studied the "motherhood," and indeed the "fatherhood," phenomena largely in the context of their effects on children. Although we have come to believe that there's something special about motherhood—and fatherhood—the "something special" is measured in terms of the child. The child derives nurturance from the mother and experiences a strong attachment that is critical to his/her development, but what does the mother derive?

Although we have begun to talk about the child's effects on the mother since Bell (1968), Lewis and Rosenblum (1974), Schaffer (1977), and others have reminded us that there is reciprocity in mother-child relationships, we have measured the child's effects on the mother almost exclusively in terms of maternal behaviors. We rarely ask the mother how motherhood feels, how it affects her life and personality, and just what motherhood means. So we know very little about the impact of motherhood on mothers except for the ways in which their behaviors are modified by this experience. The hurdles or developmental milestones of motherhood are child-related. There is pregnancy, followed by delivery, followed by feeding and the first smile, then crawling, weaning, walking, talking, terrible two's, school, adolescence, marriage, sons- or daughters-in-law, and grandchildren. Motherhood, viewed in the context of the object of moth-

ering—i.e., the infant, child, adolescent, and young adult—can be said to replicate life-span development, a fairly new area to the field of developmental research. Viewed as two or three decades in the life of an adult, motherhood is also left in a relatively unexplored area of developmental psychology—that of adulthood, a developmental stage without a journal. No one will claim motherhood, except as an independent variable, a confederate, a main effect; or perhaps, the study of the effects of motherhood on mothers is just in its infancy in the field of developmental psychology.

MOTHERHOOD BY STAGES

Pregnancy and Delivery

The perinatal, infancy, and childhood literatures feature mothers who experience stresses during pregnancy and delivery, mothers in interaction with their infants, and mothers' attitudes toward their children. In the same literatures there appear problems of mothering, all of which bear on the questions of motherhood and its impact on mothers. These, then, are the literatures we can review at this time.

Although preparation for motherhood may begin long before pregnancy—as seen in the very early pretend play of children fighting over who is to be the mother—the first real feeling of motherhood may coincide with the pregnant woman's first real sensation of the child inside her, curiously called *quickening*. While there are little data on that beginning, some researchers have recorded or asked mothers to record fetal activity (kicks, squirms, and hiccups). These studies have not focused on the effects of fetal activity on the mother as dependent variables, but rather on the changing incidence of these movements during pregnancy (Kellogg, 1941; Newberry, 1941; Walters, 1964), the relationship between fetal activity and infant development (Walters, 1965), and the high fetal activity and infant hyperactivity of those whose mothers suffered emotional trauma throughout pregnancy (Sontag, 1963). Others have stimulated fetal movements while attempting to discern the fetus's perception of sound (Sontag & Wallace, 1935), again focusing on the effects on the fetus.

The closest approximation of tapping maternal feelings during pregnancy has been the fairly extensive research on pregnancy attitudes, anxieties, and stress, focusing again on the effects of these on the fetus and neonate. Some representative studies have variously suggested that maternal anxiety and stress contribute to obstetric complications (McDonald, Gunter, & Christakos, 1963), abnormal labors (Burstein, Kinch, & Stern, 1974), premature delivery (Blau, Slaff, Easton, Welkowitz, Springarn, & Cohen, 1963; Gunter, 1963), and childbirth abnormalities (Davids & DeVault, 1962).

The belief in the "impressions" of the mother on the fetus date back to the Old Testament in which Jacob is described as having taken advantage of this phenomenon to influence profitably the color of lambs born to ewes (Genesis 30:29–43). Later Leonardo da Vinci wrote in his *Quadreni*, ". . . the same soul governs the two bodies . . . the things desired by the mother are often found impressed on the memory of the child which the mother carries at the time of the desire . . . one will, one supreme desire, one fear that the mother has, or other mental pain, has more power over the child than over the mother, since frequently the child loses its life thereby" (McMurrich, 1930). This felt power of "motherhood" persists today in even relatively civilized societies. A Greek man on the island of Skorpios once told me his birthmark, which covered half his face, derived from his mother stealing grapes while carrying him in utero.

This history and recent literature on effects of pregnancy stress and anxiety are elaborately reviewed by Ferreira (1965) and critiqued by Copans (1967) who points to methodological shortcomings of many of these studies, including the use of postnatal retrospective questionnaires, failure to control for postnatal effects, evaluation of pregnancy stress and infant behavior by the same examiner, failure to control for other obstetric variables which may covary with stress, and failure to distinguish stress factors, such as death of a husband, from intrapersonal anxiety variables. Nonetheless this literature, together with the mounting literature on prenatal drug, diet, smoking, alcohol, exercise, sex, and weight gain effects, to name only a few, undoubtedly leaves the mother feeling both very powerful and very vulnerable and very much like she might best spend her pregnancy in a deep freeze to protect the fetus from her labile emotions, hormonal changes, and health and life-style patterns.

Anecdotal reports suggest that the woman is surprisingly quite beautiful (swollen ankles aside) and quite animated (crying spells aside) during pregnancy. We say "surprisingly" because when we interviewed hundreds of mothers (who did not rate high on pregnancy anxiety or stress on traditional measures of these) about how they viewed themselves or felt about themselves during pregnancy they frequently reported feeling fat and ugly and lonely and miserable and, in general, not like themselves (Field, 1980b). In spite of these nasty feelings and their being teenaged and impoverished, these mothers-to-be anticipated their baby's birth and their own motherhood with warm feelings. The mother must experience some physical and psychological changes deriving from the life inside her and the feelings of impending motherhood which may interact with pregnancy anxiety and habits to affect herself and her fetus.

The importance of tapping the mother's feelings about herself, her pregnancy, and pending motherhood are suggested by a number of studies which point to the persistence of these maternal variables (Davids & Holden, 1970), their relationship to maternal readiness and infant status (Jones & Dlugokinski, 1978), and their ability to differentiate mothers who later have problems managing their infants (Frommer & O'Shea, 1973) or abusing and neglecting their children (Altemeier, Vietze, Sherrod, Sandler, Falsey, & O'Connor, 1979).

With fetal monitoring and ultrasound technology, mothers' feelings may never be tapped, and mothers' reports on stress and anxiety and on fetal activity may quickly be replaced by films of fetal behavior, as if those will tell the story. At this very early stage of motherhood, the research trends suggest that a primary interest is not the mother, her swelling ankles, bulging stomach, hormone levels, and feelings about all of this and the live being inside her, but the growth, activity, perception, and development of the fetus. As some have suggested we may overlook some critical predictors of mothers' later

attitudes and approaches toward mothering if we fail to tap these during pregnancy.

The birth process, too, has been buried in dozens of studies on effects on the fetus and neonate, effects of delivery medication, length of labor, type of delivery, and delivery complications. Lamaze, LeBoyer, Klaus and Kennell, and others have tried and, fortunately in many cases, succeeded in saving the mother from being "thrown out with the baby's bathwater." Although their crusade for the feelings and natural birth experiences of the mother (and father) may in some cases, carried to the extreme, jeopardize the fetus, the net effect has been to restore to the parents the joys of childbirth and the first moments of the new life created by the parents. Thus we now have, in many places, natural childbirth, father participation, early contact, and rooming-in, all of which are long overdue and widely welcomed movements, movements which a recent Swedish newspaper suggested (in reporting the work of DeChateau) might even "increase the birth rate."

These movements have proceeded in the face of very mixed research findings on the questions. A recent review of the early contact literature by Vietze (1980) suggests that the results of 12 early contact studies are as variable as the methodologies employed. Varying manipulations of early contact, such as type of contact, age of contact, and length of contact, have been assessed using mother-infant interaction behaviors, nursing behavior, medical complications, Brazelton performance, maternal attitudes and perceptions, and parenting problems as criteria. Several have reported some positive effects on mother attitudes-behavior and/or infant behavior at the neonatal period (Barnett, Leiderman, Grobstein, & Klaus, 1970; Campbell, Maloni, & Dickey, 1979; Carlsson, Fagerberg, Horneman, Hwang, Larsson, Rodholm, Schaller, Danielsson, & Gundewall, 1978; DeChateau & Wiberg, 1977a, 1977b; Hopkins & Vietze, 1977; Klaus, Jerauld, Kreger, McAlpine, Steffa, & Kennell, 1972; Sostek & Scanlon, 1979; Taylor, Taylor, Groussard, & Maloni, 1979). Others have demonstrated longer-term effects on mother-child interaction behaviors (Carlsson et al., 1978; DeChateau, 1979; Ottaviano, Campbell, & Taylor, 1979; Ringler, Trause, Klaus, & Kennell, 1978). In many of these a number of other important, uncontrolled variables, such as parity, maternal education, type of delivery, and mode of feeding, may have also affected the variability of findings. A study by Gewirtz and Hollenbeck (1979), in which these and other intervening variables were controlled either experimentally or statistically, showed minimal effects on the infant when manipulating mode and duration of contact. However, the mothers who experienced skin-to-skin contact showed more facial expressiveness than did swaddled-infant group mothers, and the mothers of the swaddled infants talked more to their infants. None of the measures was affected by length of early contact.

It is not clear whether the positive effects of early contact experiences derive from attitudinal, behavioral, and/or hormonal changes. Some have posited that the behavioral changes are mediated by hormonal changes stimulated by the infant's presence, not unlike the mechanism of an infant cry eliciting a milk "let down" reflex or breast-feeding facilitating uterine contractions. None of these hormonal-physiological effects have been assessed. The positive effects, which happen to appear more pronounced among lower-class mothers, may simply be mediated by greater attention or support directed toward the contact mothers. In any case there are some positive effects on the mother, infant, or both, and because infection, the original culprit in limiting contact, is no longer a problem, there is no urgency for research to continue to demonstrate effects.

Despite failures to replicate and many methodological problems with the research contributing to these movements (see review by Vietze, 1980), the only side effects, aside from the attendant risks to the infant of a high-risk pregnancy, appear to be the loss and mourning experienced by those who do not experience the birth process au naturel, who do not have early contact or rooming-in. Those parents are left to feel that, like mother goats, they missed their chance for "bonding," and the child, like the baby goat, may reject and be rejected. In our zealousness to restore the birth process to its rightful parents, we may have overstated our case on the deleterious effects of obstetric medications, premature deliveries, induced deliveries, Cesarean sections, and parent separation. Leaps from these preliminary data to speculation on retarded children outcomes seem ridiculous inasmuch as they suggest that many of us would be rejected and retarded. An informal survey conducted at a recent conference of developmental psychologists, for example, suggested that some 83 percent of our distinguished colleagues surveyed had experienced at least one, and many had experienced a multiple, of the preceding insults. Indeed one of our more prestigious colleagues was delivered by a mother whose legs were primitively tied together for several hours to prevent a premature delivery in the absence of a very tardy obstetrician.

A real data illustration of this point derives from studies done on Cesarean-section-delivered infants. In some of these studies the parent(s) appear to become more involved with the Cesarean-delivered infants, with the father spending more time with the infant (Pedersen, Yarrow, Anderson, & Cain, 1979) and the mother's interactions appearing more optimal (Field & Widmayer, 1980). We have speculated that for this black, lower-class sample (for which childbearing is a very routine event) the surgical delivery is a dramatic, crisis event which mobilizes family support systems around the mother and infant that are not typically mobilized by more natural deliveries and which may have contributed to the interaction effects observed.

The literature on postpartum depression suggests that depressive responses to the birth of a child often occur in the absence of support, for example, from the child's father (Herzog, 1979). If our data suggest that father support is critical and that the early contact behaviors facilitate early interactions, we might tutor or coach those early-contact–deprived parents to engage in the behaviors normally observed during early contact just as we encourage mothers of preemies who want to breast-feed to pump their milk. Delivery may be the first crisis of motherhood which has consequences for the mother and mothering, a crisis deriving not only from unnatural medical and hospital routines but also from the awesome novelty, sudden responsibilities, role changes, hormonal changes, and other physiological and psychological changes which also require understanding and support.

The Neonatal Period

In the midst of the mother's exhilaration and exhaustion over the birth experience, the neonate presents him/herself to the mother full of feeding, nurturance, and stimulation needs. The mother is faced with a multitude of immediate decisions—to room-in or not, to breast-feed or bottle-feed—and is challenged to perceive her infant's behaviors and perceptions. Although many do not realize their infants can hear and see and, in general, perceive the "booming, buzzing, confusing" world about them, many mothers behave as if their infants do all of these things and more. When we ask mothers to assess their infants on an adaptation of the Brazelton scale, the MABI or Mother's Assessment of the Behavior of Her Infant (Field, Dempsey, Hallock, & Shuman, 1978), we are frequently surprised to note that mothers' behaviors are often inconsistent with their beliefs—that is, they suggest their infants cannot see or hear, while all the time talking to them and visually stimulating them as if they do hear and see. When we ask the mothers to assess their infants on the MABI scale, their ratings on orienting, motor, and physiological-state organization and response to stress items, when summarized on the Brazelton a priori processes, are highly correlated with neonatal evaluations by Brazelton examiners (Field et al., 1978). These relationships hold even in the case of very difficult infants. So although a mother may be expecting and wanting to believe she has a "Gerber" baby, her evaluation of the baby's behaviors appears to be fairly objective. Thus mothers are able to elicit, perceive, and evaluate infant behaviors fairly effectively. These relationships which were noted for middle-class, white mothers, however, did not hold in the case of lower-class, black mothers. Perhaps the lower-class mothers viewed the MABI scale more as an evaluation of their expectations than as an objective assessment of their infants' behaviors. The mothers, for example, assigned disproportionately higher ratings to their neonates' motor behaviors (inconsistent with examiner ratings) than other behaviors, as if having given birth to future quarterbacks. Their stimulation behaviors, consistent with their expectations, were motoric, and as in a self-fulfilling prophecy, their infants were relatively more precocious motorically at four and eight months (Field, Widmayer, Stringer, & Ignatoff, 1980).

As the neonates' behaviors changed and developed over the first month of life, mothers assigned their infants more optimal ratings on the MABI, as did the examiners on the Brazelton. Again, however, the lower-class, black mothers assigned their infants more optimal motoric ratings than did the Brazelton examiners (Field et al., 1980; Widmayer & Field, 1980).

In addition to neonatal behaviors influencing mothers' perceptions, neonatal physical attractiveness and sex appear to have some influence. Mothers have notoriously, in the past, expressed a wish for a "Gerber" baby, and many of these, for a specific-sex baby. A recent study suggested that nurses accord more attention to the more attractive babies, those with "cuter" features and more hair (Corter, Trehub, Boukydis, Ford, Celhoffer, & Minde, 1978). While it is not clear whether this dimension affects mother behaviors, there are a number of studies suggesting that both nurses and mothers are able to identify the sex of the infant without any obvious sex indicators. Just as mothers are noted to perceive age differences in infant behavior and alter their own behavior accordingly during the neonatal period (Moss, 1967), they have been noted to treat girl and boy babies differentially from the start, for example, by providing more physical stimulation for boys and more visual and auditory stimulation for girls (Lewis, 1972). Thus infant behaviors, sex, and physical features appear to affect mother perceptions, attitudes, and expectations as early as the neonatal stage.

Often these perceptions are colored by contextual factors. For example mothers can identify different infant cry sounds (hunger, pain, anger), but it appears that they may use contextual clues, such as time since last feeding, to facilitate their discriminations (Wolff, 1969). Another illustration of their context-specific perceptions occurs in temperament ratings. When mothers are given the Carey Infant Temperament Questionnaire (Carey, 1970) in which a series of context-specific questions are asked referring to their infants' regularity of sleeping and feeding habits, mood, approach to novel situations, adaptability, threshold to stimulation, and activity level their responses are different from their answers to direct questions on how regular, adaptable, or moody their babies are. Their assessments are more optimal in the latter case, as if categorizing an infant as difficult on a more general attribute is more incriminating.

While there appears to be agreement between some mothers and examiners on neonatal behaviors and consistency between ratings made at birth and one month, suggesting that mothers are fairly objective in their assessments of their infants, it is not clear that mothers' perceptions of later infant temperament are objective. Although mother-examiner agreement has not been assessed on later temperament measures (probably due to the difficulty of equating mother-examiner exposure to the infant), some preliminary data suggest that nursery-teacher–mother ratings on the Carey Temperament Questionnaire are only marginally related (Field, 1979e). This, of course, could relate to these particular temperamental qualities of the infant being different in the nursery and home environments or temperament not having yet stabilized. The latter interpretation is supported by the finding of a fairly high correlation between preschool-children mothers' and teachers' ratings of temperament on another scale tapping emotionality, activity, sociability, and impulsivity (Corsini & Doyle, 1978).

Infancy

Much of the research on motherhood during infancy, again, is only tangential to the research on the infant. In the olden days psychologists spoke mostly of the ways in which parents molded their infants and children. Since Bell (1968), Lewis and Rosenblum (1974), and others have reminded us of a simple reality—mainly that interactions and relationships are reciprocal—more attention has been directed to the effects of the infant on the mother. To date this appears to be the only time period during which the mother is frequently treated as a dependent variable.

The mother's behavior appears to be dramatically altered in the presence of an infant, in fact, almost molded by the infant. The infant often appears to direct or orchestrate many of their interactions, while the mother closely attends, waiting for signals to take her turn.

Most of the mother-infant studies have used feeding and play-interaction contexts as their research material. In these contexts mothers are seen to alter their activity rhythms, behaviors, and response styles as a function of the infant's rhythms, behaviors, and response styles.

Rhythms. From the infant's birth the mother is noted to alter her pace of activity to that of her infant. She visually monitors her infant almost constantly, looking for periods of her infant's alertness and readiness to interact, then accelerates or decelerates her activity or stimulation in accord with her infant's waxing and waning attentiveness and contented-discontented or excited-lethargic arousal levels.

During feedings she quietly attends to her infant's sucking rhythms, saving her stimulation for the infant's pauses in sucking when he is otherwise unoccupied (Field, 1977b; Kaye & Brazelton, 1971).

Similarly during face-to-face interactions the mother attends to the infant's gaze-alternation rhythms. Gaze alternation or looking–looking away is intrinsic to the visual system and is affected by the type, amount, and timing of stimulation (Stern, 1974). The infant, not unlike the mother, is thought to require periods of looking away to modulate arousal and process the stimulation received during previous periods of looking (Brazelton, Koslowski, & Main, 1974; Field, 1978b; Kendon, 1967; Stern, 1974). A number of researchers have noted that the mother who does not respect the infant's looking-away periods experiences difficult or disturbed interactions with the infant (Brazelton et al., 1974; Field, 1979c; Stern, 1974).

As the infant develops an ability to modulate activity rhythms (limb movements, sucking, and gaze alternation), s/he can experience more prolonged interactions (Brazelton et al., 1974). In the interim the mother learns to attend to these rhythms, modulate her own rhythms, and thereby facilitate a rhythmical turn-taking interaction.

Evidence for modulation of infant rhythms by mother activity can be seen in a comparison between an infant relating to an adult versus an object. Although the infant's periods of looking are more sustained in the presence of an inanimate social object, such as a Raggedy Ann doll (Field, 1978c), the cycling of attention-inattention is observed to be "smoother" in the presence of mother (Brazelton et al., 1974). Limb and head movements are less pronounced when the infant is relating to his/her mother than when relating to his/her own mirror-image, another infant, or a sibling (Field, 1979c). Ways in which mothers apparently modulate infants' rhythms are by slowing down the pace of their behaviors to match the pace of infant behaviors, simplifying or "infantizing" their own behaviors, and constantly monitoring the infant's interaction signals.

Behaviors. Although mothers are observed to spend virtually all of their interaction time looking at their infants (Stern, 1974), which is very unlike the looking-looking-away patterns seen in adult-adult interactions, their repertoire includes behaviors other than constant looking at the infant or monitoring the infant's rhythms and behaviors. Much of the mother's activity has been described as "infantized" behavior (Stern, 1974). Speech is slowed down and exaggerated, and the range of pitch expanded. Ferguson (1964) examined "baby talk" in six languages and suggested that alternations occur in the range of loudness, contour of pitch, rhythms, and stress, with vowel durations being particularly elongated. Stern and Wasserman (1979) have replicated and amplified these findings for the prosodic features of mother language to infants. Since children's vowel duration is longer (Anderson & Jaffe, 1972), Stern (1974) has suggested that mothers slow down their speech to match more closely the infant's perceptual and language-production abilities.

Mothers' facial expressions are also exaggerated, slowed down in their formation, and prolonged in their duration (Stern, 1974). Again the slowing of tempo and exaggeration may enable the infant more readily to process the mother's behaviors. To illustrate the dramatic difference in adult-like and "infantized" behaviors, Trevarthen (1974), via a system of mirrors and lights, presented mothers with the face of an adult while the mother was interacting with her infant. The mothers' behaviors abruptly changed from "infantized" to adult-like behavior.

Another way in which mothers frequently enhance the communication value of their behaviors is by imitating the behaviors of their infants (Field, 1978c; Pawlby, 1977; Trevarthen, 1974). Piaget (1953) maintains that infants are more able to assimilate behaviors which are already in their own repertoire, so mothers, may be intuitively imitating their infants in order to facilitate their infants' processing of social stimulation. Still another way in which mothers alter their behavior for infants is via their frequent repetition of phrases (Stern, Beebe, Jaffe, & Bennett, 1977), as if unconsciously trying to make the infant's task easier.

The mother's repertoire also contains a number of games which appear with such frequency and universality that they might be labeled *infant games*. Infant games include "peek-a-boo," "I'm gonna get you," "So big," "Tell me a story," "crawling fingers," "itsy-bitsy spider," "pat-a-cake" (Field, 1979a), and others noted to elicit smiling and laughter in infants (Sroufe & Wunsch, 1972). Mothers modify these games as the infant develops and is able to participate more fully (Gustafson, Green, & West, 1979).

Responsivity. A number of researchers have suggested that responses must be contingent so that the partner to the interaction can feel that s/he has some influence on the interaction (Ainsworth & Bell, 1974; Goldberg, 1977b; Lewis & Goldberg, 1969; Watson, 1967). If the mother's response is appropriate and occurs within a few seconds of the infant's behavior, it is more likely to be perceived by the infant as a direct response to his/her own behavior. Many of the previously mentioned responses which are sensitively timed by mothers—e.g., ceasing activity when the infant resumes sucking or when s/he looks away—can be seen as contingent responses to the infant's signals.

Infant behaviors such as smiling, cooing, and sustained eye contact are viewed by mothers as contingent responses and encourage the mother to play more of the same game when the infant responds in such a way. For example smiling and vocalizing by infants is most frequently followed by similar behaviors on the part of the mother (Gewirtz & Gewirtz, 1969; Lewis & Wilson, 1972).

Some have argued about who conditions whom. Just as the mother's immediate responsiveness to infants' crying may reinforce crying (Gewirtz & Boyd, 1977a) in such a way that infants cry more in their mothers' presence than absence (Field, 1979b), many of the infant's behaviors are effective reinforcers of mother behaviors. Gewirtz and colleagues have convincingly demonstrated, for example, that mothers' vocalization can be conditioned both by mock infant vocalizations and staged infant head-turning (Gewirtz & Boyd, 1977b).

The mothers' frequent imitations of their infants provide a form of contingency experience for the infant (Field, 1978b; Pawlby, 1977). Imitations of infant behaviors are contingent both by being similar to the stimulus behavior and occurring with short latencies. Mothers perhaps learn at a very early time that infants both enjoy being imitated and are more able to imitate parents' imitations of their own behaviors (Piaget, 1953). Accordingly the mothers appear selectively to imitate the more frequently occurring infant behaviors—e.g., grimaces more than laughter in the very young infant since grimaces are more characteristic of the repertoire of this age infant (Field, 1978b). Videotapes of parent-infant interactions feature many sequences of an infant's behavior followed by a mother's imitation, much like a game (Field, 1978b). Conversations appear to be sustained when each member reinforces the other by a contingent or imitative response. Mothers seem to recognize that their imitations elicit "imitative" responses from their infants, and they appear to enjoy being imitated by their infants.

Another frequently observed contingency provided by the mother is termed *highlighting* of the infant's behaviors. Mothers (and fathers) frequently give a running commentary or verbally describe and pin labels on their infant's behaviors as they happen—e.g., exclaiming, "Oh, you've got the hiccups" or "Poor baby, you always spit up when you get happy" (Field, 1978b; Pawlby, 1977).

The infant games referred to earlier are another example of contingent responsivity observed in infant-adult interactions. One of the most popular games for this age infant is "Tell me a story" (Field, 1979a). The words are provided by the parent who treats the infant's vocalization as if they were words. For example the adult asks, "Do you want to tell me a story?"; the infant coos, the adult responds, "Oh yeah? And then what happened?"; the infant coos again, and the adult replies, "Oh, that's funny!" Mothers' physical games such as "peek-a-boo" and "I'm gonna get you" are typically responded to by infant smiles, vocalizations, and sometimes laughter. The parents contingently respond to these infant behaviors by playing more of the same game. The game, in turn, ceases at the point at which it no longer elicits contented responses, and the parent moves on to another game or conversation (Field, 1979a).

Other ways in which the mother's adult behaviors appear to be modified during their interactions with infants are their latency to respond and the incidence with which they interrupt. These frequently noted perturbations in adult-adult conversations—latency to respond and interrupting (Chapple, 1970)—appear to occur less frequently in mother-infant interactions. The mother usually responds immediately to her infant, as if realizing that if she does not respond immediately her response will not be registered by the infant (given his very short-term memory) as a contingent response (Field, 1978b). Similarly although she occasionally speaks at the same time as the infant (Stern et al., 1977), she rarely interrupts the infant, as if "hanging on his every word" and respecting his/her need for a turn in their turn-taking games just as she respects his/her need to pause periodically or "take a break" from the conversation. In these ways the infant affects maternal behavior in the direction of being more contingently responsive to the infant.

Other notable effects of the infant's behavior on the mother relate to her physiological activity. In a number of our interaction studies we have simultaneously recorded infant and mother heartrate and blood pressure (Field, 1978c, 1979c, 1980a, 1980c). In those situations in which the infant was attentive and interactive, the mother's heartrate was characterized by more decelerations, and in those in which the infant excessively gaze-averted or was excessively fussy, the mother's heartrate was elevated. Since elevated heartrate or heartrate accelerations are characteristic responses to aversive situations, we have speculated that aversive behaviors of the infant not only adversely affect the interaction and the mother's overt behaviors (making her appear more anxious and more active) but also her cardiac activity. Similarly Frodi and colleagues (Frodi, Lamb, Leavitt, Donovan, Neff, & Sherry, 1978) have reported elevated blood pressure and heartrate in mothers viewing videotapes of gaze-averting or fussy infants.

It should be noted that there appear to be cross-cultural differences in the ways mothers' behaviors are modified in the presence of their infants. Although there seems to be some universality in the mother's "baby talk" phenomenon (Ferguson, 1964), mothers' rhythms, eye contact, proximal and distal interaction behaviors, and infant game-playing appear to differ by culture. Callaghan (1981) and Chisholm (1981) in comparisons among Hopi, Navajo, and Caucasian mothers note differences in the acitivty, rhythms, and behaviors of these mothers. Comparisons among Navajo, black, and Caucasian mothers also yielded differences (Fajardo & Freedman, 1981). Eye contact between mothers and infants also appears to be culture-specific since eye contact is rarely seen in the infant-mother interactions of the Gusii (Dixon, Tronick, Keefer, & Brazelton, 1981), the Ua Pou (Martini, 1980), and the Fais cultures (Sostek, Zaslow, Vietze, Kreiss, Van der Waals, & Rubinstein, 1981). Proximal interaction behaviors (holding, carrying, touching) appear to be more characteristic of mothers from less industrialized cultures—e.g., Zambians (Goldberg, 1977a), Mayans (Brazelton, 1977), and Guatemalans (Klein, Lasky, Yarbrough, Habicht, & Sellers, 1977)—while distal interaction behaviors (looking, smiling, talking) are more characteristic of the repertoire of mothers in industrialized cultures. Infant games (such as "peek-a-boo," "pat-a-cake") also appear to be culture-specific; for example, British mothers play these games

less frequently and sing nursery rhymes more frequently to their infants than do American mothers (Field & Pawlby, 1980). The games of the British mothers are more "cognitive"—e.g., eliciting searching behavior for disappearing objects—and the games of American mothers are more social—e.g., attempting to elicit smiles, coos, and laughter. The British and American mothers may have different "hidden agendas" or objectives in their play with infants.

Later in infancy infants become less interested in face-to-face interactions with their mothers and more interested in object play. Thus the typical mother-infant research situation then involves objects, and as crawling and later toddling emerges, many have observed floor-play, mother-infant interactions. In a mother teaching-style study Kaye (1970) observed mothers attempting to teach their six-month-old infants a new skill (reaching round a barrier to obtain a toy). Whenever the infant looked away from the task, the mother promptly intervened and attempted to bring his/her interest back to it by demonstrating, moving his/her arm, or some other strategy. The mother continued, at this stage, to monitor all of the infant's behaviors, looking where s/he looked and capitalizing on every opportunity to turn the situation into mutual play (Collis & Schaffer, 1975).

Less formal situations involving free floor play have noted considerable variability in mothers' interactive styles, with some remaining relatively passive and responding only to initiations by the infant and others directing the infant's play (Field & Ignatoff, 1981; Goldberg, Brachfeld, & DiVitto, 1979). Although the mothers still speak "baby talk" to their infants, their mean length of utterances are longer. Our data for 4-month-old and 12-month-old infants and the data of Sherrod and colleagues (Sherrod, Friedman, Crawley, Drake, & Devieux, 1977) combine to suggest a great deal of flexibility in mother language and sensitivity to developmental change. Mothers' utterances appear to be longer to the very young (4-month-old) infants who might not be expected to comprehend, they become shorter by eight months, at which time the infants show signs of comprehension, and increase in length again by 12 months as language comprehension is presumably improving. Mothers' speech contains more imperatives (usually overprotective in nature) and more questions followed by pauses as if expecting answers at this stage, unlike an earlier stage when mothers supplied both the questions and their own "pretend" infant responses to their questions. The data of Kaye and Charney (1980) are consistent with this observation, suggesting that mothers of two-year-olds use "mands" or "turnabouts" which by reflection or content imply the mother's expectations of a response from her infant.

It is interesting that both lower-class mothers (Field & Ignatoff, 1981) and middle-class mothers (Graves & Glick, 1978) become more active and more verbal during floor-play interactions if they know they are being observed or filmed (Field & Ignatoff, 1981). It is not clear whether observing or filming merely makes mothers more anxious, and thus more active, or whether they feel that the observers expect them to be very verbal and active with their infants.

Increasingly investigators are noting fairly strong relationships between mother-infant interaction behaviors in early face-to-face interactions and later floor-play interactions (Beckwith & Cohen, 1980; Field, 1979c; Goldberg, Brachfeld, & DiVitto, 1979). Mothers, for example, who tend to be overcontrolling and less sensitive to their infant's gaze signals during early interactions tend to emit more imperatives and direct play more frequently during later floor-play interactions (Field, 1979c). This suggests that mothers may develop a style of relating to their very young infants which persists across infancy.

Another situation in which mothers and older infants are frequently studied is the Ainsworth "stranger" situation (Ainsworth et al., 1971). An entire volume could be written on the many studies using this paradigm. Basically the objective of this research has been to identify and describe the infants' responses to strangers as they are left by their mothers and the infants' responses to the mothers as they return. Infants are categorized as securely, insecurely, or ambivalently attached, based on responses such as crying or clinging. There appears to be considerable variability in infant responses depending on a host of conditions, such as the situation context—laboratory or home (Brookhart & Hock, 1976; Skarin, 1977); the style of maternal departure (Gaffuri & Lewis, 1979; Weinraub & Lewis, 1977); the way in which the stranger approaches the infant (Greenberg, Hillman, & Grice, 1973; Ross & Goldman, 1977); the amount of prior exposure to the stranger (Ross, 1975); and sex and age of stranger (Greenberg et al., 1973). Ainsworth, Bell, and Stayton (1971) have developed a maternal sensitivity-insensitivity scale on which they claim it is possible to rate mothers and demonstrate relationships between this rating and various aspects of infant behavior. Sensitive mothers are found to have secure infants who are able to explore strange situations and are able to tolerate brief separations. Infants of insensitive mothers are unable to let their mothers out of sight or else they tend to play as if she were not present. Most of the research stimulated by Ainsworth and colleagues, however, has been oriented toward infant responses in this situation, rather than assessments of mother sensitivity-insensitivity, the latter assessment being implied typically by the infant's behavior.

A final context in which mothers and older infants are studied is a situation involving other mothers and other infants in the home, laboratory, and parent cooperative nurseries. In most of these the mothers appear to serve as a secure base for infant exploration and play with other infants. Several investigators have noted in these situations that the infant engages in more proximal behaviors with the mother and more distal interaction behaviors and toy-related behaviors with the infant (Field, 1979b; Lewis, Young, Brooks, & Michalson, 1975; Rubinstein & Howes, 1976).

In a study by our own group (Field, 1979b), mothers rotated being in and out of a parents' cooperative nursery session. While the infants' mothers were present, the infant showed more negative behaviors (e.g., crying, toy snatching, and less prosocial behaviors to peers) than when the mothers were absent. Different maternal departure styles became evident, with some simply leaving as if not wanting to disrupt their infant's activity and interaction with peers. Others engaged in ritualistic leave-taking with considerable ambivalence about leaving as the infant cried. The latter mothers expressed surprise that some mothers could leave without their infants crying and suggested that "maybe the no-crying infants were less 'attached'" and were surprised that their own infants ceased crying as soon as they were out of the room, an observation anecdotally reported by babysitters with some frequency. The mothers' attitudes toward what is attachment and how it is manifested appeared to affect these mothers' departure styles.

Context also appears to influence the mothers' leave-takings and, in turn, the infant' responses. Although the least distressing departure in this familiar nursery situation appeared to be the mother who simply left without elaborating the reasons, in other studies in unfamiliar laboratory situations the least distressing departure was characterized by the mother not only informing their infants but also giving explicit instructions as to what to do in their absence (Gaffuri & Lewis, 1979; Weinraub & Lewis, 1977). Although again in much of this research the focus has been on infant responses to maternal behavior, separations are an example of an experience which undoubtedly affects mothers as much as, if not more than, their infants or children. Separations may be felt as little crises in motherhood, and there would appear to be as much variability in the way these affect mothers as there are individual differences in infant responses. Speaking of separation brings us to one of the most symbolic and painful separations—that of preschool.

Preschool and Early Childhood

In our childhoods, grade school or kindergarten was the first real departure. For many of today's children the first big departure comes much earlier. It is not clear what difference a few years makes, but the separation event, whenever it comes, is clearly a crisis and a milestone for both the child and parent. All eyes and ears are on the child, crying and clinging and evoking pangs in all those around. The mother's tears are silent and go unnoticed.

Perhaps this painful event is painful even for the researcher for, as universal as it is, there are very few studies of the separation phenomenon at school entry. A recent unpublished study (Ferguson & Freeark, 1979) did not study the physical event of school entry but the mother's anticipation of school entry and the child's subsequent adjustment to kindergarten as a functin of maternal characteristics (including self-esteem, differing role investments, child-rearing attitudes, and perception of child's competence) and the child's role as defined by gender and ordinal position. High nonmaternal role involvement (or career-role involvement) and self-esteem were positively associated with positive anticipation of school entry and with child adjustment to the classroom, but only for daughters and younger children. For mothers of oldest children and only children, nonmaternal role involvement was associated with more negative anticipations of school entry. One of the interpretations offered by these authors was that the mother who is invested in extra familial roles "views this step towards separation of her first-born child, and his or her involvement with the educational system, with feelings tinged with regret or even guilt" (p. 7). Unfortunately the sample studied was college-educated, so it is not clear to what extent these findings might generalize. However, the impact of school entry on motherhood is likely to be variable, and since it is an experience universal to motherhood, it warrants further study.

In light of the sex differences of the preceding study, another study (Martin, 1979) suggests that "girls, must be pushed by their mothers . . . perhaps pushed out of the nest . . . in order to learn to deal with the external world confidently and competently" (p. 8). In this study maternal responsiveness was positively associated with male-child exploration and compliance, but not associated with the same measure for girls. Martin (1979) draws a parallel to the Baumrind and to the Berkeley growth studies and Fels data which suggest that parental warmth and encouragement were related to high academic achievement for boys, but in the case of girls, maternal abrasiveness, coldness, and argumentativeness were associated with academic achievement. It is quite plausible that sex differences in temperament may contribute as much to these sex differences in achievement as early treatment by mothers. That either variable may have different consequences for the two sexes point to the complexity of mothering and the motherhood phenomenon.

Although the child at this stage may begin to spend more time with his/her peers and teacher, the mother's role at this time, at least the role most frequently studied, is that of teacher. A number of studies on early childhood language development suggest that mothers are generally very sensitive, versatile, language teachers (Brown & Bellugi, 1964; Cazden, 1965; Friedlander, Jacobs, Davis, & Wetstone, 1972; Whitehurst, Novak, & Zorn, 1972). A study tracing the changes in verbal child-mother interactions and increasing language skills from age two to five supports this appraisal of mothers as teachers (Moerk, 1974). For two-year-old children, mothers "very conspicuously model the encoding of objects, situations, pictures and activities" (p. 113). In the next stage the mother "seems to prod the child to encode spontaneously through questions such as "What is that? What are you doing?" If the child encodes the answer to the mother's question verbally, the mother often imitates the language product, all the while adding phonetic, semantic, or grammatical corrections. Soon the child follows the example of the mother and prods her in turn by asking the broadly observed "what" questions. Later the child (around age four or five) encodes spontaneously by explaining mechanisms, activities, and facts to the mother, this stage approximating the level of normal communication between two persons.

Nonverbal aspects of communications between preschool-aged children and their mothers have also been studied in the context of maternal teaching tasks. In one study three nonverbal variables were isolated: physical contact, body inclination, and glances (Schmidt & More, 1970). The primary focus of the study was not socioeconomic status (SES) differences, but on obtaining samples of linguistically more and less advanced children and relating linguistic to nonverbal communication development, several SES differences emerged. Physical contact was more prevalent in the low SES group. On body inclination, seen as a measure of "degree of closeness," there was no difference. The high SES mothers tended to look at their children more than low SES mothers, and high

SES children had fewer glances unreciprocated by their mothers.

That mothers of different SES and ethnic groups may have different teaching styles, strategies, and agendas for interactions with their children is further suggested by a study observing Anglos, Mexicans, and Chinese-Americans in California teaching their young sons (Steward & Steward, 1973). The single best predictor of maternal teaching or child response was ethnicity. The mothers' perceptions of themselves as teachers supported the differences in their teaching styles. The Chinese mother considered teaching to be an important maternal role with formal instruction of her preschool-age children in the home. The Mexican mother felt that she was the mother, not the teacher. The Anglo mother viewed teaching as only one of several roles and expressed ambivalence about what she should be teaching her child.

Middle Childhood

Most of the research on the role of the mother during these middle years has emphasized the degree of control which she exercises over her child. Armentrout (1972) found that mothers who were excessively controlling promoted dependency and immaturity in their children. Baldwin (1948) suggested that the children of controlling mothers tended to be quiet, well-behaved, nonresistant, socially unaggressive, and restricted in curiosity, originality, and fancifulness. The "protective" mother in a household which revolves around the child also tended to encourage dependency to a significant degree (Heathers, 1953). Schaefer (1965), using interviews with children, found that the controlling mothers interfered with the child's formation of realistic goals and of mature peer relations.

The "lax" or permissive mother, on the other hand, tends to foster lack of self-control, impulsivity, and hostility in her children (Kagan & Moss, 1962). Blatz and Griffin (1936) demonstrated that poor discipline was found more frequently among problem children who tend to be overly assertive, easily frustrated, and disobedient. Laxness and inconsistency on the part of the mother may be felt as rejection by her child, frequently resulting in more serious kinds of maladjustment and delinquency. The mother who is respectful of her child's individuality and growing sense of autonomy, conversely, tends to foster independence, interpersonal maturity, and creativity in her offspring (Baldwin, 1948, 1949). Coopersmith (1967) has suggested that the mother's establishment of reasonable expectations and limits in order to protect her child from tasks which are too difficult or frustrating is one of the most important elements in establishing adequate levels of self-esteem in her child. Jackson, Klatskin, and Wilkin (1952) studied the relationship between mothers' personal histories and their methods of raising children and found that they were highly correlated. Some children appear to model excessively anxious mothers in their nervous behaviors, while others may challenge their mothers and purposely do and say things which make the mother even more agitated (McFarlane, 1939).

A mother's attitudes toward her children are not independent of social and economic conditions (Lambie,

Bond, & Weikart, 1974). The presence or absence of the father during the child's middle years may also influence the mother's thinking and, therefore, her behaviors toward herself and her children (Anastasiow & Hanes, 1975; Marsella, Dubanoski, & Mohs, 1974).

Middle childhood appears to be a time during which parental rejection is more keenly felt and may have more longlasting effects than at other times in the child's development. Rutter (1979) maintains that maternal rejection alone is probably not predisposing to psychopathy unless it is associated with failure of the mother and child to form close bonds during early childhood. Nevertheless several studies have confirmed that maternal rejection during middle childhood may result in severe personality disturbances among children, including excessive desire for affection (Burgum, 1940), aggressiveness (Becker, 1964), suicidal tendencies (Anthony, 1970), and shyness and insecurity (Kagan & Moss, 1962).

The influence of the mother during middle childhood has been demonstrated to have significant impact on the general intellectual development of the child as well. The mother who reads to her children, helps them with homework, and discusses matters of mutual interest with them has repeatedly been shown to have children functioning at higher developmental levels than children whose mothers do not make time for such interactions (Bachman, 1970; McClelland, 1961; Morrow & Wilson, 1961).

Mother-child interactive patterns appear to be established very early in the child's life. These patterns of responsivity and sensitivity must be maintained by the mother throughout the child's middle years in order for the child's social and cognitive growth to continue, in spite of numerous external influences, such as the presence of siblings, the presence or absence of the father and/or extended family, economic, or social pressures. During the middle years given a secure, consistent, and warm relationship with his/her mother, the child may adjust successfully to peer pressure, to the demands of teachers, counselors, and other adults in his/her environment, and to the exigencies of being responsible for him/herself.

Adolescence

The period of adolescence is universally accepted as the most stressful period in a mother's life. Though many volumes have been written about the physical, emotional, and behavioral changes which occur in the teenager during these years, little has been offered to the mother who suddenly finds that the apparently close and happy relationship which she had with her son or daughter through infancy and childhood has exploded in a few words suggesting that her child can no longer "stand the nagging" and wants to go to the neighbor's to live since Mrs. Jones "understands." Few mothers survive this period unscathed, but she who has survived it with her relationship with her son or daughter intact may consider herself to have reached adulthood.

For a mother whose identity has been self-defined in terms of her children, the task of "letting go" may be a monumental one. If, however, a woman views her motherhood during infancy and childhood as the "cocoon" period, it may be possible for her to see her child's transi-

tion into adolescence as a time for more independence and involvement with her own peers.

A study by Bachman (1970) suggests that the single best indicator of adolescent adjustment is the relationship between a mother and father and their child. The majority of the other research on adolescent adjustment supports this notion, but from the point of view of the maladjusted mother's influence on her child. Mothers of delinquent teenagers, for example, have been found to be inconsistent, lax, or authoritarian in their relationship with their children, and many parents were reported to use physical punishment, to have antisocial attitudes themselves, and to have minimal aspirations for their children (Ahlstrom, 1971; Cressey & Ward, 1969; Gold, 1970).

"Overprotectiveness" and "interference" are the more typical complaints of nondelinquent adolescents. In a study by Lloyd (1954), teenagers maintained that the chief problems with their mothers included interference with their social life, especially criticism of friends, nagging about school work, dissatisfaction with their grades, and lack of adequate financial assistance. A similar investigation by Block (1937) found that mothers appeared to be more "interfering" in two-parent homes and that teenagers considered most of their mothers' criticisms to be unimportant. The following were selected from a list of 50 items by 60 percent of this group (p. 320).

> Pesters me about my table manners.
> Pesters me about my manners and habits.
> Holds my sister or brother up to me as a model.
> Scolds if my school marks are not as high as other people's.
> Objects to my going automobile riding at night with boys.
> Insists that I tell her what I spent my money for.
> Won't let me use the car.
> Insists that I eat foods that I dislike, but which are good for me.

Adolescents are reported to become rather hostile toward their mothers, continually challenging their parents' requests, rules, and behaviors. In a study of 1278 high school boys, Meissner (1965) concluded that the adolescent is gradually breaking the bonds of unqualified acceptance of maternal values and rules. While the author designates this condition as *alienation*, he does not consider that the label *rebellion* is wholly justified. The standards of the parents are ostensibly replaced by the values of the peer group, the most important of which is acceptance by one's friends (Gronlund & Holmlund, 1958). The conflict which ensues is not only between mother and teenager; it is also within the youth him/herself who is torn between dependence on his/her parents, as well as his/her love and allegiance toward them, and the desire for independence, self-determination, and acceptance by his/her peers (Lefrancois, 1973).

The area of greatest concern to many mothers traditionally has been their children's newly found sexual precocity. Studies have demonstrated that parents are more conservative with regard to the sexual activities of their children as compared to themselves. These investigators have suggested that mothers tend to focus on the relationship between the persons involved and the possible outcome of this relationship, whereas the adolescents are less conservative and see sexual behavior as a right of an independent person (Bell, 1966; Sorenson, 1973). As Mussen, Conger, Kagan, and Geiwitz (1979) point out, the mother and father do not want their child to be hurt, either by becoming involved in an emotional and sexual relationship s/he cannot handle or by becoming responsible for a precipitous marriage and/or pregnancy. In fact every year 10 percent of all teenage girls in the United States become pregnant. Many studies have demonstrated widespread ignorance of basic physiological relationships between sexual behavior, contraceptives, and pregnancy. Mothers often appear to be reluctant to discuss these matters with their teenagers, while at the same time disapproving of sex education in the schools (Kantner & Zelnick, 1974).

The ultimate goal of adolescence is the formation of a strong ego-identity. The adolescent whose behavior is consistent with his/her personal values, thoughtfully derived from those of his/her parents and peers, is well on his/her way toward an identification of his/her "real self." The mother's long-suffering fidelity to her child and her efforts to "simply stand and wait" while maintaining her personal standards are usually well rewarded by the time her adolescent daughter or son reaches young adulthood (Lynn, 1969; Martin, 1975).

DISTURBANCES IN MOTHERING

The mothering process has its share of disturbances and aberrations. An accumulating literature on early interaction disturbances and child neglect and abuse, for example, have both highlighted mothering as an important subject for study and implicated mothering disturbances as a source of developmental problems. Until recently the mother or father was implicated or blamed for everything from abuse to nervous tics. Increasingly the literature is suggesting that the disturbance lies in the relationship with each partner, the child and the parent, contributing to the problem.

Although all children and parents on occasion experience disturbed interactions, there are some who experience them fairly frequently. Disturbed interactions between mothers and children often appear as early as early infancy. Many of those reported are characterized by a hyperactive, controlling, or anxious mother and an unresponsive infant or a hypoactive, passive, or depressed mother and an unresponsive infant. It is not clear in many of the reports whether the infant is initially unresponsive and the mother's hyperactivity or hypoactivity is her response to the infant's unresponsiveness or whether the infant's unresponsiveness is a response to the over- or understimulating behaviors of the mother. Nonetheless the interaction is characterized by high levels of maternal stimulation and control (e.g., never letting the infant get a word in edgewise, not respecting his/her need to take breaks from the conversation, and escalating the level of stimulation as the infant gaze-averts, squirms, and fusses) or low levels of maternal stimulation and passivity (e.g., failing to provide stimulation for the infant and not responding to the infant's behavior). In either case low or high levels of stimulation appear to be arousing and aversive for the infant since s/he is frequently observed to gaze-avert, squirm, and fuss.

Hyperactive Mothers and Unresponsive Infants

Many of the hyperactive, controlling mother–unresponsive infant interactions have been observed among groups of infants and children who have developmental delays secondary to preterm or postterm birth, with or without perinatal complications and children who have Down's syndrome or cerebral palsy. During feeding interactions the mothers of preterm infants have been noted to stimulate their infants continuously, failing to reserve their stimulation for the nonsucking periods when the infant is otherwise unoccupied and free to interact (Brown & Bakeman, 1978; DiVitto & Goldberg, 1979; Field, 1977b). Their infants appear to be less responsive and less organized in their feeding behavior and elicited more coaxing or "stimulation-to-feed" behavior from their mothers. The increase in maternal stimulation in response to infant unresponsiveness, however, seemed to be counterproductive inasmuch as it appeared to enhance rather than diminish the infant's unresponsiveness (Field, 1979b).

Face-to-face interactions of preterm infants during the first few months of life have also been characterized by hypoactive, hyporesponsive infants and hyperactive mothers (Field, 1977a, 1979c). The preterm infants were less responsive and showed more aversive behaviors (gaze-averting, squirming, and fussing), and their mothers were more stimulating in all modes (visual, tactile, auditory, and vestibular). Similarly the mothers of postterm infants, who also gaze-averted, squirmed, and fussed, were typically hyperactive or overstimulating. A follow-up of these infants at two years (Field, 1979c) suggested that the mothers who were overactive during early face-to-face interactions were overprotective and overcontrolling during later interactions with their infants. The infants who were visually inattentive during the early interactions were verbally unresponsive and showed language delays during the two-year interactions.

Floor-play interactions of eight-month-old and one-year-old preterm infants and their parents studied by Goldberg et al. (1980) featured less playing and smiling and more fretting by the infants. The parents of the preterm infants spent more time being close to, touching, and demonstrating toys to the infants than did parents of term infants.

The picture that emerges from these analyses of different types of interactions (feeding, face-to-face, and floor play) at different stages during the first two years of life among preterm infants and their parents is a vicious cycle of the infant being relatively inactive and unresponsive and the parent trying to engage the infant by being more and more active or stimulating, which in turn leads to more inactivity and unresponsivity on the part of the infant. Although the parent's activity appears to be directed at encouraging more activity or responsivity of the infant, that strategy is counterproductive inasmuch as it leads to less, instead of more, infant responsivity.

Other groups for which similar phenomena have been observed include the Down's syndrome infant and the child with cerebral palsy. Analyses of interactions between Down's syndrome infants and their mothers suggest that the infants engaged in less eye contact and initiated fewer interactions (Jones, 1980). Their mothers were simultaneously noted to be more active and directive during these play interactions. Similarly cerebral palsied children have been noted to exhibit fewer interactive behaviors, and their mothers are more active and controlling during interactions (Kogan, 1980).

The preceding authors have speculated about the frequently observed hyperactivity of the mothers of unresponsive infants labeled *at risk* due to perinatal complications and/or handicapping conditions. The most vague interpretation suggests that the frustration of receiving minimal responses from the infant leads to a kind of aggressivity on the part of the mother. Another notion is that the mothers are more active to compensate for the relative inactivity of their infants, perhaps "to keep some semblance of an interaction going." A third relates to the mother wanting her child to perform like his/her agemates and attempting to encourage performance by more frequent modeling of behaviors. Still another interpretation is that the mothers view their infants as fragile and delayed and, as a result, tend to be overprotective. Overprotectiveness in the extreme is construed as overcontrolling behavior. Although direction of effects or causality cannot be derived from these studies of interactions, the data have evoked considerable concern since the behaviors of these dyads appear to persist over the early years of the child's life.

Hypoactive Mothers and Unresponsive Infants

Many of the hypoactive, passive mother–unresponsive infant interactions have been observed among groups of infants born to adolescent mothers, less-educated, lower-class mothers, and mothers who came from disrupted families of origin. In addition some have viewed multiple-birth infants (e.g., twins) and later-born infants as having potential interaction problems related to their caretaking situations. Frequently these infants, like the infants with developmental delays, are unresponsive, although their mothers, unlike the mothers of the developmentally delayed infants, are typically hypoactive and hyporesponsive.

A study comparing the interactions of white, middle-class and black, lower-class adult and teenage mothers and their infants revealed a very low level of activity on the part of the teenage mothers (Field, 1980b, 1980d). They were less active, less verbal, and less contingently responsive and played infant games less frequently. This was observed for both white, middle-class and black, lower-class teenage mothers, without respect to their infants' social responsivity and motor development.

Studies of older infants reveal less activity among lower-class mothers and infants than among middle-class dyads (Bee, Van Egeren, Streissguth, Nyman, & Lockie, 1969; Tulkin & Kagan, 1972). Lewis and Wilson (1972) reported less smiling and vocalizing among the lower-class infants, and Field (1980d) reported less activity, less verbal interaction, and less contingent responsivity and less frequent playing of infant games among lower-class, black mothers than among white, middle-class mothers.

A cross-cultural study comparing British working- and middle-class mothers with American lower- and middle-class mothers suggested that both in England and the United States the lower-class mothers engaged in less verbal and imitative behavior and less game-playing during early face-to-face interactions (Field & Pawlby, 1980). Their infants were simultaneously less verbal, smiled less frequently, and engaged in less eye contact. Similarly less-educated mothers are reported to talk less frequently, use less positive language, respond with less contingent vocalizations, and give less specific communications when engaging in face-to-face talk with both their one- and eight-month-old infants (Cohen & Beckwith, 1976). Interactions of infants and mothers who came from disrupted families of origin are similarly disturbed (Pawlby & Hall, 1980).

Two other groups reported to receive either less eye contact or less verbal stimulation include multiple-birth infants (twins) and higher-birth-order infants. A few investigators have reported differential behavior on the part of mothers and their two twins. Stern (1971) reported less maternal eye contact with one twin who later exhibited behavioral problems. Kubicek (1980) also reported less eye contact between one twin and his mother. In this case the twin experiencing less eye contact was later diagnosed as autistic. A study of monozygotic twins and their mothers by our group suggests that the mother is typically less active with the second-born twin (Field, 1979d). However in the case of prematurely born twins discordant on birthweight, the mother was typically overactive with the twin who had the lowest birthweight or who experienced the most perinatal complications.

Birth-order effects typically favor the first-born. Kilbride, Johnson, and Streissguth (1977) reported that later-born infants received significantly less frequent and sustained interactions during the neonatal period with respect to visual, verbal, tactile, caretaking, and play behaviors. Jacobs and Moss (1976) also found comparable birth-order differences in maternal interactions with three-month-old infants.

The dynamics contributing to lesser maternal activity and stimulation in these groups are unclear. In some of the studies neonatal assessments, as well as developmental assessments made at the same time as the interaction assessments of these infants (e.g., Field, 1979c), revealed no particular lags in development or interactive deficits which might contribute to the lesser responsivity of their mothers. The mother's condition itself—e.g., a depressed socioeconomic status or multiple infants/children to care for—may leave the mother with less time and energy for interaction. A similarly simple explanation for the lesser activity of teenage and less-educated mothers may be a limited repertoire due to lesser experience or exposure to the infants and lesser knowledge of appropriate infant stimulation. Whatever the cause, the low levels of stimulation are disconcerting given the reports that mothers of infants/children who were later diagnosed as schizophrenic or autistic engaged in less eye contact during early interactions (Massie, 1978) and that mothers of abused infants engaged in less verbal and physical interactions with their infants (Dietrich & Starr, 1980).

Interaction coaching is a term used for attempts to modify disturbed interactions (Field, 1978b). A number of manipulations have recently been tried to facilitate early interaction. They have typically been directed at the enhancement of behaviors often seen in more harmonious, synchronous interactions. The basic assumption is that the absence or infrequency of harmonious interaction behaviors in the dyad may be contributing to the disturbance. If harmonious feedings typically feature the infant gazing at the mother while vigorously sucking and the mother watching, reserving her words for the infant's breaks from sucking, then a disturbed feeding interaction might be characterized by a fussy, distracted, slow-to-suck, gaze-averting infant and a constantly coaxing-to-feed mother. Similarly if face-to-face interactions typically feature mothers "infantizing" or slowing down, exaggerating, and repeating their behaviors, contingently responding by imitating or highlighting the infant's behaviors, taking turns or not interrupting, and respecting the infant's occasional breaks from the conversation and the infant typically looking attentive and sounding contented, then the atypical or disturbed interaction might feature instead a gaze-averting, squirming, fussing infant and a mother who appears to be somewhat overactive, intrusive, controlling, and frustrated.

Since mothers' behaviors are more amenable to change than are the infants' behaviors, attempts to modify interactions have typically focused on altering the mother's behaviors. These have included asking the mother to count slowly to herself as she interacts (Tronick, Als, Wise, & Brazelton, 1978), asking her to imitate all of her infant's behaviors, to repeat her words slowly, or to be silent during her infant's sucking and looking-away periods (Field, 1977b, 1979c). These manipulations vary in their effectiveness. However each of them has resulted in longer periods of eye contact, fewer distress vocalizations, and less squirming on the part of the infant.

Other interventions include teaching the mother age-appropriate games, coaching her through an interaction via an earpiece microphone, and replaying videotapes for her viewing either with or without our running commentary (Field, 1978b). These techniques, too, have been effective in facilitating interactions. Since most mothers who are experiencing difficult interactions with their infants are aware of and concerned about those difficulties, they are usually willing to try anything. Although the interaction coaching sessions seem to alter the mother's behaviors and the infant's responsivity such that they appear to have more harmonious interactions, the degree to which this experience carries over into their day-to-day interactions is unclear.

Parent training is another intervention which has become increasingly popular. The training has usually involved the mother, and typically the mother who has been identified as having potential problems in mothering by virtue of being teenage or lower-class. A number of these programs have offered instruction in developmental milestones and modeling of child-rearing techniques. Several have reported developmental strides for the infants or children and the mother-child relationship (Badger, 1980; Field et al., 1980). However, other aspects of these programs, such as tutoring and job counseling and placement, may be more contributory to the effects

noted than is the actual parent training. Ameliorating some of the socioeconomic stresses may be the key factor in facilitating mothering among teenage and lower-class mothers.

Other parent-training programs have targeted the child with behavior problems. Training parents as behavior therapists has been a popular area of research, netting dozens of studies reviewed by Berkowitz and Graziano (1972). A representative study of this massive literature is one in which a group of mothers of four- to nine-year-olds with behavior problems was taught to respond differentially to selected behaviors that their children exhibited (Mash, Lazere, Terdal, & Garner, 1973). The altered-response repertoires of the mothers resulted in behavior changes in the children. Patterson and colleagues (Patterson, Cobb, & Ray, 1970) involved parents in the modification of behavior of boys, ages 6 to 13. Significant decreases in specific deviant behavior of the targeted children were demonstrated.

Thus parents have been noted to be not only effective teachers but also effective behavior-change agents. Although these are only a few of the many roles mothers assume in "motherhood," they are the roles most researched. For all that motherhood appears to involve, it seems a moot question to ask if mothers are really necessary, but larger social developments are leading to speculation by people like Toffler that the "mystique of motherhood" is about to be "killed off" and must soon give way to parenthood by professionals.

IS MOTHERHOOD A DYING MYSTIQUE, AND WHAT ABOUT PARENTHOOD BY PROFESSIONALS?

The recent television series "Who's raising our children?" featuring Dr. Benjamin Spock, one of us (Tiffany Field), and lots of children (and, curiously, no parents) basically concluded that parenting appeared to be more in the hands of the professionals and the television these days. Imagine how the millions of mothers who are raising their children and who were not represented on this series were made to feel. However as in disturbances in parenting, those few who have the problems in parenting are often the cause for concern and exaggeration of the problem.

In the abstract, perhaps, mothers are not critical. There are ugly experiments in nature like rehabilitated feral children and children confined to closets (Rigler & Rigler, 1975), motherless children raised in concentration camps (Freud & Dann, 1951), and institutionalized orphans (Tizard & Rees, 1975) that dramatize the point that children can survive without mothers, although the long-term effects of this deprivation are uncertain. There are controlled laboratory studies, fortunately to date only on monkey offspring, that suggest that peer-raised monkeys may develop normally (Harlow & Harlow, 1965). A more practical and relevant question for today—a period of increasing divorce, no-fault divorce, more liberal custody laws (father custody), women's lib and careers—is whether fathers can be mothers and whether institutions such as infant nurseries and preschools are adequate mother-care substitutes.

Fathers as Mothers?

Recent literature on early child development, focusing more and more on the role of fathers, suggests that, while fathers may differ somewhat from mothers, there is nothing particularly innate or exclusive to the biological mother. Although an early report suggested that Bostonian fathers averaged as little time as a mean of 37.7 seconds per day interacting with their infants (Rebelsky & Hanks, 1971), a number of investigators, mostly males and almost all fathers, have voiced their protest through their data. Chief among the father-data providers are Ban and Lewis (1971); Lamb (1977a, 1977b); Parke (1979); Pederson et al. (1979); and Yogman (1979). To legitimize the investigators' protest two females and mothers, Clarke-Stewart (1977) and Field (1978a), have provided supporting data, all of which suggests that at least during the first two years (1) fathers are no less preferred as attachment objects (Lamb, 1977a, 1977b); (2) fathers engage in more distal than proximal behaviors with their infants (Ban & Lewis, 1971); (3) fathers are more playful with their infants (Yogman, 1979); (4) fathers even use "motherese," or "baby talk" with their infants (Golinkoff & Ames, 1977); and (5) fathers, when they are the primary caregivers of infants, are more like mothers than like fathers in many of their behaviors, such as high-pitched vocalizations and infantized, imitative behaviors (Field, 1978a).

Unfortunately the literature pertaining to fathers and older children, reviewed by Biller (1974), is often confounded by the methodological problem of assessing father-influence in situations in which children have been or are deprived of fathers. At least the literature on early fathering suggests that fathers might make adequate mother substitutes and, without the need for substitution, certainly can complement the mother's role.

Institutions as Substitute Mothering

Although some orphan children institutionally reared for the first few years have not shown any unusual behavioral disturbances (Tizard & Rees, 1975), a more pertinent question for today's children is whether infants and young children suffer any consequences from early placement in infant nurseries and preschools by working mothers.

The results of an accumulating literature on infant nursery and preschool experiences are somewhat mixed but together suggest that there are no real adverse effects of "professional mothering." In one study infant-daycare-reared children at ages three and four showed more aggressive and motorically active and less cooperative behavior with adults (Schwarz, Strickland, & Krolick, 1974). In another study daycare-center children showed mildly advanced intellectual development and no social or emotional deficits but some increase in incidences of flu (Doyle, 1975). In a Swedish study children were noted to have similar experiences in home and center settings and showed no developmental differences on an infant scale or in a separation setting (Cochran, 1977). In still another study there were also no basic differences, although daycare children were less compliant and engaged in more temper tantrums (Rubinstein, Howes, & Boyle, 1979).

With respect to the mothers there is the perennial problem of there being very minimal literature on the effects on mothers. Work done by Hock (1978, 1980) suggests that working mothers as compared to nonworking mothers perceived less infant distress at separation, were less anxious about separation, and were less apprehensive about other caregivers, although the working and nonworking mothers did not differ in their child-rearing attitudes or their caregiving behaviors.

To briefly summarize, although motherhood is rarely studied for its own sake but rather for its effects on the mother's offspring, mothers appear to grow and develop with their children. Much of the experience from stage to stage appears to involve a delicate balance of attachment and separation, dependency and autonomy, in part affected by attitudes which vary by cultures and the times. Disturbances in mothering and mothering by fathers and preschools suggest that motherhood is not innate, but rather a learned phenomenon. To paraphrase Peter DeVries, the value of motherhood may not be that mothers produce children but that children produce mothers.

REFERENCES

AHLSTROM, W. M., & HAVIGHURST, R. J. *400 losers.* San Francisco: Jossey-Bass, 1971.

AINSWORTH, M.D.S., & BELL, S. M. Mother-infant interaction and the development of competence. In K. J. Connolly & J. S. Bruner (Eds.), *The growth of competence.* New York: Academic Press, 1974.

AINSWORTH, M.D.S., BELL, S. M., & STAYTON, D. J. Individual differences in strange-situation behavior of one-year-olds. In H. Schaffer (Ed.), *The origins of human social relations.* London: Academic Press, 1971.

ALTEMEIER, W. A., VIETZE, P. M., SHERROD, K. A., SANDLER, H. M., FALSEY, S., & O'CONNOR, S. Prediction of child maltreatment during pregnancy. *Journal of the American Academy of Child Psychiatry,* 1979, *18,* 205–218.

ANASTASIOW, N. J., & HANES, M. L. Identification and sex role. In J. Gallagher (Ed.), *The application of child development research to exceptional children.* Reston, Va.: Council for Exceptional Children, 1975.

ANDERSON, S. W., & JAFFE, J. *The definition, detection and timing of vocalic syllables in speech signals* (Scientific Report No. 12). Department of Communication Sciences, New York State Psychiatric Institute, 1972.

ANTHONY, E. J. The behavior disorders of children. In P. H. Mussen (Ed.), *Carmichael's manual of child psychology* (3rd ed.) (Vol. 2). New York: John Wiley, 1970.

ARMENTROUT, J. A., & BURGER, G. K. Children's reports of parental child-rearing behavior at five grade levels. *Developmental Psychology,* 1972, *7,* 44–48.

BACHMAN, J. G. *Youth in transition* (Vol. 2). The impact of family background and intelligence on tenth grade boys. Ann Arbor: Institute for Social Research, University of Michigan, 1970.

BADGER, E. Effects of parent education program on teenage mothers and their offspring. In K. Scott, T. Field, & E. Robertson (Eds.), *Teenage parents and their offspring.* New York: Grune & Stratton, 1980.

BALDWIN, A. L. Socialization and parent-child relationship. *Child Development,* 1948, *19,* 127–136.

BALDWIN, A. L. The effect of home environment on nursery school behavior. *Child Development,* 1949, *20,* 49–61.

BAN, P. L., & LEWIS, M. *Mothers and fathers, girls and boys: Attachment behavior in the one-year-old.* Paper presented at the meetings of the Eastern Psychological Association, New York, April 1971.

BARNETT, C. R., LEIDERMAN, P. H., GROBSTEIN, R., & KLAUS, M. Neonatal separation: The maternal side of interactional deprivation. *Pediatrics,* February 1970, *45*(No. 2), 197–205.

BECKER, W. C. Consequences of different kinds of parental discipline. In M. L. Hoffman & L. W. Hoffman (Eds.), *Review of child development* (Vol. 1). New York: Russell Sage Foundation, 1964.

BECKWITH, L., & COHEN, S. E. Interactions of preterm infants with their caregivers and test performance at age two. In T. Field, S. Goldberg, D. Stern, & A. Sostek (Eds.), *High-risk infants and children: Adult and peer interactions.* New York: Academic Press, 1980.

BEE, H. L., VAN EGEREN, L. F., STREISSGUTH, A. P., NYMAN, B. A., & LOCKIE, M. S. Social class differences in maternal teaching styles and speech patterns. *Developmental Psychology,* 1969, *1,* 726–734.

BELL, R. Q. A reinterpretation of the direction of effects in studies of socialization. *Psychological Review,* 1968, *75,* 81–95.

BELL, R. R. Parent-child conflict in sexual values. *Journal of Social Issues,* 1966, *22,* 34–44.

BERKOWITZ, B., & GRAZIANO, A. Training parents as behavior therapists: A review. *Behavior Research and Therapy,* 1972, *10,* 297–317.

BILLER, M. B. *Paternal deprivation.* Lexington, Mass.: D. C. Heath, 1974.

BLATZ, W. E., & GRIFFIN, J.D.M. An evaluation of the case histories of a group of pre-school children. *Child Development Series #6.* University of Toronto, Toronto, 1936.

BLAU, A., SLAFF, B., EASTON, K., WELKOWITZ, J., SPRINGARN, J., & COHEN, J. The psychogenic etiology of premature births: A preliminary report. *Psychosomatic Medicine,* 1963, *25,* 3.

BLOCK, V. L. Conflicts of adolescents with their mothers. *Journal of Abnormal and Social Psychology,* 1937, *32,* 193–206.

BOWLBY, J. *Child care and the growth of love.* Baltimore, Md.: Penguin, 1953.

BRAZELTON, T. B. Implications of infant development among the Mayan Indians of Mexico. In P. H. Leiderman, S. R. Tulkin, & A. Rosenfeld (Eds.), *Culture and infancy.* New York: Academic Press, 1977.

BRAZELTON, T. B., KOSLOWSKI, B., & MAIN, M. The origins of reciprocity: The early mother-infant interaction. In M. Lewis & L. Rosenblum (Eds.), *The effect of the infant on its caregiver.* New York: John Wiley, 1974.

BROOKHART, J., & HOCK, E. The effects of experimental context and experiential background on infants' behavior toward their mothers and a stranger. *Child Development,* 1976, *47,* 333–340.

BROWN, J. V., & BAKEMAN, R. Relationships of human mothers with their infants during the first year of life: Effect of prematurity. In R. W. Bell & W. P. Smotherman (Eds.), *Maternal influences and early behavior.* Jamaica, N.Y.: Spectrum Publ., 1978.

BROWN, R. *Psycholinguistics.* New York: Free Press, 1970.

BROWN, R., & BELLUGI, U. Three processes in the child's acquisition of syntax. *Harvard Education Review,* 1964, *34,* 133–151.

BURGUM, M. Constructive values associated with rejection. *American Journal of Orthopsychiatry,* 1940, *10,* 312–326.

BURSTEIN, I., KINCH, R.A.H., & STERN, L. Anxiety, pregnancy, labor and the neonate. *American Journal of Obstetric Gynecology,* 1974, *118,* 195–199.

CALLAGHAN, J. Face-to-face interaction styles: A comparison of Anglo, Hopi and Navajo mothers and infants. In T. Field, A. Sostek, P. Vietze, & A. Leiderman (Eds.), *Culture and early interactions.* Hillsdale, N.J.: Lawrence Erlbaum Associates, 1981.

CAMPBELL, S. G., MALONI, J., & DICKEY, D. *Early contact and maternal perceptions of infant temperament.* Paper presented at biennial meeting of the Society for Research in Child Development, San Francisco, March 1979.

CAREY, W. B. A simplified method of measuring infant temperament. *Journal of Pediatrics,* 1970, *77,* 188–194.

CARLSSON, S. G., FAGERBERG, H., HORNEMAN, G., HWANG, C. P., LARSSON, K., RODHOLM, M., SCHALLER, J., DANIELSSON, B., & GUNDEWALL, C. Effects of amount of contact between mother and child on the mother's nursing behavior. *Developmental Psychology,* 1978, *11,* 143–150.

CARLSSON, S. G., FAGERBERG, H., HORNEMAN, G., HWANG, C. P., LARSSON, K., RODHOLM, M., SCHALLER, J., DANIELSSON, B., & GUNDEWALL, C. Effects of various amounts of contact between mother and child on the mother's nursing behavior: A follow-up study. *Infant Behavior and Development,* 1979, *2,* 209–214.

CAZDEN, C. *Environmental assistance to the child's acquisition of grammar.* Unpublished doctoral dissertation, Harvard University, 1965.

CHAPPLE, E. D. Experimental production of transients in human interaction. *Nature,* 1970, *228,* 630–633.

CHISHOLM, J. Residence patterns and the environment of mother-interactions among the Navajo. In T. Field, A. Sostek, P.Vietze, & A. Leiderman (Eds.), *Culture and early interactions.* Hillsdale, N.J.: Lawrence Erlbaum Associates, 1981.

CLARKE-STEWART, K. A. *The father's impact on mother and child.* Paper presented at the biennial meetings of the Society for Research in Child Development, New Orleans, March 1977.

CLARKE-STEWART, K. A. And daddy makes three: The father's impact on mother and child. *Child Development,* 1978, *49,* 466–478.

COCHRAN, M. M. A comparison of group day and family child-rearing patterns in Sweden. *Child Development,* 1977, *48,* 702–707.

COHEN, E. S., & BECKWITH, L. Maternal language in infancy. *Developmental Psychology,* 1976, *12,* 371–372.

COLLIS, G. M., & SCHAFFER, H. R. Synchronization of visual attention in mother-infant pairs. *Journal of Child Psychology and Psychiatry,* 1975, *16,* 315–320.

CONDON, W. S., & OGSTON, W. D. A segmentation of behavior. *Journal of Psychiatric Research,* 1967, *5,* 221–235.

COOPERSMITH, S. *The antecedents of self-esteem.* San Francisco: W. H. Freeman & Company Publishers, 1967.

COPANS, S. A. Human prenatal effects: Methodological problems and some suggested solutions. *Merrill-Palmer Quarterly,* 1967, *14,* 43–52.

CORSINI, D. A., & DOYLE, K. *Temperament traits of preschool children: Across setting consistency.* Unpublished manuscript, University of Connecticut, 1978.

CORTER, C., TREHUB, S., BOUKYDIS, C., FORD, L., CELHOFFER, L., & MINDE, K. Nurses' judgments of the attractiveness of premature infants. *Infant Behavior and Development,* 1978, *1,* 373–380.

CRESSEY, D. R. & WARD, D. A. *Delinquency, crime and social pressure.* New York: Harper & Row, Pub., 1969.

DAVIDS, A., & DEVAULT, S. Maternal anxiety during pregnancy and childbirth abnormalities. *Psychosomatic Medicine,* 1962, *24,* 5, 464–470.

DAVIDS, A., & HOLDEN, R. Consistency of maternal attitudes and personality from pregnancy to eight months following childbirth. *Developmental Psychology,* 1970, *2,* 364–366.

DECHATEAU, P. The influence of early contact on maternal and infant behavior in primiparae. *Birth and the Family Journal,* 1976, *3,* 149.

DECHATEAU, P. The importance of the neonatal period for the development of synchrony in the mother infant dyad. *Birth and the Family Journal,* 1977, *4,* 10.

DECHATEAU, P. Effects of hospital practices on synchrony in the development of the infant-parent relationship. *Seminars in Perinatology III,* 1979, *1,* 45–61.

DECHATEAU, P., & WIBERG, B. Long-term effect on mother-infant behavior of extra contact during the first hours postpartum I: First observation at 36 hours. *Acta Paediatrica Scandinavica,* 1977a, *66,* 137–143.

DECHATEAU, P., & WIBERG, B. Long-term effect on mother-infant behavior of extra contact during the first hours postpartum. II: Follow-up at three months. *Acta Paediatrica Scandinavica,* 1977b, *66,* 145–151.

DIETRICH, K. N., & STARR, R. H. Maternal handling and developmental characteristics of abused infants. In T. Field, S. Goldberg, D. Stern, & A. Sostek (Eds.), *Interactions of high-risk infants and children.* New York: Academic Press, 1980.

DIVITTO, B., & GOLDBERG, S. The effects of newborn medical status on early parent-infant interaction. In T. Field, A. Sostek, S. Goldberg, & H. H. Shuman (Eds.), *Infants born at risk.* Jamaica, N.Y.: Spectrum Publ., 1979.

DIXON, S., TRONICK, E., KEEFER, C., & BRAZELTON, B. Face-to-face interaction among the Gusii. In T. Field, A. Sostek, P. Vietze, & A. Leiderman (Eds.), *Culture and early interactions.* Hillsdale, N.J.: Lawrence Erlbaum Associates, 1981.

DOYLE, B. A. Infant development in day care. *Developmental Psychology,* 1975, *11,* 655–656.

FAJARDO, B., & FREEDMAN, D. Maternal rhythmicity and mother-infant interaction among United States Black, Caucasian & Navajo. In T. Field, A. Sostek, P. Vietze, & H. Leiderman (Eds.), *Culture and early interactions.* Hillsdale, N.J.: Lawrence Erlbaum Associates, 1981.

FERGUSON, C. A. Baby talk in six languages. *American Anthropologist*, 1964, *66*, Pt. 2 (Special Issue), 103–114.

FERGUSON, L. R., & FREEARK, K. *School entry: Transition for mother and child.* Paper presented at the meeting of the Society for Research in Child Development, San Francisco, March 1979.

FERREIRA, A. The pregnant woman's emotional attitude and its reflection on the newborn. *American Journal of Orthopsychiatry*, 1960, *30*, 553–561.

FERREIRA, A. J. Emotional factors in prenatal environment: A review. *Journal of Nervous and Mental Disease*, 1965, *141*, 108–118.

FIELD, T. Effects of early separation, interactive deficits and experimental manipulations on infant-mother face-to-face interactions. *Child Development*, 1977a, *48*, 763–771.

FIELD, T. Maternal stimulation during infant feeding. *Developmental Psychology*, 1977b, *13*, 539–540.

FIELD, T. Interaction behaviors of primary versus secondary caretaker fathers. *Developmental Psychology*, 1978a, *14*, 183–184.

FIELD, T. The three Rs of infant-adult interactions: Rhythms, repertoires and responsivity. *Journal of Pediatric Psychology*, 1978b, *3*, 131–136.

FIELD, T. Visual and cardiac responses to animate and inanimate faces by young term and preterm infants. *Child Development*, 1978c, *49*, 188–195.

FIELD, T. Games parents play with normal and high-risk infants. *Child Psychiatry and Human Development*, 1979a, *10*, 41–48.

FIELD, T. Infant behaviors directed toward peers and adults in the presence and absence of mother. *Infant Behavior and Development*, 1979b, *2*, 47–54.

FIELD, T. Interaction patterns of preterm and term infants. In T. Field, A. Sostek, S. Goldberg, & H. H. Shuman (Eds.), *Infants born at risk*. Jamaica, N.Y.: Spectrum Publ., 1979c.

FIELD, T. *Interactions of twins and their mothers.* Unpublished paper, 1979d.

FIELD, T. *Temperament of infants and preschoolers as assessed by parents and teachers.* Unpublished paper, 1979e.

FIELD, T. Behavioral and cardiovascular activity during harmonious and disturbed interactions between infants and adults. In L. Lipsitt (Ed.), *Advances in Infant Development*. Hillsdale, N.J.: Lawrence Erlbaum Associates, 1980a.

FIELD, T. Early development of infants born to teenage mothers. In K. Scott, T. Field, & E. Robertson (Eds.), *Teenage parents and their offspring*. New York: Grune & Stratton, 1980b.

FIELD, T. Interactions of high-risk infants: Quantitative and qualitative differences. In D. Sawin, R. C. Hawkins, L. D. Walker, & J. H. Penticuff (Eds.), *Current perspectives on psychosocial risks during pregnancy and early infancy*. New York: Brunner/Mazel, 1980c.

FIELD, T. Interactions of preterm infants born to lower class teenage mothers. In T. Field, S. Goldberg, D. Stern, & A. Sostek (Eds.), *Interactions of high-risk infants and children*. New York: Academic Press, 1980d.

FIELD, T., DEMPSEY, J., HALLOCK, N., & SHUMAN, H. H. Mothers' assessments of the behavior of their infants. *Infant Behavior and Development*, 1978, *1*, 156–167.

FIELD, T., & IGNATOFF, E. Effects of videotaping on mother-infant interactions. *Journal of Applied Developmental Psychology*, in press.

FIELD, T., & PAWLBY, S. Early face-to-face interactions of British and American working and middle class mother-infant dyads. *Child Development*, 1980, *51*, 250–253.

FIELD, T., & WIDMAYER, S. Developmental follow-up of infants delivered by Cesarean section. *Infant Behavior and Development*, 1980, *3*, 253–264.

FIELD, T., WIDMAYER, S., STRINGER, S., & IGNATOFF, E. Teenage, lower class black mothers and their preterm infants: An intervention and developmental follow-up. *Child Development*, 1980, *51*, 426–436.

FOGEL, A. Culture and experience in scientific developmental psychology. In T. Field, A. Sostek, P. Vietze, & A. Leiderman (Eds.), *Culture and early interactions*. Hillsdale, N.J.: Lawrence Erlbaum Associates, 1980.

FRIEDLANDER, B. A., JACOBS, A. C., DAVIS, B. B., & WETSTONE, H.. S. Time-sampling analysis of infants' natural language environments in the home. *Child Development*, 1972, *43*, 730–740.

FREUD, A., & DANN, S. An experiment in group upbringing. In R. Eisler, A. Freud, H. Hartmann, & E. Kris (Eds.), *The psychoanalytic study of the child* (Vol. 6). New York: International Universities Press, 1951.

FRODI, A. M., LAMB, M. E., LEAVITT, L. A., DONOVAN, W. L., NEFF, C., & SHERRY, D. Fathers' and mothers' responses to the faces and cries of normal and premature infants. *Developmental Psychology*, 1978, *14*, 490–498.

FROMMER, E. A., & O'SHEA, G. Antenatal identification of women liable to have problems in managing their infants. *British Journal of Psychiatry*, 1973, *123*, 149–156.

GAFFURI, A. M., & LEWIS, M. *How mothers leave their infants: Developmental changes in departure style.* Paper presented at the Eastern Psychological Association Meetings, Philadelphia, April 1979.

GARDNER, J., & GARDNER, H. A note on selective imitation by a six-week-old infant. *Child Development*, 1970, *41*, 1209–1213.

GEWIRTZ, J. L., & BOYD, E. Does maternal responding imply reduced infant crying? A critique of the 1972 Bell & Ainsworth report. *Child Development*, 1977a, *48*, 1200–1207.

GEWIRTZ, J. L., & BOYD, E. F. Experiments on mother-infant interactions underlying mutual attachment-acquisition: The infant conditions the mother. In T. Alloway, L. Krames, & P. Pliner (Eds.), *Attachment behavior. Advances in the study of communication & affect* (Vol. 3). New York: Plenum, 1977b.

GEWIRTZ, H. B., & GEWIRTZ, J. L. Caretaking settings, background events and behavior differences in four Israeli child-rearing environments: Some preliminary trends. In B. Foss (Ed.), *Determinants of infant behavior* (Vol. 4). London: Methuen, 1969.

GEWIRTZ, J. L., & HOLLENBECK, A. R. *Mode and duration of post partum recovery-room contact as determinants of mother-infant interaction, maternal attachment and infant Brazelton-scale performance.* Unpublished data, 1979.

GOLD, M. *Delinquent behavior in an American city.* Monterey, Calif.: Brooks/Cole, 1970.

GOLDBERG, S. Infant development and mother-infant interaction in urban Zambia. In P. M. Leiderman, S. R. Tulkin, & A. Rosenfeld (Eds.), *Culture and infancy*. New York: Academic Press, 1977a.

GOLDBERG, S. Social competence in infancy: A model of parent-infant interaction. *Merrill-Palmer Quarterly*, 1977b, *23*, 163–177.

GOLDBERG, S., BRACHFELD, S., & DiVITTO, B. Feeding, fussing and playing: Parent-infant interaction in the first year as a function of prematurity and perinatal problems. In T. Field, S. Goldberg, D. Stern, & A. Sostek (Eds.), *High-risk infants and children: Adult and peer interactions*. New York: Academic Press, 1980.

GOLINKOFF, R. M., & AMES, G. J. *Do fathers use "motherese"?* Paper presented at Society for Research in Child Development, New Orleans, March 1977.

GRAVES, Z. R., & GLICK, J. The affect of the context on mother-child interaction: A progress report. *The Quarterly Newsletter of the Institute for Comparative Human Develoment*, 1978, *2*, 41–46.

GREENBERG, D. J., HILLMAN, D., & GRICE, D. Infant and stranger variables related to stranger anxiety in the first year of life. *Developmental Psychology*, 1973, *9*, 207–212.

GRONLUND, N. E., & HOLMLUND, W. S. The value of elementary school sociometric status scores for predicting a pupil's adjustment in high school. *Educational Administration and Supervision*, 1958, *44*, 255–260.

GUNTER, M. L. Psychopathology and stress in the life experience of mothers of premature infants. *American Journal of Obstetrics & Gynecology*, 1963, *86*, 333–340.

GUSTAFSON, G E., GREEN, J. A., & WEST, M. J. The infant's changing role in mother-infant games: The growth of social skills. *Infant Behavior and Development*, 1979, *2*, 301–308.

HALES, D. J., LOZOFF, B., SOSA, R., & KENNELL, J. H. Defining the limits of the maternal sensitive period. *Developmental Medicine and Child Neurology*, 1977, *4*, 454–461.

HARDY, J. Maternal outcomes following intervention. In K. Scott, T. Field, & E. Robertson (Eds.), *Teenage parents and their offspring*. New York: Grune & Stratton, 1980.

HARLOW, M. F., & HARLOW, M. K. The affectional systems. In A. M. Schrier, M. F. Harlow, & F. Stollwitz (Eds.), *Behavior of nonhuman primates* (Vol. 2). New York: Academic Press, 1965.

HEATHERS, G. Emotional dependence and independence in a physical threat situation. *Child Development*, 1953, *24*, 169–179.

HERZOG, J. M. Disturbances in parenting high-risk infants: Clinical impressions and hypotheses. In T. Field, A. Sostek, S. Goldberg, & H. H. Shuman (Eds.), *Infants born at risk*. Jamaica, N.Y.: Spectrum Publ., 1979.

HOCK, E. Working and nonworking mothers with infants: Perceptions of their careers, their infants' needs, and satisfaction with mothering. *Developmental Psychology*, 1978, *14*, 37–43.

HOCK, E. Working and nonworking mothers and their infants: A comparative study of maternal caregiving characteristics and infant social behavior. *Merrill-Palmer Quarterly of Behavior and Development,* 1980, *26,* 79–101.

HOPKINS, J. B., & VIETZE, P. M. *Postpartum early and extended contact: Quality, quantity or both?* Presented at biennial meeting of the Society for Research in Child Development, New Orleans, March 1977.

HRDY, S. B. The Langurs of Abu. *Time,* January 9, 1978, p. 64.

JACKSON, E. B., KLATSKIN, E. H., & WILKIN, L. C. Early child development in relation to degree of flexibility of maternal attitude. In *Psychoanalytic Study of the Child* (Vol. 7). New York: International Universities Press, 1952.

JACOBS, B. A., & MOSS, H. A. Birth order and sex of sibling as determinants of mother-infant interactions. *Child Development,* 1976, *47,* 315–322.

JONES, F. A., & DLUGOKINSKI, E. *The relationship of stress pregnancy to perinatal infant status and maternal readiness.* Unpublished manuscript, University of Oklahoma, 1978.

JONES, O. Mother-child communication in very young Down's syndrome and normal children. In T. Field, S. Goldberg, D. Stern, & A. Sostek (Eds.), *High-risk infants and children: Adults and peer interactions.* New York: Academic Press, 1980.

KAGAN, J., & MOSS, H. A. *Birth to maturity: The Fels study of psychological development.* New York: John Wiley, 1962.

KANTNER, J. F., & ZELNICK, M. Sexual experience of young unmarried women in the United States. *Family Planning Perspectives,* 1974, *4,* 9–18.

KAYE, K. *Maternal participation in infants' acquisition of a skill.* Unpublished doctoral dissertation, Harvard University, 1970.

KAYE, K., & BRAZELTON, T. B. *Mother-infant interaction in the organization of sucking.* Paper presented at the meeting of the Society for Research in Child Development, Minneapolis, April 1971.

KAYE, K., & CHARNEY, R. How mothers maintain "dialogue" with two-year-olds. In D. Olson (Ed.), *The social foundations of language and thought: Essays in honor of Jerome S. Bruner.* New York: W. W. Norton & Co., Inc., 1980.

KELLOGG, W. N. A method for recording the activity of the human fetus in utero, with specimen results. *Journal of Genetic Psychology,* 1941, *58,* 307–326.

KENDON, A. Some functions of gaze direction in social interaction. *Acta Psychologica,* 1967, *26,* 22–63.

KENNELL, J. H., JERAULD, R., WOLFE, H., CHESLER, D., KREGER, N. C., McALPINE, W., STEFFA, M., & KLAUS, M. H. Maternal behavior one year after early and extended postpartum contact. *Developmental Medicine and Child Neurology,* 1974, *16,* 172–179.

KILBRIDE, H. W., JOHNSON, D. L., & STREISSGUTH, A. P. Social class, birth order, and newborn experience. *Child Development,* 1977, *48,* 1686–1688.

KLAUS, M. H., & KENNELL, J. H. Mothers separated from their newborn infants. *Pediatric Clinics of North America,* 1970, *17,* 1015.

KLAUS, M. M., JERAULD, R., KREGER, N. C., McALPINE, W., STEFFA, M., & KENNELL, J. H. Maternal attachment: Importance of the first post-partum days. *New England Journal of Medicine.* 1972, *286,* 460–463.

KLEIN, R. E., LASKY, R. E., YARBROUGH, C., HABICHT, J. P., & SELLERS, M. J. Relationship of infant/caretaker interaction, social class and nutritional status to developmental test performance among Guatemalan infants. In P. M. Leiderman, S. R. Tulkin, & A. Rosenfeld (Eds.), *Culture and infancy.* New York: Academic Press, 1977.

KOGAN, K. L. Interaction systems between preschool aged handicapped or developmentally delayed children and their parents. In T. Field, S. Goldberg, D. Stern, & A. Sostek (Eds.), *High-risk infants and children: Adults and peer interactions.* New York: Academic Press, 1980.

KUBICEK, L. Mother interactions of twins: An autistic and nonautistic twin. In T. Field, S. Goldberg, D. Stern, & A. Sostek (Eds.), *High-risk infants and children: Adults and peer interactions.* New York: Academic Press, 1980.

LAHEY, B. B., & KAZDIN, A. E. *Advances in clinical child psychology* (Vol. 2). New York: Plenum, 1979.

LAMB, M. E. Father-infant and mother-infant interaction in the first year of life. *Child Development,* 1977a, *48,* 167–181.

LAMB, M. E. The development of mother-infant and father-infant attachments in the second year of life. *Developmental Psychology,* 1977b, *13,* 6, 637–648.

LAMBIE, D., BOND, J. T., & WEIKART, D. *Home teaching with mothers and infants.* Ypsilanti, Mich.: High/Scope Educational Research Foundation, 1974.

LEFRANCOIS, G. R. *Of children: An introduction to child development.* Belmont, Calif.: Wadsworth, 1973.

LEWIS, M. State as an infant-environment interaction: An analysis of mother-infant interaction as a function of sex. *Merrill-Palmer Quarterly,* 1972, *18,* 95–121.

LEWIS, M., & GOLDBERG, S. Perceptual-cognitive development in infancy: A generalized expectancy model as a function of the mother-infant interaction. *Merrill-Palmer Quarterly,* 1969, *15,* 81–100.

LEWIS, M., & ROSENBLUM, L. A. (Eds.), *The effect of the infant on its caregiver.* New York: John Wiley, 1974.

LEWIS, M., & WILSON, C. D. Infant development in lower-class American families. *Human Development,* 1972, *15,* 112–127.

LEWIS, M., YOUNG, G., BROOKS, T., & MICHALSON, L. The beginning of friendship. In M. Lewis & L. A. Rosenblum (Eds.), *Friendship and peer relations.* New York: John Wiley, 1975.

LLOYD, R. E. Parent-youth conflicts of college students. *Sociology and Social Research,* 1954, *38,* 227–230.

LYNN, D. B. *Parental and sex-role identification: A theoretical formulation.* Berkeley, Calif.: McCutchen, 1969.

McCLELLAND, D. C. *The achieving society.* New York: Van Nostrand Reinhold, 1961.

McDONALD, R. L., GUNTER, M. D., & CHRISTAKOS, A. C. Relations between maternal anxiety and obstetric complications. *Psychosomatic Medicine,* 1963, *25,* 357.

McFARLANE, J. W. The relation of environmental pressures to the development of the child's personality and habit patterning. *Journal of Pediatrics,* 1939, *15,* 142–154.

McMURRICH, J. P. *Leonardo da Vinci, the anatomist* (1452–1519). Baltimore, Md.: Williams & Williams, 1930.

MARSELLA, A. J., DUBANOSKI, R. A., & MOHS, K. The effects of father presence and absence upon maternal attitudes. *Journal of Genetic Psychology,* 1974, *125,* 257–263.

MARTIN, B. Parent-child relations. In F. D. Horowitz (Ed.), *Review of child development research* (Vol. 4). Chicago: University of Chicago Press, 1975.

MARTIN, J. A. *Consequences of mothers' responsiveness to boys and girls.* Paper presented at the meetings of the Society for Research in Child Development, San Francisco, March 1979.

MARTINI, M., & KIRKPATRICK, J. Interactions between caretakers and infants on the Marquesan Island of Ua Pou. In T. Field, A. Sostek, P. Vietze, & A. Leiderman (Eds.), *Culture and early interactions.* Hillsdale, N.J.: Lawrence Erlbaum Associates, 1981.

NASH, E. J., LAZERE, R., TERDAL, L., & GARNER, A. Modification of mother-child interactions: A modeling approach for groups. *Child Study Journal,* 1973, *3,* 131–145.

MASSIE, H. N. The early natural history of childhood psychosis: Ten cases studied by analysis of family home movies of the infancies of the children. *Journal of Child Psychiatry,* 1978, *17,* 29–45.

MEISSNER, S. J. Parental interaction of the adolescent boy. *Journal of Genetic Psychology,* 1965, *107,* 225–233.

MELTZOFF, A. N., & MOORE, M. K. Imitation of facial and manual gestures by human neonates. *Science,* 1977, *198,* 75–78.

MOERK, E. Changes in verbal child-mother interactions with increasing language skills of the child. *Journal of Psycholinguistic Research,* 1974, *3,* 2, 101–116.

MORROW, W. R., & WILSON, R. C. Family relations of bright high-achieving and under-achieving high school boys. *Child Development,* 1961, *32,* 501–510.

MOSS, M. A. Sex, age, and state as determinants of mother-infant interaction. *Merrill-Palmer Quarterly of Behavior and Development,* 1967, *13,* 19–36.

MUSSEN, P. H., CONGER, J. J., KAGAN, J., & GEIWITZ, J. *Psychological development: A life span approach.* New York: Harper & Row, Pub., 1979.

NEWBERRY, H. Studies in fetal behavior. IV: The measurement of three types of fetal activity. *Journal of Comparative Psychology,* 1941, *32,* 521–530.

OTTAVIANO, C., CAMPBELL, S. G., & TAYLOR, P. M. *Early contact and infant-mother attachment at one year.* Paper presented at biennial meeting of the Society for Research in Child Development, San Francisco, March 1979.

PARKE, R. D. Perspectives on father-infant interaction. In J. D.

Osofsky (Ed.), *Handbook of infant development*. New York: John Wiley, 1979.

PATTERSON, G. R., COBB, J. A., & RAY, R. S. A social engineering technology for retraining aggressive boys. In H. Adams & L. Unikel (Eds.), *Georgia Symposium in Experimental Clinical Psychology*, (Vol. 2). Oxford, England: Pergamon Press, 1970.

PAWLBY, S. Imitative interaction. In H. R. Schaffer (Ed.), *Studies in mother-infant interactions*. London: Academic Press, 1977.

PAWLBY, S., & HALL, F. Early interactions and later language development of children whose mothers come from disrupted families of origin. In T. Field, S. Goldberg, D. Stern, & A Sostek (Eds.), *High-risk infants and children: Adults and peer interactions*. New York: Academic Press, 1980.

PEDERSON, F. A., YARROW, L. J., ANDERSON, B. J., & CAIN, R. L. Conceptualization of father influences in the infancy period. In M. Lewis & L. Rosenblum (Eds.), *Genesis of behavior* (Vol. 2). The child and its family. New York: Plenum, 1979.

PIAGET, J. *The origins of intelligence in the child*. London: Routledge, 1953.

REBELSKY, F., & HANKS, C. Fathers' verbal interaction with infants in the first three months of life. *Child Development*, 1971, *42*, 63–68.

RICHMOND, A. Social interactions among Gusii infants and their child and parent caretakers. In T. Field, A. Sostek, P. Vietze, & A. Leiderman (Eds.), *Culture and early interactions*. Hillsdale, N.J.: Lawrence Erlbaum Associates, 1981.

RIGLER, D., & RIGLER, M. *Persistent effects of early experience*. Paper presented at the biennial meeting of the Society for Research in Child Development, Denver, March 1975.

RINGLER, N., TRAUSE, M. A., KLAUS, M., & KENNELL, J. The effects of extra postpartum contact and maternal speech patterns on children's IQs, speech and language comprehension at five. *Child Development*, 1978, *49*, 862–865.

ROSS, H. The effects of increasing familiarity on infants' reaction to adult strangers. *Journal of Experimental Child Psychology*, 1975, *20*, 226–239.

ROSS, S. H., & GOLDMAN, D. B. Infants' sociability toward strangers. *Child Development*, 1977, *48*, 638–642.

RUBENSTEIN, J., & HOWES, C. The effects of peers on toddler interaction with mother and toys. *Child Development*, 1976, *47*, 597–605.

RUBENSTEIN, J., HOWES, C., & BOYLE, P. *A two-year follow-up of infants in community based infant day care centers*. Paper presented at the biennial meeting of the Society for Research in Child Development, San Francisco, March 1979.

RUTTER, M. Maternal deprivation, 1972–1978: New findings, new concepts, new approaches. *Child Development*, 1979, *50*, 238–305.

SCHAEFER, E. S. A configurational analysis of children's reports of parent behavior. *Journal of Consulting Psychology*, 1965, *29*, 552–557.

SCHAFFER, H. R. (Ed.). *Studies in mother-infant interaction*. New York: Academic Press, 1977.

SCHMIDT, W.H.O., & MORE, T. Some nonverbal aspects of communication between mother and preschool child. *Child Development*, 1970, *41*, 889–896.

SCHWARZ, J. C., STRICKLAND, R. G., & KROLICK, G. Infant day care: Behavioral effects at preschool age. *Developmental Psychology*, 1974, *10*(No. 4), 502–506.

SHERROD, K. B., FRIEDMAN, S., CRAWLEY, S., DRAKE, D., & DEVIEUX, J. Maternal language to prelinguistic infants: Syntactic aspects. *Child Development*, 1977, *48*, 1662–1665.

SKARIN, K. Cognitive and contextual determinants of strange face in six- and eleven-month-old infants. *Child Development*, 1977, *48*, 537–544.

SONTAG, L. W. Somatopsychics of personality and body function. *Vita Humana*, 1963, *6*, 1–10.

SONTAG, L. W., & WALLACE, R. F. The effect of cigarette smoking during pregnancy upon the fetal heart rate. *American Journal of Obstetrics and Gynecology*, 1935, *29*, 3–8.

SORENSEN, R. C. *Adolescent sexuality in contemporary America: Personal values and sexual behavior ages 13–19*. New York: Harry N. Abrams, Inc., 1973.

SOSTEK, A. M., & SCANLON, J. W. *Effects of postpartum contact on maternal attitude*. Paper presented at Maternal Behavior Symposium, Georgetown University Family Center, Washington, D.C., June 1979.

SOSTEK, A. M., ZASLOW, M., VIETZE, P., KREISS, L., VAN DER WAALS, F., & RUBINSTEIN, D. Contribution of context to interactions with infants in Fais and the U.S.A. In T. Field, A. Sostek, P. Vietze, & A. Leiderman (Eds.), *Culture and early interactions*. Hillsdale, N.J.: Lawrence Erlbaum Associates, 1981.

SROUFE, L. A., & WUNSCH, J. P. The development of laughter in the first year of life. *Child Development*, 1972, *43*, 1326–1344.

STERN, D. N. A micro-analysis of mother-infant interaction: Behavior regulating social contact between a mother and her 3½ month-old twins. *Journal of American Academy of Child Psychiatry*, 1971, *10*, 501–517.

STERN, D. N. Mother and infant at play. In M. Lewis & L. Rosenblum (Eds.), *The effect of the infant on its caregiver*. New York: John Wiley, 1974.

STERN, D. N., BEEBE, B., JAFFE, J., & BENNETT, S. L. The infant's stimulus world during social interactions: A study of caregiver behaviours with particular reference to repetition and timing. In H. R. Schaffer (Ed.), *Studies in mother-infant interactions*. London: Academic Press, 1977.

STERN, D., & WASSERMAN, G. A. Maternal language behavior to infants: Studies of its nature, changes over the first six months, determinants and social functions. Symposium presented at Society for Research in Child Development, San Francisco, March 1979.

STEWARD, M., & STEWARD, D. The observation of Anglo, Mexican and Chinese-American mothers teaching their young sons. *Child Development*, 1973, *44*, 329–337.

TAYLOR, P. M., TAYLOR, F. H., GROUSSARD, E. R., & MALONI, J. *Effects of extra contact on early maternal attitudes, perceptions and behaviors*. Paper presented at the biennial meeting of the Society for Research in Child Development, San Francisco, March 1979.

TIZARD, B., & REES, J. The effect of early institutional rearing on the behavior problems and affectional relationships of four-year-old children. *Journal of Child Psychology and Psychiatry*, 1975, *16*, 61–73.

TOFFLER, A. *Future shock*. New York: Bantam Books, 1970.

TREVARTHEN, C. Conversations with a 2-month-old. *New Scientist*, 1974, *22*, 230–235.

TRONICK, E., ALS, H., WISE, S., & BRAZELTON, T. B. The infant's response to entrapment between contradictory messages in face-to-face interaction. *Journal of Child Psychiatry, 1978, 17*, 1–13.

TULKIN, S., & KAGAN, J. Mother-child interaction in the first few years of life. *Child Development*, 1972, *43*, 31–41.

TURNBULL, C. *The mountain people*. London: Jonathan Cape, 1973.

VIETZE, P. M. Mother-infant bonding: A review. In N. Kretchmer & J. Brasel (Eds.), *The biology of child development*. New York: Masson Publishing Inc., 1980.

WALTERS, C. E. Fetal activity, the reliability and comparison of four types of fetal activity and of fetal activity. *Child Development*, 1964, *35*, 1249–1256.

WALTERS, C. E. Prediction of postnatal development from fetal activity. *Child Development*, 1965, *36*, 801–808.

WATSON, J. S. Memory and "contingency analysis" in infant learning. *Merrill-Palmer Quarterly*, 1967, *13*, 55–76.

WEINRAUB, M., & LEWIS, M. The determinants of children's responses to separation. *Monographs of the Society for Research in Child Development*, 1977, *42*(Serial No. 172).

WHITEHURST, G. J., NOVAK, G., & ZORN, G. A. Delayed speech studied in the home. *Developmental Psychology*, 1972, *7*(No. 2), 169–177.

WIDMAYER, S., & FIELD, T. Effects of Brazelton demonstrations on early interactions of preterm infants and their mothers. *Infant Behavior and Development*, 1980, *3*, 79–89.

WILSON, E. *Sociobiology, the new synthesis*. Cambridge, Belknap Press, 1975.

WOLFF, P. M. The natural history of crying and other vocalizations in early infancy. In B. M. Foss (Ed.), *Determinants of infant behaviour* (Vol. 4). London: Methuen, 1969.

YOGMAN, M. W. *The goals and structure of face-to-face interaction between infants and fathers*. Presentation at biennial meeting of the Society for Research in Child Development, San Francisco, March 1979.

39

Fatherhood:
Implications for Child
and Adult Development

HENRY B. BILLER

Being a father can make a major contribution to a man's self-concept and personality functioning; increasing evidence shows that the expectant-father period and the birth of the first child can be particularly important sources of self-examination and psychological growth. The personal characteristics and behavior of the child can have great influence on the personality development of both fathers and mothers, as well as on the husband-wife relationship (Biller & Meredith, 1974; Heath, 1978).

Longitudinal research has indicated that the quality of a father's relationships with his children can have a significant impact on his overall life satisfaction (Levinson, 1978; Vaillant, 1977). Increasing attention has been paid to the functions that fathers can have in child-rearing (Biller, 1974c, 1977b, 1981b). The father's as well as the mother's capacity to become engrossed in and attached to the newborn infant has been clearly documented by recent research (Biller, 1974c; Greenberg & Morris, 1974; Lamb, 1976; Parke, 1979; Pedersen, 1980).

FATHERS AND INFANTS

Investigators have also found that infants form strong attachments with their fathers even during the first year of life (Lamb, 1976; Parke, 1979). These attachments are clearly reflected in the father's behavior. For example infants who are attached to their fathers spend much time looking at their fathers, react animatedly when their fathers enter or leave the room, and often make movements indicating a desire to be close to their fathers (Biller, 1974c; Pedersen & Robson, 1969). The extent of such father-attachment is highly related to the quality of the father's involvement with the infant. Although the formation of the father-infant attachment is generally similar to the mother-infant attachment, many infants tend to express their attachments differentially toward their mothers and fathers. An infant may spend more time looking at his/her father or be more interested in playing with his/her father after s/he has eaten; s/he may particularly seek out contact with his/her mother when s/he is hungry or tired and prefer cuddling with her. The crucial point, however, is that the infant may, overall, have as strong or even a stronger attachment to his/her father as to his/her mother (Biller, 1974c, 1977b; Lamb, 1976, 1981; Pedersen, 1980).

Some research has suggested that well-fathered infants are more curious in exploring their environment than are infants who are paternally deprived—e.g., they seem to relate more maturely to strangers and to react more positively to complex and novel stimuli (Biller, 1974c; Spelke, Zelazo, Kagan, & Kotelchuck, 1973). Well-fathered infants seem more secure and trustful in branching out in their explorations, and there are also indications that their motor development, in terms of crawling, climbing, and manipulating objects, is advanced. When they are involved, fathers tend to initiate more active play and to be more tolerant of physical explorations by infants than are mothers. It is common to observe involved fathers encouraging their infants to crawl a little further or reach a little higher. Fathers are usually less concerned if the child gets tired or dirty than are mothers. This generally allows them to tolerate temporary discomforts which the child may experience in his/her exploration of the environment (Biller, 1974c; Biller & Meredith, 1974).

It should also be added that, unfortunately, fathers are more likely than are mothers to institute a clearcut double standard in terms of the sex of the infant. Some fathers consistently encourage their infant sons' competence in the physical environment but inhibit their infant daughters, fearing for their "fragility." Ironically there are many cases in which the daughter was even more robust than the son was at a similar age (Biller & Meredith, 1974; Biller & Weiss, 1970/1972).

Another factor in the facilitation of the child's exploration of his/her environment is that the father provides an additional attachment figure. In many families the paternally deprived child becomes exclusively attached to the mother, often in a clinging, dependent fashion. Infants who develop an attachment to their fathers as well as their mothers appear to have an easier time relating to other people. A child who has frequent interactions with both parents has access to a wider variety of experiences and may be more adaptive to changes in his/her environment. For example there is usually less separation and stranger anxiety among well-fathered infants. The infant's positive reaction to the returning father may be a prototype to his/her reaction to the entry of other people into his/her environment (Biller, 1974c, 1977b; Biller & Meredith, 1974).

THE FATHER AND MASCULINE DEVELOPMENT

In this section there is a discussion of how various dimensions of paternal behavior may influence the boy's masculine development. Research concerning the effects of paternal masculinity, paternal nurturance, paternal limit-setting, and paternal power is reviewed. The material in this and the next three sections of this chapter focuses on the father-son relationship, and in later sections there is consideration of the importance of the father-daughter relationship. The emphasis is on adaptive dimensions of sex-role functioning. The child who evolves a positive sex-role orientation *and* the basic competencies that are associated with his/her sex is more likely to develop a firm self-confidence and a broad range of adaptive qualities that transcend narrowly defined sex-role stereotypes (Biller, 1974c, 1981b).

Paternal Masculinity

The quality of the father-son relationship appears to be a more important influence on the boy's masculine development than is the amount of time that the father spends at home (Biller, 1971a, 1981b). A crucial factor in the boy's masculine development is the degree to which his father exhibits masculine behavior in family interactions. Imitation of the father directly enhances the boy's masculine development only if the father displays masculine behavior in the presence of his son.

Biller (1969a, 1972) found a strong relationship between kindergarten boys' masculinity and the degree to which they perceived their fathers as making family decisions. In terms of measures of sex-role orientation (masculinity-femininity of self-concept), sex-role preference (masculinity-femininity of interests and attitudes), and sex-role adoption (masculinity-femininity of social and environmental interaction), a high level of perceived decision making by father was associated with strongly masculine behavior. Perceived decision making by father was particularly highly correlated with sex-role orientation. Perceived father-competence was most related to

sex-role orientation although it was also significantly related to preference and adoption (Biller, 1969a/1972). Other studies have also suggested a positive association between the son's masculinity and his perception of his father's being masculine (Bronfenbrenner, 1958; Heilbrun, 1965b, 1974; Kagan, 1958; Rychlak & Legerski, 1967).

Even though there is a consistency of findings in terms of an apparent relationship between father's and son's masculinity, the studies cited before share a common methodological shortcoming. Measurement of father and son masculinity was generally not independent, both assessments usually being deduced from the son's responses. It could be argued that such evidence is not a sufficient basis on which to conclude that father's and son's masculinity is related. An alternative explanation is that masculine sons will tend to see their fathers as highly masculine regardless of their father's actual masculinity. A boy may appear similar to his father, yet have learned his masculine behavior from his peer group rather than from his father (Bronfenbrenner, 1958).

Parental Interaction

Hetherington (1965) evaluated the relative dominance of parents by placing them in an actual decision-making situation. She found that masculinity of preschool and preadolescent boys' projective sex-role behavior (IT Scale) was positively related to paternal dominance. Moreover she discovered a general tendency for similarity between father and son and son's imitation of father to be higher in father-dominant than in mother-dominant homes (Hetherington, 1965; Hetherington & Brackbill, 1963; Hetherington & Frankie, 1967).

Using essentially the same parental interaction procedure as Hetherington, Biller (1969a/1972) found that father-dominance in father-mother interaction was positively related to kindergarten boys' sex-role orientations, preferences, and adoptions. However it is also important to point out that father-dominance in parental interaction showed weaker relationships with sex-role development than did the boys' perception of father-dominance. The boy's behavior seems to be much determined by his particular perception of family interactions, and it may be that his view of the father is the most accurate measure. The boy's perception of his father can also be influenced by his mother's behavior. In father-mother interactions some mothers encouraged their husbands to make decisions, while others appeared to prevent their husbands from serving as adequate models by constantly interfering with their attempts to assume a decision-making role. The most well-functioning families seemed to be those where both parents were competent decision makers.

Other analyses of the data suggested the complex influences of family interactions on the boy's sex-role development. Several of the boys who were low in masculinity had fathers who were dominant in terms of father-mother interaction and generally seemed masculine. However these fathers also appeared to be controlling and restrictive of their son's behavior—e.g., this type of dominant father punished his son for disagreeing with him. Masculine development is facilitated when the father is a competent masculine model *and* allows and encourages the boy to be assertive.

It is the father's sex-role adoption in family interactions that is crucial, not the degree of masculine behavior that he exhibits outside the home. Many fathers have masculine interests and are masculine in their peer and work relationships but are very ineffectual in their interactions with their wives and children. The stereotype of the hard-working father whose primary activity at home is lying on the couch, watching television, or sleeping is an all-too-accurate description of many fathers. If the boy's father is not consistently involved in family functioning, it is much more difficult for his son to learn to be appropriately assertive, active, independent, and competent (Biller, 1974b, 1981b).

Paternal Nurturance

The father's affectionate, encouraging, and attentive behavior toward his child can be seen as aspects of paternal nurturance. Such behavior may or may not be manifested in the rubric of caretaking or protective activities which appear more common in descriptions of maternal nurturance. The focus here is on paternal nurturance and masculine development; the influence of paternal nurturance on other dimensions of development is discussed in later sections of this chapter.

There is much evidence that a warm, affectionate father-son relationship can strengthen the boy's masculine development. In a study by Sears (1953), preschool boys who assumed the father role in doll-play activities (used the father doll with high frequency) tended to have warm, affectionate fathers. Mussen and Distler (1959) studied the structural doll-play of kindergarten boys. Their results revealed that boys who scored high in masculinity of projective sex-role responses perceived fathers as more warm and nurturant than did boys with low masculinity scores. Using the same methodology Mussen and Rutherford (1963) reported similar findings for first-grade boys.

Studying kindergarten boys Biller (1969a/1972) found that perceived father-nurturance was related to a fantasy game measure of sex-role orientation. Other researchers have also found evidence suggesting that paternal nurturance is related to older boys' masculinity and/or similarity to their fathers (Bandura & Walters, 1959; Bronson, 1959; Distler, 1964; Mussen, 1961; Payne & Mussen, 1956).

Paternal Limit-Setting

Findings suggesting a relationship between paternal limit-setting and masculine and/or aggressive behavior have been presented by several researchers (Lefkowitz, 1962; Moulton, Burnstein, Liberty, & Altucher, 1966). The implication of such data is that boys often learn to be aggressive and masculine by modeling themselves after their fathers, the disciplinary situation being particularly relevant. Other factors may be operating to produce a relationship between paternal limit-setting and boys' aggressive behavior—e.g., boys may be aggressive as a function of the frustration engendered by severe paternal punitiveness.

However, findings concerning the influence of paternal limit-setting on masculine development are inconsis-

tent. In Mussen and Distler's (1959) study, the kindergarten boys who manifested highly masculine projective sex-role responses perceived their fathers as somewhat more punitive and threatening in structured doll-play situations than did boys low in masculinity. Mussen and Rutherford (1963) found a similar trend for first-grade boys. In both studies perceived nurturance of father was found to be much more related to high-masculine preferences. In addition Mussen and Distler (1960) ascertained nothing to indicate that the fathers of the high-masculine kindergarten boys actually punished them more than did the fathers of the low-masculine boys. In Biller's (1969a/1972) study with kindergarten boys, perceived paternal limit-setting was slightly related to a measure of sex-role orientation but not to measures of sex-role preference or sex-role adoption. Sears, Rau, and Alpert (1965) did not find a consistent relationship between interview measures of paternal limit-setting and preschool boys' masculinity.

When the father plays a significant part in setting limits, the boy's attachment to his father seems to be facilitated *only* if there is an already established, affectionate, father-son relationship. If the father is not nurturant and is punitive, the boy is likely to display a low level of father-imitation. Bandura and Walters (1959) found that adolescent boys who had highly punitive but generally nonnurturant and nonrewarding fathers exhibited relatively low father-preference and little perception of themselves as acting and thinking like their fathers.

Paternal Power

Mussen and Distler (1959) found that boys with highly masculine projective sex-role behavior perceived their fathers as more "powerful" than did boys low in masculinity. When perceived-nurturance and perceived-punitiveness scores were combined, the difference between the masculine and nonmasculine boys was particularly clearcut. Mussen and Rutherford (1963) reported similar results for first-grade boys, but the relationship was not as strong. Freedheim and Borstelmann's (1963) data suggested that the father's total salience to the child and overall involvement in family decision making is the best predictor of the elementary school boy's masculinity. In Biller's (1969a/1972) study with kindergarten boys, the overall amount of perceived father-influence was much more important than the perception of the fathers as dominant in a particular area of family or parent-child functioning. Parent-perception and sex-role research with college students has also yielded results which are in line with formulations stressing the importance of the total father-son relationship (Distler, 1964; Moulton et al., 1966).

It is also interesting to note that Bronfenbrenner's (1961) findings indicated that the development of leadership, responsibility, and social maturity in adolescent males is closely associated with a father-son relationship which is not only nurturant but also includes a strong component of paternal limit-setting. A study by Reuter and Biller (1973) also suggests the importance of evaluating both the quality and quantity of paternal behavior. This study is discussed in more detail in a later section, but is is appropriate to note that the combination of at least moderate paternal availability with at least moderate paternal nurturance was associated with indications of positive personal adjustment among male college students.

Some Methodological Comments

The bulk of the research concerning father-child relationships and personality development can be criticized because of methodological deficiences and/or because of limited generality. In most investigations the father's behavior is not directly assessed, and maternal or child reports of paternal behavior are used. In many of the studies the sources of evidence about parental behavior and the child's behavior are not independent, leading to problems of interpretation—e.g., in many studies the child is asked to describe both his own and his parents' behavior. More studies in which there is an assessment of the amount of consistency among observer ratings of familial interactions and children's and parents' perceptions of parent-child relationships should be done.

Most of the studies done concerning the father-child relationship and personality development have been of a correlational nature. Often the child's perception of his father or some report of the father's behavior is linked to a measure of the child's personality development. When significant correlations are found between the degree to which a boy perceives his father as nurturant and the boy's masculinity, it is usually assumed that paternal nurturance has been an antecedent of masculine development, but fathers may become nurturant and accepting toward their sons when their sons are masculine and rejecting when their sons are unmasculine. Longitudinal research would be particularly helpful in determining the extent to which certain paternal behaviors precede and/or are antecedents of particular dimensions of children's behavior. Careful observations of families in various environmental settings could be especially revealing.

The focus in this section is on reviewing and integrating empirical studies relating to the father's role in sex-role development. The reader who wishes a relatively more theoretical discussion of the father's role in personality development, including an overview of the various theories of identification, should consult other sources (e.g., Biller, 1971a, 1974c; Lamb, 1976; Lynn, 1974, 1979).

FATHER-ABSENCE AND MASCULINE DEVELOPMENT

Many researchers have speculated that the primary effects of father-absence are manifested in terms of deficits and/or abnormalities in the boy's sex-role development (Biller, 1970/1971/1972, 1981a). In this section research findings concerning the relationship between father-absence and the boy's sex-role development are discussed. A comparison of the sex-role development of father-absent and father-present boys suggests some of the ways in which fathering and paternal deprivation influence personality development.

Sex-Typed Behavior

The Sears conducted a pioneering investigation of the effects of father-absence on three- to five-year-old children (Sears, 1951). Each child was given an opportunity to play with a standardized set of doll-play equipment, and the investigators recorded his behavior. Compared to the father-present boys, father-absent boys were less aggressive, and they also had less sex-role differentiation in their doll-play activity—e.g., their play contained less emphasis on the maleness of the father and the boy dolls (Sears, Pintler, & Sears, 1946). Using a similar procedure to study the effects of father-absence on six- to ten-year-old children, Bach (1946) also found that father-absent boys were less aggressive and assertive in doll-play than were father-present boys.

In a very thorough presentation Stolz et al. (1954) gathered data concerning four- to eight-year-old children who, for approximately the first two years of their lives, had been separated from their fathers. Interview results revealed that the previously father-separated boys were generally perceived by their fathers as being "sissies." Careful observation of the peer interactions of these boys supported this view. The previously father-separated boys were less assertively aggressive and independent in their peer relations than boys who had not been separated from their fathers. However, the fact that the fathers were present in the home at the time of this study and that the father-child relationships were stressful makes it difficult to specify what influence father-absence per se had on the children's personality development.

Tiller (1958) and Lynn and Sawrey (1959) conducted an extensive investigation of Norwegian children aged 8 to 9½ whose fathers were sailors absent at least nine months a year. They compared these father-separated children with a matched group of children whose fathers had jobs which did not require them to be separated from their families. The boys' responses to projective tests and interviews with their mothers indicated that father-separation was associated with compensatory masculinity (the boys at times behaving in an exaggerated masculine manner and at other times behaving in a highly feminine manner). The father-separated boys appeared to be much less secure in their masculinity than did the control-group boys. Consistent with the findings of Bach (1946) and Sears (1951), the father-separated boys were less aggressive in doll-play than were the control group.

Developmental Stages

The quality of the early father-child attachment is an important factor in the child's sex-role and personality development. The degree and quality of the father's involvement, even in the first year of life, has much influence on the child's behavior (Biller, 1974c, 1976a, 1977b).

Father-absence before the age of four or five appears to have a retarding effect on masculine development. Hetherington (1966) reported that 9- to 12-year-old father-absent boys manifested less masculine projective sex-role behavior and were rated as more dependent on their peers, less aggressive, and as engaging in fewer physical-contact games by male recreation directors than were father-present boys. However there were no consistent differences on the sex-role measures when the father-present boys were compared with boys who had become father-absent after the age of four.

Biller (1969b/1972) found that father-absent, five-year-old boys had less masculine sex-role orientations (fantasy-game measure) and sex-role preferences (game choice) than did father-present boys. Moreover the boys who became father-absent before the age of four had significantly less masculine sex-role orientations than did those who became father-absent in their fifth year. In an investigation Biller and Bahm (1971) conducted with junior high school boys, those who became father-absent before the age of five scored less masculine on an adjective checklist measure of masculinity of self-concept than did those who were father-present.

There are many other studies which suggest that early father-absence retards the young boy's development of independence and other masculine behaviors (e.g., Green, 1974; Leichty, 1960; Santrock, 1970b; Stendler, 1954). There is also cross-cultural evidence which indicates that early father-absence is often associated with sex-role conflicts among males in other societies (e.g., Burton, 1972; Burton & Whiting, 1961; Rogers & Long, 1968; Stephens, 1962; Whiting, Kluckhohn, & Anthony, 1958).

A study of lower-class fifth-grade boys by Santrock (1970b) revealed that boys who became father-absent before the age of two were more handicapped in terms of several dimensions of personality development than were boys who became father-absent at a later age. For example boys who became father-absent before age two were found to be less trusting, less industrious, and to have more feelings of inferiority than boys who became father-absent between the ages of three to five. Other evidence is consistent with the supposition that early father-absence is associated with a heightened susceptibility to a variety of psychological problems (Biller, 1971a, 1981a). Research by Wallerstein and Kelly (1974, 1975, 1976) has clearly shown that developmental stage is a crucial factor in determining the type of reaction that children have to divorce and separation from the father. Studies relating to the effects of the timing of father-absence on various dimensions of personality development are reviewed in later sections of this chapter.

Different Aspects of Sex-Role Development

As the findings relating to developmental stages have suggested, different aspects of sex role may not be affected in the same way by father-absence. It is common for young father-absent boys to seek intensely the attention of older males. Because of deprivation effects father-absent children often have a strong motivation to imitate and please potential father-figures. Father-absent boys may strive to act masculine in some facets of their behavior while continuing to behave in an unmasculine or feminine manner in others. For example a paternally deprived boy may interact only with females who encourage passivity and dependency in the first four or five years of his life, while later there is much peer pressure and societal pressure for him to behave in a masculine manner. Demands for masculine behavior may not become apparent to the boy until he reaches school age or even adolescence, but in any case under such conditions,

his sex-role preference and/or sex-role adoption may differ from his basic sex-role orientation (Biller & Borstelmann, 1967).

Barclay and Cusumano (1967) did not find any differences between father-present and father-absent adolescent males on a measure of sex-role preference (Gough Femininity Scale). However the father-absent males, as compared to the father-present males, were more field-dependent in terms of Witkin's rod and frame test. Barclay and Cusumano conceptualized the field-dependence–field-independence dimension as reflecting underlying sex-role orientation. In a study with lower-class, six-year-old children, Biller (1968b) found that father-absent boys were significantly less masculine than were father-present boys on a measure of projective sex-role behavior which was used to assess sex-role orientation. However the two groups were not consistently different in terms of their direct sex-role preferences (the toys and the games that they said they liked) or teachers' ratings of sex-role adoption. Biller's (1969b/1972) results from a study with five-year-old boys also suggested that sex-role orientation is more affected by father-absence than are sex-role preference or sex-role adoption. Even though the father-absent boys had significantly less masculine game preferences than did the father-present boys, differences between the groups were most clearcut in terms of responses to the sex-role-orientation procedure. No consistent differences were apparent with respect to the sex-role–adoption measure.

An examination of data from several other studies suggests the hypothesis that, particularly by adolescence, there is relatively little difference between lower-class father-present and father-absent boys with respect to many facets of sex-role awareness, preference, and adoption (e.g., Barclay & Cusumano, 1967; Greenstein, 1966; McCord, McCord, & Thurber, 1962; Mitchell & Wilson, 1967; Tiller, 1961).

Surrogate Models

Paternal absence or paternal inadequacy does not rule out the possible presence of other male models. A brother, uncle, grandfather, or male boarder may provide the boy with much competent adult male contact. An important role can be played by peers, neighbors, and teachers. Male teachers seem to have much potential for influencing father-absent boys (Biller, 1974a, 1974b, 1974c; Lee & Wolinsky, 1973).

Siblings. Older brothers can be very important masculine models for boys. For example paternal deprivation may have a much different effect on a five-year-old boy who is an only child than on a five-year-old boy who has two older brothers who themselves were not paternally deprived in early childhood. Obviously many other variables have to be considered, including the frequency and quality of interactions among siblings. A problem with many of the sibling studies is that they consider only the presence or absence of a particular type of sibling. This is somewhat analogous to studies which take into account only whether a child is father-present or father-absent (Biller, 1974c).

Interestingly in two-child, father-absent families, there is some evidence that boys with brothers suffer less of a deficit in academic aptitude than do boys with sisters (Sutton-Smith, Rosenberg, & Landy, 1968). In Santrock's (1970a) study, father-absent boys with only older male siblings scored more masculine (on a maternal interview measure of sex-role behavior) than did father-absent boys with only older female siblings. In an extension of Santrock's investigation, Wohlford, Santrock, Berger, and Lieberman (1971) found that father-absent children with older brothers were less dependent than were those with older sisters in terms of both doll-play and maternal-interview measures. However, the presence or absence of older female siblings was not related to the sex-role measures and did not affect the older brother's influence.

Although the presence of male siblings may lessen the effects of father-absence, data from one of Biller's (1968a) investigations were consistent with the conclusion that the presence of a father is generally a much more important factor in masculine development than is the presence of an older brother. There is evidence, in fact, that in father-present families fathers exert more consistent pressure than do either mothers, siblings, or peers for sex-typed behavior in young children (Biller, 1974a, 1981b; Langlois & Downs, 1981).

Peers. The masculine role models provided by the peer group can be particularly influential for the paternally deprived boy. In a subculture in which instrumental aggression and physical prowess are very important as a means of achieving peer acceptance, many father-absent boys are likely to emulate their masculine peers. Peer models seem especially important in lower-class neighborhoods. Miller (1958) emphasized the centrality of such traits as toughness and independence in the value system of lower-class adolescents. Lower-class boys honor aggressiveness more than do middle-class boys, and one of the types of boys that they most admire is the aggressive, belligerent youngster who earns their respect because of his toughness and strength (Pope, 1953).

The boy who is physically well-equipped may find it relatively easy to gain acceptance from his peers. Many paternally deprived boys behave in a generally effective and masculine manner. An additional case-study analysis of some of the five-year-old boys in Biller's (1968a, 1969b/1972) studies has indicated that father-absent boys who are relatively mesomorphic are less likely to be retarded in their sex-role development than are father-absent boys with unmasculine physiques. A boy's physique has important stimulus value in terms of the expectations and reinforcements it elicits from others, and it may, along with correlated constitutional factors, predispose him toward success or failure in particular types of activities. The influence of the child's anatomical, temperamental, and cognitive predispositions on parental and peer behavior must be taken into account (Biller, 1974c, 1981a, 1981b).

Methodological Issues

In addition to the obvious theoretical and practical relevance of studying the effects of father-absence, a possible methodological justification is that father-absence is a naturalistic manipulation. It can be argued that father-absence must be an antecedent rather than a conse-

quence of certain behaviors in children. However, a general problem with studies comparing father-absent and father-present children is that investigators have usually treated both father-absent children and father-present children as if they represented homogeneous groups. There has been a lack of concern for the meaning of father-absence and father-presence. For example there have been few attempts to ensure that a group of consistently father-absent boys is compared with a group of boys who have a high level and quality of father-availability.

Most researchers have treated father-absence in an overly simplistic fashion. In many studies there has been no specification of such variables as type, length, and age of onset of father-absence. Potentially important variables such as the child's sex, intelligence, constitutional characteristics, birth order, relationship with the mother, and sociocultural background as well as availability of father-surrogates are not taken into account, either in subject matching or in data analysis. When careful matching procedures are followed, more clearcut findings seem to emerge (e.g., Biller, 1969b/1972, 1971a; Blanchard & Biller, 1971; Hetherington, 1966, 1972; Hetherington, Cox, & Cox, 1978).

THE FATHER AND COGNITIVE FUNCTIONING

This section includes a description of research efforts which in some way have explored the relationship between fathering and cognitive functioning. Results from several investigations have revealed as association between inadequate father-son relationships and academic difficulties among boys.

Academic Achievement

Kimball (1952) studied highly intelligent boys enrolled in a residential preparatory school. She compared 20 boys who were failing in school with a group of boys who were randomly selected from the total school population. Interview and psychological test material consistently revealed that the underachieving boys had very inadequate relationships with their fathers. Many of the fathers were reported to work long hours and to be home infrequently or to attempt to dominate and control their sons by means of excessive discipline.

Through the use of extensive clinical interviews, Grunebaum, Hurwitz, Prentice, and Sperry (1962) examined the family life of elementary school boys who had at least average intelligence but were one to two years below expectation in their academic achievement (Metropolitan Achievement Test). These boys seemed to have very poor relationships with their fathers. Their fathers were reported to feel generally inadequate and thwarted in their own ambitions and to view themselves as failures. The fathers appeared to be particularly insecure about their masculinity and did not seem to offer their sons adequate models of male competence. This study, at best, was of an exploratory clinical nature, but it did suggest some of the ways in which the dynamics of the husband-wife relationship can affect the child's academic functioning. It is also meaningful to note that boys with inadequate sex-role development are often found in families in which the mother dominates the father and undermines his attempts to be decisive and competent (Biller, 1969a/1972).

Both Katz (1967) and Solomon (1969) reported data indicating a strong positive association between paternal interest and encouragement and academic achievement among lower-class black elementary school boys. Katz's findings were based on the boys' perceptions of their parents whereas Solomon had ratings of parent-child interactions while the boys were performing a series of intellectual tasks. Interestingly in both studies the father's behavior appeared to be a much more important factor than did the mother's behavior.

The studies so far discussed have dealt with paternal factors and their association with academic achievement. In addition there is evidence that the quality of fathering is related to the child's performance on intelligence and aptitude tests.

Radin (1972) found both the quality and quantity of father-son interactions were strongly associated with four-year-old boys' intellectual functioning. Father-son interactions during an interview with the father were recorded and later coded for frequency of paternal nurturance and restrictiveness. The overall number of father-son interactions was positively correlated to both Stanford-Binet and Peabody Picture Vocabulary Test Intelligence Test scores. However the strongest relationship observed was between paternal nurturance (seeking out the child in a positive manner, asking information of the child, meeting the child's needs) and the intelligence test measures. On the other hand paternal restrictiveness (e.g., demands for obedience) was negatively correlated with level of intellectual functioning. The quality of the father's behavior, particularly paternal nurturance, appeared to be more important than did the total number of father-son interactions.

In a subsequent study Radin (1973, 1976) reported evidence indicating that the amount of paternal nurturance at the time of the initial study was also positively related to the boys' intellectual functioning one year later. In addition a questionnaire measure of degree of paternal involvement in direct teaching activities (e.g., teaching the boy to count and read) at the time of the initial study was positively associated with the boys' intellectual functioning both at that time and one year later.

Individual Differences

Correlational data do not prove that a positive father-son relationship directly facilitates the boys' intellectual functioning. For example a father may be much more available, accepting, and nurturant to a son who is bright and performs well in school. On the other hand disappointment with the son's abilities may lead the father to reject him, and/or the son's performance may further weaken an already flimsy father-son relationship. Individual differences in the child's constitutional predispositions and behavior can have much influence on the quality of interactions between father and child (Biller, 1971a).

Fathers are reported to be much less tolerant of severely intellectually handicapped children than are mothers (Farber, 1962). The father who highly values intellectual endeavors is especially likely to reject a retarded child (Downey, 1963). Paternal deprivation lessens the probability that the retarded child will maximize his intellectual potential or have adequate sex-role development (Biller, 1971a; Biller & Borstelmann, 1965).

In addition to being the antecedents of some forms of mental retardation, constitutional predispositions and genetic factors may be related to other types of influences affecting the father-child relationship. Father and son can manifest cognitive abilities in the same area primarily as a function of a similar genetic inheritance. Poffenberger and Norton (1959) found that the attitudes of fathers and of their college freshmen sons toward mathematics were similar yet were not related to the closeness of the father-son relationship. These investigators speculated that genetic factors are involved in degree of success in mathematics and can predispose similar father-son attitudes toward mathematics. However, Hill's (1967) findings suggest that more than genetic factors are involved in the child's attitudes toward mathematics. In studying the relationship between paternal expectations and upper-middle-class seventh-grade boys' attitudes toward mathematics, Hill found that positive attitudes toward mathematics were more common among boys whose fathers viewed mathematics as a masculine endeavor and expected their sons to behave in a masculine manner.

Paternal Availability

Much of the evidence concerning the father's importance in cognitive development has come indirectly from studies in which father-absent and father-present children have been compared. Many investigators have reported evidence consistent with the supposition that father-absent children are less likely to function well on intelligence and aptitude tests than are father-present children (e.g., Biller, 1981a; Blanchard & Biller, 1971; Deutsch & Brown, 1964; Lessing, Zagorin, & Nelson, 1970; Santrock, 1972; Shinn, 1978; Sutton-Smith et al., 1968).

Sutton-Smith et al. (1968) explored the relationship between father-absence and college sophomores' aptitude test scores (American College Entrance Examination). These investigators defined father-absence as an absence of the father from the home for at least two consecutive years. Compared to father-present students those who were father-absent performed at a lower level in terms of verbal, language, and total aptitude test scores. Although father-absence appeared to affect both males and females, it seemed to have more influence on males. Some interesting variations in the effects of father-absence as a function of sex of subject and sex of sibling are also reported—e.g., in two-child, father-absent families, boys with brothers appeared to be less deficient in academic aptitude than did boys with sisters. On the other hand the father-present girl who was an only child seemed to be at a particular advantage in terms of her aptitude test scores.

Lessing et al. (1970) studied a group of nearly 500 children (ages 9 to 15) who had been evaluated at a child guidance clinic. They explored the relationship between father-absence, identified as two or more not necessarily consecutive years of separation, and functioning on the Wechsler Intelligence Test for Children. Father-absence, for both boys and girls, was associated with relatively low ability in perceptual-motor and manipulative-spatial tasks (block design and object assembly). Father-absent boys also scored lower than did father-present boys on the arithmetic subtest.

Their results suggest some rather complex interactions between father-absence and social class. Among working-class children those who were father-absent performed at a generally lower level than did those who were father-present. They were less able in their verbal functioning as well as on perceptual-motor and manipulative-spatial tasks. In comparison middle-class children did not appear to be as handicapped by father-absence. They earned lower performance scores (particularly in block design and object assembly), but they actually scored higher in verbal intelligence than did father-present children.

Early Paternal Deprivation

Blanchard and Biller (1971) attempted to specify different levels of father-availability and to ascertain their relationship to the academic functioning of third-grade boys. They examined both the timing of father-absence and the degree of father-son interaction in the father-present home. The boys were of average intelligence and were from working-class and lower-middle-class backgrounds. Four groups of boys were studied: early father-absent (beginning before age three), late father-absent (beginning after age five), low father-present (less than six hours per week), and high father-present (more than two hours per day). In order to control for variables (other than father-availability) which might affect academic performance, there was individual subject matching in terms of the characteristics of the early father-absent group. The subjects were matched so that each boy from the early father-absent group was essentially identical with a boy from each of the other three groups in terms of age, IQ, socioeconomic status, and presence or absence of male siblings.

Academic performance was assessed by means of Stanford Achievement Test scores and classroom grades. (The teachers did not have the children's achievement test scores available to them until after final classroom grades had been assigned.) The high father-present group was very superior to the other three groups. With respect to both grades and achievement test scores, the early father-absent boys were generally underachievers; the late father-absent and lower father-present boys usually functioned somewhat below grade level, and the high father-present group performed above grade level.

The early father-absent boys were consistently handicapped in their academic performance. They scored significantly lower on every achievement test index as well as in their grades. The early father-absent group functioned below grade level in both language and mathematical skills. When compared to the high father-present group, the early father-absent group appeared to be quite inferior in skills relating to reading comprehension. In a study of elementary school boys, Dyl and Biller (1973) also found early father-absence to be associated with deficits in reading comprehension.

Santrock (1972) reported additional evidence which indicated that early father-absence can have a very significant debilitating effect on cognitive functioning. Among lower-class junior high and high school students, those who became father-absent before the age of five, particularly before the age of two, generally had scored significantly lower on measures of IQ (Otis Quick Test) and achievement (Stanford Achievement Test) that had been administered when they were in the third and sixth grades than did those from intact families. The most detrimental effects occurred when father-absence was due to divorce, desertion, or separation rather than to death. The findings of this study also provided some support for the positive remedial effects of a stepfather for boys, especially when the stepfather joined the family before the child was five years of age.

Cognitive Styles

Carlsmith (1964) made an interesting discovery concerning the relationship between father-absence and differential intellectual abilities. She examined the College Board Aptitude Test scores of middle-class and upper-middle class high school males who had experienced early father-absence because of their father's military service during World War II. Boys who were father-absent in early childhood were more likely to have a feminine patterning of aptitude test scores. Compared to the typical male pattern of math score higher than verbal score, males who had experienced early separation from their fathers more frequently had a higher verbal score than math score. She found that the earlier the onset of father-absence and the longer the father-absence, the more likely was the male to have a higher verbal than math score. The effect was strongest for students whose fathers were absent at birth and/or were away for over 30 months. Higher verbal than math functioning is the usual pattern among females, and Carlsmith speculated that it reflects a feminine-global style of cognitive functioning. Results from other studies have also indicated a relationship between father-absence and a feminine patterning of aptitude test scores among males (e.g., Altus, 1958; Maccoby & Rau, 1962; Nelson & Maccoby, 1966).

A study with adolescent boys by Barclay and Cusumano (1967) supports the supposition that difficulties in analytical functioning are often related to father-absence. Using Witkin's rod and frame procedure, Barclay and Cusumano found that father-absent males were more dependent than those who were father-present. Wohlford and Liberman (1970) reported that father-separation (after the age of six) was related to field-dependency among elementary school children from an urban section of Miami. On the other hand some investigators have reported findings which suggest that warm, close father-child relationships stimulate sons to be field-independent (Bieri, 1960; Dyk & Witkin, 1965). It is also relevant to note that there is increasing evidence that paternal behavior can be an important factor in facilitating or inhibiting creative behavior in children (Biller, 1974b; Lynn, 1974).

Sex Differences

Most of the research concerning paternal influence and the child's personality development and cognitive functioning has focused on the father-son relationship. However, the quantity and quality of fathering can affect girls as well as boys (Biller, 1971a, 1974c; Biller & Weiss, 1970; Johnson, 1963, 1975). Although boys and girls are both influenced, current evidence suggests that paternal deprivation has a somewhat more negative effect on the cognitive abilities of boys (Hetherington et al., 1978; Lessing et al., 1970; Radin, 1976; Santrock, 1972).

Nevertheless there is increasing evidence that the behavior of fathers can do much to stimulate their daughter's cognitive functioning and intellectual attainment. Plank and Plank (1954) discovered that outstanding female mathematicians were particularly attached to and identified with their fathers. Bieri (1960) also reported that high analytical ability in college women was associated with father-identification. Crandall, Dewey, Katovsky, and Preston (1964) found that elementary school girls who did well in both reading and mathematics had fathers who consistently praised and rewarded their intellectual efforts.

Data from a number of studies, when taken together, indicate that high paternal expectations in the context of a warm father-daughter relationship are conducive to the development of autonomy, independence, achievement, and creativity among females (Crandall et al., 1964; Helson, 1967; Honzik, 1967; Johnson, 1975; Kundsin, 1974; Nakamura & Rogers, 1969).

On the other hand paternal rejection seems related to deficits in females functioning in certain types of cognitive tasks (Heilbrun, Harrell, & Gillard, 1967). Findings from a study by Hurley (1967) suggest that paternal hostility can be particularly detrimental to a girl's scholastic functioning. Other types of paternal behavior often interfere with the cognitive development of females. The highly nurturant father who reinforces the "feminine" stereotype of passivity, timidity, and dependency can also greatly inhibit his daughter's intellectual potential (Biller, 1974c). Much data concerning paternal influence on female personality development are reviewed in a later section of this chapter.

Social Class

Paternal deprivation is often a major factor contributing to a disadvantaged environment (Bronfenbrenner, 1967). Father-absence appears to hamper lower-class black children particularly. Some investigators have reported that among lower-class black children those who are father-absent score considerably lower on intelligence and achievement tests than do those who are father-present (e.g., Cortés & Fleming, 1968; Deutsch, 1960; Deutsch & Brown, 1964; Mackie, Maxwell, & Rafferty, 1967).

Paternal deprivation seems to be associated with much more serious consequences among lower-class children than among middle-class children (Biller, 1971a, 1974c). Some research has suggested that among father-absent children those who are from working-class backgrounds are more consistently handicapped in their cognitive functioning than are those from middle-class backgrounds (Lessing et al., 1970). A general depression in academic achievement associated with father-absence has usually been found with working-class or lower-class children (Blanchard & Biller, 1971; Santrock, 1972).

Middle-class father-absent children often do well in situations requiring verbal skills. Carlsmith's (1964) middle-class and upper-middle-class father-absent group apparently were equal or superior to her father-present group in verbal aptitude, although inferior in mathematical aptitude. Lessing et al. (1970) found that middle-class father-absent children had higher verbal scores, although lower performance (e.g., perceptual-manipulative) scores than did father-present children. Dyl and Biller (1973) found that, although lower-class father-absent boys were particularly handicapped in their reading skills, middle-class father-absent boys functioned quite adequately in reading. Because academic achievement, particularly in elementary school, is so heavily dependent on verbal and reading ability, father-absent middle-class children do not seem to be very handicapped.

Maternal Influence

The middle-class mother seems to influence strongly her father-absent son's intellectual development. In an interview study in a university town, Hilgard, Neuman, and Fisk (1960) found that men who lost their fathers during childhood tended to be highly successful in their academic pursuits despite, or maybe because of, a conspicuous overdependence on their mothers. Clinical findings presented by Gregory (1965b) also suggest that many upper-middle-class students who have been father-absent do well in college. Evidence reviewed by Nelson and Maccoby (1966) reveals that high verbal ability in boys is often associated with a close restrictive mother-son relationship. Levy (1943) reported that middle-class maternally overprotected boys did superior work in school, particularly in subjects requiring verbal facility. However their performance in mathematics was not at such a high level, which seems consistent with Carlsmith's (1964) results.

Middle-class mothers are much more likely to place strong emphasis on academic success than are lower-class mothers (Kohn, 1959). Some findings suggest that among lower-class mothers those without husbands are preoccupied with day-to-day activities and less frequently think of future goals for themselves or for their children (Heckscher, 1967; Parker & Kleiner, 1966). Compared to the middle-class mother, the lower-class mother usually puts much less emphasis on long-term academic goals and is also generally a much less adequate model for coping with the demands of the middle-class school.

In homes in which the father is absent or relatively unavailable, the mother assumes a more primary role in terms of dispensing reinforcements and emphasizing certain values. A father-absent boy who is strongly identified with an intellectually oriented mother may be at an advantage in some facets of school adjustment. He may find the transition from home to the typically feminine-oriented classroom quite comfortable. Such father-absent boys might be expected to do particularly well in tasks in which verbal skills and conformity are rewarded.

Although they may stimulate the paternally deprived child's acquisition of verbal skills and his adaptation to the typical school environment, middle-class overprotecting mothers often inhibit the development of an active problem-solving attitude toward the environment. A mother who is excessively overprotective and dominating may interfere with the development of the child's assertiveness and independence (Biller, 1969b/1972, 1971b/1972; Biller & Bahm, 1971). The psychological adjustment of the mother is a crucial factor; a mother who is emotionally disturbed and/or interpersonally handicapped can have a very negative effect on the father-absent child's self-concept and ability to relate to others (e.g., McCord et al., 1962; Pedersen, 1966). On the other hand mothers who are self-accepting, have high ego strength, and are interpersonally mature can do much to facilitate positive personality development among their paternally deprived children (Biller, 1971a, 1971b/1972, 1974c, 1981a; Hetherington et al., 1978).

Variations in fathering can influence the child's cognitive development, but it must be emphasized that fathering is only one of many factors which have an impact on the child's intellectual functioning. Sociocultural, maternal, and peer-group values are especially important. For example among children in the lower class, paternal deprivation usually intensifies lack of exposure to experiences linking intellectual activities with masculine interests. Many boys, in their desperate attempts to view themselves as totally masculine, become excessively dependent on their peer group and perceive intellectual tasks as "feminine." The school setting which presents women as authority figures and makes strong demands for obedience and conformity is particularly antithetical to such boys' fervent desires to feel masculine (Biller, 1974c).

THE FATHER AND PERSONAL AND SOCIAL ADJUSTMENT

This section includes a discussion of the influence of the father-child relationship and paternal deprivation on self-concept, anxiety, impulsiveness, moral development, delinquent behavior, interpersonal relations, and psychopathology.

Self-Esteem and Personal Adjustment

A number of investigations have revealed an association between self-esteem and various facets of paternal behavior. The father's interest and consistent participation seem to contribute strongly to the development of the child's self-confidence and self-esteem. Sears (1970) found a relationship between mother-reported paternal warmth and a questionnaire measure of sixth-grade boys' self-esteem. Medinnus (1965a) reported that college students' self-esteem was positively related to paternal love and negatively related to paternal rejection and neglect. Mussen, Young, Gaddini, and Morante (1963) presented data indicating that adolescent boys with unaffectionate relationships with their fathers were particularly likely to feel rejected and unhappy.

In Coopersmith's (1967) study with elementary school boys, paternal involvement in limit-setting was associated with high self-esteem. In contrast boys with low self-esteem were much more likely to be punished exclusively by their mothers. Coopersmith also noted that

boys who were able to confide in their fathers were likely to have high self-esteem. Rosenberg's (1965) results suggested that the early father-child relationship is particularly important for the child's self-esteem. Among adolescents those who were father-absent had lower self-esteem than those who were father-present, particularly when father-absence had begun in early childhood.

Reuter and Biller (1973) studied the relationship between various combinations of perceived paternal nurturance-availability and college males' personal adjustment. A family background questionnaire was designed to assess perceptions of father-child relationships and the amount of time the father spent at home when the subjects were children. The personal adjustment scale of Gough and Heilbrun's Adjective Checklist and the socialization scale of the California Psychological Inventory were employed as measures of personality adjustment. High paternal nurturance combined with at least moderate paternal availability and high paternal availability combined with at least moderate paternal nurturance were related to high scores on the personality adjustment measures. A male who has adequate opportunities to observe a nurturant father can imitate his behavior and develop positive personality characteristics. The father who is both relatively nurturant and relatively available may have a more adequate personality adjustment than do other types of fathers.

In contrast high paternal nurturance combined with low paternal availability and high paternal availability combined with low paternal nurturance were associated with relatively poor scores on the personality adjustment measures. The boy with a highly nurturant but seldom-home father may feel quite frustrated that his father is not home more often and/or may find it difficult to imitate such an elusive figure. Males who reported that their fathers had been home much of the time but gave them little attention seemed to be especially handicapped in their psychological functioning. The unnurturant father is an inadequate model, and his consistent presence appears to be a detriment to the boy's personality functioning. To put it another way, the boy with an unnurturant father may be better off if his father is not very available. This is consistent with evidence that suggests that father-absent boys often have better personality adjustments than do boys with passive, ineffectual fathers (Biller, 1974c).

There are some very extensive longitudinal data which underscore the importance of both the father's behavior and the father-mother relationship in the personality adjustment of the child. In general Block (1971) found that males who achieved a successful emotional and interpersonal adjustment in adulthood had both fathers and mothers who were highly involved and responsible in their unbringing. In contrast those adult males who were poorly adjusted had fathers who were typically noninvolved in child-rearing and mothers who tended to have a neurotic adjustment.

In a related investigation Block, von der Lippe, and Block (1973) reported that well-socialized and successful adult males were likely to have had highly involved fathers and come from homes in which their parents had compatible relationships. In contrast adult males who were relatively low in socialization skills and personal adjustment were likely to have grown up in homes in which the parents were incompatible and in which the fathers were either uninvolved or weak and neurotic.

Impulsive and Antisocial Behavior

Mischel (1961c) conducted a series of studies concerning the antecedents and correlates of impulse control in Caribbean children. In an earlier phase of his research, Mischel (1958) discovered that seven- to nine-year-old black West Indian children chose immediate gratification significantly more frequently than did white West Indian children. The differences between the black and white children appeared to be related to the greater incidence of father-absence among the black children. Studying eight- and nine-year-olds, Mischel (1961b) found that father-absent children showed a stronger preference for immediate gratification than did father-present children. Father-absent children, for instance, more often chose a small candy for immediate consumption rather than waiting a week for a large candy bar.

Santrock and Wohlford (1970) studied delay of gratification among fifth-grade boys. They found that boys who were father-absent because of divorce, as compared to those who were father-absent because of death, had more difficulty in delaying gratification. Boys who were father-absent because of divorce more often chose an immediately available small candy bar rather than waiting until the next day for a much larger one. Boys who became father-separated before the age of two or between the ages of six to nine were more likely to choose the immediate reward than did those who were separated from their fathers between the ages of three to five.

There is also some evidence that individuals who have been father-absent during childhood are likely to have difficulties making long-term commitments. Studying Peace Corps volunteers Suedfeld (1967) discovered that those who were father-absent during childhood were much more likely not to complete their scheduled overseas tours than were those who had not been father-absent. Premature terminations were associated with problems of adjustment and conduct and included some psychiatrically based decisions. There is other research which suggests that there is a relationship between father-absence in childhood and unemployment in adulthood (Gay & Tonge, 1967; Hall & Tonge, 1963).

Moral Development and Self-Control

Paternal dominance in discipline when combined with a high level of paternal affections is strongly associated with male children's sensitivity to their transgressions (Moulton et al., 1966). The father who is able to set limits firmly and who can also be affectionate and responsive to his child's needs seems to be a particularly good model for interpersonal sensitivity and moral development. Holstein (1972) found that adolescents who were morally mature were likely to have warm, nurturant, and highly moral fathers.

Hoffman (1971a) reported data concerning the conscience development of seventh-grade children. Father-absent boys consistently scored lower than father-present boys on a variety of moral indexes. They scored lower on measures of internal moral judgment, guilt following transgressions, acceptance of blame, moral values, and rule comformity. In addition they were rated as higher in aggression by their teachers, which may also reflect difficulties in self-control. Although there were generally not clearcut differences in terms of the measures that Hoffman had used, Santrock (1975) found that among elementary school boys those who were father-absent were consistently rated by their teachers as having a lower level of moral maturity than those who were father-present.

Hoffman (1971a, 1971b) also found that weak father-identification among father-present boys was related to less adequate conscience development than was strong father-identification. Father-identification was determined by response to questions involving the person whom the boy felt most similar to, most admired, and most wanted to resemble when he grew up. Among the seventh-graders that Hoffman studied, boys with strong father-identifications scored higher on the measures of internal moral judgment, moral values, and conformity to rules than did boys with low father-identifications.

The quality of the father-child relationship seems to have particular influence on whether the child takes responsibility for his own actions or acts as if his behavior is controlled by external forces. Children who have a warm relationship with a competent father who can constructively set limits for them are much more likely to develop a realistic internal locus of control (Biller, 1974c).

Delinquency

Antisocial behavior among children and adolescents can have many different etiologies, but paternal deprivation is a frequent contributing factor. Many researchers have noted that father-absence is more common among delinquent boys than among nondelinquent boys. Studying adolescents Glueck and Glueck (1950) reported that more than two-fifths of the delinquent boys were father-absent as compared with less than one-fourth of a matched nondelinquennt group. McCord et al. (1962) found that the lower-class father-absent boys in their study committed more felonies than did the father-present group, although the rates of gang delinquency were not different. Gregory (1965a) listed a large number of investigations linking father-absence with delinquent behavior and also detected a strong association between these variables in his study of high school students.

Early father-absence has a particularly strong association with delinquency among males. Anderson (1968) found that a history of early father-absence was much more frequent among boys committed to a training school. He also discovered that father-absent nondelinquents had a much higher rate of father substitution (stepfather, father surrogate) between the ages of four to seven than did father-absent delinquents. Kelly and Baer (1969) studied the recidivism rate among male delinquents. Compared to a 12 percent rate among father-present males, they found a 39 percent rate among males who had become father-absent before the age of six. However, boys who became father-absent after the age of six had only a 10 percent recidivism rate.

Herzog and Sudia (1970) cited much evidence indicating that lack of general family cohesiveness and supervision, rather than father-absence per se, is the most significant factor associated with juvenile delinquency.

Many familial and nonfamilial factors have to be considered, and in only some cases is father-absence directly linked to delinquent behavior. For example boys in father-absent families who have a positive relationship with their mothers seem to be less likely to become delinquent than do boys in father-present families who have inadequate fathers (Biller, 1971a, 1974c; McCord et al., 1962).

Father-present juvenile delinquents generally appear to have very unsatisfactory relationships with their fathers. Bach and Bremer (1947) reported that preadolescent delinquent boys produced significantly fewer father-fantasies on projective tests than did a nondelinquent control group. The delinquents portrayed fathers as lacking in affection and empathy. Similarly Andry (1962) found that delinquents characterized their fathers as glum and uncommunicative and as employing unreasonable punishment and little praise. Father-son communication was particularly poor.

Andry's findings are consistent with those of Bandura and Walters (1959) who reported that the relationship between delinquent sons and fathers is marked by rejection, hostility, and antagonism. McCord, McCord, and Howard (1963) found that a deviant, aggressive father in the context of general parental neglect and punitiveness was strongly related to juvenile delinquency. Medinnus (1965b) obtained data suggesting a very high frequency of poor father-child relationships among delinquent boys. The subjects in his study perceived their fathers as much more rejecting and neglecting than were their mothers.

Schaefer's (1972) data also revealed the particularly negative way delinquent boys often perceive their fathers. Compared to nondelinquent boys, delinquent boys viewed their fathers as more lax in discipline, more neglecting, and generally less involved. Surprisingly the delinquents described their mothers as more positive and loving than did the nondelinquents. It is also interesting to note that Gregory (1965a) found a higher rate of delinquency among boys living with their mothers following father-loss than among boys living with fathers following mother-loss. Such data suggest that paternal deprivation is more of a factor in the development of delinquency than is maternal deprivation.

There is considerable evidence that father-present delinquents are likely to have inadequate fathers who themselves have difficulties in impulse control. Jenkins (1968) found that the fathers of delinquent children seen at a child guidance clinic were frequently described as rigid, controlling, and prone to alcoholism. McCord et al. (1963) reported that criminal behavior in adulthood was often found among men whose fathers had been criminals, alcoholics, and/or extremely abusive to their families. Other researchers have also presented data suggesting a link between paternal inadequacy and delinquent behavior (e.g., Glueck & Glueck, 1950; Rosenthal, Ni, Finkelstein, & Berkwits, 1962).

Interpersonal Relationships

The father-infant relationship can have much impact on the child's subsequent relationships with others. For example infants who have little contact with their fathers are more likely to experience greater separation anxiety from their mothers and more negative reactions to strangers (Biller, 1974c; Spelke et al., 1973). The way the father interacts with the child presents a particularly potent modeling situation which the child is apt to generalize to his relationship with others.

Paternal deprivation can severely interfere with the development of successful peer relationships. Stoltz et al.'s (1954) observations, as well as mothers' and fathers' reports, indicated that four- to eight-year-old children who had been father-absent for the first few years of life had poorer peer relationships than did children who had not been father-absent. The Norwegian father-separated boys in Tiller's (1958) investigation were judged to have less adequate peer relationships than did non-father-separated boys. Other investigators have reported that continuously father-absent boys are less popular and have less satisfying peer relationships than do father-present boys (e.g., Leiderman, 1959; Mitchell & Wilson, 1967).

A positive father-son relationship gives the boy a basis for successful peer interactions. Rutherford and Mussen (1968) reported evidence indicating that nursery school boys who perceive their fathers as warm and nurturant are likely to be generous with other children. Payne and Mussen (1956) found that adolescent boys who were similar to their fathers in terms of responses to the California Psychological Inventory were rated as more friendly by their teachers than were boys who had responses markedly different from their fathers. Hoffman's (1961) results indicated that boys from mother-dominant homes had much more difficulty in their peer relationships than did boys from father-dominant homes. Maternal dominance was associated with impulsiveness and an inability to influence peers. On the other hand self-confidence, assertiveness, and overall competence in peer-group interactions were related to a warm father-son relationship.

Sexual and Marriage Relationships

A positive father-child relationship can greatly facilitate the boy's security in interacting with females. The boy who has developed a positive masculine self-image has much more confidence in heterosexual interactions. There is considerable evidence indicating that the male's adjustment to marriage is related to his relationship with his father and to his parents' marital relationship (Barry, 1970; Biller, 1974c).

Difficulty in forming lasting heterosexual relationships often appears to be linked to paternal deprivation. Andrews and Christensen's (1951) data suggested that college students whose parents had been divorced were likely to have frequent but unstable courtship relationships. Winch (1949, 1950) found that father-absence among college males was negatively related to degree of courtship behavior (defined as closeness to marriage). He also reported that a high level of emotional attachment to the mother was negatively related to the degree of courtship behavior. In their interview study Hilgard et al. (1960) detected that many men whose fathers died when they were children continued to be very dependent on their mothers if their mothers did not remarry. For example only one of the ten men whose mothers did not remarry seemed to manifest a fair degree of independence in his marital relationship.

Jacobson and Ryder (1969) did an exploratory interview study with young marrieds who suffered the death of a parent prior to marriage. Death of the husband's father prior to the age of 12 was associated with a high rate of marriage difficulty. Husbands, father-absent in early life, were described as immature and as lacking interpersonal competence. In general their marriages were relatively devoid of closeness and intimacy. In contrast when the husbands had lost their fathers after the age of 12 years, they were more likely to be involved in positive marriage relationships.

Other researchers have reported evidence indicating that individuals who have experienced father-absence because of a broken-home situation in childhood are more likely to have their own marriages end in divorce or separation (Landis, 1965; Rohrer & Edmondson, 1960). In many of these situations there is probably a strong modeling effect: Children see parents attempting to solve their marital conflicts by ending a marriage and are more likely to behave in a similar fashion themselves. Research by Pettigrew (1964) with lower-class blacks is also consistent with the supposition that father-absent males frequently have difficulty in their heterosexual relationships.

Homosexuality

Although no systematic studies have been made concerning the rates of homosexuality among father-absent males, some investigators have suggested that father-absent males are more prone than father-present males to become homosexual (West, 1967). Males who as children were father-absent or had ineffectual fathers, together with being involved in an intense, close-binding relationship with their mothers, seem particularly prone to develop a homosexual pattern of behavior. A close-binding, sexualized mother-son relationship seems more common in father-absent homes than in father-present homes and may, along with related factors, lessen the probability of the boy entering into meaningful heterosexual relationships. A significant proportion of homosexuals during childhood were discouraged by their mothers from participating in masculine activities and were often reinforced for feminine behavior (e.g., Bieber et al., 1962; Gundlach, 1969).

Both Bieber et al. (1962) and Evans (1969) found that more fathers of homosexuals than fathers of heterosexuals were described as detached and hostile. Mothers of homosexuals were depicted as close-binding with their sons and relatively uninvolved with their husbands. Bené (1965) reported that more male homosexuals than heterosexuals perceived their fathers as weak and were hostile toward them. Similarly studies by Apperson and McAdoo (1968) and Saghir and Robbins (1973) suggested a pattern of very negative father-child relations during the childhoods of male homosexuals.

A particularly extensive study of the family backgrounds of homosexuals was conducted by Thompson, Schwartz, McCandless, and Edwards (1973). College-age well-educated homosexuals were recruited through their friends, and their family backgrounds and childhood activities were compared with those of a control group. Homosexual men described very little interaction with their fathers and a relative lack of acceptance by their fathers during their childhood. The homosexuals generally viewed their fathers as weak, hostile, and rejecting. In general Thompson et al. found the classic male homosexual pattern of paternal deprivation coupled with an overintense mother-child relationship and early expression of avoidance of masculine activities.

Heterosexuals, as well as homosexuals, who avoided masculine activities in childhood reported more distance from both their fathers and men in general. It may be that the major difference between these homosexuals and heterosexuals was their adolescent sexual experience. For example opportunities for positive heterosexual relationships may have been more readily available for some of the boys. It should also be noted that more homosexuals than heterosexuals described themselves as frail or clumsy during childhood; again, there may be mediating constitutional factors in the development of some cases of homosexuality. The data fit well with a hypothesis suggesting that early paternal deprivation makes the individual more vulnerable to certain influences in later development. The particular form of adjustment the paternally deprived male makes is determined by a complex interaction of factors (Biller, 1974c, 1981a, 1981b).

Psychopathology

Much data relating paternal deprivation and childhood maladjustment have already been reviewed. In this section the investigations that are described generally focus on clinically diagnosed individuals. In most of the studies discussed previously, the individuals were grouped according to their test responses or behavior in specific situations and/or in terms of ratings made by others; they were not individuals who were clinically diagnosed as having some form of psychopathology or who were being treated at a clinic or hospital. It is important to emphasize that individuals who are clinically labeled are not necessarily more psychologically impaired than are individuals who have not been clinically diagnosed. Much of the time the major difference is that so-called mentally disturbed individuals have simply come into contact with a mental health facility.

The Becker and Peterson research group conducted extensive studies designed to ascertain the association between parental behaviors and specific types of clinically diagnosed psychological disturbance among 6- to 12-year-old children (Becker, Peterson, Hellmer, Shoemaker, & Quay, 1959; Becker, Peterson, Luria, Shoemaker, & Hellmer, 1962; Peterson, Becker, Hellmer, Shoemaker, & Quay, 1959). Children who had conduct problems (problems in impulse control and/or aggressiveness) frequently had fathers who were dictatorial and controlling. Children who had personality problems (shy, oversensitive, low self-concept) frequently had fathers who were insensitive and dictatorial.

Block (1969) also attempted to distinguish between the parental characteristics of children in different diagnostic groupings. Although the findings from Block's study were not specifically consistent with the Becker and Peterson studies, a picture of paternal inadequacy as a major factor in childhood psychopathology again emerged. Liverant (1959) found that fathers of disturbed children responded in a much more negative fashion on the Minnesota Multiphasic Personality Inventory (MMPI) than did fathers of nondisturbed children. The responses of the fathers of disturbed children indicated that they were impulsive, anxious, depressed, and concerned with bodily complaints. Of course such data can also be interpreted as suggesting that disturbed children can have a negative effect on the personality functioning of their parents.

Father-Absence. Garbower (1959), studying children from Navy families, found that those who were seen for psychiatric problems had more frequent and lengthy periods of father-absence than did a nondisturbed comparison group. The fathers of the disturbed children also seemed less sensitive to the effects of their being away from their families. In studying military families Pedersen (1966) found a similar amount of father-absence among 11- to 15-year-old boys, irrespective of whether they were referred for psychiatric help. However he did find that the degree of their psychopathology was highly associated with the amount of father-absence they had experienced. Trunnell (1968) studied children treated at an outpatient clinic and found that severity of psychopathology varied with the length of father-absence and the age of onset of the father's absence. The longer the absence and the younger the child at the onset of his absence, the more serious the psychopathology. Oltman and Friedman (1967) found particularly high rates of childhood father-absence among adults who had chronically disturbed personalities and inadequate moral development. In addition they found above-average rates of father-absence among neurotics and drug addicts. Rosenberg (1969) also reported extremely high rates of frequent childhood father-absence among young alcoholics and drug addicts. Maternal dominance combined with father-absence or inadequacy is common in the histories of drug addicts (Chein, Gerrard, Lee, & Rosenfeld, 1964; Wood & Duffy, 1966).

Brill and Liston (1966) reported that loss of father due to death in childhood was not unusually high among mental patients. However, the frequency of loss of father due to divorce or separation in childhood was much higher for individuals suffering from neurosis, psychosis, or personality disorders than for a number of different comparison groups. Consistent with Brill and Liston's data, father-absence due to divorce, separation, or desertion has also been found to be more highly associated with delinquency (Goode, 1961), maladjustment (Baggett, 1967), low self-esteem and sexual acting out (Hetherington, 1972), and cognitive deficits (Santrock, 1972). Other researchers who have reported that rates of childhood father-absence are higher among adult patients classified as neurotic or schizophrenic than among the general population have not done systematic analyses in terms of reason for father-absence (e.g., DaSilva, 1963; Madow & Hardy, 1947; Oltman, McGarry, & Friedman, 1952; Wahl, 1954, 1956). Gregory (1958, 1965b) critically evaluated many of the relevant studies and emphasized some of the methodological pitfalls in comparisons involving the relative incidence of mental illness among father-present and father-absent individuals. Lack of consideration of the possible effects of socioeconomic status is a major shortcoming of most of the studies. Cobliner (1963) reported some provocative findings which suggested that father-absence is more likely to be related to serious psychological disturbance in lower-class, as compared to middle-class, individuals. Middle-class families, particularly with respect to the mother-child relationship, may have more psychological, as well as economic, resources with which to cope with paternal deprivation (Biller, 1971a, 1974c, 1981a).

Family Interaction Patterns. Some of the most intriguing, as well as methodologically sound, studies have provided observations of family functioning in standardized problem-solving situations. Mishler and Waxler (1968) and Schuham (1970) found that high paternal involvement and decision making are uncommon in families in which there is a severely disturbed son. In families with nondisturbed sons, the father was most often the ascendent figure, and mutually acceptable decisions were much more common (Schuham, 1970).

In his observational study Alkire (1969) found that fathers usually dominated in families with normal adolescents, while mothers dominated in families with disturbed adolescents. Other research concerning interactions among disturbed families has indicated several subtypes of inappropriate fathering (McPherson, 1970). Paternal hostility toward the child and mother and lack of open communication among family members were very common. Leighton, Stollak, and Ferguson (1971) compared the interactions of families which had disturbed children. In general fathers in normal families were in a dominant position, and their role was accepted by family members. In contrast clinic families were usually dominated by mothers, even though the rest of the family was opposed and uncomfortable with this arrangement.

Maternal dominance has been found to be associated with a varied array of psychopathological problems, especially among males (Biller, 1974c). However it must be emphasized that many investigators have found evidence which indicates that overly dominant fathers can have just as negative an effect on their child's development as can overly dominant mothers. Researchers have reported much data relating arbitrary paternal power assertion and overcontrol to poor adjustment and psychopathology among children (Biller, 1974c). The degree of husband-wife dominance may not be a particularly good indication of degree of paternal deprivation, except where there is extreme maternal dominance. Extreme paternal dominance is indicative of inadequate fathering and squelches the child's development of independence and competence as much as does extreme maternal dominance.

Adequate personality development seems to be facilitated in families in which the father clearly represents a positive masculine role and the mother a positive feminine role. Kayton and Biller (1971) studied matched groups of nondisturbed, neurotic, paranoid schizophrenic, and nonparanoid schizophrenic adult males. They found that the nondisturbed subjects perceived their parents as exhibiting sex-appropriate behaviors to a greater extent than did the disturbed subjects. A smaller proportion of individuals in the disturbed groups viewed their fathers as possessing masculine-instrumental traits and, particularly among the schizophrenic groups, their mothers as having feminine-expressive characteristics. Severely disturbed behavior is often associated with difficulties and/or abnormalities in sex-role development (e.g., Biller, 1973; Biller & Poey, 1969; Heilbrun, 1974; Kayton & Biller, 1972; McClelland & Watt, 1968).

Types of Paternal Deprivation. There are some data which suggest that boys from father-absent homes are, in many cases, less retarded in their personality development than are boys from intact maternally dominant homes (Biller; 1968a; Reuter & Biller, 1973). In Nye's (1957) study children from broken homes were found to have better family adjustments and to have lower rates of antisocial behavior and psychosomatic illness than were children from unhappy unbroken homes. Other research has also suggested that a child may function more adequately in a father-absent home than in one in which there is a severely dysfunctional husband-wife relationship (e.g., Benson, 1968; Hetherington et al., 1978; Landis, 1962).

Father-absent children may be more influenced by factors outside the home than are children from intact but unhappy and/or maternally dominated homes. Some children may be particularly affected by attention from an adult male because of their intense feelings of paternal deprivation. Children with inadequate fathers often become resigned to their situation. For example the father-present but maternally dominated child is likely to develop a view of men as ineffectual, especially if his father is continually being controlled by his mother. In contrast the father-absent child may develop a much more flexible view of adult male behavior (Biller, 1974c).

Research which is described in this section and in other sections indicates that inadequate fathering and/or father-absence predisposes children toward certain developmental deficits. However there are many paternally deprived children who are generally well-adjusted. Such children should be more carefully studied in order to determine why they differ from less well-adjusted paternally deprived children. Investigators should include consideration of both type of child maladjustment and type of family inadequacy.

On the other hand extremely severe psychopathology, such as autism or childhood schizophrenia, does not develop simply as a function of disturbed parent-child relationships. The child's genetic and/or constitutional predispositions play an important part in determining the severity of his psychopathology as well as the quality of parent-child interactioins. Most children are handicapped if they have experienced paternal deprivation or inadequacy, and they are likely to have much difficulty in their emotional and interpersonal development. But in the great majority of cases, insufficient or inappropriate fathering (and/or mothering) per se does not account for children who are unable to develop basic communication skills and to form interpersonal attachments. For example the child's neurological malfunctioning or extreme temperamentally related hypersensitivity can make it very difficult for the parent to respond in a positive manner. In many cases constitutionally atypical children contribute to the development of psychopathol-

ogy in their parents, marital conflict and divorce, and their own paternal deprivation (Biller, 1974c, 1981a, 1981b).

THE FATHER AND FEMALE PERSONALITY DEVELOPMENT

In this section much data are reviewed which indicate that the father-daughter relationship has important effects on the female's personality development. The influence of variations in fathering and paternal deprivation with respect to the girl's emotional development and social and sexual relationships are emphasized.

Feminine Development

There has been a marked tendency to define femininity in negative terms and/or as the opposite of masculinity—e.g., stressing passivity and dependency (e.g., Salzman, 1967). Traditional femininity has often been found to be negatively associated with adjustment (Bardwick, 1971; Johnson, 1963). However since a focus of the present discussion is on ways in which the father can facilitate his daughter's personality development, it is relevant to analyze the elements of femininity which are related to psychological adjustment rather than maladjustment. It is meaningful to define feminine behavior in positive terms—e.g., femininity in social interaction can be related to skill in interpersonal communication, expressiveness of warmth, and sensitivity to the needs of others (Biller, 1971a, 1977c; Biller & Weiss, 1970/1972).

It is important to point out that femininity, according to the present definition, is based upon a positive feeling about being a female and a particular patterning of interpersonal behavior. Whether a woman enjoys housework or chooses a career should not be used as the ultimate criterion in assessing her femininity. Women, as well as men, who possess both positive feminine and positive masculine characteristics and secure sex-role orientations are most able to actualize their potential. Women who have pride in their femininity and are independent and assertive, as well as nurturant and sensitive, are likely to achieve interpersonal and creative fulfillment (Biller, 1971a, 1974c; Biller & Meredith, 1974).

Paternal Differentiation

The girl's feminine development is much influenced by how the father differentiates his "masculine" role from her "feminine" role and by what type of behavior he considers appropriate for his daughter. Mussen and Rutherford (1963) found that fathers of highly feminine girls encouraged their daughters more in sex-typed activities than did fathers of unfeminine girls. These investigators suggested that masculine fathers who actively encourage and appreciate femininity in girls are particularly able to facilitate their daughter's sex-role development. Similarly in their study with nursery school children, Sears et al. (1965) reported a significant correlation between girls' femininity and their fathers' expectations of their participation in feminine activities. Heilbrun (1965b) found that daughters who perceive themselves as feminine, as well as sons who perceive themselves as masculine, are likely to view their fathers as masculine.

Tasch (1955) interviewed fathers of boys and girls in order to learn about their conceptions of the paternal role. She found much evidence of paternal differentiation in terms of sex of child. Her results indicated that fathers viewed their daughters as more delicate than their sons. Fathers were found to use physical punishment more frequently with their sons than with their daughters. Fathers tended to define household tasks in terms of their sex-appropriateness. For example they expected girls to iron and wash clothes and babysit for siblings, while boys were expected to be responsible for taking out the garbage and helping their fathers in activities involving mechanical and physical competence. Unfortunately fathers often have rigid sex-role stereotypes, and in their zeal to "feminize" their daughters, they actively discourage the development of intellectual and physical competence (Biller & Meredith, 1974).

Nevertheless the child is not merely a passive recipient of familial and sociocultural influences. As has been stressed in earlier sections of this chapter, the child's constitutional predispositions can play a very important part in influencing parent-child and environmental interactions. For example the young girl who is temperamentally responsive to social interaction and is very attractive may make it especially easy for her father to encourage her positive feminine development. On the other hand the girl who is physically unattractive may be perceived as unfeminine by her father. The father may reject his daughter if she does not fit his conception of the physical characteristics of femininity. If the father does not have a son and his daughter is particularly vigorous and well-coordinated, he may tend to treat her as if she were a boy (Biller, 1971a, 1974c).

Personal and Social Adjustment

When the mother excessively dominates the father, the daughter is likely to have difficulties in her personality development. Hoffman (1961) found that girls from mother-dominant homes had difficulty relating to males and were disliked by boys. However Hetherington (1965) did not find a clearcut relationship between paternal dominance and girl's sex-role preferences, although girls with dominant fathers were much more likely to imitate them and to be similar to them than were girls with dominant mothers. Other studies are also consistent with the supposition that parental dominance is a less influential factor for girls than it is for boys (Biller, 1969c; Hetherington & Frankie, 1967).

Biller's (1969c) results suggested that feminine development is facilitated if the mother is seen as a generally salient controller of resources. Kindergarten girls perceived their fathers as more competent and decision-making, their mothers as more limit-setting, and both parents as similar in nurturance. There was a subgroup of girls whose femininity scores were low and who perceived their mothers as relatively high in decisionmaking and limit-setting, but quite low in nurturance and competence. In most cases at least a moderate level of paternal involvement in decision making seemed important in the girl's feminine development.

Biller and Zung (1972) reported data which suggests

that strong maternal control and dominance hampers girls' as well as boys' personality development. They found that high maternal control and intrusiveness were associated with sex-role conflict and anxiety among elementary school girls. For girls the optimal level of paternal dominance may be moderate, allowing the mother to also be viewed as a "salient controller of resources" yet in a general context of paternal involvement. It is important that the girl perceive her father as competent and as appreciating her behavior, even if she does not perceive him as the dominant parent.

Results of an investigation by Fish and Biller (1973) suggest that the father plays a particularly important role in the girl's personality adjustment. College females' perceptions of their relationships with their fathers during childhood were assessed by means of an extensive family background questionnaire. Subjects who perceived their fathers as having been very nurturant and positively interested in them scored high on the Adjective Checklist personal adjustment scale. In contrast subjects who perceived their fathers as having been rejecting scored very low on the personal adjustment measure.

Block's (1971) analysis of data collected from the Berkeley Longitudinal Study highlights the importance of both the father-daughter and father-mother relationships in the quality of the female's personality functioning. For example the females who were the most well adjusted as adults grew up in homes with two positively involved parents. Their mothers were described as affectionate, personable, and resourceful, and their fathers as warm, competent, and firm. A second group of relatively well-adjusted females came from homes with extremely bright, capable, and ambitious mothers but rather passive but warm fathers. In contrast poorly adjusted females were likely to have been reared in homes where either one or both parents were very inadequate. Even though they represented a wide range of personality adaptations, the poorly adjusted women were likely to have come from homes where there was little opportunity to view a positive mother-father relationship.

The most well-adjusted females in Block et al.'s (1973) longitudinal study tended to come from homes where both parents had been positively involved with them. Their fathers were described as warm and accepting, and their mothers appeared to be oriented toward rationality, achievement, and intellectual attainment. A variety of complex family patterns emerged among the less well-adjusted females, but it was clear that few, if any, had family backgrounds marked by a combination of a compatible father-mother relationship and a positively involved father. Their findings also suggest how difficult it is for a female to get the necessary family support to develop into a well-rounded, secure, and competent adult. It is striking to note that, according to their data, few fathers tended to be adequately involved with their daughters and to encourage both a positive feminine self-concept and instrumental competence. Again many of these problems seem to be associated with an overly rigid sex-typing and negative definition of feminine behavior. The gradually increasing flexibility in sex roles should lead to more and more women having a positive feminine self-concept, as well as a wide range of competencies and a successful, fulfilling career (Biller & Meredith, 1974).

Other data reveal the significant consequences that

the father-daughter relationship can have on marriage. In Winch's (1949, 1950) questionnaire study with college students, females who had long-term romantic relationships (who appeared near marriage) reported closer relationships with their father than did females who did not have serious heterosexual involvements. Luckey (1960) found that women who were satisfied with their marriages perceived their husbands as more similar to their fathers than did women who were not satisfied with their marriages. Fisher (1973) presented evidence indicating that paternal deprivation in early childhood is associated with infrequent orgasms among married women. The female's ability to have a successful marriage relationship is increased when she has experienced a warm, affectionate relationship with a father who has encouraged her positive feminine development (Biller, 1974c).

Inappropriate and/or inadequate fathering is a major factor in the development of homosexuality in females, as well as in males. Bené (1965) reported that female homosexuals felt that their fathers were weak and incompetent. The homosexual women were more hostile toward, and afraid of, their fathers than were the heterosexual women. Kaye et al. (1967) analyzed background data on homosexual women in psychoanalysis. These investigators found that the fathers of the homosexual women (as compared to the fathers of women in a heterosexual control group) tended to be puritanical, exploitative, and feared by their daughters, as well as possessive and infantilizing. Kaye et al. also presented evidence that suggests that female homosexuality is associated with rejection of femininity early in life. In another study lesbians described their fathers as less involved and affectionate than did heterosexual women (Gundlach & Reiss, 1968).

College-age well-educated female homosexuals were recruited by their friends in a study by Thompson et al. (1973). Compared to a control group of female heterosexuals, the female homosexuals indicated that they were less accepting of their fathers and their femininity during childhood. There was also some evidence that they perceived their fathers as more detached, weak, and hostile toward them. In general available research has suggested that inadequate fathering is more of a factor in the development of female homosexuality than is inadequate mothering. It is also relevant to note the general similarity in negative father-child relations among female and male homosexuals. Paternal deprivation makes the individual more vulnerable to difficulties in sexual development, but again it is only one of the many factors that determine the type of adjustment an adult will make (Biller, 1974c, 1981a, 1981b).

Father-Absence. Some data suggest that females are less affected by father-absence than are males (e.g., Bach, 1946; Lessing et al., 1970; Lynn & Sawrey, 1959; Santrock, 1972; Winch, 1950). However there is other research which supports the conclusion that girls are at least as much influenced in their social and heterosexual development by father-absence as are boys (e.g., Biller, 1971a, 1974c; Hetherington, 1972; Lynn, 1979; Wallerstein & Kelly, 1974, 1980). The extent and direction of the differential impact of father-absence on males and females probably varies with respect to which dimensions of personality development are considered.

Results from some studies suggest that father-absent girls are not usually inhibited in terms of their development of sex-typed interests or perceptions of the incentive value of the feminine role (Hetherington, 1972; Lynn & Sawrey, 1959; Santrock, 1970a). In fact in a study with disadvantaged black children, Santrock (1970a) found a tendency for father-absent girls to be more feminine on a doll-play sex-role measure than were father-present girls; a very high level of femininity may be associated with a rigid sex-role development which devalues males and masculine activities. In many cases father-absence seems to have more effect on the girl's ability to function in interpersonal and heterosexual relationships than it does on her sex-role preference.

In a clinical study Heckel (1963) observed frequent school maladjustment, excessive sexual interest, and social acting-out behavior in five fatherless preadolescent girls. Other investigators have also found a high incidence of delinquent behavior among lower-class father-absent girls (Monahan, 1957; Toby, 1957). Such acting-out behavior may be a manifestation of frustration associated with the girl's unsuccessful attempts to find a meaningful relationship with an adult male. Father-absence appears to increase the probability that a girl will experience difficulties in interpersonal adjustment. Many studies referred to in previous sections suggested that father-absent children are likely to have emotional and social problems, but one difficulty in interpreting some of them is that they do not differentiate between boys and girls in data analyses.

In Jacobson and Ryder's (1969) interview study, many women who had been father-absent in early life complained of difficulties in achieving satisfactory sexual relationships with their husbands. Lack of opportunity to observe meaningful male-female relationships in childhood can make it much more difficult for the father-absent female to develop the interpersonal skills necessary for adequate heterosexual adjustment. Case studies of father-absent girls are often filled with details of problems concerning interactions with males, particularly in sexual relationships (e.g., Leonard, 1966; Neubauer, 1960).

The devaluation of maleness and masculinity, so prevalent in paternally deprived, matrifocal families, adversely affects many girls as well as boys (Biller, 1974c). Children in lower-class families often do not have opportunities to interact with adequate fathers. In lower-class families father-daughter relationships are generally not very adequate. The father may be very punitive and express little affection toward his daughter. Many investigators have observed that lower-class girls in families in which the father is absent or ineffectual develop derogatory attitudes toward males (e.g., Pettigrew, 1964; Rohrer & Edmondson, 1960).

The downgrading of males in terms of their seemingly social and economic irresponsibility is common among lower-class black families. Negative attitudes toward males are transmitted by mothers, grandmothers, and other significant females and unfortunately are often strengthened by the child's observation or involvement in destructive male-female relationships. Paternal deprivation, in the rubric of the devaluation of the male role, is a major factor in the lower-class females' frequent difficulties in interacting with their male relatives, boyfriends, husbands, and children. Maternally based households seem to become like family heirlooms—passed from generation to generation (Moynihan, 1965; Rohrer & Edmondson, 1960).

Interactions with Males. The most comprehensive and well-controlled study concerning father-absence and the girl's development was conducted by Hetherington (1972). Her subjects were adolescent lower-middle-class girls (ages 13 to 17) who regularly attended a community recreation center. Hetherington was particularly interested in the possible differential effects of father-absence due to divorce or death of the father. She compared three groups of girls: girls whose fathers were absent because of divorce and who had no contact with their fathers since the divorce; girls whose fathers were absent because of death; and girls with both parents living at home. She was careful to control for sibling variables (all the girls were first-borns without brothers), and none of the father-absent children had any adult males living in their homes following the separation from the father.

The most striking finding was that both groups of father-absent girls had great difficulty in interacting comfortably with man and male peers. Hetherington discovered that the difficulties were manifested differently for the daughters of divorcées than for the daughters of widows. The daughters of divorcées tended to be very aggressive and flirtatious, while the daughters of widows tended to be very shy and timid in their interactions with males. Although their behavior was much different, most of the girls in both of the father-absent groups reported that they were very insecure with males. In contrast all three groups of girls generally appeared to have appropriate interactions with their mothers and with female adults and peers. One of the exceptions was that the father-absent girls seemed more dependent on women which is consistent with Lynn and Sawrey's (1959) findings of increased mother-dependency among father-separated girls.

Hetherington generally found that girls had the most difficulty in their heterosexual interactions when their father-absence began before the age of five. Early father-separation was usually more associated with inappropriate behavior with males than was father-absence after the age of five, although differences were not significant for every measure. Early father-absence was also associated with more maternal overprotection than was father-absence after the age of five. There is other evidence indicating that early father-absence is more associated with maternal overprotection than is father-absence beginning later in the child's life (e.g., Biller, 1969b/1972; Biller & Bahm, 1971).

There were additional findings in Hetherington's study which emphasize the importance of taking into account the context of, and reason for, father-absence. Daughters of widows recalled more positive relationships with their fathers and described them as warmer and more competent than did daughters of divorcées. The divorced mothers also painted a very negative picture of their marriages and ex-husbands. Daughters of divorcées were quite low in self-esteem, but daughters of widows did not differ significantly in their self-esteem from daughters of father-present families. Nevertheless both groups of father-absent girls had less feeling of control

over their lives and more anxiety than did father-present girls. In a longitudinal extension of her research, Hetherington has also found evidence that suggests the continuing influence of father absence on adult female development (Hetherington & Parke, 1979).

Inadequate Fathering. Inadequate fathering or mothering is frequently a reflection of difficulties in the husband-wife relationship. Such difficulties may be particularly apparent in the husband's and wife's inability to provide one another with adequate affection and sexual satisfaction. The parents' interpersonal problems are usually reflected in their interactions with their children and in their children's adjustment. Clinical studies have revealed that difficulties in parental sexual adjustment, combined with overrestrictive parental attitudes, are often associated with incestuous and acting-out behavior among adolescent females (e.g., Kaufman, Peck, & Tagiuri, 1954; Robey, Rosenwald, Snell, & Lee, 1964).

Paternal inadequacy can be a factor in the development of severe psychopathology in the female child, as well as in the male child. Unfortunately many of the studies examining the influence of paternal deprivation on childhood psychopathology reviewed earlier did not include female children or did not take the sex of the child into account in the data analyses. However there is some research which focuses on, or specifically includes, females.

In their extensive studies Lidz, Parker, and Cornelison (1956) reported a high incidence of inadequate fathering for female, as well as male, schizophrenics. The fathers of the schizophrenic females were frequently observed to be in severe conflict with their wives, to contradict their wives' decisions, and to degrade their wives in front of their daughters. These fathers made rigid and unrealistic demands on their wives. Similarly such fathers were insensitive to their daughters' needs to develop an independent self-concept. The fathers of the schizophrenic females made attempts to manipulate and mold their daughters in terms of their own unrealistic needs. Females who formed an allegiance with a disturbed father, frequently in reaction to rejection by an unloving mother, seemed mose likely to become psychotic.

Hamilton and Wahl (1948) found that almost 75 percent of the hospitalized schizophrenic women they studied had experienced some inadequacy of fathering in childhood. Prolonged father-absence, paternal rejection, and paternal abuse were very common. Baker and Holzworth (1961) compared a group of male and female adolescents who were hospitalized because of psychological disturbances with a control group who were successful in their interpersonal and school adjustments. The fathers of the hospitalized group were more likely to have had social histories involving court convictions and excessive drinking than were the fathers of the successful adolescents.

However it is important to emphasize that variations in sociocultural background may be a primary factor contributing to such findings. For example both criminal convictions and commitment to state hospitals are more frequent for lower-class individuals than for middle-class individuals. The general economic and social deprivation that lower-class children experience seems to exacerbate the effects of paternal deprivation.

Severe psychopathology is also often related to the child's constitutional predispositions and does not usually develop simply as a function of disturbed parent-child relationships. For example the girl who is temperamentally unresponsive to affection may negatively reinforce her father's attempts to form a relationship with her. Similarly if she is extremely hyperactive and aggressive, it may be very difficult for her father to relate to her.

CONCLUSIONS

Throughout this chapter it has been emphasized that paternal influence does not take place in a vacuum. Such factors as the child's constitutional characteristics and developmental status, the quality of the mother-child, father-mother, and sibling-child interactions, the family's sociocultural background, and the availability of surrogate models are frequently discussed. Methodological shortcomings in research are often noted because most investigators have not systematically considered the potential interactions of paternal influence with such factors as the quality of the mother-child and father-mother relationships and the child's constitutionally based individuality. The reader who is interested in a fuller discussion of much of the material presented in this chapter can also consult other publications by this author (e.g., Biller, 1974c, 1981a, 1981b, 1981c).

There were many issues relating to fatherhood that were not dealt with in this chapter. For example there was no systematic discussion of such topics as historical and cross-cultural factors pertaining to the father's role, genetic and animal research relevant to fatherhood, or the adjustment of unwed, single, or divorced fathers. An issue of *The Family Coordinator*, edited by James Walters (1976), includes material germane to most of these topics; relevant information can also be found in other sources (Biller & Meredith, 1974; Lynn, 1974). There is also much information that has practical implications for educational and clinical interventions that may improve the father-child relationship and prevent or lessen the effects of paternal deprivation (Biller, 1974c, 1981a, 1981b, 1981c; Biller & Meredith, 1974; Biller & Salter, 1981; Lamb, 1976, 1981; Rosenthal & Keshet, 1981; Wallerstein & Kelly, 1980; Walters, 1976).

REFERENCES

ALKIRE, A. A. Social power and communication within families of disturbed and nondisturbed adolescents. *Journal of Personality and Social Psychology*, 1969, *13*, 335–349.

ALTUS, W. D. The broken home and factors of adjustment. *Psychological Reports*, 1958, *4*, 477.

ANDERSON, R. E. Where's Dad? Paternal deprivation and delinquency. *Archives of General Psychiatry*, 1968, *18*, 641–649.

ANDREWS, R. O., & CHRISTENSEN, H. T. Relationship of absence of a parent to courtship status: A repeat study. *American Sociological Review*, 1951, *16*, 541–544.

ANDRY, R. G. Paternal and maternal roles in delinquency. Pp. 31–43 in *Deprivation of maternal care* (Public Health Paper No. 14). Geneva: World Health Organization, 1962.

APPERSON, L. B., & McADOO, W. G., JR. Parental factors in the childhood of homosexuals. *Journal of Abnormal Psychology*, 1968, *73*, 201–206.

BACH, G. R. Father-fantasies and father-typing in father-separated children. *Child Development*, 1946, *17*, 63–80.

BACH, G. R., BREMER, G. Projective father fantasies of preadolescent, delinquent children. *Journal of Psychology*, 1947, *24*, 3–17.

BAGGETT, A. T. The effect of early loss of father upon the personality of boys and girls in late adolescence. *Dissertation Abstracts*, 1967, *28*(1–B), 356–357.

BAKER, J. W., & HOLZWORTH, A. Social histories of successful and unsuccessful children. *Child Development*, 1961, *32*, 135–149.

BANDURA, A., & WALTERS, R. H. *Adolescent aggression: A study of the influence of child-rearing practices and family interrelationships.* New York: Ronald Press, 1959.

BARCLAY, A. G., & CUSAMANO, D. Father-absence, cross-sex identity and field-dependent behavior in male adolescents. *Child Development*, 1967, *38*, 243–250.

BARDWICK, J. M. *Psychology of women.* New York: Harper & Row, Pub., 1971.

BARRY, H., III, BACON, M. K., & CHILD, I. L. A cross-cultural survey of some sex differences in socialization. *Journal of Abnormal and Social Psychology*, 1957, *55*, 327–332.

BARRY, W. A. Marriage research and conflict: An integrative review. *Psychological Bulletin*, 1970, *73*, 41–55.

BECKER, W. C., PETERSON, D. R., HELLMER, L. A., SHOEMAKER, D. J., & QUAY, H. D. Factors in parental behavior and personality as related to problem behavior in children. *Journal of Consulting Psychology*, 1959, *23*, 107–118.

BECKER, W. C., PETERSON, D. R., LURIA, Z., SHOEMAKER, D. S., & HELLMER, L. A. Relations of factors derived from parent interview ratings to behavior problems of five-year-olds. *Child Development*, 1962, *33*, 509–535.

BELL, A. P. Role modeling of fathers in adolescence and young adulthood. *Journal of Counseling Psychology*, 1969, *16*, 30–35.

BENÉ, E. On the genesis of female homosexuality. *British Journal of Psychiatry*, 1965, *3*, 815–821.

BENSON, L. *Fatherhood: A sociological perspective.* New York: Random House, 1968.

BIEBER, I., et al. *Homosexuality: A psychoanalytic study.* New York: Basic Books, 1962.

BIERI, J. Parental identification, acceptability and authority, and within sex-differences in cognitive behavior. *Journal of Abnormal and Social Psychology*, 1960, *60*, 76–79.

BILLER, H. B. A multiaspect investigation of masculine development in kindergarten-age boys. *Genetic Psychology Monographs*, 1968a, *76*, 89–139.

BILLER, H. B. A note on father-absence and masculine development in young lower-class Negro and white boys. *Child Development*, 1968b, *39*, 1003–1006.

BILLER, H. B. Father dominance and sex-role development in kindergarten-age boys. *Developmental Psychology*, 1969a, *1*, 87–94. Reprinted in a slightly abridged form, pp. 73–85 in D. R. Heise (Ed.), *Personality and socialization*. New York: Rand McNally, 1972.

BILLER, H. B. Father-absence, maternal encouragement and sex-role development in kindergarten-age boys. *Child Development*, 1969b, *40*, 539–546. Reprinted, pp. 239–254 in R. C. Smart & M. S. Smart (Eds.), *Readings in child development and relationships*. New York: Macmillan, 1972.

BILLER, H. B. Maternal salience and feminine development in young girls. *Proceedings of the 77th Annual Convention of the American Psychological Association*, 1969c, *4*, 259–260.

BILLER, H. B. Father-absence and the personality development of the male child. *Developmental Psychology*, 1970, *2*, 181–201. Reprinted, pp. 120–152 in S. Chess & A. Thomas (Eds.), *Annual progress in child psychiatry and child development*. New York: Brunner/Mazel, 1971. Reprinted in slighted abridged form, pp. 407–433 in D. R. Heise (Ed.), *Personality and socialization*. New York: Rand McNally, 1972.

BILLER, H. B. *Father, child and sex role.* Lexington, Mass.: Lexington Books, Heath, 1971a.

BILLER, H. B. The mother-child relationship and the father-absent boy's personality development. *Merrill-Palmer Quarterly*, 1971b, *17*, 227–241. Reprinted in slightly abridged form, pp. 306–319 in U. Bronfenbrenner (Ed.), *Influences on human development*. Hinsdale, Ill.: Dryden Press, 1972.

BILLER, H. B. Fathering and female sexual development. *Medical Aspects of Human Sexuality*, 1971c, *5*, 116–138.

BILLER, H. B. Sex-role uncertainty and psychopathology. *Journal of Individual Psychology*, 1973, *29*, 24–25.

BILLER, H. B. Paternal and sex-role factors in cognitive and academic functioning. Pp. 83–123 in J. K. Cole & R. Dienstbier

(Eds.), *Nebraska Symposium on Motivation, 1973.* Lincoln: University of Nebraska Press, 1974a.

BILLER, H. B. Paternal deprivation, cognitive functioning and the feminized classroom. Pp. 11–52 in A. Davids (Ed.), *Child personality and psychopathology:* Current topics. New York: John Wiley, 1974b.

BILLER, H. B. *Paternal deprivation.* Lexington, Mass.: Lexington Books, Heath, 1974c.

BILLER, H. B. Syndromes of paternal deprivation in man. Pp. 147–171 in J. H. Cullen (Ed.), *Experimental behavior: A basis for the study of man.* Dublin: Irish University press, 1974d.

BILLER, H. B. The effects of intermittent but prolonged absence of the father. *Medical Aspects of Human Sexuality,* 1975, *9,* 179.

BILLER, H. B. The father-child relationship: Some crucial issues. Pp. 69–76 in V. Vaughn & B. Brazelton (Eds.), *The family—Can it be saved?* Chicago: Year Book Med. Pub. Inc., 1976a.

BILLER, H. B. The father and personality development: Paternal deprivation and sex-role development. Pp. 89–156 in M. E. Lamb (Ed.), *The role of the father.* New York: John Wiley, 1976b.

BILLER, H. B. Father absence and paternal deprivation. Pp. 7–8 in B. Wolman (Ed.), *International encyclopedia of neurology, psychiatry, psychoanalysis and psychology.* New York: Van Nostrand Reinhold, 1977a.

BILLER, H. B. Fathers and children. Pp. 9–11 in B. Wolman (Ed.), *International encyclopedia of neurology, psychiatry, psychoanalysis and psychology.* New York: Van Nostrand Reinhold, 1977b.

BILLER, H. B. Sex-role learning: Some comments and complexities from a multidimensional perspective. Pp. 201–207 in S. Cohen & T. J. Comiskey (Eds.), *Child development: A study of growth processes.* Ithaca, Ill.: Peacock, 1977c.

BILLER, H. B. Father absence and military families. Pp. 45–48 in E. J. Hunter (Ed.), *A report on the military family research conference.* San Diego: Family Studies Branch, Naval Health Research Center, 1978.

BILLER, H. B. Father absence, divorce and development. In M. E. Lamb (Ed.), *The role of the father in child development* (2nd ed.). New York: John Wiley, 1981a.

BILLER, H. B. The father and sex-role development. In M. E. Lamb (Ed.), *The role of the father in child development* (2nd ed.). New York: John Wiley, 1981b.

BILLER, H. B. *Parents and children growing together,* in preparation.

BILLER, H. B., & BAHM, R. M. Father absence, perceived maternal behavior and masculinity of self-concept among junior high school boys. *Developmental Psychology,* 1971, *4,* 178–181.

BILLER, H. B., & BARRY, W. Sex-role patterns, paternal similarity and personality adjustment in college males. *Developmental Psychology,* 1971, *4,* 107.

BILLER, H. B., & BORSTELMANN, L. J. Intellectual level and sex-role development in mentally retarded children. *American Journal of Mental Deficiency,* 1965, *70,* 443–447.

BILLER, H. B., BORSTELMANN, L. J. Masculine development: An integrative review. *Merrill-Palmer Quarterly,* 1967, *13,* 253–294.

BILLER, H. B., & DAVIDS, A. Parent-child relations, personality development and psychopathology. Pp. 48–77 in A. Davids (Ed.), *Issues in abnormal child development.* Monterey, Calif.: Brooks/Cole, 1973.

BILLER, H. B., & MEREDITH, D. L. *Father power.* New York: McKay, 1974.

BILLER, H. B., & POEY, K. An exploratory comparison of sex-role related behavior in schizophrenics and nonschizophrenics. *Developmental Psychology,* 1969, *1,* 629.

BILLER, H. B., & SALTER, M. The adolescent unwed father. In C. J. Poole (Ed.), *Children bearing children: Adolescent pregnancy and parenthood.* North Scituate, Mass.: Duxbury Press, in press.

BILLER, H. B., & WEISS, S. The father-daughter relationship and the personality development of the female. *Journal of Genetic Psychology,* 1970, *114,* 79–93. Reprinted, pp. 106–116 in D. Rogers (Ed.), *Issues in adolescent psychology.* New York: Appleton-Century-Crofts, 1972.

BILLER, H. B., & ZUNG, B. Perceived maternal control, anxiety and opposite sex-role preference among elementary school girls. *Journal of Psychology,* 1972, *81,* 85–88.

BLANCHARD, R. W., & BILLER, H. B. Father availability and academic performance among third-grade boys. *Developmental Psychology,* 1971, *4,* 301–305.

BLOCK, J. Parents of schizophrenic, neurotic, asthmatic and congenitally ill children: A comparative study. *Archives of General Psychiatry,* 1969, *20,* 659–674.

BLOCK, J. *Lives through time.* Berkeley: Bancroft Books, 1971.

BLOCK, J., VON DER LIPPE, A., & BLOCK, J. H. Sex-role and socialization: Some personality concomitants and environmental antecedents. *Journal of Consulting and Clinical Psychology,* 1973, *41,* 321–341.

BRILL, N. Q., & LISTON, E. H. Parental loss in adults with emotional disorders. *Archives of General Psychiatry,* 1966, *14,* 307–314.

BRONFENBRENNER, U. The study of identification through interpersonal perception. Pp. 110–130 in R. Tagiuri & L. Petrullo (Eds.), *Person perception and interpersonal behavior.* Stanford, Calif.: Stanford University Press, 1958.

BRONFENBRENNER, U. Some familial antecedents of responsibility and leadership in adolescents. Pp. 239–272 in L. Petrullo & B. M. Bass (Eds.), *Leadership and interpersonal behavior.* New York: Holt, Rinhart & Winston, 1961.

BRONFENBRENNER, U. The psychological costs of quality and equality in education. *Child Development,* 1967, *38,* 909–925.

BRONSON, W. C. Dimensions of ego and infantile identification. *Journal of Personality,* 1959, *27,* 532–545.

BURTON, R. V. Cross-sex identity in Barbados. *Developmental Psychology,* 1972, *6,* 365–374.

BURTON, R. V., & WHITING, J.W.M. The absent father and cross-sex identity. *Merrill-Palmer Quarterly,* 1961, *7,* 85–95.

CARLSMITH, L. Effect of early father absence on scholastic aptitude. *Harvard Educational Review,* 1964, *34,* 3–21.

CERVANTES, L. F. Family background, primary relationships and the high school drop-out. *Journal of Marriage and the Family,* 1965, *27,* 218–223.

CHEIN, I., GERRARD, D. L., LEE, B. S., & ROSENFELD, E. *The road to H.* New York: Basic Books, 1964.

CLAUSEN, J. A. Family structure, socialization, and personality. Pp. 1–53 in L. W. Hoffman & M. L. Hoffman (Eds.), *Review of child development research* (Vol. 2). New York: Russell Sage Foundation, 1966.

COBLINER, W. G. Social factors in mental disorders: A contribution to the etiology of mental illness. *Genetic Psychology Monographs,* 1963, *67,* 151–215.

COOPERSMITH, S. *The antecedents of self-esteem.* San Francisco: W. H. Freeman & Company Publishers, 1967.

CORTÉS, C. F., & FLEMING, E. The effects of father absence on the adjustment of culturally disadvantaged boys. *Journal of Special Education,* 1968, *7,* 413–420.

CRANDALL, V. J., DEWEY, R., KATKOVSKY, W., & PRESTON, A. Parents' attitudes and behaviors, and grade-school children's academic achievements. *Journal of Genetic Psychology,* 1964, *104,* 53–66.

D'ANDRADE, R. G. *Father-absence and cross-sex identification.* Unpublished doctoral dissertation, Harvard University, 1962.

D'ANDRADE, R. G. Sex differences and cultural institutions. Pp. 174–204 in E. E. Maccoby (Ed.), *The development of sex differences.* Stanford, Calif.: Stanford University Press, 1966.

DA SILVA, G. The role of the father with chronic schizophrenic patients. *Journal of the Canadian Psychiatric Association,* 1963, *8,* 190–203.

DAVIS, W. C., & PHARES, E. Parental antecedents of internal-external control of reinforcement. *Psychological Reports,* 1969, *24,* 427–436.

DEUTSCH, M. Minority group and class status as related to social and personality factors in scholastic achievement. *Monograph of the Society for Applied Anthropology,* 1960, *2,* 1–31.

DEUTSCH, M., & BROWN, B. Social influences in Negro-white intelligence differences. *Journal of Social Issues,* 1964, *20,* 24–35.

DISTLER, L. S. *Patterns of parental identification: An examination of three theories.* Unpublished doctoral dissertation, University of California, Berkeley, 1964.

DOWNEY, K. J. Parental interest in the institutionalized, severely mentally retarded child. *Social Problems,* 1963, *11,* 186–193.

DYK, T. B., & WITKIN, H. A. Family experience related to the development of differentiation in children. *Child Development,* 1965, *36,* 21–55.

DYL, A. D., & BILLER, H. B. *Paternal absence, social class and reading achievement.* Unpublished study, University of Rhode Island, 1973.

ELDER, G. H., JR. Structural variations in the child-rearing relationship. *Sociometry,* 1962, *25,* 241–262.

EVANS, R. B. Childhood parental relationships of homosexual men. *Journal of Consulting and Clinical Psychology,* 1969, *33,* 129–135.

FARBER, B. Effects of a severely mentally retarded child on the family. Pp. 227–246 in E. P. Trapp & P. Himelstein (Eds.), *Readings on the exceptional child.* New York: Appleton-Century-Crofts, 1962.

FERREIRA, A. J., WINTER, W. D., & POINDEXTER, E. J. Some interactional variables in normal and abnormal families. *Family Process,* 1966, *5,* 60–75.

FISH, K. D., & BILLER, H. B. Perceived childhood paternal relationships and college females' personal adjustment. *Adolescence,* 1973, *8,* 415–420.

FISHER, S. F. *The female orgasm: Psychology, physiology, fantasy.* New York: Basic Books, 1973.

FREEDHEIM, D. K. *An investigation of masculinity and parental role patterns.* Unpublished doctoral dissertation, Duke University, 1960.

FREEDHEIM, D. K., & BORSTELMANN, L. J. An investigation of masculinity and parental role patterns. *American Psychologist,* 1963, *18,* 339. (Abstract)

FREUD, A., & BURLINGHAM, D. T. *Infants without families.* New York: International Universities Press, 1944.

GARBOWER, G. *Behavior problems of children in Navy officers' families: As related to social conditions of Navy family life.* Washington, D.C.: Catholic University Press, 1959.

GAY, M. J., & TONGE, W. L. The late effects of loss of parents in childhood. *British Journal of Psychiatry,* 1967, *113,* 753–759.

GLUECK, S., & GLUECK, E. *Unravelling juvenile delinquency.* Cambridge, Mass.: Harvard University Press, 1950.

GOODE, W. Family disorganization. In R. K. Merton & R. A. Nisbet (Eds.), *Contemporary social problems.* New York: Harcourt Brace Jovanovich, 1961.

GOODENOUGH, E. W. Interest in persons as an aspect of sex differences in the early years. *Genetic Psychology Monographs,* 1957, *55,* 287–323.

GREEN, R. *Sexual identity conflict in children and adults.* New York: Basic Books, 1974.

GREENBERG, M., & MORRIS, N. Engrossment: The newborn's impact upon the father. *American Journal of Orthopsychiatry,* 1974, *44,* 520–531.

GREENSTEIN, J. F. Father characteristics and sex-typing. *Journal of Personality and Social Psychology,* 1966, *3,* 271–277.

GREGORY, I. Studies of parental deprivation in psychiatric patients. *American Journal of Psychiatry,* 1958, *115,* 432–442.

GREGORY, I. Anterospective data following childhood loss of a parent: I. Delinquency and high school dropout. *Archives of General Psychiatry,* 1965a, *13,* 99–109.

GREGORY, I. Anterospective data following childhood loss of a parent: II. Pathology, performance, and potential among college students. *Archives of General Psychiatry,* 1965b, *13,* 110–120.

GRUNEBAUM, M. G., HURWITZ, I., PRENTICE, N. M., & SPERRY, B. M. Fathers of sons with primary neurotic learning inhibition. *American Journal of Orthopsychiatry,* 1962, *32,* 462–473.

GUNDLACH, R. H. Childhood parental relationships and the establishment of gender roles of homosexuals. *Journal of Consulting and Clinical Psychology,* 1969, *33,* 136–139.

GUNDLACH, R. H., & REISS, B. F. Self and sexual identity in the female: A study of female homosexuals. In B. F. Riess (Ed.), *New directions in mental health.* New York: Grune & Stratton, 1968.

HALL, P., & TONGE, W. L. Long-standing continuous unemployment in male patients with psychiatric symptoms. *British Journal of Preventive and Social Medicine,* 1963, *17,* 191–196.

HAMILTON, D. M., & WAHL, J. G. The hospital treatment of dementia praecox. *American Journal of Psychiatry,* 1948, *104,* 346–352.

HEATH, D. What meaning and what effects does fatherhood have on the maturing of professional men? *Merrill-Palmer Quarterly,* 1978, *24,* 265–278.

HECKEL, R. V. The effects of fatherlessness on the preadolescent female. *Mental Hygiene,* 1963, *47,* 69–73.

HECKSCHER, B. T. Household structure and achievement orientation in lower-class Barbadian families. *Journal of Marriage and the Family,* 1967, *29,* 521–526.

HEILBRUN, A. B. Parental identification and college adjustment. *Psychological Reports,* 1962, *10,* 853–854.

HEILBRUN, A. B. The measurement of identification. *Child Development,* 1965a, *36,* 111–127.

HEILBRUN, A. B. An empirical test of the modeling theory of sex-role learning. *Child Development,* 1965b, *36,* 789–799.

HEILBRUN, A. B. Parent identification and filial sex-role behavior: The importance of biological context. Pp. 125–194 in J. K. Cole & R. Dienstbier (Eds.), *Nebraska Symposium on Motivation, 1973.* Lincoln: University of Nebraska Press, 1974.

HEILBRUN, A. B., HARRELL, S. N., & GILLARD, B. J. Perceived child-rearing attitudes of fathers and cognitive control in daughters. *Journal of Genetic Psychology,* 1967, *111,* 29–40.

HELPER, M. M. Learning theory and the self-concept. *Journal of Abnormal and Social Psychology,* 1955, *51,* 184–194.

HELSON, R. Personality characteristics and developmental history of creative college women. *Genetic Psychology Monographs,* 1967, *76,* 205–256.

HERZOG, E., & SUDIA, C. E. *Boys in fatherless families.* Washington, D.C.: Office of Child Development, 1970.

HETHERINGTON, E. M. A developmental study of the effects of sex of the dominant parent on sex-role preference, identification, and imitation in children. *Journal of Personality and Social Psychology,* 1965, *2,* 188–194.

HETHERINGTON, E. M. Effects of paternal absence on sex-typed behaviors in Negro and white preadolescent males. *Journal of Personality and Social Psychology,* 1966, *4,* 87–91.

HETHERINGTON, E. M. Effects of father-absence on personality development in adolescent daughters. *Developmental Psychology,* 1972, *7,* 313–326.

HETHERINGTON, E. M., & BRACKBILL, Y. Etiology and covariation of obstinacy, orderliness, and parsimony in young children. *Child Development,* 1963, *34,* 919–943.

HETHERINGTON, E. M., COX, M., & COX, R. Divorced fathers. *Family Coordinator,* 1976, *25,* 417–428.

HETHERING, E. M., COX, M., & COX, R. *Family interaction and the social, emotional, and cognitive development of children following divorce.* Paper presented at the Johnson and Johnson Conference on the Family. Washington, D.C., May 1978.

HETHERINGTON, E. M., & FRANKIE, G. Effects of parental dominance, warmth, and conflict on imitation in children. *Journal of Personality and Social Psychology,* 1967, *6,* 119–125.

HETHERINGTON, E. M., & PARKE, R. D. *Child psychology: A contemporary viewpoint* (2nd ed.). New York: McGraw-Hill, 1979.

HILGARD, J. R., NEUMAN, M. F., & FISK, F. Strength of adult ego following bereavement. *American Journal of Orthopsychiatry,* 1960, *30,* 788–798.

HILL, J. P. Similarity and accordance between parents and sons in attitudes towards mathematics. *Child Development,* 1967, *38,* 777–791.

HOFFMAN, L. W. The father's role in the family and the child's peer group adjustment. *Merrill-Palmer Quarterly,* 1961, *7,* 97–105.

HOFFMAN, M. L. Father absence and conscience development. *Developmental Psychology,* 1971a, *4,* 400–406.

HOFFMAN, M. L. Identification and conscience development. *Child Development,* 1971b, *42,* 1071–1082.

HOLSTEIN, C. E. The relation of children's moral judgment level to that of their parents and to communication patterns in the family. Pp. 484–494 in R. C. Smart & M. S. Smart (Eds.), *Readings in child development and relationships.* New York: Macmillan, 1972.

HONZIK, M. P. Environmental correlates of mental growth: Prediction from the family setting at 21 months. *Child Development,* 1967, *38,* 338–364.

HURLEY, J. R. Parental malevolence and children's intelligence. *Journal of Consulting Psychology,* 1967, *31,* 199–204.

JACOBSON, G., & RYDER, R. G. Parental loss and some characteristics of the early marriage relationship. *American Journal of Orthopsychiatry,* 1969, *39,* 779–787.

JENKINS, R. L. The varieties of children's behavioral problems and family dynamics. *American Journal of Psychiatry,* 1968, *124,* 1440–1445.

JOHNSON, M. M. Sex-role learning in the nuclear family. *Child Development,* 1963, *34,* 319–333.

JOHNSON, M. M. Fathers, mothers, and sex-typing. *Sociological Inquiry,* 1975, *45,* 15–26.

JOHNSON, M. M., & MEADOW, A. Parental identification among male schizophrenics. *Journal of Personality,* 1966, *37,* 300–309.

KAGAN, J. Socialization of aggression and the perception of parents in fantasy. *Child Development,* 1958, *28,* 311–320.

KATKOVSKY, W., CRANDALL, V. C., & GOOD, S. Parental antecedents of children's beliefs in internal-external control of reinforcements in intellectual achievement situations. *Child Development,* 1967, *38,* 765–766.

KATZ, I. Socialization of academic motivation in minority group children. Pp. 133–191 in D. Levine (Ed.), *Nebraska Symposium on Motivation, 1967.* Lincoln: University of Nebraska Press, 1967.

KAUFMAN, I., PECK, A. I., & TAGIURI, C. K. The family constellation and overt incestuous relations between father and daughter. *American Journal of Orthopsychiatry,* 1954, *24,* 266–277.

KAYE, H. E., et al. Homosexuality in women. *Archives of General Psychiatry,* 1967, *17,* 626–634.

KAYTON, R., & BILLER, H. B. Perception of parental sex-role behavior and psychopathology in adult males. *Journal of Consulting and Clinical Psychology,* 1971, *36,* 235–237.

KAYTON, R., & BILLER, H. B. Sex-role development and psychopathology in adult males. *Journal of Consulting and Clinical Psychology,* 1972, *38,* 308–310.

KELLY, F. J., & BAER, D. J. Age of male delinquents when father left home and recidivism. *Psychological Reports,* 1969, *25,* 1010.

KELLY, J. B., & WALLERSTEIN, J. S. The effects of paternal divorce: Experiences of the child in early latency. *American Journal of Orthopsychiatry,* 1976, *46,* 20–30.

KIMBALL, B. The Sentence Completion Technique in a study of scholastic underachievement. *Journal of Consulting Psychology,* 1952, *16,* 353–358.

KOHLBERG, L. A cognitive-developmental analysis of children's sex-role concepts and attitudes. Pp. 82–173 in E. E. Maccoby (Ed.), *The development of sex differences.* Stanford, Calif.: Stanford University Press, 1966.

KOHN, H. L. Social class and parental values. *American Journal of Sociology,* 1959, *64,* 337–351.

KOTELCHUCK, M. The infant's relationship to the father: Experimental evidence. Pp. 324–344 in M. E. Lamb (Ed.), *The role of the father in child development.* New York: John Wiley, 1976.

KUNDSIN, R. B. (Ed.). *Women and success.* New York: Morrow, 1974.

LAMB, M. E. (Ed.). *The role of the father in child development.* New York: John Wiley, 1976.

LAMB, M. E. (Ed.). *The role of the father in child development* (2nd ed.). New York: John Wiley, 1981.

LAMB, M. E., & LAMB, J. E. The nature and importance of the father-child relationship. *Family Coordinator,* 1976, *25,* 370–386.

LANDIS, J. T. The trauma of children when parents divorce. *Marriage and Family Living,* 1960, *22,* 7–13.

LANDIS, J. T. A re-examination of the role of the father as an index of family integration. *Marriage and Family Living,* 1962, *24,* 122–128.

LANDIS, P. H. *Making the most of marriage.* Englewood Cliffs, N.J.: Prentice-Hall, 1965.

LANDY, F., ROSENBERG, B. G., & SUTTON-SMITH, B. The effect of limited father-absence on cognitive development. *Child Development,* 1969, *40,* 941–944.

LANGLOIS, J. H., & DOWNS, A. C. Mothers, fathers, and peers as socialization agents of sex-typed play behaviors in young children. *Child Development,* 1980, *51,* 1237–1247.

LEE, P. C. Male and female teachers in elementary schools: An ecological analysis. *Teachers College Record,* 1973, *75,* 79–98.

LEE, P. C., & WOLINSKY, A. L. Male teachers of young children: A preliminary empirical study. *Young Children,* 1973, *28,* 342–352.

LEFKOWITZ, M. M. Some relationships between sex-role preference of children and other parent and child variables. *Psychological Reports,* 1962, *10,* 43–53.

LEICHTY, M. M. The effect of father-absence during early childhood upon the Oedipal situation as reflected in young adults. *Merrill-Palmer Quarterly,* 1960, *6,* 212–217.

LEIDERMAN, G. F. Effect of parental relationships and child-training practices on boys' interactions with peers. *Acta Psychologica,* 1959, *15,* 469.

LEIGHTON, L. A., STOLLAK, G. E., & FERGUSON, L. R. Patterns of communication in normal and clinic families. *Journal of Consulting and Clinical Psychology,* 1971, *36,* 252–256.

LEONARD, M. R. Fathers and daughters. *International Journal of Psychoanalysis,* 1966, *47,* 325–333.

LESSING, E. E., ZAGORIN, S. W., & NELSON, D. WISC subtest and IQ score correlates of father-absence. *Journal of Genetic Psychology,* 1970, *67,* 181–195.

LEVINSON, D. J. *The seasons of a man's life.* New York: Ballantine, 1978.

LEVY, D. M. *Maternal overprotection.* New York: Columbia University Press, 1943.

LEWIS, M., & WEINTRAUB, M. The father's role in the child's social network. Pp. 157–184 in M. E. Lamb (Ed.), The role of the father in child development. New York: John Wiley, 1976.

LIDZ, T., PARKER, N., & CORNELISON, A. R. The role of the father in the family environment of the schizophrenic patient. *American Journal of Psychiatry,* 1956, *13,* 126–132.

LIVERANT, S. MMPI differences between parents of disturbed children and nondisturbed children. *Journal of Consulting Psychology,* 1959, *23,* 256–260.

LUCKEY, E. B. Marital satisfaction and parental concept. *Journal of Consulting Psychology,* 1960, *24,* 195–204.

LYNN, D. B. *Parental and sex-role identification.* Berkeley, Calif.: McCutchan, 1969.

LYNN, D. B. *The father: His role in development.* Monterey, Calif.: Brooks/Cole, 1974.

LYNN, D. B. *Daughters and parents: Past, present and future.* Monterey, Calif.: Brooks/Cole, 1979.

LYNN, D. B., & SAWREY, W. L. The effects of father-absence on Norwegian boys and girls. *Journal of Abnormal and Social Psychology,* 1959, *59,* 258–262.

McCELLAND, D. C., & WATT, N. F. Sex-role alienation in schizophrenia. *Journal of Abnormal Psychology,* 1968, *73,* 226–239.

MACCOBY, E. E., & RAU, L. *Differential cognitive abilities.* Final report, Cooperative Research Project, No. 1040. Washington, D.C.: U.S. Office of Education, 1962.

McCORD, J., McCORD, W., & HOWARD, A. Family interaction as an antecedent to the direction of male aggressiveness. *Journal of Abnormal and Social Psychology,* 1963, *66,* 239–242.

McCORD, J., McCORD, W., & THURBER, E. Some effects of paternal absence on male children. *Journal of Abnormal and Social Psychology,* 1962, *64,* 631–639.

MacDONALD, A. P., JR., Internal-external locus of control: Parental antecedents. *Journal of Consulting and Clinical Psychology,* 1971, *37,* 141–147.

MACKIE, J. F., MAXWELL, A. D., & RAFFERTY, F. T. *Psychological development of culturally disadvantaged Negro kindergarten children: A study of the selective influence of family and school variables.* Paper presented at the meeting of the American Orthopsychiatric Association, Waashington, D.C., March 1967.

McPHERSON, S. Communication of intents among parents and their disturbed adolescent child. *Journal of Abnormal Psychology,* 1970, *76,* 98–105.

MADOW, L., & HARDY, S. E. Incidence and analysis of the broken family in the background of neurosis. *American Journal of Orthopsychiatry,* 1947, *17,* 521–528.

MEDINNUS, G. R. The relation between inter-parent agreement and several child measures. *Journal of Genetic Psychology,* 1965a, *102,* 139–144.

MEDINNUS, G. R. Delinquents' perception of their parents. *Journal of Consulting Psychology,* 1965b, *29,* 5–19.

MILLER, W. B. Lower-class culture as a generating milieu of gang delinquency. *Journal of Social Issues,* 1958, *14,* 5–19.

MISCHEL, W. Preference for delayed reinforcement: An experimental study of cultural observation. *Journal of Abnormal and Social Psychology,* 1959, *56,* 57–61.

MISCHEL, W. Preference for delayed reward and social responsibility. *Journal of Abnormal and Social Psychology,* 1961a, *62,* 1–7.

MISCHEL, W. Father-absence and delay of gratification. *Journal of Abnormal and Social Psychology,* 1961b, *62,* 116–124.

MISCHEL, W. Delay of gratification, need for achievement, and acquiescence in another culture. *Journal of Abnormal and Social Psychology,* 1961c, *62,* 543–552.

MISCHLER, E. G., & WAXLER, N. E. *Interaction in families.* New York: John Wiley, 1968.

MITCHELL, D., & WILSON, W. Relationship of father-absence to masculinity and popularity of delinquent boys. *Psychological Reports,* 1967, *20,* 1173–1174.

MONAHAN, T. P. Family status and the delinquent child. *Social Forces,* 1957, *35,* 250–258.

MOULTON, P. W., BURNSTEIN, E., LIBERTY, L., & ALTUCHER, N. The patterning of parental affection and dominance as a determinant of guilt and sex-typing. *Journal of Personality and Social Psychology,* 1966, *4,* 363–365.

MOYNIHAN, D. P. *The Negro family: The case for national action.* Washington, D.C.: U.S. Department of Labor, 1965.

MUSSEN, P. H. Some antecedents and consequences of masculine sex-typing in adolescent boys. *Psychological Monographs,* 1961, *75*(2, Whole No. 506).

MUSSEN, P. H., & DISTLER, L. Masculinity, identification and father-son relationships. *Journal of Abnormal and Social Psychology,* 1959, *59,* 350–356.

MUSSEN, P. H., & DISTLER, L. Child-rearing antecedents of masculine identification in kindergarten boys. *Child Development,* 1960, *31,* 89–100.

MUSSEN, P. H., & RUTHERFORD, E. E. Parent-child relationships and parental personality in relation to young children's sex-role preferences. *Child Development,* 1963, *34,* 589–607.

MUSSEN, P. H., YOUNG, H. B., GADDINI, R., & MORANTE, L. The influence of father-son relationships on adolescent personality and attitudes. *Journal of Child Psychology and Psychiatry,* 1963, *4,* 3–16.

NAKAMURA, C. V., & ROGERS, M. M. Parents' expectations of autonomous behavior and children's autonomy. *Developmental Psychology,* 1969, *1,* 613–617.

NASH, J. The father in contemporary culture and current psychological literature. *Child Development,* 1965, *36,* 261–297.

NASH, J. Historical and social changes in the perception of the role of the father. Pp. 65–87 in M. E. Lamb (Ed.), *The role of the father in child development.* New York: John Wiley, 1976.

NELSON, E. A., & MACCOBY, E. E. The relationship between social development and differential abilities on the scholastic aptitude test. *Merrill-Palmer Quarterly,* 1966, *12,* 269–289.

NEUBAUER, P. B. The one-parent child and his Oedipal development. *The Psychoanalytic Study of the Child,* 1960, *15,* 286–309.

NOWICKI, S., JR., & SEGAL, W. Perceived parental characteristics, locus of control of orientation, and behavioral correlates of locus of control. *Developmental Psychology,* 1974, *10,* 33–37.

NYE, F. I. Child adjustment in broken and unhappy unbroken homes. *Marriage and Family Living,* 1957, *19,* 356–361.

OLTMAN, J. E., & FRIEDMAN, S. Parental deprivation in psychiatric conditions: III. In personality disorders and other conditions. *Diseases of the Nervous System,* 1967, *28,* 298–303.

OLTMAN, J. E., McGARRY, J. J., & FRIEDMAN, S. Parental deprivation and the broken home in dementia praecox and other mental disorders. *American Journal of Psychiatry,* 1952, *108,* 685–694.

PARKE, R. D. Perspectives on father-infant interaction. In J. D. Osofsky (Ed.), *The handbook of infant development.* New York: John Wiley, 1979.

PARKE, R. D., & SAWIN, D. B. The father's role in infancy: A reevaluation. *Family Coordinator,* 1976, *25,* 365–371.

PARKER, S., & KLEINER, R. J. Characteristics of Negro mothers in single-headed households. *Journal of Marriage and the Family,* 1966, *28,* 507–513.

PAYNE, D. E., & MUSSEN, P. H. Parent-child relations and father-identification among adolescent boys. *Journal of Abnormal and Social Psychology,* 1956, *52,* 358–362.

PEDERSEN, F. A. Relationships between father-absence and emotional disturbance in male military dependents. *Merrill-Palmer Quarterly,* 1966, *12,* 321–331.

PEDERSEN, F. A. Does research on children reared in father-absent families yield information on father influences? *Family Coordinator,* 1976, *25,* 458–464.

PEDERSEN, F. A. *The father-infant relationship: Observational studies in the family setting.* New York: Praeger, 1980.

PEDERSEN, F. A., & ROBSON, K. S. Father participation in infancy. *American Journal of Orthopsychiatry,* 1969, *39,* 466–472.

PETERSON, D. R., BECKER, W. C., HELLMER, L. A., SHOEMAKER, D. J., & QUAY, H. C. Parental attitudes and child adjustment. *Child Development,* 1959, *30,* 119–130.

PETTIGREW, T. F. *A profile of the Negro American.* New York: D. Van Nostrand, 1964.

PLANK, E. H., & PLANK, R. Emotional components in arithmetic learning as seen through autobiographies. *The Psychoanalytic Study of the Child,* 1954, *9,* 274–293.

POFFENBERGER, T. A., & NORTON, D. Factors in the formation of attitudes towards mathematics. *Journal of Educational Research,* 1959, *52,* 171–176.

POPE, B. Socioeconomic contracts in children's peer culture prestige values. *Genetic Psychology Monographs,* 1953, *48,* 157–200.

RADIN, N. Father-child interaction and the intellectual functioning of four-year-old boys. *Developmental Psychology,* 1972, *6,* 353–361.

RADIN, N. Observed paternal behaviors as antecedents of intellectual functioning in young boys. *Developmental Psychology,* 1973, *8,* 369–376.

RADIN, N. The role of the father in cognitive, academic and intellectual development. Pp. 237–276 in M. E. Lamb (Ed.), *The role of the father in child development.* New York: John Wiley, 1976.

REUTER, M. W., & BILLER, H. B. Perceived paternal nurturance-availability and personality adjustment among college males. *Journal of Consulting and Clinical Psychology,* 1973, *40,* 339–342.

ROBEY, A., ROSENWALD, R. J., SNELL, J. E., & LEE, R. E. The run-away girl: A reaction to family stress. *American Journal of Orthopsychiatry,* 1964, *34,* 762–767.

ROGERS, W. B., & LONG, J. M. Male models and sexual identification: A case from the Out Island Bahamas. *Human Organization,* 1968, *27,* 326–331.

ROHRER, H. H., EDMONDSON, M. S. *The eighth generation.* New York: Harper & Row, Pub., 1960.

ROMNEY, A. K. Variations in household structure as determinants of sex-type behavior. Pp. 208–220 in F. Beach (Ed.), *Sex and behavior.* New York: John Wiley, 1965.

ROSENBERG, C. M. Determinants of psychiatric illness in young people: *British Journal of Psychiatry,* 1969, *115,* 907–915.

ROSENBERG, M. *Society and the adolescent self-image.* Princeton, N.J.: Princeton University Press, 1965.

ROSENTHAL, K., & KESHET, H. F. *Fathers without partners: A study of fathers and the family after marital separation.* Totowa, N.J.: Rowman & Littlefield, 1981.

ROSENTHAL, M. S., NI, E., FINKELSTEIN, M., & BERKWITS, G. K. Father-child relationships and children's problems. *Archives of General Psychiatry,* 1962, *7,* 360–373.

RUTHERFORD, E. E., & MUSSEN, P. H. Generosity in nursery school boys. *Child Development,* 1968, *39,* 755–765.

RYCHLAK, J., & LEGERSKI, A. A sociocultural theory of appropriate sex-role identification and level of personality adjustment. *Journal of Personality,* 1967, *35*(No. 1), 31–49.

SAGHIR, M. T., & ROBBINS, F. *Male and female homosexuality.* Baltimore, Md.: Williams & Wilkins, 1973.

SALZMAN, L. Psychology of the female: A new look. *Archives of General Psychiatry,* 1967, *17,* 195–203.

SANTROCK, J. W. Paternal absence, sex-typing and identification. *Developmental Psychology,* 1970a, *2,* 264–272.

SANTROCK, J. W. Influence of onset and type of paternal absence on the first four Eriksonian developmental crises. *Developmental Psychology,* 1970b, *3,* 273–274.

SANTROCK, J. W. Relation of type and onset of father-absence to cognitive development. *Child Development,* 1972, *43,* 455–469.

SANTROCK, J. W. Father absence, perceived maternal behavior, and moral development in boys. *Child Development,* 1975, *46,* 753–757.

SANTROCK, J. W., & WOHLFORD, P. Effects of father absence: Influences of, reason for, and onset of absence. *Proceedings of the 78th Annual Convention of the American Psychological Association,* 1970, *5,* 265–266.

SCHAFFER, E. S. Children's' reports of parental behavior: An inventory, *Child Development,* 1972, *43,* 413–424.

SCHLESINGER, B. The one-parent family: An overview. *Family Life Coordinator,* 1966, *15,* 133–137.

SCHUHAM, A. I. Power relations in emotionally disturbed and normal family triads. *Journal of Abnormal and Social Psychology,* 1970, *75,* 30–37.

SEARS, P. S. Doll-play aggression in normal young children: Influence of sex, age, sibling status, father's absence. *Psychological Monographs,* 1951, *65*(Whole No. 6).

SEARS, P. S. Child rearing factors related to playing of sex-typed roles. *American Psychologist,* 1953, *8,* 431 (Abstract).

SEARS, R. R. Relation of early socialization experiences to self-concepts and gender role in middle childhood. *Child Development,* 1970, *41,* 267–289.

SEARS, R. R., PINTLER, M. H., & SEARS, P. S. Effects of father-separation on preschool children's doll-play aggression. *Child Development,* 1946, *17,* 219–243.

SEARS, R. R., RAU, L., & ALPERT, R. *Identification and child rearing.* Stanford, Calif.: Stanford University Press, 1965.

SHINN, M. Father absence and children's cognitive development. *Psychological Bulletin,* 1978, *85,* 295–324.

SOLOMON, D. The generality of children's achievement related behavior. *Journal of Genetic Psychology,* 1969, *114,* 109–125.

SPELKE, D., ZELAZO, P., KAGAN, J., & KOTELCHUCK, M. Father interaction and separation protest. *Developmental Psychology,* 1973, *9,* 83–90.

STEIMEL, R. J. Childhood experiences and masculinity-femininity scores. *Journal of Consulting Psychology,* 1960, *7,* 212–217.

STENDLER, C. B. Possible causes of overdependency in young children. *Child Development*, 1954, *25*, 125–146.

STEPHENS, W. N. *The Oedipus complex: Cross cultural evidence.* Glencoe, Ill.: Free Press, 1962.

STOLZ, L. M., et al. *Father relations of war-born children.* Stanford, Calif.: Stanford University Press, 1954.

STRAUS, M. A. Conjugal power structure and adolescent personality. *Marriage and Family Living*, 1962, *24*, 17–25.

STRODTBECK, F. L. Family interaction, values and achievement. Pp. 135–194 in D. C. McClelland, A. L. Baldwin, V. Bronfenbrenner, & F. L. Strodtbeck (Eds.), *Talent and society.* New York: Van Nostrand Reinhold, 1958.

SUEDFIELD, P. Paternal absence and overseas success of Peace Corps volunteers. *Journal of Consulting Psychology*, 1967, *31*, 424–425.

SUTTON-SMITH, B., & ROSENBERG, B. G. *The sibling.* New York: Holt, Rinehart & Winston, 1970.

SUTTON-SMITH, B., ROSENBERG, B. G., & LANDY, F. Father-absence effects in families of different sibling compositions. *Child Development*, 1968, *38*, 1213–1221.

TALLMAN, I. Spousal role differentiation and the socialization of severely retarded children. *Journal of Marriage and the Family*, 1965, *17*, 37–42.

TASCH, R. J. The role of the father in the family. *Journal of Experimental Education*, 1952, *20*, 319–361.

TASCH, R. J. Interpersonal perceptions of fathers and mothers. *Journal of Genetic Psychology*, 1955, *87*, 59–65.

THOMPSON, N. L., SCHWARTZ, D. M., McCANDLESS, B. R., & EDWARDS, D. A. Parent-child relationships and sexual identity in male and female homosexuals and heterosexuals. *Journal of Consulting and Clinical Psychology*, 1973, *41*, 120–127.

TILLER, P. O. Father-absence and personality development of children in sailor families. *Nordisk Psykologi's Monograph Series*, 1958, *9*, 1–48.

TILLER, P. O. *Father separation and adolescence.* Oslo, Norway: Institute for Social Research, 1961.

TOBY, J. The differential impact of family disorganization. *American Sociological Review*, 1957, *22*, 505–512.

TRAPP, E. P., & KAUSLER, D. H. Dominance attitudes in parents and adult avoidance behavior in young children. *Child Development*, 1958, *29*, 507–513.

TRUNNELL, T. L. The absent father's children's emotional disturbances. *Archives of General Psychiatry*, 1968, *19*, 180–188.

TUCKMAN, J., & REGAN, R. A. Intactness of the home and behavioral problems in children. *Journal of Child Psychology and Psychiatry*, 1966, *7*, 225–233.

TYLER, L. E. The relationship of interests to abilities and reputation among first-grade children. *Educational Psychology Measurement*, 1951, *11*, 255–264.

VAILLANT, G. E. *Adaptation to life.* Boston: Little, Brown, 1977.

WAHL, C. W. Antecedent factors in family histories of 392 schizophrenics. *American Journal of Psychiatry*, 1954, *110*, 668–676.

WAHL, C. W. Some antecedent factors in the family histories of 568 male schizophrenics in the U.S. Navy. *American Journal of Psychiatry, 1956, 113,* 201–210.

WALLERSTEIN, J. S., & KELLY, J. B. The effects of parental divorce: The adolescent experience. In E. J. Anthony & C. Koupernick (Eds.), *The child in his family: Children at psychiatric risk.* New York: John Wiley, 1974.

WALLERSTEIN, J. S., & KELLY, J. B. The effects of parental divorce: Experiences of the preschool child. *Journal of the American Academy of Child Psychiatry*, 1975, *14*, 600–616.

WALLERSTEIN, J. S., & KELLY, J. B. The effects of parental divorce: Experiences of the child in later latency. *American Journal of Orthopsychiatry*, 1976, *46*, 256–269.

WALLERSTEIN, J. S., & KELLY, J. B. *Surviving the breakup: How children actually cope with divorce.* New York: Basic Books, 1980.

WALTERS, J. (Ed.). Special issue: Fatherhood. *Family Coordinator*, 1976, *25*, 335–520.

WEST, D. J. Parental relationships in male homosexuality. *International Journal of Social Psychiatry*, 1959, *5*, 85–97.

WEST, D. J. *Homosexuality.* Chicago: Aldine, 1967.

WESTLEY, W. A., & EPSTEIN, N. B. *Silent majority.* San Francisco: Jossey-Bass, 1970.

WHITING, J.W.M., KLUCKHOHN, R., & ANTHONY, A. The function of male initiation ceremonies at puberty. Pp. 359–370 in E. E. Maccoby, T. M. Newcomb, & E. L. Hartley (Eds.), *Readings in social psychology.* New York: Holt, Rinehart & Winston, 1958.

WINCH, R. F. The relation between loss of a parent and progress in courtship. *Journal of Social Psychology*, 1949, *29*, 51–56.

WINCH, R. F. Some data bearing on the Oedipus hypothesis. *Journal of Abnormal and Social Psychology*, 1950, *45*, 481–489.

WINCH, R. F. *Identification and its familial determinants.* Indianapolis: Bobbs-Merrill, 1962.

WOHLFORD, P., & LIBERMAN, D. Effects of father absence on personal time, field independence and anxiety. *Proceedings of the 78th Annual Convention of the American Psychological Association*, 1970, *5*, 263–264.

WOHLFORD, P., SANTROCK, J. W., BERGER, S. E., & LIBERMAN, D. Older brothers' influence on sex-typed, aggressive, and dependent behavior in father-absent children. *Developmental Psychology*, 1971, *4*, 124–134.

WOLMAN, B. B. The fathers of schizophrenic patients. *Acta Psychotherapeutic*, 1961, *9*, 193–210.

WOOD, H. P., & DUFFY, E. L. Psychological factors in alcoholic women. *American Journal of Psychiatry*, 1966, *123*, 341–345.

WYLIE, H. L., & DELGADO, R. A. A pattern of mother-son relationships involving thte absence of the father. *American Journal of Orthopsychiatry*, 1959, *29*, 644–649.

40

Adult Sexual Development

CARLFRED B. BRODERICK

The last few decades have witnessed the emergence of research on both adult development and human sexuality; yet both fields are young and ill-conceptualized. Whereas patterns of development in childhood and youth are structured by the almost irresistible forces of physical and intellectual growth, there are few constraints in the course which adult development may take. The aging process is just as real among adults, but the pace of change is slower and the responses more varied than in childhood. Taking on marital and familial statuses often imposes certain additional structure on the course of their life experiences. They typically move from single to joined, from child-free to pregnant to parent-of-young-children to parent of older-children and then to child-free once again. The pattern is flexible.

The parameters of human sexuality are equally difficult to define. Kinsey (Kinsey, Pomeroy, & Martin, 1948; Kinsey, Pomeroy, Martin, & Gebhard, 1953) taught us to count sexual events, and Masters and Johnson (1966, 1970) have shown us how human physiology responds to sexual stimulation and what the chief forms of sexual dysfunction are. No one has taught us how to measure and interpret the more important dimensions of personal and interpersonal meanings. Nevertheless in this chapter we shall attempt to focus on satisfaction as much as an orgasm and on the quality of human bonding or distancing as well as on the frequencies of intercourse or the incidence of specific dysfunctions.

MARITAL SEXUAL RELATIONSHIPS

Establishing the Marital Relationship

Only a generation or two ago the majority of American couples had their first sexual relationship on their wedding night (Kinsey et al., 1948, 1953). Today fewer than one out of five couples postpone sex until marriage (Broderick & Hicks, 1970; Levin & Levin, 1975). A substantial minority share a common residence for some period of time before their marriage (Glick & Spanier, 1980; Macklin, 1978), while others establish a sexual relationship independent of a residential one. Whatever the premarital circumstances every married couple must face the issue of establishing mutually satisfying scripts for their sexual life together.

Unfortunately there has been no research on the process of establishing the sexual relationship. The issue is dealt with to some degree in the clinical literature (e.g., Broderick, 1979a, chap. 8, 1979b, chap. 14; Masters & Johnson, 1970; Sager, 1976), but the focus, as might be expected, is on the problems associated with mismatched or pair-defeating sexual scripts. It is clear from these materials that individuals bring a very diverse set of expectations to the marital bed. Also their attempts to work out a satisfying resolution of their differences lead to a full range of possible outcomes.

It is difficult to find data specifically on newly marrieds, but a number of studies have reported on sexual morale in the general married population. In Tavris and Sadd's (1977) study of 100,000 readers of *Redbook* magazine, one-third of the sample reported that the sexual aspect of their marriage was *very good* and another third that it was *good*. The remaining third were divided between those who rated it as only *fair* (21 percent) and those who complained that is was *poor* to *very poor* (12 percent).

There is evidence that things go better at first or at least that higher morale is maintained despite whatever difficulties are encountered early in marriage. One evidence of this is the well-established datum that intercourse occurs most frequently in the early months of

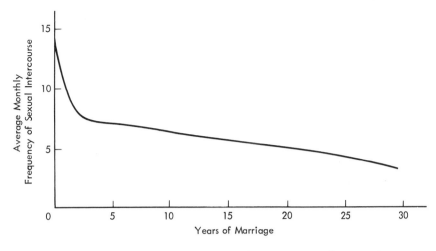

Figure 40-1 Average monthly frequency of sexual intercourse by duration of marriage. (Source: Adapted from Westoff & Westoff, 1971.)

marriage and then decreases over the length of marriage.[1] Probably the best data on frequency of intercourse over the course of the marriage came from the national probability sample obtained by Westoff and Westoff (1971). Figure 40-1 summarizes their findings. It can be seen that the biggest drop-off is in the first three years. Average monthly (four weeks) frequencies drop from about 13 to about 7 in this early period. It seems likely that at least two factors are at work beyond the oft-cited dissipation of novelty. First, this is a difficult time in marriage generally, as reflected in the fact that divorce rates peak in the third and fourth year of marriage. Second, this is also the period in which pregnancy is most likely to occur. As we shall see in more detail in Figure 40-1, frequency of intercourse decreases dramatically during the latter stages of pregnancy. Figure 40-1 shows that after the first three years of marriage the decrease continues, but at a much slower rate.

Any representation of average rates of intercourse obscures the wide range of frequencies at every stage of the marriage. This same study by Westoff and Westoff found that over the previous four weeks 6 percent reported no sexual activity at all, while at the other end of the continuum 8 percent reported 19 or more coital encounters (see Figure 40-2 for the entire distribution).

Pregnancy

Studies of couples who are experiencing the wife's pregnancy provide ample support for the idea that feelings and meanings are at least as important as biological factors. Both U.S. couples (Masters & Johnson, 1966; Pasini, 1977; Solberg, Butler, & Wagner, 1973; Tolor & DiGrazia, 1976) and couples from quite different cultural settings, such as Thailand (Morris, 1975) and Czechoslovakia (Bartova, Kolrova, Uzel, 1969), report a general decrease in sexual activity over the course of pregnancy and especially in the third trimester. The more interesting analyses, however, examine the factors that account for the great variation among couples in the way they ex-

perience pregnancy. Pasini (1977) found that women who had a positive attitude toward the pregnancy tended to maintain or even improve their sexual relationships with their husbands, while those with negative attitudes experienced a decrease in sexual satisfaction.

Several explanations have been offered for this observation. One is the principle of *stimulus generalization*—that is, the woman tends to lose enthusiasm for everything associated with the unwanted pregnancy including, preeminently, the activity that brought it about. Some research indicates that an intervening factor may be the symptoms of pregnancy (nausea, sleeplessness, fatigue). These can be shown to be greater when the attitude toward the pregnancy is negative (Semmens, 1971), and they have been shown to be an important element in the loss of sexual interest, especially during the first trimester (Landis, Poffenberger, & Poffenberger, 1950; Masters & Johnson, 1966; Poffenberger, Poffenberger, & Landis, 1952). Of course the severity of the symptoms affects the level of sexual interest no matter what the cause of the physical difficulty might be (Wolman, 1978).

Another attitudinal variable of importance is the quality of the couple's affectional life prior to the pregnancy. Solberg et al. (1973) found that women who had already established very active sexual relationships and were highly orgasmic suffered the least loss of sexual interest during their pregnancies. Masters and Johnson (1966) were able to identify two distinct patterns of adjustment. One group which had entered the pregnancy with a good affectional adjustment actually experienced an increase in sexual interest and response when they reached the relative freedom from symptoms of the second trimester. By contrast those without this positive background experienced a linear reduction in interest as the pregnancy proceeded. This may help to explain the otherwise puzzling finding by Tolor and DiGrazia (1976) that, in their cross-sectional study, the women in the second trimester group were significantly more orgasmic than were those in other groups.

All studies showed that interest in sexual intercourse waned in the third trimester, but it is worth noting that women's interest in being held did *not* diminish (Hollender & McGehee, 1974). Even when physical discomfort and concern for the unborn child dictated a shift in

[1] Nearly all studies use frequency of intercourse as their index of overall sexual activity. This seems justified by the finding that intercourse makes up 85 percent to 90 percent of all sexual activity among married adults of every age (Martin, 1977).

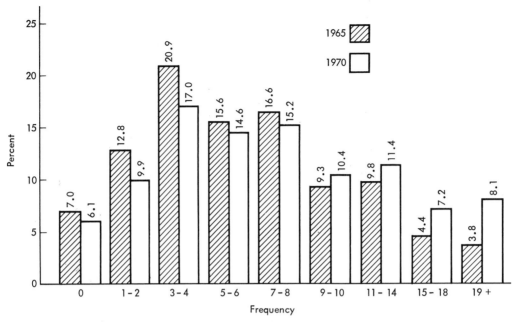

Figure 40-2 Percent of married women reporting various frequencies of intercourse in a four-week period (1965 and 1970). (Source: Adapted from Westoff, 1974.)

the form of expression of physical closeness, it seems that it in no way diminished it.

Most pregnant women apparently succeeded in negotiating a level of sexual activity that corresponded closely to their own desires. Only about one in five felt that their interest cooled faster than their husbands' in the last few weeks of the pregnancy, while an equal or larger number felt that their husbands were unnecessarily protective at that time (Tolor & DiGrazia, 1976).

Established Marriage

It was Kinsey's observation that among his subjects women reached their peak of sexual functioning in their middle years (Kinsey et al., 1953). There is little support for that view in more recent studies, and it seems likely that the phenomenon was a result of attitudes toward female sexuality at mid-century. Apparently it took many women 20 years of married life to overcome their inhibitions. The current generation is getting off to a much faster start. One of the consequences of the changing attitudes toward sex in our society in recent decades is a general increase in the amount of marital sexual activity. Westoff (1974) was able to demonstrate that in only five years (1965 to 1970) matched national samples of couples showed substantial changes (see Figure 40-2). In that period they found the percentage of women reporting sex once per week or less often dropped from 41 percent to 33 percent, while the percentage reporting frequencies of three or more times per week increased from 18 percent to 27 percent. It seems likely that this trend has continued into the 1980s and that current levels are considerably higher still.

The relationship of frequency of intercourse to marital satisfaction is not the same in every marriage and indeed may not be the same for the partners in the same marriage. There is, however, a substantial correlation between satisfaction with frequency of intercourse and overall marital satisfaction (Bell & Bell, 1972; Levinger,

1970). The causation probably works both ways. Edwards and Booth (1976b) found that the most common explanation given for extended periods of abstinence among married couples was marital discord (other reasons given were physical illness, loss of interest, and emotional stress).

Most studies find husbands' interest in sexual intimacy greater, on the average, than their wives'. One of the more novel approaches to this issue was employed by Mancini and Orthner (1978) who asked their southeastern urban sample to indicate their five most preferred leisure-time activities from a list of over 90 choices. The men in their sample ranked sexual and affectional activities among their top five choices more often than any other activity (although attendance at athletic events was only one percentage point behind). Third for men was reading independently. For women, however, reading was first, while sex and affection were tied with sewing for second place. Table 40–1 shows the percentage of husbands and wives listing sex and affection among their top five choices according to length of marriage. It can be seen that interest measured in this way declined steadily decade by decade roughly paralleling the drop in actual frequency depicted in Figure 40–1. Also men's interest exceeds women's at every age.

While husbands' interest, on the average, exceeds their wives', in individual marriages the reverse may hold true. In fact the women in Bell and Bell's (1972) volunteer sample complained of too little sex several times more often than they complained of too much.

One inevitable corollary of the increasingly positive attitude toward sex in our society is the increased pressure on men and women to perform sexually and, in the case of the woman, to have orgasm as a part of nearly every sexual encounter. Several researchers, including the author of the widely circulated *Hite Report* (1976), have condemned this view as sexist, imposing a masculine perspective on a female function. They point out, as did Masters and Johnson in their first report (1966), that

Table 40-1 Percent of Husbands and Wives Who List "Sexual and Affectional Activity" among Their Five Favorite Leisure-Time Activities, by Number of Years Married

YEARS MARRIED	HUSBANDS %	(N)	WIVES %	(N)
0–5	68	(24)	41	(27)
6–10	57	(35)	32	(37)
11–20	49	(70)	28	(72)
21–30	33	(51)	23	(54)
31–50	21	(38)	8	(37)

Source: Mancini & Orthner, 1978, Table 2.

intercourse is not necessarily the most effective stimulus for a woman since her most sensitive organ is the clitoris and this is often indifferently stimulated through vaginal thrusting. Others have noted that a substantial minority of men are premature ejaculators who may fail to provide sufficient stimulation to create sexual tension in even a highly responsive wife. Be this as it may, the majority of women (about 60 percent) report that they have orgasm during intercourse all or most of the time (Bell & Bell, 1972). Another 32 percent have orgasm occasionally, and only 8 percent never have this experience. As might be expected the more orgasmic group reports a higher frequency of intercourse and a longer average duration. They also tend to be happier with their marriage, although again it is not clear in which direction the causal influence runs.

There have been efforts to obtain a more global measure of sexual functioning. Heath(1978) administered a large number of psychological tests and questions to a group of 68 college alumni ten years after graduation. He developed a scale of *sexual compatibility* compounded from items rating one's own and one's wife's (estimated) level of sexual satisfaction during the most recent three years of their marriage, the consideration she showed for her husband's sexual needs, similarity of moral values, reciprocal fidelity, and an overall evaluation of how well-mated they were sexually. This scale proved to correlate with virtually every measure of personal maturity, stability, and effectiveness, including self-awareness, warmth, other-centeredness, responsibility, impulse control, autonomy, and tolerance. Predictably it was negatively related to moodiness, aggressiveness, anxiety, and tension. Wives of those alumni with higher scores on sexual compatibility were likely to rate their husbands as better friends and more intimate partners then did other wives. They also rated them better fathers. Were this set of findings replicated in other studies of more representative couples, it would certainly argue for the importance of a good sexual adjustment for a good overall life adjustment (or perhaps vice versa).

Most studies only hint at the variety of sexual relationships that actually occur. Some years ago Cuber and Harroff published a book, *The Significant Americans: A Study of Sexual Behavior among the Affluent* (1965). It reported on their interviews with 200 couples who were successful in most of the ways people measure success. They had been married at least 15 years and had never considered divorce. The husband was at the top of his profession or business organization. Somewhat to their own surprise the authors found that this highly homogenous group spread out along a wide continuum with respect to their marital style and the quality of their sexual relationships. Actually they distributed themselves around a normal curve with about one-sixth on the positive end reporting themselves to have a *vital* relationship. Sex was frequent and mutually rewarding; communication flourished; romance lived. At the other end were another group of equal size whom the authors characterized as *conflict-habituated*. These couples constantly quarreled and hurt each other. Sex was likely to be only one of several battlefields. They were not infrequently involved with lovers outside the marriage. In between were two groups, each of which made up about one-third of the sample. On the negative side of the center point were the *devitalized*. They were formerly vital but had lost that quality and both missed and resented it. In fact they had become cynical about marriage itself. Recognizing that the emptiness of their own relationship could be hidden from outsiders with only a little effort, they doubted the genuineness of any apparently vital relationship they saw. Sex was perfunctory or absent, and discrete affairs were common. The final category, *passive-congenial,* had settled into a comfortable, loyal relationship which, in truth, had little more intimacy in it than did the devitalized. The difference was the attitude. These couples were happy with their less intense relationships. They took each other for granted but saw this as a virtue rather than a vice. They had not expected the intensity of their early relationship to continue and so were not embittered when it did not.

There is no evidence that contemporary couples with more various backgrounds would distribute themselves along the vital-congenial-devitalized-conflicted continuum in the same proportion that this specialized sample did. On the other hand it seems to be the nature of humankind to distribute itself along a normal curve in virtually every dimension, so perhaps this pattern is quite common. In any case it seems safe to assume that a more representative contemporary sample would include at least as great a variety of marital styles as this (Wolman & Money, 1980).

One study (Ammons & Stinnett, 1980) did attempt to identify the characteristics which distinguish *vital* middle-age couples from others. Identifying the vital marriages as those with the highest scores in a standard marriage-adjustment scale, they found that high levels of mutual sexual interest and activity were among the factors most clearly distinguishing these from less happy marriages. Other important qualities included being other-oriented (rather than self-oriented) and exhibiting both the need and the capacity for nurturance, understanding, and supportiveness.

Divorce and Remarriage

Bernard (1972) and others have pointed out that the same marital relationship is often evaluated quite differently by the two participants. One cannot properly speak of a happy or unhappy marriage, but rather of how happy *he* is and how happy *she* is. The same principle applies doubly to separation and divorce. There is her experience and his experience, and it may be assumed that the marital disruption is seldom symmetrical in its effects. Studies often list infidelity and other sexually related problems as contributing importantly to marital breakups (Albrecht, 1979; Levinger, 1966). On the face of it an extramarital affair would seem to affect the sex life of the married pair in quite divergent ways. All in all we know relatively little about the effects of these experiences or of marital disruption itself upon the lifetime sexual career of the people involved, but doubtless they are various in the extreme.

Lacking research which addresses the issue directly, we must assume that for many this is a very difficult time. Various studies have shown divorced people to be among the unhappiest in our society, afflicted with problems including increased vulnerability to physical illness (Renne, 1971), mental illness (Bloom, Asher, & White, 1978), and suicide (Kitagawa & Hauser, 1973, pp. 108–112). One study found that divorced individuals who dated and maintained heterosexual friendships had fewer general adjustment problems; although again, the direction of causality is not clear (Spanier & Casto, 1979). In any case the large majority (about three out of four) maintain sufficient faith in the potential of a man-woman union that they remarry after only a few months or years (Glick & Norton, 1977). Moreover these remarriages are successful in the majority of cases both with respect to stability (Glick & Norton, 1977) and morale (Glenn & Weaver, 1977; Gove, 1972; Renne, 1971; White, 1979). I am aware of no direct measure of whether the sexual life of remarried couples is more or less satisfying than for once-married couples of the same ages. There is some evidence, however, that these remarried couples are not free from problems in their sexual adjustment. One study found this listed as the third most problematic area—after financial and emotional problems and before quarrels over children or former spouses (Albrecht, 1979).

As with other couples, however, only a minority report problems in this area, and apparently the sexual component of their marital relationships is an asset which tends to strengthen the pair bond in most cases. Since remarried people are substantially happier than are separated or divorced people (Glenn & Weaver, 1977; Gove, 1972; Renne, 1971), something must be going better.

It is clear that a great deal of work still needs to be done on the impact of separation, divorce, and remarriage upon the sexual careers of individuals.

The Aging Marriage and Widowhood

It has been well established that intimacy including physical intimacy continues to be an important part of marriage at every age and also that at every age intercourse is the preferred manifestation of this intimacy (Martin, 1977). It is equally clear that among both men and women there is some loss in the ability to respond sexually over the years.

Masters and Johnson (1966) found that among their sexually active volunteers the younger males and females responded to direct stimulation in about one-half to one-third the time that it took people in their sixties. Using erotic movie clips Skolnik and Birren (1977) found younger males (age 19 to 30) six times quicker to respond than did their older group (age 48 to 65). Whatever the exact ratio of loss, all studies are agreed that there is a gradual diminution of capacity over the adult life span. Yet the more impressive finding is that a substantial percentage

of men and women continue to function even into advanced old age.

Table 40–2 summarizes the findings of five major studies of erectile potency in aging males. It can be seen that there is little agreement as to exact percentage functioning sexually at each age. For example at age 70 the percentage active ranged from 73 percent in Kinsey et al.'s (1948) sample to 39 percent in Finkle's and in Bower's samples. A conservative conclusion extrapolating from all of the data is that most men are able to function adequately throughout their sixties; a substantial minority continue to do so into their seventies and even eighties. Women, who have no need to sustain an erection, are apparently able to function longer with less loss although supplemental lubrication may be necessary. With them the greatest obstacle to a long and happy sex life is more likely to be loss of a partner.

SEX OUTSIDE MARRIAGE

The nonmarital sexual activities of adults vary even more widely than do marital sexual patterns. They may be heterosexual or homosexual; they may involve partners who are both single, or one or the other may be married to someone else; they may be part of a casual encounter or a long-term relationship; they may occur in the context of cohabitation or separate from any such arrangement; they may be spontaneous and individually motivated or a manifestation of a commitment to a life style which promotes nonmarital sexual relationships.

Unfortunately the research in this area is not sufficiently comprehensive to maintain all of these distinctions, but we shall do what we can to avoid lumping all unmarried sexual encounters into one set of averages or frequencies.

Homosexual Relationships

Homosexual relationships may vary in their social context and personal meanings just as heterosexual relationships may. One study of men engaged in at least occasional homosexual relations (Dank, 1971) found that one-fourth of them were heterosexually married. Their homosexual activities were confined to furtive encounters or clandestine affairs. Another substantial group lived as single heterosexuals in the world of their employment and among some relatives and acquaintances, but as often as possible they escaped to the "gay" world for sociability and sex. A third and growing group chose to live openly in a frankly homosexual life style.

Perhaps the most broadly based study of homosexual life styles is the one conducted for the Kinsey Institute by Bell and Weinberg (1978). They established five categories which accounted for about 70 percent of their San Francisco sample. Some live in "closed-couple" homosexual pairs which were predicated on the principles of intimacy, continuity, and exclusivity similar to heterosexual marriages. A much larger proportion of lesbians than gay men chose this life style, yet even among the men about 14 percent lived in such an arrangement. A larger number (about 25 percent) of men and another substantial group of women lived in "open-couple" relationships which did not preclude other sexual partners even

Table 40-2 Maintenance of Sexual Potency Reported by Various Studies

AGE	KINSEY	FINKLE	BOWERS	NEWMAN	PEARLMAN & KOBASHI
	%	%	%	%	%
60–64	82	63	72	60	63
65–69	75	63	50	63	—
70–74	73	39	39	58	41
75–79	45	24	*	25	—
80+	25	*	*	*	—

Source: Adapted from Pearlman, 1972, Table 10.

though jealousy was a pervasive problem. Bell and Weinberg labeled two other groups *functional* and *dysfunctional.* The functional homosexual had many sexual partners and few commitments or regrets, while the dysfunctional had few partners and was tortured by self-doubt and guilt. The final category, *asexual,* were less active sexually than were any other groups and were defined more by their self-disclosed orientation than by their sexual life style.

Lief (1978) in his review of the Bell and Weinberg study has commented that the greatest difference between the life styles of homosexual and heterosexual males is the level of promiscuity. Among white homosexual males 28 percent reported 1000 or more partners, 15 percent more than 500, and 17 percent more than 250. In other words 60 percent reported more than 250 partners. Seventy percent reported that over half of all their partners involved single encounters with strangers. As Lief puts it, "This is non-affectionate, impersonal, shallow, perhaps compulsive sex, altogether different from most heterosexual behavior" (Lief, 1978, p. 14). The reasons for these differences are not fully clear at this time, although many have suggested that part of it may be the absence of the constraining influence of feminine attitudes toward sex. Female homosexual life styles more nearly approximate those of heterosexual females.

Nonmarital Heterosexual Relationships

Few studies of sexual life style separate out the unmarried heterosexual adult for separate analysis. Kinsey did, but his data collected in the 1930s and 1940s are virtually two generations out of date and times have changed. In any case it is a diverse group, difficult to epitomize. Included are swinging singles and celibate religious as well as committed (and very successful) professionals and those with few social or economic assets. On the face of it there appears to be a great increase in the social support of active sex lives for singles, especially for single women. Certainly there are more residential locations and recreational gathering places catering to this freer life style than there were a generation ago.

One subgroup that has received a fair amount of research attention includes those who elect to live together without marriage. Because of their greater accessibility cohabiting college students have been those most studied, but data from census surveys make it clear that they constitute only a small fraction of those choosing this life style (Carter & Glick, 1976). In fact according to one national survey, only about one out of four living in this pattern was under 25. A third were age 25 to 44, a quar-

ter were 45 to 64, and the remaining sixth were 65 or older.

Macklin (1978) in her comprehensive review of the studies in this area concludes that those who live together have a sexual life more comparable to married couples than to other singles—that is, they tend to be exclusively committed to one person with whom they share nearly every aspect of their life over a substantial time span. Among the strains experienced to a greater degree in these relationships than in marriage are the disapproval of kin and the nonsymmetrical commitment of the partners (women tend to be more committed). Another important difference is that such couples are far less likely to bring children into the world.

Extramarital Relationships

In recent years a number of studies have also examined extramarital sexual relationships—that is, relationships in which at least one partner is married to somebody else. The frequency of this type of sexual activity is not easy to determine with confidence since it is in violation of the norm of marital exclusivity, and people may be slow to admit it. Kinsey et al. (1948, 1953) with their in-depth interviews were able to determine that about 50 percent of the men in their 1940 sample and one-quarter of the women had at least one such experience. Several studies seem to indicate that men have not changed much but that women have closed the gap to a considerable extent (Bell & Peltz, 1974; Hunt, 1974; Levin & Levin, 1975; Tavris & Sadd, 1977; Wolman & Money, 1980).

Among the reasons individuals give for entering such a relationship, by far the most important is resentment and dissatisfaction with the marriage itself (Bell, Turner, & Rosen, 1975; Edwards & Booth, 1976; Tavris & Sadd, 1977). Next in importance seems to be premarital sexual patterns (the more sexual partners before marriage, the more likely to be extramaritally active) (Athanasiou & Sorkin, 1974; Bukstel, Roeder, Kilmann, Laughlin, & Sotile, 1978; Kinsey et al., 1953; Singh, Walton, & Williams, 1976). Another important issue is general traditionalism in personal attitude and life style. For example romanticism is strongly related to fidelity among women (Glass & Wright, 1977) as is a lack of interest in pornography or in oral or anal sex (Bell et al., 1975).

The consequences of extramarital activity varies according to the circumstance and attitude of the couple. At most life stages it is associated with higher rates of separation and divorce, but among older women this effect disappears. Perhaps they feel that the option of divorce is not very real for them due to their economic dependency and poor chances for remarriage (Glass & Wright, 1977).

Men are most likely to stray from the marital bed in the first 5 years, while for women it is more common after 15 or 20 years of marriage (Athanasiou, Shaver, & Tavris, 1970; Bell et al., 1975; Hunt, 1974; Kinsey et al., 1948, 1953; Levin, 1975). It may be speculated that the male pattern is tied to the pressures of pregnancy early in the marriage and perhaps to his only gradual resocialization into a married perspective. For the women it seems possible that mid-life crises, such as the empty nest or menopause, may play a role.

Despite the stresses and strains of discovered infidelity, it sometimes happens that couples utilize the pain of discovery as a stimulus to improve their own relationship.

CONCLUSIONS

This brief review of the growing literature on adult sexual development reveals many areas of ignorance. A few things, however, seem to emerge as well established even at this early point in the history of research in this area. First, if anyone ever doubted it, the research confirms the observation that for most of us our sexual life is an important element in our overall personal life style and level of life satisfaction.

Second, it is clear that there is no single, modal sexual career for adults in our society. People's sexual experience varies from celibate to intensely active, from thoroughly heterosexual to undiluted homosexual, from exclusive lifelong monogamous commitment to dedicated seekers after variety. But beyond this in the course of their adult experience, they might pass through periods of change, trauma, or growth which result in profound shifts in their sexual circumstances and choices. At the present we lack even an adequate typology for describing the most common sexual careers.

Finally, despite the pain of those suffering disruption and dysfunction, a majority of people at any given time come to terms with their own sexual situation.

REFERENCES

ALBRECHT, S. L. Correlates of marital happiness among the remarried. *Journal of Marriage and the Family*, 1979, *41*, 857–868.

AMMONS, P., & STINNETT, N. The vital marriage: A closer look. *Family Relations*, 1980, *29*, 37–42.

ATHANASIOU, R., SHAVER, P., & TAVRIS, C. Sex (A report to Psychology Today readers). *Psychology Today*, 1970, *4*, 39–52.

ATHANASIOU, R., & SORKIN, R. Premarital sexual behavior and postmarital adjustment. *Archives of Sexual Behavior*, 1974, *3*, 207–225.

BARTOVA, D., KOLROVA, O., UZEL, R., et al. Sex life during pregnancy. *Cesk Gynecol*, 1969, *34*, 560–562.

BELL, A. P., & WEINBERG, M. S. *Homosexualities: A study of diversity among men and women*. New York: Simon & Schuster, 1978.

BELL, R. R., & BELL, P. L. Sexual satisfaction among married women. *Medical Aspects of Human Sexuality*, 1972, *6, 12*, 136–144.

BELL, R. R., & PELTZ, O. Extra-marital sex among women. *Medical Aspects of Human Sexuality*, 1974, *8*, 10–31.

BELL, R. R., TURNER, S., & ROSEN, L. A multivariate analysis of female extramarital coitus. *Journal of Marriage and the Family*, 1975, *37*, 375–384.

BERNARD, J. *The future of marriage*. New York: William Collins Publishers, Inc., 1972.

BLOOM, B. L., ASHER, S. J., & WHITE, S. W. Marital disruption as a stressor: A review and analysis. *Psychiatric Bulletin*, 1978, *85*, 867–894.

BRODERICK, C. B. *Couples: How to confront problems and maintain loving relationships*. New York: Simon & Schuster, 1979a.

BRODERICK, C. B. *Marriage and the family*. Englewood Cliffs, N. J.: Prentice-Hall, 1979b.

BRODERICK, C. B., & HICKS, M. W. Toward a typology of behavior patterns in courtship in the United States of America. In G. Leaschen (Ed.), *Soziologie Der Familie*. Opladen: Westdeutcher Verlag, 1970.

BUKSTEL, L. H., ROEDER, G. D., KILMANN, R., LAUGHLIN, J., & SOTILE, W. M. Projected extramarital sexual involvement in community college students. *Journal of Marriage and the Family*, 1978, *40*, 337–340.

CARTER, H., & GLICK, P. C. *Marriage and divorce* (Rev. ed.). Cambridge, Mass.: Harvard University Press, 1976.

CUBER, J. F., & HARROFF, P. B. *The significant Americans: A study of sexual behavior among the affluent*. New York: Appleton-Century-Crofts, 1966.

DANK, B. M. Coming out in the gay world. *Psychiatry*, 1971, *34*, 180–195.

EDWARDS, J. N., & BOOTH, A. Sexual behavior in and out of marriage: An assessment of correlates. *Journal of Marriage and the Family*, 1976a, *38*, 73–81.

EDWARDS, J. N., & BOOTH, A. The cessation of marital intercourse. *American Journal of Psychiatry*, 1976b, *133*(No. 11), 1333–1336.

GLASS, S. P., & WRIGHT, T. R. The relationship of extramarital sex, length of marriage and sex difference on marital satisfaction and romanticism: Athanasiou's data reanalysed. *Journal of Marriage and the Family*, 1977, *39*, 691–703.

GLENN, N. D., & WEAVER, C. N. The marital happiness of remarried divorced persons. *Journal of Marriage and the Family*, 1977, *39*, 331–337.

GLICK, P. C., & NORTON, A. Marrying, divorcing and living together in the U.S. today. *Population Bulletin*, 1977, *32*(No. 5), 1–41.

GLICK, P. C., & SPANIER, G. B. Married and unmarried cohabitation in the United States. *Journal of Marriage and the Family*, 1980, *42*, 19–30.

GOVE, W. A. Sex, marital status and suicide. *Journal of Health and Social Behavior*, 1972, *13*, 204–213.

HEATH, D. H. Personality correlates of the marital sexual compatibility of professional men. *Journal of Sex and Marital Therapy*, 1978, *4*(No. 2), 67–82.

HITE, S. *The Hite report: A nationwide study of female sexuality*. New York: Dell Pub. Co., Inc., 1976.

HOLLENDER, M. H., & McGEHEE, J. B. The wish to be held during pregnancy. *Journal of Psychosomatic Research*, 1974, *18*, 193–197.

HUNT, M. *Sexual behavior in the seventies*. Chicago: Playboy Press, 1974.

KINSEY, A. C., POMEROY, W. B., & MARTIN, C. E. *Sexual behavior in the human male*. Philadelphia: Saunders, 1948.

KINSEY, A. C., POMEROY, W. B., MARTIN, C. E., & GEBHARD, P. H. *Sexual behavior in the human female*. Philadelphia: Saunders, 1953.

KITAGAWA, E. M., & HAUSER, P. M. *Differential mortality in the U.S.: A study in socioeconomic epidemiology*. Cambridge, Mass.: Harvard University Press, 1973.

LANDIS, J. T., POFFENBERGER, T., & POFFENBERGER, S. The effects of first pregnancy upon the sexual adjustment of 212 couples. *American Sociological Review*, 1950, *15*, 766–772.

LEVIN, R. J. The Redbook report on premarital and extramarital sex. *Redbook*, October 1975.

LEVIN, R. J., & LEVIN, A. The Redbook report: A study of female sexuality. *Redbook*, September 1975.

LEVINGER, G. Sources of marital dissatisfaction among applicants for divorce. *American Journal of Orthopsychiatry*, 1966, *36*, 803–807.

LEVINGER, G. Husbands' and wives' estimates of coital frequency. *Medical Aspects of Human Sexuality*, 1970, *4*(No. 9), 42–57.

LIEF, H. I. Homosexualities: A review. *SIECUS Report*, 1978, *7*(No. 2), 1, 13–14.

MACKLIN, E. Nonmarital heterosexual cohabitation. *Marriage and Family Review*, 1978, *1*, 1–12.

MANCINI, J. A., & ORTHNER, D. K. Recreational sexuality preferences among middle-class husbands and wives. *The Journal of Sex Research*, 1978, *14*, 96–106.

MARTIN, C. E. Sexual activity in the ageing male. Pp. 813–824 in J. Money & H. Musaph (Eds.), *Handbook of sexuality,* (Vol. 4) New York: Elsevier, 1977.

MASTERS, W., & JOHNSON, V. *Human sexual response.* Boston: Little, Brown, 1966.

MASTERS, W., & JOHNSON, V. *Human sexual inadequacy.* Boston: Little, Brown, 1970.

MORRIS, N. M. The frequency of sexual intercourse during pregnancy. *Archives of Sexual Behavior,* 1975, *4,* 501–507.

PASINI, W. Sexuality during pregnancy and post-partum frigidity. Pp. 887–893 in J. Money & J. Musaph (Eds.), *Handbook of sexology* (Vol. 5) New York: Elsevier, 1977.

PEARLMAN, C. K. Frequency of intercourse in males at different ages. *Medical Aspects of Human Sexuality,* 1972, *16*(No. 11), 92–113.

POFFENBERGER, S., POFFENBERGER, T., & LANDIS, J. T. Intent toward conception and the pregnancy experience. *American Sociological Review,* 1952, *12,* 616–620.

RENNE, K. S. Health and marital experience in an urban population. *Journal of Marriage and the Family,* 1971, *33,* 338–350.

SAGER, C. J. *Marriage contracts and couple therapy.* New York: Brunner/Mazel, 1976.

SEMMENS, J. P. Female sexuality and life situations: An etiologic psycho-socio-sexual profile of weight gain and nausea and vomiting in pregnancy. *Obstetrics and Gynecology,* 1971, *38,* 555–563.

SINGH, B. K., WALTON, B. L., & WILLIAMS, J. S. Extramarital sexual permissiveness: Conditions and contingencies. *Journal of Marriage and the Family,* 1976, *38,* 701–712.

SKOLNICK, R. C., & BIRREN, J. E. Age and male erectile responsiveness. *Archives of Sexual Behavior,* 1977, *6,* 1–9.

SOLBERG, D. A., BUTLER, J., & WAGNER, N. W. Sexual behavior in pregnancy. *New England Journal of Medicine,* 1973, *288,* 1098–1103.

SPANIER, G. G., & CASTO, R. F. Adjustments to separation and divorce. Pp. 211–229 in G. Levinger & O. C. Moles (Eds.), *Divorce and separation.* New York: Basic Books, 1979.

STACK, S. The effects of marital dissolution on suicide. *Journal of Marriage and the Family,* 1980, *42,* 83–92.

TAVRIS, C., & SADD, S. *The Redbook report on female sexuality.* New York: Delacorte, 1977.

TOLOR, A., & DiGRAZIA, P. V. Sexual attitudes and behavior patterns during and following pregnancy. *Archives of Sexual Behavior,* 1976, *5,* 539–551.

WESTOFF, C. F. Coital frequency and conception. *Family Planning Perspectives,* 1974, *3,* 136–141.

WESTOFF, L. A., & WESTOFF, C. F. *From now to zero.* Boston: Little, Brown, 1971.

WHITE, L. K. Sex differentials in the effect of remarriage on global happiness. *Journal of Marriage and the Family,* 1979, *41,* 869–876.

WOLMAN, B. B. (Ed.). *Psychological aspects of gynecology and obstetrics.* Oradell, N.J.: Medical Economics, 1978.

WOLMAN, B. B., & MONEY, J. (Eds.). *Handbook of human sexuality.* Englewood Cliffs, N.J.: Prentice-Hall, 1980.

41

Divorce:
The Adult Perspective

JOAN BERLIN KELLY

The dramatic increase in separation and divorce in the United States in the past two decades has forced substantial changes at every level of society. Not only have individuals and families been profoundly affected by the spiraling divorce rate, but also pervasive economic and social changes have occurred which seem likely to endure.

Psychologists and sociologists were largely unprepared throughout the 1960s and early 1970s to understand the complexities and consequences of this burgeoning social phenomenon. When the divorce rate started its upward turn in 1960, divorce research was sparse. Goode's (1956/1969) study of the adjustment to divorce of 425 Detroit women stood alone as the classic sociological work on adults, and while it left much of the divorce experience yet to be explored or understood, it was essentially unchallenged and unequaled in scope for the next two decades.

Despite significant annual increases in the divorce rate during the 1960s, interest in divorce research was not immediately forthcoming. As is so often the case, research follows in the wake of profound social change at a stately pace. Between 1966 and 1976 the divorce rate increased 113 percent, and as the large number of divorces made an impact professionally and personally, psychologists turned their attention to divorce as a legitimate area of research while sociologists renewed their traditional interest (see Bloom, White, & Asher, 1979; Levinger & Moles, 1979). In the early 1970s parallel to an exploding national awareness of divorce, considerable divorce literature began to appear, and now at the beginning of a new decade, the divorce literature is substantial and increasingly refined. With these newer research reports has come a growing awareness that the older divorce literature may be anachronistic. The rapid and profound changes in attitudes, values, legal constraints, economics,

and the labor market in the past decade have altered not just some of the variables associated with separation and divorce, but the very experience of divorce itself.

The need to expand our knowledge of all aspects of the divorce experience continues to be a relevant one. The increased incidence of divorce has occurred at all socioeconomic levels, for blacks as well as whites, and among couples with children as well as the childless (Norton & Glick, 1979). In the last eight years more than one million divorces have occurred each year, involving more than three million men, women, and children in each successive year. In just 1977, for example, nearly 4 percent of all married women in the United States between the ages of 14 and 44 became divorced. In 1978 for the first time in 18 years, the divorce rate showed evidence of leveling off but has not yet begun to decline. Most demographers expect the number of divorces to remain stable at a rate of 5.0 per 1000 population for the next several years.

FACTORS ASSOCIATED WITH MARITAL INSTABILITY

Much of the earliest understanding of marital instability and divorce derived from the work of demographers, sociologists, and social psychologists. More recently psychologists and family sociologists have begun to explore relationship failures from a perspective that has focused more specifically on internal processes and interactions. Certainly the variables influencing marriage and divorce are sufficiently numerous and complex to warrant a continuing multidisciplinary approach if we are to understand the causes, consequences, and experience of divorce adequately.

A selected number of external variables observed to

contribute significantly to marital instability are summarized first to provide the demographic underpinnings of the divorce experience. Such factors associated with marital instability have been perhaps the simplest to measure and understand.

Socioeconomic and Age Factors

Throughout this century there has been an inverse relationship between divorce after first marriage and level of income, education, and age at first marriage. The 1970 census showed, for example, that men who married before the age of 20 were twice as likely to divorce than were those who married after 20. The same proportion held for women who married before 18 in contrast to those who married in their early twenties. Among other married men and women those who failed to complete high school had the highest divorce rate, as did men on the lower end of the income scale.

In the past decade, however, there has been a convergence between these educational and income groups. While the relatively disadvantaged continue to have disproportionately more divorces, the gap is narrowing resulting in smaller socioeconomic differences in the divorce population (Norton & Glick, 1979).

The incidence of divorce has been consistently higher for blacks than for whites, with an even higher rate of marital disruption associated with racial intermarriages. Historically more blacks than whites reported themselves as separated but not divorced. More recently, however, as low-cost or free legal services have become available, increasing numbers of separating blacks are formally resolving their marital problems through divorce.

Premarital Pregnancy

A series of studies has shown premarital pregnancy to increase greatly the probability of eventual divorce (Lowrie, 1965; Sauber & Corrigan, 1970). Premarital pregnancies occur across all socioeconomic, racial, and religious groups, and one woman in four has been estimated to be pregnant at the time of her marriage (Hetzel & Capetta, 1973). A higher ratio of pregnancies prior to marriage may be present in the divorcing population. Fulton (Note 1) found one out of three marriages accompanied by premarital pregnancy in her sample of 560 divorcing parents, and in a study of 60 divorcing couples with children, 30 percent of the couples reported that they married because of the woman's pregnancy (Wallerstein & Kelly, 1980a). Premaritally pregnant couples in the latter study were married significantly fewer years prior to separation compared to those couples not pregnant when married (8 years versus 12 years).

Coombs and Zumeta (1970) found that 41 percent of the couples who had conceived premaritally were separated or divorced five years later, as contrasted to 18 percent of those not pregnant when married. Furstenberg (1979) found similar high rates of separation and divorce among his sample of adolescent mothers who conceived before marriage and suggested that premarital pregnancy prevents not only the necessary preparation provided by a courtship for marriage but also adversely affects young fathers' earning capacity, a factor contributing to marital dissolutions.

Work

The relationship between spousal employment and marital dissolution has received increasing attention. Although the inverse relationship between income level and incidence of divorce was well known, sociologists did not investigate *how* or *why* low income created the conditions within marriage that led to divorce. Two recent large-scale longitudinal studies have provided evidence that level of wages per se is not as centrally related to marital dissolution as previously thought (Cherlin, 1979; Ross & Sawhill, 1975); rather, the *instability* of the husband's employment and income in any given year increased the probability of dissolution, independent of income level. There was also a higher likelihood of divorce when the husband's income decreased notably from the previous year. In assessing the contribution of wives' earnings to marital stability, a variable not previously given attention, Ross and Sawhill (1975) reported that wives with higher earnings were more likely to separate or divorce than were women with lower wages. They speculated that a woman in a troubled marriage with an independent source of income was more likely to believe she could successfully divorce, or conversely, that a husband would more readily leave a marriage if his wife had her own independent income.

Expanding on these findings Cherlin (1979) then examined the ratio between the husband's wage and the wife's wage, a ratio that he labeled as the independence effect. His hypothesis that the greater the wife's wage relative to the husband's, the higher the probability of marital dissolution was supported. This was true regardless of the couple's level of overall income. Both studies indicated that the relationship between spouses' work lives and the probability of divorce was more complex than was previously thought and that the inverse correlation between husband's earning power and marital dissolutions is no longer an entirely reliable predictor.

Intergenerational Transmission

A final consideration in this limited demographic review is that of intergenerational transmission. Based essentially on role-model theory, sociologists have hypothesized that children of divorce are more likely to divorce as adults because of their earlier experience with marital dissolution. Studies have yielded mixed results. Bumpass and Sweet (1972) found that white women who experienced parental divorce as children were more likely to divorce than were women from intact families, but Duncan and Duncan (1969) found no such differences for blacks or for whites.

In a study utilizing several large data sets, Pope and Mueller (1979) found small, but real, transmission effects which were particularly consistent for whites of both sexes, for black females, and for two of the three black male samples. They speculated that marital dissolution per se has no direct causal effect on future generational marital instability but that the effect is mediated by other intervening factors.

In a five-year study of 131 children whose parents divorced, Wallerstein and Kelly (1980a) found a large number of *post*divorce factors significantly affected the child's adjustment at five years, a finding which potentially bears on this question of mediating variables. They reported that divorce *itself* did not determine outcome but rather the nature and quality of a variety of postdivorce arrangements. Relevant variables included the amount of parent-to-parent hostility that persisted, the quality of the child's relationship with both parents at five years, the frequency of the visiting pattern, the age at divorce and at the parent's remarriage if such occurred, and the quality of that remarriage from the child's viewpoint.

THE DECISION TO DIVORCE

A critical aspect of divorce largely overlooked in research studies to date is the divorce decision itself. The majority of studies of adult adjustment to divorce have failed to investigate each partner's respective role in the decision to terminate the marriage and have been unable, therefore, to examine the relationship between precipitating or opposing the divorce decision and the amount of stress in the separation period or in later adjustment to divorce. In part this omission has been the result of methodology, of studying cross-sectional samples of divorced adults rather than both members of a divorcing pair or of interviewing just women, or men, but not both. Underlying methodological considerations has been the implicit assumption, as well, that if a marriage has failed both parties move toward a divorce decision in parallel tempo and intent. A second assumption, based in part on Goode's (1956/1969) work, has been that men more often leave women in divorce. Divorce research has therefore primarily investigated women's adjustment to being abandoned, and indeed until recently, much of the literature of marital disruption has focused on women. More recently investigators are beginning to recognize that *who* makes the decision to dissolve the marriage is a worthwhile variable to consider in assessing adjustment in the early stages of the separation process.

Who Decides?

Recent research evidence has confirmed that a mutually shared decision to separate or divorce is uncommon. More often one partner wants to terminate the relationship considerably more than does the other, creating a psychological imbalance in which one spouse is actively shutting the door on a marriage while the other continues to be attached to, or dependent upon, the marriage. The consequences of such an imbalance in intent and psychological need are far-reaching, as will be discussed later. Wallerstein and Kelly (1980a) found that only one couple in 60 had made a truly mutual decision to divorce, and Fulton (Note 1) reported 13 percent of 250 fathers and 9 percent of 310 mothers similarly shared in the decision making. In Ahron's (Note 2) sample of 54 couples, the number of mutual decisions was highest (33 percent). It should be noted that all of the respondents in these three studies were parents and were married an average of 10 or 11 years.

Additional corroboration is found in research on breakups *before* marriage, in which a mutual decision to terminate the premarital relationship occurred in only 7 percent of the couples interviewed (Hill, Rubin, & Peplau, 1979). Thus it would appear that despite what the partners to a failed marriage may think of their particular relationship they are rarely in congruence in deciding to terminate the marriage.

If mutual decisions to divorce are unusual, then do men or women more often terminate relationships? It is now generally recognized that there is little, if any, relationship between the plaintiff listed on a divorce action and the spouse who actually initiated the divorce. Determining who precipitates the divorce action is not a simple matter either, as there seems to be a systematic self-bias in the reports of both men and women. Spouses of the failed marriage claim that they themselves, rather than their partners, initiated the divorce as a means of recouping damaged self-esteem. Only when researchers elicit the views of both spouses to the divorce action can this determination be accurate.

There is now convergence in a number of studies, however, which indicate that women more often take the initiative in seeking divorce (Wallerstein & Kelly, 1980a; Fulton, Note 1; Ahrons, Note 2; Bloom & Hodges, Note 3; Kitson & Sussman, Note 4). Bloom and Hodges (Note 3) found significant sex differences in the manner in which men and women reported the decision to separate. The women most commonly mentioned that the decision to divorce was a mutual one, whereas the men more often indicated that their wives had sought the divorce. Wallerstein and Kelly (1980a) in interviewing both divorcing spouses found that women sought the divorce in 75 percent of the couples studied, while 50 percent of the divorces in Ahron's (Note 2) study were initiated by women and 17 percent by men. Hill (1974) and Rubin (1969) also found a similar preponderance of female-initiated breakups in earlier studies of dating couples.

One method of determining with some certainty which spouse terminated the marriage is to assess the degree of opposition to the divorce in each spouse. Among 153 recently separated adults, Bloom and Hodges (Note 3) found men significantly more opposed to the separation than women. Wallerstein and Kelly (1980a) found that 43 percent of the men were vigorously and totally opposed to their wives' decision to divorce with an additional 19 percent expressing considerable reluctance, whereas 34 percent of the women opposed the divorce. Relationships between opposition to divorce and marital and psychological adjustment variables have been described elsewhere (Kelly, Note 5).

How Was the Decision Made?

Although there are impulsive decisions to divorce, more often the adult contemplates the possibility of divorce for months and sometimes years before there is a firm commitment. The decision is most often the culmination of accumulated grievances, instabilities, and unhappiness, accompanied by the growing recognition that the personal toll that the relationship extracts from the individual is no longer balanced by the security or gratification of being married.

Some studies report a "last-straw" phenomenon in which some specific event precipitated the decision to separate. Two-thirds of the separated men and women interviewed by Bloom and Hodges (Note 3) reported such an event. The three experiences noted most often were infidelity; outside events impinging on the relationship (moving, graduating, a new job); and some variant of the "last straw," such as a second suicide attempt or habitual drinking which was no longer tolerable.

In contrast the majority of the divorced men and women (all parents) interviewed by Fulton (Note 1) denied any specific precipitating factor and described instead a "buildup" or combination of things. This was true as well among the 60 divorcing couples interviewed in the California Divorce Study.[1] These adults, most often the women, verbalized a growing sense of dissatisfaction and emptiness which generated a slow, inexorable move toward the end of the relationship. Once these individuals admitted to themselves that divorce was a viable option, the complex process leading to separation was set in motion, almost always accompanied by turmoil, indecision, and apprehension about the future. One of the problems described by decision makers was a lack of marital interaction norms with which to compare their own relationship. Men and women alike worried that frequent conflict or the absence of intimacy and warmth in their own relationships was characteristic of all longer-term marriages. For the men and women who gradually made the decision to divorce, most often without their spouse's conscious awareness, their level of stress was noted to be very high in the preseparation period, a finding suggested by other researchers as well (Chiriboga, Roberts, & Stein, 1978; Bloom & Hodges, Note 3).

A psychotherapy or counseling experience may have figured prominently in the decision-making process for many individuals, perhaps particularly those in the middle and upper-middle classes. Bloom and Hodges (Note 3) reported that 44 percent of the separated men and women sought conjoint or couple counseling prior to separation. Most often short-term it was viewed as useful primarily in clarifying thoughts and feelings about the relationship. Of their sample 52 percent were involved in individual counseling or family therapy prior to separation, usually of longer duration. In the California Divorce Study there was also considerable participation in counseling or therapy prior to separation but with significant sex differences. Whereas 37 percent of the men sought some professional help during the marriage, most often short-term couple counseling, 57 percent of the women sought help, with a significantly greater number involved in longer-term individual psychotherapy. A number of these men and women described hard-won changes in their lives which had slowly edged them out of the psychological bonds of the marriage. The women

[1] The California Children of Divorce Project was a five-year longitudinal study of 60 families with 131 children. Family members were first seen shortly after the parental separation (average number of interviews per family was 15) in the context of a preventive intervention focusing on the child's capacity to cope with divorce. Participants returned for subsequent research follow-up at 18 months postseparation and 5 years postseparation. A full report of the five-year study and details of the sample, methodology, and data analysis can be found in Wallerstein and Kelly (1980a).

Previously unpublished data included in this chapter will be described as material from the "California Divorce Study." The author was co-principal investigator of the Children of Divorce Project from 1971 to 1980.

in particular referred to the struggle to decide to lead a life apart from a denigrating spouse who over the years had contributed centrally to the wife's severely diminished sense of competence.

The Importance of the Decision-Making Role

The spouse's respective role in terminating the marriage has been found to be significantly related to certain behaviors, feelings, and overall adjustment in the immediate postseparation period (Blair, 1970; Kelly, Note 5; Meyers, Note 6). It appears to be, for most men and women, an extraordinarily stressful experience to be told that one is no longer loved or wanted. Most often feelings of humiliation and utter powerlessness overwhelmed the rejected spouse as he or she recognized a helpless inability to make the departing spouse stay married. A common response to this pain and shattered self-esteem was immense anger, depression, and a surprising degree of regressive behavior (Wallerstein & Kelly, 1980a; Kelly, Note 5).

Many such rejected adults were completely unprepared for their partner's decision to divorce. While they may have felt as ungratified by the marital interactions as their partner, they themselves were not actively contemplating divorce and were shocked and upset by the spouse's decision. Even in those marriages where divorce threats were commonly shouted in the midst of battle, spouses did not necessarily want divorce. The finding in the California Divorce Study that marital discord, of even extreme intensity, did not equally prepare each spouse for divorce is supported as well by Spanier and Casto (1979) and in Fulton's (Note 1) work in which only 37 percent of the husbands and 30 percent of the wives reported being prepared for the divorce. The surprise and shock reported by the remaining men and women were even more remarkable in view of the finding that 53 percent of the men and 47 percent of the women had been previously separated at least once before the final separation. For the men and women in the California Divorce Study who did not participate in the spouse's decision to divorce, the period of greatest divorce-related stress more often started immediately after learning there was to be a divorce and continued at high intensity throughout the initial separation. Spanier and Casto (1979) also found a significant relationship between lack of preparation for the divorce and initial emotional problems after separation. The separation experience of such adults, to be described later, was quite different in its psychological dimensions than for those men and women who made the decision to divorce.

Spouses who initiated the divorce often did so with sadness, guilt, apprehension, relief, and sometimes anger, but a clear differentiating feature was their sense of control and the absence of profound feelings of humiliation and rejection. Further they had rehearsed and mentally prepared for their separated status. While they sometimes divorced with the diminished self-esteem characteristic of partners to a failed marriage, their self-esteem at separation was on the upswing, in stark contrast to those feeling shattered by abandonment. The enhanced self-esteem reported by these men and women was in part a result of their active role in deciding to put a miserable relationship behind them and take control of their lives.

For spouses who decide to divorce, the period of greatest stress may be *prior* to the separation, during those months spent agonizing over whether to terminate the relationship. In Bloom and Hodges's (Note 3) study, in which more women sought the divorce than did men, women reported significantly more symptoms indicating stress than did men in the six months prior to separation. Among the symptoms were weight change, upset stomach, headaches, nervousness, dizziness, and general weakness. Although such symptoms may reflect the tensions of an unhappy marriage, not apparently experienced in the same way by the men, they may be related as well to the greater prevalence of women precipitating the divorce.

Thus far research focusing on the stress associated with divorce has attempted to identify which of the periods or events in the separation and divorce process create the greatest stress but has not investigated the degree and kind of divorce-related stress in relation to the spouses' respective roles in the decision to terminate the marriage (Chiriboga & Cutler, 1977; Goode, 1956/1969; Hetherington, Cox, & Cox, 1976; Weiss, 1975; Kitson & Sussman, Note 4). Our own research would suggest that *who* terminates the relationship is an independent variable worthy of consideration in studying psychological adjustment to separation and divorce, at least during the first two years postseparation.

PERCEPTIONS OF FAILED MARRIAGES

Despite the growing body of divorce research focusing on the process of separation and divorce and divorce adjustment in men and women, only a few studies thus far have included an examination of the causes of marital failure. From these recent studies have emerged some understanding of the differences in men's and women's views of troubled marital relationships, the sources of dissatisfaction in each, and conversely, the aspects of failed marriages which seem less troublesome and may have served to prolong the marriage.

Differences in Marital Dissatisfaction

Several studies (Levinger, 1966; Wallerstein & Kelly, 1980a; Fulton, Note 1; Bloom & Hodges, Note 3) have found significant sex differences in the extent of dissatisfaction with the failed marriage. Women described their marriages more negatively than did men (Fulton, Note 1), voiced more complaints about their marriages (Levinger, 1966; Bloom & Hodges, Note 3; Kitson & Sussman, Note 4) and were more negative in their criticism of their husbands than were the husbands of these wives (California Divorce Study; Fulton, Note 1).

Despite social-class differences in samples, men were found to be more satisfied with their marriages prior to separation than were women (Chiriboga & Cutler, 1977; Fulton, Note 1; Bloom & Hodges, Note 3). In Fulton's study the men perceived their contribution to the marital effort to be equal to that of their wives', whereas the wives perceived themselves as making the most effort in the marriage. Only 6 percent of the wives, versus 19 per-cent of the husbands, described themselves as happy all or nearly all of their marriage. Conversely 43 percent of the women described three-quarters, if not all, of their married life together as unhappy, as compared to 27 percent of the men. Similar sex differences emerged when subjects were asked to describe the closeness of the family when the marriage had been going well.

The California Divorce Study found no significant sex differences in the perception of the *duration* of marital conflict or discord. There were 36 percent of the men and 42 percent of the women who reported that marital conflict and tension existed from the beginning of the marriage; for a small subgroup of each, the conflict occurred as well during the courtship. Men and women were equally congruent in reporting how long they were personally dissatisfied with the marriage, with one-fifth reporting unhappiness for at least 5 to 8 years, another one-third reporting unhappiness of 8 to 12 years' duration, and close to 15 percent reporting marital dissatisfaction for more than 12 years. The congruence may be a factor of the respondents' knowledge that the same interviewer was eliciting similar information from their spouses. Yet despite the similarity in reporting length of dissatisfaction, the women were unhappier and precipitated the divorce in a ratio of three to one.

In reporting the frequency and intensity of conflict in the marriage, however, interesting differences emerged. In marriages where conflict was rare and/or of minimal intensity, both partners were congruent in their descriptions. These couples, one-fifth of the sample, coexisted in separate emotional spheres, tending to the everyday business of family life with minimal psychological interaction. A lack of intimacy, silent disapproval, and emptiness of feeling characterized these marital relationships.

However, sex differences emerged at the other end of the scales measuring frequency and intensity of marital conflict. Women more often reported "continuous" and more intense overt conflict, whereas the men described the conflict more often as intermittent and less intense. While it was difficult to determine whether men underreported angry conflict or the women exaggerated, clear differences emerged in reports of interspousal violence which may bear on this question. Physical violence was reported in 57 percent of the marriages, with no significant differences in relation to social class or level of education. Yet the men most often did not mention the violence in their requested accounting of the failure of the marriage, and when specifically asked about violent episodes, they minimized both the frequency and intensity if violence had occurred. The many children who witnessed the violence more often corroborated the wives' accounts, particularly in regard to the intensity of the violence (Wallerstein & Kelly, 1980a). Fulton's (Note 1) respondents provided partial support for the possibility that males underplay or minimize the intensity of conflict in self-reports. Of the wives 47 percent described their marital arguments as more violent than they felt other couples to be, compared to only 23 percent of the husbands.

The Nature of Marital Complaints

In studying divorce one is presented with the opportunity to observe in rich detail many facets of marriages which failed. In the California Divorce Study the divorces were not frivolously undertaken. From a mental health standpoint the marriages were dismal and unsatisfactory by almost any reasonable criteria. In listening to vivid accountings of the marital failure, a disquieting recognition was that many individuals settled for very little in their lives. Strident incompatibilities, long unmet and competing needs, lack of respect and intimacy, dishonesty, hostility, abuse, and total failure in communication—all of these descriptions only hint at the quality of day-to-day life.

A long-term interaction between two people legally joined in psychological and economic wedlock is complex, likely to be unbalanced in gratifications, and subject to change over the years. The marriage may be dismal for one spouse but nurturing for the other; it may be perceived as a failure by both or only one of the partners. Some men and women were conscious of marital discontent from the outset; others became slowly aware of dissatisfaction over time; and some steadfastly held to the view that the marriage continued to be solid and gratifying even as the divorcing spouse departed. It was apparent that thresholds for pain and unhappiness varied widely from one individual to another and shifted as well within the individual at different times.

Also evident was that marriages terminating in divorce can and did provide the nurturance and support for at least one, if not both, of their participants at differing points in the history of the relationship, a finding reported by Weiss (1979a) as well. The gratification varied considerably in extent, source, and timing, yet clearly stood as a counterbalance to the expressed anger, hurt, and feelings of deprivation and exploitation. While much of the "marital-complaints" research by definition has focused on negative evaluations of the marriage, many spouses described how the marriage met some very basic needs and provided a modicum of support and satisfaction even as divorce was imminent.

Kitson and Sussman (Note 4) found that the marital complaints of women described by Goode (1956/1969) almost 30 years earlier differed from those mentioned by a contemporary sample of Cleveland women. Whereas Goode's women had mentioned what Kitson and Sussman called the more "serious" complaints of nonsupport, authority, drinking, and being out with the boys, the Cleveland women focused more on affective or emotional failings within the marital interaction. Reflecting perhaps the value which our society now places on individual contentedness and emotionally and sexually satisfying marriages, the complaints most frequently mentioned by the Cleveland women were those about the husband's personality, quality of home life, authority, and values.

Aside from the finding that women overall had more marital complaints than did men, Kitson and Sussman (Note 4) found some differences between sexes in the ranking of complaints using the Cleveland marital-complaint code. The most frequent complaint from both men and women was a lack of communication or understanding, a complaint most commonly voiced by respondents in two other studies as well (Granvold, Pedler, & Schellie, 1979; Bloom & Hodges, Note 3).

In the Cleveland study a second most frequent complaint of the men (but eighth for women) was joint conflict and disagreement over gender roles within the marriage and associated complaints that the spouse was too authoritarian. For the women the second highest complaint was "internal gender-role conflict," which reflected the women's own personal struggle around issues of independence and presumably a desire to have some control over their lives. If complaints about these two types of conflicts over sex-role behavior and attitudes were combined, they constituted for both sexes the second highest grouping of complaints, true as well for the women studied by Granvold et al. (1979). The second most commonly voiced complaint of Bloom and Hodges's respondents (Note 3) was of differences in values. Although the particular value differences were not specified, one might anticipate that the contemporary struggle over redefining and blending roles within marriage involved aspects of value difference. It seems plausible to suggest that the men were threatened or struggled with the outward manifestations of the women's move toward greater psychological, sexual, and economic equality and in general viewed as inappropriate their wives' wishes to blend gender roles.

Sex differences emerged in the third ranked set of complaints with men reporting, "I'm not sure what happened" (followed by various attempts to explain the marital failure), while the women complained significantly more often about extramarital affairs, drinking, and spouses' immaturity. Beyond this, significant sex differences included men more often mentioning overcommitment to work, problems with relatives and in-laws, and external events, such as death or job change. Women complained more about health, money, sexual problems, and personality problems of the spouse.

Kitson and Sussman (Note 4) found support for their hypothesis that marital complaints varied by education, social class, length of marriage, and income. Men and women of higher social status and married for more years complained more often of a lack of emotional support and deficiencies in the interpersonal relationship. Respondents married for fewer years and of lower social status had more complaints related to the spouse's failings and the performance of tasks, either within the family or outside at work, a finding reported earlier by Levinger (1966). An additional factor found by Bloom and Hodges (Note 3) was that parents had more complaints than did nonparents, particularly regarding communication difficulties, feeling unloved, verbal abuse, and infidelity. For these last two complaints female parents also had significantly more complaints than did male parents.

Using different methodology the California Divorce Study investigated the marital complaints of 106 men and women and found some overlap as well as differences in perceived causes of marital failure. Participants in Bloom and Hodges's (Note 3) study rated 16 different potential sources of marital dissatisfaction, using an expanded version of Levinger's (1966) list. Kitson and Sussman (Note 4) asked their respondents "What caused your marriage to break up?" and then coded responses on the separate marital-complaints code. California Divorce Study participants were asked in the first interview to describe the history of the failure of their marriage, and much of the first hour was devoted to the spouses' accounts, supplemented by interviewer questions and clarifications. Following the initial phase of this longitudinal research, the investigators then constructed a 27-item list which accounted for the majority of the criticisms and dissatisfactions mentioned by the divorcing spouses. The data were then coded by both investigators based on dictations of all interview sessions with the men and women (mean number of sessions was 3.4 and 5.3, respectively). Thus it represented a postinterview attempt to account for marital complaints perceived by men and women as leading to their divorce, rather than a restricted-choice method.

Clear sex differences emerged in the nature and frequency of complaints described by men and women, and similar to previously cited studies, women had more complaints about the marriage than did men. Two-thirds of the women complained of feeling unloved (compared to 37 percent of the men). This complaint ranked first in mentioned frequency for women and third for men. Most women associated these feelings with a gradual erosion of affectionate feelings for their spouse and a corresponding feeling of emptiness that led many finally to initiate divorce.

For the men the complaint mentioned most frequently (by 53 percent) was of the wife's being "inattentive," of neglecting or slighting what husbands saw as their needs and wishes. A wife's inattentiveness seemed most often to be a complaint voiced by men angered by the women's liberation movement. "Lack of love," ranked third by Bloom and Hodges's respondents, may be somewhat equivalent to the inattentiveness felt so strongly by the California men.

The second most commonly voiced complaint of the men was that of major incompatibility in interests, values, and goals from the very beginning of the marriage. Three times as many men (39 percent) as women (13 percent) complained of such longstanding incompatibility. When recent change in interests or goals is included with the longer-term incompatibility complaints, 72 percent of the men and 44 percent of the women were dissatisfied with the dissimilarity in interests and values. This complaint is most similar to that voiced second in importance by Bloom and Hodges's (Note 3) respondents, although in that study no sex difference was found.

The second and third most frequent complaints of women, almost exclusively female complaints, were closely related to each other. One-third of the women complained that their competence and intelligence were constantly belittled by their spouses, resulting not just in resentment but in the eventual feeling that they could do nothing right. One-third also reported that their spouses were hypercritical of everything about them, including their manner, clothing, physical appearance, ideas, conversations, and child-rearing practices. These two marital complaints do not appear as such on the lists of Goode, Kitson, Sussman, Levinger, or Bloom yet were central factors in the marital failure for many of the women in the California study.

Beyond these most common complaints there were few differences in the rankings for the next cluster of complaints. Sexual deprivation figured prominently for 34 percent of the men and for almost as many women. Men blamed their spouse's disinterest or frigidity; the women blamed the husband's disinterest or extramarital affairs for the sexual deprivation. Considering that 71 percent of the men had one or more extramarital affairs during the marriage (versus 15 percent of the women), it is surprising that infidelity did not rank higher. A number of couples had not had sexual intercourse for three to five years prior to separation.

Thirty-three percent of the men and 24 percent of the women complained that their spouse was chronically "bitchy" or extremely angry. Complaints of excessive nagging, of frequent outbursts of excessive anger, or an inability to enjoy anything were included in this category. Another complaint of 31 percent of the women but of very few men was that the spouse was too frequently away from home. Not necessarily "being out with the boys," as described by Goode (1956/1969), these men stayed away because of excessive attention to work and/or lovers.

Of note are those factors within the marriages not particularly seen as central to marital failure in any of the studies cited in this section. Premarital pregnancy was not mentioned by the Cleveland respondents and was not a specific marital complaint in the California study, although several men and women mentioned that they would not have married their spouse were it not for the pregnancy. Also disagreements about or problems with the children were not cited as causes of marital failure by the participants in any of the studies just considered.

A final observation is that some spouses struggled along in marriages dominated by the real mental illness of their husband or wife. In attempting to describe their failed marriages or to voice their marital complaints, these men and women understandably lacked the psychological insight and sophistication to diagnose psychological disorders. They resorted instead to descriptive phrases: "He did strange things"; "She was totally unpredictable"; "She was always down in the dumps"; "He always accused me of things I didn't do." That their mentally ill spouses were by our own observation psychotic, or severely and chronically depressed, or paranoid to a significant degree was not apparent to these bewildered men and women, and they muddled along upset, bewildered, and finally, tired of coping with the difficult and erratic behavior. While these complaints might be included under the "personality" item of other marital-complaint codes, it would be worthwhile developing a separate set of items that would specifically describe behaviors that are, for example, bizarre, irrationally accusatory, or severely depressed. Such information might shed additional light on the question of the cause-and-effect relationship between mental illness and divorce.

THE SEPARATION PERIOD

Separation and Stress

In their well-known study of stressful life events, Holmes and Rahe (1967) identified divorce as a stress second only to the death of a spouse in terms of the demands made upon the adult's need and capacity to reorganize his/her life in a major way (but see Kitson, Lopata, Holmes, & Meyerling, 1980). Recent research indicates the usefulness of differentiating several aspects of the overall divorce process in divorce research. The marital separation and ensuing period following that separation are emerging as important phenomena of their own to be studied, as distinct from divorce.

Following the lead of Goode (1956/1969) who identified the final separation as more traumatic to women than the final decree or the period after the final decree, several other investigators focused on the impact of the marital separation (Chiriboga & Cutler, 1977; Chiriboga et al., 1978; Kitson et al., 1980; Spanier & Casto, 1979; Wallerstein & Kelly, 1980a; Weiss, 1975; Bloom & Hodges, Note 3; Kelly, Note 5). Weiss (1975) noted the almost universal impact of separation on the participants in his seminars for the separated. Chiriboga and Cutler (1977) confirmed Goode's findings that the period of separation was indeed enormously stressful but found as well that "the period before the decision to divorce was equally traumatic, if not more so" (1977, p. 96). Sex differences were notable, however, with women reporting more indices of trauma or stress in the predecision period than men, similar to Bloom and Hodges's (Note 3) findings cited earlier. Men reported that they were least depressed in the predecision period, more stressed in the postseparation period, and seemed particularly vulnerable in coping with the emotional aspects of the divorce. Chiriboga and Cutler (1977) reported that the stress of the separation for the 96 men and 156 women interviewed seemed more traumatic than the stress endured in the unsatisfactory marriages, and they speculated that the many changes and new learning required by the shift to single status were responsible in part for the high level of distress.

In general social-context factors have not proven to differentiate between groups of individuals experiencing higher or lower levels of stress in the separation process. Chiriboga et al. (1978) interviewed 309 individuals between the ages of 20 and 79 separated for less than eight months and found little variation in reported happiness based on level of education, occupation, religion, ethnicity, and length of marriage and separation. Men described themselves as significantly less happy than did women, however, and older respondents were more unhappy than were the younger (see also Blair, 1970). Since length of marriage has been observed to correlate highly with age, this latter finding may suggest that the psychosocial readjustment process after separation is more difficult for older men and women. Some support for this is found in the California Divorce Study, in which older women (37 and older) were significantly more hopeless about their future and their ability to adapt when seen shortly after separation than were younger women and also as a group tended to be more angry. While the older men (39 and older) were more angry and depressed than were the younger men, the differences were not significant.

As suggested earlier evidence accumulates that the level of postseparation stress is related as well to whether the partner initiated the divorce or was not prepared for the divorce (Chiriboga & Cutler, 1977; Wallerstein & Kelly, 1980a; Bloom & Hodges, Note 3; Kelly, Note 5). Further support comes from Blair (1970), who found the postdivorce adjustment to be more difficult for middle-class women whose husbands wanted the divorce, and

Meyers (Note 6), who reported adjustment to separation to be easier for women who had an active role in the divorce decision.

Major Emotional Responses to Separation

As would be expected in any event demonstrated to be traumatic and highly stressful, the decision to divorce and subsequent marital separation precipitates intense emotional response (Herman, 1977; Wallerstein & Kelly, 1980a; Weiss, 1975, 1979a; Bloom & Hodges, Note 3; Kelly, Note 5). The varied psychological reactions are a function of the spouse's role in terminating the marriage, as well as the adult's personality and the presence of other external variables—e.g., a visible lover, the presence of children, support networks, and changed economic circumstances. The major emotional reactions to separation, described by a number of investigators and reviewed briefly in this section, include anger, depression, changes in self-esteem, regression, anxiety, relief, persisting attachment, and "new chance" feelings.

Anger. While most investigators have reported the presence of anger in divorcing spouses, few have focused on the extent or intensity of anger, its duration, or the relationship between anger and adjustment. Most often attention has been directed toward depression, loneliness, unhappiness, and other symptoms of loss. Yet it appears to be quite difficult for spouses to participate jointly in a muted, civilized divorce action. In divorce the ground rules governing behavior shift abruptly and explicitly to self-interest. Whereas the mutual ties of marriage sometimes serve to restrain hostility, in divorce the anger and resentment of the marriage is set free and fully expressed. Encouraged by a legal system which fosters hostility and extreme polarity, aggression, rather than accommodation, is more likely to be rewarded.

Indeed intense anger associated with the failed marriage and separation was one of the hallmarks of the divorce experience for the men and women interviewed in the California Divorce Study. For the majority of spouses bitterness and conflict *escalated,* rather than diminished, following separation, and for many the unexpected intensity of anger added significantly to their initial level of stress. In accounting for the overwhelming amount of anger seen in these newly separating spouses, regardless of social class or level of education, it may be that the method of interviewing both divorcing parents provides greater opportunity to observe anger and the complex array of angry interactions. What one spouse chose not to share, the other often did with alacrity, and a reasonably accurate picture of the interaction between spouses emerged over time. Further the interviews were spaced over two months, presenting an opportunity to view not just emerging and changing behaviors but repeated angry exchanges. Bloom and Hodges (Note 3) also shed light on this issue in their finding that relationships between divorcing parents were considerably more strained, with contacts significantly less pleasant, than were those between divorcing nonparents. They further noted that parents reported more difficulties overall than did nonparents after separation.

Twenty percent of the men and 44 percent of the

women in the California Divorce Study were extremely and intensely angry or bitter toward their spouses. An additional 60 percent of the men and 46 percent of the women were rated as having moderate, but not extreme, anger. Thus four-fifths of all the men and even more women were angry at separation, resulting in at least one, if not two, angry parents in each divorcing family. Women were significantly more hostile than were men, despite having initiated the divorce significantly more often.

The intense anger of the separating spouses found expression in a wide range of behaviors around a limited number of issues. Money was one such issue, and the intense hostility which accompanied the economic division of property was a reflection not just of the marital conflict but was related just as strongly to the psychology of the divorce itself for each spouse. The abandoned spouse felt not only devastated and angry at being left but also viewed his/her spouse's ability to take one-half of the community property as a final insult. Such outraged spouses were more likely to fight about every dollar or every piece of furniture in the property settlement and expend thousands of dollars in legal fees in the process. The second issue was the children. Angry parents withheld the children as a punishment or attempted to form an alliance with the child which, if successful, hostilely excluded the other parent from the child's life.

Denigrating the moral character and behavior of the spouse, often with the children as audience, was the most common form of expressing hostility postseparation, with more than half of the women and nearly half of the men openly and extremely critical of their spouses.

A small group of the men (10 percent) and women (17 percent) shared an extreme and bitter opposition to the divorce coupled with hatred toward their spouses and an often unconscious wish for the spouses' punishment and their own revenge. Described elsewhere (Wallerstein & Kelly, 1980a), the rage and vindictive behavior of these "embittered-chaotic" men and women seemed to ward. off more serious disorganizing depressions. Embittered fathers childnapped, used physical violence, and entered into custody battles for children with whom they may have had previously inadequate relationships. They attempted to convince the children and the courts that the mothers were morally bankrupt and unfit. Despite their angry denials embittered vengeful mothers were intent on destroying the father-child relationship through frequent tirades aimed at convincing the children that the father no longer loved them and by blocking visitings through any means possible. These embittered parents were more likely to turn to the court to seek redress for real or imagined grievances than were the less angry men and women. The endless litigation served to refuel and consolidate their rage, maintaining the anger at a high level of intensity for several years.

Depression. Studies linking separation or divorce with higher-than-expected rates of suicide are compelling for white females and both white and nonwhite males (see Bloom et al., 1979). On the basis of 200 interviews Herman (1977) reports divorce to be a "traumatic life crisis for women that leads to depression and feelings of hopelessness, if not suicide" (1977, p. 107). In Weiss's (1979a) discussion of "separation distress" as a response to loss of attachment, there are behavioral and emotional features similar to what some might describe either as a reactive depression or mourning. Other studies (Chiriboga et al., 1978; Wallerstein & Kelly, 1980a; Bloom & Hodges, Note 3) find evidence of depression or symptoms such as sleeplessness, decreased self-esteem, lack of energy, and weight changes that are associated clinically with depression.

A central research question is whether the depression seen in separated and divorced individuals precedes or is in response to separation. Certainly many adults experience and report a deep sadness, as distinct from depression, that the marriage has failed. They regret the loss of the social structure and family associated with marriage, the loss of real or imagined future opportunities, economically, socially, and personally, and they feel badly for themselves and their children that the cherished fantasy of "happily ever after" has exploded into fragments. However, sadness and unhappiness, while they may accompany depression, are not equivalent to depression, marked particularly by its compelling and immobilizing feelings of despair, hopelessness, poor self-esteem, self-blame, and many of the somatic equivalents described above.

On the basis of spouse and cross-spouse descriptions, ratings of presence, severity, and duration of depression *during* the marriage as well as *after* separation were made for each adult participating in the California Divorce Study. There were significant sex differences, with depression more common in the marriage for women, of greater severity and of longer duration. None of the men had attempted suicide during the marriage, contrasted to 14 percent of the women making one or several attempts. Fifty-four percent of the men and 21 percent of the women were essentially free of depression throughout the marriage. Of the remaining men 10 percent experienced severe, disabling depressions, some requiring hospitalization, and 36 percent experienced moderate depression. Among the women 31 percent were severely depressed, again with some recurrent hospitalizations in this group, and nearly half were moderately depressed at some time in their marriage. Of the women 42 percent (versus 16 percent of the men) had chronic depressions of more than five years' duration, often accompanied by psychosomatic symptoms, including numbness, vague pains, and severe and recurring migraines.

Thus a sizable proportion of the women and to a lesser extent the men entered the separation experience with a history of depression, presumably placing them at some risk for exacerbated depression in response to the stress of separation. There was *not,* however, a significant correlation between severe marital depression and severe postseparation depression. An equal number of men and women, about 30 percent, were severely or acutely depressed after the separation, most often those who had been left by their spouses.

A second group, one-third of the men and three-fifths of the women, were mildly to moderately depressed after separation, and this group included both those who had initiated the divorce and those who did not want it. Some women had been seriously depressed in a demeaning, difficult marriage, and in the process of deciding to divorce, often in the context of psychotherapy, their depression had begun to lift. After separation they were no longer severely depressed. Other adults experienced depression precipitated by the separation itself that was bothersome but did not seriously interfere with job, school, or home functioning. More than one-half of the women and one-quarter of the men experienced acute anxiety about living alone after the separation. For the women anxiety was exacerbated by the new responsibilities as head of household. Such anxieties seemed to contribute to the depression and left nearly half of the women feeling somewhat overwhelmed.

For many men the loss of daily contacts with their children engendered a moderate depressive reaction. Observed by Fulton (Note 1) as well, men deeply attached to their children were affected profoundly by their changed roles as an out-of-home parent and strongly expressed their distress: "Do you know how terrible it feels to lose a son/daughter?" One in every three men interviewed by Fulton was unhappy with the post-decree custodial and visiting arrangements and indicated a wish to have at least one, if not all, of the children living with them. Bloom and Hodges's (Note 3) male respondents felt that adapting to a new kind of parenting role was one of the two most difficult postseparation adjustments they had to make. The complexities and problems in establishing the visiting parent-child relationship have been described in detail elsewhere (Kelly, 1981; Wallerstein & Kelly, 1980a, 1980b). It may well be that the greater distress reported in men postseparation in several recent studies is in part related to the divorce-specific difficulties of coping with the loss of daily contact with children and establishing a changed, part-time parent-child relationship. Certainly the recent movement in the direction of joint legal and physical custody is in part a result of fathers' feelings that such intense loss is inappropriate and unnecessary, and not beneficial for the children as well.

Disequilibrium and Regression. Central to the inquiry regarding the demonstrated relationship between marital disruption and emotional disorder is whether the psychopathology is a significant cause for the divorce or is precipitated by the significant stress of the separation. In reviewing this literature Bloom et al. (1979) conclude that both possiblities are likely and that they may be interdependent as well. More careful cross-national and longitudinal studies will be necessary before this question is resolved.

One of the problems in current studies of separation stress is that the intensity and pervasiveness of the stress experienced by the individual is often unknown. Respondents indicate at which point they experienced the most stress or respondents check off mental-health-type symptoms experienced in separation, but it is difficult to know how disabling or disorganizing the stress of the separation is for each individual. A respondent indicating problems with lowered self-esteem, sleeplessness, and worry may be mildly depressed, whereas the next respondent reporting the same problems may be contemplating suicide. More differentiated and sophisticated measurements and interview schedules will be required to understand for whom the postseparation period is more stressful, to what degree, and in relation to which internal and external variables.

Very little such information is currently available,

even at the simple demographic level. Similar to other studies the vast majority of Fulton's (Note 1) predominantly lower-middle-class respondents reported one or more negative symptoms they experienced since divorce, but more importantly, 17 percent of the men and 19 percent of the women said their reactions were so severe that they required psychiatric attention and/or hospitalization. Of the respondents in a second study (Bloom & Hodges, Note 3), 57 percent obtained or continued counseling after separation, most often for short periods of time. Hospitalization use, if any, was not reported. Chiriboga, Coho, Stein, and Roberts (1979) found a relationship between perceived level of stress after separation and help-seeking behaviors. While utilization of support and mental health services per se may not be highly correlated with intensity or level of stress, such indices as these coupled with incidents of hospitalization, suicidal thoughts, explosive assaults, and subjective experiences such as feeling overwhelmed, worrying about "coming apart," or having a nervous breakdown would provide a richer, more complex understanding of immediate postseparation stress which one could then compare later to postdivorce outcome.

One of the startling findings of the California Divorce Study was the appearance of profoundly regressive and disturbed behavior in a broad range of men and women opposed to the divorce. The shock of rejection, the feeling of helplessness, the sense of dependence on another person for survival—all of these conjoined to cause severe disequilibrium and disorganization of immense and threatening proportions. Generally associated with intense anger and depression, these men and women seemed catapulted into a period of chaos in which primitive, regressed, and uncontrolled behavior erupted unpredictably and for which hospitalization or sedation was sometimes required.

More than a quarter of the men experienced this type of severe disorganization, some over a period of many months, others for one episode, for a few days, or for a week. Some of the men so affected had histories of well-controlled, circumspect behavior throughout the marriage and were successful as businessmen and professionals, and in a few instances they continued to function well in their occupations despite the eruption of primitive behavior outside of work hours. After separating at their wives' insistence, these men engaged in acts of spying, breaking down the doors at night, obscene and frightening phone calls, physical beatings, vandalism, and attempted childnapping.

A similar number of women became severely disorganized after the decision to divorce. Like the men their wildly fluctuating behavior reflected the severe regression precipitated by the separation. The behavior and thinking of these women was irrational and bewildering but was more often expressed verbally or through the children rather than physically.

Equally important, however, were those men and women who did not become particularly disorganized in their personality functioning. While experiencing and acknowledging varying degrees and types of stress, such as intense anxiety, anger, or economic stability, their usual state of equilibrium was not essentially affected. For almost 50 percent of the men (those seeking or not bitterly opposed to the divorce) and 42 percent of the women (all initiators of divorce), there was only mild, if any, disequilibrium generated by the separation. Because 75 percent of the women sought divorce, we can observe that being the party to initiate divorce does not in itself insure stabilized functioning, although these men and women were less likely to experience a state of acute crisis.

Attachment. Weiss (1975, 1979a) has described a persisting marital bond in separated spouses which seems unrelated to liking or respect for the spouse. The "separation distress" created by a loss of attachment was seen to be nearly universal after separation, regardless of who precipitated the divorce, and faded only slowly over time if there was no contact with the spouse.

Several recent studies have explored the frequency and type of contacts between separated and divorced men and women. Half of the respondents interviewed by Bloom and Hodges (Note 3), all separated less than six months, described a desire to spend time with their spouses. This occurred significantly more with nonparents than with parents. The majority of respondents were in contact to work out separation details, and parent communications often focused on their children. Because separation, but not filing for divorce, was a precondition for entry into this study, 45 percent of the respondents indicated that they sometimes discussed reconciliation (nonparents significantly more so than parents). Most reported a negative attitude toward reconciliation, however, particularly the women. Sexual relationships between separated spouses were rare, true as well in the California group. Despite these early and frequent contacts between separated men and women, the investigators reported there was "little evidence in this sample of the kind of general lingering attachment to the spouse reported in some earlier research" (Bloom & Hodges, Note 3, p. 22).

Spanier and Casto (1979) explored the issue of continuing attachment in their 50 separated respondents and found 36 percent to have a continuing strong attachment, 36 percent with evidence of mild attachment, and 28 percent showing no evidence of attachment. This latter group was equal in size to that reported by Goode (1956/1969). Similarly one-quarter of the men in another study showed no evidence of attachment when seen an average of five months postseparation (Kelly, Note 5). Without exception these were the men who decided to divorce their wives, who had experienced a dwindling sense of attachment years earlier, and who divorced without any particular internal conflict or anger. For the most part they negotiated the separation process with high self-esteem and little stress. Fewer women felt no particular bond or attachment to their separated spouses. More often the women who initiated the divorce did so with considerable anger and conflict, indicating some persisting attachment to the spouses but even more so to the *role* of the married woman and the benefits ascribed to this role by society. In contrast to Weiss's findings (1975), these more recent studies indicated persisting feelings of attachment to be common but by no means universal. The difference may be found in the self-selection process of the participants in Weiss's study, who came at some point after separation because of their distress. Two of the studies interviewed randomly selected respondents who agreed to participate (Spanier & Casto, 1979; Bloom & Hodges, Note 3), and the California Divorce Study participants were more often referred by lawyers, courts, and teachers than self-selected. Further they came in response to the specific child-focus of the brief intervention and included some separated men and women highly resistant and unwilling to participate, as well as those more desirous of participating.

Another study (Ahrons, Note 2) examined the nature of the continued coparental interaction at some distance from the separation. Of the couples 85 percent maintained some contact with each other postdivorce (approximately 2 to 2½ years postseparation). Two-thirds of the divorced parents spoke on the phone at least once a month, and their continued relationship involved parental, as well as nonparental, dimensions. Ahrons observed that the majority of the men and women maintained a "kin" or "quasi-kin" relationship with their former spouses which did not produce the stress of persisting marital bonds described by Weiss (1979a). Components of the continuing relationships, rooted in the past, were identified which, far from being pathological, had positive value for the former spouses and approximated a "normative attachment" involving caring, trust, and friendship.

Relief. As might be anticipated by some of the preceding data, a sense of relief obtained by the separation (and perhaps in making the decision to divorce) was also a major emotional response. Chiriboga and Cutler (1977), using nine behavioral and emotional indices indicating relief, found that close to 50 percent of their respondents were beginning to work out their problems shortly after separation. Sex differences mirrored other studies previously cited, with women more likely to feel greatest relief after separation than men.

Based on ratings of expression of relief, apart from a sense of well-being, no sex differences emerged in the California study. Nearly half of the men and women indicated considerable, if not great, relief after separation. Reported sources of relief included making one of the most difficult decisions of their lives (more difficult by far than the one to marry), as well as relief from the fear and tension that had increased in the time interval between the announced decision to divorce and the actual separation. Some men reporting relief who had not sought the divorce (almost 25 percent) were relieved at their wives' act to terminate a relationship which was more destructive and miserable than had been previously recognized.

Kitson and Sussman (Note 4) also found that separated men and women whose marital complaints reflected longstanding irritation and frustration with the spouse, in contrast to complaints that produced personal distress, were significantly more likely to feel a sense of relief and fewer symptoms of mental health disturbance after the separation.

The Feeling of a New Chance. Distinct from relief or contentedness with separation, one-fifth of the women in the California Divorce Study described a feeling and conviction that the divorce represented a chance to begin anew. They cautiously articulated their intent to improve the quality of family life for themselves and their children. Not found in women who opposed the divorce, these "new chance" women often felt guilty about the effects that their unhappy marriage may have had on their children, and indeed some had been married to emotionally disturbed men who had dominated the household and family life in erratic and destructive ways. Few of these women had plans to remarry; they intended to strike out on their own and perceived that, even with the anxiety and stress engendered by separating and setting up an independent household, a healthier atmosphere would prevail.

No men expressed this "new chance" phenomenon, in part because they, with one exception, did not have custody of their children. Those who reported a feeling of beginning anew had the immediate intention of remarrying and sought to improve their own lives rather than that of their children's. Some men, in fact, did improve the quality of relationship between themselves and their children in the year following separation, but they had not anticipated this or actively sought to bring about such positive change.

THE QUALITY OF LIFE
AFTER SEPARATION

A number of studies have focused on various aspects of postseparation adjustment in adults, apart from the emotional impact of the separation itself. Some explored the quality of life for divorced men and women, looking at social and sexual life, loneliness, support systems, and economic changes. Others studied the relationship between selected pre- and postdivorce variables and psychological adjustment to the divorce. While time elapsed since separation (or final divorce) and differences in methodology make comparisons difficult, the large number of emerging studies begin to provide composite and overlapping pictures of separated and divorced men and women.

Social and Sexual Lives
after Separation

One of the most difficult adjustments men and women must face is in their postseparation social lives and relationships. Several studies have confirmed that men and women feel that they are treated differently because of their separated or divorced status (Hetherington et al., 1976; Kitson et al., 1980; Wallerstein & Kelly, 1980a; Bloom & Hodges, Note 3). Women in particular complained that their social life was more restricted and isolated when contrasted to social life among the married (Hetherington et al., 1976) or compared to widows (Kitson et al., 1980).

Separated women reported an increased sexualization in the attitudes of others toward them and felt that married friends were jealous or suspicious of them when their spouses were present (Kitson et al., 1980; Wallerstein & Kelly, 1980a; Bloom & Hodges, Note 3). Shared friends from the disrupted marriage seemed conflicted about which spouse to call and often quietly terminated the friendship. Separated women in particular were more likely to let the social relationships collapse, feeling unwanted, vulnerable, and therefore tentative about expressing their strong need for continued support and friendship, a finding confirmed by Spanier and Casto

(1979) as well. Nearly half of the men and women in their study reported growing more distant from their close friends after separation, and the respondents seemed as responsible for the estrangement as were their friends.

Because emotional and sexual deprivation characterized so many failed marriages, separated men and women approached the postseparation period with intense longing and cautious hope for gratifying social and sexual experiences. The majority moved very quickly to establish an active heterosexual social life. Less than eight weeks after their separation, 40 percent of the Denver participants were closely involved with someone of the opposite sex. Nearly half of those relationships predated the separation, and the remainder were started an average of six weeks postseparation. The involvement included sexual activity for two-thirds of the men and 95 percent of the women. Men expressed significantly more sexual dissatisfaction than did the women.

Wallerstein and Kelly (1980a) found sex differences in heterosexual activity postseparation with men dating significantly more often than women. One-half of the men were involved in a very active or high frequency social-sexual life soon after separation, with less than half of these relationships predating the divorce. Men dating very frequently were more likely to have initiated the divorce (or were relieved when their wives filed for divorce in great anger upon discovering their husband's infidelity), were in the middle or upper classes, and had high self-esteem. They were sought-after and included as eligible males in a variety of social gatherings.

One-quarter of the men did not date at all, and an additional 25 percent dated quite infrequently in the six months after separation. Identifiable among the non-daters were men still closely attached to their predivorce families who continued to spend considerable time with their children and a second group of seriously depressed men with shattered self-esteem who seemed afraid to venture socially or sexually.

Nearly one-third of the women entered into a period of frequent dating, half of them immediately after separation. In contrast to the men they were younger, more often from lower socioeconomic classes, and self-esteem was not a relevant factor. These women were less invested in their parenting role and spent more time in social settings attempting to meet new people.

The majority of women did not have an active social life, including 40 percent who had no dates or heterosexual contact at all in the first six months after separation. In this group were those with shattered self-esteem and moderate-to-severe depression. There was a trend, as well, for older women in the sample to have no social life. Women in general were more pessimistic about their chances for finding gratifying social and sexual relationships. Aside from feeling that in contrast to men they had little control over their social life, women were more often repelled by singles bars and other social settings which they reported tended to make them feel cheapened and exploited. Level of social interaction and dating activity may be an important index of postseparation adjustment. Raschke (1974, 1977) found lower stress and Spanier and Casto (1979) found fewer adjustment problems in separated men and women who had higher levels of social interaction with relatives, friends, and the community, and in the latter study there was a significant relationship as well between regular dating or cohabitation and fewer postseparation adjustment problems.

Loneliness

Loneliness was a problem for many separated men and women, particularly for those not engaged in regular social and dating activities (Spanier & Casto, 1979; Wallerstein & Kelly, 1980a; Bloom & Hodges, Note 3). Forty percent of the men and nearly half of the women described themselves as extremely lonely in the California Divorce Study during the first six months following the separation. While one-third of the men reported no loneliness after separation, only 15 percent of the women described themselves as not lonely. The more intense loneliness of women after separation was found in other studies (Hetherington et al., 1976; Bloom & Hodges, Note 3), although several investigators found loneliness to be a preseparation problem for women as well (Chiriboga & Cutler, 1977; Bloom & Hodges, Note 3). Kitson et al. (1980) found the loneliness of divorced women to be greater than that of a sample of widows.

The loneliness of the initial postseparation period was not just related to nondating. The majority of men and women in the California study did not belong to social, community, or church organizations and thus the diminution of close friendships was perhaps even more painful. Isolation was even greater for mothers who did not work (Hetherington et al., 1976), and loneliness was in part a function of perceived discrimination against the women specifically because of their divorced status (Kitson et al., 1980; Spanier & Casto, 1979).

Support Systems

Most research investigating the extent to which separated men and women turned to various social supports has found a high use of friends, spouses, parents, clergy, counselors, and children (Chiriboga et al., 1979; Wallerstein & Kelly, 1980a; Bloom & Hodges, Note 3). Men and older respondents turned to supports less frequently than did women and younger respondents (Chiriboga et al., 1979), and women perceived the degree of support to be significantly greater than did men (Bloom & Hodges, Note 3). An interesting finding was that men were significantly more likely to name their spouses as the person who could ideally be most helpful during the stress of the separation than were women (Chiriboga et al., 1979). These investigators also found a significant relationship between respondents' *perceptions* of the amount of stress they were experiencing and the extent to which they sought out social support.

Nearly half of the men and women interviewed by Bloom and Hodges (Note 3) had family members in close geographical proximity, and generally their extended family was judged to be quite supportive. Far fewer separated adults had nearby extended family in the California Divorce Study, a factor which may have increased their sense of loneliness and distress. One-third of the women and only 13 percent of the men described their extended family as very supportive. Extended families were totally uninvolved with 58 percent of the men and

37 percent of the women, with less than 10 percent critical and rejecting of the separated men and women. Separated parents described their children as moderately supportive, although critical of each (Bloom & Hodges, Note 3), and the women in particular turned to their children for understanding, nurturance, support, advice, and increased assistance with household routines (Wallerstein & Kelly, 1980a; Weiss, 1979b).

Changed Economics

The changed family economics precipitated by separation (Bane, 1979) become a preoccupation of the vast majority of divorcing men and women regardless of income level. Significant sex differences have appeared in economic adjustment following separation (Spanier & Casto, 1979; Wallerstein & Kelly, 1980a; Bloom & Hodges, Note 3). The majority of men interviewed by Spanier and Casto reported themselves at least as well off financially after the separation, whereas significantly more women reported being in substantially worse shape. Males' incomes were significantly higher than females' in Bloom and Hodges's study (Note 3), and about one-third of the participants, especially the younger nonparents, needed to seek some form of additional financial assistance.

Three-fifths of the men and three-quarters of the women experienced a notable decline in their standard of living in the California Divorce Study. The economic decline started abruptly after separation and caught many parents unaware. The combination of limited total income and/or intense anger contributed to a prolonged period of economic instability, particularly for those women solely dependent on their spouses for regular payments. Nearly half of the women described an anxiety-filled period marked either by erratic support payments or, for those in the lower socioeconomic classes, a very marginal existence.

The decline in standard of living was accompanied for some women in the upper socioeconomic classes by the beginning slide into a lower socioeconomic class and status. These women, left by prosperous, professional men, had not worked outside the home during their marriage and derived their identity solely from their roles as wife and mother. Now cut loose entirely from their social class, as determined previously by the husbands' occupations and education, the base of social interactions was up-ended for these women, and their transition to head of household without status was extremely stressful.

ADDITIONAL FACTORS ASSOCIATED WITH ADJUSTMENT TO SEPARATION

Factors relating to postseparation adjustment cited earlier include the extent of preparation for the divorce (Spanier & Casto, 1979), the spouse's respective role in the decision making (Blair, 1970; Kelly, Note 5; Meyers, Note 6), the nature of marital complaints and reasons for divorce (Kitson & Sussman, Note 4), predivorce personality functioning (Kelly, Note 5), level of postseparation social interaction and dating activity (Spanier & Casto, 1979), being a parent (Bloom & Hodges, Note 3; Meyers,

Note 6), sex and age (Blair, 1970; Chiriboga et al., 1978; Goode, 1956/1969; Wallerstein & Kelly, 1980a; Meyers, Note 6), dramatic changes in social status for women (Wallerstein & Kelly, 1980a), and inadequate economic support (Blair, 1970). Several other variables related to marital roles also have significance.

Previous research (Goode, 1956/1969; Weiss, 1975) suggested that men and women who adhered to traditional sex roles in the marriage were more likely to have postdivorce adjustment difficulties. Chiriboga and Thurnher (1980) investigated role relationships, task sharing, and social activities during the married life of 298 newly separated respondents. Questions dealt with division of labor and authority among the spouses, independent use of leisure time, and reliance on the spouse for companionship. *Deviation* from traditional spouse-role expectations was associated with better postseparation adjustment. Younger men willing to share authority within the marriage were happier postseparation, and younger women who had been involved in marital decision making with considerable independence in work and financial matters were also more happy after the separation. Granvold et al. (1979) and Meyers (Note 6) similarly found that women with nontraditional or more equalitarian sex-role expectations were better adjusted after separation and divorce than were those less egalitarian in their attitudes.

Men and women who reported independence from their spouses in leisure-time and social activities also were better adjusted after separation (Chiriboga & Thurnher, 1980). It may well be that some of these same factors linked to greater contentedness postseparation were the focus of marital conflict prior to divorce. The reliance on independent interests and hobbies, for example, within the marriage may have reflected these spouses' growing disenchantment and move away from the marriage, and perhaps they were more likely to have initiated the divorce, a factor itself associated with better postseparation adjustment (Kelly, Note 5; Meyers, Note 6).

POSTDIVORCE ADJUSTMENT

Findings regarding postdivorce adjustment have been difficult to compare and interpret because of differing methods, measures, and time intervals between separation and the assessment of adjustment. Further complications arise in using the final divorce decree as a time reference rather than the months or years since separation. Statutes vary from state to state regarding the length of time required for filing for divorce to granting of the decree, and some states require a more prolonged separation before the divorcing spouses can even formally request divorce. Thus "after divorce" can and does range in various investigations from two months postdecree with the separation interval unspecified (Hetherington et al., 1976) to five or more years. Separation literature presented here clearly points to different intensities and sources of stress in the early stages of the divorce process for men and women who vary along a number of dimensions. Thus one might expect a differentiated recovery rate, again in relation to a range of measured variables. Cross-sectional research which samples divorced men and women at one specified point in the postdivorce period may therefore obscure real within-group differences in postdivorce adjustment.

Despite their obvious value in addressing longer-term adjustment issues, longitudinal studies of divorcing men and women have not been conducted until quite recently and continue to be few in number. Two longitudinal investigations of the impact of divorce on children and parents have been completed recently, the first observing family members at two months, one year, and two years *postdivorce* (Hetherington, 1979) and the other interviewing parents and children an average of 5 months, 18 months, and 5 years *postseparation* (Wallerstein & Kelly, 1980a). Three additional studies focusing primarily on parents or adults have completed initial contacts and are continuing with subsequent follow-up interviews and data analyses (Ahrons, Note 2; Bloom & Hodges, Note 3; Chiriboga, Note 7).

Several facets of postdivorce adjustment are of interest. Since divorce is intended as an appropriate social remedy for unsatisfactory marriages, it is reasonable to inquire how well the divorce has accomplished its purpose at some further point from the initial separation. Is the divorce successful only for those who initiated the process, or do those initially opposed to the divorce adjust to their status equally well? How long does it take men and women to restabilize their lives postseparation? And what is the quality of life for these individuals, particularly those who did not remarry?

Attitudes toward Divorce

In the California Divorce Study the intervening five years between separation and the second follow-up brought substantial change in attitudes about the divorce (Wallerstein & Kelly, 1980a; Kelly, Note 5). Nearly one-half of the men bitterly opposed the divorce at separation, but by five years two-thirds expressed a positive view of the divorce. The significant relationship observed initially between initiating the divorce action, opposition to divorce, and acute stress no longer appeared. Despite a favorable attitude among the majority of men toward divorce and its overall impact on their lives, only 30 percent perceived themselves as content.

Nearly one-fifth of the men had strongly mixed feelings about the divorce, while the remaining 17 percent had a totally negative view of divorce. Five years postseparation these bitter men continued to feel their lives had been ruined by their wives' decision to divorce. Having achieved no insight into their own behavior or possible contributions to the marital failure, their rumination about the divorce and the injustice done to them were strikingly similar to those heard five years earlier. By five years such bitterness and failure to achieve any psychological closure on the divorce experience was significantly linked to serious psychological disturbance.

In contrast to the approving men, whose numbers doubled in the five-year interval, the number of women viewing the divorce favorably had *decreased* in the corresponding time span. Fifty-six percent, equally divided between the remarried and still divorced, felt the divorce had enhanced their lives, including some who originally were shattered by their husband's decision to end the marriage. While many were lonely the majority of this group had made significant shifts in the direction of greater self-esteem. Women, and men, who approved of the divorce at five years most often relegated the divorce to the past. The divorce no longer occupied their thoughts; it had become essentially a dead issue, and for these individuals there was little, if any, remaining hostility toward their ex-spouse.

Nearly one-quarter of the women described strongly mixed feelings about the divorce at five years, most of whom sought the divorce with high hopes. For these women the combined burdens of full-time work and parenting, economic deprivation, social isolation, and loneliness compromised their continuing view that the divorce was a necessary process, and they longed for the remembered and/or fantasized gratifications of the marriage.

Of the women 21 percent viewed the divorce as a totally deplorable event at five years, including a few who initiated the divorce and now viewed their decision as a grave and irretrievable mistake. Like the men those who retained their full bitterness about the divorce more often had a history of serious psychological disturbance within the marriage, had been left by spouses, and at five years were incapable of integrating the divorce experience and restabilizing their lives. These women who continued to view the divorce in a completely negative and destructive light constituted the bulk of women (30 percent) for whom the divorce remained a live and central issue about which they were continually preoccupied.

Social-class differences and age were not significantly linked to achieving psychological closure and being able to move ahead with one's life. While men and women unable to achieve psychological closure were more likely to have been those left by their spouses, the relationship was not significant. There was, however, a significant link between continuing bitter preoccupation with the divorce and serious psychological illness in both men and women by five years postseparation.

Restabilization

Significant sex differences emerged in the length of time it took divorced men and women in the California Divorce Study to restabilize their lives postseparation, a finding noted earlier by Raschke (1974) as well. On the average it took women 3.3 years after separation before their lives assumed a sense of coherence, postdivorce reorganization, and stability, in constrast to 2.2 years postseparation for the men. Older men (43 and older) restabilized significantly earlier than did younger men, but no such difference existed for women. Being a custodial parent appeared to create more turbulence and prolonged the time needed to stabilize, but this relationship warrants further study as to other factors, such as poverty, excessive litigation, and intense bitterness, which were noted to create a sustained period of stressful and unsettled family life.

The overall psychological status of the adult preseparation was the strongest predictor of length of time to restabilize, with the more healthy or well-adjusted individuals restabilizing significantly earlier than did the most disturbed adults, regardless of who sought the divorce (Wallerstein & Kelly, 1980a). Thirty-one percent of the men and 42 percent of the women had not achieved a restructured postdivorce stability five years after separation. Individuals with a chronic or adult history of unstable or disturbed psychological functioning were significantly more likely to appear in this group, and many became even more disorganized or symptomatic after the divorce and remained so at five years.

Changes in Psychological Health

Important shifts occurred in separation and five-year follow-up in the psychological functioning of both men and women (Wallerstein & Kelly, 1980a). Whereas initially one-third of the men and women were considered to enjoy adequate to excellent psychological health or adjustment, this group had expanded by five years to include one-half of the men and 57 percent of the women, with the majority of these individuals functioning quite well. In addition to those men and women whose sound mental health continued throughout despite severe stress, this expanded group now included some previously diagnosed as having moderate psychological difficulties who experienced in the interim period a reduction or disappearance of disabling neurotic symptoms, including alcoholism, severe depression, and somatic complaints.

In contrast the group of men and women previously identified as seriously disturbed or mentally ill remained unchanged. Divorce was not helpful in the longer term for any of these troubled men (17 percent) and women (34 percent). For the most part they responded to the stress of the separation with even greater disorganization in their thinking and more erratic and bizarre behavior; restabilization, if it occurred at all, took many years.

The Quality of Life Postdivorce

Contentment and Self-Esteem. Hetherington et al. (1976) reported steady increases in happiness and self-esteem over the two-year period following the final divorce for men and women; yet in comparison to married couples, the divorced men and women were overall less happy and had lower self-esteem. Happiness and self-esteem correlated strongly with intimacy and heterosexual relationships in both samples. The California Divorce Study observed a similar rise in self-esteem, particularly in the women, and a greater sense of contentment with their lives than when initially observed. For 55 percent of the men and two-thirds of the women, life was somewhat, if not significantly, improved, whereas serious problems were created for 15 percent of the men and women. For those individuals with enhanced self-esteem and greater happiness, divorce offered not only a solution to an unsatisfactory marriage but also an opportunity to achieve a healthier and more productive level of psychological adjustment.

Social Interaction. The divorced men studied by Hetherington et al. (1976) were socially quite active in the first year after divorce, but by the second year their social activities had decreased. Divorced mothers complained of social isolation and in fact had significantly less contact with other adults than did divorced men or married couples.

Loneliness was a remaining problem for divorced individuals five years postseparation, but significantly more so for women than for men. The majority of men and women not remarried expressed disillusionment and some distaste for the shallowness of the "singles scene," and women in particular were dissatisfied and depressed by casual sexual encounters (Hetherington et al., 1976; Wallerstein & Kelly, 1980a). Those with higher self-esteem preferred their own company to a social and sexual life of continuing disappointment but spoke longingly at five years of their wish for a heterosexual relationship that involved mutual sharing, trust, and affection. Over the intervening years the intensity of loneliness had diminished somewhat as men and women constructed other social networks as alternatives to unsatisfactory dating arrangements. Thus 45 percent of the men and 63 percent of the women were moderately to acutely lonely, and a substantial number of both men and women had no social contacts at all. Severe loneliness was associated significantly more often with unstable psychological functioning in both men and women, and for men, with being in the lower socioeconomic classes. Troubled, lonely women, on the other hand, were more often previously married to upper-class men and, cut adrift from their social moorings and identifications through divorce, seemed unable to reestablish or continue a social life at any level.

CONCLUSIONS

Despite the acute stress of the separation period, the abrupt and painful economic and social changes, and the enduring loneliness of many divorced men and women far beyond the initial stages of separation, divorce has the potential not only of freeing men and women from destructive and unsatisfactory relationships but also of allowing adults to develop and change in gratifying ways in the aftermath of divorce. The majority of men and women followed beyond the separation period reported that the divorce was a positive and necessary step which resulted in greater personal contentment, increased self-esteem, and for many, healthier levels of psychological functioning. Yet the substantial minority of men and women who were overwhelmed and disorganized beyond their recuperative powers by the separation and divorce remind us that divorce is not a panacea for all. Indeed there is evidence that divorce results in clear psychological gain for just one spouse to the marriage more often than both are benefited.

With several million people newly affected each year by divorce, there is compelling need to turn further research attention to this social and psychological phenomenon that has brought far-reaching change to individuals and society at large. Virtually every facet of the divorce experience needs further exploration and replication if we are to understand with greater depth and more certainty both the immediate and longer-range impact of divorce on men and women. The complexities of failed marriages, the divorce decision, the separation period with the intense stress-engendered emotional reactions,

and the relationship between the many external and internal psychological variables and adjustments—all of these and more require our continued attention in the coming years.

REFERENCE NOTES

1. Fulton, J. A. *Factors related to parental assessments of the effect of divorce on children: A research report.* Paper presented at the NIMH conference on children and divorce, February 1978. A shortened version of this report was published in *Journal of Social Issues,* 1979, *35,* 126–139.

2. Ahrons, C. R. *The continuing coparental relationship between divorced spouses.* Paper presented at the American Orthopsychiatric Association Annual Meeting, Toronto, 1980. (Available from Constance R. Ahrons, Ph.D., School of Social Work, 425 Henry Hall, University of Wisconsin, Madison, Wisc. 53706)

3. Bloom, B. L., & Hodges, W. S. *The predicament of the newly separated.* First report of an NIMH-funded longitudinal investigation. (Available from Bernard L. Bloom, Ph.D., Dept. of Psychology, University of Colorado, Boulder, Colo. 80309)

4. Kitson, G. C., & Sussman, M. B. *Marital complaints, characteristics and symptoms of mental distress among the divorcing.* Paper presented at the Midwest Sociological Society, Minneapolis, Minn., 1977. (Available from Gay C. Kitson, Ph.D., Dept. of Family Medicine, Case Western Reserve University, 2119 Albington Rd., Cleveland, Ohio 44106)

5. Kelly, J. B. *Parent attitudes about divorce at separation and five years later.* Paper presented at the American Orthopsychiatric Association Annual Meeting, Toronto, 1980. (Available from Joan B. Kelly, Ph.D., 900 South Eliseo Drive, Greenbrae, Calif. 94904)

6. Meyers, J. C. *The adjustment of women to marital separation: The effect of sex-role identification and stage in family life.* 1976. (Unpublished manuscript, available from Judith C. Meyers, Dept. of Psychology, University of Colorado, Boulder, Colo. 80309)

7. Chiriboga, D. A. Ongoing research conducted by Dr. David Chiraboga, Human Development and Aging Program, University of California, 745 Parnassus, San Francisco, Calif. 94143.

REFERENCES

BANE, M. J. Marital disruption and the lives of children. In G. Levinger & O. Moles (Eds.), *Divorce and separation: Context, causes and consequences.* New York: Basic Books, 1979.

BLAIR, M. Divorcee's adjustment and attitudinal changes about life. *Dissertation Abstracts,* 1970, *30,* 5541–5542. (University Microfilms No. 70–11, 099)

BLOOM, B. L., WHITE, S. W., & ASHER, S. J. Marital disruption as a stressful life event. In G. Levinger & O. Moles (Eds.), *Divorce and separation: Context, causes and consequences.* New York: Basic Books, 1979.

BUMPASS, L., & SWEET, J. Differentials in marital stability: 1970. *American Sociological Review,* 1972, *37,* 754–766.

CHERLIN, A. Work life and marital dissolution. In G. Levinger & O. Moles (Eds.), *Divorce and separation: Context, causes and consequences.* New York: Basic Books, 1979.

CHIRIBOGA, D. A., & CUTLER, L. Stress responses among divorcing men and women. *Journal of Divorce,* 1977, *1,* 95–106.

CHIRIBOGA, D. A., COHO, A., STEIN, J. A., & ROBERTS, J. Divorce, stress and social supports: A study in help seeking. *Journal of Divorce,* 1979, *3,* 121–135.

CHIRIBOGA, D. A., ROBERTS, J., & STEIN, J. A. Psychological well being during marital separation. *Journal of Divorce,* 1978, *2,* 21–36.

CHIRIBOGA, D. A., & THURNHER, M. Marital lifestyles and adjustments to separation. *Journal of Divorce,* 1980, *3,* 379–390.

COOMBS, L. C., & ZUMETA, Z. Correlates of marital dissolution in a prospective fertility study: A research note. *Social Problems,* 1970, *18,* 92–101.

DUNCAN, B., & DUNCAN, O. D. Family stability and occupational success. *Social Problems,* 1969, *16,* 272–306.

FURSTENBERG, F. F. Premarital pregnancy and marital instability. In G. Levinger & O. Moles (Eds.), *Divorce and separation: Context, causes and consequences.* New York: Basic Books, 1979.

GOODE, W. J. *Women in divorce.* New York: Free Press, 1956. Republished as *Divorce and after.* New York: Free Press, 1969.

GRANVOLD, D. K., PEDLER, L. M., & SCHELLIE, S. G. A study of sex-role expectancy and female post-divorce adjustment. *Journal of Divorce,* 1979, *2,* 383–393.

HERMAN, S. J. Women, divorce and suicide. *Journal of Divorce,* 1977, *1,* 107–117.

HETHERINGTON, E. H. Divorce: A child's perspective. *American Psychologist,* 1979, *34,* 851–858.

HETHERINGTON, E. M., COX, M., & COX, R. Divorced fathers. *Family Coordinator,* 1976, *25,* 417–428.

HETZEL, A. M., & CAPETTA, M. Teenagers: Marriages, divorces, parenthood and mortality. *Vital and health statistics* (Series 21:21). Washington, D.C.: U.S. Dept. of Health, Education and Welfare, 1973.

HILL, C. T. *The ending of successive opposite-sex relationships.* Unpublished doctoral dissertation, Harvard University, 1974.

HILL, C. T., RUBIN, Z., & PEPLAU, L. A. Breakups before marriage: The end of 103 affairs. In G. Levinger & O. Moles (Eds.), *Divorce and separation: Context, causes and consequences.* New York: Basic Books, 1979.

HOLMES, T. H., & RAHE, R. H. The social readjustment rating scale. *Journal of Psychosomatic Research,* 1967, *11,* 213–218.

KELLY, J. B. Visiting after divorce: Research findings and clinical implications. In L. Abt & I. Stuart (Eds.), *Children of separation and divorce: Management and treatment.* New York: Van Nostrand Reinhold, 1981.

KITSON, G. C., LOPATA, H. Z., HOLMES, W. M., & MEYERLING, S. H. Divorcees and widows: Similarities and differences. *American Journal of Orthopsychiatry,* 1980, *50,* 291–301.

LEVINGER, G. Sources of marital dissatisfaction among applicants for divorce. *American Journal of Orthopsychiatry,* 1966, *36,* 803–807.

LEVINGER, G., & MOLES, O. C. (Eds.). *Divorce and separation: Context, causes and consequences.* New York: Basic Books, 1979.

LOWRIE, S. F. Early marriage: Premarital pregnancy and associated factors. *Journal of Marriage and the Family,* 1965, *27,* 49–56.

NORTON, A. J., & GLICK, P. G. Marital instability in America: Past, present, future. In G. Levinger & O. C. Moles (Eds.), *Divorce and separation: Context, causes and consequences.* New York: Basic Books, 1979.

POPE, H., & MUELLER, C. W. The intergenerational transmission of marital instability. In G. Levinger & O. Moles (Eds.), *Divorce and separation: Context, causes and consequences.* New York: Basic Books, 1979.

RASCHKE, H. J. *Social and psychological factors in voluntary postmarital dissolution adjustment.* Unpublished doctoral dissertation, University of Minnesota at Minneapolis, 1974.

RASCHKE, H. J. The role of social participation in post-separation and post-divorce adjustment. *Journal of Divorce,* 1977, *1,* 129–140.

ROSS, H. L., & SAWHILL, I. V. *Time of transition: The growth of families headed by women.* Washington, D.C.: The Urban Institute, 1975.

RUBIN, Z. *The social psychology of romantic love.* Doctoral dissertation, University of Michigan, 1969. (University Microfilms No. 70-4179)

SAUBER, M., & CORRIGAN, E. H. *The six-year experience of unwed mothers as parents.* New York: Community Council of Greater New York, 1970.

SPANIER, G. B., & CASTO, R. F. Adjustment to separation and divorce: An analysis of 50 case studies. *Journal of Divorce,* 1979, *2,* 241–253.

WALLERSTEIN, J. S., & KELLY, J. B. *Surviving the breakup: How children and parents cope with divorce.* New York: Basic Books, 1980a.

WALLERSTEIN, J. S., & KELLY, J. B. Effects of divorce on the visiting father-child relationship. *American Journal of Psychiatry,* 1980b, *137,* 1534–1539.

WEISS, R. S. *Marital separation.* New York: Basic Books, 1975.

WEISS, R. S. The emotional impact of marital separation. In G. Levinger & O. Moles (Eds.), *Divorce and separation: Context, causes and consequences.* New York: Basic Books, 1979a.

WEISS, R. S. *Going it alone.* New York: Basic Books, 1979b.

42

Child Effects
on Parents

CAROL R. ZEITS
ROBERT M. PRINCE

Research on parental influence on the development of children has been increasingly criticized because of its unidirectional bias (Bell, 1968; Gewirtz, 1961; Moss, 1974; Osofsky, 1971; Rossi, 1975). The assumption that the locus of influence in the parent-child relationship resided entirely in the child has come under increasing attack. Korner (1975) writes, "Mental health professionals created a generation of guilty parents who, to understand any difficulty of child development, employ the motto 'cherchez la mere' " (p. 86).

In an interesting reversal Bach and Nicholson (1976–1977) argue that infants and young children utilize "crazy making" behavior—that is, behavior designed to confuse and disorient the parent in order to limit the overwhelming power of adults. There is, in fact, evidence that the determination of which is the more important or powerful side of the relationship depends on point of view. Streib (1965), looking from the vantage of adult development, found that parents remain more emotionally attached to their adult offspring than adult children are to them.

The criticism of neglect of child effects may have been overstated or at least not universally applicable. From the point of view of *family systems theory* (Guerin, 1976), the question of the direction of effects—children on parents, parents on children—is tautological. Implicit in family systems theory is the idea of the interdependence of each member of the family unit and the idea that the behavior of one can be understood only in the context on its relation to the others. Specifically behavior is seen as effecting the homeostasis of the established system and calls into play mechanisms for reestablishing equilibrium. Clearly from this point of view the arrival of the child into the two-person marital system changes and redefines the system. The progress of the child through development results in continuing alteration in the nature

of relationships during the course of the life cycle. Similarly others (e.g., Cavan, 1974; Lidz, 1968; Rossi, 1975; Zilbach, 1968) have described schemas for stages of family development beginning with the childless couple and ending with the effects of the exit of the last child from the home.

Resolving the question of who affects whom may be more complicated than investigating "direction of effects." As Lerner and Spanier (1978) point out, the reciprocal relationships between the individuals and family units and the social and historical context in which they live need to be considered. Thus some of our psychological observations and theories about parent-child relationships must be viewed in light of childhood as a historical, as much as an ontogenetic, concept with modern research reflective of the evolution of childhood through the centuries. For example the impact of the cry of the modern infant on the modern parent is different from that of the medieval infant on the medieval parent in which the role of the child in the family unit was dramatically different from today.

As an example of the importance of the historical context, Lewis and Feiring (1978) remark that a major function of the contemporary role of the family is to raise children, by which it is understood that *raise* means to help grow, develop, and socialize. In past times, however, *raise* literally meant to lift the newborn into the air as a public act of declaring paternity and accepting the infant into the social group. Not *raising* a child literally meant to leave it on the ground to die. Thus while the concern of modern psychological research may be to establish relative subtle response patterns to infants based on, for example, sex and health, in past eras the parental response to these infant variables may have been infanticide.

The research to be reviewed is understood to occur in

a particular context. For the historian Aries (1962), the context is that of the "invention" of childhood, a concept that he feels did not develop until the modern age. De Mause (1974), though he takes issue with Aries, reviews the treatment of children in the Western world and believes it to be one of neglect alternating with abuse. He believes that the historical reaction to children has been based either on *projection* or *reversal;* the former response is based on reacting to the child as a representation of the parents' own unconscious contents and the latter on the child as a substitution for another adult figure. In a scholarly review of available historical documents, de Mause traces the evolution of adult responses to children culminating in the modern role which involves, for the first time, an empathic component. The major difference between de Mause and Aries is that for the former the modern age reflects improved conditions and for the latter an attempt to disrupt a previously happy state of affairs. However, each would be in agreement that the following review is unique to our current era's response to childhood.

The aim of this chapter is to present the various theoretical perspectives ranging from psychoanalytic to sociological, which describe and explain the child's effects on his/her caregivers. The methodological problems in studying the effects of children on adults are also discussed in order to clarify the difficulties in making interpretations from the data. Relevant research findings will be discussed to support perhaps a somewhat self-evident notion—that children do indeed affect their caregivers. Interaction studies will also be presented to illuminate the complexities of what transpires in the infant or child-parent dyad.

THE PSYCHOANALYTIC PERSPECTIVE

It needs to be noted that psychoanalysis is a body of knowledge, theory, and practice with wide and uncertain boundaries. Thus considerable differences between theorists exist with regard to both the nature and scope of child effects on parents and the type of evidence used in support of a given position.

Perhaps the center of the argument for the different theorists concerns the degree to which the specific behavior of the child influences the parents' responses beyond the preprogramming of the parents' own psychic history. It is, however, a caricature of even the most extreme psychoanalytic view that child effects on parents are exclusively a product of the parents' unconscious processes.

Coleman, Kris, and Provence (1953) make it clear that there are reality issues which enter the picture—e.g., if the child is wanted or unwanted, if the child is born to seal a happy marriage or to cement a dissolving one, if the child is born to parents in the midst of a struggle for independence. Despite the varying degrees of consideration given to reality issues, the emphasis is on the impact of children on the inner world of the parent. As Fries (1946) writes,

Parental attitudes toward the child are dictated by custom and may be consistent from birth or varied with the birth of another sibling, at different age levels, or in new situations (such as going to school, etc.). However, no matter what the cultural direction may be, the individual adult applies this pattern according to his own psychic requirements. (p. 92)

The common point of departure for the psychoanalytic approach to parent responses and attitudes to children is the unconscious meaning the child has for the parent (Coleman et al., 1953). From the analytic point of view the effect of the child on the parent is revealed not by behavior, but in the words of Coleman et al., "unconscious motivations which color this behavior and determine its nuances" (1953, p. 21).

From this common center there is considerable difference among analysts ranging from the concern about the importance of individual differences among children, the degree to which the effect of children fall within the vicissitudes of existing conflicts of the parent, and the degree to which parenting is a process that influences the basic psychic structure of the parent.

Fries is one of the first analysts to focus on child characteristics, beyond sex and health, that affect parental attitudes. Beginning in 1935 (Fries & Woolf, 1953), she began investigating the *congenital activity type,* a descriptive term referring to the amount of activity a newborn infant shows in response to certain stimuli. Her work addressed the complex reciprocal interaction between infant and parent and anticipated the work of Thomas, Chess, and Birch (1968) who addressed the response, or "fit," of parental behavior to children's temperament. Fries also antedated Escalona (1968) who also is noteworthy for her observations of the convergence and divergence of mother and infant patterns.

The emphasis of the psychoanalytic literature is the exclusive characteristics of the adult that produces child effects independent of any child variables. Freud (1914/1957) described parental love as a vicissitude of the parents' own narcissism. Zilboorg (1931) discussed the projection and displacement of the parents' need on the child. Brody (1975) believes that parents' behavior with their children had a history of unconscious conflicts and defenses intertwined with values and levels of aspiration. More specifically she feels that Oedipal conflicts are revived in the adult by the birth of a child. In this vein Benedek (1970b) comments, "Not infrequently the desire for children of the opposite sex is motivated by an intuitive awareness of the wish to avoid re-experiencing with the child the conflicts that were incorporated through the developmental interactions with the parent of the same sex" (p. 172).

Brody and Axelrad (1978) also discuss the parents' reaction to children as a function of the parents' wish to be loved. They further speculate that this wish to be loved accounts for parents' difficulties in seeing their children objectively. On the one hand excessive need for love results in a fear of destroying part of the parents' narcissistic image as well as the object on whom the parent depends for the needed love. On the other hand where the need to be loved is denied, the parent may act aggressively toward the child without conscious conflict. In the first case the parents' perception is skewed positively, while in the second it is skewed negatively.

Benedek (1970a) discusses the child's stimulation of the adult's sexuality, as for example when a father becomes aware of a genital response to a daughter or when a mother is shocked by her fascination with her son's penis.

Another thrust of the psychoanalytic literature has been the meaning of children for mothers and fathers respectively. Far more has been written with regard to the former than the latter.

Numerous writers (Bardwick, 1971; Benedek, 1959b; Bibring, Dwyer, Huntington, & Valenstein, 1961; Deutsch, 1944; Newton, 1955) have stressed the centrality of motherhood for feminine identity. Benedek (1959b) writes,

Motherhood, indeed, plays a significant role in the development of women. Physiologically, it completes maturation; psychologically, it channelizes the primarily introverted, narcissistic tendencies into many psychic qualities designated "feminine," such as responsiveness, empathy, sympathy, and the desire to do, to care for others, etc. Thus, from motherliness, it is only one step to many forms of feminine achievement since these, or many of them, represent one extension and expansion of motherliness. (p. 20)

For Benedek (1970c) motherhood is the culmination of a complex psychobiological process, with its roots in the mother's own infancy but initiated by the pregnancy. It enables the mother to regress and repeat in her mothering traces of her own infancy. Nursing has a profound significance for her insofar as it "represents a continuation of the physiologic symbiosis (of pregnancy). While the infant incorporates the breast, the mother feels united with him" (Benedek, 1970c, p. 155).

For Bibring et al. (1961) motherhood represents a major developmental step for the woman, and the process of being a mother involves shifts from representing the infant as her self, as her husband, and finally as a person in its own right.

They conclude that during pregnancy a woman moves from phases of enhanced narcissism until the baby becomes experienced as a new object within the self. The mother's relationship to the baby will be characterized by a changeable fusion of narcissistic and object-libidinal strivings.

Brody (1956) discusses different mothering patterns in terms of the transformation of developmentally prior instinctual aims into mothering. In particular she proposes that a basic contribution to the quality of maternal behavior lies in the vicissitudes of the "beating" fantasy and the defenses erected against it. This proposition followed on the

relation between the masochistic fantasy of being beaten by the father and the acceptance of femininity for the facilitation of the biological functions necessary for motherhood. It was suggested that according to the baby-penis equivalent, the impulsive demands of the baby can symbolize the impulsive "demands" on beating of the penis which the mother accepts, arouses, withdraws from, or rejects. (Brody & Axelrad, 1978, p. 11)

Bardwick (1971) stresses the different phases and gratifications of motherhood. Moving away from the formulations based on the vicissitudes of the Oedipus complex of the classical analysts, she discusses the mother's role as a source of gratification for achievement, affiliation, nurturance, and power.

Benedek (1970a) attempted to understand the infant variables of smiling and crying in terms of their impact on the mother's self-concept. She observes that the mother experiences the happy, thriving, smiling infant as a reflection of her "good self" and the crying infant as a reflection of her inadequacy and "bad," oppressive self. Benedek (1970a) further believes that the infant's imitative behavior holds up to the parent a mirror important for the parent's ontogeny as the parent's empathic mirroring is crucial for the infant's development of self.

The object-relations school stresses the interdependence of mother and infant. Michael Balint (1968) defines the mother-infant dyad and their "harmonious interpenetrating mix-up." Alice Balint (1949) similarly challenged the concept of the one-way relationship between mother and child and used the term *symbiosis* to designate a mutual instinctual need for communication between mother and child. Winnicott (1958) describes a state of "primary maternal preoccupation" defined by the mother's total absorption in the neonate.

The scope of the psychoanalytic literature on fatherhood does not, in the main, emphasize fatherhood as being as central to masculine identity as motherhood is to feminine identity. Benedek (1970b) does assert that the biological root of fatherhood is the instinctual drive for survival and that the father's function as provider makes his relationship with his children a mutual developmental experience. Benedek (1975) also discusses the origins of fatherliness in biological bisexuality and the original dependence on the mother resulting in an orientation to the world based on identification with the mother.

In terms of the gratifications of fatherhood, Brody and Axelrad (1978) note the need to be loved. Burlingham (1973) commented on the father's desire to embody his ego ideal in sons and to receive love from girls. Gurwitt (1976), citing a number of authors, notes that it has "long been recognized that the period of becoming a father is a time of important psychological transition" (p. 238). Ross (1975, 1977) reviews the evolution of generativity and nurturance in boys and men and attempts to outline the epigenesis of a prospective paternal identity during the childhood of the future parent. He makes particular note of the role of a boy's infantile sexual theories in coloring later adaptation to fatherhood.

Gurwitt (1976) presents a case in which he demonstrates the intertwining of his patients' reactions to his wife's pregnancy and the significant events in his own early life. Kramer (1978) noted that the analysis of prospective fathers reveals conflicts and regression related to the birth of their children. For these fathers children served to revive their own core issues. With others fatherhood aids resolution of conflicts, especially over masculinity, and enhances maturation, separation from the family of origin, and individuation.

Characteristic of the psychoanalytic literature is the attempt to relate the impact on the parent of the child's psychosexual stage. Flugel (1921) is cited by Anthony and Benedek (1970) as anticipating later work by observing that the development of the child requires corresponding readjustments in parents' attitudes and behavior at every stage.

Coleman et al. (1953) observe that the growth and maturation of the child, because it is accompanied by changing needs, stimulates different unconscious areas in the parent. For example a mother may delight in the infant's demands but becomes irritated when the child begins to strive for independence. Similarly Bernstein (1975) writes that children and specific emotional levels stimulate particular emotional responses. Bornstein (1948) observes that it is children's closeness to their unconscious that poses a threat to the adult.

Coleman et al. (1953) stated that unconscious parental conflicts are continually mobilized by the changing growth and development of children, and parental attitudes change accordingly. They concluded that a mother's ability to adjust to her child's growth depends on her capacity to shift from one type of identification with the child to another. They write, "The mechanism of revival of the past is operative . . . and for both parents constitutes a central point in the experience of parenthood. The relation to one's own parents is repeatedly reenacted by repetition or by avoidance" (p. 23).

Benedek (1975) believes that the related developmental conflict stimulated by each critical period in child development offers the parent an opportunity to achieve a new level of intrapsychic integration and maturation. Zetzel (1975) cautions that every important maturational challenge presents a regressive threat, as well as an opportunity for growth.

Before giving examples of some of the parental responses to child-developmental phases, it should be noted that the view that parents change in resonance to their children's progression through successive phases is not universal. In Brody and Axelrad's (1978) study of the contribution of maternal and paternal behavior to character formation in childhood, they concluded that the behavior and attitudes of parents were consistent from birth through latency and reflective of the "tenacity of the basic characterological qualities with which persons function as parents" (p. 549). Brody (1975) concludes that her early findings run counter to the assumptions that parental adequacy depends on the ability to shift identifications as the child proceeds through successive developmental phases and that "good fit" is essential to the ongoing relationship between mother and child.

Parental responses to pregnancy and parturition, particularly the mother's response, has been discussed by numerous authors (e.g., Benedek, 1970d; Bibring et al., 1961; Deutsch, 1944; Rangell, 1955; Wolff, 1971).

Liebenberg (1973) notes that for the father the pregnancy may represent proof of virility and manliness, it may produce envy of the pregnancy, or it may intensify separation issues, intensify dependency needs, or reactivate conflicts pertaining to his own parents.

Pines (1972) is impressed by the emergence of previously repressed fantasies during the analysis of pregnant women. She notes the implication of pregnancy as a crisis point in the establishment of female identity. Pines goes on to discuss "stages" of pregnancy and the implications of the early mother-child relationship for the mother's own conflicts over separation. Shereshefsky (1969) describes a study of the psychological impact of a first pregnancy and discusses characteristic patterns of response, including ambivalence, conflict rising from the mother's own needs for nurturance, and separation issues. She also notes the mother's response to the characteristics of the real infant on the basis of the fantasied expectation during infancy.

Mahler, Pine, and Bergman (1970) discuss the mother's response to the toddler's drive for individuation. They observe that the mother's response to maturational events—diminished body molding, weaning, independent locomotion, verbalization—depend on the kind and degree of intrapsychic conflict, her specific wishes, fantasies, and anxieties. They write that maternal reactions are organized around the child's increasing awareness of separateness from the mother and mostly of ego apparatuses—most notably, increasing control of motility and specificity of communications at each step. The mother may respond to the loss of the child's symbiotic dependence on her or to the gain of a new object relationship.

Anthony (1970) comments on the "silent revolution" (p. 277) of the Oedipal period in which intrapsychic shifts in parent and child occur without the conscious awareness of the former in their involvement. He writes,

The seductiveness of the oedipal child is not without effect upon the parents, although the unsophisticated among them may be hard put to say what it is specifically in the child's behavior that disquiets them. They may talk of the child's cuteness, his ability to twist them around his finger, his cajoling and wheedling ways, and his inordinate wish to remain constantly and irritatingly at the center of the stage, but they will not be able to disguise, in many cases, the vicarious gratification that the behavior affords them. (p. 276)

Anthony continues to discuss the possible detrimental consequences for the marital union of this reactivation of the parents' Oedipal concerns by the child's stimulus.

Latency likewise brings with it influences on the parent. The child's transformations during this period threaten the continuity of the parents' ego as these bring a period of alienation (Kestenberg, 1970). The morality of this period may also challenge the parents to become honest (ibid.). The child's socialization as reflected by the participation in school and community may produce parental anxiety of being exposed (Benedek, 1970e).

The storms of puberty and adolescence have also been discussed in terms of the reactions produced in adults. Friedman (1975) notes that adults frequently react with anxiety to the instability of this period because it revives the repressed feelings and conflicts of their adolescent years. The adults' authoritarianism or overpermissiveness may serve the adults' need to gratify forbidden impulses vicariously. He further notes that parents react to the "loss" of their child, the adolescent's emerging sexuality, envious feelings evoked by the vigor of youth, and adolescent skepticism toward adult values. Anthony (1969), in a paper on the reactions of adults, therapists, and parents to adolescents, calls attention to the dramatic impact of the transformation of the child into a figure who, shortly before, was helpless and in need of nourishment and who now is capable of threatening the adult.

Rachman (1975), focusing on the crucial identity formation that takes place during adolescence, calls attention to the resonance of the adults' identity confusion with the adolescents'.

We may conclude this schematic review of parental response to the child's ontogeny with Rangell's (1970) observation about the crisis that may occur when the parents are confronted by their offspring's own impending marriage and parenthood. He notes the reversal of Oedipal roles as the parent experiences decline and the child is perceived at the peak of vitality. Rangell notes that this often is the starting point of a train of neurotic symptoms in the older adult.

Colarusso and Nemiroff (1979) criticize psychoanalytic theory for its sparse contribution to the psychology of adulthood. They note that the psychoanalytic conception of adulthood is that the adult, as contrasted to the child, is free of environmental control. They go on to argue that "exchanges between organism and environment occur from birth to death, producing a continuous effect on psychic development" (p. 61). Following Colarusso and Nemiroff's argument, the child can be taken as a major influence on the psychic development of the parent. In considering from an analytic point of view the differences between the shaping forces of childhood and those of adulthood, Colarusso and Nemiroff point out, "While childhood development is focused primarily on the 'formation' of psychic structures, adult development is concerned with the continuing 'evolution' of existing psychic structures" (p. 62).

In substantial agreement with Colarusso and Nemiroff is Gould (1973) who writes that the parent is

capable of structural change because in the deep part of his mind, the experiences he has with his child are opportunities to rework intimately tied, structure determining memories of his own childhood. This is all made possible by a kind of limited regression and emotional symbiosis on the part of the adult parent to the level of the developing child. (p. 522)

In contrast to the position that the parent responds to the developmental stage the child is negotiating, Gould takes the position that the reaction of the adult is also a function of the issues pertaining to the stage of adulthood the parent is negotiating. Thus, for example, he considers the 29- to 34-year-old age group to be struggling to be accepted for "what I am" correspondingly struggling to accept their children for "what they are becoming." Similarly the 35- to 43-year-old age group is concerned with existential questions of self-values and life itself and correspondingly sees children as the "end product of parenting and reflections of their worth" (Gould, 1973, p. 526).

Erikson (1963) proposes a stage of generativity, which is essential for psychosexual and psychosocial development in the life cycle. He writes, "The fashionable insistence on dramatizing the dependence of children on adults often blinds us to the dependence of the older generation on the younger one" (p. 266).

Kestenberg (1975) believes that parenthood meets the criteria of a developmental phase because it involves a drive (reproduction), an object relation (to the child), and drive-derivative ego attitudes (of motherliness and fatherliness). She further believes that there is a principal developmental task which is to create and to care for the child. Successive subphases of parenthood have their typ-

ical anxieties, conflicts, and defense mechanisms. Finally, there is a change in psychic structure on successful completion of a subphase of parenthood, which she defines as the attainment of the task of promoting the child's growth in accordance with the particular maturational level at the time. Kestenberg believes that the roots of parenthood can be observed in the maternal interest of both sexes observable as early as the second year.

Blos (1975) feels that parenthood contributes to the tasks of achievement of ego continuity and integration of sexual identity. He also feels that it contributes to a second individuation and mastery of residual trauma.

Benedek (1959a, 1959b), who was perhaps the earliest theorist to formulate adulthood as a developmental phase, later (1975) regretted having originally formulated parenthood as a developmental phase. While still adhering to the thesis that parenthood fosters development, she preferred the term *developmental process* because it was not as time-limited or -specific. She further discusses a conflict specific to parenthood—namely that between the instinctual wish to survive in the child and the ethical command to love children in conflict with the hard task that raising children requires. She discusses a culturally accepted outcome of this conflict—namely the authority given the parent over the child.

Brody and Axelrad (1978) accept the idea of the changes of parenthood being called *developmental* as long as it is understood that progress to a higher level of emotional maturity is not implied. They dispute the idea of the existence of phase-specific behaviors essential to actual parenthood. They argue that, while parenthood requires biological maturity, it can be consciously elective. Further its gratification does not depend on any specific erogenous zone. They also argue that parenthood does not necessarily involve adult status, may serve pregenital aims, accelerate narcissism, and promote feelings of completeness based on ego or super-ego demands. Finally they point out that, while other developmental phases are accompanied by structural changes in ego and super-ego, there is no specific age of infant or child when such changes in the parent occur.

Brody (1975) also challenges the conceptualization of parenthood as a developmental phase on the basis that the biological functions involved in pregnancy, delivery, and nursing affect psychological functions of parents for limited periods; there are no universal phase-specific behaviors essential to parenthood; the structural changes in the ego and super-ego which characterize the major psychosexual or developmental phases are not invariably characteristic with parenthood.

THE ETHOLOGICAL PERSPECTIVE

Other, possibly broader, conceptualizations regarding child effects on parents and other adults have also been formulated. Bowlby (1958, 1969) discusses the specific functions of the infant's crying as a releaser mechanism for caretaking behavior. Essentially he posits that there are species-characteristic behaviors, including attachment behaviors such as crying, which have become part of the genetically programmed repertoire of the species through performing a significant survival-promoting function (Bell & Ainsworth, 1972, p. 1186). According to

Bell and Ainsworth's (1972) analysis of Bowlby's perspective, the mother-infant attachment serves the biological function of protection from danger and that "in the original environment of evolutionary adaptedness it was likely that predators were the most conspicuous danger. Attachment behaviors protect an infant by bringing him close to his mother, who can defend him from danger or help him escape from it" (p. 1186). Konner (1972) and DeVore and Konner (1974) provide support for Bowlby's notions in their study of a hunter-gatherer society in which it was found that there was virtually continuous contact between infant and mother and that infants rarely cried because mothers anticipated hunger. Infant crying was viewed as an emergency signal which was responded to with an average latency of six seconds. This may be compared to Bernal's (1972) report that in Western society response to crying is delayed between 5 and 30 minutes and that young infants cry an average of 1 to 2¾ hours per day (Bernal, 1972; Brazelton, 1962). It may be speculated that the difference is because there is no need, in Western society, to prevent predators from hearing infant cries. In summary from an ethological perspective, child effects on parents are seen as biologically determined facilitators of attachment.

THE SOCIAL-LEARNING PERSPECTIVE

Another theoretical approach to the study of child effects is that formulated by Bell and Harper (1977) who discuss offspring effects in terms of a social-learning model in which the child emits stimuli which function either to facilitate or inhibit the probability of a parental response. "Response facilitation is subdivided into 'triggering,' 'sensitizing,' and 'orienting'; response inhibition is conceptualized in terms of 'checking,' 'desensitizing,' and 'disorienting' " (Harper, 1971, p. 74). Using comparative psychology extrapolating from infrahuman studies, Harper (1975) demonstrates reciprocity of parent-offspring stimulation in other mammals.

These conceptualizations are then applied to humans in Bell and Harper's (1977) description of the mechanisms they assume regulate parent-child interaction, designated as *control theory*. In their words,

[E]ach participant in a parent-child interaction has upper and lower limits relative to the intensity, frequency or situational appropriateness of behavior shown by the other. When the upper limit for one participant is reached, the reaction of the other is to redirect or reduce the excessive, inappropriate behavior. (p. 65)

When the lower range or limit is reached, one participant stimulates the other to act. When, for example, the infant is too quiet, as defined by the parent's lower limit, the parent will modify the infant in some way.

More specifically Bell and Harper (1972) outline the progression of events that occur between parent and infant. They describe three distinct progressive periods in the evolution of social interaction between infant and caregiver. They characterize what happens initially between parent and child as *behavioral interaction*, which proceeds to *caregiving*, and ultimately leads to *true social interaction* involving mutual, reciprocal exchanges.

Immediately after birth the mother soothes distress,

responds to the infant's crying, and so on. The infant is in a cycle—sleeping, waking, feeding. "Thus, the early socialization process starts with the infant imposing its own organization on its environment" (Bell & Harper, 1977, p. 124). The caregiving system is one in which the infant emits signals about its state, to which the parent responds by attending to that state and modifying it. This first stage involves the period from birth to two months in which the compelling and demanding aspects of the infant's crying elicit a response from the parent.

The second stage, from three to six months, ushers in a period of social interaction

presumably due to a substantial reduction in fussing or crying, an increase in wakefulness that exposes the mother to another compelling (positive) effect—the infant's gaze, an increase in non-crying vocalizations, the appearance of predictable social smiles and an increase in the modifiability of its behaviors. (Bell & Harper, 1977, p. 148)

Thirdly, the period of seven to twelve months marks a new period of attachment due to the need to control and protect the infant because of his/her improved motor skills and exploratory behavior.

Bell and Harper conclude that ". . . the infant is contributing to maintaining the general behavioral interaction system by the successive production of novel responses, showing modifiability and by inducing a singular relationship with the mother" (1977, p. 148). Further they state that "early in the first year, the mother is acted upon by the infant, whose behavior plays a strong role in inducing caregiving and social interaction as well as differentiating these modes of interaction" (Bell & Harper, 1977, p. 123).

THE LIFE-SPAN PERSPECTIVE

The *interaction model,* as specifically formulated by Lerner and Spanier (1978) and others, expands Bell and Harper's (1977) perspective that children's effectuated responses on the parent should be studied as a way to balance what they justifiably observe to be a biased view—that is, that parents have extensive effects on children—that children are tabula rasa and are molded by their caretakers. Gewirtz (1961) formulated a model explaining the way in which mother and infant form attachment and showed how early social learning is an interactive process. Other researchers also perceived the need to utilize an interactive conceptualization (Bell, 1968; Hartup & Lempers, 1973; Rheingold, 1969).

Lamb (1978a) makes the observation that personality development "occurs in the context of a complex family system rather than in the context of the mother-infant dyad" (Lamb, 1978a, p. 137; Lamb, 1976b, 1977a; Lewis & Feiring, 1978). In addition, "social and psychological development is not confined to infancy and childhood but is a process that continues from birth to death" (Lamb, 1978a, p. 137). A more complex model of interaction is deemed necessary. Klein, Jorgensen, and Miller (1978) adopt, as a way to conceptualize parent-child interaction, the notion of reciprocity as cyclical causation. "Thus, the behavior of person A influences the subsequent behavior of person B, and person B's behavior completes a feedback loop by influencing the subsequent behavior of person A" (p. 109). Clark-Stewart's (1973) study exemplifies this approach. Infant's social development and language competency were positively correlated with positive maternal emotion; mother's affection and verbal responsiveness, in turn, fostered the development of social skills in their infants.

Rather than demonstrating child effects on parents, Lerner and Spanier (1978) opt for a complex model of seeing interaction as reciprocally affecting behaviors, forming a history or set of experiences as if it were a cycle with no beginning and no end which continued over the life span of each of the participants. Biological and social events are also to be considered as part of what the individual brings to each situation.

THE SOCIOLOGICAL PERSPECTIVE

The importance of including the sociological perspective in this review of child effects on parents is that it locates observed phenomenon in a family and social context. Lamb (1978a), in a review of the literature on the influence of the child on marital quality and family interaction during the prenatal, perinatal, and infancy periods, points to the importance of the complex interactions between micro and macro levels of analysis and establishing the influence of pregnancy and parenthood within the ecological context of the family and society.

Cross-cultural studies give evidence of the specificity of parental response to cultural, rather than either parent or child, variables. Salisbury (1962) notes that among certain New Guinea groups adult men do not develop the intense and exclusive emotional concerns for their own children that characterize American fathers but act as fathers to all children in the group. Similarly Pearlin and Kohn (1966) observe that, while American families are more child-oriented, Italian families are more adult-centered and stress conformity to adult standards.

Another sociological contribution is that it identifies features of social organization that mediate the parents' response. Blake (1961) observes that the matrifocal family structure in Jamaica results in the biological father having no role in raising his offspring but a role in raising his mother's and sisters'. Homans (1962) notes that in a patrilinear society the father has jural authority but the uncle is the formal helper and advisor to the children. Rossi (1975) calls attention to the social context for child effects when she accounts for the fact that ethnographic accounts give little evidence of postpartum depression in simpler societies by pointing out that these societies provide numerous adults to care for the infant in contrast to the total responsibility enjoined by a family system of isolated households in industrial societies.

Similarly the child's effects on the parent may depend on the parent's relationship to the environment. Henry (1963) and Benson (1967) believe that fathers react to children as a source of refuge from the outer world and that the worth of the parents may be reflected by the public behavior of the children. Madsen (1973) provides the example of the Mexican family in which the father's response to children is based on his role as preserving the family's public image by policing it. Parsons and Bales (1955) note that the response of mothers and fathers to deviance in their children is based on their social roles.

The father may be more embarrassed than is the mother by deviants because he is the representative to the non-family world. Parsons (Parsons & Bales, 1955) develops a distinction between husband's and wife's roles with the former having an "instrumental" and the latter an "expressive" function.

Benson (1967) presents evidence that shifts in parental responsiveness and involvement in children parallel shifts in sex roles in society. Durkheim (1892/1965) states that the expanding social environment brings with it a decrease in family size with an increase in family ties.

Another approach to child effects on parents is the social-class perspective. Bronfenbrenner (1975) reviews the effects of social class on the parent-child relationship and observes that the responsibility for upbringing has shifted from the family to other settings in society. Kohn (1975) notes that social class has a decided influence on the techniques parents use to raise their children. For example working-class parents punish for the consequences of their children's acts, while middle-class parents tend to punish on the basis of interpretation of the child's intent. Benson (1967) reported that fathers in a middle-class suburb evaluated their children's behavior in terms of aggressiveness and competitiveness expected by their own occupations. Nunn (1964) concluded that middle-class fathers were less likely to be annoyed by their children than were either upper- or lower-class fathers.

Another thrust of the sociological approach is in terms of the effect of children on family roles and relationships. Rossi (1975) describes four *role-cycle stages* of parenthood and emphasizes the cultural pressures influencing parenthood as a social role.

One area that has received particular attention is that of *parenthood as crisis*. LeMasters (1957) regards the first child as posing a crisis to the marital dyad. Dyer (1963) supports LeMasters and observes that there is no evidence that a child enhances a couple's marriage. Hobbs (1965) disputes LeMasters and Dyer and concludes that parenthood is not a crisis and that while there may be difficulties adjusting these are not severe unless the baby has health problems.

Murrell and Stachowiak (1965) observe that parenthood ushers in a new interpersonal situation for the couple by destroying the two-person patterns of interaction. Childless couples, they observe, are likely to have clear-cut divisions of labor that become ambiguous with the addition of children.

Lamb (1978a), on the other hand, suggests that the first child influences the couple by moving them toward more traditional sex roles. He further suggests that the father becomes more active in the care of subsequent children resulting in diminished role segregation brought on by the first child. Similarly Geiken (1964) reports that the longer the couples have been married, the greater the cooperation of father with mother in selected childcare activities.

Koos (1950) reports that family crisis resulting from strained parent-child relationships occur more than twice as often as from strained husband-wife relationships and that this ratio persists as the children grow older. Powell (1963) reports that marital relationships develop new vulnerabilities as children reach adolescence.

Hoffman and Manis (1978) report a survey that also studies the impact of children at various ages on the marital relationship and marital adjustment and conclude that, while the impact is dramatic and undeniable, the effect is complex resulting in both satisfactions and frustrations throughout the family cycle.

Rollins and Galligan (1978) have reviewed the literature on the influence of presence, density, and age of children on the marital relationship. On the basis of an exhaustive review, they developed a theory of the influence of children on role accumulation and strain and marital satisfaction throughout the course of family transitions beginning with the arrival of the first child and continuing through the departure of the last child from the home.

METHODOLOGICAL ISSUES

Bell and Harper (1977) indicate that "there are few definitive research findings in studies of human socialization and that there is ambiguity in the interpretation of even these few findings that have some claim of generality" (p. 85). In studies of human socialization Bell feels that the important dimension is to be able to demonstrate that parent and child are a true social system such that the responses of each individual serve as stimuli for the other and that modifications in one would be likely to have an impact on the other. Among the kinds of studies that elucidate these interactions are descriptive studies of recorded data, longitudinal studies, and sequence analysis, although Bell points out that the data generated sometimes do not meet the assumption of independence required for certain statistical analyses (e.g., chi square, analysis of variance). Correlational studies which indicate degree of relationship do not provide information regarding the direction of the effect, so that it is unclear whether the study reports an effect of the parent on the child or vice versa. In addition the correlations obtained tend to be of low magnitude, and thus the amount of variance explained is lower still.

Among some of the typical problems in child-effects research are the common genetic background between parent and child, the failure to delineate specific contingencies in the parent-child interaction, the reliance on interviews with parents for information on both parent and child behavior, lack of adequate operational definitions of types of behavior such as dependency and aggression, and unrepresentative samples. According to Bell's analysis of research methodology, other more illuminating strategies included videotape or observational data regarding initiation, maintenance, and termination of interaction bouts or the study of experimenter-child dyads instead of parent-child dyads.

Historically both interviews and questionnaires were utilized to study parent-child relationships; but as Yarrow, Campbell, and Burton (1968) report, the interview had limited success as a predictor of *anything* (Hartup, 1978, p. 30). Field-based observational studies have been done (Barker & Wright, 1949), but generally speaking these studies do not shed light on long-term child-parent interaction.

In addition to interviews and home observations, social science experiments are devised to further the study of parent-child interaction. In the laboratory situation behaviors are studied under controlled circumstances in order to reduce unwanted chance effects. Aside from these situational experiments, intervention studies are designed, although the emphasis has been on studying how the parent influences or affects the child.

Hartup (1978) discusses the use of analogue experiments designed to "simulate in the laboratory the conditions of childhood socialization using individuals who were not related to one another" (p. 32). Lerner and Spanier (1978) call for a more sophisticated examination of child-family interactions which they suggest should include an evaluation of the child-family interactions over the life span of both, utilizing different sources of data.

Only through collaborative, interdisciplinary work will the nature, direction, and extent of social and behavioral change be explained.... Moreover, research in human development must go beyond merely detailing patterns of covariation among behaviors and age and, instead, consider how the confluence of all potential contributions to change functions influences development. (p. 14)

Sequential research strategies, delineated by Schaie (1965) and Baltes (1968), are viewed as useful paradigms by Lerner and Spanier. In addition they suggest that experimentally produced "short-term change patterns as simulations of naturalistic long-term change phenomena" (1978, p. 15) and causal-modeling procedures would provide more sophisticated complex data that would be useful in looking at theories of behavior change linked to multiple levels of analysis. In their view part of the complexity of "dynamic interactionism" is that each component of development "is a source of each of the other components with which it interacts" (p.15). Because of the nonlinear character of these notions, Lerner and Spanier (1978) indicate the need for new statistical models for these analyses, since the linear statistical procedures would not be applicable—i.e., the variables involved may not be appropriately seen as antecedent or consequent. Development is seen as constantly changing; therefore, the research methodologies should reflect this. They state,

Our model leads to a conception of development that is interdisciplinary, dynamic, and involves multiple sources of change. For example, we have raised the issue of the continual reciprocities between components of development and we have formulated the research problem of what are the reciprocal contributions of a child and a family over the life-span. (Lerner & Spanier, 1978, p. 17)

Development is conceptualized as a probabilistic phenomenon, "that is, the nature, direction, and extent of developmental change are relative to the changing boundaries imposed by the ever-changing context within which it exists" (ibid., p. 18).

REVIEW OF RESEARCH

What follows is a review of studies that demonstrate the range and scope of child effects on parents. The studies to be reported arise out of both unidirectional and interactional models.

Pregnancy and Parturition

Procreation, pregnancy, and parturition have a profound impact for both parents. Bell and Harper (1977) write, "In many cultures a woman's sense of adequacy and physical integrity—her feeling of personal worth—is intimately linked with her ability to bear and rear offspring successfully" (p. 194). Arbeit (1975) found that during pregnancy women are preoccupied with analyzing and working through issues related to their own mothers. In Gurwitt's (1976) report of a single case, the father-to-be experienced a similar process of self-examination, although his focus was how to be a better father to his child than his own father was to him. Lamb (1978b) indicates that pregnancy may trigger dramatic changes in the roles of family members, and particularly in the relationship between husband and wife. In addition subsequent pregnancies lead to maternal changes toward older children in terms of decreasing maternal warmth, intensity, and duration of contact, lessening of their effectiveness in child-rearing, and declining infantilization; however, restrictiveness, severity of punishment, and coercion increased (Baldwin, 1947).

Pregnancy, and thus the presence of the fetus (Eichorn, 1970), makes for many physical changes in the mother: weight gain (Singer, Westphal, & Niswander, 1968), nausea, and anxiety (Grimm, 1967; Gruenberg, 1967). Gruenberg (1967) states that the complications of pregnancy often reflect fetal abnormalities, and Petre-Quadens (1967) reports that even the mother's sleep pattern is affected by the fetus. The length of gestation may be under fetal influence in that the sensitivity of the uterus to the hormones controlling contraction is affected by fetal mass (Bulmer, 1970). In addition pregnancy brings with it enormous and complex hormonal changes (Hamburg, Moos, & Yalom, 1968; Klopper, 1973). The fetus's position influences the duration and difficulty of labor (Peiper, 1963), and suckling facilitates the expulsion of the placenta (Caldeyro-Barcia, 1961). In order to maintain lactation the infant's suckling is necessary (Meites, 1966; Newton & Newton, 1967). Since the amount of suckling determines the amount of milk produced (Meites, 1966), the infant regulates its mother's state as well (Harper, 1975). In elaborating the physiological changes that occur during pregnancy and lactation, Harper emphasizes that it is the fetus, and later the infant, who stimulates or causes these events.

Beyond the physical changes that occur, this is a period of great emotional change. Grimm (1967) reports frequent episodes of crying, feelings of vulnerability, sensitivity to feelings of rejection, and anxiety in pregnant women. Pregnancy is viewed by some investigators as a biologically determined psychological crisis because it heralds a new set of growth experiences, particularly for the mother-to-be (Bibring, 1959; Caplan, 1961). Adjustment to the newborn is difficult. In fact a third of women were found to have special difficulty in the early period of caring for the first-born infant. Intense, sometimes disruptive, anxiety about the care of the infant was evident (Hubert, 1974; Shereshefsky, Liebenberg, & Lockman, 1973). Women expressed surprise at the degree of fatigue they experienced and at the demands involved in caring for the infant. Shereshefsky et al. (1973) emphasize the women's developmental gains at a first pregnancy.

The finding that a substantial proportion achieved an improved level of personality integration, when taken in conjunction with the statistically significant increase of the nurturance factor between the pre- and post-natal periods, suggests that the experience of a first pregnancy and of the first months of mothering an infant may accentuate developmental changes for a substantial proportion of women. (p. 179)

The experience of pregnancy is reflected in a variety of attitudes. Jessner, Weigart, and Foy (1970), in their study of the development of parental attitudes during pregnancy, report that the experience of fetal movements makes the fetus "real"; however, women also experience a feeling of "otherness within" which makes it feel like a stranger. The attitudes which women report are generally those of fulfillment and delight, what Erikson (1964) calls the "relevance of the productive interior . . . a sense of vital inner potential" (p. 13).

Women also report changes in attitudes toward eating and the loss of its spontaneous pleasure. Dietary restrictions are commonly placed on pregnant women (Hubert, 1974; Mead & Newton, 1967), and the frequency of cravings and food aversions were present in 30 percent to 70 percent of pregnant women, according to Trethowan and Dickens (1972). Attitudes toward sex, beauty, and youth are also changed (Jessner et al., 1970).

As pregnancy neared term women report fears of death for themselves or their infants, as well as fears of deformities in the infant or damage to themselves. Childbirth itself is reported as an extremely moving emotional experience for both parents (Greenberg, 1973; Greenberg & Morris, 1974; Klaus & Kennell, 1976).

After delivery some of the mothers complained that they could not immediately feel love for the baby. Some felt resentful at this little creature for the anxiety and pain they suffered (Jessner et al., 1970). Robson and Moss (1970) state that primiparous mothers describe feelings of strangeness, distance, and unfamiliarity at initial contact with their infants.

Emotional changes also occur after the birth of the infant. Yalom (1968) reports that two-thirds of all postparturitional women experience some kind of postpartum "blues" in the ten days following delivery, although the effects are most often transient. Other researchers report lower, yet substantial, percentages (Hamburg et al., 1968; Jacobsen, Kaij, & Nilsson, 1965; Jarrahi-Zaden, Kane, Van de Castle, Lachenbruch, & Ewing, 1969; Kaij & Nilsson, 1972; Pitt, 1968).

It is Harper's (1975) conclusion that "having or caring for a child may either precipitate an emotional breakdown or lead to enhanced personality functioning" (p. 793).

Fatherhood

For the father, as well, having a child may enhance self-esteem and provide proof of both his masculinity and his relationship with his wife (Howells, 1971). Although there are no overt physical indications of impending fatherhood, "sixty-five percent of expectant fathers develop physical complaints similar to pregnancy symptoms" (Shereshefsky, 1973, p. 239). Trethowan (1972) reports a lower percentage of 20 percent to 25 percent.

The impact of pregnancy on expectant fathers' emotional states is evident in the findings reported by Curtis (1955) that psychosomatic symptoms were the most important distinguishing psychiatric features of the men he studied. Psychiatric disturbance in fathers was also noted in Hartman and Nicolay's (1966) study which reported that in a group of men arraigned in criminal court sexual crimes were more likely among expectant fathers than among married men whose wives were not expecting. In another study fatherhood was reported to be a precipitant of mental illness (Wainwright, 1966).

Less dramatic emotional reactions have also been reported. In their study of expectant fathers, Bittman and Zalk (1978) state that men experience feelings of envy in relation to their wife's pregnancy—there are disruptions in sexual intercourse with fantasies that the fetus is looking at them and that the fetus will bite the penis off. Men report that sexual intercourse is interrupted by their infant's crying and that, for them, too, life style changes during pregnancy and afterward. There are even instances of postpartum depression in men.

In addition breast-feeding also elicits a range of reactions in fathers from identifying with the infant to feeling envious and excluded (Lerner, 1979; Waletzky, 1979).

Recently there has been some discussion of the implications of the increased involvement of the father during the duration of pregnancy and childbirth. On one hand Greenberg and Morris (1974) reported that fathers begin developing an attachment to their infants by the first three days after birth, although they found no evidence that the father's presence at delivery facilitates father-infant bonding. However, Parke and O'Leary (1975) found that fathers who were present at birth were better able to distinguish their infants and were more comfortable holding them.

Peterson, Mehl, and Leiderman (1979) report even more emphatically that the "father's experience of birth and his behavior toward his spouse and his baby during delivery are more important than the prenatal attitude in determining the father's involvement" (p. 337). Their study also supports animal data that the birth experience acts as a powerful catalyst for nurturing behavior from any observer. They conclude that the father's participation in and attitude toward the birth was the most significant variable in predicting future attachment.

Attachment

The next question to be considered, it would seem, is how attachment occurs. According to Murray's (1979) review, exposure to the young is a major component in the development of human parenting behavior. Females, however, are further sensitized to infants by hormonal influences, although babyness tends to elicit positive responses from both males and females; females respond at an earlier age with a stronger preference than that evidenced by males (Fullard & Reiling, 1976).

Gewirtz (1961) has put forth the notion that the infant's growth and attainment of skills are inherently reinforcing for parents. "If something new is happening each week or so, the caregivers' motivation to remain in the behavior interaction system with the infant receives general strengthening" (Bell & Harper, 1977, p. 134). More specifically Klaus, Jerauld, Kreger, McAlpine,

Steffa, and Kennell (1972) and Kennell, Jerauld, Wolfe, Chester, Kreger, McAlpine, Steffa, and Klaus (1974) posit a special attachment period, "a maternal sensitive period," shortly after birth during which separations result in disturbances in caring, analogous to those found in animals. In the human these disturbances might be manifested as child abuse or "deprivation failure to thrive" (Kennell et al., 1974, p. 178). Leifer, Leiderman, Barnett, and Williams's (1972) work supports the notion that disturbances in maternal caretaking occur for mothers of premature infants who were separated from their infants. Enduring differences were found in caregiving behavior between mothers who were allowed early contact with their premature infants and mothers who were allowed late contact (Klaus & Kennell, 1970). In further studies of mothers of full-term infants, Klaus et al. (1972) found that the early-contact mothers responded to their infant's crying by picking them up more frequently than did the traditional-contact mothers.

When her infant was introduced to the mother experimentally (for 16 hours in the first four days), responsiveness and attentiveness were enhanced when measured again one month later (Klaus et al., 1972) and persisted one year later (Kennell et al., 1974). Klaus and co-workers conclude that early separation affects the mother's commitment and attachment to her infant (Barnett, Leiderman, Grobstein, & Klaus, 1970).

Similar findings are reported in studies of older children. A certain amount of exposure to the infant is necessary to consolidate maternal responsiveness. It was not until the infant appeared to be looking at its mother and smiling at her that strong maternal bonds were reported (Robson & Moss, 1970). By the third month when smiling and vocalization increased, mothers reported an increase in affectionate behavior (Moss, 1967). In nine- to twelve-month-old infants, the amount of time they spent in looking and smiling at their mothers was predictive of the amount of time mothers spent in contact with them at a later time (Clarke-Stewart, 1973). Both David and Appell (1961) and Stevens (1971) found that extended care to infants in residential nurseries led to nurse-infant attachments that were apparently initiated by the infants, so that exposure to the young appears to lead to an increase in adult responsiveness.

The infant is seen as initiating and maintaining attachment through the use of attachment behaviors, defined by Ainsworth (1969) and Bowlby (1958, 1969) as two types: "active behaviors through which an infant himself achieves proximity or maintains contact once it has been attained, and signaling behaviors that stimulate his mother to come into closer proximity or contact with him" (Bell & Ainsworth, 1972, p. 1172). These eliciting behaviors are crying, supplemented by vocalization, smiling, and gesturing. To reiterate, the infant's cry is seen as a releaser of caregiving behavior (Ainsworth, 1969; Bowlby, 1969).

Crying and Parental Response

According to Bell and Ainsworth (1972), crying "is the most conspicuous of early attachment behaviors" (p. 1172) because it arouses alarm or displeasure and evokes maternal responses designed to terminate it. Contrary to learning theory ignoring infants' crying during its first year does not extinguish crying but rather increases the likelihood that the infant will cry more frequently from the fourth month on. By her responses the mother bridges the distance between the baby and herself, thereby indicating that infants' crying evokes proximity. Bell and Ainsworth indicate that, at first, crying is "expressive and indiscriminate. It is activated by states such as hunger, but it also seems likely to be activated by the condition of being alone and out of visual, auditory and physical contact with others" (ibid., pp. 1183–1184).

By the end of the first year, crying appears to be a form of communication designed to influence the behavior of others, particularly the mother. What results is the formation of a dyad: "The more responsive she is (mother), the less likely he is to cry and the more likely he is to develop varied modes of communication" (ibid., p. 1184).

Crying elicits a holding response from the mother or caretaker and it is the most effective of the infant's behaviors in eliciting a response (Bell & Ainsworth, 1972). Fretting and crying were likely to initiate mother's vocalization and rocking (Lewis & Lee-Painter, 1974).

Moss (1974) reported that some mothers responded to crying to provide relief, while others responded to terminate a noxious stimulus. Rheingold (1966) states, "So aversive, especially to humans, is the crying of the infant, that there is almost no effort we will not expend, no device we will not employ, to change a crying baby into a smiling one—or just a quiet one" (p. 1243). Crying evokes intense emotional reactions (Ostwald, 1963; Stone, Smith, & Murphy, 1973) or an experience of stress (Bell & Ainsworth, 1972; Parmalee, 1972).

However, Murray (1979) reports evidence to the contrary—i.e., that, at least in Western cultures, the infant's cry does not always elicit a response from the caregiver. Bell and Ainsworth (1972) reported that 46 percent of crying episodes were ignored by primiparous mothers. Moss and Robson (1968) and Bernal (1972) reported figures of 17 percent and 18 percent. Response latencies or delays were 3.83 minutes in Bell and Ainsworth's (1972) study. Bernal (1972) reported an average of ten minutes. In fact Bernal's findings on mother's unresponsiveness to crying in a Western culture led Richards (1974) to remark that "the important lesson for the infant is how little effect his crying has on his caretakers" (p. 98).

Another response to crying was the abuse and battering of children under the age of 12 months. Eighty percent of parents gave excessive crying as their reason for battering (Weston, 1968). Ostwald (1963) and Moss and Robson (1968) emphasize that the motivation for the parent's response is self-serving—i.e., to terminate a noxious stimulus. Hoffman (1975), on the other hand, postulates a theory of empathic distress as the basis for altruism and motivation to respond to the cry. Empathic distress is described as the "involuntary, forceful experiencing of another person's painful emotional state" (Hoffman, 1975, p. 613), or as Murray (1979) states,

The response to the cry likewise consists of an isomorphic response of distress in the observer. . . . Egoistic or self-serving motives for responses to the cry, that is, to reduce the parent's own distress, may account for attempts to avoid or escape from the crying infant. On the other hand, altruistic motives, that is, to reduce the baby's distress, may underlie parental responses at removing the source of discomfort." (p. 212)

There has been some discussion of the notion that mothers are able to make discriminations about the meaning of their infant's cries—i.e., to be able to understand the meaning of the infant's communications. Valanne, Vuorenkoski, Partanen, Lind, and Wasz-Hockert (1967) reported that a third of multiparous mothers were able to distinguish the hunger cries of their child from those of the other infants within their infant's first week of life. In a 1964 study Wasz-Hockert, Partanen, Vuorenkoski, Valanne, and Michelson demonstrated that caretakers can make discriminations between infants crying because of hunger or discomfort. Experienced caretakers were better able to make the discriminations (Michelson, Vuorenkoski, Partanen, Valanne, & Wasz-Hockert, 1965), indicating that prior caretaking experience may increase efficiency and sensitivity. Formby (1967) found that within 48 hours postpartum only 12 of 22 mothers could identify their infant's cry. However after 48 hours every one of the eight mothers they tested could make the differentiation.

However in a recent report Muller, Hollien, and Murry (1974) found that mothers were generally unable to match the cries of their infants and those of unfamiliar infants with the cry-evoking stimulus.

Parental Responses to Infant Behavior

There is an impressive body of findings documenting the influence of infants on their parents. Korner (1974) and Sander (1962) present evidence that the infants' state of arousal, the infants' sex, and the infants' ontogenetic stage of development should, and does, affect the caregiver. Korner (1970) found reliable differences among newborns in how frequently they were spontaneously alert and how readily infants respond to maternal behaviors with alertness. Other researchers found arousal level and activity level of the infant as having an impact on maternal behavior (Korner, 1974; Korner & Thoman, 1972; Levy, 1958; Osofsky & Danzger, 1973; Thoman, Becker, & Freese, 1978; Wolff, 1971; Yarrow, 1963).

The Effects of Gender on Parental Responses

There is a growing body of research to indicate that the sex of the infant results in differential treatment by its caregivers (Condry & Condry, 1976; Lamb, 1977b, 1977c; Lewis & Weintraub, 1974; Moss, 1967; Rubin, Provenzano, & Luria, 1974). Thoman, Leiderman, and Olson (1972) found that primiparous mothers talked to infant girls more during feeding than they did to boys. Lewis's (1972) results were similar in that mothers vocalized to infant girls more than to boys and responded to boys by holding them more than girls. Moss and Robson (1968) reported similar findings in that mothers talked to their fretting infant daughters, while holding fretting infant boys or offering them distractions. Similarly Goldberg, Godfrey, and Lewis (1967) rated mothers of female infants as vocalizing more than mothers of male infants. There were no differences between male and female infants in terms of vocalizing or any of the other eliciting behaviors. Korner (1974) points out, however, that these findings may be a function of differential maternal treatment, so that clearcut sex differences ought to be demonstrated shortly after birth.

The child's age (Brody, 1956; Rheingold, 1961; Van den Berghe, 1973) and sex are related to caregiving practices. The child's gender determines which set of cultural expectations are elicited (Becker, 1964; Kagan, 1971; Minton, Kagan, & Levine, 1971; Rebelsky & Hanks, 1971; Sears, Maccoby, & Levin, 1957; Serbin, O'Leary, & Tonick, 1973).

Bell and Harper (1977) concluded, "Although social expectations are involved in such gender-specific responsiveness, it is still the child who is the 'discriminant stimulus' to which the caregiver reacts" (p. 181). Not only does the infant's irritability have an effect on the caregiver, but his/her soothability does as well. Mothers' ability to soothe is deemed an important challenge, one which provides an estimate of her effectiveness. In addition mothers whose children were easily cared for developed strong attachments far more easily than mothers of difficult children (Chess, 1967).

Infant colic also had significant effects on the mother-infant relationship. By the end of the first three months, mothers were less confident, and somewhat less accepting of the infant, suggesting that colic makes it harder for mothers to cope. However, by six months these mothers were no longer seen as less confident (Shaver, 1973).

Mothers' interpretations of infant's muscle tonus had a profound effect on their movements and manner of holding their infants. Stiffness was interpreted as rejection (Wolff, 1971). Wolff concluded that congenital differences in muscle tonus, motility, duration of wakefulness, and sleep-waking patterns contribute as much to the mother-infant relationship as does the mother's individuality.

There exist an entire range of infant behaviors which affect their caregivers and elicit reactions. For example smiling is likely to elicit caretaking responses, usually in the form of talking or smiling (Gewirtz & Gewirtz, 1969). Emde, Gaenbauer, and Harmon (1976) and Wolff (1971) indicate that smiling is also likely to evoke parental feelings of delight, bringing with it a sense that the infant is "human; before, he was more of a doll-like object, to be protected and taken care of" (Emde et al., 1976, p. 86). By the fifth month most mothers felt that their infants vocalized and smiled discriminatively more toward them than toward others (Emde et al., 1976).

Perhaps one of the most compelling examples of the importance of the smile is provided by Fraiberg's (1974) report of the lengths to which parents of blind infants would go in order to elicit a smile.

As one would expect, infant feeding patterns have an impact upon their caregivers. Pauses in feeding lead to maternal responses such as moving the nipple and stroking the infants' cheeks (Kaye & Brazelton, 1971). Infant vocalizations and looking at the mother tend to result in pauses in feeding activity on the part of mothers and the introduction of social interaction. In addition mothers attempt to gain feedback from their infants as to whether they had enough to eat (Olley, 1973). Bernal (1972) reports that breast-feeding mothers respond more quickly to infants' crying and are more likely to respond by feeding. Prompt responding to crying may be related to the letdown reflex (Mead & Newton, 1967) and/or to

changes in breast temperature (Vuorenkoski, Wasz-Hockert, Koivisto, & Lind, 1969). Mothers tend to open their own mouths while feeding their infants (Blauvelt & McKenna, 1961; O'Toole & Dubin, 1968). Infants' vocalizations are mimicked by their mothers (Millar, 1968; Slobin, 1968).

Another study which demonstrates to some degree the centrality of the infant to the mother is that of Collis and Schaffer (1975) who demonstrate that mothers are drawn to peer at objects of the infant's interest more than infants are likely to peer at the mother's object of interest.

By the infant's sixth month s/he becomes increasingly responsive to novelty, which according to Bruner (1972) facilitates mother's play and thus social interaction. Babbling may also acquire discriminative value for the initiation of reciprocal play. Periods of quiescence may pique the mother's curiosity as well and bring her into proximity with her infant (Bell & Harper, 1977).

In addition to initiating interaction bouts, infants are active in terminating them. Stern (1974) found that the infant initiates or terminates 94 percent of all mutual gaze interactions.

Initiation, or termination of interactions, involves both self-regulation as well as inter-regulation, cycling between "stimulus hunger and pleasure with decreasing periods of unmanageable excitement as development proceeds" (Bell & Harper, 1977, p. 142).

Up to this point research has been presented to document the impact of the infant upon its caregiver. Maternal behavior can be modified by the infant (Gewirtz & Boyd, 1976), and the infant is active in his/her mother's socialization (Bell & Harper, 1977; Gewirtz & Boyd, 1976; Rheingold, 1969).

Another major area of interest, in part made possible by the availability of film and videotape technology, involves the study of the infant's caregiver *interactions*. As Lewis and Lee-Painter (1974) point out, the model of caregiver-infant relationship is often implicit in the observation and measurement techniques of the study. The designation of a given behavior as stimulus or response leads to alternative interpretations. The use of film and videotape permits the analysis of the flow of interaction rather than the designation of a given behavior as the dependent or independent variable. The thrust of interaction studies is to elucidate an interactive model in which "interaction is viewed as a dyadic system in which influences flow in both directions between mother and infant" (Stern, 1974, p. 187). Microanalysis of recorded interaction makes it possible to demonstrate how, in Stern's words, "mutually elicited behavior of each member in turn influences the behavior of the other member" (ibid., p. 187).

The infant has available a large number of behaviors from birth that influence the interaction with the caretaker. Bennett (1971) found that neonates display differences in rhythms of wakefulness, arousal, alertness, and facial expressions during alertness which result in the caretaker constructing a fantasy about the infant's personality and using this fantasy personality as the basis for handling the infant.

Stern (1971) traces the difference in a mother's characteristic interaction with each of her fraternal twins and the characteristic infant behaviors of each infant as they regulate social contact with the mother.

Beebe (1973) using a frame-by-frame analysis of mother-infant interaction demonstrates a range of infant facial and postural behavior during the third and fourth month which produces joy in the mother.

Brazelton (Brazelton, Koslowster, & Main, 1974) describes his attempt to use detailed film studies to document observations from his pediatric practice of the rhythmic, cyclic quality of mother-infant interaction. In such a film study Brazelton et al. (1974) present evidence that infants possess a regulatory system that enables management of the mother's activator in response to stimulation. Their analysis reveals that mothers endow neonate behavior with meaning and react effectively. Mothers learn rules for reacting to infants, the most important of which is sensitivity to the baby's capacity for attention and nonattention.

Stern (1974) reviews the literature on the mutually regulating function of gaze and presents a microanalysis of a mother-infant play situation and documents the patterns of gaze and gaze aversion that contribute to the behavior of each participant in particular. Stern (1974) demonstrated that the infant's behavior has a powerful influence on components of maternal behavior such as gaze, facial expression, and vocalization.

At the center of the interactive approach to the study of the caretaker-infant dyad is Stern's (1977) observation that mothers act differently with infants than they do with others—i.e., the adult's social behavior with infants is specific to them. Among what Stern (1977) calls "infant-elicited social behaviors" are facial expressions which are exaggerated in time and space; prolonged gaze and variations on face presentations and other head movements; vocal alterations involving pitch, variations in loudness, more pronounced rhythms, and syncopations of speech; simplifications of syntax; and overall timing and rhythm of behaviors.

A large number of facial expressions are available at birth, including pleasure, displeasure, fear, joy, sorrow, disgust, and anger and even more specifically, expressions of humor, rejection, intense visual involvement, cunning and quizzical frowns, and smiles. A milestone of the infant's visual motor system occurs during the sixth week when the infant becomes capable of visually fixating his/her mother's eyes.

Mothers experience for the first time the very certain impression that the infant is really looking at *her,* even more, into her eyes. Most often mothers cannot identify this change. At best, most observers say this infant looks at her differently. In any event, the mother's behavior becomes markedly more social. (Stern, 1977, p. 37)

By the end of the third month the visual system is sufficiently mature to regulate the visual stimulation creating more control over the interaction. Stern (1977) concludes,

Gazing, head movements and facial expression are integrated into behavioral packages which function as communicative units. . . . These integrated innate motor patterns are for the mother (or any average adult) the crucial stimulus which once received and processed, lead her to act in a specific

way. . . . Very clearly then, . . . the infant is well equipped with a large repertoire of behaviors to engage and disengage his caregivers. (p. 68)

The finding that by as early as three to four months infants are actively involved in a communication with their caretakers permits a shift from the relatively naive question of whether children influence parents to a microanalysis of the infant-adult interchange which in turn reveals an unanticipated richness and complexity to the interaction. Stern, Jaffe, Beebe, and Bennett (1975) examined the integration of the vocal and kinesic behaviors during the course of development. They found that, in addition to alternating vocalization, mothers and three-to four-month-old infants vocalize simultaneously to a far greater extent than had been anticipated with the mother-infant dyad representing a coaction system. They present evidence that there is a "parallel emergence of two separate modes of vocal communication which differ structurally and functionally" (Stern et al., 1975, p. 96). The coactional mode "is not simply an early developmental pattern that later transforms into the alternating pattern of conversational dialogue, but that it is also an enduring mode of human communication that shares much structurally and functionally with the kinesic systems of mutual gaze, posture sharing, and rhythm sharing" (ibid., p. 90).

Parental Reactions to Characteristics of Children

Other characteristics of the child evoke differential responses in adults. Yarrow, Waxler, and Scott (1971) found that adults returned to imitate positive contacts more readily with children who, in previous interactions, showed interest or compliance. Rothbart and Maccoby (1966) studied the effects of the child's sex on the reactions of parents to the child's voice in situations simulating dependency, aggression, and independence. Fathers were permissive toward girls and mothers toward boys in response to both aggression and dependency. Maccoby and Masters (1970) also found an association between dependence and parental rejection. Osofsky and O'Connell (1972) designed a study in which children participate in independence- and dependence-producing situations. The results demonstrated that dependence in children elicited controlling and interactive behavior from both mothers and fathers.

Besides responding to children's dependency, parents also react to their aggression. Feshbach (1970) indicates the parental response to children's aggression does not occur in a vacuum.

[T]heir response to a particular act may be influenced by the history of their interaction with the child. . . . Although one can exaggerate the influence of the child's aggression upon the parents' disciplinary practices, the possible contribution of the child's behavior to the parent-child interaction has been largely ignored. (p. 228)

Aggression in the child may elicit rejection from the parent which may lead to further aggression. The child's aggression "must be considered as having the capability of affecting the parent" (ibid., p. 217). Schulman, Shoemaker, and Moelis (1962) support Feshbach in that they found that parents of conduct-problem children exhibit significantly more hostile behavior toward their child and reject their children more than do parents of non-conduct-problem children. Parents are apt to respond to aggression with aggression.

Children also affect caregiver speech patterns (Rebelsky & Hanks, 1971), and the age of the child may affect vocal behavior of adults (Ferguson, 1964; Honig, Caldwell, & Tannenbaum, 1970; Landreth, Gardner, Eckhardt, & Prugh, 1943; Philip, 1973; Siegel, 1963; Slobin, 1968; Snow, 1972). Subtler child effects can also be demonstrated.

Rosenblatt (1974) reported that when one or more children were present there was less adult-adult touching, smiling, or talking in public situations, which suggests that when more than two individuals are studied there are indirect effects to be considered. Lamb (1976) found that when the father was present mother-infant interaction was different.

Child Abuse

That the child plays a role in stimulating parental abuse is relevant to our review since it illustrates the dramatic effect that infants have on their families and how they themselves influence the nature of their experience. Gill (1970) reported that demands or specific acts of the child were part of the sequence of events in abuse. In fact parents stated that they felt abused by their child. In his factor analyses, "deviance in the child was at least as substantial a factor in explaining the incidents as deviance in the parents" (pp. 130–131). Klaus and Kennell (1970) found that battered children had medical problems which may have overburdened the limited resources of certain parents. A crying infant, as Berkowitz (1974) reports, may become an aversive stimulus and as such may provoke aggressive behavior on the part of the parent. Often these infants are inconsolable, their moods are labile and not often positive (Thomas et al., 1968, 1970; Thomas, Chess, Birch, Hertzig, & Korn, 1963). Through a process of conditioning the infant becomes an aversive stimulus.

Premature infants appear to be "at risk" for potential abuse. Lamb (1978a) observes that the characteristics of premature infants, their "high-pitched cry, their distorted head-to-body ratio, their fragility and size, their wizened appearance, make them less effective as elicitors of the 'cute response' " (Jolly, 1972, p. 155). In addition they do not smile for a long period after birth and thereby do not provide positive feedback to the parent, which leaves the parent with predominantly aversive stimulation in the form of crying.

Steele's (1970) analysis of child abuse involves the role of the infant as a satisfier of parental ungratified infantile needs. As long as the parent is proven "loved" with the infant providing pleasure and cooperation

all goes well. Should the infant be uncooperative, however, continuing to cry, or persist in wriggling and thwarting parental caretaking efforts, the parent may feel disappointed, disapproved of, unloved and criticized, and will respond with attack in the form of yanking, slapping, hitting and throwing about in an effort to make the baby behave." (p. 452)

The Impact of the Disabled Child on the Parent

Handicapped or disabled children also elicit parental reactions. Depression and grief are the foremost symptoms and reactions to the birth of a handicapped child (Evans, 1976; Fraiberg & Freedman, 1964; Sieffert, 1978; Weiner, 1970). Since the child is seen as an extension of themselves (Illingworth, 1967; Kohut, 1966), there are personal reactions of inadequacy, as well as anticipation of social rejection and ridicule.

Mothers of handicapped children suffer a decrement in self-esteem (Cummings, Bayley, & Rie, 1966; Morris, 1972; Richards, 1974). If the child was unwanted, feelings of guilt may be engendered. If the mother attempted to self-abort, the handicapped infant is seen as an extension of her "bad self." Sometimes guilt about sexual thoughts or acts, or even childhood fantasies, may reemerge if the child is born impaired (Jamison, 1965).

A vivid example of the effect of a handicap upon the parent is deafness of the child. Deaf infants are unable to respond to the sound of the parent's approach or voice or to verbal attempts at soothing. The deaf infant ceases to babble because of lack of auditory feedback. These characteristics naturally have an impact on the parent's emotional and behavioral responses. Parents begin to feel deprived and rejected because of the deaf infant's failure to respond, which results in lack of parental stimulation and a decrease in parental-child interaction (Harris, in press).

Another example of child-elicited rejection is reported in Prechtl's (1963) study in which he followed the development of neurologically impaired infants and found that, at the end of three months, seven of the eight mothers were overanxious or rejecting toward their youngsters, while only one of the ten mothers in the control was. Mitchell and Schroers (1973) report similar findings. Handicapped children may also stress family resources, both financial and emotional, as well as require extended care (Korn, Chess, & Fernandez, 1978). In addition the cries of atypical children are said to be so unpleasant that they override maternal style (Ostwald, 1973; Wolff, 1969). In the nursery handicapped babies are kept out of earshot because their cries are so unbearable to their caretakers (Milowe & Lourie, 1964).

The child's disability itself affects the parent's handling of the child. D'Antonio (1976) reported that mothers of congenitally impaired cardiac preschoolers were more sensitive to their children's biological functions than to their behaviors. There was an overconcern with nutrition and growth and pervasive fears of the child's death; avoidance of conflict and leniency in discipline were also distinguishing characteristics of the mother's response to the child's disability.

The Impact of the Child on Lifestyle

Beyond specific experimental effects of the young, Bell and Harper (1977) report on a wide range of social effects that are due to the presence of the young. For example planning for children may result in changes in residence (Davenport, 1965; Mead & Newton, 1967); parents may support organized religion or other social institutions (i.e., schools), or they may take their children to places they would not frequent by themselves (Harper, 1970, 1975). There are economic strains, as well as changes in the work force, when mothers leave the labor force; grandparents sometimes return to caregiving roles as a way to help their children (Bell & Harper, 1977; Money & Ehrhardt, 1972).

Changes in the marital relationship occur after the birth of a child (Nye, Carlson, & Garrett, 1970; Ryder, Kafka, & Olson, 1971; Sears et al., 1957). The presence or prospect of children affects sexual practices of parents (Davenport, 1965; Ford & Beach, 1951; Mead, 1935/1950; Mead & Newton, 1967). In addition there are changes in relationships with extended family. Ryder et al. (1971) indicate that mothers have more contact with their own mothers as a result of having a child. Other social relationships change: New mothers have more contact with other new mothers.

Parental patterns of consumption are affected by the presence of offspring (Fimrite, 1970), as reflected in the buying of toys, diaper services, and formula.

There are even changes in adults' values due to the presence of the young. Kestenberg (1970) suggests "that when parents fail to conform, they are often confronted by their latency-age children with reminders of the culture's standards" (Harper, 1975, p. 796).

These examples are not meant to be exhaustive, only illustrative of the range of the impact the young have on the adult and the adult's world. "Caregiving can influence patterns of interaction and responsibilities within the wider group and sometimes across groups" (Bell & Harper, 1977, p. 205).

CONCLUSIONS

The preceding review has addressed the issue of child effects on parents from various theoretical perspectives and has summarized relevant research. Each of these points of view is more or less supported by hard evidence and leads to an interpretation that infants and children (1) from the psychoanalytic perspective, contribute to the structural development of the parent's personality and activate past conflicts which are met with either regression or resolution; (2) from an ethological (attachment-theory) perspective, emit a range of stimuli that release caregiving behaviors which lead to mutual attachment; (3) from a social-learning perspective, have the capacity to socialize the parent; (4) from a life-span perspective, contribute to a complex, interdependent, reciprocal, and mutually evolving relationship over the course of the life span; (5) from a sociological perspective, contribute to the organization of parents' relationship with each other and society and to their role definition. The research which is summarized supports these points of view but does not always resolve conflicts between theorists who espouse a particular point of view.

A number of theorists have been especially critical of what they see as a past emphasis on parent effects on children at the expense of child effects on parents. This criticism may have been overstated since the latter position has been at least implicit in a number of theoretical approaches. Nevertheless its much-hailed "discovery" is

an important and welcome contribution of the past 10 to 15 years. It should, however, be remembered that the issue is more complex than a reversal of the direction of effects. As hard as it may be to investigate, and as difficult as the conceptual model may be, there seems to be a mutually interpenetrating, reverberating influence between parent and child. Thus parent-child interaction, rather than direction of effect, is the true subject of this review. As has been discussed the methodological complications and the difficulty of statistical analysis challenge the investigator.

In conclusion it may be speculated that the call for increased attention to the effect of children on parents may itself be data. First, it parallels wide-ranging shifts in society from one which, through its child orientation, defines the role of women to one in which traditional sex roles are being reevaluated. Second, it may be concomitant to the shift, anticipated by Mead (1970), from a postfigurative to cofigurative and prefigurative culture —that is, a shift from intergenerational relations in which the older generation provides a model for a way of life to the younger one, to a situation in which rapid change leads to each generation's discovery of a model together, to finally a situation in which change has been so rapid that the young must reeducate the old.

REFERENCES

AINSWORTH, M.D.S. Object relations, dependency and attachment: A theoretical review of the infant-mother relationship. *Child Development*, 1969, *40*, 969–1025.

ANTHONY, E. J. The reactions of adults to adolescents and their behavior. In G. Caplan & S. Lebovici (Eds.), *Adolescence: Psychosocial perspective*. New York: Basic Books, 1969.

ANTHONY, E. J. The reactions of parents to the Oedipal child. In E. J. Anthony & T. Benedek (Eds.), *Parenthood*. Boston: Little, Brown, 1970.

ANTHONY, E. J., & BENEDEK, T. *Parenthood*. Boston: Little, Brown, 1970.

ARBEIT, S. A. *A study of women during their first pregnancy*. Unpublished doctoral dissertation, Yale University, 1975.

ARIES, P. [*Centuries of childhood: A social history of family life*] (R. Balolick, Trans.). New York: Knopf, 1962. (Originally published, 1960).

BACH, G., & NICHOLSON, L. The cradle of crazymaking or how children drive their parents crazy. *Voices: Journal of the American Academy of Psychotherapy*, 1976-1977, *12*(No. 4), 33–42.

BALDWIN, A. L. Changes in parent behavior during pregnancy: An experiment in longitudinal analysis. *Child Development*, 1947, *18*, 29–39.

BALINT, A. Love for the mother and mother love. *International Journal of Psychoanalysis*, 1949, *30*, 256–259.

BALINT, M. *The basic fault: Therapeutic aspects of regression*. London: Tavistock, 1968.

BALTES, P. B. Longitudinal and cross-sectional references in the study of age and generation effects. *Human Development*, 1968, *11*, 145–171.

BARDWICK, J. *Psychology of woman*. New York: Harper & Row, Pub., 1971.

BARKER, R. G., & WRIGHT, H. F. Psychological ecology and the problem of psychosocial development. *Child Development*, 1949, *20*, 131–143.

BARNETT, C. R., LEIDERMAN, P. H., GROBSTEIN, R., & KLAUS, M. Neonatal separations: The maternal side of interactional deprivation. *Pediatrics*, 1970, *45*, 197–205.

BECKER, W. C. Consequences of different kinds of parental discipline. In M. L. Hoffman & L. W. Hoffman (Eds.), *Review of child development research* (Vol. 1). New York: Russell Sage Foundation, 1964.

BEEBE, B. *Ontogeny of positive affect in the third and fourth months of the life of one infant.* Unpublished doctoral dissertation, Columbia University, 1973.

BELL, R. Q. The effect on the family of a limitation in coping ability in the child: A research approach and a finding. *Merrill-Palmer Quarterly,* 1964, *10,* 129–142.

BELL, R. Q. A reinterpretation of the direction of effects in studies of socialization. *Psychological Review,* 1968, *75,* 81–95.

BELL, R. Q., & HARPER, L. V. *Child effects on adults.* New York: John Wiley, 1977.

BELL, S. M., & AINSWORTH, M. D. Infant crying and maternal responsiveness. *Child Development,* 1972, *43,* 1171–1190.

BENEDEK, T. Parenthood as a developmental phase: A contribution to the libido theory. *Journal of the American Psychoanalytic Association,* 1959a, *7,* 389–417.

BENEDEK, T. Climacterium: A developmental phase. *Psychoanalytic Quarterly,* 1959b, *19,* 1–27.

BENEDEK, T. The psychobiologic approach to parenthood—The family as a psychologic field. In E. J. Anthony & T. Benedek (Eds.), *Parenthood.* Boston: Little, Brown, 1970a.

BENEDEK, T. Fatherhood and providing. In E. J. Anthony & T. Benedek (Eds.), *Parenthood.* Boston: Little, Brown, 1970b.

BENEDEK, T. Motherhood and nurturing. In E. J. Anthony & T. Benedek (Eds.), *Parenthood.* Boston: Little, Brown, 1970c.

BENEDEK, T. The psychobiology of pregnancy. In E. J. Anthony & T. Benedek (Eds.), *Parenthood.* Boston: Little, Brown, 1970d.

BENEDEK, T. Parenthood during the life cycle. In E. J. Anthony & T. Benedek (Eds.), *Parenthood.* Boston: Little, Brown, 1970e.

BENEDEK, T. In H. Parens (Reporter), Parenthood as a developmental phase. In Panel Reports. *Journal of the American Psychoanalytic Association,* 1975, *23,* 154–165.

BENNETT, S. L. Infant-caretaker interactions. *Journal of the American Academy of Child Psychiatry,* 1971, *10,* 321–335.

BENSON, L. *Fatherhood: A sociological perspective.* New York: Random House, 1967.

BERKOWITZ, L. A. Some determinants of impulsive aggression: Role of mediated associations with reinforcements for aggression. *Psychological Review,* 1974, *81,* 165–176.

BERNAL, J. F. Crying during the first ten days of life and maternal responses. *Developmental Medicine and Child Neurology,* 1972, *14,* 362–372.

BERNSTEIN, I. On the technique of child and adolescent analysis. *Journal of the American Psychoanalytic Association,* 1975, *23,*190–232.

BIBRING, G. L. Some considerations of the psychological process in pregnancy. *Psychoanalytic Study of the Child,* 1959, *14,* 113–121.

BIBRING, G., DWYER, T., HUNTINGTON, D., & VALENSTEIN, A. Some considerations of the psychological processes in pregnancy. *Psychoanalytic Study of the Child,* 1961, *16,* 15–24.

BITTMAN, S., & ZALK, S. R. *Expectant fathers.* New York: Hawthorn, 1978.

BLAKE, J. *Family structure in Jamaica.* New York: Free Press, 1961.

BLAUVELT, H., & McKENNA, J. Mother-neonate interaction: Capacity of the human newborn for orientation. In B. M. Foss (Ed.), *Determinants of infant behaviour I.* New York: John Wiley, 1961.

BLOS, P. In H. Parens (Reporter), Parenthood as a developmental phase. In Panel Reports. *Journal of the American Psychoanalytic Association,* 1975, *23,* 154–165.

BORNSTEIN, B. Emotional barriers in the understanding and treatment of children. *American Journal of Orthopsychiatry,* 1948, *18,* 691–697.

BOWLBY, J. The nature of the child's tie to his mother. *International Journal of Psychoanalysis,* 1958, *39,* 1–34.

BOWLBY, J. *Attachment and loss* (Vol. 1). London: Hogarth, 1969.

BRAZELTON, T. Crying in infancy. *Pediatrics,* 1962, *29,* 579–588.

BRAZELTON, T. B., KOSLOWSTER, B., & MAIN, M. The origins of reciprocity: The early mother-infant interaction. In M. Lewis & L. Rosenblum (Eds.), *The effect of the infant on its caregiver.* New York: John Wiley, 1974.

BREIN, O. Family structure and sex-role learning by children. *Sociometry,* 1958, *21,* 1–16.

BRIM, O. The parent-child relation as a social system: I. Parent and child roles. *Child Development,* 1957, *28,* 343–364.

BRODY, S. *Patterns of mothering.* New York: International Universities Press, 1956.

BRODY, S. In H. Parens (Reporter), Parenthood as a develop-

mental phase. In Panel Reports. *Journal of the American Psychoanalytic Association,* 1975, *23,* 154–165.

BRODY, S., & AXELRAD, S. *Mothers, fathers, and children.* New York: International Universities Press, 1978.

BRONFENBRENNER, U. The changing American child. *Journal of Social Issues,* 1961, *17,* 6–18.

BRONFENBRENNER, U. The split level American family. In W. Sze (Ed.), *Human life cycle.* New York: Jason Aronson, 1975.

BRUNER, J. S. Nature and uses of immaturity. *American Psychologist,* 1972, *27,* 687–708.

BULMER, M. G. *The biology of twinning in man.* London: Oxford University Press, 1970.

BURLINGHAM, D. The preoedipal infant-father relationship. *The Psychoanalytic Study of the Child,* 1973, *28,* 23–48.

CALDEYRO-BARCIA, R. Factors controlling the actions of the pregnant human uterus. In M. Knowlessar (Ed.), *The physiology of prematurity.* New York: Josiah Macy Foundation, 1961.

CAPLAN, G. *An approach to community mental health.* London: Tavistock, 1961.

CAVAN, R. Stages of the family life cycle. In R. Cavan (Ed.), *Marriage and family in the modern world: A book of readings.* New York: Harper & Row, Pub., 1974.

CHESS, S. Temperament in the normal infant. In J. Hellmuth (Ed.), *The Exceptional Infant* (Vol. 1). The normal infant. New York: Brunner/Mazel, 1967.

CLARKE-STEWART, K. A. Interactions between mothers and their children: Characteristics and consequences. *Monographs of the Society for Research in Child Development,* 1973, *38*(6–7, Serial No. 153).

COLARUSSO, C., & NEMIROFF, R. Some observations and hypotheses about the psychoanalytic theory of adult development. *International Journal of Psychoanalysis,* 1979, *60,* 59–71.

COLEMAN, R. W., KRIS, E., & PROVENCE, S. The study of variations of early parental attitudes: A preliminary report. *The Psychoanalytic Study of the Child,* 1953, *8,* 20–27.

COLLIS, G. M., & SCHAFFER, H. R. Synchronization of visual attention in mother-infant pairs. *Journal of Child Psychology and Psychiatry,* 1975, *16,* 315–320.

CONDON, W. S., & SANDER, L. W. Neonate movement is synchronized with adult speech: Interactional participation and language acquisition. *Science,* 1974, *183,* 99–101.

CONDRY, J., & CONDRY, S. Sex differences: A study of the eye of the beholder. *Child Development,* 1976, *47,* 812–819.

CUMMINGS, S., BAYLEY, H., & RIE, H. Effects of the child's deficiency on the mother: A study of mothers of mentally retarded, chronically ill and neurotic children. *American Journal of Orthopsychiatry,* 1966, *36*(No. 4), 595–608.

CURTIS, J. L. A psychiatric study of 55 expectant fathers. *U.S. Armed Forces Medical Journal,* 1955, *6,* 937–950.

D'ANTONIO, I. J. Mothers' responses to the functioning and behavior of cardiac children in child-rearing situations. *Maternal-Child Nursing Journal,* 1976, *5*(No. 4), 207–264.

DAVENPORT, W. Sexual patterns and their regulation in a society of the southwest Pacific. In F. A. Beach (Ed.), *Sex and behavior.* New York: John Wiley, 1965.

DAVID, M., & APPELL, G. A study of nursing care and nurse-infant interaction. In B. M. Foss (Ed.), *Determinants of infant behavior* (Vol. 1). New York: John Wiley, 1961.

DAVID, M., & APPELL, G. Mother-child relationship. In J. Howells (Ed.), *Modern perspectives in international child psychiatry.* New York: Brunner/Mazel, 1971.

DE MAUSE L. The evolution of childhood. In L. de Mause (Ed.), *The history of childhood.* New York: Harper & Row, Pub., 1974.

DEUTSCH, H. *The psychology of women: A psychoanalytic interpretation.* New York: Grune & Stratton, 1944.

DEVORE, I., & KONNER, M. Infancy in a hunter-gatherer life: An ethological perspective. In N. White (Ed.), *Ethology and psychiatry.* Toronto: University of Toronto Press, 1974.

DURKHEIM, E. [Lecture on the family.] In *American Journal of Sociology,* 1965, *70,* 527–536. (M. Mauss, Recorder, & G. Simpson, Transcriber.) (Originally published, 1892)

DYER, E. Parenthood as crisis: A re-study. *Marriage and Family Living,* 1963, *25,* 196–201.

EICHORN, D. Physiological development. In P. H. Mussen (Ed.), *Carmichael's manual of child psychology* (3rd ed., Vol. 1). New York: John Wiley, 1970.

EMDE, R. N., GAENBAUER, T. J., & HARMON, R. J. Emotional expression in infancy: A biobehavioral study. *Psychological Issues,* 1976, *10*(1, Monograph 37).

ERIKSON, E. *Childhood and society.* New York: W. W. Norton & Co., Inc., 1963.

ERIKSON, E. H. Inner and outer space: Reflections on womanhood. In R. J. Lifton (Ed.), *The woman in America.* Boston: Beacon Press, 1964.

ESCALONA, S. *The roots of individuality.* Chicago: Aldine, 1968.

EVANS, E. C. The grief reaction of parents of the retarded and the counselor's role. *Australian Journal of Mental Retardation,* 1976, *4,* 8–12.

FERGUSON, C. A. Baby talk in six languages. In J. Gumperz & D. Hymes (Eds.), The ethnography of communication. *American Anthropologist,* 1964, *66,* 103–114.

FESHBACH, S. Parental discipline and aggression. In P. H. Mussen (Ed.), *Carmichael's manual of child psychology.* New York: John Wiley, 1970.

FIMRITE, R. Dish night at the ball park. *San Francisco Chronicle,* July 3, 1970, p. 48.

FLUGEL, J. C. *The psychoanalytic study of the family.* London: Hogarth, 1921.

FORD, C. S., & BEACH, F. A. *Patterns of sexual behavior.* New York: Harper & Row, Pub., 1951.

FORMBY, D. Maternal recognition of infant's cry. *Developmental Medicine and Child Neurology,* 1967, *9,* 293–298.

FRAIBERG, S. Blind infants and their mothers: An examination of the effects of the sign system. In M. Lewis & L. Rosenblum (Eds.), *Effect of infant on its caregivers.* New York: John Wiley, 1974.

FRAIBERG, S., & FREEDMAN, D. A. Studies in the ego development of the congenitally blind. *Psychoanalytic Study of the Child,* 1964, *195,* 113–169.

FREUD, S. *On narcissism* (Standard Ed., Vol. 14). London: Hogarth Press, 1957. (Originally published, 1914)

FRIEDMAN, R. The vicissitudes of adolescent development and what it activates in adults. *Adolescence,* 1975, *10*(No.4), 520–526.

FRIES, M. The child's ego development and the training of adults in his environment. *Psychoanalytic Study of the Child,* 1946, *2,* 85–112.

FRIES, M., & WOOLF, P. Some hypotheses on the role of the congenital activity type in personality development. *The Psychoanalytic Study of the Child,* 1953, *8,* 48–64.

FULLARD, W., & REILING, A. M. An investigation of Lorenz's "babyness." *Childhood Development,* 1976, *47,* 1191–1193.

GEIKEN, R. Expectations concerning husband-wife responsibilities in the home. *Journal of Marriage and the Family,* 1964, *26,* 349–352.

GEWIRTZ, H. B., & GEWIRTZ, J. L. Caretaker settings, background events and background differences in 4 Israeli child rearing environments. Some preliminary trends. In B. M. Foss (Ed.), *Determinants of infant behavior* (Vol. 4). London: Methuen, 1969.

GEWIRTZ, J. A learning analysis of the effects of normal stimulation, privation and deprivation on the acquisition of social motivation and attachment. In B. M. Foss (Ed.), *Determinants of infant behavior* (Vol. 1). New York: John Wiley, 1961.

GEWIRTZ, J. L., & BOYD, E. F. Experiments in mother-infant interactions, mutual attachment, acquisition. The infant conditions his mother. In T. Alloway, L. Krames, & P. Pliner (Eds.), *Advances in the study of communication and affect* (Vol. 3). New York: Plenum, 1976.

GILL, D. G. *Violence against children.* Cambridge, Mass.: Harvard University Press, 1970.

GOLDBERG, S., GODFREY, L., & LEWIS, M. *Play behavior in the year-old infant: Early sex differences.* Paper presented at biennial meeting of the Society for Research in Child Development, New York, March 1967.

GOULD, R. L. The phases of adult life: A study in developmental psychology. *American Journal of Psychiatry,* 1973, *129,* 521–531.

GREENBERG, M. First mothers rooming-in with their newborns: Its impact on the mother. *American Journal of Orthopsychiatry,* 1973, *45,* 783–788.

GREENBERG, M., & MORRIS, N. Engrossment: The newborn's impact upon the father. *American Journal of Orthopsychiatry,* 1974, *44,* 520–531.

GRIMM, E. Psychological and social factors in pregnancy, delivery and outcome. In S. A. Richardson & A. F. Guttmacher (Eds.), *Childbearing: Its social and psychological aspects.* Baltimore, Md.: Williams & Wilkins, 1967.

GRUENBERG, E. M. On the psychosomatics of the not-so-perfect fetal parasite. In S. A. Richardson & A. F. Guttmacher (Eds.), *Childbearing: Its social and psychological aspects.* Baltimore, Md.: Williams & Wilkins, 1967.

GUERIN, P. Family therapy: The first twenty-five years. In P. Guerin (Ed.), *Family therapy: Theory and practice.* New York: Gardner Press, 1976.

GURWITT, A. R. Aspects of prospective fatherhood. A case report. *Psychoanalytic Study of the Child,* 1976, *31,* 237–271.

HAMBURG, D. A., MOOS, R. F., & YALOM, I. D. Studies of distress in the menstrual cycle and the post-partum period. In R. P. Michael (Ed.), *Endocrinology and human behavior.* London: Oxford University Press, 1968.

HARPER, L. V. Ontogenetic & phylogenetic functions of the parent-offspring relations in mammals. In D. S. Lehrman, R. A. Hinde, & E. Shaw (Eds.), *Advances in the study of behavior* (Vol. 3). New York: Academic Press, 1970.

HARPER, L. V. The young as a source of stimuli. Controlling caretaker behavior. *Developmental Psychology,* 1971, *4,* 73–88.

HARPER, L. V. The scope of offspring effects. From caregiver to culture. *Psychological Bulletin,* 1975, *82,* 784–801.

HARRIS, A. E. Language in the deaf community and the deaf individual: Communicational competence and control. In L. S. Liven (Ed.), *Theoretical and practical implications of the development of deaf children.* New York: Academic Press, in press.

HARTMAN, A. A., & NICOLAY, R. C. Sexually deviant behavior in expectant fathers. *Journal of Abnormal Psychology,* 1966, *71,* 232–234.

HARTUP, W. W. Perspectives on child and family interaction: Past, present and future. In R. M. Lerner & G. B. Spanier (Eds.), *Child influences on marital and family interaction: A life-span perspective.* New York: Academic Press, 1978.

HARTUP, W. W., & LEMPERS, J. A problem in life-span development: The interactional analysis of family attachments. In P. B. Baltes & K. W. Schaie (Eds.), *Life-span developmental psychology* (Vol. 3). New York: Academic Press, 1973.

HENRY, J. *Culture against man.* New York: Random House, 1963.

HOBBS, D. Parenthood as crisis: A third study. *Journal of Marriage and the Family,* 1965, *27,* 367–372.

HOFFMAN, L. W., & MANIS, J. D. Influences of children on marital interactions and parental satisfactions and dissatisfactions. In R. M. Lerner & G. B. Spanier (Eds.), *Child influences on marital and family interactions: A life-span perspective.* New York: Academic Press, 1978.

HOFFMAN, M. Developmental synthesis of affect and cognition and its implications for altruistic motivation. *Developmental Psychology,* 1975, *11,* 607–622.

HOMANS, G. *Sentiments and activities.* New York: Free Press, 1962.

HONIG, A. S., CALDWELL, B. M., & TANNENBAUM, J. Patterns of information processing used by and with young children in a nursery school setting. *Child Development,* 1970, *41,* 1045–1066.

HOWELLS, J. G. Fathering. In J. G. Howells (Ed.), *Modern perspectives in international child psychiatry.* New York:Brunner/Mazel, 1971.

HUBERT, J. Belief and reality: Social factors in pregnancy and childbirth. In M.P.M. Richards (Ed.), *The integration of a child into a social world.* Cambridge, England: Cambridge University Press, 1974.

ILLINGWORTH, R. Counseling the parents of the mentally handicapped child. *Clinical Pediatrics,* 1967, *6*(No. 6), 340–347.

JACOBSON, L., KAIJ, L., & NILSSON, A. Post-partum mental disorders in an unselected sample. *British Medical Journal,* 1965, *1,* 16407.

JAMISON, J. The impact of mental retardation on the family and some directions of help. *Journal of the National Medical Association,* 1965, *57*(No. 2), 136–138.

JARRAHI-ZADEN, A., KANE, F. J., JR., VAN DE CASTLE, R. L., LACHENBRUCH, P. A., & EWING, J. A. Emotional and cognitive changes in pregnancy and early puerperium. *British Journal of Psychiatry,* 1969, *115,* 797.

JESSNER, L., WEIGART, E., & FOY, J. L. The development of parental attitudes during pregnancy. In E. J. Anthony & T. Benedek (Eds.), *Parenthood.* Boston: Little, Brown, 1970.

JOLLY, A. *The evolution of primate behavior.* New York: Macmillan, 1972.

KAGAN, J. *Change and continuity in infancy.* New York: John Wiley, 1971.

KAIJ, L., & NILSSON, A. Emotional and psychotic illness following childbirth. In J. G. Howells (Ed.), *Modern perspectives in psycho-obstetrics.* New York: Brunner/Mazel, 1972.

KAYE, K., & BRAZELTON, T. B. *Mother-infant interaction in the organization of sucking.* Paper presented at the Society for Research in Child Development, Minneapolis, Minn., March 1971.

KENNELL, J., JERAULD, R., WOLFE, H., CHESTER, D., KREGER, N. C., MCALPINE, W., STEFFA, M., & KLAUS, M. H. Maternal behavior one year after early and extended post-partum contact. *Developmental Medicine and Child Neurology, 1974, 16,* 172–179.

KESTENBERG, J. S. The effect on parents of the child's transition into and out of latency. In E. J. Anthony & T. Benedek (Eds.), *Parenthood.* Boston: Little, Brown, 1970.

KESTENBERG, J. S. In H. Parens (Reporter), Parenthood as a developmental phase. In Panel Reports. *Journal of the American Psychoanalytic Association, 1975, 23,* 154–165.

KLAUS, M. H., JERAULD, R., KREGER, N. C., MCALPINE, W., STEFFA, M., & KENNELL, J. H. Maternal attachment, importance of the first post-partum days. *New England Journal of Medicine, 1972, 286,* 460–463.

KLAUS, M. H., & KENNELL, J. Mothers separated from their infants. *Pediatric Clinics of North America, 1970, 17,* 1015–1037.

KLAUS, M., & KENNELL, J. *Maternal infant bonding.* St. Louis, Mo.: C. V. Mosby, 1976.

KLEIN, D. M., JORGENSEN, S. R., & MILLER, B. C. Research methods and developmental reciprocity in families. In R. M. Lerner & G. B. Spanier (Eds.), *Child influences on marital and family interaction: A life-span perspective.* New York: Academic Press, 1978.

KLOPPER, A. The role of oestrogens in the onset of labor. In A. Klopper & J. Gardner (Eds.), Endocrine factors in labor. *Memoirs of the Society for Endocrinology* (No. 20). Cambridge, England: Cambridge University Press, 1973.

KOHN, M. Social class and parent-child relationship. In W. Sze (Ed.), *Human life cycle.* New York: Jason Aronson, 1975.

KOHUT, S. The abnormal child: His impact on the family. *Journal of the American Physical Therapy Association, 1966, 66*(No. 5), 1062–1065.

KONNER, M. Aspects of a developmental ethology of a foraging people. In N. Blurton-Jones (Ed.), *Ethological studies of child behavior.* Cambridge, England: Cambridge University Press, 1972.

KOOS, E. Class differences in family reactions to crisis. *Marriage and Family Living, 1950, 12,* 77–78.

KORN, S. J., CHESS, S., & FERNANDEZ, P. The impact of children's physical handicaps. In R. H. Lerner & G. B. Spanier (Eds.), *Child influences on marital and family interaction: A life-span perspective.* New York: Academic Press, 1978.

KORNER, A. F. Visual alertness in neonates: Individual differences and their correlates. *Perceptual and Motor Skills, 1970, 31,* 67–78.

KORNER, A. F. The effect of the state, level of arousal, sex and ontogenetic stage on the caregiver. In M. Lewis & L. A. Rosenblum (Eds.), *The effect of the infant on its caregiver.* New York: John Wiley, 1974.

KORNER, A. Mother-child interaction. In W. Sze (Ed.), *Human life cycle.* New York: Jason Aronson, 1975.

KORNER, A. F., & THOMAN, E. B. The relative efficacy of contact and vestibular proprioceptive stimulation in soothing neonates. *Child Development, 1972, 43,* 443–453.

KRAMER, S. In R. Prall (Reporter), The role of the father in the preoedipal years. *Journal of the American Psychoanalytic Association, 1978, 26,* 143–161.

LAMB, M. E. The role of the father: An overview. In M. E. Lamb (Ed.), *The role of the father in child development.* New York: John Wiley, 1976a.

LAMB, M. E. Interaction between eight-month-old children and their fathers and mothers. In M. E. Lamb (Ed.), *The role of the father in child development.* New York: John Wiley, 1976b.

LAMB, M. E. A reexamination of the infant social world. *Human Development, 1977a, 20,* 65–85.

LAMB, M. E. The development of mother-infant and father-infant attachments in the second year of life. *Developmental Psychology, 1977b, 13,* 637–648.

LAMB, M. E. The development of parental preferences in the first two years of life. *Sex Roles, 1977c, 3,* 495–497.

LAMB, M. E. Influence of the child on marital quality and family interaction during the prenatal, perinatal and infancy periods. In R. M. Lerner & G. B. Spanier (Eds.), *Child influences on marital*

and family interaction: A life-span perspective. New York: Academic Press, 1978a.

LAMB, M. E. Psychosocial development: A theoretical overview and a look into the future. In M. E. Lamb (Ed.), *Social and personality development.* New York: Holt, Rinehart & Winston, 1978b.

LANDRETH, C., GARDNER, G. M., ECKHARDT, B. C., & PRUGH, A. D. Teacher-child contacts in nursery school. *Journal of Experimental Education, 1943, 12,* 65–91.

LEIFER, A. D., LEIDERMAN, D. H., BARNETT, C. R., & WILLIAMS, J. A. Effects of a mother-infant separation on maternal attachment behavior. *Child Development, 1972, 43,* 1203–1218.

LEMASTERS, E. Parenthood as crisis. *Marriage and Family Living, 1957, 19,* 352–355.

LERNER, D. Effects of the nursing mother-infant dyad on my family. *American Journal of Orthopsychiatry, 1979, 49,* 339–348.

LERNER, R. M., & SPANIER, G. B. A dynamic interactional view of child and family development. In R. M. Lerner & G. B. Spanier (Eds.), *Child influences on marital and family interaction: A life-span perspective.* New York: Academic Press, 1978.

LEVY, D. M. *Behavioral analysis: Analysis of clinical observations of behavior as applied to mother-newborn relationship.* Springfield, Ill.: Charles C Thomas, 1958.

LEWIS, M. State as an infant-environment interaction: An analysis of mother-infant behavior as a function of sex. *Merrill-Palmer Quarterly, 1972, 18,* 95–121.

LEWIS, M., & FEIRING, C. The child's social world. In R. M. Lerner & G. B. Spanier (Eds.), *Child influences on marital and family interaction: A life-span perspective.* New York: Academic Press, 1978.

LEWIS, M., & LEE-PAINTER, S. An interactional approach to the mother-infant dyad. In M. Lewis & L. Rosenblum (Eds.), *The effect of the infant on its caregiver.* New York: John Wiley, 1974.

LEWIS, M., & WEINTRAUB, M. Sex of parent × sex of child: Socioemotional development. In R. Friedman, R. Richart, & R. Vande Wiele (Eds.), *Sex differences in behavior.* New York: John Wiley, 1974.

LIDZ, T. *The person: His development throughout the life cycle.* New York: Basic Books, 1968.

LIEBENBERG, B. Expectant fathers. In P. M. Shereshefsky & L. J. Yarrow (Eds.), *Psychological aspects of a first pregnancy and early postnatal adaptation.* New York: Raven Press, 1973.

MACCOBY, E. E., & MASTERS, J. C. Attachment and dependency. In P. H. Mussen (Ed.), *Carmichael's manual of child psychology.* New York: John Wiley, 1970.

MADSEN, W. *The Mexican Americans of South Texas.* New York: Holt, Rinehart & Winston, 1973.

MAHLER, M., PINE, F., & BERGMAN, A. The mother's reaction to her toddler's drive for individuation. In E. J. Anthony & T. Benedek (Eds.), *Parenthood.* Boston: Little, Brown, 1970.

MEAD, M. *Sex and temperament in three primitive societies.* New York: Mentor, 1950. (Originally published, 1935)

MEAD, M. *Culture and commitment: A study of the generation gap.* Garden City, N.Y.: Doubleday, 1970.

MEAD, M., & NEWTON, N. Cultural patterning of perinatal behavior. In S. A. Richardson & A. F. Guttmacher (Eds.), *Childbearing: Its social and psychological aspects.* Baltimore, Md.: Williams & Wilkins, 1967.

MEITES, J. Control of mammary growth and lactation. In L. Martini & W. F. Ganong (Eds.), *Neuroendocrinology* (Vol. 1). New York: Academic Press, 1966.

MICHELSON, K., VUORENKOSKI, V., PARTANEN, T., VALANNE, E., & WASZ-HOCKERT, O. [Identification of the baby's preverbal communication] (Translated by Division of Research Services, National Institute of Mental Health). *Finsk Lakaresellsk Handl, 1965, 109,* 43–47.

MILLAR, S. *The psychology of play.* Baltimore, Md.: Penguin Books, 1968.

MILOWE, I., & LOURIE, R. The child's role in the battered child syndrome. *Society for Pediatric Research, 1964, 65,* 1079–1081.

MINTON, C., KAGAN, J., & LEVINE, J. A. Maternal control and obedience in the two-year-old. *Child Development, 1971, 42,* 1873–1894.

MITCHELL, G., & SCHROERS, L. Birth order and parent experience in monkeys and in man. In H. W. Reese (Ed.), *Advances in child development behavior* (Vol. 8). New York: Academic Press, 1973.

MONEY, J., & EHRHARDT, A. *Man and women, boy and girl.* Baltimore, Md.: Johns Hopkins University Press, 1972.

MORRIS, D. The psychological management of handicapped children in the first part of life. In J. C. Howelles (Ed.), *Modern perspectives in psycho-obstetrics*. New York: Brunner/Mazel, 1972.

MOSS, H. A. Sex, age, and state as determinants of mother-infant interaction. *Merrill-Palmer Quarterly*, 1967, *13*, 19–36.

MOSS, H. A. Communication in a mother-infant interaction. In L. Kramer, P. Pliner, & T. Alloway (Eds.), *Non-verbal communication: Comparative aspects*. New York: Plenum Press, 1974.

MOSS, H. A., & ROBSON, K. S. The role of protest behavior in the development of the mother-infant attachment. In J. L. Gewirtz (Chm.), *Attachment behaviors in humans and animals*. Symposium presented at the meeting of the American Psychological Association, San Francisco, September 1968.

MULLER, E., HOLLIEN, H., & MURRY, T. Perceptual responses to infant crying: Identification of any types. *Journal of Child Language*, 1974, *1*, 89–95.

MURRAY, A. Infant crying as an elicitor of parental behavior: An examination of two models. *Psychological Bulletin*, 1979, *86*, 191–215.

MURRELL, S., & STACHOWIAK, J. The family group: Development, structure and theory. *Journal of Marriage and the Family*, 1965, *27*, 13–18.

NEWTON, N. *Maternal emotions*. New York: Hoeber, 1955.

NEWTON, N., & NEWTON, M. Psychologic aspects of lactation. *New England Journal of Medicine*, 1967, *277*, 1179–1188.

NUNN, L. Child-control through a coalition with god. *Child Development*, 1964, *35*, 417–432.

NYE, I., CARLSON, J., & GARRETT, G. Family size, interaction, affect and stress. *Journal of Marriage and the Family*, 1970, *32*, 216–226.

OLLEY, G. *Mother-infant interactions during feeding*. Paper presented at the biennial meeting of the Society for Research in Child Development, Philadelphia, March 1973.

OSOFSKY, J. D. Children's influences upon parental behavior. An attempt to define the relationship utilizing laboratory tasks. *Genetic Psychology Monographs*, 1971, *83*, 147–169.

OSOFSKY, J. D., & DANZGER, B. *Relationship between neonatal characteristics and mother-infant interaction*. Paper presented at the biennial meeting of the Society for Research in Child Development, Philadelphia, March 1973.

OSOFSKY, J. D., & O'CONNELL, E. J. Parent-child interaction. Daughters' effects upon mothers' and fathers' behaviors. *Developmental Psychology*, 1972, *7*, 157–168.

OSTWALD, P. *Soundmaking: The acoustic communication of emotion*. Springfield, Ill.: Chas. C Thomas, 1963.

OSTWALD, P. *The semiotics of human sounds*. The Hague: Mouton, 1973.

O'TOOLE, R., & DUBIN, R. Baby feeding and body sway: An experiment in George Herbert Mead's "Taking the role of the mother." *Journal of Personality and Social Psychology*, 1968, *10*, 59–65.

PARENS, H. (Reporter). Parenthood as a developmental mode. In Panel Reports. *Journal of the American Psychoanalytic Association*, 1975, *23*, 154–165.

PARKE, R. D., & O'LEARY, S. Father-mother-infant interaction in the newborn period. Some findings, some observations and some unresolved issues. In K. F. Riegel & J. Meacham (Eds.), *The developing individual in a changing world* (Vol. 2). Social and environmental issues. The Hague: Mouton, 1975.

PARMALEE, A. H., JR. Development states in infants. In C. Clemente, D. Purpura, & F. Mayor (Eds.), *Maturation of brain mechanisms related to sleep behavior*. New York: Academic Press, 1972.

PARSONS, T., & BALES, R. *Family socialization and interaction process*. New York: Free Press, 1955.

PEARLIN, L., & KOHN, M. Social class, occupation and parental values: A cross-national study. *American Sociological Review*, 1966, *31*, 466–479.

PEIPER, A. *Cerebral functioning in infancy and childhood*. New York: Consultant's Bureau, 1963.

PERRY, J., & STERN, D. Gaze duration frequency distributions during mother-infant interaction. *Journal of Genetic Psychology*, 1976, *129*, 45–55.

PETERSON, G., MEHL, L., & LEIDERMAN, P. The role of some birth related variables in father attachment. *American Journal of Orthopsychiatry*, 1979, *49*, 330–338.

PETRE-QUADENS, O. Sleep in pregnancy: Evidence of fetal sleep characteristics. *Journal of Neurological Science*, 1967, *4*, 600–605.

PHILIP, J. R. Syntax and vocabulary of mother's speech to young children: Age and sex comparisons. *Child Development*, 1973, *44*, 182–185.

PINES, D. Pregnancy and motherhood: Interaction between fantasy and reality. *British Journal of Medical Psychology*, 1972, *45*, 333–343.

PITT, B. Atypical depression following childbirth. *British Journal of Psychiatry*, 1968, *114*, 1325.

POWELL, K. Family variables. In F. Nye & L. Hoffman (Eds.), *The employed mother in America*. Skokie, Ill.: Rand McNally, 1963.

PRALL, R. (Reporter). The role of the father in the preoedipal years. *Journal of the American Psychoanalytic Association*, 1978, *26*, 143–161.

PRECHTL, H.F.R. The mother-child interaction in babies with minimal brain dysfunction. In B. M. Foss (Ed.), *Determinants of infant behavior* (Vol. 2). New York: John Wiley, 1963.

RACHMAN, A. W. *Identity group psychotherapy with adolescents*. Springfield, Ill.: Charles C Thomas, 1975.

RANGELL, L. The role of the parent in the Oedipus complex. *Bulletin of the Menninger Clinic*, 1955, *19*, 9–15.

RANGELL, L. The return of the repressed "Oedipus." In E. J. Anthony & T. Benedek (Eds.), *Parenthood*. Boston: Little, Brown, 1970.

REBELSKY, F., & HANKS, C. Father's verbal interaction with infants in the first three months of life. *Child Development*, 1971, *42*, 63–67.

RHEINGOLD, H. L. The effects of environmental stimulation upon social and exploration of behavior in the human infant. In B. M. Foss (Ed.), *Determinants of infant behavior* (Vol. 1). New York: John Wiley, 1961.

RHEINGOLD, H. L. The development of social behavior in the human infant. In H. W. Stevenson (Ed.), Concept of development: A report of a conference commemorating the 40th anniversary of the Institute of Child Development, University of Minnesota. *Monographs of the Society for Research in Child Development*, 1966, *31*(Whole No. 107).

RHEINGOLD, H. L. The social and socializing infant. In D. A. Goslin (Ed.), *Handbook of socialization theory and research*. Skokie, Ill.: Rand McNally, 1969.

RICHARDS, M. P. First steps in becoming social. In M. D. Richards (Ed.), The integration of a child into a social world. Cambridge, England: Cambridge University Press, 1974.

ROBSON, K. S., & MOSS, H. A. Patterns and determinants of maternal attachment. *Journal of Pediatrics*, 1970, *77*, 976–985.

ROLLINS, B. C., & GALLIGAN, R. The developing child and marital satisfaction of parents. In R. M. Lerner & G. B. Spanier (Eds.), *Child influences on marital and family interaction. A life-span perspective*. New York: Academic Press, 1978.

ROSENBLATT, P. C. Behavior in public places: Comparison of couples accompanied and unaccompanied by children. *Journal of Marriage and the Family*, 1974, *36*, 750–755.

ROSS, J. The development of paternal identity: A critical review of the interactions and nurturance and generativity in boys and men. *Journal of the American Psychoanalytic Association*, 1975, *23*, 783–822.

ROSS, J. Toward fatherhood: The epigenesis of paternal identity during a baby's first decade. *International Journal of Psychoanalysis*, 1977, *58*, 327–347.

ROSSI, A. Transition to parenthood. In W. Sze (Ed.), *Human life cycle*. New York: Jason Aronson, 1975.

ROTHBART, M. K., & MACCOBY, E. E. Parents' differential reactions to sons and daughters. *Journal of Personality and Social Psychology*, 1966, *3*, 237–243.

RUBIN, J. Z., PROVENZANO, F. J., & LURIA, Z. The eye of the beholder: Parents' views on sex of newborns. *American Journal of Orthopsychiatry*, 1974, *44*, 512–519.

RYDER, R. G., KAFKA, J. S., & OLSON, D. H. Separating and joining influences in courtship and early marriage. *American Journal of Orthopsychiatry*, 1971, *41*, 450–467.

SALISBURY, R. *From stone to steel*. New York: Cambridge University Press, 1962.

SANDER, L. W. Issues in early mother-child interaction. *Journal of the American Academy of Child Psychiatry*, 1962, *1*, 141–166.

SCHAIE, K. W. A general model for the study of developmental problems. *Psychological Bulletin*, 1965, *64*, 92–107.

SCHULMAN, R. E., SHOEMAKER, D. J., & MOELIS, I. Laboratory measurement of parental behavior. *Journal of Consulting Psychology*, 1962, *26*, 109–114.

SEARS, R. R., MACCOBY, E. E., & LEVIN, H. *Patterns of child rearing.* Evanston, Ill.: Rows, Peterson, 1957.

SERBIN, L. H., O'LEARY, K. D., KENT, R. N., & TONICK, I. J. A comparison of teacher responsibilities to the preacademic and problem behavior of boys and girls. *Child Development,* 1973, *44,* 796–804.

SHAVER, B. A. Maternal personality and early adaptation as related to infantile colic. In P. M. Shereshefsky & L. J. Yarrow (Ed.), *Psychological aspects of a first pregnancy and early postnatal adaptations.* New York: Raven Press, 1973.

SHERESHEFSKY, P. The child bearing experience. *Journal of the Otto Rank Association,* 1969, *4,* 88–116.

SHERESHEFSKY, P. M., LIEBENBERG, B., & LOCKMAN, R. F. Maternal adaptation. In P. M. Shereshefsky & L. J. Yarrow (Eds.), *Psychological aspects of a first pregnancy and early postnatal adaptation.* New York: Raven Press, 1973.

SHERESHEFSKY, P. M., & YARROW, L. J. (Eds.). *Psychological aspects of a first pregnancy and early postnatal adaptation.* New York: Raven Press, 1973.

SIEFFERT, A. Parents' initial reactions to having a mentally retarded child: A concept and model for social workers. *Clinical Social Worker Journal,* 1978, *6,* 33–43.

SIEGEL, G. M. Adult verbal behavior with retarded children labeled as high or low in verbal ability. *American Journal of Mental Deficiency,* 1963, *68,* 417–424.

SINGER, J. E., WESTPHAL, M., & NISWANDER, K. Relationship of weight gain during pregnancy to birth weight and infant growth and development in the first year of life. *Obstetrics and Gynecology,* 1968, *31,* 417–423.

SLOBIN, D. I. Imitation and grammatical development in children. In N. S. Endler, L. R. Boulter, & H. Osser (Eds.). *Contemporary issues on developmental psychology.* New York: Holt, Rinehart & Winston, 1968.

SNOW, C. Mothers speech to children. Learning language. *Child Development,* 1972, *43,* 549–565.

STEELE, B. F. Parent abuse of infants and small children. In E. J. Anthony & T. Benedek (Eds.), *Parenthood.* Boston: Little, Brown, 1970.

STERN, D. A micro analysis of mother-infant interaction: Behaviors regulating social contact between a mother and her 3½ month-old twins. *Journal of the American Academy of Child Psychiatry,* 1971, *10,* 501–517.

STERN, D. Mother and infant at play: The dyadic interaction involving social, vocal, and gaze behaviors. In M. Lewis & G. L. Rosenblum (Eds.), *The effect of the infant on its caregiver.* New York: John Wiley, 1974.

STERN, D. *The first relationship: Infant and mother.* Cambridge, Mass.: Harvard University Press, 1977.

STERN, D., JAFFE, J., BEEBE, B., & BENNETT, S. Vocalizing in unison and in alternation: Two modes of communication within the mother-infant dyad. *Annals of the New York Academy of Sciences,* 1975, *263,* 89–100.

STEVENS, A. G. Attachment behavior, separation anxiety and stranger anxiety. In H. R. Schaffer (Ed.), *The origins of human social relationships.* London: Academic Press, 1971.

STONE, L., SMITH, H., & MURPHY, L. (Eds.). The competent infant. New York: Basic Books, 1973.

STREIB, G. F. Intergenerational relations: Perspectives of the two generations on the older parent. *Journal of Marriage and the Family,* 1965, *27,* 469–476.

SZE, W. (Ed.). *Human life cycle.* New York: Jason Aronson, 1975.

THOMAN, E. B., BECKER, P. T., & FREESE, M. P. Individual patterns of mother-infant interaction. In G. P. Sackett (Ed.), *Observing behavior.* Baltimore, Md.: University Park Press, 1978.

THOMAN, E. B., LEIDERMAN, P. H., & OLSON, J. R. Neonate-mother interaction during breast feeding. *Developmental Psychology,* 1972, *6,* 110–118.

THOMAS, A., CHESS, S., & BIRCH, H. *Temperament and behavior disorders in children.* New York: New York University Press, 1968.

THOMAS, A., CHESS, S., & BIRCH, H. G. The origin of personality. *Scientific American,* 1970, *223,* 102–109.

THOMAS, A., CHESS, S., BIRCH, H. G., HERTZIG, M., & KORN, S. *Behavioral individuality in early childhood.* New York: New York University Press, 1963.

TRETHOWAN, W. H. The couvade syndrome. In J. C. Howells (Ed.), *Modern perspectives in psycho-obstetrics.* New York: Brunner/Mazel, 1972.

TRETHOWAN, W. H., & DICKENS, G. Cravings, aversion and pica of pregnancy. In J. G. Howells (Ed.), *Modern perspectives in psycho-obstetrics.* New York: Brunner/Mazel, 1972.

VALANNE, E. H., VUORENKOSKI, V., PARTANEN, T. J., LIND, J., & WASZ-HOCKERT, O. The ability of human mothers to identify hunger by signals of their own new-born infants during the lying in period. *Experientia,* 1967, *23,* 1–4.

VAN DEN BERGHE, P. *Age and sex in human societies, a biosocial perspective.* Belmont, Calif.: Wadsworth, 1973.

VUORENKOSKI, V., WASZ-HOCKERT, O., KOIVISTO, E., & LIND, J. The effects of cry stimulus on the temperature of the lactating breast of primipara: A thermographic study. *Experientia,* 1969, *25,* 1286–1287.

WAINWRIGHT, W. H. Fatherhood as a precipitant of mental illness. *American Journal of Psychiatry,* 1966, *123,* 40–44.

WALETSKY, L. Husbands' problems with breast feeding. *American Journal of Orthopsychiatry,* 1979, *49,* 349–352.

WASZ-HOCKERT, O., PARTANEN, T. J., VUORENKOSKI, V., VALANNE, E. H., & MICHELSON, K. Effect of training on ability to identify pre-verbal vocalizations. *Developmental Medicine and Child Neurology,* 1964, *6,* 393–396.

WEINER, P. S. Mothers' reactions to delayed language development in their children. *Exceptional children,* 1970, *36,* 277–279.

WESTON, J. The pathology of child abuse. In R. Helfer & C. Kempe (Eds.), *The battered child.* Chicago: University of Chicago Press, 1968.

WINNICOTT, D. Primary maternal preocupation. In D. Winnicott, *From pediatrics to psychoanalysis.* New York: Basic Books, 1958.

WOLFF, P. The natural history of crying and other vocalizations in early infancy. In B. Foss (Ed.), *Determinants of infant behavior* (Vol. 4). London: Methuen, 1969.

WOLFF, P. H. Mother-infant relationships at birth. In J. G. Howells (Ed.), *Modern perspectives in international psychiatry.* New York: Brunner/Mazel, 1971.

YALOM, I. D. Postpartum blues syndrome. *Archives of General Psychiatry,* 1968, *28,* 16–27.

YARROW, L. J. Research in dimensions of early maternal care. *Merrill-Palmer Quarterly,* 1963, *9,* 101–114.

YARROW, M. R., CAMPBELL, J. D., & BURTON, R. V. *Child rearing: An inquiry into research and methods.* San Francisco: Jossey-Bass, 1968.

YARROW, M. R., WAXLER, C. Z., & SCOTT, P. M. Child effects on adult behavior. *Developmental Psychology,* 1971, *5,* 300–311.

ZETZEL, E. In H. Parens (Reporter), Parenthood as a developmental phase. In Panel Reports. *Journal of the American Psychoanalytic Association,* 1975, *23,* 154–165.

ZILBACH, J. Family development. In J. Marmor (Ed.), *Modern psychoanalysis.* New York: Basic Books, 1968.

ZILBOORG, G. Depressive reactions related to parenthood. *American Journal of Psychiatry,* 1931, *10,* 927–962.

43

The World of Work

ROBERT J. HAVIGHURST

Every human society has its own ways of earning its living—of getting its food and clothing and shelter. To use a modern term, it has its own peculiar technology. This was true of the cave men and women and their society. It was true of the Hebrews of biblical times and of the Egyptians who ruled over them until they crossed the Red Sea to dwell in the Promised Land. It was true of the native Americans, whom we call Indians and Eskimos, who lived in a large number of tribes with technologies that depended on the nature of the climate, the soil, and the water in the area which they inhabited.

When we look at the European societies which sent people to live in North America between 1600 and 1900, we note that most of these people engaged in what we now call extractive technologies—agriculture, fishing, forestry, and mining. People worked with crude muscle power, a few simple tools, and some domesticated animals. However, they had developed what we call *division of labor,* which permitted some people to specialize in making clothes or shoes or furniture or weapons, while other people collected goods and transported and traded them. Others managed the religious ceremonies. Others worked out the rules for living together in families and in villages and cities and nations, thus forming governments.

We call the society which made up the United States in the nineteenth century a *preindustrial society.* The majority of families lived on the land as farmers or engaged in other extractive industries. The family members worked together, if they lived on a farm, and we speak of the family as the *unit of production.* Some townspeople worked as family units, with one or more sons learning from their fathers to be blacksmiths or carpenters or merchants.

In most of the world today—in most of Africa, Latin America, and Asia—this is still the condition of human society. By the end of the nineteenth century, the United States was becoming urbanized and industrialized. In 1910 only about one-third of men in the labor force were farmers or farm laborers.

We may date the beginning of the *industrial society* in the United States at about 1910, just before World War I. Factories and steel mills multiplied. The labor force changed rapidly, so that by 1950 half of all male workers were engaged in manufacturing or construction. The proportion of men who were farmers or farm laborers dropped to 15 percent.

The industrial society invents and uses machines which operate with mechanical energy. Coal and petroleum and natural gas are the fuels of the twentieth-century industrial society. With cheap fuel the productivity per worker rose rapidly, as did his/her real income. At the same time the profits of industrial owners rose rapidly, making the United States the most affluent of societies.

We are now in the midst of a transition to a *postindustrial society.* This is signified by the broad change in the occupational structure which is observed in Table 43–1. Today between 65 percent and 70 percent of workers are engaged in services. Daniel Bell, professor of sociology at Harvard University, predicts that by the year 2000 only 10 percent of the labor force will be in manufacturing—producing goods for the other 90 percent.

The word *services* covers many different economic activities. In earlier societies the common services were mainly domestic and household work and transportation and distribution of goods. In the postindustrial society there has been a multiplication of *human services,* such as education and health, and of *professional and technical services,* such as research and development, data processing, and communications. There is a vigorous growth in white-collar and middle-class occupations. In the postin-

Table 43-1 Occupational Distribution in the United States, 1910–1976

OCCUPATIONAL CLASS	PERCENT OF MEN						PERCENT OF WOMEN					
	1910	1930	1950	1960	1970	1976	1910	1930	1950	1960	1970	1976
Professional and technical	3.1	4.0	6.4	10.7	14.0	14.7	9.2	13.6	10.0	12.2	14.5	15.9
Managers, proprietors, and officials	7.9	9.0	12.9	13.4	14.2	14.1	1.6	2.2	5.7	5.0	4.5	5.5
Clerical	9.2[a]	12.8[a]	7.2	7.1	7.1	6.2	13.9[a]	28.8[a]	26.2	29.8	34.5	35.4
Sales			5.7	6.1	5.6	6.1			8.3	7.6	7.0	6.7
Craftsmen and foremen	14.5	16.4	17.7	18.7	20.1	20.2	1.2	0.8	1.1	1.0	1.1	1.5
Service workers, including private household workers	2.0	2.7	6.4	6.6	6.7	9.0	24.9	21.6	22.0	24.6	21.6	20.9
Farmers and farm managers	19.9	15.2	9.4	6.4	3.2	4.6[b]	3.5	2.5	1.5	0.5	0.3	1.2[b]
Farm laborers	14.0	9.5	5.3	3.5	1.9		16.4	5.4	5.5	3.9	1.5	
Operatives (semiskilled)	11.2	14.4	20.8	19.4	19.6	17.6	27.9	23.7	19.1	15.0	14.5	11.9
Nonfarm laborers (unskilled)	18.2	16.1	8.1	8.1	7.3	7.4	1.4	1.5	0.5	0.4	0.5	1.1
Number employed (millions)	29.5	37.9	42.2	44.5	49.0	51.8	7.8	10.7	17.5	22.2	29.7	34.7

[a] Clerical and Sales are combined.

[b] Farmers and farm laborers

Source: Statistical Abstract of the United States, 1976.

dustrial society education and professional training provide access to higher status and income, rather than inheritance of property.

The move from the *industrial* to the *service* base of the occupational structure is portrayed graphically in Figure 43-1, which shows the changes in proportions since 1900 in the manual-worker categories and in the white-collar categories. Most of the blue-collar workers are producing goods through manufacturing, construction, agriculture, and mining. Most of the white-collar workers are in the service occupations. The blue-collar workers and farm workers decreased from 73 percent in 1900 to 37 percent in 1977. The service and white-collar occupations increased from 27 percent to 63 percent during the same period.

The postindustrial society provides an economic base for the employment and advancement of women in the labor force. The new service economy has a growing proportion of jobs which are sought by women. Table 43-2 shows that the number of women in the labor force has increased by 60 percent between 1960 and 1975, contrasting with a 20 percent increase in the number of men in the labor force.

A PSYCHOLOGICAL PERSPECTIVE ON CAREERS

There is an interaction between values, attitudes, and careers. It seems obvious that a person with certain values will tend to select a career that fits those values. For example a person with a strong desire to help people is not likely to choose a career in a physics laboratory. Conversely a person who has been working in a certain occupation will adapt his/her values and attitudes to it or shift to a more congenial type of work.

Donald Super, in his book entitled *The Psychology of Careers* (1957), describes the progress of a person through the work and career aspect of his/her adult life. We will summarize this in the next few pages.

Work Molds Values and Attitudes

An occupation can be seen as a complex *social role,* which is a set of behaviors, skills, and attitudes which society expects of a person in that role. Lawyers, physicians, and insurance salespersons have differing social roles. Young men and women as graduate students or students in professional schools of law, business, social welfare, or medicine are learning skills, habits, and attitudes from their professors, as well as the specific knowledge and technology of the occupation.

The physical conditions of work in a hospital, a bank, or a building under construction teach people habits of work, of cooperation, and of association with fellow workers.

The social climate varies from one occupation to another. The faculty members of a college or university tend to have easy, informal, and democratic relations among deans, chairpersons, and teachers. This contrasts with the social climate of a hospital, where the physicians have a more authoritarian role. A large-city bank with several departments and a hierarchy of staff may have different dining rooms or cafeterias for clerical staff and for department heads.

Finding One's Place in the World of Work

Young people generally try themselves out in several different jobs in their early vocational history unless they have elected a professional career which involves university training. This has been called the *trial work period.* At the same time they may be newly married, and they may be adapting to life in a new and different community from the one that has been "home" to them.

There may be some *floundering* and certainly some error in the process of trial and error which may last several years. Vocational guidance in high school or college may be helpful.

Miller and Form (1951) have made a sociological

772 ROBERT J. HAVIGHURST

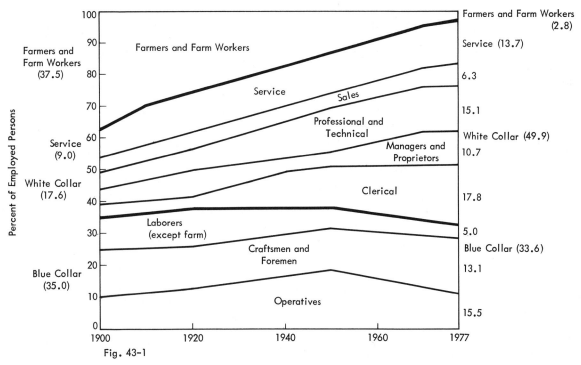

Figure 43-1 Occupational Trends in the United States (Source: U.S. Census, *Occupational Trends in the United States, 1900–1959; Manpower Report of the President, 1968; Employment and Training Report of the President, 1979.*)

analysis of career development through the life span. They see the *initial work period* beginning at about age 14 with part-time or summer work experience, usually on a marginal job. The *trial work period* follows, with entry to the regular labor market sometime between 16 and 25 and continuing with job changes until a *stable work period* comes from about 35 to 60. The *retirement period* follows sometime during the sixties.

Career Patterns of Men

Four types of career patterns were identified by Miller and Form (1951) in taking work histories from a sample of men in Ohio.

1. *The Conventional Career Pattern.* The sequence of jobs follows the typical course from initial through trial to stable em-

ployment. This is fairly typical of managerial, skilled, and clerical workers.
2. *The Stable Career Pattern.* In this category are most professional careers, many managers, some skilled, semiskilled, and clerical workers. They have gone directly from school or college into the type of work they now follow.
3. *The Unstable Career Pattern.* The sequence is trial-stable-trial. The worker may not stabilize his career. This is most frequently seen in semiskilled, clerical, and domestic workers.
4. *The Multiple-Trial Career Pattern.* This involves frequent job changes, with no one type dominant or prolonged. This is observed most frequently in domestic, clerical, and semiskilled workers.

Miller and Form (1951) found that 73 percent of white-collar workers had stable or conventional career patterns. Only 46 percent of blue-denim workers had such patterns, and only 29 percent of unskilled workers had stable histories.

The Maintenance Stage

At about age 40 to 45 the average man has established himself in a stable career, whether it be professional, managerial, clerical, sales, or the career of a blue-collar worker. He then maintains this career for some 20 years. He has acquired a family and a position or status in a local neighborhood. His is a stable existence, and he feels as successful as he will ever feel. He will still have to keep up with changes in the details of his job, but the pattern of his work is well established. His place in the community as a citizen and a family man is tied to his role as a competent worker.

For the minority of people who do not succeed in stabilizing their occupational career, this period of middle age is likely to be one of frustration. Coping with com-

Table 43-2 Civilian Labor Force, by Age and Sex

	NUMBERS OF PEOPLE IN THE LABOR FORCE		
	(MILLIONS)		
Men	1960	1975	1990
Total, 16 and over	46.4	55.6	65.2
16–24	6.9	12.2	10.7
25–44	21.3	24.2	35.1
45 and over	18.3	19.3	19.4
Women			
Total, 16 and over	23.2	37.0	48.6
16–24	4.7	10.1	10.3
25–44	9.4	15.0	24.8
45 and over	9.2	11.8	13.6

Source: Fullerton & Flaim, *Monthly Labor Review,* 99 (December 1966), 3–13; *Employment and Training Report of the President,* 1977.

munity and home expectations is difficult. A blue-collar worker may be laid off by his employer when business is slack. He may collect unemployment insurance which helps to pay the bills, but any prolonged period of unemployment undermines morale.

Adjustment to Retirement

During the middle years there are physical changes such as the loss of elasticity in the lens of the eye, making special glasses for reading necessary for some people; graying of the hair; expanding waistline; and a general slowing-down that warns the man that he will have to retire from his occupational role. He faces the possible need to make adjustments and perhaps to find a new and more interesting or appropriate job for a few years before actually leaving the labor force. He will think about finding a satisfactory substitute way of life for the next age period.

SHORTENING THE WORK LIFE

The productivity of American industry has increased greatly during the last hundred years. This greater productivity resulted from the greater use of machines fed by cheap energy (petroleum and coal) and by more efficient use of machines and labor in factories and farms. Consequently wages and salaries increased, as did profits to owners of industry.

A major result of growing productivity was the shortening of the work week and of the working life of American workers. The average number of hours in the work week was about 60 hours in 1870 and is now about 39 hours. Also there has been some reduction in the number of weeks worked in a year, due to holidays and longer vacations.

During the past century the number of days or years spent in formal schooling by the average person has increased greatly, and the amount of time spent in leisure activities during the adult life span has increased, as has the amount of time lived after retirement from work.

Some complex studies of the extent and nature of the working life for various groups of workers in the past and present have been made under the auspices of the U.S. Department of Labor. Figure 43–2 shows the results of this work as applied to men for the period since 1900. This shows the lifetime distribution of education, work, and leisure in relation to life expectancy (average length of life).

Life expectancy increased substantially between 1900 and 1950, due to prevention of contagious diseases and to a limited gain in the reduction of diseases of the heart and cardiovascular system. Consequently the period since 1950 has seen the work life made fairly stable, with projections by demographers indicating no great change for the remainder of this century.

It is clear that Figure 43–2 does not describe the actual use of time by men. They do not move from a period of full-time schooling to full-time work and on to full-time retirement; rather, they combine education, work, leisure, and retirement activities in different proportions at various periods after about the age of 16.

A similar chart for the use of time by women is more difficult to make, since most women have the role of homemaker, while a growing proportion also have the role of worker outside the home. The changing work life of women will be described in a special section of this chapter.

WORK IN THE ADULT LIFE SPAN

When we think of the 50 years from age 18 to age 68, we know at once that this age period is so complex and so long that it should be seen as a series of stages or phases

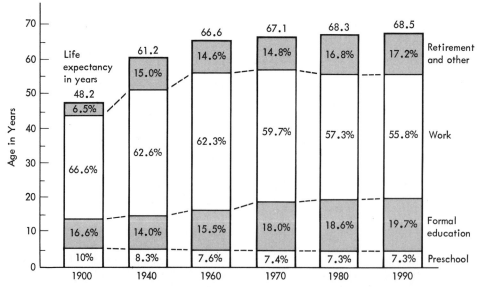

Figure **43-2** U.S. men's lifetime distribution of work, education, and leisure, 1900–1990. (Source: Fred Best and Barry Stern, "Education, Work, and Leisure—Should They Come in That Order?" *Monthly Labor Review,* July 1977, p. 4. Constructed from data cited from Howard N. Fullerton and James J. Byrne, "Length of Working Life for Men and Women, 1970." *Monthly Labor Review,* February 1976; *Projected Years of Education: Current Population Reports,* Series P-20, Nos. 243 and 293, Series P-25, No. 476; U.S. Bureau of the Census, *Life Expectancy: Statistical Abstract of the United States,* 1974.)

that present different challenges and opportunities to a person.

For each phase or stage we can identify a set of *developmental tasks*. The tasks the individual must learn—the developmental tasks of life—are those things that constitute healthy and satisfactory growth in our society. They are the things a person must learn if s/he is to be judged and to judge him/herself to be a reasonably happy and successful person. *A developmental task arises at or about a certain period in the life of the individual, successful achievement of which leads to his/her happiness and to success with later tasks, while failure leads to unhappiness in the individual, disapproval by the society, and difficulty with later tasks.*

Developmental tasks originate from forces inside and outside of the individual. Internal forces are primarily biological and are seen most clearly in the early years of human growth. The infant's legs grow larger and stronger, enabling him/her to achieve the task of walking. The child's nervous system grows more complex, enabling him/her to reason more subtly and to understand the complexities of subjects such as arithmetic. At puberty the sex glands develop rapidly and pour sex hormones into the blood stream, making the young adult more aware of his/her sexuality and more interested in the opposite sex. In the forties the human body undergoes a series of changes in the eyes, in the distribution of fat, and (for women) in the organs of reproduction, which require adjustments of various kinds.

Other tasks arise primarily from the cultural pressure of society, such as learning to read, for a child, and learning to participate as a socially responsible citizen in society, for a young adult. In contemporary society young people are expected to prepare for a career as a worker.

There is a third source of developmental tasks —namely, the personal values and aspirations of the individual, which are part of his/her personality or *self*. The personality or self emerges from the interaction of organic and environmental forces. As the self evolves it becomes increasingly a force in its own right in the subsequent development of the individual.

Thus developmental tasks may arise from physical maturation, from the pressure of the surrounding society upon the individual, from the desires, aspirations, and values of the emerging personality, and they arise in most cases from combinations of these factors acting together. During early and middle adulthood the social demands and personal aspirations dominate in setting and defining developmental tasks, with the biological changes of late middle age asserting a major force in the years after age 50.

Developmental Tasks with Major Career Involvement

The developmental tasks most directly related to career and to work will be described briefly, in the order of their appearance, commencing with adolescence.

Preparing for an Economic Career. The goal is to organize one's plans and energies in such a way as to begin an orderly career and to feel able to make a living when necessary.

During the period of adolescence in a modern urban society, there is an enforced delay between the desire for adult status and its fulfillment, and the adolescent needs somehow to become sure of his/her ability to function as an adult. Until about 1930 in the United States, boys and girls aged 15 to 20 could generally find employment and thus earn money which they could call their own. This gave them the assurance they needed that they could assert their independence of their parents if they had need to do so. As the labor force reduced its supply of unskilled jobs which juveniles could fill, however, this source of assurance was available to very few adolescents.

An alternative was to depart from the parental home, with or without money from home, and live independently for a time. This alternative seems to have been adopted by many middle-class youth in the 1960s and 1970s. For example an article appearing in the Paris edition of an American newspaper in 1971 was entitled "Hitting the Road in America" and described the phenomenon of American adolescents hitchhiking or traveling at the lowest possible cost, with sleeping bag, knapsacks, long hair, and grubby blue jeans—girls and boys alike. This was not limited to the United States. It was visible all over Europe, from southern Spain to Stockholm and Copenhagen, with Copenhagen the center of attraction in 1971. Two 16-year-old boys were interviewed as they sat by the coastal highway in southern California. They were third-year students in an upper-middle-class suburban high school on the outskirts of Chicago. "I want to learn how to function without my parents. Our parents are two thousand miles away now, and anything we do is on us. Back home, if I'm really in a jam, they'll help me out. Here, there's no such thing. I don't know if I really like that feeling, but it's good preparation."

Nevertheless it remains a fact that the great majority of young people, especially boys, in modern societies do choose an occupation and start work in it or start a formal educational preparation for it. Studies of the interests of adolescents show that occupational planning and preparation are the principal interests of boys and of many girls aged 15 to 20.

Studies made with the Strong Vocational Interest Inventory show that interests which have an occupational significance stabilize by about 16, so that guidance into a general family of occupations may safely be given at that age on the basis of an interest inventory.

Testing for vocational aptitudes shows much promise, especially for aptitudes related to clerical and mechanical work. Aptitude tests for the various kinds of professional work are not as satisfactory.

In a modern democratic society where choice and entrance to occupations are relatively free and open, the career has been the organizing center for the lives of most men and many women. A career in which a person can grow in responsibility and competence as well as income, can plan for the future, and can invest his/her time and energy with the certainty of future gain has been called by Wilensky (1961) an "orderly career." With such careers increasingly open to women, it appears that even with the possible reduction of the value placed upon work in the postindustrial societies adolescents will continue to find that getting started on an orderly career is a crucial task for them.

For middle-class youth this task is especially important. Yet there is a great deal of fumbling about, without guidance, which results in a substantial number of vocational misfits. Those who go to college are often encouraged to put off a vocational choice until they have completed two years of "general education." Yet college is definitely a vocational school for this group. The two largest vocational outlets for college graduates are business and teaching. Those who are going into teaching prepare explicitly for this occupation in college. Many of those who are going into business major in business administration or in economics in college.

For girls college is increasingly a vocational school. There are very few college girls who do not plan their college courses with half an eye to a job after college. The proportion who definitely plan on a business or professional career is increasing.

The long period of preparation required for many middle-class occupations makes this task take precedence over others for young men and women in their twenties. Thus this task may interfere with the successful performance of other developmental tasks, such as those of becoming a responsible citizen and the head of a family.

Getting Started in an Occupation.

This task takes an enormous amount of the young man's time and energy during young adulthood. Often he becomes so engrossed in this particular task that he neglects others.

This task is much more difficult for middle-class than for upper- or lower-class men. For the middle-class man success in an occupation is essential to holding his middle-class social position. He will usually subordinate all other tasks of life to this one, if it seems necessary in order to make a vocational success.

Some women find this task to conflict with the tasks of finding a mate and starting a family. This may be the major problem of early adulthood for some middle-class women.

Reaching and Maintaining Satisfactory Performance in One's Occupational Career.

During the middle adult years most men attain the highest status and income of their careers. Women do likewise, if they have been employed all their adult lives. This is a natural outcome of successful choice and application of one's energy to a productive career; but there are some interesting exceptions of people in middle adulthood who start over to fashion new careers for themselves.

There are men and women who have held more or less routine jobs and deliberately make a change in search of work that is more interesting or more rewarding to them in other ways. At present it appears that approximately 53 percent of women aged 40 to 59 are in the American labor force, many of them having sought jobs after raising a family. Also approximately 10 percent of men change the nature of their work between the ages of 40 and 60, either of their own volition or because their jobs disappear through no act of their own.

Also a number of men change their jobs because they are not physically fit for such work after a certain age. They may be professional athletes, policemen, firemen, or army officers whose work requires a level of physical skill and strength they cannot maintain. Some of them move into supervisory or executive positions in the same kind of organization, but others must find new career avenues.

Thus the career task for many people is not so much that of reaching and maintaining their peak of prestige and income as it is the task of achieving a flexible work role that is interesting, productive, and financially satisfactory.

Changes in the worker role during the middle years often require some retraining which can be obtained in public or private school systems and universities. Additionally some large employers in public service and private enterprise make provision for change of jobs with related training to serve those of their employees who wish to change or whose jobs are discontinued.

Adjusting to Retirement and Reduced Income.

Sometime between the ages of 60 and 70, the great majority of people must give up their occupation, whether they be professional or manual workers. For people to whom the job is the axis of life, this is a most difficult and unwelcome task. Others rejoice in their new "freedom" and fill the space of their lives with interesting leisure activities or with social and civic services. The goal of our society is to make the retirement process flexible enough to suit people with a variety of attitudes toward work.

There may also be a problem of living comfortably on the reduced income that comes with retirement, particularly in a period of economic inflation which reduces the purchasing power of a retirement income.

WOMEN IN THE LABOR FORCE

Much has been said and written about the "changing lives of women" during the most recent decades. Women who are marrying in the late 1970s and early 1980s are having relatively fewer children, and the consensus of researchers on women is that the average number of children born per woman in the United States during the remainder of this century will be slightly less than two and therefore not enough to replace their mothers and fathers when they grow up.[1]

Career Patterns of Women

The last 35 years have seen major changes in the labor force participation and significance of work to women. Most of the change consists of greater employment of women between the ages 20 and 65 and of married women with children. By 1975 of the female work force 58 percent were married and living with their husbands; another 19 percent were widowed, divorced, or separated from their husbands. By 1975 there were 37 million women workers, or 40 percent of the total labor force. The figures in Table 43–3 show the numbers of women workers in 1975 in comparison to the total population.

The patterns described by Mueller in 1954 are still in existence, though the proportions of women in the various patterns have changed substantially since 1950.

[1] This section draws upon the chapter entitled "Women and Education" in the book *Society and Education* (5th ed.) by Robert J. Havighurst and Daniel U. Levine. The chapter was written by Prof. Bernice L. Neugarten, a long-time colleague of Professor Havighurst.

Table 43-3 Women Workers as Percent of All Women: By Age Group, 1975

AGE	NUMBER	PERCENT OF WOMEN OF THAT AGE
18–64	34.3 million	54.3
18–19	2.4	58.1
20–24	6.1	64.1
25–34	8.5	54.6
35–44	6.5	55.8
45–54	6.7	54.6
55–64	4.2	41.0
65 Plus	1.0	8.3

Source: U.S. Department of Commerce. Bureau of the Census, *Statistical Abstract of the United States, 1976.* Table 570, page 355.

1. *The Stable Homemaking Career Pattern.* Women marry shortly after leaving school or college and devote themselves to homemaking.
2. *The Conventional Career Pattern.* Women are employed for some months or several years after leaving school or college; marriage and full-time homemaking follow this relatively brief career of work experience.
3. *Stable Working Career Pattern.* The career becomes the woman's life work. School, college, or professional school may have provided preparation for the job.
4. *The Double-Track Career Pattern.* The woman goes to work after completing her education, then marries, and continues with a double career of working and homemaking.
5. *The Interrupted Career Pattern.* The sequence is one of working, homemaking, and working while or instead of homemaking. The resumption of employment depends upon the age of children and the interests and economic needs of the woman.
6. *The Unstable Career Pattern.* This consists of alternate working and homemaking, with the amount of employment dependent upon economic needs or health. This is most frequent for women in low-income family situations.

The Work Roles of Women

Being "in the labor force" for a women means working for pay outside the home. The proportion of people in the labor force who are women has doubled in the last 50 years, from one in five members of the labor force to two in five. At present nine out of ten women are in the labor force at one or more times in their lives. As is seen in Table 43–3 there were 63 percent of all women ages 18 to 64 in the labor force in 1975. Even women with young children are now working—over a third of all working mothers have children under the age of six.

Before World War II married women workers were nearly all in low-income families working at relatively low-paying jobs. Since that time middle-class wives are as likely to be employed as working-class wives. In 1976 there were 65 percent of women with four or more years of college employed, compared with 40 percent of women with one to three years of high school. Just as true for men, women at higher educational levels find their work intrinsically satisfying as well as economically rewarding.

Occupational Status of Women

Table 43–4 shows how the proportions of women have changed in the various occupational categories since 1950. Increasing proportions of women are found in professional-technical, managerial-administrative, clerical, and service occupations other than private household services. The largest proportions of women in professional and managerial occupations, as seen in Table 43–5, continue to work in lower-paying jobs, such as registered nurses or elementary or secondary school teachers, but there have been significant increases of women in occupations such as lawyers, accountants, physicians, bankers, and college teachers.

Comparison of Earnings

It is well known that women get lower pay than do men for similar jobs. According to the Bureau of Labor Statistics, in 1977 women in professional and technical occupations earned 73 percent of men's earnings in those occupations, but in sales work, their earnings were 45 percent of the earnings of men.

Some antidiscrimination legislation has been passed by Congress recently to improve the economic status of women workers. The Equal Pay Act of 1963 provides that employers may not discriminate in salaries on the basis of sex where equal skill, effort, and responsibility are required. In the Civil Rights Act of 1964, Title VII prohibits discrimination in employment on the basis of sex. Title IX of the Education Amendments of 1972 forbids sex discrimination in employment on any education activity receiving federal government assistance.

Table 43-4 Occupational Distribution of Employed Women (Percent Distribution)

OCCUPATION GROUP	1950	1970	1976	WOMEN AS PERCENT OF ALL WORKERS IN OCCUPATION GROUP, 1976
Total	100	100	100	40
Professional–technical	13	15	16	42
Managerial–administrative	4	5	6	21
Sales	9	7	7	43
Clerical	28	35	35	79
Craft	1.5	1	2	5
Operatives including transport	20	15	12	31
Nonfarm laborers	0.8	0.5	1	9
Service, except private household	12	17	18	58
Private household	9	5	3	97
Farm	4	2	1	16

Source: Adapted from *U.S. Working Women: A Databook,* 1977, Table 7, U.S. Bureau of Labor Statistics.

Table 43-5 Women in Professional and Managerial Occupations

OCCUPATION	WOMEN: PERCENT OF ALL WORKERS IN OCCUPATION		
	1950	1970	1976
Accountants	15	25	27
Engineers	1	2	2
Lawyers–judges	4	5	9
Physicians–osteopaths	7	9	13
Registered nurses	98	97	97
School teachers	75	70	71
College faculty	23	28	31
Technicians	21	15	14
Bank officials–financial managers	12	18	25
Food service managers	27	34	35
Sales managers–department heads; retail trade	25	24	35

Source: Adapted from *U.S. Working Women: A Databook,* 1977, Table 8, U.S. Bureau of Labor Statistics.

Women Employed in Education

It is well known that elementary and secondary school teaching offer opportunities especially to women. In 1974 women were 83 percent of elementary school teachers, and 46 percent of teachers in secondary schools. As Table 43–6 indicates the administrative positions in the field of education went mainly to men. In the field of higher education, women made up 18 percent of the faculty of colleges and universities in 1970, but they have been gaining in relative numbers and status during the 1970s. They occupy about 16 percent of faculty positions with tenure, about 16 percent of associate professorships, and about 8 percent of full professorships.

Expanding Professional Opportunities for Women

Women have been moving increasingly into fields that have traditionally belonged to men. The number of

Table 43-6 Full-Time Employees in Public Elementary and Secondary Education, 1974

	MEN	WOMEN
Administrators	3	.2
Principals	5	.4
Assistant principals	2	.3
Elementary teachers	13	37
Secondary teachers	39	18
Other teachers	3	4
Other professionals	6	7
Teachers aides	.8	9
Technicians	.5	.4
Clerical/secretarial	.4	9
Service workers	21	14
Skilled craft	4	.2
Laborers	2	.5
Total percent	100	100
Total number	1,230,914	2,220,967

Source: Adapted from Equal Employment Opportunity Commission, 1976, Table 6, "Job Patterns of Minorities and Women in Public Elementary and Secondary Schools." Research Report No. 51. U.S. Govt. Printing Office.

women studying engineering has multiplied by four during the 1970s with women in 1977 constituting 9 percent of first-year engineering enrollment. In 1975 laws were passed to permit women to be appointed to Army, Navy, and Air Force Academies. Law schools and medical schools admit women more readily. Women's enrollment in law schools increased from 8 percent in 1971 to 27 percent in 1978. In medical schools the increase was from 10 percent to 26 percent.

Some 35 associations of professional workers have established committees to examine the special problems of women in their respective fields. They aim to eliminate dual standards of admission and quota systems. The Carnegie Commission on Higher Education, in its report on *Opportunities for Women in Higher Education* (1973), makes the following broad statement:

The second most fundamental revolution in the affairs of mankind on earth is now occurring. The first came when man settled down from hunting, fishing, herding, and gathering to sedentary agricultural and village life. The second is now occurring as women, no longer so concentrated on and sheltered for their childbearing and childrearing functions, are demanding equality of treatment in all aspects of life, are demanding a new sense of purpose. (p. iii)

ATTITUDES TOWARD WORK

The psychological significance or the meaning of work in the life of the individual is best understood by exploring two different questions. One is the very specific question of the individual's attitudes toward his/her current job. What does s/he like and what does s/he dislike about this job? How could the job become more satisfactory to him/her? The other question is the broad concept of the *meaning* of work in his/her life, not just this month or this year, but throughout his/her adult years. Here it is the *career*, rather than the *job*, which is the target of concern.

Work Satisfaction

The widely held "common man view" of the growing-up process in America sees the secondary school providing for the cognitive and social-civic development of youth, with various forms of work experience—summer, after school, or full-time work at age 16 or thereabouts—giving experience that leads into the roles of worker and citizen. As secondary school and college came to fill up more of the time of more young people, some persons interested in youth development called for more work experience. The report of a White House Advisory Panel on Youth, entitled *Youth: Transition to Adulthood,* directed and edited by Coleman (1974) proposed that the American public secondary school provides too narrow and age-limited a social environment to be adequate as a maturing educational experience for youth after the age of 15. They call for a kind of experience in the world of work and adult service which they argue will help young people develop skills and attitudes that are needed for competent participation in the adult roles of worker and citizen. They suggest that participation in the adult work world is valuable and should be encouraged by work-study programs and internship activities. They also favor the expansion of Youth Service Corps programs, which enable young people to interact with and to serve people of all ages and social classes.

A special issue of the journal *School Review* printed a number of essays on the *Youth: Transition to Adulthood* report. Some were favorable, and some were quite critical. Among the latter was a direct attack written by Behn, Carnoy, Carter, Crain, and Levin (1974), members of the Stanford University Center for Economic Studies, entitled "School is Bad! Work is Worse." They espoused what is generally called the Neo-Marxist position which argues that the system of work and production in the American economy tends to make workers into conformists and willing slaves to their upper-middle-class supervisors. They say that the work environment to which young people are subject if they do go to work is inhuman, stunting their social and moral growth. Therefore it is better to keep them out of work experience unless and until a different economic order produces a different work role that will encourage greater freedom, initiative, and life satisfaction.

They conclude their critique as follows:

The desirable portrait of youth that has been painted in the report cannot be achieved in a society which alienates worker from worker and worker from his product. Young people apparently understand this better than the authors of the report, for the rise of the present youth culture is in part a reaction to a hierarchical, dehumanized adult world. We suggest that, rather than deemphasize the youth culture by an earlier incorporation of youth into the adult world, we should humanize and democratize the workplace and the institutions which prepare people for work. (Behn et al., 1974, pp. 66–67)

In the course of their critique, Behn et al. argue that the schools tend to reinforce the class structure.

For example, school environments tend to differ according to the social class origins of students so that students from lower-class families are inculcated with the traits requisite for being workers while children from more lofty class backgrounds are socialized to be managers and professionals.... The lower-class school and curricula are characterized by a high degree of external discipline.... Decisions about each child's studies are made impersonally by counsellors with little input from the student, and alternatives are few anyway in such schools. This socialization pattern corresponds to the requirements of industry for unskilled workers who need primarily to defer to authority, respond passively to orders, accept alienation from work, and become one of the faceless multitudes at the bottom of the work hierarchy. (ibid., p. 57)

In order to subject this proposition about the nature of work in America to empirical test, we might explore the large body of social science research on the subject of work satisfaction. Quinn, Staines, and McCullough of the Survey Research Center at the University of Michigan reported in 1974 on national surveys of attitudes by people toward their work. They report that

... despite the numerous tales of blue-collar blues and white-collar woes which have cried out from the pages of the most respectable periodicals in the country during the past 15 years, the average American worker has not spent his time cursing his lot. Even groups often thought to be seething with discontent—the young, blacks, women—have felt an almost unchanging degree of satisfaction with the jobs they held during this 15-year span. Nor has dissatisfaction grown among any of these groups over the last decade. (p. 7)

Quinn et al. studied data from 15 national surveys conducted from 1958 through 1973 by the National Opinion Research Center, by ISR's Survey Research Center, by the Survey Research Center at the University of California, and by George Gallup. The seven surveys conducted by the research centers asked essentially the same single question to gauge job satisfaction: All in all, how satisfied are you with your job? The responses show that between 1962 and 1964 job satisfaction increased, particularly in workers under 30, and remained at a high level until early 1973 (Quinn et al., 1974).

In 1972 Kahn brought together the results of ten major studies of work attitudes, published between 1935 and 1967. The percentages who said they were dissatisfied with their jobs varied from 10 to 21 percent. Blauner, writing in 1960 on "Work Satisfaction and Industrial Trends in Modern Society," summarized his conclusions from six research studies as follows: "The studies of job satisfaction reviewed in this paper further question the prevailing thesis that most workers in modern society are alienated and estranged.... There is remarkable consistency in findings that the vast majority of workers, in virtually all occupations and industries, are moderately or highly satisfied, rather than dissatisfied, with their jobs" (p. 353).

The 1973 study on *Work in America,* written by a special Task Force of the U.S. Department of Health, Education and Welfare, found the quality of working life to be one of the major contemporary social issues. This book comments, "It is clear that classically alienating jobs (such as on the assembly line) that allow the worker no control over the conditions of work and that seriously affect his mental and physical functioning off the job probably comprise less than 2 percent of the jobs in America" (Upjohn Institute for Employment Research, p. 13). The authors of this book give a thoughtful and useful analysis of the difference between *extrinsic* and *intrinsic* rewards that a person may gain from his/her work. In this they give some support to the Neo-Marxist philosophy of intrinsic value in work where the worker has a certain amount of control over the schedule and organization of his/her work. The experiment of the VOLVO factory in Sweden, where a team of workers takes responsibility for planning their work in assembling an automobile, is one which sounds interesting and useful and which may have some value for American technology, but it seems probable that extrinsic rewards (money and good working conditions) will persist in modern society and that work experience will continue to be regarded as valuable for the maturing of American youth.

A Recent Decline in Job Satisfaction

The 1977 *Quality of Employment Survey* showed an appreciable drop in job satisfaction between 1973 and 1977. Responses to a number of statements about their jobs, given by workers in 1973 and in 1977, are reported in Table 43–7. The number of workers who believed their job skills would be useful and valuable five years from now declined from 68 percent in 1973 to 62 percent in 1977. Also in 1977 there were 36 percent of the respondents who reported that their skills were not fully utilized in their job, compared to 25 percent reporting underutilization in 1973.

Table 43-7 Attitudes toward the Job: 1977 versus 1973

	PERCENT AGREEING	
STATEMENT	1973	1977
Very satisfied with my job	52	47
Would prefer a different job	52	60
Job is very much like the job respondent wants	58	53
Would strongly recommend this job to a friend	64	62
Has skills that cannot be used in this job	25	36
Is overeducated for this job	28	32
Very likely will seek another job	14	16
Easy to find a job with similar income and fringe benefits	27	20
There is a shortage of workers with my experience, training, and skills	48	37

Source: Institute for Social Research: University of Michigan, 1979; Quinn & Staines, *1977 Quality of Employment Survey.*

Probably the economic recession of the 1973–1977 period was responsible for the rather general decline in job satisfaction which is seen in Table 43-7. There was a slight, but noticeable, decrease in morale among American workers, as indicated by the fact that a set of questions about life satisfaction, also asked in 1973 and 1977, showed a reduction in life satisfaction score of 8 percent.

Factors Affecting Work Satisfaction

The research on job satisfaction that has been reported in the previous pages has generally been focused on national samples of adults of all ages who are in the labor force. However it is useful to examine age differences and differences between the sexes and between races. It turns out that age of the workers and the status level of the job bring variation in attitudes toward the job. In a study of male white workers who are members of trade unions, Sheppard and Herrick (1977) found substantial age differences among men in blue-collar occupations. Dividing their men into three age groups (under 30, 30 to 55, and over 55), they found that 62 percent of the young workers rated their job as of little importance, but only 45 percent of the oldest group said that almost anyone or a good many people could do their job. Only a third of the under-30 workers said that they were satisfied with their jobs most of the time, contrasted with 64 percent of the oldest group who were satisfied most of the time. The middle-aged group was intermediate in job satisfaction.

Other age differences were

1. Thirty-eight percent of the younger workers thought very often about changing their occupations compared with 10 percent of the older workers.
2. Only 14 percent of the younger workers were so attached to their current jobs that they would not change jobs even for more money—compared to 45 percent of the oldest group.
3. The youngest group were less likely to consider their current jobs as very much like the kind they wanted when they first took them.

Another contrast between younger and older workers was the extent to which they express *authoritarian* social-civic attitudes. Of the under-30 workers, 53 percent scored in the lowest fourth on *scale of authoritarianism,* compared with only 14 percent of the oldest group. The young workers were much more antiauthoritarian.

THE MEANINGS OF WORK

We know, of course, that the job fills a large portion of the worker's time. However, the job is not only a time-filling activity. It is, more importantly, a purposeful activity which is expected of most adult males and increasing proportions of females in our society. The job, or rather the productive system of which the job is a part, orients and controls the behavior of those persons who participate in it. It sets a goal for the worker, determines the manner in which the goal may be attained and the reward offered for its achievement, and affects the whole range of his/her participation in the society of which s/he is a member. Its influence extends even beyond the actual work life of the individual. We also find that the part of his/her adult life not spent in work is, nonetheless, affected by whether or not s/he holds a job, the nature of the job s/he may hold, and the manner in which s/he performs it. In short the job in our society exerts an influence which pervades the whole of the adult life span.

Thus the job—or work activity—can be regarded as an axis along which the worker's pattern of life is organized. It serves to maintain him/her in his/her group, to regulate his/her life-activity, to fix his/her position in his/her society, and is a source of many of his/her satisfactions and affective experiences. In this sense work can be said to perform certain *functions* in the life of the individual.

Certainly we can expect that in our culture practically all workers recognize their job as a way of earning a living. However, we may also discover that many individuals have come to recognize other functions of the job as well. For example some may view it in terms of the prestige (or lack of prestige) it gives them in the community; for others it may be the chief source of contact they have with the outside world, or it may be regarded as the locus of association with friends and fellow workers. The recognitions made of the functions of work, therefore, would vary according to the individual's conception of the part which the job has played in his/her life.

The individual's interpretation of the job experience varies according to the type of evaluation s/he makes of his/her work. Around all the work functions cluster a variety of emotional experiences. From the job the worker derives such feelings as success, failure, accomplishment, frustration, good fellowship, aesthetic pleasure, and boredom. Thus work may be welcomed by him/her as a joy or dreaded as a burden.

Although we have described work as having certain functions for all workers, we find that it does not have the same meaning for all individuals. We can gather this impression merely by listening to people talk about their jobs—the insurance salesperson telling about his/her excitement in "cracking" a tough customer, the executive describing the responsibilities and worries of his/her job, the assembly-line worker complaining about the monotony of his/her job yet bragging that s/he is the best worker in the plant. Meanings vary as jobs vary and as people vary. Yet there are some common threads which run through the diversity.

In speaking of the meanings of work, then, we are speaking both of the individual's recognition of the part the job has played in his/her life and of the type of affective response s/he has made to it. It would be hard to conceive of a neutral recognition of work function without any feeling tone attached to it.

Table 43–8 presents an illustrative list of some of the meanings which the individual may assign to his/her job and shows how they may be related to the more universal functions of work.

Studying the Meanings of Work

Friedmann and Havighurst studied the positive meanings that people in several different occupations find in their work. They studied people who were past age 55 (with a few exceptions) because they were interested in the process of retirement and they wanted to find out how job satisfactions are related in the worker's mind to questions of retirement when retirement has already come or is clearly visible. They studied people in several occupational groups by interviewing samples of workers in these groups. They expected to find differences between occupations in the meanings recognized and emphasized.

Studies of Occupational Groups

In 1950 interviews were conducted with workers, nearly all of them between the ages of 55 and 80, some employed and some retired, in the following categories.

1. Men (union members) working or retired from a steel mill in the area southeast of Chicago
2. Men (union members) nearly all working in one or another of 12 mines in southern Illinois
3. Men and women (about equal numbers) of salespersons in a Chicago department store, age range 55 to 70, all employed

Table 43–8 The Relation between the Functions and Meanings of Work

WORK FUNCTION	WORK MEANING
Income	Maintaining a minimum sustenance level of existence Achieving some higher level or group standard
Expenditure of time and energy	Something to do A way of filling the day or passing time
Identification and status	Source of self-respect Way of achieving recognition or respect from others Definition of role
Association	Friendship relations Peer-group relations Subordinate-superordinate relations
Source of meaningful life experience	Gives purpose to life Creativity; self-expression New experience Service to others

Source: Friedmann & Havighurst, 1954, p. 7.

4. Skilled craftsmen in one of the printing trades, all over 65 years of age, about half of them retired, answered a questionnaire distributed by mail under union auspices
5. Physicians, all over 65 years of age, and members of the American Medical Association in Chicago or Cook County, Illinois, mostly respondents to a questionnaire, but 39 of them were interviewed.

In 1975 a questionnaire study was made of college and university administrators and of social scientists (sociologists and psychologists) who had held academic positions between the ages of 45 and 60. National samples were drawn from national directories of college presidents and deans and membership directories of the American Psychological Association and the American Sociological Association. The sample consisted of men with dates of birth between 1893 and 1903 and of women whose dates of birth were between 1893 and 1906.

One of the items of the questionnaire read as follows:

Please check the *three* statements which come closest to indicating the principal meanings that work has for you.
1. Self-respect
2. Respect of others
3. Makes the time pass
4. New and interesting experiences
5. Gives me a chance to be useful
6. Gives the money I need
7. Association with friends
8. Enables me to serve others
9. Gives a chance to be creative

Table 43–9 shows the data from the two sets of studies, in crudely comparable form. However, the format varied a great deal from one group to another with interviews and questionnaires. A strict ordering of the "meanings" according to importance to the respondent was not always attained.

A rough comparison of the several occupational groups shows the following things:

1. The workers of lower skill and socioeconomic status are more likely to see their work as having no other meaning than that of earning money.
2. The five occupational groups all value "association" about equally as a meaning of work.
3. Work as a routine which makes the time pass is recognized about equally by all five groups.
4. All groups discover self-respect and secure respect or recognition from others by means of their work, and there is probably no reliable difference among them in the prevalence of this meaning. While it seems to be highest among the skilled craftsmen, this may have resulted from the fact that the category "service to others" was not used in that particular study, and anyone to whom this meaning was especially significant may have mentioned self-respect or the respect of others which s/he obtained as a result of the service element in his/her work.
5. The physicians show a high awareness of the "service to others" meaning in their work. This may be characteristic of the "service" professions.
6. Work is important as a source of interesting, purposeful activity and as a source of intrinsic enjoyment for all groups, but there may be reliable differences between them in this respect.

Table 43-9 Meanings of Work[a]

| | CATEGORY OF WORKER (PERCENT CHOOSING) | | | | | | SOCIAL SCIENTISTS | |
MEANINGS	Steel Workers	Miners	Photo-Engravers over 65	Sales Persons	Senior Physicians	College Administrators	Male	Female
1. Income, for my needs	28	18	11	0	0	4	6	5
2. Routine: Makes time pass	28	19	15	21	15	1	1	1
3a. Brings self-respect				12	7	14	12	8
3b. Brings prestige				11	13	11	14	5
3a + 3b	16	18	24					
4. Association with fellows	15	19	20	20	19	11	10	17
5. Self-expression; new experience; creativity	13	11	30	26	15	27	39	41
6. Service to others; useful	N.D.[b]	16	N.D.	10	32	31	17	22

[a] The interview or questionnaire format varied from one group to another, making strict comparisons questionable. The data are reported in percentages within groups; assuming each respondent to have given his/her favored response.

[b] N.D. = No data

Source: Friedmann & Havighurst, 1954; Havighurst et al., 1976.

The skilled craft and white-collar groups stressed the extra-financial meanings of work to a much greater extent than did the workers in heavy industry, thus bearing out our hypothesis that these meanings of work become more and more important as we ascend the occupational and skill ladders. However it is not only the extent to which these meanings were stressed but also the patterns in which they occurred that reveal the nature of work experience.

OCCUPATIONS RELATED TO ABILITIES AND LEVEL OF FUNCTION

The various groups of occupations tend to differ not only in the nature of the work but also in the kinds of abilities that are required for success. For example the professions (law, medicine, teaching) require more abstract (verbal or cognitive) ability than do the skilled crafts or the construction industry. An attempt at judging the significance of three types of ability for occupational groups was made by Lorge and Blau (1942), with results shown in Table 43-10. The three types of ability are abstract or cognitive verbal, mechanical, and social (relating well to people).

Roe, in her book on *The Psychology of Occupations,* has classified occupations according to what she calls *level of function,* or degrees of responsibility, capacity, and skill. The concept of level of function is close to the well-known concept of socioeconomic status. It includes the level of difficulty and complexity of the decisions to be made as well as the different kinds of problems that must be resolved.

Table 43-11 presents Roe's two-way classification of occupations. The eight groups are classified according to what Roe calls *primary focus.* Thus group I (called *Service*) consists of occupations where the primary emphasis is upon person-to-person relationships. These range from psychotherapy and counseling to social work, police detectives, barbers, nurses, taxidrivers, and chambermaids. Obviously they cover the entire range of socioeconomic status.

All of the groups include a range of socioeconomic status. For example in the outdoor group, farm owners are at level 3, farm tenants at level 5, and farm laborers at level 6.

Level of education tends to be closely related to level of function in all of the groups except group VIII, *Arts and Entertainment.* Here a wide variety of talents are central, and formal education is not an essential criterion. Thus a creative artist, in sculpture or in music, is in the same broad group as an interior decorator and a driver of a racing car. They must have special talents, which may or may not require formal educational training.

FLEXIBLE CAREERS DURING MIDDLE AGE

The "typical" career that starts in early adulthood and carries through middle ages into retirement is centered in a single occupational category. A person gets the training or the work experience that enables him/her to become, for example, a lawyer, physician, teacher, banker, salesperson, secretary, factory manager, owner of a retail business, plumber, or tailor. Even the not unusual case of Dave Johnson shows a degree of stability and orderliness that enables us to call his career "typical." Aged 72 Dave

Table 43-10 Estimated Ability Requirements of Major Occupational Groups

| | RANK IN ESTIMATED ABILITY | | |
OCCUPATIONS	Abstract	Mechanical	Social
Professional	1	4	3
Managerial	2	6	2
Semiprofessional	3	2	5
Sales	4	14	1
Clerical	5	13	8
Skilled	6	1	9
Protective services	7	11	4
Agriculture, horticulture	8	5	13
Semiskilled	9	3	12
Personal service	11	9	6
Domestic service	11	8	7
Fishery	11	11	14
Building services	13	11	10.5
Unskilled	14	7	10.5

Source: Adapted from Lorge & Blau, 1942, p. 293.

Table 43–11 Two-Way Classification of Occupations

GROUP

LEVEL	I. Service	II. Business Contact	III. Organization	IV. Technology	V. Outdoor	VII. Science	VII. General Cultural	VII. Arts and Entertainment
1	Personal therapists, Social work supervisors, Counselors	Promoters	United States President and Cabinet officers, Industrial tycoons, International bankers	Inventive geniuses, Consulting or chief engineers, Ships' commanders	Consulting specialists	Research scientists, University, college faculties, Medical specialists, Museum curators	Supreme Court Justices, University, college faculties, Prophets, Scholars	Creative artists, Performers, great, Teachers, university equivalent, Museum curators
2	Social workers, Occupational therapists, Probation, truant officers (with training)	Promoters, Public relations counselors	Certified public accountants, Business and government executives, Union officials, Brokers, average	Applied scientists, Factory managers, Ships' officers, Engineers	Applied scientists, Landowners and operators, large, Landscape architects	Scientists, semi-independent, Nurses, Pharmacists, Veterinarians	Editors, Teachers, high school and elementary	Athletes, Art critics, Designers, Music arrangers
3	YMCA officials, Detectives, police sergeants, Welfare workers, City inspectors	Salesmen: auto, bond, insurance, etc., Dealers, retail and wholesale, Confidence men	Accountants, average, Employment managers, Owners, catering, dry-cleaning, etc.	Aviators, Contractors, Foremen, Radio operators	County agents, Farm owners, Forest rangers, Fish, game wardens	Technicians, medical, X-ray, museum, Weather observers, Chiropractors	Justices of the Peace, Radio announcers, Reporters, Librarians	Ad writers, Designers, Interior decorators, Showmen
4	Barbers, Chefs, Practical nurses, Policemen	Auctioneers, Buyers, House canvassers, Interviewers, poll	Cashiers, Clerks, credit, express, etc., Foremen, warehouse, Salesclerks	Blacksmiths, Electricians, Foremen, Mechanics, average	Laboratory testers, dairy products, etc., Miners, Oil well drillers	Technical assistants	Law clerks	Advertising artists, Decorators, window, etc., Photographers, Racing car drivers
5	Taxi drivers, General houseworkers, Waiters, City firemen	Peddlers	Clerks, file, stock, etc., Notaries, Runners, Typists	Bulldozer operators, Deliverymen, Smelter workers, Truck drivers	Gardeners, Farm tenants, Teamsters, cowpunchers, Miners' helpers	Veterinary hospital attendants		Illustrators, greeting cards, Showcard writers, Stagehands
6	Chambermaids, Hospital attendants, Elevator operators, Watchmen		Messenger boys	Helpers, Laborers, Wrappers, Yardmen	Dairy hands, Farm laborers, Lumberjacks	Nontechnical helpers in scientific organizations		

Source: Anne Roe, *The Psychology of Occupations* New York: John Wiley & Sons, Inc., 1956, p. 151.

has lived all his life in a north central state. He had a tenth-grade education from the public high school in the small city of 30 thousand where he grew up. His first job, at 16, was in a grocery store where he did a variety of work, arranging food stock, waiting on customers, and making deliveries in the neighborhood. He says he had no career plans. At 19 he shifted to a factory job as a "helper" to a machinist. Three years later he moved to a larger city where a brother-in-law helped him to get a job in a furniture factory. Here he was promoted as he learned the work and eventually became a foreman. He was married when he was 22 years old and has lived for the last 25 years in his own home which he values at $45,-000. He retired at the age of 64, at a time when business was slack. He keeps a productive orchard and vegetable garden on a two-acre lot which he owns on the edge of the city.

However there is a considerable group of people who have a sequence of different jobs during the age period from 40 to 60. Without a close definition of the concept of *different jobs,* we estimate that about 10 percent of men are in this category. Many of the women who enter or reenter the labor force after age 40 could be placed in this category.

Conditions that lead to this type of movement of people within the labor force are either external to the persons or individual personal factors, such as health, becoming dissatisfied with the current job, wanting to move to a more pleasant climate, and widowhood. External factors are changes in the local job market, with closing of some work-places and opening of new ones, lengthening unemployment, and the creation of new service jobs, such as computer applications and services to elderly people.

Examples of Flexible Careers

To get some idea of the nature of the job changes of people with flexible careers, one may inspect a set of three studies of men and women aged 45 to 75 who spent their middle adult years in very different settings. The people were not representative samples but were found and interviewed by researchers who wanted to get some useful general information about the phenomenon of changing jobs during the middle adult years.

The three studies may be described briefly as follows:

Urban Women—Lopata and Steinhart (1971). Interviews with 20 women in Chicago, one married and the others widowed or divorced or never married. Seventeen of them live in a retirement hotel or a Chicago Housing Authority building for the elderly.

Kansas City Blacks—Hearn (1971). Interviews with 18 men and 4 women, generally of lower-middle-class status. Twenty of the 22 live in homes they own outright or are paying for.

Migrants to the Ozarks—Oliver (1971). Thirty persons, four of them women, had migrated to the Ozark region from a city larger than 50,000 within a period of three years prior to the interviews (May, 1971). Oliver describes his study group and his research interests as follows:

While the sample is biased in terms of a greater likelihood of successful adjustment (since the resort area is the choice for retirement), it is useful in that the respondents all come from large metropolitan centers—from those decaying and densely populated settings in which there are not only major social problems, in general, but also special problems of the aged, in particular. Thus, we can ask, why does a man pack up his bags and migrate to a rural non-farm area prior to the usual age of retirement? What sort of leisure-activities does he pursue? How does his income, health, and educational background affect his adjustment? What are the attitudes of his friends toward his escape from the city? What problems are associated with early retirement, semi-retirement, or the taking up of a second career? (p. 13)

This research project is described in a general way by Murray, Powers, and Havighurst (1971) under the title "Personal and Situational Factors Producing Flexible Careers." The age range of the people studied was 45 to 70, except for the Chicago women, 14 of whom were over 70.

The number of jobs held by these people after the age of 41 is shown in Table 43-12. More than half of the respondents held three or more different jobs. The migrants to the Ozarks are a special type who want to combine leisure activities with work in ways that are interesting and that lead to a comfortable retirement.

Maximizing the Options

A sizable number of people who have held jobs that required certain sensory or muscular skills find themselves in difficulty as they move into their fifties and early sixties because their skills are decreasing due to aging of the body or to accidents. For example a person who inspects a manufactured product as it comes off the assembly line may find his/her eyesight deteriorating, or a person who must lift a heavy piece of equipment and attach other pieces to it may find that his/her back muscles or his/her thigh muscles are losing some of their strength.

Such employees might be laid off because they are losing their effectiveness. On the other hand their experience and their long association with the employer would make it desirable to keep them on in some capacity for which they are still well fitted.

Some employers ask their personnel staff to try to find jobs for such people which are well within their physical abilities. This happened at deHavilland Aircraft, Ltd., in Toronto, Canada. Dr. Leon Koyl, an industrial physi-

Table 43-12 Number of Different Jobs: Age 41 to 70. Three Samples

NUMBER OF JOBS	STUDY GROUP		
	Ozarks	Kansas City Blacks	Chicago Women
1	3	6	6
2	11	7	7
3	9	5	3
4	3	3	2
5	1	1	0
6	0	0	0
7	0	0	0
Over 7	1	0	1
Total persons	30	22	20

Source: Murray, Powers, & Havighurst, 1971, Table 3.

cian, developed a plan for studying and measuring the abilities of middle-aged workers and matching them to jobs for which their abilities were suitable. He developed a set of tests known as GULHEMP—tests of seven major functional areas.

G—General physique
U—Upper extremities
L—Lower extremities
H—Hearing
E—Eyesight
M—Mentality (intelligence)
P—Personality

A worker who felt uncomfortable in his/her current job or whose efficiency was falling off, as seen by his/her foreman or supervisor, could volunteer to take the GULHEMP tests or might be urged to do so by his/her foreman. S/he would be ranked on each of the seven GULHEMP tests, thus getting a profile showing where s/he was low, high, or average. At the same time the jobs which exist in sizable numbers each have a profile of desirable scores on the GULHEMP battery. Thus the actual profile of the worker can be compared with the desired profiles for a variety of jobs, and job profiles that are reasonably similar to his/her profile can be identified. Possible shifts to one or another of these jobs can be discussed with him/her.

The National Council on the Aging, collaborating with Dr. Koyl, set up the Industrial Health Counselling Service and secured funds from the U.S. Department of Labor to try out this method in the Portland (Maine) metropolitan area. More than 100 firms in the Portland area participated (private and public, including the Post Office). From 1971 to 1974 more than 2400 persons were examined and GULHEMP profiles completed. These people varied over the entire adult age range. Some of them were referred by their employers. Others were clients of the Maine State Employment Service and were seeking jobs.

Approximately 51 percent of the examinees were placed in jobs, and almost half of this group were over 40 years of age. Three large employers, after more than a year's experience, compared workers screened and placed through the project with similar workers not examined with GULHEMP. There was substantially less "sick leave" time among the GULHEMP group.

We may conclude that this technique tends to shift the emphasis of employers from chronological to functional age and thus can assist middle-aged and older workers to get and keep the jobs for which they are well-fitted. (Batten, 1973; Koyl, 1974; Quirk & Skinner, 1973).

Flexible Retirement

There are several forces or trends in the contemporary society that tend to favor greater flexibility in the working life of people beyond the age of 50. One of these is the desire of some people to change the nature of their job assignments as they grow older. This may come from biological changes in strength and sensory acuity that reduce their fitness for certain types of work. It may also come from changes in interests and in the personal situations of men and women as they grow older. Another is the fact that certain jobs are decreasing and others are increasing in numbers in the working force, thus reducing or increasing the need for workers in those particular jobs.

Another factor is the need for income to supplement Social Security and pension income in a period of inflation or increasing cost of living. This affects the desire of people to retire, take part-time work, or continue with full-time employment.

The most desirable situation is one which *maximizes the options* of people past 50, with respect to employment.

In this treatment of the participation of older people in the labor force, we will deliberately set aside the major social problem of unemployment in the 1970s and the 1980s, a problem especially of young adults due to the relatively large numbers of births in the 1950–1965 period which now crowd the entrance to the labor force. In spite of the broad social problem of unemployment, there are needs and opportunities for employment of older people in rather special and limited categories that do not conflict with the need of young people for more employment.

Conditions Facilitating Work and Employment of Older People. There has been a growing need for services that are socially valuable but are not appropriate for young adults who are seeking stable careers. The federal government has funded such programs through the Comprehensive Employment and Training Act (CETA), the Older Americans Act, and the Action Agency. Examples are *Foster Grandparents, Senior Companions,* and the Older Americans Community Service Employment Act, which provided $42 million for use in fiscal year 1975. Federal government funds for these purposes were reduced under the Reagan administration in 1981.

There is the growing field of services for the elderly which involves the staffing of senior centers and the provision of home-care services to assist older people to live independently in their own homes. Those jobs pay at relatively low rates and are not likely to attract college graduates. Also there will certainly be a growing number of professional jobs in the field of services for the elderly—jobs as directors of senior centers, counselors, administrators of homes for the aged, and administrators of nursing homes. These are generally full-time jobs, and many of them may be second-career jobs for people, themselves past 50, who become interested in this kind of service.

Part-Time Employment Combined with Partial Pension. People past 55 or 60 who have pension rights which do not yield enough to live on may need part-time employment to supplement their income. The average Social Security benefit is not enough to place a married couple above the poverty level, and a good many private pension plans pay relatively low benefits to many pensioners. For people in this situation, a part-time job extending past age 65 and even past 70 may be a good solution. Furthermore a good many people would prefer to go on working on a part-time basis until they are 70 or over.

A combination of pension income with part-time employment has attracted favorable attention, partly because of its economic value to some people and partly because it would support and strengthen the movement toward extensive part-time employment for people in their sixties.

The Swedish Partial-Pension Plan is attracting attention in this connection. The Swedish Parliament in 1975 adopted this plan to facilitate the transition from active work life to full retirement during the decade from age 60 to age 70. All Swedish people are eligible for the national old-age pension at age 65, this pension being approximately 65 percent of the average annual earned income during the 15 best years before retirement. The new Partial-Pension plan permits a worker between 60 and 65 to take a job with 17 to 35 hours of work a week and to draw a partial pension which will bring him/her up to 85 or 90 percent of the average full-income earnings. Furthermore the part-time work can be continued until age 70, with total income at about this same level and with some credits that will increase his/her full pension at the age of 70. In the first two years of this plan, approximately 20 percent of workers between 60 and 65 chose the partial pension by taking part-time work.

Work in the Year 2000

We began this chapter with a description of three periods of American industrial history—the preindustrial, the industrial, and the postindustrial. The change from industrial to postindustrial is now in full swing, with changing occupational structure and changing life styles.

If we attempt to look ahead as much as 20 years we must devote attention to the cost of energy and its effects on the work life. Between 1900 and 1970 the technology of the United States was based on cheap energy, coming mainly from petroleum. It was an energy-intensive technology, with relatively high wages, salaries, and profits. Then came the rise in the cost of petroleum and petroleum products. This doubled during the 1970s, and most experts expect it to double again by the year 2000, in dollars of 1980 purchasing power.

The Future Cost and Supply of Energy. The United States in 1975 consumed about 30 percent of the energy used in the entire world, for its 6 percent of the world's population. The United States secured about 20 percent of its energy supply from coal, about 40 percent from petroleum, about 30 percent from natural gas, about 4 percent from hydroelectric plants and miscellaneous sources, and the remaining 6 percent from nuclear or atomic energy. Nuclear reactors are now being built by the major energy-selling companies and with very large capital costs.

Alternatives to nuclear energy are solar energy and synthetic fuels made from coal. Solar energy is the best hope, since it will continue as long as the sun continues, but the most optimistic experts do not expect to provide generally usable forms of solar energy at less than four times the 1980 costs of oil and gas. Approximately 30 percent of the cost of living in modern society is the cost of energy used in heating, lighting, travel, and transporting and manufacturing goods.

Basically the cost of energy will control the socioeconomic structure of the twenty-first century. It will determine the numbers and age structure of the labor force. It will affect the distribution of the population between big cities and smaller cities. It will affect the structure and size of dwelling units.

There is almost no expert on the problem of energy sources and energy uses who now believes that we will, in the next 75 years, have energy as cheap as it was between 1900 and 1970. We may hope for it, and we will of course support research to produce cheaper energy.

Material Standard of Living. A major increase of cost of energy will tend to lower the material standard of living. People will probably respond by working more years or longer hours to increase the production of goods and services and thus to maintain their present standard of living. Therefore it appears likely that elderly people will be encouraged to stay in the labor force as long as they are reasonably productive. One may even imagine that the notion of mandatory retirement at a fixed age will be forgotten, and the average age of retirement may go up to about age 70. There may be a considerable development of part-time employment.

REFERENCES

American Association for Higher Education: 1978. National Conference Series: *The Adult Learner*, K. Patricia Cross; and *Life Stages and Learning Interests*, Rita Weathersby. Washington, D.C.: American Association for Higher Education.

BALTES, P. B., & SCHAIE, K. (Eds.). *Life-span developmental psychology: Personality and socialization.* New York: Academic Press, 1973.

BARFIELD, R. E., & MORGAN, J. N. *Early retirement: The decision and the experience and a second look.* Ann Arbor, Mich.: Institute for Social Research, 1974.

BATTEN, M. D. Application of a unique industrial health system. *Industrial Gerontology* 1973, *19*, 13–18.

BECKER, H. *Boys in white.* Chicago: University of Chicago Press, 1961.

BEHN, W. H., CARNOY, M., CARTER, M. A., CRAIN, J. C., & LEVIN, H. M. School is bad: Work is worse. *School Review*, 1974, *83*, 49–69.

BELL, D. *The coming of post-industrial society.* New York: Basic Books, 1973.

BEST, F. The future of retirement and lifetime distribution of work. *Aging and Work*, 1979, *2*, 173–181.

BLAUNER, R. Work satisfaction and industrial trends in modern society. In W. Galenson & S. Lipset (Eds.), *Labor and trade unionism.* New York: John Wiley, 1960.

Carnegie Commission on Higher Education. *Opportunities for women in higher education.* New York: McGraw-Hill, 1973.

COLEMAN, J. S. (Ed.). *Youth: Transition to adulthood.* Chicago: University of Chicago Press, 1974.

COMMONER, B. The solar transition: I & II. *New Yorker*, April 23 & 30, 1979.

EPSTEIN, C. F. *Women's place: Options and limits in professional careers.* Berkeley, Calif.: University of California Press, 1971.

FORM, W. H., & MILLER, D. C. Occupational career pattern as a sociological instrument. *American Journal of Sociology*, 1949, *54*, 317–329.

FRIEDMANN, E., & HAVIGHURST, R. J. *The meaning of work and retirement.* Chicago: University of Chicago Press, 1954.

FULLERTON, H. N., JR., & BYRNE, J. J. Length of working life for men and women. *Monthly Labor Review*, February 1976, pp. 31–35.

HAVIGHURST, R. J. (Ed.). Flexible careers and life styles. *The Gerontologist*, Winter 1971, *11*(No. 4, Pt. 2).

HAVIGHURST, R. J. *Developmental tasks and education* (3rd ed.). New York: David McKay, 1972.

HAVIGHURST, R. J., MCDONALD, W. J., PERUN, P. J., & SNOW, R. B. *Social scientists and educators: Lives after sixty.* Chicago: Committee on Human Development, University of Chicago, 1976.

HAVIGHURST, R. J., & LEVINE, D. U. *Society and education* (5th ed.). Boston: Allyn & Bacon, 1979.

HEARN, H. L. Career and leisure patterns of middle-aged urban blacks. *Gerontologist,* 1971, *11*(No. 4), 21–26.

KAHL, J. Educational and occupational aspirations of "common man" boys. *Harvard Educational Review,* 1953, *23,* 186–203.

KAHN, R. L. The meaning of work: Interpretation and proposals for measurement. In A. A. Campbell & P. E. Converse (Eds.), *The human meaning of social change.* New York: Basic Books, 1972.

KENISTON, K. *Youth and dissent.* New York: Harcourt Brace Jovanovich, 1970.

KNOX, A. *Adult development and learning.* San Francisco: Jossey-Bass, 1977.

KOYL, L. F. *Employing the older worker: Matching the employee to the job.* Washington, D.C.: National Council on the Aging, 1974.

KREPS, J. *Sex in the marketplace.* Baltimore, Md.: Johns Hopkins University Press, 1971.

LEVINSON, D. *The seasons of a man's life.* New York: Knopf, 1978.

LOPATA, H. Z. *Widowhood in an American city.* Boston: Schenkman Publishing Co., 1972.

LOPATA, H. Z. *Women as widows: Support systems.* Amsterdam: Elsevier Publishing Company, 1978.

LOPATA, H. Z., & STEINHART, F. Work histories of American urban women. *Gerontologist,* 1971, *11*(No. 4), 27–36.

LORGE, I., & BLAU, R. D. Broad occupational groupings by estimated abilities. *Occupations,* 1942, *21,* 289–295.

LOVINS, A. B. Energy strategy: The road not taken? *Foreign Affairs,* 1976, *55,* 65–96.

MILLER, D. C., & FORM, W. H. *Industrial sociology.* New York: Harper & Row, Pub., 1951.

MUELLER, K. H. *Educating women for a changing world.* Minneapolis: University of Minnesota Press, 1954.

MURRAY, J. R., POWERS, E. A., & HAVIGHURST, R. J. Personal and situational factors producing flexible careers. *Gerontologist,* 1971, *11*(No. 4), 4–12.

National Society for the Study of Education. Seventy-fourth yearbook. YOUTH. Chicago: University of Chicago Press, 1975.

OLIVER, D. B. Career and leisure patterns of middle-aged metropolitan out-migrants. *Gerontologist,* 1971, *11*(No. 4), 13–20.

QUINN, R. P., & STAINES, G. L. The 1977 quality of employment survey. Ann Arbor, Mich.: Institute for Social Research, 1979.

QUINN, R. P., STAINES, G. L., & McCULLOUGH, M. R. *Job satisfaction: Is there a trend?* Washington, D.C.: U.S. Government Printing Office, 1974.

QUIRK, D. A., & SKINNER, J. H. IHCS: Physical capacity, age and employment. *Industrial Gerontology,* 1973, *19,* 18–22.

ROE, A. *The psychology of occupations.* New York: John Wiley, 1956.

SHEPPARD, H. L., & HERRICK, N. Q. *Worker dissatisfaction in the '70s.* New York: Free Press, 1977.

SUPER, D. E. *The psychology of careers: An introduction to vocational development.* New York: Harper & Row, Pub., 1957.

U.S. Bureau of Labor Statistics. *U.S. working women: A databook, 1977.* Washington, D.C.: U.S. Government Printing Office, 1977.

Upjohn Institute for Employment Research. *Work in America.* Cambridge, Mass.: MIT Press, 1973.

WILENSKY, H. Orderly careers and social participation: The impact of work history on social integration in the middle mass. *American Sociological Review,* 1961, *26,* 521–530.

Aging

PART SIX

44

Old Age
and
Biobehavioral Changes

ASENATH LA RUE
LISSY F. JARVIK

Centuries ago Galen described old age as a state midway between illness and health (cf. de Beauvoir, 1973). Indeed the frequency of physical illness increases with age, so that in the United States 86 percent of the elderly have chronic health problems (U.S. Department of Health, Education and Welfare, 1972). Mental illness also appears to increase with advancing age, being estimated to affect between 15 percent and 25 percent of older persons living in the community, and often mental and physical illness coexist. Nonetheless aging is *not* synonymous with disease—either physical or mental—and the question remains largely unanswered as to which "age changes" in psychological performance might better be attributed to disease processes than to growing old per se.

This chapter examines interrelationships between biological changes and cognitive performance in old age, looking first at neuroanatomical and neurophysiological changes, second at chromosome and immune variables, and finally at the effects of systemic illness on intellectual performance. An attempt is made to distinguish between normal and pathological age changes, although such differentiation is complicated by overlap between the types of changes which characterize physiologic and pathologic aging and by the fact that most psychological studies of "healthy" elderly adults probably include individuals with subclinical, if not clinical, diseases. The review is restricted to studies of cognitive performance, since in the gerontological literature this aspect of behavior has been most frequently examined in relation to biological variables. Similarly some biological changes characteris-

tic of old age, such as increasing frequency of lipofuscin deposits in various brain areas, will not be mentioned since they have not been related to changes in mental functioning. Others, like cerebral infarcts or tumors, will be omitted because they are clearly pathological and not generally considered to be on a continuum with normal aging.

Before summarizing specific biobehavioral investigations, however, some discussion of models of aging and cognition is in order. Such models, though rudimentary at the present time, serve to underscore the causal role of biological changes but also suggest ways in which biological aging combines with other factors to produce psychological stability or change.

MODELS OF AGING AND COGNITION

Schaie (1973) described three general models of aging changes, each with implications for research methodology. One, the *stability of adult behavior model,* predicts no change with age in the behavior under study or cyclic fluctuation around a mean. Schaie states that this model is most appropriate for studies in which the sample of interest is restricted to selected, pathology-free subjects or to aspects of behavior (e.g., crystallized intelligence) for which a zero correlation between age-correlated pathology and performance might be assumed.

Flavell (1970) provides an example of this type of theoretical interpretation in his discussion of cognitive changes in adulthood. He states that, in childhood, biologic variables contribute significantly to cognitive maturation and growth, with the effect that basic changes in levels of thought emerge in a fixed order, with uniform directionality, and are largely irreversible. By contrast he suggests that adulthood is the closest thing to a pure ex-

The authors wish to recognize the assistance of Dr. Steven Matsuyama in the writing of the sections on chromosome and immune changes, as well as that of Clara Neves and Anna Waldbaum in the preparation of the manuscript.

periment in nature for assessing the change-making power of experience alone, there presumably being no biological changes in maturity sufficient to impose strong constraints on cognitive growth. It is important to note that Flavell restricts his interpretation to such aspects of cognition as judgments, attitudes, and beliefs, and it is not clear how late into the life span he would expect such assumptions to hold true.

A second of Schaie's (1973) models is that of *irreversible decrement.* He considers this model to be applicable to psychological processes (e.g., reaction time) for which there is relatively direct biological determination of performance. It is further assumed that such behaviors are relatively unaffected by immediate environmental inputs (hence the term *irreversible*).

Unfortunately this conceptualization of aging changes is known to many psychologists as the *medical model,* under the assumption that investigators who focus on behavioral manifestations of age-correlated biological changes, either normal or pathological, also assume such changes to be irremediable. In fact the opposite is true, as illustrated by the rapidly expanding field of the discipline concerned with diseases disproportionately affecting older adults (e.g., cardiovascular illness or dementia). Today the geriatrician is generally seen as the starting point for a series of medical and psychosocial interventions designed to reverse, arrest, or at least ameliorate the underlying biological condition and its noxious behavioral manifestations.

The third model proposed by Schaie (1973) is that of *decrement with compensation.* Here it is assumed that environmental inputs may partially compensate for biologically determined decrements. Such environmental inputs may consist of life-style changes and supports (e.g., improved nutrition or physical exercise) or specific training programs designed to enhance performance in specific problematic areas (e.g., recent memory). Schaie considers this model to be the most practical one for approaching many of the problems of aging, perhaps because it is applicable to a broader range of behavioral processes and/or ascribes a more optimistic and aggressive role to mental health professionals than do the other models.

The assumption that no one model is likely to incorporate all aspects of cognitive change in adulthood is exemplified by Horn and Cattell's (Cattell, 1963; Horn, 1970, 1976) theory of fluid versus crystallized intelligence. Fluid intelligence (*Gf*) involves organization and reorganization of information in the process of problem solving; it is believed to be closely tied to neurological and general physiological processes and is likely to decline after adolescence. Crystallized intelligence, by contrast, may be thought of as the body of knowledge acquired from living in a particular culture; tied to the quality and quantity of one's life experiences, it is believed to increase with age, at least until the mid-life point. General intelligence, reflecting both fluid and crystallized components, is predicted by Horn to be stable through much of adulthood, a prediction supported by most recent longitudinal and sequential follow-up studies (see Botwinick, 1977, for a review).

Attempts to extend traditional developmental models of cognition (e.g., Piagetian theory) to the last half of life have thus far had unsatisfying results. In an early paper relating Piagetian theory to processes of aging, Hooper, Fitzgerald, and Papalia (1971) speculated that late in life there may be "a sequential order of regression which would involve the formal period tasks first and the concrete operations skills at a still later point" (p. 15). Since that time a small number of studies (e.g., Chap & Sinnott, 1977–1978; Clayton & Overton, 1976; Kuhn, Langer, Kohlberg, & Hahn, 1977; Sinnott, 1975; Tomlinson-Keasey, 1972) have contrasted the performance of younger and older adults on formal operations tasks, and most have reported that middle-aged and elderly subjects are indeed less likely to display formal thought than are young adults. However, because of methodological limitations, such studies cannot be viewed as supporting the notion of regression with age. In the first place, no longitudinal or cross-sequential studies have been reported; since the data base is thus entirely cross-sectional, discussion of results in terms of age *changes* is inappropriate. Second, it is likely that these cross-sectional studies confounded differences in age with other variables, such as health and education, and in that manner are subject to the same inferential errors as earlier investigations of age differences in IQ test performance. Ultimately regression through stages may prove to be a more appropriate model for cognitive changes accompanying neurodegenerative diseases (see Baro, 1972, regarding Huntington's disease) than for normal aging changes.

In our current state of knowledge with regard to aging processes, it may be most useful to retreat from specific theoretical models to a more basic "metatheoretical" framework as advanced by Baltes (1973) and Baltes and Willis (1977). These latter authors state,

It is our judgment . . . that the nature of behavioral change at all stages of life can take many forms in terms of directionality, range, or intensity, depending upon the class of behavior and theoretical orientation chosen. Therefore, it is desirable to refrain from the application of strict generic criteria such as unidirectionality, irreversibility, and universality when delineating aging change although these attributes may apply to *some* behavioral changes at *some* historical periods for *some* organisms. (p. 136)

They go on to propose a paradigm for *change-oriented explanations* in which behavior, at all life-span points, is viewed as some unspecified function of three classes of variables: organismic or biological, stimulus or environmental, and response or behavioral. They assert further that different determinants (e.g., organismic versus environmental) may operate to lesser or greater degrees at different points in the life span and that the nature of the causal relationship among antecedents, or between antecedents and consequents, may change over time. Their focus, then, is on accounting for aging changes "in terms of time-ordered (sequential) but potentially changing systems of explanatory determinants" (ibid., p. 141). In such a metatheoretical system, biological variables can be assumed to be causally related to some degree to behavior throughout the life span. It is our contention that in advanced age, as in early childhood, a rapidly changing physiological substrate exerts a relatively major impact on changes in cognition, as well as other behaviors. The remainder of this chapter will, therefore, address some of the more significant age-linked biological developments hypothesized to explain a portion of the differences in cognition observed among elderly individuals.

NEUROANATOMICAL AND NEUROPHYSIOLOGICAL CHANGES

The area which has been studied more intensively and over a longer period of time than any other is that relating neuroanatomical changes to behavioral deficits.

Neuronal Degeneration

Neuronal degenerative changes, particularly accumulation of neurofibrillary tangles, senile plaques, and granulovacuolar degeneration, as well as loss of neurons, are typical of the most common form of dementia affecting older people (primary degenerative or Alzheimer-type dementia) and occur to a lesser extent in apparently normal individuals of advanced age (cf. Brody, 1978; Katzman, 1976; Terry & Davies, 1980; Wells, 1978). At the extreme such changes appear to be correlated with impairment in activities of daily living and social functioning as well as basic cognitive abilities, including orientation, attention-concentration, and recent and remote memory. Tomlinson, Blessed, and Roth (1968) administered a quantitative mental status questionnaire to 50 senile dementia patients and subsequently examined post-mortem the number of senile plaques. The correlation ($r = .63$) was significant, suggesting that problems with concentration, orientation, and memory reflect neurodegenerative changes. It is not known, however, to what extent, if any, mild degrees of neurodegenerative change are correlated with individual differences in cognitive performance among the aged.

Since loss of neurons and neuronal degeneration are hallmarks of normal aging, it has been argued that the more pronounced changes characterizing senile dementia indicate a quantitative, rather than qualitative, difference between senile dementia and normal aging. However, Roth (1978) has proposed a threshold model to account for the fact that significant neuropathological changes may be observed in the brains of individuals who, prior to death, appeared to function normally. According to this model the concentration of neuropathological changes must exceed threshold values at a given location before behavioral deficits become manifest.

Inferences relating behavior to neurodegenerative changes always suffer from the uncertainty due to the time lapse between psychological testing and autopsy. This source of uncertainty has been removed by the emergence of computerized axial tomography (CT scans) which allows visualization of the brain in the living human being. Most studies (cf. Fox, Topel, & Huckman, 1975; Huckman, Fox, & Topel, 1975; Kaszniak, Garron, Fox, Huckman, & Ramsey, 1975; Roberts, Caird, Grossart, & Steven, 1976) report a greater incidence of atrophy, defined on the basis of either enlarged cortical sulci or ventricles, or both, among patients diagnosed as demented compared to age-matched controls. However, enough exceptions to this association exist, both in terms of normal-functioning persons with brain atrophy and impaired individuals without atrophy, to indicate that CT scans cannot be used to either confirm or reject the diagnosis of senile dementia, unless a specific lesion is discovered to account for the symptoms of dementia. This observation is not surprising since the correlation between cerebral atrophy ascertained at autopsy and antemortem cognitive functioning is far from perfect and since CT scans do not measure the density of neuritic plaques or neurofibrillary tangles in the hippocampus or cortex, changes which do correlate highly with cognitive functioning.

Cortical atrophy as measured by CT scans, particularly ventricular enlargement, has also been related to age, with a gradual increase in ventricle size from the first through the seventh decades, followed by sharper increases in decades eight and nine (Barron, Jacobs, & Kinkei, 1976). Whether such cortical changes relate to cognitive performance among normal older persons is a matter of debate, however.

Earnest, Heaton, Wilkinson, and Manke (1979) assessed CT scan findings and neuropsychological test performance among a sample of 59 middle- to upper-middle-class elderly residents of retirement communities, all of whom were free of obvious neurologic disease. Several measures were computed from the CT scans, including widths of the four largest sulci and ventricle-to-skull diameter ratios. Neuropsychological tests, administered approximately one year after the CT scans, consisted of the Trail-Making Test from the Halstead-Reitan battery, the Digit Symbol and Block Design subtests from the WAIS, and the visual reproduction subtest from the Wechsler Memory Scale. Evidence for age differences in psychological performance was provided by analyses comparing scores of younger (60 to 79 years old) and older (80 to 99 years old) elderly subjects and also by contrasting performance of the total elderly sample with that of a group of education-matched young adults (16 to 40 years old); on all tests greater age was associated with lower mean scores. Age differences, contrasting the 60- to 79-year-old and 80- to 99-year-old subgroups, were also noted on each of the CT measures, increased age being associated with wider sulci and higher ventricle-to-skull ratios. With the effects of age differences partialled out, however, correlations between CT measures and psychological test performance were generally not significant. The authors interpreted their findings as suggesting that cerebral atrophy and lower psychological performance may be independent correlates of advancing age, since individual differences in degree of atrophy were essentially unrelated to test scores when age was statistically controlled. Several factors limit confidence in this interpretation, however, including the gap of a year's time between CT scans and mental assessment. In addition this sample appeared to be an intellectually exceptional one, age-corrected scaled scores for the 80- to 99-year olds being 13 and 12 for Digit Symbol and Block Design, respectively. Finally, the neuropsychological test battery was limited to timed perceptual-motor tests, leaving the question of atrophy-performance relationships open for such functions as short- or long-term verbal memory, abstract reasoning, or arithmetic calculation.

A related, but more thorough, investigation was performed by Kaszniak, Garron, Fox, Bergen, and Huckman (1979). Subjects were 78 patients aged 52 to 86 years, referred for neuropsychological evaluation of suspected dementia. All were free of focal neurological abnormalities, history of stroke, toxic or metabolic delirium, systemic disease, or psychosis. CT scans and clinical EEG's were performed, and a neuropsychological test battery was administered (including the Wechsler Memory Scale, a memory span for objects test, picture vocabulary and sentence production measures, aphasia and apraxia screening tests, the Benton Right-Left Discrimination Battery, and the Picture Absurdities Subtest from the Stanford-Binet). Results were examined separately for each cognitive measure in a series of stepwise multiple regression analyses in which effects of educational differences were statistically controlled. EEG slowing affected performance on all tasks except Sentence Production even though the range on the EEG variable was restricted to a simple three-point scale. Cerebral atrophy (based on measurement of both sulci and ventricles) was independently related to performance on tests assessing recall of verbal material (Paragraphs, Paired-Associates, Information, and Mental Control subtests from the Wechsler Memory Scale and the Sentence Production and Memory Span for Objects tests). Age effects, independent of EEG and CT differences, were observed on memory tasks for both verbal and nonverbal material.

Kaszniak and associates (1975, 1979) interpreted their results as indicating that cerebral atrophy may be linked to difficulties in some mental functions, particularly verbal recall, but that EEG slowing is more disruptive of a wider range of cognitive abilities. It is difficult to ascertain the implications of these findings for variations in performance within the normal range since all subjects were referred because of symptoms of dementia and the authors do not report how many subjects were judged to be free of dementia after evaluation. Also patterns of results might have been different if predictor variables had been entered into the regression analyses in another order. In comparison to the study by Earnest and collaborators (1979), it is interesting to note that the tasks correlated with CT findings of cerebral atrophy in the study by Kaszniak and colleagues were not part of the battery used by Earnest and colleagues.

Newer, more refined analyses of CT scans may eventually be of assistance in resolving questions regarding age-correlated cerebral atrophy and psychological functioning. Thus Naeser, Gebhardt, and Levine (1980) used CT number, a measure related to the coefficient of attenuation of brain material at a particular scanning location, in comparing patients with presenile or senile dementia and normal age-matched controls. They examined mean CT number in white matter from the centrum semiovale and reported that all dementia patients (senile and presenile) had lower mean CT numbers in healthy tissue samples than did controls; in fact, the distributions of this quantitative index of tissue attrition showed no overlap. CT number discriminated even those dementia cases without prominent sulci or enlarged ventricles, suggesting this measure may provide the sensitivity which the more traditional gross measures (sulcal width and ventricular size) lack. The finding may also be important in pointing to changes in white matter as key correlates of mental functioning accompanying, or possibly even preceding, changes in gray matter. Age was not significantly correlated with CT number, but it should be noted that all but one of the control cases were relatively young (age range = 50 to 64 years). If larger samples of normal individuals representing a broader range of ages were to be studied, it is possible that correlations between CT number, age, and cognitive impairment might be observed. It also remains to be established whether CT number correlates with the less pronounced cognitive changes characteristic of normal aging, as opposed to senile dementia. In line with Roth's (1978) threshold model, it is possible, of course, that there are no reliable behavioral correlates of cerebral degenerative changes until some threshold of loss is obtained, at which time the individual exhibits dementia rather than the milder impairments of cognitive performance typical of advancing age.

Cerebral Electrophysiology

The most reliable change in EEG late in life is a diffuse slowing of the dominant alpha rhythm from a mean frequency of 10 cps to 8 or 9 cps (Obrist, 1963, 1975; Wang & Busse, 1969). The extent of slowing is related to general health, being greatest among persons with cardiac or cerebrovascular disease (Obrist, 1974). It is also related to dementia; a majority of demented patients, compared to only about 7 percent of healthy aged persons (Wang & Busse, 1969), show generalized slowing into the theta range (5 to 7 cps). Delta rhythms ($\leq$ 4 cps) are also observed among dementia patients (Muller & Kral, 1967; Obrist & Henry, 1958a, 1958b; Short & Wilson, 1971; Swain, 1959) but generally not among the normal elderly (Hughes & Cayaffa, 1977; Wang & Busse, 1969).

Significant correlations between diffuse EEG slowing and cognitive performance have been reported for patients with dementia or suspected dementia (Barnes, Busse, & Friedman, 1956; Kasniak et al., 1979; Obrist, Busse, Eisdorfer, & Kleemeier, 1962; Wang, 1973), and the presence or absence of such slowing has been used as an ancillary test for differentiating organic from functional disorders in old age (cf. Obrist, 1975). Among healthy old persons, however, the slight EEG slowing observed is generally unrelated to performance on intelligence tests (Birren, Butler, Greenhouse, Sokoloff, & Yarrow, 1963; Obrist, 1975), and so is localized EEG slowing. Approximately one-third of normal elderly persons show slow activity in the anterior temporal region (Busse & Obrist, 1965; Kooi, Guvener, Tupper, & Bagchi, 1964), but individuals with these focal changes apparently do not differ from age-matched controls on memory or intelligence tests (Obrist, 1975). Some middle-aged and older women have an increase in rhythmic beta activity (fast waves) over the precentral areas (Busse & Obrist, 1965), and this change has been reported to be related to maintenance of intellectual abilities (Busse, 1978).

There has been an upsurge of interest in event-related electrophysiological responses in relation to both normal and pathological aging. Unlike the clinical EEG, event-related responses (ERP's) or evoked potentials (EP's) are correlated in time with the processing of specific stimuli and are believed to represent a limited set of cognitive operations, most often sensory discrimination and decision making (cf. John et al., 1977; Regan, 1979). One component of ERP's is the P300, a late-occurring endogenous wave most often elicited when a subject detects an infrequent stimulus embedded at irregular intervals in a series of more common stimuli. Goodin, Squires, Henderson, and Starr (1978) presented series of tonal stimuli to normal subjects ranging in age from 6 to 76 years. Eighty-five percent of the tones had a frequency of 1000 Hz; and 15 percent, a frequency of 2000 Hz. Subjects were asked to count the infrequent tones. Consistent with the results of previous investigations (Brent, Smith, Michalewski, & Thompson, 1976; Ford, Hink, Hopkins, Roth, Pfefferbaum, & Kopell, 1979; Marsh & Thompson, 1972), there was a shift toward longer latencies of the P300 with advancing adult age, from a mean of 300 msec for young adults (15 to 20 years) to 400 msec or more by the seventh decade. By contrast the initial (N1) component, most likely reflecting activation of the sensory pathways as opposed to cognitive processing, did not increase significantly with age. The authors suggested that longer latencies of cognitive-processing operations, as reflected in the P300, might underlie some of the commonly observed age-linked changes in psychomotor speed, but they did not directly investigate this possibility.

In a related investigation Squires et al. (1979) compared the auditory ERP's of dementia patients (aged 25 to 84 years) and normal controls (aged 19 to 78 years). A quantitative mental status examination (Folstein, Folstein, & McHugh, 1975), assessing orientation, registration, attention-concentration, delayed three-item recall, language and visuographic function, was also administered. The mean score of the patient group was 20.7 (out of a possible 30), a level considered by Folstein and colleagues to be suggestive of global cognitive impairment; normal controls generally received a score of 29 or 30. Significant slowing of the P300 component, as well as a decrease in amplitude, was observed for the dementia patients in contrast to the controls, with 83 percent of the latencies for the patients exceeding the normal, age-controlled regression line by two or more standard deviations. Because of the marked differences observed, Starr and collaborators suggested that auditory ERP's might be helpful in the clinical differentiation of normal and cognitively impaired elderly. John and colleagues (1977) also reported differences in latencies and amplitudes of late-occurring components of ERP's for aged dementia patients and controls, suggesting further that differing subgroups of cognitively impaired elderly (perhaps with differing etiologies of their problems) could be distinguished on the basis of ERP waveforms.

Thus like the clinical EEG, ERP's show some changes with normal aging but even more marked changes with senile dementia. It remains to be seen whether or not slowing of particular ERP components is associated with impaired cognitive functions (e.g., reaction time or short-term memory) in normal aged persons.

Autonomic Nervous System Function

Several hypotheses have been proposed relating changes in cognitive performance to age-associated changes in autonomic nervous system activity. Prominent among them is the hypothesis that elderly persons are "underaroused" compared to younger individuals (e.g., Botwinick & Kornetsky, 1960; Thompson & Now-lin, 1973) and its converse, that the aged are "overaroused" compared to the young (Eisdorfer, 1968; Eisdorfer, Nowlin, & Wilkie, 1970). In general support for the underarousal hypothesis is found in studies of reaction time using electrophysiological measures of autonomic nervous system function, while overarousal is supported by studies of verbal learning with free fatty acid levels used as indicators of autonomic state.

Powell, Eisdorfer, and Bogdonoff (1964) used free fatty acid (FFA) mobilization as an indicator of autonomic nervous system activity, finding that the older subjects had the higher FFA levels before a learning task was given; this higher FFA level was maintained in the older group for at least one hour after the task was completed. Eisdorfer's hypothesis that the learning decrements found among the elderly are at least partially attributable to heightened autonomic nervous system arousal was supported (Eisdorfer et al., 1970) when a group of older subjects receiving propranolol (Inderal), an adrenergic blocking agent, made significantly fewer errors on a learning task than did a placebo group and had lowered FFA levels and heartrates as well.

Froehling (1974) was unable to replicate these findings, however. She reported decreases in FFA levels for the propranolol group but no differences in performance on the learning task between the treatment and the control groups. It has been pointed out that this study differs from that of Eisdorfer's group in that different drug dosages were used and the subjects had trial runs in the laboratory, thus gaining familiarity with the situation.

To explain some of the inconsistencies, Powell, Milligan, and Furchtgott (1980) hypothesized that tasks that elicit phasic changes (e.g., reaction time) might be expected to produce a different pattern of correlations between autonomic nervous system function and age than are tasks which elicit sustained (i.e., tonic) alterations in arousal level (e.g., multi-trial learning paradigms). To test this hypothesis the performance of young (mean age = 27.8 years) and older (mean age = 63.2 years) men was examined on reaction-time and verbal serial-learning tasks. Subjects were hospitalized VA patients drawn from acute surgical wards or a nursing home care unit; all were nonmedicated and free from acute medical illness. Individuals with histories of alcoholism, brain damage, or psychiatric disorder were excluded. Tasks consisted of simple and two-choice reaction-time and two eight-item verbal serial-learning lists, one with items presented at a four-second rate and the other at a ten-second rate. Systolic and diastolic blood pressure were recorded immediately before and after each task, and heartrate and electrodermal activity were recorded continuously.

Age differences were observed on both behavioral measures and on baseline heartrate and blood pressure measures. Older subjects made significantly more errors and required more trials to criterion on the serial-learning tasks and had slower reaction times compared to the younger subjects. Baseline blood pressure was higher and heartrate lower among older, as opposed to younger, subjects. There were no significant correlations, however, between behavioral performance and baseline physiologic measures in either age group.

Analyses of changes in physiologic measures during task performance indicated that tonic autonomic changes were greater and phasic changes smaller among elderly, as opposed to younger, subjects. On the serial-learning tasks increases in systolic blood pressure were greater and frequency of unelicited electrodermal responses higher in the older as compared to the younger group. By contrast phasic electrodermal responses during the reaction-time tasks were smaller in the elderly, compared to younger, subjects. Changes in physiologic measures were generally unrelated to behavioral performance, the exception being that increases in systolic blood pressure were associated with higher serial-learning scores among older, but not among younger, subjects.

The results of this study substantiate earlier investigations regarding age differences in autonomic nervous system functioning and suggest, in addition, that age may differentially affect tonic and phasic responses. This study provides little support, however, for the hypothesis that age differences in cognitive performance are mediated by autonomic nervous system changes. With the exception of a positive correlation between serial learning and increases in systolic blood pressure among elderly subjects, neither baseline physiologic measures nor change scores were related to individual differences in behavioral performance.

CHROMOSOME AND IMMUNE VARIABLES

Chromosome Loss

A number of cross-sectional investigations (Cadotte & Fraser, 1970; Court-Brown, Buckton, Jacobs, Tough, Kuenssberg, & Knox, 1966; Demoise & Conrad, 1972; Fitzgerald, 1975; Goodman, Feicheimer, Miller, Miller, & Zartman, 1969; Hamerton, Taylor, Angell, & McGuire, 1961; Jacobs, Court-Brown, & Doll, 1961; Jarvik & Kato, 1970; Jarvik, Yen, & Moralishvili, 1974; Mattevi & Salzano, 1975; Neurath, DeRemer, Bell, Jarvik, & Kato, 1970; Nielsen, 1970; Sandberg, Cohen, Rimm, & Levin, 1967) and one longitudinal study (Jarvik, Yen, Fu, & Matsuyama, 1976) reported increasing proportions of aneuploid cells (abnormal chromosome number) with advancing age. Age differences in chromosome number have been found more reliably among women than men, with the typical observation for women being an increased frequency of hypodiploidy (loss of chromosomes) with increasing age, probably resulting from the loss of an X chromosome. For men loss of the Y chromosome has been the predominant finding. Since age-related chromosome loss has typically been demonstrated in peripheral leukocytes, it is unclear in what manner, if any, such changes might be linked to variations in mental performance among older persons. One hypothesis (Jarvik, 1971) has been that hypodiploid cells among peripheral leukocytes reflect similar losses among other dividing cellular systems (e.g., glial cells), and assuming that aneuploid cells operate at suboptimal levels, hypodiploidy among glial cells would interfere with brain homeostasis and neuronal functioning.

Several studies do suggest an association between leukocyte hypodiploidy and dementia. Jarvik, Altshuler, Kato, and Blumner (1971), as well as Nielsen (1970), reported that women with senile, but not with arteriosclerotic (multi-infarct), dementia had a significantly higher frequency of chromosome loss than did normal women of comparable age. These findings were not present in men, but the data base for men was small. More recently increased hypodiploidy, as well as increased frequency of acentric fragments, was reported for ten patients with the sporadic form of Alzheimer disease (Nordenson, Adolfsson, Beckman, Bucht, & Winbled, 1980), and in another study a higher percentage of aneuploid cells was reported for patients with familial Alzheimer disease and their affected relatives than for controls matched by age and sex (Ward, Cook, Robinson, & Austin, 1979). The suggestion that aneuploidy may be useful as a predictor of Alzheimer disease (Cook, Ward, & Austin, 1979) is premature even though there is additional evidence linking Alzheimer disease and aneuploidy. Thus patients with Down's syndrome (a disorder due to extra chromosomal material) show premature signs of aging, including the development of dementia in their thirties and forties with characteristic Alzheimer-type brain changes (Jervis, 1970; Olson & Shaw, 1969). By contrast such brain changes are rare (14 percent) among those whose mental retardation has causes other than Down's syndrome (Malamud, 1972).

Significant correlations between chromosome loss and psychological test performance on the Graham-Kendall Memory-for-Designs Test and the Stroop Color-Word Test have been reported for community residents ranging in age from 77 to 93 years (Jarvik, 1971; Jarvik & Kato, 1969), suggesting that hypodiploidy may be related to individual differences in mental functioning of the normal aged as well as to dementia. Correlations with a number of other cognitive measures (Wechsler-Bellevue subtests, Stanford-Binet Vocabulary, and a tapping test of psychomotor speed) were not significant, however, and further studies of chromosome loss and normal mental functioning are needed to clarify the relationship.

Immunological Changes

Aging appears to affect immune system functioning in a number of ways. The production of antibodies reaches a peak during adolescence and then progressively declines with advancing age (Makinodan, 1973). In some species senescent animals retain only about one-tenth of the immune capabilities of younger ones (Shock, 1977). Such changes reduce the individual's ability to protect itself against microorganisms and also to deactivate mutant cells originating within its own body. The resultant increase in susceptibility to systemic illness may be indirectly responsible for intellectual losses observed with advancing age, since disease has been related not only to declining psychomotor speed but also to impairments of learning and memory as discussed later in this chapter.

Indeed there is an autoimmune theory (Blumenthal & Berns, 1964; Walford, 1969) which attributes aging to the development of antibodies which destroy normal cells (Shock, 1977). It has long been known that autoimmune diseases increase with age, and Walford (1969) reported age-related increases in autoimmune serum antibodies. More recently evidence has been accumulated suggesting that autoimmune reactions may play a role in neuronal degeneration. Thus Nandy and colleagues (cf.

Nandy, 1977) have identified brain-reactive antibodies (BRA) in the gamma globulin fraction of serum from old, but not young, mice. These BRA increase progressively with age and react equally with neurons from young and old mice. The report by Ingram, Phegan, & Blumenthal (1974) of an age-associated increase in a neuron-binding gamma globulin fraction in human serum suggests that a similar brain-reactive antibody exists in aged humans, and in fact, Nandy's (1978) preliminary human data show an increase with age in BRA.

Evidence of a link between immunological changes and cognitive performance is as yet only tentative. Rapport (1978; Rapport & Karpiak, 1976) found that in rats injections of antiserum against synaptic membrane fractions resulted in changes in EEG patterns and interfered with cognitive performance. Relationships between serum immunoglobulin levels and intellectual function in the elderly humans have been reported by at least three groups.

Roseman and Buckley (1975) were the first to note an association between cognition and serum immunoglobulin concentration. Their subjects, participants in the Duke longitudinal study, showed an inverse relationship between serum Ig concentration and certain measures of intelligence. Subsequently Cohen, Matsuyama, and Jarvik (1976) reported a direct relationship between serum Ig levels and vocabulary score in survivors of the New York State Psychiatric Institute longitudinal study of normal aging twins (Jarvik, 1967; Kallman & Sander, 1949). The same group of investigators (Matsuyama, Deckard, & Jarvik, 1978), in a recent study of 20 elderly women who exhibited mild to moderate organic brain syndrome, found a significant positive correlation between serum IgG level and cognition as measured by the Hooper Test of Visual Organization, the four symptom areas of the Sandoz Clinical Assessment Scale (Geriatric-SCAG) which assess impairment in cognitive functioning, and the orientation item on the Plutchik Geriatric Assessment Scale. Similarly a positive association between Ig levels and cognitive performance in nursing home residents as well as community elderly was reported by a third group of investigators (Cohen & Eisdorfer, 1977; Eisdorfer, Cohen, & Buckley, 1978), who suggest that a curvilinear function may best describe the relation between immune response and cognition.

In general as with many of the other biological changes discussed in this section, evidence for immune dysfunction as related to cognitive decline is stronger in the case of dementia than in normal aging. Thus components or fragments of immunoglobulins have been localized in senile plaques by the fluorescent antibody technique (Ishii, Haga, & Shimizu, 1975) and through immunoelectron microscopy more specifically localized in amyloid fibrils of senile plaques (Ishii & Haga, 1976). As mentioned earlier senile plaques are present in increasing numbers with increasing age (Matsuyama, Wamiki, & Watanabe, 1966), and their concentrations are significantly higher in demented than in nondemented patients (Blessed, Tomlinson, & Roth, 1968; Dayan, 1970a, 1970b; Morimatsu, Hirai, Muramatsu, & Yoshikawa, 1975). Nandy (1978) found higher concentrations of brain-reactive antibodies in persons with Alzheimer-type dementia than in control subjects of similar ages, and a significantly elevated mean serum IgG level has

been reported for cognitively impaired elderly (Cohen & Eisdorfer, 1980) and for late-onset Alzheimer-dementia patients (Hensche, Bell, & Cape, 1979) as compared to age-matched control subjects.

Immune changes are consistent with the postulated involvement of an infectious agent in the etiology of senile dementia. Viruses have been implicated in Down's syndrome and leukemia (seasonal fluctuations and variations in geographic distribution), both of which have been related to Alzheimer disease (Heston & Mastri, 1977). There is tentative evidence for a viral role in Alzheimer disease from the report (deBoni & Crapper, 1978) that cultured neurons from fetal human cerebral cortex, exposed to an extract of Alzheimer brain, developed the paired helical filaments characteristic of neurofibrillary tangles. If confirmed it would be the first successful experimental laboratory production of neurofibrillary degeneration and could aid considerably in the elucidation of the pathogenesis of senile dementia. Caution is indicated in interpreting these results, not only in terms of reproducibility but also because brains damaged by some other underlying pathology may be attacked by a transmissible viral agent not directly involved in their pathogenesis. This explanation was proposed by Traub, Gajdusek, and Gibbs (1977) for the transmission to squirrel monkeys of the spongiform encephalopathy characteristic of Creutzfeldt-Jakob disease by an inoculum from two patients with familial Alzheimer disease (transmission attempted from many other Alzheimer patients had been unsuccessful).

THE EFFECTS OF SYSTEMIC ILLNESS

Though known to play a crucial role in late-life adaptation, health status has often been ignored in psychosocial research. Thus between 1963 and 1974 only 11 percent of the studies reported in the *Journal of Gerontology* controlled for health variables (Abrahams, Hoyer, Elias, & Bradigan, 1975), and little seems to have changed since then. In the behavioral and social sciences section of the 1978 volumes of this journal, for example, 68 percent of the articles made no mention of subjects' health, and 23 percent more stated that subjects were in good health but failed to specify the procedures used to assess health status. In only 9 percent of the articles, then, was health status well specified.

The cardiovascular and cerebrovascular diseases are particularly relevant to the cognitive functioning of the aged. The prevalence of atherosclerosis approaches 100 percent among the very old. Mortality due to heart disease doubles each decade past mid-life for men and triples for women (Hendricks & Hendricks, 1977). Cardiac output declines by about one percent a year past the age of 30 (Freeman, 1965), and there is accumulation of subpericardial fat and lipofuscin, as well as less efficient valvular function with advancing age. Moreover blood pressure tends to rise with age, and hypertension is common among the elderly. Cerebrovascular accidents or strokes rank third among the causes of death in the second half of life (National Center for Health Statistics, 1971), and the incidence of transient ischemic episodes is undoubtedly significantly higher still.

The subsequent sections review the limited literature

available relating general health, cardiovascular, and cerebrovascular diseases to intellectual performance. Reaction time has been the most commonly used behavioral measure in these investigations, but scattered reports concerning problem solving, learning and memory, and IQ test performance are also available.

General Health Status

As part of a longitudinal study of healthy aged men, Botwinick and Birren (1963) divided their sample into two groups. One group consisted of exceptionally healthy men (i.e., no medical problems were detected by extensive screening) and the other of men with mild, asymptomatic conditions. Performance of the disease-free group was superior to that of the other group on all but two of the 23 tests (derived from WAIS subscales and other cognitive measures, including speed of word and digit copying, Raven's Progressive Matrices, and arithmetic caculation), the differential tending to be greater on WAIS performance rather than verbal subtests. Botwinick (1973) interpreted these findings as suggesting that "... even slight alterations of optimum health of the elderly can adversely affect their intellectual functioning" (p. 194).

In another study (Correll, Rokosz, & Blanchard, 1966), health was one of the variables related to WAIS performance. Participants were selected from two residential facilities, a hospital unit for the aged and a housing facility operated by a nonsectarian Protestant organization; the latter group was somewhat younger, better educated, and of higher socioeconomic status than the former. A three-point health classification based on medical examinations and laboratory tests was used: (1) apparently healthy, nonmedicated, unrestricted activity; (2) known illnesses, well-controlled, restricted activity; and (3) known illnesses, poorly controlled, restricted activity. Health status was most consistently related to WAIS performance as opposed to verbal subscales with much of the variance due to health status apparently attributable to the presence or absence of cardiovascular or cerebrovascular disease. Current social activity was also related to a variety of verbal and nonverbal scores. Education was related to scores on verbal scales, but more so in the hospitalized group than among residents of the housing project. Age and prior social activity correlated with performance on comparatively few measures and then only for the housing project subjects, while current social activity was consistently related to WAIS performance. The authors interpreted their results as indicating that environmental and physiological variables, including general health, account for more of the individual differences in cognitive function among old persons than does age per se. They also noted, however, that the percent of variance attributable to a given factor is likely to differ from sample to sample, depending on the absolute level of scores.

The effects of differences in general health on problem-solving or decision-making styles were examined in 60 middle-aged (40 to 59 years) and 60 elderly (60 to 79 years) community residents (La Rue, 1979; La Rue & Waldbaum, 1980) classified as either in "excellent" or "good-to-fair" health on the basis of medical examinations performed within three weeks of psychological testing. Subjects in the "excellent" category were generally asymptomatic, free of any evidence of cardiovascular, cerebrovascular, neoplastic, metabolic, endocrine, hematologic, or skeletal-muscular disease. The middle-aged group contained a somewhat greater percentage of subjects in excellent health than did the elderly group (53.3 percent versus 45.0 percent, respectively), and a greater frequency of highly educated persons (56.7 percent versus 48.3 percent), reflecting current trends in the general U.S. adult population.

Problem-solving styles were assessed in a series of six formal operational reasoning tasks similar to those used by Piaget to measure adolescents' thought. Two of Inhelder and Piaget's (1958) tasks were used: the pendulum problem (assessing hypothetico-deductive thought) and the colorless-liquids problem (assessing combinatorial analysis); a third task involved proportional reasoning (measurement), and three others represented familiar analogues to the traditional formal thought tasks (building a tire swing for a grandchild, suggesting new blends of pipe-smoking tobacco, and adjusting proportions of ingredients in a cake recipe). Answers to each problem were scored as either preoperational, concrete operational, or formal operational, and scores were summed across the set of six tasks to arrive at a composite estimate of problem-solving style. Formal operational style was more characteristic of those in "excellent" than those in "good-to-fair" health, of men rather than women, and of the better educated rather than the less well educated. The effect of age was not significant. Since the most frequent type of ill health in this sample was some form of vascular disease (e.g., hypertension, cardiac arrhythmia, past history of stroke, or myocardial infarction), the present study suggests that higher-order Piagetian tasks are sensitive to general cardiovascular integrity. This notion is further supported by the observation of a low, but significant, negative correlation ($r = -.28$, $p = .007$) between systolic blood pressure and composite formal thought scores.

Cardiovascular and Cerebrovascular Disease

Earlier studies had already suggested a link between hypertension and cognitive impairment. Apter, Halstead, and Heimburger (1951) reported that hypertensives, while free of neurological signs, showed impaired cerebral functioning "equivalent to that seen in patients with surgical removal of both frontal lobes" (p. 812), and Reitan (1954) found the frequency of "organic" signs on the Rorschach test to be greater among hypertensives than among matched neurotic patients but less than among individuals with known brain damage. Subsequent studies, involving more extensive standardized psychometric measures, provide equivocal evidence for cognitive concomitants of hypertension and, in general, suggest that hypertension alone represents the lower end of a continuum of cardio- and cerebrovascular diseases affecting intellectual performance.

Spieth (1965) studied the performance of middle-aged men (35 to 59 years) on speeded tasks (serial reaction time, WAIS digit symbol substitution and block design, and the trail-making and tactual performance tests from the Halstead-Reitan battery) as a function of cardiovascular or cerebrovascular diseases. The subjects were federal civil servants, primarily pilots or air controllers, the majority of whom were in good general health and above average in intelligence, education, and occupational status. The slowest performance was observed in a subgroup with cerebrovascular disease, while individuals with arteriosclerotic cardiovascular disease were also significantly slower than were controls, as were nonmedicated subjects with essential hypertension. The performance of medicated hypertensives, with normal blood pressures at the time of testing, was similar to that of the normal controls. Differences between control subjects and those with cerebrovascular or cardiovascular disease increased with task complexity, suggesting that these conditions affected decision-making speed in addition to sensory or motor processes.

In another study Goldman, Kleinman, Snow, Bidus, and Korol (1974) reported a mean error score indicative of cerebral impairment on the Halstead-Reitan category test for a small ($n = 14$) group of male essential hypertensives (mean age = 47.6 years), carefully screened to rule out other forms of cardiovascular disease. There was a significant positive correlation between diastolic, but not systolic, blood pressure and error scores, even when age and WAIS IQ had been partialled out. The absence of matched, nonhypertensive controls limits interpretation of these findings, as does the lack of information on other potentially confounding factors, such as occupation or socioeconomic status.

Hypertension has also been related to losses in overall intellectual ability among older adults. In a ten-year follow-up of adults first tested in their sixties, Wilkie and Eisdorfer (1971) observed greater declines in WAIS scores on the part of subjects with diastolic hypertension as compared to normotensives or those with mild blood pressure elevations. Differential decline was greatest on performance, as opposed to verbal, subscales. The same group of investigators (Wilkie, Eisdorfer, & Nowlin, 1976) examined the relationship between diastolic blood pressure and memory (as measured by the Wechsler memory scale) in a subsample of participants from the Duke longitudinal study. They noted that previous investigations suggested that effects of high blood pressure were more likely to be observed on tasks involving complex nonverbal material, time limits, and psychomotor components as opposed to processing of highly meaningful verbal material and, therefore, hypothesized that differences as a function of blood pressure would be obtained on the visual reproduction subscale of the Wechsler battery, but not on the paired-associate or paragraph-recall sections. No differences in performance between normotensive subjects (diastolic BP between 66 and 95 mm Hg) and those with mild elevations (96 to 105 mm Hg) or hypertension (105 mm Hg) were noted on initial testing (mean age of subjects being 67.7 years), but on follow-up testing 6.5 years later, hypertensive subjects performed more poorly than did normotensives on the visual reproduction task. As predicted there were generally no differences as a function of blood pressure on the verbal memory tasks at the time of follow-up, although subjects in the high blood pressure group had the lowest mean scores on all measures and performed significantly more poorly than did the other groups on an immediate recall test. Based on analyses of the types of tasks

presenting difficulty to the hypertensive subjects, Wilkie and colleagues (1976) hypothesized that performance factors (e.g., increased state anxiety or difficulty in shifting sets), rather than memory per se, accounted for the deficits associated with increased blood pressure. They also suggested that the emergence of group differences at retest, when none had been present initially, implicated duration of cardiovascular disease as a potentially important determinant of cognitive impairment in hypertension.

Data on the effects of antihypertensive medication on cognitive performance are conflicting. Spieth (1962, 1964, 1965) found that serial RT's of medicated young and middle-aged hypertensives were similar to those of normotensives and faster than were those of subjects with uncontrolled hypertension, but Light (1975) reported RT slowing among medicated hypertensives. In a more extensive investigation of medication effects, Light (1978) studies 271 adults aged 18 to 77 years with one of six types of cardiovascular or cerebrovascular disorder: normotensive, treated or untreated hypertensive, coronary heart disease (CHD), transient ischemic attack (TIA), and recovered stroke. Subjects with more than one vascular problem were classified according to their most severe problem, so that, for example, individuals who met the blood pressure criteria for hypertension (diastolic BP > 90 mm Hg or systolic BP > 140 or 150 mm Hg for subjects younger or older than 60 years, respectively) and also had evidence of angina, myocardial infarction, coronary artery disease, or previous heart failure, were assigned to the CHD group. All TIA patients were neurologically asymptomatic at testing, the most recent TIA's having occurred 2 to 30 days prior to assessment. All stroke patients were at least two months poststroke, and none were aphasic at the time of testing. All medicated hypertensives and CHD patients discontinued drug use 3 to 21 days prior to testing but immediately before assessment were treated with furosemide, a diuretic, which lowered BP to near normal levels. A subsample of normotensive control subjects also received the furosemide treatment. Mean arterial blood pressures at the time of testing were 78.6 for normotensives treated with furosemide, 93.2 for untreated normotensives, 103.9 for previously unmedicated hypertensives, and 107.7 for previously medicated hypertensives (both hypertensive groups having received furosemide). Results, based on 12 serial reaction-time tasks, indicated slowing of RT with age for all groups, those with cerebrovascular disorders responding most slowly, those with untreated hypertension or CHD performing similarly to normotensive controls, but previously medicated hypertensives performing more slowly than did controls. An additional trend in the data was toward greater slowing among untreated hypertensives with high plasma renin levels as compared to those with normal or low plasma renin, consistent with the findings of a previous study by Light (1975). No differences in RT between normotensives treated with furosemide and those without such treatment were obtained, suggesting that mild, acute reductions in blood pressure may not greatly influence psychomotor speed.

Effects of chronic use of antihypertensive medications remain unclear after this investigation, and further studies of individuals who have not discontinued use of these drugs are required. The greater slowing of previously medicated subjects observed in this investigation did not appear to reflect direct drug action of any specific class of medications but instead might have been due to common factors in the action of these medications, decreased autoregulatory activity, or personality differences between individuals who seek treatment for hypertension and those who do not.

Schultz, Dineen, Elias, Pentz, and Wood (1979) also examined effects of antihypertensive medication history on cognitive performance, using WAIS performance rather than reaction time as the dependent variable. Subjects included younger (21 to 39 years) and older adults (45 to 65 years) with or without hypertension (defined as mean arterial BP > 105 mm Hg, roughly equivalent to a diastolic BP > 90 mm Hg or a systolic BP > 140 mm Hg). Screening procedures excluded individuals with histories of cardiac, cerebrovascular, or renal disease. As in Light's investigation all hypertensives and a subset of controls were treated with furosemide prior to testing, having stopped all previous antihypertensive medications 3 to 21 days earlier. Results included a significant age-by-blood-pressure interaction for verbal scale scores, with lower scores observed for hypertensives as compared to normotensives in the younger, but not the older, age group. Analyses of performance scale scores were computed with subjects being matched on verbal ability. A significant main effect of blood pressure was obtained on performance scores with both younger and older hypertensives performing more poorly than normotensives on the overall performance scale score and on digit symbol, block design, picture arrangement, and object assembly subtests. Contrary to Light's (1978) findings on reaction time, there were no significant differences as a function of antihypertensive medication history, nor were plasma renin levels associated with performance.

No effect of cardiovascular disease on cognitive performance could be detected in another examination of a subset of subjects participating in the Duke longitudinal study (Thompson, Eisdorfer, & Estes, 1970). Approximately half (n = 43) of the group (aged 60 to 93 years) had symptoms of cardiovascular disease (based on physical examination, EKG interpretation, estimates of heart size, extent of aortic calcification, hypertension, and cardiac decompensation), and half (n = 41) did not. Individuals with essential hypertension alone or with evidence of cerebrovascular or pulmonary disease were excluded from comparisons. Initial analyses suggested that WAIS performance IQs were lower in the group with cardiovascular disease than in the symptom-free group, but the differences disappeared when variations in race and socioeconomic status were taken into account. No significant change in IQ occurred for subjects in either group during a three-year test-retest interval. Since none of the subjects was severely restricted in activities as a result of disease, the authors suggested that only the initial stages of cardiovascular disease may have been present, and indeed subsequent analyses of data from the Duke longitudinal study (e.g., Wilkie & Eisdorfer, 1971; Wilkie et al., 1976), involving longer test-retest intervals and a wider range of impairments, provided evidence for negative effects of cardiovascular disease on cognition. The long interval between clinically manifest cardiovascular disease and the appearance of impaired cognition is a hopeful indication as it offers an opportunity for preventive intervention.

Longitudinal changes in cognitive performance as a function of cardiovascular disease were also noted in another study (Hertzog, Schaie, & Gribbin, 1978). Subjects were 156 community residents representing two 14-year age cohorts (birth years 1886 to 1899 and 1900 to 1913) who were tested in 1956 and again in 1963. Tests included five subtests from the primary mental abilities battery, two composite measures (intellectual ability and educational aptitude) computed from the same subtests, and three factor scales from the Test of Behavioral Rigidity. Presence and absence of cardiovascular disease were determined by examination of medical histories from 1956 and 1963, and the mean performances of subjects with cardiovascular disease was found to be lower than that of normals in both cohort groups for all dependent variables, including a greater decline in speed over time, for those with, as opposed to those without, disease. Subjects with hypertension only, however, generally performed similarly, or increased over time, relative to normals, the exception being hypertensives' greater decline in psychomotor speed. The findings of this study, then, generally support the notion that presence of cardiovascular disease exerts a negative influence on intellectual performance and substantiate earlier findings (e.g., Wilkie & Eisdorfer, 1971) of generally positive correlations between mild hypertension and certain aspects of cognitive functioning.

Botwinick and Storandt (1974) examined the effects of self-reported symptoms of cardiovascular disease, depressive affect, and education on simple reaction time among young (mean age approximately 23 years) and elderly (mean age approximately 68 years) subjects. Participants rated themselves on the cardiovascular scale of the Cornell Medical Index, and the sample was dichotomized into those reporting three to seven symptoms of cardiovascular disease and those with two or fewer symptoms. Self-ratings of depression were obtained on the Zung scale, and data were compared for those with scaled scores greater than or equal to 50 and those with lower scores. All of the younger subjects had completed at least 15 years of formal education, but elderly subjects represented two education subgroups, those with 8 to 11 years of education and those with 15 or more years. Behavioral assessment consisted of a series of simple auditory-reaction-time tasks with preparatory intervals of 0.5 or 6.0 seconds. Young subjects had significantly faster reaction times, and among the older subjects, those with more education were faster than were those with less education. Higher depression scores were associated with slower reaction times within both age groups, as were higher numbers of cardiovascular symptoms. Among the elderly, however, cardiovascular symptoms failed to relate significantly to reaction time when education was taken into account.

The preceding results are similar to those of several other studies in showing relationships between cardiovascular status and psychomotor speed; Botwinick and Storandt (1974), however, made the important observation that cardiovascular status, as well as depressive affect, account for relatively little of the variance in reaction time scores when compared to the effects of age. A major problem in comparing results of this investigation with those of other studies is that only the frequency, not the types, of cardiovascular symptoms was reported and that no information on use of medications is available.

Finally, there is a study examining reaction time as a function of behavioral predisposition to coronary heart disease (Abrahams & Birren, 1973). Subjects, all men, aged 25 to 59 years, were given the Standard Situation Interview (Friedman, 1969) assessing drive, competitiveness, aggressiveness, time-consciousness, and feelings of work-related pressure as well as expressions such as grimacing, fist-clenching, and fidgeting. Individuals scoring high on these characteristics were classified as Type *A* personalities (a coronary-prone pattern) and those scoring low, as Type *B*. Type *A* normotensive subjects, free of clinical signs and symptoms of coronary heart disease as confirmed by medical examination, had significantly longer response latencies on both simple and choice reaction-time tasks than did Type *B* subjects; moreover, Type *A* persons were disproportionately slower on the more difficult choice reaction-time task. The authors interpreted their results as suggesting that psychomotor slowing may be in part a result of those behavioral factors shown to precede the development of coronary heart disease. Alternative explanations included the possibility that coronary-prone (Type *A*) individuals undergo accelerated aging changes and/or exhibit different patterns of activation and arousal (indicative of differential integration of autonomic and central nervous system feedback) than do Type *B* individuals. Even though the possibility that Type *A* subjects were experiencing central nervous system circulatory insufficiency as a result of early, subclinical cardiovascular pathology was discounted on the basis of their normal medical screenings, it is well known that a normal medical examination may be followed almost immediately by myocardial infarction and that medical screenings generally fail to detect TIA's unless the history of such attacks is provided.

Mortality

It has been a common finding in longitudinal studies that participants with the lowest test scores are less likely to survive for repeated testing than those with higher initial scores. First described by Kleemeier (1962) and soon confirmed by Jarvik and colleagues (e.g., Jarvik & Falek, 1963), this finding has been reported from nearly every longitudinal study (e.g., Birren, 1968; Granick, 1971; Hertzog et al., 1978; Riegel, 1971; Riegel, Riegel, & Meyer, 1967). It is not known whether the static correlation between survival and test scores at a given time represents a general relation between intelligence and viability or whether individuals with the lowest test scores are those who already experienced the decline in mental function presaging death (*terminal decline*).

A few studies have directly investigated *changes* in cognitive performance as related to nearness of death (see Siegler, 1975, for a review). Among these is the New York State Psychiatric Institute Study of senescent twins, in the course of which 134 twin pairs were given a battery of psychological tests (Similarities, Digits Forward and Backward, Block Design, and Digit Symbol Substitution from the Wechsler-Bellevue, Vocabulary from the Stanford-Binet, and a psychomotor tapping test) beginning in the late 1940s and at intervals thereafter (Blum, Clark,

& Jarvik, 1973; Jarvik, 1962; Jarvik & Blum, 1971; Jarvik & Falek, 1963; Jarvik, Kallman, & Falek, 1962a; Jarvik, Kallman, Lorge, & Falek, 1962b; Kallmann & Jarvik, 1959). All of the twins were over 60 years old at the time of entrance into the study, and all of them have been followed for the remainder of their lives. Survivors were retested several times, most recently in 1973, and changes in psychological performance were examined in relation to survival. From these data emerged the concept of *critical loss,* defined as two or more of the following: any loss in vocabulary score, an annual rate of decline of 10 percent on the similarities test, and an annual rate of decline of 2 percent on the Digit Symbol Substitution test. Twins showing a critical loss during the seventh and eighth decades of life were significantly more likely to die within five years of testing than were those without such loss. Even stronger evidence was obtained when monozygotic twin pairs discordant for critical loss were compared: In all 11 such pairs, the partner with the critical loss died earlier. Investigators following other samples (e.g., Hall, Savage, Bolton, Pidwell, & Blessed, 1972; Reimanis & Green, 1971) have also reported significant associations between rate of cognitive loss and nearness to death, but there is disagreement among the various sets of findings as to whether verbal or perceptual motor tests are the better predictors. To our knowledge the other data have not been analyzed in terms of critical loss. Nonetheless these studies suggest that changes in cognitive performance may serve as early markers of shifts in viability.

The causal mechanisms underlying terminal decline are not as yet known. Since arteriosclerotic disease was the predominant type of terminal illness in the New York twins, as it was for the comparable general population, it was postulated that the decline in those specific psychological functions constituting critical loss may reflect subclinical cerebral dysfunction. This conjecture is indirectly supported by the research on the relation between cardiovascular-cerebrovascular disease and cognitive function reviewed in the preceding section.

In the ninth decade and beyond, however, critical loss no longer predicted mortality among the aging twins (Steuer, La Rue, Jarvik, & Blum, 1980), possibly for reasons similar to those which explain why, in contradistinction to earlier decades, physical health variables become poor predictors of mortality in the eighth decade of life and beyond (La Rue, Bank, Jarvik, & Hetland, 1979).

Preventive Interventions

Our rationale for focusing on disease in relation to changes in mental functioning was the fact that such an approach permits, and even dictates, attempts at preventive intervention. Data reviewed in the preceding sections suggest that declines in abstract reasoning, verbal intelligence, and to some extent, memory and psychomotor speed may be linked to remediable diseases, rather than being a part of normal aging. Certain risk factors have already been identified, such as the finding that dietary habits and tobacco use influence the incidence of atherosclerotic disease. Indeed it has been argued that the 20 percent decline observed in coronary heart disease mortality during the past decade may be attributable, at least in part, to public awareness of and response to these risk factors (Havlik & Feinleib, 1979).

Our society's awareness of the importance of physical exercise is also increasing, and there are data suggesting that, as we grow older, continued exercise might well reduce the decline in speed so common in old age. Botwinick and Thompson (1968) observed that reaction times of an elderly sample were not significantly different from those of a young adult group with little or no regular exercise, although the elderly were slower than were young adults who exercised regularly.

Botwinick and Storandt (1974) also examined the effects of physical exercise on reaction time as part of a larger investigation (pp. 30–31). When young (approximately 23 years old) and elderly (approximately 68 years old) men and women were divided into four groups on the basis of their habits of physical exercise (none; very little, or irregularly; one or more hours, two or three times a week; one or more hours at least four days a week, or being a team athlete), a significant correlation between degree of exercise and reaction time was found for the young, but not the elderly, participants. The authors interpreted their results as suggesting that beneficial effects of exercise on psychomotor speed may be limited to the young, but it is possible that there was greater restriction of range of exercise within the elderly group (the probability of inclusion of team athletes being low, for example). Duration of participation in regular exercise was also not reported in this investigation, and this may prove to be an important variable.

In another study (Elsayed, Ismail, & Young, 1980) of the effects of physical fitness on intellectual functioning in young (mean age = 34.78 years) and older (mean age = 52.95 years) men, subjects in each age group were classified at the beginning of the investigation as either high- or low-fit on the basis of a series of physiological measures. Performance on measures of fluid and crystallized intelligence (Scale 3 of Cattell's Culture Fair Intelligence Test and Factor *B* of the Cattell Sixteen Personality Factor Questionnaire, respectively) was assessed before and after participation in a four-month physical fitness program consisting of three 90-minute sessions per week of jogging, calisthenics, progressive running, and self-selected recreational activities. Pretest scores on the fluid intelligence measures varied significantly with fitness (high-low) and age (young-old). Gains in fluid intelligence following the exercise program were observed on two of four submeasures of fluid intelligence (series and matrices). There were no significant differences in crystallized intelligence as a function of age, initial fitness, or participation in the exercise program. The authors speculated that the facilitative effects of exercise may have been mediated by increased availability of circulating glucose and/or psychological factors (e.g., increased feelings of self-worth).

No risk factors, either dietary- or exercise-related, have as yet been detected for senile dementia. Even though genetic factors undoubtedly play a part in the etiology of Alzheimer-type senile dementia, they do so also in hypertension and coronary heart disease, yet treatment and/or preventive efforts have had a dramatic effect on mortality due to the last two conditions. Thus there is every reason to believe that appropriate interventions, once identified, should be equally successful in preventing senile dementia and perhaps also the benign senescent forgetfulness (Kral, 1978) so often seen among the aged.

CONCLUSIONS

Considered together, the studies reviewed point toward a number of conclusions.

First, evidence relating neurodegenerative changes, EEG slowing, chromosome changes, and immune dysfunctions to cognitive impairment in old age is stronger in the case of dementia than in normal aging. In part this may be due to the fact that only a few studies, comprising relatively small numbers of individuals, have attempted to correlate individual differences on biological and behavioral measures within the normal range. Failure to examine multiple biological indices may also have contributed to the apparent lack of biobehavioral linkage in the case of normal aging, as may the relative insensitivity of the behavioral measures (e.g., mental status exams) commonly employed.

Second, cardiovascular and cerebrovascular diseases generally have a negative impact on cognition, but the extent of the effect differs widely depending on the severity of illness and type of behavior examined. Studies contrasting patients with cardiovascular or cerebrovascular conditions (e.g., history of myocardial infarction, transient ischemic attacks, stroke, or congestive heart failure) with normal controls almost invariably report poorer performance for the patients on both verbal and nonverbal measures. By contrast when patients with hypertension only are compared with age-matched normals, the pattern of outcomes is more complex. Hypertension impairs speeded psychomotor performance more than untimed verbal abilities. Occasionally mild hypertension appears to enhance performance relative to that of normals and has been postulated to improve cerebral perfusion. If the hypertension is more severe, however, the outcome is ultimately lowered intellectual performance. It is unclear whether chronic use of antihypertensive medications influences cognitive abilities in a systematic way.

Finally, in our opinion it would be premature to argue in favor of either continuity or discontinuity in biobehavioral relationships at different points in the adult life span. However, we might offer the following speculations in support of discontinuity. There are scattered suggestions in the studies reviewed that psychological factors, especially personality, may play a greater role in mediating relations between cardiovascular disease and cognition early, as opposed to later, in adulthood. For example Type *A* versus Type *B* personality has been found to be a more powerful predictor of cardiac pathology among younger (39 to 49 years) as opposed to older (50 to 59 years) subjects (Rosenman, Friedman, Straus, Jenkins, Zyzanski, & Wurm, 1970). Similarly detrimental effects of hypertension (a condition closely tied to psychological states such as anxiety) on cognition are found more reliably among young and middle-aged, rather than elderly, subjects. With advancing age and its attendant physiological declines, variables such as duration of disease and severity of clinical symptoms, in combination with factors roughly subsumed under the label of socioeconomic status (affecting diet and patterns of intellectual, as well as physical, stimulation), appear to account for more of the variance in observed disease-cognition relations than do personality or attitudinal variables. Regarding old age it is only half in jest that one might say that "Health + Wealth = Happiness," with happiness predicated in part on the retention of those mental abilities which enable attainment of pleasure.

REFERENCES

ABRAHAMS, J. P., & BIRREN, J. E. Reaction time as a function of age and behavioral predisposition to coronary heart disease. *Journal of Gerontology*, 1973, *28*, 471–478.

ABRAHAMS, J. P., HOYER, W. J., ELIAS, M. F., & BRADIGAN, B. Gerontological research in psychology published in the *Journal of Gerontology*, 1963–1974: Perspectives and progress. *Journal of Gerontology*, 1975, *30*, 668–673.

APTER, N. S., HALSTEAD, W. C., & HEIMBURGER, R. F. Impaired cerebral functions in essential hypertension. *American Journal of Psychiatry*, 1951, *107*, 808–813.

BALTES, P. B. Prototypical paradigms and questions in life-span research on development and aging. *Gerontologist*, 1973, *13*, 458–467.

BALTES, P. B., & WILLIS, S. L. Toward psychological theories of aging and development. In J. E. Birren & K. W. Schaie (Eds.), *Handbook of the psychology of aging*. New York: Van Nostrand Reinhold, 1977.

BARNES, R. H., BUSSE, E. W., & FRIEDMAN, E. L. The psychological function of aged individuals with normal and abnormal electroencephalograms. II. A study of hospitalized individuals. *Journal of Nervous Mental Disease*, 1956, *124*, 585–593.

BARO, F. *Huntington's chorea.* Unpublished dissertation, Belgium, Katholieke Universiteit de Leuven, 1972.

BARRON, S. A., JACOBS, L., & KINKEI, W. R. Changes in size of normal lateral ventricles during aging determined by computerized tomography. *Neurology*, 1976, *26*, 1011–1013.

BIRREN, J. E. Increment and decrement in the intellectual status of the aged. *Psychiatric Research Reports*, 1968, *23*, 207–214.

BIRREN, J. E., BUTLER, R. N., GREENHOUSE, S. W., SOKOLOFF, L., & YARROW, M. R. Interdisciplinary relationships: Interrelations of physiological, psychological and psychiatric findings in healthy elderly men. In J. E. Birren, R. N. Butler, S. W. Greenhouse, L. Sokoloff & M. R. Yarrow (Eds.), *Human aging: A biological and behavioral study.* Washington, D.C.: U.S. Government Printing Office, 1963.

BLESSED, G., TOMLINSON, B. E., & ROTH, M. The association between quantitative measures of dementia and of senile change in the cerebral grey matter of elderly subjects. *British Journal of Psychiatry*, 1968, *114*, 797–811.

BLUM, J. E., CLARK, E. T., & JARVIK, L. F. The New York State Psychiatric Institute study of aging twins. In L. F. Jarvik, C. Eisdorfer, & J. E. Blum (Eds.), *Intellectual functioning in adults.* New York: Springer, 1973.

BLUMENTHAL, H. T., & BERNS, A. W. Autoimmunity and aging. In B. L. Strehler (Ed.), *Advances in gerontological research* (Vol. 1). New York: Academic Press, 1964.

BOTWINICK, J. *Aging and behavior.* New York: Springer, 1973.

BOTWINICK, J. Intellectual abilities. In J. E. Birren & K. W. Schaie (Eds.), *Handbook of the psychology of aging.* New York: Van Nostrand Reinhold, 1977.

BOTWINICK, J., & STORANDT, M. Cardiovascular status, depressive affect, and other factors in reaction time. *Journal of Gerontology*, 1974, *29*, 543–548.

BOTWINICK, J., & BIRREN, J. E. Cognitive processes: Mental abilities and psychomotor responses in healthy aged men. In J. E. Birren, R. N. Butler, S. W. Greenhouse, L. Sokoloff, & M. Yarrow (Eds.), *Human aging: A biological and behavioral study.* Washington, D.C.: U.S. Government Printing Office, 1963.

BOTWINICK, J., & KORNETSKY, C. Age differences in the acquisition and extinction of GSR. *Journal of Gerontology*, 1960, *15*, 83–84.

BOTWINICK, J., & THOMPSON, L. W. Age difference in reaction time: An artifact? *Gerontologist*, 1968, *8*, 25–28.

BRENT, G., SMITH, D., MICHALEWSKI, H., & THOMPSON, L. Differences in evoked potentials in young and old subjects during habituation and dishabituation procedures. *Psychophysiology*, 1976, *14*, 96–97.

BRODY, H. Cell counts in cerebral cortex and brainstem. In R. Katzman, R. D. Terry, & K. L. Bick (Eds.), *Aging* (Vol. 7), Alzheimer's disease: Senile dementia and related disorders. New York: Raven Press, 1978.

BUSSE, E. W. The Duke longitudinal study I: Senescence and senility. In R. Katzman, R. D. Terry, & K. L. Bick (Eds.), *Alzheimer's disease: Senile dementia and related disorders.* New York: Raven Press, 1978.

BUSSE, E. W., & OBRIST, W. D. Pre-senescent electroencephalographic changes in normal subjects. *Journal of Gerontology*, 1965, *20*, 315–320.

CADOTTE, M., & FRASER, D. Etude de l'aneuploidie observee dans les cultures de sang et de moelle en fonction du nombre et de la longeur des chromosomes da chaque groups et de l'age et du sexe des sujets. *L'Union Medicale du Canada*, 1970, *99*, 2003–2007.

CATTELL, R. B. Theory of fluid and crystallized intelligence: A critical experiment. *Journal of Educational Psychology*, 1963, *54*, 1–22.

CHAP, J., & SINNOTT, J. Performance of institutionalized and community-active old persons on concrete and formal Piagetian tasks. *International Journal of Aging and Human Development*, 1977–1978, *8*, 269–278.

CLAYTON, V., & OVERTON, W. F. Concrete and formal operational thought processes in young adulthood and old age. *International Journal of Aging and Human Development*, 1976, *7*, 237–248.

COHEN D., & EISDORFER, C. Behavioral-immunologic relationships in older men and women. *Experimental Aging Research*, 1977, *3*, 225–229.

COHEN, D., & EISDORFER, C. Serum immunoglobulins and cognitive status in the elderly: A population study. *British Journal of Psychiatry*, 1980, *136*, 33–39.

COHEN, D., MATSUYAMA, S. S., & JARVIK, L. F. Immunoglobulin levels and intellectual functioning in the aged. *Experimental Aging Research*, 1976, *2*, 345–348.

COOK, R. H., WARD, B. E., & AUSTIN, J. A. Studies in aging of the brain: IV. Familial Alzheimer disease: Relation to transmissible dementia, aneuploidy, and microtubular defects. *Neurology*, 1979, *29*, 1402–1412.

CORRELL, R. E., ROKOSZ, S., & BLANCHARD, B. M. Some correlates of WAIS performance in the elderly. *Journal of Gerontology*, 1966, *21*, 544–549.

COURT-BROWN, W. M., BUCKTON, K. E., JACOBS, P. A., TOUGH, I. M., KUENSSBERG, E. V., & KNOX, J.D.E. *Chromosome studies on adults.* London: Cambridge University Press, 1966.

DAYAN, A. D. Quantitative histological studies on the aging human brain. I. Senile plaques and neurofibrillary tangles in "normal" patients. *Acta Neuropathologia*, 1970a, *16*, 85–94.

DAYAN, A. D. Quantitative histological studies on the aging human brain. II. Senile plaques and neurofibrillary tangles in senile dementia. *Acta Neuropathologia*, 1970b, *16*, 95–102.

DE BEAUVOIR, S. *The coming of age.* New York: Warner Paperback Library, 1973.

DE BONI, U., & CRAPPER, D. R. Paired helical filaments of the Alzheimer type in cultured neurons. *Nature*, 1978, *271*, 566–568.

DEMOISE, C. F., & CONRAD, R. A. Effects of age and radiation exposure in a Marshall Island population. *Journal of Gerontology*, 1972, *27*, 197–201.

EARNEST, P. E., HEATON, R. K., WILKINSON, W. E., & MANKE, W. F. Cortical atrophy, ventricular enlargement and intellectual impairment in the aged. *Neurology*, 1979, *29*, 1138–1143.

EISDORFER, C. Arousal and performance: Experiments in verbal learning and a tentative theory. In G. Talland (Ed.), *Human behavior and aging: Recent advances in research and theory.* New York: Academic Press, 1968.

EISDORFER, C., COHEN, D., & BUCKLEY, C. E., III. Serum immunoglobulins and cognition in the impaired elderly. In R. Katzman, R. D. Terry, & K. L. Bick (Eds.), *Alzheimer's disease: Senile dementia and related disorders.* New York: Raven Press, 1978.

EISDORFER, C., NOWLIN, J. B., & WILKIE, F. Improvement of learning in the aged by modification of autonomic nervous system activity. *Science*, 1970, *170*, 1327–1329.

ELSAYED, M., ISMAIL, A. H., & YOUNG, R. J. Intellectual differences of adult men related to age and physical fitness before and after an exercise program. *Journal of Gerontology*, 1980, *35*, 383–387.

FITZGERALD, P. H. A mechanism of X chromosome aneuploidy in lymphocytes of aging women. *Humangenetik*, 1975, *28*, 153–158.

FLAVELL, J. H. Cognitive changes in adulthood. In L. R. Goulet & P. B. Baltes (Eds.), *Life span developmental psychology: Research and theory.* New York: Academic Press, 1970.

FOLSTEIN, M. F., FOLSTEIN, S. E., & McHUGH, P. R. "Mini Mental State": A practical method of grading the cognitive state of patients for the clinician. *Journal of Psychiatric Research*, 1975 *12*, 189–198.

FORD, J. M., HINK, R. F., HOPKINS, W. F., III, ROTH, W. T., PFEFFERBAUM, A., & KOPELL, B. S. Age effects on event-related potentials in a selective attention task. *Journal of Gerontology*, 1979, *34*, 388–395.

FOX, J. H., TOPEL, J. L., & HUCKMAN, M. S. Use of computerized tomography in senile dementia. *Journal of Neurology, Neurosurgery, and Psychiatry.* 1975, *38*, 948–953.

FREEMAN, J. T. *Clinical features of the older patient.* Springfield, Ill.: Chas. C Thomas, 1965.

FRIEDMAN, M. The general causes of coronary artery disease. In M. Friedman (Ed.), *The pathogenesis of coronary artery disease.* New York: McGraw-Hill, 1969.

FROEHLING, S. *Effects of propranolol on behavior and physiological measures in elderly males.* Unpublished doctoral dissertation, University of Miami, 1974.

GOLDMAN, H., KLEINMAN, K. M., SNOW, M. Y., BIDUS, D. R., & KOROL, B. Correlation of diastolic blood pressure and signs of cognitive dysfunction in essential hypertension. *Diseases of the Nervous System*, 1974, *35*, 571–572.

GOODIN, D., SQUIRES, K., HENDERSON, B., & STARR, A. Age related variations in evoked potentials to auditory stimuli in normal human subjects. *Electroencephalography and Clinical Neurophysiology*, 1978 , *44*, 447–458.

GOODMAN, R. M., FEICHEIMER, N. S., MILLER, F., MILLER, R., & ZARTMAN, D. Chromosomal alterations in three age groups of human females. *American Journal of Medical Science*, 1969, *258*, 26–31.

GRANICK, S. Psychological test functioning. In S. Granick & R. D. Patterson (Eds.), *Human Aging II. An eleven-year followup biomedical and behavioral study.* Washington, D.C.: U.S. Government Printing Office, 1971.

HALL, E. H., SAVAGE, R.D., BOLTON, N., PIDWELL, D.M., & BLESSED, G. Intellect, mental illness, and survival in the aged: A longitudinal investigation. *Journal of Gerontology*, 1972, *27*, 237–244.

HAMERTON, J. L., TAYLOR, A. E., ANGELL, R., & McGUIRE, M. P. Chromosome investigations of a small isolated human population: Chromosome abnormalities and distribution of chromosome counts according to age and sex among the population. *Nature*, 1961, *191*, 1178–1180.

HAVLIK, R. J., & FEINLEIB, M. (Eds.). Proceedings of the Conference on the Decline in Coronary Heart Disease Mortality, (NIH Publication No. 79-1610). Washington, D.C.: U.S. Department of Health, Education, and Welfare, May 1979.

HENDRICKS, J., & HENDRICKS, C. D. *Aging in mass society.* Cambridge, Mass.: Winthrop, 1977.

HENSCHKE, P. J., BELL, D. A., & CAPE, R.D.T. Immunologic indices in Alzheimer dementia. *Journal of Experimental Gerontology*, 1979, *1*, 23–37.

HERTZOG, C., SCHAIE, K. W., & GRIBBIN, K. Cardiovascular disease and changes in intellectual functioning from middle to old age. *Journal of Gerontology*, 1978, *33*, 872–883.

HESTON, L. L., & MASTRI, A. R. The genetics of Alzheimer's disease: Associations with hematologic malignancy and Down's syndrome. *Archives of General Psychiatry*, 1977, *34*, 976–981.

HOOPER, F. H., FITZGERALD, J., & PAPALIA, D. Piagetian theory and the aging process: Extensions and speculations. *Aging and Human Development*, 1971, *2*, 3–20.

HORN, J. L. Organization of data on life-span development of human abilities. In R. L. Goulet & P. B. Baltes (Eds.), *Life span developmental psychology: Research and theory.* New York: Academic Press, 1970.

HORN, J. L. Human abilities: A review of research and theories in the early 1970's. *Annual Review of Psychology*, 1976, *27*, 437–485.

HUCKMAN, M. S., FOX, J., & TOPEL, J. The validity of criteria for the evaluation of cerebral atrophy by computed tomography. *Radiology*, 1975, *116*, 85–92.

HUGHES, J. R., & CAYAFFA, J. J. The EEG in patients at different ages without organic cerebral disease. *Electroencephalography and Clinical Neurophysiology*, 1977, *42*, 776–784.

INGRAM, C. R., PHEGAN, K. J., & BLUMENTHAL, H. T. Significance of an age-linked neuron binding gamma-globulin fraction of human sera. *Journal of Gerontology*, 1974, *29*, 20–27.

INHELDER, B., & PIAGET, J. *The growth of logical thinking from childhood to adolescence.* New York: Basic Books, 1958.

ISHII, T., & HAGA, S. Immuno-electron microscopic localization of immunoglobulins in amyloid fibrils of senile plaques. *Acta Neuropathologia*, 1976, *36*, 243–249.

ISHII, T., HAGA, S., & SHIMIZU, F. Identification of components of immunoglobulins in senile plaques by means of flourescent antibody techniques. *Acta Neuropathologia*, 1975, *32*, 157–162.

JACOBS, P. A., COURT-BROWN, W. M., & DOLL, A. Distribution of human chromosome count in relation to age. *Nature*, 1961, *191*, 1178–1180.

JARVIK, L. F. Biological differences in intellectual functioning. *Vita Humana*, 1962, *5*, 195–203.

JARVIK, L. F. Survival and psychological aspects of aging in man. *Symposium of the Society for Experimental Biology*, 1967, *21*, 463–482.

JARVIK, L. F. Mental functioning related to chromosome findings in the aged. *Excerpta Medica International Congress Series* No. 274, *Psychiatry* (Part II), 1971, 851–855.

JARVIK, L. F., ALTSHULER, K. Z., KATO, T., & BLUMNER, B. Organic brain syndrome and chromosome loss in aged twins. *Diseases of the Nervous System*, 1971, *32*, 159–170.

JARVIK, L. F., & BLUM, J. E. Cognitive decline as predictor of mortality in twin pairs. A twenty-year-long study of aging. In E. Palmore & F. C. Jeffers (Eds.), *Prediction of life-span.* Lexington, Mass.: Heath, 1971.

JARVIK, L. F., & FALEK, A. Intellectual stability and survival in the aged. *Journal of Gerontology*, 1963, *18*, 173–176.

JARVIK, L. F., KALLMAN, F. J., & FALEK, A. Intellectual changes in aged twins. *Journal of Gerontology*, 1962a, *17*, 289–294.

JARVIK, L. F., KALLMANN, F. J., LORGE, I., & FALEK, A. Longitudinal study of intellectual changes in senescent twins. In C. Tibitts & W. Donahue (Eds.), *Social and psychological aspects of aging.* New York: Columbia University Press, 1962b.

JARVIK, L. F., & KATO, T. Chromosomes and mental changes in octogenarians. *British Journal of Psychiatry*, 1969, *115*, 1193–1194.

JARVIK, L. F., & KATO, T. Chromosome examinations in aged twins. *American Journal of Human Genetics*, 1970, *22*, 562–573.

JARVIK, L. F., YEN, F. S., FU, T. K., & MATSUYAMA, S. S. Chromosomes in old age: A six-year longitudinal study. *Human Genetics*, 1976, *33*, 17–22.

JARVIK, L. F., YEN, F. S., & MORALISHVILI, E. Chromosome examinations in aging institutionalized women. *Journal of Gerontology*, 1974, *29*, 269–276.

JERVIS, G. A. Premature senility in Down's syndrome. *Annals of the New York Academy of Sciences*, 1970, *171*, 559–561.

JOHN, E. R., KARMEL, B. Z., CORNING, W. C., EASTON, P., BROWN, D., AHN, H., JOHN, M., HARMONEY, T., PRICHEP, L., TORO, A., GERSON, I., BARTLETT, F., THATCHER, R., KAYE, H., VALDES, P., & SCHWARTZ, E. Neurometrics. *Science*, 1977, *196*, 1393–1409.

KALLMANN, F. J., & JARVIK, L. F. Individual differences in constitution and genetic background. In J. E. Birren (Ed.), *Handbook of aging and the individual.* Chicago: University of Chicago Press, 1959.

KALLMANN, F. J., & SANDER, G. Twin studies on senescence. *American Journal of Psychiatry*, 1949, *106*, 29–36.

KASZNIAK, A. W., GARRON, D. C., FOX, J. H., BERGEN, D., & HUCKMAN, M. Cerebral atrophy, EEG slowing, age, education, and cognitive functioning in suspected dementia. *Neurology*, 1979, *29*, 1273–1279.

KASZNIAK, A. W., GARRON, D. C., FOX, J. H., HUCKMAN, S., & RAMSEY, R. G. Relation between dementia and cerebral atrophy as measured by computerized tomography. *Neurology*, 1975, *25*, 387.

KATZMAN, R. The prevalence and malignancy of Alzheimer disease. *Archives of Neurology*, 1976, *33*, 217–218.

KLEEMEIER, R. W. Intellectual changes in the senium. *Proceedings of the American Statistical Association*, 1962, *1*, 290–295.

KOOI, K. A., GUVENER, A. M., TUPPER, C. J., & BAGCHI, B. K. Electroencephalographic patterns of the temporal region in normal adults. *Neurology*, 1964, *14*, 1029–1035.

KRAL, V. A. Benign senescent forgetfulness. In R. Katzman, R. D. Terry, & K. L. Bick (Eds.), *Alzheimer's disease: Senile dementia and related disorders*. New York: Raven Press, 1978.

KUHN, D., LANGER, J., KOHLBERG, L., & HAAN, N. The development of formal operations in logical and moral judgment. *Genetic Psychology Monographs*, 1977, *95*, 97–188.

LA RUE, A. *Older women and younger men: Differing cognitive approaches.* Paper presented at a meeting of the American Psychological Association, New York, September 1979.

LA RUE, A., BANK, L., JARVIK, L., & HETLAND, M. Health in old age: How do physicians' ratings and self-ratings compare? *Journal of Gerontology*, 1979, *34*, 687–691

LA RUE, A., & WALDBAUM, A. *Aging vs. illness as predictors of Piagetian problem solving in older adults.* Paper presented at the 10th annual Interdisciplinary International Conference on Piagetian Theory and the Helping Professions, Los Angeles, February 1980.

LIGHT, K. C. Slowing of response time in young and middle-aged hypertensive patients. *Experimental Aging Research*, 1975, *1*, 209–227.

LIGHT, K. C. Effects of mild cardiovascular and cerebrovascular disorders on serial reaction time performance. *Experimental Aging Research*, 1978, *4*, 3–22.

MAKINODAN, T. Cellular basis of immunosenescence. In *Molecular and cellular mechanisms of aging* (Vol. 27). Paris: INSERM, 1973.

MALAMUD, N. Neuropathology of organic brain syndromes associated with dying. In C. M. Gaitz (Ed.), *Aging and the brain*. New York: Plenum, 1972.

MARSH, G. R., & THOMPSON, L. W. Age differences in evoked potentials during an auditory discrimination task. *Gerontologist*, 1972, *12*, 44.

MATSUYAMA, H., WAMIKI, H., & WATANABE, I. Senile changes in the brain in the Japanese. Incidence of Alzheimer's neurofibrillary change and senile plaques. In F. Luthy & A. Bischoff (Eds.), *Proceedings of the 5th International Congress of Neuropathology*, Excerpta Medica, 1966, Series No. 100, 979–980.

MATSUYAMA, S. S., DECKARD, B. S., & JARVIK, L. F. *Immunoglobulins and cognition in impaired elderly women.* Paper presented at the 11th International Congress of Gerontology, Tokyo, August 1978.

MATTEVI, M. S., & SALZANO, F. M. Senescence and human chromosome changes. *Humangenetik*, 1975, *27* 1–8.

MORIMATSU, M., HIRAI, S., MURAMATSU, A., & YOSHIKAWA, M. Senile degenerative brain lesions and dementia. *Journal of the American Geriatrics Society.* 1975, *23*, 390–406.

MULLER, H. F., & KRAL, V. A. The electroencephalogram in advanced senile dementia. *Journal of the American Geriatrics Society*, 1967, *15*, 415–426.

NAESER, M. A., GEBHARDT, C., & LEVINE, H. L. Decreased computerized tomography numbers in patients with presenile dementia. Detection in patients with otherwise normal scans. *Archives of Neurology*, 1980, *38*, 401–409.

NANDY, K. Immune reactions in aging brain and senile dementia. In K. Nandy & I. Sherwin (Eds.), *The aging brain and senile dementia*. New York: Plenum, 1977.

NANDY, K. *Neuroanatomical changes in the aging brain.* Paper presented at a South Central RMEC symposium ("Biomedical Aspects of Senile Dementia and Related Disorders"), St. Louis, Mo., March 1978.

NATIONAL CENTER FOR HEALTH STATISTICS. Department of Health, Education, and Welfare. *Health in the later years of life.* Washington, D.C.: U.S. Government Printing Office, 1971.

NEURATH, P., DEREMER, K., BELL, B., JARVIK, L., & KATO, T. Chromosome loss compared with chromosome size, age, and sex of subjects. *Nature*, 1970, *225*, 281–282.

NIELSEN, J. Chromosomes in senile, presenile, and arteriosclerotic dementia. *Journal of Gerontology*, 1970, *25*, 312–315.

NORDENSON, I., ADOLFSSON, R., BECKMAN, G., BUCHT, G., & WINBLED, B. Chromosomal abnormality in dementia of Alzheimer type. *Lancet*, 1980, *1*, 481–482.

OBRIST, W. D. The electroencephalogram of healthy aged males. In J. E. Birren, R. N. Butler, S. W. Greenhouse, L. Sokoloff, & M. Yarrow (Eds.), *Human aging: A biological and behavioral study*. Washington, D.C.: U.S. Government Printing Office, 1963.

OBRIST, W. D. Problems of aging. In A. Remond (Ed.), *Handbook of electroencephalography and clinical neurophysiology* (Vol. 6). Amsterdam: Elsevier Publishing Co., 1974.

OBRIST, W. D. Cerebral physiology of the aged: Relation to psychological function. In N. R. Burch & H. L. Altshuler (Eds.), *Behavior and brain electrical activity*. New York: Plenum, 1975.

OBRIST, W. D., BUSSE, E. W., EISDORFER, C., & KLEEMEIER, R. W. Relation of the electroencephalogram to intellectual function in senescence. *Journal of Gerontology*, 1962, *17*, 197–207.

OBRIST, W. D., & HENRY, C. E. Electroencephalographic findings in aged psychiatric patients. *Journal of Nervous and Mental Disorders*, 1958a, *126*, 254–267.

OBRIST, W. D. & HENRY, C. E. Electroencephalographic frequency analysis of aged psychiatric patients. *Electroencephalography and Clinical Neurophysiology*, 1958b, *10*, 621–632.

OBRIST, W. D., SOKOLOFF, L., LASSEN, M. A., LANE, M. H., BUTLER, R. N., & FEINBERG, I. Relation of EEG to cerebral blood flow and metabolism in old age. *Electroencephalography and Clinical Neurophysiology*, 1963, *15*, 610–619.

OLSON, M. I., & SHAW, C. M. Presenile dementia and Alzheimer's disease in mongolism. *Brain*, 1969, *92*, 147–156.

POWELL, A. H., EISDORFER, C., & BOGDONOFF, M. D. Physiologic response patterns observed in a learning task. *Archives of General Psychiatry*, 1964, *10*, 192–195.

POWELL, D. A., MILLIGAN, W. L., & FURCHTGOTT, E. Peripheral autonomic changes accompanying learning and reaction time performance in older people. *Journal of Gerontology*, 1980, *35*, 57–65.

RAPPORT, M. M. *Immunological perturbations of neurological functions.* Paper presented at South Central RMEC symposium ("Biomedical Aspects of Senile Dementia and Related Disorders"), St. Louis, Mo., March 1978.

RAPPORT, M. M., & KARPIAK, S. E. Discriminative effects of antisera to brain constituents on behavior and EEG activity in the rat. *Research Communications in Psychology, Psychiatry, and Behavior*, 1976, *1*, 115–124.

REGAN, D. Electrical responses evoked from the human brain. *Scientific American*, 1979, *241*, 134–146.

REIMANIS, G., & GREEN, R. R. Imminence of death and intellectual decrement in the aging. *Developmental Psychology*, 1971, *5*, 270–272.

REITAN, R. M. Intellectual and affective changes in essential hypertension. *American Journal of Psychiatry*, 1954, *110*, 817–824.

RIEGEL, K. F. The prediction of death and longevity in longitudinal research. In E. Palmore & F. C. Jeffers (Eds.), *Prediction of the life span*. Lexington, Mass.: Heath, 1971.

RIEGEL, K. F., RIEGEL, R. M., & MEYER, M. A study of the dropout rate in longitudinal research on aging and the prediction of death. *Journal of Personality and Social Psychology*, 1967, *5*, 342–348.

ROBERTS, M. A., CAIRD, F. I., GROSSART, K. W., & STEVEN, J. L. Computerized tomography in the diagnosis of cerebral atrophy. *Journal of Neurology, Neurosurgery, and Psychiatry*, 1976, *39*, 909–915.

ROSEMAN, J. M. & BUCKLEY, C. E. Inverse relationship between serum IgG concentrations and measures of intelligence in elderly persons. *Nature*, 1975, *254*, 55–56.

ROSENMAN, R. H., FRIEDMAN, M., STRAUS, R., JENKINS, C. D., ZYZANSKI, S., & WURM, M. Coronary heart disease in the western collaborative study: A follow-up experience of 4½ years. *Journal of Chronic Diseases*, 1970, *23*, 173–190.

ROTH, M. Diagnosis of senile and related forms of dementia. In R. Katzman, R. D. Terry & K. L. Bick (Eds.), *Alzheimer's disease: Senile dementia and related disorders*. New York: Raven Press, 1978.

SANDBERG, A. A., COHEN, M. M., RIMM, A. A., & LEVIN, M. L. Aneuploidy and age in a population survey. *American Journal of Human Genetics*, 1967, *19*, 633–643.

SCHAIE, K. W. Methodological problems in descriptive developmental research on adulthood and aging. In J. R. Nesselroade & H. W. Reese (Eds.), *Life-span developmental psychology: Methodological issues*. New York: Academic Press, 1973.

SCHLUTZ, N. R., JR., DINEEN, J. T., ELIAS, M. F., PENTZ, C. A., & WOOD, W. G. WAIS performance for different age groups of hypertensive and control subjects during the administration of a diuretic. *Journal of Gerontology*, 1979, *34*, 246–253.

SHOCK, N. W. Biological theories of aging. In J. E. Birren & K. W. Schaie (Eds.), *Handbook of the psychology of aging*. New York: Van Nostrand Reinhold, 1977.

SHORT, M. J., & WILSON, W. P. The electroencephalogram in dementia. In C. E. Wells (Ed.), *Dementia*. Philadelphia: F. A. Davis, 1971.

SIEGLER, I. C. The terminal drop hypothesis: Fact or artifact? *Experimental Aging Research*, 1975, *1*, 169–185.

SINNOTT, J. D. Everyday thinking and Piagetian operativity in adults. *Human Development*, 1975, *18*, 430–443.

SPIETH, W. Abnormal slow perceptual-motor task performances in individuals with stable mild to moderate heart disease. *Aerospace Medicine*, 1962, *33*, 270.

SPIETH, W. Cardiovascular health status, age and psychological performance. *Journal of Gerontology*, 1964, *19*, 277–284.

SPIETH, W. Slowness of task performance and cardiovascular disease. In A. T. Welford & J. E. Birren (Eds.), *Behavior, aging, and the nervous system*. Springfield, Ill.: Chas. C Thomas, 1965.

SQUIRES, K., GOODIN, D., & STARR, A. Event related potentials in development, aging and dementia. In D. Lehmann & E. Callaway (Eds.), *Human evoked potentials: Applications and problems*. New York: Plenum, 1979.

STEUER, J., LA RUE, A., BLUM, J. E., & JARVIK, L. F. "Critical loss" in the eighth and ninth decades. *Journal of Gerontology*, 1980, *36*, 211–213.

SWAIN, J. M. Electroencephalographic abnormalities in presenile atrophy. *Neurology*, 1959, *9*, 722–727.

TERRY, R. D. Dementia: A brief and selective review. *Archives of Neurology*, 1976, *33*, 1–4.

TERRY, R. D., & DAVIES, P. Dementia of the Alzheimer type. *Annual Review of Neuroscience*, 1980, *3*, 77–95.

THOMPSON, L. W., EISDORFER, C., & ESTES, E. H. Cardiovascular disease and behavioral changes in the elderly. In E. Palmore (Ed.), *Normal aging*. Durham, N.C.: Duke University Press, 1970.

THOMPSON, L. W., & NOWLIN, J. B. Relation of increased attention to central and autonomic nervous system states. In L. F. Jarvik, C. Eisdorfer, & J. E. Blum (Eds.), *Intellectual functioning in adults*. New York: Springer, 1973.

TOMLINSON, B. E., BLESSED, G., & ROTH, M. Observations on the brains of nondemented old people. *Journal of Neurological Science*, 1968, *7*, 331–356.

TOMLINSON-KEASEY, C. Formal operations in females from eleven to fifty-four years of age. *Developmental Psychology*, 1972, *6*, 364.

TRAUB, R., GAJDUSEK, D. C., & GIBBS, C. J. Transmissible virus dementia: The relation of transmissible spongi-form encephalopathy to Creutzfeldt-Jakob disease. In W. L. Smith & M. Kinsbourne (Eds.), *Aging and dementia*. Jamaica, N.Y.: Spectrum Publ., 1977.

U.S. Department of Health, Education and Welfare. Public Health Service, Series 10. *Limitation of activity due to chronic conditions*. Washington, D.C.: U.S. Government Printing Office, 1972.

WALFORD, R. L. *The immunologic theory of aging*. Baltimore, Md: Williams & Wilkins, 1969.

WANG, H. S. Cerebral correlates of intellectual function in senescence. In L. F. Jarvik, C. Eisdorfer, & J. E. Blum (Eds.), *Intellectual functioning in adults*. New York: Springer, 1973.

WANG, H. S., & BUSSE, E. W. EEG of healthy old persons—A longitudinal study: I. Dominant background activity and occipital rhythm. *Journal of Gerontology*, 1969, *24*, 419–426.

WARD, B. E., COOK, R. H., ROBINSON, A., & AUSTIN, J. H. Increased aneuploidy in Alzheimer disease. *American Journal of Medical Genetics*, 1979, *3*, 137–144.

WELLS, C. E. Chronic brain disease: An overview. *American Journal of Psychiatry*, 1978, *135*, 1–12.

WILKIE, F., & EISDORFER, C. Intelligence and blood-pressure. *Science*, 1971, *172*, 959–962.

WILKIE, F., EISDORFER, C., & NOWLIN, J. B. Memory and blood pressure in the aged. *Experimental Aging Research*, 1976, *2*, 3–16.

45

Aging
and
Cognitive Changes

NANCY WADSWORTH DENNEY

The topic of this chapter is that of cognitive change during the adult years and especially during the later adult years. Thinking, reasoning, and problem solving will be emphasized rather than learning and memory since learning and memory are covered in a separate chapter in this volume. The focus of this chapter will be on whether there are age changes in cognition during the adult years, whether there are cohort differences in adult cognition, whether the changes that are found are important in any practical sense, whether the changes that are found can be reversed through a variety of intervention techniques, and whether such intervention techniques actually eliminate age differences. In addition an attempt will be made to integrate what is currently known about adult cognition into a preliminary theoretical formulation to guide further research in the area. The issue of whether there are changes in adult cognition will be dealt with first.

ARE THERE AGE CHANGES IN ADULT COGNITION?

There is currently a controversy among gerontologists over whether there are age-related declines during the adult years in cognitive abilities. The debate over this issue was stated most clearly in a series of articles that appeared in the *American Psychologist.* The first article by Horn and Donaldson (1976) was a critique of two earlier articles, one by Baltes and Schaie entitled "Aging and I.Q.: The Myth of the Twilight Years" (1974) and one by Schaie (1974) in which Schaie concluded "that the major finding produced in the gerontology laboratory in the area of intellectual functioning is the demolishing (of the idea of) serious intellectual decrement in the aged"

(p. 806). In their article Horn and Donaldson (1976) concluded that,

... it is premature to argue that existing results clearly indicate the myth of intellectual decline; such clarity as the results possess often indicates decline. There are results which caution against the view that all of the abilities which are believed to be involved in intelligence necessarily decline or decline in the same way; some abilities may decline little or not at all. Also, there are results which caution against supposing that decline necessarily occurs for all subjects or necessarily sets in as early as might be supposed from considerations of cross-sectional data alone. But such cautions are quite different from dogmatic assertions that ideas about intellectual decline are mythical or based only on "methodological artifacts" or "misunderstanding of the relation between individual development and sociocultural change" (Schaie, 1974, p. 802). (p. 715)

Baltes and Schaie (1976) responded by saying,

It is correct to say that our effort has been to debunk the myth of general and universal decline in intellectual performance because it is not supported by the data. Our key theoretical position, however, is not one of creating a new monolithic view on aging, that is, that there is no intellectual decline during adulthood and old age. Our central argument is one for plasticity of intelligence in adulthood and old age as evidenced by large interindividual differences, multidirectionality, multidimensionality, the joint significance of ontogenetic and historical change components, and emerging evidence on modifiability via intervention research. (p. 724)

In response to the Baltes and Schaie reply, Horn and Donaldson (1977) conclude,

The Baltes-Schaie non sequitor does not seriously contest the criticism made by Horn and Donaldson. This is unfortunate, for the criticisms are constructive and designed to improve statements of a theory of generational influence. Many would like a solid basis for believing such a theory. It is, therefore, unfortunate indeed that Baltes and Schaie have not made good use of our invitation to put their ideas in this area into a credible theoretical position, for no one can be satisfied with mere assurances of continued belief that "our major conclusions are unchallenged." To repeat this litany, fortissimo, may well suffice for believers. But it's a funny thing about litanies: They don't make sense to nonbelievers. Quite simply, faith is not enough. (p. 373)

And so the debate continues.

This debate has not been limited to the area of intellectual functioning. In a paper entitled "Memory and Learning Do Decline Late in Life," Arenberg (1977) stated,

Before I describe these studies, I would like to explain why I believe it is important to tell you about them. A pervasive belief among people in the field of aging in the United States is that intellectual functioning does not decline even late in life except shortly before death. Much of this kind of thinking is based primarily on longitudinal psychometric data, particularly the papers by Dr. Warner Schaie and his colleagues. These data have been characterized by the term "the myth of intellectual decline." Recently, in response to a critical paper, Drs. Baltes and Schaie clarified their use of the term "myth." The meaning of "myth" they use is "an uncritically accepted belief." Unfortunately, many of us interpreted "myths" to mean "imaginary" or "contrary to fact." As a result, many gerontologists and people who work in the aging field now believe that intellectual functioning is maintained even late in life.

Furthermore, it is very easy to say "cognitive functioning" for "intellectual functioning" which is a short step from "cognitive decline" instead of "intellectual decline." Then we have gerontologists, even some who are in cognitive gerontology, believing that *memory* and *learning* and *reasoning* do not decline late in life. It is a very appealing belief, and it is understandable why it is so readily accepted. But I am convinced at this time it is WRONG! Let me hasten to add that I am not referring only to speed or cognitive performance based upon speed; I am talking about *learning*, and *memory*, and *problem solving*—aspects of behavior we so cherish and would like to maintain. (p. 1)

There is a fair amount of research related to this controversy over whether there are age declines in cognitive abilities during the adult years. The research evidence relevant to this issue will be reviewed with the results of cross-sectional studies being presented first, followed by the results of longitudinal studies.

CROSS-SECTIONAL RESEARCH

The cross-sectional research that has been conducted in three main areas of investigation—problem solving, performance on Piagetian tasks, and psychometric intelligence—will be reviewed here. A word of caution regarding the interpretation of the results of cross-sectional studies is, however, necessary at this point. As has been pointed out by both Schaie (1965) and Baltes (1968), age and cohort are confounded in cross-sectional research. If, for example, 70-year-olds are compared with 30-year-olds in a cross-sectional study conducted in 1980, the 70-year-olds would be in the 1910 cohort while the

30-year-olds would be in the 1950 cohort. As a result in comparing the 70-year-olds with the 30-year-olds, one is comparing not only 70-year-olds with 30-year-olds but also 1910 cohort members with 1950 cohort members. In this case it is not possible to determine whether differences between the 70-year-olds and the 30-year-olds are a result of the differences in their ages or a result of their membership in different cohorts—that is, it is not clear whether the 70-year-olds were like the 30-year-olds when they were younger but changed with age or whether individuals in the 1910 cohort were always different from individuals in the 1950 cohort. As a result of this confounding, valid conclusions regarding *age change* cannot be drawn on the basis of such cross-sectional research; only conclusions regarding *age differences* can be drawn— that is, you can conclude that the 70-year-olds are different from the 30-year-olds, but you cannot conclude that the 70-year-olds changed with age. It is important to keep this fact in mind when reviewing the cross-sectional studies that follow.

Piagetian Research

A number of cross-sectional studies have been conducted with various Piagetian tasks. In most cases these studies have yielded age differences with elderly adults performing less well than do younger adults. Such age differences have been obtained with classification tasks (Annett, 1959; Cicirelli, 1976; Denney, 1974a, 1974b, 1974c; Denney & Lennon, 1972). While younger adults tend to classify items that are related according to similarity, elderly adults tend to classify items that are related in a complementary fashion much as young children do. When asked more constrained questions about classification based on similarity in studies of class inclusion and multiple classification, elderly adults are less likely to answer correctly than are younger adults (Denney & Cornelius, 1975). Elderly adults have also been reported to be more egocentric (Bielby & Papalia, 1975; Comalli, Wapner, & Werner, 1959; Looft & Charles, 1971; Rubin, 1974; Rubin, Attewell, Tierney, & Tumolo, 1973) and more animistic (Dennis & Mallinger, 1949) in their thinking than are younger adults. Likewise there appear to be age differences on various formal operational tasks as well (Clayton, 1972; Tomlinson-Keasey, 1972).

Whereas the results of the preceding studies seem to indicate strongly age differences among adults in performance on Piagetian tasks, the results of studies on conservation are not nearly so consistent. In several studies elderly individuals were found to conserve less than did younger adults. Sanders, Laurendeau, and Bergeron (1966) found that elderly individuals conserved less on a conservation-of-surfaces test than did young or middle-aged individuals. Papalia (1972) found that elderly individuals conserved less than did college-aged or middle-aged individuals on tests of substance, weight, and volume conservation. However she found no difference between these age groups on a test of conservation of number. Rubin et al. (1973) also found that elderly individuals showed less evidence of conservation on two-dimensional space, number, substance, weight, and continuous quantity tests than did young and middle-aged adults.

Several correlational studies have been presented as evidence of a decline in conservation ability in old age because of the low level of performance of the individuals tested. Papalia, Salverson, and True (1973) found that the proportions of individuals between ages 64 and 85 passing substance, weight, and volume conservation tasks were 66.9 percent, 43.7 percent, and 20.9 percent, respectively. Since the tasks traditionally considered to be more difficult were passed less frequently than were the easier tasks, the authors concluded that elderly individuals lose their abilities to conserve in the reverse order in which they are acquired. However, the fact that there was not a significant correlation between age and performance might lead one to question that assumption. Storck, Looft, and Hooper (1972) tested individuals between the ages of 55 and 79 on both weight and volume conservation tasks. While all individuals obtained perfect scores on the weight conservation tasks, relatively low scores were obtained on the volume conservation tasks. Storck et al. also concluded that their results provided evidence that elderly individuals exhibit performance decrements on more advanced Piagetian tasks. Again, however, their correlation between age and performance on the volume conservation task was not significant.

Although both Storck et al. (1972) and Papalia et al. (1973) concluded that the rather low-level conservation performance exhibited by their elderly individuals supported the notion that there is a decline in conservation ability in old age, there is a problem with such a conclusion. The conclusion is based on the assumption that younger adults would have performed better on the same conservation tasks. However since no middle-aged control group was included in either of these studies, there it no evidence that middle-aged adults would have performed any better. Thus these studies are inconclusive with respect to age differences in conservation.

In contrast to the studies which indicate that there may be age differences in conservation ability, there are also studies which suggest that there may not be such age differences during the adult years. In addition to the studies previously discussed in which elderly individuals obtained perfect scores on weight conservation tasks (Storck et al., 1972) and on number conservation tasks (Papalia, 1972), there is also evidence that elderly individuals perform less well on continuous and discontinuous quantity conservation tasks than do younger adults. Rubin (1976) reported that 92 percent of his elderly subjects reached criterion on a test of these two types of conservation. The remaining 8 percent received scores closely approaching criterion. Selzer and Denney (1980) found that elderly adults performed as well on tests of conservation of substance, weight, and volume as did middle-aged adults.

The results of research with Piagetian tasks tend to indicate definite age differences among adults on most Piagetian tasks, with the possible exception of conservation tasks. It is possible that elderly individuals are more likely to maintain their ability to conserve because they frequently exercise conservation abilities in conducting their everyday activities. In order to cook, for example, an individual would have to realize that a cup of milk was a cup of milk whether it was in the measuring cup or in the bottom of a bowl. The fact that conservation ap-pears to be maintained in old age better than are some of the other Piagetian abilities suggests that practice or exercise may facilitate the maintenance of cognitive abilities in old age.

Problem-Solving Research

A number of different types of problem-solving tasks have been administered to adults of different ages. Virtually all of these studies have resulted in age differences in performance with elderly adults performing less well than do middle-aged or younger adults. Such age differences have been obtained with studies of concept learning. In these studies the subjects are presented with stimuli which vary on a number of dimensions and are told that it is their task to determine what the "concept" is. As the stimuli are presented the subject is told which instances are examples of the concept and which are not. From this procedure the subject is supposed to be able to determine what the concept is. Studies by Arenberg (1968), Brinley, Jovick, and McLaughlin (1974), Carpenter (1971), and Hayslip and Sterns (1979) have demonstrated that elderly adults perform less well than do younger adults on such concept-learning tasks.

Age differences have also been found with cross-sectional studies of performance on a variety of "search" tasks. In these tasks individuals are presented with an array of stimuli and are told that they are supposed to figure out which stimulus or combination of stimuli are "correct." The subjects are supposed to find the correct stimulus or combination of stimuli by selecting stimulus alternatives and then being told whether the "correct" stimulus or combination of stimuli are included in the selected sample. The object is to find the correct solution in as few selections of stimulus alternatives as possible. Older adults have been found to be less efficient and to use less efficient strategies on both nonverbal problems in which the subjects are to select stimuli with, and receive feedback from, a mechanical apparatus (e.g., Arenberg, 1974; Jerome, 1962; Young, 1966, 1971) and verbal problems in which the subjects ask verbal questions of, and receive verbal feedback from, the experimenter (e.g., Denney & Denney, 1973; Kesler, Denney, & Whitely, 1976; Rimoldi & Woude, 1971).

Age differences have also been obtained on tasks which require that subjects change the concept or strategy that they are using during the experimental session. Heglin (1956) found that elderly adults had more difficulty overcoming set in problems similar to the Luchins' water-jar problems than did younger adults. Likewise Wetherick (1965) found that elderly adults were less able to change an established concept in a typical concept-learning session than were young adults even when they were given feedback that indicated that the concept they were using was no longer correct.

Elderly adults have also been found to perform more poorly than do younger adults on tests of verbal reasoning. Morgan (1956) found that elderly adults performed at a lower level than did younger adults on a test of logical reasoning. Bromley (1957) reported that elderly adults performed less well on proverb interpretation tasks than did younger adults. Likewise Friend and Zubek (1958) reported that elderly adults performed less well on a test of "critical thinking" which was composed of a number of practical problems.

Not only do there appear to be age differences with most problem-solving tasks, but there is also evidence that age differences increase with problem complexity. There are at least two cross-sectional studies of the relationship between problem complexity and age differences. Both Kay (1954) and Clay (1954) found that as the complexity of the problems increased the difference between the performance of middle-aged and elderly adults also increased.

Cross-sectional studies have also been conducted with the Matching Familiar Figures test which tests one's ability to choose the stimulus figure that matches a standard figure exactly from among an array of similar figures. Performance is measured in terms of the number of errors an individual makes before s/he arrives at the correct figure and of the time taken to select the first alternative. Denney and List (1979) found that between the ages of 30 and 80 both errors and latency increased with age. Although Coyne, Whitbourne, and Glenwick (1978) did not find the same increase in latency with increasing age, they did find that elderly adults made more errors on a modified version of the Matching Familiar Figures test than did young adults. Thus it seems clear that elderly adults make more errors in trying to select the figure that looks exactly like the standard from an array of alternatives, although it is not clear whether they respond more or less quickly than do younger adults on such a task.

While the majority of the studies on age differences in traditional problem-solving performance have yielded age differences with elderly adults performing less well than do younger adults, there are a few studies in which such age differences were not obtained. Most of the studies in which age differences were not obtained were studies in which the younger and older adults were matched in nonverbal intelligence (e.g., Smith, 1967; Wetherick, 1964), and as a result, they are difficult to interpret. Since there are age differences in nonverbal intelligence, it is not surprising that when age groups are equated with respect to nonverbal intelligence age differences on other dimensions are eliminated as well.

Thus studies emanating from different theoretical and historical backgrounds indicate that there are age differences among adults in problem-solving abilities. Elderly individuals tend to perform less well than do younger individuals. However, as with the Piagetian studies there is evidence that there may be less decline in problem-solving abilities that are frequently exercised. Denney and Palmer (1980) found that, while performance on an abstract "search" task decreased linearly from early adulthood through old age, performance on a set of more realistic, practical problems increased to a peak in the 40- and 50-year-old groups and decreased thereafter. Although there was a decrease with age even in practical problem solving, it began at a much later age than did the decrease associated with the more abstract problem-solving measure.

Intelligence Research

A number of cross-sectional studies of performance on intelligence tests have been conducted. This research suggests that there are different developmental patterns for different abilities. The performance subtests (subtests which measure perceptual-motor, spatial, and other nonverbal abilities) show greater age differences than do the verbal subtests (subtests which measure vocabulary, information, verbal reasoning, and other verbal abilities). Cross-sectional studies indicate either very little decline or sometimes even slight increases in verbal abilities throughout most of the life span (e.g., Birren & Morrison, 1961; Doppelt & Wallace, 1955; Horn & Cattell, 1967) with a possible drop in verbal abilities in the sixties or thereafter (Doppelt & Wallace, 1955). With performance abilities, on the other hand, there seems to be a decline that begins in the early adult years and continues throughout the life span (e.g., Birren & Morrison, 1961; Doppelt & Wallace, 1955; Horn & Cattell, 1967). While these studies indicate that there are eventual declines in virtually all intellectual abilities, they also clearly indicate that the point at which such abilities begin to decline and the rate of decline may vary considerably depending on the type of ability tested. Nonverbal and novel types of intellectual abilities appear to begin to decline much earlier than do more verbal and experience-related types of intellectual abilities. These results again suggest that those abilities that are frequently used are maintained better than those that are not frequently used.

Summary

The results of cross-sectional studies in all of the research areas reviewed clearly indicate that there are age differences in cognitive abilities during the adult years with the performance of younger adults typically being better than that of older adults. However since age-change effects are confounded with cohort-difference effects in cross-sectional studies, one cannot conclude that the age differences obtained in cross-sectional studies actually reflect age changes. Thus it is important to look at longitudinal studies to determine whether there are, in fact, actual age changes in cognitive abilities.

LONGITUDINAL RESEARCH

In longitudinal studies age-change effects and cohort-difference effects are not confounded. Thus one can draw conclusions regarding the actual age changes of the individuals tested in a longitudinal study. There are, however, other interpretation difficulties associated with longitudinal studies. The first problem is that the longitudinal developmental patterns observed in one cohort are confounded with time-of-testing effects. For illustration assume that an investigator follows one cohort over a number of years. Assume also that something occurs in the environment that tends to change individuals' behavior in a certain direction at some point during those years. The change in individuals' behavior that results from the environmental event might be attributed incorrectly to some universal, maturationally determined process rather than to the external event. The second problem is that of selective survival. It has been found that those individuals who remain to be retested in longitudinal studies tend to be those individuals who were brighter to begin with, while the less able subjects are more likely to drop out of the study before it is completed. As a result the final longitudinal study will be a study of more able, as opposed to less able, individuals. If the results of studies of more able individuals differ from those of less able individuals, the longitudinal studies will not be representative of the population in general. With these limitations in mind, longitudinal studies of cognitive abilities will be examined next.

Most of the longitudinal studies that have been conducted have involved intellectual abilities. However, Arenberg (1974) conducted a longitudinal study of the more traditional type of problem solving. He tested individuals between the ages of 24 and 87 on logical problem solving and then six years later retested the same individuals. His cross-sectional comparisons showed an increase in errors with increasing age. The largest age differences occurred between groups under 60 and groups over 60. On the other hand his longitudinal trends revealed a decline only in individuals over the age of 70. These results support the cross-sectional research results presented earlier. However, the results of this study indicate that the decline in problem-solving ability may occur much later than most of the cross-sectional research would indicate.

The results of longitudinal research on intellectual abilities tend to indicate the same types of developmental patterns as those indicated by the cross-sectional research on intellectual abilities. Verbal abilities tend to remain stable or increase slightly across the adult years until about the age of 65 when they begin to decline (Bayley & Oden, 1955; Eisdorfer & Wilkie, 1973; Gilbert, 1973; Jarvik, Kallmann, & Falek, 1962; Owens, 1953, 1966; Rhudick & Gordon, 1973). Performance abilities, on the other hand, begin to show decline much earlier (Blum, Fosshage, & Jarvik, 1972; Eisdorfer & Wilkie, 1973; Gilbert, 1973; Jarvik et al., 1962). While longitudinal studies indicate the same types of developmental patterns as cross-sectional studies, the longitudinal studies tend to show less decline than do the cross-sectional ones, and they show the declines starting later in life.

Summary

The results of both the cross-sectional and longitudinal studies tend to indicate the same pattern—that is, most of the cognitive abilities exhibit age differences that are reflective of age changes. Cross-sectional and longitudinal studies differ in the age at which decline begins and the extent of the decline. Cross-sectional studies suggest that the decline begins at an earlier age and is more extensive than what longitudinal studies indicate. It is not clear whether the quantitative discrepancies in the cross-sectional and longitudinal studies are a result of the cross-sectional studies overestimating age change because age change is confounded with cohort differences or whether the longitudinal studies underestimate age change because of the problems associated with selective survival. In any case the discrepancy is not a major one. Both types of study indicate the same general developmental pattern.

Thus in answer to the question of whether there are age changes in adult cognition, the data currently available indicate that the answer should be "yes." There appear to be age changes in virtually all abilities. Verbal abilities, particularly scores on tests such as vocabulary and information scales, may either increase or remain stable across most of the life span while declining only in late adulthood. Other abilities such as those tapped on performance intelligence measures, Piagetian tasks, and traditional problem-solving tasks may begin to decline at much earlier ages. However, there may be individual differences in adult cognition and changes in cognition during the adult years. Some individuals may exhibit a great deal of change, while others may show little or no change. Further research is needed on individual differences in cognitive change during the adult years.

ARE THERE COHORT DIFFERENCES IN ADULT COGNITION?

In the controversy over whether there are age changes in adult cognition, Baltes and Schaie (Baltes & Schaie, 1976; Schaie, 1974) and others have suggested that some of the age differences observed in cognitive performance among adults may be a result of cohort effects rather than of actual age change. The literature reviewed in the last section suggests that there are, in fact, actual age changes in cognitive performance during the adult years. This, however, does not eliminate the possibility that there are cohort differences as well. The data relevant to the existence of cohort differences will be reviewed in this section.

The data most directly relevant to the issue of cohort effects come from studies of intelligence test performance. In 1956 Schaie and colleagues administered the Primary Mental Abilities Test to a number of adults of different ages. The same adults were retested in 1963 and 1970. The subjects were divided into seven cohorts. The youngest cohort was approximately age 25 when they were first tested in 1956, while the oldest cohort was approximately age 67 when they were first tested in 1956. Schaie and Labouvie-Vief (1974) performed a cross-sequential analysis on the data. This is an analysis such as those proposed by both Schaie (1965) and Baltes (1968) which is aimed at differentiating the effects of age change and cohort differences. These analyses consist of a combination of cross-sectional and longitudinal comparisons on the same data. Schaie and Labouvie-Vief reported substantial cohort effects. In fact Schaie and Labouvie-Vief concluded that the cross-sectional age differences involved primarily cohort, rather than age-change, components. This conclusion, however, should not be given too much importance since the age-change differences involved a 14-year span from the first to the last testing, while the difference between cohorts covered a 40-year span. As a result of these differences it is not surprising that the cohort effects might appear larger than the age effects. Further because of these differences it is difficult to make comparisons between the relative effects of age-change versus cohort differences. However, as Botwinick (1977) has pointed out, the cross-sectional curves and the longitudinal curves obtained with this study were roughly the same with the exception of the cross-sectional indicating earlier age decline. It appears that there are significant cohort effects in performance on intelligence tests although it is not yet possible to determine whether these cohort effects are, in fact, larger than the age-change effects.

There is further evidence of the importance of cohort effects in cognitive performance among adults. Kesler et al. (1976) performed regression analyses with performance on various problem-solving tasks as criterion variables and age, sex, education, occupation, and nonverbal intelligence as predictor variables. They found that education and nonverbal intelligence were the only significant predictors of problem-solving performance. Nonverbal intelligence could have components of both age-change effects and cohort-difference effects and is therefore difficult to interpret. However since the number of years of education a person has obtained is partly a function of his/her cohort because individuals from older cohorts tend to have less education, education would have to be classified as a variable that is indicative of cohort effects rather than age-change effects. Selzer and Denney (1980) included age, education, residence (institution versus community), and sex as predictor variables in a regression analysis with conservation as the criterion variable. They found that education was the only significant predictor among the middle-aged and elderly adults. This suggests that there may be cohort effects in performance on Piagetian abilities as well as on intellectual and problem-solving abilities. Other studies have also indicated the importance of education when age is controlled (e.g., Birren & Morrison, 1961; Chap & Sinnot, 1977–1978; Papalia, Kennedy, & Sheehan, 1973; Papalia et al., 1973).

In answer to the question of whether there are cohort differences in adult cognition, the data currently available indicate that there probably are. There is less data bearing on this issue than on the issue of actual age change, but there is enough to suggest that there probably are cohort differences in adult cognition. Further the research indicates that education *may* be one of the prime causes of such cohort effects. However since the relationship between education and cognitive performance is correlational, one cannot be sure that the relationship is not caused by a third variable such as intelligence or even cohort differences in nutrition, physical exercise, or reading. The rather consistent finding that education is related to cognitive performance during the adult years, however, suggests that this is one of the prime variables for investigation as a potential cause of cohort effects.

ARE THE OBSERVED COGNITIVE CHANGES IMPORTANT?

A number of investigators have suggested that the types of tasks that are typically employed in research might not tap abilities that are relevant to the life styles of elderly individuals or that are indicative of changes that have any real significance in their lives (e.g., Labouvie-Vief & Chandler, 1978; Schaie, 1976). It has further been suggested that elderly individuals do not perform well on these types of tasks *because* they are not relevant to their lives. The implication is that elderly individuals would be less likely to exhibit performance decrements in more realistic circumstances. As a consequence it is important to look at the research on abilities that are directly relevant to real-life performance.

One line of research that is relevant to this question is that in which the "meaningfulness" of the tasks has been manipulated. With a few exceptions (e.g., Demming & Pressey, 1957; Zaretsky & Halberstam, 1968), most of the researchers who have used meaningful stimuli in learning and memory tasks have found that elderly individuals perform less well than do younger adults. Such results have been found with paired-associates tasks (e.g., Hulicka, 1967; Wittels, 1972), serial memorization tasks (e.g., Craik & Masani, 1967; Heron & Craik, 1964), and prose memorization tasks (Gordon & Clark, 1974). Arenberg (1968) found similar results with a problem-solving task. He first attempted to study concept learning in young and old adults employing the geometric stimuli traditionally used. However, he reported that "preliminary work with the old Ss however, dramatically indicated that dimensions of color, form, and number and the entire task were too abstract to be understood" (p. 279). As a consequence he made the stimuli and task less abstract. In the less abstract task the subject was presented with the names of nine foods written across the top of a sheet of paper and was told that one of these foods was poison. The subject was then presented with "meals" of a list of three foods at a time. After each presentation of a meal the subject was told if the person who ate it lived or died. The subject's task was to determine which of the foods was poison. Arenberg found that elderly adults performed less well than did younger adults on this task in spite of the fact that it was more meaningful. Thus the research in which the meaningfulness of the tasks was manipulated in order to facilitate the learning, memory, and problem-solving performance of elderly adults indicates that elderly adults tend to perform less well than do younger adults on these tasks as well as on the more traditional tasks.

In a recent comparison of performance on a less realistic task which has frequently been used in problem-solving research and performance on a task composed of practical problems that adults might encounter in their daily lives, Denney and Palmer (1980) found that performance on the traditional problem-solving task decreased linearly across the adult years, while performance on the practical problems increased to a peak in the 40- and 50-year-old groups and decreased thereafter. These results indicate that the developmental function obtained for problem-solving during the adult years depends on the type of problems that are presented. However, these results also indicate that even performance on practical problems decreases during the later adult years. Whereas it is possible that elderly adults might perform at a higher level on a different type of practical problem, the evidence to date indicates that middle-aged adults perform better than do older adults even on practical problems.

Another line of research that is relevant to the question of the importance of the cognitive changes during the later adult years is that in which one's professional productivity is mapped across the life span. In a series of studies Lehman (1953, 1962, 1965, 1966) has investigated the productivity and creativity in professional careers across the life span. Although he notes that the peak years with respect to both productivity and creativity occur at different ages for individuals in different professions, he rather consistently finds a peak during the young or middle adult years with a decline during the later adult years. For example his research shows that the peak years in professions such as mathematics and chemistry are attained relatively early (in the late twenties or early thirties), while those in professions such as literature and history are obtained later (between the mid-forties and mid-fifties). Lehman found that in most professions the maximum production rate for quality work occurred between the ages of 30 and 39.

Although there are a number of methodological problems with Lehman's work (Dennis, 1956, 1958), other research yields similar results. Manniche and Falk (1957) investigated the age at which Nobel prize winners did their award-winning work. They found that, although there were differences for different fields, most of the Nobel prize-winning work was conducted in the scientists' late twenties or thirties. Elo (1965) investigated the ability of master chess players across the life span. He reported a peak in ability at about age 35 with a decline thereafter.

Although many of these studies suffer from methodological difficulties, they do tend to suggest that ability in one's profession increases during the early adult years and decreases during the later adult years. Because of the methodological difficulties, one should not conclude that this fact has been proven. However since most of the data point in the same direction it must be seen as the safest conclusion given the data to date. These data suggest that the age declines in cognitive ability that have been obtained in laboratory studies reflect changes that are not limited to abilities that are not relevant to one's life; there appear to be declines in performance and/or abilities that are directly relevant to one's occupation during the later adult years as well.

Relevant to this issue is Hebb's (1978) account of the effect of his own aging on his intellectual abilities. Hebb, a very prominent psychologist, at the age of 74 reported, "Today, I have none of that drive, that engrossing, dominating need to fiddle with and manipulate ideas and data in psychology" (p. 23). He attributed this change in motivation to a change in cognitive ability; "The real change, I conclude, is a lowered ability to think; the loss of interest in psychological problems is secondary to that" (p. 23). In summary he states his view of cognitive change during the later adult years, "But—between you and me, privately—the picture is one of a slow, inevitable loss of cognitive capacity" (p. 23). Certainly Hebb's statements suggest that he has experienced some age-related decrements in abilities which are very relevant to his own life.

In summary the experimental studies of the effect of "meaningfulness" and the studies of professional productivity across the life span, as well as Hebb's personal experience, all point in the same direction. There appear to be declines in cognitive ability during the later adult years on meaningful, relevant tasks as well as on less meaningful, laboratory tasks.

CAN COGNITION IN ELDERLY ADULTS BE FACILITATED?

Once it is established that there are age changes and cohort differences in adult cognition, it is important to determine whether these age differences can be reduced or eliminated through a variety of intervention techniques. Thus the literature on whether the cognitive functioning of elderly adults can be facilitated will be examined. The intervention techniques that have been employed can be divided into two groups: *cognitive intervention techniques* which provide the individual with direct training or practice on the ability in question and *noncognitive techniques* which involve the manipulation of some noncognitive characteristic of the individual (e.g., motivation) that is thought to be responsible for the less-than-optimal cognitive performance. Research with both types of intervention techniques will be reviewed.

Cognitive Training

Piagetian and Problem-Solving Research. A variety of different intervention techniques have been employed to facilitate the Piagetian and problem-solving performance of elderly individuals. One of the types of intervention techniques that has been used is that in which the subject views a model using efficient cognitive strategies similar to those employed by younger adults. This intervention approach is typically a very effective means of modifying the performance of elderly individuals on a variety of tasks. Denney and Denney (1974) found that the performance of elderly individuals on the Twenty Questions task could be improved through a modeling technique. In this task the subject is presented with a picture of several different objects and is instructed to identify the object that the experimenter is thinking of by asking questions that can be answered either "yes" or "no." The subject is encouraged to try to find the solution by asking as few questions as possible. Without training many elderly adults tend to ask questions that eliminate only one item at a time and, thus, solve the problem more slowly than do younger adults whose questions often exclude a whole group of items at a time (Denney & Denney, 1973). However, after simply observing a model ask questions that eliminate more than one item at a time, elderly individuals begin to ask such questions themselves (Denney & Denney, 1974).

Similar modeling techniques have been successfully used with other types of tasks as well. Denney (1974a) was able to facilitate abstract classification through modeling. Meichenbaum (1972) was, likewise, able to facilitate the performance of elderly adults on concept-learning problems with a modeling procedure, and Crovitz (1966) found that elderly individuals were better able to learn to sort a deck of cards according to the relevant dimension after having observed a model sort the cards.

A second intervention technique has been called *direct instruction*. Direct instruction is similar in many ways to modeling. However rather than being shown how to perform as is done in the modeling studies, the participant in direct instruction studies is told how to perform on the task under investigation. In spite of the similarity of direct instruction and modeling, what little research has been conducted indicates that direct instruction may be less effective than modeling. Heglin (1956) compared young, middle-aged, and elderly adults on set induction tasks both before and after training. Training consisted of telling the subjects, after they had finished the first series of problems, that their difficulty on some of the latter problems was due to their continued use of a method that they had used for solving the earlier problem when that method was no longer efficient or effective. The subjects were then told that they would be presented with another series of problems and were warned to try to avoid using just one method for solving the problems. Heglin reported that the middle-aged individuals gained more from the training than did either the younger or older adults; the older adults gained the least. Young (1966) also used direct instruction in an attempt to facilitate the performance of elderly adults on a nonverbal search task. She included both middle-aged and elderly adults in her study. She found that, even after rather explicit instructions on how to follow an orderly search strategy and how to take notes to lessen the memory load, the elderly adults still performed at a lower level than did the younger adults.

It is difficult to draw conclusions on the basis of the results of the direct-instruction studies because of various methodological problems. Heglin did not compare pretraining results with posttraining results, and thus it is not possible to tell whether the elderly subjects in his study increased from pre- to posttest. Young, on the other hand, did not include a control group of individuals who were not given instructions, and thus it is not possible to determine whether the instructions had a beneficial effect for either her middle-aged or her elderly subjects. As a result of these problems it is not possible to determine whether the direct-instruction training techniques employed in either of these studies actually facilitated the performance of elderly adults.

It would be surprising if direct instruction were not effective in facilitating the performance of elderly individuals when modeling appears to be so effective; direct instruction involves telling a subject how to perform, while modeling involves showing the subjects how to perform. However since there is evidence that elderly individuals function at a more concrete level than do younger individuals (e.g., Arenberg, 1968; Bromley, 1957; Hulicka & Grossman, 1967), it is possible that the verbal instructions may be too abstract for the elderly individuals to comprehend as well as they comprehend the more concrete modeling instructions in which they are actually shown how to perform.

A third group of intervention techniques can be labeled *feedback* techniques. These techniques all involve some form of feedback to the subject regarding the correctness of his/her responses. Hornblum and Overton (1976) attempted to train elderly individuals to conserve by providing them with feedback contingent upon their responses to conservation problems. The control subjects received the same problems but were not given feedback as to the correctness of their answers. Significantly more conservation responses were obtained on the posttest in the feedback condition than in the control condition. Schutz and Hoyer (1976) found that feedback facilitated the performance of elderly individuals on a spatial egocentrism task. Likewise Sanders, Sterns, Smith, and Sanders (1975) found that feedback facilitated performance on a concept-learning task.

A final type of intervention technique is that of providing the subjects with practice on similar types of problems. Some researchers have suggested that elderly individuals may not perform well on cognitive tasks because they are not frequently required to perform at a high cognitive level in their everyday living (e.g., Denney & Denney, 1974; Selzer & Denney, 1980). If this were indeed the case, then practice on similar problems alone might facilitate performance. A number of studies have included practice-only control groups which are relevant to this issue. In a couple of these studies, practice resulted in improved cognitive performance (e.g., Labouvie-Vief & Gonda, 1976; Panicucci, 1975). However there are also studies that show no significant practice effects (e.g., Hoyer, Hoyer, Treat, & Baltes, 1978; Sanders et al., 1975; Schutz & Hoyer, 1976). Thus the effects of practice on cognitive abilities in the elderly are difficult to assess. It may be that practice is more beneficial for some types of tasks than for others, or it may be that the specifics of the practice procedures determine whether the practice is effective.

From the results of the preceding studies, it appears that modeling and feedback are especially effective intervention techniques whereas direct instruction may be less effective. Practice appears to be more equivocal; some studies indicate significant practice effects, while others do not. It appears that the particular training technique involved in an intervention program may, to a certain extent, determine whether the intervention program is successful. However it is also possible that the particular types of ability under investigation may determine the effectiveness of intervention as well.

One particular cognitive ability has seemed to be particularly resistant to training efforts. Denney (1979b) has conducted a series of studies in which she has attempted to change elderly individuals' performance on the Matching Familiar Figures test. The two dependent measures obtained from this test are latency to first response and total number of errors. In all three of her studies, Denney attempted to modify the response latency of elderly individuals. In the first study the subjects were given either instructions to take as much time as they needed, instructions to respond as quickly as they could, or no instructions regarding response speed. In the second experiment the subjects observed a model who either responded more slowly, more quickly, or at the same speed typically used by elderly adults. In the third experiment the subjects were either forced to respond very slowly, forced to respond very quickly, or allowed to respond at their own rate. Only one of these experimental manipulations affected response latency. The subjects who were forced to respond very quickly in the third study exhibited a decrease in response latency from pretest to posttest, while the subjects in the other two conditions did not. There was a corresponding effect for errors; the subjects in the fast condition exhibited very little change in error rate from pretest to posttest, while the subjects in the other two conditions made fewer errors on the posttest than on the pretest. In the third study an attempt was made to modify the error rate by training the subjects in the use of a thorough and systematic scanning strategy. The strategy training had no effect on either errors or latency.

The results of this series of studies indicate that performance on the Matching Familiar Figures test may be somewhat less responsive to intervention than on some of the other cognitive tasks that have been investigated. This is somewhat surprising since most of the studies in which young children have been given training have resulted in changes in their performance (e.g., Briggs & Weinberg, 1973; Debus, 1970; Denney, 1972; Heider, 1971; Meichenbaum & Goodman, 1971; Ridberg, Parke, & Hetherington, 1971). However, one should not draw conclusions regarding the relative trainability of young children and elderly adults unless they have been compared in the same study under the same experimental conditions. It was earlier postulated that elderly adults might be more responsive to modeling effects on the Twenty Questions Task than are young children (e.g., Denney & Wright, 1976) until Denney, Jones, and Krigel (1979) compared young children and elderly adults in the same study. When given exactly the same training procedures, the young children and elderly adults responded in exactly the same way.

Only further research can determine whether some abilities are more susceptible to training effects than are others. For example it may be that speed of response is less responsive to training than are strategies. Or it may be that perceptual-cognitive abilities are less responsive to training than are cognitive abilities which do not rely so much on perceptual processes. Further research is also needed to determine whether children's perceptual-cognitive abilities are more responsive to training than are those of elderly adults.

Intelligence-Test Research. The training of intelligence-test performance has recently been discussed as an important theoretical area of concern. However, the studies that have been conducted have not provided very clearcut evidence of the effectiveness of the training techniques used on intelligence-test performance. The data have not been inconsistent; rather, the studies have not been designed so as to provide unambiguous evidence for the effectiveness of the training techniques, and some of the conclusions of the researchers have not adequately reflected what can be found in their data.

Several investigators have used modeling approaches in an attempt to improve performance on inductive-reasoning problems. Labouvie-Vief and Gonda (1976) employed two modeling procedures—one aimed at facilitating cognitive strategies and one aimed at reducing anxiety. Labouvie-Vief and Gonda's data indicate that on an immediate posttest on the task on which training was given both the cognitive- and the anxiety-training groups performed significantly better than a no-training group, while a group that was given unspecific training (practice with the problems) did not perform better than the no-training group. On a delayed posttest both the unspecific-training and the anxiety-training groups performed better than did the no-training group. On a transfer task (Raven Progressive Matrices), only the unspecific-training group performed significantly better than did the no-training group on the immediate posttest, while the cognitive-training and the unspecific-training groups performed better than did the no-training group on the delayed posttest. These results provide no clear evidence that cognitive or anxiety training was any better than practice alone (unspecific training) over all types of tasks and posttests. Further the cognitive and anxiety groups should have been compared with the unspecific-training group in order for the authors to conclude that cognitive and anxiety training were effective; these comparisons were not reported. Also the authors

did not use standard statistical analyses, but rather they stated that "... intersubject variability tends to be so great that it is often difficult to demonstrate treatment effects. Thus, in order to increase the power of the analysis, pair-wise directional planned contrasts were performed by Dunn's method between the no-training group on the one hand, and the three remaining groups on the other" (Labouvie-Vief & Gonda, 1976, p. 330). Presumably standard analyses were performed first, and when they proved to be insignificant, Dunn's method was employed. A further problem with the study was the fact that a pretest was not included. Any differences that were obtained between the groups on the posttests could be a result of differences that occurred when subjects were assigned to conditions, rather than as a result of treatment effects. Thus it is not possible to conclude from this study that the training techniques employed had an effect on either of the measures of intelligence-test performance. These data neither suggest that there are training effects nor that there are not. Rather the best conclusion might be that there *may* be training effects, that there *may* be practice effects, and that there is no indication that the training effects are any greater than the practice effects.

Plemons, Willis, and Baltes (1978) attempted to modify the performance of elderly individuals on a measure of "fluid" intelligence with a modeling procedure. The subjects in their training group were presented with eight one-hour practice sessions in which they were presented with the rules that are required for solution of a figural-relations test. The subjects in their control condition were given no training between pretest and posttest. The results indicate a significant training effect only for the figural-relations test which was almost identical to the test items on which the subjects were given training. No training effect was obtained on a different figural-relations test, an induction test, or a verbal-comprehension test. However there were significant practice effects for the figural-relations test that was similar to the one on which training was given, the other figural-relations test, and the verbal-comprehension test. These practice effects were more highly significant than were the training effects for the original figural-relations test. Although Plemons et al. conclude that their study demonstrated the effectiveness of their training procedure, their results do not correspond with this conclusion. Their results indicate that there are very strong practice effects for virtually all of the intelligence-tests measures. Further since their training group was given a great deal of practice with the figural-relations items that were similar to the ones on the posttest on which a training effect was found, there is no reason to conclude that training had any effect on performance; rather, practice effects could account for all the significant effects obtained in their study.

A second set of studies was conducted to determine whether intelligence-test performance could be facilitated by changing response speed. Hoyer and colleagues (Hoyer, Labouvie, & Baltes, 1973; Hoyer et al., 1978) tried to facilitate intelligence-test performance by first training elderly individuals to respond very rapidly on an unrelated task. In the first study Hoyer et al. (1973) found that, whereas response speed on the unrelated task increased dramatically with practice, their reinforcement training treatment did not have a significant effect on response speed on the unrelated task beyond the effects of practice alone. With respect to intelligence-test performance, Hoyer et al. (1973) found that there were practice effects from pre- to posttest but there were no treatment condition effects. Thus the results of this study indicate that both response speed and intelligence-test performance exhibit practice effects; this study presents no evidence that the training procedure employed facilitated performance beyond those practice effects. In the second study Hoyer et al. (1978) increased the number of training sessions and changed the reinforcement procedure to one that they thought might be more effective. In spite of these procedural changes, no treatment-condition effects were found for either response time on the training tasks or performance on the intelligence subtests. Both of these studies then indicate that response speed and intelligence-test performance may be facilitated through practice. Both of them also indicate that reinforcing response speed has no effect on response speed above and beyond practice effects and, further, that reinforcing response speed has no effect on intelligence-test performance.

In conclusion the studies in which an attempt has been made to facilitate intelligence-test performance indicate that at least some of the abilities measured by intelligence tests improve as a result of practice. There is no indication that intelligence-test performance is facilitated by any specific type of training technique. The fact that practice facilitates performance demonstrates that intelligence-test performance can be improved. Further research is needed to determine whether any specific types of training might facilitate performance beyond the level obtained by practice alone. It is clear that future studies in this area need to include training groups, practice-only control groups, and no-practice control groups in order to separate the effects of practice and training. Further as with all intervention studies with aging, it would be best if future studies included younger age groups in addition to groups of elderly individuals. Only when such age groups are included in the same study can one conclude that age deficits are being eliminated as a result of training.

Noncognitive Training

The intervention techniques discussed so far were designed to give the subjects some form of direct training in the cognitive ability under investigation. The subjects were either shown how to perform, told how to perform, given feedback regarding their performance, given practice on the task in question, and/or given feedback regarding response speed. There is another group of intervention techniques which does not involve direct training on the cognitive ability in question. Some of these less direct intervention techniques have been used because investigators have hypothesized that the elderly have the ability to perform at a higher level than they sometimes exhibit on their own. They suggest that, for reasons such as lack of motivation, lack of self-confidence, and insufficient consideration of the task demands, the elderly do not perform as well as they are capable of. Thus these techniques are aimed at trying to change the characteristics which the investigators think may be responsible for the less-than-optimal performance in the elderly.

The author conducted a series of studies to determine whether such noncognitive variables might indirectly influence problem-solving performance on the Twenty Questions Task (Denney, 1980). She hypothesized that elderly individuals might not use efficient problem-solving strategies on the Twenty Questions Task because they are not motivated to try to perform efficiently, because they lack confidence in their ability to perform well, or because they do not take enough time to consider the strategy they are going to use on the task. Denney manipulated each of these variables before presenting elderly individuals with the Twenty Questions Task in order to see if these manipulations would have an effect on their performance. She attempted to increase motivation by setting up a system in which the elderly received more money the fewer questions they had to ask in order to solve the Twenty Questions Task. She found no difference between the performance of subjects who were reinforced with money for efficient performance and those who were not reinforced.

Denney tried to manipulate self-confidence in a study in which the elderly were presented with a series of problems, the Raven Progressive Matrices, before the Twenty Questions Task. The individuals in one condition were told throughout the administration of the Raven that they were doing extremely well. The experimenter acted pleasantly surprised at how well they were doing in order to give them the impression that they were doing much better than one might expect. The individuals in the other condition were given the same problems but with no feedback. No difference was obtained between the two experimental groups in their performance on the Twenty Questions Task which was administered immediately after the Raven.

Denney also proposed that elderly individuals may not use efficient strategies on the Twenty Questions Task because they do not take the time necessary to consider the demands of the task and to think of the most appropriate strategy given these demands. Because she felt that elderly individuals may require more time than do younger adults to decide upon the most appropriate strategy, she gave one group of elderly adults a forced three-minute delay between the time when the experimenter gave the instructions for the task and the time when the elderly individuals were allowed to begin asking questions. The other group was allowed to begin asking questions as soon as the experimenter finished giving the instructions. Again no differences between experimental and control groups were obtained on the Twenty Questions Task.

The results of the present series of studies indicate that it is not easy to facilitate cognitive performance among elderly individuals through the manipulation of noncognitive variables such as motivation, self-confidence, and time to plan a strategy. However, the results of the present series of studies certainly do not prove that manipulation of such variables could not be more effective. First, it is possible that better manipulations of the same variables might be more effective. Second, it is possible that the manipulations of other noncognitive variables might be more successful. However, until more research is done in this area, we must conclude that it does not appear as if short-term manipulation of such noncognitive variables is a very effective means of facilitating cognitive performance in the elderly.

Summary

In summary research indicates that the cognitive performance of elderly individuals on at least some tasks can be facilitated with at least some types of direct-training techniques. Both the modeling and the feedback-training techniques appear to be rather effective. Since several of the feedback procedures that have been used have included modeling components as well, it is difficult to determine whether the feedback itself is effective or whether the modeling component of these procedures is also necessary. It is difficult to evaluate some of the direct-instruction studies because the research designs used do not permit one to draw any clear conclusions regarding the effectiveness of the training procedures. The effects of practice on similar or identical problems alone are not clear; in some studies practice seems to facilitate performance, while in others it does not. In the studies in which attempts were made to manipulate some noncognitive variable, no facilitative effect on problem-solving performance was obtained. Thus it seems clear that it is much easier to facilitate cognitive performance in the elderly by trying to manipulate cognitive, as opposed to noncognitive, variables.

DOES INTERVENTION REDUCE AGE DIFFERENCES?

Since it is clear that the cognitive performance of elderly adults can be facilitated with a variety of intervention techniques, it is now important to ask whether the obtained facilitation actually reduces age differences. It has frequently been asserted that old age is marked by a great deal of plasticity in intellectual and cognitive abilities (e.g., Baltes & Schaie, 1976; Labouvie-Vief, 1977; Labouvie-Vief & Gonda, 1976). For example in one recent article Baltes, Reese, and Lipsitt (1980) stated that

. . . there is growing evidence for large intraindividual plasticity or modifiability in intellectual performance, particularly in late life. Although cognitive intervention in childhood has often led to equivocal outcomes, intervention research in late adulthood and old age presents generally a rather consistent pattern of positive outcomes. Relatively short-term interventions are successful in increasing intellectual performance, including its maintenance and transfer to other related abilities (Denney, 1979; Labouvie-Vief, 1976; Plemons, Willis, & Baltes, 1978; Sanders & Sanders, 1978). Such results suggest not only that many older persons function below their maximal level of performance but also that a life-long capacity for intellectual change exists. (pp. 91–92)

It is clear that all living organisms, in particular human beings, have a certain degree of plasticity at any age. Thus the question of plasticity must not be a question of absolute plasticity, but rather, as Baltes et al. point out, a question of relative plasticity. Thus the question of the relative plasticity of intellectual and cognitive functioning needs to be examined. Are elderly individuals more susceptible to intervention effects than other age groups, and if so, do such intervention effects compensate for the deficit that elderly individuals have in various cognitive abilities and, thus, bring them up to the level of performance of younger adults? In order to answer these questions, only the studies that have included more than one age group will be reviewed. There are only a handful of studies in this category.

One of the studies which compared different-aged adults was that of Heglin (1956). As reported previously Heglin compared the effect of training in young, middle-aged, and elderly adults on set induction tasks. Heglin reported that his middle-aged adults gained more from the training than did either his younger or older subjects; the older adults gained the least. Heglin did not analyze pretraining versus posttraining differences within each age group. However, from the means he presented, it does not look as if his training procedure reduced the elderly adults' susceptibility to set at all. The results of this study demonstrated only that middle-aged adults improved from the first series of set induction problems to the second set of problems.

Another study which compared groups of different-aged subjects was that of Young (1966). Again as mentioned previously Young compared the responses of middle-aged and elderly adults to direct instruction aimed at facilitating their performance on a nonverbal search task. She found that, even after rather explicit instructions on how to follow an orderly strategy and how to take notes to lessen the memory load, the elderly subjects still performed at a lower level than did the younger adults.

Hoyer et al. (1978–1979) compared the effectiveness of reinforcement for reponse speed in young and older women. They found that their reinforcement and their practice conditions resulted in increased response speed as compared to a control condition. However, they reported that their young adults showed greater training effects than did their elderly adults.

These three studies indicate that young and middle-aged adults may be more responsive to training effects on cognitive abilities than are elderly individuals. This fact does not convincingly demonstrate that there is ". . . large intraindividual plasticity or modifiability, particularly in late life" (Baltes et al., 1980). Instead it appears that not only does cognitive performance on many types of tasks decrease with increasing age during the adult years, but in addition what little research there is indicates that plasticity also *decreases* during the adult years.

In summary although the intervention research does indicate that the cognitive performance of elderly individuals can be facilitated through training, the few studies in which elderly adults have been compared with younger adults indicates that there is a decrease in plasticity with increasing age. Thus the evidence that the performance of elderly individuals can be facilitated through intervention should not be taken to mean that age differences can be eliminated with various intervention techniques or that elderly individuals are somehow more responsive than other age groups to the effects of training.

DO COGNITIVE CHANGES IN OLD AGE MIRROR EARLY DEVELOPMENTAL CHANGES?

The discussion of the relative plasticity of cognition in adults leads naturally to a discussion of the comparison of the performance of elderly individuals with other age groups. The research on age differences suggests that elderly individuals perform, at least in some ways, like young children rather than like older children and younger adults. Research indicates that both young children and elderly adults are responsive to training on a variety of cognitive abilities, and what little research has been done suggests that young children and elderly adults respond to training in virtually the same way (Denney et al., 1979). In one study Denney et al. (1979) provided both six-year-old children and elderly adults with training on the Twenty Questions Task. Their subjects received training in either how to classify the stimuli, how to ask efficient questions, or how to use the information gained from the answers to their questions. In a second study Denney et al. (1979) compared four- to six-year-old children and elderly adults in their response to training which included either providing an example of an efficient question or providing the rule for generating efficient questions. In the first study both six-year-old children and elderly adults asked more efficient questions when they were given training in how to ask an efficient question; the other training conditions had no effect on performance. In the second study both providing an example of an efficient question and providing the rule for generating efficient questions facilitated the performance of both the young children and the elderly adults. The results of this study indicate that young children and elderly adults have the same needs with respect to training. Denney et al. (1979) concluded that "the fact that young children and elderly adults do not differ in their training needs suggests that the elderly may be using the same processes as the young children in performing on the Twenty Questions Task" (p. 34). As a result of the fact that elderly adults tend to perform like young children and, according to the research to date, to respond to intervention programs in the same way, one might be tempted to conclude that development during the latter part of the life span mirrors development that takes place during the early part of a life span.

Another line of research which suggests that development during the latter part of a life span may mirror development during the first part of the life span is research on structural changes in intelligence. Although the research is not unequivocal, there is a growing consensus that, as the child develops, his/her cognitive abilities become more differentiated—that is, with increasing age during childhood there appear to be a larger number of factors representing cognitive ability, with lower correlations between the factors and a weaker general factor (e.g., Asch, 1936; Burt, 1954; Garrett, 1946). Although less research has been done on structural changes in adults, there is some evidence that there is a reintegration of cognitive abilities during later adulthood—that is, there are fewer factors, higher correlations between factors, and a much stronger general factor (e.g., Balinsky, 1941; Green & Berkowitz, 1964). Although there is not enough data on structural change to draw any strong conclusions, these data suggest that older adults may be similar to young children not only in their level of performance and their response to training but also in the structure of their abilities. This evidence suggests again that development during the latter part of the life span may mirror development during childhood.

Although there is a fair amount of research that suggests that development during the late adult years might mirror development during childhood, it is important that researchers do not accept that conclusion without further research which looks much more closely at the performance of both young children and elderly adults. To date very few studies have included both young children and elderly adults in the same study, and as a consequence, comparisons of the performance of young children with that of elderly adults are often made between different studies in which different procedures, experimenters, testing conditions, and types of subjects were used. In order to determine whether there are differences in their performance, it is necessary that young children and elderly adults be compared with exactly the same conditions. Further it would be beneficial if the responses of young children and elderly adults were compared at a very precise level rather than at the more global level typically used, such as the total number of correct responses or the total amount of time taken. It would be more informative, for example, to look at the specific types of errors that subjects make rather than looking only at the total number of errors committed. When young children and elderly adults make an error, is it the same type of error? It seems very unlikely that elderly adults and young children would respond in exactly the same way given the fact that the elderly adults have had so much more experience than have young children. Presumably this background of experience would have an effect on performance even though the absolute level of performance of elderly individuals might be the same as that of young children. Certainly more research is needed before any strong conclusions can be drawn regarding whether development during adulthood mirrors development during childhood.

THEORY

With a few exceptions (e.g., Arlin, 1975; Riegel, 1973; Schaie, 1977/1978), there has been very little theoretical work done in the area of cognitive development during the adult years. In the remainder of this chapter an attempt will be made to integrate some of the empirical findings into a theoretical framework that will encompass the entire life span. This framework is based on empirical findings that are currently available rather than on any previously available theoretical position. It is being presented in an attempt to integrate what is already known and to stimulate further research.

The data presented so far in this chapter clearly indicate that there is an increase in cognitive ability during childhood until a peak is reached in late adolescence or early adulthood; after that age there appears to be a decline in cognitive ability, at least in those abilities that are not exercised very much. There is also evidence that practice and experience have a very definite influence on cognitive ability. Thus in the present formulation two developmental functions will be considered—the developmental function of untrained or unpracticed ability and the developmental function of optimally trained or optimally exercised ability. Untrained or unpracticed ability reflects what a normal, healthy individual would be able to do if that individual were not given any training or exercise in the particular ability in question. This aspect of ability will be referred to as *unexercised ability* throughout the remainder of this chapter. Unexercised ability is proposed to be a function of *both* biological potential and normal, standard environmental experience. It is not possible to separate the effects of normal biological development from the effects of normal environmental experience. However, it is assumed that the unexercised ability curve reflects fairly accurately the biological potential given a normal environment without specific exercise and/or training in the ability in question. The other developmental function that will be considered along with unexercised ability will be labeled *optimally exercised ability;* it reflects the maximal ability attainable by a normal, healthy individual under conditions of optimal training and/or exercise. It is assumed that this curve reflects the maximum biological potential given a normal environment and optimal exercise and/or training in the ability in question.

The proposed curves for each of these two functions are presented in Figure 45-1. As can be seen in Figure 45-1, both unexercised and optimally exercised ability levels increase up to late adolescence or early adulthood and decline thereafter. These two aspects of ability will first be illustrated by using the noncognitive example of running ability. The unexercised ability curve indicates how well an individual could run at any given age if that individual had never had any training or practice in running. If the curve were the same as that presented in Figure 45-1, an individual would be best at running under these conditions during his/her twenties. The optimally exercised ability curve indicates how well that individual could run if s/he were given optimal training and exercise. The space between the unexercised and the optimally exercised ability curves indicates the degree to which specific training and practice can affect an individual's performance. If the unexercised and the optimally exercised running curves were the same as those presented in Figure 45-1, a person could run better at the age of 50 if s/he were given enough training and

practice to reach his/her maximum potential (optimally exercised ability) than s/he could at the age of 20 if s/he had not been running at all. The curves also indicate that a 70-year-old individual who had been running enough to reach his/her maximum potential (optimally exercised ability) would not be a better runner than s/he would have been at the age of 20 if s/he were not practicing, because the optimally exercised ability curve is lower at the age of 70 than is the unexercised ability curve at the age of 20. While these hypothetical curves probably do represent the developmental functions of unexercised and optimally exercised running ability in a general way, research would obviously be needed to draw the curves more precisely.

With respect to cognitive abilities the curves have the same meaning. The curve for unexercised ability reflects how an individual would perform on a cognitive task if that individual were given no exercise or training on that particular ability, while the curve for optimally exercised ability reflects how an individual would perform on a cognitive task if that individual were given optimal exercise and optimal training on that particular ability. The curve for unexercised ability has been drawn to decrease starting in early adulthood because the literature indicates that abilities that are not often exercised, such as those measured by performance subtests on intelligence tests and abstract problem-solving tasks, begin to decline in early adulthood. It is only the more frequently exercised abilities which tend to remain relatively stable during the adult years. The potential effect of exercise is represented by the area between the unexercised and the optimally exercised curves. Through exercise and training, individuals can improve their performance substantially over the unexercised ability level. However, the optimally exercised ability curve has also been drawn to decrease starting in early adulthood because research indicates that there are probably declines, at least in later adulthood, even in the abilities that are most resistant to age-change effects, such as verbal abilities and practical problem-solving abilities.

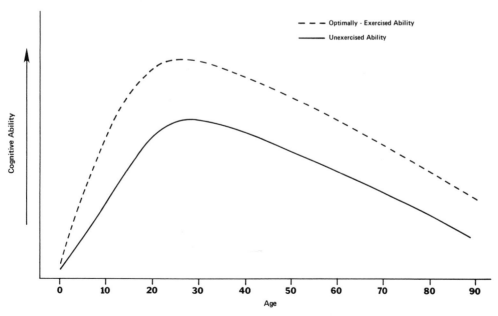

Figure 45-1 Developmental functions of unexercised and optimally exercised cognitive abilities

The two curves are drawn closer together during childhood and old age and farther apart during the young and middle adult years because of the data on both the structural changes in cognitive abilities across the life span and the relative effectiveness of training on various age groups. As was mentioned previously there is evidence that cognitive abilities differentiate as the child develops and reintegrate again in old age. This evidence suggests that there may be more room for experience to have an effect on cognitive ability in young and middle-aged adults than in either younger or older individuals. When abilities differentiate it may be because those abilities that are exercised show improvement, while those that are not exercised fall behind. The relative integration of abilities that is observed in early childhood and later adulthood may, thus, indicate that there is less room for experience (exercise and training) to make a difference. Further the training research that has been conducted also suggests that elderly adults may benefit less from training than do younger adults, again suggesting that there may be less room for experience to have an effect during the latter part of the life span. Comparable studies comparing the relative effectiveness of training on young children and young adults have not as yet been conducted.

Different Developmental Courses for Different Abilities

As was reported earlier different abilities take different developmental courses across the life span. The formulation presented in Figure 45–1 is not inconsistent with this fact. Consider first the different courses taken by the verbal and performance measures obtained from standard intelligence tests. As can be seen in Figure 45–2 the performance abilities tend to follow a developmental pattern very similar to that of unexercised ability. This may be because many of these abilities are not exercised very much during the adult years of the typical individ-

ual. It is not often that adults perform tasks similar to the block design, picture completion, or digit symbol substitution subtests of the Wechsler Adult Intelligence Scale. As a result of very little exercise during the adult years, the curve for performance abilities decreases steadily after early adulthood just as the curve for unexercised ability does.

Verbal abilities, on the other hand, take a somewhat different developmental course than either the unexercised or the optimally exercised curves. As can be seen in Figure 45–2 the verbal abilities tend to remain stable during the middle adult years with a decline only in later adulthood. This may be because individuals get a lot more exercise in verbal abilities than in performance abilities. The curve is drawn to indicate that most individuals do not reach their maximum potential during the early adult years but that they do exercise their verbal abilities enough to maintain the level which they attained during early adulthood throughout most of their adult years. They exercise their verbal abilities enough so that they do not lose any of their abilities *until the age at which the optimally exercised ability level drops below the level at which the person has been functioning.* At this point the individual's verbal abilities are limited by the decline in optimally exercised ability level and a drop in verbal ability results.

So far verbal and performance abilities have been discussed in a very global fashion as if all verbal and all performance abilities show similar developmental trends. This has been done for the sake of simplicity in order to illustrate how the fact that different abilities take different developmental courses would be explained in the framework of the proposed model. Things, however, are not so simple. Certainly not all verbal abilities follow the same developmental course; likewise not all performance abilities follow the same developmental course.

In addition to the data on the developmental course of different intellectual abilities, the present formulation is also consistent with the recent data obtained by Denney

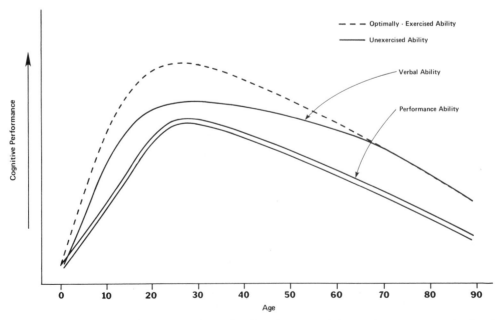

***Figure* 45-2** Developmental functions of verbal and performance abilities relative to unexercised and optimally exercised functions

and Palmer (1980) in a study of problem solving. In order to determine whether there are different developmental functions for different types of problem-solving abilities, they compared performance on a traditional problem-solving task with performance on a set of practical problems. They found that between the ages of 20 and 79 the performance on the traditional problem-solving task decreased linearly, while there was an increase in performance on the practical problems until the forties and fifties and a decline thereafter. These data are presented in Figure 45–3 along with the hypothetical curves for unexercised and optimally exercised ability.

According to the present formulation the ability tested by the traditional problem-solving task is one that is not exercised very much during the adult years, and thus it follows the unexercised-ability curve rather closely. Practical problem-solving ability is, of course, exercised throughout life, and thus performance on practical problems increases up until the age at which the decline in the optimally exercised ability actually limits performance. The reason the performance of the 20-year-olds was lower than that of the 30-, 40-, and 50-year-olds is because 20-year-olds have less frequently had to deal with the types of practical problems involved in maintaining a house, maintaining appliances, or taking care of children that were tested in the Denney and Palmer study. Since they typically have not had very much experience with these types of problems, they do not approach their optimally exercised ability level. Of course older individuals do not perform as well as the 30-, 40-, and 50-year-olds because the declining level of optimally exercised ability limits their performance during the later adult years.

Developmental Precursors of Different Abilities

Different cognitive abilities are often proposed to be differentially influenced by biological and environmental factors. In a recent article Horn (1978) describes two types of intellectual abilities—fluid and crystallized—as having different determinants. He states that fluid intelligence

is characterized by processes of perceiving relationships, educing correlates, maintaining span of immediate awareness in reasoning, abstracting concept formation, and problem-solving. It is measured in unspeeded as well as speeded tasks involving figural symbolic or semantic content, but tasks in which relatively little advantage accrues from intensive or extended education and acculturation. (p. 220)

Fluid abilities, he suggests, are primarily determined by biological factors. On the other hand he states that crystallized intelligence

also involves the processes of perceiving relationships, educing correlates, reasoning, etc., just as does Gf (fluid intelligence), and Gc (crystallized intelligence), too, can be measured in unspeeded tasks involving various kinds of content (semantic, figural, symbolic), but the content of the tasks that best characterize Gc indicates relatively advanced education and acculturation either in the fundaments of the problem or in the operations that might be performed on the fundaments. (p. 221)

Thus according to Horn some abilities are determined primarily by biological factors, whereas others are influenced more by experiential factors.

According to the present formulation, however, different abilities are not seen as *necessarily* under the control of different determinants. Rather in the present formulation all abilities are treated the same; they are all dependent upon, and capable of being influenced by, both biological and environmental factors. As can be seen in Figure 45–2 it is true that the curves of the performance measures of intelligence are more closely related to the curves of biological functioning than are the curves of the verbal measures. (Both the unexercised and opti-

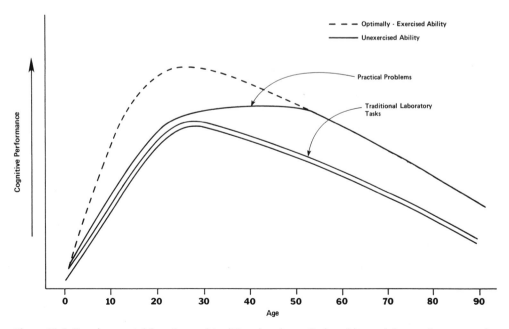

***Figure* 45–3** Developmental functions of traditional and practical problem-solving performance relative to unexercised and optimally exercised functions

mally exercised curves can be seen as indices of biological functioning under conditions of no exercise and optimal exercise, respectively.) But according to the present formulation this only reflects the fact that, in our culture, the verbal abilities are more highly exercised by the average adult during the middle adult years than are the performance abilities; it does not reflect the fact that verbal abilities are necessarily more influenced by experience, while performance abilities are necessarily more influenced by biological factors. According to the present formulation those abilities that are not frequently exercised will follow a developmental path very similar to that of biological functioning because there is no influence to direct them away from such a development course. Abilities that are frequently exercised, on the other hand, may be influenced by such exercise to follow a different developmental course than that followed by biological functioning. The developmental course followed by the exercised abilities will be determined by both the biologically determined limits on performance and the degree and timing of the exercise; there is no one developmental course that will be taken by all exercised abilities.

Differential Effects of Training on Different Abilities

These two conceptions of the relationship between different cognitive abilities and both biological and environmental determinants result in different predictions regarding the effects of training on different abilities. According to the present formulation all abilities are more or less equally amenable to the influence of both biological and environmental factors. However, those abilities that are most frequently exercised will be less responsive to training than will those abilities that are less frequently exercised because there is more room for improvement in the exercised abilities since they are farther from their optimal level while there is very little room for improvement in the highly exercised abilities because they are much closer to their maximum level. This fact is illustrated in Figure 45-4. Two age levels have been selected for illustration—age 30 and age 50. As can be seen from the figure, the amount of improvement possible in performance abilities is much greater than is the amount of improvement possible in verbal abilities at both of these two age levels.

This prediction is in direct contradiction to the prediction that would be made if the verbal abilities were seen as more amenable to the influence of experiential factors while performance abilities were seen as more amenable to the influence of biological factors. If the performance abilities were seen as more dependent upon the biological functioning of the individual, they would be seen as less susceptible to training than are the verbal abilities if the verbal abilities were seen as more dependent upon learning and experience. Research on the relative effectiveness of training on different abilities is needed to resolve this issue.

Differential Effects for Different Difficulty Levels

So far the discussion has focused on cognitive tasks that are difficult enough to be challenging to any age group. However, the current formulation would make different predictions for cognitive tasks of varying difficulty levels. In Figure 45-5 three levels of task difficulty are represented. When the line representing a difficulty level is in the area below the curve of unexercised ability, an individual in those age ranges has the ability required by the task without being given training. When the line representing a difficulty level is in the area below the curve of optimally exercised ability and above the curve for unexercised ability, the individual in those age ranges is able to achieve the ability required by the task through

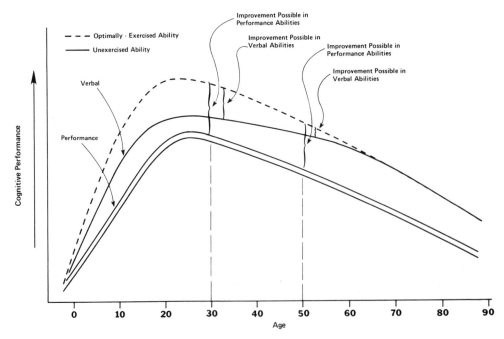

Figure **45-4** Amount of improvement possible in both verbal and performance abilities at ages 30 and 50

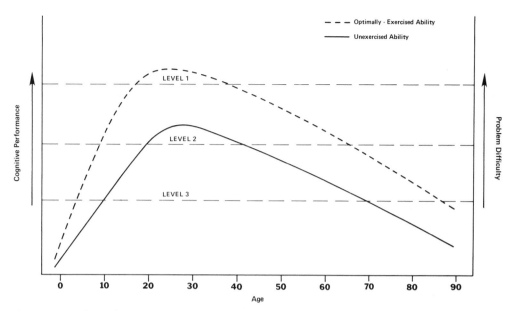

Figure 45-5 Relationship between problem difficulty and unexercised and optimally exercised ability functions

either practice or training. If the line for the difficulty level is above the optimally exercised ability level, the individual in those age ranges is unable to acquire the level of ability required for optimal performance on the task.

As can be seen from Figure 45–5, tasks of the lowest level of difficulty illustrated (level 3) could be performed by the individual between the ages of 10 and 70 without training and by the individual between the ages of about 4 and 10 and the ages of about 70 and 90 if the individual were given optimal learning experiences and optimal exercise. Tasks at difficulty level 2, on the other hand, could be performed by the individual between the ages of about 18 and 40 without training and by the individual between the ages of 8 and 18 and the ages of 40 and 65 with training and exercise. Below the age of 8 and above the age of 65, the individual would, according to this formulation, never be able to acquire the ability required for optimal performance on tasks of this difficulty level. Tasks of the highest difficulty level (level 1), on the other hand, could not be performed optimally by the individual at any age without training and exercise and could only be performed optimally by the individual between the ages of 15 and 35 with training.

As can be seen from Figure 45–5, different predictions would be made regarding the effect of training on tasks of different difficulty levels. Training on tasks of rather low difficulty levels, such as level 2 and level 3 tasks, would result in improvement only in the performance of older adults and young children because individuals between these two age ranges would be performing at ceiling. On tasks of difficulty level 1 individuals of all ages would improve as a result of optimal training, but older adults and young children would not, even after training, reach the optimal level of performance; only individuals between the ages of 15 and 35 would reach optimal performance. However, individuals in the teens and the late thirties and early forties would actually show the most improvement. Thus the effect of training is proposed to be determined by age and level of problem diffi-

culty. Quality of training would, of course, also be a factor, but this variable is not considered here.

Relationship between Integration of Abilities and Interindividual Variability

The unexercised and the optimally exercised ability curves that have been presented are meant to represent the life-span curves for one individual. The levels of the curves will, of course, vary as a result of interindividual factors that determine different ability levels. The slopes of the curves will also vary between individuals; some individuals will develop more quickly and/or decline more quickly than others. The differences in levels and differences in slopes would, in addition to differences in experience, result in interindividual variability. Since there is some evidence that, at least with respect to intelligence-test performance, interindividual variability is higher during young childhood and later adulthood (Matarazzo, 1972) than during the middle years, there is reason to suspect that variability may be greatest during periods of most rapid developmental change, possibly because of individual differences in the slopes of the curves of unexercised and optimally exercised ability. However it is difficult to determine whether the increase in interindividual variability in both young childhood and later adulthood is a result of the integration of abilities within individuals during these ages or whether the reverse is true—that is, that the seeming integration of abilities during young childhood and later adulthood is a result of larger interindividual differences during these age ranges. Since the variance of a total test score is equal to the variances of each of the individual subtests plus the intercorrelations among the subtests (Magnusson, 1967), the variability of the entire test would tend to increase as the intercorrelations among the subtests increase. As a result high within-subject variability in subtest scores will tend to be associated with low between-subject variability in total test scores and vice versa. It is important to recognize this relationship so that one does not incorrectly assume that large interindividual variability must reflect large intraindividual variability as some researchers in the field are currently doing. It is not clear whether the intraindividual integration which is observed in childhood and old age occurs first, with the interindividual variability that is observed during these ages resulting only as a byproduct, or whether the interindividual variability occurs first, with the intraindividual integration resulting only as a byproduct. Either trend could be primary with the other being an artifactual result, or both trends could occur simultaneously.

The present theoretical formulation deals exclusively with intraindividual development and change. Further research will be needed to extend this model to deal with interindividual factors such as ability-level differences, cohort differences, and sex differences.

Summary

In the present formulation a distinction is made between unexercised ability and optimally exercised ability. Unexercised ability reflects how an individual would perform on a cognitive task if that individual were given no exercise or training in that particular ability. Optimally exercised ability reflects how an individual would perform on a cognitive task if that individual were given optimal exercise and/or optimal training in that particular ability. Both unexercised ability and optimally exercised ability increase up to late adolescence or early adulthood and decrease thereafter. At all age levels there is a difference between unexercised ability and optimally exercised ability, indicating that exercise and training can facilitate performance at any age level. According to the present formulation, however, there is less difference between unexercised and optimally exercised ability levels during childhood and old age than there is between these two age extremes. Thus exercise and training can have less impact during childhood and old age than at other ages.

According to this formulation different predictions would be made regarding the life-span developmental functions of abilities that are exercised frequently as compared to those that are not exercised frequently. Abilities that are not often exercised would be expected to follow a developmental function similar to that which has been proposed for unexercised abilities—i.e., to increase up to early adulthood and decline thereafter. Abilities that are frequently exercised, however, would be expected to follow a different developmental course depending on the degree and timing of the exercise. According to the present formulation different predictions would be made for the effectiveness of training and exercise on different abilities; those abilities that are frequently exercised should be less responsive to training than are those abilities that are infrequently exercised. Further according to the present formulation different predictions regarding age differences in susceptibility to training would be made for abilities of different difficulty levels. For example on very easy tasks young children and elderly adults would be expected to be more responsive to training than would young adults who would be performing near ceiling. On extremely difficult tasks, on the other hand, young adults would be expected to benefit more from training than would either young children or elderly adults who would lack the ability required to reach the optimal performance level.

CONCLUSIONS

From a review of the literature available on cognitive changes during the adult years, it was concluded that, on the basis of both cross-sectional and longitudinal research, there are age-related declines in most, if not all, cognitive abilities during the adult years. However, the declines that are observed in abilities which are used frequently appear to begin at a later age and to be less drastic than are the declines in abilities which are exercised less frequently. In addition to age changes research also suggests that there are cohort differences in cognitive abilities as well. Further, research indicates that the cognitive changes that take place during the adult years are not limited to relatively unimportant, laboratory settings. Research on career performance suggests that there are probably declines during the latter adult years in professional performance as well.

Research indicates that the performance of elderly adults can be facilitated through various training techniques. However, comparative research indicates that age differences are not eliminated through such training; in fact, the few studies that have been done indicate that younger adults are likely to benefit more from training than are older adults.

In order to integrate the research findings, a theoretical formulation was presented. According to this formulation there is an increase up until early adulthood in both one's unexercised and one's optimally exercised ability levels. Both levels decline after early adulthood. A distinction was made between these two developmental functions in order to account for the fact that experience and training have very definite effects on performance. According to this formulation the potential for experience to affect performance is greater during the young adult years than during either childhood or old age. Predictions based on this formulation regarding the developmental functions of different abilities, the relative effectiveness of training on different abilities, and the relative effectiveness of training on abilities of different difficulty levels were discussed.

REFERENCES

ANNETT, M. The classification of instances of four common class concepts by children and adults. *British Journal of Educational Psychology*, 1959, *29*, 223–236.

ARENBERG, D. Concept problem solving in young and old adults. *Journal of Gerontology*, 1968, *23*, 279–282.

ARENBERG, D. A longitudinal study of problem solving in adults. *Journal of Gerontology*, 1974, *29*, 650–658.

ARENBERG, D. *Memory and learning do decline late in life.* Presented at the conference on "Aging: A challenge to science and social policy" at the Institute de la Vie, Vichy, France, 1977.

ARLIN, P. K. Cognitive development in adulthood: A fifth stage? *Developmental Psychology*, 1975, *11*, 602–605.

ASCH, S. E. A study of change in mental organization. *Archives of Psychology*, 1936, *28*(Whole No. 195).

BALINSKY, B. An analysis of the mental factors of various age groups from nine to sixty. *Genetic Psychology Monographs*, 1941, *23*, 191–234.

BALTES, P. B. Longitudinal and cross-sectional sequences in the study of age and generation effects. *Human Development*, 1968, *11*, 145–171.

BALTES, P. B., REESE, H. W., & LIPSITT, L. P. Life-span developmental psychology. *Annual Review of Psychology*, 1980, *31*, 65–110.

BALTES, P. B., & SCHAIE, K. W. Aging and I.Q.: The myth of the twilight years. *Psychology Today*, 1974, *7*, 35–40.

BALTES, P. B., & SCHAIE, K. W. On the plasticity of intelligence in adulthood and old age: Where Horn and Donaldson fail. *American Psychologist*, 1976, *31*, 720–725.

BAYLEY, N., & ODEN, M. H. The maintenance of intellectual ability in gifted adults. *Journal of Gerontology*, 1955, *10*, 91–107.

BIELBY, D. D., & PAPALIA, D. E. Moral development and egocentrism: Their development and interrelationship across the life-span. *International Journal of Aging and Human Development*, 1975, *6*, 293–308.

BIRKHILL, W. R., & SCHAIE, K. W. The effect of differential reinforcement of cautiousness in intellectual performance among the elderly. *Journal of Gerontology*, 1975, *30*, 578–583.

BIRREN, J. E., & MORRISON, D. F. Analysis of the WAIS subtests in relation to age and education. *Journal of Gerontology*, 1961, *16*, 363–369.

BLUM, J. E., FOSSHAGE, J. L., & JARVIK, L. F. Intellectual changes and sex differences in octogenarians: A twenty-year longitudinal study of aging. *Developmental Psychology*, 1972, *7*, 178–187.

BOTWINICK, J. *Aging and behavior.* New York: Springer, 1977.

BRENT, S. B. Individual specialization, collective adaptation, and rate of environmental change. *Human Development*, 1978, *21*, 21–33.

BRIGGS, C. H., & WEINBERG, R. A. Effects of reinforcement in training children's conceptual tempos. *Journal of Educational Psychology*, 1973, *65*, 383–394.

BRINLEY, J. F., JOVICK, T. J., & McLAUGHLIN, L. M. Age, reasoning, and memory in adults. *Journal of Gerontology*, 1974, *29*, 182–189.

BROMLEY, D. B. Some effects of age on the quality of intellectual output. *Journal of Gerontology*, 1957, *12*, 318–323.

BURT, C. The differentiation of intellectual abilities. *British Journal of Psychology*, 1954, *24*, 76–90.

CARPENTER, W. L. The relationship between age and information processing capacity of adults. *Industrial Gerontology*, 1971, *8*, 55–57.

CHAP, J. B., & SINNOTT, J. C. Performance of institutionalized and community-active old persons on concrete and formal Piagetian tasks. *Aging and Human Development*, 1977–1978, *8*, 269–278.

CICIRELLI, V. G. Categorization behavior in aged subjects. *Journal of Gerontology*, 1976, *31*, 676–680.

CLAY, H. M. Changes of performance with age on similar tasks of varying complexity. *British Journal of Psychology*, 1954, *45*, 7–13.

CLAYTON, V. *The role of formal operational thought in the aging process.* Unpublished manuscript, State University of New York at Buffalo, 1972.

COMALLI, P. E., WAPNER, S., & WERNER, H. Perception of verticality in middle and old age. *Journal of Psychology*, 1959, *47*, 259–266.

COYNE, A. C. WHITBOURNE, S. K., & GLENWICK, D. S. Adult age differences in reflection-impulsivity. *Journal of Gerontology*, 1978, *33*, 402–407.

CRAIK, F.I.M., & MASANI, P. A. Age differences in temporal integration of language. *British Journal of Psychology*, 1967, *58*, 291–299.

CROVITZ, E. Reversing a learning deficit in the aged. *Journal of Gerontology*, 1966, *21*, 236–238.

DEBUS, R L. Effects of brief observation of model behavior on conceptual tempo of impulsive children. *Developmental Psychology*, 1970, *2*, 22–32.

DEMMING, J. A., & PRESSEY, S. L. Tests "indigenous" to adult and older years. *Journal of Counseling Psychology*, 1957, *4*, 144–148.

DENNEY, D. R. Modeling effects upon conceptual style and cognitive tempo. *Child Development*, 1972, *43*, 105–119.

DENNEY, D. R., & DENNEY, N. W. The use of classification for problem solving: A comparison of middle and old age. *Developmental Psychology*, 1973, *9*, 275–278.

DENNEY, N. W. Classification abilities in the elderly. *Journal of Gerontology*, 1974a, *29*, 309–314.

DENNEY, N. W. Classification criteria in middle and old age. *Developmental Psychology*, 1974b, *10*, 901–906.

DENNEY, N. W. Evidence for developmental change in categorization criteria for children and adults. *Human Development*, 1974c, *17*, 41–53.

DENNEY, N. W. Problem solving in later adulthood: Intervention research. In P. B. Baltes & O. J. Brim, Jr. (Eds.), *Life-span development and behavior.* New York: Academic Press, 1979a.

DENNEY, N. W. *Attempts to modify cognitive tempo in elderly adults.* Unpublished manuscript, University of Kansas, 1979b.

DENNEY, N. W. The effect of the manipulation of peripheral, non-cognitive variables on problem-solving performance among the elderly. *Human Development*, 1980, *23*, 268–277.

DENNEY, N. W., & CORNELIUS, S. Class inclusion and multiple classification in middle and old age. *Developmental Psychology*, 1975, *11*(No. 4), 521–522.

DENNEY, N. W., & DENNEY, D. R. Modeling effects on the questioning strategies of the elderly. *Developmental Psychology*, 1974, *10*, 400–404.

DENNEY, N. W., JONES, F. W., & KRIGEL, S. W. Modifying the questioning strategies of young children and elderly adults. *Human Development*, 1979, *22*, 23–36.

DENNEY, N. W., & LENNON, M. L. Classification: A comparison of middle and old age. *Developmental Psychology*, 1972, *7*, 210–213.

DENNEY, N. W., & LIST, J. A. Adult age differences in performance on the matching familiar figures test. *Human Development*, 1979, *22*, 137–144.

DENNEY, N. W., & PALMER, A. M. *Adult age differences in traditional and practical problem-solving measures.* Unpublished manuscript, University of Kansas, 1980.

DENNEY, N. W., & WRIGHT, J. C. Cognitive changes during the adult years: Implications for developmental theory and research. In H. W. Reese (Ed.), *Advances in child development and behavior.* New York: Academic Press, 1976.

DENNIS, W. Age and achievement: A critique. *Journal of Gerontology*, 1956, *11*, 331–333.

DENNIS, W. The age decrement in outstanding scientific contributions: Fact or artifact? *American Psychologist*, 1958, *13*, 457–460.

DENNIS, W., & MALLINGER, B. Animism and related tendencies in senescence. *Journal of Gerontology*, 1949, *4*, 218–221.

DOPPELT, J. E., & WALLACE, W. L. Standardization of the Wechsler adult intelligence scale for older persons. *Journal of Abnormal and Social Psychology*, 1955, *51*, 312–330.

EISDORFER, C., & WILKIE, F. Intellectual changes with advancing age. In L. F. Garvik, C. Eisdorfer, & J. E. Blum (Eds.), *Intellectual functioning in adults.* New York: Springer, 1973.

ELO, A. E. Age changes in master chess performance. *Journal of Gerontology*, 1965, *20*, 289–299.

FRIEND, C. M., & ZUBEK, J. P. The effects of age on critical thinking ability. *Journal of Gerontology*, 1958, *13*, 407–413.

GARRETT, H. E. A developmental theory of intelligence. *American Psychologist*, 1946, *1*, 372–378.

GILBERT, J. G. Thirty-five year follow-up study of intellectual functioning. *Journal of Gerontology*, 1973, *28*, 68–72.

GORDON, S. K., & CLARK, W. C. Application of signal detection theory to prose recall and recognition in elderly and young adults. *Journal of Gerontology*, 1974, *29*, 64–72.

GREEN, R. F., & BERKOWITZ, B. Changes in intellect with age: II. Factorial analyses of Wechsler-Bellevue scores. *The Journal of Genetic Psychology*, 1964, *104*, 3–18.

HAYSLIP, B., JR., & STERNS, H. L. Age differences in relationships between crystallized and fluid intelligences and problem-solving. *Journal of Gerontology*, 1979, *34*, 404–414.

HEBB, D. O. On watching myself get old. *Psychology Today*, 1978, *12*, 15, 20–23.

HEGLIN, H. J. Problem solving set in different age groups. *Journal of Gerontology*, 1956, *11*, 310–317.

HEIDER, E. R. Information processing and the modification of an "impulsive conceptual tempo." *Child Development*, 1971, *42*, 1276–1281.

HERON, A., & CRAIK, F. Age differences in cumulative learning of meaningful and meaningless material. *Scandinavian Journal of Psychology*, 1964, *5*, 209–217.

HORN, J. L. Human ability systems. In P. B. Baltes (Ed.), *Life-span development and behavior* (Vol. 1). New York: Academic Press, 1978.

HORN, J. L., & CATTELL, R. B. Age differences in fluid and crystallized intelligence. *Acta Psychologica,* 1967, *26,* 107–129.

HORN, J. L., & DONALDSON, G. On the myth of intellectual decline in adulthood. *American Psychologist,* 1976, *31,* 701–719.

HORN, J. L., & DONALDSON, G. Faith is not enough. A response to the Baltes-Schaie claim that intelligence does not wane. *American Psychologist,* 1977, *32,* 369–373.

HORNBLUM, J. N., & OVERTON, W. F. Area and volume conservation among the elderly: Assessment and training. *Developmental Psychology,* 1976, *12,* 68–74.

HOYER, F. W., HOYER, W. J., TREAT, N. J., & BALTES, P. B. Training response speed in young and elderly women. *International Journal of Aging and Human Development,* 1978–1979, *9,* 247–253.

HOYER, W., LABOUVIE, G., & BALTES, P. Modification of response speed and intellectual performance in the elderly. *Human Development,* 1973, *16,* 233–242.

HULICKA, I. M. Age differences in retention as a function of interference. *Journal of Gerontology,* 1967, *22,* 180–184.

HULICKA, I. M., & GROSSMAN, J. L. Age-group comparisons for the use of mediators in paired-associate learning. *Journal of Gerontology,* 1967, *22,* 46–51.

JARVIK, L. F., KALLMANN, F. J., & FALEK, A. Intellectual changes in aged twins. *Journal of Gerontology,* 1962, *17,* 289–294.

JEROME, E. A. Decay of heuristic processes in the aged. In C. Tibbitts & W. Donahue (Eds.), *Social and psychological aspects of aging.* New York: Columbia University Press, 1962.

KAY, H. The effects of position in a display upon problem solving. *Quarterly Journal of Experimental Psychology,* 1954, *6,* 155–169.

KESLER, M. S., DENNEY, N. W., & WHITELY, S. E. Factors influencing problem solving in middle-aged and elderly adults. *Human Development,* 1976, *19,* 310–320.

LABOUVIE-VIEF, G. Toward optimizing cognitive competence. *Educational Gerontology,* 1976, *1,* 75–92.

LABOUVIE-VIEF, G. Adult cognitive development: In search of alternative interpretations. *Merrill-Palmer Quarterly,* 1977, *23,* 227–263.

LABOUVIE-VIEF, G., & CHANDLER, M. J. Cognitive development and life-span developmental theory: Idealistic versus contextual perspectives. In P. B. Baltes (Ed.), *Life-span development and behavior* (Vol. 1). New York: Academic Press, 1978.

LABOUVIE-VIEF, G., & GONDA, J. N. Cognitive strategy training and intellectual performance in the elderly. *Journal of Gerontology,* 1976, *31,* 327–332.

LEHMAN, H. C. *Age and achievement.* Princeton, N.J.: Princeton University Press, 1953.

LEHMAN, H. C. The creative production rates of present versus past generations of scientists. *Journal of Gerontology,* 1962, *17,* 409–417.

LEHMAN, H. C. The production of masters' works prior to age 30. *Gerontologist,* 1965, *5,* 24–30.

LEHMAN, H. C. The most creative years of engineers and other technologists. *Journal of Genetic Psychology,* 1966, *108,* 263–277.

LOOFT, W. R., & CHARLES, D. C. Egocentrism and social interaction in young and old adults. *International Journal of Aging and Human Development,* 1971, *2,* 21–28.

MAGNUSSON, D. *Test theory.* Reading, Mass.: Addison-Wesley, 1967.

MANNICHE, E., & FALK, G. Age and the Nobel prize. *Behavioral Science,* 1957, *2,* 301–307.

MATARAZZO, J. D. *Wechsler's measurement and appraisal of adult intelligence.* Baltimore, Md.: Williams & Wilkins Co., 1972.

MEICHENBAUM, D. *Training the aged in verbal control of behavior.* Paper presented at the International Congress on Gerontology, Kiev, Russia, 1972.

MEICHENBAUM, D. H., & GOODMAN, J. Training impulsive children to talk to themselves: A means of developing self-control. *Journal of Abnormal Psychology,* 1971, *77,* 115–126.

MORGAN, A. B. Differences in logical reasoning associated with age and higher education. *Psychological Reports,* 1956, *2,* 235–240.

OWENS, W. A., JR. Age and mental abilities: A longitudinal study. *Genetic Psychology Monographs,* 1953, *48,* 3–54.

OWENS, W. A., JR. Age and mental abilities: A second adult follow-up. *Journal of Educational Psychology,* 1966, *51,* 311–325.

PANICUCCI, C. L. *The effect of training on inductive reasoning behavior in young and old adults.* Paper presented at the 28th annual meeting of the American Gerontological Society, Louisville, Ky., October 1975.

PAPALIA, D. E. The status of several conservation abilities across the life-span. *Human Development,* 1972, *15,* 229–243.

PAPALIA, D. E., KENNEDY, E., & SHEEHAN, N. Conservation of space in noninstitutionalized old people. *Journal of Psychology,* 1973, *84,* 75–79.

PAPALIA, D. E., SALVERSON, S. M., & TRUE, M. An evaluation of quantity conservation performance during old age. *Aging and Human Development,* 1973, *4,* 103–109.

PLEMONS, J. K., WILLIS, S. L., & BALTES, P. B. Modifiability of fluid intelligence in aging: A short-term longitudinal training approach. *Journal of Gerontology,* 1978, *33,* 224–231.

RHUDICK, P. J., & GORDON, C. The age center of New England study. In L. F. Jarvik, C. Eisdorfer, & J. E. Blum (Eds.), *Intellectual functioning in adults.* New York: Springer, 1973.

RIDBERG, E. H., PARKE, R. D., & HETHERINGTON, E. M. Modification of impulsive and reflective cognitive styles through observation of film-mediated models. *Developmental Psychology,* 1971, *5,* 369–377.

RIEGEL, K. F. Dialectic operations: The final period of cognitive development. *Human Development,* 1973, *16,* 346–370.

RIMOLDI, H.G.A., & WOUDE, K.W.V. Aging and problem solving. *Industrial Gerontology,* 1971, *8,* 68–69.

RUBIN, K. The relationship between spatial and communicative egocentrism in children and young and old adults. *Journal of Genetic Psychology,* 1974, *125,* 295–301.

RUBIN, K. Extinction of conservation: A life-span investigation. *Developmental Psychology,* 1976, *12,* 51–56.

RUBIN, K. H., ATTEWELL, P., TIERNEY, M., & TUMOLO, P. The development of spatial egocentrism and conservation across the life-span. *Developmental Psychology,* 1973, *9,* 432.

SANDERS, J. C., STERNS, H. L., SMITH, M., & SANDERS, R. E. Modification of concept identification performance in older adults. *Developmental Psychology,* 1975, *11,* 824–829.

SANDERS, R. E., & SANDERS, J. C. Long term durability and transfer of enhanced conceptual performance in the elderly. *Journal of Gerontology,* 1978, *33,* 408–412.

SANDERS, S., LAURENDEAU, M., & BERGERON, J. Aging and the concept of space: The conservation of surfaces. *Journal of Gerontology,* 1966, *21,* 281–285.

SCHAIE, K. W. A general model for the study of developmental problems. *Psychological Bulletin,* 1965, *64,* 92–107.

SCHAIE, K. W. Translation in gerontology—from lab to life: Intellectual functioning. *American Psychologist,* 1974, *29,* 802–807.

SCHAIE, K. W. External validity in the assessment of intellectual development in adulthood. *Proceedings of the 84th Annual Convention of the American Psychological Association,* 1976.

SCHAIE, K. W. Toward a stage theory of adult cognitive development. *Aging and Human Development,* 1977–1978, *8,* 129–138.

SCHAIE, K. W., & LABOUVIE-VIEF, G. Generational versus ontogenetic components of change in adult cognitive behavior: A fourteen-year cross-sequential study. *Developmental Psychology,* 1974, *10,* 305–320.

SCHUTZ, N. R., & HOYER, W. J. Feedback effects on spatial egocentrism in old age. *Journal of Gerontology,* 1976, *31,* 72–75.

SELZER, S. C., & DENNEY, N. W. Conservation abilities among middle-aged and elderly adults. *Aging and Human Development,* 1980, *11,* 135–146.

SMITH, D. K. The Einstellung effect in relation to the variables of age and training (Doctoral dissertation, Rutgers: The State University, 1967). *Dissertation Abstracts,* 1966, *27B,* 4115.

STORCK, P. A., LOOFT, W. R., & HOOPER, F. H. Interrelationships among Piagetian tasks and traditional measures of cognitive abilities in mature and aged adults. *Journal of Gerontology,* 1972, *27,* 461–465.

STREHLER, B. L. *Time, cells, and aging.* New York: Academic Press, 1977.

TOMLINSON-KEASEY, C. Formal operations in females from eleven to fifty-six years of age. *Developmental Psychology,* 1972, *6,* 364.

WETHERICK, N. E. A comparison of the problem-solving ability of young, middle-aged and old subjects. *Gerontologia,* 1964, *9,* 164–178.

WETHERICK, N. E. Changing an established concept: A comparison of the ability of young, middle-aged and old subjects. *Gerontologia,* 1965, *11,* 82–95.

WITTELS, I. Age and stimulus meaningfulness in paired-associate learning. *Journal of Gerontology*, 1972, *27*, 372–375.

YOUNG, M. L. Problem-solving performance in two age groups. *Journal of Gerontology*, 1966, *21*, 505–509.

YOUNG, M. L. Age and sex differences in problem solving. *Journal of Gerontology*, 1971, *26*, 330–336.

ZARETSKY H. H., & HALBERSTAM, J. L. Age differences in paired-associate learning. *Journal of Gerontology*, 1968, *23*, 165–168.

46

Learning and Memory in Later Life

GISELA LABOUVIE-VIEF
DAVID A. SCHELL

Investigators studying the aging of learning and memory functions have, since their beginning around the turn of the century, amassed a wide and fairly consistent data field. In general the process of individual aging has appeared to be characterized by sweeping deficits. Nevertheless interpretations of such decrement patterns have tended to polarize around two principal sources or causes of such deficits. On the one hand deficits have been seen to reflect a regressive breakdown or restriction of biophysical brain structures (e.g., Hebb, 1978; Horn, 1978, this volume)—the *hardware* (Hunt, 1978) of the cognitive apparatus. In this view aging is characterized by a restriction of *capacity*, of flexible cognitive structure (see Horn, Chap. 47, this volume). On the other hand occasional doubts have been raised at the stringency of this interpretation. Many deficits in information analysis and processing, for example, may arise from the fact that research subjects differ in the familiarity with certain knowledge structures from which assessment tasks are derived (e.g., Hultsch, 1981; Labouvie-Vief & Chandler, 1978)—what Hunt (1978) has termed the *software* of the cognitive apparatus.

The resulting polarization is not unique to the field of aging, but it is a recurrent one in other areas as well. Such distinctions as fluid versus crystallized intelligence (Horn, Chap. 47, this volume), data versus knowledge based limits on information processing (Norman & Bobrow, 1976), or mechanistic versus knowledge-related deficits (Hunt, 1978) are but a few examples. Yet despite their wide acceptance such polarizations have increasingly raised theoretical puzzles to models of information processing which are converging on a view where the two actually engage in intimate interaction (Marslen-Wilson & Welsh, 1978; Masson & Sala, 1978; Norman & Bobrow, 1976). It is a basic tenet of this chapter that such interactive views provide a much more general and com-prehensive framework in the analysis of aging changes (and indeed, more generally, developmental changes) in learning and memory.

The difficulty may be best exemplified by referring to two extreme prototypes of memory models. The first is Ebbinghaus's (1885/1965), who made a deliberate attempt to bracket culture and varied individual experience out of the definition of memory. Quite conscious of the complexities introduced by the historicity of subjects' memory, Ebbinghaus resolved to table the problem until learning and retention of very simple material (i.e., nonsense syllables) in rigidly controlled laboratory settings were better understood. This, he believed, offered "a possibility of indirectly approaching the problem . . . in a small and definitely limited sphere and, by means of keeping aloof for a while from any theory, perhaps of constructing one" (Ebbinghaus, 1885/1965, p. 65).

Ebbinghaus's is a nomothetic process view which hopes to construct by proceeding from the simple to the complex, a comprehensive theory of memory. It contrasts, at the other extreme, with that of Bartlett (1932) for whom the idiosyncratic historicity of the individual is an integral part of a comprehensive theory of memory. In his view the complexity of knowledge codes will covary with the degree to which the individual has learned to apply cognitive schemata to specific content domains. Thus cultural heritage, interest, and motivation must be part and parcel of a structural analysis of mnemonic process. Low-level recall (rote emphasis on detail, for instance, or purely temporal-sequential organization) is likely to operate in the absence of socially provided schemata or where recall is not particularly vital. High-level recall, alternatively, is likely if materials and experimental conditions fit ecological demands. In other words nomothetic laws of information processing become apparent only in ideographically fluctuant situations.

We will argue in this chapter that these polar views imply profoundly different conceptions of the ordering of difficulty levels of developmental complexity and, since such levels serve as gauges of what are to be called regressive changes, on conceptualizations of changes in learning and memory with advanced age as well. Moreover we will attempt to show that the second prototype—here called *nonlinear*—provides, in fact, a generalized formulation of the first type—here called *linear*.

This distinction will provide a convenient organization for this chapter. In the first part we will provide a review of models and research subsumed under the linear model. Due to the enormous body of research, we must restrict ourselves to a mere highlighting of some of the issues it has raised and kept unresolved. In the second part we will briefly summarize the assumptions of nonlinear models and discuss their heuristic and interpretive emphases.

LINEAR MODELS
OF MNEMONIC AGING

Linear models of mnemonic functioning and information processing have, thus far, provided the backbone of interpretations of mnemonic aging. Such models are based on a principle of linear cumulation (Piaget, 1971) which derives from the traditions of logical positivism and Wundtian elementarism. This principle holds that complex, abstract cognitions are an extension of the processing of more basic, direct, and veridical sensory and perceptual data. The latter are seen as providing a direct link with an experiential context, while the former are seen as deriving from a sensory basis by a process of secondary synthesis. The resulting view of mnemonic aging could be likened to a pyramid which, as it structurally weakens at the bottom, causes the top to erode.

Models of memory fashioned after this type therefore assume that the mnemonic system can be subdivided into different stages. From stage to stage information is transferred through a series of channels, each of which becomes successively more removed from a phenomenal world, and each of which is capable of performing characteristic mnemonic retention and transformation functions (Haber, 1969). Thus a first contact is made at a sensory register, a preattentive and preconceptual system of exceedingly low stability. A second system, the *short-term store* or *primary memory* displays somewhat higher stability. It too is limited, however, and information will quickly be lost unless it is passed on to the highly stable *long-term store*.

In general these systems are conceived as stages of processing and the information flow as moving through them in a one-directional manner. Each stage will display specific processes characterized in the main by different temporal durations or *memories* (see Craik & Lockhart, 1972). Wide variations occur, however, where different authors locate the bottleneck of processing deficits. Broadbent's (1958) and Sperling's (1963, 1967) models have primarily focused on early stages of sensory registering. Since these early stages are assumed to be preattentive and precategorical, they are thought to leave little, if any, room for individual's knowledge structures.

In contrast Waugh and Norman's (1965) model of primary and secondary memory has placed higher emphasis on the bottleneck created by the somewhat more stable, though still restricted (in terms of temporal span, structural capacity, and forgetting rates), transferring function of the primary-memory system. A further extension was provided by Atkinson and Shiffrin's (1968) model in which a differentiation is made between the structural features of these stores and the different control operations they are capable of. The primary memory, for example, is characterized by very simple operations of rehearsal. The secondary memory, in contrast, is capable of all the control operations that derive from our preexperimental knowledge of semantic organization, such as "chunking" and categorization. Thus a bottleneck could result either from limitations on the capacity of short-term processing mechanisms or else from a failure or inefficiency to apply the control operations of the long-term store.

Craik and Lockhart's (1972) depth of processing formulation has similarly pushed the bottleneck into the long-term store proper—at least, potentially so. In these authors' model an item in primary memory will be least memorable if it receives only shallow sensory processing. More retention results if it is processed to deeper semantic levels by relating it to existing knowledge structures. Thus though Craik and Lockhart do not depart from the idea of a linear, one-directional information transfer, they do maintain that the fate, as it were, of an item will depend on the degree and type of processing it receives through different processing levels.

While the preceding synopsis is only sketchy, it nevertheless provides a convenient framework for summarizing the bulk of the evidence on aging changes in the assimilation and storage of information. It has been a recurrent question to ask where in the sequence age-related deficits may have a primary locus. We will survey this evidence, separately discussing the roles of the sensory-register, primary-memory, and secondary-memory systems.

At each of these stages aging deficits may arise from three sources that have been distinguished on a conceptual level (although, as we will argue later, they are in fact interrelated). First, each system may show changes in structural capacity—e.g., the biophysical substrate of the system concerned might undergo deteriorative changes which will reduce the amount of information capable of being stored. Second, changes might primarily affect the temporal processes (e.g., duration, decay) of the system. Finally—and this is thought to be especially important at later stages—deficits might arise from a failure to employ processes of transfer and transformation from one system to another.

Sensory Register

It is a well-documented fact that aging brings a number of deteriorative changes in the sensory system (for a broad current review, see Birren & Schaie, 1977). In the visual system, for example, these changes will, among others, imply an age-related decrease of the perceived intensity of constant light sources, a slowing of dark adaptation, and a gradual shrinkage of the visual field (see McFarland, 1968). It is surprising, therefore, that age-related deficits in the capacity of the sensory register have not been demonstrated with any consistency (for recent reviews, see Botwinick, 1978). The technique used to assess the capacity of the sensory register has been developed by Sperling (1960), and it rests on the observation that we perceive more in a brief display than we can later report. Sperling (1960) used tones to cue subjects as to which row of a matrix, presented for 50 msec, should be reported. Subjects who were cued within 500 msec could report 76 percent of the items; if delayed to 1 second, they could only report 36 percent of the items. This partial-report technique has not been applied with much success with older subjects (Walsh & Prasse, 1981; Walsh & Thompson, 1978), who may not be able to complete the task. It is not clear at present why this difficulty should arise; however, it is interesting to note that results of the partial-report technique are highly affected by subjects' strategies (Sperling, 1960, Experiment 4).

On the other hand age-related changes have been demonstrated in the persistence of the information stored—i.e., the icon. Walsh and Thompson (1978) presented a flashing circle to both young and old subjects. The subjects' task was to decide when they could no longer perceive the circle disappear or reappear—i.e., when the circle appeared continuous or discontinuous. With this method Walsh and Thompson found that the older subjects needed less time than did the younger subjects, suggesting that the icon is of a shorter duration for the older subjects.

Divergent results have been obtained with another technique: the stimulus-half procedure. This procedure consists of presenting dot fragments of words for a brief duration, followed by a variable interstimulus interval, after which the complement fragments are presented (Eriksen & Collins, 1967). Kline and Orme-Rogers (1978) modified the technique by using straight-line segments (see, however, Kline & Baffa, 1976). Kline and Orme-Rogers found that the young and the old subjects did not differ in word identification at 0 msec, but that older subjects identified more words at longer intervals than did younger subjects, suggesting that the icon persists longer in the older subject. It is possible that this divergence reflects the involvement of different biostructural processing subsystems (see Hoyer & Plude, 1980); it is also possible, however, that the discrepancy occurs because the different tasks (geometric versus linguistic symbols) may differentially involve processing interactions with more stable stores.

There are very few studies examining transfer processes from the sensory register to primary and/or secondary memory. Walsh and Prasse (1981) report preliminary findings that older subjects require more time for a single-letter readout and that each additional readout of a letter requires 15 msec more time than that for younger subjects (35 msec compared to 20 msec). Walsh, Vletas, and Thompson (as reported in Walsh & Prasse, 1981) presented brief displays consisting of a single letter or a marker. In their first condition subjects had to identify a single letter that appeared in the center of the display. The second condition randomly varied the position of the marker in one of four quadrants of the display, and the subject had to identify the location of the marker. The third condition combined the first two; the subjects had to both identify and locate a single letter that was

randomly placed in one of the four quadrants. In all conditions the older subjects required more time to complete the task. Moreover the younger subjects required approximately a constant 65 msec for each task, while the older subjects required increasing times for each (100 msec, 140 msec, and 220 msec, respectively). Walsh and Prasse state that these readout and attentional processes have a profound effect on later memory stages, in essence by creating a bottleneck. Conversely they assume that any of the differences in icon duration may be too insignificant to affect later memory stages.

If Walsh and Prasse's bottleneck hypothesis were correct, large age differences in primary memory should be expected. This expectation does not, however, bear out (see following and Craik, 1977). It is possible that this discrepancy is because in the readout tasks subjects do not behave in accordance with a model of linear unidirectional information transfer. For example while the sensory register is defined to refer to precategorical, preattentive processes, it is not certain that this exclusive emphasis on peripheral processes continues to be heuristic. Shiffrin and Schneider (1977) have shown that tasks similar to the one used by Walsh, Vletas, and Thompson (cf. Walsh & Prasse, 1981) is subject to massive practice effects. Moreover readout rates for letters are themselves highly influenced by the word context in which they are embedded (e.g., Massaro, 1975).

Mnemonic process located at the level of the sensory register, in other words, may well be strongly affected by the expectations and knowledge schemata available to a subject (see also Posner, 1979). A good example of this view is that of Neisser (1976) who holds that the pickup of information at any stage is a result of an interaction between knowledge schemata and the information to which these schemata direct the perceiver. Many displays utilized in research, therefore, may have limited applicability as they interrupt this normal cycle.

Such displays come very close to not existing at all. They last for only a fragment of a second, and lack all temporal coherence with what preceded or what will follow them. They also lack any spatial link with their surroundings, being physically as well as temporally disconnected from the rest of the world. They cannot be touched, cannot be heard, and cannot be glanced at more than once. The subject is isolated, cut off from ordinary environmental support, able to do nothing but initiate and terminate trials that run their magical course whatever he may do. Although the data obtained under such conditions can serve as the basis of much ingenious theorizing, the resulting theories may mislead us. (Neisser, 1976, pp. 35–36)

It is possible, however, that some useful information may be derived from such displays. It may well bear, for example, on changes in receptors at an anatomical level (Sakitt, 1975). Nevertheless it may be of little significance in the context of a normal cycle of information pickup.

. . . by definition it does not exist while a given fixation continues, and it is destroyed by masking after every eye movement. Although the exact retinal arrangement of still unperceived forms may be briefly stored under tachistoscopic conditions, this storage is not persistent or robust enough to affect the perceptual cycle. (Neisser, 1976, p. 48)

Primary Memory

Similar to the research on the sensory register, both structural capacity and decay or duration times of the primary memory show slight, if any, differences between young and old subjects, while process differences have been demonstrated (Botwinick, 1978; Craik, 1977; Eysenck, 1977).

The usual method of assessing the capacity of primary memory in older subjects is the forward-span task. In this task the subject is presented serial lists of items (digits, letters, or words) to repeat back immediately in their order of presentation. The lists are presented in varying lengths (i.e., number of items), and the longest list a subject reproduces in correct serial order is usually considered the span of primary memory. Using this method little or no differences are found between young and old subjects (Botwinick & Storandt, 1974; Bromley, 1958; Craik, 1968a; Drachman & Leavitt, 1972; Friedman, 1974; Talland, 1965).

Age-related differences in rate of forgetting or decay of items in primary memory have been assessed by several variations on forward-span-type tasks. One, the recognition-probe technique, is a modification of Waugh and Norman's (1965) probe-digit experiment. In it a series of items are presented auditorily to the subject, followed by a test probe. The subjects' task is to decide whether the probe was on the list. The resulting recognition value at a given serial position is taken as an index of forgetting. Recognition is usually highest at the end of the list and lowest at earlier positions. The studies using this technique have not found rate differences between young and old (Craik, 1971).

A second method for assessing forgetting rates is a comparison of the recency portion of a free-recall list (Crowder, 1976). Again there is no evidence for a difference between young and old (Craik, 1968b).

A third technique is motivated by an early assumption that the older organism might be more susceptible to forgetting if the items held in primary memory are interfered with by subsequent incoming information (Talland, 1967). By using the Brown-Peterson paradigm in which the interference of subsequent counting activity on the recall of previously presented word lists is assessed, however, no compelling evidence is found to suggest that older subjects are more susceptible to interference (Talland, 1967).

In contrast to these studies which may not place high demands on the transfer operations to be applied to incoming material is another group of studies which have reported marked age differences in primary-memory performance under conditions where such control operations must be applied. There are two methods by which age differences in primary-memory performance have been demonstrated: backward span (reviewed by Craik, 1977) and the Sternberg (1969) reaction-time scan task (reviewed by Craik, 1977; Fozard & Popkin, 1978).

Backward span can be considered a method for demonstrating process constraints since the subject must manipulate or reorganize the information already present in primary memory by repeating it in reverse order. The research strongly suggests that the old perform significantly poorer than do the young (Botwinick & Storandt, 1974; Bromley, 1958).

In the modal application of Sternberg's (1969) reaction-time task, the subjects are presented a short list of items (varying from one to seven) to hold in memory, called the *memory set*. After the presentation of the memory set, the subjects are presented a single item, called the *probe item*. The subjects' task is to quickly decide whether the probe item was a member of the memory set. The intercept of the resulting linear function is conceived to reflect perceptual-motor time and decision time, while the slope reflects search rate—i.e., comparison time per item in the memory set (Sternberg, 1969). In the three experiments using this task (Anders & Fozard, 1973; Anders, Fozard, & Lillyquist, 1972; Eriksen, Hamlin, & Daye, 1973), the older subjects typically have larger intercept and slope values, suggesting that older subjects require a longer time for all processes: perceptual-motor, decision, and comparison.

Nevertheless it appears that such age-related deficits do not universally extend to all tasks. In particular facility at performing a Sternberg task is affected by one's experience with task materials, and age differences may therefore vary considerably if this factor is taken into consideration. Thomas, Waugh, and Fozard (1978) tested subjects using sets that differed in assumed familiarity. In a control condition where the subjects responded if any letter was present on the screen, no age differences were found. In a single-letter set condition the subjects responded "yes" any time the letter *b* was presented and "no" to any other letter; the older subjects took longer to respond than did the younger subjects. In a familiar set condition consisting of the set *a b c d e f*, again the older subjects took longer to respond than did the younger subjects. In the fourth condition an unfamiliar set consisting of *p g k t r i* was presented. This set produced the largest age differences, thus demonstrating an interaction of age and set familiarity.

While the results of Thomas et al. (1978) should lead one to exercise some caution as far as any absolute statements about age-related processing deficits on Sternberg tasks are concerned, suggestive evidence for a similar relativistic interpretation emerges even more strongly from studies performed on college students. Jonides and Gleitman (1972) changed the context in which a shape (i.e., *O*) was embedded. Such variations drastically altered slope values and indeed reduced them to zero in some instances (see also Schiffrin & Schneider, 1977). Slope values, in other words, may not always indicate "valid" age deficits.

Once more we are led, then, to the problem that questions about the efficiency of a processing system—the primary memory in this case—are not entirely independent of the knowledge schemata of a subject. A particularly dramatic example of this interdependence can be seen in research of mnemonic capacity in children and adults who may or may not play chess (Chase & Simon, 1973; Chi, 1978). Adult chess players, for example, may have an astounding capacity to memorize configurations which correspond to actual moves; this is not due, however, to a phenomenal short-term storage capacity, as they are no better than are chess novices at memorizing random moves. Similarly Chi (1978) has demonstrated that child chess players have a superior memory span for chess positions than do adult novices. However, the results of a digit-span task demonstrate the reverse—i.e., adults are superior. Again the question arises: To what extent are deficits in the older organism a result of their having evolved different ways of organizing knowledge?

Secondary Memory

In contrast to the two systems just discussed, the secondary memory subsumes mechanisms of such variety and temporal extension that it is not usually practicable to talk about functional capacity limits. An implicit assumption, therefore, of many memory models is that there is no such limit to secondary memory. This assumption has constrained the hypotheses that were entertained about the profound aging changes in secondary memory that have been consistently demonstrated since the beginning of this century (see Riegel, 1977)—namely, most hypotheses of the mechanisms underlying such changes have not focused on capacity limits per se but rather on processes of transfer of information to and from secondary memory. Thus limitations in old subjects are viewed as processing deficits located either at encoding (Eysenck, 1974, 1977), storage (Welford, 1958), and retrieval (Craik, 1977; Schonfield & Robertson, 1966) or in the interaction of encoding-retrieval, specifically organizational processes (Smith, 1979, 1981; Smith & Fullerton, 1980). In essence this view implies that somewhere along the input-output sequence of secondary memory the older subjects fail to apply some critical abstract control operation or are limited in resources to apply such operations as encoding, storage, and retrieval.

Encoding-Storage versus Retrieval. Theoretically, poor performance on recall tasks could have their basis in one of three mechanisms. First, the individual may fail to assimilate, or encode, material that s/he learned. Second, material—although it has been encoded and stored—may not be accessible. Third, deficits might result from an interaction of encoding and retrieval processes.

One example of an early theoretical position that associates aging deficits in mnemonic performance to failures to store information properly is Welford's (1958) hypothesis that aging brings increased susceptibility to interference. This hypothesis has stimulated a large body of research. However it is now generally thought to lack support (see Craik, 1977; Smith, 1979, 1981; Smith & Fullerton, 1980).

The *retrieval*-difficulty explanation of observed memory deficits is based on the observation that the provision of information at the time of retrieval increases the number of items recalled (as in cued-recall and recognition tests), hence the items must have been in storage but were inaccessible for retrieval (see Smith, 1979; Tulving, 1974).

Similar to the research on primary-memory span, typically nonsignificant differences in recognition scores are found in intentional learning between young and old subjects (Craik, 1971; Harkins, Chapman, & Eisdorfer, 1979; Schonfield & Robertson, 1966; Smith, 1975) or results suggest that recognition produces smaller differences than recall scores (Botwinick & Storandt, 1974; Erber, 1974; Perlmutter, 1979; White, in Craik, 1977). Recent studies do suggest that if only correct recognition is considered then there will be little difference. However, if response bias is taken into consideration a somewhat

different picture emerges—that is, older subjects are actually poorer at discriminating old and new items (Harkins et al., 1979). They are more likely to say wrongly that a new item occurred on the study list (Rankin & Kausler, 1979).

Further support for the retrieval-deficit hypothesis derives from the comparison of free- and cued-recall conditions: If provision of cues at recall increases recall performance over a free-recall base line, it is concluded that subjects fail to employ effective retrieval mechanisms. Research has shown that this manipulation attenuates the profound free-recall differences between young and old adults (Hultsch, 1975; Laurence, 1967; Smith, 1977). Craik (1968a, 1968b) provides evidence that when the words to be studied are taken from small pools of possible alternatives (e.g., digits) as compared to larger pools (e.g., animal names) the age decrement in recall is somewhat attenuated. Craik suggests "that when good retrieval information is made available—either by the provision of retrieval cues or by the use of a limited set of items—older subjects' retention is less impaired" (1977, p. 400). Conversely the increased dependence on such information is said to expose the aging individual's retrieval difficulty.

Encoding deficits, finally, are evidenced in research providing orienting tasks at the time of encoding. The type of orienting task used is itself important in determining the pattern of age differences obtained. Typical orienting tasks may use (1) orthographic or structural processing (e.g., *E* or *G* checking, or capital letter verification), (2) phonemic processing (rhyme verification), and (3) semantic processing (category verification). Craik states that semantic processings are "deeper," result in more elaborate encoding, and hence yield superior retention than either structural or phonemic processing (Craik, 1979; Craik & Lockhart, 1972; Craik & Simon, 1981; Craik & Tulving, 1975; Jacoby & Craik, 1979.)

The results of the recall studies using this paradigm to compare young and old subjects are fairly consistent in demonstrating that when the tasks involve shallow or less elaborative processing there is typically no difference between the young and old (Eysenck, 1974; Mason, in Smith, 1979; White, in Craik, 1977). When orienting tasks require deeper or more elaborative processing, the recall of the young typically exceeds that of the older subject (Craik & Simon, 1981; Eysenck, 1974; Lauer, 1975; Mason, in Smith, 1979; Perlmutter, 1978, 1979; White, in Craik, 1977). Zelinski, Walsh, and Thompson (1978) demonstrated somewhat similar effects except that they found no differences in immediate recall between the young (age 18 to 30) and young-old (age 55 to 70). However, an old-old group (age 71 to 85) did have poorer subsequent recall. The results of their delayed (48-hour) recall test showed that the youngest group had the best recall, while the two older groups did not differ. Further on the delayed test the type of orienting task performed by the older groups did not differentially effect recall, while for the younger group semantic tasks resulted in higher recall than the nonsemantic tasks.

Encoding-Retrieval Interactions. One conceptual difficulty raised by the encoding-storage-retrieval trichotomy is the fact that differences in encoding strategies themselves will affect retrieval efficiency (see Smith,

1981). This interaction is shown particularly well in a study by Smith (1977) in which the presence and absence of cues at input and output were factorially combined with cue type. Either taxonomic (category label) or structural (first letter of the word) cues were used. When there were no cues at either input or output (free recall), the older subjects performed significantly poorer than did the young. When cues were provided at output (typical cued recall), there was a main effect of both age and cue type. Older subjects recalled significantly fewer words than did the young, and category cueing resulted in higher recall than did structural cueing. When cues were provided at input, and at *both* input and output, there was a significant age-by-cue-type interaction: The differences between age groups in recall with category cues was nonsignificant, while with structural cues the young recalled significantly more words than did the older subjects. Thus in effect input cueing seemed to be the most critical variable. Indeed input cueing with structural cues actually depressed performance below the free-recall base line for both the young and the old (see also Craik & Simon, 1981).

Smith (1981; Smith & Fullerton, 1980) has therefore recently proposed a more specific hypothesis. He proposes that older subjects have an organizational processing deficit (i.e., interrelating items together at input) in that the older subjects do not spontaneously organize the words presented to them (Hultsch, 1971, 1974, 1975). This deficit hypothesis is a restatement, in fact, of the older hypothesis that the older individual fails to interrelate material spontaneously by means of relational schemata (see Goulet, 1973; Horn, this volume) of all kinds. Such schemata may not only refer to the size of the linguistic categories but also to the use of imagery (e.g., Hulicka & Grossman, 1967; Treat & Reese, 1976) or the imposition of rather idiosyncratic ordering strategies (e.g., Hultsch, 1971, 1974; Laurence, 1966).

Hypothesized Mechanisms. It may be useful to pause at this juncture and attempt some preliminary synthesis of the material discussed thus far. In general it has proven difficult to locate any single one bottleneck that might account for the older adult's difficulty with mnemonic tasks of the nature discussed. In particular it does not seem to be the case that such deficits can in general be predicted in a unilinear, bottom-up fashion. Rather most authors agree that one must be dealing here with a phenomenon of a more central nature and one that affects processes of abstraction and relational synthesis that may bear on all stages of mnemonic integration but that nevertheless affect more central, or deeper, modes of analysis in the most dramatic fashion. This view is congruent with, in fact, a law formulated by Ribot a century ago (Ribot, 1882, in Rubinstein, 1968).

Regression first affects more complex organizations. In mnemonic organization, the "new" dies prior to the "old," the complex before the simple. Thus in old age one will often remember events long past while forgetting recent ones.... Volitional control is lost first, the control of automatic action later. In this way cognitive disorganization follows the reverse order of its development through sequential stages. (cf., Rubinstein, 1968, p. 409; first author's translation)

In agreement with this general view of cognitive aging, several biological mechanisms have been postu-

lated to account for such processes. In general most of the available models emphasize deteriorative processes in the brain which may affect the "hardware" of the mnemonic apparatus in a more or less diffuse fashion. Horn (this volume) hypothesizes that cumulative random assaults and normative deteriorative damage to central nervous system structures may be responsible. Terry (e.g., Wisniewski & Terry, 1976) more specifically calls attention to cell deterioration and death in the hippocampal structures, which would indeed affect the integration of new material. The general effect of such neurophysiological damage has been thought to either create more "neural noise" by random firing of neurons (thus decreasing the signal-to-noise ratio of incoming stimulation) (e.g., Welford, 1977) and/or possibly to create disturbances in mechanisms of inhibiting neural system activation (Birren, 1974; Hebb, 1978).

A further major hypothesis, the *central*-speed hypothesis (Birren, 1974; reviewed by Botwinick, 1978), is based on the almost universal observation that older subjects are slower in performing many behaviors. While younger subjects' psychomotor speed depends upon variations in experience and specific demands, the slowness in the older subjects appears instead to be marked by the emergence of a general speed factor (Botwinick & Storandt, 1974; Chown, 1961). If the loss-of-speed hypothesis was only based on peripheral limitations set by the sense organs and muscles, it would not be of crucial importance in limiting cognitive functioning (Botwinick, 1978; Salthouse, 1976); however, the central-speed hypothesis does posit that the changes within the nervous system which support cognitive abilities do occur and that cognitive decline reflects neurophysiological decline (Marsh & Thompson, 1977).

Other hypotheses, in turn, have emphasized the effects of aging of other organismic structures, such as the cardiovascular system, which may cause decreased efficiency of brain functioning (e.g., Botwinick, 1978; Eisdorfer & Wilkie, 1973; Wang, 1973).

However, while all of these factors may play an important role in a subpopulation of the elderly (particularly those institutionalized or hospitalized as a function of strokes or senility), some authors have argued that they may not be as significant in the majority (up to 95 percent of the elderly population) which lives in the community in fairly good health. Despite claims of the widespread occurrence of neuronal death in aging, a number of recent reports have claimed either stability of neuronal populations over the adult life span of various species (e.g., Dayan, 1971; Diamond, 1978), including humans (e.g., Brody, 1955), or else that losses affect specific areas of the brain rather than being diffuse. Moreover the behavioral significance of the loss of brain cells is not at all clear. First of all, the brain is able to tolerate enormous loss with little apparent effect on normal functioning (Timiras, 1972), as information is stored with great redundancy. Second, there appears to be considerable dendritic growth in the *normal* aging human brain (in at least the parahippocampal gyrus), whereas regression and cell death may be limited to senile pathology (Buell & Coleman, 1979). Third, even in the adult brain, lost functioning may be replaced by new systems (Lund, 1978). Finally, even stable neuronal populations are able to reorganize their interconnections through processes of reactive synaptic regrowth (Scheff, Bernardo, & Cotman, 1978).

Despite a proliferation of hypothesized biological mechanisms for cognitive-mnemonic regression, therefore, it is not at all a foregone conclusion that such regression must be a normative component of aging. Any hypothesis of a central location of deficit must also contend, of course, with the fact that the older person by virtue of his/her position at a particular life stage and the cumulative effect of his/her sociocultural milieu must have developed specific modes of organization by which information is processed (Bartlett, 1932; Hultsch, 1981; Labouvie-Vief, 1981; Schaie, 1965). This is reminiscent, of course, of Horn's (this volume) assertion of a separate life-course development of fluid and crystallized processes. Nevertheless this distinction, by erecting a dualism between biophysical structure on the one hand and knowledge structures on the other, may not offer a satisfactory integration of known biological and experiential processes. For example psychobiological approaches to cognition and development tend to emphasize the fact that biologically based structures for dealing with information develop in interaction with specific sets of experience and thus are specialized to deal with those experiences (e.g., Jacobson, 1978). Furthermore it appears that mnemonic deficits of the kind surveyed thus far are quite specific to the tasks by which they have been assessed and may not at all have any significant bearing on processes of more real-life linguistic integration of high complexity (see following). It is not surprising, therefore, to find an increasing interest in a more developmental, historically oriented account of mechanisms of memory and aging.

MNEMONIC AGING:
A DEVELOPMENTAL VIEW

Often questions about the location of mnemonic deficits may not have any determinate answers since, in order to provide such answers, it would be necessary to have information about the subject's specific mode of organizing experience. It is because of this correlative relationship that many authors (e.g., Baltes, Reese, & Lipsitt, 1980; Hultsch, 1981; Labouvie-Vief, 1980a, 1980b, 1981; Schaie, 1978) are urging for an account of mnemonic aging that is less oriented toward deficit interpretations.

In pursuing such interpretations one must, however, walk a fine line between asserting on the one hand that mnemonic aging is to be equated *by fiat* with deterioration and, on the other, ruling deterioration out of court. To adopt the second stance entails the danger of a defensive rigidity of a theoretical account that integrates a small portion of available evidence, at best. There are nevertheless a number of strong reasons for adopting such a posture, if only as a tentative and heuristic one.

A first reason is exemplified particularly well by a Piagetian approach to the study of children. In this view it is not sufficient to conceptualize children as "deficient," quantitatively reduced adults. To do so would fail to expose the fact that the organization of thinking and memorizing of children nevertheless forms a whole which—however much it may deviate from that of adults—is coherent and logically interrelated. Further by failing to expose a normative unfolding of this organiza-

tion over time, it traps us by a static notion of normalcy rather than by offering a concept of normalcy as deviations from a developmental trajectory. Normalcy, in other words, is a concept to be scaled by a view of the capacities characteristic of sequential life stages.

Second, the notion of deficit thereby attains a certain relativisitic, rather than absolute, quality, and this quality is expressed both in individual trajectories over time and in their interindividual variation. Intraindividually, for example, some authors (e.g., Kummer, 1971; Seitelberger, 1978) claim that the function of mnemonic reorganization in aging individuals may serve certain adaptive functions, despite whatever losses may be apparent. Also interindividually individuals may become specialized for different modes of information intake through the historicity of their experience (e.g., Bartlett, 1932; Scribner, 1979; Werner, 1948); thus mnemonic efficiency, rather than being gauged by a single standard, may better be expressed in relation to the idiosyncratic modes of having organized one's experience.

Finally, however, this view of cognitive aging as continued developmental reorganization offers unique advantages for a theoretical account in which both gains and losses over the course of time have their place. In this section this view will first be outlined. We will then review additional evidence congruent with this view, as well as a reinterpretation of the evidence thus far discussed.

Nonlinear Models of Information Processing

Most of the models discussed thus far, and the research emanating from them, have assumed a one-directional causal flow from the intake of sensory information which, by the superimposition of more and more processing, eventually make contact with higher-level representations. These higher-level representations, in turn, are not usually assumed to control the perception of sensory events. Many recent models, however, have questioned this one-directional process and instead have proposed more interactive views in which knowledge structures acquired in the past may guide all stages of information analysis in a top-down fashion. Such top-down processes are necessary as they allow for the resolution of degraded, missing, or ambiguous lower-level information (Lindsay & Norman, 1977; Marslen-Wilson & Welsh, 1978; Masson & Sala, 1978; Norman & Bobrow, 1976). Thus a word (e.g., *watch*) may take on different meanings when embedded into different linguistic contexts (see Lindsay & Norman, 1977; Miller, 1962) and the likelihood of being remembered also will be influenced by this context (Solso, 1974). This view, then, maintains that what we perceive of the context may not be a mere recording of objective events but rather a constructive process by which these events are enriched with the memories of past actions and concepts.

Top-Down Processes. A first assumption, then, of many recent models of information intake is that input stimuli may make contact directly with secondary memory and that the knowledge (e.g., semantic) structure associated with the stimulus becomes available to primary memory (Hayes-Roth, 1977; Shiffrin & Schneider, 1977).

Structures that are highly complex and conceptual (e.g., chess) then may be automatically activated for top-down processing rather than by a bottom-up process of directed elaboration, and structures that appear simple at face value, vice versa, may involve a process of directed search (Hayes-Roth, 1977).

Piaget (e.g., 1972, in particular) has similarly rejected the view that concepts arise from percepts by a process of abstractive elaboration. In fact the reverse is usually true. In Piaget's words,

There is immediate perception as totality and sensations are now mere structured elements and no longer structuring. . . . When I perceive a house, I do not see at first the color of the tile, the height of the chimney, and the rest, and finally the house! . . . The neurologist Weizsaecker said . . . "When I perceive a house, I do not see an image which enters through the eye; on the contrary, I see a solid into which I can enter!" (Piaget, 1972, pp. 65–66; emphasis is added)

Thus once the individual has abstracted the salient dimensions, the assimilation of information proceeds not from elements (microstructure) to their transformation (macrostructure), but the process is usually the reverse: A transformation determines what elements are perceived. This is not to say, of course, that such transformations operate *in vacuo,* detached from a perceptual context. However, the role of the context may be restricted to a signaling function which immediately activates a more general structure.

Second, one may ask from where this "more general structure" receives its power to direct information analysis in a top-down fashion. In Piaget's (e.g., 1970) system this property is always a result of a temporal process, and the answer thus always forces one to look at structures with a view toward their past. In this view the functioning of structures is profoundly different depending on whether one examines them from a process perspective (i.e., the process of their formation) or a product perspective (i.e., as an already finished product). From a process perspective one must refer to an earlier stage in which the components are structur*ing*—i.e., more readily available or activated than the eventual "more general" structure. From a product perspective, however, the structure has become dominant such that even only a component process may activate it.

The creation and buildup of these structures can be viewed as a *recursive* process: Knowledge organization and reorganization is seen as a process through which a number of previously independent knowledge structures come to be subordinated under a new knowledge structure (see Hayes-Roth, 1977). Eventually the superordinating knowledge structure is established. This new knowledge structure then will be automatically activated.

The process of sub- and superordination is best exemplified in research examining the integration of new information into existing (already unitized) knowledge structures (e.g., Anderson, 1976; Hayes-Roth, 1977; Hayes-Roth & Hayes-Roth, 1975; Lewis & Anderson, 1976). The general procedure involves having subjects learn a series of facts (propositions) about real or fictitious people. At various stages in the learning process, subjects are timed as they verify these propositions as well as false propositions. During the intial stages of

learning, the time it takes to verify a proposition about a real or fictitious person increases with the number of propositions that the subject has learned about that person (Anderson, 1976; Hayes-Roth, 1977; Hayes-Roth & Hayes-Roth, 1975; Lewis & Anderson, 1976). However, as the new propositions become over-learned—that is, as the new information becomes integrated and unitized into the knowledge structure—verification time no longer depends on the total number of propositions (Hayes-Roth, 1977).

This process of hierarchical sub- and superordination also implies that knowledge structures may be automatically activated at different levels. Note that this assumption leads to predicting an ordering of the contents or task components in the various stores at different levels of depth which is different from the ordering assumed in most current research on adult memory. Given sufficient practice and a sufficiently salient context, an automatic, quasi-"perceptual" match may be established at the level of what would appear to be a very complex structure. Mandler (1962) has described this process.

First, the organism makes a series of discrete responses, often interrupted by incorrect ones. However, once errors are dropped out and the sequence of behavior becomes relatively stable—as in running a maze, speaking a word, reproducing a visual pattern—the various components of the total behavior required in the situation are "integrated." Integration refers to the fact that previously discrete parts of a sequence come to behave functionally as a unit; the whole sequence is elicited as a unit and behaves as a single component response has in the past; any part of it elicits the whole sequence. (p. 417)

Hayes-Roth (1977) has reviewed evidence pertinent to this proposition. Thus three-word idioms may be recalled faster than are their single-word constituents (Johnson, 1975) or sentence meanings more reliably than are the specific constituent words (e.g., Bransford & Franks, 1971). At much higher levels yet, texts may be encoded in terms of a string of interrelated propositions (e.g., Kintsch, 1974; Rumelhart, 1975), social information in terms of broad social action schemata (Carroll & Payne, 1976), or typical action sequences in scripts (Schank & Abelson, 1977).

Such broad knowledge structures are seen to subordinate their constituent components. Initially (at an early stage of learning) the constituent units may be activated singly in accordance with their own contexts and feedback properties and more readily activated than the superordinating task structures they are structur*ing*. Given sufficient practice, however, the information about a complete set, or structure, is more readily available than is any component part—which is now structur*ed*. The evidence cited before is consistent with this interpretation. Hayes-Roth (1977) similarly has argued that a knowledge structure usually will be automatically activated, even if only a component is presented. The process of recall then can be represented by one of decomposition or reconstructive activation of lower levels.

Dominance and Flexibility. The discussion thus far suggests a low degree of flexibility by which the individual can access information—namely, information is always accessed through a top node in top-down fashion. It is possible sometimes, however, to present contexts which may highlight the need for a particular level of analysis. A study conducted by McNeill and Lindig (1973) may serve as an example. College students were presented a target of one level (e.g., phoneme) and a search list consisting of phonemes, syllables, words, and sentences. Fastest reaction times for target detection resulted from target-list match conditions (i.e., phoneme-phoneme, syllable-syllable), while mismatches between target and search lists resulted in longer reaction times. Further the larger the mismatch (i.e., phoneme-sentence), the more reaction time increased. Thus task difficulty was directly ordered by matches in level.

However, there is a limit to such flexibility. Much experimental evidence suggests that individuals may establish strong directional preferences by which a unidirectional mode of information processing becomes a dominant one. A striking example of this phenomenon is offered in a study by Ozier (1978) which utilized a crossing of different encoding and cueing conditions. When words were category-coded during learning, categories provided near-perfect recall cues, while orthographic cues produced intermediate recall only, no better than category cueing. Collins and Loftus (1975) have reviewed similar evidence and explained it by the assumption that superordinate categories tend to push a decision criterion over a critical limit so as to eliminate search of the subordinate set.

A second example can be seen developmentally in a study by Bisanz, Danner, and Resnick (1979). Children (aged 8, 10, and 12 years) performed a variant of Posner's matching task (Posner, Boies, Eichelman, & Taylor, 1969) by deciding whether two drawings were the same or different based on either physical or name information. As with the Posner task results, physical matching was faster than name matching. However, parameter estimation revealed two sources of interference that showed different effects across the age groups: Interference due to irrelevant physical information *decreased with age* (open and closed umbrella SAME under name-identity instructions), while interference due to irrelevant name information *increased with age* (open and closed umbrella DIFFERENT under physical-identity instructions).

The degree to which flexibility is thus lost in favor of the establishment of superordinate categories may be strongly influenced by ecological variables. Thus Hayes-Roth (1977) has reasoned that "perfectly flexible," bidirectional processing will obtain only if ecological conditions (e.g., practice) demand bidirectional analysis. If, on the other hand, they favor unidirectional analysis, flexibility may be lost altogether (see also Hayes-Roth & Hayes-Roth, 1975).

Similarly a series of experiments by Schneider and Shiffrin (1977) demonstrated that flexibility of processing is not only dependent upon the length of learning trials but also upon the type of training. In their consistent mapping conditions where memory set items stayed constant across trials, *automatic detection* was developed. In varied mapping conditions where targets and distractors are interchanged trial to trial, controlled processing resulted. Later experiments by the same authors (Shiffrin & Schneider, 1977) demonstrated that such automatic processes are extremely resistant to change (requiring

2400 trials to produce a level of efficiency which had previously been established with only 1500 original training trials).

Nonlinear Ordering. It is important to realize that from the view of structures as a mode of dominant, recursive, and transformative information assimilation follows an ordering property that is nonlinear: Once the child has attained, for example, a concept of an object as a series of invariant temporal and spatial transformations, it becomes almost unthinkable to revert back to perceiving merely a series of isolated images.

The implication of this process is perhaps best demonstrated by referring to the domain of mnemonic transformations. Most research in aging has examined memory changes with tasks that were fashioned after a view of memory as a passive event recorder. Thus in examining the retention of verbal material, "accuracy" was scored by the ability to retain the verbatim content of such verbal messages as lists of words and, less frequently, sentences or paragraphs. The nonlinear view rejects, however, any single criterion of accuracy; rather, it starts with the assumption that individuals may perform different kinds of transformation on the messages given. In sentence memory, for example, coding may be primarily in terms of verbatim content (e.g., "A rolling stone gathers no moss"), or it may be in terms of a meaning preserving transformation such as a paraphrase (e.g., "Only a resting stone gathers moss"), or it may even be in terms of a meaning-expanding transformation (e.g., "A restless soul remains rootless"). The important point is that different criteria for accuracy may be partially *exclusive.*

It is because of this property of structures that acquisitions of a higher level of functioning may imply a loss of ability to reproduce the surface detail that is assimilated into the structure. Information is encoded in conformity with the constraints of the formal or deep-structural (top node) properties, and so it will be decoded in conformance with the same rules of transformation. To exemplify let us call first two modes of the example just given *Modes A and B,* and let us assume that a particular individual functions at *Mode B.* We may then say that the mapping of A to B or B to A is stochastic since a variety of verbatim surface forms can express the same meaning. However, if we apply a criterion appropriate to *B,* we face a one-to-one mapping: The meaning-preserving constraints of level *B* permit us, with relative facility, to discern between transformations that preserve meaning and those that do not. It is when we mix levels of analysis, however, that a degree of stochastic slippage is inherently introduced.

The view expressed in this example is one which is profoundly different from the linear view often held about development. Elsewhere (Labouvie-Vief, 1980a, 1981) we have called it the *nonlinear* view to capture the fact that, as we develop, we not only achieve integrations of higher spatio-temporal order, but we also tend to give up those of lower order unless they can be integrated into higher-order concepts. Thus the *linear* view of development is profoundly misleading in suggesting that throughout development we become better and better information processors. Hence development is often represented by the Guttman Scalogram (e.g., Wohlwill, 1973). In contrast the nonlinear principle proposes a view of life-course development in which different periods are characterized by dominant modes which supersede and replace earlier ones. The whole course of the life span thus can be conceptualized as a succession of single peaked functions (Coombs & Smith,1973) of different modes, each of which undergoes a period of growth, achievement of a functionally mature form, and then decline as it is superseded by a new mode.

It is also apparent that the meaning of context varies from level to level: The context is defined by the individual's modal level, not something absolute "out there." In the mnemonic example given, one individual may define the context at a concrete, verbatim level in conformity with his/her structural capacities; for a second individual the context may be defined by all possible meaning-preserving transformations; for a third the context may be broader yet and include all metaphoric permutations of the verbatim surface form. The sentence per se, in other words, may convey all kinds of different meanings.

Nonlinear orderings of the kind postulated are rarely attended to by developmental psychologists. Still the literature is replete with examples which show that with each new level not only a gain is achieved but also a loss. Piaget (1972) has shown that a loss of accuracy in simple perceptual judgments accompanies the movement from a two-dimensional to a three-dimensional perspective concept of space. Weir (1964) has reported that on a simple probability task, consisting of three targets with different hit probabilities, young children will very quickly adopt the strategy with the highest payoff—i.e., to always hit the target with the highest probability. College students, conversely, find this task exceedingly difficult, presumably due to the interference of more complex hypotheses.

Other nonlinear relationships are to be found more specifically in the children's mnemonic literature. In a variety of learning tasks, for example, young children pick up a vast array of material not bearing on the task proper—they may encode the position of the stimulus (Hagen, 1967; Maccoby & Hagen, 1965) or other detail that does not bear on the central issue of the task (see Stevenson, 1972, for review). Older children, on the contrary, show a *de*cline in such incidental learning. Of course this decline is not usually interpreted as a net decrement.

The decrease in incidental learning may represent an active attempt by the child to disregard the aspects of the situation that he has discovered to be irrelevant in his pursuit of a particular goal. He may demonstrate this disregard by failing to look at or label the irrelevant stimuli in an effort to improve his performance. (Stevenson, 1972, p. 213)

Another way to describe this state of affairs is to say that one deals with a trade-off. The older child is more selective but thereby also disregards many perceptual features.

The point is made even more cogently in research aimed at showing what features of words children of different ages encode. In general children before approximately sixth grade are highly susceptible to acoustic interference (i.e., an acoustically similar word is selected instead of a target word), while older children make more association errors (i.e., select semantically related foils) (e.g., Bach & Underwood, 1970; Freund & Johnson,

1972; Means & Rohwer, 1976; Underwood, 1969). Similarly in free recall younger children tend to cluster along acoustic dimensions and older ones along semantic dimensions (Hasher & Clifton, 1974; Naron, 1978; Rossi & Wittrock, 1971). Hence we see a trade-off both within and across levels. Across levels semantic encoding superordinates (and thereby decreases attention to) acoustic codes; within a level, attention to a mode of encoding causes a loss of differentiation between similar codes.

More generally pronounced nonlinearities appear to mark the establishment of linguistic control over the motor and perceptual behavior of young children (over an approximate interval of four to seven years of age). The reader is referred to Luria (1976), Reese (1962), and White (1965) for extensive examples of such nonlinearities which are indexed, among others, by (1) a relative increase in the difficulty of using simple perceptual codes as more complex linguistic codes become available (e.g., Kendler & Kendler, 1962; Underwood, 1975) and (2) a concomitant relative decline in the efficiency of simple perceptual discrimination (Kendler & Kendler, 1962; Weir & Stevenson, 1959). Suffice it to state here that decreasing age-performance functions are the rule throughout the whole process of development (see Labouvie-Vief, 1980a, 1980b, 1981, for a more extensive theoretical discussion).

Developmental Directions. The preceding view has served to argue that declining age-performance functions per se do not of necessity imply any absolute restrictions of developmental adaptability. Instead they are part and parcel of the process of cognitive restructuring at any segment of the life span. It is for this reason that, when attempting to judge whether changes in mnemonic aging can be interpreted within a model of further growth, an additional set of criteria is necessitated. Here we will borrow from the work of Piaget (1970, 1971, 1972; Werner, 1948, 1957) in pointing out such a set.

First, the process of development in general is characterized as a move from potential of extreme plasticity to one where potential is lost but realized in structures of higher specialization and spatio-temporal permanence. This principle applies not just to psychological development but to biological development as well (e.g., Jacobson, 1978; Lund, 1978). It is similar, of course, to Horn's (this volume) principle of fluidity versus crystallization. It does, however, contain a shift in emphasis: Specialization and stability are not seen as a loss in developmental adaptability but rather a gain, as the very functioning of the mature organism hinges on it.

Second, the process of development is one in which structures of relatively higher stability supersede structures of relatively lower stability. It is known, for example, that people are more likely to retain the gist of a sentence for a longer period of time than their verbatim surface form, or the kernel propositions of discourse material longer than lower-order data (e.g., Bartlett, 1932; Dooling & Christiaansen, 1977). By this virtue we would expect that if an individual were to perform a task that corresponds to a developmentally prior mode, deficits would be apparent. Nevertheless we are not really concerned in that case with "valid" deficits but rather with questions of developmental flexibility.

A Nonlinear Stage View of Mnemonic Aging

The view outlined before implies that questions about the aging of the information-processing system can never be all-or-none questions. Instead they require that we view such aging just as we view any other developmental transition: As new modes of information analysis supersede old ones, a trade-off is being made by which old modes lose in efficiency. It is important, however, to examine such restructuring with a view toward potential gains as well. Thus we would predict that adults, even ones quite advanced in age, will display modes of information processing which are not only coherent but also highly efficient in selected circumstances.

It is possible, in fact, from the previous discussion to predict the conditions under which the older adult will be relatively ineffective in information analysis but also those under which s/he will be relatively effective if compared to younger adults.

However, a note of caution is in order. These predictions are formulated as tentative, but heuristic, tools, not as firm statements of fact. First, we would expect that if materials to be learned and memorized are adjusted for ecological salience age differences will largely disappear or even reverse under special manipulations. Second, we predict that part of mnemonic deficit resides in the fact that younger and older individuals come to the experimental situation with different ways of structuring the tasks to be recalled. Therefore if it were possible to tap into these structures, age differences again should largely disappear. Third, we can hypothesize that presumptive deficits in abstractive ability are not an absolute matter; indeed, they should not invariably occur in media of information processing, such as linguistic structure, which continue to be of prime adaptive salience. Indeed we expect that in linguistic material continued movement to higher abstractive ability will be discerned as long as materials are well related to subjects' real-world knowledge. Finally, we may propose that presumptive deficits in depth of processing reflect a normative loss of developmental flexibility which may, however, be counteracted by specific contextual pressures toward flexibility. The following four predictions will form the major categories for reviewing additional evidence.

Ecological Salience. Research that manipulates the ecological salience or familiarity of task materials strongly supports the contention that stimulus material can be selected such that performance differences between age groups are either eliminated or reversed (i.e., Botwinick & Storandt, 1980; Gardner & Monge, 1977; Poon & Fozard, 1978). In an early study manipulating familiarity of stimulus material, Howell (1972) tested both recognition performance and sorting time of young and old subjects using material that consisted of (1) meaningless and unfamiliar patterns, (2) objects from a 1908 Sears and Roebuck catalogue, and (3) current objects which were assumed to be highly familiar and meaningful for both age groups. Also included in the design was an easy and difficult condition in which the distractors were either very similar (difficult) or very different (easy) from the targets. The results revealed nonsignificant differences between young and old for both easy and difficult recognition tests on the 1908 objects and for the easy recognition test of unfamiliar patterns. The remaining conditions (easy and difficult tests of current objects and the difficult test for unfamiliar patterns) showed that the young had significantly fewer recognition errors.

With more precise reaction-time data, a rather elegant study using naming latency conducted by Poon and Fozard (1978) further demonstrates the effect of familiarity and datedness of the objects to be named. The objects in this study were classified as (1) unique dated objects consisting of items that were used in the early 1900s (e.g., spittoon), (2) unique contemporary items consisting of items used during the 1960s and 1970s (e.g., calculator), (3) common dated objects consisting of the 1900s version of objects still in use (e.g., an old typewriter), and (4) common contemporary items consisting of today's version of the same objects in condition 3 (e.g., a new typewriter). The naming latency for unique dated objects showed that the oldest group (ages 60 to 70) named the unique dated items faster than did the youngest group (18 to 22), and the youngest group named the unique contemporary items fastest. A middle-aged group (45 to 54) fell between the youngest and oldest in both conditions. The naming latency for common items showed nonsignificant differences in performance for the contemporary versions of the objects, but the oldest group had the fastest naming latency for the dated versions of the same objects. The analysis of priming conditions showed a main effect of age, but by subtracting the priming data from the naming-latency data, an estimate of retrieval time from secondary memory was compared. The differences between age groups on this measure were nonsignificant (see, however, Poon & Fozard, 1980).

The results of the latency analyses were consistent with the hypothesis that the over-all age-related differences in response time were due to the perceptual-motor components of the NL (naming latency) and that the properties of the test stimuli were the major determiners of the magnitude and direction of age differences in the time required to retrieve the name from long-term memory. (Poon & Fozard, 1978, p. 714)

This view has been echoed in a review of the literature by Fozard and Popkin (1978) who conclude that "available research findings make it clear that older persons take longer to retrieve information from both short- and long-term memory" (1978, p. 981), but that "the age differences in slowness of retrieving familiar information are related to the perceptual-motor rather than the mental operations required to search long-term memory" (1978, pp. 980–981).

Other studies provide support for this conclusion: Kirsner (1972) used both decision latency (Sternberg, 1969) and naming latency with words as the stimuli in comparing groups across the life span (mean ages 9.1, 13.1, 24.4, and 59.9). Kirsner found that with an auditory presentation and test, both decision and naming latencies are longest for the 9.1 age group, improve (decrease) from ages 13.1 to 24.4, and then increase for the 59.3 age group. However, with corrected decision latency (decision latency minus naming latency), age effects were eliminated. On the basis of these corrected-decision-latency results, Kirsner concluded that the difference between age groups must be in perceptual and response factors. This hypothesis has also received support from a study conducted by Thomas, Fozard, and Waugh (1977). These authors tested groups (ages 25 to 74) on a naming-latency task and found significant effects of both age and trial blocks, as well as a near-significant interaction ($p = .051$), demonstrating that the difference between age groups decreased over blocks. The difference between age groups was further reduced on a priming task, suggesting again that the differences between groups can be largely attributed to the perceptual-motor component of the tasks (Thomas et al., 1977).

Finally the effect of familiarity can also be seen in a recent study by Jacewicz and Hartley (1979). Testing Birren's (1974) hypothesis of a central-speed deficit (see earlier), they presented young and old college students (mean ages 21.6 and 55.9) with capital letters in varying orientations from an upright position. The subjects' task was to decide if the letter presented was in regular or mirror-image form. In general the research with young college students has shown that reaction time increases as absolute deviance from an upright position increases; further, it has been suggested that subjects mentally rotate the stimulus until it is upright for comparison to the target letter (Cooper & Shepard, 1973; Shepard & Metzler, 1971). Jacewicz and Hartley (1979) also found that reaction time increased with absolute deviance; however, the differences between young and old were nonsignificant (i.e., nonsignificant age, rate of rotation, and base-time differences). Subjects (mean ages 56.5 and 21.2) in a second experiment performed the same task using unfamiliar material (lower-case Greek letters). Reaction-time results showed the typical orientation effect. Unlike the first experiment older subjects were significantly slower overall and also had a significantly longer base time than did younger subjects. It should be noted that both the young and old subjects in these studies were college students.

In summary this evidence shows clear support of the first prediction. Whether assessed by more global measures of recall accuracy or more analytic measures of retrieval speed, older adults do not appear to suffer from a generalized central deficit. Indeed it appears that their processing efficiency is lawfully related to their familiarity with task materials, just as it is for the young.

Categorization. The research on familiarity is only one epiphenomenon of the nonlinear model. Another, even more enlightening, aspect can be seen in the research on strategies of categorization and organizing behavior. This research can be interpreted as demonstrating that knowledge organization of young and old differ.

While much of the literature relating to categorization and conceptualization styles of older adults has been interpreted within a Piagetian framework as indicating regressive phenomena (Denney, 1974; Papalia & Del Vento Bielby, 1974), Kogan (1974) raised the question of whether this research has not virtually guaranteed that older subjects would be at a disadvantage. Often, for example, Kogan claims the materials employed are bare of meaning, and there are minimal attempts at controlling for the all-pervasive education differences between young and old subjects. Exploring the problem of presumed age deficits within a more meaningful context and

from a more stylistic perspective, no evidence was found to indicate that the older adults' performance had a regressive quality. In fact Kogan suggests that the older subjects' preference for thematic groupings offered a greater imaginative scope. Hence Kogan (1974) proposes it is possible

that judicious selection of tasks can yield stylistic differences between age groups that are equally adaptive for both. It is no surprise that college students should strongly favor the superordinate inferential groupings typical of high-level abstract functioning. It is doubtful, however, whether educated healthy older adults have lost the capacity for such groupings. Rather, they appear more willing to indulge an alternative mode when circumstances permit. (p. 228)

Further support for Kogan's (1974) position is seen in research by Sabatini and Labouvie-Vief (1979). Formal reasoning tasks based on Piagetian formal operational and hierarchical classification tasks were given to young college students (20.1 years) and older subjects (68.8 years). Half of these subjects were either majoring in science or had a degree in science. The analysis of the reasoning-task scores only showed an effect of specialization; age had no effect. However, the analysis of the scores based on the hierarchical structures formed by subjects revealed no specialization effect—only an age effect. Qualitatively

a comparison of the structures demonstrates the tendency of the older subjects to form more symmetrical structures, to include more items per category and to leave fewer unelaborated categories (i.e., empty end nodes). The younger subjects appeared to form more stereotyped classifications . . . while the older subjects produced more unique or unusual structures. (Sabatini & Labouvie-Vief, 1979, pp. 4–5)

Thus the research on categorization suggests that in selected, meaningful situations the older subject has well-developed modes of categorizing material which are distinctly different from those of young adults. This fact, if upheld, is important since the effect of cognitive structures is a keystone to most of the current theories in learning and memory. This is because most isolated words are multiply embedded into different meaning structures: With such stimuli any meaning or attribute of the word, therefore, can be activated (e.g., Collins & Loftus, 1975). Solso (1974) has presented suggestive evidence that when subjects have a different semantic organization cues that are effective for one subject may not be as effective for another subject. Thus the word *pot* may be interpreted and encoded in different cognitive structures depending upon the individual, other words on the list, and a whole host of other contextual variables.

The importance of this argument can be seen in data from word-association and production studies that also tentatively support the hypothesis of differences in cognitive structures between young and old (Perlmutter, 1978; Riegel, 1968). Riegel's study, designed to investigate developmental changes in word association (1968), found evidence for large longitudinal and cross-sectional differences in response data. His results showed (1) that response variability increases with age (i.e., a greater number of different responses to a stimulus word), (2) that while young subjects gave associative responses of the same-form class (noun-noun, verb-verb) older subjects' responses were more syntagmatic (more usage-meaning-based responses). In his vocal-latency studies Riegel found that the responses of the older subject were comparable to that of a younger subject reacting to low-frequency stimuli. On the basis of his studies he concluded that "young *Ss* tie a smaller number of different responses to a set of stimuli than old *Ss:* but the strength of these is higher; for old *Ss* the input-output matrix is more equalized and the strength of ties are lower" (Riegel, 1968, p. 249). Perlmutter (1978) also conducted an association-production task, and while finding that there were no differences in the number of associates made to a word by young and old, she found that there were differences in the type of associations made. The older subjects displayed greater response variability than did the younger subjects (large variance both within and between groups).

In recognition of some of these problems, Hultsch (1971) had one group of young (ages 20 to 29), middle-aged (ages 40 to 49), and older subjects (ages 60 to 69) perform Mandler's (1967) sorting-and-recall tasks, while another comparable group just studied and recalled the words. In Mandler's task a list of words is given to the subject to form into two to seven categories. Subjects perform successive sorts until the criterion of two identical sorts is reached. Typically Mandler (1967) has found a strong correlation between number of categories formed and subsequent recall of those words. Hultsch (1971) found that in the sorting condition the young group recalled significantly more words than did the oldest group, while with no sorting the young recalled significantly more than did both the older groups. Further the differences between the youngest and oldest groups were decreased under the sorting condition. Contrary to Mandler's (1967) finding Hultsch only found a low correlation between number of categories formed and amount recalled. Hultsch suggests that this may have occurred "for the older subject since he has to search through a larger repertory, even after he has recalled a category" (Hultsch, 1971, p. 342; see, however, Craik & Masani, 1969; Hultsch, 1975).

In general these data are congruent with the hypothesis that difficulties encountered by older individuals are due to their highly complex association networks. However, this statement must remain tentative as no current semantic network model has yet appropriately addressed the question of how developmental changes bear on a restructuring of associative structures, and indeed, there is barely any knowledge of the hierarchic networks which older individuals do in actuality use. Nevertheless the data by Kogan (1974), Riegel (1968), and Sabatini and Labouvie-Vief (1979) do suggest that this issue deserves intensive study.

Memory of Discourse. The most dramatic evidence thus far of the nonlinear pattern outlined here can be found in studies of the processing and retention of discourse. While linear views of aging might lead one to expect profound deficits in the processing of fairly abstract linguistic material, evidence thus far is altogether in conflict with this prediction.

However, statements about the recall of such material will depend on the criterion of accuracy applied (see earlier section). Craik and Masani (1967) tested ten individuals in each decade from ages 20 to 70 on the retention of either scrambled proverbs or coherent sentences and found clear age differences. The older individuals consistently recalled significantly less words than did the younger subjects. Gilbert and Levee (1971) have also found that younger subjects have better *rote* recall scores of paragraphs than do older subjects.

A different pattern emerges, however, if individuals are tested on the comprehension and retention of gist rather than verbatim surface structure. Walsh and Baldwin (1977) used Bransford and Frank's (1971) semantic-integration task and found no age differences in linguistic integration across unit sentences between their young (ages 18 to 20) and old (ages 60 to 90) subjects, even though the two groups differed markedly on rote recall of words (with the young recalling about twice as many words as the old). Hurlbut (1976), more specifically, instructed her subjects to either memorize or comprehend sentences. With verbatim instructions the young (ages 18 to 25) recalled significantly more than did the old (ages 64 to 85). With comprehension instructions the young and old did not differ.

Similar results have also been obtained in the recall of text passages, where age differences disappear if recall is in terms of higher-order units of gist or propositions (e.g., Gordon & Clark, 1974; Labouvie-Vief, Schell, & Weaverdyck, 1980; Taub & Kline, 1978).

It is possible, indeed, to suggest that the loss of specific, low-structure detail is a trade-off that goes along with attention to higher-order units of meaning.

The Soviet researcher Istomina and her associates (1967, in Loewe, 1977, pp. 119–120) advanced such an interpretation. When using isolated words as test items, young subjects were much better than were the old; but when recall was scored for higher-order propositions and inferences, the old were better. Istomina et al. suggested on this basis that ". . . with increasing age different aspects of memory change in different ways. While memory for immediate detail shows marked decline in later life, memory for logical relationships which are mediated by a process of active abstraction, not only fails to show any deficit, but does in fact improve" (cf. Loewe, 1977, p. 120; first author's translation). More recently Zelinski, Gilewski, and Thompson (1981) have also reported that elderly subjects tend to focus on such higher-order propositions.

Istomina's interpretation also is congruent with the results of two recent studies on the memory and/or interpretation of metaphoric sentences. One is a study by Boswell (1978) who asked high school students (age 18.0) and old subjects (age 70.1) to give an explanation or create a story which would make a given metaphor meaningful. These explanations were then rated as to their abstract-synthesizing versus analytic-literal nature. These ratings showed that the elderly subjects produced synthesizing integrative explanations, while the high school students produced explanations that were more literal and analytic (i.e., based on surface form). A second is a memory study by Labouvie-Vief, Campbell, Weaverdyck, and Tanenhaus (1979) who compared college students (mean age 23.6) and elderly adults (mean age 76.5). In this study the young excelled in memory for verbatim surface form, but the old were highest on the retention of meaning-preserving transformations. Indeed when the two recall modes were combined, the age differences disappeared altogether, indicating a trade-off between verbatim and meaning retention on the part of the old.

From a developmental perspective it is not too speculative to maintain that this position is an adaptively useful strategy. This adaptive interpretation of the adult's attention to higher-order units of meaning, captured by Birren (1969) by the notion of an age-related race between the "bit and the chunk," receives support from several further empirical sources. First, it is known that if recall is followed over a prolonged period of time, lower-order information tends to decay rather rapidly, while the recall of meaning-preserved kernel transformations displays more temporal stability (e.g., Bartlett, 1932; Dooling & Christiaansen, 1977). Second, it does appear that this decline of lower-order or detail information is particularly pronounced in elderly subjects (Gordon & Clark, 1974; Labouvie-Vief et al., 1980). Finally, two studies also have demonstrated that the elderly may have acquired more accurate knowledge of the functioning of their mnemonic system (Lachman & Lachman, 1981; Zelinski et al., 1981). Thus it is possible that they have learned to attend selectively to more informative, or temporally stable, units of meaning.

Nevertheless this interpretation must remain tentative as yet. Indeed Cohen (1979) has reported just the opposite finding, claiming that the older individual is most profoundly hampered in carrying out interpretive and abstract processes. It must be noted, however, that these two views are not necessarily irreconcilable. This is because specialization due to occupation or interest is so pronounced in the elderly that it is necessary to tailor task contents to specific subject groups (e.g., Bartlett, 1932; Sabatini & Labouvie-Vief, 1979). This again will be an important research endeavor for the future.

Flexibility and Plasticity. The interpretation so far advanced certainly is at variance with the view that older individuals suffer from a failure to process information to a deep level. It is important, therefore, to discuss briefly how in the present framework the apparently contradictory claims are integrated.

The general position taken here is that different life stages are characterized by relatively broad, dominant levels of information analysis. Apparent deficits, therefore, can enter by either of two assumptions. The first, mostly closely represented by Craik's (1977) position, is that a mode of processing which was presumably once present in the aging individual's repertoire, has become impaired and thereby reduces the individual's general efficiency as an information processor. The second, in contrast, asserts that an earlier mode may have been merely superordinated by a more recent mode. Thus in many instances we may be concerned not with developmental deficit, but rather with the issue of *flexibility*—or, if the experiment calls for an altogether new mode, of *plasticity*.

The differentiation between these two cases is important as it asserts that the aging individual when presented with certain stimulus materials may tend to relate them to a current modal level and thus be fairly inefficient when the experimental setting calls for a different mode. However if the experimenter clarifies this ambiguity, a different picture may emerge. In particular we would expect that orienting instructions and/or brief pre-experimental practice should result in relatively quick performance improvements.

The effect of instructional conditions on raising performance levels in the elderly has been discussed previously (see also Botwinick, 1978). Specifically when informing the elderly that the issue at hand in a particular study is to use specific semantic category systems or other organizational strategies, performance increases are usually instantaneous and dramatic, often eliminating age differences altogether.

Even if no specific instructions are given, we usually observe that the older individual may accommodate fairly quickly to the strategy the experimenter is calling for. An example is provided by Riegel and Birren (1966) who tested young and old on both their latency to produce a single word given a discrete first syllable (i.e., *can → candy*) and in addition asked the subjects to write as many words as they could given the same constraints (i.e., *can → candy, cancer, candid*). In the initial trials of the experiments, the researchers found that the older subjects were slower in responding and that their responses were more random that those of the younger subjects (again demonstrating structure differences). However, as the test continued the older subjects finally achieved the same response latency as the younger subjects. Concomitantly, though, there was also a decrease in the randomness of the older subjects' responses. As Riegel and Birren state, "By restricting their responses to the most common ones and by avoiding unique and original answers, they (the older subjects) increase their speed during continual performance" (1966, p. 169). This general type of performance is not strictly limited to the older subjects and can often be seen in studies conducted on college students (see Shiffrin & Schneider, 1977).

Similar time-related improvements are not usually reported in research on aging and information processing. Nevertheless in studies which have extended over a substantial series of trials, age-by-trial interaction indicating a reduction of age differences over time appears to be ubiquitous (e.g., Labouvie-Vief, 1977; Poon & Fozard, 1978; Thomas, Fozard, & Waugh, 1977). Botwinick (1978) also has reviewed a series of studies on the effect of practice (e.g., Botwinick, Robbin, & Brinley, 1960; Erber, 1976; Grant, Storandt, & Botwinick, 1978). These studies demonstrate that both the old and young continue to increase their performance over trials and that the rate of improvement appears not to be different for the various age groups. However, these studies have not trained subjects of different age groups to asymptotic levels and, as pointed out by Goulet (1973), they do not therefore permit statements about absolute levels of competence.

CONCLUSIONS

This chapter has reviewed much of the available evidence on memory and aging by interpreting it within two general prototype models. Within the linear model aging deficits in mnemonic functioning have appeared dramatic and in general of a regressive nature. Within the second, the nonlinear view, however, such regressive changes may form a part of continued developmental reorganization over the life span.

The two views, to be sure, are not necessarily in conflict as far as most available evidence is concerned. Indeed we have argued that the nonlinear view may provide a generalization of the linear view—one that both changes emphasis and calls for specific research implimentations.

As far as interpretive focus is concerned, a nonlinear view maintains that a loss of flexibility, increasing specialization, and an increasing integration of the mnemonic system with ecological demands are a regular concomitant of developmental progression. Therefore many of the changes observed in aging adults are not, in principle, different from those observed at other developmental periods.

This change in emphasis may appear somewhat idealistic. It is not, however, proposed that all aging changes fall into this normative and adaptive pattern—much as to talk about normative stages of childhood does not deny that deviations may be frequent. Instead it may be seen to call for a heuristic reorientation of research—that is, rather than studying aging changes as deviations from patterns of memory and information processing typical of college students, a more vigorous focus may be desirable on basic developmental processes by which the capacities of the old emerge in time from those of the young. Thus several avenues of investigation which have remained fairly inactive so far may hold much promise for the future.

A first area of needed research relates to the necessity to define how adults and aging individuals organize materials such as word lists, rather than defining apparent deficits by models of semantic organization which are themselves static. Thus many of the questions raised in this review call for the formulation of developmental mnemonic network models which outline changes in association strength as old knowledge systems become superordinated by new ones.

A second general area concerns a more direct attention to the effects of specialization (e.g., one's work) in accounting for the wide variability among adults. Certainly some of the tentative conclusions of this chapter will need to be modified as researchers direct more attention to the intricate relationship between mnemonic capacities and real-life adaptive pressures.

Third, by such a socioecological emphasis a change in focus is possible from a pure descriptive account of age-related decreases in flexibility and plasticity to a more explanatory analysis of the conditions under which flexibility is lost or maintained. Thus some authors have argued that a potential for plasticity and flexibility is apparent until late in life (Baltes & Baltes, 1977; Labouvie-Vief, 1980a, 1980b, 1981) and that its systematic explication is of high theoretical and practical import.

Fourth, the interpretations suggested call for a systematic investigation of the nature of hierarchically organized mnemonic systems. For example the theoretical status of research on speed of retrieval from secondary memory will require investigations of how such temporal processes are moderated by their location in hierarchically organized mnemonic systems. While it might be predicted that in linguistically integrated material (e.g.,

texts) the older adult will handle higher-order codes with greater facility, as yet there are no studies that have examined such *hierarchical* temporal orders in populations other than college students.

A fifth issue similarly related to a hierarchical interpretation of aging changes relates to the fact that items in secondary memory are subject to differential decay rates or else less likely to be activated as time proceeds. Thus much as more mature children will selectively focus on information that is temporally more stable than do less mature ones (Liben & Posnansky, 1977), older adults may favor codes of yet higher temporal stability.

Finally, there are many situations in which deviations from the "adaptive" aging pattern outlined here can be expected. For example certain brain lesions may result in an inability to integrate linguistic discourse (e.g., Luria, 1973) and/or to assimilate semantic material (e.g., Wisniewski & Terry, 1976). Such a differentiation between normative and pathological aging changes is a central one in clarifying the theoretical and empirical status of the concept of regression—that is, a differentiation of performance declines due to continued processes of growth and hierarchical superordination from those that reflect traumatic insults to the organism constitutes a much-needed area of investigation.

REFERENCES

ANDERS, T. R., & FOZARD, J. L. Effects of age upon retrieval from primary and secondary memory. *Developmental Psychology*, 1973, *9*, 411–415.

ANDERS, T. R., FOZARD, J. L., & LILLYQUIST, T. D. The effects of age upon retrieval from short-term memory. *Developmental Psychology*, 1972, *6*, 214–217.

ANDERSON, J. R. *Language, memory, and thought.* Hillsdale, N.J.: Lawrence Erlbaum Associates, 1976.

ATKINSON, R. C., & SHIFFRIN, R. M. Human memory: A proposed system and its control processes. Pp. 89–195 in K. W. Spence & J. T. Spence (Eds.), *The psychology of learning and motivation* (Vol. 2). New York: Academic Press, 1968.

BACH, M. J., & UNDERWOOD, B. J. Developmental changes in memory attributes. *Journal of Educational Psychology*, 1970, *61*, 292–296.

BALTES, M. M., & BALTES, P. B. The ecopsychological relativity and plasticity of psychological aging: Convergent perspectives of cohort effects and operant psychology. *Zeitschrift fuer experimentelle und angewandte Psychologie*, 1977, *24*, 179–197.

BALTES, P. B., REESE, H. W., & LIPSITT, L. P. Life-span developmental psychology. In M. R. Rosenzweig & L. W. Porter (Eds.), *Annual review of psychology* (Vol. 31). Palo Alto, Calif.: Annual Reviews Inc., 1980.

BALTES, P. B., REESE, H. W., & NESSELROADE, J. R. *Life-span developmental psychology: Introduction to research methods.* Monterey, Calif.: Brooks-Cole, 1977.

BALTES, P. B., & SCHAIE, K. W. On the plasticity of adult and gerontological intelligence: Where Horn and Donaldson fail. *American Psychologist*, 1976, *31*, 720–725.

BARTLETT, F. C. *Remembering: A study in experimental and social psychology.* Cambridge, England: Cambridge University Press, 1932.

BIRREN, J. E. Psychophysiological relations. In J. E. Birren, R. N. Bulter, S. W. Greenhouse, L. Sokoloff, & M. R. Yarrow (Eds.), *Human aging: A biological and behavioral study.* Washington, D.C.: U.S. Government Printing Office, 1963.

BIRREN, J. E. Age and decision strategies. In A. T. Welford & J. E. Birren (Eds.), *Interdisciplinary topics in gerontology* (Vol. 4). Basel, Switzerland: S. Karger, 1969.

BIRREN, J. E. Translations in gerontology—From lab to life: Psychophysiology and speed of response. *American Psychologist*, 1974, *29*, 808–815.

BIRREN, J. E., & SCHAIE, K. W. (Eds.). *Handbook of the psychology of aging.* New York: Van Nostrand Reinhold, 1977.

BISANZ, J., DANNER, F., & RESNICK, L. B. Changes with age in measures of processing efficiency. *Child Development,* 1979, *50,* 132–141.

BOSWELL, D. A. *Metaphoric processing in the mature years.* Paper presented at the 1978 annual meeting of the Gerontological Society, Dallas, November 1978.

BOTWINICK, J. *Aging and behavior* (2nd ed.). New York: Springer, 1978.

BOTWINICK, J., ROBBIN, J. S., & BRINLEY, J. F. Age difference in cardsorting performance in relation to task difficulty, task set, and practice. *Journal of Experimental Psychology,* 1960, *59,* 10–18.

BOTWINICK, J., & STORANDT, M. *Memory related functions and age.* Springfield, Ill.: Chas. C Thomas, 1974.

BOTWINICK, J., & STORANDT, M. Recall and recognition of old information in relation to age and sex. *Journal of Gerontology,* 1980, *35,* 70–76.

BRANSFORD, J. D., & FRANKS, J. J. The abstraction of linguistic ideas. *Cognitive Psychology,* 1971, *2,* 331–350.

BROADBENT, D. E. *Perception and communication.* Elmsford, N.Y.: Pergamon Press, 1958.

BRODY, H. Organization of the cerebral cortex. *Journal of Comparative Neurology,* 1955, *102,* 551–556.

BROMLEY, D. B. Some effects of age on short-term learning and memory. *Journal of Gerontology,* 1958, *13,* 398–406.

BUELL, S. J., & COLEMAN, P. D. Dendrite growth in the aged human brain and failure of growth in senile dementia. *Science,* 1979, *206,* 854–856.

CARROLL, J. S., & PAYNE, J. W. *Cognition and social behavior.* New York: John Wiley, 1976.

CHASE, W. G., & SIMON, H. A. Perception in chess. *Cognitive Psychology,* 1973, *4,* 55–81.

CHI, M.T.H. Knowledge structures and memory development. In R. S. Siegler (Ed.), *Children's thinking: What develops?* Hillsdale, N.J.: Lawrence Erlbaum Associates, 1978.

CHOWN, S. M. Age and the rigidities. *Journal of Gerontology,* 1961, *16,* 353–362.

COHEN, G. Language comprehension in old age. *Cognitive Psychology,* 1979, *11,* 412–429.

COLLINS, A. M., & LOFTUS, E. F. A spreading-activation theory of semantic processing. *Psychological Review,* 1975, *82,* 407–428.

COOMBS, C. H., & SMITH, J.E.K. Detection of structure in attitudes and developmental process. *Psychological Review,* 1973, *80,* 337–351.

COOPER, L. A., & SHEPARD, R. N. Chronometric studies in rotation of mental images. In W. G. Chase (Ed.), *Visual information processing.* New York: Academic Press, 1973.

CRAIK, F.I.M. Short-term memory and the aging process. In G. A. Talland (Ed.), *Human aging and behavior.* New York: Academic Press, 1968a.

CRAIK, F.I.M. Two components in free recall. *Journal of Verbal Learning and Verbal Behavior,* 1968b, *7,* 996–1004.

CRAIK, F.I.M. Age differences in recognition memory. *Quarterly Journal of Experimental Psychology,* 1971, *23,* 316–323.

CRAIK, F.I.M. Age differences in human memory. In J. E. Birren & K. W. Schaie (Eds.), *Handbook of the psychology of aging.* New York: Van Nostrand Reinhold, 1977.

CRAIK, F.I.M. Levels of processing: Overview and closing comments. In L. S. Cermak and F.I.M. Craik (Eds.), *Levels of processing in human memory.* Hillsdale, N.J.: Lawrence Erlbaum Associates, 1979.

CRAIK, F.I.M., & LOCKHART, R. S. Levels of processing: A framework for memory research. *Journal of Verbal Learning and Verbal Behavior,* 1972, *11,* 671–684.

CRAIK, F.I.M., & MASANI, P. A. Age differences in the temporal integration of language. *British Journal of Psychology,* 1967, *58,* 291–299.

CRAIK, F.I.M., & MASANI, P. A. Age and intelligence differences in coding and retrieval of word lists. *British Journal of Psychology,* 1969, *60,* 315–319.

CRAIK, F.I.M., & SIMON, E. Age differences in memory: The roles of attention and depth of processing. In L. W. Poon, J. L. Fozard, L. S. Cermak, D. Arenberg, & L. W. Thompson (Eds.), *New directions in memory and aging: Proceedings of the George Talland memorial conference.* Hillsdale, N.J.: Lawrence Erlbaum Associates, 1981.

CRAIK, F.I.M., & TULVING, E. Depth of processing and the reten-

tion of words in episodic memory. *Journal of Experimental Psychology: General,* 1975, *104,* 268–294.

CROWDER, R. C. *Principles of learning and memory.* Hillsdale, N.J.: Lawrence Erlbaum Associates, 1976.

DAYAN, A. D. Comparative neuropathology of aging: Studies of the brains of 47 species of vertebrates. *Brain,* 1971, *94,* 31–42.

DENNEY, N. Classification abilities in the elderly. *Journal of Gerontology,* 1974, *29,* 309–314.

DIAMOND, M. C. The aging brain: Some enlightening and optimistic results. *American Scientist,* 1978, *66,* 66–71.

DOOLING, J. D., & CHRISTIAANSEN, R. E. Levels of encoding and retention of prose. In G. H. Bower (Ed.), *The psychology of learning and motivation* (Vol. 2). New York: Academic Press, 1977.

DRACHMAN, D., & LEAVITT, J. Memory impairment in the aged: Storage versus retrieval deficit. *Journal of Experimental Psychology,* 1972, *93,* 302–308.

EBBINGHAUS, H. [*Memory*] (H. Ruger & C. Bussenius, trans.). New York: Dover, 1965. (Originally published, 1885; translation originally published, 1913.)

EISDORFER, C., & WILKIE, F. Intellectual changes with advancing age. In L. F. Jarvik, C. Eisendorfer, & J. C. Blum (Eds.), *Intellectual functioning in adults.* New York: Springer, 1973.

ERBER, J. T. Age differences in recognition memory. *Journal of Gerontology,* 1974, *29,* 177–181.

ERBER, J. T. Age differences in learning and memory on a digit-symbol substitution task. *Experimental Aging Research,* 1976, *2,* 45–54.

ERIKSEN, C. W., & COLLINS, J. F. Some temporal characteristics of visual pattern perception. *Journal of Experimental Psychology,* 1967, *74,* 476–484.

ERIKSEN, C. W., HAMLIN, R. M., & DAYE, C. Aging adults and rate of memory scan. *Bulletin of the Psychonomic Society,* 1973, *1,* 259–260.

EYSENCK, M. W. Age differences in incidental learning. *Developmental Psychology,* 1974, *10,* 936–941.

EYSENCK, M. W. *Human memory.* Elmsford, N.Y.: Pergamon Press, 1977.

FOZARD, J. L., & POPKIN, S. J. Optimizing adult development: Ends and means of an applied psychology of aging. *American Psychologist,* 1978, *33,* 975–989.

FREUND, J. S., & JOHNSON, J. W. Changes in memory attribute dominance as a function of age. *Journal of Educational Psychology,* 1972, *63,* 386–389.

FRIEDMAN, H. Interrelation of two types of immediate memory in the aged. *Journal of Psychology,* 1974, *87,* 177–181.

GARDNER, E. F., & MONGE, R. H. Adult age differences in cognitive abilities and educational background. *Experimental Aging Research,* 1977, *3,* 337–383.

GILBERT, J. G., & LEEVE, R. F. Patterns of declining memory. *Journal of Gerontology,* 1971, *26,* 70–75.

GORDON, S. K., & CLARK, W. C. Application of signal detection theory to prose recall and recognition in elderly and young adults. *Journal of Gerontology,* 1974, *29,* 64–72.

GOULET, L. R. The interfaces of acquisition: Models and methods for studying the active developing organism. In J. R. Nesselroade & H. W. Reese (Eds.), *Life-span developmental psychology: Methodological issues.* New York: Academic Press, 1973.

GRANT, E. A., STORANDT, M., & BOTWINICK, J. Incentive and practice in psychomotor performance of the elderly. *Journal of Gerontology,* 1978, *33,* 413–415.

HABER, R. N. *Information-processing approaches to visual perception.* New York: Holt, Rinehart & Winston, 1969.

HAGEN, J. W. The effect of distraction on selective attention. *Child Development,* 1967, *38,* 685–694.

HARKINS, S. W., CHAPMAN, C. R., & EISDORFER, C. Memory loss and response bias in senescence. *Journal of Gerontology,* 1979, *34,* 66–72.

HASHER, L., & CLIFTON, D. A developmental study of attribute encoding in free recall. *Journal of Experimental Child Psychology,* 1974, *17,* 332–346.

HAYES-ROTH, B. Evolution of cognitive structures and processes. *Psychological Review,* 1977, *84,* 260–278.

HAYES-ROTH, B., & HAYES-ROTH, F. Plasticity in memorial networks. *Journal of Verbal Learning and Verbal Behavior,* 1975, *14,* 506–522.

HEBB, D. O. On watching myself get old. *Psychology Today,* 1978, *12,* 15–23.

HORN, J. L. Human ability systems. In P. B. Baltes (Ed.), *Life-span development and behavior* (Vol. 1). New York: Academic Press, 1978.

HORN, J. L., & DONALDSON, G. On the myth of intellectual decline in adulthood. *American Psychologist,* 1976, *31,* 701–719.

HOWELL, S. C. Familiarity and complexity in perceptual recognition. *Journal of Gerontology,* 1972, *27,* 364–371.

HOYER, W. J., & PLUDE, D. J. Attentional and perceptual processes in the study of cognitive aging. In L. W. Poon (Ed.), *Aging in the 1980's.* Washington, D.C.: American Psychological Association, 1980.

HULICKA, I. M., & GROSSMN, J. L. Age group comparisons for the use of mediators in paired-associate learning. *Journal of Gerontology,* 1967, *22,* 46–51.

HULTSCH, D. F. Adult age differences in free classification and free recall. *Developmental Psychology,* 1971, *4,* 338–342.

HULTSCH, D. F. Learning to learn in adulthood. *Journal of Gerontology,* 1974, *29,* 302–308.

HULTSCH, D. F. Adult age differences in retrieval: Trace-dependent and cue-dependent forgetting. *Developmental Psychology,* 1975, *11,* 197–201.

HULTSCH, D. F. Encoding, storage, and retrieval in adult memory: The role of model assumptions. In L. W. Poon, J. L. Fozard, L. S. Cermak, D. Arenberg, & L. W. Thompson (Eds.), *New directions in memory and aging: Proceedings of the George Talland memorial conference.* Hillsdale, N.J.: Lawrence Erlbaum Associates, 1981.

HUNT, E. Mechanics of verbal ability. *Psychological Review,* 1978, *85,* 109–130.

HURLBUT, N. L. *Adult age differences in sentence memory.* Unpublished doctoral dissertation, University of Wisconsin, 1976.

JACEWICZ, M. M., & HARTLEY, A. A. Rotation of mental images by young and old college students: The effects of familiarity. *Journal of Gerontology,* 1979, *34,* 396–403.

JACOBSON, M. *Developmental neurobiology* (2nd ed.). New York: Plenum, 1978.

JACOBY, L. L., & CRAIK, F.I.M. Effects of elaboration of processing at encoding and retrieval: Trace distinctiveness and recovery of initial context. In L. S. Cermak & F.I.M. Craik (Eds.), *Levels of processing in human memory.* Hillsdale, N.J.: Lawrence Erlbaum Associates, 1979.

JOHNSON, N. F. On the function of letters in word identification: Some data and a preliminary model. *Journal of Verbal Learning and Verbal Behavior,* 1975, *14,* 17–29.

JONIDES, J., & GLEITMAN, H. A conceptual category effect in visual search: O as letter or as digit. *Perception and Psychophysics,* 1972, *12,* 457–460.

KENDLER, H. H., & KENDLER, T. S. Vertical and horizontal processes in human problem solving. *Psychological Review,* 1962, *69,* 1–18.

KINTSCH, W. *The representation of meaning in memory.* Hillsdale, N.J.: Lawrence Erlbaum Associates, 1974.

KIRSNER, K. Developmental changes in short-term recognition memory. *British Journal of Psychology,* 1972, *63,* 109–117.

KLINE, D. W., & BAFFA, G. Differences in the sequential integration of form as a function of age and interstimulus interval. *Experimental Aging Research,* 1976, *2,* 333–343.

KLINE, D. W., & ORME-ROGERS, C. Examination of stimulus persistence as the basis for superior visual identification performance among older adults. *Journal of Gerontology,* 1978, *33,* 76–81.

KOGAN, N. Categorizing and conceptualizing styles in younger and older adults. *Human Development,* 1974, *17,* 218–230.

KUMMER, H. *Primate societies: Group techniques of ecological adaptation.* Chicago: Aldine, 1971.

LABOUVIE-VIEF, G. Adult cognitive development: In search of alternative interpretations. *Merrill-Palmer Quarterly,* 1977, *23,* 227–263.

LABOUVIE-VIEF, G. Adaptive dimensions of adult cognition. In N. Datan & N. Lohmann (Eds.), *Transitions of aging.* New York: Academic Press, 1980a.

LABOUVIE-VIEF, G. Beyond formal operations: Uses and limits of pure logic in life-span development. *Human Development,* 1980b, *23,* 141–161.

LABOUVIE-VIEF, G. Pro-active and re-active aspects of constructivism: Growth and aging in life-span perspective. In R. M. Lerner & N. A. Busch (Eds.), *Individuals as products of their development: A life-span perspective.* New York: Academic Press, 1981.

LABOUVIE-VIEF, G., CAMPBELL, S. O., WEAVERDYCK, S. E., & TANENHAUS, M. K. *Metaphoric processing in young and old adults.*

Paper presented at the 1979 annual meeting of the Gerontological Society, Washington, D.C., November 1979.

LABOUVIE-VIEF, G., & CHANDLER, M. Cognitive development and life-span development theory: Idealist versus contextual perspectives. In P. B. Baltes (Ed.), *Life-span development and behavior.* New York: Academic Press, 1978.

LABOUVIE-VIEF, G., SCHELL, D. A., & WEAVERDYCK, S. E. *Levels of organization in adult discourse processing.* Paper presented at the 1980 annual meeting of the Gerontological Society, San Diego, November 1980.

LACHMAN, J. L., & LACHMAN, R. Age and the actualization of world knowledge. In L. W. Poon, J. L. Fozard, L. Cermak, D. Arenberg, & L. Thompson (Eds.), *New directions in memory and aging: Proceedings of the George Talland memorial conference.* Hillsdale, N.J.: Lawrence Erlbaum Associates, 1981.

LAUER, P. A. *The effects of different types of word processing on memory performance in young and elderly adults.* Doctoral dissertation, University of Colorado, 1975. (University Microfilms No. 76–11, 591)

LAURENCE, M. W. Age differences in performance and subjective organization in the free recall of pictorial material. *Canadian Journal of Psychology,* 1966, *20,* 388–399.

LAURENCE, M. W. Memory loss with age: A test of two strategies for its retardation. *Psychonomic Science,* 1967, *9,* 209–210.

LEWIS, C. H., & ANDERSON, J. R. Interference with real world knowledge. *Cognitive Psychology,* 1976, *8,* 311–335.

LIBEN, L. S., & POSNANSKY, C. J. Inferences on inference: The effects of age, transitive ability, memory load, and lexical factors. *Child Development,* 1977, *48,* 1490–1497.

LINDSAY, P. H., & NORMAN, D. A. *Human information processing* (2nd ed.). New York: Academic Press, 1977.

LOEWE, H. *Lernpsychologie: Einfuehrung in die Lernpsychologie des Erwachsenenalters.* Berlin: Verlag, 1977.

LUND, R. D. *Development and plasticity of the brain.* New York: Oxford University Press, 1978.

LURIA, A. R. *The working brain.* New York: Basic Books, 1973.

LURIA, A. R. *Cognitive development: Its cultural and social foundations.* Cambridge, Mass.: Harvard University Press, 1976.

MACCOBY, E. E., & HAGEN, J. W. Effects of distraction upon central vs. incidental recall. *Journal of Experimental Child Psychology,* 1965, *2,* 280–289.

McFARLAND, R. A. The sensory and perceptual processes in aging. In K. W. Schaie (Ed.), *Theory and methods of research on aging.* Morgantown: West Virginia University Press, 1968.

McNEILL, D., & LINDIG, K. The perceptual reality of phonemes, syllables, words, and sentences. *Journal of Verbal Learning and Verbal Behavior,* 1973, *12,* 419–430.

MANDLER, G. From association to structure. *Psychological Review,* 1962, *69,* 415–427.

MANDLER, G. Organization and memory. In K. W. Spence & J. T. Spence (Eds.), *The psychology of learning and motivation* (Vol. 1). New York: Academic Press, 1967.

MARSH, G., & THOMPSON, L. W. Psychophysiology of aging. In J. E. Birren & K. W. Schaie (Eds.), *Handbook of the psychology of aging.* New York: Van Nostrand Reinhold, 1977.

MARSLEN-WILSON, W. D., & WELSH, A. Processing interactions and lexical access during word recognition in continuous speech. *Cognitive Psychology,* 1978, *10,* 29–63.

MASSARO, D. W. *Understanding language: An information processing analysis of speech, perception, reading, and psycholinguistics.* New York: Academic Press, 1975.

MASSON, M.E.J., & SALA, L. S. Interactive processes in sentence comprehension and recognition. *Cognitive Psychology,* 1978, *10,* 244–270.

MEANS, B. M., & ROHWER, W. D., JR. Attribute dominance in memory development. *Developmental Psychology,* 1976, *12,* 411–417.

MILLER, G. A. Decision units in the perception of speech. *IRE Transactions on Information Theory,* 1962, *8,* 81–83.

NARON, N. K. Developmental changes in word attribute utilization for organization and retrieval in free recall. *Journal of Experimental Child Psychology,* 1978, *25,* 279–297.

NEISSER, U. *Cognition and reality.* San Francisco: W. H. Freeman & Company Publishers, 1976.

NORMAN, D. A., & BOBROW, D. G. On the role of active memory processes in perception and cognition. In C. N. Cofer (Ed.), *The structure of human memory.* San Francisco: W. H. Freeman & Company Publishers, 1976.

OZIER, M. Access to the memory trace through orthographic and categoric information. *Journal of Experimental Psychology: Human Learning and Memory, 4,* 469–485.

PAPALIA, D. E., & DEL VENTO BIELBY, D. Cognitive functioning in middle and old adults: A review of research based on Piaget's theory. *Human Development,* 1974, *17,* 424–443.

PERLMUTTER, M. What is memory aging the aging of? *Developmental Psychology,* 1978, *14,* 330–345.

PERLMUTTER, M. Age differences in adults' free recall, cued recall, and recognition. *Journal of Gerontology,* 1979, *34,* 533–539.

PIAGET, J. *Structuralism.* New York: Basic Books, 1970.

PIAGET, J. *Biology and knowledge.* Chicago: University of Chicago Press, 1971.

PIAGET, J. Intellectual evolution from adolescence to adulthood. *Human Development,* 1972, *16,* 1–12.

POON, L. W., & FOZARD, J. L. Speed of retrieval from long-term memory in relation to age, familiarity, and datedness of information. *Journal of Gerontology,* 1978, *33,* 711–717.

POON, L. W., & FOZARD, J. L. Age and word frequency effects in continuous recognition memory. *Journal of Gerontology,* 1980, *35,* 77–86.

POSNER, M. I. *Movements of visual attention.* Address presented at the annual meeting of the Midwestern Psychological Association, Chicago, May 1979.

POSNER, M. I., BOIES, S. J., EICHELMAN, W. H., & TAYLOR, R. L. Retention of visual and name codes of single letters. *Journal of Experimental Psychology Monograph,* 1969, *79*(No. 1, Pt. 2).

RANKIN, J. L., & KAUSLER, D. H. Adult age differences in false recognitions. *Journal of Gerontology,* 1979, *34,* 58–65.

RAYMOND, B. Free recall among the aged. *Psychological Reports,* 1971, *29,* 1179–1182.

REESE, H. W. Verbal mediation as a function of age level. *Psychological Bulletin,* 1962, *59,* 502–509.

RIEGEL, K. F. Changes in psycholinguistic performances with age. In G. A. Talland (Ed.), *Human aging and behavior.* New York: Academic Press, 1968.

RIEGEL, K. F. History of psychological gerontology. In J. E. Birren & K. W. Schaie (Eds.), *Handbook of the psychology of aging.* New York: Van Nostrand Reinhold, 1977.

RIEGEL, K. F., & BIRREN, J. E. Age differences in verbal associations. *The Journal of Genetic Psychology,* 1966, *108,* 153–170.

ROSSI, S. I., & WITTROCK, M. C. Developmental shifts in verbal recall between mental ages 2 and 5. *Child Development,* 1971, *42,* 333–338.

RUBINSTEIN, S. L. *Grundlagen der allgemeinen Psychologie.* Berlin: Volkseigner Verlag Berlin, 1968.

RUMELHART, D. Notes on a schema for stories. In D. Bobrow & A. Collins (Eds.), *Representation and understanding: Studies in cognitive sciences.* New York: Academic Press, 1975.

SABATINI, P., & LABOUVIE-VIEF, G. *Age and professional specialization in formal reasoning.* Paper presented at the 1979 annual meeting of the American Gerontological Society, Washington, D.C., November 1979.

SAKITT, B. Locus of short-term visual storage. *Science,* 1975, *190,* 1318–1319.

SALTHOUSE, T. A. Speed and age: Multiple rates of age decline. *Experimental Aging Research,* 1976, *2,* 349–359.

SCHAIE, K. W. A general model for the study of developmental problems. *Psychological Bulletin,* 1965, *64,* 92–107.

SCHAIE, K. W. External validity in the assessment of intellectual development in adulthood. *Journal of Gerontology,* 1978, *33,* 695–701.

SCHANK, R. C., & ABELSON, R. P. *Scripts, plans, goals and understanding.* New York: Halsted Press, 1977.

SCHEFF, S. W., BERNARDO, L. S., & COTMAN, C. W. Decrease in adrenergic axon sprouting in the senescent rat. *Science,* 1978, *202,* 775–778.

SCHNEIDER, W., & SHIFFRIN, R. M. Controlled and automatic human information processing: 1. Detection, search, and attention. *Psychological Review,* 1977, *84,* 1–66.

SCHONFIELD, D., & ROBERTSON, B. A. Memory storage and aging. *Canadian Journal of Psychology,* 1966, *20,* 228–236.

SCRIBNER, S. Modes of thinking and ways of speaking: Culture and logic reconsidered. In R. O. Freedle (Ed.), *New directions in discourse processing* (Vol. 2). Norwood, N.J.: Albex Publishing Co., 1979.

SEITELBERGER, F. Lebensstadien des Gehirns—Strukturelle und Funktionale Aspekte. In L. Rosenmayr (Ed.), *Die Menschlichen Lebensalter.* Munich, W. Germany: R. Piper and Co. Verlag, 1978.

SHEPARD, R. N., & METZLER, J. Mental rotation of three-dimensional objects. *Science,* 1971, *171,* 701–703.

SHIFFRIN, R. M., & SCHNEIDER, W. Controlled and automatic human information processing: II. Perceptual learning, automatic attending, and a general theory. *Psychological Review,* 1977, *84,* 127–190.

SMITH, A. D. Partial learning and recognition memory in the aged. *International Journal of Aging and Human Development,* 1975, *6,* 359–365.

SMITH, A. D. Adult age differences in cued recall. *Developmental Psychology,* 1977, *13,* 326–331.

SMITH, A. D. The interaction between age and list length in free recall. *Journal of Gerontology,* 1979, *34,* 381–387.

SMITH, A. D. Age differences in encoding, storage, and retrieval. In L. W. Poon, J. L. Fozard, L. S. Cermak, D. Arenberg, & L. W. Thompson (Eds.), *New directions in memory and aging: Proceedings of the George Talland memorial conference.* Hillsdale, N.J.: Lawrence Erlbaum Associates, 1981.

SMITH, A. D., & FULLERTON, A. M. Age differences in episodic and semantic memory: Implications for language and cognition. In D. S. Beasley & G. A. Davis (Eds.), *Speech, language, and hearing: The aging process.* New York: Grune & Stratton, 1980.

SOLSO, R. L. Memory and the efficacy of cues or "Yes, I know!" vs. "Why didn't I think of that?" In R. L. Solso (Ed.), *Theories in cognitive psychology: The Loyola symposium.* Hillsdale, N.J.: Lawrence Erlbaum Associates, 1974.

SPERLING, G. The information available in brief visual presentations. *Psychological Monographs,* 1960, *74*(Whole No. 11).

SPERLING, G. A model for visual memory tasks. *Human Factors,* 1963, *5,* 19–31.

SPERLING, G. Successive approximations to a model for short-term memory. *Acta Psychologica,* 1967, *27,* 285–292.

STERNBERG, S. Memory-scanning: Mental processes revealed by reaction-time experiments. *American Scientist,* 1969, *57,* 421–457.

STEVENSON, H. W. *Children's learning.* Englewood Cliffs, N.J.: Prentice-Hall, 1972.

TALLAND, G. A. Three estimates of the word span and their stability over the adult years. *Quarterly Journal of Experimental Psychology,* 1965, *17,* 301–307.

TALLAND, G. A. Age and the immediate memory span. *The Gerontologist,* 1967, *7,* 4–9.

TAUB, H. A., & KLINE, G. E. Recall of prose as a function of age and input modality. *Journal of Gerontology,* 1978, *33,* 725–730.

THOMAS, J. C., FOZARD, J. L., & WAUGH, N. C. Age-related differences in naming latency. *American Journal of Psychology,* 1977, *90,* 499–509.

THOMAS, J. C., WAUGH, N. C., & FOZARD, J. L. Age and familiarity in memory scanning. *Journal of Gerontology,* 1978, *33,* 528–533.

TIMIRAS, P. S. *Developmental physiology and aging.* New York: Macmillan, 1972.

TREAT, N. J., & REESE, H. W. Age, pacing, and imagery in paired-associate learning. *Developmental Psychology,* 1976, *12,* 119–124.

TULVING, E. Cue-dependent forgetting. *American Scientist,* 1974, *62,* 74–82.

UNDERWOOD, B. J. Attributes of memory. *Psychological Review,* 1969, *76,* 559–573.

UNDERWOOD, B. J. Individual differences as a crucible in theory construction. *American Psychologist,* 1975, *30,* 128–134.

WALSH, D. A., & BALDWIN, M. Age differences in integrated semantic memory. *Developmental Psychology,* 1977, *13,* 509–514.

WALSH, D. A., & PRASSE, M. J. Iconic memory and attentional processes in the aged. In L. W. Poon, J. L. Fozard, L. Cermak, D. Arenberg, & L. Thompson (Eds.), *New directions in memory and aging: Proceedings of the George Talland memorial conference.* Hillsdale, N.J.: Lawrence Erlbaum Associates, 1981.

WALSH, D. A., & THOMPSON, L. W. Age differences in visual sensory memory. *Journal of Gerontology,* 1978, *33,* 383–387.

WANG, H. S. Cerebral correlates of intellectual functioning in senescence. In L. F. Jarvik, C. Eisdorfer, & J. E. Blum (Eds.), *Intellectual functioning in adults.* New York: Springer, 1973.

WAUGH, N. C., & NORMAN, D. A. Primary memory. *Psychological Review,* 1965, *72,* 89–104.

WEIR, M. W. Developmental changes in problem-solving strategies. *Psychological Review,* 1964, *71,* 473–490.

WEIR, M. W., & STEVENSON, H. W. The effect of verbalization in children's learning as a function of chronological age. *Child Development,* 1959, *30,* 143–149.

WELFORD, A. T. *Aging and human skill.* London: Oxford University Press, 1958.

WELFORD, A. T. Motor performance. In J. E. Birren & K. W. Schaie (Eds.), *Handbook of the psychology of aging.* New York: Van Nostrand Reinhold, 1977.

WERNER, H. *Comparative psychology of mental development.* New York: International Universities Press, 1948.

WERNER, H. The concept of development from a comparative and organismic point of view. In D. B. Harris (Ed.), *The concept of development.* Minneapolis: University of Minnesota Press, 1957.

WHITE, S. Evidence for a hierarchial arrangement of learning processes. In L. P. Lipsitt & C. C. Spiker (Eds.), *Advances in child development and behavior* (Vol. 2). New York: Academic Press, 1965.

WISNIEWSKI, H. M., & TERRY, R. D. Neuropathology of the aging brain. In R. D. Terry & S. Gershon (Eds.), *Neurobiology of aging.* New York: Raven Press, 1976.

WOHLWILL, J. F. *The study of behavioral development.* New York: Academic Press, 1973.

ZELINSKI, E. H., GILEWSKI, M. J., & THOMPSON, L. W. Do laboratory tests relate to self-assessment of memory ability in the young and the old? In L. W. Poon, J. L. Fozard, L. Cermak, D. Arenberg, & L. Thompson (Eds.), *New directions in memory and aging: Proceedings of the George Talland memorial conference.* Hillsdale, N.J.: Lawrence Erlbaum Associates, 1981.

ZELINSKI, E. M., WALSH, D. A., & THOMPSON, L. W. Orienting task effects on EDR and free recall in three age groups. *Journal of Gerontology,* 1978, *33,* 239–245.

47

The Aging
of Human Abilities

JOHN L. HORN

QUESTIONS TO BE CONSIDERED
AND APPROACHES TO BE TAKEN

Is there aging of human abilities? That is the question. But wait! What does the question mean? What is meant by the term *aging,* and in this context what are *human abilities?*

What Is Aging?

At a rather high level of abstraction, adult aging can be thought of as "a series of time-related changes in a set of interconnected variables" (Bromley, 1966, p. 17). This broad meaning can thus include both *development,* in the sense of growth or improvement, and *deterioration,* in the sense of decline from a more elaborated, fully grown, or adequate condition. More often than not, it seems, deterioration is meant when the word *aging* is used. Most of the material considered in this chapter pertains to aging in this sense. A major question to be considered is: Do human abilities decline as age increases in adulthood? It seems that most people believe that the answer to this question is "yes," but prominent developmental psychologists have said that such belief is myth (Baltes & Schaie, 1974; Schaie, 1974). Are we to believe these prominent developmental psychologists? Probably not, but that is an issue to be addressed: Research results will be reviewed to provide an empirical basis for dealing with this issue. We shall see that answers to questions about deterioration of human abilities must be qualified by considerations of "what abilities?" Some abilities improve with

adult age, at least for some parts of adulthood, while others decline. Thus we shall be concerned with a broad meaning of aging. Although more attention will be given to decrements than to increments, both kinds of changes will be considered.

What Human Abilities?

What shall we mean when we speak of human abilities? There is so much that might be meant. Humans have abilities in music, in all the arts, in social interactions, in athletics, in tiddlywinks and philosophy, in talking and drinking, in relaxing, in deceit and empathy, in thinking, in memorizing, in sensing, in cognitive processing, and so on: There is a myriad of human abilities. Some abilities are very broad in the sense that they involve a host of subabilities. Most definitions of intelligence specify such a broad ability. Other abilities are very narrow. In the work of Shiffrin and Schneider (1977), an automated ability that is a major focus of study involves merely indicating whether a letter of a previous presentation of two or three or four letters (the memory set) is among a display set of two or three or four letters. Each year scores, perhaps hundreds, of new operational definitions of abilities are introduced into the research literature through the hundreds of studies that are reported in journals, academic theses, and technical reports. In major theories of psychology some abilities are said to indicate features of perception; others are said to indicate sensory processes; still others represent attention . . . central processing . . . peripheral processing . . . secondary memory . . . cognition . . . problem solving . . . decentration . . . conservation . . . formal operations . . . verbal comprehension . . . and so on, and on again. Thus even the theories of our field do not give us thoroughly acceptable or even generally accepted ways of slicing up

The research of this chapter was supported by a grant from the National Institute on Aging, #R01 AG00583, and the National Institute of Mental Health, #R01 HD13251. I am particularly indebted to my co-workers Gary Donaldson, Bob Engstrom, Ralph Mason, Jack McArdle, and Steven Poltrock for help in preparing my thinking for this chapter.

the myriad of human abilities into independent pieces. Restating the problem in terms of development does not lead to solution. Very broad and very narrow abilities develop, often in similar ways. Change in a simple ability can be a critical feature of the aging of a very complex ability (e.g., Hoyer & Plude, 1980). There is no simple answer to the question: To what human abilities shall we attend?

How then might we circumscribe a meaningful, not entirely arbitrary, domain of abilities for purposes of accurately characterizing human aging? How might this domain differ from the ability domains considered in other chapters of this book—under such rubrics as "Cognitive Change" (Denney, Chap. 45, this volume), "Learning and Memory" (Labouvie-Vief & Schell, Chap. 46, this volume), and "Memory" (Kail & Hagen, Chap. 20, this volume)?

To deal with these questions we will build on results from a particular line of research, here labeled *structure-of-intellect* (SI) research. This research has two major characteristics. First, it is directed at describing covariation patterns among rather large samples of task performances. For this description the methods of common-factor analysis (seeking minimum rank and simple structure) have been used. Second, the tasks of this work have been designed to indicate what are referred to as "higher mental processes of human intellect." Verbal definitions of *higher processes* and *intellect* require essays of explanation. It is sufficient here to recognize that in a general way these terms have directed SI research away from narrow operationalism and measurement of elementary process toward broad, abstract concepts based on measurement operations that permit a variety of different kinds of behaviors to be indicative of an ability. A principal purpose of the research has been to describe the organization (which is assumed to exist) among large numbers of abilities thus defined.

Primary Mental Abilities. SI research is not easily summarized. There have been hundreds of studies. Integrating the results from these studies involves the problems (mentioned previously) of comparing large numbers of abilities that pertain to different levels of function. Some SI studies have focused on perceptual behavior, some on memory alone, some on broad problem-solving skills. The studies can be classified in any number of ways.

Despite this variety several investigators have been able to assemble the results of SI research in ways that suggest that the same distinct abilities have been identified in different studies, based on different samples of subjects and somewhat different samples of variables. The abilities thus identified as replicated in adequate and independent studies have come to be known as *primary mental abilities* (PMA), a term suggested by Thurstone (1938) in a pioneering study in this area of research. The most recent of several summaries and evaluations of the evidence for the PMA system is provided by Ekstrom, French, and Harman). Table 47–1 is a listing of the PMA's that these investigators found to be reasonably well established on a basis of replicated findings from satisfactory studies.

The system of primary mental abilities provides a starting point for developing a scientific theory about human abilities. It does not entirely solve the problems that stem from the large number and great variety of human abilities, but it does bring some order to considerations of these problems. Over a thousand different tests, representing nearly as many different abilities, have entered into the hundreds of SI studies on which the summaries of PMA findings are based. The findings mean that different operations of measurement (i.e., different tests) indicate the same abilities, that a new test does not necessarily measure a new ability. With qualifications this means that the major abilities manifested in performances on the hundreds of tests that have been studied in SI research are well represented by the 25 abilities listed in Table 47–1. This means, too, that very likely what is presented as a newly found measure of ability is merely a somewhat different set of operations for measuring an ability that is already among the 25 primary abilities. New labels do not change the contents of old bottles.

There are a number of qualifications that need to accompany these generalizations. We need to recognize that a summary of many studies involving hundreds of tests is not equivalent to a definitive study of the hundreds of tests, as such (Undheim & Horn, 1977). We need to remember that SI research has tended to focus on the broad "higher mental abilities of intellect" to the neglect of many other kinds of abilities. Only common variance, representing a condition of more than one test recording the same variability, not unique variance, is considered in the summaries of SI research. The replications identified in these summaries were not perfect: Factors identified as the "same" are never quite the same. The methods in some SI studies have not been fully adequate, and there have been notable failures in trying to ensure that specifications and tests of hypotheses are satisfactorily independent (Horn & Knapp, 1973, 1974). We also need to acknowledge that there can be something new under the sun. Some of what are described as new tests probably do indicate human abilities that are not well represented in the list of primary abilities.

With provisos of this kind, however, we can recognize that the system of primary abilities is the kind of foundation on which a scientific account of the aging of human abilities can be built. The system is empirically based. It derives from confirmed findings. Although it represents only a small part of the domain of human abilities, that part is important in the totality of human functioning. In short the PMA system provides a reasonable way to begin to deal with the question of what abilities change with age in adulthood.

Second-Order Mental Abilities. The PMA foundation for organizing information about ability development is very broad. It is extremely difficult to bring all of the 25 abilities of this system into an internally consistent, coherent, and empirically founded theory of development. It is perhaps even more difficult to design and conduct studies in which each of the 25 abilities is taken properly into account. The different primaries may relate to age in subtly different ways (Horn & Cattell, 1966b), and thus a very complex theory may be needed to account for aging phenomena at the PMA level of analysis.

For these reasons it has seemed desirable to move up the abstraction ladder from the PMA system to a sec-

Table 47–1 Primary Mental Ability Factors Indicated by Replicated Research

FACTOR	FACTOR LABEL	EXAMPLES OF TESTS THAT DEFINE THE FACTOR
V	Verbal Comprehension	Vocabulary, Reading Comprehension, Understanding Grammar and Syntax
CV	Verbal Closure	Scrambled Words, Hidden Words, Incomplete Words
FW	Word Fluency	Word Endings, Word Beginnings, Rhymes
FA	Associational Fluency	Controlled Associations, Inventive Opposites, Figures of Speech
FE	Expressional Fluency	Making Sentences, Rewriting, Simile Interpretations
O	Object Flexibility	Substantive Uses, Improving Things, Combining Objects
SP	Sensitivity to Problems	Improvements For Common Objects, Listing Problems, Finding Deficiencies
CA	Concept Formation	Picture-Group Naming, Word Grouping, Verbal Relations
RL	Logical Reasoning	Nonsense Syllogisms, Diagramming Relationships, Deciphering Languages
I	Induction	Letter Sets, Locating Marks, Classifications
RG	General Reasoning	Word Problems, Ship Destination, Language Rules
ES	Estimation	Width Determination, Spatial Judgment, Quantitative Estimation
N	Number Facility	Addition, Division, Mixed Numerical Operations
S	Spatial Orientation	Card Rotations, Cube Comparisons, Boat Positions
CS	Speed (Gestalt) Closure	Gestalt Completion, Incomplete Pictures, Concealed Objects
CF	Flexibility of Closure	Hidden Figures, Embedded Figures, Copying Figures
VZ	Visualization	Form Board, Paper Folding, Surface Development
P	Perceptual Speed	Finding a's, Number Comparisons, Identical Pictures
FF	Figural Flexibility	Toothpicks, Planning Patterns, Storage
FL	Figural Fluency	Decorations, Alternate Signs, Make a Figure
IT	Integration	Following Directions, Internalizing Rules, Manipulating Numbers
MV	Visual Memory	System-Shape Recognition, Monogram Recall, Orientation Memory
MS	Span Memory	Digit Span-Visual, Letter Span-Auditory, Tone Reproduction
MA	Associative Memory	Picture-Number Pairs, First-Last Names, Serial Recall
MM	Meaningful Memory	Recalling Limericks, Sentence Completion, Sentence Recall

Source: After Ekstrom, French, & Harman, 1979.

ond-order system that includes the primary abilities as components of broader abilities. Research directed at specifying a second-order system has been based on the same common-factor procedures as were used to indicate the PMA's, but the variables of the second-order studies have been marker-tests and factor-score composites designed to estimate the primary abilities. At least 15 such second-order studies have been completed (see Cattell, 1971; Horn, 1976, 1978a, 1980; Horn & Donaldson, 1980, for reviews). A summary of the major ability concepts indicated by this work is provided in Table 47–2. Figure 47–1 is an outline of a theory that deals with the functional and developmental interrelationships among the second-order abilities. The evidence on which this theory is based will be considered briefly in the context of introducing the second-order abilities in the next section.

Theoretical Orientation

As was suggested in the previous section, the second-order factors are, in one sense, simply empirical generalizations. They represent conditions of covariance among different kinds of abilities: When an ability J is high in a particular individual, then abilities $K, L, \ldots, N$ of the same factor are also likely to be high in that individual, but abilities of other factors are not likely to be correspondingly high. Such conditions of covariation can be important elements of scientific understanding, but in

themselves they have little descriptive or explanatory power. They need to be fitted into a theory before they can effectively serve to describe or explain or generate hypotheses.

The Gc and Gf factors (Table 47–2) are similar to, respectively, the verbal IQ (VIQ) and performance IQ (PIQ) dimensions of the Wechsler Adult Intelligence Scale (WAIS) (Matarazzo, 1972). It might seem that the theory on which the WAIS is based would provide the needed framework for fitting the second-order abilities into a scientific account of human functioning. This is partly true, because many of the fingings obtained with the WAIS can be brought to bear in understanding the Gc and Gf factors. Matarazzo (1972) summarizes a wealth of information of this kind. It is particularly important to recognize that the age relationships for Gc and Gf are similar to the corresponding, well-established relationships for VIQ and PIQ.

In general, however, theory associated with the WAIS does not provide a sufficient framework for understanding the second-order structure among primary abilities. The WAIS was not designed to represent such a structure. The verbal-performance labeling does not provide a very useful theoretical distinction, and it can be a bit misleading. Any measured ability is based on performance and thus is a performance ability; it is misleading to designate a particular ability with the performance label because this incorrectly suggests that other abilities are

Table 47-2 Operational and Verbal Descriptions of Major Second-Order Ability Functions

Gc, Crystallized Intelligence. This form of intelligence is indicated by a very large number of performances indicating breadth of knowledge and experience, sophistication, comprehension of communications, judgment, understanding conventions, and reasonable thinking. The factor that provides evidence of Gc is defined by primary abilities such as verbal comprehension, concept formation, logical reasoning, and general reasoning. Tests used to measure the ability include vocabulary (what is a word near in meaning to temerity?), esoteric analogies (Socrates is to Aristotle as Sophocles is to _____?), remote associations (what word is associated with Bathtub, Prizefighting, and Wedding?), and judgment (determine why a foreman is not getting the best results from workers). As measured, the factor is a fallible representation of the extent to which an individual has incorporated, through the systematic influences of acculturation, the knowledge and sophistication that constitutes the intelligence of a culture.

Gf, Fluid Intelligence. The broad set of abilities of this intelligence include those of seeing relationships among stimulus patterns drawing inferences from relationships and comprehending implications. The primary abilities that best represent the factor, as identified in completed research, include induction, figural flexibility, integration, and cooperatively with Gc, logical reasoning and general reasoning. Tasks that measure the factor include letter series (what letter comes next in the following series d f i m r x e ═), matrices (discern the relationships among elements of 3-by-3 matrices), and topology (from among a set of figures in which circles, squares, and triangles overlap in different ways, select a figure that will enable one to put a dot within a circle and square but outside a triangle). The factor is a fallible representation of such fundamental features of mature human intelligence as reasoning, abstracting, problem solving. In Gf these features are not imparted through the systematic influences of acculturation but instead are obtained through learning that is unique to an individual or is in other ways not organized by the culture.

Gv, Visual Organization. This dimension is indicated by PMA's such as visualization, spatial orientation, speed of closure, and flexibility of closure, measured by tests such as Gestalt Closure (identify a figure in which parts have been omitted), Form Board (show how cut-out parts fit together to depict a particular figure), and Embedded Figures (find a geometric figure within a set of intersecting lines). To distinguish this factor from Gf, it is important that relationships among visual patterns be clearly manifest so performances reflect primarily fluency in perception of these patterns, not reasoning in inferring the patterns.

Ga, Auditory Organization. This factor has been identified on the basis of studies by Horn (1972b), Horn and Stankov (1981), Stankov (1978), and Stankov and Horn (1980) in which PMA abilities of temporal tracking, auditory cognition of relations, and speech perception under distraction-distortion were first defined among other primary abilities and then found to indicate a broad dimension at the second order. Tasks that measure Ga include repeated tones (identify the first occurrence of a tone when it occurs several times), tonal series (indicate which tone comes next in an orderly series of tones), and cafeteria noise (identify a word amid a din of surrounding noise). As in the case of Gv, this ability is best indicated when the relationships among stimuli are not such that one needs to reason for understanding but instead are such that one can fluently perceive patterns among the stimuli.

SAR, Short-Term Acquisition and Retrieval. This ability is comprised of processes of becoming aware and processes of retaining information long enough to do something with it. Almost all tasks that involve short-term memory have variance in the SAR factor. Span-memory, associative-memory, and meaningful-memory primary abilities define the factor, but measures of primary and secondary memory also can be used to indicate the dimension.

TSR, Long-Term Storage and Retrieval. Formerly this dimension was regarded as a broad factor among fluency tasks, such as those of the primary abilities labeled associational fluency, expressional fluency, and object flexibility. In recent work, however, these performances have been found to align with others indicating facility in storing information and retrieving information that was acquired in the distant past. It seems, therefore, that the dimension mainly represents processes for forming encoding associations for long-term storage and using these associations, or forming new ones, at the time of retrieval. These associations are not so much correct as they are possible and useful; to associate *tea kettle* with *mother* is not to arrive at a truth so much as it is to regard both concepts as sharing common attributes (e.g., *warmth*).

Other Possible Dimensions. The dotted-line circles in Figure 47–1 indicate factors that have been found in more than one study but are not yet regarded as well established as independent dimensions. In regard to speediness, for example, several studies have suggested that there is a cohesiveness among speed of performance measures that is broader than the perceptual-speed primary ability (which, however, is at the core of the broader, Gs, dimension). This broad form of speediness emerges when tests become so easy that all people would get all items (problems) correct or have essentially the same score if the test were not highly speeded. It seems to be indicated also by tasks of speed of writing and printing. In two recent studies Gs was found to be largely independent of quickness in obtaining correct answers (CDS) and quickness in deciding to abandon a problem (QDS). These latter two forms of speediness may also represent broad independent processes (factors). However, the main point of results indicating speediness factors is that speediness (of one form or another) is separate from major dimensions of intelligence, memory, and perception. There is considerable evidence to indicate that speediness is important for understanding age differences in ability test performances (see Birren, 1965, 1974, for reviews).

Dotted-line rectangles in Figure 47–1 also indicate that sensory detector functions are largely independent of major indicants of intelligence (Gf and Gc) and memory (SAR and TSR). Sda and Sdv represent findings that measures of immediate apprehension, as derived from dichotic listening tasks and an adaptation of Sperling's (1960) matrix-element recognition task, are reliably independent of the measures that define Gf, Gc, SAR, and TSR. The sensory detector measures seem to represent the human's capacities for becoming aware, but only for a very short time (a second or two), of a large number of the events that constantly compete for one's attention.

---

not performance abilities. Similarly there are many verbal abilities, so it can be misleading to single out one ability and label it as if it were *the* verbal ability. Although Gc and VIQ do indeed involve verbal skills to a considerable extent, they involve other skills as well, and, conversely, Gf and PIQ involve verbal skills. Thus neither the distinction between Gc and Gf nor the distinction between the two IQ dimensions of the WAIS is well characterized as a contrast between verbal and performance abilities. To fit the second-order factors into a comprehensive theoretical framework, it is necessary to look beyond the WAIS.

Several lines of research provide information that can be of use in specifying the desired theoretical framework for second-order abilities. In addition to results from studies of covariational structure and the evidence on age differences (the principal concern of this chapter), there is information from a wide variety of studies pertaining to (1) levels of psychological functioning, (2) relationships between psychological test performance and indicants of brain damage, genetic structure, child-rearing influences, educational experiences, and socioeconomic circumstances, and (3) age differences in brain structure and function. Rather extensive reviews and discussions of this evidence are available (Cattell, 1971; Horn, 1968, 1970a, 1972a, 1976, 1977, 1978a, 1978b, 1981; Horn & Donaldson, 1980), so it is probably not necessary to review the material in detail here. Several major conclusions should be considered, however, to set the stage properly for examining correlates of aging.

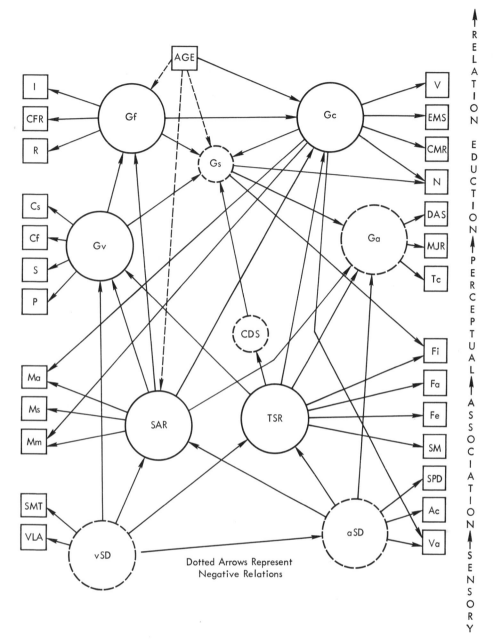

Dotted Arrows Represent
Negative Relations

Figure 47-1 Function organizations of intellect

First, as concerns level of function, we have almost 100 years of research suggesting that it is useful to divide a nearly continuous, and certainly a very interdependent, stream of human capacities into sets that are referred to as *sensory processes, perception, memory,* and *thinking.* There are many ways to divide the stream of psychological functions, but in most systems four or five broad categories, such as are suggested in Figure 47–1, are seen to represent major levels of organization underlying observed patterns of human behavior.

The idea of *levels* of organization has several connotations in these systems. We will not consider these meanings in any detail, but it is useful to notice that often we think in terms of hierarchical interdependence among the categories of function. Processes organized at the sensory level prepare elementary input information for perceptual processes, which in turn send information on to storage (memory) functions that hold information in

awareness for processing by thinking functions. It is recognized that processing at higher levels feeds back to influence processing at lower levels and that such interdependence is complex and prevalent, but it is useful nevertheless to regard functioning at higher levels as dependent on functioning at lower levels. A well-regarded hypothesis about aging, for example, stipulates that losses of sensory or perceptual functions affect performances that are believed to reflect thinking, so we may incorrectly conclude that there is loss in ability to think when in fact the loss is in ability to sense or perceive. More about this later.

The levels of function depicted in Figure 47–1 are, for purposes of this review, specified operationally and empirically; the levels are represented by the second-order ability factors to which we referred earlier and which are described verbally in Table 47–2. Each circle drawn with solid lines in Figure 47–1 represents a factor that is regarded as established because it has been identified in at least five technically adequate and satisfactorily independent studies. The circles drawn with dotted lines also represent factors—identified in at least one study—but factors that have not been found in enough studies, under varied enough conditions in the context of other second-order factors, to be regarded as established.

Even the factors depicted with dotted lines, as well as those regarded as established, represent function organizations that have been indicated by evidence other than merely that of covariational studies of structure. For example, Birren (1965, 1974) has assembled a large amount of evidence indicating that speed of reaction is a pervasive feature of human performance and a feature associated with aging—i.e., in many performances we tend to get slower as we get older. The work of Morrison (1960) and Meredith (1971) suggests that there may be more than one broad organization among speed-of-reaction functions. Such evidence adds to indications from covariational studies that there is a second-order factor, or possibly more than one such factor, representing speediness in a wide array of ability performances. Similarly evidence from several sources adds credence to the view that functions of short-term acquisition and retrieval (SAR) are organized somewhat independently of the relation-eduction and inference functions of Gf and Gc. As early as 1938, for example, in studies of learning followed by retention after periods ranging from a few seconds to 30 days, Woodrow (1938) found that short-term memory measures are rather closely interrelated relative to the rather weak relationships they have with learning-retention over long periods of time and measures of intelligence and academic achievement (see also Hunt, Frost, & Lunneborg, 1973). Thus seen in studies that were not directed at indicating factor structure are the same kinds of findings as are indicated by results showing that the SAR functions form a second-order factor that is independent of the factors of Gf and Gc (e.g., Horn & Bramble, 1976; Hundal & Horn, 1977; Rossman & Horn, 1972; Shucard & Horn, 1972; Stankov, Horn, & Roy, 1980).

Independence in this context, as in most scientific discussion, does not mean *correlated zero* or *orthogonal*, as sometimes seems to be assumed. SAR and Gf are correlated about .35, for example, when the respective reliabilities are about .8, and this correlation is statistically significant in samples of the sizes that are typical in psychological research. This does not mean that the two factors do not represent independent scientific constructs. Height and weight in humans are correlated well above .35, but they still represent different concepts. If constructs are orthogonal in the universe of inference (the population), they are found to be correlated in samples drawn from the universe, even when the samples are drawn in a perfectly representative manner (i.e., randomly). Our working definition of independence has been that the squared multiple correlation of the measure in question with all other measures of different constructs in the domain must be at least .10 less than the squared correlation of the fallible measure with its own true-score component (i.e., the measure's reliability).

As can be seen in Table 47–2, the concepts specified at each level of function in Figure 47–1 are defined operationally in terms of varied collections of performances.

Visual organization (Gv), for example, is defined, not by a single test, such as visual rotations, but by peformances as varied as those of achieving closure of disparate parts of an incomplete figure, finding a form embedded among distracting lines, and imagining rearrangements of figural parts, as well as estimating visual rotations. The variety of performances entering into definition of a function is indicative of a variety of separate processes of the function. Just as the function of the human heart involves separate processes, such as those of the left and right ventricle and the right and left auricle, the function of Gv visual organization involves separate processes of search, closure, and figure-ground discrimination. An assumption of the theoretical orientation of this chapter (somewhat in contrast to other chapters of this section) is that it may prove useful to approach the task of comprehending adult development by first considering aging in terms of the broad operational definitions of function that are indicated in Table 47–2 and then attempting to describe any trends that may be indicated by looking to see if the trends can be described in terms of other such functions and/or subprocesses of the broad functions. The focus will be on the relation-eduction functions near the top in Figure 47–1, particularly Gf, because it seems that the major practical concerns about aging pertain to the question of whether intelligence declines.

Concepts of function can provide a reasonable starting point for understanding human aging; it is useful to think of the human as a machine with functions. However, it is desirable in theory to extend this view of the matter by recognizing that the human "machine" regenerates, changes into a different machine, restructures—in general, develops. We need to consider how functional organizations come into existence and change over time, first in childhood, because this development can indicate changes to be expected, and then in adulthood. We need to consider relationships between performances representing the functional categories of Figure 47–1 and developmental influences such as can be associated with conditions of child-rearing, the school, and the subculture of origin. To fully review such evidence, however, would require much more space than a chapter. All we can do here is to cite a few major conclusions that are particularly important for characterizing the functional concepts that thus far have been briefly described.

One important conclusion is that the abilities we see and measure in adulthood are outcomes of extended periods of learning. Ferguson (1954, 1956) has characterized the primary abilities as asymptotic levels of learning. Of course learning is not the only determinant of an ability, and individual differences in an ability need not be due primarily to individual differences in learning. However, we base our inferences about an ability on a complex set of acts (sensing, perceiving, remembering, thinking), and such "sets" do not spring into function without there being a considerable amount of learning. This is true for relatively narrow abilities for which a major part of the needed learning may occur early in life—e.g., the ability to walk—as well as for abilities that are commonly regarded as notably changing with learning even in adulthood—e.g., ability in use of vocabulary.

It follows from these considerations that the abilities of Tables 47–1 and 47–2 are not well classified as *learned* and *unlearned*. Indeed they are not even well classified as *largely learned* and *largely unlearned*. This is not to ignore the possibility that some abilities derive from more extensive programs of learning than do other abilities. Rather it is to recognize that we have virtually no information, and very little insight, about the amount of learning which goes into formation of a primary ability or one of the broader functions of Table 47–2. Some of the evidence from developmental study does suggest, however, that the Gc and Gf abilities differ, in part, in terms of the *kind* of learning on which they are based.

Gc reflects largely acculturational learning. The society in which one is raised is organized to provide a huge series of "lessons" designed to convert the intellectual capacities of its members, particularly its youthful members, into a form of intelligence that is useful for maintaining and enhancing that society. These lessons are provided pervasively throughout the society, although they are most intensively administered in institutions designed for acculturation, such as homes and schools. The lessons are accompanied by rewards and punishments that are part of a subtle, but powerful, system of promotions and exclusions that bring some individuals to more advanced levels of acculturation than others. For a large variety of reasons acculturation is more effective in shaping the abilities of some individuals than in shaping the abilities of others. Those for whom the system is highly effective develop the abilities of Gc to a high degree relative to the individual's innate potential and relative to what remains of this potential after the ravages of physiological damages (occurring throughout life, from conception to death) have taken their toll. The systematic influences of acculturation thus shape the extremely broad collection of abilities that we identify as crystallized intelligence and measure, very imperfectly, in the second-order factor symbolized as Gc (see Table 47–2).

Acculturation represents a very extensive and powerful set of learning experiences, but it does not represent all of the learning that occurs in development and that is important in the shaping of abilities. Much learning occurs that is not part of the systematic plan of acculturation. For example a child acquires ideas about conservation, in the sense that Piaget discussed this concept, without being exposed to systematic efforts by parents or other teachers to instill these ideas. A person may learn much about the regularities of time and space without being well indoctrinated with the particular views on these matters that are a part of a given culture. Indeed the views sponsored within a culture were at one time the views of individuals who introduced them into the culture. We do not have a particularly appropriate term for designating a pattern of learning that leads to idiosyncratic views and concepts. Here we refer to it as *casual learning*. No matter how we designate it, the important point is that abilities are learned somewhat independently of the systematic influence of acculturational learning. Casual learning and acculturation are even to some extent antagonistic, or at least mutually exclusive, in the sense that if one is persistently exposed to acculturation there can be relatively little time and resource left for the idiosyncratic, self-directed explorations of casual learning.

Casual learning accumulates in a broad set of capabilities that aid in dealing effectively with some of the tasks that are accepted as requiring exercise of human intelligence. The second-order factor identified as Gf provides a fallible indication of this broad set of capabilities.

This developmental view of the distinction between Gf and Gc does not, in itself, point to a difference in the neurological foundations for the two forms of intelligence. We have little reason to believe that casual and acculturational learning should produce different neural circuitry. Nevertheless evidence from several sources suggests that the Gf and Gc factors reflect somewhat different patterns of neurological organization. Thus the two broad factors of intelligence seem to represent influences in addition to those that operate through different histories of learning.

One set of evidence that is of relevance in this regard suggests that brain damage has a more nearly irreversible and lasting effect on the abilities of Gf than on the abilities of Gc. Some of the abilities that are immediately affected by stroke, for example, recuperate with time or a bit of retraining, and these abilities often characterize Gc. Other abilities affected by brain damage do not recuperate with time, and it is questionable whether even extensive retraining can do much to restore them to former levels. Often these are abilities that define the Gf factor. (See Horn, 1970a, 1981; Horn & Donaldson, 1980; and LaRue & Jarvik, Chap. 44, this volume, for reviews of this evidence.)

Also of relevance in this context is a swath of evidence indicating that some of the abilities that are well accepted as indicating intelligence decline with age in adulthood, while other such abilities do not decline. The abilities that decline often characterize Gf, while those that do not decline frequently are components of Gc. This does not necessarily indicate a difference in the neurological foundations of Gf and Gc, but other evidence indirectly supports the idea of such a difference.

Several kinds of evidence suggest that aging in adulthood is accompanied by a number of neurological alterations that can be expected to result in lowered intellectual performance. For example there is evidence of decrease in the number of active neurons in the central nervous system. Other neurological alterations are similar to changes associated with brain damage (Horn, 1970a; Reitan, 1955). Also some forms of brain damage, such as stroke, occur with increasing frequency as age increases. Collectively such indirect bits of evidence add up to suggest that the observed aging decline of Gf abilities probably reflects damage of neurological structures and functions.

It is difficult on the basis of present evidence to discern the neurological concomitants of maintenance and enhancement of the abilities of Gc. We know that out neural processes are constantly active as long as we live and that neural systems continuously are being restructured as we continuously take in new experiences and learn. It seems that the trend throughout development is toward building ever more efficient neural systems for directing behavior, and this trend is manifested in enhancement of some intellectual abilities—those of Gc—even as the absolute amount of neural support decreases (and is registered in decline of other abilities).

Questions about genetic influences also are of some relevance in considering age-related changes. There is interest in knowing whether an observed change is a maturational necessity of genetic structure or if it is a result of environmental or experiential factors. The evidence in regard to such matters is extremely limited, partly because it is almost impossible to separate maturational and other influences with the designs that are possible in our studies of development (see Horn & Donaldson, 1980, for a more extended discussion of this problem).

There are some results suggesting that genetic influences may be more important in determining individual differences in Gf than in determining individual differences in Gc, particularly if only between-family, not within-family, differences are considered (Cattell, 1980). However, other evidence points to larger heritabilities for the primary abilities of Gc than for the principal markers of Gf (DeFries, Kuse, & Vandenberg, 1979; Martin, 1975; Vandenberg, 1962, 1971). In the DeFries et al. (1979) study, for example, midchild verbal-comprehension measures were predicted from midparent scores in the range of about .60, whereas the comparable predictions for figural-reasoning (matrices) measures averaged around .40.

Genetic influence in ability development is not equivalent to "physiological influence" or "lack of acculturational learning influence." In an open, egalitarian society individual differences in highly learned abilities that derive primarily from acculturation can mainly reflect genetic differences, as Herrnstein (1973) has pointed out in some detail (see also Jencks, Smith, Acland, Bane, Cohen, Gentis, Heyns, & Michelson, 1972). In particular if the development of an ability depends on both genetic and acculturational determinants and individuals of a given society have (on the average) the same chance of being affected by the acculturational determinants, then individual differences in the ability will mainly reflect differences in genetic influences; the heritability will thus be found to be high. Such conditions might (we do not know) be fairly well approximated in the societies of Europe and America where heritability studies have been done. Thus the high heritability estimates that have been obtained for Gc abilities, such as verbal comprehension, need not be regarded as inconsistent with evidence indicating that these abilities are largely determined by learning and evidence indicating that individual differences in these abilities largely reflect individual differences in acculturation. On the other hand if the development of an ability depends on both genetic structure and favorable conditions for neurological development and there are notable individual differences in these latter conditions, the manifest differences in the ability need not relate very strongly to genetic differences. Under these conditions heritability could be rather small. For this reason results indicating rather low heritabilities for the abilities of Gf need not be regarded as inconsistent with the evidence suggesting that these abilities are not closely related to acculturation and are closely related to influences associated with brain damage and other such physiological factors.

Cattell's (1980) results indicating higher within-family heritability for Gc than for Gf suggest that acculturational influences are similar for different children raised within the same family—i.e., similar relative to casual learning and physiology-altering influences that also operate within families. On the other hand Cattell's finding that between-family heritability was larger for Gf than for Gc suggests that acculturation varies notably from one family to another (as from one social class to another or from one ethnic group to another) relative to the between-family variability in casual learning and factors that enhance or injure the neurological structures on which intelligence is based. As noted previously, however, this conclusion is not indicated in all studies. Also, the results in any such study reflect, in part, the nature of the society in which the heritability estimates are obtained.

There are many things that should be considered in properly interpreting heritability results. They do not necessarily imply rejection of an hypothesis that Gf is more fully determined by heredity than is Gc, but in toto they do not strongly support this hypothesis either. Perhaps the most reasonable conclusion to draw at this time is that we do not have sufficient reason to believe that differences in aging trends for Gf and Gc reflect differences in genetic influences that operate through maturation.

The ideas and bits of evidence that have been outlined in this section add up to a preview of much of what will be considered in subsequent sections of the chapter. Abilities will be considered in terms of broad levels of function. Our major objective will be to describe aging trends for these functions in terms of component abilities and processes and in terms of plausible determinants of the trends.

A BRIEF LOOK AT SOME IMPORTANT METHODOLOGICAL ISSUES

Before looking at results as such, it can be worthwhile to pause for a moment to consider a few major features of measurement and data-gathering that condition the inferences that legitimately can be drawn from studies of age differences and age changes in adulthood.

The Fallible Nature of Measurements

Operational definitions provide only very fallible indications of the concepts that factors (in theory) represent. The concept of *crystallized intelligence,* for example, refers to a huge repertoire of skills and understandings—all that individuals can learn under the press of a huge number of acculturation influences. There is no way that the totality of these skills and understandings can be assessed in practice. The different tests that are used to measure the Gc factor in a particular study are only a sample of tests that might be used. This sample is almost certainly not representative of the population of tests that truly represent the factor. Just how a particular sample is biased is not known. (The items within a particular test also provide only a sample, biased in unknown ways, of the process that is said to be measured by that test.) For these reasons the factor measures obtained in particular studies are perturbated; the true positions of the concepts are not ascertained because the measurement operations are not fully adequate. The problem in this regard is not one of unreliability of measurement (although that enters, too); it is one of lack of concept (or construct) validity.

The problem of fallibility of measurement is augmented by the fact that no sample of subjects is representative of people in general, and measurement devices are never quite appropriate for the people on which they are used. What a test measures depends, in part, on the sample in which it is used. Among Ph.D. mathematicians a test of numerical operations (addition, subtraction, division) mainly measures carefulness, speediness, and the like, whereas the same test used in a sample of grade-school children measures abilities in forming quantitative concepts. Such extremes exemplify a general rule: In any heterogeneous sample of people, any test measures somewhat different processes in each different person. What we see in the averages (the results of published studies) are merely dominant trends in the operation of different processes. Particular tests reliably measure more than one factor. This means that people are using different abilities to deal with the problems presented by a particular test. When we analyze the age differences for such measures, the results reflect the operation of such different influences. We can isolate and distinguish between some of the influences, but results are always to some extent confounded. It is particularly important to keep these qualifications in mind when considering information pertaining to adult aging because adults of different ages also may come from different cohorts, live in different circumstances, and differ in other ways that can pertain to their performances.

Problems and Perspectives in Sampling Subjects

There has been considerable discussion of the differences between cross-sectional and longitudinal data-gathering methods (see Horn & Donaldson, 1980, and Nesselroade & Baltes, 1979, for recent, rather different analyses of issues in this regard). In a cross-sectional (CS) sample all the subjects are tested at a particular time (in history). Individuals of different ages thus would have been born in different years; they are said to belong to different cohorts. Differences between age groupings are also differences between cohorts. In a repeated-measures longitudinal (RL) sample, the subjects tested at one time are located and tested again at a later (historical) time (or at several later times). In an independent-measures longitudinal (IL) sample, groups believed to belong to the same population are tested at different (historical) times. When a CS sample is followed up in the manner of either RL or IL sampling, the data-gathering (or *design*) may be referred to as a mixed CS-RL or mixed CS-IL (or CS-RL-IL).

Investigators talk about representative sampling for these different methods of drawing samples, but it never occurs. Investigators also refer to such subject-sampling procedures as *designs* and thereby imply that various possible confounding influences have been controlled, but such talk usually is closer to hyperbole than to fact. Samples drawn in these different ways can represent quite different influences, however, and results obtained with one subject-sampling procedure can differ substantially from results based on another procedure. The findings of several comparative studies indicate systematic (average) ability differences in samples drawn in these different ways (see Nesselroade & Baltes, 1979; Willis & Baltes, 1980, for review).

The possibility that the results from CS, RL, and IL samples can differ and the evidence that, indeed, samples drawn in these different ways do differ (in some cases, with respect to some variables) have led some investigators to argue that conclusions about the aging of human abilities are notably different for CS studies than for studies based on other subject-sampling procedures (e.g., Baltes & Schaie, 1974). Some writers have extolled the virtues of RL and IL data-gathering methods relative to CL methods. It has been suggested that CS studies provide no basis for inferences about development and that results from such studies give a mistaken ("mythical") impression of aging decline in abilities, but RL, IL, and mixed CS-RL-IL studies give the correct impression that there is no decline (Baltes & Schaie, 1974, 1976; Schaie, 1974). Such claims are not well founded.

Each method of data-gathering has strengths and weaknesses that need to be carefully considered when drawing inferences about development. Depending on the nature of the variables studied, the kinds of analyses carried out, and the extent and representativeness of the subject-sampling, cross-sectional study can provide a better basis for inference about development than can RL studies (or IL or mixed studies). Subjects of low ability and the unhealthy tend to drop out of repeated-measures longitudinal studies, for example. Thus the averages for ability and health (and related variables, such as socioeconomic level) tend to be high in (what remains in) RL samples relative to CL studies (as well as IL studies). The less able are less likely to volunteer for any testing, that of CS studies as well as of other studies, and those who do not volunteer are more likely to die in the years immediately following testing than are those who do volunteer (the so-called death-drop phenomenon). Many factors of this kind operate in any of the different systems for gathering subjects. Inferences should be conditioned by careful considerations of how such factors might affect results (for discussions of the kinds of qualifications that should be taken into account, see Baltes, 1968, Botwinick, 1977; Botwinick & Arenberg, 1976; Horn, 1976; Horn & Donaldson, 1976, 1977; Kendler, 1979; as well as the aforementioned articles). No data-gathering procedure and no particular study is without limitations. Fortunately the limitations of one study usually are not repeated in other studies, so there is a sense in which truth can be sifted through collation over several studies, particularly different kinds of studies. This is why it is not correct to assert that only one kind of data-gathering is appropriate for developmental studies.

As for statements about the myth of ability decline, careful analyses of logical possibilities, evidence of sampling influences, and the data on which the statements are based lead to a conclusion that results from RL, IL, and mixed studies are not seriously discrepant from conclusions based on CS results (Horn, 1970; Horn & Donaldson, 1976, 1977, 1980). In major respects results derived from CS studies are consistent with results obtained in other kinds of studies. The results from CS studies may suggest that decline in some abilities starts at an earlier age than is suggested by results from some other studies, but as noted previously, such differences reflect somewhat different influences and should be qualified in several ways. When analyzed carefully the different results point to the operation of the same basic laws.

Assertions that results are contradictory usually have

been based on one or more of the following (among several other) failures: (1) failure to consider differences in the abilities compared (e.g., when RL results for Gc abilities are compared with CS results for Gf abilities), (2) failure to take account of the amount of change to be expected (on the basis of CS studies) and to draw samples that are large enough to demonstrate statistical significance for this amount of change, and (3) failure to make comparisons for age categories for which change reasonably could be expected (e.g., when teenagers are compared with 35-year-olds, a group that would not have reached peak performance is compared with a group that, in accordance with CS findings, would not have declined very much from peak performance).

It is important to realize, also, that the results on which most of our scientific inferences are based derive from studies of *averages,* not from analyses for individuals. This is no less true of longitudinal studies than of cross-sectional studies. Our inferences thus refer to what is typical (in the sense that an average is typical); they do not refer to what might be true for Grandma Moses (or Georgia O'Keefe). Also in most cases (but not all—e.g., Birren, Butler, Greenhouse, Sokoloff, & Yarrow, 1963), our inferences do not pertain to samples of exceptionally healthy people or people who are believed to have avoided some of the "natural shocks that flesh is heir to." Thus when we speak of "lawful regularities in the aging process," we may be referring to phenomena that occur with statistical, rather than necessary, regularity and under the conditions of particular societies at a particular time in history, all of which will change.

When qualifications of these kinds are kept in mind as one evaluates results from studies based on different subject-sampling procedures, the conclusions that emerge, overall, are very much the same. Let us now turn to a consideration of some of these conclusions.

AGE CHANGES IN THE BROAD FUNCTIONS OF INTELLECT

We have mentioned the prevalent finding that some of the major functions of intelligence appear to be characterized by decline, while other of these functions seem to improve over at least a substantial period of adulthood, if not throughout this phase of life. What are the features of the functions that decline, and in what important ways are these different from the features of the functions that improve?

Functions That Deteriorate

Just as our eyes are drawn relentlessly to a bloody accident that we would just as soon not witness, so our interests can be drawn compellingly but reluctantly to the spectacle of humans losing with aging the capabilities about which they are most proud. Such capabilities are exemplified by Gf. As described in Table 47-2, Gf is a collection of abilities in reasoning, comprehending complex relationships, drawing sound inferences, problem solving, concept formation, abstracting, and in general, thinking intelligently. It is indeed sobering to learn that older adults, on the average, display less of these abilities than do younger adults. What are the features of this decline?

Tasks that measure the induction primary ability are particularly consistent markers for the Gf function; a particularly good test for measuring the induction PMA is Inventive Letter Series. A measure having reliability of about .7 can be obtained with this test by administering roughly 15 items of the form SUXBGM?, where the task is to fill in the letter that comes next in the series.[1] Mathematicians tell us that most such series are indeterminant and that therefore the best answer usually should be "I don't know" (Hoffmann, 1962); however, most people play the game (mathematicians included) and try to find a regularity in the series that will enable them to provide a letter that "continues the series." Older adults provide answers that are less adequate in this regard than are the answers given by younger adults. This is not a matter of older adults failing to work quickly to find answers when younger adults do (although this occurs as well); in the results to which reference is made, scores were based on items that all subjects attempted (e.g., Horn & Cattell, 1966a; Horn, Donaldson, & Engstrom, 1981). Also the decline does not appear to be merely a condition of very old age; there is gradual decline beginning perhaps as early as the mid-twenties. Expressed in scale values in which one standard deviation equals 15 units (a common scaling for IQ tests), the decline is about 5 units from age 25 to age 40 and roughly 5 units for every 10 years of living from age 40 onward (perhaps accelerating with advancing age).

The induction primary ability and the letter series test are no more than examples. Other primary abilities that help to indicate features of fluid intelligence and that decline with adult age to about the same extent as induction, include figural flexibility, integration, and figural relations. Tests that measure these abilities, and show the decline, include match problems, directions, and matrices.[2] Other primary abilities that decline with adult age and have nontrivial relations to Gf include logical reasoning, spatial orientation, speed of closure, visualization, span memory, and associative memory. These abilities have substantial relations with functions other than Gf, however, so their aging curves may pertain as much to these other functions as to Gf. Several of the subtests of the WAIS also indicate the Gf function and adult decline of this function. Block designs (also known as Kohs Blocks) is perhaps the best exemplar of these relationships. The aging effects for several of the WAIS subtests that have some relation to Gf (digit symbol, object assembly) are larger than for block designs, but these tests also have large unique-factor variances and relations to broad visualization and speediness factors, so it is questionable whether they best indicate Gf decline or the decline of other functions (or both, which seems most likely).

Many measures and paradigms that indicate learning and retention over short periods of time—a few seconds up to a few minutes—also decline with age in adulthood and to about the same extent as Gf. Collectively these

---

[1] In choice letter series four or five possible answers are provided, and the task is to select the best of these alternatives. Our experience has been that this test is not quite as pure a marker for Gf, or quite as good an indicator of Gf decline, as is inventive letter series.
[2] A particular set of matrices problems, called Raven's Matrices, has been used in many studies of aging.

measures and paradigms define the SAR functions. Because these functions are important for complete expression of human intelligence and because they decline in much the same way as the functions of Gf, it is often assumed that the decline indicated for memory functions is equivalent to the decline of intelligence. This is not the case, however. As we have seen in our considerations of evidence derived from factor-analytic research, SAR and Gf are correlated but independent. Their aging trends are also independent. This means that, although the functions of the respective factors are interrelated (probably representing functional interdependencies), individual differences collectively in the functions of SAR do not convary, one to one, with individual differences collectively in the functions of Gf, and this is true for individual differences associated with differences in age as well as for individual differences among people of the same age. In other words people who are high or low in the SAR functions are not correspondingly high or low in the functions of Gf, and this is true for individuals who differ in age as well as for those who do not. People who exemplify the aging decline of Gf do not in general exemplify, to the same extent, the aging decline of SAR, even though the aging decline indicated in the averages (over several people at each age) is about the same for SAR as for Gf.

These conditions of independent variation and development for SAR and Gf can seem to be in some sense contradictory or only anomalies of particular measures. The conditions can indeed represent only anomalies of particular measures; but this seems not to be the case, and the results are not necessarily contradictory. In fact the results are typical of conditions that obtain for aging phenomena. For example we observe that, on the average, people become more wrinkled as they grow older and they also become heavier; but those who exemplify the wrinkling concomitant of aging do not necessarily, or in general, exemplify the weight gain that accompanies aging. In this example the aging trends for the two manifest variables reasonably could be thought to represent quite different developmental phenomena. Many things are associated with aging. Although in a very abstract sense such things are related, most of them are not related in the sense that they are part of the same lawful descriptions of particular phenomena. SAR and Gf probably are related in the sense that they pertain to the same general phenomena of human intelligence, but the necessity of even this relation can be questioned and, in any case, the two functions appear to represent independent features of intelligence.

The measures of short-term acquisition and retrieval can be age-related in different ways and related in different ways to other functions, such as Gf and Gc, that are related to age. For example the primary ability of *Meaningful memory* (Mm) is measured with tasks in which a subject can perceive meaningful relations between the elements to be remembered and the retrieval cues, and these relations can be more or less aided by the knowledge system of Gc. If an item requires one to remember *Dane* when the retrieval cue is *Fetid*, a person familiar with Shakespeare's plays might use this element of Gc to relate the two words and thereby remember better than would one who did not have this element of Gc. If the measure of Mm were largely comprised of such

items, then even if other measures of SAR were more closely related to Gf and aging decline than to Gc and aging improvements, this particular measure could show the opposite relationships. Similarly some of the tasks that measure a particular primary ability of memory require retrieval after only a few seconds, while in other such tasks there may be many seconds between presentation and retrieval. These task features can also relate to age and to Gf and Gc in any of several ways.

These possibilities for variations in memory tasks make it hazardous to venture generalizations about the features of short-term acquisition and retrieval that best characterize SAR and the aging decline of this collection of functions. Contrary to what seems to be widely believed, however, simple span memory—as in remembering a telephone number long enough to dial it—does not appear to be the central feature of SAR that declines with age (see the reviews of Craik, 1977, and Reese, 1977). List learning, on the other hand, is relatively strongly related to SAR and to aging.

In general it seems that as the interval between presentation and retrieval in a memory task becomes very small and as the task becomes merely one of clang memory the relation of the resulting measures to aging and to SAR decreases, so extremely short-term clang memory is not much different in older than in younger people and is not very indicative of the SAR functions. When the presentation-retrieval interval is in a range somewhere between 30 seconds and a minute or two and when there are several things to remember but these are not entirely nonsensical elements, the resulting measures do relate to aging and to SAR.

The SAR functions are more indicative of secondary memory than of primary memory, as these concepts are operationally defined in the research of cognitive psychology (Craik, 1977; Horn, 1975, 1976; Hundal & Horn, 1977; Kintsch, 1970; Reese, 1977). Secondary memory represents a form of information processing in which a person retains the information for time periods of at least 30 seconds, whereas primary memory represents only a condition of holding information for short periods of time (e.g., as long as it takes to dial a telephone number). Craik and Lockhart (1972) have attempted to call attention to some of the features of secondary memory processing by characterizing it as *in-depth processing*. Such processing occurs when one attempts to make sense out of information or in other such ways does "work" with information (e.g., as in rehearsing).

A concept of working memory is also used to help describe the phenomena of maintaining awareness and retention (e.g., Hunt, 1978; Massaro, 1975; Resnick & Glaser, 1976). The thought is that in a learning or problem-solving or memory task a person must code the information of the task into a holding memory, where the information is worked on with the knowledge store (also referred to as *long-term memory*, LTM). After information in working memory is used or as it is being used, it is overlayed with new information that constantly pours into awareness, and so awareness at one instant tends to be lost to awareness at a following instant. Usually the experimental operations designed to indicate working memory define the retention periods of time as very short (i.e., less than 30 seconds), so the concept turns out to be very similar to primary memory. As noted before, such short-term awareness is not a central feature of SAR, nor does it seem to decline very much with aging (Craik, 1977; Reese, 1977).

Functions That Improve

Just as Gf represents many qualities of thinking that are widely accepted as being indicative of intelligence, so Gc is defined by a set of abilities that people in general and psychologists in particular often refer to in their attempts to specify what they mean by *intelligence*. As can be seen in Table 47–2, the tasks that exemplify Gc require that subjects use good judgment, abstract information, form concepts, solve problems, draw reasonable inferences, detect relations among stimuli, and in other such ways display intellectual abilities. Thus the Gc factor represents intelligence as surely as does Gf. Unlike Gf, however, the abilities that define Gc increase (on the average over numbers of subjects at each age) throughout most of adulthood, at least from the twenties to the sixties. This increase in Gc is approximately equal (in absolute value) to the decrease in Gf over the same age period when the two shifts in averages are identified in the same samples of subjects. Thus a measure that was comprised of about equal parts of Gf and Gc (i.e., a measure that could well be regarded as a good indicator of general intelligence) would show no systematic rise or fall with aging (Horn & Cattell, 1967).

The abilities of *tertiary storage and retrieval* (TSR) are related to and supportive of, but also independent from, Gc in much the same manner as SAR is related to and supportive of, but independent from Gf. Throughout most of life the averages for TSR abilities rise or at least do not decline. If one looked at only the means for groups of adults of different ages, it might be concluded that the TSR abilities represent the same facts about development as are represented by the age changes for Gc. Also the abilities of TSR are correlated with the abilities of Gc, so again it might seem that both sets of abilities represent the same functions. However, as in the case of SAR and Gf, the within-factor intercorrelations for TSR and Gc are larger than the between-factor correlations; the two factors appear to represent different functions. This is suggested by evidence in addition to that of factor analysis. Also the age differences for one factor are not highly predicted by the age differences for the other factor. Thus TSR represents functions that improve in adulthood, and this development is separate from the comparable development for Gc.

The abilities that define TSR indicate fluent access to the knowledge system, perhaps particularly that part of the system that is represented by Gc. As can be seen in Table 47–2, specific TSR abilities involve retrieving words that are similar in meaning to a given word, putting together different ideas about a particular event (such as a man going up a ladder), finding new ways to express an idea, and imagining new uses for old objects. These kinds of abilities are sometimes regarded as indicative of creativity (e.g., Getzels & Jackson, 1962; Guilford, 1967; Rossman & Horn, 1972), so in this sense, contrary to what often seems to be assumed, we may get more creative as we get older. Also most of the measures of TSR are obtained under speeded conditions, which

means that these abilities reflect speediness of intellectual function. Thus again contrary to what often seems to be assumed, people may come to think more rapidly (in one sense) as they become older.

The knowledge system of humans might be characterized as a net in which each knot is a bit of information and each string between knots is an association pathway to retrieval of information. Continuously throughout life such a net would be altered; it would be torn in some places, become worn out in other places, be rebuilt and repaired, and be expanded along a number of different edges. Also the net probably needs to be regarded as at least three-dimensional, perhaps many-dimensional, and quite irregular and different for one person as compared to another. By this analogy individual differences in TSR might reflect either differences in the efficiency or directedness with which one can move through the net to a particular node of knowledge or differences in the number of nodes that can be accessed (size of net). Probably both features are represented in any fallible measure of TSR. It seems that Gc and Gf may best represent the size-of-net feature and that TSR is mainly indicative of an ease-of-access function for retrieving learned information.

Attrition and Restructuring in Loss and Gain

We have considered the likelihood that all complex human abilities are heavily determined by learning. We have not considered the likelihood, however, that each such ability is characterized by the antithesis of learning—namely, forgetting. Yet the fading of human abilities, as in forgetting, is no less a feature of human development (at all ages) than is the enhancement of abilities through learning. The enhancement of Gc in the adult period of development thus should be comprehended within a context of understanding that some features of these abilities are also being lost as we become older.

To become aware of losses in Gc, all one need do is remember that some things are forgotten that once were known very well—e.g., completing the square in developing the solution for a quadratic equation or the middle parts of the "to be or not to be" soliloquy of Hamlet. The limited evidence now available suggests that the curve for loss of knowledge over periods of months and years has the same negatively accelerated form as the familiar forgetting curves so often seen in studies of short-term learning and memory (Riegel, 1973). A large amount of what is learned in one month is not retrievable in the month that immediately follows. Of that which is still available, a substantial amount is not retrievable in the next month. Similar attrition occurs in subsequent months.

Even after very extended periods of time, however, some previously learned information is retrievable. How much is retrievable depends on how well the information was learned initially and a number of other factors. Sometimes if special care is taken to build a well overdetermined network of retrieval cues, a rather surprising amount of early learned information can be recovered even after very long periods of time (Graesser & Mandler, 1978; Norman, 1979). Also for many items of knowledge there is repeated use over time and repeated reexamination and restructuring. By *restructuring* we mean that the network of knowledge is relearned—reinforced where it has become worn, rebuilt where it has been torn, elaborated with new information nodes, rearranged to improve access to information, and in general, improved. What was initially learned in the distant past thus can be reinforced and kept fresh and become more firmly integrated into an individual's knowledge system. This is true of both the Gf and the Gc parts of the knowledge system. What the evidence suggests, however, is that Gc represents knowledge that is most assiduously maintained and enhanced, while Gf represents knowledge that tends to be lost or to wear down and not to be replaced. It seems that the Gc-TSR abilities are more commonly used and restructured in everyday living; in consequence, they become the more dominant features of the complex network of a person's total knowledge system, while the Gf-SAR abilities become merely the "kept" elements of this system, not the elements "promoted" to more involved levels of influence.

The "more dominant" or "influential" features of a knowledge network can be thought of in terms of overdetermination in learning and in neural concomitants of, and support for, learning. There can be several kinds of overdetermination. For example a given item of information almost always is regarded as related to (associated with) several other items of information; thus, there are usually several pathways of association to retrieval of any piece of information. This condition of several ways to achieve a particular end is overdetermination. If a particular pathway to retrieval is destroyed—e.g., by loss of neuronal support for an acquired association—other pathways in an overdetermined system may still remain open to enable one to retrieve, and to refurbish, particular pieces of information. Nodes and pathways that are much used and restructured into the knowledge system bring about overdetermination. Information in such areas of the knowledge network continues to be available even when particular pathways and nodes are lost to function. Gc and TSR represent these overdetermined parts of the network. On the other hand Gf and SAR represent parts of the network that are not overdetermined. If pathways and nodes are lost to these parts, there is decline in corresponding abilities. This does not necessarily mean that the deteriorated functions cannot be restored by repairing or adding to the knowledge network through new learning, but existing evidence suggests that ordinarily such refurbishing does not occur and that it may be very difficult to do in any case, particularly if the new learning pertains primarily to in-laboratory kinds of performances, not to in-life coping mechanisms. (See Denney, Chap. 45, this volume, for a good review of evidence in this area of inquiry.)

INTELLIGENCE DEFICITS DESCRIBED IN TERMS OF OTHER VARIABLES

Much of the talk and some of the research pertaining to the aging of intellectual abilities has been directed at supporting hypotheses specifying that what appear to be decreases in intelligence are not really losses in the fundamental capacities for intellectual functioning but in-stead are decreases in performance that reflect only losses in motivation or in processes of sensing, perceiving, and/or attending—i.e., factors that are regarded as peripheral to the central features of intelligence. Existing research results do not provide a sufficient basis for either accepting or dismissing this hypothesis. One can conclude, however, that some interpretations of the hypothesis are not supported by the evidence and are not likely to be supported by new results. Also simple optimistic interpretations are not likely to find support. If decreases in Gf-test performances are manifestations of low motivation, for example, then the evidence suggests that the low motivation is no less a problem for behaving intelligently than is the problem that exists if the low test performance indicates loss of an ability to behave intelligently. In other words the problem is not simply peripheral in the sense that all a low-scorer need do is "buck up and try." There is great difficulty in separating the chicken and the egg in these kinds of considerations. Taking the results all in all, however, it seems that there are losses in processes of attending (perhaps reflecting losses in motivation), as well as losses in sensing and perceiving. Some of these losses are related to decline in performances on intellectual tasks, but it is not possible to argue convincingly either that these losses are peripheral, or are not peripheral, to basic capacities for intellectual functioning.

Part of the problem of drawing firm conclusions in regard to these hypotheses is that there are so many possible peripheral functions that could conceivably be at the core of noteworthy decline in an intellectual process. How can we bring some system into a program for considering this multitude of alternatives? Here the approach is to reconnoiter the territory with a broad sweep from consideration of rather elementary sensory-detector variables through consideration of variables at each of the levels of function suggested in Figure 47–1. Such an exploratory survey can perhaps serve to indicate where more intensive investigations are likely to lead to genuine advances in understanding.

Sensory-Detector Functions

William James observed that at the level of sensation we are vaguely aware of a buzzing, blooming confusion of energy changes—lights, sounds—that surround us and compete for full entry into our awareness. It seems that we are very briefly aware of a large part of this confusion of events and that this awareness is virtually automatic, uncontrolled by efforts to turn it off or on (Broadbent, 1958; Hasher & Zacks, 1979; Keele, 1973; Madden & Nebes, 1980; Norman & Bobrow, 1975; Rabbitt, 1979a; Shiffrin & Schneider, 1977; Sperling, 1960). The ways in which such automatic processes of attending can be distinguished from controlled processes of almost equally short duration is a topic of considerable current interest in both general psychology and the psychology of aging.

Very short-term apprehension is sometimes referred to as *iconic* if the material is visual or *echoic* if the stimuli are auditory. A detection or awareness that is referred to in this manner has a duration of only a couple of seconds—a bit longer for auditory than for visual stimulation. Usually it is localized in the sense organ of stimulus detection. For example if a subject is presented with the numbers 7, 6, 5 on a screen and the numbers 4, 9, 2 through ear phones, s/he tends to recall the numbers in the sets 765 and 492—the sets presented to the eye and ear respectively—rather than as odd numbers 759 and even numbers 642. The recall thus indicates detection at the level of sensory function. As time between presentation and recall is increased, then if there is recall at all, it tends to be organized in terms of what Broadbent (1966) characterized as *meaningful detection* in contrast to *sensory detection.* For example if two minutes elapse between presentation of the numbers mentioned before and subjects are not encouraged to rehearse the presentation orders, then recall (if there was any) is likely to be produced in sets of odd numbers and even numbers.

It is reasonable to suppose that aging deficits in performances on intellectual tasks reflect loss of awareness of the kind indicated by sensory-detector paradigms. Perhaps the spectrum of awareness automatically attained by older people is not as broad as the spectrum attained by younger people. Perhaps age differences in Gf or SAR might be altered by controlling for sensory-awareness differences. If it were true, for example, that older persons have greater difficulty than do younger persons in becoming aware of the totality of the stimulus array presented in letter-series problems, then by partialling out the variance associated with a sensory-awareness measure in the relationship between age and performance on letter-series problems, the aging decline indicated for this latter would be reduced, perhaps eliminated, and thus be shown to reflect a sensory-awareness deficit. This is a reasonable hypothesis, but the extant evidence gives scant support for it.

Research reviewed by Botwinick (1977), Bromley (1966), Craik (1977), Horn (1970a, 1975, 1976), Walsh (1975), and Welford (1958) suggests that there are, to be sure, aging decrements in sensory-detector functions. Representative of this evidence is a recent study by Walsh and Thompson (1978) in which the mean duration of iconic memory was found to be 15 percent greater for a sample of young people (mean age 24 years) than for a sample of old people (mean age 67 years). But such sensory deficits do not seem to be responsible for comparable deficits in intellectual test performances. This is the conclusion of much research (see reviews mentioned before) dating from an early period in the study of aging (see particularly Welford, 1958).

The conclusion is illustrated concretely by results from an investigation by Horn et al. (1981) in which sensory detection was measured by a modification of a paradigm developed by Sperling (1960). A subject was shown 3-by-3 matrices containing letters (or numbers). A matrix would remain in the field of vision for a few seconds, then vanish, and be replaced by an empty matrix in which a particular row or column would be designated by an arrow; the subject's task was to reproduce the particular letters of the original matrix that were in the row or column that was designated in the empty matrix. The time between disappearance of the original matrix and appearance of the empty matrix was very short (less than 2 seconds), the demand on working memory (i.e., the memory of "hold while reproduce") was very small (3 elements), and the subject could not know which part of the matrix array s/he would be required to reproduce, so the adequacy of reproduction could be in-

terpreted as indicating the extent of a subject's awareness of the full matrix array. A measure having reliability in excess of .7 was obtained with 15 matrix pairings of the kind described.

There was aging decline for this measure of sensory-detector awareness (SDA), and this decline was approximately the same as the decline seen in measures of fluid intelligence. However when SDA was controlled in Gf by estimating Gf from SDA (using the linear relation between the two variables) and subtracting this estimated part from Gf, the resulting residual variable had practically the same aging decline as the uncontrolled measure of Gf. Thus, correcting for SDA deficits (which were more common in older adults) did not correct for the Gf deficits that were associated with aging. The sensory-detector defects of older adults were not found to be responsible for findings that older adults, on the average, perform less well on fluid intelligence tasks than do younger adults.

Results of this kind were also found in other studies of this program of research when measures based on a dichotic-listening paradigm designed to represent Broadbent's (1966) concept of sensory detection was used to effect control of Gf decline. Walsh (1981) has obtained similar results in a series of tightly designed studies of somewhat narrower scope. In general, evidence from several sources now adds up to suggest that probably the aging deficits seen in performances on fluid-intelligence tasks are not merely manifestations of defects in sensory awareness (even as such defects are associated with aging).

Association Functions

Defects in sensory detection *do* appear to be implicated in aging losses of short-term memory even as they are not, as we have seen, involved in Gf decline. Yet the totality of short-term memory functions, as indicated by SAR, appears to be a part of the fluid-intelligence functions that decline with age. The component of SAR and Gf that is shared in aging decline appears to be closely related to a capacity, or inclination, for maintaining close attention and/or for allocating attention to different things. The interrelationships in this regard are complex and not easily interpreted. Let us consider some of the main features of these interrelationships.

First, there is the suggestion that sensory detection is related to short-term memory and the aging decline of SAR, even as it is unrelated to the aging decline of Gf. This suggestion is illustrated by some of the findings from the Horn et al. (1981) studies. In one of these studies a memory-span backward (MsB) test was used to estimate ability to hold information in mind while doing something with it: In a particular item of MsB, the subject would be presented with several numbers, one after another, as 7-6-9-4-8-2, and be required after a few seconds to reproduce the numbers in the opposite of the order in which they were presented, as 2-8-4-9-6-7. This measure of working memory was found to decline with age in adulthood—to about the same extent as Gf and SDA. A substantial portion of this aging decline was eliminated by controlling for SDA in the manner indicated before for Gf. This was the finding also when SDA was controlled in the decline for a measure of memory span forward (MsF)—the ability to remember a telephone number long enough to dial it. Thus defects of sensory detection that were associated with aging appeared to be partly responsible for aging defects in short-term (i.e., working) memory.

Next, and most interesting, control for the kind of working memory that is represented by the MsB variable produced a significant reduction in the intelligence decline recorded with measures of Gf. Thus a part of the ability to hold information in awareness while doing something with it appears to be implicated in aging losses in the abilities to reason, to abstract, and to educe relations. As noted before sensory awareness is implicated in MsB working ability, but this part of MsB is not involved in the decline of Gf. This uninvolved part is also represented by MSF, which itself declines with age, but control of which does little to alter Gf decline. But what is the nature of the involved part—the part of MsB working memory that is also a part of the decline of fluid intelligence.

A number of studies are relevant to consideration of this question. Rabbitt (1979) has summarized several studies, the results of which suggest that important aging decrements in intellectual activities may stem from "failures in control processes by means of which information stored in memory is used to optimize attentional selectivity from moment to moment during the course of contemporary tasks" (p. 93). Earlier Broadbent and Heron (1962), Clay (1957), Kay (1959), Rabbitt (1964, 1965), and Welford (1958), among others, demonstrated that abilities in dividing attention, in the sense of holding some aspects of a problem in mind while dealing with other aspects of the problem, and abilities in ignoring irrelevant information are a part of the picture of aging decline and appear to be linked to losses in the abilities of short-term memory and intelligence. Welford (1980) summed up results from this area of research rather well.

Thinking seems to consist of a series of "stages" in which a "leap" is made from one idea or partial solution of a problem to another. Between these stages, verbal, visual, and other images seem to store the data already gathered and the partial solutions already attained while the next leap is being made. It is a fair guess that a major limitation in thinking is the amount of data that can be stored in this way, and there is evidence that this is so in older people (Rabbitt, 1977; Welford, 1958, Chap. 8). It seems fair to argue that many, if not all, items that test "fluid" intelligence involve some form of thinking of this kind and that their demands might be quantified in terms of the amount of data to be carried and the attentional demands of other operations over which they have to be retained. (Welford, 1980, pp. 618–619)

Hunt (1978) has argued that it is only when demand is put on capacities for maintaining attention that controlled mechanistic processes relate to measures of intelligence. In related work Botwinick and Storandt (1974), Horn and Cattell (1967), and Horn et al. (1981) have found that abilities in maintaining concentration in very simple clerical tasks are related to the features of memory that decline with age in adulthood and are implicated in the decline of fluid intelligence. Still other work suggests that concentration (or attention) fluctuates on and off and that periods of "off" might increase in length and/or frequency as age increases (Fozard, Thomas, & Waugh,

1976; Thomas, Waugh, & Fozard, 1978; Waugh, Fozard, & Thomas, 1978). In general qualities of maintaining and allocating attention, even when measured in tests that are not ordinarily thought of as intelligence tests, seem to be at the core of aging deficits that are recorded in both SAR and Gf.

The results outlined in the previous paragraph are illustrated in study 3 of the Horn et al. (1981) report. A measure of concentration (COS) was obtained using an adaptation of the Botwinick-Storandt (1974) slow-tracing paradigm. A measure of ability to divide attention (ATD) was based on the Broadbent-Heron (1962) procedures in which a particular symbol had to be located while one also attempted to remember the facts of a story. Controlling for either ATD or COS reduced the aging decline of Gf by about one IQ unit per decade of adulthood. Controlling for both of these influences or controlling for one or the other with measures of primary and secondary memory did not bring about a worthwhile further change in Gf-age relationship. Thus it seems that a basic part of working memory that is associated with aging decline or intelligence is a process that is closely related to abilities in dividing attention and focusing concentration.

In sensory detection virtually no meaningful relationship is perceived or worked out; virtually no depth of processing occurs. Consequently events that are thus detected are retained for only very short periods of time, a second or two. At the other extreme if one explicates a poem or writes a sonnet, the essential ideas and even the exact wording of the piece may be recalled after months or years. This is depth of processing at the level of eduction of relations and correlates, as in the exercise of Gf or Gc (or both). In between eduction of relations and sensory detection are levels of processing that are responsible, in part, for the SAR factor (as well as for the Gv, Ga, and TSR factors). These levels of processing also seem to be implicated in the aging decline of fluid intelligence.

Short-term tasks that require meaningful organization of the material that is to be remembered are indicative of functions that decline with age in adulthood (Hultsch, 1969, 1971, 1974; Laurence, 1967). This short-term memory usually is on the "long side"—i.e., retrieval is required after 30 seconds or more. What is meant by the term *meaningful organization* in this context is not precisely specified, but some of the important features are suggested by studies such as those of Mandler (1967, 1977). He required subjects to classify words under several different conditions. He found that if subject classified under instructions to form a system "that makes sense to you" they remembered better with fewer learning trials than if they classified in accordance with another system, in particular a system that "made sense" to someone else. This result was obtained whether or not the subject was instructed that retrieval would be required. In the Horn et al. (1981) studies, controls with measures based on Mandler's paradigms were found (1) to account for a substantial portion of the variance of SAR and, in particular, the aging decline of SAR and (2) to reduce by noteworthy and significant amounts the aging decline of Gf that was also associated with SAR.

We see then that aging losses in abilities of intelligence that are also losses in short-term memory appear in one form to be linked to abilities in spreading and focusing attention and appear in another form to be linked to abilities in organizing incoming information in meaningful ways. In these accounts of the data it is as if the trunk and the tail of the elephant might be roughly described by two blind men. There is more to the beast than this. In particular it seems that a kind of spontaneous awareness, at first glance similar to sensory awareness, is to some extent involved in the aging decline of both SAR and Gf.

Tulving (1972) distinguished semantic and episodic memory in a parallel-processing theory of retention. *Semantic memory* is, for the purposes at hand, the same concept as we have already described under the heading of *secondary memory*. The idea is that organized knowledge about referents, rules, and generalized problem-solving procedures permits good storage and retrieval, and this is functionally different from storage and retrieval of events or episodes. *Episodic memory* differs from primary memory particularly in the fact that it is not specified in terms of shortness of time of retention. As we have seen primary memory is defined as a very short-term temporary storage, and this appears to be relatively unrelated to the aging decline of intelligence. The retention time for episodic memory need not be short, but it is analogously trivial in the sense that "meaningful organization" does not seem to be paramount (as per Mandler's paradigm and the Craik-Lockhart notion of depth processing). The phenomena of episodic memory are similar to what were identified in rather hoary attempts to specify *incidental memory* (e.g., Jones, Conrad, & Horn, 1928; Willoughby, 1930). In more recent uses of incidental memory (e.g., Estes & DaPolito, 1967; Postman, 1964), it has come to refer to a contrast between conditions in which subjects are *not* told that they will later be asked to recall (the incidental memory conditions) and conditions in which there are explicit instructions to expect a recall trial. The sorting tasks of Mandler's (1967) work can be regarded as incidental memory tasks in this sense because subjects are not told that they will be asked to recall after sorting. However, the concept of *episodic memory* and the older concept of *incidental memory* not only imply that subjects will not be instructed to remember but also suggest that subjects will have only very vague ideas about what constitutes an episode or what might be relevant to retain for future reference.

It is interesting in this regard that the studies of Jones et al. (1928) and Willoughby (1930) indicated an aging loss in such incidental or episodic memory. Interestingly, too, using a measure that was designed to represent Tulving's concept of *subjective organization* of episodic information, Hultsch (1974) found that older adults do not retain such information as well as do younger adults.[3] A similar result was obtained in the Horn et al. (1981) study with an entirely different paradigm. The paradigm involved staging a number of rather trivial events (i.e., episodes) at different times during the administration of other tests. An example of an "event" is a male wearing a bright red tie entering the testing room and asking the test administrator a question. To measure memory of

this "event," subjects would be asked the color of the tie worn by the person who appeared and asked a question (and approximate time and place in the testing would be indicated). Episodes of this kind were spread over a period of about 2.5 hours, after which the subject's memory for the eipisodes was determined. This memory declined with age in adulthood (a replication of earlier work) and also accounted for a noteworthy portion of decline of both SAR and Gf.

In regarding the aging of memory processes consideration should be given also to what is called *recognition memory*. This latter is similar in one respect to the incidental memory of the Horn et al. (1981) study. In both cases memory is measured by a questionnaire in which the subject is required merely to recognize information that had been presented before. But incidental memory and recognition memory differ in a major respect: the subject is not at all primed to remember the material of an incidental memory task, whereas s/he is so primed in the usual tests for recognition memory.

It is well established that one can rather easily recognize material that is not all that easily recalled (e.g., Deese,1969). The literature also suggests that there is little or no aging decline in recognition memory (Hultsch, 1971; Schonfield, 1965; Walsh & Baldwin, 1977). It is possible that this result mainly indicates that recognition-memory tasks tend to be too easy (relative to recall tasks) to record aging deficits sensitively—that is, more difficult recognition-memory tasks may be found to show aging decline (Walsh & Baldwin, 1977).

Also of relevance in this context are findings pertaining to very long-term, or tertiary, memory. This form of memory is represented in part by the TSR factor but in part also by other factors, such as Gc and Gf, that are based on measures in which the subject must retrieve information of a variety of kinds in order to do the tests of the factors.

Botwinick (1977) and Fozard (1980) refer to results showing that vocabulary scores do not decline with age as evidence that tertiary memory does not decline. The finding of this kind that emerges from studies based on a variety of different kinds of paradigms is that if material is learned reasonably well, then it seems to be retrieved as well by older adults as by younger ones (see Botwinick, 1977; Fozard, 1980; Horn, 1970a, for reviews of results dating from at least as early as Shakow, Dolkart, & Goldman, 1941).

People learn and retain information that is peculiar to their age cohort. For example people who were adults at the time are inclined to remember where the Hindenberg burned and crashed, but younger adults who have heard about this event only secondhand, if at all, are less likely to "remember" the place of the event. This example illustrates that much of the aging difference in "retrieval" from tertiary memory can be merely difference in what was learned and stored initially, not retrieval at all.

Differences in amount and kind of material initially learned may be what is measured, at least in part, in TSR. The factor is a broad indication of the facility with which one can retrieve different kinds of information under different kinds of task demands—get words similar in meaning to a given word, come up with ideas about a situation, or provide a different way of expressing an idea. If learning or storage of information continues

---

[3] Laurence (1966) and Horn et al. (1981) found no age differences for measures of subjective organization that were similar to the Hultsch measure. There were problems with the Laurence and Horn et al. measures that might account for their discrepant findings, however (see Horn, 1978a; Hultsch, 1974).

throughout life and if the rate of such storage is generally faster than the rate of loss of storage, then if TSR is regarded as mainly indicative of amount of storage, it is not surprising that results from a number of studies converge to suggest that there is no aging decline for the abilities of TSR (e.g., Botwinick, 1977; Botwinick & Storandt, 1974; Fozard, 1980; Horn, 1970a, 1976; Horn & Cattell, 1967; Lachman & Lachman, 1980).

What is perhaps surprising is that the TSR abilities do not improve very much throughout adulthood; perhaps there is some improvement, but if so it is not large (not as large as for Gc). Since the measures of the factor are usually obtained under moderately speeded conditions and since speediness in many activities decreases with adult age (Birren, 1974), it might be reasoned that the aging increase that might otherwise be expected for TSR is damped by a decrease in speediness that is also a part of the factor. This does not seem to be the case, however. Although older adults produce fewer responses in TSR tests during the first few seconds—up to approximately the first minute—their rate of responding continues to be high during the next minute or two relative to the corresponding rate for younger adults, so that, over the period of roughly three minutes per item that is typical for TSR measures, older adults produce more responses than do younger adults (Horn, 1970a, 1978a, 1978b; Horn & Cattell, 1967; Lachman & Lachman, 1980). Such results are consistent with findings that if only the first minute or so of responding is recorded (e.g., in naming objects) older adults may seem to retrieve information at a slower rate than do younger adults (Thomas, Fozard, & Waugh, 1977).

In anecdotal accounts of memory failures that accompany aging, it is often suggested that inability to retrieve a particular item from stored information is a major feature of aging. It is not always recognized that instances of this inability are common in people of any age. However, some of the research literature does support the idea that such inability increases with age in adulthood (Schonfield, 1972). There is no necessary inconsistency between results of this kind and results suggesting that older adults retrieve more than do younger adults in tests that define TSR. If the older adult's network of information is larger and more variegated than is the information network of the younger adult, it could well be more difficult for the older adult to get directly to a specific element in the network even when, and perhaps partly because, s/he had more elements in his/her information categories and more categories than did the younger adult.

Perhaps enough has been said to indicate the general features of the aging of association functions and the relation of this aging to the adulthood decline of fluid intelligence. It seems that very short-term retention processes, perhaps well characterized as automatic (Shiffrin & Schneider, 1977) or data-driven (Rabbitt, 1979), are very little affected by adulthood aging. Similarly retrieval from the knowledge network seems not to decline and may improve (on the average) in adulthood. On the other hand aging memory losses that appear to be important features of aging loss of fluid intelligence occur in tasks which

1. Require (or allow) one to impose organization (at the time of encoding) on the to-be-remembered material;

2. Require that one maintain close attention to the details of the to-be-remembered material;
3. Require that one divide attention among several aspects of the to-be-remembered material, perhaps particularly when this material comes in a continuous stream over time;
4. Require that one be spontaneously aware of material that would not seem relevant (but subsequently becomes relevant).

The discussion of this section is merely illustrative of a very large body of work. More research has been done on memory processes than on any other aspect of intelligence, and this is true also of work on adulthood development. Other summaries of this work are provided by Arenberg and Robertson-Tchabo (1977), Carroll and Maxwell (1979), Craik (1977), Fozard (1980), Hartley, Harker, and Walsh (1980), Horn (1970a, 1978a), Hoyer and Plude (1980), Hunt (1978), Reese (1977), and Sternberg (1977), among others.

Perceptual-Organization Functions

There is no clear line of demarcation between sensory-detector functions and perceptual-organization functions, nor is the line between these latter and associative processes clearly drawn. However, operational definitions of perceptual-organization functions can be obtained with factor measures that involve visual and auditory performances of a fairly complex kind. These definitions are measurement-independent of factors representing other functions. Thus fairly clear operational distinctions can be drawn between perceptual organization and associative organization even though the precise nature of the distinction, in terms of essential processes, is not made evident. We have a few clues about these matters, however.

Perceptual organization involves recognition of pattern, but the recognition does not necessarily involve the use of semantic relationships; if the recognition does involve use of semantic relationships, it represents *associational organization*. A melody can be comprehended better than a random set of notes because there is a recognizable pattern to the melody, but this comprehension need not involve any ability in the use of a conventional language (even the language of mathematics). Thus perceptual organization occurs even when one does not, or cannot, verbalize it. Perceptual processing is indicated when one comprehends pattern, but the processing is not expressed, or understood, in terms of semantic associations. It is in this sense that classes of behavior define the functions of Gv and Ga independently of SAR and TSR. Intuitively these factor distinctions represent the idea that people understand music and sculpture and painting without being able to express this understanding very well in ordinary language.

In research, somewhat in contrast to theory, it has proven more difficult to keep Gv separate from Gf than to keep it separate from SAR. Typically Gv tasks can be dealt with by reasoning, even though they have been designed to indicate visual fluency in different forms of perception of pattern. In the Gestalt closure test, for example, the usual (and usually the best) way to deal with an item is to merely sit back, as it were, and let the closure happen—e.g., let the disparate parts of a figure "congeal" in one's mind's eye to reveal a man kneeling to take a picture with a reflex camera. However, sometimes the closure does not take place in this manner. One may then resort to reasoning: "Well, that looks like a part of a shoe, and that part of a hat, so it seems to be a man." When this occurs the task measures Gf (or Gc) rather than Gv (i.e., the alternate mechanism principle—Horn, 1970a—is indicated). In several studies it has been virtually impossible to distinguish Gv from Gf because the Gv factor has not been sufficiently overdetermined and the Gv tasks have, in the sample under study, called for too much of the reasoning and other processes of Gf.

The distinction between Gv and other factors has been indicated in several studies (e.g., Horn, 1972b; Horn & Bramble, 1967; Horn & Cattell, 1966; Horn & Stankov, 1981; Shucard & Horn, 1972). A particularly broad, and in that sense valid, measure of the Gv-organization was obtained in the Horn and Cattell (1967) study of adult development. The primary abilities identified as *spatial orientation, speed of closure, flexibility of closure, visualization,* and *figural flexibility* (see Table 47–1) were combined by summing scores obtained on factor-marker tests labeled *cards, figures, Gestalt completion, designs, form boards, backward reading,* and *match arrangements.* The factor was well distinguished from Gf in an objectively rotated solution. In analyses to indicate features of aging, this estimate of the Gv factor was found to improve (on the average) until the early thirties, to level off until the late forties, and to decline gradually thereafter. When entered as a covariate in analyses of covariance of the age differences for estimates of Gf, very little alteration in Gf decline was produced by the Gv covariate "control."

Thus while there is little doubt that notable changes in vision occur with aging in adulthood (see Hultsch & Deutsch, 1981, for a concise, comprehensive review), these alterations seem to have only moderate and late-occurring effects on visual-perceptual organization, and these latter changes in turn do not seem to account for any notable portion of the aging decline of fluid intelligence.

In the available studies of adulthood changes in the broad Ga factor that represents auditory perception of pattern, only narrow spans of age have been considered (Stankov & Horn, 1980, and unpublished results based on the data of this report). The results from this early work are similar to the results obtained for the Gv factor. The age changes are small, and they do not appear to be responsible for the aging decline of Gf.

These results should not be regarded as definitive. Insofar as they go, however, they suggest that perceptual organization is not greatly affected by aging and is not highly associated with the aging decline in Gf.

Relation-Eduction Functions

Much of what can be said about the aging changes of Gf and Gc already has been outlined in previous sections: What can be added? How can we speak about these factors in new ways that reveal nuances of meaning about the functions?

One thought is that Gf and Gc involve using existing information to anticipate, to form hypotheses, and to educe consequences. Ideas of this kind have been discussed and researched for years under headings such as *temporal integration* (Hearnshaw, 1956), *long-circuiting* (Cattell, 1957), and *eduction of correlates* (Spearman, 1927). In studies of aging, phenomena of this kind have been looked at by considering how a person uses information that is available at a given moment to formulate questions and thus elicit information that can aid solution of a problem (e.g., Denney & Denney, 1973; Denney, Chap. 45, this volume; Sanford & Maule, 1973). The familiar twenty-questions game is an example of the kind of task that can be used to indicate this process. In this game person *A* (the test administrator) thinks of an object, and the task for person *B* (the subject) is to discover what the object is by asking questions to which person *A* must answer truthfully either "yes" or "no." The number of questions person *B* asks to discover the object is an indication of ability in forming and testing hypotheses. The usual finding has been that older subjects use more such questions than do younger ones; in particular, they ask more irrelevant questions and relatively fewer of the kind of question that efficiently eliminates possibilities. Measures of this kind have been found to account for part of the age-decline variance of fluid intelligence (e.g., Horn et al., 1981).

In twenty-questions tasks it appears that the older person does not educe relationships and implications—does not initially comprehend—as well as the younger person and for this reason does not develop the most satisfactory organization of information and the best basis for seeking new information. The scoring decisions on which these measurements are based are reasonable, but they leave open the question of whether mainly style or mainly capacity is represented by the differences in the questioning behavior. It seems, however, that capacity is implicated.

Questions about style vis-à-vis capacity have been addressed in studies in which subjects are asked to classify words or objects, and measurements are taken of the types of classification provided. Investigators have looked at several features of the classifications that people provide—e.g., whether the classifications are made in terms of exemplars, in terms of properties, or in terms of function (Gardner & Schoen, 1962; Kogan, 1974). Some studies have focused on the "goodness" of classification, defined in a particular way—e.g., the proportion of objects successfully classified or the "abstractness" of the system (Goldstein & Scheerer, 1941). The typical finding is that older people differ from younger people in more frequent use of functional classification relative to exemplar classification—that is, the older person tends to classify a coffee pot, a skillet, and a toaster as "a thing in which to make coffee," "a thing in which to fry eggs," and "a thing in which to make toast," whereas the younger person more frequently classifies the objects as "cooking utensils." Similarly the older person scores lower than does the younger person on "abstractness" and "number of objects adequately classified."

The behavior observed in classification and question-asking tasks is similar in important respects to the behavior observed in tasks that are variously referred to as indicating concept formation, concept attainment, concept awareness, problem solving, and reasoning. The attainment of concepts is a major feature of intellectual development.

Throughout ontogenetic development one forms concepts in order to comprehend and retain awareness of the welter of stimulation that constantly impinges. Words are "tags" for concepts, and so the development of language can be seen to be an important part of the development of intelligence. It is for this reason that tests of understanding of language provide measures of an important part of intelligence. Such tests indicate the products of concept attainment. They define the verbal-comprehension primary ability that is central to the measure of crystallized intelligence.

Concepts are not always tagged with words, and awareness of a word is not always a good indication of comprehension of a concept, so language development is only an indirect indication of the development of intelligence. More nearly direct measures of the capacity for attaining concepts can be obtained with concept-formation tasks. Some of these tasks pertain to features of fluid intelligence and its decline. As we grow older we seem to lose some of our capacities for concept attainment. Several qualifiers are needed to put this statement in proper perspective, however.

For one thing some reasoning tasks provide good measures of Gc, not Gf. In particular the tasks of the primary abilities identified as *general reasoning, logical evaluation, judgment,* and *experiential evaluation* are good markers for the Gc factor. Such tasks indicate the processes of concept attainment under conditions in which one may use "cultural aids" (also known as strategies and operations) (see Cattell, 1957, 1971; Horn, 1968, 1970a, 1978a). One might, for example, use mathematics—i.e., the strategies of problem solving within mathematics—to facilitate solution to a concept-formation problem. In contrast a major feature of Gf is that it is indicated by tasks in which cultural aids are not readily applied to facilitate eduction of the relationships. Thus it is not the capacity for concept attainment per se that is the essence of the distinction between Gf and Gc; rather, it is the nature of the concept attainment—in particular, whether it depends largely on use of cultural aids or on idiosyncratic techniques for educing relationships and drawing inferences.

It is interesting in this respect that the twenty-question game indicates aging decline of Gf rather than aging increase in Gc, for the game is commonly played, strategies for effectively playing it are developed in playing, and it is not unreasonable to suppose that these strategies would be learned and retained throughout adulthood. For example parents (and grandparents) commonly play the game with young children when traveling long distances by auto. As noted earlier, however, the forgetting curve for concepts and aids can decline steeply if these elements are not integrated into the knowledge system. If the strategies of the twenty-question game are not regarded as real knowledge and thus are not integrated into the knowledge system for that reason or are not frequently used and reintegrated into the knowledge system, the game can represent very nearly a novel task for most adults.

It may be relevant in this respect to consider the possibility (reported in anecdote as fact) that peak performance in games such as chess and "Go" is reached in the early years of adulthood even when the games are played intensively throughout adulthood (e.g., by professional

chess players). Performance in such games depends primarily on acculturation, but at the limits of accultural development, capacities of Gf may be the main determinants of individual differences. It seems that a principal determinant of top-notch performance in chess is a capacity for intensive concentration. Such a capacity is not unlike that considered earlier in the discussion of how a measure of concentration-on-slowness can account for some of the aging decline of both SAR and Gf.

The rise of crystallized intelligence over a substantial portion of the period of adulthood must also be considered in any comprehensive theory of development. This rise indicates that intellectual development in the adult years is not merely a matter of maintaining the status quo nor only accretion of isolated facts or simply a staving-off of pirates intent on stealing our capacities for focusing concentration and avoiding distraction. Adult development is all of these things, to be sure, but in addition it has a dynamic quality. There is growth of new and better ways of thinking.

As already noted some of the variables that indicate the dynamic features of Gc, and the growth of these features in adulthood, pertain to reasoning. Crystallized intelligence is not simply a store of knowledge: It is measured in abilities that involve use of knowledge to deal with problems and form new knowledge. These abilities indicate the outlines of how we restructure our knowledge systems. There is increase in information or in the number of nodes in our knowledge networks, and there are also changes in the means whereby information becomes accessible (see, particularly, Broadbent, 1966). The net effect is improvement in many of the abilities that are important for dealing with the problems of living.

It seems that some features of what some people mean by creativity improve with adulthood development. In the Horn et al. (1981) study correlational control with a test known as common-uses accounted for a notable amount of aging increment of crystallized intelligence. When the linear effect associated with common-uses was removed from the relationship between age and Gc, a three-point IQ improvement per decade was cut roughly in half. In the common-uses test one must propose new, and yet reasonable, ways of using everyday objects. The test is often regarded as a measure of creativity (Barron & Harrington, 1981). Although this performance itself improved only slightly with aging in the Horn et al. (1981) study, the finding that it accounted for some of the adulthood rise in Gc suggests that this latter involves capacities for generating novel conceptions of everyday events. The finding is interesting partly because an ability to generate new ways of regarding phenomena is often thought to be an exclusive feature of Gf. The finding suggests that capacities for novel reconceptualization may be features of both Gf and Gc. This view of the matter is similar to a conclusion arrived at by Kogan (1974) in his evaluation of results from classification tests (as discussed earlier in this section).

Other subprocesses of Gc that appear to improve with aging involve retrieving concepts that are similar to given concepts, comprehending arguments of the kind presented in newspaper editorials, and judging how best to deal with problems for which there are no clearly right answers but only better and worse answers.

In general the development of intelligence over the adult years is a matter of increase in some of the relation-eduction abilities and decrease in others. Perhaps these two developments are to some extent antagonistic. The tasks that define Gc indicate reasoning that enables one to attain concepts; the Gf tasks are also of this ilk. Perhaps as the former of these skills develop, there is less and less need for the latter. Many of the problems one encounters in normal, everyday living can be solved as readily by exercise of crystallized intelligence as by application of fluid intelligence. Future research should look closely at possibilities of these kinds.

SOME CONCLUDING THOUGHTS ABOUT PHYSIOLOGICAL CORRELATES

Three major lines of evidence appear to converge to suggest some interesting possibilities for further important research. The three lines are (1) evidence reviewed here indicating that aging defects in intelligence are intimately linked to losses in capacities for intense concentration and spread of attention to several activities, (2) evidence pertaining to the behavioral concomitants of damage to an area of the brain that may be rather loosely designated as the *limbic area,* and (3) evidence of age-related changes in blood flow and oxygen use in different parts of the brain, particularly the limbic area. Together these sets of data suggest that aging losses of intelligence may result, in part, from ischemic damage that shows up first, but with profound implications, in the limbic area. We have already considered the first of these lines of evidence. Let us now give brief attention to the brain-damage and blood-flow evidence.

The brain malfunctions to which we refer are not neatly pinpointed. This is true partly because people usually do not arrange to have brain damage in a nicely circumscribed area. The damage of a particular study may be described as having occurred primarily in the hippocampus, the fornix, the thalamus, the mammillary bodies, the limbic-diencephalic structures, or even the temporal lobe.

Regardless of which of these areas is said to be primarily affected (and it is recognized that usually several areas are affected in part), there is a similar ring to descriptions of the kinds of behavior that accompany the damage. In particular there is description of loss of abilities in dividing attention, encoding, organizing, concentrating, and being spontaneously alert—that is, abilities similar to those described as associated with aging decline of Gf (see Barbizet, 1963; Brion, 1969; Butters & Cremak, 1975; Drachman & Arbit, 1966; Hachinski, 1980; Jahro, 1973; Milner, 1967; Scoville & Milner, 1957; Turner, 1969). Much of the evidence suggests that damage to the hippocampus, particularly, produces behavior of the kind we have mentioned, but descriptions of Korsakoff's syndrome, in which the major damage often is thought to be in the mammillary bodies, also characteristically make reference to behavior deficits of the kind we have mentioned. In extreme cases these deficits produce an inability to learn to a point where material can be retained over periods of several minutes or hours.

Some abilities remain largely intact, however, despite the previously mentioned losses. The abilities of Gc, for example, appear to be well retained. Also the very short-term memory and apprehension abilities seem to be spared. In the reported cases the patients were able to respond to instructions and in other ways demonstrate that their immediate awareness and short-term retention capabilities were functioning. Also although some problems in recall from the distant past were reported, these did not seem to be paramount. Thus it seems that TSR may be largely unaffected.

Despite these capabilities the patients were deeply confused. This confusion was related to inability to deal effectively with relatively simple problems of comprehending relations in a manner that would permit retention and help guide future behavior. Patients could not seem to form new, even simple, concepts about time and space. A patient could be "talked through" the stages of a problem (e.g., how to get back to his/her bed) and s/he might seem to comprehend at each stage (thus suggesting that sensory detection and SAR were intact), but in the end s/he would not know how to deal with the problem.

Such behavior is similar to that observed when a subject fails to solve a matrices or letter-series problem of the fluid-intelligence factor. As different relations of such a problem are explained, the person seems to be aware of the train of thought—perhaps to comprehend particular relations. However, after several steps in the solution are explained, the person seems to draw a total blank in understanding the overall problem. The answers and the suggestions made to indicate possible answers are arbitrary (i.e., as if random) relative to any reasonable inference.

Hachinski (1980) has pointed out that the vascular anatomy of the hippocampus makes this area particularly vulnerable to a variety of injuries that can result from changes in blood pressure. He notes that

the arteries supplying the hippocampus are arranged in rake-like fashion, branching at right angles to the main trunks and penetrating the hippocampus as end arteries. This feature has led Sharrer (1940) to suggest that whereas a drop in blood pressure is distributed equally in blood vessels branching dichotomously, in the rake-like pattern of the hippocampus, the blood pressure would drop critically before this condition occurs elsewhere in the brain. Hence the hippocampus would be damaged earlier and more severely than the rest of the brain. Furthermore, Coceani and Gloor (1966) point out that the hippocampus lies in the watershed between the carotid and vertebro-basilar arteries territories; any drop in blood pressure renders the hippocampus susceptible to ischemic damage, since the blood flow would cease earliest at the branches furthest away from the blood supply. It is well established that the hippocampus is one of the areas selectively vulnerable to severe falls in blood pressure (Brierly, 1976). . . . It is possible . . . that multiple small areas of brain softenings (infarcts) may occur in patients prone to repeated bouts of profound falls in blood pressure. . . . Corsellis (1976) has noted that atherosclerosis and small infarcts are more common in the hippocampus than elsewhere in the brain. (Hachinski, 1980, p. 2)

Thus a prima facie case exists for a hypothesis that over the course of a lifetime any of a number of things can happen to bring about decreases—perhaps profound decreases—in blood pressure, which decreases would register first and most noticeably in the hippocampi and be detected in losses in the abilities to concentrate and organize information in fluid intelligence. Such events could be the incipient initiators of the cascade of neuropathology that is seen in clearcut cases of dementia, such as Alzheimer's.

This scenario cannot outline the whole story of intellectual decline, of course, and while the case is built here for the hippocampus, damage that occurs to areas other than the hippocampi may also be important. Also while encoding organization, concentration, and spontaneous alertness appear to be very central to the functioning of fluid intelligence, they are not the whole of this functioning, and several malfunctions in addition to any in the hippocampal areas could be responsible for some of the breakdowns of this form of intelligence.

This possible account of one aspect of the aging of important intellectual abilities is particularly interesting because of recent developments in the technology of measuring blood flow and oxygen consumption in the brain (e.g., Lassen, Ingvar, & Skinhøj, 1978; Yamaguchi, Meyer, Yamamoto, Sakai, & Shaw, 1980). These new methods are inobtrusive and safe (although expensive). They now make it feasible to design research that might, by direct correlation, demonstrate relations between age, the Gf abilities of concentration, and attention-distribution that appear to be affected by aging, and features of blood flow and O_2 utilization in the hippocampal regions. Existing evidence suggests that there is decrease in blood flow with age and aging injuries (Yamaguchi et al., 1980). The suggestion here is that this decrease should appear early, accumulate in the hippocampal regions, and be at the root of observed behavioral deficits associated with aging. Tests of the hypotheses that derive from this reasoning could have important practical and theoretical ramifications.

REFERENCES

ARENBERG, D., & ROBERTSON-TCHABO, E. A. Learning and aging. Pp. 421–499 in J. E. Birren & K. W. Schaie (Eds.), *Handbook of the psychology of aging.* New York: Van Nostrand Reinhold, 1977.

BALTES, P. B. Longitudinal and cross-sectional sequences in the study of age and generation effects. *Human Development,* 1968, *11,* 145–171.

BALTES, P. B. Life-span models of psychological aging: A white elephant? *Gerontologist,* 1973, *13,* 458–492.

BALTES, P. B., & SCHAIE, K. W. The myth of the twilight years. *Psychology Today,* 1974, *40,* 35–40.

BALTES, P. B., & SCHAIE, K. W. On the plasticity of intelligence in adulthood and old age: Where Horn & Donaldson fail. *American Psychologist,* 1976, *31,* 720–723.

BARBIZET, J. Defect of memorizing of hippocampal-mammillary origin: A review. *Journal of Neurology, Neurosurgery and Psychiatry,* 1963, *26,* 126–135.

BARRON, F., & HARRINGTON, D. M. Creativity, intelligence, and personality. *Annual Review of Psychology,* 1981, *32,* 439–476.

BIRREN, J. E. Age changes in speed of behavior: Its central nature and physiological correlates. Pp. 191–216 in A. T. Welford & J. E. Birren (Eds.), *Behavior, aging and the nervous system.* Springfield, Ill.: Chas. C Thomas, 1965.

BIRREN, J. E. Psychophysiology and speed of response. *American Psychologist,* 1974, *29,* 808–815.

BIRREN, J. E., BUTLER, R. N., GREENHOUSE, S. W., SOKOLOFF, L., & YARROW, M. R. (Eds.). *Human aging: A biological and behavioral study.* Washington, D.C.: U.S. Government Printing Office, 1963.

BOTWINICK, J. Aging and intelligence. Pp. 580–605 in J. E. Birren & K. W. Schaie (Eds.), *Handbook of the psychology of aging.* New York: Van Nostrand Reinhold, 1977.

BOTWINICK, J., & ARENBERG, D. Disparate time spans in sequential studies of aging. *Experimental Aging Research,* 1976, *2,* 55–66.

BOTWINICK, J., & STORANDT, M. *Memory, related functions and age.* Springfield, Ill.: Chas. C Thomas, 1974.

BRIERLY, J. B. Cerebral hypoxia. In W. Blackwood & J.A.N. Corsellis (Eds.), *Greenfield's neuropathology.* London: Arnold, 1976.

BRION, S. Korsakoff's syndrome. Clinico-anatomical and physiopathological considerations. In G. A. Talland & N. Waugh (Eds.), *The pathology of memory.* New York: Academic Press, 1969.

BROADBENT, D. E. *Perception and communication.* Oxford, England: Pergamon, 1958.

BROADBENT, D. E. The well ordered mind. *American Educational Research Journal,* 1966, *3,* 281–295.

BROADBENT, D. E., & HERON, A. Effects of a subsidiary task on performance involving immediate memory in younger and older men. *British Journal of Psychology,* 1962, *53,* 189–198.

BROMLEY, D. B. *The psychology of human aging* (2nd ed.). London: Penguin, 1966.

BUTTERS, N., & CERMAK, L. Some analyses of amnesic syndromes in brain-damaged patients. *The Hippocampus,* 1975, *2,* 377–409.

CARROLL, J. B. Defining language comprehension: Some speculations. Pp. 1–29 in R. O. Freedle & J. B. Carroll (Eds.), *Language comprehension and the acquisition of knowledge.* New York: John Wiley, 1972.

CARROLL, J. B., & MAXWELL, S. E. Individual differences in cognitive abilities. *Annual Review of Psychology,* 1979, *30,* 603–640.

CATTELL, R. B. *Personality.* New York: McGraw-Hill, 1950.

CATTELL, R. B. *Personality and motivation structure and measurement.* New York: World Book, 1957.

CATTELL, R. B. *Abilities: Their structure, growth and action.* Boston: Houghton-Mifflin, 1971.

CATTELL, R. B. The heritability of fluid, gf, and crystallized, gc, intelligence, estimated by least squares use of the MAVA method. *British Journal of Educational Psychology,* 1980, *50,* 253–265.

CLAY, H. M. The relationship between time and accuracy on similar tasks of varying complexity. *Gerontologia,* 1957, *1,* 41–49.

COCEANI, F., & GLOOR, P. The distribution of the internal carotid circulation in the brain of the macaque monkey (Macaca mulatta). *Journal of Comparative Neurology,* 1966, *128,* 419.

CORSELLIS, J.A.N. Aging and the dementias. In W. Blackwood & J.A.N. Corsellis (Eds.), *Greenfield's neuropathology.* London: Arnold, 1976.

CRAIK, F.I.M. Age differences in human memory. Pp. 384–420 in J. E. Birren & K. W. Schaie (Eds.), *Handbook of the psychology of aging.* New York: Van Nostrand Reinhold, 1977.

CRAIK, F.I.M., & LOCKHART, R. S. Levels of processing: A framework for memory research. *Journal of Verbal Learning and Verbal Behavior,* 1972, *11,* 671–684.

DEESE, J. Frequency of usage and number of words in free recall: The role of association. *Psychological Reports,* 1969, *7,* 337–344.

DeFRIES, J. C., KUSE, R. R., & VANDENBERG, S. G. Genetic correlations, environmental correlations and behavior. In J. R. Royce (Ed.), *Theoretical advances in behavior genetics.* Alphen aan den Rijn, Netherlands: Sijthoff Noordhoff International, 1979.

DENNEY, D. R., & DENNEY, N. W. The use of classification for problem solving: A comparison of middle and old age. *Developmental Psychology,* 1973, *9,* 275–278.

DONALDSON, G. Conditions of adequacy for abilities intervention studies as applied to a particular case. *Journal of Gerontology,* in press.

DRACHMAN, D. A., & ARBIT, J. Memory and the hippocampal complex. II. Is memory a multiple process? *Archives of Neurology,* 1966, *15,* 52–61.

EKSTROM, R. B., FRENCH, J. W., & HARMAN, H. H. Cognitive factors: Their identification and replication. *Multivariate Behavior Research Monographs,* 1979, No. 79.2.

ESTES, W. K., & DaPOLITO, F. Independent variation in information storage and retrieval processes in paired-associate learning. *Journal of Experimental Psychology,* 1967, *75,* 18–26.

EYSENCK, M. W. *Human memory: Theory, research and individual differences.* Oxford, England: Pergamon Press, 1977.

FERGUSON, G. A. On learning and human ability. *Canadian Journal of Psychology,* 1954, *8,* 95–112.

FERGUSON, G. A. On transfer and the abilities of man. *Canadian Journal of Psychology,* 1956, *10,* 121–131.

FOZARD, J. L. The time for remembering. Pp. 273–290 in L. W.

Poon (Ed.), *Aging in the 1980's.* Washington, D.C.: American Psychological Association, 1980.

FOZARD, J. L., THOMAS, J. C., & WAUGH, N. C. Effects of age and frequency of stimulus repetitions on two-chance reaction time. *Journal of Gerontology,* 1976, *31,* 556–563.

GARDNER, R. W., & SCHOEN, R. A. Differentiation and abstraction in concept formation. *Psychological Monographs,* 1962, *41,* 560.

GETZELS, J. W., & JACKSON, P. W. *Creativity and intelligence.* New York: John Wiley, 1962.

GOLDSTEIN, K., & SCHEERER, M. Abstract and concrete behavior. *Psychological Monographs,* 1941, *53*(No. 2), 1–28.

GRAESSER, A., & MANDLER, G. Limited processing capacity constrains the storage of unrelated sets of words and retrieval from natural categories. *Journal of Experimental Psychology: Human Learning and Memory,* 1978, *4,* 86–100.

GUILFORD, J. P. *The nature of human intelligence.* New York: McGraw-Hill, 1967.

HACHINSKY, V. Relevance of cerebrovascular changes in mental function. *Mechanisms of Aging and Development,* 1980, *10,* 1–11.

HARTLEY, J. T., HARKER, J. O., & WALSH, D. A. Contemporary issues and new directions in adult development of learning and memory. Pp. 239–252 in L. W. Poon (Ed.), *Aging in the 1980's.* Washington, D.C.: American Psychological Association, 1980.

HASHER, L., & ZACKS, R. T. Automatic and effortful processes in memory. *Journal of Experimental Psychology: General.* 1979, *108,* 356–388.

HEARNSHAW, L. S. Temporal integration and behavior. *Bulletin of British Psychological Society,* 1956, *9,* 1–20.

HEBB, D. O. *The organization of behavior: A neuropsychological theory.* New York: John Wiley, 1949.

HERRNSTEIN, R. J. *IQ in the meritocracy.* Boston: Little, Brown, 1973.

HOFFMANN, B. *The tyranny of testing.* New York: Collier, 1962.

HORN, J. L. Organization of abilities and the development of intelligence. *Psychological Review,* 1968, *75,* 242–259.

HORN, J. L. Organization of data on life-span development of human abilities. Pp. 423–466 in L. R. Goulet & P. B. Baltes (Eds.), *Life-span development psychology.* New York: Academic Press, 1970a.

HORN, J. L. Review of J. P. Guilford's "The Nature of Human Intelligence." *Psychometrika,* 1970b, *35,* 273–277.

HORN, J. L. The structure of intellect: Primary abilities. Pp. 451–511 in R. M. Dreger (Ed.), *Multivariate Personality Research.* Baton Rouge, La.: Claitor, 1972a.

HORN, J. L. State, trait and change dimensions of intelligence. *British Journal of Educational Psychology,* 1972b, *42,* 159–185.

HORN, J. L. Psychometric studies of aging and intelligence. Pp. 19–43 in S. Gershon & A. Raskin (Eds.), *Aging* (Vol. 2). Genesis and treatment of psychologic disorders in the elderly. New York: Raven, 1975.

HORN, J. L. Human abilities: A review of research and theories in the early 1970's. *Annual Review of Psychology,* 1976, *27,* 437–485.

HORN, J. L. Personality and ability theory. Pp. 139–165 in R. B. Cattell & R. M. Dreger (Eds.), *Handbook of modern personality theory.* London: Hemisphere, 1977.

HORN, J. L. Human ability systems. Pp. 211–256 in P. B. Baltes (Ed.), *Life-span development and behavior.* New York: Academic Press, 1978a.

HORN, J. L. The nature and development of intellectual abilities. Pp. 107–136 in R. T. Osborne, C. E. Noble, & N. Weyl (Eds.), *Human variation: The biopsychology of age, race and sex.* New York: Academic Press, 1978b.

HORN, J. L. Some correctible defects in research on intelligence. *Intelligence,* 1979, *3,* 307–322.

HORN, J. L. Concepts of intellect in relation to learning and adult development. *Intelligence,* 1980, *4,* 285–317.

HORN, J. L. The theory of fluid and crystallized intelligence in relation to apprehension, memory, speediness, laterality, and physiological functioning through the "vital years" of adulthood. In F.I.M. Craik & S. E. Trehub (Eds.), *Aging and cognitive processes.* New York: Plenum, 1981.

HORN, J. L., & BRAMBLE, W. J. Second order ability structure revealed in right and wrong scores. *Journal of Educational Psychology,* 1967, *58,* 115–122.

HORN, J. L., & CATTELL, R. B. Age differences in primary mental ability factors. *Journal of Gerontology,* 1966a, *21,* 210–220.

HORN, J. L., & CATTELL, R. B. Refinement and test of the theory of fluid and crystallized intelligence. *Journal of Educational Psychology,* 1966b, *57,* 253–270.

HORN, J. L., & CATTELL, R. B. Age differences in fluid and crystallized intelligence. *Acta Psychologica,* 1967, *26,* 107–129.

HORN, J. L., & DONALDSON, G. On the myth of intellectual decline in adulthood. *American Psychologist,* 1976, *31,* 701–719.

HORN, J. L., & DONALDSON, G. Faith is not enough: A response to the Baltes-Schaie claim that intelligence will not wane. *American Psychologist,* 1977, *32,* 369–373.

HORN, J. L., & DONALDSON, G. Cognitive development II: Adulthood development of human abilities. Pp. 445–529 in O. G. Brim & J. Kagan (Eds.), *Constancy and change in human development: A volume of review essays.* Cambridge, Mass.: Harvard University Press, 1980.

HORN, J. L., DONALDSON, G., & ENGSTROM, R. Apprehension, memory and fluid intelligence decline through the "vital years" of adulthood. *Research On Aging,* 1981, *3,* 33–84.

HORN, J. L., & KNAPP, J. R. On the subjective character of the empirical base of Guilford's structure-of-intellect model. *Psychological Bulletin,* 1973, *80,* 33–43.

HORN, J. L., & KNAPP, J. R. Thirty wrongs do not make a right: A reply to Guilford. *Psychological Bulletin,* 1974, *81,* 502–504.

HORN, J. L., & STANKOV, L. Auditory and visual factors of intelligence. *Intelligence,* 1981, *5.*

HOYER, W. J., & PLUDE, D. J. Attention and perceptual processes in the study of cognitive aging. Pp. 227–238 in L. W. Poon (Ed.), *Aging in the 1980's.* Washington, D.C.: American Psychological Association, 1980.

HULTSCH, D. F. Adult age differences in the organization of free recall. *Developmental Psychology,* 1969, *1,* 673–678.

HULTSCH, D. F. Adult age differences in free classification and free recall. *Developmental Psychology,* 1971, *4,* 334–342.

HULTSCH, D. F. Learning to learn in adulthood. *Journal of Gerontology,* 1974, *29,* 302–308.

HULTSCH, D., & DEUTSCH, T. *Adult development and aging: A life-span perspective.* New York: McGraw-Hill, 1981.

HUMPHREYS, L. G. Doing research the hard way: Substituting analysis of variance for a problem in correlational analysis. *Journal of Educational Psychology,* 1978, *70*(No. 6), 873–876.

HUNDAL, P. S., & HORN, J. L. On the relationship between short-term learning and fluid and crystallized intelligence. *Applied Psychological Measurement,* 1977, *1,* 11–21.

HUNT, E. Mechanics of verbal ability. *Psychological Review,* 1978, *85,* 109–130.

HUNT, E., FROST, N., & LUNNEBORG, C. Individual differences in cognition. A new approach to intelligence. Pp. 87–120 in G. Bower (Ed.), *The psychology of learning and motivation* (Vol. 7). New York: Academic Press, 1973.

JAHRO, L. Korsakoff-like amnesic syndrome in penetrating brain injury: A study of Finnish war veterans. *Acta Neurological Scandinavia Supplement,* 1973, *54,* 3–156.

JENCKS, C., SMITH, M., ACLAND, H., BANE, M. J., COHEN, D., GENTIS, H., HEYNS, B., & MICHELSON, S. *Inequality: A reassessment of the effect of family and schooling in America.* New York: Harper & Row, 1972.

JONES, H. E., CONRAD, H. S., & HORN, A. Psychological studies of motion pictures. II. Observation and recall as a function of age. *University of California Publications in Psychology,* 1928, *3,* 225–243.

KAY, H. Theories of learning and aging. Pp. 614–654 in J. E. Birren (Ed.), *Handbook of aging and the individual.* Chicago: University of Chicago Press, 1959.

KEELE, S. W. *Attention and human performance.* Santa Monica, Calif.: Goodyear, 1973.

KINTSCH, W. *Learning, memory and conceptual processes.* New York: John Wiley, 1970.

KENDLER, T. S. Cross-sectional research, longitudinal theory, and a discriminative transfer ontogeny. *Human Development,* 1979, *22,* 235–254.

KOGAN, N. Categorization and conceptualizing styles in younger and older adults. *Human Development,* 1974, *17,* 218–230.

LACHMAN, J. L., & LACHMAN, R. Age and the actualization of world knowledge. In L. W. Poon, J. L. Fozard, L. S. Germak, D. Arenberg, & L. W. Thompson (Eds.), *New directions in memory and aging.* Proceedings of the George A. Talland Memorial conference, Hillsdale, N.J., 1980.

LASSEN, N. A., INGVAR, D. H., & SKINHØJ, E. Brain function and blood flow. *Scientific American,* 1978, *239,* 62–71.

LAURENCE, M. W. Memory loss with age: A test of two strategies for its retardation. *Psychonomic Science,* 1967, *9*(No. 4), 209–210.

MADDEN, D. J., & NEBES, R. D. Aging and the development of automaticity in visual search. *Developmental Psychology,* 1980, *16,* 377–384.

MANDLER, G. Organization and memory. In K. W. Spence & J. T. Spence (Eds.), *The psychology of learning and motivation: Advances in research and theory* (Vol. 1). New York: Academic Press, 1967.

MANDLER, G. Organized recall: Individual functions. *Psychonomic Science,* 1968, *13,* 23–236.

MANDLER, G. Commentary on "Organization and memory." In G. H. Bower (Ed.), *Human memory: Basic process.* New York: Academic Press, 1977.

MARTIN, N. G. The inheritance of scholastic abilities in a sample of twins. II. *Annals of Human Genetics,* 1975, *39,* 219–229.

MASSARO, D. W. *Experimental psychology and information processing.* Skokie, Ill.: Rand McNally, 1975.

MATARAZZO, J. D. *Wechsler's measurement and appraisal of adult intelligence* (5th ed.). Baltimore, Md.: Williams & Wilkins, 1972.

MEREDITH, W. Poisson distributions of error in mental test theory. *British Journal of Mathematical and Statistical Psychology,* 1971, *21,* 49–82.

MILNER, B. Amnesia following operation on the temporal lobes. In O. L. Langwill & C.M.W. Whitty (Eds.), *Amnesia.* London: Buttersworth, 1967.

MORRISON, J. R. *Effects of time limits on the efficiency and factorial composition of reasoning measures.* Unpublished doctoral dissertation, University of Illinois, Urbana, 1960.

NESSELROADE, J. R., & BALTES, P. B. (Eds.). *Longitudinal research and study of behavior and development.* New York: Academic Press, 1979.

NORMAN, D. A. Perception, memory and mental processes. Pp. 121–144 in L. G. Nilsson (Ed.), *Perspectives in memory research.* Hillsdale, N.J.: Lawrence Erlbaum Associates, 1979.

NORMAN, D. A. *Research considerations in the assessment of the (impaired) elderly.* Conference on Cognition and Aging, Battelle Research Center, Seattle, Wash., January 1977.

NORMAN, D. A., & BOBROW, D. G. On data-limited and resource-limited processes. *Cognitive Psychology,* 1975, *7,* 44–64.

POSTMAN, L. Short-term memory and incidental learning. Pp. 146–201 in A. W. Melton (Ed.), *Categories of human learning.* New York: Academic Press, 1964.

RABBITT, P.M.A. Ignoring irrelevant information. *British Journal of Psychology,* 1964, *35,* 403–414.

RABBITT, P.M.A. An age-decrement in the ability to ignore irrelevant information. *Journal of Gerontology,* 1965, *20,* 233–238.

RABBITT, P.M.A. Changes in problem solving ability in old age. In J. E. Birren & K. W. Schaie (Eds.), *Handbook of the psychology of aging.* New York: Van Nostrand Reinhold, 1977.

RABBITT, P.M.A. Some experiments and a model for changes in attentional selectivity with old age. Pp. 82–94 in *Brain function in old age.* West Germany: Springer-Verlag, 1979a.

RABBITT, P.M.A. How old and young subjects monitor and control responses for accuracy and speed. *British Journal of Psychology,* 1979b, *70,* 305–311.

REESE, H. W. Memory development through the lifespan. In L. Montada (Ed.), *Brennpunkte der Entwicklungspsychologie.* Stuttgart: Kohlhammer, 1977.

REITAN, R. M. The distribution according to age of psychologic measure dependent upon organic brain functions. *Journal of Gerontology,* 1955, *10,* 338–340.

RESNICK, L. B., & GLASER, P. Problem solving and intelligence. Pp. 205–230 in R. L. Resnick (Ed.), *The nature of intelligence.* Hillsdale, N.J.: Lawrence Erlbaum Associates, 1976.

RIEGEL, K. F. The recall of historical events. *Behavioral Science,* 1973, *18,* 354–363.

ROSSMAN, B. B., & HORN, J. L. Cognitive, motivational and temperamental indicants of creativity and intelligence. *Journal of Educational Measurement,* 1972, *9,* 265–286.

SANFORD, A. J., & MAULE, A. J. The concept of general experience: Age and strategies in guessing future events. *Journal of Gerontology,* 1973, *28,* 81–88.

SCHAIE, K. W. Transitions in gerontology—from lab to life: Intellectual functioning. *American Psychologist,* 1974, *29,* 802–807.

SCHONFIELD, D. Memory changes with age. *Nature,* 1965, *208,* 918.

SCHONFIELD, D. Theoretical nuances and practical old questions: The psychology of aging. *Canadian Psychologist,* 1972, *13,* 252–266.

SCHULMAN, A. I. Word length and rarity in recognition memory. *Psychonomic Science,* 1967, *9,* 211–212.

SCOVILLE, W., & MILNER, B. Loss of recent memory after bilateral hippocampal lesions. *Journal of Neurology, Neurosurgery and Psychiatry,* 1957, *20,* 11.

SHAKOW, D., DOLKART, M. B., & GOLDMAN, R. The memory function in psychoses of the aged. *Disorders of the Nervous System,* 1941, *2,* 43–48.

SHARRER, E. Vascularization and vulnerability of the cornu arrmonis in the opposum. *Journal of Neurology, Neurosurgery, and Psychiatry,* 1940, *44,* 483.

SHEPARD, R. N. Recognition memory for words, sentences, and pictures. *Journal of Verbal Learning and Verbal Behavior,* 1967, *6,* 156–163.

SHIFFRIN, R. M., & SCHNEIDER, W. Controlled and automatic human information processing. II. Perceptual learning, automatic attending, and a general theory. *Psychological Review,* 1977, *84,* 127–190.

SHUCARD, D. W., & HORN, J. L. Cortical evoked potentials and measurement of human abilities. *Journal of Comparative and Physiological Psychology,* 1972, *78,* 59–68.

SPEARMAN, C. *The abilities of man.* New York: Macmillan, 1927.

SPERLING, G. The information available in brief visual presentations. *Psychological Monographs,* 1960, *74,* 498.

STANKOV, L. Fluid and crystallized and broad perceptual factors among the 11 to 12 year olds. *Journal of Educational Psychology,* 1978, *70,* 324.

STANKOV, L., & HORN, J. L. Human abilities revealed through auditory tests. *Journal of Educational Psychology,* 1980, *72,* 21–44.

STANKOV, L., HORN, J. L., & ROY, T. On the relationship between Gf/Gc theory and Jensen's Level I/Level II Theory. *Journal of Educational Psychology,* 1980, *72,* 796–809.

STERNBERG, R. J. Intelligence, information processing, and analogical reasoning: The componential analysis of human abilities. Hillsdale, N.J.: Lawrence Erlbaum Associates, 1977.

SWEET, W. H., TALLAND, G. A., & ERVIN, F. R. Loss of recent memory following section of fornix. *Transactions of the American Neurological Association,* 1959, *84,* 76–79.

THOMAS, J. C., FOZARD, J. L., & WAUGH, N. C. Age-related differences in naming latency. *American Journal of Psychology,* 1977, *90,* 499–509.

THOMAS, J.C., WAUGH, N. C., & FOZARD, J. L. Age and familiarity in memory scanning. *Journal of Gerontology,* 1978, *33,* 528–533.

THURSTONE, L. L. Primary mental abilities. *Psychometric Monographs,* Number 1. Chicago: University of Chicago Press, 1938.

TULVING, E. Episodic and semantic memory. In E. Tulving & W. Donaldson (Eds.), *Organization and memory.* New York: Academic Press, 1972.

TURNER, E. Hippocampus and memory. *Lancet,* 1969, *2,* 1123–1126.

TYLER, L. E. The psychology of human differences. Englewood Cliffs, N.J.: Prentice-Hall, 1965.

UNDHEIM, J. O., & HORN, J. L. Critical evaluation of Guilford's structure-of-intellect theory. *Intelligence,* 1977, *1,* 65–81.

VANDENBERG, S. G. The hereditary abilities study: Hereditary components in a psychological test battery. *American Journal of Human Genetics,* 1962, *14,* 220–237.

VANDENBERG, S. G. What do we know today about the inheritance of intelligence and how do we know it? In R. Cancro (Ed.), *Intelligence: Genetic and environmental influences.* New York: Grune & Stratton, 1971.

WALSH, D. A. Age differences in learning and memory. In D. S. Woodruff & J. E. Birren (Eds.), *Aging: Scientific perspectives and social issues.* New York: Van Nostrand Reinhold, 1975.

WALSH, D. A. Age differences in visual information processing. In F.I.M. Craik & S. E. Trehub (Eds.), *Aging and cognitive processes.* Boston: Plenum, 1981.

WALSH, D. A., & BALDWIN, M. Age differences in integrated semantic memory. *Developmental Psychology,* 1977, *13,* 509–514.

WALSH, D. A., & THOMPSON, L. W. Age differences in visual sensory memory. *Journal of Gerontology,* 1978, *33,* 383–387.

WAUGH, N. C., FOZARD, J. L., & THOMAS, J. C. Age-related differences in serial binary classification. *Experimental Aging Research,* 1978, *4,* 433–442.

WELFORD, A. T. *Aging and human skill.* Oxford, England: Oxford University Press, 1958.

WELFORD, A. T. Where do we go from here? In L. W. Poon (Ed.),

Aging in the 1980's. Washington, D.C.: American Psychological Association, 1980.

WILLIS, S. L., & BALTES, P. B. Intelligence in adulthood and aging: Contemporary issues. In L. W. Poon (Ed.), *Aging in the 1980's.* Washington, D.C.: American Psychological Association, 1980.

WILLOUGHBY, R. R. Incidental learning. *Journal of Educational Psychology,* 1930, *21,* 12–23.

WOODROW, H. The relation between abilities and improvement with practice. *Journal of Educational Psychology,* 1938, *29,* 215–230.

YAMAGUCHI, F., MEYER, J. S., YAMAMOTO, M., SAKAI, F., & SHAW, T. Noninvasive regional cerebral blood flow measurements in dementia. *Archives of Neurology,* 1980, *37,* 410–418.

48

Social Behavior
and Aging

BOAZ KAHANA

With the recognition that increasing numbers of older persons are living decades past retirement age, the importance of the older years has been increasingly noted within scientific circles and by the public as well. The later years are no longer seen as a brief period of physical and intellectual decline between retirement and death.

This recognition has been reflected in increased attention to the older years as part of human development. Initially life-span developmental psychology tended to focus on the study of decrements which may be viewed as the reverse side of development during the early years. With the coming of age of life-span developmental psychology came the realization that aging cannot be equated with "negative development." In terms of intrinsic change we now know that most aspects of cognitive and psychological functioning remain intact in healthy older people (Jarvik & Cohen, 1973).

The phenomenon of aging, however, takes place in a social context. Much of what we think about the effects of aging, both as individuals and as a society, is based not only on laboratory research but also on the real-life adaptations which older persons have to make to their environment and to their internal changes. The perception and attitudes held by younger people and by the aged themselves are very much a part of this process, as are the personal, social, and environmental resources available to older individuals. The focus of this chapter is on recent orientations and research on the social aspects of aging.

Social integration of the aged represents a major focus of the chapter. This broad topic of social integration subsumes the areas of social interaction and participation within the family, informal networks, and organizational participation. The focus here will be on adaptations that older persons make while navigating in the social world. The environmental, situational, and psy-

chological context of social behavior for older people will also be considered.

In exploring social behavior of the aged, the effort will be to identify meaningful issues, concepts, and theoretical frameworks in light of empirical research evidence. The orientation of the chapter is interdisciplinary, drawing heavily on the work of sociologists and social psychologists but also keeping in mind special concerns of life-span developmental psychology.

Life-span developmental theory contends that personality and behavior continue to evolve in the adult years. If indeed such development takes place, the question arises whether it is intrinsic to the aging process or merely a correlate of life events which usually accompany the later years. Thus loss of spouse and of significant others, physical decline, increased incidence of chronic illness, and loss of adequate income could precipitate change in personality and in social behavior. Thus gerontologists have come to distinguish between *biological, psychological,* and *sociological* aging (Birren, 1964). One may argue that whatever differences in personality or behavior may be found at different points in the adult life span may be the result of losses and changes of status rather than of the aging process per se. These changes need not occur if physical and social losses may be prevented or ameliorated by therapy or through environmental change.

Social and personal constraints during the later years may alter or limit social behavior. In fact studies of social gerontologists have traditionally concerned themselves with the vulnerable older person. Nevertheless a perusal of the most recent research on life satisfaction and life styles of older persons reveals that the later years present many new opportunities and that most elderly individuals can look forward to gratifying social experiences (Larson, 1978).

The age-old controversy regarding the relative roles of environment and heredity may be revisited in evaluating social behavior of the aged. We may also view changes in social behavior as they relate to life history or environmental and situational influences in the adaptations to aging.

Social behavior in the later years, just as in youth, is governed by two important vectors: personal characteristics as they have unfolded through the life cycle (Beck & Leviton, 1976) and the special situations in which the aged find themselves. The issue of personality development in later life is specifically addressed elsewhere in this volume. It is relevant to note here, however, that the later years have been associated with increasing introversion, cautiousness (Botwinick, 1973), rigidity and lack of flexibility (Schaie & Strother, 1968), and a shift from active to passive mastery (Gutmann, 1969). Some of the critical individual underpinnings of social behavior will be touched upon here. While the writer generally agrees with others in the field of gerontology who have emphasized the basic continuity of self throughout the life cycle, he also ventures to explore discontinuities of age both as opportunities and as stresses. We will therefore consider the elderly who survive psychologically through life events which bring discontinuity and those who seek a brand-new life style in later life. Social groups may be viewed as providing the individual with a sense of self during his/her early development and as serving important functions in maintaining his/her sense of self during the later years. Even when older persons experience a lifelong series of discontinuities, the family and the ethnic or cultural group can help buttress a sense of identity through these discontinuities (Myerhoff, 1978).

SOCIAL INTEGRATION VERSUS ISOLATION

Social integration may be viewed as a basic process through which the individual finds a sense of meaning outside of him/herself by getting involved in a group. Such integration has been postulated as an important prerequisite of adjustment in the later years (Maddox, 1963).

On a societal level lack of social integation may be viewed as a major source of the low status and diminished power of the aged. In his original formulation regarding the elderly, Parsons (1949) contended that in comparison with other societies the United States isolates the aged from participation in the most important social structures and interests. Dowd (1972) has examined the situation of the elderly in contemporary U.S. society from a vantage point of exchange theory. He suggests that this decreased social interaction is the eventual result of a series of exchange relationships in which the relative power of the aged vis-à-vis their social environment is gradually diminished until all that remains of their power resources is the humble capacity to comply.

Rosow (1967), in his treatise of the social integration of the aged, contends that with the loss of social roles and memberships the social participation of the elderly is increasingly channeled from formal to informal organizations and is diminished in scope. Social participation of the elderly is thus increasingly directed toward informal groups of family members, relatives, friends, and neighbors.

On an individual level empirical studies have generally supported the notion that social integration in its various forms has a positive relationship with morale and/or well-being. It is important to note, however, that definitions of both social integration and the adjustment factors to which it is related vary widely. Thus social integration of the aged has been defined in terms of organizational participation, social activity, social networks, residential integration, and friendship patterns. Adjustment, in turn, has been defined as morale, life satisfaction, happiness, competence, environmental satisfaction, or even as positive mental health.

George (1980) distinguishes between social networks and social support systems. While the former are seen as reflecting patterns of social involvement, the latter are composed of individuals who may provide support at times of stress. Social-support networks operate either based on a sense of obligation (formal service providers) or on a sense of affection (family and friends) or at times on both. Maintenance of meaningful social ties is likely to promote the development of social-support networks. Thus the individual who has isolated him/ herself from social interaction and who has seldom provided help to others is unlikely to receive assistance during times of need.

In terms of integration into an informal social network, studies by Lowenthal and Haven (1968), Mariwaki (1973), and Beck and Leviton (1976) have all found significant relationships between having a confidante or significant other and positive adjustment in diverse populations. Edwards and Klemmack (1973) found morale to be significantly related to social interaction with persons outside of the family but observed no significant relationship between family interactions and morale.

Hochschild (1975) has argued that social integration has not been adequately conceptualized in gerontological research and cautions against the use of "umbrella" variables such as disengagement, which classify numerous distinct phenomenan under one title. Futhermore social-integration research typically considered only objective indices of integration. Accordingly Lowenthal and Robinson (1976) contend that subjective and objective social factors need to be considered simultaneously in order to understand the effects of integration versus isolation on adjustment of older persons. In recent research the subjective meaning of integration to the older individual has been demonstrated to serve as an important mediator between objective aspects of integration and morale (Liang, Dvorkin, Kahana, & Mazian, 1980). Based on a survey of 402 urban aged in Michigan and 961 older persons in North Carolina, these authors found morale to be significantly related to the individual's subjective sense of integration, even when other factors such as socioeconomic status, financial satisfaction, and health status were held constant.

Family and Kin Relations

Until the early 1960s sociologists had described the typical U.S. family as consisting of nuclear units including grown children and their adult parents (Parsons, 1949; Sussman, 1953). This position has been revised, however, based on later research which has demonstrated that the extended family does operate even where residential arrangements are limited to the nuclear family. Students of aging have consistently pointed to the maintenance of close ties between the elderly and family members as well as friends and neighbors (Litwak, 1964; Lowenthal, 1964; Shanas, 1962; Streib, 1970; Troll, 1979).

Data on kinship patterns points to considerable interaction between the aged and their families. Adult children are the major providers of emotional support for their parents, especially their widowed parents (Lopata, 1973). Emotional support for the nonmarried elderly population emanates from family and friendship networks (Kahana, 1974; Rosow, 1967). In terms of assistance in everyday issues of living, the elderly receive most of their help from children and other relatives and from friends and neighbors. The peer group is the major source of companionship for the elderly, followed by adult children and family (Rosow, 1967; Shanas et al., 1968). Literature on the aged as providers of supports and help exist but is sparse (Harel, Kahana, & Felton, 1972). Cantor (1979) considered helping networks of the elderly in the inner city of New York and presented findings indicating that a viable, informal support network exists among a significant portion of the elderly in this area. The network is composed of (in the order of importance) kin, friends, and neighbors. Major findings provide evidence of reciprocity in exchanges of the aged with kin with friends and neighbors. In considering the implications of her study for provision of formal services, Cantor argues that the preferences of the elderly for obtaining aid from friends and neighbors does not negate the acceptance by the elderly and their families of public service.

The importance of companionship for older persons has been illustrated in the work of McKain (1969). In his research on couples who married during their later years, the most frequently given reason for marrying was a desire for companionship. This "companionship" motive, however, needs greater scrutiny since many of this age cohort may find it unacceptable to verbalize feelings of love and intimacy as influencing marriage in the later years.

The incidence of widowhood is far greater among women (because of higher mortality rates of older men and age differences between couples). Nevertheless due to the increasing longevity rates and to earlier marriages, more and more couples survive jointly to old age (Shanas, 1965).

Social and Organizational Participation

Organizational participation reflects a measure of integration into formal organizations. Numerous studies have pointed to a positive relationship between organizational membership or participation and diverse indices of morale. Early studies in this area were those by Burgess (1954), Havighurst and Albrecht (1953), and Pihlblad and McNamara (1965). Later work by Palmore and Luikart (1972) also supported the notion that involvement in social activity has a positive effect on life satisfaction.

Social Isolation and Disengagement

Studies linking social involvement, integration, and well-being among the aged are numerous. However, much less is known about the effects of social isolation on the elderly (Lowenthal & Robinson, 1976). Considerable research evidence reveals that there is an age-related decline in social interaction and in a variety of social contacts (Riley & Foner, 1968). Self-initiated reduction in social interaction may take place in terms of "sloughing off" of unwanted relationships in the later years (Lowenthal, Thurner, & Chiriboga, 1975). A similar phenomenon has been observed by Kahana and Kahana (1980) among residents of retirement communities who report among the advantages of long-distance migration the ability to leave behind unwanted social relationships—e.g., problem children, difficult neighbors, or a divorced spouse. This type of freedom to rid oneself of unwanted social relationships or to substitute new ones should be distinguished from the type of mutual withdrawal between the older individual and society which has been posited by classical disengagement theory (Cumming & Henry, 1961). Lowenthal and Robinson (1976), in their reviews of studies of social networks and isolation among the aged, cite the important distinctions among isolation, loneliness, and aloneness.

The desire for privacy represents another relevant concept in considering the social life of the older person. It is generally assumed that privacy represents an important liability of congregate living arrangements. A study by Kiyak, Kahana, and Fairchild (1977), however, demonstrated that it is not the actual amount of privacy available but rather the congruence between privacy desired and opportunities for privacy that predicts morale in homes for the aged.

Empirical Evidence Regarding Disengagement

The classical theoretical controversy related to social behavior of the aged revolves around the relative roles of activity versus disengagement in characterizing older persons and in predicting well-being in later years. The disengagement theory of aging (Cummings & Henry, 1961) has been predicated on a notion of mutual withdrawal between the aged and society. Such withdrawal has been seen as both normative and desirable. Numerous studies have been generated by the disengagement-activity theory. None has been able to either substantiate or conclusively dismiss the original formulations, but most have pointed to the need for more complex formulations in considering the relationship between disengagement and well-being (Hochschild, 1975). Havighurst, Neugarten, and Tobin (1968) demonstrated that personality is an important intervening variable between activity and morale. Lemon, Bengtson, and Peterson (1972) explored tenets of the activity theory among new residents of a retirement community. Activity per se was not found to be significantly related to life satisfaction. Neither was frequency of social interaction found by these investigators to relate to life satisfaction, but belonging to an informal friendship network was found to be a significant predictor.

The distinction between voluntary and involuntary

withdrawal is an important one if we are to understand social behavior of the aged (Lowenthal & Boler, 1975). Accordingly, Kahana (1965a) found that older persons who retired voluntarily portrayed less expansiveness on intrapsychic measures than did those who retired against their will.

SELF-CONCEPTIONS OF THE AGED

Self theories have argued that one's self-concept is built on the views, perceptions, and attitudes that others hold of one's behavior, value, and character (Mead, 1934). At any one life stage we may view the self-concept as the function of personal characteristics, traits (biological, cognitive, and personality), and stage-related expectations of the culture. Allport (1961) has viewed the self as an internal integrating structure which gives organization and purpose to one's behavior. Reference groups of the aged importantly include their own former selves as well as others of similar ages. Rose (1965) calls this the "subculture of the aged." Different types of social conditions may necessitate playing different social roles. Acting according to social and role prescription may be seen as self-deception according to some existential theories (Beck & Leviton, 1976). At later stages of life according to this view, attachments to society diminish, and the real self may emerge. With old age this becomes a period of maximal self-actualization.

In a recent survey which the author conducted on 483 older persons living in a Florida retirement community, older persons expressed optimism about their own changing status, with 80 percent indicating that their status has improved (Kahana, Kahana, & McLenigan, 1980). The majority of community-dwelling older persons identify with an image of "young-old," with less than 10 percent considering themselves young or elderly. While self-concepts of these aged were generally good, a certain degree of mistrust of one's own age cohort is nonetheless discernible. Thus over one-fourth of the respondents reported that they would not want a person over age 65 to become president of the United States (Kahana et al., 1980).

It has been suggested by a number of studies that stereotypes of aging and negative attitudes are shared by older persons who apparently accept negative cultural expectations and endorse stereotypes as applied to themselves (Tuckman & Lorge, 1953). Some recent data indicate, however, that the aged devalue their own age far less than the young and middle-aged devalue it (Kahana, Kahana, & Kiyak, 1979). Furthermore it has been argued that persons who have held positive self-concepts throughout life are far less likely to accept negative stereotypes of old age than are persons with a less secure self-concept. Even those elderly who endorse negative views of their cohorts tend to view themselves more favorably than they view other members of their age group.

Attitudes of the elderly toward themselves differ based on age, sex, geographic location, and a host of other factors. Among urban aged the old-old have been found to be more satisfied and to have a more positive self-image, whereas there were few differences among groups in rural areas (Youman, 1977). The elderly who suffer the most

from old age are those who see themselves as very old, in poor health, and a burden to others and who are socially isolated. Research has debunked many of the myths of aging. There is sufficient evidence to show that as people age they do not normally become disengaged, rigid, or senile. In contrast to the portrait of the timid aged who are afraid to take risks, many elderly in fact voluntarily undertake major changes in their life patterns. There are increasing numbers of "adventurous" aged who adopt new careers, residences, and life styles during late life (Kahana et al., 1980). For a long time the public, even many gerontologists viewed age as a great homogenizer. However, it is now recognized that tremendous variability exists among the aged. The search for an optimal environment or program for all older people cannot be very useful. The real challenges for those seeking to understand and assist older persons is in developing increased options and life styles for our increasing and diverse older population (who after all will be us in the future).

ATTITUDES TOWARD THE AGED

Attitudes held by young people toward the elderly serve as an important social context for behavior of the elderly and their self-concept. It is important to consider commonly held attitudes and stereotypes about the aged in order to understand their social behavior. It is also likely to define social opportunities open to older persons. Thus if older persons are commonly viewed as reclusive, this will likely diminish social interactions initiated with the aged. The study of attitudes of individuals who provide direct services to the elderly is even more critical from a very practical orientation. Thus it has been demonstrated that the care and treatment of the elderly is mediated by attitudes of staff working with older clients. It has been shown in several studies that stereotyped attitudes toward the aged result in negative staff behavior (Davis, 1968; Jaeger & Simmons, 1970; Schwartz, 1974).

However, other studies have shown, surprisingly enough, that stereotypic attitudes produce a greater desire to work with the aged. Campbell (1971) found a greater willingness to work with the aged among those with stereotyped attitudes; however, these studies did not evaluate the effectiveness of workers with stereotyped attitudes in dealing with the elderly. Troll and Schlossberg (1970) found an "age bias" among members of various helping professions (counselors, psychologists). Most preferred to work with young clients and were less inclined to work with the aged.

Some evidence indicates that increased social contact with the aged improves attitudes. Others argue that merely more information about them is obtained, but little positive feeling or desire for further interaction is generated. One important issue for evaluating the significance of holding negative attitudes is the relationship between attitudes toward the elderly and actual behaviors. Based on findings of numerous studies from within and outside the field of aging, the relationship between attitudes and overt behaviors is at best modest. Results of many early studies (conducted before 1971) pointed to older persons as ill and devoid of energy and sexual interest. The aged were also often portrayed as grouchy, defensive, withdrawn, and living with self-pity. Their activities were seen as limited and unproductive, except for religious participation. They were viewed as deficient in resources and as largely dependent on the younger generation. Considering that many of the studies reflecting such negative attitudes and stereotypes toward the aged were based on opinions of well-educated persons, it is not likely that the general population hold more positive views. Nevertheless some positive attitudes and stereotypes regarding the aged have also come to light. The elderly have thus been perceived as wiser and more stable than other age groups. It is interesting to note that in a broad array of surveys the same set of personality dimensions has been designated by respondents as distinguishing different age groups.

Threatening aspects of old age are revealed in some studies which showed that to young persons old age is unpleasant, dangerous, and lacking in value. Perceived conflict between generations was revealed in other attitude studies during the 1950s and 1960s. Thus young people viewed the aged as resentful of the young and suggested that they would prefer to limit contact with the old. It is ironic in this context that, typically, each generation overestimates the gap between itself and others and tends to think that other groups view them more negatively.

Most studies of attitudes toward the aged have been based on groups of college students who are an accessible group for study. Other studies have focused specifically on service providers, while a third group of studies sought to unravel the development of attitudes by focusing on young children. At a different level of analysis some studies have sought to explore cultural manifestations of social attitudes toward the aged.

One study conducted by the author examined how people of different ages view one another. People of different ages, representing childhood (9 to 11 years), adolescence (15 to 17 years), young adults (20 to 25 years), mid-adulthood (30 to 40 years), and the elderly (65+ years), were asked to rate all ages as well as themselves on dimensions of hopefulness, activity, independence, involvement, heartiness, stability, and wisdom.

Young adulthood was almost unanimously regarded as the most desirable age, followed by middle adulthood and by adolescence. Old age was seen as most undesirable by everyone, including the elderly. The elderly were seen as hopeless, helpless, passive, uninvolved, and fragile (although also wise and stable). Interestingly people viewed themselves as better off than others of the same age (Kahana, 1970).

Among children there is some evidence that children from lower socioeconomic backgrounds hold more negative views of the aged. The commonly held notion that as children get older they hold more negative views of the aged, however, has not been conclusively demonstrated.

Cross-cultural studies have found that attitudes toward the aged are more favorable in primitive societies and tend to get worse with modernization. It has been argued (Cowgill, 1972) that the status of the aged is highest in those societies where they continue to perform useful and valued functions. Aged persons were also respected where they hold useful information for their society. In modern industrial societies, however, the aged have been increasingly excluded from many meaningful social roles. Retirement and loss of friends and family members also often lead to social isolation for many aged individuals.

One must recognize, however, that people do not live to very old ages in primitive societies, and the small number of older individuals reduces competition for social resources. Studies of literature suggest that portrayals of the aged have become somewhat more negative during the 90 years between 1870 and 1960. In all, however, negative historical changes were found to be less marked than one would expect.

ATTITUDES OF OLDER PERSONS TOWARD THE YOUNG

In focusing on attitudes of society and of members of the younger generation toward the old, we must not neglect to consider reciprocal attitudes: those of the old toward younger persons. Very few studies have specifically explored this relationship. We have learned, nevertheless, that these attitudes are influenced by the older person's life satisfaction and by his/her present or past relationship with his/her children (Cyrus & Monk, 1972). It has been argued that individuals with high levels of life satisfaction may have less need to release frustration through aggression and may be more accepting toward others. Furthermore those with positive family ties may generalize these positive feelings toward others. When we consider perceptions within the framework of the family, the older generation tends to minimize "generational differences" and, unlike the younger family members, often overestimates the extent of family closeness. Adult children also report more family disagreements than do members of the parent generation. These data tend to support the view that attitudes of older persons toward the young are more favorable than are reciprocal attitudes by the young.

Changing Attitudes

Recent studies indicate that some of the negative stereotypes of aging among young people seem to be breaking down. In a classic study conducted in 1959, older people were viewed in negative and distant terms. Students tended to feel sorry for the aged. Depression was frequently seen as characteristic of the aged. The fear of dying was seen as their greatest fear while their kindness was seen as their best feature. A follow-up study of a similar student group in 1974 reveals a far more interactive view. Friendship with the aged is now a frequent theme. While in 1959 the suggestion of sitting next to an aged person on a bus brought responses like "I wouldn't mind," in 1974 the typical student response suggests striking up a conversation and getting to know the older person. Another very significant change is the changing view from having seen the aged as sexless in 1959 to a recognition that sex can be an important and pleasurable part of an older person's life (Kahana, 1975b).

Kahana's (1975b) survey found generally favorable images of the elderly among medical students. An open-ended format was used asking respondents to use three words to describe men and women of various age groups. Most used similar adjectives for all age groups: *happy, friendly, stable, responsible.* Other words were unique to the

70-year-old: *dependent, reflective, wide, lonely, morbid.* Using the sentence-completion technique of eliciting attitudes toward the elderly revealed rather positive views. To the stem "working with elderly people is _____" most said "rewarding," "interesting," and "pleasing," although some used the adjectives, "difficult," "trying," and "sad." Other sentence-completion items ("When I'm with an older person, I _____") produced equally favorable responses ("try to listen," "pay attention," "talk to him," "try to relate").

More positive perceptions of older people have also emerged from studies of children than those reflected in earlier studies. Recent studies found far more favorable attitudes toward the aged on the part of school children than had emerged in studies done seven years prior. Children's impressions of the elderly were found to be more positive and more flexible than had been previously thought.

Another study in 1973 has found uniformly positive attitudes toward the aged by groups of school children and college students. In two recent experimental studies, college students rated elderly persons more favorably than they rated younger persons. In a 1975 study by the National Council on Aging which used random nationwide samples of young and old, more positive than negative attitudes toward the aged were found.

One reason for recent changes toward more positive attitudes may be a new tolerance which has come about regarding various minority groups in society, including the aged. There may also be an increased awareness of the potentials, as well as the plight, of the elderly in our society.

SOCIAL BEHAVIOR AND WELL-BEING OF THE AGED

The disengagement theory, as originally posed, suggested that older persons who are less involved in social relationships and responsibilities and those who have fewer attachments would have higher morale (Cumming & Henry, 1961). The social life space of older persons is seen as shrinking due to retirement, widowhood, death of friends, and children leaving the home. This shrinking of social life space is also seen to be paralleled by psychological withdrawal. The disengagement theory has been widely criticized both on conceptual grounds (Hochschild, 1975) and on empirical findings supporting the importance of activity in promoting psychosocial well-being. The initial evidence supporting the value of activity comes from studies of Havighurst et al. (1968) based on a reanalysis of the original Kansas City studies of adult life on which the disengagement theory was based. In the following years the disengagement theory has generated an extensive literature which attempted to, and succeeded in, refuting it.

Recently Palmore (1979) presented data exemplifying this trend and supporting the activity theory. He utilized data from the first Duke Longitudinal Study of Aging. He defined successful aging as "survival to age 75 with good health and happiness." The author presents findings supporting the activity theory. Two of the strongest explanatory predictors of successful aging for both men and women were group activity and physical activity.

The value of social behaviors in the later years may be best understood by considering relationships of various forms of social interaction and participation as possible determinants of morale and life satisfaction of the aged.

Larson (1978) has reviewed the last 30 years of research on life satisfaction, morale, and related constructs. He reveals a consistent body of findings: Subjective well-being is most strongly related to health, socioeconomic factors, and the degree of social interaction in older populations. Based on the study of 109 males and 192 females, age 65 and over, from a national probability sample, Medley (1976) underscored the importance of family-life satisfaction for life-satisfaction as a whole. The study points out the value of examining interrelationships among variables using a path-analytic model. Markides and Martin (1979) applied path analysis to data from interviews with 141 persons, 60 years and older, with predictor variables: self-reported health, income, education, and activity index. The results indicated that for both sexes activity was strongly related to life satisfaction. Income was found to be only indirectly significant via activity. Education was found to be the least significant variable. Medley's use of "health satisfaction, with standard of living and satisfaction with family life" as determinants of satisfaction with life in general has been questioned however. Conner, Powers, and Bultena (1979) studied the role of social interaction in affecting life satisfaction. Their results show that "the number of persons interacted with" and "frequency" of interaction in and of themselves have little importance. Controlling for the effects of income, health, and status produced significant relationships between life satisfaction and (1) the number of siblings and other relatives seen; (2) exclusivity in scope of interaction with immediate family members; and (3) exclusivity in scope of interaction with siblings and other relatives. These results prompted the authors to suggest that it is the quality of the interactions rather than the quantity that is the important determinant of life satisfaction. Similarly a study by Mancini (1979) stressed the role of quality of family interaction in influencing well-being and results of this study indicated that qualitative variables, such as "perceptions concerning marital satisfaction and effectiveness and involvement as a spouse or parent" are strongly related to morale rather than the quantitative variables. These authors suggest that the helping professions begin to see the aged as having "the potential for more productive relationships" and work to strengthen the family relationships of the elderly.

In reviewing the literature concerning the social determinants of life satisfaction among older people, there is a growing recognition of the need to measure more adequately the complex interrelationships of various determinants of well-being and morale in the elderly. Such a trend is seen in the call for the application of more sophisticated multivariate and path-analysis techniques to past, present, and future studies. There is also a growing awareness of the importance of operationalizing qualitative variables such as the quality of social interactions rather than merely their quantity. This is seen in the studies on social supports for the elderly which question the roles and desirability of both informal and formal support systems.

Adaptation

Although the importance of adaptive strategies for psychosocial well-being is implicit in theories of personality (Hall & Lindsey, 1970), there has been relatively little specific research exploring adaptive strategies of older people. Until recently conceptualizations of adaptation tended to be fragmented. Styles of coping were often equated with personality traits and were seldom differentiated from success of coping or adjustment (Kahana, 1975a; Moos, 1974). Furthermore environmental demands for coping or constraints on coping were seldom considered. The emphasis of most investigations seeking to understand adjustment has been on the individual (Busse & Pfeiffer, 1969; Butler, 1968; Lieberman, 1969; Lowenthal, 1971; Reichard, Livson, & Peterson, 1962) or on the environment (Carp, 1974; Kahana & Kahana, 1970; Lawton, 1979; Lowenthal et al., 1975; Pincus, 1968).

Consideration of individual adaptation has not only included the personality dimension but also the individual-response dimension (Lazarus, Averill, & Opton, 1974). The importance of the individual-response dimension for understanding coping revolves around the difficulty in interpreting seeming contradictions in response patterns and then inferring from these samples of coping behavior a total pattern of coping. Personality measures have been the the focus of Lieberman and Cohler's (1976) attempt to measure adaptive strategies. Assessments of relevant personality characteristics include such dimensions as locus of control, frustration tolerance, affective equilibrium, and defense mechanisms called upon in response to stressful circumstances. Focus on the effects of environmental influences on adaptation has included diverse ecological variables. This may be represented by the effects of physical environment (e.g., climate), the suprapersonal environment (age integration), and situation factors (e.g., type of problem to be dealt with). Within gerontology, examples of this orientation may be seen in studies of institutional factors as they affect adaptation (Kahana & Kahana, 1970) or readjustment to housing environments (Carp, 1974; Lawton, 1975). Only recently has there been a trend in the study of adaptation to recognize the interaction of individual and environmental characteristics (Hamburg, Coelho, & Adams, 1974; Kahana & Kahana, 1979; Lawton, 1975; Lazarus, Averill, & Opton, 1974; Mechanic, 1974).

Within the psychological literature, coping has been regarded as an individualized defense or way of handling threats aroused in individualized situations (Lazarus et al., 1974). Many of the psychological measurement approaches have emerged from recent developments in personality theory (Moos, 1974) which have emphasized personal striving toward environmental mastery and competence and emphasized an adaptative-ego process (Erikson, 1950; Hartmann, Kris, & Lowenstein, 1949; White, 1959).

Psychologists studying adaptation have focused on processes for handling both everyday life stresses and major life crises and transitions (Allser, 1968). Haan (1963) distinguished between adaptive strategies characterized by a quality of positive problem solving (i.e., coping) and strategies which are essentially maladaptive (i.e., defenses). Allser (1968), in elaborating on Haan's model, suggests that coping is flexible, differentiated, reality oriented, purposive, effective and permissive of open, ordered impulsive satisfaction. In contrast, defensive behavior is seen as rigid, essentially distorting, maladaptive and permissive of impulse gratification by subterfuge. Both kinds of ego functioning are assumed to handle conflicts.

In considering these conceptualizations one questionable assumption is that appropriate need gratification is typically within the individual's control. Thus it may be seen as far more functional to change one's undesirable environment in order to obtain gratification than to deny existing problems. In the case of elderly persons whose personal and environmental options may be severely limited, the demarcation between coping and defensive behavior may be blurred.

Within sociology Mechanic (1974) has focused on the fit between social structure and environmental demands as influencing coping behavior and has emphasized the importance of culturally provided adaptive strategies. Lazarus et al. (1974) stress a broad range of problem-solving efforts exercised by people in response to environmental demands. Both Lazarus et al. (1974) and Hamburg et al. (1974) consider the concept of adaptive tasks as useful in providing a more thorough view of adaptation. It should be noted, however, that much of the work cited before is limited to presentation of conceptual frameworks without empirical investigations to test the utility of the concepts proposed. Conceptual schemes for the study of coping have been presented by sociologists, especially in the framework of hospitals and other "total institutions." Thus Goffman (1959) and Merton (1957) offer four essential patterns of coping with institutional environments. These include (1) withdrawal, (2) aggression (3) integration, and (4) acquiescence. While most of these discussions lack empirical validation, they have helped to provide a framework for the study of adaptation.

Pearlin and Schooler's (1978) work has been a major attempt within the field of sociology to study adaptive processes empirically. Pearlin and Schooler argue that coping behavior is normatively learned from groups to which people belong. One may, therefore, fruitfully use concepts such as *norms, values,* and *social rituals* for understanding individual coping behavior. Thus one can look outside of traditional psychological profiles for understanding the etiology of coping behavior. For the aged social expectation in norms and statuses are drastically changed. Coping behavior may be seen as a most sensitive index of the changed status of older persons in society.

Pearlin and Schooler's (1978) conceptualization directly ties coping to problematic life circumstances or social-role conflicts. They attempt to specify the array of coping mechanisms which people use to deal with these problems and also seek to assess the efficiency of various coping strategies. Lastly using a sociological model they suggest linkages between social characteristics of persons and their coping behavior. The importance of sex and socioeconomic status for coping strategies is stressed.

In another empirical study of adaptation using a structural framework similar to Merton's, Sharma and Kahana (1977) examined sex differences in adaptation patterns of urban ethnic aged using Merton's theoretical framework of typologies of adaptation. Structural constraints on the use of socially endorsed means of activity and socially endorsed goals of morale were examined in operationalizing Merton's adaptive modes of conformity, ritualism, innovation, and retreatism.

Existing studies in gerontology have often focused on adaptation as an outcome (Carp, 1974; Lieberman & Cohler, 1976). Adaptation is considered to be similar to adjustment—a product—rather than reflecting the process of trying to adjust. Although some of these authors define adaptation in terms of behavioral or intrapsychic *processes*, their techniques of assessment are closer to definitions of *outcome*—well-being, mental health, emotional equilibrium—rather than focusing on the process by which these ends may be achieved.

Within gerontology Lawton and Nahemow (1973) and Carp (1974) have developed theoretical approaches which view adaptation as a response to the environment. Lowenthal et al. (1975) studied adaptation in response to major life transitions and focused on personal control as a major aspect of adaptation. They have focused on typologies on adaptation to life transitions, while Quayhagen and Chiriboga (1976) have considered antecedents of different styles of adaptation among institutionalized aged.

Gerontological research on adaptation patterns of the aged has also used theoretical perspectives of activity and of disengagement (Stephens, 1976). Some studies have suggested that personality types provide more informative predictions of various patterns of adaptation (Neugarten, 1964; Reichard, Livson, & Peterson, 1962). Various styles of aging were also analyzed in terms of their adaptive value in the cross-cultural work of Goldstein and Gutmann (1972) and Gutmann (1969).

Having reviewed a number of conceptual approaches to the study of adaptation, the question still remains: How can the older person successfully cope with situations and settings which may be incongruent with his/her needs and expectations? The disadvantages of the older years in terms of reduced income, frequently impaired health, and loss of social roles reduce the options and choices available to the older person in maintaining or finding an environment in keeping with his/her preferences. Major discontinuities with earlier life patterns often occur and pose major challenges to adaptive strategies of the older person. Typical examples of such discontinuities are retirement, widowhood, and institutionalization. How can the older person handle the disruption of his/her previous life style and the frustration inherent in the reduced options which result from aging?

Based on Lewin's (1935) theoretical formulations and appraisal of prior research evidence, four *generalized* or *typical styles* of handling noncongruence or discontinuity between older persons' expectations and needs and the environment have been postulated by Kahana and Kahana (1979). In an ongoing longitudinal study, coping strategies of older persons are considered in terms of instrumental, cognitive restructuring; effective and escape approaches to problem solving; and self reported inability to cope with stress.

The adaptive strategies marshaled by the older person may be seen on the one hand as rooted in earlier types of adaptation and coping; on the other hand, coping strategies may be reponsive to changing demands of the environment. Thus they may be viewed as having both *trait-like* and *dynamic* components.

Although adaptive strategies are often outlined as typologies, it should be recognized that they overlap and that all individuals will engage in a variety of coping methods.

The variables of adaptation and coping have been recognized as valuable conceptual tools in understanding how persons deal with stresses and daily problems by both psychologists and sociologists. In fact Pearlin and Schooler (1978) have suggested that the study of adaptation may represent a potentially useful point of convergence in sociological and psychological approaches for understanding the functioning and well-being of older persons.

Environmental Context of Social Behavior

If we are to understand social behavior of the aged, it is important to understand the context in which this occurs. Several formulations have been proposed in focusing on the special transaction between environmental and situational factors in the later years and social behavior.

A broad environmental context for enhancing or constraining social behaviors of the aged may be found in the community in which they live. In this setting the residential environment exerts the most direct influence on social behavior.

To the extent that personal financial resources of the aged diminish, the impact of their environment becomes especially important. Lawton (1980) has termed this phenomenon of increasing environmental susceptibility of the vulnerable aged the *environmental docility hypothesis*. This phenomenon is likely to increase in importance in future years as the vulnerable old–old aged represent the fastest growing segment of the U.S. population. Older persons who live in crime-ridden neighborhoods are likely to limit their social interactions and limit their activities to remain within their homes as much as possible. Fear of victimization has been shown to have an even greater impact on social life space of older persons than have the actual crime rates or the actual personal experience of crime. Furthermore neighborhood problems play a major role among social problems reported by the urban aged (Kahana, Liang, Felton, Fairchild, & Harel, 1977), surpassing in importance both reported discrimination and problems with governmental and social agencies. Use of resources by the aged within a given neighborhood has been found to be associated with distance from the resources (Newcomer, 1975). Friendship formations have also been affected by physical proximities (Lawton & Simon, 1968), with best friends in new housing developments for the aged most likely to be neighbors living next door or across the hall. Lack of environmental satisfaction represents a major reason for relocation of the aged (Mezneck, Liang, & Kahana, 1980).

Classification of Environments Relevant in Social Behaviors

Lawton (1980) has provided a classification scheme of environments which is useful for consideration of the impact of environments on social behavior. The *personal environment* refers to significant others surrounding or available to the older person. The *group environment* refers to social phenomena exerted by the environment which transcend individual characteristics of persons or physical attributes of the milieu. These include social norms, reference groups, or group pressures for conformity. The *suprapersonal environment* refers to the aggregate characteristics of persons in a given environment—e.g., age concentration or cultural background. The *social environment* is represented by characteristics of the larger society—e.g., political climate or social institutions. The *physical environment* refers to the natural or artificially created surroundings of the person. Definitions of environment in predicting social behavior must incorporate objective aspects of the milieu (Wohlwill & Carson, 1972) and subjective representations of the environment. In the following review we will not address research on each of these classifications but rather will select important and theoretical-research issues which are relevant to the impact of diverse aspects of the environment on social behavior.

Age integration versus age segregation represents one important aspect of the suprapersonal environment. In his classical study of the effects of age density in residential environments, Rosow (1967) found increased social interaction among elderly tenants of housing facilities which have high concentrations of older persons (i.e., 50 percent or more). Age homogeneity should be distinguished, however, from total age segregation. Effects of the latter have been found to be deleterious to the elderly. Kahana and Kahana (1970), in a study of age integration-segregation in psychiatric hospitals, found significant improvement in affective and cognitive functioning and in activity among elderly patients randomly assigned to wards with young patients when compared to those assigned to strictly age-segregated wards.

In some of the noninstitutional populations, the concept of age integration also has some common-sense appeal. Living in age-integrated environments keeps older persons within the mainstream of society and allows greater social contact between young and old. There is considerable evidence (Kahana, Kahana, & Kiyak, 1979) that social contact between the generations leads to improved attitudes toward older persons and reduces stereotypes about aging.

Studies considering age integration-segregation in housing sites typically focused on public-housing environments (Teaff, Lawton, Nahemow, & Carlson, 1978). Within such environments age integration also implies mixing of older persons with problem families and exposing them to potential victimization by juveniles. The latter, however, is unlikely to emerge as a problem in age-segregated settings.

The high levels of satisfaction found among older persons in age-segregated environments (as well as in retirement communities) may thus reflect self-selection of those aged who enjoy age-homogeneous life styles (Kahana, Kahana, & McLenigan, 1979).

Residential arrangements—i.e., living alone, with spouse, or with other relatives—could have a pervasive impact on social life and interaction patterns of the elderly. In this context it is important to note that most older persons live alone or with a spouse—i.e., in both cases independently. Among those living in someone else's household, there are substantial sex differences with only about 4 percent of elderly men and 13 percent of elderly women having such residential arrangements. Important sex differences also exist in likelihood of older persons to be living alone (U.S. Census Bureau, 1975). Older persons in the United States tend to be fiercely independent, opting in favor of solitary living arrangements rather than moving in with children or with other family members. There appears to be a pervasive fear among the old, as well as the rest of society, regarding intergenerational living arrangements. Nevertheless there is some evidence that those families opting for three-generational living arrangements do not suffer negative psychological consequences (Bresver, 1975). There is, at the present time, little research bearing on the specific social consequences of living alone. Some research points to greater service needs of older persons, especially women living alone (Kahana & Kiyak, 1976). Studies of older persons living in SRO (single room occupancy) hotels suggest that social interaction, norms, and supports exist even in spite of isolated living arrangements (Stephens, 1976). Residential proximity has been found to be an important determinant of interaction of the aged with family members. Rosenberg (1970) found that distant relatives living in close proximity interact more with older persons than do closer relatives living far away. Congregate housing programs for the elderly which have proliferated in recent years are offering diverse living accommodations to low- and moderate-income elderly (Lawton, 1980). Most of these housing sites offer nutritional programs on the premises, thereby also presenting opportunities for social interaction among tenants.

Effects of Housing

An in-depth study on the effects of relocation to a senior-citizen housing site indicated increased social interaction and participation in activities as well as improved morale subsequent to relocation and even at the time of an eight-year follow-up (Carp, 1965, 1976). More limited positive consequences of moves to senior-citizen residences were observed by Lawton and Cohen (1974) and Sherwood, Greer, and Morris (1979). This was especially so in terms of increased activity and morale. These studies focused on overall well-being and dealt only tangentially with social behavior.

Physical Space and Social Behavior

Lawton (1980) has reviewed studies of personal space and the aged. Interestingly it has been found that proximity to friends and relatives is not an important determinant of older persons' general satisfaction with their neighborhood (Peterson, Hamovitch, & Larson, 1973). An interesting interaction between homegeneity of age, sex, racial background and residence was observed by Nahemow and Lawton (1975).

Areas of high activity have been found to be sought out by residents of special housing sites as well as those in institutions for the aged (Lawton, 1980).

Institutionalization and Social Behavior

In considering those characteristics of residential facilities for the aged which affect the well-being of residents, the focus has traditionally been on the physical inadequacies and on the absence of basic services. Yet there is evidence that residents often show better adjustment and have higher morale in relatively modest residential environments and are dissatisfied or show maladaptive behavior in costly and modern facilities (Kahana & Harel, 1972). Even those entrusted with providing services or planning for improving the quality of environments for the aged usually consider environments in physical or managerial terms. In determining the effects on the social behavior of the elderly living in those environments, the social-psychological milieu may be just as important as the physical features of the setting. Social and psychological aspects of residential environments may be considered independent of traditionally perceived indices of physical amenities.

Continuity with previous environments has been assumed to be a very important aspect of residential context (Rosow, 1967). Older persons want to maintain contact with old friends and enjoy familiar surroundings. To the extent that continuity with the past is important to older persons, residential facilities that are located in unfamiliar neighborhoods or in areas from which peers have moved away present problems to older persons. Conversely new housing may place the aged far out in suburbia, away from familiar stores, transportation, friends, family, and neighbors. Such data point to a need for residents to retain meaningful personal possessions in new residential facilities and meaningful ties with people, places, and things in the resident's previous world. There must be an effort to bridge several gaps: (1) those between the residents' past and their present situation; (2) between the old familiar and the new or often strange situation; and (3) between the previous personal and social existence and the institutional definitions (Kahana, 1975a).

The social-psychological milieu which would respond to these needs would be one where residents can be alone without being lonely, where people are available to each other without crowding one another, where personal attention is available without surveillance, where one can be cared for without giving up the feeling of caring for one's self and for relevant others, where one can depend on others without giving up one's independence.

Consideration of effects of institutional environments on older people underscores the importance of recognizing the complexity of person-environment interactions. Thus a complex situation exists in which the fit between the individual and society becomes an important issue. An overview of social gerontological research during the last 20 years reveals initial emphasis on the individual, then on the environment, and more recently, on the interactions between the two, effecting satisfaction among the aged (Lawton, 1968). The relative importance of environmental or individual characteristics in determining outcome has engendered considerable controversy—not unlike the heredity-environment debate in child development.

When old people enter institutions, the social relationships that previously sustained their identities in the community become less accessible (Hendricks, Kahana, & Kahana, 1978). New social opportunities and constraints on social relationships are determined by the policies and procedures of the institutions into which they have moved (Kiyak, Kahana, & Lev, 1978). At the same time by entering a home for the aged, people who previously were isolated due to limitations of mobility are nearer to others and in a social context where there is a potential for developing new relationships.

It has generally been argued that homes for the aged have a depersonalizing effect upon residents which diminish patterns of social interaction (Coe, 1965; Lieberman, 1969). However it should be noted that many socially isolated persons are, in fact, provided with more opportunities for social relationships after they enter a congregate setting. Residents in institutional facilities express a desire for privacy. This need is often coupled with a preference to be sociable and to have the company of other people. It is important, in this context, to distinguish between potentially problematic aspects of environments, such as crowding or surveillance (Goffman, 1959) and congregation (Kleemeier, 1959). On the other hand, opportunities for interaction, availability of peers or a confidante (Lowenthal & Haven, 1968), or group activities (Hendricks, Kahana, & Kahana, 1978) all represent potential features of the environment for enhancing social behavior. A study by Smith and Bengtson (1979) based on open-ended interviews with 100 institutionalized elderly and their middle-aged children indicated that a majority expressed improvement or continuation of family ties; only 10 percent expressed a negative affect. Generalizability of these findings may be limited since the institutions studied maintained unusually high standards. The study does show that in certain circumstances institutionalization can "support the family structure." Data on relocation of the older person into special housing environments indicate that the interpersonal environment of a congregate setting can provide opportunities for interaction with others of similar characteristics (Carp, 1968).

Two important factors may be expected to influence changes in social networks. Initiatives from others (i.e., family, friends, staff, or even other residents) represent one of these. Initiative from the older person him/herself represents the other. These two factors interact in a complex fashion to shape the interpersonal world of the older resident. In a longitudinal study of adaptation of the aged to institutional settings, correlates of changes in social-interaction patterns following institutionalization were considered. With regard to age older respondents were found to live alone, to have fewer casual friends, and to engage in solitary activities, more so than younger respondents. They were also more lonely and reported lack of friends more often. Yet they also preferred to do things alone more so than with other people (Hendricks et al., 1978).

Data on relocation of the older person into special housing environments indicate that the interpersonal environment of a congregate setting can provide opportunities for interaction with others of similar characteristics (Carp, 1968). In her in-depth study on the effects of relocation to a senior citizen housing site, Carp (1965, 1974) indicated increased social interaction and participation in activities as well as improved morale subsequent to relocation and even at the time of an eight-year follow-up. Similar, though limited, positive consequences of moves to senior citizen residences were observed by Sherwood et al. (1979), Kahana and Kahana (1979), and Lawton and Cohen (1974). Improvements tended to occur especially in terms of increased activity and morale. It should be noted that these studies focused on overall well-being and dealt only tangentially with social behavior.

Two important factors may be expected to influence changes in social networks. Initiatives from others (i.e., family, friends, staff, or even other residents) represent one of these. Initiative from the older person him/herself represents the other. These two factors interact in a complex fashion to shape the interpersonal world of the older resident. In a longitudinal study of adaptation of the aged to institutional settings, correlates of changes in social interaction patterns following institutionalization were considered (Hendricks, Kahana, & Kahana, 1978).

Focus on Interaction between Person and Environment—Matching Environment and Needs of the Aged

In considering environmental influences on social behavior and adjustment of the aged, it is important to note that apparently helpful environmental characteristics may be harmful to some elderly people, while apparently undesirable features may benefit others. The importance of a fit between environmental characteristics and individual needs is explicitly or implicitly expected to contribute to adjustment (Goffman, 1961; Hunt, 1961; Kleemeier, 1961). A conceptual model for considering and measuring congruence between environmental characteristics and personal preferences of the aged has been proposed by Kahana (1980). The congruence model of environment–individual interaction has its roots in Lewin's (1951) notion that behavior is a function of the relationship between the person and his/her environment and in Murray's (1938) need-press model of human behavior. It is assumed that environmental press provides a situational counterpart to internalized needs; environmental press may facilitate or hinder the gratification of needs. According to the congruence model older people are most likely to seek and be found in environments which are congruent with their needs. Lack of fit between press and need leads to modification of the press or to the individual leaving the field in a free-choice situation. When such a choice is unavailable and the individual must function in a dissonant milieu, stress and discomfort follow (Stern, 1970).

In the field of social ecology a congruence model of person-environment interaction has been discussed by French, Rodgers, and Cobb (1974). They define *adjustment* as the goodness of fit between characteristics of the person and properties of his/her environment. These authors emphasize the notion first proposed by Lewin (1951) that quantification of person-environment fit requires that characteristics of persons and environments be considered along commensurate dimensions—i.e., common terms must be used to describe person and environments. When there is a lack of congruence between the individual's needs and his/her life situation, due to either a change in environment (e.g., housing or institutionalization) or to a change in needs or capacities, various adaptive strategies must be marshaled to increase the person-environment congruence.

In an empirical test of the congruence model (Kahana, Liang, & Felton, 1980), morale was examined in relation to the effects of person and environmental characteristics as well as that of the congruence along commensurate dimensions. Seven commensurate dimensions of person and environment have been proposed. They are (1) segregation, (2) congregation, (3) institutional control, (4) structure, (5) stimulation, (6) affect, and (7) impulse control. The first three dimensions represent areas along which settings for the aged have been characterized. The segregate, congregate, and institutional-control dimensions used by Kleemeier (1961) and the elaborations presented by Pincus (1968) provide a comprehensive schema for classifying the impact of the setting on the life style of the residents. The last four dimensions represent personal characteristics along which older persons may experience changes. In areas where an older individual has experienced changes in needs and preferences, s/he may be especially vulnerable to environmental incongruence. Thus a person who can no longer delay gratification as s/he once did may find it especially problematic to be placed in an environment where a great delay is expected. An empirical study based on institutionalized older persons (Kahana et al., 1980) compared the importance of person-environment fit in the areas of congregation, impulse control, and segregation. Person-environment fit proved to be the most important predictor of morale in areas of segregation and impulse control. In contrast personal and/or environmental characteristics, rather than fit, were found to be more important along the dimensions of affective expression and institutional control in explaining morale.

An interesting application of the person-environment fit conceptualization to issues of sociability and social behavior may be found in the work of Carp and Carp (1978). These investigators assert that to the extent that older persons prefer privacy and solitude (Pastalan, 1970) efforts to provide them with opportunities for enhanced social interaction may be useless or even deleterious. In contrast when social behavior has been limited by life events (e.g., bereavement) or environmental constraints (e.g., high crime neighborhoods) increasing opportunities for social interaction should result in higher satisfaction. They postulate that the degree of congruence between sociability needs of the older person and environmental opportunities for sociability must be considered to predict outcomes.

In the framework of a longitudinal study of the person relocating into public housing sites for the elderly, these authors found that the importance of person-situation congruence for outcomes was supported, with older persons of greatest sociability needs improving most and those with minimal sociability needs benefiting least from a congregate living situation.

The desire for privacy represents another relevant concept in considering the social life of the older person. It is generally assumed that privacy represents an important liability of congregate living arrangements. A study by Kiyak, Kahana, and Fairchild (1977), however, demonstrated that it is not the actual amount of privacy available but rather the congruence between privacy desired and opportunities for privacy that predicts morale in homes for the aged.

RESIDENTIAL RELOCATION, PERSONAL CHANGE, AND SOCIAL BEHAVIOR

Relocation among the elderly has been typically seen as resulting in negative physical and psychological consequences (Lieberman, 1969). The body of knowledge stressing the negative consequences of relocation may be viewed as a specific case of the more general notion that significant life changes are stressful and lead to negative psychosocial and psychological outcomes for the aged (Dohrenwend & Dohrenwend, 1974).

More recently it has been recognized that under some circumstances, relocation need not result in negative outcomes (Carp, 1968, Lawton & Yaffe, 1970). In attempting to reconcile contradictory findings about the impact of relocation on older persons, Schultz and Brenner (1977) argue that controllability and predictability serve as the major mediators of the older person's response to stress. They borrow from the stress paradigm utilized in psychology and suggest that behavioral control may reduce uncertainty about the nature and timing of the threatening event.

Shultz and Brenner (1977) have made an important contribution toward providing a conceptual framework for understanding the impact of relocation and environmental changes on older persons. Nevertheless it is interesting to note that they still consider environmental change as representing a noxious stimulus and a potentially negative event which may be rendered less problematic when control and predictability are introduced.

This generally negative view of environmental or personal changes during the later years is also reflected in work concerned with personal and/or environmental continuity during late life approached from diverse conceptual and empirical perspectives within the field of gerontology.

In contrast to the prevailing view on the general negative impact of change on older people, a few researchers have recognized the potential value of personal and an environmental change during late life. Spence (1975) outlines a dynamic model of engagement in the late years. He suggests that there is a constant reinterpretation of self and situation with consequent modification of actions which comprises the dynamic nature of major life roles. He refers to these dynamic aspects of roles as changing careers. He suggests that with termination of major work and family careers a new flexibility develops during the later years. Geographic moves and life style changes are facilitated by this new flexibility.

In a study of life transitions, Lowenthal (1971) investigated different life styles which constitute adaptive strategies after relocation. New leisure roles assumed by older persons were found to assume greater importance. Lowenthal (1971) suggests that following role losses which may have been experienced prior to relocation, new environments may afford many opportunities for

reengagement primarily in social and leisure activities.

Tobin and Lieberman (1976), based on their longitudinal study, suggested that the major predictor of postrelocation functioning and adjustment was the degree of environmental change. In their paradigm of responses to stress, they consider characteristics of the person (i.e., personal and social resources, crisis management techniques) and degree and types of stress. They found the stress factors to be most clearly predictive of outcomes. Tobin and Lieberman's (1976) results suggest that personal resources, coping strategies, and subjective aspects of stress have relatively little significance for adjustment of older persons to crises.

A subsequent longitudinal study by Kahana and Kahana (1979) focused on the specific role of diverse strategies of adaptation to postrelocation and outcomes for less impaired older persons entering special housing for the aged, as well as a variety of homes for the aged. Analyses of the relative distributions of coping styles of institutionalized aged reveal that instrumental and affective coping styles predominate across a number of measures. Far fewer persons portrayed an escapist orientation or an inability to cope. The relative prevalence of coping styles did not show any significant change over the first three months of institutional living. Some respondents, however, portrayed a greater inability to cope after three months, whereas another group followed the opposite pattern with better ability to cope subsequent to three months of institutional living. Overall data, however, underscore the stability of coping strategies over time. Findings in this regard support notions about trait-like characteristics of adaptive strategies.

When considering the morale of respondents after three or four months of institutionalization, only effective coping strategies were significant predictors of morale. Persons who said they were likely to use affective coping strategies were significantly more likely to have low morale than were those portraying instrumental or cognitive coping strategies.

Relatively little research has been done on social networks, behavior, and adjustment of people who migrate within the United States after retirement (Lemon et al., 1972; Sheley, 1974). Rates of migration of older persons to warm climates (Golant, 1975) has been increasing in recent years. A large proportion of these older persons settle in retirement communities. When older persons move to retirement communities, however, the social networks that previously sustained their social identities in the community are disrupted. Although in some instances moving to a retirement community, in fact, brings one closer to children (Bultena & Wood, 1969), typically family and old friends are left behind, and long-term social supports are no longer available. At the same time the importance of such support networks for well-being among the aged has been well documented in the gerontological literature. Along with health and financial adequacy, continuing social relationships have consistently demonstrated a positive relationship with life satisfaction or well-being (Lemon et al., 1972). On the other hand, by entering a retirement community, people have the opportunity for developing new social relationships. In fact in a study by Sherman (1971) on the reasons why older persons moved into each of six retirement sites in California, it was found that the best-liked aspect was the presence of friends. Christopherson (1972) also found that older persons who relocate to retirement communities claimed that one of the most positive aspects of such environments is the ease with which new friends are made.

A recent study of Kahana, Kahana, and McLenigan (1979) considered the relationship of demographic variables and social-network factors among 451 residents of a Florida retirement community. When the relationship between demographic factors and objective, as well as perceived, interaction variables was considered, an interesting cluster of relationships emerged. Women, unmarried respondents, and older respondents portrayed a pattern of relative social deprivation as compared to men, married respondents, and younger respondents. Social networks were viewed as more significant for women and for unmarried respondents while at the same time these groups portrayed a more limited array of social interactions and felt more socially deprived. In contrast older respondents preferred solitary activities, although they also made fewer casual friends and felt more lonely.

In terms of marital status significant associations emerged between unmarried status, living alone, fewer casual friends, fewer close friends, feelings of loneliness, and duration of friendships. Women placed significantly greater value on friendships than did men, and unmarried persons placed significantly greater value on friendships and good personal relations than did married persons. Thus older unmarried women are characterized as the most socially deprived among those in the retirement community. These data confirm earlier findings regarding the special vulnerabilities of widowed older women (Kahana & Kiyak, 1981).

Among objective indices of social-network supports, living alone proved to be a significant predictor of both life satisfaction and service needs. Those living alone showed less life satisfaction and higher service needs. Participation in more interpersonal than solitary activities also mitigated against high service needs.

The most consistent predictor which had a significant effect on three sets of outcome variables was perceived lack of friends. In addition loneliness proved to be a significant determinant of service needs. It should be noted that similar sets of predictors emerged for both life satisfaction and service needs, although the two are not highly correlated.

Interestingly living alone, loneliness, and not enough friends, which could comprise a social-deprivation index, affected both life satisfaction and service needs.

As older persons lose major role support through relocation, death of spouse, retirement, or other reasons, the need for social supports among the elderly becomes more important. It has been suggested that the lack of such supports may lead to loneliness and concomitant feelings of uselessness among the aged. This, in turn, has a negative impact upon the older person's self-esteem (Gordon, 1976). This kind of effect is demonstrated by the comments written by one of the respondents in this sample. A 65-year-old woman who has lived in Florida for 3½ years with her second husband says,

If we did not go up north for 5 to 6 months, I would find it boring, lonely, and depressing. I need to have a chance to see my children—I need the feelings of being needed—always having held responsible positions—have feelings about rejection or not being needed by children which disturbs and hurts. Without my new husband's companionship, I would be a very sad and lonely person. (Kahana, Kahana, & McLenigan, 1979)

On the whole our results emphasize the importance of subjective feelings and attitudes toward social networks subsequent to relocation to retirement communities. The variables such a loneliness represent an individual's interpretation of, or response to, his/her social circumstance and are not necessarily a direct reflection of one's social reality. These subjective evaluations of one's social context and the congruence between what is available and what one desires emerge as important predictors of morale, self-image, and service needs.

Data from our longitudinal study of adaptation of voluntary long-distance movers (Kahana, Kahana, & McLenigan, 1979), reveal that long-distance relocation typically represents the combination of long years of planning and preparation for older persons and often involve some trial periods, such as being a "snow bird" in Florida or temporary resident in some country abroad. Relocaters portray a wide range of adaptive styles. New activities and life styles are often portrayed representing changes in macro-adaptations. In contrast coping strategies with concrete stresses and problem situations appear to be rooted in trait-like constellations of coping. Interestingly many long-term relocaters seek this continuity and adventure, and they measure their success by new challenges faced and and interest levels of new lives rather than by the lack of adaptive tasks. Relocation usually takes place based on the pull of the new environment rather than due to the dissatisfactions with previous living arrangements. Readaptations are most difficult for persons who are not enthusiastic about the move at the onset.

Our findings have generally confirmed hypotheses about different life styles subsequent to the relocation for Florida-bound and Israel-bound persons. These different life styles represent alternative pathways to self-actualization and to Erickson's stage of integrity. It was typical for the Florida-bound respondents to say, "All of my life I have done for my children and family, now it is time to do for me." This orientation was then followed by various efforts toward self-improvement: education, diet, exercise, or learning new skills (Kahana & Kahana, 1981).

In contrast the Israel-bound respondents in our study typically reasoned, "All of my life I have done for my children and my family, now it is time that I do for others." Although many migrants to Israel opted for a leisure-oriented life style, this group appeared more altruistic and often gravitated toward social and volunteer activities. Israel-bound respondents often moved for ideological reasons, seeking fulfillment of a dream to live in this state. Florida-bound repondents appeared more pragmatic about their moves, citing concrete, environmental, and even financial advantages, with the minority moving for health reasons. Both Israel and Florida-bound respondents were generally satisfied with their new location, as portrayed in their readiness to encourage a friend who wanted to move there.

SERVICE NEEDS, UTILIZATION, AND PLANNING—THE SOCIAL CONTEXT

In understanding service needs of the aged living in the community and of those seeking institutional care, the interpersonal context of the aged person presents a prominent influence. Significant others must be considered as a source of potential services to aged persons, often providing the essential support for maintaining them in the community (Linn, 1968; Shanas, 1962).

Numerous studies have examined the frequency of interactions and the helping patterns which characterize the relationships between older people and their significant others (see review by Troll, 1971). Relatively little attention, however, has been given to the integration of the older people into an informal social network as related to the older person's needs for formal services.

In day-to-day planning of service delivery to older individuals, opinions of kin frequently constitute the basis for providing or withholding services. The elderly, as consumers, are seldom consulted in decisions made about service priorities. Nevertheless it is important to note that there may be a disparity in the perception of needs of older people and their significant others. In a study by Kahana (1974) significant others tended to reiterate the traditional service priorities for older people—namely, health and financial concerns. In contrast self-reports by older people called attention to such previously underemphasized needs such as housing and domestic services. Older people perceived greater community needs among the aged than did significant others, and older people perceived themselves as being in greater need than did their significant others.

Help Available with Service Needs

Most older people indicated that they did have people available to them for both helping roles and for more general emotional support. Only 3.9 percent of the 154 older people questioned stated that there was no family member to whom they felt particularly close. In view of the relatively high proportion of older people who had no children (18.8 percent), it appears that familial bonds persist despite the absence of children. A similarly small proportion of older people (3.9 percent) stated that they had no one with whom they could discuss important problems. However 16.9 pecent indicated that they had no one to help them with everyday problems. The difference in these proportions seems to lend support to the notion developed by Langford (1962) and Shanas (1962) that friends and family members respond supportively to crisis situations but are less available for day-to-day support and assistance. Furthermore it appears that family members, especially children, are more frequently turned to for assistance for the important problems than for help with everyday problems; 53.9 percent of our sample of older people named their child as their source of help with problems, although children comprised only 42.2 percent of those named by older people as the source of help with everyday problems. Neighbors and friends emerge as highly important in terms of social interaction but of little moment for emotional or practical support. The older adult is more likely to socialize with friends but turns to family for help with problems. Of all signifi-

cant others named by the older persons, friends comprise only 21 percent and neighbors only 23 percent. Interestingly agencies or professionals were hardly mentioned at all by our sample as sources of help. Less than 2 percent of older persons spontaneously mentioned professionals in response to our questions. This finding is consistent with much previous research (e.g., Gurin, Veroff, & Field, 1960) indicating that self-help and informal sources of support are overwhelmingly preferred to professional help services.

SOCIAL VICTIMIZATION

Both professionals in the field and social consciousness have recently called attention to discrimination against the aged by social agencies, organizations, and groups. There has been evidence of job discrimination, consumer fraud, rejection by organizations, problems with government agencies, indifference of police, and even physical abuse by family (Butler, 1975; Lawton & Kleban, 1971). There is also evidence for avoidance of older persons in formal and informal associations as well as discriminatory practices in employment and services of all kinds (Butler, 1975). Findings have recently also been reported regarding criminal victimization of older people and their fears of crime (Clemente & Kleinman, 1976; Sundeen & Mathieu, 1976). Recent research indicates that stereotypes of vulnerability and fears of victimization are actually greater than personally experienced problems by the aged (Kahana, Liang, Felton, Fairchild, & Harel, 1977; Liang & Sengstock 1980). Among antecedents of fear of crime among the aged, fear has been found to be most closely related to sex and community size, with women in urban residence showing greatest fear (Brown, 1975; Clemente & Kleinman, 1976). Availability of social supports and age-homogeneous living arrangements have also been identified as reducing fear of victimization (Gubrium, 1974; Sundeen & Mathieu, 1976). It has also been argued that a subculture of aging may protect older persons from vulnerability and social victimization (Rose, 1965).

PLANNING FOR SERVICES TO THE AGED

The research reviewed underlines the importance of soliciting input from several sources, including the aged themselves in planning services. Possible disparity between perception of need by the aged, their significant others, service professionals, and planners must be recognized and acknowledged.

The determinants of service needs comprise a dynamic, rather than a static, system with needs of the aged changing as time goes on. Consequently models of service delivery must be flexible if they are to accommodate changing needs and demands. Existing services must be carefully evaluated in each area of service development in terms of availability, accessibility, and quality. The cost-effectiveness of modifying existing services must be weighed against the advantages of a new service which is specifically designed to meet existing needs. In this regard the utility of expanding services of existing hospitals and institutions to serve the needs of older persons outside their walls deserves attention.

For many adventurous aged the later years pose a new opportunity for freedom from obligations and role prescriptions, affording them with a second career in living. This may be a chance to get in shape, fight for one's favorite cause or even try to make the world a little better place to live. The adventurous aged in fact may be seen as embodying and giving substance to the old adage: Life begins at 60. Although the search for new life styles exemplified by this group may be relatively infrequent among the elderly, they pose a challenge to gerontologists to reexamine our stereotypes and to consider alternative pathways to integrity in the later years.

CONTRIBUTIONS TO SOCIETY DURING LATE LIFE— AN UPBEAT VIEW

Gerontological literature dealing with the vulnerable aged and focusing on provision of services to the elderly generally tends to emphasize dependency and vulnerability of that group. Nevertheless older persons living independently in the community often act as resources and providers of assistance to children, to other friends, and to family members. A study of service needs of urban aged (Kahana, 1974) found that community elderly provide more services than they receive. In contrast older persons living in sheltered housing or in public housing reported receiving more assistance than they gave to friends and neighbors. A recent demonstration program by Ehrlich (1980) has illustrated the usefulness of elderly neighbors in the context of a comprehensive neighborhood-based service program.

Rosow (1974) proposes a theory of role transition/continuity in his work on socialization to old age. He argues that, contrary to all other age-related role transitions and status sequences in American society, socialization to old age does not have complementary rites of passage, social gains, and normative preparation. In this sense he views old age as characterized by major role discontinuity. Discontinuities in late life are primarily comprised of social losses. According to Rosow there is little cultural preparation and facilitation or attribution of meaning to these discontinuities. Role losses are not seen by Rosow as encompassing potentially desirable freedoms from responsibility. While focusing on the reduction in social roles and interpersonal involvements often characterizing older persons, psychologists have seldom focused on the reverse pattern of seeking engagement, involvement and stimulation during the later years (Kahana & Kahana, 1981). Yet Wohlwill (1966) argues that a large portion of everyday human activity is related to heightening the level of incoming stimulation "by voluntary exposure to stimulus objects or situations that are novel, incongruous, surprising or complex."

CONCLUSIONS

The focus of this chapter has been on social behaviors of older people. Studies and theoretical formulations were reviewed which deal with social integration of older

adults and with the personal and societal context of such integration. It is recognized that in selecting areas for review only a sampling of relevant issues could be presented and that oftentimes research reviewed was illustrative rather than comprehensive. In recent years there has been a rapid growth of research in the field of gerontology and especially on the topic of social relations covered in this chapter. The subject of social behavior also crosscuts disciplinary lines of all the social and behavioral sciences, with relevant studies found in the fields of psychology, sociology, social welfare, political science, and others.

In the last decade as social gerontology has become firmly established as a recognized area of inquiry, there have been a number of important changes in orientation of social gerontologists toward the elderly which have been implicitly noted in this chapter. Having established that age is an important determinant of behavior well into late life and having undertaken diverse studies of the elderly, gerontologists are increasingly focusing on diversity rather than homogeneity inherent in the older years. Attention has been directed toward vast differences in concerns of the active young old of postretirement years and the more fragile and vulnerable old-old. Differences in needs and life styles of the rural and urban elderly have recently also received greater recognition (Pihlblad & McNamara, 1965; Rowles, 1978).

Because of the great variation of cultural-ethnic background among U.S. aged, their social integration must also be considered within the context of their own cultures and value systems. Different life styles and activity patterns may best suit older persons coming from different ethnic backgrounds and having different expectations. Thus, social interaction with family members tends to be more frequent and important for older persons coming from French-American backgrounds then those with a Scandinavian origin (Greely, 1974). The latter group, however, is more used to individual living and may seek social integration through organizational participation. Studies of the elderly have only recently begun to recognize and investigate empirically the role of ethnicity in social behavior. Examples of such studies include studies of Italian and Polish aged (Fandetti & Gelfand, 1976), black aged (Jackson, 1971), and Jewish aged (Kahana & Felton, 1977; Myerhoff, 1979).

Much of the research on social behavior has been conducted in a sociological framework. Nevertheless social behavior has very important psychological determinants as well. Not only do personality factors affect social behavior, but social experiences also have an effect on psychological functioning of the aged. Personality changes relevant to social behavior are discussed elsewhere in this volume. Nevertheless the special relevance of extroversion-introversion, nurturance-succorance, and capacity for intimacy or mutuality should be specifically noted in considering social behaviors in the later years.

In concluding this chapter, the reader is urged to consider the immense range of reactions to the aging process while at the same time focusing on some of the regularities of development manifested in the course of aging. Recognition of such diversity allows for appreciation of opportunities and potentials as well as vulnerabilities of the later years. To the extent that older persons are viewed as able to transcend biological decline and progression toward inevitable death, an optimistic view of the later years may prevail. Similarly, to the degree that the older individual is seen as able to extricate him/herself from the presses and limited expectations of society, old age may be viewed as a period of positive potential. Ultimately it is the belief that the individual psyche can achieve mastery over both negative biological and societal influences which give us the most potentially positive view of old age.

REFERENCES

ALLPORT, G. W. *Patterns and growth in personality.* New York: Holt, Rinehart & Winston, 1961.

ALLSER, H. A. Coping, defense and socially desirable responses. *Psychological Reports,* 1968, *22,* 985–988.

BECK, A. A., & LEVITON, B. *Social support mediating factors in widowhood and life satisfaction among the elderly.* Paper presented at the Gerontological Society Meetings, New York, 1976.

BIRREN, J. E. *The psychology of aging.* Englewood Cliffs, N.J.: Prentice-Hall, 1964.

BIRREN, J. E. The concept of functional age. *Human Development,* 1969, *12,* 214–215.

BOTWINICK, J. Geropsychology. *Annual Review of Psychology,* 1970, *21,* 239–272.

BRESVER, B. *A psychological comparison of two generation and three-generation families.* Doctoral dissertation, University of Toronto (Canada), 1975.

BROWN, E. *Fear of assault among the elderly.* Paper presented at Gerontological Society Meeting, Kentucky, 1975.

BULTENA, G. L., & WOOD, V. The American retirement community: Bane or blessing? *Journal of Gerontology,* 1969, *24,* 209–217.

BURGESS, E. W. Social relations, activities and personal adjustment. *American Journal of Sociology,* 1954, *59,* 352–360.

BUSSE, E., & PFEIFFER, E. *Behavior and adaptation in late life.* Boston: Little, Brown, 1969.

BUTLER, R. N. The facade of chronological age. In B. Neugarten (Ed.), *Middle age and aging.* Chicago: University of Chicago Press, 1968.

BUTLER, R. N. *Why survive?* New York: Harper & Row, 1975.

CAMPBELL, M. E. Studies of attitudes of nursing personnel toward geriatric patients. *Nursing Research,* 1971, *20,* 147–151.

CANTOR, M. K. Neighbors and friends—an overlooked resource in the informal support system. *Research on Aging,* 1979, *1,* 434–463.

CARP, F. M. Effects of improved housing on the lives of older people. In U.S. Department of Health, Education and Welfare, *Patterns of living and housing of middle-aged and older people.* Washington, D.C.: U.S. Government Printing Office, 1965.

CARP, F. M. Person-environment congruence in engagement. *Gerontologist,* 1968, *8,* 184–188.

CARP, F. M. Short-term and long-term prediction of adjustment to a new environment. *Journal of Gerontology,* 1974, *29,* 444–453.

CARP, F. M. Impact of improved housing on morale and life satisfaction. *Gerontologist,* 1975, *15,* 511–515.

CARP, F. M. Housing and Living environments of older people. In R. Binstock & E. Shanas (Eds.), *Handbook of aging and the social sciences.* New York: Van Nostrand Reinhold, 1976.

CARP, F. M., & CARP, A. *Person-environment congruence and sociability.* Unpublished manuscript. Berkeley: The Wright Institute, 1980.

CHRISTOPHERSON, V. A. Retirement communities: The cities of two tales. *Social Science,* 1972, *47,* 82–86.

CLEMENTE, F., & KLEINMAN, M. B. Fear of crime among the aged. *Gerontologist,* 1976, *16,* 207–210.

COE, R. M. Self-conception and institutionalization. In A. M. Rose & W. A. Peterson (Eds.), *Older people and their social world.* Philadelphia: Davis, 1965.

CONNER, K. S., POWERS, E. A., & BULTENA, G. L. Social interaction and life satisfaction: An empirical assessment of late life patterns. *Journal of Gerontology,* 1979, *34,* 116–121.

COWGILL, D. O. *Aging and modernization.* New York: Appleton-Century-Crofts, 1972.

CYRUS, A., & MONK, A. Attitudes of the aged toward the young: A multivariate study in intergenerational perception. *Journal of Gerontology,* 1972, *27,* 107–112.

CUMMING, E., & HENRY, W. *Growing Old.* New York: Basic Books, Inc., 1961.

DAVIS, R. W. Psychological aspects of geriatric nursing. *American Journal of Nursing,* 1968, *68,* 802–804.

DOWD, J. *Aging as exchange: A preface to theory.* Los Angeles: Southern California Gerontology Center, 1972.

DOHRENWEND, B., & DOHRENWEND, B. *Stressful life events: Their nature and effects.* New York: John Wiley, 1974.

EDWARDS, J. N., & KLEMMACK, D. L. Correlates of life satisfaction: A re-examination. *Journal of Gerontology,* 1973, *28,* 497–502.

EHRLICH, P. *Mutual help for community elderly: A demonstration and research project.* Paper presented at Institute of Gerontology, Wayne State University, Detroit, October 1980.

ERIKSON, E. *Childhood and society.* New York: W. W. Norton & Co., Inc., 1950.

FAIRCHILD, T., CHANG, V., & KAHANA, E. *Influence of expectations on environmental satisfaction of institutionalized aged.* Paper presented at the 11th International Congress of Gerontology, Tokyo, August 1978.

FANDETTI, D. V., & GELFAND, D. E. Care of the aged: Attitudes of white ethnic families. *Gerontologist,* 1976, *16,* 544–549.

FELTON, B., & KAHANA, E. Adjustment and situationally bound locus of control among institutionalized aged. *Journal of Gerontology,* 1974, *29* (No. 3), 295–301.

FRENCH, J. P. R., Jr., RODGERS, W., & COBB, S. Adjustment as person environment fit. In G. V. Coelho, D. A. Hamburg, & J. E. Adams (Eds.), *Coping and adaptation.* New York: Basic Books, 1974.

GEORGE, L. K. *Roles transition in later life.* Monterey, Calif.: Brooks/Cole, 1980.

GOFFMAN, E. The characteristics of total institutions. In Walter Reed Institute of Research, *Symposium on Preventive and Social Psychiatry.* Washington, D.C.: U.S. Government Printing Office, 1959.

GOFFMAN, E. *Asylums.* Garden City, N.Y.: Anchor Books, 1961.

GOFFMAN, E. B., & WOOG, P. Mental health in nursing homes training project, 1972–1973. *Gerontologist,* 1975, *15,* 119–124.

GOLANT, S. M. Residential concentrations of the future elderly. *Gerontologist,* 1975, *15,* 16–23.

GOLDSTEIN, T., & GUTMANN, D. A. T.A.T. study of Navajo indians. *Psychiatry,* 1972, *35,* 373–384.

GORDON, S. *Lonely in America.* New York: Simon & Schuster, 1976.

GREELY, A. M. *Ethnicity in the United States.* New York: John Wiley, 1974.

GUBRIUM, J. *Late life, communities and environmental policy.* Springfield, Ill.: Chas. C Thomas, 1974.

GURIN, G., VEROFF, J., & FIELD, S. *Americans view their mental health.* New York: Basic Books, 1960.

GUTMANN, D. the country of old men: Crosscultural studies in the psychology of later life. In *Occasional papers in gerontology series.* Ann Arbor: Institute of Gerontology, 1969.

HAAN, N. Proposed model of ego functioning: Coping and defense mechanisms in relationship to IQ change. *Psychological Monographs,* 1963, *77,* 1–23.

HALL, C., & LINDSEY, G. *Theories of personality.* New York: John Wiley, 1970.

HAMBURG, D. A., COELHO, G. V., & ADAMS, J. E. Coping and adaptation: Steps toward a synthesis of biological and social perspectives. In G. V. Coelho, D. A. Hamburg, & J. E. Adams (Eds.), *Coping and adaptation.* New York: Basic Books, 1974.

HAREL, Z., KAHANA, E., & FELTON, B. *Correlates and predictors of morale and life satisfaction in residential settings for the aged.* Paper presented at the Gerontological Society Meeting, San Juan, 1972.

HARTMANN, H., KRIS, E., & LOWENSTEIN, R. Notes on the theory of regression. *Psychoanalytic Study of the Child,* 1949, *4,* 9–36.

HAVIGHURST, R. J., & ALBRECHT, R. *Older people.* New York: Longmans, Green, 1953.

HAVIGHURST, R. J., NEUGARTEN, B. L., & TOBIN, S. S. Disengagement and patterns of aging. In B. L. Neugarten (Ed.), *Middle age and aging: A reader in social psychology.* Chicago: University of Chicago Press, 1968.

HENDRICKS, J., KAHANA, E., & KAHANA, B. *Correlates of expanded and contracted social relationships in homes for the aged.* Paper from the proceedings of the 31st annual Scientifical Meeting of the Gerontological Society, Dallas, November 1978.

HOCHSCHILD, A. R. Disengagement theory: A critique and proposal. *American Sociological Review*, 1975, *40*, 553–569.

HUNT, J. *Intelligence and experience*. New York: Ronald Press, 1961.

JACKSON, J. J. Compensatory care for the black aged. In Occasional paper #10, Institute of Gerontology (Ed.), *Minority Aged in America*. University of Michigan, 1971.

JAEGER, D., & SIMMONS, L. W. *The aged ill: Coping with problems in geriatric care*. New York: Appleton-Century-Crofts, 1970.

JARVIK, L. F., & COHEN, D. A biobehavioral approach to intellectual changes with aging. In C. Eisdorfer (Ed.), *The psychology of adult development and aging*. Washington, D.C.: APA Publications, 1973.

KAHANA, B. The young and old view each other. *Geriatric Focus*, 1970, *9*(No. 10).

KAHANA, B., & KAHANA, E. *Age changes in impulsivity among chronic schizophrenics*. Paper presented at the International Congress of Gerontology, Vienna, 1966.

KAHANA, B., & KAHANA, E. Changes in mental status of elderly patients in age integrated and age segregated hospital milieus. *Journal of Abnormal Psychology*, 1970, *75* (No. 2), 177–181.

KAHANA, B., & KAHANA, E. The role of impulse control in cognitive functioning and morale of institutionalized aged women. *Journal of Gerontology*, 1975, *30*(No. 6), 679–687.

KAHANA, B., & KAHANA, E. *Strategies of coping in institutional environments*. Final progress report, NIH Grant No. 24959–04, August 1979.

KAHANA, B., & KAHANA, E. *Grandparents attitudes toward divorce of children and grandchildren*. Paper presented at the American Orthopsychiatric Association Meetings, Toronto, April 1980.

KAHANA, B., KAHANA, E., & KIYAK, A. Changing attitudes toward the aged. *National Journal*, November 1979, pp. 1913–1919.

KAHANA, B., KAHANA, E., & MCLENIGAN, P. *The adventurous aged: Voluntary relocation in the later years*. Paper presented at the 33rd Annual Scientific Meeting of the Gerontological Society, San Diego, November 1980.

KAHANA, E. *Aging and involvement in interpersonal relationships*. Paper presented at the American Psychological Association Meetings, Chicago, 1965a.

KAHANA, E. Profile analysis as a method of measuring adult personality change. *Essays on development*. Chicago: Committee on Human Development, 1965b.

KAHANA, E. Emerging issues in institutional services for the aging. *Gerontologist*, 1971, *11* (No. 1), 51–58.

KAHANA, E. *The role of homes for the aged in meeting community needs. Final Report*. Detroit, Mich.: Elderly Care Research Center, Wayne State University, 1974.

KAHANA, E. Matching environments to needs of the aged: A conceptual scheme. In J. Gubrium (Ed.), *Late life: Recent developments in the sociology of aging*. Springfield, Ill.: Chas. C Thomas, 1975a.

KAHANA, E. *Intergenerational relations: Perspectives of the grandparent generation*. Paper presented at the annual meeting of the St. Louis Family and Children's Services, St. Louis, Mo., May 1975b.

KAHANA, E. *A congruence model of person-environment fit*. Paper presented at Gerontological Society Meeting, Washington, D.C., November 1979.

KAHANA, E. A congruence model of person-environment interaction. In M. P. Lawton, P. G. Windley, & T. O. Byerts (Eds.), *Aging and the environment: Theoretical approaches*. New York: Garland Publishing, 1980.

KAHANA, E., & COE, R. M. Self and staff conceptions and institutionalized aged. *Gerontologist*, 1969, *9* (No. 4), 264–277.

KAHANA, E., FAIRCHILD, T., & KAHANA, B. Measurement of adaptation to changes in health and environmental changes among the aged. In R. Mangen & W. Peterson (Eds.), *Handbook to research instruments in social gerontology*. Minneapolis: University of Minnesota Press, in press.

KAHANA, E., & FELTON, B. *Continuity and change in coping strategies in a longitudinal analysis*. Paper presented at Gerontological Society Meetings, New York, October 1976.

KAHANA, E., & FELTON, B. Social context and personal needs–a study of Polish and Jewish aged. *Journal of Social Issues*, 1977, *33* (No. 4), 56–74.

KAHANA, E., & HAREL, Z. Social psychological milieu in residential care settings for the aged. *Gerontologist*, 1971, *11* (No. 3), 47.

KAHANA, E., & HAREL, Z. *Social and behavioral principles in residential care settings for the aged: The residents' perspective. Part II*. Position paper prepared for presentation at the annual meeting of the American Orthopsychiatric Association, Detroit, Mich., April 1972.

KAHANA, E., & KAHANA, B. Parenting and personality in three-generational families. In T. Williams (Ed.), *Infant care*. Washington, D.C.: Department of Health, Education and Welfare, 1972.

KAHANA, E., KAHANA, B., & HASEGAWA, K. *Adaptive strategies and institutionalization of the aged: U.S. and Japanese perspective*. Paper from the proceedings of the 11th International Congress of Gerontology, Tokyo, August 1978.

KAHANA, E., KAHANA, B., & MCLENIGAN, M. *Support network of long distance movers*. Paper presented at the Gerontological Society meetings, Washington, D.C., November 1979.

KAHANA, E., & KIYAK, A. Service needs of older women. In L. Troll & J. Israel (Eds.), *Looking ahead: A woman's guide to problems and the joys of growing older*. Englewood Cliffs, N.J.: Prentice-Hall, 1976.

KAHANA, E., & KIYAK, A. *Service needs of older women in urban areas*. Papers given at Cornell University Conference on Women in Midlife, Ithaca, N.Y., October, 1976.

KAHANA, E., & KIYAK, A. The older woman: Impact of widowhood and independent living on service needs. *Journal of Gerontological Social Work*, 1981.

KAHANA, E., LIANG, J., FELTON, B., FAIRCHILD, T., & HAREL, Z. Perspectives of aged on victimization: "Ageism" and their problems in urban society. *Gerontologist*, 1977, *17* (No. 2), 121–129.

KAHANA, E., LIANG, J., & FELTON, B. Alternative models of person-environment fit: Prediction of morale in three homes for the aged. *Journal of Gerontology*, 1980, *35*, 584–595.

KIYAK, A., KAHANA, B., & FAIRCHILD, T. *Privacy as a salient aspect of P-E fit: Implications for institutional planning*. Paper presented at Symposium on Implications of Environmental Features in the Design of Intervention Programs for the Aged. Gerontological Society Meeting, San Francisco, 1977.

KIYAK, A., KAHANA, E., & LEV, N. The role of informal norms in determining institutional totality in homes for the aged. *Long Term Care and Health Administration Quarterly*, 1978, *2*, 100–110.

KLEEMEIER, R. W. Behavior and the organization of the bodily and external environment. In J. E. Birren (Ed.), *Handbook of aging and the individual*. Chicago: University of Chicago Press, 1959.

KLEEMEIER, R. W. *Aging and leisure*. New York: Oxford University Press, 1961.

LANGFORD, M. *Community aspects of housing for the aged*. Ithaca, N.Y.: Center for Housing and Environmental Studies, Cornell University, 1962.

LARSON, R. Thirty years of research on the subjective well-being of older Americans. *Journal of Gerontology*, 1978, *33*, 109–125.

LAWTON, M. P. *Ecology and aging*. Unpublished paper, 1968.

LAWTON, M. P. The Philadelphia Geriatric Center morale scale: A revision. *Journal of Gerontology*, 1975, *30*, 85–89.

LAWTON, M. P. (Ed.). *Environmental context of aging: Life-styles, environmental quality and living arrangements*. New York: Garland STPM Press, 1979.

LAWTON, M. P. *Environment and aging*. Monterey, Calif.: Brooks/ Cole, 1980.

LAWTON, M. P., & COHEN, J. The generality of housing impact on the well-being of older people. *Journal of Gerontology*, 1974, *29*, 194–204.

LAWTON, M. P., & KLEBAN, M. H. The aged resident of the inner city. *Gerontologist*, 1971, *11*, 277–283.

LAWTON, M. P., & NAHEMOW, L. Ecology and the aging process. In C. Eisdorfer & M. P. Lawton (Eds.), *Psychology of adult development and aging*. Washington, D.C.: APA Publication, 1973.

LAWTON, M. P., & SIMON, B. The ecology of social relationships in housing for the elderly. *Gerontologist*, 1968, *8*, 108–115.

LAWTON, M. P., & YAFFE, S. Mortality, morbidity, and voluntary change of residence by older people. *Journal of the American Gerontological Society*, 1970, *18*, 823–831.

LAZARUS, R., AVERILL, J., & OPTON, E. The psychology of coping: Issues of research and assessment. In G. V. Coelho, D. A. Hamburg, & J. A. Adams (Eds.), *Coping and adaptation*. New York: Basic Books, 1974.

LEMON B. W., BENGTSON, V. L., & PETERSON, J. A. An exploration of the activity theory of aging: Activity types and life satisfaction among in-movers to a retirement community. *Journal of Gerontology,* 1972, *27,* 511–523.

LEWIN, K. *A dynamic theory of personality.* New York: McGraw-Hill, 1935.

LEWIN, K. *Field theory in social science.* New York: Harper & Row, 1951.

LIANG, J., DVORKIN, L., KAHANA, E., & MAZIAN, F. Social integration and morale: A re-examination. *Journal of Gerontology,* 1980, *35* (No. 5), 726–757.

LIANG, J., KAHANA, E., & DVORKIN, L. Morale and dimensions of social integration. *Gerontologist,* 1977, *17* (No. 5), 79.

LIANG, J., & SENGSTOCK, M. C. *The liklihood of victimization among the elderly.* Paper presented to the American Society of Criminology, San Francisco, 1980.

LIEBERMAN, M. Institutionalization of the aged: Effects on behavior. *Journal of Gerontology,* 1969, *24,* 330–339.

LIEBERMAN, M., & COHLER, B. *Constructing personality measures for older people.* Final Report Administration on Aging, Grant No. 93:P: 57425/5, 1976.

LINN, N. W. *Determinants of family involvement and family attitude in nursing home placement.* Paper presented at the 21st Annual Meeting of the Gerontological Society, Denver 1968.

LITWAK, E. Extended kin relations in industrial democratic societies. In G. Streib & E. Shanas (Eds.), *The family intergenerational relationship and social structure.* Englewood Cliffs, N.J.: Prentice-Hall, 1964.

LOPATA, H. A. *Widowhood in an American city.* Cambridge, Mass.: Schenkman, 1973.

LOWENTHAL, M. Social isolation and mental illness in old age. *American Sociological Review,* 1964, *29,* 54–70.

LOWENTHAL, M. Intentionality: Toward a framework for the study of adaptation in adulthood. *Aging and Human Development,* 1971, *2,* 79–95.

LOWENTHAL, M., & BOLER, D. Voluntary vs. involuntary social withdrawal. *Journal of Gerontology,* 1975, *20,* 363–371.

LOWENTHAL, M., & HAVEN, C. Interaction and isolation: Intimacy as a critical variable. *American Sociological Review,* 1968, *33,* 20–30.

LOWENTHAL, M., & ROBINSON, B. Social networks and isolation. In R. Binstock & E. Shanas (Eds.), *Handbook of aging and the social sciences.* New York: Van Nostrand Reinhold, 1976.

LOWENTHAL, M., THURNHER, M., & CHIRIBOGA, D. *Four stages of life.* San Francisco: Jossey-Bass, 1975.

McKAIN, W. C. *Retirement marriage.* Storrs Agricultural Experiment Station Monograph, University of Connecticut, 1969, *3.*

MADDOX, G. L. Activity and morale: A longitudinal study of selected elderly subjects. *Social Forces,* 1963, *14,* 226–232.

MANCINI, J. Family relationships and morale among people 65 years of age and older. *American Journal of Orthopsychiatry,* 1979, *49,* 292–300.

MARIWAKI, S. Y. Self-disclosure, significant others and psychological well-being in old age. *Journal of Health and Social Behavior,* 1973, *14,* 226–232.

MARKIDES, K., & MARTIN, H. A causal model of life satisfaction among the elderly. *Journal of Gerontology,* 1979, *34,* 89–93.

MEAD, G. H. *Mind, self and society.* Chicago: University of Chicago Press, 1934.

MECHANIC, D. Social structure and personal adaptation, some neglected dimensions. In G. V. Coelho, D. A. Hamburg, & J. E. Adams (Eds.), *Coping and adaptation.* New York: Basic Books, 1974.

MEDLEY, M. L. Satisfaction with life among persons sixty-five years and older: A casual model. *Journal of Gerontology,* 1976, *31,* 448–455.

MERTON, K. *Social theory and social structure.* New York: Free Press, 1957.

MEZNECK, J., LIANG, J., & KAHANA, E. Definition of a situation and desire to relocate among the elderly. *Sociological Symposium,* No. 29, Winter 1980.

MOOS, R. Psychological techniques in the assessment of adaptive behavior. In G. V. Coelho, D. A. Hamburg, & J. E. Adams (Eds.), *Coping and adaptation.* New York: Basic Books, 1974.

MURRAY, H. A. *Explorations in personality.* New York: Oxford University Press, 1938.

MYERHOFF, B. *Life's career: Aging.* Beverly Hills, Calif.: Sage Publications, Inc., 1978.

MYERHOFF, B. *Number our days.* New York: Dutton, 1979.

NAHEMOW, L., & LAWTON, M. P. Similarity and propinquity in friendship formation. *Journal of Personality and Social Psychology,* 1975, *32,* 205–213.

NEUGARTEN, B. L. A developmental view of adult personality. In J. E. Birren (Ed.), *Relations of development and aging.* Springfield, Ill.: Chas. C. Thomas, 1964.

NEWCOMER, R. *Group housing for the elderly: Defining neighborhood service convenience for public housing and section 202 residences.* Unpublished doctoral dissertation, University of Southern California, Los Angeles, 1975.

PALMORE, E. Predictors of successful aging. *Gerontologist,* 1979, *19,* 427–431.

PALMORE, E., & LUIKART, C. Health and social factors related to life satisfaction. *Journal of Health and Social Behavior,* 1972, *13,* 68–80.

PARSONS, T. Age and sex in the social structure of the United States. In *Essays in sociological theory, pure and applied.* Gencoe, Ill.: Free Press, 1949.

PARSONS, T. The social structure of the family. In R. Anshen (Ed.), *The family: Its function and destiny.* New York: Harper & Row, Pub., 1949.

PASTALAN, L. *Spatial behavior of older people.* Ann Arbor: University of Michigan—Wayne State University Institute of Gerontology, 1970.

PEARLIN, L. I., & SCHOOLER, C. The structure of coping. *Journal of Health and Social Behavior,* 1978, *19,* 2–21.

PETERSON, J. A., HAMOVITCH, M., & LARSON, A. E. *Housing needs and satisfaction of the elderly.* Los Angeles: Ethel Percy Andrus Gerontology Center, University of Southern California, 1973.

PIHLBLAD, C. T., & McNAMARA, R. L. Social adjustment of elderly people in three small towns. In A. M. Rose & W. A. Peterson (Eds.), *Older people and their social world.* Philadelphia: F. A. Davis, 1965.

PINCUS, A. The definition and measurement of the institutional environment in homes for the aged. *Gerontologist,* 1968, *8,* 207–210.

QUAYHAGEN, M., & CHIRIBOGA, D. *Geriatric coping schedule: Potential and problems.* Paper presented at meeting of Gerontological Society of New York, October 1976.

REICHARD, S., LIVSON, F., & PETERSON, P. G. *Aging and personality: A study of eighty-seven older men.* New York: John Wiley, 1962.

RILEY, M., & FONER, A. *Aging and society* (Vol. 1). New York: Russell Sage Foundation, 1968.

ROSE, A. M. The subculture of aging. In A. M. Rose & W. A. PETERSON (Eds.), *Older people and their soical world.* Philadelphia: F. A. Davis, 1965.

ROSENBERG, G. *The worker grows old.* San Francisco: Jossey-Bass, 1970.

ROSOW, I. *Socialization to old age.* Berkeley: University of California Press, 1974.

ROSOW, I. *Social integration of the aged.* Glencoe, Ill.: Free Press, 1967.

ROWLES, G. *Prisoners of space.* Boulder, Colo.: Westview Press, 1978.

SCHAIE, K. W., & STROTHER, C. R. Cognitive and personality variables in college graduates of advanced age. In G. A. Tolland (Ed.), *Human aging and behavior.* New York: Academic Press, 1968.

SCHULZ, R., & BRENNER, G. Relocation of the aged: A review and the theoretical analysis. *Journal of Gerontology,* 1977, *32*(No. 3), 323–333.

SCHWARTZ, A. N. Staff development and morale building in nursing homes. *Gerontologist,* 1974, *14,* 50–55.

SHANAS, E. *The health of older people.* Cambridge, Mass.: Harvard University Press, 1962.

SHANAS, E. Health care and health services for the aged. *Gerontologist,* 1965, *5,* 240–276.

SHANAS, E., TOWNSEND, P., WEDDERBURN, D., FRIIS, H., MILHOJ, P., & STEHOUWER, J. *Old people in three industrial societies.* New York: Atherton Press, 1968.

SHARMA, S., & KAHANA, E. *Sex differences in adaptation patterns of urban aged.* Paper presented at meeting of Society for the Study of Social Problems (SSSP), Chicago, 1977.

SHELEY, J. Mutuality and retirement community success: An interactionist perspective in gerontological research. *Aging and Human Development,* 1974, *5,* 71–80.

SHERMAN, S. The choice of retirement housing among the well elderly. *Aging and Human Development,* 1971, *2,* 118–138.

SHERWOOD, W., GREER, D. S., & MORRIS, T. N. A study of the Highland Heights apartments for the physically impaired and elderly in Fall River. In T. D. Byerts, L. A. Pastalan, & S. C. Howell (Eds.), *The environmental context of aging.* New York: Garland STPM Press, 1979.

SMITH, K. F., & BENGTSON, V. L. Positive consequences of institutionalization: Solidarity between elderly parents and their middle-aged children. *Gerontologist,* 1979, *5,* 438–447.

SPENCE, D. The meaning of engagement. *International Journal of Aging and Human Development,* 1975, *6*(No. 3), 193–198.

STEPHENS, B. J. *Loners, losers, and lovers.* Seattle: University of Washington Press, 1976.

STERN, G. G. *People in context,* New York: John Wiley, 1970.

STREIB, G. Old age and the family. In E. Shanas (Ed.), *Aging in contemporary society.* Beverly Hills, Calif.: Sage Publications, Inc., 1970.

SUNDEEN, R. A., & MATHIEU, J. T. The fear of crime and its consequences among the elderly in three urban communities. *Gerontologist,* 1976, *16,* 211–219.

SUSSMAN, M. The helping pattern in the middle class family. *American Sociological Review,* 1953, *18,* 22–28.

TEAFF, J. D., LAWTON, M. P., NAHEMOW, L., & CARLSON, D. Impact of age integration on the well-being of elderly tenants in public housing. *Journal of Gerontology,* 1978, *33,* 126–133.

TOBIN, S., & LIEBERMAN, M. *Last home for the aged.* San Francisco: Jossey-Bass, 1976.

TROLL, L. E. Family in later life: A decade review. *Journal of Marriage and Family,* 1971, *33,* 263–290.

TROLL, L. E. *Families in later life.* Belmont, Calif.: Wadsworth, 1979.

TROLL, L. E., & SCHLOSSBERG, N. A preliminary investigation of "age bias" in the helping professions. *Gerontologist,* 1970, *10,* 14–20.

TUCKMAN, J., & LORGE, I. Attitudes toward older people. *Journal of Social Psychology,* 1953, *37,* 249–260.

U.S. Bureau of the Census. Demographics aspects of aging and the older population in the United States. *Current Populations Reports,* Series P-23, No. 59. Washington, D.C.: Government Printing Office, 1976.

WHITE, R. Motivation reconsidered: The concept of competence. *Psychological Review,* 1959, *66,* 297–333.

WOHLWILL, J., & CARSON, D. *Environment and the social sciences: Perspectives and applications.* Washington, D.C.: American Psychological Association, Inc., 1972.

YOUMAN, E. G. Attitudes: Young-old and old-old. *Gerontologist,* 1977, *17,* 175–178.

49

Intergenerational Relations throughout the Life Span

LILLIAN E. TROLL
VERN L. BENGTSON

CONCEPTS AND METHODS

The literature shows us the necessity of distinguishing between *generations within the family* and *generations outside the family.* In the first case we deal with parents and children; in the second, with people of different ages who, because they have lived through different events, are shaped by changes in history and society. Mediating between these two constructs of generations is that of the *developmental generations of the individual life span.*

The prototypic generational system is the chain of grandparent-parent-child. The first generation could be either the oldest still living or the oldest in the memory of living descendants. An esteemed grandfather or grandmother could be a model for 100 years and more, and most parents leave a legacy to their children which lasts at least as long as the children survive (Sussman, Cates, & Smith, 1971; Troll, 1972). If self-reports or observations are used, however, only living people can be used.

It is significant that family-generation rank or lineage position is independent of chronological age. The second-oldest generation could be anywhere from two seconds to 72 years old, depending in part on the longevity of that family. Lineage positions tend also to differ along maternal and paternal lines. A person could be second generation on the maternal side and first generation on the paternal side, influenced by three generations of ancestors on one side and only one on the other. Not only do women in our society now tend to live longer than do men, but they have usually married younger, married men older than themselves, and become parents at younger ages. Thus women, relative to men, can now have a doubled impact upon later generations. They are likely

to have been more involved than men in child-rearing; there are likely to be more generations of them around; and they are likely to continue their interactions with their children in a more overt manner than are men.

Time between generations—which affects the number of coexistent generations—is related to such biological factors as age of sexual maturity and to such social factors as age of marriage. There have been secular trends for both earlier age of sexual maturity (Tanner, 1961) and earlier age of marriage. Fertility is also a factor—number of children per set of parents and time between their births. If the time span between the oldest and youngest child is 30 years and many children are spread over those 30 years, the distinction between lineage generations itself can be blurred.

Any consideration of generations must take into account the developmental status of the people in each lineage position. A parent's influence on a child of 10—or, reciprocally, that child's influence on its parent—is different if the parent is a young adult from what it would be if that parent were middle-aged (Hagestad, 1979; Nydegger, 1973). Adolescents interact differently with their parents from the way they did when they were young children and the way they are going to when they are adults. Grandparents who are youthful, vigorous, and involved in the world have a different impact than if they are feeble and withdrawn. The effect can go both ways; belonging to the oldest living generation in a five-generation family, knowing that one is next in line to die, or looking down at many steps of descendants could make a person feel, think, and act very "old." Another person the same age or even in the same physical condition whose first child has just gotten married could feel much younger. From the perspective of the younger generations, having a long line of living grandparents and great-grandparents could have a profound effect on one's

Vern L. Bengtson was assisted in the original study by Dianne McFarland.

890

relations with and feelings toward one's parents, one's children, and, in fact, almost anybody else.

Age- and culture-homogenous groups include all people born at the same time *who have been raised under comparable historical and cultural circumstances.* Members of such an age cohort may share many attitudes and values, perceive themselves as belonging together, and be recognized as belonging together by others. The particular age cohort to which a grandparent, a parent, or a child belongs conceivably affects all their relationships. Parents who grew up in the Depression probably treat their children differently from those who grew up after World War II, even if they are dealing with children the same age who have many other characteristics in common.

Mannheim (1923/1952) makes a distinction between *lifelong* and *temporary* age groups. In the former, membership is maintained throughout life. Even though the members get older, they continue to belong to the group into which they were born. This kind of cohort usually has a historical derivation (Braungart, 1974). We can speak of the generation of those born at the turn of the century or of the Depression generation. Pinder (1926) emphasizes the "noncontemporaneity of the contemporaneous." All people living at the same time do not necessarily share the same history. Critical events have affected them at different points in their life and thus affected them differently. Americans born at the beginning of the century, today's grandparents or great-grandparents, were adolescents at the time of World War I. That war was a different kind of experience for them than it was for their parents. Experiencing the war as adolescents affected many of their future relationships and attitudes and made them a different group of people from those before or after them.

Mannheim (1923/1952) suggests that the function of the *temporary* age group, on the other hand, whose membership lasts only for a limited period of the life span, seems to be largely that of easing a transition from one period of life to another one that is very different. Such age groups seem to emerge at times of developmental crises, particularly during the transition from youth to adulthood but also recently, according to many writers, during a mid-life transition. Once the transition is over, this temporary "generation" may dissolve. The "youth culture" of the late 1960s is in part an example of a temporary age group even though its members could well retain a lifelong feeling of kinship. Eisenstadt (1956) has argued that youth groups arise in societies with sharp differences between the kinds of interpersonal associations customary in children's early life in the family and those prevailing in the wider social system in which they must function after maturity. It has been suggested that a parallel case may be arising today among older people in our society (Bengtson & Cutler, 1976; Rose, 1962). As greater numbers of individuals live longer, their shared experiences could induce a meaningful "senior-citizen" cohort or a "gerontological-generation" unit (Laufer & Bengtson, 1974).

On the basis of modal cultural characteristics or *Zeitgeist* (Mannheim, 1923/1952), a series of current age groups might be distinguished. There is a cohort born shortly before the turn of the century that started out life in a spirit of expanding economy where conventional "Protestant-ethic" virtues such as thrift, industry, re-

spect, and obedience might be rewarded (Neugarten, 1968). Then there are those who came of age during the economic depression of the thirties who might be less optimistic and value material gains more. Those who grew up in the shadow of the atom bomb, the present child-rearing generation, could, as Mead (1970) asserts, have found both the present and the future precarious and turned to radical political action, become alienated, or resorted to violence, depending in part on family background and personality. Their current adult life will differ from that of earlier and later adult generations. Finally there is a new youth group, marked by cynicism consequent to the Watergate scandals and neofundamentalism. To illustrate the effects of historical periods on age cohorts, consider the interactions between a father and son in which the father's attitudes were formed during the Depression and the son's in facing the possibility of world atomic destruction.

The "generation gap" was an important issue in the late 1960s. In general most generational theorists reviewed by Mannheim (1923/1952) and more recently by Bengtson, Furlong, and Laufer (1974) focus on political and value shifts evident among contemporary age groups. Many assume that differences would necessarily be accompanied by conflict. Mannheim himself considered conflict between age groups usual but not inevitable. Davis (1940), however, suggested that conflict is unavoidable, especially in present technological societies. Universals such as the developmental difference between parent and child and a decreasing rate of socialization with the coming of maturity (so that youth changes more rapidly than later adulthood) would result in physiological, sociological, and psychological differences that would amount to confrontations.

Bengtson (1970) described three positions on this issue: "great gap," "nothing really new," and "selective continuity."

Great Gap. One of the most eloquent exponents of the "great gap" orientation has been Friedenberg (1959, 1965, 1969), who noted, "Young people aren't rebelling against their parents; they're abandoning them" (p. 23). He saw a "real and serious conflict of interest" between generations rather than mutual misunderstanding, with youth a discriminated-against minority and parents the discriminating majority. Freudians have long asserted that sons must rebel against their fathers in order to achieve the power and independence essential to adult masculinity. Bettelheim (1965) saw this rebellion assuming truly divisive proportions in modern-day life. Like Mead (1970) and others (e.g., Slater, 1970), he suggested that, in the face of rapid social change, generational discontinuity is adaptive because old responses become inappropriate to radically new situations.

Nothing Really New. The opposite position emphasizes continuities across generations. It points to within-family similarities in basic political attitudes (e.g., Thomas, 1971; Troll, Neugarten, & Kraines, 1969; Westby & Braungart, 1966), to the importance of parents compared with peers as reference persons for adolescents (Kandel & Lesser, 1972), and to closeness of communication between parents and children of all ages (Troll, 1971). Adelson (1970) suggested that we have translated the basic ideological differences which exist in our deeply divided society into generational conflict and differences—that the "generation gap" is just a projection of other social contrasts.

Selective Continuity. An intermediate position is presented by researchers such as Hill, Foote, Aldous, Carlson, and MacDonald (1970), who, in their impressive study of consumership and life style of three generation lineages of couples, found that some characteristics tend to be continuous over generations in certain kinds of families, and others not. For some this position means that most conflicts between generations are over secondary issues and that substantial continuity and solidarity prevail. While the rapid pace of social change encourages new ways of expressing old values, it is largely old values that are expressed. Some writers who originally concluded that change was overwhelming or that really nothing had changed have since moved over to this more balanced viewpoint. Some make a distinction between central or core values and peripheral values (Angres, 1975; Hess & Torney, 1967; Jennings & Niemi, 1968; Keniston, 1968; Tedin, 1974). In a 1965 study of student activists (Troll et al., 1969), a variable called "dedication to causes" showed the highest parent-child correlations—around .50. However, the parents may have been dedicated to "modernizing" the practices of the Catholic Church or eliminating reading problems by adopting a phonetic method of teaching and their children to promoting interracial housing or opposing the war in Vietnam. The *modus vivendi* of the parents may have been committee meetings and public speaking and of their children, marches and "sit-ins," but for both generations in these dedicated families, the core value of righting wrongs and improving the world seemed to be the same. Dedication to causes was a "family theme" (cf. Hess & Handel, 1959).

Methodological Problems

As Hagestad (1979) has documented, many methodological problems beset existing empirical data on generations in the family and make it hazardous to draw firm conclusions. We will list six here.

Measurement at One Time Only. Generational studies suffer from the same problems as research in life-span development; we must rely primarily on cross-sectional data when we need cross-sequential, time-sequential, or at least longitudinal (Schaie, 1965, 1973). Where present cross-sectional data show low parent-child correlations for high school or college students and their middle-aged parents, we might find much higher congruence if we could study these dyads again 20 years later or compare a comparable group of high school students and their parents 20 years from now. So far the only longitudinal reports of lineage-generational comparisons are those of Angres (1975) from the Chicago Youth and Social Change Project; Clausen (1974) from the Berkeley longitudinal files; and Jennings and Niemi (1975) from a seven-year follow-up of a national sample of high school seniors and their parents.

Equilibration across Families. In evaluating parent-child resemblances the centrality of values or other characteristics measured should be taken into account. If

there is such a thing as a "family theme" (Hess & Handel, 1959) and if children resemble their parents more in central or core characteristics than in peripheral ones, then the first step in comparing generations should be to ascertain value hierarchies. Ultimately we should need to evaluate each family individually, as Hess and Handel (1959) did in their pioneering study of "family worlds"—since to some extent each has a unique culture. In current empirical literature perhaps only Tedin (1974) and Thomas (1971) can be said to have approached this criterion.

Thomas and Stankiewicz (1974) have followed the general typology of "core" and "peripheral" values utilized by Rokeach (1960, 1968). Unfortunately this procedure confronts further problems. Judging values only from overt behavior has long been known to be risky, if not invalid. A few investigators have made preliminary steps toward weighting for centrality. Some have asked all respondents to rank-order a list of goals or values (e.g., Angres, 1975; Bengtson, 1975a: Flacks, 1967; Furstenberg, 1967; Goldsmid, 1972). Tedin (1974) used issue prominence as an independent or intervening variable.

Most of the studies reviewed in this chapter chose a less direct course toward considering centrality of values. They assumed that certain categories of attitudes or values would be equally prominent throughout our culture. An example is political orientation, which has been studied more than other values (Cutler, 1977; Jennings & Niemi, 1968, 1974, 1975). Because it is assumed to be central to most citizens' ideology and because most respondents are willing to talk about it—more than they are about money—a large part of family-transmission research deals with political-party preference and political beliefs.

Statistical Analysis. The majority of studies on generations in the family have utilized either inappropriate, nonrigorous, or naive analytic procedures. Correlation coefficients are probably among the most appropriate measures of pair correspondence (Connell, 1972). However they do not indicate causal direction—who influences whom (Hagestad, 1979; Lerner & Spanier, 1978). Transmission is not necessarily all from parent to child. Similar values and beliefs could be the result of the child influencing the parent as much as the other way around or of both parent and child being exposed to the same milieu (Bandura, 1969). For more precise determination of direction of influence or of relative influence of societal, family, or developmental processes, some form of recursive analysis might be better.

A further problem is that covariation does not necessarily reflect agreement or similarity (Acock & Bengtson, 1978). Parents and children may exhibit high covariation (correlation) but low absolute agreement. Absolute pair correspondence is the extent to which the scale scores of the sons are exactly the same as the scale scores of their fathers. This correspondence is usually measured by percentage agreement. A measure of group correspondence is used to compare cohorts as aggregates, parents as a group with children as a group. Group correspondence can be reported by giving each cohort's percentage agreement on the variable measured or by the mean agreement scores of each cohort, and cohort differences can be represented by means of a *t*-test or analysis of variance (Bengtson & Acock, 1977). Sigel and Reynolds (1979/1980) demonstrated dramatically the complicated relationship between aggregate and lineage data on women's attitudes toward women's movement issues.

As Connell (1972) points out, the distinctions between the types of intergenerational correspondence have often been blurred in actual practice. One particular difficulty is that several early studies reported group correspondence in terms of correlation coefficients. In addition to the correlation being a poor statistic for group correspondence, group data presented in this manner are easily misconstrued as measures of pair correspondence (Acock & Bengtson, 1980; Bengtson, 1975a).

Sampling. Problems in sampling include poor sampling methods, low response rates, and reliance on only one parent in estimating parental influences. These problems are prevalent in the early studies of parent-child political congruence reported in Hyman's (1959) comprehensive review of the early political socialization research. Connell (1972) argues that the samples of many of these early studies, which depended on children for obtaining their parents' responses, were likely to have been biased (Duffy, 1941; Fisher, 1948; Himmelhoch, 1950; Hirschberg & Gilliland, 1942; Stagner, 1936; Weltman & Remmers, 1946). It is possible that those children who were able to get their parents to fill out a questionnaire had a closer relationship with their parents than those who could not and thus were likely to share more of their parents' opinions.

Reliability and Validity of Measures. Most data on parent-child similarity consist of either self-descriptions, descriptions by others, or behavioral ratings. Self-descriptions are susceptible to response biases which may artificially inflate or diminish congruence scores. If the same person rates both self and parent, rater contamination is particularly likely. Questionnaire techniques, which tend to focus on self-descriptions, may give little information about actual behavior or attitudes, as is demonstrated by Bengtson and Acock (1977) in parent-child comparisons. In addition questionnaires are subject to problems of response set, item ambiguity, measurement unreliability, and social desirability of response. Behavioral ratings (seldom found in the generational literature) are similarly subject to problems of reliability and validity and of response bias. For a discussion of these and similar problems in examining parent-child agreement or levels of prediction, see Acock and Bengtson (1980).

In light of these grave methodological handicaps, it is clear that we must observe extreme caution in considering most of the generational literature. The following two sections will, therefore, be limited to those studies which are based on research designs that appear both appropriate and sound. In view of the earlier intense interest in the "generation gap," it is indeed surprising that relatively few studies can meet these criteria, even marginally.

Major Questions

Six major questions are persistently encountered in the generational literature. These are listed briefly here;

they will be treated in more detail in the following two sections of this chapter.

1. What (if indeed anything) is transmitted across family generations? Is it a general orientation to life, or is it particular values, attitudes, or personality characteristics?
2. What is the effect of historical events or societal changes upon family transmission and interpersonal bonds?
3. Is there a gender difference in either transmission or attachment? Are mothers closer and more influential than fathers, and are daughters closer to and more like their parents than sons?
4. What is the relative influence of parents, or conversely, children, as compared with friends or age peers in the socialization of orientations and behaviors?
5. What is the effect of family emotional climate or quality of interrelationships among family members on transmission or consensus?
6. What is the effect of ontogenetic developmental processes upon transmission and interpersonal bonds?

TRANSMISSION

The topic of intergenerational transmission focuses on the degree of similarity—or difference—between parents and children and, to a lesser extent, between grandparents and grandchildren. To what extent do people in different generations replicate each other? Do differences indicate different developmental statuses, coming of age at different times, or differential influence of sociohistorical trends?

At the extreme of family transmission—the "no gap" position—children would be expected to differ from their parents only because of ontogenetic developmental state. To be adolescent is to be different from older adults, but when youths in turn become middle-aged or old, they will then presumably resemble their parents and grandparents at these equivalent times of life. Relevant to this position is the concept of the *generational stake* (Bengtson & Kuypers, 1971). The effort and commitment now middle-aged parents have invested in raising their children combined with their present diminished influence on them, as well as the shortening of their own future, make it important to them that the next generation "carry on." Their children, on the other hand, look forward to a whole life ahead and need to express their uniqueness at least with respect to their parents. The parents' tendency will be to exaggerate similarities between themselves and their children. Their children's tendency will be to exaggerate differences.

Question 1: What Is Transmitted?

Almost all the research on this question has dealt with attitudes, value, and orientations in five areas: politics, religion, sex, work, and life-style characteristics. The following summary statements are based primarily on an earlier review of the literature (Troll & Bengtson, 1979). This earlier report contains tables of findings to which the reader is referred.

Politics. It is strategic to consider political-party identification, general political orientation, and specific attitudes separately. All five of the studies investigating parent-child similarity in *political-party preference* that met our criteria for inclusion found substantial cross-generational continuity, although each used a different kind of analysis. In a study of Illinois high school students and their parents (Levin, 1961), party preference of parents accounted for 68 percent of the variance in party choice of children. In a national probability sample of high school students and their parents (Jennings & Niemi, 1968), the correlation was .59. Two other studies of high school students and parents (Blumenfield, 1964; Tedin, 1974) report a contingency correlation of .54 and a product-moment correlation of .48, respectively. The data of Dodge and Uyeki (1962) are based on college students; they found much more agreement for Republican than for Democratic families: 68 percent versus 32 percent. Significantly we found no studies comparing party-affiliation concordance among older parent-child dyads. General political orientations studied include liberalism, cynicism, egalitarianism, Bengtson's (1975a) statistically derived "humanitarianism-materialism" and "collectivism-individualism," and Troll's (Troll et al., 1969) "dedication to causes." We find mixed support for transmission here.

Parent-child congruence on liberalism (Angres, 1975; Thomas & Stankiewicz, 1974), egalitarianism (Angres, 1975, but only for activists in Time 1), "dedication to causes" (Troll et al., 1969), "collectivism-individualism" (Bengtson, 1975a), "humanitarianism" (Troll et al., 1969), and "political-participation obligation" (Thomas & Stankiewicz, 1974) are consistent with a hypothesis of moderate transmission. Furthermore Thomas (1971) reports that children of liberal parents are significantly more likely to have taken part in left-wing causes (11 out of 30 families), while none of the children of liberal parents had taken part in right-wing causes. Only 5 out of 30 children of conservative parents took part in conservative causes, but none took part in liberal activities. In Bengtson's (1975a) data family membership did not contribute significantly to agreement on "humanitarianism-materialism." Sigel and Reynolds (1979/1980), though, found high mother-daughter consistency on women's movement orientation.

On some specific attitudes and opinions, there is high agreement; on others, virtually none. Sigel and Reynolds (1979/1980) report that agreement is highest on those issues which show most aggregate generational consistency. This will be discussed further with reference to dynamics of transmission.

Religion. Parent-child agreement on religious affiliation is consistently high—74 percent in Jennings and Niemi's data (1968); 58 percent to 79 percent in Hill et al.'s (1970); and 72 percent in Acock and Bengtson's (1975). Sixty-four percent of Hill's sample showed not only two- but three-generation continuity.

Generational agreement in general religious orientation is substantial in most investigations, although not as high as for denominational affiliation. There are two ambiguous findings, though. Thomas and Stankiewicz (1974) found a mother-daughter correlation of .47 for "belief in God" but only −.04 for "belief in the Bible." Angres (1975) found no significant mother-child correla-

tion for "conventional moralism," although Troll et al. (1969) found significant correlations for all cross-generation dyads on the same sample seven years earlier.

While Linder and Nahemow (1970) found relatively low family continuity in religious behavior, Acock and Bengtson (1980) report generally high levels of parent-child similarity on frequency of church attendance, self-rated religiosity, and traditional religious beliefs.

Sex Roles and Sexual Behavior. Almost all investigators agree that there has been a notable generational shift in sex-role affiliation (same-sex identity), in sexual restrictiveness (conformance to sex-role stereotypes), and in orientation and attitudes toward sex-role behavior (Bengtson & Starr, 1975; Sigel & Reynolds, 1979/1980). However, there have been few intrafamily comparisons.

In general generational shifts within the family seem to parallel those in the larger society. A negative correlation between mother and daughter on "femininity" found by Parkman (1965) is relevant. Similarly Acock and Bengtson (1980) report low parent-child correspondence on attitudes toward sexual permissiveness and Sigel and Reynolds (1979/1980) on definitions of womanhood.

Work and Achievement. In the face of an occupationally upwardly mobile society over the past century, the fact that Hill et al. (1970) found some three-generational continuity in husband's occupation (47 percent over three generations), particularly for fathers and sons, is notable. One might expect to find greater similarity in orientation toward achievement (need) than in actual educational or occupational attainment, since the latter is contingent upon economic opportunity. The Hill study did not measure achievement orientation or motivation as such. Those studies that did look at vocational interest, plans, or motivation (Kandel & Lesser, 1972; Sandis, 1970; Switzer, 1974; Troll et al., 1969) report parent-child agreement in these characteristics. In fact the only deviating results are those of Thomas and Stankiewicz (1974) and of Angres (1975). Because their populations are more "avant-garde," they may be picking up the beginnings of a new historical shift away from the "Protestant ethic." A possible "forerunner effect" will be discussed later.

Life-Style Characteristics. It is particulary in life style that one might expect wide generational differences, especially in a time of rapid social change. Intrafamily comparisons tend to be consistent with this generalization, but there are some interesting exceptions. Clausen (1974) reports high parent-child similarity in order of life values in his Berkeley longitudinal sample. Hill et al. (1970) found 60 percent parent-child agreement in consumership style on their Minneapolis three-generation sample and 47 percent in neighborhood grade. Brook, Lukoff, and Whiteman (1977) report a correlation of .40 between parental drug use and adolescent drug use.

Conclusion. In answer to our first question, the evidence available suggests that there is substantial but selective intergenerational continuity within the family. Parent-child similarity is mot noticeable in religious and political areas, least in sex roles, life style, and work orientation.

Question 2: What Is the Effect of Societal Processes upon Lineage Transmission?

As noted earlier similarities between parents and children could be the result of their joint exposure to what goes on around them rather than the result of specific within-family socialization. Three kinds of societal generation processes can be differentiated: a period effect, a cohort effect, and a "generational-unit" effect. To illustrate a period effect Cutler and Bengtson (1974) point out that "trends in alienation can be attributed to the societal events which comprise social and political history" (p. 140). This reflects changes in the population as a whole, changes which cannot be attributed to age, region, sex, education, or income. Mannheim (1923/1952) related social change to cohort effects. Because there is a "continuous emergence of new participants in the cultural process" (p. 293), one "comes to live within a specific, individually acquired, framework of useable past experience, so that every new experience has its form and its place largely marked out for it in advance" (p. 296). Mannheim further pointed out that "members of any one generation can only participate in a temporally limited section of the historical process" (p. 296). It is because each new cohort comes afresh upon the social scene and can see it with new perspective that new variations of old themes can occur.

Mannheim (1923/1952) also mentioned the independent effect of the "generational unit." Not all people born at the same time share the same socialization or perceive historical events in the same way. "Only where contemporaries are in a position to participate as an integrated group in certain common experiences can we rightly speak of community of location of a generation" (p. 298). No single characterization of youth in the 1960s would be completely descriptive of all members of that cohort. Rather there was a range of styles that included political activists, religious revivalists, communalists, and "freaks" (Laufer & Bengtson, 1974). While they all characterized members of the same generational cohort, they defined different generational units. Social structural variables like social class, race, and geographic location would be expected to influence "generational-unit" membership.

Bengtson and Cutler (1976) argue that all three of these generation-in-society processes interact with each other (as well as with generation-in-the-family processes) to influence values, attitudes, and behaviors. The effects of period and cohort are apparent in Tables 49–1 and 49–2. In Table 49–1 cohorts A through E, born at different times and thus of different ages in 1968 when alienated feelings permeated our country, show correspondingly different levels of susceptibility to the alienated mood (period effect). However, all the cohorts are more alienated in 1968 than at other times (period effect). Similarly both people in their twenties and in their sixties were more in favor of federal medical aid in 1960 than they were in 1952 and 1968 (period effect), although the older cohort (E) endorsed the idea more than did younger ones in each of these years (cohort effect).

Politics. Riesman (1950) suggested three decades ago that political attitudes and preferences are substantially

Table 49–1 Cohort Analysis of Political Alienation 1952–1968 (Percent Giving Alienated Response)[a]

AGE GROUP	COHORT LABEL	1952	1960	1968
21–28	A	31	10	31
29–36	B	28	26	34
37–44	C	25	25	37
45–52	D	29	29	40
53–60	E	35	27	49
61–68		40	32	54
69+		41	37	53
TOTAL		31	27	41

[a] Percentage agreeing with the statement, "People like me don't have any say about what the government does."

Source: Adapted from Cutler & Bengtson, 1974, Table 1, p. 169.

influenced by the particular historical era in which a person comes of age. Similarly Hyman (1959) concluded that a generation tends to become affiliated with the political party in power during the period of its socialization. Are they right?

Parent-child congruence in political party affiliation (see discussion under Question 1) shows fluctuations over the years in which studies have been done. These fluctuations seem to be synchronized with fluctuations in the political climate of the country. From the 1950s to the 1970s, the voting majority shifted from Democrat to Republican to Democrat to Republican, loosely corresponding to a left-right-left-right alternation. In times of Republican or conservative victory, conservative parents were more likely to have children who were in political agreement with them. In times of Democratic victory, the children of the Democrats were more likely to vote like their parents. During the late 1950s when Republicans were on top, Levin (1961) found that 95 percent of the children of Republicans voted Republican and only 75 percent of the children of Democrats voted Democrat. Dodge and Uyeki (1962), who also collected their data in the mid-1950s, found that 96 percent of Republicans' children voted Republican, while only 51 percent of Democrats' children voted Democrat. The converse obtained during the more liberal 1960s. Jennings and Langton (1969) found 68 percent of Republican offspring were Republican and 85 percent of Democratic offspring were Democratic. Thomas (1971a) reports that in 1965 the college-age children of politically active liberal parents were somewhat more congruent with them than were the children of conservative parents. The left-wing college students investigated by the University of Chicago Youth and Social Change Project in 1965 (Goldsmid, 1972) were, as a group, more in political agreement with their liberal parents than were the less active, more conservative students with their more conservative parents.

The same data show that the influence of generations in society, while clear, is not absolute. In Republican

Table 49-2 Attitudes toward Federal Governmental Medical Aid Programs (Percent in Favor)

AGE GROUP	1956[a]	1960	1964	1968	1972
21–24	70	77	67	67	
25–28		69	62	56	56
Change		−1	−15	−12	−11
61–64	69	84	64	72	
65–68		85	73	76	69
Change		+16	−11	+12	−4
Total sample	70	77	65	67	61
Change		+7	−12	+2	−6

[a] The questions read, for 1956 and 1960: "The government ought to help people get doctors and hospital care at low cost." For 1964 and 1968: "Some people say the government in Washington ought to help people get doctors and hospital care at low cost; others say the government should not get into this. Have you been interested enough in this to favor one side or the other?" For 1972: "There is much concern about the rapid rise in medical and hospital costs. Some feel there should be a government insurance plan which would cover all medical expenses. Others feel that medical expenses should be paid by individuals through private insurance like the Blue Cross. Which side do you favor?"

Source: Bengtson and Cutler (1976). Data were made available by the Inter-University Consortium for Political and Social Research, through the USC Political and Social Data Laboratory.

years not all the children of Democrats vote Republican. In fact a majority still keep to the party affiliation of their parents. Jennings and Langton (1969) found that 57 percent of their mother–father–high-school-child triads all favored the same party, and only 17 percent had agreeing parents and deviating child.

So far as politics is concerned, we can conclude that social climate can be said to have an intervening or tempering effect upon family transmission rather than an overriding influence.

Religion. Since the early 1960s there has been a historical shift in this country away from organized religion (Bengtson & Starr, 1975). Middle-aged parents as a group show wide differences in religiosity from their college-age children as a group (Acock & Bengtson, 1975; Armstrong & Sotzin, 1974; Payne, Summers, & Stewart, 1973; Weinstock & Lerner, 1972; Wieting, 1975; Yankelovich, 1970, 1972). What do lineage data show?

As noted earlier with reference to Question 1, family continuity in religious beliefs and practices, while substantial, is not as great as in denominational affiliation. The younger generation mostly adheres to the religious identity of its parents and grandparents but gives the actual working out of practices new meaning and new structure (Acock & Bengtson, 1975; Braun & Bengtson, 1972; Jennings & Niemi, 1968; Kalish & Johnson, 1972; Linder & Nahemow, 1970).

Family continuity in denominational affiliation is impressive (Acock & Bengtson, 1975; Hill et al., 1970; Jennings & Niemi, 1968); the same is true for lineage continuity in the related general orientation of conventional moralism, where Troll et al. (1969), Troll and Smith (1972), and Friedman, Gold, and Christie (1972) found both dyadic and three-generational family similarity, even though aggregate data (pooled parents versus pooled children) show cohort shifts.

In general we conclude that cohort changes may not override lineage transmission in religious identification, but they do seem to modify religious expression.

Sex Roles and Sexual Behavior. A marked shift toward liberalization of both sex-role definitions and sexual behavior has taken place in this country since the middle 1960s. Both acceptance of premarital sex in general and admission of having engaged in it have increased signifi-

cantly. Attitudes of acceptance increased even more rapidly than did practices. Comparisons between aggregates of parent and of youth show wide differences (Armstrong & Sotzin, 1974; Freeman, 1972; Lesser & Steininger, 1975; Walsh, 1970; Yankelovich, 1972). Changes between 1969 and 1973 suggest a period effect as noticeable as a cohort effect. What do the lineage data show?

We have few data on lineage comparisons of sexual norms, but those which we do have point to greater lineage differences than in either politics or religion. This is true for sexual permissiveness (Thomas & Stankiewicz, 1974) and sex-role stereotyping (Aldous & Hill, 1965; Angres, 1975; Thomas & Stankiewicz, 1974; Troll et al., 1969). Angres's findings could be interpreted as suggesting that the influence of the larger society can override that of parents but more so for those children who themselves are most influenced by—or most likely to influence—social trends (see ensuing discussion of the "forerunner effect"). The political activists whom Angres (and earlier, Troll et al., 1969) interviewed were as ready to espouse a liberal view of sex-role equality and, to a lesser extent, sexual permissiveness as they were to espouse a more liberal political view. They would thus tend to differ more from their parents than would the nonactivists. One might also conclude from Sigel and Reynolds's (1979/1980) data that sex-role attitudes have partly been a period effect and partly the result of mother-daughter negotiation within the boundaries of family values.

Work and Achievement. The cohort of the mid-1960s—or at least the college youth unit of that cohort—adopted a different orientation not only toward politics and sexual matters but also toward work (Bengtson & Starr, 1975; Flacks, 1967). Flacks observed that "the dissatisfaction of socially advantaged youth with conventional career opportunities is a significant social trend, the most important single indicator of restlessness among sectors of the youth population" (p. 58). While only a small portion of that cohort actually turned its back upon jobs as such, most of the cohort moved toward a different orientation toward work.

Over three-fourths of the students surveyed by Yankelovich (1970) in 1969 agreed that "commitment to a meaningful career is a very important part of a person's life." However, they no longer believed in inevitable rewards for hard work; only 39 percent said they did in Yankelovich's (1972) survey, and they were more concerned with personal fulfillment and social service than with financial rewards. In 1969 only 56 percent of college youth agreed that "hard work will always pay off," as opposed to 76 percent of their parents, 79 percent of noncollege youth, and 85 percent of parents of noncollege youth (Yankelovich, 1972). The youth observed by Flacks in 1965 were still, seven years later, looking for personal fulfillment in their work. Angres (1975) noted significant aggregate generational differences in their work attitudes in 1972. However, this change in work attitudes did not seem to affect achievement motivations. In their late twenties they still wanted to do well, although doing well was defined differently. How do within-family comparisons look?

Hill et al.'s (1970) data on three-generational families, who all—even the youngest couples—predate the cohort shift described before, point sharply to the strong influence of sociohistorical conditions in providing differential climates for achievement. Upgrading in education and income (of the husbands) over the three generations was allied to greater opportunities. Even so relative consumership achievement level shows 80 percent continuity over three generations.

The aggregate generational differences in work-ethic attitudes reported by Angres are duplicated in lineage generational differences; mother-child correlations are not significant. Thomas and Stankiewicz (1974) found similar lack of agreement between parents and college-age children on work-achievement values; Acock and Bengtson (1980), however, found mothers' scores on work ethic to be highly predictive of youths' orientations—much more so than fathers' scores. An interesting sex difference emerges between lineage similarities of men (Hill et al., 1970) and of women (Troll & Smith, 1972). This will be discussed further with reference to sex differences.

As far as achievement orientation and achievement motivation are concerned, we see more continuity than we do for work ethic. The young children studied by Furstenberg (1967) tended to duplicate their parents' desires for status mobility if they perceived these goals correctly, parents' aspirations for their later college attendance contributed significantly to high school students' intentions for further education (Sandis, 1970). Two other studies of high school students (Kandel & Lesser, 1972; Kerckhoff & Huff, 1974) show substantial correlations between youth and their parents' achievement goals. The achievement need of the college students who were interviewed seven years later by Angres correlated significantly in achievement need with their parents (Troll et al., 1969) and so do the three-generation women's lineages in Troll's later Detroit sample (Switzer, 1974).

In conclusion, period and cohort influences may override family influence in work orientation and belief in conventional work ethic more than they do in general achievement orientation. While high–achievement-motivated parents still tend to have high–achievement-motivated children, the areas in which achievement is sought varies from one generation to the other.

A Special Look at Forerunners. Earlier in the discussion of Question 2, reference was made to *generational*

units. It is possible to consider *forerunners* as a kind of generational unit. Mannheim (1923/1952) remarks that the "nucleus of attitudes particular to a new generation is first evolved and practiced by older people who are isolated in their own generation (forerunners)" (p. 308), and Adelson (1970) makes a similar point. In a somewhat speculative vein, we suggest that there is a relationship between forerunners, defined in terms of societal cohorts, and lineage transmission. The following three-step process could occur. (See Bengtson and Black, 1973a, for a similar formulation based on systems theory and focusing on generational cohorts instead of on the family.)

1. A new age cohort of forerunners, on coming of age developmentally, turns to new and vigorous ways of expressing the general political orientation—a dedication to causes, say—it has gotten from its family. If this is in tune with basic political processes going on in the country, it can start a swing in a new direction. In its first move toward this new direction, the forerunners inevitably decrease their congruence with both their parents and their age-mates who come from different kinds of families—and perhaps should not truly be called peers.

2. If this new ideology has appeal for peers and parents of the forerunners, both these groups are influenced to shift toward it. This shift increases the congruence again between parents and children in the forerunner families. At the same time it decreases the congruence between the second wave of youth which joins the forerunners and *its* parents.

3. If this new ideology is really in tune with the times, the parents of the second wave of youth are in turn influenced by their children, and their family congruence increases again. In effect each lineage generation plays both mediator and recipient roles. This multiple-generation effect would then become manifest in political change that surfaces in the country as a whole.

Conclusion. In response to Question 2 the evidence suggests that social and historical forces—cohort or period effects—serve as moderator variables in family-lineage transmission. Transmission is enhanced where social forces encourage particular values or behavior. It is reduced in areas where social forces discourage them, as where particular characteristics become "keynotes" of a new rising generational unit.

Question 3: Are There Gender Differences in Transmission?

Several somewhat conflicting assumptions pervade the socialization and family-transmission literature. The first is that fathers have more influence on the ideology of their children than do mothers. Second, mothers affect noncognitive belief areas more than do fathers. Third, same-sex lineages are more alike than are cross-sex lineages. Fourth, daughters are more susceptible to parental influence than are sons. Obviously sex-role stereotypes of the powerful father and the warm, close mother, of the adventurous son and the compliant daughter, are at the bottom of these assumptions. Freud (1963) and Parsons (1968) are the underlying theorists. Let us look at these assumptions in the light of available empirical data.

Politics. Jennings and Langton (1969) counter the prevailing view that the father is the dominant influence in shaping his child's political orientations with the fact that most mothers have closer ties with their children than do fathers. Therefore, they postulate, the mother is the primary influence. In a study of political-party affiliation of high school students and their parents, Jennings and Langton did indeed find that the students were slightly more likely to share their mother's affiliation than their father's. This is particularly pronounced in families where parents do not agree on party affiliation—even though such disagreement occurred in only 26 percent of the sample. Democratic mothers were most likely to have Democratic children. Remember this was a period of rising Democratic power (see discussion under Question 2). However, even during a Democratic tide, Republican mothers rallied 45 percent of their children to their side (Democratic mothers only rallied 6 percent more). Fengler and Wood's (1973) findings on college students' liberalism are similar. While the majority of the University of Wisconsin students they surveyed were liberal at the time of the study, more of those whose mothers were liberal were themselves liberal than were those whose fathers were liberal. Earlier Helfant (1952) had reported that in two out of three specific political attitudes children were more in agreement with their mothers than with their fathers. Similar conclusions concerning the greater impact of mothers' influence are noted by Acock and Bengtson (1980).

Most other investigations in the political area, however, show no evidence for gender difference (Friedman et al., 1972; Jennings & Langton, 1969; Jennings & Niemi, 1968; Thomas, 1971b; Thomas & Stankiewicz, 1973; Troll et al., 1969).

Political-party affiliation, which shows more evidence of family transmission than do other aspects of political orientation, also shows more evidence of gender effects. Mothers have greater effect on their children than do fathers if the two are split in their voting. No other findings about political transmission support a hypothesis of gender differences.

Religion. It has been held that socialization of religion is the domain of the mother, and it is in this area that most writers, following Hill and colleagues (1970), see gender effects. What do other data show?

Four independent investigations concur with Hill's generalization (Braun & Bengtson, 1972; Fengler & Wood, 1973; Hill et al., 1970; Thomas & Stankiewicz, 1973). In these studies agreement between mothers and children tends to be higher than that between fathers and children. Continuity along three-generational female lineages and even predominantly female lineages is greater than along male and predominantly male lineages. Only one finding would be consistent with the more-susceptible-daughter hypothesis, though—that of Thomas and Stankiewicz (1974) on "belief in God."

Conventional or traditional moralism might be considered a type of religious orientation. Neither Troll et al. (1969) nor Friedman et al. (1972) found any differences in conventional moralism among four possible dyadic combinations (mother-daughter, mother-son, father-daughter, or father-son). Similar absence of gender influence on general religious orientation and on specific beliefs is found in the four studies which present relevant data (Aldous & Hill, 1965; Braun & Bengtson, 1972; Thomas & Stankiewicz, 1974; Troll et al., 1969). On the other hand Acock and Bengtson (1980) found that fathers had considerably more influence than did mothers on religious *practices.*

While there seems to be greater female continuity in denominational affiliation, there is no support for a conclusion of particular female influence in religious values, attitudes, or behaviors.

Sex Roles and Sexual Behavior. If, in popular belief, politics and jobs are the domains of the man and religion of the woman, transmission of sex roles should be same-sex-linked, with fathers socializing sons and mothers socializing daughters into proper male and female behavior. What do the data show?

Aldous and Hill (1965) found that three-generation female and "predominantly female" lineages show more agreement on "role-task specialization" than do male and predominantly male lineages. The difference is between 38 percent agreement in the female line and 29 percent in the male line. Whether this difference is statistically significant is not clear. More impressive evidence for maternal influence can be found in Fengler and Wood's (1973) data, particularly those related to sexual norms and boundaries. Where the mother is liberal and the father is conservative on this issue, 80 percent of their children are also liberal. On the other hand when the father is liberal and the mother is conservative, only 42 percent of their children are liberal.

In summary most gender differences in cross-generational similarity in sex roles and sexual behavior are not significant. Exceptions are the greater maternal influence reported by Aldous and Hill and Fengler and Wood. There is no evidence for greater daughter susceptibility or of same-sex specialization.

Work and Achievement. The extensive research literature on achievement motivation and attitude toward jobs has been notably sex determined. Early socialization patterns can be related to later need for achievement motivation in boys and men but not in girls and women (Troll, 1975). This is not hard to understand, since the world of jobs has until very recently been considered the domain of men. In view of this bivalence one would predict that if there were generational continuity in this area it would obtain for men and not for women.

The three-generational investigation of Hill et al. (1970) supports this prediction, finding impressive continuity in occupation and educational level in male lineages. They do not even provide figures for wife's occupation and education.

Most other studies that have looked at work and achievement have either been focused on college students or upon women and children. None of these found sex differences, either for job attitudes, achievement motivation, or achievement level (Kerckhoff & Huff, 1974; Thomas & Stankiewicz, 1974; Troll et al., 1969). Kandel and Lesser (1972), in fact, report greater mother-daughter than mother-son consensus on educational goals. Mothers' attitudes were much more influential than were fathers' in predicting work-ethic orientations of their children in one study (Acock & Bengtson, 1978).

We can conclude that, while there may be marked sex differences in most populations with reference to work and achievement values, these appear to be subject to period effects from changing societal attitudes toward women in the labor force. Mothers are generally as influential as fathers, daughters as affected as sons, in the socialization of orientations to work and achievement.

Conclusion. In response to Question 3 at the present time we cannot conclude that gender is an important variable in transmission. While some studies support the common assumption that fathers are more influential than are mothers, other studies do not. Sex of child does not appear to be a relevant variable.

Question 4: How Does Family Influence Compare with That of Peers or Friends?

According to the traditional view of socialization, family members exert a major influence in early childhood—but gradually school and peers become more important. By adolescence the peer group is believed to be more powerful than the family (see Campbell, 1969; Coleman, 1961; McCandless, 1969). Campbell says that the casual relationships which exist among age-mates, as compared with the intense, intimate relationships of family or close friends, help to prepare for the casual relationships of business and community interactions. Kandel and Lesser (1972), however, found that, while Danish adolescents turn to both their parents and friends, American youth have diffuse relationships with a peer reference group rather than with friends and are closer to their parents, mainly their mothers.

Concordance between both Danish and American high school students and their mothers on educational plans—ways to get ahead in life and life goals—was higher than that between the students and their best school friend (Kandel & Lesser, 1972); it should be noted that all correlations are high. The investigators suggest that youth do not choose friends in opposition to parents but are likely to select the children of their parents' friends or those who come from similar families as their friends. Two studies on the relative influence of parents and friends on adolescent marijuana use (Brook et al., 1977; Kandel, 1974) found disparate evidence. In Kandel's study, while parents' use of alcohol had virtually no relation to their children's use of marijuana, friends' use of marijuana correlated (tau beta =.48) with their own use of marijuana. Brook et al. (1977) found that both peer and parent drug use were important correlates, although peers were more influential.

Beyond adolescence close ties to a spouse tend to overshadow, though not usually replace or erase, family cross-generational ties. Recent interest in adulthood and old-age social relationships (e.g., Adams, 1968; Hess, 1972; Knipscheer, 1979; Stueve & Fisher, 1978) show a separation of functions into sharing of recreational and topical activities with friends and of more functional activities with parents—in old age with children. Nonmarried adults and older people lean more heavily upon cross-generational relationships and friends than those who have a spouse available, women more than men.

It would obviously be presumptuous to generalize from present meager data, beyond saying that parents (and children) may be more influential in some areas of socialization and peers or friends in others (cf. Hagestad & Snow, 1977). Perhaps it is primarily in "generation keynote" issues like the use of marijuana that peers' influence predominates.

Conclusion. The conclusion with regard to Question 4 is that friends or peers may serve as a moderating influence on family transmission in some areas, such as recreation, sexual behavior, or use of marijuana, which are prominent issues for a cohort. Parental—or child—influences seem strong in achievement, work and political orientations, however (see Bengtson & Troll, 1978; Hagestad, 1979; Troll, 1981). In general peer and parent influences appear complementary rather than oppositional.

Question 5: What Is the Effect of Intrafamily Relationships upon Generational Similarities?

The quality of family interrelationships varies widely. Some families are tightly knit, with strong boundaries keeping members in and nonmembers out; others are loose-knit with little distinction between family members and nonkin. Are variations in the quality of family relationships related to lineage transmission? Does closeness lead to greater similarity? Such questions have been asked since the time of Davis (1940) and before. However, partly because the variables considered are so diverse, the available data are not easy to integrate or interpret.

Politics. Three studies support the hypothesis that the quality of family relationships might influence political transmission. One is that of Jennings and Langton (1969), who looked at families in which parents differed in party affiliation. In these families the high school students were more likely to choose the same party as their mother if they felt closer to her than to their father (51 percent as compared with 26 percent). Another is that of Troll et al. (1969), who found that "family power balance" and "family integration" contributed significantly (in a multiple stepwise regression analysis) to parent-child similarity—but only in "dedication to causes."

Tedin (1974) systematically investigated family factors that might influence political-attitude transmission. He looked at three family variables: perceptual accuracy by the high school seniors of their parents' attitudes; salience of their political position to the parents; and "attractiveness" of the parents to the child. He concluded that "the influence of parents on the party identification and public-policy attitudes of their children . . . at any point in time, will be highly dependent on the distribution of issue salience and perceptual accuracy for the particular attitude object in question" (p. 1952). While "attractiveness of parents to children" did not predict high school seniors' party affiliation or political attitudes, as well as the other two variables, it did affect attitudes about racial integration and China.

In contrast to these three studies, most other investigators show remarkable independence between quality of family relationships and parent-child similarity in politics (Acock & Bengtson, 1978; Angres, 1975; Jennings & Niemi, 1968; Thomas, 1971b; Thomas & Stankiewicz, 1973; Troll et al., 1969). The intervening variables studied include parental power styles (Jennings & Niemi, 1968); parent-child closeness (Angres, 1975; Jennings & Niemi, 1968); affectual solidarity (Acock & Bengtson, 1978); family expression of affect and parents' approval of each other (Troll et al., 1969); intrafamily conflict (Thomas, 1971b; Thomas & Stankiewicz, 1974; Troll et al., 1969); family integration or solidarity (Thomas & Stankiewicz, 1974; Troll et al., 1969); permissiveness and warmth (Thomas, 1971b; Thomas & Stankiewicz, 1974); parental understanding and quality and frequency of communication (Thomas & Stankiewicz, 1974); and maternal satisfaction with child (Angres, 1975). All of these variables—based on data from both children and parents—have little effect on parent-child similarity in politics.

Religion. Acock and Bengtson (1978) report that associational solidarity (activities shared by parent and child) is significantly related to congruence in church membership and church attendance. Affectual solidarity is related to congruence in religiosity. Troll et al. (1969) found "family integration" related to conventional moralism, and in Angres's (1975) follow-up of the same sample, she found mother-child "bondedness" related to moralism.

Most of the other findings for religion are similar to those for politics: no relation between family-closeness variables and lineage continuity (Acock & Bengtson, 1978; Angres, 1975; Jennings & Niemi, 1968; Thomas & Stankiewicz, 1974; Troll et al., 1969).

Other Characteristics. In neither the 1965 round of interviewing with Chicago college students and their parents (Troll, 1967) nor in the 1972 follow-up (Angres, 1975) did family-relationship variables show any influence on parent-child similarity in achievement motivation.

There is somewhat more support for a connection between family quality and similarity in life style than there is in the other areas. Both Furstenberg (1967) and Clausen (1974) show that family climate affects children's and adolescents' agreement with their parents. In Furstenberg's study the quality of interaction, the use of parents as reference persons, low interaction with peers, and minimal family conflict were all positively related to consensus on social-mobility goals. An inspection of Clausen's (1974) data suggests that there are noticeably higher correlations when the relationship is considered "close," at least in same-sex dyads.

There is also contrary evidence. Kandel and Lesser (1972) found that none of the maternal-relationship variables had any influence on mother-child concordance in educational goals. The variables they investigated included maternal authority, extent of explanations for decisions, child's feelings of closeness to mother, reliance on her for advice, adolescent peer orientation, and respect for mother's opinions. Angres (1975) also found no relation between mother-child bondedness and consensus on goals of life.

Overall it is the minimal influence of family interrelationships as such upon transmissions of life-style characteristics that is most striking. Consensus seems to be relatively independent of quality of family behavior and practices. Lack of consensus does not seem to interfere ⸱ ᵗʰe strength of parent-child bonds. In fact both

Troll (1971) and Hagestad (1979) observed an interesting process of what Hagestad called "demilitarized zones" used by family members to preserve family harmony and avoid damaging conflict in sensitive areas. Fights are over minor matters.

Conclusion. In summarizing evidence for Question 5, qualitative aspects of family relationships, such as "closeness," do not seem to affect lineage transmission.

Question 6: What Is the Effect of Developmental Levels upon Family Transmission?

Up to now the bulk of the writing on generations has focused on comparisons of youth and middle age, on the emergence of new cohorts, or on the individual's transition into adulthood. Yet many theoretical questions arise from a consideration of change over the course of life. The behavior of parents at any given moment comes not only from their lineage and social position but also from their position along their own life course. One of the earlier findings from the Berkeley longitudinal studies was the lack of constancy in maternal and child behaviors (Bayley, 1964), even during the early part of the child's life. Bengtson and Black (1973a) point out that in any intergenerational relationship the actors in each generation are dynamically acting out their own developmental agenda. Further "the gap between young and old sometimes represents differences in maturational level and life stage responsibilities. Thus, in many instances, the differences between parents and their children are temporary phenomena rooted in developmental process" (p. 140).

The possibly temporary nature of parent-child differences may be most clearly illustrated for adolescents. Basic similarities might be obscured by adolescents' needs to "try on" attitudes and behaviors different from those of their parents as part of their "search for identity." It is possible that when they pass into a more stable developmental period their values and attitudes may more closely resemble those of their parents, particularly if cohort changes do not override lineage transmission.

Several writers (e.g., Angres, 1975; Bengtson & Black, 1973a; Goslin, 1969; Lerner, 1978) point out that socialization is not always from parent to child but also from child to parent. Also both generations learn together from their location within the same social structure under the impact of historical or period effects. Greater similarity between older adults and their parents than between adolescents and their parents (or vice versa) may represent either developmental effects, lineage effects, cohort effects, or period effects. The two older generations could be at more stable points in their lives—unless the oldest generation is in a terminal decline. Differential expectations and responsibilities could produce different values, attitudes, or personality characteristics. These differences may intertwine with cohort effects; the middle generation could express its separateness from its parents in the area of religion; and the younger generation, in the area of life style or politics. Particular historical circumstances could have induced one kind of change in the growing up of the middle generation and another kind in the growing up of the 1960s youth.

Since sophisticated cross-sequential or time-sequential

designs are not yet available in generational research, developmental effects on lineage transmission must be estimated from comparisons of different lineage dyads or triads: of grandparents with their children and those children with the grandchildren. There have been few investigations of three-generation family lineages—Hill et al., Bengtson and colleagues, Fengler and Wood, Troll's Detroit study, Kalish and Johnson, and Hagestad, Cohler, and Neugarten in Chicago. The only longitudinal data available on lineage transmission are those of Angres (1975), Clausen (1974), and Jennings and Niemi (1975).

Two questions are involved here. First, do adolescents or college-age youth differ from their parents more than adults differ from their parents? Second, are parents more like their children than grandparents are like their grandchildren? These questions will be discussed in terms of the content areas delineated previously.

Politics. Arranging the generational studies by the age of the younger or youngest generation suggests that parent-child agreement in the area of politics decreases steadily from childhood through young adulthood (Jennings & Niemi, 1975). It is, of course, impossible with present data to separate cohort or period effects from developmental effects. The only preadolescent data available are indirect. For example Hess and Torney (1967) studied family similarity but among siblings, not cross-generationally, and Radke-Yarrow, Trager, and Miller (1952) used only parents' reports so their findings of strong family similarities are not directly relevant. Most studies of high school students (Blumenfeld, 1964; Douvan & Adelson, 1966; Helfant, 1952; Jennings & Langton, 1969; Jennings & Niemi, 1968; Levin, 1961; Remmers & Weltman, 1947; Tedin, 1974) show agreement on political-party preference but less agreement on attitudes. College-age youth show even less consensus with their parents (Friedman et al., 1972; Goldsmid, 1972; Troll & Smith, 1972; Troll et al., 1969). Agreement on these data varies with forerunner status and political climate, as well as with specificity of measure. Thus in Angres's (1975) follow-up of the Chicago student-activist sample, the young adults seem to be in less agreement with their mothers on political issues than they had been seven years earlier. This diminishing similarity may even continue into later life. Middle-aged children (Bengtson, 1975a; Kalish & Johnson, 1972) show less congruence with their parents than with their children. An exception is the greater congruence for collectivism versus individualism (Bengtson, 1975a) in the middle-age–old-age dyad. Supporting evidence for increasing differentiation comes from grandparent-grandchild agreement (Kalish & Johnson, 1972), which is lower than either parent-child dyad (grandparent-parent or parent-grandchild).

Religion. Much less research has been done in lineage continuity in religion that in politics and most of that since 1960. While Hill et al. (1970) found relatively little developmental effect in religious affiliation (remember the high level of three-generational continuity), Kalish and Johnson (1972), Troll and Smith (1972), and Braun and Bengtson (1972) all found more agreement on religious belief between young adults and their parents than between middle-aged adults and theirs. Similarly Angres found that consensus on moralism decreased over seven

years. Grandparents and their grandchildren are in less agreement than are parents and children of any age.

Sex Roles and Sexual Behavior. Because of an overriding period or historical effect journalistically titled *the sexual revolution* (Bengtson & Starr, 1975), developmental effects are impossible to determine. Aggregate data from surveys (Yankelovich, 1970) show sharp generational differences, but Angres's (1975) interviews with middle-aged mothers found that 60 percent said they had been influenced by their daughters' behavior. Against a background of low three-generational continuity (Aldous & Hill, 1965), there appears to be more agreement between youth and their parents than between the two older generations (Fengler & Wood, 1972). Possible developmental effects are suggested by the data of Reiss (1968); while 44 percent of single adults surveyed approved of premarital sexual intercourse, only 23 percent of married adults and only 13 percent of adults whose children were teenage or older approved of this behavior. Angres's (1975) findings further support the three-step "forerunner" effect as proposed under Question 2. It was the mothers of activists who were most open to the influence of youth. When asked under what circumstances they would consider premarital intercourse for college women, the modal response of the young women was "if there was some emotion," but of their mothers, "if there was deep emotional involvement." On the basis of existing studies (cf. Sigel & Reynolds, 1979/1980), we might predict that a new sample of college students (non-forerunners) and their mothers investigated five years from now would move toward increased congruence again.

Work and Achievement. The available data suggest greater similarity in work and achievement orientations and behavior between the two younger generations than between the two older. However, in line with our earlier discussion, these may represent period instead of developmental effects (Bengtson & Starr, 1975; Hill et al., 1970). Changed attitudes toward work and sex seem to characterize the "youth revolt" of the 1960s when generational means are compared, but Kandel and Lesser (1972) report that parental influence does not seem to decrease during adolescence, either for Danish or American youth. In Troll's three-generation Detroit study (Switzer, 1974), the general level of achievement motivation correlated .42 between young adults and their parents but only .26 between the middle and oldest generations. Finally Hill et al. (1970) report greater congruence between the oldest and middle family generations for "middle-level achievers" and between the middle and youngest generations for "low-level achievers" but no difference among generational dyads for "high-level achievers." Grandparents and grandchildren are less congruent than contiguous generational dyads.

Hill et al. (1970) report larger shifts in child-rearing values between the two older generations than between the two younger ones, as do Miller and Schvaneveldt (1977) for fertility-related attitudes of Mormon women. Kalish and Johnson (1972) found more agreement between the two younger generations on attitudes toward students and old people and no difference in other dimensions. Bengtson (1975a) found no dyadic difference in humanism versus materialism but close agreement between the youngest and middle generations on collectivism versus individualism.

When Bengtson and Kuypers (1971) suggested the term *generational stake* to describe the differences in perception of a generational gap on the part of youth and their parents, they were referring to different perspectives one has at different parts of one's own individual and family life course. Youths appear eager to express uniqueness and independence and thus tend to exaggerate the difference between themselves and their parents, even with middle-aged people in general. The middle-aged, about to relinquish some of the authority and responsibility for the actions of their maturing children, are anxious that these children not abandon the values which guided them—the parents—in their child-rearing labors. The oldest generation "senses their finitude and fears loss of their own significance" (Bengtson, Olander, & Haddad, 1976, p. 242). These different perspectives may reflect cohort or aggregate differences more than within-lineage differences and perception of difference more than actual difference.

Conclusion. In response to Question 6 the effect of variation in individual life-span developmental levels (aging or maturation) upon lineage transmission is thus neither general nor obvious. It is a prime example of "selective continuity" and cannot at present be separated from period effects.

CLOSENESS AND AFFECT

A variety of labels have been used to conceptualize family interrelationships. Most of these deal with the separate concepts of *closeness* and *affect*. For example *solidarity* between generations has been conceptualized in terms of associations, affect, and consensus (Bengtson et al., 1976). So far we have focused upon consensus. Now we will turn to such topics as *attachment, conflict, interaction,* and *communication.*

Unfortunately data on this subject are even more inadequate than they are for intergenerational transmission (Hagestad, 1979). There are fewer studies altogether, and these suffer from many of the same methodological problems noted earlier. They tend to rely on reports of only one family member. They are almost all self-report rather than observational or experimental. They are restricted in age, focusing on either middle-aged parents and their high school or college-aged children or on aged parents and their middle-aged children. Until recently, we were faced with a gap of about 30 years of the life span unexplored. Studies of interaction between parents and their infant and preschool children (e.g., Cherry & Lewis, 1976; Lewis & Freedle, 1973; Moss, 1967) are now proliferating.

Research approaches are generally stereotyped and narrow; few look beyond social expectations and surface behavior to more complex variables. In an area most needful of creative design and measurement—that of long-standing affective bonds between clinically normal people—little application of clinical expertise or theory has been evident. Where clinical approaches have been used, they have too often followed a dogmatic, rather ~ an empirical, perspective—e.g., the body of studies

dealing with "schizophrenic" or "problem" families (see review by Riskin & Faunce, 1972).

Concepts and operationalized measures differ so widely that it is dangerous to generalize. Sampling also makes it difficult to generalize, particularly since many studies focus on institutionalized old people or families with mentally ill members. Empirical analyses, with a few exceptions (Adams, 1968; Andersson, 1973; Angres, 1975; Kandel & Lesser, 1972; Troll, 1975; Troll et al., 1969) are often primitive. Finally the dimensions we are interested in—family closeness and affect—have been treated mostly as independent or intervening variables (e.g., Clausen's use of "closeness" as an intervening variable for measuring family similarity) rather than as dependent variables. The data on the relation between perceived similarity to perceived closeness, treated in Question 5, are among the few exceptions.

Question 7: Are There Variations in Parent-Child Attachment through the Life Course?

A commonly held belief among family theorists is that a child's development is accompanied by a progressive severing of bonds with family members. Some writers believe this must occur, that parents must "let go" and children must "achieve independence" or both they and society will suffer. According to this view the break with the family should be completed by late adolescence. Families of orientation should give way to families of procreation. Adults should be devoted to their new families, free of interference from the old. Yet we are faced with a growing body of data on adult kinship interactions that suggests such a picture may be simplistic and misleading. In fact it is the amazing lifelong persistence of some parent-child bonds in the fact of geographic separation, socioeconomic differences, and even value conflict that we must explain (cf. Gewirtz, 1972; Kalish & Knudsen, 1976; Troll, 1971; Troll & Smith, 1976).

Granted that there are variations in closeness and amount of affect between parents and their very young children, what can we say about the extent of such "attachments" at later points in the life course? Four kinds of evidence are available: data on residential propinquity, patterns of interaction, helping behaviors, and self-reports of feelings.

Residential Propinquity. Since the norm in our society is that children reside in their parents' home until they finish high school, only information about post–high school families is relevant. Assumptions that families today are split apart by geographic separation have not been substantiated by most survey data (Shanas, Townsend, Wedderburn, Friis, Milhoj, & Stehouwer, 1968; Sussman & Burchinal, 1962). In a review of the literature on the family of later life, Troll, Miller, and Atchley (1979) report that young adults as well as their parents and grandparents want to live near each other, though not in the same quarters. This seems to be particularly true after the young are married and even more true after they have children. As Litwak (1969) pointed out extended family ties are not broken by migration in the service of better economic opportunities. In fact, he concludes, it is the support of the family back home that enables trial explorations into new territory, and where yonder fields *are* greener, the "family scouts" are followed by other kin. In middle-class careers where executives and professionals are transferred or look for promotion to other parts of the country, ties are maintained in other ways than by living nearby and frequent visiting. In many cases eventual return of the younger generation or migration of the older tends to reunite the separated generations. While late adolescents and young adults may live far from parents, this kind of separation may be temporary. The studies cited and many others (e.g., Harris, 1975; Shanas et al., 1968) show that old people, whenever possible, live in their own homes but near their children. Moreover moving in with children is resorted to only when there is not enough money to live alone, when health is so poor that self-care is impossible, or—to a lesser extent—when a spouse has died. Even so one-third of all people over 65 who have living children do live with one of them. Such joint households, though, are usually two-generation, not three-generation. It is usually post–child-rearing couples and their very old parents who live together after the younger generation is out of the house.

Interaction. Interaction and communication may also follow a life-course pattern. They are presumably all highest in early childhood, gradually diminishing through the school years, and then increasing again as young adults form their own "families of procreation." The findings of Bayley (1964) and Hill et al. (1970) are consistent with such a hypothesis. According to Hill's data it is the middle-aged generation that has the most interaction, combining contacts with both parents and children (and probably also grandchildren). In fact the authors call this generation the *lineage bridge.* Nydegger and Mitteness (1979) show that fathers, at least, believe they progressively reduce control over their children after adolescence, shifting instead to companionship. Hagestad and Snow (1977) found that "empty-nest" parents said their children were now their friends.

Parents and adult children see each other often or keep in touch by telephone, letter-writing, and intermittent lengthy visits (e.g., Adams, 1968; Bengtson, 1975b; Berardo, 1967; Shanas et al., 1968; Sussman, 1965; Troll et al., 1979). In the three generations of couples studied by Hill et al. (1970), 70 percent of the married young adults saw their parents weekly and 10 percent saw their grandparents weekly. Forty percent of *their* parents (the middle generation) saw their parents weekly, and 70 percent saw their children weekly. Neither socioeconomic mobility nor social class diminished the effect of massive cross-generational contact. Even though areas open for communication and activities shared vary, contact remains high (Angres, 1975). A recent study of "academic gypsies" found as high a level of contact with parents as among more settled Americans (Bedford, 1980).

Helping. Most parents and children continue to help each other throughout life. The peak of giving help is probably in middle age and of receiving help in childhood and late old age. Aid may be in the form of services, such as babysitting, shopping, housecleaning, or in money or gifts. In some families the flow of support seems to be stronger down the generation line than up. Like the reversal in living arrangements, which only occurs where

old parents who are poor or disabled give up their independence to move in with their children, a shift from parental giving to children giving may occur only when parents can no longer give (see Gibson, 1969; Hawkinson, 1965; Hill et al., 1970; Kerckhoff, 1965; Schorr, 1960; Shanas et al., 1968; Streib, 1965; Sussman, 1965; Sussman & Burchinal, 1962; Winch & Greer, 1968). The amount of help exchanged does not seem to be closely related either to residential nearness or to frequency of visiting. When parents and children live farther apart (more frequent with middle-class and not-so-old parents), they are more likely to exchange money and serviceable gifts like appliances and cars (see Troll et al., 1979).

Unfortunately most of the information in this area relies on reports from only one family member. A notable exception is the research of Hill and associates (1970), who conclude that "in mutual aid as well as in visiting patterns and sharing in common activities the three generations are linked together in a symbiotic network of multiple services and transfers" (p. 66). All three generations in Hill's Minneapolis study said they preferred to get help from family members over other sources. Hill et al. (1970) draw two propositions concerning intergenerational helping patterns. These relate to kinds of help sought and to dependency status. The oldest generation looks to the younger ones for help with problems of illness and household management; it is in a relatively dependent status, receiving more than giving. The middle generation looks for emotional gratification and is in a patron status, giving more than receiving. The youngest adult generation looks for help with problems of childcare and economic assistance and is in a reciprocal status, high in both giving and receiving.

In spite of widespread beliefs that old people are isolated from—or even deserted by—their families, almost all surveys find that the oldest generation is an integral and active part of the family structure (Hill et al., 1970; Martin & Bengtson, 1971; review in Troll et al., 1979).

Affect or Sentiment. Many writers assume that closeness is synonymous with positive affect or sentiment and estrangement with negative affect. In the present chapter we are assuming another perspective: that where affect runs high, it is rarely only positive or negative (Bengtson et al., 1976; Lowenthal, Thurnher, & Chiriboga, 1975; Troll & Smith, 1976). Where there is love, there is also hate. Bengtson et al. (1976) found high correlations between positive and negative affect, particularly for youth and so did Lowenthal et al. (1975). Feldman (1964) found the same mixture for husband-wife relationships.

Most of the data on this topic are self-reports and even more likely to be biased than those relating to residence or visiting. Therefore, unfortunately, they must be treated as tentative.

The youngest subjects for whom parent-child feelings have been reported are high school students. Just as it is rare to find a young child not attached to his/her parents (Ainsworth, 1972)—and vice versa, presumably—so does it seem to be rare to find a high school student who does not report feeling close to his/her parents. In comparisons of Danish and American adolescents (Kandel & Lesser, 1972), only 11 percent of American high school students and 13 percent of Danish students did not feel close to their mothers, while 13 percent of Americans and 14 percent of Danes did not feel close to their fathers. Over a third of both groups said they enjoyed doing many things with their parents and wanted to be like them in many ways. Andersson (1973) found that only one-quarter of Swedish youth stated that they did not have warm feelings for their parents. Several other studies of high school students indicate that parent-child relationships are usually perceived as satisfying (Bengtson, 1969; Douvan & Adelson, 1966; Larson & Myerhoff, 1965; Lubell, 1968).

In support of the "generational-stake" hypothesis (Bengtson & Kuypers, 1971) described earlier in this chapter, middle-aged parents consistently overestimated the degree of closeness, understanding, and communication compared to the responses of their college-aged children. Mothers expressed more concern for their children's welfare than children expressed for their mothers' welfare (Angres, 1975). Nonetheless Hill et al. (1970) report that their youngest adult generation was the strongest endorser of kinship obligations and contact, while the oldest generation was the weakest endorser of these values. Studies of college students (Bengtson & Black, 1973b; Freeman, 1972) show that they and their parents may think there is a generation gap in society as a whole, but they rarely perceive there is one in their own family. This was as true of student radicals as of more general samples (Angres, 1975).

Lowenthal et al. (1975) state that most of the middle-aged parents in their San Francisco sample felt good about their children. About half had only positive things to say about them, and only about 10 percent of the middle-aged and almost none of those in their sixties had any strong negative comments. "The remaining descriptions can most accurately be described as 'mixed indulgent,' recognizing frailties or irritating idiosyncrasies— often viewed as temporary—but stressing the overall likeableness of the child" (p. 41). However, they also included problems of tidiness, lackadaisical attitudes toward studies, difficulties in communication, and troublesome personality traits. Differences in goals and values played a lesser role than anticipated, being mentioned no more than any of the other problem areas.

For older ages Bengtson and Black (1973b), who examined trust, understanding, fairness, respect, and affection, found that high levels of regard were reported by both old parents and their middle-aged children. On the other hand the old parents reported higher levels of sentiment, while their children reported higher levels of giving help. Bengtson and Cutler (1976) suggest that this is another instance of the "generational stake." It seems that parents remain important to their children throughout the life of the children. When adults of all ages were asked to describe a person, they tended spontaneously to refer to their parents more frequently than to any other person (Troll, 1972a). The oldest members of the sample, in their seventies and eighties, were still using parents as reference persons.

Bengtson and Black (1973b) found a gradual increase in perception of family solidarity among four age groups of adolescents and young adults. The younger respondents may still have been trying to achieve independence from parents and thus minimized their ties to them. The

older youth, having achieved job and marriage, could feel freer to recognize their feelings of closeness—or to once more feel close. This finding was replicated by Angres (1975). She found that when the younger generation had been in college they had reported more differences with their mothers than the mothers themselves did. Troll (1972b) had noted, though, that these overt conflicts tended to center on apparently superficial concerns like style of dress or hair length rather than apparently major issues like political and social values. These "superficial" concerns, incidentally, are the ones that adolescents say they would refer to peers rather than to parents (Britain, 1963; Larson, 1972). Can it be that this is a displacement of anger into areas where it can be handled without disrupting family relations? Hagestad (1979) uses the term *demilitarized zones* to describe topics mutually avoided in the service of family harmony. Newlyweds surveyed by Feldman (1964) reported that their relations with their parents had improved since they left home. On the other hand a San Francisco sample of newlyweds (Lowenthal et al., 1975) showed some rejection of their parents.

Grandparents. So far almost no attention has been paid to grandparent-grandchild relations. This relationship may also be affected by the "generational stakes" of each of the parents (cf. Hill et al., 1970). Under recently prevailing conditions of early marriage and childbirth, people most commonly become grandparents in their forties. Not only are they likely to be middle-aged rather than old and to perceive themselves as youthful, but they are also likely to be working.

Of five different styles of grandparenting found by Neugarten and Weinstein (1964)—formal, fun-seekers, surrogate parents, reservoirs of family wisdom, and distant figures—young grandparents are mostly fun-seekers and distant figures. They see grandparenting as a recreational activity or they are benevolent, but infrequent, visitors who emerge from the shadows on holidays and ritual occasions. In fact grandparents interviewed by Cumming and Henry (1961) did not feel particularly close to their grandchildren. As one of their respondents said, "I'm always glad to see them come and equally glad to see them go" (p. 60). Gilford and Black (1972) found that geographic separation, which was not an important variable in the adult relationship between parents and children who had once lived together, is important in the grandparent-grandchild relationship, but the effect of separation is not simple. Grandparents' feelings toward their grandchildren have a direct effect on the feelings of the grandchildren when they have the opportunity for frequent interpersonal interaction. However, when they live far apart, their relationship is contingent upon the intervening parent-child dyadic bonds. In other words when grandparents are close to their own children, they are likely to be important to their grandchildren even if they do not see each other very often. Hagestad (1978) found that both grandparents and grandchildren perceive that they exert influence upon each other.

On the whole the "valued grandparent" is an earned and acquired status, involving personal qualities not automatically ascribed to the role. Family solidarity is built up from parent-child dyadic bonds—or personal dyadic bonds where contact is possible. Also feelings about grandchildren seem to change as a function of the changes in the developing grandchildren. Clark (1969) found that grandparents liked their grandchildren better when they were small. As the children got older, they were less interested in their grandparents, and this feeling was then reciprocated.

Kahana and Kahana (1970) found that children of different ages emphasize different aspects of grandparent-grandchild relations. They also found that maternal grandmothers and paternal grandfathers show closeness and warmth toward their grandchildren, view them as if they were their own children, and approve of their upbringing. In contrast maternal grandfathers and paternal grandmothers express negative attitudes.

Aging family members do not feel as "left out" of the family as some observers would contend. Brown (1960) reports that the majority of elderly subjects in his sample did not feel neglected by their children, and Martin, Bengtson, and Acock (1974) report that men over 57 might feel alienated from political and economic institutions in the social structure but not from their families. On the other hand observational data (Scott, 1962) suggest that grandparents are singularly unimportant to the interactions between parents and adolescent children.

Conclusion. In summary our analysis of research relevant to Question 7 suggests that parent-child "attachments" are perceived as exceptionally strong interpersonal bonds throughout the life course. Where variations in perceived level of affect appear, they may be related to the ontogenetic status of generation members involved.

Question 8: Does Gender of Parent or Child Influence either Closeness or Affect?

Do parents relate differently to sons and daughters or children relate differently to fathers and mothers? The psychoanalytic school has long maintained that this is so (cf. Freud, 1963). It has also struck many investigators in the field of kinship interactions that families seem to be linked through females (Troll, 1971).

Accumulating observations suggest that gender differences in parent-child interactions appear at the very beginning of life (Lamb, 1978; Maccoby & Jacklin, 1974; Malatesta, 1980; Walters & Stinnett, 1971). For example, boys are allowed to ask for more comforting and get more praise, particularly if they are first-born (Walters & Stinnett, 1971). Mothers of two-year-old girls asked them more questions, used longer statements when talking with them, and repeated their statements more often than did mothers of two-year-old boys (Cherry & Lewis, 1976). Loving or hating a child is more persistent over the child's life than is permissiveness or controlling (Bayley, 1964), but mothers show even greater consistency in how they feel about their sons. They are also less consistent in how much they control their sons than their daughters—that is, mothers' control over daughters does not decrease with age as much as their control over sons. Fathers, on the other hand, tend to exercise more control over sons than over daughters (Straus, 1967).

We noted earlier that this effort to control diminishes during the adult years (Nydegger, 1979). Cross-national differences in control over adolescents were found by Kandel and Lesser (1972). In the United States the giving of orders and the disciplining tends to be the tasks of mothers more than fathers; in Denmark both parents share control.

Most families around the world seem to be linked through women (Adams, 1968; Bengtson et al., 1976; Kahana, Perez, Tagore, & Kahana, 1973; Troll, 1971). Ties between mother and daughter are closer than those between mother and son or between father and either daughter or son (Adams, 1968; Blenkner, 1965; Bott, 1957; Gans, 1962; Hagestad, 1974; Reiss, 1962; Townsend, 1957; Young & Geertz, 1961; Young & Willmott, 1964). Daughters have also been found to be affectionately closer to both parents than are sons (Andersson, 1973; Gray & Smith, 1960; Komarovsky, 1964; Sweetser, 1963). In the San Francisco study of Lowenthal et al. (1973), adolescents and young adults—both men and women—as well as older women reported closer ties to their mother than to any other family member, although other parts of the sample were not so consistent. Mothers report more affectional feelings for their young adult daughters than for their young adult sons (Angres, 1975). In fact over the seven years of the Chicago study, mothers' attachment to daughters increased relative to that to sons. According to Hill et al. (1970), cohesiveness in same-sex three-generation lineages is greater than in mixed-sex lineages, and this is particularly true for the female lineages.

One of the early findings of ongoing three-generation research in Chicago (Hagestad, 1979) is the gender difference in influencing among parents and children as well as grandparents and grandchildren. Mothers and grandmothers try to influence both sons and daughters the same way on the same issues—and this is reciprocal. Fathers and grandfathers differentiate more, dealing with money and success issues with sons and grandsons and more expressive, "feminine" issues with daughters and granddaughters. The young generation, however, does not make this gender distinction toward the old.

In his North Carolina sample, Adams (1968) found that daughters' affections for their fathers were related to the fathers' occupational position; they appreciated their fathers more if they had higher status. The more successful sons appreciated their mothers more. While most of the San Francisco respondents (Lowenthal et al., 1975) said they had closer ties to their mothers and daughters, the older men accorded preferred position to their oldest sons, suggesting an emergent concern for succession reminiscent of the concept of "generational stake" proposed by Bengtson and Kuypers (1971). On the other hand while they evaluated their mothers in terms of nurturance, caring and understanding, they were more likely to evaluate their fathers in terms of moods and other personality characteristics.

Conclusion. We might conclude in response to Question 8 that gender differences are apparent in research on cross-sectional family relationships. Parents feel differently about daughters and sons; and daughters and sons relate differently to mothers and fathers. In general females have stronger kinship ties, and more affection is reported for female family members than for male.

Question 9: Does Consensus Influence Closeness or Affect?

Do parents and children—or grandparents and grandchildren—feel closer to each other or like each other better if they hold the same values or see the world through similar eyes? Apparently not. Just as in Question 5 the quality of family interrelationships does not seem to affect value consensus, and the converse also seems to hold. None of the studies in this area have found significant correlations between similarities among family members and any of the dimensions of family closeness or affect (Adams, 1968; Angres, 1975; Bengtson, 1969; Jennings & Niemi, 1968; Kandel & Lesser, 1972; Thomas, 1971a). Whether or not family members see eye to eye, they continue to live near each other, visit and help each other, and like or feel obligated to each other.

There are two possible exceptions to this conclusion. First, when it is perceived congruence that is measured rather than actual comparisons of responses of both questions, the younger generation's perception of value differences does seem to be associated with reporting of less family closeness (Andersson, 1973; Angres, 1975; Kandel & Lesser, 1972). Only when youth like their parents do they recognize similarity. Second, it seems possible that extreme socialization differences or social discontinuity resulting in marked changes in attitudes and values may also induce feelings of estrangement between generations (Campisi, 1948; Davis, 1940; Gans, 1962; Senior, 1957). This has been noted particularly for immigrant families and seen most in the relations between middle-aged children and their old parents, more of whom were immigrants. Clark (1969) points out that, in many cases, the model of old age that immigrants learned in their youth is regarded as strange by their Americanized offspring, even leading in extreme cases to parents' being institutionalized.

Conclusion. The available evidence suggests that, in the absence of extreme social discontinuity, value congruence does *not* seem to be related to degree of parent-child attachment. Ties tend to remain close even when there is little consensus.

Question 10: How Do Family Relationships Compare with Those between Friends or Peers?

Question 4 of this chapter dealt with the relative influence of parents and peers on transmission. At this point we are interested in the relative quality or quantity of relationships. From later childhood on are individuals more likely to turn to friends or members of their own age cohort for meaningful interactions than they are to lineage members—parents or grandparents, children or grandchildren?

In his review of childhood socialization literature, McCandless (1969) concludes that "peer group supplies important confirmation-disconfirmation of self-judgments of competence and self-esteem, although the foundation of these is probably more influenced by the family" (p. 809). In the United States it is the same-sex peer group that is important. Further peers are more important for lower-class than for middle-class children.

According to Eisenstadt (1956) societies like ours which are regulated by values which differ from those of the family make it necessary for individuals who are nearing the transition from childhood familial roles to adult societal roles to establish more extensive social relations outside the family. In fact, says Coleman (1961), because the youth group emphasizes the difference between youth and parental values, adolescents are exposed to constant conflict. Thus they live "more and more in a society of [their] own; [they] find the family a less and less satisfying psychological home" (p. 312).

Campbell (1969) points to the tremendous amount of time that adolescents spend with each other and to the interpersonal prominence they hold for each other, but whether such association and prominence attest to loss of association and importance for parents is not clearly demonstrated. When Coleman (1961) asked adolescents, "Which one of these things would be hardest for you to take: your parents' disapproval, your teacher's disapproval, or breaking with your friend?" 53 percent selected parents as against 43 percent who selected friends. Coleman interpreted this balance as a sign of transitional status, of leaving family behind and moving over to friends. Campbell, however, concludes that adolescent peer-group loyalties do not threaten the emotional bond between adolescent and family. Andersson (1973) found that it was those Swedish youth who had very low self-esteem who were most likely to see friends set off against parents; this finding was replicated in the United States by Condry and Simon (1974), who found that highly peer-oriented children were less likely to come from families having a climate of "passive neglect." As Kandel and Lesser (1972) note, "In critical areas, interaction with peers support, express, and specify for the peer context the values of parents and other adults" (p. 168). In both Denmark and the United States, parents were turned to for help in solving problems, and peers were turned to for companionship. While the subjective peer orientation of youth is related to the directiveness of the family (adolescents in democratic families more often prefer their parents' company over that of their friends), adolescents' actual peer-interaction patterns are not related to family-relationship patterns.

The data—equally scarce—that we have for adults suggest that there are qualitative differences between parent-child relationships and friendships in maturity. As noted earlier in this chapter, adults turn to family for help in times of trouble more than they do to friends (Hill et al., 1970; Troll et al., 1979). Adult respondents in Greensboro, N.C. (Adams, 1968) say they feel intimate with their parents, have "positive regard" for them, and above all feel obligated and dutiful to them. They are more likely to share attitudes, interests, and recreational activities with friends. A study of relationships of old people in Holland (Knipscheer, 1978) found that children were most likely to visit on their birthday (86 percent as compared with 65 percent by friends), friends were slightly more likely to share recreational activities like card playing (35 percent as compared with 32 percent of children), children were more likely to help (30 percent as compared with 12 percent of friends), and children were equally likely to be intimate (65 percent as compared with 64 percent for friends). Relations with parents persist, while those with friends are vulnerable to mobility and other kinds of changes. Some of this difference may be a function of different developmental patterns of attraction and attachment.

In the beginning of any relationship, attraction seems to be high but attachment to be low. Novelty creates interest, but bonds are not yet cemented. A breakup in such a relationship would cause only temporary distress, and substitutions of loved objects would be relatively easy—"there are many more fish in the sea." In the course of repeated interaction, however, novelty is gone and attraction reduced, but attachment may have become very strong. A breakup at this time may never be overcome. Support for such a proposal comes from a variety of disparate data: studies of marital satisfaction over time (Adams, 1968; Feldman, 1964; Pineo, 1961), of experimentally organized groups (Taylor, 1968), and of qualitative differences in relationships with parents, siblings, and friends (Adams, 1968). Friendships are likely to be of shorter association and thus more interesting, but it is parents—who may be less interesting—who remain important even when one moves away or up the social ladder (Troll & Smith, 1976).

Among older people relationships with both family and friends tend to be of long duration. Some older people maintain close ties with both (Knipscheer, 1978; Lopata, 1977), and when they do, intimate relationships may be the strongest survival mechanism possible (Lowenthal & Haven, 1968). Retired teachers surveyed by Candy (1976) found no difficulty in listing five close friends, all of whom they had known for many years. However, other investigators find that the older years are characterized more by disengagement *into* the family (Troll, 1971), though this may be a cohort effect, influenced by the large numbers of old women of today whose relationships were traditionally restricted to family members (Lopata, 1977).

Conclusion. The evidence concerning Question 10 suggests that relationships with friends or peers are more likely to be complementary than in opposition to relationships with family members of other generations. Age peers or friends are not substitutes for family-lineage relations.

CONCLUSIONS

Relations between generations are central issues in theory concerning individual development, family processes, and societal changes or stability. Yet despite the body of empirical studies cited here, theory development in this area is primitive. One basic problem is methodological. We need more longitudinal and particularly cross-sequential research that would distinguish between effects of a short-term nature and more enduring ones. We also need replication of findings and more observational or ethnographic studies. We need to examine the effects of various structural variables on the parent-child bond.

The research reviewed in this chapter can be summarized in the following ten tentative statements, as presented in the text.

1. There is substantial but selective intergenerational continuity within the family. Parent-child similarity is most noticeable in religious and political areas, least in sex roles, life style, and work orientation.

2. Social and historical forces—cohort or period effects—serve as moderator variables in family-lineage transmission. Transmission is enhanced in areas where social forces encourage particular values or behavior. It is reduced where social forces discourage them, as where particular characteristics become "keynotes" of a new rising generational unit.

3. At the present time we cannot conclude that gender is an important variable in transmission. While some studies support the common assumption that fathers are more influential than are mothers, other studies do not. Sex of child does not appear to be a relevant variable in parent-child similarity.

4. Friends or peers may serve as a moderating influence on family transmission in some areas, such as sexual behavior or use of marijuana, which are prominent issues for their cohort. Parental influences seem strong in achievement, work, and educational orientations, however. In general peer and parent influences appear complementary rather than oppositional.

5. Qualitative aspects of family relationships, such as "closeness," do not seem to affect lineage transmission.

6. The effect of variation in individual life-span developmental levels (aging or maturation) upon lineage transmission is neither general nor obvious. It is a prime example of "selective continuity" and cannot at present be separated from period effects.

7. Parent-child "attachments" are perceived as exceptionally strong interpersonal bonds throughout the life course. Where variations in perceived level of affect appear, they may be related to the ontogenetic status of generation members involved.

8. Gender differences are apparent in research on cross-sectional family relationships. Parents feel differently about daughters and sons; daughters and sons relate differently to mothers and fathers. In general females have stronger kinship ties, and more affection is reported for female family members than for males.

9. In the absence of extreme social discontinuity, value congruence does *not* seem to be related to degree of parent-child attachments. Ties tend to remain close even where there is little consensus.

10. Relationships with friends or peers are more likely to be complementary than in opposition to relationships with family members of other generations. Age peers or friends are not substitutes for family-lineage relations.

Two general conclusions stand out. First, it is noteworthy that so many studies show a high degree of intergenerational attachment or cohesion. Despite differentials in maturational levels, geographic propinquity, gender, and socioeconomic mobility, as well as possibly confounding effects of cultural change and peer interaction, *parent-child solidarity appears to represent consistently an important interpersonal bond in contemporary American culture.* This appears true at all stages of the life course and among individuals from varying locations in the social structure.

Second, it is of interest that *high levels of intergenerational cohesion do not necessarily reflect high levels of similarity* in general orientations or specific opinions. This generalization must, of course, continue to be tested in empirical work specifying arenas of similarity (transmission) as well as various aspects of parent-child cohesion, but if this proposition remains substantiated, its implications for theory are significant.

Psychoanalytic theory, learning theory, balance theory, and symbolic interactionist theory appear to have one common assumption in their application to family socialization: that the stronger (closer, more attractive) the bond to the parent, the more similar is the behavior or orientation of the offspring to that of the parent. This assumption can now be considered unwarranted. Similarly many theoretical statements concerning social change assume a generational base rooted in the desire of emergent generations to be independent of existing social institutions (embodied by their parents). Many of the data reviewed here suggest such an explanation to be, at best, simplistic and at worst, distorting of actual parent-child relationships.

REFERENCES

ACOCK, A. C., & BENGTSON, V. L. *Intergenerational transmission of religious behavior and beliefs.* Paper presented at the Pacific Sociological Association Annual Meeting, Victoria, B.C., 1975.

ACOCK, A. C., & BENGTSON, V. L. On the relative influence of mothers and fathers: A covariance analysis of political and religious socialization. *Journal of Marriage and the Family,* 1978, *40*(No. 3), 519–530.

ACOCK, A. C., & BENGTSON, V. L. Socialization and attribution processes: Actual vs. perceived similarities among parents and youth. *Journal of Marriage and the Family,* 1980, *42*(No. 3), 501–515.

ADAMS, B. *Kinship in an urban setting.* Chicago: Markham, 1968.

ADELSON, J. What generation gap? *New York Times Magazine,* January 18, 1970, pp. 10–11, 34–36, 45–46.

AINSWORTH, M. Attachment and dependency: A comparison. In J. Gewirtz (Ed.), *Attachment and dependency.* Washington, D.C.: D. H. Winston & Sons, 1972.

ALDOUS, J., & HILL, R. Social cohesion, lineage type, and intergenerational transmission. *Social Forces,* 1965, *43,* 371–382.

ANDERSSON, B. *The generation gap: Imagination or reality?* Paper presented to the biennial meeting of the International Society for the Study of Behavioral Development, Institute of Education, Goteborg, Sweden, 1973.

ANGRES, S. *Intergenerational relations and value congruence between young adults and their mothers.* Unpublished doctoral dissertation, University of Chicago, 1975.

ARMSTRONG, B., & SOTZIN, M. Intergenerational comparison of attitudes toward basic life concepts. *Journal of Psychology,* 1974, *87,* 293–304.

BANDURA, A. Social-learning theory of identificatory processes. In D. Goslin (Ed.), *Handbook of socialization theory and research.* Skokie, Ill.: Rand McNally, 1969.

BAYLEY, N. Consistency of maternal and child behaviors in the Berkeley growth study. *Vita Humana,* 1964, *7,* 73–95.

BEDFORD, V. *Academic gypsies.* Unpublished manuscript, 1980.

BENGTSON, V. L. *The generation gap: Differences by generation and by sex in the perception of parent-child relations.* Paper presented at annual meeting of Pacific Sociological Association, Seattle, Wash., 1969.

BENGTSON, V. L. The generation gap: A review and typology of social-psychological perspectives. *Youth and Society,* 1970, *2,* 7–32.

BENGTSON, V. L. Inter-age differences in perceptions of the generation gap. *The Gerontologist,* 1971, pt. 2, 85–89.

BENGTSON, V. L. Generation and family effects in value socialization. *American Sociological Review,* 1975a, *40,* 358–371.

BENGTSON, V. L. Perceptions of intergenerational solidarity: Attitudes of elderly parents and middle-aged children. *Proceedings of the 10th International Congress of Gerontology,* Jerusalem, 1975b, *1,* 106–110.

BENGTSON, V. L., & ACOCK, A. C. *Attribution within the family: Actual vs. perceived similarity among parents and youth.* Paper presented at the annual meeting of The American Sociological Association, Chicago, 1977.

BENGTSON, V. L., & BLACK, K. D. Intergenerational relations and continuities in socialization. In P. Baltes & W. Schaie (Eds.), *Life-span developmental psychology: Personality and socialization.* New York: Academic Press, 1973a.

BENGTSON, V. L., & BLACK, K. D. *Solidarity between parents and children: Four perspectives on theory development.* Paper presented at the Theory Development Workshop, National Council on Family Relations Annual Meeting, Toronto, October 16, 1973b.

BENGTSON, V. L., & CUTLER, N. Generations and intergenerational relations: Perspectives on age groups and social change. In R. Binstock & E. Shanas (Eds.), *Handbook of aging and the social sciences.* New York: Van Nostrand Reinhold, 1976.

BENGTSON, V. L., FURLONG, M. J., & LAUFER, R. S. Time, aging, and the continuity of social structures: Themes and issues in generational analysis. *Journal of Social Issues,* 1974, *30,* 6–11.

BENGTSON, V. L., & KUYPERS, J. A. Generational differences and the developmental stake. *Aging and Human Development,* 1971, *2,* 249–260.

BENGTSON, V. L., OLANDER, E., & HADDAD, E. The generation gap and aging family members: Toward a conceptual model. In J. F. Gubrium (Ed.), *Time, roles, and self in old age.* New York: Human Sciences Press, 1976.

BENGTSON, V. L., & STARR, J. M. Contrast and consensus: A generational analysis of youth in the 1970s. In R. J. Havighurst (Ed.), *Youth. The seventy-fourth yearbook of the National Society for the Study of Education* (Pt. 1). Chicago: University of Chicago Press, 1975.

BENGTSON, V. L., & TROLL, L. E. Youth and their parents. Feedback and intergenerational influence in socialization. In R. Lerner & G. Spanier (Eds.), *Child influences on marital and family interactions.* New York: Academic Press, 1978.

BERARDO, F. Kinship interaction and communications among space-age migrants. *Journal of Marriage and the Family,* 1967, *29,* 541–554.

BETTELHEIM, B. The problem of generations. In E. Erikson (Ed.), *The challenge of youth.* New York: Anchor Press, 1965.

BLENKNER, M. Social work and family relationships in later life with some thoughts on filial maturity. In E. Shanas & G. Streib (Eds.), *Social structure and the family: Generational relationships.* Englewood Cliffs, N.J.: Prentice-Hall, 1965.

BLUMENFELD, W. S. Note on the relationship of political performance between generations within a household. *Psychological Reports,* 1964, *15,* 976.

BOTT, E. *Family and social network.* London: Tavistock, 1957.

BRAUN, P., & BENGTSON, V. *Religious behavior in three generations: Cohort and lineage effects.* Paper presented at the Gerontological Society meetings, San Juan, P.R., 1972.

BRAUNGART, R. G. A sociology of generations and student politics: A comparison of the functionalist and generational unit models. *Journal of Social Issues,* 1974, *30,* 31–54.

BRITTAIN, V. Adolescent choices and parent-peer cross-pressures. *American Sociological Review,* 1963, *28,* 385–391.

BRITTON, J., MATHER, W., & LANSING, K. Expectations for older persons in a rural community: Living arrangements and family relationships. *Journal of Gerontology,* 1961, *16,* 156–162.

BROOK, J., LUKOFF, I., & WHITEMAN, M. Peer, family and personality domains as related to adolescents' drug behavior. *Psychological Reports,* 1977, *41,* 1095–1102.

BROWN, P. G. Family structure and social isolation of older persons. *Journal of Gerontology,* 1960, *15,* 170–174.

CAMPBELL, E. Q. Adolescent socialization. In D. A. Goslin (Ed.), *Handbook of socialization theory and research.* Skokie, Ill.: Rand McNally, 1969.

CAMPISI, P. Ethnic family patterns: The Italian family in the United States. *American Journal of Sociology,* 1948, *53,* 443–449.

CANDY, S. *An exploration of the development of the functions of friendship in women.* Unpublished master's thesis, Wayne State University, 1976.

CHERRY, L., & LEWIS, M. Mothers and two-year-olds: A study of sex-differentiated aspects of verbal interaction. *Developmental Psychology,* 1976, *12,* 278–282.

CLARK, M. Cultural values and dependency in later life. In R. Kalish (Ed.), *The dependencies of old people.* Ann Arbor, Mich.: Institute for Gerontology, 1969.

CLAUSEN, J. *Value transmission and personality resemblance in two generations.* Paper presented at American Sociological Association meeting, Montreal, 1974.

COLEMAN, J. S. *The adolescent society.* New York: Free Press, 1961.

CONDRY, J., & SIMON, M. Characteristics of peer and adult oriented children. *Journal of Marriage and the Family*, 1974, *36*, 543–554.

CONNELL, R. W. Political socialization in the American family. *Public Opinion Quarterly*, 1972, *36*, 323–333.

CUMMING, E., & HENRY, W. *Growing old: The process of disengagement*. New York: Basic Books, 1961.

CUTLER, N. Demographic, social psychological, and political factors in the politics of age: A call for research in political gerontology. *American Political Science Review*, 1977, *71*(No. 3), 1011–1025.

CUTLER, N., & BENGTSON, V. Age and political alienation: Maturation, generation and period effects. *Annals of American Academy of Political and Social Sciences*, 1974, *415*, 160–175.

DAVIS, K. The sociology of parent-youth conflict. *American Sociological Review*, 1940, *5*, 523–535.

DODGE, R. W., & UYEKI, E. S. Political affiliation and imagery across two related generations. *Midwest Journal of Political Science*, 1962, *6*, 266–276.

DOUVAN, E., & ADELSON, J. *The adolescent experience*. New York: John Wiley, 1966.

DUFFY, E. Attitudes of parents and daughters toward war and toward the treatment of criminals. *Psychological Record*, 1941, *4*, 366–372.

EISENSTADT, S. N. *From generation to generation*. New York: Free Press, 1956.

FELDMAN, H. Development of the husband-wife relationship. *Preliminary report, Cornell studies of marital development: Study in the transition to parenthood*. Ithaca, N.Y.: Cornell University, 1964.

FENGLER, A. P., & WOOD, V. The generation gap: An analysis of attitudes on contemporary issues. *The Gerontologist*, 1972, *12*, 124–128.

FENGLER, A. P., & WOOD, V. Continuity between the generations: Differential influence of mothers and fathers. *Youth and Society*, 1973, *4*, 359–372.

FISHER, S. C. *Relationships in attitudes, opinions, and values among family members*. Berkeley: University of California Press, 1948.

FLACKS, R. The liberated generation: An exploration of the roots of student protest. *Journal of Social Issues*, 1967, *23*, 52–75.

FREEMAN, H. The generation gap: Attitudes of students and of their parents. *Journal of Counseling Psychology*, 1972, *19*, 441–447.

FREUD, S. On narcissism: An introduction (1914). In S. Freud, *General psychological theory* (Philip Rieff, Ed.). New York: Collier Books, 1963.

FRIEDENBERG, E. *The vanishing adolescent*. Boston: Beacon Press, 1959.

FRIEDENBERG, E. *Coming of age in America*. New York: Random House, 1965.

FRIEDENBERG, E. Current patterns of a generation conflict. *Journal of Social Issues*, 1969, *25*, 21–38.

FRIEDMAN, L. N., GOLD, A. R., & CHRISTIE, R. Dissecting the generation gap: Intergenerational and intrafamilial similarities and differences. *Public Opinion Quarterly*, 1972, *36*, 334–346.

FURSTENBERG, F., JR. *Transmission of attitudes in the family*. Unpublished doctoral dissertation, Columbia University, 1967.

GANS, H. J. *The urban villagers: Group and class life of Italian-Americans*. New York: Free Press, 1962.

GEWIRTZ, J. L. (Ed.). *Attachment and dependence*. Washington, D.C.: D. H. Winston & Sons, 1972.

GIBSON, G. Kin family network: Overheralded structure in past conceptualizations of family functioning. *Journal of Marriage and the Family*, 1969, *34*, 13–23.

GILFORD, R., & BLACK, D. *The grandchild-grandparent dyad: Ritual or relationship*. Paper presented at Gerontological Society, San Juan, P.R., 1972.

GOLDSMID, P. *Intergenerational similarity in political attitudes: The effects of parent-child relations and exposure to politics*. Unpublished doctoral dissertation, University of Chicago, 1972.

GOSLIN, D. A. *Handbook of socialization theory and research*. Skokie, Ill.: Rand McNally, 1969.

GRAY, R., & SMITH, T. C. Effect of employment on sex differences in attitudes toward the parental family. *Marriage and Family Living*, 1960, *22*, 36–38.

HAGESTAD, G. Personal communication, 1974.

HAGESTAD, G. *Patterns of communication and influence between grandparents and grandchildren in a changing society*. Paper presented at the World Congress of Sociology, Sweden, 1978.

HAGESTAD, G. Problems and promises in the social psychology of intergenerational relations. In R. Fogel, E. Hatfield, S. Kiesler, & T. March (Eds.), *Stability and change in the family*. Annapolis: National Research Council, 1979.

HAGESTAD, G., & SNOW, R. *Young adult offspring as interpersonal resources in middle age*. Presented at Gerontological Society meeting, San Francisco, 1977.

HARRIS, L., & ASSOCIATES. *The myth and reality of aging in America*. Washington, D.C.: National Council on Aging, 1975.

HAWKINSON, W. Wish expectancy and practice in the interaction of generations. In A. Rose & W. Peterson (Eds.), *Older people and their social world*. Philadelphia: F. A. Davis, 1965.

HELFANT, K. Parents' attitudes vs. adolescent hostility in the determination of adolescents' sociopolitical attitudes. *Psychological Monographs: General and Applied*, 1952, *66* (13, Whole No. 345), 1–23.

HESS, B. Friendship. In M. W. Riley, M. W. Johnson, & A. Foner (Eds.), *Aging and society* (Vol. 3). A sociology of age stratification. New York: Russell Sage Foundation, 1972.

HESS, R., & HANDEL, G. *Family worlds*. Chicago: University of Chicago Press, 1959.

HESS, R. D., & TORNEY, J. V. *The development of political attitudes among children*. Chicago: Aldine, 1967.

HILL, R. N., FOOTE, J., ALDOUS, R., CARLSON, R., & MACDONALD, R. *Family development in three generations*. Cambridge, Mass.: Schenkman, 1970.

HIMMELHOCH, J. Tolerance and personality needs. *American Sociological Review*, 1950, *15*, 79–88.

HIRSCHBERG, G., & GILLILAND, A. Parent-child relationships in attitudes. *Journal of Abnormal and Social Psychology*, 1942, *37*, 125–130.

HYMAN, H. H. *Political socialization*. New York: Free Press, 1959.

JENNINGS, M., & LANGTON, K. Mothers versus fathers: The formation of political orientations among young Americans. *Journal of Politics*, 1969, *31*, 329–358.

JENNINGS, M., & NIEMI, R. The transmission of political values from parent to child. *American Political Science Review*, 1968, *42*, 169–184.

JENNINGS, M., & NIEMI, R. *The political character of adolescents*. Princeton, N.J.: Princeton University Press, 1974.

JENNINGS, M., & NIEMI, R. Continuity and change in political orientations: A longitudinal study of two generations. *American Political Science Review*, 1975, *69*, 1316–1335.

KAHANA, B., & KAHANA, E. Grandparenthood from the perspective of the developing grandchild. *Developmental Psychology*, 1970, *1*, 98–105.

KAHANA, B., PEREZ, R., TAGORE, A., & KAHANA, E. *Cross-cultural perspectives in intergenerational relations*. Paper presented at the American Psychological Association, Montreal, 1973.

KALISH, R., & JOHNSON, A. Value similarities and differences in three generations of women. *Journal of Marriage and the Family*, 1972, *34*, 49–54.

KALISH, R., & KNUDSON, F. W. Attachment vs. disengagement: A life-span conceptualization. *Human Development*, 1976, *19*, 171–181.

KANDEL, D. Inter- and intragenerational influences on adolescent marijuana use. *Journal of Social Issues*, 1974, *30*, 107–135.

KANDEL, D., & LESSER, G. *Youth in two worlds*. San Francisco: Jossey-Bass, 1972.

KENISTON, K. *Young radicals: Notes on committed youth*. New York: Harcourt Brace Jovanovich, 1968.

KERCKHOFF, A. C. Nuclear and extended family relationships: Normative and behavioral analysis. In E. Shanas & G. Streib (Eds.), *Social structure and the family*. Englewood Cliffs, N.J.: Prentice-Hall, 1965.

KERCKHOFF, A. C., & HUFF P. Parental influence on educational goals. *Sociometry*, 1974, *30*, 307–327.

KNIPSCHEER, K. *The primary relations in old age: Children, brothers, sisters, other relatives, friends and neighbors*. Presented at 11th Congress of the International Society of Gerontology, Tokyo, August 1978.

KOMAROVSKY, M. *Blue-collar marriage*. New York: Random House, 1964.

LAMB, M. Influence of the child on marital quality and family interaction during the prenatal, perinatal, and infancy periods. Pp. 137–163 in R. Lerner & G. Spanier (Eds.), *Child influences on marital and family interaction: A life span perspective*. New York: Academic Press, 1978.

LARSON, L. E. The influence of parents and peers during adolescence: The situations hypothesis revisited. *Journal of Marriage and the Family*, 1972, *34*, 67–76.

LARSON, W. R., & MYERHOFF, B. Primary and formal family organization and adolescent socialization. *Sociology and Social Research*, 1965, *50*, 63–71.

LAUFER, R., & BENGTSON, V. L. Generations, aging, and social stratification: On the development of generational units. *Journal of Social Issues*, 1974, *30*, 181–205.

LERNER, R. M. Nature, nurture, and dynamic interactionism. *Human Development*, 1978, *21*, 1–20.

LERNER, R. M., & KNAPP, J. R. Actual and perceived intrafamilial attitudes of late adolescents and their parents. *Journal of Youth and Adolescence*, 1975, *4*, 17–36.

LERNER, R. M., & SPANIER, G. B. (Eds.), *Child influences on marital and family interaction: A life-span perspective.* New York: Academic Press, 1978.

LESSER, H., & STEININGER, M. Family patterns in dogmatism. *Journal of Genetic Psychology*, 1975, *126*, 155–156.

LEVIN, M. L. Political climates and political socialization. *Public Opinion Quarterly*, 1961, *25*, 596–606.

LEWIS, M., & FREEDLE, R. Mother-infant dyad: The cradle of meaning. In P. Piner, L. Krames, & T. Alloway (Eds.), *Communication and affect language and thoughts.* New York: Academic Press, 1973.

LINDER, C., & NAHEMOW, N. *Continuity of attitudes in three-generation families.* Paper presented at the Gerontological Society Meeting, Toronto, 1970.

LITWAK, E. Geographic mobility and extended family cohesion. *American Sociological Review*, 1960, *25*, 385–394.

LOPATA, H. Friendships among widows. In L. Troll, J. Israel, & K. Israel (Eds.), *Looking ahead.* Englewood Cliffs, N.J.: Prentice-Hall, 1977.

LOWENTHAL, M. F., & HAVEN, C. Interaction and adaptation: Intimacy as a critical variable. *American Sociological Review*, 1968, *33*, 20–30.

LOWENTHAL, M. F., THURNHER, M., & CHIRIBOGA, D. *Four stages of life.* San Francisco: Jossey-Bass, 1975.

LUBELL, S. That generation gap. *The Public Interest*, 1968, *13*, 52–60.

McCANDLESS, B. R. Childhood socialization. In D. A. Goslin (Ed.), *Handbook of socialization theory and research.* Skokie, Ill.: Rand McNally, 1969.

MACCOBY, E., & JACKLIN, C. *The psychology of sex differences.* Stanford, Calif.: Stanford University Press, 1974.

MALATESTA, C. *Affective development over the life span. Involution of growth.* Unpublished paper, 1980.

MANNHEIM, K. The problem of generations. In K. Mannheim, *Essays on the sociology of knowledge.* London: Routledge & Keagan, 1952. (Originally published, 1923.)

MARTIN, W. C., & BENGTSON, V. L. *Alienation of the aged: Its nature and correlates.* Paper presented at the meetings of the Gerontological Society, Houston, 1971.

MARTIN, W. C., BENGTSON, V. L., & ACOCK, A. C. Alienation and age: A context-specific approach. *Social Forces*, 1974, *53*, 266–274.

MAXWELL, P., CONNOR, R., & WALTER, J. Family member perception of parent role performance. *Merrill-Palmer Quarterly*, 1961, *7*, 31–37.

MEAD, M. *Culture and commitment: A study of the generation gap.* New York: Basic Books, 1970.

MILLER, B. C., & SCHVANEVELDT, J. D. Fertility-related attitudes of Mormon women across three generations. In P. R. Kuntz (Ed.), *The Mormon family.* Provo, Utah: Brigham Young University, 1977.

MOSS, H. Sex, age, and state as determinants of mother-infant interaction. *Merrill-Palmer Quarterly*, 1967, *13*, 19–36.

NEUGARTEN, B. *Middle age and aging.* Chicago: University of Chicago Press, 1968.

NEUGARTEN, B., & WEINSTEIN, K. K. The changing American grandparent. *Journal of Marriage and the Family*, 1964, *26*, 199–204.

NYDEGGER, C. N. *Late and early fathers.* Paper presented at the annual meeting of the Gerontological Society, Miami Beach, 1973.

NYDEGGER, C. N., & MITTENESS, L. Transitions in fatherhood. *Generations*, 1979, *4*(No. 1), 14–15.

PARKMAN, M. *Identity, role and family functioning.* Unpublished doctoral dissertation, University of Chicago, 1965.

PARSONS, T. The stability of the American family system. In N. W. Bell & E. F. Vogel (Eds.), *A modern introduction to the family.* New York: Free Press, 1968.

PAYNE, S., SUMMERS, D., & STEWART, T. Value differences across three generations. *Sociometry*, 1973, *36*, 20–30.

PINDER, A. *Kunstgeschichte nach Generaionen, Zwischen Philosophie und Kunst.* Johann Volkelt zum 100. Lehrsemester dargebracht. Leipzig, 1926.

PINEO, P. Disenchantment in the later years of marriage. *Marriage and Family Living*, 1961, *2*, 3–11.

RADKE-YARROW, M., TRAGER, H. G., & MILLER, J. The role of parents in the development of children's ethnic attitudes. *Child Development*, 1952, *23*, 13–53.

REISS, I. L. How and why America's sex standards are changing. *Transaction*, 1968, *5*, 26–32.

REISS, P. J. Extended kinship system: Correlates of and attitudes on frequency of interaction. *Marriage and Family Living*, 1962, *24*, 333–339.

REMMERS, H. H., & WELTMAN, N. Attitude interrelationships of youth, their parents, and teachers. *Journal of Social Psychology*, 1947, *26*, 61–68.

RIESMAN, D. *The lonely crowd.* New Haven, Conn.: Yale University Press, 1950.

RISKIN, J., & FAUNCE, E. E. An evaluation review of family interaction research. *Family Process*, 1972, *11*, 365–455.

ROKEACH, M. *The open and closed mind: Investigations into the nature of belief systems and personality systems.* New York: Basic Books, 1960.

ROKEACH, M. *Beliefs, attitudes, and values: A theory of organization and change.* San Francisco: Jossey-Bass, 1968.

ROSE, A. M. The subculture of the aging: A topic for sociological research. *The Gerontologist*, 1962, *2*, 123–127.

SANDIS, E. The transmission of mothers' educational ambitions, as related to specific socialization techniques. *Journal of Marriage and the Family*, 1970, *32*, 204–210.

SCHAIE, K. W. A general model for the study of developmental problems. *Psychological Bulletin*, 1965, *64*, 92–107.

SCHAIE, K. W. Developmental process and aging. In C. Eisdorfer & Powell-Lawton (Eds.), *The psychology of adult development and aging.* Washington, D.C.: American Psychological Association, 1973.

SCHORR, A. *Filial responsibility in the modern American family.* Washington, D.C.: Social Security Administration, Department of Health, Education and Welfare, 1960.

SCOTT, F. G. Family group structure and patterns of social interaction. *American Journal of Sociology*, 1962, *68*, 214–228.

SENIOR, C. Research on the Puerto Rican family in the United States. *The Gerontologist*, 1957, *1*, 27–29.

SHANAS, E. Family-kin networks and aging in cross-cultural perspective. *Journal of Marriage and the Family*, 1973, *35*, 505–511.

SHANAS, E., TOWNSEND, P., WEDDERBURN, D., FRIIS, H., MILHOJ, P., & STEHOUWER, J. *Older people in three industrial societies.* New York: Lieber-Atherton, Inc., 1968.

SIGEL, R., & REYNOLDS, J. Generational differences and the women's movement. *Political Science Quarterly*, 1979–1980, *94*, 635–648.

SLATER, P. *The pursuit of loneliness.* Boston: Beacon Press, 1970.

STAGNER, R. Fascist attitudes: Their determining conditions. *Journal of Social Psychology*, 1936, *7*, 447–448.

STRAUS, M. A. The influence of sex of children and social class on instrumental and expressive family roles in a laboratory setting. *Sociology and Social Research*, 1967, *52*, 7–21.

STREIB, G. F. Intergenerational relations: Perspectives of the two generations on the older parent. *Journal of Marriage and the Family*, 1965, *27*, 469–476.

STUEVE, A., & FISHER, C. S. *Social networks and older women.* Presented at HEW Workshop on Older Women, Washington, D.C., September 1978.

SUSSMAN, M. B. Relationships of adult children with their parents in the United States. In E. Shanas & G. Streib (Eds.), *Social structure and the family: Generational relations.* Englewood Cliffs, N.J.: Prentice-Hall, 1965.

SUSSMAN, M. B., & BURCHINAL, L. Kin family network: Unheralded structure in current conceptualizations of family functioning. *Marriage and Family Living*, 1962, *24*, 231–240.

SUSSMAN, M. B., CATES, J., & SMITH, D. *The family and inheritance.* New York: Russell Sage Foundation, 1970.

SWEETSER, D. A. A symmetry in intergenerational family relationships. *Social Forces*, 1963, *41*, 346–352.

SWITZER, K. A. *Achievement motivation in women: A three generational study.* Unpublished master's thesis, Wayne State University, 1974.

TANNER, J. M. *Education and physical growth.* London: University of London Press, 1961.

TAYLOR, D. A. Some aspects of the development of interpersonal relations: Social penetration process. *Journal of Social Psychology,* 1968, *75,* 79–98.

TEDIN, K. L. The influence of parents on the political attitudes of adolescents. *American Political Science Review,* 1974, *68,* 1579–1592.

THOMAS, L. E. Family correlates of student political activism. *Developmental Psychology,* 1971a, *4,* 206–214.

THOMAS, L. E. Political attitude congruence between politically active parents and college age children. *Journal of Marriage and the Family,* 1971b, *32,* 375–386.

THOMAS, L. E., & STANKIEWICZ, J. F. *Correspondence between related generations on a range of attitudes and values: An attempt to map the domain.* Paper presented at the meeting of the American Psychological Association, Montreal, 1973.

THOMAS, L. E., & STANKIEWICZ, J. F. Family correlates of parent-child attitude congruence: Is it time to throw in the towel? *Psychological Reports,* 1974, *34,* 10–38.

TOWNSEND, P. *The family life of old people.* London: Routledge & Kegan, 1957.

TROLL, L. E. *Personality similarities between college students and their parents.* Unpublished doctoral dissertation, University of Chicago, 1967.

TROLL, L. E. Issues in the study of generations. *Aging and Human Development,* 1970, *1,* 199–218.

TROLL, L. E. The family of later life: A decade review. In C. Broderick (Ed.), *A decade of family research and action.* Minneapolis, Minn.: National Council on Family Relations, 1971.

TROLL, L. E. *Salience of family members in three generations.* Paper presented at the meeting of the American Psychological Association, Honolulu, 1972a.

TROLL, L. E. Is parent-child conflict what we mean by the generation gap? *Family Coordinator,* 1972b, *21,* 347–349.

TROLL, L. E. *Early and middle adulthood.* Monterey, Calif.: Brooks/Cole, 1975.

TROLL, L. E. *Development after 20.* Monterey, Calif.: Brooks/Cole, 1981.

TROLL, L. E. & BENGTSON, V. Generations in the family. In W. Burr, G. Nye, R. Hill, & I. Riess (Eds.), *Contemporary theories about the family* (Vol. 1). New York: Free Press, 1979.

TROLL, L. E., MILLER, S., & ATCHLEY, R. *Families of later life.* Belmont, Calif.: Wadsworth, 1979.

TROLL, L. E., NEUGARTEN, B. L., & KRAINES, R. J. Similarities in values and other personality characteristics in college students and their parents. *Merrill-Palmer Quarterly,* 1969, *15,* 323–336.

TROLL, L. E., & SMITH, J. *Three-generation lineage changes in cognitive style and value traits.* Paper presented at Gerontological Society meeting, San Juan, P.R., 1972.

TROLL, L. E. & SMITH, J. Attachment through the life-span: Some questions about dyadic bonds among adults. *Human Development,* 1976, *19,* 156–170.

WALSH, H. *The generation gap in sexual beliefs.* Paper presented at the American Sociological Association, Washington, D.C., 1970.

WALTERS, J., & STINNETT, N. Parent-child relationships: A decade review of research. In C. Broderick (Ed.), *A decade of family research and action.* Minneapolis, Minn.: National Council on Family Relations, 1971.

WEINSTOCK, A., & LERNER, R. M. Attitudes of late adolescents and their parents toward contemporary issues. *Psychological Reports,* 1972, *30,* 239–244.

WELTMAN, N., & REMMERS, H. H. Pupils, parents and teachers attitudes: Similarities and differences. *Studies in Higher Education,* 1946, *56,* 72–84.

WESTBY, D. L., & BRAUNGART, R. G. Class and politics in the family background of student political activists. *American Sociological Review,* 1966, *31,* 690–692.

WIETING, S. G. An examination of intergenerational patterns of religious belief and practice. *Sociological Analysis,* 1975, *36,* 137–149.

WINCH, R. F., & GREER, S. A. Urbanism, ethnicity, and extended families. *Marriage and Family Living,* 1968, *30,* 40–45.

YANKELOVICH, D. *Generations apart: A study of the generation gap.* A survey conducted for CBS News, 1970.

YANKELOVICH, D. *The changing values on campus.* New York: Simon & Schuster, 1972.

YOUNG, M., & GEERTZ, H. Old age in London and San Francisco. *British Journal of Sociology,* 1961, *12,* 124–141.

YOUNG, M., & WILLMOTT, P. *Family and kinship in East London.* Baltimore, Md.: Penguin, 1964.

50

Sex-Related Differences
in Aging

BARBARA F. TURNER

The focus of this chapter is the review of sex-related differences in the psychological changes that occur in late life. Primary attention will be focused on the age groups that Neugarten (1975) referred to as young-old (55 to 74 years) and old-old (75+ years). It is a truism, however, that aging cannot be understood without reference to earlier life periods. Research studies, furthermore, vary considerably in the age ranges of the samples studied. Because of the especially valuable information on sex-related differences in aging that longitudinal studies provide, special attention will be devoted to longitudinal studies, many of which deal with earlier life periods.

The political and social implications of research results in studies of sex differences (Unger, 1979) suggest the importance of differentiating sex differences and gender differences. The term *sex* implies genetic or biological mechanisms, while *gender* refers to the social-psychological dimension of sex status that is culturally defined. It is likely that many so-called sex differences are actually gender differences. The nature of the causal mechanisms underlying female-male differences remain unclear in virtually every instance. The term *sex-related*, therefore, will generally be used throughout this chapter when referring to differences in aging between females and males.

It is worth noting that there are not many unequivocally demonstrable female-male differences in the psychological literature for early life periods (Maccoby & Jacklin, 1974). Similarly the characteristics that are associated with old age in present-day America—such as relatively poor health and the effects of age stereotyping

Portions of this chapter are drawn from L. E. Troll & B. F. Turner, Sex differences in problems of aging. In E. S. Gomberg & V. Franks (Eds.), *Gender and disordered behavior: Sex differences in psychopathology.* New York: Brunner/Mazel, 1979.

and bias—are shared by both women and men. That women and men are far more similar than different, however, is not considered compelling psychological news. Similarities between the sexes are less likely to be published than are differences and, if published, may pass unnoticed by readers (Lipman-Blumen & Tickamyer, 1975; Unger, 1979).

The focus of this chapter, nevertheless, is on sex-related differences rather than similarities. Sex status is so powerful an influence on the life chances and life styles of individuals throughout life that patterns of aging tend to be very different for women than for men. The following pages will attend to these sex-related differences in aging.

Sex-related differences in aging that are of interest to developmental psychologists cover a broad range of topics. This chapter is organized into three main sections: (1) mortality and health or morbidity; (2) psychology as a natural science, including the following topics: learning, memory, and intelligence; and (3) psychology as a social science, including personality, coping and adaptation, and family relationships.

MORTALITY AND HEALTH

Sex-related differences in health in later life are of compelling interest to psychologists because of the important influence of health upon psychological measures such as cognitive performance (Birren, Butler, Greenhouse, Sokoloff, & Yarrow, 1963; Botwinick & Birren, 1963; Eisdorfer & Wilkie, 1977; Palmore & Jeffers, 1971; Siegler, 1980; Spieth, 1964), self-concepts (Kaplan & Pokorny, 1970; Palmore & Luikart, 1972; Riley & Foner, 1968; Turner, 1979; Ward, 1977), morale (Campbell, Converse, & Rodgers, 1976; Larson, 1978; Palmore & Luikart, 1972), and general adaptation (Maas & Kuypers,

1974). Female-male differences in mortality are important since they necessarily form the context for examining sex-related differences in morbidity (Nathanson, 1977).

Mortality

At all ages mortality rates of males in economically developed countries are well above those for females (Preston, 1977; Siegel, 1978). Expectation of life at birth in the United States in 1976 was 76.7 years for women and 69.0 years for men, a difference of nearly eight years (U.S. Bureau of Census, 1978). A large part of this difference is accounted for by differential death rates for women and men over the age of 65. In 1975 white women at age 65 could expect to live for another 18.1 years and nonwhite women for 17.5 years, but men, regardless of race, could expect only 13.7 more years (Kovar, 1978). The mortality differential between women and men over 65 has widened since 1900. In 1900 the death rate for men 65 years and over was 6 percent higher than for women (Linder & Grove, 1947). By 1950 the elderly male death rate was 27 percent higher than that for elderly women; it was 41 percent higher by 1975.

Heart disease is responsible for 44 percent of the deaths of people 65 years and over. Together heart disease, cancer, and cerebrovascular disease (primarily stroke) account for 75 percent of all deaths of people over 65 (Kovar, 1978). Males die more frequently and also more readily from the leading causes of death. At any older age men are likely to suffer from lethal conditions, while women are prone to more chronic conditions that are rarely lethal (Siegel, 1978; Verbrugge, 1977).

Both hereditary (genetic and nongenetic) and environmental factors have been advanced to explain the female-male mortality differential. A biological explanation of the differential is favored by Madigan (1957), Rose (1971), and in part, by Siegel (1978, 1979). Females outlive males in most sexually differentiated species (Kallmann & Jarvik, 1959), and this has been cited as evidence for a genetic contribution to the higher mortality of men (Waldron, 1976). Among birds and mammals, however, higher female mortality is as common as higher male mortality (Caughley, 1966). On the other hand male fetal and infant mortality is considerably higher than that of females (Dublin, Lotka, & Spiegelman, 1949), strengthening the tenability of the genetic hypothesis. Females generally have more resistance than do males to infectious disease because the X chromosome carries quantitative genes for the production of immunoglobin M, resulting in higher serum levels of immunoglobin M in females (Goble & Konopka, 1973). Waldron (1976) suggests that the genetic difference in immune resistance contributes to the female-male differential in pneumonia, which is a leading cause of death among the elderly and accounts for 3 percent of men's excess mortality at all ages.

The study most widely cited in support of the importance of genetic factors is Madigan's (1957) examination of the mortality rates of nuns and brothers in Catholic teaching orders. The men and women had similar life styles, yet the nuns lived longer. As Waldron (1976) points out, however, genetic factors are not the sole cause of the brothers' higher mortality. The brothers drank and smoked more than did the nuns, which would also contribute to higher male mortality.

In support of the importance of hereditary factors, Siegel (1978) suggests that

One tenable hypothesis regarding the basis of the difference in life expectation of the sexes is that women have superior vitality and, with the virtual elimination of the infectious and parasitic illnesses and the consequent emergence of the "chronic degenerative" diseases, such as diseases of the heart, cerebrovascular diseases, and malignant neoplasms, as the leading causes, this vital superiority has been increasingly evidenced. (p. 30)

In contrast most writers (Enterline, 1961; Palmore, 1971; Retherford, 1972; Waldron, 1976; Waldron & Johnston, 1976) suggest that the female-male mortality differential results largely or even wholly from differences in the socialization, environment, social roles, and life styles of women and men. Waldron (1976) offers an especially clear exposition of the behavioral factors underlying higher male mortality in leading causes of death. Although she analyzed causes of death without regard to age at death, much of her argument is pertinent to the female-male mortality differential at older ages.

Cigarette smoking appears to account for the greatest portion of the mortality differential. Retherford (1972) estimates that cigarette smoking accounted for 47 percent of the sex mortality differential between the ages of 37 and 87 in 1962, almost entirely through the relationship of smoking to heart disease and lung cancer, as well as to emphysema. Waldron (1976) attributes one-third of the mortality differential to smoking. She suggests that the sex differential in smoking, at least during the early part of this century, primarily reflects the rebelliousness that adolescents associate with cigarette smoking. The majority of smokers begin to smoke during adolescence (National Clearinghouse for Smoking & Health, 1973), and boys are permitted more rebelliousness and independence than are girls. Hence sex-role socialization leads to higher rates of smoking among males, which then produces higher male mortality.

The behavioral factors related to disease that have been of most interest to psychologists are the behaviors that typify the Type A or Coronary Prone Behavior Pattern (Siegler, Nowlin, & Blumenthal, 1980). In research done in the United States, the pattern of several psychosocial traits that comprise Type A behavior makes a substantial contribution to the higher rate of coronary heart disease among men, and Type A behavior is more prevalent among men than among women (Friedman & Rosenman, 1974). The pattern of Type A traits include a chronic, driving sense of time pressure and *excessive* competitiveness and aggressiveness (Friedman & Rosenman, 1974). Friedman and Rosenman (1974) suggest that a looming sense of time urgency, or "hurry sickness," is the most significant lethal trait of the Type A individual. Huyck (1980) has noted, however, that secondary sources often erroneously describe the Type A individual as merely "aggressive and competitive." Aggressive and competitive behaviors, however, are frequently displayed by Type B individuals, whose incidence of coronary disease is quite low (Friedman & Rosenman, 1974). Unaccompanied by time pressures aggressiveness may in fact *improve* survival chances in later life—as we shall see in a later section. Although genetic factors appear to contribute to the greater aggressiveness of males, socialization and cultural pressures related to adult male social roles are probably primary contributors to the development of the Coronary Prone Behavior Pattern (Waldron, 1976). It is apparent, in any case, that further research should focus upon disentangling the relationships of each of the traits that comprise Type *A* behavior to coronary heart disease.

Behavioral factors are clearly implicated in deaths caused by accidents, suicide, and cirrhosis of the liver (Waldron, 1976). All of these were among the ten leading causes of death among persons 65 years and over in 1975 (Kovar, 1978), and males predominate in each. Excessive alcohol consumption is a major contributor to cirrhosis of the liver (Goodman & Gilman, 1970), as well as to many accidents and some suicides (Blum, 1967). Male drivers are involved in far more fatal accidents per mile driven than are female drivers (National Safety Council, 1972), in part because men have less safe driving habits than do women (Waldron, 1976). In the United States males are about two and a half times more likely to commit suicide than are females (Kastenbaum, 1977). This is the average across all age groups. At age 85 and over the suicide rate of white males is ten times higher than that of white female age-mates (Linden & Breed, 1976). Societal expectations for sex-role behavior account for at least a part of the sex difference in suicide (Lester, 1979). In one study students rated "masculine" males and females as far more likely to commit suicide than "feminine" males and females (Linehan, 1971). The "masculine" males were judged most likely to commit suicide; the "feminine" females, the least likely. Viewing the behavioral factors related to accidents, suicide, and cirrhosis of the liver together, the higher fatalities of men are attributed to behaviors culturally encouraged in males more than in females: risk-taking, aggressiveness, and heavy use of alcohol (Waldron, 1976).

Exposure to greater occupational hazards among men also makes a small contribution to the sex mortality differential (Siegel, 1978; Waldron, 1976), primarily through the effects of industrial carcinogens, respiratory irritants, and accidents.

In summary both cultural and genetic factors appear to contribute to the shorter life expectancy of men. Cultural factors no doubt interact with genetic or biological factors in accounting for the female-male mortality differential. Waldron (1976) concludes that

. . . sex differences in behavior are a more important cause of higher male mortality than are any inherent sex differences in physiology. Furthermore, although these sex differences in behavior may be due in part to genetic differences, cross-cultural and developmental studies clearly show that child-rearing practices and cultural factors strongly influence behavioral differences in both children and adults. (p. 358)

What of future trends? Higher male mortality has been attributed to (1) the higher rates of cigarette smoking among men and (2) higher rates of labor-force participation among men which, presumably, is more stress-inducing than the homemaking role of women (Ehrenreich, 1979; Friedman & Rosenman, 1974). Will the increased rates of cigarette smoking (USDHEW,

1979) and labor-force participation of women (U.S. Bureau of the Census, 1978) appreciably diminish the sex differential in mortality?

Cigarette smoking affects mortality rates primarily through the relationship of smoking to coronary heart disease and, secondarily, to lung cancer. The 1979 report of the Surgeon General on smoking and health indicates that the ". . . mortality rate from lung cancer for women in 1978 was almost three times as high as in 1964, and the ratio of male to female mortality from lung cancer has decreased by almost one-half" (USDHEW, 1979, p. 8). It is unlikely, however, that female mortality rates from lung cancer will overtake those of males. Although women are beginning to smoke at as early an age as men, the former are more likely to use filter cigarettes, inhale less deeply, select brands with lower tar and nicotine yields, and smoke fewer cigarettes per day (USDHEW, 1979). Furthermore in 1976 women were even *less* likely than men to die of coronary heart disease than was true in 1960 (Nathanson, cited in Ehrenreich, 1979). Although the 1979 Surgeon General's report indicates that women smokers are more likely than nonsmokers to die of coronary heart disease, this has not been reflected in the overall change between 1960 and 1976 in the sex mortality differential for this cause of death.

Friedman and Rosenman (1974) suggest that the lethal essence of the American work ethic comprises deadlines, competition, and hostility (p. 78). They argue, therefore, that as women enter the labor force, they too will suffer a greater incidence of coronary heart disease, presumably mediated by the increased Type *A* behavior that the work ethic encourages. The mortality differential would thereby diminish. Most research on Type *A* behavior has sampled only men, but at least one study (cited in Friedman & Rosenman, 1974) found that Type *A* women suffered as much coronary heart disease as their male counterparts. The labor-force participation of American women has increased rapidly since 1940, from 27 percent in 1940 to 48 percent in 1977 (U.S. Bureau of the Census, 1978). During this period, however, the death rates of women from coronary heart disease have fallen more rapidly than the death rates of men (Siegel, 1978). It is, of course, possible that there have not been large enough numbers of women in the labor force for a sufficient number of years to show up in the death rates. In the U.S.S.R., however, where rates of female labor-force participation have been high for many decades, there is an even greater gap in life expectancy at birth (9.2 years in 1970) than in the U.S. (Siegel, 1978). In the Framingham Heart Study Type *A* women between 45 and 74 who had worked for pay for more than half of their adult lives were not more likely to have developed heart disease than were Type *A* homemakers (Haynes, Feinleib, Levine, Scotch, & Kannel, 1979). Haynes (cited in Ehrenreich, 1979) also found a higher incidence of coronary heart disease among women clerical and sales workers than among women in blue-collar or professional and business positions. But the Coronary Prone Behavior Pattern was *not* associated with heart disease among these "pink-collar" women. Instead the psychological factors related to heart disease among the clerical and sales workers were those of having a nonsupportive boss and having suppressed hostility.

Women are, on the average, less likely than are men to

invest themselves fully (and stressfully) in the work ethic (Troll & Turner, in preparation). Sex-role norms for women, internalized during the process of socialization, decree that even employed women should find their major satisfactions within the family. This socialized norm is buttressed by ubiquitous discrimination against women in the labor force, which ensures that women cannot reap the rewards, material or intrapsychic, from labor-force participation that are available to men (Bart, 1971; Dibner, Barnett, & Baruch, 1976). Although the overall occupational status of employed women is similar to that of employed men, women are underrepresented in high-status occupations (Treiman & Terrell, 1975) and are concentrated in low-paying white-collar occupations. Even within occupation groups women earn less for equivalent work and effort (Suter & Miller, 1973). The earnings gap between employed women and men widened appreciably between 1962 and 1973 (U.S. Department of Labor, 1975). When Featherman and Hauser (1976) controlled family-background variables, occupation, education, hours worked, and experience, sexual discrimination was found to account for 85 percent of the earnings gap in 1962 and 84 percent in 1973. Although women are slowly filtering into higher-paying, skilled blue-collar trades and the old professions such as medicine and law (U.S. Department of Labor, 1975), discrimination against women in pay and relative status within these occupational groups is unlikely to abate appreciably over the next two decades. Since women cannot reap the rewards from paid work that men can, women are less likely than are men to invest themselves fully in the work ethic. Hence in comparison to husbands, wives are more likely to continue to search for major satisfactions within the family, despite higher rates of labor-force participation and more investment in occupational careers. The Coronary Prone Behavior Pattern, therefore, should continue to be less common among women than among men.

As the Framingham findings regarding women indicate, however, Type *A* behavior is not the only cluster of psychological factors mediating work-related stresses and coronary heart disease. The multiple responsibilities of employed women who are wives and mothers may also increase stress (and stress-related diseases). Indeed Haynes (cited in Ehrenreich, 1979) found that marriage and child-rearing increased the incidence of heart disease among employed women.

Increased rates of labor force participation and cigarette smoking among women are likely, therefore, to produce some diminution in the sex differential in mortality over the next two decades. The diminution, however, is unlikely to be substantial.

Health

Although males have higher death rates, females, paradoxically, appear to have worse health. As Table 50-1 indicates, women aged 65 and over report more days of restricted activity and more days in bed for an illness than do men. A higher percentage of older women than men report one or more chronic conditions (Kovar, 1978). Males, however, are more likely to have more serious and incapacitating chronic conditions (Nathanson, 1975, 1977; Verbrugge, 1977). Common experience corroborates Health Information Survey reports that older men are considerably more likely than are older women to report limitation of major work and maintenance activities due to chronic health problems (see Table 50-1). Men with chronic conditions also report more mobility limitation than similarly afflicted women, suggesting that males' chronic conditions are more severe than females' (Verbrugge, 1977). Women display more vitality than men in almost any group of older people, even when the women are as old as the men. This sex-related difference in vitality is accentuated in groups of married couples by the typical age differential between spouses in which the husband is older than the wife.

The apparent contradiction between the sex differences in morbidity and mortality largely disappears when data on specific disorders are examined. As Verbrugge (1977) reports,

... when we consider chronic ailments that force a person to restrict activity, a pronounced male excess appears for the majority of conditions. Among them are several leading causes of death. Females have excess morbidity for one major killer (diabetes mellitus) and for less fatal conditions such as mental/nervous conditions, varicose veins, arthritis/rheumatism, and genitourinary conditions—causes of much greater morbidity than mortality. (p. 285)

Diabetes mellitus is the only major cause of death for which women have a higher mortality rate than do men, consistent with women's higher morbidity rate. In general, males have both greater mortality *and* morbidity for

Table 50-1 Selected Health Indicators for Total Population and Population 65 Years and Over, by Sex: 1977 (Civilian noninstitutional population)

	BOTH SEXES		MALE		FEMALE	
INDICATOR	All ages	65 years and over	All ages	65 years and over	All ages	65 years and over
Total population (thousands)	212,153	22,266	102,384	9,197	109,769	13,070
Percent with activity limitation	13.5	43.0	13.9	47.7	13.1	39.7
In major activity	10.4	37.3	10.9	43.8	9.9	32.8
Days of restricted activity per person per year	17.8	36.5	15.8	33.0	19.6	38.9
Days of bed disability per person per year	6.9	14.5	5.8	12.7	7.9	15.8
Persons injured per 100 persons per year	34.8	21.4	41.3	18.7	28.8	23.3
Days of bed disability with injury per 100 persons per year	89.4	192.9	87.6	155.1	91.1	219.5

Source: U.S. Department of Health, Education and Welfare, National Center for Health Statistics, *Vital and Health Statistics,* Series 10, No. 126. U.S. Bureau of the Census, 1979.

most leading causes of death. The apparent poorer health of women is based primarily on higher rates of mild acute disorders (such as the common cold) as well as nonlethal chronic conditions (such as arthritis and hypertension without heart disease).

Consequences of Sex-Related Differences in Health and Longevity

These sex-related differences in health and longevity have many behavioral and interpersonal consequences. Female superiority in longevity, for example, is a mixed blessing. As Huyck (1977) has commented, it increases a woman's chances of living to be very old, alone, and ill. In 1975 there were 69 men aged 65 and over for every 100 women of that age group in the United States (Siegel, 1979). (This ratio is expected to fall further by the year 2000, to 65 males per 100 females.) Due to the female-male difference in life expectancy and the social expectation that women will marry men older than themselves, the ratio of married women increases sharply in later years. Over 65 years of age 75 percent of men but only 37 percent of women are married (U.S. Bureau of Census, 1979). Singled women thus find fewer men available for remarriage, while singled men have many women from whom to choose. In 1970 there were fewer than three brides per 1000 single women 65 and over, compared to 17 grooms per 1000 single men in this age group (NCHS, 1974).

There are many psychological consequences of the sex-related health differential. The cognitive performance of older women appears to be less affected by physiological pathology than that of older men. Poor health—especially cardiovascular disease—has been shown to be related to poorer cognitive performance. In a longitudinal study of the effects of cardiovascular disease (CVD) upon intellectual performance from middle to old age (Hertzog, Schaie, & Gribbin, 1978), men with CVD were significantly more likely than men free of disease to drop out of the study. Proportions of women dropouts and participants with CVD did not differ significantly, probably indicating a more benign course of CVD among women (USDHEW, 1971).

Good health in later years is both directly (Edwards & Klemmack, 1973; Medley, 1976; Palmore & Luikart, 1972; Spreitzer & Snyder, 1974; Tornstam, 1975) and indirectly (Markides & Martin, 1979) related to life satisfaction. We have seen that really poor health is less common among older women than among men. Thus older women, being less likely to suffer from poor health, should enjoy a happier, more vigorous outlook on life than do older men.

Sex-related differences in health in the later years are exaggerated by the differential interpretation of good and poor health for the two sexes. If a woman experiences a reduction in vigor associated with health decrements, she is not perceived as defeminized. The physical image of masculinity for adult males, however, requires an active, vigorous presentation of the total body. The self-esteem of older men is especially vulnerable to health-related decrements in activity level (Nowak, 1976), which represent a blow to the image of masculinity. Huyck (1977) notes that middle-aged men may be especially likely to find illness threatening. "Some un-doubtedly respond with denial of the symptoms, because illness is equated with passivity and the femininity they wish to deny in themselves; they may threaten their health of later years by postponing care and sabotaging medical treatment" (p. 3). Elderly men are also more likely than are women to deny ill health. In the Duke University studies of Durham residents aged 60 and over, men were more likely than were women to deny clear signs of poor health (Maddox, 1964; Maddox & Douglass, 1973)—that is, men predominated among the one-fourth of the sample whose self-rated health was more favorable than physician-rated health despite painstaking feedback to respondents regarding their objective health status.

The sex-related differential in health has many consequences for marital interaction. Given the tendency for many middle-aged men to deny even life-threatening signs of ill health, it is not surprising that Glick, as quoted by Bernard (1973, p. 18), should comment, "Most men profit greatly from having a wife to help them to take care of their health." Both Neugarten (1968) and Deutscher (1964) noted that middle-aged women monitor not only their own health but that of their husbands, a rational response to seeing the deaths of so many middle-aged men in their social networks. When men experience health problems, many wives are drawn back into a repetition of the mother-nurse role they experienced while raising children. It becomes the wife's responsibility to see that her husband goes to the doctor, watches his diet, takes his medication, and alters his activities as indicated. The health services of wives range from maternal nurturance ("Dear, don't forget to take your medicine") to terminal nursing care at home. In her study of middle-aged urban widows, Lopata (1973) was surprised to find that as many as 46 percent of the widows had cared for their husbands at home during their final illnesses. Indeed in fully 40 percent of these instances (p. 48), the wife had cared for her husband at home for over one year. Since the incidence of chronic health conditions rises with age, it is hardly surprising that Feldman (1964) found that health was a major topic of conversation between couples over 65 years of age and that wives at this time had the highest degree of power. It seems likely that at least part of the enhanced power position of wives of this age resides in their physical vigor relative to that of their husbands. The open dependency of such men upon their wives, no longer disguised as it was in earlier stages of marriage, is based in part upon the men's actual physical dependence upon the health services of their wives. Wifely power that is based upon an elderly husband's ill health, however, does not extend to the social structure outside the home, and the nurse role severely curtails a wife's freedom of movement, if not virtually enslaving her. The end result for women of the sex-related differential in health can be a paradoxically continued servitude and caring function instead of new freedom and individuation.

A related consequence of the health differential is the absence of a healthy spouse to nurse the older woman who is unlucky enough to become ill. Women are thus more likely than are men to enter nursing homes (U.S. Bureau of Census, 1979). About 60 percent of persons over 65 are female, but about 70 percent of persons over 65 in nursing homes are female. The predominance of older women in nursing homes is largely attributable to the much greater incidence of widowhood among women and to their older age.

Many older women turn to physicians for the attention they cannot find at home. Unfortunately as Butler and Lewis (1973) point out,

Old women cannot count on the medical profession. Few doctors are interested in them. Their physical and emotional discomforts are often characterized as "postmenopausal syndromes" until they have lived too long for this to be an even faintly reasonable diagnosis. After that, they are assigned the category of "senility." Doctors complain about being harassed by their elderly female patients, and it is true that many are lonely and seeking attention. Yet more than 85% have some kind of chronic health problem, and both depression and hypochondriasis commonly accompany the physical ailments. (p. 91)

Indeed authorities (e.g., Busse & Blazer, 1980; Pfeiffer, 1977) have concluded that hypochondriasis is more common among older women than among men. *Hypochondriasis* is defined as excessive and unwarranted preoccupation with the body (Busse & Blazer, 1980; Pfeiffer, 1977), in conjunction with a pattern of prolonged and frequent medical contacts (Busse, Dovenmuehle, & Brown, 1960). In studies that have compared self-rated with physician-rated health, between 8 to 12 percent of the elderly, on the average, rate their physical health as poorer than their objective health status (Blazer & Houpt, 1979; La Rue, Bank, Jarvik, & Hetland, 1979; Maddox, 1964; Maddox & Douglass, 1973). Women in the Duke University longitudinal studies (Maddox, 1964; Maddox & Douglass, 1973) are more likely than are men to rate their health as poorer than it actually is. In a community survey of nearly 1000 Durham County residents conducted in 1972, however, no sex-related differences in "health pessimism" appeared (Blazer & Houpt, 1979). Similarly La Rue et al. (1979) also failed to report a sex-related difference in "health pessimism" in their sample of aged twins. Hypochondriasis, in short, may *not* be more common among older women than among men; the evidence is equivocal.

LEARNING, MEMORY, AND INTELLECTUAL PERFORMANCE

Sex-related differences in cognition among the elderly have recently received penetrating reviews by Cohen and Wilkie (1979) and by Kramer and Jarvik (1979). Since most measures of cognition increase in variability with increasing age, one might expect that the gerontological literature would devote considerable attention to sources of individual differences in performance. Indeed, sex-related differences in cognitive functioning among the young have been widely studied (Maccoby & Jacklin, 1974; Petersen & Wittig, 1979). As Cohen and Wilkie (1979) point out, however, sex-related differences during adulthood and aging have been relatively neglected in the study of cognition. The topic *sex differences* is not indexed in the appendix of the *Handbook of the Psychology of Aging* (Birren & Schaie, 1977), which contains reviews of gerontological research from 1959 to 1977. The chapters

in that volume on aging and memory (Craik, 1977) and learning (Arenberg & Robertson-Tchabo, 1977) do not mention female-male differences, while the chapter on intellectual functioning (Botwinick, 1977) contains one reference to a sex-related difference in performance. In an excellent comprehensive review of the psychological changes that occur in adulthood and in aging, Siegler (1980) made no references to sex-related differences in memory and learning and cited one study on differences in intellectual performance. Despite the substantial predominance of women in the population aged 55 and over, subjects in cognition research are largely males. Even when both women and men have been studied, sex-related differences may go unreported (Abrahams, Hoyer, Elias, & Bradigan, 1975), although, as Maccoby and Jacklin (1974) and Unger (1979) note, this may simply mean that sex-related differences were tested, found statistically nonsignificant, and thus not mentioned.

The major issue in this section is whether differences between older women and men, if any, reveal qualitative differences or whether the cognitive behaviors are essentially the same but perhaps differ quantitatively.

Verbal Learning

Paired-associate-learning and serial-rote-learning paradigms are most frequently used in verbal-learning research, and old subjects generally do more poorly than do young subjects with both types of learning (Arenberg, 1965; Canestrari, 1963; Hulicka, Sterne, & Grossman, 1967; Monge & Hultsch, 1971; Talland, 1966; Witte, 1975). The age effect diminishes when slow or self-paced presentation rates are used (Arenberg, 1965; Eisdorfer, 1965, 1968; Eisdorfer, Axelrod, & Wilkie, 1963; Taub, 1967).

In childhood females generally outperform males on tests with high verbal loadings (Maccoby & Jacklin, 1974). When sex-related differences in adult populations have been noted on verbal-learning tasks, females also generally outperform males (Kramer & Jarvik, 1979). On tests with high verbal loadings, females respond faster (Elias & Kinsbourne, 1974), more frequently (Harkins, Nowlin, Ramm, & Schroeder, 1974), and more correctly (Bromley, 1958). Wilkie and Eisdorfer (1977) studied serial-rote learning among elderly women and men with high and average verbal ability, using fast and slow stimulus presentation rates. At the fast pacing speed, males with average verbal skills made more omission errors (failure to respond) and total errors than did average-ability women and high-ability women and men. When presentation was slowed no sex-related differences appeared.

In summary since females tend to excel in tests of verbal ability, the literature appears to indicate that elderly women tend to perform better than do male agemates on tests of verbal learning, especially under fast-paced conditions. Males, on the other hand, tend to outperform females on tests of spatial abilities (cf. Cohen & Wilkie, 1979). The mechanisms underlying these sex-related performance differences are unclear. Cohen and Wilkie (1979), however, observe that

Sex-related differences in motivation may partially account for the differences in verbal learning observed among elderly males and females. In unpublished findings Wilkie and Eisdorfer analyzed a postlearning questionnaire and reported that elderly females attached greater importance to "doing well" on a verbal learning test than elderly males. Elderly females believed that their performance was indicative of their general abilities and appeared to be more sensitive to feedback pertaining to their performance. Unlike elderly males, they associated incorrect responses (commission errors) with poor performance. (p. 151)

Arousal, health, performance factors, and inherent abilities may, separately or in combination, account for the sex-related differences in performance that have been observed.

Memory

Few studies of information processing in the aged have addressed sex-related differences in performance, leading Cohen and Wilkie (1979) to conclude that the literature is too limited to improve our understanding of sex-related differences. It seems likely that sex-related differences have been ignored because, as Botwinick and Storandt (1980) suggest, there is no theoretical reason to believe that there are sex-related differences in permanent memory.

In a study of word-association recall among individuals in their twenties and sixties, Perlmutter (1979) found that females performed better than did males on both free and cued recall. Sex-related differences in recognition memory did not appear, however, in Gordon and Clark's (1974) study of individuals in their twenties and seventies using meaningful words and nonsense syllables. Similarly Storandt, Grant, and Gordon (1978) and Botwinick and Storandt (1980) failed to find female-male differences in recall of information about the entertainment world among adults between 20 and 80. In a study of visual short-term memory of simple and complex visual patterns among subjects in their twenties and mid-fifties, Adamowicz (1976) found that females performed better than did males under the fastest-paced condition (3 seconds) but less well under the slower-paced conditions. Adamowicz suggested that the superior overall performance of the males was consistent with Hutt's (1972) conclusion that males perform better on perceptual motor tasks than do females.

The extremely limited literature on sex-related differences in memory with increasing age reveals no consistent findings on quantitative or qualitative female-male differences.

Intelligence

Two sets of findings suggest that women *may* decline less in intelligence than do men in old age. First, the classic aging pattern (Botwinick, 1977) of intellectual change is that verbal intelligence tends to increase until age 50 or 60 before falling off gradually. Performance intelligence, on the other hand, increases till the late thirties or slightly beyond, with a gradual decline until the sixties and a sharper decline after that (Botwinick, 1977; Siegler, 1980; also see Denney, Chap. 45, this volume). Second, although total scores on intelligence-test batteries are similar for females and males at all ages, females tend to excel on nonsymbolic reasoning tasks and

on tests with high verbal loadings, while males tend to excel on spatial abilities. These sex-related differences have been found to hold in middle and old age (Blum, Fosshage, & Jarvik, 1972; Doppelt & Wallace, 1955; Hayslip & Sterns, 1979; Nesselroade, Schaie, & Baltes, 1972; Schaie & Strother, 1968; Wilson, DeFries, McClearn, Vandenberg, Johnson, & Rashad, 1975) as well as in adolescence and young adulthood (Anastasi, 1964; Broverman, Klaiber, Kobayashi, & Vogel, 1968; Buffery & Gray, 1972; Garai & Scheinfeld, 1968; Maccoby & Jacklin, 1974; Tyler, 1965)—that is, verbal subtest scores tend to comprise a greater proportion of women's total intelligence score, whereas performance subtest scores tend to make up a greater proportion of men's total intelligence score. Since verbal abilities are maintained well into old age while performance abilities begin to decline in mid-life, one implication is that women are likely to maintain overall levels of intellectual functioning to a later age than are men. Women may decline less than men do even though the classic aging pattern, with higher verbal than performance scores obtained by elderly subjects, appears to hold for both sexes (Eisdorfer, Busse, & Cohen, 1959). What, now, are the empirical findings bearing on this assertion?

Sex-related differences in intellectual change have been largely neglected (Jarvik & Cohen, 1974). In a 20-year follow-up of twins who were 60 to 73 years of age at initial testing, women initially scored significantly higher than did men on the Wechsler-Bellevue tapping and digit-symbol substitution subtests (Blum et al., 1972). When retested 20 years later, women significantly outperformed men on tapping, digit-symbol substitution, vocabulary, and similarities. When annual rates of decline were computed for the 20-year follow-up, men declined more rapidly than did women on all subtests except tapping and digit-symbol substitution. Blum et al. (1972) regarded the decrements for males as substantial compared with those for females; none of the sex-related differences on rate of decline, however, were statistically significant.

Rhudick and Gordon (1973) tested 50 women and 36 men aged 58 to 88 and retested them one to eight years later. Among those retested within two years, males dropped significantly on the WAIS performance scale, while females did not. When overall change scores were computed for each individual, 43 subjects declined, and 40 improved. Women were more likely to improve than were men. Change was *not* accounted for by age, education, health, retirement status, or initial test scores. Change *was* related to personality variables. On the Leary Interpersonal Checklist, improvers tended to increase their dominance score (reflecting force, power, efficiency, and mastery) over time, while decreasing their love score (reflecting a decrease in overconventionality, overconformity, and "weakness" in interpersonal relations); the opposite pattern occurred for decliners. It is noteworthy that improvement in WAIS scores, more characteristic of women in this study, was related to a pattern of personality change that has frequently been found to characterize older women (Gutmann, 1964, 1975, 1977; Livson, 1976a; Lowenthal, Thurnher, Chiriboga, & Associates, 1975; Neugarten & Gutmann, 1964).

If women do, indeed, decline less in intelligence than do men in old age, the differential decline is unlikely to represent true ontogenetic change. Cardiovascular disease (CVD) produces cognitive decrement (Botwinick & Birren, 1963; Eisdorfer & Wilkie, 1977; Obrist, 1972; Spieth, 1964, 1965). Men are more likely than are women to die of CVD, and CVD appears to take a more benign course in women (USDHEW, 1971), producing less behavioral and psychological decrement than in men. In Hertzog et al.'s (1978) cross-sequential study of CVD and changes in intellectual functioning from middle to old age, men with CVD were significantly more likely than men free of disease to drop out of the study. Proportions of women dropouts and participants with CVD did not differ significantly. Thus considerably more women than men participants had CVD. Participants with CVD, as anticipated, showed poorer performance on several cognitive subtests; nevertheless, the intellectual functioning of the women studied was substantially similar to that of the men. Since it is the less able who tend to drop out of longitudinal studies, subjects with CVD who dropped out of this study very likely showed even more intellectual decrement, on the average, than those with CVD who continued. Thus the poorer health of older men also implies greater cognitive deficit among men than among women in the elderly population at large. (It should be noted that the findings of Hertzog et al., 1978, do not necessarily imply that women are better able than men are to withstand the negative effects of equivalent severity of CVD. The women in this study may well have had less severe forms of CVD, on the average, than the men.)

Cohen and Wilkie (1979) review evidence (e.g., Cohen & Eisdorfer, 1977; Cohen, Matsuyama, & Jarvik, 1976; Roseman & Buckley, 1975) suggesting that immune reactivity may indicate subclinical changes underlying cognitive impairment in older adults. Females tend to resist infectious disease more effectively than do males because the X chromosome carries quantitative genes for the production of immunoglobin M, resulting in higher serum levels of immunoglobin M in females (Goble & Konopka, 1973). There may be direct or indirect linkages between immunoglobulins and cognitive functioning (Cohen & Wilkie, 1979), such that older females are more successful than are older males in combating somatic insults that impair cognition. Cohen and Wilkie (1979) speculate,

If females are more successful in combating somatic insults, heightened serum Ig levels would be a less likely response in the immunocompetent female. Immunoglobulin levels may reflect the result of a different immunological mechanism in males and females with senile dementia. Females, with the CNS changes of dementia, would be more immunoresponsive (i.e., show higher levels of serum immunoglobulins) and perform better on cognitive tasks. Males with a diagnosis of dementia could show a lack of immunoresponsiveness, possibly as a result of immunological depletion. (p. 156)

The sex-related differences in immune reactivity, measuring resistance to disease, and cognitive functioning clearly warrant further study.

Given the well-documented sex-related differences in spatial dimensions and verbal abilities, are the cognitive structures of older women and men dissimilar? Cohen, Schaie, and Gribbin (1977) tested the cognitive identity of the elderly using score, factor, and factor-score measures of spatial and verbal performance. The subjects, 100 women and 96 men who averaged 70 years of age, were matched for age, education, and WAIS vocabulary score. Analyses of variance on the factor scores generated from three verbal and six spatial cognitive tests revealed the typical female-male differences. Women scored significantly higher than did men on the verbal component, while men outperformed women on two of the three spatial components. Jöreskog's (1971) procedures were applied to test the identity of the covariance structure. The best fit for the data turned out to be a model specifying equivalent factor structure, means, coefficients, and correlations—that is, the two sexes in this sample had the same cognitive organization, with no female-male differences on the latent constructs of verbal and spatial abilities.

PSYCHOLOGY AS A SOCIAL SCIENCE

In this section studies of sex-related differences in patterns of personality change, coping and adaptation, and family relationships are reviewed. There is no one theory or paradigm for studying changes in personality and coping over the adult life span that enjoys consensus. There *is* consensus that the differences in life course of women and men are so pervasive that patterns of aging are very different for women and for men (Neugarten & Hagestad, 1976). The metatheoretical and theoretical issues surrounding the explication of developmental change in adulthood (cf. the volumes edited by Baltes, 1978; Baltes & Brim, 1979; Baltes & Schaie, 1973; Datan & Ginsberg, 1975; Datan & Reese, 1977; Goulet & Baltes, 1970) generally apply as well to the study of individual differences in aging, including sex-related differences. A variety of metamodels (developmental-organismic, mechanistic, dialectical) underlie the theory and research from which data on sex-related differences have emerged. Important contributions have come from psychologists (e.g., psychoanalysis and ego psychology) as well as from sociologists and social psychologists (e.g., social-role theory, symbolic interactionism, social learning). Patterns of change in adulthood occur within a complex and dynamic matrix of biological, social, contextual, and historical events, and age-related change must be disentangled from cohort and historical effects. One must keep in mind that most studies are cross-sectional, indicating age differences (if any) or cohort differences rather than age changes. Nor are longitudinal studies free of confounding effects. The changes that appear in longitudinal studies may reflect time-of-measurement effects, including the effects of cultural change within the span of years that a longitudinal sample is studied, rather than effects of maturation. Rapid social change also makes the generalization of longitudinal findings to later cohorts problematic.

Given these complexities in the study and interpretation of changes in adulthood and the theoretical and methodological diversity in approaches to its study, what sex-related differences in aging have appeared in the literature?

Personality

The focus of this section is upon the patterning of sex-related differences in personality in the second half of life. Since few longitudinal studies have followed individuals from middle through old age, attention will be directed to studies which deal with earlier life periods as well.

The empirical literature in this area is difficult to summarize, in part because sex-related personality differences in aging are often discussed under the rubric of *sex role*. For psychologists the latter concept has become an omnibus term used to refer to female-male differences in behaviors, such as role enactments, as well as in internal dispositions, such as personality, abilities, values, attitudes, and other characteristics (Angrist, 1969); theoretical and empirical confusion is the result. Since behavior has multiple determinants, however, it is a mistake to *assume* a close correspondence between stereotypic sex-related personality characteristics and a particular behavior or other psychological characteristic (Constantinople, 1973; Spence & Helmreich, 1978).

The research evidence reviewed herein is diverse. Data sources range from intrapsychic measures of covert personality processes and traits based on projective tests and dream analysis, to personality typologies and personality *Q*-sort ratings based on clinical interviews, to self-reports such as self-concept ratings, paper-and-pencil inventories of "masculine" and "feminine" attributes and other objective personality measures. Both longitudinal and cross-sectional studies are represented. After the evidence is reviewed theoretical explanations for the apparent shifts in gender-linked personality characteristics will be addressed.

Several lines of evidence suggest that personality characteristics stereotypically considered to differentiate women and men are most pronounced in early adulthood (Douvan & Adelson, 1966; Livson, 1976a) and that women and men become progressively more "androgenous" as they move from middle to old age (e.g., Gutmann, 1975, 1977; Livson, 1976a; Lowenthal et al., 1975; Neugarten & Associates, 1964).

Dramatic sex-related differences in personality appeared in the Kansas City Studies of Adult Life, based upon cross-sectional and longitudinal analyses of nearly one thousand women and men aged 40 to 90 from all social class levels, studied between 1953 and 1962 (Neugarten, 1973; Neugarten & Associates, 1964). These urban respondents were born during the closing decades of the nineteenth century and the first decade of the twentieth century. Data sources included lengthy clinical interviews and thematic apperception test (TAT) responses. In a classic study on this project, Neugarten and Gutmann (1964) analyzed the responses of women and men aged 40 to 70 to a TAT-type card depicting an intergenerational family scene. Respondents under 55 tended to describe the old man in this card as dominant and the old woman as nurturant and submissive, while older respondents, in contrast, described the old man as submissive and the old woman as dominant. For the older women and men respondents, Neugarten and Gutmann (1964) concluded, "it is almost always the old woman, not the old man, to whom impulsivity, aggressivity, and hostile dominance are ascribed. This consistency cannot be explained by chance. The assumption seems warranted that there is something common to the actual role behaviors of older women that elicits this consistency in respondents' fantasies" (p. 88). They noted,

however, that the behavior attributed by older respondents to the old woman and man in the projective stimulus was not apparent in the social behavior of these respondents and warned against applying their findings directly to actual behavior. Summarizing these cross-sectional findings with regard to modes of dealing with impulse life, Neugarten (1973) concluded,

Differences between the sexes appeared with age. Older men seemed more receptive than younger men of their affiliative, nurturant, and sensual promptings; older women, more receptive than younger women of aggressive and egocentric impulses. Men appeared to cope with the environment in increasingly abstract and cognitive terms; women, in increasingly affective and expressive terms. . . . In both sexes, however, older people seemed to move toward more eccentric, self-preoccupied positions and to attend increasingly to the control and satisfaction of personal needs. (p. 320)

Gutmann (1975) reports that these age trends in sex-role perceptions, with men perceived as more receptive and accommodating and women as more dominant as respondents approach old age, appear in longitudinal as well as in cross-sectional data. Shifts in sex-role perceptions in TAT responses were found among Druze and Navaho men restudied after five years. Men over 60 at first testing were more likely than were younger men to assign dominance to female figures. When retested men then over 60 shifted toward a view of women as dominant (Gutmann, 1975). Gutmann suggests that these findings represent an ontogenetic age change rather than a cohort effect.

Gutmann's later research (1964, 1969, 1971, 1974, 1975) focused on the construct of *ego mastery style* which, he suggests, shifts in opposite directions for women and men in later adulthood. Since ego mastery style is viewed as an aspect of covert personality, Gutmann has used TAT responses, dreams, and clinical analysis of interview material to assess it. It is important to note that the mastery styles are assessed in terms of the intrapsychic need or motive underlying behavior, not in terms of the behavior itself. Aggressive motives directed toward autonomy and control of the external environment characterize the *active mastery* ego style. In the *passive-accommodative mastery* style (cf. Huyck & Hoyer, in press), the self, rather than the world, is the focus of control. The individuals exemplifying this style are uncomfortable with aggression and, instead, passively acquire external power by accommodating themselves to those seen as controlling power. *Magical mastery* is characterized by marked distortions of external reality that permit the illusion of control.

Summarizing the results of his cross-cultural studies, Gutmann (1977) concludes that, across cultures, men shift from active to passive-accommodative mastery modes in later life and sometimes shift again, into magical mastery. Women, on the other hand, shift from passive-accommodative mastery to active mastery and sometimes again into magical mastery. It is noteworthy that women and men differ in expression of the active mastery and magical mastery styles in particular (Gutmann, 1964). Consistent with traditional definitions of *femininity* and *masculinity*, women with the active-mastery ego style in this early study tend to view conflicts as interpersonal ones, while men with this ego style tend to struggle against an impersonal environment. Interestingly within the magical-mastery ego style, men are unable to act instrumentally to alter the world, whereas women seem zestfully engaged in the external deployment of aggressive energy (Gutmann, 1964).

Investigators at the Institute of Human Development in Berkeley (e.g., Block in collaboration with Haan, 1971; Livson, 1975, 1976a, 1976b) have followed the Berkeley Guidance (born 1927–1928) and/or the Oakland Growth (born 1921) samples over four time periods from early adolescence until the Oakland Growth group was nearly age 50, using the 90-item California Q-sort rated from clinical interview material (Block in collaboration with Haan, 1971) as a primary data source. These project findings imply (1) the continuity of genotypic—but not always phenotypic—personality over time; (2) the importance of sex status in determining developmental patterns; and (3) within each sex group, the *diversity* of recognizably continuous patterns of development. Unfortunately for the purpose of this chapter, these respondents have yet to be followed up as they approach age 60, let alone 70 or 80. Questions regarding consistency and change in sex-related personality characteristics through old age cannot yet be answered in this sample.

Maas and Kuypers (1974), however, followed up the parents of the Berkeley sample when they averaged 70 years of age, comparing data on personality and life style to data collected when they averaged 30 years of age. Maas and Kuypers concluded that the young-adult antecedents of personality at 70 showed more continuity for women than for men, especially for the one-fourth of the women who showed low adaptive capacity at 70. The continuity in personality shared by these women focused on gender-nonspecific traits indicative of psychological difficulties—i.e., depression and low self-esteem. (Although depression and low self-esteem are more common among women than men—cf. Turner, 1979, Weissman & Klerman, 1979—neither is commonly viewed as a central stereotypic component of femininity.)

When the personality profiles of the Oakland Growth and Berkeley Guidance respondents in their thirties were compared to their profiles in adolescence, group trends for both sexes showed considerably enhanced coping capacity and less narcissistic impulsivity (Block in collaboration with Haan, 1971). Since adolescence the men compared to the women had become more obsessive and detached and less interesting; the women more than the men had become psychologically minded, tender in interpersonal attachments, and prone to guilt and worry.

A different approach to the question of how personality is organized over the adult years was taken by applying a cluster-analytic technique to data from the Berkeley samples when the respondents were in their forties. More than 70 percent of both the women and the men revealed a *common* personality organization representing a psychologically healthy, comfortable, well-socialized style of functioning (Haan, 1976). (In early adolescence 48 percent of these men showed this personality organization; in late adolescence, 43 percent; and in their thirties, 37 percent. The corresponding figures for women were 33 percent, 26 percent and 48 percent, respectively. The overall age trend reflects movement toward enhanced personal comfort and competence. Women were least likely to belong to this cluster in late adolescence, a

time of turmoil for many; while the low point for men was in their thirties, when some were still establishing themselves occupationally. The increased psychological comfort for *women* in their forties was especially marked.) This personality cluster was then compared to the primary cluster for physically healthy, well-functioning older women and men (average age 69). Like these middle-aged respondents the older people of both sexes were dependable and productive, but the older group placed much more emphasis on close interpersonal relationships. The older men differed from the middle-aged and from their female age-mates in greater self-satisfaction, masculinity, clarity and consistency of personality, and conventional thoughts; the older women were more uncomfortable with uncertainty, were more undercontrolled, projective, and gregarious, and showed *less* bodily concern than did the middle-aged.

A report of 40 women and 40 men (born in 1921) who remained in the Oakland Growth study until the time of the latest follow-up, when they were almost 50, traces patterns of similarity and divergence in personality ratings at four time periods, from early adolescence to the age of 50 (Livson, 1976a). When they were rated in their early teens, the girls were at least as assertive as the boys. By late adolescence these girls had exchanged their self-assertion for flirtatious, seductive behavior, while the boys had learned to express competence, dominance, and coolness and to suppress spontaneity and tender feelings. Using the personality ratings done when the respondents were 50, the women and men were divided at the mean on Block's (1961) Q-sort of psychological health. By the age of 50 all of the men, but only some of the women, added characteristics traditionally assigned to the other sex, thereby becoming, according to ratings by clinical psychologists on the project, more effective people than they had been at 37 and younger. All of the men became more expressive, but while those above the mean on psychological health or adjustment became more nurturant and giving, those below the mean became more openly dependent. Women above the mean on psychological health at 50 had become more assertive and sharp of mind than earlier; they maintained the nurturant and expressive aspects of "femininity." Women below the mean on psychological health at 50 had been rated as dependent and unassertive in early adolescence; at 47 they continued to be fearful and dependent, and they were more anxious than any of the other age-sex groups. It appears, then, that oversocialization to the passive, socially undesirable aspects of the feminine stereotype inhibits later-life development (Livson, 1976a).

In short an important effect of these changes was to increase the similarity over time of the personality profiles of the psychologically healthy women and men. Correlations between their personality profiles were .73 in early adolescence, .56 in late adolescence, .78 at age 40, and a striking .91 at age 50. An increase in socially desirable, well-socialized traits among both sexes accounts for the increase in similarity. The less psychologically healthy women and men, on the other hand, showed no change in personality resemblance to each other from late adolescence to age 50.

In related analyses focusing only on the women and men above the mean in psychological health at age 50, Livson (1975, 1976b) found that 7 women and 7 men had also been high on psychological health at 40, while 17 women and 14 men had markedly improved on psychological health between 40 and 50. In adolescence as well as at 40 and 50, the stable women and men evinced conventional sex-related personality characteristics. Their personalities appeared well suited to traditional female and male roles. In contrast the women and men whose psychological adjustment improved in mid-life had, as adolescents, shown personality characteristics inconsistent with traditional gender roles. In adolescence the women were intellectual and the men emotionally expressive. At 40, however, these women were depressed, irritable, and prone to daydream, while the men evinced a form of hostile, exploitative hypermasculinity. The latter had suppressed their adolescent emotionality, Livson (1975) suggested, in order to fulfill sex-role expectations for high-achieving men. For both sexes, then, the price of the suppression of genotypic personality characteristics was a diminution of psychological health at 40. By age 50, however, the men had integrated their emotional expressiveness with their sense of masculinity and were nurturant and sensual rather than anxiously hypermasculine. The women at 50, by then disengaged from the mother role, were autonomous, trusting, and goal-oriented.

Lowenthal et al. (1975) studied lower-middle-class women and men in four adult-life transitional stages. In a cross-sectional analysis differences between female and male respondents indicative of gender stereotypes appeared on 34 percent of 70 self-concept items. It appears, then, that a very considerable proportion of people's self-concepts reflects cultural definitions of femininity and masculinity—although the apparent importance of gender stereotypes to self-concepts may be an artifact of instrumentation (Turner, 1979). At all ages the men ascribed "masculine" instrumental characteristics to themselves. The older women, however, were less likely to ascribe "feminine" characteristics to themselves than were the younger women, such that the preretired women (average age 58), the oldest group of women studied, were no more "feminine" in self-conception than were the preretired men (average age 60). In general the preretired women perceived themselves as more assertive, competent, independent, and effective in interpersonal relations than did the younger women (launching-stage women, who averaged 48 years of age; newlyweds; and high school seniors). The assertive self-image of the preretired women further contrasted with the expressive orientation of the preretired men, consistent with developmental changes in intrapsychic functioning for both sexes described by Gutmann (1977). Compared to the controlling and self-controlled orientation of the middle-aged men (average age 50), the preretired men described themselves as more mellow and interested in warm interpersonal relations. Indeed the preretired women's emphasis on competence and self-control in their self-description was more like that of the middle-aged men than like that of their male age-mates (Lowenthal et al., 1975).

In a five-year longitudinal follow-up of self-concepts on this project, middle-aged men decreased significantly in assertiveness, regardless of whether the transition anticipated at Time 1 had been made (Chiriboga & Pierce, 1978).

Gender reversal in dominance with increasing age also appeared on a cross-sectional measure most nearly reflecting overt sex-typed behavior (Lowenthal et al., 1975). In response to the question, "Who's the boss in your family?" husbands were less likely to subscribe to male dominance across the three life stages, while wives were markedly more likely across the stages to report that they themselves were dominant. This provocative finding is unlikely to represent a cohort effect rather than a developmental trend, for there is no compelling reason to believe that lower-middle-class respondents born around 1910 would be more likely than later-born cohorts to subscribe to a norm of female dominance from the outset of their marriages.

The developmental hypothesis is strengthened and also specified by longitudinal analyses of self-concept data from the same project (Thurnher, 1979). The hypothesized "developmental" change with age in self-concept for the two oldest groups restudied after eight years—toward more instrumental assertiveness for women and less assertiveness for men—did indeed occur but only for respondents who evaluated the outcomes of the adult-life transitions that they had recently traversed in *positive* terms. Those who evaluated the outcomes of the recently experienced normative transition in negative terms did *not* evidence the "developmental" change in self-concepts. Among those whose transitional outcomes were negatively evaluated, the women continued to describe themselves as unassertive, while the men tended to describe themselves as even more assertive than they had eight years earlier. Stress experience, therefore, may mediate the hypothesized developmental shift in sex-related personality characteristics.

Age-related shifts in the *overt behavior* of women and men have also been reported. In a study by Gold (1960), 26 anthropologists reported on age-related shifts in sex-typed behavior in the cultures they had studied. Fourteen reported a shift toward greater female dominance in later life; in no case did male authority over women increase with advancing age. It is essential to note, however, that the shift to greater female dominance was not registered in the formal rules of any of the societies. The dominance of old women is without institutional support and does not extend outside the home.

Although evidence of similar age-sex interactions in sex-typed attributes appear in many studies (e.g., Clark & Anderson, 1967; Hubbard, Santos, & Farrow, 1979), many cross-sectional studies do *not* produce evidence for such age-related reversals (Ryff & Baltes, 1976; Urberg & Labouvie-Vief, 1976; Zaks, Karuza, Domurath, & Labouvie-Vief, 1979). Urberg and Labouvie-Vief (1976) suggest that the appearance of reversals in sex-typed attributes in longitudinal studies is a function of differential drop-out rates, since it is the better educated, more mature individuals—those most likely to continue participating in a longitudinal study—who are less likely to show distinct sex-typed differences.

What of theoretical explanations for the postulated shifts in sex-related personality characteristics?

Jung (1933), who described stages of development in adulthood, proposed a dualistic conception of feminity and masculinity. Both the masculine *animus* and the feminine *anima,* he suggested, coexist in everyone. Jung proposed that the process of individuation in the second half of life balances the one-sided development of masculinity or of feminity in the first half. Specifically, he suggested, men after 40 "take back" the feminine aspects of self they had previously repressed, while women reclaim the masculine, assertive aspects represented in the animus. As in personality theories generally (cf. Huyck & Hoyer, in press; Riegel, 1975), the determinants of the shifts in Jung's internally based developmental progression in adulthood are not explained. The process by which individuals shift from one developmental phase to another in this and other psychodynamic models is also inadequately explained (Huyck & Hoyer, in press).

The viewpoint that intrapsychic change in the second half of life reflects inner developmental realities more than sociocultural constraints is most fully developed in the work of Gutmann (1964, 1969, 1971, 1974, 1975, 1977). He suggests that cultures have arranged the formal age-grading of male passivity and the informal age-grading of female dominance in patterns consistent with the *intrinsic* developmental trajectory of each sex (Gutmann, 1977). Young men must vigorously struggle in the world outside the home, while men in late life are expected to accommodate to external forces. Young women, on the other hand, are expected to trade submission to their husbands for security; in later life, they become more domineering. Indeed Gutmann (1977) suggests that the male mid-life crisis is most likely to emerge in societies in which social arrangements do not permit the smooth unfolding of male passivity in mid-life.

In explaining the determinants of these shifts in sex-role modalities, Gutmann (1975) has integrated psychoanalytic concepts with aspects of role theory in a schema he terms the *parental imperative*. He suggests that each sex in young adulthood represses characteristics ascribed to the other sex so as to provide an environment maximally conducive to the survival of offspring. After the children have reached adulthood, adults are free to release and express the repressed characteristics—for women, assertiveness and independence; for men, expressiveness, dependency, and nurturance. In short, stage of life—especially that of active parenting, a role nearly universal until recently in the human species and which is rather uniform in content of sex-role expectations across cultures—as well as one's sex status determine the dualistic, sequentially patterned emergence of "masculine" and "feminine" traits in both sexes (Gutmann, 1977).

Gutmann's rich and provocative model remains to be tested. Unlike other psychodynamic theorists he does propose a determinant—the experience of the social role of parenthood—for the personality changes proposed. The linkage between covert personality processes and actual behavior assumed in this theory, however, requires testing. There is a minimal relationship between people's conscious self-descriptions and their actual behavior (Mischel, 1975); behavioral motives expressed in TAT stories also often bear slight relationship to actual behavior. The elderly Kansas City women who expressed primitive, unbridled aggressive motives in TAT protocols, for example, "were often described by interviewers as warm, friendly, intelligent, full of civic spirit and concern for their families" (Gutmann, 1964, p. 143). Nor is it necessarily the case that adequate parenting *requires* the suppression of cross-gender psychological characteristics. Ten years of research based upon a dualistic conception of masculinity and feminity has amply demonstrated the

possibility of being high in both masculine and feminine attributes (cf. Kaplan & Sedney, 1980; Spence & Helmreich, 1978) and that the responsibilities of motherhood require "instrumental" strengths (Rossi, 1968), as well as "expressive" skills. It is essential, in further research on Gutmann's model as well as those of other investigators, to distinguish both empirically and conceptually between femininity and masculinity as properties of personality and as properties of *roles*.

Livson's work (1975, 1976a, 1976b, 1981) assumes the genotypic continuity of personality. Among those high in psychological health at 50, phenotypic continuity from adolescence to the age of 50 holds for those women and men, about one-third of the group studied, whose basic personalities in adolescence "fit" the definitions of characteristics required for excellent performance in traditional feminine and masculine social roles as the role demands changed from adolescence to mid-life. The cross-gender adolescent characteristics displayed by the remaining women and men high on psychological health at 50 had been suppressed at 40, Livson suggests, in order to conform to traditionally sex-typed role definitions. These genotypic cross-gender characteristics, however, emerged by the age of 50. Among those somewhat lower in psychological health at 50, both women and men manifested sex-typed, but socially undesirable, personality characteristics in adolescence. At 50 only the men were more androgenous and better adjusted than they were earlier. The mechanism for the overall shift in gender-related personality characteristics in this sample is unclear. Changes in social roles (launching of children for women, coming to terms with occupational goals for men) are obvious possibilities, but change in time perspective or other age-related changes may also be involved (Livson, 1981). Consistent with Gutmann's (1975) propositions, Livson suggests that the sex-role polarization of young adult roles, at least for the birth cohort studied, tends to lead individuals to polarize role-related personality characteristics as well.

Lowenthal et al. (1975) relate the gender and stage differences in self-concepts found in their study to role demands tied to social stage of life. Some of the preretired women, for example, still had children at home, and their self-concepts more closely resembled those of the somewhat younger launching-stage mothers than those of the child-free preretired women. Back (1971) similarly noted that the presence or absence of children had more effect upon the content of the self-concepts of women than did their chronological age. With children at home women's responses to a "Who Am I?" test cited family relationships; with children gone women's identities focused on personal characteristics and values. The latter group of women, it would seem, were finally free to become more truly themselves. Abrahams, Feldman, and Nash (1978) similarly found that gender-related self-concepts of both women and men in varied life situations conformed to the degree of masculine or feminine behavior required in each life situation.

Consistent with the overall masculine bias of psychological research, research and theory in adult development and aging has focused far more on men than women. As the research findings reviewed in this chapter make clear, however, findings on personality development drawn from research on males cannot safely be generalized to females. The same point holds, of course, for development of theory. In commenting on Levinson's (1978) theory of adult male development, Baruch and Barnett (1979) conclude that the theory would be very different if the study of mid-life had begun with women. Because they deal with development only in males, this chapter has not reviewed findings of the longitudinal Normative Aging Study of some 2000 men of all ages in Boston, the Baltimore Longitudinal Study of Aging, Levinson's (1978) dialectical model of adult male development, or Vaillant's (1977) study of adaptation among Harvard graduates. It is worth noting, however, that analyses of males' responses when only one objective personality test is used (e.g., the Cattell 16PF or the Guilford-Zimmerman Temperament Survey) over periods of 6, 10, and 12 years in the Boston and Baltimore studies reveal remarkable stability of mean level and rank-ordering at all ages on the various subscales (Costa & McCrae, 1977, Costa & McCrae, 1978; Costa, McCrae, & Arenberg, 1980). Test-retest stability over a longer, 30-year period from middle to old age is less impressive, however, though still substantial (Leon, Gillum, Gillum, & Gouze, 1979). Not all investigators report invariant stability. Using a cross-sequential design Douglas and Arenberg (1978) found evidence for maturational decline over a seven-year period on the Guilford-Zimmerman masculinity scale (reflecting "masculine interests" and emotional inexpressiveness) for men at all ages, but no age change in ascendance (reflecting social assertiveness). Certain methodological problems associated with research on aging are, perhaps, especially acute in studies using single objective personality tests: increased response bias with age; increased variability in response with age; uncertain validity of instruments for older individuals.

Despite the rich data base of the longitudinal studies of adult personality cited in this section, the findings cannot be generalized to larger populations or to other cohorts. Several lines of evidence characterize the young adult (postadolescent) males studied as emotionally inexpressive (Douglas & Arenberg, 1978; Gutmann, 1977; Livson, 1976a; Vaillant, 1977), consistent with sex-role expectations for high-achieving males. Subcultural expectations for young black men in the United States, however, include considerably more warmth and expressiveness (Turner & Turner, 1974). The samples of the longitudinal studies cited in this section are small, predominantly middle-class, white, well educated, and generally blessed with supportive environments. Californians and respondents born in the 1920s are overrepresented. As Neugarten (1977) has pointed out, it is possible to regard these investigations as nothing more than groups of case studies, albeit as valuable sources of data on continuity and change in adult personality.

Investigators of sex-related differences in adult personality, regardless of data source, agree that patterns of personality development differ for women and men. Studies using single objective personality tests in a follow-up design report no or almost no gender × time interactions over the period of a few years—that is, sex-related differences are stable over time, with little evidence for age-related changes in personality for either women or men (e.g., Schaie & Parham, 1976; Siegler, George, & Okun, 1979). In research using personality Q-sort ratings based on clinical interviews, the general trend of personality development for both genders reflects an increase in socially adaptive traits and a corresponding decrease in maladaptive characteristics, such that psychologically healthy women and men resemble each other far more at 50 than at 18. Increasing similarity in personality does not, however, characterize women and men who are less well adapted in mid-life. It is unclear whether continuity of maladaptive traits characterizes one gender more than the other.

Dissension reigns on whether personality change in later life is mediated by sex-related differences, with decreasing "femininity" among women and declining "masculinity" among men. This debated age-related shift is most frequently associated with data based on projective tests (Gutmann, 1975) and with self-concept data (e.g., Chiriboga & Pierce, 1978; Thurnher, 1979). Drawing together the findings of both longitudinal and cross-sectional studies using data amenable to conscious control, it appears that older men are more likely to add characteristics stereotypically associated with femininity (Hyde & Phillis, 1979; Livson, 1976b) or decline in stereotypically masculine traits (Chiriboga & Pierce, 1978; Douglas & Arenberg, 1978) than older women are to add characteristics stereotypically associated with masculinity (Chiriboga & Pierce, 1978; Hyde & Phillis, 1979; Livson, 1976b).

It is premature to conclude that continuity in personality over the adult life span is similar for women and men. As the different investigators note, the men studied have stable and advantageous life circumstances; few, for example, are widowed or divorced. Few have incomes below the poverty line. Women are far more likely to experience normative role discontinuities that may interact with personality development, and the developmental tasks of women in later life vary more than those of men. Further research on both sexes might well combine objective personality tests with other types of data on personality *and* behavior and contrast those individuals who show the most personality change with those who are stable to ascertain the determinants of relative stability and change.

Coping and Adaptation

The literature reviewed herein overlaps considerably with that reviewed in the previous section, reflecting the strong focus of gerontologists interested in personality upon adaptive processes in general and "successful aging" in particular.

A variety of theoretical and empirical approaches (e.g., Hultsch & Plemons, 1979; Livson, 1975, 1976a, 1976b, in press; Lowenthal & Chiriboga, 1973; Maas & Kuypers, 1974; Neugarten, 1977; Srole, 1978; Turner, Tobin, & Lieberman, 1972) appear in the literature on coping and adaptation in later life that also reveal sex-related differences.

In several studies (e.g., Livson, 1975, 1976a, 1976b, 1981; Maas & Kuypers, 1974), adaptation is viewed as itself an aspect of personality. Maas and Kuypers (1974) derived life styles and personality types for the 70-year-old parents of the Berkeley sample. Life styles since the age of 30 were more continuous for fathers than for mothers, in part because the men remained married while the women became widowed. These data suggest that the late-life personal adaptation of highly feminine, other-oriented women is dependent upon their marital status and proximity to children. With no interests and involvements outside the family circle, such women are more vulnerable than more autonomous women to the changes in life style and life focus wrought by widowhood. Continuity from age 30 to 70 in personality (reviewed in the previous section) was greater for mothers, especially those poorly adapted, than for fathers. The continuity of neurotic indicators in this study contrasts with the conclusions of Moss and Susman (1980) who reviewed research on life-span constancy and change in personality and suggested that undesirable traits show more change than do other variables. The young adult data on personality for the fathers in the Maas and Kuypers study, however, is so sparse as not to justify a weighty burden of interpretation.

In Livson's research (reviewed in the previous section), a measure of psychological health similar to *ego strength* is used to assess adaptation. Her findings indicate that, for many of the women and men studied, suppression of cross-gender personality traits in the service of conformity to sex-role expectations exacts the price, early in mid-life, of a diminution in psychological health. At the age of 50 same-sex characteristics were the dominant mode for all, but all the men and some of the women in this affluent, predominantly upper-middle-class group had either added or reclaimed cross-gender characteristics that enhanced their overall functioning. The men became more expressive and nurturant, or dependent— the women, more assertive. For some of the women, however, early life socialization to the passive, negatively evaluated psychological aspects of femininity inhibited psychological growth, at least to the age of 50. In summarizing her work Livson (1980) suggests that women actualize their autonomy and sense of identity much later than men do, often not before the middle years of life; and that improved adaptation for both sexes is regulated, in part, by changing definitions of masculinity and femininity in later life. Women's life styles, Livson (1980) further suggests, may permit more role flexibility and more ability to tolerate the losses of later life than is true for men.

In 1974 Srole and Fischer (1978) reinterviewed 695 of the 1660 white adults first interviewed in 1954, aged 20 to 59, for the Midtown Manhattan Study. Compared to women aged 40 to 59 in 1954, the mental health ratings of women aged 40 to 59 in 1974 were significantly higher. In 1954, for example, 26 percent of the women 50 to 59 had been impaired versus only 15 percent of the men. Twenty years later only 11 percent of the women who were now in their fifties were impaired, compared with 9 percent of the men. The male superiority in mental health in 1954 for that age group, as well as for those aged 40 to 49, had all but disappeared. This finding does not necessarily herald similarly high levels of mental health for younger cohorts of women when they reach middle age. Women aged 35 to 39 when sampled in a National Health Survey in the early 1970s, for example, were more likely to report symptoms of nervous breakdown than were women at that age 12 years earlier (cited in Bird, 1979).

Two of the measures used by Lowenthal et al. (1975)

in a complex model of adaptive capacity revealed interesting sex-related differences. Among the men 30 percent of the middle-aged (age 50) and 40 percent of the preretired (age 60) in this lower-middle-class group were rated as prone to give in to the needs or demands of others rather than dominate them, compared to 56 percent of the women at these stages. (Eighty percent of newlywed women were accommodating rather than dominating.) At the preretired stage men and women did not differ in level of accommodation. Interestingly the oldest group of men rated low on capacity for mutuality in relationships compared to female age-mates, despite these men's professed interest in warm interpersonal relationships. There were also sex-related differences in response to stress. Among the middle-aged and preretired, highly stressed women were preoccupied with the stresses they had experienced, while highly stressed men simply reported the stresses and made nothing more of them.

The explication of sex-related differences in adaptation to aging is complicated by the fact that the salient psychological issues of adulthood change over time (Neugarten, 1977). In middle age, for example, the personalization of death leads women to rehearse for widowhood, while men rehearse for illness (Neugarten, 1968). Not only do social roles and role combinations vary across the life span, but many social roles themselves, according to social-role theory (Lopata, 1973), have a life cycle which is predictable and foreseen by those entering the role. Sex-role expectations for performance may diverge and converge along the life cycle of important social roles. In a study of men's perceptions of their role as father vis-à-vis the role of mother, convergence in father-mother role definitions was *positively* related to age of father (ages 45 to 75), contrary to predictions based on cohort membership (Mitteness & Nydegger, 1979). Regardless of the age of father, convergence in role definitions accompanied the maturing of the men's children—that is, the father and mother of an infant are seen as divergent in role behavior, compared to the father and mother of a 15-year-old.

Self-Esteem

Psychological researchers frequently use self-esteem as a measure of adaptation. Voluminous literature indicates that, regardless of age, females in our culture have lower self-esteem than do males (Crain & Weisman, 1972; Dinitz, Dynes, & Clarke, 1954; Gove & Geerken, 1977; Lynn, 1959; Sherriffs & McKee, 1957). Self-criticism is closely related to self-esteem, and women are also more self-critical than men are (Gove & Geerken, 1977; Gove & Tudor, 1973; Gurin, Veroff, & Feld, 1960). From the politics of caste perspective (Hochschild, 1973), the relationship between the sexes is a political one in which men (and male characteristics) are superior and women (and female characteristics) are inferior. Hence the lower self-esteem and higher self-criticism of women.

Gender differences in self-criticism, however, appear to diminish by late middle age (Turner, 1979). In the Gurin et al. (1960) large sample survey, women over 55 were less self-critical, relative to men of the same age, than were women under 55, although the older women were still more self-critical than were their male age-mates. Similar findings emerged in Lowenthal et al.'s

(1975) study of lower-middle-class women and men in four adult-life transitional stages. Using an adjective-rating list, high school senior women circled many more attributes that they disliked about themselves than did high school men, whereas gender differences in self-criticism were minimal in the preretirement stage, the oldest group studied. What accounts for this diminution in late middle age of gender differences in self-esteem? (It is possible, of course, that the findings of these studies indicate cohort differences rather than age changes.)

Because so many stereotypically feminine traits are rated as socially undesirable by both women and men (Broverman, Broverman, Clarkson, Rosenkrantz, & Vogel, 1970; Lowenthal et al., 1975), it follows that if femininity in self-concept declines and masculinity increases as women grow older self-acceptance should also increase. Indeed masculinity in self-concept facilitates self-esteem among both sexes (cf. Spence & Helmreich, 1978). In the Lowenthal et al. (1975) study, preretired women with highly feminine self-concepts were considerably more self-critical; conversely, women in this stage who were higher on masculinity were also lower in self-criticism.

The Adaptive Value of Assertiveness in Late Life

Since the demands of social roles, the psychological issues and preoccupations of adulthood, social settings, and the body itself change with increasing age, adaptive characteristics may be specific to settings and life stages. In a study of adaptation to the stress of entering an institution for the aged, a model was developed which assumed that congruence between a person's coping style and the demands of the specific environment would facilitate adaptation (Turner, 1969; Turner et al., 1972). For *both* men and women an aggressive, even combative stance predicted survival and adaptation within the institutional setting. Pugnaciousness—and rejection of passivity—are central characteristics of long-lived men in preliterate societies (Gutmann, 1977). Gutmann suggests that active mastery, and perhaps also longevity, require the capacity to externalize· aggression. The resulting stance of active vigilance may also tune up the cardiovascular system, thereby avoiding death (Gutmann, 1977). Interesting also is that the elderly in a longitudinal study who improved their WAIS scores also tended to increase their dominance scores and decrease their love scores on the Leary Interpersonal Checklist (Rhudick & Gordon, 1973). Women in this study were more likely to improve their WAIS scores than were men (change was not accounted for by health). Aggressiveness, when unaccompanied by the sense of time pressure that forms part of the Coronary Prone Behavior Pattern, may thus be adaptive in old age for *both* sexes, at least in the sense of improving survival chances and intellectual functioning.

To be sure, aggressive and competitive behavior may limit smooth interpersonal relations. The social disapproval meted out in white America to assertive women at any age, however, surely inhibits the expression of aggressive tendencies in white women more than in men. Even highly desirable "instrumental" masculine traits are viewed by white men as undesirable for women (Broverman et al., 1970; Turner & Turner, 1974), and women

tend to concur (Lowenthal et al., 1975). Huyck (1977) points out that jokes and social unease accompany tales of strong, dominant old women. "The old battle-axe" is deprecated; much more acceptable is the meek, kindly, "feminine" old man. (These considerations do not hold among black Americans and also may not hold in other places or at other times.) Among whites, however, the aggressive older woman is viewed with alarm by the younger generation—and by her husband. With few realistic social possibilities for expression of newly experienced self-assertion among the lower-middle-class white women studied by Lowenthal et al. (1975), the oldest women apparently responded by becoming more dominant in relation to their husbands and also sometimes to their adult children. At least part of the enhanced power position of older wives, as we have seen in an earlier section, is based on their physical vigor relative to that of their husbands. In any case the dominance of old wives does not extend outside the home.

FAMILY RELATIONSHIPS

Family relationships in later life include those between spouses, between parents and children, and between extended kin. These are considered in the following sections.

Marital Relations

The effects of differential health status on marital relationships in later life have already been discussed.

Most research on husband-wife relationships across the adult life span has focused on marital satisfaction. The many thorny methodological issues in this area of research have been reviewed by Hudson and Murphy (1980), Spanier, Lewis, and Cole (1975), and Troll and Turner (in preparation). Almost all these studies, both cross-sectional and longitudinal, find a decline in satisfaction from the peak of the honeymoon to the nadir of middle age (e.g., Blood & Wolfe, 1960; Campbell et al., 1976; Feldman, 1964; Paris & Luckey, 1966; Pineo, 1961). Most studies that compare couples before and after the "launching" period report a curvilinear trend, with an upswing in marital satisfaction usually following the departure of the last child from home (Blood & Wolfe, 1960; Campbell et al., 1976; Deutscher, 1964; Feldman, 1964; Rollins & Feldman, 1970; Stinnett, Carter, & Montgomery, 1972). Other studies, however, report a leveling off in satisfaction at some point in midlife, without a subsequent rise (e.g., Spanier, Lewis, & Cole, 1975). Using a two-dimensional measure of marital satisfaction reflecting positive interaction and negative sentiment in a large-sample cross-sectional study of three age groups of married individuals who averaged 22, 44, and 67 years of age, Gilford and Bengtson (1979) found that negative sentiment declined linearly by age, while positive interaction revealed a U-shaped curve. The oldest group had moderately low levels of positive interaction but considerably lower levels of negative sentiment. Hudson and Murphy (1980) suggest, however, that virtually all such findings of a nonlinear relationship between marital satisfaction and age or stage of the family life cycle may be based on statistical artifacts. The strikingly positive marital evaluations of elderly spouses in several studies may also, in part, reflect response-bias tendencies among older persons (Campbell et al., 1976; Gove & Geerken, 1977).

The array of findings are reviewed by Rollins and Cannon (1974), Spanier et al. (1975), Troll (1971, 1975), and Troll and Turner (in preparation). That the drop in marital satisfaction with length of marriage may be associated with child-rearing is suggested by its acceleration after the birth of the first child, its relative absence in couples without children, its greater strength and consistency among women than among men, and its possible reversal—at least temporarily—after the children are "launched." Data derived from husbands are both rarer and less consistent than those derived from wives. Some studies show no life-course change in marital satisfaction among men (Hamilton, 1929; Luckey, 1961; Paris & Luckey, 1966); some show no sex-related differences across the adult life course (e.g., Gilford & Bengtson, 1979); while other studies show different time patterns in marital satisfaction for husbands and wives (Bossard & Boll, 1955; Hicks & Platt, 1970; Lowenthal et al., 1975).

In the Lowenthal et al. (1975) study, sex-related differences in marital satisfaction were primarily confined to the launching-stage respondents (whose youngest child was a high school senior). While four-fifths of the men at all stages (newlywed through preretired) as well as newlywed and preretired women reported high marital satisfaction and positive regard for their spouses, the launching-stage women were much more critical. Only two-fifths portrayed their husbands and their marriages in predominantly positive terms. On the other hand when they were asked, "How do you think your spouse would describe you?," over half of the women, but only one-third of the men, at that stage expected predominantly positive descriptions. (The men and women in this sample were not married to each other.) While the men stressed their wives' virtues, they knew that they did not meet their wives' expectations. Thurnher (1975) notes,

In terms of fulfilling emotional needs, these sex differences appear to mirror actuality. Middle-aged men, by and large, did not question their adequacy as family providers but seemed aware—though not necessarily contrite about it or moved to change—that they were often inconsiderate and unheeding of the wife's desires for attention, companionship, or diversion. (p. 28)

In describing daily activities these women spoke about their husbands more than the men spoke about their wives. Similar to the working-class and upper-middle-class fathers described by Rubin (1975), these lower-middle-class middle-aged men tended to be psychologically absent from their homes even when physically present in them.

This study also employed TAT responses to tap covert perceptions of marital relationships. Although launching-stage men's interview descriptions of their wives focused upon instrumental role performance, in fantasy these men revealed a need for reciprocal nurturance with their wives, from whom they wanted love and support and toward whom they expressed tenderness. The fantasy responses of launching-stage women, in contrast, were consistent with those they gave to direct questions—that

is, women were more aware of their feelings and more able to express them than were men. The women's fantasy responses indicated that their husbands were failing to meet their wives' emotional needs but that the women anticipated more dependency and more closeness in the future. Launching-stage women's feelings about the dependent marital relationships they anticipated were less sanguine than those of their male age-mates: Where men described such relationships as "tender," women described them as "clinging." Although in their fantasy responses both sexes at this stage of the family life cycle yearned for warmth and intimacy in the marital relationship, women seemed less hopeful of its promise, expecting at best a relationship that provided support and staved off loneliness. The marital relationships depicted in the somewhat older, preretired men's fantasies differed from the satisfying companionable bonds described in interview responses on their actual marriages: Comfort was present, but nurturance and warmth were not. Preretired women's TAT responses were less likely than those of other groups to portray affiliation themes. Instead consolation and dependency themes depicted stoicism and the notion of "leaning on one another." Their fantasies commented more coldly, even cynically, on male-female relationships than did those of the somewhat younger launching-stage women.

Many launching-stage and preretired women in this study felt that their husbands were overdependent. (Among the newlyweds it was the men who were more likely to express such feelings about their wives.) Many of these middle-aged women were looking forward to expressing themselves autonomously in the world outside the family. The emotional support this might require from their husbands, however, did not seem to be forthcoming. Husbands in this sample, as in the samples of other studies, were not ready to fulfill this need. Instead many of the women were being drawn into mothering their husbands—and few of the women seemed to want this.

Among the launching-stage respondents in this study, both sexes expected that the departure of the last child would improve marital relations, emphasizing companionship and mutual dependency rather than better understanding. Both women and men in the preretired group noted improved marital relationships since the departure of children; the greater companionship and closeness that had occurred were attributed to more opportunities to spend time together and to the renewal of the wife's undivided attention. Men, however, expressed more satisfaction than did women. Data from six U.S. national surveys corroborate the finding of improved marital relationships following the departure of children (Glenn, 1975). Middle-aged women whose children have left home generally report somewhat greater happiness and enjoyment of life and substantially greater marital happiness than do middle-aged women still in the launching stage. In general respondents report that the time after children leave home is like a second honeymoon, a recapturing of the joys of undivided companionship (e.g., Deutscher, 1964).

Nonetheless wives look forward less than husbands do to marital togetherness following husbands' retirement (Lowenthal et al., 1975), and after husbands have retired, wives enjoy togetherness less than husbands do. In a study of husbands and wives following the husbands' retirement, three-fourths of the women but almost no men reported a disadvantage of retirement that was related to the marital relationship (Keating & Cole, 1980). Wives complained of loss of personal freedom, too much togetherness, and too many demands on their time. They accommodated to their husbands' retirement by rescheduling their own household tasks and orchestrating their husbands' leisure activities in response to what they perceived as their husbands' needs. Women viewed these accommodations as nurturant and supportive of their husbands; some felt guilty if they continued their own preretirement social activities without taking responsibility for meeting their husbands' perceived social needs. Most wives were compensated, fully or in part, by the increased centrality of the marital relationship or by a sense of being needed; a minority simply suffered in silence. A striking finding was that wives' accommodations were made unilaterally; few discussed these issues with their husbands. As a result many men were unaware of the "supportive" changes that their wives had made in scheduling their own activities.

In summary sex-related differences in marital satisfaction after the departure of children and through very old age are not large in studies that use omnibus measures of satisfaction; when differences do occur, men are more satisfied. Before retirement women wish for more companionship and communication than do men; after retirement, at least some women wish for *less* companionship than do men, although women may still be less satisfied with the degree of communication with spouse. From the age of 50 onward, the increasing psychological and physical dependency of men upon their wives leads women to behave more like mothers and less like wives in the marital relationship. Not many women find this desirable.

Explanations of the sex-related differences found in marital satisfaction in later life may be drawn from the role perspective and the politics of caste, or sexual-politics, paradigms (Hochschild, 1973). The sexual-politics paradigm assumes that sex-related differences are due to socialization, which in turn is linked to power and status differences: Men are superior and women, inferior. Bernard (1972) suggests that because women's happiness is more dependent on marriage than is men's, women have to pay more for it. Normative expectations for marital roles are that women will make more concessions in marriage than will men, both early and late in life. The demands of marriage are more stringent for wives than for husbands; thus, the psychological costs of marriage to wives, evidenced in the higher rates of depression and other symptoms for married women than for married men, are greater than to husbands.

Another explanation is that women and men expect and want different things from marriage and that women are less likely than men are to have their expectations and wishes fulfilled (Laws, 1971). There is evidence in studies conducted over the past 20 years that conversation in marriage is more important to the marital satisfaction of wives than of husbands. Although it seems that as social class rises, husbands talk more to their wives, the classic plea of wives to husbands in all social classes—and age groups—is still, "Talk to me!" (Bernard, 1972; Cuber & Harroff, 1965; Komarovsky,

1964; Lowenthal et al., 1975; Rubin, 1975). The proverbial silence of husbands, so frustrating to their wives, has been attributed to differential socialization of expressiveness by sex. The "inexpressive male" is a stock figure in the research literature on self-disclosure. Inarticulate men who are unable to share their feelings, or even to be aware of them, are more common in lower socioeconomic classes but are far from rare at any social class level. Not all the middle-aged men in Cuber and Harroff's (1965) upper-middle-class sample, however, were psychologically obtuse; yet most communicated very little to their wives. A second common explanation of the silence of husbands is immersion in upper-middle-class occupational roles; to these men, their careers are far more engrossing than their families are. Even lower-middle-class men, many of whom are bored with their jobs, may become preoccupied with work to the exclusion of other roles. Lowenthal et al. (1975) reported that launching-stage men, 10 to 15 years away from retirement, were strongly, even frantically, concerned with ensuring financial security for their retirement years. The preretired men, in contrast, expressed considerable interest in warm, intimate interpersonal relationships; their professed interest in mutuality, unfortunately, was greater than their capacity for it. Even after retirement, therefore, men may be less able to meet their wives' intimacy needs than vice versa. Indeed, men depend on their wives for fulfillment of their intimacy needs; women report a greater variety of others as intimates (Harris & Associates, 1975; Huyck, 1975) and are less likely to identify spouses as primary confidantes (Lowenthal & Robinson, 1976). Restriction of an older wife's social activities in accommodating to her retired husband's needs and interests may result, therefore, in relative nonfulfillment of her intimacy needs.

Household division of labor is notoriously unequal between the two sexes. In an early cross-sectional study, Blood and Wolfe (1960) found that household-task specialization by gender increased over the life span, reaching its highest point during retirement. Departure of children from the home and even retirement did not increase the husband's share of household work. Lipman (1961, 1962) reported that many retired husbands participated in chores that required little specialized skill and knowledge and which could be done jointly with their wives, such as washing dishes and shopping for groceries. On the other hand Ballweg (1967) did not find that retired husbands shared more work with their wives than did employed husbands of the same age. Instead the retired husbands were slightly more likely to assume full responsibility for a few tasks already socially defined as "masculine"; they did not perform any "feminine" tasks. This traditional division of household labor apparently corresponded with the values of both wives and husbands in Ballweg's study. In a more recent study many couples increased their sharing of household tasks in the immediate postretirement period, but most soon reverted to their preretirement task division (Keating-Groen, 1977). Now that husbands spent more time at home, however, wives had more household tasks to do than before their husbands retired (Keating & Cole, 1980).

In very old age when both spouses may find the tasks of household maintenance beyond their strength, they may shift to what has been called a *symbiotic* relationship

(Troll, 1971), in which each contributes what s/he best can. The fact that people who have been married many years tend to die within a short time of each other suggests that they are holding each other up as in the form of an arch, which collapses when either side falls.

Widowhood

As we have seen, women are far more likely to be widowed than are men. In 1970 more than one-third of women were widows by the age of 65; men reached 75 before one-third were widowed. Widows have far lower incomes than do widowers (Lopata, 1973), especially in the working class (Atchley, 1977). Older widowers are much more likely to remarry than are older widows, in part because men are more dependent on their spouses in meeting intimacy needs than are women.

During the last decade there has been much controversy over whether widowhood is more difficult for women or for men. Berardo (1968, 1970) suggested that widowers faced greater adjustment problems, while Bell (1971) concluded that widows had a harder time. Subsequent research indicates minimal sex-related differences in overall adjustment when adjustment is defined in terms of morale, loneliness, life satisfaction, or positive and negative indices of well-being (Arens, 1979; Atchley, 1977; Kunkel, 1979). The majority of both widows and widowers adjust well to loss of spouse. An analysis of national survey data indicated that among men the negative impact of widowhood was interpreted by low levels of social participation; among women, adverse effects of widowhood were interpreted by their low economic resources (Arens, 1979).

Parent-Child Relations

In this selective review the *Cassandra function* (Troll & Turner, 1980) of older women as daughters, wives, and mothers is used to bridge sex-related differences in (1) middle-aged parents' relationships with adolescent and young adult children and (2) middle-aged and aged children's relationships with very aged parents. Research trends over the last decade have shifted away from the supposed "empty-nest" tribulations of middle-aged women toward issues involved in what Neugarten (1978) has termed the *parent-caring* activities of middle-aged children.

Findings from several small-sample studies indicate that, rather than dreading the "empty nest" and feeling bereft by the departure of children, neither the anticipation nor the experience of the last child's departure has negative effects upon the well-being of the great majority of middle-aged women (Harkins, 1978; Lowenthal et al., 1975; Neugarten, 1970; Rubin, 1979). Among most women the negative effects that do appear are extremely minor and transitory (Harkins, 1978; Rubin, 1979). Large-sample surveys indicate substantially greater marital happiness and somewhat greater general happiness among women whose children have left home compared to those still in the launching stage (Glenn, 1975). Research on fathers' reactions is uncommon, but they also expect improved marital relations when the children depart and look forward to their wives' undivided attention (Lowenthal et al., 1975).

The minority of middle-aged mothers who experience stereotypical suffering after their children depart are those whose child did not become successfully independent *when expected* (Harkins, 1978), who were overinvolved or overprotective with their children (Bart, 1971), or who blamed themselves for their children's unacceptable life styles (Rubin, 1979).

Overinvolvement, in the sense of concern with the problems of family members, characterizes middle-aged and older women more than men and younger women. Bernard (1972) has suggested that the supportive or stroking function is the quintessential social-psychological sex-role function of women. Socialization shapes personality and behavior patterns in girls so that as women they will assume a nurturant role in interaction with others: Women comply, understand, accept, allay the anxiety of others, and promote solidarity and emotional bonds. It appears that older women perform a function that is a specialized dimension of the supportive role: They worry about the well-being of other family members. An apt designation for this work of worry is the *Cassandra function* (Troll & Turner, 1980).

For launching-stage and preretired women in the Lowenthal et al. (1975) study—but not for men or younger women—stresses experienced by others (almost always a family member) were identified as sources of personal stress. Stresses focused on others involved children, husbands, and aged parents. Launching-stage women were twice as likely as preretired women to mention children as a source of stress. Mothers (rarely fathers) worried about many aspects of their children's lives: educational and occupational problems, marital and parental changes in the children's lives, the children's health problems, and conflict with other family members. More than one-third of the preretired women worried about their husbands, while only two preretired husbands mentioned a stress that centered on their wives.

Other researchers have also noticed a tendency for middle-aged women to be stressed by the problems of others. In a study of coping ability in middle age, Sedney (1976) reported that a number of women respondents commented that Paykel, Prusoff, and Uhlenhuth's (1971) Life Events Scale, which each filled out, did not contain several important and stressful life events. Most of the events they suggested adding to the scale involved children (e.g., daughter's divorce) or parents (e.g., decision to place parent in a nursing home).

In a report on her study of working-class marriages, Rubin (1975) comments that many wives in the middle years of marriage felt burdened by the sense that they bore the responsibility for the present and future of their families, especially with regard to "the emotional work in the family" (p. 160). According to one wife,

He just goes to work and brings some money home, but I have all the responsibilities. I tell him what the bills are. I know when something's wrong in the family. I know when his brother and sister-in-law are splitting up. I know when his mother's unhappy. I know when there's a problem with the kids. Why, I'm even the one who knows when there's a problem in our marriage. I have to tell him about all those things and most of the time he just listens to a few words and tunes it out. I'm the one who knows about it; and I'm the one who gets stuck worrying what to do about it. (Ibid., p. 105)

Like this working-class woman's husband, most launching-stage men in Lowenthal et al.'s (1975) sample enacted their family roles in terms of their economic function. Even though as a group these men were described as family-oriented more than work-oriented, few responded to their family roles in terms of the interpersonal responsibilities and relationships involved.

Women, on the other hand, are kinkeepers, responsible for maintaining relationships and facilitating communication among family members. In mid-life these responsibilities run in multiple directions, and the internalization of these responsibilities may be a problem in increasing vulnerability to stress (Huyck, 1977). The Cassandra function operates, however, to promote solidarity and emotional bonding among family members. Adult children may be intensely irritated by their mother's worry but are attached to her by it; attachment is composed of both positive and negative emotions (Troll & Smith, 1976).

Recent research indicates that it is not the departure of the children that distresses most mothers but their refusal to leave or their repeated return for shorter or longer stays after having nominally moved out (Troll, 1975). Parental expectations appear to be the key element. Distress, worry, and a strained relationship with the child are most likely when the child is late—off-time (Neugarten, 1968)—in negotiating the many tasks that define the transition to adulthood. Fathers as well as mothers report a strained relationship with a child who has failed to leave home on time (Wilen, 1979). Since mothers bear the primary responsibility for the outcome of child-rearing, however, fathers should be less likely than mothers are to react to their children's delayed independence with worry and self-blame.

The intersection of psychoanalytic personality theory, social-role theory, and historical change shed light on the propensity of mothers to worry about their young adult children. Benedek (1959, 1970) points out that in normal development parents identify with their children as well as vice versa—parents aim at self-realization, according to current cultural standards, through the development of their children, and they hope to be "good parents." Current cultural standards require completion of a minimum educational level, dependent on parental socioeconomic class; the establishment of economic independence, including occupational stability and establishing an independent household; and marriage, followed by parenthood. Children's desultory progress in meeting these tasks may threaten both parental self-realization and the self-definition of "good parent," with consequent parental depression and at least covert parent-child conflict.

In terms analogous to social-role theory, Back (1976) points out that the departure of children from the parental household is a developmental event that is part of the identity of parents; it is an expected development. People expect to have children, raise them to adulthood, watch them leave home and establish their own families, and live independently in old age without children. Mothers whose adult children live in the parental household are suspected of having inculcated excessive dependency in their children. Such mothers may be regarded as having failed as mothers; their children, too, have "failed" in the task of achieving adult independence.

There is evidence that the average age (and, therefore, the socially normative age) of leaving the parental home has decreased since 1950 (Glick, 1977). Before 1950 when the middle-aged parents now studied were approaching adulthood, children left home to go to college, join the military, or marry. In the working class economic circumstances required even many newlyweds to live with parents (Komarovsky, 1964). General increasing economic affluence in the last three decades has permitted increasing numbers of youth to establish households independent of their parents so that the average age of departure from the parental household has dropped to 18 years (Glick, 1977). Conversely parents are less likely to need the additional income provided by the contributions of working adult children who live in the parental home. The interlocking of the historical effect of increasing economic affluence with social-role theory and psychoanalytic personality theory explains both the general relief of mothers when their children depart and parental tension regarding subsequent signs of their children's failure to achieve full adult independence. Historical effects related, in part, to the sheer size of the "baby boom" cohort also explain their delayed transition to adulthood and their willingness to return to the parental household. The age at marriage has risen, and among those who marry, parenthood is increasingly postponed; the divorce rate has risen as well. When education is prolonged, postponing economic maturity, young adults may accept considerable material aid from parents which may continue until the former are into their thirties. Cohort-related experiences of underemployment may also prolong the flow of aid from middle-aged parents to young adult children. Returning home for a while to the parental household is a comfortable option; the young adults know that their parents can afford to support them. The young adult experiences of these two cohorts, in short, are quite different, and the younger cohort is at a disadvantage in meeting the expectations of their parents.

The increasing numbers of old-old individuals in the American population has increased the salience of parent-caring—the provision of services by middle-aged children to dependent aged parents. There are now more than 2 million Americans 85 years of age and older (Siegel, 1978) so that an increasing number of adult children in their sixties and even seventies are involved in parent-caring. Most of these services are provided to elderly widows, since men are far more likely to be married and services of various kinds are most likely to be provided by a spouse, if there is one. When there is no spouse most research indicates that almost all services (household maintenance, transportation, cooking, shopping, personal care, medically related care, and emotional support) are provided by daughters and daughters-in-law (Litman, 1971; Shanas, 1961; Stehouwer, 1968; Sussman, 1965). Parent-caring is a highly salient issue for middle-aged women (Lieberman, 1978) who are more stressed by these tasks than are men (Wilen, 1979). It is worth noting that middle-aged daughters who are employed outside the home do not differ from women not so employed in the provision of instrumental services to dependent aged mothers (Brody, Davis, Fulcomer, & Johnsen, 1979), although only the nonemployed provided personal services.

The overinvolvement, worry, and guilt characteristic

of the Cassandra function of middle-aged women appear in relationships with dependent elderly parents as well as with young adult children. In a report on the parent-caring activities of middle-aged women and men, Robinson and Thurnher (1979) note that the men

... appeared to have greater ability in distancing themselves physically and emotionally from their parents and they appeared to experience less guilt and more readily accept the fact that it was not within their power to make the parent much happier. When men did have a high degree of contact with dependent parents, however, our data suggest that they were more likely to have negative perceptions of parents than were women. Possibly, contact with an aged parent is less rewarding for men than for women and results in greater irritability and impatience. Over the five years men recognized economic responsibilities and instrumental tasks but unlike women seldom felt responsible for the emotional well-being of the parent. They were also more likely, not always unselfishly, to counsel the wife not to become overly involved with her own mother. (p. 591)

The Cassandra function of middle-aged women increases their own vulnerability to stress but has a generally beneficent effect upon others. Middle-aged wives' concern with their husbands' health, for example, probably functions to enhance the longevity of many husbands.

Grandparenthood

From the point of view of grandchildren in the United States at the present time, there are few sex-related differences in the roles of grandmother and grandfather. Both roles are described as feminine. In response to an essay assignment, a third-grader wrote, "A grandfather is a man Grandmother" (Huyck, 1974, p. 77). When asked to list their images of the roles of grandmother and grandfather, college students made few distinctions between the roles (Hess & Markson, 1980). The characteristics ascribed to both roles emphasized loving interest in others—i.e., feminine traits. But where grandfathers were described as impatient and chauvinistic, grandmothers were characterized as "stronghold of family," fragile (despite the superior longevity of women), and most understanding. The masculine traits ascribed to grandfathers encompass a refusal to take the viewpoint of the young, which grandmothers are seen as able to do; the one nonfeminine attribute ascribed to grandmothers emphasizes their central position in the family.

In the majority of American families at the present time, neither grandparent wields instrumental power over their children or grandchildren. Thus although many grandparents are middle-aged rather than elderly and employed rather than retired, these characteristics probably describe quite well the behavior of both grandmother and grandfather toward grandchildren; therefore, grandparenting approaches a unisex role.

CONCLUSIONS

Sex-related differences in the psychological changes that occur in later life pervade the topics reviewed in this chapter. Within each topic it is apparent that both the differences and, especially, their causes are poorly under-

stood (cf. the exchange of Verbrugge [1980], Mechanic [1980], and Gove & Hughes [1980] on sex-related differences in physical health; Jacklin's [1979] conclusions regarding sex-related differences in cognitive functioning; and Neugarten's [1977] remarks on research on personality and aging, which are relevant to research on sex-related differences as well).

In the area of personality this chapter has noted that large-sample longitudinal investigations have studied males far more than females, have typically relied on single objective personality tests, and have generally focused on overall group differences by age or gender without regard to the life events or cultural change that occurred between times of measurement. (The Kansas City Study of Adult Life is an exception, in having studied both genders using a variety of measures.) The small-sample longitudinal studies have sampled both genders, used a variety of measures, have noted or focused upon life events and cultural change, and have analyzed subgroup patterns within their samples but have not employed the particular objective personality tests used in the large-sample studies. It is no surprise that the two sets of studies report findings that are inconsistent with each other.

Unclear terminology is a major obstacle in the study of sex-related differences in personality in later life. The omnibus definition of *sex role* has created theoretical and empirical confusion. Further research should distinguish both empirically and conceptually between femininity and masculinity as properties of personality and as properties of roles.

REFERENCES

ABRAHAMS, B., FELDMAN, S. S., & NASH, S. C. Sex role self-concept and sex role attitudes: Enduring personality characteristics or adaptations to changing life situations? *Developmental Psychology,* 1978, *14,* 393–400.

ABRAHAMS, J. P., HOYER, W. J., ELIAS, M. F., & BRADIGAN, B. Gerontological research in psychology published in the Journal of Gerontology 1963–1974: Perspectives and progress. *Journal of Gerontology,* 1975, *30,* 668–673.

ADAMOWICZ, J. K. Visual short-term memory and aging. *Journal of Gerontology,* 1976, *31,* 39–46.

ANASTASI, A. *Differential psychology: Individual and group differences in behavior.* New York: Macmillan, 1964.

ANGRIST, S. A. The study of sex-roles. *Journal of Social Issues,* 1969, *15,* 215–232.

ARENBERG, D. Anticipation interval and age differences in verbal learning. *Journal of Abnormal Psychology,* 1965, *70,* 419–425.

ARENBERG, D., & ROBERTSON-TCHABO, E. A. Learning and aging. In J. E. Birren & K. W. Schaie (Eds.), *Handbook of the psychology of aging.* New York: Van Nostrand Reinhold, 1977.

ARENS, D. A. *Well-being and widowhood: Interpreting sex differences.* Paper presented at the 32nd Annual Scientific Meeting of the Gerontological Society, Washington, D.C., November 1979.

ATCHLEY, R. C. *The social forces in later life: An introduction to social gerontology* (2nd ed.). Belmont, Calif.: Wadsworth, 1977.

BACK, K. W. Transition to aging and the self-image. *International Journal of Aging and Human Development,* 1971, *2,* 296–304.

BACK,, K. W. Personal characteristics and social behavior: Theory and method. In R. H. Binstock & E. Shanas (Eds.), *Handbook of aging and the social sciences.* New York: Van Nostrand Reinhold, 1976.

BALLWEG, J. A. Resolution of conjugal role adjustment after retirement. *Journal of Marriage and the Family,* 1976, *29,* 277–281.

BALTES, P. B. (Ed.). *Life-span development and behavior* (Vol. 1). New York: Academic Press, 1978.

BALTES, P. B., & BRIM, O. G., JR., (Eds.). *Life-span development and behavior* (Vol. 2). New York: Academic Press, 1979.

BALTES, P. B., & SCHAIE, K. W. (Eds.). *Life-span developmental psychology: Personality and socialization.* New York: Academic Press, 1973.

BART, P. B. Depression in middle-aged women. In V. Gornick & B. K. Moran (Eds.), *Woman in sexist society.* New York: Basic Books, 1971.

BARUCH, G., & BARNETT, R. *If the study of midlife had begun with women.* Paper presented at the 32nd Annual Scientific Meeting of the Gerontological Society, Washington, D.C., November 1979.

BELL, R. *Marriage and family interaction* (3rd ed.). Homewood, Ill.: Dorsey Press, 1971.

BENEDEK, T. Parenthood as a developmental phase. *Journal of the American Psychoanalytic Association,* 1959, *7,* 389–417.

BENEDEK, T. Chapters 4, 5, 6, & 7. In E. J. Anthony & T. Benedek (Eds.), *Parenthood.* Boston: Little, Brown, 1970.

BERARDO, F. M. Widowhood status in the U.S.: Perspectives on a neglected aspect of the family life cycle. *The Family Coordinator,* 1968, *17,* 191–203.

BERARDO, F. M. Survivorship and social isolation: The case of the aged widower. *The Family Coordinator,* 1970, *19,* 11–15.

BERNARD, J. *The sex game.* New York: Atheneum, 1972.

BERNARD, J. *The future of marriage.* New York: Bantam, 1973.

BIRD, C. The best years of a woman's life. *Psychology Today,* June 1979, pp. 20–22, 26.

BIRREN, J. E., BUTLER, R. N., GREENHOUSE, S. W., SOKOLOFF, L., & YARROW, M. R. (Eds.). *Human aging* (Publication No. 986). Washington, D.C.: Public Health Service, 1963.

BIRREN, J. E., & SCHAIE, K. W. (Eds.). *Handbook of the psychology of aging.* New York: Van Nostrand Reinhold, 1977.

BLAZER, D. G., & HOUPT, J. Perception of poor health in the healthy elderly. *Journal of the American Geriatrics Society,* 1979, *27,* 330–334.

BLOCK, J. *The Q-sort method in personality assessment and psychiatric research.* Springfield, Ill.: Chas. C Thomas, 1961.

BLOCK, J., in collaboration with Haan, N. *Lives through time.* Berkeley, Calif.: Bancroft Books, 1971.

BLOOD, R. O., & WOLFE, D. M. *Husbands and wives.* Glencoe, Ill.: Free Press, 1960.

BLUM, J. E., FOSSHAGE, J. L., & JARVIK, L. F. Intellectual changes and sex differences in octogenarians: A twenty-year longitudinal study of aging. *Developmental Psychology,* 1972, *7,* 178–187.

BLUM, R. H. Mind-altering drugs and dangerous behavior: Alcohol. In President's Commission on Law Enforcement and Administration of Justice, *Task force report: Drunkenness* (Appendix B). Washington, D.C.: U.S. Government Printing Office, 1967.

BOSSARD, J.H.S., & BOLL, E. S. Marital unhappiness in the life cycle of marriage. *Marriage and Family Living,* 1955, *17,* 10–14.

BOTWINICK, J. Intellectual abilities. In J. E. Birren & K. W. Schaie (Eds.), *Handbook of the psychology of aging.* New York: Van Nostrand Reinhold, 1977.

BOTWINICK, J., & BIRREN, J. E. Mental abilities and psychomotor responses in healthy aged men. In J. E. Birren, R. N. Butler, S. W. Greenhouse, L. Sokoloff, & M. R. Yarrow (Eds.), *Human aging* (Publication No. 986). Washington, D.C.: Public Health Service, 1963.

BOTWINICK, J., & STORANDT, M. Recall and recognition of old information in relation to age and sex. *Journal of Gerontology,* 1980, *35,* 70–76.

BRODY, E., DAVIS, L., FULCOMER, M., & JOHNSEN, P. *Formal and informal service providers: Preferences of three generations of women.* Paper presented at the 32nd Annual meeting of the Gerontological Society, Washington, D.C., November 1979.

BROMLEY, D. B. Some effects of aging on short-term learning and remembering. *Journal of Gerontology,* 1958, *13,* 398–406.

BROVERMAN, D. M., KLAIBER, E. L., KOBAYASHI, Y., & VOGEL, W. Roles of activation and inhibition in sex differences in cognitive abilities. *Psychological Review,* 1968, *75,* 23–50.

BROVERMAN, I., BROVERMAN, D. M., CLARKSON, F. E., ROSENKRANTZ, P. S., & VOGEL, S. R. Sex-role stereotypes and clinical judgments of mental health. *Journal of Consulting and Clinical Psychology,* 1970, *34,* 1–7.

BUFFERY, A., & GRAY, J. A. Sex differences in the development of spatial and linguistic skills. In C. Ounsted & D. C. Taylor (Eds.), *Gender differences: Their ontogeny and significance.* Edinburgh: Churchill Livingstone, 1972.

BUSSE, E. W., & BLAZER, D. G. Disorders related to biological functioning. In E. W. Busse & D. G. Blazer (Eds.), *Handbook of geriatric psychiatry.* New York: Van Nostrand Reinhold, 1980.

BUSSE, E. W., DOVENMUEHLE, R. H., & BROWN, R. G. Psychoneurotic reactions of the aged. *Geriatrics,* 1960, *15,* 97–105.

BUTLER, R. N., & LEWIS, M. I. *Aging and mental health.* St. Louis, Mo.: C. V. Mosby, 1973.

CAMPBELL, A., CONVERSE, P. E., & RODGERS, W. L. *The quality of American life.* New York: Russell Sage Foundation, 1976.

CANESTRARI, R. E. Paced and self-paced learning in young and elderly adults. *Journal of Gerontology,* 1963, *18,* 165–180.

CAUGHLEY, G. Mortality patterns in mammals. *Ecology,* 1966, *47,* 906.

CHIRIBOGA, D. A., & PIERCE, R. *Of time and transitions.* Unpublished manuscript, 1978.

CLARK, M., & ANDERSON, B. *Culture and aging.* Springfield, Ill.: Chas. C Thomas, 1967.

COHEN, D., & EISDORFER, C. Behavior-immunologic relationships in older men and women. *Experimental Aging Research,* 1977, *3,* 225–229.

COHEN, D., MATSUYAMA, D., & JARVIK, L. F. Immunoglobulin levels and intellectual functioning in the aged. *Experimental Aging Research,* 1976, *2,* 345–348.

COHEN, D., SCHAIE, K. W., & GRIBBIN, K. The organization of spatial abilities in older men and women. *Journal of Gerontology,* 1977, *32,* 578–585.

COHEN, D., & WILKIE, F. Sex-related differences in cognition among the elderly. In M. A. Wittig & A. C. Petersen (Eds.), *Sex-related differences in cognitive functioning.* New York: Academic Press, 1979.

CONSTANTINOPLE, A. Masculinity-femininity: An exception to a famous dictum? *Psychological Bulletin,* 1973, *80,* 389–407.

COSTA, P. T., JR., & MCCRAE, R. R. Age differences in personality structure revisited: Studies in validity, stability and change. *International Journal of Aging and Human Development,* 1977, *8,* 261–275.

COSTA, P. T., JR., & MCCRAE, R. R. Objective personality assessment. In M. Storandt, I. C. Siegler, & M. F. Elias (Eds.), *The clinical psychology of aging.* New York: Plenum, 1978.

COSTA, P. T., JR., MCCRAE, R. R., & ARENBERG, D. Enduring dispositions in adult males. *Journal of Personality and Social Psychology,* 1980, *38,* 793–800.

CRAIK, F.I.M. Age differences in human memory. In J. E. Birren & K. W. Schaie (Eds.), *Handbook of the psychology of aging.* New York: Van Nostrand Reinhold, 1977.

CRAIN, R. L., & WEISMAN, C. S. *Discrimination, personality and achievement.* New York: Seminar Press, 1972.

CUBER, J. F., & HARROFF, P. B. *The significant Americans.* New York: Appleton-Century-Crofts, 1965.

DATAN, N., & GINSBERG, L. H. (Eds.). *Life-span developmental psychology: Normative life crises.* New York: Academic Press, 1975.

DATAN, N., & REESE, H. W. (Eds.). *Life-span developmental psychology: Dialectical perspectives on experimental research.* New York: Academic Press, 1977.

DEUTSCHER, I. The quality of post-parental life. *Journal of Marriage and the Family,* 1964, *26,* 52–60.

DIBNER, S. S., BARNETT, R., & BARUCH, G. Women in the middle years: Toward a theoretical understanding. In B. F. Turner (Chair), *The double standard of aging: A question of sex differences.* Symposium presented at the 29th Annual Scientific Meeting of the Gerontological Society, New York City, 1976.

DINITZ, S., DYNES, R. R., & CLARKE, A. Preference for male or female children—traditional or affectional. *Marriage and Family Living,* 1954, *16,* 128–130.

DOPPELT, J. E., & WALLACE, W. L. Standardization of the Wechsler adult intelligence scale for older persons. *Journal of Abnormal and Social Psychology,* 1955, *51,* 321–330.

DOUGLAS, K., & ARENBERG, D. Age changes, cohort differences, and cultural change on the Guilford-Zimmerman temperament survey. *Journal of Gerontology,* 1978, *33,* 737–747.

DOUVAN, E., & ADELSON, J. *The adolescent experience.* New York: John Wiley, 1966.

DUBLIN, L. I., LOTKA, A. J., & SPEIGELMAN, M. *Length of life.* New York: Ronald Press, 1949.

EDWARDS, J. N., & KLEMMACK, D. L. Correlates of life satisfaction: A re-examination. *Journal of Gerontology,* 1973, *28,* 497–502.

EHRENREICH, B. Is success dangerous to your health? The myths—and facts—about women and stress. *Ms.,* May 1979, pp. 51–54, 97–101.

EISDORFER, C. Verbal learning and response time in the aged. *Journal of Genetic Psychology*, 1965, *107*, 15–22.

EISDORFER, C. Arousal and performance: Experiments in verbal learning and a tentative theory. In G. Talland (Ed.), *Human behavior and aging*. New York: Academic Press, 1968.

EISDORFER, C., AXELROD, S., & WILKIE, F. L. Stimulus exposure time as a factor in serial learning in an aged sample. *Journal of Abnormal and Social Psychology*, 1963, *67*, 594–600.

EISDORFER, C., BUSSE, E. W., & COHEN, L. D. The WAIS performance of an aged sample: The relationship between verbal and performance I.Q.s *The Journal of Gerontology*, 1959, *14*, 197–201.

EISDORFER, C., & WILKIE, F. Stress, disease, aging, and behavior. In J. E. Birren & K. W. Schaie (Eds.), *Handbook of the psychology of aging*. New York: Van Nostrand Reinhold, 1977.

ELIAS, M. F., & KINSBOURNE, M. Age and sex differences in the processing of verbal and nonverbal stimuli. *Journal of Gerontology*, 1974, *29*, 162–171.

ENTERLINE, P. E. Cause of death responsible for recent increases in sex mortality differentials in the United States. *Milbank Memorial Fund Quarterly*, 1961, *39*, 312–328.

FEATHERMAN, D. L., & HAUSER, R. M. Sexual inequalities and socio-economic achievement in the United States, 1962–1973. *American Sociological Review*, 1976, *41*, 462–483.

FELDMAN, H. *Development of the husband-wife relationship: A research report*. New York: Cornell University Press, 1964.

FRIEDMAN, M., & ROSENMAN, R. H. *Type A behavior and your heart*. New York: Fawcett Books Group—CBS Publications, 1974.

GARAI, J. E., & SCHEINFELD, A. Sex differences in mental and behavioral traits. *Genetic Psychology Monographs*, 1968, *77*, 169–299.

GILFORD, R., & BENGTSON, V. Measuring marital satisfaction in three generations: Positive and negative dimensions. *Journal of Marriage and the Family*, 1979, *41*, 387–398.

GLENN, N. D. Psychological well-being in the postparental stage: Some evidence from national surveys. *Journal of Marriage and the Family*, 1975, *37*, 15–27.

GLICK, P. Updating the family life cycle. *Journal of Marriage and the Family*, 1977, *39*, 5–13.

GOBLE, F. C., & KONOPKA, E. A. Sex as a factor in infectious disease. *Transactions of the New York Academy of Science*, 1973, *35*, 325.

GOLD, S. Cross-cultural comparisons of role change with aging. *Student Journal of Human Development*, 1960, *1*, 11–15.

GOODMAN, L. S., & GILMAN, A. *The pharmacological basis of therapeutics* (4th ed.). New York: Macmillan, 1970.

GORDON, S. D., & CLARK, W. C. Adult age differences in word and nonsense syllable recognition memory and response criterion. *Journal of Gerontology*, 1974, *29*, 659–665.

GOULET, L. R., & BALTES, P. B. (Eds.). *Life-span developmental psychology: Research and theory*. New York: Academic Press, 1970.

GOVE, W. R., & GEERKEN, M. R. Response bias in surveys of mental health: An empirical investigation. *American Journal of Sociology*, 1977, *82*, 1289–1317.

GOVE, W. R., & HUGHES, M. Sex differences in physical health and how medical sociologists view illness (A reply to Mechanic and Verbrugge). *American Sociological Review*, 1980, *45*, 514–522.

GOVE, W. R., & TUDOR, J. Adult sex roles and mental illness. *American Journal of Sociology*, 1973, *78*, 812–835.

GURIN, G., VEROFF, J., & FELD, S. *Americans view their mental health*. New York: Basic Books, 1960.

GUTMANN, D. An exploration of ego configurations in middle and later life. In B. L. Neugarten (Ed.), *Personality in middle and later life*. New York: Lieber-Atherton, 1964.

GUTMANN, D. The country of old men: Cross-cultural studies in the psychology of later life. *Occasional Papers in Gerontology*, No. 5, Institute of Gerontology, University of Michigan–Wayne State University, April 1969.

GUTMANN, D. Female ego styles and generational conflict. In E. Walker (Ed.), *Female psychology and conflict*. Monterey, Calif.: Brooks/Cole, 1971.

GUTMANN, D. Alternatives to disengagement: The old men of the Highland Druze. In R. LeVine (Ed.), *Culture and personality: Contemporary readings*. Chicago: Aldine, 1974.

GUTMANN, D. L. Parenthood: A key to the comparative psychology of the life cycle. In N. Datan & L. Ginsberg (Eds.), *Life-span developmental psychology: Normative life crises*. New York: Academic Press, 1975.

GUTMANN, D. L. The cross-cultural perspective: Notes toward a comparative psychology of aging. In J. Birren & K. W. Schaie

(Eds.), *Handbook of the psychology of aging*. New York: Van Nostrand Reinhold, 1977.

HAAN, N. Personality organizations of well-functioning younger people and older adults. *International Journal of Aging and Human Development*, 1976, *7*, 117–127.

HAMILTON, G. V. *A research in marriage*. New York: Boni, 1929.

HARKINS, E. B. Effects of empty nest transition on self-report of psychological and physical well-being. *Journal of Marriage and the Family*, 1978, *40*, 549–558.

HARKINS, S. W., NOWLIN, J. B., RAMM, D., & SCHROEDER, S. Effects of age, sex, and time-on-watch on a brief continuous performance task. In E. Palmore (Ed.), *Normal aging II*. Durham, N.C.: Duke University Press, 1974.

HARRIS, L., & Associates, Inc. *The myth and reality of aging in America*. Washington, D.C.: The National Council on the Aging, Inc., 1975.

HAYNES, S. G., FEINLEIB, M., LEVINE, S., SCOTCH, N., & KANNEL, W. B. The relationship of psychosocial factors to coronary heart disease in the Framingham study: II. Prevalence of coronary heart disease. *American Journal of Epidemiology*, 1978, *107*, 384–402.

HAYSLIP, B., JR., & STERNS, H. L. Age differences in relationships between crystallized and fluid intelligences and problem solving. *Journal of Gerontology*, 1979, *34*, 404–414.

HERTZOG, C., SCHAIE, K. W., & GRIBBIN, K. Cardiovascular disease and changes in intellectual functioning from middle to old age. *Journal of Gerontology*, 1978, *33*, 872–883.

HESS, B. B., & MARKSON, E. W. *Aging and old age: An introduction to social gerontology*. New York: Macmillan, 1980.

HICKS, M. W., & PLATT, M. Marital happiness and stability: A review of the research in the sixties. *Journal of Marriage and the Family*, 1970, *32*, 553–574.

HOCHSCHILD, A. R. A review of sex role research. *American Journal of Sociology*, 1973, *78*, 1011–1029.

HUBBARD, R., SANTOS, J. F., & FARROW, B. J. *Age differences in sex role diffusion: A study of middle aged and older adult married couples*. Paper presented at the 32nd Annual Meeting of the Gerontological Society, New York City, November 1979.

HUDSON, W. W., & MURPHY, G. J. The non-linear relationship between marital satisfaction and stages of the family life cycle: An artifact of Type I errors? *Journal of Marriage and the Family*, 1980, *42*, 263–268.

HULICKA, I. M., STERNE, H., & GROSSMAN, J. Age-group comparisons of paired-associate learning as a function of paced and self-paced association and response time. *Journal of Gerontology*, 1967, *22*, 274–280.

HULTSCH, D. F., & PLEMONS, J. K. Life events and life-span development. In P. B. Baltes & O. G. Brim, Jr. (Eds.), *Life-span development and behavior* (Vol. 2). New York: Academic Press, 1979.

HUTT, C. Sex differences in human development. *Human Development*, 1972, *15*, 153–170.

HUYCK, M. H. *Growing older*. Englewood Cliffs, N.J.: Prentice-Hall, 1974.

HUYCK, M. H. *Friendships and coping among United States adults 18–65*. Paper presented at the International Congress of Gerontology, Jerusalem, June 1975.

HUYCK, M. H. Sex, gender and aging. *Humanitas*, 1977, *13*.

HUYCK, M. H. Personal communication, September 1, 1980.

HUYCK, M. H., & HOYER, W. J. *The psychology of adult development*. Belmont, Calif.: Wadsworth, in press.

HYDE, J. S., & PHILLIS, D. E. Androgeny across the life span. *Developmental Psychology*, 1979, *15*, 334–336.

JACKLIN, C. N. Epilogue. In M. A. Wittig & A. C. Petersen (Eds.), *Sex-related differences in cognitive functioning*. New York: Academic Press, 1979.

JARVIK, L. F., & COHEN, D. Relevance of research to work with the aged. In A. N. Schwartz & I. N. Mensh (Eds.), *Professional obligations and approaches to the aged*. Springfield, Ill.: Chas. C Thomas, 1974.

JÖRESKOG, K. G. Simultaneous factor analysis in several populations. *Psychometrika*, 1971, *36*, 409–426.

JUNG, C. *Modern man in search of a soul*. New York: Harcourt Brace Jovanovich, 1933.

KALLMANN, F. J., & JARVIK, L. F. Individual differences in constitution and genetic background. In J. E. Birren (Ed.), *Handbook of aging and the individual*. Chicago: University of Chicago Press, 1959.

KAPLAN, A. G., & SEDNEY, M. A. *Psychology and sex roles: An androgenous perspective.* Boston: Little, Brown, 1980.

KAPLAN, H. B., & POKORNY, A. D. Aging and self-attitude, a conditional relationship. *Aging and Human Development,* 1970, *1,* 241–250.

KASTENBAUM, R. G. *Death, society, and human experience.* St. Louis, Mo.: C. V. Mosby, 1977.

KEATING, N. C., & COLE, P. What do I do with him 24 hours a day? Changes in the housewife role after retirement. *The Gerontologist,* 1980, *20,* 84–89.

KEATING-GROEN, N. *Marital satisfaction and retirement.* Unpublished doctoral dissertation, Syracuse University, 1977.

KOMAROVSKY, M. *Blue-collar marriage.* New York: Random House, 1964.

KOVAR, M. G. Elderly people: The population 65 years and over. In U.S. Department of Health, Education and Welfare, *Health•United States 1976–1977* (DHEW Publication No. 77–1232). Washington, D.C.: U.S. Government Printing Office, 1978.

KRAMER, N. A., & JARVIK, L. F. Assessment of intellectual changes in the elderly. In A. Raskin & L. F. Jarvik (Eds.), *Psychiatric symptoms and cognitive loss in the elderly.* Washington, D.C.: Hemisphere Publishing, 1979.

KUNKEL, S. *Sex differences in adjustment to widowhood.* Paper presented at the 32nd Annual Scientific meeting of the Gerontological Society, Washington, D.C., November 1979.

LARSON, R. Thirty years of research on subjective well-being of older Americans. *Journal of Gerontology,* 1978, *33,* 109–125.

LARUE, A., BANK, L., JARVIK, L., & HETLAND, M. Health in old age: How do physicians' ratings and self-ratings compare? *Journal of Gerontology,* 1979, *34,* 687–691.

LAWS, J. L. A feminist review of the marital adjustment literature: The rape of the Locke. *Journal of Marriage and the Family,* 1971, *33,* 483–516.

LEON, G. R., GILLUM, B., GILLUM, R., & GOUZE, M. Personality stability and change over a 30-year period—middle age to old age. *Journal of Consulting and Clinical Psychology,* 1979, *47,* 517–524.

LESTER, D. Sex differences in suicidal behavior. In E. S. Gomberg & V. Franks (Eds.), *Gender and disordered behavior: Sex differences in psychopathology.* New York: Brunner/Mazel, 1979.

LEVINSON, D. J. *The seasons of a man's life.* New York: Knopf, 1978.

LIEBERMAN, G. L. Children of the elderly as natural helpers: Some demographic differences. *American Journal of Community Psychology,* 1978, *6,* 489–498.

LINDEN, L. L., & BREED, W. The demographic epidemiology of suicide. In E. S. Schneidman (Eds.), *Suicidology: Contemporary developments.* New York: Grune & Stratton, 1976.

LINDER, F. E., & GROVE, R. D. *Vital statistics rates in the United States, 1900–1940.* Washington, D.C.: U.S. Government Printing Office, 1947.

LINEHAN, M. Sex differences in suicide and attempted suicide. *Dissertation Abstracts International,* 1971, *32B,* 3036.

LIPMAN, A. Role conceptions and morale of couples in retirement. *Journal of Gerontology,* 1961, *16,* 267–271.

LIPMAN, A. Role conceptions of couples in retirement. In C. Tibbetts & W. Donahue (Eds.), *Social and psychological aspects of aging: Aging around the world.* New York: Columbia University Press, 1962.

LIPMAN-BLUMEN, J., & TICKAMYER, A. R. Sex roles in transition: A ten-year perspective. In A. Inkeles, J. Coleman, & N. Smelser (Eds.), *Annual review of sociology* (Vol. 1). Palo Alto, Calif.: Annual Reviews, 1975.

LITMAN, T. J. Health care and the family: A three-generational analysis. *Medical Care,* 1971, *9,* 67–81.

LIVSON, F. B. *Sex differences in personality development in the middle adult years: A longitudinal study.* Paper presented at the 28th Annual Scientific Meeting of the Gerontological Society, Louisville, October 1975.

LIVSON, F. B. Coming together in the middle years: A longitudinal study of sex role convergence. In B. F. Turner (Chair), *The double standard of aging: A question of sex differences.* Symposium presented at the 29th Annual Scientific Meeting of the Gerontological Society, New York City, 1976a.

LIVSON, F. B. Patterns of personality development in middle-aged women: A longitudinal study. *International Journal of Aging and Human Development,* 1976b, *7,* 107–115.

LIVSON, F. B. Paths to mental health in later life: His and hers. In F. B. Livson (Organizer) & L. E. Troll (Chair), *Sex differences in later life: Physical, mental, developmental.* Symposium presented at the 88th Annual Convention of the American Psychological Association, Montreal, 1980.

LIVSON, F. B. Paths to psychological health in the middle years: Sex differences. In D. H. Eichorn, J. A. Clausen, N. Haan, M. P. Honzik, & P. Mussen (Eds.), *Present and past in middle life.* New York: Academic Press, 1981.

LOPATA, H. Z. *Widowhood in an American city.* Cambridge, Mass.: Schenkman, 1973.

LOWENTHAL, M. F., & CHIRIBOGA, D. Social stress and adaptation: Toward a life-course perspective. In C. Eisdorfer & M. P. Lawton (Eds.), *The psychology of adult development and aging.* Washington, D.C.: American Psychological Association, 1973.

LOWENTHAL, M. F., & ROBINSON, B. Social networks and isolation. In R. H. Binstock & E. Shanas (Eds.), *Handbook of aging and the social sciences.* New York: Van Nostrand Reinhold, 1976.

LOWENTHAL, M. F., THURNHER, M., CHIRIBOGA, D., & Associates. *Four stages of life.* San Francisco: Jossey-Bass, 1975.

LUCKEY, E. B. Perceptual congruence of self and family concepts as related to marital interaction. *Sociometry,* 1961, *24,* 234–250.

LYNN, D. B. A note on sex differences in the development of masculine and feminine identification. *Psychological Review,* 1959, *66,* 126–135.

MAAS, H. S., & KUYPERS, J. A. From thirty to seventy. San Francisco: Jossey-Bass, 1974.

MACCOBY, E. E., & JACKLIN, C. N. *The psychology of sex differences.* Stanford, Calif.: Stanford University Press, 1974.

MADDOX, G. Self assessment of health status. *Journal of Chronic Diseases,* 1964, *17,* 449–460.

MADDOX, G. L., & DOUGLASS, E. B. Self-assessments of health. *Journal of health and Social Behavior,* 1973, *14,* 87–93.

MADIGAN, F. C. Are sex mortality differentials biologically caused? *Milbank Memorial Fund Quarterly,* 1957, *35,* 203–223.

MARKIDES, K. S., & MARTIN, H. W. A causal model of life satisfaction among the elderly. *Journal of Gerontology,* 1979, *34,* 86–89.

MECHANIC, D. Comment on Gove and Hughes, *ASR,* February, 1979. *American Sociological Review,* 1980, *45,* 513–514.

MEDLEY, M. L. Satisfaction with life among persons 65 years and older. *Journal of Gerontology,* 1976, *31,* 448–455.

MISCHEL, W. On the future of personality measurement. In *The future of personality measurement.* Symposium presented at the 83rd Annual Convention of the American Psychological Association, Chicago, 1975.

MITTENESS, L., & NYDEGGER, C. *Determinants of parental role convergence.* Paper presented at the 32nd Annual Scientific Meeting of the Gerontological Society, Washington, D.C., November 1979.

MONGE, R. H., & HULTSCH, D. F. Paired associate learning as a function of adult age and the length of the anticipation and inspection intervals. *Journal of Gerontology,* 1971, *26,* 157–162.

MOSS, H. A., & SUSMAN, E. J. Constancy and change in personality development. In O. G. Brim, Jr. & J. Kagan (Eds.), *Constancy and change in human development.* Cambridge, Mass.: Harvard University Press, 1980.

NATHANSON, C. Illness and the feminine role: A theoretical review. *Social Science and Medicine,* 1975, *9,* 57–62.

NATHANSON, C. Sex, illness and medical care: A review of data, theory and method. *Social Science and Medicine,* 1977, *11,* 13–25.

National Center for Health Statistics. *Vital statistics of the United States: 1970* (Vol. 3). Marriage and divorce. Washington, D.C.: U.S. Government Printing Office, 1974.

National Clearinghouse for Smoking and Health. *Adult use of tobacco—1970* (USDHEW, Public Health Service.) Washington, D.C.: U.S. Government Printing Office, 1973.

National Safety Council. *Accident facts, 1972.* Chicago: Author, 1972.

NESSELROADE, J. R., SCHAIE, K. W., & BALTES, P. B. Ontogenetic and generational components of structural and quantitative change in adult cognitive behavior. *Journal of Gerontology,* 1972, *27,* 222–228.

NEUGARTEN, B. L. The awareness of middle age. In B. L. Neugarten (Ed.), *Middle age and aging.* Chicago: University of Chicago Press, 1968.

NEUGARTEN, B. L. Adaptation and the life cycle. *Journal of Geriatric Psychiatry,* 1970, *4,* 71–100.

NEUGARTEN, B. L. Personality change in late life: A developmental perspective. In C. Eisdorfer & M. P. Lawton (Eds.), *The psychology of adult development and aging.* Washington, D.C.: American Psychological Association, 1973.

NEUGARTEN, B. L. The future and the young old. *The Gerontologist,* 1975, *15*(Pt. 2), 4–9.

NEUGARTEN, B. L. Personality and aging. In J. E. Birren & K. W. Schaie (Eds.), *Handbook of the psychology of aging.* New York: Van Nostrand Reinhold, 1977.

NEUGARTEN, B. L. *Personality changes in adulthood.* In American Psychological Association (Organizer), *Master lectures on the psychology of aging.* Paper presented at the 86th Annual Convention of the American Psychological Association, Toronto, Canada, 1978.

NEUGARTEN, B. L., & Associates. *Personality in middle and late life.* New York: Leiber-Atherton, 1964.

NEUGARTEN, B. L., & GUTMANN, D. L. Age-sex roles and personality in middle age: A thematic apperception study. In B. L. Neugarten & Associates, *Personality in middle and late life.* New York: Leiber-Atherton, 1964.

NEUGARTEN, B. L., & HAGESTAD, G. O. Age and the life course. In R. H. Binstock & E. Shanas (Eds.), *Handbook of aging and the social sciences.* New York: Van Nostrand Reinhold, 1976.

NOWAK, C. A. Age and sex differences in the perception of personal age and self-esteem. In B. F. Turner (Chair), *The double standard of aging: A question of sex differences.* Symposium presented at the 29th Annual Scientific Meeting of the Gerontological Society, New York City, 1976.

OBRIST, W. D. Cerebral physiology of the aged: Influence of circulatory disorders. In C. M. Gaitz (Ed.), *Aging and the brain.* New York: Plenum, 1972.

PALMORE, E. Summary and the future. In E. Palmore & F. C. Jeffers (Eds.), *Prediction of life span.* Lexington, Mass.: Heath, 1971.

PALMORE, E., & JEFFERS, F. (Eds.). *Prediction of lifespan.* Lexington, Mass.: Heath, 1971.

PALMORE, E., & LUIKART, C. Health and social factors related to life satisfaction. *Journal of Health and Social Behavior,* 1972, *13,* 68–80.

PARIS, B. L., & LUCKEY, E. B. A longitudinal study of marital satisfaction. *Sociology and Social Research,* 1966, *50,* 212–223.

PAYKEL, E. S., PRUSOFF, B. A., & UHLENHUTH, E. H. Scaling of life events. *Archives of General Psychiatry,* 1971, *25,* 340–347.

PERLMUTTER, M. Age differences in adults' free recall, cued recall, and recognition. *Journal of Gerontology,* 1979, *34,* 533–539.

PETERSEN, A. C., & WITTIG, M. A. Sex-related differences in cognitive functioning: An overview. In M. A. Wittig & A. C. Petersen (Eds.), *Sex-related differences in cognitive functioning.* New York: Academic Press, 1979.

PFEIFFER, E. Psychopathology and social pathology. In J. E. Birren & K. W. Schaie (Eds.), *Handbook of the psychology of aging.* New York: Van Nostrand Reinhold, 1977.

PINEO, P. Disenchantment in the later years of marriage. *Marriage and Family Living,* 1961, *23,* 3–11.

PRESTON, S. H. Mortality trends. In A. Inkeles, J. Coleman, & N. Smelser (Eds.), *Annual review of sociology* (Vol. 3). Palo Alto, Calif.: Annual Reviews, 1977.

RETHERFORD, R. D. Tobacco smoking and the sex mortality differential. *Demography,* 1972, *9,* 203–216.

RHUDICK, P. J., & GORDON, C. The age center of New England study. In L. F. Jarvik, C. Eisdorfer, & J. E. Blum (Eds.), *Intellectual functioning in adults.* New York: Springer, 1973.

RIEGEL, K. F. Adult life crises: A dialectic interpretation of development. In N. Datan & L. H. Ginsberg (Eds.), *Life-span developmental psychology: Normative life crises.* New York: Academic Press, 1975.

RILEY, M. W., & FONER, A. *Aging and society* (Vol. 1). New York: Russell Sage Foundation, 1968.

ROBINSON, B., & THURNHER, M. Taking care of aged parents: A family cycle transition. *The Gerontologist,* 1979, *19,* 586–593.

ROLLINS, B. C., & CANNON, K. L. Marital satisfaction over the family life cycle: A re-evaluation. *Journal of Marriage and the Family,* 1974, *36,* 271–282.

ROLLINS, B. C., & FELDMAN, H. Marital satisfaction over the family life cycle. *Journal of Marriage and the Family,* 1970, *32,* 20–28.

ROSE, C. L. Critique of longevity studies. In E. Palmore & F. C. Jeffers (Eds.), *Prediction of life span.* Lexington, Mass.: Heath, 1971.

ROSEMAN, J. M., & BUCKLEY, C. E. Inverse relationship between serum Ig concentrations and measures of intelligence in elderly persons. *Nature,* 1975, *254,* 55–56.

ROSSI, A. S. Transition to parenthood. *Journal of Marriage and the Family,* 1968, *30,* 26–39.

RUBIN, L. B. *Worlds of pain.* New York: Basic Books, 1975.

RUBIN, L. B. *Women of a certain age: The midlife search for self.* New York: Harper & Row, Pub., 1979.

RYFF, C., & BALTES, P. B. Value transition and adult development in women: The instrumentality-terminality sequence hypothesis. *Developmental Psychology,* 1976, *12,* 567–568.

SCHAIE, K. W., & PARHAM, I. A. Stability of adult personality: Fact or fable? *Journal of Personality and Social Psychology,* 1976, *34,* 146–158.

SCHAIE, K. W., & STROTHER, C. R. Cognitive and personality variables in college graduates of advanced age. In G. A. Talland (Ed.), *Human behavior and aging.* New York: Academic Press, 1968.

SEDNEY, M. A. *Use and effectiveness of rumination as a cognitive coping strategy following stressful life events in middle-aged women.* Unpublished doctoral dissertation, University of Massachusetts at Amherst, 1976.

SHANAS, E. *Family relationships of older people.* Chicago: Health Information Foundation, Research Series 20, University of Chicago, 1961.

SHERRIFFS, A. C., & McKEE, J. P. Qualitative aspects of beliefs about men and women. *Journal of Personality,* 1957, *25,* 451–464.

SIEGEL, J. S. *Demographic aspects of aging and the older population in the United States.* U.S. Bureau of the Census, Current Population Reports (Special Studies Series P-23, No. 59, Second Printing, revised). Washington, D.C.: U.S. Government Printing Office, 1978.

SIEGEL, J. S. *Prospective trends in the size and structure of the elderly population, impact of mortality trends, and some implications.* U.S. Bureau of the Census, Current Population Reports (Special Studies Series P-23, No. 78). Washington, D.C.: U.S. Government Printing Office, 1979.

SIEGLER, I. C. The psychology of adult development and aging. In E. W. Busse & D. G. Blazer (Eds.), *Handbook of geriatric psychiatry.* New York: Van Nostrand Reinhold, 1980.

SIEGLER, I. C., GEORGE, L. K., & OKUN, M. A. Cross-sequential analysis of adult personality. *Developmental Psychology,* 1979, *15,* 350–351.

SIEGLER, I. C., NOWLIN, J. B., & BLUMENTHAL, J. A. Health and behavior: Methodological considerations for adult development and aging. In L. W. Poon (Ed.), *Aging in the 1980's: Psychological issues.* Washington, D.C.: American Psychological Association, 1980.

SPANIER, G. B., LEWIS, R. A., & COLE, C. L. Marital adjustment over the family life cycle: The issue of curvilinearity. *Journal of Marriage and the Family,* 1975, *37,* 263–276.

SPENCE, J. T., & HELMREICH, R. L. *Masculinity and femininity: Their psychological dimensions, correlates and antecedents.* Austin: University of Texas Press, 1978.

SPIETH, W. Cardiovascular health status, age, and psychological performance. *Journal of Gerontology,* 1964, *19,* 277–284.

SPIETH, W. Slowness of task performance and cardiovascular disease. In A. T. Welford & J. E. Birren (Eds.), *Behavior, aging, and the nervous system.* Springfield, Ill.: Chas. C Thomas, 1965.

SPREITZER, E., & SNYDER, E. E. Correlates of life satisfaction among the aged. *Journal of Gerontology,* 1974, *29,* 454–458.

SROLE, L., & FISCHER, A. K. The midtown Manhattan study: Longitudinal focus on aging. In R. E. Weber (Organizer), *Lives in transition: Advancements in theory and research.* Symposium presented at the 31st Annual Meeting of the Gerontological Society, Dallas, 1978.

STEHOUWER, J. The household and family relations of old people. In E. Shanas (Ed.), *Old people in three industrial societies.* New York: Lieber-Atherton, 1968.

STINNETT, N., CARTER, L. M., & MONTGOMERY, J. E. Older persons' perceptions of their marriages. *Journal of Marriage and the Family,* 1972, *34,* 665–670.

STORANDT, M., GRANT, E. A., & GORDON, B. C. Remote memory as a function of age and sex. *Experimental Aging Research,* 1978, *4,* 365–375.

SUSSMAN, M. B. Relationships of adult children with their parents in the United States. In E. Shanas & G. F. Streib (Eds.), *Social structure and the family: Generational relations.* Englewood Cliffs, N.J.: Prentice-Hall, 1965.

SUTER, L., & MILLER, H. Income differences between men and career women. *American Journal of Sociology,* 1973, *78,* 962–974.

TALLAND, G. A. Performance studies in human aging and their theoretical significance. *Psychiatric Digest,* 1966, *27,* 37–53.

TAUB, H. A. Paired associates learning as a function of age, rate and instructions. *Journal of Genetic Psychology,* 1967, *111,* 41–46.

THURNHER, M. Family confluence, conflict and affect. In M. Lowenthal, M. Thurnher, D. Chiriboga, & Associates, *Four stages of life.* San Francisco: Jossey-Bass, 1975.

THURNHER, M. *Turning points across the life course: Subjective perspectives.* Paper presented at the 32nd Annual meeting of the Gerontological Society, New York City, November 1979.

TORNSTAM, L. Health and self-perception: A systems theoretical approach. *Gerontologist,* 1975, *15,* 264–270.

TREIMAN, D. J., & TERRELL, K. Sex and the process of status attainment. *American Sociological Review,* 1975, *40,* 174–200.

TROLL, L. The family of later life: A decade review. *Journal of Marriage and the Family,* 1971, *33,* 263–290.

TROLL, L. *Development in early and middle adulthood.* Monterey, Calif.: Brooks/Cole, 1975.

TROLL, L. E., & SMITH, J. Attachment through the life span: Some questions about dyadic relations in later life. *Human Development,* 1976, *19,* 156–171.

TROLL, L. E., & TURNER, B. F. The secular trends in sex roles and the family of later life. In B. F. Turner & L. E. Troll (Eds.), *Socialization to become an old woman,* in preparation.

TURNER, B. F. *Psychological predictors of adaptation to the stress of institutionalization in the aged.* Unpublished doctoral dissertation, University of Chicago, 1969.

TURNER, B. F. The self-concepts of older women. *Research on Aging,* 1979, *1,* 464–480.

TURNER, B. F., TOBIN, S. S., & LIEBERMAN, M. A. Personality traits as predictors of institutional adaptation among the aged. *Journal of Gerontology,* 1972, *27,* 61–68.

TURNER, B. F., & TURNER, C. B. Evaluations of women and men among black and white college students. *Sociological Quarterly,* 1974, *15,* 442–456.

TYLER, L. E. *The psychology of human differences.* Englewood Cliffs, N.J.: Prentice-Hall, 1965.

UNGER, R. K. Toward a redefinition of sex and gender. *American Psychologist,* 1979, *34,* 1085–1094.

U.S. Bureau of the Census. *Statistical abstract of the United States: 1978*(99th ed.). Washington, D.C.: U.S. Government Printing Office, 1978.

U.S. Bureau of the Census. *Social and economic characteristics of the older population: 1978.* Current Population Reports (Special Studies Series P-23, No. 85). Washington, D.C.: U.S. Government Printing Office, 1979.

U.S. Department of Health, Education and Welfare. *Health in the later years of life* (Public Health Service, National Center for Health Statistics No. 1722–0178). Washington, D.C.: U.S. Government Printing Office, 1971.

U.S. Department of Health, Education and Welfare. *Smoking and health: A report of the Surgeon General* (Public Health Service Publication No. 79-50066). Washington, D.C.: U.S. Government Printing Office, 1979.

U.S. Department of Labor. *1975 Handbook on women workers* (Bulletin 297). Washington, D.C.: U.S. Government Printing Office, 1975.

URBERG, K. A., & LABOUVIE-VIEF, G. Conceptualizations of sex roles: A life-span developmental study. *Developmental Psychology,* 1976, *12,* 15–23.

VAILLANT, G. E. *Adaptation to life.* Boston: Little, Brown, 1977.

VERBRUGGE, L. M. Sex differences in morbidity and mortality in the United States. *Social Biology,* 1977, *23,* 275–296.

VERBRUGGE, L. M. Comment on Walter R. Gove and Michael Hughes, *ASR,* February, 1979: Possible causes of the apparent sex differences in physical health. *American Sociological Review,* 1980, *45,* 507–513.

WALDRON, J. Why do women live longer than men? *Social Science and Medicine,* 1976, *10,* 349–362.

WALDRON, J., & JOHNSTON, S. Why do women live longer than men? *Journal of Human Stress,* 1976, *2,* 19–29.

WARD, R. A. The impact of subjective age and stigma on older persons. *Journal of Gerontology,* 1977, *32,* 227–232.

WEISSMAN, M. M., & KLERMAN, G. L. Sex differences and the epidemiology of depression. In E. S. Gomberg & V. Franks (Eds.), *Gender and disordered behavior: Sex differences in psychopathology.* New York: Brunner/Mazel, 1979.

WILEN, J. B. *Changing relationships among grandparents, parents, and their young adult children.* Paper presented at the 32nd Annual Meeting of the Gerontological Society, Washington, D.C., November 1979.

WILKIE, F., & EISDORFER, C. Sex, verbal ability and pacing differences in serial learning. *Journal of Gerontology,* 1977, *32,* 63–67.

WILSON, J. R., DeFRIES, J. C., McCLEARN, G. E., VANDENBERG, S. G., JOHNSON, R. C., & RASHAD, M. N. Cognitive abilities: Use of family data as a control to assess sex and age differences in two ethnic groups. *International Journal of Aging and Human Development,* 1975, *6,* 261–276.

WITTE, K. L. Paired associate learning in young and elderly adults as related to presentation rate. *Psychological Bulletin,* 1975, *82,* 975–985.

ZAKS, P., KARUZA, J., DOMURATH, K., & LABOUVIE-VIEF, G. *Sex role orientation across the adult life span.* Paper presented at the 32nd Annual Meeting of the Gerontological Society, Washington, D.C., November 1979.

Author Index

Malpass, R. S., 77
Mamnheimer, S., 480
Manaster, G. J., 554
Mancini, J., 728, 876
Mandler, G., 345, 835, 840, 858, 861, 862
Mandler, J. M., 358, 360
Mangurten, H. H., 181
Mangus, A. H., 655
Manis, J. D., 670, 675, 757
Manke, W. F., 793
Mann, A. J., 454, 457, 459, 464
Mann, I., 246
Mann, L., 248
Mannheim, K., 890, 895
Manniche, E., 813
Manniello, R. L., 184
Manosevitz, M., 31, 420
Mans, L., 245
Maratsos, M., 341
Maratsos, M. P., 369, 372, 375, 377, 383
Marcia, J. E., 30, 31, 508, 509, 510, 511, 547, 551
Marcus, D. E., 424
Maresh, M., 474, 478
Margolin, G., 667, 677, 678
Marini, M. M., 672
Mariwaki, S. Y., 872
Markel, N. N., 303
Markides, K., 876, 916
Markman, E. M., 338, 341, 390
Markman, H. J., 678
Markson, E. W., 931
Marmarou, A., 232
Marmorale, A. M., 86
Marolla, F., 178
Marquis, A. L., 377
Marschark, M., 10
Marsella, A. J., 693
Marsh, G. R., 626, 795, 833
Marshall, R. N., 480
Marshall, W. A., 472, 473, 474, 625, 627
Marslen-Wilson, W. D., 828, 834
Marston, P. T., 455
Martin, B., 676, 677, 692, 694
Martin, C. E., 562, 570, 576, 579, 585, 586, 624, 726, 727, 730
Martin, H. W., 916
Martin, J., 508
Martin, N. G., 854
Martin, R. D., 211
Martin, W. C., 903
Martin, W. H., 263
Martindale, L., 582, 586
Martini, M., 690
Martorano, C. S., 491
Marvin, R. S., 393, 394
Marx, G. F., 184
Marx, M. H., 20
Masani, P. A., 812, 840
Masankay, Z. S., 392, 394, 396
Mash, E. J., 696
Masica, D. N., 416
Maslow, A. H., 550
Mason, K. O., 104, 105
Mason, W. A., 70, 72, 121
Mason, W. M., 104, 105
Massad, C. M., 341
Massarik, F., 54
Massaro, D. W., 830, 857
Massie, H. N., 695
Massie, P., 128
Masson, M.E.J., 828, 832, 834
Mast, A., 417
Masters, J., 190, 191, 192, 196, 215
Masters, J. C., 448
Masters, R. D., 603
Masters, W. H., 217, 643, 645, 726, 727, 730, 763
Masterson, B., 222
Masterson, J. F., 541
Mastri, A. R., 797
Masur, E. F., 344, 353
Matarazzo, J. D., 80, 823, 849
Matarese, G., 481

Matarese, S., 481
Matas, L., 218, 240
Mathews, M. E., 358
Mathews, S. R., 339
Mathieu, J. T., 884
Matlin, N., 608
Matsuyama, H., 796, 797, 919
Matsuyama, S. S., 796, 797, 919
Matteson, D. R., 511, 512, 518
Mattessich, P., 668, 670
Mattevi, M. S., 796
Matthews, N., 585
Mattingly, I. G., 266
Mattsson, I., 108
Maturana, H. R., 187
Matza, D., 162
Mauer, D., 244, 245, 246, 247, 248, 252
Maule, A. J., 864
Maurer, D., 324, 355
Maxwell, P., 710
May, M. A., 448
May, R. D., 457, 784
Mayer, F. E., 559
Maynard, J., 256
Mayr, E., 215, 224
Mazian, F., 872
Meacham, J. A., 351
Mead, G. H., 650, 759
Mead, M., 77, 86, 406, 534, 762, 880, 891
Means, B. M., 837
Mears, C., 64
Mechanic, D., 877, 931
Medawar, P. B., 222
Medinnus, G. R., 711, 713
Medley, M. L., 876, 916
Mednick, M., 605
Medvid, L., 180
Meehl, P., 6, 196
Mehl, L., 760
Mehler, J., 374
Meichenbaum, D., 337, 340, 343, 344, 813, 815
Meir, E. I., 607
Meir, G. W., 217
Meisels, M., 505
Meissner, J. A., 393
Meissner, S. J., 693
Meissner, W. J., 676, 677, 693
Meissner, W. W., 543
Meites, J., 759
Melamed, L. E., 230–241
Melson, W. H., 236
Meltzoff, A., 315
Meltzoff, A. N., 328, 700
Mendel, M. I., 263, 264
Mendelson, M. J., 245, 246, 278
Mendoza, J. L., 108
Mening-Peterson, C., 393
Menken, J., 590
Mentz, L., 262, 264
Menzel, E. W., 123, 130
Menzneck, J., 878
Meredith, D. L., 702, 703, 716, 717, 720
Meredith, H. V., 77, 559
Meredith, W., 111, 852
Merlino, F. J., 56
Merton, K., 877
Mervis, C., 59
Mervis, C. B., 377, 381, 383
Mesibov, G., 351
Messent, P. R., 417
Messerly, L., 678
Messick, S. J., 408
Metcalf, D., 272
Metcalf, L. E., 556
Metzler, J., 839
Meux, M., 556
Meyer, M., 801, 867
Meyer, W. J., 404, 419
Meyerhoff, B., 904
Meyerling, S., 740
Meyerowitz, J., 587, 589
Meyers, H., 746, 747
Meyers, W., II, 232, 233, 234
Mezneck, J., 888

Michael, J. A., 149
Michael, S. T., 541
Michaleweski, H., 795
Michalson, L., 691
Michel, G. F., 246, 287
Michela, J. L., 552
Michelson, K., 761, 854
Michielutte, R., 592
Milburn, J. F., 460
Milewski, A. E., 245, 246, 248, 249, 250
Milgram, N. A., 356
Milgram, S., 165, 444
Milhoj, P., 902
Millar, S., 762
Miller, B. C., 901
Miller, C., 305, 306
Miller, D. C., 756, 772, 773, 796
Miller, D. J., 249, 337
Miller, D. R., 514
Miller, G. A., 308, 374, 382, 834
Miller, H., 915
Miller, J., 306
Miller, J. L., 265
Miller, J. W., 338
Miller, L. B., 453, 457, 459, 464
Miller, M. I., 607
Miller, N. E., 191
Miller, P., 182
Miller, P. H., 335, 397
Miller, S. A., 341
Miller, S. I., 180
Miller, W. B., 303, 575, 577, 578, 579, 581, 707
Milligan, W. L., 795
Mills, K., 595
Milner, B., 860
Milowe, I., 764
Mindick, B., 567, 568, 582, 583
Minifie, F., 306
Minifie, F. D., 266
Minton, C., 418, 762
Miranda, S., 248, 250
Mirande, A., 573, 577
Mirels, H. L., 552
Mischel, H. N., 343, 442, 447, 448
Mischel, W., 56, 58, 59, 342, 343, 417, 442, 446, 447, 448, 711, 923
Mishkin, B., 162
Mishler, E. G., 715
Mitchell, D., 706, 713
Mitchell, G., 66, 764
Mitteness, L., 903, 925
Mittler, P., 219
Modgil, C., 489
Modgil, S., 489
Moelis, I., 763
Moely, B. E., 351, 356
Moerk, E., 314, 692
Moerk, E. L., 377, 381
Moffitt, A., 305
Mokros, J. R., 448
Moles, O. C., 734
Molfese, D. L., 265, 266, 301–318, 370, 373, 414
Molfese, V. J., 265, 266, 301–318
Monahan, T. P., 718
Moncrieff, R. W., 270
Money, J., 177, 219, 403, 404, 406, 416, 417, 419, 424, 559, 560, 565, 729, 731, 765
Monge, R. H., 838, 917
Monk, A., 875
Monson, R. R., 177
Monsour, K., 581, 586
Montemayor, R., 425, 508, 537
Montgomery, J. E., 926
Montgomery, R. G., 477
Montoye, H. J., 477
Montpetit, R. R., 477
Moore, C., 287
Moore, D., 436, 552, 677, 678
Moore, J., 306
Moore, J. M., 265, 266
Moore, K., 587, 588, 589
Moore, M., 245, 253, 254, 315
Moore, M. K., 324, 328

Moore, R. W., 250
Moore, S. G., 420
Moos, R., 759, 877
Moralishvili, E., 796
Morante, L., 711
More, T., 692
Moreau, T., 246, 273
Morehead, A., 314
Morehead, D., 314
Morgan, A. B., 809
Morgan, J. N., 650
Morgan, K., 307
Morgan, S. T., 184
Morimatsu, M., 797
Morris, C., 550, 552, 555
Morris, C. D., 339
Morris, D., 759, 760, 764
Morris, N. M., 570, 579, 702, 727
Morris, R. C., 149
Morris, T. N., 879
Morrison, D. F., 142, 143, 145
Morrison, F. J., 335
Morrison, J. R., 810, 812, 852
Morrow, W. R., 693
Morsbach, G., 315
Morse, P., 250, 305, 306, 307
Morse, P. A., 234, 265, 266
Morse, W. C., 454, 455, 456
Moser, H. P., 605, 606
Moshman, D., 488, 494, 495
Moskowitz, H. R., 267
Moss, H. A., 233, 308, 405, 418, 688, 692, 695, 751, 760, 761, 902, 925
Mossler, D. G., 393, 394
Mosteller, F., 160, 168, 170
Mott, J. C., 66
Motta, E., 568, 582
Motz, S. C., 637
Moulton, D. G., 271
Moulton, P. W., 712
Mowbray, J. B., 68, 70
Moynahan, E. D., 352, 353
Moynahan, T. P., 719
Mueller, C. W., 735
Mueller, E., 284–298, 340, 425
Muir, D., 256, 273
Muir, D. W., 245
Mulaik, S. A., 111
Muller, E., 315, 761
Muller, M. F., 794
Mundy-Castle, A., 81
Munroe, R. H., 77, 78, 81, 82
Munroe, R. L., 77, 78, 81, 82
Muntjewerf, W., 265
Murimatsu, A., 797
Murphy, D. P., 182
Murphy, G. J., 926
Murphy, L., 761
Murphy, M. D., 315, 361
Murray, A., 760, 761
Murray, F., 355
Murray, H. A., 655, 784, 881
Murray, T. H., 164
Murrell, S., 757
Murry, T., 315, 761
Murstein, B. I., 652–665, 667, 676, 677
Muslin, H. L., 541
Mussen, P., 519
Mussen, P. H., 417, 421, 422, 539, 540, 560, 694, 704, 711, 713, 716
Mutterer, M. L., 448
Muuss, R. E., 537, 604
Myerhoff, B., 872, 885
Myers, M., 339, 343, 353, 356
Myers, N. A., 335, 357
Myrianthopoulos, N. C., 180

Naditch, S. F., 425
Naeser, M. A., 794
Naeye, R. L., 178, 179
Nahemow, L., 878, 879, 894, 896
Nakamura, C. Y., 418
Nandy, K., 797
Naron, N. K., 837

Nash, J., 209, 220, 724
Nash, S. C., 424, 425, 428, 923
Nash, W. R., 462, 464
Nass, G., 573, 575
Nathanson, C., 913, 914, 915
Naus, M. J., 336, 351, 352, 358
Neff, C., 690
Neimark, E. D., 336, 486–502, 518
Neisser, U., 3, 830
Nelsen, E. A., 398, 448
Nelson, C. A., 250
Nelson, D., 708, 709, 710
Nelson, D. D., 512
Nelson, F., 584
Nelson, K., 4, 290, 291, 298, 314, 317, 318, 328, 329, 379, 380, 382
Nelson, K. E., 313, 314, 352, 377
Nelson, M. N., 234
Nelson, S., 427
Nesselroade, J. R., 54, 60, 92, 93, 95, 97, 98, 100, 144, 145, 504, 517, 522, 553, 605, 855, 918
Neubauer, P. B., 718
Neugarten, B. L., 54, 56, 57, 618, 623, 670, 776, 873, 891, 901, 912, 918, 919, 924, 925, 929, 930, 931
Neuman, M. F., 710
Neurath, P., 796
Neville, M. H., 338
Newberry, H., 685
Newcomb, T. M., 531, 549
Newcomb, R. G., 178
Newcombe, N., 353
Newcomer, R., 878
Newell, A., 487
Newhoff, M., 382
Newman, B. M., 617–634
Newman, G., 635
Newman, L. S., 550
Newman, P., 526–535
Newport, E. L., 308, 309, 313, 314
Newson, E., 419
Newson, J., 419
Newton, N., 753, 759, 762
Nicholich, L., 317
Nichols, C. R., 624
Nichols, I. A., 611
Nichols, P. L., 179
Nicholson, L., 751
Nickerson, R. J., 177
Nicol, T. L., 532
Nicolay, R. C., 760
Nicholson, A. B., 472, 473
Nielsen, J., 796
Niemi, R., 892, 894, 896, 898, 899, 901, 906
Nietzel, M. T., 678
Nilsen, A. P., 426
Nilsson, A., 759
Ninio, A., 316, 382
Nisbett, E. R., 345
Nisbett, R., 267, 268
Niskanen, P., 185
Niswander, K. R., 178, 179, 759
Noam, G. G., 23–40
Nock, S. L., 636–650
Nodine, C. F., 492
Norcia, A., 253
Nordenson, I., 796
Norman, D. A., 361, 363, 828, 829, 834
Norman, R., 550
Norris, J., 607
Norton, A. J., 708, 730, 734, 735
Novak, C. A., 692, 916
Novick, M. N., 111
Nowicki, S., Jr., 724
Nowlin, J. B., 795, 799, 913, 917
Nowlis, G. H., 268
Nugent, J., 678
Nunn, L., 757
Nunnally, J. C., 133–148
Nydegger, C. N., 890, 905, 925
Nye, F. I., 667, 716, 765
Nyman, B. A., 419, 695

Oatley, D. A., 492
Oberg, C., 253
Obmascher, P., 190
O'Brien, P. C., 495
Obrist, P. A., 231, 232, 235
Obrist, W. D., 794, 919
O'Connell, E. J., 419, 763
O'Connell-Higgins, R., 23–40
O'Connor, S., 686
Oden, M. H., 634, 811
O'Donnell, W. J., 251, 511
Oetzel, R., 428
Offer, D., 518, 540, 541, 542, 544
Offir, C., 406
Ohlrich, E. S., 263
Okamoto, N., 316
Okun, M., 924
Olander, E., 902
Oldfield, S., 419
O'Leary, D. K., 419
O'Leary, K., 85
O'Leary, K. D., 427
O'Leary, S., 294, 295, 760, 762
O'Leary, V. E., 516
Olejnik, A. B., 398, 553
Oliver, C. M., 230–241
Oliver, D. B., 784
Olkin, I., 413
Olley, G., 762
Olsen, M. G., 335, 352
Olsen, P. N., 179
Olson, D. H., 665, 765
Olson, F. A., 351
Olson, M. I., 761, 796
Olsson, V., 112
Oltman, J. E., 714
Oltman, P. K., 79
O'Malley, P. M., 673
Omark, D. R., 226
Omvig-Clayton, P., 609
Opler, M. K., 541
Oppel, W., 585
Oppenheimer, L., 396
Opper, S., 481
Opton, E., 877
Ordy, J. M., 247
Orlando, V. P., 339
Orlofsky, D. E., 452, 453
Orlofsky, J. L., 31, 511
Orme-Rogers, C., 830
Orne, M. T., 123
Ornstein, P. A., 336, 351, 356, 358
Orpen, C., 552
Orpin, J., 263
Orti, E., 271
Osgood, C. E., 6, 7, 373, 549
O'Shea, G., 686
Osherson, D., 390
Osherson, D. N., 489, 493
Oshman, H., 31
Osipow, S. H., 608
Oskamp, S., 567, 568, 575, 582, 583
Osler, S. F., 12
Osofsky, H., 586
Osofsky, J. D., 419, 586, 751, 761, 763
Ostrea, E. M., 182, 210
Ostrom, T. M., 549, 550
Ostwald, P., 761, 764
O'Toole, R., 762
Ottaviano, C., 686
Ottinger, D., 184, 185
Otto, L. B., 671, 672
Overall, J. E., 107
Overstreet, P. L., 605, 606
Overton, W. F., 55, 56, 57, 284, 424, 492, 603, 792, 814
Owens, W. A., 811
Owings, R. A., 339
Owsley, C. J., 245, 250 259, 274
Ozier, M., 845

Packard, R., 425
Packard, V., 566
Padgug, E. J., 307
Paille, W., 265, 414

Painter, P., 183
Paivio, A., 10
Pajot, N., 231
Palermo, D. S., 265, 304, 370, 372, 373, 383
Palm, J., 352
Palmer, R., 560, 810, 812, 821
Palmore, E., 876, 912, 913, 916
Palmore, J., 585
Pamcucci, C. L., 826
Panko, J. S., 462, 465
Papalia, D. E., 491, 792, 808, 809, 812, 839
Parens, H., 769
Parham, I. A., 924
Paris, B. L., 926, 927
Paris, S. G., 127, 333–347, 353, 357, 362, 494
Park, B., 463
Parke, R. D., 293, 294, 295, 328, 637, 702, 760, 815
Parker, G. H., 267
Parker, S. T., 222, 719
Parker, T., 353, 359
Parkman, M., 894
Parks, M. M., 253
Parlee, M. B., 560
Parmelee, A. H., Jr., 326, 761
Parrow, A. A., 672
Parsons, C. K., 491
Parsons, T., 637, 639, 769, 872, 897
Parsons, T. M., 551
Partanen, T. J., 761
Pasamanick, B., 182, 552
Pascual-Leone, J., 488, 491, 496, 497, 498
Pasini, W., 727
Passer, M. W., 552
Pastalan, L., 881
Patker, J., 584
Patterson, C. J., 341, 342
Patterson, G. R., 463, 677, 678, 696
Patterson, H. F., 497
Patterson, J. G., 324
Patterson, J. R., 554
Pattullo, E. L., 168, 170
Paully, P. W., 71
Pavlov, I. P., 46
Pawlby, S. J., 689, 690, 695
Paykel, E. S., 929
Payne, D. E., 422, 704
Payne, J. W., 835
Payne, S., 896
Payne, T.R.S., 398
Pearlin, L., 757, 877, 878
Pearlman, C. K., 733
Pears, C., 607
Peck, A. I., 719
Peck, M. B., 267
Peck, R. F., 455, 464
Pedersen, F. A., 294, 418, 423, 687, 697, 702, 714
Pederson, D. M., 425, 427
Pedhazur, E. J., 102
Pedler, L. M., 739
Peel, E. A., 492
Peiper, A., 267, 759
Pellegrino, J. W., 356
Peltz, O., 731
Pennoyer, M. M., 183
Pentz, C. A., 800
Peplau, L. A., 736
Peretti, P. O., 532
Perez, R., 905
Perez-Reyes, M., 232, 586
Perkins, G. M., 245
Perlman, S. M., 416, 417
Perlmutter, M., 324, 335, 357, 832, 839, 840, 918
Perry, J., 769
Persky, H., 416
Pertjelan, A., 480
Peskin, H., 539, 540
Pessel, D., 180
Peter, N., 552
Peters, D. G., 9

Petersen, A. C., 412, 415, 539, 917
Petersen, G. A., 323–329
Peterson, C. C., 341, 318
Peterson, D. R., 714
Peterson, G., 760
Peterson, J. A., 873, 877, 878, 879
Peterson, J. L., 418
Peterson, L., 245, 254, 255, 256, 444
Peterson, R. A., 519, 573, 575
Petre-Quadens, O., 759
Petroni, F. A., 527
Pettigrew, T. F., 718
Pfaff, D., 417
Pfaffman, C., 417
Pfefferbaum, A., 795
Pfeiffer, E., 877
Phelps, E., 496
Philip, J. R., 764
Philips, J. R., 293, 308, 309, 310, 312
Phillips, B., 458, 464
Phillips, L. S., 480
Phillips, W., 359
Phillis, D. E., 924
Phoenix, C. H., 72
Piaget, J., 4, 5, 12, 13, 14, 15, 16, 17, 18, 19, 20, 21, 39, 40, 45, 48, 58, 59, 78, 79, 192, 193, 201, 210, 219, 259, 272, 287, 290, 291, 316, 317, 323, 324, 326, 327, 328, 336, 344, 354, 355, 388, 389, 391, 393, 397, 398, 399, 437, 438, 440, 441, 442, 443, 488, 489, 490, 496, 506, 518, 519, 520, 540, 602, 606, 631, 689, 798, 829, 835, 837
Pick, H. L., 240, 335, 352
Picone, T. A., 179
Picton, T. W., 263, 264
Pidwell, H., 80
Piel, E., 609
Pierce, R., 924
Pietras, R. J., 271
Pihlblad, C. T., 873, 885
Pilkington, G. W., 552
Pincus, A., 877
Pincus, J., 464
Pinder, A., 891
Pine, F., 537
Pineo, P., 672, 907, 926
Pines, D., 754
Pinkston, E. M., 427
Pintler, M. H., 705
Pion, R., 575
Piontrowski, D., 334
Pipp, S., 255
Pitt, B., 759
Pizzamiglio, L., 413
Plank, E. H., 710
Platt, J. J., 447
Platt, L., 512
Platt, M., 927
Pleck, J., 425
Plemons, J. K., 94, 815, 817, 924
Plimpton, E. H., 72
Plomin, R., 219
Ploog, D., 67
Plotkin, H. C., 222
Plude, D. J., 830, 848, 863
Plummer, G., 182
Pocaro, E. T., 162, 163
Podd, M., 31
Podd, M. H., 511, 519
Poey, K., 716
Poffenberger, S., 708, 727
Poffenberger, T. A., 708, 727
Pohly, S. R., 425
Pokorny, A. D., 912
Polany, P. E., 412
Polanyi, M., 117
Polikanina, R., 238
Polit, D. F., 648
Pollack, E. A., 44
Pollack, S. B., 179
Pomerleau-Malcuit, A., 233, 234, 235, 240

Subject Index

Sex and aging. *See* Aging: Sex related differences
Sex and sexual behavior in adolescence, 559–601
  abortions, 584
  attitudes, 565, 566
  behavior, 568–584
  childbirth to adolescent mothers, 584–595
  contraception, 575–584
  homosexuality, 564
  marriage, 595, 596
  masturbation, 564
  physiological development, 559–562
  research methods, 562–564
  secular trend, 561–562
  Sullivan, on, 621, 622
Sex and sexual behavior in adulthood, 726, 733
  and aging, 730
  climacterium, 622–624
  in divorce, 729–730
  of homosexuality, 730, 731
  in marriage, 726–729
  and menopause, 622–624
  nonmarital and extramarital sex relations, 731, 732
  and pregnancy, 727, 728
  satisfaction in sex, 624
Sex and sexuality in childhood and infancy
  biological determinants, 403, 407, 408, 412–417
  cognitive factors, 424, 425
  cultural factors, 85, 403–408
  emotional factors, 410–412, 620, 621
  gender identity, 421, 424
  in infancy, 215, 216, 225
  intellectual aspects, 408–410
  learning of sex roles, 462–464
  parental influence, 417–424, 705–707
  peer influence, 707
  research, 406–407, 562–564
  school influence, 426–428
  sexual maturation, 471, 473, 480, 559–562
  sex roles, 403–433
Smiling
  in infancy, 286, 287
Smoking, 178, 179, 913, 914
Social behavior and aging, 871–889
  adaptation, 877–878
  attitudes of aged people, 874, 875
  attitudes toward, 874, 884
  disengagement and isolation, 872, 873, 876
  environmental factors, 878–882
  family, 872, 873
  integration and involvement, 872
  institutionalization, 880–884

Social behavior and aging (*cont.*)
  morale and life satisfaction, 876, 877, 881
  mortality, 871
  residential relocation, 882, 883
  retirement, 871
  services for the aged, 884–886
  social roles of the aged, 877
Social behavior in adolescence. *See* Adolescence: social behavior
Social-cognitive development in childhood, 387–402
  attachment to mother, 190
  concrete operations, 394–397
  egocentricity, 388, 390, 391
  knowledge, 389, 390
  moral issues, 397–400
  Piaget's views, 388, 389
  social role taking, 388–391
  socionomous phase (Wolman), 51, 52
Social development, socialization, 190–207, 284–300
  in adolescence, 503–536
  in adulthood, 669
  and aging, 871–889
  in childhood, 342, 343, 387–402
  education and social development, 459–461
  in infancy, 284–300
  infant-father interaction, 293, 295
  infant-mother interaction, 190–207, 284–295
  social deprivation, 217
Social development in infancy, 284–300
  attachment to mother, 190–207, 291
  crying, 287
  developmental approach, 284, 285
  eye contact, 288
  father-infant interaction, 293–295
  feeding, 289
  game playing, 292
  language, 293
  newborns, 285
  peer interaction, 295–297
  smiling, 286, 287, 289, 292
Society for Research in Child Development, 149, 164
S-O-R theory (Woodworth), 6
Spatial orientation
  in infancy, 259–261
Speech perception
  in infancy, 264–266
  structure-function principle (Gesell), 46
Statistical methods, 105–113, 141, 142
Stereotypy, 217, 218
Stimulus-half procedure, 830
"Strange Situation" studies, 196–198
Strong Vocational Interest Inventory, 775

Superego
  Freud, on, 49
  Hartmann, on, 49
Syntax, 369–378

T

Taste perception
  in infancy, 267–269
  textural ecology (Brunswik), 119
  thalidomide, 180
Thematic Apperception Test (TAT), 920, 927
Theories in development
  cognitive theories, 3–22
  cross-cultural theories, 76–90
  interactional theory, 44–53
  life-span theory, 54–62
  Piaget's theory, 4, 5, 12–20, 48
  psychoanalytic theories, 23–43
Thought processes
  in adolescence, 486–502
  in adulthood, 628–630
Transformational grammar (Chomsky), 368–369, 372, 374
Twenty Questions Task, 816, 818, 865

V

Values, value system
  in adolescence, 530, 531
  cultural, 533
  parental, 530, 531
Vector-ego (Wolman), 52, 53
Vectorialism (Wolman), 48
Visual perception
  in infancy, 246–260
Vocational guidance, 608, 609, 772
Vocational role development
  in adolescence, 602–614
  career choice, 604
  Career Pattern Study, 606, 607
  demographic changes, 610, 611
  maternal employment, 611
  vocational guidance, 608, 609
  vocational maturity, 606, 607
  vocational role development, 604–608, 612, 613

W

Wechsler Adult Intelligence Scale (WAIS), 793, 798, 799, 849, 850, 856
We-ego (Wolman), 51, 52
World Medical Association, 152